Exploring Premium Media Site

Improve your grade with hands-on tools and resources!

- Master *Key Terms* to expand your vocabulary.
- Prepare for exams by taking practice quizzes in the *Online Chapter Review*.
- Download *Student Data Files* for the applications projects in each chapter.

And for even more tools, you can access the following Premium Resources using your Access Code. Register now to get the most out of ***Exploring!***

- *Hands-On Exercise Videos* accompany each Hands-On Exercise in the chapter. These videos demonstrate both how to accomplish individual skills as well as why they are important.*
- *Soft Skills Videos* are necessary to complete the Soft Skills Beyond the Classroom Exercise, and introduce students to important professional skills.*

*Access code required for these premium resources

Your Access Code is:

EMOV1-CLINK-RICCI-CALIF-WERSH-FAMES

Note: If there is no silver foil covering the access code, it may already have been redeemed, and therefore may no longer be valid. In that case, you can purchase online access using a major credit card or PayPal account. To do so, go to **www.pearsonhighered.com/exploring**, select your book cover, click on "Buy Access" and follow the on-screen instructions.

To Register:

- To start you will need a valid email address and this access code.
- Go to **www.pearsonhighered.com/exploring** and scroll to find your text book.
- Once you've selected your text, on the Home Page, click the link to access the Student Premium Content.
- Click the Register button and follow the on-screen instructions.
- After you register, you can sign in any time via the log-in area on the same screen.

System Requirements

Windows 7 Ultimate Edition; IE 8
Windows Vista Ultimate Edition SP1; IE 8
Windows XP Professional SP3; IE 7
Windows XP Professional SP3; Firefox 3.6.4
Mac OS 10.5.7; Firefox 3.6.4
Mac OS 10.6; Safari 5

Technical Support

http://247pearsoned.custhelp.com

SERIES

(ex·ploring)

1. Investigating in a systematic way: examining. 2. Searching into or ranging over for the purpose of discovery.

Microsoft® Office 2013

VOLUME 1

Series Editor Mary Anne Poatsy

Mulbery | Hogan | Rutledge | Krebs | Cameron

Series Created by Dr. Robert T. Grauer

PEARSON

Boston Columbus Indianapolis New York San Francisco Upper Saddle River
Amsterdam Cape Town Dubai London Madrid Milan Munich Paris Montréal Toronto
Delhi Mexico City São Paulo Sydney Hong Kong Seoul Singapore Taipei Tokyo

Editor in Chief: Michael Payne
Senior Editor: Samantha McAfee Lewis
Editorial Project Manager: Keri Rand
Product Development Manager: Laura Burgess
Development Editor: Jennifer Lynn
Editorial Assistant: Laura Karahalis
Director of Marketing: Maggie Moylan Leen
Marketing Manager: Brad Forrester
Marketing Coordinator: Susan Osterlitz
Marketing Assistant: Darshika Vyas
Managing Editor: Camille Trentacoste
Production Project Manager: Ilene Kahn
Senior Operations Specialist: Maura Zaldivar
Senior Art Director: Jonathan Boylan
Interior Design: Studio Montage
Cover Design: Studio Montage
Cover Photo: Courtesy of Shutterstock® images
Associate Director of Design: Blair Brown
Digital Media Editor: Eric Hakanson
Director of Media Development: Taylor Ragan
Media Project Manager, Production: Renata Butera
Full Service Project Management: Andrea Stefanowicz/PreMediaGlobal
Composition: PreMediaGlobal

Credits and acknowledgments borrowed from other sources and reproduced, with permission, in this textbook appear on the appropriate page within text.

10 9 8 7 6 5

ISBN 10: 0-13-314267-1
ISBN 13: 978-0-13-314267-9

Dedications

For my husband, Ted, who unselfishly continues to take on more than his share to support me throughout the process; and for my children, Laura, Carolyn, and Teddy, whose encouragement and love have been inspiring.

Mary Anne Poatsy

I dedicate this book in memory to Grandpa Herman Hort, who dedicated his life to his family and to the education field as a teacher and administrator. He inspired a daughter and several grandchildren to become passionate educators and provide quality curriculum to students.

Keith Mulbery

I dedicate this work to my wonderful family—my husband, Paul, and my daughters, Jenn and Alli. You have made this adventure possible with your support, encouragement, and love. You inspire me!

Lynn Hogan

To my husband Dan, whose encouragement, patience, and love helped make this endeavor possible. Thank you for taking on the many additional tasks at home so that I could focus on writing. To Michelle and Stephanie, thank you so much for your hard work and dedication on this project. The long hours we all spent together did not go unnoticed. I have very much enjoyed working with you and I wish you the best in your future careers. To all my family and friends for their love and support. I want to thank Jennifer, Keri, Sam, and the entire Pearson team for their help and guidance and for giving me this amazing opportunity. Also, a big thanks to Cynthia and her family for her photos and videos.

Amy Rutledge

To my students—you continue to inspire me. Thank you for all you have taught me and shared with me.

Cynthia Krebs

I dedicate this book to my fiancée, Anny, for encouraging me throughout the writing process and for being the person she is, to Sonny, to Drs. Hubey, Boyno, Bredlau, and Deremer at Montclair State University for educating and inspiring me, and to my students, who I hope will inspire others someday.

Eric Cameron

For my wife, Patricia, whose patience, understanding, and support continue to make this work possible … especially when I stay up past midnight writing! And to my parents, Jackie and Dean, who taught me the best way to achieve your goals is to constantly strive to improve yourself through education.

Alan Evans

This book is dedicated to my children and to my students to inspire them to never give up and to always keep reaching for their dreams.

Rebecca Lawson

About the Authors

Mary Anne Poatsy, Series Editor

Mary Anne is a senior faculty member at Montgomery County Community College, teaching various computer application and concepts courses in face-to-face and online environments. She holds a B.A. in Psychology and Education from Mount Holyoke College and an M.B.A. in Finance from Northwestern University's Kellogg Graduate School of Management.

Mary Anne has more than 12 years of educational experience. She is currently adjunct faculty at Gwynedd-Mercy College and Montgomery County Community College. She has also taught at Bucks County Community College and Muhlenberg College, as well as conducted personal training. Before teaching, she was Vice President at Shearson Lehman in the Municipal Bond Investment Banking Department.

Dr. Keith Mulbery, Excel Author

Dr. Keith Mulbery is the Department Chair and a Professor in the Information Systems and Technology Department at Utah Valley University (UVU), where he currently teaches systems analysis and design, and global and ethical issues in information systems and technology. He has also taught computer applications, C# programming, and management information systems. Keith served as Interim Associate Dean, School of Computing, in the College of Technology and Computing at UVU.

Keith received the Utah Valley State College Board of Trustees Award of Excellence in 2001, School of Technology and Computing Scholar Award in 2007, and School of Technology and Computing Teaching Award in 2008. He has authored more than 17 textbooks, served as Series Editor for the Exploring Office 2007 series, and served as developmental editor on two textbooks for the Essentials Office 2000 series. He is frequently asked to give presentations and workshops on Microsoft Office Excel at various education conferences.

Keith received his B.S. and M.Ed. in Business Education from Southwestern Oklahoma State University and earned his Ph.D. in Education with an emphasis in Business Information Systems at Utah State University. His dissertation topic was computer-assisted instruction using Prentice Hall's Train and Assess IT program (the predecessor to MyITLab) to supplement traditional instruction in basic computer proficiency courses.

Lynn Hogan, Word Author

Lynn Hogan teaches at the University of North Alabama, providing instruction in the area of computer applications. With over 30 years of educational experience at the community college and university level, Lynn has taught applications, programming, and concepts courses in both online and classroom environments. She received an M.B.A. from the University of North Alabama and a Ph.D. from the University of Alabama.

Lynn is a co-author of *Practical Computing* and has served on the authoring team of *Your Office* as well as the *Exploring Office 2010* series. She resides in Alabama with her husband and two daughters.

Amy Rutledge, PowerPoint Author

Amy Rutledge is a Special Instructor of Management Information Systems at Oakland University in Rochester, Michigan. She coordinates academic programs in Microsoft Office applications and introductory management information systems courses for the School of Business Administration. Before joining Oakland University as an instructor, Amy spent several years working for a music distribution company and automotive manufacturer in various corporate roles including IT project management. She holds a B.S. in Business Administration specializing in Management Information Systems, and a B.A. in French Modern Language and Literature. She holds an M.B.A from Oakland University. She resides in Michigan with her husband, Dan.

Cynthia Krebs, Access Author

Cynthia Krebs is the Director of Business and Marketing Education at Utah Valley University. She is a professor in the Information Systems and Technology Department at Utah Valley University (UVU). In 2008, she received the UVU College of Technology and Computing Scholar Award. She has also received the School of Business Faculty Excellence Award twice during her tenure at UVU. Cynthia teaches the Methods of Teaching Digital Media class to future teachers, as well as classes in basic computer proficiency, business proficiency applications, and business graphics.

Cynthia is active in the Utah Business and Computer Education Association, the Western Business Education Association, the National Business Education Association, and the Utah Association of Career and Technical Educators. She was awarded the WBEA Outstanding Educator at the University Level in 2009. Cynthia has written multiple texts on Microsoft Office software, consulted with government and business, and has presented extensively at the local, regional, and national levels to professional and business organizations.

Cynthia lives by a peaceful creek in Springville, Utah. When she isn't teaching or writing, she enjoys spending time with her children, spoiling her grandchildren Ava, Bode, Solee, and Morgan. She loves traveling and reading.

Eric Cameron, Access Author

Eric holds a M.S. in computer science and a B.S. degree in Computer Science with minors in Mathematics and Physics, both from Montclair State University. He is a tenured Assistant Professor at Passaic County Community College, where he has taught in the Computer and Information Sciences department since 2001. Eric is also the author of the *Your Office: Getting Started with Web 2.0* and *Your Office: Getting Started with Windows 8* textbooks. Eric maintains a professional blog at **profcameron.blogspot.com**.

Alan Evans, Windows 8 Author

Alan is currently a faculty member at Moore College of Art and Design and Montgomery County Community College teaching a variety of computer science and business courses. He holds a B.S. in Accounting from Rider University and an M.S. in Information Systems from Drexel University, and he is a certified public accountant. After a successful career in business, Alan finally realized his true calling is education. He has been teaching at the college level since 2000. Alan enjoys giving presentations at technical conferences and meets regularly with computer science faculty and administrators from other colleges to discuss curriculum development and new methods of engaging students.

Rebecca Lawson, Office Fundamentals Author

Rebecca Lawson is a professor in the Computer Information Technologies program at Lansing Community College. She coordinates the curriculum, develops the instructional materials, and teaches for the E-Business curriculum. She also serves as the Online Faculty Coordinator at the Center for Teaching Excellence at LCC. In that role, she develops and facilitates online workshops for faculty learning to teach online. Her major areas of interest include online curriculum quality assurance, the review and development of printed and online instructional materials, the assessment of computer and Internet literacy skill levels to facilitate student retention, and the use of social networking tools to support learning in blended and online learning environments.

Brief Contents

Contents

Windows 8

CHAPTER ONE Getting Started with Windows 8 1

Microsoft Office 2013

CHAPTER ONE Office Fundamentals and File Management: Taking the First Step 55

Microsoft Office Word 2013

CHAPTER ONE **Introduction to Word:** Organizing a Document 137

CHAPTER TWO **Document Presentation:** Editing and Formatting 197

CHAPTER THREE **Document Productivity:** Working with Tables and Mail Merge 259

CHAPTER FOUR **Collaboration and Research:** Communicating and Producing Professional Papers 313

Microsoft Office Excel 2013

CHAPTER ONE **Introduction to Excel:** What Is a Spreadsheet? 373

CHAPTER TWO **Formulas and Functions:** Performing Quantitative Analysis 447

CHAPTER THREE **Charts:** Depicting Data Visually 505

CHAPTER FOUR **Datasets and Tables:** Managing Large Volumes of Data 555

Microsoft Office Access 2013

CHAPTER ONE **Introduction to Access:** Finding Your Way Through an Access Database 617

■ CHAPTER TWO **Tables and Queries in Relational Databases:** Designing Databases and Extracting Data 675

■ CHAPTER THREE **Customize, Analyze, and Summarize Query Data:** Creating and Using Queries to Make Decisions 745

■ CHAPTER FOUR **Creating and Using Professional Forms and Reports:** Moving Beyond Tables and Queries 791

Microsoft Office PowerPoint 2013

CHAPTER ONE **Introduction to PowerPoint:** Creating a Basic Presentation 843

CHAPTER TWO **Presentation Development:** Planning and Preparing a Presentation 899

CHAPTER THREE **Presentation Design:** Illustrations and Infographics 943

Acknowledgments

The Exploring team would like to acknowledge and thank all the reviewers who helped us throughout the years by providing us with their invaluable comments, suggestions, and constructive criticism.

We'd like to especially thank our Focus Group attendees and User Diary Reviewers for this edition:

Stephen Z. Jourdan
Auburn University at Montgomery

Ann Rovetto
Horry-Georgetown Technical College

Jacqueline D. Lawson
Henry Ford Community College

Diane L. Smith
Henry Ford Community College

Sven Aelterman
Troy University

Suzanne M. Jeska
County College of Morris

Susan N. Dozier
Tidewater Community College

Robert G. Phipps Jr.
West Virginia University

Mike Michaelson
Palomar College

Mary Beth Tarver
Northwestern State University

Alexandre C. Probst
Colorado Christian University

Phil Nielson
Salt Lake Community College

Carolyn Barren
Macomb Community College

Sue A. McCrory
Missouri State University

Lucy Parakhovnik
California State University, Northridge

Jakie Brown Jr.
Stevenson University

Craig J. Peterson
American InterContinental University

Terry Ray Rigsby
Hill College

Biswadip Ghosh
Metropolitan State University of Denver

Cheryl Sypniewski
Macomb Community College

Lynn Keane
University of South Carolina

Sheila Gionfriddo
Luzerne College

Dick Hewer
Ferris State College

Carolyn Borne
Louisiana State University

Sumathy Chandrashekar
Salisbury University

Laura Marcoulides
Fullerton College

Don Riggs
SUNY Schenectady County Community College

Gary McFall
Purdue University

James Powers
University of Southern Indiana

James Brown
Central Washington University

Brian Powell
West Virginia University

Sherry Lenhart
Terra Community College

Chen Zhang
Bryant University

Nikia Robinson
Indian River State University

Jill Young
Southeast Missouri State University

Debra Hoffman
Southeast Missouri State University

Tommy Lu
Delaware Technical Community College

Mimi Spain
Southern Maine Community College

We'd like to thank everyone who has been involved in reviewing and providing their feedback, including for our previous editions:

Adriana Lumpkin
Midland College

Alan S. Abrahams
Virginia Tech

Ali Berrached
University of Houston–Downtown

Allen Alexander
Delaware Technical & Community College

Andrea Marchese
Maritime College, State University of New York

Andrew Blitz
Broward College; Edison State College

Angel Norman
University of Tennessee, Knoxville

Angela Clark
University of South Alabama

Ann Rovetto
Horry-Georgetown Technical College

Astrid Todd
Guilford Technical Community College

Audrey Gillant
Maritime College, State University of New York

Barbara Stover
Marion Technical College

Barbara Tollinger
Sinclair Community College

Ben Brahim Taha
Auburn University

Beverly Amer
Northern Arizona University

Beverly Fite
Amarillo College

Bonita Volker
Tidewater Community College

Bonnie Homan
San Francisco State University

Brad West
Sinclair Community College

Brian Powell
West Virginia University

Carol Buser
Owens Community College

Carol Roberts
University of Maine

Carolyn Barren
Macomb Community College

Cathy Poyner
Truman State University

Charles Hodgson
Delgado Community College

Cheri Higgins
Illinois State University

Cheryl Hinds
Norfolk State University

Chris Robinson
Northwest State Community College

Cindy Herbert
Metropolitan Community College–Longview

Dana Hooper
University of Alabama

Dana Johnson
North Dakota State University

Daniela Marghitu
Auburn University

David Noel
University of Central Oklahoma

David Pulis
Maritime College, State University of New York

David Thornton
Jacksonville State University

Dawn Medlin
Appalachian State University

Debby Keen
University of Kentucky

Debra Chapman
University of South Alabama

Derrick Huang
Florida Atlantic University

Diana Baran
Henry Ford Community College

Diane Cassidy
The University of North Carolina at Charlotte

Diane Smith
Henry Ford Community College

Don Danner
San Francisco State University

Don Hoggan
Solano College

Doncho Petkov
Eastern Connecticut State University

Donna Ehrhart
State University of New York at Brockport

Elaine Crable
Xavier University

Elizabeth Duett
Delgado Community College

Erhan Uskup
Houston Community College–Northwest

Eric Martin
University of Tennessee

Erika Nadas
Wilbur Wright College

Floyd Winters
Manatee Community College

Frank Lucente
Westmoreland County Community College

G. Jan Wilms
Union University

Gail Cope
Sinclair Community College

Gary DeLorenzo
California University of Pennsylvania

Gary Garrison
Belmont University

George Cassidy
Sussex County Community College

Gerald Braun
Xavier University

Gerald Burgess
Western New Mexico University

Gladys Swindler
Fort Hays State University

Heith Hennel
Valencia Community College

Henry Rudzinski
Central Connecticut State University

Irene Joos
La Roche College

Iwona Rusin
Baker College; Davenport University

J. Roberto Guzman
San Diego Mesa College

Jan Wilms
Union University

Jane Stam
Onondaga Community College

Janet Bringhurst
Utah State University

Jeanette Dix
Ivy Tech Community College

Jennifer Day
Sinclair Community College

Jill Canine
Ivy Tech Community College

Jim Chaffee
The University of Iowa Tippie College of Business

Joanne Lazirko
University of Wisconsin–Milwaukee

Jodi Milliner
Kansas State University

John Hollenbeck
Blue Ridge Community College

John Seydel
Arkansas State University

Judith A. Scheeren
Westmoreland County Community College

Judith Brown
The University of Memphis

Juliana Cypert
Tarrant County College

Kamaljeet Sanghera
George Mason University

Karen Priestly
Northern Virginia Community College

Karen Ravan
Spartanburg Community College

Kathleen Brenan
Ashland University

Ken Busbee
Houston Community College

Kent Foster
Winthrop University

Kevin Anderson
Solano Community College

Kim Wright
The University of Alabama

Kristen Hockman
University of Missouri–Columbia

Kristi Smith
Allegany College of Maryland

Laura McManamon
University of Dayton

Leanne Chun
Leeward Community College

Lee McClain
Western Washington University

Linda D. Collins
Mesa Community College

Linda Johnsonius
Murray State University

Linda Lau
Longwood University

Linda Theus
Jackson State Community College

Linda Williams
Marion Technical College

Lisa Miller
University of Central Oklahoma

Lister Horn
Pensacola Junior College

Lixin Tao
Pace University

Loraine Miller
Cayuga Community College

Lori Kielty
Central Florida Community College

Lorna Wells
Salt Lake Community College

Lorraine Sauchin
Duquesne University

Lucy Parakhovnik (Parker)
California State University, Northridge

Lynn Mancini
Delaware Technical Community College

Mackinzee Escamilla
South Plains College

Marcia Welch
Highline Community College

Margaret McManus
Northwest Florida State College

Margaret Warrick
Allan Hancock College

Marilyn Hibbert
Salt Lake Community College

Mark Choman
Luzerne County Community College

Mary Duncan
University of Missouri–St. Louis

Melissa Nemeth
Indiana University-Purdue University Indianapolis

Melody Alexander
Ball State University

Michael Douglas
University of Arkansas at Little Rock

Michael Dunklebarger
Alamance Community College

Michael G. Skaff
College of the Sequoias

Michele Budnovitch
Pennsylvania College of Technology

Mike Jochen
East Stroudsburg University

Mike Scroggins
Missouri State University

Muhammed Badamas
Morgan State University

NaLisa Brown
University of the Ozarks

Nancy Grant
Community College of Allegheny County–South Campus

Nanette Lareau
University of Arkansas Community College–Morrilton

Pam Brune
Chattanooga State Community College

Pam Uhlenkamp
Iowa Central Community College

Patrick Smith
Marshall Community and Technical College

Paul Addison
Ivy Tech Community College

Paula Ruby
Arkansas State University

Peggy Burrus
Red Rocks Community College

Peter Ross
SUNY Albany

Philip H. Nielson
Salt Lake Community College

Ralph Hooper
University of Alabama

Ranette Halverson
Midwestern State University

Richard Blamer
John Carroll University

Richard Cacace
Pensacola Junior College

Richard Hewer
Ferris State University

Rob Murray
Ivy Tech Community College

Robert Dušek
Northern Virginia Community College

Robert Sindt
Johnson County Community College

Robert Warren
Delgado Community College

Rocky Belcher
Sinclair Community College

Roger Pick
University of Missouri at Kansas City

Ronnie Creel
Troy University

Rosalie Westerberg
Clover Park Technical College

Ruth Neal
Navarro College

Sandra Thomas
Troy University

Sheila Gionfriddo
Luzerne County Community College

Sherrie Geitgey
Northwest State Community College

Sophia Wilberscheid
Indian River State College

Sophie Lee
California State University, Long Beach

Stacy Johnson
Iowa Central Community College

Stephanie Kramer
Northwest State Community College

Stephen Jourdan
Auburn University Montgomery

Steven Schwarz
Raritan Valley Community College

Sue McCrory
Missouri State University

Susan Fuschetto
Cerritos College

Susan Medlin
UNC Charlotte

Suzan Spitzberg
Oakton Community College

Sven Aelterman
Troy University

Sylvia Brown
Midland College

Tanya Patrick
Clackamas Community College

Terri Holly
Indian River State College

Thomas Rienzo
Western Michigan University

Tina Johnson
Midwestern State University

Tommy Lu
Delaware Technical and Community College

Troy S. Cash
NorthWest Arkansas Community College

Vicki Robertson
Southwest Tennessee Community

Weifeng Chen
California University of Pennsylvania

Wes Anthony
Houston Community College

William Ayen
University of Colorado at Colorado Springs

Wilma Andrews
Virginia Commonwealth University

Yvonne Galusha
University of Iowa

Special thanks to our development and technical team:

Barbara Stover

Cheryl Slavick

Elizabeth Lockley

Heather Hetzler

Jennifer Lynn

Joyce Nielsen

Linda Pogue

Lisa Bucki

Lori Damanti

Mara Zebest

Susan Fry

Preface

The Exploring Series and You

Exploring is Pearson's Office Application series that requires students like you to think "beyond the point and click." In this edition, we have worked to restructure the Exploring experience around the way you, today's modern student, actually use your resources.

The goal of Exploring is, as it has always been, to go further than teaching just the steps to accomplish a task—the series provides the theoretical foundation for you to understand when and why to apply a skill.

As a result, you achieve a deeper understanding of each application and can apply this critical thinking beyond Office and the classroom.

You are practical students, focused on what you need to do to be successful in this course and beyond, and want to be as efficient as possible. Exploring has evolved to meet you where you are and help you achieve success efficiently. Pearson has paid attention to the habits of students today, how you get information, how you are motivated to do well in class, and what your future goals look like. We asked you and your peers for acceptance of new tools we designed to address these points, and you responded with a resounding "YES!"

Here Is What We Learned About You

You are goal-oriented. You want a good grade in this course—so we rethought how Exploring works so that you can learn the how and why behind the skills in this course to be successful now. You also want to be successful in your future career—so we used motivating case studies to show relevance of these skills to your future careers and incorporated Soft Skills, Collaboration, and Analysis Cases in this edition to set you up for success in the future.

You read, prepare, and study differently than students used to. You use textbooks like a tool—you want to easily identify what you need to know and learn it efficiently. We have added key features such as Step Icons, Hands-On Exercise Videos, and tracked everything via page numbers that allow you to navigate the content efficiently, making the concepts accessible and creating a map to success for you to follow.

You go to college now with a different set of skills than students did five years ago. The new edition of Exploring moves you beyond the basics of the software at a faster pace, without sacrificing coverage of the fundamental skills that you need to know. This ensures that you will be engaged from page 1 to the end of the book.

You and your peers have diverse learning styles. With this in mind, we broadened our definition of "student resources" to include Compass, an online skill database; movable Student Reference cards; Hands-On Exercise videos to provide a secondary lecture-like option of review; Soft Skills video exercises to illustrate important non-technical skills; and the most powerful online homework and assessment tool around with a direct 1:1 content match with the Exploring Series, MyITLab. Exploring will be accessible to all students, regardless of learning style.

Providing You with a Map to Success to Move Beyond the Point and Click

All of these changes and additions will provide you with an easy and efficient path to follow to be successful in this course, regardless of your learning style or any existing knowledge you have at the outset. Our goal is to keep you more engaged in both the hands-on and conceptual sides, helping you to achieve a higher level of understanding that will guarantee you success in this course and in your future career. In addition to the vision and experience of the series creator, Robert T. Grauer, we have assembled a tremendously talented team of Office Applications authors who have devoted themselves to teaching you the ins and outs of Microsoft Word, Excel, Access, and PowerPoint. Led in this edition by series editor Mary Anne Poatsy, the whole team is equally dedicated to providing you with a **map to success** to support the Exploring mission of **moving you beyond the point and click**.

Key Features

- **White Pages/Yellow Pages** clearly distinguish the theory (white pages) from the skills covered in the Hands-On Exercises (yellow pages) so students always know what they are supposed to be doing.
- **Enhanced Objective Mapping** enables students to follow a directed path through each chapter, from the objectives list at the chapter opener through the exercises in the end of chapter.
  - **Objectives List:** This provides a simple list of key objectives covered in the chapter. This includes page numbers so students can skip between objectives where they feel they need the most help.
  - **Step Icons:** These icons appear in the white pages and reference the step numbers in the Hands-On Exercises, providing a correlation between the two so students can easily find conceptual help when they are working hands-on and need a refresher.
  - **Quick Concepts Check:** A series of questions that appear briefly at the end of each white page section. These questions cover the most essential concepts in the white pages required for students to be successful in working the Hands-On Exercises. Page numbers are included for easy reference to help students locate the answers.
  - **Chapter Objectives Review:** Appears toward the end of the chapter and reviews all important concepts throughout the chapter. Newly designed in an easy-to-read bulleted format.
- **Key Terms Matching:** A new exercise that requires students to match key terms to their definitions. This requires students to work actively with this important vocabulary and prove conceptual understanding.
- **Case Study** presents a scenario for the chapter, creating a story that ties the Hands-On Exercises together.

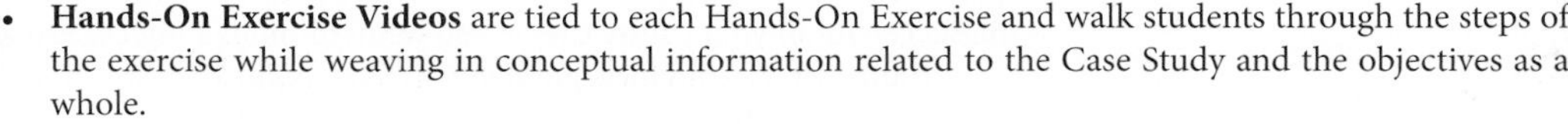

- **Hands-On Exercise Videos** are tied to each Hands-On Exercise and walk students through the steps of the exercise while weaving in conceptual information related to the Case Study and the objectives as a whole.

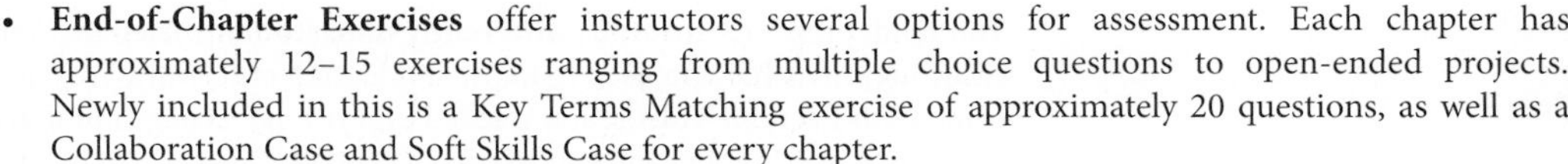

- **End-of-Chapter Exercises** offer instructors several options for assessment. Each chapter has approximately 12–15 exercises ranging from multiple choice questions to open-ended projects. Newly included in this is a Key Terms Matching exercise of approximately 20 questions, as well as a Collaboration Case and Soft Skills Case for every chapter.

- **Enhanced Mid-Level Exercises** include a **Creative Case** (for PowerPoint and Word), which allows students some flexibility and creativity, not being bound by a definitive solution, and an **Analysis Case** (for Excel and Access), which requires students to interpret the data they are using to answer an analytic question, as well as **Discover Steps**, which encourage students to use Help or to problem-solve to accomplish a task.

- **MyITLab** provides an auto-graded homework, tutorial, and assessment solution that is built to match the book content exactly. Every Hands-On Exercise is available as a simulation training. Every Capstone Exercise and most Mid-Level Exercises are available as live-in-the-application Grader projects. Icons are included throughout the text to denote which exercises are included.

Instructor Resources

The Instructor's Resource Center, available at **www.pearsonhighered.com**, includes the following:

- **Instructor Manual** provides an overview of all available resources as well as student data and solution files for every exercise.
- **Solution Files with Scorecards** assist with grading the Hands-On Exercises and end-of-chapter exercises.
- **Prepared Exams** allow instructors to assess all skills covered in a chapter with a single project.
- **Rubrics** for Mid-Level Creative Cases and Beyond the Classroom Cases in Microsoft® Word format enable instructors to customize the assignments for their classes.
- **PowerPoint® Presentations** with notes for each chapter are included for out-of-class study or review.
- **Lesson Plans** provide a detailed blueprint to achieve chapter learning objectives and outcomes.
- **Objectives Lists** map chapter objectives to Hands-On Exercises and end-of-chapter exercises.
- **Multiple Choice and Key Terms Matching Answer Keys**
- **Test Bank** provides objective-based questions for every chapter.
- **Grader Projects** textual versions of auto-graded assignments for Grader.
- **Additional Projects** provide more assignment options for instructors.
- **Syllabus Templates**
- **Scripted Lectures** offer an in-class lecture guide for instructors to mirror the Hands-On Exercises.
- **Assignment Sheet**
- **File Guide**

Student Resources

Companion Web Site

www.pearsonhighered.com/exploring offers expanded IT resources and self-student tools for students to use for each chapter, including:

- Online Chapter Review
- Glossary
- Chapter Objectives Review
- Web Resources
- Student Data Files

In addition, the Companion Web Site is now the site for Premium Media, including the videos for the Exploring Series:

- Hands-On Exercise Videos*
- Soft Skills Exercise Videos*
- Audio PPTs*

*Access code required for these premium resources.

Student Reference Cards

A two-sided card for each application provides students with a visual summary of information and tips specific to each application.

Windows 8

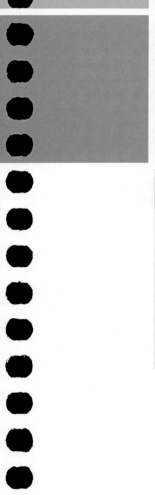

Getting Started with Windows 8

CHAPTER 1

OBJECTIVES

AFTER YOU READ THIS CHAPTER, YOU WILL BE ABLE TO:

1. Understand the Start screen p. 2
2. Configure the Start screen p. 4
3. Run Windows 8 apps p. 7
4. Close apps p. 9
5. Understand the desktop p. 9
6. Manage Windows 8 apps and windows p. 14
7. Identify Windows accessories p. 24
8. Work with security settings and software p. 27
9. Perform a search p. 36
10. Use targeted searches p. 36
11. Get help p. 37

CASE STUDY | Cedar Grove Elementary School

Your good friend recently graduated with a degree in Elementary Education and is excited to begin her first job as a fifth-grade teacher at Cedar Grove Elementary School. The school has a computer lab for all students as well as a computer system in each classroom. The computers were acquired through a state technology grant so they are new models running Windows 8. Your friend's lesson plans must include a unit on operating system basics and an introduction to application software. Because you have a degree in Computer Information Systems, she has called on you for assistance with the lesson plans. She also hopes you will occasionally visit her classroom to help present the material.

You cannot assume that all students have been exposed to computers at home, especially to those configured with Windows 8. Your material will need to include very basic instruction on Windows 8, along with a general overview of application software. You will probably focus on application software that is included with Windows 8, including WordPad, Paint, and Calculator. Your friend's lesson plans must be completed right away, so you are on a short timeline but are excited about helping students learn!

Windows 8 Fundamentals

Computer activities that you enjoy might include e-mail, games, social networking, and digital photo management. If you have a computer at work, you probably use software such as spreadsheet, database, word processing, and other job-specific applications. Those applications are necessary for your enjoyment or career, but they would not be possible without an ***operating system***. The operating system is software that directs computer activities such as checking all components, managing system resources, and communicating with application software.

Windows 8 is a Microsoft operating system released in 2012 and is available on laptops, desktops, and tablet computers. Because you are likely to encounter Windows 8 on computers at school, work, and home, it is well worth your time to explore and learn about its computer management and security features. In this section, you will explore the Start screen and desktop, the two areas in which you will spend the most time when working with Windows 8. You will also learn to customize the Start screen and desktop to suit your needs.

Understanding the Start Screen

Windows 8 is a departure from previous versions of Windows because it is designed to operate on touch-screen devices in addition to traditional laptops and desktops. To enable Windows 8 to function on all types of devices, there are often three different ways to accomplish tasks in Windows 8:

1. Using a mouse
2. Touching the screen (on touch-enabled devices)
3. Using keystrokes

The method you use depends on the type of device you are using and, to a large extent, on your personal preferences. In this text, we will focus mainly on mouse and keystroke commands because initially most users will be using Windows 8 with mouse-activated devices. If you are using a touch-screen device, you should refer to the common touch gestures shown in Figure 1.1. For instance, when an instruction in this text says to click a screen element, on a touch-screen device, you would tap the screen element with your finger.

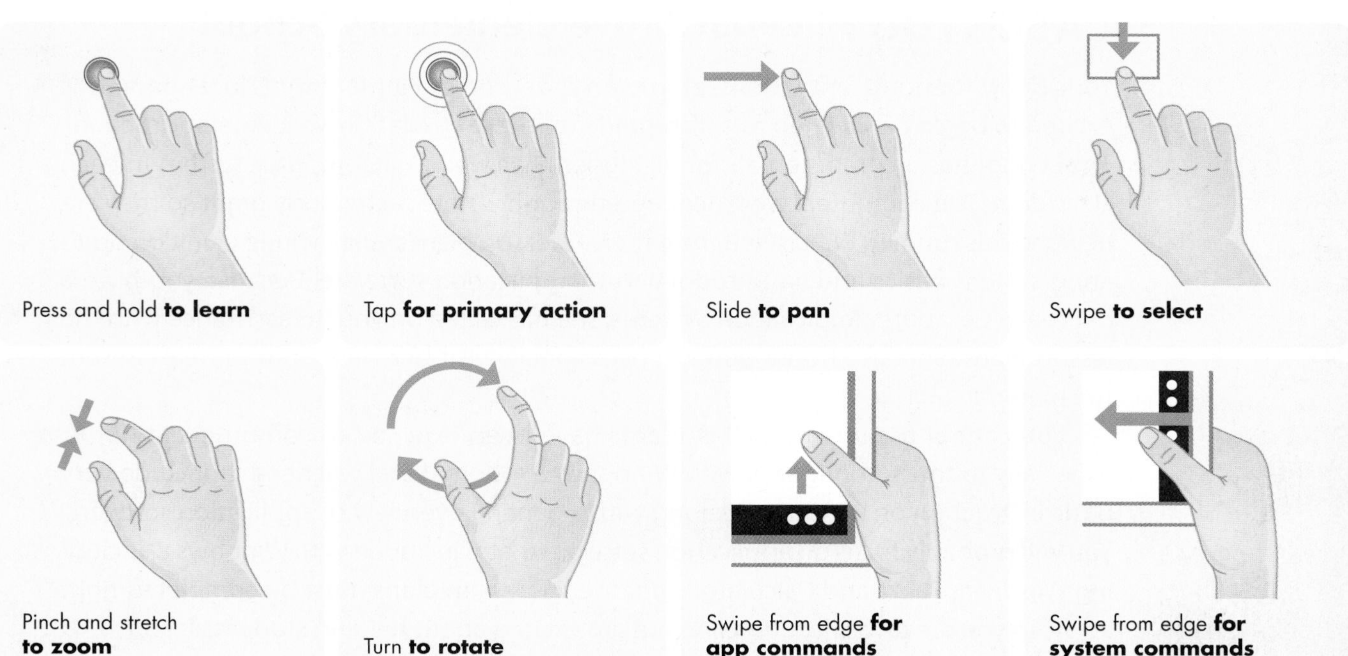

FIGURE 1.1 Common Touch Gestures in Windows 8

The ***Start screen***, as shown in Figure 1.2, is the display that you see after you turn on your computer and respond to any username and password prompts. Windows 8 defaults to logging you in with a Windows ID, although you can also log in as a local user. However, a local user does not gain all the benefits of being connected to Microsoft's resources on the Internet, so it is preferable to log in with a Windows ID. If you do not have a Windows ID, Windows 8 will guide you through obtaining one and it is free. As the name implies, the Start screen is the place where you begin all of your computing activities. The Windows 8 Start screen provides you with access to your most used applications in one convenient location.

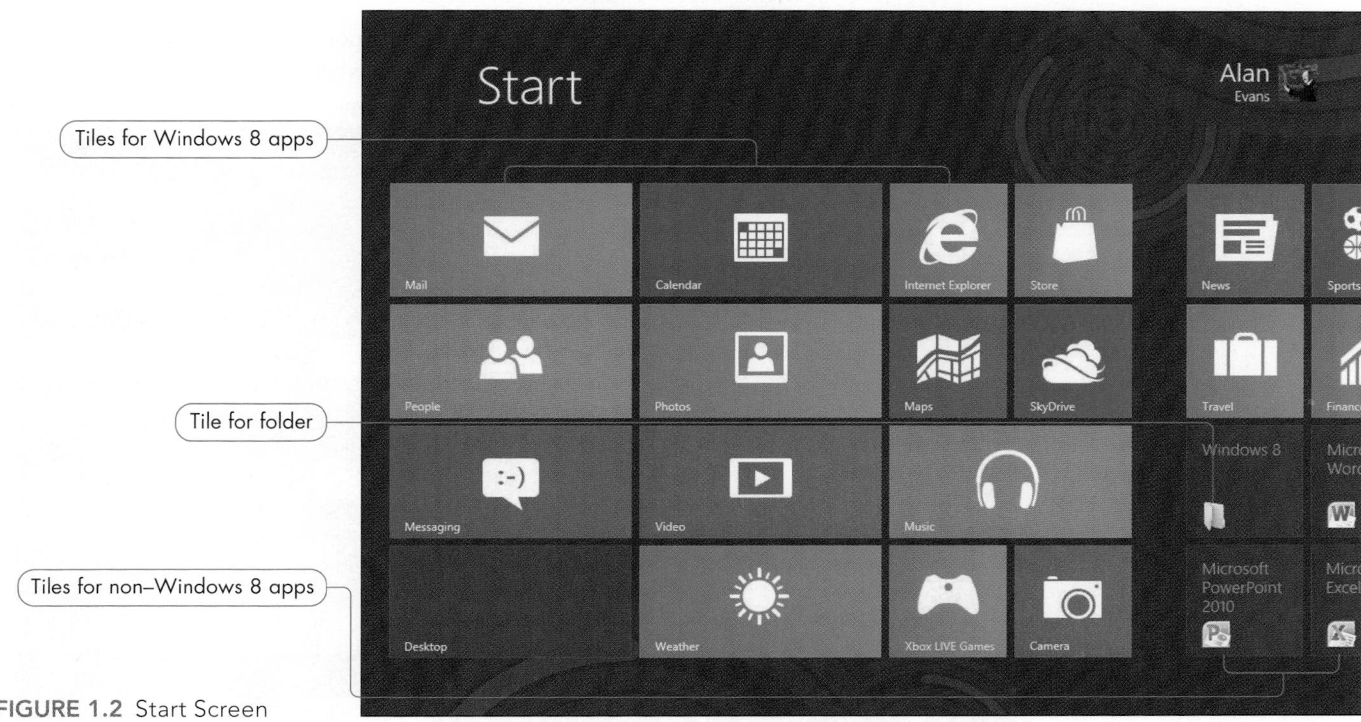

FIGURE 1.2 Start Screen

Identify Start Screen Components

The ***Windows 8 interface*** is the name given to the Start screen and features large type with clean, readable block images (called ***tiles***) inspired by metropolitan service signs such as those found on bus stations and subways. ***Windows 8 apps*** are applications specifically designed to run in the Start screen interface of Windows 8. The tiles represent programs, files, folders, or other items related to your computer. When you log in to Windows 8 with your Windows ID, you should see the same Start screen configuration no matter what Windows 8 device you are using, because your Windows ID stores your preferences and settings for your Start screen on the Internet. Your work computer and your home computer should look exactly the same.

Windows 8 apps are either preinstalled with Windows 8 (such as Photos, Messaging, and Calendar) or are available for download from the Windows Store (Microsoft's apps marketplace). You can launch Windows 8 apps by clicking or tapping their tiles on the Start screen. Applications designed for previous versions of Windows, such as Microsoft Office 2010, can also be installed and will run in Windows 8. Tiles for older versions of software look more transparent than Windows 8 tiles.

Display the Charms Bar

If you have been using previous versions of Windows, one thing you may notice that is missing right away is the Start button that used to be in the bottom left-hand corner of the desktop. The Start button is still used in Windows 8 but its functionality and position has changed. In Windows 8, the ***Charms bar*** has been introduced, as shown in Figure 1.3. The

Charms bar provides quick access to actions that most users perform frequently. To access the Charms bar, move your mouse to the top- or bottom-right corner of the screen or press the Windows key+C. Five icons are on the Charms bar:

- Search—takes you to the Search screen to facilitate locating applications and files.
- Share—accesses tools to allow you to easily share information with others within the application that is running.
- Start—takes you to the Start screen.
- Devices—provides access and control of devices connected to your computer.
- Settings—provides different options for configuring your computer which change depending upon which application you are accessing when you display the Charms bar.

FIGURE 1.3 Charms Bar

Configuring the Start Screen

STEP 3» Not everyone uses Windows in the same fashion. You probably will want to set up your Start screen so the apps (programs) you use most often are readily available. Windows 8 makes it easy to add and remove application tiles on the Start screen, to group tiles, name the groups, and to display tiles to access areas of the computer to which you need frequent access, such as folders which you can use to organize files.

For non–Windows 8 applications you need to install, such as the Firefox browser, you may find you need to add a tile to the Start screen to access these apps. Adding a tile to the Start screen is known as ***pinning*** the app to the screen (see Figure 1.4). To pin an application to the Start screen:

- Display the Start screen by pressing the Windows key or clicking the Start button on the Charms bar.
- Right-click any blank area of the Start screen and click the *All apps* icon located in the bottom-right corner of the screen. This takes you to the Apps screen.
- Find the application that you wish to pin to the Start screen and right-click the app. This displays the options bar at the bottom of the screen.
- Click the *Pin to Start* icon. An icon for the app will now display on the Start screen.

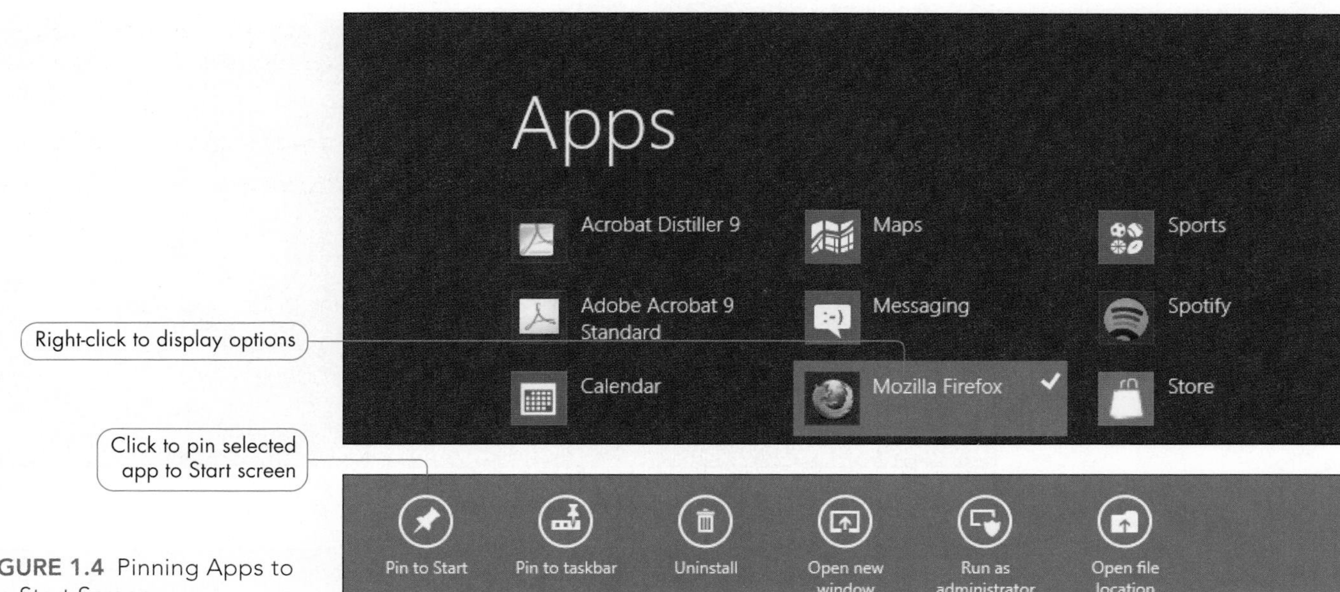

FIGURE 1.4 Pinning Apps to the Start Screen

However, when you view the Start screen, you may not see the tile for the program you just added. This is because Windows adds the tile at the very end of your app tiles, so you may have to scroll right to find the new tile you added. Tiles on the Start screen are organized in groups separated by a small amount of dividing space, as shown in Figure 1.5. You can easily move tiles from one group to another by clicking a tile and dragging it into another group. Or you can rearrange tiles in a group by dragging them around within the group. But what if you want to create a new group?

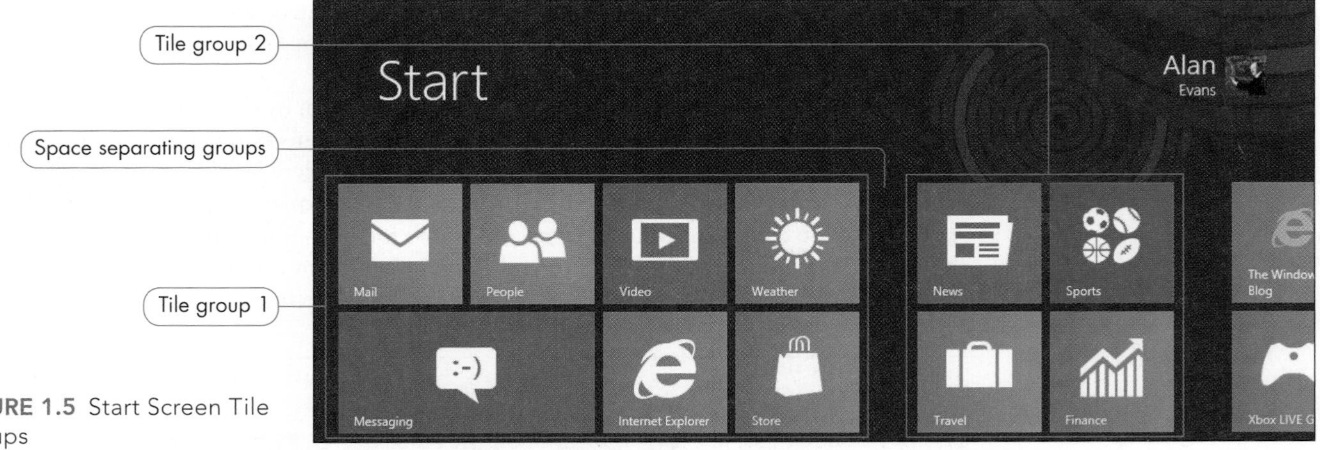

FIGURE 1.5 Start Screen Tile Groups

To create a new group of tiles, click and drag the first tile for the new group to the space to the left or right of an existing tile group, as shown in Figure 1.6. A light grey bar displays, indicating where the new group will be located. Release the mouse and the tile will now be in its own new group.

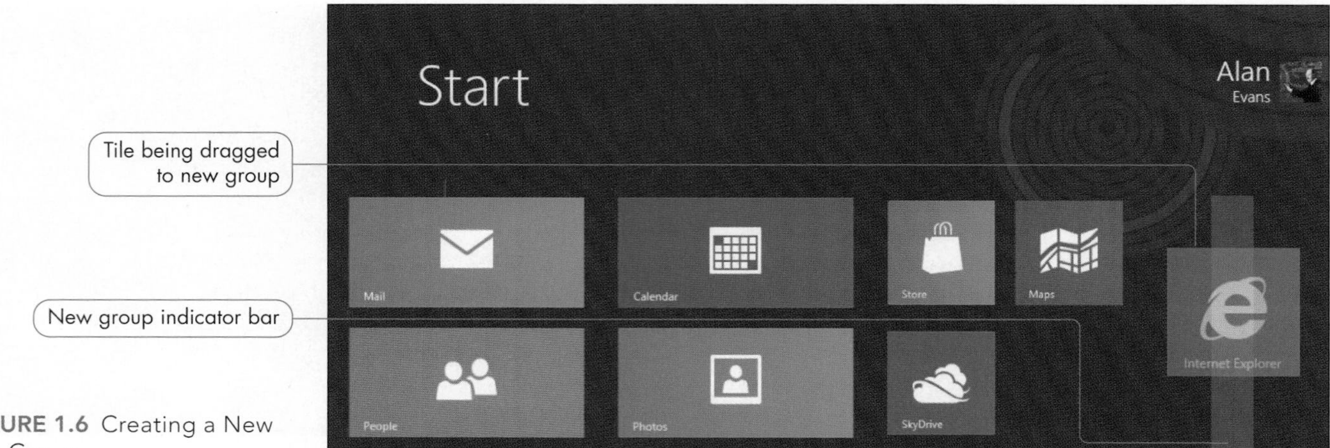

FIGURE 1.6 Creating a New Tile Group

TIP Name Tile Groups

You can also name groups, which makes it easier to keep track of and find similar apps. Click the minus sign in the bottom-right corner of the Start screen. This zooms the Start screen out so you can see more tiles. Right-click the group of tiles you wish to name and click the Name group icon in the bottom-left corner. Then enter a name for the group in the dialog box that displays. Your group name will display above the group of tiles on the Start screen.

Some tiles are small and others are large on the default Start screen. You can change the size of the tiles by right-clicking them and selecting either the larger or smaller icon as appropriate. Also, right-clicking a tile provides you with the option of removing the tile for a program you will not use frequently from the Start screen. Clicking the *Unpin from Start* icon will remove the tile from your Start screen.

STEP 4» You can personalize your Start screen to a limited extent by changing the colors and patterns displayed on it. On the Start screen, display the Charms bar, click the Settings option, and then select Change PC Settings at the bottom of the screen. This takes you to the PC settings screen, as shown in Figure 1.7. If you click the Personalize option and then the *Start screen* link, you can change the patterns and colors for your Start screen. You can also access the settings for your Account picture and Lock screen from the Personalize screen as well. These are just a few of the settings. You can explore other settings on your own.

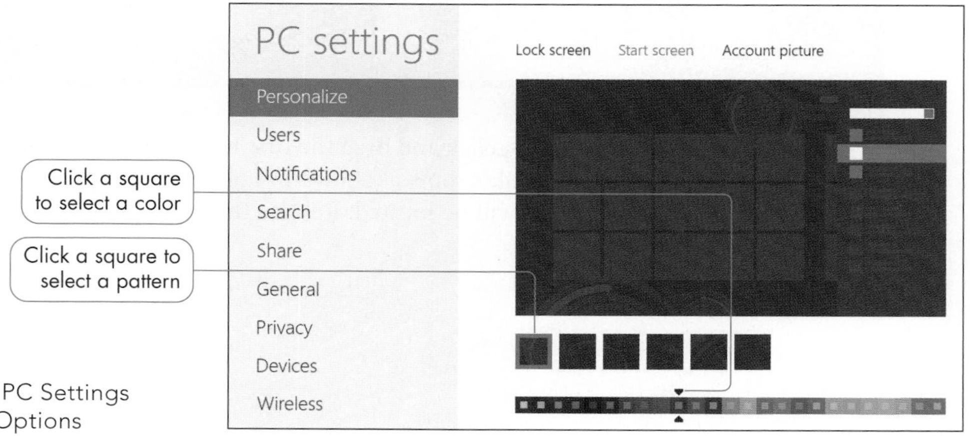

FIGURE 1.7 PC Settings Personalize Options

Running Windows 8 Apps

To launch an app from the Start screen, merely click the app tile. Windows 8 apps, such as Internet Explorer 10, are displayed full screen, without the distractions of borders or controls (such as scroll-bars or menus). Notice that unlike non–Windows 8 apps, such as Firefox shown in Figure 1.8, there are no window borders or menus visible as the application fills the entire screen. This design was implemented to provide advantages on devices with smaller screens such as tablets. Controls and settings are contained on ***app bars***, such as the Tabs bar and Address bar (Figure 1.9), which float on a screen above the app when you summon them or you need them. Right-clicking a Windows 8 app screen displays available app bars such as the Tabs and Address bars.

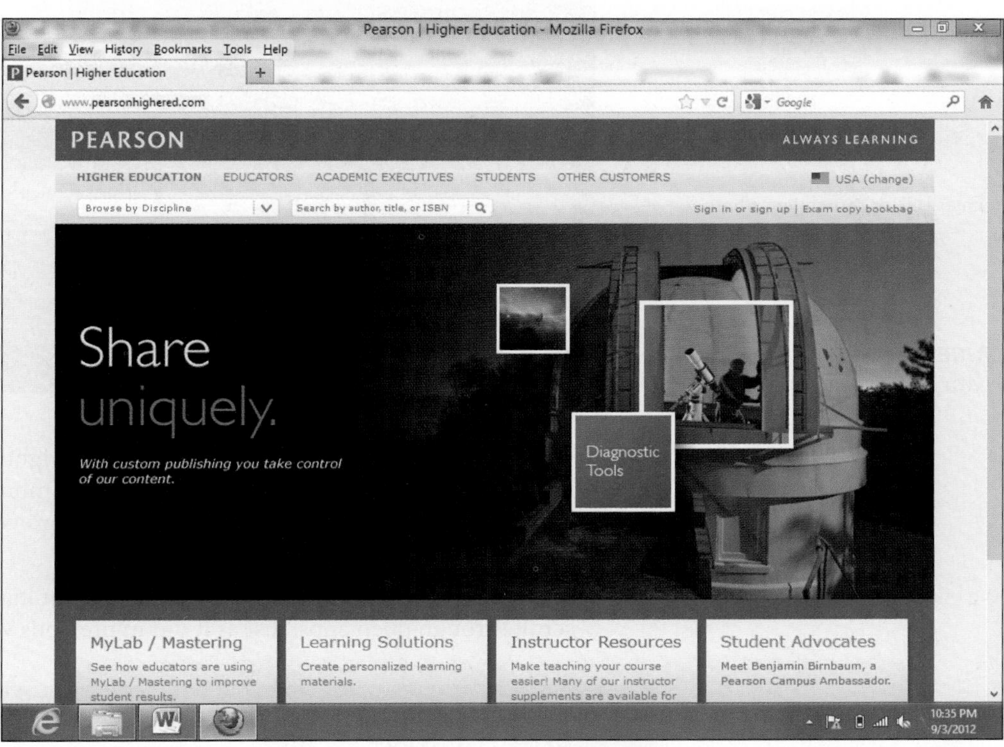

FIGURE 1.8 Firefox (non–Windows 8 app)

Click the plus sign on the Tabs bar to open a new tab. Enter URLs or search terms in the box on the Address bar at the bottom of the screen. If there is a Web site that you use frequently, you may wish to create a tile on the Start screen to access it immediately. Just click the *Pin to Start* icon on the Address bar to create a tile for the currently displayed Web site on the Start screen.

STEP 1

Switching between open applications is relatively easy:

- If you want to go back to the last program or screen you were using, just point your pointer to the top-left corner of the screen and drag your mouse from the left. Drag the thumbnail image of your previous program to the middle of your screen and it will be available.

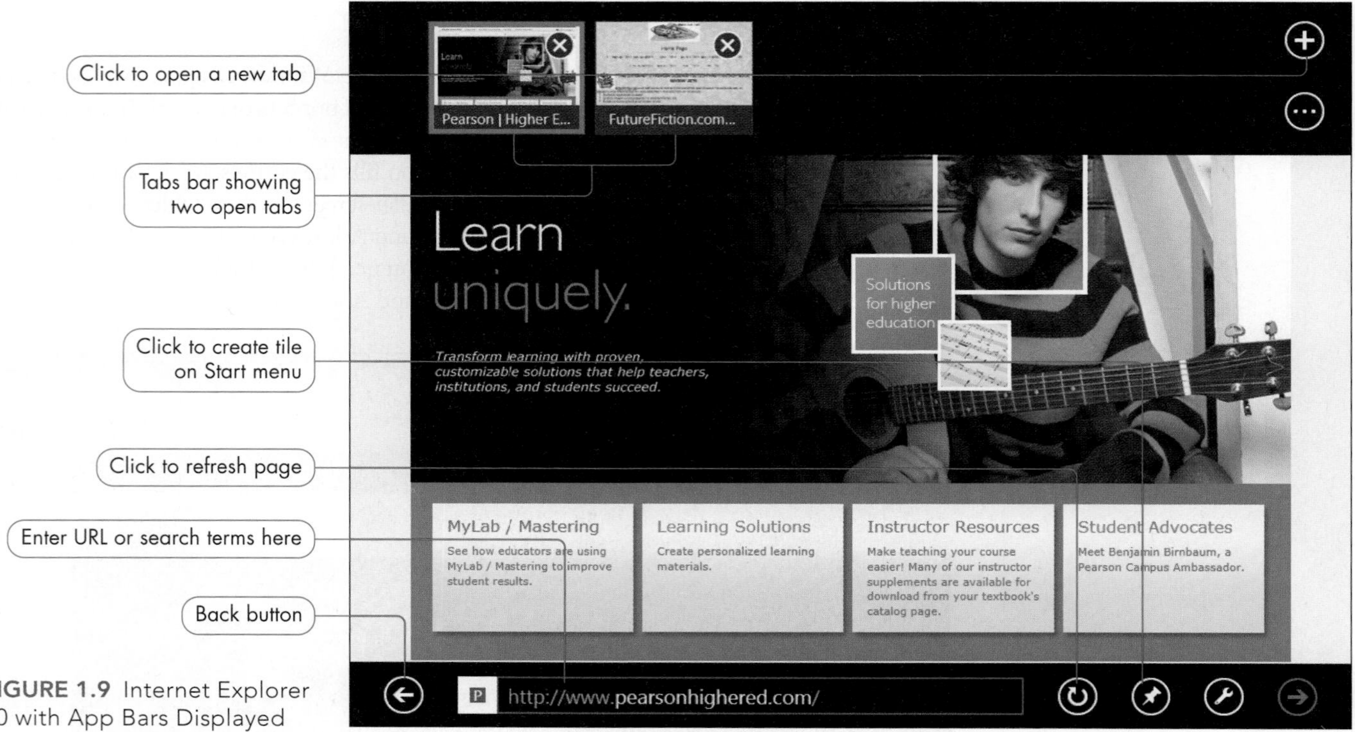

FIGURE 1.9 Internet Explorer 10 with App Bars Displayed

- For a list of open programs—so you can jump right to the correct one—position your pointer in the top-left corner until the thumbnail displays, then move the pointer down to display a list of thumbnails of previous programs called a ***Switch list*** (see Figure 1.10).
- Alternatively, pressing the Alt and Tab keys simultaneously will also allow you to scroll through open apps, just as it did in previous versions of Windows.

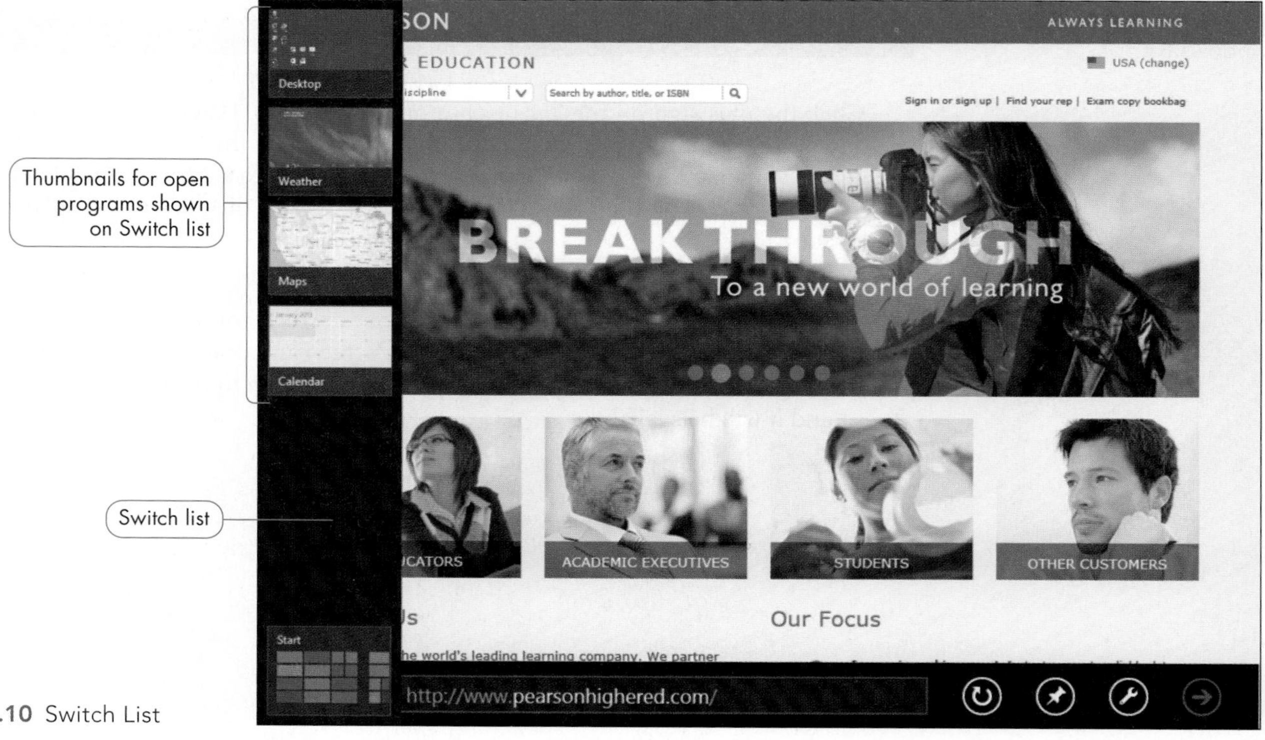

FIGURE 1.10 Switch List

In previous versions of Windows, you could display multiple windows simultaneously. With Windows 8, you can only display two apps on the screen at once with a feature known as ***snap***. You can snap an app to the left or right side of the screen and display it alongside the current app by right-clicking the app's thumbnail in the Switch list and selecting *Snap left* or *Snap right* from the shortcut menu. Figure 1.11 shows the weather app snapped to the left side of the screen with Internet Explorer.

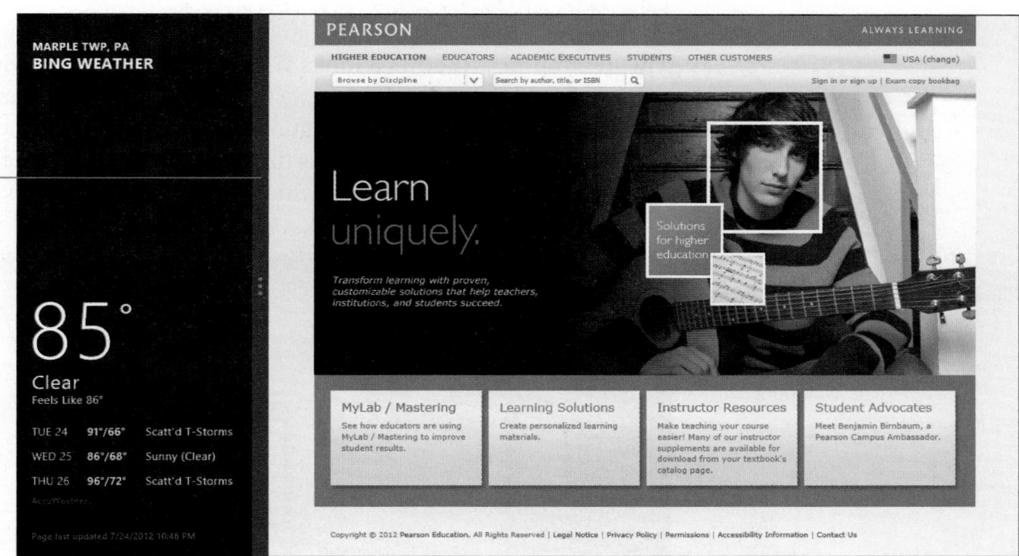

FIGURE 1.11 Snapping Apps

To remove one of the apps from the screen, move your pointer in between the apps until it turns into a double-headed arrow, then click and drag the pointer either left or right to remove the appropriate app.

Closing Apps

When Windows 8 apps are not displayed on the screen, Windows will suspend them temporarily so they do not use much memory or power. Therefore, theoretically, you do not ever need to shut down Windows 8 apps. However, most people prefer not to have endless apps running, and it may be inconvenient to scroll through a huge list of running apps to find the one you want.

To close a Windows 8 app, you do not need to click an X or closing icon. Instead, you can close a Windows 8 app from within the app, by pressing Alt+F4. Alternatively, you can move your pointer to the top of the screen until it turns into a hand, then click and drag down. The app will shrink to a small window. Drag it down to the bottom of the screen and release the mouse button to close the app. Right-clicking a thumbnail of the app on the Switch list also allows you to close an app.

Understanding the Desktop

If you have worked with a previous version of Windows, you are used to seeing the desktop when you first start up Windows. In Windows 8, the Start screen is your initial access, but a modified version of the desktop still exists. It is called a ***desktop*** because it serves the purpose of a desk, on which you can manage tasks and complete paperwork. Just as you can work with multiple projects on a desk, you can work with several software applications, each occupying a ***window***, or area of space, on the desktop.

Unlike previous versions of Windows, where you only worked on the desktop, in Windows 8, you will work both in the Start screen (Windows 8) environment and on the desktop depending upon the app you are using. If you are using a Windows 8 app, you will be working in the Start screen environment. However, programs and apps that have not been optimized for Windows 8, such as Microsoft Office 2010, will run on the desktop. To get to the desktop, click the Desktop tile on the Start screen or press the Windows key+D. You should expect to be jumping back and forth between the Start screen and the desktop frequently as you use Windows 8.

Identify Desktop Components

The desktop in Windows 8 looks very much like the desktop in Windows 7, except there is no Start button! Those pictures, or ***icons***, represent programs, files, folders, or other items related to your computer (see Figure 1.12). You can easily add and remove icons so that the desktop includes only those items that are important to you or that you access often. You can even include desktop folders in which you can organize files and programs.

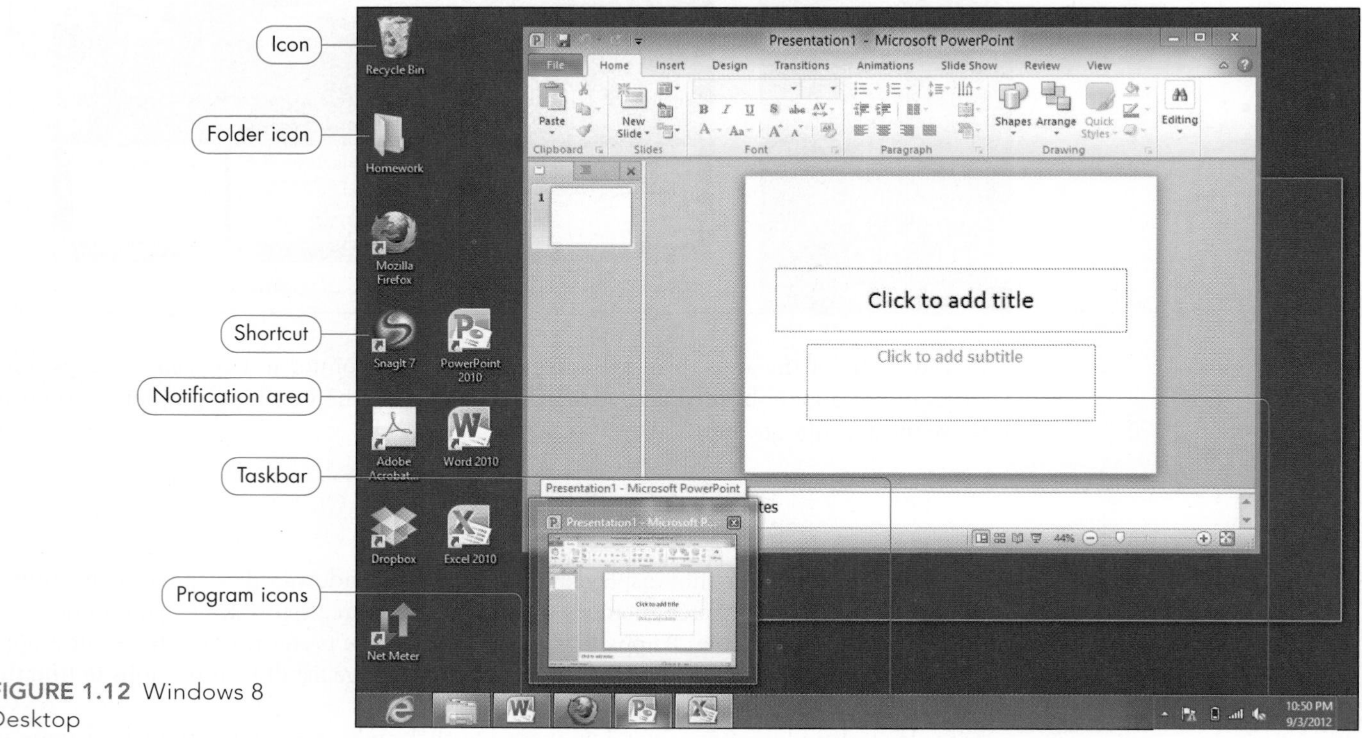

FIGURE 1.12 Windows 8 Desktop

Icons provide quick access to programs or features just like the tiles on the Start screen. Some icons, which are identified by a small arrow in the bottom left-hand corner, are ***shortcuts*** to programs. Another element on the desktop screen is a folder icon. A computer provides a large amount of storage space, some of which you might use to house files, such as documents, worksheets, and digital photos related to particular projects or work-related activities. Because the desktop is so convenient to access, you could create a folder, identified by a folder icon, on the desktop to organize such files. If you save files to the desktop, you should organize them in desktop folders. That way, the desktop will not become too cluttered and you can easily find related files later. You can easily add icons to the desktop, but the way in which you add an icon depends on the icon's purpose. You can also delete and rename icons, as described below.

- *To add a program shortcut to the desktop*, you must first locate the program. Right-click an empty area of the desktop, point to New, and then click Shortcut. This will open the Create Shortcut dialog box. Click Browse and navigate to the folder that contains the program for which you wish to create a shortcut. Click the program file and click OK. Then click Next. Type a name for the shortcut in the box and click Finish to place the shortcut icon on your desktop.

- *To add a folder to the desktop*, right-click an empty area of the desktop. Point to New and click Folder. Type a folder name and press Enter.
- *To delete an icon*, right-click the icon and click Delete. Deleting a program shortcut icon does not remove, or uninstall, the program itself. You simply remove the desktop pointer (shortcut) to the program.
- *To rename an icon*, right-click the icon and click Rename. Type the new name and press Enter.

TIP Auto Arrange Icons

A desktop can easily become cluttered and disorganized. To avoid clutter, make sure that you maintain only desktop icons that are accessed often or that are important to keep handy. To neatly organize the desktop, you can auto arrange the icons. Right-click an empty area of the desktop, point to View, and then click *Auto arrange icons* (unless *Auto arrange icons* already has a checkmark). Icons are maintained in straight columns and cannot be moved out of line.

Explore the Taskbar

The Windows Desktop provides a tool for keeping track of open computer programs or files—the ***taskbar***. The taskbar is a long horizontal bar located at the bottom of the desktop. The taskbar is the location of the toolbars, open window buttons, and the ***Notification area***.

The taskbar simplifies the task of keeping track of what programs and files are open on the desktop. Every open window has a corresponding icon on the taskbar. Icons represent programs, such as Excel and PowerPoint. To move from one window to another, simply click the taskbar icon representing the window. Figure 1.13 shows two windows open on the desktop, with corresponding taskbar program icons. Although several windows can be open at one time, only one is active (in front of other windows). If several programs are open, you will see a taskbar icon for each open window.

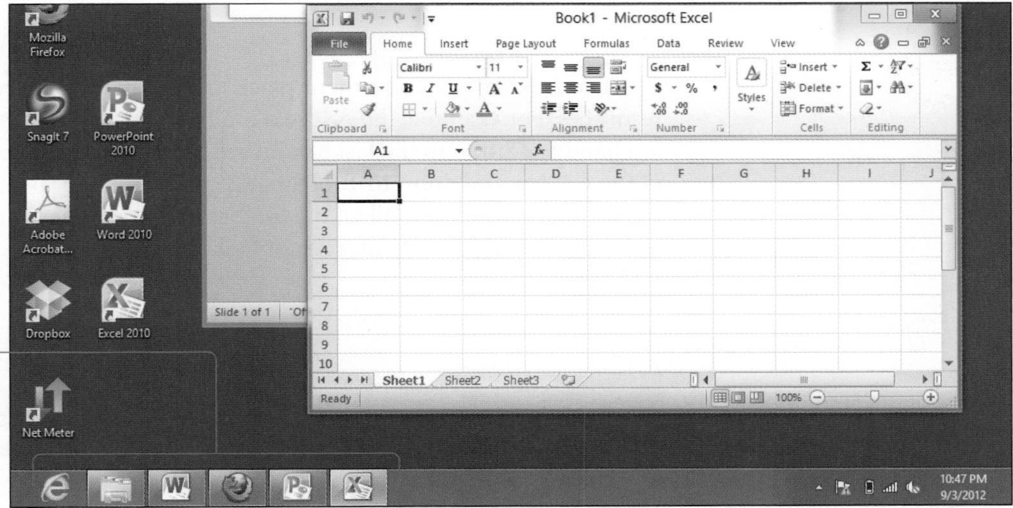

FIGURE 1.13 Desktop with Open Application Windows

To get a sneak preview of any open window, even if it is obscured by another, place the pointer over the program's icon on the taskbar. The resulting preview is called ***Aero Peek***. Place the pointer over the thumbnail (previewed window), without clicking, to temporarily view the window in full size. When you move the pointer away, the active window reappears. If you click the thumbnail (window preview), you will switch to the previewed window. See Figure 1.14 for an example of Aero Peek.

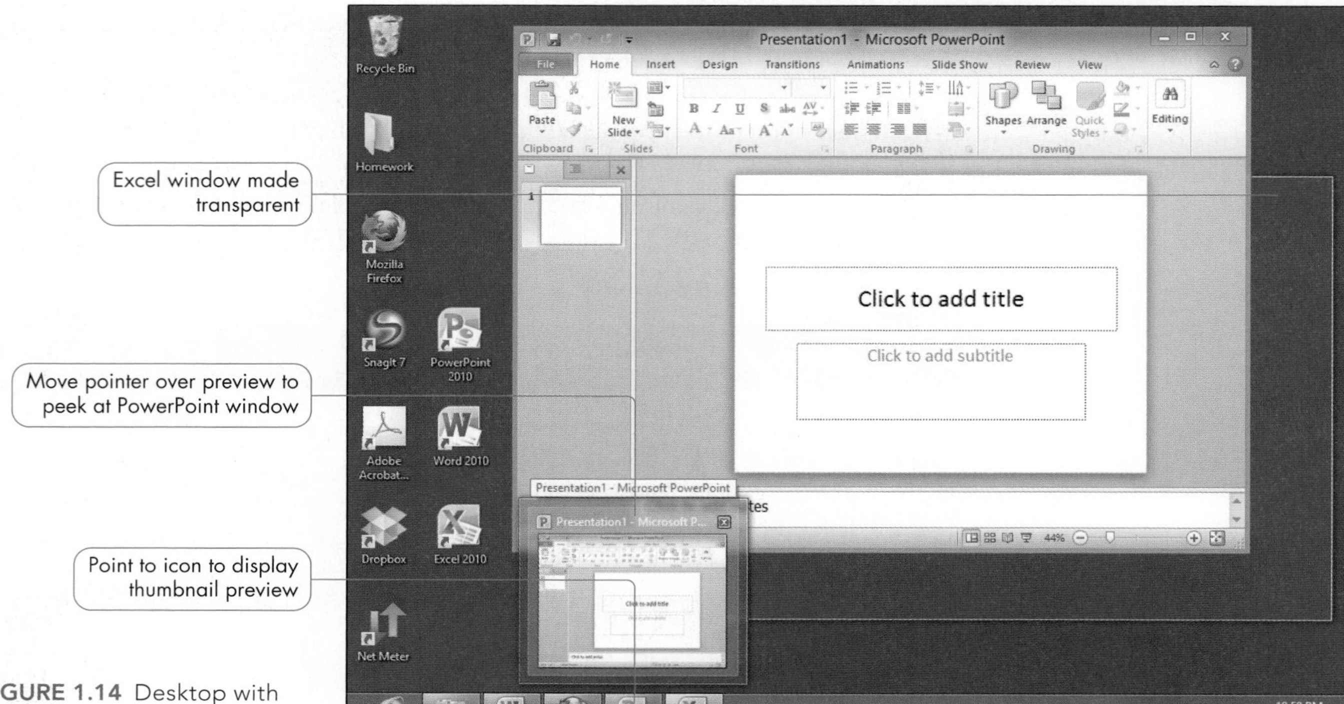

FIGURE 1.14 Desktop with Aero Peek

TIP Hide the Taskbar

Although it is very helpful, the taskbar can occupy space on your work area that you may need. To temporarily hide the taskbar, right-click an empty area of the taskbar. Click Properties. In the Taskbar Properties dialog box, click to select *Auto-hide the taskbar*, and then click OK. The taskbar immediately disappears. When you move the pointer to the previous location of the taskbar, it will appear, but only until you move the pointer away. To return the taskbar to view, reverse the process described above, clicking to deselect *Auto-hide the taskbar.*

The taskbar is a convenient place to display ***toolbars***, which provide shortcuts to Web resources. For example, the Address toolbar, which allows you to easily enter Web addresses, is a handy addition to the taskbar. To see a list of available toolbars, right-click an empty part of the taskbar and point to Toolbars. Click any item in the list to add or remove it. If you see a checkmark beside a toolbar, the toolbar is already open on the taskbar. Figure 1.15 shows a taskbar that includes an Address toolbar.

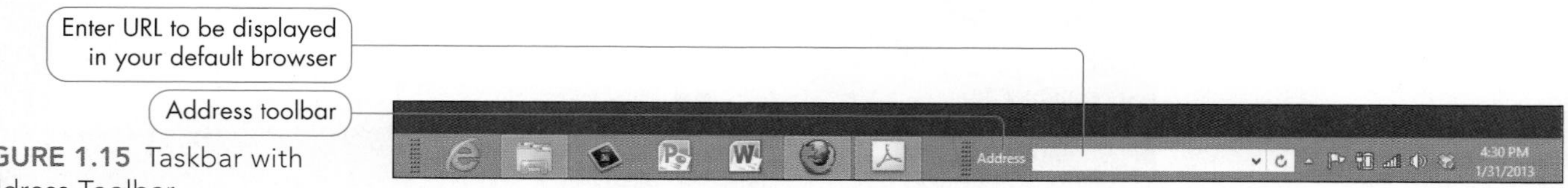

FIGURE 1.15 Taskbar with Address Toolbar

You can place, or pin, icons of frequently used programs on the taskbar for quick access later. When you pin a program to the taskbar, the program icon becomes a permanent part of the taskbar. You can then open the program by clicking its icon. If the program that you want to pin is not already open, right-click its desktop shortcut and click *Pin to taskbar*. If the program that you want to pin is already open, right-click the program icon on the taskbar to open its ***Jump List*** (see Figure 1.16). Click *Pin this program to taskbar*. A Jump List is a list of program shortcuts, which show recently opened files, the program name, an option to pin or unpin an item, and a close option.

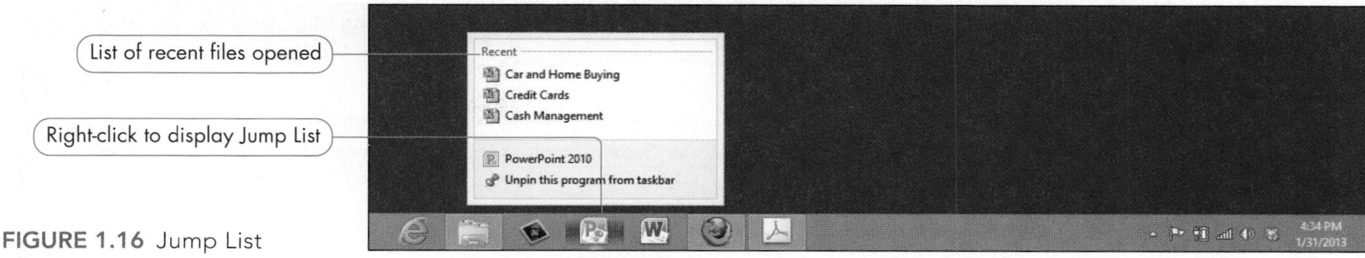

FIGURE 1.16 Jump List

You will find the Notification area (see Figure 1.17) on the right side of the taskbar. It displays icons for programs running in the background, such as a virus scanner, and provides access to such system activities as managing wireless networks and adjusting volume. A major purpose of the Notification area is to provide important status information that displays in pop-up windows. Status information could include the detection of new devices, the availability of software updates, or recommended maintenance and security tasks. An example of a pop-up notification is shown in Figure 1.17. If the notification is a recommended update or maintenance task, you can click the message to perform the recommended task.

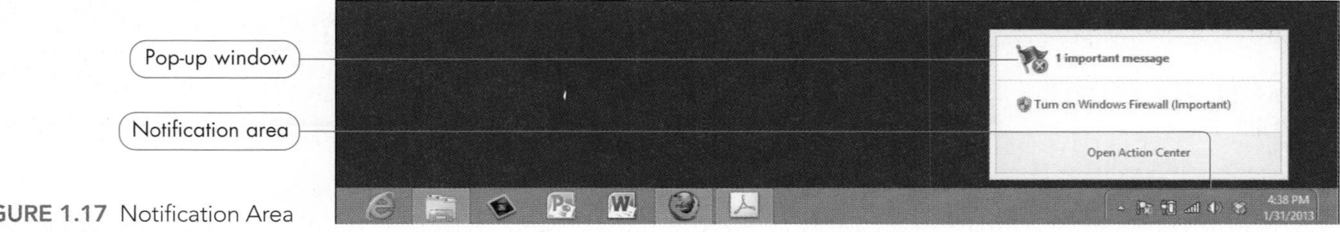

FIGURE 1.17 Notification Area

Customize the Desktop

For a little variety, you can customize the desktop with a different background or color theme. You can even include a slide show of favorite photos to display when your computer is idle. Customizing the desktop can be fun and creative. Windows 8 provides a wide selection of background and color choices.

To change the desktop background, or change the color theme, right-click an empty area of the desktop and click Personalize (see Figure 1.18). If you choose to change the background, click Desktop Background. You can choose from built-in categories such as Windows Desktop Backgrounds, or you can browse for a folder containing your personal pictures. Click Window Color to change the color of window borders and the taskbar. You can also select a ***screen saver***. A screen saver is a moving series of pictures or images that displays when your computer has been idle for a specified period of time.

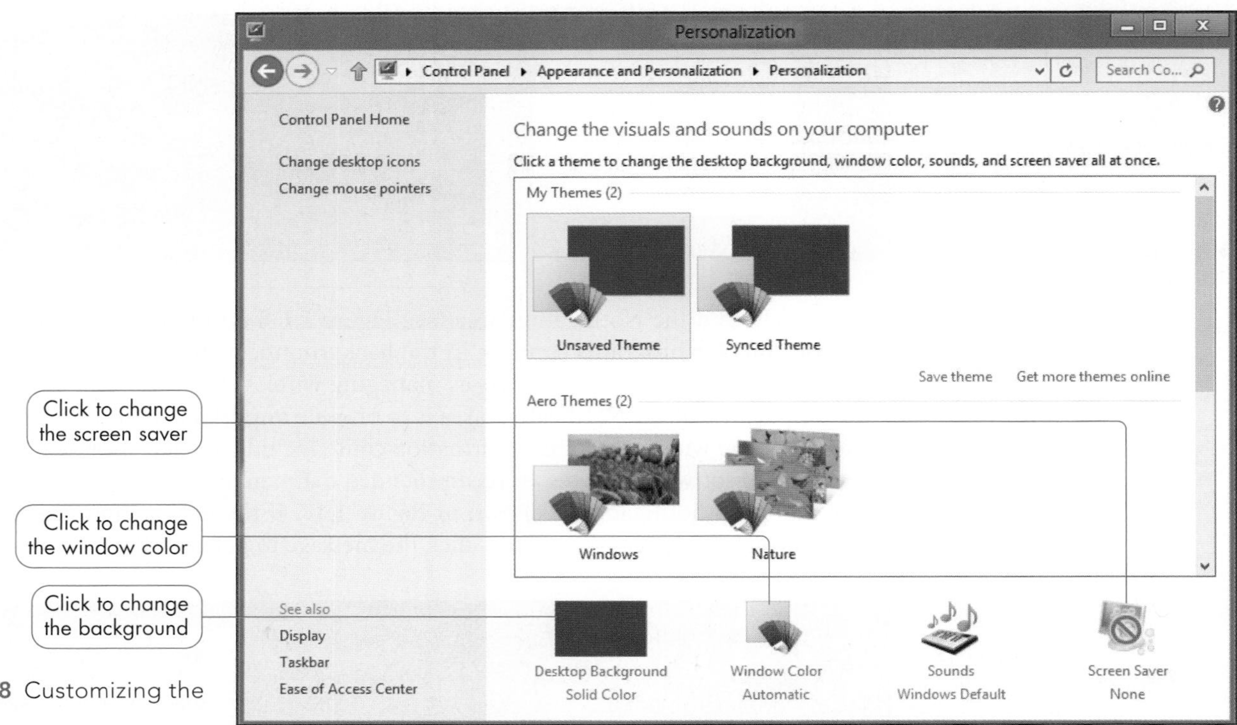

FIGURE 1.18 Customizing the Desktop

Managing Windows 8 Apps and Windows

Using the taskbar, you can move among open windows with ease, but you will also need to know how to move, resize, and close windows. Windows 8 makes it easy to automatically arrange windows, even snapping them quickly to the desktop borders.

Identify Window Components

All windows share common elements including a title bar and control buttons, as shown in Figure 1.19. Although each window's contents vary, those common elements make it easy for you to manage windows appropriately so that you make the best use of your time and computer resources.

The ***title bar*** is the long bar at the top of each window. The title bar always displays the name of the folder, file, or program. Control buttons are found on the right side of the title bar. Those control buttons enable you to minimize, maximize (or restore down), or close any open window.

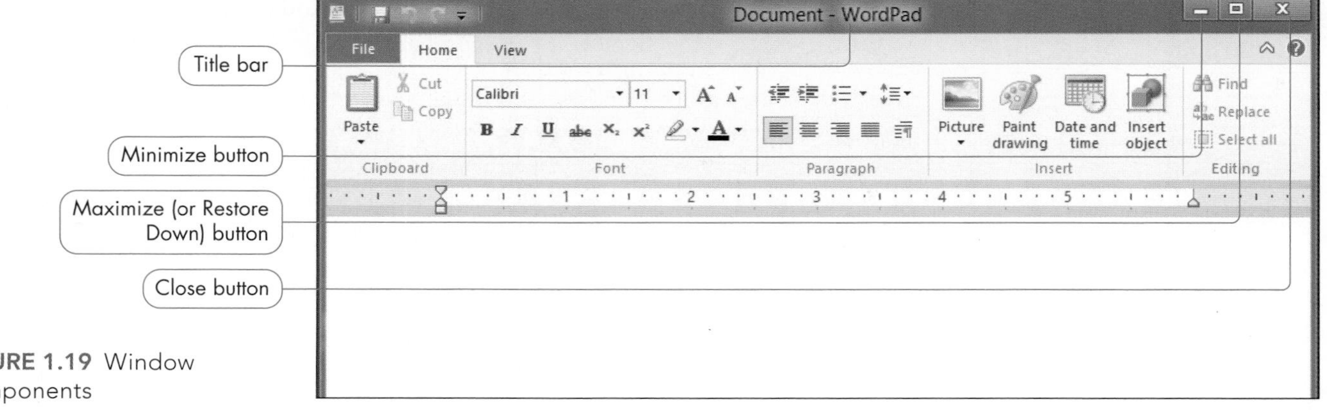

FIGURE 1.19 Window Components

The first control button is used to minimize a window and displays as a horizontal line. When you minimize a window, you hide it from view but do not close it. That means that the window becomes a taskbar icon that you can click to view.

The middle control button shares two functions, depending on the current size of the window. One is to maximize a window to its full size, and one is to restore down a window to a smaller size. If a window is less than full size, click the middle button to maximize the window so that it occupies the entire desktop. The Maximize button looks like a small box. The Restore Down button appears as two overlapped boxes. Restoring down a window returns it to the size it was before the windows was maximized. You can also maximize or restore down a window by double-clicking the title bar of the open window.

Maximize a Window and Expand a Window Vertically

You can quickly maximize a window by clicking and dragging the title bar to the top of the desktop. The window immediately becomes full sized. To expand a window vertically without changing the window's width, place the pointer on the top or bottom edge of a window to display a double-headed arrow. Then click and drag the border to the corresponding top or bottom edge of the desktop. Release the mouse button to expand the window vertically.

The button on the far right side of the title bar is used to close a window. It is always displayed as an X. When you close a window, you remove the file or program from the computer's random access memory (RAM). RAM is temporary (or volatile) storage, meaning files stored in RAM are not permanently saved. To save a file so you can access it later, the file must be saved to a permanent storage device such as the computer's hard drive or a flash drive. If you have not saved a file that you are closing, Windows 8 will prompt you to save it before closing.

Move and Resize Windows

STEP 2》 Multitasking involves working with multiple open windows at the same time, and this often requires moving or resizing windows. If multiple windows are open, you will need to know how to switch between windows and how to rearrange them.

You can only move or resize a window that is not maximized. To move a window, click and drag the title bar. To resize a window, place the pointer on a border of the window. The pointer will become a double-headed arrow. Click and drag to make the window larger or smaller. If the pointer is on a corner of the window, forming a diagonal double-headed arrow, you can resize two adjacent sides of the window at once by clicking and dragging.

You can also use the keyboard to switch to another window. To cycle through all open windows, stopping at any one, hold down Alt on the keyboard and repeatedly press Tab. Release Alt when you see the window that you want to display. Note that any Windows 8 apps that are running are also displayed in this list, so you may leave the desktop and go to Windows 8 view when selecting a window.

You might prefer to let Windows 8 arrange your windows automatically. Windows 8 can arrange any open windows in a cascading fashion, vertically stacked, or side by side. To automatically arrange open windows on the desktop, right-click an empty part of the taskbar. Click *Cascade windows*, *Show windows stacked*, or *Show windows side by side* (see Figure 1.20).

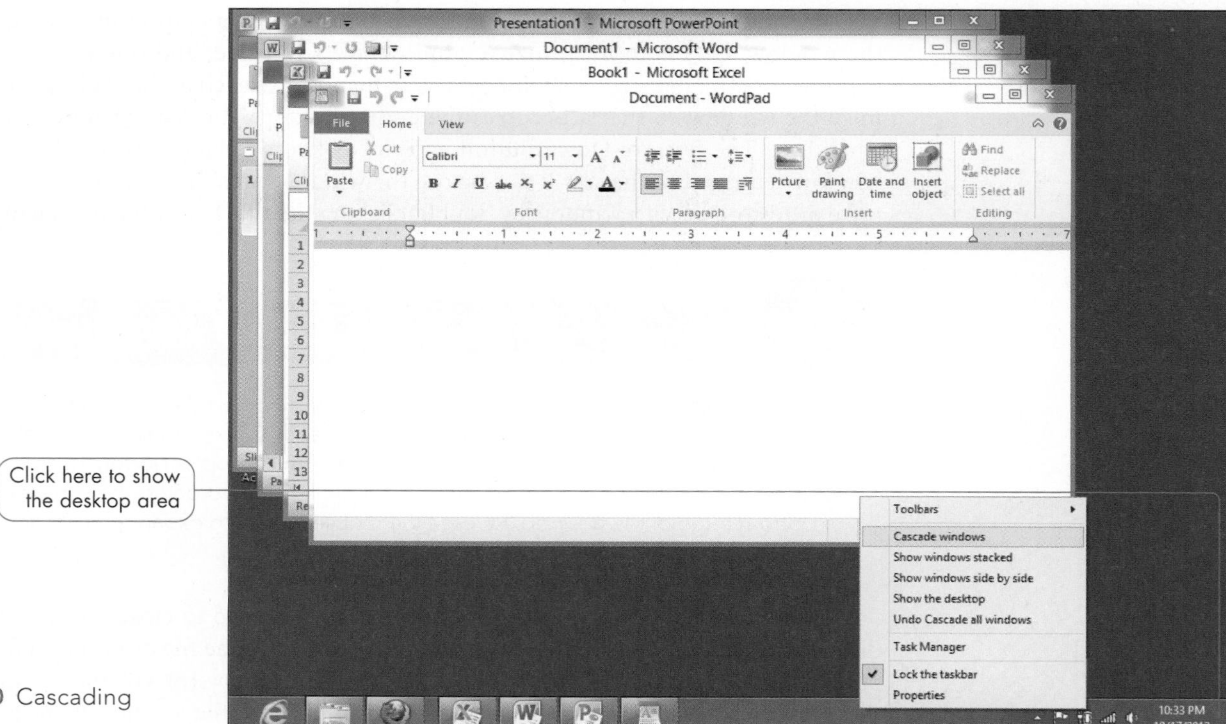

FIGURE 1.20 Cascading Windows

Snap also works with windows on the desktop as well as with Windows 8 apps. Snap will automatically place a window on the side of the desktop, resulting in a well-ordered arrangement of windows. Simply click and drag the title bar of a window to the left or right side of the desktop until an outline of the window displays. Release the mouse button. Do the same with another window to the opposite side of the desktop.

Another function of Aero Peek is to provide a quick way to show the desktop without actually removing or minimizing windows. Simply click in the *Show desktop* area, as shown in Figure 1.20, to view the desktop. Click the *Show desktop* area again to return the windows to view (or click an icon on the taskbar).

The preceding discussion of windows focused on those windows that represent programs, files, or folders. Those could be considered standard windows. In addition to displaying programs, files, or folders as described earlier, another type of window is a dialog box. A ***dialog box*** is a window that displays when a program requires interaction with you, such as inputting information, before completing a procedure. Figure 1.21 shows a typical dialog box. By responding to areas of the dialog box, you can indicate how you want an operation to occur and how the program should behave. You cannot minimize or maximize a dialog box, but you can move it or close it using the same actions described earlier. To get help on a feature in the dialog box, click the ? button, if present. Typical components of a dialog box are as follows:

- *Option buttons* indicate mutually exclusive choices, one of which *must* be chosen, such as the page range. In this example, you can print all pages, the selection, the current page, or a specific set of pages (such as pages 3–12). When you select an option, any previously selected option is deselected.
- A *text box*, such as the one shown beside the *Pages* option in Figure 1.21, enables you to enter specific information. In this case, you could type 3-12 in the text box if you wanted only those pages to print.
- A *spin arrow* is a common component of a dialog box, providing a quick method of increasing or decreasing a setting. For example, clicking the spin arrow beside *Number of copies* enables you to increase or decrease the number of copies of the document to print.

- *Check boxes* are used instead of option buttons if you may make more than one selection. You can select or clear options by clicking the appropriate check box, which toggles the selection on and off. In Figure 1.21, you can select the option of printing to a file by checking the box.
- All dialog boxes also contain one or more *command buttons* that provide options to either accept or cancel your selections. The Print button, for example, initiates the printing process shown in Figure 1.21. The Cancel button does just the opposite and ignores (cancels) any changes made to the settings, closing the dialog box.

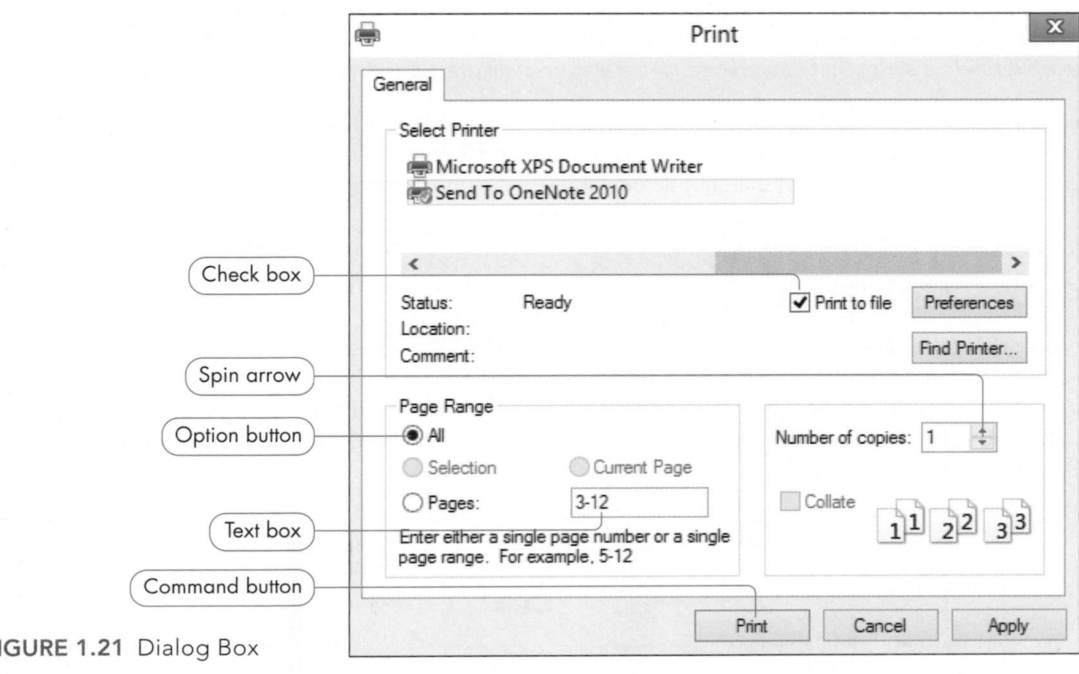

FIGURE 1.21 Dialog Box

Hands-On Exercises

1 Windows 8 Fundamentals

Tomorrow, you will meet with the Cedar Grove class to present an introduction to Windows 8. The classroom has only one computer, which is connected to a projector. You plan to demonstrate a few basics of working with the operating system including managing Windows 8 apps and working with non–Windows 8 apps on the desktop. Above all, you want to keep it simple so that you encourage class enthusiasm. You have prepared a script that you plan to follow and you will practice it in the steps that follow.

Skills covered: Open Multiple Windows 8 Apps, Display Two Apps Together, and Close an App • Manage Multiple Windows, Arrange Windows Automatically, and Arrange Windows Using Snap on the Desktop • Add and Remove Tiles from the Start Screen and Add Shortcuts to the Desktop • Customize the Appearance of the Start Screen and Change the Desktop Background and Screen Saver

STEP 1 » OPEN MULTIPLE WINDOWS 8 APPS, DISPLAY TWO APPS TOGETHER, AND CLOSE AN APP

Before the students can work with software, they must learn to work with the Windows 8 interface. Specifically, they must understand that programs and apps optimized for the Windows 8 interface will display full-screen and not in windows with which they are probably familiar. They need to be comfortable launching, managing and closing Windows 8 apps. You will stress the importance of the Start screen as the location starting point for all Windows 8 apps. Refer to Figure 1.22 as you complete Step 1.

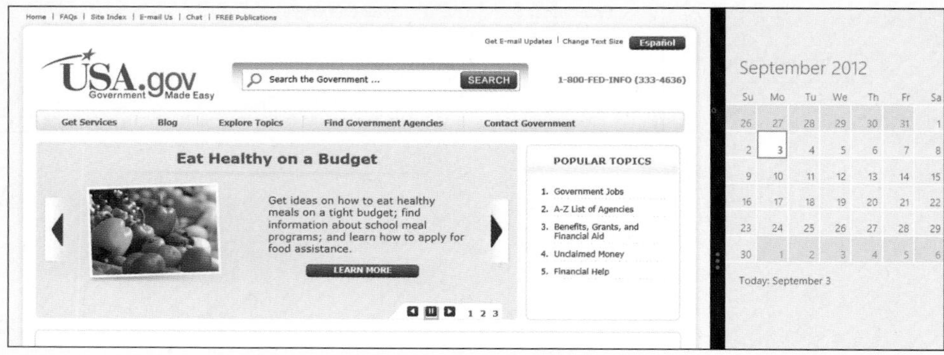

FIGURE 1.22 Internet Explorer and Calendar Apps

a. Open a new, blank Microsoft Word document. Save this document as **win01h1Basics_LastFirst**, replacing *LastFirst* with your own last name and first name. You will capture screenshots of your progress in this exercise and paste them into this document to submit to your instructor.

b. Click the **Internet Explorer tile** on the Start screen, enter **usa.gov** in the **search box**, and then press **Enter**.

   You have opened the Internet Explorer application and navigated to usa.gov, the United States official Web portal.

c. Press the **Windows key** to return to the Start screen.

   You will now be returned to the Start screen. You need to feel comfortable launching multiple apps and displaying two apps at once.

d. Click the **Calendar tile** on the Start screen.

   You have now launched the Calendar app. Most likely, the calendar will not have any data on it, unless you have previously entered items in the calendar app.

e. Point to the top-left corner of the screen to display the Switch list and drag the pointer down to display all of the open apps.

f. Find the Internet Explorer app thumbnail image on the Switch list and click the image to make the Internet Explorer app the active app (filling the entire screen).

g. Display the switch list again, find the Calendar thumbnail image on the switch list, and then click and drag the **Calendar thumbnail image** to the right side of the screen. Release the mouse button. The Calendar app should snap into place on the right side of the screen with the Internet Explorer app displayed on the left side. You will now capture an image of this screen to show your instructor you successfully completed this exercise.

h. Press the **Windows key+PRTSC**. This captures the current screen and places a copy of it on the clipboard. Press the **Windows key+D** to return to the desktop. Place your pointer at the beginning of the *win01h1Basics_LastFirst* file and press **Ctrl+V**. This will paste an image of your screen into your file. Save the file.

i. Place the pointer at the top of the Calendar app until the pointer turns into a hand, click the app, and then drag it down—noticing that the app shrinks—and off the bottom of the screen. You have now closed the Calendar app.

j. Repeat Step i to close the Internet Explorer app.

k. Keep the *win01h1Basics_LastFirst* file open if you are proceeding to Step 2. Otherwise, save and close the file.

STEP 2 » MANAGE MULTIPLE WINDOWS, ARRANGE WINDOWS AUTOMATICALLY, AND ARRANGE WINDOWS USING SNAP ON THE DESKTOP

Because there will be occasions when several windows are open simultaneously on the desktop, students must learn to arrange them. You will show them various ways that Windows 8 can help arrange open windows. Refer to Figure 1.23 as you complete Step 2.

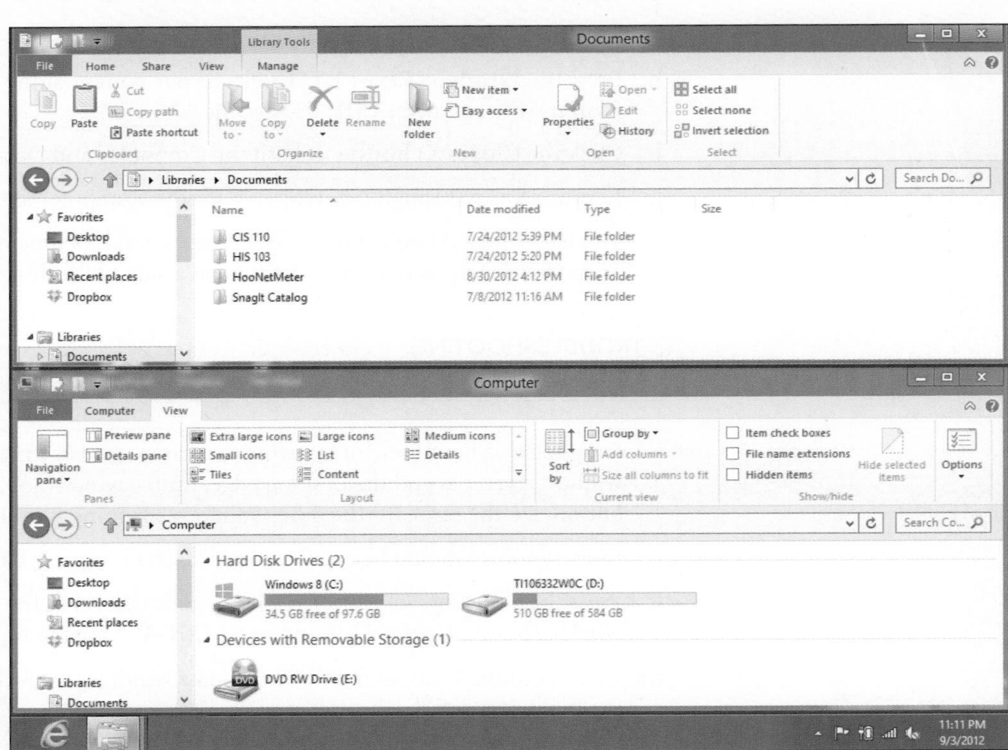

FIGURE 1.23 Stacked Windows on the Desktop

a. Open the *win01h1Basics_LastFirst* file, if it is not open from the previous step.

b. Point to the bottom-left corner of the screen. The Start screen thumbnail will display. Right-click the **Start screen thumbnail** to display a shortcut menu. Select **File Explorer** from the menu.

File Explorer displays on the desktop.

c. Click **Computer** in the left-hand pane to display the Computer information screen.

d. Move the pointer to the bottom-left corner of the screen to display a thumbnail image, right-click the thumbnail image to display a shortcut menu, and then select **File Explorer** from the menu to display a second instance of File Explorer on the desktop. In the left-hand pane, click **Documents**.

   You have opened two windows—Computer and Documents. You are going to show students various ways to arrange the open windows.

> **TROUBLESHOOTING:** If the two windows open so that one is directly on top of the other, the window underneath will be obscured. Drag the title bar of the top most window to move the window so that you can see both.

e. Right-click an empty part of the taskbar and click **Show windows stacked**. Compare your desktop with Figure 1.23.

   The contents of the windows will vary, but the arrangement should be similar.

> **TROUBLESHOOTING:** If your desktop displays more than three stacked windows, you have more than three windows open. You should make sure that only the Computer, Documents, and Word windows are open. Close any other open windows by right-clicking the corresponding taskbar icon and clicking *Close window.*

f. Press the **Windows key+PRTSC**. Place your pointer at the end of the *win01h1Basics_LastFirst* file and press **Ctrl+V**. Save the file.

g. Right-click an empty part of the taskbar and click **Show windows side by side**.

   The three windows should line up vertically.

h. Press the **Windows key+PRTSC**. Place your pointer at the end of the *win01h1Basics_LastFirst* file and press **Ctrl+V**. Save the file.

i. Click the **Close (X) button** in both the Computer and Documents windows to close them.

j. Repeat Steps b through d to reopen both the Computer and the Documents windows.

   You have opened two windows—Computer and Documents. You will use the Windows Snap feature to position each window on a side of the desktop.

> **TROUBLESHOOTING:** If either window opens at full size (maximized), click the Restore Down button (middle button) at the top-right corner of the title bar to make the window smaller.

k. Drag the title bar of one of the windows to one side of the desktop. Keep dragging the window, even beyond the desktop edge, until a window outline displays. Release the mouse button. Do the same for the other window, snapping it to the opposite side of the desktop.

   Both windows should be evenly spaced, each occupying half of the desktop.

l. Press the **Windows key+PRTSC**. Place your pointer at the end of the *win01h1Basics_LastFirst* file and press **Ctrl+V**. Save the file.

m. Close both the Computer and Documents windows by clicking the **Close (X) button** in the top-right corner of each.

n. Keep the *win01h1Basics_LastFirst file* open if you are proceeding to Step 3. Otherwise, save and close the file.

STEP 3 » ADD AND REMOVE TILES FROM THE START SCREEN AND ADD SHORTCUTS TO THE DESKTOP

Not only do you want students to understand the basics of managing apps and windows, but you know that they will also enjoy customizing the Start screen and the desktop. They will also benefit from creating program shortcuts.

a. Open the *win01h1Basics_LastFirst* file if it is not open from the previous step.

b. Go to the Start screen, right-click an empty area of the screen, and then select **All apps** to display the Apps screen. Scroll to the right and under *Windows Accessories*, look for the Snipping Tool icon.

c. Right-click the **Snipping Tool icon** to display the Options bar at the bottom of the screen, and then click **Pin to Start** to create a tile on the Start screen for the Snipping Tool.

d. Right-click again and click **Pin to taskbar** to pin the Snipping Tool to the taskbar on the desktop.

e. Press the **Windows key** to display the Start screen. Scroll to the right to find the Snipping Tool tile. Click the **Snipping Tool tile** and drag it over on top of the first group of tiles at the far left of the Start screen. Release the mouse button. The Snipping Tool tile should now be part of the first group of tiles.

f. Press the **Windows key+PRTSC**. Place your pointer at the end of the *win01h1Basics_LastFirst* file and press **Ctrl+V**. Save the file.

g. Right-click the **Video tile** to display the Options bar and click **Unpin from Start**. Notice that the tile disappears from the Start screen.

h. Click the **Desktop tile** to go to the desktop.

   Notice that the Snipping Tool is now pinned to the Taskbar.

i. Right-click an empty area of the taskbar, click **Properties**, and then click the **Auto-hide the taskbar check box** (unless a checkmark already displays). Click **OK**.

   The taskbar will only show if you place the pointer near where it should show. When you move the pointer away, the taskbar disappears. You will explain to students that they can use the Taskbar Properties dialog box to customize the appearance and behavior of the taskbar.

j. Move the pointer to the location of the taskbar, right-click an empty area of the taskbar, and then click **Properties**. Click to deselect the **Auto-hide the taskbar check box** and click **OK**.

k. Right-click an empty area of the desktop. Select **New** and **Shortcut** from the menu that displays. This will display the Create Shortcut dialog box. Click **Browse** and navigate to the Windows directory on your hard drive (usually the C: drive). Scan the directory for the notepad file. Click this file to select it. Click **OK**, and click **Next**. Type a name for the shortcut in the box and click **Finish**. You should now have a shortcut for Notepad on your desktop.

l. Press the **Windows key+PRTSC**. Place your pointer at the end of the *win01h1Basics_LastFirst* file and press **Ctrl+V**. Save the file.

m. Right-click the **Notepad shortcut icon** on the desktop and click **Delete** to remove the icon from your desktop. Right-click the **Snipping Tool icon** on the taskbar. Select **Unpin this program from taskbar** to remove the Snipping Tool icon from the taskbar.

   Because you want to leave the classroom's computer just as you found it, you deleted the Notepad shortcut from the desktop and the Snipping Tool icon from the taskbar.

n. Leave the *win01h1Basics_LastFirst* file open if you are proceeding to Step 4. Otherwise, save and close the file.

STEP 4 » CUSTOMIZE THE APPEARANCE OF THE START SCREEN AND CHANGE THE DESKTOP BACKGROUND AND SCREEN SAVER

To end the class session on a creative note, you want the students to have fun changing the Start screen and desktop background and experimenting with screen savers. Refer to Figure 1.24 as you complete Step 4.

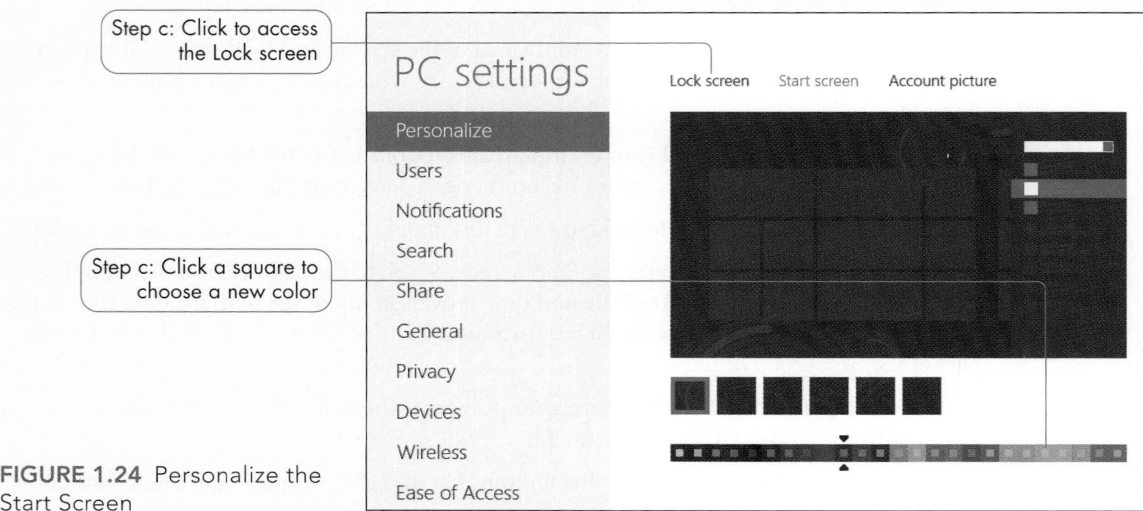

FIGURE 1.24 Personalize the Start Screen

> **TROUBLESHOOTING:** If you are working in a campus lab, you might not be able to change the Start screen, desktop background, or screen saver. In this case, you cannot complete this step of the Hands-On Exercises.

a. Open the *win01h1Basics_LastFirst* file, if it is not open from the previous step.

b. Display the Charms bar, click **Settings**, and then click **Change PC settings**. On the PC settings screen, click the **Personalize option**. Click **Start screen** in the top-right pane. As shown in Figure 1.24, choose a new pattern and color for your Start screen.

c. Click the **Lock screen link** to access your lock screen. This is the screen to which your PC defaults when you leave it for a period of time. Browse through your computer's hard drive and pick a new background image for this screen.

d. Press the **Windows key** to display the Start screen and notice that your Start screen has now changed to reflect your personalization choices.

e. Press the **Windows key+PRTSC**. Place your pointer at the end of the *win01h1Basics_LastFirst* file and press **Ctrl+V**. Save the file.

f. Display the desktop. Right-click an empty area of the desktop and select **Personalize**. Click the **Desktop Background link** and make sure *Windows Desktop Backgrounds* displays in the Picture location. If not, click the **Picture location arrow** and select **Windows Desktop Backgrounds**.

g. Click to select one of the backgrounds that you like. Click the **Picture position arrow** and click **Fill** if necessary. If your instructor allows you to change the background, click **Save changes**. Otherwise, click **Cancel**.

h. Press the **Windows key+D** to display the desktop and view your new background image.

i. Press the **Windows key+PRTSC**. Place your pointer at the end of the *win01h1Basics_LastFirst* file and press **Ctrl+V**. Save the file.

j. Redisplay the Desktop Background dialog box. This time, click **Browse** and navigate to a folder on your computer (or flash drive) where you have pictures stored. Select a personal picture and set it as your background. Click the **Picture position arrow** and select **Center**. If your instructor allows you to change the background, click **Save changes**. Otherwise, click **Cancel**.

k. Click the **Screen Saver link** in the Personalization dialog box, click the **Screensaver arrow**, and then select a screen saver. Click **Preview**. Press **Esc** to remove the screen saver from view. Note that you can also change the Wait time to specify the number of minutes the computer must remain idle before the screen saver displays. Click **Cancel** to avoid making the change permanent or **OK** if you are allowed to change the screen saver. Close any open windows.

   Unless you saved the screen saver change and wait the required wait time for the screen saver to display, you will see no changes.

l. Save and close the *win01h1Basics_LastFirst* file and submit it to your instructor.

Windows Programs and Security Features

Windows 8 is a full-featured operating system, including built-in programs for tasks such as word processing, creating graphics, and system security. With only a little effort, you can learn to use those programs. Regardless of how many programs you install on your computer system, you can take comfort in knowing that you will always have access to software supporting basic tasks and that your computer is securely protected against spyware and hacking.

Identifying Windows Accessories

You use your computer by interacting with computer programs. A program (app) is software that accomplishes a specific task. You use a word processing program to prepare documents, an e-mail program to compose and send e-mail, and a database program to maintain records. You can customize a computer by installing programs of your choice. Windows 8 provides many programs for basic tasks, as well. Those programs include WordPad, Notepad, Paint, Calculator, and Snipping Tool, some of which you have opened and will now learn how to use.

Use Notepad and WordPad

STEP 1》

Notepad and ***WordPad*** are programs that enable you to create documents. Notepad is a basic text editing program used primarily to edit text files—files that are identified with a .txt extension. Programmers sometimes use Notepad to prepare basic program statements. Notepad is not at all concerned with style and does not include the features of typical word processing software such as document formatting and character design.

WordPad, on the other hand, is a basic word processing program and includes the capability of formatting text and inserting graphics. Not as full-featured as Microsoft Word, WordPad is still a handy alternative when you do not have access to Word or when you want to quickly create a simple document. WordPad saves documents in a rich text format, so you can open WordPad files in any word processing program (like Word) that can handle rich text format.

Figure 1.25 shows both WordPad and Notepad windows. Note the bare-bones appearance of Notepad when compared with WordPad. Access either program by right-clicking the Start screen and clicking *All apps*. Under the Windows accessories group, click the appropriate icon.

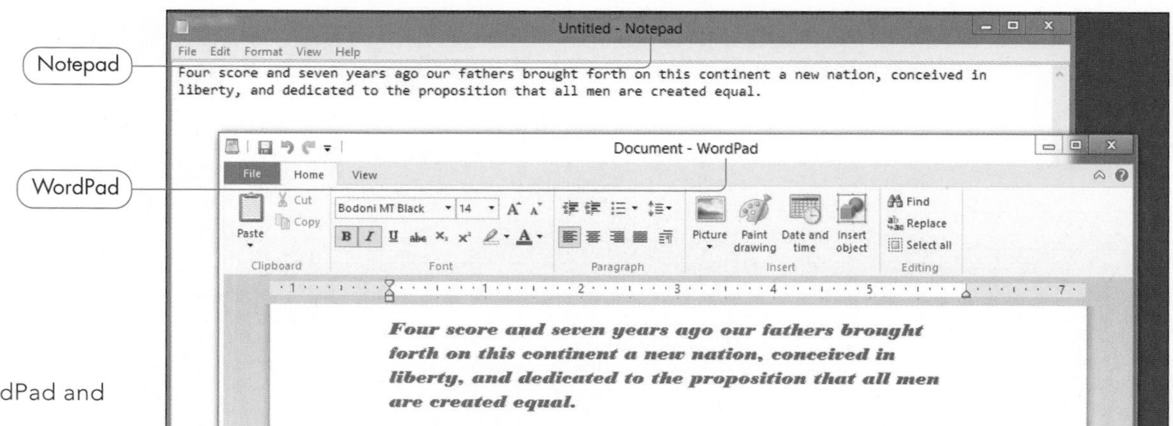

FIGURE 1.25 WordPad and Notepad

Use Paint

Paint is a Windows 8 program that enables you to create drawings and to open digital pictures. Figure 1.26 shows the Paint interface. Note the Ribbon at the top of the Paint window that includes such items as the Pencil tool, Brushes, Colors, and Shapes. Open Paint by right-clicking the Start screen, clicking *All apps*, and then clicking the Paint icon under the Windows Accessories group. The canvas in the center of the Paint window acts as an easel on which you can draw.

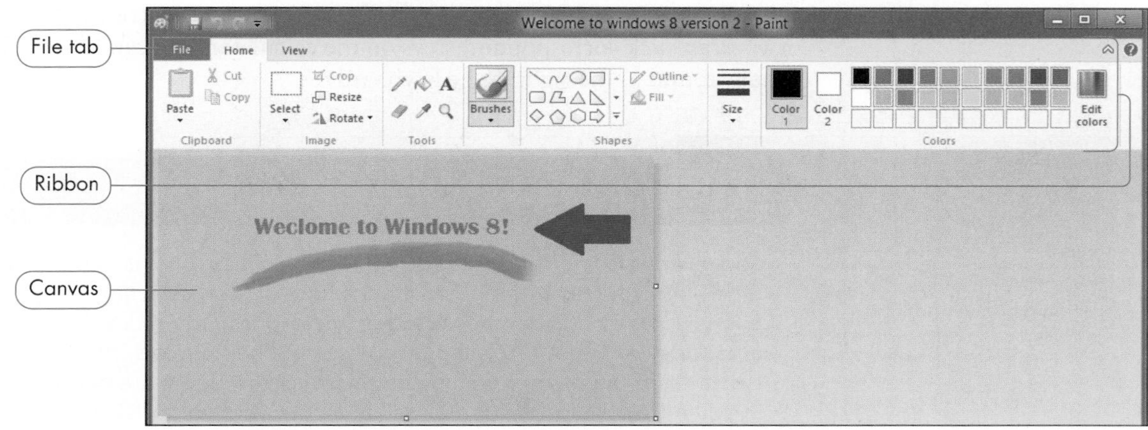

FIGURE 1.26 Paint

When you open Paint, you can create and save a colorful drawing, including text, shapes, and background color. You can also open a digital photo and add comments, shapes, or drawings. If you want to work with an existing picture, open the photo by clicking the File tab on the Ribbon (see Figure 1.26). Click Open, browse to the location of the picture, and double-click the picture. Then use the Paint tools to add to the picture, saving it when done.

Use the Calculator

The ***Calculator*** tool lets you perform simple addition, subtraction, multiplication, and division to advanced scientific, programming, and statistical functions. Open Calculator by right-clicking the Start screen, selecting *All apps*, and then clicking the Calculator icon under the Windows Accessories group. Figure 1.27 shows all four Calculator versions. Change from one version to another by clicking View and making a selection.

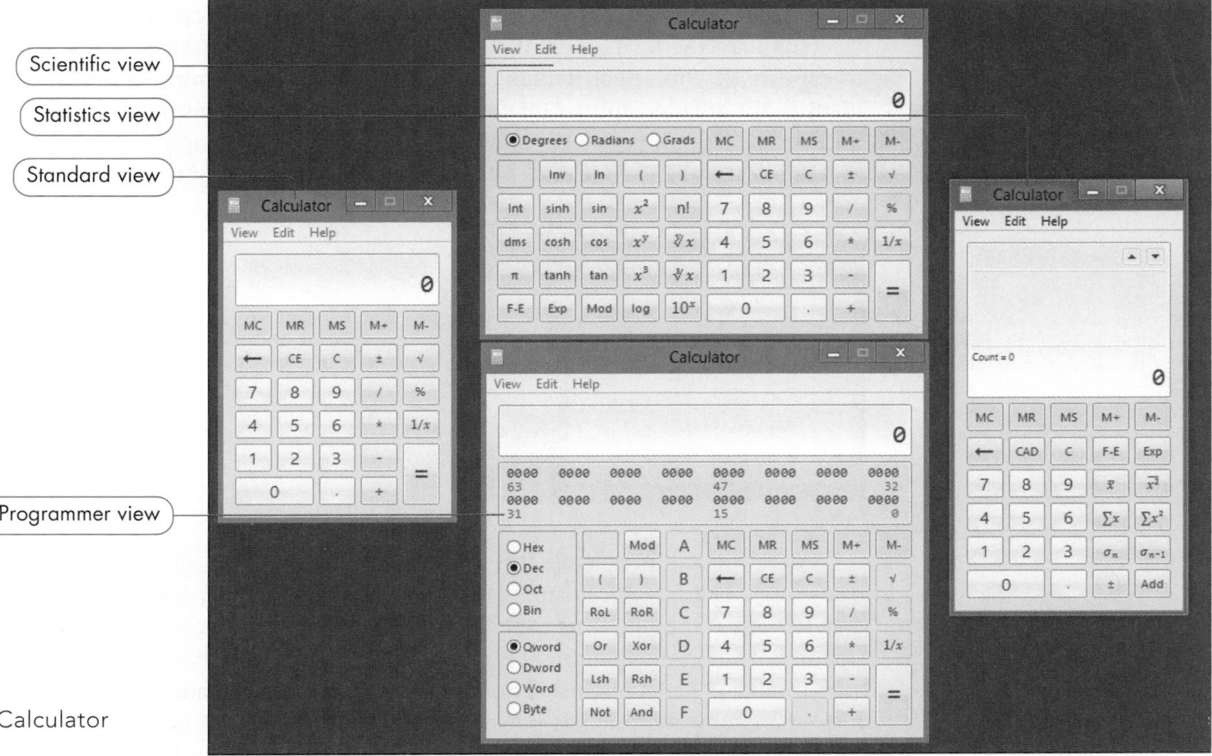

FIGURE 1.27 Calculator Views

When using Calculator, you can either type numeric entries and operators (+, –, *, and /) or you can click corresponding keys on the calculator. You can also use the numeric keypad, usually found to the right of the keyboard.

TIP Use Sticky Notes and Quick Note

Sticky Notes is a fun and useful Windows 7 accessory that is also available in Windows 8. Open Sticky Notes by right-clicking the Start screen, selecting *All apps*, and clicking the Sticky Notes icon under the Windows Accessories group. Use the program as you would a paper sticky note, recording to-do lists, phone numbers, or anything else. Your notes display as stick-up notes on the desktop. Click the New Note button to add another note, click the Delete Note button to delete a note, and right-click a note to change the color. Because Sticky Notes is not a Windows 8 app, you cannot pin notes to the Start screen. Instead, use Quick Note which is a similar app available for free in the Windows Store which does provide the option of pinning notes to the Start screen.

Use the Snipping Tool

STEP 3

The ***Snipping Tool*** is a Windows 8 accessory program that enables you to capture, or ***snip***, a screen display so that you can save, annotate, or share it. Up to this point, you have been capturing your entire screen with the Windows key+PRTSC. Using the Snipping Tool (see Figure 1.28) provides you with additional options such as capturing screen elements in a rectangular, free-form, window, or full-screen fashion. You can then also draw on or annotate the screen captures, save them, or send them to others.

Open the Snipping Tool on the Start screen by right-clicking in any empty area and clicking the *All apps* icon that is displayed in the bottom-right corner of the screen. In the group of icons labeled *Windows Accessories*, click the Snipping Tool icon. This launches the Snipping tool and places you on the desktop. Click the New arrow and select a snip type (rectangular, free-form, etc.). If you select the Window Snip type, you will click the window to capture. If you select Rectangular Snip or Free-form Snip, you must click and drag to identify the area to capture. Of course, it is not necessary to specify an area when you select Full-screen Snip. If you need to take a snip of a Windows 8 app or the Start screen, switch to that application, and then click Ctrl+PRTSC to start your capture.

FIGURE 1.28 Snipping Tool

After you capture a snip, it is displayed in the mark-up window, where you can write or draw on it. The screen capture is also copied to the Clipboard, which is a temporary holding area in your computer's memory. You can then paste the screen capture in a word processing document when the document is displayed by clicking the Paste button on the word processor's toolbar. The Clipboard is temporary storage only. Because the Clipboard's contents are lost when your computer is powered down, you should immediately paste a copied screen image if it is your intention to include the screen capture in a document or other application. Otherwise, you can save a screen capture by clicking the Save Snip button and indicating a location and file name for the snip.

Working with Security Settings and Software

Windows 8 monitors your security status, providing recommendations for security settings and software updates as needed. Windows 8 includes basic security features. ***Windows Defender*** is antispyware and antivirus software included with Windows 8. It identifies and removes ***viruses*** and ***spyware***. A computer virus is a computer program that attaches itself to another computer program (known as the host program) and attempts to spread to other computers when files are exchanged. Viruses can have effects ranging from minor annoyances such as displaying amusing images on your screen to devasting effects such as wiping out the contents of your computer's hard drive.

Spyware is software that is usually downloaded without your awareness, and collects personal information from your computer. Windows 8 also includes a ***firewall*** which is a software program that helps to protect against unauthorized access (hacking) to your computer. Although Windows Defender and Windows Firewall provide basic protection, many computer users opt for the purchase of third-party software, such as Norton Internet Security, to provide an even greater level of protection.

Understand the Action Center

STEP 2»

Windows 8 monitors your system for various maintenance and security settings, recommending action through the ***Action Center*** when necessary. When the status of a monitored item changes, perhaps when your files need backing up, Action Center will display a message in an alert box (pop-up) on the Notification area. For a quick summary of Action Center items, you can click the Action Center icon in the Notification area (see Figure 1.29) to display the Action Center alerts box. You can click a link on the summary list to explore a recommended action.

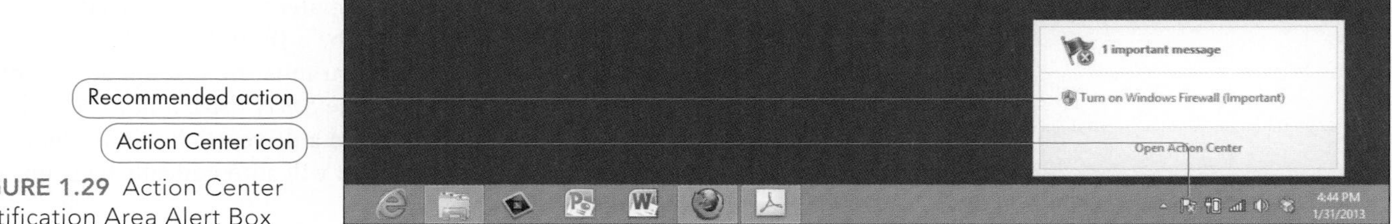

FIGURE 1.29 Action Center Notification Area Alert Box

If you wish, you can display the full Action Center (see Figure 1.30) either by clicking the Open Action Center link in the alert box or by pointing to the bottom-left corner of your screen until the thumbnail image appears and right-clicking the thumbnail image. On the shortcut menu that appears, select Control Panel, System and Security, and then Action Center. The Action Center gives messages in order of severity. Red items are for potentially serious or important alerts that should be addressed immediately. Yellow items are suggested tasks, usually maintenance, such as backing up files. Usually action buttons are provided to take you where you need to go to address the security issues.

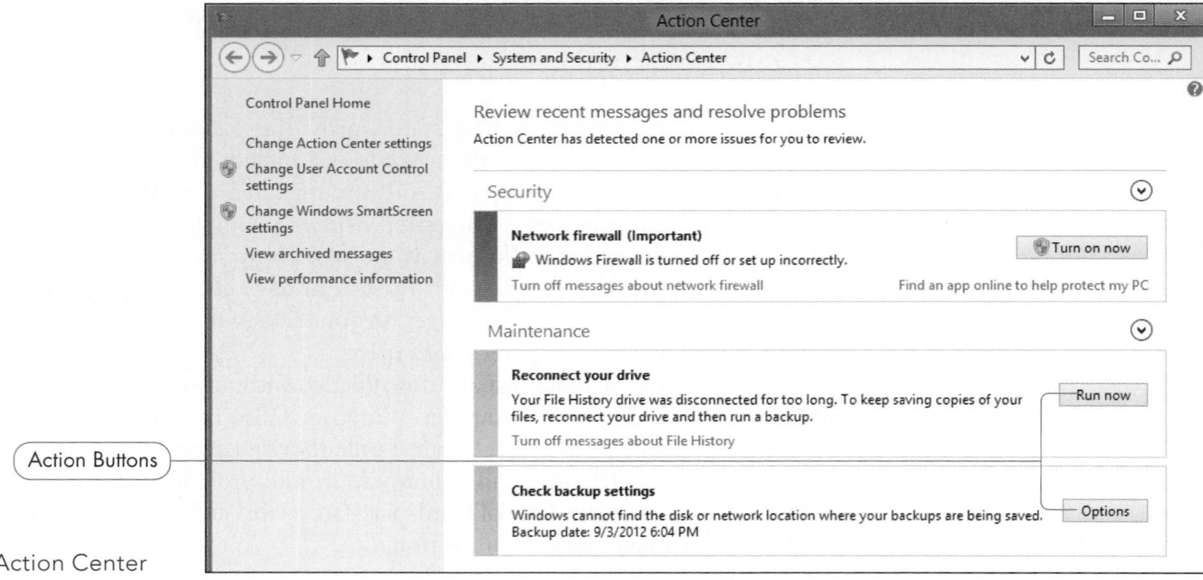

FIGURE 1.30 Action Center

Use File History

Many things can accidently happen to your files. You might mistakenly delete a file or a file might become corrupted, meaning it is damaged and therefore unusable by your software programs.

Windows 8 File History is a utility that will constantly make copies of your important files so that you can recover them if you ever encounter a file problem. You can access the File History screen (see Figure 1.31) by right-clicking the Start screen thumbnail in the bottom-left corner of the screen and selecting Control Panel, System and Security, and File History.

The File History utility will save files to a drive that you designate, perhaps an external hard drive or a separate partition (section) of your computer's internal hard drive. Most likely this will be an external hard drive but it could also be a flash drive, as shown in the example here. To set up File History for the first time, you must first designate the drive where File History will save backups of your files. Click the *Select drive* link to see a list of drives connected to your computer. Once you have selected a drive, click the *Run now* link to back up your files. As long as File History is turned on, it will automatically back up your files from your libraries, desktop, contacts, and favorites.

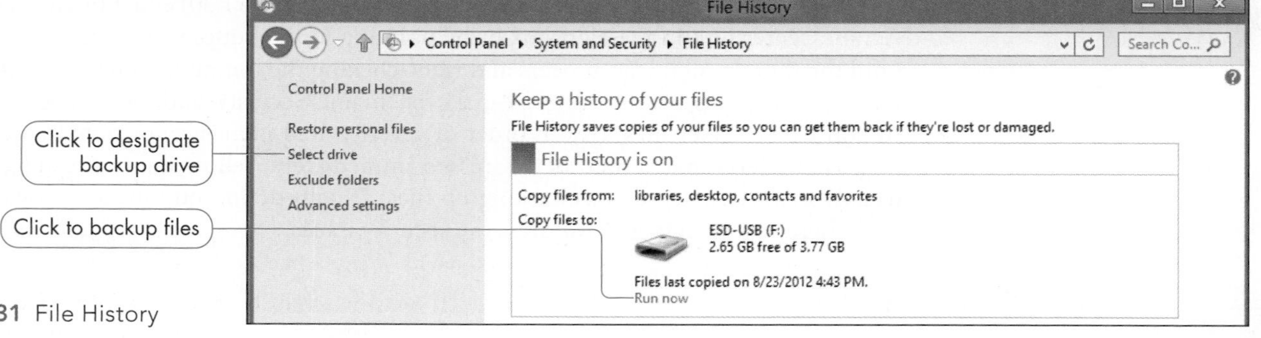

FIGURE 1.31 File History

Use Windows Defender

Viruses and spyware can be installed on your computer whenever you connect to the Internet, regardless of whether you download anything, just by visiting a Web site set up to infect your computer. Spyware and viruses are installed without your knowledge. They can do many unpleasant things such as:

- Keeping track of Web sites you visit (for marketing purposes)
- Changing browser settings to direct you to dangerous Web sites

- Recording keystrokes for stealing sensitive information
- Erasing or corrupting files on your hard drive

Obviously, viruses and spyware are unwelcome and potential security risks.

Windows Defender is antivirus and antispyware software that is included with Windows 8. Windows Defender can be set to run with real-time protection, which means that it is always on guard against threats, alerting you when malicious programs attempt to install themselves or change your computer settings. You can also schedule routine scans so that Windows Defender checks your system for malicious software. Open Windows Defender by right-clicking the Start screen thumbnail in the bottom-left corner of the screen, selecting Control Panel, typing Windows Defender in the Search Control Panel box, and then clicking the corresponding link in the Results list. Figure 1.32 shows the Windows Defender program window.

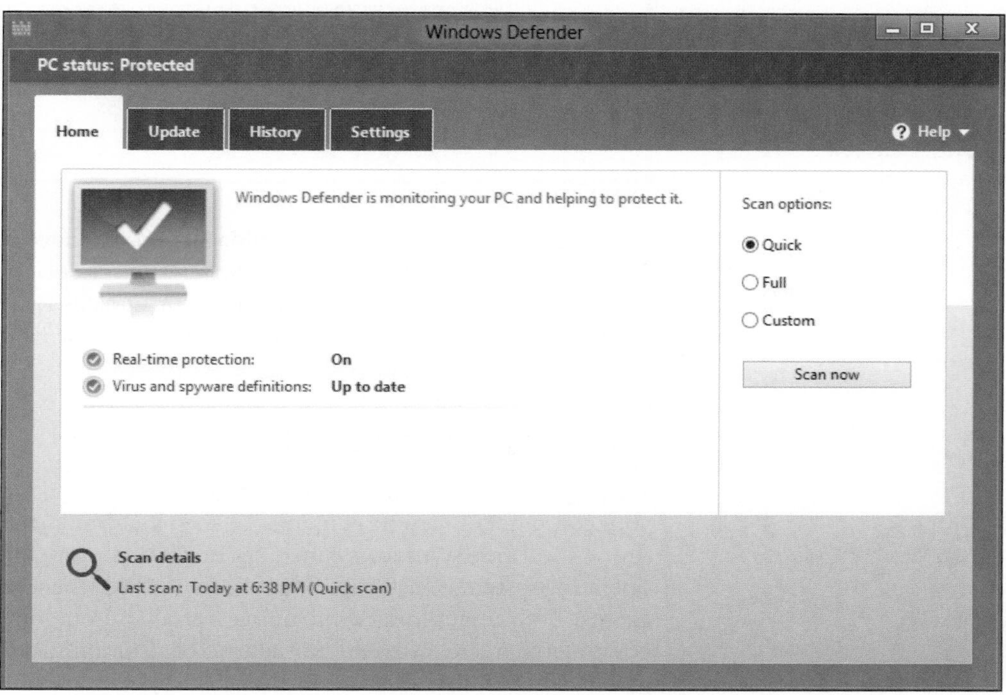

FIGURE 1.32 Windows Defender

Access Windows Update

Microsoft constantly identifies ways to enhance Windows security or fix problems that occur. There is no need to download or purchase an updated operating system each time changes are necessary; instead, you can simply make sure that your computer is set to automatically download any updates (fixes). Such modifications to the operating system are called ***Windows Updates***.

Microsoft strongly recommends that you configure your computer to automatically download and install any updates. That way, you do not have to remember to check for updates or manually download them. This is the default setting for Windows Update in Windows 8. To check your settings for updates, right-click the Start screen thumbnail in the bottom-left corner of the screen, and then select Control Panel, *System and Security*, and Windows Update. Click Change settings. As shown in Figure 1.33, you can click to select the level of updates. You can have Windows both download and install updates automatically (strongly recommended), only download but let you install them, or never check for updates (certainly not recommended!).

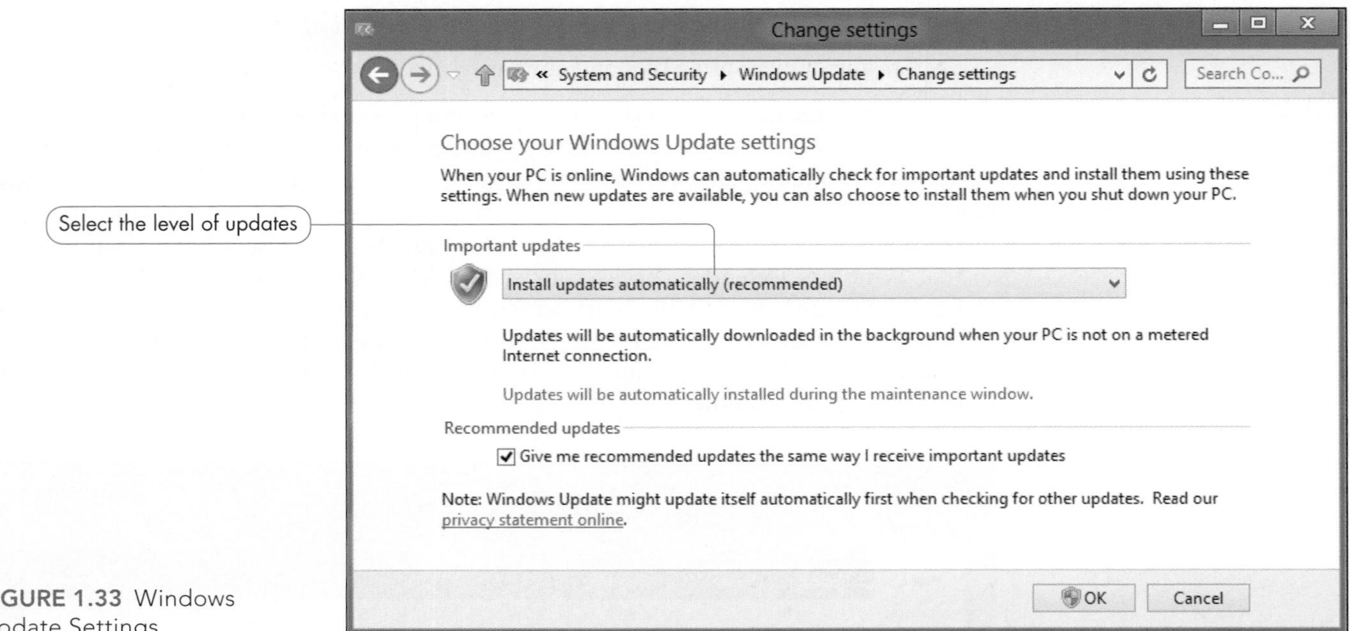

FIGURE 1.33 Windows Update Settings

Even between scheduled downloads, you can have your computer check for updates. Display the Control Panel, choose *System and Security* and Windows Update, and then Check for updates. If you want to check for updates for other Microsoft products, such as Microsoft Office, open Windows Update and click the *Find out more* link next to *Get updates for other Microsoft products*.

Use Windows Firewall

When you work with the Internet, there is always a possibility that a hacker could disable your computer or view its contents. To keep that from occurring, it is imperative that you use firewall software. Windows 8 includes firewall software that is turned on by default when the operating system is installed. It remains on guard whenever your computer is on, protecting against both unauthorized incoming traffic and outgoing. That means that other people, computers, or programs are not allowed to communicate with your computer unless you give permission. Also, programs on your system are not allowed to communicate online unless you approve them.

Periodically, you might want to check to make sure your firewall has not been turned off accidentally. If you have another security program installed, such as Norton Internet Security, these programs have their own firewall software and therefore may recommend that Windows Firewall be turned off. This is because two active firewall programs can sometimes interfere with each other. But you should ensure that one firewall program is turned on at all times.

Display the Control Panel, choose *System and Security*, and then *Check firewall status* (under *Windows Firewall*). From the dialog box (see Figure 1.34), you can turn the firewall on or off. You can also adjust other firewall settings.

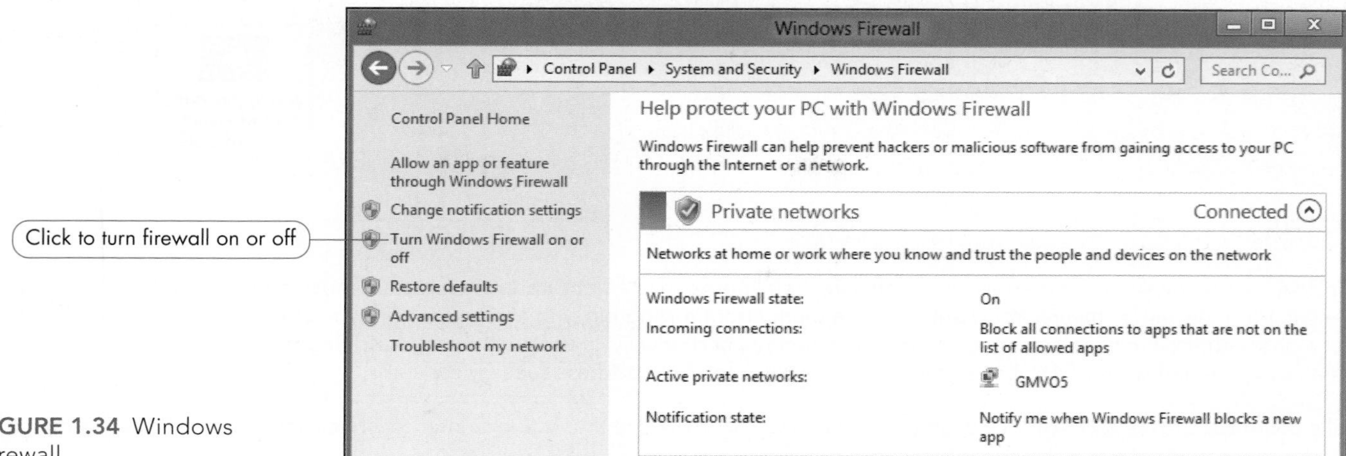

FIGURE 1.34 Windows Firewall

TIP Set Up Family Safety

If children in your household have user accounts on your computer, you can use the Family Safety utility to limit the hours they can use the computer, choose what they can see online, and limit the apps they can run. Open the Control Panel to create user accounts. To apply controls to an account, open the Control Panel and click *Set up Family Safety for any user* (under *User Accounts and Family Safety*). After selecting the user account to limit, apply the desired Family Safety limitations.

Hands-On Exercises

2 Windows Programs and Security Features

Windows is a gateway to using application software. You know that the fifth-grade students are most interested in the "fun" things that can be done with software. You want to excite them about having fun with a computer but you also want them to understand that along with the fun comes some concern about security and privacy. In this section of your demonstration, you will encourage them to explore software and to understand how Windows can help address security concerns.

Skills covered: Create a WordPad Document and Use Calculator • Use the Action Center to Check Security and Privacy Settings • Use the Snipping Tool

STEP 1 » CREATE A WORDPAD DOCUMENT AND USE CALCULATOR

Because all computers are configured with different software, your demonstration to the class will focus on only those programs (software) that are built into Windows (those that students are most likely to find on any computer). Specifically, you will use WordPad and Calculator for your brief discussion. Refer to Figure 1.35 as you complete Step 1.

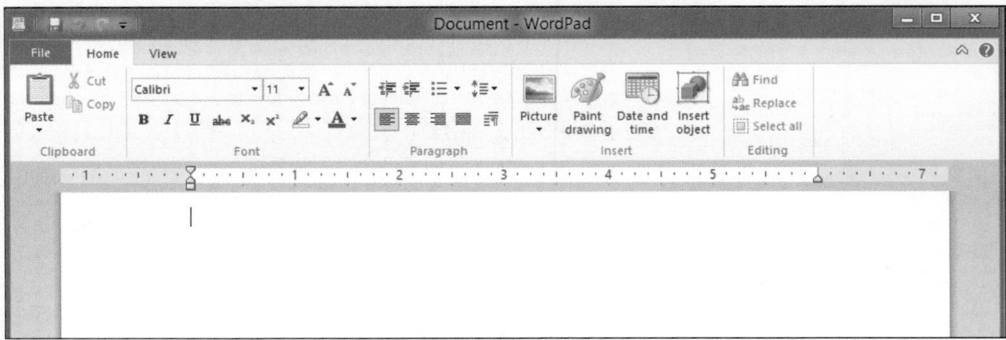

FIGURE 1.35 WordPad

a. Open a new, blank Microsoft Word document. Save this document as **win01h2Programs-Security_LastFirst**, replacing *LastFirst* with your own last name and first name.

b. Right-click in any blank area on the Start screen and click **All apps**. Scroll to the right to find the Windows Accessories group and click **WordPad**. The WordPad window opens, as shown in Figure 1.35.

   WordPad is a word processing program that is installed along with Windows 8 (and earlier Windows versions).

c. Click in the document area to position the insertion point (blinking black bar) at the top left of the WordPad window. Type your first and last names and press **Enter**. Type your street address and press **Enter**. Type your city, state, and ZIP.

d. Press the **Windows key+PRTSC**. Place your pointer at the beginning of your Word document and press **Ctrl+V**. Save your Word document.

e. Close the WordPad document. Click **Don't Save** when prompted to save your changes.

   Having demonstrated the use of a word processor, you will close the document without saving it.

f. Right-click in any blank area on the Start screen. Click **All apps**. Scroll to the right to find the Windows Accessories group, click **Calculator**, and then click **View**. If you do not see a bullet beside *Standard*, click **Standard**. If you do see a bullet beside *Standard*, press **Esc** (on the keyboard).

g. Click the corresponding keys on the calculator to complete the following formula: **87+98+100/3**. Click the **= sign** when you have typed the formula.

   You use the calculator to show how a student might determine his exam average, assuming he has taken three exams (weighted equally) with scores of 87, 98, and 100. The result should be 95.

h. Press the **Windows key+PRTSC**. Place your pointer at the end of your Word document and press **Ctrl+V**. This will paste another image of your screen into your Word document. Save your Word document.

i. Close the Calculator.

j. Keep the *win01h2Programs-Security_LastFirst* file open if you are proceeding to Step 2. Otherwise, save and close the file.

STEP 2 » USE THE ACTION CENTER TO CHECK SECURITY AND PRIVACY SETTINGS

The Action Center will occasionally display messages regarding security and privacy settings. You want the Cedar Grove students to be aware of how important those messages are, so you will show them how to use the Action Center. Refer to Figure 1.36 as you complete Step 2.

TROUBLESHOOTING: If you are working in a campus lab, you might not have access to the Action Center or Windows Update. In that case, you should proceed to Step 3 of this Hands-On Exercise.

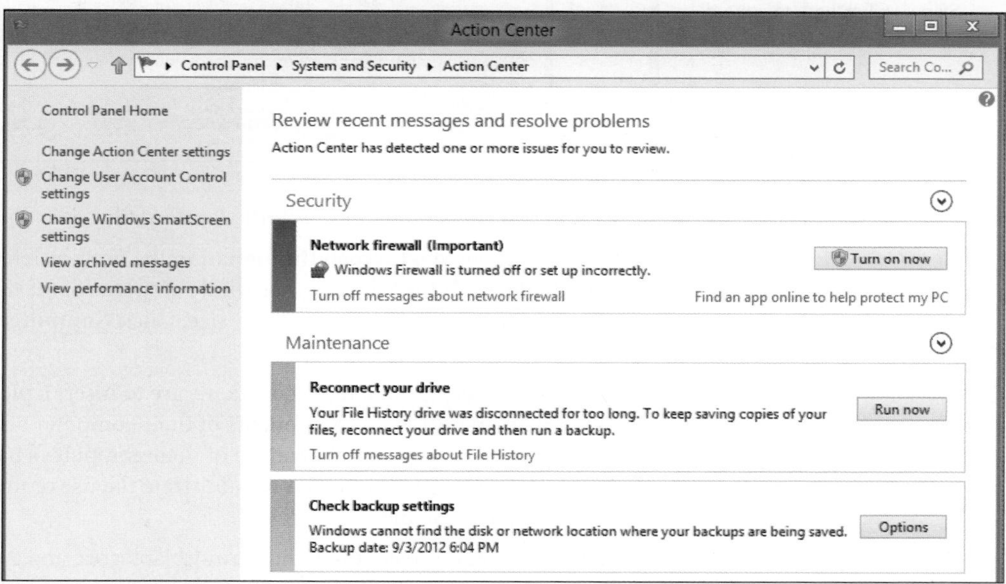

FIGURE 1.36 Action Center

a. Open the *win01h2Programs-Security_LastFirst* file if it is not open from the previous step.

b. Right-click the **Start screen thumbnail** in the bottom-left corner of the screen, select **Control Panel**, and then click **System and Security**. Click *Action Center*.

   Although any alerts displayed on your computer may vary from those shown in Figure 1.36, the general appearance should be similar.

c. Press the **Windows key+PRTSC**. Place your pointer at the end of your Word document and press **Ctrl+V**. Save your Word document.

d. Click **Change Action Center settings**. Take a look at the items monitored by the Action Center. Note that you can select or deselect any of them. Click **Cancel**. Close the Action Center window.

e. Right-click the **Start screen thumbnail** in the bottom-left corner of the screen, select **Control Panel**, and then click **System and Security**. Click **Windows Update** and click **Change settings**. Is your system scheduled for a routine check for installation of updates? Click the **Back button** (arrow pointing left at the top-left corner of the window).

f. Press the **Windows key+PRTSC**. Place your pointer at the end of your Word document, and then press **Ctrl+V**. Save your Word document.

g. Click **View update history**. You should see a summary of recent updates and their level of importance. Click **OK**. Close all open Control Panel windows.

h. Keep the *win01h2Programs-Security_LastFirst* file open if you are proceeding to Step 3. Otherwise, save and close the file.

STEP 3 » USE THE SNIPPING TOOL

Windows 8 includes a Snipping Tool that enables you to select any part of the screen and save it as a picture file. You plan to present the Snipping Tool to the Cedar Grove class. Refer to Figure 1.37 as you complete Step 3.

FIGURE 1.37 Saving a Snip

a. Open the *win01h2Programs-Security_LastFirst* file if it is not open from the previous step.

b. Right-click the **Start screen thumbnail** in the bottom-left corner of the screen and select **File Explorer**. If the File Explorer window opens in full size (maximized), click the **Restore Down button** to reduce the window size. Click **Computer** in the left-hand panel to display the Computer window.

   Assume that as part of a report, students are to insert a picture of the Computer window. Perhaps the report is on components of their computer and the student wants to include the Computer window as an illustration of their computer's hardware configuration. After opening the Computer window, you will illustrate the use of the Snipping Tool to capture the screen in a picture file.

c. Display the Start screen, right-click in any blank area, and then click **All apps**. In the Windows Accessories group, click **Snipping Tool**. The Snipping Tool displays. Click the **New arrow**, click **Window Snip**, and then click in the **Computer window** to select it.

   You have selected a window as a screen capture, which now appears in the Snipping Tool markup window.

d. Click the **Save Snip icon** in the Snipping Tool window, as shown in Figure 1.37. Scroll up in the left pane of the Save As dialog box, if necessary and click **Favorites**. Click **Desktop** (in the left pane, not the right) click in the **File name box** (where you most likely see the word *Capture*), and then click and drag to select the word *Capture* (if it is not already selected). Type **Computer window** (to change the file name). Click **Save**.

   You have saved the picture of the Computer window to the desktop.

e. Click in the *win01h2Programs-Security_LastFirst* file to position the insertion point at the end of the file. On the Insert tab of the Ribbon, click the **Picture icon**. In the Insert Picture dialog box that displays, click **Desktop** in the left-hand pane. Browse through the right-hand pane and find the **Computer window file** and click it. Click **Insert** at the bottom of the dialog box to insert the file into your Word document. Save your word document.

f. Close any open windows. You should see the *Computer window* file on the desktop. Double-click to open it. Close the file.

g. Right-click the **Computer window file** on the desktop. Click **Delete**. Confirm the deletion.

You have removed the file from the desktop.

Windows Search and Help

No matter how careful you are to save files in locations that will be easily located later, you will sometimes lose track of a file or folder. In this case, Windows 8 can help as you can easily search for items. In this section, you will learn to search for items such as files, folders, and programs. Sometimes, you may not be sure how to accomplish certain tasks within Windows. We will also cover utilizing the Help feature of Windows to fill in any gaps in your knowledge.

You can locate any file, folder, or application on your computer by using all or part of the file name, the file type, or a bit of the contents. Windows 8 provides several ways to search. The two most useful are the Search screen accessed from the Charms bar and the Search tools located in File Explorer. Although the Search screen is fast, the search tools in File Explorer are more full-featured. You can customize a search to look at specific folders, libraries, or storage media, and you can narrow the search using filters (file type, date modified, etc.). After conducting a search, you can save it so that you can access it later without re-creating search criteria.

Performing a Search

STEP 1» The Search option on the Charms bar takes you to the Search screen (see Figure 1.38). You will probably find this the most convenient place to begin a search. You can find files, folders, programs, and e-mail messages saved on your computer by entering one or more keywords in the Search box. Items that match your search term will be grouped into three categories: Apps, Settings, and Files. Apps are programs that match the search term. Settings are Windows options that are somehow related to your search term. Files show all files that contain a reference to your search term based on text in the file, text in the file name, file tags, and other file properties.

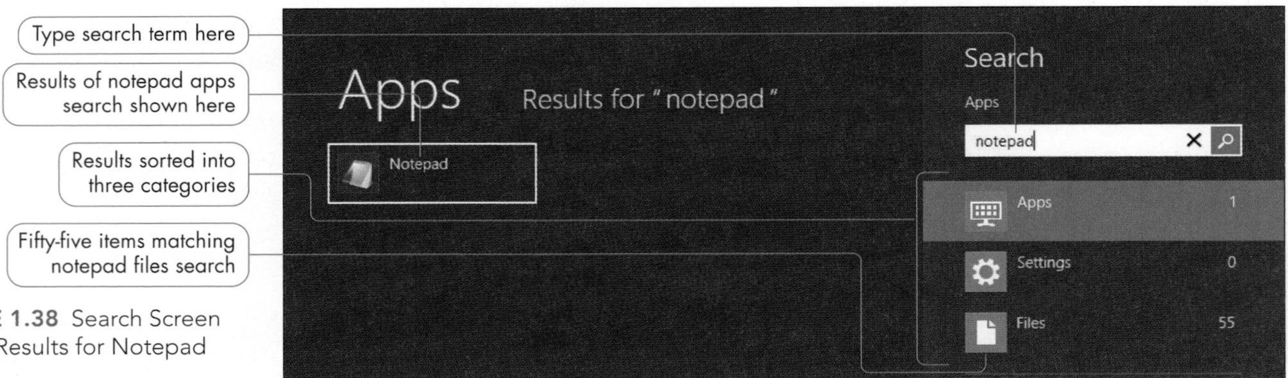

FIGURE 1.38 Search Screen Search Results for Notepad Search

If you are certain a program is installed on your computer, but you cannot find the program on the Start screen, you can type some or all of the program name in the Search box on the Search screen. Immediately, because Apps is selected in the right pane, you will see any matching program names on the left side of the screen, such as the Notepad search shown in Figure 1.38. Simply click the name in the list of results to open the program. But notice also that there are 46 files which contain a reference to Notepad. Clicking the Files icon would display a list of those 46 files. You could then click any one of those files to open it. Searches conducted through the Search screen search the entire contents of your computer. This could take some time if you have a lot of data on your computer!

Using Targeted Searches

STEP 2» To perform more targeted searches, you may wish to use the search features of File Explorer (see Figure 1.39). To launch File Explorer, click the File Explorer tile on the Start screen or move the pointer to the bottom-left corner of your screen until the thumbnail image displays and right-click. From the shortcut menu, select File Explorer.

FIGURE 1.39 File Explorer Search Tools

Suppose you are looking for a report you did on the history of rocketry for your CIS class. You know it covers Robert Goddard one of the early rocket pioneers. Most likely the file is stored in one of your libraries. So click Libraries in the left-hand pane to select it and narrow the search to this part of your computer. You could also use the search options to further restrict your search to certain types of files. The search results shown in Figure 1.39 show four files that mention Robert Goddard. Two are picture files. One is the report you are looking for on the History of Rocketry. The other is a report on NASA you did for a history class that also happens to mention Robert Goddard. You can click any files in the search results list to access them. Notice that additional information is shown about the files such as their location, size, and file type.

You could use many advanced options to further narrow the search if the results are extensive such as restricting the search to files generated or modified within certain date ranges. The search feature of File Explorer is a very powerful, yet easy-to-use tool.

Save a Search

If you know that you will conduct the same search often, you might find it helpful to save the search so that you do not have to continually enter the same search criteria. Perform the search once. On the Search tab on the Ribbon, click *Save search*. Type a name for the search and click Save. The next time you want to conduct the search, open File Explorer. The saved search name is displayed in the *Favorites* section, as shown in Figure 1.39. Simply click the link to get new results.

Getting Help

STEP 3»

No matter how well prepared you are or how much you know about your computer, you will occasionally have questions about a process or tool. Fortunately, help on almost any Windows topic is only a click away using ***Help and Support***. It is probably a good idea to conduct a search for the Help and Support App and pin it to your Start screen. Then, as you find that you need assistance on a topic or procedure, you can click the *Help and Support* tile to display the *Help and Support* app (see Figure 1.40).

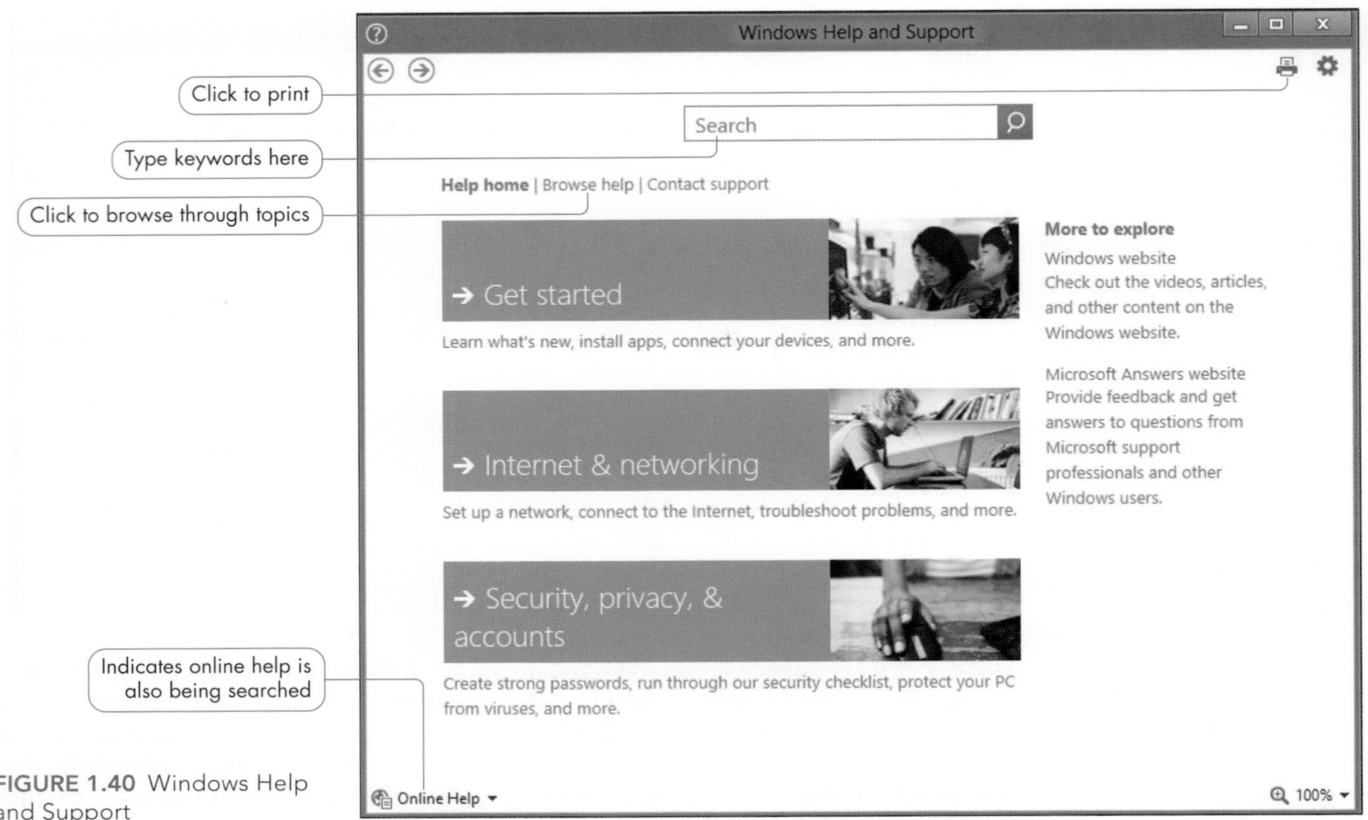

FIGURE 1.40 Windows Help and Support

You can then browse the help library by topic or search the library by typing keywords. You can even take advantage of Microsoft's extensive online help if you have an Internet connection.

Search and Browse Help

If you know exactly what you need assistance with, click in the Search box of *Help and Support* and type your topic. For example, if you are seeking information on resizing desktop icons, type *resize desktop icons*. Press Enter or click the magnifying glass icon next to the Search box. A list of results displays, arranged in order of usefulness. Click any topic to view more detail. You can print results by clicking the Printer icon.

Help topics are also available when you browse help by clicking Browse help (see Figure 1.40). By browsing the subsequent list of topics, you can learn a lot about Windows. You might browse *Help and Support* when you have no particular need for topic-specific assistance or when your question is very general. Figure 1.41 shows a list of topics that you can select from when you browse Help.

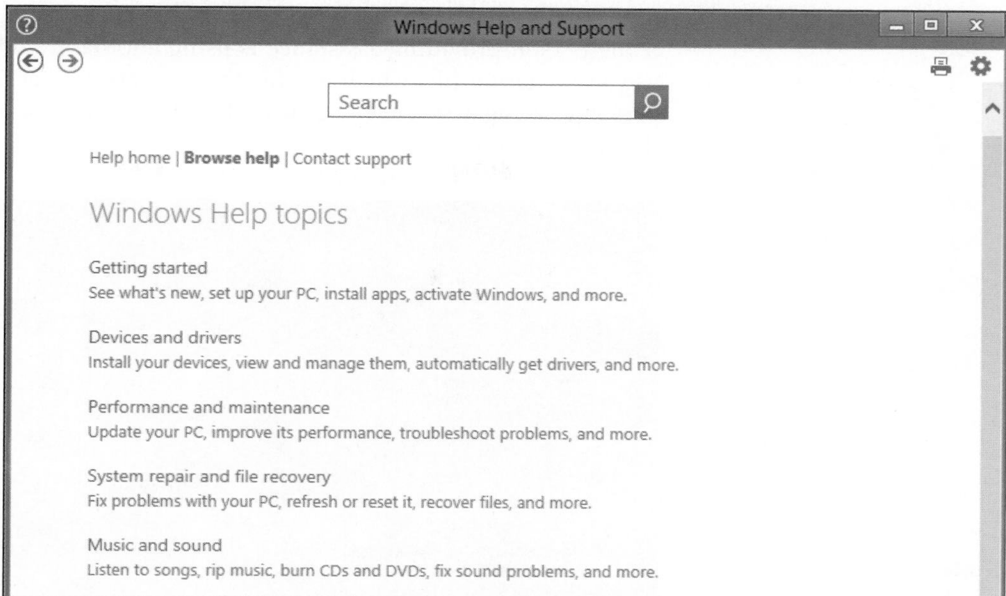

FIGURE 1.41 Browsing Help and Support

Windows *Help and Support* is an excellent tool when you need assistance on general topics related to the operating system, but you might also need help with a specific application, as well. For example, you will be working with a software application, such as a word processing program, and find that you have a question. Invariably, you can locate a Help button that enables you to type search terms or browse application-specific help topics. When you are working with a task in an application, you will often be responding to a dialog box. If you have a question at that time, click the ? button, usually located in the top-right corner of a window, for help related to the specific task. Some dialog boxes, but not all, include a Help button. Figure 1.42 shows a dialog box from Microsoft Word with a Help button.

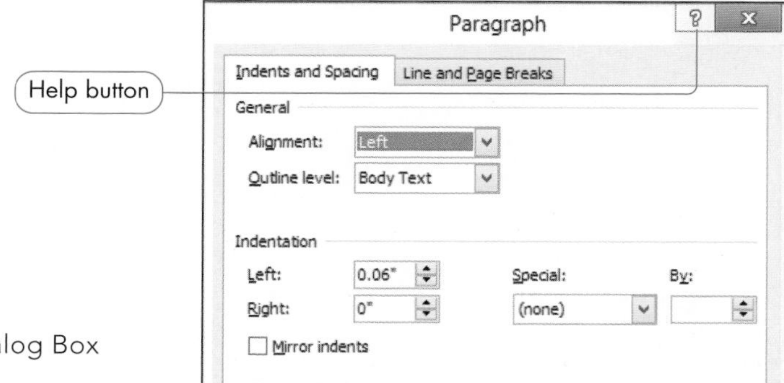

FIGURE 1.42 Dialog Box Help

Get Remote Assistance

Undoubtedly, you will have trouble with your computer at some time and need some assistance. You might consider getting someone to help you by letting them connect to your computer remotely to determine the problem. Of course, you will only want to ask someone that you trust because that person will temporarily have access to your files.

To access Remote Assistance in Windows 8, display the Charms bar, click the Search option, and then type Remote Assistance in the search term box. The settings for Remote Assistance will be listed as shown in Figure 1.43 as a set of steps. You should go through these steps in order to enable remote assistance on your computer. If the person who is helping you is also using Windows 8, you can use a method called Easy Connect. The first time you use Easy Connect to request assistance, you will receive a password that you then give to the person offering assistance. Using that password, the helper can remotely connect to your computer and exchange information. Thereafter, a password is not necessary—you simply click the contact information for the helper to initiate a session. If the person providing assistance is using another Windows operating system, you can use an invitation file, which is a file that you create that is sent (usually by e-mail) to the person offering assistance. The invitation file includes a password that is used to connect the two computers.

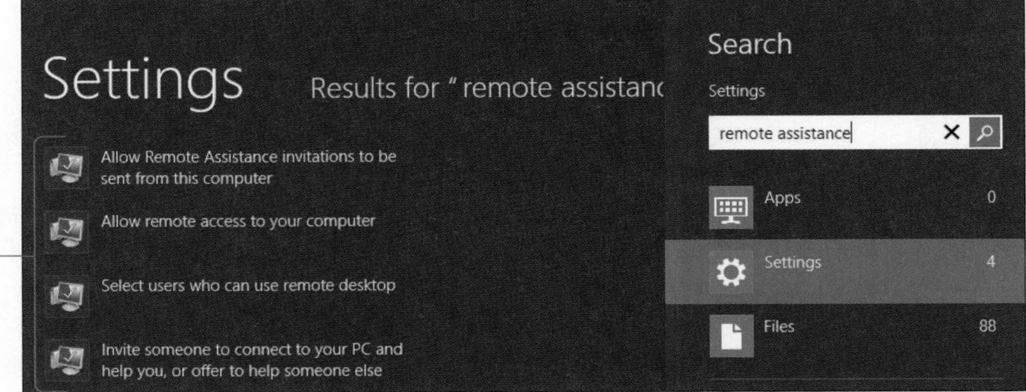

FIGURE 1.43 Remote Assistance

Get Online Help

So that you are sure to get the latest help, you will probably want to include online Help files in your searches for assistance. To make sure that is happening, open *Help and Support*, and check that *Online help* is visible at the bottom of the screen (it is selected by default). Of course, you must be connected to the Internet before accessing online help.

Hands-On Exercises

3 Windows Search and Help

As you close your presentation to the Cedar Grove class, you want the students to be confident in their ability, but well aware that help is available. You plan to demonstrate several ways they can get assistance. You also want them to know how to conduct searches for files and folders. Although they might not give it much thought, you know that there will be many times when they will forget where they saved a very important file. Therefore, it is imperative that you include the topic of searching in your presentation.

Skills covered: Explore Windows Help and Search Using Keywords • Use the Search Box to Conduct a Search and Expand a Search • Get Help in an Application and a Dialog Box

STEP 1 » EXPLORE WINDOWS HELP AND SEARCH USING KEYWORDS

As students in your class progress to middle and high school, they may have opportunities to use laptops for class work. They also are likely to find themselves in locations where they can connect to the Internet wirelessly. Using that example, you will help the class understand how to use Windows Help and Support to learn how to find and safely connect to an available wireless network. Refer to Figure 1.44 as you complete Step 1.

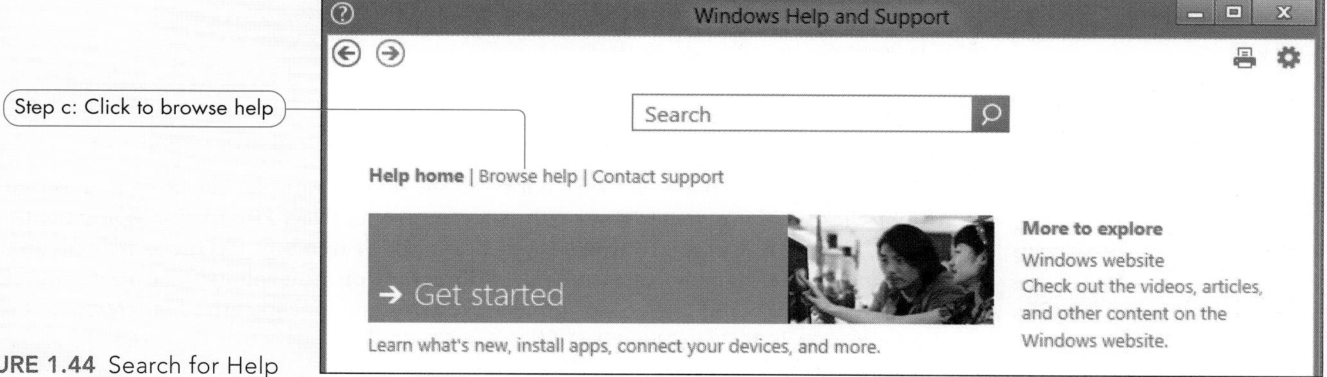

FIGURE 1.44 Search for Help

a. Open a new, blank Microsoft Word document. Save this document on the drive where you normally save files as **win01h3Help-Search_LastFirst**, replacing *LastFirst* with your own last name and first name.

b. Display the Start screen, right-click an empty section of the screen, and then click **All apps**. Click the **Help and Support icon**. Maximize the Windows Help and Support window.

> **TROUBLESHOOTING:** Your computer should be connected to the Internet before completing this exercise.

c. Click the **Browse help link**, click **Security, privacy and accounts**, and then click **Why Use Windows Defender?**. Read through the topic.

   You will show students how to use Help and Support browsing to locate help on a topic—in this case, why they should use Windows Defender.

d. Press the **Windows key+PRTSC**. Place your pointer at the beginning of the *win01h3Help-Search_LastFirst* file and press **Ctrl+V**. Save the file.

e. Click the **Help and Support home link**, click in the **Search Help box**, and then type **Windows Defender**. Press **Enter**. Click **Why Use Windows Defender**. Note that you arrived at the same topic as in the previous step, but took a different route. Close the Windows Help and Support window.

f. Use any method of getting Help and Support to answer the question *How can I protect myself from viruses?* What did you find?

g. Press the **Windows key+PRTSC** with the virus information still displayed. Place your pointer at the end of the *win01h3Help-Search_LastFirst* file and press **Ctrl+V**. Save the file.

h. Keep the *win01h3Help-Search_LastFirst* file open if you are proceeding to Step 2. Otherwise, save and close the file.

STEP 2 » USE THE SEARCH BOX TO CONDUCT A SEARCH AND EXPAND A SEARCH

You want to show students how to search for files, but you are not familiar enough with the classroom computer to know what files to search for. You know, however, that Windows-based computers will include some picture files so you feel certain you can use the example of searching for files with a .jpg (picture) file type. You will also illustrate expanding and narrowing a search. Refer to Figure 1.45 as you complete Step 2.

FIGURE 1.45 Narrow a Search

a. Open the *win01h3Help-Search_LastFirst* file if it is not open from the previous step.

b. Move the pointer to the bottom-left corner of the screen to display the thumbnail image. Right-click the thumbnail to display the shortcut menu, select **File Explorer**, and then click **Computer**. Maximize the window. Click in the **Search box**. On the Search tab on the Ribbon, click **Other properties** and select **file extension**. You will now see *file extension:* displayed in the search box. Click in the **Search box** and type **jpg** after *file extension:*. Press **Enter** to search. Note the long list of files found.

c. Press the **Windows key+PRTSC**. Place your pointer at the end of the *win01h3Help-Search_LastFirst* file and press **Ctrl+V**. This will paste an image of your screen into the file. Save the file.

d. Close the Computer window.

e. Point to the bottom-left corner of the screen to display the *Start screen* thumbnail. Right-click the thumbnail to display the shortcut menu, select **File Explorer**, and then click **Computer**. Maximize the window. Type **Tulips** in the **Search box**. Click **Other properties** and select **type**. Enter **jpg** in the **Search box** after the word *type*. Press **Enter** to search. You will probably only find one jpg of tulips now that you have restricted the search.

f. Press the **Windows key+PRTSC**. Place your pointer at the end of the *win01h3Help-Search_LastFirst* file and press **Ctrl+V**. This will paste an image of your screen into the file. Save the file.

g. Keep the *win01h3Help-Search_LastFirst* file open if you are proceeding to Step 3. Otherwise, save and close the file.

STEP 3 » GET HELP IN AN APPLICATION AND A DIALOG BOX

As you complete the session with the fifth-graders, you want them to understand that they will never be without assistance. If they need help with general computer and operating system questions, they can access Help and Support from the Apps screen. If they are working with an application, such as a word processor, they will most likely find a Help link that will enable them to search for help related to keywords. Within an application, if they have a dialog box open, they can sometimes get help related to the dialog box's activities. You will demonstrate application help and dialog box help.

a. Display the Charms bar and click **Search**. On the Search screen, type **Windows Defender** in the **Search box**. Click the **Windows Defender icon** that displays in the results list to display Windows Defender.

b. Click the **question mark (?)** on the right side of the Windows Defender screen. Maximize the Windows Help and Support window. Read about why you should use Windows Defender.

c. Press the **Windows key+PRTSC**. Place your pointer at the end of the *win01h3Help-Search_LastFirst file* and press **Ctrl+V**. This will paste an image of your screen into the file. Save the file.

d. Close the Windows Help and Support window and Windows Defender.

e. Move the pointer to the bottom-left corner of the screen until the thumbnail image displays and right-click the thumbnail image. Select **Control Panel** from the shortcut menu. Click **Appearance and Personalization**. Click **Change the theme** in the *Personalization* section. Click **?** in the top-right corner of the dialog box to open the Help dialog box. Read about themes.

f. Press the **Windows key+PRTSC**. Place your pointer at the end of the *win01h3Help-Search_LastFirst* file and press **Ctrl+V**. Save the file and submit it to your instructor.

g. Close any open windows.

Chapter Objectives Review

After reading this chapter, you have accomplished the following objectives:

1. **Understand the Start screen.**
   - The Start screen is the display that appears when you turn on a computer. It contains tiles (icons) that represent programs, files, folders, and system resources.
   - Windows 8 optimized programs are designed to run full screen to take advantage full advantage of small screens on portable devices.
2. **Configure the Start screen.**
   - You can easily add and remove tiles from the Windows 8 Start screen.
   - Adding a tile to the start screen is known as "pinning" a tile.
   - You can organize the tiles into groups by dragging them around the screen with your mouse.
   - You can also assign appropriate names for each group of tiles.
3. **Run Windows 8 apps.**
   - Clicking a tile on the Start screen will launch an app.
   - Windows 8 apps are displayed full screen without borders or scroll bars.
   - Displaying the Switch list will allow you to easily switch from one open app to another.
4. **Close apps.**
   - You can close Windows 8 apps by pressing Alt+F4 from within the app.
   - You can click at the top of an app and drag it down off the bottom of the screen.
5. **Understand the desktop.**
   - Windows 8 still includes a modified version of the Windows 7 desktop.
   - Non–Windows 8 programs will still run on the desktop.
   - The taskbar is the horizontal bar along the bottom of the desktop. It includes pinned icons, icons of open windows and the Notification area.
   - You can customize the desktop to include a background and screen saver.
6. **Manage Windows 8 apps and windows.**
   - Windows 8 apps run full screen without the distraction of borders.
   - Older programs and folders open in individual windows on the desktop, much like papers on a desk.
   - You can manage windows by moving, resizing, stacking, or snapping them into position so that multiple windows are easier to work with and identify.
   - Windows 8 apps can only be displayed two at a time.
7. **Identify Windows accessories.**
   - Windows 8 provides several accessory programs, including a word processor (WordPad), text editor (Notepad), calculator (Calculator), and screen capture tool (Snipping Tool).
   - You will find accessory programs when you access the Apps screen by clicking the *All apps* icon on the Start screen.
8. **Work with security settings and software.**
   - Windows 8 takes computer security seriously, providing monitoring and software that helps keep your computer safe from viruses, spyware, and hackers.
   - Windows Defender, an antivirus and antispyware program, is included with Windows and works to identify and remove malicious software.
   - The Action Center monitors the status of your security and maintenance settings, alerting you when maintenance tasks (such as backing up your system) are overlooked or when your security is at risk (when antivirus software is out of date, for example).
   - A Windows firewall protects against unauthorized access to your computer from outside entities and prohibits Internet travel by programs from your computer without your permission.
   - The File History utility can be configured to automatically make backups of your important files while you work.
9. **Perform a search.**
   - As you work with a computer, it is inevitable that you will forget where you saved a file. Windows 8 provides ample support for finding such items, providing a Search utility accessible from the Charms bar and in every open window. As you type search keywords in either of those areas, Windows immediately begins a search, showing results.
   - From File Explorer, you can begin a search and then narrow it by file type or other criteria unique to the searched folders or libraries. You might, for example, narrow a search by Date Taken if you are searching in the Pictures folder. You can also expand a search to include more search areas than the current folder or library.
10. **Use targeted searches.**
    - File Explorer provides tools to do focused (targeted searches).
    - Using the search tools within File Explorer, you can tailor your searches to restrict searches by file types, file date ranges, and file size.
11. **Get help.**
    - You can learn a lot about Windows by accessing the *Help and Support* features available with Windows 8.
    - The *Help and Support* center is accessible from the Apps screen.
    - If you are looking for specific answers, you can type search keyword(s) in the Search box and then click any resulting links.
    - If your question is more general, you can browse Help by clicking the *Browse help* link and then working through various links, learning as you go.
    - Help is also available within an application by clicking a Help button and phrasing a search.
    - If you are working with a dialog box, you can click a ? button for specific assistance with the task at hand.

Key Terms Matching

Match the key terms with their definitions. Write the key term letter by the appropriate numbered definition.

- **a.** App bars
- **b.** Charms bar
- **c.** Desktop
- **d.** Dialog box
- **e.** Help and support
- **f.** Icon
- **g.** Jump list
- **h.** Notification area
- **i.** Operating system
- **j.** Pinning
- **k.** Shortcut
- **l.** Snipping tool
- **m.** Start screen
- **n.** Switch list
- **o.** Taskbar
- **p.** Windows 8 apps
- **q.** Windows 8 Interface
- **r.** Windows Defender
- **s.** Windows updates
- **t.** Wordpad

1. _____ An icon with an arrow in the left-hand corner. **p. 10**
2. _____ Floats on the screen above an app when summoned. **p. 7**
3. _____ The workspace for non–Windows 8 apps. **p. 9**
4. _____ A picture that represents programs or folders. **p. 10**
5. _____ Shows recently opened files and other options for a program. **p. 12**
6. _____ Software that directs computer activities. **p. 2**
7. _____ An accessory program that facilitates screen captures. **p. 26**
8. _____ Contains thumbnail images of open programs. **p. 8**
9. _____ Programs designed to run in the Start screen interface. **p. 3**
10. _____ Detects and removes viruses and spyware. **p. 27**
11. _____ A basic word processing program included with Windows. **p. 24**
12. _____ Provides quick access to frequently performed actions. **p. 3**
13. _____ A window that facilitates user input. **p. 16**
14. _____ An app that provides user assistance on topics or procedures. **p. 37**
15. _____ Provides system status alerts in pop-up boxes. **p. 11**
16. _____ Adding a tile to the Start screen. **p. 4**
17. _____ The first thing you see after your Windows 8 computer boots up. **p. 3**
18. _____ Helps track open programs on the desktop. **p. 11**
19. _____ Another name for the Start screen. **p. 3**
20. _____ Delivers modifications to the operating system to fix problems. **p. 29**

Multiple Choice

1. The Windows 8 feature that alerts you to any maintenance or security concerns is the:
   (a) Action Center.
   (b) Security Center.
   (c) Windows Defender.
   (d) Control Panel.

2. Snapping apps means that you:
   (a) Minimize all open apps simultaneously so that the Start screen displays.
   (b) Auto arrange all open apps so that they are of uniform size.
   (c) Manually reposition all open apps so that you can see the content of each.
   (d) Move a second app to the left or right side of the screen so it displays along with the first app.

3. Which of the following accessory programs is primarily a text editor?
   (a) Notepad
   (b) Snipping Tool
   (c) Journal
   (d) Calculator

4. Apps on the Start screen are represented by rectangular icons known as:
   (a) Tiles.
   (b) Thumbnails.
   (c) Gadget.
   (d) Bricks.

5. Open apps are displayed as thumbnails on the:
   (a) Desktop.
   (b) Start screen.
   (c) Notification area.
   (d) Switch list.

6. A shortcut icon on the desktop is identified by:
   (a) An arrow at the bottom-left corner of the icon.
   (b) The word *shortcut* included as part of the icon name.
   (c) A checkmark at the bottom-left corner of the icon.
   (d) Its placement on the right side of the desktop.

7. Help and Support is available from which of the following?
   (a) Switch list
   (b) Dialog boxes with ? buttons
   (c) Notification area
   (d) Taskbar

8. Which of the following is a method of switching between open windows?
   (a) Alt+Tab
   (b) Shift+Tab
   (c) Click an open app icon on the Start screen.
   (d) Windows key+Tab

9. When you maximize a window, you:
   (a) Fill the screen with the window.
   (b) Prioritize the window so that it is always placed on top of all other open windows.
   (c) Expand the window's height but leave its width unchanged.
   (d) Expand the window's width but leave its height unchanged.

10. When you enter search keywords in the Search box of File Explorer and the Computer option is selected:
    (a) The search is limited to a specific library.
    (b) The search cannot be further narrowed.
    (c) The search is automatically expanded to include every folder on the hard drive.
    (d) The search is limited to the selected folder, but can be expanded if you like.

Practice Exercises

1 Senior Academy

FROM SCRATCH

As a requirement for completing graduate school, you must submit a thesis, which is a detailed research report. Your degree is in education with a minor in information technology. Your thesis will center on generational learning styles, comparing the way students learn across the generations. Although you have not yet conducted your research, you suspect that students aged 55 and older have a very different way of learning than do younger students. You expect the use of technology in learning to be much more intimidating to older students who have not been exposed to such learning at a high level. As a researcher, however, you know that such suppositions must be supported or proven incorrect by research. As part of your thesis preparation, you are surveying a group of senior adults and a group of college students who are less than 25 years old. The local senior center will distribute your survey to seniors who are currently enrolled in a non-credit computer literacy course sponsored by the senior center. The same survey will be given to students enrolled in a computer literacy college course. The survey covers Windows 8 basics and includes the following steps. You should go over the steps before finalizing the survey instrument. This exercise follows the same set of skills as used in Hands-On Exercises 1–3 in the chapter. Refer to Figure 1.46 as you complete this exercise.

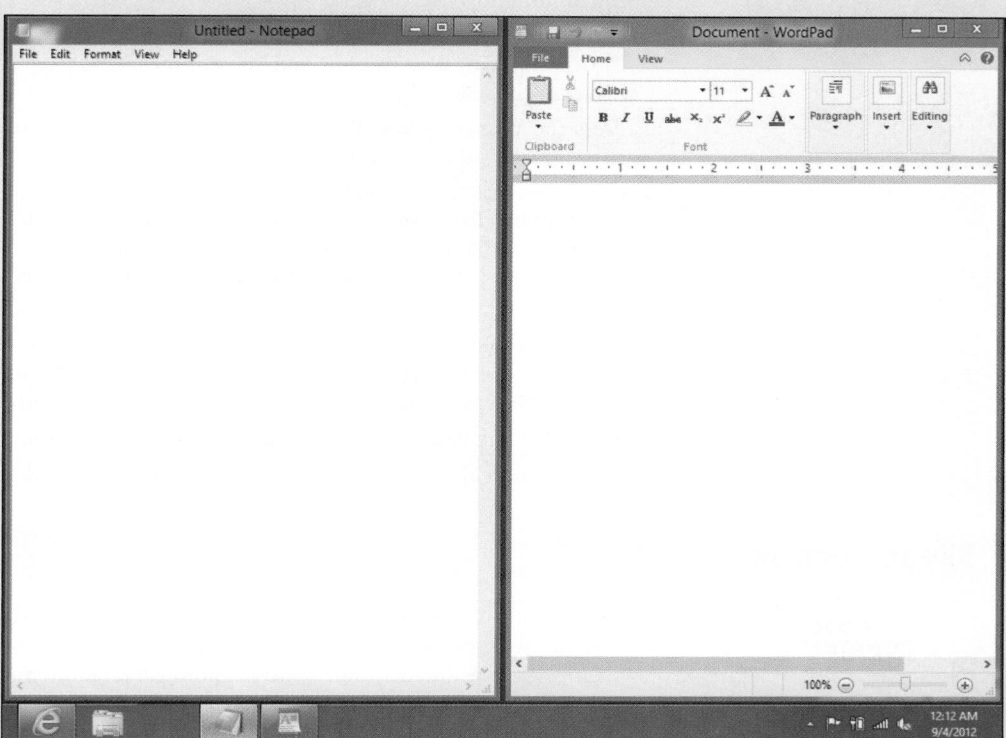

FIGURE 1.46 Notepad and WordPad

a. Open a new, blank Microsoft Word document. Save this document on the drive where you normally save files as **win01p1senioracademy_LastFirst**, replacing *LastFirst* with your own last name and first name.

b. Display the desktop, right-click an empty portion of the desktop, select **Personalize** from the shortcut menu, and then click the **Desktop Background link**. Make sure *Picture location* shows *Windows Desktop Backgrounds*. Scroll through the picture choices and select one.

c. Press the **Windows key+PRTSC**. Place your pointer at the beginning of the *win01p1senioracademy_LastFirst* file and press **CTRL+V**. Save the file.

d. Click **Save Changes** if you are allowed to make a change to the desktop or **Cancel** if you are not. Close all open windows (except Word).

e. Go to the Start screen, right-click and select **All apps**, and then right-click the **WordPad icon**. Click **Pin to Taskbar**.

f. Go to the Start screen, right-click and select **All apps**, and then right-click the **Paint icon**. Click **Pin to Start screen**.
g. Go to the Start screen, right-click and select **All apps**, and then right-click the **Notepad icon**. Click **Pin to Taskbar**.
h. Go to the desktop and click the **Notepad icon** on the taskbar. With Notepad still open, click the **WordPad icon** on the taskbar.
i. Right-click an empty area of the taskbar and click **Show windows side by side**. Compare your screen to Figure 1.46.
j. Press the **Windows key+PRTSC**. Place your pointer at the end of the *win01p1senioracademy_LastFirst* file and press **CTRL+V**. Save the file.
k. Click the **Close (X) button** at the top-right corner of the Notepad window to close the program.
l. Click the **Maximize button** on the right side of the WordPad window to maximize the window.
m. Go to the Start screen, right-click an empty portion of the screen, and then select **All apps**. Click the **Help and Support icon**, click **Browse Help**, and then click **Security, privacy and accounts**. Scroll down the list if necessary and click **How can I help protect my PC viruses?**. Click **How do I find and remove a virus?**.
n. Display the desktop. Right-click an empty area of the taskbar and click **Show windows stacked**. Click in the WordPad window and, in your own words, type a description of how to protect your PC from viruses.
o. Press the **Windows key+PRTSC**. Place your pointer at the end of the *win01p1senioracademy_LastFirst* file and press **CTRL+V**. Save the file.
p. Go to the Start screen, right-click an empty portion of the screen, and then select **All apps**. Click the **Snipping Tool icon**, click the **New arrow**, and then click **Full-screen Snip**. Click the **Save Snip button**. Scroll down the left side of the Save As dialog box and click to select the disk drive where you will save your student files. Click in the **File name box** and type **win01p1survey_LastFirst**. Click **Save**.
q. Close all open windows without saving.
r. Right-click the **WordPad icon** on the taskbar and click **Unpin this program from taskbar**. Right-click the **Notepad icon** on the taskbar and click **Unpin from taskbar**.
s. Right-click the **Paint tile** on the Start screen and click **Unpin from Start screen**.
t. Save and close the *win01p1senioracademy_LastFirst* file and submit it to your instructor.

2 Silent Auction

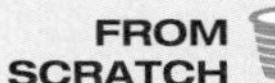

As part of your responsibility as vice president of the National Youth Assembly of College Athletes, you are soliciting donated items for a silent auction at the national conference. You accept items and tag them with an estimated value and a beginning bid requirement. You will use a computer to keep a record of the donor, value, and minimum bid requirement. Because you will not always be in the office when an item is donated, you will configure the desktop and taskbar of the computer to simplify the job of data entry for anyone who happens to be at the desk. This exercise follows the same set of skills as used in Hands-On Exercises 1–3 in the chapter. Refer to Figure 1.47 as you complete this exercise.

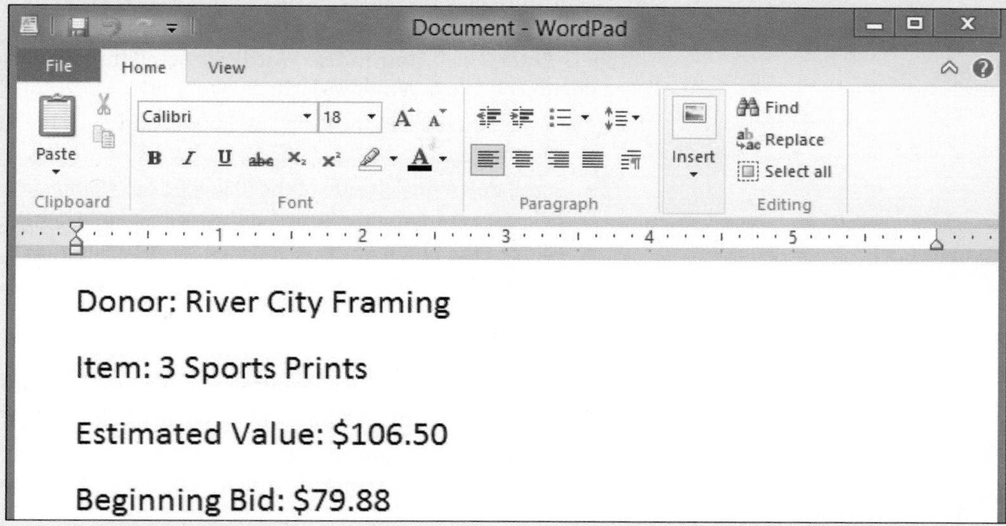

FIGURE 1.47 WordPad Auction Listing

a. Open a new, blank Microsoft Word document. Save this document on the drive where you normally save files as **win01p2silentauction_LastFirst**, replacing *LastFirst* with your own last name and first name.

b. Go to the **Start screen**. Right-click and select **All apps**, right-click the **WordPad icon**, and then click **Pin to Taskbar**.

c. Display the desktop. Right-click an empty area of the taskbar, click **Properties**, and then click the **Auto-hide the taskbar check box** (if no checkmark displays). Click **OK**.

d. Click the **WordPad icon** on the taskbar. WordPad will open.
   - Click the **Maximize button**. If no insertion point (blinking bar) displays in the top-left corner of the white space, click to position it there.
   - Type **Donor: River City Framing**. Press **Enter**.
   - Type **Item: 3 Sports Prints**. Press **Enter**.
   - Type **Estimated Value:**. Press **Spacebar**.

e. Go to the Start screen. Right-click and select **All apps**, right-click **Calculator**, and then select **Pin to Taskbar**. Press the **Windows key+D** to go to the desktop. Click the **Calculator icon** on the taskbar to launch Calculator.

   The estimated value of each print is $35.50, but the frames will be sold as a unit. Therefore, you need to determine the total value ($35.50 multiplied by 3). Because you are in the middle of typing a WordPad document, you do not want to close it. Instead, you will open the Calculator program and compute the value.

f. Use the mouse to click **35.50*3** and click =. The total value should show on the calculator. Minimize the calculator.

g. Type the total in the WordPad document. Press **Enter** and type **Beginning Bid:**. Press **Spacebar**.

h. Click the **Calculator icon** on the taskbar. The amount from step e should still be displayed on the calculator. Click the **multiplication key** (*) and **.75**. Click =. Jot down the value shown on the calculator and close the calculator.

   The beginning bid will be 75% of the estimated value. So the calculation should be Estimated Value multiplied by .75.

i. Click after the word *Bid:* in the WordPad window, if necessary. Type the value that you recorded in step h, rounded up to the nearest hundredth. Press **Enter**. Compare your screen to Figure 1.47.

j. Press the **Windows key+PRTSC**. Place your pointer at the beginning of the *win01p2silentauction_LastFirst* file and press **CTRL+V**. Save the file.

k. Go to the **Start screen**. Right-click and select **All apps**, and then click **Help and Support**. Maximize the Windows Help and Support window. Click in the **Search box** and type **WordPad**. Press **Enter**. Click **How to Use WordPad**. Scroll through the document to determine how to save a document. Close Windows Help and Support.

l. As you were directed in the Help and Support tip, click the **File tab**.
   - Click **Save**.
   - Scroll down the left side of the dialog box to *Computer* and click the disk drive where you save your student files. Proceed through any folder structure, as directed by your instructor.
   - Click in the **File name box** and type **win01p2auction_LastFirst**. You might first need to remove the current file name before typing the new one.
   - Click **Save**.
   - Close WordPad.

m. Right-click the taskbar, click **Properties**, and then click **Auto-hide the taskbar**. Click **OK**.

n. Right-click the **WordPad icon** on the taskbar. Click **Unpin from Taskbar**.

o. Save the *win01p2silentauction_LastFirst* file and close Word. Submit both the *win01p2silentauction_LastFirst* and the *win01p2auction_LastFirst* files to your instructor.

Mid-Level Exercises

1 Junk Business

FROM SCRATCH 

You and a college friend have signed on as a franchise for JUNKit, a company that purchases unwanted items and disposes of or recycles them. A recent pickup included a desktop computer that appeared to be reusable. Because you had a few spare parts and some hardware expertise, you rebuilt the computer and installed Windows 8. Now you will check the system to verify that it is workable and configured correctly. Pretend your lab computer (or your home computer) is the computer you rebuilt.

a. Open WordPad and, in a new document, type as directed when you complete the following items.

b. Open the Action Center. Are there any alerts? Make note of them and close the Action Center. In the WordPad document, type **Step b:** and list any alerts or indicate that there are none. Press **Enter**.

c. Open Windows Defender and check to see when the last scan occurred. Click the **WordPad icon** on the taskbar, click in the document on the line following your response for step b, type **Step c:**, and then record when the last scan occurred. Press **Enter**. Close the Windows Defender window.

d. Check the firewall status. Is the firewall on? Close the System and Security window. If necessary, click in the WordPad document on the line following your response for step c. Type **Step d:** and record whether the firewall is on or off. (Note that the firewall may not be on for the lab computer because the campus lab is likely to be behind another campus-wide firewall. Your computer at home is more likely to have the firewall turned on.) Press **Enter**.

e. Check Windows Update. When did the last update occur? Click the **WordPad icon** on the taskbar. If necessary, click in the WordPad document on the line following your response for step d. Type **Step e:** and record the date of the last update. Press **Enter**. Close the Windows Update window.

f. Check for available desktop backgrounds. Identify one that you plan to use and make a note of it, but click **Cancel** without selecting it. Close any open windows other than WordPad. If necessary, click in the WordPad document on the line following your response for step e. Type **Step f:** and list the name of the background that you would have selected in the WordPad document. Press **Enter**.

g. Save the file as **win01m1junk_LastFirst**, replacing *LastFirst* with your own last name and first name. Leave WordPad open.

DISCOVER 

h. Open Help and Support. Find information on backup options for Windows 8. Going a little further, research backup strategies for home computers on the Web. Click the **WordPad icon** on the taskbar, type **Step g:**, and then summarize your findings in the WordPad document. Press **Enter**. Save the file.

i. Close the Windows Help and Support window. Save the WordPad document on the drive where you normally save files as **win01m1junk_LastFirst**. Close WordPad. Submit the file to your instructor.

2 Technical Writing

CREATIVE CASE 

FROM SCRATCH

You are employed as a software specialist with Wang Design, a firm that provides commercial and residential landscape design and greenscape services. The landscape designers use a wide array of software that assists with producing detailed plans and lawn layouts. The firm has just purchased several new computers and tablets, configured with Windows 8. Because the operating system is new to all employees, you have been assigned the task of producing a small easy-to-follow manual summarizing basic Windows 8 tasks.

a. Use WordPad or Microsoft Word to produce a report, no more than 10 pages, based on the following topic outline. Where appropriate, use the Snipping Tool to include screen captures that illustrate a topic or process. Use this chapter and Windows Help and Support to find information for your report.
   1. Start Screen Components and Navigation
   2. Customizing the Start Screen and Desktop
   3. Windows Accessories
   4. Windows Search

b. Save your report as **win01m2writing_LastFirst**.

Beyond the Classroom

Campus Chatter

As a reporter for the college newspaper *Campus Chatter,* you are responsible for the education section. Each month, you contribute a short article on an educational topic. This month, you will summarize a feature of Windows 8. You are having writer's block, however, and need a nudge, so you will use the Internet for an idea. Go online and locate the Windows 8 Web site or the Windows 8 blog. Browse some links, locate a topic of interest, and use WordPad to write a minimum one-page typed report on a topic related to Windows 8. Save the report as **win01b2chatter_LastFirst** in a location as directed by your instructor.

Laptop Logic

Your job in sales with an educational software company requires a great deal of travel. You depend on a laptop computer for most of what you do, from keeping sales records to connecting with an overhead projector when you make presentations to groups. In short, you would be lost without your computer. A recent scare, when you temporarily misplaced the laptop, has led you to consider precautions you can take to make sure your computer and its data are protected. Since you have a little free time before leaving for your next trip, you will use Windows 8 Help and Support to explore some suggestions on protecting your laptop. Open Help and Support and search for information on protecting a laptop. Create a one- to two-page typed report covering two topics. First, describe how you would protect data (including passwords and financial information) on your laptop. Second, provide some suggestions on steps you can take to make sure you do not lose your laptop or have it stolen. Use WordPad to record the report, saving the report as **win01b3laptop_LastFirst** in a location as directed by your instructor.

Capstone Exercise

You are enrolled in a Directed Studies class as one of the final courses required for your degree. The class is projects-based, which means that the instructor assigns open-ended cases for students to manage and report on. You will prepare teaching materials for a Windows 8 community education class. The class is a new effort for the college and, given early enrollment figures, it appears that most students are over the age of 50 with very little computer background. Most students indicate that they have recently purchased a laptop or tablet with Windows 8 and want to learn to work with the operating system at a minimal level. The class is short, only a couple of Saturday mornings, and it is fast approaching. In this exercise, you will prepare and test class material, introducing students to using the Start screen and desktop, managing apps and windows, working with accessory programs and security settings, getting help, and finding files. Your instructor wants screen shots of your progress, so you will use the Snipping Tool to prepare those.

Explore the Start Screen and Desktop/ Manage Apps and Windows

The instructor will spend the first hour of class introducing students to the Windows 8 Start screen and reviewing desktop operations (since these should be familiar to users of previous versions of Windows). He will assume that students are complete novices, so he wants an outline that begins with the basics. You have prepared the series of steps given below. You will go through those steps, preparing a screen shot to accompany your submission.

a. Add a tile to the Start screen for the Notepad program.

b. Rearrange tiles on the Start screen including making new tile groups.

c. Pin the WordPad program to the Start screen and the taskbar.

d. Open the Notepad shortcut. If necessary, restore down the window so that it is not maximized.

e. Open WordPad from the taskbar. If necessary, restore down the window so that it is not maximized.

f. Display two Windows 8 apps on the screen at one time and snap two open windows to opposing sides of the desktop.

g. Switch between open Windows 8 apps.

h. Use the Snipping Tool to capture a copy of the Start screen. Save it as **win01c1desktop_LastFirst**.

i. Close all open apps and windows.

Work with Accessory Programs and Security Settings

The instructor wants to make sure students understand that some software is included with a Windows 8 installation. Because using any type of software most often involves Internet access, you know that the class must include instruction on security risks and solutions. You have prepared some notes and will test them in the steps that follow.

a. Open WordPad. Maximize the window, if necessary. Students in class will be instructed to type a paragraph on Windows 8 security features. Use Windows 8 Help and Support if necessary to identify Windows 8 security features, and then compose a paragraph in the WordPad document. Minimize WordPad but do not close it.

b. Open Paint. Maximize the window, if necessary. Click the top half of the **Brushes button**. Click and drag to write your name in the Paint area. Click the top half of the **Select button**. Click and drag in a rectangle around your name. Click **Copy**. Close Paint without saving.

c. Click the **WordPad icon** on the taskbar. Click the top half of the **Paste button** to add your "signature" to the paragraph.

d. Save the WordPad document as **win01c1paragraph_LastFirst**.

e. Close WordPad.

Get Help and Find Files

You know from personal experience that things usually work well when an instructor is available to help. You also know that as students leave the Windows 8 class, they will have questions and must know how to find help themselves. They will also undoubtedly misplace files. The steps that follow should help them understand how to get help and how to find files, programs, and folders.

a. Browse *Help and Support* to find information on the Start screen.

b. Search *Help and Support* to find a description of remote assistance.

c. Minimize the Windows *Help and Support* window.

d. Display the Charms bar, click **Search**, and then type **Word** in the **Search screen Search box**. You will search for any app with the word *word* in the app name. At the very least, you should see *WordPad* in the results list. Click the program name to open it. If WordPad is maximized, restore it down to less than full size.

e. Click the **Help and Support tile** on the Apps screen to open the window.

f. Show all open windows stacked.

g. Use the Snipping Tool to capture the screen, saving it as **win01c1help_LastFirst**. Close all open windows.

h. Unpin the WordPad icon from the taskbar.

i. Unpin the NotePad tile from the Start screen.

Office

Office Fundamentals and File Management

CHAPTER 1

Andresr/Shutterstock

Taking the First Step

OBJECTIVES

AFTER YOU READ THIS CHAPTER, YOU WILL BE ABLE TO:

CASE STUDY | Spotted Begonia Art Gallery

You are an administrative assistant for Spotted Begonia, a local art gallery. The gallery deals in local artists' work, including fiber art, oil paintings, watercolors, prints, pottery, and metal sculptures. The gallery holds four seasonal showings throughout the year. Much of the art is on consignment, but there are a few permanent collections. Occasionally, the gallery exchanges these collections with other galleries across the country. The gallery does a lot of community outreach and tries to help local artists develop a network of clients and supporters. Local schools are invited to bring students to the gallery for enrichment programs. Considered a major contributor to the local economy, the gallery has received both public and private funding through federal and private grants.

As the administrative assistant for Spotted Begonia, you are responsible for overseeing the production of documents, spreadsheets, newspaper articles, and presentations that will be used to increase public awareness of the gallery. Other clerical assistants who are familiar with Microsoft Office will prepare the promotional materials, and you will proofread, make necessary corrections, adjust page layouts, save and print documents, and identify appropriate templates to simplify tasks. Your experience with Microsoft Office 2013 is limited, but you know that certain fundamental tasks that are common to Word, Excel, and PowerPoint will help you accomplish your oversight task. You are excited to get started with your work!

Windows 8.1.1 Startup

You use computers for many activities for work, school, or pleasure. You probably have never thought too much about what makes a computer function and allows you to do so many things with it. But all of those activities would not be possible without an operating system running on the computer. An ***operating system*** is software that directs computer activities such as checking all components, managing system resources, and communicating with application software. ***Windows 8.1.1*** is a Microsoft operating system released in April 2014 and is available on laptops, desktops, and tablet computers.

The ***Start screen*** is what you see after starting your computer and entering your username and password. It is where you start all of your computing activities. See Figure 1.1 to see a typical Start screen.

FIGURE 1.1 Typical Start Screen Components and Charms

In this section, you will explore the Start screen and its components in more detail. You will also learn how to log in with your Microsoft account and access the desktop.

Logging In with Your Microsoft Account

Although you can log in to Windows 8.1.1 as a local network user, you can also log in using a Microsoft account. When you have a Microsoft account, you can sign in to any Windows 8.1.1 computer and you will be able to access the saved settings associated with your Microsoft account. That means the computer will have the same familiar look that you are used to seeing. Your Microsoft account will allow you to be automatically signed in to all of the apps and services that use a Microsoft account as the authentication. You can also save your sign-in credentials for other Web sites that you frequently visit.

Logging in with your Microsoft account not only provides all of the benefits just listed, but also provides additional benefits such as being connected to all of Microsoft's resources on the Internet. These resources include a free Outlook account and access to cloud storage at OneDrive. ***Cloud storage*** is a technology used to store files and to work with programs that are stored in a central location on the Internet. ***OneDrive*** is an app used to store, access, and share files and folders. It is accessible using an installed desktop app or as cloud storage using a Web address. Files and folders in either location can be synced. For Office 2013 applications, OneDrive is the default location for saving files. Documents saved in OneDrive are accessible from any computer that has an Internet connection. As long as the document has been saved in OneDrive, the most recent version of the document will be accessible from any computer connected to the Internet. OneDrive allows you to collaborate with others. You can easily share your documents with others or add Reply Comments next to the text that you are discussing together. You can work with others on the same document simultaneously.

STEP 1 » You can create a Microsoft account at any time by going to live.com. You simply work through the Sign-up form to set up your account by creating a username from your e-mail address and creating a password. After filling in the form, you will be automatically signed in to Outlook and sent to your Outlook Inbox. If you already have a Microsoft account, you can just go ahead and log in to Outlook. See Figure 1.2 to see the Sign-up page at live.com.

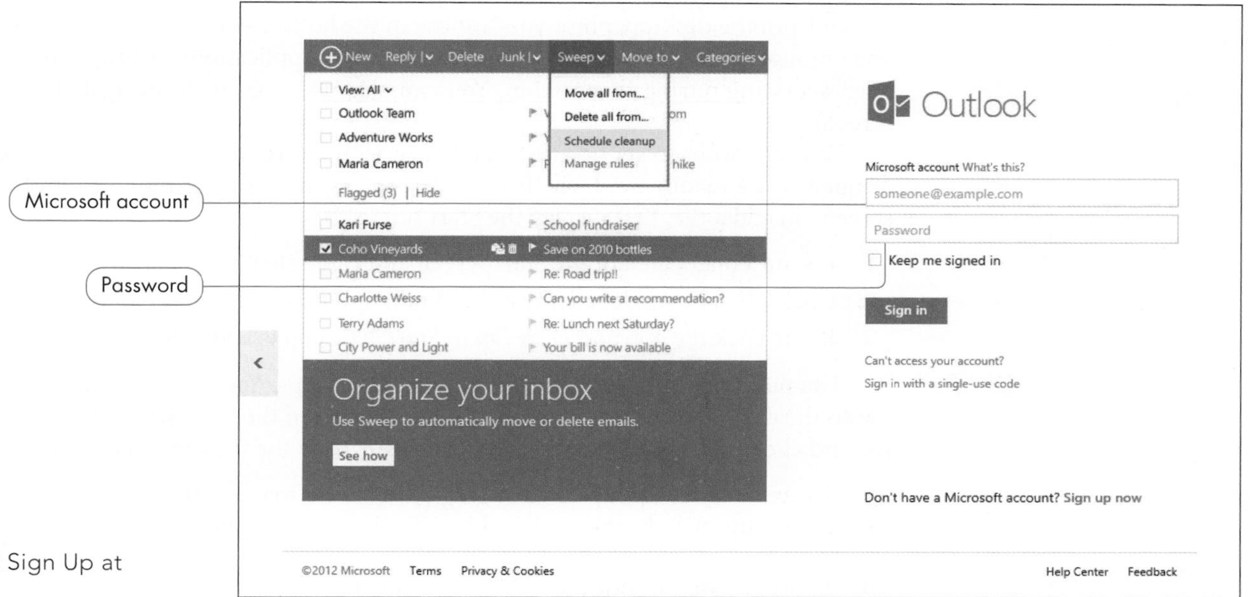

FIGURE 1.2 Sign Up at live.com

Identifying the Start Screen Components

The first thing you will notice when you turn on a computer running Windows 8.1.1 is that the Start screen has a new sleek, clean look and large readable type (refer to Figure 1.1). The user is identified in the top-right corner of the screen. You can click the user's name to access settings such as locking or signing out of the account. You can also change the picture associated with the account here.

You will notice that the Start screen is made up of several colorful block images called ***tiles***. When you click a tile, you will be taken to a program, file, folder, or other ***Windows 8.1.1 app***. Windows 8.1.1 apps are applications specifically designed to run in the Start screen interface of Windows 8.1.1. Some Windows 8.1.1 apps, such as desktop, Mail, and OneDrive, are already installed and ready to use. Others can be downloaded from the Windows Store. The default apps are brightly colored. Tiles for programs that run on the traditional Windows desktop are smaller and more transparent. The look of the tiles is customizable, but all tiles include the name of the app or program. Depending on the number of apps that you have installed, as you move your mouse to the bottom of the screen, you will see a horizontal scroll bar display. This can be used to access any app that does not display within the initial view of the Start screen.

STEP 2 » The traditional Start button is not present in Windows 8.1.1. Instead, the ***Charms*** are available (refer to Figure 1.1). The Charms are made up of five icons that provide similar functionality to the Start button found in previous versions of Windows. The icons are Search, Share, Start, Devices, and Settings. Using the Charms, you can search for files and applications, share information with others within an application that is running, or return to the Start screen. You can also control devices that are connected to your computer or modify various settings depending on which application is running when accessing the Setting icon. To display the Charms, point to the top-right or bottom-right corners of the screen. Refer to Figure 1.1 to view the Start screen components and the Charms.

Interacting with the Start Screen

To interact with any tile on the Start screen (refer to Figure 1.1), simply click it. If you have signed in with your Microsoft account, you will automatically be able to access any of the Internet-enabled programs. For example, if you click Mail, you will go straight to your Outlook Inbox. If you right-click a tile, you will see several contextual options displayed. For example, the option to unpin the tile from the Start screen displays. To return to the Start screen from the desktop, point your mouse in the bottom-left corner of the screen. Pointing your mouse to the top-left corner reveals the open applications or programs that you have been accessing during this session. You can also use Charms to navigate back to the Start screen.

You may want to set up the Start screen so that programs and apps that you use most frequently are readily available. It is very easy to add tiles to or remove tiles from the Start screen. To add a tile, first display the Start screen.

1. Locate a blank area of the Start screen and right-click to display the *All apps* icon.
2. Click *All apps* and locate the desired new app that you want to add.
3. Right-click the app and click *Pin to Start*. The app is added to the Start screen.

The new app's tile is added at the end of your apps. You can move tiles by dragging the tile to the desired location. You can remove a tile from the Start screen by right-clicking the tile and clicking *Unpin from Start*. You can also group the tiles and name the groups:

1. To create a new group of tiles, drag a tile to the space to the left or right of an existing tile group. A light gray vertical bar displays to indicate where the new group will be located.
2. Add more tiles to this new group as needed.
3. To name the group, right-click any blank area of the Start screen and click Name groups. Type in the space provided to name a group. If a name is not entered for a group, the horizontal Name group bar disappears.

Accessing the Desktop

Although the Start screen is easy to use, you may want to access the more familiar desktop that you used in previous versions of Windows. The Desktop tile is available on the Start screen. Click the tile to bring up the desktop. Alternatively, you can be pushed to the desktop when you click other tiles such as Word. In Windows 8.1.1, the desktop is simplified to accommodate use on mobile devices where screen space is limited. However, on a laptop or desktop computer, you may want to have more features readily available. The familiar Notification area is displayed in the bottom-right corner. You will see the Windows Start screen, File Explorer, and Internet Explorer icons. See Figure 1.3 to locate these desktop components.

FIGURE 1.3 Desktop Components

STEP 3»

You can add more toolbars, such as the Address bar, to the taskbar by right-clicking the taskbar, pointing to Toolbars, and then selecting Address. The Address bar can be used to locate Web sites using the URL or to perform a keyword search to locate Web sites about a specific topic. You can also add programs such as the ***Snipping Tool***. The Snipping Tool is a Windows 8.1.1 accessory program that allows you to capture, or ***snip***, a screen display so that you can save, annotate, or share it. You can remove all of the icons displayed on the taskbar by right-clicking the icon you want to remove and selecting *Unpin this program from taskbar*.

TIP Using the Snipping Tool

The Snipping Tool can be used to take all sizes and shapes of snips of the displayed screen. Options include Free-form Snip, Rectangle Snip, Window Snip, and Full-screen Snip. You can save your snip in several formats, such as PNG, GIF, JPEG, or Single file HTML. In addition, you can use a pen or highlighter to mark up your snips. This option is available after taking a snip and is located under the Tools menu in the Snipping Tool dialog box.

You can return to the Start screen by clicking the Start screen icon on the taskbar.

1. Logging in to Windows 8.1.1 with your Microsoft account provides access to Internet resources. What are some benefits of logging in this way? ***p. 56***
2. OneDrive allows you to collaborate with others. How might you use this service? ***p. 57***
3. What is the Start screen, and how is it different from the desktop? ***p. 57***
4. The desktop has been a feature of previous Windows operating systems. How is the Windows 8.1.1 desktop different from previous versions? ***p. 58***

Hands-On Exercises

1 Windows 8.1.1 Startup

The Spotted Begonia Art Gallery has just hired several new clerical assistants to help you develop promotional materials for the various activities coming up throughout the year. It will be necessary to have a central storage space where you can save the documents and presentations for retrieval from any location. You will also need to be able to collaborate with others on the documents by sharing them and adding comments. To begin, you will get a Microsoft account. Then you will access the desktop and pin a toolbar and a Windows 8.1.1 accessory program to the taskbar.

Skills covered: Log In with Your Microsoft Account • Identify the Start Screen Components and Interact with the Start Screen • Access the Desktop

STEP 1 ›› LOG IN WITH YOUR MICROSOFT ACCOUNT

You want to sign up for a Microsoft account so you can store documents and share them with others using the resources available with a Microsoft account, such as OneDrive. Refer to Figure 1.4 as you complete Step 1.

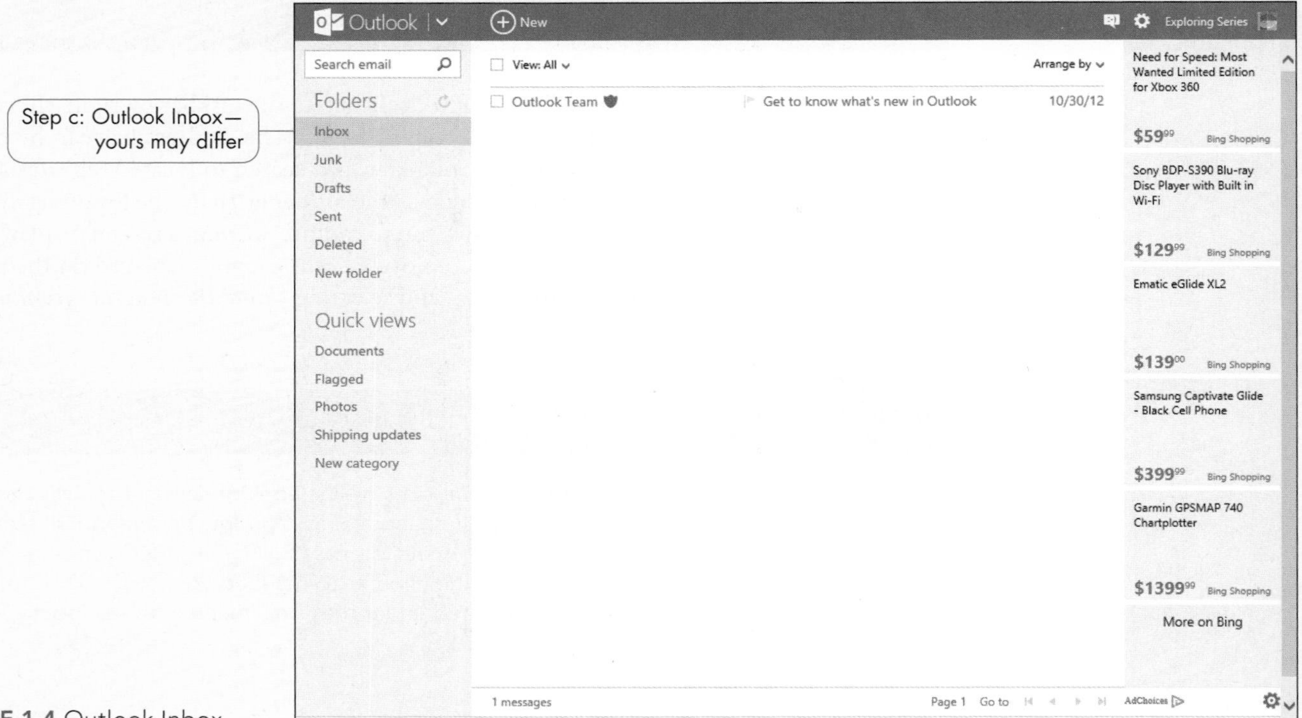

FIGURE 1.4 Outlook Inbox

a. Start your computer and enter your local username and password. On the Start screen, click the **Internet Explorer tile**. Click in the **Address bar** at the bottom of the screen. Type **live.com** and press **Enter**.

Internet Explorer displays, and you are taken to the Sign-up page for Outlook. This is where you can create a username and password for your Microsoft account.

> **TROUBLESHOOTING:** If you already have a Microsoft account, you can skip Step 1 and continue with Step 2. If someone else was already signed in at your computer, you can locate your username and click it to begin to log in.

b. Click the **Sign up now** link at the bottom of the screen. Fill in all text boxes and make all menu selections on the screen. Scroll down as needed. Type the **CAPTCHA code** carefully.

CAPTCHA is a scrambled code used with online forms to prevent mass sign-ups. It helps to ensure that a real person is requesting the account. You can choose not to accept e-mail with promotional offers by clicking the check box near the bottom of the screen to remove the check.

> **TROUBLESHOOTING:** You may want to write down your username and password so that you do not forget it the next time you want to log in with your Microsoft account. Keep this information in a safe and confidential location.

c. Click **I accept**. Your screen should display similarly to Figure 1.4.

Your Microsoft account is created, and you are taken to your Outlook Inbox.

d. Keep Internet Explorer open if you plan to continue using Outlook. Otherwise, sign out of Outlook and close Internet Explorer.

STEP 2 » IDENTIFY THE START SCREEN COMPONENTS AND INTERACT WITH THE START SCREEN

You decide to explore the Start screen components. Then you use the Desktop tile on the Start screen to access the desktop. Refer to Figure 1.5 as you complete Step 2.

FIGURE 1.5 Desktop

a. Point to the top-right corner to display the Charms. Click the **Start screen charm**.

Because you finished on the desktop after completing Step 1, clicking the Start screen charm takes you to the Start screen.

> **TROUBLESHOOTING:** If you skipped Step 1, log in to Windows with your username and password to display the Start screen.

b. Point to the bottom of the Start screen to display the horizontal scroll bar. Drag the scroll bar to the right to view all of the tiles available. Then drag the scrollbar back to the left to its original position.

Many components of the Start screen do not display until they are needed. This saves screen space on mobile devices. In this case, the horizontal scroll bar is hidden until needed.

c. Point to the bottom-right corner of the screen to display the Charms.

The Charms will display whenever you point to the top-right or bottom-right corners of the screen, regardless of the application you are using.

d. Locate and click the **Desktop tile**. See Figure 1.5.

STEP 3 » ACCESS THE DESKTOP

You would like to add some components to make the desktop easier to use. You customize the desktop by adding the Address toolbar and the Snipping Tool to the taskbar. Refer to Figure 1.6 as you complete Step 3.

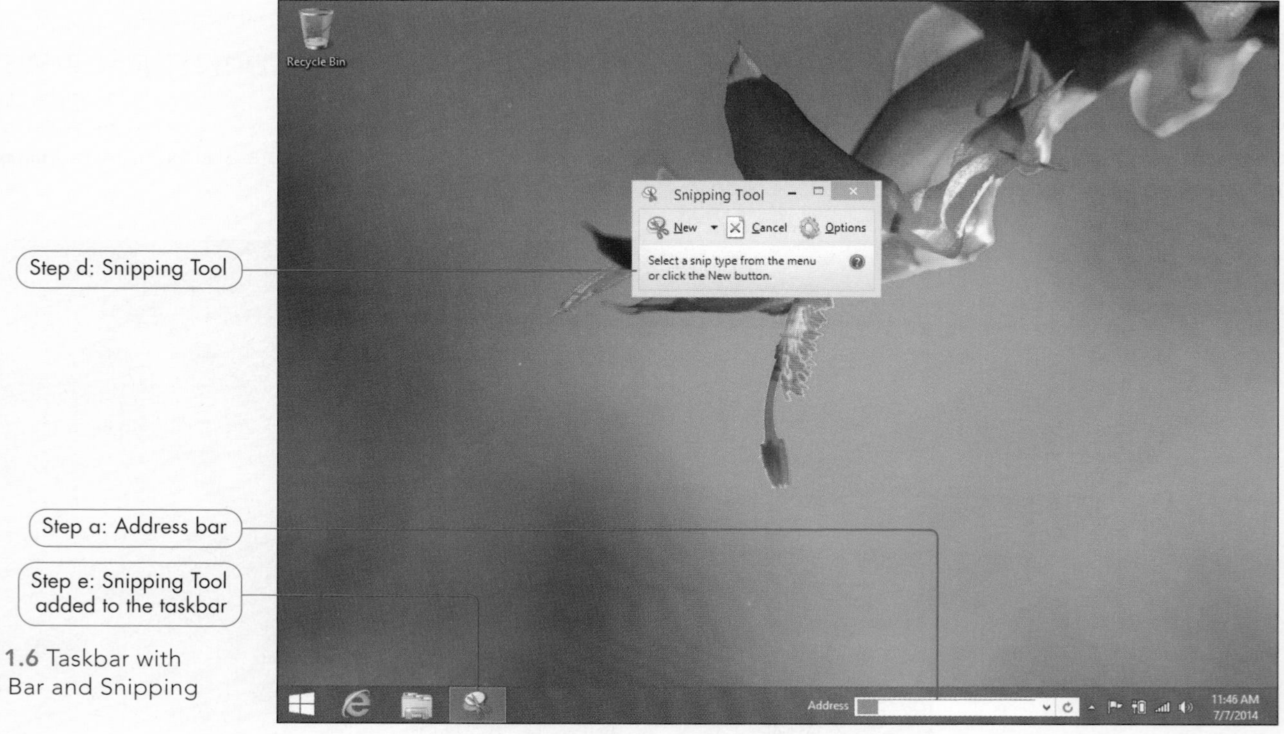

FIGURE 1.6 Taskbar with Address Bar and Snipping Tool

a. Locate and right-click the taskbar. Point to *Toolbars* and select **Address**.

The Address bar now displays on the right side of the taskbar.

b. Point to the top-right corner of the screen to display the Charms. Click the **Search charm**.

The Search pane displays on the right. The Search pane is organized into categories that you may want to search. For whatever category is selected, the relevant content is displayed.

Viewing Dialog Box Components

In Windows 8.1.1, many dialog boxes have been changed to panes. This is in keeping with the sleek, clean look of Windows 8.1.1. Even though the look is different, the functionality remains the same.

c. Type **Sn** in the **Search box**. Below the search box, the results listed display everything that begins with Sn.

d. Click the **Snipping Tool app** in the results list.

   The Snipping Tool app displays on the desktop and the Snipping Tool icon displays on the taskbar.

e. Right-click the **Snipping Tool icon** on the taskbar. Click **Pin this program to taskbar**. See Figure 1.6.

   The Snipping Tool and the Address bar will now be part of your taskbar.

TROUBLESHOOTING: If you are in a lab and cannot keep these changes, you can remove the Snipping Tool icon from the taskbar. Right-click the icon and click *Unpin this program from taskbar*. You can remove the Address bar by right-clicking the taskbar, pointing to Toolbars, and then clicking Address to remove the check mark.

f. Click the **Snipping Tool icon**. Click the **New arrow** in the Snipping Tool on the desktop. Click **Full-screen Snip**.

   A snip of your desktop displays in the Snipping Tool program.

g. Click **File** and click **Save As**. Navigate to the location where you are saving your student files. Name your file **f01h1Desktop_LastFirst** using your own last name and first name. Check to see that *Portable Network Graphic file (PNG)* displays in the *Save as type* box. Click **Save**.

   You have created your first snip. Snips can be used to show what is on your screen. Notice the Snipping Tool app does not display in your snip. When you save files, use your last and first names. For example, as the Office Fundamentals author, I would name my document *f01h1Desktop_LawsonRebecca*.

TROUBLESHOOTING: If PNG does not display in the *Save as type* box, click the arrow on the right side of the box and select *Portable Network Graphic file (PNG)*.

h. Close the Snipping Tool. Submit the file based on your instructor's directions.

i. Shut down your computer if you are ready to stop working. Point to the top-right corner to display the Charms. Click the **Settings charm**, click the **Power icon**, and then click **Shut down**. Otherwise, leave your computer turned on for the next Hands-On Exercise.

Files and Folders

Most activities that you perform using a computer produce some type of output. That output could be games, music, or the display of digital photographs. Perhaps you use a computer at work to produce reports, financial worksheets, or schedules. All of those items are considered computer ***files***. Files include electronic data such as documents, databases, slide shows, and worksheets. Even digital photographs, music, videos, and Web pages are saved as files.

You use software to create and save files. For example, when you type a document on a computer, you first open a word processor such as Microsoft Word. In order to access files later, you must save them to a computer storage medium such as a hard drive or flash drive, or in the cloud at OneDrive. And just as you would probably organize a filing cabinet into a system of folders, you can organize storage media by ***folders*** that you name and into which you place data files. That way, you can easily retrieve the files later. Windows 8.1.1 provides tools that enable you to create folders and to save files in ways that make locating them simple.

In this section, you will learn to use File Explorer to manage folders and files.

Using File Explorer

File Explorer is an app that you can use to create and manage folders and files. The sole purpose of a computer folder is to provide a labeled storage location for related files so that you can easily organize and retrieve items. A folder structure can occur across several levels, so you can create folders within other folders—called ***subfolders***—arranged according to purpose. Windows 8.1.1 uses the concept of libraries, which are folders that gather files from different locations and display the files as if they were all saved in a single folder, regardless of where they are physically stored. Using File Explorer, you can manage folders, work with libraries, and view favorites (areas or folders that are frequently accessed).

Understand and Customize the Interface

You can access File Explorer in any of the following ways:

- Click the File Explorer icon from the taskbar on the desktop.
- Click File Explorer from the Start screen.
- Display the Charms (refer to Figure 1.1) and click the Search charm. Type F in the Search box and in the results list on the left, click File Explorer.

Figure 1.7 shows the File Explorer interface containing several areas. Some of those areas are described in Table 1.1.

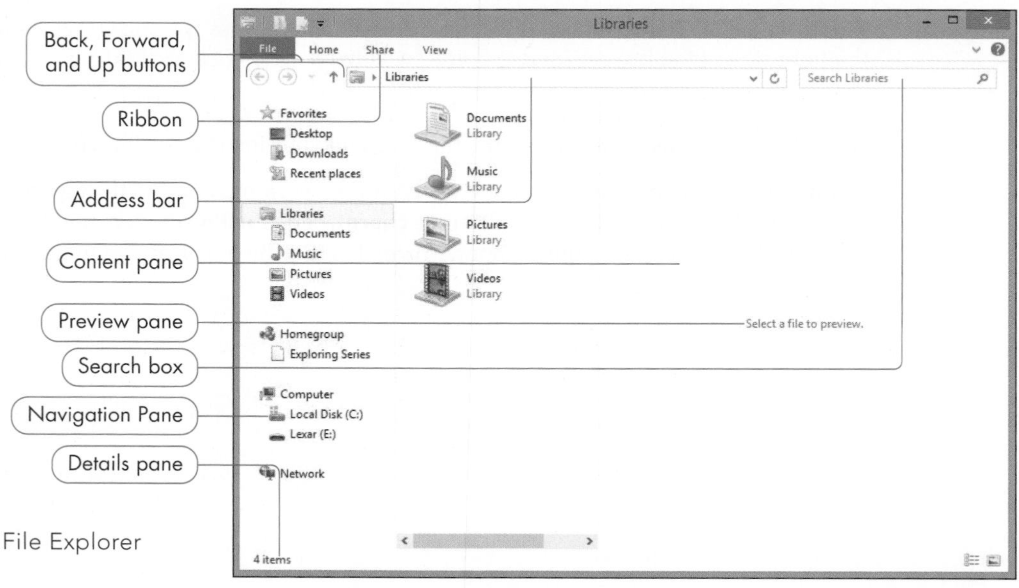

FIGURE 1.7 File Explorer Interface

TABLE 1.1 File Explorer Interface

Navigation Pane	The Navigation Pane contains five areas: Favorites, Libraries, Homegroup, Computer, and Network. Click an item in the Navigation Pane to display contents and to manage files that are housed within a selected folder.
Back, Forward, and Up Buttons	Use these buttons to visit previously opened folders or libraries. Use the Up button to open the parent folder for the current location.
Ribbon	The Ribbon includes tabs and commands that are relevant to the currently selected item. If you are working with a music file, the Ribbon commands might include one for burning to a CD, whereas if you have selected a document, the Ribbon would enable you to open or share the file.
Address bar	The Address bar enables you to navigate to other folders or libraries.
Content pane	The Content pane shows the contents of the currently selected folder or library.
Search box	Find files and folders by typing descriptive text in the Search box. Windows immediately begins a search after you type the first character, further narrowing results as you type.
Details pane	The Details pane shows properties that are associated with a selected file. Common properties include information such as the author name and the date the file was last modified. This pane does not display by default but can display after clicking the View tab.
Preview pane	The Preview pane provides a snapshot of a selected file's contents. You can see file contents before actually opening the file. The Preview pane does not show the contents of a selected folder. This pane does not display by default but can display after clicking the View tab.

File Explorer has a Ribbon like all the Office applications. As you work with File Explorer, you might want to customize the view. The file and folder icons might be too small for ease of identification, or you might want additional details about displayed files and folders. Modifying the view is easy. To make icons larger or to provide additional detail, click the View tab (refer to Figure 1.7) and select from the views provided in the Layout group. If you want additional detail, such as file type and size, click Details. You can also change the size of icons by selecting Small, Medium, Large, or Extra Large icons. The List view shows the file names without added detail, whereas Tiles and Content views are useful to show file thumbnails (small pictures describing file contents) and varying levels of detail regarding file locations. To show or hide File Explorer panes, click the View tab and select the pane to hide or show in the Panes group. You can widen or narrow panes by dragging a border when the mouse changes to a double-headed arrow.

Work with Groups on the Navigation Pane

The ***Navigation Pane*** provides ready access to computer resources, folders, files, and networked peripherals such as printers. It is divided into five areas: Favorites, Libraries, Homegroup, Computer, and Network. Each of those components provides a unique way to organize contents. In Figure 1.8, the currently selected area is Computer.

Earlier, we used the analogy of computer folders to folders in a filing cabinet. Just as you would title folders in a filing cabinet according to their contents, computer folders are also titled according to content. Folders are physically located on storage media such as a hard drive or flash drive. You can also organize folders into ***libraries***, which are collections of files from different locations that are displayed as a single virtual folder. For example, the Pictures library includes files from the My Pictures folder and from the Public Pictures folder, both of which are physically housed on the hard drive. Although the library content comes from two separate folders, the contents are displayed as a single virtual folder.

Windows 8.1.1 includes several libraries that contain default folders or devices. For example, the Documents library includes the My Documents and Public Documents folders, but you can add subfolders if you wish so that they are also housed within the Documents library. To add a folder to a library, right-click the library, point to New, and then select Folder. You can name the folder at this point by typing the folder name. To remove a folder from the Documents library, open File Explorer, right-click the folder, and then select Delete.

The Computer area provides access to specific storage locations, such as a hard drive, CD/DVD drives, and removable media drives, including a flash drive. Files and folders housed on those storage media are accessible when you click Computer. For example, click drive C, shown under Computer in the Navigation Pane, to view its contents in the Content pane on the right. If you simply want to see the subfolders of the hard drive, click the arrow to the left of drive C to expand the view, showing all subfolders. The arrow is filled in and pointing down. Click the arrow again to collapse the view, removing subfolder detail. The arrow is open and pointing right. It is important to understand that clicking the arrow—as opposed to clicking the folder or area name—does not actually select an area or folder. It merely displays additional levels contained within the area. Clicking the folder or area, however, does select the item. Figure 1.8 illustrates the difference between clicking the folder or area name in the Navigation Pane and clicking the arrow to the left.

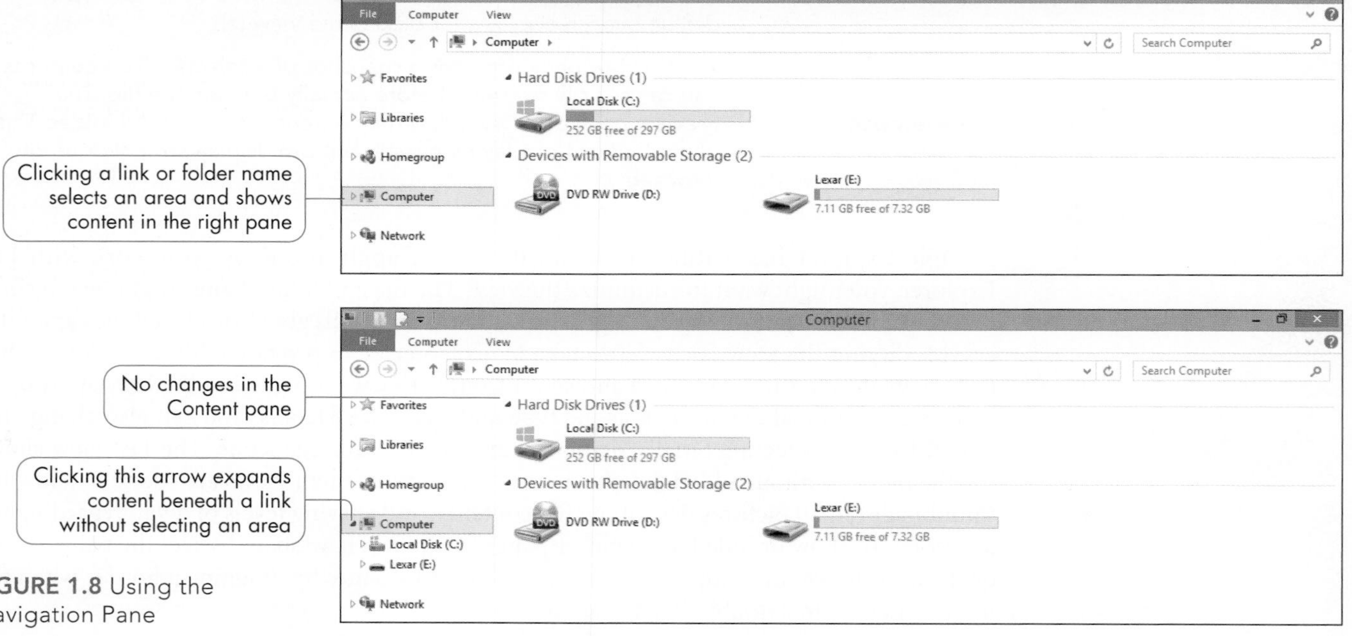

FIGURE 1.8 Using the Navigation Pane

To locate a folder using File Explorer:

1. Click the correct drive in the Navigation Pane (or double-click the drive in the Content pane).
2. Continue navigating through the folder structure until you find the folder that you want.
3. Click the folder in the Navigation Pane (or double-click the folder in the Content pane) to view its contents.

The Favorites area contains frequently accessed folders and recent searches. You can drag a folder, saved search, library, or disk drive to the Favorites area. To remove a favorite, simply right-click the favorite and select Remove. You cannot add files or Web sites as favorites.

Homegroup is a Windows 8.1.1 feature that enables you to share resources on a home network. You can easily share music, pictures, videos, and libraries with other people in your home through a homegroup. It is password protected, so you do not have to worry about privacy.

Windows 8.1.1 makes creating a home network easy, sharing access to the Internet and peripheral devices such as printers and scanners. The Network area provides quick access to those devices, enabling you to see the contents of network computers.

Working with Folders and Files

As you work with software to create a file, such as when you type a report using Microsoft Word, your primary concern will be saving the file so that you can retrieve it later if necessary. If you have created an appropriate and well-named folder structure, you can save the file in a location that is easy to find later.

Create a Folder

You can create a folder a couple of different ways. You can use File Explorer to create a folder structure, providing appropriate names and placing the folders in a well-organized hierarchy. You can also create a folder from within a software application at the time that you need it. Although it would be wonderful to always plan ahead, most often you will find the need for a folder at the same time that you have created a file. The two methods of creating a folder are described next.

STEP 1

Suppose you are beginning a new college semester and are taking four classes. To organize your assignments, you plan to create four folders on a flash drive, one for each class. After connecting the flash drive and closing any subsequent dialog box (unless the dialog box is warning of a problem with the drive), open File Explorer. Click Computer in the Navigation Pane. Click the removable (flash) drive in the Navigation Pane or double-click it in the Content pane. You can also create a folder on the hard drive in the same manner, by clicking drive C instead of the removable drive. Click the Home tab on the Ribbon. Click *New folder* in the New group. Type the new folder name, such as Biology, and press Enter. Repeat the process to create additional folders.

Undoubtedly, you will occasionally find that you have just created a file but have no appropriate folder in which to save the file. You might have just finished the slide show for your speech class but have forgotten first to create a speech folder for your assignments. Now what do you do? As you save the file, a process that is discussed later in this chapter, you can click Browse to bring up the Save As dialog box. Navigate to the drive where you want to store your file. Click *New folder* (see Figure 1.9), type the new folder name, and then double-click to save the name and open the new folder. After indicating the file name, click Save.

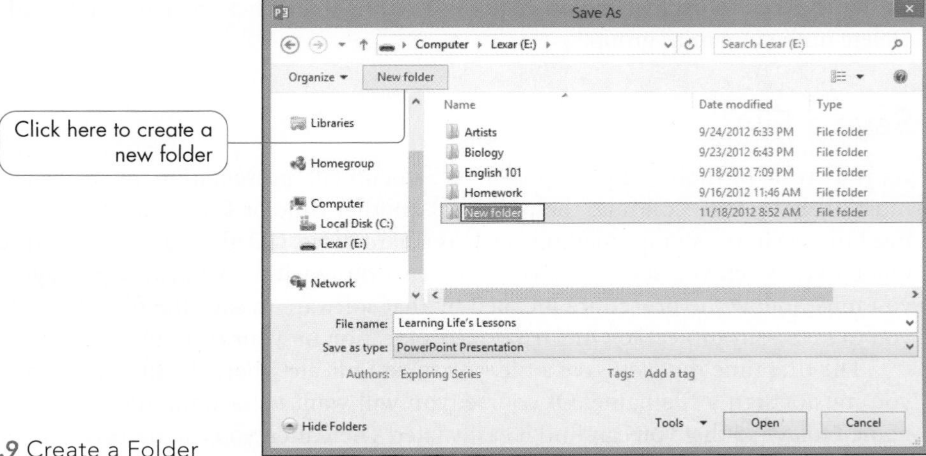

FIGURE 1.9 Create a Folder

OneDrive makes it easy to access your folders and files from any Internet-connected computer or mobile device. You can create new folders and organize existing folders just as you would when you use File Explorer. Other tasks that can be performed at OneDrive include opening, renaming, and deleting folders and files. To create a new folder at OneDrive, you can simply click the OneDrive tile on the Start screen. By default, you will see three items: Documents, Pictures, and Public Shared. You can right-click any of these three items to access icons for creating a new folder or to upload files. Once files and folders are added or created here, you can access them from any computer with Internet access at onedrive.live.com. Similarly, you can create folders or upload files and folders at OneDrive and then access them using the OneDrive tile on your Start screen.

Open, Rename, and Delete Folders and Files

You have learned that folders can be created in File Explorer but files are more commonly created in other ways, such as within a software package. File Explorer can create a new file, and you can use it to open, rename, and delete files just as you use it for folders.

Using the Navigation Pane, you can locate and select a folder containing a file that you want to open. For example, you might want to open the speech slide show so that you can practice before giving a presentation to the class. Open File Explorer and navigate to the speech folder. In your storage location, the file will display in the Content pane. Double-click the file. The program that is associated with the file will open the file. For example, if you have the PowerPoint program associated with that file type on your computer, then PowerPoint will open the file. To open a folder and display the contents, just click the folder in the Navigation Pane or double-click it in the Content pane.

STEP 3»

At times, you may want to give a different name to a file or folder than the one that you originally gave it. Or perhaps you made a typographical mistake when you entered the name. In these situations, you should rename the file or folder. In File Explorer, move through the folder structure to find the folder or file. Right-click the name and select Rename. Type the new name and press Enter. You can also rename an item when you click the name twice—but much more slowly than a double-click. Type the new name and press Enter. Finally, you can click a file or folder once to select it, click the Home tab, and then select Rename in the Organize group. Type the new name and press Enter.

It is much easier to delete a folder or file than it is to recover it if you remove it by mistake. Therefore, be very careful when deleting items so that you are sure of your intentions before proceeding. When you delete a folder, all subfolders and all files within the folder are also removed. If you are certain you want to remove a folder or file, the process is simple. Right-click the item, click Delete, and then click Yes if asked to confirm removal to the Recycle Bin. Items are placed in the Recycle Bin only if you are deleting them from a hard drive. Files and folders deleted from a removable storage medium, such as a flash drive, are immediately and permanently deleted, with no easy method of retrieval. You can also delete an item (file or folder) when you click to select the item, click the Home tab, and then click Delete in the Organize group.

Save a File

STEP 2»

As you create or modify a project such as a document, presentation, or worksheet, you will most likely want to continue the project at another time or keep it for later reference. You need to save it to a storage medium such as a hard drive, CD, flash drive, or in the cloud with OneDrive. When you save a file, you will be working within a software package. Therefore, you must follow the procedure dictated by that software to save the file. Office 2013 allows you to save your project to OneDrive or to a location on your computer.

The first time that you save a file, you must indicate where the file should be saved, and you must assign a file name. Of course, you will want to save the file in an appropriately named folder so that you can find it easily later. Thereafter, you can quickly save the file with the same settings, or you can change one or more of those settings, perhaps saving the file to a different storage device as a backup copy. Figure 1.10 shows a typical Save As pane for Office 2013 that enables you to select a location before saving the file.

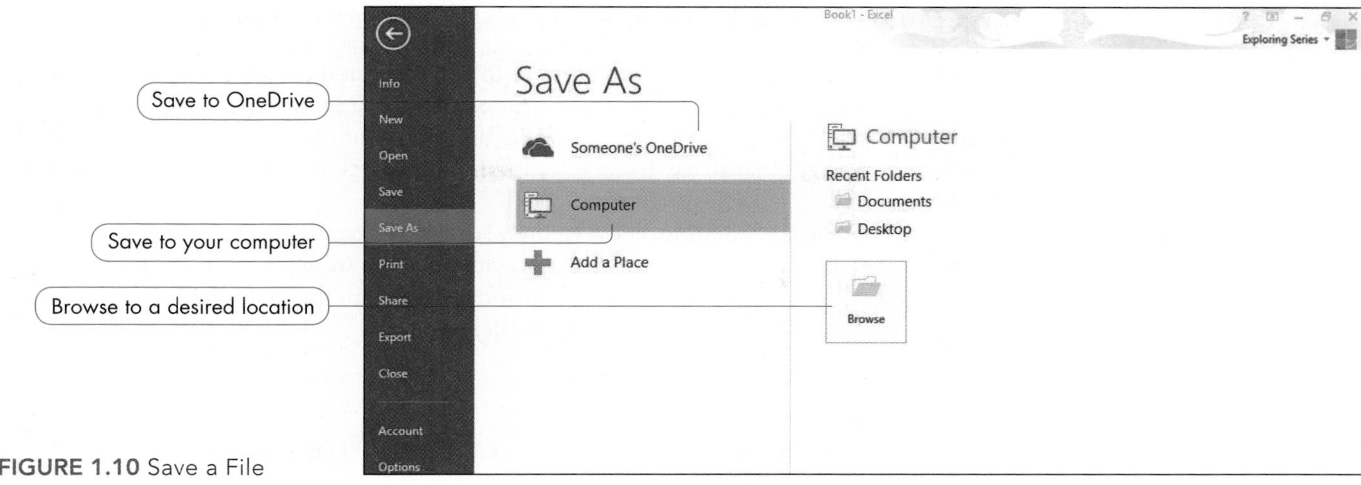

FIGURE 1.10 Save a File

Selecting, Copying, and Moving Multiple Files and Folders

You will want to select folders and files when you need to rename, delete, copy, or paste them, or open files and folders so that you can view the contents. Click a file or folder to *select* it; double-click a file or folder (in the Content pane) to *open* it. To apply an operation to several files at once, such as deleting or moving them, you will want to select all of them.

Select Multiple Files and Folders

You can select several files and folders, regardless of whether they are adjacent to each other in the file list. Suppose that your digital pictures are contained in the Pictures folder. You might want to delete some of the pictures because you want to clear up some hard drive space. To select pictures in the Pictures folder, open File Explorer and click the Pictures library. Locate the desired pictures in the Content pane. To select the adjacent pictures, select the first picture, press and hold Shift, and then click the last picture. All consecutive picture files will be highlighted, indicating that they are selected. At that point, you can delete, copy, or move the selected pictures at the same time.

If the files or folders to be selected are not adjacent, click the first item. Press and hold Ctrl while you click all desired files or folders, releasing Ctrl only when you have finished selecting the files or folders.

To select all items in a folder or disk drive, use File Explorer to navigate to the desired folder. Open the folder, press and hold Ctrl, and then press A on the keyboard. You can also click the Home tab, and in the Select group, click *Select all* to select all items.

TIP Using a Check Box to Select Items

In Windows 8.1.1, it is easy to make multiple selections, even if the items are not adjacent. Open File Explorer and select your drive or folder. Click the View tab and select Item check boxes in the Show/Hide group. As you move the mouse pointer along the left side of files and folders, a check box displays. Click in the check box to select the file. If you want to quickly select all items in the folder, click the check box that displays in the Name column heading.

Copy and Move Files and Folders

When you copy or move a folder, you move both the folder and any files that it contains. You can move or copy a folder or file to another location on the same drive or to another drive. If your purpose is to make a ***backup***, or copy, of an important file or folder, you will probably want to copy it to another drive. It can be helpful to have backup copies saved in the cloud at OneDrive as well.

STEP 4»

To move or copy an item in File Explorer, select the item. If you want to copy or move multiple items, follow the directions in the previous section to select them all at once. Right-click the item(s) and select either Cut or Copy on the shortcut menu. In the Navigation Pane, locate the destination drive or folder, right-click the destination drive or folder, and then click Paste.

1. The File Explorer interface has several panes. Name them and identify their characteristics. ***p. 65***
2. After creating a file, such as a PowerPoint presentation, you want to save it. However, as you begin to save the file, you realize that you have not yet created a folder in which to place the file. Is it possible to create a folder as you are saving the file? If so, how? ***p. 67***
3. What should you consider when deleting files or folders from a removable storage medium such as a flash drive? ***p. 68***
4. Office 2013 enables you to save files to OneDrive or your computer. Why might it be helpful to save a file in both locations? ***p. 67***
5. You want to delete several files, but the files are not consecutively listed in File Explorer. How would you select and delete them? ***p. 69***

Hands-On Exercises

2 Files and Folders

You will soon begin to collect files from volunteers who are preparing promotional and record-keeping material for the Spotted Begonia Art Gallery. It is important that you save the files in appropriately named folders so that you can easily access them later. You can create folders on a hard drive, flash drive, or at OneDrive. You will select the drive on which you plan to save the various files. As you create a short document, you will save it in one of the folders. You will then make a backup copy of the folder structure, including all files, so that you do not run the risk of losing the material if the drive is damaged or misplaced.

Skills covered: Create Folders and Subfolders • Create and Save a File • Rename and Delete a Folder • Open and Copy a File

STEP 1 » CREATE FOLDERS AND SUBFOLDERS

You decide to create a folder titled *Artists* and then subdivide it into subfolders that will help categorize the artists' artwork promotional files as well as for general record keeping for the art gallery. Refer to Figure 1.11 as you complete Step 1.

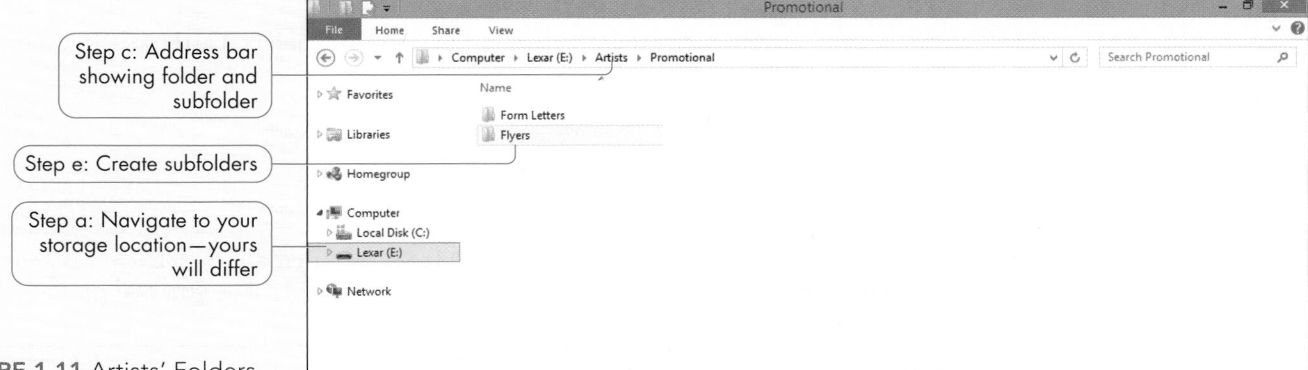

FIGURE 1.11 Artists' Folders

a. Navigate to the location where you are storing your files. If storing on your computer or a flash drive, navigate to the desktop. Click **File Explorer** on the taskbar and maximize the window. Click the **VIEW tab** and click to display the **Preview pane**, if necessary.

A removable drive is shown in Figure 1.11 and is titled *Lexar (E:)*, describing the drive manufacturer and the drive letter. Your storage area will be designated in a different manner, perhaps also identified by manufacturer (or perhaps you are saving your files on OneDrive). The storage area identification is likely to be different because the configuration of disk drives on your computer is unique.

TROUBLESHOOTING: If you do not have a flash drive, you can use the hard drive. In the next step, simply click drive C in the Navigation Pane instead of the removable drive. You can also create and save folders and files at OneDrive.

b. Click the removable drive in the Navigation Pane (or click **drive C** if you are using the hard drive). Click the **HOME tab**, click **New folder** in the New group, type **Artists**, and then press **Enter**.

You create a folder where you can organize subfolders and files for the artists and their promotional materials and general record-keeping files.

TROUBLESHOOTING: If the folder you create is called *New folder* instead of *Artists*, you probably clicked away from the folder before typing the name, so that it received the default name. To rename it, right-click the folder, click Rename, type the correct name, and then press Enter.

c. Double-click the **Artists folder** in the Content pane. The Address bar at the top of the File Explorer window should show that it is the currently selected folder. Click the **HOME tab**, click **New folder** in the New group, type **Promotional**, and then press **Enter**.

   You decide to create subfolders of the *Artists* folder to contain promotional material, presentations, and office records.

d. Check the Address bar to make sure *Artists* is still the current folder. Using the same technique, create a new folder named **Presentations** and create a new folder named **Office Records**.

   You create two more subfolders, appropriately named.

e. Double-click the **Promotional folder** in the Navigation Pane. Right-click in a blank area, point to *New*, and then click **Folder**. Type **Form Letters** and press **Enter**. Using the same technique, create a new folder named **Flyers** and press **Enter**.

   To subdivide the promotional material further, you create two subfolders, one to hold form letters and one to contain flyers (see Figure 1.11).

f. Take a full-screen snip of your screen and name it **f01h2Folders_LastFirst**. Close the Snipping Tool.

g. Close File Explorer.

STEP 2 » CREATE AND SAVE A FILE

To keep everything organized, you assign volunteers to take care of certain tasks. After creating an Excel worksheet listing those responsibilities, you will save it in the Office Records folder. Refer to Figure 1.12 as you complete Step 2.

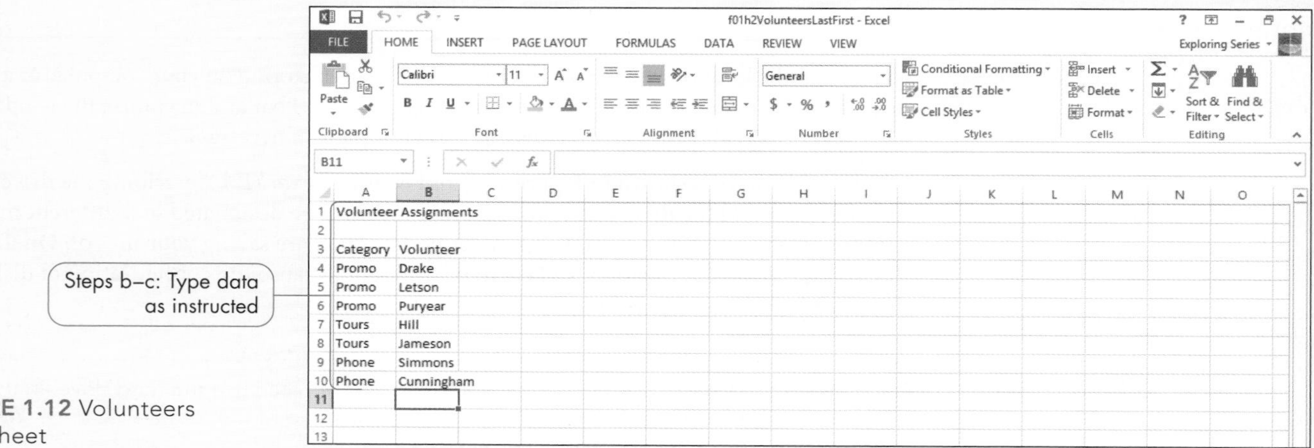

FIGURE 1.12 Volunteers Worksheet

a. Navigate to the Start screen. Scroll across the tiles and click **Excel 2013**. If necessary, use the Search charm to locate Excel.

   You use Excel 2013 to create the Volunteers worksheet.

b. Click **Blank workbook** in the Excel 2013 window that displays. Type **Volunteer Assignments** in **cell A1**. Press **Enter** twice.

   Cell A3 is the active cell, as indicated by a green box that surrounds the cell.

c. Type **Category**. Press **Tab** to make the next cell to the right the active cell and type **Volunteer**. Press **Enter**. Complete the remaining cells of the worksheet as shown in Figure 1.12.

> **TROUBLESHOOTING:** If you make a mistake, click in the cell and retype the entry.

d. Click the **FILE tab** and click **Save**.

The Save As pane displays. The Save As pane is where you determine the location where your file will be saved, either your Computer or OneDrive.

e. Click **Browse** to display the Save As dialog box. Scroll down if necessary and click **Computer** or the location where you are saving your files in the Navigation Pane. In the Content pane, locate the Artists folder that you created in Step 1 and double-click to open the folder. Double-click **Office Records**. Click in the **File name box** and type **f01h2Volunteers_LastFirst**. Click **Save**. Refer to Figure 1.12.

The file is now saved as *f01h2Volunteers_LastFirst*. The workbook is saved in the Office Records subfolder of the Artists folder. You can check the title bar of the workbook to confirm the file has been saved with the correct name.

f. Click the **Close (X) button** in the top-right corner of the Excel window to close Excel.

STEP 3 ›› RENAME AND DELETE A FOLDER

As often happens, you find that the folder structure you created is not exactly what you need. You will remove the Flyers folder and the Form Letters folder and will rename the Promotional folder to better describe the contents. Refer to Figure 1.13 as you complete Step 3.

FIGURE 1.13 Artists Folder Structure

a. Navigate to the desktop, if necessary. Click **File Explorer** on the taskbar. Click the location where you are saving your files. Double-click the **Artists folder** in the Content pane.

b. Click the **Promotional folder** to select it.

> **TROUBLESHOOTING:** If you double-click the folder instead of using a single-click, the folder will open and you will see its title in the Address bar. To return to the correct view, click Artists in the Address bar.

c. Click the **HOME tab**. In the Organize group, click **Rename**, type **Promotional Print**, and then press **Enter**.

Because the folder will be used to organize all of the printed promotional material, you decide to rename the folder to better reflect the contents.

d. Double-click the **Promotional Print folder**. Click **Flyers**. Press and hold **Shift** and click **Form Letters**. Both folders should be selected (highlighted). Right-click either folder and click **Delete**. If asked to confirm the deletion, click **Yes**. Click **Artists** in the Address bar.

Your screen should appear as shown in Figure 1.13. You decide that dividing the promotional material into flyers and form letters is not necessary, so you deleted both folders.

e. Take a full-screen snip of your screen and name it **f01h2Artists_LastFirst**. Close the Snipping Tool.

f. Leave File Explorer open for the next step.

STEP 4 » OPEN AND COPY A FILE

You hope to recruit more volunteers to work with the Spotted Begonia Art Gallery. The Volunteers worksheet will be a handy way to keep up with people and assignments, and as the list grows, knowing exactly where the file is saved will be important for easy access. You will modify the Volunteers worksheet and make a backup copy of the folder hierarchy. Refer to Figure 1.14 as you complete Step 4.

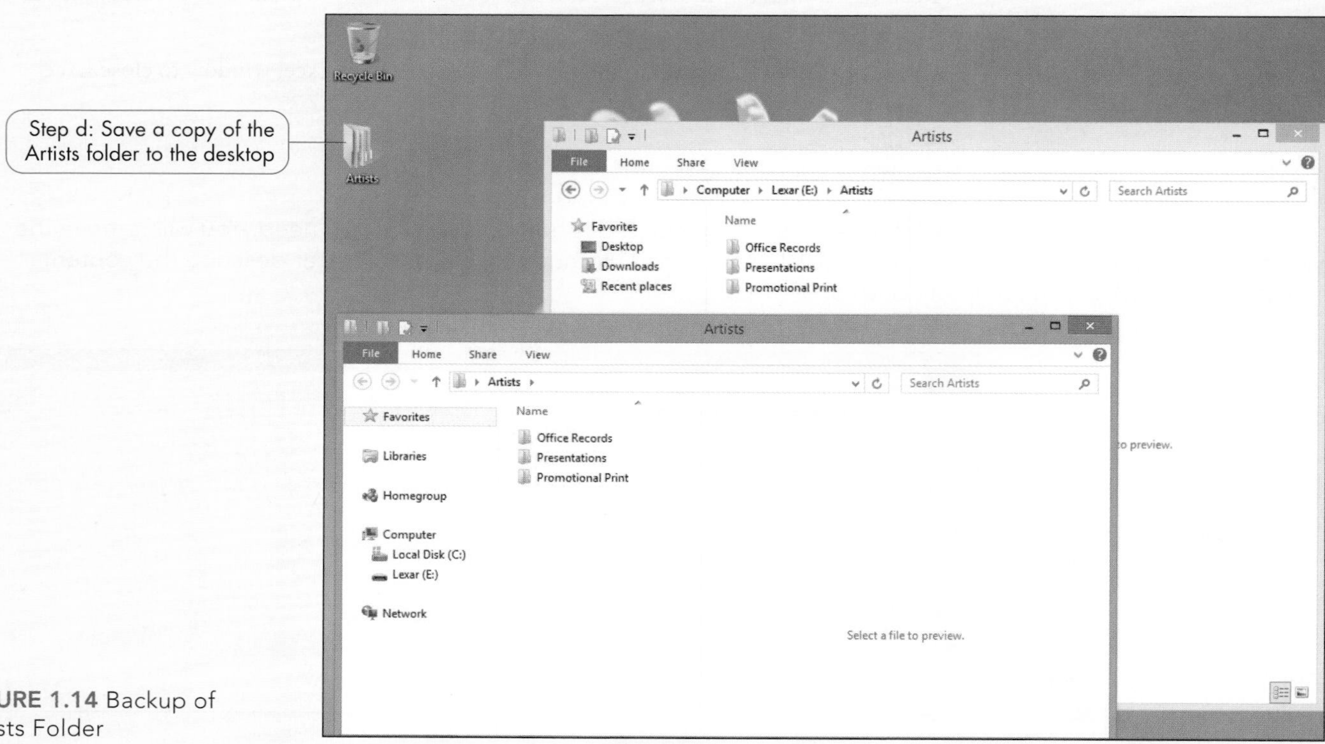

FIGURE 1.14 Backup of Artists Folder

a. Double-click the **Office Records folder**. Double-click *f01h2Volunteers_LastFirst*. Save the file with the new name **f01h2Stp4Volunteers_LastFirst** in the same location.

Because the file was created with Excel, that program opens, and the Volunteers worksheet is displayed.

b. Click **cell A11**, if necessary, and type **Office**. Press **Tab**, type **Adams**, and then press **Enter**. Click the **FILE tab** and click **Save**. The file is automatically saved in the same location with the same file name as before. Close Excel.

A neighbor, Sarah Adams, has volunteered to help in the office. You record that information on the worksheet and save the updated file in the Office Records folder.

c. Click the location where you save files in the Navigation pane in File Explorer so that the Artists folder displays in the Content pane. Right-click the **Artists folder** and click **Copy**.

d. Right-click **Desktop** in the Favorites group on the Navigation Pane and click **Paste**. Close File Explorer. If any other windows are open, close them also.

   You made a copy of the Artists folder on the desktop.

e. Double-click the **Artists folder** on the desktop. Double-click the **Office Records folder**. Verify that the *f01h2Stp4Volunteers_LastFirst* worksheet displays in the folder. Take a full-screen snip of your screen and name it **f01h2Backup_LastFirst**. Close the Snipping Tool and close File Explorer.

f. Right-click the **Artists folder** on the desktop, select **Delete**, and then click **Yes** if asked to confirm the deletion.

   You deleted the Artists folder from the desktop of the computer because you may be working in a computer lab and want to leave the computer as you found it. You may also want to empty the Recycle Bin.

g. Submit your files based on your instructor's directions.

Microsoft Office Software

Organizations around the world rely heavily on ***Microsoft Office*** software to produce documents, spreadsheets, presentations, and databases. Microsoft Office is a productivity software suite including a set of software applications, each one specializing in a particular type of output. You can use ***Word*** to produce all sorts of documents, including memos, newsletters, forms, tables, and brochures. ***Excel*** makes it easy to organize records, financial transactions, and business information in the form of worksheets. With ***PowerPoint***, you can create dynamic presentations to inform groups and persuade audiences. ***Access*** is relational database software that enables you to record and link data, query databases, and create forms and reports.

You will sometimes find that you need to use two or more Office applications to produce your intended output. You might, for example, find that a Word document you are preparing for your investment club should also include a summary of stock performance. You can use Excel to prepare the summary and then incorporate the worksheet in the Word document. Similarly, you can integrate Word tables and Excel charts into a PowerPoint presentation. The choice of which software applications to use really depends on what type of output you are producing. Table 1.2 describes the major tasks of these four primary applications in Microsoft Office.

TABLE 1.2 Microsoft Office Software

Office 2013 Product	Application Characteristics
Word 2013	Word processing software used with text to create, edit, and format documents such as letters, memos, reports, brochures, resumes, and flyers.
Excel 2013	Spreadsheet software used to store quantitative data and to perform accurate and rapid calculations with results ranging from simple budgets to financial analyses and statistical analyses.
PowerPoint 2013	Presentation graphics software used to create slide shows for presentation by a speaker, to be published as part of a Web site, or to run as a stand-alone application on a computer kiosk.
Access 2013	Relational database software used to store data and convert it into information. Database software is used primarily for decision making by businesses that compile data from multiple records stored in tables to produce informative reports.

As you become familiar with Microsoft Office, you will find that although each software application produces a specific type of output, all applications share common features. Such commonality gives a similar feel to each software application so that learning and working with Microsoft Office software products is easy. In this section, you will identify features common to Microsoft Office software, including such interface components as the Ribbon, the Backstage view, and the Quick Access Toolbar. You will also learn how to get help with an application.

Identifying Common Interface Components

As you work with Microsoft Office, you will find that each application shares a similar ***user interface***. The user interface is the screen display through which you communicate with the software. Word, Excel, PowerPoint, and Access share common interface elements, as shown in Figure 1.15. One of the feature options includes the availability of templates as well as new and improved themes when each application is opened. A ***template*** is a predesigned file that incorporates formatting elements, such as a theme and layouts, and may include content that can be modified. A ***theme*** is a collection of design choices that includes colors, fonts, and special effects used to give a consistent look to a document, workbook, or presentation. As you can imagine, becoming familiar with one application's interface makes it that much easier to work with other Office software.

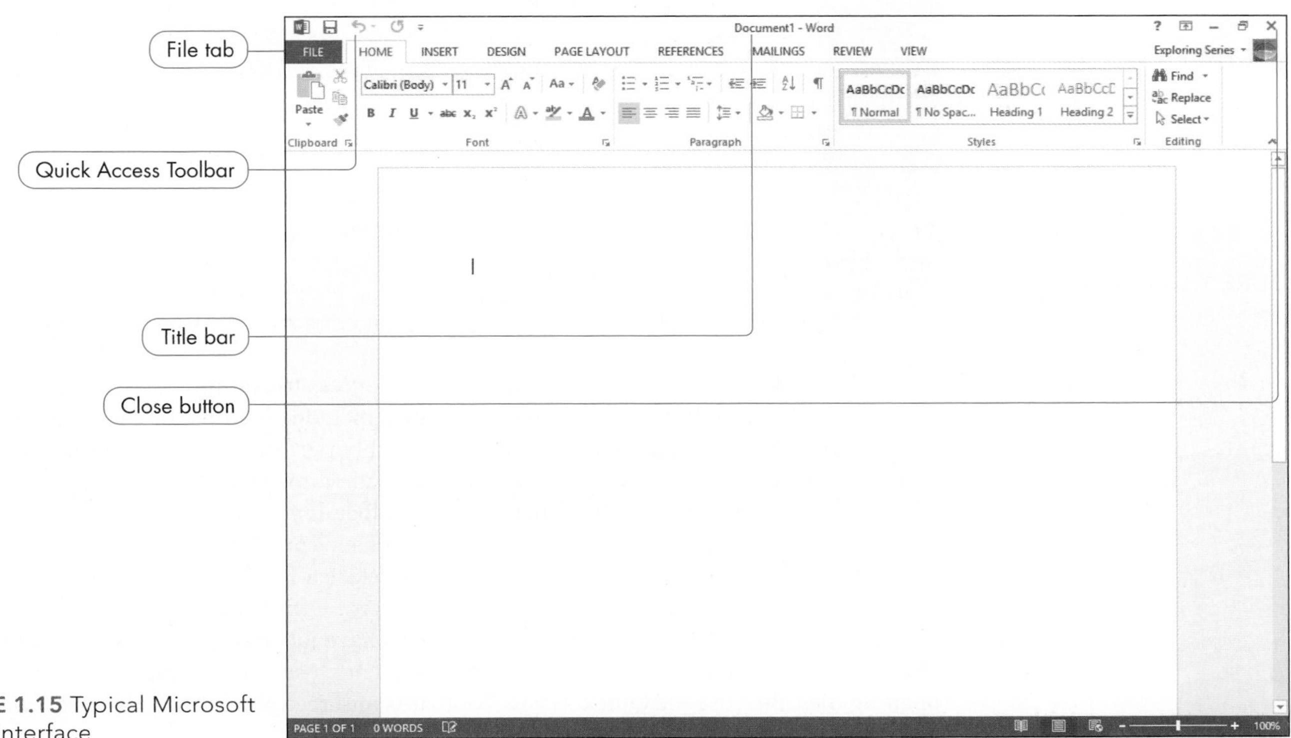

FIGURE 1.15 Typical Microsoft Office Interface

Use the Backstage View and the Quick Access Toolbar

The ***Backstage view*** is a component of Office 2013 that provides a concise collection of commands related to an open file. Using the Backstage view, you can find out information such as protection, permissions, versions, and properties. A file's properties include the author, file size, permissions, and date modified. You can create a new document or open, save, print, share, export, or close. The ***Quick Access Toolbar***, located at the top-left corner of any Office application window, provides fast access to commonly executed tasks such as saving a file and undoing recent actions. The ***title bar*** identifies the current file name and the application in which you are working. It also includes control buttons that enable you to minimize, maximize, restore down, or close the application window (see Figure 1.15).

You access the Backstage view by clicking the File tab. When you click the File tab, you will see the Backstage view (see Figure 1.16). Primarily focusing on file activities such as opening, closing, saving, printing, and beginning new files, the Backstage view also includes options for customizing program settings, signing in to your Office account, and exiting the program. It displays a file's properties, providing important information on file permission and sharing options. When you click the File tab, the Backstage view will occupy the entire application window, hiding the file with which you might be working. For example, suppose that as you are typing a report you need to check the document's properties. Click the File tab to display a Backstage view similar to that shown in Figure 1.16. You can return to the application—in this case, Word—in a couple of ways. Either click the Back arrow in the top-left corner or press Esc on the keyboard.

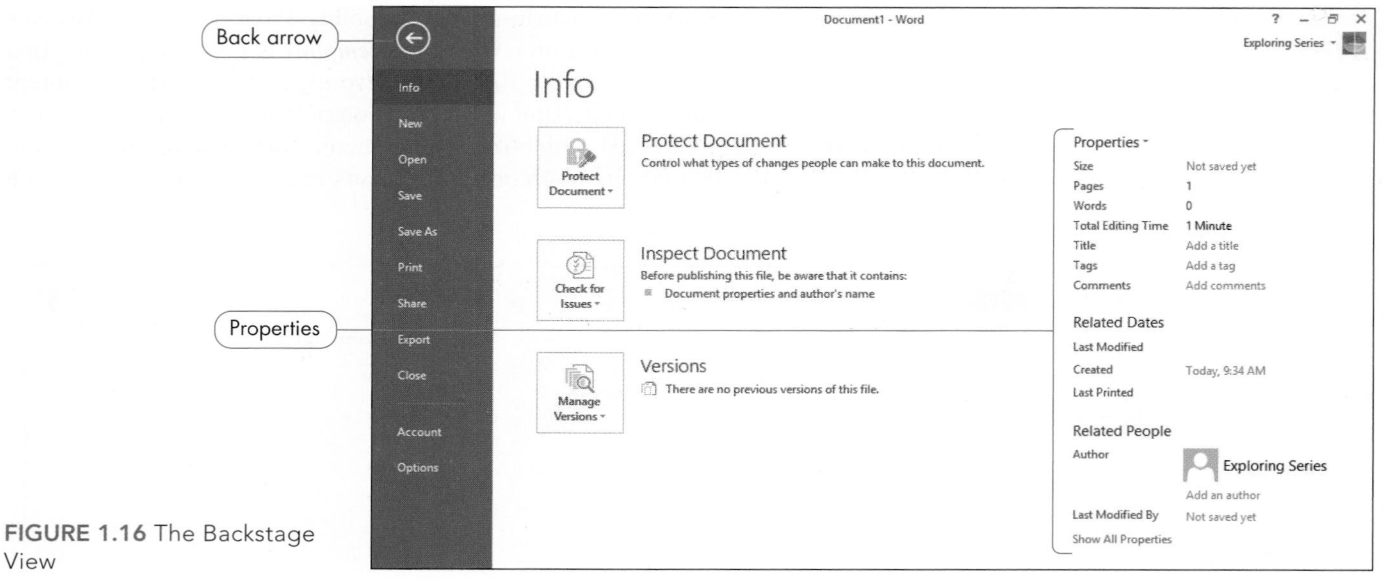

FIGURE 1.16 The Backstage View

STEP 4» The Quick Access Toolbar provides one-click access to common activities, as shown in Figure 1.17. By default, the Quick Access Toolbar includes buttons for saving a file and for undoing or redoing recent actions. You will probably perform an action countless times in an Office application and then realize that you made a mistake. You can recover from the mistake by clicking Undo on the Quick Access Toolbar. If you click the arrow beside Undo—known as the Undo arrow—you can select from a list of previous actions in order of occurrence. The Undo list is not maintained when you close a file or exit the application, so you can erase an action that took place during the current Office session only. Similar to Undo, you can also Redo (or Replace) an action that you have just undone. You can customize the Quick Access Toolbar to include buttons for frequently used commands such as printing or opening files. Because the Quick Access Toolbar is onscreen at all times, the most commonly accessed tasks are just a click away.

To customize the Quick Access Toolbar, click Customize Quick Access Toolbar (see Figure 1.17) and select from a list of commands. You can also click More Commands near the bottom of the menu options. If a command that you want to include on the toolbar is not on the list, you can right-click the command on the Ribbon and click *Add to Quick Access Toolbar*. Similarly, remove a command from the Quick Access Toolbar by right-clicking the icon on the Quick Access Toolbar and clicking *Remove from Quick Access Toolbar*. If you want to display the Quick Access Toolbar beneath the Ribbon, click Customize Quick Access Toolbar (see Figure 1.17) and click *Show Below the Ribbon*.

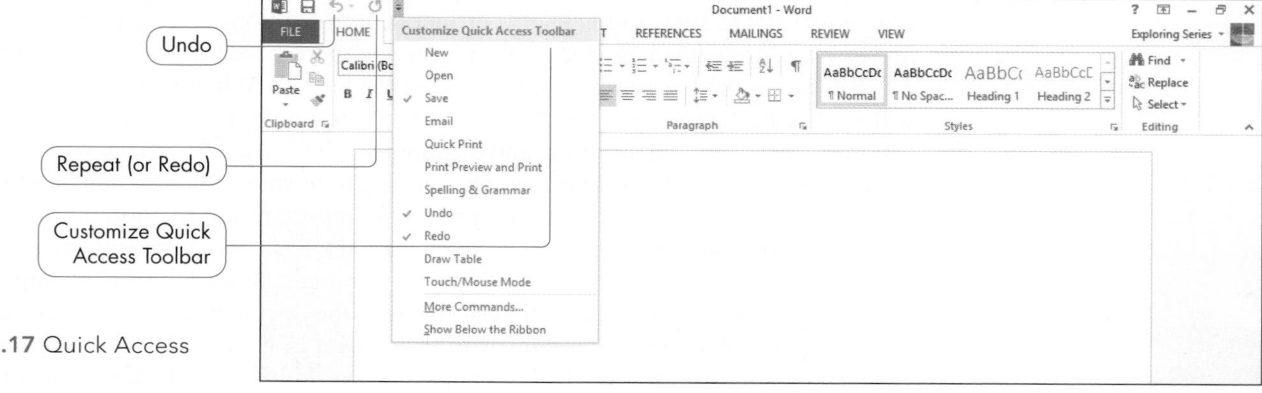

FIGURE 1.17 Quick Access Toolbar

Familiarize Yourself with the Ribbon

The ***Ribbon*** is the command center of Office applications. It is the long bar located just beneath the title bar, containing tabs, groups, and commands. Each ***tab*** is designed to appear much like a tab on a file folder, with the active tab highlighted. The File tab is always a darker shade than the other tabs and a different color depending on the application. Remember that clicking the File tab opens the Backstage view. Other tabs on the Ribbon enable you to modify a file. The active tab in Figure 1.18 is the Home tab.

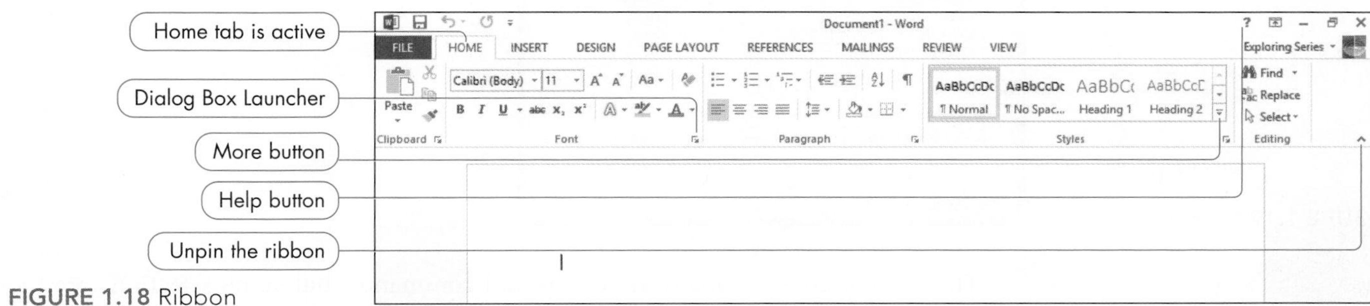

FIGURE 1.18 Ribbon

When you click a tab, the Ribbon displays several task-oriented ***groups***, with each group containing related ***commands***. A group is a subset of a tab that organizes similar tasks together. A command is a button or area within a group that you click to perform tasks. Microsoft Office is designed to provide the most functionality possible with the fewest clicks. For that reason, the Home tab, displayed when you first open an Office software application, contains groups and commands that are most commonly used. For example, because you will often want to change the way text is displayed, the Home tab in each Office application includes a Font group with activities related to modifying text. Similarly, other tabs contain groups of related actions, or commands, many of which are unique to the particular Office application.

Because Word, PowerPoint, Excel, and Access all share a similar Ribbon structure, you will be able to move at ease among those applications. Although the specific tabs, groups, and commands vary among the Office programs, the way in which you use the Ribbon and the descriptive nature of tab titles is the same regardless of which program you are working with. For example, if you want to insert a chart in Excel, a header in Word, or a shape in PowerPoint, you will click the Insert tab in any of those programs. The first thing that you should do as you begin to work with an Office application is to study the Ribbon. Take a look at all tabs and their contents. That way, you will have a good idea of where to find specific commands and how the Ribbon with which you are currently working differs from one that you might have used previously in another application.

If you are working with a large project, you might want to maximize your workspace by temporarily hiding the Ribbon. You can hide the Ribbon in several ways. Double-click the active tab to hide the Ribbon and double-click any tab to redisplay it. You can click *Unpin the ribbon* (see Figure 1.18), located at the right side of the Ribbon, and click any tab to redisplay the Ribbon.

The Ribbon provides quick access to common activities such as changing number or text formats or aligning data or text. Some actions, however, do not display on the Ribbon because they are not so common but are related to commands displayed on the Ribbon. For example, you might want to change the background of a PowerPoint slide to include a picture. In that case, you will need to work with a ***dialog box*** that provides access to more precise, but less frequently used, commands. Figure 1.19 shows the Font dialog box in Word, for example. Some commands display a dialog box when they are clicked. Other Ribbon groups include a ***Dialog Box Launcher*** that, when clicked, opens a corresponding dialog box (refer to Figure 1.18).

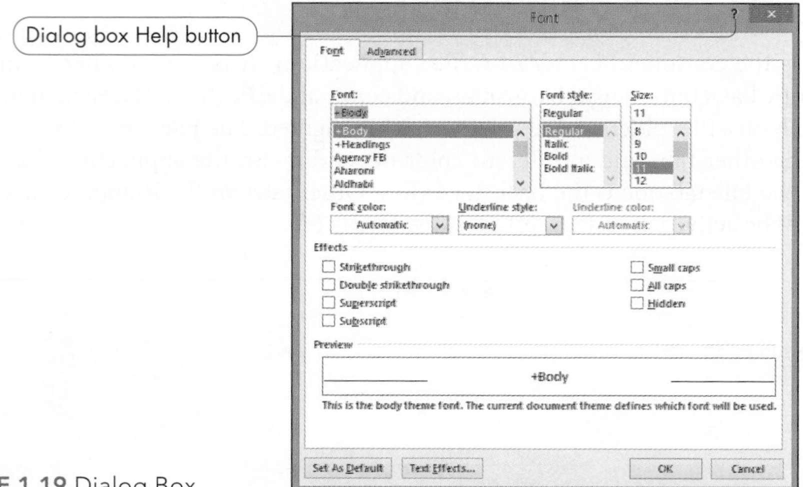

FIGURE 1.19 Dialog Box

The Ribbon contains many selections and commands, but some selections are too numerous to include in the Ribbon's limited space. For example, Word provides far more text styles than it can easily display at once, so additional styles are available in a ***gallery***. A gallery also provides a choice of Excel chart styles and PowerPoint transitions. Figure 1.20 shows an example of a PowerPoint Themes gallery. Most often, you can display a gallery of additional choices by clicking the More button (refer to Figure 1.18) that is found in some Ribbon selections.

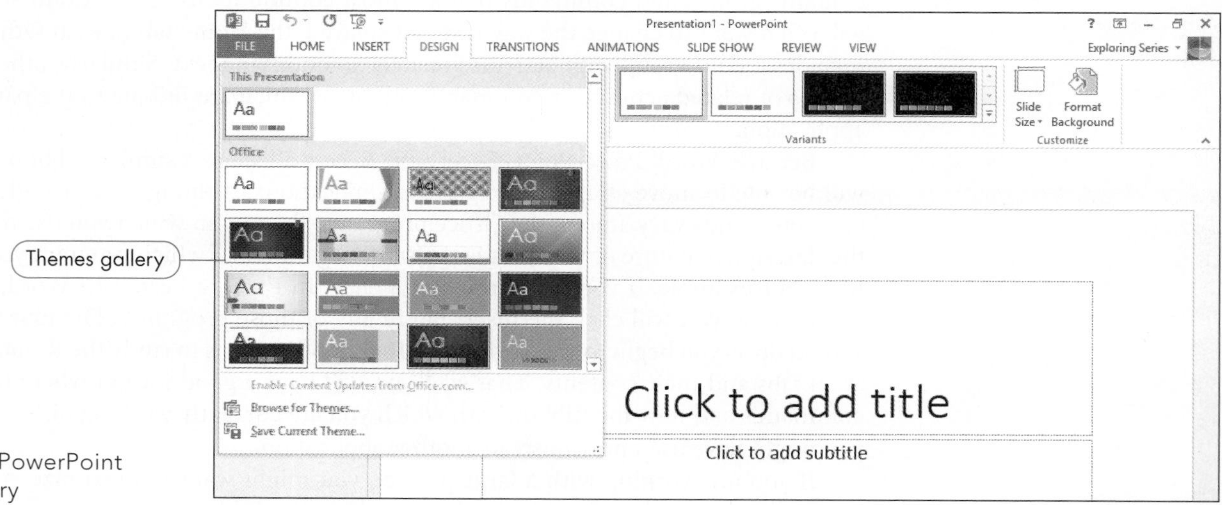

FIGURE 1.20 PowerPoint Themes Gallery

STEP 3» When editing a document, worksheet, or presentation, it is helpful to see the results of formatting changes before you make final selections. The feature that displays a preview of the results of a selection is called ***Live Preview***. You might, for example, be considering changing the font color of a selection in a document or worksheet. As you place the mouse pointer over a color selection in a Ribbon gallery or group, the selected text will temporarily display the color to which you are pointing. Similarly, you can get a preview of how color designs would display on PowerPoint slides by pointing to specific themes in the PowerPoint Themes group and noting the effect on a displayed slide. When you click the item, such as the font color, the selection is applied. Live Preview is available in various Ribbon selections among the Office applications.

Office applications also make it easy for you to work with objects such as pictures, ***clip art***, shapes, charts, and tables. Clip art is an electronic illustration that can be inserted into an Office project. When you include such objects in a project, they are considered separate components that you can manage independently. To work with an object, you must click to select it. When you select an object, the Ribbon is modified to include one or more ***contextual tabs*** that contain groups of commands related to the selected object. Figure 1.21 shows a contextual tab related to a selected SmartArt object in a Word document. When you click outside the selected object, the contextual tab disappears.

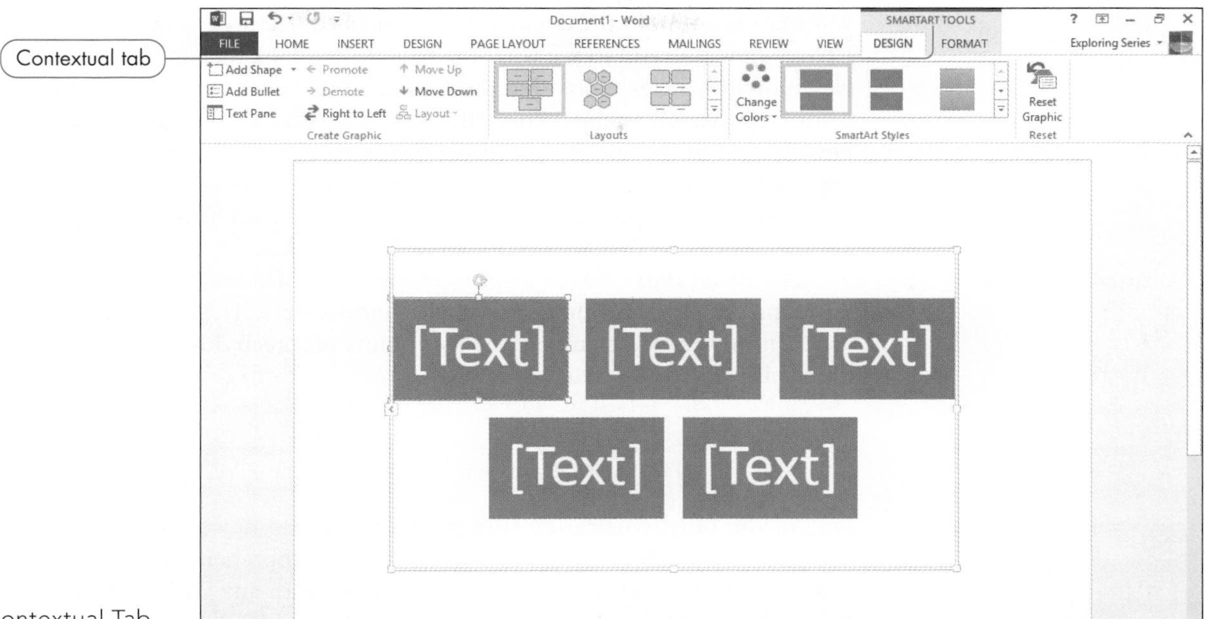

FIGURE 1.21 Contextual Tab

TIP Using Keyboard Shortcuts

You might find that you prefer to use keyboard shortcuts, which are keyboard equivalents for software commands, when they are available. Universal keyboard shortcuts include Ctrl+C (copy), Ctrl+X (cut), Ctrl+V (paste), and Ctrl+Z (undo). To move to the beginning of a Word document, to cell A1 in Excel, or to the first PowerPoint slide, press Ctrl+Home. To move to the end of those items, press Ctrl+End. Press Alt to display keyboard shortcuts, called a ***Key Tip***, for items on the Ribbon and Quick Access Toolbar. You can press the letter or number corresponding to Ribbon items to invoke the action from the keyboard. Press Alt again to remove the Key Tips.

Use the Status Bar

The ***status bar*** is located at the bottom of the program window and contains information relative to the open file. It also includes tools for changing the view of the file and for changing the zoom size of onscreen file contents. Contents of the status bar are unique to each specific application. When you work with Word, the status bar informs you of the number of pages and words in an open document. The Excel status bar displays summary information, such as average and sum, of selected cells. The PowerPoint status bar shows the slide number, total slides in the presentation, and the applied theme. It also provides access to notes and comments.

STEP 3»

Regardless of the application in which you are working, the status bar includes view buttons and a Zoom slider. You can also use the View tab on the Ribbon to change the current view or zoom level of an open file. The status bar's view buttons (see Figure 1.22) enable you to change the ***view*** of the open file. When creating a document, you might find it helpful to change the view. You might, for example, view a PowerPoint slide presentation with multiple slides displayed (Slide Sorter view) or with only one slide in large size (Normal view). In Word, you could view a document in Print Layout view (showing margins, headers, and footers), Web Layout view, or Read Mode.

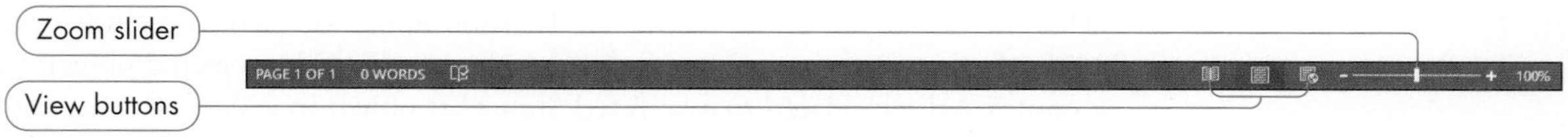

Zoom slider

View buttons

PAGE 1 OF 1 0 WORDS 100%

FIGURE 1.22 Word Status Bar

Additional views are available in the View tab. Word's Print Layout view is useful when you want to see both the document text and such features as margins and page breaks. Web Layout view is useful to see what the page would look like on the Internet. The Read Mode view provides a clean look that displays just the content without the Ribbon or margins. It is ideal for use on a tablet where the screen may be smaller than on a laptop or computer. PowerPoint, Excel, and Access also provide view options, although they are unique to the application. The most common view options are accessible from *View shortcuts* on the status bar of each application. As you learn more about Office applications, you will become aware of the views that are specific to each application.

STEP 1

The ***Zoom slider*** always displays at the far right side of the status bar. You can drag the tab along the slider in either direction to increase or decrease the magnification of the file. Be aware, however, that changing the size of text onscreen does not change the font size when the file is printed or saved.

Getting Office Help

One of the most frustrating things about learning new software is determining how to complete a task. Thankfully, Microsoft includes comprehensive help in Office so that you are less likely to feel such frustration. As you work with any Office application, you can access help online as well as within the current software installation. Help is available through a short description that displays when you rest the mouse pointer on a command. Additionally, you can get help related to a currently open dialog box by clicking the question mark in the top-right corner of the dialog box, or when you click Help in the top-right corner of the application.

Use Office Help

STEP 2

To access the comprehensive library of Office Help, click the Help button, displayed as a question mark on the far right side of the Ribbon (refer to Figure 1.18). The Help window provides assistance with the current application as well as a direct link to online resources and technical support. Figure 1.23 shows the Help window that displays when you click the Help button while in Excel. For general information on broad topics, click a link in the window. However, if you are having difficulty with a specific task, it might be easier to simply type the request in the Search online help box. Suppose you are seeking help with using the Goal Seek feature in Excel. Simply type *Goal Seek* or a phrase such as *find specific result by changing variables* in the Search box and press Enter (or click the magnifying glass on the right). Then select from displayed results for more information on the topic.

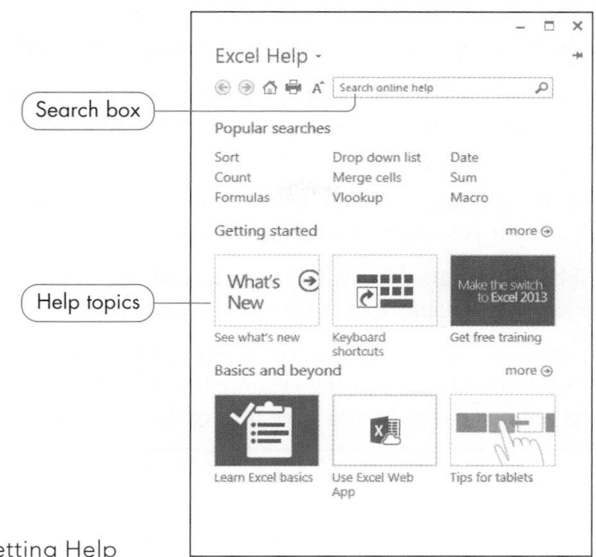

FIGURE 1.23 Getting Help

Use Enhanced ScreenTips

For quick summary information on the purpose of a command button, place the mouse pointer over the button. An ***Enhanced ScreenTip*** displays, giving the purpose of the command, short descriptive text, and a keyboard shortcut if applicable. Some ScreenTips include a suggestion for pressing F1 for additional help. The Enhanced ScreenTip in Figure 1.24 provides context-sensitive assistance.

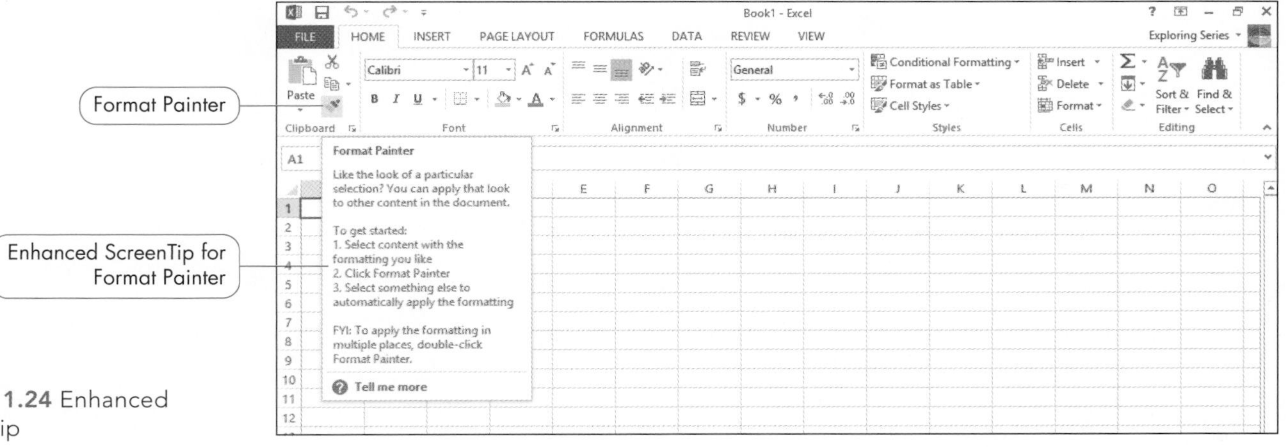

FIGURE 1.24 Enhanced ScreenTip

Get Help with Dialog Boxes

Getting help while you are working with a dialog box is easy. Simply click the Help button that displays as a question mark in the top-right corner of the dialog box (refer to Figure 1.19). The subsequent Help window will offer suggestions relevant to your task.

1. How do you access the Backstage view, and what can you do there? ***p. 77***
2. What is the purpose of the Quick Access Toolbar? Suppose you often engage in an activity such as printing. What steps would you take to add that command to the Quick Access Toolbar? ***pp. 77–78***
3. The Ribbon is an important interface component of Office applications. What can you do with it? How is it organized? Is it always visible? ***pp. 79–80***
4. Occasionally, the Ribbon is modified to include a contextual tab. Define a contextual tab and give an example of when a contextual tab is displayed. ***pp. 80–81***
5. After using Word to develop a research paper, you learn that the margins you used are incorrect. You plan to use Word's built-in Help feature to obtain information on how to change margins. Explain the process of obtaining help on the topic. ***pp. 82–83***

Hands-On Exercises

Watch the Video for this Hands-On Exercise!

MyITLab®
HOE3 Training

3 Microsoft Office Software

As the administrative assistant for the Spotted Begonia Art Gallery, you need to get the staff started on a proposed schedule of gallery showings worksheet. Although you do not have access to information on all of the artists and their preferred media, you want to provide a suggested format for a worksheet to keep up with showings as they get booked. You will use Excel to begin design of the worksheet.

Skills covered: Open an Office Application, Get Enhanced ScreenTip Help, and Use the Zoom Slider • Get Help and Use the Backstage View • Change the View and Use Live Preview • Use the Quick Access Toolbar and Explore PowerPoint Views

STEP 1 » OPEN AN OFFICE APPLICATION, GET ENHANCED SCREENTIP HELP, AND USE THE ZOOM SLIDER

Because you will use Excel to create the gallery showings worksheet, you will open the application. You will familiarize yourself with items on the Ribbon by getting Enhanced ScreenTip Help. For a better view of worksheet data, you will use the Zoom slider to magnify cell contents. Refer to Figure 1.25 as you complete Step 1.

Step b: Enter data

FIGURE 1.25 Gallery Showings Worksheet

a. Navigate to the Start screen. Scroll across the tiles, if necessary, and click **Excel 2013**. Click **Blank workbook** in the Excel 2013 window that displays.

You have opened Microsoft Excel because it is the program in which the gallery showings worksheet will be created.

b. Type **Date** in **cell A1**. As you type, the text appears in the current worksheet cell. Press **Tab** and type **Artist**. Press **Tab** and type **Media Used**. Press **Enter**. See Figure 1.25.

The worksheet that you create is only a beginning. Your staff will later suggest additional columns of data that can better summarize the upcoming gallery showings.

c. Hover the mouse pointer over any command on the Ribbon and note the Enhanced ScreenTip that displays, informing you of the purpose of the command. Explore other commands and identify their purpose.

d. Click the **PAGE LAYOUT tab**, click **Orientation** in the Page Setup group, and then select **Landscape**.

The PAGE LAYOUT tab is also found in Word, enabling you to change margins, orientation, and other page settings. Although you will not see much difference in the Excel screen display after you change the orientation to landscape, the worksheet will be oriented so that it is wider than it is tall when printed.

e. Drag the tab on the Zoom slider, located at the far right side of the status bar, to 190% to temporarily magnify the text. Take a full-screen snip of your screen and name it **f01h3Showings_LastFirst**.

f. Click the **VIEW tab** and click **100%** in the Zoom group to return the view to its original size.

When you change the zoom, you do not change the text size that will be printed or saved. The change merely magnifies or decreases the view while you work with the file.

g. Keep the workbook open for the next step in this exercise. Submit the file based on your instructor's directions.

STEP 2 ›› GET HELP AND USE THE BACKSTAGE VIEW

Because you are not an Excel expert, you occasionally rely on the Help feature to provide information on tasks. You need assistance with saving a worksheet, previewing it before printing, and printing the worksheet. From what you learn, you will find that the Backstage view enables you to accomplish all of those tasks. Refer to Figure 1.26 as you complete Step 2.

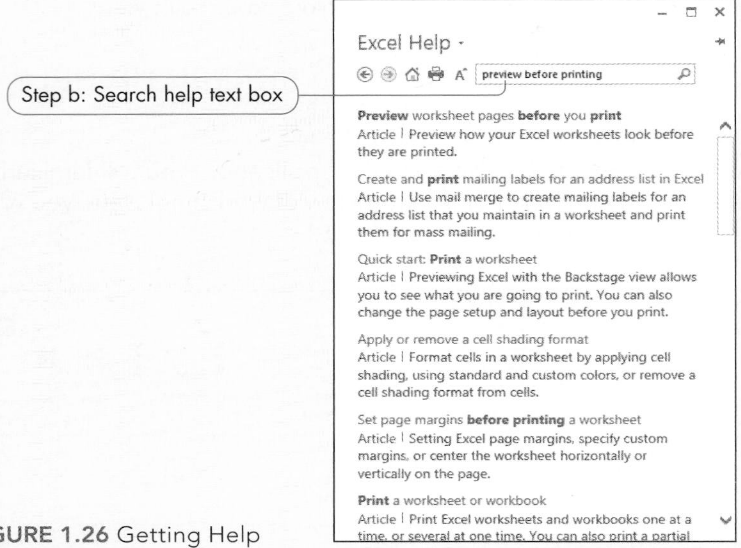

FIGURE 1.26 Getting Help

a. Click **Help**, which is the question mark in the top-right corner of the Ribbon.

The Help dialog box displays.

TIP Using Shortcuts to Access Help

You can discover alternative ways to access Help. For example, the ScreenTip that displays as you point to the Help button suggests that you could press the F1 key.

b. Click in the **Search online help text box** at the top of the Help dialog box. Type **preview before printing** and press **Enter** (see Figure 1.26). In the Excel Help window, click **Preview worksheet pages before you print**. Read about how to preview a worksheet before printing. From what you read, can you identify a keyboard shortcut for previewing worksheets? Click the **Close (X) button**.

Before you print the worksheet, you would like to see how it will look when printed. You used Help to find information on previewing before printing.

c. Click the **FILE tab** and click **Print**.

Having used Office Help to learn how to preview before printing, you follow the directions to view the worksheet as it will look when printed. The preview of the worksheet displays on the right. To print the worksheet, you would click Print. However, you can first select any print options, such as the number of copies, from the Backstage view.

d. Click the **Back arrow** on the top left of the screen. Click **Help**. Excel Help presents several links related to the worksheet. Explore any that look interesting. Return to previous Help windows by clicking **Back** at the top-left side of the Help window. Close the Help dialog box.

e. Click the **HOME tab**. Point to *Bold* in the Font group.

You will find that, along with Excel, Word and PowerPoint also include formatting features in the Font group, such as Bold and Italic. When the Enhanced ScreenTip appears, identify the shortcut key combination that could be used to bold a selected text item. It is indicated as Ctrl plus the letter B.

f. Click the **Close (X) button** in the top-right corner of the Excel window to close both the workbook and the Excel program. When asked whether you want to save changes, click **Don't Save**.

You decide not to print or save the worksheet right now because you did not change anything during this step.

STEP 3 » CHANGE THE VIEW AND USE LIVE PREVIEW

It is important that the documents you prepare or approve are error free and as attractive as possible. Before printing, you will change the view to get a better idea of how the document will look when printed. In addition, you will use Live Preview to experiment with font settings before actually applying them. Refer to Figure 1.27 as you complete Step 3.

FIGURE 1.27 Word Views

a. Navigate to the Start screen. Scroll across the tiles, if necessary, and click **Word 2013**. Click **Blank document**.

You have opened a blank Word document. You plan to familiarize yourself with the program for later reference.

b. Type your first and last names and press **Enter**. Drag to select your name.

Your name should be highlighted, indicating that it is selected. You have selected your name because you want to experiment with using Word to change the way text looks.

c. Click the **Font Size arrow** in the Font group. If you need help locating Font Size, check for an Enhanced ScreenTip. Place the mouse pointer over any number in the list, but do not click. As you move to different font sizes, notice the size of your name changes. The feature you are using is called Live Preview. Click **16** in the list to change the font size of your name.

d. Click any white space to deselect your name. Click **Read Mode** in the *View shortcuts* group on the status bar to change the view (see Figure 1.27). Click **Print Layout** to return to the original view.

e. Save the file as **f01h3Read_LastFirst** and click the **Close (X) button** to close the Word program. Submit the file based on your instructor's directions.

STEP 4 » USE THE QUICK ACCESS TOOLBAR AND EXPLORE POWERPOINT VIEWS

In your position as administrative assistant, you will be asked to review documents, presentations, and worksheets. It is important that you explore each application to familiarize yourself with operations and commonalities. Specifically, you know that the Quick Access Toolbar is common to all applications and that you can place commonly used commands there to streamline processes. Also, learning to change views will enable you to see the project in different ways for various purposes. Refer to Figure 1.28 as you complete Step 4.

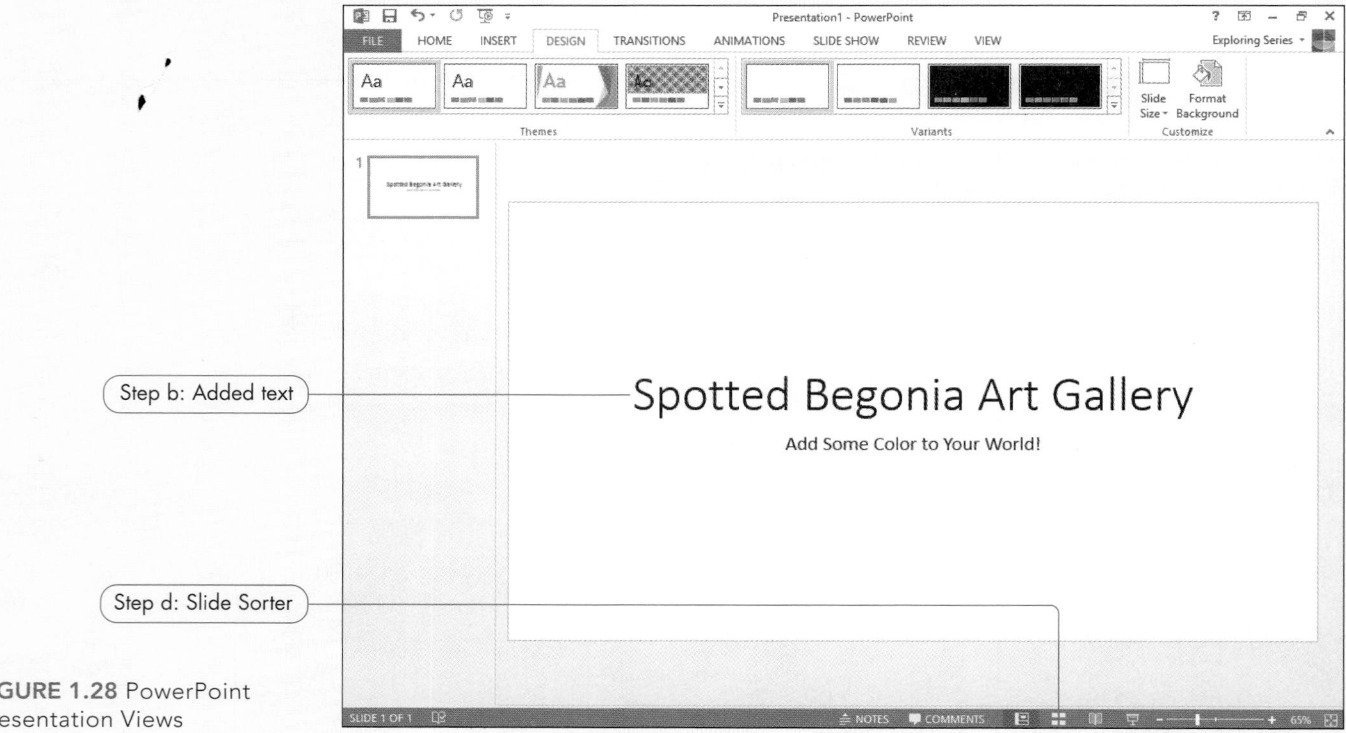

FIGURE 1.28 PowerPoint Presentation Views

a. Navigate to the Start screen. Scroll across the tiles, if necessary, and click **PowerPoint 2013**. Click **Blank Presentation**.

   You have opened PowerPoint. A blank presentation displays.

b. Click **Click to add title** and type **Spotted Begonia Art Gallery**. Click in the bottom, subtitle box and type **Add Some Color to Your World!** Click the bottom-right corner of the slide to deselect the subtitle. Your PowerPoint presentation should look like that shown in Figure 1.28.

c. Click **Undo** two times on the Quick Access Toolbar.

   The subtitle on the current slide is selected and removed because those are the most recent actions.

TROUBLESHOOTING: If all of the subtitle text is not removed after two clicks, you should continue clicking until it is removed.

d. Click **Slide Sorter** in the *View shortcuts* group on the status bar.

The Slide Sorter view shows thumbnails of all slides in a presentation. Because this presentation has only one slide, you see a small version of one slide.

e. Move the mouse pointer to any button on the Quick Access Toolbar and hold it steady. See the tip giving the button name and the shortcut key combination, if any. Move to another button and see the description.

The Quick Access Toolbar has at least three buttons: Save, Undo, and Redo. In addition, a small arrow is included at the far-right side. If you hold the mouse pointer steady on the arrow, you will see the ScreenTip Customize Quick Access Toolbar.

f. Click **Customize Quick Access Toolbar** and select **New**. The New button is added to the toolbar. The New button enables you to quickly create a new presentation (also called a document).

g. Right-click **New** and click **Remove from Quick Access Toolbar**. The button is removed from the Quick Access Toolbar.

You can customize the Quick Access Toolbar by adding and removing items.

h. Click **Normal** in the *View shortcuts* group on the status bar.

The presentation returns to the original view in which the slide displays full size.

i. Click **Slide Show** in the *View shortcuts* group on the status bar.

The presentation is shown in Slide Show view, which is the way it will be presented to audiences.

j. Press **Esc** to end the presentation.

k. Save the presentation as **f01h3Views_LastFirst** and click the **Close (X) button** to close the PowerPoint program. Submit the presentation based on your instructor's directions.

The Backstage View Tasks

When you work with Microsoft Office files, you will often want to open previously saved files, create new ones, print items, and save and close files. You will also find it necessary to indicate options, or preferences, for settings. For example, you might want a spelling check to occur automatically, or you might prefer to initiate a spelling check only occasionally. Because those tasks are applicable to each software application within the Office 2013 suite, they are accomplished through a common area in the Office interface—the Backstage view. Open the Backstage view by clicking the File tab. Figure 1.29 shows the area that displays when you click the File tab in PowerPoint. The Backstage view also enables you to exit the application and to identify file information, such as the author or date created.

In this section, you will explore the Backstage view, learning to create, open, close, and print files.

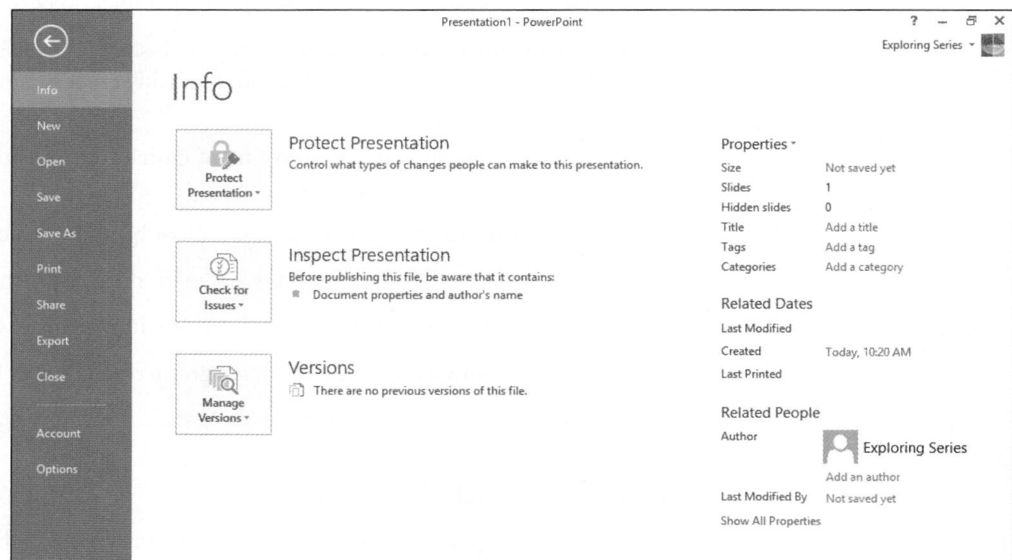

FIGURE 1.29 The Backstage View

Opening a File

When working with an Office application, you can begin by opening an existing file that has already been saved to a storage medium, or you can begin work on a new file. Both actions are available when you click the File tab. When you first open an application within the Office 2013 suite, you will need to decide which template you want to work with before you can begin working on a new file. You can also open a project that you previously saved to a disk.

Create a New File

After opening an Office application, such as Word, Excel, or PowerPoint, you will be presented with template choices. Click *Blank document* to start a new blank document. The word *document* is sometimes used generically to refer to any Office file, including a Word document, an Excel worksheet, or a PowerPoint presentation. Perhaps you are already working with a document in an Office application but want to create a new file. Simply click the File tab and click New. Click *Blank document* (or *Blank presentation* or *Blank workbook*, depending on the specific application).

Open a File Using the Open Dialog Box

STEP 1

You may choose to open a previously saved file, such as when you work with the data files for this book or when you want to access any previously created file. You will work with the Open dialog box, as shown in Figure 1.30. The Open dialog box displays after you click Open from the File tab. You will click Computer and the folder or drive where your document is stored.

If it is not listed under Recent Folders, you can browse for it. Using the Navigation Pane, you will make your way to the file to be opened. Double-click the file or click the file name once and click Open. Most likely, the file will be located within a folder that is appropriately named to make it easy to find related files. Obviously, if you are not well acquainted with the file's location and file name, the process of opening a file could become quite cumbersome. However, if you have created a well-designed system of folders, as you learned to do in the "Files and Folders" section of this chapter, you will know exactly where to find the file.

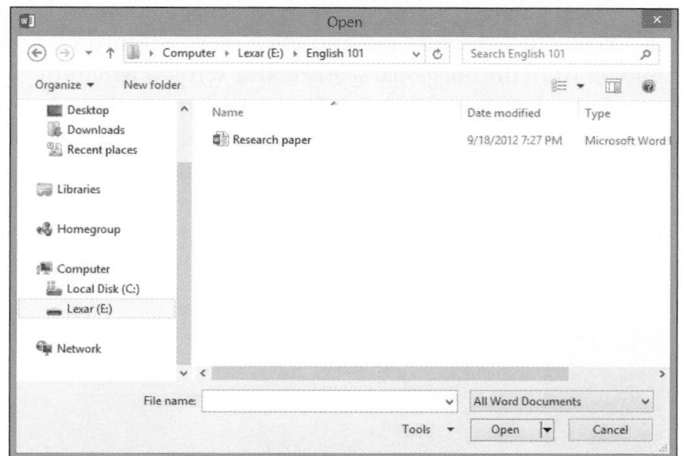

FIGURE 1.30 Open Dialog Box

Open a File Using the Recent Documents List

STEP 3

You will often work with a file, save it, and then continue the project at a later time. Office simplifies the task of reopening the file by providing a Recent Documents list with links to your most recently opened files (see Figure 1.31). To access the list, click the File tab, click Open, and then select Recent Documents. Click any file listed in the Recent Documents list to open that document. The list constantly changes to reflect only the most recently opened files, so if it has been quite some time since you worked with a particular file, you might have to work with the Open dialog box instead of the Recent Documents list.

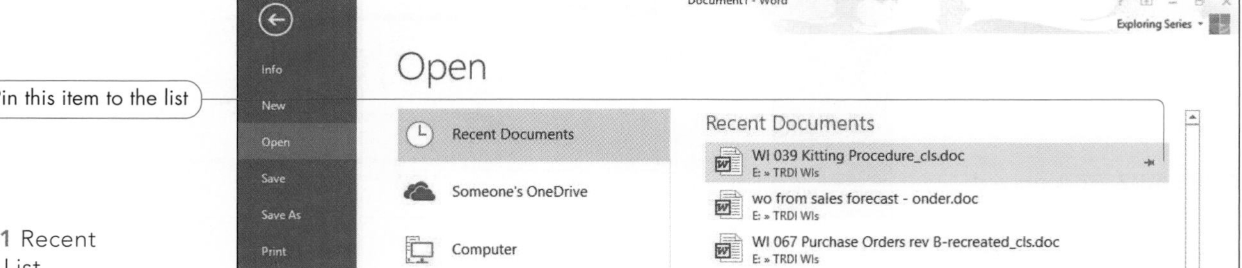

FIGURE 1.31 Recent Documents List

TIP Keeping Files on the Recent Documents List

The Recent Documents list displays a limited list of only the most recently opened files. You might, however, want to keep a particular file in the list regardless of how recently it was opened. In Figure 1.31, note the *Pin this item to the list* icon displays to the right of each file. Click the icon to pin the file to the list. At that point, you will always have access to the file by clicking the File tab and selecting the file from the Recent Documents list. The pushpin of the "permanent" file will change direction so that it appears to be inserted, indicating that it is a pinned item. If later you want to remove the file from the list, click the inserted pushpin, changing its direction and allowing the file to be bumped off the list when other, more recently opened, files take its place.

Open a File from the Templates List

You do not need to create a new file if you can access a predesigned file that meets your needs or one that you can modify fairly quickly to complete your project. Office provides templates, making them available when you click the File tab and New (see Figure 1.32). The Templates list is comprised of template groups available within the current Office installation on your computer. The Search box can be used to locate other templates that are available from Office.com. When you click one of the Suggested searches, you are presented with additional choices.

For example, you might want to prepare a home budget. After opening a blank worksheet in Excel, click the File tab and click New. From the template categories, you could click Budget from the *Suggested searches* list, scroll down until you find the right template, such as Family Budget, and then click Create to display the associated worksheet (or simply double-click Family Budget). If a Help window displays along with the worksheet template, click to close it or explore Help to learn more about the template. If you know only a little bit about Excel, you could then make a few changes so that the worksheet would accurately represent your family's financial situation. The budget would be prepared much more quickly than if you began the project with a blank workbook, designing it yourself.

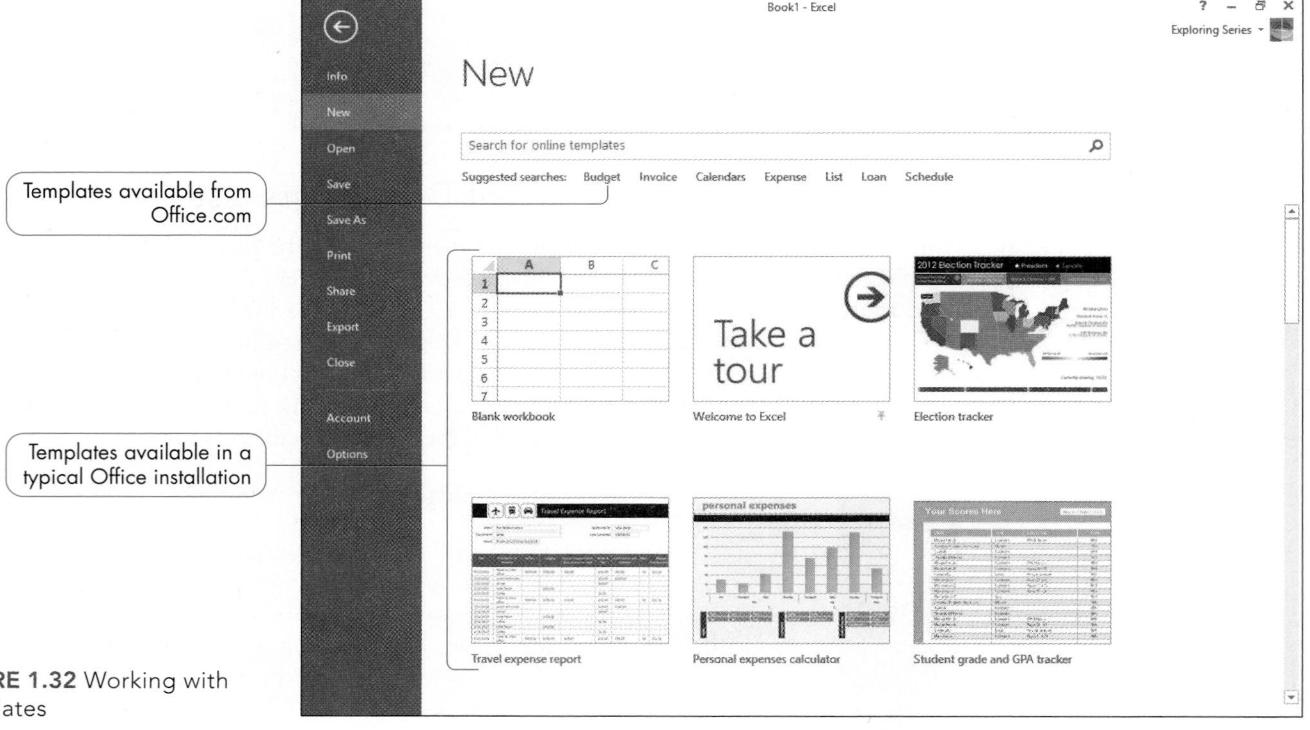

FIGURE 1.32 Working with Templates

Printing a File

There will be occasions when you will want to print an Office project. Before printing, you should preview the file to get an idea of how it will look when printed. That way, if there are obvious problems with the page setup, you can correct them before wasting paper on something that is not correct. When you are ready to print, you can select from various print options, including the number of copies and the specific pages to print. If you know that the page setup is correct and that there are no unique print settings to select, you can simply print the project without adjusting any print settings.

STEP 2»

It is a good idea to take a look at how your document will appear before you print it. The Print Preview feature of Office enables you to do just that. In the Print pane, you will see all items, including any headers, footers, graphics, and special formatting. To view a project before printing, click the File tab and click Print. The subsequent Backstage view shows the file preview on the right, with print settings located in the center of the Backstage screen. Figure 1.33 shows a typical Backstage Print view.

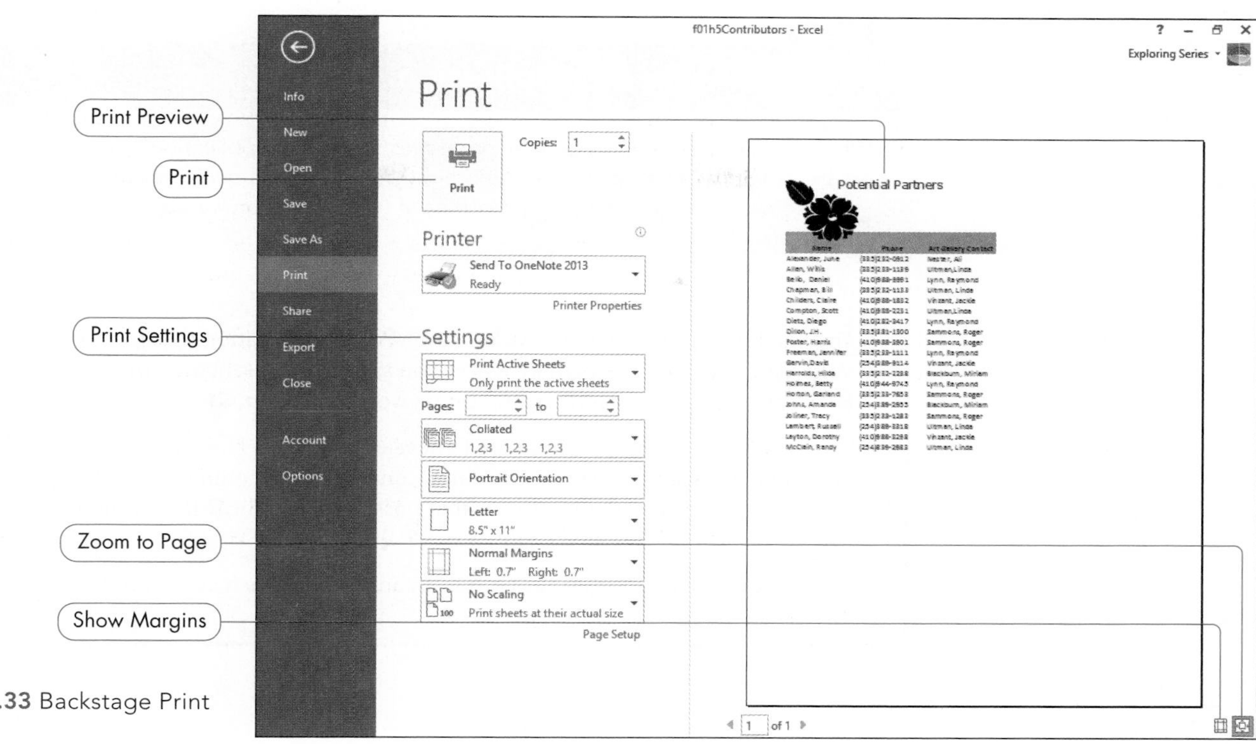

FIGURE 1.33 Backstage Print View

To show the margins of the document, click Show Margins (see Figure 1.33). To increase the size of the file preview, click *Zoom to Page* (see Figure 1.33). Both are found on the bottom-right corner of the preview. Remember that increasing the font size by adjusting the zoom applies to the current display only; it does not actually increase the font size when the document is printed or saved. To return the preview to its original view, click *Zoom to Page* once more.

Other options in the Backstage Print view vary depending on the application in which you are working. Regardless of the Office application, you will be able to access Settings options from the Backstage view, including page orientation (landscape or portrait), margins, and paper size. You will find a more detailed explanation of those settings in the "Page Layout Tab Tasks" section later in this chapter. To print a file, click Print (see Figure 1.33).

The Backstage Print view shown in Figure 1.33 is very similar across all Office applications. However, you will find slight variations specific to each application. For example, PowerPoint's Backstage Print view includes options for printing slides and handouts in various configurations and colors, whereas Excel's focuses on worksheet selections and Word's includes document options. Regardless of software, the manner of working with the Backstage view print options remains consistent.

Closing a File and Application

Although you can have several documents open at one time, limiting the number of open files is a good idea. Office applications have no problem keeping up with multiple open files, but you can easily become overwhelmed with them. When you are done with an open project, you will need to close it.

You can easily close any files that you no longer need. With the desired file on the screen, click the FILE tab and click the Close (X) button. Respond to any prompt that might display suggesting that you save the file. The application remains open, but the selected file is closed. To close the application, click the Close (X) button in the top-right corner.

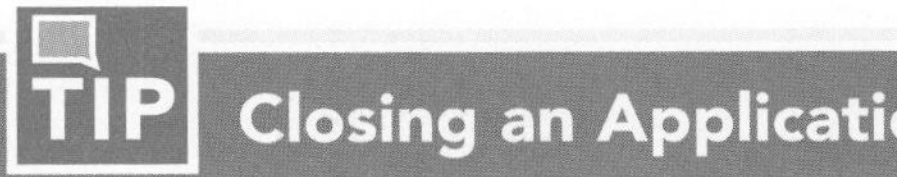

Closing an Application

When you close an application, all open files within the application are also closed. You will be prompted to save any files before they are closed. A quick way to close an application is to click the X in the top-right corner of the application window.

1. You want to continue to work with a PowerPoint presentation that you worked with yesterday, but cannot remember where you saved the presentation on your hard drive. How can you open a file that you recently worked with? ***p. 91***
2. As part of your job search, you plan to develop a resume. However, you find it difficult to determine the right style for your resume, and wish you could begin with a predesigned document that you could modify. Is that possible with Word? If so, what steps would you take to locate a predesigned resume? ***p. 92***
3. Closing a file is not the same as closing an application, such as closing Excel. What is the difference? ***p. 93***

Hands-On Exercises

4 The Backstage View Tasks

Projects related to the Spotted Begonia Art Gallery's functions have begun to come in for your review and approval. You have received an informational flyer to be distributed to schools and supporting organizations around the city. It contains a new logo along with descriptive text. Another task on your agenda is to keep the project moving according to schedule. You will identify a calendar template to print and distribute. You will explore printing options, and you will save the flyer and the calendar as directed by your instructor.

Skills covered: Open and Save a File • Preview and Print a File • Open a File from the Recent Documents List and Open a Template

STEP 1 » OPEN AND SAVE A FILE

You have asked your staff to develop a flyer that can be used to promote the Spotted Begonia Art Gallery. You will open a Word document that may be used for the flyer, and you will save the document to a disk drive. Refer to Figure 1.34 as you complete Step 1.

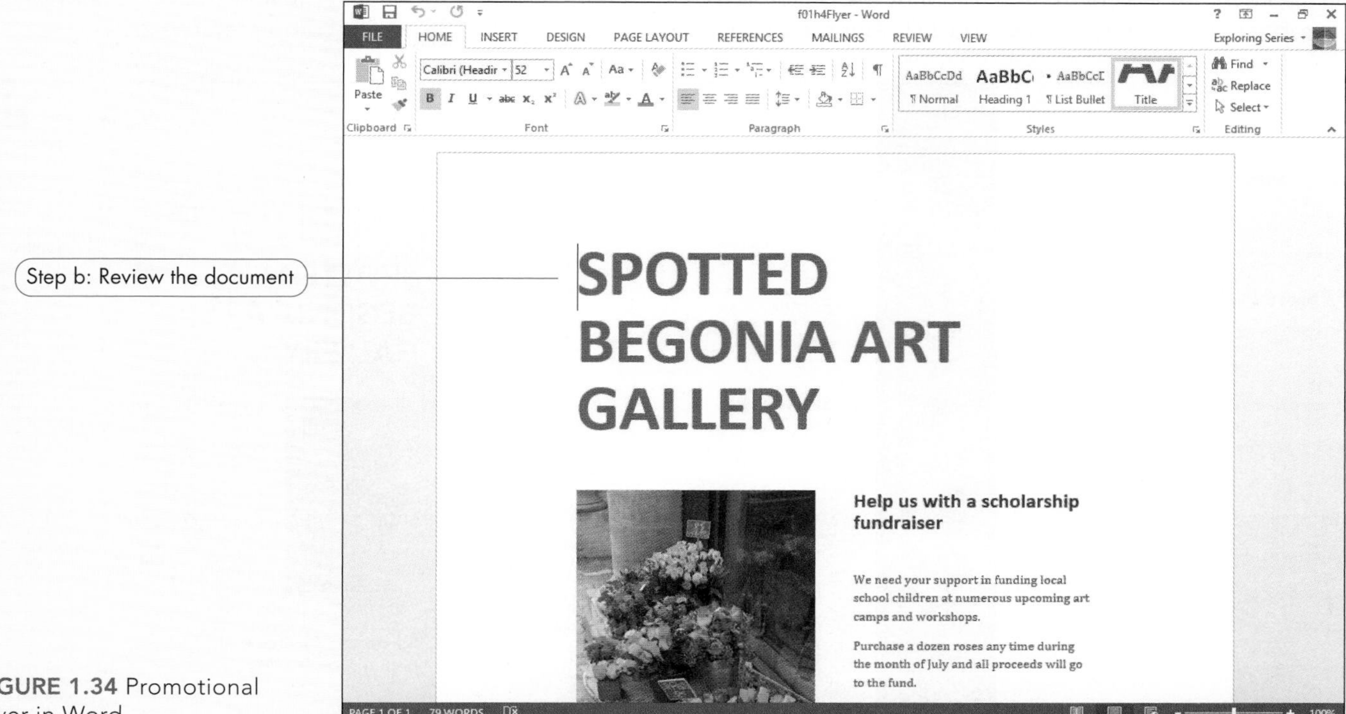

FIGURE 1.34 Promotional Flyer in Word

a. Navigate to the Start screen. Scroll across the tiles, if necessary, and click **Word 2013**. Click **Open Other Documents** at the bottom-left corner of the Word 2013 window.

You have opened Microsoft Word because it is the program in which the promotional flyer is saved.

b. Click **Computer** and click **Browse**. Navigate to the location of your student files. Double-click *f01h4Flyer* to open the file shown in Figure 1.34. Familiarize yourself with the document. Then, if necessary, click **Read Mode** in the *View shortcuts* group on the Status bar to change to that view. Read through the document.

The graphic and the flyer are submitted for your approval. A paragraph next to the graphic will serve as the launching point for an information blitz and the beginning of the fundraising drive.

TIP Using Read Mode

Read Mode displays the document. If the document is large enough, multiple screens may display. You can use the arrows found on the middle edges of the document to navigate and view the entire document.

c. Click **Print Layout** on the Status bar to change to that view. Click the **FILE tab** and click **Save As**.

   You choose the Save As command because you know that it enables you to indicate the location to which the file should be saved, as well as the file name.

d. Click **Browse**, navigate to the drive where you save your files, and then double-click the **Artists folder** you created earlier. Double-click **Office Records**, click in the **File name box**, type **f01h4Flyer_LastFirst**, and then click **Save**.

STEP 2 » PREVIEW AND PRINT A FILE

You approve of the flyer, so you will print the document for future reference. You will first preview the document as it will appear when printed. Then you will print the document. Refer to Figure 1.35 as you complete Step 2.

FIGURE 1.35 Backstage Print

a. Click the **FILE tab** and click **Print**.

   Figure 1.35 shows the flyer preview. It is always a good idea to check the way a file will look when printed before actually printing it.

b. Drag the **Zoom slider** to increase the document view. Click **Zoom to Page** to return to the original size.

c. Click **Portrait Orientation** in the Print settings area in the center of the screen. Click **Landscape Orientation** to show the flyer in a wider and shorter view.

d. Click **Landscape Orientation** and click **Portrait Orientation** to return to the original view.

You decide that the flyer is more attractive in portrait orientation, so you return to that setting.

e. Click the **Copies spin arrow** repeatedly to increase the copies to **5**.

You will need to print five copies of the flyer to distribute to the office assistants for their review.

f. Click **Close** on the left side of the screen. When asked, click **Don't Save** so that changes to the file are not saved. Keep Word open for the next step.

STEP 3 » OPEN A FILE FROM THE RECENT DOCUMENTS LIST AND OPEN A TEMPLATE

A large part of your responsibility is proofreading Spotted Begonia Art Gallery material. You will correct an error by adding a phone number in the promotional flyer. You must also keep the staff on task, so you will identify a calendar template on which to list tasks and deadlines. Refer to Figure 1.36 as you complete Step 3.

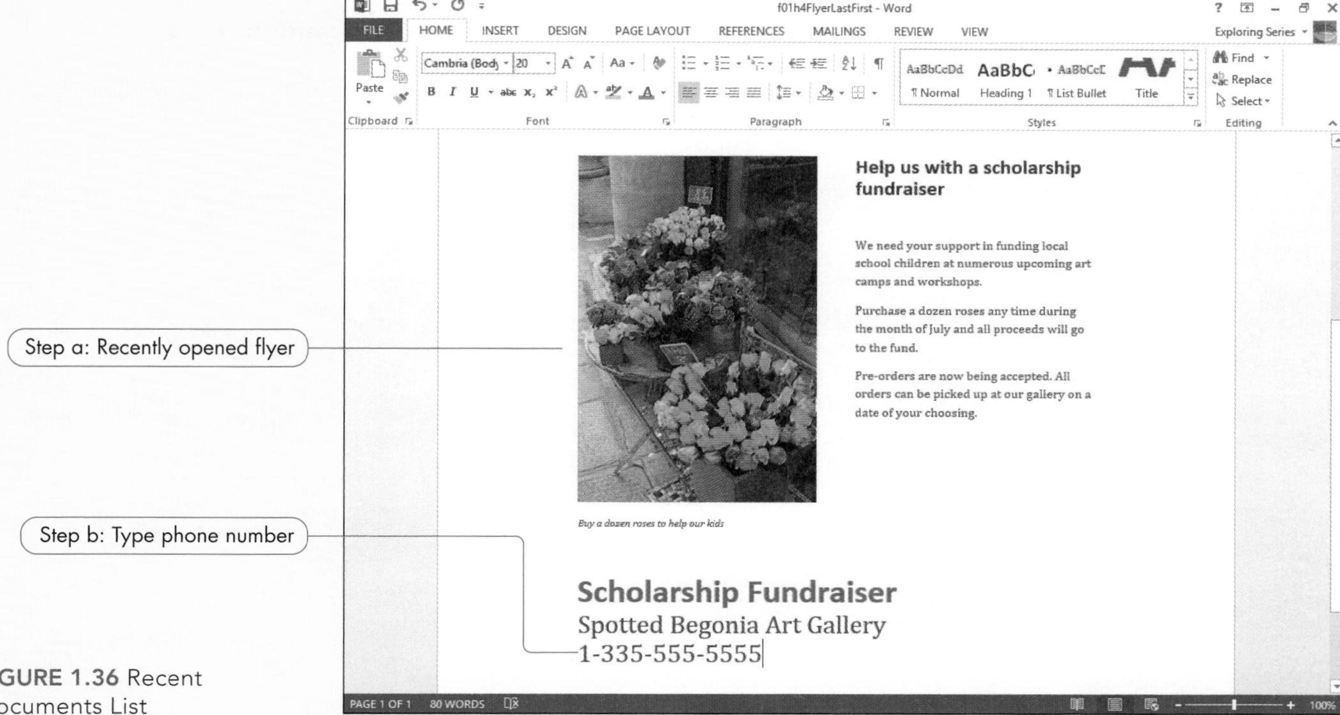

FIGURE 1.36 Recent Documents List

a. Click the **FILE tab**, click **Recent Documents** if necessary, and then click **f01h4Flyer_LastFirst** in the **Recent Documents list**.

> **TROUBLESHOOTING:** If the file opens in Read Mode, use the status bar to change to the Print Layout view.

b. Press **Ctrl+End** to move the insertion point to the end of the document and press **Enter**. Type **1-335-555-5555**.

Figure 1.36 shows the phone number correction.

c. Click **Save** on the Quick Access Toolbar, click the **FILE tab**, and then click **Close**.

When you click Save on the Quick Access Toolbar, the document is saved in the same location with the same file name as was indicated in the previous save.

d. Click the **FILE tab** and click **New**. Click **Calendar** from the list of the *Suggested searches* category just beneath the *Search online templates* box.

Office.com provides a wide range of calendar choices. You will select one that is appealing and that will help you keep projects on track.

e. Click a calendar of your choice from the gallery and click **Create**. Respond to and close any windows that may open.

The calendar that you selected opens in Word.

TROUBLESHOOTING: It is possible to select a template that is not certified by Microsoft. In that case, you might have to confirm your acceptance of settings before you click Download.

f. Click **Save** on the Quick Access Toolbar. If necessary, navigate to your Office Records subfolder (a subfolder of Artists) on the drive where you are saving your student files. Save the document as **f01h4Calendar_LastFirst**. Because this is the first time to save the calendar file, the Save button on the Quick Access Toolbar opens a dialog box in which you must indicate the location of the file and the file name.

g. Click **Save** and exit Word. Submit your files based on your instructor's directions.

Home Tab Tasks

You will find that you will repeat some tasks often, whether in Word, Excel, or PowerPoint. You will frequently want to change the format of numbers or words, selecting a different ***font*** or changing font size or color. A font is a complete set of characters, both upper- and lowercase letters, numbers, punctuation marks, and special symbols, with the same design including size, spacing, and shape. You might also need to change the alignment of text or worksheet cells. Undoubtedly, you will find a reason to copy or cut items and paste them elsewhere in the document, presentation, or worksheet. And you might want to modify file contents by finding and replacing text. All of those tasks, and more, are found on the Home tab of the Ribbon in Word, Excel, and PowerPoint. The Access interface is unique, sharing little with other Office applications, so this section will not address Access.

In this section, you will explore the Home tab, learning to format text, copy and paste items, and find and replace words or phrases. Figure 1.37 shows Home tab groups and tasks in the various applications. Note the differences and similarities between the groups.

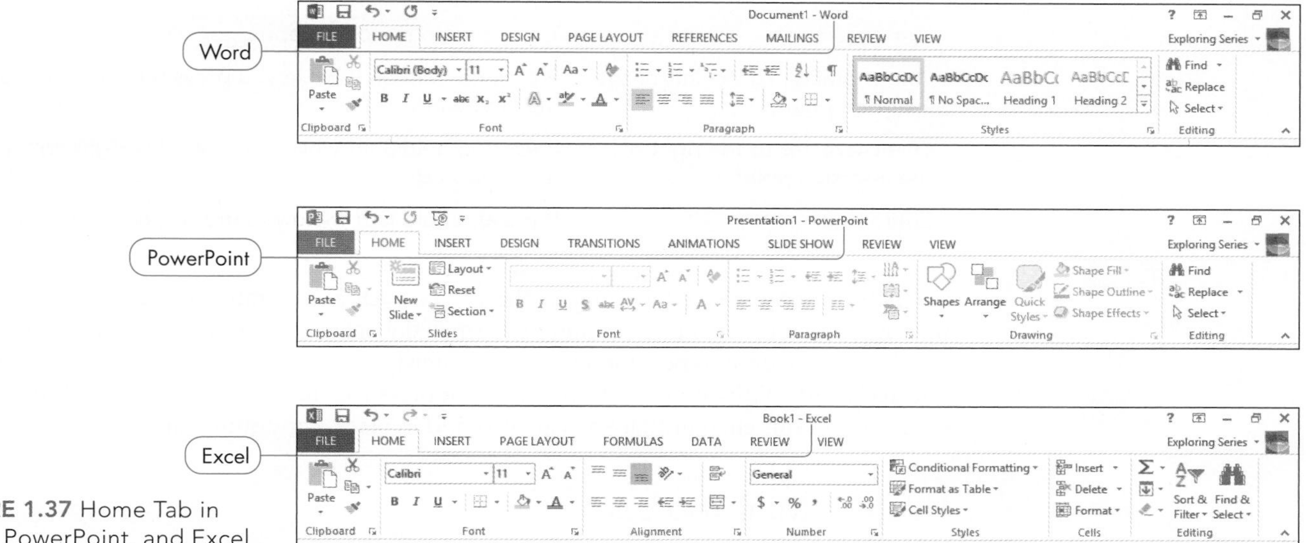

FIGURE 1.37 Home Tab in Word, PowerPoint, and Excel

Selecting and Editing Text

After creating a document, worksheet, or presentation, you will probably want to make some changes. You might prefer to center a title, or maybe you think that certain budget worksheet totals should be formatted as currency. You can change the font so that typed characters are larger or in a different style. You might even want to underline text to add emphasis. In all Office applications, the Home tab provides tools for selecting and editing text. You can also use the Mini toolbar for making quick changes to selected text.

Select Text to Edit

Before making any changes to existing text or numbers, you must first select the characters. A general rule that you should commit to memory is "Select, then do." A foolproof way to select text or numbers is to place the mouse pointer before the first character of the text you want to select, and then drag to highlight the intended selection. Before you drag, be sure that the mouse pointer takes on the shape of the letter *I*, called the *I-bar*. Although other methods for selecting exist, if you remember only one way, it should be the click-and-drag method. If your attempted selection falls short of highlighting the intended area, or perhaps highlights too much, simply click outside the selection and try again.

Sometimes it can be difficult to precisely select a small amount of text, such as a single character or a single word. Other times, the task can be overwhelming, such as when selecting an entire 550-page document. Shortcut methods for making selections in Word and PowerPoint are shown in Table 1.3. When working with Excel, you will more often need to select multiple cells. Simply drag the intended selection, usually when the mouse pointer displays as a large white plus sign. The shortcuts shown in Table 1.3 are primarily applicable to Word and PowerPoint.

TABLE 1.3 Shortcut Selection in Word and PowerPoint

Item Selected	Action
One word	Double-click the word.
One line of text	Place the mouse pointer at the left of the line, in the margin area. When the mouse changes to a right-pointing arrow, click to select the line.
One sentence	Press and hold Ctrl while you click in the sentence to select.
One paragraph	Triple-click in the paragraph.
One character to the left of the insertion point	Press and hold Shift while you press the left arrow on the keyboard.
One character to the right of the insertion point	Press and hold Shift while you press the right arrow on the keyboard.
Entire document	Press and hold Ctrl while you press A on the keyboard.

After having selected a string of characters, such as a number, word, sentence, or document, you can do more than simply format the selection. Suppose you have selected a word. If you begin to type another word, the newly typed word will immediately replace the selected word. With an item selected, you can press Delete to remove the selection. You will learn later in this chapter that you can also find, replace, copy, move, and paste selected text.

Use the Mini Toolbar

STEP 3»

You have learned that you can always use commands on the Ribbon to change selected text within a document, worksheet, or presentation. All it takes is locating the desired command on the Home tab and clicking to select it. Although using the Home tab to perform commands is simple enough, an item called the ***Mini toolbar*** provides an even faster way to accomplish some of the same formatting changes. When you select any amount of text within a worksheet, document, or presentation, you can move the mouse pointer only slightly within the selection to display the Mini toolbar (see Figure 1.38). The Mini toolbar provides access to the most common formatting selections, such as adding bold or italic, or changing font type or color. Unlike the Quick Access Toolbar, the Mini toolbar is not customizable, which means that you cannot add or remove options from the toolbar.

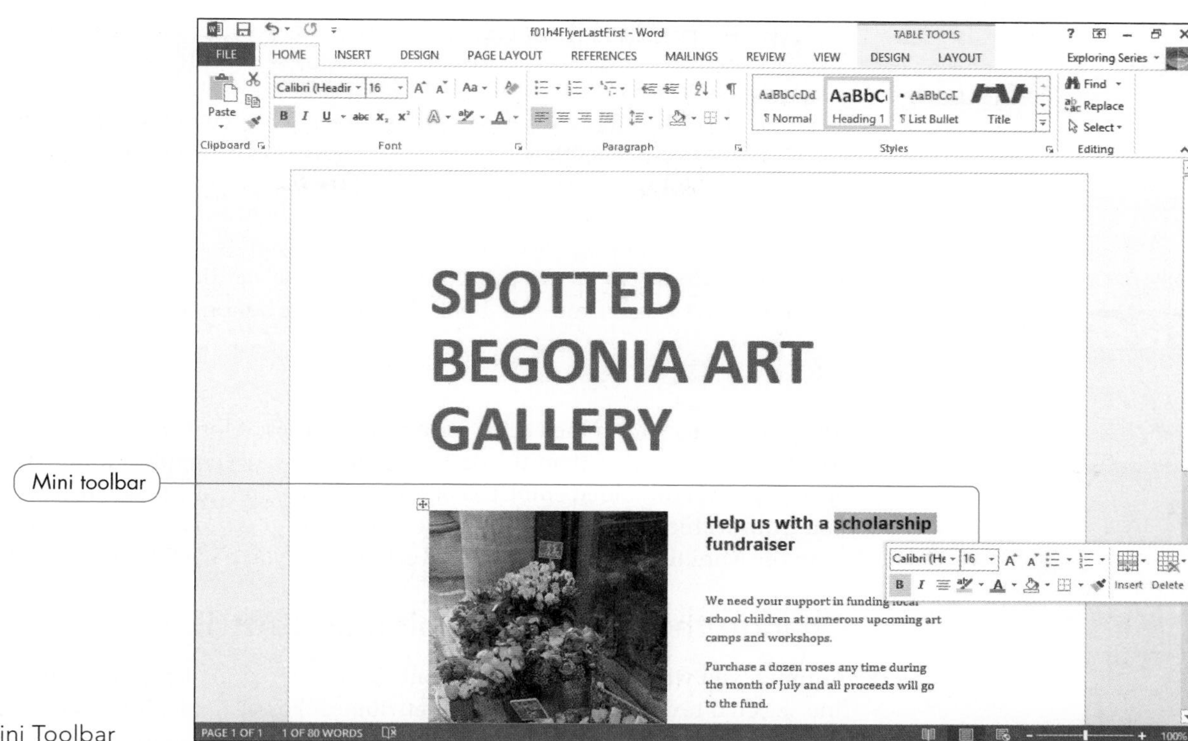

FIGURE 1.38 Mini Toolbar

The Mini toolbar will display only when text is selected. The closer the mouse pointer is to the Mini toolbar, the darker the toolbar becomes. As you move the mouse pointer away from the Mini toolbar, it becomes almost transparent. Make any selections from the Mini toolbar by clicking the corresponding button. To temporarily remove the Mini toolbar from view, press Esc.

If you want to permanently disable the Mini toolbar so that it does not display in any open file when text is selected, click the FILE tab and click Options. As shown in Figure 1.39, click General, if necessary. Deselect the *Show Mini Toolbar on selection* setting by clicking the check box to the left of the setting and clicking OK.

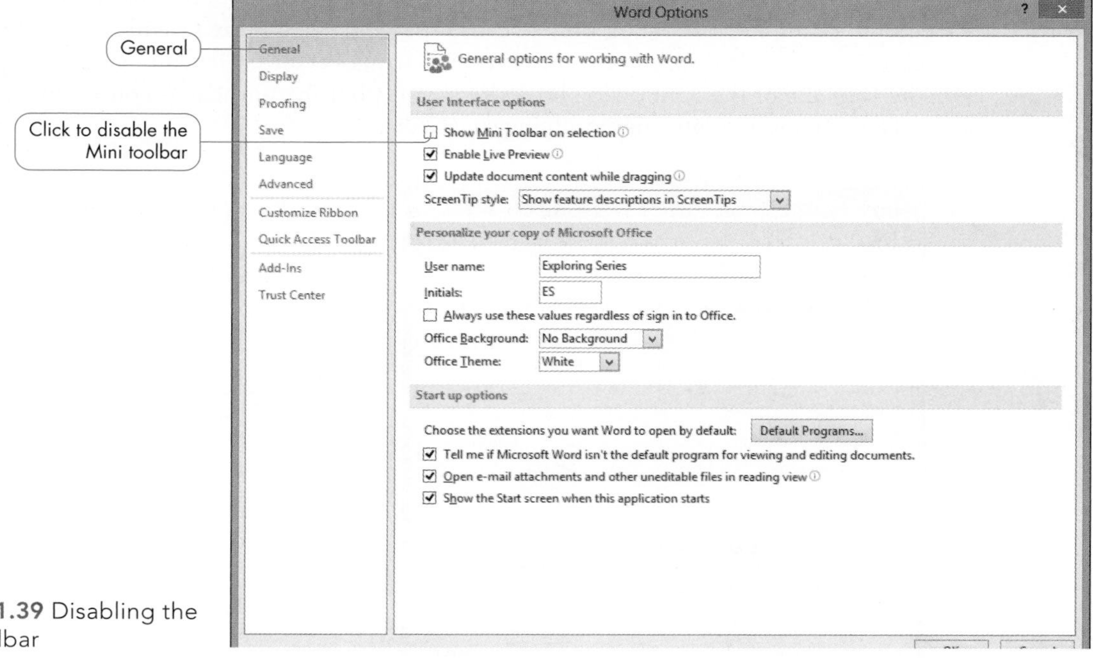

FIGURE 1.39 Disabling the Mini Toolbar

Apply Font Attributes

The way characters appear onscreen, including qualities such as size, spacing, and shape, is determined by the font. Each Office application has a default font, which is the font that will be in effect unless you change it. Other font attributes include boldfacing, italicizing, and font color, all of which can be applied to selected text. Some formatting changes, such as Bold and Italic, are called ***toggle*** commands. They act somewhat like light switches that you can turn on and off. For example, after having selected a word that you want to add bold to, click Bold in the Font group of the Home tab to turn the setting "on." If, at a later time, you want to remove bold from the word, select it again and click Bold. This time, the button turns "off" the bold formatting.

Change the Font

All applications within the Office suite provide a set of fonts from which you can choose. If you prefer a font other than the default, or if you want to apply a different font to a section of your project for added emphasis or interest, you can easily make the change by selecting a font from within the Font group on the Home tab. You can also change the font by selecting from the Mini toolbar, although that works only if you have first selected text.

Change the Font Size, Color, and Attributes

STEP 2»

At times, you will want to make the font size larger or smaller, change the font color, underline selected text, or apply other font attributes. For example, if you are creating a handout for a special event, you may want to apply a different font to emphasize key information such as dates and times. Because such changes are commonplace, Office places those formatting commands in many convenient places within each Office application.

You can find the most common formatting commands in the Font group on the Home tab. As noted earlier, Word, Excel, and PowerPoint all share very similar Font groups that provide access to tasks related to changing the character font (refer to Figure 1.37). Remember that you can place the mouse pointer over any command icon to view a summary of the icon's purpose, so although the icons might at first appear cryptic, you can use the mouse pointer to quickly determine the purpose and applicability to your desired text change. You can also find a subset of those commands plus a few additional choices on the Mini toolbar.

If the font change that you plan to make is not included as a choice on either the Home tab or the Mini toolbar, you can probably find what you are looking for in the Font dialog box. Click the Dialog Box Launcher in the bottom-right corner of the Font group. Figure 1.40 shows a sample Font dialog box. Because the Font dialog box provides many formatting choices in one window, you can make several changes at once. Depending on the application, the contents of the Font dialog box vary slightly, but the purpose is consistent—providing access to choices related to modifying characters.

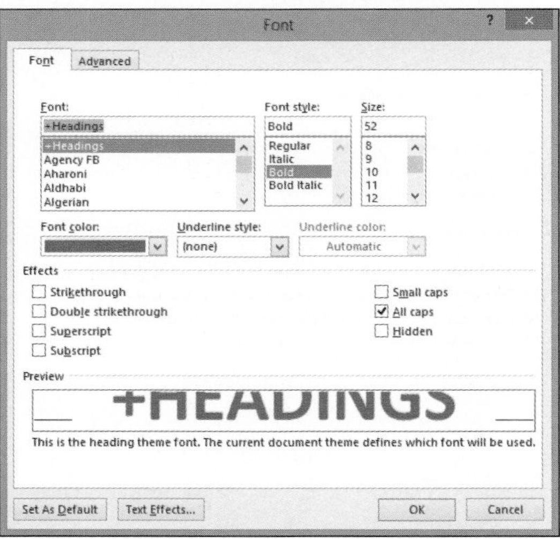

FIGURE 1.40 Font Dialog Box

Using the Clipboard Group Commands

On occasion, you will want to move or copy a selection from one area to another. Suppose that you have included text on a PowerPoint slide that you believe would be more appropriate on a different slide. Or perhaps an Excel formula should be copied from one cell to another because both cells should be totaled in the same manner. You can easily move the slide text or copy the Excel formula by using options found in the Clipboard group on the Home tab. The Office ***Clipboard*** is an area of memory reserved to temporarily hold selections that have been ***cut*** or ***copied*** and allows you to paste the selections. To cut means to remove a selection from the original location and place it in the Office Clipboard. To copy means to duplicate a selection from the original location and place a copy in the Office Clipboard. Although the Clipboard can hold up to 24 items at one time, the usual procedure is to ***paste*** the cut or copied selection to its final destination fairly quickly. To paste means to place a cut or copied selection into another location. When the computer is shut down or loses power, the contents of the Clipboard are erased, so it is important to finalize the paste procedure during the current session.

The Clipboard group enables you not only to copy and cut text and objects but also to copy formatting. Perhaps you have applied a font style to a major heading of a report and you realize that the same formatting should be applied to other headings. Especially if the heading includes multiple formatting features, you will save a great deal of time by copying the entire set of formatting options to the other headings. In so doing, you will ensure the consistency of formatting for all headings because they will appear exactly alike. Using the Clipboard group's ***Format Painter***, you can quickly and easily copy all formatting from one area to another in Word, PowerPoint, and Excel.

In Office, you can usually accomplish the same task in several ways. Although the Ribbon provides ample access to formatting and Clipboard commands (such as Format Painter, Cut, Copy, and Paste), you might find it convenient to access the same commands on a ***shortcut menu***. Right-click a selected item or text to open a shortcut menu such as the one shown in Figure 1.41. A shortcut menu is also called a *context menu* because the contents of the menu vary depending on the location at which you right-clicked.

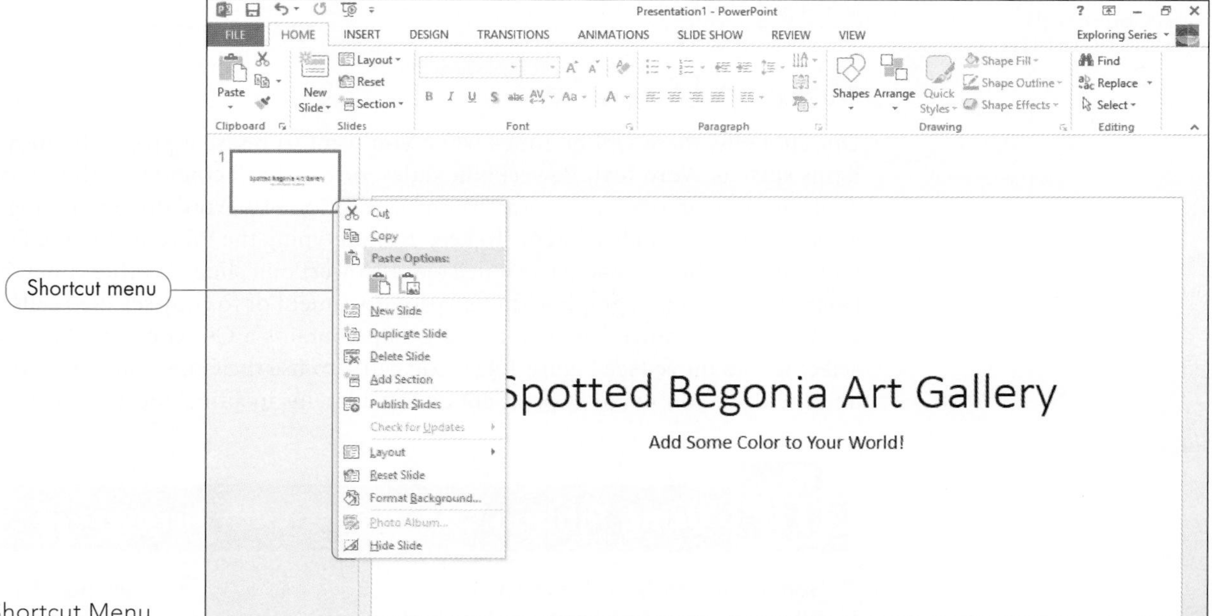

FIGURE 1.41 Shortcut Menu

Copy Formats with the Format Painter

STEP 3»

As described earlier, the Format Painter makes it easy to copy formatting features from one selection to another. You will find the Format Painter command conveniently located in the Clipboard group of the Home tab (see Figure 1.42). To copy a format, you must first select the text containing the desired format. If you want to copy the format to only one other selection, *single-click* Format Painter. If, however, you plan to copy the same format to multiple areas, *double-click* Format Painter. As you move the mouse pointer, you will find that it has the appearance of a paintbrush with an attached I-bar. Select the area to which the copied format should be applied. If you single-clicked Format Painter to copy the format to one other selection, Format Painter turns off once the formatting has been applied. If you double-clicked Format Painter to copy the format to multiple locations, continue selecting text in various locations to apply the format. Then, to turn off Format Painter, click Format Painter again or press Esc.

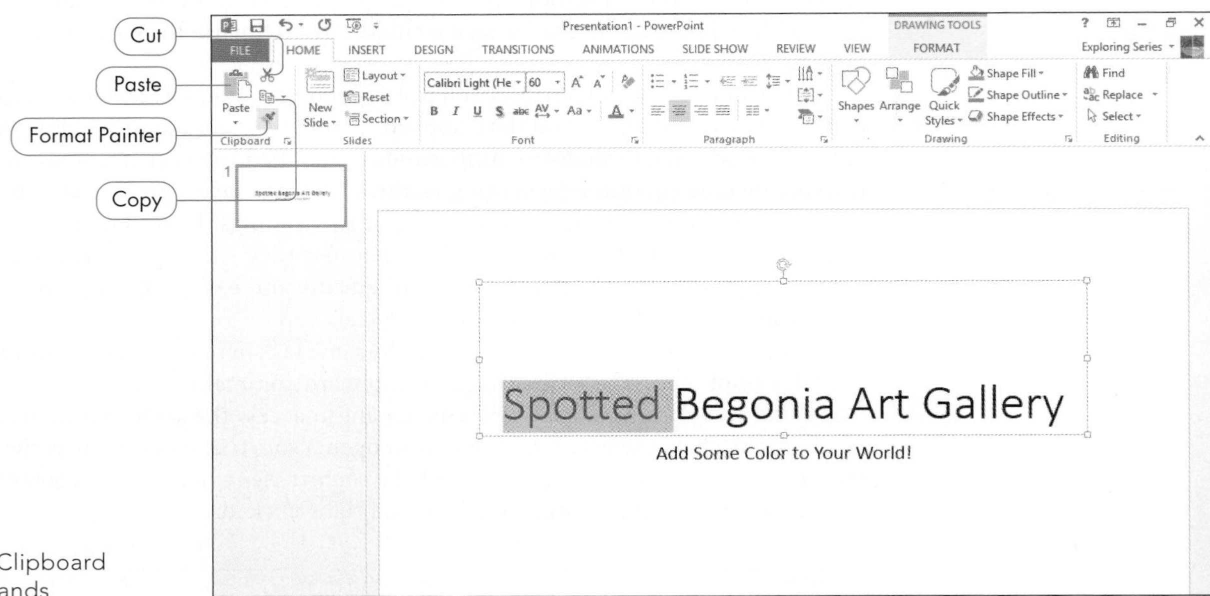

FIGURE 1.42 Clipboard Group Commands

Move and Copy Text

Undoubtedly, there will be times when you want to revise a project by moving or copying items such as Word text, PowerPoint slides, or Excel cell contents, either within the current application or among others. For example, a section of a Word document might be appropriate as PowerPoint slide content. To keep from retyping the Word text in the PowerPoint slide, you can copy the text and paste it in a blank PowerPoint slide. At other times, it might be necessary to move a paragraph within a Word document or to copy selected cells from one Excel worksheet to another. The Clipboard group contains a Cut command with which you can select text to move (see Figure 1.42). You can also use the Copy command to duplicate items and the Paste command to place cut or copied items in a final location (see Figure 1.42).

TIP Using Ribbon Commands with Arrows

Some commands, such as Paste in the Clipboard group, contain two parts: the main command and an arrow. The arrow may be below or to the right of the command, depending on the command, window size, or screen resolution. Instructions in the *Exploring* series use the command name to instruct you to click the main command to perform the default action (e.g., Click Paste). Instructions include the word *arrow* when you need to select the arrow to access an additional option (e.g., Click the Paste arrow).

STEP 1»

The first step in moving or copying text is to select the text. Then do the following:

1. Click the appropriate icon in the Clipboard group either to cut or copy the selection. Remember that cut or copied text is actually placed in the Clipboard, remaining there even after you paste it to another location. It is important to note that you can paste the same item multiple times, because it will remain in the Clipboard until you power down your computer or until the Clipboard exceeds 24 items.
2. Click the location where you want the cut or copied text to be placed. The location can be in the current file or in another open file within any Office application.
3. Click Paste in the Clipboard group on the HOME tab.

In addition to using the Clipboard group icons, you can also cut, copy, and paste in any of the ways listed in Table 1.4.

TABLE 1.4 Cut, Copy, and Paste Options

Command	Actions
Cut	• Click Cut in Clipboard group. • Right-click selection and select Cut. • Press Ctrl+X.
Copy	• Click Copy in Clipboard group. • Right-click selection and select Copy. • Press Ctrl+C.
Paste	• Click in destination location and select Paste in Clipboard group. • Right-click in destination location and select Paste. • Click in destination location and press Ctrl+V. • Click the Clipboard Dialog Box Launcher to open the Clipboard task pane. Click in destination location. With the Clipboard task pane open, click the arrow beside the intended selection and select Paste.

Use the Office Clipboard

When you cut or copy selections, they are placed in the Office Clipboard. Regardless of which Office application you are using, you can view the Clipboard by clicking the Clipboard Dialog Box Launcher, as shown in Figure 1.43.

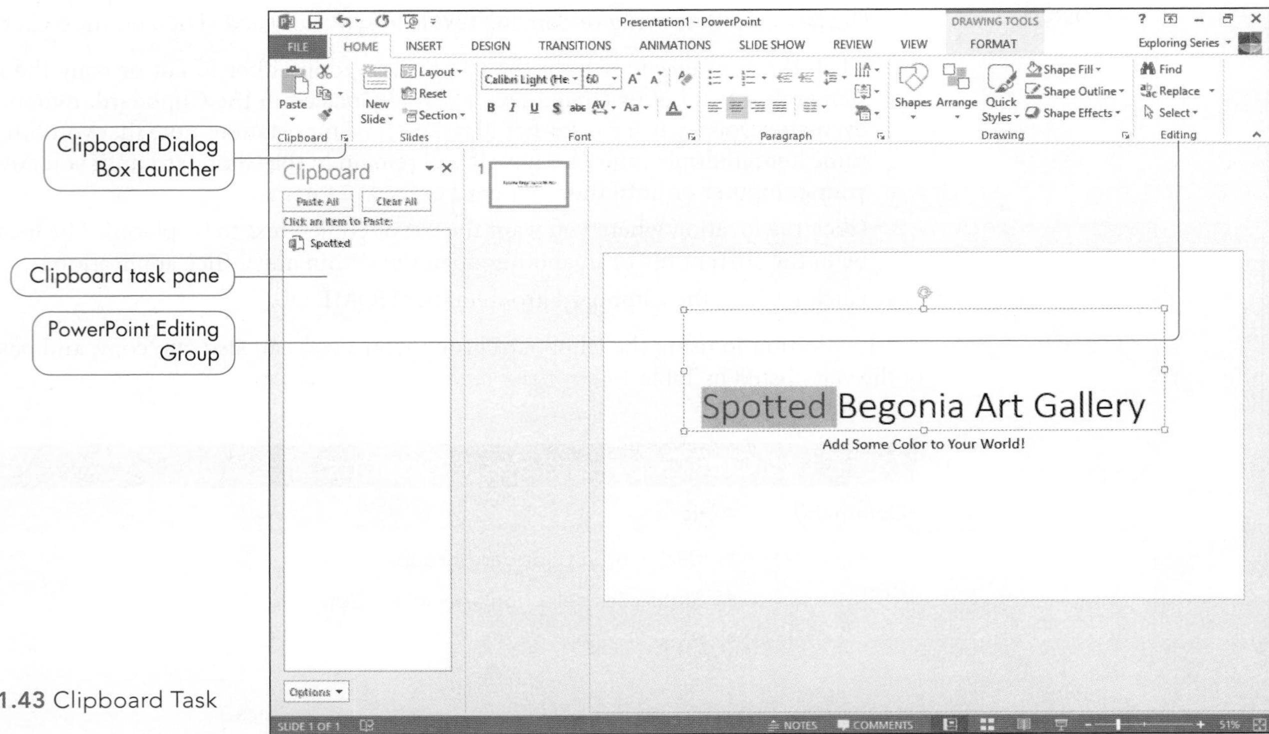

FIGURE 1.43 Clipboard Task Pane

Unless you specify otherwise when beginning a paste operation, the most recently added Clipboard item is pasted. You can, however, select an item from the Clipboard task pane to paste. Similarly, you can delete items from the Clipboard by making a selection in the Clipboard task pane. You can remove all items from the Clipboard by clicking Clear All. The Options button in the Clipboard task pane enables you to control when and where the Clipboard is displayed. Close the Clipboard task pane by clicking the Close (X) button in the top-right corner of the task pane or by clicking the arrow in the title bar of the Clipboard task pane and selecting Close.

Using the Editing Group Commands

The process of finding and replacing text is easily accomplished through options in the Editing group of the Home tab. The Editing group also enables you to select all contents of a project document, all text with similar formatting, or specific objects, such as pictures or charts. The Editing group is found at the far-right side of the Home tab in Excel, Word, and PowerPoint.

The Excel Editing group is unique in that it also includes options for sorting, filtering, and clearing cell contents; filling cells; and summarizing numeric data. Because those commands are relevant only to Excel, this chapter will not address them specifically.

Find and Replace Text

STEP 4

Especially if you are working with a lengthy project, manually seeking a specific word or phrase can be time-consuming. Office enables you not only to ***find*** each occurrence of a series of characters, but also to ***replace*** what it finds with another series. You will at times find it necessary to locate each occurrence of a text item so that you can replace it with another or so that you can delete, move, or copy it. If you have consistently misspelled a person's name throughout a document, you can find the misspelling and replace it with the correct spelling in a matter of a few seconds, no matter how many times the misspelling occurs in the document. To begin the process of finding and replacing a specific item:

1. Click Replace in the Editing group on the HOME tab of Word or PowerPoint.
2. Or click Find & Select in the Editing group on the HOME tab of Excel. Then click Replace. The dialog box that displays enables you to indicate the word or phrase to find and replace.

The Advanced Find feature is one that you will use often as you work with documents in Word. It is beneficial to find each occurrence of a word you are searching for. But it is also very helpful to see all the occurrences of the word at once. Click Reading Highlight in the *Find and Replace* dialog box and select Highlight All to display each word highlighted, as shown in Figure 1.44. Click Reading Highlight again and select Clear Highlighting to remove the illumination.

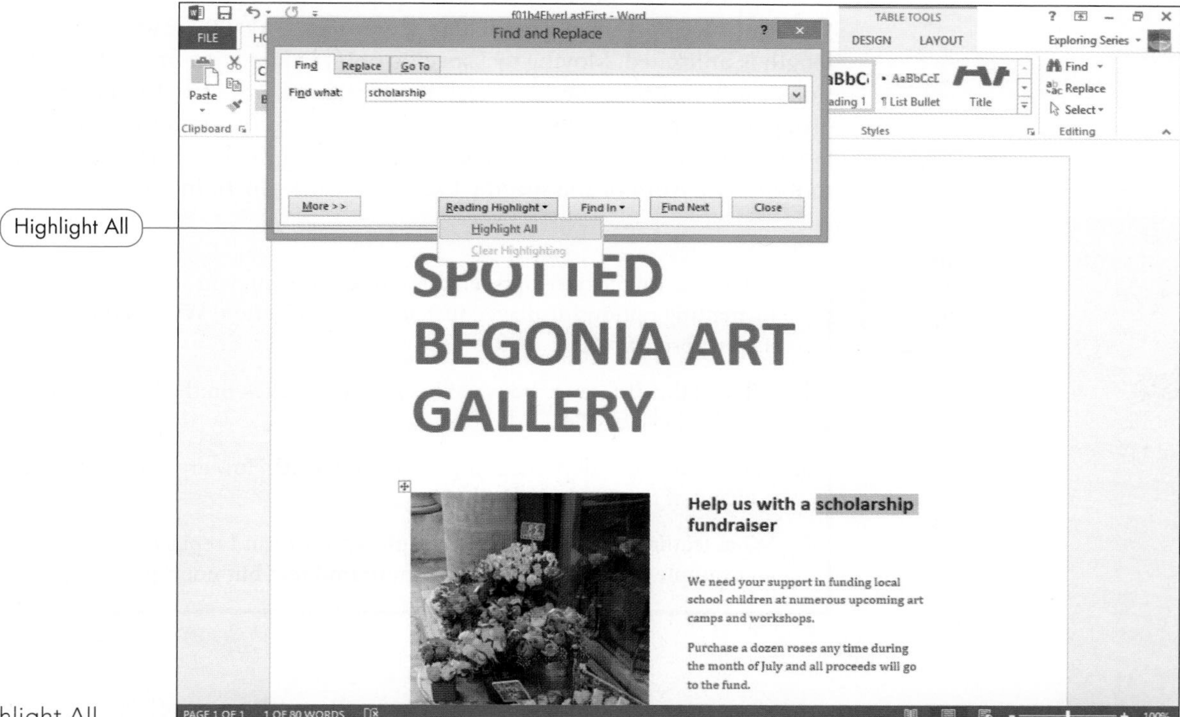

FIGURE 1.44 Highlight All

TIP Using a Shortcut to Find Items

Ctrl+F is a shortcut used to find items in a Word, Excel, or PowerPoint file. When you press Ctrl+F, the *Find and Replace* dialog box displays in Excel and PowerPoint. Pressing Ctrl+F in Word displays a feature—the Navigation Pane—at the left side of a Word document. When you type a search term in the Search Document area, Word finds and highlights all occurrences of the search term. The Navigation Pane also makes it easy to move to sections of a document based on levels of headings.

To find and replace selected text, type the text to locate in the *Find what* box and the replacement text in the *Replace with* box. You can narrow the search to require matching case or find whole words only. If you want to replace all occurrences of the text, click Replace All. If you want to replace only some occurrences, click Find Next repeatedly until you reach the occurrence that you want to replace. At that point, click Replace. When you are finished, click the Close button (or click Cancel).

Use Advanced Find and Replace Features

The *Find and Replace* feature enables you not only to find and replace text, but also to restrict and alter the format of the text at the same time. To establish the format criteria associated with either the *Find or Replace* portion of the operation:

1. Click the More button to expand the dialog box options. Click Format in the bottom-left corner of the dialog box.
2. Add formatting characteristics from the Font dialog box or Paragraph dialog box (as well as many other formatting features).

In addition to applying special formatting parameters on a *Find and Replace* operation, you can specify that you want to find or replace special characters. Click Special at the bottom of the *Find and Replace* dialog box to view the punctuation characters from which you can choose. For example, you might want to look for all instances in a document where an exclamation point is being used and replace it with a period.

An Excel worksheet can include more than 1,000,000 rows of data. A Word document's length is unlimited. Moving to a specific point in large files created in either of those applications can be a challenge. That task is simplified by the Go To option, found in the Editing group as an option of the Find command in Word (or under Find & Select in Excel). Click Go To and enter the page number (or other item, such as section, comment, bookmark, or footnote) in Word or the specific Excel cell. Click Go To in Word (or OK in Excel).

Quick Concepts

1. After selecting text in a presentation or document, you see a small transparent bar with formatting options displayed just above the selection. What is the bar called and what is its purpose? ***p. 100***
2. What is the difference between using a single-click on the Format Painter and using a double-click? ***p. 104***
3. What is the first step in cutting or copying text? How are cutting and copying related to the concept of the Clipboard? ***p. 105***
4. What feature can you use to very quickly locate and replace text in a document? Provide an example of when you might want to find text but not replace it. ***p. 106***

Hands-On Exercises

5 Home Tab Tasks

You have created a list of potential contributors to the Spotted Begonia Art Gallery. You have used Excel to record that list in worksheet format. Now you will review the worksheet and format its appearance to make it more attractive. You will also modify a promotional flyer. In working with those projects, you will put into practice the formatting, copying, moving, and editing information from the preceding section.

Skills covered: Move, Copy, and Paste Text • Select Text, Apply Font Attributes, and Use the Mini Toolbar • Use Format Painter and Work with the Mini Toolbar • Use the Font Dialog Box and Find and Replace Text

STEP 1 » MOVE, COPY, AND PASTE TEXT

Each contributor to the Spotted Begonia Art Gallery is assigned a contact person. You manage the worksheet that keeps track of those assignments, but the assignments sometimes change. You will copy and paste some worksheet selections to keep from having to retype data. You will also reposition a clip art image to improve the worksheet's appearance. Refer to Figure 1.45 as you complete Step 1.

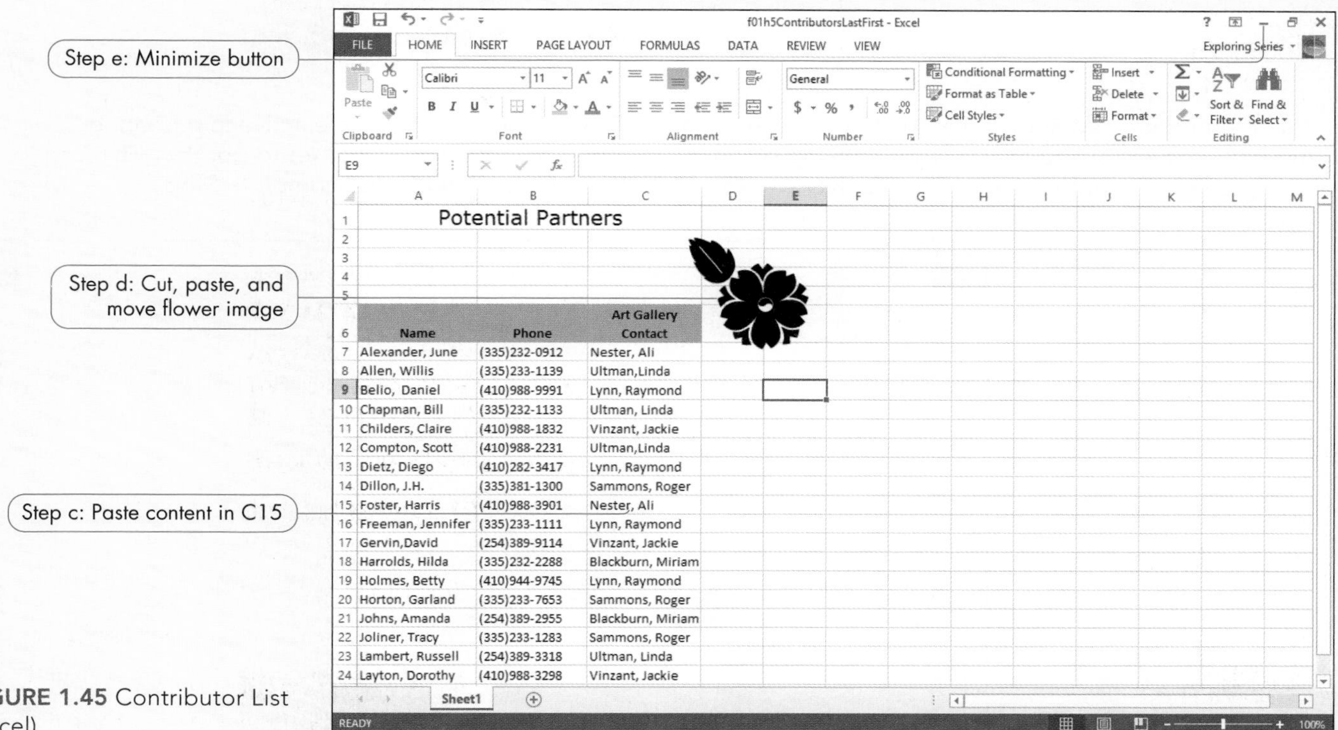

FIGURE 1.45 Contributor List (Excel)

a. Navigate to the Start screen. Scroll across the tiles, if necessary, and click **Excel 2013**. Click **Open Other Workbooks**.

   You have opened Microsoft Excel because it is the program in which the contributors list is saved.

b. Open the student data file *f01h5Contributors*. Save the file as **f01h5Contributors_LastFirst** in the Office Records folder (a subfolder of Artists) you created.

   The potential contributors list shown in Figure 1.45 is displayed.

c. Click **cell C7** to select the cell that contains *Nester, Ali*, and click **Copy** in the Clipboard group on the HOME tab. Click **cell C15** to select the cell that contains *Sammons, Roger*, click **Paste** in the Clipboard group, and then press **Esc** to remove the selection from *Nester, Ali*.

Ali Nester has been assigned as the Spotted Begonia Art Gallery contact for Harris Foster, replacing Roger Sammons. You make that replacement on the worksheet by copying and pasting Ali Nester's name in the appropriate worksheet cell.

d. Click the picture of the begonia. A box displays around the image, indicating that it is selected. Click **Cut** in the Clipboard group, click **cell D2**, and then click **Paste**. Drag the picture to resize and position it as needed (see Figure 1.45) so that it does not block any information in the list. Click anywhere outside the begonia picture to deselect it.

You decide that the picture of the begonia will look better if it is placed on the right side of the worksheet instead of the left. You move the picture by cutting and pasting the object.

> **TROUBLESHOOTING:** A Paste Options icon might display in the worksheet after you have moved the begonia picture. It offers additional options related to the paste procedure. You do not need to change any options, so ignore the button.

e. Click **Save** on the Quick Access Toolbar. Click **Minimize** to minimize the worksheet without closing it.

STEP 2 » SELECT TEXT, APPLY FONT ATTRIBUTES, AND USE THE MINI TOOLBAR

As the opening of a new showing at the Spotted Begonia Art Gallery draws near, you are active in preparing promotional materials. You are currently working on an informational flyer that is almost set to go. You will make a few improvements before approving the flyer for release. Refer to Figure 1.46 as you complete Step 2.

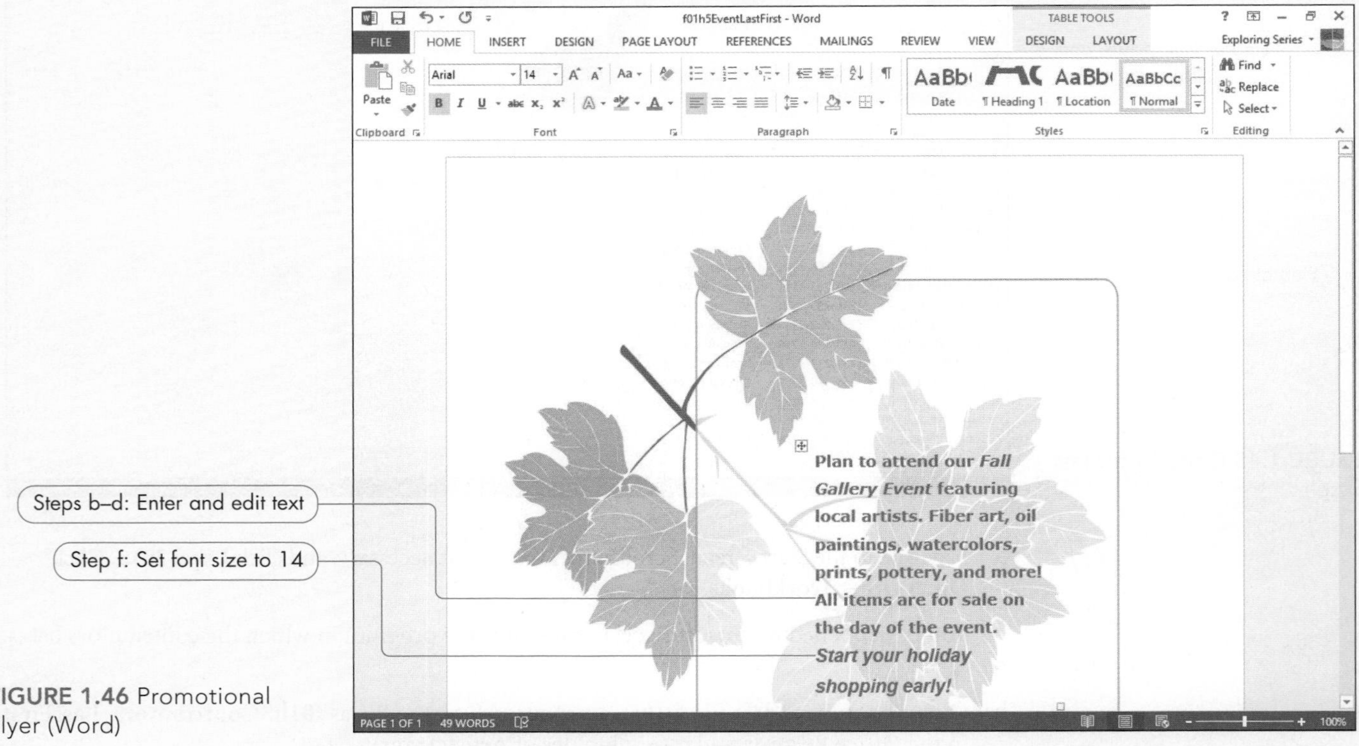

FIGURE 1.46 Promotional Flyer (Word)

a. Navigate to the Start screen. Scroll across the tiles, if necessary, and click **Word 2013**. Click **Open Other Documents**. Open *f01h5Event* and save the document as **f01h5Event_LastFirst** in the Promotional Print folder (a subfolder of Artists) you created.

You plan to modify the promotional flyer slightly to include additional information about the Spotted Begonia Art Gallery.

> **TROUBLESHOOTING:** If you make any major mistakes in this exercise, you can close the file without saving it, open *f01h5Event* again, and then start this exercise over.

b. Click after the exclamation mark after the word *more* at the end of the first paragraph. Press **Enter** and type the following text. As you type, do not press Enter at the end of each line. Word will automatically wrap the lines of text.

All items are for sale on the day of the event. Start your holiday shopping early! You'll find gifts for everyone on your list.

> **TROUBLESHOOTING:** If you make any mistakes while typing, press Backspace and correct them.

c. Select the sentence beginning with *You'll find gifts*. Press **Delete**.

When you press Delete, selected text (or characters to the right of the insertion point) is removed. Deleted text is not placed in the Clipboard.

d. Select the words *Start your holiday shopping early!* Click **Italic** in the Font group on the HOME tab and click anywhere outside the selection to see the result.

e. Select both paragraphs but not the final italicized line. While still within the selection, move the mouse pointer slightly to display the Mini toolbar, click the **Font arrow** on the Mini toolbar, and then scroll to select **Verdana**.

> **TROUBLESHOOTING:** If you do not see the Mini toolbar, you might have moved too far away from the selection. In that case, click outside the selection and drag to select it once more. Without leaving the selection, move the mouse pointer slightly to display the Mini toolbar.

You have changed the font of the two paragraphs.

f. Click after the period following the word *event* before the last sentence in the second paragraph. Press **Enter** and press **Delete** to remove the extra space before the first letter, if necessary. Drag to select the new line, click **Font Size arrow** in the Font group, and then select **14**. Click anywhere outside the selected area. Your document should appear as shown in Figure 1.46.

You have increased font size to draw attention to the text.

g. Save the document and keep open for Step 3.

STEP 3 ›› USE FORMAT PAINTER AND WORK WITH THE MINI TOOLBAR

You are on a short timeline for finalizing the promotional flyer, so you will use a few shortcuts to avoid retyping and reformatting more than is necessary. You know that you can easily copy formatting from one area to another using Format Painter. The Mini toolbar can also help you make changes quickly. Refer to Figure 1.47 as you complete Step 3.

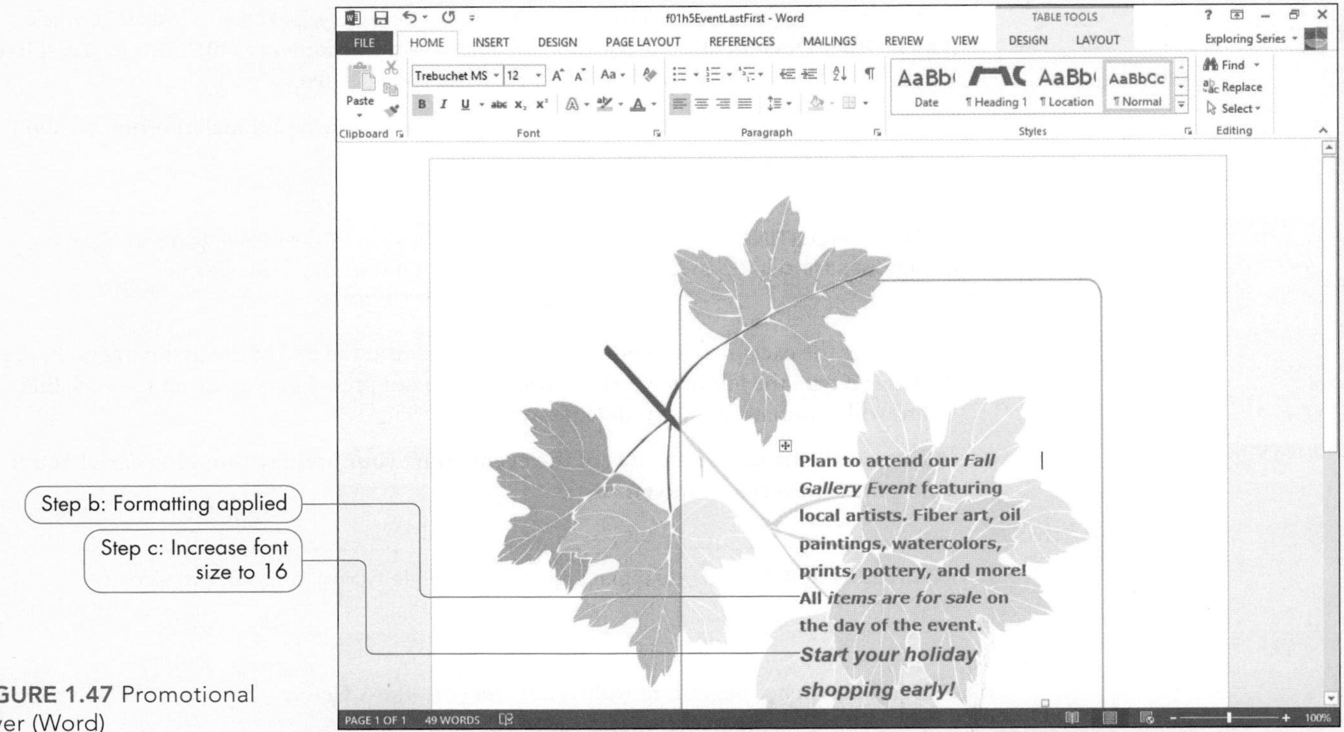

FIGURE 1.47 Promotional Flyer (Word)

a. Select the words *Fall Gallery Event* in the first paragraph and click **Format Painter** in the Clipboard group.

b. Select the words *items are for sale* in the sixth line. Click anywhere outside the selection to deselect the phrase.

The format of the area that you first selected (*Fall Gallery Event*) is applied to the line containing the phrase.

c. Select the text *Start your holiday shopping early!* in the Mini toolbar, click in the **Font Size box**, and then select **16** to increase the font size slightly. Click outside the selected area.

Figure 1.47 shows the final document as it should now appear.

d. Save the document as **f01h5Stp3Event_LastFirst** in the Promotional Print folder you created and close Word. Submit your file based on your instructor's directions.

The flyer will be saved with the same file name and in the same location as it was when you last saved the document in Step 2. As you close Word, the open document will also be closed.

STEP 4 » USE THE FONT DIALOG BOX AND FIND AND REPLACE TEXT

The contributors worksheet is almost complete. However, you first want to make a few more formatting changes to improve the worksheet's appearance. You will also quickly change an incorrect area code by using Excel's *Find and Replace* feature. Refer to Figure 1.48 as you complete Step 4.

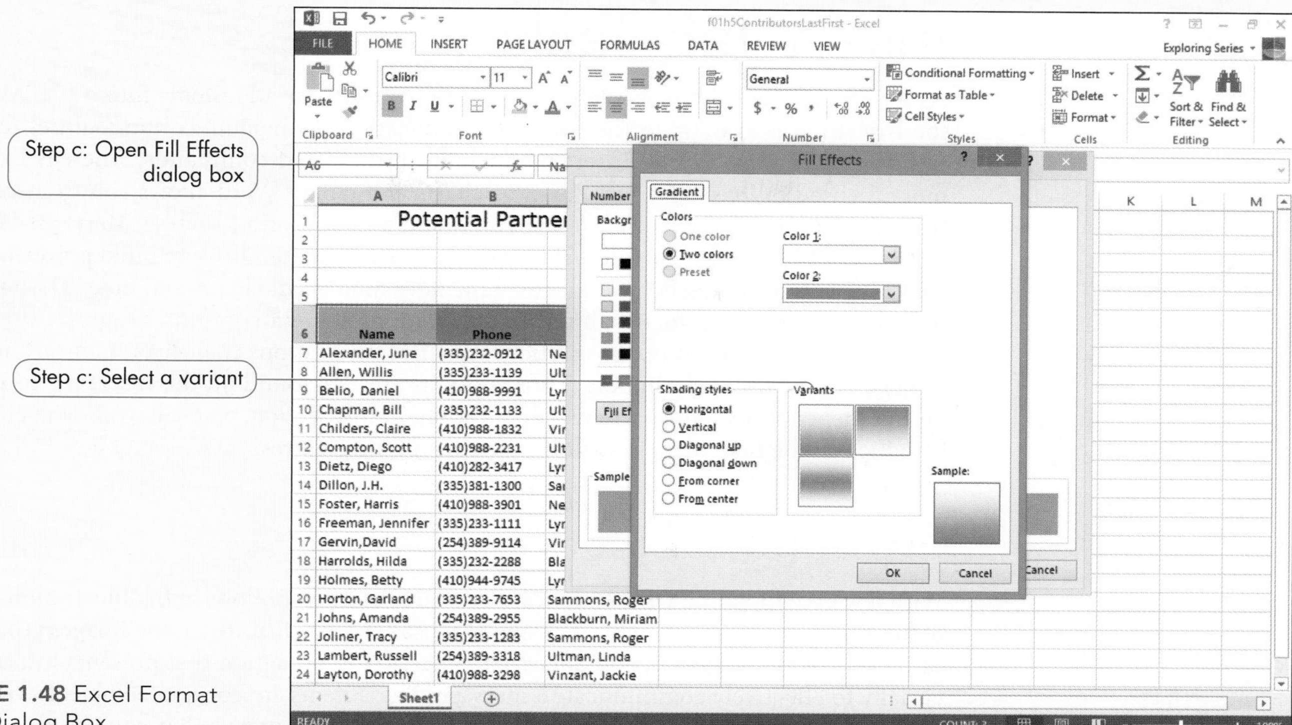

FIGURE 1.48 Excel Format Cells Dialog Box

a. Click the **Excel icon** on the taskbar to redisplay the contributors worksheet that you minimized in Step 1.

The Excel potential contributors list displays.

> **TROUBLESHOOTING:** If you closed Excel, you can find the correct worksheet in your Recent Documents list.

b. Drag to select **cells A6** through **C6**.

> **TROUBLESHOOTING:** Make sure the mouse pointer looks like a large white plus sign before dragging. It is normal for the first cell in the selected area to be a different shade. If you click and drag when the mouse pointer does not resemble a white plus sign, text may be moved or duplicated. In that case, click Undo on the Quick Access Toolbar.

c. Click the **Dialog Box Launcher** in the Font group to display the Format Cells dialog box. Click the **Fill tab** and click **Fill Effects**, as shown in Figure 1.48. Click any style in the *Variants* section, click **OK**, and then click **OK** once more to close the Format Cells dialog box. Click outside the selected area to see the final result.

The headings of the worksheet are shaded more attractively.

d. Click **Find & Select** in the Editing group and click **Replace**. Type **410** in the **Find what box**. Type **411** in the **Replace with box**, click **Replace All**, and then click **OK** when notified that Excel has made seven replacements. Click **Close** in the *Find and Replace* dialog box.

You discovered that you consistently typed an incorrect area code. You used Find and Replace to make the corrections quickly.

e. Save the workbook as **f01h5Stp4Contributors_LastFirst** in the Office Records folder you created. Exit Excel, if necessary. Submit your files based on your instructor's directions.

Insert Tab Tasks

As its title implies, the Insert tab enables you to insert, or add, items into a file. Much of the Insert tab is specific to the particular application, with some commonalities to other Office applications. Word's Insert tab includes text-related commands, whereas Excel's is more focused on inserting such items as charts and tables. Word allows you to insert apps from the Microsoft app store, so you could add an application such as Merriam-Webster Dictionary. Both Word and Excel allow you to insert Apps for Office to build powerful Web-backed solutions. PowerPoint's Insert tab includes multimedia items and links. Despite their obvious differences in focus, all Office applications share a common group on the Insert tab—the Illustrations group. In addition, all Office applications enable you to insert headers, footers, text boxes, and symbols. Those options are also found on the Insert tab in various groups, depending on the particular application. In this section, you will work with common activities on the Insert tab, including inserting online pictures.

Inserting Objects

With few exceptions, all Office applications share common options in the Illustrations group of the Insert tab. PowerPoint places some of those common features in the Images group. You can insert pictures, shapes, and ***SmartArt***. SmartArt is a diagram that presents information visually to effectively communicate a message. These items are considered objects, retaining their separate nature when they are inserted in files. That means that you can select them and manage them independently of the underlying document, worksheet, or presentation.

After an object has been inserted, you can click the object to select it or click anywhere outside the object to deselect it. When an object is selected, a border surrounds it with handles, or small dots, appearing at each corner and in the middle of each side. Figure 1.49 shows a selected object, surrounded by handles. Unless an object is selected, you cannot change or modify it. When an object is selected, the Ribbon expands to include one or more contextual tabs. Items on the contextual tabs relate to the selected object, enabling you to modify and manage it.

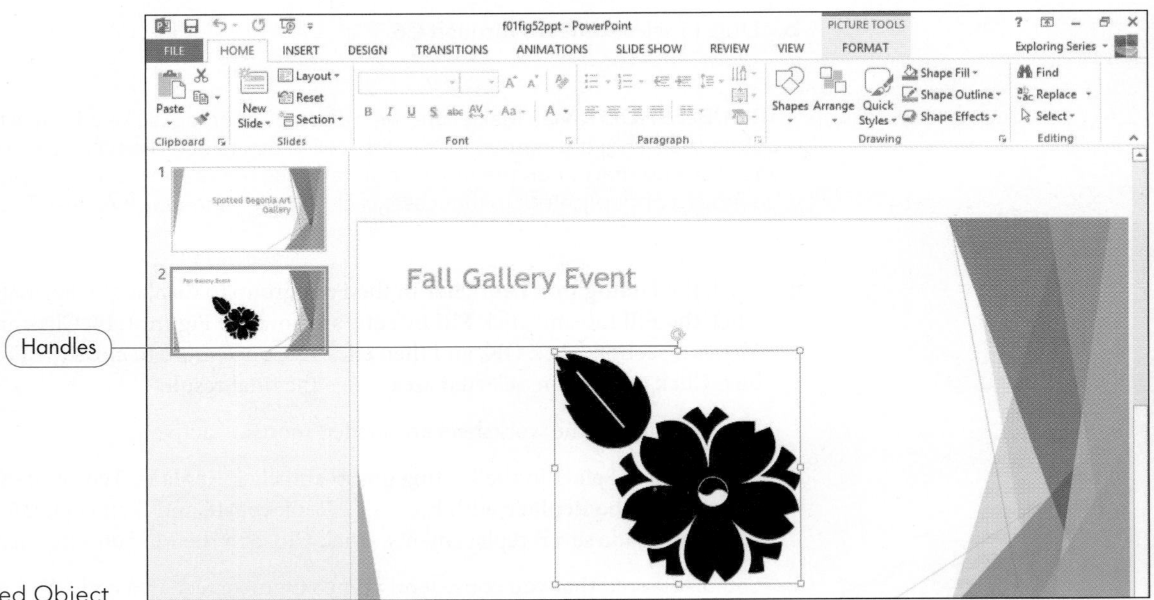

FIGURE 1.49 Selected Object

You can resize and move a selected object. Place the mouse pointer on any handle and drag (when the mouse pointer looks like a two-headed arrow) to resize the object. Be careful! If you drag a side handle, the object is likely to be skewed, possibly resulting in a poor image. Instead, drag a corner handle to proportionally resize the image. To move an object, drag the object when the mouse pointer looks like a four-headed arrow.

Insert Pictures

STEP 2»

Documents, worksheets, and presentations can include much more than just words and numbers. You can easily add energy and additional description to the project by including pictures and other graphic elements. Although a ***picture*** is usually just that—a digital photo—it is actually defined as a graphic element retrieved from storage media such as a hard drive or a CD. A picture could actually be a clip art item that you saved from the Internet onto your hard drive.

The process of inserting a picture is simple.

1. Click in the project where you want the picture to be placed. Make sure you know where the picture that you plan to use is stored.
2. Click the INSERT tab.
3. Click Pictures in the Illustrations group (or Images group in PowerPoint). The Insert Picture dialog box is shown in Figure 1.50. You can also use Online Pictures to search for and insert pictures.
4. Navigate to where your picture is saved and click Insert (or simply double-click the picture).

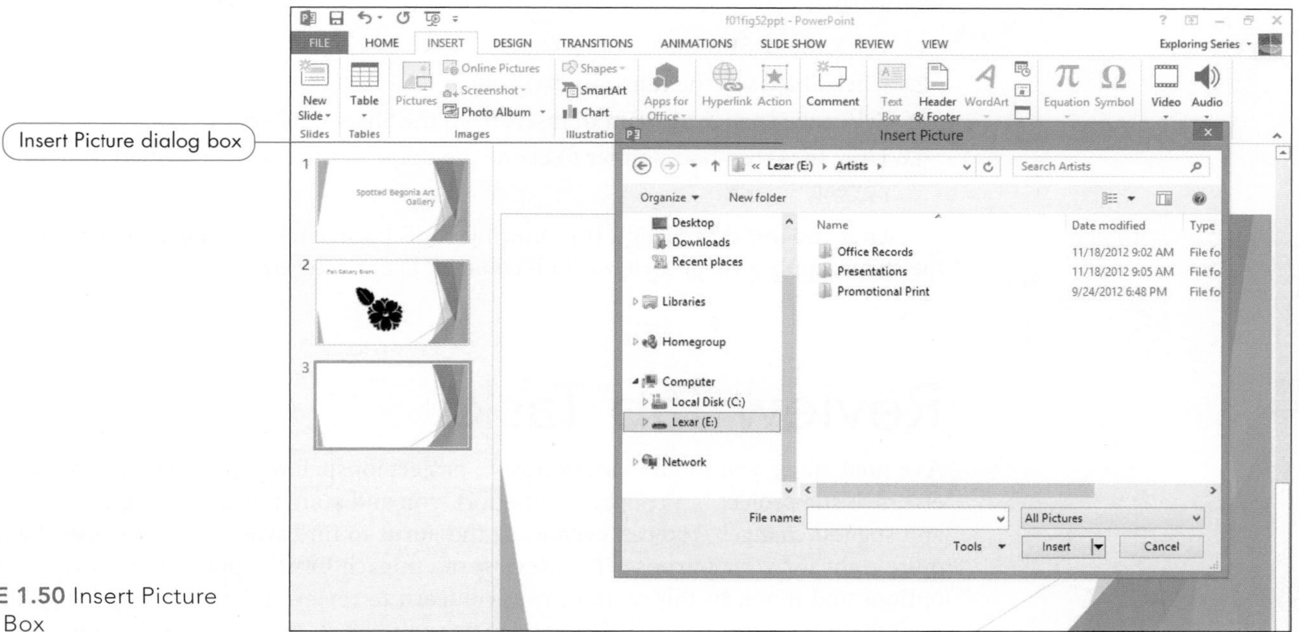

FIGURE 1.50 Insert Picture Dialog Box

In addition, on some slide layouts, PowerPoint displays Pictures and Online Pictures buttons that you can click to search for and select a picture for the slide.

Insert and Modify SmartArt

The SmartArt feature enables you to create a diagram and to enter text to provide a visual representation of data. To create a SmartArt diagram, choose a diagram type that fits the purpose: List, Process, Cycle, Hierarchy, Relationships, Matrix, Pyramid, and Picture. You can get additional SmartArt diagrams at Office.com. To insert a SmartArt object, do the following:

1. Click the INSERT tab.
2. Click SmartArt in the Illustrations group to display the Choose a SmartArt Graphic dialog box.
3. Click the type of SmartArt diagram you want in the left pane of the dialog box.
4. Click the SmartArt subtype from the center pane.
5. Preview the selected SmartArt and subtype in the right pane and click OK.

Once you select the SmartArt diagram type and the subtype, a Text pane opens in which you can enter text. The text you enter displays within the selected object. If the SmartArt diagram contains more objects than you need, click the object and press Delete.

The SmartArt Tools Design tab enables you to customize the design of a SmartArt diagram. You can modify the diagram by changing its layout, colors, and style. The layout controls the construction of the diagram. The style controls the visual effects, such as embossing and rounded corners of the diagram. The SmartArt Tools Format tab controls the shape fill color, border, and size options.

Insert and Format Shapes

You can insert a shape to add a visual effect to a worksheet. You can insert various types of lines, rectangles, basic shapes (such as an oval, a pie shape, or a smiley face), block arrows, equation shapes, flowchart shapes, stars and banners, and callouts. You can insert shapes, such as a callout, to draw attention to particular worksheet data. To insert a shape, do the following:

1. Click the INSERT tab.
2. Click Shapes in the Illustrations group.
3. Select the shape you want to insert from the Shapes gallery.
4. Drag the cross-hair pointer to create the shape in the worksheet where you want it to appear.

After you insert the shape, the Drawing Tools Format tab displays so that you can change the shape, apply a shape style with fill color, and adjust the size.

Review Tab Tasks

As a final touch, you should always check a project for spelling, grammatical, and word usage errors. If the project is a collaborative effort, you and your colleagues might add comments and suggest changes. You can even use a thesaurus to find synonyms for words that are not quite right for your purpose. The Review tab in each Office application provides all these options and more. In this section, you will learn to review a file, checking for spelling and grammatical errors. You will also learn to use a thesaurus to identify synonyms.

Reviewing a File

As you create or edit a file, you will want to make sure no spelling or grammatical errors exist. You will also be concerned with wording, being sure to select words and phrases that best represent the purpose of the document, worksheet, or presentation. On occasion, you might even find yourself at a loss for an appropriate word. Not to worry. Word, Excel, and PowerPoint all provide standard tools for proofreading, including a spelling and grammar checker and a thesaurus.

Check Spelling and Grammar

STEP 1

In general, all Office applications check your spelling and grammar as you type. If a word is unrecognized, it is flagged as misspelled or grammatically incorrect. Misspellings are identified with a red wavy underline, grammatical problems are underlined in green, and word usage errors (such as using *bear* instead of *bare*) have a blue underline. If the word or phrase is truly in error—that is, it is not a person's name or an unusual term that is not in the application's dictionary—you can correct it manually, or you can let the software correct it for you. If you right-click a word or phrase that is identified as a mistake, you will see a shortcut menu similar to that shown in Figure 1.51. If the application's dictionary can make a suggestion as to the correct spelling, you can click to accept the suggestion and make the change. If a grammatical rule is violated, you will have an opportunity to select a correction. However, if the text is actually correct, you can click Ignore or Ignore All (to bypass all occurrences of the flagged error in the current document). Click *Add to Dictionary* if you want the word to be considered correct whenever it appears in all documents. Similar selections on a shortcut menu enable you to ignore grammatical mistakes if they are not errors.

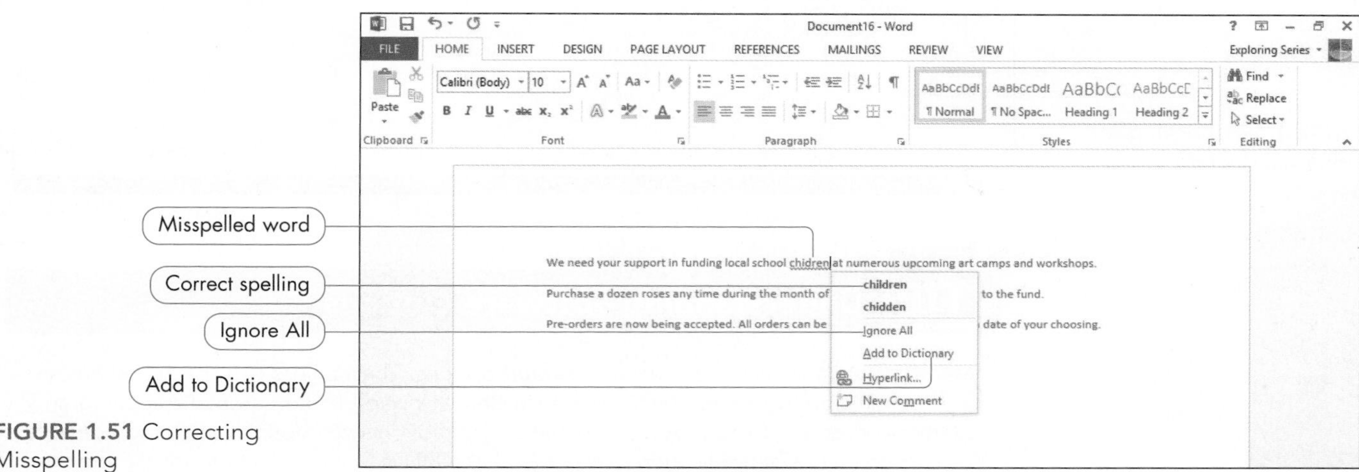

FIGURE 1.51 Correcting Misspelling

You might prefer the convenience of addressing possible misspellings and grammatical errors without having to examine each underlined word or phrase. To do so, click Spelling & Grammar in the Proofing group on the Review tab. Beginning at the top of the document, each identified error is highlighted in a pane similar to Figure 1.52. You can then choose how to address the problem by making a selection from the options in the pane.

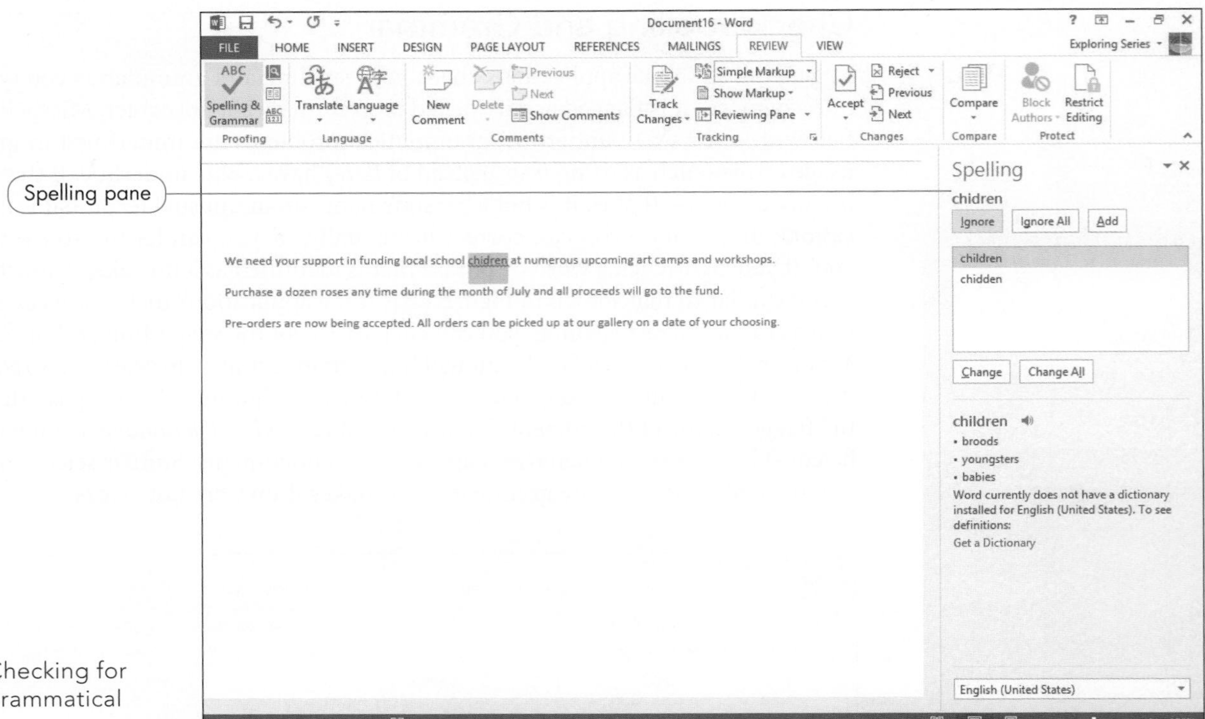

FIGURE 1.52 Checking for Spelling and Grammatical Errors

TIP Understanding Software Options

Many Office settings are considered ***default*** options. Thus, unless you specify otherwise, the default options are in effect. One such default option is the automatic spelling and grammar checker. If you prefer to enable and disable certain options or change default settings in an Office application, you can click the FILE tab and select Options. From that point, you can work through a series of categories, selecting or deselecting options at will. For example, if you want to change how the application corrects and formats text, you can select or deselect settings in the Proofing group.

Use the Thesaurus

As you write, there will be times when you are at a loss for an appropriate word. Perhaps you feel that you are overusing a word and want to find a suitable substitute. The Thesaurus is the Office tool to use in such a situation. Located in the Proofing group on the Review tab, Thesaurus enables you to search for synonyms, or words with similar meanings. Select a word and click Thesaurus in the Proofing group on the Review tab. A task pane displays on the right side of the screen, and synonyms are listed similar to those shown in Figure 1.53. You can also use the Thesaurus before typing a word to find substitutes. Simply click Thesaurus and type the word for which you are seeking a synonym in the Search box. Press Enter or click the magnifying glass to the right of the Search box for some suggestions. Finally, you can also identify synonyms when you right-click a word and point to Synonyms (if any are available). Click any word from the options offered to place it in the document.

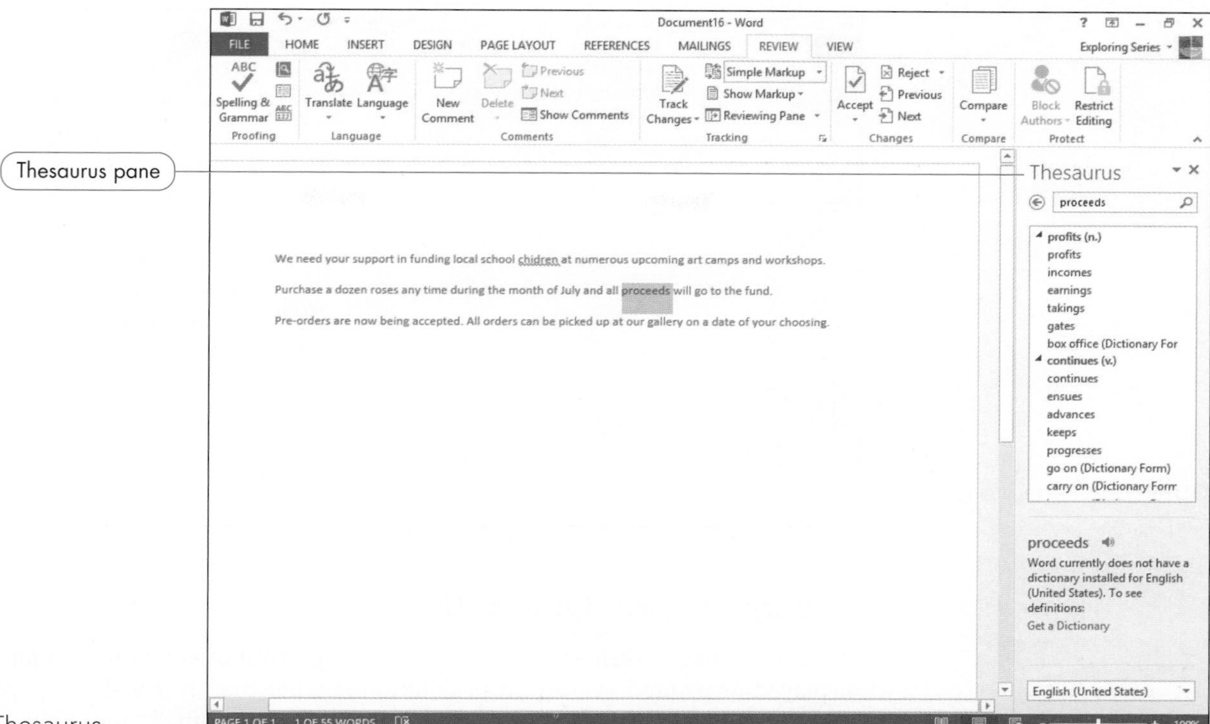

FIGURE 1.53 Thesaurus

Page Layout Tab Tasks

When you prepare a document or worksheet, you are concerned with the way the project appears onscreen and possibly in print. Unlike Word and Excel, a PowerPoint presentation is usually designed as a slide show, so it is not nearly as critical to concern yourself with page layout settings. The Page Layout tab in Word and Excel provides access to a full range of options such as margin settings and page orientation. In this section, you will identify page layout settings that are common to Office applications.

Because a document is most often designed to be printed, you will want to make sure it looks its best in printed form. That means that you will need to know how to adjust margins and how to change the page orientation. Perhaps the document or spreadsheet should be centered on the page vertically or the text should be aligned in columns. By adjusting page settings, you can do all these things and more. You will find the most common page settings, such as margins and page orientation, in the Page Setup group on the Page Layout tab. For less common settings, such as determining whether headers should print on odd or even pages, you can use the Page Setup dialog box.

Changing Margins

A ***margin*** is the area of blank space that displays to the left, right, top, and bottom of a document or worksheet. Margins are evident only if you are in Print Layout or Page Layout view or if you are in the Backstage view, previewing a document to print. To set or change margins, click the Page Layout tab. As shown in Figure 1.54, the Page Setup group enables you to change such items as margins and orientation. To change margins:

1. Click Margins in the Page Setup group on the PAGE LAYOUT tab.
2. If the margins that you intend to use are included in any of the preset margin options, click a selection. Otherwise, click Custom Margins to display the Page Setup dialog box in which you can create custom margin settings.
3. Click OK to accept the settings and close the dialog box.

You can also change margins when you click Print on the File tab.

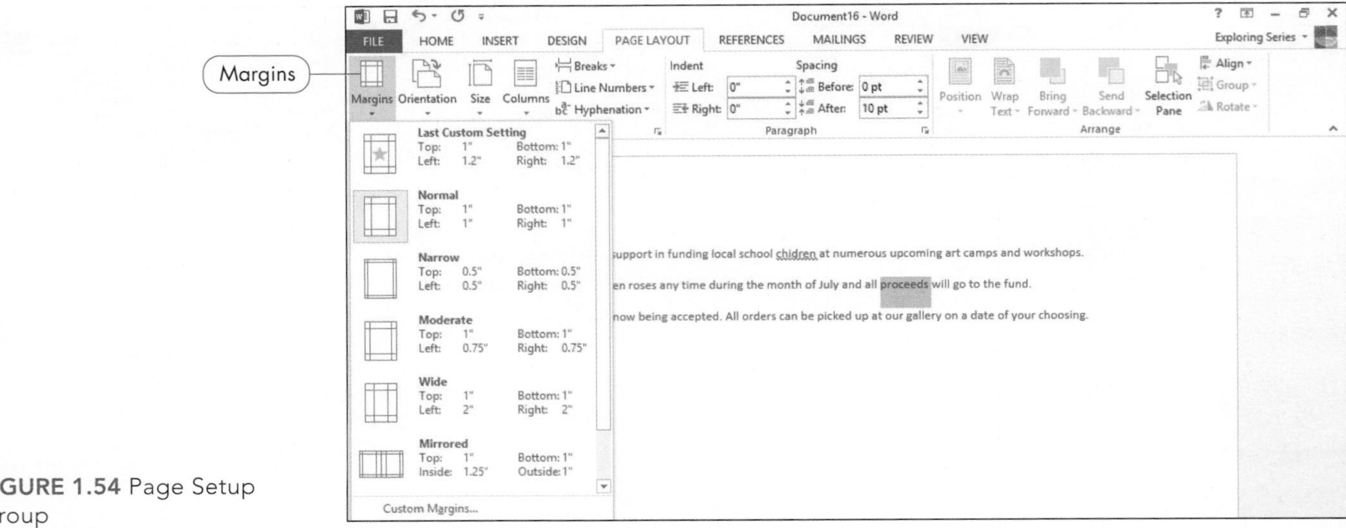

FIGURE 1.54 Page Setup Group

Changing Page Orientation

STEP 3》 Documents and worksheets can be displayed in ***portrait*** orientation or in ***landscape***. A page displayed or printed in portrait orientation is taller than it is wide. A page in landscape orientation is wider than it is tall. Word documents are usually more attractive displayed in portrait orientation, whereas Excel worksheets are often more suitable in landscape. To select page orientation, click Orientation in the Page Setup group on the Page Layout tab (see Figure 1.55). Orientation is also an option in the Print area of the Backstage view.

Using the Page Setup Dialog Box

The Page Setup group contains the most commonly used page options in the particular Office application. Some are unique to Excel, and others are more applicable to Word. Other less common settings are available in the Page Setup dialog box only, displayed when you click the Page Setup Dialog Box Launcher. The subsequent dialog box includes options for customizing margins, selecting page orientation, centering vertically, printing gridlines, and creating headers and footers, although some of those options are available only when working with Word; others are unique to Excel. Figure 1.55 shows both the Excel and Word Page Setup dialog boxes.

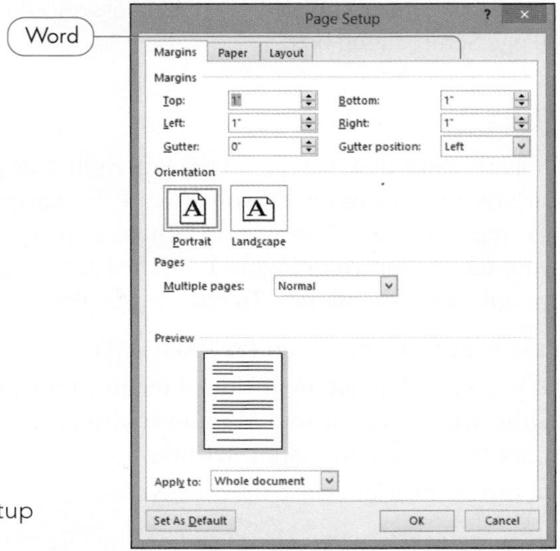

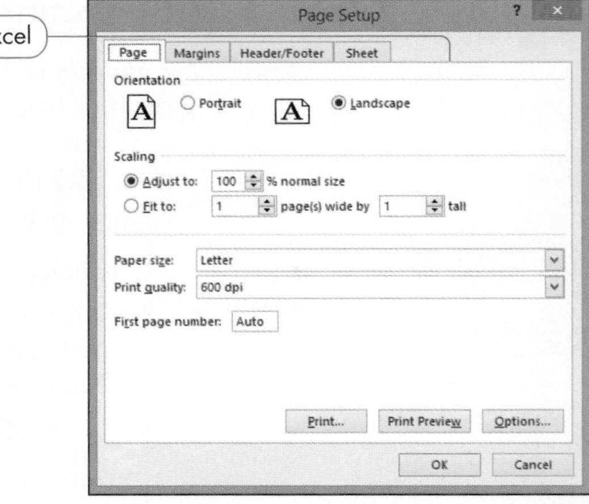

FIGURE 1.55 Page Setup Dialog Boxes

1. Give two ways to resize an object, such as a picture, that has been inserted in a document. ***p. 115***
2. Often, an Office application will identify a word as misspelled that is not actually misspelled. How can that happen? If a word is flagged as misspelled, how can you correct it (or ignore it if it is not actually an error)? ***p. 117***
3. Give two ways to change a document from a portrait orientation to landscape. Identify at least one document type that you think would be better suited for landscape orientation rather than portrait. ***p. 120***
4. What dialog box includes options for selecting margins, centering vertically, and changing page orientation? ***p. 120***

Hands-On Exercises

MyITLab®
HOE6 Training

6 Insert Tab Tasks, Page Layout Tab Tasks, and Review Tab Tasks

A series of enrichment programs at the Spotted Begonia Art Gallery is nearing kickoff. You are helping plan a ceremony to commemorate the occasion. To encourage interest and participation, you will edit a PowerPoint presentation that is to be shown to civic groups, the local retiree association, and to city and county leaders to solicit additional funding. You know that pictures add energy to a presentation when used appropriately, so you will check for those elements, adding whatever is necessary. A major concern is making sure the presentation is error free and that it is available in print so that meeting participants can review it later. As a reminder, you also plan to have available a handout giving the time and date of the dedication ceremony. You will use the Insert tab to work with illustrations and the Review tab to check for errors, and you will use Word to generate an attractive handout as a reminder of the date.

Skills covered: Check Spelling and Use the Thesaurus • Insert Pictures • Change Margins and Page Orientation

STEP 1 » CHECK SPELLING AND USE THE THESAURUS

As you check the PowerPoint presentation that will be shown to local groups, you make sure no misspellings or grammatical mistakes exist. You also use the Thesaurus to find a suitable substitution for a word you feel should be replaced. Refer to Figure 1.56 as you complete Step 1.

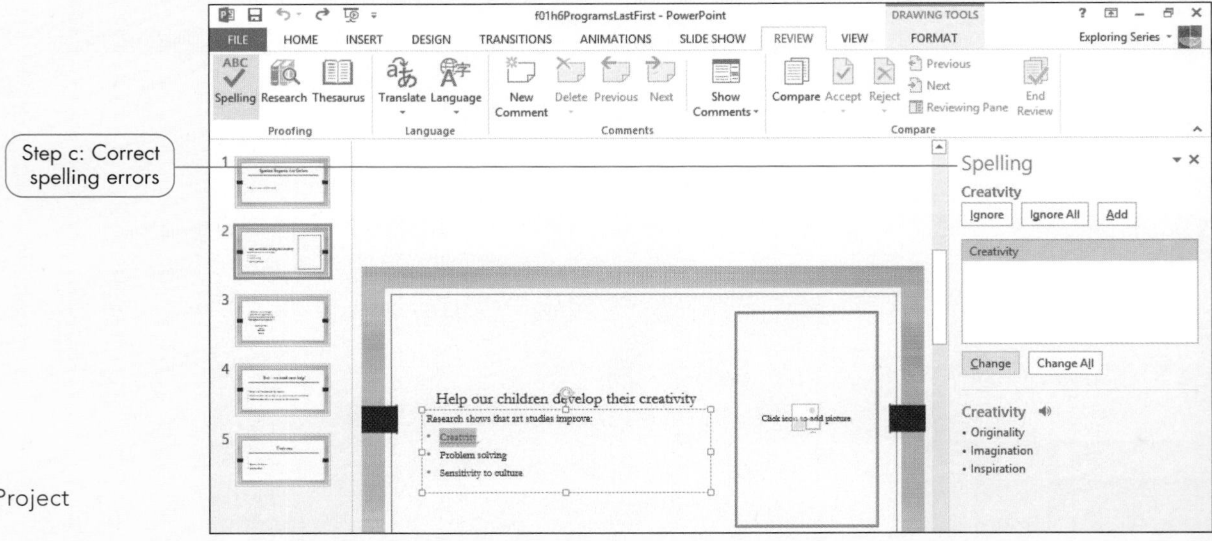

FIGURE 1.56 Project Presentation

a. Navigate to the Start screen. Scroll across the tiles, if necessary, and click **PowerPoint 2013**. Click **Open Other Presentations**. Open *f01h6Programs* and save the document as **f01h6Programs_LastFirst** in the Promotional Print folder (a subfolder of Artists) you created.

   The PowerPoint presentation opens, with Slide 1 shown in Normal view.

b. Click the **SLIDE SHOW tab** and click **From Beginning** in the Start Slide Show group to view the presentation. Click to advance from one slide to another. After the last slide, click to return to Normal view.

c. Click the **REVIEW tab** and click **Spelling** in the Proofing group. Correct any words that are misspelled by clicking the correction and clicking Change or Ignore in the Spelling pane. Click **Change** to accept *Creativity* on Slide 2, click **workshops** and click **Change** on Slide 3, and click **Change** to accept *Thank* for Slide 5. Refer to Figure 1.56. Click **OK** when the spell check is complete and close the pane.

d. Click **Slide 2** in the Slides pane on the left. Double-click the bulleted word *Creativity*, click **Thesaurus** in the Proofing group, point to *Imagination* in the Thesaurus pane, click the arrow to the right of the word, and then select **Insert**.

   The word *Creativity* is replaced with the word *Imagination*.

e. Click the **Close (X) button** in the top-right corner of the Thesaurus pane.

f. Save the presentation.

STEP 2 » INSERT PICTURES

Although the presentation provides the necessary information and encourages viewers to become active participants in the enrichment programs, you believe that pictures might make it a little more exciting. Where appropriate, you will include a picture. Refer to Figure 1.57 as you complete Step 2.

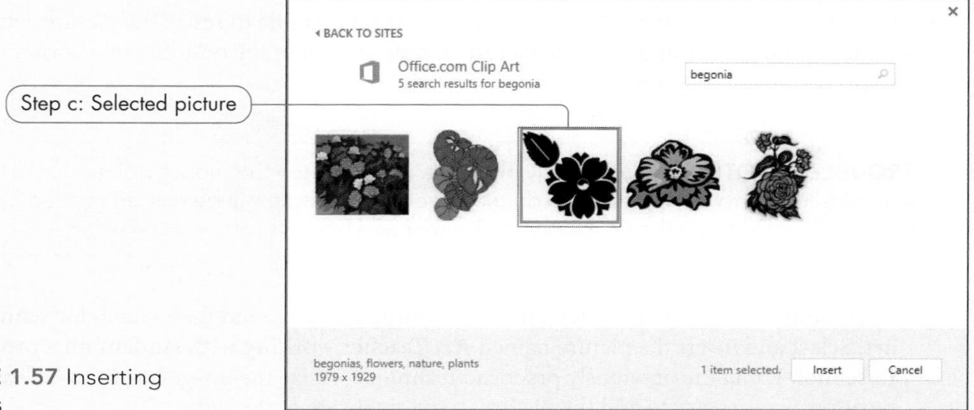

FIGURE 1.57 Inserting Pictures

a. Click **Slide 2** in the Slides pane on the left, if necessary. Click the **INSERT tab** and click **Online Pictures** in the Images group.

   The Insert Pictures pane displays on the screen.

> **TROUBLESHOOTING:** You can add your own pictures to slides using the Pictures command. Or you can copy and paste images directly from a Web page.

b. Type **begonia** in the **Office.com Clip Art search box** and press **Enter**.

   You will identify pictures that may be displayed on Slide 2.

c. Click to select the black flower shown in Figure 1.57 or use a similar image. Click **Insert**.

   The picture may not be placed as you would like, but you will move and resize it in the next substep as necessary. Also, notice that the picture is selected, as indicated by the box and handles surrounding it.

> **TROUBLESHOOTING:** It is very easy to make the mistake of inserting duplicate pictures on a slide, perhaps because you clicked the image more than once in the task pane. If that should happen, you can remove any unwanted picture by clicking to select it and pressing Delete.

d. Click a corner handle—the small square on the border of the picture. Make sure the mouse pointer appears as a double-headed arrow. Drag to resize the image so that it fits well on the slide. Click in the center of the picture. The mouse pointer should appear as a four-headed arrow. Drag the picture slightly to the right corner of the slide. Make sure the picture is still selected (it should be surrounded by a box and handles). If it is not selected, click to select it.

TROUBLESHOOTING: You may not need to perform this substep if the picture came in as desired. Proceed to the next substep if this occurs.

e. Click **Slide 5** in the Slides pane on the left. Click the **INSERT tab** and select **Online Pictures**. Type **happy art** in the **Office.com Clip Art search box** and press **Enter**. Click the **Three handprints picture** and click **Insert**.

   A picture is placed on the final slide.

f. Click to select the picture, if necessary. Drag a corner handle to resize the picture. Click the center of the picture and drag the picture to reposition it in the bottom-right corner of the slide, as shown in Figure 1.57.

TROUBLESHOOTING: You can only move the picture when the mouse pointer looks like a four-headed arrow. If instead you drag a handle, the picture will be resized instead of moved. Click Undo on the Quick Access Toolbar and begin again.

g. Click **Slide 3**. Click the **INSERT tab**, click **Online Pictures**, and then search for **school art**. Select and insert the picture named **Art Teacher working with student on a project in school**. Using the previously practiced technique, resize the image height to **3.9"** and position as necessary to add the picture to the right side of the slide.

h. Save the presentation and exit PowerPoint. Submit your file based on your instructor's directions.

STEP 3 » CHANGE MARGINS AND PAGE ORIENTATION

You are ready to finalize the flyer promoting the workshops, but before printing it you want to see how it will look. You wonder if it would be better in landscape or portrait orientation, so you will try both. After adjusting the margins, you are ready to save the flyer for later printing and distribution. Refer to Figure 1.58 as you complete Step 3.

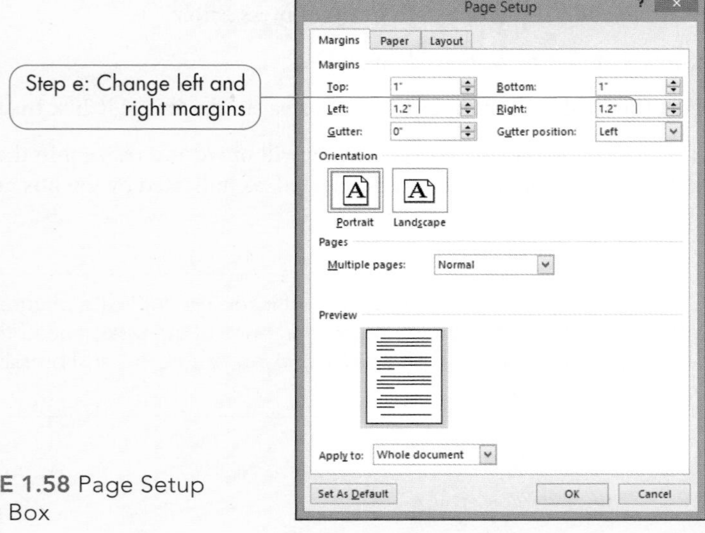

FIGURE 1.58 Page Setup Dialog Box

a. Navigate to the Start screen. Scroll across the tiles, if necessary, and click **Word 2013**. Click **Open Other Documents**. Open *f01h6Handout* and save the document as **f01h6Handout_LastFirst** in the Promotional Print folder (a subfolder of Artists) you created.

b. Click the **PAGE LAYOUT tab**, click **Orientation** in the Page Setup group, and then select **Landscape** to view the flyer in landscape orientation.

   You want to see how the handout will look in landscape orientation.

c. Click the **FILE tab**, click **Print**, and then click **Next Page** and click **Previous Page** (right- and left-pointing arrows at the bottom center of the preview page).

   The second page of the handout shows only the last two bullets and the contact information. You can see that the two-page layout is not an attractive option.

d. Click the **Back arrow** in the top-left corner. Click **Undo** on the Quick Access Toolbar. Click the **FILE tab** and click **Print**.

   The document fits on one page. Portrait orientation is a much better choice for the handout.

e. Click the **Back arrow** in the top-left corner. Click the **PAGE LAYOUT tab** if necessary, click **Margins** in the Page Setup group, and then select **Custom Margins**. Click the **spin arrow** beside the left margin box to increase the margin to **1.2**. Similarly, change the right margin to **1.2**. Refer to Figure 1.58. Click **OK**.

f. Save the document and exit Word. Submit your file based on your instructor's directions.

Chapter Objectives Review

After reading this chapter, you have accomplished the following objectives:

1. **Log in with your Microsoft account.**
   - Your Microsoft account connects you to all of Microsoft's Internet-based resources.
2. **Identify the Start screen components.**
   - The Start screen has a sleek, clean interface that is made up of tiles and Charms.
3. **Interact with the Start screen.**
   - Customize the Start screen to access programs and apps.
4. **Access the desktop.**
   - Simplified to accommodate mobile devices, laptops, and desktops.
5. **Use File Explorer.**
   - Understand and customize the interface: Change the view to provide as little or as much detail as you need.
   - Work with groups on the Navigation Pane: Provides access to all resources, folders, and files.
6. **Work with folders and files.**
   - Create a folder: A well-named folder structure can be created in File Explorer or within a program as you save a file.
   - Open, rename, and delete folders and files: File Explorer can be used to perform these tasks.
   - Save a file: When saving a file for the first time, you need to indicate the location and the name of the file.
7. **Select, copy, and move multiple files and folders.**
   - Select multiple files and folders: Folders and files can be selected as a group.
   - Copy and move files and folders: Folders and the files within them can be easily moved to the same or a different drive.
8. **Identify common interface components.**
   - Use the Backstage view and the Quick Access Toolbar: The Backstage view can perform several commands.
   - Familiarize yourself with the Ribbon: Provides access to common tasks.
   - Use the status bar: The status bar provides information relative to the open file and quick access to View and Zoom level options.
9. **Get Office Help.**
   - Use Office Help: The Help button links to online resources and technical support.
   - Use Enhanced ScreenTips: Provides the purpose of a command button as you point to it.
   - Get help with dialog boxes: Use the Help button in the top-right corner of a dialog box to get help relevant to the task.
10. **Open a file.**
    - Create a new file: A document can be created as a blank document or with a template.
    - Open a file using the Open dialog box: Previously saved files can be located and opened using a dialog box.
    - Open a file using the Recent Documents list: Documents that you have worked with recently display here.
    - Open a file from the Templates list: Templates are a convenient way to save time when designing a document.
11. **Print a file.**
    - Check and change orientation or perform other commands related to the look of your file before printing.
12. **Close a file and application.**
    - Close files you are not working on to avoid becoming overwhelmed.
13. **Select and edit text.**
    - Select text to edit: Commit to memory: "Select, then do."
    - Use the Mini toolbar: Provides instant access to common formatting commands after text is selected.
    - Apply font attributes: These can be applied to selected text with toggle commands.
    - Change the font: Choose from a set of fonts found within all Office applications.
    - Change the font size, color, and attributes: These commands are located in the Font group on the Ribbon.
14. **Use the Clipboard group commands.**
    - Copy formats with the Format Painter: Copy formatting features from one section of text to another.
    - Move and copy text: Text can be selected, copied, and moved between applications or within the same application.
    - Use the Office Clipboard: This pane stores up to 24 cut or copied selections for use later on in your computing session.
15. **Use the Editing group commands.**
    - Find and replace text: Finds each occurrence of a series of characters and replaces them with another series.
    - Use advanced find and replace feature: Change the format of every occurrence of a series of characters.
16. **Insert objects.**
    - Insert pictures: You can insert pictures from a CD or other media, or from an online resource such as Office.com.
    - Insert and modify SmartArt: Create a diagram and to enter text to provide a visual of data.
    - Insert and format shapes: You can insert various types of lines and basic shapes.
17. **Review a file.**
    - Check spelling and grammar: All Office applications check and mark these error types as you type for later correction.
    - Use the Thesaurus: Enables you to search for synonyms.
18. **Use the Page Setup dialog box.**
    - Change margins: You can control the amount of blank space that surrounds the text in your document.
    - Change margins and page orientations, and create headers and footers.

Key Terms Matching

Match the key terms with their definitions. Write the key term letter by the appropriate numbered definition.

- **a.** Backstage view
- **b.** Charms
- **c.** Cloud storage
- **d.** Find
- **e.** Font
- **f.** Format Painter
- **g.** Group
- **h.** Mini toolbar
- **i.** Navigation Pane
- **j.** Operating system
- **k.** Quick Access Toolbar
- **l.** Ribbon
- **m.** OneDrive
- **n.** Snip
- **o.** Snipping Tool
- **p.** Start screen
- **q.** Subfolder
- **r.** Tile
- **s.** Windows 8.1.1
- **t.** Windows 8.1.1 app

1. ______ A tool that copies all formatting from one area to another. **p. 103**

2. ______ Software that directs computer activities such as checking all components, managing system resources, and communicating with application software. **p. 56**

3. ______ A task-oriented section of the Ribbon that contains related commands. **p. 79**

4. ______ An app used to store, access, and share files and folders. **p. 56**

5. ______ Any of the several colorful block images found on the Start screen that when clicked takes you to a program, file, folder, or other Windows 8.1.1 app. **p. 57**

6. ______ A component of Office 2013 that provides a concise collection of commands related to an open file. **p. 77**

7. ______ A tool that displays near selected text that contains formatting commands. **p. 100**

8. ______ A level of folder structure indicated as a folder within another folder. **p. 64**

9. ______ An application specifically designed to run in the Start screen interface of Windows 8.1.1. **p. 57**

10. ______ A command used to locate each occurrence of a series of characters. **p. 106**

11. ______ A Windows 8.1.1 accessory program that allows you to capture a screen display so that you can save, annotate, or share it. **p. 59**

12. ______ What you see after starting your Windows 8.1.1 computer and entering your username and password. **p. 56**

13. ______ Provides handy access to commonly executed tasks such as saving a file and undoing recent actions. **p. 77**

14. ______ A Microsoft operating system released in 2012 that is available on laptops, desktops, and tablet computers. **p. 56**

15. ______ A component made up of five icons that provide similar functionality to the Start button found in previous versions of Windows. **p. 57**

16. ______ The captured screen display created by the Snipping Tool. **p. 59**

17. ______ The long bar located just beneath the title bar containing tabs, groups, and commands. **p. 79**

18. ______ Provides access to computer resources, folders, files, and networked peripherals. **p. 65**

19. ______ A technology used to store files and to work with programs that are stored in a central location on the Internet. **p. 56**

20. ______ A character design or the way characters display onscreen. **p. 99**

Multiple Choice

1. The Recent Documents list shows documents that have been previously:
   (a) Printed.
   (b) Opened.
   (c) Saved in an earlier software version.
   (d) Deleted.

2. Which of the following File Explorer features collects related data from folders and gives them a single name?
   (a) Network
   (b) Favorites
   (c) Libraries
   (d) Computer

3. When you want to copy the format of a selection but not the content, you should:
   (a) Double-click Copy in the Clipboard group.
   (b) Right-click the selection and click Copy.
   (c) Click Copy Format in the Clipboard group.
   (d) Click Format Painter in the Clipboard group.

4. Which of the following is *not* a benefit of using OneDrive?
   (a) Save your folders and files in the cloud.
   (b) Share your files and folders with others.
   (c) Hold video conferences with others.
   (d) Simultaneously work on the same document with others.

5. What does a red wavy underline in a document, spreadsheet, or presentation mean?
   (a) A word is misspelled or not recognized by the Office dictionary
   (b) A grammatical mistake exists
   (c) An apparent word usage mistake exists
   (d) A word has been replaced with a synonym

6. When you close a file:
   (a) You are prompted to save the file (unless you have made no changes since last saving it).
   (b) The application (Word, Excel, or PowerPoint) is also closed.
   (c) You must first save the file.
   (d) You must change the file name.

7. Live Preview:
   (a) Opens a predesigned document or spreadsheet that is relevant to your task.
   (b) Provides a preview of the results of a choice you are considering before you make a final selection.
   (c) Provides a preview of an upcoming Office version.
   (d) Enlarges the font onscreen.

8. You can get help when working with an Office application in which one of the following areas?
   (a) Help button
   (b) Status bar
   (c) The Backstage view
   (d) Quick Access Toolbar

9. The *Find and Replace* feature enables you to do which of the following?
   (a) Find all instances of misspelling and automatically correct (or replace) them
   (b) Find any grammatical errors and automatically correct (or replace) them
   (c) Find any specified font settings and replace them with another selection
   (d) Find any character string and replace it with another

10. A document or worksheet printed in landscape orientation is:
    (a) Taller than it is wide.
    (b) Wider than it is tall.
    (c) A document with 2" left and right margins.
    (d) A document with 2" top and bottom margins.

Practice Exercises

1 Designing Web Pages

You have been asked to make a presentation to the local business association. With the mayor's renewed emphasis on growing the local economy, many businesses are interested in establishing a Web presence. The business owners would like to know a little bit more about how Web pages are designed. In preparation for the presentation, you need to proofread and edit your PowerPoint file. This exercise follows the same set of skills as used in Hands-On Exercises 1–6 in the chapter. Refer to Figure 1.59 as you complete this exercise.

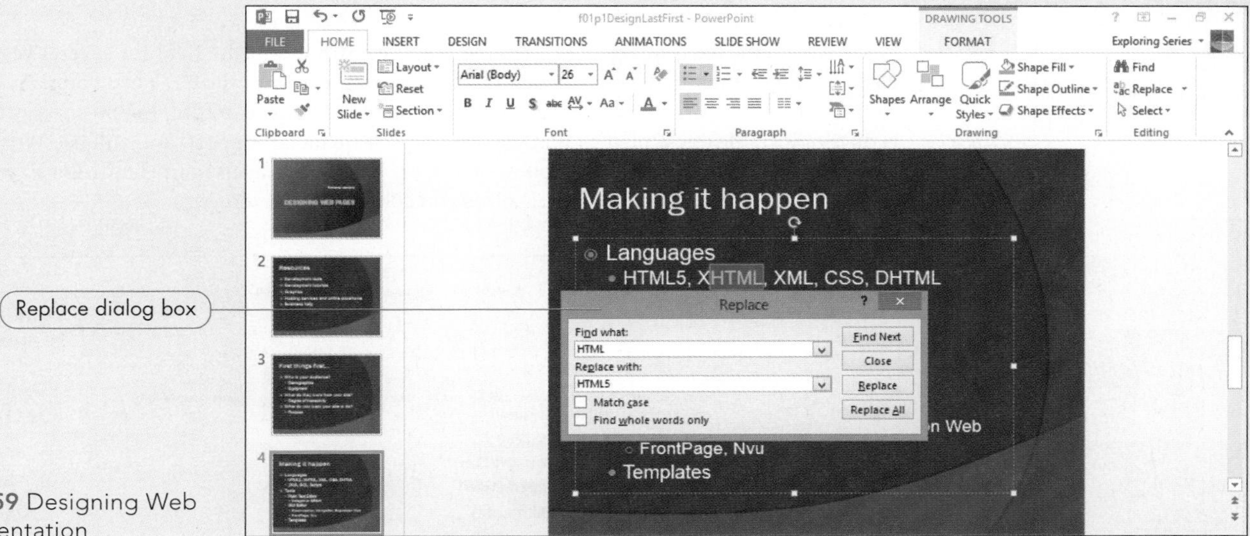

FIGURE 1.59 Designing Web Pages Presentation

a. Click **File Explorer** on the taskbar and select the location where you save your files. Click the **HOME tab** and click **New folder** in the New group. Type **Designing Web Pages** and press **Enter**.
Take a snip, name it **f01p1DesignSnip_LastFirst**, and then save it in the Designing Web Pages folder. Close File Explorer.

b. Point to the bottom-right corner of your screen to display the Charms and click the **Start charm**. Scroll if necessary and click **PowerPoint 2013** to start PowerPoint. Open *f01p1Design* and save it as **f01p1Design_LastFirst** in the Designing Web Pages folder. In Slide 1, drag to select the text *Firstname Lastname* and type your own first and last names. Click an empty area of the slide to cancel the selection.

c. Click the **REVIEW tab** and click **Spelling** in the Proofing group. In the Spelling pane, click **Change** or **Ignore** to make or not make a change as needed. Most identified misspellings should be changed. The words *KompoZer* and *Nvu* are not misspelled, so you should ignore them when they are flagged. Click **OK** to end the spell check.

d. Click the **SLIDE SHOW tab**. Click **From Beginning** in the Start Slide Show group. Click each slide to view the show and press **Esc** on the last slide.

e. Click **Slide 2** in the Slides pane on the left. Drag to select the *Other tools* text and press **Backspace** on the keyboard to delete the text.

f. Click **Slide 4** in the Slides pane. Click the **HOME tab** and click **Replace** in the Editing group. Type **HTML** in the **Find what box** and **HTML5** in the **Replace with box**. Click **Find Next**. Read the slide and click **Replace** to change the first instance of *HTML*. Refer to Figure 1.59. Click **Close**.

g. Click **Replace** in the Editing group. Type **CSS** in the **Find what box** and **CSS5** in the **Replace with box**. Click **Replace All** and click **OK**. Click **Close**.

h. Drag to select the *FrontPage, Nvu* text and press **Backspace** on the keyboard to delete the text.

i. Press **Ctrl+End** to place the insertion point at the end of *Templates* and press **Enter**. Type **Database Connectivity** to create a new bulleted item.

j. Click the **FILE tab** and click **Print**. Click the **Full Page Slides arrow** and click **6 Slides Horizontal** to see a preview of all of the slides as a handout. Click the **Back arrow** and click the **HOME tab**.

k. Click **Slide 1** in the Slides pane to move to the beginning of the presentation.

l. Drag the **Zoom slider** on the status bar to the right to **130%** to magnify the text. Then use the **Zoom Slider** to return to **60%**.

m. Save and close the file. Submit your files based on your instructor's directions.

2 Upscale Bakery

You have always been interested in baking and have worked in the field for several years. You now have an opportunity to devote yourself full time to your career as the CEO of a company dedicated to baking cupcakes, pastries, and catering. One of the first steps in getting the business off the ground is developing a business plan so that you can request financial support. You will use Word to develop your business plan. This exercise follows the same set of skills as used in Hands-On Exercises 1, 3, 4, and 5 in the chapter. Refer to Figure 1.60 as you complete this exercise.

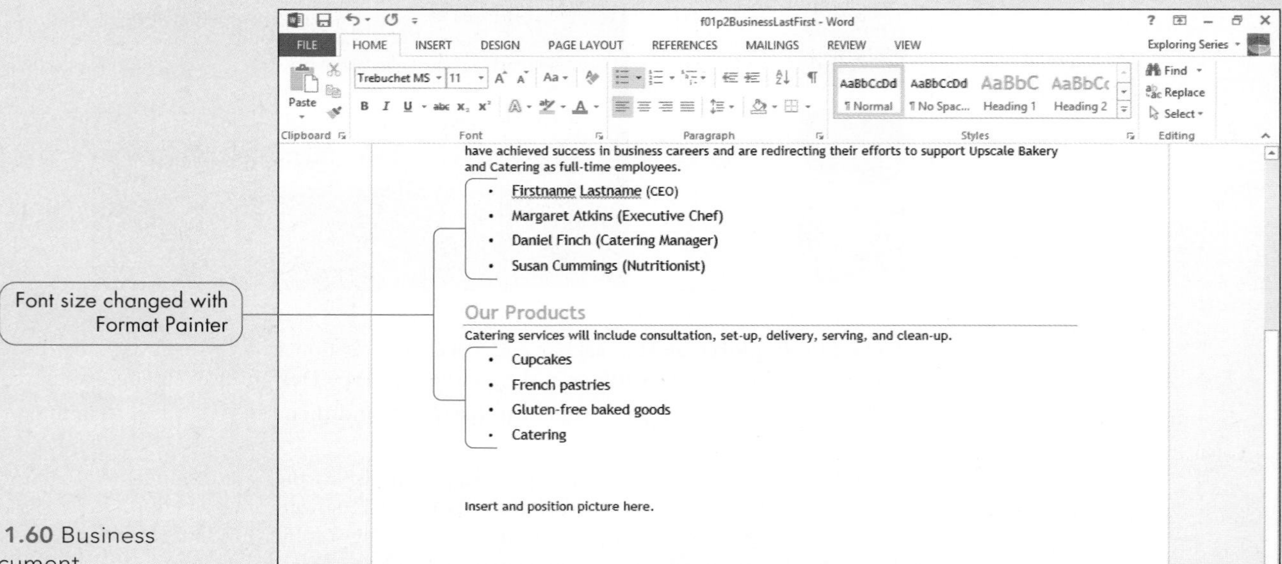

FIGURE 1.60 Business Plan Document

a. Click **File Explorer** on the taskbar and select the location where you save your files. Click the **HOME tab** and click **New folder** in the New group. Type **Business Plan** and press **Enter**.

   Take a snip, name it **f01p2BusinessSnip_LastFirst**, and save it in the Business Plan folder. Close File Explorer.

b. Point to the bottom-right corner of your screen to display the Charms and click the **Start charm**. Scroll if necessary and click **Word 2013** to start Word. Open *f01p2Business* and save it as **f01p2Business_LastFirst** in the Business Plan folder.

c. Click the **REVIEW tab** and click **Spelling & Grammar** in the Proofing group. Click **Change** for all suggestions.

d. Drag the paragraphs beginning with *Our Staff* and ending with *(Nutritionist)*. Click the **HOME tab** and click **Cut** in the Clipboard group. Click to the left of *Our Products* and click **Paste**.

e. Select the text *Your name* in the first bullet and replace it with your first and last names. Select that entire bullet and use the Mini toolbar to use Live Preview to see some other Font sizes. Then click **11** to increase the size.

f. Double-click the **Format Painter** in the Clipboard group on the HOME tab. Drag the Format Painter to change the other *Our Staff* bullets to **11**. Drag all four *Our Products* bullets. Click the **Format Painter button** to toggle it off and click outside of the text to deselect it. Refer to Figure 1.60.

g. Select the last line in the document, which says *Insert and position picture here.*, and press **Delete**. Click the **INSERT tab** and click **Online Pictures** in the Illustrations group.

- Click in the **Office.com Clip Art search box**, type **Cupcakes**, and then press **Enter**.
- Select **Cupcake with a single birthday candle** or select any image and click **Insert**. Do not deselect the image.
- Click the **PICTURE TOOLS FORMAT tab**, if necessary, click the **More button** in the Picture Styles group, and then click the **Soft Edge Rectangle** (sixth from the left on the top row).
- Click outside the picture.

h. Click the **FILE tab** and click **Print**. Change *Normal Margins* to **Moderate Margins**. Click the **Back arrow**.

i. Click the picture and click **Center** in the Paragraph group on the HOME tab.

j. Save and close the file. Submit your files based on your instructor's directions.

3 Best Friends Pet Care

You and a friend are starting a pet sitting service and have a few clients already. Billing will be a large part of your record keeping, so you are planning ahead by developing a series of folders to maintain those records. This exercise follows the same set of skills as used in Hands-On Exercises 1, 2, and 5 in the chapter. Refer to Figure 1.61 as you complete this exercise.

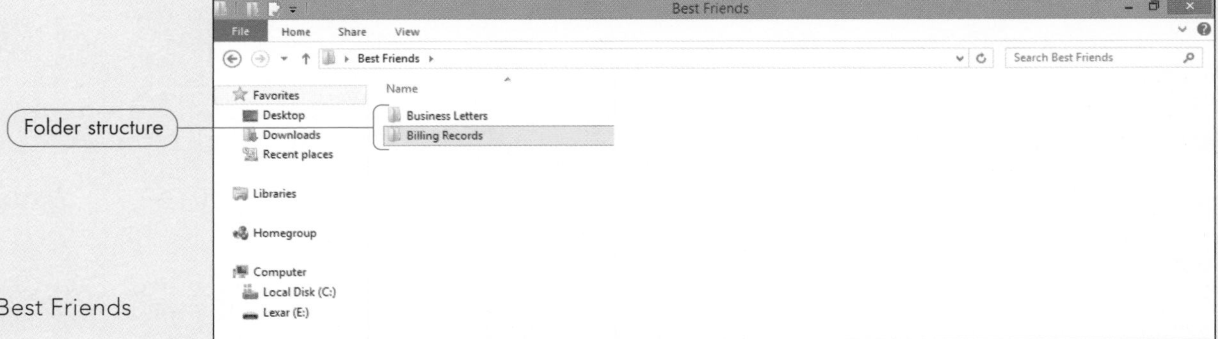

FIGURE 1.61 Best Friends Pet Care

a. Click **File Explorer** on the taskbar and select the location where you save your files. Click the **Home tab** and click **New folder** in the New group. Type **Best Friends** and press **Enter**.

b. Double-click **Best Friends** in the Content pane to open the folder. Create new subfolders as follows:

- Click the **Home tab** and click **New folder** in the New group. Type **Business Letters** and press **Enter**.
- Click the **Home tab** and click **New folder** in the New group. Type **Billing Records** and press **Enter**. Compare your results to Figure 1.61. Take a snip and name it **f01p3FriendsSnip_LastFirst**. Save it in the Billing Records subfolder of the Best Friends folder. Close File Explorer.

c. Navigate to the Start screen and click on **Word 2013**. Click **Open Other Documents** and open *f01p3Friends*. Save it as **f01p3Friends_LastFirst** in the Business Letters subfolder of the Best Friends folder.

d. Use *Find and Replace* to replace the text *Your Name* with your name by doing the following:

- Click **Replace** in the Editing group on the HOME tab.
- Type **Your name** in the **Find what box**. Type your first and last names in the **Replace with box**.
- Click **Replace** and click **OK**. Close the *Find and Replace* dialog box. Close, save changes to the document, and exit Word.

e. Click **File Explorer** on the taskbar so that you can rename one of your folders:

- Click **Computer** in the Navigation Pane.
- In the Content pane, navigate to the drive where you earlier created the Best Friends folder. Double-click the **Best Friends folder**.
- Right-click **Billing Records**, click **Rename**, type **Accounting Records**, and then press **Enter**.

f. Take a snip and name it **f01p3FolderSnip_LastFirst**. Save it in the Business Letters subfolder of the Best Friends folder. Submit your files based on your instructor's directions.

Mid-Level Exercises

1 Reference Letter

You are an instructor at a local community college. A student has asked you to provide her with a letter of reference for a job application. You have used Word to prepare the letter, but now you need to make a few changes before it is finalized.

a. Open File Explorer. Create a new folder named **References** in the location where you are saving your student files. Take a snip, name it **f01m1ReferencesSnip_LastFirst**, and save it in the References folder. Close File Explorer.
b. Start Word. Open *f01m1Letter* and save it in the References folder as **f01m1Letter_LastFirst**.
c. Select the date and point to several font sizes in the Mini toolbar. Use the Live Preview to compare them. Click **11**.
d. Double-click the date and use the **Format Painter** to change the rest of the letter to font size 11.
e. Apply bold to the student's name, *Stacy VanPatten*, in the first sentence.
f. Correct all errors using Spelling & Grammar. Her last name is spelled correctly. Use the Thesaurus to find a synonym for *intelligent* and replace wih **gifted**. Change the *an* to *a* just before the new word. Replace each occurrence of *Stacy* with **Stacey**.
g. Move the last paragraph—beginning with *In my opinion*—to position it before the second paragraph—beginning with *Stacey is a gifted*.
h. Move the insertion point to the beginning of the document.
i. Change the margins to **Narrow**.
j. Preview the document as it will appear when printed.
k. Save and close the file. Submit your files based on your instructor's directions.

2 Medical Monitoring

You are enrolled in a Health Informatics program of study in which you learn to manage databases related to health fields. For a class project, your instructor requires that you monitor your blood pressure, recording your findings in an Excel worksheet. You have recorded the week's data and will now make a few changes before printing the worksheet for submission.

a. Open File Explorer. Create a new folder named **Medical** in the location where you are saving your student files. Take a snip, name it **f01m2MedicalSnip_LastFirst**, and save it in the Medical folder. Close File Explorer.
b. Start Excel. Open *f01m2Tracker* and save it as **f01m2Tracker_LastFirst** in the Medical folder.
c. Preview the worksheet as it will appear when printed. Change the orientation of the worksheet to **Landscape**. Preview the worksheet again.
d. Click in the cell to the right of *Name* and type your first and last names. Press **Enter**.
e. Change the font of the text in **cell C1** to **Verdana**. Use Live Preview to try some font sizes. Change the font size to **20**.
f. Check the spelling for the worksheet.

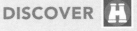

g. Get help on showing decimal places. You want to increase the decimal places for the values in **cells E22**, **F22**, and **G22** so that each value shows two places to the right of the decimal. Use Excel Help to learn how to do that. You might use *Increase Decimals* as a Search term. When you find the answer, select the three cells and increase the decimal places to **2**.
h. Click **cell A1** and insert a picture of your choice related to blood pressure. Be sure the image includes content from Office.com. Resize and position the picture so that it displays in an attractive manner. Format the picture with **Soft Edges** set to **4 pt**. Change the margins to **Wide**.
i. Open the Backstage view and adjust print settings to print two copies. You will not actually print two copies unless directed by your instructor.
j. Save and close the file. Submit your files based on your instructor's directions.

3 Today's Musical Artists

COLLABORATION CASE 

CREATIVE CASE  ★

With a few of your classmates, you will use PowerPoint to create a single presentation on your favorite musical artists. Each student must create at least one slide and then all of the slides will be added to the presentation. Because everyone's schedule is varied, you should use either your Outlook account or OneDrive to pass the presentation file among the group.

a. Open File Explorer. Create a new folder named **Musical** in the location where you are saving your student files. Take a snip, name it **f01m3MusicalSnip_LastFirst**, and then save it in the Musical folder. Close File Explorer.

b. Start PowerPoint. Create a new presentation and save it as **f01m3Music_GroupName** in the Musical folder.

c. Add one slide that contains the name of the artist, the genre, and two or three interesting facts about the artist.

d. Insert a picture of the artist or clip art that represents the artist.

e. Put your name on the slide that you created. Save the presentation.

f. Pass the presentation to the next student so that he or she can perform the same tasks and save the presentation before passing it on to the next student. Continue until all group members have created a slide in the presentation.

g. Save and close the file. Submit your file based on your instructor's directions.

Beyond the Classroom

Fitness Planner

RESEARCH CASE 

You will use Microsoft Excel to develop a fitness planner. Open *f01b2Exercise* and save it as **f01b2Exercise_LastFirst**. Because the fitness planner is a template, the exercise categories are listed, but without actual data. You will personalize the planner. Change the orientation to **Landscape**. Move the contents of **cell A2** (*Exercise Planner*) to **cell A1**. Click **cell A8** and use the Format Painter to copy the format of that selection to **cells A5** and **A6**. Increase the font size of **cell A1** to **26**. Use Excel Help to learn how to insert a header and put your name in the header. Begin the fitness planner, entering at least one activity in each category (warm-up, aerobics, strength, and cool-down). Submit as directed by your instructor.

Household Records

DISASTER RECOVERY 

FROM SCRATCH

Use Microsoft Excel to create a detailed record of your household appliances and other items of value that are in your home. In case of burglary or disaster, an insurance claim is expedited if you are able to itemize what was lost along with identifying information such as serial numbers. You will then make a copy of the record on another storage device for safekeeping outside your home (in case your home is destroyed by a fire or weather-related catastrophe). Connect a flash drive to your computer and then use File Explorer to create a folder on the hard drive titled **Home Records**. Design a worksheet listing at least five fictional appliances and electronic equipment along with the serial number of each. Save the workbook as **f01b3Household_LastFirst** in the Home Records folder. Close the workbook and exit Excel. Use File Explorer to copy the Home Records folder from the hard drive to your flash drive. Use the Snipping Tool to create a full-screen snip of the screen display. Save it as **f01b3Disaster_LastFirst** in the Home Records folder. Close all open windows and submit as directed by your instructor.

Meetings

SOFT SKILLS CASE 

FROM SCRATCH

After watching the Meetings video, you will use File Explorer to create a series of folders and subfolders to organize meetings by date. Each folder should be named by month, day, and year. Three subfolders should be created for each meeting. The subfolders should be named **Agenda**, **Handouts**, and **Meeting Notes**. Use the Snipping Tool to create a full-screen snip of the screen display. Save it as **f01b4Meetings_LastFirst**. Submit as directed by your instructor.

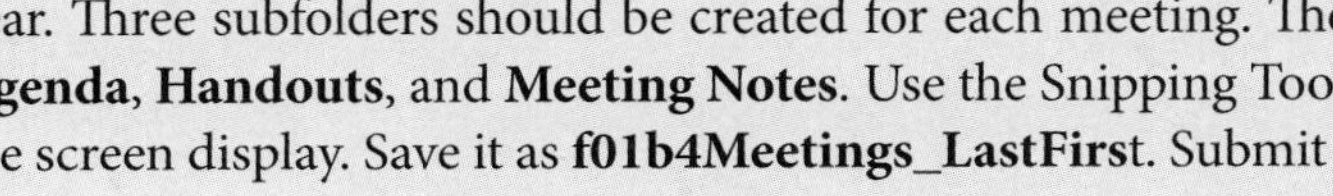

Capstone Exercise

MyITLab® Grader

You are a member of the Student Government Association (SGA) at your college. As a community project, the SGA is sponsoring a Stop Smoking drive designed to provide information on the health risks posed by smoking cigarettes and to offer solutions to those who want to quit. The SGA has partnered with the local branch of the American Cancer Society as well as the outreach program of the local hospital to sponsor free educational awareness seminars. As the secretary for the SGA, you will help prepare a PowerPoint presentation that will be displayed on plasma screens around campus and used in student seminars. You will use Microsoft Office to help with those tasks.

Manage Files and Folders

You will open, review, and save an Excel worksheet providing data on the personal monetary cost of smoking cigarettes over a period of years.

a. Create a folder called **SGA Drive**.

b. Start Excel. Open *f01c1Cost* from the student data files and save it in the SGA Drive folder as **f01c1Cost_LastFirst**.

c. Click **cell A10** and type your first and last names. Press **Enter**.

Modify the Font

To highlight some key figures on the worksheet, you will format those cells with additional font attributes.

a. Draw attention to the high cost of smoking for 10, 20, and 30 years by changing the font color in **cells G3 through I4** to **Red**.

b. Italicize the Annual Cost cells (**F3 and F4**).

c. Click **Undo** on the Quick Access Toolbar to remove the italics. Click **Redo** to return the text to italics.

Insert a Picture

You will add a picture to the worksheet and then resize it and position it.

a. Click **cell G7** and insert an online picture appropriate for the topic of smoking.

b. Resize the picture and reposition it near cell B7.

c. Click outside the picture to deselect it.

Preview Print, Change Page Layout, and Print

To get an idea of how the worksheet will look when printed, you will preview the worksheet. Then you will change the orientation and margins before printing it.

a. Preview the document as it will appear when printed.

b. Change the page orientation to **Landscape**. Click the **PAGE LAYOUT tab** and change the margins to **Narrow**.

c. Preview the document as it will appear when printed.

d. Adjust the print settings to print two copies. You will not actually print two copies unless directed by your instructor.

e. Save and close the file.

Find and Replace

You have developed a PowerPoint presentation that you will use to present to student groups and for display on plasma screens across campus. The presentation is designed to increase awareness of the health problems associated with smoking. The PowerPoint presentation has come back from the reviewers with only one comment: A reviewer suggested that you spell out Centers for Disease Control and Prevention, instead of abbreviating it. You do not remember exactly which slide or slides the abbreviation might have been on, so you use *Find and Replace* to make the change quickly.

a. Start PowerPoint. Open *f01c1Quit* and save it in the SGA Drive folder as **f01c1Quit_LastFirst**.

b. Replace all occurrences of *CDC* with **Centers for Disease Control and Prevention**.

Cut and Paste and Insert a Text Box

The Mark Twain quote on Slide 1 might be more effective on the last slide in the presentation, so you will cut and paste it there in a text box.

a. On Slide 1, select the entire Mark Twain quote by clicking on the placeholder border. When the border is solid, the entire placeholder and its contents are selected.

b. On Slide 22, paste the quote, reposition it more attractively, and then format it in a larger font size.

Check Spelling and Change View

Before you call the presentation complete, you will spell check it and view it as a slide show.

a. Check spelling. The word *hairlike* is not misspelled, so it should not be corrected.

b. View the slide show and take the smoking quiz. Click after the last slide to return to the presentation.

c. Save and close the presentation. Exit PowerPoint. Submit both files included in this project as directed by your instructor.

Word

Introduction to Word

CHAPTER 1

Organizing a Document

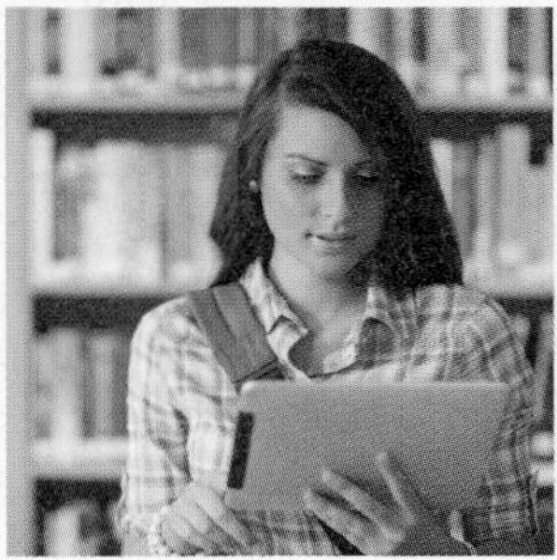

OBJECTIVES AFTER YOU READ THIS CHAPTER, YOU WILL BE ABLE TO:

1. Begin and edit a document p. 139
2. Customize Word p. 148
3. Use features that improve readability p. 157
4. View a document in different ways p. 162
5. Prepare a document for distribution p. 174
6. Modify document properties p. 178

CASE STUDY | Swan Creek National Wildlife Refuge

You have always been fascinated with wildlife in its natural habitat. For that reason, you are excited to be working with Swan Creek National Wildlife Refuge, assigned the task of promoting its educational programs to area schools and preparing documents to support the refuge's educational outreach. The wildlife refuge is situated near a large urban area that is dominated by a thriving industry of steel production. Emily Traynom, Swan Creek's site director, is concerned that children in the city have little opportunity to interact with nature. In fact, many spend their days indoors or on city streets, seldom having an opportunity to enjoy nature. She fears that a generation of children will mature into adults with little appreciation of the role of our country's natural resources in the overall balance of nature. Her passion is encouraging students to visit Swan Creek and become actively involved in environmental activities.

Ms. Traynom envisions summer day camps in which children will explore the wildlife refuge and participate in learning activities. She wants to provide internships for students, encouraging an ongoing relationship with nature. For those efforts and others, you will use your expertise in Microsoft Word to produce documents such as flyers, brochures, memos, contracts, and letters. As the school year draws to a close, Ms. Traynom has asked you to design and produce an article about a series of summer camps available to children from 5th through 8th grades. She has given you a rough draft of the article from which you will create an attractive document for distribution to schools and for posting on Swan Creek's Web site.

Introduction to Word Processing

Word processing software, often called a word processor, is one of the most commonly used types of software in homes, schools, and businesses. People around the world—students, office assistants, managers, and professionals in all areas—use word processing programs such as ***Microsoft Word*** for a variety of tasks. Microsoft Word 2013, included in the Microsoft Office suite of software, is the most current version of the popular word processor. You can create letters, reports, research papers, newsletters, brochures, and all sorts of documents with Word. You can even create and send e-mail, produce Web pages, post to social media sites, and update blogs with Word. Figure 1.1 shows examples of documents created in Word. If a project requires collaboration online or between offices, Word makes it easy to share documents, track changes, view comments, and efficiently produce a document to which several authors can contribute. By using Word to create a research paper, you can easily create citations, a bibliography, a table of contents, a cover page, an index, and other reference pages. To enhance a document, you can change colors, add interesting styles of text, insert graphics, and use tables to present data. With emphasis on saving documents to the cloud, Word enables you to share these documents with others or access them from any device. To say the least, Word is a very comprehensive word processing solution.

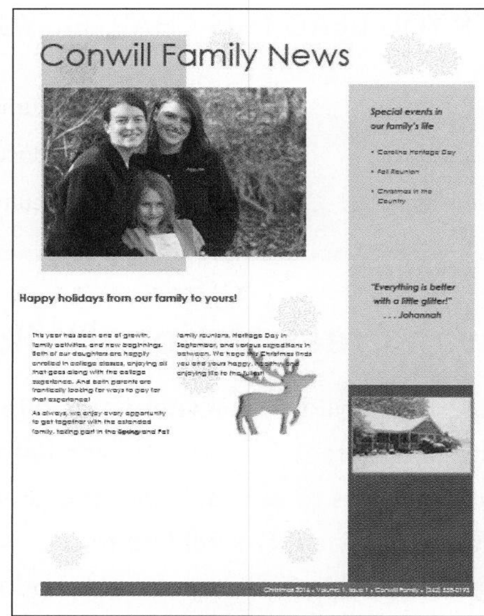

Conwill Family News

Special events in our family's life

- Carolina Heritage Day
- Fall Reunion
- Christmas in the Country

Happy holidays from our family to yours!

This year has been one of growth, family activities, and new beginnings. Both of our daughters are happily enrolled in college classes, enjoying all that goes along with the college experience. And both parents are frantically looking for ways to pay for that experience!

As always, we enjoy every opportunity to get together with the extended family, taking part in the Spring and Fall family reunions, Heritage Day in September, and various expeditions in between. We hope this Christmas finds you and yours happy, healthy and enjoying life to the fullest!

"Everything is better with a little glitter!" . . . Johannah

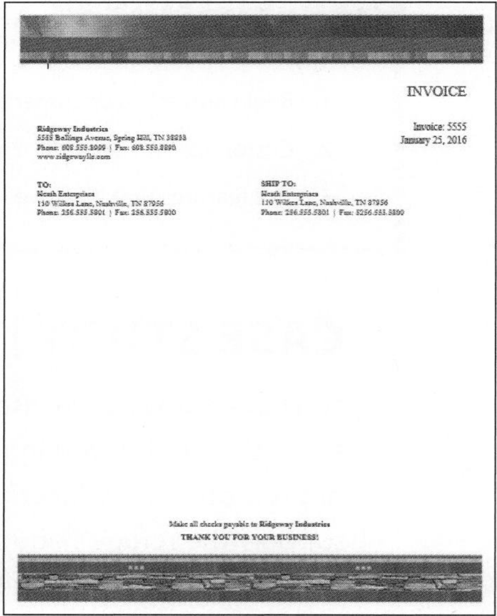

INVOICE

Invoice: 5555
January 25, 2016

Ridgeway Industries
5555 Ballings Avenue, Spring Hill, TN 38238
www.ridgewayllc.com

TO:
Heath Enterprises
110 Wilkes Lane, Nashville, TN 87956

SHIP TO:
Heath Enterprises
110 Wilkes Lane, Nashville, TN 87956

Make all checks payable to Ridgeway Industries
THANK YOU FOR YOUR BUSINESS!

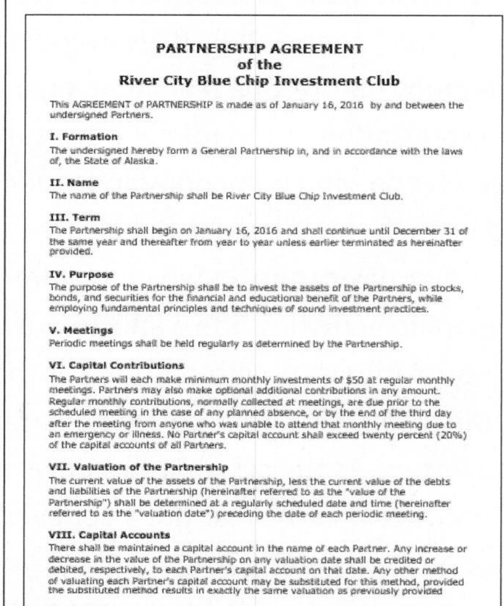

PARTNERSHIP AGREEMENT
of the
River City Blue Chip Investment Club

This AGREEMENT of PARTNERSHIP is made as of January 16, 2016 by and between the undersigned Partners.

I. Formation
The undersigned hereby form a General Partnership in, and in accordance with the laws of, the State of Alaska.

II. Name
The name of the Partnership shall be River City Blue Chip Investment Club.

III. Term
The Partnership shall begin on January 16, 2016 and shall continue until December 31 of the same year and thereafter from year to year unless earlier terminated as hereinafter provided.

IV. Purpose
The purpose of the Partnership shall be to invest the assets of the Partnership in stocks, bonds, and securities for the financial and educational benefit of the Partners, while employing fundamental principles and techniques of sound investment practices.

V. Meetings
Periodic meetings shall be held regularly as determined by the Partnership.

VI. Capital Contributions
The Partners will each make minimum monthly investments of $50 at regular monthly meetings. Partners may also make optional additional contributions in any amount. Regular monthly contributions, normally collected at meetings, are due prior to the scheduled meeting in the case of any planned absence, or by the end of the third day after the meeting from anyone who was unable to attend that monthly meeting due to an emergency or illness. No Partner's capital account shall exceed twenty percent (20%) of the capital accounts of all Partners.

VII. Valuation of the Partnership
The current value of the assets of the Partnership, less the current value of the debts and liabilities of the Partnership (hereinafter referred to as the "value of the Partnership") shall be determined at a regularly scheduled date and time (hereinafter referred to as the "valuation date") preceding the date of each periodic meeting.

VIII. Capital Accounts
There shall be maintained a capital account in the name of each Partner. Any increase or decrease in the value of the Partnership on any valuation date shall be credited or debited, respectively, to each Partner's capital account on that date. Any other method of valuating each Partner's capital account may be substituted for this method, provided the substituted method results in exactly the same valuation as previously provided

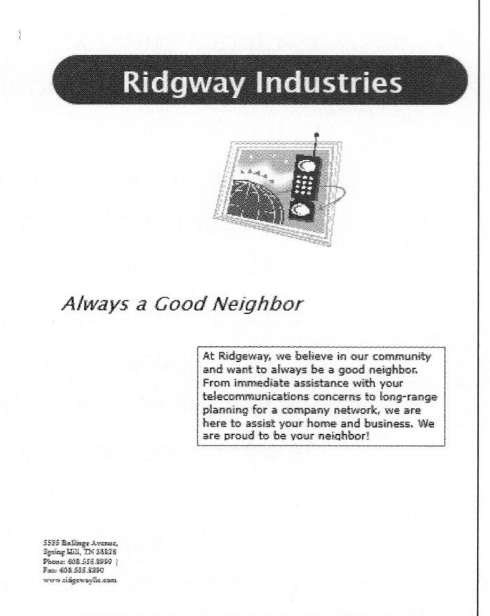

Ridgway Industries

Always a Good Neighbor

At Ridgeway, we believe in our community and want to always be a good neighbor. From immediate assistance with your telecommunications concerns to long-range planning for a company network, we are here to assist your home and business. We are proud to be your neighbor!

www.ridgewayllc.com

FIGURE 1.1 Word Documents

Communicating through the written word is an important task for any business or organization. In fact, it would be almost impossible to conduct business without written and oral communication. Word processing software, such as Word, simplifies the technical task of preparing documents, but a word processor does not replace the writer. Be careful when wording a document so you are sure it is appropriate for the intended audience. Always remember that once you distribute a document, either on paper or electronically, you cannot retract the words. Therefore, you should never send a document that you have not carefully checked several times to be sure it conveys your message in the best way possible. Also, you cannot depend completely on a word processor to identify all spelling and grammatical errors, so be sure to closely proofread every document you create. Although several word processors, including Word, provide predesigned documents (called *templates*) that include basic wording for various tasks, it is ultimately up to you to compose well-worded documents. The role of business communication, including the written word, in the success or failure of a business cannot be overemphasized.

In this section, you will explore Word's interface, learn how to create and save a document, explore the use of templates, and perform basic editing operations. You will learn how to move around in a document and to review spelling and word usage. Using Word options, you will explore ways to customize Word to suit your preferences, and you will learn to customize the Ribbon and the Quick Access Toolbar.

Beginning and Editing a Document

When you open Word 2013, your screen will be similar to Figure 1.2. You can create a blank document, or you can select from several categories of templates. Recently viewed files are shown on the left, for ease of access should you want to open any again.

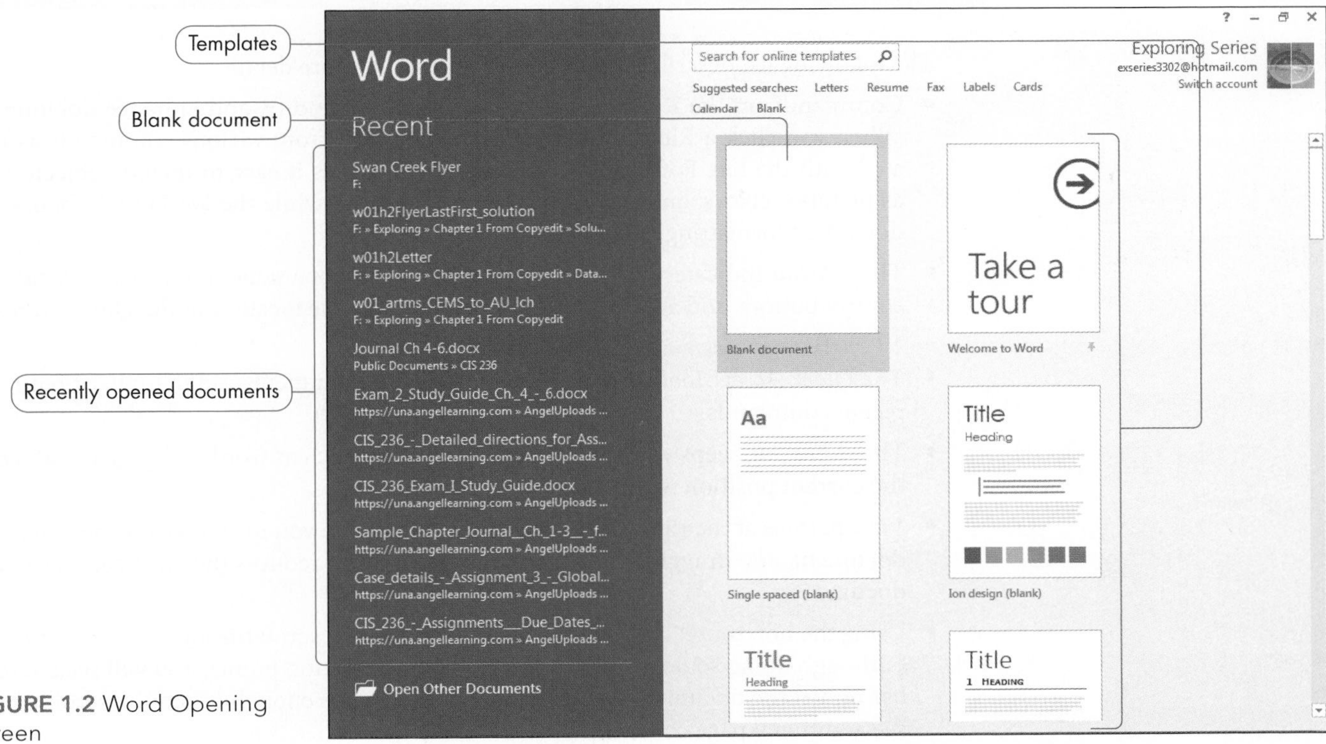

FIGURE 1.2 Word Opening Screen

To begin a blank document, click *Blank document* (or simply press Enter, if *Blank document* is selected). Word provides a clean, uncluttered area in which to type, with minimal distraction at the sides and across the top. Unlike earlier Word versions, Word 2013 provides a large, almost borderless area for your document, with an interface closely aligned with that of Windows 8.1.1. Using several basic features, including the Ribbon, Quick Access Toolbar, vertical and horizontal scroll bars, and the status bar, you can easily create an attractive document. Figure 1.3 shows a typical Word document.

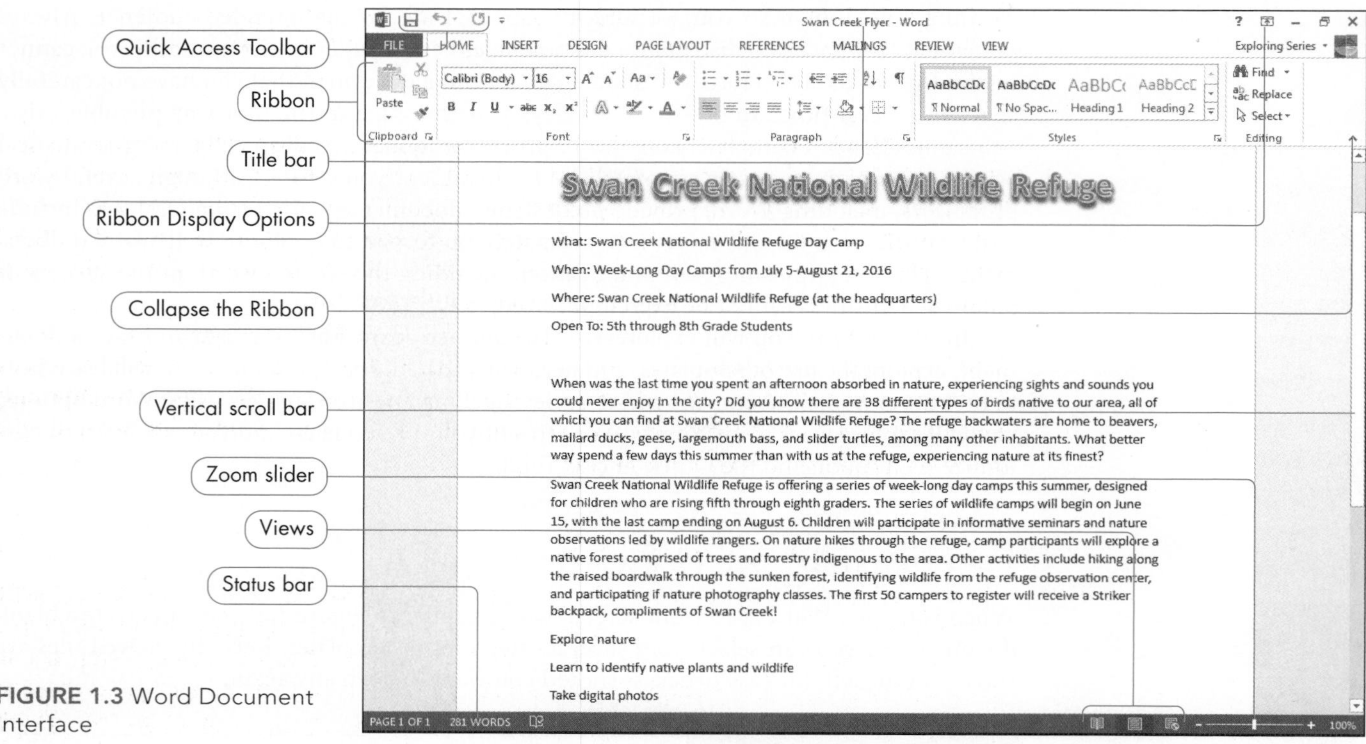

FIGURE 1.3 Word Document Interface

The following list describes Word's basic features in more detail:

- Commands on the ***Ribbon*** enable you to create, modify, and enhance documents. When you click a Ribbon tab, you can then select from various commands associated with the tab. For example, the Insert tab makes it easy to include objects such as pictures, charts, and screenshots in a document, while the Design tab focuses on document formatting and color selections.
- The *title bar* indicates the file name of the current document and includes Windows control buttons and access to Word Help. It is also the location of the Quick Access Toolbar.
- The *Quick Access Toolbar* makes it easy to save a document, and to undo or redo recent commands.
- The *status bar* keeps you apprised of information such as word and page count, and the current position within the document.
- *View buttons* at the right side of the status bar enable you to change the view of a document, and dragging the *Zoom slider* enlarges or reduces the onscreen size of a document.
- Using the horizontal and vertical *scroll bars*, you can scroll through a document (although doing so does not actually move the insertion point). You will see a scroll bar only if the document is long enough and/or wide enough to require scrolling to see additional page content.

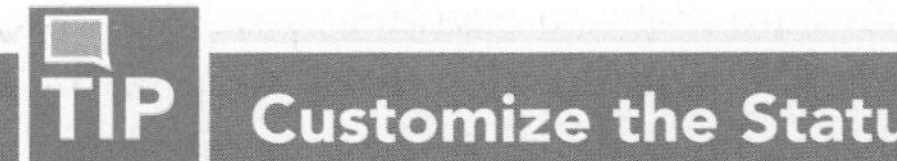

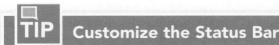

TIP Customize the Status Bar

You can customize the status bar to include even more items of information. Simply right-click an empty area of the status bar and select one or more items from the list.

Many people enjoy having the Ribbon close at hand when developing or editing a document. Others might prefer an uncluttered workspace, free of distractions. Temporarily remove the Ribbon from view by clicking *Collapse the Ribbon* (see Figure 1.3). Tabs remain displayed, but all detail beneath them is hidden, resulting in a large amount of uncluttered typing space. To display the Ribbon again, click any tab and click *Pin the ribbon* (the toggle of *Collapse the Ribbon*) or simply double-click a tab on the Ribbon.

Ribbon Display Options (Figure 1.3) enables you to adjust the Ribbon view. You can choose to hide the Ribbon, providing a clear document space in which to edit or read a document. Click at the top of the Ribbon to show it again. You can also choose to show only the Ribbon tabs. Click a tab to display its options. Finally, you can choose to show all Ribbon tabs and commands, which is the default.

Use a Template

STEP 2» Wording a document can be difficult, especially if you are struck with writer's block! With that in mind, the developers of Word have included a library of ***templates*** from which you can select a predesigned document. You can then modify the document to suit your needs. Categories of templates are displayed when you first open Word, or when you click the File tab and click New. In addition to local templates—those that are available offline with a typical Word installation—Microsoft provides many more through Office.com. All of those templates are displayed or searchable within Word, as shown in Figure 1.4. Microsoft continually updates content in the template library, so you are assured of having access to all the latest templates each time you open Word.

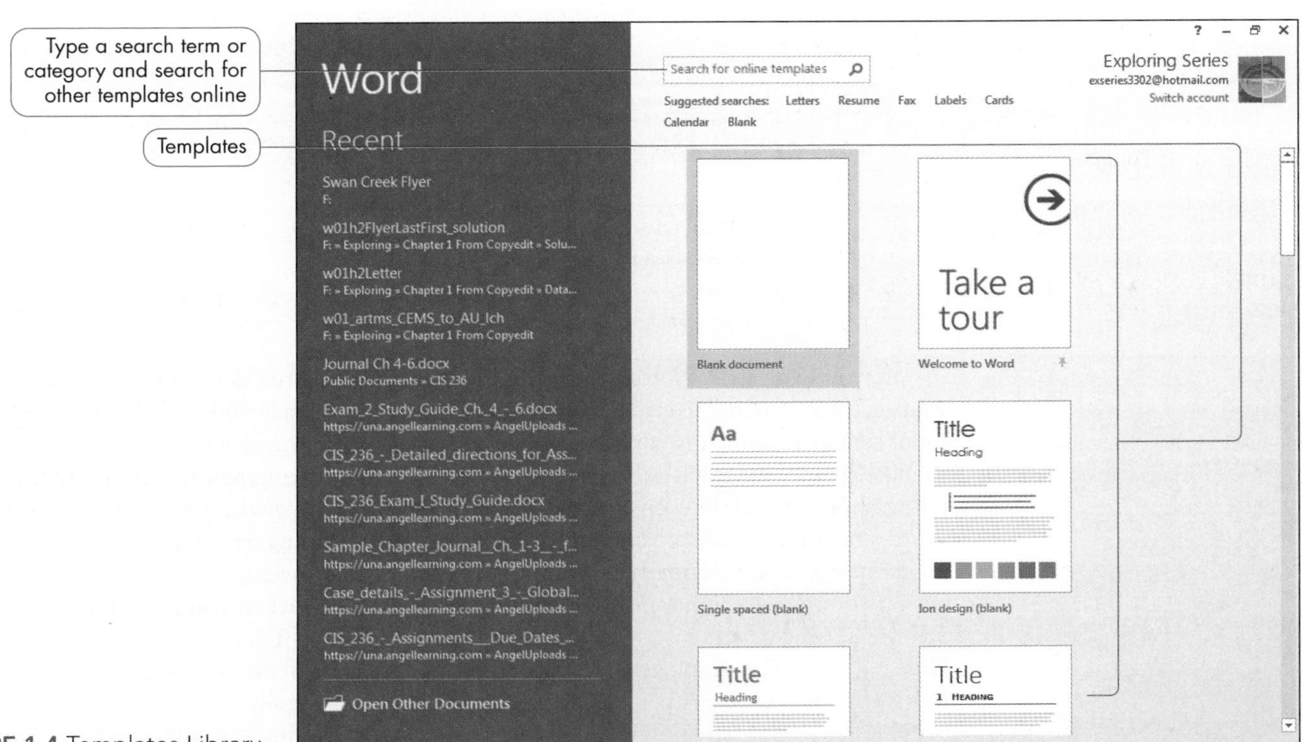

FIGURE 1.4 Templates Library

Some templates are likely to become your favorites. Because you will want quick access to those templates, you can pin them to the top of the templates menu so they will always be available. Simply right-click a favorite template and click *Pin to list*. To unpin a previously pinned template, repeat the process but select *Unpin from list*.

Create a Document

STEP 1

To create a blank document, click *Blank document* when Word opens (refer to Figure 1.2). As you type text, you will not need to think about how much text can fit on one line or how sentences progress from one line to the next. Word's ***word wrap*** feature automatically pushes words to the next line when you reach the right margin.

Word wrap is closely associated with another concept: the hard return and soft return. A *hard return* is created when you press Enter at the end of a line or paragraph. A *soft return* is created by Word as it wraps text from one line to the next. The locations of soft returns change automatically as text is inserted or deleted, or as page features or settings, such as objects or margins, are added or changed. Soft returns are not considered characters and cannot be deleted. However, a hard return is actually a nonprinting character, called a *paragraph mark*, that you can delete, if necessary. To display nonprinting characters, such as paragraph marks and tabs, click Show/Hide (¶) (see Figure 1.5). Just as you delete any other character by pressing Backspace or Delete (depending on whether the insertion point is positioned to the right or left of the item to remove), you can delete a paragraph mark. To remove the display of nonprinting characters, click Show/Hide (¶) again.

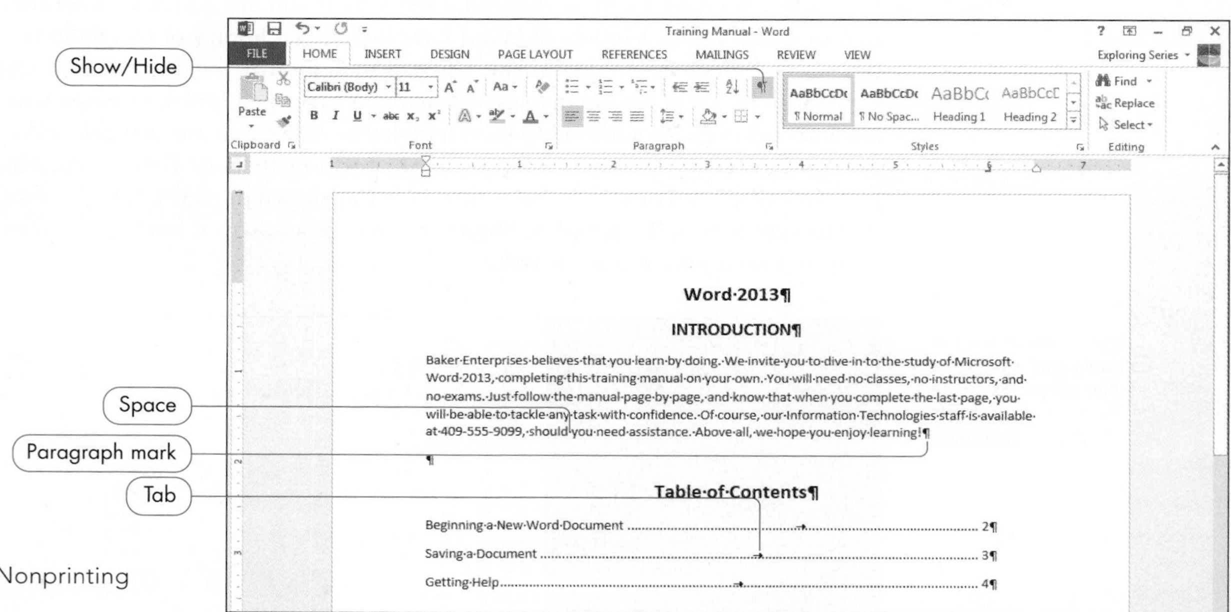

FIGURE 1.5 Nonprinting Characters

As you work with Word, you must understand that Word's definition of a paragraph and your definition are not likely to be the same. You would probably define a paragraph as a related set of sentences, which is correct in a literary sense. When the subject or direction of thought changes, a new paragraph begins. However, Word defines a paragraph as text that ends in a hard return. Even a blank line, created by pressing Enter, is considered a paragraph. Therefore, as a Word student, you will consider every line that ends in a hard return a paragraph. When you press Enter, a paragraph mark is displayed in the document (refer to Figure 1.5).

In addition to the nonprinting mark that Word inserts when you press Enter, other nonprinting characters are inserted when you press keys such as Tab or the Spacebar. Click Show/Hide (¶) in the Paragraph group on the Home tab to reveal all nonprinting characters in a document (refer to Figure 1.5). Nonprinting characters are generally not viewed when working in a document and will not be included when a document is printed, but they can assist you with troubleshooting a document and modifying its appearance before printing or distributing. For example, if lines in a document end awkwardly, some not even extending to the right margin, you can click Show/Hide (¶) to display nonprinting characters and check for the presence of poorly placed, or perhaps unnecessary, hard returns. Deleting the hard returns might realign the document so that lines end in better fashion.

Reuse Text

You might find occasion to reuse text from a previously created document because the wording fits well in a document on which you are working. For example, a memo to employees describing new insurance benefits might borrow wording from another document describing the same benefits to company retirees. In that case, you would simply insert text from a saved document into the currently open memo. With the insertion point positioned where the inserted text is to be placed, complete the following steps:

1. Click the INSERT tab.
2. Click the Object arrow (see Figure 1.6).
3. Click *Text from File.*
4. Navigate to the location of the saved document and double-click the file name.

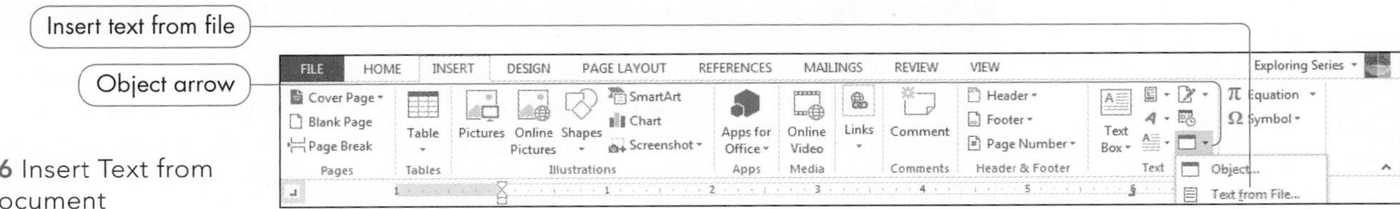

FIGURE 1.6 Insert Text from Another Document

Save a Document

Saving a document makes it possible for you to access it later for editing, sharing, or printing. In fact, it is a good idea not to wait until a document is complete to save it, but to save a document periodically as you develop it. That way, you risk losing only what you created or edited since the last save operation if you experience a disruption of power. If you have ever worked with a word processor, you are probably familiar with the process of saving a document. Word 2013 recognizes not only the need to save files, but also the need to make them available on any device you might have access to and the need to share documents with others so you can collaborate on projects. To make that possible, Word encourages you to save documents to the cloud, or Internet, instead of a local drive, such as a hard drive or flash drive. It is always a good idea, however, to save a document in several places so that you always have a backup copy. You might save a document to a hard drive as well as OneDrive, which is free online storage space provided by Microsoft. If you plan to use the document on another computer, you could also save it to a flash drive for ease of transporting. To save a document, click the File tab and click Save (or Save As). You can also click Save on the Quick Access Toolbar.

If you are using Windows 8.1.1 as your operating system, you most likely provided a Windows Live ID, or e-mail address, when you installed the operating system. In that case, the address connects to your associated OneDrive storage and enables Word, and other Microsoft programs, to save files in that location by default. (A default setting is one that is automatically set unless you specify otherwise.) If you choose to share documents from your OneDrive storage, collaborators can easily access and edit them.

As you save a file, Word enables you to select a location to save to. Although OneDrive is the default, you can select another drive on your computer (see Figure 1.7).

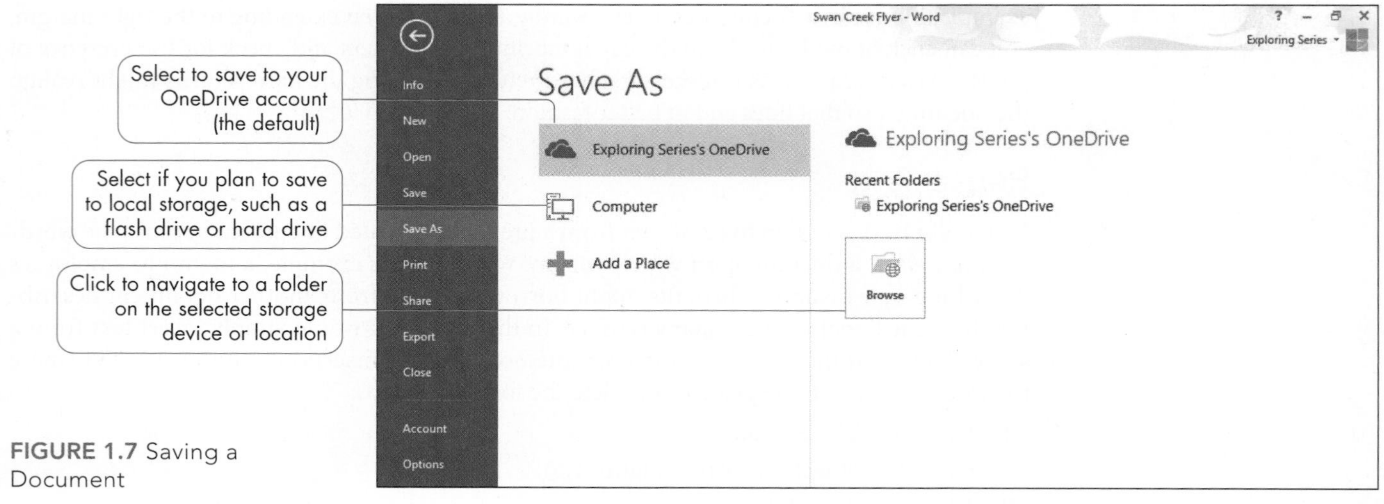

FIGURE 1.7 Saving a Document

Remember to save files often. If you open a document and plan to save it with the same file name and in the same location from which it was opened, click Save on the Quick Access Toolbar. You can also click the File tab and click Save. Otherwise, click the File tab and click Save As to change either the save location or the file name.

To save a document to local storage, such as a flash drive, hard drive, or local network location, click Computer (refer to Figure 1.7) and click Browse to navigate to the desired location. Provide a file name and either accept the default type (Word Document) or click the *Save as type* arrow (see Figure 1.8) and select another format. Users of Word 2007 and Word 2010 will be able to open a document saved in Word 2013 format, but some Word 2013 features might be disabled. However, if you plan to distribute a document to someone using a Word version earlier than Word 2007, change the type to Word 97-2003 Document. You will learn more about file compatibility later in this chapter.

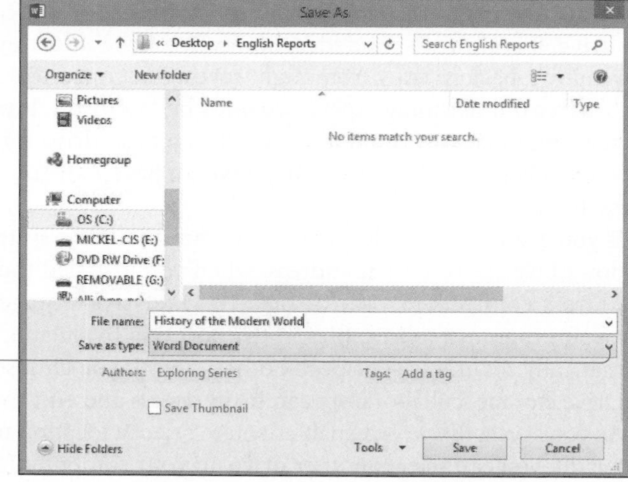

FIGURE 1.8 Changing File Type

Open a Document

STEP 3» Having saved a document, you can open it later when you start Word and then either select the document from the Recent list or click Open Other Documents and navigate to the saved file. Word remembers the position of the insertion point when you previously saved the file and suggests that you return to that same location (see Figure 1.9). Just click the link to return, or ignore it if you prefer the current display.

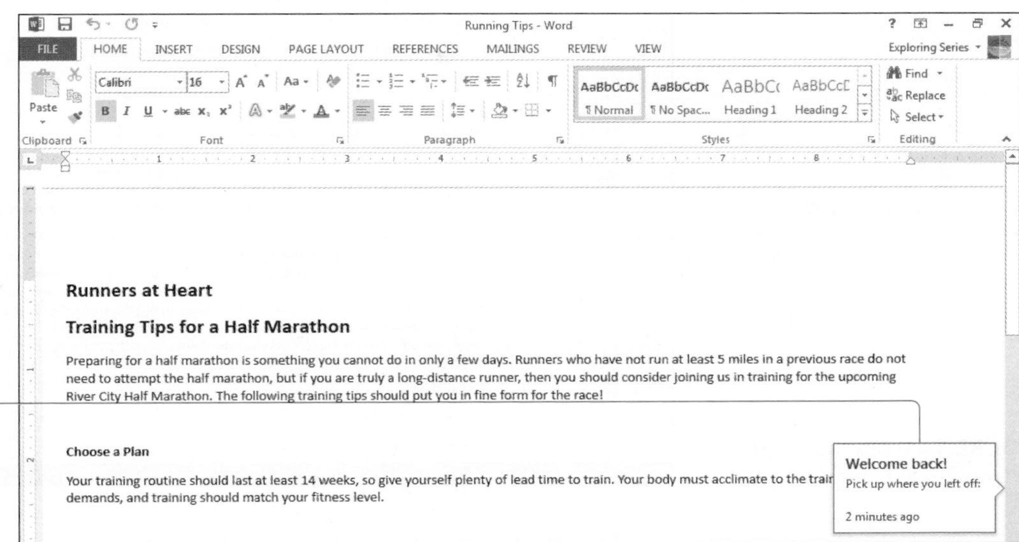

FIGURE 1.9 Opening a Previously Viewed Document

Move Around a Document and Edit a Document

The ***insertion point*** indicates where the text you type will be inserted. It is important to remain aware of the location of the insertion point and to know how to move it so that you can control where text is typed. Probably the easiest way to move the insertion point within a document is to simply click in the desired location. When you reposition the insertion point within existing text in a document and then type text, the text is inserted between pieces of existing text.

If a document contains more text than will display onscreen at one time, you can click the horizontal or vertical scroll arrows (or drag a scroll bar) to view different parts of the document. Then, when the desired text is shown onscreen, click to position the insertion point and continue editing the document. Be aware that using the scroll bar or scroll arrows to move the display does not reposition the insertion point. It merely lets you see different parts of the document, leaving the insertion point where it was last positioned. Only when you click in the document, or use a keyboard shortcut, is the insertion point moved.

Review Word Usage in a Document

It is important to create a document that is free of typographical and grammatical errors. One of the easiest ways to lose credibility with readers is to allow such errors to occur. You will also want to choose words that are appropriate and that best convey your intentions in writing or editing a document. Word provides tools on the Review tab that simplify the tasks of reviewing a document for errors, identifying proper wording, and defining words with which you are unfamiliar.

With the automated spelling and grammar tools in Word, it is relatively easy to produce an error-free document. A word that is considered by Word to be misspelled is underlined with a red wavy line. A possible grammatical mistake or word usage error is underlined in blue. Both types of errors are shown in Figure 1.10. Never depend completely on Word to catch all errors; always proofread a document yourself. For example, typing the word *fee* when you meant to type *free* is not an error that Word would typically catch, because the word is not actually misspelled and might not be flagged as a word usage error, depending upon the sentence context.

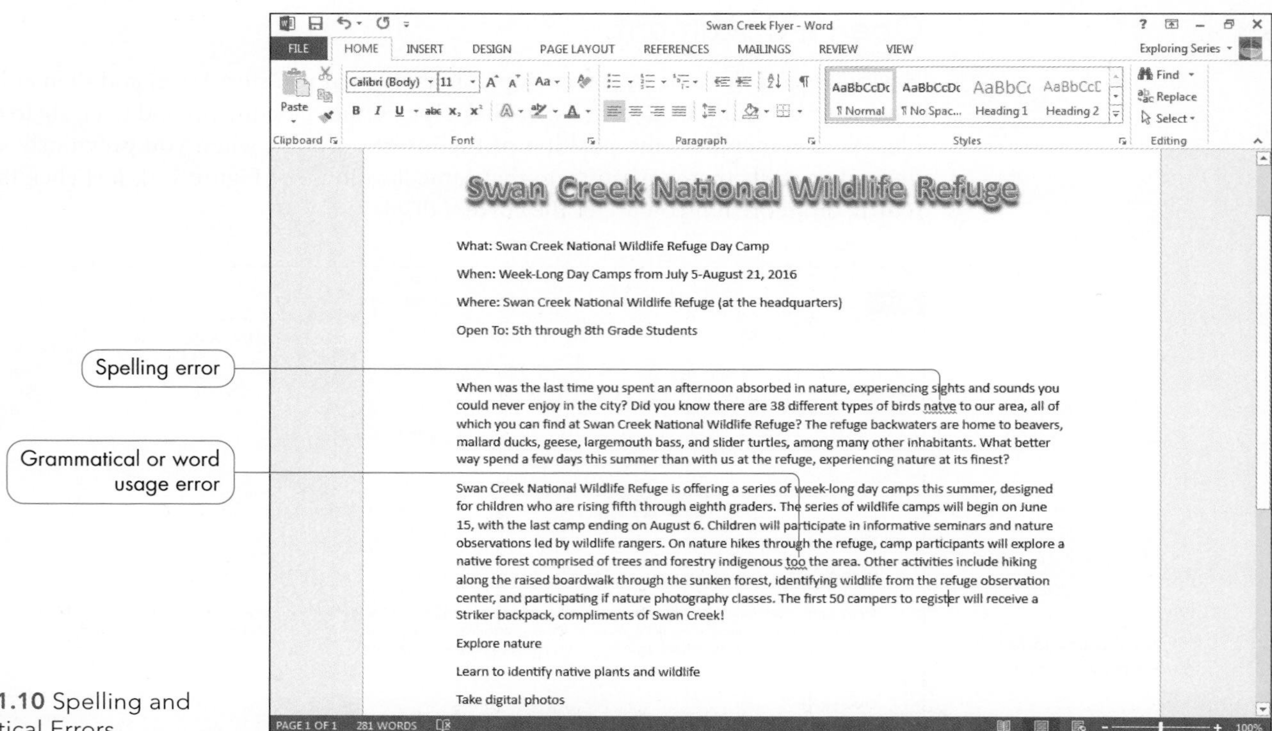

FIGURE 1.10 Spelling and Grammatical Errors

To correct possible spelling, grammatical, or word usage errors in a document, you can right-click an underlined error and select an option from a shortcut menu. If possible, Word will attempt to provide a correction that you can select from the menu. If the word or text is not actually an error, you can choose to ignore it by making an appropriate selection from the shortcut menu.

STEP 4» Correcting each error by right-clicking can become time-consuming, especially if the mistakes are many. In that case, Word can check an entire document, pausing at each identified error so that you can determine whether to correct or ignore the problem. To check an entire document, click the Review tab and click Spelling & Grammar in the Proofing group (see Figure 1.11). For even quicker error identification, check the Proofing errors button on the status bar (see Figure 1.11). By default, Word will automatically check an entire open document for spelling, grammatical, and word usage errors, displaying an *X* on the Proofing errors button if errors are found. Click the button to either change or ignore all errors, one at a time. If, instead, you see a check mark on the Proofing errors button, the document appears to be error free. The document in Figure 1.11 contains errors, as indicated by the *X* on the Proofing errors button. Note that at a higher screen resolution than that shown in Figure 1.11, buttons in the Proofing group will be spelled out (Thesaurus, Define, and Word Count).

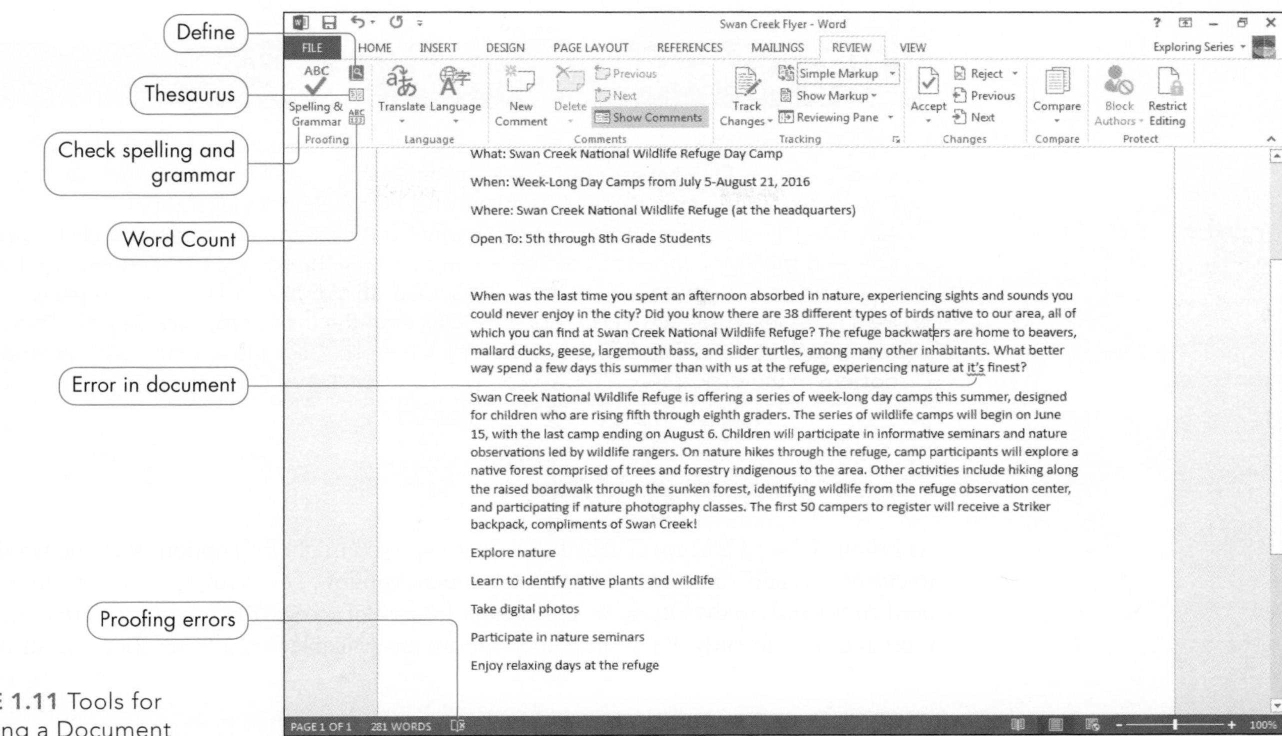

FIGURE 1.11 Tools for Reviewing a Document

Words do not always come easily. Occasionally, you might need to find a synonym (a word with the same meaning as another) for a particular word but are unable to do so quickly. Word provides a handy ***thesaurus*** for just such an occasion. Select a word in a document and click the Review tab. Click Thesaurus (refer to Figure 1.11) and select from a group of synonyms. If you have installed a dictionary, you will see a definition of the selected word at the bottom of the Thesaurus pane. Otherwise, you can click a link to get a dictionary app.

TIP Counting Words

Occasionally, you might need to know how many words are included in a document. For example, your English instructor might require a minimum word count for an essay. Click the Review tab and click Word Count (refer to Figure 1.11) to get a quick summary of words, characters, lines, pages, and paragraphs.

Especially when editing or collaborating on a document created by someone else, you might come across a word with which you are unfamiliar. After selecting a word, click the Review tab and click Define (refer to Figure 1.11). If a dictionary app is installed, the definition will display in the Dictionary pane.

Using Apps

New to Office 2013 is an online app store, providing replacements and additions to add-ins of previous Office versions. Several are especially useful for Word, such as Britannica Researcher, Merriam-Webster Dictionary, and Pingar Summaries (preparing a document summary). Locate those apps and more when you click the Insert tab and click *Apps for Office* in the Apps group. Click See All and click Featured Apps to view featured apps. You can find even more at the Office Store. Click an app link and follow prompts to download it. To insert the app, click *Apps for Office* on the Insert tab, click See All, Click *Find more apps at the Office Store*, and then click Refresh. Click the app and click Insert at the bottom of the dialog box.

Customizing Word

As installed, Word is immediately useful. However, you might find options that you would prefer to customize, add, or remove from the document window. For example, you can add frequently used commands to the Quick Access Toolbar for ease of access. You might prefer that the Ribbon is organized differently. These and other options are available for customization within Word.

Explore Word Options

STEP 5»

By default, certain Word settings are determined and in place when you begin a Word document. For example, unless you specify otherwise, Word will automatically check spelling as you type. Similarly, the Mini toolbar will automatically display when text is selected. Although those and other settings are most likely what you will prefer, there may be occasions when you want to change them. When you change Word options, such as those just described, you change them for all documents—not just the currently open file. To modify Word options, click the File tab and click Options. As shown in Figure 1.12, you can select from several categories and then make appropriate adjustments. Word options that you change will remain in effect until you change them again, even after Word is closed and reopened. Keep in mind that if you are working in a school computer lab, you might not have permission to change options permanently.

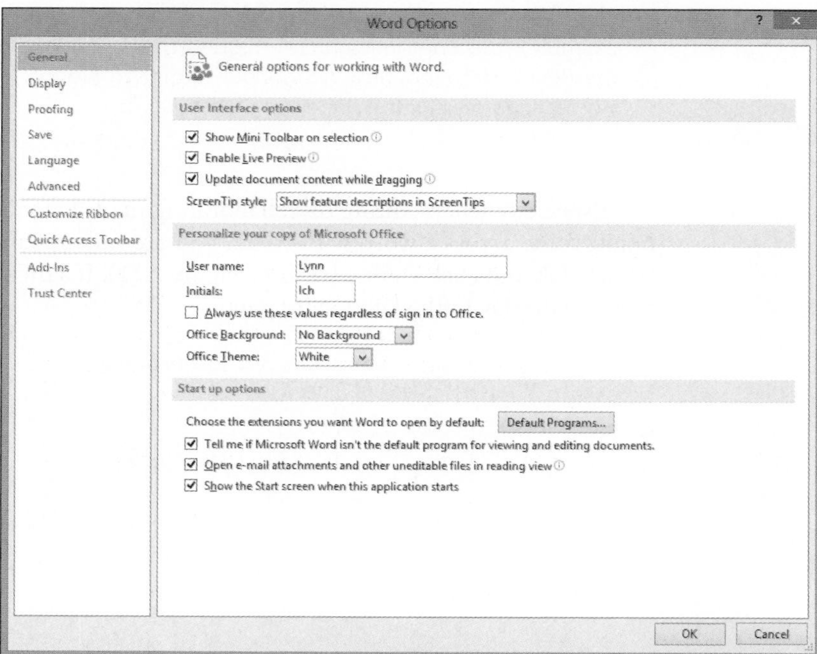

FIGURE 1.12 Word Options

TIP Leaving the File Menu

If you click the File tab and then decide to return to the document without making a selection on the File menu, click the Back arrow at the top of the File menu or press Esc.

Customize the Ribbon

STEP 6

The Word 2013 Ribbon provides access to commands that make it easy to develop, edit, save, share, and print documents. If necessary, you can add and remove Ribbon tabs, as well as rename them. Simply click the File tab and click Options. Click Customize Ribbon. By deselecting a tab name (see Figure 1.13), you can remove a Ribbon tab. Later, you can select it again to redisplay it. Click a tab name and click Rename to change the name of the tab. Type a new name and press Enter. To return to showing all original tabs, click Reset and click *Reset all customizations*.

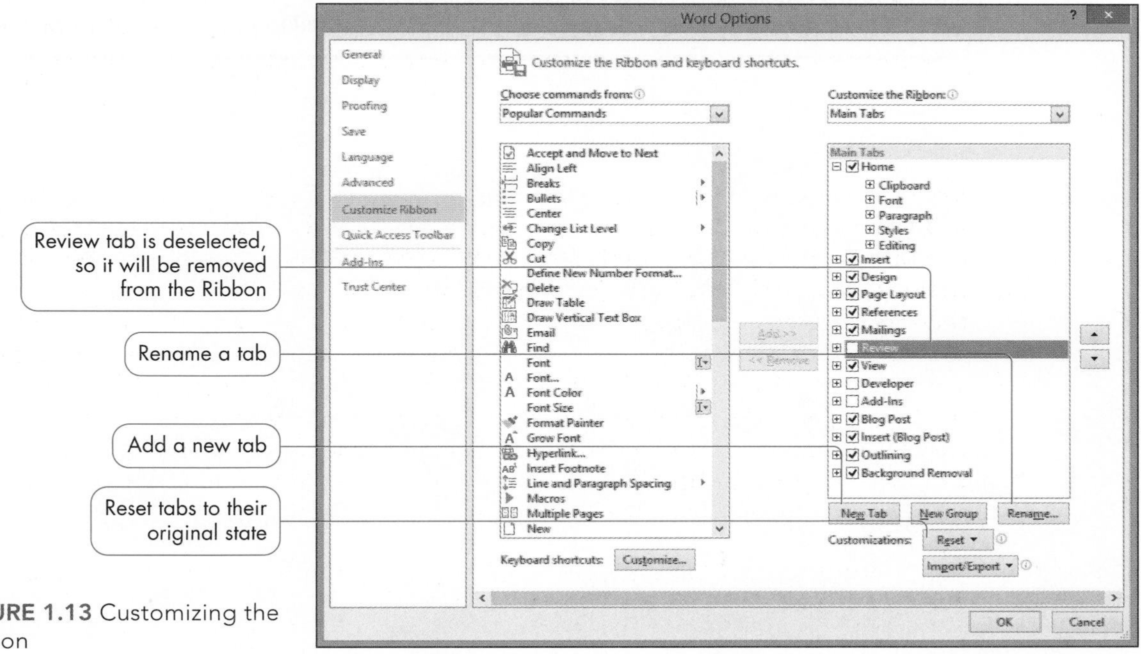

FIGURE 1.13 Customizing the Ribbon

Customize the Quick Access Toolbar

STEP 7

The ***Quick Access Toolbar (QAT)*** contains only a few commands, by default. With one click, you can save a document. Another QAT command enables you to undo a recent command, whereas another is the Redo command. Although it is helpful to have those options close at hand, you might want to include even more on the QAT. You can even remove commands that you do not use often. To customize the QAT, click Customize Quick Access Toolbar (see Figure 1.14) and select from a menu of options (or click More Commands for even more choices). You can also add a Ribbon command when you right-click it and select *Add to Quick Access Toolbar*. To remove a command from the QAT, right-click the command on the QAT and select *Remove from Quick Access Toolbar*.

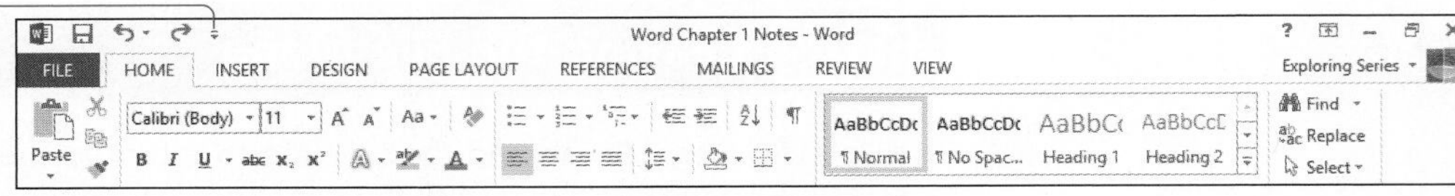

FIGURE 1.14 Customizing the Quick Access Toolbar

***Quick* Concepts**

1. When creating or editing a document, you can show nonprinting characters. In what ways might the display of nonprinting characters assist you with developing a document? ***p. 142***
2. Word 2013 strongly encourages saving documents to a OneDrive account. In fact, OneDrive is the default save location. Provide at least two advantages of using OneDrive as a storage location for your documents. ***p. 143***
3. It is very important to check a document for spelling, grammatical, and word usage errors—a task that Word 2013 can help you with. However, Word 2013 might not identify every error in a document. Why not? Provide an example of an error that Word might not identify. ***p. 145***
4. In your position of employment, you must print documents often. Describe a way to customize Word to minimize the number of steps required to print a document. ***p. 149***

Hands-On Exercises

1 Introduction to Word Processing

As an office assistant working with the wildlife refuge, you will prepare a document publicizing the summer day camps at Swan Creek. Your supervisor has worded a few paragraphs that you will modify and add to, creating an article for distribution to schools in the area. You will also open a document from a template, creating a calendar. Because you plan to use the office computer for future projects as well, you will explore ways to customize Word for ease of use.

Skills covered: Create and Save a Document • Use a Template • Move Around a Document and Edit a Document • Review Word Usage in a Document • Explore Word Options • Customize the Ribbon • Customize the Quick Access Toolbar

STEP 1 » CREATE AND SAVE A DOCUMENT

As you create a new document, you will insert text provided by your supervisor at the wildlife refuge and then save the document for later editing. Refer to Figure 1.15 as you complete Step 1.

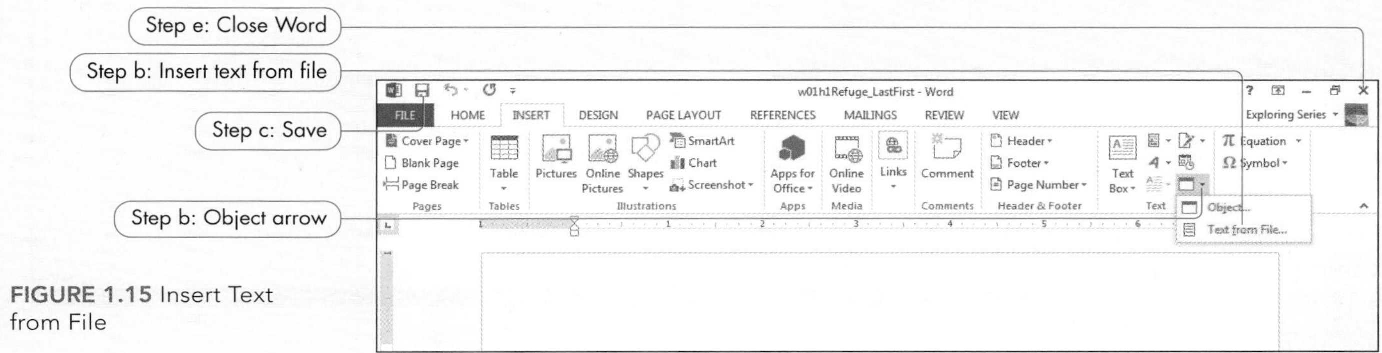

FIGURE 1.15 Insert Text from File

a. Open Word. Click **Blank document**. Click **Save** on the Quick Access Toolbar. In the right pane, click the location where you save your files and change the file name to **w01h1Refuge_LastFirst**. Click **Save**.

When you save files, use your last and first names. For example, as the Word author, I would name my document *w01h1Refuge_HoganLynn*.

b. Click the **INSERT tab** and click the **Object arrow**. Click **Text from File**. Navigate to *w01h1Camps.docx* in the location of your student data files and double-click the file name. Press **Ctrl+Home** to move the insertion point to the beginning of the document.

c. Click **Save** on the Quick Access Toolbar.

This saves the document with the same name and in the same location as the previous save.

d. Click the **FILE tab** and click **Close** to close the document.

You will use this document again later in this Hands-On Exercise.

e. Click **Close** to exit Word.

STEP 2 »» USE A TEMPLATE

As a multitasker, you are accustomed to working with several projects at once. Ms. Traynom, your supervisor, has asked that you print a calendar for the current year. She often must plan ahead and needs an at-a-glance calendar showing each month. You know that Word provides calendar templates, so you will locate one. Refer to Figure 1.16 as you complete Step 2.

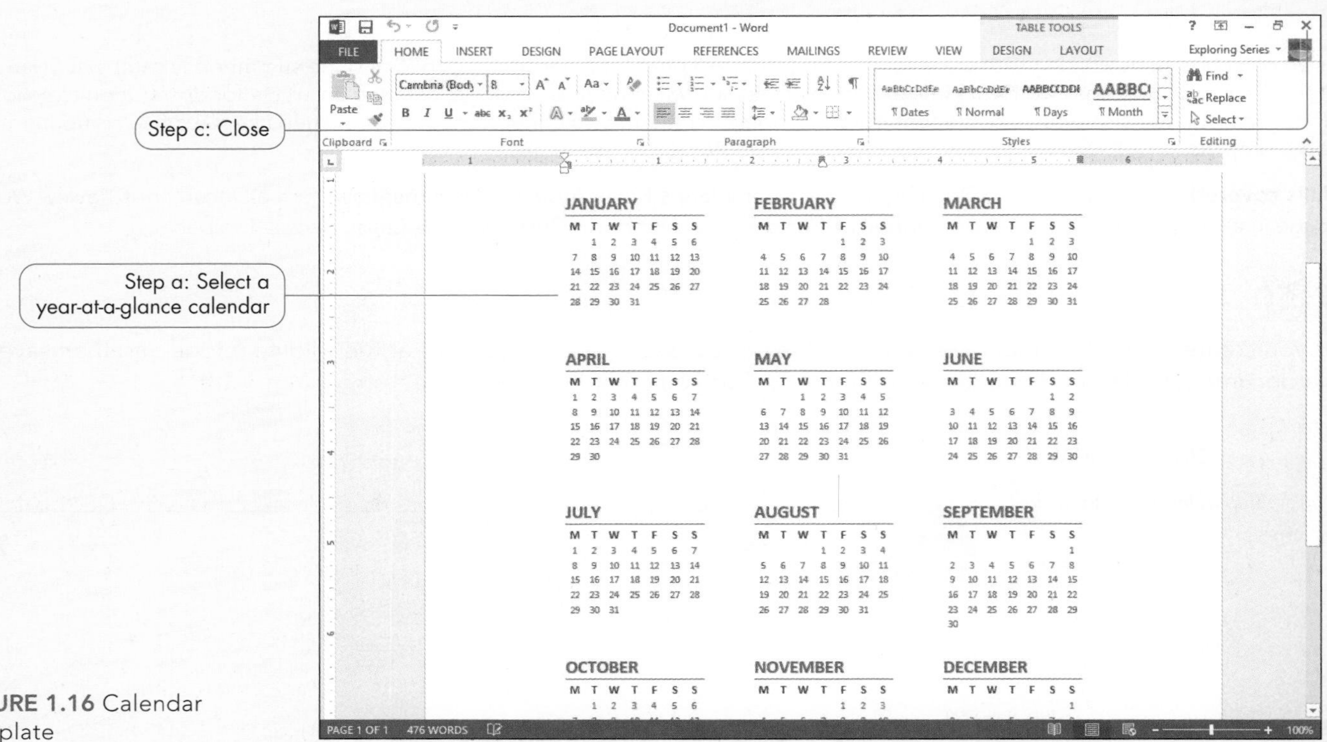

FIGURE 1.16 Calendar Template

a. Open Word. Click the **Search for online templates box** and type **Calendar**. Press **Enter**. Click **Year-at-a-Glance** in the *Filter by* pane on the right. Scroll through the calendar templates presented and click to select one that presents the current year.

> **TROUBLESHOOTING:** The calendar template is only available if you are currently connected to the Internet.

b. Click **Create**. Save the calendar as **w01h1Calendar_LastFirst.**

The location of your student files should display in the Recent Folders list on the right side of the Save As window. Click to select the location.

c. Click **Close** to exit Word.

STEP 3 »» MOVE AROUND A DOCUMENT AND EDIT A DOCUMENT

Although Ms. Traynom provided you with a good start, you will add a bit more detail to the w01h1Refuge_LastFirst article. Refer to Figure 1.17 as you complete Step 3.

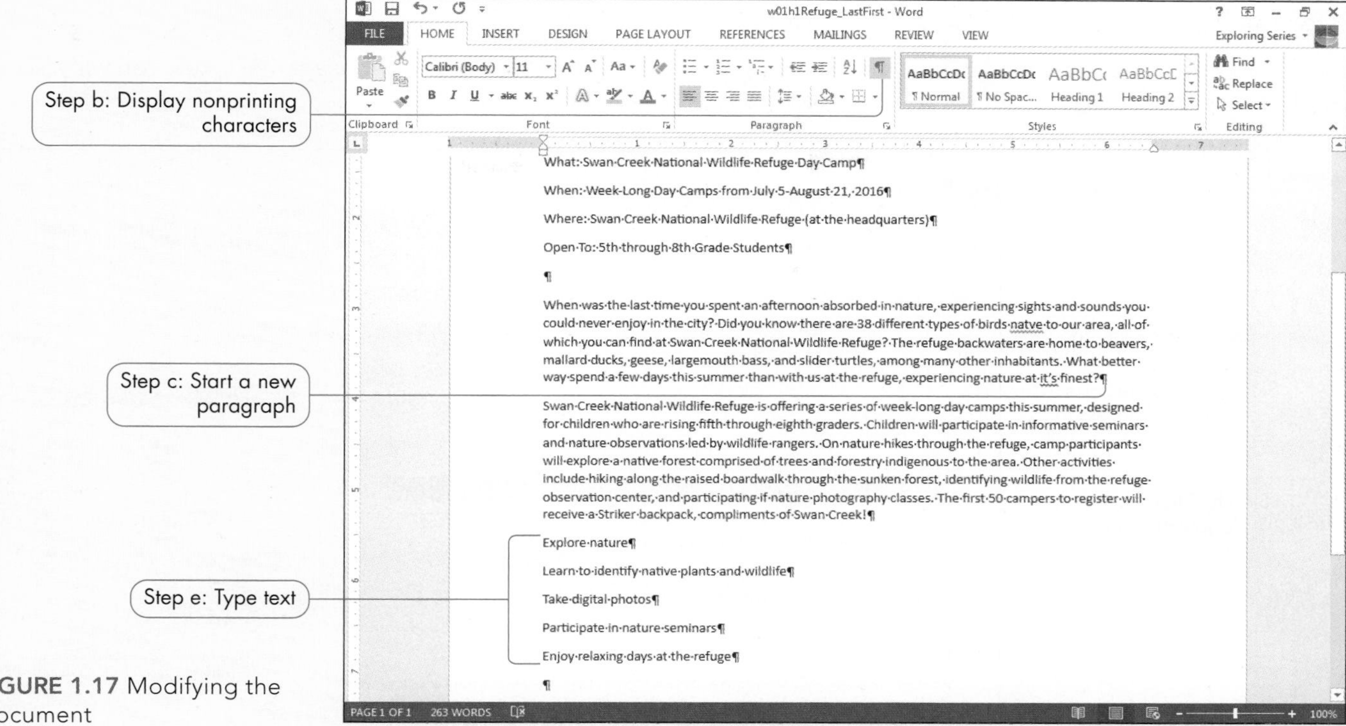

FIGURE 1.17 Modifying the Document

a. Open Word. In the Recent list, click **w01h1Refuge_LastFirst**.

b. Click the **HOME tab**, if necessary, and click **Show/Hide (¶)** in the Paragraph group, if necessary, to display nonprinting formatting marks.

c. Click after the sentence ending in *finest?*—immediately after the question mark at the end of the fourth sentence in the body text—and press **Enter** to insert a hard return. Press **Delete** to remove the space before the word *Swan*.

> **TROUBLESHOOTING:** There will be no space before Swan if you clicked after the space instead of before it when you pressed Enter. In that case, there is no space to delete, so leave the text as is.

d. Scroll down and click after the word *Creek!*—immediately after the exclamation point after the second body paragraph—and press **Enter** to insert a hard return.

e. Type the following text, pressing **Enter** at the end of each line:

explore nature

learn to identify native plants and wildlife

take digital photos

participate in nature seminars

enjoy relaxing days at the refuge

As you type each line, the first letter is automatically capitalized. Unless you specify otherwise in Word Options, words that begin new paragraphs and sentences are capitalized. In this case, the capitalization is correct, so leave the words as they are capitalized by Word.

f. Press **Ctrl+End**. Press **Delete** to delete the final paragraph mark in the document.

STEP 4 ›› REVIEW WORD USAGE IN A DOCUMENT

As you continue to develop the article, you will check for spelling, grammar, and word usage mistakes. You will also identify a synonym and get a definition. Refer to Figure 1.18 as you complete Step 4.

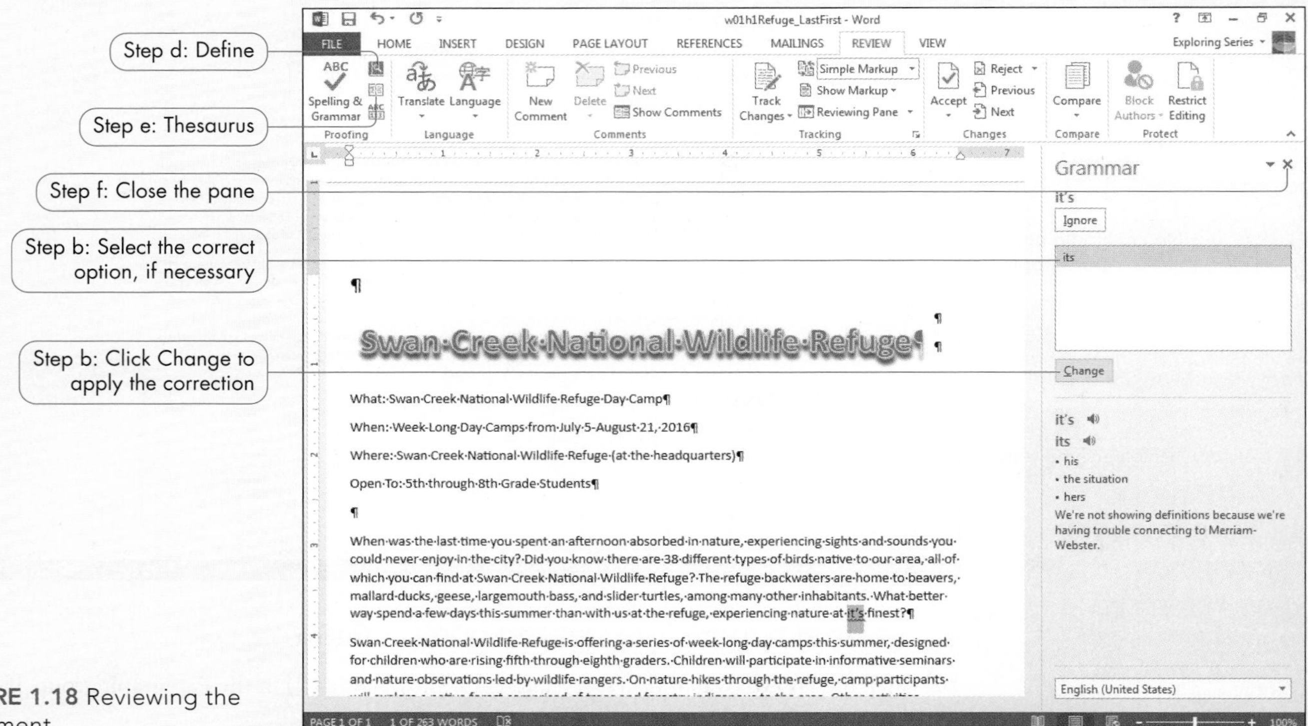

FIGURE 1.18 Reviewing the Document

a. Press **Ctrl+Home** to move to the beginning of the document. Right-click the red underlined word *natve* in the second line of the first body paragraph in the document. Click **native** on the shortcut menu to select the correct spelling.

b. Click the **REVIEW tab** and click **Spelling & Grammar** in the Proofing group. As each error is presented, click to select the correct option. The word *it's* should not include an apostrophe, so ensure the correct option is selected (see Figure 1.18) and click **Change**. The word *fo* should be *for*. Click **OK** when the check is complete.

c. At least one error in the document is not identified as a spelling or word usage error by Word. Read through the document to identify and correct the error.

d. Drag to select the word *immersed* in the first sentence of the first body paragraph (or double-click the word to select it). Click **Define** in the Proofing group. If a dictionary app is installed, you should see a definition of the word in the pane on the right. If a dictionary app is not installed, follow the prompts to install a dictionary app.

e. Close the pane on the right. With the word *immersed* still selected, click **Thesaurus** in the Proofing group. Point to the word *absorbed*, click the arrow at the right, and then select **Insert**.

f. Close the Thesaurus pane. Save the document.

STEP 5 ›› EXPLORE WORD OPTIONS

You will explore some Word options that will enable you to customize the computer assigned to you at the refuge. Such customization ensures that Word is configured to suit your preferences. Refer to Figure 1.19 as you complete Step 5.

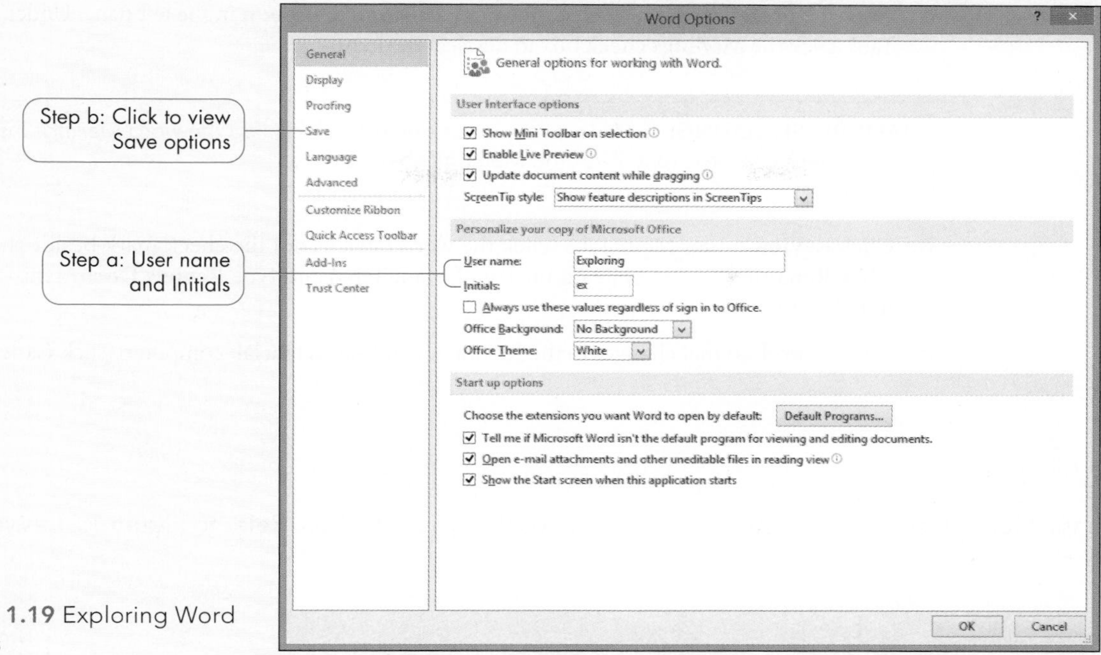

FIGURE 1.19 Exploring Word Options

a. Click the **FILE tab** and click **Options**. Ensure that the General category in the left pane is selected.

   Note that you can change the User name and Initials that identify you as the author of documents you create. Because you might be working in a computer lab, you will not actually change anything at this time.

b. Click **Save** in the left pane of the Word Options dialog box.

   Note that you can adjust the AutoRecover time, a feature covered later in this chapter, by typing in the text box, replacing existing text, or by clicking the up or down arrow repeatedly.

c. Click **Cancel**, so you do not actually make changes.

STEP 6 » CUSTOMIZE THE RIBBON

As you continue to explore ways to customize Word preferences, you will identify Ribbon tabs that you can add or remove. Refer to Figure 1.20 as you complete Step 6.

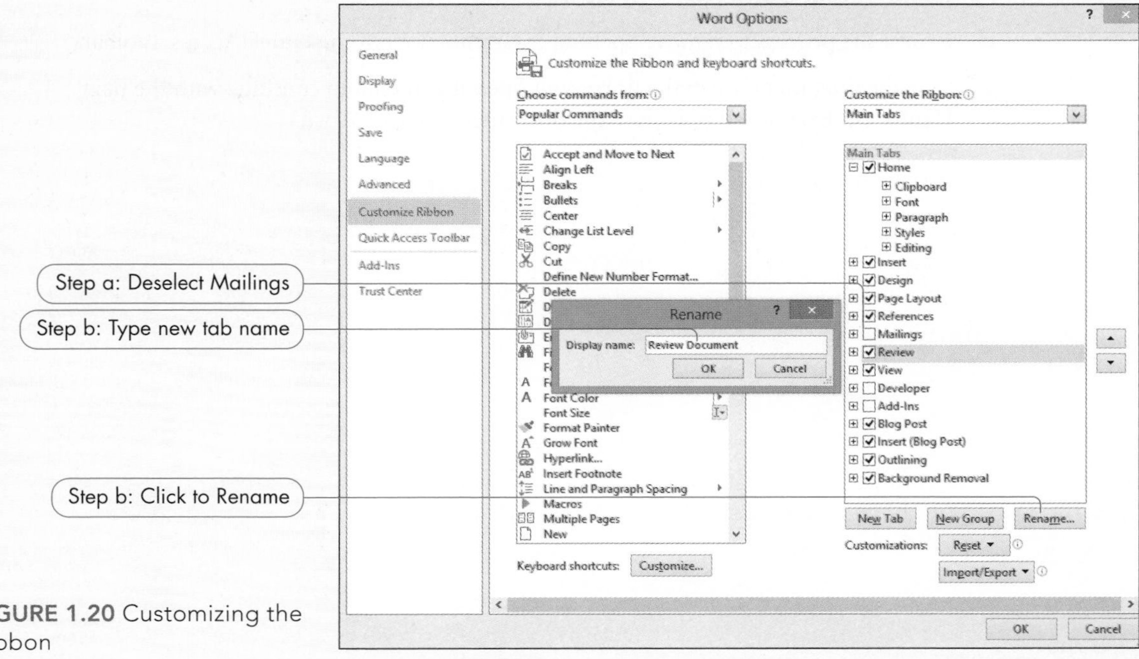

FIGURE 1.20 Customizing the Ribbon

a. Click the **FILE tab** and click **Options**. Click **Customize Ribbon** in the left pane. Under Main Tabs, click the **Mailings check box** to deselect the item.

> **TROUBLESHOOTING:** If *Mailings* is not deselected, you clicked the word *Mailings* instead of the check box next to it. Click the **Mailings check box**.

b. Click **Review** under Main Tabs (click the word *Review*, not the check mark beside the word). Click **Rename** (located beneath the list of Main Tabs) and type **Review Document**—but do not click OK.

c. Click **Cancel**, so that changes to the Ribbon are not saved to a lab computer. Click **Cancel** again.

STEP 7 ›› CUSTOMIZE THE QUICK ACCESS TOOLBAR

You will customize the Quick Access Toolbar to include commands that you use often. Refer to Figure 1.21 as you complete Step 7.

Step a: Customize Quick Access Toolbar

Step b: New buttons

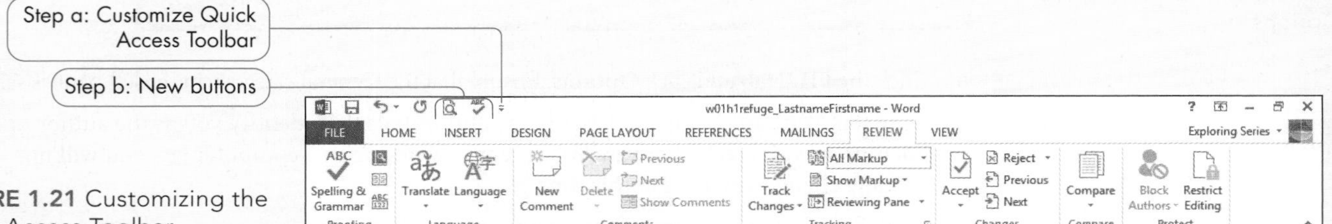

FIGURE 1.21 Customizing the Quick Access Toolbar

a. Click **Customize Quick Access Toolbar**, located at the right side of the QAT, and select **Print Preview and Print** from the shortcut menu.

   As shown in Figure 1.21, an additional button appears on the QAT, enabling you to preview and print a document when you click the button.

b. Click the **REVIEW tab**, if necessary, and right-click **Spelling & Grammar** in the Proofing group. Click **Add to Quick Access Toolbar**.

c. Right-click the **Print Preview and Print button** on the Quick Access Toolbar and select **Remove from Quick Access Toolbar**.

d. Repeat the process to remove Spelling & Grammar from the Quick Access Toolbar.

e. Save the document. Keep the document open if you plan to continue with the next Hands-On Exercise. If not, close the document and exit Word.

Document Organization

Most often, the reason for creating a document is for others to read; therefore, the document should be designed to meet the needs of the reading audience. It should not only be well worded and structured, but also might include features that better identify it, such as headers, footers, and ***watermarks***. A watermark is text or graphics that displays behind text. In addition, adjusting margins and changing page orientation might better suit a document's purposes and improve its readability. Depending on its purpose, a document might need to fit on one page, or it could be very lengthy.

Before printing or saving a document, you will want to review it to ensure that it is attractive and appropriately organized. Word has various views, including Read Mode, Print Layout, Web Layout, Outline, and Draft, that you can use to get a good feel for the way the entire document looks in a variety of uses, regardless of its length. The view selected can also give a snapshot of overall document organization so you can be assured that the document is well structured and makes all points. In this section, you will explore features that improve readability, and you will learn to change the view of a document.

Using Features That Improve Readability

Choosing your words carefully will result in a well-worded document. However, no matter how well worded, a document that is not organized in an attractive manner so that it is easy to read and understand is not likely to impress the audience. Consider not only the content, but also how a document will look when printed or displayed. Special features that can improve readability, such as headers, footers, and symbols, are located on Word's Insert tab. Other settings, such as margins, page orientation, and paper size, are found on the Page Layout tab. The Design tab provides access to watermarks, which can help convey the purpose or originator of a document.

Insert Headers and Footers

Headers and ***footers*** can give a professional appearance to a document. A header consists of one or more lines at the top of each page. A footer displays at the bottom of each page. One advantage of using headers and footers is that you have to specify the content only once, after which it displays automatically on all pages. Although you can type the text yourself at the top or bottom of every page, it is time-consuming, and the possibility of making a mistake is great. Typically, the purpose of including a header or footer is to better identify the document. As a header, you might include an organization name or a class number so that each page identifies the document's origin or purpose. A page number is a typical footer, although it could just as easily be included as a header.

STEP 1»

To insert a header or footer, click the Insert tab and click Header (or Footer) in the Header & Footer group. Select from a gallery of predefined header or footer styles or click Edit Header (or Edit Footer), as shown in Figure 1.22, to create an unformatted header or footer. After typing a header or footer, click *Close Header and Footer* to leave the header and footer area and return to the document (see Figure 1.23). In Print Layout view, you can also double-click in the document to close the header or footer. A header or footer can be formatted like any other text. It can be center, left, or right aligned, and formatted in any font or font size. When working with a header or footer, the main body text of the document is grayed out temporarily. When you return to the document, the body text is active, but the header or footer text is dim.

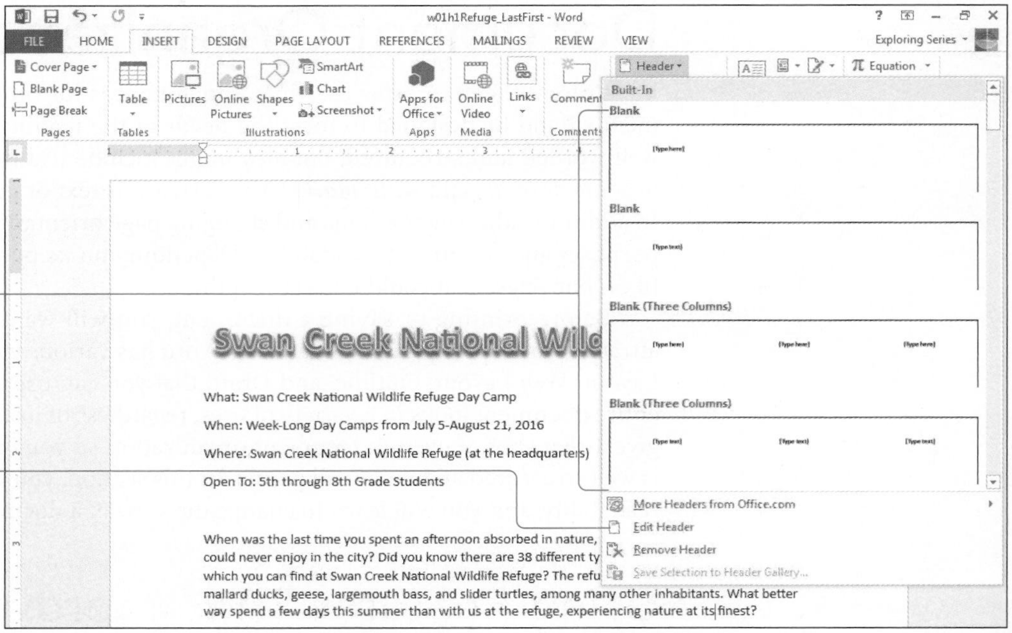

Choose from predesigned headers

Create an unformatted header

FIGURE 1.22 Inserting a Header

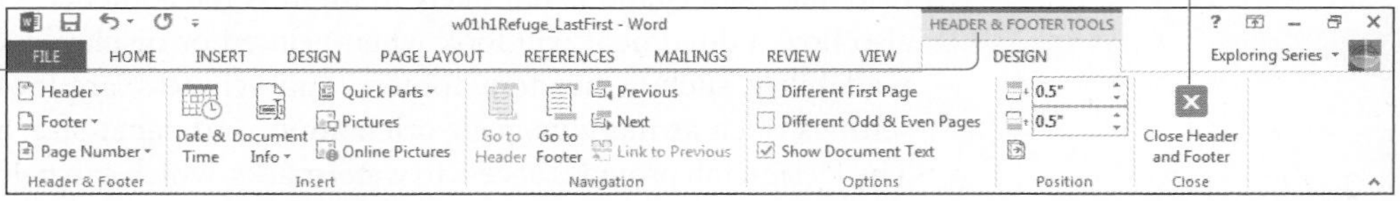

Click to close a header or footer

Header & Footer Tools contextual tab

FIGURE 1.23 Close a Header or Footer

Word provides fields, such as author, date, and file name, that you can choose to include in headers and footers. Some header and footer fields, such as page numbers, will actually change from one page to the next. Other fields, such as author name and date, will remain constant. Regardless, selecting fields (instead of typing the actual data) simplifies the task of creating headers and footers. Some of the most frequently accessed fields, such as Date & Time and Page Number, are available on the Header & Footer Tools Design contextual tab as separate commands (see Figure 1.24). Others, including Author, File Name, and Document Title, are available when you click Document Info in the Insert group. Depending on the field selected, you might have to indicate a specific format and/or placement. For example, you could display the date as *Monday, August 12, 2016*, or you might direct that a page number is centered.

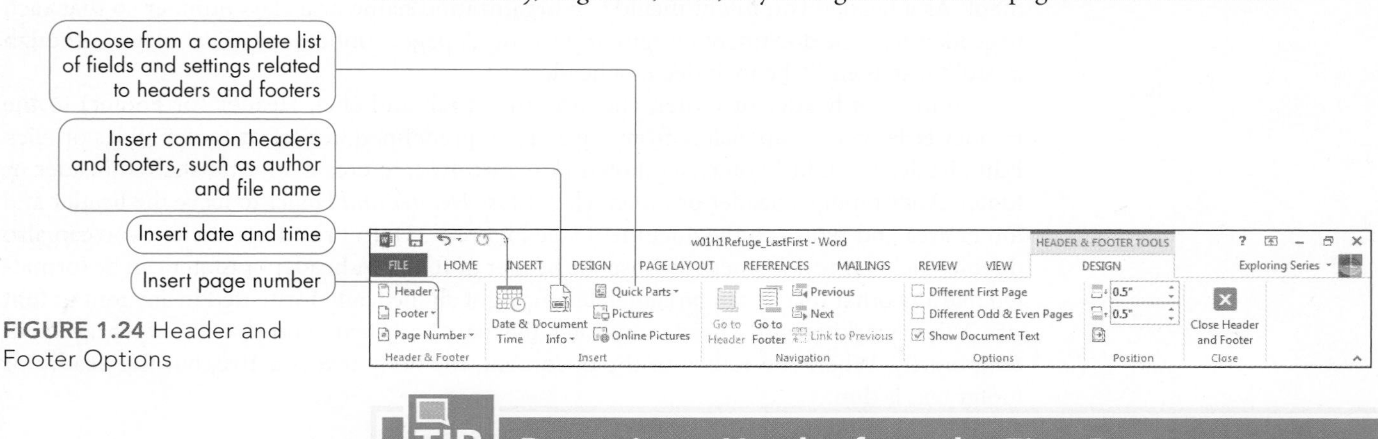

FIGURE 1.24 Header and Footer Options

TIP Removing a Header from the First Page

Occasionally, you will want a header or footer on all pages except the first, such as when the first page is a report's cover page. In that case, select Different First Page in the Options group on the Header & Footer Tools Design tab (when a header or footer is selected).

You will find that you use some fields more often than others as headers and footers. Word 2013 provides one-click access to common fields such as Author, File Name, File Path, and Document Title when you click Document Info in the Insert group on the Header & Footer Tools Design tab. You can click Field for a complete list of fields to choose from (see Figure 1.25). The same fields are available when you click Quick Parts in the Insert group and click Field.

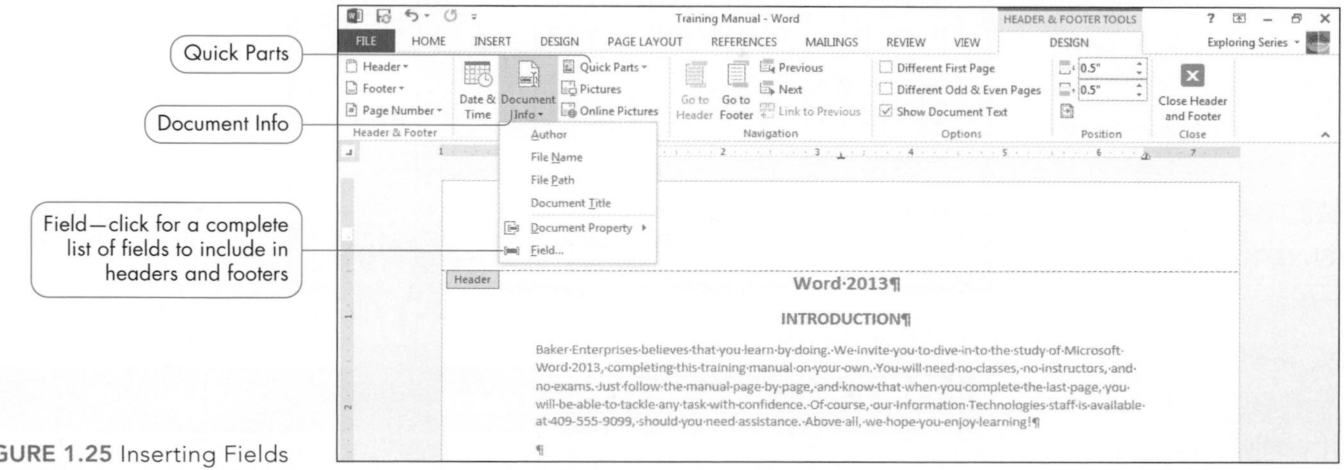

FIGURE 1.25 Inserting Fields

Insert a Symbol

A ***symbol*** is text, a graphic, or a foreign language character that can be inserted into a document. Most symbols are not located on the keyboard and are available only from Word's collection of symbols. Symbols such as © and ™ can be an integral part of a document; in fact, those particular symbols are necessary to properly acknowledge a source or product. Because they are typically not located on the keyboard, you need to find them in Word's library of symbols or use a shortcut key combination, if available.

Some symbols serve a very practical purpose. For example, it is unlikely you will want a hyphenated word to be divided between lines in a document. In that case, instead of typing a simple hyphen between words, you can insert a *nonbreaking hyphen*, which is available as a symbol. Similarly, you can insert a *nonbreaking space* when you do not want words divided between lines. For example, a person's first name on one line followed by the last name on the next line is not a very attractive placement. Instead, make the space between the words a nonbreaking space by inserting the symbol, so the names are never divided. Select a nonbreaking hyphen, nonbreaking space, and other special characters when you click the Insert tab, Symbol, More Symbols, and Special Characters. Click a special character and click Insert to place it in a document.

STEP 5»

A typical Microsoft Office installation includes a wide variety of fonts. To view and select a symbol, click the Insert tab and click Symbol. A gallery of frequently accessed symbols displays, from which you can choose. If the symbol you seek is not in the list, click More Symbols. Figure 1.26 shows the dialog box from which you can search for a symbol. Depending upon the font selected (normal text is shown in Figure 1.26), your symbol choices will vary. Fonts such as Wingdings, Webdings, and Symbol contain a wealth of special symbols, many of which are actually pictures.

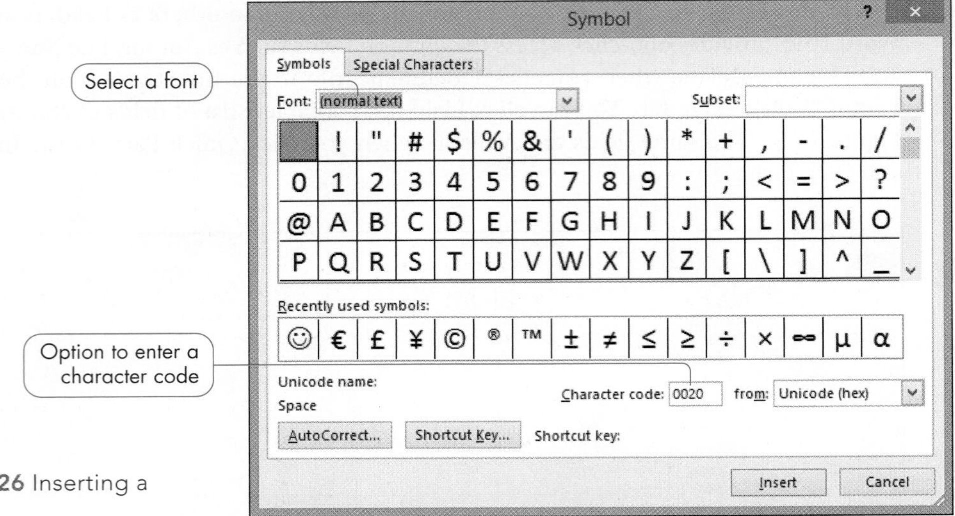

FIGURE 1.26 Inserting a Symbol

Using Symbol Shortcuts

You can insert some symbols, such as ©, ™, and ☺, as keyboard shortcuts. For example, type (c) to insert ©, (tm) for ™, and :) for ☺.

Each symbol is assigned a character code. If you know the character code, you can type the code (refer to Figure 1.26) instead of searching for the symbol itself or using a keyboard shortcut.

Adjust Margins

A ***margin*** is the area of blank space that displays to the left, right, top, and bottom of a document, between the text and the edge of the page. Although a 1" margin all around the document is the normal setting, you can easily adjust one or more margins for a particular document. You might adjust margins for several reasons. You can change a document's appearance and readability, perhaps even causing it to fit attractively on one page, by adjusting margins. Also, a style manual, such as you might use in an English class, will require certain margins for the preparation of papers and publications.

You can change margins in a couple of ways:

STEP 2

- Click the PAGE LAYOUT tab and click Margins in the Page Setup group. Select from one of the predefined margin settings (see Figure 1.27) or click Custom Margins to adjust each margin (left, right, top, and bottom) individually.
- Click the FILE tab and click Print. Click Normal Margins (or the previous margin setting) to change one or more margins.

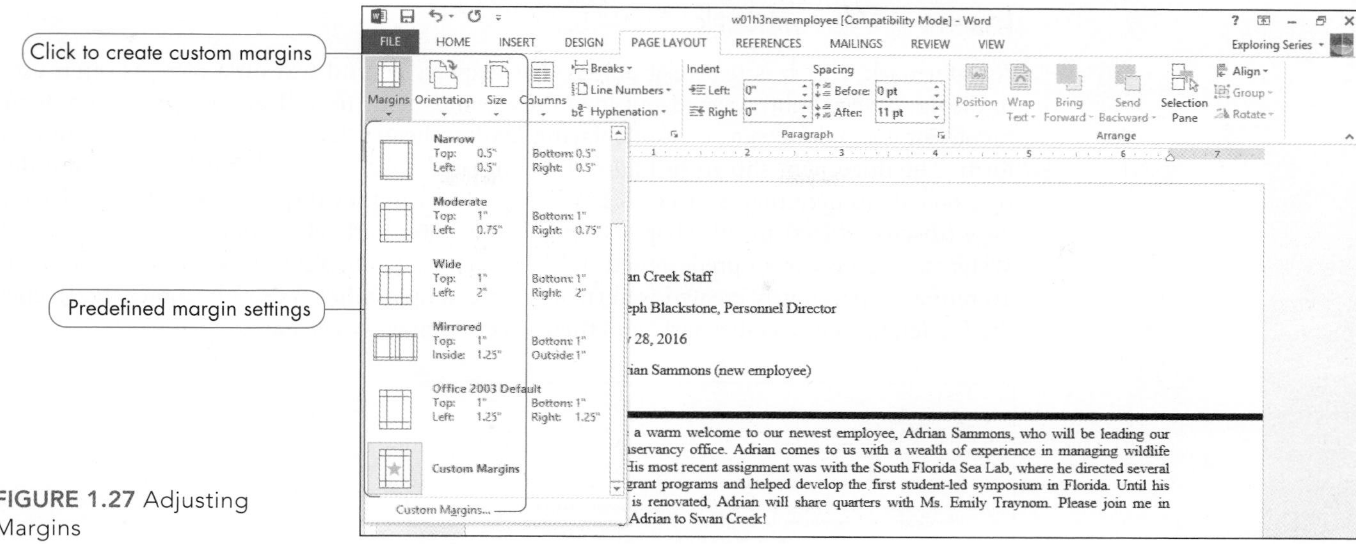

FIGURE 1.27 Adjusting Margins

Change Page Orientation

You will find that some documents are more attractive in either ***portrait*** or ***landscape orientation***. A document displayed in portrait orientation is taller than it is wide, whereas a document shown in landscape is wider than it is tall. Most certificates are designed in landscape orientation; letters and memos are typically presented in portrait orientation. You can change page orientation in several ways:

STEP 3»

- Click Orientation on the PAGE LAYOUT tab to select either Portrait or Landscape.
- Click Margins on the PAGE LAYOUT tab and click Custom Margins to display the Page Setup dialog box (see Figure 1.28). From there, select either Portrait or Landscape.
- Click the FILE tab, click Print, and then click Portrait Orientation (or Landscape Orientation if the document is in landscape orientation). Select either Portrait Orientation or Landscape Orientation.

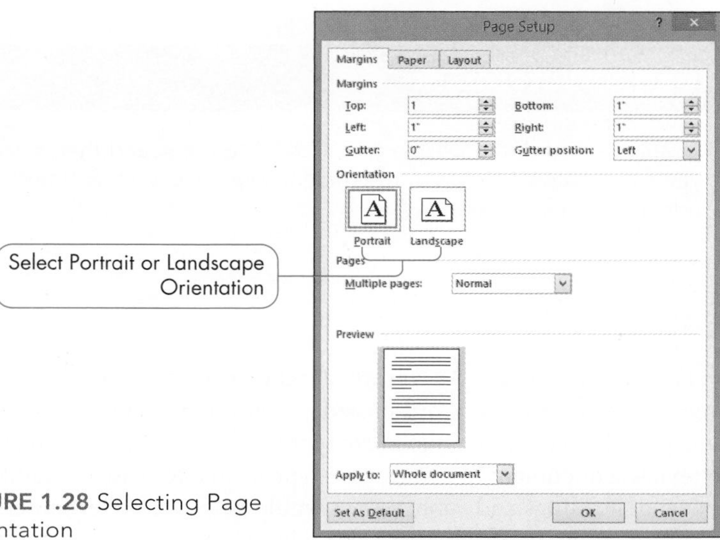

FIGURE 1.28 Selecting Page Orientation

Insert a Watermark

A watermark, which is text or graphics that displays behind text on a page, is often used to display a very light, washed-out logo for a company or to indicate the status of a document. For example, a watermark displaying *Draft* indicates that the document is not in final form. The document shown in Figure 1.29 contains a watermark. Watermarks do not display on a document that is saved as a Web page, nor will they display in Word's Web Layout view (discussed later in this chapter). To insert a watermark, click the Design tab and click Watermark. Select from predesigned styles, or click Custom Watermark to create your own. To remove a previously created watermark (for example, when a draft becomes final), click the Design tab, click Watermark, and then select Remove Watermark.

STEP 4 »

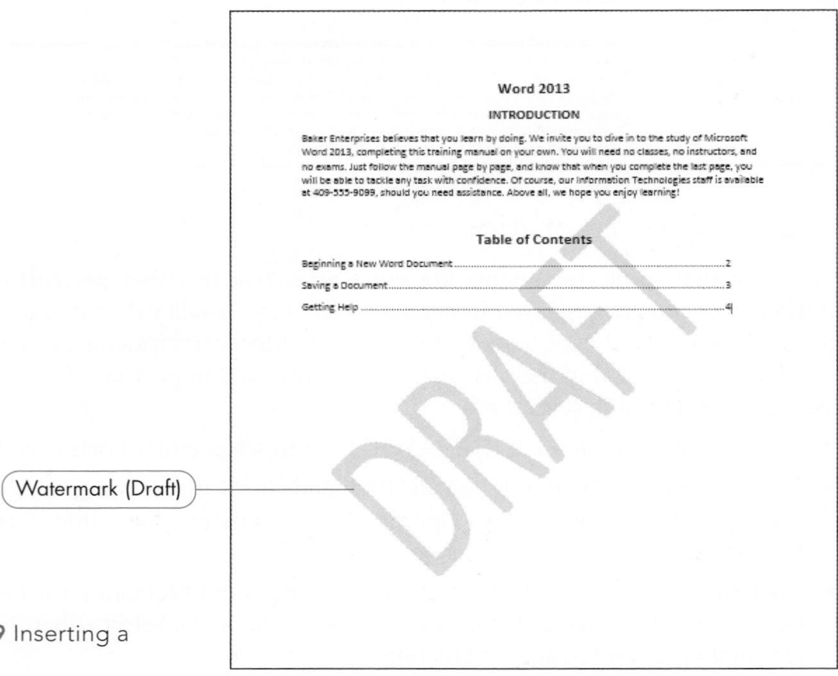

Word 2013

INTRODUCTION

Baker Enterprises believes that you learn by doing. We invite you to dive in to the study of Microsoft Word 2013, completing this training manual on your own. You will need no classes, no instructors, and no exams. Just follow the manual page by page, and know that when you complete the last page, you will be able to tackle any task with confidence. Of course, our Information Technologies staff is available at 409-555-9099, should you need assistance. Above all, we hope you enjoy learning!

Table of Contents

Beginning a New Word Document 2
Saving a Document 3
Getting Help 4

FIGURE 1.29 Inserting a Watermark

TIP Formatting a Watermark

In selecting a custom watermark (click the Design tab, click Watermark, and then select Custom Watermark), you can select or change a watermark's color, size, font, and text. In addition, you can include a picture as a watermark.

Viewing a Document in Different Ways

Developing a document is a creative process. As you create, edit, or review a project, you will want to view the document in various ways. Word provides a view that enables you to see a document as it will print, as well as views that maximize typing space by removing page features. You might like to review a document in a magazine-type format for ease of reading, or perhaps a hierarchical view of headings and subheadings would help you better understand and proof the structure of a document. The ability to zoom in on text and objects can make a document easier to proofread, while viewing a document page by page helps you manage page flow—perhaps drawing attention to awkward page endings or beginnings. Taking advantage of the various views and view settings in Word, you will find it easy to create attractive, well-worded, and error-free documents.

Select a Document View

When you begin a new document, you will see the top, bottom, left, and right margins. The document view is called ***Print Layout view***, and it is the default view. You can choose to view a document differently, which is something you might do if you are at a different step in its production. For example, as you type or edit a document, you might prefer ***Draft view***, which provides the most typing space possible without regard to margins and special page features. Word's ***Read Mode*** facilitates proofreading and comprehension, whereas ***Outline view*** displays a document in hierarchical fashion, clearly delineating levels of heading detail. If a document is destined for the Web, you would want to view it in ***Web Layout view***.

To change document view, click the View tab and select a view from the Views group (see Figure 1.30). Although slightly more limited in choice, the status bar also provides views to choose from (Read Mode, Print Layout, and Web Layout). Word views are summarized in Table 1.1.

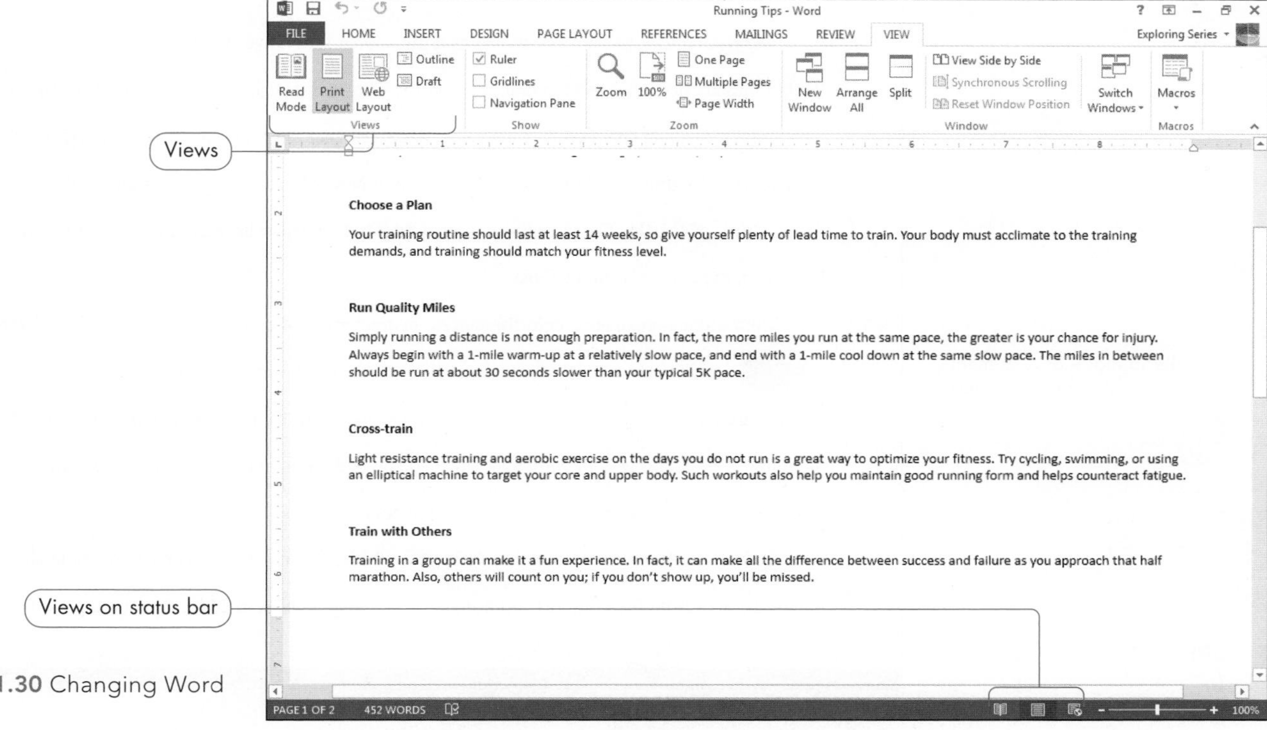
Views
Views on status bar
Running Tips - Word
FILE
HOME
INSERT
DESIGN
PAGE LAYOUT
REFERENCES
MAILINGS
REVIEW
VIEW
Exploring Series
Read Mode
Print Layout
Web Layout
Outline
Draft
Ruler
Gridlines
Navigation Pane
Zoom
100%
One Page
Multiple Pages
Page Width
New Window
Arrange All
Split
View Side by Side
Synchronous Scrolling
Reset Window Position
Switch Windows
Macros
Choose a Plan
Your training routine should last at least 14 weeks, so give yourself plenty of lead time to train. Your body must acclimate to the training demands, and training should match your fitness level.
Run Quality Miles
Simply running a distance is not enough preparation. In fact, the more miles you run at the same pace, the greater is your chance for injury. Always begin with a 1-mile warm-up at a relatively slow pace, and end with a 1-mile cool down at the same slow pace. The miles in between should be run at about 30 seconds slower than your typical 5K pace.
Cross-train
Light resistance training and aerobic exercise on the days you do not run is a great way to optimize your fitness. Try cycling, swimming, or using an elliptical machine to target your core and upper body. Such workouts also help you maintain good running form and helps counteract fatigue.
Train with Others
Training in a group can make it a fun experience. In fact, it can make all the difference between success and failure as you approach that half marathon. Also, others will count on you; if you don't show up, you'll be missed.
PAGE 1 OF 2
452 WORDS
100%

FIGURE 1.30 Changing Word View

TABLE 1.1 Word Views

View	Appearance
Read Mode	Primarily used for reading, with a document shown in pages, much like a magazine. The Ribbon is hidden, with only a limited number of menu selections shown.
Print Layout	Shows margins, headers, footers, graphics, and other page features—much like a document will look when printed.
Web Layout	Shows a document as it would appear on a Web page.
Outline	Shows level of organization and detail. You can collapse or expand detail to show only what is necessary. Often used as a springboard for a table of contents or a PowerPoint summary.
Draft	Provides the most space possible for typing. It does not show margins, headers, or other features, but it does include the Ribbon.

The Read Mode is new to Word 2013. Designed to make a document easy to read and to facilitate access across multiple devices, Read Mode presents a document in a left to right flow, automatically splitting text into columns, if necessary, for a magazine-like appearance. Text often displays in a two-page format. Text adjusts to fit any size screen, flowing easily from page to page with a simple flick of a finger (if using a tablet or touch-sensitive device) or click of the mouse. Users of touch-based devices can rotate the device between landscape and portrait modes, with the screen always divided into equally sized columns. When in Read Mode (see Figure 1.31), you will note that the Ribbon is removed from view. Instead, you have access to only three menu items: File, Tools, and View. One of the most exciting features of Read Mode is object zooming. Simply double-click an object, such as a table, chart, picture, or video, to zoom in. Press Esc to leave Read Mode. Although you can also leave Read Mode when you click the View tab and click Edit Document, doing so causes subsequently opened Word documents to automatically display in Read Mode when opened.

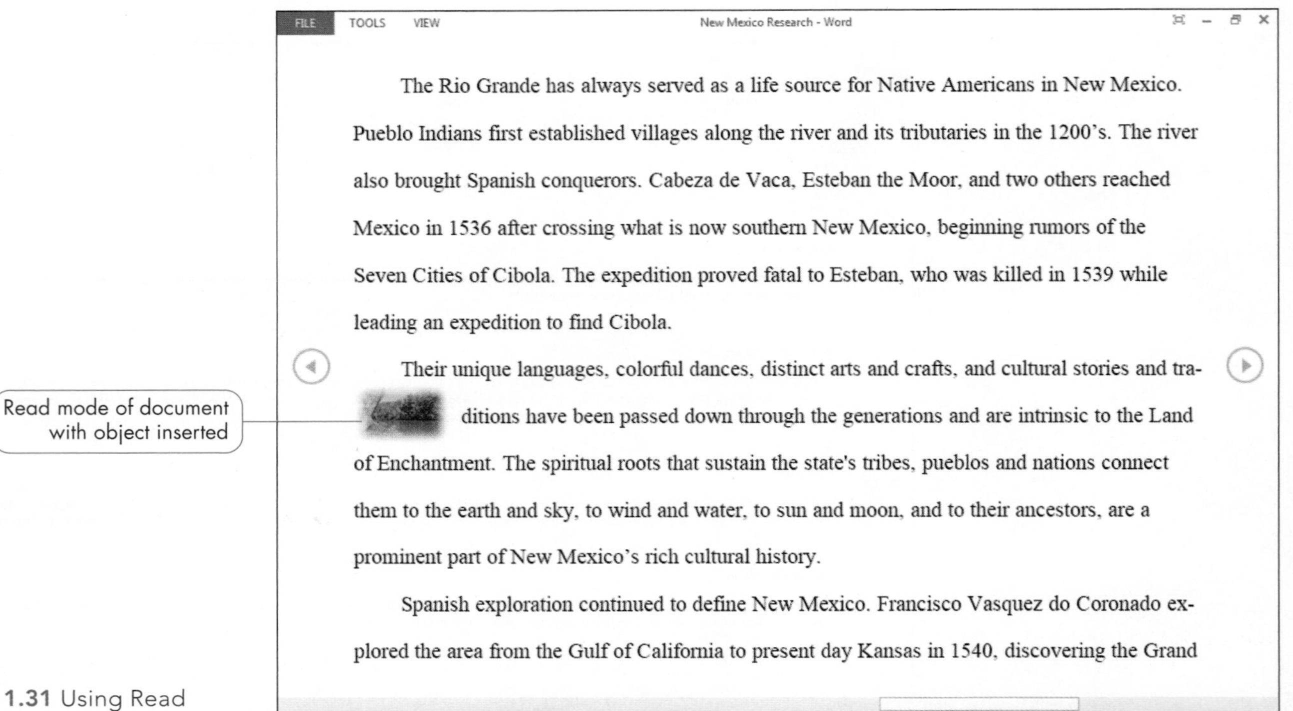

FIGURE 1.31 Using Read Mode

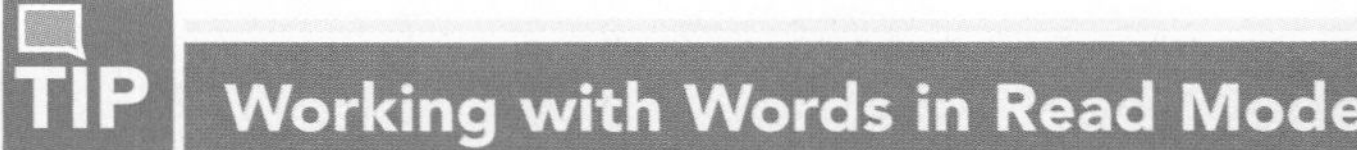

Working with Words in Read Mode

In Read Mode, right-click a word and choose Define from the shortcut menu for a quick definition and synonym. Select Translate, if the document is not in your native language.

Change the Zoom Setting

Regardless of the view selected, you can use Word's zoom feature to enlarge or reduce the view of text. Unlike zooming in on an object in Read Mode, the zoom feature available on the View tab enables you to enlarge text, not objects or videos. Enlarging text might make a document easier to read and proofread. However, changing the size of text onscreen does not actually change the font size of a document. Zooming in or out is simply a temporary change to the way a document appears onscreen. The View tab includes options that change the onscreen size of a document (see Figure 1.32). You can also enlarge or reduce the view of text by dragging the Zoom slider on the status bar. Click Zoom In and Zoom Out on the status bar to change the view incrementally by 10% for each click.

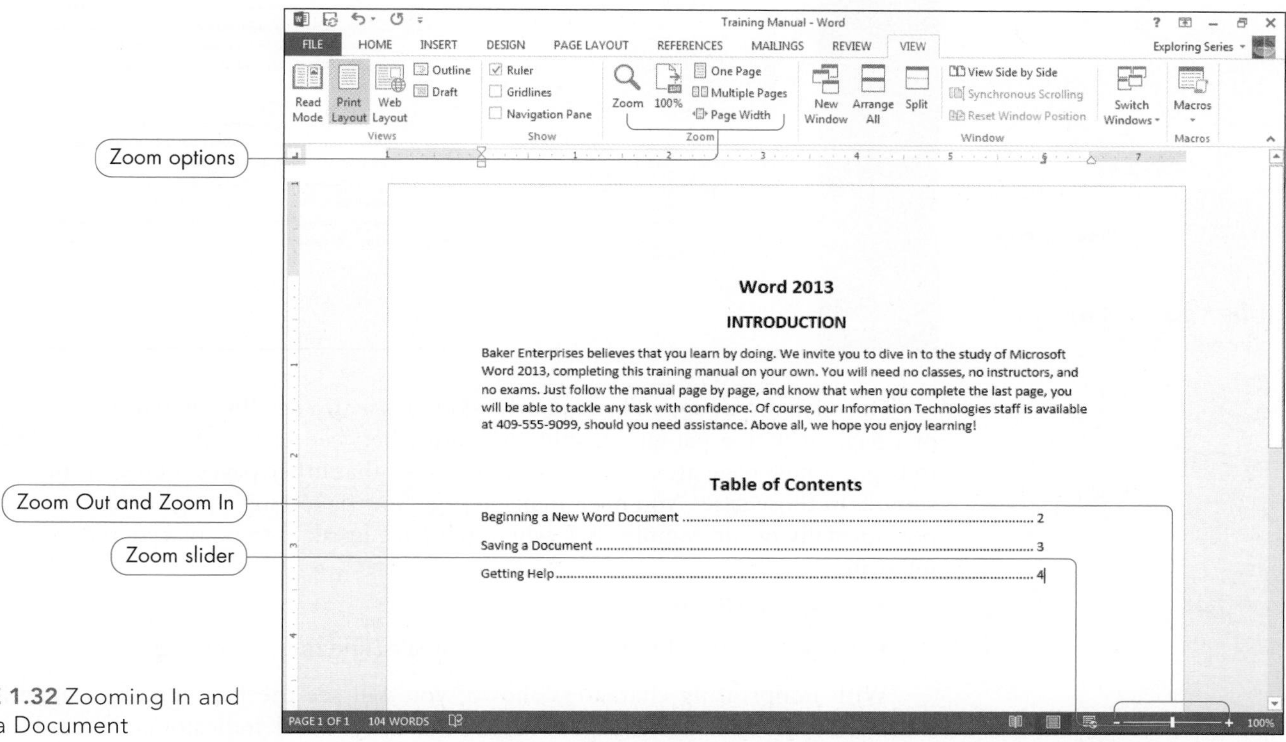

FIGURE 1.32 Zooming In and Out of a Document

Use the Zoom command on the View tab to select a percentage of zoom or to indicate a preset width (page width, text width, or whole page). Preset widths are also available as individual options in the Zoom group on the View tab (refer to Figure 1.32).

View a Document and Manage Page Flow

Document lengths can vary greatly. A research paper might span 20 pages, whereas a memo is seldom more than a few pages (most often, only one). Obviously, it is easier to view a memo onscreen than an entire research paper. Even so, Word enables you to get a good feel for the way a document will look when printed or distributed, regardless of document length.

STEP 6

Before printing, it is a good idea to view a document in its entirety. One way to do that is to click the File tab and click Print. A document is shown one page at a time in print preview (see Figure 1.33). Click the Next Page or Previous Page navigation arrow to proceed forward or backward in pages. You can also view a document by using options on the View tab (refer to Figure 1.32). Clicking One Page provides a snapshot of the current page, while Multiple Pages shows pages of a multiple-page document side by side (and on separate rows, in the case of more than two pages).

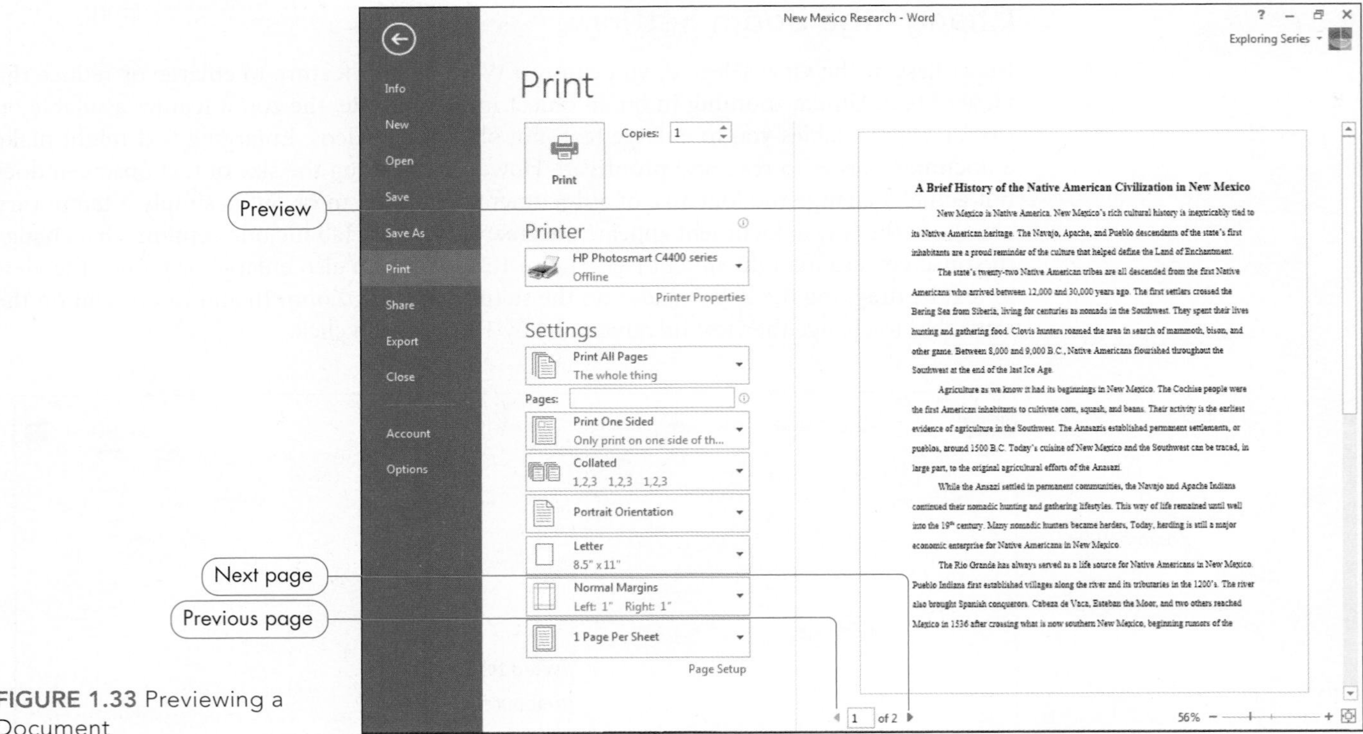

FIGURE 1.33 Previewing a Document

Occasionally, a page will end poorly—perhaps with a heading shown alone at the bottom of a page or with a paragraph split awkwardly between pages. Or perhaps it is necessary to begin a new page after a table of contents, so that other pages follow in the order they should. In those cases, you must manage page flow by forcing a page break where it would not normally occur. Simply click where the page break is to be placed and do one of the following:

- Press Ctrl+Enter.
- Click the PAGE LAYOUT tab, click Breaks, and then select Page.

With nonprinting characters shown, you will see the Page Break designation (see Figure 1.34). To remove the page break, click the Page Break indicator and press Delete.

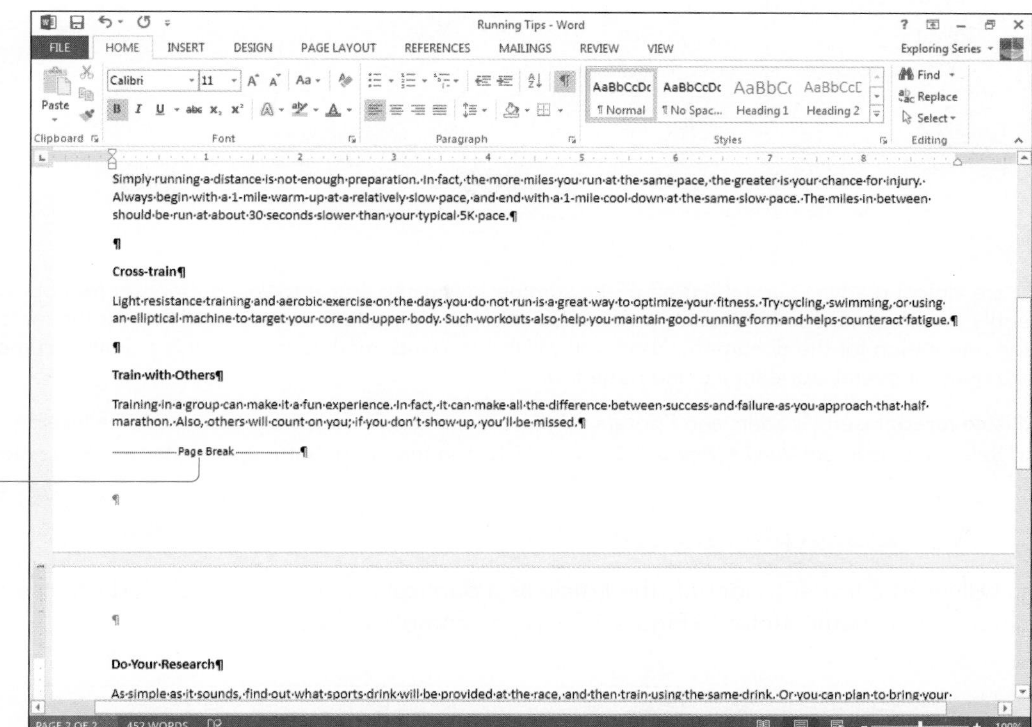

Running Tips - Word
FILE
HOME
INSERT
DESIGN
PAGE LAYOUT
REFERENCES
MAILINGS
REVIEW
VIEW
Exploring Series
Paste
Clipboard
Font
Paragraph
Styles
Editing
¶ Normal
¶ No Spac...
Heading 1
Heading 2
Find
Replace
Select
Simply·running·a·distance·is·not·enough·preparation.·In·fact,·the·more·miles·you·run·at·the·same·pace,·the·greater·is·your·chance·for·injury.·Always·begin·with·a·1-mile·warm-up·at·a·relatively·slow·pace,·and·end·with·a·1-mile·cool-down·at·the·same·slow·pace.·The·miles·in·between·should·be·run·at·about·30·seconds·slower·than·your·typical·5K·pace.¶
Cross-train¶
Light·resistance·training·and·aerobic·exercise·on·the·days·you·do·not·run·is·a·great·way·to·optimize·your·fitness.·Try·cycling,·swimming,·or·using·an·elliptical·machine·to·target·your·core·and·upper·body.·Such·workouts·also·help·you·maintain·good·running·form·and·helps·counteract·fatigue.¶
Train·with·Others¶
Training·in·a·group·can·make·it·a·fun·experience.·In·fact,·it·can·make·all·the·difference·between·success·and·failure·as·you·approach·that·half·marathon.·Also,·others·will·count·on·you;·if·you·don't·show·up,·you'll·be·missed.¶
Page Break
Page break indicator
Do·Your·Research¶
PAGE 2 OF 2
452 WORDS
100%

FIGURE 1.34 Forcing a Page Break

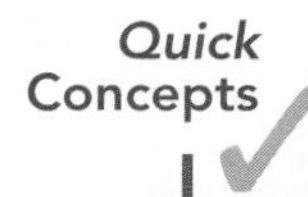

Quick Concepts

1. Some header and footer items, such as author name and file name, serve to identify the document and its origin. Other header and footer fields portray data that changes. Provide at least two examples of fields that contain variable data. When would you want to exclude headers and footers from the first page of a document, and how would you do that? ***p. 158***
2. A watermark is often in the form of text, such as the word *Draft*, which indicates that a document is not in its final form. What other text and/or graphic watermarks might you include in a document? ***p. 162***
3. The status bar includes selections that change a document view. Compare and contrast the view selections on the status bar. ***p. 163***
4. You have just completed a multiple-page research paper, including a cover page. Before printing the paper, you will check it onscreen to determine how text flows from one page to the next, assuring attractive page endings (no heading shown alone at the end of a page, for example). Provide two ways to view the multiple-page document, so that at least one entire page is shown at a time. Also, assume that you find it necessary to break a page before a solo heading at the bottom of a page. How would you force a page break at that location? ***p. 165***

Hands-On Exercises

MyITLab® HOE2 Training

2 Document Organization

You are almost ready to submit a draft of the summer day camp article to your supervisor for approval. After inserting a footer to identify the document as originating with the U.S. Fish and Wildlife Service, you will adjust the margins and determine the best page orientation for the document. Next, you will insert a watermark to indicate it is a draft document. Finally, you will review the document for overall appearance and page flow.

Skills covered: Insert Headers and Footers • Adjust Margins • Change Page Orientation • Insert a Watermark • Insert a Symbol and Select a Document View • View a Document, Change the Zoom Setting, and Manage Page Flow

STEP 1 » INSERT HEADERS AND FOOTERS

You will insert a footer to identify the article as a publication of the U.S. Fish and Wildlife Service. The footer will also include the file name. Refer to Figure 1.35 as you complete Step 1.

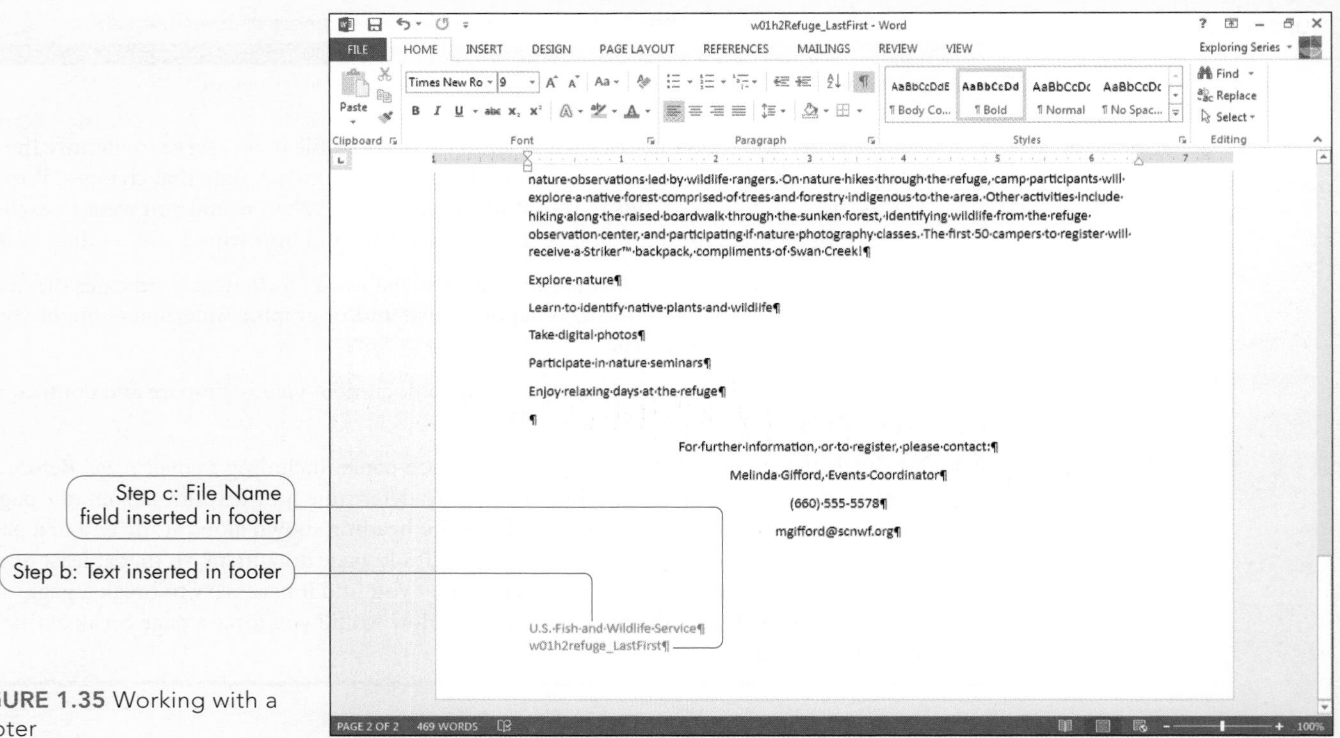

FIGURE 1.35 Working with a Footer

a. Open *w01h1Refuge_LastFirst* if you closed it at the end of Hands-On Exercise 1 and save it as **w01h2Refuge_LastFirst**, changing *h1* to *h2*.

> **TROUBLESHOOTING:** If you make any major mistakes in this exercise, you can close the file, open *w01h1Refuge_LastFirst* again, and then start this exercise over.

b. Click the **INSERT tab**, click **Footer** in the Header & Footer group, and then select **Edit Footer**. Type **U.S. Fish and Wildlife Service**. Press **Enter**.

TROUBLESHOOTING: If you select a predefined footer instead of clicking *Edit Footer*, click **Undo** on the Quick Access Toolbar and repeat step b.

c. Click **Document Info** in the Insert group and select **File Name**.

d. Click **Close Header and Footer** in the Close group.

e. Click after the first sentence of the second body paragraph, ending with *through eighth graders*. Be sure to click after the period ending the sentence. Press the **Spacebar** and type the following sentence: **The series of wildlife camps will begin on June 15, with the last camp ending on August 6.**

f. Save the document.

STEP 2 » ADJUST MARGINS

The article fits on one page, but you anticipate adding text. You suspect that with narrower margins, you might be able to add text while making sure the article requires only one page. You will experiment with a few margin settings. Refer to Figure 1.36 as you complete Step 2.

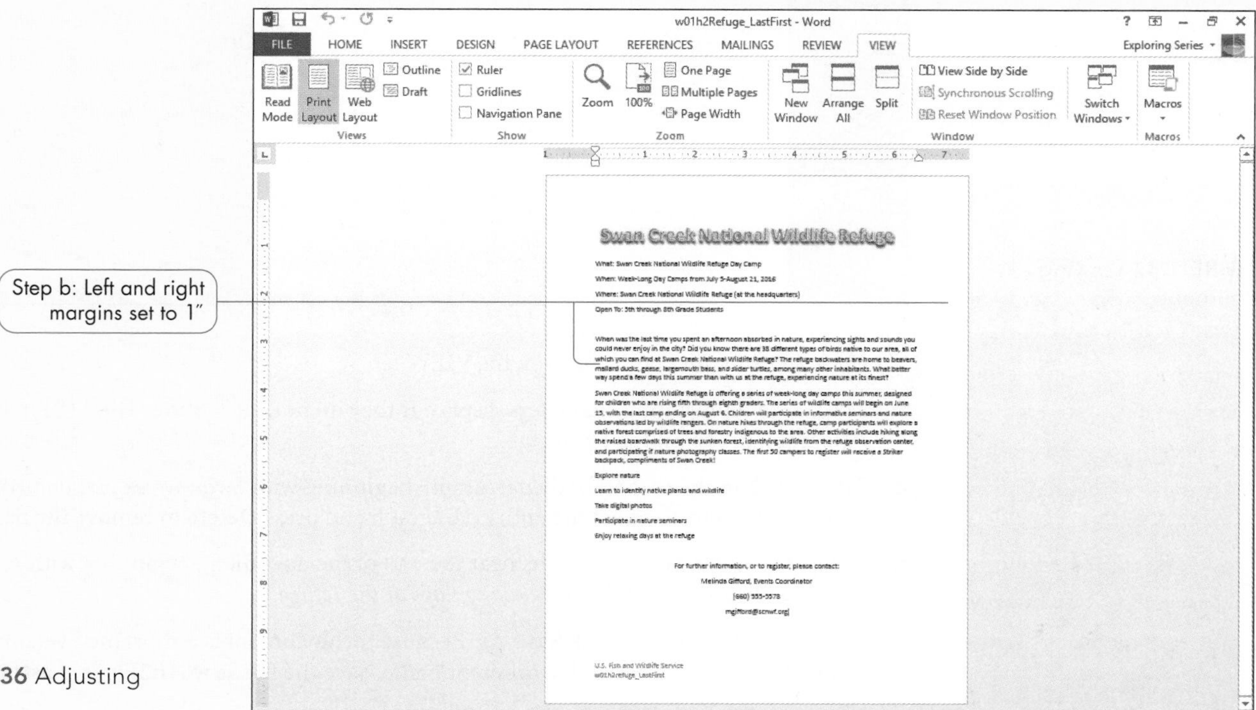

FIGURE 1.36 Adjusting Margins

a. Click the **PAGE LAYOUT tab**, click **Margins** in the Page Setup group, and then select **Narrow**.

   At a glance, you determine the right and left margins are too narrow, so you will adjust them.

b. Click **Margins** and select **Custom Margins**. Adjust the Left and Right margins to **1"** and click **OK**.

c. Click the **VIEW tab** and click **One Page** in the Zoom group.

   The document appears to be well positioned on the page, with what appears to be room for a small amount of additional text, if necessary.

d. Save the document.

STEP 3 ›› CHANGE PAGE ORIENTATION

Ms. Traynom has asked that you prepare an abbreviated version of the article, retaining only the most pertinent information. You will prepare and save the shortened version, but you will also retain the lengthier version. The shortened article will provide a snapshot of the summer activity in an at-a-glance format. Refer to Figure 1.37 as you complete Step 3.

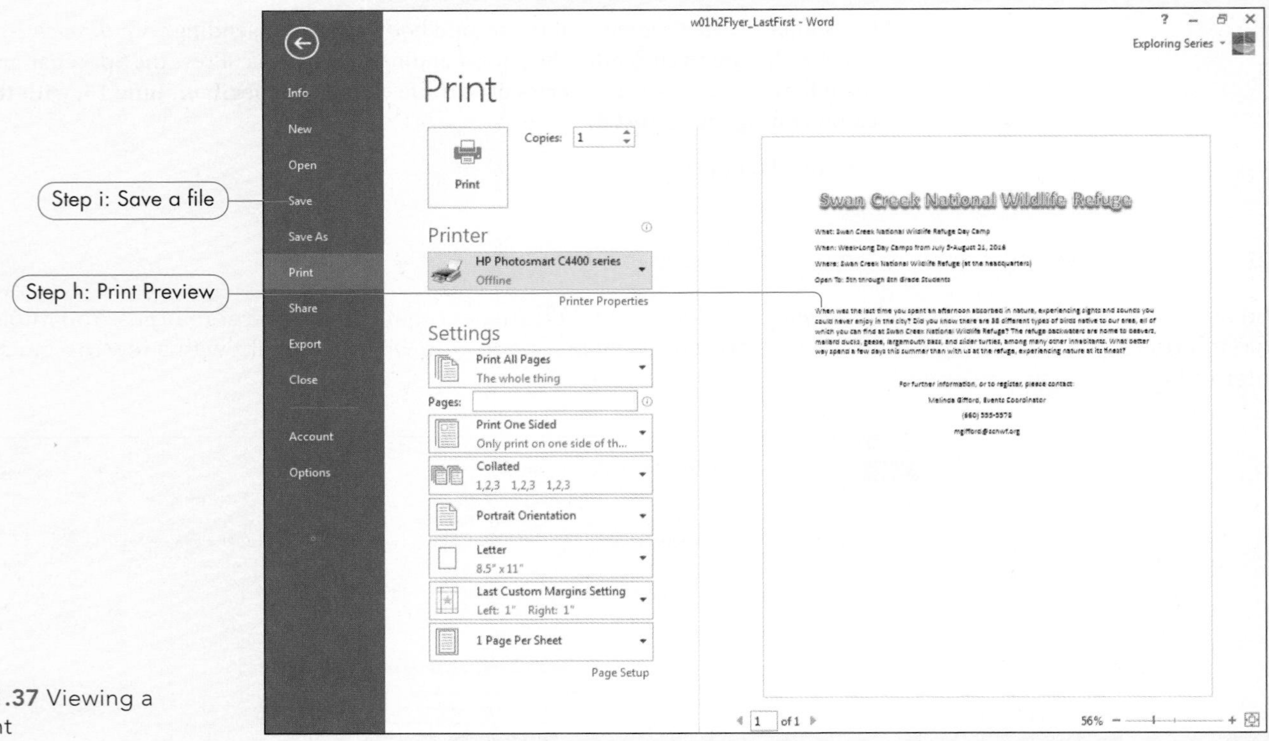

FIGURE 1.37 Viewing a Document

a. Click **100%** in the Zoom group on the VIEW tab.

b. Make sure nonprinting characters display. If they do not, click **Show/Hide (¶)** in the Paragraph group on the Home tab.

c. Triple-click in the second body paragraph, beginning with *Swan Creek National Wildlife Refuge is offering*, to select the entire paragraph and press **Delete** to remove the paragraph.

d. Delete the single line paragraphs near the end of the document, beginning with *Explore nature* and ending with *Enjoy relaxing days at the refuge.*

e. Click the **FILE tab** and click **Save As**. Because the document is a shortened version of the original, you will save it with a different name. Save the file as **w01h2Flyer_LastFirst**.

Given the shortened nature of the document, you will see whether landscape orientation provides a more attractive view.

f. Click the **PAGE LAYOUT tab** and click **Orientation** in the Page Setup group. Click **Landscape**. Click the **VIEW tab,** and click **One Page**. The new orientation is not attractive, so click **Undo** on the Quick Access Toolbar.

The flyer is attractive, but you do not think it requires a footer. You will remove the footer.

g. Scroll down and double-click in the footer area. Select both footer lines and press **Delete** to remove the footer. Double-click in the document to close the footer.

h. Click the **FILE tab** and click **Print** to confirm the footer is removed.

i. Click **Save** in the left pane to save the document. Click the **FILE tab** and click **Close** to close the flyer without exiting Word.

STEP 4 ≫ INSERT A WATERMARK

You will open the original article so that you can add the finishing touches, making sure to identify it as a draft and not the final copy. To do so, you will insert a DRAFT watermark, which can be removed after your supervisor has approved the document for distribution. Refer to Figure 1.38 as you complete Step 4.

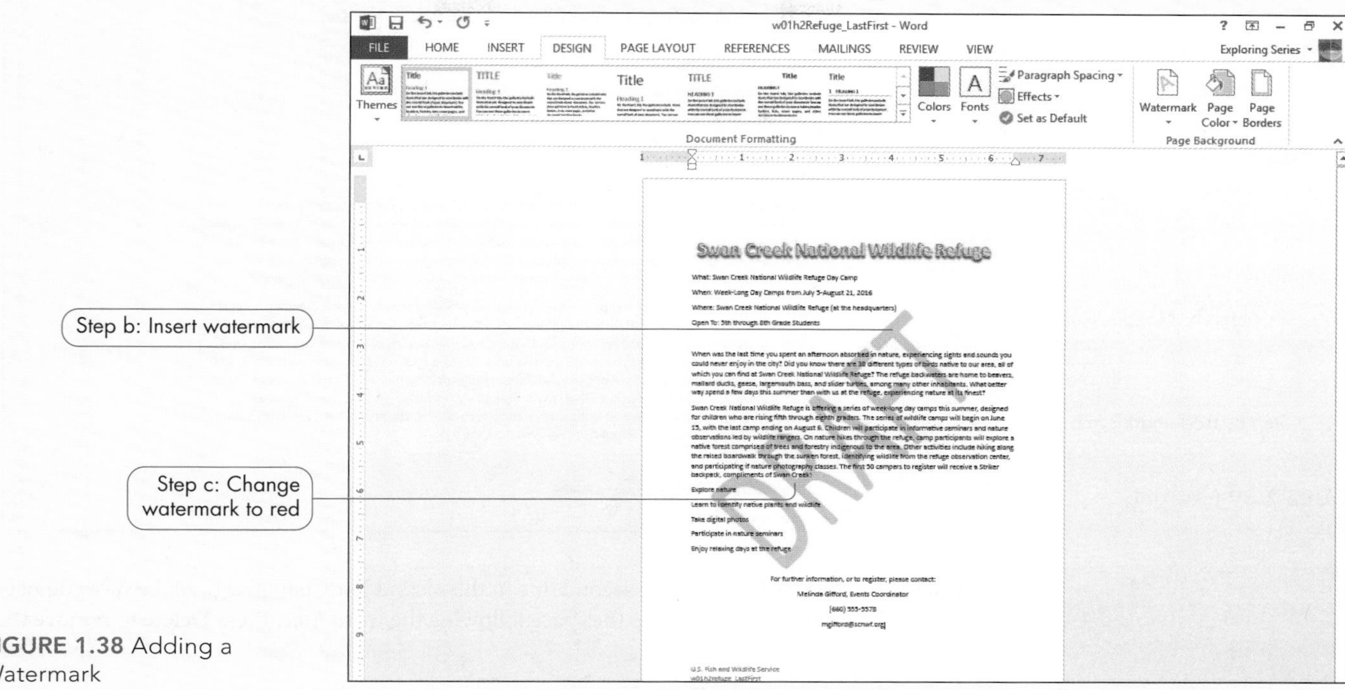

FIGURE 1.38 Adding a Watermark

a. Click the **FILE tab** and click **w01h2Refuge_LastFirst** in the list of recent documents.

b. Click the **DESIGN tab** and click **Watermark** in the Page Background group. Scroll through the gallery of watermarks and click **DRAFT 1** (under *Disclaimers*).

The watermark is not as visible as you would like, so you will change the color.

c. Click **Watermark** again and select **Custom Watermark**. Click the **Color arrow** in the Printed Watermark dialog box and click **Red** (under *Standard Colors*). Click **OK**.

d. Save the document.

STEP 5 ≫ INSERT A SYMBOL AND SELECT A DOCUMENT VIEW

The article you are preparing will be placed in numerous public venues, primarily schools. Given the widespread distribution of the document, you must consider any legality, such as appropriate recognition of name brands or proprietary mentions by inserting a trademark symbol. You will also ensure that words flow as they should, with no awkward or unintended breaks between words that should remain together. Refer to Figure 1.39 as you complete Step 5.

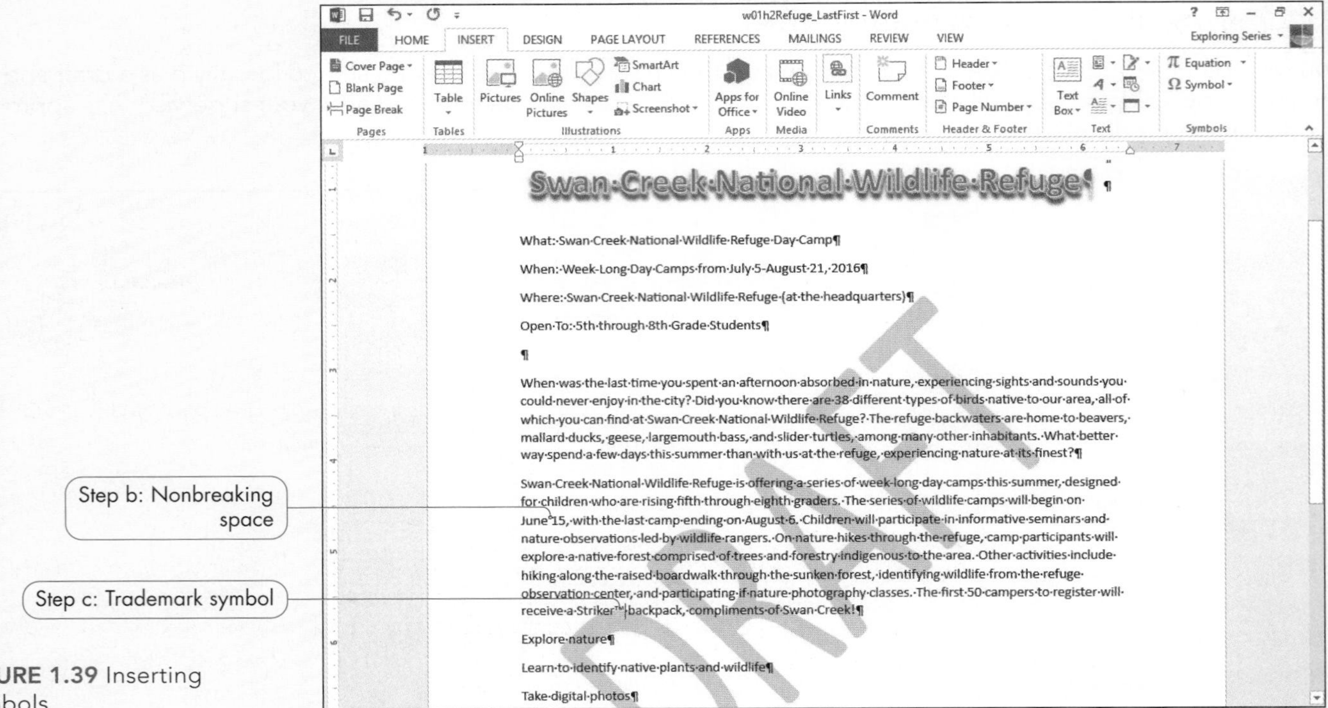

FIGURE 1.39 Inserting Symbols

a. Click after the word *June* on the second line in the second body paragraph. Make sure you have placed the insertion point before the space following the word *June*. Press **Delete** to remove the space.

Regardless of where the line ends, you want to make sure the phrase *June 15* is not separated, with the month on one line and the day on the following line. Therefore, you will insert a nonbreaking space.

b. Click the **INSERT tab** and click **Symbol** in the Symbols group. Click **More Symbols**. Click the **Special Characters tab**. Click **Nonbreaking Space**. Click **Insert** and click **Close**.

c. Click after the word *Striker* in the last sentence of the same paragraph. Click **Symbol** in the Symbols group and click **More Symbols**. Click **Special Characters**. Click **Trademark** to insert the Trademark symbol. Click **Insert** and click **Close**.

You use the Trademark symbol to indicate that *Striker* is a brand name.

d. Click the **VIEW tab** and click **Draft** in the Views group. Click **Print Layout** in the Views group.

e. Save the document.

STEP 6 » VIEW A DOCUMENT, CHANGE THE ZOOM SETTING, AND MANAGE PAGE FLOW

Ms. Traynom has provided you with a cover letter to include with the article. You will incorporate the letter text into the article as the first page, remove the footer from the first page, proofread the document, and ensure that both pages are attractively designed. Refer to Figure 1.40 as you complete Step 6.

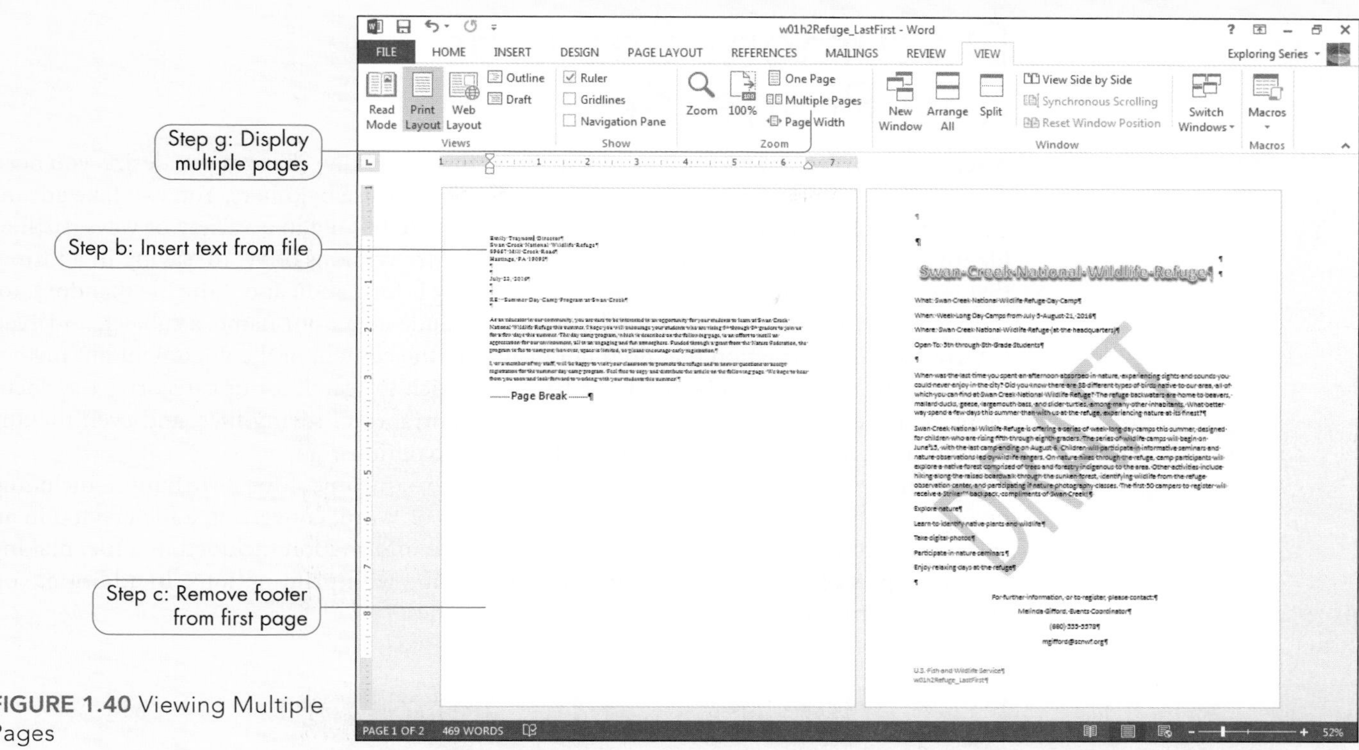

FIGURE 1.40 Viewing Multiple Pages

a. Press **Ctrl+Home** to position the insertion point at the top of the article. Press **Ctrl+Enter** to insert a blank page at the top. Press **Ctrl+Home** to move to the top of the new page.

Note that both the watermark and the footer display on the new page. That is because those features are designed to appear by default on all pages of a document.

b. Click the **INSERT tab**, if necessary, and click the **Object arrow** in the Text group. Click **Text from File**. Navigate to *w01h2Letter* in your student data files and double-click the file name.

c. Double-click in the footer area of the first page. Click **Different First Page** in the Options group of the HEADER & FOOTER TOOLS DESIGN tab.

You have indicated that the watermark and footer are not to appear on the first page, but will remain on all others.

d. Click **Close Header and Footer** in the Close group.

e. Press **Ctrl+Home**. Click the **VIEW tab** and click **Zoom** in the Zoom group. Click in the **Percent box** and change the Zoom to **125%**. Click **OK**.

f. Scroll through the document, proofreading for spelling and grammatical errors. Right-click any underlined error and either correct or ignore it. Manually correct any errors that Word has not flagged.

g. Click **Multiple Pages** in the Zoom group.

h. Click the **FILE tab** and click **Print**. Click **Next Page** (the arrow that follows *1 of 2* at the bottom of the screen) to view the article. Click **Previous Page** to return to the letter.

The letter appears to be too high on the page, so you will move the text down a bit.

i. Click **Back** (the arrow at the top left) to return to the document. Click **100%** in the Zoom group. Press **Ctrl+Home** to move to the top of the document. Press **Enter** three times to move the text down the page.

j. Click the **FILE tab** and click **Print**. The first page should be better situated on the page, with additional space at the top.

k. Save the document. Keep the document open if you plan to continue with the next Hands-On Exercise. If not, close the document and exit Word.

Document Settings and Properties

After you organize your document and make all the formatting changes you desire, you need to save the document in its final form and prepare it for use by others. You can take advantage of features in Word that enable you to manipulate the file in a variety of ways, such as identifying features that are not compatible with older versions of Word, saving in a format that is compatible with older versions, and including information about the file that does not display in the document. For example, you can include an author name, a subject, and even keywords—all information that does not display in the content of the document but further identifies the file, and can be used as a basis on which to search for or categorize the document later. Because you are well aware of the importance of saving files, and even making backup copies of those files, you will explore backup options.

In this section, you will explore ways to prepare a document for distribution, including saving in a format compatible with earlier versions of Word, converting a file created in an earlier version to Office 2013, checking for sensitive information included in a file, making backup copies of important documents, and working with print options. In addition, you will learn to customize and print document properties.

Preparing a Document for Distribution

Seldom will you prepare a document that you do not intend to distribute. Whether it is a report to submit to your instructor or a memo on which you collaborated, most likely the document is something that will be shared with others. Regardless of how you plan to develop, save, and distribute a document, you will not want to chance losing your work because you did not save it properly or failed to make a backup copy. Inevitably, files are lost, systems crash, and viruses infect a system. That said, the importance of saving work frequently and ensuring that backup copies exist cannot be overemphasized.

With the frequency of new Word versions, there is always a chance that someone who needs to read your document is working with a version that is not compatible with yours, or perhaps the person is not working with Word at all. You can eliminate that source of frustration by saving a document in a compatible format before distributing it. Another source of concern when distributing a document is the hidden or personal data that might be stored in document properties, such as the author's or organization's name. Backing up documents, ensuring their compatibility with other software versions, and removing document information that is either unnecessary or has the potential for too much disclosure should definitely be considered before finalizing a project or allowing others to see it.

Ensure Document Compatibility

Earlier in this chapter, in the section on saving files, you learned how to save a document in an earlier Word version so that someone without access to Word 2013 might still open the file. You might also consider saving a file in Rich Text Format, which adds even more flexibility, as such a file can be opened by other word processing software in addition to Word. Be aware, however, that doing so might compromise the document somewhat because Rich Text Format, and even earlier Word versions, cannot accommodate all of the current Word version's special features. (See the section in this chapter on saving a file for information on how to change the file type.)

When you open a file created in an earlier Word version, the words *Compatibility Mode* are included in the title bar, advising you that some of Word 2013's features will not be available or viewable in the document. While in Compatibility Mode, you might not be able to use new and enhanced features of the most current Word version; by keeping the file in Compatibility Mode, you ensure that people with earlier Word versions will still have full editing capability when they receive the document. However, if you want to convert the file to Office 2013, complete the following steps:

1. Click the FILE tab. Info should be selected; if not, click to select it.
2. Click Convert (beside Compatibility Mode). The Convert option will not be displayed if the file is currently in Office 2013 format.
3. Click OK.

When you convert a file, you change the original file to a newer version of Word. When you subsequently save the file, it is saved in the newest Word version.

Documents saved in Word 2013 can be opened by users of Word 2010 and Word 2007. Even so, documents developed in Word 2013 might contain features that are not recognizable by those or earlier versions. In some cases, it might be necessary for a user of Word 2007 or Word 2010 to install a service pack or otherwise download a software solution in order to view a Word 2013 file in its entirety.

Before distributing a document, you can check it for compatibility, ensuring that it can be read in its entirety by users of earlier Word versions. To check a document for compatibility, do the following:

STEP 1»

1. Click the FILE tab.
2. Click Check for Issues (beside Inspect Document).
3. Click Check Compatibility.
4. Click *Select versions to show* and then select one or more versions of Word to check (or simply leave them all selected).
5. After reading a summary of any features that are incompatible, click OK.

Understand Backup Options

Word enables you to back up files in different ways. One option is to use a feature called ***AutoRecover***. If Word crashes when AutoRecover is enabled, the program will be able to recover a previous version of your document when you restart the program. The only work you will lose is anything you did between the time of the last AutoRecover operation and the time of the crash, unless you happen to save the document in the meantime. By default, file information is saved every 10 minutes (see Figure 1.41), but you can adjust the setting so that the AutoRecover process occurs more or less frequently.

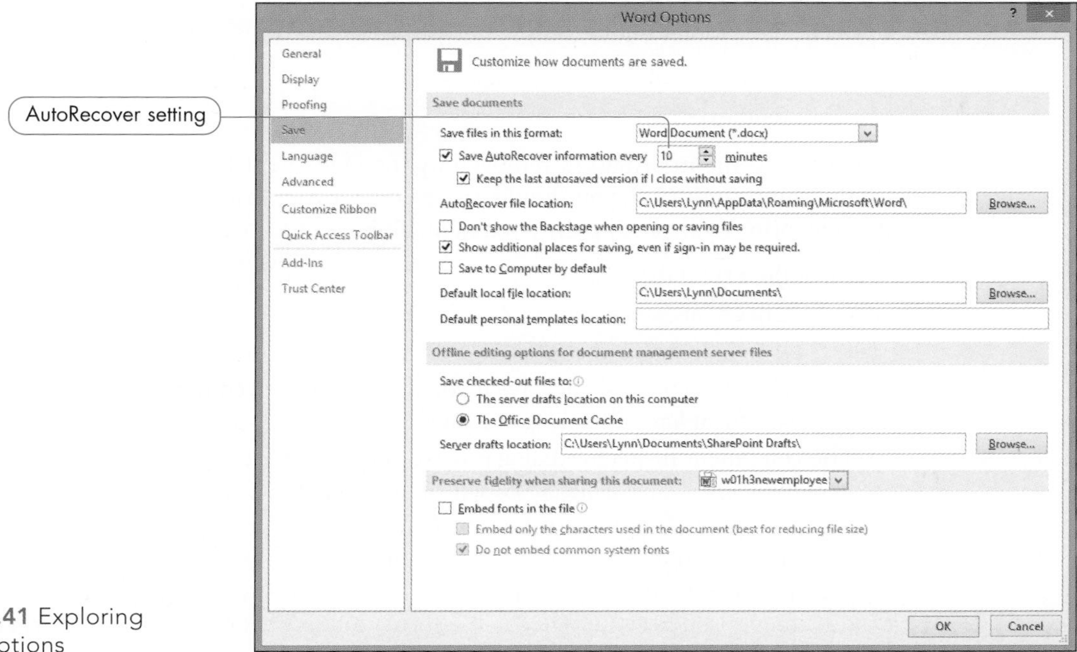

FIGURE 1.41 Exploring Backup Options

You can also configure Word to create a backup copy each time a document is saved. Although the setting to always create a backup copy is not enabled by default, you can enable it from Word Options in the Advanced category. Scroll through categories under Advanced options to locate the Save group, in which you can choose to always create a backup copy. Word will create a backup copy in this way. Assume that you have created the simple document with the phrase *The fox jumped over the fence*, and have saved it under the name *Fox*. Assume further that you edit the document to read *The quick brown fox jumped over the fence*, and that you save it a second time. The second Save command changes the name of the original document (containing the text *The fox jumped over the fence*) from *Fox* to *Backup of Fox*, then saves the current contents (*The quick brown fox jumped over the fence*) as *Fox*. In other words, the disk now contains two instances of the document: the current *Fox* document and the document containing the original text—*Backup of Fox*.

The cycle goes on indefinitely, with *Fox* always containing the current document and *Backup of Fox* the most recent instance. So, if you revise and save the document a third time, the original wording of the document is no longer available, because only two instances of the document are kept. The contents of *Fox* and *Backup of Fox* are different, but the existence of the latter enables you to retrieve the previous iteration if you inadvertently edit beyond repair or accidentally erase the current *Fox* document. To enable an automatic backup:

STEP 2»

1. Click the FILE tab.
2. Click Options.
3. Click Advanced.
4. Scroll to the Save group and click *Always create backup copy*. Click OK.

Run the Document Inspector

Before you send or give a document to another person, you should run the ***Document Inspector*** to reveal any hidden or personal data in the file. For privacy or security reasons, you might want to remove certain items contained in the document such as author name, comments made by one or more persons who have access to the document, or document server locations. Word's Document Inspector will check for and enable you to remove various types of identifying information, including:

- Comments, revisions, versions, and annotations
- Document properties and personal information
- Custom XML data
- Headers, footers, and watermarks
- Invisible content
- Hidden text

Because some information removed by the Document Inspector cannot be recovered with the Undo command, you should save a copy of your original document, using a different name, prior to inspecting the document. To inspect a document:

STEP 3»

1. Click the FILE tab.
2. Click Check for Issues.
3. Click Inspect Document.
4. If a dialog box appears, click Yes if you have not yet saved the file and want to do so (or click No if you have already saved the file).
5. The Document Inspector dialog box (see Figure 1.42) enables you to confirm the types of content you want to check. Deselect any categories you do not want to check.
6. Click Inspect to begin the process. When the check is complete, Word lists the results and enables you to choose whether to remove the content from the document. For example, if you are distributing a document to others, you might want to remove all document properties and personal information. In that case, you can instruct the Document Inspector to remove such content.

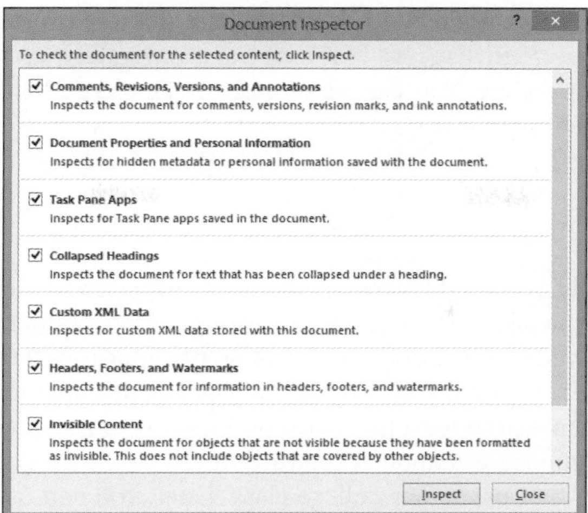

FIGURE 1.42 Document Inspector

Select Print Options

It is far too easy to print an entire document when you intend to print only a few pages. That is because you might not pay enough attention to print options, one of which enables you to print the entire document unless you specify otherwise. You will find that print setting, and others, when you click the File tab and click Print. The current printer is shown, although you can change to another installed printer, if you like (see Figure 1.43). The Print settings shown in Figure 1.43 enable you to select the number of copies, the pages or range of pages to print, the printer to use, whether to collate pages, whether to print on only one side of the paper, and how many pages to print per sheet. In addition, you can adjust page orientation, paper size, and even customize a document's margins—all by paying attention to print options. Please note that the wording of some Print options will vary, depending on whether you have previously selected the option and indicated a custom setting. For example, if you recently selected Print All Pages and indicated a specific range to print, then the Print All Pages option will display the most recent range of pages printed or selected.

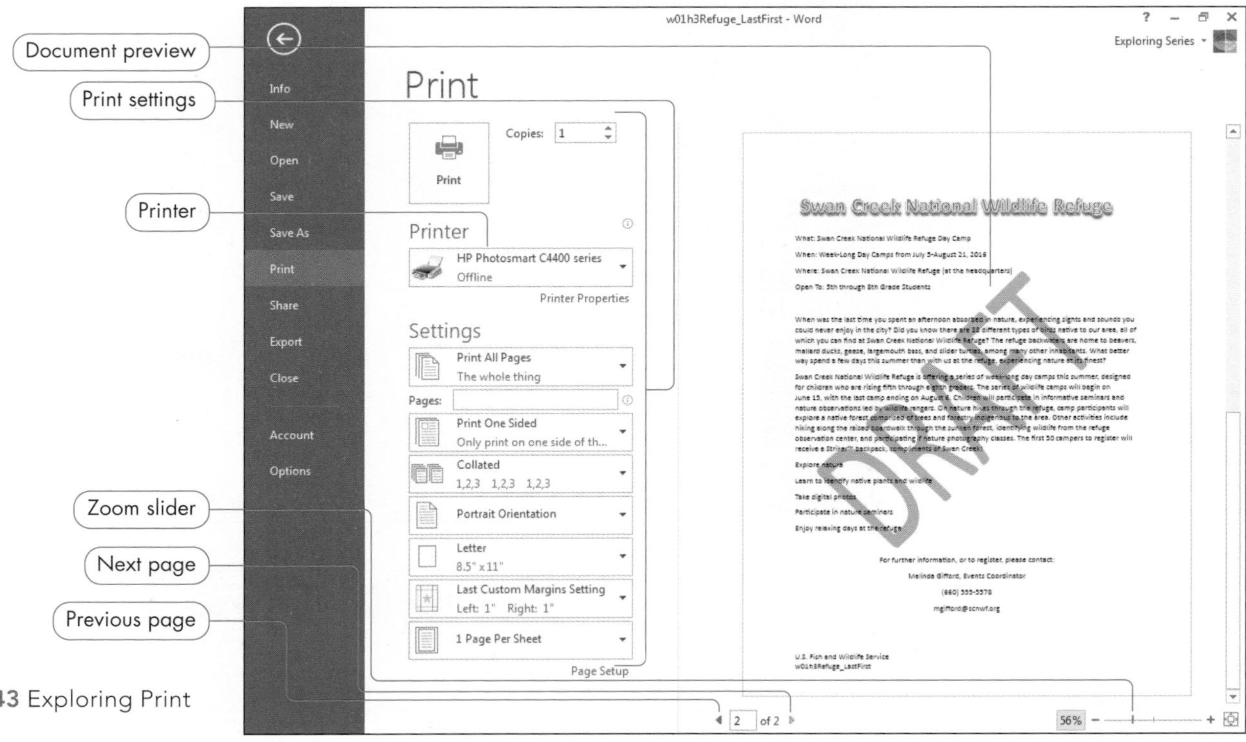

FIGURE 1.43 Exploring Print Settings

Print options display to the left of the document preview (refer to Figure 1.43). You can click the Next Page or Previous Page navigation arrow to move among pages in the document preview. You can also drag the Zoom slider to enlarge or reduce the size of the document preview.

Modifying Document Properties

Occasionally, you might want to include information to identify a document, such as author, document purpose, intended audience, or general comments. Those data elements, or *metadata*, are saved with the document, but do not appear in the document as it displays onscreen or is printed. Instead, you can use the ***Document Panel*** to display descriptive information. You can even search for a file based on identifying information you assign a document. For example, suppose you apply a keyword of *CIS 225* to all documents you create that are associated with that particular college class. Later, you can use that keyword as a search term, locating all associated documents.

For statistical information related to the current document, click the File tab and make sure that Info is selected. Data such as file size, number of pages, and total words are presented (see Figure 1.44). You can modify some document information in this view, such as adding a title or comments, but for more possibilities, display the full Document Panel (see Figure 1.45). To display the Document Panel:

1. Click the FILE tab.
2. Click the Properties arrow.
3. Click Show Document Panel.

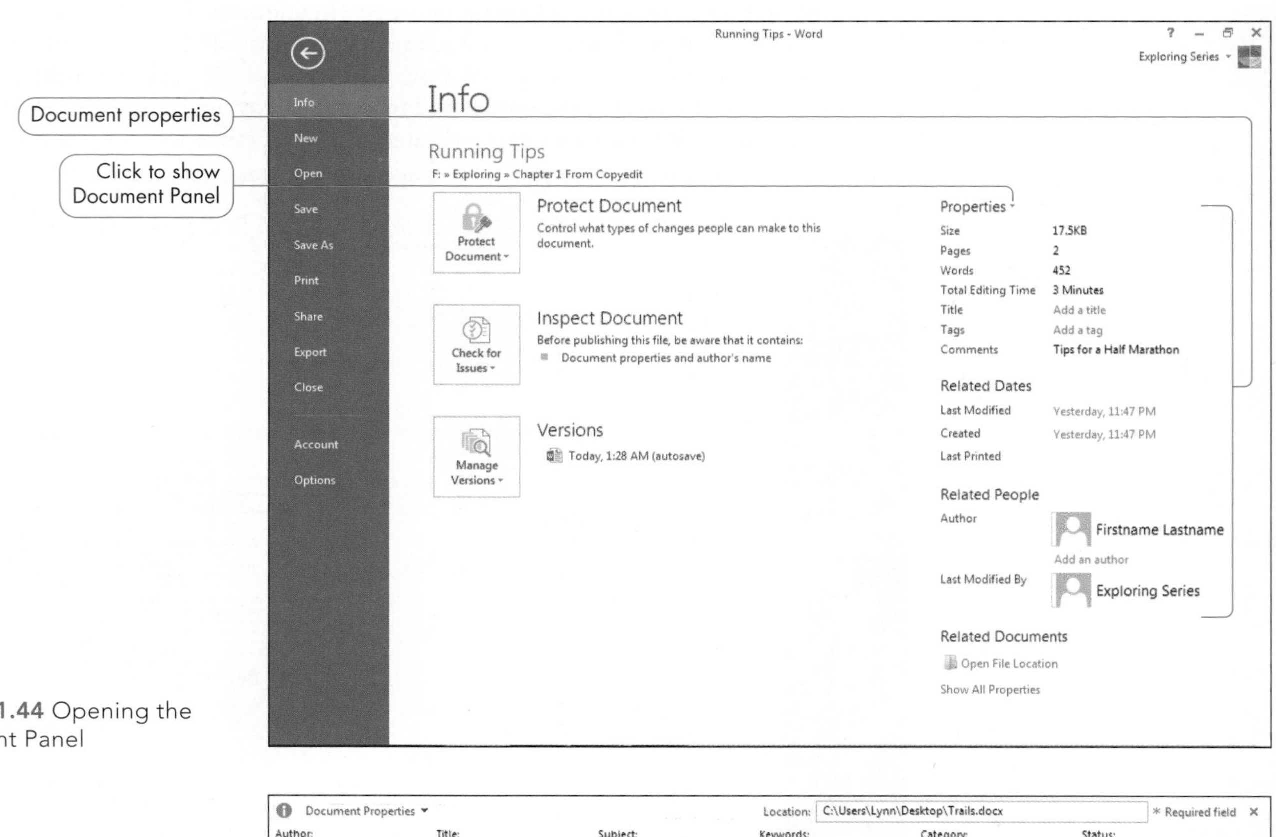

FIGURE 1.44 Opening the Document Panel

FIGURE 1.45 Viewing the Document Panel

When you save the document, Word saves this information with the document. You can update the descriptive information at any time by opening the Document Panel for the respective document.

Customize Document Properties

In addition to creating, modifying, and viewing a document summary, you may want to customize document properties in the Document Panel. For example, you might want to add a *Date completed* property and specify an exact date for reference. This date would reflect the completion date, not the date the file was last saved. You also might create a field to track company information such as warehouse location or product numbers.

To customize document properties:

STEP 4

1. Click the FILE tab and click Info, if necessary. Click Properties and click Advanced Properties. The Properties dialog box displays, showing commonly used properties on the General tab.
2. Click the Custom tab of the Properties dialog box to add custom property categories and assign values to them.
3. Click Add, after assigning a value to a custom category, and click OK.

TIP Checking Statistics

When working with Advanced Properties, you might want to check document statistics, such as the date the document was created, the total editing time, or the word count. Click the File tab, select Info, and then click Properties. Click Advanced Properties and click the Statistics tab to view statistics related to the current document.

Print Document Properties

You can print document properties to store hard copies for easy reference. To do this:

1. Click the FILE tab.
2. Click Print.
3. Click Print All Pages.
4. Click Document Info.
5. Click Print.

Quick Concepts

1. A coworker who uses Office 2007 has sent you a document for review. When you open the document, the words *[Compatibility Mode]* display in the title bar after the file name. Is there any reason you might want to remove the document from Compatibility Mode? And if so, how would you convert the document to Word 2013 format? ***p. 174***
2. You are aware that it is very important to create backup copies of important documents. Describe the process of using Word 2013 options to ensure that backup copies are automatically created. ***p. 176***
3. Before distributing a document, you want to make sure any personally identifying information, such as author and comments, are removed. How would you accomplish that? ***p. 176***
4. Before printing pages 3 through 5 of the current document, you want to preview the document and then print only those pages. In a separate print procedure, you also want to print document properties that are associated with the current document. What steps would you follow to preview and print those pages? ***pp. 177 and 179***

Hands-On Exercises

Watch the Video for this Hands-On Exercise!

MyITLab® HOE3 Training

3 Document Settings and Properties

As the office assistant for Swan Creek National Wildlife Refuge, you are responsible for the security, management, and backup of the organization's documents. The article promoting the summer day camps is ready for final approval. Before that happens, however, you want to check it one last time yourself, making sure it is saved in a format that others can read and that you have sufficient backup copies. You will also include appropriate document properties for additional identification, and you will consider print options. Privacy and security are to be considered as well, so you will check for identifiers that should be removed before distributing the document.

Skills covered: Ensure Document Compatibility • Understand Backup Options • Run the Document Inspector and Select Print Options • Customize and Print Document Properties

STEP 1 ›› ENSURE DOCUMENT COMPATIBILITY

You know Ms. Traynom is anxious to review a copy of this document; however, she has not yet upgraded to Office 2013. Instead, her office computer has Office 2007 installed. To make sure she can open and read the document, you will check the document for compatibility with earlier Word versions. Refer to Figure 1.46 as you complete Step 1.

Memo

To: Swan Creek Staff

From: Joseph Blackstone, Personnel Director

Date: July 28, 2016

Re: Adrian Sammons (new employee)

Please give a warm welcome to our newest employee, Adrian Sammons, who will be leading our Nature Conservancy office. Adrian comes to us with a wealth of experience in managing wildlife programs. His most recent assignment was with the South Florida Sea Lab, where he directed several successful grant programs and helped develop the first student-led symposium in Florida. Until his new office is renovated, Adrian will share quarters with Ms. Emily Traynom. Please join me in welcoming Adrian to Swan Creek!

FIGURE 1.46 Converted Document

a. Open *w01h2Refuge_LastFirst* if you closed it at the end of Hands-On Exercise 2 and save it as **w01h3Refuge_LastFirst**, changing *h2* to *h3*.

b. Click the **FILE tab**, make sure that *Info* is selected, and then click **Check for Issues** (beside *Inspect Document*).

c. Click **Check Compatibility**. Click **Select versions to show** and deselect **Word 97-2003** to make sure only *Word 2007* and *Word 2010* are selected.

   Note that some formatting features are not supported and will not be available in the version you are preparing for Ms. Traynom.

d. Click **OK**. Save the document.

   Because the compatibility issues are few and are restricted to what appear to be minor text effects, you feel confident that Ms. Traynom will be able to open the document in Word 2007. You will also provide her with a printed copy, just in case.

e. Click the **FILE tab** and close the document.

   The personnel director has prepared a draft of a memo introducing a new employee. He has asked that you proof the document and prepare it for printing. However, he created and saved the memo using Word 2007. You will open the file and convert it to Word 2013 format.

f. Open *w01h3NewEmployee* from your data files.

   The title bar displays *[Compatibility Mode]* following the file name *w01h3NewEmployee*, indicating that it is not a file saved with Word 2013.

g. Click the **FILE tab** and click **Convert** (beside *Compatibility Mode*). A message box displays explaining the consequences of upgrading the document. Click **OK**.

   The Compatibility Mode designation is removed from the title bar.

h. Save the document as **w01h3NewEmployee_LastFirst**.

STEP 2 » UNDERSTAND BACKUP OPTIONS

The timeline for preparing for the summer day camps is short. Given the time spent in developing the article, you know that if it were lost, recreating it in a timely fashion would be difficult. In fact, it is critical to ensure appropriate backups for *all* files for which you are responsible at Swan Creek. You will explore backup options on your computer to verify that files are saved periodically and that backups are automatically created. Refer to Figure 1.47 as you complete Step 2.

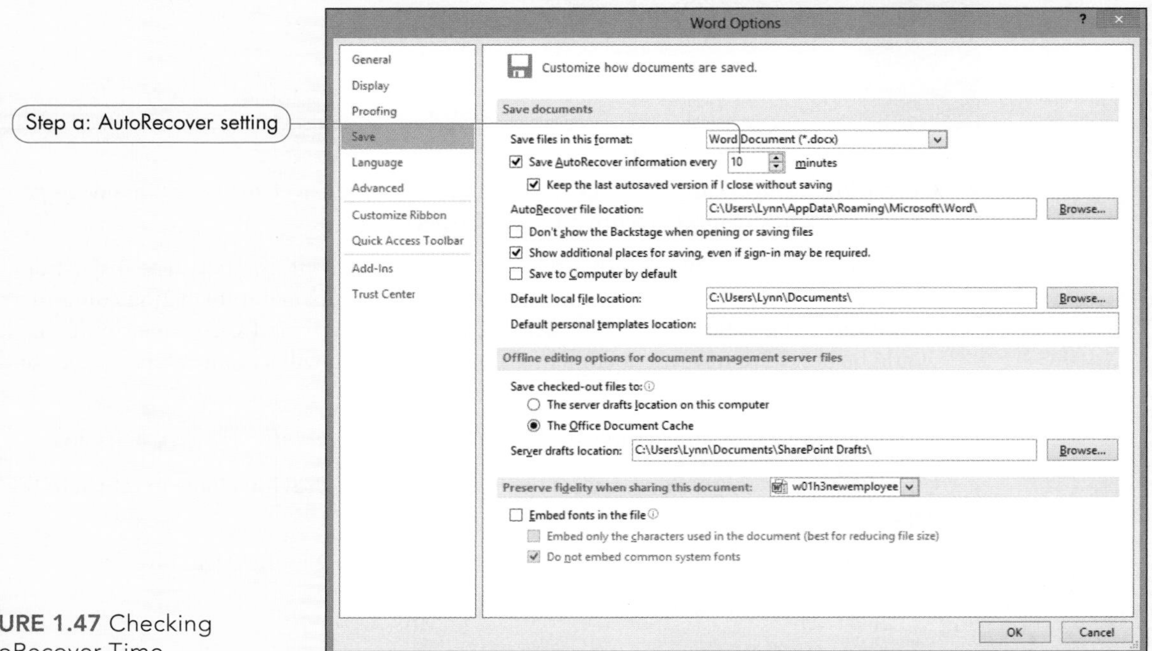

FIGURE 1.47 Checking AutoRecover Time

a. Click the **FILE tab** and click **Options**. Click **Save** in the left pane of the Word Options dialog box. If *Save AutoRecover information every* is checked, note the number of minutes between saves.

b. Click **Advanced**. Scroll to the Save area and note whether *Always create backup copy* is selected.

   You will not select the setting at this time, although you should consider doing so on your own computer or a computer at a workplace.

c. Click **Cancel**. Close the document.

STEP 3 ≫ RUN THE DOCUMENT INSPECTOR AND SELECT PRINT OPTIONS

Before distributing the article, you will run the Document Inspector to identify any information that should first be removed. You will also prepare to print the document. Refer to Figure 1.48 as you complete Step 3.

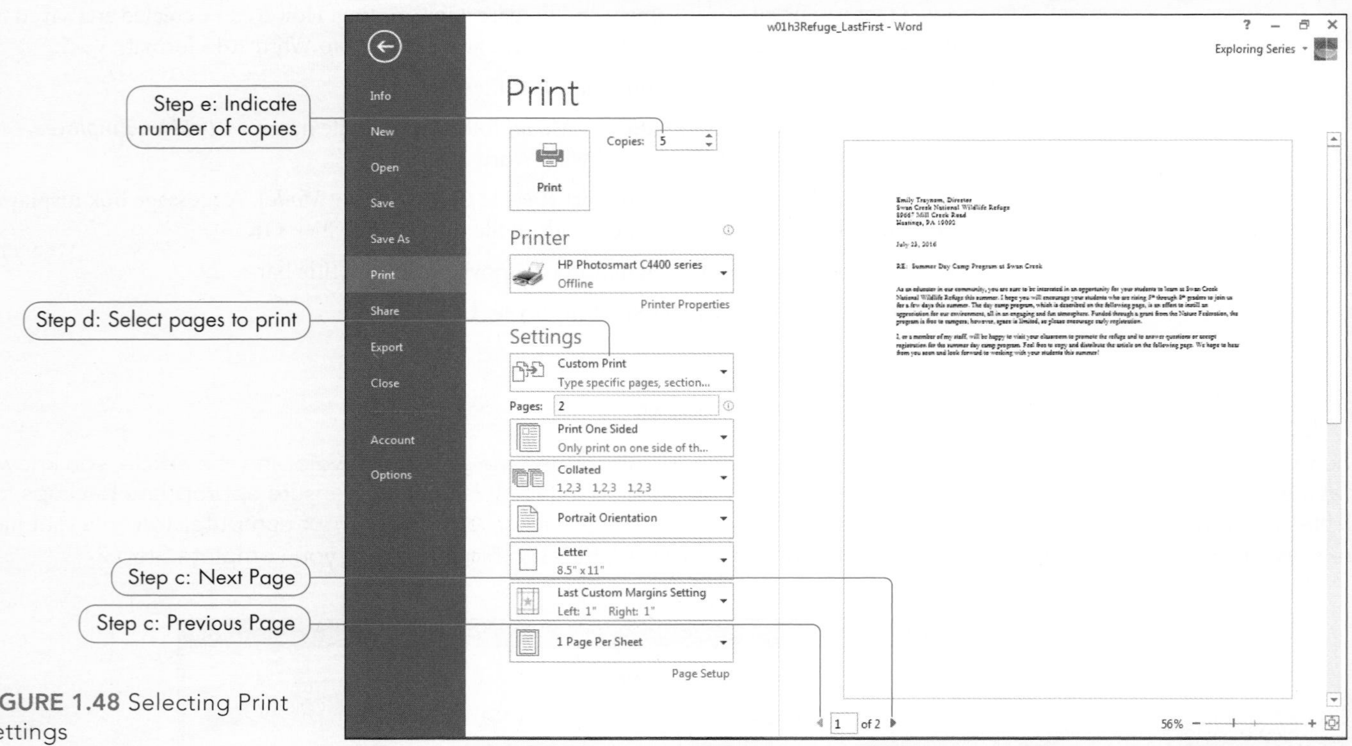

FIGURE 1.48 Selecting Print Settings

a. Open *w01h3Refuge_LastFirst*. Click the **FILE tab** and click **Check for Issues** (beside *Inspect Document*). Click **Inspect Document**. Click **Inspect**.

   You check for document areas that might display sensitive information. The inspection suggests that the category of Document Properties and Personal Information contains identifying data, as does that of Headers, Footers, and Watermarks. You determine that it would be best to remove all document properties, but you will leave headers, footers, and watermarks.

b. Click **Remove All** beside *Document Properties and Personal Information*. Click **Close**.

c. Click **Print**. Click **Next Page** to view the next page. Click **Previous Page** to return to the first page.

d. Click **Print All Pages**, click **Custom Print**, and then type **2** in the Pages box.

   You indicate that you want to print page 2 only.

e. Click the **Copies up arrow** repeatedly to print five copies.

You have indicated that you want to print five copies of page 2.

f. Press **Esc** to return to the document without printing.

STEP 4 » CUSTOMIZE AND PRINT DOCUMENT PROPERTIES

You will assign document properties to the document to identify its author and purpose. You will also create an additional property to record a project identifier. Finally, you will prepare to print document properties. Refer to Figure 1.49 as you complete Step 4.

FIGURE 1.49 Advanced Document Properties

a. Save the document as **w01h4Refuge_LastFirst**, changing *h3* to *h4*. Click the **FILE tab**, click **Properties** in the right pane, and then click **Show Document Panel**.

The Document Panel displays above your document.

b. Ensure that the Author box contains your name. Type your name, if necessary. Click one time in the **Comments box** and type **Summer Camp Information**.

c. Click the **Document Properties arrow** in the top-left of the Document Properties panel and click **Advanced Properties** to display the w01h4Refuge_LastFirst Properties dialog box.

d. Create a custom property by completing the following steps:

- Click the **Custom tab** and select **Project** in the **Name list**.
- Type **School Information** in the **Value box**, as shown in Figure 1.56, and click **Add**.
- Click **OK** to close the dialog box.

You want to catalog the documents you create for Swan Creek National Wildlife Refuge, and one way to do that is to assign a project scope using the custom properties that are stored with each document. Because you set up a custom field in the Document Properties, you can later perform searches and find all documents in that Project category.

e. Click **Close the Document Information Panel** in the top-right corner of Document Properties. Save the document.

f. Click the **FILE tab**, click **Print**, click **Custom Print**, and then click **Document Info**. If your computer is in communication with, or connected to, a printer, click **Print**. Otherwise, continue to step g.

g. Save and close *w01h4Refuge_LastFirst* and submit based on your instructor's directions.

Chapter Objectives Review

After reading this chapter, you have accomplished the following objectives:

1. **Begin and edit a document.**
   - Use a template: Predesigned documents save time by providing a starting point.
   - Create a document: Create a blank document by clicking *Blank document* when Word opens.
   - Save a document: Saving a document makes it possible to access it later for editing, sharing, or printing.
   - Open a document: Open a saved document by selecting the document from the Recent Documents List or browsing for other documents.
   - Move around a document and edit a document: Use scroll bars or keyboard shortcuts to move around in a document.
   - Review Word usage in a document: Use the Review tab to make sure all documents are free of typographical and grammatical errors.
2. **Customize Word.**
   - Explore Word options: Word options are global settings you can select, such as whether to check spelling automatically, or where to save a file by default.
   - Customize the Ribbon: Customize the Ribbon, using Word Options, to add, remove, or rename Ribbon tabs.
   - Customize the Quick Access Toolbar: The Quick Access Toolbar contains a few commands by default, but you can add more when you click *Customize the Quick Access Toolbar* and select from a menu.
3. **Use features that improve readability.**
   - Insert headers and footers: Headers and footers provide information, such as page number and organization name, in the top and bottom margins of a document.
   - Insert a symbol: A symbol is typically a character or graphic that is not found on the keyboard, such as ©.
   - Adjust margins: You can change margins, selecting predefined settings or creating your own.
   - Change page orientation: Select Landscape (located on the Page Layout tab) to show a document that is wider than it is tall, or Portrait to show a document taller than it is wide.
   - Insert a watermark: A watermark is text or a graphic that displays behind text to identify such items as a document's purpose, owner, or status.
4. **View a document in different ways.**
   - Select a document view: A view is the way a document displays onscreen; available Word views include Print Layout, Read Mode, Outline, Web Layout, and Draft.
   - Change the zoom setting: By changing the zoom setting (available on the View tab as well as the status bar), you can enlarge or reduce text size onscreen.
   - View a document and manage page flow: Forcing a page break is useful to divide document sections (for example, to separate a cover page from other report pages), or to better manage page flow so that pages do not end awkwardly.
5. **Prepare a document for distribution.**
   - Ensure document compatibility: Using Word 2013, you can convert documents to the most recent version and you can also ensure a document's compatibility with earlier versions.
   - Understand backup options: Backup options include AutoRecover and the ability to always create a backup copy of a saved document.
   - Run the Document Inspector: Word's Document Inspector reveals any hidden or personal data in a file and enables you to remove sensitive information.
   - Select print options: Using Word's print options (available when you click the File tab and click Print), you can specify the pages to print, the number of copies, and various other print selections.
6. **Modify document properties.**
   - Customize document properties: Document properties are items you can add to a document to further describe it, such as author, keywords, and comments.
   - Print document properties: For documentation purposes, you might want to print Document Properties.

Key Terms Matching

Match the key terms with their definitions. Write the key term letter by the appropriate numbered definition.

a. AutoRecover
b. Document Inspector
c. Document Panel
d. Draft view
e. Header and Footer
f. Insertion point
g. Landscape orientation
h. Microsoft Word
i. Outline view
j. Portrait orientation
k. Print Layout view
l. Quick Access Toolbar
m. Read Mode
n. Ribbon
o. Symbol
p. Template
q. Watermark
r. Word processing software
s. Word wrap

1. _______ The long bar of tabs, groups, and commands located just beneath the Title bar. **p. 140**
2. _______ Text or graphic that displays behind text. **p. 157**
3. _______ A structural view of a document or presentation that can be collapsed or expanded as necessary. **p. 163**
4. _______ Area that provides one-click access to commonly used commands. **p. 149**
5. _______ Document that is displayed taller than it is wide. **p. 161**
6. _______ The feature that automatically moves words to the next line if they do not fit on the current line. **p. 142**
7. _______ Enables Word to recover a previous version of a document. **p. 175**
8. _______ A computer application, such as Microsoft Word, used primarily with text to create, edit, and format documents. **p. 138**
9. _______ View in which text reflows to screen-sized pages to make it easier to read. **p. 163**
10. _______ Word processing application included in the Microsoft Office software suite. **p. 138**
11. _______ A predesigned document that may include format and wording that can be modified. **p. 141**
12. _______ Document that is displayed wider than it is tall. **p. 161**
13. _______ View that closely resembles the way a document will look when printed. **p. 163**
14. _______ A character or graphic not normally included on a keyboard. **p. 159**
15. _______ Checks for and removes certain hidden and personal information from a document. **p. 176**
16. _______ Information that displays at the top or bottom of each document page. **p. 157**
17. _______ View that shows a great deal of document space, but no margins, headers, footers, or other special features. **p. 163**
18. _______ Blinking bar that indicates where text that you next type will appear. **p. 145**
19. _______ Provides descriptive information about a document, such as a title, subject, author, keywords, and comments. **p. 178**

Multiple Choice

1. The view that presents a document in screen-sized pages with two shown at a time, for ease of comprehension and sharing, is the:
   (a) Read Mode
   (b) Print Layout view
   (c) Draft view
   (d) Full Screen Mode

2. One reason to display nonprinting characters is to:
   (a) Simplify the process of converting a document to an earlier Word version.
   (b) Enable spell checking on the document.
   (c) Enable document properties to be added to a document.
   (d) Assist with troubleshooting a document and modifying its appearance.

3. You are the only person in your office to upgrade to Word 2013. Before you share documents with coworkers, you should do which of the following?
   (a) Print out a backup copy.
   (b) Run the Compatibility Checker.
   (c) Burn all documents to CD.
   (d) Have no concerns that coworkers can open your documents.

4. Word 2013 encourages saving files so they can be accessed from multiple devices. One way that is accomplished is by:
   (a) Creating an automatic backup copy of every file, regardless of where it is saved.
   (b) Saving to your OneDrive account.
   (c) Shortening the AutoRecover interval so save operations occur more frequently and in various locations.
   (d) Saving all files to flash storage by default, so files can then be transferred to other devices.

5. Which of the following is detected by the contextual spelling check feature?
   (a) Incorrectly divided words that flow from one line to the next
   (b) Use of the word *their* when you should use *there*
   (c) Irregular capitalization
   (d) Improper use of commas

6. Suppose you are preparing a report that requires a cover page followed by text on the next page. To keep the cover page on its own page, you would position the insertion point at the end of the cover page and do which of the following?
   (a) Press Enter.
   (b) Click the PAGE LAYOUT tab, click Breaks, and then select Line Numbers.
   (c) Press Ctrl+Enter.
   (d) Press Ctrl+Page Down.

7. You need to prepare a resume to assist in your job search but are challenged with the design of the document. You have a classic case of writer's block! Word provides assistance in the form of a predesigned document called a:
   (a) Template.
   (b) Pattern.
   (c) Document Inspector.
   (d) Shell.

8. You have just opened a document provided by a coworker, and the title bar includes not only the file name but also the words *Compatibility Mode*. What does that mean?
   (a) The file was created in an earlier version of Word but saved as a Word 2013 file.
   (b) The file was created using another operating system, but opened under a version of Windows.
   (c) Word 2013 has placed the document in read-only mode, which means you will not be able to edit it.
   (d) The file was created in an earlier version of Word and might not be able to accommodate newer Word 2013 features unless you convert it.

9. To identify a document as a draft, and not in final form, which of the following could you add to the document?
   (a) Symbol
   (b) Watermark
   (c) Template
   (d) Document property

10. You plan to print only the current page of a Word document. Instead, the entire document prints. What should you have done to print only one page?
    (a) Click Print on the PRINT LAYOUT tab and click Current Page.
    (b) Click Print on the Quick Access Toolbar.
    (c) Click Print on the FILE tab and change the print setting to print only the current page.
    (d) Click Info on the FILE tab and change the print document property to only the current page.

Practice Exercises

1 Interview Tips

You are a student assistant in your college's Career Placement Center (CPC). The CPC provides assistance with job searches, hosts job fairs on campus, collects student resumes for inclusion in departmental "resume yearbooks," and encourages many other forms of college-to-career activities. The newest project is the preparation of a guidebook for students who are nearing graduation or are otherwise seeking a career track. You are charged with the task of modifying a description of interview skills that was actually included in an earlier guidebook. The only problem is that the document was saved in Word 2007 format, so you must make sure it is converted to the most current Word version before beginning to modify it (in case you want to include any special features of the newest version). This exercise follows the same set of skills as used in Hands-On Exercises 1–3 in the chapter. Refer to Figure 1.50 as you complete this exercise.

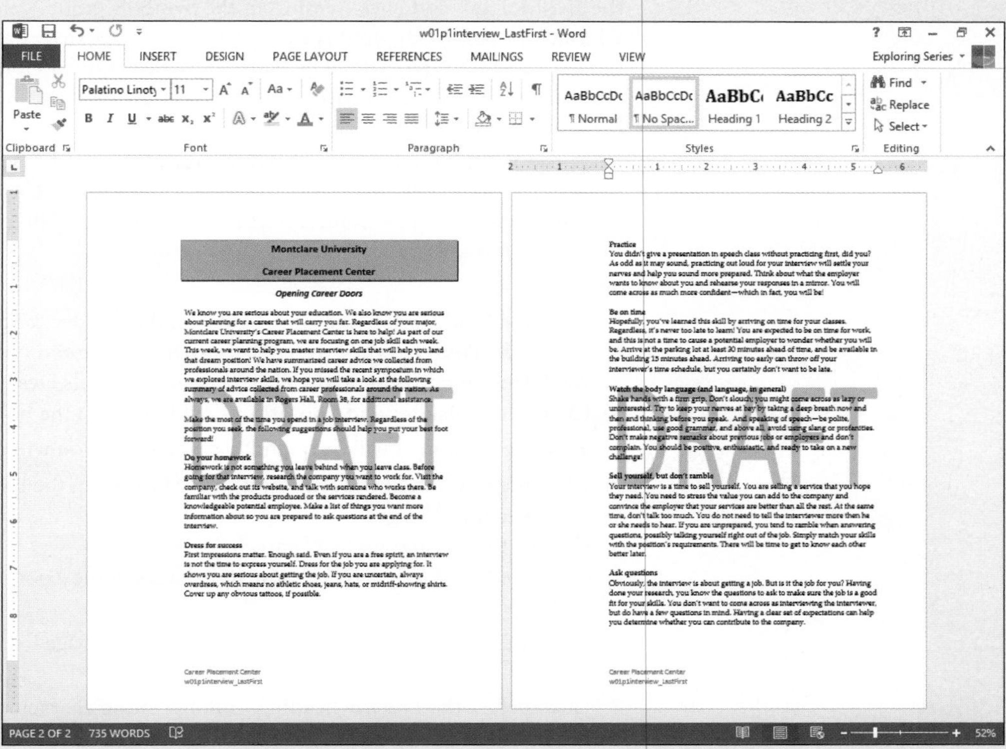

FIGURE 1.50 Modifying Interview Skills

a. Open the *w01p1Interview* document.

The words *[Compatibility Mode]* inform you the document was created in an earlier version of Word.

b. Click the **FILE tab**, and then click **Save As**. Save the document as **w01p1Interview_LastFirst**. Click **Save**. You will be presented with a dialog box letting you know the document will be upgraded to the newest file format. Click **OK**.

c. Press **Ctrl+Home** to make sure the insertion point is at the beginning of the document and check the document for errors:

- Click the **REVIEW tab** and click **Spelling & Grammar** in the Proofing group. The university's name is Montclare, so it is not misspelled. Click **Ignore All**.
- Correct any other identified errors, if they are actually incorrect.
- Read over the document again, checking for errors the spell check might have missed.

d. Double-click to select the word *ongoing* in the paragraph that begins with *We know you are serious* and click **Define** in the Proofing group to get a definition. If a definition does not display, you might not have a dictionary app installed. Follow the prompts to install a dictionary. Close the Define pane on the right. Click **Thesaurus** in the Proofing group to get an alternative word for *ongoing*. Locate the word *current* in the Thesaurus pane, click its arrow, and then click **Insert**. Close the Thesaurus pane.

e. Make the following edits in the document:

- Remove the words *if possible* (including the following comma and space) from the paragraph following the *Do your homework* heading by selecting the text and pressing **Delete**.
- Begin the same sentence with the capitalized word *Visit*.
- Rearrange the words *first practicing* in the *Practice* paragraph, so they read **practicing first**.

f. Select the hyphen between the words *midriff* and *showing* in the *Dress for success* paragraph. Click the **INSERT tab** and click **Symbol** in the Symbols group. Click **More Symbols**. Click the **Special Characters tab**. Click **Nonbreaking Hyphen**. Click **Insert** and click **Close**. You have made sure the words will not be divided between lines. Select the double "hyphen" between the words *confident* and *which* in the *Practice* paragraph. Following the same steps, insert an em dash. Close the Symbols dialog box.

g. Click the **DESIGN tab** and click **Watermark** in the Page Background group. Scroll through the watermarks and click **Draft 2**. Click **Watermark**, click **Custom Watermark**, and then deselect **Semitransparent**. Click **Color**, select **Red**, **Accent 2**, and then click **OK**. You have inserted a watermark that indicates the document is not yet final.

h. Set up a footer:

- Click the **INSERT tab** and click **Footer** in the Header & Footer group.
- Click **Edit Footer**. Type **Career Placement Center** and press Enter.
- Click **Document Info** on the Header & Footer Tools Design tab and select **File Name**.
- Click **Close Header and Footer** (or double-click in the body of the document).

i. Because the document will be bound in a notebook, you will make the left margin larger:

- Click the **PAGE LAYOUT tab** and click **Margins** in the Page Setup Group.
- Click **Custom Margins**.
- Change the left margin to **2"** and click **OK**.
- Click the **VIEW tab** and click **Multiple Pages** in the Zoom group to see how the text is lining up on the pages.

j. Because the *Practice* paragraph is split between two pages, you will insert a page break before the paragraph heading:

- Click before the *Practice* heading. If nonprinting characters are not displayed, click the **HOME tab** and click **Show/Hide (¶)**.
- Press **Ctrl+Enter** to insert a page break.

k. Press **Ctrl+Home**. Click the **VIEW tab** and click **Read Mode** in the Views group. Click the arrow on the right to move from one page to the next. Press **Esc** to return to the previous document view.

l. Save the document. Before distributing the document, you will check it for sensitive information:

- Click the **FILE tab** and click **Check for Issues**.
- Click **Inspect Document** and click **Inspect**.
- Click **Remove All** beside *Document Properties and Personal Information*. Click **Close**.

m. Finally, you will check the document for compatibility with earlier Word versions:

- Click **Check for Issues** and click **Check Compatibility**.
- Click **Select versions to show** and make sure that all earlier Word versions are selected. Click **Select versions to show again** to close the list. One compatibility issue is found.
- Click **OK**.

n. Click **Save** on the Quick Access Toolbar to save the document. It is saved as a Word 2013 file. One of your coworkers is still using Word 2003, so you will also save the document in that format:

- Click the **FILE tab** and click **Save As**.

- Click the location where you save your files in the Recent Folders list (or click **Computer** and navigate to the location).
- Click the **Save as type box** and click **Word 97-2003 Document**. Click **Continue**.
- Click **Save**. Although the file name remains the same, you have actually saved two files in this step. One is named *w01p1Interview_LastFirst.docx* (the Word 2013 version), and the other is called *w01p1Interview_LastFirst.doc* (the Word 97-2003 version).

o. Close the file and submit based on your instructor's directions.

2 Aztec Computers

As the co-owner of Aztec Computers, you are frequently asked to provide information about computer viruses and backup procedures. You are quick to tell anyone who asks about data loss that it is not a question of if it will happen, but when—hard drives fail, removable disks are lost, and viruses may infect systems. You advise customers and friends alike that they can prepare for the inevitable by creating an adequate backup before the problem occurs. Because people appreciate a document to refer to about this information, you have started one that contains information that should be taken seriously. After a few finishing touches, you will feel comfortable about passing it out to people who have questions about this topic. This exercise follows the same set of skills as used in Hands-On Exercises 1–3 in the chapter. Refer to Figure 1.51 as you complete this exercise.

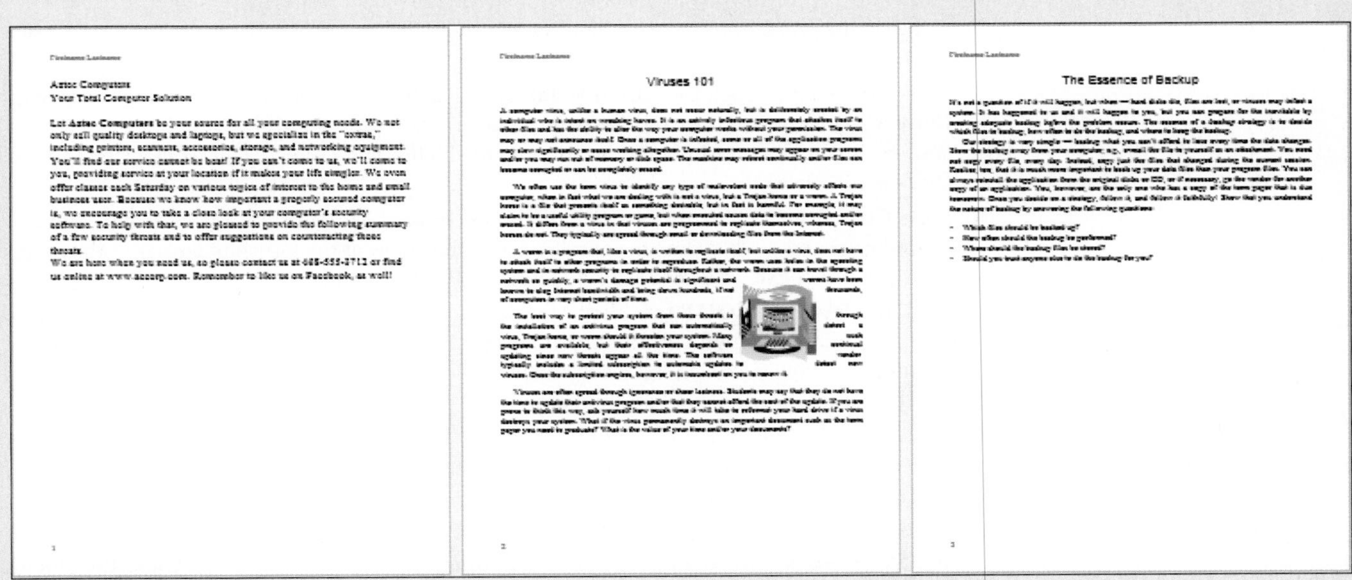

Aztec Computers
Your Total Computer Solution

Let **Aztec Computers** be your source for all your computing needs. We not only sell quality desktops and laptops, but we specialize in the "extras," including printers, scanners, accessories, storage, and networking equipment. You'll find our service cannot be beat! If you can't come to us, we'll come to you, providing service at your location if it makes your life simpler. We even offer classes each Saturday on various topics of interest to the home and small business user. Because we know how important a properly secured computer is, we encourage you to take a close look at your computer's security software. To help with that, we are pleased to provide the following summary of a few security threats and to offer suggestions on counteracting those threats.
We are here when you need us, so please contact us at [illegible] or find us online at www.accorp.com. Remember to like us on Facebook, as well!

Viruses 101

The Essence of Backup

FIGURE 1.51 Multiple Pages View

a. Open *w01p2Virus* and save it as **w01p2Virus_LastFirst**.

b. Press **Ctrl+Enter** to insert a page break, creating a blank page at the beginning. Press **Ctrl+Home** to move the insertion point to the beginning of the first page.

c. You will insert a short paragraph prepared by your partner, promoting the company and encouraging the use of computer security tools. The paragraph will be shown on a page by itself, as a lead-in to the article. To insert the paragraph:

- Click the **INSERT tab** and click the **Object arrow** in the Text group.
- Click **Text from File**.
- Locate and click **w01p2Summary** and click **Insert**.

d. Press **Ctrl+Home**. You want to add a heading above the paragraph, so type **Aztec Computers**. Press **Enter**. Type **Your Total Computer Solution**. Press **Enter** twice.

e. Scroll to the bottom of the second page and click before the title *The Essence of Backup*. Click the **PAGE LAYOUT tab**, click **Breaks** in the Page Setup group, and then click **Page**. Click the **VIEW tab** and click **Multiple Pages** in the Zoom group. Scroll to view all pages. Click **100%** in the Zoom group.

f. You will add a footer to better identify the document:
   - Click the **INSERT tab** and click **Footer** in the Header & Footer group.
   - Click **Edit Footer**.
   - Click **Page Number** in the Header & Footer group, point to **Current Position**, and then click **Plain Number**. You have created a page number footer.

g. Scroll to the top of the current page and click in the Header area. Type your first name and last name. Double-click in the document to close the header.

h. Click the **FILE tab** and click **Print**. Click **Previous Page** to view the previous page. Click **Back** (the arrow at the top left) to return to the document.

i. If nonprinting characters are not displayed, click the **HOME tab** and click **Show/Hide (¶)**. You will make edits to the text:
   - The second to last sentence in the first body paragraph on page 2 should begin with the word *Unusual* instead of *Usual*. Make that change.
   - Click before the paragraph mark after the word *worm* in the second body paragraph. Delete the paragraph mark so the two paragraphs become one.
   - Locate the words *will it* in the last paragraph on the second page (in the sentence beginning with *If you are prone to think this way*). Reverse those words so the sentence reads *it will* instead of *will it*.

j. Press **Ctrl+Home**. Click the **REVIEW tab** and click **Spelling & Grammar** in the Proofing group. Correct any identified errors, if they are actual errors. The word *Trojan* should be capitalized and *backup* should be two words, in the context in which it is presented. Click **OK** when the spelling check is complete.

k. Press **Ctrl+Home**. Click the **VIEW tab** and click **Read Mode** in the Views group. Move to the second page and double-click the graphic. Click the arrow at the top-right corner of the graphic to enlarge it. Press **Esc**. Press **Esc** again to return to Print Layout view.

l. Click the **PAGE LAYOUT tab**, click **Margins** in the Page Setup group, and then select **Custom Margins**. Change the left and right margins to **0.75"**. Click **Landscape** and click **OK**. Because the document is adjusted to landscape orientation, the newly created left and right margins (0.75") are now considered the top and bottom margins.

m. Click the **FILE tab** and click **Print**. Click **Next Page** and/or **Previous Page** repeatedly to view all pages. You decide portrait orientation is a better choice for this document. Click **Landscape Orientation** and click **Portrait Orientation**.

n. Click **Info**, click **Properties**, and then click **Show Document Panel**. Click in the **Comments box** and type **General information for understanding computer viruses**. Click **Close the Document Information Panel** (on the top-right side of the Document Panel).

o. Save the document. Click the **FILE tab**, click **Check for Issues**, and then click **Check Compatibility**. There are no compatibility issues with earlier Word versions, so click **OK**.

p. Click the **FILE tab**, click **Check for Issue**s, click **Inspect Document**, click **No**, and then click **Inspect**. Click **Close** after you review the results.

q. Click **Print**. Click **Print All Pages**, click **Custom Print**, and then type **2-3** to indicate that you want to print only the second and third pages. Because you are likely in a lab setting, you will not print the pages.

r. Press **Esc** twice to return to the document. Save and close the file, and submit based on your instructor's directions.

Mid-Level Exercises

1 Runners at Heart

CREATIVE CASE 

A local cross-country team, Runners at Heart, is comprised of people who are recovering from a heart ailment or who support the cause of fitness for former heart patients. A half marathon is coming up in five months, and the Runners at Heart cross-country team wants to be prepared. A half marathon is a run/walk of 13 miles. You and others have researched tips on preparing for a half marathon. You have begun a document containing a few of those tips, and will collect ideas from other club members as well. You will finalize the tips document and make it available in plenty of time for the runners to prepare.

a. Open *w01m1Running* and save it as **w01m1Running_LastFirst**.

b. Move to the end of the document and press **Enter**. Insert the text from *w01m1Tips*, a list of running tips provided by another club member.

c. Make sure nonprinting characters display. View each page of the document and note that the first page ends awkwardly, with a single heading at the bottom. Insert a page break before the *Prepare mentally* heading.

d. The headings from the *w01m1Tips* file should be capitalized to be consistent with those you typed earlier. Make that correction. They should read: *Train with Others, Do Your Research, Rest, What to Wear*, and *Prepare Mentally*.

e. Insert a hard return before each heading except *Prepare Mentally* (beginning with *Choose a Plan* and ending with *What to Wear*) to increase the space between them. Make sure you are in Print Layout view. Because the page break is no longer necessary in its current position, click on the **Page Break line** and press **Delete**. Insert a hard return before the *Prepare Mentally* heading.

f. View the document and insert a page break, if necessary, wherever a heading stands alone.

g. Identify synonyms for the word *regimen* in the *Choose a Plan* section. Insert the word *routine*. Check for spelling and word usage errors, correcting any that are identified. The brand of clothing is correctly spelled *Dri-Fit*. Proofread the document carefully to identify any errors that Word might have missed.

h. Insert a page number footer as a **Plain Number** in the current position (on the left side of the footer). As a header, include the file name as a field.

i. Select the hyphen between the words *long* and *distance* in the paragraph following *Training Tips for a Half Marathon*. Insert a nonbreaking hyphen. Insert a trademark symbol immediately after the words *Nike Dri-Fit* in the *What to Wear* paragraph.

 j. Add a custom watermark, with a text or graphic of your choice. The watermark should be clearly visible, and colored, if you like.

k. Change the page orientation to landscape. Preview the document to determine if the orientation is appropriate. Return to the document and delete the page break before the *Rest* heading. Remove one of the blank paragraphs before the *Rest* heading.

l. Save the document. Because one of your club members, who will contribute to the document later, uses Word 2003, save the document in that format, with the same file name. Click **Continue** if warned of unsupported features. Save it again as a Word 2013 file by changing the file type (during the save operation) to **Word Document**. Agree to replace the existing file and click **OK**. Click **OK** when advised that the file will be upgraded to the newest format.

m. Open the **Document Panel** and replace the current author with your first and last names. In the *Comments* section, type **Tips for a Half Marathon**. Close the Document Panel.

n. Preview the document and then remove the watermark. Print the document properties if approved by your instructor.

o. Save and close the file, and submit based on your instructor's directions.

2 Health Fair

You are a pediatric health assistant in a pediatrician's office. The local community college is hosting a health fair and has asked that your office staff a table promoting childhood vaccinations. Having worked in the office for several years, you are well aware of the benefits of immunization against a host of serious illnesses, so you are happy to help. You want to prepare a document summarizing in an at-a-glance fashion the advantages of immunization and the problems with avoiding it. However, because you are not a physician, you will depend on the doctor you work with to provide a bit of research and statistics that you will then compile into a more complete document for distribution.

a. Open *w01m2Vaccines* and save it as **w01m2Vaccines_LastFirst**.
b. Preview the document to get a feel for the text flow.
c. Check for spelling and word usage errors. Proofread the document to identify and correct errors that Word might have missed. (Hint: Most, but not all, vaccines have a low risk of side effects.)
d. Remove the words *as well* from the last sentence in the second body paragraph. The sentence should end with *child*, so you should also remove the comma and space before the words *as well*. Remove the word *actually* from the last sentence of the third body paragraph. In the same paragraph, click before the word *Vaccines* in the sentence beginning *Vaccines contain a weak form*. Insert a hard return.
e. Identify a synonym for the word *counteracted* in the third sentence of the third body paragraph. Replace the word with **thwarted.** Your document is limited to 500 words. Check the status bar for a word count (or click **Word Count** in the Proofing group) to see if you are above or below the limit.
f. Select the hyphen between the words *day* and *a* in the third body paragraph. Replace the selection with an **em dash symbol**.

g. Select the word *Vaccines* anywhere in the document and use Word's Translate Language tool to identify the equivalent word in Spanish. You do not need to make the change in the document.
h. Change all margins to **0.75"**. Preview the document.
i. Include the file name in the footer area. On a separate line in the footer, type your first name and last name.
j. View each page of the document and make any adjustments necessary to ensure that only two pages are included, with the required vaccinations shown on the second page.
k. Add a watermark with the text **Health Fair** shown in red. The watermark should be horizontal. Save the document.
l. List yourself as the author in Document Properties. The subject is **Childhood Vaccinations**.
m. Run the Compatibility Checker to make sure the file is compatible with earlier Word versions.
n. Save and close the file, and submit based on your instructor's directions.

3 College Events

COLLABORATION CASE

FROM SCRATCH 

You and a group of your fellow students are assigned the project of preparing a document describing several upcoming events at your college or university. Identify a few events to highlight, and assign each event to a student. Although each student will conduct independent research on an event, all event descriptions will be collected and combined into one document for submission to your instructor. To complete the project:

a. Identify a unique name for the group (perhaps assigned by your instructor).
b. Identify events (perhaps conduct research online) and assign one event to each student.
c. Each student will collect information on the event (general description, location, cost, etc.).
d. Compose a cover letter to the instructor, identifying group members and noting events to be included in the document. The cover letter should be attractive and error-free.
e. Insert a hard return at the end of the cover letter so that the first event description begins on a new page.

f. Save the document to OneDrive as **w01m3Events_GroupName** (replacing *GroupName* with the actual group name). Go to http://onedrive.live.com, sign in, and then open *w01b3EventsGroupName*. Click **Share** and click **Get link**. Click **Shorten** to get a shorter version of the URL. Provide the URL to group members so each member can access and edit the file.

g. Each group member will access the file from the URL. When the document opens, click **Edit Document**, and then click **Edit in Word**. Enter any login information (Windows Live ID) and edit the document to add event information. When a description is complete, insert a hard return so that the next description begins on a new page. Click **Save** on the Quick Access Toolbar to save the document back to OneDrive.

h. Submit the completed document based on your instructor's directions.

Beyond the Classroom

Dream Destination

RESEARCH CASE

FROM SCRATCH

You work with a local radio station that will award a dream vacation of one week in a resort area to a lucky listener. Select a destination and conduct some research to determine approximately how much it will cost your employer to make the vacation available. What travel arrangements are possible? What type of accommodations do you recommend? What activities are there to enjoy in the area, and what are some outstanding restaurants? Prepare a one- to two-page document, outlining what you think are the best selling points for the area and approximately how much the travel and hotel accommodations will cost the radio station. Because the document is for internal distribution in draft format, you do not need to be overly concerned with format. However, you should use skills from this chapter to properly identify the document (headers, footers, and watermarks) and to position it on the page. The document should be error-free. Modify document properties to include yourself as the author. Save the file as **w01b2Vacation_LastFirst** and submit based on your instructor's directions.

Logo Policy

DISASTER RECOVERY

Open *w01b3Policy* and save it as a Word 2013 file with the file name **w01b3Policy_LastFirst**. The document was started by an office assistant, but was not finished. You must complete the document, ensuring that it is error-free and attractive. The current header includes a page number at the top right. Remove the page number from the header and create a footer with a centered page number instead. Remove the word *copyright* where it appears in the document and replace it with the copyright symbol. Show nonprinting characters and remove any unnecessary or improperly placed paragraph marks. Insert hard returns where necessary to better space paragraphs. The hyphenated word *non-Association* should not be divided between lines, so use a nonbreaking hyphen, if necessary. Modify document properties to include yourself as the author and assign relevant keywords. Finally, use a watermark to indicate that the document is not in final form. Save the document as a Word 2013 file and as a separate Word 97-2003 document with the same file name. Submit both files based on your instructor's directions.

Time Management

SOFT SKILLS CASE

FROM SCRATCH

After watching the video on time management and organization skills, think about how you could put into practice some of the tips suggested in the video. Specifically, consider how you might better manage your time with respect to completing class assignments, studying for quizzes and exams, and preparing for class. Then write an informal one-to-two page paper, saving it as **w01b4Time_LastFirst**, outlining changes you plan to make. You will use Word's default line and paragraph spacing settings, but you should make sure the document also includes the following items:

- A left-aligned header with your name, and a centered footer including the page number.
- Top and bottom margins of 1" and left and right margins of 1.5".
- A *Draft* watermark of your choice.
- A smiley face symbol in an appropriate place within the document.
- Your name in the Document Properties Author area.
- No spelling or grammatical errors.

Capstone Exercise

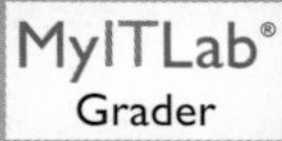

Ethical conflicts occur all the time and result when one person or group benefits at the expense of another. Your Philosophy 101 instructor assigned a class project whereby students must consider the question of ethics and society. The result of your research includes a collection of questions every person should ask him- or herself. Your paper is nearly complete but needs a few modifications before you submit it.

Spelling, Margins, Watermarks, and Editing

You notice Word displays spelling and grammatical errors with colored underlines, so you must correct those as soon as possible. Additionally, you want to adjust the margins and then insert a watermark that displays when you print so that you will remember that this is not the final version.

a. Open *w01c1Ethics* and save it as **w01c1Ethics_LastFirst**.

b. Run the Spelling & Grammar tool to correct all misspelled words and contextual errors. Identify and insert a synonym for the word *whereas* in the *$50 Bill* paragraph.

c. Change the margins to **0.75"** on all sides.

d. Insert a diagonal watermark that displays **Version 1**. (Hint: Insert a Custom watermark, select Text watermark, and then type **Version 1** in the text box.) Color the watermark blue.

e. Remove the word *new* from the first body paragraph, beginning with *Ethics refers to the principals or standards*. You realize that the word *principals* is incorrectly used in the first sentence of the same paragraph. Change the word to **principles**. Proofread the document to find any spelling or word usage errors that Word missed.

Headers, Footers, and Features That Improve Readability

You will set up page numbering and will include a descriptive header. Because you are going to customize headers and footers precisely, you must use several of the custom settings available for headers and footers.

a. Insert a centered page number at the bottom of the report. Type your first name and last name in the header area. The header and footer should not display on the first page.

b. Insert a space and then a frownie face symbol after the word *exam* in the first sentence of the *Honor Code* section. You can find a frownie face symbol in the Wingdings font.

c. Insert a ™ symbol after *Office 2013*, in the *Office CD* paragraph.

Set Properties and Finalize Document

After improving the readability of the document, you remember that you have not yet saved it. Your professor still uses an older version of Word, so you save the document in a compatible format that will display easily.

a. Save the document.

b. Run the Compatibility Checker and Document Inspector, but do not take any suggested actions at this time.

c. Add **Ethics**, **Responsibility**, and **Morals** to the Keywords field in the document properties. Change the author to your first name and last name. Close the Document Panel.

d. Preview the document.

e. Save and close the file, and submit based on your instructor's directions.

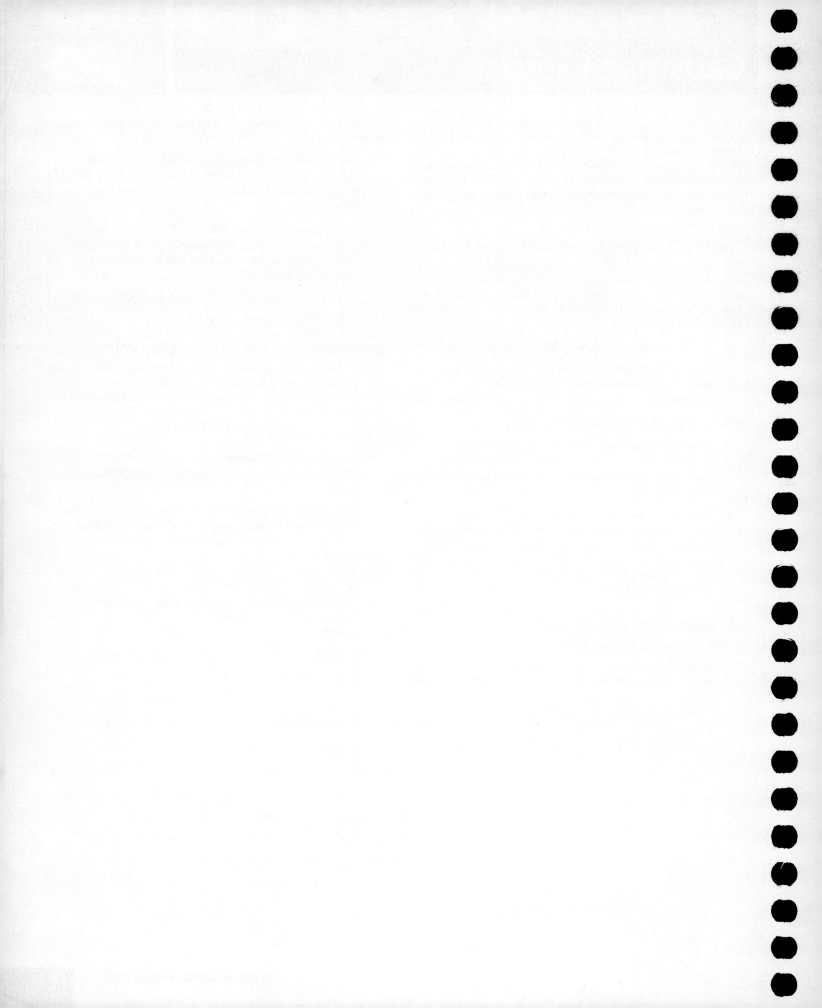

Word

Document Presentation

CHAPTER 2

Editing and Formatting

OBJECTIVES AFTER READING THIS CHAPTER, YOU WILL BE ABLE TO:

CASE STUDY | Phillips Studio L Photography

Having recently opened your own photography studio, you are involved in marketing the business. Not only do you hope to attract customers from the local community who want photos of special events, but also you will offer classes in basic photography for interested amateur photographers. You have even designed a Web site to promote the business and provide details on upcoming events and classes. You are not yet a large enough business to employ an office staff, so much of the work of developing promotional material falls to you.

Among other projects, you are currently developing material to include in a quarterly mailing to people who have expressed an interest in upcoming studio events. You have prepared a rough draft of a newsletter describing photography basics—a document that must be formatted and properly organized before it is distributed to people on your mailing list. You will modify the document to ensure attractive line and paragraph spacing, and you will format text to draw attention to pertinent points. Formatted in columns, the document will be easy to read. The newsletter is somewhat informal, and you will make appropriate use of color, borders, and pictures so that it is well received by your audience.

Text and Paragraph Formatting

When you format text, you change the way it looks. Your goal in designing a document is to ensure that it is well received and understood by an audience of readers. Seldom will your first attempt at designing a document be the only time you work with it. Inevitably, you will identify text that should be reworded or emphasized differently, paragraphs that might be more attractive in another alignment, or the need to bold, underline, or use italics to call attention to selected text. As you develop a document, or after reopening a previously completed document, you can make all these modifications and more. That process is called ***formatting***.

In this section, you will learn to change font and font size, and format text with character attributes, such as bold, underline, and italics. At the paragraph level, you will adjust paragraph and line spacing, set tabs, change alignment, and apply bullets and numbering.

Applying Font Attributes

A ***font*** is a combination of typeface and type style. The font you select should reinforce the message of the text without calling attention to itself, and it should be consistent with the information you want to convey. For example, a paper prepared for a professional purpose, such as a resume, should have a standard font, such as Times New Roman, instead of one that looks funny or frilly, such as Comic Sans. Additionally, you will want to minimize the variety of fonts in a document to maintain a professional look. Typically, you should use three or fewer fonts within a document. A header might be formatted in one font, while body text is shown in another. Word enables you to format text in a variety of ways. Not only can you change a font, but you can apply text attributes, such as bold, italic, or underline, to selected text, or to text that you are about to type. Several of the most commonly used text formatting commands are located in the Font group on the Home tab.

Select Font Options

When you begin a new, blank document, a default font is applied, which you can change for the current document if you like. The default font is Calibri 11 pt. To change the font for selected text, or for a document you are beginning, click the Font arrow and select a font from those displayed (see Figure 2.1). Each font shown is a sample of the actual font. With text selected, you can point to any font in the list, without clicking, to see a preview of the way selected text will look in that particular font. The feature whereby you can preview the effect of a formatting selection is called ***Live Preview***.

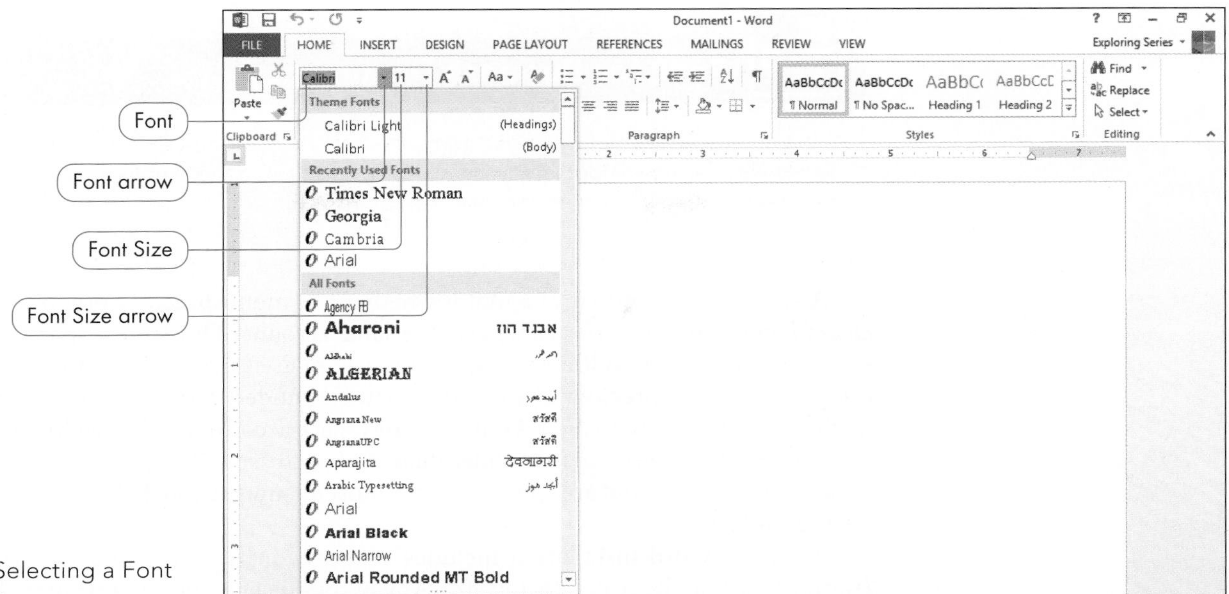

FIGURE 2.1 Selecting a Font and Font Size

You can also change font size when you click the Font Size arrow (refer to Figure 2.1) and select a point size. Each point size is equivalent to 1/72 of an inch; therefore, the larger the point size, the larger the font. A document often contains various sizes of the same font. For example, a document that includes levels of headings and subheadings might have major headings formatted in a larger point size than lesser headings.

A definitive characteristic of any font is the presence or absence of thin lines that end the main strokes of each letter. A ***serif font*** contains a thin line or extension at the top and bottom of the primary strokes on characters. Times New Roman is an example of a serif font. A ***sans serif font*** (*sans* from the French word meaning *without*) does not contain the thin lines on characters. Arial is a sans serif font.

Serifs (the thin lines that begin and end each character formatted in a serif font) help the eye connect one letter with the next and generally are used with large amounts of text. The paragraphs in this book, for example, are set in a serif font. Body text of newspapers and magazines is usually formatted in a serif font, as well. A sans serif font, such as Arial or Verdana, is more effective with smaller amounts of text such as titles, headlines, corporate logos, and Web pages. For example, the heading *Select Font Options*, at the beginning of this section, is set in a sans serif font. Web developers often prefer a sans serif font because the extra strokes that begin and end letters in a serif font can blur or fade into a Web page, making it difficult to read. Examples of serif and sans serif fonts are shown in Figure 2.2.

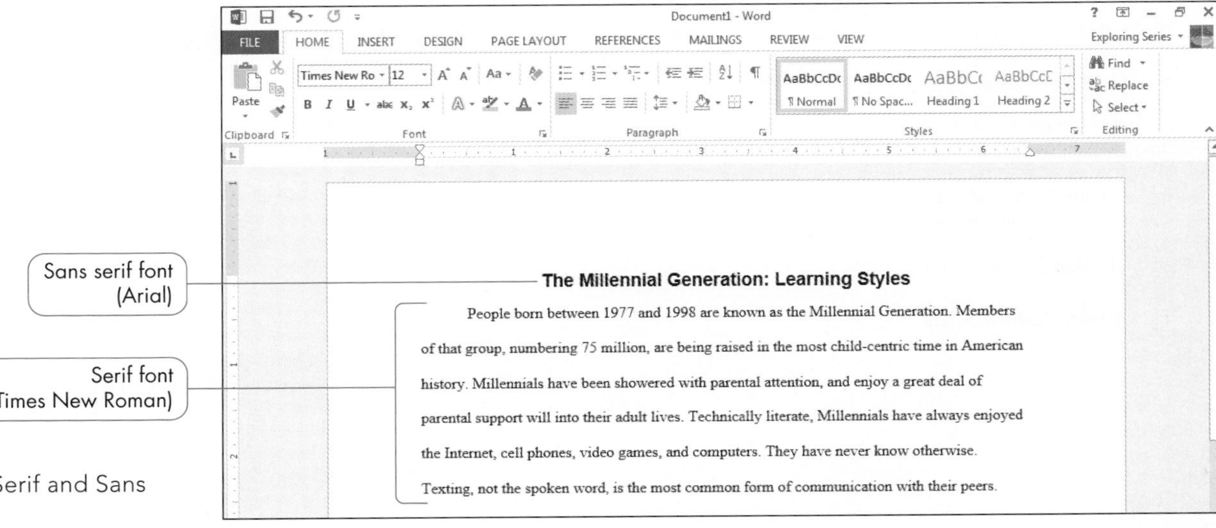

FIGURE 2.2 Serif and Sans Serif Fonts

TIP Font for Business Documents

Most business documents are best formatted in 11- or 12-point serif font. A good choice is Times New Roman. A document designed for display on the Web is attractive in a blocky sans serif font, such as Arial, regardless of point size.

A second characteristic of a font is whether it is monospaced or proportional. A *monospaced font* (such as Courier New) uses the same amount of horizontal space for every character regardless of its width. Monospaced fonts are used in tables and financial projections where text must be precisely aligned, one character underneath another. A *proportional font* (such as Times New Roman or Arial) allocates space according to the width of the character. For example, the lowercase *m* is wider than the lowercase *i*. Proportional fonts create a professional appearance and are appropriate for most documents, such as research papers, status reports, and letters.

A typical Word installation includes support for TrueType and OpenType fonts. A *TrueType font* can be scaled to any size. Any output device, such as a printer, that Windows supports can recognize a TrueType font. An *OpenType font* is an advanced form of font that is designed for all platforms, including Windows and Macintosh. OpenType fonts incorporate a greater extension of the basic character set. Most fonts included in a typical Word installation are OpenType.

Change Text Appearance

Commonly accessed commands related to font settings are located in the Font group on the Home tab (see Figure 2.3). Word 2013 enables you to bold, underline, and italicize text, apply text highlighting, change font color, and work with various text effects and other formatting options from commands in the Font group. For even more choices, click the Font Dialog Box Launcher in the Font group and select from additional formatting commands available in the Font dialog box (see Figure 2.4). With text selected, you will see the Mini Toolbar when you move the pointer near the selection. The ***Mini Toolbar*** (see Figure 2.5), which contains several of the most commonly accessed formatting and alignment commands, makes it convenient to quickly select a format (instead of locating it on the Ribbon or using a keyboard shortcut).

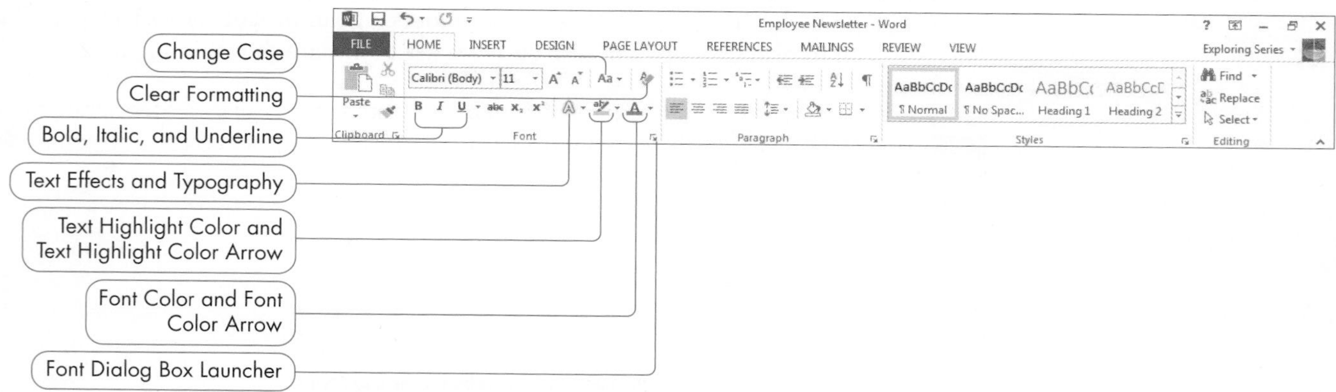

FIGURE 2.3 Font Commands

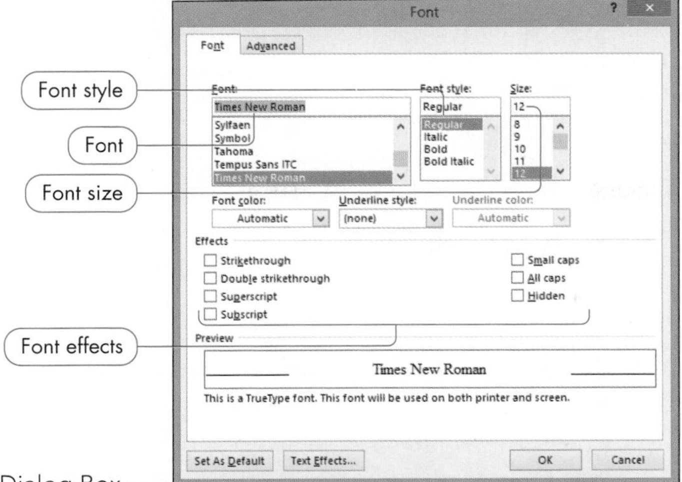

FIGURE 2.4 Font Dialog Box

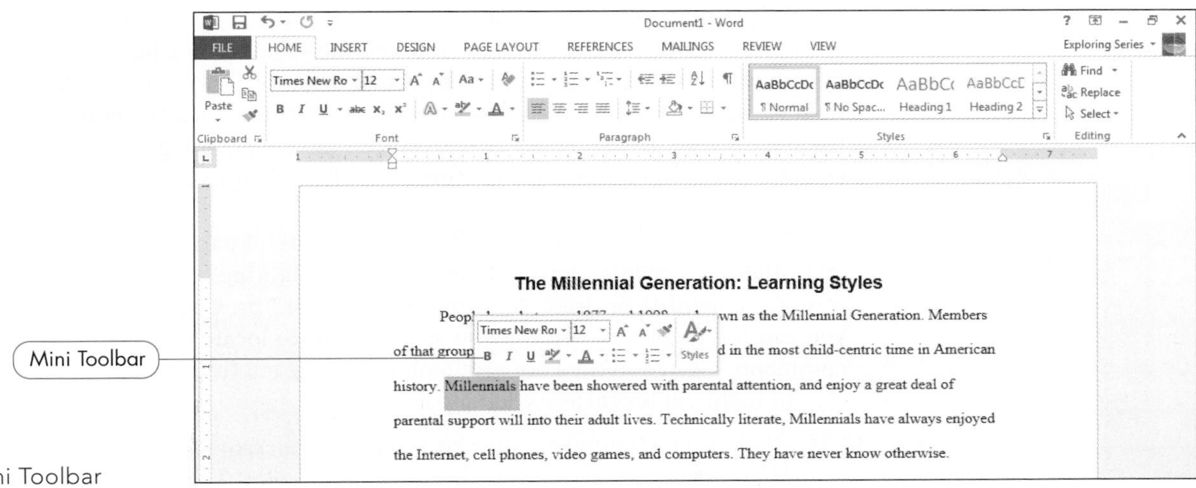

FIGURE 2.5 Mini Toolbar

STEP 1

To bold, underline, or italicize text, do either of the following:

- Select text to be formatted. Click Bold, Italic, or Underline in the Font group on the HOME tab.
- Click Bold, Italic, or Underline in the Font group on the HOME tab and type text to be formatted. Click the same command to turn off the formatting effect.

Word 2013 includes a variety of text effects that enable you to add a shadow, outline, reflection, or glow to text. The *Text Effects and Typography* gallery (see Figure 2.6) provides access to those effects as well as to WordArt styles, number styles, ligatures, and stylistic sets that you can apply to text.

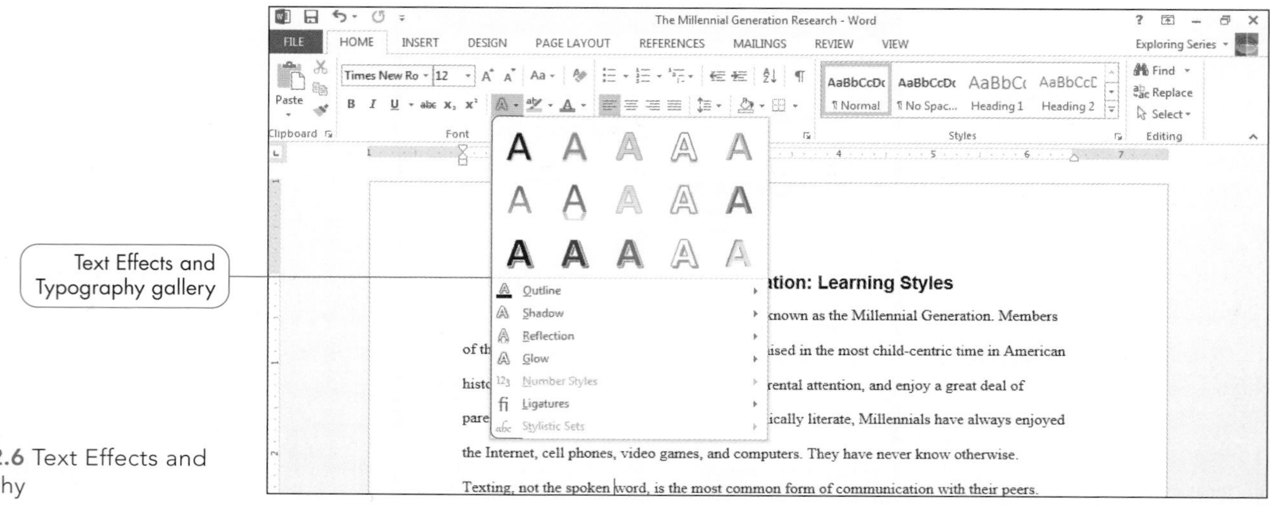

FIGURE 2.6 Text Effects and Typography

A *ligature* is two letters that are crafted together into a single character, or *glyph*. For example, you often see the letters *f* and *i* bound together in a ligature. A *stylistic set* is a collection of letter styles that you can apply to OpenType fonts. Some fonts include more stylistic sets than others. To explore advanced font settings, click the Font Dialog Box Launcher (refer to Figure 2.3) and click the Advanced tab (refer to Figure 2.4). Select a ligature and stylistic set. Stylistic sets and ligatures are often used in the preparation of formal documents such as wedding invitations.

As a student, you are likely to highlight important parts of textbooks, magazine articles, and other documents. You probably use a highlighting marker to shade parts of text you want to remember or draw attention to. Word 2013 provides an equivalent tool with which you can highlight text you want to stand out or to locate easily—the Text Highlight Color command, located in the Font group on the Home tab (refer to Figure 2.3).

To highlight text *before* selecting it:

1. Click Text Highlight Color to select the current highlight color or click the Text Highlight Color arrow and choose another color. The mouse pointer resembles a pen when you move it over the document.
2. Drag across text to highlight it.
3. Click Text Highlight Color or press Esc to stop highlighting.

To highlight text *after* selecting it, click Text Highlight Color or click the Text Highlight Color arrow and choose another color. To remove highlights, select the highlighted text, click the Text Highlight Color arrow, and then select No Color.

When creating a document, you must consider when and how to capitalize text. Titles are occasionally in all caps, sentences begin with a capital letter, and each key word of a heading is typically capitalized. Use the Change Case option in the Font group on the Home tab to quickly change the capitalization of document text (refer to Figure 2.3).

By default, text is shown in black as you type a document. For a bit of interest, or to draw attention to text within a document, you can change the font color of previously typed text or of text that you are about to type. Click the Font Color arrow (refer to Figure 2.3) and select from a gallery of colors. For even more choices, click More Colors and select from a variety of hues or shades. As shown in Figure 2.7, you can click the Custom tab in the Colors dialog box and click to select a color hue, while honing in on a variation of that hue by dragging along a continuum.

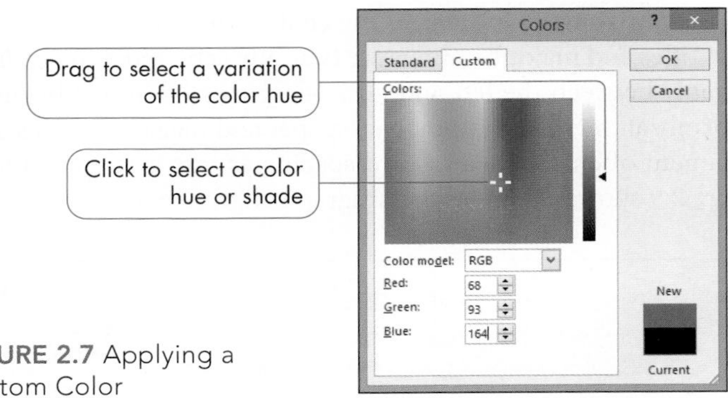

FIGURE 2.7 Applying a Custom Color

Matching Font Color

If you have created a custom font color, matching text that you type later to that particular shade can be a challenge. It is easy to match color, however, when you click the Font Color arrow and select the shade from the Recent Colors area.

Formatting a Paragraph

Formatting selected text is only one way to alter the appearance of a document. You can also change the alignment, indentation, tab stops, or line spacing for any paragraph within the document. Recall that Word defines a paragraph as text followed by a hard return, or even a hard return on a line by itself (indicating a blank paragraph). You can include borders or shading for added emphasis around selected paragraphs, and you can number paragraphs or enhance them with bullets. The Paragraph group on the Home tab contains several paragraph formatting commands (see Figure 2.8). If you are formatting only one paragraph, you do not have to select the entire paragraph. Simply click to place the insertion point within the paragraph and apply a paragraph format. However, if you are formatting several paragraphs, you must select them before formatting.

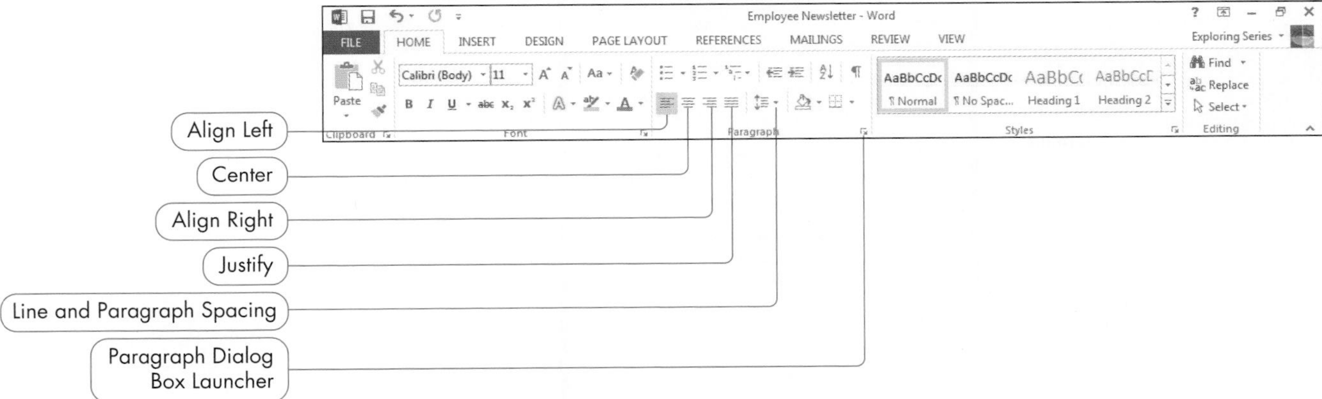

FIGURE 2.8 Paragraph Commands

Select Paragraph Alignment

Left alignment is the most common alignment, often seen in letters, reports, and memos. When you begin a new blank Word document, paragraphs are left aligned by default. Text begins evenly at the left margin and ends in an uneven right edge. The reverse of left alignment is ***right alignment***, a setting in which text is aligned at the right margin with a ragged left edge. Short lines including dates, figure captions, and headers are often right aligned. A ***centered*** paragraph is horizontally located in the center, an equal distance from the left and right edges. Report titles and major headings are typically centered. Finally, ***justified alignment*** spreads text evenly between the left and right margins so that text begins at the left margin and ends uniformly at the right margin. Newspaper and magazine articles are often justified. Such text alignment often causes awkward spacing as text is stretched to fit evenly between margins. Figure 2.9 shows examples of paragraph alignments.

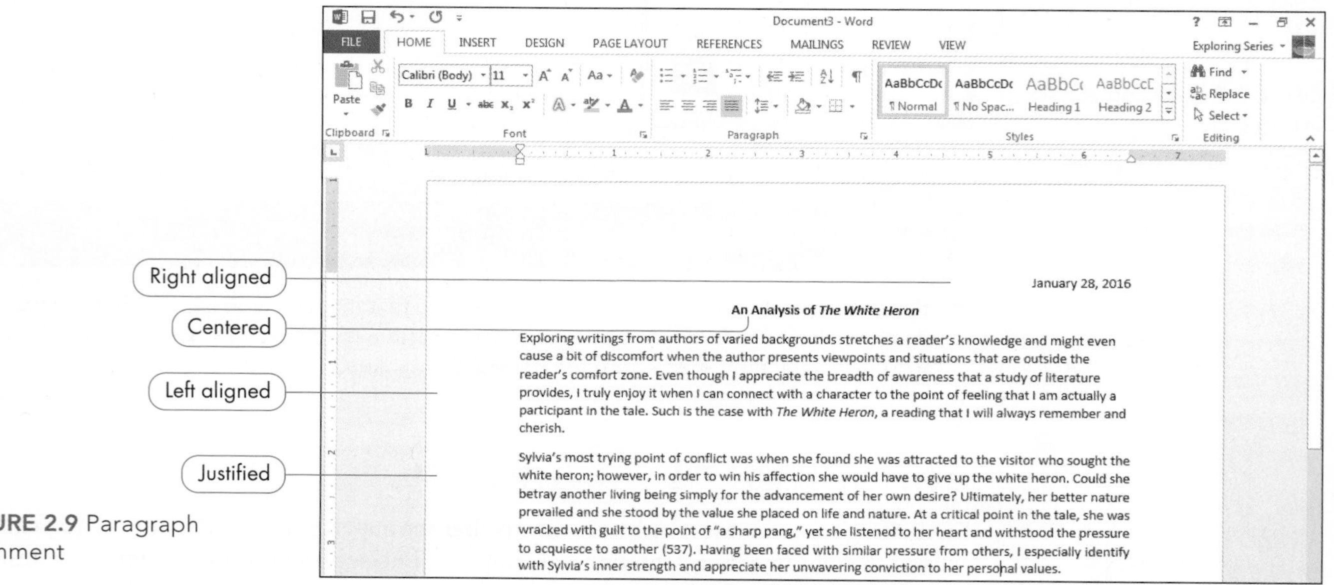

FIGURE 2.9 Paragraph Alignment

STEP 2» To change paragraph alignment, select text (or click to position the insertion point in a paragraph, if only one paragraph is to be affected) and select an alignment from the Paragraph group on the Home tab (refer to Figure 2.8). You can also change alignment by making a selection from the Paragraph dialog box (see Figure 2.10), which opens when you click the Paragraph Dialog Box Launcher (refer to Figure 2.8).

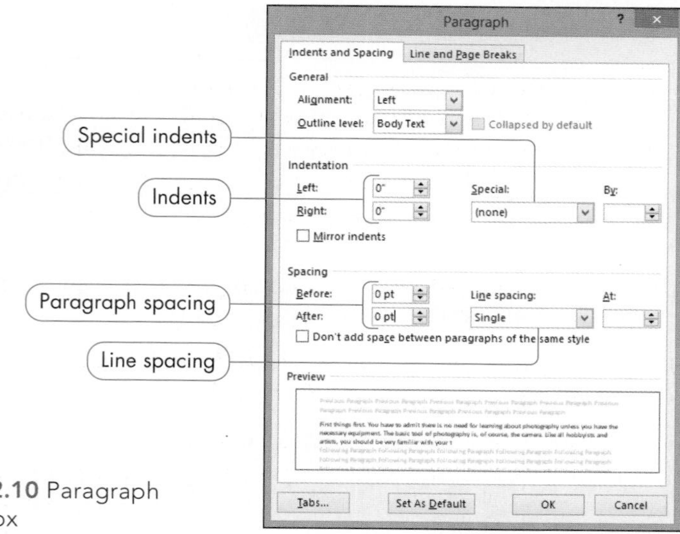

FIGURE 2.10 Paragraph Dialog Box

Select Line and Paragraph Spacing

Paragraph spacing is the amount of space between paragraphs, measured in points. (Recall that one point is 1/72 of an inch.) Paragraph spacing is a good way to differentiate between paragraphs, especially if the beginning of each paragraph is not clearly identified by an indented line. In such a case, paragraph spacing makes it clear where one paragraph ends and another begins. Spacing used to separate paragraphs usually comes *after* each affected paragraph, although you can specify that it is placed *before*. Use the Paragraph dialog box to select paragraph spacing (refer to Figure 2.10).

Word provides several ways to select paragraph spacing, as described in the following steps:

- Click the HOME tab. Click *Line and Paragraph Spacing* in the Paragraph group on the HOME tab (see Figure 2.11). Click to Add Space Before Paragraph (or to Remove Space After Paragraph).
- Click the Paragraph Dialog Box Launcher in the Paragraph group on the HOME tab. Type spacing Before or After in the respective areas (refer to Figure 2.10) or click the spin arrows to adjust spacing. Click OK.
- Click the PAGE LAYOUT tab. Change the Before or After spacing in the Paragraph group (see Figure 2.12).

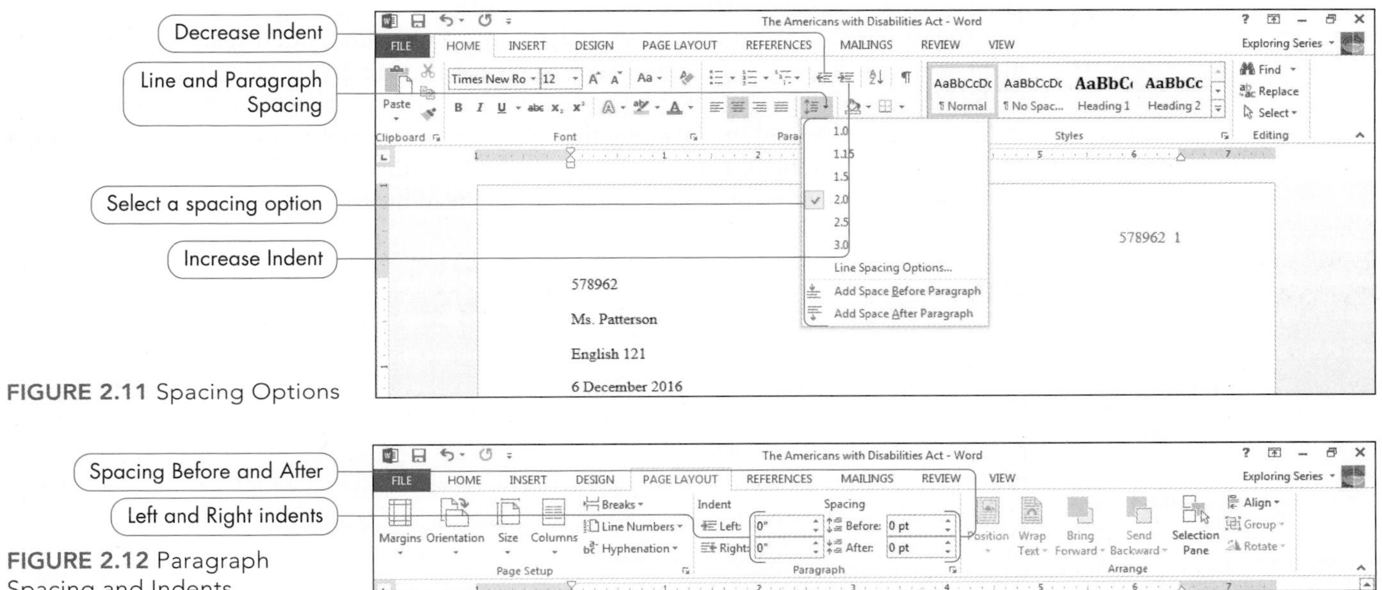

FIGURE 2.11 Spacing Options

FIGURE 2.12 Paragraph Spacing and Indents

Just as paragraph spacing is the amount of space between paragraphs, ***line spacing*** is the amount of space between lines. Typically, line spacing is determined before beginning a document, such as when you know that a research paper should be double-spaced, so you identify that setting before typing. Of course, you can change line spacing of a current paragraph or selected text at any point as well. Change line spacing in one of the following ways:

- Click the HOME tab. Click *Line and Paragraph Spacing* (refer to Figure 2.11). Select line spacing or click Line Spacing Options for more choices.
- Click the Paragraph Dialog Box Launcher on the HOME tab. Click the *Line spacing* arrow and select spacing (refer to Figure 2.10). Click OK.

The most common line spacing options are single, double, or 1.5. Word provides those options and more. From the Paragraph dialog box (refer to Figure 2.10), you can select Exactly, At Least, or Multiple. To specify an exact point size for spacing, select Exactly. If you select At Least, you will indicate a minimum line spacing size while allowing Word to adjust the height, if necessary, to accommodate such features as drop caps (oversized letters that sometimes begin paragraphs). The Multiple setting enables you to select a line spacing interval other than single, double, or 1.5.

Select Indents

An ***indent*** is a setting associated with how part of a paragraph is distanced from one or more margins. One of the most common indents is a ***first line indent***, in which the first line of each paragraph is set off from the left margin. For instance, your English instructor might require that the first line of each paragraph in a writing assignment is indented 0.5" from the left margin, a typical first line indent. If you have ever prepared a bibliography for a research paper, you have most likely specified a ***hanging indent***, where the first line of a source begins at the left margin, but all other lines in the source are indented. Indenting an entire paragraph from the left margin is a ***left indent***, while indenting an entire paragraph from the right margin is a ***right indent***. A lengthy quote is often set apart by indenting from both the left and right margins.

Using the Paragraph dialog box (refer to Figure 2.10), you can select an indent setting for one or more paragraphs. First line and hanging indents are considered special indents. You can select left and right indents from either the Paragraph dialog box or from the Paragraph group on the Page Layout tab (refer to Figure 2.12).

STEP 2»

You can use the Word ruler to set indents. If the ruler does not display above the document space, click the View tab and click Ruler (see Figure 2.13). The three-part indicator at the left side of the ruler enables you to set a left indent, a hanging indent, or a first line indent. Drag the desired indent along the ruler to apply the indent to the current paragraph (or selected paragraphs). Figure 2.13 shows the first line indent moved to the 0.5" mark, resulting in the first line of a paragraph being indented by 0.5".

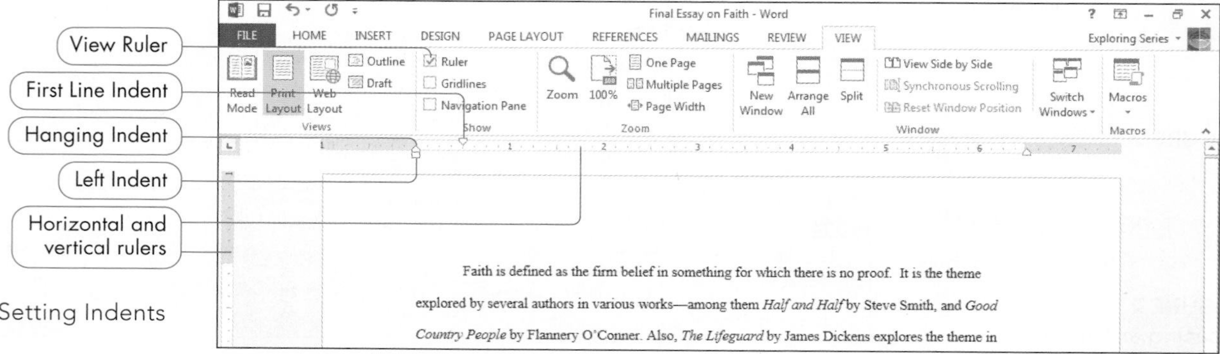

FIGURE 2.13 Setting Indents on the Ruler

Set Tabs

A tab is a marker that specifies a position for aligning text. By using ***tabs***, you can easily arrange text in columns or position text a certain distance from the left or right margins. Tabs enable you to add organization to a document, arranging text in easy-to-read columns. A table of contents is an example of tabbed text, as is a restaurant menu. You can select from various types of tabs, with the most common being *left*, *right*, *center*, and *decimal*. By default, a left tab is set every 0.5" when you start a new document. Each time you press Tab on the keyboard, the insertion point will move to the left by 0.5". Typically, you would set a first line indent or simply press Tab to indent the first line of each new paragraph within a document. Table 2.1 describes various types of tabs.

TABLE 2.1 Tab Markers

Tab Icon on Ruler	Type of Tab	Function
∟	Left tab	Sets the start position on the left so as you type; text moves to the right of the tab setting.
⊥	Center tab	Sets the middle point of the text you type; whatever you type will be centered on that tab setting.
┘	Right tab	Sets the start position on the right so as you type; text moves to the left of that tab setting and aligns on the right.
⊥.	Decimal tab	Aligns numbers on a decimal point. Regardless of how long the number, each number lines up with the decimal point in the same position.
|	Bar tab	This tab does not position text or decimals; but inserts a vertical bar at the tab setting. This bar is useful as a separator for text printed on the same line.

STEP 3» Tabs that you set override default tabs. For example, suppose you set a left tab at 1". That means the default tab of 0.5" is no longer in effect, nor is any other 0.5" default tab still in place. Perhaps the easiest way to set tabs, if not the most precise, is to use the ruler. Click the tab selector (see Figure 2.14) repeatedly to cycle through tabs, including left, center, right, decimal, bar, first line indent, and hanging indent. Then simply click a position on the ruler to set a tab. You can drag a tab along the ruler to reposition it, or you can drag a tab off the ruler to remove it. Figure 2.14 shows a left tab at 1" and a right tab at 5.5". To apply one or more tabs, you can select text and set tabs (applying tabs to the selected text), or you can set a tab and type text (applying tabs to text typed after setting tabs).

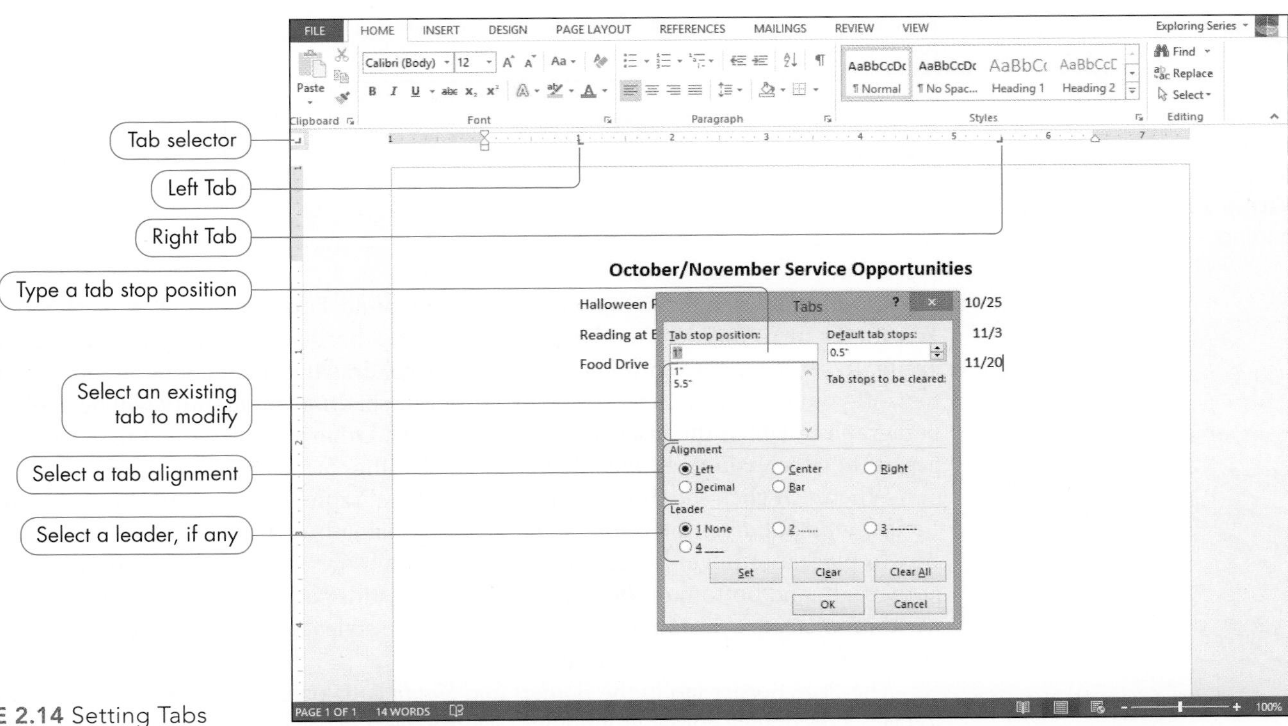

FIGURE 2.14 Setting Tabs

To include *leaders* (the series of dots or hyphens that leads the reader's eye across the page to connect two columns of information), use the Tabs dialog box, shown in Figure 2.14.

The row of dots that typically connects a food item with its price on a restaurant menu is an example of a leader. To set a tab with a leader:

1. Click the Paragraph Dialog Box Launcher in the Paragraph group on the HOME tab and click Tabs from the *Indents and Spacing* tab. Alternatively, double-click a tab on the ruler.
2. Type the location where you want to set the tab. The number you type is assumed to be in inches, so typing *2* would place a tab at 2".
3. Select a tab alignment (Left, Right, etc.).
4. Specify a leader, if desired.
5. Click OK (or click Set and continue specifying tabs).

Deleting Tabs

To manually delete a tab you have set, simply drag it off the ruler. An alternative is to click the Paragraph Dialog Box Launcher, click Tabs, select the tab (in the Tab stop position box), and then click Clear. Click OK.

Apply Borders and Shading

You can draw attention to a document or an area of a document by using the *Borders and Shading* command. A ***border*** is a line that surrounds a paragraph, a page, a table, or an image, similar to how a picture frame surrounds a photograph or piece of art. A border can also display at the top, bottom, left, or right of a selection. ***Shading*** is a background color that appears behind text in a paragraph, a page, or a table. Figure 2.15 illustrates the use of borders and shading.

October/November Service Opportunities

Halloween Fun Run	10/25
Salvation Army Fundraiser	11/3
Reading at Brandon Elementary	11/18
Food Drive	11/20

FIGURE 2.15 Borders and Shading

Borders are used throughout this text to surround Tip boxes and Troubleshooting areas. You might surround a particular paragraph with a border, possibly even shading the paragraph, to set it apart from other text on the page, drawing the reader's attention to its contents. If you have not selected text, any border or shading you identify will be applied to the paragraph in which the insertion point is located. Otherwise, you must first select all paragraphs to which you will apply the border or shading formats.

STEP 4»

When you click the Borders arrow in the Paragraph group on the Home tab and select *Borders and Shading*, the *Borders and Shading* dialog box displays (see Figure 2.16). Click Box to place a uniform border around a paragraph or select Shadow to place thicker lines at the right and bottom of the bordered area. 3D adds some dimension to the border. Click Custom to create a custom border by selecting the style, color, width, and side. The Preview area displays a diagram of your border.

The Page Border tab in the *Borders and Shading* dialog box provides controls that you use to place a decorative border around one or more selected pages. As with a paragraph border, you can place the border around the entire page, or you can select one or more sides. The Page Border tab also provides an additional option to use preselected clip art as a border instead of ordinary lines. Note that it is appropriate to use page borders on documents such as flyers, newsletters, and invitations, but not on formal documents such as research papers and professional reports.

To apply shading to one or more selected paragraphs, click the Shading arrow in the Paragraph group on the Home tab. You can select a solid color, or a lighter or darker variation of the color, for the shaded background. Click More Colors for even more selection. You can also select shading from the Shading tab of the *Borders and Shading* dialog box (see Figure 2.16).

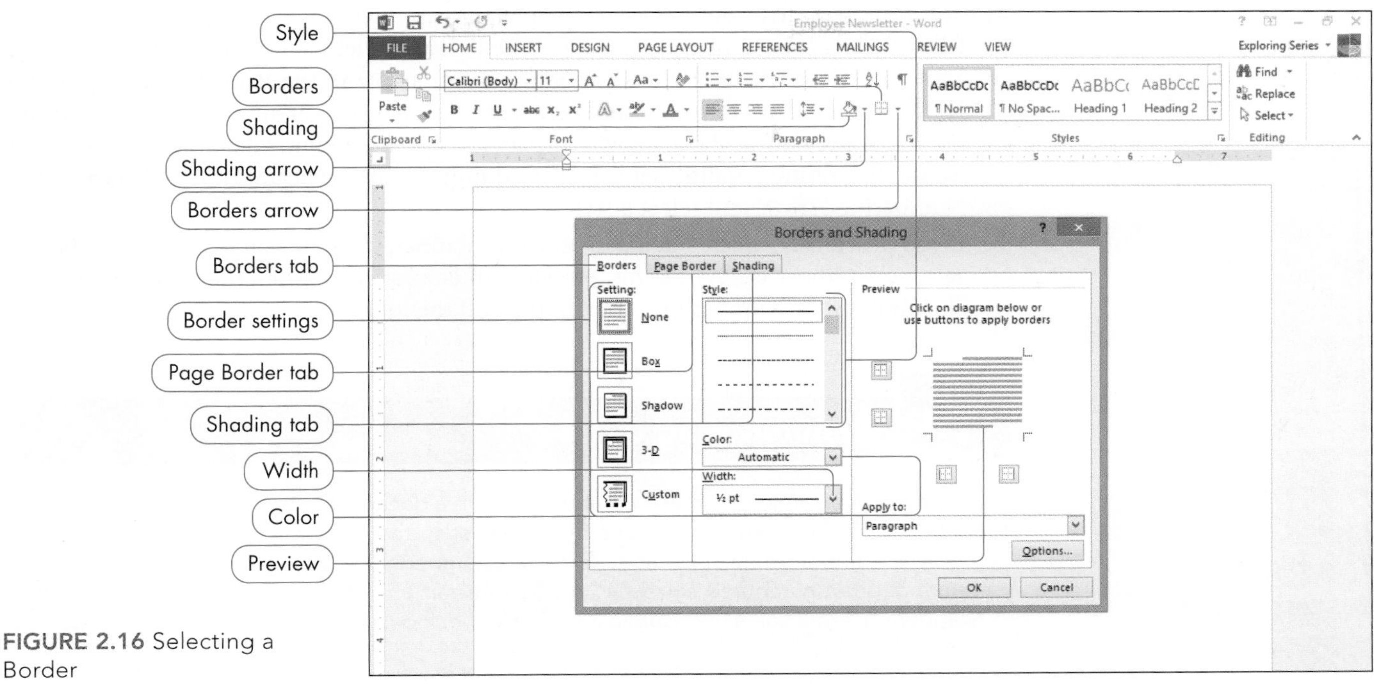

FIGURE 2.16 Selecting a Border

Create Bulleted and Numbered Lists

A list organizes information by topic or in a sequence. Use a ***numbered list*** if the list is a sequence of steps. If the list is not of a sequential nature, but is a simple itemization of points, use a ***bulleted list*** (see Figure 2.17). The numerical sequence in a numbered list is automatically updated to accommodate additions or deletions, which means that if you add or remove items, the list items are renumbered. A *multilevel list* extends a numbered or bulleted list to several levels, and it, too, is updated automatically when topics are added or deleted. You create each of these lists from the Paragraph group on the Home tab.

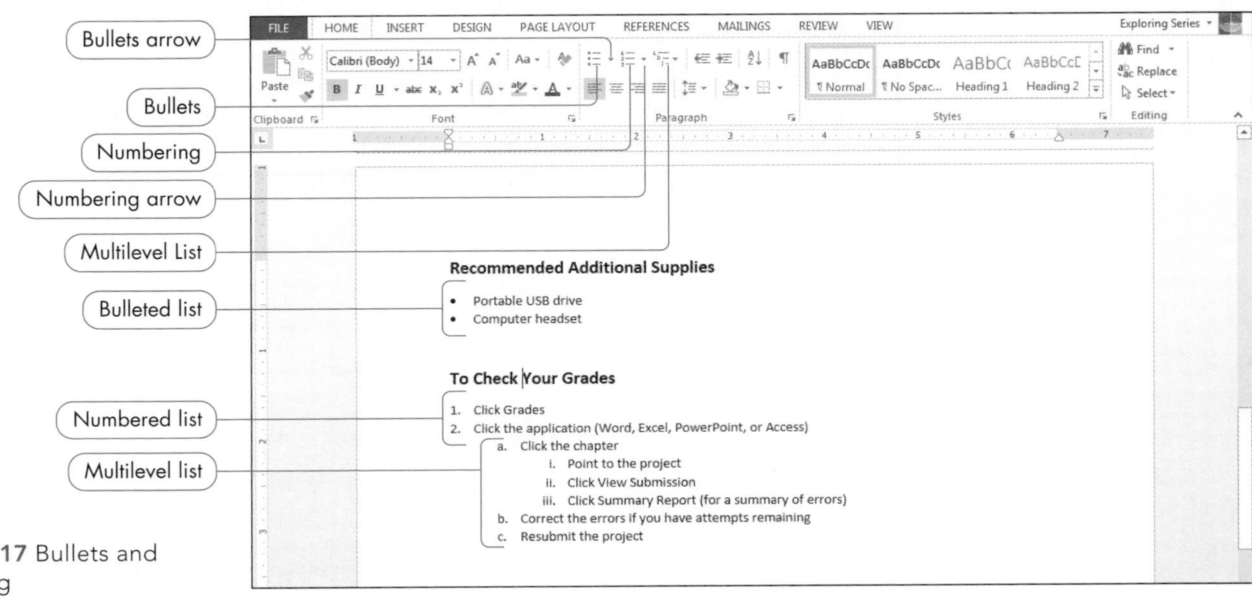

FIGURE 2.17 Bullets and Numbering

To define a new bullet or customize the formatting (such as color or special effect) of a selected bullet, click the Bullets arrow in the Paragraph group on the Home tab and click Define New Bullet. Make selections from the Define New Bullet dialog box and click OK.

To apply bullets, numbering, or multiple levels to a list:

1. Select the items to be bulleted or numbered, or click where you will begin typing the items. Click Bullets (or Numbering) to apply the default bullet or numbering style. To select another style, click the Bullets (or Numbering) arrow in the Paragraph group on the HOME tab and point to one of the predefined symbols or numbering styles in the library. A preview of the style will display in your document. Click the style you want to use. If creating a multilevel list, click Multilevel List (instead of the Bullets arrow or Numbering arrow) and select a style.
2. If you previously selected items to bullet or number, the style will be applied to the selection. Otherwise, type items, pressing Enter after each; when the list is complete, click Bullets (or Numbering) again to turn off the toggle.

TIP Renumbering a List

Especially when creating several numbered lists in a document, you might find that Word continues the numbering sequence from one list to the next, when your intention was to begin numbering each list at 1. To restart numbering at a new value, right-click the item that is not numbered correctly, and click *Restart at 1*. Alternatively, you can click the Numbering arrow and select Set Numbering Value. Indicate a starting value in the subsequent dialog box.

1. Describe the difference between a serif and sans serif font. Give examples of when you might use each. ***p. 199***
2. Suppose a document is single spaced. However, when you type a series of bulleted lines, the lines are not single spaced; instead there is a much larger distance between each. What could cause the larger space, and how would you correct it so that the bulleted items are also single spaced? ***p. 205***
3. You are working with a campus organization, helping plan a charity dinner. You will use Word to create the menu. What type of tabs would you use, and approximately how would you space them? ***p. 207***
4. You are preparing a document of tips for an upcoming camping trip. You will include a list of items to bring along for the overnight adventure. What Word feature could you use to draw attention to the list? ***p. 209***

Hands-On Exercises

1 Text and Paragraph Formatting

The newsletter you are developing needs a lot of work. The first thing to do is to make sure it is error free, and to format it so it is much easier to read. After selecting an appropriate font and font size, you will emphasize selected text with bold and italic text formatting. Paragraphs must be spaced so they are easy to read. You know that to be effective, a document must capture the reader's attention while conveying a message. You will begin the process of formatting and preparing the newsletter in this exercise.

Skills covered: Select Font Options and Change Text Appearance • Select Paragraph Alignment, Spacing, and Indenting • Set Tabs • Apply Borders and Shading • Create Bulleted and Numbered Lists

STEP 1 » SELECT FONT OPTIONS AND CHANGE TEXT APPEARANCE

The newsletter will be printed and distributed by mail. As a printed document, you know that certain font options are better suited for reading. Specifically, you want to use a serif font in an easy-to-read size. Refer to Figure 2.18 as you complete Step 1.

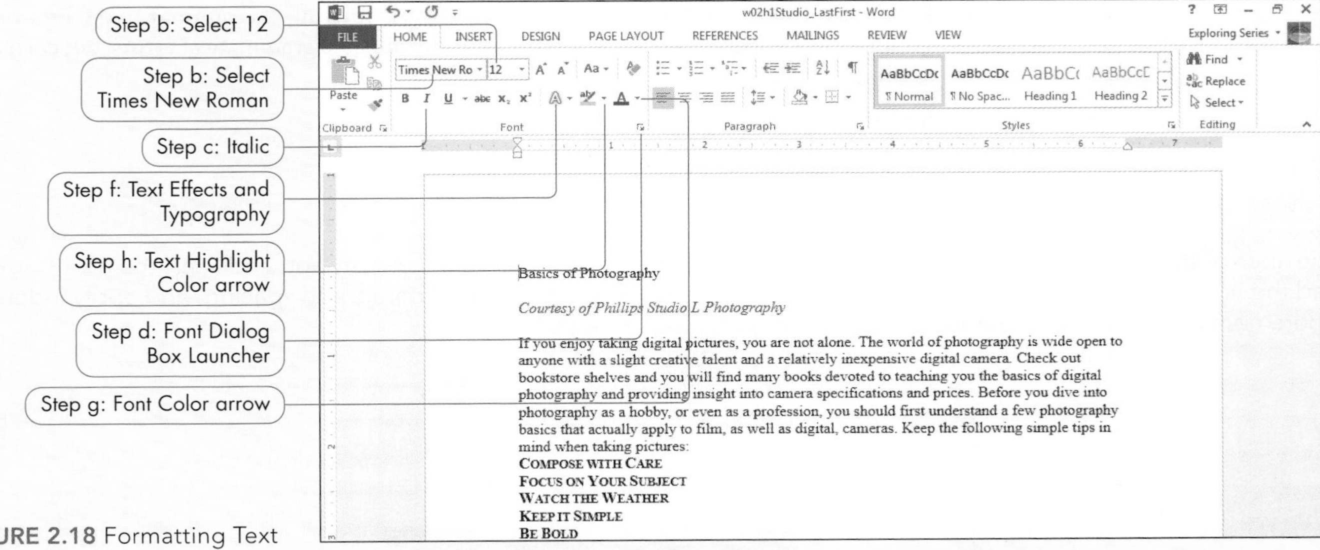

FIGURE 2.18 Formatting Text

a. Open *w02h1Studio* and save it as **w02h1Studio_LastFirst**.

When you save files, use your last and first names. For example, as the Word author, I would name my document *w02h1Studio_HoganLynn*.

> **TROUBLESHOOTING:** If you make any major mistakes in this exercise, you can close the file, open *w02h1Studio* again, and then start this exercise over.

b. Press **Ctrl+A** to select all of the text in the document. Click the **Font arrow** in the Font group on the HOME tab and scroll, if necessary, to select **Times New Roman**. Click the **Font Size arrow** in the Font group and select **12**.

You use a 12-pt serif font on the whole document because it is easier to read in print.

c. Select the second line of text in the document, *Courtesy of Phillips Studio L Photography*. Click **Italic** on the Mini Toolbar. Scroll down, if necessary, and double-click *boxy* in the paragraph below *Camera Body*. Click **Italic** in the Font group.

TROUBLESHOOTING: If the Mini Toolbar does not display or disappears, click Italic in the Font group on the HOME tab.

d. Select the five paragraphs beginning with *Compose with Care* and ending with *Be Bold*. Click the **Font Dialog Box Launcher** in the Font group.

   The Font dialog box displays with font options.

e. Click the **Font tab**, if necessary, and click **Bold** in the Font style box. Click to select the **Small caps check box** under *Effects*. Click **OK**.

f. Press **Ctrl+End** to move the insertion point to the end of the document. Select the last line in the document, *Let Phillips Studio L Photography Preserve Your Memories!* Click **Text Effects and Typography** in the Font group. Select **Fill – Blue, Accent 1, Outline – Background 1, Hard Shadow – Accent 1** (third row, third column). Change the font size of the selected text to **16**. Click anywhere to deselect the text.

g. Press **Ctrl+Home** to position the insertion point at the beginning of the document. Select the second line in the document, *Courtesy of Phillips Studio L Photography*. Click the **Font Color arrow** and select **Blue, Accent 5, Darker 25%** (fifth row, ninth column).

h. Select the words *you should consider how to become a better photographer* in the paragraph under the *Composition* heading. Click the **Text Highlight Color arrow** and select **Yellow**.

i. Press **Ctrl+Home**. Click the **REVIEW tab** and click **Spelling & Grammar** in the Proofing group to check spelling and grammar. Ignore any possible grammatical errors, but correct spelling mistakes.

j. Save the document.

STEP 2 » SELECT PARAGRAPH ALIGNMENT, SPACING, AND INDENTING

The lines of the newsletter are too close together. It is difficult to tell where one paragraph ends and the next begins, and the layout of the text is not very pleasing. Overall, you will adjust line and paragraph spacing, and apply indents where necessary. Refer to Figure 2.19 as you complete Step 2.

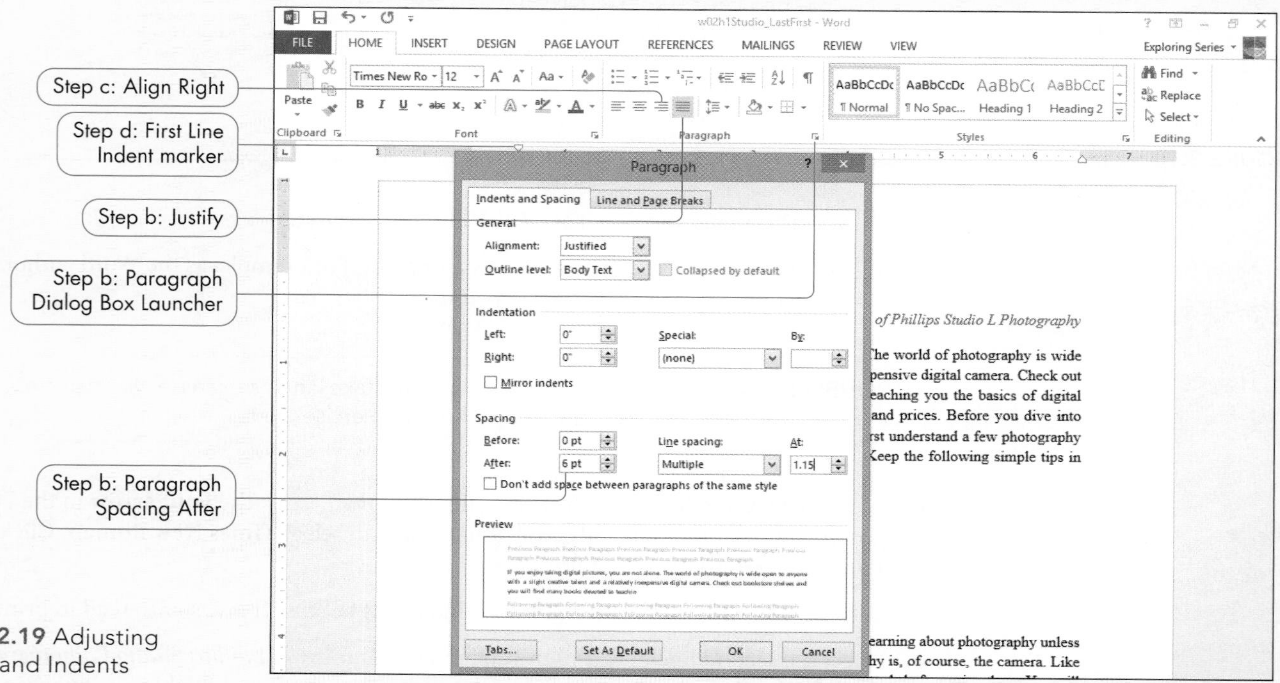

FIGURE 2.19 Adjusting Spacing and Indents

a. Select most of the document beginning with the sentence *If you enjoy taking digital pictures* and ending with *emotion expressed before even greeting Santa*. Click the **HOME tab**. Click **Line and Paragraph Spacing** in the Paragraph group. Select **1.15**. Do not deselect the text.

All lines within the selected text are spaced by 1.15.

b. Click **Justify** in the Paragraph group. Click the **Paragraph Dialog Box Launcher**. With the Indents and Spacing tab selected, click the **After spin arrow** in the *Spacing* section once to increase spacing after to **6 pt**. Click **OK**. Click anywhere to deselect the text.

You have placed 6 pt spacing after each paragraph in the selected area. Selected paragraphs are also aligned with justify, which means text is evenly distributed between the left and right margins.

c. Press **Ctrl+End**. Click anywhere on the last line in the document, *Let Phillips Studio L Photography Preserve Your Memories!* Click **Center** in the Paragraph group. Press **Ctrl+Home**. Click anywhere on the second line of text in the document, *Courtesy of Phillips Studio L Photography*. Click **Align Right** in the Paragraph group.

d. Click the **VIEW tab** and click **Ruler** in the Show group to display the ruler, if necessary. Click anywhere in the first body paragraph, beginning with *If you enjoy taking digital pictures*. Click the **HOME tab**, if necessary, and click the **Paragraph Dialog Box Launcher**. Click the **Special arrow** in the Indentation group and select **First line**. Click **OK**. Click anywhere in the second multiline paragraph—the paragraph beginning with *First things first*. Position the mouse pointer on the First Line Indent marker and drag the marker to the **0.5"** mark on the horizontal ruler.

The first line of both multiline paragraphs that begin the document are indented by 0.5 inches.

e. Save the document.

STEP 3 » SET TABS

You realize that you left off the studio hours and want to include them at the end of the document. Refer to Figure 2.20 as you complete Step 3.

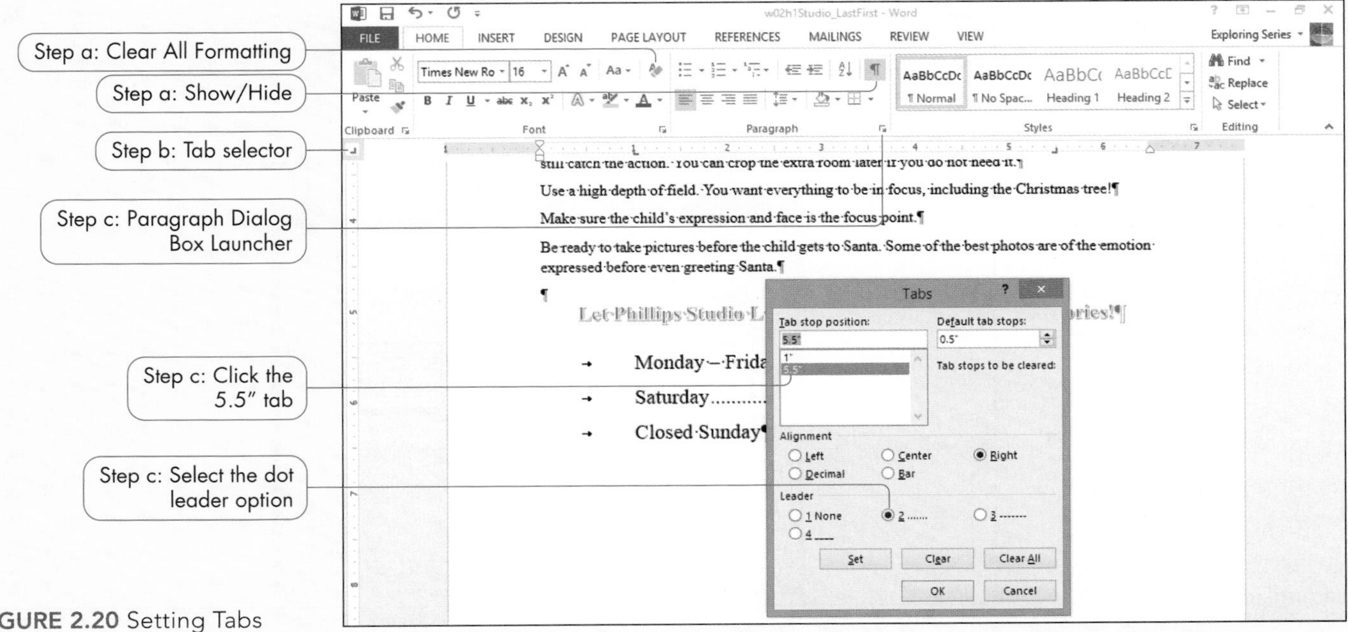

FIGURE 2.20 Setting Tabs

a. Press **Ctrl+End**. If necessary, click **Show/Hide** in the Paragraph group to display nonprinting characters. Press **Enter** twice. Click **Clear All Formatting** in the Font group on the HOME tab. Select **Times New Roman font** and **16 pt size**.

   You clicked Clear All Formatting so that the text effect formatting from the line above the insertion point is not carried forward to text that you will type next.

b. Make sure the tab selector (shown at the top of the vertical ruler) specifies a Left Tab and click at **1"** on the ruler to set a left tab. Click the tab selector twice to select a right tab and click at **5.5"** on the ruler to set a right tab.

   You set a left tab at 1" and a right tab at 5.5".

> **TROUBLESHOOTING:** If the tabs you set are incorrectly placed on the ruler, click Undo in the Quick Access Toolbar and repeat step b. You can also simply drag a tab off the ruler to remove it, or drag it along the ruler to reposition it.

c. Click the **Paragraph Dialog Box Launcher** and click **Tabs** at the bottom-left corner. Click **5.5"** in the Tab stop position box. Click **2** in the *Leader* section and click **OK**.

   You modified the right tab to include dot leaders, which means dots will display before text at the right tab.

d. Press **Tab**. Type **Monday – Friday** and press **Tab**. Type **9:00 – 4:00**. Press **Enter**. Press **Tab**. Type **Saturday** and press **Tab**. Type **9:00 – 2:00**. Press **Enter**. Press **Tab**. Type **Closed Sunday**.

e. Save the document.

STEP 4 » APPLY BORDERS AND SHADING

To draw attention to the business hours, you will shade and border the information you typed. Refer to Figure 2.21 as you complete Step 4.

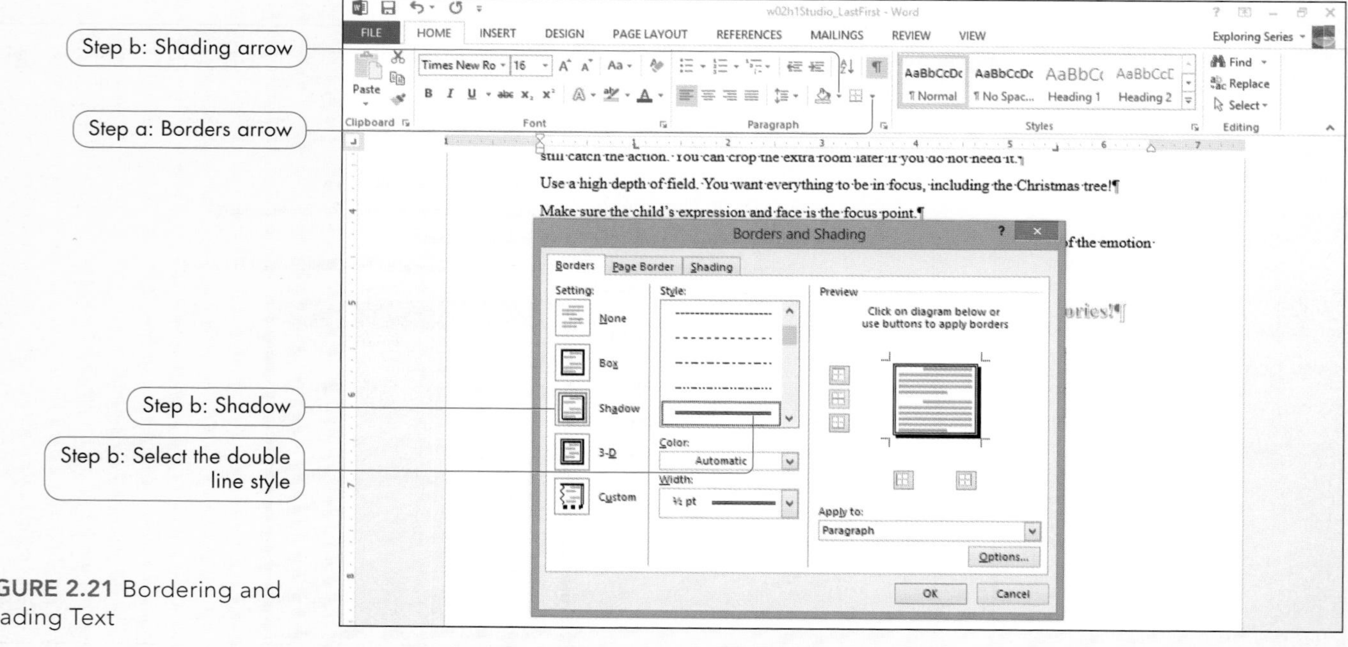

FIGURE 2.21 Bordering and Shading Text

a. Select the three lines at the end of the document, beginning with *Monday – Friday* and ending with *Closed Sunday*. Click the **Borders arrow** in the Paragraph group on the HOME tab and select **Borders and Shading**.

> **TROUBLESHOOTING:** If you click Borders instead of the Borders arrow, you will not see the *Borders and Shading* dialog box and the most recent border will be applied to selected text. Click Undo on the Quick Access Toolbar and click the Borders arrow. Then click *Borders and Shading*.

b. Click **Shadow** in the *Setting* section. Scroll through the **Style box** and select the seventh style—double line. Click **OK**. Do not deselect text. Click the **Shading arrow** and select **Blue, Accent 1, Lighter 60%** (third row, fifth column). Click anywhere to deselect the text.

Studio hours are bordered and shaded.

c. Save the document.

STEP 5 » CREATE BULLETED AND NUMBERED LISTS

At several points in the newsletter, you include either a list of items or a sequence of steps. You will add bullets to the lists and number the steps. Refer to Figure 2.22 as you complete Step 5.

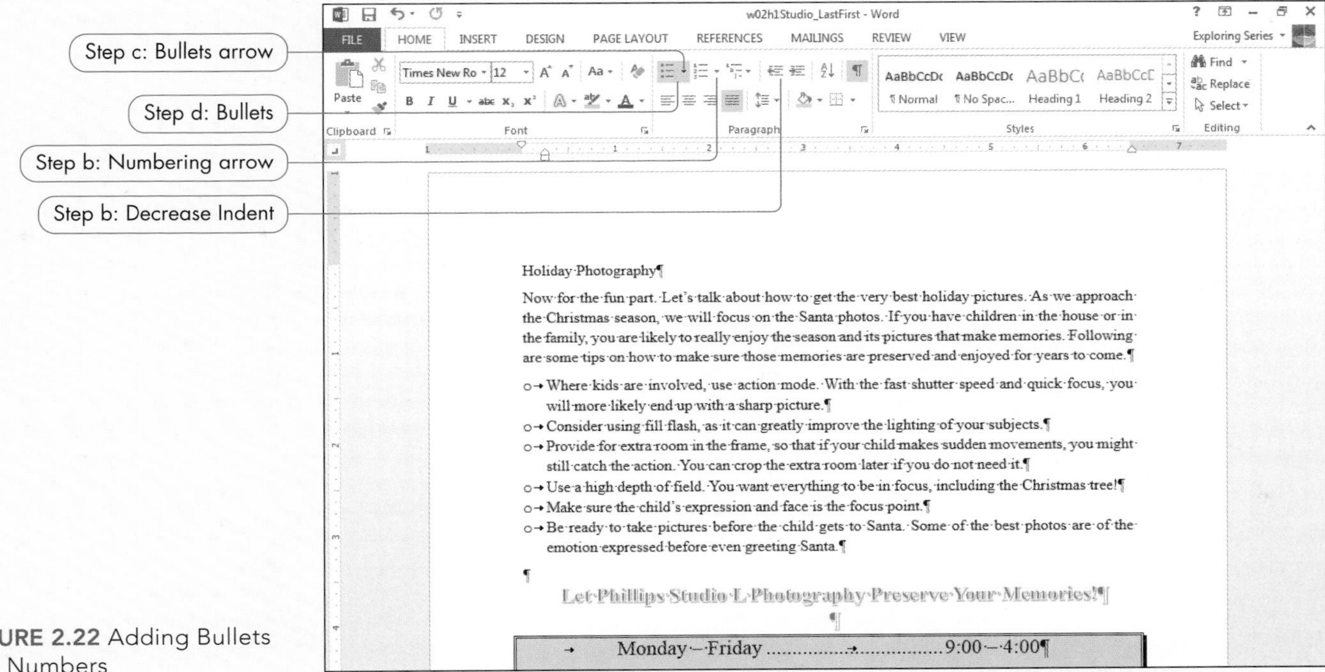

FIGURE 2.22 Adding Bullets and Numbers

a. Press **Ctrl+Home**. Select the five boldfaced paragraphs, beginning with *Compose with Care* and ending with *Be Bold*.

b. Click the **Numbering arrow** and select **Number alignment: Left** (third option on the first row in the Numbering Library, showing each number followed by a right parenthesis). Click **Decrease Indent** in the Paragraph group to move the numbered items to the left margin. Click anywhere to deselect the text.

c. Scroll to the second page and select four paragraphs following the sentence *Depth of field is determined by several factors:*, beginning with *Aperture/F-Stop* and ending with *Point of View*. Click the **Bullets arrow** and select the hollow round bullet. Decrease the indent to move the selected text to the left margin. Deselect the text.

d. Press **Ctrl+End** and select the six paragraphs beginning with *Where kids are involved*, and ending *even greeting Santa*. Click **Bullets** to apply a hollow round bullet to the selected paragraphs. Decrease the indent so the bullets begin at the left margin.

Clicking Bullets applied the most recently selected bullet style to selected text. You did not have to click the Bullets arrow and select from the Bullet Library.

e. Save the document. Keep the document open if you plan to continue with the next Hands-On Exercise. If not, close the document and exit Word.

Document Appearance

The overall appearance and organization of a document is the first opportunity to effectively convey your message to readers. You should ensure that a document is formatted attractively with coordinated and consistent style elements. Not only should a document be organized by topic, but also it should be organized by design, so that it is easy to read and so that topics of the same level of emphasis are similar in appearance. For example, major headings are typically formatted identically, with subheadings formatted to indicate a subordinate relationship—in a smaller font, for example. Word 2013 includes tools on the Design tab that help you create a polished and professional-looking document. You will find options for creating a themed document, with color-coordinated design elements, as well as ***style sets***, which are predefined combinations of font, style, color, and font size that can be applied to selected text. Organizing a document into sections enables you to combine diverse units into a whole, formatting sections independently of one another.

In this section, you will explore document formatting options, including themes and style sets. In addition, you will learn to create and apply styles. You will work with sections and columns, learning to organize and format sections independently of one another, to create an attractive document that conveys your message.

Formatting a Document

A ***document theme*** is a set of coordinating fonts, colors, and special effects, such as shadowing or glows that are combined into a package to provide a stylish appearance. Applying a theme enables you to visually coordinate various page elements. In some cases, adding a page border or page background can also yield a more attractive and effective document. All these design options are available on the Design tab, which is new to Word 2013. As you consider ways to organize a document, you might find it necessary to divide it into sections, with each section arranged or formatted independently of others. For example, a cover page (or section) might be centered vertically, while all other pages are aligned at the top. By arranging text in columns, you can easily create an attractive newsletter or brochure. The Page Layout tab facilitates the use of sections and formatting in columns. When formatting a document, you should always keep in mind the document's purpose and its intended audience. Whereas a newsletter might use more color and playful text and design effects, a legal document should be more conservative. With the broad range of document formatting options available in Word, you can be as playful or conservative as necessary.

Select a Document Theme

A document theme combines color, font, and graphics, simplifying the task of creating a professional, color-coordinated document. When you select a theme for a document, a unified set of design elements, including font style, color, and special effects, is applied to the entire document. The Design tab includes selections related to themes (see Figure 2.23). Themes are not limited to Word, but are also available in other Office 2013 applications. A Word document, color-coordinated to match a supporting PowerPoint presentation, adds professionalism and encourages continuity of purpose between the two projects. Even a new blank Word document is based on a theme by default—the Office theme. Click the Font arrow in the Font group on the Home tab to see the theme fonts (both Heading and Body) for the Office theme. Of course, you can select from other fonts in the list if you prefer. Similarly, you will see Office theme font colors when you click the Font Color arrow.

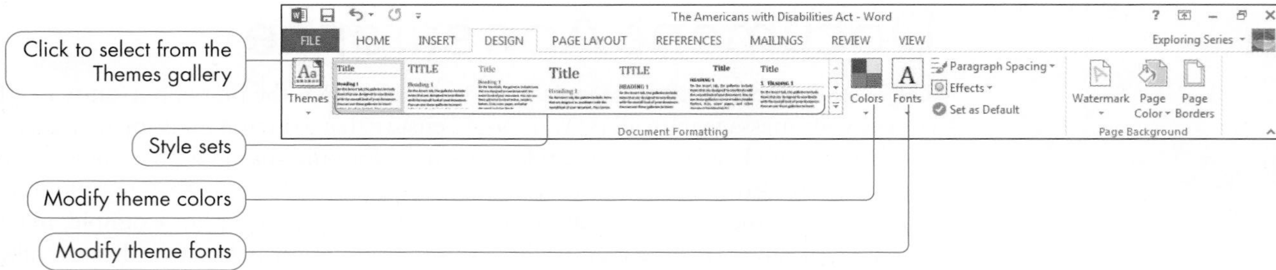

FIGURE 2.23 Design Tab

STEP 1» Themes are located in the Document Formatting group on the Design tab (refer to Figure 2.23). Click Themes to select from the Themes gallery. As you point to a theme, you will see a preview of the effect on document text. Depending on document features and color selections already in place, you might not see an immediate change when previewing or selecting a document theme. Click a theme to select it. Perhaps you are pleased with most of the theme effects, but want to modify the color or font selection. Click Colors or Fonts in the Document Formatting group on the Design tab to adjust the theme slightly. Each group of coordinated colors or font selections is summarized and identified by a unique name. Click to select a color or font group to adjust the selected theme in the document. To apply themed effects to objects in a document, click Effects in the Document Formatting group on the Design tab and select from a gallery of effects.

Work with Sections

It sometimes becomes necessary to vary the layout of a document within a page or between pages, and incorporate sections into a document. A headline of an article might center horizontally across the width of a page, while remaining article text is divided into columns. The headline could be situated in one section, while article text resides in another. So that sections can be managed separately, you must indicate with section breaks where one section ends and another begins. A ***section break*** is a marker that divides a document into sections. Word stores the formatting characteristics of each section within the section break at the end of a section. Therefore, if you delete a section break, you also delete the formatting for that section, causing the text above the break to assume the formatting characteristics of the previous section. To delete a section break, click the section break indicator (see Figure 2.24) and press Delete.

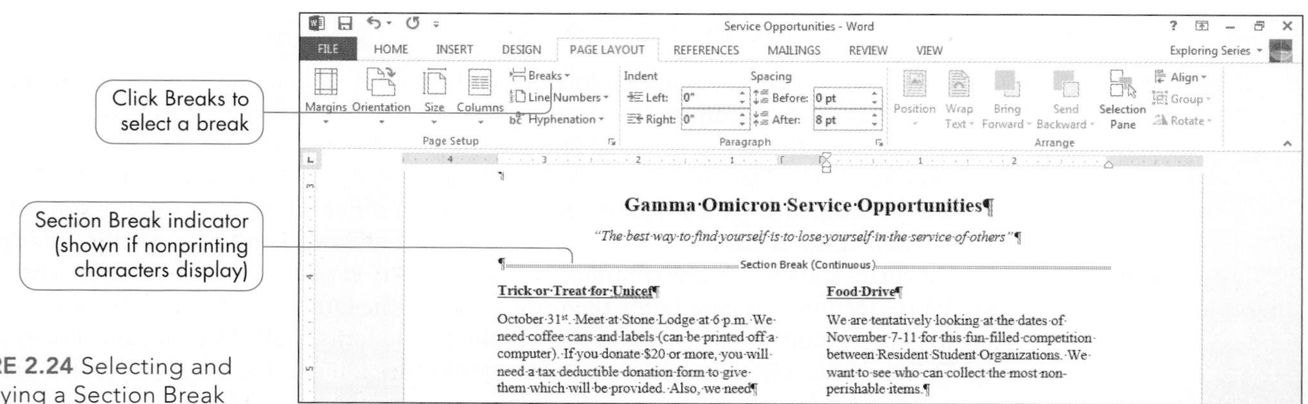

FIGURE 2.24 Selecting and Displaying a Section Break

You can choose from four types of section breaks, as shown in Table 2.2. You can select a section break type when you click the Page Layout tab and click Breaks in the Page Setup group. Before inserting a break, the insertion point should be at the point where the break is to occur.

TABLE 2.2 Section Breaks		
Type	**Description**	**Example**
Next Page	Text that follows must begin at the top of the next page.	Use to force a chapter to start at the top of a page.
Continuous	Text that follows can continue on the same page.	Use to format text in the middle of the page into columns.
Even Page	Text that follows must begin at the top of the next even-numbered page.	Use to force a chapter to begin at the top of an even-numbered page.
Odd Page	Text that follows must begin at the top of the next odd-numbered page.	Use to force a chapter to begin at the top of an odd-numbered page.

To place a section break in a document:

1. Click at the location where the section break should occur.
2. Click the PAGE LAYOUT tab. Click Breaks in the Page Setup group.
3. Select a section break type (see Table 2.2). If nonprinting characters display, you will see a section break (refer to Figure 2.24).

Format Text into Columns

STEP 2»

Columns format a document or section of a document into side-by-side vertical blocks in which the text flows down the first column and continues at the top of the next column. To format text into columns, click the Page Layout tab and click Columns in the Page Setup group. Specify the number of columns or select More Columns to display the Columns dialog box. The Columns dialog box (see Figure 2.25) provides options for setting the number of columns and spacing between columns.

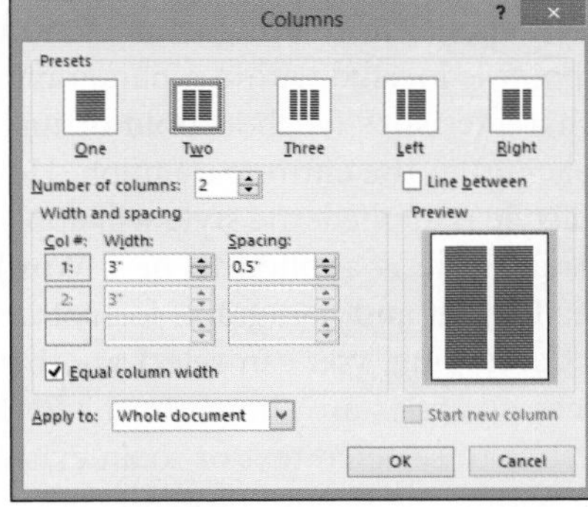

FIGURE 2.25 Columns Dialog Box

Having created a two-column document, you should preview the document to ensure an attractive arrangement of columns. Try to avoid columns that end awkwardly, perhaps with a column heading at the bottom of one column, while remaining text continues at the top of the next column. In addition, columns should be somewhat balanced, if possible, so that one column is not lengthy, while the next is very short. To force a column break, click in the document where the break is to occur, click the Page Layout tab, click Breaks, and then click Column in the *Page Breaks* section. With nonprinting characters displayed, you will see the Column break indicator at the location where one column ends and the next begins.

Applying Styles

As you complete reports, assignments, and other projects, you probably apply the same text, paragraph, table, and list formatting for similar documents. Instead of formatting each element of each document individually, you can create your own custom format for each element—called a style—to save time in designing titles, headings, and paragraphs. A characteristic of a professional document is uniform formatting. All major headings look the same, with uniform subheadings. Even paragraphs can be styled to lend consistency to a document. If styles are appropriately assigned, Word can automatically generate reference pages such as a table of contents and indexes.

A ***style*** is a named collection of formatting characteristics. Styles automate the formatting process and provide a consistent appearance to a document. It is possible to store any type of character or paragraph formatting within a style, and once a style is defined, you can apply it to any element within a document to produce identical formatting. Word provides a gallery of styles from which you can choose, or you can create your own style. For example, having formatted a major report heading with various settings, such as font type, color, and size, you can create a style from the heading, calling it *Major_Heading*. The next time you type a major heading, simply apply the *Major_Heading* style so that the two headings are identical in format. Subsequent major headings can be formatted in exactly the same way. If you later decide to modify the *Major_Heading* style, all text based on that style will automatically adjust as well.

Select and Modify Styles

Some styles are considered either character or paragraph styles. A *character* style formats one or more selected characters within a paragraph, often applying font formats found in the Font group on the Home tab. A *paragraph* style changes the entire paragraph in which the insertion point is located, or changes multiple selected paragraphs. A paragraph style typically includes paragraph formats found in the Paragraph group on the Home tab, such as alignment, line spacing, indents, tabs, and borders. Other styles are neither character nor paragraph, but are instead *linked* styles in which both character and paragraph formatting are included. A linked style applies formatting dependent upon the text selected. For example, when the insertion point is located within a paragraph, but no text is selected, a linked style applies both font characteristics (such as bold or italic) and paragraph formats (such as paragraph and line spacing) to the entire paragraph. However, if text is selected within a paragraph when a linked style is applied, the style will apply font formatting only.

By default, the Normal style is applied to new Word documents. Normal style is a paragraph style with specific font and paragraph formatting. If that style is not appropriate for a document you are developing, you can select another style from Word's style gallery. The most frequently accessed styles are shown in the Styles group on the Home tab (see Figure 2.26). To apply a style to selected text or to an existing paragraph, select the text (or place the insertion point within the paragraph) and click a style in the Styles group on the Home tab. For even more style choice, click the Styles Dialog Box Launcher (see Figure 2.26) to display the Styles pane (see Figure 2.26) and click to select a style.

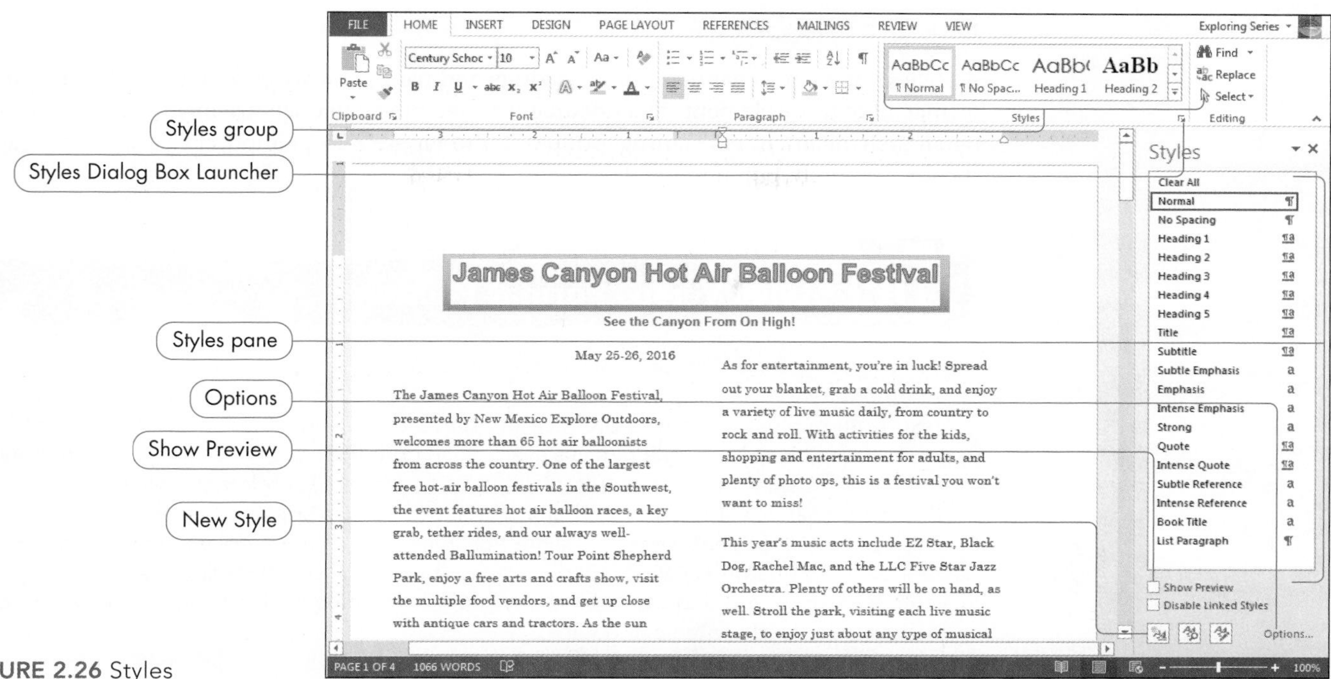

FIGURE 2.26 Styles

STEP 3

To modify a style:

1. Click the Styles Dialog Box Launcher.
2. Point to a style in the Styles pane and click the arrow on the right.
3. Click Modify. The Modify Style dialog box displays (see Figure 2.27).
4. Change any font and paragraph formatting or click Format for even more choices.
5. Click *Add to the Styles gallery* if the style is one you are likely to use often.
6. Indicate whether the style should be available only in the current document, or in new documents based on the current template.
7. Click OK.

Modifying a style, or even creating a new style, affects only the current document, by default. However, you can cause the style to be available to all documents that are based on the current template when you select *New documents based on this template* in the Modify Style dialog box (see Figure 2.27). Unless you make that selection, however, the changes are not carried over to new documents you create or to others that you open. As an example, the specifications for the Title style are shown in Figure 2.27.

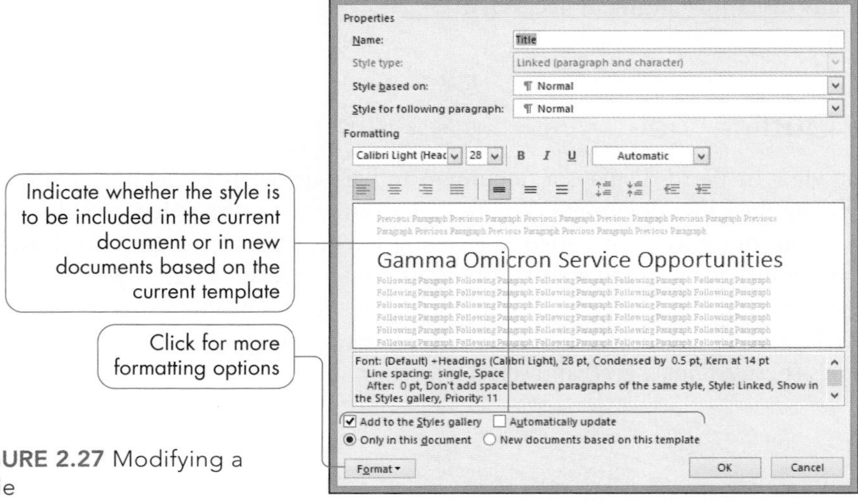

FIGURE 2.27 Modifying a Style

Use a Style Set

A style set is a combination of title, heading, and paragraph styles. Using a style set, you can format all of those elements in a document at one time. Style sets are included on the Design tab in the Document Formatting group (refer to Figure 2.23). Simply click a style set to apply the format combination to the document.

TIP Styles Versus Format Painter

To copy formatting from one selection to another, you can certainly use Format Painter. Another alternative is to create a new style from the selection and apply it to additional text. Both processes seem to produce the same results. However, unlike changes made using Format Painter, a style remains available in both the current document and in other documents based on the same template, if you indicate that preference when you create the style. That way, the same formatting changes can be applied repeatedly in various documents or positions within the same document, even after a document is closed and reopened. Formatting changes made as a result of using Format Painter are not available later. Also, styles that indicate a hierarchy (such as Heading 1, Heading 2) can be used to prepare a table of contents or outline.

Create a New Style from Text

Having applied several formatting characteristics to text, you might want to repeat that formatting on other selections that are similar in purpose. For example, suppose you format a page title with a specific font size, font color, and bordering. Subsequent page titles should be formatted identically. You can select the formatted page title and create a new style based on the formatting of the selected text. Then simply select the next title to which the formatting should be applied and choose the newly created style name from the Styles group or from the Styles pane.

STEP 4»

To create a new style from existing text:

1. Select the text from which the new style should be created or click in a paragraph containing paragraph characteristics you want to include in the new style.
2. Click the Styles Dialog Box Launcher (refer to Figure 2.26) to open the Styles pane.
3. Click New Style, located in the bottom-left corner of the Styles pane (refer to Figure 2.26).
4. Enter a name for the new style. Do not use the name of an existing style.
5. Click the *Style type* arrow and select a style type (paragraph, character, or linked, among others).
6. Adjust any other formatting, if necessary.
7. Click OK.

Use the Outline View

The Outline view in Word displays a document in various levels of detail, according to heading styles applied in a document. Figure 2.28 shows the Outline view of a document in which major headings were formatted in Heading 1 style, with subheadings in Heading 2 style. You can modify the heading styles to suit your preference; however, if you plan to use Outline view to summarize a document, you must apply Word's heading styles (even if you have modified them) to your text. To select a level to view, perhaps only first-level headings, click All Levels (beside *Show Level*) and select a level.

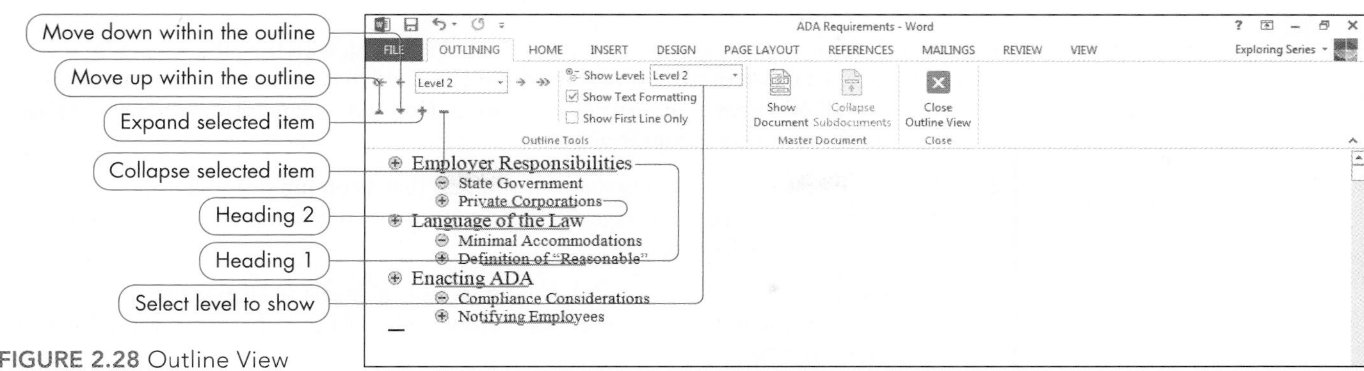

FIGURE 2.28 Outline View

STEP 5» To collapse or expand a single heading, click the heading in Outline view and click + (to expand) or – (to collapse) on the Ribbon. For example, having clicked text formatted as Heading 1, click + to show any lower-level headings associated with the particular heading (refer to Figure 2.28). Text other than that associated with the selected heading will remain unaffected. As shown in Figure 2.28, you can move a heading (along with all associated sub-headings) up or down in the document. In Outline view, you can also drag the + or – beside a heading to move the entire group, including all sublevels, to another location.

In Print Layout view, you can quickly collapse everything except the section you want to work with. Point to a heading and click the small triangle that displays beside the heading (see Figure 2.29) to collapse or expand the following body text and sublevels. Collapsing text in that manner is a handy way to provide your readers with a summary.

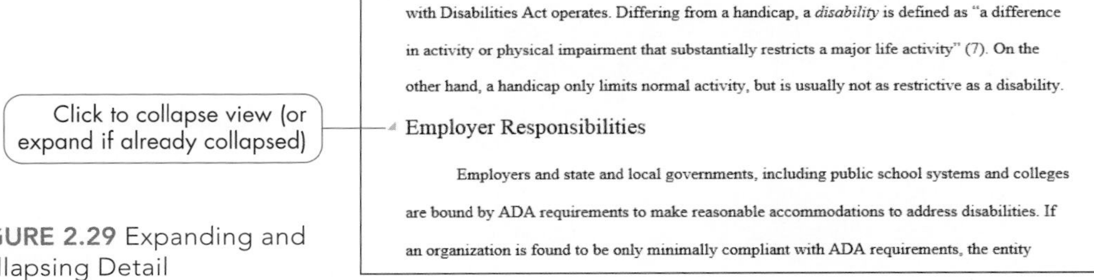

FIGURE 2.29 Expanding and Collapsing Detail

Use Outline view to glimpse or confirm a document's structure. Especially when developing lengthy reports, you will want to make sure headings are shown at the correct level of detail. A document shown in Outline view can also be easily converted to a PowerPoint presentation, with each level shown as a point on a slide. Also, a table of contents is automatically generated when you click *Table of Contents* on the References tab.

You can also quickly move through a document in Outline view, and you can restructure a document:

- With levels collapsed so that body text does not display, just click a heading to move to and change the view to Print Layout or another view. The document will expand, and the insertion point will be in the section identified by the heading you clicked. Using Outline view to move through a lengthy document can save a great deal of time because it is not necessary to page through a document looking for a particular section heading.
- Use Outline view to restructure a document. Simply drag and drop a heading to reposition it within a document, or use the Move Up or Move Down buttons. If subheadings are associated, they will move with the heading as well.

1. You will include a table on the second page of a document, with the table taking up the entire page. You determine that the table is best situated in landscape orientation, with the text on all other pages in portrait orientation. How would you format the second page separately from the other pages? ***p. 219***
2. As you develop a two-column newsletter, you find that a column heading displays alone at the end of a column on one page, with remaining text continuing on the next. How can you correct that problem? ***p. 219***
3. Although both Format Painter and the use of styles enable you to change the appearance of text in a document, what is the benefit of using styles when formatting several different areas of text? ***p. 222***
4. How is the concept of styles related to the Outline view? ***p. 222***

Hands-On Exercises

2 Document Formatting

The next step in preparing the photography newsletter for distribution is to apply document formatting to several areas of the document that will make it easier to read. By applying a theme and formatting the document in columns, you will add to the visual appeal. Using styles, you can ensure consistent formatting of document text. Finally, you will check the document's organization by viewing it in Outline view.

Skills covered: Select a Document Theme • Work with Sections and Format Text into Columns • Select and Modify Styles • Use a Style Set and Create a New Style • Use the Outline View

STEP 1 » SELECT A DOCUMENT THEME

A document theme provides color and font coordination, simplifying your design task. You will apply a document theme to the newsletter as a simple way to ensure that yours is an attractive document with well-coordinated features. Refer to Figure 2.30 as you complete Step 1.

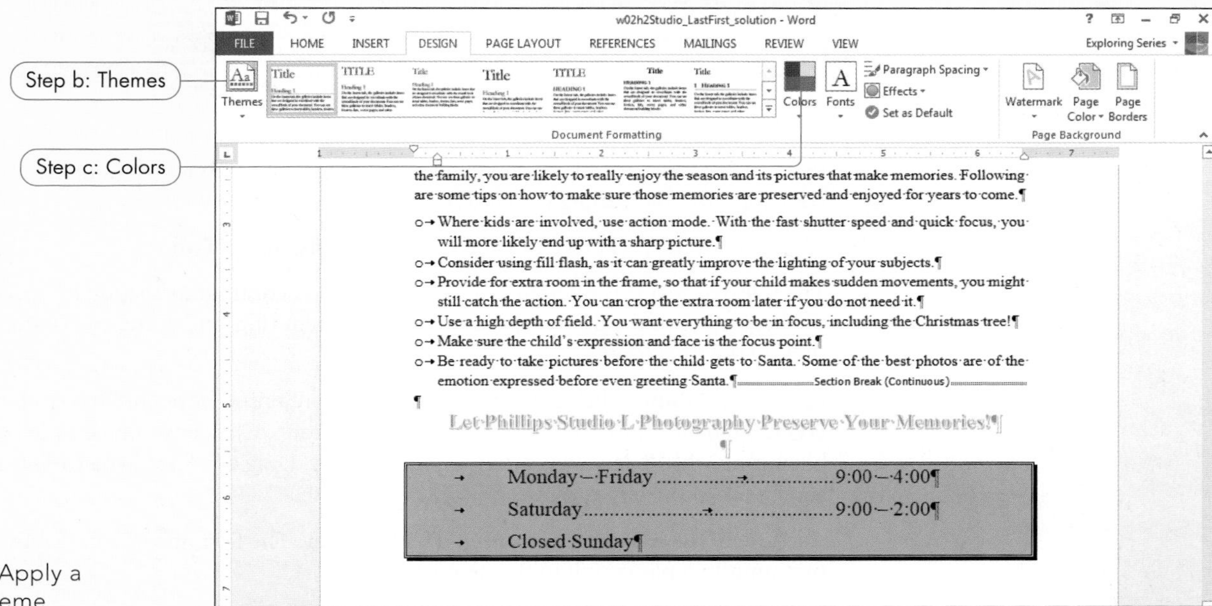

FIGURE 2.30 Apply a Document Theme

a. Open *w02h1Studio_LastFirst* if you closed it at the end of Hands-On Exercise 1 and save it as **w02h2Studio_LastFirst**, changing *h1* to *h2*.

b. Press **Ctrl+Home**. Click the **DESIGN tab** and click **Themes** in the Document Formatting group. Select **Organic**.

   Note the color change applied to the second line of the document, *Courtesy of Phillips Studio L Photography*.

c. Click **Colors** in the Document Formatting group and select **Violet II**.

   The second line of the document, *Courtesy of Phillips Studio L Photography*, has changed colors because you selected a new color scheme within the theme. The table of studio hours on the last page of the document also changed colors.

d. Save the document.

STEP 2 » WORK WITH SECTIONS AND FORMAT TEXT INTO COLUMNS

The document should be formatted as a newsletter. Most often, newsletters display in columns, so you will apply columns to the newsletter. A few items, such as the newsletter heading and the store hours at the end of the document, should be centered horizontally across the page instead of within a column. Using sections, you will format those items differently from column text. Refer to Figure 2.31 as you complete Step 2.

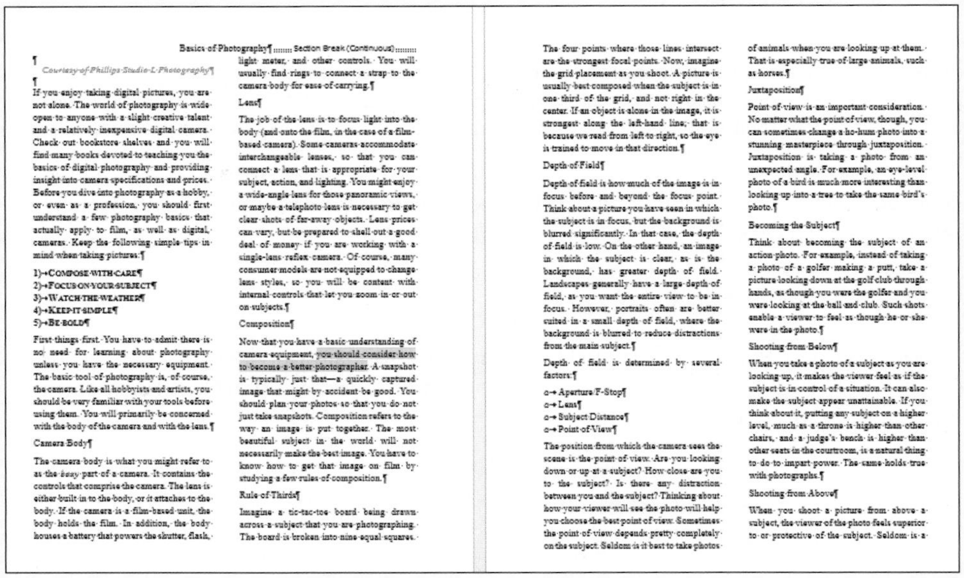

FIGURE 2.31 Formatting in Columns

a. Press **Ctrl+Home**. Select most of the document text, beginning with *Courtesy of Phillips Studio L Photography* and ending with *before even greeting Santa*.

b. Click the **PAGE LAYOUT tab** and click **Columns**. Select **Two**.

   The selected text is formatted into two columns. A continuous section break is inserted at the beginning of the document, after the document title, and at the end of the document (before the final line).

c. Press **Ctrl+Home**. Click anywhere on the line containing *Basics of Photography*. Click the **HOME tab** and click **Center** in the Paragraph group. Click anywhere in the paragraph beginning with *If you enjoy taking digital pictures*. Drag the **First Line Indent marker** on the ruler back to the left margin.

   The title of the newsletter is centered horizontally. The first line indent is removed from the first multiline paragraph in the newsletter.

d. Click anywhere in the paragraph beginning with *First things first*. Drag the **First Line Indent marker** to the left margin to remove the indent.

e. Click the **VIEW tab** and click **Multiple Pages** in the Zoom group. Scroll down to view all pages, getting an idea of how text is positioned on all pages. Click **100%** in the Zoom group.

f. Save the document.

STEP 3 » SELECT AND MODIFY STYLES

The newsletter is improving in appearance, but you note that the headings (Camera, Composition, etc.) are not as evident as they should be. Also, some headings are subordinate to others, and should be identified accordingly. You will apply heading styles to headings in the newsletter. Refer to Figure 2.32 as you complete Step 3.

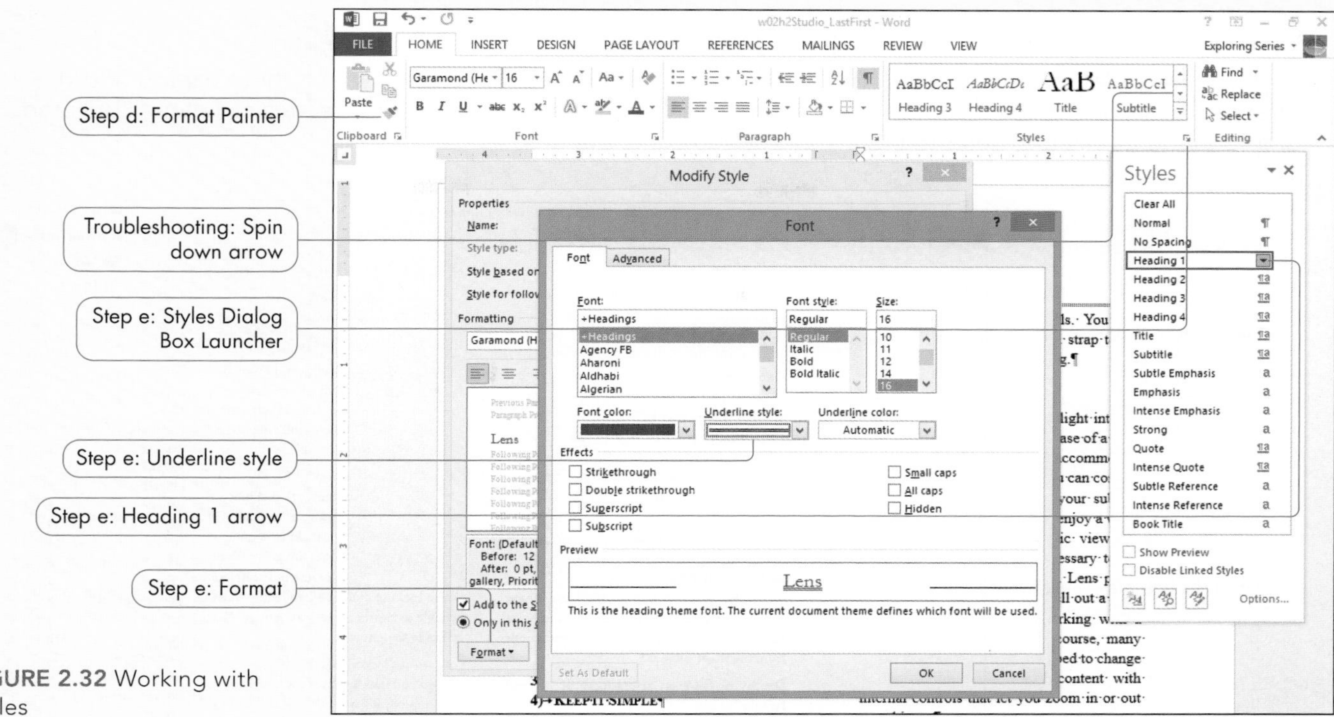

FIGURE 2.32 Working with Styles

a. Select the text *Camera Body* on the first page of the newsletter. Click the **HOME tab** and select **Heading 1** in the Styles group. On the same page, in the column on the right, select *Lens* and apply **Heading 1**. Select *Composition* and apply **Heading 1**.

b. Apply **Heading 1** to *Juxtaposition*, *Common Photography Mistakes*, and *Holiday Photography* on the second and third pages of the newsletter.

c. Select *Rule of Thirds* on the first page and press and hold **Ctrl** on the keyboard as you also select *Depth of Field*, *Becoming the Subject*, *Shooting from Below*, and *Shooting from Above* on the second page. Release Ctrl. Click **Heading 2** in the Styles group on the HOME tab. Do not deselect text.

d. Double-click **Format Painter** in the Clipboard group. Select *Dark Photos* on the third page. Select *Blurry Images*. Press **Esc**. Select *Blurry Images Due to Focus* on the third page. Click **Heading 3** in the Styles group. Select *Blurry Images Due to Camera Shake* on the third page and apply **Heading 3** style.

> **TROUBLESHOOTING:** If you do not see Heading 3 in the Styles group, click the More arrow beside the styles in the Styles group and select Heading 3.

Using Format Painter, you copied the format of the Heading 2 style to a few headings. Headings throughout the newsletter are formatted according to their hierarchy, with major headings in Heading 1 style and others in correct order beneath the first level.

e. Click the **Styles Dialog Box Launcher** to display the Styles pane. Point to *Heading 1* and click the **Heading 1 arrow**. Click **Modify**. Click **Format** in the Modify Style dialog box and click **Font**. Click the **Underline style arrow** and click the second underline style (double underline). Click **OK**. Click **OK** again.

You modified Heading 1 style to include a double underline. Every heading formatted in Heading 1 style is automatically updated to include an underline.

f. Save the document.

STEP 4 ›› USE A STYLE SET AND CREATE A NEW STYLE

Although you are pleased with the heading styles you selected in the previous step, you want to explore Word's built-in style sets to determine if another style might be more attractive. You will also create a style for all bulleted paragraphs in the newsletter. Refer to Figure 2.33 as you complete Step 4.

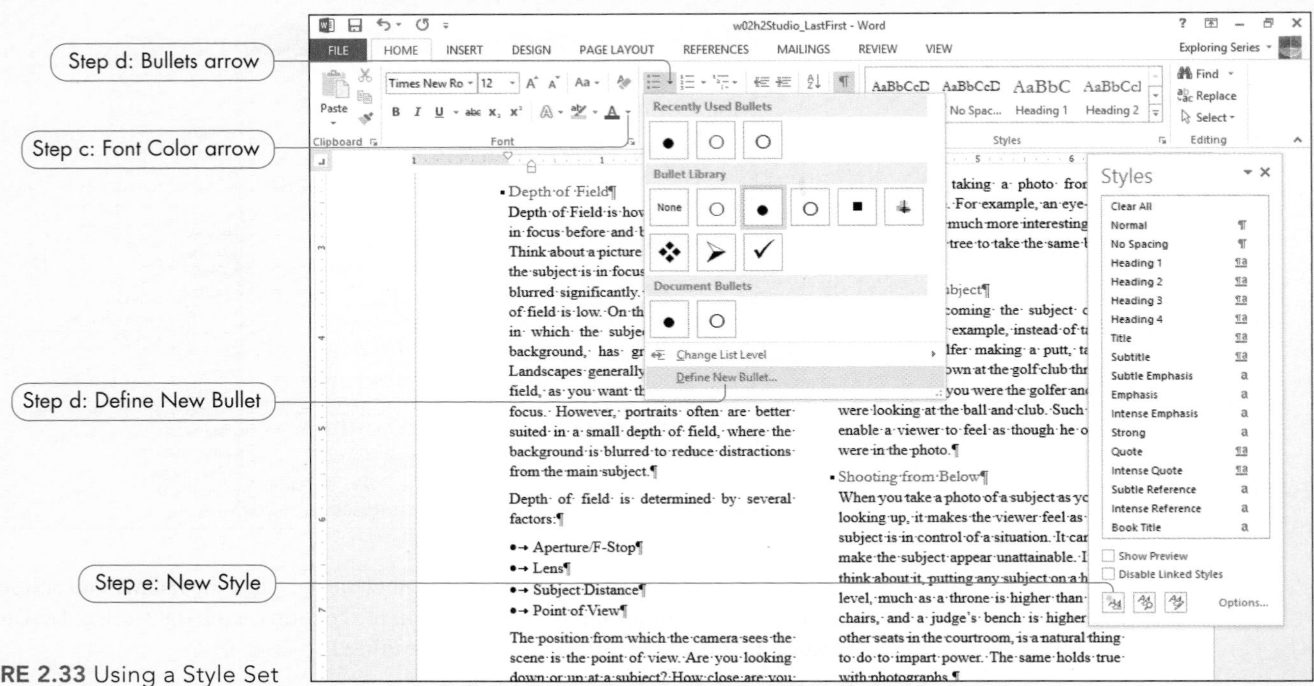

FIGURE 2.33 Using a Style Set

a. Press **Ctrl+Home**. Click the **DESIGN tab**. Point to any style set in the Document Formatting group, without clicking, to view the effect on the document. Specifically, see how the previewed style affects the *Lens* heading shown in the right column. Click the **More arrow** beside the style sets and select **Lines (Simple)** (second row, third column under *Built-In*).

When you apply a style set, headings are formatted according to the style settings, overriding any formatting characteristics you might have set earlier.

b. Click the **VIEW tab** and click **One Page** in the Zoom group to view the first page.

Note the format of the major headings—*Camera Body*, *Lens*, and *Composition*—has been modified, removing the underline you set earlier, and now displays the format of the Lines (Simple) style set.

c. Click **100%** in the Zoom group. Select the second line in the document, *Courtesy of Phillips Studio L Photography*. Click the **HOME tab**. Click the **Font Color arrow** and select **Plum, Accent 1, Darker 25%** (fifth row, fifth column).

You select a coordinating text color for the second line in the document.

d. Scroll to the second page and click anywhere in the bulleted paragraph containing the text *Aperture/F-Stop*. Click the **Bullets arrow** and select a solid round black bullet. Click the **Bullets arrow** and click **Define New Bullet**. Click **Font**. Click the **Font color arrow** and select **Plum, Accent 1, Darker 25%**. Click **OK**. Click **OK** again.

Having modified the format of one bulleted item, you will create a style from that format to apply to all other bulleted items in the document.

e. Click **New Style** in the Styles pane. Type **Bullet Paragraph** in the **Name box** and click **OK**.

You should see a new style in the Styles pane titled *Bullet Paragraph*.

f. Select the three bulleted paragraphs below *Aperture/F-Stop* and click **Bullet Paragraph** in the Styles pane. Scroll to the third page, select the three bulleted paragraphs at the bottom of the right column, and then click **Bullet Paragraph** in the Styles pane. Scroll to the fourth page, select the three bulleted paragraphs at the top of the page (in both columns), and then apply the **Bullet Paragraph style**. Close the Styles pane.

g. Save the document.

STEP 5 » USE THE OUTLINE VIEW

The newsletter spans four pages, with headings identifying various levels of detail. You will check to make sure you have formatted headings according to the correct hierarchy. To do so, you will view the newsletter in Outline view. Refer to Figure 2.34 as you complete Step 5.

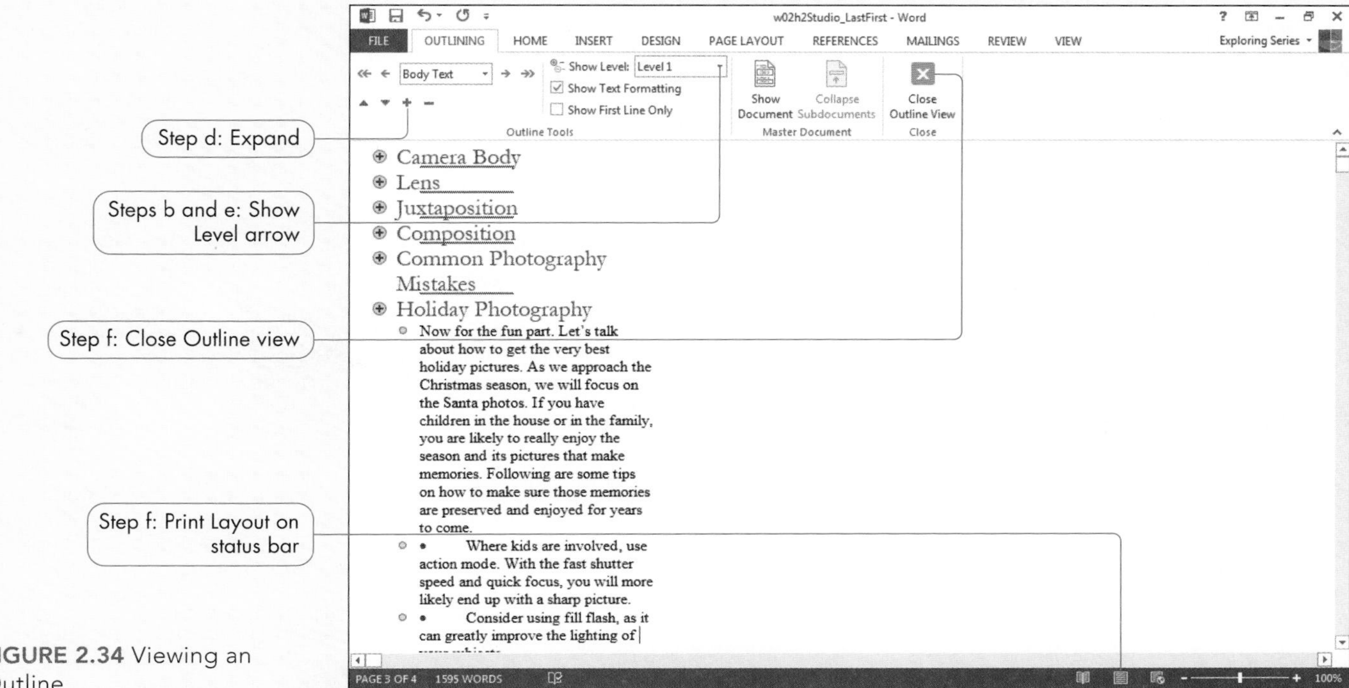

FIGURE 2.34 Viewing an Outline

a. Press **Ctrl+Home**. Click the **VIEW tab** and click **Outline** in the Views group. Scroll down slightly to see the first major heading (with a + on the left)—*Camera Body*.

b. Click the **Show Level arrow** and click **Level 3**.

   You formatted headings in the newsletter as headings, in three levels of detail. Because you did so, you are able to view the document structure according to the hierarchy of headings.

c. Position the pointer on the + that precedes *Blurry Images Due to Camera Shake* (so the pointer becomes a four-headed arrow). Drag the heading above the preceding level (*Blurry Images Due to Focus*). When you see a small black triangle above the preceding level, release the mouse button to reposition the section.

d. Using the same procedure as in step c, move the *Juxtaposition* section above *Composition*. Click **Expand** in the Outline Tools group to view the content of the *Juxtaposition* section.

e. Click the **Show Level arrow** and select **Level 1** to display Level 1 headings only. Select *Holiday Photography* and click **Expand** in the Outline Tools group.

   The *Holiday Photography* section is expanded. Other Level 1 headings remain collapsed.

f. Click **Close Outline View** in the Close group on the Outlining tab. If both columns do not display, click **Print Layout** on the status bar.

g. Save the document. Keep the document open if you plan to continue with the next Hands-On Exercise. If not, close the document and exit Word.

Objects

An ***object*** is an item that can be individually selected and manipulated within a document. Objects, such as pictures, text boxes, tables, clip art, and other graphic types are often included in documents to add interest or convey a point (see Figure 2.35). Newsletters typically include pictures and other decorative elements to liven up what might otherwise be a somewhat mundane document. As you work with a document, you can conduct a quick search for appropriate pictures and graphics online—all without ever leaving your document workspace.

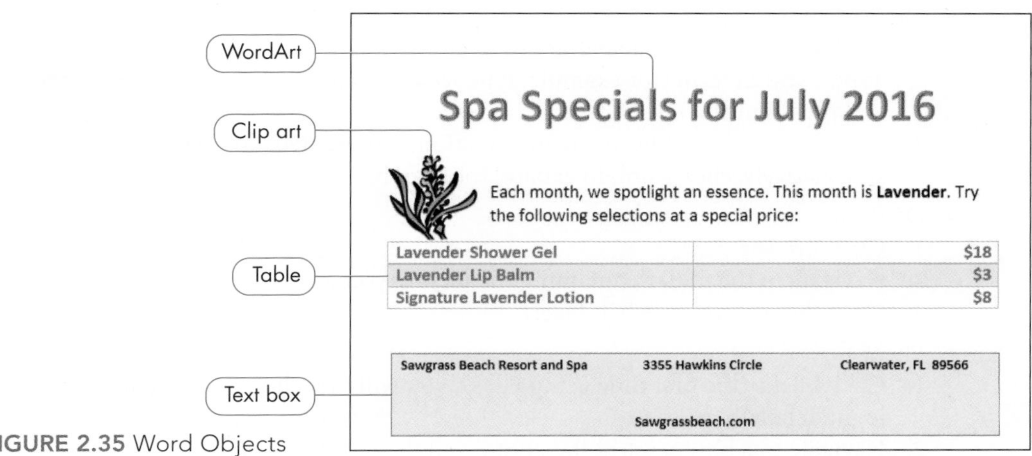

FIGURE 2.35 Word Objects

One thing all objects have in common is that they can be selected and worked with independently of surrounding text. You can resize them, add special effects, and even move them to other locations within the document. Word 2013 includes convenient text wrapping controls so that you can quickly adjust the way text wraps around an object. With Live Layout and alignment guides, you can easily line up pictures and other diagrams with existing text.

In this section, you will explore the use of objects in a Word document. Specifically, you will learn to include pictures, searching for them online as well as obtaining them from your own storage device. You will learn to create impressive text displays with WordArt. A text box is a bordered area you can use to draw attention to specific text. You will create text boxes, as well.

Inserting and Formatting Objects

Objects can be collected from the Web or from a storage device, as with pictures and illustrations. You can create other objects, such as WordArt, text boxes, charts, and tables. When you insert an object, it is automatically selected so that you can manipulate it independently of surrounding text. A contextual tab displays on the Ribbon with options related to the selected object, making it easy to quickly modify and enhance an object.

Insert a Picture

A ***picture*** is a graphic image, such as a drawing or photograph. You can insert pictures in a document from your own library of digital pictures you have saved, or you can access Microsoft's abundant picture resources at Office.com. From within a document, you can conduct a Web search to locate even more picture possibilities. Microsoft refers to its royalty-free photos and illustrations as ***clip art***. Inserting a picture is only the first step in the process. Once incorporated into your document, a picture can be resized and modified with special bordering and artistic effects. Other options enable you to easily align a picture with surrounding text, rotate or crop it, if necessary, and even recolor it so it blends in with an existing color scheme.

You might find it necessary to include a picture within an open document. If you do not have a picture already saved on your computer, you can go online to locate a suitable image. Without closing or minimizing the document, and without opening a browser to search the Web, you can immediately peruse Office.com, Bing Image Search, OneDrive, and even your Flickr account for a picture. It is not necessary to obtain an image from the Web and save it to a storage device before inserting it in the document. The picture is inserted directly from the Web, after which you can resize and reposition it.

To insert an online picture, click to place the insertion point in the document in the location where the picture is to be inserted. Click the Insert tab and click Online Pictures (see Figure 2.36) to insert a picture from:

- Office.com or Bing:
  1. Click the box beside the picture source.
  2. Type a search term (for example, type *school* to identify school-related images) and press Enter.
  3. Review any relevant licensing information, if presented, and select an image. Alternatively, click a link to expand the search.
- OneDrive:
  1. Click Browse.
  2. Navigate to the folder containing the picture you want to insert.
  3. Click the picture and click Insert.
- Flickr:
  1. Click Flickr (the first time using Flickr, you will first click Connect and provide login details).
  2. Navigate to a photo, select the photo, and then click Insert.

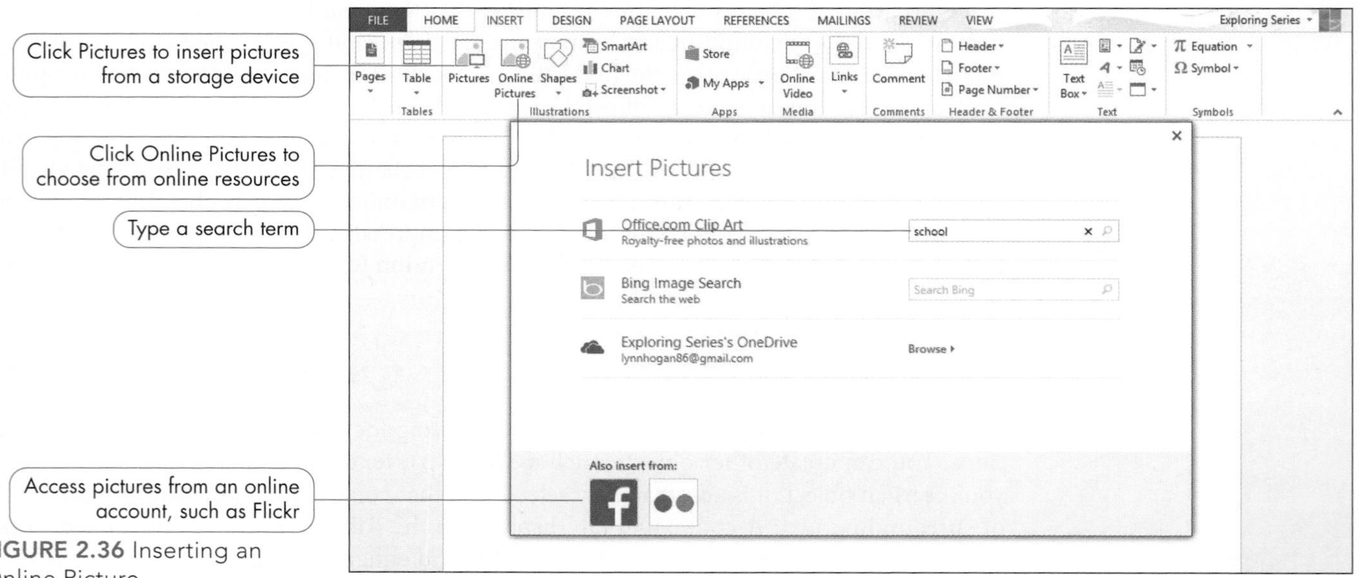

FIGURE 2.36 Inserting an Online Picture

TIP Insert a Screenshot

When describing a process, you might find occasion to include a screenshot of a computer display in a document. You can capture a screenshot and insert it in a document as an object. With the item to capture displayed on the computer screen, open the document in which you plan to place the screenshot. Click the Insert tab and click Screenshot in the Illustrations group. Click Screen Clipping. The document is removed from view, leaving the original screen display. Drag to select any part of the screen display. The document displays again, with the selection included as an object.

STEP 1

If you enjoy taking digital pictures, you most likely have a great many of your pictures saved to a storage device you can access with a computer. Suppose you are using Word to prepare a flyer or newsletter. In that case, you might want to insert one or more of your pictures into the document. Inserting pictures from a storage device is a simple process. To do so:

1. Position the insertion point in the document where the picture is to be inserted.
2. Click the INSERT tab.
3. Click Pictures in the Illustrations group (refer to Figure 2.36).
4. Navigate to the folder in which your photos are stored.
5. Select a photo to insert.
6. Click Insert.

Resize, Move, and Align a Picture

A new Ribbon tab, with one or more associated tabs beneath it, is added to the Ribbon when you insert and select an object. The new Ribbon tab, called a ***contextual tab***, includes commands relevant to the type of object selected. As shown in Figure 2.37, the Picture Tools Format tab includes settings and selections related to the inserted picture.

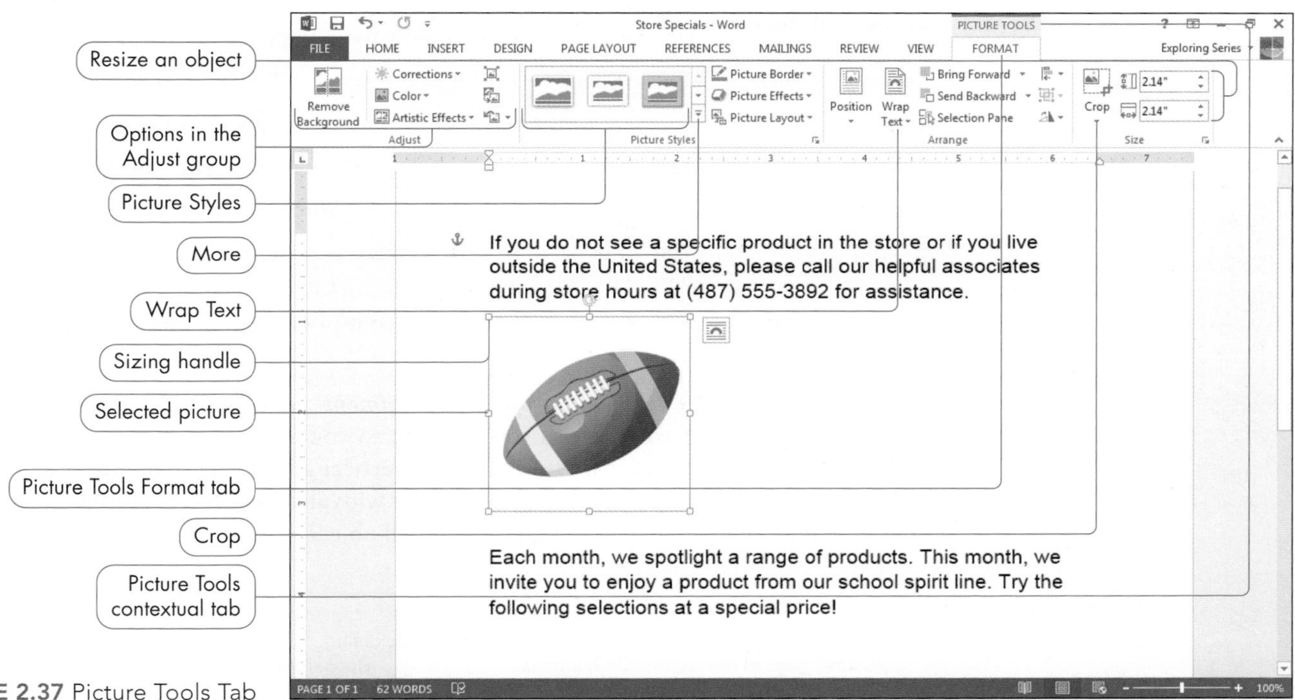

FIGURE 2.37 Picture Tools Tab

STEP 2

Although an inserted picture is considered a separate object, you will want to position it so that it flows well with document text and does not appear to be a separate unit. One way to make that happen is to wrap text around the picture. The Format tab includes an option to wrap text around a selected picture (refer to Figure 2.37). You can select from the text wrapping styles shown in Table 2.3 when you click Wrap Text. You can also choose to allow the object to move with text as text is added or deleted, or you can keep the object in the same place on the page, regardless of text changes.

Word 2013 includes a new feature that simplifies text wrapping around an object—Layout Options. Located next to a selected object, the Layout Options control (see Figure 2.38) includes the same selections shown in Table 2.3. The close proximity of the control to the selected object makes it easy to quickly adjust text wrapping.

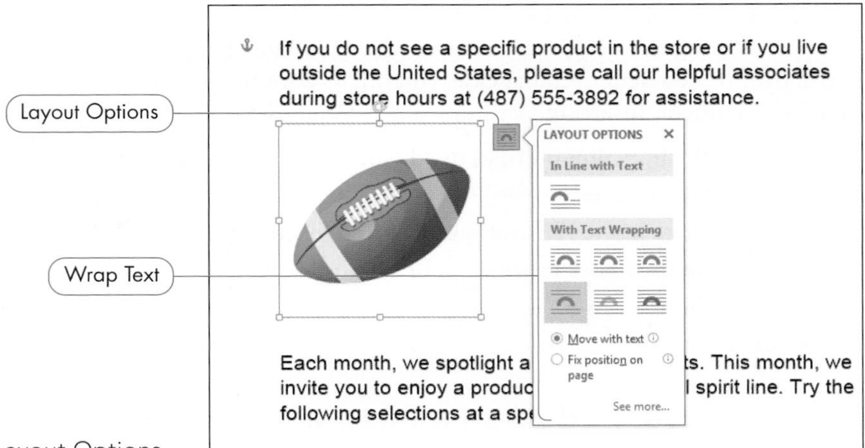

FIGURE 2.38 Layout Options

TABLE 2.3 Text Wrap Options

Type	Effect
In Line with Text	The image is part of the line of text in which it is inserted. Typically, text wraps above and below the object.
Square	Text wraps on all sides of an object, following an invisible square.
Tight	Text follows the shape of the object, but does not overlap the object.
Through	Text follows the shape, filling any open spaces in the shape.
Top and Bottom	Text flows above and below the borders of the object
Behind Text	The object is positioned behind text. Both the object and text are visible (unless the fill color exactly matches the text color).
In Front of Text	The object is positioned in front of text, often obscuring the text.

New to Word 2013 are *Live Layout* and *alignment guides*. ***Live Layout*** enables you to watch text flow around an object as you move it, so you can position the object exactly as you want it. ***Alignment guides*** are horizontal or vertical green bars that appear as you drag an object, so you can line up an object with text or with another object. The green alignment guide shown in Figure 2.39 helps align the football object with paragraph text.

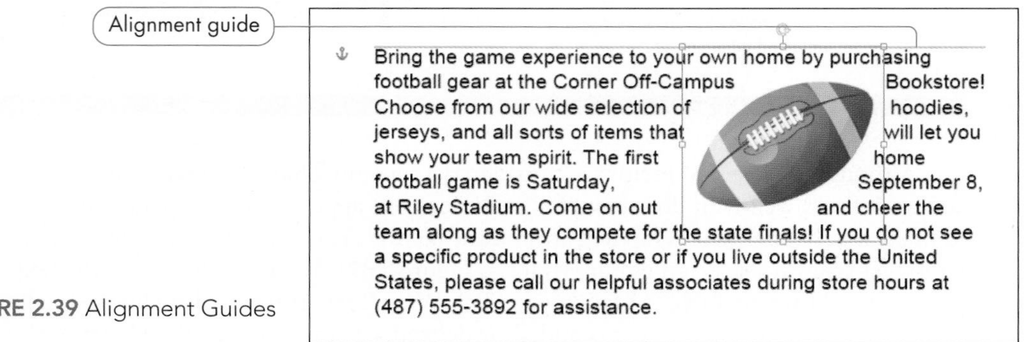

FIGURE 2.39 Alignment Guides

Often, a picture is inserted in a size that is too large or too small for your purposes. To resize a picture, you can drag a corner ***sizing handle***. You should never resize a picture by dragging a center sizing handle, as doing so would skew the picture. You can also resize a picture by adjusting settings in the Size group of the Picture Tools Format tab (refer to Figure 2.37).

Modify a Picture

The Picture Tools Format tab (refer to Figure 2.37) includes options for modifying a picture. You can apply a picture style or effect, as well as add a picture border, from selections in the Picture Styles group. Click More (refer to Figure 2.37) to view a gallery of picture styles. As you point to a style, the style is shown in Live Preview, but the style is not applied until you click it. Options in the Adjust group (refer to Figure 2.37) simplify changing a color scheme, applying creative artistic effects, and even adjusting the brightness, contrast, and sharpness of an image.

STEP 3》

If a picture contains more detail than is necessary, you can ***crop*** it, which is the process of trimming edges that you do not want to display. The Crop tool is located on the Picture Tools Format tab (refer to Figure 2.37). Even though cropping enables you to adjust the amount of a picture that displays, it does not actually delete the portions that are cropped out. Therefore, you can later recover parts of the picture, if necessary. Cropping a picture does not reduce the file size of the picture and the Word document in which it displays.

Other common adjustments to a picture include contrast and/or brightness. Adjusting *contrast* increases or decreases the difference in dark and light areas of the image. Adjusting *brightness* lightens or darkens the overall image. These adjustments often are made on a picture taken with a digital camera in poor lighting or if a picture is too bright or dull to match other objects in your document. The Brightness/Contrast adjustment is available when you click Corrections in the Adjust group on the Format tab (refer to Figure 2.37).

Insert a Text Box

Text in a ***text box*** is bordered, sometimes shaded, and set apart from other text in a document. Depending on the outline selected, a border might not even be visible, so it is not always possible to identify a text box in a document. In most cases, however, you will find a text box as a boxed area of text—usually providing additional details or drawing attention to an important point. A text box could contain a *pull quote*, which is a short text excerpt that is reinforced from a report, or a text box could be used as a banner for a newsletter. Place any text you want to draw attention to or set apart from the body of a document in a text box. Figure 2.40 shows a simple text box that provides business information. Remember that a text box is an object. As such, you can select, move, resize, and modify it, much as you learned you could do with pictures in the preceding sections of this chapter. Layout Options enable you to wrap text around a text box, and alignment guides assist with positioning a text box within existing text.

Removing Background

Word 2013 makes it easy to remove the background or portions of a picture you do not want to keep. When you select a picture and click the Remove Background tool in the Adjust group on the Format tab, Word creates a marquee selection area in the picture that determines the *background*, or area to be removed, and the *foreground*, or area to be kept. Word identifies the background selection with magenta coloring. Using tools on the Background Removal tab, you can mark areas to keep or mark additional areas to remove. Click Keep Changes to remove the background.

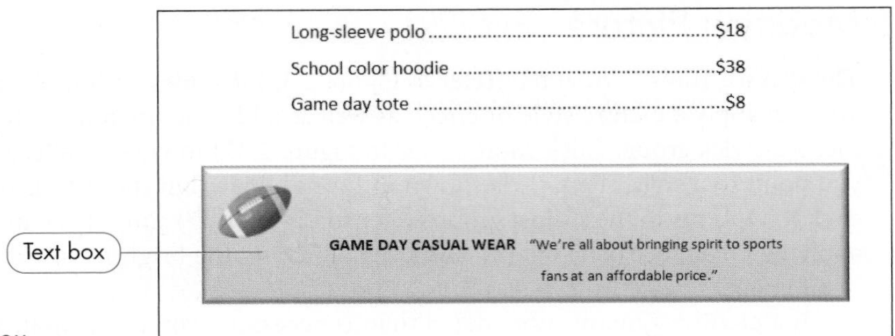

FIGURE 2.40 Text Box

STEP 4

To insert a text box:

1. Click the INSERT tab.
2. Click Text Box in the Text group.
3. Click Draw Text Box or select a predefined text box style (see Figure 2.41).
4. Drag to draw a box (unless you selected a predefined text box style, in which case, the text box will be automatically drawn). The dimensions of the text box are not that critical, as you can adjust the size using the Ribbon.
5. Type text in the text box.

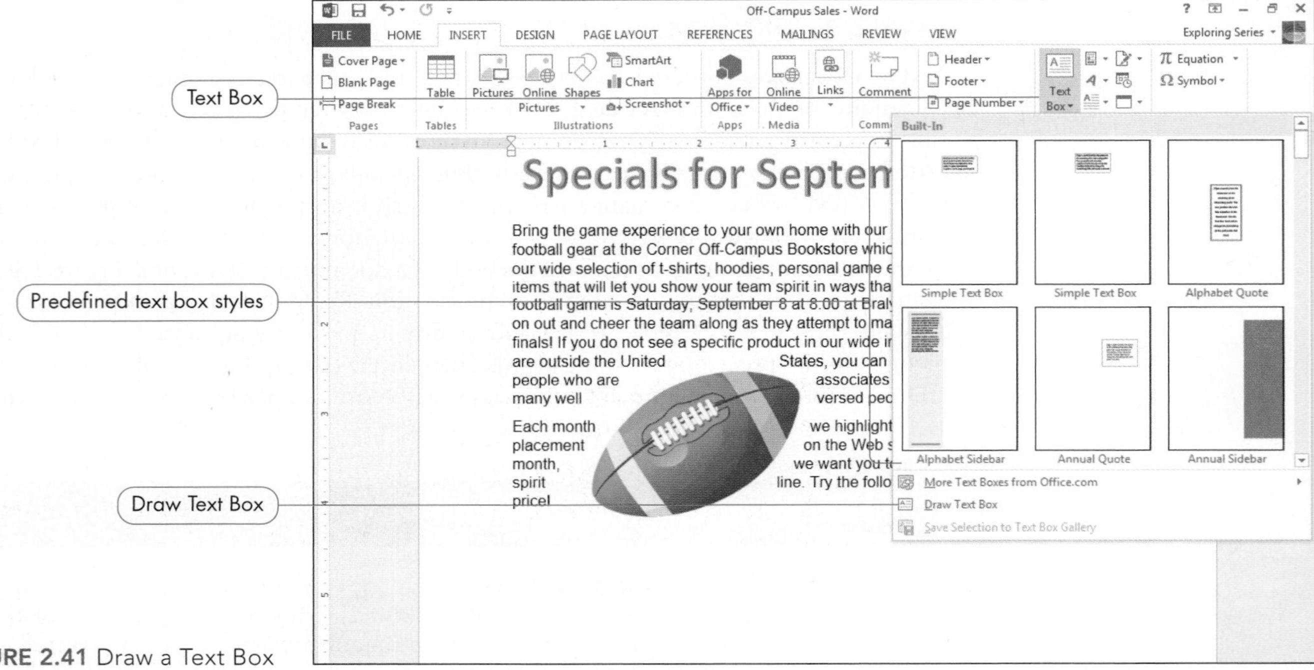

FIGURE 2.41 Draw a Text Box

TIP Formatting Text in a Text Box

Before formatting text in a text box, you should select the text to be affected. To do so, drag to select the text to be formatted. Or, if you want to select *all* text, you might appreciate learning a shortcut. You can select all of the text when you click the dashed border surrounding the text box (when the pointer is a small four-headed shape). The dashed line should become solid, indicating that all text is selected. At that point, any formatting selections you make related to text are applied to all text in the text box.

Resize, Move, and Modify a Text Box

The Drawing Tools Format tab includes a multitude of options for adding color, background, and style to a text box. In addition, you can select from predefined text styles or design your own text fill, outline, and text effects. Positioning a text box is a simple task, with text wrap options available to arrange text evenly around the text box. You can even indicate the exact height and width of a text box using the Format tab (see Figure 2.42).

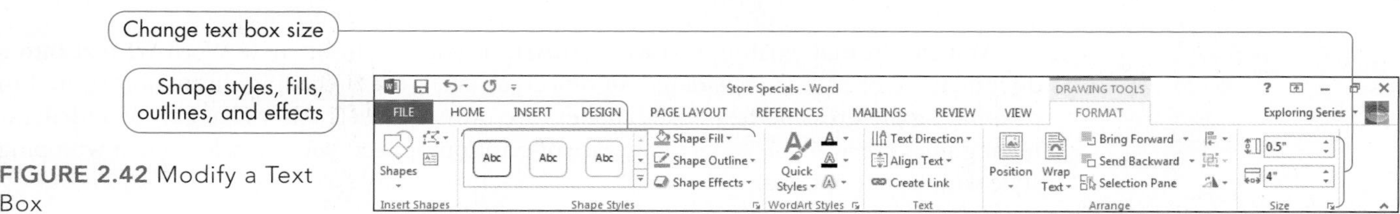

FIGURE 2.42 Modify a Text Box

One way to resize a text box is to drag a sizing handle. Although not as precise as using the Size group on the Format tab to indicate an exact measurement, dragging to resize a text box is done quickly. Depending on how you want to resize the object, you can either drag a corner handle (to resize two sides at once) or a center handle (to adjust the size in only one direction). Although you should not drag a center handle when resizing a *picture* (because doing so will skew the picture), dragging a center handle in a *text box* is an appropriate way to resize a text box.

You can be as creative as you like when designing a text box. Options on the Format tab enable you to add color and definition to a text box with shape fill and outline selections, or select from a gallery of shape styles. Select text within a text box and select an alignment option on the Home tab to left align, right align, center, or justify text.

You can move a text box by dragging it from one area to another. You should first select or confirm a text wrapping option. Text will then wrap automatically around the text box as you move it. Position the pointer on a border of the text box so it appears as a black, four-headed arrow. Drag to reposition the text box. As you drag the box, green alignment guides assist in positioning it neatly. The Format tab includes a Position option in the Arrange group that enables you to align the text box in various ways within existing text.

Insert WordArt

WordArt is a feature that modifies text to include special effects, including colors, shadows, gradients, and 3-D effects (see Figure 2.43). It is a quick way to format text so that it is vibrant and eye-catching. Of course, WordArt is not appropriate for all documents, especially more conservative business correspondence, but it can give life to newsletters, flyers, and other more informal projects, especially when applied to headings and titles. WordArt is well suited for single lines, such as document headings, where the larger print and text design draws attention and adds style to a document title. However, it is not appropriate for body text, because a WordArt object is managed independently of surrounding text and cannot be formatted as a document (with specific margins, headers, footers, etc.). In addition, if WordArt were incorporated into body text, the more ornate text design would adversely affect the readability of the document.

WordArt

Off-Campus School Spirit Sale

We welcome the opportunity to serve you, especially during the football season at the university. Our store is filled with special sales this time of year.

FIGURE 2.43 WordArt

You can format existing text as WordArt, or you can insert new WordArt text into a document. WordArt is considered an object; as such, the preceding discussion related to positioning pictures and text boxes applies to WordArt as well. Also, Live Layout and alignment guides are available to facilitate ease of positioning, and you can select a text wrapping style with layout options.

STEP 5» To format existing text as WordArt:

1. Select text to be formatted.
2. Click the INSERT tab.
3. Click WordArt in the Text group.
4. Select a WordArt style.

To insert new text as WordArt:

1. Place the insertion point at the point where WordArt should appear.
2. Click the INSERT tab.
3. Click WordArt in the Text group.
4. Select a WordArt style.
5. Type text.

Depending upon the purpose of a document and its intended audience, objects such as pictures, text boxes, and WordArt can help convey a message and add interest. As you learn to incorporate objects visually within a document so that they appear to flow seamlessly within existing text, you will find it easy to create attractive, informative documents that contain an element of design apart from simple text.

Quick Concepts

1. How would you determine what type of text wrapping to use when positioning a picture in a document? ***p. 234***
2. Describe two methods to modify the height and width of a picture. ***p. 234***
3. Although a text box can appear similar to text in a document that has simply been bordered and shaded, a text box is actually an object. What does that fact tell you about a text box that makes it very different from simple shaded text? ***p. 235***
4. Why is WordArt most often used to format headings or titles, and not text in the body of a document? ***p. 237***

Hands-On Exercises

3 Objects

You will add interest to the newsletter by including pictures that illustrate points, a text box with business information, and WordArt that livens up the newsletter heading.

Skills covered: Insert a Picture • Resize, Move, and Align a Picture • Modify a Picture • Insert and Modify a Text Box • Insert WordArt

STEP 1 » INSERT A PICTURE

You will include pictures in the newsletter to represent photographs shot from various angles, as well as holiday graphics. Pictures will be formatted with appropriate picture styles and effects and positioned within existing text. Refer to Figure 2.44 as you complete Step 1.

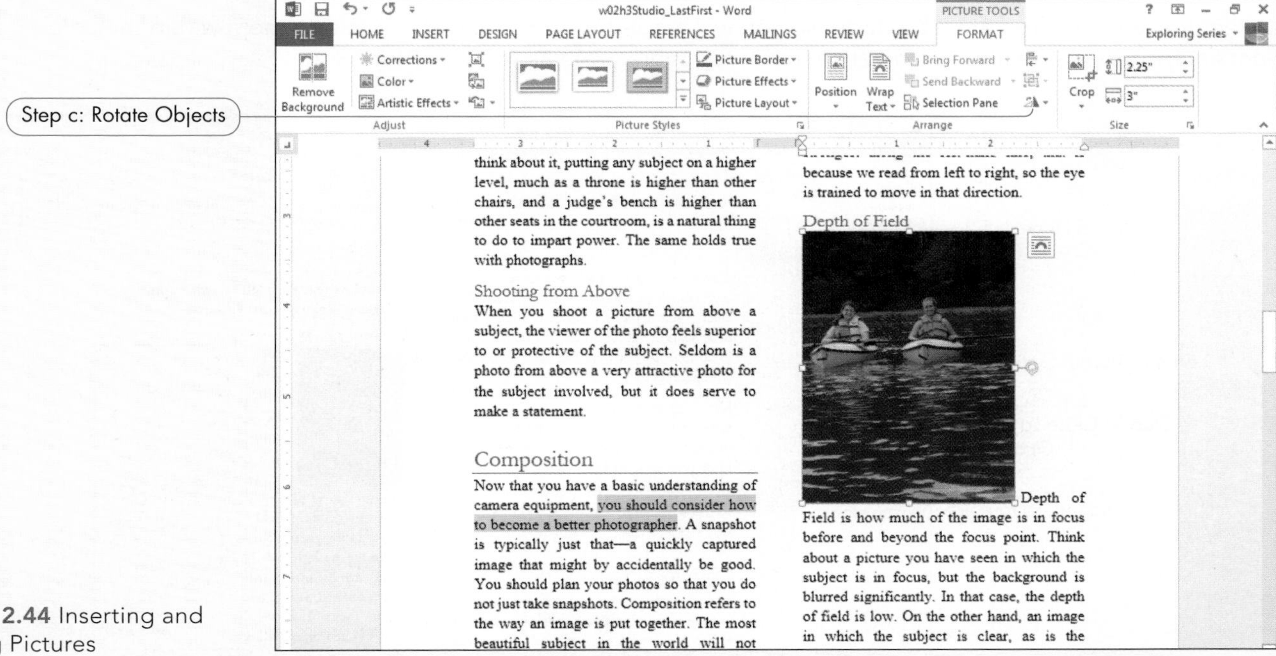

FIGURE 2.44 Inserting and Rotating Pictures

a. Open *w02h2Studio_LastFirst* if you closed it at the end of Hands-On Exercise 2 and save it as **w02h3Studio_LastFirst**, changing *h2* to *h3*.

b. Scroll to the second page of the document and click to place the insertion point before the words *Depth of Field is how much of the image*. Click the **INSERT tab** and click **Pictures** in the Illustrations group. Navigate to the location of your student data files and double-click *w02h3Kayak*.

   The picture is inserted, but must be rotated.

c. With the picture selected (surrounded by a border and sizing handles), click **Rotate Objects** in the Arrange group on the PICTURE TOOLS FORMAT tab and click **Rotate Right 90°**. Click outside the picture to deselect it.

TROUBLESHOOTING: If you do not see Rotate Objects or the Format tab, click the picture to select it. Then click the Format tab, if necessary.

d. Scroll to the third page and click to place the insertion point before *The most common reason for a blurred image* under the *Blurry Images Due to Focus* heading. Click the **INSERT tab**, click **Pictures** in the Illustrations group, and then double-click *w02h3Float* in your student data files. If necessary, rotate the picture to the right. Click outside the picture to deselect it.

> **TROUBLESHOOTING:** The placement of the picture will vary, so it is OK if it is not positioned directly below the *Blurry Images Due to Focus* heading. You will move it later.

e. Scroll to the *Holiday Photography* section and click to place the insertion point before *Now for the fun part*. Click the **INSERT tab**. Click **Online Pictures** in the Illustrations group. In the box beside Office.com, type **Ski** and press **Enter**. Select the picture shown in Figure 2.45b (or one that is very similar). Click **Insert**.

The picture is placed within or very near the *Holiday Photography* section. You will reposition it and resize it later.

f. Save the document.

STEP 2 ≫ RESIZE, MOVE, AND ALIGN A PICTURE

The pictures you inserted are a bit large, so you will resize them. You will also position them within the column and select an appropriate text wrapping style. Refer to Figures 2.45 as you complete Step 2.

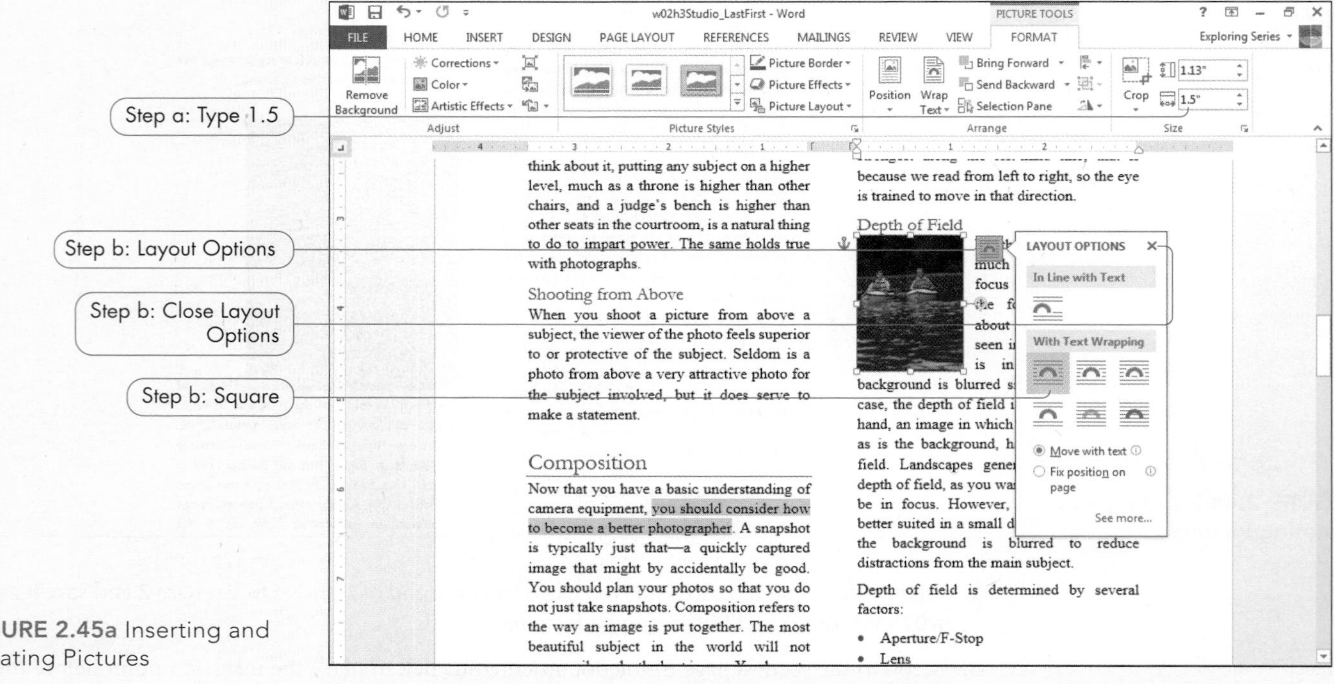

FIGURE 2.45a Inserting and Rotating Pictures

Holiday Photography

Now for the fun part. Let's talk about how to get the very best holiday pictures. As we approach the Christmas season, we will focus on the Santa photos. If you have children in the house or in the family, you are likely to really enjoy the season and its pictures that make memories. Following are some tips on how to make sure those

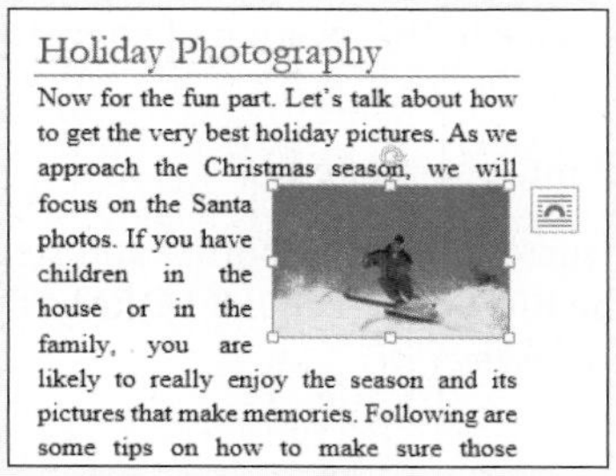

FIGURE 2.45b Inserting and Rotating Pictures

a. Scroll up and click to select the picture near the *Depth of Field* section. Click in the **Width box** in the Size group on the FORMAT tab and type **1.5**. Press **Enter**.

   By default, the *Lock aspect ratio* setting is on, which means that when you change a dimension—either width or height—of a picture, the other dimension is automatically adjusted as well. To confirm, or deselect the Lock aspect ratio, click the **Size Dialog Box Launcher** and adjust the setting in the Layout dialog box. Unless you deselect the setting, you cannot change both width and height manually, as that would skew the picture.

b. Click **Layout Options** (beside the selected picture) and select **Square** (first selection under *With Text Wrapping*). Close Layout Options. Check the placement of the image with that shown in Figure 2.45a, and adjust if necessary.

c. Scroll down and select the second picture near the *Blurry Images Due to Focus* heading. Change the text wrapping to **Square** and change the width to **1.5**. Close Layout Options. If necessary, drag the picture (when the pointer is a four-headed arrow) so it displays immediately beneath the section heading.

d. Scroll down and select the ski picture in, or near, the *Holiday Photography* section. Change text wrapping to **Tight**, change the width to **1.5**, close Layout Options, and then drag to position the picture as shown in Figure 2.45b. Words may not wrap exactly as shown in Figure 2.45b, but they should be approximately as shown.

e. Save the document.

STEP 3 » MODIFY A PICTURE

You will apply a picture style and picture effects to the pictures included in the newsletter. You will also crop a picture to remove unnecessary detail. Refer to Figure 2.46 as you complete Step 3.

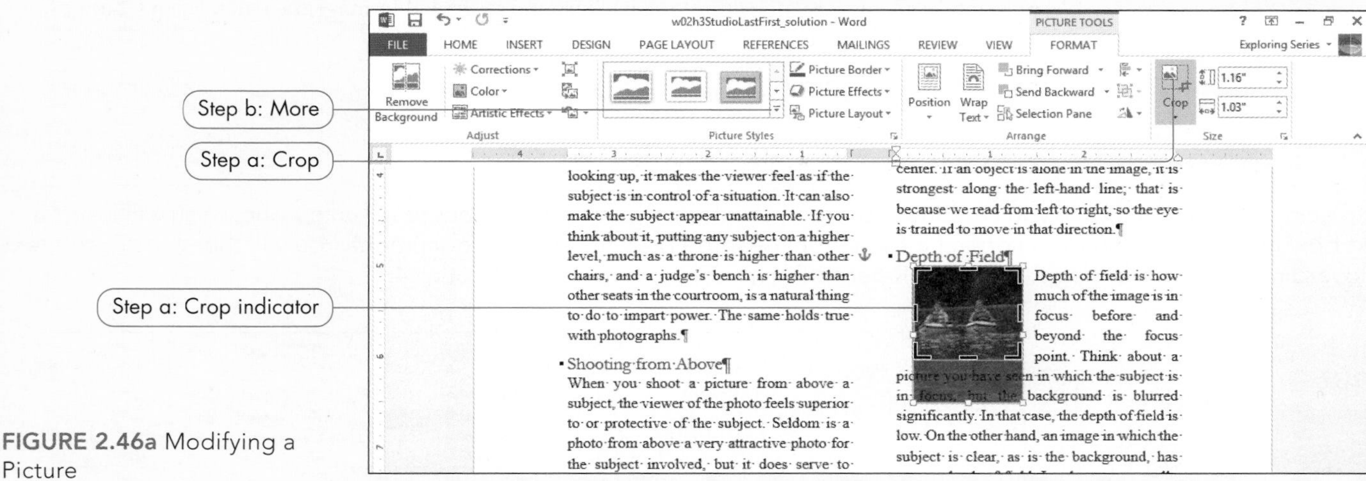

FIGURE 2.46a Modifying a Picture

hands, as though you were the golfer and you were looking at the ball and club. Such shots enable a viewer to feel as though he or she were in the photo.¶

• Shooting from Below¶

When you take a photo of a subject as you are looking up, it makes the viewer feel as if the subject is in control of a situation. It can also make the subject appear unattainable. If you think about it, putting any subject on a higher level, much as a throne is higher than other chairs, and a judge's bench is higher than other seats in the courtroom, is a natural thing to do to impart power. The same holds true with photographs.¶

• Shooting from Above¶

When you shoot a picture from above a subject, the viewer of the photo feels superior to or protective of the subject. Seldom is a photo from above a very attractive photo for the subject involved, but it does serve to make a statement.¶

• Composition¶

across a subject that you are photographing. The board is broken into nine equal squares. The four points where those lines intersect are the strongest focal points. Now, imagine the grid placement as you shoot. A picture is usually best composed when the subject is in one third of the grid, and not right in the center. If an object is alone in the image, it is strongest along the left-hand line; that is because we read from left to right, so the eye is trained to move in that direction.¶

• Depth of Field¶

Depth of Field is how much of the image is in focus before and beyond the focus point. Think about a picture you have seen in which the subject is in focus, but the background is blurred significantly. In that case, the depth of field is low. On the other hand, an image in which the subject is clear, as is the background, has greater depth of field. Landscapes generally have a large depth of field, as you want the entire view to be in focus. However, portraits often are

FIGURE 2.46b Modifying a Picture

a. Select the picture in the *Depth of Field* section. Click the **FORMAT tab**, if necessary. Click **Crop** in the Size group on the FORMAT tab. Be sure to click *Crop*, not the *Crop arrow*. Drag the crop indicator in the bottom center of the photograph up slightly to remove some of the water, as shown in Figure 2.46a. Click **Crop** to toggle the selection off. If necessary, drag to position the picture as shown in Figure 2.46b.

> **TROUBLESHOOTING:** If the picture becomes skewed as you drag, instead of simply shading the water to remove, you are dragging a sizing handle instead of the crop indicator. Only drag when the pointer is a thick black T, not a two-headed arrow. Click Undo and repeat the crop.

b. If necessary, click to select the picture in the *Depth of Field* section. Click **More** beside the Picture Styles gallery in the Picture Styles group. Select **Soft Edge Rectangle**.

> **TROUBLESHOOTING:** If you do not see options related to the picture, make sure the picture is selected and click the Format tab, if necessary.

c. Select the picture in the *Blurry Images Due to Focus* section. Click **Corrections** in the Adjust group on the FORMAT tab. Select **Brightness: 0% (Normal), Contrast: +20%** (fourth row, third column under *Brightness/Contrast*).

   You used Word's image editing feature to change brightness and contrast.

d. Select the ski picture. Click **Remove Background** in the Adjust group on the FORMAT tab. Wait a few seconds until the background is shaded in magenta. Click **Keep Changes**. Deselect the picture.

e. Save the document.

STEP 4 ≫ INSERT AND MODIFY A TEXT BOX

By placing text in a text box, you can draw attention to information you want your readers to notice. You will insert a text box, including the studio's contact information, near the beginning of the document. You will then modify the text to coordinate with other page elements. Refer to Figure 2.47 as you complete Step 4.

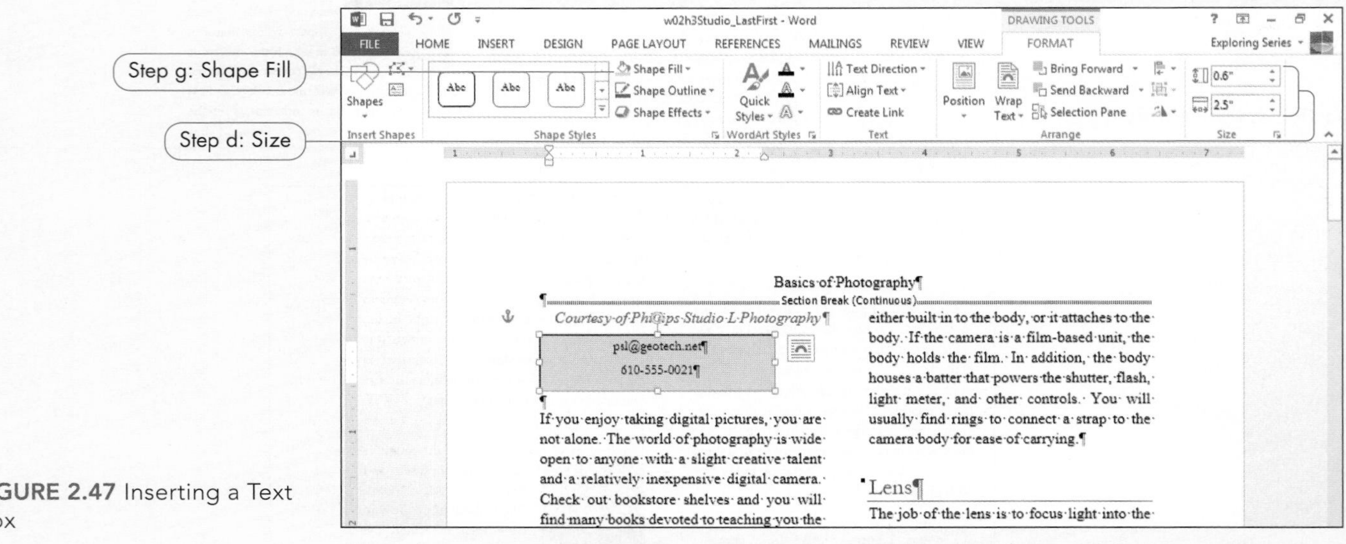

FIGURE 2.47 Inserting a Text Box

a. Press **Ctrl+Home**. If nonprinting characters do not display, click **Show/Hide** in the Paragraph group on the HOME tab.

b. Click the **INSERT tab** and click **Text Box** in the Text group. Click **Draw Text Box**. Point to the blank paragraph mark below *Courtesy of Phillips Studio L Photography* and drag to draw a small box. The dimensions are not important, as you will resize the text box later.

   A small text box is drawn in the document.

c. Click **Layout Options** (beside the text box) and select **Top and Bottom** (second row, first column under *Text Wrapping*). Close Layout Options.

   Text wraps above and below the text box.

d. Click the **Height box** in the Size group on the FORMAT tab and type **0.6**. Click the Width box and type **2.5**. Press **Enter**.

e. Click in the text box, if necessary, to position the insertion point. Type **psl@geotech.net** and press **Enter**. Type **610-555-0021**. Right-click the underlined e-mail link in the text box and select **Remove Hyperlink**.

f. Click the dashed line surrounding the text box to make it solid, so that all text in the text box is selected (although it is not shaded). Click the **HOME tab** and click **Center** in the Paragraph group.

   All text is centered in the text box.

g. Click the **FORMAT tab**. Click **Shape Fill** in the Shape Styles group. Select **Plum, Accent 1, Lighter 80%** (second row, fifth column).

   The text box background is shaded to match the document theme.

h. Position the pointer near a border of the text box so that the pointer appears as a four-headed arrow. Drag to the left edge of the column, until the green alignment guide indicates the text box is aligned at the left edge of the column. Release the mouse button. The text box should appear as shown in Figure 2.47.

i. Save the document.

STEP 5 » INSERT WORDART

The newsletter is near completion, but you need to work with the heading—*Basics of Photography*. You will format the heading with WordArt to add some visual appeal. Refer to Figure 2.48 as you complete Step 5.

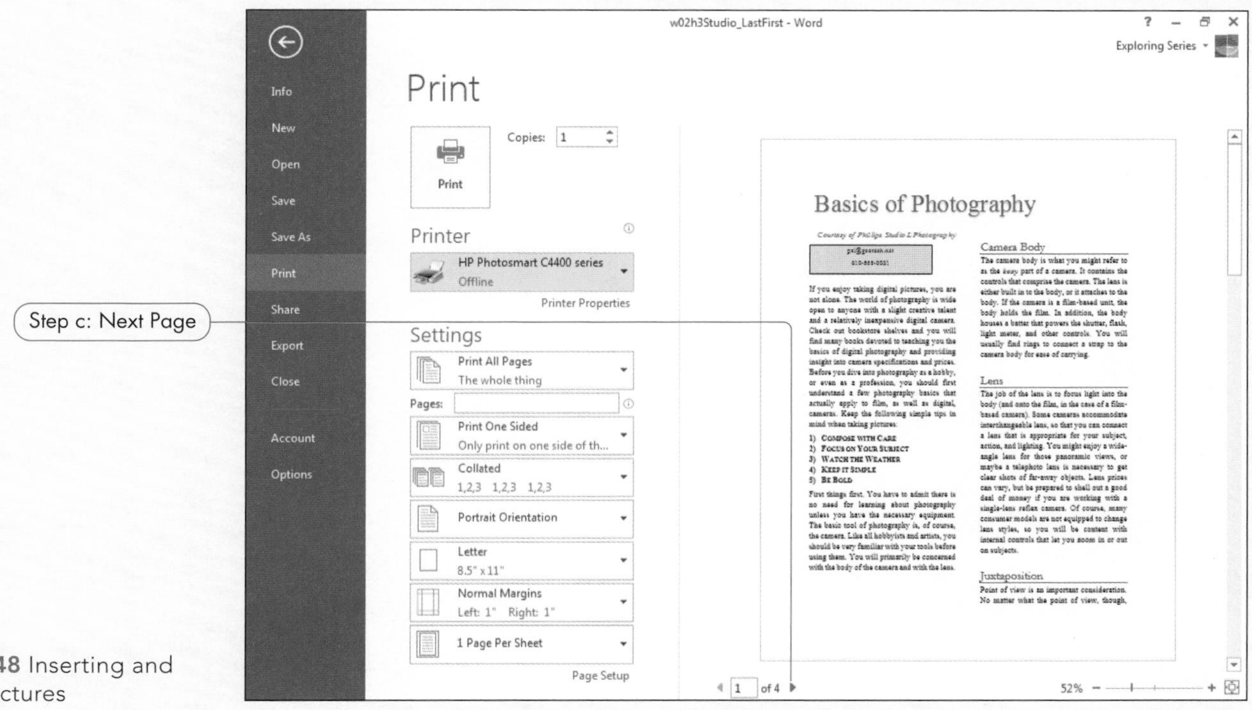

FIGURE 2.48 Inserting and Rotating Pictures

a. Select *Basics of Photography* on the first line of the newsletter, including the following paragraph mark. Be careful not to select the Section Break indicator following the paragraph mark. Click the **INSERT tab** and click **WordArt** in the Text group. Select **Fill – Plum, Accent 1, Shadow** (first row, second column).

> **TROUBLESHOOTING:** If you do not see a Section Break indicator, click Show/Hide in the Paragraph group on the Home tab.

The heading is formatted in WordArt, in a shade that coordinates with other text formatting in the newsletter.

b. Click **Layout Options** and click **Top and Bottom**. Close Layout Options.

c. Click outside the WordArt object to deselect it. Click the **FILE tab** and click **Print**. The first page shows in preview in the right pane (refer to Figure 2.48). Click **Next Page** (at the bottom of the preview page) to move to the next page.

d. Save and close the file, and submit the file based on your instructor's directions.

Chapter Objectives Review

After reading this chapter, you have accomplished the following objectives:

1. **Apply font attributes.**
   - Select font options: Font options include serif or sans serif font, as well as monospaced or proportional font. The Font group on the Home tab includes font selections.
   - Change text appearance: Format characters by applying bold, italics, underline, font color, text highlighting, and text effects.
2. **Format a paragraph.**
   - Select paragraph alignment: Align paragraphs to be left or right aligned, centered, or justified.
   - Select line and paragraph spacing: Line spacing refers to the amount of space between lines within a paragraph, whereas paragraph spacing is concerned with the amount of space between paragraphs.
   - Select indents: Options for indenting paragraphs include left indent, right indent, hanging indent, and first line indent.
   - Set tabs: Use tabs to arrange text in columns, including leaders if desired.
   - Apply borders and shading: Draw attention to selected paragraphs when you add borders and shading.
   - Create bulleted and numbered lists: Itemized lists can be set apart from other text with bullets, while sequential lists are often formatted with numbers.
3. **Format a document.**
   - Select a document theme: Use a theme to create a color-coordinated document, with page elements based on themed settings.
   - Work with sections: Divide a document into sections, so that each area can be formatted independently of others.
   - Format text into columns: Some documents, such as newsletters, are formatted in columns.
4. **Apply styles.**
   - Select and modify styles: Styles enable you to apply identical formatting to page features, such as headings. When a style is modified, changes apply to all text formatted in that style.
   - Use a style set: Select a style set to quickly format page elements, such as headers and paragraph text.
   - Create a new style from text: Format text and create a style from the text so that formatting characteristics can be easily applied to other text in the document.
   - Use the Outline view: Expand and collapse sections, view document structure, and easily rearrange document sections in Outline view.
5. **Insert and format objects.**
   - Insert a picture: Insert pictures from online sources or from a storage device connected to your computer.
   - Resize, move, and align a picture: Reposition objects easily using Live Layout and alignment guides. You can also resize objects and wrap text around objects.
   - Modify a picture: Apply a picture style or effect, adjust the color, contrast, and brightness of a picture, and crop a picture to modify a picture's appearance.
   - Insert a text box: Include text in a bordered area when you insert a text box. You can format a text box with shape styles and effects, and you can align text within a text box.
   - Resize, move, and modify a text box: As an object, a text box can be moved, resized, and modified with options on the Format tab.
   - Insert WordArt: A WordArt object displays text with special effects, such as color, size, gradient, and 3-D appearance.

Key Terms Matching

Match the key terms with their definitions. Write the key term letter by the appropriate numbered definition.

- **a.** Alignment guide
- **b.** Border
- **c.** Bulleted list
- **d.** Column
- **e.** Document theme
- **f.** First line indent
- **g.** Font
- **h.** Indent
- **i.** Line spacing
- **j.** Live Layout
- **k.** Object
- **l.** Paragraph spacing
- **m.** Picture
- **n.** Section break
- **o.** Sizing handles
- **p.** Style
- **q.** Style set
- **r.** Tab
- **s.** Text box
- **t.** WordArt

1. ______ An item, such as a picture or text box, that can be individually selected and manipulated. **p. 231**

2. ______ The small circles and squares that appear around a selected object and enable you to adjust its size. **p. 234**

3. ______ A list of points that is not sequential. **p. 209**

4. ______ A feature that modifies text to include special effects, such as color, shadow, gradient, and 3-D appearance. **p. 237**

5. ______ The vertical space between the lines in a paragraph. **p. 205**

6. ______ A typeface or complete set of characters. **p. 198**

7. ______ The horizontal or vertical green bar that appears as you move an object, assisting with lining up an object. **p. 234**

8. ______ Marks the location to indent only the first line in a paragraph. **p. 206**

9. ______ A named collection of formatting characteristics that can be applied to characters or paragraphs. **p. 220**

10. ______ A combination of title, heading, and paragraph styles that can be used to format all of those elements at one time. **p. 217**

11. ______ A format that separates document text into side-by-side vertical blocks, often used in newsletters. **p. 219**

12. ______ A marker that specifies the position for aligning text, sometimes including a leader. **p. 206**

13. ______ The amount of space before or after a paragraph. **p. 204**

14. ______ A feature that enables you to watch text flow around an object as you move the object. **p. 234**

15. ______ A setting associated with the way a paragraph is distanced from one or more margins. **p. 206**

16. ______ An indicator that divides a document into parts, enabling different formatting in each section. **p. 218**

17. ______ A boxed object that can be bordered and shaded, providing space for text. **p. 235**

18. ______ A line that surrounds a paragraph or a page. **p. 208**

19. ______ A graphic file that is obtained from the Internet or a storage device. **p. 231**

20. ______ A unified set of design elements, including font style, color, and special effects, that is applied to an entire document. **p. 217**

Multiple Choice

1. How does a document theme differ from a style?
   (a) A theme applies an overall design to a document, with no requirement that any text is selected. A style applies formatting characteristics to selected text or to a current paragraph.
   (b) A theme applies color-coordinated design to selected page elements. A style applies formatting to an entire document.
   (c) A theme and a style are actually the same feature.
   (d) A theme applies font characteristics, whereas a style applies paragraph formatting.

2. To identify a series of sequential steps, you could use:
   (a) Outlining.
   (b) Bullets.
   (c) Tabs.
   (d) Numbering.

3. The feature that modifies text to include special effects, such as color, shadow, and gradients, is:
   (a) WordArt.
   (b) Themes.
   (c) Live Layout.
   (d) Text box.

4. If you have not selected text when you identify a shading color, what part of a document is shaded?
   (a) The paragraph in which the insertion point is located.
   (b) The entire document.
   (c) The currently displayed page.
   (d) The most recent selection of text.

5. Having applied a particular heading style to several headings within a document, you modify the style to include bold and italic font formatting. What happens to the headings that were previously formatted in that style, and why?
   (a) They remain as they are. Changes in style affect only text typed from that point forward.
   (b) They remain as they are. You cannot modify a style that has already been applied to text in the current document.
   (c) They are updated to reflect the modified heading style settings. When a heading style is modified, all text formatted in that style is updated.
   (d) Each heading reverts to its original setting. When you modify styles, you make them unavailable to previously formatted styles.

6. To divide a document so that one area can be formatted independently of the next, you can use a(n):
   (a) Column.
   (b) Indent.
   (c) Section break.
   (d) Page break.

7. If you select text and apply a linked style, what happens?
   (a) Paragraph formats are applied, but not character formats.
   (b) Both paragraph and character formats are applied.
   (c) Linked formats are applied.
   (d) Character formats are applied, but not paragraph formats.

8. To draw attention to such items as contact information or store hours, you could place text in a bordered area called a:
   (a) Text box.
   (b) Dot leader.
   (c) Section.
   (d) Tabbed indent.

9. Viewing a document in Outline view can be helpful in which one of the following ways?
   (a) It simplifies the application of formatting to entire sections.
   (b) It streamlines the process of applying heading styles to selected text.
   (c) It color coordinates various heading levels.
   (d) It enables you to expand and collapse levels, dragging to reposition them within the document.

10. The feature that enables you to watch text flow around an object as you move the object is called:
    (a) Alignment guide.
    (b) Live Layout.
    (c) Text wrap.
    (d) Layout Options.

Practice Exercises

1 Campus Safety

You are the office assistant for the police department at a local university. As a service to students, staff, and the community, the police department publishes a campus safety guide, available both in print and online. With national emphasis on homeland security, and local incidents of theft and robbery, it is obvious that the safety guide should be updated and distributed. You will work with a draft document, formatting it to make it more attractive and ready for print. This exercise follows the same set of skills used in Hands-On Exercises 1–3 in the chapter. Refer to Figure 2.49 as you complete this exercise.

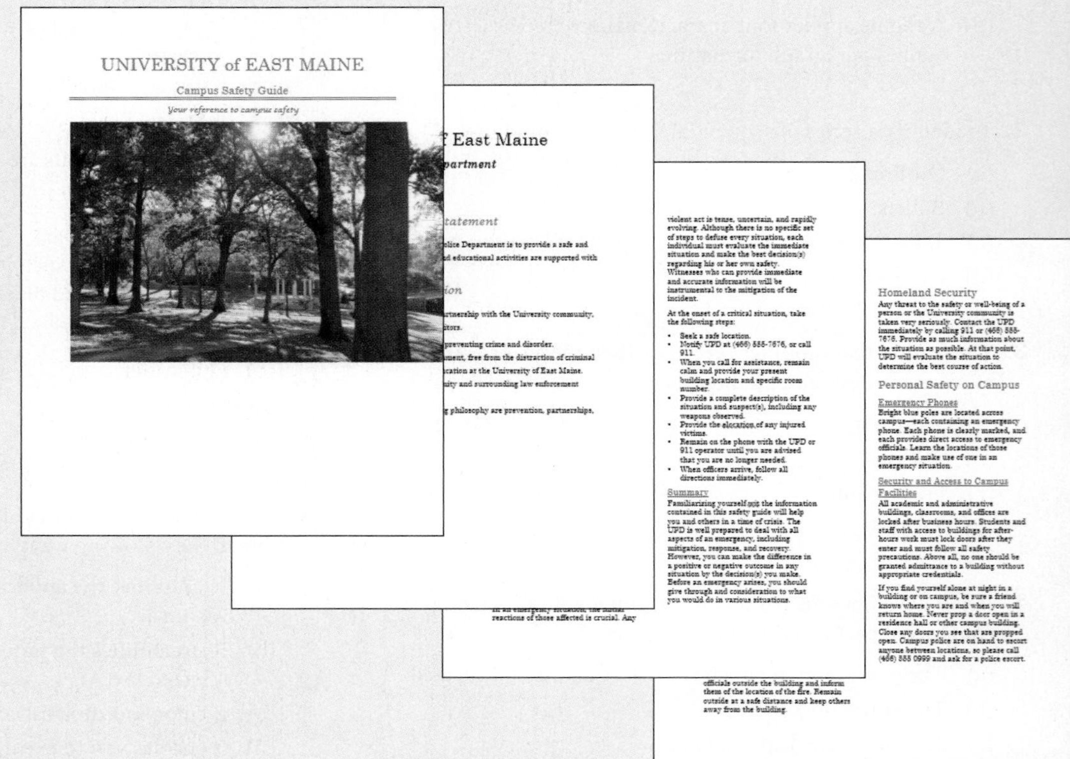

FIGURE 2.49 Format a Document

a. Open *w02p1Safety* and save the document as **w02p1Safety_LastFirst**. Click **Show/Hide** in the Paragraph group to show nonprinting characters, if necessary.

b. Click the **DESIGN tab**. Click **Themes** in the Document Formatting group and select **Retrospect**. Click **Colors** in the Document Formatting group and select **Blue**. Click **Fonts** in the Document Formatting group and select **Century Schoolbook**.

c. Click the **HOME tab**. Select the first line in the document and click **Center** in the Paragraph group. Click the **Font Color arrow** in the Font group and select **Blue, Accent 1**. Click the **Font Size arrow** and select **26**. Click **Change Case** in the Font group and select **UPPERCASE**. Double-click *of* in the first line in the document, click **Change Case**, and then select **lowercase**. Select the second line in the document. Center the line, change the font color to **Blue, Accent 1**, change the font size to **16**, and then change the case to **Capitalize Each Word**. Do not deselect the text.

d. Click the **Borders arrow** in the Paragraph group and click **Borders and Shading**. Click **Custom** in the *Setting* section of the Borders and Shading dialog box. Click the **Color arrow** and select **Blue, Accent 1**. Scroll through styles in the Style box and select the seventh style (double line). Click the **Width arrow** and select **1 1/2 pt**. Click **Bottom** in the Preview group and click **OK**.

e. Select the line containing the text *Your reference to campus safety*. Click **Font Color** on the Mini toolbar to apply the most recent font color selection. Use either the Mini toolbar or selections on the HOME tab to change the font to **Lucida Calligraphy** and center the selection.

f. Click at the end of the currently selected line to position the insertion point immediately after *Your reference to campus safety*. Click the **INSERT tab** and click **Pictures** in the Illustrations group. Navigate to the location of your student data files and double-click *w02p1Campus*.

g. Click **Height** in the Size group on the FORMAT tab and type **5**. Press **Enter**. Click **Corrections** in the Adjust group and select **Brightness: 0% (Normal), Contrast: +20%** under *Brightness/Contrast*.

h. Click before the words *University of East Maine* immediately below the picture and press **Ctrl+Enter** to insert a manual page break. Scroll up and select the first line on page 1 of the document. Click the **Home tab**, if necessary, and click **Format Painter** in the Clipboard group. Scroll to the second page and select the first line (*University of East Maine*) to copy the formatting. Change the font color of the selected line to **Black, Text 1**.

i. Select the second line on page 2, containing the text *Police Department*. Apply **Center**, **Bold**, and **Italic** to the selection. Change the font size to **16 pt**. Select text in the document beginning with *Mission Statement* and ending with *prevention, partnerships, and problem solving* (on the same page). Click **Line and Paragraph Spacing** in the Paragraph group and select **1.5**. Click the **Paragraph Dialog Box Launcher** and change **Spacing After** to **6 pt**. Click **OK**. Click to position the insertion point after the words *Police Department* and press **Enter** twice.

j. Select the *Mission Statement* heading near the top of page 2 and change the font color to **Blue, Accent 1**. Center the selection and change the font size to **16** and the font to **Lucida Calligraphy**. Copy the format of the selection to the *Vision* heading on the same page. Insert a page break after the sentence ending with the words *problem solving* on page 2.

k. Select the paragraphs on page 2 beginning with *University police officers are committed to* and ending with *prevention, partnerships, and problem solving*. Click the **Bullets arrow** in the Paragraph group and select the square filled bullet. Click **Decrease Indent** in the Paragraph group to move bullets to the left margin.

l. Scroll to page 3. Click the **Styles Dialog Box Launcher**. Complete the following steps to apply styles to selected text.
   - Click in the line containing *Emergency Notifications*. Click **Heading 1** in the Styles pane. Scroll down and apply Heading 1 style to the headings *Personal Safety*, *Medical Emergencies*, *Fire Emergencies*, *Homeland Security*, and *Personal Safety on Campus*.
   - Click in the line on page 4 containing the text *Summary*. Click **Heading 2** in the Styles pane. Scroll down and apply Heading 2 style to the headings *Security and Access to Campus Facilities* and *Emergency Phones*.

m. Point to *Heading 2* in the Styles pane, and click the **Heading 2 arrow**. Click **Modify**. Click **Underline** and click **OK**.

   Heading 2 is modified to include an underline. All text previously formatted in Heading 2 style now includes an underline.

n. Scroll to page 3 and select the five paragraphs in the *Emergency Notifications* section, beginning with *Phone* and ending with *provide additional information*. Apply square filled bullets to the selection. Decrease indent to the left margin. Click **New Style** in the Styles pane, type **Bulleted Text** in the **Name box**, and then click **OK**.

o. Select the seven paragraphs in the *Personal Safety* section, beginning with *Seek a safe location* and ending with *follow all directions immediately*. Click **Bulleted Text** in the Styles pane to apply the style to the selection. Apply the same style to the seven paragraphs in the *Medical Emergencies* section, beginning with *The victim should not be moved* and ending with *information is needed*. Close the Styles pane.

p. Press **Ctrl+Home** to move to the beginning of the document. Spell check the document. The word *of* in the university name is correct in lowercase, so do not correct it.

q. Scroll to page 3 and select all text beginning with *The University of East Maine* and ending at the end of the document. Click the **PAGE LAYOUT tab**, click **Columns**, and then select **Two**. Click the **VIEW tab** and click **Multiple Pages** in the Zoom group to view pages of the document. Scroll up or down to check the document for text positioning and any awkward column endings. Click **100%** in the Zoom group.

r. Click **Outline** in the Views group. Click the **Show Level arrow** in the Outline Tools group and click **Level 1**. Click + beside *Personal Safety on Campus* and click **Expand** in the Outline Tools group. Point to + beside *Emergency Phones* and drag to position the *Emergency Phones* section above *Security and Access to Campus Facilities.* Click **Print Layout** on the status bar.

s. Press **Ctrl+Home** to move to the beginning of the document. Click the **FILE tab** and click **Print** to preview the document. Click **Next Page** to move through the pages of the document. Click **Back** at the top-left corner of the screen to leave print preview.

t. Compare your work to Figure 2.49. Save and close the file, and submit based on your instructor's directions.

2 Alcohol Awareness

You have been employed to oversee a grant program that your city has been awarded to develop material on alcohol awareness. The purpose of the grant is to increase awareness among youth of the dangers of abusing alcohol and the long-term repercussions of alcohol dependency. You will make presentations to various groups around the city, including civic clubs and student organizations. Along with using a PowerPoint presentation to support your discussions, you also have on hand articles, flyers, and brochures that help convey the message. One such document, a summary of medical facts regarding alcohol abuse, is near completion. However, your assistant was called away and you must finish it. It is in need of proofreading, formatting, and a few other features that will result in a polished handout for your next presentation. This exercise follows the same set of skills as used in Hands-On Exercises 1–3 in the chapter. Refer to Figure 2.50 as you complete this exercise.

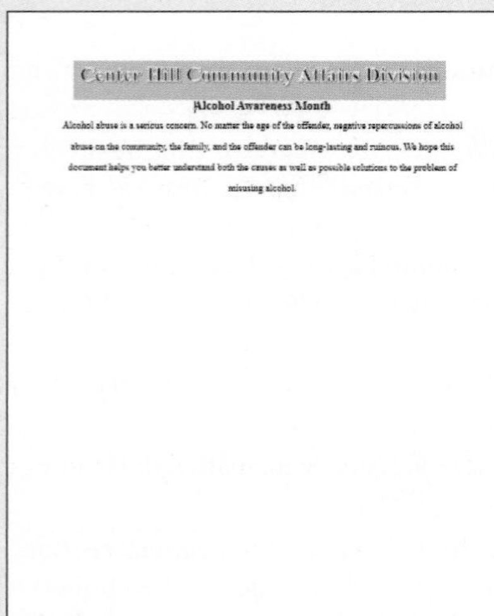

Center Hill Community Affairs Division

Alcohol Awareness Month

Alcohol abuse is a serious concern. No matter the age of the offender, negative repercussions of alcohol abuse on the community, the family, and the offender can be long-lasting and ruinous. We hope this document helps you better understand both the causes as well as possible solutions to the problem of misusing alcohol.

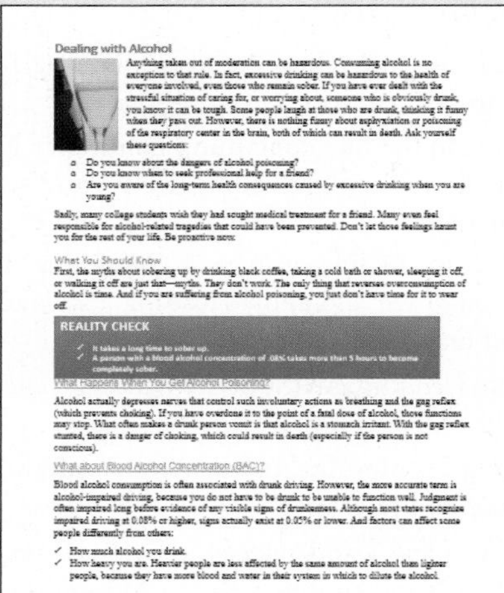

Dealing with Alcohol

Anything taken out of moderation can be hazardous. Consuming alcohol is no exception to that rule. In fact, excessive drinking can be hazardous to the health of everyone involved, even those who remain sober. If you have ever dealt with the stressful situation of caring for, or worrying about, someone who is obviously drunk, you know it can be tough. Some people laugh at those who are drunk, thinking it funny when they pass out. However, there is nothing funny about asphyxiation or poisoning of the respiratory center in the brain, both of which can result in death. Ask yourself these questions:

- Do you know about the dangers of alcohol poisoning?
- Do you know when to seek professional help for a friend?
- Are you aware of the long-term health consequences caused by excessive drinking when you are young?

Sadly, many college students wish they had sought medical treatment for a friend. Many even feel responsible for alcohol-related tragedies that could have been prevented. Don't let those feelings haunt you for the rest of your life. Be proactive now.

What You Should Know

First, the myths about sobering up by drinking black coffee, taking a cold bath or shower, sleeping it off, or walking it off are just that—myths. They don't work. The only thing that reverses overconsumption of alcohol is time. And if you are suffering from alcohol poisoning, you just don't have time for it to wear off.

REALITY CHECK

- It takes a long time to sober up.
- A person with a blood alcohol concentration of .08% takes more than 5 hours to become completely sober.

What Happens When You Get Alcohol Poisoning?

Alcohol actually depresses nerves that control such involuntary actions as breathing and the gag reflex (which prevents choking). If you have overdone it to the point of a fatal dose of alcohol, those functions may stop. What often makes a drunk person vomit is that alcohol is a stomach irritant. With the gag reflex stunted, there is a danger of choking, which could result in death (especially if the person is not conscious).

What about Blood Alcohol Concentration (BAC)?

Blood alcohol consumption is often associated with drunk driving. However, the more accurate term is alcohol-impaired driving, because you do not have to be drunk to be unable to function well. Judgment is often impaired long before evidence of any visible signs of drunkenness. Although most states recognize impaired driving at 0.08% or higher, signs actually exist at 0.05% or lower. And factors can affect some people differently from others:

- How much alcohol you drink.
- How heavy you are. Heavier people are less affected by the same amount of alcohol than lighter people, because they have more blood and water in their system in which to dilute the alcohol.

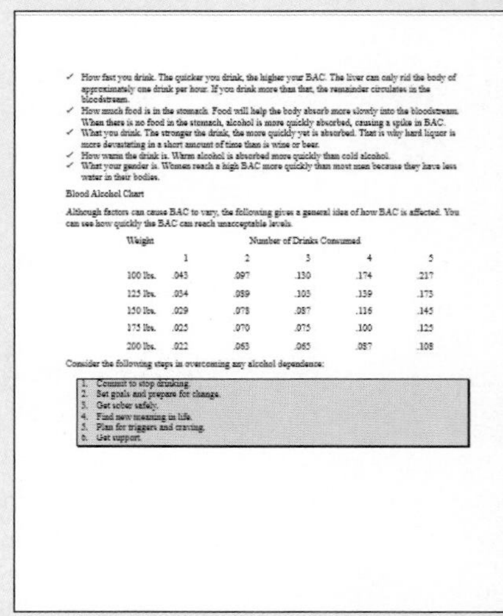

- How fast you drink. The quicker you drink, the higher your BAC. The liver can only rid the body of approximately one drink per hour. If you drink more than that, the remainder circulates in the bloodstream.
- How much food is in the stomach. Food will help the body absorb more slowly into the bloodstream. When there is no food in the stomach, alcohol is more quickly absorbed, causing a spike in BAC.
- What you drink. The stronger the drink, the more quickly yet is absorbed. That is why hard liquor is more devastating in a short amount of time than is wine or beer.
- How warm the drink is. Warm alcohol is absorbed more quickly than cold alcohol.
- What your gender is. Women reach a high BAC more quickly than most men because they have less water in their bodies.

Blood Alcohol Chart

Although factors can cause BAC to vary, the following gives a general idea of how BAC is affected. You can see how quickly the BAC can reach unacceptable levels.

Weight	Number of Drinks Consumed				
	1	2	3	4	5
100 lbs.	.043	.097	.130	.174	.217
125 lbs.	.034	.089	.103	.139	.173
150 lbs.	.029	.078	.087	.116	.145
175 lbs.	.025	.070	.075	.100	.125
200 lbs.	.022	.063	.065	.087	.108

Consider the following steps in overcoming any alcohol dependence:

1. Commit to stop drinking.
2. Set goals and prepare for change.
3. Get sober safely.
4. Find new meaning in life.
5. Plan for triggers and craving.
6. Get support.

FIGURE 2.50 Finish a Handout

a. Open *w02p2Alcohol* and save it as **w02p2Alcohol_LastFirst**.

b. Click the **HOME tab** and click **Show/Hide** if nonprinting characters are not displayed. Press **Ctrl+A** to select all document text. Click the **Font arrow** and select **Times New Roman**. Click anywhere to deselect the text. Check the document for spelling and grammatical errors. Ignore the identified grammatical mistake.

c. Press **Ctrl+Home** to move to the beginning of the document. Select the first line in the document, *Center Hill Community Affairs Division*. Click the **INSERT tab** and select **WordArt** in the Text group. Click **Fill – Black, Text 1 – Outline – Background 1, Hard Shadow – Background 1** (third row, first column). Click the **Shape Fill arrow** in the Shape Styles group on the DRAWING TOOLS FORMAT tab. Select **White, Background 1, Darker 25%** (fourth row, first column). Click the **HOME tab** and change the font size to **24**.

d. Click **Layout Options** and click **Top and Bottom**. Close Layout Options. Point to the WordArt object and drag to visually center it. You should drag when the mouse pointer resembles a four-headed arrow.

e. Select the second line in the document, *Alcohol Awareness Month*. When you select the text, the WordArt is also selected because it is anchored to the selected paragraph. Center and bold the selected text and change the font size to **14**.

f. Click anywhere in the paragraph that begins *Alcohol abuse is a serious concern*. Center the paragraph. Click **Line and Paragraph Spacing** in the Paragraph group and select **2.0**. Click before the paragraph mark ending the paragraph that begins *Alcohol abuse is a serious concern*. Click the **PAGE LAYOUT tab** and click **Breaks**. Click **Next Page** in the Section Breaks group. Press **Delete** to remove the paragraph mark at the top of page 2.

g. Click the **HOME tab**. Select the first line on page 2, *Dealing with Alcohol*. Click **Heading 1** in the Styles group. Select *What You Should Know* and select **Heading 2**.

h. Select *What Happens When You Get Alcohol Poisoning?* Change the font to **Arial**, click **Underline** in the Font group, click the **Font Color arrow**, and change the font color to **Blue, Accent 1**. Click the **Styles Dialog Box Launcher**. Click **New Style**. Type **Lower Item** in the **Name box** and click **OK**. Select the heading *What about Blood Alcohol Concentration (BAC)?* Click **Lower Item** in the Styles pane to apply the newly created style to the selected text.

i. Point to *Heading 1* in the Styles pane and click the **Heading 1 arrow**. Click **Modify**. Click **Bold** and click **OK**. Scroll up, if necessary, to see that the heading *Dealing with Alcohol* is bold. Close the Styles pane.

j. Select three paragraphs in the *Dealing with Alcohol* section, beginning with *Do you know about the dangers* and ending with *excessive drinking when you are young?* Click the **Bullets arrow** and select the hollow round bullet.

k. Select seven paragraphs in the *What about Blood Alcohol Concentration (BAC)?* section, beginning with *How much alcohol you drink* and ending with *because they have less water in their bodies*. Apply a check mark bullet to the selected paragraphs. Click **Decrease Indent** to move bulleted items to the left margin.

l. Scroll to page 3 and select the last six paragraphs, beginning with *Commit to stop drinking* and ending with *Get support*. Click **Numbering** in the Paragraph group to apply default numbers to the selection.

m. Click after the sentence ending with *unacceptable levels* on the same page. Press **Enter**. If the ruler is not displayed above the document area, click the **VIEW tab** and click **Ruler** in the Show group. Ensure that the tab selector, shown just above the vertical ruler, shows a left tab. Click **1"** to set a left tab. Click **3"** to set another left tab. Press **Tab**. Type **Weight**. Press **Tab**. Type **Number of Drinks Consumed**. Press **Enter**.

n. Drag the 3" left tab off the ruler to remove it. Click the tab selector twice to select a right tab. Click **2"** to set a right tab. Click **3"**, **4"**, **5"**, and **6"** to set four more right tabs.

o. Press **Tab**. Press **Tab** again. Type **1**. Press **Tab**. Type **2**. Press **Tab**. Type **3**. Press **Tab**. Type **4**. Press **Tab**. Type **5**. Press **Enter**. Press **Tab**. Type the following data, pressing **Tab** between each entry and pressing **Enter** at the end of each line except the last line:

100 lbs.	**.043**	**.097**	**.130**	**.174**	**.217**
125 lbs.	**.034**	**.089**	**.103**	**.139**	**.173**
150 lbs.	**.029**	**.078**	**.087**	**.116**	**.145**
175 lbs.	**.025**	**.070**	**.075**	**.100**	**.125**
200 lbs.	**.022**	**.063**	**.065**	**.087**	**.108**

p. Scroll to page 2 and click before the first sentence in the *What You Should Know* section. Click the **INSERT tab** and click **Online Pictures** in the Illustrations group. Type **alcohol** in the **Office.Com Clip Art box**. Press **Enter**. Double-click the image shown in Figure 2.50 (or select one very similar if it is unavailable). Change the height of the picture to **1.5** in the Size group on the PICTURE TOOLS FORMAT tab. Click **Layout Options** and select **Square**. Close Layout Options. Drag to position the image as shown in Figure 2.50.

q. Press **Ctrl+End** to move to the end of the document. Select the six numbered paragraphs. Click the **HOME tab** and click the **Borders arrow** in the Paragraph group. Click **Borders and Shading**. Click **Shadow** in the *Setting* section. Click the **Shading tab**. Click the **Color arrow** in the *Fill* section and select **White, Background 1, Darker 15%**. Click **OK**.

r. Click after the last sentence in the *What You Should Know* section. Click the **INSERT tab** and click **Text Box** in the Text group. Click **Draw Text Box**. Drag to draw a box approximately 1" high and 6" wide below the *What You Should Know* section. If necessary, change the height to **1"** and the width to **6"** in the Size group on the DRAWING TOOLS FORMAT tab. Click **Layout Options**. Click **Top and Bottom**. Click to place the insertion point in the text box, if necessary.

s. Click the **HOME tab** and click **Bold** in the Font group. Change the font size to **16**. Type **REALITY CHECK** and press **Enter**. Click **Line and Paragraph Spacing** in the Paragraph group and click **1.0**. Click the **Paragraph Dialog Box Launcher**. Change **Paragraph Spacing After** to **0 pt**. Click **OK**. Change the font size to **10**. Type the following, pressing **Enter** after each line:

It takes a long time to sober up.

A person with a blood alcohol concentration of .08% takes more than 5 hours to become completely sober.

t. Apply check mark bullets to the two sentences you just typed. Click the **FORMAT tab**. Click **More** beside Shape Styles. Select **Subtle Effect – Blue, Accent 5** (fourth row, sixth column). Point in the text box so that the pointer displays as a four-headed arrow. Drag to position the text box as shown in Figure 2.50.

u. Compare your work to Figure 2.50. Save and close the file, and submit based on your instructor's directions.

Mid-Level Exercises

1 Balloon Festival

As chair of the James Canyon Balloon Festival, you are responsible for promoting the upcoming event. You have begun a document providing details on the festival. You plan to distribute the document both in print and online. First, you must format the document to make it more attractive and well designed. You will use styles, bullets, and line and paragraph spacing to coordinate various parts of the document. In addition, you will add interest by including objects, such as pictures, text boxes, and WordArt.

a. Open *w02m1Balloons* and save it as **w02m1Balloons_LastFirst**.

b. Change the document theme to **Slice**. Select the first line in the document, *James Canyon Balloon Festival*. Insert WordArt, selecting **Fill – Dark Purple, Accent 2, Outline – Accent 2** (first row, third column). Change the font size of the WordArt object to **20**.

c. Wrap text around the WordArt object as **Top and Bottom**. Format the WordArt object with Shape Style **Subtle Effect – Dark Purple, Accent 2** (fourth row, third column). Visually center the WordArt object on the first line of the document.

d. Select the second line in the document, *See the Canyon From on High!* Center and bold the text and apply a font color of **Dark Purple, Accent 2**.

e. Select the remaining text on page 1, beginning with *May 25-26, 2016* and ending with *on the festival grounds*. Format the selected text into two columns. Insert a page break (not a section break) after the sentence ending with *on the festival grounds*. Change the font of the columned text on page 1 to **Century Schoolbook**.

f. Check spelling and grammar—the word *Ballumination* is not misspelled (for the purposes of this document).

g. Click in the third line on page 1—*May 25-26, 2016*—and right align it. Select all columned text, including the line containing festival dates, and select a line spacing of **1.5** and paragraph spacing after of **6 pt**. Insert a column break before the paragraph beginning with *And don't forget the dogs!*

h. Click to place the insertion point before the paragraph beginning *As for the kids*. Insert an online picture from Office.com relating to hot air balloons. Size the picture with a height of **1.5"**. Select **Square text wrapping** and a picture style of **Rotated, White**. Position the picture so that it is on the left side of the paragraph beginning with *As for the kids*, but still in the right column.

i. Select the picture and recolor it to coordinate with the purple theme of the document. Choose an artistic effect of **Photocopy**.

j. Scroll to page 3 and select the heading, *When is the best time to see balloons?* Bold the selection and change the font color to **Dark Purple, Accent 2**. Do not deselect the heading. Open the Styles pane and create a new style named **Questions**. Apply the **Questions style** to other questions (headings) on page 3.

k. Scroll to page 4 and apply solid round bullets to the first nine paragraphs on the page. Decrease the indent so the bullets begin at the left margin. With the bulleted items selected, click the **Bullets arrow** and click **Define New Bullet**. Click **Font** and change the font color to **Dark Purple, Accent 2**. Click **OK**. Click **OK** again.

l. Insert a page break (not a section break) before the heading *How can I plan for the best experience?* on page 3.

m. Select the schedule of items under the heading *Saturday (5/25/16)*, beginning with *6:00 AM* and ending with *Balloon Glow*. Set a left tab at **1"**. Press **Tab** to move selected paragraphs to the left tab. Select the schedule of items under *Sunday (5/26/16)*, set a left tab at **1"**, and then tab selected paragraphs.

n. Save and close the file, and submit based on your instructor's directions.

2 Dental Information Meeting

You are the office manager for a pediatric dentist who periodically conducts informational sessions for young children. You have written a letter to children in the neighborhood reminding them about the upcoming monthly session, but you want to make the letter more professional looking. You decide to use paragraph formatting such as alignment, paragraph spacing, borders and shading, and bullets that describe some of the fun activities of the day. You will also want to add the dentist's e-mail address and appropriate clip art to the letter.

a. Open the document *w02m2Dentist* and save it as **w02m2Dentist_LastFirst**.

b. Change the capitalization of the recipient *Ms. Catherine Ellis* and her address so that each word is capitalized and the state abbreviation displays in uppercase. Change Dr. Block's name to your full name in the signature block. Type your e-mail address (or a fictitious e-mail address) on the next line below your name.

c. Show nonprinting characters, if they are not already displayed. Apply **Justify alignment** to body paragraphs beginning with *On behalf* and ending with *July 14*. At the paragraph mark under the first body paragraph, create a bulleted list, selecting a bullet of your choice. Type the following items in the bulleted list. Do not press Enter after the last item in the list.

   Participating in the dental crossword puzzle challenge
   Writing a convincing letter to the tooth fairy
   Digging through the dental treasure chest
   Finding hidden toothbrushes in the dental office

d. Select text from the salutation *Dear Catherine*: through the last paragraph that ends with *seeing you on July 14*. Set **12 pt Spacing After paragraph**.

e. Use small caps on *Dr. Block Pediatric Dental Center* in the first paragraph.

f. Select the italicized lines of text that give date, time, and location of the meeting. Remove the italics, do not deselect the text, and then complete the following:
   - Increase left and right indents to **1.25** and set **0 pt Spacing After paragraph**.
   - Apply a **double-line box border** with the color **Red, Accent 2, Darker 50%** and a line width of **3/4 pt**. Shade selected text with the **Red, Accent 2, Lighter 40% shading color**.
   - Delete the extra tab formatting marks to the left of the lines containing *July 14, 2012; 4:00 p.m.*; and *Dr. Block Pediatric Dental Center* to align them with other text in the bordered area.
   - Remove the paragraph mark before the paragraph that begins with *Please call our office*.

g. Click the line containing the text *Glen Allen, VA 23060*, and set **12 pt Spacing After** the paragraph. Click the line containing *Sincerely* and set **6 pt Spacing Before** the paragraph. Add **6 pt Spacing Before** the paragraph beginning with the text *Dr. Block is pleased to let you know*.

h. Select the entire document and change the font to **12-pt Bookman Old Style**.

i. Move to the beginning of the document. Search online for a picture related to *tooth*. Insert the picture and apply a square text wrap. Position the picture in the top-right corner of the document, just below the header area. Resize the graphic to **1.1"** high. Apply the **Bevel Perspective Left, White picture style** (fourth row, third column).

j. Move to the end of the document. Insert a Next Page section break. Change the orientation to **Landscape**. Change **Paragraph Spacing After** to **6 pt**. Change the font size to **14**. Center the first line. Type **Ariat Lake Water Park Fun Day!** Press **Enter** and type **July 5, 2016**. Press **Enter** and change the alignment to **Left**. Change the font size to **12**. Set a left tab at **2"** and a right tab at **7"**. Type the following text, with the first column at the 2" tab and the next column at the 7" tab. Do not press Enter after typing the last line.

Check-in	**9:00**
Water slide	**9:30-11:00**
Lunch at the pavilion	**11:00-12:00**
Wave pool	**12:00-2:00**
Bungee	**2:00-3:00**
Parent pickup at the gate	**3:00-3:30**

k. Select **Ariat Lake Water Park Fun Day!** on page 2 and insert WordArt with the style **Fill – Aqua, Accent 1, Outline – Background 1, Hard Shadow – Accent 1** (third row, third column). Wrap text around the WordArt object at **Top and Bottom**, change the font size of the WordArt object to **24**, and drag to center the object horizontally on the first line.

l. Select the tabbed text, beginning with *Check-in* and ending with *3:00-3:30*. Modify the 7" right tab to include a dot leader.

m. Change the theme to **Integral**. Check spelling and grammar, correcting any errors and ignoring those that are not errors.

n. Save and close the file, and submit based on your instructor's directions.

3 A Music CD Cover

COLLABORATION CASE 

FROM SCRATCH 

You play bass guitar with a local band, Twilight Hour. You love playing with the band, but you also enjoy the business side of music, and plan to pursue a career in music production. To that end, you are completing requirements for a B.S. degree. This semester, you are participating in a seminar on music marketing and production. You are in a group that is required to design the front and back of a CD cover for a band, real or fictitious, and your group decides to create a cover for your band, Twilight Hour. You will begin a document and share it with members of the group, who will each contribute to the CD cover. Your group will first locate a music CD case to use as a model. The front of the CD typically displays the band or artist name, along with a graphic or background design.

Before continuing with this case, all group members must have a Microsoft account. An account can be obtained at www.outlook.com.

a. One person in your group should complete the following two steps:
   - Open a new Word document. Include the group name in the header. Click the **FILE tab** and click **Share**. Click **Save to Cloud** and click the **OneDrive link**. Select a recently accessed folder, or click **Browse**, and navigate to, or create, another folder.
   - Change the file name to **w02m3Cover_GroupName** and click **Save**. Click **Get a Link**. Click **Create Link** beside the *Edit Link* section. Share the link with group members so that they can access the document online.

b. Each group member should enter the link in a browser to access the shared document. When the document opens in Word Online, click **Edit Document** and click **Edit in Word**.
   - One or more group members will focus on developing the front cover, including WordArt, pictures, and/or text boxes where appropriate. Use font and paragraph formatting, as needed, to produce an attractive front cover. The front cover should occupy the first page, or first section, of the shared document. Save the document often, ensuring the save location is OneDrive.
   - One or more group members will focus on the back cover, including a list of songs, numbered and in two columns. In addition, give attention to the design of text and headings, formatting all items to produce an attractive back cover. The back cover will occupy the second page, or second section, of the shared document. Save the document often, ensuring the save location is OneDrive.
   - The dimensions of the final document will not necessarily be that of an actual CD. You are concerned with the design only.

c. The final version of the CD cover should be saved to OneDrive and printed and submitted according to your instructor's directions.

Beyond the Classroom

Invitation

RESEARCH CASE

FROM SCRATCH

Search the Internet for an upcoming local event at your school or in your community and produce the perfect invitation. You can invite people to a charity ball, a fun run, or to a fraternity party. Your color printer and abundance of fancy fonts, as well as your ability to insert page borders, enable you to do anything a professional printer can do. Save your work as **w02b2Invitation_LastFirst** and submit based on your instructor's directions.

Fundraising Letter

DISASTER RECOVERY

Each year, you update a letter to several community partners soliciting support for an auction. The auction raises funds for your organization, and your letter should impress your supporters. Open *w02b3Auction* and notice how unprofessional and unorganized the document looks so far. You must make changes immediately to improve the appearance. Consider replacing much of the formatting that is in place now and instead using columns for auction items, bullets to draw attention to the list of forms, page borders, and pictures or clip art—and that is just for starters! Save your work as **w02b3Auction_LastFirst** and submit based on your instructor's directions.

Job Search Strategies

SOFT SKILLS CASE

FROM SCRATCH

After watching the video on Job Search Strategies, develop a two-page document providing suggestions on searching for a job and listing numbered and/or bulleted strategies that you would suggest. The document should be error-free and must include at least one graphic (picture, clip art, text box, or WordArt). Use appropriate paragraph and line spacing, and include appropriate heading styles for sections within the paper. Save your work as **w02b4Strategy_LastFirst** and submit based on your instructor's directions.

Capstone Exercise

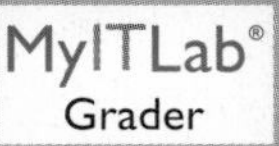

In this project, you work with a document prepared for managers involved in the hiring process. This report analyzes the validity of the interview process and suggests that selection does not depend only on quality information, but on the quality of the interpretation of information. The document requires formatting to enhance readability and important information; you will use skills from this chapter to format multiple levels of headings, arrange and space text, and insert graphics.

Applying Styles

This document is ready for enhancements, and the styles feature is a good tool that enables you to add them quickly and easily.

a. Open *w02c1Interview* and save it as **w02c1Interview_LastFirst**.

b. Press **Ctrl+Home**. Create a paragraph style named **Title_Page_1** with these formats: **22-pt font size** and **Dark Blue, Text 2, Darker 50% font color**. Ensure that this style is applied to the first line of the document, *Understanding the Personal Interview*.

c. Select the second line, *A Study for Managers Involved in the Hiring Process*. Change the font size to **16** and apply a font color of **Dark Blue, Text 2, Darker 50%**.

d. Click the line following *Updated by:* and type your first and last names. Change the capitalization for your name to uppercase.

e. Select the remainder of the text in the document that follows your name, starting with *The Personal Interview*. Justify the alignment of all paragraphs and change line spacing to **1.15**. Place the insertion point on the left side of the title *The Personal Interview* and insert a page break (not a section break).

f. Apply **Heading 1 style** to *The Personal Interview*. Apply **Heading 2 style** to paragraph headings, including *Introduction, Pre-interview Impression Effects, The Bias of Information Processing, Interviewer Decision Styles, Nonverbal Communications, Physical Characteristics*, and *Stereotypes*.

g. Modify the Heading 2 style to use **Dark Red font color**.

Formatting the Paragraphs

Next, you will apply paragraph formatting to the document. These format options will further increase the readability and attractiveness of your document.

a. Apply a bulleted list format for the five-item list in the *Introduction*. Use the symbol of a four-sided star.

b. Select the second paragraph in the *Introduction* section, which begins with *Personal interviewing continues*, and apply these formats: **0.6" left and right indents**, **6 pt spacing after the paragraph**, **boxed 1 1/2 pt border** using the color **Dark Blue, Text 2, Darker 25%**, and the shading color **Dark Blue, Text 2, Lighter 80%**.

c. Apply the first numbered-list format (1., 2., 3.) to the three phases in the *Pre-interview Impression Effects* section.

d. Select the last two multiline paragraphs in the *Pre-Interview Impression Effects* section and display them in two columns with a line between the columns. To do so, click the **PAGE LAYOUT tab**, click **Columns**, and then select **More Columns**. Click **Two** and select **Line between**. Click **OK**.

Inserting Graphics

To put the finishing touches on your document, you will add graphics that enhance the explanations given in some paragraphs.

a. Insert the picture file *w02c1Perceptions.jpg* at the beginning of the line that contains *First, we discuss some of the psychological pitfalls*, near the bottom of page 2. Change the height of the picture to **3"**. Change text wrapping to **Top and Bottom**. Position the picture so that it appears at the top of page 3. Click **Align Objects** in the Arrange group and click **Align Center** to center the graphic horizontally. Apply the **Rounded Diagonal Corner, White picture style**.

b. Insert the picture file *w02c1_Phases.jpg* at the beginning of the line on page 3 that begins with *Hakel, in 2002*. Ensure that text wrapping is **Top and Bottom**, position the picture so it appears immediately above the line beginning *Hakel, in 2002*. Apply **Offset Center Shadow Picture Effect** (second row, second column under *Outer*) to the graphic.

c. Spell check and review the entire document—no author names are misspelled.

d. Display the document in Outline view. Collapse all paragraphs so only lines formatted as Heading 1 or Heading 2 display. Move the *Stereotypes* section above *Physical Characteristics*. Close Outline view.

e. Save and close the file, and submit based on your instructor's directions.

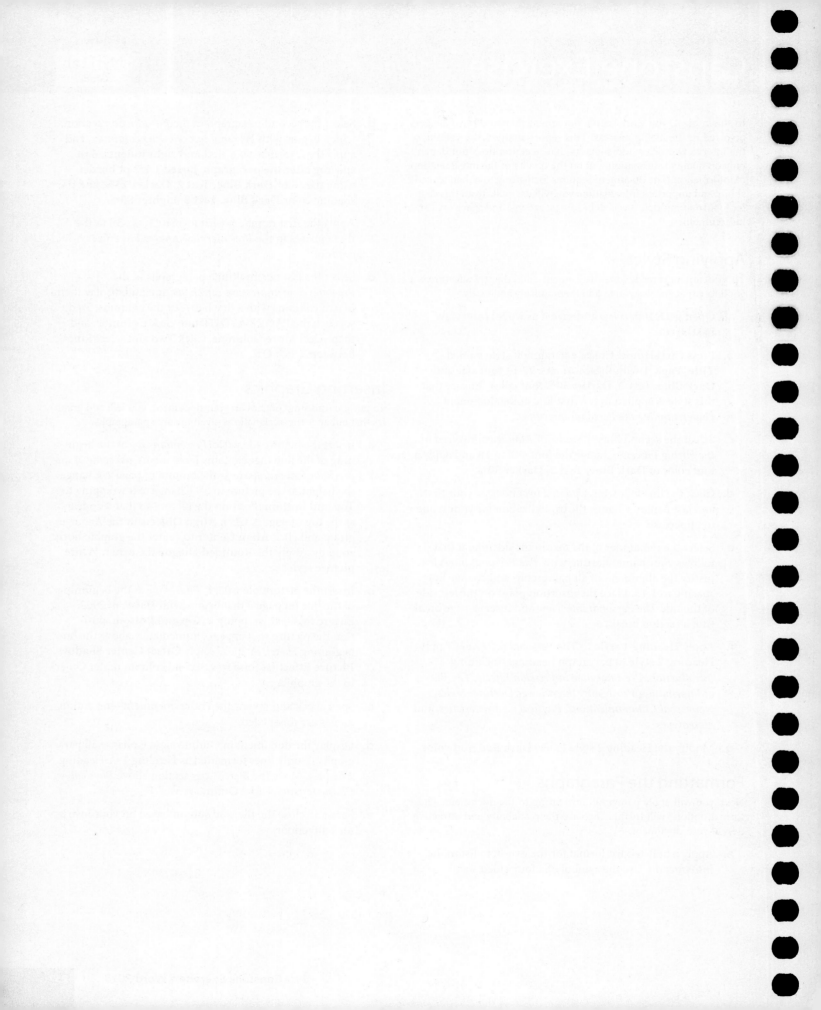

Word

Document Productivity

CHAPTER 3

Working with Tables and Mail Merge

OBJECTIVES AFTER YOU READ THIS CHAPTER, YOU WILL BE ABLE TO:

CASE STUDY | Traylor University Economic Impact Study

As director of marketing and research for Traylor University, a mid-sized university in northwest Nebraska, you have been involved with an economic impact study during the past year. The study is designed to measure as closely as possible the contribution of the university to the local and state economy. The scale of the study is large, measuring direct, indirect, and induced effects on employment, employee compensation, and spending. An evaluation of data led university researchers to conclude that Traylor University serves as a critical economic driver in the local community and, to a lesser extent, the state of Nebraska. It is your job to summarize those findings and see that they are accurately reflected in the final report.

Your assistant has prepared a draft of an executive summary that you will present to the board of trustees, outlining the major findings and conclusions. The summary is designed to provide a snapshot of the study process and findings. The best way to present some of the data analysis will be through tables, which your assistant is not very familiar with, so you will take responsibility for that phase of the summary preparation. The economic impact study is of interest to community leaders and groups throughout the university's service area, so you will send the executive summary, along with a cover letter, to those individuals. You will use Word's mail merge feature to prepare personalized letters and mailing labels.

Tables

A ***table*** is a grid of columns and rows that organizes data. As shown in Figure 3.1, a table is typically configured with headings in the first row and related data in following rows. The intersection of each column and row is a ***cell***, in which you can type data. A table is an excellent format in which to summarize numeric data because you can easily align numbers and even include formulas to sum or average numbers in a column or row. Text can be included in a table as well. Although you can use tabs to align text in columns in a Word document, you might find it quicker to create a table than to set tabs, and you have more control over format and design when using a table.

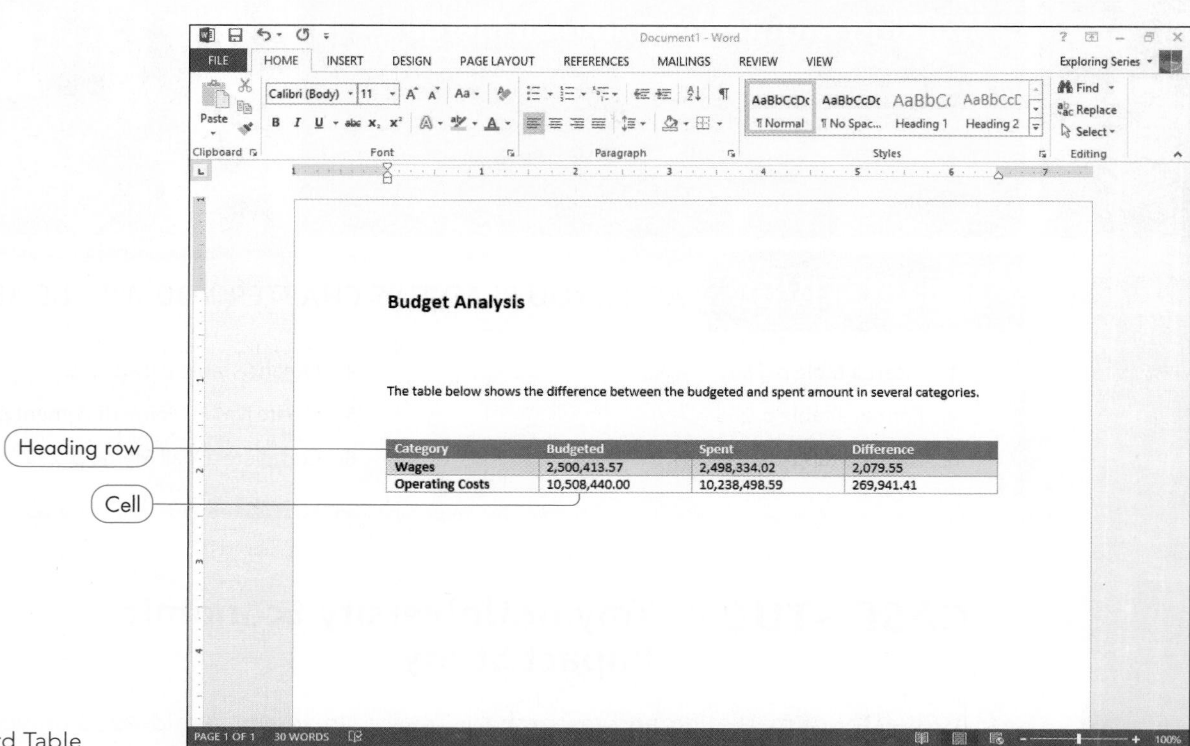

FIGURE 3.1 Word Table

Word's Table feature is a comprehensive but easy-to-use tool, enabling you to create a table, add and remove rows and columns, format table elements, include formulas to summarize numbers in a table, and customize borders and shading. When you create a table, you specify the number of columns and rows that should be included. For example, the table shown in Figure 3.1 is a 4x3 table, which means it contains 4 columns and 3 rows. Often, the number that you indicate turns out to be more or less than is actually necessary. Adding and deleting columns and rows is a simple task. In addition, you can merge cells, adjust row height and column width, and change alignment within cells.

In this section, you will learn to create a table. After positioning the table within a document, you will explore inserting and deleting columns and rows, merging and splitting cells, and adjusting row height and column width. Using Table styles, you will modify the appearance of a table, and you will adjust table position and alignment.

Inserting a Table

Inserting a table in a document is an easy task. You can either create a table with uniformly spaced rows and columns, or you can draw a table with the mouse pointer, creating rows and columns of varying heights and widths. Regardless of how a table is created, you can always change table settings so that rows and columns fit the data included in the table.

A table is an object; as such, it can be selected and manipulated independently of surrounding text. Although you can indicate precise table settings, such as column width and row height, you can also simply drag to increase or reduce the size of table elements, or adjust table settings by making selections from a dialog box. After selecting a column or row, you can delete or resize the item. You can even drag the entire table to reposition it, if necessary.

TIP Insert an Excel Spreadsheet

If you are familiar with Microsoft Excel, you can insert an Excel spreadsheet into a document and format it as a Word table. The advantage is that when you double-click a cell in the table, it reverts to an Excel spreadsheet, so you can use Excel commands and functionality with which you are familiar to modify the table and create formulas. To insert an Excel spreadsheet, click the Insert tab, click Table, and then click Excel Spreadsheet. Enter data in the Excel spreadsheet and click outside the spreadsheet to view it as a Word table. Double-click any cell to return to Excel.

Create or Draw a Table

STEP 1» To insert a table with identically sized rows and columns, click Table in the Tables group on the Insert tab. Drag to select the number of columns and rows to include in the table, as shown in Figure 3.2, or click Insert Table to display the Insert Table dialog box, where you can indicate the number of rows and columns you want to include.

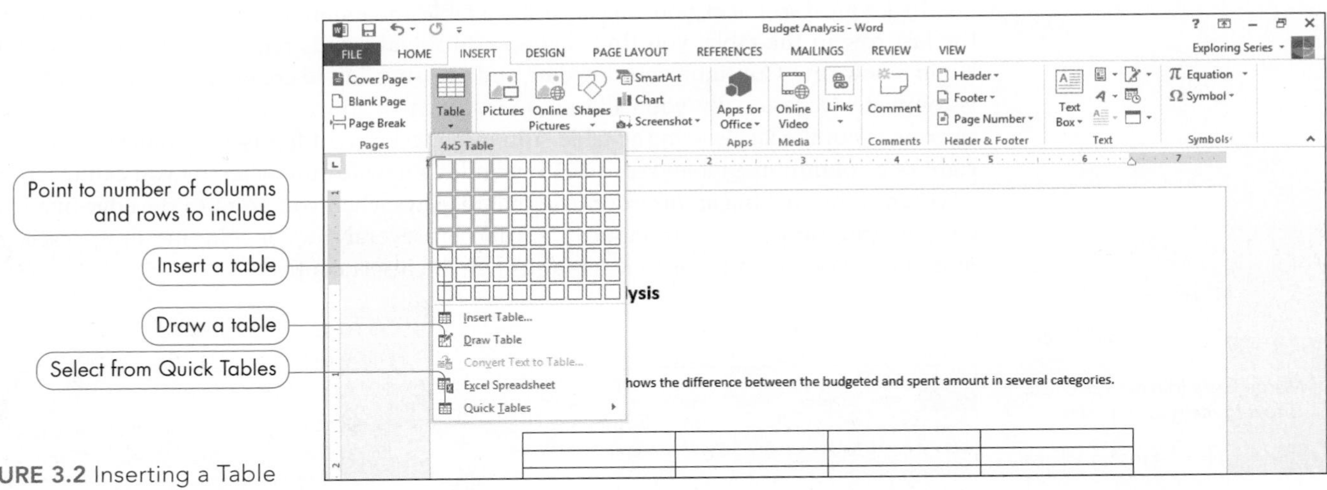

FIGURE 3.2 Inserting a Table

Instead of inserting a table, you can draw a table. You might choose to draw a table if you know that rows and/or columns should have varying heights or widths. It is sometimes easier to draw rows and columns of varying dimensions when a table is created rather than to modify the dimensions later, as would be necessary if you inserted a table instead of drawing it. To draw a table, click the Insert tab, click Table in the Tables group, and then select Draw Table. As you move the mouse pointer over the document, it resembles a pencil. Drag a rectangle and then draw horizontal and vertical lines to create rows and columns within the rectangular table space. Press Esc when the table is complete. To erase a grid line, click the Table Tools Layout contextual tab and click Eraser in the Draw group (see Figure 3.3). Click a grid line to erase. When the line is erased, press Esc.

TIP Quick Tables

Word 2013 provides easy access to several types of tables, including calendars, tabular lists, and matrices. Click the Insert tab, point to Quick Tables, and then select from a gallery of table types. Modify the table content to personalize it.

After the table structure is created, you can enter characters, numbers, or graphics in cells, moving from one cell to another when you press Tab or a directional arrow key. You can also simply click a cell to move to. As you type text in a cell, Word will wrap text to the next line when it reaches the right edge of the cell, adjusting row height if necessary to accommodate cell contents. To force text to a new line in a cell (before reaching the right cell border), press Enter.

Seldom will you create a table that is in final form as soon as data is entered. Instead, you are likely to find that additional rows or columns are necessary or that you have too many rows or columns. You might want to apply a table design to enhance the appearance or modify borders or text alignment. All of those activities are possible if you know how to select a table or individual table components.

Insert and Delete Rows and Columns

Having inserted a table, you might find the need for additional rows or columns. Or perhaps you overestimated the number of rows or columns needed and want to remove some. Word makes it easy to insert and delete rows and columns.

In a typical scenario, you have inserted a table and entered text in cells. As you complete the last row in the table, you find that an additional row is required. Simply press Tab to begin a new row. Continue entering data and pressing Tab to create new rows until the table is complete. Occasionally, you will want to insert a row above or below an existing row, when the row is not the last row in the table. You might even want to insert a column to the left or right of a column in a table. Word 2013 includes a new feature whereby you can insert rows or columns by clicking an ***insert control*** that displays when you point to the edge of a row or column gridline, as shown in Figure 3.3. To insert several rows or columns, drag to select the number of rows or columns to insert and click the insert control.

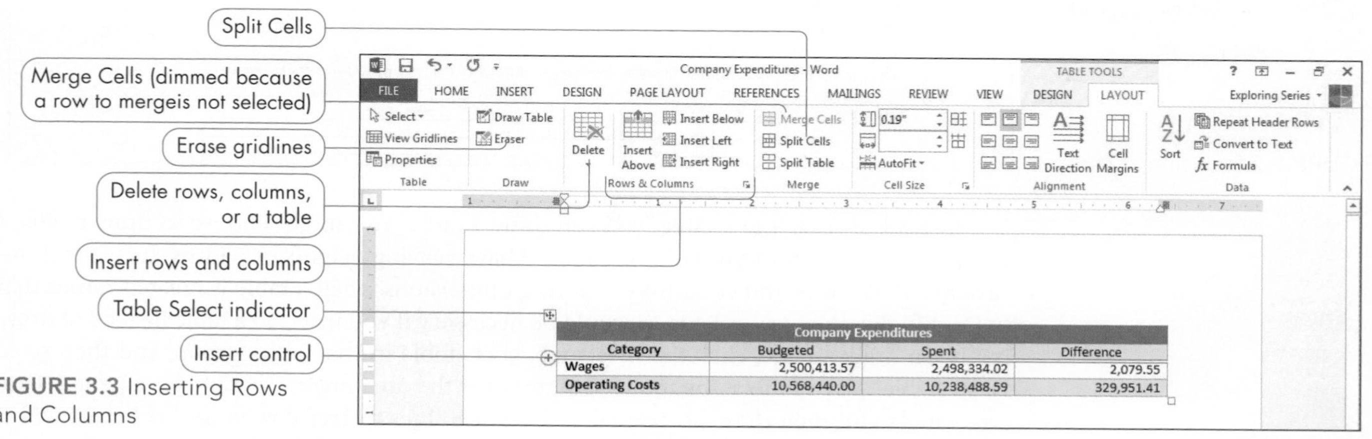

FIGURE 3.3 Inserting Rows and Columns

TIP Delete a Table

If you find you no longer need a particular table in a document, you can delete the table. Click the Table Select indicator (visible at the top-left corner of the table when you move the mouse pointer over any cell in the table or click a cell in the table), shown in Figure 3.3. Click the Table Tools Layout tab, if necessary, and click Delete in the Rows & Columns group. Click Delete Table.

You can also use commands on the Table Tools Layout tab to insert rows or columns, as described in the following steps:

1. Click in the row that is to appear *above* the new row or the row that is to appear *below* the new row. If inserting a column, click in the column that is to appear to the *left* of the new column or click in the column that is to appear to the *right* of the new column.
2. To insert a new row, click Insert Above or Insert Below in the Rows & Columns group. To insert a new column, click Insert Left or Insert Right in the Rows & Columns group.

As you develop a table, you might determine that one or more rows or columns are unnecessary. If you want to delete an entire row or column (not merely the cell contents of a row or column), complete the following steps:

1. Select the row or column to delete (or drag to select multiple rows or columns). Position the pointer just outside the left edge of a row or just above the top edge of a column and click to select the row or column.
2. Click Delete in the Rows & Columns group (see Figure 3.3).
3. Click Delete Columns or Delete Rows. Additional selections on the Delete menu enable you to delete individual cells or an entire table.

OR

1. Select the row or column to delete (or drag to select multiple rows or columns).
2. Right-click the selected row(s) or column(s) and click Delete Rows or Delete Columns.

TIP Delete Cell Contents

To delete cell contents without removing a row or column, position the pointer just inside the left edge of the cell so that the pointer appears as a small right-directed black arrow. Click to select all cell contents (or drag to saelect contents of multiple adjacent cells). Press Delete.

Merge and Split Cells

The first row of the table shown in Figure 3.3 is actually a merged cell. If you want to place a title across the top of a table or center a label over columns or rows of data, you can merge cells. Align data in a merged cell, perhaps by centering it, and change the font size to create a table title. Merging cells is a simple process, as described in the following steps:

STEP 2»

1. Select the row or column in which to merge cells (or drag to select multiple rows or columns).
2. Click the TABLE TOOLS LAYOUT tab and click Merge Cells in the Merge group (see Figure 3.3).

Conversely, you might find occasion to split a single cell into multiple cells. You might find it necessary to split a row or column to provide additional detail in separate cells. Splitting cells is an option on the Table Tools Layout tab. Select a row or column to split and click Split Cells in the Merge group. Respond to selections in the Split Cells dialog box and click OK. Especially when splitting a previously merged cell, it is likely that you will have to reposition text in cells (by retyping, or cutting and pasting).

Change Row Height and Column Width

When you create a table by inserting it, Word builds a grid with evenly spaced columns and rows. If text that you type requires more than one row within a cell, Word automatically wraps the text and adjusts row height to accommodate the entry. Row height is the vertical distance from the top to the bottom of a row, whereas column width is the horizontal space from the left to the right edge of a column. On occasion, you might want to manually adjust row height or column width to modify the appearance of a table, perhaps making it more readable or more attractive. Increasing row height can better fit a header that has been enlarged for emphasis. You might increase column width to display a wide area of text, such as a first and last name, to prevent wrapping of text in a cell.

You can distribute selected columns and rows to ensure that they are the same size and width. Simply select the columns and rows to affect and click Distribute Rows (or Distribute Columns) in the Cell Size group on the Table Tools Layout tab. Distributing rows and columns is an easy way to ensure uniformity within a table.

A simple, but not very precise way to change row height or column width is to position the pointer on a border so that it displays as a double-headed arrow and drag to increase or reduce height or width. For more precision, select a row or column to be adjusted (or select multiple rows or columns). Then change the row height or column width in the Cell Size group on the Table Tools Layout tab. You can also simply right-click the selected row or column and select Table Properties on the shortcut menu. Click the Column tab or Row tab and indicate a measurement in inches, as shown in Figure 3.4.

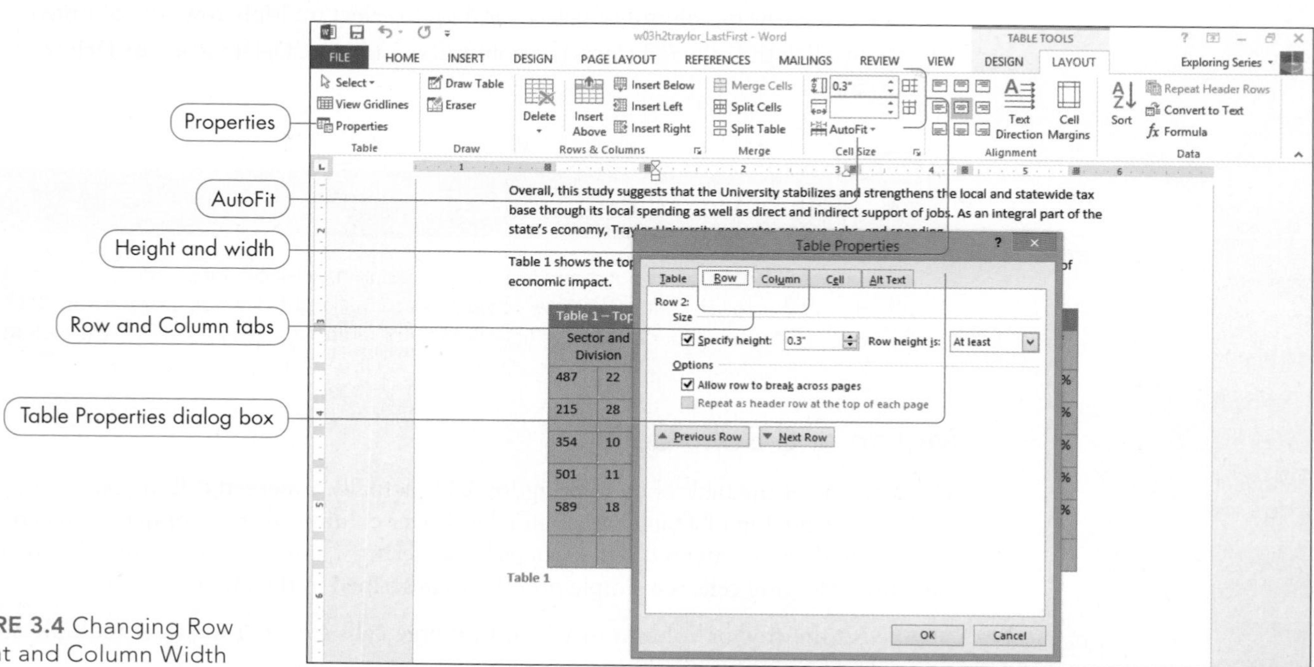

FIGURE 3.4 Changing Row Height and Column Width

TIP AutoFit Columns and Rows

Instead of adjusting individual columns and rows, you can let Word format a table with column and row dimensions that accommodate all cell entries. Click in any table cell and click AutoFit in the Cell Size group on the Table Tools Layout tab (see Figure 3.4). Click AutoFit Contents. Columns and rows are automatically adjusted.

Formatting a Table

After a table is inserted in a document, you can enhance its appearance by applying a predesigned ***table style***, in which colors, borders, shading, and other design elements are coordinated. Edit text within a table by underlining, boldfacing, or italicizing it. You can also align text within cells by selecting an alignment from the Alignment group on the Table Tools Layout tab. Lists or series within cells can be bulleted or numbered, and you can indent table text. Use the Properties control on the Table Tools Layout tab, or right-click a table and select Table Properties, to reposition a table by centering it horizontally or vertically, or simply drag a table to change its position on the page.

Apply Table Styles

Word provides several predesigned table styles that contain borders, shading, font sizes, and other attributes that enhance the readability of a document. Use a table style when:

- You want to create a color-coordinated, professional document.
- You are coordinating a table with elements of Word, Excel, or PowerPoint files, so that the table can be shared among the Office applications.
- You do not have time to design your own custom borders and shading.

As shown in Figure 3.5, the Table Styles gallery provides styles that work well for presenting lists and others that are suited for displaying data in a grid (which typically includes a shaded first row and/or column with headings). Word 2013 has added black-and-white styles to the gallery as well.

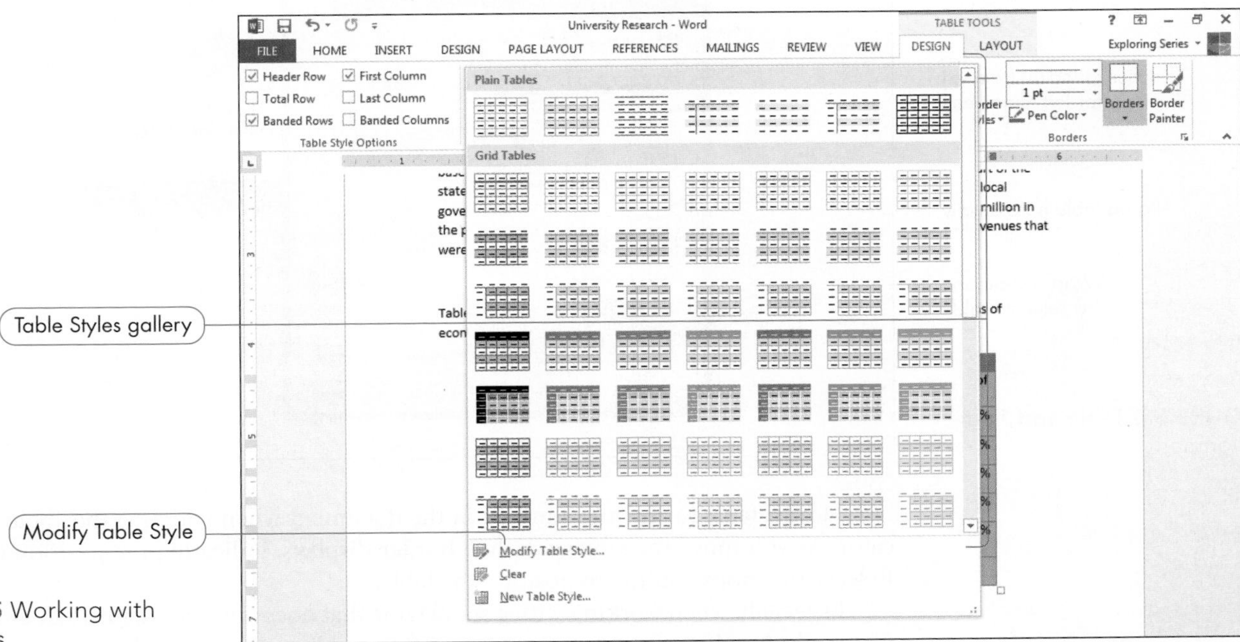

FIGURE 3.5 Working with Table Styles

STEP 3 To apply a table style, click anywhere in a table and click the Table Tools Layout tab, if necessary. Select a style from the Table Styles group (see Figure 3.5) or click More for even more choices. When you point to a style in the gallery, Live Preview shows the result of the style selection in the table.

TIP Modify a Table Style

Having selected a table style, you can modify it when you click Modify Table Style (see Figure 3.5) and adjust the format in the Modify Table Style dialog box. As you modify a table style, you can apply changes to the entire table or to elements such as the header row. In that way, you can adjust a style so that it better suits your purposes for the current table as well as for others that are based on the style. Save the changes for use in the current document only, or in new documents based on the current template.

Adjust Table Position and Alignment

Table alignment refers to the position of a table between the left and right document margins. When you insert a table, Word automatically aligns it at the left margin. To change table alignment, as well as to adjust text wrapping around a table, right-click an empty area of a table cell and select Table Properties. You can also select Properties from the Table Tools Layout tab. The Table tab of the Table Properties dialog box shown in Figure 3.6 includes options to align a table horizontally on the left, center, or right side of a document. If you select left alignment but want the table positioned slightly away from the left margin, you can indicate the number of inches to indent the table from the left.

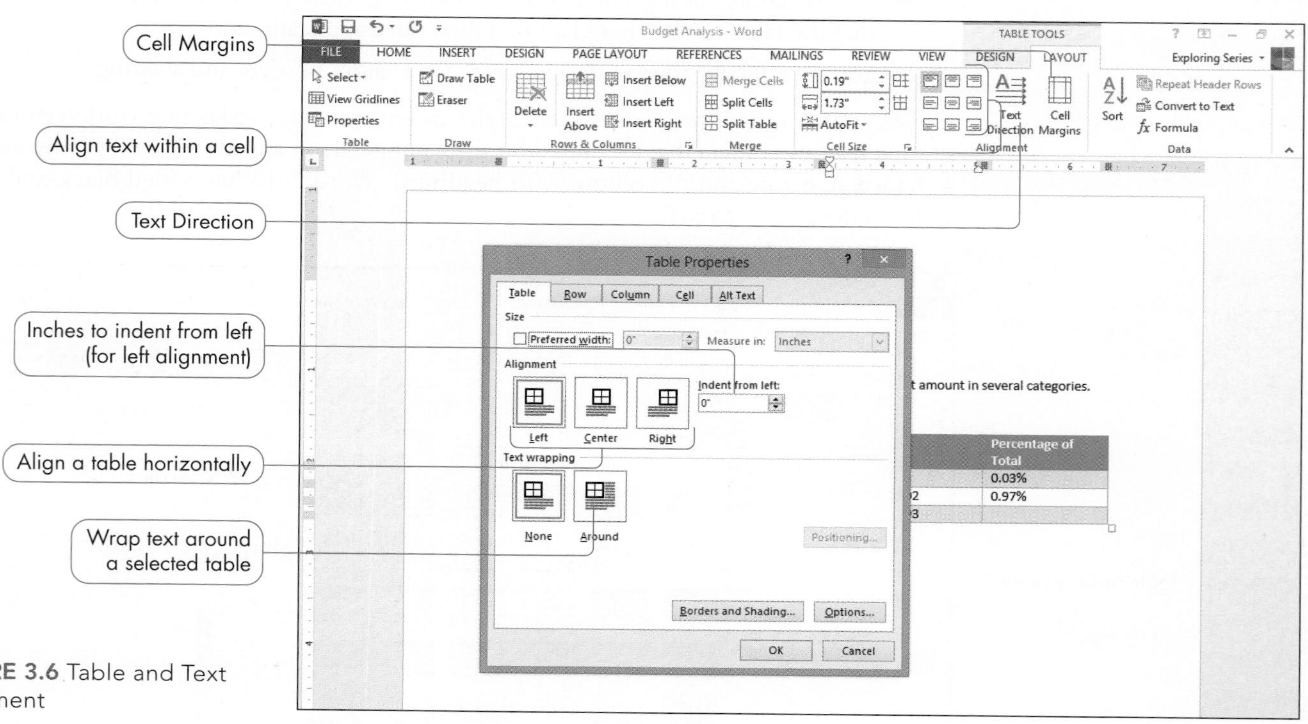

FIGURE 3.6 Table and Text Alignment

Move a table to any location within the document when you drag the Table Select indicator. As you move the table, a dashed border displays, indicating the position of the table. Release the mouse button to position the table.

Especially when working with a small table that does not require much document space, you might find it useful to wrap text around the table so that the table is better incorporated visually into the document. Select Around in the *Text wrapping* section of the Table tab of the Table Properties dialog box (refer to Figure 3.6) to wrap text around a table. Text will wrap on the right side of a left-aligned table, on both sides of a centered table, and on the left side of a right-aligned table. If you select None in the *Text wrapping* section, text is prevented from wrapping, ensuring that text displays only at the top and bottom of a table.

Text within cells can be aligned as well. To align text in a cell, click the cell and select an alignment option in the Alignment group on the Table Tools Layout tab. You can align cell contents both vertically and horizontally within the current cell, as indicated in Figure 3.6.

Format Table Text

Text within a cell can be formatted just as any other text in a document. Select text to format and apply one or more font attributes such as font type, font size, underline, boldface, or italics. Although you can drag text to select it, you can also quickly select all cell contents when you click just inside the left edge of a cell. Select a font attribute to apply to the selected cell text.

By default, text within a cell is oriented horizontally so that it reads from left to right. On occasion, you might want to change that direction. Lengthy column headings can be oriented vertically, so that they require less space. Or perhaps a table includes a row of cells repeating a business telephone number, with each cell designed to be ripped off. Such cells are often in a vertical format for ease of removal. To change cell orientation, click Text Direction in the Alignment group on the Table Tools Layout tab (see Figure 3.6). Each time you click the Text Direction option, text in the current cell or selection rotates.

The Cell Margins command in the Alignment group enables you to adjust the amount of white space inside a cell as well as spacing between cells. With additional empty space shown between typed entries, a table can appear more open and readable.

1. Assume you are describing a table to someone who has never worked with one. Using correct terminology, explain the basics of how a table is organized. ***p. 260***
2. You can create a table by inserting it or by drawing it. When might you prefer one method over the other? ***p. 261***
3. You can align a table and the text within each cell in various ways. Discuss the ways you can apply alignment to a table and its content. ***p. 266***

Hands-On Exercises

Watch the Video
for this Hands-
On Exercise!

MyITLab®
HOE1 Training

1 Tables

The executive summary is the first section of the complete economic impact report for Traylor University. You will present the executive summary at the upcoming board of trustees meeting. Although the summary is already well organized, the data analysis part of the summary needs some attention. Specifically, you will develop tables to organize major findings so the trustees will understand the general outcome of the study.

Skills covered: Create a Table and Insert and Delete Rows and Columns • Merge and Split Cells and Change Row Height and Column Width • Apply Table Styles, Adjust Table Position and Alignment, and Format Table Data

STEP 1 ›› CREATE A TABLE AND INSERT AND DELETE ROWS AND COLUMNS

You will create a couple of tables to summarize study findings, including those tables in the executive summary. As you develop the tables, you will find it necessary to insert rows to accommodate additional data and to delete columns that are not actually required. Refer to Figure 3.7 as you complete Step 1.

Key Findings

Table 1 shows the top industry sectors in which Traylor University makes a difference in terms of economic impact.

Step c: Insert Table 1

Table 1 – Top Industry Sectors		
Sector	Description	Economic Impact
487	Colleges and universities	1,770,281,355
354	Private hospitals	544,871,166
215	Retail interests	1,256,390,688
589	Food services and drinking establishments	321,381,992
501	Real estate companies	348,999,342

Table 2 presents impact sources, with a description of each.

Step g: Draw Table 2

Table 2 – Impact Sources	
Employee Compensation	Salary and wages to faculty and staff circulate in the local and regional economy
Other Expenditures	Non-salary expenditures for goods and services needed to support ongoing operations
Capital Investment	New construction expenditures, creating additional "indirect" and "induced" jobs

FIGURE 3.7 Report Tables

a. Open *w03h1Traylor* and save it as **w03h1Traylor_LastFirst**.

> **TROUBLESHOOTING:** If you make any major mistakes in this exercise, you can close the file, open *w03h1Traylor* again, and then start this exercise over.

b. Click the **VIEW tab** and click **Ruler** in the Show group, if necessary. Scroll through the document to view its contents. Press **Ctrl+End** to move to the end of the document. Type **Table 1 shows the top industry sectors in which Traylor University makes a difference in terms of economic impact.** Press **Enter**.

c. Click the **INSERT tab** and click **Table** in the Tables group. Drag to select a four column by five row table and click.

   A four column by five row table is inserted. The insertion point is located in the top-left cell.

d. Type **Sector** and press **Tab**. Type **Description** and press **Tab**. Type **Category**, press **Tab**, and then type **Economic Impact**.

e. Press **Tab** and type the following entries, tabbing between each item, but not tabbing after the last cell on the last row. Text will wrap, where necessary, in each cell.

487	**Colleges and universities**	**Education**	**1,770,281,355**
354	**Private hospitals**	**Health**	**544,871,166**
589	**Food services and drinking establishments**	**Retail**	**321,381,992**
501	**Real estate companies**	**Land**	**348,999,342**

   You entered data in the table to indicate community and state interests positively impacted by the presence of Traylor University.

> **TROUBLESHOOTING:** If you press Tab after the last entry, a new row is created. Click Undo.

> **TROUBLESHOOTING:** If the insertion point returns to a new line within a cell instead of advancing to another cell or row, you pressed Enter instead of Tab between entries. Press Backspace and press Tab.

f. Press **Ctrl+End** and press **Enter**. Type **Table 2 presents impact sources, with a description of each.** Press **Enter**.

g. Click the **INSERT tab**, click **Table** in the Tables group, and then click **Draw Table**. The mouse pointer appears as a pencil. Drag a box approximately 6 inches wide and 4 inches tall, using the vertical and horizontal rulers as guides. Draw grid lines to create three approximately evenly spaced columns of about 2 inches each. Draw horizontal grid lines to divide the table into four approximately evenly spaced rows of about 1 inch each. Press **Esc**.

> **TROUBLESHOOTING:** It is possible that the lines you draw to form the table are in a color or style other than black. That occurs if someone using the same computer previously selected a different pen color. For this exercise, it will not matter what color the table borders are.

   It is OK if the height and width of rows and columns is not identical. Simply approximate the required height and width for each.

h. Click **Eraser** in the Draw group and click to erase the third vertical gridline from the left in each cell. The table design should result in a two-column, four-row table, although the columns will not be evenly spaced. With the Eraser tool still selected, erase the vertical gridline in the first row, so that the row includes only one column. Click **Eraser** to toggle off the eraser or press **Esc**.

> **TROUBLESHOOTING:** If you make any mistakes while erasing gridlines, press Esc. Then click Undo (repeatedly, if necessary) to undo your actions.

i. With the insertion point in the first row, type **Table 2 - Impact Sources**. (Do not type the period.) Press **Tab** and complete the table as follows:

Employee Compensation	**Salary and wages to faculty and staff circulate in the local and regional economy**
Other Expenditures	**Non-salary expenditures for goods and services needed to support ongoing operations**
Capital Investment	**New construction expenditures, creating additional "indirect" and "induced" jobs**

   Text you type may wrap within a cell. You will resize the columns later, so leave the text as it appears.

j. Position the pointer just above the Category column in Table 1, so that the pointer resembles a downward-directed black arrow. Click to select the column. Click **Delete** in the Rows & Columns group on the TABLE TOOLS LAYOUT tab and select **Delete Columns**.

k. Click anywhere in row 1 of Table 1. Click **Insert Above** in the Rows & Columns group. Click in the first cell in the new row and type **Table 1 - Top Industry Sectors**.

l. Point to the left edge of the horizontal gridline dividing Sector 354 from 589 to display an insert control. Click the + indicator on the end of the insert control to insert a new row. Click the first cell in the new row and type the following. Press Tab between cells. Do not press Tab after the last entry.

215 Retail interests 1,256,390,688

m. Click anywhere in Table 2 to select the table. Use the **insert control** to insert a row above row 2 (*Employee Compensation*). Leave the row blank, for now.

n. Save the document.

STEP 2 » MERGE AND SPLIT CELLS AND CHANGE ROW HEIGHT AND COLUMN WIDTH

As you work with the tables in the executive summary, you notice that the first row of Table 1 is not very attractive. The title in that row should not be limited to one small cell. Instead, you will merge cells in the row to provide more space for the entry. More uniformity of row height and column width might also improve the appearance of Table 2, and you need to add data to the second row. You will explore ways to modify both tables by merging and splitting cells and changing row height and column width. Refer to Figure 3.8 as you complete Step 2.

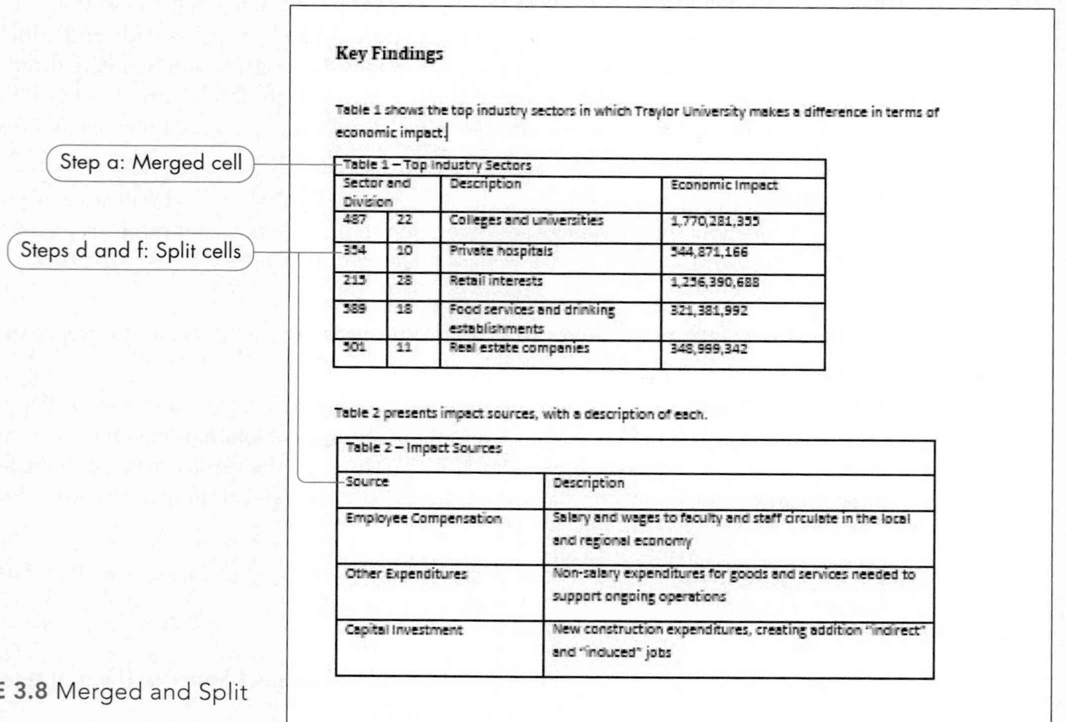

Key Findings

Table 1 shows the top industry sectors in which Traylor University makes a difference in terms of economic impact.

Table 1 – Top Industry Sectors			
Sector and Division		Description	Economic Impact
487	22	Colleges and universities	1,770,281,355
354	10	Private hospitals	344,871,166
215	28	Retail interests	1,256,390,688
589	18	Food services and drinking establishments	321,381,992
501	11	Real estate companies	348,999,342

Table 2 presents impact sources, with a description of each.

Table 2 – Impact Sources	
Source	Description
Employee Compensation	Salary and wages to faculty and staff circulate in the local and regional economy
Other Expenditures	Non-salary expenditures for goods and services needed to support ongoing operations
Capital Investment	New construction expenditures, creating addition "indirect" and "induced" jobs

FIGURE 3.8 Merged and Split Cells

a. Position the mouse pointer just outside the left edge of the first row of Table 1, so that it resembles a right-directed diagonal arrow. Click to select row 1. Click the **TABLE TOOLS LAYOUT tab**, if necessary. Click **Merge Cells** in the Merge group.

You merge the cells in row 1 to create one cell in which text can be better positioned across the table.

b. Position the mouse pointer in row 2 on the border between the first and second column of Table 1. The pointer appears as a double-headed arrow. Click and drag to the left to reduce the column width to approximately 1 inch to better accommodate the contents of the column.

c. Position the mouse pointer just outside the left edge of row 2 in Table 1 and drag down to select row 2 as well as all remaining rows. With the TABLE TOOLS LAYOUT tab selected, click the **top spin arrow** beside Height in the Cell Size group to change the height to **0.3"**.

Row height of rows 2, 3, 4, 5, and 7 is adjusted to 0.3". However, because text wraps in row 6, the height of that row is not adjusted to 0.3".

> **TROUBLESHOOTING:** If items in the first column are selected instead of every cell in every row, you selected cells instead of rows. Repeat step c, making sure to position the mouse pointer *outside* the table and very near the left edge.

The first column of Table 1 lists a sector in which an area of economic impact is identified. Each sector should be further identified by a division, which you now need to add. You will split column 1 into two columns so that the first column includes the sector, and the second contains the associated division.

d. Position the mouse pointer just *inside* the left edge of the third row of Table 1 (containing *487*). The pointer should resemble a right-directed black arrow. Drag down to select the contents of the first column in row 3 as well as all remaining rows. Click **Split Cells** in the Merge group. Check to ensure that *2* displays as the number of columns and *5* displays as the number of rows. Make adjustments, if necessary. Deselect **Merge cells before split**. Click **OK**.

> **TROUBLESHOOTING:** If all sector numbers appear in the first cell, instead of remaining in separate cells, you did not deselect *Merge cells before split*. Click Undo and repeat step d.

e. Click in the first cell on the second row in Table 1 (containing *Sector*). Type **and Division** after *Sector*. Complete the data underneath the heading as follows, using Figure 3.8 as a guide:

487	**22**
354	**10**
215	**28**
589	**18**
501	**11**

f. Click in the second row of Table 2. Click **Split Cells** in the Merge group. Check to ensure that *2* displays as the number of columns and *1* displays as the number of rows. Adjust, if necessary. Click **OK**. Place the mouse pointer on the vertical gridline dividing the two columns in row 2. The pointer displays as a double-headed arrow. Click and drag to the left to align the gridline with the vertical gridline in row 3.

g. Click in the first cell of row 2 in Table 2 and type **Source**. Press **Tab**. Type **Description**.

h. Click the **Table Select indicator** (at the top-left corner of Table 2) to select the entire table. Click the **bottom spin arrow** beside *Height* in the Cell Size group to reduce the height to **0.01"**.

Row height of all rows in Table 2 is reduced, resulting in a more attractive table.

i. Save the document.

STEP 3 » APPLY TABLE STYLES, ADJUST TABLE POSITION AND ALIGNMENT, AND FORMAT TABLE DATA

The tables included in the *Key Findings* section are complete with respect to content, but you realize that they could be far more attractive with a bit of color and appropriate shading. You will explore Word's gallery of table styles. You will bold and center column headings and explore aligning the tables horizontally on the page. Refer to Figure 3.9 as you complete Step 3.

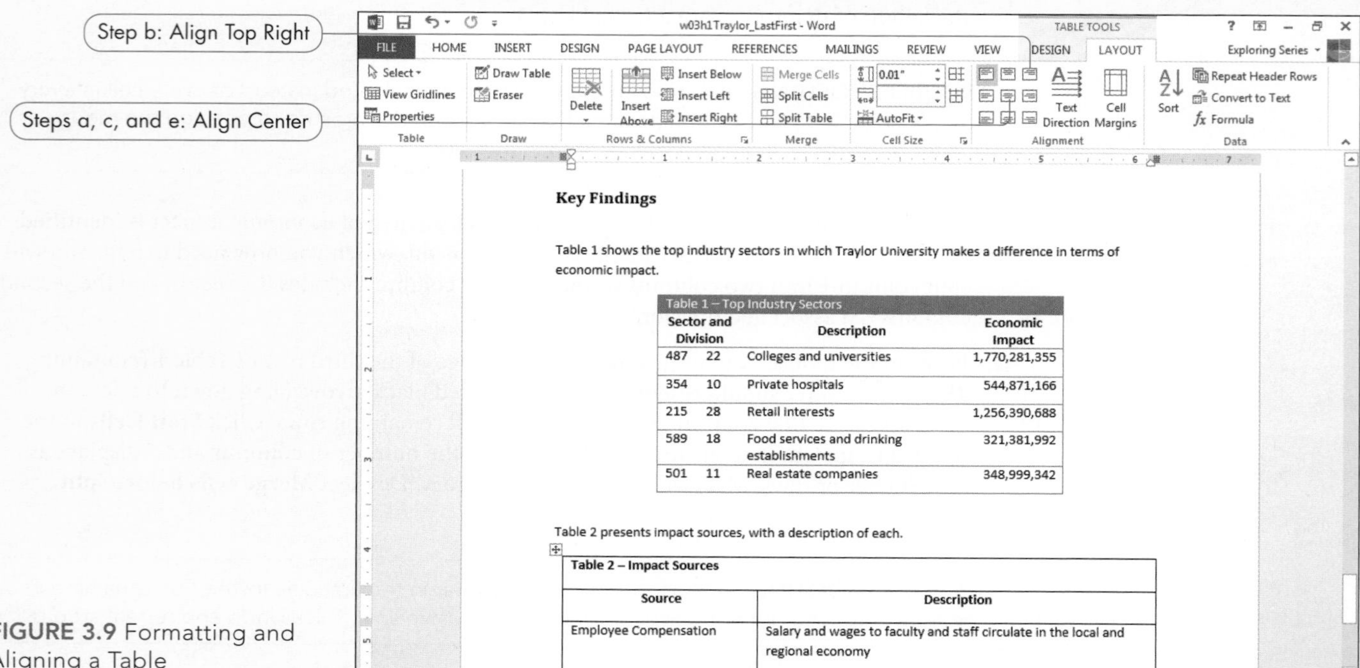

FIGURE 3.9 Formatting and Aligning a Table

a. Select the second row in Table 1. Click the **TABLE TOOLS LAYOUT tab,** if necessary. Click **Align Center** in the Alignment group to center text in row 2 both vertically and horizontally within each cell.

b. Select the cells containing numbers in the rightmost column of Table 1 (beginning with *1,770,281,355* and ending with *348,999,342*). Click **Align Top Right** in the Alignment group. Click anywhere to deselect the cells. Position the mouse pointer on the right border of the rightmost column so that it resembles a double-headed arrow. Drag to the left to reduce the column so that the width is approximately 1", better accommodating the contents of the column.

Numbers are usually right aligned, so you right align numbers in Table 1.

c. Select the second row in Table 2, containing column headings. Click **Align Center** in the Alignment group. With the column headings selected, click the **HOME tab** and click **Bold** in the Font group. Bold the contents of row 1 in Table 2. Bold the contents of the first two rows in Table 1.

d. Click anywhere in Table 1. Click the **TABLE TOOLS DESIGN tab** and click **More** in the Table Styles group. Scroll through the gallery and select **List Table 3 - Accent 1** (third row, second column under *List Tables*).

The table style removed some of the formatting from step c, applying color-coordinated font color, shading, and a colored border. The style also removed the inside vertical borders.

e. Remove bold formatting from all numeric entries in column 1 of Table 1 (*Sector and Division*). Click the **TABLE TOOLS LAYOUT tab**. Select row 2 in Table 1 (containing column headings) and click **Align Center** in the Alignment group. Ensure that all entries in row 2 of Table 1 are bold.

f. Click the **VIEW tab** and click **One Page** in the Zoom group to view the current page. Note that the tables are not centered on the page horizontally. Click **100%** in the Zoom group.

g. Right-click anywhere in Table 1 and select **Table Properties**. Click **Center** in the Alignment group of the Table tab in the Table Properties dialog box to center the table horizontally. Click **OK**. Repeat this technique to center Table 2 horizontally. Click **One Page** in the Zoom group to view the effects of the realignment. Click **100%**.

h. Save the document and keep it onscreen if you plan to continue with the next Hands-On Exercise. If not, close the document and exit Word.

Advanced Table Features

Developing a basic Word table to organize data in columns is a fairly simple task. With a bit more effort, you can enhance a table using features that improve its readability and summarize table data. Many of the tasks typically associated with an Excel spreadsheet can be accomplished in a Word table, such as summing or averaging a numeric column or row. By using advanced table features in Word, you can create tables that not only organize data, but also present table contents in an attractive, easy-to-read format.

In this section, you will use Word to enhance tables with borders and shading of your choice. In addition, you will sort table data and learn to total and average numbers in a table. You will learn to include captions with tables, so that tables are correctly identified. By indicating that a heading row should recur on each printed page in which a table displays, you will ensure that table contents are easily identified, even if table rows are carried over to another page. Finally, you will simplify the task of creating a table by converting plain text into a table, and you will learn to convert a table to plain text.

Managing Table Data

A table is often used to summarize numeric data. For example, the table shown in Figure 3.10 organizes a list of students receiving a particular college scholarship. Scholarship amounts vary, so there is no standard amount awarded. The last row of the table shows a total scholarship amount, although for illustration, the formula that produces the total is shown in Figure 3.10. The table is sorted by student last name. Because the company awards many individual scholarships, there is a likelihood that the table could extend beyond one page. In that case, the first row (containing table headings) should be set to recur across all pages so that table data is identified by column headings, regardless of the page on which the table is continued. Using Word, you can manage table data to include calculations, sort table contents, and cause heading rows to recur across pages. Planning a table ahead of time is always preferable to recognizing the need for a table after text has already been typed. However, in some cases, you can convert plain text into a table. Conversely, after a table has been created, you can convert table text back to plain text.

Calculate Using Table Formulas and Functions

Organizing numbers in columns and rows within a Word table not only creates an attractive and easy-to-read display, but also simplifies the task of totaling, averaging, or otherwise summarizing those numbers. A ***formula*** is a calculation that can add, subtract, divide, or multiply cell contents. Although Word is not designed to perform heavy-duty statistical calculations, it is possible to determine basic items, such as a sum, an average, or a count, of items in cells. Word provides ***functions***, which are built-in formulas, to simplify the task of performing basic calculations. A function uses values in a table to produce a result. For example, the SUM function totals values in a series of cells, whereas the COUNT function identifies the number of entries in a series of cells. The total scholarship amount shown in Figure 3.10 was calculated with a SUM function. In most cases, a function provides an alternative to what would otherwise be a much lengthier calculation.

Recipient Name	Major	Date Awarded	Amount Awarded	Amount Spent	Amount Left
Alim, Nisheeth	Accounting	5/15/2016	1,850	650	
Blair, Walter	Finance	4/23/2016	1,200	1,200	
Diminsha, Ahmed	Management	2/1/2016	1,350	728	
Don, Clarice	Finance	6/4/2016	2,550	1,014	
Edge, Latisha	Accounting	2/16/2016	1,500	0	
Gonzalez, Patricia	Entrepreneurship	3/12/2016	1,225	1,225	
Green, Amber	CIS	5/10/2016	2,890	856	
James, Greg	Marketing	4/23/2016	2,335	2,010	
McDonald, Barbara	Accounting	5/15/2016	1,675	981	
Marish, Tia	CIS	2/10/2016	1,895	1,400	
Pintlala, Sarah	Management	6/2/2016	2,350	2,482	
Tellez, Anthony	Finance	8/1/2016	3,950	2,100	
Wallace, April	Marketing	2/28/2016	1,100	250	
		TOTAL	=SUM(ABOVE)		

Function to show total scholarship amount

FIGURE 3.10 Managing Table Data

Use a Formula

To use formulas, you must understand the concept of cell addresses. A Word table is very similar to an Excel worksheet, so if you are familiar with Excel, you will understand how Word addresses cells and develops formulas. Each cell in a Word table has a unique address. Columns are labeled with letters (although such labeling is understood—letters do not actually display above each column) and rows with numbers. For example, Nisheeth Alim's award amount, shown in Figure 3.10, is in cell D2 (second row fourth column). The amount he has spent is in cell E2, and the amount left is to be calculated in cell F2. The formula to calculate the amount left is =D2-E2, which subtracts the amount spent from the award amount. When indicating a cell reference, you do not have to capitalize the address. For example, =A10+A11 is evaluated identically to =a10+a11.

Unlike the way you would manage formulas in an Excel worksheet, you do not actually type a formula or function in a cell. Instead, you use a Formula dialog box to build a formula or use a function. To create a formula in a Word table:

STEP 1»

1. Click in the cell that is to contain the result of the calculation. For example, click in cell F2 to begin the formula to determine the amount of scholarship award left.
2. Click the TABLE TOOLS LAYOUT tab, if necessary.
3. Click Formula in the Data group.
4. The Formula dialog box (see Figure 3.11) displays with a suggested function in the Formula box. The suggested =SUM formula is not appropriate because you are not summing the two values in row 2; instead, you are subtracting one from the other. Backspace to remove the function from the box, but leave the = (because all formulas must begin with =).
5. In calculating Nisheeth's remaining amount, you would subtract his amount spent from his amount awarded. Type D2-E2, subtracting the contents of cell E2 from those of cell D2. The resulting formula should read *=D2-E2*. Because you began the formula in cell F2, the resulting amount left will be shown there when the formula is complete.
6. Click the *Number format* arrow and select a format. Click OK.

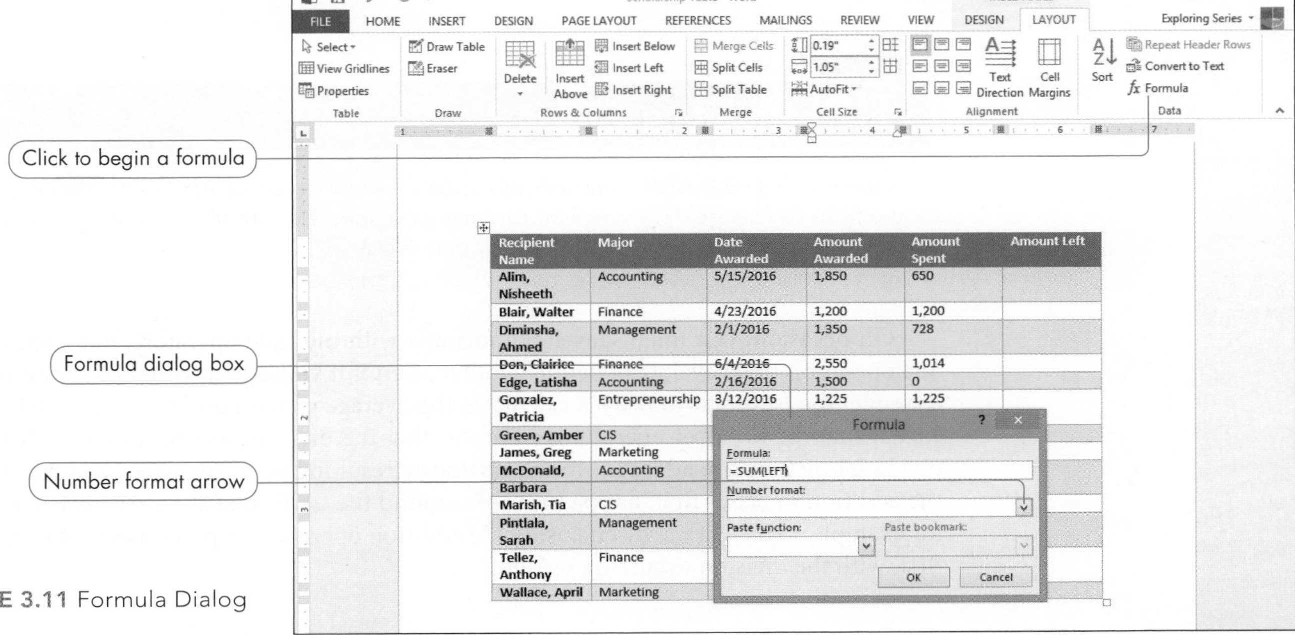

FIGURE 3.11 Formula Dialog Box

Number Format

When identifying a number format, you have several options to select from when you click Number Format in the Formula dialog box. A # in a format indicates that leading zeroes will be suppressed. A *0* in a format indicates that leading zeroes will be displayed. Other format options enable you to display dollar signs or percent signs in the formula result.

A formula can contain more than one mathematical operator. The minus sign in the formula described in the preceding steps is considered an *operator*. Mathematical operators that you can use in creating formulas are described below.

- Exponentiation: ^
- Multiplication: *
- Division: /
- Addition: +
- Subtraction: -

When more than one operator is included in a formula, evaluation of the formula follows a set procedure, called the ***order of operations***, or ***order of precedence***. The order of operations requires that the following operations be evaluated in order from highest to lowest.

1. Parenthetical information (anything in parentheses)
2. Exponentiation
3. Multiplication and Division—evaluated from left to right if both operators are present in a formula
4. Addition and Subtraction—evaluated from left to right if both operators are present in a formula

As an example, the expression =C12+C15*1.8 is evaluated as follows: Multiply cell C15 by 1.8 and add the result to cell C12.

Updating a Table

A formula in a table is not automatically updated when the contents of cells referenced by the formula change. However, you can manually update a formula. Simply right-click the cell containing the formula and select Update Field.

On occasion, you might develop a formula with multiple operators, but want to force one operation to be evaluated before another, even if it violates the order of operations. For example, the formula =B3+B4/2 calculates the average of the numbers in cells B3 and B4, except that the order of operations indicates that the division will occur first. That would divide B4 by 2 before adding it to B3, obviously resulting in an incorrect average. To force the addition to occur first, use parentheses around the terms that should be calculated first, for example, =(B3+B4)/2. By enclosing the addition operation in parentheses, it is evaluated first, with the division occurring second.

TIP Inserting Equations in a Document

Occasionally, you might find it necessary to include a formula, or complicated equation, in a document, even outside a table. Most math symbols and operators are not located on the keyboard; however, you can create a formula so that it seamlessly integrates with surrounding text when you make selections from the Symbols group on the Insert tab. Word even makes common equations, such as the area of a circle, available with a single click.

To use Word's equation tools to assist in developing a formula in a document (or to insert a common equation), click the Insert tab and click Equation in the Symbols group. Select from options on the Equation Tools Design tab to create a formula, no matter how complex. A formula is created in a placeholder, so you can manage it independently of surrounding text. To insert a common equation, such as the Quadratic Formula, click Equation on the Equation Tools Design tab.

Use a Function

To determine a final scholarship amount in the Total row of the table shown in Figure 3.10, you could click in the cell underneath the last scholarship award amount and add all cells in the fourth column, as in =D2+D3+D4+D5+D6…, continuing to list cells in the range through D14. A ***range*** is a series of adjacent cells. Although the formula would produce a final total, the formula would be extremely lengthy. Imagine the formula length in a more realistic situation in which hundreds of students received a scholarship! A much more efficient approach would be to include a SUM function, in which you indicate, by position, the series of cells to total. For example, the function to produce a total scholarship amount is =SUM(ABOVE). Similarly, a function to produce an average scholarship amount is =AVERAGE(ABOVE). In fact, you can select from various table functions, as shown in Table 3.1. The positional information within parentheses is referred to as an ***argument***. Positional information refers to the position of the data being calculated. You can use positional notation of ABOVE, BELOW, LEFT, or RIGHT as arguments. An argument of ABOVE indicates that data to be summarized is located above the cell containing the function. A similar function to determine an average scholarship amount is =AVERAGE(ABOVE). Although not a comprehensive list, the functions shown in Table 3.1 are commonly used. Note that an argument will be included within parentheses in each function.

TABLE 3.1 Table Functions

Function	Action
=SUM(argument)	Totals a series of cells
=AVERAGE(argument)	Averages a series of cells
=COUNT(argument)	Counts the number of entries in a series of cells
=MAX(argument)	Displays the largest number in a series of cells
=MIN(argument)	Displays the smallest number in a series of cells

To place a function in a table cell:

1. Click in the cell that is to contain the result of the calculation. For example, click in cell D15 of the table shown in Figure 3.10 to include a function totaling all scholarship amounts.
2. Click the TABLE TOOLS LAYOUT tab, if necessary.
3. Click Formula in the Data group.
4. The Formula dialog box (see Figure 3.11) displays with a suggested =SUM function in the Formula box. To select a different function, press Backspace or delete the existing function and click *Paste function*. Select a function and type an argument. Click OK.

Combining Arguments

Combine arguments in a function to indicate cells to include. For example, =SUM(ABOVE,BELOW) totals numeric cells above and below the current cell. =SUM(LEFT,ABOVE) totals numeric cells to the left and above the current cell, whereas =SUM(RIGHT,BELOW) totals numeric cells to the right and below the current cell. Combine any two arguments, separated by a comma, to indicate cells to include.

Sort Data in a Table

Columns of text, dates, or numbers in a Word table can be sorted alphabetically, chronologically, or numerically. The table shown in Figure 3.10 is sorted alphabetically in ascending order by student name. It might be beneficial to sort the data in Figure 3.10 by date, so that scholarship awards are shown in chronological order. Or you could sort table rows numerically by award amount, with highest awards shown first, followed in descending order by lesser award amounts. You might even want to sort awards alphabetically by major, with scholarship award amounts within programs of study shown in order from low to high. Such a sort uses a primary category (major, in this case) and a secondary category (award amount). You can sort a Word table by up to three categories.

To sort table rows:

STEP 2»

1. Click anywhere in the table (or select the column to sort by) and click the TABLE TOOLS LAYOUT tab.
2. Click Sort in the Data group.
3. Indicate or confirm the primary category, or column, to sort by (along with the sort order, either ascending or descending), as shown in Figure 3.12.
4. Select any other sort columns and indicate or confirm the sort order.
5. Specify whether the table includes a header row and click OK.

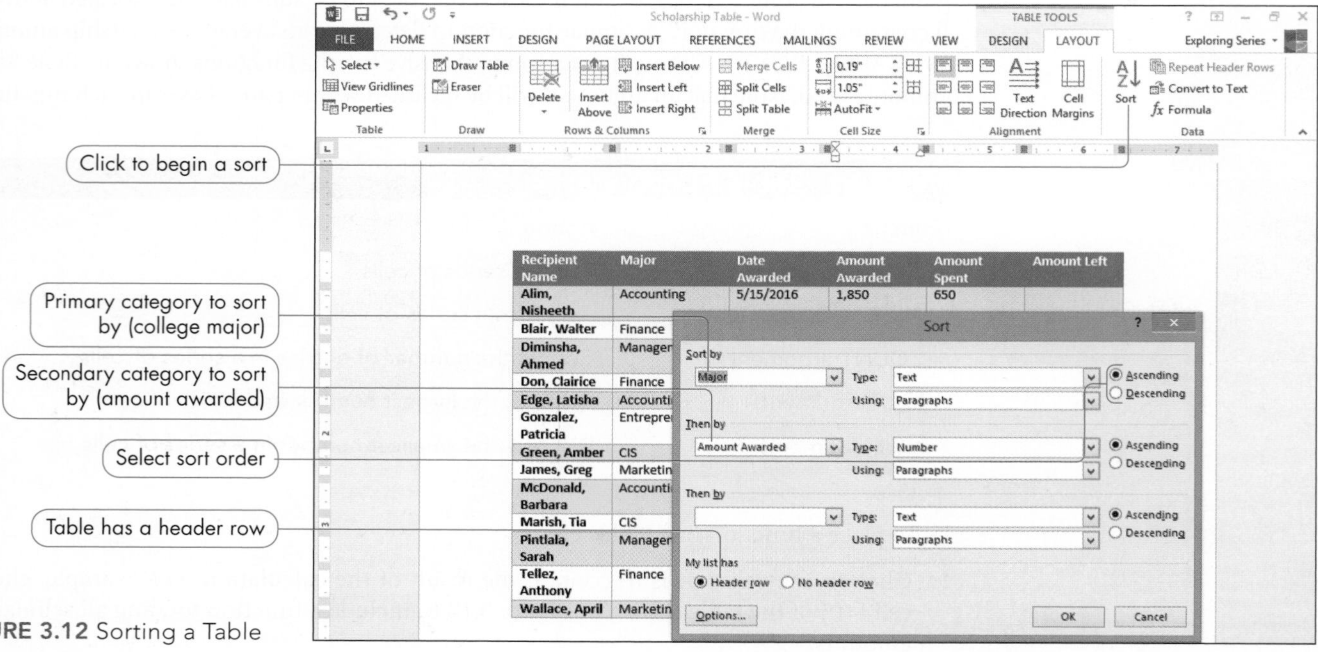

FIGURE 3.12 Sorting a Table

Include a Recurring Table Header

A table is typically comprised of a heading row followed by several rows of data. The heading row in Figure 3.10 includes text identifying the first column as *Recipient Name*, the second as *Major*, and so forth. With a large number of students receiving scholarships, the table could easily extend beyond one page. In that case, table rows on the additional pages would have no identifying heading row. To remedy that situation, you can cause one or more rows of headings to repeat at the top of every page on which a table extends. Repeated table heading rows are visible only in Print Layout view. To cause one or more header rows to recur:

1. Select the heading row(s).
2. Click the TABLE TOOLS LAYOUT tab, if necessary, and click Repeat Header Rows in the Data group.

Converting Text to a Table (and Converting a Table to Text)

Suppose you are working with a list of items organized into two columns, separated by a tab. You know that if the columns were organized as a table, you could easily apply a table style, sort rows, and even use formulas to summarize numeric information. Conversely, you might identify a need to convert table text to plain text, removing special table features and organizing columns into simple tabbed columns.

To convert text into a table:

STEP 4

1. Select text to be converted.
2. Click the INSERT tab and click Table in the Tables group.
3. Click *Convert Text to Table.*
4. Select options from the Convert Text to Table dialog box (see Figure 3.13), including the number of columns and rows to include.
5. Click OK.

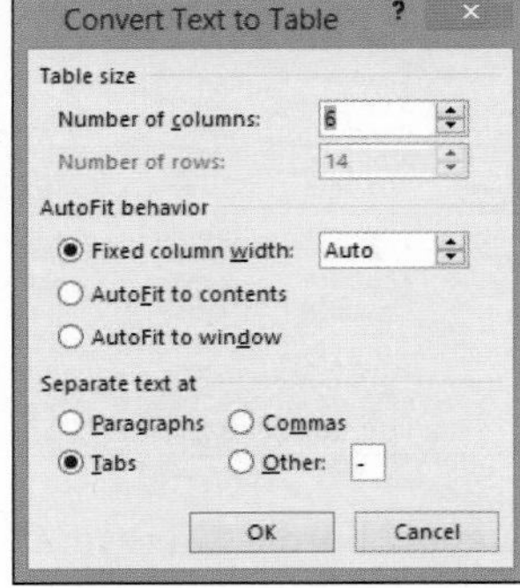

FIGURE 3.13 Converting Text to a Table

To convert a table into text:

1. Click anywhere in the table.
2. Click the TABLE TOOLS LAYOUT tab, if necessary.
3. Click *Convert to Text* in the Data group.
4. In the *Convert Table to Text* dialog box, indicate how table text is to be divided (see Figure 3.14).
5. Click OK.

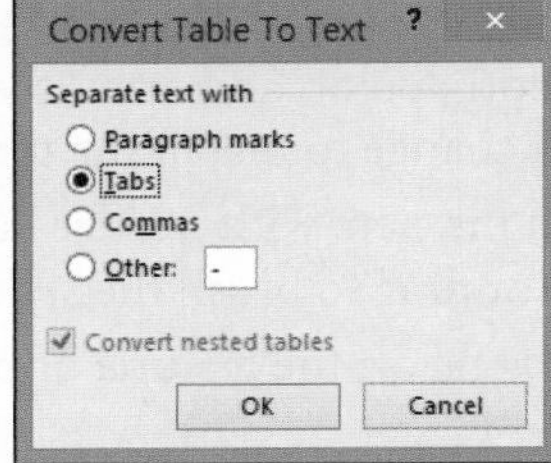

FIGURE 3.14 Converting a Table to Text

Enhancing Table Data

You include data in a table to organize it in a way that makes it easy for a reader to comprehend. Using table styles and table formulas, you have learned to configure a table so it is attractive and so that it provides any necessary summary information. To further enhance table data, you can select custom shading and borders, and you can include images in cells. Certain writing styles require the use of captions to identify tables included in reports; you will learn to work with captions in this section.

Include Borders and Shading

Enhancing a table with custom borders and shading is a simple task when you use Word 2013's Border tools. A ***border*** is a line style you can apply to individual cells, an entire table, or to individual areas within a table. You can design your own border, selecting a pen color, line style, and line weight, or you can select from a gallery of predesigned borders that coordinate with existing table styles. New to Word 2013 is ***Border Painter***, a tool that enables you to easily apply border settings you have identified (or a border style selected from the Borders gallery) to one or more table borders. Using Border Painter, you can apply preselected borders by simply "brushing" them on a table border with the mouse. Figure 3.15 shows various border selections that are available on the Table Tools Design tab when a table is selected.

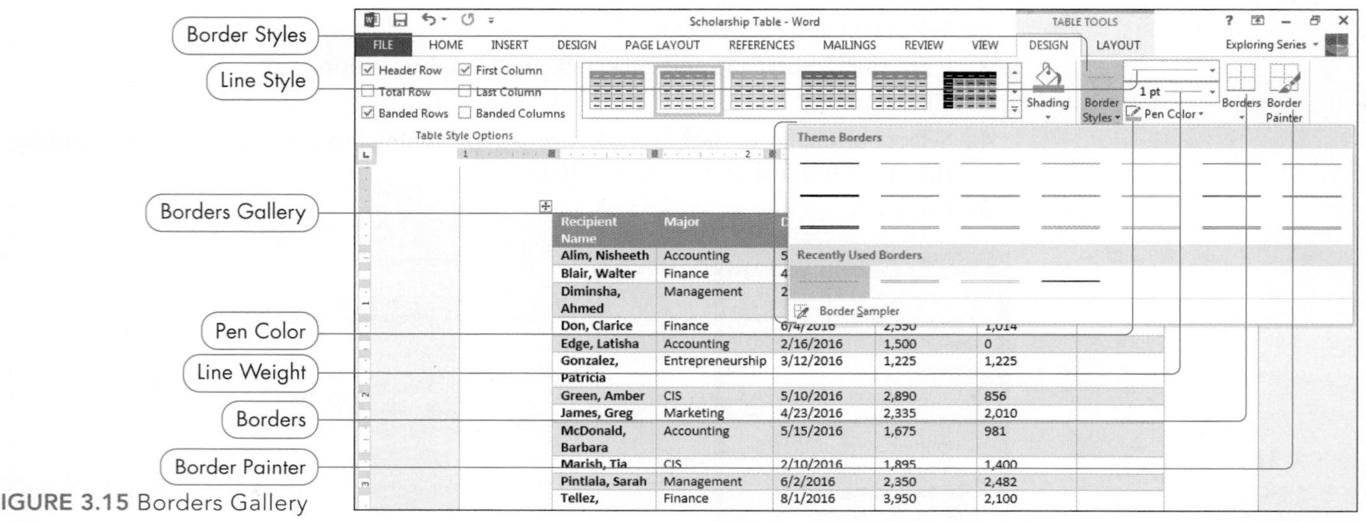

FIGURE 3.15 Borders Gallery

With a table selected, you can apply borders in several ways:

- To create a *custom* border:
  1. Choose a pen color, line style, and line weight (refer to Figure 3.15).
  2. The pointer displays as an ink pen, with Border Painter active. Click a table border to apply the border selection (or click and drag to brush the selection on several borders).
  3. Click Border Painter to toggle off the feature, or press Esc.
- To apply a border *style*:

STEP 3

  1. Click Border Styles (refer to Figure 3.15) and select a border style. Each border style combines border width, color, and size. If you change the document theme later, the border style will change to match the theme.
  2. The pointer displays as an ink pen, with Border Painter active. Click a table border to apply the border style (or drag to brush the style on several borders).
  3. Click Border Painter to toggle off the feature, or press Esc.

Regardless of whether you are applying a custom border or a predesigned style, you can select the borders to which to apply the selection when you click Borders (see Figure 3.15) and select a type (Outside Borders, Right Border, Left Border, etc.).

As shown in Figure 3.16, the Design tab also includes options for selecting shading. ***Shading*** applies color or a pattern to the background of a cell or group of cells. You might want to apply shading to a heading row to emphasize it, setting it apart from the rows beneath. Click the Borders arrow in the Table Styles group and select a border position, or click *Borders and Shading* to display the *Borders and Shading* dialog box, which includes additional options related to border and shading design.

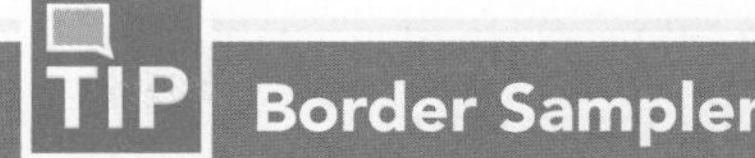

TIP Border Sampler

Having applied a custom border or border style to one or more borders in a table, you might want to copy the selection to other table borders. Using Border Sampler, you can easily accomplish that task. Click the Border Styles arrow and click Border Sampler. The mouse pointer becomes an eyedropper tool; click a table border that you want to copy. Automatically, the pointer switches to the Border Painter tool, as indicated by the ink pen designation, so you can brush another border to apply the border selection.

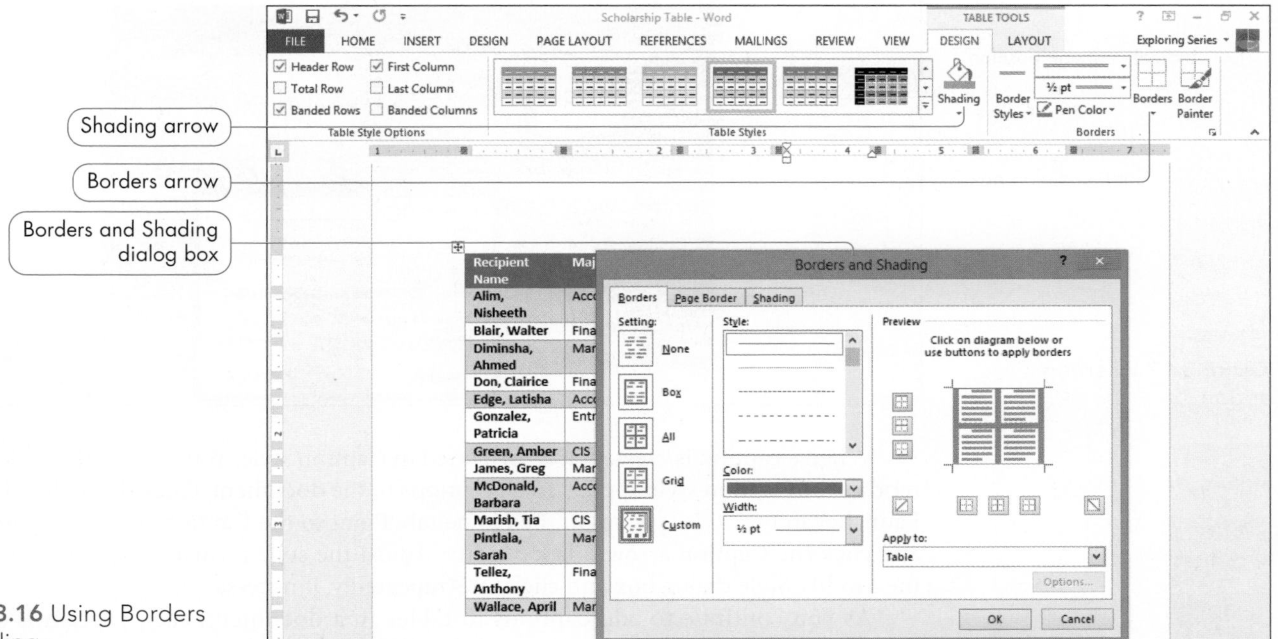

FIGURE 3.16 Using Borders and Shading

When a table is created, it is automatically formatted in Table Grid style, with all cells bordered with a 1/2 pt single line border. To use the *Borders and Shading* dialog box to change borders in a table:

1. Select the cells to modify (or click the Table Select indicator to select the entire table).
2. Click the Borders arrow in the Table Styles group on the TABLE TOOLS DESIGN tab. Click *Borders and Shading* to display the *Borders and Shading* dialog box (see Figure 3.16).
3. Select from options in the dialog box to add, remove, or modify table and cell borders. In addition, you can select shading when you click the Shading tab in the dialog box.

Include a Table Caption

A ***caption***, such as *Table 1*, is a numbered item of text that identifies a table, figure, or other object in a Word document. A caption typically includes a *label*, such as the word *Figure* or *Table*, followed by a sequential number that can be automatically updated with the addition of new tables or captioned objects.

To include a table caption:

1. Click a cell in the table.
2. Click the REFERENCES tab and click Insert Caption in the Captions group. The Caption dialog box displays, as shown in Figure 3.17.

3. Click the Label arrow and select a type (Table, Figure, or Equation), or click New Label and type a new label.
4. Click the Position arrow and indicate a caption position—above or below the table.
5. If you prefer that the label is excluded from display, select *Exclude label from caption.*
6. Click Numbering to select a numbering style (*1, 2, 3*, or *A, B, C*, for example).
7. Click OK (repeatedly, if necessary).

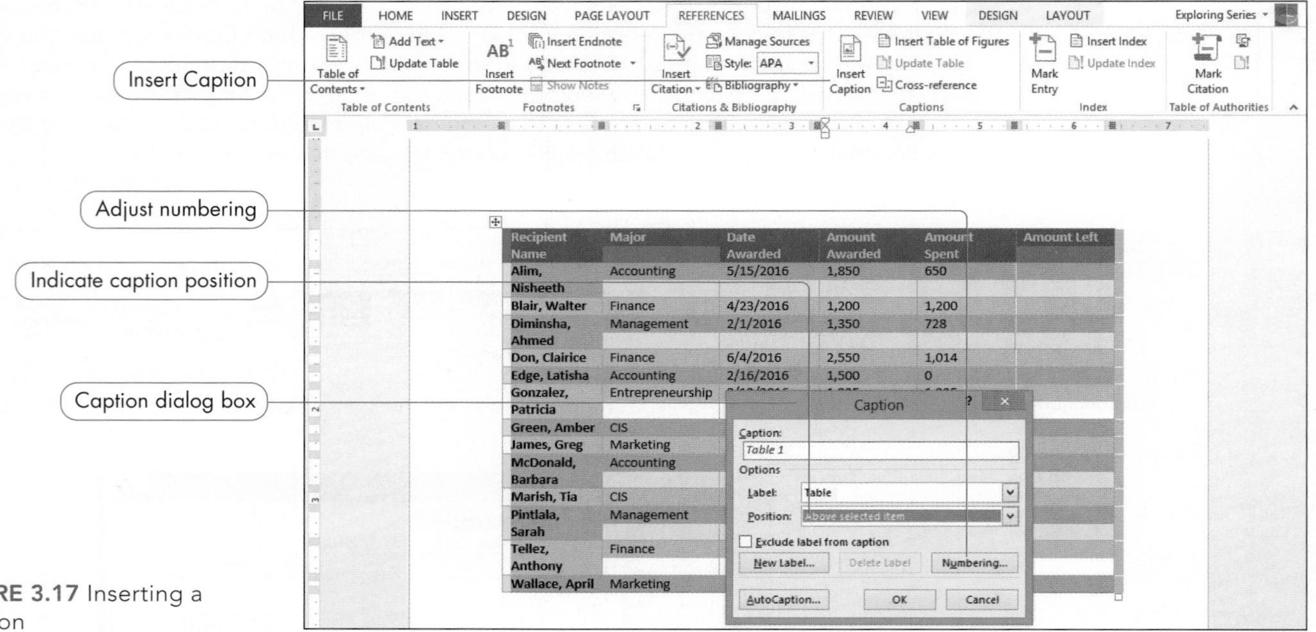

FIGURE 3.17 Inserting a Caption

When a caption is created, it is formatted in Caption style. You can use the Styles pane to modify the Caption style applied to all captions in the document. Click the Styles Dialog Box Launcher in the Styles group on the Home tab. Point to the Caption style in the Styles pane and click the Caption arrow. Click Modify. Adjust the style format by making selections in the Modify Style dialog box and click OK (repeatedly, if necessary).

As you continue to add captions to tables in a document, each caption is shown in sequence. For example, if the first caption is *Table 1*, then the second caption you add will automatically be labeled *Table 2*. If you should insert a table between existing tables, the caption you add to the table will automatically be shown in sequence, with captions on following tables updated accordingly. However, if you delete a table from a document, remaining captions are not automatically renumbered. To update all captions in a document, press Ctrl+A to select all document text, right-click anywhere in the selection, and then select Update Field. To update only one caption, right-click the caption number and click Update Field.

***Quick* Concepts**

1. When summing a long column of values in a Word table, would you use a function or a formula? In general terms, how would the function or formula be developed? ***p. 277***
2. A table contains several columns; among them is one containing employee last name and another containing department. You want to sort the table so that departments are shown in alphabetical order, with employee last names sorted alphabetically within departments. What steps would you follow to complete that sort operation? ***p. 278***
3. A table is split between two pages, with a heading row identifying columns on the first page. However, the heading row does not display above the table rows that continue on the second page, so it is difficult to determine what each column represents. How would you remedy that situation? ***p. 278***
4. What steps would you take to convert a list of names and addresses into a table? ***p. 279***

Hands-On Exercises

Watch the Video for this Hands-On Exercise!

MyITLab®
HOE2 Training

2 Advanced Table Features

As you continue to work with the *Key Findings* section of the executive summary, you will modify the two tables you previously created. The first table, showing major areas in which the university contributed to the economy, will be modified to include a total row and to indicate the percentage represented by each category. You will explore Word's Borders Gallery as you customize the tables to reflect the color scheme of the university. Adding a caption to each table will serve to identify the table and will be useful for your assistant when she prepares a Table of Figures later. You will also apply a sort order to each table to organize each in a more understandable manner.

Skills covered: Calculate Using Table Formulas • Sort Data in a Table and Include Recurring Rows • Include Borders and Shading and a Table Caption • Convert Text to a Table

STEP 1 » CALCULATE USING TABLE FORMULAS

Table 1 includes a numeric column showing Traylor University's economic impact in several sectors. You will add a row showing the total for all of the sectors. You will also insert a column showing the percentage of the total represented by each sector's value. Refer to Figure 3.18 as you complete Step 1.

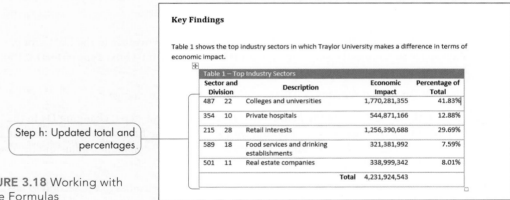

Key Findings

Table 1 shows the top industry sectors in which Traylor University makes a difference in terms of economic impact.

Table 1 – Top Industry Sectors

Sector and Division		Description	Economic Impact	Percentage of Total
487	22	Colleges and universities	1,770,281,355	41.83%
354	10	Private hospitals	544,871,166	12.88%
215	28	Retail interests	1,256,390,688	29.69%
589	18	Food services and drinking establishments	321,381,992	7.59%
501	11	Real estate companies	338,999,342	8.01%
		Total	4,231,924,543	

Step h: Updated total and percentages

FIGURE 3.18 Working with Table Formulas

a. Open the *w03h1Traylor_LastFirst* document if you closed it after the last Hands-On Exercise and save it as **w03h2Traylor_LastFirst**, changing *h1* to *h2*.

b. Scroll to page 5, if necessary, to display Table 1 and Table 2. Click in the last row of Table 1 and click the **TABLE TOOLS LAYOUT tab**, if necessary. Click **Insert Below** in the Rows & Columns group on the TABLE TOOLS LAYOUT tab. Click in the third column of the new row (the Description column) and type **Total**. Bold the word *Total*. With Total still selected, click the **TABLE TOOLS LAYOUT tab**, if necessary, and click **Align Top Right** in the Alignment group.

   You have added a row in which to place a total economic impact figure.

c. Click in the cell immediately below the last economic impact number. Click **Formula** in the Data group. The suggested function, *=SUM(ABOVE)*, will total all values in the row. Click the **Number format arrow** and select **(#,##0)**. Click **OK**.

   The total economic impact is 4,241,924,543.

TROUBLESHOOTING: If the total is incorrect, you most likely typed a number incorrectly in the column above. Refer to Figure 3.9 in the previous Hands-On Exercise for the correct numbers. Make any necessary corrections in Table 1. The total will not show the correct number until you complete step h to update the field.

d. Click **Insert Right** in the Rows & Columns group. Click the last cell in the second row of the new column and type **Percentage of Total**. If necessary, center align the new entry.

Text will wrap in the cell. You have added a new column that will show the percentage each sector's value represents of the total economic impact. You will create a formula to obtain that result.

e. Click in the third row of the last column (in the *Colleges and universities* row). Click **Formula** in the Data group. Press **Backspace** repeatedly to remove the suggested function from the Formula box. Type **=D3/D8*100**. Click the **Number format arrow**, scroll through the options, and then select **0.00%**. Click **OK**.

The formula divides the value in the cell to the left (cell D3) by the total value of economic impact in the last row of the table (cell D8). The result is multiplied by 100 to convert it to a percentage. The format you chose displays the result with a percent sign and two places to the right of the decimal. The percentage represented by *Colleges and universities* is 41.73%.

TROUBLESHOOTING: If an error message displays in the cell instead of a percentage, or if the percentage is incorrect, click Undo and repeat step e.

f. Click in the last column of the *Private hospitals* row. Click **Formula** in the Data group. Press **Backspace** to remove the suggested function from the Formula box. Type **=D4/D8*100**. Click **OK**.

The number format remains at 0.00%, so there is no need to change it.

g. Click in the last column of the *Retail interests* row and repeat step f, changing *D4* in the formula to **D5** (because you are working with a value on the fifth row). Create a formula for *Food services and drinking establishments* and *Real estate companies,* adjusting the row reference in each formula.

h. Change the number in Economic Impact for *Real estate companies* in the second to last row in the table from *348,999,342* to **338,999,342**. Right-click the total in the next row, *4,241,924,543*, and click **Update Field** to update the total. Right-click the percentage of total for *Real estate companies* in the last column of the second to last row. Click **Update Field**. Right-click each remaining percentage figure in the last column, updating each field.

i. Save the document.

STEP 2 ›› SORT DATA IN A TABLE AND INCLUDE RECURRING ROWS

You will sort Table 1 so that the dollar amounts in Table 1 are arranged in descending order. That way, it is very clear in which sectors the university had the most impact. You will sort Table 2 in alphabetical order by Source. The resulting table will appear well organized. After inserting text from another file, Table 2 will be split between two pages. You will repeat Table 2 heading rows to better identify table rows that are carried over to another page. Refer to Figure 3.19 as you complete Step 2.

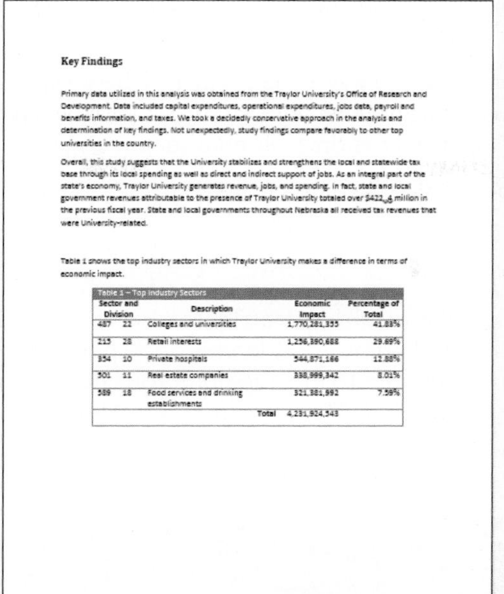

Key Findings

Primary data utilized in this analysis was obtained from the Traylor University's Office of Research and Development. Data included capital expenditures, operational expenditures, jobs data, payroll and benefits information, and taxes. We took a decidedly conservative approach in the analysis and determination of key findings. Not unexpectedly, study findings compare favorably to other top universities in the country.

Overall, this study suggests that the University stabilizes and strengthens the local and statewide tax base through its local spending as well as direct and indirect support of jobs. As an integral part of the state's economy, Traylor University generates revenue, jobs, and spending. In fact, state and local government revenues attributable to the presence of Traylor University totaled over $422.4 million in the previous fiscal year. State and local governments throughout Nebraska all received tax revenues that were University-related.

Table 1 shows the top industry sectors in which Traylor University makes a difference in terms of economic impact.

Table 1 – Top Industry Sectors				
Sector and Division		Description	Economic Impact	Percentage of Total
487	22	Colleges and universities	1,770,281,355	41.83%
215	28	Retail interests	1,256,390,688	29.69%
354	10	Private hospitals	544,871,166	12.88%
501	11	Real estate companies	338,999,342	8.01%
589	18	Food services and drinking establishments	321,381,992	7.59%
		Total	4,231,924,543	

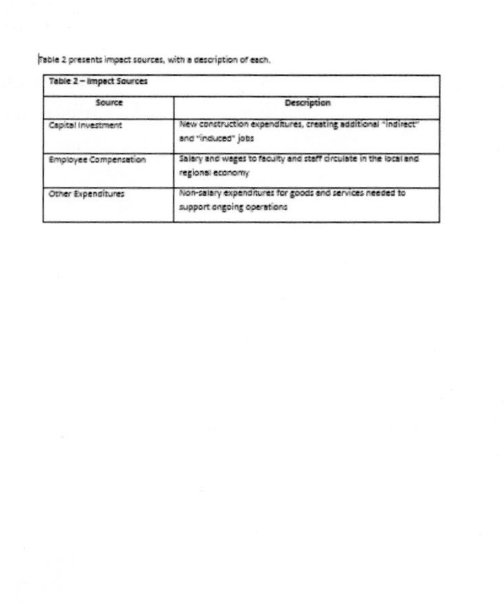

Table 2 presents impact sources, with a description of each.

Table 2 – Impact Sources	
Source	Description
Capital Investment	New construction expenditures, creating additional "indirect" and "induced" jobs
Employee Compensation	Salary and wages to faculty and staff circulate in the local and regional economy
Other Expenditures	Non-salary expenditures for goods and services needed to support ongoing operations

FIGURE 3.19 Sorted Tables

a. Show nonprinting characters if they are not already displayed. Position the mouse pointer just outside the left edge of the third row of Table 1 (beginning with *487*). The pointer should be a right-oriented white arrow. Drag down to select the five rows containing a description. Do not include the final total row.

You have selected the table rows that are to be sorted. You do not want to include the first two rows or the final total row in the sort because they do not contain individual values to sort.

b. Click the **TABLE TOOLS LAYOUT tab**, if necessary. Click **Sort** in the Data group. Click the **Sort by arrow** and select **Column 4**. Click **Descending** (in the *Column 4* section). Click **OK**.

You have sorted the five rows containing a sector name (*Colleges and universities*, *Retail interests*, etc.) in descending order by the value in the fourth column (Economic Impact). It is clear that the sector most affected is *Colleges and universities*.

c. Position the mouse pointer just outside the left edge of the third row of Table 2. Drag to select the remaining rows. Click **Sort** in the Data group. Make sure *Column 1* displays in the **Sort by box**. Click **Ascending** and click **OK**.

You have sorted the three rows containing a source (Capital Investment, etc.) in ascending order alphabetically.

d. Click before the words *Table 1* in the first multi-line paragraph on page 5. Press **Enter**. Click before the second blank paragraph under *Key Findings*. Click the **INSERT tab**, click the **Object arrow** in the Text group, and then select **Text from File**. Navigate to your student data files and double-click **w03h2KeyFindings**.

> **TROUBLESHOOTING:** If you see an Object dialog box instead of text from the inserted file, you clicked *Object* instead of the *Object arrow*. Close the dialog box and repeat step d.

e. Scroll to the bottom of page 5 and note that Table 2 is now split between pages, with several rows on page 6. Those rows are not identified by column headings (Source and Description). Select the first two rows of Table 2 (on page 5). Click the **TABLE TOOLS LAYOUT tab**, if necessary. Click **Repeat Header Rows** in the Data group.

The first two rows of Table 2 repeat above the remaining rows of Table 2 shown on page 6.

f. Click **Undo**. Click before the words *Table 2 presents impact sources* on page 5. Press **Ctrl+Enter** to insert a manual page break.

You determine that the way Table 2 is divided between pages 5 and 6 is very unattractive, even with repeating heading rows, so you remove the repeating rows and insert a manual page break to force the entire table onto another page.

g. Save the document.

STEP 3 » INCLUDE BORDERS AND SHADING AND A TABLE CAPTION

You expect to add more tables later, but will go ahead and format Tables 1 and 2 so they are more attractive and color-coordinated. You will explore border and shading options, learning to "paint" borders and considering border selections from the Borders Gallery. Because you expect to include numerous figures throughout the report, you will insert captions to identify those tables. Refer to Figure 3.20 as you complete Step 3.

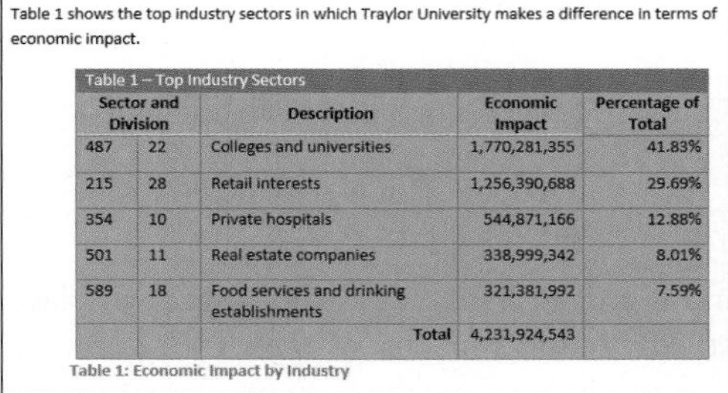

Table 1 shows the top industry sectors in which Traylor University makes a difference in terms of economic impact.

Table 1 – Top Industry Sectors				
Sector and Division		Description	Economic Impact	Percentage of Total
487	22	Colleges and universities	1,770,281,355	41.83%
215	28	Retail interests	1,256,390,688	29.69%
354	10	Private hospitals	544,871,166	12.88%
501	11	Real estate companies	338,999,342	8.01%
589	18	Food services and drinking establishments	321,381,992	7.59%
		Total	4,231,924,543	

Table 1: Economic Impact by Industry

Table 2 presents impact sources, with a description of each.

Table 2 – Impact Sources	
Source	Description
Capital Investment	New construction expenditures, creating addition "indirect" and "induced" jobs
Employee Compensation	Salary and wages to faculty and staff circulate in the local and regional economy
Other Expenditures	Non-salary expenditures for goods and services needed to support ongoing operations

Table 2: Sources of Economic Impact

FIGURE 3.20 Including Borders, Shading, and Captions

a. Scroll to page 6. Click the **Table Select indicator** to select Table 2. Click the **TABLE TOOLS DESIGN tab** and click **Border Styles** in the Borders group. Click **Double solid lines, 1/2 pt, Accent 4** (third row, fifth column under *Theme Borders*). Click the **Borders arrow** in the Borders group and click **All Borders**.

> **TROUBLESHOOTING:** If you do not see the Table Select indicator, click any cell in the table and move to the top-left corner of the table to click the Table Select indicator.

Traylor University's school colors are purple and gold, so you will design tables with that color combination. Here, you apply a border style (double solid line) to all cells in Table 2.

b. Select row 1 in Table 2. Click the **Shading arrow** in the Table Styles group and select **More Colors**. Click the **Custom tab** and adjust Red to **240**, Green to **239**, and Blue to **29**. Click **OK**.

c. Select rows 2, 3, 4, and 5 in Table 2. Click the **Shading arrow** and click **Purple, Accent 4, Lighter 40%** (fourth row, eighth column).

d. Click **Pen Color** in the Borders group. Click the **Yellow color** shown under *Recent Colors*. The mouse pointer displays as an ink pen, indicating that Border Painter is active. Drag the pen along the horizontal border dividing row 1 from row 2. Next, drag the pen along the horizontal border dividing row 2 from row 3. Do the same for the next two horizontal borders dividing row 3 from row 4, and row 4 from row 5. Drag the pen along the vertical border dividing the first column from the second (in the purple shaded area). Press **Esc** to turn off the Border Painter.

> **TROUBLESHOOTING:** If you make a mistake as you color borders, press Esc to turn off the pen and click Undo (repeatedly, if necessary) to undo your action(s). Repeat step d.

e. Select the first two rows in Table 2. Right-click the selection and click **Table Properties**. Click the **Row tab**. Make sure *Specify height* is checked and change the height to **0.4"**. Click **OK**.

The first two rows in Table 2 are resized slightly.

f. Click **Border Painter** in the Borders group. Scroll to page 5 and drag the pen along the horizontal border dividing row 2 from 3 in Table 1. Do the same for the horizontal borders dividing all other rows, but do not drag the bottom border of the table or the horizontal border dividing row 1 from row 2. Drag the pen along the vertical gridlines dividing all columns, but do not drag the outside borders of the table. Press **Esc**.

> **TROUBLESHOOTING:** If you make a mistake as you color borders, press Esc to turn off the pen and click Undo (repeatedly, if necessary) to undo your action(s). Repeat step f.

You used Border Painter to "paint" the currently selected yellow border on the gridlines dividing rows and columns in Table 1.

g. Click anywhere in Table 1 and click the **Table Select indicator** to select Table 1. Click the **Border Styles arrow**. Select **Double solid lines, 1/2 pt, Accent 4** (third row, fifth column). Click the **Borders arrow** and click **Outside Borders**.

You selected a border style and applied it to the outside borders of the selected table.

h. Select **row 1** in Table 1. Click the **Shading arrow** in the Table Styles group and click **Purple Accent 4** (first row, eighth column). Select **rows 2 through 8** in Table 1. Click the **Shading arrow** and click **Purple, Accent 4, Lighter 40%** (fourth row, eighth column under *Theme Colors*).

i. Click the **Table Select indicator** to select Table 1. Click the **Borders arrow** and click **Borders and Shading**. Click **All** in the Setting area and scroll up and click the first selection in the Style box (single purple line). Click **Width** and select **1 pt**. Click **OK**.

You decide a more conservative format would be attractive, so you use the *Borders and Shading* dialog box to apply a purple border between all cells.

j. Click anywhere in Table 1. Click the **References tab**. Click **Insert Caption** in the Captions group. With the insertion point immediately after Table 1 in the Caption box, type : and press the **Spacebar**. Type **Economic Impact by Industry**. Click the **Position arrow** and select **Below selected item**. Click **OK**. Click the **HOME tab** and click **Increase Indent** in the Paragraph group. Click anywhere in Table 2 and insert a caption below the selected item. The caption should read **Table 2: Sources of Economic Impact**.

k. Click the **HOME tab**. Click the **Styles Dialog Box Launcher**. Scroll down and point to *Caption* in the Styles pane. Click the **Caption arrow** and click **Modify**. Change the font size to **11** and the font color to **Purple, Accent 4**. Click **OK**. Close the Styles pane.

You modified the Caption style to include purple font so the caption text coordinates with the table color scheme.

l. Save the document.

STEP 4 » CONVERT TEXT TO A TABLE

One additional table is necessary to complete the executive summary, but the necessary data are arranged in a tabbed format instead of a table. You will convert the columns of data into a table. Refer to Figure 3.21 as you complete Step 4.

Table 2 presents impact sources, with a description of each.

Table 2 – Impact Sources	
Source	**Description**
Capital Investment	New construction expenditures, creating addition "indirect" and "induced" jobs
Employee Compensation	Salary and wages to faculty and staff circulate in the local and regional economy
Other Expenditures	Non-salary expenditures for goods and services needed to support ongoing operations

Table 2: Sources of Economic Impact

Table 3 summarizes the total employment impact of Traylor University.

Description	Total Employment
Colleges and universities	902 jobs
Nursing and residential care facilities	420 jobs
Offices of physicians and health practitioners	319 jobs
Retail stores – general merchandise	311 jobs
Retail stores – food and beverage	281 jobs
Private hospitals	178 jobs

Table 3: Economic Impact by Employment

FIGURE 3.21 Caption Dialog Box

a. Press **Ctrl+End** to move to the end of the document. Press **Enter** twice. Click the **INSERT tab**, click the **Object arrow**, and then select **Text from File**. Navigate to the location of your student data files and double-click **w03h2Text**.

   Columned text is inserted in the document, with each column separated by a tab.

b. Select the newly inserted text, beginning with *Description* and ending with *178 jobs*. Click **Table** in the Tables group and click **Convert Text to Table**. Click **OK** to accept the default settings of 2 columns and 7 rows.

c. Click **More** in the Table Styles group. Click **Grid Table 2 - Accent 4** (second row, fifth column in the *Grid Tables* section).

d. Click in the newly created table, click the **REFERENCES tab**, and then click **Insert Caption** in the Captions group. The caption should read **Table 3: Economic Impact by Employment**. Ensure that the position is *Below selected item*. Click **OK**.

   Note that the caption is formatted with the purple font that you indicated earlier.

e. Click before the blank paragraph preceding Table 3 and type **Table 3 summarizes the total employment impact of Traylor University.**

f. Save the document and exit Word. Submit the file based on your instructor's directions.

Mail Merge

At some point in your personal or professional life, you will need to send the same document to a number of different people. The document might be an invitation, a letter, or a memo. For the most part, document text will be the same, regardless of how many people receive it. However, certain parts of the document are likely to be unique to the recipient, such as the inside address included in a letter. Consider the task of conducting a job search. Having prepared a cover letter to accompany your résumé for a job search, you will want to include the recipient's name and address in the letter so that the document appears to have been prepared especially for the company to which you are applying. Word's ***Mail Merge*** feature enables you to easily generate those types of documents. Mail Merge is a process that combines content from a ***main document*** and a ***data source***, with the option of creating a new document.

Mail merge is often used to send personalized e-mail messages to multiple recipients. Unlike sending e-mail to a group of recipients or listing recipients as blind carbon copies, creating a mail-merged e-mail makes it appear as if each recipient is the sole addressee. You can also use mail merge to send an e-mail in which the message is personalized for each recipient, perhaps referring to the recipient by name within the body of the message.

You might use Mail Merge to create a set of form letters, personalizing or modifying each one for the recipient. A ***form letter*** is a document that is often mass produced and sent to multiple recipients. The small amount of personal information included in the form letter—perhaps the salutation or the recipient's address—can be inserted during the mail merge procedure. In this section, you will learn to use Mail Merge to create a main document and select a recipient list. You will then combine, or merge, the main document and data source to produce a document that is personalized for each recipient.

Creating a Mail Merge Document

The mail merge process begins with a document that contains wording that remains the same for all recipients. In the case of the cover letter used in your job search, the main document would include paragraphs that are intended for all recipients to read—perhaps those that describe your qualifications and professional goals. ***Merge fields*** are also included in the main document. A merge field is a placeholder for variable data, which might include a recipient's address or a salutation directed to a particular person. During the mail merge process, a ***data source*** that contains variable data is combined with the main document to produce personalized documents. You might merge a data source of employer addresses with a main document to produce a personalized letter for each potential employer. Mail merge also enables you to print labels or envelopes, obtaining addresses from a data source.

To begin a mail merge, open a main document, which you might have prepared earlier. The main document is likely to contain merge fields for combining with a data source. You will learn to create merge fields later in this chapter. The main document can also be blank, as would be the case when preparing mailing labels that you intend to merge with an address data source. Click the Mailings tab and click Start Mail Merge in the Start Mail Merge group. Although you can select from several document types, including Letters, E-mail Messages, Envelopes, Labels, or a Directory, you can simply click Start Mail Merge Wizard for a step-by-step approach to developing a merged document. A ***wizard*** guides you through a process one step at a time, asking questions and using the responses to direct the end result. In the case of the Mail Merge wizard, step-by-step directions display in the Mail Merge pane on the right side of the main document. The self-explanatory options for the current step appear in the top portion of the pane, with a link to the next step shown at the bottom of the same pane. Figure 3.22 shows the first step in the Mail Merge process.

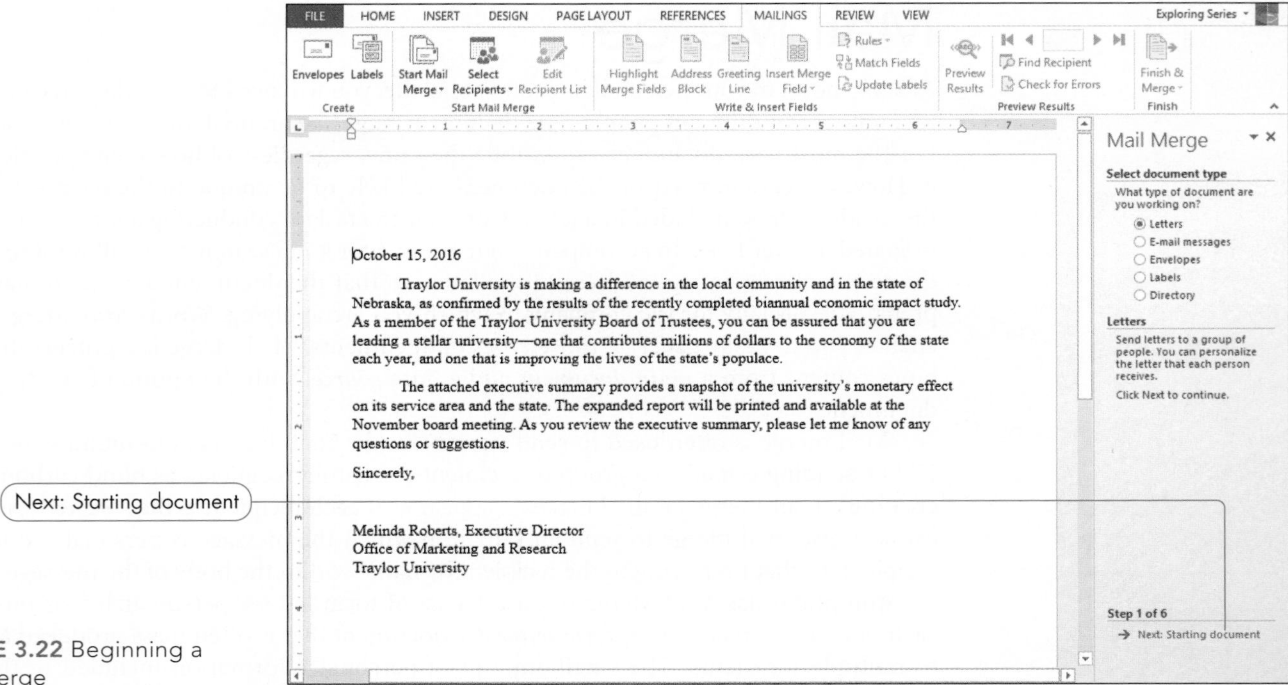

FIGURE 3.22 Beginning a Mail Merge

Click the link to the next step at the bottom of the pane to move forward in the mail merge process. In subsequent steps, you can click a link to the previous step to correct any mistakes you might have made. As is typical of wizards, the Mail Merge wizard simplifies a task so you can follow obvious links to complete the process.

Select or Create a Recipient List

STEP 1

The first step in the mail merge process, shown in Figure 3.22, is to identify the type of document you are producing—letters, e-mail messages, envelopes, labels, or directory. If creating a form letter in which certain variable data will be inserted, you can begin with the main document, or letter, open (if you have already included merge fields in the document). If you have not yet created the form letter, you will begin with a blank document. Similarly, you would begin with a blank document when creating envelopes or labels. After indicating the document type, click *Next: Starting document* at the bottom of the Mail Merge task pane (refer to Figure 3.22). To use the current document, which is the default selection, click *Next: Select recipients*. Otherwise, you can select *Start from existing document* to begin the mail merge with an existing mail merge document, making changes to the content or recipients. If a template is available, you can also begin with a template.

The data source provides variable data to include in the document, such as recipient name, address, phone number, and company information. Each item of information is referred to as a ***field***. For example, the data source might include a last name field, a first name field, a street address field, etc. A group of fields for a particular person or thing, presented as a row in the data source, is called a ***record***. Figure 3.23 illustrates a sample data source. Note that each record in the data source represents a person, with each record subdivided into fields. The data source shown in Figure 3.23 is an Access database table.

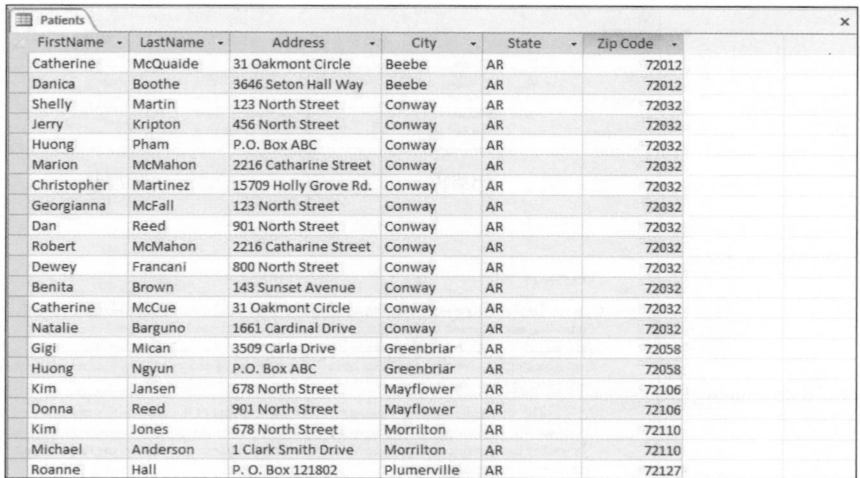

FirstName	LastName	Address	City	State	Zip Code
Catherine	McQuaide	31 Oakmont Circle	Beebe	AR	72012
Danica	Boothe	3646 Seton Hall Way	Beebe	AR	72012
Shelly	Martin	123 North Street	Conway	AR	72032
Jerry	Kripton	456 North Street	Conway	AR	72032
Huong	Pham	P.O. Box ABC	Conway	AR	72032
Marion	McMahon	2216 Catharine Street	Conway	AR	72032
Christopher	Martinez	15709 Holly Grove Rd.	Conway	AR	72032
Georgianna	McFall	123 North Street	Conway	AR	72032
Dan	Reed	901 North Street	Conway	AR	72032
Robert	McMahon	2216 Catharine Street	Conway	AR	72032
Dewey	Francani	800 North Street	Conway	AR	72032
Benita	Brown	143 Sunset Avenue	Conway	AR	72032
Catherine	McCue	31 Oakmont Circle	Conway	AR	72032
Natalie	Barguno	1661 Cardinal Drive	Conway	AR	72032
Gigi	Mican	3509 Carla Drive	Greenbriar	AR	72058
Huong	Ngyun	P.O. Box ABC	Greenbriar	AR	72058
Kim	Jansen	678 North Street	Mayflower	AR	72106
Donna	Reed	901 North Street	Mayflower	AR	72106
Kim	Jones	678 North Street	Morrilton	AR	72110
Michael	Anderson	1 Clark Smith Drive	Morrilton	AR	72110
Roanne	Hall	P. O. Box 121802	Plumerville	AR	72127

FIGURE 3.23 Mail Merge Data Source

A data source can be obtained from:

- A Word document that contains records stored in a table, where each row after the first is a record and the top row contains headings (field names)
- An Access database table
- An Excel worksheet, where each row after the first contains records and the top row shows headings (field names)
- A group of Outlook Contacts

The first row in the data source is called the ***header row*** and identifies the fields in the remaining rows. Each row beneath the header row contains a record, and every record contains the same fields in the same order—for example, Title, FirstName, LastName, etc.

If you do not have a preexisting list to use as a data source, you can create one. Select *Type a New List* in the Mail Merge pane to create a data source. Click Create in the *Type a new list* area. A New Address List dialog box displays with the most commonly used fields for a mail merge. You can enter data immediately or click Customize Columns to add, delete, or rename the fields to meet your particular needs. The data source is saved as an Access database file.

Use an Excel Worksheet as a Data Source

Because an Excel worksheet organizes data in columns and rows, it can be used to develop a data source that can be merged with a main document during a mail merge. With only a bit of introduction, you can learn to enter data in an Excel worksheet, designing columns and rows of data so that a lengthy address list can be easily maintained. With millions of columns and rows available in a single worksheet, Excel can store a huge number of records, making them available as you create a mail merge document. Figure 3.24 shows an Excel worksheet that can be used as a data source. Note the header row, with records beneath.

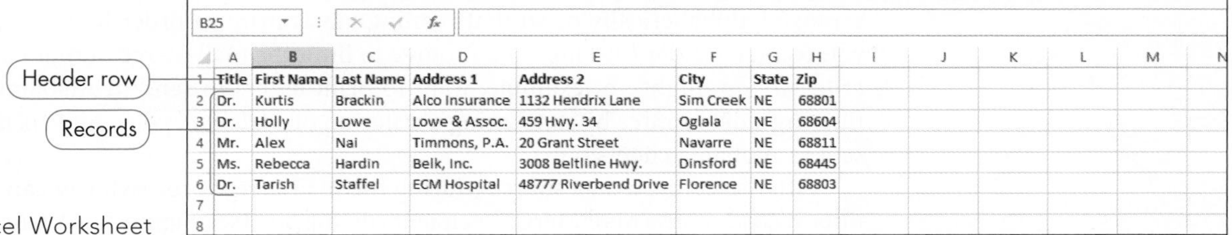

	A	B	C	D	E	F	G	H
1	Title	First Name	Last Name	Address 1	Address 2	City	State	Zip
2	Dr.	Kurtis	Brackin	Alco Insurance	1132 Hendrix Lane	Sim Creek	NE	68801
3	Dr.	Holly	Lowe	Lowe & Assoc.	459 Hwy. 34	Oglala	NE	68604
4	Mr.	Alex	Nai	Timmons, P.A.	20 Grant Street	Navarre	NE	68811
5	Ms.	Rebecca	Hardin	Belk, Inc.	3008 Beltline Hwy.	Dinsford	NE	68445
6	Dr.	Tarish	Staffel	ECM Hospital	48777 Riverbend Drive	Florence	NE	68803
7								
8								

FIGURE 3.24 Excel Worksheet

To merge a Word document with an Excel data source, select *Use an existing list* in Step 3 of the mail merge process (see Figure 3.25). Click Browse. Navigate to the Excel workbook and double-click the file.

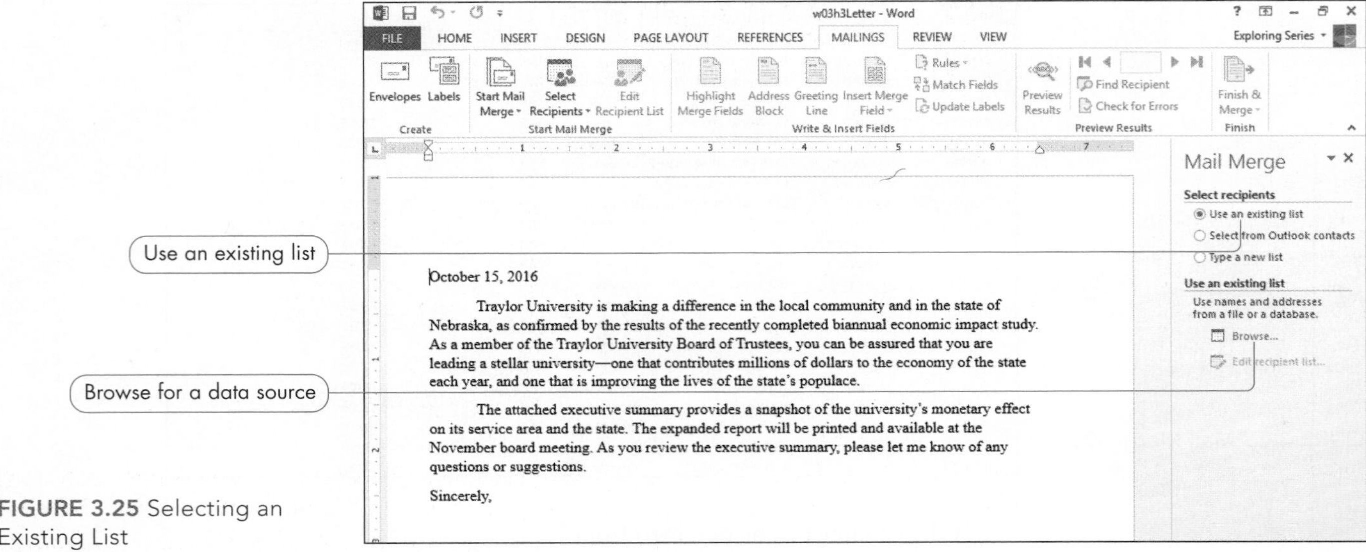

FIGURE 3.25 Selecting an Existing List

Use an Access Database as a Data Source

As a database program, Microsoft Access is designed to manage large amounts of data. An Access database typically contains one or more tables; each table is a collection of related records that contain fields of information. Access enables you to *query* a table, which is the process of filtering records to show only those that meet certain search criteria. For example, you might want to view only the records of employees who work in the Accounting department. If you want to send a personalized communication, such as a letter or e-mail, to all employees in the Accounting department, you could use the query as a basis for a mail merge. An Access table is well suited for use as a mail merge data source, due to its datasheet design (approximating an Excel worksheet) and its propensity for filtering records. Figure 3.23 shows a sample Access table that could be used as a data source.

Use a Word Table or an Outlook List as a Data Source

A Word table is organized in rows and columns, which is ideal for use as a data source in a mail merge. The first row in the Word table should include descriptive headers, with each subsequent row including a record from which data can be extracted during a mail merge process. The document used in a mail merge must contain a single table. You can also use a list of Outlook contacts as a data source. Select the list during the mail merge process.

Sort and Filter Records in a Data Source

Before merging a data source with the main document, you might want to rearrange records in the data source so that output from a mail merge is arranged accordingly. For example, you might want to sort the data source in alphabetical order by last name so that letters are arranged alphabetically or so that mailing labels print in order by last name. In addition, you could consider filtering a data source to limit the mail merge output based on particular criteria. You might, for example, want to print letters to send to Alabama clients only. By filtering a data source by state, using a criterion of *Alabama*, you could ensure that letters are sent to Alabama clients only.

STEP 2»

After selecting a data source (during the mail merge process), you can choose to sort or filter records in the Mail Merge Recipients dialog box (see Figure 3.26). Click Sort to indicate one or more fields to sort by. Click Filter to specify criteria for including records that meet certain conditions during the merge process.

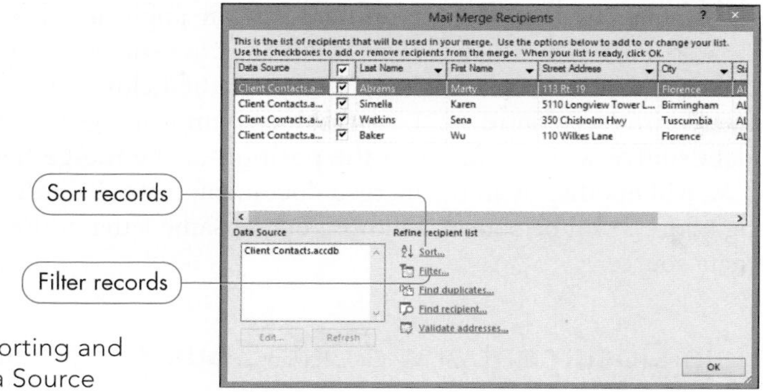

FIGURE 3.26 Sorting and Filtering a Data Source

Completing a Mail Merge

The goal of a mail merge is often to produce a personalized document or e-mail that can be sent to multiple recipients. As the document is prepared, you will indicate locations of variable data, such as a mailing address or a personalized greeting. Such areas of information are called merge fields. After inserting merge fields, you will combine the main document with a data source, a process that results in a single document that includes items (often letters or labels) that are personalized for each recipient. For example, if a data source contains 60 recipient addresses that are then merged with a main document (a letter with placeholders for variable data such as recipient name and address), the resulting merged document will contain 60 letters.

Insert Merge Fields

STEP 3»

When you write a letter or create an e-mail in preparation for a mail merge, you will insert one or more merge fields in the main document in the location(s) of variable data. As shown in Figure 3.27, the Mail Merge wizard enables you to select an Address block, Greeting line, or other item that can be included as a placeholder in the main document. The data source must contain fields that are recognizably named. For example, a field containing last names should be given a field name that is likely to be recognized as containing a person's last name, such as Last Name. Because a merge field corresponds with a field in the data source, matching the two fields guarantees that the right data will be inserted into the main document when you complete the merge.

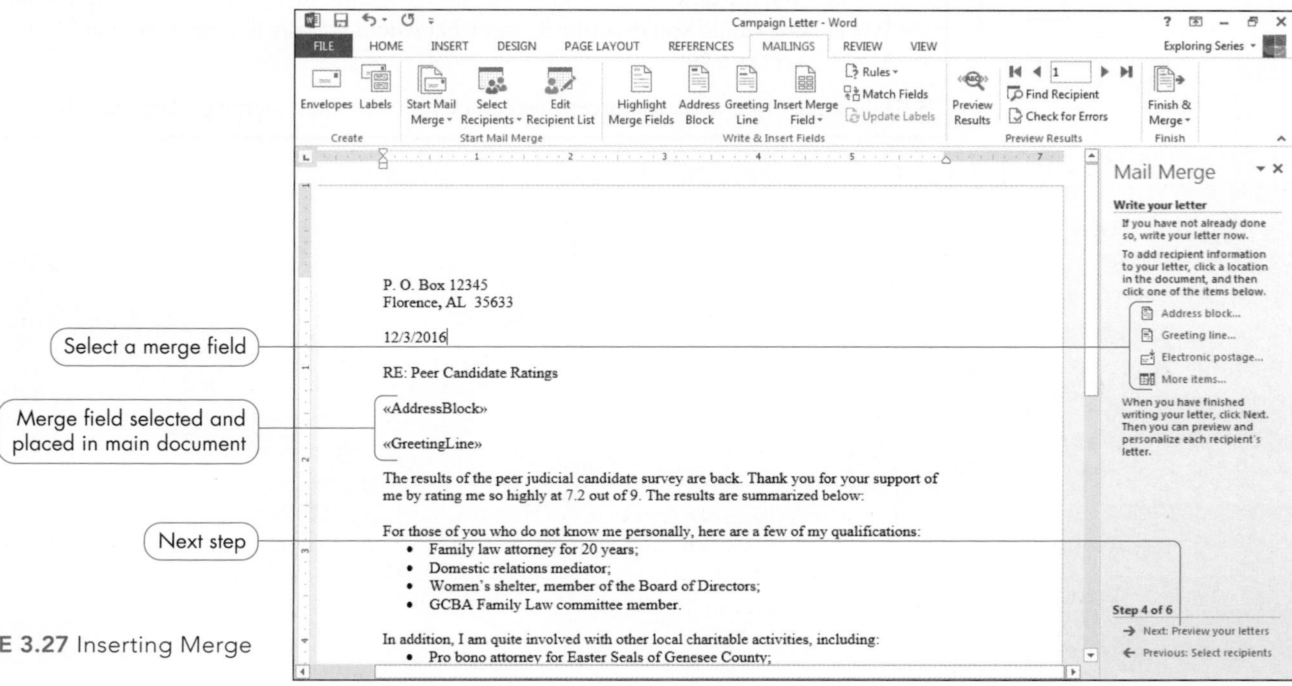

FIGURE 3.27 Inserting Merge Fields

Merge fields display in the main document within angle brackets, for example <<AddressBlock>>, <<FirstName>>, or <<Donation>>. Those entries are not typed explicitly but are entered automatically when you select one of the fields that displays in Step 4 of the Mail Merge wizard (see Figure 3.27). As the document is merged with a data source, data from the data source will be placed in the position of the merge fields. Therefore, <<AddressBlock>> will not display in the merged document; instead a particular recipient's multiline mailing address will be shown, followed by the same letter addressed to another recipient in the data source.

Merge a Main Document and a Data Source

After you create the main document and identify the source data, you are ready to begin the merge process. The merge process examines each record in the data source, and when a match is found, it replaces the merge field in the main document with the information from the data source. A copy of the main document is created for each record in the data source, creating individualized documents.

STEP 4»

To complete the merge, click *Next: Preview your letters* (see Figure 3.27). You can view each merged document, making changes to the recipient list, if necessary. Click *Next: Complete the merge.* Two options display: *Edit individual letters* (or other document) and Print. To create a merged document, select *Edit individual letters.* This enables you to preview each page of the merged document prior to saving or printing. If you select Print, you will have the opportunity to specify which pages to print; however, you cannot preview the document prior to printing. To conserve paper, you should choose *Edit individual letters* and use Print only when you are ready to print.

The same data source can be used to create multiple sets of form documents. You could, for example, create a marketing campaign in which you send an initial letter to the entire list, and then send follow-up letters at periodic intervals to the same mailing list. Alternatively, you could filter the original mailing list to include only a subset of names, such as the individuals who responded to the initial letter. You could also create a different set of documents, such as envelopes, labels, or e-mail messages.

Quick Concepts

1. What forms of output can you create as an end result of a mail merge? ***p. 289***
2. Assume you are describing Word's Mail Merge feature to a person who is unfamiliar with Word. How would you describe it, and what would you say is a major reason for using Mail Merge? ***p. 289***
3. List three types of data sources that can be used in a mail merge process. ***p. 291***

Hands-On Exercises

3 Mail Merge

This executive summary is ready to send to members of the board of trustees. You will merge a form letter with a data source of addresses, merging fields in the process to personalize each letter.

Skills covered: Create a Recipient List • Sort and Filter Records in a Data Source • Insert Merge Fields • Merge a Main Document and a Data Source

STEP 1 » CREATE A RECIPIENT LIST

You will use Word to create a recipient list, including the names and addresses of members of the board of trustees. Refer to Figure 3.28 as you complete Step 1.

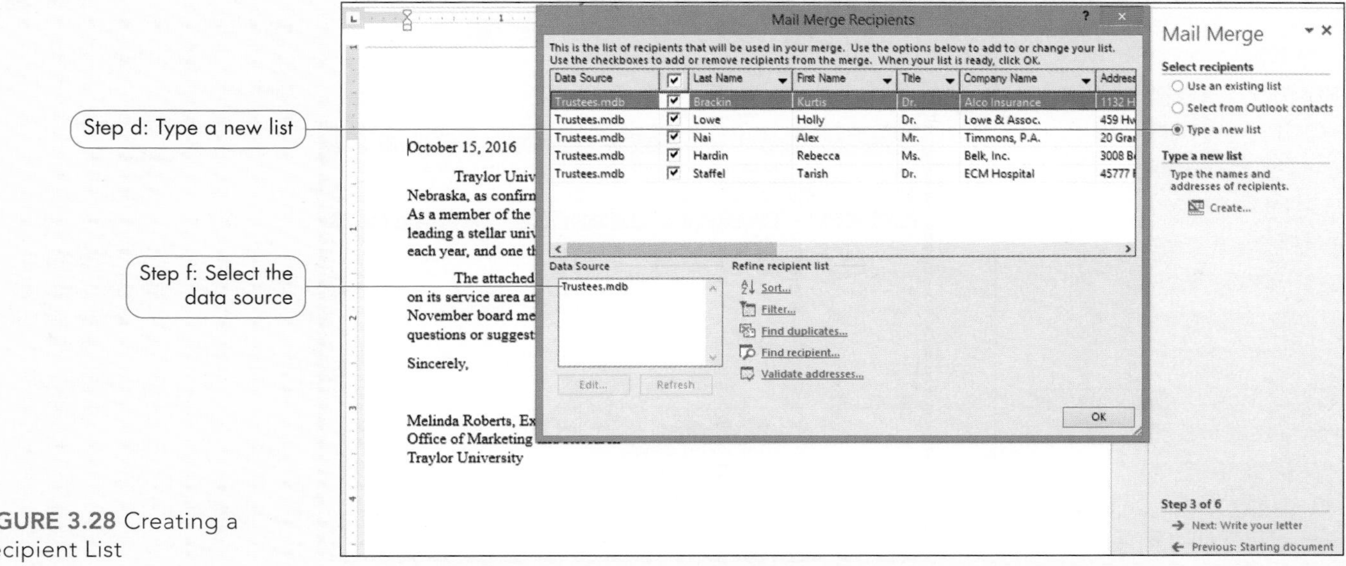

FIGURE 3.28 Creating a Recipient List

a. Open *w03h3Letter*.

b. Click the **MAILINGS tab** and click **Start Mail Merge** in the Start Mail Merge group. Click **Step-by-Step Mail Merge Wizard**. Ensure that *Letters* is selected in the *Select document type* area of the Mail Merge pane and click **Next: Starting document** at the bottom of the Mail Merge pane.

c. Ensure that *Use the current document* is selected in the *Select starting document* area. Click **Next: Select recipients**.

d. Select **Type a new list** in the *Select recipients* area and click **Create**. Type the information in the table below, pressing **Tab** to move from one field (column) to another. You will not include data in the country, phone, or e-mail fields. Tab through all fields and continue entering data on a new row for a new record. After typing the last record, click **OK**.

Title	First Name	Last Name	Company	Address 1	Address 2	City	State	ZIP
Dr.	Kurtis	Brackin	Alco Insurance	1132 Hendrix Lane		Sim Creek	NE	68801
Dr.	Holly	Lowe	Lowe & Assoc.	459 Hwy. 34		Oglala	NE	68604
Mr.	Alex	Nai	Timmons, P.A.	20 Grant Street		Navarre	NE	68811
Ms.	Rebecca	Hardin	Belk, Inc.	3008 Beltline Hwy.	Suite 10	Dinsford	NE	68445
Dr.	Tarish	Staffel	ECM Hospital	45777 Riverbend Drive		Florence	NE	68803

e. Type **Trustees** in the **File name box** and click **Save** to save the data source with your student files.

The address list displays as shown in Figure 3.28, with all recipients checked. It is an Access database. Note that you can deselect any recipients to which you do not want to send the letter. In this case, you will send the letter to all.

f. Click **Trustees.mdb** in the Data Source box. Click **Edit**. Click **New Entry** and add the following record. After typing the record, click **OK**. Click **Yes**. Click **OK**.

Mr. Robert Cobb Tremont Insurance Rt. 19 Navarre NE 68811

You inadvertently left off one of the trustees, so you add him to the data source.

STEP 2 » SORT AND FILTER RECORDS IN A DATA SOURCE

You will sort the records alphabetically by city and then by recipient last name. Refer to Figure 3.29 as you complete Step 2.

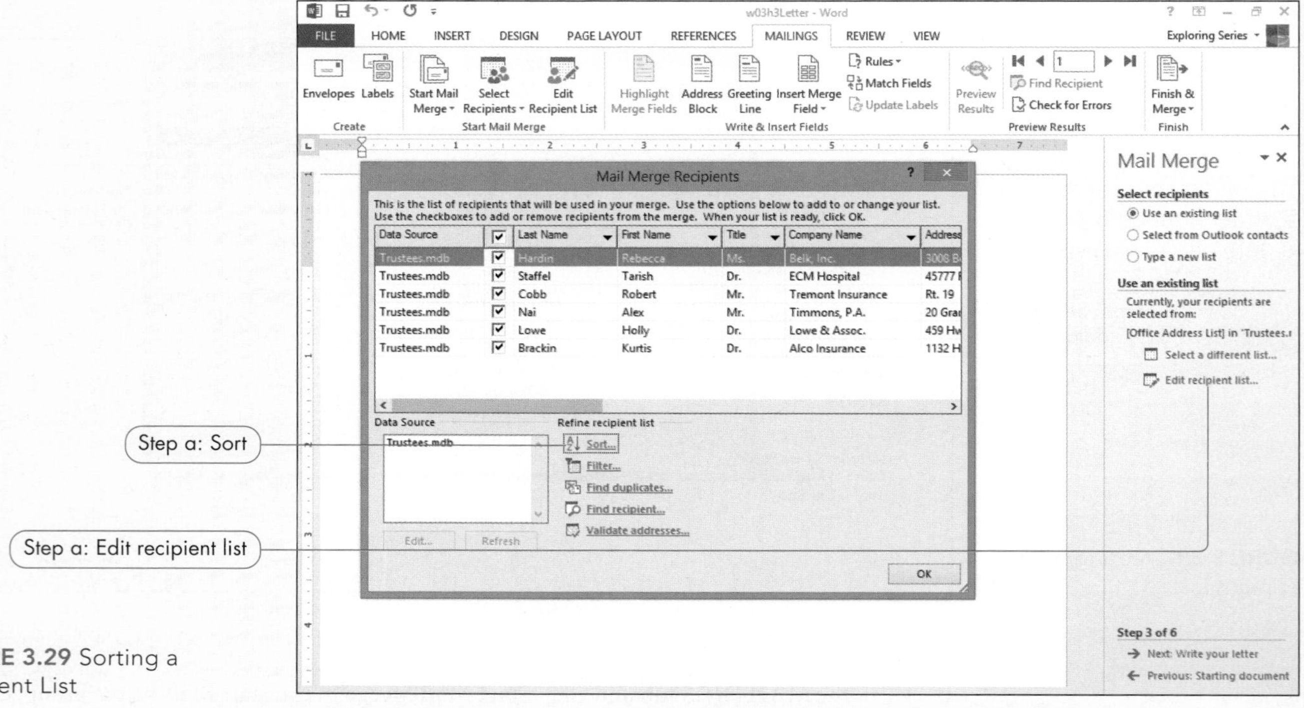

FIGURE 3.29 Sorting a Recipient List

a. Click **Edit recipient list** in the *Use an existing list* area on the Mail Merge pane. Click **Sort** in the *Refine recipient list* area of the Mail Merge Recipients dialog box.

You open the data source in order to sort it.

b. Click the **Sort by arrow**, scroll down, and then click **City**. Sort order is *Ascending*. Click the **Then by arrow** and click **Last Name**. Sort order should be *Ascending*. Click **OK**.

c. Scroll to the right to confirm that records are sorted by City. Scroll back to the left and confirm that the two records with a city of *Navarre* (records 3 and 4) are also sorted by Last Name. Click **OK**.

STEP 3 ›› INSERT MERGE FIELDS

Although the body of the letter will be the same for all recipients, you will create merge fields to accommodate variable data, including each recipient's name and address. Refer to Figure 3.30 as you complete Step 3.

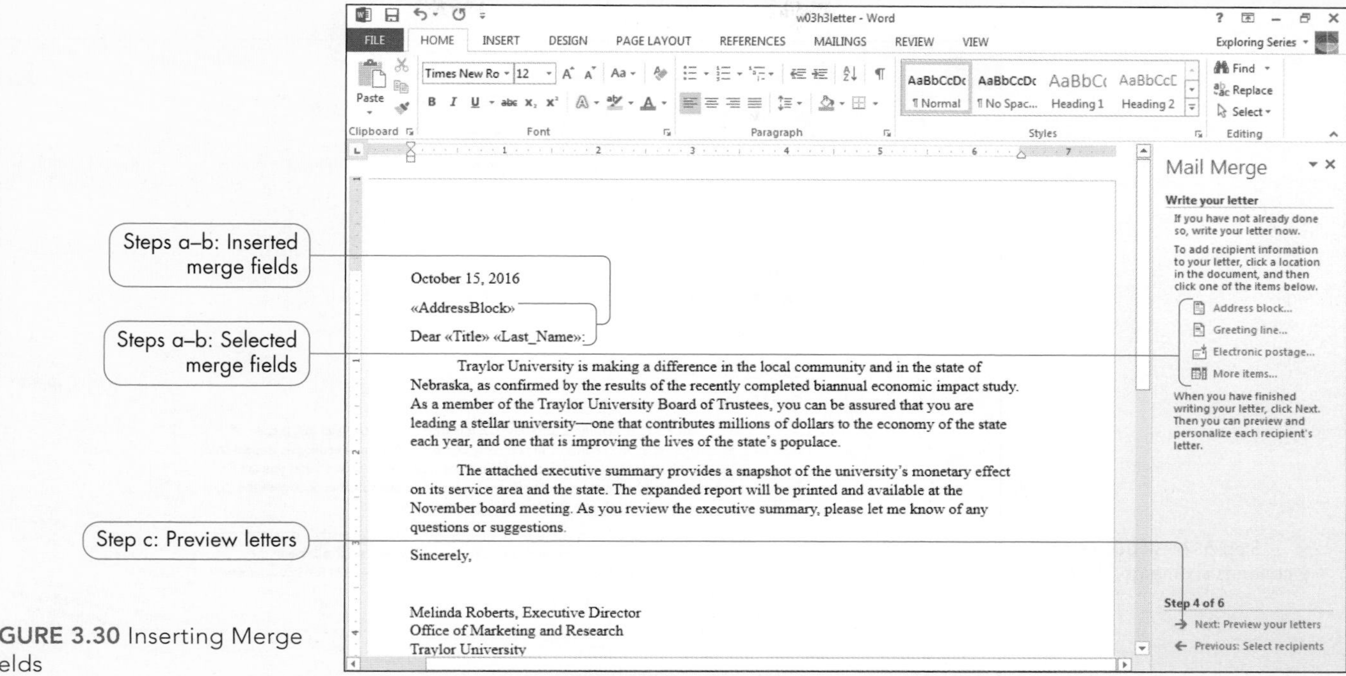

FIGURE 3.30 Inserting Merge Fields

a. Click after *2016* in the first line of the document. Press **Enter**. Click **Next: Write your letter** at the bottom of the Mail Merge pane. Click **Address block** in the Mail Merge pane. Note the address in the Preview area. Ensure that *Insert recipient's name in this format*, *Insert company name*, and *Insert postal address* are selected. Click **OK**.

The AddressBlock merge field is inserted, with double chevrons on each side, indicating its status.

b. Press **Enter**. Type **Dear** and press **Space**. Click **More items** in the Mail Merge pane. With *Title* selected, click **Insert**. Click **Close**. Press **Space**. Click **More items**, click **Last Name**, click **Insert**, and then click **Close**. Type **:**.

You add a salutation, including the title and last name, followed by a colon (:).

> **TROUBLESHOOTING:** If you make a mistake when entering merge fields, you can backspace or otherwise delete a field.

c. Click **Next: Preview your letters** in the Mail Merge pane. Select the address block, from the recipient name through the line preceding the city and state. Do not select the line containing the city, state, and ZIP code. Click the **HOME tab**, click the **Paragraph Dialog Box Launcher**, and then change the paragraph spacing after to **0 pt**. Click **OK**.

One letter is shown. Note the personalized inside address and salutation.

STEP 4 ≫ MERGE A MAIN DOCUMENT AND A DATA SOURCE

Having inserted merge fields into the form letter, the letter is complete. You will now merge the main document with the data source so that each letter is personally addressed and ready to be printed. Refer to Figure 3.31 as you complete Step 4.

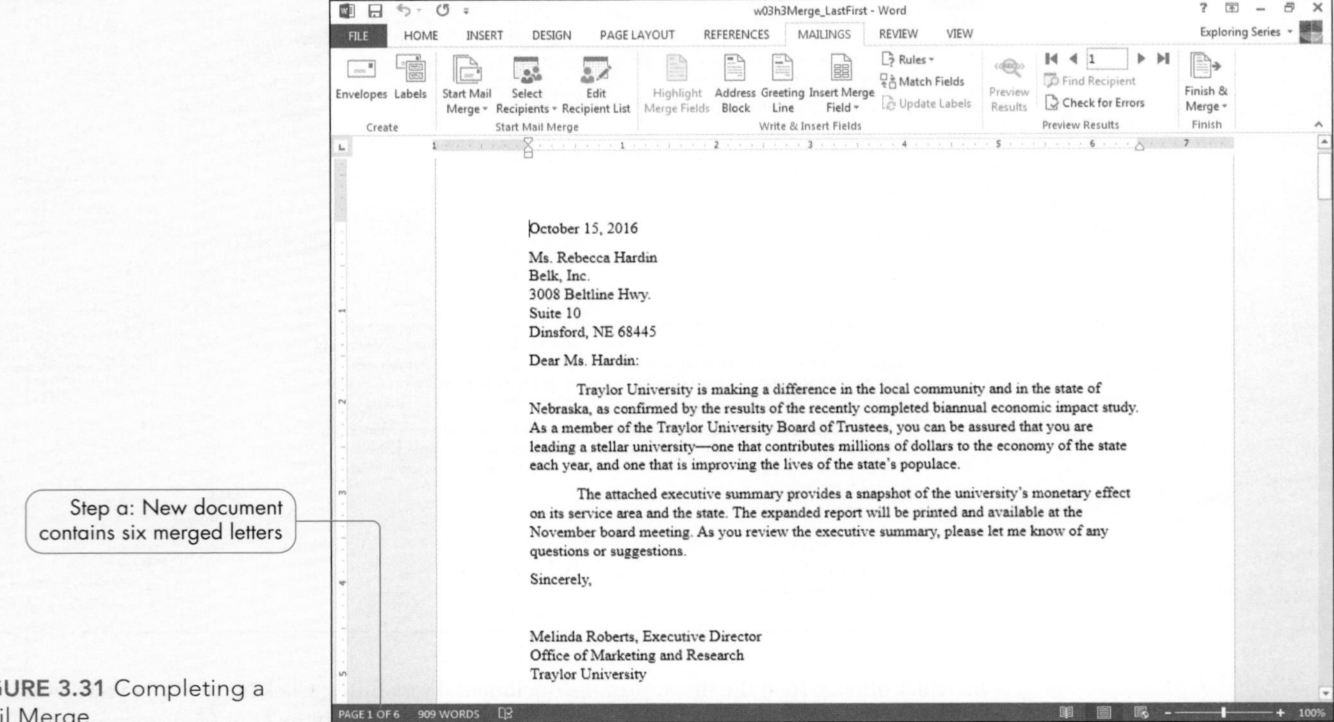

FIGURE 3.31 Completing a Mail Merge

a. Click **Next: Complete the merge** at the bottom of the Mail Merge pane. Click **Edit individual letters**. Ensure that *All* is selected in the *Merge to New Document* dialog box and click **OK**.

Scroll through the letters, noting that each address and salutation is unique to the recipient. The main document and data source were merged to create a new document titled *Letters1*. You will save the document.

b. Click the **FILE tab** and click **Save As**. Navigate to the location where you save your files and change the file name to *w03h3Merge_LastFirst*. Click **Save**. Close the document. Close *w03h3Letter* without saving it.

c. Exit Word and submit the merged document as directed by your instructor.

Chapter Objectives Review

1. **Insert a table.**
   - Create or draw a table: You can include a table in a document by indicating the number of rows and columns, allowing Word to create the table, or you can draw the table, designing rows and columns of varying height and width.
   - Insert and delete rows and columns: You will often find it necessary to insert or delete rows and columns in a table to accommodate additional data or to otherwise update a table.
   - Merge and split cells: As you update a table, you can merge cells in a row, accommodating text that is to be aligned within the row, and you can split cells within an existing column as well.
   - Change row height and column width: You can increase or decrease row height and column width in several ways—using selections on the Table Tools Layout tab as well as manually dragging column or row borders.
2. **Format a table.**
   - Apply table styles: Apply predesigned color, borders, and shading to a table by selecting a table style.
   - Adjust table position and alignment: A table can be aligned horizontally on a page; in addition, you can align cell contents within each cell horizontally and vertically.
   - Format table text: Format text included in a cell just as you would format text outside a table, with bold, italics, underlining, etc. You can also apply paragraph formatting, such as alignment, bullets, and numbering.
3. **Manage table data.**
   - Use a formula: A formula includes table cells and mathematical operators to calculate data in a table.
   - Use a function: A function is a simplified formula, such as SUM or AVERAGE, that can be included in a table cell.
   - Sort data in a table: You can sort table columns in ascending or descending order, including up to three sort categories. For example, you can sort a table by department name, and then by employee name within department.
   - Include a recurring table header: When table rows are divided between pages, you can repeat heading rows so that they display at the top of table rows on a new page.
   - Convert text to a table (and convert a table to text): Text that is arranged in columns, with tabs separating columns, can be converted to a table. Conversely, text arranged in a table can be converted to text that is tabbed or otherwise divided into columns.
4. **Enhance table data.**
   - Include borders and shading: Use borders and shading to customize a table's design. You can use Word's Borders Styles Gallery, Border Painter, or the *Borders and Shading* dialog box to enhance a table with borders and shading.
   - Include a table caption: A table caption identifies a table, numbering each table in a document sequentially. You can modify the caption style and update caption numbering when tables are deleted.
5. **Create a Mail Merge document.**
   - Select or create a recipient list: To prepare a form letter or other document type so that it is personalized with variable data, such as recipient name and address, you will select or create a recipient list that will be merged with the main document.
   - Use an Excel worksheet as a data source: A worksheet, comprised of columns and rows, can be used as a data source containing records used in a mail merge.
   - Use an Access database as a data source: An Access table or query, containing records with data that can be merged with a main document, is often used as a data source for a mail merge.
   - Use a Word table or an Outlook list as a data source: A Word table is often used as a data source, with data merged into a main document. Similarly, Outlook contacts can be incorporated into a main document during a mail merge.
   - Sort and filter records in a data source: Records in a data source can be sorted or filtered before they are merged with the main document.
6. **Complete a Mail Merge.**
   - Insert merge fields: Merge fields are placeholders in a main document to accommodate variable data obtained from a data source.
   - Merge a main document and a data source: As you complete a mail merge procedure, you will update a main document with variable data from a data source, resulting in a new document that is a combination of the two.

Key Terms Matching

Match the key terms with their definitions. Write the key term letter by the appropriate numbered definition.

a. Argument
b. Border
c. Border Painter
d. Caption
e. Cell
f. Data source
g. Form letter
h. Formula
i. Function
j. Insert control
k. Mail Merge
l. Main document
m. Merge field
n. Order of operations
o. Record
p. Shading
q. Table
r. Table alignment
s. Table style
t. Wizard

1. _______ The position of a table between the left and right document margins. **p. 266**
2. _______ A descriptive title for a table. **p. 281**
3. _______ A document with standard information that you personalize with recipient information, which you might print or e-mail to many people. **p. 289**
4. _______ A line that surrounds a Word table, cell, row, or column. **p. 280**
5. _______ A named collection of color, font, and border design that can be applied to a table. **p. 265**
6. _______ A background color that displays behind text in a table, cell, row, or column. **p. 280**
7. _______ A combination of cell references, operators, and values used to perform a calculation. **p. 274**
8. _______ The intersection of a column and row in a table. **p. 260**
9. _______ A process that combines content from a main document and a data source. **p. 289**
10. _______ Contains the information that stays the same for all recipients in a mail merge. **p. 289**
11. _______ An indicator that displays between rows or columns in a table; click the indicator to insert one or more rows or columns. **p. 262**
12. _______ Organizes information in a series of rows and columns. **p. 260**
13. _______ A list of information that is merged with a main document during a mail merge procedure. **p. 289**
14. _______ A tool that makes a process easier by asking a series of questions, then creates a structure based on your answers. **p. 289**
15. _______ Determines the sequence by which operations are calculated in an expression. **p. 276**
16. _______ Serves as a placeholder for the variable data that will be inserted into the main document during a mail merge procedure. **p. 289**
17. _______ A pre-built formula that simplifies creating a complex calculation. **p. 274**
18. _______ Feature that enables you to choose border formatting and click on any table border to apply the formatting. **p. 280**
19. _______ A positional reference contained in parentheses within a function. **p. 277**
20. _______ A group of related fields representing one entity, such as a person, place, or event. **p. 290**

Multiple Choice

1. Having applied custom borders to a table, you can use this feature to copy the border style to another table:
   (a) Borders Gallery
   (b) Format Painter
   (c) Border Painter
   (d) Border Style

2. When used in a table, an insert control enables you to insert a(n):
   (a) Blank row or column.
   (b) Table in a document.
   (c) Caption above or below a table.
   (d) Image in a cell.

3. A mail merge procedure combines two items—a main document and a(n):
   (a) Merge field.
   (b) Data table.
   (c) Data source.
   (d) Address list.

4. To center a table heading in row 1 across several columns of data (when row 1 is *not* already merged):
   (a) Select row 1 and click Align Center on the Table Tools Layout tab.
   (b) Click the Home tab and click Center in the Font group.
   (c) Merge the cells in row 1 and center the contents of the merged cell.
   (d) Split the cells in row 1 and center the contents of the split cells.

5. Which of the following documents is not included as an option in the mail merge procedure?
   (a) Directory
   (b) Labels
   (c) Envelopes
   (d) Report

6. You plan to place a function or formula in cell C4 of a Word table to total the cells in the column above. How would that function or formula appear?
   (a) =SUM(ABOVE)
   (b) -C1+C2+C3+C4
   (c) =TOTAL(ABOVE)
   (d) =SUM(C1-C3)

7. If a table with a heading row extends from one page to another, rows on the second page will not be identified by a heading row. How would you correct that situation?
   (a) Drag the heading row(s) to the top of the second page.
   (b) Insert a manual page break at the top of the second page.
   (c) Select the heading row(s) and cut and paste them to the top of the rows on the second page.
   (d) Select the heading row(s) and click Repeat Header Rows on the Table Tools Layout tab.

8. You have created a table containing numerical values and have entered the =SUM(ABOVE) function at the bottom of a column. You then delete one of the rows included in the sum. Which of the following is *true*?
   (a) The row cannot be deleted because it contains a cell that is referred to in the =SUM function.
   (b) The sum is updated automatically.
   (c) The sum cannot be updated.
   (d) The sum will be updated after you right-click the cell and click the Update Field command.

9. During a mail merge process, what operation can you perform on a data source so only data that meet specific criteria, such as a particular city, are included in the merge?
   (a) Sort
   (b) Propagate
   (c) Delete
   (d) Filter

10. What happens when you press Tab from within the last cell of a table?
    (a) A Tab character is inserted just as it would be for ordinary text.
    (b) Word inserts a new row below the current row.
    (c) Word inserts a new column to the right of the current column.
    (d) The insertion point displays in the paragraph below the table.

Practice Exercises

1 Rental Car Business

As an executive assistant working for the state of Arkansas, you are involved with a project in which the state has selected a rental car company to supply rental cars for state employees. An employee conducting state business will be assigned a rental car if a state car is not available. Roadway Rentals was awarded the contract and has provided a price list for daily and weekly rentals. You will prepare Word tables to summarize the bid process and the subsequent contract award. This exercise follows the same set of skills as used in Hands-On Exercises 1 and 2 in the chapter. Refer to Figure 3.32 as you complete this exercise.

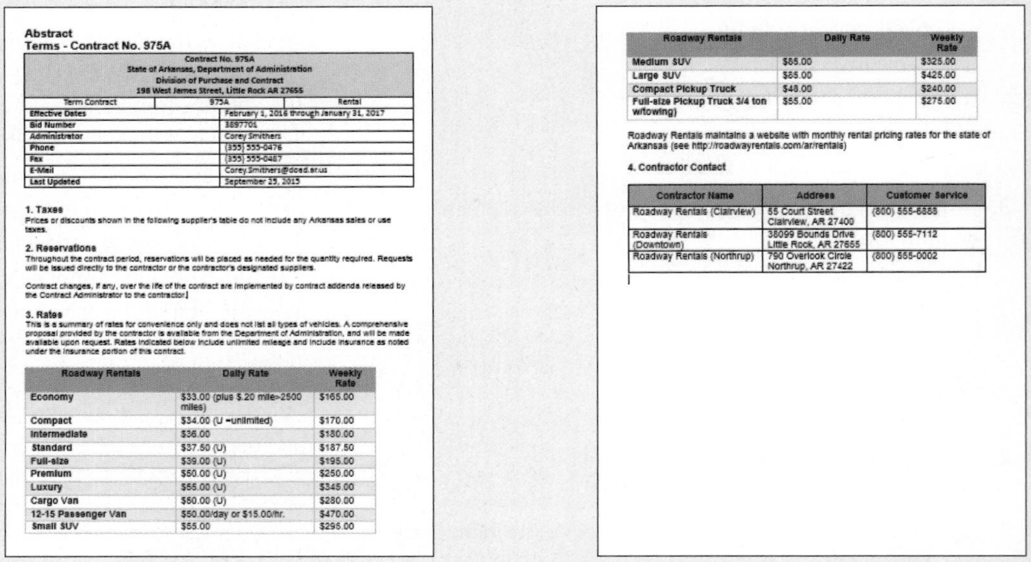

Abstract
Terms - Contract No. 975A

Contract No. 975A State of Arkansas, Department of Administration Division of Purchase and Contract 198 West James Street, Little Rock AR 27655		
Term Contract	975A	Rental
Effective Dates	February 1, 2016 through January 31, 2017	
Bid Number	3897701	
Administrator	Corey Smithers	
Phone	(355) 555-0476	
Fax	(355) 555-0487	
E-Mail	Corey.Smithers@doad.ar.us	
Last Updated	September 25, 2015	

1. Taxes
Prices or discounts shown in the following supplier's table do not include any Arkansas sales or use taxes.

2. Reservations
Throughout the contract period, reservations will be placed as needed for the quantity required. Requests will be issued directly to the contractor or the contractor's designated suppliers.

Contract changes, if any, over the life of the contract are implemented by contract addenda released by the Contract Administrator to the contractor.

3. Rates
This is a summary of rates for convenience only and does not list all types of vehicles. A comprehensive proposal provided by the contractor is available from the Department of Administration, and will be made available upon request. Rates indicated below include unlimited mileage and include insurance as noted under the insurance portion of this contract.

Roadway Rentals	Daily Rate	Weekly Rate
Economy	$33.00 (plus $.20 mile>2500 miles)	$165.00
Compact	$34.00 (U =unlimited)	$170.00
Intermediate	$36.00	$180.00
Standard	$37.50 (U)	$187.50
Full-size	$39.00 (U)	$195.00
Premium	$50.00 (U)	$250.00
Luxury	$55.00 (U)	$345.00
Cargo Van	$50.00 (U)	$280.00
12-15 Passenger Van	$50.00/day or $15.00/hr.	$470.00
Small SUV	$55.00	$295.00

Roadway Rentals	Daily Rate	Weekly Rate
Medium SUV	$65.00	$325.00
Large SUV	$85.00	$425.00
Compact Pickup Truck	$48.00	$240.00
Full-size Pickup Truck 3/4 ton w/towing)	$55.00	$275.00

Roadway Rentals maintains a website with monthly rental pricing rates for the state of Arkansas (see http://roadwayrentals.com/ar/rentals)

4. Contractor Contact

Contractor Name	Address	Customer Service
Roadway Rentals (Clairview)	55 Court Street Clairview, AR 27400	(800) 555-6888
Roadway Rentals (Downtown)	38099 Bounds Drive Little Rock, AR 27655	(800) 555-7112
Roadway Rentals (Northrup)	790 Overlook Circle Northrup, AR 27422	(800) 555-0002

FIGURE 3.32 Rental Car Contract

a. Open *w03p1Rental* and save the document as **w03p1Rental_LastFirst**. Click **Show/Hide** in the Paragraph group to show nonprinting characters, if necessary.

b. Click before the blank paragraph mark after the Terms heading and press **Enter**. Click the **INSERT tab** and click **Table** in the Tables group. Drag to insert a 2x11 table. Beginning in the top-left cell, enter the following text, pressing **Tab** after each entry. However, do not press Tab after the last entry on the last row. The e-mail address will be formatted as a hyperlink.

Contract No. 975A	
State of Arkansas, Department of Administration	
Division of Purchase and Contract	
198 West James Street, Little Rock AR 27655	
Term Contract	975A
Bid Number	3897701
Administrator	Corey Smithers
Phone	(355) 555-0476
Fax	(355) 555-0487
E-Mail	Corey.Smithers@doad.ar.us
Last Updated	September 25, 2016

c. Point to the border dividing the Term Contract row from the Bid Number row, slightly outside the left edge of the table. Click the **Insert control**. Click in the left cell of the new row. Type the following text, tabbing to position each entry in a separate cell on the new row:

Effective Dates **February 1, 2016 through January 31, 2017**

d. Select the first four rows. Click the **TABLE TOOLS LAYOUT tab** and click **Merge Cells** in the Merge group. Click **Align Center** in the Alignment group. Click the **HOME tab** and click **Bold**. Do not deselect the first row.

e. Click the **TABLE TOOLS DESIGN tab,** click the **Shading arrow**, and then click **White Background 1, Darker 15%** (third row, first column). Select all text in the first column under the merged row, beginning with *Term Contract* and ending with *Last Updated*. Bold the selection.

f. Right-click the e-mail hyperlink, *Corey.Smithers@doad.au.us*, and select **Remove Hyperlink**. Select the second row, beginning with *Term Contract*. Click the **TABLE TOOLS LAYOUT tab** and click **Split Cells** in the Merge group. Change the number of columns to **3** and ensure that the number of rows is 1. Make sure *Merge cells before split* is checked. Click **OK**.

g. Click in the third cell in the newly split row and type **Rental**. Select the newly split row and click **Align Center** in the Alignment group. Remove the bold formatting from *Term Contract*.

h. Scroll down to the *Rates* section and select all text from *Roadway Rentals* through *$275.00*. Do not select the paragraph mark following *$275.00*. Click the **Insert tab** and click **Table** in the Tables group. Click **Convert Text to Table**. Accept the default settings of 3 columns and 15 rows in the *Convert Text to Table* dialog box and click **OK**.

i. Deselect the table. Place the pointer above the first column so that it appears as a downward-pointing black arrow. Click to select the first column. Right-click in the selected column and select **Table Properties**. Click the **Column tab** in the Table Properties dialog box. Change the width to **2.5"**. Click **OK**.

j. Select the first row. Click the **TABLE TOOLS LAYOUT tab**. Click **Align Center** in the Alignment group. Click the **TABLE TOOLS DESIGN tab** and click **More** beside *Table Styles* to display the Table Styles gallery. Select **Grid Table 4 - Accent 3** (fourth row, fourth column under *Grid Tables*).

k. Click the **TABLE TOOLS LAYOUT tab** and click **Repeat Header Rows** in the Data group.

l. Display the ruler, if it is not already shown. (Click the **VIEW tab** and click **Ruler**.) Click before the second blank paragraph under *4. Contractor Contact*. Click the **INSERT tab**, click **Table** in the Tables group, and then select **Draw Table**. Use the mouse to draw a box, beginning at the second blank paragraph mark, extending to approximately 6" on the ruler, and down approximately 2".

TROUBLESHOOTING: If the pen color that displays when you draw the table is not black, click the Table Tools Design tab and click Pen Color. Click Black, Text 1 (first row, second column under *Theme Colors*). Click Border Painter. Click the Borders arrow and select Outside Borders. Click the Insert tab, click Table, and then select Draw Table. Continue to step m.

m. Draw three vertical borders in the box, each beginning approximately 1.5" from the previous border. Draw three horizontal borders in the table area, each beginning approximately 0.5" from the previous. The borders do not have to be precise, as they will be adjusted later. Press **Esc**.

n. Click **Eraser** in the Draw group on the TABLE TOOLS LAYOUT tab. Click the left border of the last cell on the first row. The left border of that cell is removed. Click the left border of the last cell on the second row to remove it. Similarly, remove the left border of the last cell in the third and fourth rows. Press **Esc**.

o. Point to the vertical grid line dividing the second column from the third so that the pointer displays as a double-headed arrow. Drag to the right to resize the last column to approximately 2". Resize the remaining columns to approximately 2".

p. Type the following text in the table. Press **Enter** to place the address on two rows within each cell in the second column, and after typing the table, adjust the width of the first column to display all text on a single line. The table appearance should be similar to that shown below.

Contractor Name	Address	Customer Service
Roadway Rentals (Clairview)	55 Court Street Clairview, AR 27400	(800) 555-6888
Roadway Rentals (Downtown)	38099 Bounds Drive Little Rock, AR 27655	(800) 555-7112
Roadway Rentals (Northrup)	790 Overlook Circle Northrup, AR 27422	(800) 555-0002

q. Select the first row. Click the **TABLE TOOLS LAYOUT tab**, if necessary, and click **Align Center** in the Alignment group. Click the **TABLE TOOLS DESIGN tab** and click the **Shading arrow**. Select **Gray - 25%, Background 2, Darker 25%** (third row, third column). Click the **HOME tab** and bold the text in row 1.

r. Save the document and exit Word. Submit *w03p1Rental_LastFirst* according to your instructor's directions.

2 Restaurant Letter

You are the manager of a local steak and seafood restaurant. At the end of each month, you balance the books and process the accounts payable. You then write a letter to all your suppliers, thank them for the prompt delivery services, and enclose a check for the monthly balance. Because you already have the suppliers' information stored in a spreadsheet, you decide to create a mail merge document that you can use to quickly create letters to send to each supplier. There is no need to send payments to suppliers with a zero balance, so you use a filter to remove their names from the merge process. This exercise follows the same set of skills as used in Hands-On Exercise 3 in the chapter. Refer to Figure 3.33 as you complete this exercise.

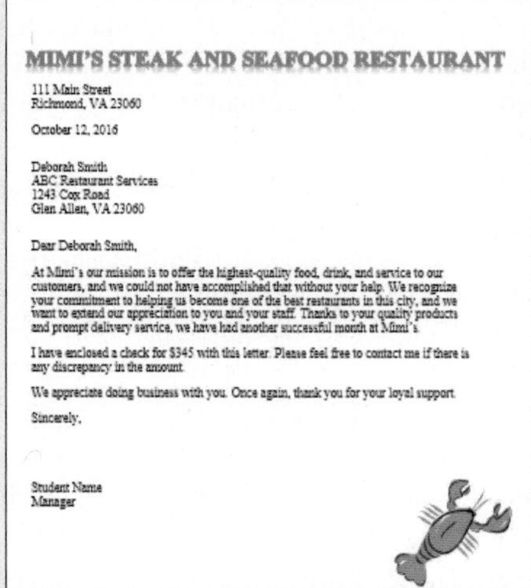

MIMI'S STEAK AND SEAFOOD RESTAURANT

111 Main Street
Richmond, VA 23060

October 12, 2016

Deborah Smith
ABC Restaurant Services
1243 Cox Road
Glen Allen, VA 23060

Dear Deborah Smith,

At Mimi's our mission is to offer the highest-quality food, drink, and service to our customers, and we could not have accomplished that without your help. We recognize your commitment to helping us become one of the best restaurants in this city, and we want to extend our appreciation to you and your staff. Thanks to your quality products and prompt delivery service, we have had another successful month at Mimi's.

I have enclosed a check for $345 with this letter. Please feel free to contact me if there is any discrepancy in the amount.

We appreciate doing business with you. Once again, thank you for your loyal support.

Sincerely,

Student Name
Manager

FIGURE 3.33 Completed Letter

a. Open *w03p2Letter*. Show nonprinting characters if they are not already displayed.

b. Click the **MAILINGS tab** and click **Start Mail Merge** in the Start Mail Merge group. Click **Step-by-Step Mail Merge Wizard**. Make sure *Letters* is selected in the *Select document type* area of the Mail Merge pane and click **Next: Starting document**. Make sure *Use the current document* is selected in the *Select starting document* area and click **Next: Select recipients**.

c. Make sure *Use an existing list* is selected and click **Browse**. Navigate to the location where data files are stored and double-click **w03p2Suppliers.xlsx**. Make sure *Sheet1$* is selected in the Select Table dialog box and click **OK**. Click **OK** again. Click **Next: Write your letter**.

d. Insert merge fields by completing the following steps:
   - Click before the blank paragraph mark below the date. Click **Address block** in the Mail Merge pane and click **OK** to insert the default format of the supplier's address at the top of the letter.
   - Place the insertion point at the left of the comma in the salutation line beginning with *Dear*. Click **More items** in the Mail Merge pane. Click **FirstName**, click **Insert**, and then click **Close**. With the insertion point at the right of *FirstName*, press **Space** and click **More items**. With *LastName* selected, click **Insert** and click **Close**.
   - Place the insertion point at the right side of the dollar sign in the first sentence of the second body paragraph. Click **More items** and click **Balance**. Click **Insert** and click **Close**.

e. Click **Next: Preview your letters**. To correct the extra lines around the address block, complete these steps:
   - Select the four lines that comprise the address block (the address block is located beneath *October 12, 2016*).
   - Click the **PAGE LAYOUT tab**.
   - Change the paragraph spacing Before and After to **0 pt**.

f. Click **Next: Complete the merge**. Click **Edit individual letters**. Click **All**, if necessary, and click **OK**. The letters are shown in a new document, titled *Letters1*, with one letter shown for each recipient (10 letters in all). Save the new document as **w03p2SupplierLetters1_LastFirst**. Close the document.

g. You are returned to the original document, *w03p2Letter*. Close the Mail Merge pane. Filter the recipient list in preparation for limiting letters to include only suppliers with a positive balance by completing the following steps:
   - Click the **MAILINGS tab** and click **Edit Recipient List** in the Start Mail Merge group.
   - Click **Filter** to display the *Filter and Sort* dialog box. Click the **Filter Records tab**, if necessary.
   - Click the **Field arrow** and click **Balance**.
   - Click the **Comparison arrow** and click **Greater than**.
   - Type **0** in the **Compare to box** and click **OK**.
   - Click **OK** again to close the Mail Merge Recipients dialog box.

h. Click **Finish & Merge** in the Finish group on the right side of the Ribbon, click **Edit Individual Documents**, click **All**, if necessary, and then click **OK**.

i. The new document, titled *Letters2*, contains eight letters—each recipient's balance is greater than 0. Save the new document as **w03p2SupplierLetters2_LastFirst**. Close the document.

j. Close *w03p2Letter* without saving it and exit Word. Submit *w03p2SupplierLetters1_LastFirst* and *w03p2SupplierLetters2_LastFirst* based on your instructor's directions.

Mid-Level Exercises

1 Football Statistics

CREATIVE CASE 

As an intern for the Southern Athletic Conference, you are preparing a summary of football statistics for inclusion in material published and placed online by the conference. Specifically, you will highlight stats from the offensive units of leading teams in the conference. A Word table is an ideal way to summarize those statistics, so you will prepare and populate several tables. Where appropriate, you will include formulas to summarize table data. The tables must be attractively formatted, so you will use Word's design and bordering tools as well.

a. Open *w03m1Football* and save it as **w03m1Football_LastFirst**.

DISCOVER 

b. Select text in the document from # (in the top-left corner) to *13.4* (in the bottom-right corner) and convert the text to a table. The number of columns is 15, and the number of rows is 18. Table data are separated by tabs. After creating the table, change page orientation to **Landscape**.

c. Delete column 1. Change the font of all table data to **Cambria**. Change the font size of all table text to **10**. AutoFit the contents of the table.

d. Change the font of the first two lines (*Southern Athletic Conference* and *Season Statistics*) to **Cambria 16 pt**.

e. Insert a row above row 1 in the table. Complete the following activities to populate and format the new row:
   - Type **Offensive Statistics** in the first cell on the new row.
   - Type **Rushing Statistics** in the next cell on the first row.
   - Select the second, third, fourth, fifth, and sixth cells on the first row. Merge the selected cells.
   - Align *Rushing Statistics* in the center of the merged cell.
   - Type **Passing Statistics** in the next cell on the first row.
   - Select the cell containing *Passing Statistics* and the next three cells on the first row. Merge the cells.
   - Align *Passing Statistics* in the center of the merged cell.
   - Merge the remaining cells on row 1, type **Total** in the merged cell, and then center *Total*.

f. Insert a row between *HARKINSVILLE* and *DAKOTA STATE* and type the following data in the new row.

JAMES COLLEGE	38.2	41.0	220.5	4.2	19.7	32.7	0.601	199.2	7.6	57.9	449.3	5.9	12.7

g. Select a table style of **Grid Table 5 Dark - Accent 2** (fifth row, third column under *Grid Tables*). Click the **Table Select indicator** to select all table text. Change the Pen Color to **Orange, Accent 2, Darker 50%** (sixth row, sixth column under *Theme Colors*). Click **Borders** and apply the color to Outside Borders.

h. Select a border style of your choice and apply it to the border along the horizontal line separating row 1 from row 2, and also along the vertical line separating the first column from the second.

i. Move to the end of the document. Press **Enter** twice and insert a 3x5 table. Enter the following data in the table.

Calvin Spraggins	SPR	1428
Demaryius Schuster	DEN	1197
Brandon Marchant	CHI	1182
Wayne McAnalley	IND	1156
Sparky Hall	HOU	1114

j. Insert a new blank row at the top of the table and complete the following steps:
   - Type **Receiving Yards** in the first cell on row 1.
   - Change the font size of the entry on row 1 to **14 pt**.
   - Merge all cells on row 1.
   - Align Center *Receiving Yards*.

k. Manually adjust each column of data to approximately 1.5" wide. Center all entries in the last two columns.

l. Select the first row and apply a shading of **Orange, Accent 2, Lighter 60%** (third row, sixth column under *Theme Colors*).

m. Add a new blank row at the end of the table and type **Total** in the first cell of the new row. Enter a formula in the last cell of the new row to sum all entries in the column above. You do not need to select a number format.

n. Align both tables horizontally in the center of the page.

o. Change the receiving yards for *Calvin Spraggins* to **1451**. Update the formula to reflect the change.

p. Add a caption below the bottom of the first table. The caption should read **Table 1: Southern Athletic Conference Offensive Statistics**. Add a caption below the bottom of the second table that reads **Table 2: Total Receiving Yards**. Modify the Caption style to include a font color of **Orange, Accent 2, Darker 50%** (sixth row, sixth column under *Theme Colors*). Change the Caption style font to **Bold** (not italicized) and **Centered**.

q. Save and submit *w03m1Football_LastFirst* based on your instructor's directions.

2 Pool Places

You own a swimming pool company, installing in-ground pools, providing pool services (such as replacing liners and repairing pumps), and selling pool supplies and covers. Each month, you bill for sales and services. Traditionally, you type the total amount of your services in the document, but after a discussion with another business owner you discover how to use table formulas and begin to use them to calculate total fees on the invoice. In this exercise, you develop a professional-looking invoice and use formulas to calculate totals within the table. You will also create a mail merge document.

a. Begin a blank document and save it as **w03m2Pool_LastFirst**.

b. Insert a 1x3 table. Type **Party Pools, LLC** in the first cell of the first row. Change the font size of the text in row 1 to **28** and center the text.

c. Select the second and third rows. Split cells, resulting in 2 columns by 2 rows.

d. Complete the table as shown below, adding rows where necessary:

Invoice Number: 300	**Invoice Date: 8/20/2016**
Bill to:	**Submit Payment to:**
Ladean Murphy	**Party Pools, LLC**
33252 S. Campbell Ave.	**2048 S. Glenn Ave.**
Springfield, MO 65807	**Springfield, MO 65807**

e. Change the font size of the text you just typed to **14**.

f. Select the second row of the table, click the **PAGE LAYOUT tab**, and increase both **Spacing before** and **Spacing after** to **6 pt**. Bold entries in the second row.

g. Format the table as follows:
- Select the table. Open the *Borders and Shading* dialog box and select the **Box setting**. Accept default line selections and click **OK**.
- Select the second row of the table. Change the pen color to **Blue, Accent 1, Darker 25%** (fifth row, fifth column under *Theme Colors*). Apply the color to outside borders of the selection. Press **Esc**.
- Shade the first row with **Blue, Accent 1, Lighter 40%**.

h. Move to the end of the document and press **Enter** twice. Insert a 4x5 table. Type the following column headings in the first row.

File #	**Service Date**	**Property Address**	**Service Charge**

i. Change the column width of all columns to **1"**. Center align all entries on row 1 so that entries are centered both horizontally and vertically. Adjust the column width of only the third column (Property Address) to **2"**.

j. Type the following information in rows 2 through 4.

65	**8/4/2016**	**2402 E. Lee St., Republic**	**300.00**
70	**8/2/2016**	**105 Amanda Ln., Nixa**	**300.00**
75	**8/1/2016**	**335 Valley Vista Dr., Springfield**	**800.00**

k. Adjust the width of the third column to accommodate the longest entry, if necessary. Create a total row in row 5 by completing the following steps:
   - Merge the first three cells in row 5.
   - Type **Total** in the first cell in row 5 and right align the entry.
   - Insert a formula or function in the last cell on row 5 to total the service charges in the column above. The number format should show a dollar sign and two decimal places. Right align all numbers in the last column of the table. However, the words *Service Charge* should remain centered in the top cell of the last column.

l. Add another row to the end of the table. Merge all cells in the final row and type **Thank you for your business.** (Include the period.) Center the entry in the last row.

m. Insert a row after the row containing File # 75. Add the following text to the new row:

77	**8/4/2016**	**3324 N. Hickory Hills Ct., Nixa**	**100.00**

n. Update the total on the last row to include the new row information. Sort the rows containing service charges by Service Date and then by Service Charge, both in ascending order. *Do not include the header row, total row, or last row in the table in the sort selection.*

o. Center both tables horizontally on the page. Save and close the document.

p. Open *w03m2BillLetter*. Begin a mail merge, using the Step-by-Step Mail Merge Wizard. Complete the following steps:
   - Ensure that *Letters* is selected and click **Next: Starting document**.
   - Ensure that *Use the current document* is selected and click **Next: Select recipients**.
   - Browse and select **w03m2Clients.xlsx** from your data files as the data source. Select **Sheet1** and click **OK**. Sort the data source by **Last Name** in ascending order.
   - Click **Next: Write your letter**. Click before the second blank paragraph after the inside address. Insert an Address Block, using default settings.
   - Click after the space following the word *Dear* (and before the colon). Click **More items**. Click **First Name**, click **Insert**, and then click **Close**. Press **Space**. Click **More items** and insert the **Last Name**.
   - Click **Next: Preview your letters**. Adjust the paragraph spacing of the address block (beginning with *Ashley Dugan* and ending with *Midlothian, VA 23113*) to **0 pt** paragraph spacing before and after. Click **Next: Complete the merge**. Click **Edit individual letters** and ensure that all letters will be merged to a new document. Click **OK**.

q. Save the merged document, containing four pages, as **w03m2Merge_LastFirst** and close it. Close *w03m2BillLetter* without saving it.

r. Submit *w03m2Pool_LastFirst* and *w03m2Merge_LastFirst* based on your instructor's directions.

3 Remodeling

COLLABORATION CASE

FROM SCRATCH

As a general contractor, you are often called upon to help plan remodeling projects. A local shelter for women and children is considering updating a bathroom and has asked for your help in identifying necessary construction materials and an estimated cost for the equipment. The shelter is run by a board of directors to whom you will send a letter of introduction that includes a table of materials. This project is designed to be completed by a group of three students. The project is completed as follows:

a. The team will decide on a shared location in which to place files, such as OneDrive, Dropbox, or server space allotted by the college or university. All team members should become familiar with the shared space and any login requirements.
b. Determine a group name to be used throughout this project, or use one assigned by your instructor. Allocate one of three major tasks to each team member. One student will develop a main document to be used in a mail merge, one student will develop a data source to merge with the main document, and one student will develop a table of building materials to include in the main document before it is merged.

Student 1:

c. Develop an introduction letter to each member of the board of trustees. The letter will be designed as the main document in a mail merge; as such it will include fields for variable data such as each board member's name and mailing address. Indicate in the letter that the included table of materials outlines an estimated cost for each item as well as a total estimate for the remodeling project. The letter should be worded so that another student can easily insert the table of materials.
d. Format the letter attractively, using appropriate alignment, line spacing, and paragraph spacing. The letter should be error-free and grammatically correct. When complete, although without the table that will be inserted later, save the letter as **w03m3Introduction_GroupName**. Upload the letter to the shared location and contact the next student.

Student 2:

e. Develop a data source containing the names and addresses of all six board members. The data source can be a Word table, an Access database table or query, or an Excel worksheet.
f. Use descriptive field names and design the data source so it can be merged with a Word document. Include at least six records. Save the data source as **w03m3Trustees_GroupName** and upload the document to the shared location. Contact Student 3.

Student 3:

g. Convert the text found in *w03m3Construction* into a Word table and format the table so it is attractive, well structured, and descriptive. The table initially contains three columns, including description, quantity, and unit cost. A fourth column should be added to include a formula for each item (multiplying the quantity by the unit cost). Save the table as **w03m3Construction_GroupName** and upload the document to the shared location. Contact Student 2.

Student 2:

h. From the shared location, access or download *w03m3Introduction_GroupName* and *w03m3Construction_GroupName*. Insert text from (or copy and paste) the table into *w03m3Introduction_GroupName*, adjusting wording within the letter, if necessary, to assimilate the table. Save the revised letter as **w03m3Introduction_GroupName** and upload the file to the shared location, replacing the previous version with the new. Contact Student 1.

Student 1:

i. Download *w03m3Introduction_GroupName* and *w03m3Construction_GroupName*. Merge the two documents through Word's mail merge process, incorporating variable data where indicated in the letter. Save the merged document as **w03m3ConstructionLetter_GroupName**.
j. Submit the document based on your instructor's directions.

Beyond the Classroom

Personal Budget Report

RESEARCH CASE 

FROM SCRATCH

You are taking a personal finance class this semester and one of the assignments is to provide a report about your income, expenses, and spending habits for a 12-month period. Begin a new document and type two paragraphs that describe your spending habits. Be as general as you like, and feel free to create a fictional account of your spending, if you prefer. In the first paragraph, include your primary sources of income and how you allocate your income to different sources such as savings accounts and expenses. In the second paragraph, describe your major expenses. Create a Word table that details your budget under various major categories such as **Income**, **Expenses**, and **Savings**. Include subcategories such as **Fixed Expenses** and **Variable Expenses**. Examples of fixed expenses include tuition, rent, auto insurance, cable, and cell phone subscriptions. Variable expenses include food, books, school supplies, and utilities. Create multiple columns that enable you to break down your income and costs by category and by month, and then add formulas to show subtotals for each month and the grand total for the 12-month period. Save your report as **w03b2Budget_LastFirst**. Close the document and submit based on your instructor's directions.

Assignment Planner

DISASTER RECOVERY 

Your computer applications instructor has assigned the task of using your Word skills to design an assignment planner. She has challenged you to use what you have learned about Word tables to design an attractive document, with a table grid set up so you can enter class assignments for each week. The assignment is a group project, so you and your classmates decide to pattern the assignment planner table after a notebook you already use to record assignments. The first attempt at table design did not go so well, and the classmate who began the project needs help. Open *w03b3Planner* and redesign the document to produce an attractive planner that you could actually use. Do not settle for a mundane table. Use what you have learned about table styles, creating borders, adjusting row height and column width, and alignment to create a stunning table. Make sure your table has enough space for a five-day week and six subjects. Complete the table with a sample week of assignments in classes in which you are enrolled. Save the completed document as **w03b3Planner_LastFirst** and submit based on your instructor's directions.

Pre-Interview Activities

SOFT SKILLS CASE

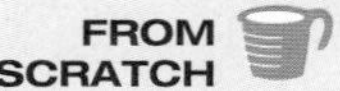

FROM SCRATCH

As an assistant in the Office of Student Development, you will create a short document for mailing to all graduating seniors. The document is in the form of a memo, with a placeholder for each student recipient's first and last names, as indicated by the starred placeholders in the sample below:

MEMO
TO: *First Name* *Last Name*
FROM: Office of Student Development
DATE: Current Date
Memo Text

Develop the memo as a main document for inclusion in a mail merge, containing a table you will create after watching the video on pre-interview skills. In the memo, you will let students know how important it is to prepare for an interview, and you will develop a table within the memo with at least three columns and several rows. Column headings might include such categories as Activities, Timeline, and Expected Outcome. The table should be attractively formatted, using appropriate column width, headings, and style. Be creative, designing your own style with shading and border tools. When the memo is complete, develop a data source with the first and last names as well as major program of study for at least eight fictional graduating seniors. Finally, merge the main document with the data source. Save the final merged document as **w03b4PreInterview_LastFirst**. Submit the file based on your instructor's directions.

Capstone Exercise

You work as the business manager for the local Sports Medicine Clinic and are responsible for many forms of correspondence. This week, you want to send a letter of welcome to three physical therapists recently hired at the clinic. Additionally, you need to send your weekly reminders to patients who are scheduled for upcoming treatment or consultations. In the past, the letters were generated manually and names were typed in each letter separately. However, because you now use Word 2013, you decide to create and use source data documents and implement a mail merge so you can produce the letters quickly and accurately.

Create a Table Containing Therapist Information

You will create a new document that includes a table of information about the new physical therapists. Then you will personalize the welcome letter created for the therapists and use information from the table to create a personal letter for each person.

a. Open a new blank document and save it as **w03c1Therapists_LastFirst**.

b. Create a table with the following information:

Name	Credentials	Street Address	Days Working	Salary
Mike Salat	**M.S., ATC**	**2342 W. Cardinal Street**	**Monday-Thursday**	**$65,000**
Justin Ebert	**M.S., ATC**	**34234 S. Callie Place**	**Monday-Friday**	**$68,000**
Karen Rakowski	**ATC, PT**	**98234 E. Shepherd Lane**	**Monday-Friday**	**$65,000**

c. Separate each name, including the column heading, into two columns, because it will be easier to use in form letters using mail merge features. (Hint: Uncheck the option *Merge cells before split* in the Split Cells dialog box.) Make necessary changes to the table to display the therapists' first and last names in two separate columns. The first column should include first names, while the second column contains last names. The first cell in the first row should include **First Name**, and the second cell in the first row should include **Last Name**.

d. Insert three new columns after the Street column for the City, State, and Zip information. Add a column heading to each new column, with **City**, **State**, and **Zip**, from left to right. Center entries in row 1 both horizontally and vertically. Populate each cell in the City column with **Conway**. Each cell in the State column should contain **AR**, and each cell in the Zip column should contain **72032**. Center all entries in rows 2, 3, and 4 both horizontally and vertically.

e. Create a new row at the end of the table. Type the word **Average** in the eighth cell on the last row and right align it. Use a formula to average the Salary column in the next cell on the last row. (Hint: In the Formula dialog box, remove the suggested function, but leave the = and paste an Average function, indicating that the average should include the numbers *Above*.) Select a currency number format, displaying a dollar sign and two places to the right of the decimal.

f. Select a table style of **Grid Table 6 Colorful - Accent 6** (sixth row, seventh column, under *Grid Tables*). Select a pen color of **Green, Accent 6** and a double underline line style (seventh selection under *Line Style*). Brush the border dividing the first row from the second. Press **Esc**. Remove bold formatting from the first names in column 1.

g. Click the **Border Styles arrow** and select **Border Sampler**. Click to sample the new border dividing the first and second rows and brush it along the bottom border of the table. Press **Esc**.

h. Sort the data in the table (but do not include the header or total rows) by Last Name in ascending order. Save and close the document.

Merge Therapist Information into a Welcome Letter

You have documented information about the new physical therapists; you can use it as a source for the welcome letter.

a. Open *w03c1Welcome*. Start a mail merge using the welcome letter as the source document. The recipient information will come from *w03c1Therapists_LastFirst*. Be sure to deselect the last record in the data source so the Average row is not included in the merge.

b. Replace the bracketed *Current Date* with today's date. Replace the starred placeholders in the letter with fields from the recipient table. Insert an Address Block using the default settings. Include a first name in the salutation and replace *days of week* in the body of the letter with data from the Days_Working field. Replace *Firstname Lastname* in the closing with your first and last names.

c. Complete the merge of all records, producing a document containing three letters, each addressed to a recipient in the data source. Save the merged letters as **w03c1MergedWelcome_LastFirst** and close the document. Close *w03c1Welcome* without saving it.

Produce a Reminder Letter for Patients

Your second project for the day is the generation of a letter to remind patients of their appointment with therapists. For this project, you will use an Access database as the source because that is how your office stores patient information.

a. Begin a new document. You do not need to save the document at this time. Start a mail merge letter, using the current document, and pull your recipients from *w03c1Patients.accdb*. When you select the database file, use the Patients table.

b. Press **Enter** twice and insert today's date, aligned at the left margin. Press **Enter** three times and insert an Address Block, using default settings. Press **Enter** twice and type **RE: Upcoming Appointment**.

c. Press **Enter** twice and type **Please remember that you have an appointment at the Sports Medicine Clinic of Conway on *date*, at *time*. If you have paperwork to fill out, please arrive at our office 15 minutes prior to your appointment time stated above. Thank you!**

d. Press **Enter** twice and finish the letter by typing:
Sincerely,
The Sports Medicine Clinic of Conway
(501) 555-5555

e. Insert the fields for date and time in the first sentence and remove the markers. Change the formatting of the document so the letter is single spaced with no additional spacing before or after any paragraph. Insert three blank paragraphs between *Sincerely* and *The Sports Medicine Clinic of Conway*.

f. Merge all records from the data source into a new document. Save the document as **w03c1Appointments_LastFirst** and close it. Close the original mail merge document without saving it. Exit Word.

g. Submit *w03c1Welcome_LastFirst*, *w03c1MergedWelcome_LastFirst*, and *w03c1Appointments_LastFirst* based on your instructor's directions.

Word

Collaboration and Research

CHAPTER 4

Communicating and Producing Professional Papers

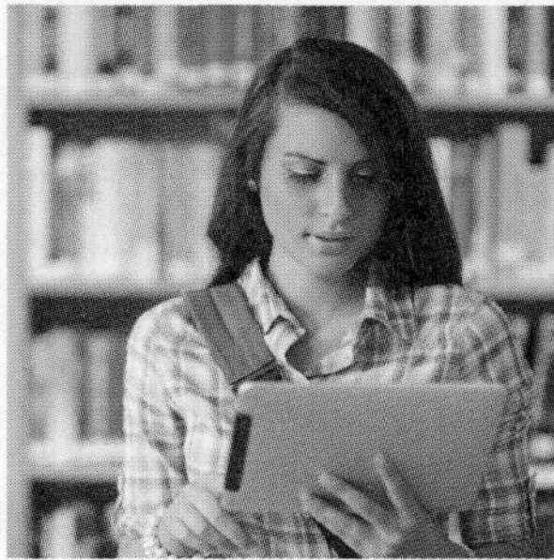

OBJECTIVES AFTER YOU READ THIS CHAPTER, YOU WILL BE ABLE TO:

CASE STUDY | Literature Analysis

You are a college student enrolled in several classes in which you are required to write papers. One is a literature class, and the other is a business management class. Each class requires that you adhere to a specific writing style; each style differs with respect to writing guidelines and the use of citations. As a requirement for the literature class in which you are enrolled, you will prepare an analysis of *The White Heron*, a short story by Sarah Orne Jewett. The analysis is a group effort, completed by five students, including you. You are required to develop the paper based on a particular writing style, and you will include citations and a bibliography. Your instructor will provide feedback in the form of comments that the group will then incorporate into the paper. Because you are a commuting student with a part-time job, you are not always on campus and your time is very limited. As is typical of many college students, even those in your literature group, time and availability are in short supply. The group is quick to realize that much of the coordination on the project must be done from a distance. You will share the project in such a way that each student can contribute, although not in a group setting. Instead, the document will be available online, with each student reviewing, contributing, and reposting the project. Another project involves a short paper for your business management class in which you will include a cover page as well as footnotes.

Research Paper Basics

Researching a topic and preparing a research paper is a common component of most college degrees. The task of writing a research paper is often met with dread by many college students, and although Word cannot replace the researcher, it can provide a great deal of support for properly citing sources and adhering to specific style manuals. A ***style manual***, or style guide, is a set of standards for designing documents. In addition, Word assists with preparing footnotes and endnotes and preparing a bibliography. Although the research and wording of a research paper are up to you, Word is an excellent tool in the production of an attractive, well-supported document.

In this section, you will explore the use of Word features that support the preparation of a research paper. Specifically, you will understand the use of style manuals, create source references and insert citations, develop a bibliography, and work with footnotes and endnotes.

Using a Writing Style and Acknowledging Sources

As you write a research paper, you will develop content that supports your topic. The wording you use and the way you present your argument are up to you; however, you will be expected to adhere to a prescribed set of rules regarding page design and the citing of sources. Those rules are spelled out in a style guide that you can refer to as you develop a research paper. A style guide prescribes such settings as margins, line and paragraph spacing, the use of footnotes and endnotes, the way sources are cited, and the preparation of a bibliography.

It is common practice to use a variety of ***sources*** to supplement your own thoughts when writing a paper, report, legal brief, or other type of document. In fact, the word *research* implies that you are seeking information from other sources to support or explore your topic when writing a research paper. Properly citing or giving credit to your sources of information ensures that you avoid plagiarizing. Merriam-Webster's Collegiate Dictionary's definition of ***plagiarizing*** is "to steal and pass off (the ideas or words of another) as one's own." Not limited to failure to cite sources, plagiarism includes buying a paper that is already written and asking (or paying) someone else to write a paper for you. In addition to written words, plagiarism applies to spoken words, multimedia works, or graphics. Plagiarism has serious moral and ethical implications and is typically considered academic dishonesty in a college or university.

Select a Writing Style

When assigning a research paper, your instructor will identify the preferred ***writing style***. Various writing styles are available and described in style manuals that are available both in print and online; however, the choice of writing style is often a matter of the academic discipline in which the research is conducted. For example, MLA style is often used in the humanities, while the field of social science typically prefers APA style. Those styles and others are described in this section.

A style manual does not require specific wording within a research paper. It will not assist with developing your topic or collecting research. However, it does provide a set of rules that results in standardized documents that present citations in the same manner and that include the same general page characteristics. In that way, research documents contain similar page features and settings so a reader can focus on the content of a paper without the distraction of varying page setups. Among the most commonly used style manuals are ***MLA (Modern Language Association)***, ***APA (American Psychological Association)***, and ***Chicago***.

If you have recently been assigned the task of writing a research paper as a requirement for an English class, you most likely were instructed to use *MLA writing style*. The humanities disciplines, including English, foreign languages, philosophy, religion, art, architecture, and literature, favor the MLA style, which has been in existence for more than 50 years. Brief parenthetical citations throughout a paper identify sources of information, with those sources arranged alphabetically in a works cited page. MLA style is used in many countries around the world, including the United States, Brazil, China, India, and Japan. Current MLA guidelines are published in *MLA Handbook for Writers of Research Papers* and *MLA Style Manual and Guide to Scholarly Publishing*.

Such disciplines as business, economics, communication, and social sciences promote the use of *APA writing style*. Developed in 1929, APA attempts to simplify the expression of scientific ideas and experiment reports in a consistent manner. Its focus is on the communication of experiments, literature reviews, and statistics. The *Publication Manual of the American Psychological Association* provides current rules and guidelines associated with the writing style.

Chicago writing style is an excellent choice for those who are preparing papers and books for publication. In fact, it is one of the most trusted resources within the book publishing industry. True to its name, the Chicago writing style was developed at the University of Chicago in 1906. It is described in *The Chicago Manual of Style*, currently in its 16th edition. The style is often referred to as *CMS* or *CMOS*. Often associated with the Chicago writing style, the ***Turabian*** writing style originated as a subset of Chicago. The dissertation secretary at the University of Chicago, Kate Turabian, narrowed the Chicago writing style to focus on writing papers. To do so, she omitted much of the information that is relevant for publishing. Currently, Turabian style is used mainly for the development of papers in the field of history.

Regardless of the writing style used, most research papers share common formatting features, as described below. With minor tweaks, a research paper generated according to these suggestions will be well on the way to completion.

- Align text at the left.
- Double-space lines.
- Include no paragraph spacing before or after.
- Set all margins (top, bottom, left, and right) at 1".
- Indent the first line of all body paragraphs by 1/2".
- Separate sentences by only one space.
- Use a serif font, such as Times New Roman, at 12 pt size.
- Create a right-aligned header, including the page number, positioned 1/2" from the top of the page.

Create a Source and Include a Citation

By its very nature, a research paper is a collection of ideas and statements related to a topic. Many of those ideas are your own, summarizing your knowledge and conclusions. However, you will often include facts and results obtained from other sources. When you quote another person, glean ideas from others, or include information from another publication, you must give credit to the source by citing it in the body of your paper and/or including it in a bibliography. A ***citation*** is a brief, parenthetical reference placed at the end of a sentence or paragraph. Word 2013 enables you to select a writing style upon which all citations, sources, and bibliographic entries will be based. Before using Word to create a research paper, you should select a writing style:

STEP 1»

1. Click the REFERENCES tab.
2. Click the Style arrow in the Citations & Bibliography group (see Figure 4.1).
3. Click a writing style to use.

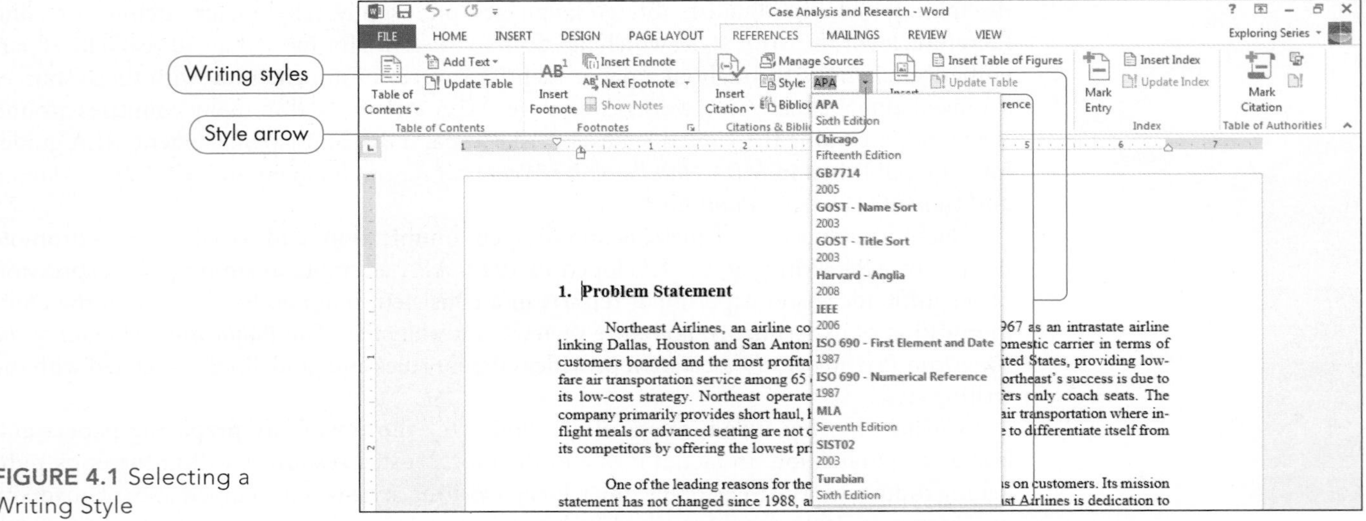

FIGURE 4.1 Selecting a Writing Style

Whenever you quote or paraphrase another person or publication, you should reference the source with a citation. Typically, a citation includes an author or publication name, with an optional page number. A citation directs a reader to a source of information you used. For more information, the reader can check the source on your bibliography or works cited page. Word 2013 formats sources and citations according to the writing style you specify, freeing you from the task of constantly checking a writing style for guidance. Even so, you should always compare citations and bibliographic entries created by Word with the most current writing style guidelines to ensure accuracy.

Proper placement of a citation within a research paper is critical. A citation should appear near a source of reference without interrupting the flow of a sentence. Use your judgment in placing a citation. For example, a long section of text that comes from one source should be cited at the end of the section—not after every sentence within the section. In other cases, a sentence that includes a quote or a direct reference to a particular source should be cited at the end of the sentence. Check a writing style manual for assistance with determining where to place a citation. Citations are typically placed before a punctuation mark that ends a sentence. As you create a citation, you will either add a new source or select a previously defined source as the reference. A cited reference includes the type of source (book, journal article, report, Web site, etc.), title, publisher, page number(s), and other items specific to the type of source. At the conclusion of a report, you can use Word to create a bibliography, listing all of the sources you have cited.

To insert a citation and source:

1. Click at the end of a sentence or phrase that you want to cite.
2. Click the REFERENCES tab.
3. Click Insert Citation in the Citations & Bibliography group.
4. If inserting a previously defined source, click the source. If creating a new source, click Add New Source and type the new source information (see Figure 4.2).

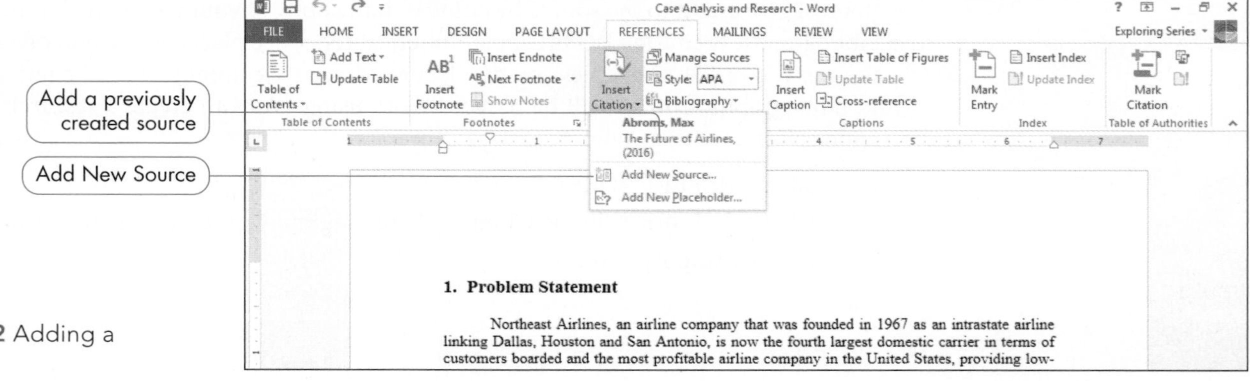

FIGURE 4.2 Adding a Source

Depending on the writing style in use, the way a citation is worded may vary. Although Word 2013 automatically formats citations, you might need to modify the wording or placement of items to accommodate the writing style. For example, if a sentence you are citing includes the author's name, most writing styles require only the page number in the citation, not the author's name. However, Word 2013 will place the author's name in the citation, so you must edit the citation to remove the name. A parenthetical citation is considered a field, which can be selected as a unit within a paper, with actions that can be taken after selecting (such as editing or removing). As such, you can simply click the citation to select it.

To edit a citation:

1. Click the parenthetical citation.
2. Click the Citation Options arrow.
3. Click Edit Citation.
4. Add a page reference and/or suppress the Author, Year, or Title by selecting the appropriate boxes.
5. Click OK.

Editing a Citation and Source

When you click a parenthetical citation and click the Citation Options arrow, you can do more than simply edit the citation. You can also choose Edit Source (updating the source citation wherever it appears in the document) or Convert citation to static text (removing the field designation from the citation so that you can treat it like normal text). When you convert the citation to text, however, it is no longer included in a bibliography generated by Word unless it also appears elsewhere in the paper.

Share and Search for a Source

When you create a source, it is available for use in the current document, saved in the document's ***Current List***. It is also placed in a ***Master List***, which is a database of all sources created in Word on a particular computer. Sources saved in the Master List can be shared in any Word document. This feature is helpful to those who use the same sources on multiple occasions. Suppose you are working with a research paper that addresses a topic similar to that of another paper you created on the same computer. To access a source from the Master List of previously defined sources:

1. Click the REFERENCES tab.
2. Click Manage Sources.
3. Select a source in the Master List that you intend to use in the current document (see Figure 4.3).
4. Click Copy to move it to the Current List.
5. Click Close.
6. Click in the location of the citation in the current document and click Insert Citation.
7. Select the source reference.

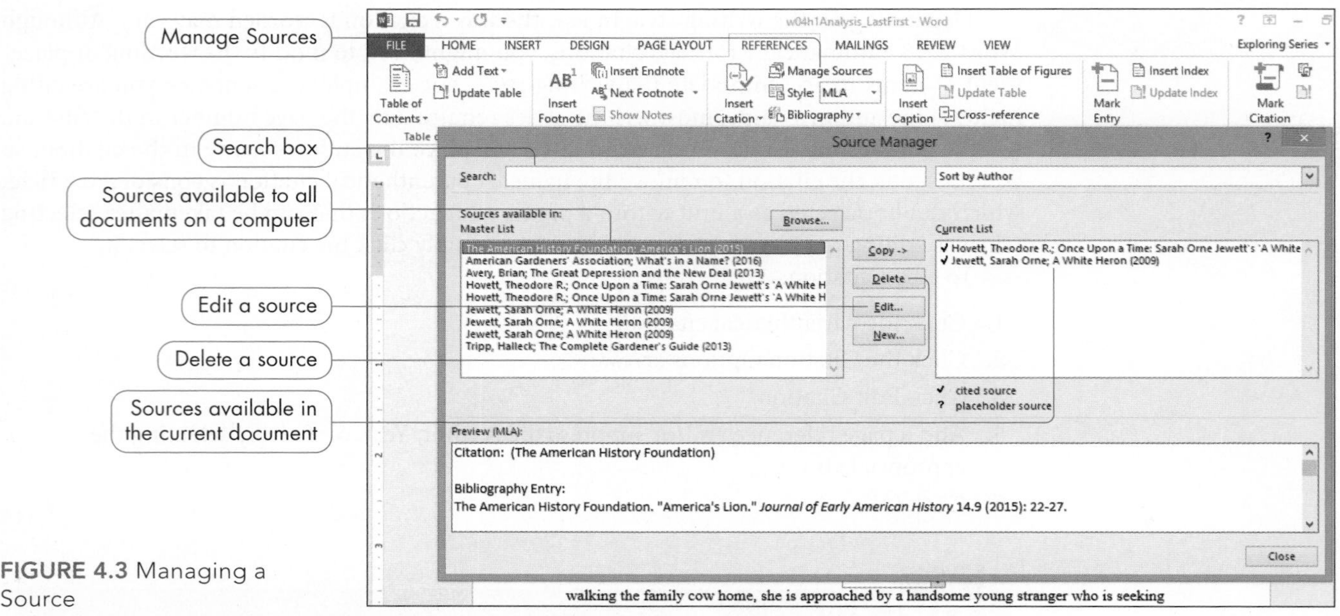

FIGURE 4.3 Managing a Source

The Source Manager not only enables you to share sources among several documents, but it also makes it easy to delete and edit sources. Click Manage Sources on the References tab, select a source from either the Master or Current List, and then click Delete or Edit (refer to Figure 4.3).

Especially if sources are numerous, you might appreciate a quick way to search for a particular source. You can search by author, title, or year. Type a search term in the Search box of the Source Manager dialog box (refer to Figure 4.3). As you type, Word narrows the results so you can more easily determine if a source exists that meets your search criteria.

Create a Bibliography

A ***bibliography*** is a list of documents or sources consulted by an author during research for a paper. It not only guides a reader to sources of your research for additional study, but it also provides a reader with an opportunity to validate your references for accuracy. In theory, a bibliography lists not only those references that were cited in parenthetical terms throughout the paper but also those that were not cited but were helpful as you prepared the paper. However, Word includes in a bibliography (or ***works cited*** page) only those sources that were cited in the paper, which is the way most research documents are expected to be prepared. Therefore, a bibliography and a works cited page (which is designed to contain only cited references) are considered synonymous terms when working with Word. After a bibliography is prepared, you can always edit it to add additional references if required. Figure 4.4 shows a bibliography developed in Word. The bibliography is formatted according to the MLA writing style, which requires the use of *Works Cited* as a title. Note that all sources include a hanging indent, which is typical of all writing style requirements. In addition, entries are listed in alphabetical order by last names of authors or editors, or by first words of titles.

Works Cited

Hovet, Theodore R. "Once Upon a Time: Sarah Orne Jewett's 'A White Heron' as a Fairy Tale." *Studies in Short Fiction* 25 Sept. 2011: 63-68.

Jewett, Sarah Orne. "A White Heron." *The American Tradition in Literature*. Ed. George Perkins and Barbara Perkins. Vol. 2. New York: McGraw-Hill, 2009. 531-537.

Propp, Vladimir. *Morphology of a Folk Tale*. New York: Anniston, 1994.

FIGURE 4.4 Bibliography

Depending on the writing style you are following, the term used for the list of references varies. MLA uses the term *Works Cited*, whereas APA requires *References*. Still others prefer *Bibliography*. You should be familiar with the preferred term and organization before using Word to develop the list of references. At that point, Word simplifies the addition of the reference page:

STEP 2»

1. Insert a page break at the end of the research paper.
2. Click the REFERENCES tab.
3. Click Bibliography.
4. Select Bibliography, References, or Works Cited (depending on the particular writing style requirement). If you want no heading but simply the formatted references, click Insert Bibliography.

Regardless of which approach you take, you should always confirm that the resulting page meets all requirements of the particular style to which you are writing. Just as you would proofread a document instead of relying solely on Word's spelling checker, you should also consult a writing style manual to make sure your bibliography is correct.

When Word creates a bibliography page, it places all citations in a single field. As shown in Figure 4.5, when you click a bibliography list that Word has prepared, the entire list is shown as a unit, called a Citations field. The field can be updated; for example, if at a later time you include additional sources within the paper, click *Update Citations and Bibliography* (see Figure 4.5) to include the new sources in the bibliography. You can also choose to format the existing bibliography with a different title (perhaps changing from *Works Cited* to *References*), and you can convert the bibliography to static text, removing the field designation from the bibliography so that you can edit and delete references as you like. At that point, however, you cannot update the bibliography with additional sources.

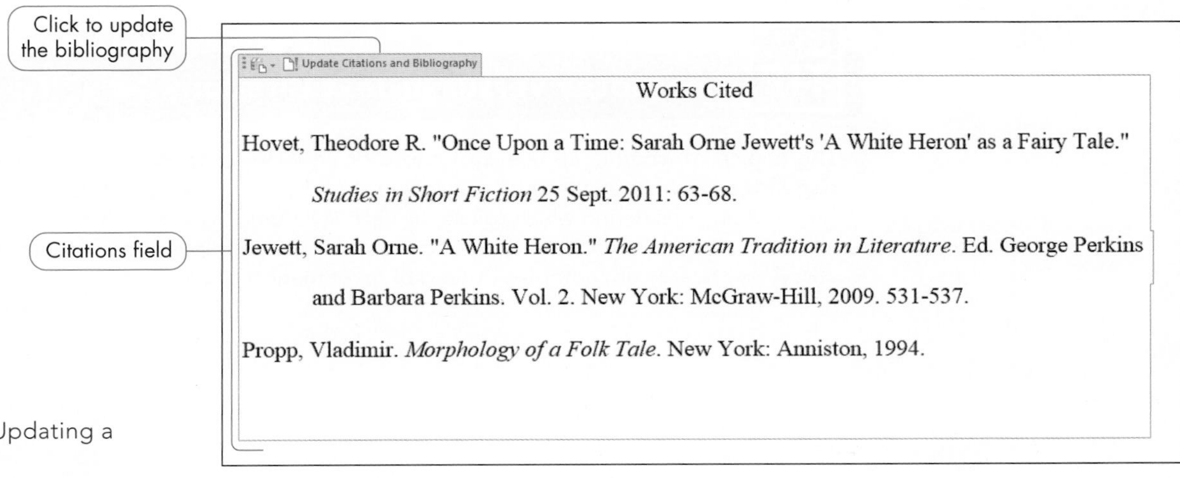

Works Cited

Hovet, Theodore R. "Once Upon a Time: Sarah Orne Jewett's 'A White Heron' as a Fairy Tale." *Studies in Short Fiction* 25 Sept. 2011: 63-68.

Jewett, Sarah Orne. "A White Heron." *The American Tradition in Literature*. Ed. George Perkins and Barbara Perkins. Vol. 2. New York: McGraw-Hill, 2009. 531-537.

Propp, Vladimir. *Morphology of a Folk Tale*. New York: Anniston, 1994.

FIGURE 4.5 Updating a Bibliography

Creating and Modifying Footnotes and Endnotes

A ***footnote*** is a citation or note that appears at the bottom of a page, while an ***endnote*** serves the same purpose but appears at the end of a document. Like in-text parenthetical citations, the purpose of a footnote and endnote is to draw a reader's attention to a specific source of information. In addition, footnotes and endnotes are often used to further describe a statistic or statement used in the report without including additional detail in the text. A footnote, providing clarification of a statistic, is shown in Figure 4.6. Note that the footnote is linked by superscript (elevated number) to the corresponding reference in the paper.

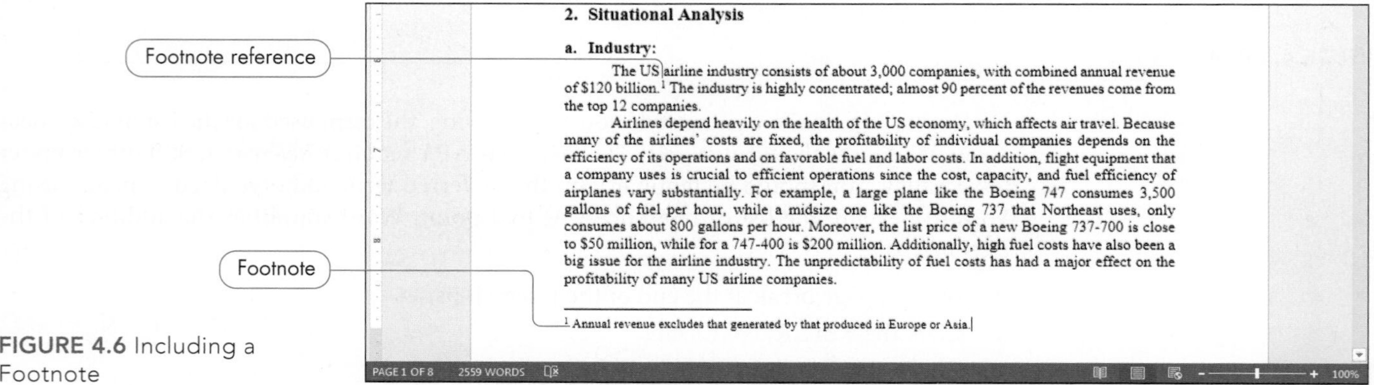

2. Situational Analysis

a. Industry:

The US airline industry consists of about 3,000 companies, with combined annual revenue of $120 billion.[1] The industry is highly concentrated; almost 90 percent of the revenues come from the top 12 companies.

Airlines depend heavily on the health of the US economy, which affects air travel. Because many of the airlines' costs are fixed, the profitability of individual companies depends on the efficiency of its operations and on favorable fuel and labor costs. In addition, flight equipment that a company uses is crucial to efficient operations since the cost, capacity, and fuel efficiency of airplanes vary substantially. For example, a large plane like the Boeing 747 consumes 3,500 gallons of fuel per hour, while a midsize one like the Boeing 737 that Northeast uses, only consumes about 800 gallons per hour. Moreover, the list price of a new Boeing 737-700 is close to $50 million, while for a 747-400 is $200 million. Additionally, high fuel costs have also been a big issue for the airline industry. The unpredictability of fuel costs has had a major effect on the profitability of many US airline companies.

[1] Annual revenue excludes that generated by that produced in Europe or Asia.

FIGURE 4.6 Including a Footnote

You should never use both footnotes and endnotes in the same paper. Choosing whether to use footnotes or endnotes, if at all, depends in part on the number of citations included and the way you want your reader to process the report's information. Because endnotes are included as a list at the end of the document, they do not add clutter to the end of pages. In addition, they might make the report easier to read because a reader's gaze is not constantly shifting back and forth from the bottom of a page to the text. Conversely, a footnote provides immediate clarification of a source and enables the writer to make additional comments related to a statement on the same page as the footnote.

Although you might choose to include footnotes to provide additional information related to a statement on the same page, you will most likely use a bibliography or works cited page to provide a complete list of referenced sources in a paper. An advantage to using a bibliography for that task is that each source is listed only once. In contrast, a footnote or endnote appears each time a source is referenced, regardless of how many times the same source is cited in a paper. Although subsequent footnotes and endnotes referencing the same source are abbreviated, they are still listed, often resulting in a cluttered, possibly distracting, arrangement of repetitive information.

TIP Footnotes Versus In-Text Citations

The choice of whether to use a footnote or an in-text citation to reference a source depends somewhat on the writing style you are following. Always refer to the writing style guide when considering which to use, as each style tends to prefer one to the other. The choice is also related to the type of document. For example, legal documents almost always rely heavily on footnotes instead of parenthetical citations.

Including a bibliography does not mean that you cannot use footnotes to provide more detailed descriptions of statements or facts in the paper. You might use a footnote to provide an explanation of statistics. For example, a statistic on the number of victims in a natural disaster or the amount of money given through a government program could be further detailed in a footnote. You might also define or illustrate a concept included in the report, providing a personal comment. Much of business writing is actually persuasive text, in which you explain a situation or encourage others to take some action. Using a footnote is a great way to further describe a statistic used in your text without having to incorporate it into the written paragraph. That way, you do not risk cluttering the manuscript with overly explanatory text, perhaps losing or diverting the attention of the reader. You should be aware, however, that most writing styles limit a footnote to only one sentence. Therefore, any planned explanation of a report statement must be condensed to just one sentence.

Create Footnotes and Endnotes

Source information in a document that you reference with a footnote or endnote includes a number or symbol in superscript. The reference is then keyed to the same number or symbol at the end of the page (footnote) or at the end of the document (endnote).

The References tab includes the Insert Footnote and Insert Endnote options. To insert a footnote or endnote:

STEP 3»

1. Click beside the text to reference (or after ending punctuation, if referencing a sentence)
2. Click the REFERENCES tab.
3. Click Insert Footnote (or Insert Endnote) in the Footnotes group.
4. Type footnote text.

A footnote is automatically positioned at the end of the page, with the same superscript as that assigned to the in-text reference. An endnote is automatically positioned sequentially with other endnotes on a page at the end of the document. By default, Word sequentially numbers footnotes with Arabic numerals (1, 2, and 3). Endnotes are numbered with lowercase Roman numerals (i, ii, and iii). If you add or delete footnotes or endnotes, Word renumbers remaining notes automatically.

Although Word automatically assigns numbers to footnotes or endnotes, you can specify the use of a symbol instead. Click where the reference is to be placed and click the References tab. Click the Footnotes Dialog Box Launcher. Click Symbol in the *Footnote and Endnote* dialog box, select a symbol, click OK, and then click Insert.

Modify Footnotes and Endnotes

Occasionally, you will determine that different wording better suits a particular footnote or endnote. Or perhaps you want to remove a footnote or endnote completely. You can even change the format of a footnote or endnote, changing the font, font size, or character formatting. To modify a footnote or endnote, you can double-click the numeric reference in the body of the document. The insertion point will be placed to the left of the corresponding footnote or endnote text.

To insert a footnote or endnote while specifying settings other than those selected by default, use the *Footnote and Endnote* dialog box. Click the Footnotes Dialog Box Launcher to open the dialog box. As shown in Figure 4.7, you can modify the placement, number format, symbol, and initial number before you insert a new footnote or endnote.

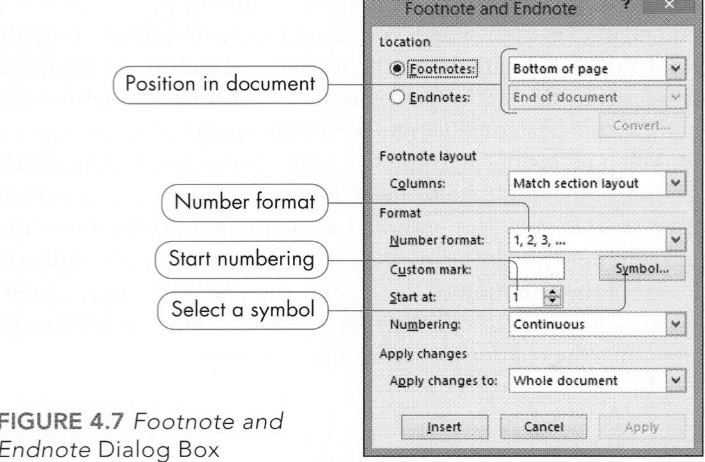

FIGURE 4.7 *Footnote and Endnote* Dialog Box

You can remove note text and replace it with alternate wording, just as you would adjust wording in a document. If you plan to change the format of a single note, instead of affecting all footnotes or endnotes in a document, you can select text and apply different formatting—perhaps italicizing or bolding words.

More often, you might want to adjust the format of every footnote or endnote in a document. Footnotes are formatted in Footnote Text style, and endnotes are formatted in Endnote Text style. Those styles include a specific font and font size. To modify the style of either a footnote or endnote so that the formatting changes you make are applied to all notes in a document:

1. Right-click a footnote or endnote and click Style.
2. Click Modify (in the Style dialog box).
3. Adjust font and alignment settings or click Format for more selections.
4. Click OK (repeatedly, if necessary) to accept settings and return to the document.

Deleting a Footnote or Endnote

To delete a footnote or endnote, select the numeric footnote or endnote indicator in the document. Press Delete.

Exploring Special Features

Although writing a research paper is a typical requirement of a college class, it is not the only type of paper you are likely to write. In the workplace, you might be asked to contribute to technical reports, grant proposals, and other types of business documents. Those reports are not likely to be as strictly bound to writing style rules as are reports written for academic purposes. In fact, you might find it necessary to include special features such as a table of contents, an index, and even a cover page to properly document a paper and make it easier to navigate. Such features are not usually included in a college research report or required by academic writing style guides, but they are common components of papers, chapters, and articles to be published or distributed.

Create a Table of Contents

A ***table of contents*** lists headings in the order they appear in a document, along with the page numbers on which the entries begin. The key to enabling Word to create a table of contents is to apply heading styles to headings in the document at appropriate levels. You can apply built-in styles, Heading 1 through Heading 9, or identify your own custom styles to use when generating the table of contents. For example, if you apply Heading 1 style to major headings, Heading 2 style to subordinate headings, and lesser numbered heading styles to remaining headings as appropriate, Word can create an accurate table of contents. At your request, Word will update the table of contents when you change heading text, sequence, or level.

STEP 4

To insert a predefined table of contents, ensure that headings in the document are formatted with heading styles according to level. Then:

1. Click the REFERENCES tab.
2. Click *Table of Contents* in the *Table of Contents* group.
3. Select an Automatic table style to create a formatted table of contents that can be updated when heading text or positioning changes (or select Manual Table to create a table of contents that is not updated when changes occur).

For more flexibility as you design a table of contents, you can click *Table of Contents* (on the References tab) and then select *Custom Table of Contents*. From the *Table of Contents* dialog box, select options related to page numbering and alignment, general format, level of headings to show, and leader style (the characters that lead the reader's eye from a heading to its page number). The subsequent table of contents can be updated when changes occur in headings within the document.

A table of contents created by Word is inserted as a field. When you click a table of contents, the entire table is shown as an entity that you can update or remove. As shown in Figure 4.8, controls at the top of the selection enable you to update, modify, or remove a table of contents. As you make changes to a document, especially if those changes affect the number, positioning, or sequencing of headings, you will want to update any associated table of contents. You will indicate whether you want to update page numbers only or the entire table.

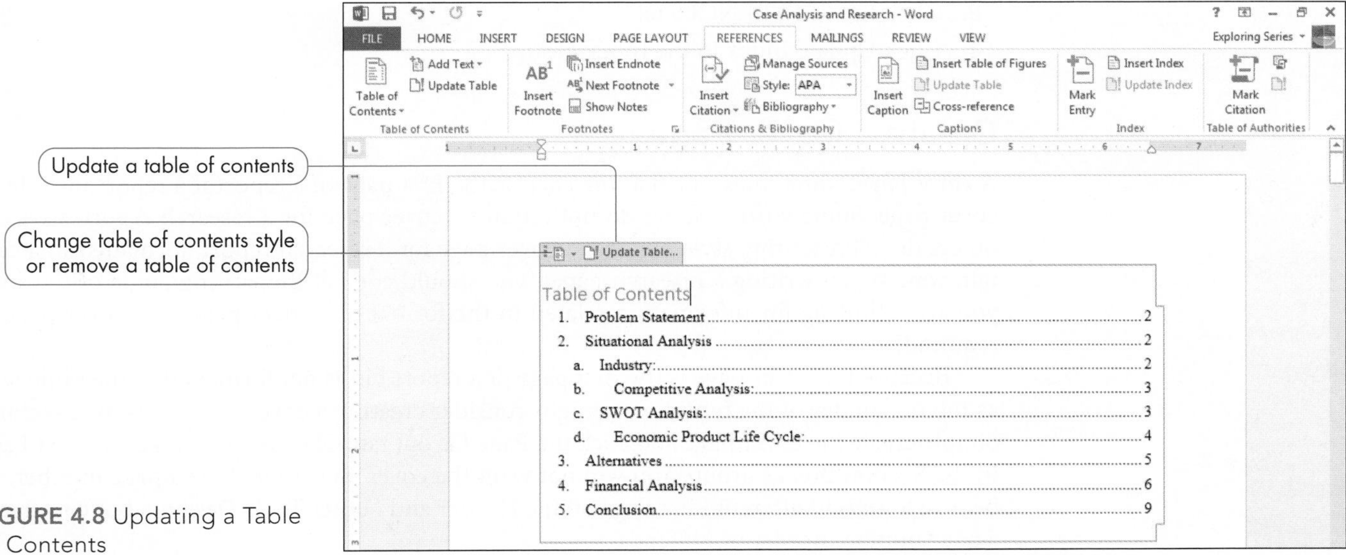

FIGURE 4.8 Updating a Table of Contents

Create an Index

No doubt you have used an ***index*** to locate a topic of interest in a book. In doing so, you were able to move quickly to the topic. Most books and many lengthy papers include an index. Typically located at the end of a book or document, an index provides an alphabetical listing of topics included in a document, along with related page numbers. Using Word 2013, you can mark items to include and then have them automatically formatted as an index.

To mark items to include in an index:

1. Select a word or phrase to include in an index.
2. Click the REFERENCES tab and click Mark Entry in the Index group.

3. Select or confirm settings in the Mark Index Entry dialog box.
    - Ensure that text in the Main entry box is stated exactly as it should appear in the index.
    - If only one occurrence of the selected text is to be noted in the index, click Mark. Otherwise, click Mark All to include all occurrences of the selected text.
    - Include a cross reference, if necessary. For example, an index entry for *appetizers* could be cross-referenced with *hors d'oeuvres.* Click Mark.
4. Repeat steps 1 and 3 for any additional terms to mark as index entries. Close the dialog box when all items have been marked.

As you mark entries for inclusion in the index, they will be coded in the document with a tag. After marking entries to include in an index, you are ready to create the index, typically among the last pages of a document. Word 2013 arranges the index entries in alphabetical order and supplies appropriate page references. To create an index:

1. Insert a blank page at the end of the document or at a location where the index is to display. Position the insertion point on the blank page.
2. Click the REFERENCES tab and click Insert Index in the Index group.
3. Adjust settings in the Index dialog box, including the format style, number of columns, language, and alignment.
4. Click OK.

Creating an index is usually among the last tasks related to preparing a paper, chapter, or book. However, even if an index has been created, you can still update the index with new entries. New entries are alphabetized along with the original entries in the index. To update an index so that newly marked entries are included:

1. Click in the index to select it.
2. Click the REFERENCES tab.
3. Click Update Index in the Index group.

Create a Cover Page

A ***cover page***, sometimes called a *title page*, is the first page of a report if a report includes a cover page. Some writing styles do not require a cover page for a research report, whereas others do. APA writing style requires a cover page for a research report, formatted in a certain way. When writing a research paper, you should consult the writing guide of the style you are following for information related to the format of a cover page (if a cover page is required).

STEP 5»

Because the cover page is the first page of a report but is not formatted in the same way as the remainder of the report, you might consider creating a cover page in its own section. Simply create the cover page and click the Page Layout tab. Click Breaks and click Next Page in the Section Breaks group. You will not want the cover page to include a page number, so be sure to select Different First Page on the Header and Footer Tools Design tab if you create a page number header or footer.

Creating a Cover Page

If the writing style allows it or if you are not following a writing style, you can use Word 2013 to create a cover page in any of a variety of styles. Click the Insert tab and click Cover Page in the Pages group. Select from a number of designs, or click More Cover Pages from Office.com for even more choice. Personalize the cover page with your name, report title, and any other variable data.

Quick Concepts

1. What type of writing style would you expect to be required to use for a writing assignment in a business class? ***p. 315***
2. How would you edit a citation to remove an author name and add a page number? ***p. 317***
3. You find that you can use some of the same sources in the research paper you are currently working on were used in your previous research paper. How can you pull sources from the previous paper so that you do not have to recreate them? ***p. 317***
4. You have developed a table of contents for a research paper. After having done that, you rearrange a few headings and add others. How can you make sure a table of contents is updated to reflect the current content of a document, especially if content has changed? ***p. 323***

Hands-On Exercises

1 Research Paper Basics

You have completed a draft of an analysis of the short story *A White Heron*. As a requirement for the literature class in which you are enrolled, you must format the paper according to MLA style, including citations and a bibliography. In addition to the literature analysis, you have also completed a marketing plan for a fictional company, required for a business management class. The instructor of that class has asked that you consider submitting the paper for inclusion in a collection of sample papers produced by the School of Business at your university. For that project, you will include a cover page, table of contents, and an index.

Skills covered: Select a Writing Style and Create a Source • Share and Search for a Source and Create a Bibliography • Create and Update Footnotes • Create a Table of Contents and an Index • Create a Cover Page

STEP 1 » SELECT A WRITING STYLE AND CREATE A SOURCE

You will format the analysis of *A White Heron* in MLA style and include citations where appropriate. Refer to Figure 4.9 as you complete Step 1.

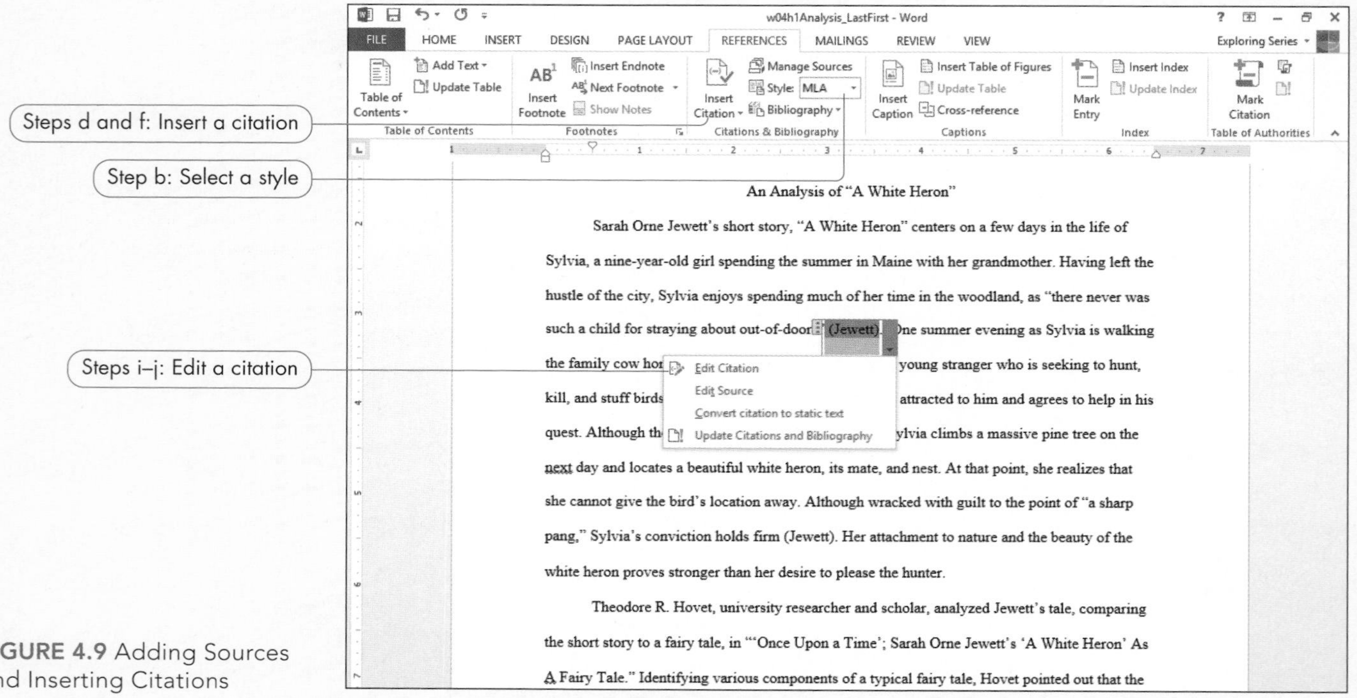

FIGURE 4.9 Adding Sources and Inserting Citations

a. Start Word. Open *w04h1Analysis* and save it as **w04h1Analysis_LastFirst**.

b. Click the **REFERENCES tab** and click the **Style arrow** in the Citations & Bibliography group. Select **MLA Seventh Edition**. Ensure that the following settings, required by the MLA writing style, are in place, adjusting any that may be missing or incorrect:

- Document is double-spaced.
- The font is Times New Roman 12 pt.
- There is no paragraph spacing before or after any paragraph.
- Margins are 1" at the top, bottom, left, and right.
- All body paragraphs are indented .5".
- The report title is centered.

c. Insert a right-aligned header that includes your last name, followed by a space and a plain page number. Make sure the page number is inserted as a field, not simply typed. The header should be formatted as Times New Roman 12 pt.

d. Place the insertion point after the ending quotation mark and before the ending period in the second sentence of the first body paragraph, ending in *straying about out-of-doors*. Click the **REFERENCES tab** and then click **Insert Citation** in the Citations & Bibliography group. Click **Add New Source**. Click the **Type of Source arrow** and click **Book Section**. Complete the citation as follows, but do not click OK after completing the source.

   Author: **Jewett, Sarah Orne**

   Title: **A White Heron**

   Book Title: **The American Tradition in Literature**

   Year: **2009**

   Pages: **531–537**

   City: **New York**

   Publisher: **McGraw-Hill**

e. Click **Show All Bibliography Fields**. Click in the **Editor box** and type **Perkins, George**. Click **Edit** beside *Editor*. Type **Perkins** in the **Last box**. Click in the **First box** and type **Barbara**. Click **Add** and click **OK**. Click in the **Volume box** and type **2**. Click **OK**.

   You have added a source related to a section of a book in which the short story is printed.

f. Click after the word *firm* and before the ending period in the sentence that ends in *Sylvia's conviction holds firm* in the same paragraph. Click **Insert Citation** in the Citations & Bibliography group and click **Jewett, Sarah Orne** to insert a citation to the same source as that created earlier.

g. Place the insertion point after the ending quotation mark and before the ending period in the sentence in the second body paragraph ending in *functions that are also present in "A White Heron"*. Add a new source, selecting **Article in a Periodical** as the source type:

   Author: **Hovet, Theodore R.**

   Title: **Once Upon a Time: Sarah Orne Jewett's 'A White Heron' as a Fairy Tale**

   Periodical Title: **Studies in Short Fiction**

   Year: **2011**

   Month: **Sept.**

   Day: **25**

   Pages: **63–68**

h. Click **Show All Bibliography Fields**, complete the following, and then click **OK**.

   Volume: **15**

   Issue: **1**

i. Click the parenthetical citation in the first body paragraph beside the words *straying about out-of-doors*. Click the **Citation Options arrow** and click **Edit Citation**. Type **532** in the **Pages box**. Click **OK**.

   You have added a page number to identify the source as required by MLA writing style.

j. Edit the next citation in the first body paragraph, following the sentence that ends in *Sylvia's conviction holds firm*, to include page number **537**. Click the only citation in the second body paragraph. Click the **Citation Options arrow** and click **Edit Citation**. Suppress the display of Author, Year, and Title, but include a Page Number of **63**. Click **OK**.

k. Save the document.

STEP 2 » SHARE AND SEARCH FOR A SOURCE AND CREATE A BIBLIOGRAPHY

Now that sources are cited and stored in the document, you can quickly insert the bibliography at the end. You will also explore the sharing of sources. Refer to Figure 4.10 as you complete Step 2.

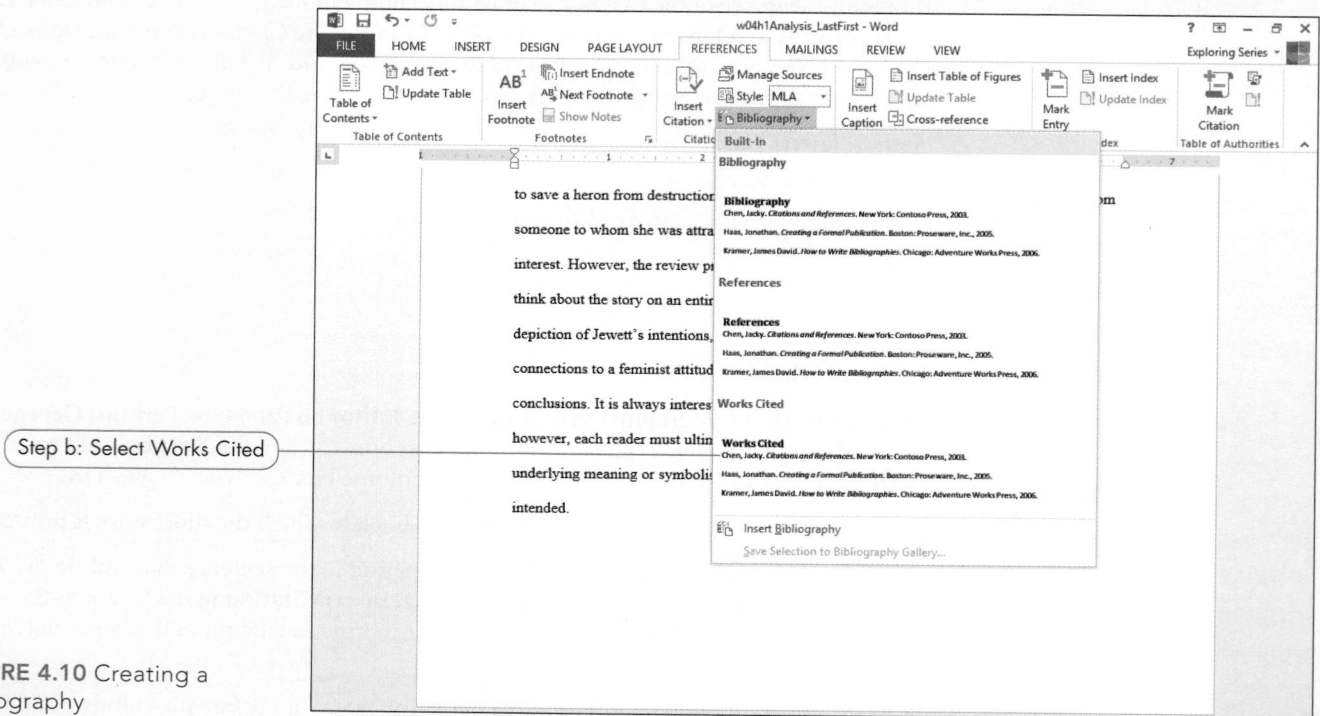

FIGURE 4.10 Creating a Bibliography

a. Click **Manage Sources.**

Note that the sources you created in the previous step are shown in the Master List as well as in the Current List. They are available for use in other documents, as well as in the current document.

> **TROUBLESHOOTING:** It is possible that sources other than those you just added are also shown in the Master List. The list includes all sources you have included in other documents as well as those in the current document.

b. Click **Close**. Press **Ctrl+End** to move to the end of the document. Press **Ctrl+Enter** to insert a page break. Click **Bibliography** in the Citations & Bibliography group and click **Works Cited.**

A bibliography is always included as a separate page at the end of the document. Therefore, you insert a page break before adding the bibliography. The bibliography includes the heading *Works Cited*. The two sources you used in your analysis are listed, although you may have to scroll up to see them.

c. Drag to select all text on the Works Cited page, including the heading *Works Cited* and all sources. Change the line spacing to **2.0** (or double), the paragraph spacing Before and After to **0**, and the font to **Times New Roman 12 pt**. Select the *Works Cited* heading, remove the bold format, and center the line.

The Works Cited page adheres to MLA writing style guidelines.

d. Save and close the document. Leave Word open for the next step.

STEP 3 ›› CREATE AND UPDATE FOOTNOTES

You are a business major enrolled in a business management class. As a final project, you have prepared a case analysis of a fictional airline. Due to the large amount of statistical data included, you expect to use footnotes to provide additional clarification. Because footnotes and endnotes are mutually exclusive—you only use one or the other in a single paper—you will not use endnotes. However, you know that the way in which endnotes and footnotes are added is very similar. Refer to Figure 4.11 as you complete Step 3.

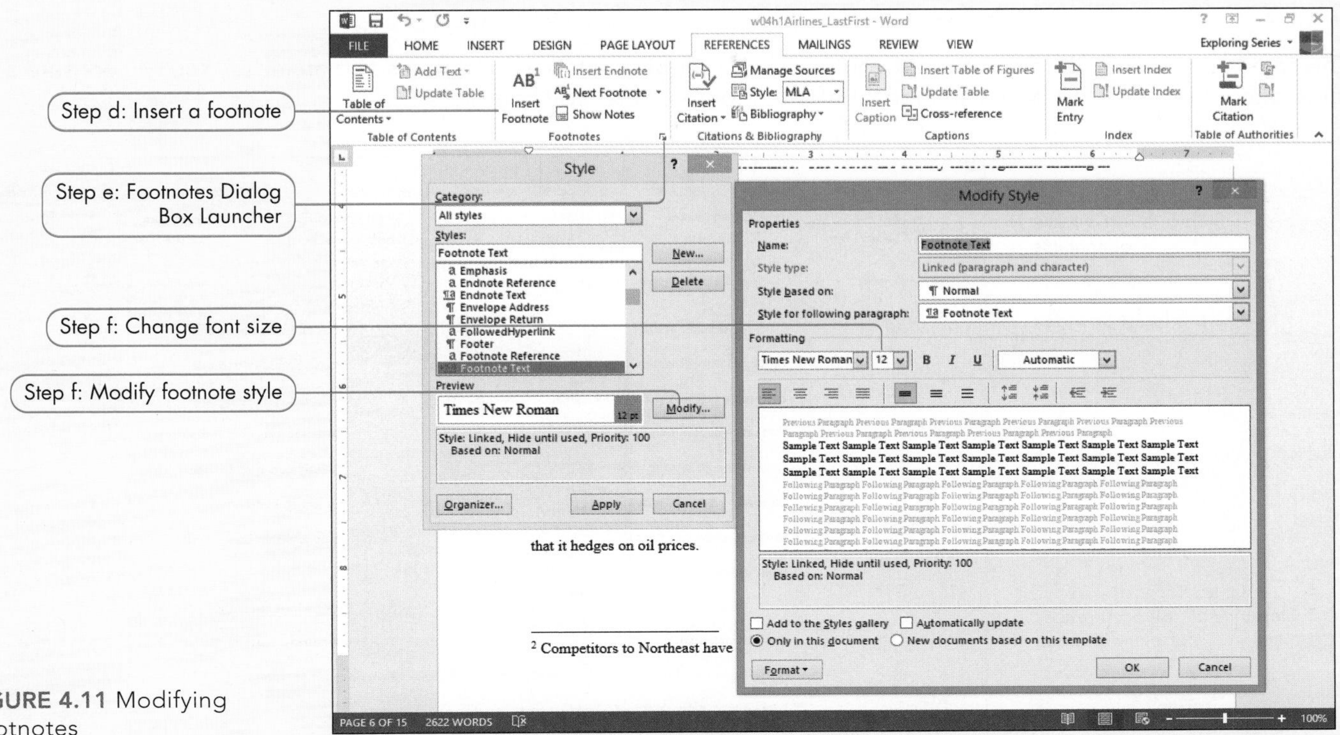

FIGURE 4.11 Modifying Footnotes

a. Open *w04h1Airlines* and save it as **w04h1Airlines_LastFirst**.

b. Click the **Select arrow** in the Editing group on the HOME tab, click **Select All**, and then apply the following formatting:

- Line spacing is 2.0 (or double)
- Paragraph spacing Before and After is 0
- Font is Times New Roman at 12 pt size
- Alignment is left aligned

c. Deselect the text.

d. Click **Find** in the Editing group. The Navigation Pane opens on the left. Type **200 million** in the Search box and press **Enter**. Click after the period ending the sentence that ends in *$200 million*, which is shown highlighted. Close the Navigation Pane. Click the **REFERENCES tab** and click **Insert Footnote** in the Footnotes group. Type **This statistic is obtained from the 2015 U.S. Air Transportation Log.** (include the period).

You insert a footnote, numbered with a superscript, further clarifying the information stated.

e. Scroll to page 4 and place the insertion point after the period ending the first paragraph, ending in *34 years*. Click the **Footnotes Dialog Box Launcher** and click **Insert**. Type **Competitors to Northeast have proven slightly less profitable.** (include the period).

You insert another footnote, numbered sequentially after the first footnote. Using the *Footnote and Endnote* dialog box, you have options to specify various choices, including numbering and formatting.

f. Right-click the footnote at the bottom of page 4 and click **Style**. Click **Modify**. Change the font size to **12**. Click **OK**. Click **Apply**.

You changed the footnote style for this document to include a font size of 12. The new format applies to all footnotes in the document.

g. Save the document.

STEP 4 » CREATE A TABLE OF CONTENTS AND AN INDEX

The case study is almost complete, but your instructor requires a table of contents and an index. You will prepare a table of contents and will begin an index. Refer to Figure 4.12 as you complete Step 4.

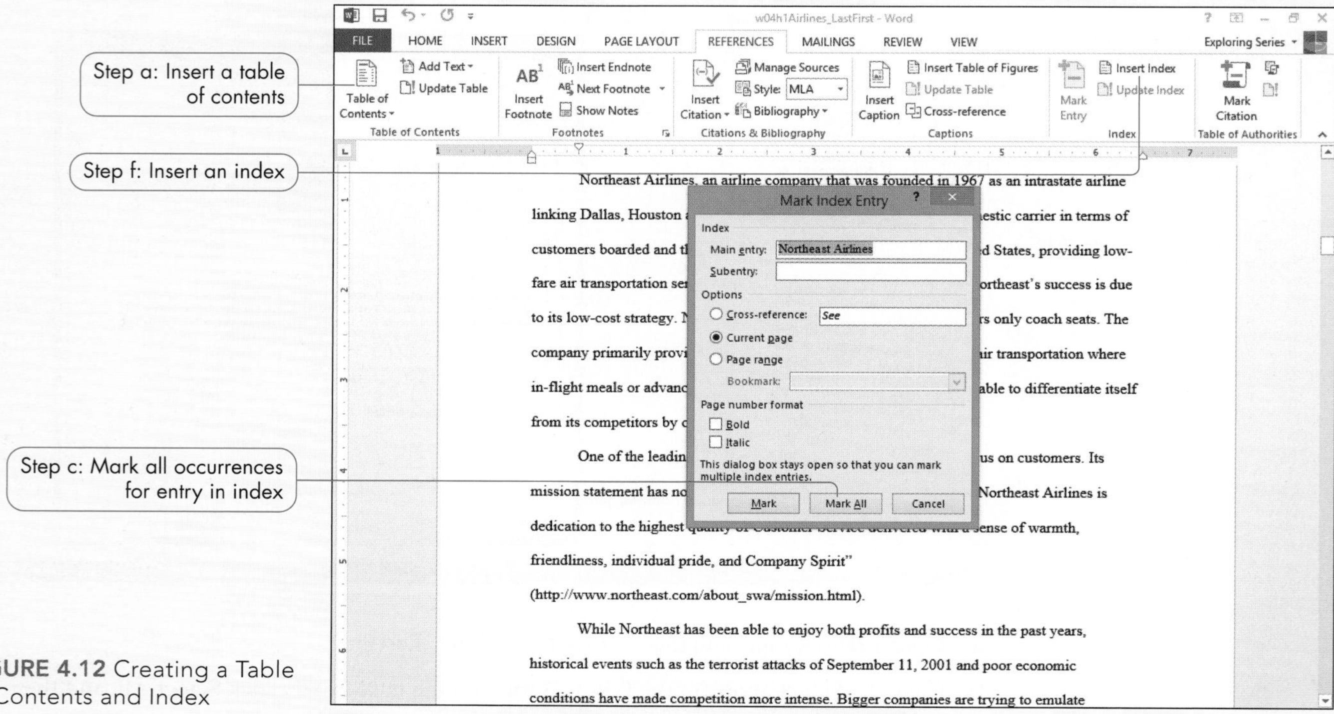

FIGURE 4.12 Creating a Table of Contents and Index

a. Press **Ctrl+Home** to move to the beginning of the document. Press **Ctrl+Enter** to insert a page break. Move to the beginning of the new page and press **Enter** twice. Click the **REFERENCES tab**, if necessary, and click **Table of Contents** in the Table of Contents group. Select **Automatic Table 2**.

You inserted a table of contents comprising headings and page numbers from the report.

b. Scroll to page 3 and change the heading *Situational Analysis* to **Data Analysis**. Press **Ctrl+Home** to move to the beginning of the document and ensure that the table of contents is selected. If not, click to select the table of contents. Click **Update Table** at the top-left corner of the table. Click **Update entire table**. Click **OK**.

You changed the wording of a heading in the report. After updating the table of contents, the new wording is also included there.

c. Click outside the table of contents to deselect it. Click the **REFERENCES tab**, if necessary. Scroll to page 2 and select **Northeast Airlines** in the first sentence of the first body paragraph. Click **Mark Entry** in the Index group, click **Mark All** in the Mark Index Entry dialog box, and then click **Close**.

You have marked the phrase *Northeast Airlines* for inclusion in the index. By selecting *Mark All*, you have instructed Word to include a page reference to the phrase wherever it occurs in the document.

d. Select the word **Northeast** in the sentence that begins *Northeast operates solely Boeing 737s* in the same paragraph. Click **Mark Entry** in the Index group. Select **Cross-reference** and type **Northeast Airlines** beside the word *See*. Click **Mark**. Click **Close**.

Because you refer to Northeast Airlines throughout the document as either *Northeast Airlines* or *Northeast*, you will cross-reference the term so that it appears appropriately in the index.

e. Scroll to page 4 and mark the first word on the page, **Code-sharing**, as an index entry, making sure to mark all occurrences. Place the insertion point at the end of the document and insert a page break. Ensure the insertion point is at the top of the new blank page.

f. Click **Insert Index** in the Index group. Click **OK** to accept all default settings and insert the index.

You inserted an index comprising the three terms you marked earlier. A complete index would most likely consist of many more terms, with all terms referenced to pages in the document.

g. Save the document.

STEP 5 » CREATE A COVER PAGE

As a final touch, you will create a cover page with information related to the report title, your name, the course number, and the current date. Refer to Figure 4.13 as you complete Step 5.

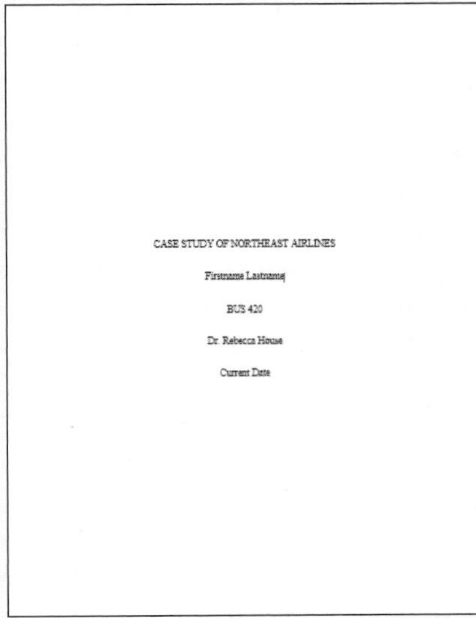

CASE STUDY OF NORTHEAST AIRLINES
Firstname Lastname
BUS 420
Dr. Rebecca House
Current Date

FIGURE 4.13 Creating a Cover Page

a. Insert a page break at the beginning of the document and place the insertion point at the top of the new blank page. Click the **HOME tab** and click **Center alignment**. Change the font size to **16 pt**. Change the font color to **Black, Text 1**. Toggle off **Italic**, if necessary.

b. Type **CASE STUDY OF NORTHEAST AIRLINES**. Press **Enter** three times. Type your first and last names. Press **Enter** three times. Type **BUS 420**. Press **Enter** three times. Type **Dr. Rebecca House**. Press **Enter** three times. Type the current date. Ensure that text on the cover page is neither bold nor italicized.

Although Word 2013 provides many more colorful choices of cover pages, you design a more conservative cover page to accompany this business report.

c. Click the **PAGE LAYOUT tab** and click the **Page Setup Dialog Box Launcher**. Click the **Layout tab**. Click the **Vertical Alignment arrow** and click **Center**. Click **OK**.

You centered the cover page vertically.

d. Click the **VIEW tab** and click **One Page**.

The cover page is centered vertically on the page.

e. Save the document and exit Word. Submit as directed by your instructor.

Document Tracking

Whether in a college class or in the workplace, it is likely that you will seek feedback from others or that you will collaborate with others on the completion of a project. Word 2013 provides a clutter-free way to make comments, reply to comments, and track changes that might have been made to a document by others during a review process. Called ***Simple Markup***, Word 2013's approach to group editing makes it easy to track changes and review any comments that have been made. Documents are often saved in ***PDF*** format to share with others. PDF (portable document format) is a file format that captures all of the elements of a page and stores them in electronic format. Especially useful for documents like magazine articles, brochures, and flyers, PDF format accurately represents all page elements, including graphics and text effects. Using Word 2013, you can now convert a PDF document into a Word document and edit the content.

In this section, you will explore reviewing documents, adding and replying to comments in the process. As you track changes in a document, you will learn to control the level of detail that shows, and you can accept or reject changes made by others. Finally, you will explore ways that Word enables you to work with PDF documents.

Reviewing a Document

In today's organizational environment, teams of people with diverse backgrounds, skills, and knowledge prepare documents. Team members work together while planning, developing, writing, and editing important documents. A large part of that process is reviewing work begun or submitted by others. No doubt you have focused on a document so completely that you easily overlooked obvious mistakes or alternative wording. A reviewer can often catch mistakes, perhaps even suggesting ways to improve readability. In reviewing a document, you will most often find ways to change wording or otherwise edit the format, and you might find an opportunity to provide ***comments*** related to the content. Although comments are most often directed to the attention of another author or editor, you can even include comments to remind yourself of a necessary action.

Add a Comment

The Review tab includes options related to adding and replying to comments, as well as tracking changes and changing the markup view. Using Simple Markup, a feature new to Word 2013, you can minimize the clutter of multiple comments, viewing only those that you choose. Adding a comment is an easy process. Simply click in the document or select a word or phrase to comment on and click New Comment in the Comments group on the Review tab. In the subsequent ***comment balloons***, type a comment. You will be identified as the author in the comment balloon. If you do not select anything prior to clicking New Comment, Word assigns the comment to the word or object closest to the insertion point. Figure 4.14 shows a document in the All Markup view with a few comments. All replies to original comments are indented beneath the original, which makes it easy to follow the progression of a comment through its replies, if any.

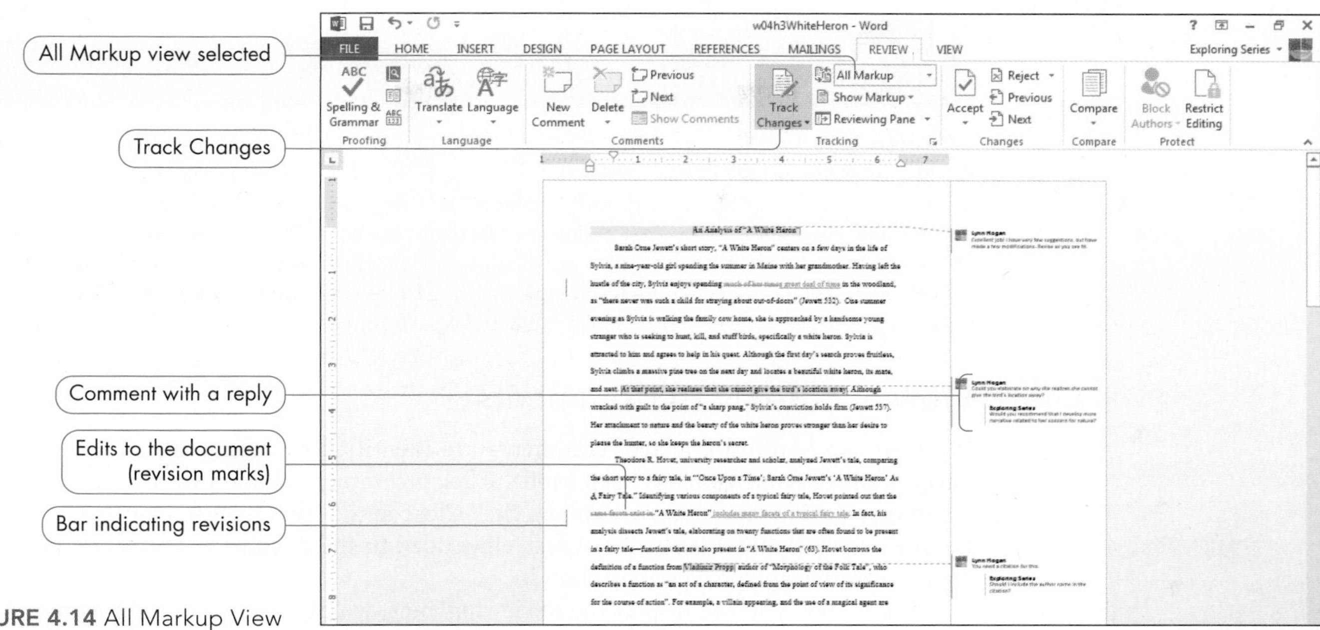

FIGURE 4.14 All Markup View

The document in Figure 4.14 is shown with All Markup selected in the Tracking group. Other options for markup views include Simple Markup, which is shown in Figure 4.15, as well as No Markup. The same document with the same comments, shown in Simple Markup, is much less cluttered. A small balloon on the right side of a paragraph in which a comment has been made provides access to the comment. A red vertical bar on the left side of a paragraph in which edits have been made alerts a reader to the existence of edits. Click a balloon to view a comment or click the red vertical bar to view edited text.

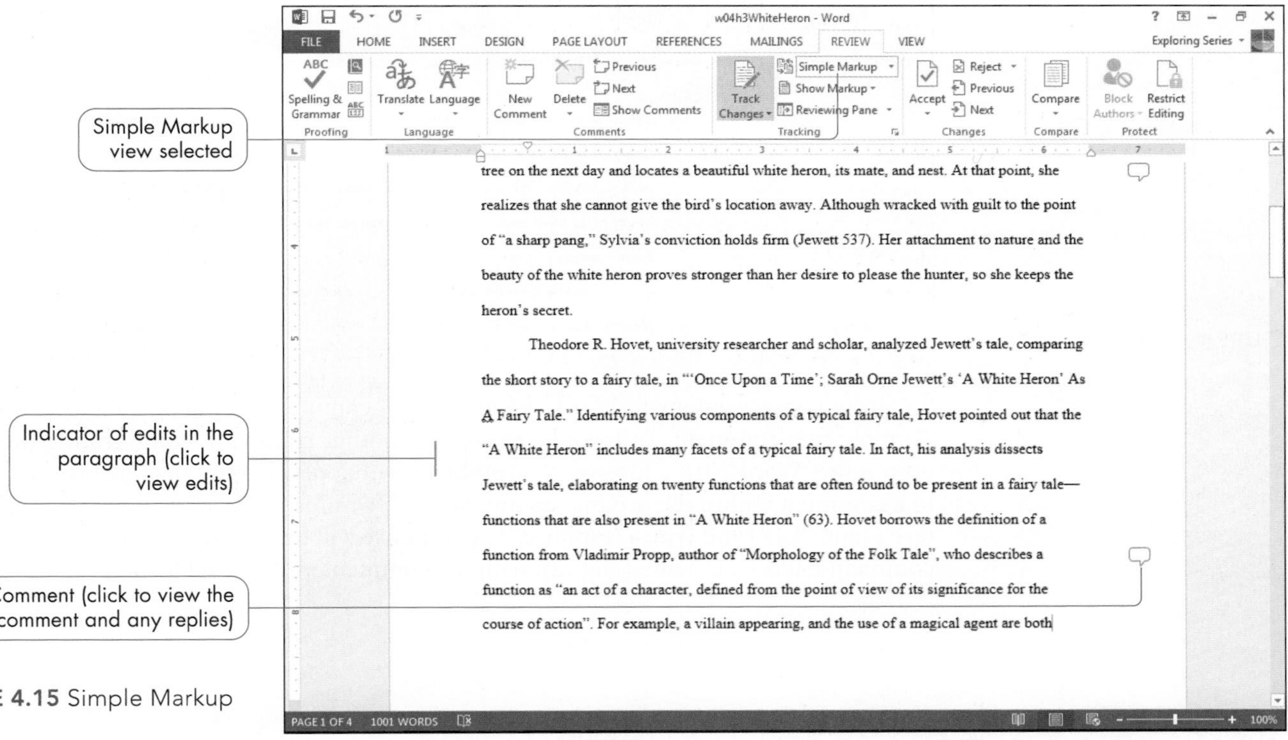

FIGURE 4.15 Simple Markup View

TIP Confirming the User Name

Before you use the Comments feature, make sure your name appears as you want it to in any comments. To do so, click the File tab and click Options. In the *General* section, confirm that your name and initials display as the user. Word uses that information to identify the person who uses collaboration tools, such as Comments. If you are in a lab environment, you might not have permission to modify settings or change the user name; however, you should be able to change those settings on a home computer.

View and Reply to Comments

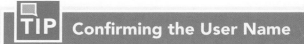

With Simple Markup selected, comments are identified by comment balloons in Print Layout, Web Layout view, or Read Mode. Click a comment balloon to read the associated comment. Having viewed the comment, click Close in the comment to remove it from view. In Draft view, comments appear as tags embedded in the document; when you hover the cursor over the tag, the comment shows.

STEP 1 In any view, you can display the Reviewing Pane, which displays all comments and editorial changes made to the document, as well as statistics regarding the number of changes made. You will find the Reviewing Pane useful when contents of comments are too lengthy to display completely in a comment balloon. Figure 4.16 shows the Reviewing Pane on the left. To display the Reviewing Pane:

1. Click the Reviewing Pane arrow on the REVIEW tab.
2. Select Reviewing Pane Vertical or Reviewing Pane Horizontal.

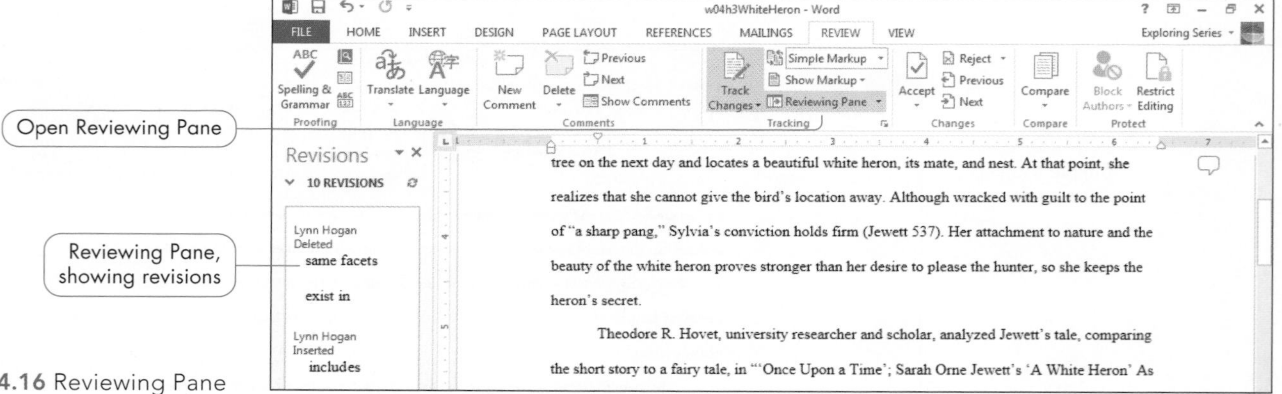

FIGURE 4.16 Reviewing Pane

In previous versions of Word, the number of comments could become overwhelming. To reply to a comment, you would create yet another comment, complicating the display even more. Word 2013 addresses that problem with a new feature that enables you to reply to a comment within the original comment. Each comment has a Reply option. Click Reply (see Figure 4.17) and type a response. The response will be placed in the original comment's comment balloon, indented slightly, with the commenter identified by name.

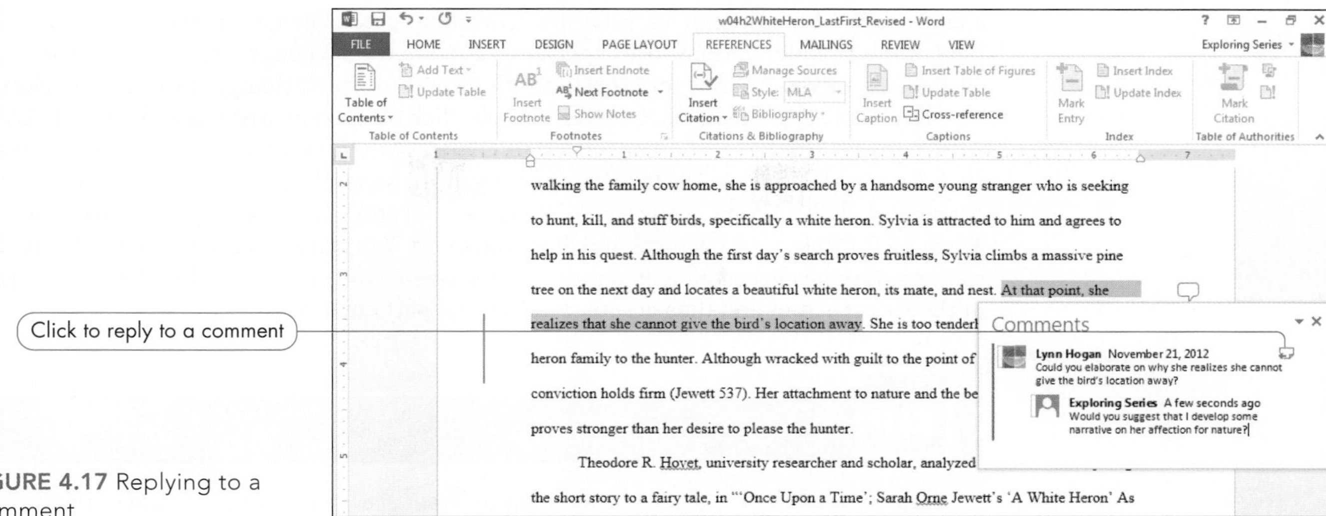

FIGURE 4.17 Replying to a Comment

When a comment has been addressed, it may no longer be relevant to the review process, and you might want to prohibit any further replies to the original comment. To deactivate a comment, right-click the open comment and select Mark Comment Done. Although the balloon remains in Simple Markup, the comment is grayed out when you click the balloon, so it is evident that it has been addressed. Further replies to the original comment are prohibited.

Tracking Changes

Whether you work individually or with a group, you can monitor any revisions you make to a document. The ***Track Changes*** feature keeps track of all additions, deletions, and formatting changes made to the document. Click Track Changes (refer to Figure 4.14) to track all changes made to a document. Click it again to toggle the feature off so that changes are no longer tracked. It is particularly useful in situations in which a document must be reviewed by several people—each of whom can offer suggestions or change parts of the document—and then returned to one person who will finalize the document.

Use Track Changes

When Track Changes is not active, any change you make to a document is untraceable, and no one will know what you change unless he or she compares your revised document with the previous version. When Track Changes is active, it applies ***revision marks***, which indicate where a person added, deleted, or formatted text. In addition, a bar displays on the left side of any paragraph in which edits have occurred (refer to Figure 4.14).

STEP 3» In Simple Markup, you will not see changes, even with Track Changes toggled on. Instead, a red bar on the left side of a modified paragraph will alert you to the fact that something is different. Click the red bar (refer to Figure 4.15) to show the changes. Click the bar again to remove them from view.

For a completely clean view of a document, temporarily hiding all comments and revisions, click the Markup arrow in the Tracking group on the Review tab and click No Markup. Although no revisions or comments show, keep in mind that they are only hidden. To remove them permanently, you have to accept or reject all changes.

Accept and Reject Changes

As you complete revision on a document, you will have reviewed all comments and acted on them or otherwise replied to the reviewer. You will also have had an opportunity to view all edits, including changes in wording and formatting. At that point, you will want to produce a clean copy of the document, incorporating all accepted changes or rejecting others. The Review tab includes options to accept changes and to reject changes. You can accept or reject all changes, or you can be more specific with respect to which changes to accept or reject.

To accept all changes, click the Review tab, click the Accept arrow, and then click Accept All Changes. Similarly, you can reject all changes when you click the Reject arrow and click Reject All Changes. To turn off tracking at the same time that you accept or reject all changes, click the Accept arrow (or the Reject arrow) and select Accept All Changes and Stop Tracking (or Reject All Changes and Stop Tracking). You can also accept or reject individual changes. Having clicked an edited area in a document, you can click either the Accept arrow or the Reject arrow, and then accept or reject that particular edit.

TIP Using Show Markup

Click Show Markup in the Tracking group on the Review tab to view document revisions organized by the type of revision (such as comments, formatting, insertions, and deletions) as well as by reviewer. You can toggle each selection on or off, so you can view several at the same time.

Work with PDF Documents

PDF Reflow is a feature that produces editable Word documents from PDF files—documents that retain the intended formatting and page flow of the original PDF document. PDF Reflow seeks to convert recognizable features of a PDF document into items that are native to Word. For example, a table in a PDF document is converted into a table in a Word document so you can use Word's table feature to modify and update the item. Similarly, bulleted lines in a PDF file become bulleted paragraphs in a Word document. Although using PDF Reflow does not always convert every feature flawlessly, the result is usually a close imitation of the original. PDF Reflow is more attuned to converting text than graphics.

STEP 2»

To convert a PDF document to Word 2013, start Word, click the File tab, click Open, and then browse for the PDF document to open. Within a few seconds, the PDF file opens as a Word document. At that point, you can edit it as you would any Word document. To save a Word document as a PDF file, click the File tab and click Export. Click Create PDF/XPS and click Publish.

Quick Concepts

1. When you reply to a comment, where is your reply placed? ***p. 334***
2. In Simple Markup, how can you tell that edits have been made to a paragraph? How can you see the changes that have been made? ***p. 335***
3. As you complete a research paper that has been marked up by several reviewers (with Track Changes on), you now want to provide a clean copy. What steps might you follow to do that? ***p. 336***
4. Briefly describe the Word feature that converts a PDF file into a Word document so that you can edit the document. ***p. 336***

Hands-On Exercises

2 Document Tracking

Your literature group submitted a draft copy of the analysis of *A White Heron*. Your literature instructor will make comments and suggest any additional editing before the paper is considered complete. Even at this early stage, however, your instructor is very pleased with your group's initial analysis. In fact, she suggested that you prepare to submit the paper to the campus Phi Kappa Phi Honor Society for judging in a writing contest. She will provide a copy of the entry form in PDF format so you can have it on hand when you submit the paper. At this point, you will review her comments and changes and act on her suggestions.

Skills covered: Add, View, and Reply to Comments • Work with a PDF Document • Use Track Changes and Accept or Reject Changes

STEP 1 » ADD, VIEW, AND REPLY TO COMMENTS

Your instructor has returned to you an electronic copy of the analysis with a few comments and edits. You will review the suggestions, make a few changes, and save the document for final review and group collaboration later. Refer to Figure 4.18 as you complete Step 1.

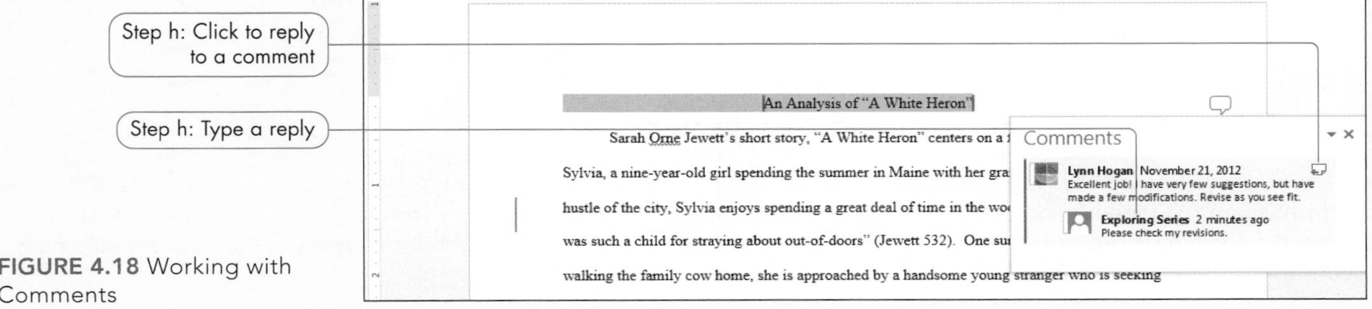

FIGURE 4.18 Working with Comments

a. Open *w04h2WhiteHeron* and save it as **w04h2WhiteHeron_LastFirst.**

b. Click the **REVIEW tab**, click the **Simple Markup arrow** in the Tracking group, and then click **All Markup**. Review the comments made by your instructor, as well as the tracked edits in the document. Click the **All Markup arrow** in the Tracking group and click **Simple Markup** to return to an uncluttered view.

> **TROUBLESHOOTING:** It is possible that All Markup is selected as the markup view before you begin this exercise. In that case, review the comments and edits, click the All Markup arrow, and then click Simple Markup. Continue to step c.

c. Click the **Reviewing Pane arrow** in the Tracking group and click **Reviewing Pane Vertical**. Scroll through the comments and edits shown in the Reviewing Pane. Close the Reviewing Pane (titled *Revisions*).

d. Click the vertical red bar on the left side of the first body paragraph to view all edits and comments. Click the bar again to hide the tracked changes. Point to the first comment balloon on the right of the report title and note the highlighted text. Click the comment balloon, if necessary, to view the comment. Click the comment balloon again to close the comment.

e. View the third comment on the first page and note that you need to add a citation. Click **Close** in the markup balloon to close it. Click after the quotation mark and before the period in the sentence in the last paragraph on the first page, ending with *for the course of action.* Add a new source for the following book:

   Author: **Propp, Vladimir**

   Title: **Morphology of a Folk Tale**

   Year: **1994**

   City: **New York**

   Publisher: **Anniston**

f. Scroll to the end of the document and click to select the **Works Cited field**. Click **Update Citations and Bibliography**.

   You added a new source and updated the Works Cited page to include the newly added source.

g. Scroll to page 1 and click the second comment balloon to view the comment. Close the markup balloon. Click before the word *Although* in the sentence in the first body paragraph that begins with *Although wracked with guilt*. Type **She is too tenderhearted to give up the heron family to the hunter.** Press **spacebar**.

h. Click the first comment on page 1, point to the comment text, and then click **Reply** (see Figure 4.18) at the right side of the instructor name. Type **Please check my revisions.** Close the comment.

i. Save and close the document. Keep Word open for the next step.

STEP 2 ›› WORK WITH A PDF DOCUMENT

You are ready to finalize the paper, and your instructor has let you know that you must include an entry form with the submission. You are not on campus, so your instructor has e-mailed the entry form as a PDF document. You will convert the form to Word and then complete it with your name and report information. You will then save it as a PDF document for later submission. Refer to Figure 4.19 as you complete Step 2.

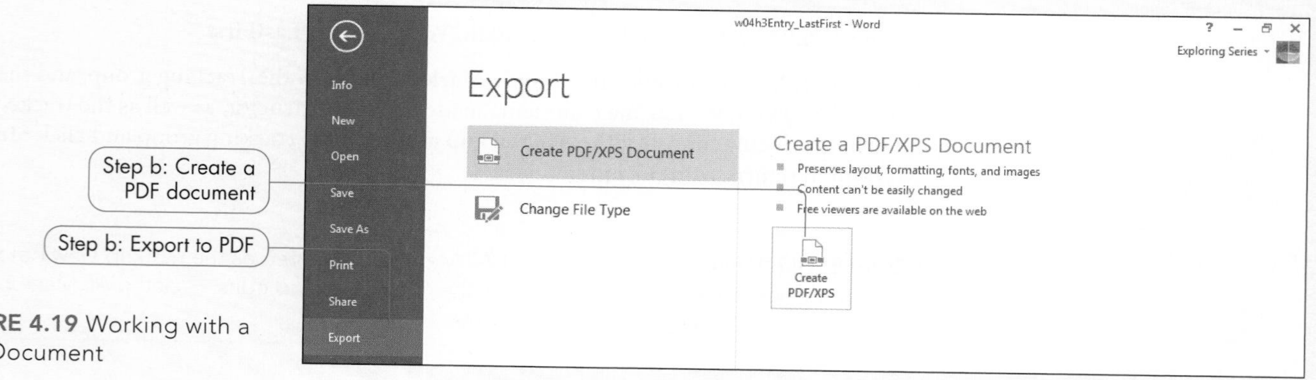

FIGURE 4.19 Working with a PDF Document

a. Click the **FILE tab** and click **Open**. Open *w04h2Entry.pdf* from your student files. Click **OK** if warned that the conversion might take a while. Click after **Date** and type today's date. Complete the remaining information, including your name, instructor's name, college level, e-mail, and report title, **An Analysis of "A White Heron"**.

   PDF Reflow has converted the original PDF version of the entry form and opened it in Word so you can modify it.

TROUBLESHOOTING: If the document opened as an Adobe PDF file instead of as a Word document, you opened the file from File Explorer. Instead, you should open the document from within Word when you click the File tab and click Open.

b. Click the **FILE tab** and click **Export**. Click **Create PDF/XPS**. Navigate to the location where you save your assignments and ensure that *Open file after publishing* is checked. Click **Publish**. After the PDF version of the completed entry form opens, close the document. Close the Word version of the entry form without saving it.

You saved the entry form you completed in Word as a PDF file for later submission with the entry.

STEP 3 » USE TRACK CHANGES AND ACCEPT AND REJECT CHANGES

You are ready to submit the paper, but you must first accept or reject changes and remove all comments. Refer to Figure 4.20 as you complete Step 3.

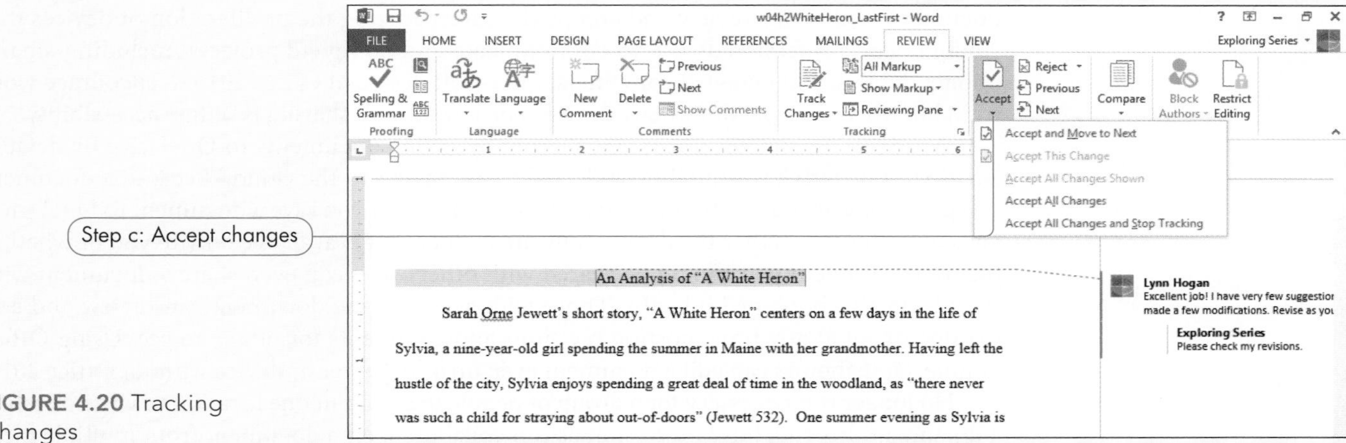

FIGURE 4.20 Tracking Changes

a. Open *w04h2WhiteHeron_LastFirst*. Click the **REVIEW tab** and click the **Simple Markup arrow**, unless All Markup is already selected. Click **All Markup**.

b. Click anywhere in the sentence you added on the first page, *She is too tenderhearted to give up the heron family to the hunter*. Click the **Reject arrow** in the Changes group and click **Reject Change**.

You decide the additional sentence is not necessary, so you reject the change you made earlier.

c. Click the **Accept arrow** and click **Accept All Changes and Stop Tracking**.

You have accepted all remaining changes and deleted all comments. The document is now ready for the group to finalize.

d. Click **Save** on the Quick Access Toolbar to save the document with the same name and in the same location. Save the document and submit based on your instructor's directions.

Online Document Collaboration

Word 2013 is changing the way education and the workforce expect projects to be completed. At one time, students primarily worked independently, completing projects on their own and being graded accordingly. Business professionals relied on their skills to produce projects that were often prepared at one site—typically by working independently in an office, coordinating efforts with others only occasionally. The global marketplace and the ease with which communication can occur worldwide have changed all that, creating a new dynamic in which collaboration on projects is the norm rather than the exception. Marketing proposals, company reports, and all sorts of other documents are often prepared by a group of people working with shared documents to which all can contribute at any time. Similarly, group projects that are assigned as part of a class requirement can often be completed by sharing documents online for review and completion. Recognizing the proliferation of devices that students and professionals use to communicate and complete projects, including smartphones, tablets, and personal computers, Microsoft designed Office 2013 to encourage work from anywhere and on almost any device. The key to such sharing is online accessibility.

Word 2013 facilitates document sharing by saving documents to OneDrive by default. Saving to OneDrive is sometimes referred to as "saving to the cloud," because a document saved in that way is available online (in the cloud). When you save a document to OneDrive, you can indicate whether the document is in a folder that is available only to you or whether the folder or document should be shared with others. You can even share a document with friends on Facebook or LinkedIn. Those with access to the document can review and edit the document at any time, posting revisions and comments for others to see. Using Office Online, contributors can edit a document even on a computer or device without Office 2013.

No longer is it necessary for a group of people to gather in one location to write or refine a document. Instead, busy professionals can collaborate on a document from multiple locations at the same time. The conference leader can present the document online using the Office Presentation service. At that point, users can comment, edit, and collaborate on the document although not simultaneously.

In this section, you will explore the use of Word Online, as it coordinates with OneDrive to facilitate the sharing and editing of documents. In addition, you will learn to present a document online.

Using OneDrive

Provided by Microsoft, ***OneDrive*** is an online storage system and sharing utility. More than a simple file storage location, OneDrive is an integral component of Microsoft's total solution to "anywhere computing." It is the backbone behind Microsoft's push for providing access to files from any location and from any mobile device, such as a laptop, tablet, or smartphone. You can use OneDrive to share documents with others, facilitating online collaboration in the production of documents and the completion of projects, or as a repository for backup copies of files. With 7GB of free storage made available to users, OneDrive is a viable storage alternative to a local drive. In fact, it is often used in lieu of a flash drive because it makes files available from any Internet-connected location.

When you save a Word document, you can indicate OneDrive as the storage location. In fact, OneDrive is the default storage location for Office 2013; documents are automatically saved there unless you specify otherwise (see Figure 4.21).

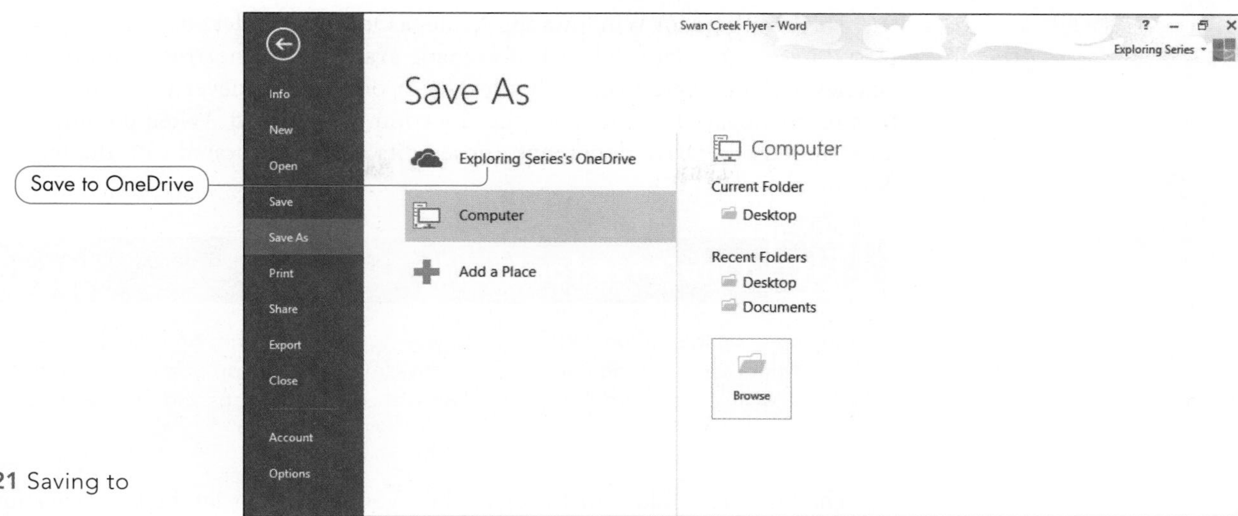

FIGURE 4.21 Saving to OneDrive

TIP Using a Microsoft Account

To use Microsoft services such as OneDrive, Zune, or Office Live or to participate in online presentations (discussed later in this chapter), you must have a Microsoft account. If you use Outlook, Hotmail, OneDrive, or Xbox LIVE, or if you have a Windows Phone, you already have a Microsoft account. If you do not have an account, you can create one at http://www.outlook.com.

Understand OneDrive Apps

Word 2013 encourages the use of OneDrive as a storage location so that you can retrieve documents from any Internet-connected device and so that you can share documents with others. You are also likely to use OneDrive as a location for backing up documents. For example, you might save an important document on your hard drive and upload or save the document to OneDrive as a backup. If you grant access, others can view and edit the document. The inherent challenge in that scenario is that as you edit the local copy of the document or as co-authors edit the OneDrive copy, both copies of the document should be synchronized so that they are identical. Microsoft provides *apps* to simplify the process of organizing and managing OneDrive folders (and contents), as well as ensuring that files are synchronized.

Windows 8.1.1 includes a OneDrive app that displays OneDrive folders and files on your desktop. The ***Windows 8.1.1 OneDrive app*** enables you to access files from your OneDrive folders and upload others to OneDrive. However, it *does not include automatic synchronization of files* (maintaining up-to-date versions of files between OneDrive and copies of files saved on your computer). The purpose of the Windows 8.1.1 OneDrive app is to provide access to items you have saved to OneDrive and to facilitate uploading new files. In addition, the OneDrive app enables you to delete files and folders and create folders in OneDrive.

STEP 1» To ensure that OneDrive files are always up to date and that you can easily access them from your computer, you might consider downloading the ***OneDrive for Windows app***. If you work with Windows 8.1.1, Windows 7, or Windows Vista, you can download the app (available at https://apps.live.com/onedrive), which *automatically synchronizes* files between your personal computer and your OneDrive account. The Windows 8.1.1 OneDrive app (described in the preceding paragraph) and the OneDrive for Windows app are separate entities with differing purposes.

The OneDrive for Windows app creates a OneDrive folder on your computer. Everything placed in the OneDrive folder is also made available in OneDrive, with files synchronized whenever changes are made either locally or online. Whenever you add, change, or delete files in one location, files in another location are updated. When co-authors collaborate on a shared OneDrive document, those edits are incorporated into the local copy of the document.

OneDrive for Mobile Devices

You can download a OneDrive app on your Windows Phone, Android, iPhone, or iPad at http://windows.microsoft.com/is-IS/onedrive/mobile. The app enables you to easily access your OneDrive files from the mobile device and upload videos and pictures to OneDrive.

The OneDrive folder that is created on your computer by the OneDrive for Windows app is a subfolder of your personal Users folder (C:/Users/your name/OneDrive). Although you can navigate to the OneDrive folder through File Explorer, Windows provides easy access to the OneDrive folder in the Notification area on the taskbar. Click OneDrive to confirm that it is up to date and click Open your OneDrive folder for immediate access to files saved on OneDrive (and synced locally so they are also available on your computer). In the File Explorer interface, shown in Figure 4.22, you can simply drag and drop files between folders, including OneDrive.

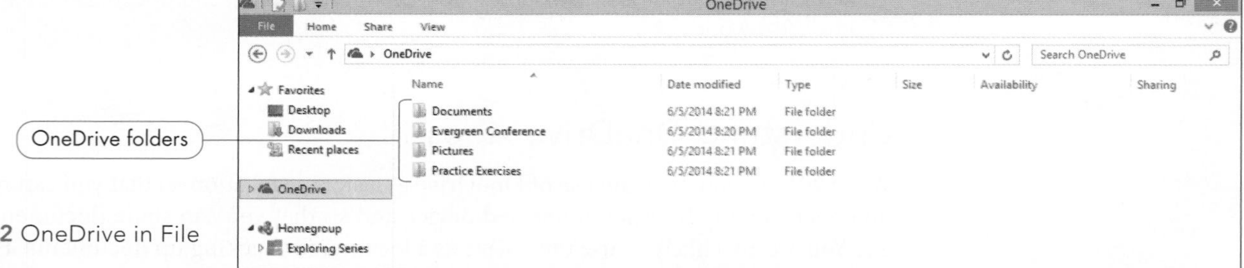

FIGURE 4.22 OneDrive in File Explorer

Regardless of whether you have downloaded the OneDrive for Windows app, you can save or upload documents to OneDrive. Simply save a Word file to OneDrive or upload it to http://onedrive.live.com.

To save a Word file to OneDrive:

1. Click the FILE tab and click Save As.
2. Confirm that OneDrive is selected in the Places section and navigate to the OneDrive folder to save to (or click Browse to create a new folder or select another storage location on OneDrive).
3. Click Save.

To upload a file (not restricted to Word 2013 files) to OneDrive:

1. Go to http://onedrive.live.com.
2. Sign in using your login information (or click Sign Up to create a new account).
3. Follow all prompts to upload the file, creating a new OneDrive folder if desired.

Sharing and Collaborating on Documents

For various reasons, you might want to share folders or files. In the educational environment and in the workplace, one of the most common reasons to share files is to facilitate collaborative projects. Because a document saved on OneDrive is available online, you can share the document with others who have access to the Internet. Although you are likely to use Word 2013 to share documents, you can also share a document that opens in Word Online (discussed later in this chapter). You might even find it convenient to share a file other than one created with a Microsoft Office application, such as a picture or a PDF file. You can access your files directly at http://onedrive.live.com.

Share Documents in Word 2013

After saving a document to OneDrive, you can share it with others in several ways and with varying levels of permission. You may be sharing a file for informational purposes only; you do not intend to ask others to edit or collaborate on the document. Other times, you will invite collaboration. You can share a document through a link, by posting to a social network, through e-mail, as a blog post, or even as an online presentation. As you share a document, you can indicate whether those you share with can edit the document or simply view it.

Invite Others to Share a Document or Share a Link

Perhaps the simplest way to share a document using Word 2013 is to *invite* others to edit or view the document. You can also share a link to a document that you have saved to OneDrive. To save a Word document to OneDrive while also inviting others to share the document (or sharing a link), create or open a document in Word 2013, then:

1. Click the FILE tab and click Share. As shown in Figure 4.23, you can invite people to access the document you will save to OneDrive.
2. Click Save to Cloud.
3. Navigate to the OneDrive folder in which to save the file and click Save.
4. Click Share
   - If you plan to invite others to share the document, type the e-mail addresses of invitees, include a message, and indicate whether the recipient can edit or only view the shared document. Select *Require user to sign-in before accessing document* if you want to provide the utmost privacy for your document. Click Share.
   - Instead of inviting others, you can create a sharing link when you click *Get a Sharing Link* and click *Create link* (indicating whether to limit a user to view or edit privileges). Copy the resulting link to share with others.

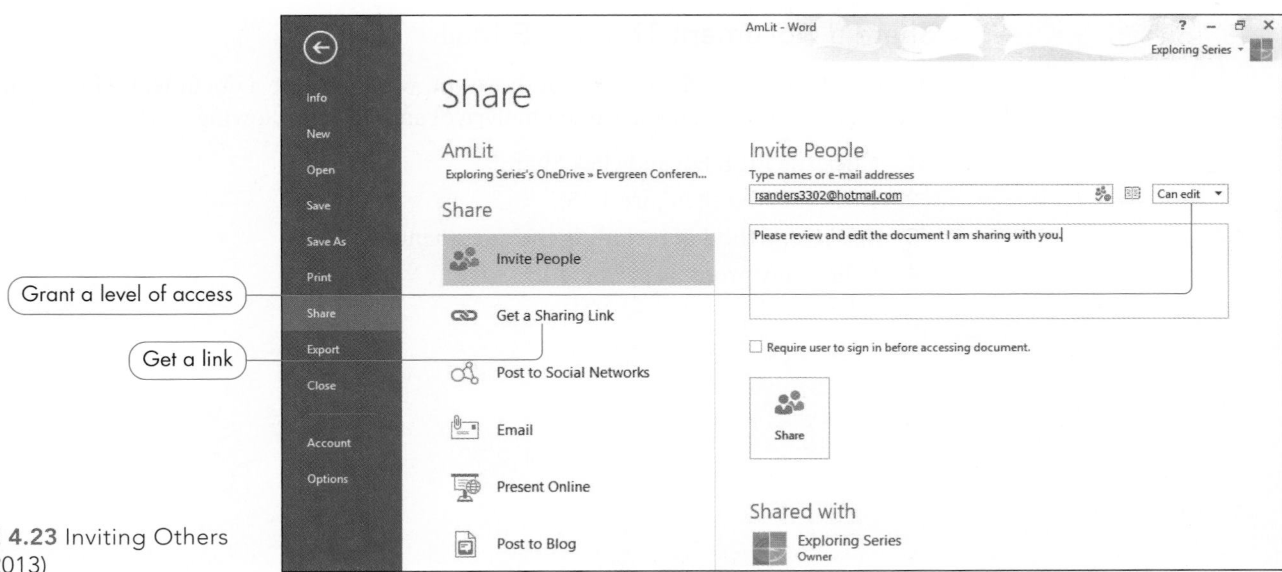

FIGURE 4.23 Inviting Others (Word 2013)

Post to a Social Network

You can post a Word document to a social network, including Facebook, LinkedIn, Flickr, Google+, and Twitter, indicating whether your contacts can only view the document or can also edit it. With a Word document open (that you have saved to OneDrive):

1. Click the FILE tab and then click Share.
2. Click Post to Social Networks (see Figure 4.24).
3. Click a link to connect to a social network, if necessary. You can share a document through a social network only if you have affiliated the network with your OneDrive account. You will connect the account by following Word prompts as you share the post.
4. Indicate a level of permission (*Can edit* or *Can view*) and include a brief message.
5. Click Post.

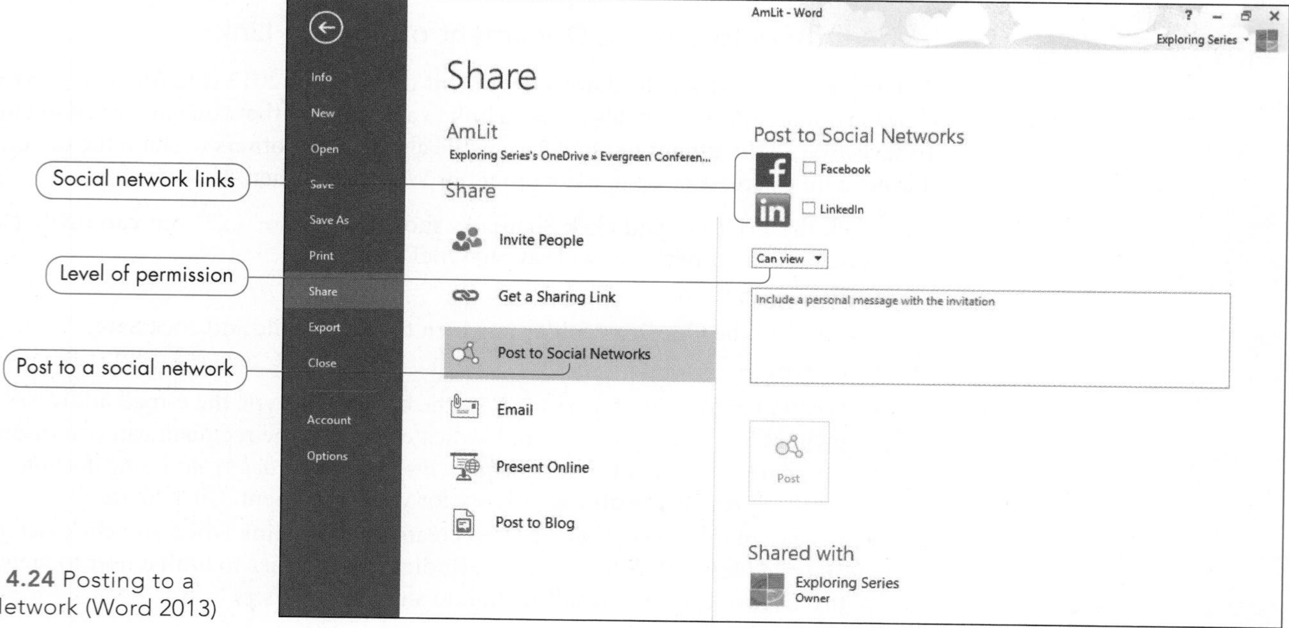

FIGURE 4.24 Posting to a Social Network (Word 2013)

Share a Document Through E-Mail

If you know the *e-mail* addresses of those you want to share a document with, open a Word document (that you have saved to OneDrive) and do the following:

1. Click the FILE tab and click Share.
2. Click Email (see Figure 4.25).
3. Select a method of including the document.
4. Follow any prompts presented.

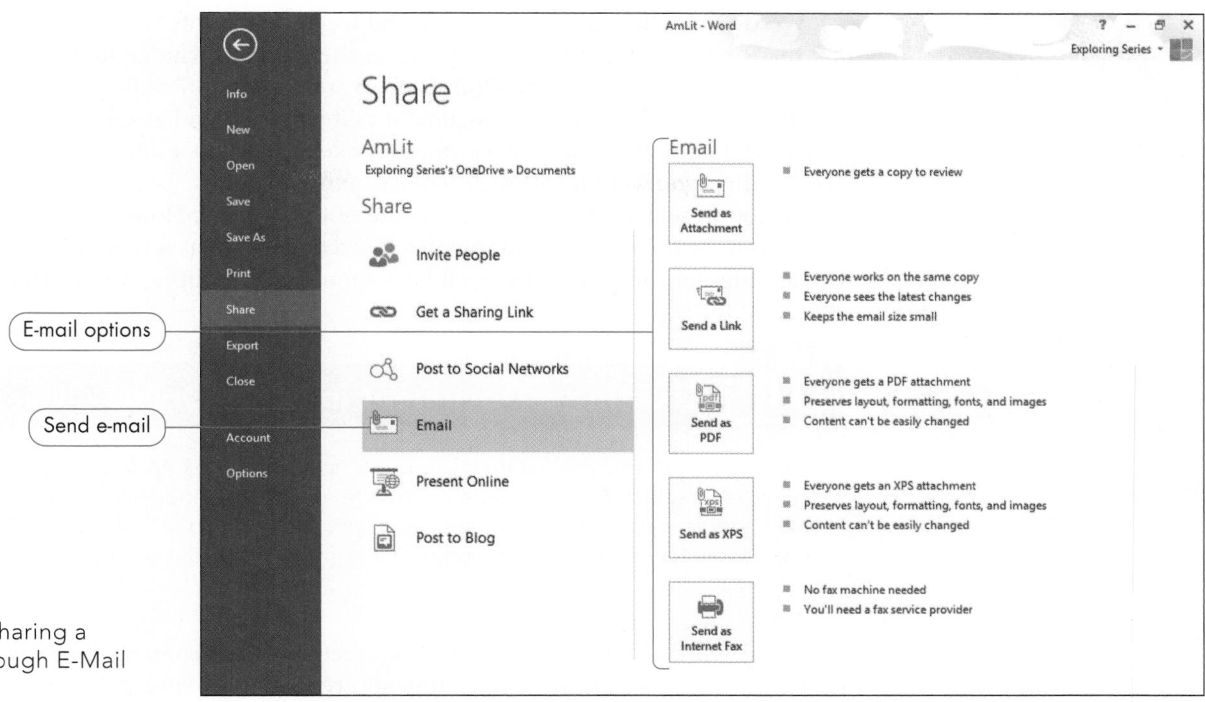

FIGURE 4.25 Sharing a Document Through E-Mail (Word 2013)

Share Documents in Word Online

Word Online is a limited version of Word, enabling you to edit and format a document online. As a component of Office Online, which also includes Excel, PowerPoint, and OneNote, Word Online is free and accessible when you sign in to or create a OneDrive account. You are not required to install software to use Word Online. Neither are you required to have purchased a copy of Word 2013. That means that you can use Word Online, creating and editing Word documents, from any Internet-connected computer regardless of whether Word is installed on the computer. Although not as full-featured as Word 2013, Word Online enables you to create basic documents and share documents with others.

Word Online is available to you when you access a OneDrive account and either begin a new document or open a document previously saved in OneDrive and choose to use Word Online to edit the document. For example, when you sign in to your OneDrive account (http://onedrive.live.com), you can click a previously saved Word document to open it. As shown in Figure 4.26, the document opens in a browser window with a very limited selection of tabs. On the Edit Document tab, select Edit in Word (to open the document in a full Word version if installed on your computer) or Edit in Word Online (to open the document for editing in Word Online). You are not required to have Word 2013 installed on your computer in order to open a document using Word Online. In fact, that is an advantage of using Word Online—you can share and collaborate on Word documents with others, regardless of whether anyone has a version of Word installed.

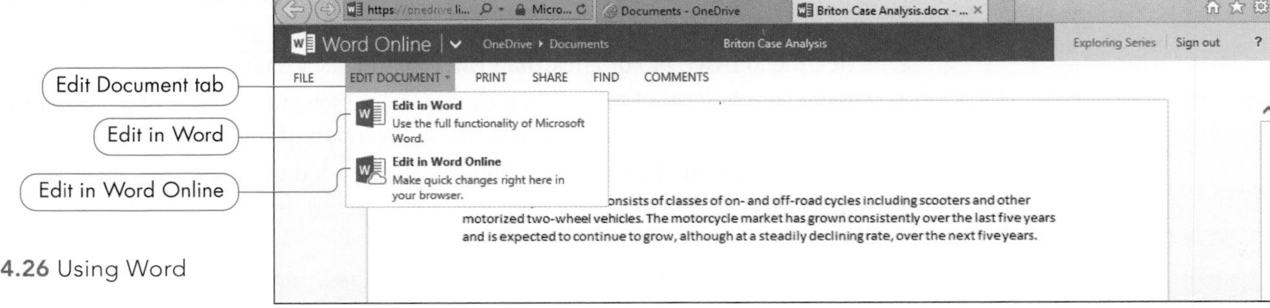

FIGURE 4.26 Using Word Online

Word Online has the familiar look and feel of Microsoft Word; however, you will note that the Ribbon is much more limited than the Ribbon included in a standard Word 2013 installation. In addition, Word Online views are limited to Reading view and Editing view, with Reading view showing the document as it will print and enabling the addition of comments, while Editing view enables you to make changes to a document. As you work with Word Online, you will find other differences and limitations; for example, dialog box launchers are not present, and certain features are not supported. However, it can be the solution to encouraging online collaboration on a Word document, as it is readily available to anyone with an Internet connection and facilitates simultaneous editing with others.

TIP Creating a Document in Word Online

You can create a Word document using Word Online. At http://onedrive.live.com, click Create and select Word document. Provide a file name and click Create. Type a document, saving it to OneDrive. At any point, you can click *Open in Word* to take advantage of the more full-featured Word version if it is installed on your computer.

Using Word Online, you can open or create Word documents that you can share with others. In much the same way as documents are shared in Word 2013, through a link, social network, or e-mail, you can share documents through Word Online.

Share a Link

A very straightforward way to share access to a document is by providing a link. The link can be included in an e-mail or any other form of electronic or written communication. As you create a link, you can mark it as *View only*, *Edit*, or *Public*, depending upon the level of access you want to grant. A *View only* link enables a recipient to view but not edit a shared document. An *Edit* link enables a recipient to view the document and make changes to it. A *Public* link is the same as an Edit link, except that anyone can search for publicly shared files, whereas only those with whom you have shared a link can access those designated for viewing and editing.

TIP Sharing a Link

Be careful when sharing a link to a document, especially if it is a *Edit* or *Public* link. Anyone can forward the link to others, opening the document for editing by people to whom you did not intend to grant permission.

To use Word Online to create a link to a shared document:

STEP 3»

1. Open the document in Word Online. To do so, simply click the document in your OneDrive account.
2. Click the SHARE tab or click the FILE tab and click Share.
3. Click *Get a link* (see Figure 4.27). Click Create (selecting a level of permission). Click Shorten, if desired, to generate a shortened version of the link.
4. Copy the generated link for distribution to intended recipients.
5. Click Done.

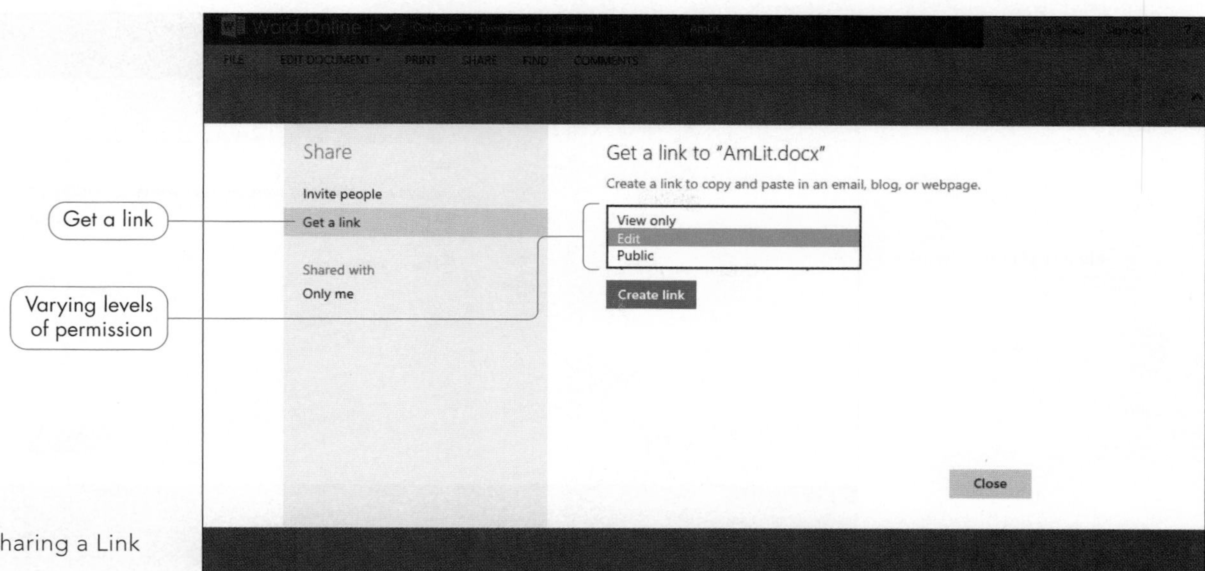

FIGURE 4.27 Sharing a Link (Word Online)

Sharing with Embedded HTML

You can embed a shared document in a blog or Web site that you manage. To do so, right-click the document in OneDrive and select Embed. Click Generate. OneDrive will create HTML code that you can copy and paste into your blog or Web page.

Post to a Social Network

Using Word Online, you can share documents with your contacts on several social networks, including Facebook, Twitter, Google+, and LinkedIn.

To share a document link to a social network:

1. Open the document in Word Online. To do so, click the document in your OneDrive account.
2. Click SHARE on the toolbar or click the FILE tab and click Share.
3. Click Get a link (see Figure 4.28).
4. Indicate whether recipients can edit the document. Click Create link.
5. Select the social network. Click Share Link. Type a short message, if you like, to accompany the posted document.

   A link to the document appears on the social media site, along with a message if you chose to include one. Follow the social network site's rules to advise intended recipients of the document's availability.

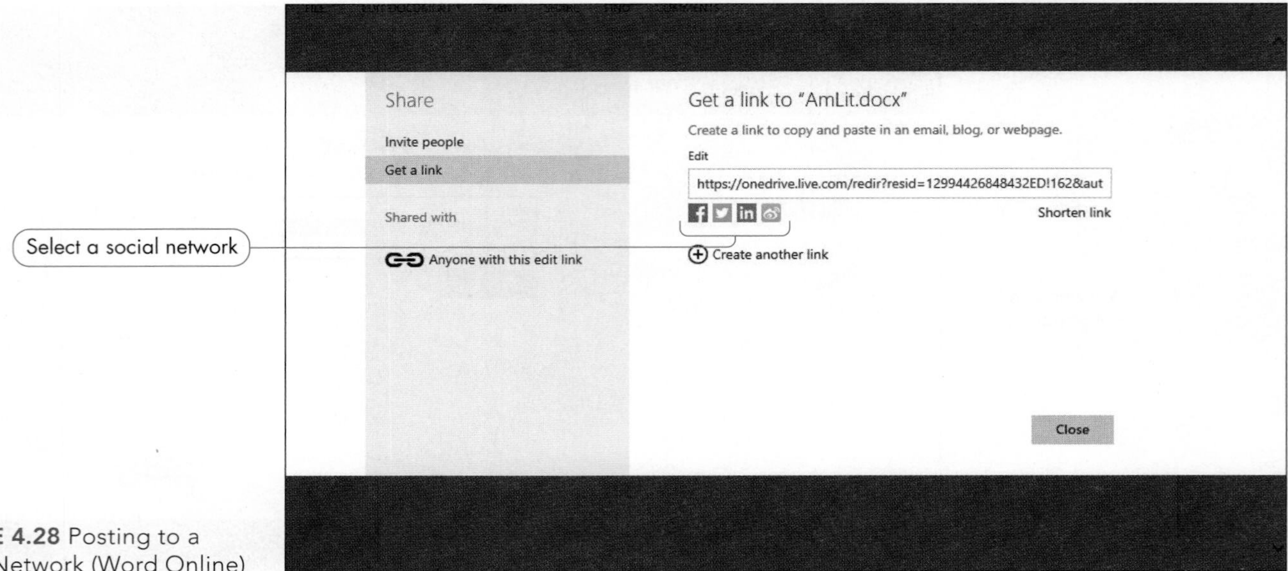

FIGURE 4.28 Posting to a Social Network (Word Online)

Share a Document Through E-Mail

Word Online enables you to share a document with e-mail contacts:

1. Click SHARE on the toolbar or click the FILE tab and click Share.
2. Click Invite people (see Figure 4.29).
3. Type the e-mail addresses of those with whom you will share the document and a short note if desired.
4. Click the *Recipients can edit* link to display an additional option that enables you to limit recipients to viewing the document only. In addition, you can specify whether recipients need a Microsoft account to access the document.
5. Click Share to send invitations to all recipients with a link to the shared file.

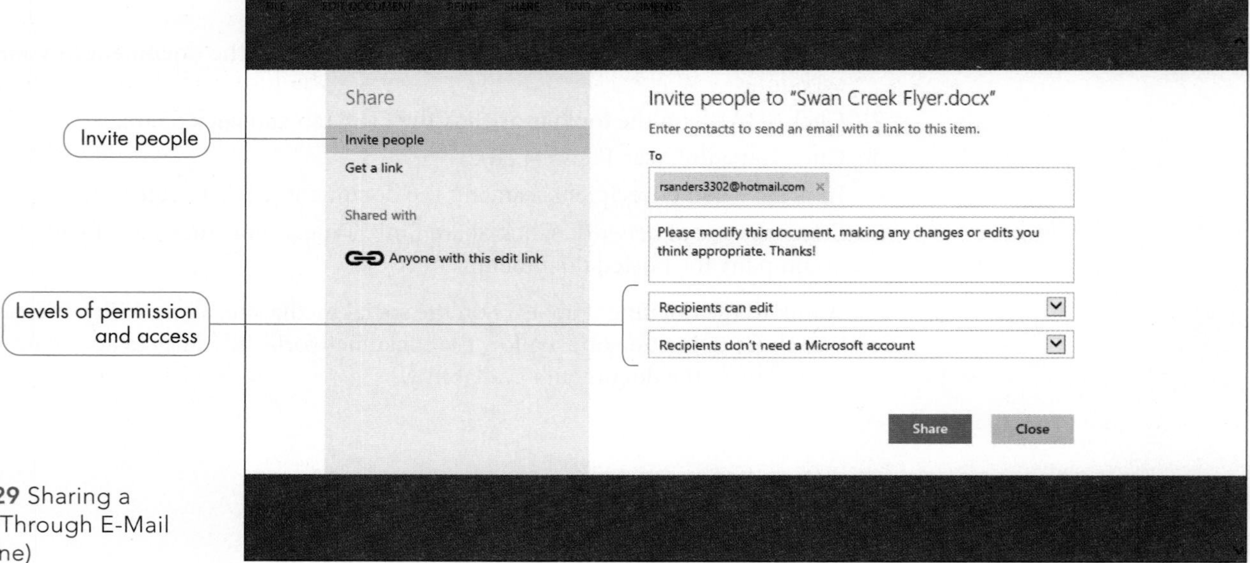

FIGURE 4.29 Sharing a Document Through E-Mail (Word Online)

TIP Share a File on OneDrive

When viewing a list of files in OneDrive at http://onedrive.live.com, you can right-click a file and click Share to open a Share dialog box from which you can select a method of sharing.

Collaborate on a Document

Co-authoring a document is simple, with no specific commands required to begin editing. Simply open a shared document from OneDrive and use either Word Online or Word 2013 to modify the document. Of course, the document must be shared in such a way that editing by other authors is permitted.

STEP 4

When you save or post a Word document to OneDrive, anyone with whom you share the document (with editing privileges) can access and edit the document, even if you are also editing the document at the same time. The most straightforward approach to co-editing a document, especially if you will be doing so simultaneously, is to open the document in Word Online. Simply click a shared link or click a shared document in OneDrive to open it in Word Online. At that point, click Edit Document and select Edit in Word or Edit in Word Online (see Figure 4.30).

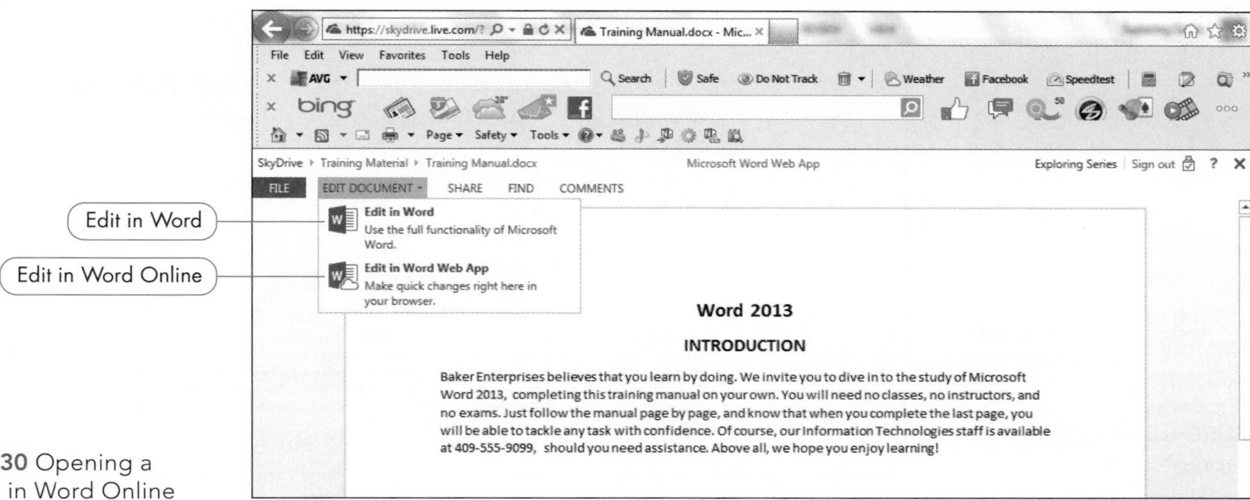

FIGURE 4.30 Opening a Document in Word Online

As you edit a shared document, you will be made aware of others who are editing the same document (see Figure 4.31). If using Word Online, you can edit a document simultaneously with other co-authors, with all changes occurring immediately. As you or others with whom the document is shared edit the document, the changes are immediately shown. In that way, it is possible for several people to work with the same document, each viewing changes made by others as those changes are being typed. You can check the right side of the toolbar for notification of others who might be editing the document at the same time (see Figure 4.32). As a co-author makes changes to a document, the area in which he or she is working will be identified with a colored flag (see Figure 4.33). When you point to the flag, the identity of the co-author is revealed.

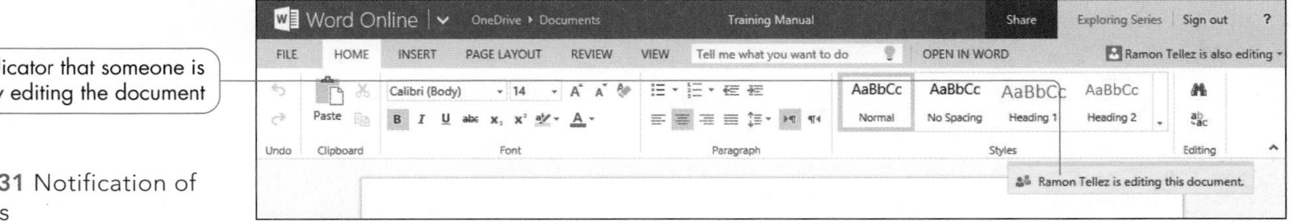

FIGURE 4.31 Notification of Co-Authors

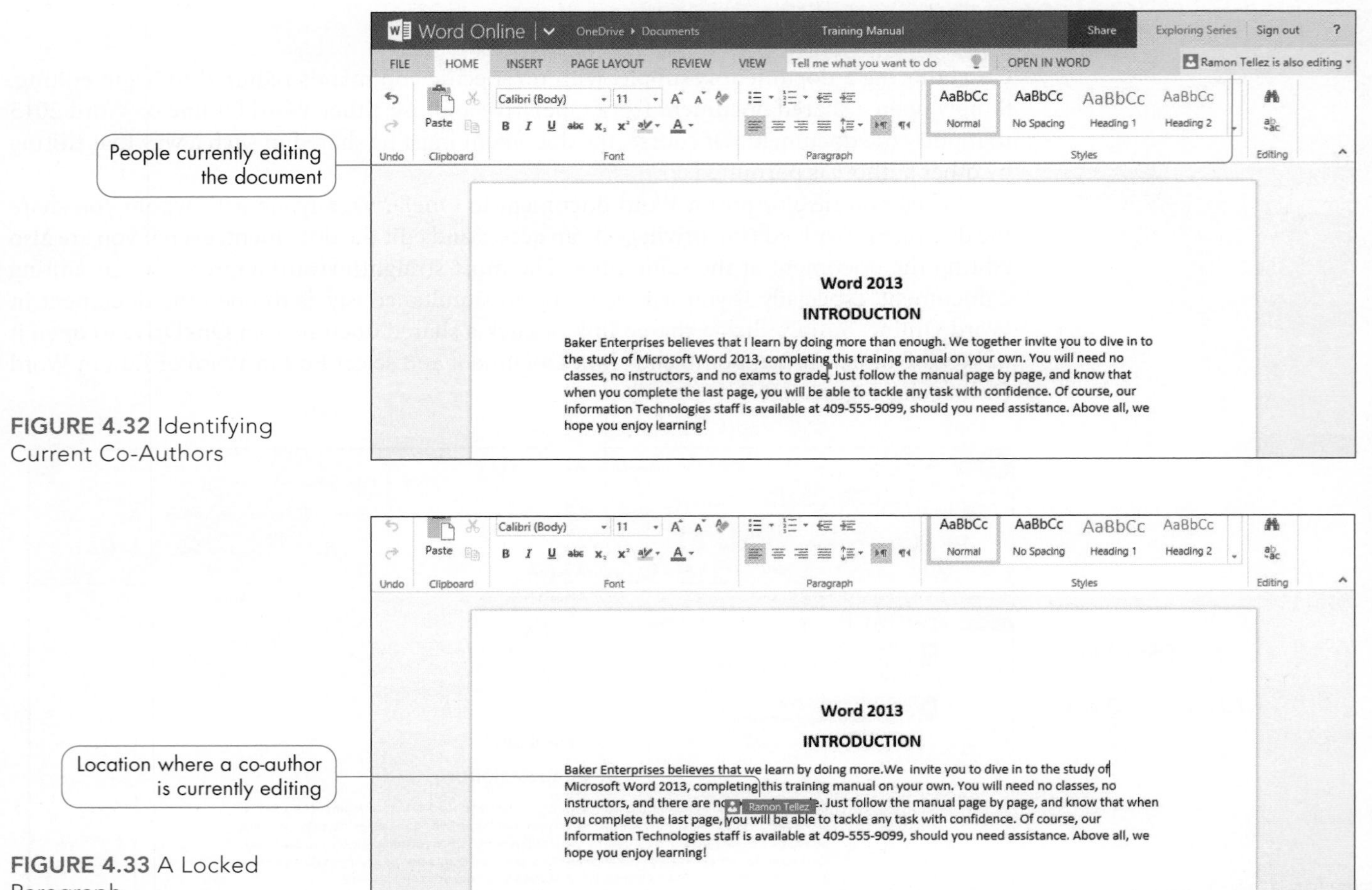

FIGURE 4.32 Identifying Current Co-Authors

FIGURE 4.33 A Locked Paragraph

As you edit a document, even if others are editing the same document simultaneously, the document is being saved automatically. Therefore, you do not need to save the document periodically. The updated document is available to all co-authors in its most current form. If you like, you can download the document when you click the FILE tab, click Save As, and then click Download a Copy (see Figure 4.34). In that way, you can place a copy of the document on a form of local storage, such as your hard drive or a flash drive. The document is also saved on OneDrive so that it is available to everyone who collaborated on the document.

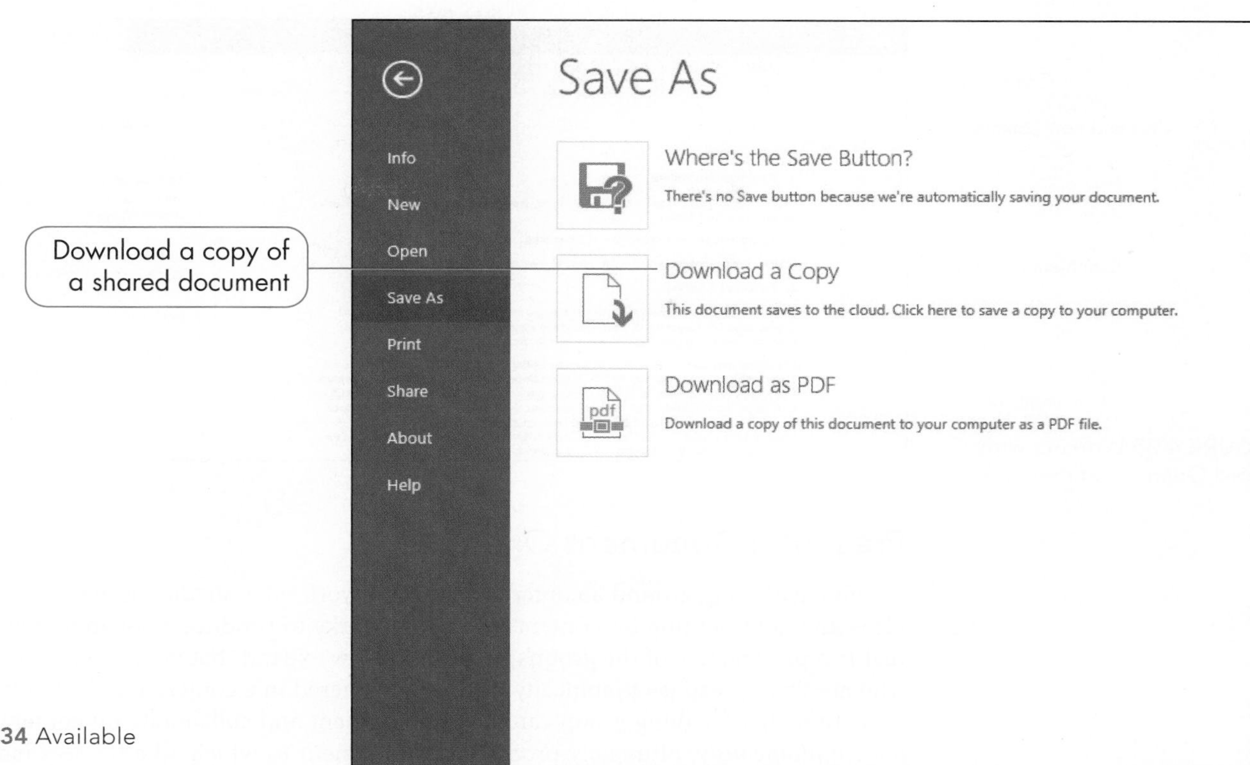

FIGURE 4.34 Available Updates

At any point, you can switch to Word 2013 to continue working with a shared document. Because Word Online is somewhat limited, you might find that you need to edit a document in Word 2013 to access a feature not found in Word Online. For example, you might want to add a bibliography or check a document in Outline view. Even when working in Word 2013, you will be apprised of other editors.

When you work with a shared document, you will often want to make comments about the content or ask questions of co-authors. Often, the purpose of sharing a document is to seek feedback. Those with whom you share a document might not make any edits at all—they could simply comment on the document so that you can improve or validate the content. Using Word 2013 or Word Online, you can create comments as well as reply to comments others might include.

When using Word Online, you must be in Reading View to create or respond to comments. If in Editing View, click the View tab and click Reading View in the Document Views group. To create or reply to a comment:

1. Select a line of text (or double-click to select a paragraph).
2. Click COMMENTS (see Figure 4.35).
3. Click New Comment in the Comments pane on the right or click an existing comment and click Reply.
4. Type a comment and click Post.

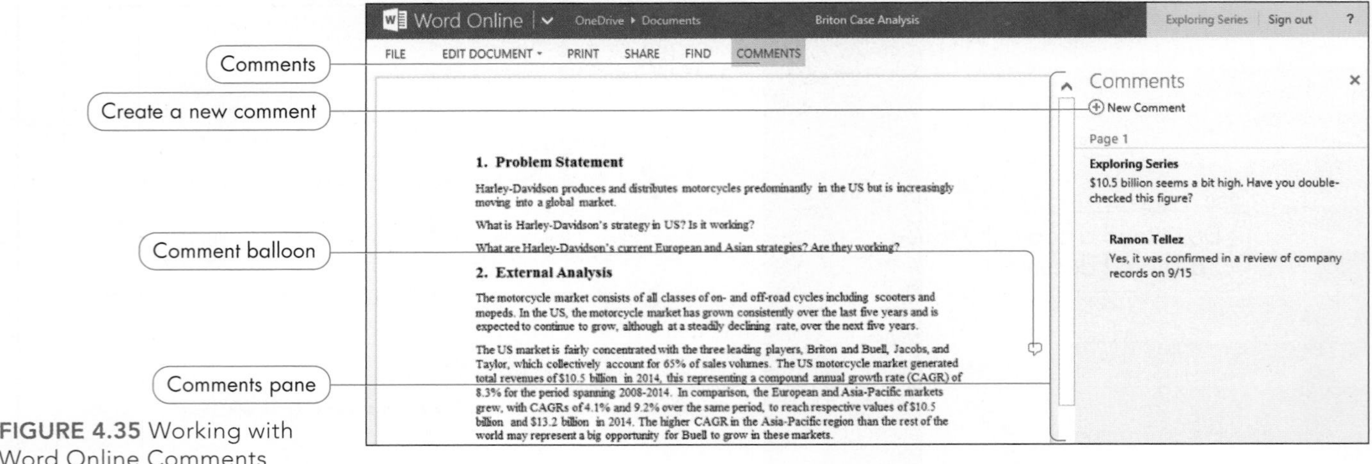

FIGURE 4.35 Working with Word Online Comments

Present a Document Online

Imagine gathering around a conference table to work on a document with others. Sharing ideas and commenting on content, the group works to produce a collaborative document that is representative of the group's best effort. Now expand that view to include co-authors who are widespread geographically instead of gathered in a conference room. Online at the same time, the far-flung group can view a document and collaborate on content, although *not simultaneously*, ultimately producing a document to which all attendees have had the opportunity to contribute. After a document presentation, conference attendees can download a copy of the document for additional editing if necessary. Word 2013 enables you to invite attendees and present a document online. Whether your goal is to present a document for discussion (but no editing) or to seek input from a group after the conference, you will appreciate the ease with which Word 2013 facilitates that task.

Begin an Online Presentation

During an online presentation, a conference leader will present a document. Although attendees can navigate the document independently during the presentation, they cannot edit the document. If an attendee independently navigates the document during the presentation, he or she will stop following the presenter but can rejoin the presentation at any time. As the conference leader, you can make a document available for download, inviting an audience to view the document as you work with it if desired. As the conference leader, you will open the document that you intend to share in Word 2013. Then complete the following steps:

STEP 2»

1. Click the FILE tab, Share, Present Online, and then Present Online (see Figure 4.36). You will need a Microsoft account in order to begin the presentation.
2. Click Connect.
3. Click Copy Link (to copy and paste the meeting hyperlink, perhaps in a Skype chat window) or *Send in Email* (to e-mail the hyperlink in your e-mail client). If you have an IM chat client, you can click *Send in IM*.
4. Click Start Presentation. Your attendees can click the hyperlink or paste it in a browser window to view the document. Attendees can view the document even if they do not have a version of Word installed.

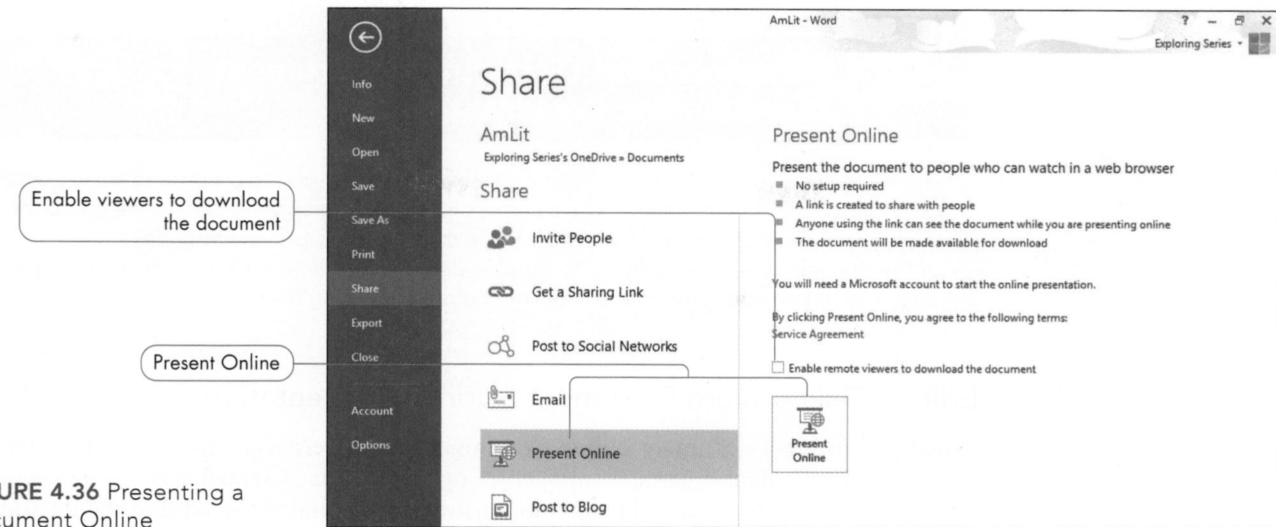

FIGURE 4.36 Presenting a Document Online

Figure 4.37 shows a presenter's view as well as an attendee's. If the presenter's goal is to inform an audience without inviting participation, he or she can simply navigate through the document as the audience follows along online. When the presentation is complete, the presenter will click End Online Presentation.

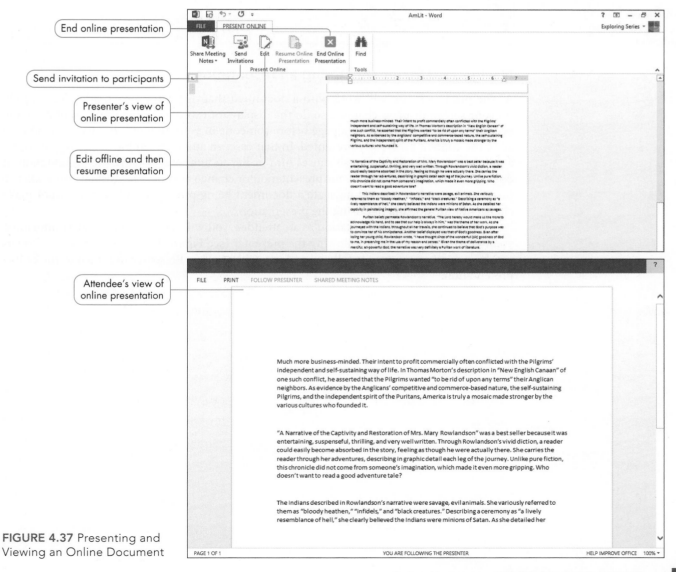

End online presentation

Send invitation to participants

Presenter's view of online presentation

Edit offline and then resume presentation

Attendee's view of online presentation

FIGURE 4.37 Presenting and Viewing an Online Document

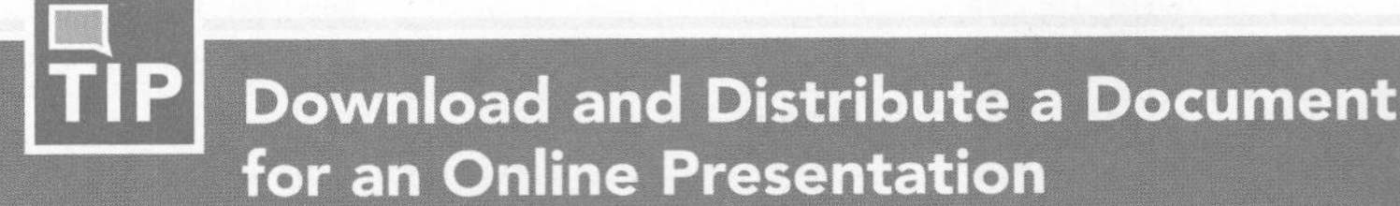

Download and Distribute a Document for an Online Presentation

An online presentation can serve several purposes. Perhaps you are presenting a completed document for informational purposes, or maybe you and a group of students are collaborating on a research paper. In the latter case, you might want to provide attendees with a copy of the document for later editing. To do so, select *Enable remote viewers to download the document* when you select Present Online (before beginning the presentation).

Edit an Online Word Document During a Presentation

While presenting a document online, you might identify errors or modifications that you want to make. Perhaps a name is misspelled, or you see that a sentence could be reworded for better readability. Click Edit to temporarily move offline. After editing the document, click Resume, as shown in Figure 4.38, to return to the online presentation. Attendees will be informed that the presenter has made changes to the file.

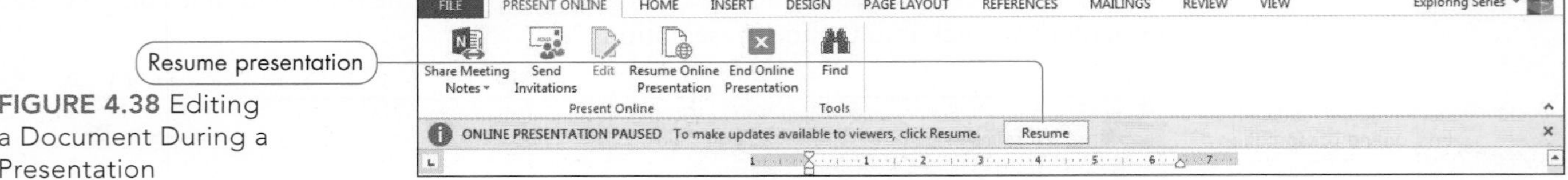

FIGURE 4.38 Editing a Document During a Presentation

Navigate a Document During a Presentation

As the presenter, you will work with a document that displays on each attendee's screen. As your screen displays changes, so do the displays of those watching the presentation. On occasion, you might move to a page before someone in your audience has had time to read all of the content previously presented. In that case, an attendee can independently navigate a document, although doing so causes him or her to temporarily leave the presentation. It does not, however, interrupt your presentation or change anyone else's display. An audience member can independently navigate a document being presented online but cannot make changes to the document during the presentation.

When you leave a presentation as an attendee, you will see a temporary alert informing you that you are no longer following the presenter (see Figure 4.39). The status bar also lets you know you are no longer following along. Click Follow Presenter to return to the online presentation.

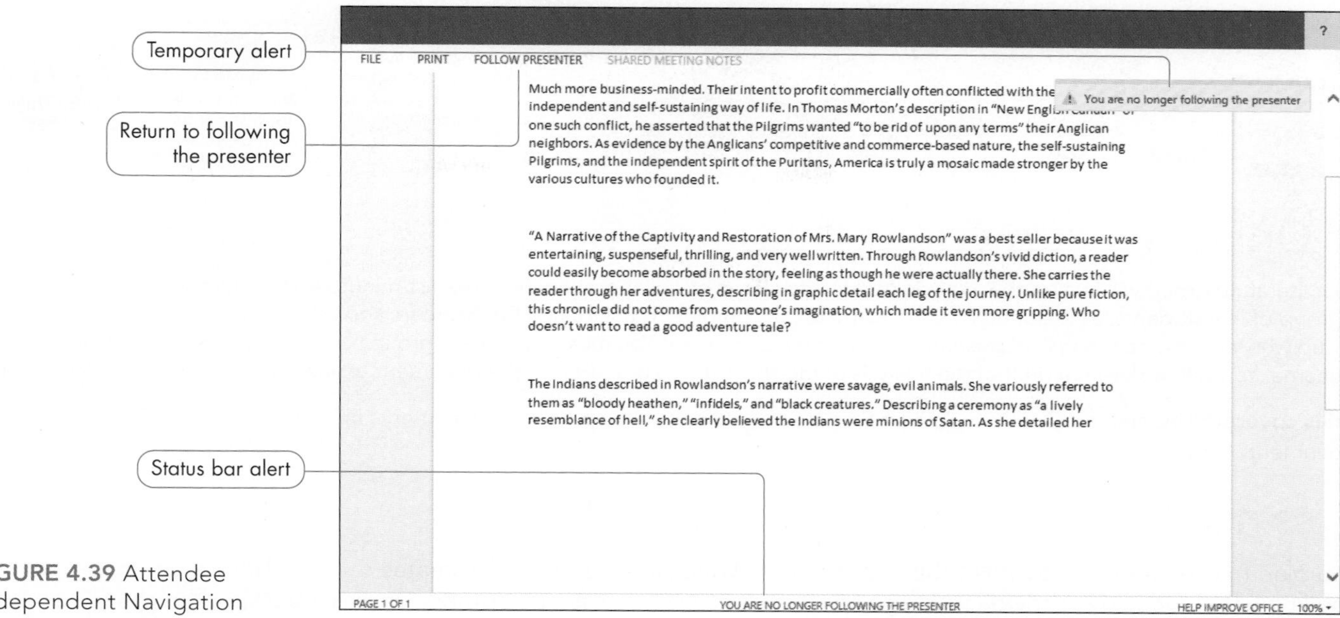

FIGURE 4.39 Attendee Independent Navigation

1. As you save a document to OneDrive, you will most likely want to also have a copy on your computer for backup purposes. How can you make sure that as you modify one copy, the other is also updated? ***p. 341***
2. Both Word 2013 and Word Online enable you to create and edit a document. When might one be preferred over the other? ***p. 345***
3. After editing a shared document online, you want to make your edits available to co-authors who might be editing the same file. How would you do that? ***p. 350***
4. The Editing view and the Reading view of Word Online serve different purposes. Aside from enabling you to easily read a document, what purpose does the Reading view serve? ***p. 351***

Hands-On Exercises

MyITLab®
HOE3 Training

3 Online Document Collaboration

Your literature group will finalize the analysis of *A White Heron* by collaborating on a few last-minute edits online. You will work in a group of five students, as assigned by your instructor, in completing this Hands-On Exercise. You will select a chairperson of your group who will assume the task of posting and sharing a document. You must also have a group name that you will include in the filename. You will work with a draft of the analysis of the short story, co-authoring the document online with classmates in your group.

Skills covered: Understand OneDrive Apps • Present a Document Online • Share Documents in Word Online • Collaborate on a Document

STEP 1 » UNDERSTAND ONEDRIVE APPS

You plan to use OneDrive to share the analysis of *A White Heron* so that classmates can collaborate on the project. You know that OneDrive provides storage space that can be accessed by others, and as a backup, the chairperson of your group will save a copy of the analysis on a hard drive. In doing so, you will want to make sure that edits made to the paper at either location are synchronized with the other location so that both copies remain current. You can use a OneDrive app to accomplish that goal, but first you will learn a bit more about the app. Because you are likely to be in a computer lab, you will not actually download the app, although you can do so on your home computer at http://apps.live.com/onedrive. Before beginning this exercise, you should have a Microsoft account. If you do not have a Microsoft account, create one at www.outlook.com. Refer to Figure 4.40 as you complete Step 1.

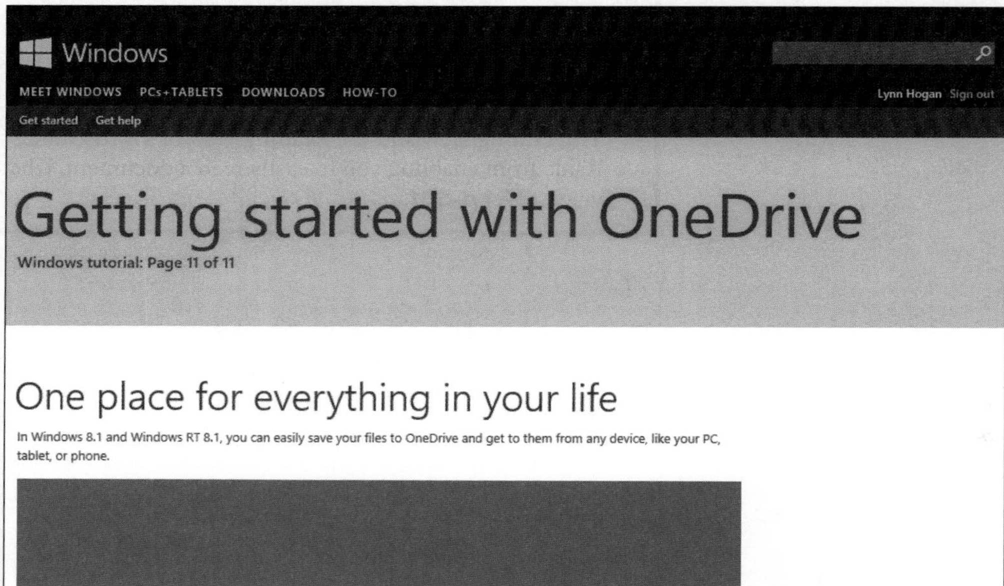

FIGURE 4.40 OneDrive for Windows App

a. Start Word and open a new blank document. Open an Internet browser window. Go to http://windows.microsoft.com/en-gb/windows-8/getting-started-onedrive-tutorial?ocid=onedrive_site_supportlink. Scroll through the Web page, learning more about OneDrive.

b. Having learned a bit more about the app, go to the new blank Word document and type **OneDrive Desktop App** for Windows. Press **Enter**. Type your first name and last name. Press **Enter**. Provide an example of when you might use OneDrive and how the OneDrive for Windows app would help with file coordination and organization. In your description, include system requirements for running the OneDrive Desktop App for Windows. Save the document as **w04h3OneDrive_LastFirst** and close the document.

c. Close the browser window.

STEP 2 » PRESENT A DOCUMENT ONLINE

Before collaborating on the analysis that is to be shared and edited by the group, the chairperson will present the document online to group members, highlighting areas to be edited in a later step. The group chairperson will make the presentation, sharing it with group members who will watch the presentation from their own Internet-connected computers. The group chairperson will use Word 2013 to prepare the online presentation, providing a link to attendees so they can watch. All group members must have a Microsoft account before beginning this exercise. You can create an account at http://www.outlook.com. Your instructor should assign your group a name. Refer to Figure 4.41 as you complete Step 2.

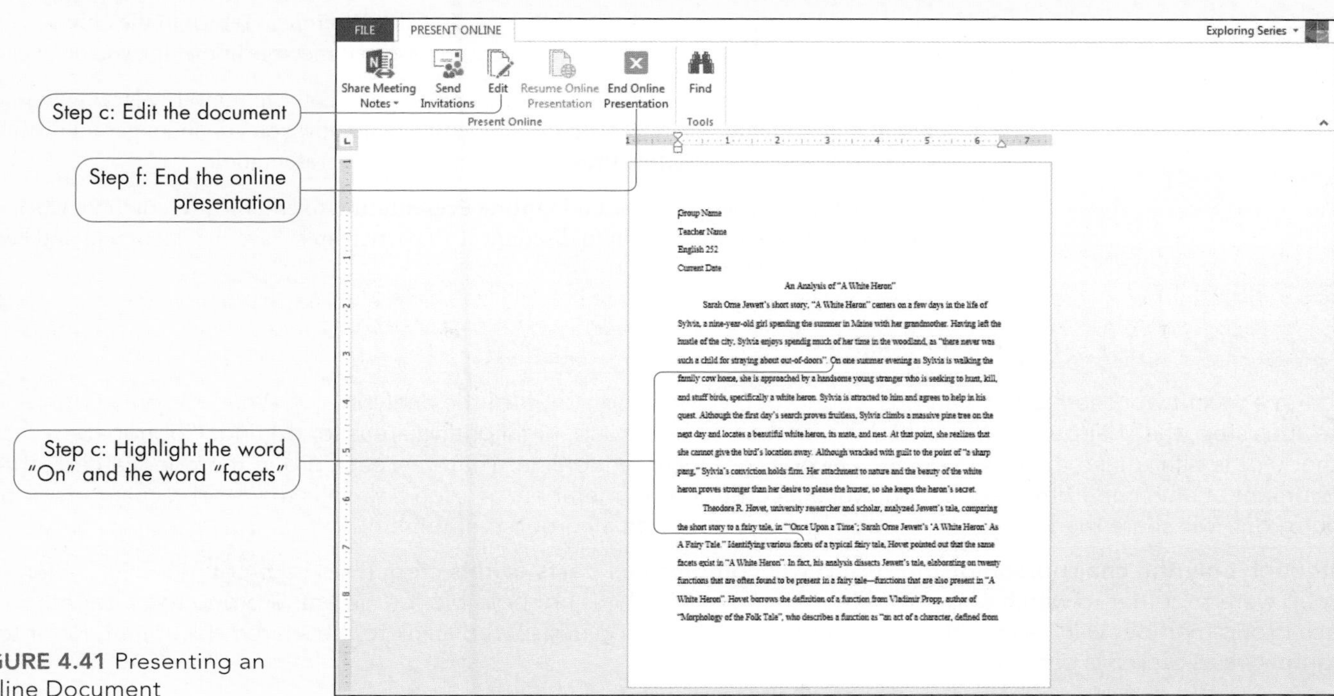

FIGURE 4.41 Presenting an Online Document

a. Start Word. Open *w04h3Analysis* and save it as **w04h3Analysis_GroupName,** replacing *GroupName* with the name assigned the group by your instructor. Keep the document open.

> **TROUBLESHOOTING:** To complete all steps of this exercise, every group member must have a Microsoft account. If you do not have a Microsoft account, create one at http://www.outlook.com.

b. Click the **FILE tab** and click **Share**. Click **Present Online** and click **Present Online** again. Log in to your Microsoft account if necessary and provide a copy of the link to all group members. Click **START PRESENTATION**.

> **TROUBLESHOOTING:** If you are unable to connect, proceed directly to Step 3, skipping all of the following parts of Step 2. However, you should check spelling first, correcting all mistakes (note that author names are not misspelled).

c. If you are the chairperson, scroll through the document, presenting it to the group. Each group member should see the document on individual computers as it is being presented. You will then click **Edit** to temporarily pause the presentation to make edits. Click the **HOME tab** and click **Text Highlight Color**. Highlight the following areas in the document, indicating that they are to be edited later (toggle off Text Highlight Color when highlighting is complete):

- Highlight the word *On* in the third sentence of the first paragraph.
- Highlight the word *facets* in the second paragraph.
- Highlight the words *by killing the white heron* after the word *nature* near the end of the paragraph that begins *On an even deeper level* on page 3.
- Highlight the word *helpful* in the last paragraph of the document.

d. Check the document for spelling errors. All authors' names are correctly spelled, so you should ignore flagged errors of names. The essay begins with a capital *A*, so ignore the apparent grammatical error. Correct any misspelled words. Click **Resume** to return to the online presentation. As a group member, you will see an onscreen message informing you of an edit.

e. If you are a group member, scroll the document independently, temporarily leaving the presentation. A temporary alert will display, letting you know you are no longer following the presentation. Click **Follow Presenter** to return to the presentation.

f. If you are the chairperson, click **End Online Presentation** to end the presentation. Click **End Online Presentation** again to disconnect all participants. Save the document and keep it open for the next step.

STEP 3 » SHARE DOCUMENTS IN WORD ONLINE

During a recent work session on campus, your group developed a draft of the analysis of *A White Heron*. In the previous step, the chairperson presented the analysis to the group, highlighting areas for editing. Coordinating schedules is difficult, so the group decides to edit the document online. That way, each group member can edit the document at any time from any location, while all other group members can see any edits made. The chairperson of your group will share the document through Word Online with all group members.

Although **only the chairperson of the group will complete all parts of this step**, it would be beneficial if the entire group were together to watch or participate in that process. If it is not possible for the entire group to be together, each group member will begin with Step 4, after the chairperson has shared a link to the shared document. Refer to Figure 4.42 as Step 3 is completed.

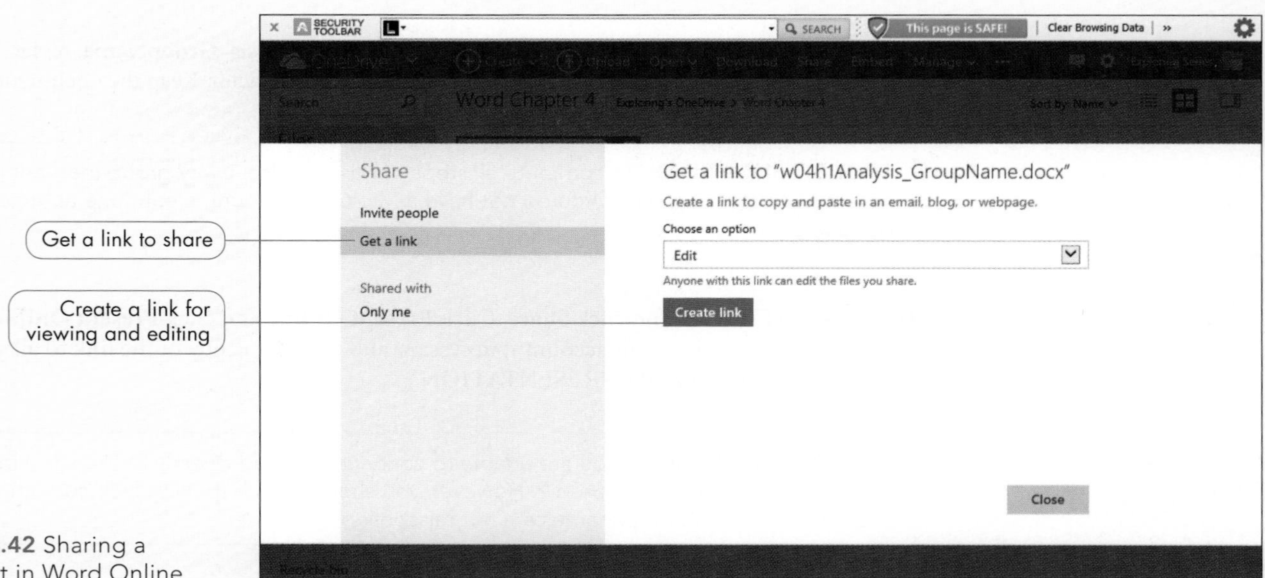

FIGURE 4.42 Sharing a Document in Word Online

a. If you are the chairperson, save *w04h3Analysis_GroupName* in a new folder on OneDrive. Open the document if it is not already open. To save the document to OneDrive, click the **FILE tab** and click **Save As**. Ensure that **OneDrive** is selected and click **Browse**. Click **New Folder**, type **Word Chapter 4**, and then press **Enter**. Double-click **Word Chapter 4** and click **Save**. Close the document.

> **TROUBLESHOOTING:** If you have difficulty saving the file to OneDrive, make sure the file is saved to a local drive and complete the following steps:
>
> 1. Go to http://onedrive.live.com and log in, if necessary.
> 2. Click Create, click Folder, type Word Chapter 4, and then press Enter. Click the new folder.
> 3. Click Upload and click *select them from your computer.* Navigate to the *w04h3Analysis_GroupName* file on your computer and double-click the file. After the file is uploaded, close the OneDrive information window at the bottom-right corner of the browser if necessary.
> 4. Click *w04h3Analysis_GroupName* to open it.
> 5. Proceed to step c.

b. Go to http://onedrive.live.com and sign in. Navigate to the Word Chapter **4** folder. Right-click **w04h3Analysis_GroupName** to open a shortcut menu.

> **TROUBLESHOOTING:** If you cannot find the document in OneDrive, click in the Search OneDrive box at the top left side of the display. Type w04h3Analysis_GroupName (replacing *GroupName* with your group's name, as you saved it in step a). Press Enter. Click the file name, if found, to open the document in Word Online.

c. Click **Share** and click **Get a link**. Click **Create Link**. Click **Shorten link** to display a shorter version of the link. Copy the link for distribution to team members, or have each team member (including the chairperson) make note of the link for later reference. You might include the link in an e-mail to group members or otherwise post it where group members can access it. Click **Done**.

d. Close the browser.

STEP 4 ≫ COLLABORATE ON A DOCUMENT

Each team member has a link to a shared document—*w04h3Analysis_GroupName*. Each person will access *w04h3Analysis_GroupName*, reviewing and editing the report individually. You do not have to access the report simultaneously, although that is an option. All team members will complete all parts of this step (with the exception of the last sentence of part b and all of part c). Refer to Figure 4.43 as you complete Step 4.

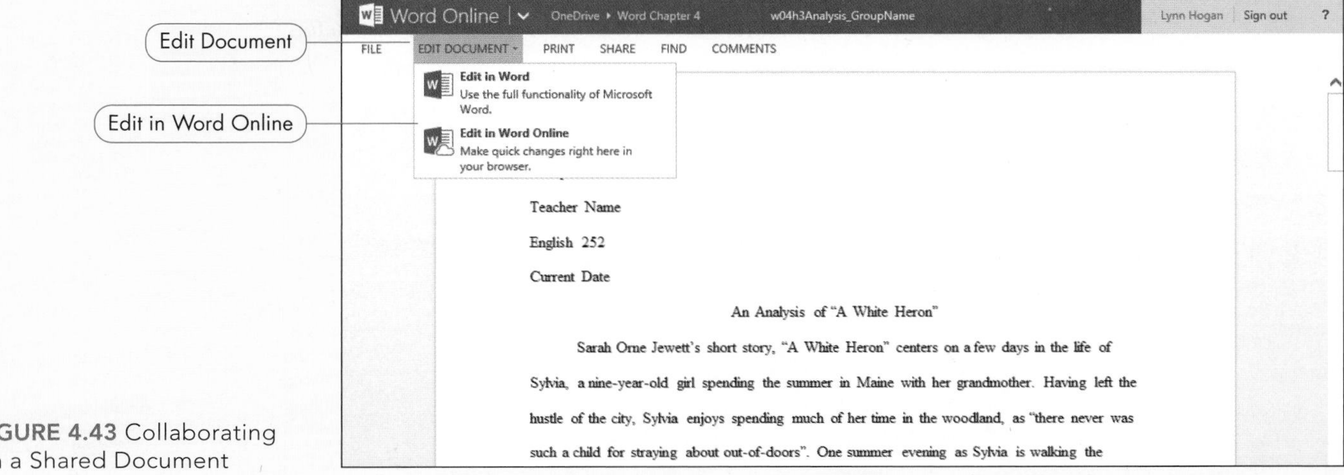

FIGURE 4.43 Collaborating on a Shared Document

a. Open a browser window and type or paste the link provided in part c of the previous step. Press **Enter**.

> **TROUBLESHOOTING:** If the link you use does not display the shared document, the chairperson can repeat Step 3 to produce another link.

b. Click **Edit Document**. Click **Edit in Word Online**. Provide login information related to your Windows account if required. As the chairperson, change the words *Group Name* in the first line of the document to the actual group name assigned by your instructor in Step 2 of this Hands-On Exercise.

c. Divide the following tasks among group members, excluding the chairperson, with each task completed by only one team member (unless there are fewer team members than tasks; in that case, assign the tasks as appropriate). As each group member completes a task, click Save in the upper left corner of the Word Online window. These tasks can be done simultaneously because they are in different paragraphs.

   Task 1: Remove the word *On* from the third sentence of the first paragraph. The sentence should begin with the word *One*.

   Task 2: Change the word *facets* in the second paragraph to *components*. Remove the text highlight if present.

   Task 3: Change the words *by killing the white heron* to *by revealing the white heron* after the word *nature* near the end of the paragraph that begins *On an even deeper level*. Remove the text highlight if present.

   Task 4: Change the word *helpful* to *interesting* in the last paragraph of the document. Remove the text highlight if present.

d. As you complete your edit, click **Save** in the upper left corner of the Word Online window.

e. When all edits are complete, click the **FILE tab**. Click **Save As** and click **Download**. Click the **Save arrow** and click **Save As**. Navigate to an offline storage location, change the file name to **w04h3Analysis_LastFirst**, replacing *LastFirst* with your name, and then click **Save**. Close the browser.

f. Start Word and open **w04h3Analysis_LastFirst**. Change the group name on the first page to your own first and last names and include a real or fictitious instructor name. Make sure the current date shows today's date. Save the file.

g. Submit *w04h3Analysis_LastFirst* as directed by your instructor.

Chapter Objectives Review

After reading this chapter, you have accomplished the following objectives:

1. **Use a writing style and acknowledge sources.**
   - Select a writing style: A research paper is typically written to adhere to a particular writing style, often dictated by the academic discipline.
   - Create a source and include a citation: Each source consulted for a paper must be cited, according to the rules of a writing style.
   - Share and search for a source: Sources are included in a Master List, available to all documents created on the same computer, and a Current List, available to the current document.
   - Create a bibliography: A bibliography, also known as *works cited* or *references*, lists all sources used in the preparation of a paper.
2. **Create and modify footnotes and endnotes.**
   - Create footnotes and endnotes: Footnotes (located at the end of a page) and endnotes (located at the end of a paper) enable you to expand on a statement or provide a citation.
   - Modify footnotes and endnotes: You can change the format or style of footnotes and endnotes, or delete them.
3. **Explore special features.**
   - Create a table of contents: If headings are formatted in a heading style, Word 2013 can prepare a table of contents listing headings and associated page numbers.
   - Create an index: Mark entries for inclusion in an index, which is an alphabetical listing of marked topics and associated page numbers.
   - Create a cover page: Some writing styles require a cover page, which you can create as the first page, listing a report title and other identifying information.
4. **Review a document.**
   - Add a comment: A comment is located in a comment balloon in the margin of a report, providing a note to the author.
   - View and reply to comments: Simple Markup enables you to view comments and reply to them in an unobtrusive manner.
5. **Track Changes.**
   - Use Track Changes: With Track Changes active, all edits in a document are traceable so you can see what has been changed.
   - Accept and reject changes: With Track Changes active, you can evaluate each edit made, accepting or rejecting it.
   - Work with PDF documents: PDF Reflow is a Word feature that converts a PDF document into an editable Word document.
6. **Use OneDrive.**
   - Understand OneDrive apps: Windows 8.1.1 OneDrive app and OneDrive for Windows app simplify the use of OneDrive for saving documents.
7. **Share and collaborate on documents.**
   - Share documents in Word 2013: Use Word 2013 to share documents through links, social media, or e-mail.
   - Share documents in Word Online: Use Word Online to share documents through links, social media, or e-mail.
   - Collaborate on a document: With an online document shared, multiple authors can collaborate on the document, editing it simultaneously.
   - Present a document online: Word 2013 enables you to present a document online, although those viewing the presentation cannot edit it at the same time as the presentation.

Key Terms Matching

Match the key terms with their definitions. Write the key term letter by the appropriate numbered definition.

a. Bibliography
b. Citation
c. Comment
d. Cover page
e. Endnote
f. Footnote
g. Index
h. MLA
i. PDF Reflow
j. Plagiarism
k. Revision mark
l. Simple Markup
m. OneDrive for Windows app
n. Source
o. Style manual
p. Table of contents
q. Track Changes
r. Windows 8.1.1 OneDrive app
s. Word Online
t. Works Cited

1. ______ Word feature that converts a PDF document into an editable Word document. **p. 336**
2. ______ A list of works cited or consulted by an author in his or her work; the listing preferred by MLA. **p. 318**
3. ______ A note recognizing a source of information or a quoted passage. **p. 315**
4. ______ A downloadable app that synchronizes documents between a computer and OneDrive storage so that documents in both locations remain up to date. **p. 341**
5. ______ An alphabetical listing of topics covered in a document along with the page numbers where the topic is discussed. **p. 323**
6. ______ Word feature that monitors all additions, deletions, and formatting changes you make in a document. **p. 335**
7. ______ A citation that appears at the end of a document. **p. 320**
8. ______ Word feature that simplifies the display of comments and revision marks, resulting in a clean, uncluttered look. **p. 332**
9. ______ Page that lists headings in the order they appear in a document and the page numbers where the entries begin. **p. 322**
10. ______ A note, annotation, or additional information to the author or another reader about the content of a document. **p. 332**
11. ______ A list of works cited or consulted by an author in his or her work. **p. 318**
12. ______ An online component of Office Online presenting a free, although limited, version of Word 2013. **p. 345**
13. ______ A guide to a particular writing style outlining required rules and conventions related to the preparation of papers. **p. 314**
14. ______ The act of using and documenting the works of another as one's own. **p. 314**
15. ______ A citation that appears at the bottom of a page. **p. 320**
16. ______ Writing style established by the Modern Language Association with rules and conventions for preparing research papers (used primarily in the area of humanities). **p. 314**
17. ______ App included in Windows 8.1.1 displaying in File Explorer all documents and folders saved to OneDrive. **p. 341**
18. ______ Indicates where text is added, deleted, or formatted while the Track Changes feature is active. **p. 335**
19. ______ The first page of a report, including the report title, author or student, and other identifying information. **p. 324**
20. ______ A publication, person, or media item that is consulted in the preparation of a paper and given credit. **p. 314**

Multiple Choice

1. What Word Online view is required when you are adding comments to a shared document?
   (a) Editing
   (b) Reading
   (c) Print Layout
   (d) Web Layout

2. A major difference between sharing a document through Word Online and sharing a document as an online presentation is that:
   (a) You cannot simultaneously edit a document shared through Word Online; you can simultaneously edit a document shared as an online presentation.
   (b) A document shared as an online presentation must be saved in PDF format; a document shared through Word Online must be a Word document.
   (c) A person viewing an online presentation of a document can edit the document; a document shared through Word Online is available for viewing only, not editing.
   (d) A document shared through Word Online is available for simultaneous editing and collaboration; viewers of an online document presentation cannot edit the document during the presentation.

3. The choice of whether to title a list of sources *bibliography*, *works cited*, or *references* is dependent upon:
   (a) The writing style in use.
   (b) The version of Word you are using.
   (c) Whether the sources are from academic publications or professional journals.
   (d) Your own preference.

4. When working with Word Online, how can you tell that someone is editing a shared document at the same time that you are?
   (a) A note displays on the right side of the status bar.
   (b) A comment balloon displays in the left margin.
   (c) The Reviewing Pane displays, providing the names of others who are editing the document.
   (d) There is no way to tell who is editing at the same time.

5. Which of the following is *not* an option on Word's Reference tab?
   (a) Update a Table of Contents
   (b) Create a Cover Page
   (c) Insert a Citation
   (d) Insert an Index

6. The writing style you are most likely to use in a college English composition class is:
   (a) APA
   (b) Chicago
   (c) Turabian
   (d) MLA

7. To ensure that documents you save on OneDrive are synchronized with copies of the same documents saved on your hard drive, you could use a(n):
   (a) Backup setting in Word Options.
   (b) Windows 8.1.1 OneDrive app.
   (c) OneDrive for Windows app.
   (d) AutoRecover option.

8. This feature ensures a simple, uncluttered, view of comments and tracked changes made to a document.
   (a) Track Changes
   (b) Show Markup
   (c) Show/Hide
   (d) Simple Markup

9. After you create and insert a table of contents into a document:
   (a) Any subsequent page changes arising from the insertion or deletion of text to existing paragraphs must be entered manually.
   (b) Any additions to the entries in the table arising due to the insertion of new paragraphs defined by a heading style must be entered manually.
   (c) An index cannot be added to the document.
   (d) You can select a table of contents and click Update Table to bring the table of contents up to date.

10. You are participating in a group project in which each member makes changes to the same document, although not simultaneously. Which feature should you suggest the members use so each can see the edits made by fellow group members?
    (a) Mark Index Entries
    (b) Track Changes
    (c) Accept Changes
    (d) Create Cross-References

Practice Exercises

1 Social Media and Marketing

As a graduate student, you are nearing completion of an M.B.A. degree. You and several friends plan to start a small business after graduation, offering business and Web design consulting services. Having been an active participant in all sorts of social networking and having studied the use of social media to promote businesses in several marketing classes, you are well aware of the benefits of using social media to help build a client base. You decide to conduct a bit of research to determine which social networks seem to be effective and how to incorporate them into a marketing strategy. The bonus is that you are involved in a group project to develop a research paper for a marketing class, so you will be able to use the paper to complete that objective as well. You will share the paper online so that others in your group can contribute and comment. This exercise follows the same set of skills as used in Hands-On Exercises 1–2 in the chapter. Refer to Figure 4.44 as you complete this exercise.

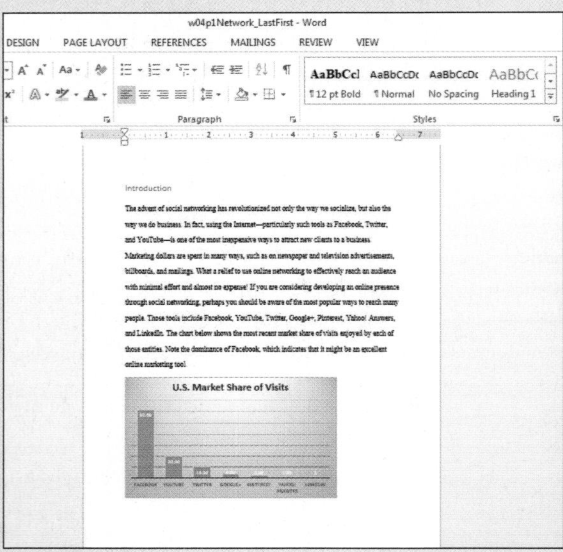

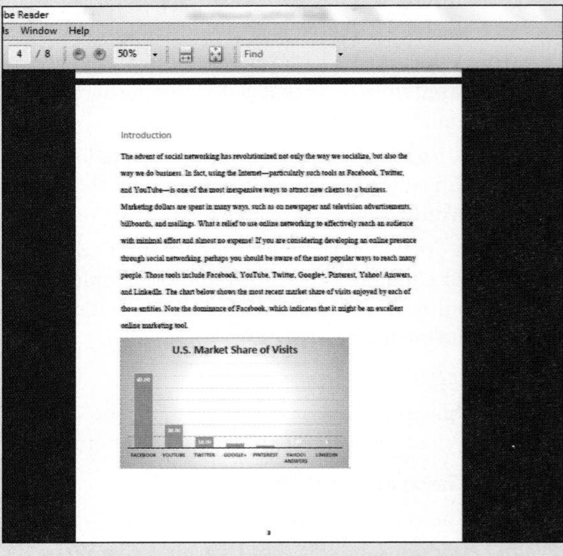

FIGURE 4.44 Social Media Documents

a. Open *w04p1Network* and save it as **w04p1Network_LastFirst**.

b. Press **Ctrl+Home**. Click the **Insert tab**, click **Cover Page**, and then select **Austin**. Complete the cover page by completing the following:
   - Click **Document title** and type **Using Social Media**.
   - Click **Document subtitle** and type **Market Your Business**.
   - Remove the current author (unless the current author shows your first and last names) and type your first and last names.
   - Right-click the **Abstract paragraph** at the top of the page and click **Remove Content Control**.

c. Click the **REVIEW tab**. Click the **Track Changes arrow** and click **Track Changes**. All of your edits will be marked as you work. Change the view to **All Markup**, if necessary.

d. Make the following changes to the document:
   - Change the heading *Social Networking Sites* on page 2 (following the cover page) to **Social Media Sites**.
   - Select all text except the cover page. Change line spacing to **Double** (or **2.0**).
   - Click the **PAGE LAYOUT tab** and ensure that paragraph spacing Before and After is **0.**
   - Scroll to page 5 and select the heading *Maintain a blog*. Click the **REVIEW tab** and click **New Comment**. Type **Tricia – Would you please expand on this subject? It seems too short.**

e. Insert a page break at the beginning of the document and move to the beginning of the new page. Insert text from the file *w04p1Invitation*. Replace *Firstname Lastname* with your first and last names. Because Track Changes is on, the text you inserted is colored to indicate it is a new edit.

f. Scroll through the document, noting the edits that were tracked. On page 6, you should see the comment you made earlier. Press **Ctrl+Home** to move to the beginning of the document. Click the **REVIEW tab** and change the view to **No Markup**. Scroll through the document to note that revision marks (indicating edits) do not display. Move to the beginning of the document and select **Simple Markup**. Scroll through the document once more. Click a bar beside an edited paragraph to display the edits. Click the bar again to remove them from view.

g. Check the document for spelling errors. All names of people and Web sites are correctly spelled. Scroll to page 6 and click the comment balloon beside the *Maintain a blog* section. Click **Reply** in the expanded markup balloon. Type **I'll make my edits by Tuesday evening**. Close the comment balloon.

h. On page 4, click after the period at the end of the second sentence under *Social Media Sites*. The sentence ends in *growing audience of users*. Click the **REFERENCES tab** and click **Insert Footnote** in the Footnotes group. Type **See http://www.socialstats.org for current social media usage statistics.** (include the period). Right-click the hyperlink in the footnote and click **Remove Hyperlink**.

i. Click the **REVIEW tab**, if necessary, and change the view to **No Markup**. Right-click the footnote at the bottom of page 4 and click **Style**. Click **Modify**. Change the font to **Times New Roman**. The font size should be **10**. Click **OK** and click **Close**.

j. Move to the top of page 3 (beginning with *Introduction*) and insert a page break at the top of the page. Move to the top of the new page (page 3). Click the **REFERENCES tab**. Click **Table of Contents** in the *Table of Contents* group and click **Automatic Table 2**.

k. Scroll to page 7 and delete the *Downsides of Social Networking* section (removing the heading and the paragraph below the heading). Scroll to page 3 and click the **Table of Contents** to select the field. Click **Update Table** in the content control and select **Update entire table**. Click **OK**. Note that the *Downsides of Social Networking* section is no longer included in the table of contents.

l. Click the **REVIEW tab** and change the view to **Simple Markup**. Click the **Accept arrow** and click **Accept All Changes and Stop Tracking**. Click the **Delete arrow** in the Comments group and click **Delete All Comments in Document**. Scroll through the document and note that edits are no longer marked.

m. Click after the year *2010* and before the period in the sentence in the *Facebook* section that ends *$2 billion in 2010*. Click the **REFERENCES tab** and click the **Style arrow** in the Citations & Bibliography group. Select **APA Sixth Edition**. Click **Insert Citation** in the Citations & Bibliography group and click **Add New Source**. Add the following source from a *Journal Article* and click **OK.**

   Author: **Amberley, Anna Leigh**

   Title: **Growing More Social**

   Journal Name: **Journal of Internet Studies**

   Year: **2015**

   Pages: **18–20**

   Volume: **2**

   Issue: **8**

   (Hint: Click **Show All Bibliography Fields** to enter the volume and issue.)

n. Click the citation you just created, click the **Citation Options arrow**, and then click **Edit Citation**. Type **18** in the **Pages box**. Click **OK**.

o. Save the document as **w04p1Network_LastFirst**. Click the **FILE tab** and click **Export**. Ensure that *Create PDF/XPS Document* is selected and click **Create PDF/XPS**. Leave the file name as *w04p1Network_LastFirst* and ensure that the type is *PDF*. Click **Publish** to save the document as a PDF file. Close all open files, saving a file if prompted to do so.

p. Submit *w04p1Network_LastFirst.docx* and *w04p1Network_LastFirst.pdf* as directed by your instructor.

2 Dream Act Letter

You are a partner in a law firm that deals with a large number of potential DREAM Act beneficiaries. The DREAM Act (Development, Relief, and Education for Alien Minors) provides conditional permanent residency to undocumented residents under certain conditions (good moral character, completion of U.S. high school degree, arrival in the United States as minors, etc.). Supporters of the Act contend that it provides social and economic benefits, whereas opponents label it as an amnesty program that rewards illegal immigration. Your law firm has partnered with leading law professors across the country to encourage the U.S Executive Branch (Office of the President) to explore various options related to wise administration of the DREAM Act. In a letter to the president, you outline your position. Because it is of legal nature, the letter makes broad use of footnotes and in-text references. Because the letter is to be signed and supported by law professors across the country, you will share the letter online, making it possible for others to edit and approve of the wording. This exercise follows the same set of skills as used in Hands-On Exercises 1–3 in the chapter. Refer to Figure 4.45 as you complete this exercise.

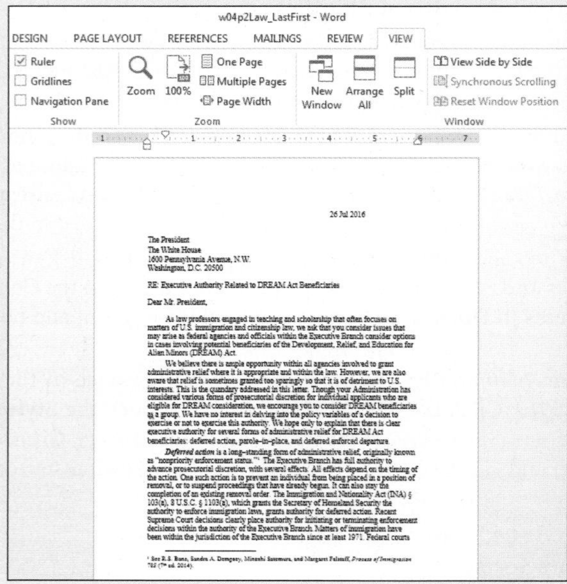

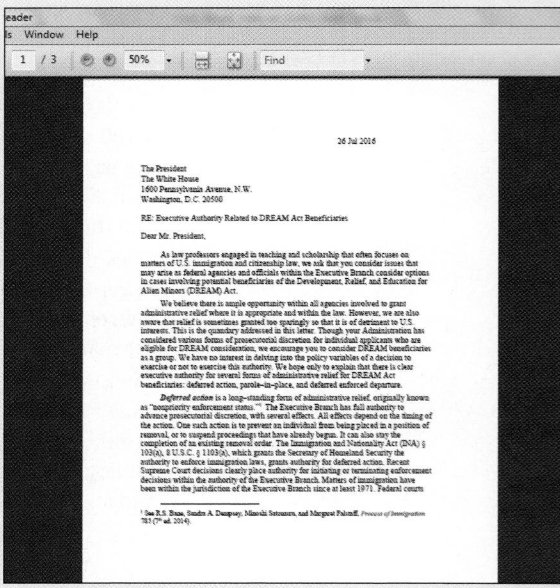

26 Jul 2016

The President
The White House
1600 Pennsylvania Avenue, N.W.
Washington, D.C. 20500

RE: Executive Authority Related to DREAM Act Beneficiaries

Dear Mr. President,

As law professors engaged in teaching and scholarship that often focuses on matters of U.S. immigration and citizenship law, we ask that you consider issues that may arise as federal agencies and officials within the Executive Branch consider options in cases involving potential beneficiaries of the Development, Relief, and Education for Alien Minors (DREAM) Act.

We believe there is ample opportunity within all agencies involved to grant administrative relief where it is appropriate and within the law. However, we are also aware that relief is sometimes granted too sparingly so that it is of detriment to U.S. interests. This is the quandary addressed in this letter. Though your Administration has considered various forms of prosecutorial discretion for individual applicants who are eligible for DREAM consideration, we encourage you to consider DREAM beneficiaries as a group. We have no interest in delving into the policy variables of a decision to exercise or not to exercise this authority. We hope only to explain that there is clear executive authority for several forms of administrative relief for DREAM Act beneficiaries: deferred action, parole–in–place, and deferred enforced departure.

Deferred action is a long–standing form of administrative relief, originally known as "nonpriority enforcement status."[1] The Executive Branch has full authority to advance prosecutorial discretion, with several effects. All effects depend on the timing of the action. One such action is to prevent an individual from being placed in a position of removal, or to suspend proceedings that have already begun. It can also stay the completion of an existing removal order. The Immigration and Nationality Act (INA) § 103(a), 8 U.S.C. § 1103(a), which grants the Secretary of Homeland Security the authority to enforce immigration laws, grants authority for deferred action. Recent Supreme Court decisions clearly place authority for initiating or terminating enforcement decisions within the authority of the Executive Branch. Matters of immigration have been within the jurisdiction of the Executive Branch since at least 1971. Federal courts

[1] See R.S. Bane, Sandra A. Dempsey, Minoshi Satomura, and Margaret Falstaff, *Process of Immigration* 785 (7th ed. 2014).

FIGURE 4.45 Dream Act Letter

a. Start Word and open a blank document. Click the **FILE tab** and click **Open**. Navigate to your data files and double-click the PDF file *w04p2Law.pdf.* Click **OK** when advised that Word will convert the document into an editable Word document. Save it as a Word document with the file name **w04p2Law_LastFirst**.

b. Scroll through the document and change *Firstname Lastname* in the closing to your first and last names. Check the document for spelling errors. All names are spelled correctly. The word *parol* should be spelled *parole*. The word *nonpriority* is not misspelled. Select text in the document from *As law professors engaged in teaching and scholarship* through *historically and recently*. Make sure paragraph spacing After is **6 pt**. Deselect the text.

c. Scroll down and select text from *Respectfully Yours* through the end of the document. Format the selected text in two columns. Deselect the text. Scroll to the last page and place the insertion point to the left of *Richard Hill*. Click **Breaks** in the Page Setup group on the PAGE LAYOUT tab. Click **Column**.

d. Place the insertion point after the ending quotation mark that ends the first sentence in the third body paragraph on page 1. Click the **REFERENCES tab** and click **Insert Footnote** in the Footnotes group. Type ***See* R.S. Bane, Sandra A. Dempsey, Minoshi Satomura, and Margaret Falstaff, *Process of Immigration* 785 (7th ed. 2014).** (include the period).

e. Scroll to page 2 and place the insertion point after the quotation mark that ends the second sentence in the paragraph that begins *Parole-in-place is defined.* Click the **Footnotes Dialog Box Launcher** in the Footnotes group and click **Insert**. Type ***See* Lani Parosky, Comment, *Congressional Policy*, 64 U. Buffalo L. Rev. 578, 56–58 (2003).** (include the period).

f. Save the document. Next, save the document to a OneDrive account in a new folder called **Word Practice Exercises**. After saving the file to OneDrive, close the document and exit Word.

g. Go to http://onedrive.live.com and sign in to your Windows account if necessary. Navigate to the Word Practice Exercises folder and click **w04p2Law_LastFirst**. Click **EDIT DOCUMENT** and click **Edit in Word Online**. Scroll through the document and note that Word Online shows a placeholder for the footnotes you created. However, you cannot edit or work with footnotes in Word Online because it is limited in features. Point to a footnote placeholder to read a comment to the effect that you must open Word to work with footnotes.

h. Click **View** and select **Reading View**. Select the date at the top of the letter. Click **Comments** and click **New Comment**. Type **Please review this document in its entirety and make any edits you feel necessary.** Click **Post**. Close the Comments pane. Click **EDIT DOCUMENT** and click **Edit in Word Online**. Click **Save** in the top left corner.

i. Click the **FILE tab** and click **Open in Word**. Click **Yes** in the warning dialog box. When the document opens in Word, click the **REVIEW tab** and change the view to Simple Markup, if necessary.

j. Click the **Track Changes arrow** in the Tracking group and click **Track Changes**. Click **Reviewing Pane** (not the Reviewing Pane arrow). Reverse the words *to* and *not* in the second body paragraph on page 1. Note the changes in the Reviewing Pane as well as the vertical bar on the right side of the affected paragraph indicating that edits have been made. Click the vertical bar to view the changes. Click it again to return to Simple Markup. Close the Reviewing (Revisions) Pane.

k. Click the **FILE tab** and click **Save As**, saving the file to the location of your student files, not to OneDrive. Keep the file open. Click the **FILE tab** and click **Export**. Ensure that *Create PDF/XPS Document* is selected and click **Create PDF/XPS**. Leave the file name as *w04p2Law_LastFirst* and ensure that the type is *PDF*. Click **Publish** to save the document as a PDF file. Scroll through the PDF file and note that the edits and the comment were saved as part of the PDF document. Close the PDF document.

l. With *w04p2Law_LastFirst.docx* open, click the **REVIEW tab**, click the **Accept arrow** in the Changes group, and then click **Accept All Changes and Stop Tracking**. Right-click the comment and click **Delete Comment**.

m. Save the document. Close all open files.

n. Submit *w04p2Law_LastFirst.docx* and *w04p2Law_LastFirst.pdf* as directed by your instructor.

Mid-Level Exercises

1 WWW Web Services Agency

You work as a Web designer at WWW Web Services Agency and have been asked to provide some basic information to be used in a senior citizens' workshop. You want to provide the basic elements of good Web design and format the document professionally. Use the basic information you have already prepared in a Word document and revise it to include elements appropriate for a research-oriented paper.

a. Start Word and begin a blank document. Open the PDF file *w04m1Web*, agreeing that Word will enable the document as a Word document. Save the subsequent Word document as **w04m1Web_LastFirst**.

b. Change the author name to **Shannon Lee**.

c. Place the insertion point at the end of the *Proximity and Balance* paragraph (after the period) on the second page of the document. The paragraph ends with *indicates less proximity*. Insert the following footnote: **Max Rebaza, Effective Web Sites, Chicago: Windy City Publishing, Inc. (2014)**. Do not include the period.

d. Insert a table of contents on a new page after the cover page. Use a style of your choice.

e. You will add a bibliography to the document, inserting citation sources from the footnotes already in place. Because you will not use in-text citations, you will use the Source Manager to create the sources: To add new sources:
- Click the **REFERENCES tab** and click **Manage Sources** in the Citations & Bibliography group.
- Begin by adding a source for the footnote you created in step c (a Book). Click **New** in the Source Manager dialog box and add the source to both the Current and the Master list.
- Create citation sources for the two additional sources identified in the document footnotes. The footnote on the fourth page is from an article in a periodical (issue 7), and the footnote on the fifth page cites a journal article.

f. Insert a bibliography at the end of the document on a separate page using the Chicago style. Select **Bibliography**. Apply **Heading 2 style** to the *Bibliography* heading and center the heading. Double space the bibliography and ensure that there is no paragraph spacing before or after.

g. Mark all occurrences of *Web*, *content*, and *site* as index entries. Create an index on a separate page after the bibliography using the **Formal** format.

h. Click the **FILE tab** and share the document, saving it to a folder of your choice on OneDrive in the process. After the document has been saved, click the **FILE tab** and get a sharing link that can be edited by anyone with whom you share the link. Copy the link and paste it as a footer in *w04m1Web_LastFirst*.

i. Begin to track changes. Select the heading *Proximity and Balance* on the third page. Add a new comment, typing **This section seems incomplete. Please check and add content.**

j. Add the following sentence as the second sentence in the *Contrast and Focus* section: **You are most likely familiar with the concept of contrast when working with pictures in an image editor.**

k. Save the document in the location of your student files (not OneDrive), replacing the existing file, and submit based on your instructor's directions.

2 New York City Trip

Your family is planning a seven-day trip to New York City next summer. Your responsibility is to research the city and develop a list of activities that your family will enjoy. You used the Internet to complete your research. Now you want to format the Word document to impress your family with your word-processing skills by incorporating different styles and formats and including a cover page, table of contents, and index.

a. Open *w04m2NYC* and save it as **w04m2NYC_LastFirst**.

b. Accept all formatting changes in the document. Turn on **Track Changes** so any further changes will be flagged.

c. Apply **Heading 1 style** to section headings that display in all capital letters. Apply **Heading 2 style** (scroll to locate the style) to section headings that display alone on a line in title case (the first letter of each word is capitalized).

d. Check all comments in the report, acting on them, if necessary. Reply to each comment after you have read and/or taken action on the item.

e. Create a footer for the document consisting of the title **Trip to New York City**, followed by a space and a page number. If the page number already appears as a footer, adjust it so that it follows *Trip to New York City*. Left align the footer in the footer area. Do not display the footer on the first page.

f. Create a page specifically for the table of contents and generate a table of contents.

g. Mark all occurrences of the following text for inclusion in the index: *New York City*, *Bronx Zoo*, and *Liberty Island*. Cross-reference *Big Apple* with *New York City*. On a separate page at the end of the document, create the index in **Classic format**.

h. Save and close the file and submit based on your instructor's directions.

3 American History

COLLABORATION CASE

FROM SCRATCH

You are working on a group project in an American history class. You and two other students will prepare an informal paper on favorite presidents, including a brief history of the United States and a summary of American government.

a. Determine a group name to be used throughout this project, or use one assigned by your instructor.

b. Allocate one of three tasks to each team member. One student will develop a paragraph describing a favorite president (along with a photo), another will compose a paragraph giving a very brief history of the United States, and a third will describe our system of government. All paragraphs will be included in one shared document that will be submitted to your instructor.

Student 1:

c. Begin a blank document, turn on Track Changes, and include three headings, formatted in Heading 1 style: **Favorite President, History,** and **American Government**. Save the document as **w04m3History_GroupName**, replacing Group Name with the name assigned by your instructor. In a paragraph beneath the *Favorite President* heading, format text as Times New Roman 12 pt. Type a paragraph about your favorite president, including a photo of the president. Type your name in the footer, save the document, and share it with the next student.

Student 2:

d. In a paragraph beneath the *History* heading, format text as Times New Roman 12 pt. Include a paragraph providing a brief description of American history. Type your name in the footer, save the document, and share it with the next student.

Student 3:

e. In a paragraph beneath the *American Government* heading, format text as Times New Roman 12 pt. Include a paragraph providing a brief description of American government. Type your name in the footer and save the document. Select the *Favorite President* heading and insert a new comment. In the comment, provide the names of group members and the date of submission. Turn Track Changes off, save, and submit the file based on your instructor's directions.

Beyond the Classroom

An Ethics Paper on Cheating

Cheating and the violation of schools' honor codes have become major problems in many school systems. We often hear stories of how high school and college students can easily cheat on tests or written papers without being caught. You will use the Internet to research the topic of plagiarism, honor codes, and the honor and judicial program at your university and several other universities in your state. You should use more than five sources, with at least one each from the Internet, a book, and a journal. After your research is complete, you will write a three-page, double-spaced report describing your findings. Include the definition of plagiarism, the penalty for violating the honor code at your school, and the statistics for cheating in high schools and colleges. Cite all the sources in your paper, insert at least one footnote, and develop a bibliography for your paper based on the APA Sixth Edition writing style. Save the report as **w04b2Cheating_LastFirst**. Also save the report on OneDrive and create a sharing link. Include the link as a footnote in the paper you will submit. Save and close the file and submit based on your instructor's directions.

Computer History

You are preparing a brief history of computers for inclusion in a group project. Another student began the project, but ran completely out of time and needs your help. Open *w04b3Computers* and save it as **w04b3Computers_LastFirst**. Turn on Track Changes and respond to all comments left for you by the previous student. Save the document and submit based on your instructor's directions.

Making Ethical Choices

SOFT SKILLS CASE

After watching the video on making ethical choices, prepare a two- to five-page research paper, using MLA style, on making ethical choices in the workplace or at school. Include at least three sources, cited in text and included in a bibliography. If directed by your instructor, you might work on the research paper with one or more fellow students, sharing the document online for co-editing. The document should be error-free. Save the document as **w04b4Ethics_LastFirst** (or **GroupName** if working in a group). Submit the document as directed by your instructor.

Capstone Exercise

You are a member of the Horticulture Society and have been asked to assist in the development of information packets about a variety of flowers and plants. A report about tulips has been started, and you are responsible for completing the document so that it is ready for the fall meeting.

Track Revisions

The document you receive has a few comments and shows the last few changes by the author. You will accept or reject the changes and then make a few of your own.

a. Open *w04c1Tulip* and save it as **w04c1Tulip_LastFirst**.

b. Ensure that the markup view is *All Markup*. Review the comments. Move to the third page and reject the insertion of a sentence about squirrels. (Hint: Click anywhere in the edited text. Click the **REVIEW tab**, click the **Reject arrow**, and click **Reject Change**.)

c. Accept all other tracked changes in the document and stop tracking. Keep all comments.

d. Change all headings that use Heading 3 style so they use **Heading 1 style**, as per the comment left by the author.

e. Click the first comment balloon and reply to the comment by typing **I have made the style replacement.**

f. Select the first tulip picture on the left on page 1, click the **REFERENCES tab**, and then click **Insert Caption** in the Captions group. Modify the caption text to read **Figure 1: Angelique**. Make sure the caption displays below the selected item. Assign captions below the remaining tulip photos using information in the comments. The photos are numbered from left to right, with the first row of pictures identified as *Figure 1, Figure 2,* and *Figure 3*. Delete all comments except the first one (to which you replied).

g. Add a caption below the image on page 3 showing *Figure 6: Planting Guide*.

Credit Sources

You are now ready to add the citations for resources that the author used when assembling this report.

a. Select **MLA Seventh Edition style**. Click before the period ending the second paragraph in the *Planting* section. The sentence ends in *5 to 6 inches apart*. Insert the following Book citation:

   Author: **Tripp, Halleck**
   Title: **The Complete Gardener's Guide**
   Year: **2012**
   City: **Houston**
   Publisher: **Halpern**

b. Click before the period ending the first sentence in the document, ending in *turban*. Insert the following citation:

   Corporate Author: **American Gardeners' Association**
   Title: **What's in a Name?**
   Journal Name: **Journal of American Gardeners**
   Year: **2016**
   Pages: **22–27**
   Volume: **14**
   Issue: **9**

c. Modify the book source (*The Complete Gardener's Guide*) to change the year to **2013**. To do so, click **Manage Sources** and edit the source in both the Current List and the Master List.

d. Click after the word *Tripp* in the last paragraph on page 2 (but before the period). Insert the Tripp citation you created in step a in this section. Edit the citation to include page 23 but no author, year, or title.

e. Insert a footnote on page 2 at the end of the third paragraph in the *Planting* section (after the period), which ends with *made by the planter*. Type the following for the footnote: **Stanley, Meredith Parelli, A Guide to Tulips (Sunrise, October 2009)**. (Do not include the period.) Change the number format for footnotes to **a, b, c** in the Footnotes dialog box. (Click **Apply**, not Insert.)

f. Insert a blank page at the end of the report and insert a bibliography in MLA style on the blank page with the title **Works Cited**. The bibliography should be double spaced, with no paragraph spacing and a font of Times New Roman 12 pt. The title *Works Cited* should be centered, 12 pt, and not bold. All text in the bibliography should be Black, Text 1 font color.

Finish with Table of Contents and Index

To put the finishing touches on your document, you add a table of contents and an index.

a. Automatically generate a table of contents and display it on a page between the cover page and page 2. The style is **Automatic Table 1**.

b. Mark the following words as index entries, selecting *Mark All* for each: *Holland*, *perennials*, *deadheading*, and *soil*. Create an index cross-reference entry using the word *dirt* in the index to indicate where the word *soil* is used.

c. Add an index on a blank page at the end of the document. Use the **Classic format**. Use all other default settings.

d. Display a centered page number, using **Plain Number 2** format, in the footer of the document. Do not display the page number footer on the first page. Numbering begins with page 2 on the Table of Contents page.

e. Save the file, then save it again as a PDF document with the file name **w04c1Tulip_LastFirst.pdf**. Close both files and submit them based on your instructor's directions.

Introduction to Excel

CHAPTER 1

What Is a Spreadsheet?

OBJECTIVES

AFTER YOU READ THIS CHAPTER, YOU WILL BE ABLE TO:

CASE STUDY | OK Office Systems

You are an assistant manager at OK Office Systems (OKOS) in Oklahoma City. OKOS sells a wide range of computer systems, peripherals, and furniture for small- and medium-sized organizations in the metropolitan area. To compete against large, global, big-box office supply stores, OKOS provides competitive pricing by ordering directly from local manufacturers rather than dealing with distributors.

Alesha Bennett, the general manager, asked you to calculate the retail price, sale price, and profit analysis for selected items on sale this month. Using markup rates provided by Alesha, you need to calculate the retail price, the amount OKOS charges its customers for the products. For the sale, Alesha wants to give customers between a 10% and 30% discount on select items. You need to use those discount rates to calculate the sale prices. Finally, you will calculate the profit margin to determine the percentage of the final sale price over the cost.

After you create the initial pricing spreadsheet, you will be able to change values and see that the formulas update the results automatically. In addition, you will be able to insert data for additional sale items or delete an item based on the manager's decision.

Although your experience with Microsoft Office Excel 2013 may be limited, you are excited to apply your knowledge and skills to your newly assigned responsibility. In the Hands-On Exercises for this chapter, you will create and format the analytical spreadsheet to practice the skills you learn.

Introduction to Spreadsheets

Organizing, calculating, and evaluating quantitative data are important skills needed today for personal and managerial decision making. You track expenses for your household budget, maintain a savings plan, and determine what amount you can afford for a house or car payment. Retail managers create and analyze their organizations' annual budgets, sales projections, and inventory records. Charitable organizations track the donations they receive, the distribution of those donations, and overhead expenditures.

You can use a spreadsheet to maintain data and perform calculations. A ***spreadsheet*** is an electronic file that contains a grid of columns and rows used to organize related data and to display results of calculations, enabling interpretation of quantitative data for decision making.

Performing calculations using a calculator and entering the results into a ledger can lead to inaccurate values. If an input value is incorrect or needs to be updated, you have to recalculate the results manually, which is time-consuming and can lead to inaccuracies. A spreadsheet makes data entry changes easy. If the formulas are correctly constructed, the results recalculate automatically and accurately, saving time and reducing room for error.

In this section, you will learn how to design spreadsheets. In addition, you will explore the Excel window and learn the name of each window element. Then, you will enter text, values, and dates in a spreadsheet.

Exploring the Excel Window

In Excel, a ***worksheet*** is a single spreadsheet that typically contains descriptive labels, numeric values, formulas, functions, and graphical representations of data. A ***workbook*** is a collection of one or more related worksheets contained within a single file. By default, new workbooks contain one worksheet. Storing multiple worksheets within one workbook helps organize related data together in one file and enables you to perform calculations among the worksheets within the workbook. For example, you can create a budget workbook of 13 worksheets, one for each month to store your personal income and expenses and a final worksheet to calculate totals across the entire year.

Excel contains the standard interface of Microsoft Office applications:

- **Quick Access Toolbar:** Save, Undo, and Redo/Repeat commands
- **Title bar:** File name (such as Book1) and software name (such as Excel)
- **Control buttons:** Microsoft Excel Help, Full Screen Mode, Minimize, Restore Down, and Close
- **Ribbon:** Commands (such as Align Left) organized within groups (such as Alignment) on various tabs (such as Home)
- **Scroll bars:** Tools to scroll vertically and horizontally through a worksheet

Identify Excel Window Elements

Figure 1.1 identifies elements specific to the Excel window, and Table 1.1 lists and describes the Excel window elements.

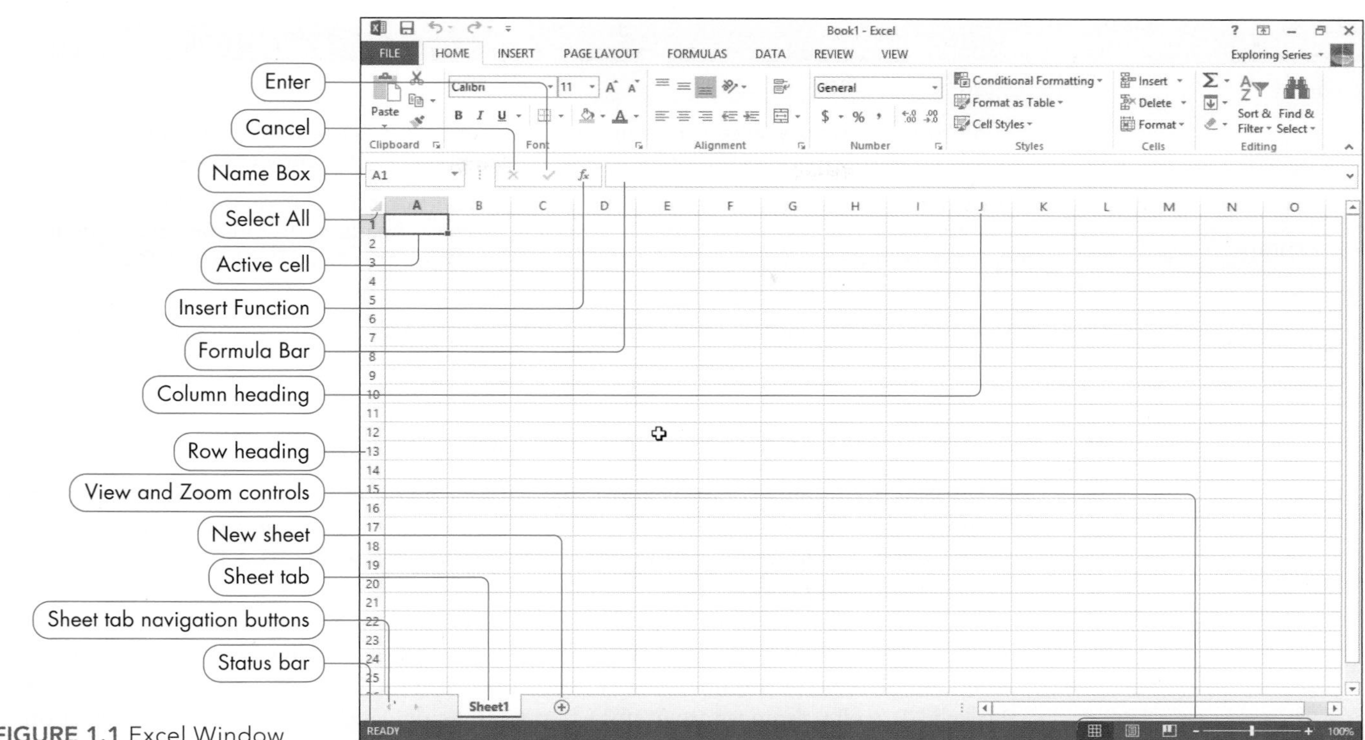

FIGURE 1.1 Excel Window

TABLE 1.1 Excel Elements

Element	Description
Name Box	The ***Name Box*** is an identifier that displays the address of the current cell in the worksheet. Use the Name Box to go to a cell, assign a name to one or more cells, or select a function.
Cancel ☒	When you enter or edit data, click Cancel to cancel the data entry or edit and revert back to the previous data in the cell, if any. The Cancel icon changes from gray to red when you position the mouse pointer over it.
Enter ☑	When you enter or edit data, click Enter to accept data typed in the active cell and keep the current cell active. The Enter icon changes from gray to blue when you position the mouse pointer over it.
Insert Function *fx*	Click to display the Insert Function dialog box to search for and select a function to insert into the active cell. The Insert Function icon changes from gray to green when you position the mouse pointer over it.
Formula Bar	The ***Formula Bar*** shows the contents of the active cell. You can enter or edit cell contents here or directly in the active cell. Drag the bottom border of the Formula Bar down to increase the height of the Formula Bar to display large amounts of data or a long formula contained in the active cell.
Select All ◢	The triangle at the intersection of the row and column headings in the top-left corner of the worksheet. Click it to select everything contained in the active worksheet.
Column headings	The letters above the columns, such as A, B, C, and so on.
Row headings	The numbers to the left of the rows, such as 1, 2, 3, and so on.
Active cell	The active cell is the current cell, which is indicated by a dark green border.
Sheet tab	A ***sheet tab*** shows the name of a worksheet contained in the workbook. When you create a new Excel workbook, the default worksheet is named Sheet1.
New sheet ⊕	Inserts a new worksheet to the right of the current worksheet.
Sheet tab navigation buttons	If your workbook contains several worksheets, Excel may not show all the sheet tabs at the same time. Use the buttons to display the first, previous, next, or last worksheet.

TABLE 1.1 Excel Elements *(continued)*	
Element	**Description**
Status bar	Displays information about a selected command or operation in progress. For example, it displays *Select destination and press ENTER or choose Paste* after you use the Copy command.
View controls	Click a view control to display the worksheet in Normal, Page Layout, or Page Break Preview. Normal view displays the worksheet without showing margins, headers, footers, and page breaks. Page Layout view shows the margins, header and footer area, and a ruler. Page Break Preview indicates where the worksheet will be divided into pages.
Zoom control	Drag the zoom control to increase the size of the worksheet onscreen to see more or less of the worksheet data.

Identify Columns, Rows, and Cells

A worksheet contains columns and rows, with each column and row assigned a heading. Columns are assigned alphabetical headings from columns A to Z, continuing from AA to AZ, and then from BA to BZ until XFD, which is the last of the possible 16,384 columns. Rows have numeric headings ranging from 1 to 1,048,576.

The intersection of a column and row is a ***cell***; a total of more than 17 billion cells are available in a worksheet. Each cell has a unique ***cell address***, identified by first its column letter and then its row number. For example, the cell at the intersection of column A and row 9 is cell A9. Cell references are useful when referencing data in formulas, or in navigation.

Navigate In and Among Worksheets

The ***active cell*** is the current cell. Excel displays a dark green border around the active cell in the worksheet, and the cell address of the active cell appears in the Name Box. The contents of the active cell, or the formula used to calculate the results of the active cell, appear in the Formula Bar. You can change the active cell by using the mouse to click in a different cell. If you work in a large worksheet, use the vertical and horizontal scroll bars to display another area of the worksheet and click in the desired cell to make it the active cell.

To navigate to a new cell, click it or use the arrow keys on the keyboard. When you press Enter, the next cell down in the same column becomes the active cell. Table 1.2 lists the keyboard navigation methods. The Go To command is helpful for navigating to a cell that is not visible onscreen.

TABLE 1.2 Keystrokes and Actions	
Keystroke	**Used to**
↑	Move up one cell in the same column.
↓	Move down one cell in the same column.
←	Move left one cell in the same row.
→	Move right one cell in the same row.
Tab	Move right one cell in the same row.
Page Up	Move the active cell up one screen.
Page Down	Move the active cell down one screen.
Home	Move the active cell to column A of the current row.
Ctrl+Home	Make cell A1 the active cell.
Ctrl+End	Make the rightmost, lowermost active corner of the worksheet—the intersection of the last column and row that contains data—the active cell. Does not move to cell XFD1048576 unless that cell contains data.
F5 or Ctrl+G	Display the Go To dialog box to enter any cell address.

To display the contents of another worksheet within the workbook, click the sheet tab at the bottom-left corner of the workbook window. The active sheet tab has a white background color. After you click a sheet tab, you can then navigate within that worksheet.

Entering and Editing Cell Data

You should plan the structure before you start entering data into a worksheet. Using the OKOS case presented at the beginning of the chapter as an example, use the following steps to plan the worksheet design, enter and format data, and complete the workbook:

Plan the Worksheet Design

1. **State the purpose of the worksheet.** The purpose of the OKOS worksheet is to store data about products on sale and to calculate important details, such as the retail price based on markup, the sales price based on a discount rate, and the profit margin.
2. **Decide what input values are needed.** Input values are the initial values, such as variables and assumptions. You may change these values to see what type of effects different values have on the end results. For the OKOS worksheet, the input values include the costs OKOS pays the manufacturers, the markup rates, and the proposed discount rates for the sale. In some worksheets, you can create an ***input area***, a specific region in the worksheet to store and change the variables used in calculations. For example, if you applied the same Markup Rate and same Percent Off for all products, it would be easier to create an input area at the top of the worksheet to change the values in one location rather than in several locations.
3. **Decide what outputs are needed to achieve the purpose of the worksheet.** Outputs are the results you need to calculate. For the OKOS worksheet, the outputs include columns to calculate the retail price (i.e., the selling price to your customers), the sale price, and the profit margin. In some worksheets, you can create an ***output area***, the region in the worksheet to contain formulas dependent on the values in the input area.

Enter and Format the Data

4. **Enter the labels, values, and formulas in Excel.** Use the design plan (steps 2–3) as you enter labels, input values, and formulas to calculate the output. In the OKOS worksheet, descriptive labels (the product names) appear in the first column to indicate that the values on a specific row pertain to a specific product. Descriptive labels appear at the top of each column, such as Cost and Retail Price, to describe the values in the respective column. Change the input values to test that your formulas produce correct results. If necessary, correct any errors in the formulas to produce correct results. For the OKOS worksheet, change some of the original costs and markup rates to ensure the calculated retail price, selling price, and profit margin percentage results update correctly.
5. **Format the numerical values in the worksheet.** Align decimal points in columns of numbers and add number formats and styles. In the OKOS worksheet, use Accounting Number Format and the Percent Style to format the numerical data. Adjust the number of decimal places as needed.
6. **Format the descriptive titles and labels so that they stand out.** Add bold and color to headings so that they stand out and are attractive. Apply other formatting to headings and descriptive labels. In the OKOS worksheet, you will center the main title over all the columns, bold and center column labels over the columns, and apply other formatting to the headings. Figure 1.2 shows the completed OKOS worksheet.

Complete the Workbook

7. **Document the workbook as thoroughly as possible.** Include the current date, your name as the workbook author, assumptions, and purpose of the workbook. You can provide this documentation in a separate worksheet within the workbook. You can also add some documentation in the *Properties* section when you click the File tab.
8. **Save and share the completed workbook.** Preview and prepare printouts for distribution in meetings, send an electronic copy of the workbook to those who need it, or upload the workbook on a shared network drive or in the cloud.

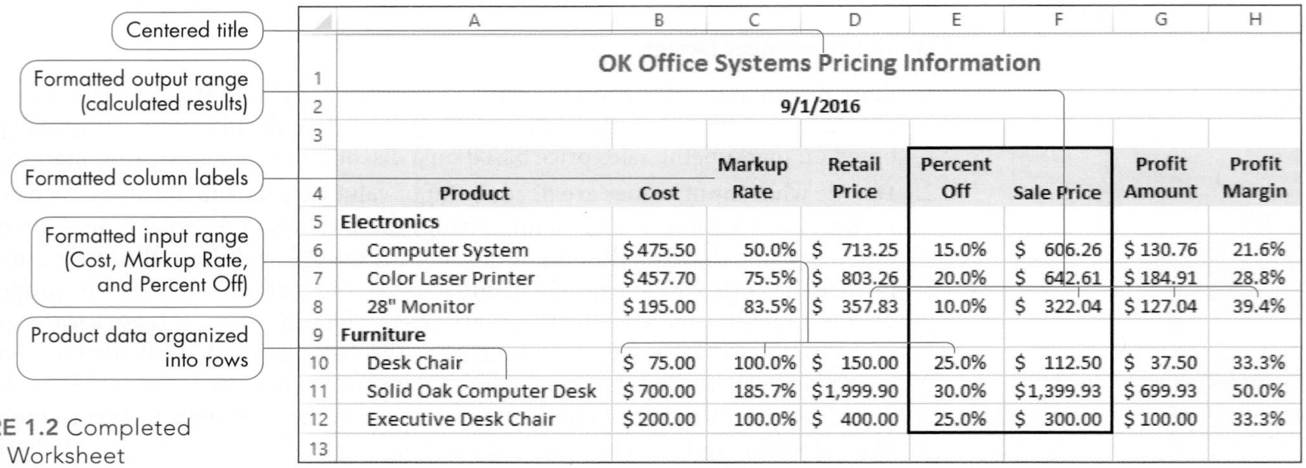

Centered title
Formatted output range (calculated results)
Formatted column labels
Formatted input range (Cost, Markup Rate, and Percent Off)
Product data organized into rows

	A	B	C	D	E	F	G	H
1	OK Office Systems Pricing Information							
2	9/1/2016							
3								
4	Product	Cost	Markup Rate	Retail Price	Percent Off	Sale Price	Profit Amount	Profit Margin
5	Electronics							
6	Computer System	$ 475.50	50.0%	$ 713.25	15.0%	$ 606.26	$ 130.76	21.6%
7	Color Laser Printer	$ 457.70	75.5%	$ 803.26	20.0%	$ 642.61	$ 184.91	28.8%
8	28" Monitor	$ 195.00	83.5%	$ 357.83	10.0%	$ 322.04	$ 127.04	39.4%
9	Furniture							
10	Desk Chair	$ 75.00	100.0%	$ 150.00	25.0%	$ 112.50	$ 37.50	33.3%
11	Solid Oak Computer Desk	$ 700.00	185.7%	$1,999.90	30.0%	$1,399.93	$ 699.93	50.0%
12	Executive Desk Chair	$ 200.00	100.0%	$ 400.00	25.0%	$ 300.00	$ 100.00	33.3%
13								

FIGURE 1.2 Completed OKOS Worksheet

Enter Text

Text is any combination of letters, numbers, symbols, and spaces not used in calculations. Excel treats phone numbers, such as 555-1234, and Social Security numbers, such as 123-45-6789, as text entries. You enter text for a worksheet title to describe the contents of the worksheet, as row and column labels to describe data, and as cell data. In Figure 1.2, the cells in column A, row 1, and row 4 contain text, such as *Product.* Text aligns at the left cell margin by default. To enter text in a cell, do the following:

STEP 1

1. Make sure the cell is active where you want to enter text.
2. Type the text.
3. Do one of the following to make another cell the active cell after entering data:
   - Press Enter on the keyboard.
   - Press an arrow key on the keyboard.
   - Press Tab on the keyboard.

   Do one of the following to keep the current cell the active cell after entering data:
   - Press Ctrl+Enter.
   - Click Enter (the check mark between the Name Box and the Formula Bar).

As soon as you begin typing a label into a cell, the ***AutoComplete*** feature searches for and automatically displays any other label in that column that matches the letters you typed. For example, *Computer System* is typed in cell A6 in Figure 1.2. When you start to type *Co* in cell A7, AutoComplete displays *Computer System* because a text entry previously typed starts with *Co.* Press Enter to accept the repeated label, or continue typing to enter a different label, such as *Color Laser Printer*.

TIP Line Break in a Cell

If a long text label does not fit well in a cell, you can insert a line break to display the text label on multiple lines within the cell. To insert a line break while you are typing a label, press Alt+Enter where you want to start the next line of text within the cell.

Enter Values

STEP 2 Values are numbers that represent a quantity or a measurable amount. Excel usually distinguishes between text and value data based on what you enter. The primary difference between text and value entries is that value entries can be the basis of calculations, whereas text cannot. In Figure 1.2, the data below the *Cost*, *Markup Rates*, and *Percent Off* labels are values. Values align at the right cell margin by default. After entering values, you can align decimal places and apply formatting by adding characters, such as $ or %.

Enter Dates

STEP 3 You can enter dates and times in a variety of formats in cells, such as 9/1/2016; 9/1/16; September 1, 2016; or 1-Sep-16. You can also enter times, such as 1:30 PM or 13:30. You should enter a static date to document when you create or modify a workbook or to document the specific point in time when the data were accurate, such as on a balance sheet or income statement. Later, you will learn how to use formulas to enter dates that update to the current date. In Figure 1.2, cell A2 contains a date. Dates are values, so they align at the right cell margin. However, the date in Figure 1.2 has been centered by the user.

Excel displays dates differently from the way it stores dates. For example, the displayed date 9/1/2016 represents the first day in September in the year 2016. Excel stores dates as serial numbers starting at 1 with January 1, 1900, so 9/1/2016 is stored as 42614 so that you can create formulas, such as to calculate how many days exist between two dates.

Enter Formulas

Formulas combine cell references, arithmetic operations, values, and/or functions used in a calculation. You must start the formula with an equal sign (=). In Figure 1.3, the data below the *Retail Price*, *Sale Price*, *Profit Amount*, and *Profit Margin* labels contain formulas. When a cell containing a formula is the active cell, the formula displays in the Formula Bar, and the result of the formula displays in the cell.

Edit and Clear Cell Contents

You can edit a cell's contents by doing one of the following:

- Click the cell, click in the Formula Bar, make the changes, and then click Enter (the check mark between the Name Box and the Formula Bar) to keep the cell the active cell.
- Double-click the cell, make changes in the cell, and then press Enter.
- Click the cell, press F2, make changes in the cell, and then press Enter.

You can clear a cell's contents by doing one of the following:

- Click the cell and press Delete.
- Click the cell, click Clear in the Editing group on the HOME tab, and then select Clear Contents.

1. What are two major advantages of using an electronic spreadsheet instead of a paper-based ledger? ***p. 374***
2. What visual indicators let you know which cell is the active cell? ***p. 376***
3. What steps should you perform before entering data into a worksheet? ***p. 377***
4. What are four major things you can enter into a cell? Give an example (different from those in the book) for each type. ***pp. 378–379***

Hands-On Exercises

Watch the Video for this Hands-On Exercise!

MyITLab®
HOE1 Training

1 Introduction to Spreadsheets

As the assistant manager of OKOS, you need to create a worksheet that shows the cost (the amount OKOS pays its suppliers), the markup percentage (the amount by which the cost is increased), and the retail selling price. You also need to list the discount percentage (such as 25% off) for each product, the sale price, and the profit margin percentage.

Skills covered: Enter Text • Enter Values • Enter a Date and Clear Cell Contents

STEP 1 » ENTER TEXT

Now that you have planned the OKOS worksheet, you are ready to enter labels for the title, column labels, and row labels. You will type a title in cell A1, product labels in the first column, and row labels in the fourth row. Refer to Figure 1.3 as you complete Step 1.

Step b: Title
Step f: Labels for other columns
Step e: Label for second column
Step c: Label for first column
Step d: Name of products

	A	B	C	D	E	F	G	H
1	OK Office Systems Pricing Information							
2								
3								
4	Product	Cost	Markup Ra	Retail Pric	Percent O	Sale Price	Profit Margin	
5	Computer System							
6	Color Laser Printer							
7	Filing Cabinet							
8	Desk Chair							
9	Solid Oak Computer Desk							
10	28" Monitor							
11								
12								

FIGURE 1.3 Text Entered in Cells

a. Start Excel and open a new blank workbook. Save the new workbook as **e01h1Markup_LastFirst**.

When you save files, use your last and first names. For example, as the Excel author, I would save my workbook as *e01h1Markup_MulberyKeith*.

b. Type **OK Office Systems Pricing Information** in **cell A1** and press **Enter**.

When you press Enter, the next cell down—cell A2 in this case—becomes the active cell. The text does not completely fit in cell A1, and some of the text appears in cells B1, C1, D1, and possibly E1. If you make cell B1, C1, D1, or E1 the active cell, the Formula Bar is empty, indicating that nothing is stored in those cells.

c. Click **cell A4**, type **Product**, and then press **Enter**.

d. Continue typing the rest of the text in **cells A5** through **A10** as shown in Figure 1.4. Text in column A appears to flow into column B.

When you start typing *Co* in cell A6, AutoComplete displays a ScreenTip suggesting a previous text entry starting with *Co—Computer System*—but keep typing to enter *Color Laser Printer* instead. You just entered the product labels to describe the data in each row.

e. Click **cell B4** to make it the active cell. Type **Cost** and press **Tab**.

Instead of pressing Enter to move down column B, you pressed Tab to make the cell to the right the active cell.

f. Type the following text in the respective cells, pressing **Tab** after typing each of the first four column labels and pressing **Enter** after the last column label:

- **Markup Rate** in **cell C4**
- **Retail Price** in **cell D4**
- **Percent Off** in **cell E4**
- **Sale Price** in **cell F4**
- **Profit Margin** in **cell G4**

The text looks cut off when you enter data in the cell to the right. Do not worry about this now. You will adjust column widths and formatting later in this chapter.

> **TROUBLESHOOTING:** If you notice a typographical error, click in the cell containing the error and retype the label. Or press F2 to edit the cell contents, move the insertion point using the arrow keys, press Backspace or Delete to delete the incorrect characters, type the correct characters, and then press Enter. If you type a label in an incorrect cell, click the cell and press Delete.

g. Save the changes you made to the workbook.

You should develop a habit of saving periodically. That way if your system unexpectedly shuts down, you will not lose everything you worked on.

STEP 2 » ENTER VALUES

Now that you have entered the descriptive labels, you need to enter the cost, markup rate, and percent off for each product. Refer to Figure 1.4 as you complete Step 2.

Steps e–f: Percent Off values

Steps c–d: Markup Rate values

Steps a–b: Cost values

	A	B	C	D	E	F	G	H
1	OK Office Systems Pricing Information							
2								
3								
4	Product	Cost	Markup Ra	Retail Pric	Percent O	Sale Price	Profit Margin	
5	Computer	400	0.5		0.15			
6	Color Lase	457.7	0.75		0.2			
7	Filing Cab	68.75	0.905		0.1			
8	Desk Chai	75	1		0.25			
9	Solid Oak	700	1.857		0.3			
10	28" Monit	195	0.835		0.1			
11								
12								

FIGURE 1.4 Values Entered in Cells

a. Click **cell B5**, type **400**, and then press **Enter**.

b. Type the remaining costs in **cells B6** through **B10** shown in Figure 1.4.

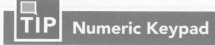

TIP Numeric Keypad

To improve your productivity, use the number keypad (if available) on the right side of your keyboard. It is much faster to type values and press Enter on the number keypad rather than using the numbers on the keyboard. Make sure Num Lock is active before using the number keypad to enter values.

c. Click **cell C5**, type **0.5**, and then press **Enter**.

You entered the markup rate as a decimal instead of a percentage. You will apply Percent Style later, but now you can concentrate on data entry. When you enter decimal values less than zero, you can type the period and value without typing the zero first, such as .5. Excel will automatically add the zero. You can also enter percentages as 50%, but the approach this textbook takes is to enter raw data without typing formatting such as % and to use number formatting options through Excel to display formatting symbols.

d. Type the remaining markup rates in **cells C6** through **C10** as shown in Figure 1.4.

e. Click **cell E5**, type **0.15**, and then press **Enter**.

You entered the Percent Off or markdown sale value as a decimal.

f. Type the remaining Percent Off values in **cells E6** through **E10** as shown in Figure 1.4 and save the workbook.

STEP 3 ENTER A DATE AND CLEAR CELL CONTENTS

As you review the worksheet, you realize you need to provide a date to indicate when the sale starts. Refer to Figure 1.5 as you complete Step 3.

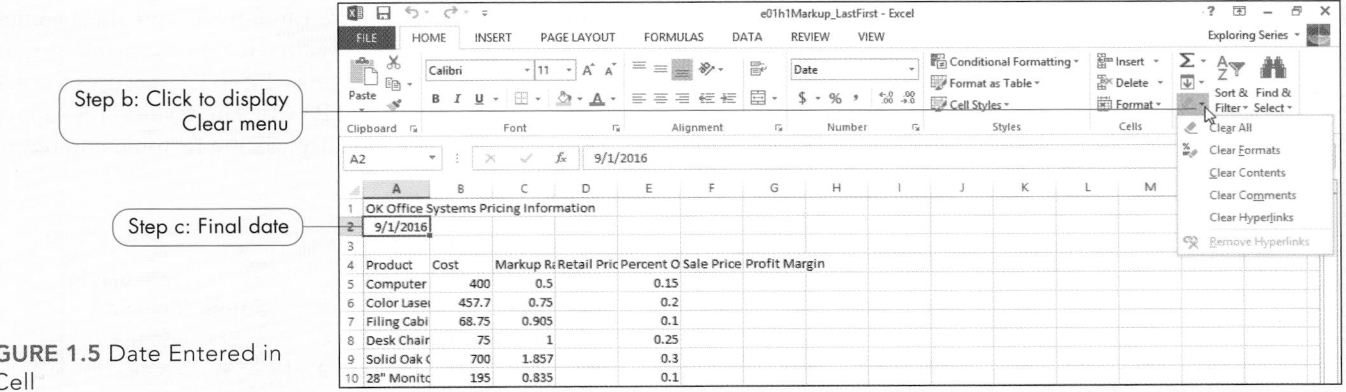

FIGURE 1.5 Date Entered in a Cell

a. Click **cell A2**, type **9/1**, and then press **Enter**.

The date aligns on the right cell margin by default. Excel displays *1-Sep* instead of *9/1*.

b. Click **cell A2**, click **Clear** in the Editing group on the HOME tab, and then select **Clear All**.

The Clear All command clears both cell contents and formatting in the selected cell(s).

c. Type **9/1/2016** in **cell A2** and press **Enter**.

TROUBLESHOOTING: If you did not use Clear All and typed 9/1/2016 in cell A2, Excel would have retained the previous date format and displayed 1-Sep again.

d. Save the workbook. Keep the workbook open if you plan to continue with the next Hands-On Exercise. If not, close the workbook and exit Excel.

Mathematics and Formulas

Formulas transform static numbers into meaningful results that can update as values change. For example, a payroll manager can build formulas to calculate the gross pay, deductions, and net pay for an organization's employees, or a doctoral student can create formulas to perform various statistical calculations to interpret his or her research data.

You can use formulas to help you analyze how results will change as the input data change. You can change the value of your assumptions or inputs and explore the results quickly and accurately. For example, if the interest rate changes from 4% to 5%, how would that affect your monthly payment? Analyzing different input values in Excel is easy after you build formulas. Simply change an input value and observe the change in the formula results.

In this section, you will learn how to use mathematical operations in Excel formulas. You will refresh your memory of mathematical order of precedence and how to construct formulas using cell addresses so that when the value of an input cell changes, the result of the formula changes without you having to modify the formula.

Creating Formulas

Start a formula by typing the equal sign (=), followed by the arithmetic expression. Do not include a space before or after the arithmetic operator. Figure 1.6 shows a worksheet containing data and results of formulas. The figure also displays the actual formulas used to generate the calculated results. For example, cell B6 contains the formula =B2+B3. Excel uses the value stored in cell B2 (10) and adds it to the value stored in cell B3 (2). The result—12—appears in cell B6 instead of the actual formula. The Formula Bar displays the formula entered into the active cell.

	A	B	C	D	E	F
1	**Description**	**Values**		**Description**	**Results**	**Formulas in Column E**
2	First input value	10		Sum of 10 and 2	12	=B2+B3
3	Second input value	2		Difference between 10 and 2	8	=B2-B3
4				Product of 10 and 2	20	=B2*B3
5				Results of dividing 10 by 2	5	=B2/B3
6				Results of 10 to the 2nd power	100	=B2^B3

FIGURE 1.6 Formula Results

> **TROUBLESHOOTING:** If you type B2+B3 without the equal sign, Excel does not recognize that you entered a formula and stores the data as text.

Use Cell References in Formulas

STEP 1》 **STEP 2》** **STEP 3》**

You should use cell references instead of values in formulas where possible. You may include values in an input area—such as dates, salary, or costs—that you will need to reference in formulas. Referencing these cells in your formulas, instead of typing the value of the cell to which you are referring, keeps your formulas accurate if the values change.

When you create a formula, you can type the cell references in uppercase, such as =B2+B3, or lowercase, such as =b2+b3. Excel changes cell references to uppercase.

In Figure 1.6, cell B2 contains 10, and cell B3 contains 2. Cell E2 contains =B2+B3 but shows the result, 12. If you change the value of cell B3 to 5, cell E2 displays the new result, which is 15. However, if you had typed actual values in the formula, =10+2, you would have to edit the formula each time an input value changes. This would be problematic, as you might forget to edit the formula or you might have a typographical error if you edit the formula. Always design worksheets in such a way as to be able to change input values without having to modify your formulas if an input value changes later.

TIP Constants in Formulas

Use cell references instead of actual values in formulas, unless the value is a constant. For example, assume that 25% is stored in cell D10. To calculate the reciprocal of 25%, type =1-D10. The constant, 1, represents 100%, a value that never changes, although the percentage in cell D10 might change. In this situation, 100% – 25% is 75%.

Apply the Order of Precedence

The ***order of precedence*** (also called order of operations) is a rule that controls the sequence in which arithmetic operations are performed, which affects the results of the calculation. Excel performs mathematical calculations left to right in this order: **P**ercent, **E**xponentiation, **M**ultiplication or **D**ivision, and finally **A**ddition or **S**ubtraction. Some people remember the order of precedence with the phrase ***P****lease* ***E****xcuse* ***M****y* ***D****ear* ***A****unt* ***S****ally*.

Table 1.3 lists the complete order of precedence. This chapter focuses on orders 4, 5, and 6.

TABLE 1.3 Order of Precedence

Order	Description	Symbols
1	Reference Operators	colon (:), space, and comma (,)
2	Negation	-
3	Percent	%
4	Exponentiation	^
5	Multiplication and Division	* and / (respectively)
6	Addition and Subtraction	+ and – (respectively)
7	Concatenation	ampersand symbol (&) to connect two text strings
8	Comparison	Equal sign (=), greater than (>), and less than (<)

TIP Parentheses in Formulas

You can change the order of operations by using parentheses. For example, to add the values in cells A1 and A2 and multiply that result by the value in cell A3, enclose parentheses around the addition operation: =(A1+A2)*A3. Without parentheses, multiplication has a higher order of precedence than addition and will be calculated first.

Figure 1.7 shows formulas, the sequence in which calculations occur, calculations, the description, and the results of each order of precedence. The highlighted results are the final formula results. This figure illustrates the importance of symbols and use of parentheses.

	A	B	C	D	E	F
1	Input		Formula	Sequence	Description	Result
2	2		=A2+A3*A4+A5	1	3 (cell A3) * 4 (cell A4)	12
3	3			2	2 (cell A2) + 12 (order 1)	14
4	4			3	14 (order 2) + 5 (cell A5)	19
5	5					
6			=(A2+A3)*(A4+A5)	1	2 (cell A2) + 3 (cell A3)	5
7				2	4 (cell A4) + 5 (cell A5)	9
8				3	5 (order 1) * 9 (order 2)	45
9						
10			=A2/A3+A4*A5	1	2 (cell A2) / 3 (cell A3)	0.666667
11				2	4 (cell A4) * 5 (cell A5)	20
12				3	0.666667 (order 1) + 20 (order 2)	20.66667
13						
14			=A2/(A3+A4)*A5	1	3 (cell A3) + 4 (cell A4)	7
15				2	2 (cell A2) / 7 (order 1)	0.285714
16				3	0.285714 (order 2) * 5 (cell A5)	1.428571
17						
18			=A2^2+A3*A4%	1	4 (cell A4) is converted to percentage	0.04
19				2	2 (cell A2) to the power of 2	4
20				3	3 (cell A3) * 0.04 (order 1)	0.12
21				4	4 (order 2) + 0.12 (order 3)	4.12

FIGURE 1.7 Formula Results Based on Order of Precedence

Use Semi-Selection to Create a Formula

To decrease typing time and ensure accuracy, you can use ***semi-selection***, a process of selecting a cell or range of cells for entering cell references as you create formulas. Semi-selection is often called ***pointing*** because you use the mouse pointer to select cells as you build the formula. To use the semi-selection technique to create a formula, do the following:

1. Click the cell where you want to create the formula.
2. Type an equal sign (=) to start a formula.
3. Click the cell or drag to select the cell range that contains the value(s) to use in the formula. A moving marquee appears around the cell or range you select, and Excel displays the cell or range reference in the formula.
4. Type a mathematical operator.
5. Continue clicking cells, selecting ranges, and typing operators to finish the formula. Use the scroll bars if the cell is in a remote location in the worksheet, or click a worksheet tab to see a cell in another worksheet.
6. Press Enter to complete the formula.

Using Auto Fill

Auto Fill enables you to copy the contents of a cell or a range of cells by dragging the ***fill handle*** (a small green square appearing in the bottom-right corner of the active cell) over an adjacent cell or range of cells. To use Auto Fill, do the following:

1. Click the cell with the content you want to copy to make it the active cell.
2. Point to the fill handle in the bottom-right corner of the cell until the mouse pointer changes to the fill pointer (a thin black plus sign).
3. Drag the fill handle to repeat the content in other cells.

Copy Formulas with Auto Fill

STEP 4»

After you enter a formula in a cell, you can duplicate the formula without retyping it by using the fill handle to copy the formula in the active cell down a column or across a row, depending on how the data are organized. Excel adapts each copied formula based on the type of cell references in the original formula.

Complete Sequences with Auto Fill

You can also use Auto Fill to complete a sequence. For example, if you enter January in a cell, you can use Auto Fill to enter the rest of the months in adjacent cells. Other sequences you can complete are quarters (Qtr 1, etc.), weekdays, and weekday abbreviations, by typing the first item and using Auto Fill to complete the other entries. For numeric sequences, however, you must specify the first two values in sequence. For example, if you want to fill in 5, 10, 15, and so on, you must enter 5 and 10 in two adjacent cells, select the two cells, and then use Auto Fill so that Excel knows to increment by 5. Figure 1.8 shows the results of filling in months, abbreviated months, quarters, weekdays, abbreviated weekdays, and increments of 5.

	A	B	C	D	E	F	G	H	I
1	January	Jan	Qtr 1	Monday	Mon	5			
2	February	Feb	Qtr 2	Tuesday	Tue	10			
3	March	Mar	Qtr 3	Wednesday	Wed	15			
4	April	Apr	Qtr 4	Thursday	Thu	20			
5	May	May		Friday	Fri	25			
6	June	Jun		Saturday	Sat	30			
7	July	Jul		Sunday	Sun	35			
8	August	Aug							
9	September	Sep							
10	October	Oct							
11	November	Nov							
12	December	Dec							
13									
14									
15									

FIGURE 1.8 Auto Fill Examples

Immediately after you use Auto Fill, Excel displays the Auto Fill Options button in the bottom-right corner of the filled data (see Figure 1.8). Click Auto Fill Options to display five fill options: Copy Cells, Fill Series, Fill Formatting Only, Fill Without Formatting, or Flash Fill.

TIP Double-Clicking the Fill Handle

You can double-click the fill handle to quickly copy a formula down a column. Excel will copy the formula in the active cell for each row of data to calculate in your worksheet.

Displaying Cell Formulas

Excel shows the result of the formula in the cell (see the top half of Figure 1.9); however, you might want to display the formulas instead of the calculated results in the cells (see the bottom half of Figure 1.9). To display cell formulas, do one of the following:

STEP 5

- Press Ctrl and the grave accent (`) key, sometimes referred to as the tilde key, in the top-left corner of the keyboard, below the Esc key.
- Click Show Formulas in the Formula Auditing group on the FORMULAS tab.

To hide the formulas and display the formula results again, repeat the preceding process.

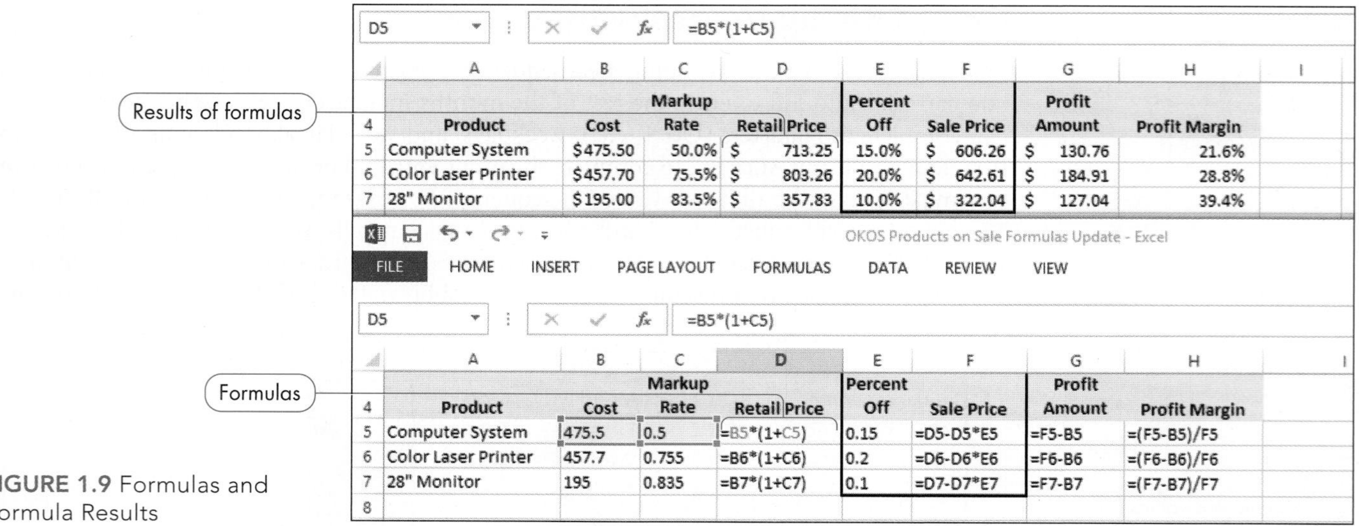

Results of formulas
D5
=B5*(1+C5)
	A	B	C	D	E	F	G	H
4	Product	Cost	Markup Rate	Retail Price	Percent Off	Sale Price	Profit Amount	Profit Margin
5	Computer System	$475.50	50.0%	$ 713.25	15.0%	$ 606.26	$ 130.76	21.6%
6	Color Laser Printer	$457.70	75.5%	$ 803.26	20.0%	$ 642.61	$ 184.91	28.8%
7	28" Monitor	$195.00	83.5%	$ 357.83	10.0%	$ 322.04	$ 127.04	39.4%

OKOS Products on Sale Formulas Update - Excel
FILE
HOME
INSERT
PAGE LAYOUT
FORMULAS
DATA
REVIEW
VIEW
Formulas
D5
=B5*(1+C5)
	A	B	C	D	E	F	G	H
4	Product	Cost	Markup Rate	Retail Price	Percent Off	Sale Price	Profit Amount	Profit Margin
5	Computer System	475.5	0.5	=B5*(1+C5)	0.15	=D5-D5*E5	=F5-B5	=(F5-B5)/F5
6	Color Laser Printer	457.7	0.755	=B6*(1+C6)	0.2	=D6-D6*E6	=F6-B6	=(F6-B6)/F6
7	28" Monitor	195	0.835	=B7*(1+C7)	0.1	=D7-D7*E7	=F7-B7	=(F7-B7)/F7
8								

FIGURE 1.9 Formulas and Formula Results

1. What is the order of precedence? Provide and explain two examples that use four different operators, one with parentheses and one without. ***p. 385***
2. What is the purpose of Auto Fill? Provide an example of data you can complete using Auto Fill. ***p. 386***
3. Why would it be useful to display formulas instead of formula results in a worksheet? ***p. 387***

Hands-On Exercises

MyITLab®
HOE2 Training

2 Mathematics and Formulas

In Hands-On Exercise 1, you created the basic worksheet for OKOS by entering text, values, and a date for items on sale. Now you need to insert formulas to calculate the missing results—specifically, the retail (before sale) value, sale price, and profit margin. You will use cell addresses in your formulas, so when you change a referenced value, the formula results will update automatically.

Skills covered: Use Cell References in a Formula and Apply the Order of Precedence • Use the Semi-Selection Method to Enter a Formula • Use Cell References in a Formula and Apply the Order of Precedence • Copy Formulas with Auto Fill • Change Values and Display Cell Formulas

STEP 1 » USE CELL REFERENCES IN A FORMULA AND APPLY THE ORDER OF PRECEDENCE

The first formula you need to create will calculate the retail price. The retail price is the price you originally charge. It is based on a percentage of the original cost so that you earn a profit. Refer to Figure 1.10 as you complete Step 1.

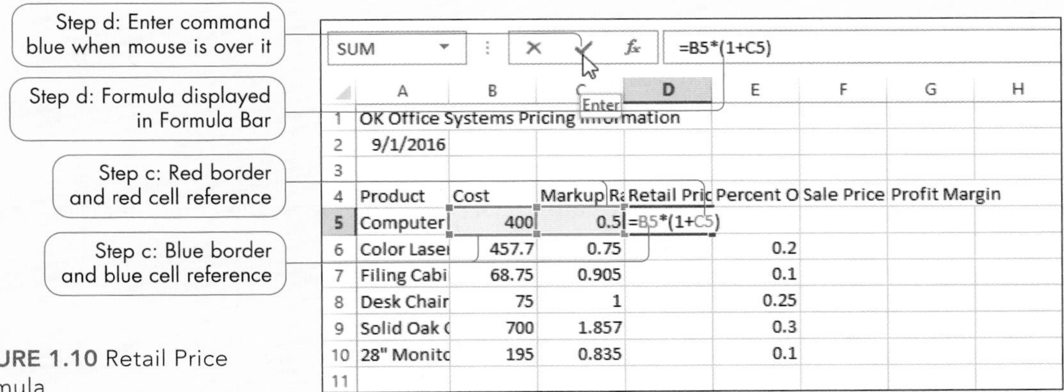

FIGURE 1.10 Retail Price Formula

a. Open *e01h1Markup_LastFirst* if you closed it at the end of Hands-On Exercise 1 and save it as **e01h2Markup_LastFirst**, changing *h1* to *h2*.

> **TROUBLESHOOTING:** If you make any major mistakes in this exercise, you can close the file, open *e01h1Markup_LastFirst* again, and then start this exercise over.

b. Click **cell D5**, the cell where you will enter the formula to calculate the retail selling price of the first item.

c. Type **=B5*(1+C5)** and view the formula and the colored cells and borders on the screen.

As you type or edit a formula, each cell address in the formula displays in a specific color, and while you type or edit the formula, the cells referenced in the formula have a temporarily colored border. For example, in the formula =B5*(1+C5), B5 appears in blue, and C5 appears in red. Cell B5 has a temporarily blue border and cell C5 has a temporarily red border to help you identify cells as you construct your formulas (see Figure 1.10).

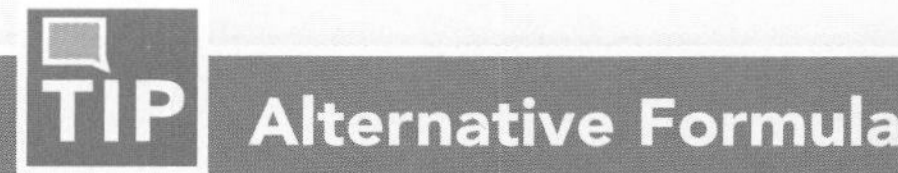

Alternative Formula

An alternative formula also calculates the correct retail price: =B5*C5+B5 or =B5+B5*C5. In this formula, 400 (cell B5) is multiplied by 0.5 (cell C5); that result (200) represents the dollar value of the markup. Excel adds the value 200 to the original cost of 400 to obtain 600, the retail price. You were instructed to enter =B5*(1+C5) to demonstrate the order of precedence.

d. Click **Enter** (the check mark ✓ between the Name Box and the Formula Bar) and view the formula in the Formula Bar to check it for accuracy.

The result of the formula, 600, appears in cell D5, and the formula displays in the Formula Bar. This formula first adds 1 (the decimal equivalent of 100%) to 0.5 (the value stored in cell C5). Excel multiplies that sum of 1.5 by 400 (the value stored in cell B5). The theory behind this formula is that the retail price is 150% of the original cost.

TROUBLESHOOTING: If the result is not correct, click the cell and look at the formula in the Formula Bar. Click in the Formula Bar, edit the formula to match the formula shown in Step c, and then click Enter (the check mark between the Name Box and the Formula Bar). Make sure you start the formula with an equal sign.

e. Save the workbook with the new formula.

STEP 2 ›› USE THE SEMI-SELECTION METHOD TO ENTER A FORMULA

Now that you have calculated the retail price, you need to calculate a sale price. This week, the computer is on sale for 15% off the retail price. Refer to Figure 1.11 as you complete Step 2.

Step b: Formula in Formula Bar

Step b: Result of formula in cell

F5 | =D5-D5*E5

	A	B	C	D	E	F	G	H
1	OK Office Systems Pricing Information							
2	9/1/2016							
3								
4	Product	Cost	Markup Ra	Retail Pric	Percent O	Sale Price	Profit Margin	
5	Computer	400	0.5	600	0.15	510		
6	Color Lase	457.7	0.75		0.2			
7	Filing Cabi	68.75	0.905		0.1			
8	Desk Chair	75	1		0.25			
9	Solid Oak (	700	1.857		0.3			
10	28" Monitc	195	0.835		0.1			
11								

FIGURE 1.11 Sale Price Formula

a. Click **cell F5**, the cell where you will enter the formula to calculate the sale price.

b. Type =, click **cell D5**, type -, click **cell D5**, type *, and then click **cell E5**. Notice the color-coding in the cell addresses. Press **Ctrl+Enter** to keep the current cell the active cell.

You used the semi-selection method to enter a formula. The result is 510. Looking at the formula, you might think D5–D5 equals zero; remember that because of the order of precedence rules, multiplication is calculated before subtraction. The product of 600 (cell D5) and 0.15 (cell E5) equals 90, which is then subtracted from 600 (cell D5), so the sale price is 510. If it helps to understand the formula better, add parentheses: =D5-(D5*E5).

c. Save the workbook with the new formula.

TIP Spot-Check Your Work

You should check the result for logic. Use a calculator to spot-check the accuracy of formulas. If you mark down merchandise by 15% of its regular price, you are charging 85% of the regular price. You can spot-check your formula to ensure that 85% of 600 is 510 by multiplying 600 by 0.85.

STEP 3 » USE CELL REFERENCES IN A FORMULA AND APPLY THE ORDER OF PRECEDENCE

After calculating the sale price, you want to know the profit margin OKOS will earn. OKOS paid $400 for the computer and will sell it for $510. The profit of $110 is then divided by the $400 cost, which gives OKOS a profit margin of 21.57%. Refer to Figure 1.12 as you complete Step 3.

Step b: Formula in Formula Bar

Step b: Result of formula in cell

G5 =(F5-B5)/F5

	A	B	C	D	E	F	G	H
1	OK Office Systems Pricing Information							
2	9/1/2016							
3								
4	Product	Cost	Markup Ra	Retail Pric	Percent O	Sale Price	Profit Margin	
5	Computer	400	0.5	600	0.15	510	0.215686	
6	Color Laser	457.7	0.75		0.2			
7	Filing Cabi	68.75	0.905		0.1			
8	Desk Chair	75	1		0.25			
9	Solid Oak (	700	1.857		0.3			
10	28" Monitc	195	0.835		0.1			
11								

FIGURE 1.12 Profit Margin Formula

a. Click **cell G5**, the cell where you will enter the formula to calculate the profit margin.

The profit margin is the profit (difference in sales price and cost) percentage of the sale price.

b. Type **=(F5-B5)/F5** and notice the color-coding in the cell addresses. Press **Ctrl+Enter**.

The formula must first calculate the profit, which is the difference between the sale price (510) and the original cost (400). The difference (110) is then divided by the sale price (510) to determine the profit margin of 0.215686, or 21.6%.

TROUBLESHOOTING: If you type a backslash (\) instead of a forward slash (/), Excel will display an error message box. Make sure you type / as the division operator.

c. Look at the Formula Bar and save the workbook with the new formula.

STEP 4 » COPY FORMULAS WITH AUTO FILL

After double-checking the accuracy of your calculations for the first product, you are ready to copy the formulas down the columns to calculate the retail price, sale price, and profit margin for the other products. Refer to Figure 1.13 as you complete Step 4.

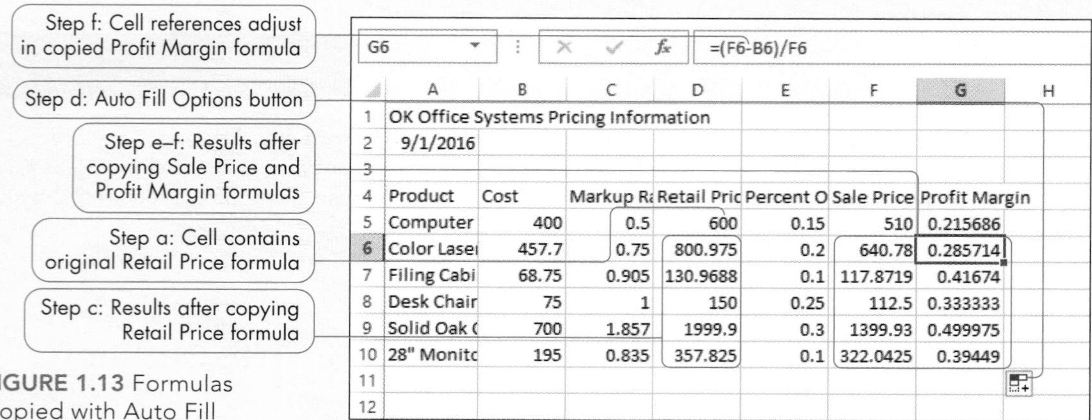

	A	B	C	D	E	F	G	H
1	OK Office Systems Pricing Information							
2	9/1/2016							
3								
4	Product	Cost	Markup Ra	Retail Pric	Percent O	Sale Price	Profit Margin	
5	Computer	400	0.5	600	0.15	510	0.215686	
6	Color Lasei	457.7	0.75	800.975	0.2	640.78	0.285714	
7	Filing Cabi	68.75	0.905	130.9688	0.1	117.8719	0.41674	
8	Desk Chair	75	1	150	0.25	112.5	0.333333	
9	Solid Oak (	700	1.857	1999.9	0.3	1399.93	0.499975	
10	28" Monitc	195	0.835	357.825	0.1	322.0425	0.39449	
11								
12								

FIGURE 1.13 Formulas Copied with Auto Fill

a. Click **cell D5**, the cell containing the formula to calculate the retail price for the first item.

b. Position the mouse pointer on the **cell D5 fill handle**. When the pointer changes from a white plus sign to a thin black plus sign, double-click the **fill handle**.

Excel's Auto Fill feature copies the retail price formula for the remaining products in your worksheet. Excel detects when to stop copying the formula when it encounters a blank row, such as in row 11.

c. Click **cell D6**, the cell containing the first copied retail price formula, and look at the Formula Bar.

The formula in cell D5 is =B5*(1+C5). The copied formula in cell D6 is =B6*(1+C6). Excel adjusts the cell addresses in the formula as it copies the formula down a column so that the results are based on each row's data rather than using the original formula's cell addresses for other products.

> **TROUBLESHOOTING:** The result in cell D7 may show more decimal places than shown in Figure 1.13. This may be due to different screen resolutions. Do not worry about this slight difference.

d. Select the **range F5:G5**. Double-click the **fill handle** in the bottom-right corner of **cell G5**.

Auto Fill copies the selected formulas down their respective columns. Auto Fill Options are available down and to the right of the cell G10 fill handle, indicating you could select different fill options if you want.

> **TROUBLESHOOTING:** If Excel displays pound symbols, such as ####, instead of results, that means the column is not wide enough to show results. You will learn how to adjust column widths in the third section.

e. Click **cell F6**, the cell containing the first copied sale price formula, and view the Formula Bar.

The original formula was =D5-D5*E5. The copied formula in cell F6 is adjusted to =D6-D6*E6 so that it calculates the sales price based on the data in row 6.

f. Click **cell G6**, the cell containing the first copied profit margin formula, and look at the Formula Bar. Save the workbook.

The original formula was =(F5-B5)/F5, and the copied formula in cell G6 is =(F6-B6)/F6.

STEP 5 ›› CHANGE VALUES AND DISPLAY CELL FORMULAS

You want to see how the prices and profit margins are affected when you change some of the original cost values. For example, the supplier might notify you that the cost to you will increase. In addition, you want to see the formulas displayed in the cells temporarily. Refer to Figures 1.14 and 1.15 as you complete Step 5.

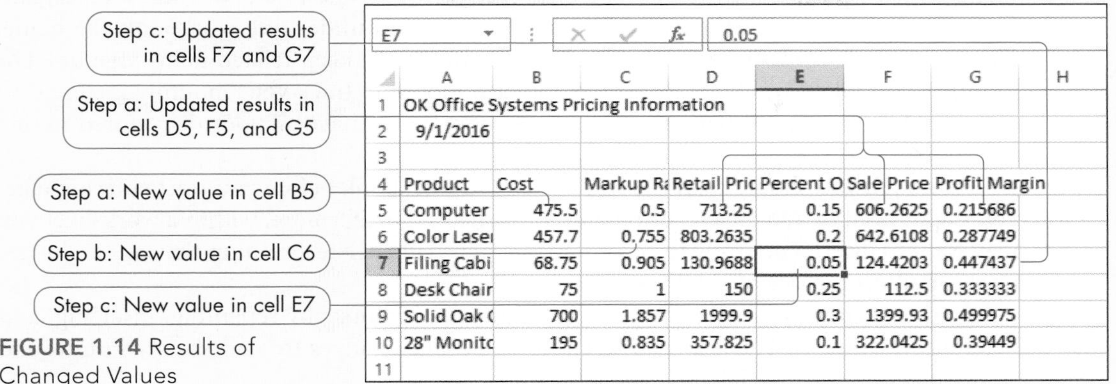

	A	B	C	D	E	F	G	H
1	OK Office Systems Pricing Information							
2	9/1/2016							
3								
4	Product	Cost	Markup Ra	Retail Pric	Percent O	Sale Price	Profit Margin	
5	Computer	475.5	0.5	713.25	0.15	606.2625	0.215686	
6	Color Lase	457.7	0.755	803.2635	0.2	642.6108	0.287749	
7	Filing Cabi	68.75	0.905	130.9688	0.05	124.4203	0.447437	
8	Desk Chair	75	1	150	0.25	112.5	0.333333	
9	Solid Oak (	700	1.857	1999.9	0.3	1399.93	0.499975	
10	28" Monitc	195	0.835	357.825	0.1	322.0425	0.39449	
11								

FIGURE 1.14 Results of Changed Values

a. Click **cell B5**, type **475.5**, and then press **Enter**.

The results of the retail price, sale price, and profit margin formulas change based on the new cost.

b. Click **cell C6**, type **0.755**, and then press **Enter**.

The results of the retail price, sale price, and profit margin formulas change based on the new markup rate.

c. Click **cell E7**, type **0.05**, and then press **Ctrl+Enter**.

The results of the sale price and profit margin formulas change based on the new markdown rate. Note that the retail price did not change, since that formula is not based on the markdown rate.

d. Press **Ctrl+`** (the grave accent mark).

The workbook now displays the formulas rather than the formula results (see Figure 1.15). This is helpful when you want to review several formulas at one time.

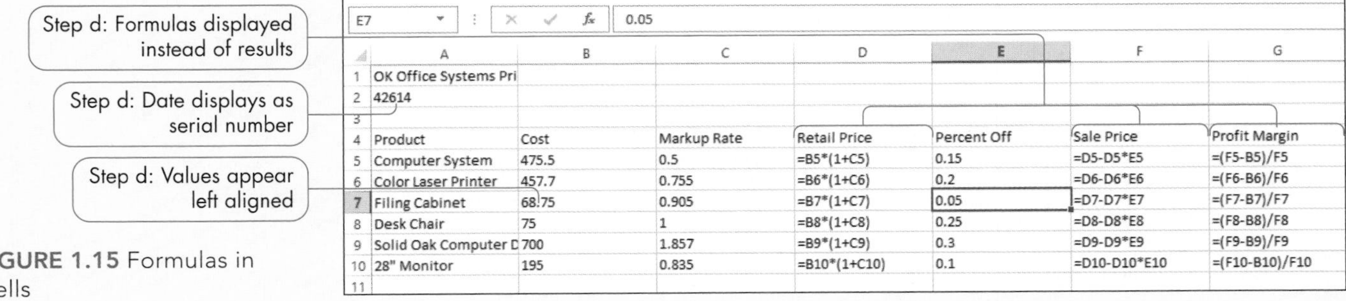

	A	B	C	D	E	F	G
1	OK Office Systems Pri						
2	42614						
3							
4	Product	Cost	Markup Rate	Retail Price	Percent Off	Sale Price	Profit Margin
5	Computer System	475.5	0.5	=B5*(1+C5)	0.15	=D5-D5*E5	=(F5-B5)/F5
6	Color Laser Printer	457.7	0.755	=B6*(1+C6)	0.2	=D6-D6*E6	=(F6-B6)/F6
7	Filing Cabinet	68.75	0.905	=B7*(1+C7)	0.05	=D7-D7*E7	=(F7-B7)/F7
8	Desk Chair	75	1	=B8*(1+C8)	0.25	=D8-D8*E8	=(F8-B8)/F8
9	Solid Oak Computer D	700	1.857	=B9*(1+C9)	0.3	=D9-D9*E9	=(F9-B9)/F9
10	28" Monitor	195	0.835	=B10*(1+C10)	0.1	=D10-D10*E10	=(F10-B10)/F10
11							

FIGURE 1.15 Formulas in Cells

e. Press **Ctrl+`** (the grave accent mark).

The workbook now displays the formula results in the cells again.

f. Save the workbook. Keep the workbook open if you plan to continue with the next Hands-On Exercise. If not, close the workbook and exit Excel.

Workbook and Worksheet Management

When you start a new blank workbook in Excel, the workbook contains one worksheet named Sheet1. However, you can add additional worksheets. The text, values, dates, and formulas you enter into the individual sheets are saved under one workbook file name. Having multiple worksheets in one workbook is helpful to keep related items together. For example, you might want one worksheet for each month to track your monthly income and expenses for one year. When tax time comes around, you have all your data stored in one workbook file.

Although you should plan the worksheet and workbook before you start entering data, you might need to add, delete, or rename worksheets. Furthermore, within a worksheet you may want to insert a new row to accommodate new data, delete a column that you no longer need, or adjust the size of columns and rows.

In this section, you will learn how to manage workbooks by renaming, inserting, and deleting worksheets. You will also learn how to make changes to worksheet columns and rows, such as inserting, deleting, and adjusting sizes.

Managing Worksheets

Creating a multiple-worksheet workbook takes some planning and maintenance. Worksheet tab names should reflect the contents of the respective worksheets. In addition, you can insert, copy, move, and delete worksheets within the workbook. You can even apply background color to the worksheet tabs so that they stand out onscreen. Figure 1.16 shows a workbook in which the sheet tabs have been renamed, colors have been applied to worksheet tabs, and a worksheet tab has been right-clicked so that the shortcut menu appears.

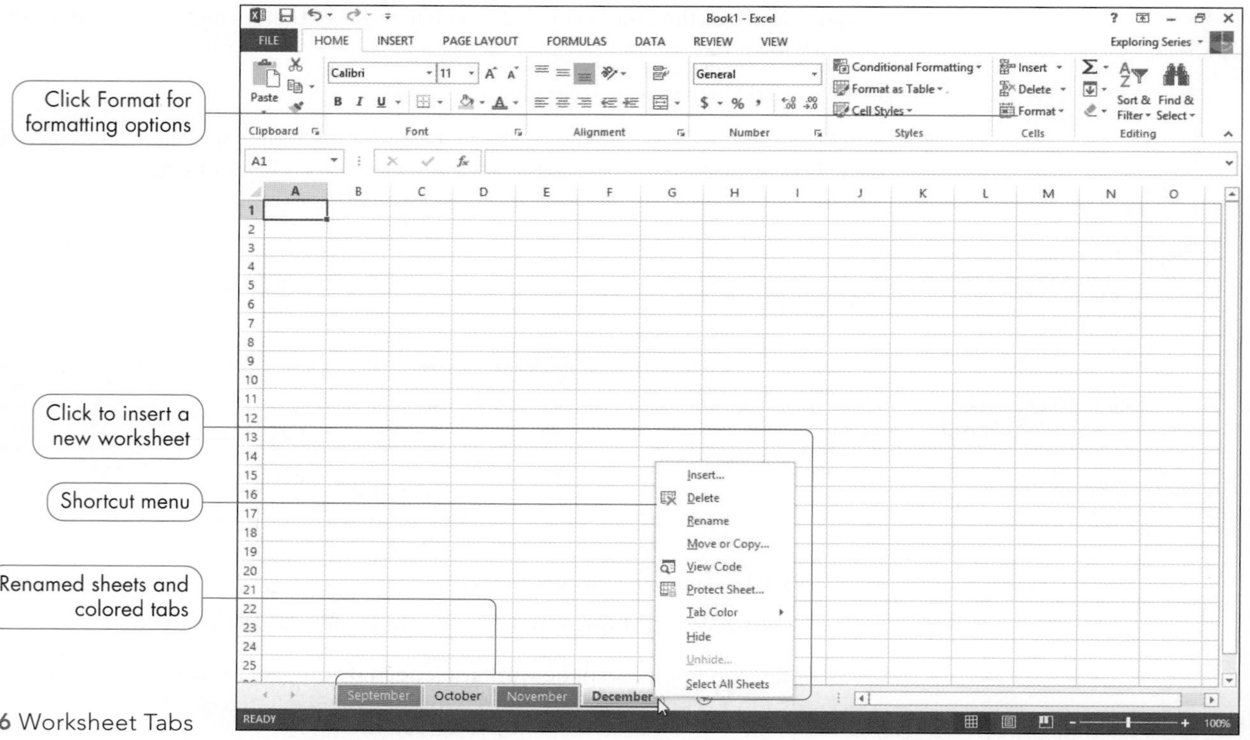

FIGURE 1.16 Worksheet Tabs

Rename a Worksheet

STEP 1》 The default worksheet name Sheet1 does not describe the contents of the worksheet. You should rename worksheet tabs to reflect the sheet contents. For example, if your budget workbook contains monthly worksheets, name the worksheets September, October, etc. Although you can have spaces in worksheet names, keep worksheet names relatively short. The longer the worksheet names, the fewer sheet tabs you will see at the bottom of the workbook window without scrolling.

To rename a worksheet, do one of the following:

- Double-click a sheet tab, type the new name, and then press Enter.
- Click the sheet tab for the sheet you want to rename, click Format in the Cells group on the HOME tab (refer to Figure 1.16), select Rename Sheet (see Figure 1.17), type the new sheet name, and then press Enter.
- Right-click the sheet tab, select Rename from the shortcut menu (see Figure 1.16), type the new sheet name, and then press Enter.

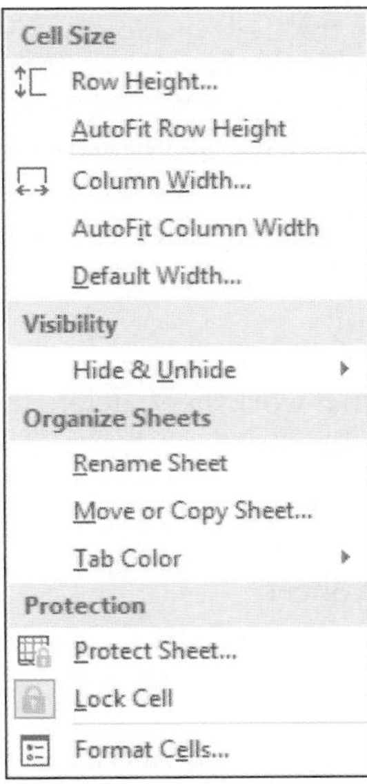

FIGURE 1.17 Format Menu

Change Worksheet Tab Color

STEP 1》 The active worksheet tab is white with a green bottom border. When you use multiple worksheets, you might want to apply a different color to each worksheet tab to make the tab stand out or to emphasize the difference between sheets. For example, you might apply red to the September tab, green to the October tab, dark blue to the November tab, and purple to the December tab.

To change the color of a worksheet tab, do one of the following:

- Click the sheet tab for the sheet you want to rename, click Format in the Cells group on the HOME tab (refer to Figure 1.16), point to Tab Color (refer to Figure 1.17), and then click a color on the Tab Color palette.
- Right-click the sheet tab, point to Tab Color on the shortcut menu (refer to Figure 1.16), and then click a color on the Tab Color palette.

Insert and Delete a Worksheet

STEP 2»

Sometimes you need more than one worksheet in the workbook. For example, you might create a workbook that contains 12 worksheets—a worksheet for each month of the year. To insert a new worksheet, do one of the following:

- Click *New sheet* to the right of the last worksheet tab.
- Click the Insert arrow—either to the right or below Insert—in the Cells group on the HOME tab and select Insert Sheet.
- Right-click any sheet tab, select Insert from the shortcut menu (refer to Figure 1.16), click Worksheet in the Insert dialog box, and then click OK.
- Press Shift+F11.

TIP Ribbon Commands with Arrows

Some commands, such as Insert in the Cells group, contain two parts: the main command and an arrow. The arrow may be below or to the right of the command, depending on the command, window size, or screen resolution. Instructions in the Exploring Series use the command name to instruct you to click the main command to perform the default action, such as *Click Insert in the Cells group* or *Click Delete in the Cells group.* Instructions include the word arrow when you need to select an additional option, such as *Click the Insert arrow in the Cells group* or *Click the Delete arrow in the Cells group.*

If you no longer need the data in a worksheet, delete the worksheet. Doing so will eliminate extra data in a file and reduce file size. To delete a worksheet in a workbook, do one of the following:

- Click the Delete arrow—either to the right or below Delete—in the Cells group on the HOME tab and select Delete Sheet.
- Right-click any sheet tab and select Delete from the shortcut menu (refer to Figure 1.16).

If the sheet you are trying to delete contains data, Excel will display a warning: *You can't undo deleting sheets, and you might be removing some data. If you don't need it, click Delete.* If you try to delete a blank worksheet, Excel will not display a warning; it will immediately delete the sheet.

Move or Copy a Worksheet

After inserting and deleting worksheets, you can arrange the worksheet tabs in a different sequence, especially if the newly inserted worksheets do not fall within a logical sequence. To move a worksheet, do one of the following:

- Drag a worksheet tab to the desired location. As you drag a sheet tab, the pointer resembles a piece of paper. A down-pointing triangle appears between sheet tabs to indicate where the sheet will be placed when you release the mouse button.
- Click Format in the Cells group on the HOME tab (refer to Figure 1.16) and select *Move or Copy Sheet*, or right-click the sheet tab you want to move and select *Move or Copy* to display the *Move or Copy dialog box* (see Figure 1.18). You can move the worksheet within the current workbook, or you can move the worksheet to a different workbook. In the *Before sheet* list, select the worksheet you want to come after the moved worksheet and click OK. For example, you have just created a new worksheet named August and you want it to come before the September worksheet. You would select September in the *Before sheet* list.

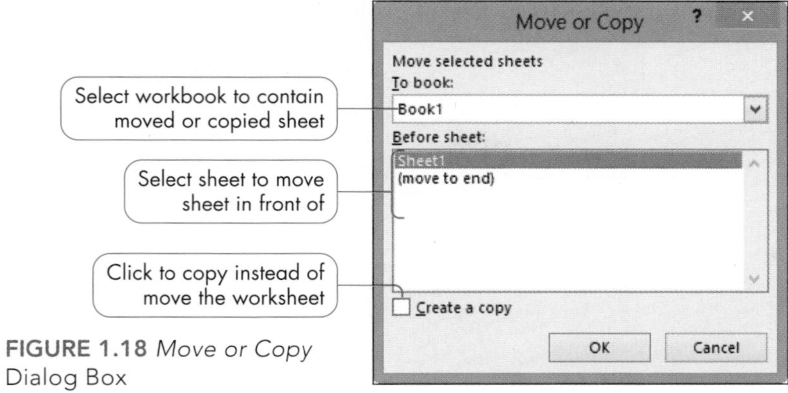

FIGURE 1.18 *Move or Copy* Dialog Box

After creating a worksheet, you may want to copy it to use as a template or starting point for similar data. For example, if you create a worksheet for your September budget, you can copy the worksheet and then easily edit the data on the copied worksheet to enter data for your October budget. Copying the entire worksheet would save you a lot of valuable time in entering and formatting the new worksheet. The process for copying a worksheet is similar to moving a sheet. To copy a worksheet, press and hold Ctrl as you drag the worksheet tab. Alternatively, display the *Move or Copy* dialog box, select the *To book* and *Before sheet* options (refer to Figure 1.18), click the *Create a copy* check box, and then click OK.

Managing Columns and Rows

As you enter and edit worksheet data, you can adjust the row and column structure. You can add rows and columns to add new data, or you can delete data you no longer need. Adjusting the height and width of rows and columns, respectively, can present the data better.

Insert Cells, Columns, and Rows

STEP 3»

After you construct a worksheet, you might need to insert cells, columns, or rows to accommodate new data. For example, you might need to insert a new column to perform calculations or a new row to list a new product. When you insert cells, rows, and columns, cell addresses in formulas adjust automatically.

To insert a new column or row, do one of the following:

- Click in the column or row for which you want to insert a new column to the left or a new row above, respectively. Click the Insert arrow in the Cells group on the HOME tab and select Insert Sheet Columns or Insert Sheet Rows.
- Right-click the column (letter) or row (number) heading for which you want to insert a new column to the left or a new row above, respectively, and select Insert from the shortcut menu.

Excel inserts new columns to the left of the current column and new rows above the active row. If the current column is column C and you insert a new column, the new column becomes column C, and the original column C data are now in column D. Likewise, if the current row is 5 and you insert a new row, the new row is row 5, and the original row 5 data are now in row 6.

Inserting a cell is helpful when you realize that you left out an entry in one column after you have entered columns of data. Instead of inserting a new row for all columns, you just want to move the existing content down in one column to enter the missing value. You can insert a single cell in a particular row or column. To insert a cell, click in the cell where you want the new cell, click the Insert arrow in the Cells group on the Home tab, and then select Insert Cells. Select an option from the Insert dialog box (see Figure 1.19) to position the new cell and click OK. Alternatively, click Insert in the Cells group. The default action of clicking Insert is to insert a cell at the current location, which moves existing data down in that column only.

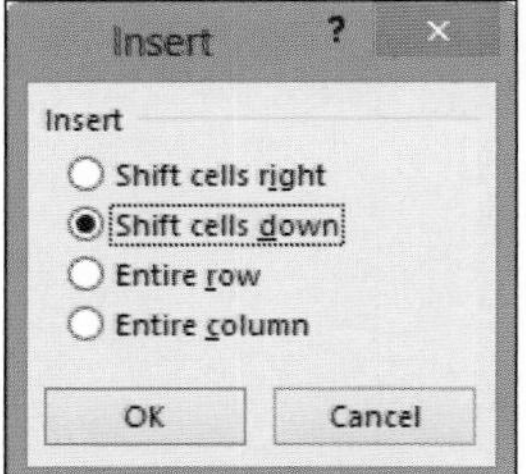

FIGURE 1.19 Insert Dialog Box

Delete Cells, Columns, and Rows

STEP 4»

If you no longer need a cell, column, or row, you can delete it. In these situations, you are deleting the entire cell, column, or row, not just the contents of the cell to leave empty cells. As with inserting new cells, any affected formulas adjust the cell references automatically. To delete a column or row, do one of the following:

- Click the column or row heading for the column or row you want to delete. Click Delete in the Cells group on the HOME tab.
- Click in any cell within the column or row you want to delete. Click the Delete arrow in the Cells group on the HOME tab and select Delete Sheet Columns or Delete Sheet Rows, respectively.
- Right-click the column letter or row number for the column or row you want to delete and select Delete from the shortcut menu.

To delete a cell or cells, select the cell(s), click the Delete arrow in the Cells group, and then select Delete Cells to display the Delete dialog box (see Figure 1.20). Click the appropriate option to shift cells left or up and click OK. Alternatively, click Delete in the Cells group. The default action of clicking Delete is to delete the active cell, which moves existing data up in that column only.

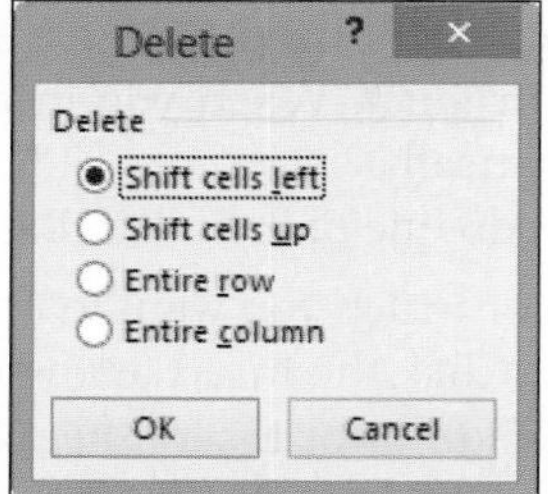

FIGURE 1.20 Delete Dialog Box

Adjust Column Width

STEP 5»

After you enter data in a column, you often need to adjust the ***column width***—the number of characters that can fit horizontally using the default font or the number of horizontal pixels—to show the contents of cells. For example, in the worksheet you created in Hands-On Exercises 1 and 2, the labels in column A displayed into column B when those adjacent cells were empty. However, after you typed values in column B, the labels in column A appeared cut off. You will need to widen column A to show the full name of all of your products.

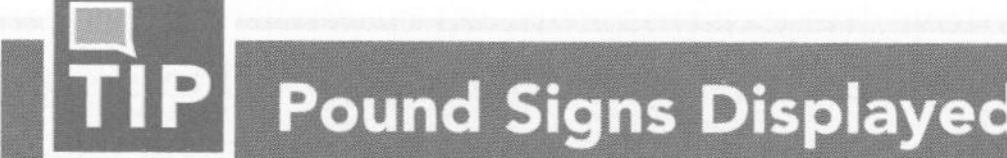

Numbers appear as a series of pound signs (######) when the cell is too narrow to display the complete value, and text appears to be truncated.

To widen a column to accommodate the longest label or value in a column, do one of the following:

- Position the pointer on the vertical border between the current column heading and the next column heading. When the pointer displays as a two-headed arrow, double-click the border. For example, if column B is too narrow to display the content in that column, double-click the border between the column B and C headings.
- Click Format in the Cells group on the HOME tab (refer to Figure 1.16) and select AutoFit Column Width (refer to Figure 1.17).

To widen a column to an exact width, do one of the following:

- Drag the vertical border to the left to decrease the column width or to the right to increase the column width. As you drag the vertical border, Excel displays a ScreenTip specifying the width (see Figure 1.21) from 0 to 255 characters and in pixels.
- Click Format in the Cells group on the HOME tab (refer to Figure 1.16), select Column Width (refer to Figure 1.17), type a value in the Column width box in the Column Width dialog box, and then click OK.

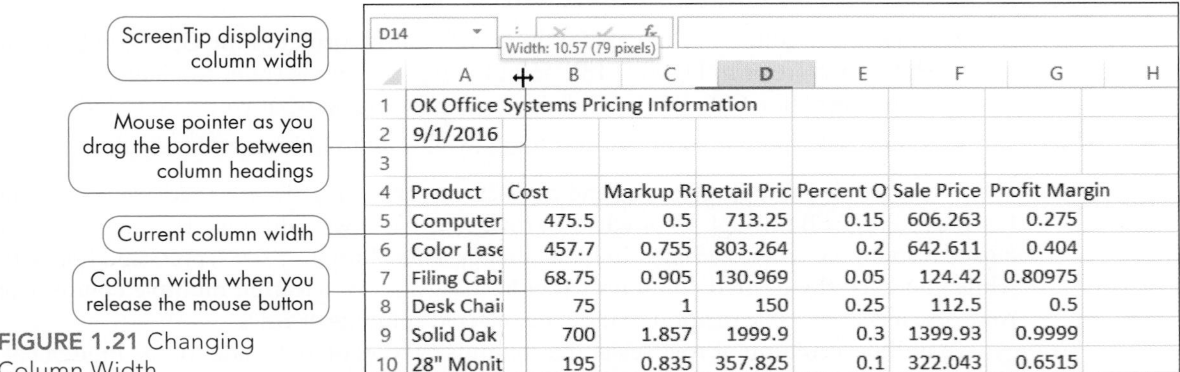

	A	B	C	D	E	F	G	H
1	OK Office Systems Pricing Information							
2	9/1/2016							
3								
4	Product	Cost	Markup Ra	Retail Pric	Percent O	Sale Price	Profit Margin	
5	Computer	475.5	0.5	713.25	0.15	606.263	0.275	
6	Color Lase	457.7	0.755	803.264	0.2	642.611	0.404	
7	Filing Cabi	68.75	0.905	130.969	0.05	124.42	0.80975	
8	Desk Chai	75	1	150	0.25	112.5	0.5	
9	Solid Oak	700	1.857	1999.9	0.3	1399.93	0.9999	
10	28" Monit	195	0.835	357.825	0.1	322.043	0.6515	

FIGURE 1.21 Changing Column Width

Adjust Row Height

When you increase the font size of cell contents, Excel automatically increases the ***row height***—the vertical measurement of the row. However, if you insert a line break or wrap text to create multiple lines of text in a cell, Excel might not increase the row height. You can adjust the row height in a way similar to how you change column width by double-clicking the border between row numbers or by selecting Row Height or AutoFit Row Height from the Format menu (refer to Figure 1.17). In Excel, row height is a value between 0 and 409 based on point size (abbreviated as pt) and pixels. Whether you are measuring font sizes or row heights, one point size is equal to 1/72 of an inch. Your row height should be taller than your font size. For example, with an 11-pt font size, the default row height is 15.

TIP Multiple Column Widths and Row Heights

You can set the size for more than one column or row at a time to make the selected columns or rows the same size. Drag across the column or row headings for the area you want to format, and then set the size using any method.

Hide and Unhide Columns and Rows

STEP 6 » If your worksheet contains confidential information, you might need to hide some columns and/or rows before you print a copy for public distribution. However, the column or row is not deleted. If you hide column B, you will see columns A and C side by side. If you hide row 3, you will see rows 2 and 4 together. Figure 1.22 shows that column B and row 3 are hidden. Excel displays a double line between column headings (such as between A and C), indicating one or more columns are hidden, and a double line between row headings (such as between 2 and 4), indicating one or more rows are hidden.

Double vertical line indicates hidden column

Double horizontal line indicates hidden row

	A	C	D
1			
2			
4			
5			

FIGURE 1.22 Hidden Column and Row

To hide a column or row, do one of the following:

- Click in the column or row you want to hide, click Format in the Cells group on the HOME tab (refer to Figure 1.16), point to Hide & Unhide (refer to Figure 1.17), and then select Hide Columns or Hide Rows, depending on what you want to hide.
- Right-click the column or row heading(s) you want to hide and select Hide.

You can hide multiple columns and rows at the same time. To select adjacent columns (such as columns B through E) or adjacent rows (such as rows 2 through 4), drag across the adjacent column or row headings. To hide nonadjacent columns or rows, press and hold Ctrl while you click the desired column or row headings. After selecting multiple columns or rows, use any acceptable method to hide the selected columns or rows.

To unhide a column or row, select the columns or rows on both sides of the hidden column or row. For example, if column B is hidden, drag across column letters A and C. Then do one of the following:

- Click Format in the Cells group on the HOME tab (refer to Figure 1.16), point to Hide & Unhide (refer to Figure 1.17), and then select Unhide Columns or Unhide Rows, depending on what you want to display again.
- Right-click the column(s) or row(s) you want to hide and select Unhide.

TIP Unhiding Column A, Row 1, and All Hidden Rows/Columns

Unhiding column A or row 1 is different because you cannot select the row or column on either side. To unhide column A or row 1, type A1 in the Name Box and press Enter. Click Format in the Cells group on the Home tab, point to Hide & Unhide, and then select Unhide Columns or Unhide Rows to display column A or row 1, respectively. If you want to unhide all columns and rows, click Select All and use the Hide & Unhide submenu.

1. What is the benefit of renaming a worksheet? ***p. 395***
2. What are two ways to insert a new row in a worksheet? ***p. 397***
3. How can you delete cell B5 without deleting the entire row or column? ***p. 398***
4. When should you adjust column widths instead of using the default width? ***p. 398***

Hands-On Exercises

3 Workbook and Worksheet Management

After reviewing the OKOS worksheet, you decide to rename the worksheet, change the worksheet tab color, insert a worksheet, and delete an empty worksheet. In addition, you need to insert a column to calculate the amount of markup and delete a row containing data you no longer need. You also need to adjust column widths to display the labels in the columns.

Skills covered: Rename a Worksheet and Select a Tab Color • Insert, Move, and Delete a Worksheet • Insert a Column and Rows • Delete a Row • Adjust Column Width and Row Height • Hide and Unhide Columns

STEP 1 » RENAME A WORKSHEET AND SELECT A TAB COLOR

You want to rename Sheet1 to describe the worksheet contents and add a color to the sheet tab. Refer to Figure 1.23 as you complete Step 1.

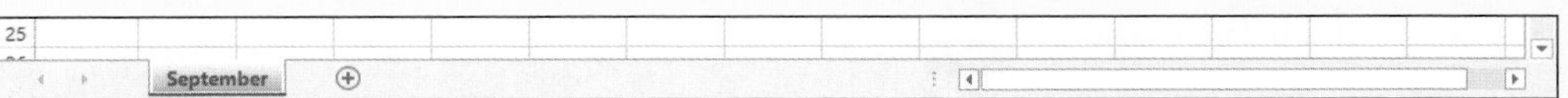

FIGURE 1.23 Renamed Worksheet with Tab Color

a. Open *e01h2Markup_LastFirst* if you closed it at the end of Hands-On Exercise 2 and save it as **e01h3Markup_LastFirst**, changing *h2* to *h3*.

b. Double-click the **Sheet1 sheet tab**, type **September**, and then press **Enter**.

You renamed Sheet1 September.

c. Right-click the **September sheet tab**, point to *Tab Color*, and then click **Red** in the *Standard Colors* section.

The worksheet tab color is red.

d. Save the workbook.

STEP 2 » INSERT, MOVE, AND DELETE A WORKSHEET

Your supervisor asks you to add another worksheet to the workbook. She wants you to place it before the September worksheet so that she can add August data. After you do this, she calls you on the phone and tells you that she won't be adding the August data after all. Therefore, you will delete that worksheet. Refer to Figure 1.24 as you complete Step 2.

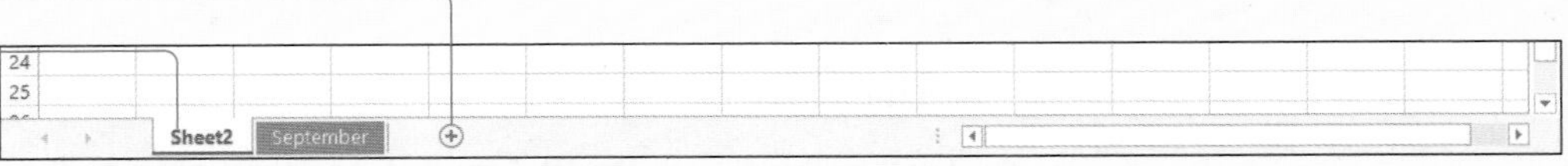

FIGURE 1.24 New Sheet Inserted

a. Click **New sheet**, the plus icon to the right of the September sheet tab.

Excel adds a new worksheet named either Sheet1 or Sheet2 to the right of the previously active sheet.

b. Drag the **Sheet tab** to the left of the September sheet tab.

c. Click the **Sheet tab**, click the **Delete arrow** in the Cells group on the HOME tab, and then select **Delete Sheet**.

You deleted the blank worksheet from the workbook.

> **TROUBLESHOOTING:** Delete in the Cells group, like some other commands in Excel, contains two parts: the main command icon and an arrow. Click the main command icon when instructed to click Delete to perform the default action. Click the arrow when instructed to click the Delete arrow for additional command options.

> **TROUBLESHOOTING:** Notice that Undo is unavailable on the Quick Access Toolbar. You cannot undo deleting a worksheet. It is deleted!

d. Save the workbook.

STEP 3 ›› INSERT A COLUMN AND ROWS

You decide that you need a column to display the amount of profit. Because profit is a dollar amount, you want to keep the profit column close to another column of dollar amounts. Therefore, you will insert the profit column before the profit margin (percentage) column. You also want to insert new rows for product information and category names. Refer to Figure 1.25 as you complete Step 3.

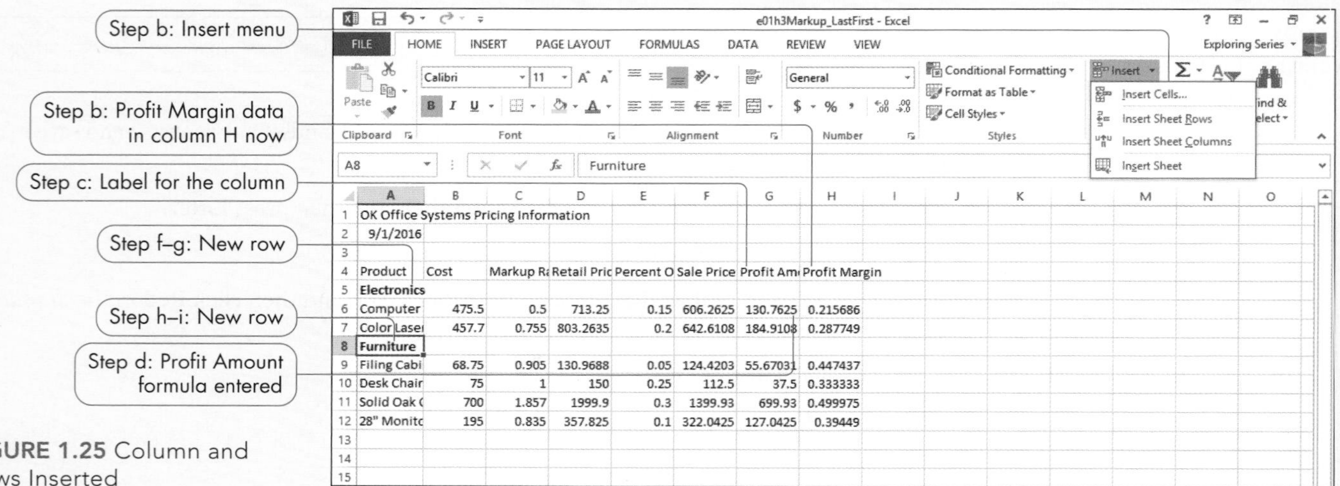

FIGURE 1.25 Column and Rows Inserted

a. Click **cell G5** (or any cell in column G), the column containing the Profit Margin.

You want to insert a column between the Sale Price and Profit Margin columns so that you can calculate the profit amount in dollars.

b. Click the **Insert arrow** in the Cells group and select **Insert Sheet Columns**.

You inserted a new, blank column G. The data in the original column G are now in column H.

c. Click **cell G4**, type **Profit Amount**, and then press **Enter**.

d. Make sure the active cell is **cell G5**. Type **=F5-B5** and click **Enter** (the check mark between the Name Box and the Formula Bar). Double-click the **cell G5 fill handle** to copy the formula down the column.

You calculated the profit amount by subtracting the original cost from the sale price. Although steps e and f below illustrate one way to insert a row, you can use other methods presented in this chapter.

e. Right-click the **row 5 heading**, the row containing the Computer System data.

Excel displays a shortcut menu consisting of commands you can perform.

f. Select **Insert** from the shortcut menu.

   You inserted a new blank row 5, which is selected. The original rows of data move down a row each.

g. Click **cell A5**. Type **Electronics** and press **Ctrl+Enter**. Click **Bold** in the Font group on the HOME tab.

   You typed and bolded the category name *Electronics* above the list of electronic products.

h. Right-click the **row 8 heading**, the row containing the Filing Cabinet data, and select **Insert** from the shortcut menu.

i. Click **cell A8**. Type **Furniture** and press **Ctrl+Enter**. Click **Bold** in the Font group on the HOME tab.

   You typed and bolded the category name *Furniture* above the list of furniture products.

j. Save the workbook.

STEP 4 » DELETE A ROW

You just realized that you do not have enough filing cabinets in stock to offer on sale, so you need to delete the Filing Cabinet row. Refer to Figure 1.26 as you complete Step 4.

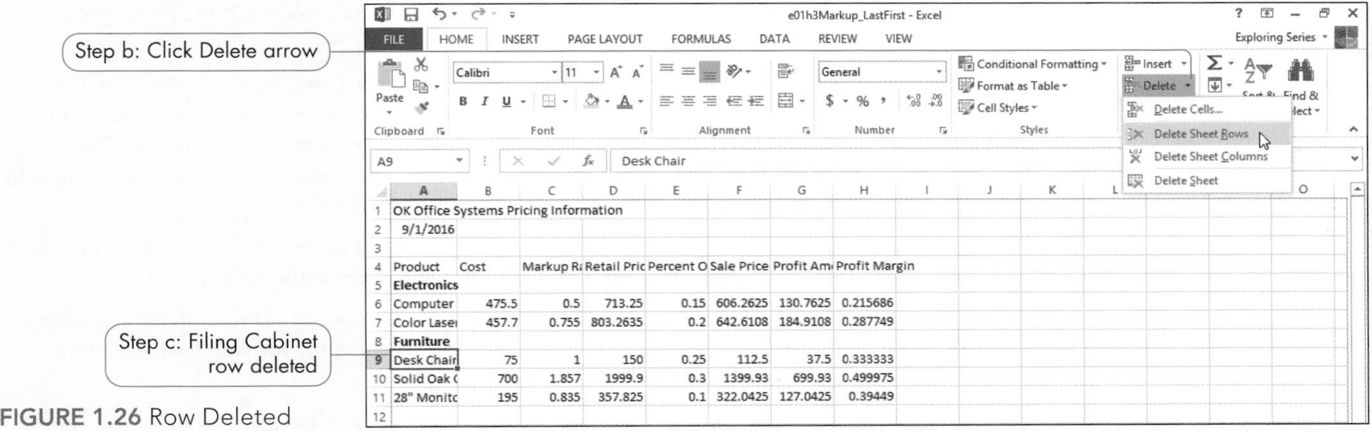

	A	B	C	D	E	F	G	H
1	OK Office Systems Pricing Information							
2	9/1/2016							
3								
4	Product	Cost	Markup R	Retail Pric	Percent O	Sale Price	Profit Am	Profit Margin
5	**Electronics**							
6	Computer	475.5	0.5	713.25	0.15	606.2625	130.7625	0.215686
7	Color Lase	457.7	0.755	803.2635	0.2	642.6108	184.9108	0.287749
8	**Furniture**							
9	Desk Chair	75	1	150	0.25	112.5	37.5	0.333333
10	Solid Oak (	700	1.857	1999.9	0.3	1399.93	699.93	0.499975
11	28" Monitc	195	0.835	357.825	0.1	322.0425	127.0425	0.39449
12								

FIGURE 1.26 Row Deleted

a. Click **cell A9** (or any cell on row 9), the row that contains the Filing Cabinet data.

b. Click the **Delete arrow** in the Cells group.

c. Select **Delete Sheet Rows** and save the workbook.

   The Filing Cabinet row is deleted and the remaining rows move up one row.

> **TROUBLESHOOTING:** If you accidentally delete the wrong row or accidentally select Delete Sheet Columns instead of Delete Sheet Rows, click Undo on the Quick Access Toolbar to restore the deleted row or column.

STEP 5 » ADJUST COLUMN WIDTH AND ROW HEIGHT

As you review your worksheet, you notice that the labels in column A appear cut off. You need to increase the width of that column to display the entire product names. In addition, you want to make row 1 taller. Refer to Figure 1.27 as you complete Step 5.

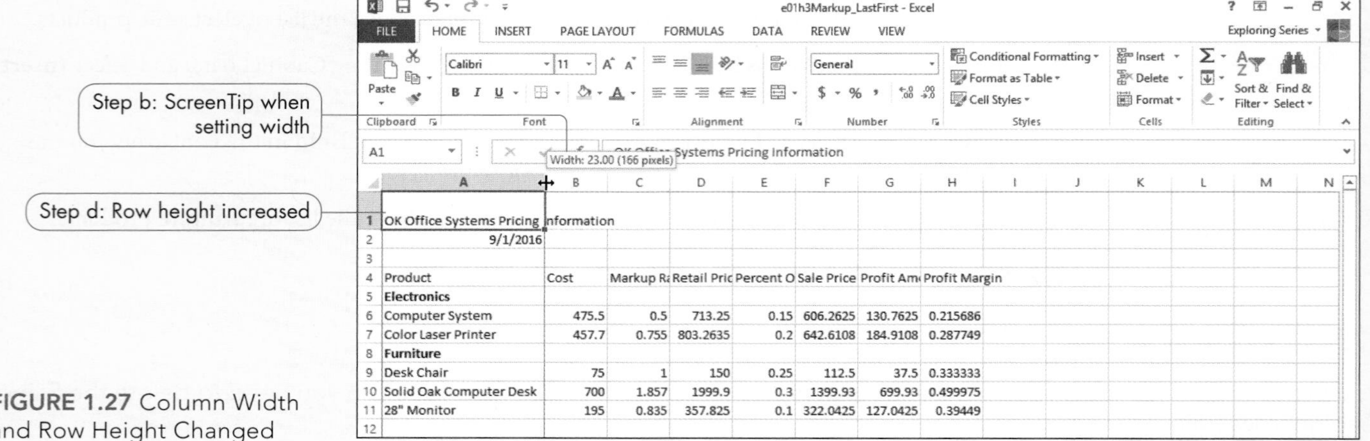

FIGURE 1.27 Column Width and Row Height Changed

a. Position the pointer between the column A and B headings. When the pointer looks like a double-headed arrow, double-click the border.

When you double-click the border between two columns, Excel adjusts the width of the column on the left side of the border to fit the contents of that column. Excel increased the width of column A based on the cell containing the longest content (the title in cell A1, which will eventually span over all columns). Therefore, you want to decrease the column to avoid so much empty space in column A.

b. Position the pointer between the column A and B headings again. Drag the border to the left until the ScreenTip displays **Width: 23.00 (166 pixels)**. Release the mouse button.

You decreased the column width to 23 for column A. The longest product name is visible. You will not adjust the other column widths until after you apply formats to the column headings in Hands-On Exercise 5.

c. Click **cell A1**. Click **Format** in the Cells group and select **Row Height** to display the Row Height dialog box.

d. Type **30** in the **Row height box** and click **OK**. Save the workbook.

You increased the height of the row that contains the worksheet title so that it is more prominent.

STEP 6 » HIDE AND UNHIDE COLUMNS

To focus on the dollar amounts, you decide to hide the markup rate, discount rate, and profit margin columns. Refer to Figure 1.28 as you complete Step 6.

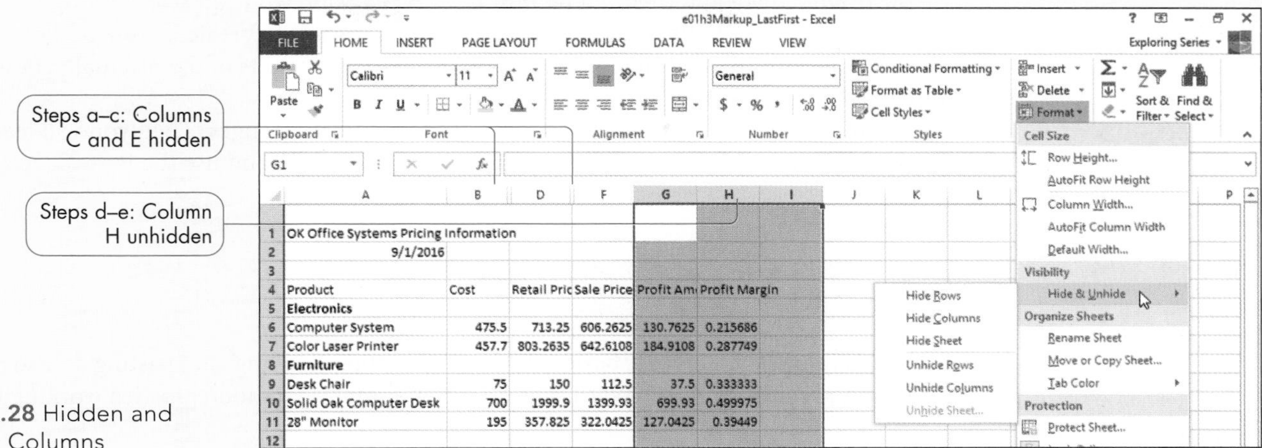

FIGURE 1.28 Hidden and Unhidden Columns

a. Click the **column C heading**, the column containing the Markup Rate values.

b. Press and hold **Ctrl** as you click the **column E heading** and the **column H heading**. Release Ctrl after selecting the headings.

Holding down Ctrl enables you to select nonadjacent ranges. You want to hide the rate columns temporarily.

c. Click **Format** in the Cells group, point to *Hide & Unhide*, and then select **Hide Columns**.

Excel hides the selected columns. You see a gap in column heading letters, indicating columns are hidden (refer to Figure 1.28).

d. Drag to select the **column G and I headings**.

You want to unhide column H, so you must select the columns on both sides of the hidden column.

e. Click **Format** in the Cells group, point to *Hide & Unhide*, and then select **Unhide Columns**.

Column H, which contains the Profit Margin values, is no longer hidden. You will keep the other columns hidden and save the workbook as evidence that you know how to hide columns. You will unhide the remaining columns in the next Hands-On Exercise.

f. Save the workbook. Keep the workbook open if you plan to continue with the next Hands-On Exercise. If not, close the workbook and exit Excel.

Clipboard Tasks

Although you plan worksheets before entering data, you might decide to move data to a different location in the same worksheet or even in a different worksheet. Instead of deleting the original data and then typing it in the new location, you can select and move data from one cell to another. In some instances, you might want to create a copy of data entered so that you can explore different values and compare the results of the original data set and the copied and edited data set.

In this section, you will learn how to select different ranges. Then you will learn how to move a range to another location, make a copy of a range, and use the Paste Special feature.

Selecting, Moving, Copying, and Pasting Data

You may already know the basics of selecting, cutting, copying, and pasting data in other programs, such as Microsoft Word. These tasks are somewhat different when working in Excel.

Select a Range

STEP 1》

A ***range*** refers to a group of adjacent or contiguous cells. A range may be as small as a single cell or as large as the entire worksheet. It may consist of a row or part of a row, a column or part of a column, or multiple rows or columns, but will always be a rectangular shape, as you must select the same number of cells in each row or column for the entire range. A range is specified by indicating the top-left and bottom-right cells in the selection. For example, in Figure 1.29, the date is a single-cell range in cell A2, the Color Laser Printer data are stored in the range A6:G6, the cost values are stored in the range B5:B10, and the sales prices and profit margins are stored in range F5:G10. A ***nonadjacent range*** contains multiple ranges, such as C5:C10 and E5:E10. At times, you need to select nonadjacent ranges so that you can apply the same formatting at the same time, such as formatting the nonadjacent range C5:C10 and E5:E10 with Percent Style.

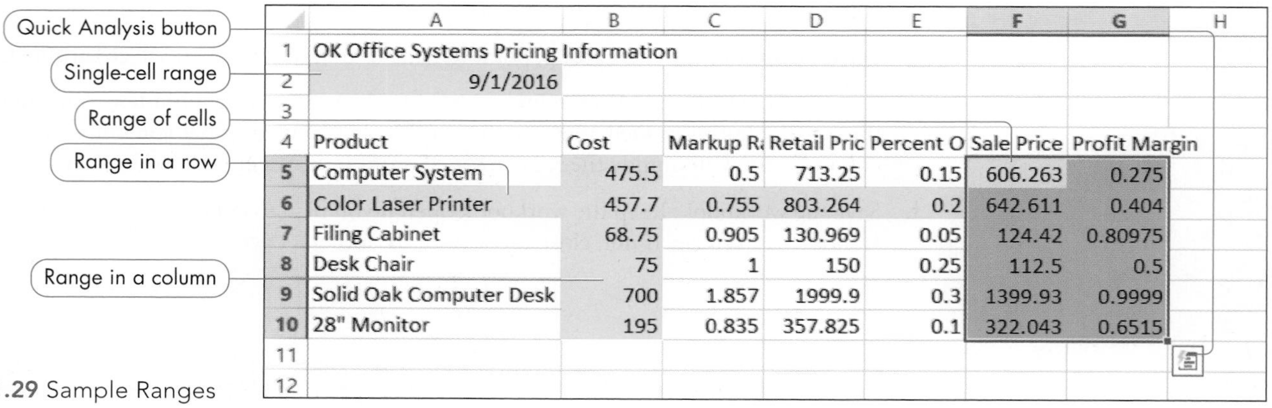

Quick Analysis button
Single-cell range
Range of cells
Range in a row
Range in a column

	A	B	C	D	E	F	G	H
1	OK Office Systems Pricing Information							
2	9/1/2016							
3								
4	Product	Cost	Markup R	Retail Pric	Percent O	Sale Price	Profit Margin	
5	Computer System	475.5	0.5	713.25	0.15	606.263	0.275	
6	Color Laser Printer	457.7	0.755	803.264	0.2	642.611	0.404	
7	Filing Cabinet	68.75	0.905	130.969	0.05	124.42	0.80975	
8	Desk Chair	75	1	150	0.25	112.5	0.5	
9	Solid Oak Computer Desk	700	1.857	1999.9	0.3	1399.93	0.9999	
10	28" Monitor	195	0.835	357.825	0.1	322.043	0.6515	
11								
12								

FIGURE 1.29 Sample Ranges

Table 1.4 lists methods you can use to select ranges, including nonadjacent ranges.

TABLE 1.4 Selecting Ranges	
To Select:	**Do This:**
A range	Drag until you select the entire range. Alternatively, click the first cell in the range, press and hold Shift, and then click the last cell in the range.
An entire column	Click the column heading.
An entire row	Click the row heading.
Current range containing data	Click in the range of data and press Ctrl+A.
All cells in a worksheet	Click Select All or press Ctrl+A twice.
Nonadjacent range	Select the first range, press and hold Ctrl, and then select additional range(s).

A green border appears around a selected range, and the Quick Analysis button displays in the bottom-right corner of the selected range. Any command you execute will affect the entire range. The range remains selected until you select another range or click in any cell in the worksheet.

Name Box

You can use the Name Box to select a range by clicking in the Name Box, typing a range address such as B15:D25, and then pressing Enter.

Move a Range to Another Location

STEP 1 You can move cell contents from one range to another. For example, you might need to move an input area from the right side of the worksheet to above the output range. When you move a range containing text and values, the text and values do not change. However, any formulas that refer to cells in that range will update to reflect the new cell addresses. To move a range, do the following:

1. Select the range.
2. Use the Cut command to copy the range to the Clipboard. Unlike cutting data in other Microsoft Office applications, the data you cut in Excel remain in their locations until you paste them elsewhere. After you click Cut, a moving dashed green border surrounds the selected range and the status bar displays *Select destination and press ENTER or choose Paste.*
3. Make sure the destination range—the range where you want to move the data—is the same size or greater than the size of the cut range. If any cells within the destination range contain data, Excel overwrites that data when you use the Paste command.
4. Click in the top-left corner of the destination range, and then use the Paste command to insert the data contained in the selected range and remove that data from the original range.

Copy and Paste a Range

STEP 2 You may need to copy cell contents from one range to another. For example, you might copy your January budget to another worksheet to use as a model for creating your February budget. When you copy a range, the original data remain in their original locations. Cell references in copied formulas adjust based on their relative locations to the original data. To copy a range, do the following:

1. Select the range.
2. Use the Copy command to copy the contents of the selected range to the Clipboard. After you click Copy, a moving dashed green border surrounds the selected range and the status bar displays *Select destination and press ENTER or choose Paste.*
3. Make sure the destination range—the range where you want to copy the data—is the same size or greater than the size of the copied range. If any cells within the destination range contain data, Excel overwrites that data when you use the Paste command.
4. Click in the top-left corner of the destination range where you want the duplicate data, and then use the Paste command. The original range still has the moving dashed green border, and the pasted copied range is selected with a solid green border. Figure 1.30 shows a selected range and a copy of the range.
5. Press Esc to turn off the moving dashed border around the originally selected range.

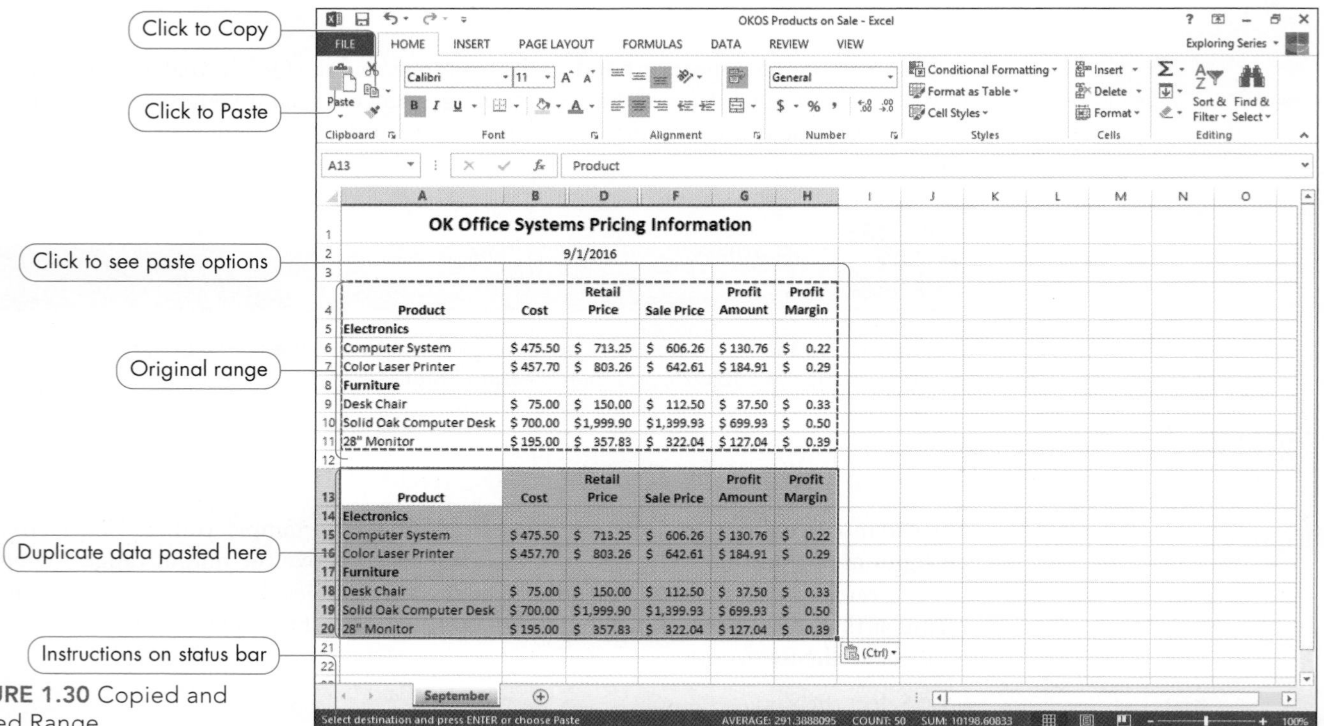

FIGURE 1.30 Copied and Pasted Range

TIP Copy as Picture

Instead of clicking Copy, if you click the Copy arrow in the Clipboard group, you can select Copy (the default option) or Copy as Picture. When you select Copy as Picture, you copy an image of the selected data. You can then paste the image elsewhere in the workbook or in a Word document or PowerPoint presentation. However, when you copy the data as an image, you cannot edit individual cell data after you paste the image.

Use Paste Options and Paste Special

STEP 3»

Sometimes you might want to paste data in a different format than they are in the Clipboard. For example, you might want to copy a range containing formulas and cell references, and paste the range as values in another workbook that does not have the referenced cells. If you want to copy data from Excel and paste them into a Word document, you can paste the Excel data as a worksheet object, as unformatted text, or in another format. To paste data from the Clipboard into a different format, click the Paste arrow in the Clipboard group, and hover over a command to see a ScreenTip and a preview of how the pasted data will look. In Figure 1.31, the preview shows that a particular paste option will maintain formulas and number formatting; however, it will not maintain the text formatting, such as font color and centered text. After previewing different paste options, click the one you want in order to apply it.

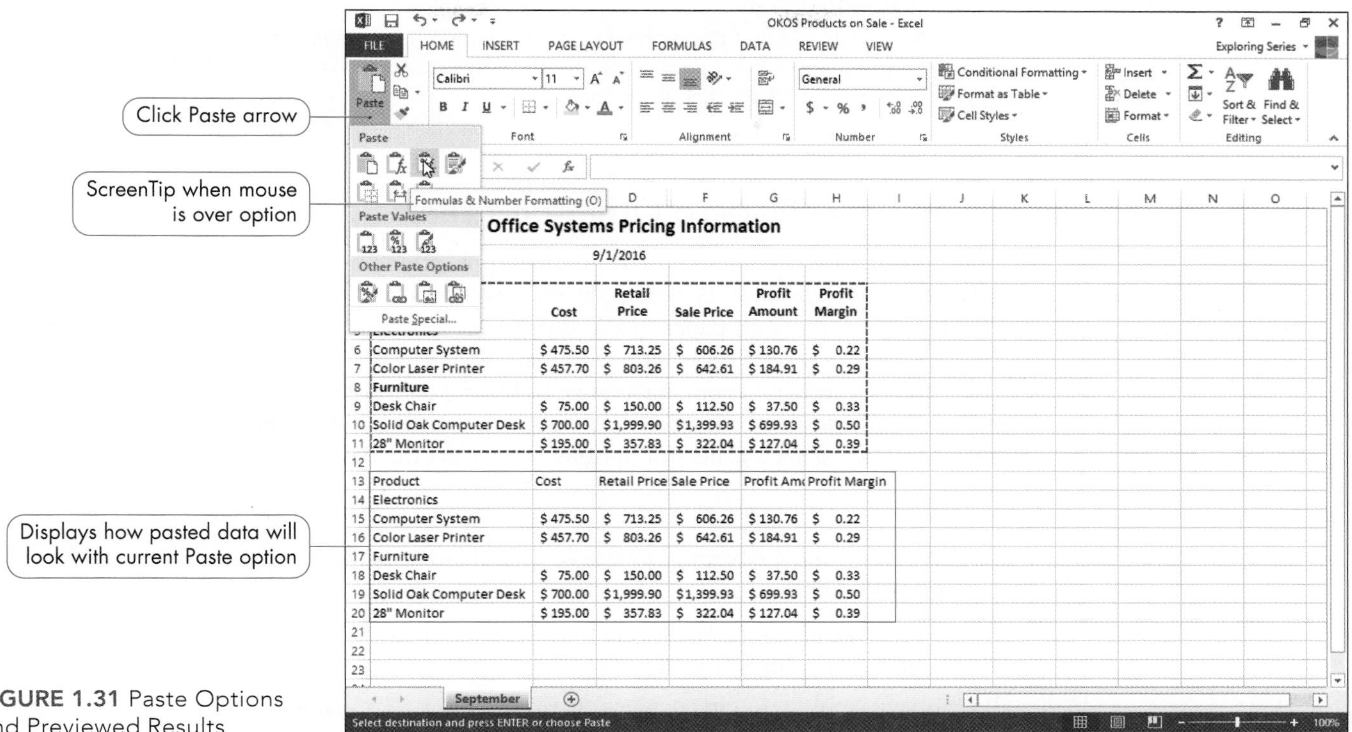

FIGURE 1.31 Paste Options and Previewed Results

For more specific paste options, click the Paste arrow, and then select Paste Special to display the Paste Special dialog box (see Figure 1.32). This dialog box contains more options than the Paste menu. Click the desired option and click OK.

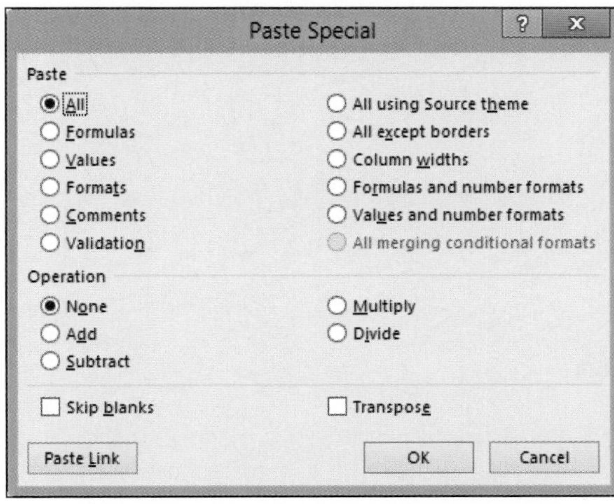

FIGURE 1.32 Paste Special Dialog Box

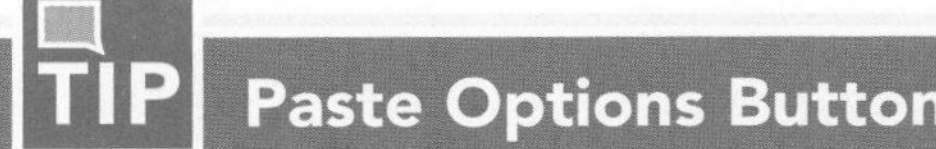

Paste Options Button

When you copy or paste data, Excel displays the ***Paste Options button*** in the bottom-right corner of the pasted data (refer to Figure 1.30). Click Paste Options to see different results for the pasted data.

Transposing Columns and Rows

After entering data into a worksheet, you might want to transpose the columns and rows so that the data in the first column appear as column labels across the first row, or the column labels in the first row appear in the first column. To transpose worksheet data, select and copy the original range, click the top-left corner of the destination range, click the Paste arrow, and then click Transpose.

Copy Excel Data to Other Programs

You can copy Excel data and use it in other applications, such as in a Word document or in a PowerPoint slide show. For example, you might perform statistical analyses in Excel, copy the data into a research paper in Word or create a budget in Excel, and then copy the data into a PowerPoint slide show for a meeting.

After selecting and copying a range in Excel, you must decide how you want the data to appear in the destination application. Click the Paste arrow in the destination application, such as Word, to see a gallery of options or to select the Paste Special option.

Quick Concepts

1. When you move or copy a worksheet, what are some of the decisions you must make? ***pp. 407–408***
2. How can you select nonadjacent ranges, such as B5:B10 and F5:F10? Why would you select nonadjacent ranges? ***pp. 406–407***
3. Why would you use the Paste Special options in Excel? ***p. 408***

Hands-On Exercises

4 Clipboard Tasks

You realize the 28" Monitor data is in the Furniture category instead of the Electronics category. You need to move the product to its appropriate location. In addition, your supervisor will ask you to enter data for a new product. Because it is almost identical to an existing product, you can copy the original data and edit the copied data to save time. You also want to experiment with the Paste Special option to see the results of using it in the OKOS workbook.

Skills covered: Select a Range and Move a Row to a New Location • Copy and Paste a Range • Use Paste Special

STEP 1 » SELECT A RANGE AND MOVE A ROW TO A NEW LOCATION

You want to move the 28" Monitor product to be immediately after the Color Laser Printer product. Before moving the 28" Monitor row, you need to insert a blank row between the Color Laser Printer and Furniture rows. Refer to Figure 1.33 as you complete Step 1.

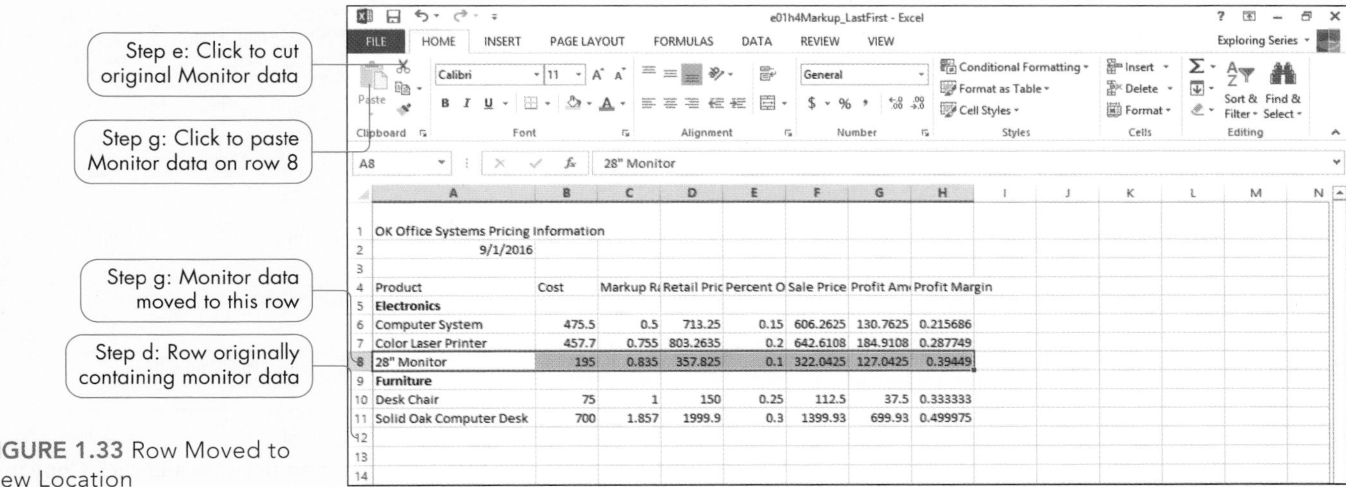

FIGURE 1.33 Row Moved to New Location

a. Open *e01h3Markup_LastFirst* if you closed it at the end of Hands-On Exercise 3 and save it as **e01h4Markup_LastFirst**, changing *h3* to *h4*.

b. Select the **column B, D, and F headings**. Unhide columns C and E as you learned in Hands-On Exercise 3.

You kept those columns hidden when you saved the *e01h3Markup_LastFirst* workbook to preserve evidence that you know how to hide columns. Now you need the columns visible to continue.

c. Right-click the **row 8 heading** and select **Insert** from the menu.

You need to insert a blank row so that you can move the *28" Computer Monitor* data to be between the *Color Laser Printer* and *Furniture* rows.

d. Select the **range A12:H12**.

You selected the range of cells containing the 28" Monitor data.

e. Click **Cut** in the Clipboard group.

A moving dashed green border outlines the selected range. The status bar displays the message *Select destination and press ENTER or choose Paste.*

f. Click **cell A8**, the new blank row you inserted in step c.

This is the first cell in the destination range.

g. Click **Paste** in the Clipboard group and save the workbook.

The 28" Monitor data are now located on row 8.

> **TROUBLESHOOTING:** If you cut and paste a row without inserting a new row first, Excel will overwrite the original row of data, which is why you inserted a new row in step c. If you forgot to do step c, click Undo until the 28" Monitor data is back in its original location and start with step c again.

STEP 2 COPY AND PASTE A RANGE

Alesha told you that a new chair is on its way. She asked you to enter the data for the Executive Desk Chair. Because most of the data is the same as the Desk Chair data, you will copy the original Desk Chair data, edit the product name, and then change the cost to reflect the cost of the second chair. Refer to Figure 1.34 as you complete Step 2.

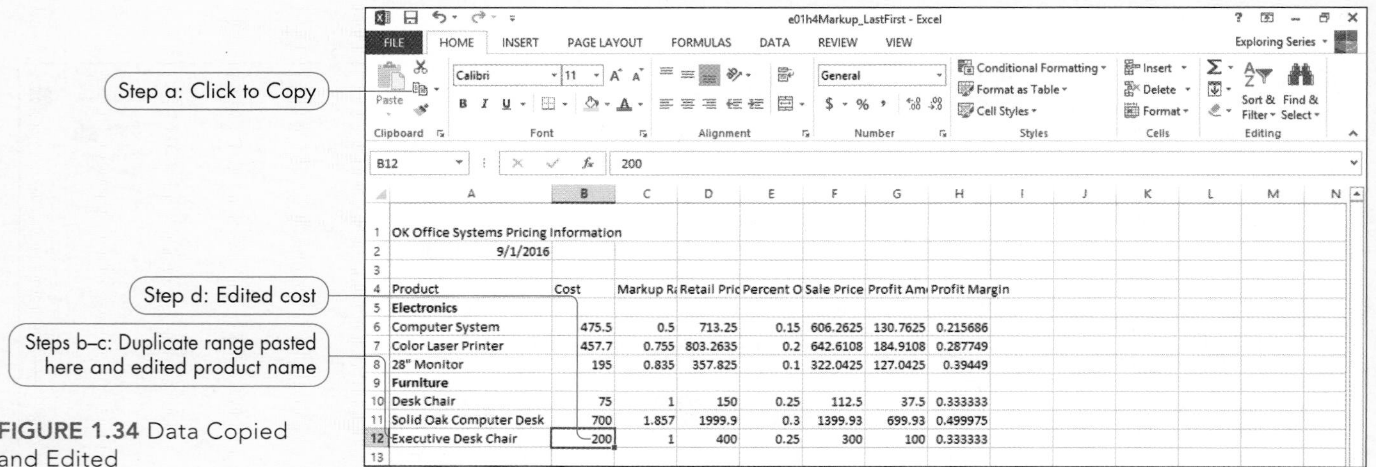

FIGURE 1.34 Data Copied and Edited

a. Select the **range A10:H10**, the row containing the Desk Chair product data, and click **Copy** in the Clipboard group.

b. Click **cell A12**, the location for the duplicate data, and click **Paste** in the Clipboard group. Press **Esc**.

The pasted range is selected in row 12.

c. Click **cell A12**, press **F2** to activate Edit Mode, press **Home**, type **Executive**, press **Spacebar**, and then press **Enter**.

You edited the product name.

d. Change the value in **cell B12** to **200**. Save the workbook.

The formulas calculate the results based on the new cost of 200 for the Executive Desk Chair.

STEP 3 ›› USE PASTE SPECIAL

During your lunch break, you want to experiment with some of the Paste Special options. Particularly, you are interested in pasting Formulas and Value & Source Formatting. First, you will bold the title and apply a font color to help you test these Paste Special options. Refer to Figure 1.35 as you complete Step 3.

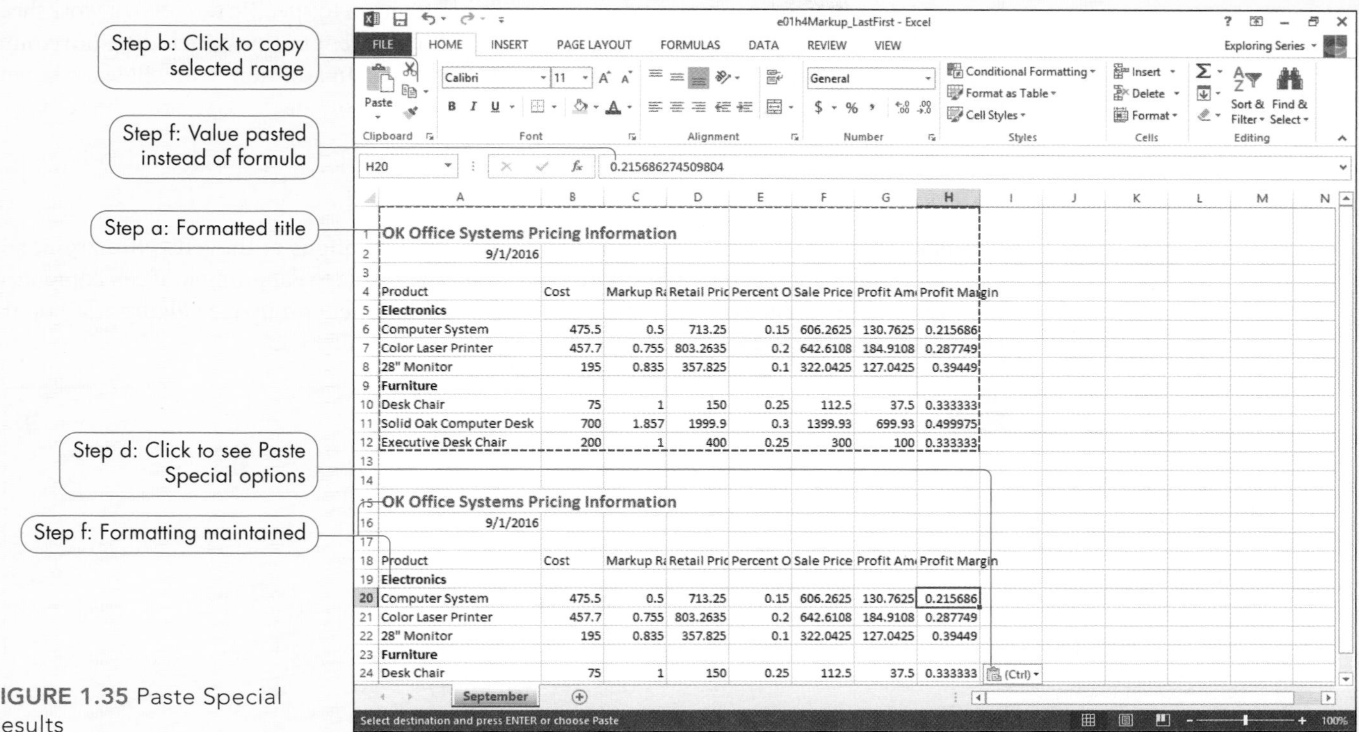

FIGURE 1.35 Paste Special Results

a. Click **cell A1**. Apply these font formats to the title: **14 pt**, **Bold**, and **Gold, Accent 4, Darker 50% font color** in the Font group on the HOME tab.

   You need to format text to see the effects of using different Paste Special options.

b. Select the **range A1:H12** and click **Copy** in the Clipboard group.

c. Click **cell A15**, the top-left corner of the destination range.

d. Click the **Paste arrow** in the Clipboard group and position the mouse pointer over *Formulas*.

   Without clicking the command, Excel shows you a preview of what that option would do. The pasted copy would not contain the font formatting you applied to the title or the bold on the two category names. In addition, the pasted date would appear as a serial number. The formulas would be maintained.

e. Position the mouse pointer over *Values & Source Formatting*.

   This option would preserve the formatting, but it would convert the formulas into the current value results.

f. Click **Values & Source Formatting**, click **cell H6** to see a formula, and then click **cell H20**. Press **Esc** to turn off the border.

   Cell H6 contains a formula, but in the pasted version, the equivalent cell H20 has converted the formula result into an actual value. If you were to change the original cost on row 20, the contents of cell H20 would not change. In a working environment, this is useful only if you want to capture the exact value in a point in time before making changes to the original data.

g. Save the workbook. Keep the workbook open if you plan to continue with the next Hands-On Exercise. If not, close the workbook and exit Excel.

Formatting

After entering data and formulas, you should format the worksheet. A professionally formatted worksheet—through adding appropriate symbols, aligning decimals, and using fonts and colors to make data stand out—makes finding and analyzing data easy. You apply different formats to accentuate meaningful details or to draw attention to specific ranges in a worksheet.

In this section, you will learn to apply different alignment options, including horizontal and vertical alignment, text wrapping, and indent options. In addition, you will learn how to format different types of values.

Applying Alignment and Font Options

Alignment refers to how data are positioned in cells. Text aligns at the left cell margin, and dates and values align at the right cell margin. You can change the alignment of cell contents to improve the appearance of data within the cells. The Alignment group (see Figure 1.36) on the Home tab contains several features to help you align and format data.

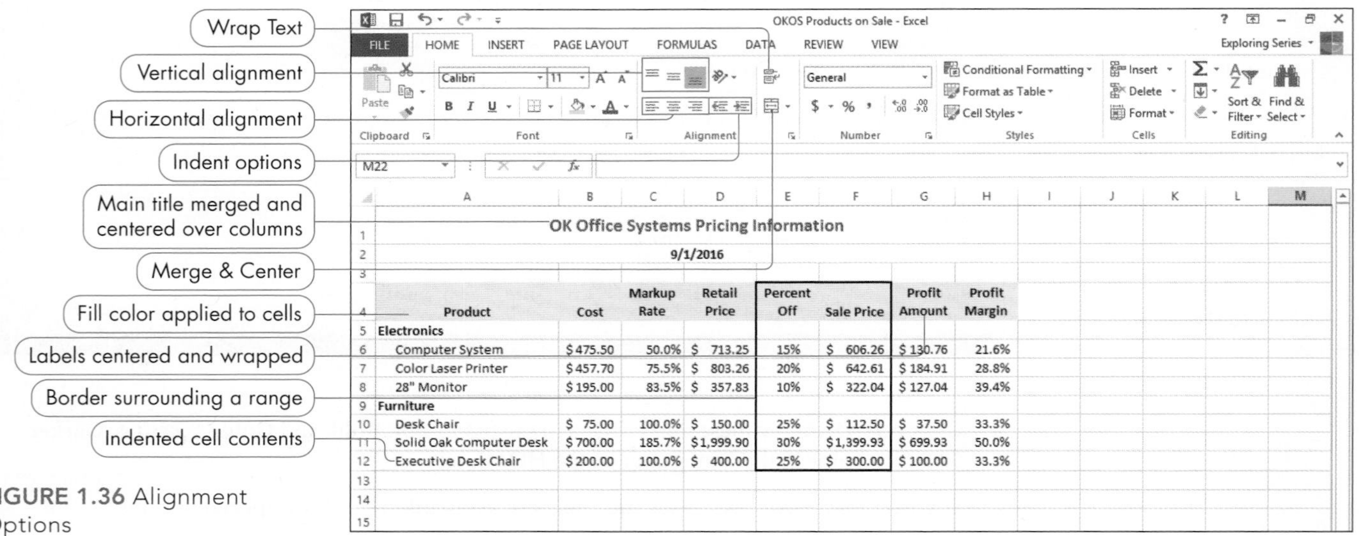

FIGURE 1.36 Alignment Options

> **TIP Alignment Options**
>
> The Format Cells dialog box contains additional alignment options. To open the Format Cells dialog box, click the Dialog Box Launcher in the Alignment group on the Home tab. The Alignment tab in the dialog box contains the options for aligning data.

Merge and Center Labels

STEP 1

You may want to place a title at the top of a worksheet and center it over the columns of data in the worksheet. You can center main titles over all columns in the worksheet, and you can center category titles over groups of related columns. To create a title, enter the text in the far left cell of the range. Select the range of cells across which you want to center the title and click Merge & Center in the Alignment group on the Home tab. Only data in the far left cell (or top right cell) are merged. Any other data in the merged cells are deleted. Excel merges the selected cells together into one cell, and the merged cell address is that of the original cell on the left. The data are centered between the left and right sides of the merged cell.

If you merge too many cells and want to split the merged cell back into its original multiple cells, click the merged cell and click Merge & Center. Unmerging places the data in the top-left cell.

For additional options, click the Merge & Center arrow. Table 1.5 lists the four merge options.

TABLE 1.5 Merge Options

Option	Results
Merge & Center	Merges selected cells and centers data into one cell.
Merge Across	Merges the selected cells but keeps text left aligned or values right aligned.
Merge Cells	Enables you to merge a range of cells on multiple rows as well as in multiple columns.
Unmerge Cells	Separates a merged cell into multiple cells again.

Change Horizontal and Vertical Cell Alignment

STEP 2»

Horizontal alignment specifies the position of data between the left and right cell margins, and ***vertical alignment*** specifies the position of data between the top and bottom cell margins. Bottom Align is the default vertical alignment (as indicated by the light green background), and Align Left is the default horizontal alignment for text. In Figure 1.36, the labels on row 4 have Center horizontal alignment and the title in row 1 has Middle Align vertical alignment.

If you increase row height, you might need to change the vertical alignment to position data better in conjunction with data in adjacent cells. To change alignments, click the desired alignment setting(s) in the Alignment group on the Home tab.

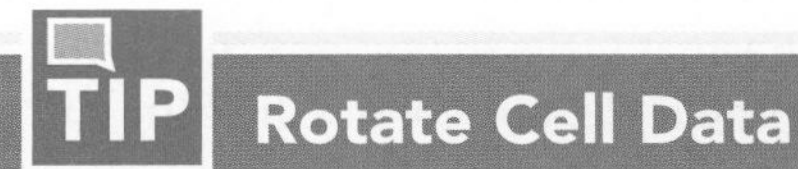

TIP Rotate Cell Data

People sometimes rotate headings in cells. You can rotate data in a cell by clicking Orientation in the Alignment group and selecting an option, such as Angle Clockwise.

Wrap Text

STEP 2»

Sometimes you have to maintain specific column widths, but the data do not fit entirely. You can use ***wrap text*** to make data appear on multiple lines by adjusting the row height to fit the cell contents within the column width. When you click Wrap Text in the Alignment group, Excel wraps the text on two or more lines within the cell. This alignment option is helpful when the column headings are wider than the values contained in the column. In Figure 1.36, the *Markup Rate* and *Percent Off* labels on row 4 are examples of wrapped text.

Increase and Decrease Indent

STEP 3»

To offset labels, you can indent text within a cell. ***Indenting*** helps others see the hierarchical structure of data. Accountants often indent the word *Totals* in financial statements so that it stands out from a list of items above the total row. To indent the contents of a cell, click Increase Indent in the Alignment group on the Home tab. The more you click Increase Indent, the more text is indented in the cell. To decrease the indent, click Decrease Indent in the Alignment group. In Figure 1.36, *Computer System* and *Desk Chair* are indented.

Indenting Values

Values right align by default. You should align the decimal places in a column of values. If the column label is wide, the values below it appear too far on the right. To preserve the values aligning at the decimal places, use the Align Right horizontal alignment and click Increase Indent to shift the values over to the left a little for better placement.

Apply Borders and Fill Color

STEP 4》 You can apply a border or fill color to accentuate data in a worksheet. A ***border*** is a line that surrounds a cell or a range of cells. You can use borders to offset some data from the rest of the worksheet data. To apply a border, select the cell or range that you want to have a border, click the Borders arrow in the Font group, and then select the desired border type. In Figure 1.36, a border surrounds the range E4:F12. To remove a border, select No Border from the Borders menu.

To add some color to your worksheet to add emphasis to data or headers, you can apply a fill color. ***Fill color*** is a background color that displays behind the data. You should choose a fill color that contrasts with the font color. For example, if the font color is Black, you might want to choose Yellow fill color. If the font color is White, you might want to apply Blue or Dark Blue fill color. To apply a fill color, select the cell or range that you want to have a fill color, click the Fill Color arrow on the Home tab, and then select the color choice from the Fill Color palette. In Figure 1.36, the column labels in row 4 contain the Gold, Accent 4, Lighter 80% fill color. If you want to remove a fill color, select No Fill from the bottom of the palette.

For additional border and fill color options, click the Dialog Box Launcher in the Font group to display the Format Cells dialog box. Click the Border tab to select border options, including the border line style and color. Click the Fill tab to set the background color, fill effects, and patterns.

Applying Number Formats

Values have no special formatting when you enter data. You should apply ***number formats*** based on the type of values in a cell, such as applying either the Accounting or Currency number format to monetary values. Changing the number format changes the way the number displays in a cell, but the format does not change the number's value. If, for example, you enter 123.456 into a cell and format the cell with the Currency number type, the value shows as $123.46 onscreen, but the actual value 123.456 is used for calculations. When you apply a number format, you can specify the number of decimal places to display onscreen.

Apply a Number Format

STEP 5》 The default number format is General, which displays values as you originally enter them. General does not align decimal points in a column or include symbols, such as dollar signs, percent signs, or commas. Table 1.6 lists and describes the primary number formats in Excel.

TABLE 1.6 Number Formats

Format Style	Display
General	A number as it was originally entered. Numbers are shown as integers (e.g., 12345), decimal fractions (e.g., 1234.5), or in scientific notation (e.g., 1.23E+10) if the number exceeds 11 digits.
Number	A number with or without the 1,000 separator (e.g., a comma) and with any number of decimal places. Negative numbers can be displayed with parentheses and/or red.
Currency	A number with the 1,000 separator and an optional dollar sign (which is placed immediately to the left of the number). Negative values are preceded by a minus sign or are displayed with parentheses or in red. Two decimal places display by default.
Accounting Number Format	A number with the 1,000 separator, an optional dollar sign (at the left border of the cell, vertically aligned within a column), negative values in parentheses, and zero values as hyphens. Two decimal places display by default. Changes alignment slightly within the cell.
Comma	A number with the 1,000 separator. Used in conjunction with Accounting Number Style to align commas and decimal places.
Date	The date in different ways, such as Long Date (March 14, 2016) or Short Date (3/14/16 or 14-Mar-16).
Time	The time in different formats, such as 10:50 PM or 22:50.
Percent Style	The value as it would be multiplied by 100 (for display purpose), with the percent sign. The default number of decimal places is zero if you click Percent Style in the Number group or two decimal places if you use the Format Cells dialog box. However, you should typically increase the number of decimal points to show greater accuracy.
Fraction	A number as a fraction; use when no exact decimal equivalent exists. A fraction is entered into a cell as a formula such as =1/3. If the cell is not formatted as a fraction, the formula results display.
Scientific	A number as a decimal fraction followed by a whole number exponent of 10; for example, the number 12345 would appear as 1.23E+04. The exponent, +04 in the example, is the number of places the decimal point is moved to the left (or right if the exponent is negative). Very small numbers have negative exponents.
Text	The data left aligned; is useful for numerical values that have leading zeros and should be treated as text, such as postal codes or phone numbers. Apply Text format before typing a leading zero so that the zero displays in the cell.
Special	A number with editing characters, such as hyphens in a Social Security number.
Custom	Predefined customized number formats or special symbols to create your own customized number format.

The Number group on the Home tab contains commands for applying ***Accounting Number Format***, ***Percent Style***, and ***Comma Style*** numbering formats. You can click the Accounting Number Format arrow and select other denominations, such as English pounds or euros. For other number formats, click the Number Format arrow and select the numbering format you want to use. For more specific numbering formats than those provided, select More Number Formats from the Number Format menu or click the Number Dialog Box Launcher to open the Format Cells dialog box with the Number tab options readily available. Figure 1.37 shows different number formats applied to values.

	A	B
1	General	1234.567
2	Number	1234.57
3	Currency	$1,234.57
4	Accounting	$ 1,234.57
5	Comma	1,234.57
6	Percent	12%
7	Short Date	3/1/2016
8	Long Date	Tuesday, March 1, 2016

FIGURE 1.37 Number Formats

Increase and Decrease Decimal Places

STEP 5»

After applying a number format, you may need to adjust the number of decimal places that display. For example, if you have an entire column of monetary values formatted in Accounting Number Format, Excel displays two decimal places by default. If the entire column of values contains whole dollar values and no cents, displaying *.00* down the column looks cluttered. You can decrease the number of decimal places to show whole numbers only.

To change the number of decimal places displayed, click Increase Decimal in the Number group on the Home tab to display more decimal places for greater precision or Decrease Decimal to display fewer or no decimal places.

Quick Concepts

1. What is the importance of formatting a worksheet? ***p. 414***
2. Describe five alignment and font formatting techniques used to format labels that are discussed in this section. ***pp. 414–416***
3. What are the main differences between Accounting Number Format and Currency format? Which format has its own command on the Ribbon? ***p. 417***

Hands-On Exercises

Watch the Video for this Hands-On Exercise!

MyITLab®
HOE5 Training

5 Formatting

In the first four Hands-On Exercises, you entered data about products on sale, created formulas to calculate markup and profit, and inserted new rows and columns to accommodate the labels *Electronics* and *Furniture* to identify the specific products. You are ready to format the worksheet. Specifically, you need to center the title, align text, format values, and then apply other formatting to enhance the readability of the worksheet.

Skills covered: Merge and Center the Title • Align Text Horizontally and Vertically and Wrap Text • Increase Indent • Apply Borders and Fill Color • Apply Number Formats and Increase and Decrease Decimal Places

STEP 1 » MERGE AND CENTER THE TITLE

To make the title stand out, you want to center it over all the data columns. You will use the Merge & Center command to merge cells and center the title at the same time. Refer to Figure 1.38 as you complete Step 1.

Step e: Date merged, centered, and bold A2:H2

	A	B	C	D	E	F	G	H	I
1	OK Office Systems Pricing Information								
2	9/1/2016								
3									
4	Product	Cost	Markup Ra	Retail Pric	Percent O	Sale Price	Profit Am	Profit Margin	
5	**Electronics**								
6	Computer System	475.5	0.5	713.25	0.15	606.2625	130.7625	0.215686	
7	Color Laser Printer	457.7	0.755	803.2635	0.2	642.6108	184.9108	0.287749	
8	28" Monitor	195	0.835	357.825	0.1	322.0425	127.0425	0.39449	
9	**Furniture**								
10	Desk Chair	75	1	150	0.25	112.5	37.5	0.333333	
11	Solid Oak Computer Desk	700	1.857	1999.9	0.3	1399.93	699.93	0.499975	
12	Executive Desk Chair	200	1	400	0.25	300	100	0.333333	
13									

FIGURE 1.38 Title and Date Merged and Centered

a. Open *e01h4Markup_LastFirst* if you closed it at the end of Hands-On Exercise 4 and save it as **e01h5Markup_LastFirst**, changing *h4* to *h5*.

b. Select the **range A15:H26** and press **Delete**.

You maintained a copy of your Paste Special results in the *e01h4Markup_LastFirst* workbook, but you do not need it to continue.

c. Select the **range A1:H1**.

You want to center the title over all columns of data.

d. Click **Merge & Center** in the Alignment group.

Excel merges cells in the range A1:H1 into one cell and centers the title horizontally within the merged cell, which is cell A1.

> **TROUBLESHOOTING:** If you merge too many or not enough cells, you can unmerge the cells and start again. To unmerge cells, click in the merged cell. The Merge & Center command is shaded in green when the active cell is merged. Click Merge & Center to unmerge the cell. Then select the correct range to merge and use Merge & Center again.

e. Select the **range A2:H2**. Merge and center the date and bold it.

> **TROUBLESHOOTING:** If you try to merge and center data in the range A1:H2, Excel will keep the top-left data only and delete the date. To merge separate data on separate rows, you must merge and center data separately.

f. Save the workbook.

STEP 2 » ALIGN TEXT HORIZONTALLY AND VERTICALLY AND WRAP TEXT

You will wrap the text in the column headings to avoid columns that are too wide for the data, but which will display the entire text of the column labels. In addition, you will horizontally center column labels between the left and right cell margins. Refer to Figure 1.39 as you complete Step 2.

Step d: Title with Middle (vertical) Align

Steps b–c: Column labels wrapped, centered, and bold

	A	B	C	D	E	F	G	H	I
1	OK Office Systems Pricing Information								
2	9/1/2016								
3									
4	**Product**	**Cost**	**Markup Rate**	**Retail Price**	**Percent Off**	**Sale Price**	**Profit Amount**	**Profit Margin**	
5	**Electronics**								
6	Computer System	475.5	0.5	713.25	0.15	606.2625	130.7625	0.215686	
7	Color Laser Printer	457.7	0.755	803.2635	0.2	642.6108	184.9108	0.287749	
8	28" Monitor	195	0.835	357.825	0.1	322.0425	127.0425	0.39449	
9	**Furniture**								
10	Desk Chair	75	1	150	0.25	112.5	37.5	0.333333	
11	Solid Oak Computer Desk	700	1.857	1999.9	0.3	1399.93	699.93	0.499975	
12	Executive Desk Chair	200	1	400	0.25	300	100	0.333333	
13									

FIGURE 1.39 Formatted Column Labels

a. Select the **range A4:H4** to select the column labels.

b. Click **Wrap Text** in the Alignment group.

   The multiple-word column headings are now visible on two lines within each cell.

c. Click **Center** in the Alignment group. Bold the selected column headings.

   The column headings are centered horizontally between the left and right edges of each cell.

d. Click **cell A1**, which contains the title, click **Middle Align** in the Alignment group, and then save the workbook.

   Middle Align vertically centers data between the top and bottom edges of the cell.

STEP 3 » INCREASE INDENT

As you review the first column, you notice that the category names, Electronics and Furniture, do not stand out. You decide to indent the labels within each category to better display which products are in each category. Refer to Figure 1.40 as you complete Step 3.

Step d: Column A width increased to 26.00

Step b: Electronics product labels indented twice

Step c: Furniture product labels indented twice

	A	B	C	D	E	F	G	H	I
1	OK Office Systems Pricing Information								
2	9/1/2016								
3									
4	Product	Cost	Markup Rate	Retail Price	Percent Off	Sale Price	Profit Amount	Profit Margin	
5	Electronics								
6	Computer System	475.5	0.5	713.25	0.15	606.2625	130.7625	0.215686	
7	Color Laser Printer	457.7	0.755	803.2635	0.2	642.6108	184.9108	0.287749	
8	28" Monitor	195	0.835	357.825	0.1	322.0425	127.0425	0.39449	
9	Furniture								
10	Desk Chair	75	1	150	0.25	112.5	37.5	0.333333	
11	Solid Oak Computer Desk	700	1.857	1999.9	0.3	1399.93	699.93	0.499975	
12	Executive Desk Chair	200	1	400	0.25	300	100	0.333333	
13									

FIGURE 1.40 Indented Cell Contents

a. Select the **range A6:A8**, the cells containing electronic products labels.

b. Click **Increase Indent** in the Alignment group twice.

The three selected product names are indented below the *Electronics* heading.

c. Select the **range A10:A12**, the cells containing furniture products, and click **Increase Indent** twice.

The three selected product names are indented below the *Furniture* heading. Notice that the one product name appears cut off.

d. Increase the column A width to **26.00**. Save the workbook.

STEP 4 » APPLY BORDERS AND FILL COLOR

You want to apply a light gold fill color to highlight the column headings. In addition, you want to emphasize the percent off and sale prices. You will do this by applying a border around that range. Refer to Figure 1.41 as you complete Step 4.

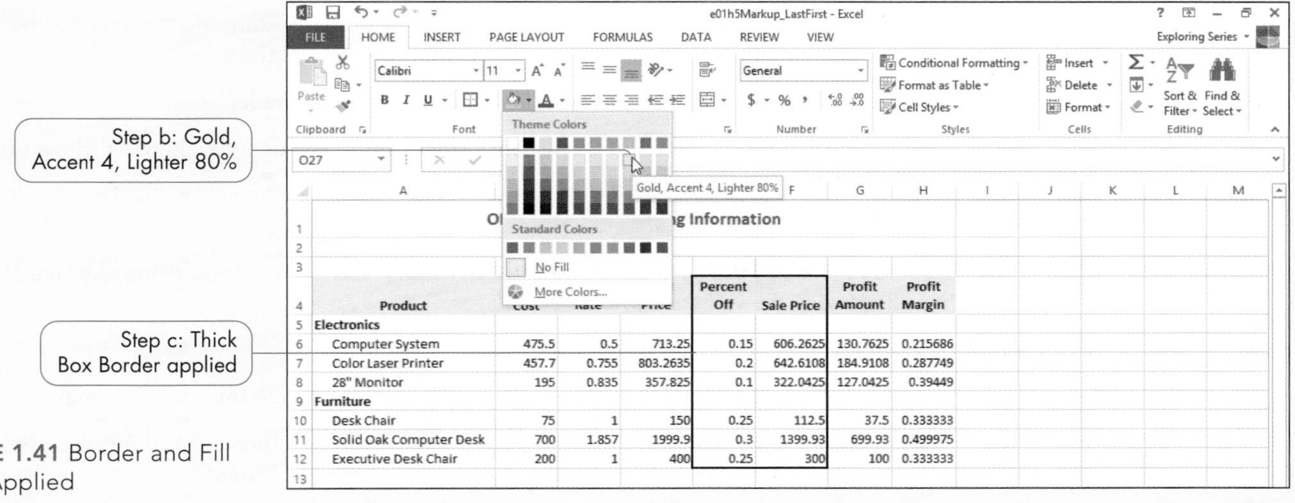

FIGURE 1.41 Border and Fill Color Applied

a. Select the **range A4:H4** and click the **Fill Color arrow** in the Font group.

b. Click **Gold, Accent 4, Lighter 80%** in the *Theme Colors* section. It is the second color down in the third column from the right.

You applied a fill color to the selected cells to draw attention to these cells.

c. Select the **range E4:F12**, click the **Border arrow** in the Font group, and then select **Thick Box Border**.

   You applied a border around the selected cells.

d. Click in an empty cell below the columns of data to deselect the cells. Save the workbook.

STEP 5 » APPLY NUMBER FORMATS AND INCREASE AND DECREASE DECIMAL PLACES

You need to format the values to increase readability and look more professional. You will apply number formats and adjust the number of decimal points displayed. Refer to Figure 1.42 as you complete Step 5.

Step f: Percent Style, Align Right, Indent twice

Step e: Percent Style

Steps c–d: Percent Style with one decimal place

Step b: Accounting Number Format

	A	B	C	D	E	F	G	H	I
1	OK Office Systems Pricing Information								
2	9/1/2016								
3									
4	Product	Cost	Markup Rate	Retail Price	Percent Off	Sale Price	Profit Amount	Profit Margin	
5	Electronics								
6	Computer System	$ 475.50	50.0%	$ 713.25	15%	$ 606.26	$ 130.76	21.6%	
7	Color Laser Printer	$ 457.70	75.5%	$ 803.26	20%	$ 642.61	$ 184.91	28.8%	
8	28" Monitor	$ 195.00	83.5%	$ 357.83	10%	$ 322.04	$ 127.04	39.4%	
9	Furniture								
10	Desk Chair	$ 75.00	100.0%	$ 150.00	25%	$ 112.50	$ 37.50	33.3%	
11	Solid Oak Computer Desk	$ 700.00	185.7%	$1,999.90	30%	$1,399.93	$ 699.93	50.0%	
12	Executive Desk Chair	$ 200.00	100.0%	$ 400.00	25%	$ 300.00	$ 100.00	33.3%	
13									

FIGURE 1.42 Number Formats and Decimal Places

a. Select the **range B6:B12.** Press and hold **Ctrl** as you select the **ranges D6:D12** and **F6:G12.**

   Because you want to format nonadjacent ranges with the same formats, you hold down Ctrl.

b. Click **Accounting Number Format** in the Number group. If some cells contain pound signs, increase the column widths as needed.

   You formatted the selected nonadjacent ranges with the Accounting Number Format. The dollar signs align on the left cell margins and the decimals align.

c. Select the **range C6:C12** and click **Percent Style** in the Number group.

   You formatted the values in the selected ranges with Percent Style, showing whole numbers only.

d. Click **Increase Decimal** in the Number group.

   You increased the decimal to show one decimal place to avoid misleading your readers by displaying the values as whole percentages.

e. Apply **Percent Style** to the **range E6:E12**.

f. Select the **range H6:H12**, apply **Percent Style**, and then click **Increase Decimal**.

g. Select the **range E6:E12**, click **Align Right**, and then click **Increase Indent** twice. Select the **range H6:H12**, click **Align Right**, and then click **Increase Indent**.

   With values, you want to keep the decimal points aligned, but you can then use Increase Indent to adjust the indent so that the values appear more centered below the column labels.

h. Save the workbook. Keep the workbook open if you plan to continue with the next Hands-On Exercise. If not, close the workbook and exit Excel.

Page Setup and Printing

Although you might distribute workbooks electronically as e-mail attachments or you might upload workbooks to a corporate server, you should prepare the worksheets in the workbook for printing. You should prepare worksheets in case you need to print them or in case others who receive an electronic copy of your workbook need to print the worksheets. The Page Layout tab provides options for controlling the printed worksheet (see Figure 1.43).

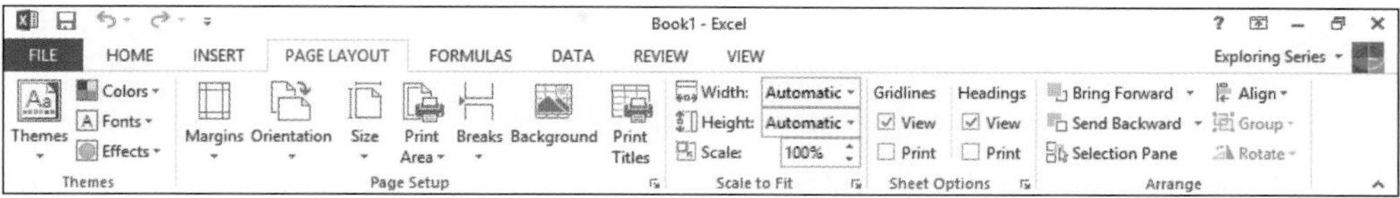

FIGURE 1.43 Page Layout Tab

In this section, you will select options on the Page Layout tab. Specifically, you will use the Page Setup, Scale to Fit, and Sheet Options groups. After selecting page setup options, you are ready to print your worksheet.

Selecting Page Setup Options

The Page Setup group on the Page Layout tab contains options to set the margins, select orientation, specify page size, select the print area, and apply other options. The *Scale to Fit* group contains options for adjusting the scaling of the spreadsheet on the printed page. When possible, use the commands in these groups to apply page settings. Table 1.7 lists and describes the commands in the Page Setup group.

TABLE 1.7 Page Setup Commands

Command	Description
Margins	Displays a menu to select predefined margin settings. The default margins are 0.75" top and bottom and 0.7" left and right. You will often change these margin settings to balance the worksheet data better on the printed page. If you need different margins, select Custom Margins.
Orientation	Displays orientation options. The default page orientation is portrait, which is appropriate for worksheets that contain more rows than columns. Select landscape orientation when worksheets contain more columns than can fit in portrait orientation. For example, the OKOS worksheet might appear better balanced in landscape orientation because it has eight columns.
Size	Displays a list of standard paper sizes. The default size is 8 1/2" by 11". If you have a different paper size, such as legal paper, select it from the list.
Print Area	Displays a list to set or clear the print area. When you have very large worksheets, you might want to print only a portion of that worksheet. To do so, select the range you want to print, click Print Area in the Page Setup group, and then select Set Print Area. When you use the Print commands, only the range you specified will be printed. To clear the print area, click Print Area and select Clear Print Area.
Breaks	Displays a list to insert or remove page breaks.
Background	Enables you to select an image to appear as the background behind the worksheet data when viewed onscreen (backgrounds do not appear when the worksheet is printed).
Print Titles	Enables you to select column headings and row labels to repeat on multiple-page printouts.

Specify Page Options

STEP 1» To apply several page setup options at once or to access options not found on the Ribbon, click the Page Setup Dialog Box Launcher. The Page Setup dialog box organizes options into four tabs: Page, Margins, Header/Footer, and Sheet. All tabs contain Print and Print Preview buttons. Figure 1.44 shows the Page tab.

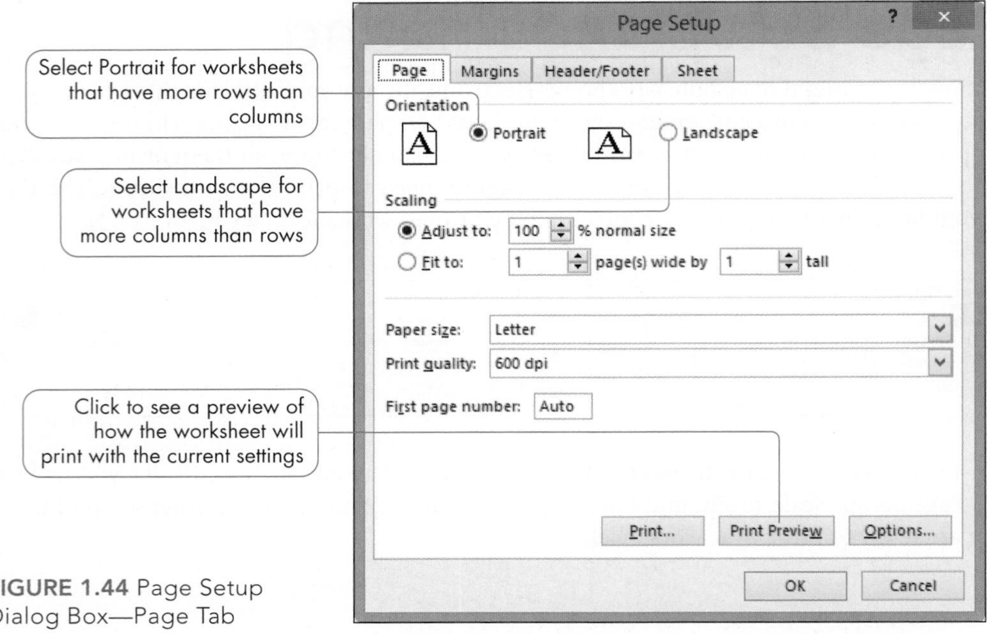

FIGURE 1.44 Page Setup Dialog Box—Page Tab

The Page tab contains options to select the orientation and paper size. In addition, it contains scaling options that are similar to the options in the *Scale to Fit* group on the Page Layout tab. You use scaling options to increase or decrease the size of characters on a printed page, similar to using a zoom setting on a photocopy machine. You can also use the *Fit to* option to force the data to print on a specified number of pages.

Set Margins Options

STEP 2»

The Margins tab (see Figure 1.45) contains options for setting the specific margins. In addition, it contains options to center the worksheet data horizontally or vertically on the page. To balance worksheet data equally between the left and right margins, Excel users often center the page horizontally.

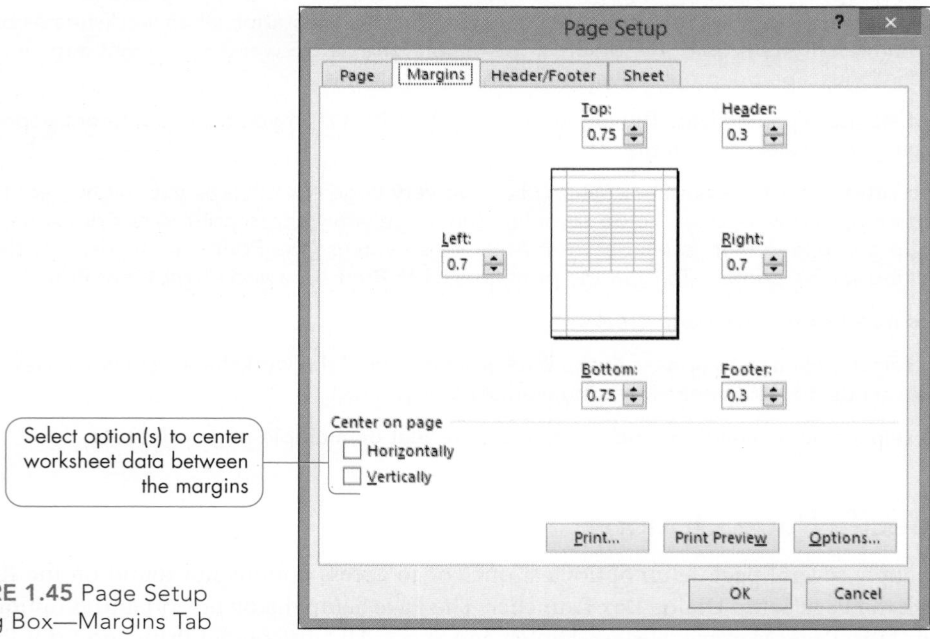

FIGURE 1.45 Page Setup Dialog Box—Margins Tab

Create Headers and Footers

STEP 3»

The Header/Footer tab (see Figure 1.46) lets you create a header and/or footer that appears at the top and/or bottom of every printed page. Click the arrows to choose from several preformatted entries, or alternatively, you can click Custom Header or Custom Footer, insert text and other objects, and then click the appropriate formatting button to customize your headers and footers. You can use headers and footers to provide additional information about the worksheet. You can include your name, the date the worksheet was prepared, and page numbers, for example.

You can create different headers or footers on different pages, such as one header with the file name on odd-numbered pages and a header containing the date on even-numbered pages. Click the *Different odd and even pages* check box in the Page Setup dialog box (see Figure 1.46).

You might want the first page to have a different header or footer from the rest of the printed pages, or you might not want a header or footer to show up on the first page but want the header or footer to display on the remaining pages. Click the *Different first page* check box in the Page Setup dialog box to specify a different first page header or footer (see Figure 1.46).

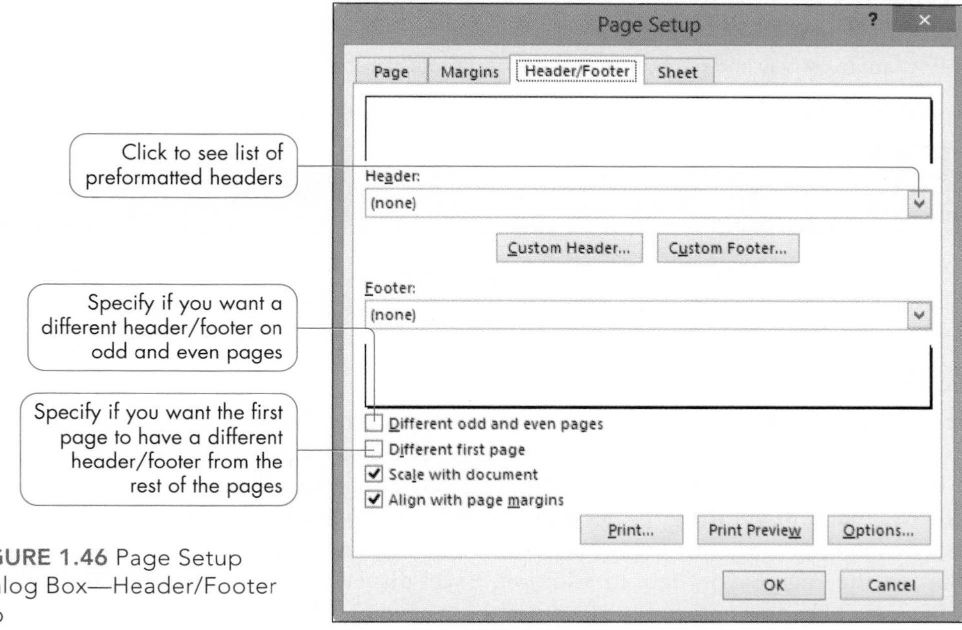

FIGURE 1.46 Page Setup Dialog Box—Header/Footer Tab

Instead of creating headers and footers using the Page Setup dialog box, you can click the Insert tab and click Header & Footer in the Text group. Excel displays the worksheet in Page Layout view with the insertion point in the center area of the header. You can click inside the left, center, or right section of a header or footer. When you do, Excel displays the Header & Footer Tools Design contextual tab (see Figure 1.47). You can enter text or insert data from the Header & Footer Elements group on the tab. Table 1.8 lists and describes the options in the Header & Footer Elements group. To get back to Normal view, click any cell in the worksheet and click Normal in the Workbook Views group on the View tab.

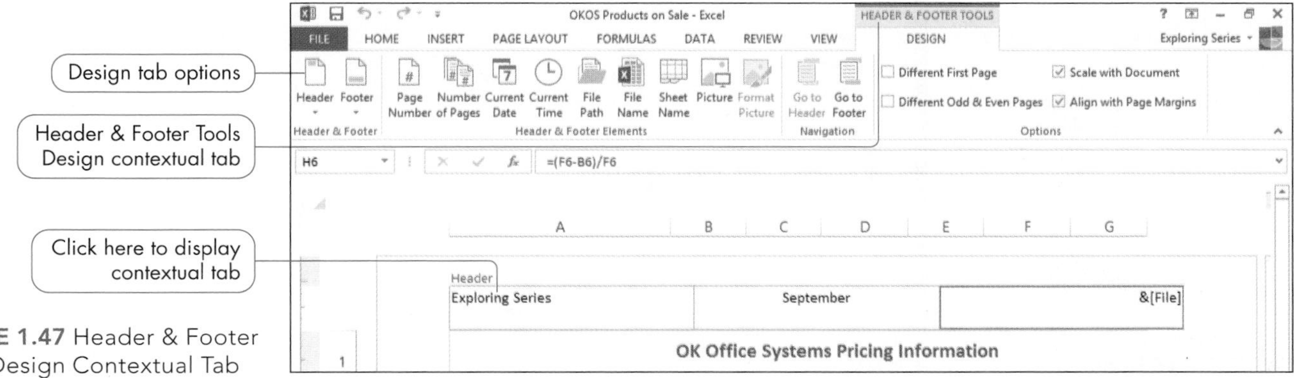

FIGURE 1.47 Header & Footer Tools Design Contextual Tab

TABLE 1.8 Header & Footer Elements Options	
Option Name	**Result**
Page Number	Inserts the code &[Page] to display the current page number.
Number of Pages	Inserts the code &[Pages] to display the total number of pages that will print.
Current Date	Inserts the code &[Date] to display the current date, such as 5/19/2016. The date updates to the current date when you open or print the worksheet.
Current Time	Inserts the code &[Time] to display the current time, such as 5:15 PM. The time updates to the current time when you open or print the worksheet.
File Path	Inserts the code &[Path]&[File] to display the path and file name, such as C:\Documents\e01h4Markup. This information changes if you save the workbook with a different name or in a different location.
File Name	Inserts the code &[File] to display the file name, such as e01h4Markup. This information changes if you save the workbook with a different name.
Sheet Name	Inserts the code &[Tab] to display the worksheet name, such as September. This information changes if you rename the worksheet.
Picture	Inserts the code &[Picture] to display and print an image as a background behind the data, not just the worksheet.
Format Picture	Enables you to adjust the brightness, contrast, and size of an image after you use the Picture option.

TIP View Tab

If you click the View tab and click Page Layout, Excel displays an area *Click to add header* at the top of the worksheet.

Select Sheet Options

STEP 5» The Sheet tab (see Figure 1.48) contains options for setting the print area, print titles, print options, and page order. Some of these options are also located in the Sheet Options group on the Page Layout tab on the Ribbon. By default, Excel displays gridlines onscreen to show you each cell's margins, but the gridlines do not print unless you specifically select the Gridlines check box in the Page Setup dialog box or the Print Gridlines check box in the Sheet Options group on the Page Layout tab. In addition, Excel displays row (1, 2, 3, etc.) and column (A, B, C, etc.) headings onscreen. However, these headings do not print unless you click the *Row and column headings* check box in the Page Setup dialog box or click the Print Headings check box in the Sheet Options group on the Page Layout tab.

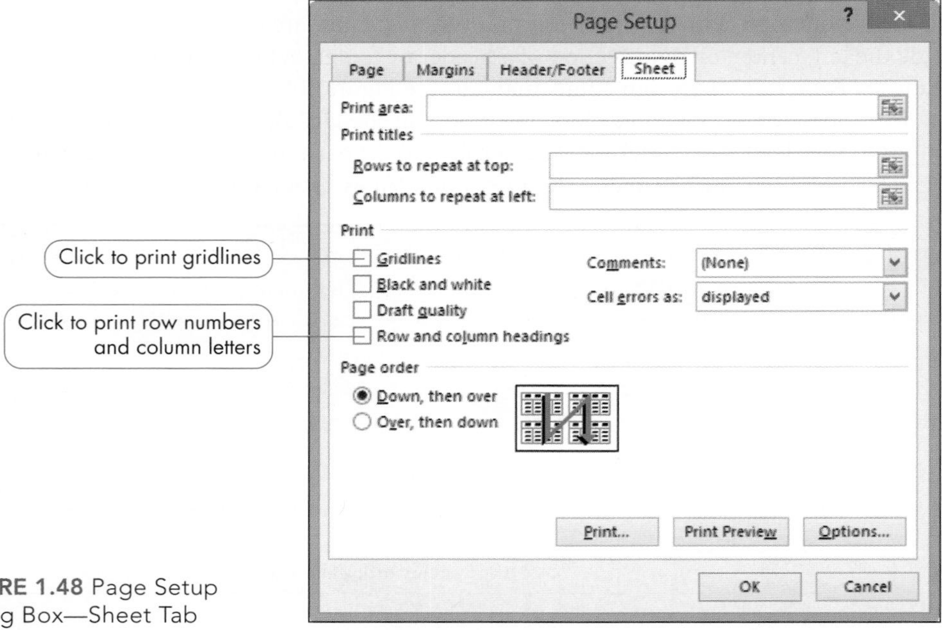

FIGURE 1.48 Page Setup Dialog Box—Sheet Tab

TIP Printing Gridlines and Headings

For most worksheets, you do not need to print gridlines and row/column headings. However, when you want to display and print cell formulas instead of formula results, you might want to print the gridlines and row/column headings. Doing so will help you analyze your formulas. The gridlines help you see the cell boundaries, and the headings help you identify what data are in each cell. At times, you might want to display gridlines to separate data on a regular printout to increase readability.

Previewing and Printing a Worksheet

STEP 4»

Before printing a worksheet, you should click the File tab and select Print. The Microsoft Office Backstage view displays print options and displays the worksheet in print preview mode. This mode helps you see in advance if the data are balanced on the page or if data will print on multiple pages.

You can specify the number of copies to print and which printer to use to print the worksheet. The first option in the Settings area enables you to specify what to print. The default option is Print Active Sheets. You can choose other options, such as Print Entire Workbook or Print Selection. You can also specify which pages to print. If you are connected to a printer capable of duplex printing, you can print on only one side or print on both sides. You can also collate, change the orientation, specify the paper size, adjust the margins, and adjust the scaling.

The bottom of the Print window indicates how many pages will print. If you do not like how the worksheet will print, click the Page Layout tab so that you can adjust margins, scaling, column widths, and so on until the worksheet data appear the way you want them to print.

TIP Printing Multiple Worksheets

To print more than one worksheet at a time, select the sheets you want to print. To select adjacent sheets, click the first sheet tab, press and hold Shift, and then click the last sheet tab. To select nonadjacent sheets, press and hold Ctrl as you click each sheet tab. When you display the Print options in the Microsoft Office Backstage view, Print Active Sheets is one of the default settings. If you want to print all of the worksheets within the workbook, change the setting to Print Entire Workbook.

Quick Concepts

1. What helps determine whether you use portrait or landscape orientation for a worksheet? ***p. 424***
2. Why would you select a *Center on page* option if you have already set the margins? ***p. 424***
3. List at least five elements you can insert in a header or footer. ***p. 426***
4. Why would you want to print gridlines and row and column headings? ***p. 427***

Hands-On Exercises

Watch the Video for this Hands-On Exercise!

MyITLab®
HOE6 Training

6 Page Setup and Printing

You are ready to complete the OKOS worksheet. Before printing the worksheet for your supervisor, you want to make sure the data will appear professional when printed. You will adjust some page setup options to put the finishing touches on the worksheet.

Skills covered: Set Page Orientation • Set Margin Options • Create a Header • View in Print Preview and Print • Adjust Scaling and Set Sheet Options

STEP 1 » SET PAGE ORIENTATION

Because the worksheet has several columns, you decide to print it in landscape orientation.

a. Open *e01h5Markup_LastFirst* if you closed it at the end of Hands-On Exercise 5 and save it as **e01h6Markup_LastFirst**, changing *h5* to *h6*.

b. Click the **PAGE LAYOUT tab**.

c. Click **Orientation** in the Page Setup group.

d. Select **Landscape** from the list. Save the workbook.

   If you print the worksheet, the data will print in landscape orientation.

STEP 2 » SET MARGIN OPTIONS

You want to set a 1" top margin and center the data between the left and right margins.

a. Click **Margins** in the Page Setup group on the PAGE LAYOUT tab.

   As you review the list of options, you notice the list does not contain an option to center the worksheet data horizontally.

b. Select **Custom Margins**.

   The Page Setup dialog box opens with the Margins tab options displayed.

c. Click the **Top spin arrow** to display **1**.

   You set a 1" top margin. For the OKOS worksheet, you do not need to change the left and right margins because you will center the worksheet data horizontally between the original margins.

d. Click the **Horizontally check box** in the *Center on page* section and click **OK**. Save the workbook.

   The worksheet data are centered between the left and right margins.

TIP

Page Setup Dialog Box

You can click the Page Setup Dialog Box Launcher in the Page Setup group to quickly display the Page Setup dialog box. From there, you can click the Margins tab and set the desired margins.

STEP 3 » CREATE A HEADER

To document the worksheet, you want to include your name, the current date, and the worksheet tab name in a header. Refer to Figure 1.49 as you complete Step 3.

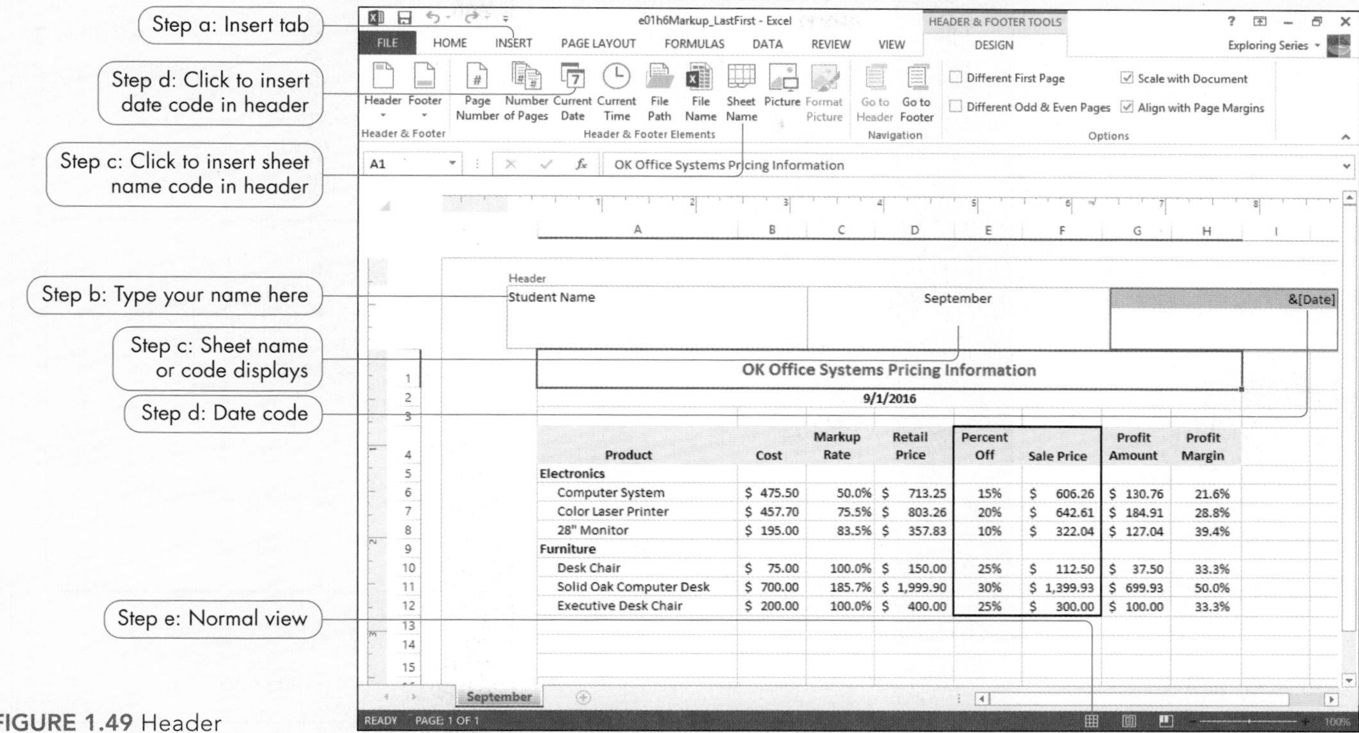

FIGURE 1.49 Header

a. Click the **INSERT tab** and click **Header & Footer** in the Text group.

Excel displays the DESIGN tab and the worksheet displays in Page Layout view, which displays the header area, margin space, and ruler. The insertion point blinks inside the center section of the header.

b. Click in the left section of the header and type your name.

c. Click in the center section of the header and click **Sheet Name** in the Header & Footer Elements group on the DESIGN tab.

Excel inserts the code &[Tab]. This code displays the name of the worksheet. If you change the worksheet tab name, the header will reflect the new sheet name.

d. Click in the right section of the header and click **Current Date** in the Header & Footer Elements group on the DESIGN tab.

Excel inserts the code &[Date]. This code displays the current date based on the computer clock when you print the worksheet. If you want a specific date to appear regardless of the date you open or print the worksheet, you would have to type that date manually. When you click in a different header section, the codes, such as &[Tab], display the actual tab name instead of the code.

e. Click in any cell in the worksheet, click **Normal** on the status bar, and then save the workbook.

Normal view displays the worksheet, but does not display the header or margins.

STEP 4 » VIEW IN PRINT PREVIEW AND PRINT

Before printing the worksheet, you should preview it. Doing so helps you detect margin problems and other issues, such as a single row or column of data flowing onto a new page. Refer to Figure 1.50 as you complete Step 4.

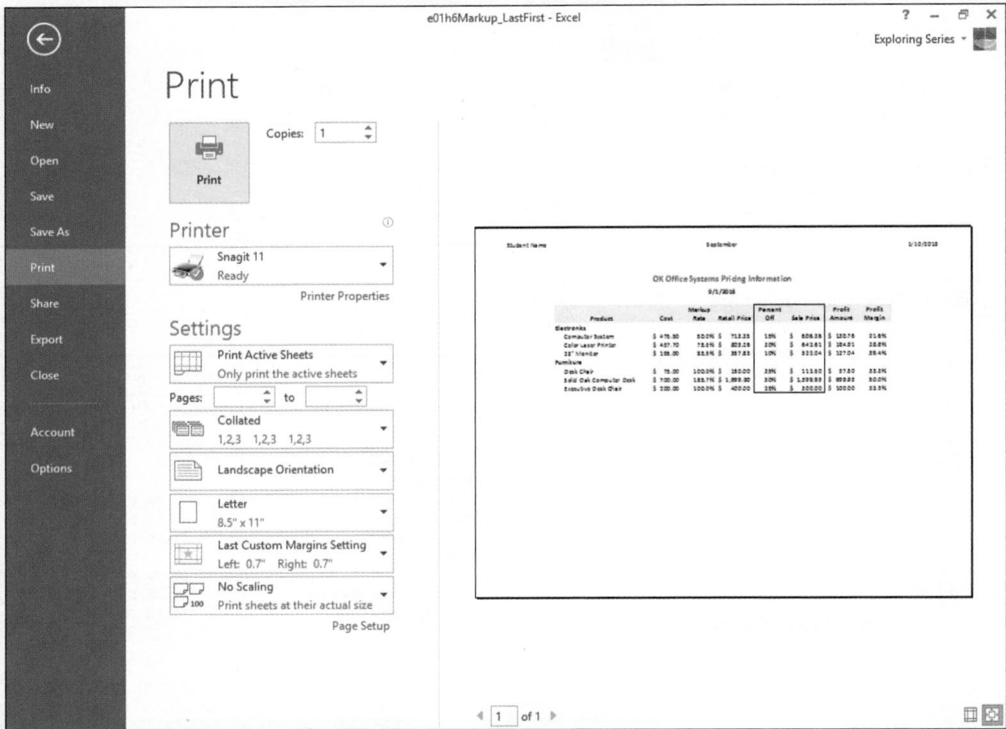

FIGURE 1.50 Worksheet in Print Preview

a. Click the **FILE tab** and click **Print**.

   The Microsoft Office Backstage view displays print options and a preview of the worksheet.

b. Verify the Printer box displays the printer that you want to use to print your worksheet.

c. Click **Print** to print the worksheet and save the workbook.

   Check your printed worksheet to make sure the data are formatted correctly. After you click Print, the HOME tab displays. If you decide not to print at this time, click the **Back arrow** to display the Ribbon again.

STEP 5 » ADJUST SCALING AND SET SHEET OPTIONS

You want to print a copy of the worksheet formulas to check the logic of the formulas. You need to display the formulas, select options to print gridlines and headings, and then decrease the scaling so that the data print on one page. Refer to Figure 1.51 as you complete Step 5.

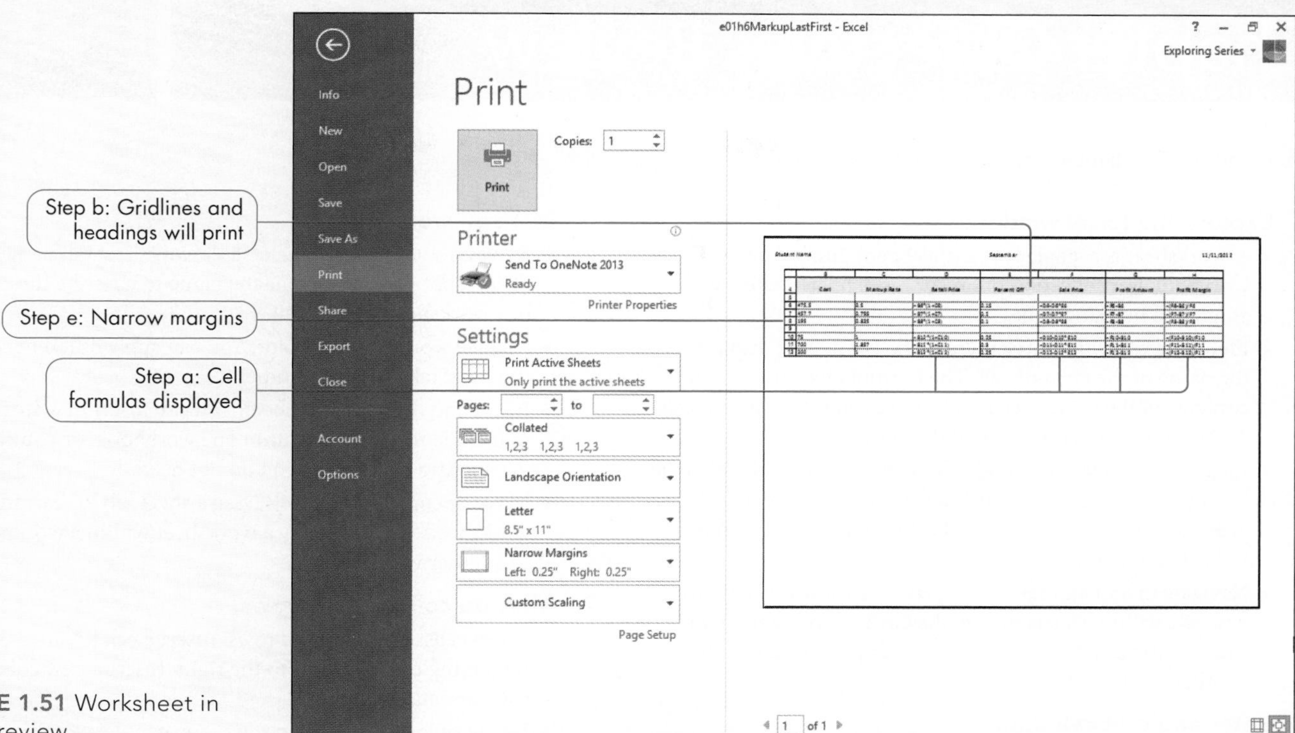

FIGURE 1.51 Worksheet in Print Preview

a. Press **Ctrl+`** to display cell formulas.

b. Click the **PAGE LAYOUT tab**. Click the **Print Gridlines check box** in the Sheet Options group and click the **Print Headings check box** in the Sheet Options group.

   Because you want to print cell formulas, it is helpful to display the gridlines and row and column headings on that printout.

c. Click the **FILE tab** and click **Print**.

   The bottom of the Print Preview displays 1 of 2, indicating the worksheet no longer prints on one page.

d. Click **Next Page** (the right triangle at the bottom of the Microsoft Office Backstage view) to view the contents of the second page and click the **Back arrow** to display the Ribbon again.

e. Click **Margins** in the Page Setup group and select **Narrow**.

f. Select the **range B4:H12**, click **Print Area** in the Page Setup group, and then select **Set Print Area**.

g. Click the **Scale spin arrow** in the *Scale to Fit* group on the PAGE LAYOUT tab until it displays **90%**.

   If you want to verify that the worksheet will print on one page, display it in print preview.

h. Save and close the workbook and submit based on your instructor's directions.

   Check your printed worksheet to make sure the data are formatted correctly.

Chapter Objectives Review

After reading this chapter, you have accomplished the following objectives:

1. **Explore the Excel window.**
   - A worksheet is a single spreadsheet containing data. A workbook is a collection of one or more related worksheets contained in a single file.
   - Identify Excel window elements: The Name Box displays the name of the current cell. The Formula Bar displays the contents of the current cell. The active cell is the current cell. A sheet tab shows the name of the worksheet.
   - Identify columns, rows, and cells: Columns have alphabetical headings, such as A, B, C. Rows have numbers, such as 1, 2, 3. A cell is the intersection of a column and row and is indicated like A5.
   - Navigate in and among worksheets: Use the arrow keys to navigate within a sheet, or use the Go To command to go to a specific cell. Click a sheet tab to display the contents on another worksheet.
2. **Enter and edit cell data.**
   - You should plan the worksheet design by stating the purpose, deciding what input values are needed, and then deciding what outputs are needed. Next, you enter and format data in a worksheet. Finally, you document, save, and then share a workbook.
   - Enter text: Text may contain letters, numbers, symbols, and spaces. Text aligns at the left side of a cell.
   - Enter values: Values are numbers that represent a quantity. Values align at the right side of a cell by default.
   - Enter dates: Excel stores dates as serial numbers so that you can calculate the number of days between dates.
   - Enter formulas: A formula is used to perform calculations. The formula results display in the cells.
   - Edit and clear contents: You can clear the cell contents and/or formats.
3. **Create formulas.**
   - Use cell references in formulas: Use references, such as =B5+B6, instead of values within formulas.
   - Apply the order of precedence: The most commonly used operators are performed in this sequence: Exponentiation, Multiplication, Division, Addition, and Subtraction. Use parentheses to perform a lower operation first.
   - Use semi-selection to create a formula: When building a formula, you can click a cell containing a value to enter that cell reference in the formula.
4. **Use Auto Fill.**
   - Copy formulas with Auto Fill: To copy a formula down a column or across a row, double-click or drag the fill handle.
   - Complete sequences with Auto Fill: Use Auto Fill to copy formulas, number patterns, month names, etc.
5. **Display cell formulas.**
   - By default, the results of formulas appear in cells.
   - You can display formulas by pressing Ctrl+`.
6. **Manage worksheets.**
   - Rename a worksheet: The default worksheet tab name is Sheet1, but you can change the name to describe the contents of a worksheet.
   - Change worksheet tab color: You can apply different colors to the sheet tabs so they stand out.
   - Insert and delete a worksheet: You can insert new worksheets to include related data within one workbook, or you can delete extra worksheets you do not need.
   - Move or copy a worksheet: Drag a sheet tab to rearrange the worksheets. You can copy a worksheet within a workbook or to another workbook.
7. **Manage columns and rows.**
   - Insert cells, columns, and rows: Insert a cell to move the remaining cells down or to the right. Insert a new column or row for data.
   - Delete cells, columns, and rows: You can delete cells, columns, and rows you no longer need.
   - Adjust column width: Double-click between the column headings to widen a column based on the longest item in that column, or drag the border between column headings to increase or decrease a column width.
   - Adjust row height: Drag the border between row headings to increase or decrease the height of a row.
   - Hide and unhide columns and rows: Hiding rows and columns protects confidential data from being displayed.
8. **Select, move, copy, and paste data.**
   - Select a range: A range may be a single cell or a rectangular block of cells.
   - Move a range to another location: After selecting a range, cut it from its location. Then make the top-left corner of the destination range the active cell and paste the range there.
   - Copy and paste a range: After selecting a range, click Copy, click the top-left corner of the destination range, and then click Paste to make a copy of the original range.
   - Use Paste Options and Paste Special: The Paste Special option enables you to specify how the data are pasted into the worksheet.
   - Copy Excel data to other programs: You can copy Excel data and paste it in other programs, such as in Word or PowerPoint.
9. **Apply alignment and font options.**
   - Merge and center labels: Type a label in the left cell, select a range including the data you typed, and then click Merge & Center to merge cells and center the label within the newly merged cell.
   - Change horizontal and vertical cell alignment: The default horizontal alignment depends on the data entered, and the default vertical alignment is Bottom Align.

- Wrap text: Use the Wrap Text option to present text on multiple lines in order to avoid having extra-wide columns.
- Increase and decrease indent: To indicate hierarchy of data or to offset a label you can increase or decrease how much the data are indented in a cell.
- Apply borders and fill colors: Borders and fill colors help improve readability of worksheets.

10. Apply number formats.

- The default number format is General, which does not apply any particular format to values. Apply appropriate formats to values to present the data with the correct symbols and decimal alignment. For example, Accounting Number Format is a common number format for monetary values.
- Increase and decrease decimal places: After applying a number format, you can increase or decrease the number of decimal places displayed.

11. Select page setup options.

- The Page Layout tab on the Ribbon contains options for setting margins, selecting orientation, specifying page size, selecting the print area, and applying other settings.
- Specify page options: Page options include orientation, paper size, and scaling.
- Set margin options: You can set the left, right, top, and bottom margins. In addition, you can center worksheet data horizontally and vertically on a page.
- Create headers and footers: You can insert a header or footer to display documentation, such as your name, date, time, and worksheet tab name.
- Select sheet options: Sheet options control the print area, print titles, print options, and page order.

12. Preview and print a worksheet.

- Before printing a worksheet, you should display a preview to ensure the data will print correctly. The Print Preview helps you see if margins are correct or if isolated rows or columns will print on separate pages.
- After making appropriate adjustments, you can print the worksheet.

Key Terms Matching

Match the key terms with their definitions. Write the key term letter by the appropriate numbered definition.

- **a.** Alignment
- **b.** Auto Fill
- **c.** Cell
- **d.** Column width
- **e.** Fill color
- **f.** Fill handle
- **g.** Formula
- **h.** Formula Bar
- **i.** Input area
- **j.** Name Box
- **k.** Order of precedence
- **l.** Output area
- **m.** Range
- **n.** Row height
- **o.** Sheet tab
- **p.** Text
- **q.** Value
- **r.** Workbook
- **s.** Worksheet
- **t.** Wrap text

1. _______ A spreadsheet that contains formulas, functions, values, text, and visual aids. **p. 374**
2. _______ A file containing related worksheets. **p. 374**
3. _______ A range of cells containing values for variables used in formulas. **p. 377**
4. _______ A range of cells containing results based on manipulating the variables. **p. 377**
5. _______ Identifies the address of the current cell. **p. 375**
6. _______ Displays the content (text, value, date, or formula) in the active cell. **p. 375**
7. _______ Displays the name of a worksheet within a workbook. **p. 375**
8. _______ The intersection of a column and row. **p. 376**
9. _______ Includes letters, numbers, symbols, and spaces. **p. 378**
10. _______ A number that represents a quantity or an amount. **p. 379**
11. _______ Rules that control the sequence in which Excel performs arithmetic operations. **p. 385**
12. _______ Enables you to copy the contents of a cell or cell range or to continue a sequence by dragging the fill handle over an adjacent cell or range of cells. **p. 386**
13. _______ A small green square at the bottom-right corner of a cell. **p. 386**
14. _______ The horizontal measurement of a column. **p. 398**
15. _______ The vertical measurement of a row. **p. 399**
16. _______ A rectangular group of cells. **p. 406**
17. _______ The position of data between the cell margins. **p. 414**
18. _______ Formatting that enables a label to appear on multiple lines within the current cell. **p. 415**
19. _______ The background color appearing behind data in a cell. **p. 416**
20. _______ A combination of cell references, operators, values, and/or functions used to perform a calculation. **p. 379**

Multiple Choice

1. What is the first step in planning an effective worksheet?
   (a) Enter labels, values, and formulas.
   (b) State the purpose of the worksheet.
   (c) Identify the input and output areas.
   (d) Decide how to format the worksheet data.

2. What Excel interface item displays the address of the current cell?
   (a) Quick Access Toolbar
   (b) Formula Bar
   (c) Status bar
   (d) Name Box

3. Given the formula =B1*B2+B3/B4^2 where B1 contains 3, B2 contains 4, B3 contains 32, and B4 contains 4, what is the result?
   (a) 14
   (b) 121
   (c) 76
   (d) 9216

4. Why would you press Ctrl+` in Excel?
   (a) To display the print options
   (b) To undo a mistake you made
   (c) To display cell formulas
   (d) To enable the AutoComplete feature

5. Which of the following is a nonadjacent range?
   (a) C15:D30
   (b) L15:L65
   (c) A1:Z99
   (d) A1:A10, D1:D10

6. If you want to balance a title over several columns, what do you do?
   (a) Enter the data in the cell that is about midway across the spreadsheet.
   (b) Merge and center the data over all columns.
   (c) Use the Increase Indent command until the title looks balanced.
   (d) Click Center to center the title horizontally over several columns.

7. Which of the following characteristics is not applicable to the Accounting Number Format?
   (a) Dollar sign immediately on the left side of the value
   (b) Commas to separate thousands
   (c) Two decimal places
   (d) Zero values displayed as hyphens

8. You selected and copied worksheet data containing formulas. However, you want the pasted copy to contain the current formula results rather than formulas. What do you do?
   (a) Click Paste in the Clipboard group on the Home tab.
   (b) Click the Paste arrow in the Clipboard group and select Formulas.
   (c) Click the Paste arrow in the Clipboard group and select Values & Source Formatting.
   (d) Display the Paste Special dialog box and select *Formulas and number formats.*

9. Assume that the data on a worksheet consume a whole printed page and a couple of columns on a second page. You can do all of the following except what to force the data to print all on one page?
   (a) Decrease the Scale value.
   (b) Increase the left and right margins.
   (c) Decrease column widths if possible.
   (d) Select a smaller range as the print area.

10. What should you do if you see a column of pound signs (###) instead of values or results of formulas?
    (a) Increase the zoom percentage.
    (b) Delete the column.
    (c) Adjust the row height.
    (d) Increase the column width.

Practice Exercises

1 Mathematics Review

You want to brush up on your math skills to test your logic by creating formulas in Excel. You realize that you should avoid values in formulas most of the time. Therefore, you created an input area that contains values you will use in your formulas. To test your knowledge of formulas, you will create an output area that will contain a variety of formulas using cell references from the input area. You also need to include a formatted title, the date prepared, and your name. After creating and verifying formula results, you will change input values and observe changes in the formula results. You want to display cell formulas, so you will create a picture copy of the formulas view. This exercise follows the same set of skills as used in Hands-On Exercises 1–4 and 6 in the chapter. Refer to Figure 1.52 as you complete this exercise.

	A	B	C	D	E
1	**Excel Formulas and Order of Precedence**				
2	Date Created:	42614		Student Name	
3					
4	**Input Area:**			**Output Area:**	
5	First Value	2		Sum of 1st and 2nd values	=B5+B6
6	Second Value	4		Difference between 4th and 1st values	=B8-B5
7	Third Value	6		Product of 2nd and 3rd values	=B6*B7
8	Fourth Value	8		Quotient of 3rd and 1st values	=B7/B5
9				2nd value to the power of 3rd value	=B6^B7
10				1st value added to product of 2nd and 4th values and difference between sum and 3rd value	=B5+B6*B8-B7
11				Product of sum of 1st and 2nd and difference between 4th and 3rd values	=(B5+B6)*(B8-B7)
12				Product of 1st and 2nd added to product of 3rd and 4th values	=(B5*B6)+(B7*B8)

FIGURE 1.52 Formula Practice

a. Open *e01p1Math* and save it as **e01p1Math_LastFirst**.

b. Type the current date in **cell B2** in this format: 9/1/2016. Type your first and last names in **cell D2**.

c. Adjust the column widths by doing the following:
   - Click in any cell in column A and click **Format** in the Cells group.
   - Select **Column Width**, type **12.57** in the **Column width box**, and then click **OK**.
   - Click in any cell in column B and set the width to **11**.
   - Click in any cell in column D and set the width to **35.57**.

d. Select the **range A1:E1**, click **Merge & Center** in the Alignment group, click **Bold**, and then apply **14 pt font size**.

e. Select the **range B5:B8** and click **Center** in the Alignment group.

f. Select the **range D10:D12** and click **Wrap Text** in the Alignment group.

g. Enter the following formulas in column E:
   - Click **cell E5**. Type **=B5+B6** and press **Enter**. Excel adds the value stored in cell B5 (1) to the value stored in cell B6 (2). The result (3) appears in cell E5, as described in cell D5.
   - Enter appropriate formulas in **cells E6:E8**, pressing **Enter** after entering each formula. Subtract to calculate a difference, multiply to calculate a product, and divide to calculate a quotient.
   - Type **=B6^B7** in **cell E9** and press **Enter**. Calculate the answer: 2*2*2 = 8.
   - Enter **=B5+B6*B8-B7** in **cell E10** and press **Enter**. Calculate the answer: 2*4 = 8; 1+8 = 9; 9–3 = 6. Multiplication occurs first, followed by addition, and finally subtraction.
   - Enter **=(B5+B6)*(B8-B7)** in **cell E11** and press **Enter**. Calculate the answer: 1+2 = 3; 4–3 = 1; 3*1 = 3. This formula is almost identical to the previous formula; however, calculations in parentheses occur before the multiplication.
   - Enter **=B5*B6+B7*B8** in **cell E12** and press **Enter**. Calculate the answer: 1*2 = 2; 3*4 = 12; 2+12 = 14.

h. Edit a formula and the input values:
   - Click **cell E12** and click in the Formula Bar to edit the formula. Add parentheses as shown: **=(B5*B6)+(B7*B8)** and click **Enter** to the left side of the Formula Bar. The answer is still 14. The parentheses do not affect order of precedence because multiplication occurred before the addition. The parentheses help improve the readability of the formula.
   - Type **2** in **cell B5**, **4** in **cell B6**, **6** in **cell B7**, and **8** in **cell B8**.
   - Double-check the results of the formulas using a calculator or your head. The new results in cells E5:E12 should be 6, 6, 24, 3, 4096, 28, 12, and 56, respectively.

i. Double-click the **Sheet1 tab**, type **Results**, and then press **Enter**. Right-click the **Results tab**, select **Move or Copy**, click **(move to end)** in the *Before sheet* section, click the **Create a copy check box**, and then click **OK**. Double-click the **Results (2) tab**, type **Formulas**, and then press **Enter**.

j. Click the **FORMULAS tab** and click **Show Formulas** in the Formula Auditing group. Double-click between the column A and column B headings to adjust the column A width. Double-click between the column B and column C headings to adjust the column B width. Set **24.0 width** for column D.

k. Select the **range A1:E12**, click the **HOME tab**, click the **Copy arrow** in the Clipboard group, and then select **Copy as Picture**. In the Copy Picture dialog box, click **As shown on screen** and click **OK**.

l. Press **Delete** to delete the selected worksheet data and click **Paste**.

> **TROUBLESHOOTING:** If you do not delete the worksheet data, the pasted picture image will display over the data, creating a double effect.

m. Make sure the Formulas worksheet is active, click the **PAGE LAYOUT tab**, and then do the following:
   - Click **Orientation** in the Page Setup group and select **Landscape**.
   - Click the **View Gridlines check box** in the Sheet Options group to deselect it. The worksheet gridlines are hidden, but the gridlines in the picture still display.

n. Click the **FILE tab** and click **Print**. Verify that the worksheet will print on one page. Press **Esc** to close the Print Preview.

o. Save and close the file, and submit based on your instructor's directions.

2 Calendar Formatting

FROM SCRATCH 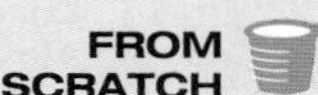

You want to create a calendar for May 2016. The calendar will enable you to practice alignment settings, including center, merge and center, and indents. In addition, you will need to adjust column widths and increase row height to create cells large enough to enter important information, such as birthdays, in your calendar. You will create a formula and use Auto Fill to complete the days of the week and the days within each week. To improve the appearance of the calendar, you will add fill colors, font colors, borders, and clip art. This exercise follows the same set of skills as used in Hands-On Exercises 1–6 in the chapter. Refer to Figure 1.53 as you complete this exercise.

	A	B	C	D	E	F	G
1	May 2016						
2	Sunday	Monday	Tuesday	Wednesday	Thursday	Friday	Saturday
3	1	2	3	4	5	6	7
4	8	9	10	11	12	13	14
5	15	16	17	18	19	20	21
6	22	23	24	25	26	27	28
7	29	30	31				

FIGURE 1.53 May 2016 Calendar

a. Click the **FILE tab**, select **New**, and then click **Blank workbook**. Save the workbook as **e01p2May2016_LastFirst**.

b. Type **'May 2016** in **cell A1** and click **Enter** on the left side of the Formula Bar.

> **TROUBLESHOOTING:** If you do not type the apostrophe before *May 2016*, the cell will display *May-16* instead of *May 2016*.

c. Format the title:
- Select the **range A1:G1** and click **Merge & Center** in the Alignment group.
- Apply **48 pt font size**.
- Click the **Fill Color arrow** and click **Green, Accent 6, Lighter 40%** in the *Theme Colors* section of the color palette.

d. Complete the days of the week:
- Type **Sunday** in **cell A2** and click **Enter** on the left side of the Formula Bar.
- Drag the **cell A2 fill handle** across the row through **cell G2** to use Auto Fill to complete the rest of the weekdays.
- Click the **Fill Color arrow** and select **Green, Accent 6, Lighter 60%**. Click the **Font Color arrow** and click **Green, Accent 6, Darker 50%**. Apply bold and **14 pt font size**. Click **Middle Align** and click **Center** in the Alignment group.

e. Complete the days of the month:
- Type **1** in **cell A3** and press **Ctrl+Enter**. Drag the **cell A3 fill handle** across the row through **cell G3**. Click **Auto Fill Options** in the bottom-right corner of the filled data and select **Fill Series**.
- Type **=A3+7** in **cell A4** and press **Ctrl+Enter**. Usually you avoid numbers in formulas, but the number of days in a week is always 7. Drag the **cell A4 fill handle** down through **cell A7** to get the date for each Sunday in May.
- Keep the **range A4:A7** selected and drag the fill handle across through **cell G7**. Select the **range D7:G7** and press **Delete** to delete the extra days.

f. Format the columns and rows:
- Select **columns A:G**. Click **Format** in the Cells group, select **Column Width**, type **16** in the **Column width box**, and then click **OK**.
- Select **row 2**. Click **Format** in the Cells group, select **Row Height**, type **54**, and then click **OK**.

- Select **rows 3:7**. Set an **80 row height**.
- Select the **range A2:G7**. Click the **Borders arrow** in the Font group and select **All Borders**.
- Select the **range A3:G7**. Click **Top Align** and **Align Left** in the Alignment group. Click **Increase Indent**. Bold the numbers and apply **12 pt font size**.

g. Double-click the **Sheet1 tab**, type **May**, and then press **Enter**.

h. Deselect the range and click the **PAGE LAYOUT tab**. Click **Orientation** in the Page Setup group and select **Landscape**.

i. Click the **INSERT tab** and click **Header & Footer** in the Text group. Click in the left side of the header and type your name. Click in the center of the header and click **Sheet Name** in the Header & Footer Elements group on the DESIGN tab. Click in the right side of the header and click **File Name** in the Header & Footer Elements group on the DESIGN tab. Click in any cell in the workbook and click **Normal** on the status bar.

j. Save and close the file, and submit based on your instructor's directions.

3 Bricktown Theatre

You are the assistant manager at Downtown Theatre, where touring Broadway plays and musicals are performed. You need to complete a spreadsheet to help you analyze ticket sales by seating chart for each performance. The spreadsheet will identify the seating sections, total seats in each section, and the number of seats sold for a performance. You will then calculate the percentage of seats sold and unsold. This exercise follows the same set of skills as used in Hands-On Exercises 1–6 in the chapter. Refer to Figure 1.54 as you complete this exercise.

	A	B	C	D	E
1	**Downtown Theatre**				
2	Ticket Sales by Seating Section				
3	3/31/2016				
4					
5	**Section**	**Available Seats**	**Seats Sold**	**Percentage Sold**	**Percentage Unsold**
6	Box Seats	25	12	48.0%	52.0%
7	Front Floor	120	114	95.0%	5.0%
8	Back Floor	132	108	81.8%	18.2%
9	Tier 1	40	40	100.0%	0.0%
10	Mezzanine	144	138	95.8%	4.2%
11	Balcony	106	84	79.2%	20.8%

FIGURE 1.54 Theatre Seating Data

a. Open *e01p3TicketSales* and save it as **e01p3TicketSales_LastFirst**.

b. Double-click the **Sheet1 tab**, type **Seating**, and then press **Enter**.

c. Type **3/31/2016** in **cell A3** and press **Enter**.

d. Adjust alignments and font attributes by doing the following from the Alignment and Font groups on the HOME tab:

- Select the **range A1:E1**, click **Merge & Center**, click **Bold**, click the **Font Size arrow**, and then select **16**.
- Use the Merge & Center command to merge the **range A2:E2** and center the subtitle.
- Use the Merge & Center command to merge the **range A3:E3** and center the date.
- Select the **range A5:E5**, click **Wrap Text**, click **Center**, and then click **Bold** to format the column labels.

e. Right-click the **row 9 heading** and select **Insert** from the shortcut menu to insert a new row. Type the following data in the new row: **Back Floor**, **132**, **108**.

f. Move the Balcony row to be the last row by doing the following:
   - Click the **row 6 heading** and click **Cut** in the Clipboard group on the HOME tab.
   - Right-click the **row 12 heading** and select **Insert Cut Cells** from the menu.
g. Adjust column widths by doing the following:
   - Double-click between the column A and column B headings.
   - Select **columns B** and **C headings** to select the columns, click **Format** in the Cells group, select **Column Width**, type **9** in the **Column width box**, and then click **OK**. Because columns B and C contain similar data, you set the same width for these columns.
   - Set the width of columns D and E to **12**.
h. Select the **range B6:C11**, click **Align Right** in the Alignment group on the HOME tab, and then click **Increase Indent** twice in the Alignment group.
i. Calculate and format the percentage of sold and unsold seats by doing the following:
   - Click **cell D6**. Type **=C6/B6** and press **Tab** to enter the formula and make cell E6 the active cell. This formula divides the number of seats sold by the total number of Box Seats.
   - Type **=(B6-C6)/B6** and click **Enter** on the left side of the Formula Bar to enter the formula and keep cell E6 the active cell. This formula must first subtract the number of sold seats from the available seats to calculate the number of unsold seats. The difference is divided by the total number of available seats to determine the percentage of unsold seats.
   - Select the **range D6:E6**, click **Percent Style** in the Number group on the HOME tab, and then click **Increase Decimal** in the Number group. Keep the range selected.
   - Double-click the **cell E6 fill handle** to copy the selected formulas down their respective columns. Keep the range selected.
   - Click **Align Right** in the Alignment group and click **Increase Indent** twice in the Alignment group. These actions will help center the data below the column labels. Do not click Center; doing so will center each value and cause the decimal points not to align. Deselect the range.
j. Display and preserve a screenshot of the formulas by doing the following:
   - Click **New sheet**, double-click the **Sheet1 tab**, type **Formulas**, and then press **Enter**.
   - Click **Select All** in the top-left corner above the row headings and to the left of the column headings, click the **Fill Color arrow** in the Font group, and then click **White, Background 1**. Applying this fill color will prevent the cell gridlines from bleeding through the screenshot you are about to embed.
   - Click the **Seating sheet tab**, click the **FORMULAS tab**, and then click **Show Formulas** in the Formula Auditing group to display cell formulas.
   - Click **cell A1** and drag down to **cell E11** to select the range of data. Click the **HOME tab**, click **Copy arrow** in the Clipboard group, select **Copy as Picture**, and then click **OK**.
   - Click the **Formulas sheet tab**, click **cell A1**, and then click **Paste**.
   - Click the **PAGE LAYOUT tab**, click **Orientation** in the Page Setup group, and then select **Landscape**.
   - Click the **Seating sheet tab**, click the **FORMULAS tab**, and then click **Show Formulas** in the Formula Auditing group to hide the cell formulas.
k. Click **cell A1**. Click the **PAGE LAYOUT tab**, click **Margins** in the Page Setup group, and then select **Custom Margins**. Click the **Horizontally check box** and click **Print Preview**. Excel centers the data horizontally based on the widest item. Press **Esc** to leave the Print Preview mode.
l. Click the **Page Setup Dialog Box Launcher**, click the **Header/Footer tab** in the Page Setup dialog box, click **Custom Footer**, type your name in the **Left section box**, click in the **Center section box**, click **Insert File Name**, click in the **Right section box**, click **Insert Sheet Name**, and then click **OK**. Click **OK**.
m. Save and close the file, and submit based on your instructor's directions.

Mid-Level Exercises

1 Restaurant Receipt

FROM SCRATCH

Matt, the owner of Matt's Sports Grill in Toledo, Ohio, asked you to help him create a receipt spreadsheet that he can use until his new system arrives. He wants an input area for the total food and beverage purchases, the sales tax rate, and the tip rate. The formatted receipt should include the subtotal, tax, tip, and total amount for a customer. Refer to Figure 1.55 as you complete this exercise.

	A	B	C	D	E
1	**Input Area**			**Matt's Sports Grill**	
2	Food & Beverages	$ 9.39		Toledo, Ohio	
3	Sales Tax Rate	6.5%			
4	Tip Rate	18.0%		Food & Beverages	$ 9.39
5				Sales Tax Amount	0.61
6				Subtotal	$ 10.00
7				Tip Amount	1.69
8				**Total Bill**	**$ 11.69**
9					
10				*Thank you for dining with us.*	

FIGURE 1.55 Matt's Sports Grill Receipt

a. Open a new Excel workbook, save it as **e01m1Receipt_LastFirst**, and then rename *Sheet1* as **Receipt**.

b. Enter the four labels in the **range A1:A4** in the Input Area as shown in Figure 1.56. Type **9.39**, **0.065**, and **.18** in the **range B2:B4**. Apply these formats to the Input Area:
   - Merge and center the *Input Area* title over both columns. Apply bold and **Blue, Accent 1, Lighter 40% fill color** to the title. Adjust the width of the first column.
   - Apply the **Accounting Number Format** and **Percent Style** format with the respective decimal places as shown in the **range B2:B4**.

c. Enter the labels in the receipt area in column D. Use Format Painter to copy the formats of the title in **cells A1** and **D1**. Merge and center the city and state in the **range D2:E2**. Change the width of column D to **17**. Indent the *Subtotal* and *Tip Amount* labels twice each. Apply bold to *Total Bill* and apply italic to *Thank you for dining with us*.

d. Enter the following formulas for the receipt:
   - **Food & Beverages:** Enter a formula that reads the value in the Input Area; do not retype the value in cell E4.
   - **Sales Tax Amount:** Calculate the product of the food & beverages and the sales tax rate.
   - **Subtotal:** Determine the formula needed.
   - **Tip Amount:** Calculate the tip based on the pretax amount and the tip rate.
   - **Total Bill:** Determine the formula needed.

e. Apply **Accounting Number Format** to the *Food & Beverages*, *Subtotal*, and *Total Bill* values, if necessary. Apply **Comma Style** and underline to the *Sales Tax Amount* and *Tip Amount* values. Apply the **Double Underline style** to the *Total Bill* value.

f. Set **1.5"** top margin and center the data horizontally on the page.

g. Insert a footer with your name on the left side, the sheet name code in the center, and the file name code on the right side.

h. Create a copy of the Receipt worksheet, move the new sheet to the end, and then rename the copied sheet **Formulas**. Display cell formulas on the Formulas worksheet, select **Landscape orientation**, and then select the options to print gridlines and headings. Adjust column widths so that the data will fit on one page.

i. Open the Excel Options dialog box while displaying the Formulas worksheet. In the Advanced category, under *Display options for this worksheet:*, select the **Show formulas in cells instead of their calculated results check box.** This option will make sure the active worksheet will display the formulas when you open the workbook again. The Receipt worksheet will continue showing the results.

j. Save and close the file, and submit based on your instructor's directions.

2 Guest House Rental Rates

ANALYSIS CASE 

You manage a beach guest house in Ft. Lauderdale containing three types of rental units. Prices are based on peak and off-peak times of the year. You need to calculate the maximum daily revenue for each rental type, assuming all units are rented. In addition, you need to calculate the discount rate for off-peak rental times. Finally, you will improve the appearance of the worksheet by applying font, alignment, and number formats.

a. Open *e01m2Rentals* and save it as **e01m2Rentals_LastFirst**.

b. Merge and center *Peak Rentals* in the **range C4:D4**, over the two columns of peak rental data. Apply **Dark Red fill color** and **White, Background 1 font color**.

c. Merge and center *Off-Peak Rentals* in the **range E4:G4** over the three columns of off-peak rental data. Apply **Blue fill color** and **White, Background 1 font color**.

d. Center and wrap the headings on row 5. Adjust the width of columns D and F, if needed. Center the data in the **range B6:B8**.

e. Create and copy the following formulas:
   - Calculate the Peak Rentals Maximum Revenue by multiplying the number of units by the peak rental price per day.
   - Calculate the Off-Peak Rentals Maximum Revenue by multiplying the number of units by the off-peak rental price per day.
   - Calculate the Discount rate for the Off-Peak rental price per day. For example, using the peak and off-peak per day values, the studio apartment rents for 75% of its peak rental rate. However, you need to calculate and display the off-peak discount rate, which is .24975.

f. Format the monetary values with **Accounting Number Format**. Format the Discount Rate formula results in **Percent Style** with one decimal place.

g. Apply **Blue, Accent 1, Lighter 80% fill color** to the **range E5:G8**.

h. Select the **range C5:D8** and apply a custom color with **Red 242**, **Green 220**, and **Blue 219**.

i. Answer the four questions below the worksheet data. If you change any values to answer the questions, change the values back to the original values.

j. Set **1"** top, bottom, left, and right margins. Center the data horizontally on the page.

k. Insert a footer with your name on the left side, the sheet name code in the center, and the file name code on the right side.

l. Create a copy of the Rental Rates worksheet, place the new sheet to the right side of the original worksheet, and rename the new sheet **Formulas**. On the Formulas worksheet, select **Landscape orientation** and the options to print gridlines and headings. Delete the question and answer section on the Formulas sheet.

DISCOVER 

m. Open the Excel Options dialog box while displaying the Formulas worksheet. In the Advanced category, under *Display options for this worksheet:*, select the **Show formulas in cells instead of their calculated results check box**. This option will make sure the active worksheet will display the formulas when you open the workbook again. The Rental Rates worksheet will continue showing the results. Adjust column widths so that the data will fit on one page.

n. Save and close the file, and submit based on your instructor's directions.

3 Real Estate Sales Report

You own a small real estate company in Indianapolis. You want to analyze sales for selected properties. Your assistant has prepared a spreadsheet with sales data. You need to calculate the number of days that the houses were on the market and their sales percentage of the list price. In one situation, the house was involved in a bidding war between two families that really wanted the house. Therefore, the sale price exceeded the list price.

a. Open *e01m3Sales* and save it as **e01m3Sales_LastFirst**.
b. Delete the row that has incomplete sales data. The owners took their house off the market.
c. Calculate the number of days each house was on the market. Copy the formula down that column.
d. Format prices with **Accounting Number Format** with zero decimal places.
e. Calculate the sales price percentage of the list price. The second house was listed for $500,250, but it sold for only $400,125. Therefore, the sale percentage of the list price is 79.99%. Format the percentages with two decimal places.
f. Wrap the headings on row 4.
g. Insert a new column between the *Date Sold* and *List Price* columns. Move the *Days on Market* column to the new location. Apply **Align Right** and increase the indent on the days on market formula results. Then delete the empty column B.
h. Edit the list date of the 41 Chestnut Circle house to be **4/22/2016**. Edit the list price of the house on Amsterdam Drive to be **$355,000**.
i. Select the property rows and set a **20 row height**. Adjust column widths as necessary.
j. Select **Landscape orientation** and set the scaling to **130%**. Center the data horizontally and vertically on the page.
k. Insert a header with your name, the current date code, and the current time code.
l. Save and close the file, and submit based on your instructor's directions.

4 Problem-Solving with Classmates

Your instructor wants all students in the class to practice their problem-solving skills. Pair up with a classmate so that you can create errors in a workbook and then see how many errors your classmate can find in your worksheet and how many errors you can find in your classmate's worksheet.

a. Create a folder named **Exploring** on your OneDrive and give access to that drive to a classmate and your instructor.
b. Open *e01h6Markup_LastFirst*, which you created in the Hands-On Exercises, and save it as **e01m4Markup_LastFirst**.
c. Edit each main formula to have a deliberate error (such as a value or incorrect cell reference) in it and then copy the formulas down the columns.
d. Save the workbook to your shared folder on your OneDrive.
e. Open the workbook your classmate saved on his or her OneDrive and save the workbook with your name after theirs, such as *e01m4Markup_MulberyKeith_KrebsCynthia*.
f. Find the errors in your classmate's workbook, insert comments to describe the errors, and then correct the errors.
g. Save the workbook back to your classmate's OneDrive and submit based on your instructor's directions.

Beyond the Classroom

Credit Card Rebate

RESEARCH CASE 

FROM SCRATCH

You recently found out the Costco TrueEarnings® American Express credit card earns annual rebates on all purchases. You want to see how much rebate you would have received had you used this credit card for purchases in the past year. Use the Internet to research the percentage rebates for different categories. Plan the design of the spreadsheet. Enter the categories, rebate percentages, amount of money you spent in each category, and a formula to calculate the amount of rebate. Use the Excel Help feature to learn how to add several cells using a function instead of adding cells individually and how to apply a Double Accounting underline. Insert the appropriate function to total your categorical purchases and rebate amounts. Apply appropriate formatting and page setup options for readability. Underline the last monetary values for the last data row and apply the **Double Accounting underline style** to the totals. Insert a header. Save the workbook as **e01b2Rebate_LastFirst**. Close the workbook and submit based on your instructor's directions.

Net Proceeds from House Sale

DISASTER RECOVERY 

Garrett Frazier is a real estate agent. He wants his clients to have a realistic expectation of how much money they will receive when they sell their houses. Sellers know they have to pay a commission to the agent and pay off their existing mortgages; however, many sellers forget to consider they might have to pay some of the buyer's closing costs, title insurance, and prorated property taxes. The realtor commission and estimated closing costs are based on the selling price and the respective rates. The estimated property taxes are prorated based on the annual property taxes and percentage of the year. For example, if a house sells three months into the year, the seller pays 25% of the property taxes. Garrett created a worksheet to enter values in an input area to calculate the estimated deductions at closing and calculate the estimated net proceeds the seller will receive. However, the worksheet contains errors. Open *e01b3Proceeds* and save it as **e01b3Proceeds_LastFirst**.

Use Help to learn how to insert comments into cells. As you identify the errors, insert comments in the respective cells to explain the errors. Correct the errors, including formatting errors. Apply **Landscape orientation**, **115% scaling**, **1.5" top margin**, and center horizontally. Insert your name on the left side of the header, the sheet name code in the center, and the file name code on the right side. Save and close the workbook, and submit based on your instructor's directions.

Goal Setting

SOFT SKILLS CASE 

FROM SCRATCH

After watching the Goal Setting video, start a new Excel workbook and save it as **e01b4Goals_LastFirst**. List three descriptive goals in column A relating to your schoolwork and degree completion. For example, maybe you usually study three hours a week for your algebra class, and you want to increase your study time by 20%. Enter *Algebra homework & study time (hours)* in column A, *3* in column B, the percentage change in column C, and create a formula that calculates the total goal in column D. Adjust column widths as needed.

Insert column labels above each column. Format the labels and values using information you learned earlier in the chapter. Merge and center a title at the top of the worksheet. Use the Page Setup dialog box to center the worksheet horizontally. Rename Sheet1 using the term, such as *Fall 2016*. Create a footer with your name on the left side, sheet name code in the center, and file name code on the right side. Save and close the workbook, and submit based on your instructor's directions.

Capstone Exercise

You manage a publishing company that publishes and sells books to bookstores in Austin. Your assistant prepared a standard six-month royalty statement for one author. You need to insert formulas, format the worksheets, and then prepare royalty statements for other authors.

Enter Data into the Worksheet

You need to format a title, enter the date indicating the end of the statement period, and delete a blank column. You also need to insert a row for the standard discount rate, a percentage that you discount the books from the retail price to sell to the bookstores.

a. Open *e01c1Royalty* and save it as **e01c1Royalty_LastFirst**.

b. Merge and center the title over the **range A1:D1**.

c. Type **6/30/2016** in **cell B3** and left align the date.

d. Delete the blank column between the Hardback and Paperback columns.

e. Insert a new row between Retail Price and Price to Bookstore. Enter **Standard Discount Rate**, **0.55**, and **0.5**. Format the two values as **Percent Style**.

Calculate Values

You need to insert formulas to perform necessary calculations.

a. Enter the Percent Returned formula in **cell B10**. The percent returned indicates the percentage of books sold but returned to the publisher.

b. Enter the Price to Bookstore formula in **cell B15**. This is the price at which you sell the books to the bookstore. It is based on the retail price and the standard discount. For example, if a book has a $10 retail price and a 55% discount, you sell the book for $4.50.

c. Enter the Net Retail Sales formula **in cell B16**. The net retail sales is the revenue from the net units sold at the retail price. Gross units sold minus the returned units equals net units sold.

d. Enter the Royalty to Author formula in **cell B20**. Royalties are based on net retail sales and the applicable royalty rate.

e. Enter the Royalty per Book formula in **cell B21**. This amount is the author's earnings on every book sold but not returned.

f. Copy the formulas to the Paperback column.

Format the Values

You are ready to format the values to improve readability.

a. Apply **Comma Style** with zero decimal places to the **range B8:C9**.

b. Apply **Percent Style** with one decimal place to the **range B10:C10** and **Percent Style** with two decimal places to the **range B19:C19**.

c. Apply **Accounting Number Format** to all monetary values.

Format the Worksheet

You want to improve the appearance of the rest of the worksheet.

a. Select the **range B6:C6**. Apply bold, right alignment, and **Purple font color.**

b. Click **cell A7**, apply **Purple font color**, and then apply **Gray-25%, Background 2, Darker 10% fill color**. Select the **range A7:C7** and select **Merge Across**.

c. Use Format Painter to apply the formats from **cell A7** to **cells A12** and **A18**.

d. Select the **ranges A8:A10**, **A13:A16**, and **A19:A21**. Indent the labels twice. Widen column A as needed.

e. Select the **range A7:C10** (the *Units Sold* section) and apply the **Outside Borders** border style. Apply the same border style to the *Pricing* and *Royalty Information* sections.

Manage the Workbook

You will apply page setup options insert a footer, and, then duplicate the royalty statement worksheet to use as a model to prepare a royalty statement for another author.

a. Select the margin setting to center the data horizontally on the page. Insert a footer with your name on the left side, the sheet name code in the center, and the file name code on the right side.

b. Copy the Jacobs worksheet, move the new worksheet to the end, and then rename it **Lopez**.

c. Change the Jacobs sheet tab to **Red**. Change the Lopez sheet tab to **Dark Blue**.

d. Make these changes on the Lopez worksheet: **Lopez** (author), **5000** (hardback gross units), **14000** (paperback gross units), **400** (hardback returns), **1925** (paperback returns), **19.95** (hardback retail price), and **6.95** (paperback retail price).

Display Formulas and Print the Workbook

You want to print the formatted Jacobs worksheet to display the calculated results. To provide evidence of the formulas, you want to display and print cell formulas in the Lopez worksheet.

a. Display the cell formulas for the Lopez worksheet.

b. Select options to print the gridlines and headings.

c. Change the Options setting to make sure the formulas display instead of cell results on this worksheet when you open it again.

d. Adjust the column widths so that the formula printout will print on one page.

e. Save and close the workbook, and submit based on your instructor's directions.

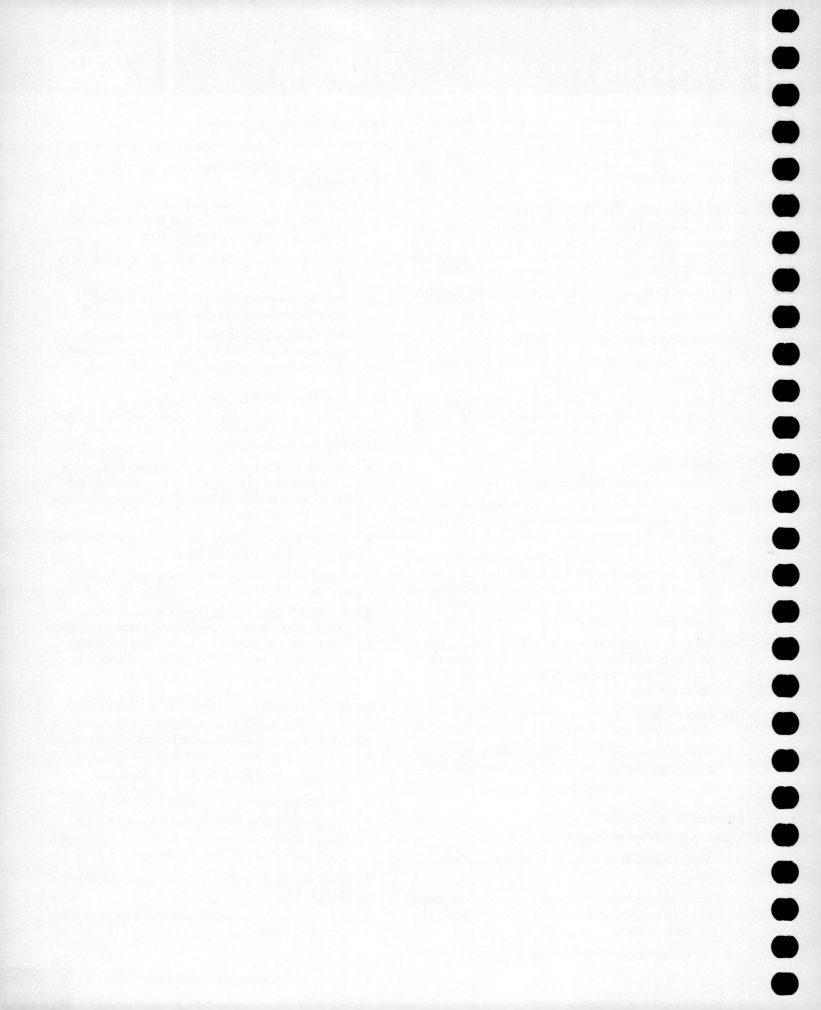

Excel

Formulas and Functions

CHAPTER 2

Performing Quantitative Analysis

OBJECTIVES AFTER YOU READ THIS CHAPTER, YOU WILL BE ABLE TO:

CASE STUDY | Townsend Mortgage Company

You are an assistant to Erica Matheson, a mortgage broker at the Townsend Mortgage Company. Erica spends her days reviewing mortgage rates and trends, meeting with clients, and preparing paperwork. She relies on your expertise in using Excel to help analyze mortgage data.

Today, Erica provided you with sample mortgage data: loan number, house cost, down payment, mortgage rate, and the length of the loan in years. She asked you to perform some basic calculations so that she can check the output provided by her system to verify if it is calculating results correctly. She needs you to calculate the amount financed, the periodic interest rate, the total number of payment periods, the percent of the house cost that is financed, and the payoff year for each loan. In addition, you will calculate totals, averages, and other basic statistics.

Furthermore, you need to complete another worksheet that uses functions to look up interest rates from another table, calculate the monthly payments, and determine how much (if any) the borrower will have to pay for private mortgage insurance (PMI).

Formula Basics

When you increase your understanding of formulas, you can build robust workbooks that perform a variety of calculations for quantitative analysis. Your ability to build sophisticated workbooks and to interpret the results increases your value to any organization. By now, you should be able to build simple formulas using cell references and mathematical operators and using the order of precedence to control the sequence of calculations in formulas.

In this section, you will create formulas in which cell addresses change or remain fixed when you copy them. Finally, you will learn how to identify and prevent circular references in formulas.

Using Relative, Absolute, and Mixed Cell References in Formulas

When you copy a formula, Excel either adjusts or preserves the cell references in the copied formulas based on how the cell references appear in the original formula. Excel uses three different ways to reference a cell in a formula: relative, absolute, and mixed. When you create a formula that you will copy to other cells, ask yourself the following question:

> Do the cell references need to adjust for the copied formulas, or should the cell references always refer to the same cell location, regardless of where the copied formula is located?

Use a Relative Cell Reference

STEP 1»

A ***relative cell reference*** indicates a cell's relative location, such as five rows up and one column to the left, from the cell containing the formula. When you copy a formula containing a relative cell reference, the cell references in the copied formula change relative to the position of the copied formula. Regardless of where you copy the formula, the cell references in the copied formula maintain the same relative distance from the cell containing the copied formula, as the cell references the relative location to the original formula cell.

In Figure 2.1, the formulas in column F contain relative cell references. When you copy the original formula =D2-E2 from cell F2 down to cell F3, the copied formula changes to =D3-E3. Because you copy the formula *down* the column to cell F3, the column letters in the formula stay the same, but the row numbers change to reflect the row to which you copied the formula. Using relative cell addresses to calculate the amount financed ensures that each borrower's down payment is subtracted from his or her respective house cost.

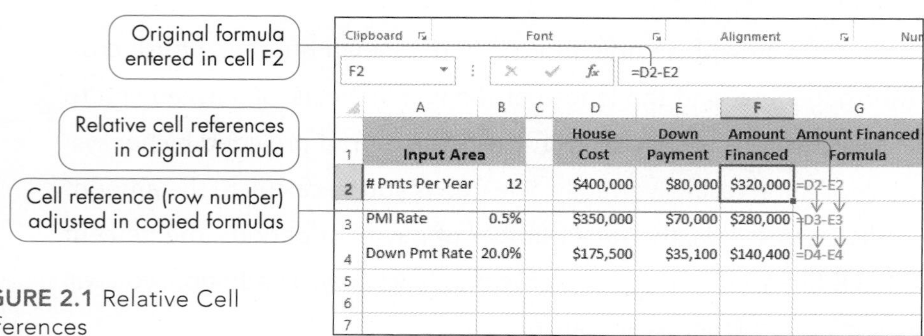

FIGURE 2.1 Relative Cell References

Use an Absolute Cell Reference

STEP 2»

An ***absolute cell reference*** provides a permanent reference to a specific cell. When you copy a formula containing an absolute cell reference, the cell reference in the copied formula does not change, regardless of where you copy the formula. An absolute cell reference appears with a dollar sign before both the column letter and row number, such as $B$4.

In Figure 2.2, each down payment is calculated by multiplying the respective house cost by the down payment rate (20%). Cell E2 contains =D2*$B$4 ($400,000*20.0%) to calculate the first borrower's down payment ($80,000). When you copy the formula down to the next row, the copied formula in cell E3 is =D3*$B$4. The relative cell reference D2 changes to D3 (for the next house cost) and the absolute cell reference $B$4 remains the same to refer to the 20.0% down payment rate. This formula ensures that the cell reference to the house cost changes for each row but that the house cost is always multiplied by the rate in cell B4.

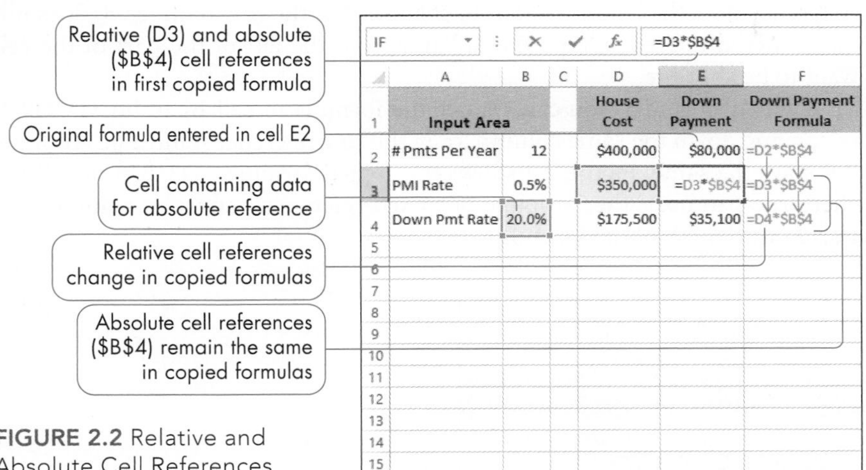

FIGURE 2.2 Relative and Absolute Cell References

TIP Input Area and Absolute Cell References

Figure 2.2 illustrates an input area, a range in a worksheet that contains values that you can change. You build formulas using absolute references to the cells in the input area. By using cell references from an input area, you can change the value in the input area and the formulas that refer to those cells will update automatically. If an input value changes (e.g., the down payment rate changes from 20% to 25%), enter the new input value in only one cell (e.g., B4), and Excel recalculates the amount of down payment for all the formulas.

Figure 2.3 shows what happens if the down payment formula used a relative reference to cell B4. If the original formula in cell E2 is =D2*B4, the copied formula becomes =D3*B5 in cell E3. The relative cell reference to B4 changes to B5 when you copy the formula down. Because cell B5 is empty, the $350,000 house cost in cell D3 is multiplied by 0, giving a $0 down payment, which is not a valid down payment amount.

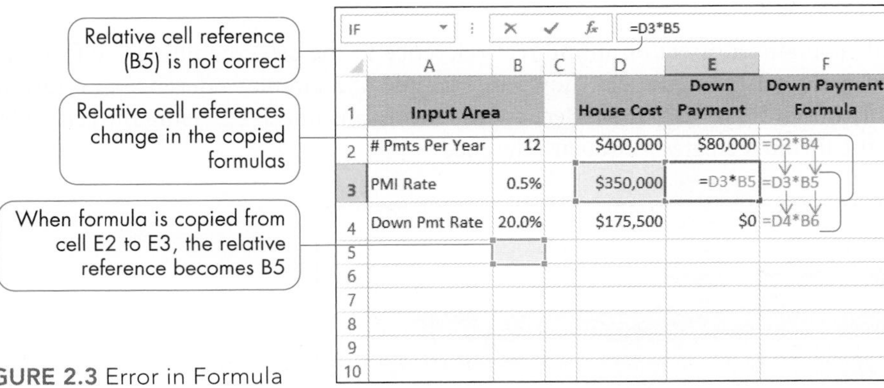

FIGURE 2.3 Error in Formula

Use a Mixed Cell Reference

STEP 3» A ***mixed cell reference*** combines an absolute cell reference with a relative cell reference. When you copy a formula containing a mixed cell reference, either the column letter or the row number that has the absolute reference remains fixed while the other part of the cell reference that is relative changes in the copied formula. $B4 and B$4 are examples of mixed cell references. In the reference $B4, the column B is absolute, and the row number is relative; when you copy the formula, the column letter, B, does not change, but the row number will change. In the reference B$4, the column letter, B, changes, but the row number, 4, does not change. To create a mixed reference, type the dollar sign to the left of the part of the cell reference you want to be absolute.

In the down payment formula, you can change the formula in cell E2 to be =D2*B$4. Because you are copying down the same column, only the row reference 4 must be absolute; the column letter stays the same. Figure 2.4 shows the copied formula =D3*B$4 in cell E3. In situations where you can use either absolute or mixed references, consider using mixed references to shorten the length of the formula.

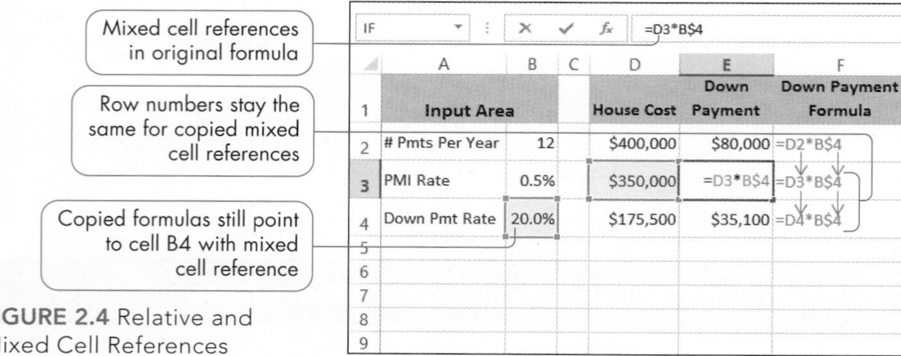

FIGURE 2.4 Relative and Mixed Cell References

> **TIP** The F4 Key
>
> The F4 key toggles through relative, absolute, and mixed references. Click a cell reference within a formula on the Formula Bar and press F4 to change it. For example, click in B4 in the formula =D2*B4. Press F4 and the relative cell reference (B4) changes to an absolute cell reference ($B$4). Press F4 again and $B$4 becomes a mixed reference (B$4); press F4 again and it becomes another mixed reference ($B4). Press F4 a fourth time and the cell reference returns to the original relative reference (B4).

Correcting Circular References

If a formula contains a direct or an indirect reference to the cell containing the formula, a ***circular reference*** exists. Figure 2.5 shows an example of a circular reference in a formula. The formula in cell E2 is =E2*$B$4. Because the formula is in cell E2, using the cell address E2 within the formula creates a circular reference.

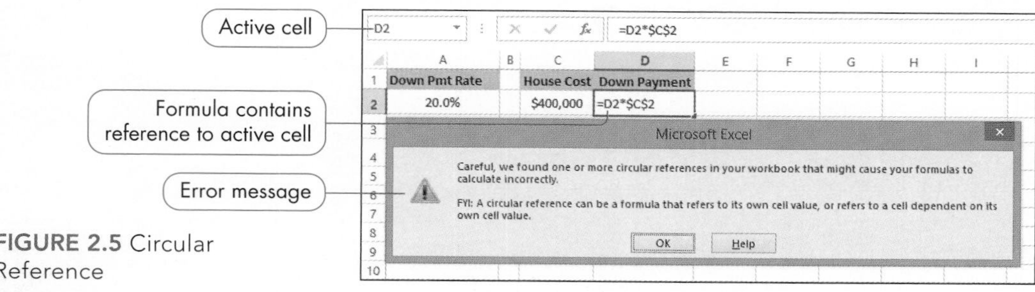

FIGURE 2.5 Circular Reference

STEP 4» Circular references usually cause inaccurate results. Excel displays a warning message when you enter a formula containing a circular reference or when you open an Excel workbook that contains an existing circular reference. Click Help to display the *Find and fix a circular reference* Help topic or click OK to accept the circular reference. Until you resolve a circular reference, the status bar indicates the location of a circular reference, such as CIRCULAR REFERENCES: E2.

TIP Green Triangles

Excel displays a green triangle in the top-left corner of a cell if it detects a potential error in a formula. Click the cell to see the Trace Error button (yellow diamond with exclamation mark). When you click Trace Error, Excel displays information about the potential error and how to correct it. In some cases, Excel may anticipate an inconsistent formula or the omission of adjacent cells in a formula. For example, if a column contains values for the year 2016, the error message indicates that you did not include the year itself. However, the year 2016 is merely a label and should not be included; therefore, you would ignore that error message.

Quick Concepts

1. What happens when you copy a formula containing a relative cell reference one column to the right? *p. 448*
2. Why would you use an absolute reference in a formula? *p. 449*
3. What is a circular reference? Provide an example. *p. 450*

Hands-On Exercises

MyITLab®
HOE1 Training

1 Formula Basics

Erica prepared a workbook containing data for five mortgages financed with the Townsend Mortgage Company. The data include house cost, down payment, mortgage rate, number of years to pay off the mortgage, and the financing date for each mortgage.

Skills covered: Use a Relative Cell Reference in a Formula • Use an Absolute Cell Reference in a Formula • Use a Mixed Cell Reference in a Formula • Correct a Circular Reference

STEP 1 » USE A RELATIVE CELL REFERENCE IN A FORMULA

You need to calculate the amount financed by each borrower by creating a formula with relative cell references that calculates the difference between the house cost and the down payment. After verifying the results of the amount financed by the first borrower, you will copy the formula down the Amount Financed column to calculate the other borrowers' amounts financed. Refer to Figure 2.6 as you complete Step 1.

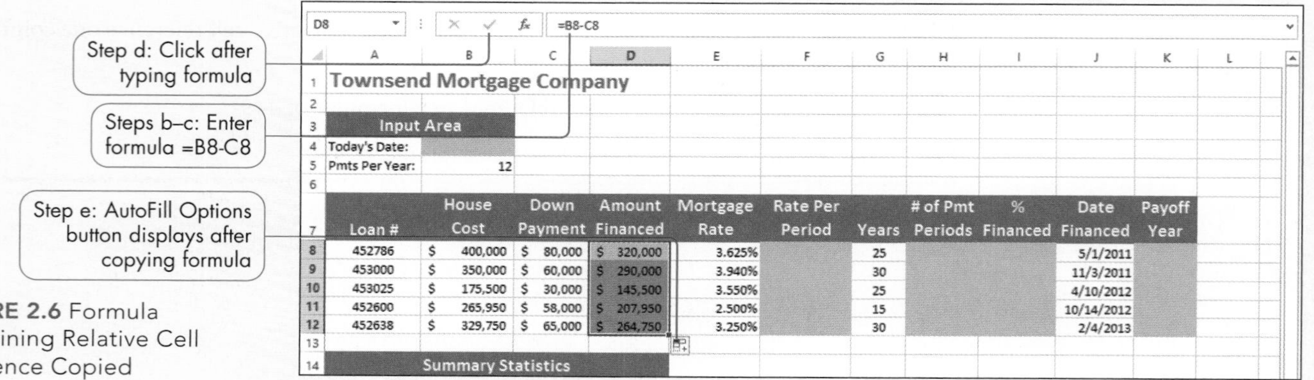

FIGURE 2.6 Formula Containing Relative Cell Reference Copied

a. Open *e02h1Loans* and save it as **e02h1Loans_LastFirst**.

> **TROUBLESHOOTING:** If you make any major mistakes in this exercise, you can close the file, open *e02h1Loans* again, and then start this exercise over.

The workbook contains two worksheets: Details (for Hands-On Exercises 1 and 2) and Payment Info (for Hands-On Exercises 3 and 4). You will enter formulas in the shaded cells.

b. Click **cell D8** in the Details sheet. Type = and click **cell B8**, the cell containing the first borrower's house cost.

c. Type - and click **cell C8**, the cell containing the down payment by the first borrower.

d. Click **Enter** (the check mark between the Name Box and Formula Bar) to complete the formula.

The first borrower financed (i.e., borrowed) $320,000, the difference between the cost ($400,000) and the down payment ($80,000).

e. Double-click the **cell D8 fill handle**.

You copied the formula down the Amount Financed column for each mortgage row.

TIP Auto Fill Options

The Auto Fill Options button appears in the bottom-right corner of the copied formulas. If you click it, you can see that the default is Copy Cells. If you want to copy only formatting, click Fill Formatting Only. If you want to copy data only, click Fill Without Formatting.

f. Click **cell D9** and view the formula in the Formula Bar.

   The formula in cell D8 is =B8-C8. The formula pasted in cell D9 is =B9-C9. Because the original formula contained relative cell references, when you copy the formula down to the next row, the row numbers for the cell references change. Each result represents the amount financed for that particular borrower.

g. Press [↓] and look at the cell references in the Formula Bar to see how the references change for each formula you copied. Save the workbook with the new formula you created.

STEP 2 » USE AN ABSOLUTE CELL REFERENCE IN A FORMULA

Column E contains the annual percentage rate (APR) for each mortgage. Because the borrowers will make monthly payments, you need to calculate the monthly interest rate by dividing the APR by 12 (the number of payments in one year) for each borrower. Refer to Figure 2.7 as you complete Step 2.

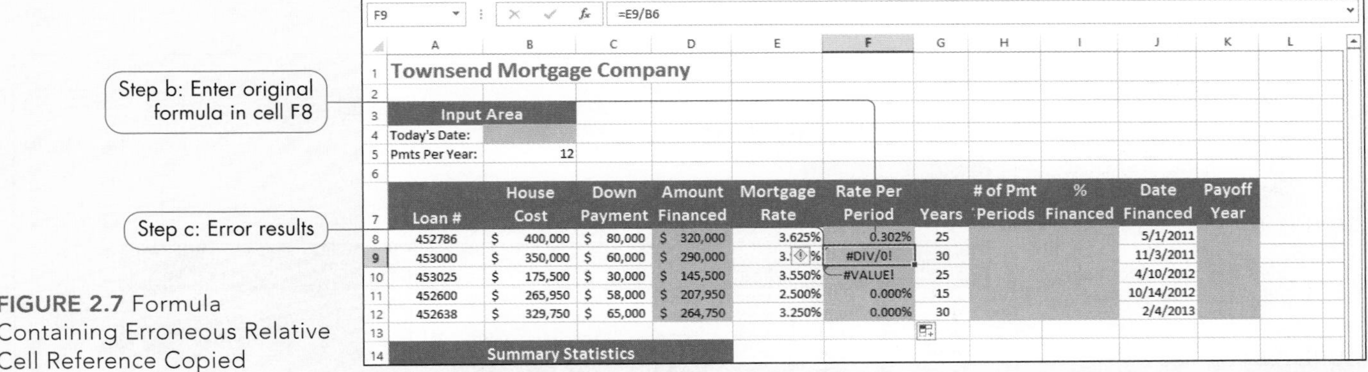

FIGURE 2.7 Formula Containing Erroneous Relative Cell Reference Copied

a. Click **cell F8**.

   You need to create a formula to calculate the monthly interest rate for the first borrower.

b. Type **=E8/B5** and click **Enter** (the checkmark between the Name Box and the Formula Bar).

   Typically, you should avoid typing values directly in formulas. Although the number of months in one year is always 12, use a reference to cell B5, where the number of payments per year is placed in the input area, so that the company can change the payment period to bimonthly (24 payments per year) or quarterly (four payments per year) without adjusting the formula.

c. Double-click the **cell F8 fill handle**, click **cell F9**, and then view the results (see Figure 2.7).

   An error icon displays to the left of cell F9, cell F9 displays #DIV/0!, and cell F10 displays #VALUE!. The original formula was =E8/B5. Because you copied the formula =E8/B5 down the column, the first copied formula is =E9/B6, and the second copied formula is =E10/B7. Although you want the mortgage rate cell reference (E8) to change (E9, E10, etc.) from row to row, you do not want the divisor (cell B5) to change. You need all formulas to divide by the value stored in cell B5, so you will edit the formula to make B5 an absolute reference.

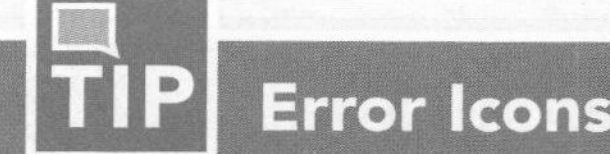

TIP Error Icons

You can position the mouse pointer over the error icon to see a tip indicating what is wrong, such as *The formula or function used is dividing by zero or empty cells.* You can click the icon to see a menu of options to learn more about the error and how to correct it.

d. Click **Undo** in the Quick Access Toolbar to undo the Auto Fill process. Click within or to the right of **B5** in the Formula Bar.

e. Press **F4** and click **Enter** (the checkmark between the Name Box and the Formula Bar).

Excel changes the cell reference from B5 to $B$5, making it an absolute cell reference.

f. Copy the formula down the Rate Per Period column. Click **cell F9** and view the formula in the Formula Bar. Save the workbook.

The formula in cell F9 is =E9/$B$5. The reference to E9 is relative and the reference to B5 is absolute.

STEP 3 ›› USE A MIXED CELL REFERENCE IN A FORMULA

The next formula you create will calculate the total number of payment periods for each loan. Refer to Figure 2.8 as you complete Step 3.

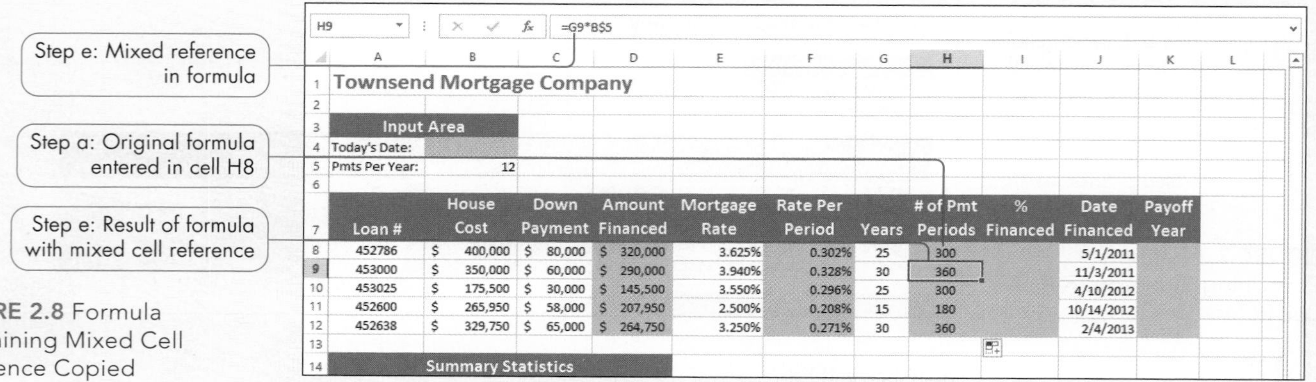

Loan #	House Cost	Down Payment	Amount Financed	Mortgage Rate	Rate Per Period	Years	# of Pmt Periods	% Financed	Date Financed	Payoff Year
452786	$ 400,000	$ 80,000	$ 320,000	3.625%	0.302%	25	300		5/1/2011	
453000	$ 350,000	$ 60,000	$ 290,000	3.940%	0.328%	30	360		11/3/2011	
453025	$ 175,500	$ 30,000	$ 145,500	3.550%	0.296%	25	300		4/10/2012	
452600	$ 265,950	$ 58,000	$ 207,950	2.500%	0.208%	15	180		10/14/2012	
452638	$ 329,750	$ 65,000	$ 264,750	3.250%	0.271%	30	360		2/4/2013	

FIGURE 2.8 Formula Containing Mixed Cell Reference Copied

a. Click **cell H8** and type **=G8*B5**.

You need to multiply the number of years (25) by the number of payment periods in one year (12) using cell references.

b. Press **F4** to make the B5 cell reference absolute and click **Enter** (the checkmark between the Name Box and Formula Bar).

You want B5 to be absolute so that the cell reference remains B5 when you copy the formula. The product of 25 years and 12 months is 300 months or payment periods.

c. Copy the formula down the # of Pmt Periods column.

The first copied formula is =G9*$B$5, and the result is 360. You want to see what happens if you change the absolute reference to a mixed reference and copy the formula again. Because you are copying down a column, the column letter B can be relative because it will not change either way, but the row number 5 must be absolute.

d. Click **Undo** on the Quick Access Toolbar to undo the copied formulas.

Cell H8 is the active cell.

e. Click within the **$B$5 cell reference** in the Formula Bar. Press **F4** to change the cell reference to a mixed cell reference: B$5. Press **Ctrl+Enter** and copy the formula down the # of Pmt Periods column. Click **cell H9**. Save the workbook.

The first copied formula is =G9*B$5 and the result is still 360. In this situation, using either an absolute reference or a mixed reference provides the same results.

STEP 4 ›› CORRECT A CIRCULAR REFERENCE

Erica wants to know what percentage of the house cost each borrower will finance. As you create the formula, you enter a circular reference. After studying the results, you correct the circular error and plan future formulas that avoid this problem. Refer to Figure 2.9 as you complete Step 4.

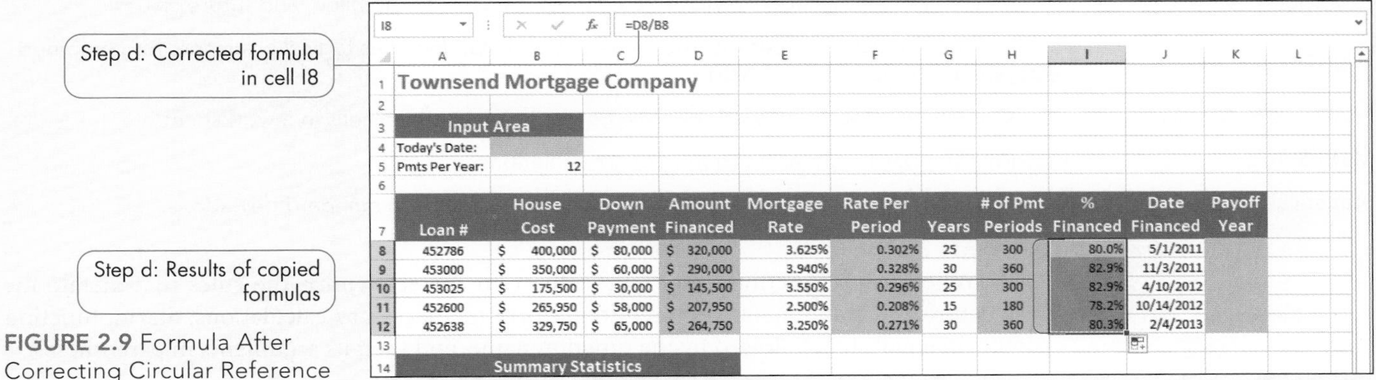

FIGURE 2.9 Formula After Correcting Circular Reference

a. Click **cell I8**, type **=I8/B8**, and then press **Enter**.

The Circular Reference Warning message box displays.

> **TROUBLESHOOTING:** If the message box does not display, close the workbook and exit Excel. Start Excel, open the workbook again, and then repeat Step 4a. Sometimes the message box appears only once while Excel is running. If you had previously experimented with a circular reference during a work session, the message box might not display. However, exiting Excel and opening it again will enable the message box to display.

b. Read the description of the error and click **Help**.

The Excel Help window opens, displaying information about circular references.

c. Read the circular reference information, close the Excel Help window, and then click **OK** in the message box.

The left side of the status bar displays *CIRCULAR REFERENCES: I8*.

Because the formula is stored in cell I8, the formula cannot refer to the cell itself. You need to divide the value in the Amount Financed column by the value in the House Cost column.

d. Click **cell I8** and edit the formula to be **=D8/B8**. Copy the formula down the % Financed column.

The first borrower financed 80% of the cost of the house: $320,000 financed divided by $400,000 cost.

e. Save the workbook. Keep the workbook open if you plan to continue with the next Hands-On Exercise. If not, close the workbook and exit Excel.

Function Basics

An Excel ***function*** is a predefined computation that simplifies creating a formula that performs a complex calculation. Excel contains more than 400 functions, which are organized into 14 categories. Table 2.1 lists and describes the primary function categories used in this chapter.

TABLE 2.1 Function Categories and Descriptions

Category	Description
Date & Time	Provides methods for manipulating date and time values.
Financial	Performs financial calculations, such as payments, rates, present value, and future value.
Logical	Performs logical tests and returns the value of the tests. Includes logical operators for combined tests, such as AND, OR, and NOT.
Lookup & Reference	Looks up values, creates links to cells, or provides references to cells in a worksheet.
Math & Trig	Performs standard math and trigonometry calculations.
Statistical	Performs common statistical calculations, such as averages and standard deviations.

When using functions, you must adhere to correct ***syntax***, the rules that dictate the structure and components required to perform the necessary calculations. Start a function with an equal sign, followed by the function name, and then its arguments in parentheses.

- The function name describes the purpose of the function. For example, the function name SUM indicates that the function sums, or adds, values.
- A function's ***arguments*** specify the inputs—such as cells, values, or arithmetic expressions—that are required to complete the operation. In some cases, a function requires multiple arguments separated by commas.

In this section, you will learn how to insert common functions using the keyboard and the Insert Function and Function Arguments dialog boxes.

Inserting a Function

To insert a function by typing, first type an equal sign, and then begin typing the function name. ***Formula AutoComplete*** displays a list of functions and defined names that match letters as you type a formula. For example, if you type =SU, Formula AutoComplete displays a list of functions and names that start with *SU* (see Figure 2.10). You can double-click the function name from the list or continue typing the function name. You can even scroll through the list to see the ScreenTip describing the function.

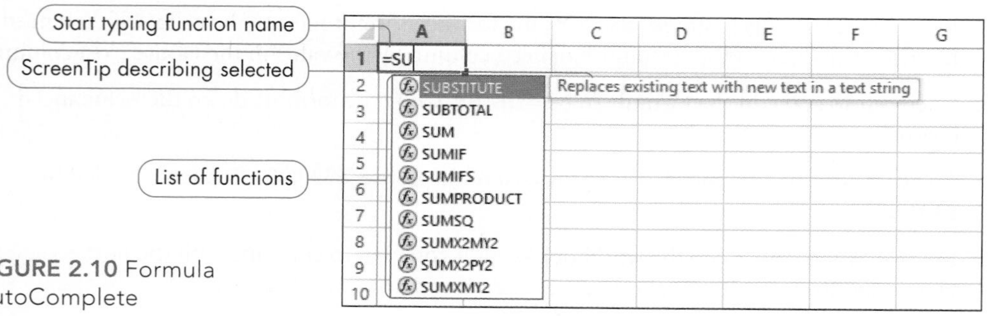

FIGURE 2.10 Formula AutoComplete

After you type the function name and opening parenthesis, Excel displays the ***function ScreenTip***, a small pop-up description that displays the function's arguments. The argument you are currently entering is bold in the function ScreenTip (see Figure 2.11). Square brackets indicate optional arguments. For example, the SUM function requires the number1 argument, but the number2 argument is optional. Click the argument name in the function ScreenTip to select the actual argument in the formula you are creating if you want to make changes to the argument.

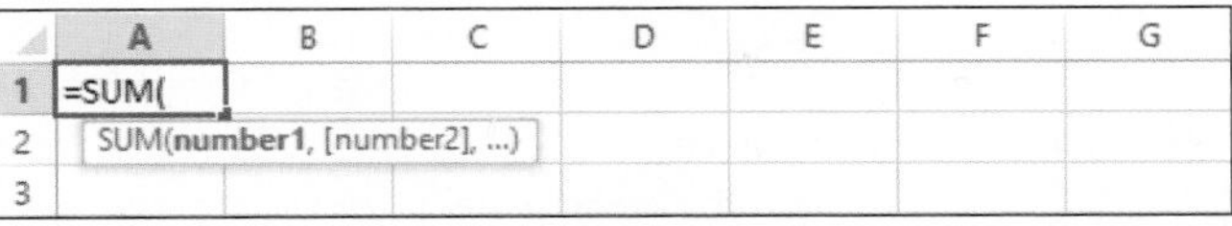

FIGURE 2.11 Function ScreenTip

You can also use the Insert Function dialog box to search for a function, select a function category, and select a function from the list (see Figure 2.12). The dialog box is helpful if you want to browse a list of functions, especially if you are not sure of the function you need and want to see descriptions.

To display the Insert Function dialog box, click Insert Function f_x (located between the Name Box and the Formula Bar) or click Insert Function in the Function Library group on the Formulas tab. From within the dialog box, select a function category, such as Most Recently Used, and select a function to display the syntax and a brief description of that function. Click *Help on this function* to display details about the selected function.

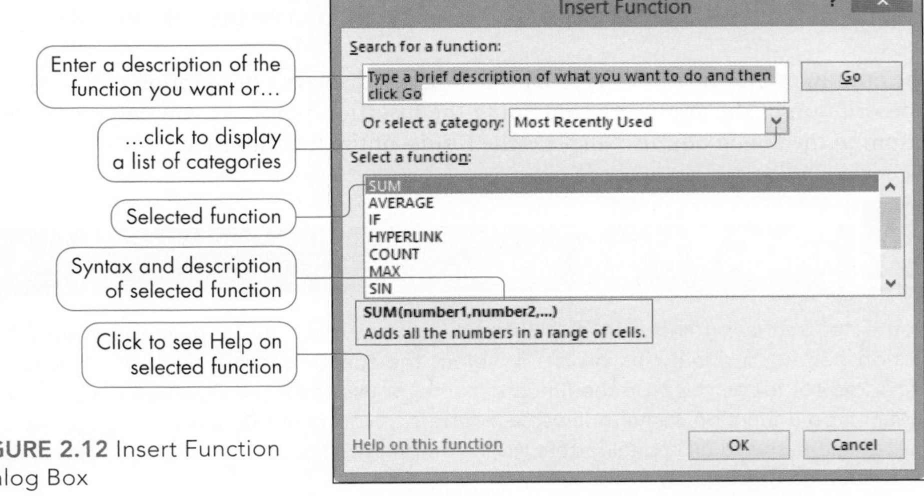

FIGURE 2.12 Insert Function Dialog Box

When you find the function you want, click OK. The Function Arguments dialog box opens so that you can enter the arguments for that specific function (see Figure 2.13). The following list explains the arguments in the Function Arguments dialog box:

- Argument names in **bold** (such as Number1 in the SUM function) are required.
- Argument names that are not bold (such as Number2 in the SUM function) are optional. The function can operate without the optional argument, which is used when you need additional specifications to calculate a result.

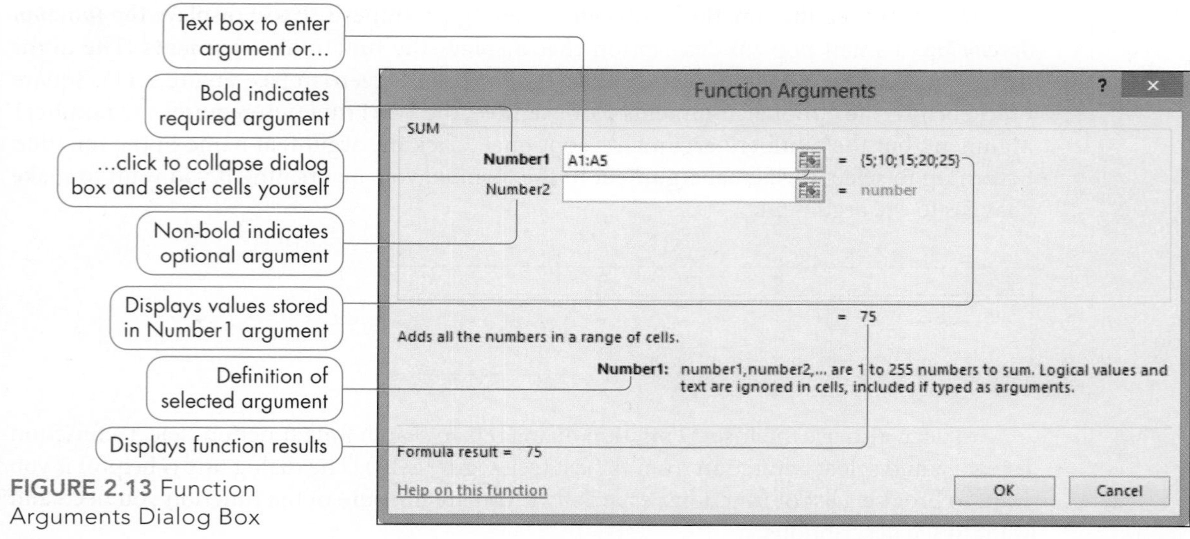

FIGURE 2.13 Function Arguments Dialog Box

Type the cell references in the argument boxes or click a collapse button to the right side of an argument box to collapse the dialog box and select the cell or range of cells in the worksheet to designate as that argument. If you click the collapse button to select a range, you need to click the expand button to expand the dialog box again. The value, or results, of a formula contained in the argument cell displays on the right side of the argument box (such as 5; 10; 15; 20; 25—the values stored in the range A1:A5 used for the Number1 argument). If the argument is not valid, Excel displays an error description on the right side of the argument box.

The bottom of the Function Arguments dialog box displays a description of the function and a description of the argument containing the insertion point. As you enter arguments, the bottom of the dialog box also displays the results of the function, such as 75.

If you enter a function and #NAME? displays in the cell, you might have mistyped the function name. To avoid this problem, select the function name from the Formula AutoComplete list as you type the function name, or use the Insert Function dialog box. You can type a function name in lowercase letters. If you type the name correctly, Excel converts the name to all capital letters when you press Enter, indicating that you spelled the function name correctly.

Inserting Basic Math and Statistics Functions

Excel includes commonly used math and statistical functions that you can use for a variety of calculations. For example, you can insert functions to calculate the total amount you spend on dining out in a month, the average amount you spend per month downloading music from iTunes®, your highest electric bill, and your lowest time to run a mile this week.

Calculate a Total with the SUM Function

STEP 1

The ***SUM function*** totals values in two or more cells and displays the result in the cell containing the function. This function is more efficient to create when you need to add the values contained in three or more cells. For example, to add the contents of cells A2 through A14, you could enter =A2+A3+A4+A5+A6+A7+A8+A9+A10+A11+A12+A13+A14, which is time-consuming and increases the probability of entering an inaccurate cell reference, such as entering a cell reference twice or accidentally leaving out a cell reference. Instead, you should use the SUM function, =SUM(A2:A14).

=SUM(number 1, [number 2],...)

Function Syntax

In this book, the function syntax lines are highlighted. Brackets [ ] indicate optional arguments; however, do not actually type the brackets when you enter the argument.

The SUM function contains one required argument (Number1) that represents a range of cells to add. The range, such as A2:A14, specifies the first and last cells containing values to SUM. Excel will sum all cells within that range. The Number2 optional argument is used when you want to sum values stored in nonadjacent cells or ranges, such as =SUM(A2:A14,F2:F14). The ellipsis in the function syntax indicates you can add as many additional ranges as desired, separated by commas.

Avoiding Functions for Basic Formulas

Do not use a function for a basic mathematical expression. For example, although =SUM(B4/C4) produces the same result as =B4/C4, the SUM function is not needed to perform the basic arithmetic division. Furthermore, someone taking a quick look at that formula might assume it performs addition instead of division. Use the most appropriate, clear-cut formula, =B4/C4.

To insert the SUM function (for example, to sum the values in the range A2:A14), do one of the following:

- Type =SUM(A2:A14) and press Enter.
- Type =SUM(and drag to select the range A2:A14 with the mouse. Type the ending #) and press Enter.
- Click in cell A15, click Sum in the Editing group on the HOME tab, press Enter to select the suggested range or type (or drag to select) A2:A14, and then press Enter.
- Click in cell A15, click Sum in the Function Library group on the FORMULAS tab, press Enter to select the suggested range or type A2:A14, and then press Enter.

Figure 2.14 shows the result of using the SUM function in cell D2 to total scores (898).

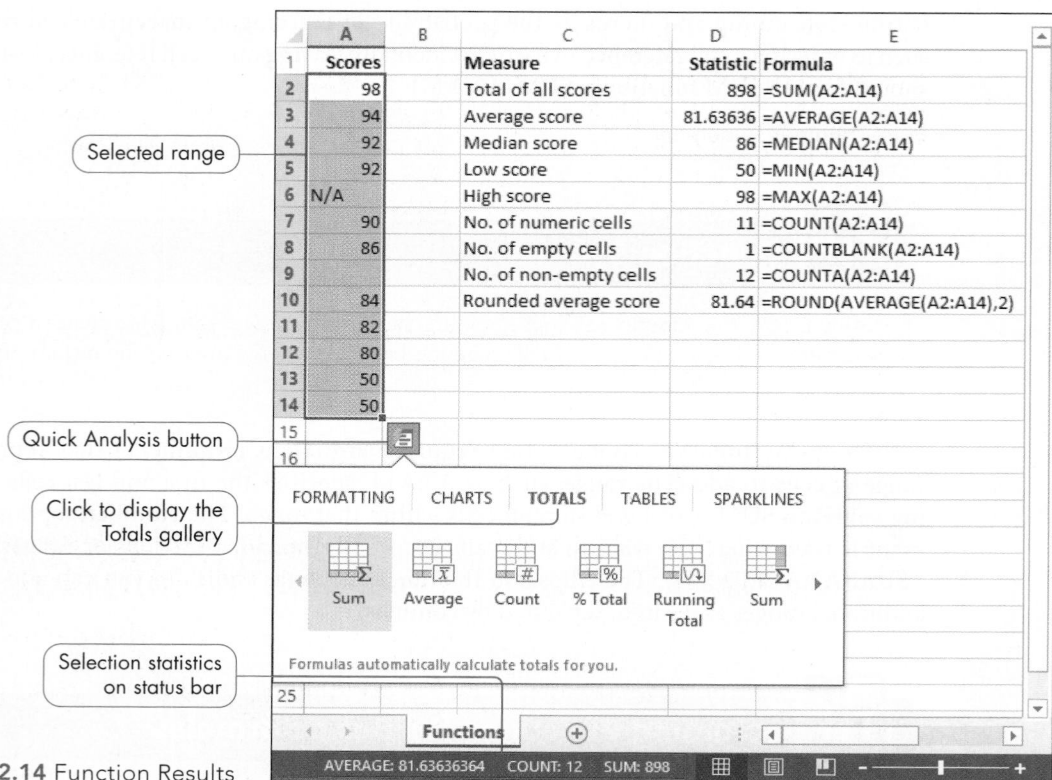

FIGURE 2.14 Function Results

TIP Sum Arrow

If you click Sum, Excel inserts the SUM function. However, if you click the Sum arrow in the Editing group on the Home tab or in the Function Library group on the Formulas tab, Excel displays a list of basic functions to select: Sum, Average, Count Numbers, Max, and Min. If you want to insert another function, select More Functions from the list.

Find Central Tendency with AVERAGE and MEDIAN

STEP 2»

People often describe data based on central tendency, which means that values tend to cluster around a central value. Excel provides two functions to calculate central tendency: AVERAGE and MEDIAN. The ***AVERAGE function*** calculates the arithmetic mean, or average, for the values in a range of cells. You can use this function to calculate the class average on a biology test or the average number of points scored per game by a basketball player. In Figure 2.14, =AVERAGE(A2:A14) in cell D3 returns 81.63636 as the average test score. The AVERAGE function ignores empty cells and cells containing N/A or text.

```
=AVERAGE(number 1,[number2],...)
```

STEP 3»

The ***MEDIAN function*** finds the midpoint value, which is the value that one half of the data set is above or below. The median is particularly useful because extreme values often influence arithmetic mean calculated by the AVERAGE function. In Figure 2.14, the two extreme test scores of 50 distort the average. The rest of the test scores range from 80 to 98. Cell D4 contains =MEDIAN(A2:A14). The median for test scores is 86, which indicates that half the test scores are above 86 and half the test scores are below 86. This statistic is more reflective of the data set than the average is. The MEDIAN function ignores empty cells and cells containing N/A or text.

```
=MEDIAN(number 1,[number 2],...)
```

Identify Low and High Values with MIN and MAX

STEP 4》 The ***MIN function*** analyzes an argument list to determine the lowest value, such as the lowest score on a test. Manually inspecting a range of values to identify the lowest value is inefficient, especially in large spreadsheets. If you change values in the range, the MIN function will identify the new lowest value and display it in the cell containing the MIN function. In Figure 2.14, =MIN(A2:A14) in cell D5 identifies that 50 is the lowest test score.

```
=MIN(number 1,[number 2],...)
```

The ***MAX function*** analyzes an argument list to determine the highest value, such as the highest score on a test. Like the MIN function, when the values in the range change, the MAX function will display the new highest value within the range of cells. In Figure 2.14, =MAX(A2:A14) in cell D6 identifies 98 as the highest test score.

```
=MAX(number 1,[number 2],...)
```

Nonadjacent Ranges

You can use multiple ranges as arguments, such as finding the largest number within two nonadjacent (nonconsecutive) ranges. For example, you can find the highest test score where some scores are stored in cells A2:A14 and others are stored in cells K2:K14. Separate each range with a comma in the argument list, so that the formula is =MAX(A2:A14,K2:K14).

Identify the Total Number with COUNT Functions

Excel provides three basic count functions—COUNT, COUNTBLANK and COUNTA—to count the cells in a range that meet a particular criterion. The ***COUNT function*** tallies the number of cells in a range that contain values you can use in calculations, such as numerical and date data, but excludes blank cells or text entries from the tally. In Figure 2.14, the selected range spans 13 cells; however, =COUNT(A2:A14) in cell D7 returns 11, the number of cells that contain numerical data. It does not count the cell containing the text *N/A* or the blank cell.

The ***COUNTBLANK function*** tallies the number of cells in a range that are blank. In Figure 2.14, =COUNTBLANK(A2:A14) in cell D8 identifies that one cell in the range A2:A14 is blank. The ***COUNTA function*** tallies the number of cells in a range that are not blank, that is, cells that contain data, whether a value, text, or a formula. In Figure 2.14, =COUNTA(A2:A14) in cell D9 returns 12, indicating the range A2:A14 contains 12 cells that contain some form of data. It does not count the blank cell.

```
=COUNT(number 1,[number 2],...)
=COUNTBLANK(number 1,[number 2],...)
=COUNTA(number 1,[number 2],...)
```

Status Bar Statistics: Average, Count, and Sum

When you select a range of cells containing values, by default Excel displays the average, count, and sum of those values on the status bar (see Figure 2.14). You can customize the status bar to show other selection statistics, such as the minimum and maximum values for a selected range. To display or hide particular selection statistics, right-click the status bar and select the statistic.

Perform Calculations with Quick Analysis Tools

Excel 2013 contains a new feature called ***Quick Analysis***, which is a set of analytical tools you can use to apply formatting, create charts or tables, and insert basic functions. When you select a range of data, the Quick Analysis button displays in the bottom-right corner of the selected range. Click the Quick Analysis button to display the Quick Analysis gallery and select the analytical tool to meet your needs.

Figure 2.14 shows the TOTALS options so that you can sum, average, or count the values in the selected range. Select % Total to display the percentage of the grand total of two or more columns. Select Running Total to provide a cumulative total at the bottom of multiple columns.

Use Other Math and Statistical Functions

In addition to the functions you have learned in this chapter, Excel provides more than 100 other math and statistical functions. Table 2.2 lists and describes some of these functions that you might find helpful in your business, education, and general statistics courses.

TABLE 2.2 Math and Statistical Functions

Function Syntax	Description
=ABS(number)	Displays the absolute (i.e., positive) value of a number.
=FREQUENCY(data_array,bins_array)	Counts how often values appear in a given range.
=INT(number)	Rounds a value number down to the nearest whole number.
=MODE.SNGL(number1,[number2],...)	Displays the most frequently occurring value in a list.
=RANK.AVG(number,ref,[order])	Identifies a value's rank within a list of values; returns an average rank for identical values.
=RANK.EQ(number,ref,[order])	Identifies a value's rank within a list of values; the top rank is identified for all identical values.
=ROUND(number,num_digits)	Rounds a value to a specific number of digits. Rounds numbers of 5 and greater up and those less than 5 down.

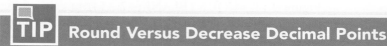

Round Versus Decrease Decimal Points

When you click Decrease Decimal in the Number group to display fewer or no digits after a decimal point, Excel still stores the original value's decimal places so that those digits can be used in calculations. The ROUND function changes the stored value to its rounded state.

Nest Functions as Arguments

A ***nested function*** occurs when one function is embedded as an argument within another function. Each function has its own set of arguments that must be included. For example, cell D10 in Figure 2.14 contains =ROUND(AVERAGE(A2:A14),2). The ROUND function requires two arguments: number and num_digits.

The AVERAGE function is nested in the *number* argument of the ROUND function. AVERAGE(A2:A14) returns 81.63636. That value is then rounded to two decimal places, indicated by 2 in the *num_digits* argument. The result is 81.64. If you change the second argument from 2 to 0, such as =ROUND(AVERAGE(A2:A14),0), the result would be 82.

Using Date Functions

Because Excel treats dates as serial numbers, you can perform calculations using dates. For example, assume today is January 1, 2016, and you graduate on May 6, 2016. To determine how many days until graduation, subtract today's date from the graduation date. Excel uses the serial numbers for these dates (42370 and 42494) to calculate the difference of 126 days.

Insert the TODAY Function

STEP 5»

The ***TODAY function*** displays the current date, such as 6/14/2016, in a cell. Excel updates the function results when you open or print the workbook. The TODAY() function does not require arguments, but you must include the parentheses. If you omit the parentheses, Excel displays #NAME? in the cell with a green triangle in the top-left corner of the cell. When you click the cell, an error icon appears that you can click for more information.

```
=TODAY()
```

Insert the NOW Function

The ***NOW function*** uses the computer's clock to display the date and military time, such as 6/14/2016 15:30, that you last opened the workbook. (Military time expresses time on a 24-hour period where 1:00 is 1 a.m. and 13:00 is 1 p.m.) The date and time will change every time the workbook is opened. Like the TODAY function, the NOW function does not require arguments, but you must include the parentheses. Omitting the parentheses creates a #NAME? error.

```
=NOW()
```

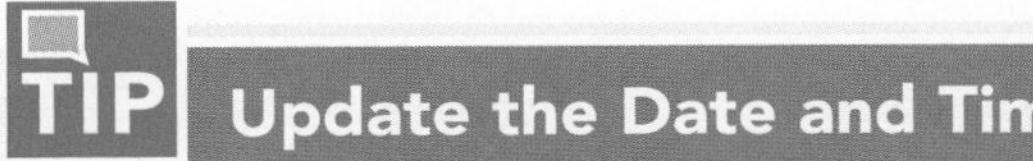

TIP Update the Date and Time

Both the TODAY and NOW functions display the date/time the workbook was last opened or last calculated. These functions do not continuously update the date and time while the workbook is open. To update the date and time, press F9 or click the Formulas tab and click *Calculate now* in the Calculation group.

Use Other Date & Time Functions

Excel contains a variety of other date functions. You can use these functions to calculate when employees are eligible for certain benefits, what the date is six months from now, or what day of the week a particular date falls on. Table 2.3 describes and Figure 2.15 shows examples of some date functions.

TABLE 2.3 Date Functions

Function Syntax	Description
=DATE(year,month,day)	Returns the serial number for a date.
=DAY(serial_number)	Displays the day (1–31) within a given month for a date or its serial number.
=EDATE(start_date,months)	Displays the serial number using the General format of a date a specified number of months in the future (using a positive value) or past (using a negative value). Displays the actual future or past date in Short Date format.
=EOMONTH(start_date,months)	Identifies the serial number of the last day of a month using General format or the exact last day of a month using Short Date format for a specified number of months from a date's serial number.
=MONTH(serial_number)	Returns the month (1–12) for a serial number, where 1 is January and 12 is December.
=WEEKDAY(serial_number, [return_type])	Identifies the weekday (1–7) for a serial number, where 1 is Sunday and 7 is Saturday (the default with no second argument); can specify a second argument for different numbers assigned to weekdays (see Help).
=YEAR(serial_number)	Identifies the year for a serial number.
=YEARFRAC(start_date,end_date,[basis])	Calculates the fraction of a year between two dates based on the number of whole days.

	A	B	C	D	E	F
1	**Inputs:**	**7**	**11**	**2016**	**10/17/2016**	
2						
3	**Description**			**Format**	**Result**	**Formula**
4	Today's Date			Short Date	10/17/2016	=TODAY()
5	Today's Date			Other Date	October 17, 2016	=TODAY()
6	Today's Date and Military Time			Date/Time	10/17/2016 17:15	=NOW()
7	Serial # of Date			General	42562	=DATE(D1,B1,C1)
8	Serial # of Date			Short Date	7/11/2016	=DATE(D1,B1,C1)
9	Day within the Month			General	17	=DAY(E4) or =DAY(TODAY())
10	Serial # of Date 3 Months in Future			General	42752	=EDATE(E4,3)
11	Date 3 Months in Future			Short Date	1/17/2017	=EDATE(E4,3)
12	Date 3 Years in Future			Short Date	10/17/2019	=EDATE(E4,3*12)
13	Date 2 Months Ago			Short Date	8/17/2016	=EDATE(E4,-2)
14	Serial # of Date 6 Months in Future			General	42746	=EDATE(DATE(D1,B1,C1),6)
15	Serial # of Last Day in 6 Months			General	42855	=EOMONTH(E4,6) or =EOMONTH(TODAY())
16	Last Day of 6 Months in Future			Short Date	4/30/2017	=EOMONTH(E4,6) or =EOMONTH(TODAY())
17	Month Number (where 6=June)			General	10	=MONTH(E5) or =MONTH(TODAY())
18	Week day (1=Sunday; 7=Saturday)			General	2	=WEEKDAY(E4)
19	Week day (1=Monday; 7=Sunday)			General	1	=WEEKDAY(E4,2)
20	Year for a Serial Date			General	2016	=YEAR(E4) or =YEAR(TODAY())
21	Fraction of Year 7/11/2016-10/17/2016			General	0.266666667	=YEARFRAC(DATE(D1,B1,C1),E1)

FIGURE 2.15 Date Function Examples

You can nest a date function inside another date function, such as =DAY(TODAY()). This nested function TODAY() first identifies today's date, and from that date, the DAY function identifies the day of the month. In Figure 2.15, cell E21 contains =YEARFRAC(DATE(D1,B1,C1),E1). The DATE function is nested to combine values in three cells (D1, B1, and C1) to build a date (7/11/2016). Excel finds the number of days between that date and 10/17/2016, the date stored in cell E1. From there, the YEARFRAC function calculates the fraction of a year (26.667%) between those two dates. Had 7/11/2016 been stored as a date in a single cell, the formula would simplify to something like =YEARFRAC(D1,E1).

TIP Date Functions and Arithmetic Operations

You can combine date functions with arithmetic operations. For example, you sign a lease on June 14, 2016, for three years. The starting date is stored in cell E4. What date does your lease expire? Enter =EDATE(E4,3*12)-1 to calculate the expiration date. The first argument, E4, is the cell containing the start date, and the second argument, 3*12, equals three years containing 12 months each, or 36 months. (In an actual worksheet, you should store the value 36 in a cell instead of typing numbers in the argument.) That result is June 14, 2019, but the lease actually expires the day before. So you must then subtract 1 from the function result to calculate the June 13, 2019, date.

Quick Concepts

1. What visual features help guide you through typing a function directly in a cell? ***pp. 456–457***
2. What type of data do you enter in a Function Arguments dialog box, and what are four things the dialog box tells you? ***pp. 457–458***
3. What is the difference between the AVERAGE and MEDIAN functions? ***p. 460***
4. What is a nested function, and why would you create one? ***p. 462***
5. Provide three examples of using date functions to determine something specific. ***p. 464***

Hands-On Exercises

2 Function Basics

The Townsend Mortgage Company's worksheet contains an area in which you must enter summary statistics. In addition, you need to include today's date and identify the year in which each mortgage will be paid off.

Skills covered: Use the SUM Function • Use the AVERAGE Function • Use the MEDIAN Function • Use the MIN, MAX, and COUNT Functions • Use the TODAY and YEAR Functions

STEP 1 » USE THE SUM FUNCTION

The first summary statistic you need to calculate is the total value of the houses bought by the borrowers. You will use the SUM function. Refer to Figure 2.16 as you complete Step 1.

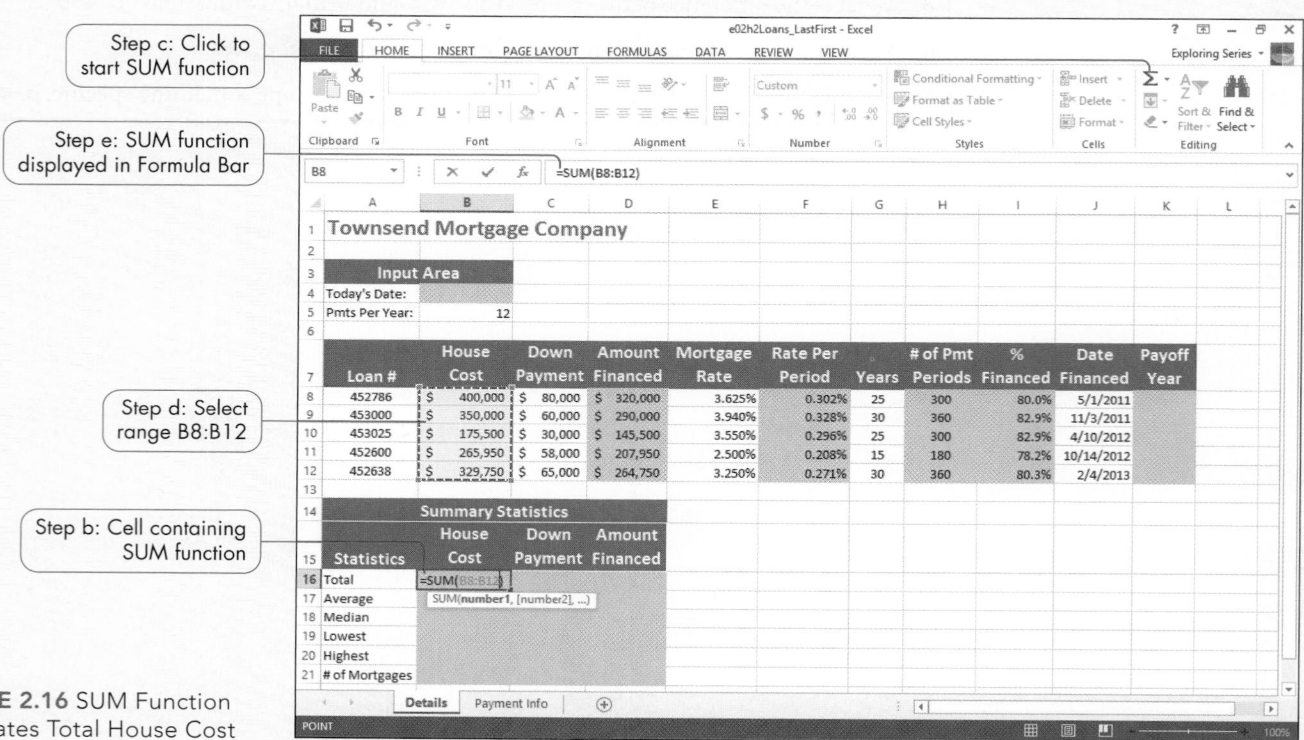

FIGURE 2.16 SUM Function Calculates Total House Cost

a. Open *e02h1Loans_LastFirst* if you closed it at the end of Hands-On Exercise 1 and save it as **e02h2Loans_LastFirst**, changing *h1* to *h2*.

b. Make sure the Details worksheet is active and click **cell B16**, the cell where you will enter a formula for the total house cost.

c. Click **Sum** in the Editing group on the HOME tab.

> **TROUBLESHOOTING:** Click the main part of the Sum command. If you click the Sum arrow, select Sum.

Excel anticipates the range of cells containing values you want to sum based on where you enter the formula—in this case, A8:D15. This is not the correct range, so you must enter the correct range.

d. Select the **range B8:B12**, the cells containing house costs.

As you use the semi-selection process, Excel enters the range in the SUM function.

> **TROUBLESHOOTING:** If you entered the function without changing the arguments, repeat steps b–d or edit the arguments in the Formula Bar by deleting the default range, typing B8:B12 between the parentheses and pressing Enter.

e. Click **Enter** (the checkmark between the Name Box and Formula Bar) and save the workbook.

Cell B16 contains the function = SUM(B8:B12), and the result is $1,521,200.

STEP 2 » USE THE AVERAGE FUNCTION

Before copying the functions to calculate the total down payments and amounts financed, you want to calculate the average house cost bought by the borrowers in your list. Refer to Figure 2.17 as you complete Step 2.

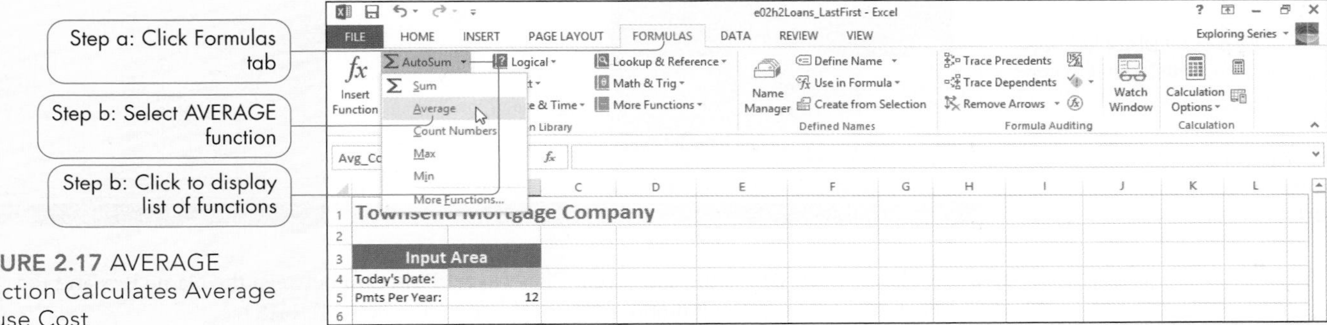

FIGURE 2.17 AVERAGE Function Calculates Average House Cost

a. Click the **FORMULAS tab** and click **cell B17**, the cell where you will display the average cost of the houses.

b. Click the **Sum arrow** in the Function Library group and select **Average**.

Excel selects cell B15, which is the total cost of the houses. You need to change the range.

> **TROUBLESHOOTING:** Sum, like some other commands in Excel, contains two parts: the main command icon and an arrow. Click the main command icon when instructed to click Sum to perform the default action. Click the arrow when instructed to click the Sum arrow for additional options. If you accidentally clicked Sum instead of the arrow, press Esc to cancel the SUM function from being completed and try step b again.

c. Select the **range B8:B12**, the cells containing the house costs.

The function is =AVERAGE(B8:B12).

d. Press **Enter**, make **cell B18** the active cell, and save the workbook.

The average house cost is $304,240.

STEP 3 » USE THE MEDIAN FUNCTION

You realize that extreme house costs may distort the average. Therefore, you decide to identify the median house cost to compare it to the average house cost. Refer to Figure 2.18 as you complete Step 3.

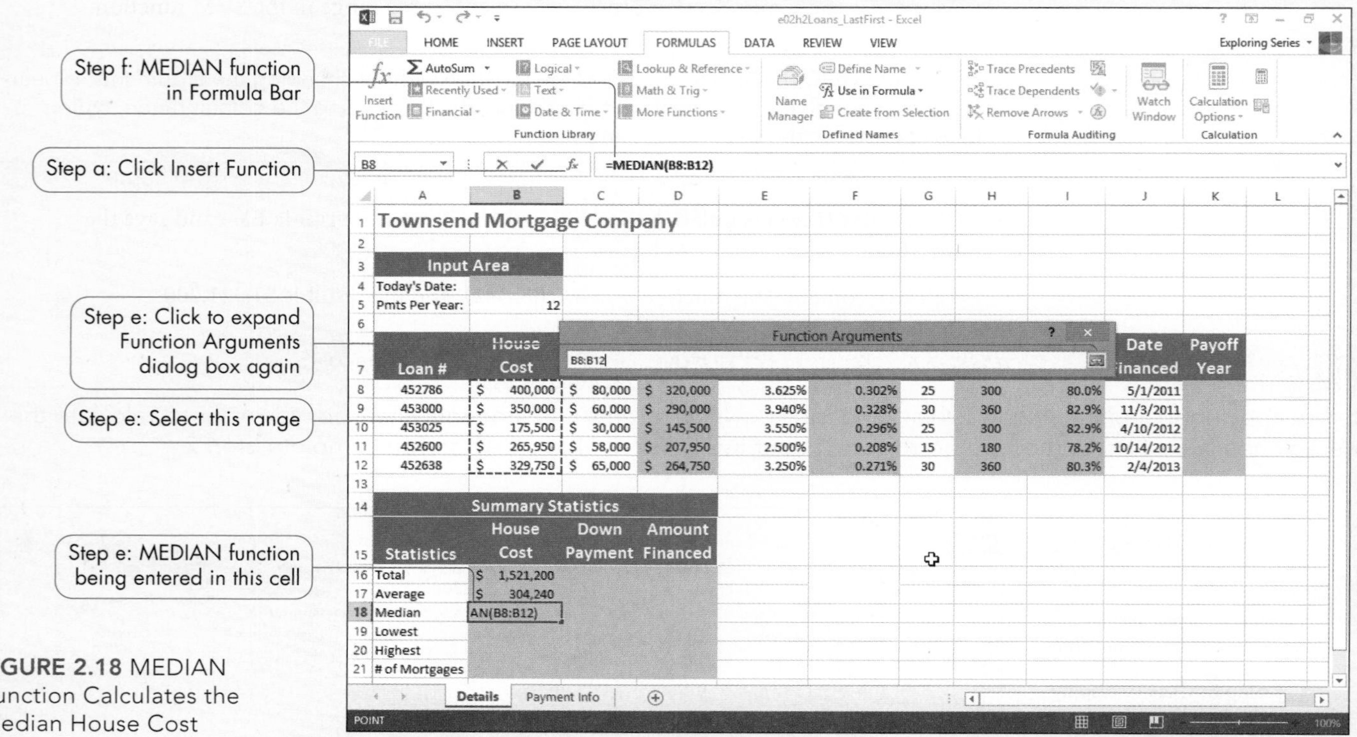

FIGURE 2.18 MEDIAN Function Calculates the Median House Cost

a. Make sure **cell B18** is the active cell. Click **Insert Function** between the Name Box and the Formula Bar, or in the Function Library group on the FORMULAS tab.

The Insert Function dialog box opens. Use this dialog box to select the MEDIAN function since it is not available on the Ribbon.

b. Type **median** in the **Search for a function box** and click **Go**.

Excel displays a list of functions in the *Select a function* list. The MEDIAN function is selected at the top of the list; the bottom of the dialog box displays the syntax and the description.

c. Read the MEDIAN function's description and click **OK**.

The Function Arguments dialog box opens. It contains one required argument, Number1, representing a range of cells containing values. It has an optional argument, Number2, which you can use if you have nonadjacent ranges that contain values.

d. Click the **collapse button** to the right of the Number1 box.

You collapsed the Function Arguments dialog box so that you can select the range.

e. Select the **range B8:B12** and click the **expand button** in the Function Arguments dialog box.

The Function Arguments dialog box expands, displaying B8:B12 in the Number1 box.

f. Click **OK** to accept the function arguments and close the dialog box. Save the workbook.

Half of the houses purchased cost more than the median, $329,750, and half of the houses cost less than this value. Notice the difference between the median and the average: The average is lower because it is affected by the lowest-priced house, $175,500.

STEP 4 » USE THE MIN, MAX, AND COUNT FUNCTIONS

Erica wants to know the least and most expensive houses so that she can analyze typical customers of the Townsend Mortgage Company. You will use the MIN and MAX functions to obtain these statistics. In addition, you will use the COUNT function to tally the number of mortgages in the sample. Refer to Figure 2.19 as you complete Step 4.

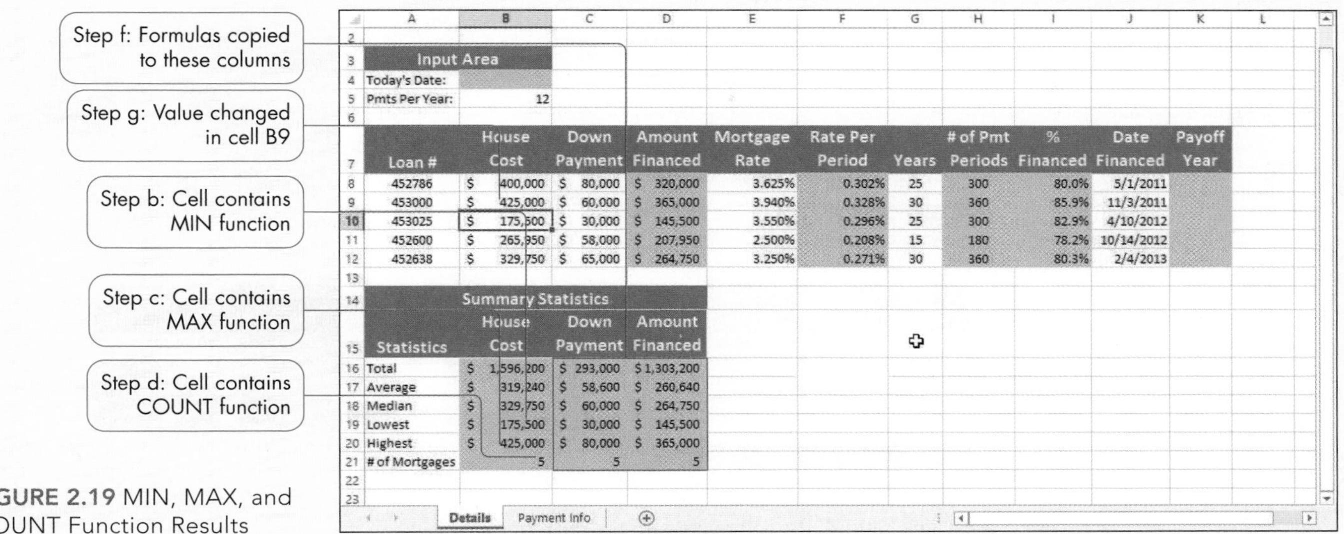

Loan #	House Cost	Down Payment	Amount Financed	Mortgage Rate	Rate Per Period	Years	# of Pmt Periods	% Financed	Date Financed	Payoff Year
452786	$ 400,000	$ 80,000	$ 320,000	3.625%	0.302%	25	300	80.0%	5/1/2011	
453000	$ 425,000	$ 60,000	$ 365,000	3.940%	0.328%	30	360	85.9%	11/3/2011	
453025	$ 175,500	$ 30,000	$ 145,500	3.550%	0.296%	25	300	82.9%	4/10/2012	
452600	$ 265,950	$ 58,000	$ 207,950	2.500%	0.208%	15	180	78.2%	10/14/2012	
452638	$ 329,750	$ 65,000	$ 264,750	3.250%	0.271%	30	360	80.3%	2/4/2013	

Summary Statistics			
Statistics	House Cost	Down Payment	Amount Financed
Total	$ 1,596,200	$ 293,000	$ 1,303,200
Average	$ 319,240	$ 58,600	$ 260,640
Median	$ 329,750	$ 60,000	$ 264,750
Lowest	$ 175,500	$ 30,000	$ 145,500
Highest	$ 425,000	$ 80,000	$ 365,000
# of Mortgages	5	5	5

FIGURE 2.19 MIN, MAX, and COUNT Function Results

a. Click **cell B19**, the cell to display the cost of the lowest-costing house.

b. Click the **Sum arrow** in the Function Library group, select **Min**, select the **range B8:B12**, and then press **Enter**.

The MIN function identifies that the lowest-costing house is $175,500.

c. Click **cell B20**, if necessary. Click the **Sum arrow** in the Function Library group, select **Max**, select the **range B8:B12**, and then press **Enter**.

The MAX function identifies that the highest-costing house is $400,000.

d. Click **cell B21**, if necessary. Type **=COUNT(B8:B12)** and press **Enter**.

As you type the letter *C*, Formula AutoComplete suggests functions starting with *C*. As you continue typing, the list of functions narrows. After you type the beginning parenthesis, Excel displays the function ScreenTip, indicating the arguments for the function. The range B8:B12 contains five cells.

e. Select the **range B16:B21**.

You want to select the range of original statistics to copy the cells all at one time to the next two columns.

f. Drag the fill handle to the right by two columns to copy the functions. Click **cell D21**.

Because you used relative cell references in the functions, the range changes from =COUNT(B8:B12) to =COUNT(D8:D12).

g. Change the value in **cell B9** to **425000**. Save the workbook.

The results of several formulas and functions change, including the total, average, and max house costs.

STEP 5 » USE THE TODAY AND YEAR FUNCTIONS

You have two date functions (TODAY and YEAR) to enter to complete the first worksheet. The TODAY function will display today's date, and you will use the YEAR function in a formula to calculate the payoff year for each mortgage. Refer to Figure 2.20 as you complete Step 5.

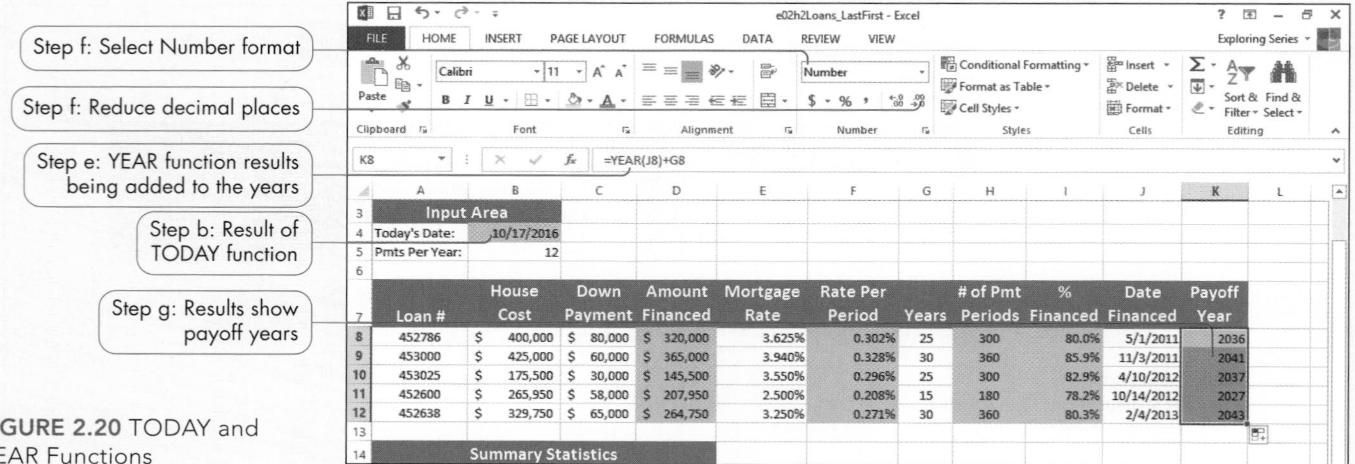

FIGURE 2.20 TODAY and YEAR Functions

a. Click **cell B4**, the cell to contain the current date.

b. Click **Date & Time** in the Function Library group, select **TODAY** to display the Function Arguments dialog box, and then click **OK** to close the dialog box.

The Function Arguments dialog box opens, although no arguments are necessary for this function. Excel inserts the current date in Short Date format, such as 1/2/2016, based on the computer system's date.

c. Click **cell K8**, click **Date & Time** in the Function Library group, scroll through the list, and then select **YEAR**.

The Function Arguments dialog box opens so that you can enter the argument, a serial number for a date.

d. Click **cell J8** to enter it in the **Serial_number box**. Click **OK**.

The function returns 2011, the year the first mortgage was taken out. However, you want the year the mortgage will be paid off. The YEAR function returns the year from a date. You need to add the years to the result of the function to calculate the year that the borrower will pay off the mortgage.

e. Press **F2** to edit the formula stored in **cell K8**. With the insertion point on the right side of the closing parenthesis, type **+G8** and press **Ctrl+Enter**.

Pressing Ctrl+Enter is the alternative to clicking Enter by the Formula Bar. It keeps the current cell as the active cell. The results show a date: 7/28/1905. You need to apply the Number format to display the year.

f. Click the **HOME tab**, click the **Number Format arrow** in the Number group, and then select **Number**. Decrease the number of decimal places to show the value as a whole number.

You applied the Number format instead of the Comma format because although the Comma format is correct for quantities, such as 2,036 units, it is not appropriate for the year 2036.

g. Copy the formula down the Payoff Year column.

h. Save the workbook. Keep the workbook open if you plan to continue with the next Hands-On Exercise. If not, close the workbook and exit Excel.

Logical, Lookup, and Financial Functions

As you prepare complex spreadsheets using functions, you will frequently use three function categories: logical, lookup and reference, and finance. Logical functions test the logic of a situation and return a particular result. Lookup and reference functions are useful when you need to look up a value in a list to identify the applicable value. Financial functions are useful to anyone who plans to take out a loan or invest money.

In this section, you will learn how to use the logical, lookup, and financial functions.

Determining Results with the IF Function

STEP 3»

The most common logical function is the ***IF function***, which returns one value when a condition is met or is true and returns another value when the condition is not met or is false. For example, a company gives a $500 bonus to employees who sold *over* $10,000 in merchandise this week, but no bonus to employees who did not sell over $10,000 in merchandise. Figure 2.21 shows a worksheet containing the sales data for three representatives and their bonuses, if any.

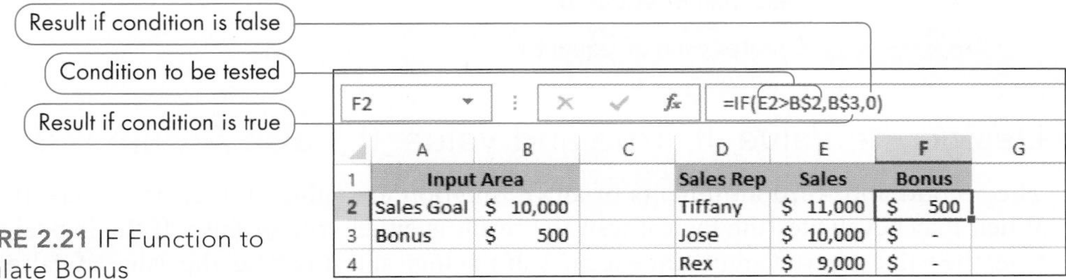

	A	B	C	D	E	F	G
1	Input Area			Sales Rep	Sales	Bonus	
2	Sales Goal	$ 10,000		Tiffany	$ 11,000	$ 500	
3	Bonus	$ 500		Jose	$ 10,000	$ -	
4				Rex	$ 9,000	$ -	

FIGURE 2.21 IF Function to Calculate Bonus

The IF function has three arguments: (1) a condition that is tested to determine if it is either true or false, (2) the resulting value if the condition is true, and (3) the resulting value if the condition is false.

=IF(logical_test,value_if_true,value_if_false)

You might find it helpful to create two flowcharts to illustrate an IF function. First, construct a flowchart that uses words and numbers to illustrate the condition and results. For example, the left flowchart in Figure 2.22 illustrates the condition to see if sales are greater than $10,000, and the $500 bonus if the condition is true or $0 if the condition is false. Then, create a second flowchart similar to the one on the right side of Figure 2.22 that replaces the words and values with actual cell references. Creating these flowcharts can help you construct the IF function that is used in cell F2 in Figure 2.21.

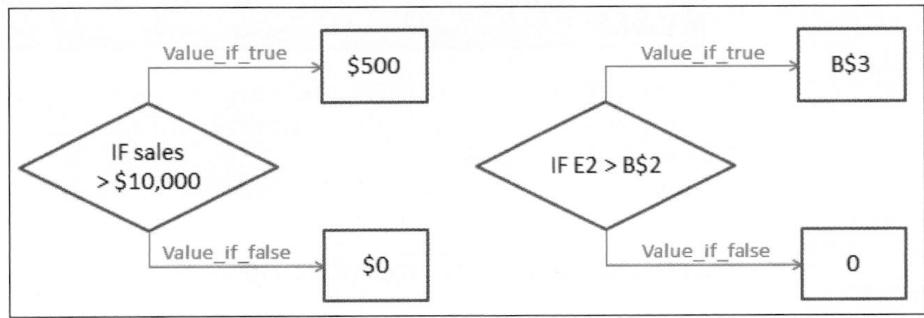

FIGURE 2.22 Flowcharts Illustrating IF Function

Design the Logical Test

The first argument for the IF function is the logical test. The ***logical test*** is a formula that contains either a value or an expression that evaluates to true or false. The logical expression is typically a binary expression, meaning that it requires a comparison between at least two variables, such as the values stored in cells E2 and B2. Table 2.4 lists and describes the logical operators to make the comparison in the logical test.

In Figure 2.21, cell F2 contains an IF function where the logical test is E2>B$2 to determine if Tiffany's sales in cell E2 are greater than the sales goal in cell B2. The reference to cell B2 can be mixed B$2 or absolute $B$2. Either way, copying the function down the column will compare each sales representative's sales with the $10,000 value in cell B2.

TABLE 2.4 Logical Operators

Operator	Description
=	Equal to
<>	Not equal to
<	Less than
>	Greater than
<=	Less than or equal to
>=	Greater than or equal to

Design the Value_If_True and Value_If_False Arguments

The second and third arguments of an IF function are value_if_true and value_if_false. When Excel evaluates the logical test, the result is either true or false. If the logical test is true, the value_if_true argument executes. If the logical test is false, the value_if_false argument executes. Only one of the last two arguments is executed; both arguments cannot be executed, because the logical test is either true or false but not both.

The value_if_true and value_if_false arguments can contain text, cell references, formulas, or constants (not recommended unless –1, 1, or 0). In Figure 2.21, cell F2 contains an IF function in which the value_if_true argument is B$3 and the value_if_false argument is 0. Because the logical test (E2>B$2) is true—that is, Tiffany's sales of $11,000 are greater than the $10,000 goal—the value_if_true argument is executed, and the result displays $500, the value that is stored in cell B3.

Jose's sales of $10,000 are not *greater than* $10,000, and Rex's sales of $9,000 are not *greater than* $10,000. Therefore, the value_if_false argument is executed and returns no bonus in cells F3 and F4.

At Least Two Possible Right Answers

Every IF function can have at least two right solutions to produce the same results. For example, if the logical test is E2<=B$2 for Figure 2.21, the value_if_true is 0, and the value_if_false is B$3.

Create Other IF Functions

Figure 2.23 illustrates several IF functions, how they are evaluated, and their results. The input area contains values that are used in the logical tests and results. You can create this worksheet with the input area and IF functions to develop your understanding of how IF functions work.

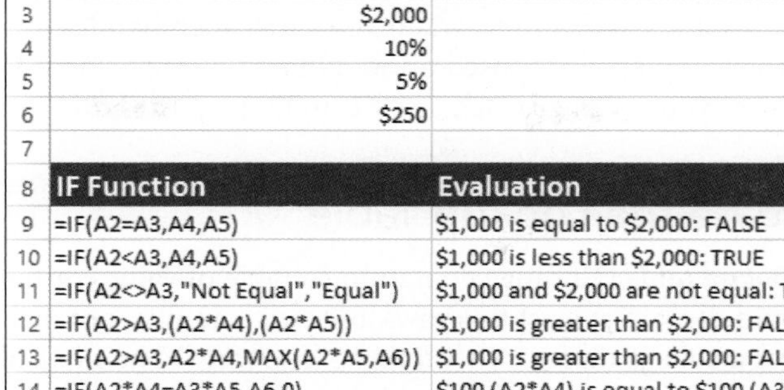

	A	B	C
1	Input Values		
2	$1,000		
3	$2,000		
4	10%		
5	5%		
6	$250		
7			
8	IF Function	Evaluation	Result
9	=IF(A2=A3,A4,A5)	$1,000 is equal to $2,000: FALSE	5%
10	=IF(A2<A3,A4,A5)	$1,000 is less than $2,000: TRUE	10%
11	=IF(A2<>A3,"Not Equal","Equal")	$1,000 and $2,000 are not equal: TRUE	Not Equal
12	=IF(A2>A3,(A2*A4),(A2*A5))	$1,000 is greater than $2,000: FALSE	$50
13	=IF(A2>A3,A2*A4,MAX(A2*A5,A6))	$1,000 is greater than $2,000: FALSE	$250
14	=IF(A2*A4=A3*A5,A6,0)	$100 (A2*A4) is equal to $100 (A3*A5): TRUE	$250

FIGURE 2.23 Sample IF Functions

- **Cell A9.** The logical test A2=A3 compares the values in cells A2 and A3 to see if they are equal. Because $1,000 is not equal to $2,000, the logical test is false. The value_if_false argument is executed, which displays 5%, the value stored in cell A5.
- **Cell A10.** The logical test A2<A3 determines if the value in cell A2 is less than the value in A3. Because $1,000 is less than $2,000, the logical test is true. The value_if_true argument is executed, which displays the value stored in cell A4, which is 10%.
- **Cell A11.** The logical test A2<>A3 determines if the values in cells A2 and A3 are not equal. Because $1,000 and $2,000 are not equal, the logical test is true. The value_if_true argument is executed, which displays the text *Not Equal.*
- **Cell A12.** The logical test A2>A3 is false. The value_if_false argument is executed, which multiplies the value in cell A2 ($1,000) by the value in cell A5 (5%) and displays $50. The parentheses in the value_if_true (A2*A4) and value_if_false (A2*A5) arguments are optional. They are not required but may help you read the function arguments better.
- **Cell A13.** The logical test A2>A3 is false. The value_if_false argument, which contains a nested MAX function, is executed. The MAX function, MAX(A2*A5,A6), multiplies the values in cells A2 ($1,000) and A5 (5%) and returns the higher of the product ($50) and the value stored in cell A6 ($250).
- **Cell A14.** The logical test A2*A4=A3*A5 is true. The contents of cell A2 ($1,000) are multiplied by the contents of cell A4 (10%) for a result of $100. That result is then compared to the result of A3*A5, which is also $100. Because the logical test is true, the function returns the value of cell A6 ($250).

TIP Using Text in Formulas

You can use text within a formula. For example, you can build a logical test comparing the contents of cell A1 to specific text, such as A1="Input Values". The IF function in cell A11 in Figure 2.23 uses "Not Equal" and "Equal" in the value_if_true and value_if_false arguments. When you use text in a formula or function, you must enclose the text in quotation marks. However, do not use quotation marks around formulas, cell references, or values.

TIP Nest Functions in IF Functions

You can nest functions in the logical test, value_if_true, and value_if_false arguments of the IF function. When you nest functions as arguments, make sure the nested function contains the required arguments for it to work and that you nest the function in the correct argument to calculate accurate results. For example, cell C13 in Figure 2.23 contains a nested MAX function in the value_if_false argument.

Using Lookup Functions

You can use lookup and reference functions to look up values to perform calculations or display results. For example, when you order merchandise on a Web site, the Web server looks up the shipping costs based on weight and distance, or at the end of a semester, your professor uses your average, such as 88%, to look up the letter grade to assign, such as B+.

Create the Lookup Table

A ***lookup table*** is a range containing a table of values or text that can be retrieved. The table should contain at least two rows and two columns, not including headings. Figure 2.24 illustrates a college directory with three "columns." The first column contains professors' names. You look up a professor's name in the first column to see his or her office (second "column") and phone extension (third "column").

Brazil, Estivan	GT 218b	7243
Fiedler, Zazilia	CS 417	7860
Lam, Kaitlyn	SC 124a	7031
Rodriquez, Lisa	GT 304	7592
Yeung, Bradon	CS 414	7314

FIGURE 2.24 College Directory Lookup Table Analogy

It is important to plan the table so that it conforms to the way in which Excel can utilize the data in it. Excel cannot interpret the structure of Table 2.5. To look up a value in a range (such as the range 80–89), you must arrange data from the lowest to the highest value and include only the lowest value in the range (such as 80) instead of the complete range. If the values you look up are *exact* values, you can arrange the first column in any logical order. The lowest value for a category or in a series is the ***breakpoint***. The first column contains the breakpoints—such as 60, 70, 80, and 90—or the lowest values to achieve a particular grade. The lookup table contains one or more additional columns of related data to retrieve. Table 2.6 shows how to construct the lookup table in Excel.

TABLE 2.5 Grading Scale

Range	Grade
90–100	A
80–89	B
70–79	C
60–69	D
Below 60	F

TABLE 2.6 Grades Lookup Table

Range	Grade
0	F
60	D
70	C
80	B
90	A

Understand the VLOOKUP Function Syntax

STEP 1»

The ***VLOOKUP function*** accepts a value, looks the value up in a vertical lookup table, and returns a result. Use VLOOKUP to search for exact matches or for the nearest value that is less than or equal to the search value, such as assigning a B grade for an 87% class average. The VLOOKUP function has the following three required arguments and one optional argument: (1) lookup_value, (2) table_array, (3) col_index_number, and (4) range_lookup.

```
=VLOOKUP(lookup_value,table_array,col_index_number,[range_lookup])
```

Figure 2.25 shows a partial grade book that contains a vertical lookup table, as well as the final scores and letter grades. The function in cell F3 is =VLOOKUP(E3,$A$3:$B$7,2).

F3 =VLOOKUP(E3,$A$3:$B$7,2)

Value (final score) to look up

Table array range

Use second column within the table to return letter grade

	A	B	C	D	E	F	G
1	Grading Scale			Partial Gradebook			
2	Breakpoint	Grade		Names	Final Score	Letter Grade	
3	0	F		Abbott	85	B	
4	60	D		Carter	69	D	
5	70	C		Hon	90	A	
6	80	B		Jackson	74	C	
7	90	A		Miller	80	B	
8				Nelsen	78	C	

FIGURE 2.25 VLOOKUP Function for Grade Book

The ***lookup value*** is the cell reference of the cell that contains the value to look up. The lookup value for the first student is cell E3, which contains 85. The ***table array*** is the range that contains the lookup table: $A$3:$B$7. The table array range must be absolute and cannot include column labels for the lookup table. The ***column index number*** is the column number in the lookup table that contains the return values. In this example, the column index number is 2.

TIP Using Values in Formulas

You know to avoid using values in formulas because the input values in a worksheet cell might change. However, the value 2 is used in the col_index_number argument of the VLOOKUP function. The 2 refers to a particular column within the lookup table and is an acceptable use of a number within a formula.

Understand How Excel Processes the Lookup

Here is how the VLOOK function works:

1. The function identifies the value-stored cell used as the lookup value argument.
2. Excel searches the first column of the lookup table until it (a) finds an exact match (if possible) or (b) identifies the correct range if the lookup table contains breakpoints for range.
3. If Excel finds an exact match, it returns the value stored in the column designated by the column index number on that same row. If breakpoints are used and the lookup value is larger than the breakpoint, it looks to the next breakpoint to see if the lookup value is larger than that breakpoint also. When Excel detects that the lookup value is not greater than the next breakpoint, it stays on that row. It then uses the column index number to identify the column containing the value to return for the lookup value. Because Excel goes sequentially through the breakpoints, it is mandatory that the breakpoints are arranged from the lowest value to the highest value for ranges.

In Figure 2.25, the VLOOKUP function assigns letter grades based on final scores. Excel identifies the lookup value (85 in cell E3) and compares it to the values in the first column of the lookup table (range A3:B7). It tries to find an exact match of 85; however, the table contains breakpoints rather than every conceivable score. Because the lookup table is arranged from the lowest to the highest breakpoints, Excel detects that 85 is greater than the 80 breakpoint but is not greater than the 90 breakpoint. Therefore, it stays on the 80 row. Excel looks at the second column (column index number of 2) and returns the letter grade of B. The B grade is then stored in cell F3.

Use the Range_Lookup Argument

Instead of looking up values in a range, you can look up a value for an exact match using the optional range_lookup argument in the VLOOKUP function. By default, the range_lookup is set implicitly to TRUE, which is appropriate to look up values in a range. Omitting the optional argument or typing TRUE in it enables the VLOOKUP function to find the closest match in the table to the lookup value.

To look up an exact match, enter FALSE in the range_lookup argument. For example, if you are looking up product numbers, you must find an exact match to display the price. The function would look like this: =VLOOKUP(D15,$A$1:$B$50,2,FALSE). The function returns a value for the first lookup value that matches the first column of the lookup table. If no exact match is found, the function returns #N/A.

Nest Functions Inside the VLOOKUP Function

You can nest functions as arguments inside the VLOOKUP function. For example, Figure 2.26 illustrates shipping amounts that are based on weight and location (Boston or Chicago). In the VLOOKUP function in cell C3, the lookup_value argument looks up the weight of a package in cell A3. That weight (14 pounds) is looked up in the table_array argument, which is $E$3:$G$5. To determine which column of the lookup table to use, an IF function is nested as the column_index_number argument. The nested IF function compares the city stored in cell B3 to the text *Boston*. If cell B3 contains *Boston*, it returns 2 to use as the column_index_number to identify the shipping value for a package that is going to Boston. If cell B3 does not contain *Boston* (i.e., the only other city in this example is *Chicago*), the column_index_number is 3.

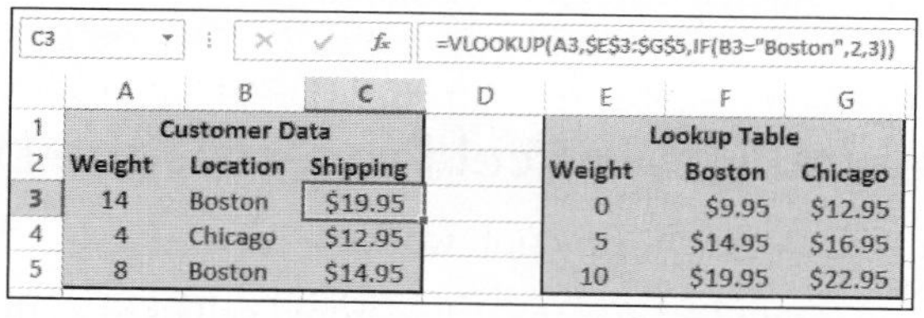

C3 =VLOOKUP(A3,$E$3:$G$5,IF(B3="Boston",2,3))

	A	B	C	D	E	F	G
1	Customer Data				Lookup Table		
2	Weight	Location	Shipping		Weight	Boston	Chicago
3	14	Boston	$19.95		0	$9.95	$12.95
4	4	Chicago	$12.95		5	$14.95	$16.95
5	8	Boston	$14.95		10	$19.95	$22.95

FIGURE 2.26 IF Function Nested in VLOOKUP Function

Use the HLOOKUP Function

You can design a lookup table horizontally where the first row contains the values for the basis of the lookup or the breakpoints, and additional rows contain data to be retrieved. With a horizontal lookup table, use the ***HLOOKUP function***. Table 2.7 shows how the grading scale would look as a horizontal lookup table.

TABLE 2.7 Horizontal Lookup Table

0	60	70	80	90
F	D	C	B	A

The syntax is almost the same as the syntax for the VLOOKUP function, except the third argument is row_index_number instead of col_index_number.

```
=HLOOKUP(lookup_value,table_array,row_index_number,[range_lookup])
```

Calculating Payments with the PMT Function

STEP 2

Excel contains several financial functions to help you perform calculations with monetary values. If you take out a loan to purchase a car, you need to know the monthly payment, which depends on the price of the car, the down payment, and the terms of the loan, in order to determine if you can afford the car. The decision is made easier by developing the worksheet in Figure 2.27 and by changing the various input values as indicated.

B9 | =PMT(B6,B8,-B3)

	A	B	C	D
1	Purchase Price	$25,999.00		
2	Down Payment	$ 5,000.00		
3	Amount to Finance	$20,999.00		
4	Payments per Year	12		
5	Interest Rate (APR)	3.500%		
6	Periodic Rate (Monthly)	0.292%		
7	Term (Years)	5		
8	No. of Payment Periods	60		
9	Monthly Payment	$ 382.01		
10				

FIGURE 2.27 Car Loan Worksheet

Creating a loan model helps you evaluate options. You realize that the purchase of a $25,999 car is prohibitive because the monthly payment is $382.01. Purchasing a less expensive car, coming up with a substantial down payment, taking out a longer-term loan, or finding a better interest rate can decrease your monthly payments.

The ***PMT function*** calculates payments for a loan with a fixed amount at a fixed periodic rate for a fixed time period. The PMT function uses three required arguments and up to two optional arguments: (1) rate, (2) nper, (3) pv, (4) fv, and (5) type.

```
=PMT(rate,nper,pv,[fv],[type])
```

The ***rate*** is the periodic interest rate, the interest rate per payment period. If the annual percentage rate (APR) is 12% and you make monthly payments, the periodic rate is 1% (12%/12 months). With the same APR and quarterly payments, the periodic rate is 3% (12%/4 quarters). Divide the APR by the number of payment periods in one year. However, instead of dividing the APR by 12 within the PMT function, calculate the periodic interest rate in cell B6 in Figure 2.27 and use that calculated rate in the PMT function.

The ***nper*** is the total number of payment periods. The term of a loan is usually stated in years; however, you make several payments per year. For monthly payments, you make 12 payments per year. To calculate the nper, multiply the number of years by the number of payments in one year. Instead of calculating the number of payment periods in the PMT function, calculate the number of payment periods in cell B8 and use that calculated value in the PMT function.

The ***pv*** is the present value of the loan. The result of the PMT function is a negative value because it represents your debt. However, you can display the result as a positive value by typing a minus sign in front of the present value cell reference in the PMT function.

Quick Concepts

1. Describe the three arguments for an IF function. ***pp. 471–472***
2. How should you structure a vertical lookup table if you need to look up values in a range? ***p. 474***
3. What are the first three arguments of a PMT function? Why would you have to divide by or multiply an argument by 12? ***p. 477***

Hands-On Exercises

MyITLab®
HOE3 Training

3 Logical, Lookup, and Financial Functions

Erica wants you to complete another model that she might use for future mortgage data analysis. As you study the model, you realize you need to incorporate logical, lookup, and financial functions.

Skills covered: Use the VLOOKUP Function • Use the PMT Function • Use the IF Function

STEP 1 » USE THE VLOOKUP FUNCTION

Rates vary based on the number of years to pay off the loan. Erica created a lookup table for three common mortgage years, and she entered the current APR. The lookup table will provide efficiency later when the rates change. You will use the VLOOKUP function to display the correct rate for each customer based on the number of years of the respective loans. Refer to Figure 2.28 as you complete Step 1.

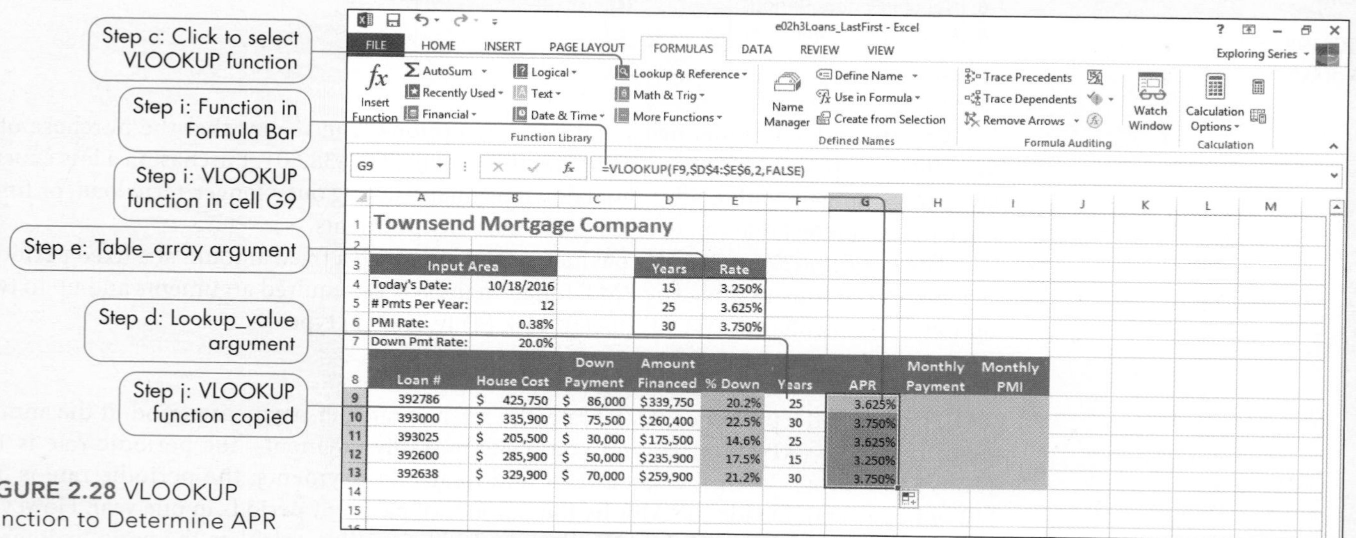

FIGURE 2.28 VLOOKUP Function to Determine APR

a. Open *e02h2Loans_LastFirst* if you closed it at the end of Hands-On Exercise 2 and save it as **e02h3Loans_LastFirst**, changing *h2* to *h3*.

b. Click the **Payment Info worksheet tab** to display the worksheet containing the data to complete. Click **cell G9**, the cell that will store the APR for the first customer.

c. Click the **FORMULAS tab**, click **Lookup & Reference** in the Function Library group, and then select **VLOOKUP**.

   The Function Arguments dialog box opens.

d. Click **F9** to enter F9 in the **Lookup_value box**.

   Cell F9 contains the value you need to look up from the table: 25 years.

> **TROUBLESHOOTING:** If you cannot see the cell you need to use in an argument, click the Function Arguments dialog box title bar and drag the dialog box on the screen until you can see and click the cell you need for the argument. Alternatively, you can click the collapse button to the right of the argument box to collapse the dialog box so that you can select the range. After selecting the range, click the expand button to expand the dialog box.

e. Press **Tab** and select the **range D4:E6** in the **Table_array box**.

This is the range that contains that data for the lookup table. The Years values in the table are arranged from lowest to highest. Do **not** select the column labels for the range.

Anticipate what will happen if you copy the formula down the column. What do you need to do to ensure that the cell references always point to the exact location of the table? If your answer is to make the table array cell references absolute, then you answered correctly.

f. Press **F4** to make the range references absolute.

The Table_array box now contains $D$4:$E$6.

g. Press **Tab** and type **2** in the **Col_index_num box**.

The second column of the lookup table contains the APRs that you want to return and display in the cells containing the formulas.

h. Press **Tab** and type **False** in the **Range_lookup box**.

You want the formula to display an error if an incorrect number of years has been entered. To ensure an exact match to look up in the table, you enter *False* in the optional argument.

i. Click **OK**.

The VLOOKUP function looks up the first person's years (25), finds an exact match in the first column of the lookup table, and then returns the corresponding APR, which is 3.625%.

j. Copy the formula down the column and save the workbook.

Spot check the results to make sure the function returned the correct APR based on the number of years.

STEP 2 ›› USE THE PMT FUNCTION

The worksheet now has all the necessary data for you to calculate the monthly payment for each loan: the APR, the number of years for the loan, the number of payment periods in one year, and the initial loan amount. You will use the PMT function to calculate the monthly payment, which includes paying back the principal amount with interest. This calculation does not include escrow amounts, such as property taxes or insurance. Refer to Figure 2.29 as you complete Step 2.

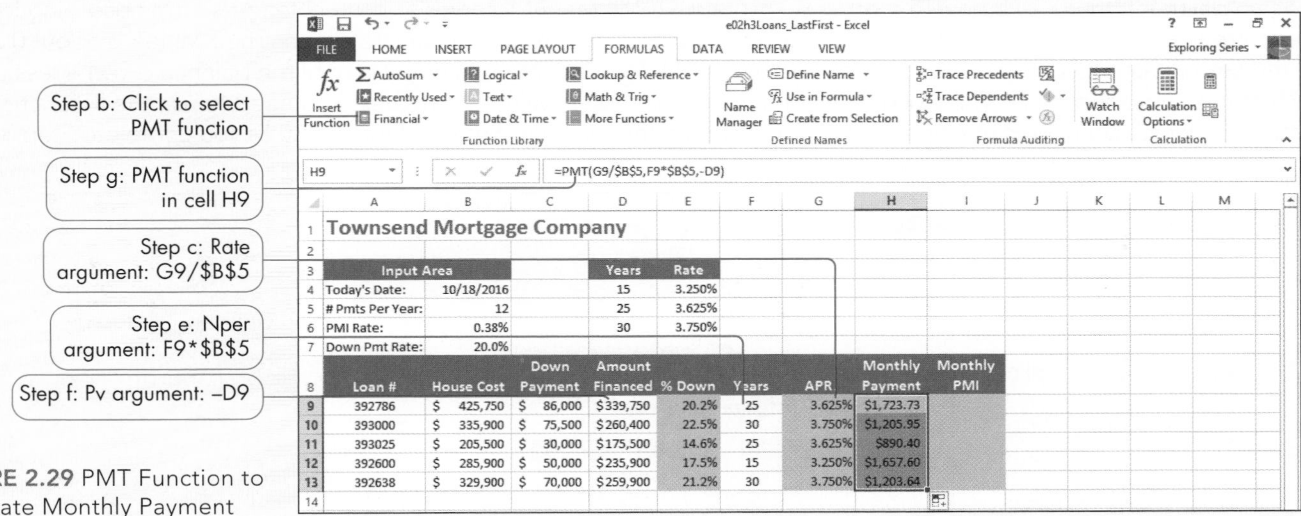

FIGURE 2.29 PMT Function to Calculate Monthly Payment

a. Click **cell H9**, the cell that will store the payment for the first customer.

b. Click **Financial** in the Function Library group, scroll through the list, and then select **PMT**.

> **TROUBLESHOOTING:** Make sure you select PMT, not PPMT. The PPMT function calculates the principal portion of a particular monthly payment, not the total monthly payment itself.

The Function Arguments dialog box opens.

c. Type **G9/B5** in the **Rate box**.

Think about what will happen if you copy the formula. The argument will be G10/B6 for the next customer. Are those cell references correct? G10 does contain the APR for the next customer, but B6 does not contain the correct number of payments in one year. Therefore, you need to make B5 an absolute cell reference because the number of payments per year does not vary.

d. Press **F4** to make the reference to cell B5 absolute.

e. Press **Tab** and type **F9*$B$5** in the **Nper box**.

You calculate the nper by multiplying the number of years by the number of payments in one year. You must make B5 an absolute cell reference so that it does not change when you copy the formula down the column.

f. Press **Tab** and type **-D9** in the **Pv box**.

The bottom of the dialog box indicates that the monthly payment is 1723.73008 or $1,723.73.

> **TROUBLESHOOTING:** If the payment displays as a negative value, you probably forgot to type the minus sign in front of the D9 reference in the Pv box. Edit the function and type the minus sign in the correct place.

g. Click **OK**. Copy the formula down the column and save the workbook.

STEP 3 ≫ USE THE IF FUNCTION

Lenders often want borrowers to have a 20% down payment. If borrowers do not put in 20% of the cost of the house as a down payment, they pay a private mortgage insurance (PMI) fee. PMI serves to protect lenders from absorbing loss if the borrower defaults on the loan, and it enables borrowers with less cash to secure a loan. The PMI fee is about 0.38% of the amount financed. Some borrowers have to pay PMI for a few months or years until the balance owed is less than 80% of the appraised value. The worksheet contains the necessary values input area. You need to use the IF function to determine which borrowers must pay PMI and how much they will pay. Refer to Figure 2.30 as you complete Step 3.

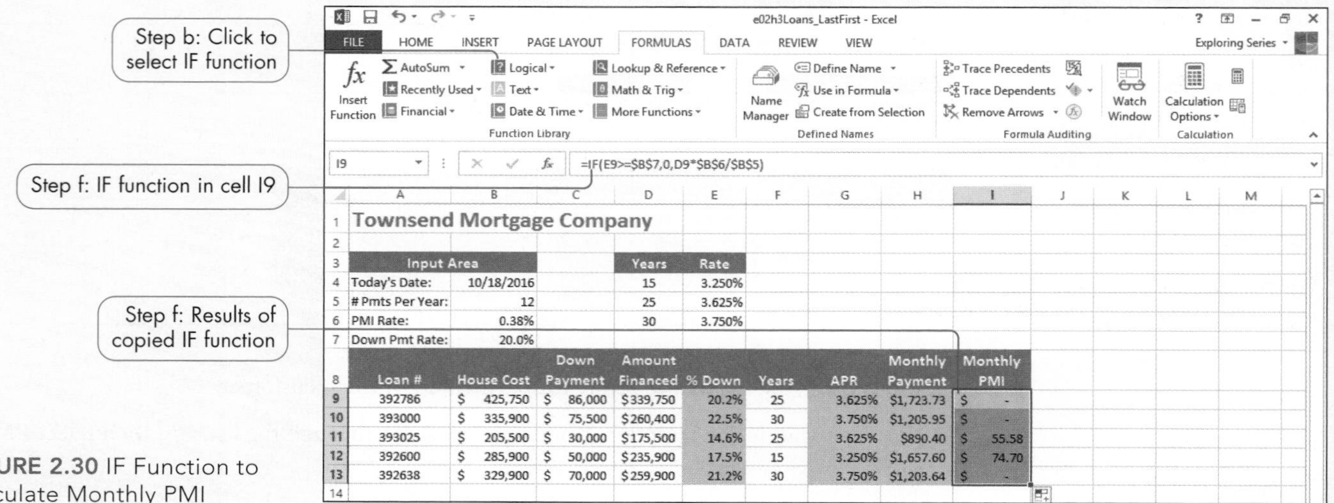

FIGURE 2.30 IF Function to Calculate Monthly PMI

a. Click **cell I9**, the cell that will store the PMI, if any, for the first customer.

b. Click **Logical** in the Function Library group and select **IF**.

   The Function Arguments dialog box opens. You need to enter the three arguments.

c. Type **E9>=$B$7** in the **Logical_test box**.

   The logical test compares the down payment percentage to see if the customer's down payment is at least 20%, the threshold stored in B7, of the amount financed. The customer's percentage cell reference needs to be relative so that it will change when you copy it down the column; however, cell B7 must be absolute because it contains the threshold value.

d. Press **Tab** and type **0** in the **Value_if_true box**.

   If the customer makes a down payment that is at least 20% of the purchase price, the customer does not pay PMI. The first customer paid 20% of the purchase price, so he or she does not have to pay PMI.

e. Press **Tab** and type **D9*$B$6/$B$5** in the **Value_if_false box**.

   If the logical test is false, the customer must pay PMI, which is calculated by dividing the yearly PMI (0.38%) by 12 and multiplying the result by the amount financed.

f. Click **OK** and copy the formula down the column.

   The third and fourth customers must pay PMI because their respective down payments were less than 20% of the purchase price.

TROUBLESHOOTING: If the results are not as you expected, check the logical operators. People often mistype < and > or forget to type = for >= situations. Correct any errors in the original formula and copy the formula again.

g. Save the workbook. Keep the workbook open if you plan to continue with the next Hands-On Exercise. If not, close the workbook and exit Excel.

Range Names

To simplify entering ranges in formulas, you can use range names. A ***range name*** is a word or string of characters assigned to one or more cells. Think of range names in this way: Your college identifies you by your student ID; however, your professors call you by an easy-to-remember name, such as Micah or Vanessa. Similarly, instead of using cell addresses, you can use descriptive range names in formulas. Going back to the VLOOKUP example shown in Figure 2.25, you can assign the range name *Grades* to cells A3:B7 and modify the VLOOKUP function to be =VLOOKUP(E3,Grades,2), using the range name *Grades* in the formula. Another benefit of using range names is that they are absolute references, which helps ensure accuracy in your calculations.

In this section, you will work with range names. First, you will learn how to create and maintain range names. Then you will learn how to use a range name in a formula.

Creating and Maintaining Range Names

Each range name within a workbook must be unique. For example, you cannot assign the name *COST* to ranges on several worksheets or on the same sheet. After you create a range name, you might need to change its name or range. If you no longer need a range name, you can delete it. You can also insert in the workbook a list of range names and their respective cell ranges for reference.

Create a Range Name

STEP 1 A range name can contain up to 255 characters, but it must begin with a letter or an underscore. You can use a combination of upper- or lowercase letters, numbers, periods, and underscores throughout the range name. A range name cannot include spaces or special characters. You should create range names that describe the range of cells being named, but names cannot be identical to the cell contents. Keep the range names short to make them easier to use in formulas. Table 2.8 lists acceptable and unacceptable range names.

TABLE 2.8 Range Names

Name	Description
Grades	Acceptable range name
COL	Acceptable abbreviation for cost-of-living
Tax_Rate	Acceptable name with underscore
Commission Rate	Unacceptable name; cannot use spaces in names
Discount Rate %	Unacceptable name; cannot use special symbols and spaces
2016_Rate	Unacceptable name; cannot start with a number
Rate_2016	Acceptable name with underscore and numbers

To create a range name, select the range you want to name and do one of the following:

- Click in the Name Box, type the range name, and then press Enter.
- Click the FORMULAS tab, click Define Name in the Defined Names group to open the New Name dialog box (see Figure 2.31), type the range name in the Name Box, and then click OK.
- Click the FORMULAS tab, click Name Manager in the Defined Names group to open the Name Manager dialog box, click New, type the range name in the Name Box, click OK, and then click Close.

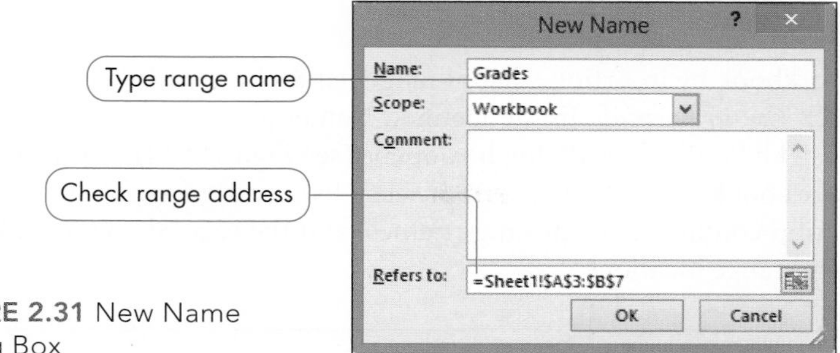

FIGURE 2.31 New Name Dialog Box

You can create several range names at the same time if your worksheet includes ranges with values and descriptive labels. To do this, select the range of cells containing the labels that you want to become names and the cells that contain the values to name, click *Create from Selection* in the Defined Named group on the Formulas tab, and then select an option in the *Create Names from Selection* dialog box (see Figure 2.32).

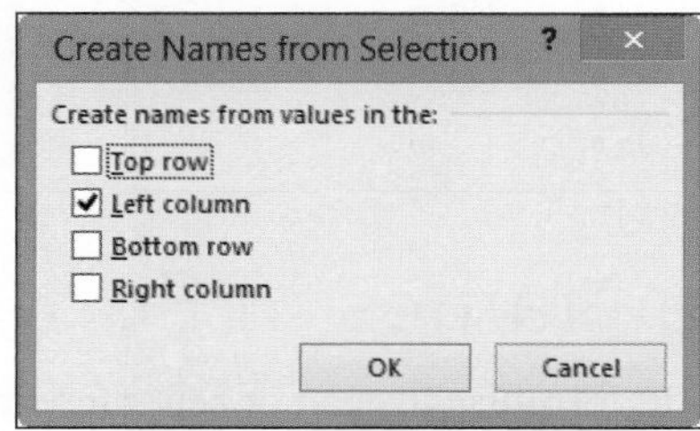

FIGURE 2.32 Create Names from Selection Dialog Box

Edit or Delete a Range Name

STEP 2

Use the Name Manager dialog box to edit, delete, and create range names. To open the Name Manager dialog box shown in Figure 2.33, click Name Manager in the Defined Names group on the Formulas tab. To edit a range or range name, click the range name in the list and click Edit. In the Edit Name dialog box, make your edits and click OK.

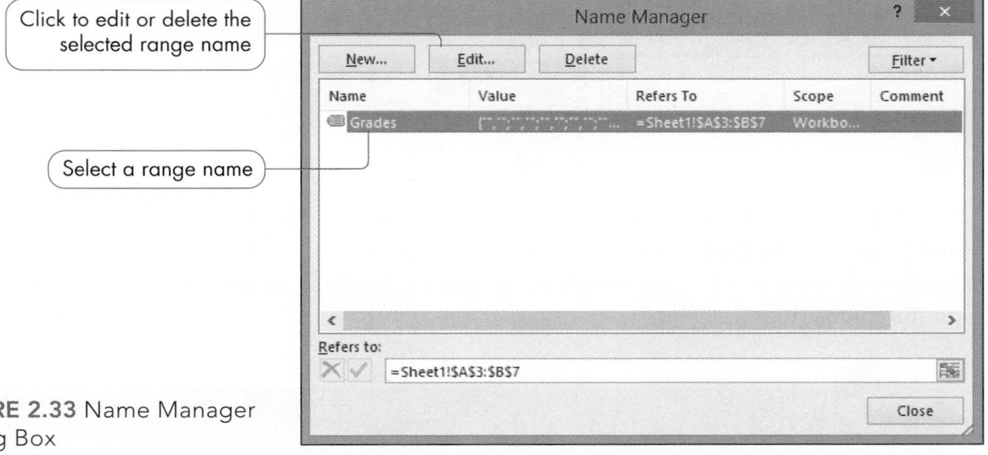

FIGURE 2.33 Name Manager Dialog Box

To delete a range name, open the Name Manager dialog box, select the name you want to delete, click Delete, and then click OK in the confirmation message box.

If you change a range name, any formulas that use the range name reflect the new name. For example, if a formula contains =cost*rate and you change the name rate to tax_rate, Excel updates the formula to be =cost*tax_rate. If you delete a range name and a formula depends on that range name, Excel displays #NAME?—indicating an Invalid Name Error.

Insert a Table of Range Names

STEP 4» You can document a workbook by inserting a list of range names in a worksheet. To insert a list of range names, click *Use in Formula* in the Defined Names group on the Formulas tab and select Paste Names. The Paste Name dialog box opens (see Figure 2.34), listing all range names in the current workbook. Click Paste List to insert a list of range names in alphabetical order. The first column contains a list of range names, and the second column contains the worksheet names and range locations.

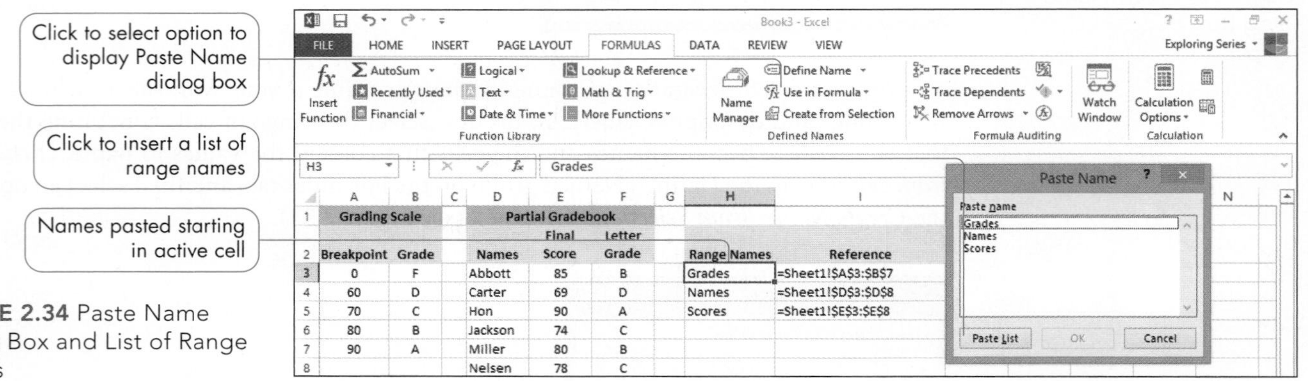

FIGURE 2.34 Paste Name Dialog Box and List of Range Names

Using Range Names in Formulas

STEP 3» You can use range names in formulas instead of cell references. For example, if cell C15 contains a purchase amount, and cell C5 contains the sales tax rate, instead of typing =C15*C5, you can type the range names in the formula, such as =purchase*tax_rate. When you type a formula, Formula AutoComplete displays a list of range names, as well as functions, that start with the letters as you type (see Figure 2.35). Double-click the range name to insert it in the formula.

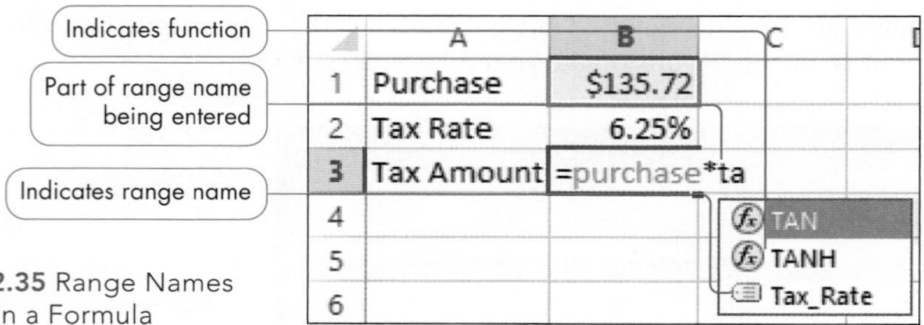

FIGURE 2.35 Range Names Inserted in a Formula

Another benefit of using range names is that if you have to copy the formula, you do not have to make the cell reference absolute in the formula. Furthermore, if you share your workbook with others, range names in formulas help others understand what values are used in the calculations.

TIP Go to a Range Name

Use the Go To dialog box to go to the top-left cell in a range specified by a range name.

Quick Concepts

1. What is a range name? ***p. 482***
2. List at least five guidelines and rules for naming a range. ***p. 482***
3. What is the purpose of inserting a list of range names in a worksheet? What is contained in the list, and how is it arranged? ***p. 484***

Hands-On Exercises

MyITLab®
HOE4 Training

4 Range Names

You decide to simplify the VLOOKUP function by using a range name for the APR rates lookup table instead of the actual cell references. After creating a range name, you will modify some range names Erica created and create a list of range names.

Skills covered: Create a Range Name • Edit and Delete Range Names • Use a Range Name in a Formula • Insert a List of Range Names

STEP 1 » CREATE A RANGE NAME

You want to assign a range name to the lookup table of years and APRs. Refer to Figure 2.36 as you complete Step 1.

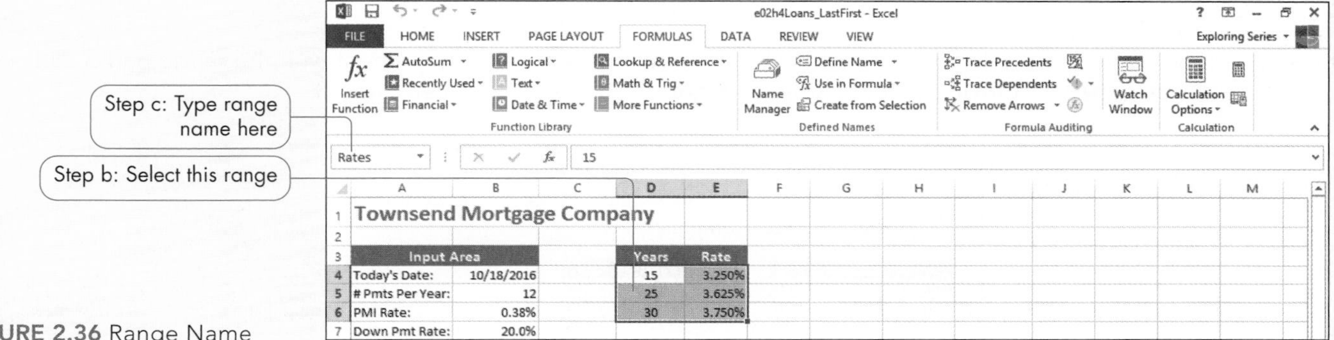

FIGURE 2.36 Range Name

a. Open *e02h3Loans_LastFirst* if you closed it at the end of Hands-On Exercise 3 and save it as **e02h4Loans_LastFirst**, changing *h3* to *h4*.

b. Make sure the **Payment Info worksheet tab** is active. Select **range D4:E6** (the lookup table).

c. Click in the **Name Box**, type **Rates**, and then press **Enter**. Save the workbook.

STEP 2 » EDIT AND DELETE RANGE NAMES

You noticed that Erica added some range names. You will use the Name Manager dialog box to view and make changes to the range names, such as reducing the length of two range names and deleting another range name. Refer to Figure 2.37 as you complete Step 2.

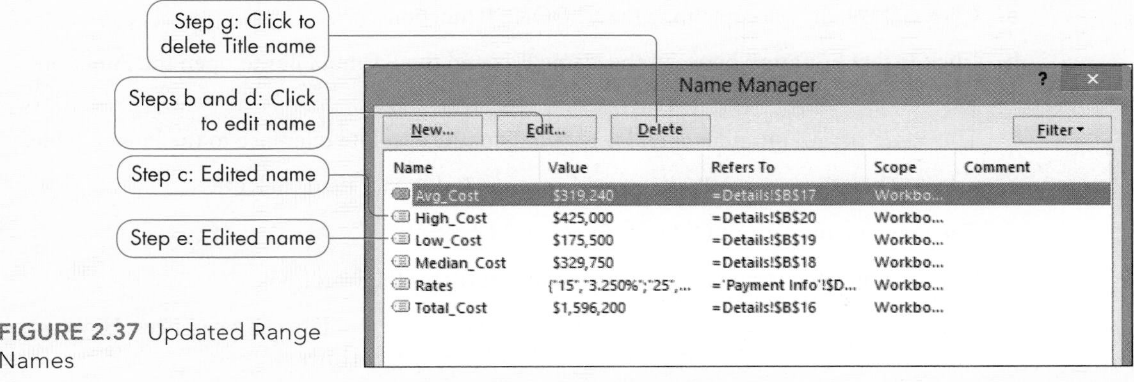

FIGURE 2.37 Updated Range Names

a. Click **Name Manager** in the Defined Names group on the FORMULAS tab.

The Name Manager dialog box opens.

b. Select **Highest_House...** and click **Edit** to open the Edit Name dialog box.

c. Type **High_Cost** in the **Name Box** and click **OK**.

d. Select **Lowest_House...** and click **Edit**.

e. Type **Low_Cost** in the **Name Box** and click **OK**.

f. Select **Title** in the Name Manager dialog box.

This range name applies to a cell containing text, which does not need a name as it cannot be used in calculations. You decide to delete the range name.

g. Click **Delete**, read the warning message box, and then click **OK** to confirm the deletion of the Title range name.

h. Click **Close** and save the workbook.

STEP 3 » USE A RANGE NAME IN A FORMULA

You will modify the VLOOKUP function by replacing the existing Table_array argument with the range name. This will help Erica interpret the VLOOKUP function. Refer to Figure 2.38 as you complete Step 3.

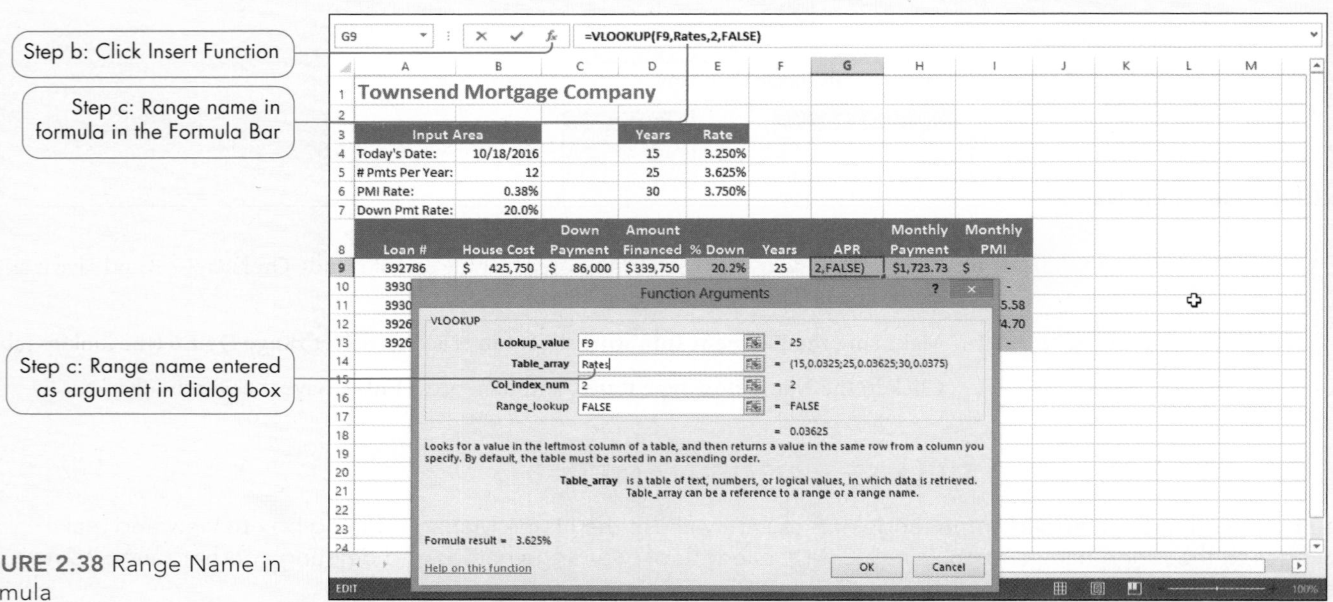

FIGURE 2.38 Range Name in Formula

a. Click **cell G9**, the cell containing the VLOOKUP function.

b. Click **Insert Function** between the Name Box and the Formula Bar to open the Function Arguments dialog box.

The Table_array argument contains $D$4:$E$6, the absolute reference to the lookup table.

c. Select **$D$4:$E$6** in the **Table_array box**, type **Rates**, and then click **OK**.

The new function is =VLOOKUP(F9,Rates,2,FALSE).

d. Copy the updated formula down the column and save the workbook.

The results are the same as they were when you used the absolute cell references. However, the formulas are shorter and easier to read with the range names.

STEP 4 ›› INSERT A LIST OF RANGE NAMES

Before submitting the completed workbook to Erica, you want to create a documentation worksheet that lists all of the range names in the workbook. Refer to Figure 2.39 as you complete Step 4.

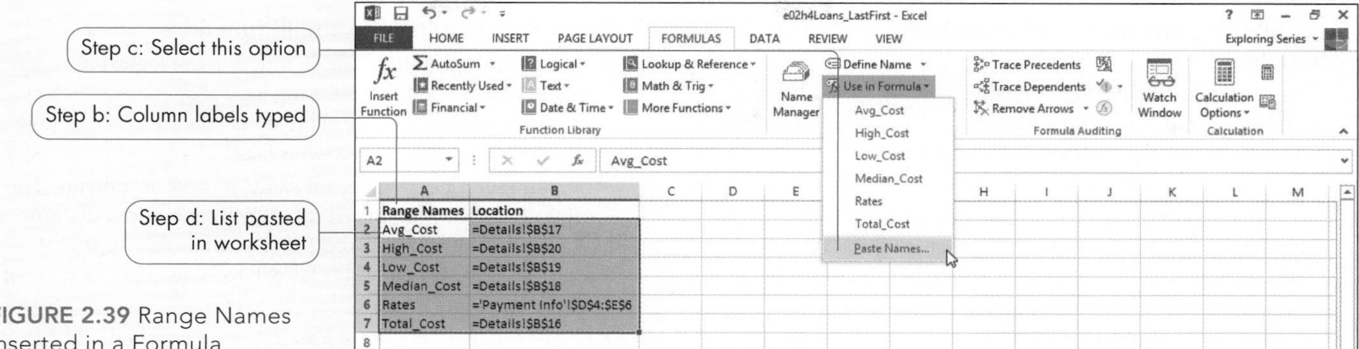

FIGURE 2.39 Range Names Inserted in a Formula

a. Click **New sheet** to the right of the worksheet tabs and double-click the default sheet name, **Sheet1**. Type **Range Names** and press **Enter**.

You inserted and renamed the new worksheet to reflect the data you will add to it.

b. Type **Range Names** in **cell A1** and type **Location** in **cell B1**. Bold these headings.

These column headings will display above the list of range names.

c. Click **cell A2**, click **Use in Formula** in the Defined Names group on the FORMULAS tab, and then select **Paste Names**.

The Paste Name dialog box opens, displaying all of the range names in the workbook.

d. Click **Paste List**.

Excel pastes an alphabetical list of range names starting in cell A2. The second column displays the locations of the range names.

e. Increase the widths of columns A and B to fit the data.

f. Save and close the workbook, and submit based on your instructor's directions.

TIP List of Range Names

When you paste range names, the list will overwrite any existing data in a worksheet, so consider pasting the list in a separate worksheet. If you add, edit, or delete range names, the list does not update automatically. To keep the list current, you would need to paste the list again.

Chapter Objectives Review

After reading this chapter, you have accomplished the following objectives:

1. **Use relative, absolute, and mixed cell references in formulas.**
   - Use a relative cell address: A relative reference indicates a cell's location relative to the formula cell. When you copy the formula, the relative cell reference changes.
   - Use an absolute cell reference: An absolute reference is a permanent pointer to a particular cell, indicated with $ before the column letter and row number, such as $B$5. When you copy the formula, the absolute cell reference does not change.
   - Use a mixed cell reference: A mixed reference contains part absolute and part relative reference, such as $B5 or B$5. Either the column or row reference changes, while the other remains constant when you copy the formula.
2. **Correct circular references.**
   - A circular reference occurs when a formula refers to the cell containing the formula. The status bar indicates the location of a circular reference.
3. **Insert a function.**
   - A function is a predefined formula that performs a calculation. It contains the function name and arguments. Formula AutoComplete, function ScreenTips, and the Insert Function dialog box help you select and create functions. The Function Arguments dialog box guides you through entering requirements for each argument.
4. **Insert basic math and statistics functions.**
   - Calculate the total with the SUM function: The SUM function calculates the total of a range of values. The syntax is =SUM(number1,[number2],...).
   - Find central tendency with AVERAGE and MEDIAN: The AVERAGE function calculates the arithmetic mean of values in a range. The MEDIAN function identifies the midpoint value in a set of values.
   - Identify low and high values with MIN and MAX: The MIN function identifies the lowest value in a range, whereas the MAX function identifies the highest value in a range.
   - Identify the total number with COUNT functions: The COUNT function tallies the number of cells in a range, whereas the COUNTBLANK function tallies the number of blank cells in a range.
   - Use other math and statistical functions: Excel contains other math and statistical functions, such as and MODE.
   - Nest functions as arguments: You can nest one function inside another function's argument, such as nesting the AVERAGE function inside the ROUND function: =ROUND(AVERAGE(A2:A14),2).
5. **Use date functions.**
   - Insert the TODAY function: The TODAY function displays the current date.
   - Insert the NOW function: The NOW function displays the current date and time.
   - Use other date functions: Excel contains a variety of date and time functions.
6. **Determine results with the IF function.**
   - Design the logical test: The IF function is a logical function that evaluates a logical test using logical operators, such as <, >, and =, and returns one value if the condition is true and another value if the condition is false.
   - Design the value_if_true and value_if_false arguments: The arguments can contain cell references, text, or calculations. If a logical test is true, Excel executes the value_if_true argument. If a logical test is false, Excel executes the value_if_false argument.
   - Create other IF functions: You can nest or embed other functions inside one or more of the arguments of an IF function to create more complex formulas.
7. **Use lookup functions.**
   - Create the lookup table: Design the lookup table using exact values or the breakpoints for ranges. If using breakpoints, the breakpoints must be in ascending order.
   - Understand the VLOOKUP syntax: The VLOOKUP function contains the required arugments lookup_value, table_array, and col_index_num and one optional argument, range_lookup.
   - Understand how Excel processes the lookup: The VLOOKUP function looks up a value for a particular record, compares it to a lookup table, and returns a result in another column of the lookup table.
   - Use the range_lookup argument: If an exact match is required, the optional fourth argument should be FALSE; otherwise, the fourth argument can remain empty.
   - Nest functions inside the VLOOKUP function: You can nest functions inside one or more arguments.
   - Use the HLOOKUP function: The HLOOKUP function looks up values by row (horizontally) rather than by column (vertically).
8. **Calculate payments with the PMT function.**
   - The PMT function calculates periodic payments for a loan with a fixed interest rate and a fixed term. The PMT function requires the periodic interest rate, the total number of payment periods, and the original value of the loan.
9. **Create and maintain range names.**
   - Create a range name: A range name may contain letters, numbers, and underscores, but must start with either a letter or an underscore.
   - Edit or delete a range name: Use the Name Manager dialog box to edit, create, or delete range names.
   - Insert a table of range names: The first column contains an alphabetical list of range names, and the second column contains a list of their ranges.
10. **Use range names in formulas.**
    - You can use range names in formulas to make the formulas easier to interpret by using a descriptive name for the value(s) contained in a cell or range.

Key Terms Matching

Match the key terms with their definitions. Write the key term letter by the appropriate numbered definition.

- **a.** Absolute cell reference
- **b.** Argument
- **c.** AVERAGE function
- **d.** Circular reference
- **e.** COUNT function
- **f.** IF function
- **g.** Logical test
- **h.** Lookup table
- **i.** MAX function
- **j.** MEDIAN function
- **k.** MIN function
- **l.** Mixed cell reference
- **m.** NOW function
- **n.** PMT function
- **o.** Range name
- **p.** Relative cell reference
- **q.** SUM function
- **r.** Syntax
- **s.** TODAY function
- **t.** VLOOKUP function

1. _______ A set of rules that governs the structure and components for properly entering a function. **p. 456**
2. _______ Displays the current date. **p. 463**
3. _______ Indicates a cell's specific location; the cell reference does not change when you copy the formula. **p. 448**
4. _______ Occurs when a formula directly or indirectly refers to itself. **p. 450**
5. _______ An input, such as a cell reference or value, needed to complete a function. **p. 456**
6. _______ Identifies the highest value in a range. **p. 461**
7. _______ Tallies the number of cells in a range that contain values. **p. 461**
8. _______ Looks up a value in a vertical lookup table and returns a related result from the lookup table. **p. 474**
9. _______ A range that contains data for the basis of the lookup and data to be retrieved. **p. 474**
10. _______ Calculates the arithmetic mean, or average, of values in a range. **p. 460**
11. _______ Identifies the midpoint value in a set of values. **p. 460**
12. _______ Displays the current date and time. **p. 463**
13. _______ Evaluates a condition and returns one value if the condition is true and a different value if the condition is false. **p. 471**
14. _______ Calculates the total of values contained in two or more cells. **p. 458**
15. _______ Calculates the periodic payment for a loan with a fixed interest rate and fixed term. **p. 477**
16. _______ Indicates a cell's location from the cell containing the formula; the cell reference changes when the formula is copied. **p. 448**
17. _______ Contains both an absolute and a relative cell reference in a formula; the absolute part does not change but the relative part does when you copy the formula. **p. 450**
18. _______ A word or string of characters that represents one or more cells. **p. 482**
19. _______ An expression that evaluates to true or false. **p. 472**
20. _______ Displays the lowest value in a range. **p. 461**

Multiple Choice

1. If cell D15 contains the formula =$C$5*D$15, what is the D15 in the formula?
   (a) Relative reference
   (b) Absolute reference
   (c) Circular reference
   (d) Range name

2. What function would most appropriately accomplish the same thing as =(B5+C5+D5+E5+F5)/5?
   (a) =SUM(B5:F5)/5
   (b) =AVERAGE(B5:F5)
   (c) =MEDIAN(B5:F5)
   (d) =COUNT(B5:F5)

3. When you start =AV, what displays a list of functions and defined names?
   (a) Function ScreenTip
   (b) Formula AutoComplete
   (c) Insert Function dialog box
   (d) Function Arguments dialog box

4. A formula containing the entry =$B3 is copied to a cell one column to the right and two rows down. How will the entry appear in its new location?
   (a) =$B3
   (b) =B3
   (c) =$C5
   (d) =$B5

5. Cell B10 contains a date, such as 1/1/2016. Which formula will determine how many days are between that date and the current date, given that the cell containing the formula is formatted with Number Format?
   (a) =TODAY()
   (b) =CURRENT()-B10
   (c) =TODAY()-B10
   (d) =TODAY()+NOW()

6. Given that cells A1, A2, and A3 contain values 2, 3, and 10, respectively, and B6, C6, and D6 contain values 10, 20, and 30, respectively, what value will be returned by the function =IF(B6>A3,C6*A1,D6*A2)?
   (a) 10
   (b) 40
   (c) 60
   (d) 90

7. Given the function =VLOOKUP(C6,$D$12:$F$18,3), the entries in:
   (a) Range D12:D18 are in ascending order.
   (b) Range D12:D18 are in descending order.
   (c) The third column of the lookup table must be text only.
   (d) Range D12:D18 contain multiple values in each cell.

8. The function =PMT(C5,C7,-C3) is stored in cell C15. What must be stored in cell C5?
   (a) APR
   (b) Periodic interest rate
   (c) Loan amount
   (d) Number of payment periods

9. Which of the following is *not* an appropriate use of the SUM function?
   (a) =SUM(B3:B45)
   (b) =SUM(F1:G10)
   (c) =SUM(A8:A15,D8:D15)
   (d) =SUM(D15-C15)

10. Which of the following is *not* an acceptable range name?
    (a) FICA
    (b) Test_Weight
    (c) Goal for 2016
    (d) Target_2015

Practice Exercises

1 Blue Canadian Skies Airlines

You are an analyst for Blue Canadian Skies Airlines, a regional airline headquartered in Victoria. Your assistant developed a template for you to store daily flight data about the number of passengers per flight. Each regional aircraft can hold up to 70 passengers. You need to calculate the occupancy rate (the percent of each flight that is occupied), daily statistics (such as total number of passengers, averages, least full flights, etc.), and weekly statistics per flight number. This exercise follows the same set of skills as used in Hands-On Exercises 1 and 2 in the chapter. Refer to Figure 2.40 as you complete this exercise.

	A	B	C	D	E	F	G	H	I	J	K	L	M	N	O	P
1	Blue Canadian Skies Airlines															
2	Aircraft Capacity:		70													
3			Daily Flight Information													
4	Flight Info		Sunday		Monday		Tuesday		Wednesday		Thursday		Friday		Saturday	
5	Flight #	Destination	# Pass	% Full	# Pass	% Full	# Pass	% Full	# Pass	% Full	# Pass	% Full	# Pass	% Full	# Pass	% Full
6	4520	YEG	60	85.7%	65	92.9%	55	78.6%	65	92.9%	62	88.6%	50	71.4%		
7	3240	YYC	35	50.0%	57	81.4%			60	85.7%			55	78.6%		
8	425	YDA	50	71.4%	70	100.0%	48	68.6%	66	94.3%	68	97.1%			55	78.6%
9	345	YMM	69	98.6%	70	100.0%	61	87.1%	66	94.3%	70	100.0%	68	97.1%	67	95.7%
10	3340	YWG	45	64.3%	61	87.1%	64	91.4%	45	64.3%	48	68.6%	66	94.3%		
11	418	YZF	65	92.9%	67	95.7%	58	82.9%	66	94.3%	55	78.6%	69	98.6%	66	94.3%
12	4526	YYZ	68	97.1%	70	100.0%	58	82.9%			63	90.0%	70	100.0%	68	97.1%
13	300	YXE	70	100.0%	70	100.0%			61	87.1%	70	100.0%	59	84.3%		
14	322	YOW	70	100.0%	60	85.7%	48	68.6%			65	92.9%	68	97.1%	69	98.6%
15	349	YMX	70	100.0%	64	91.4%	67	95.7%			66	94.3%	70	100.0%	55	78.6%
16																
17			Daily Statistics													
18	Total # of Passengers		602		654		459		429		567		575		380	
19	Averages		60.2	86%	65.4	93%	57.375	82%	61.2857	88%	63	90%	63.8889	91%	63.3333	90%
20	Medians		66.5	95%	66	94%	58	83%	65	93%	65	93%	68	97%	66.5	95%
21	Least Full Flights		35	50%	57	81%	48	69%	45	64%	48	69%	50	71%	55	79%
22	Most Full Flights		70	100%	70	100%	67	96%	66	94%	70	100%	70	100%	69	99%
23	# of Flights per Day		10		10		8		7		9		9		6	

Stats

FIGURE 2.40 Blue Canadian Skies Airlines

a. Open *e02p1Flights* and save it as **e02p1Flights_LastFirst**.

b. Click **cell D6**, the cell to display the occupancy percent for Flight 4520 on Sunday, and do the following:
   - Type **=C6/$C$2** and click **Enter** (the checkmark between the Name Box and the Formula Bar). The occupancy rate of Flight 4520 is 85.7%.
   - Double-click the **cell D6 fill handle** to copy the formula down the column.

c. Click **cell D7**. When you copy a formula, Excel also copies the original cell's format. The cell containing the original formula did not have a bottom border, so when you copied the formula down the column, Excel formatted it to match the original cell with no border. To reapply the border, click **cell D15**, click the **Border arrow** in the Font group on the HOME tab, and then select **Bottom Border**.

d. Select the **range D6:D15**, click **Copy**, click **cell F6**, and then click **Paste**. The formula in cell F6 is =E6/$C$2. The first cell reference changes from C6 to E6, maintaining its relative location from the pasted formula. $C$2 remains absolute so that the number of passengers per flight is always divided by the value stored in cell C2. The copied range is still in the Clipboard. Paste the formula into the remaining % Full columns (columns H, J, L, N, and P). Press **Esc**.

e. Clean up the data by deleting *0.0%* in cells, such as H7. The 0.0% is misleading, as it implies the flight was empty; however, some flights do not operate on all days. Check your worksheet against the *Daily Flight Information* section in Figure 2.40.

f. Calculate the total number of passengers per day by doing the following:
   - Click **cell C18** and click **Sum** in the Editing group.
   - Select the **range C6:C15** and press **Enter**.

g. Calculate the average number of passengers per day by doing the following:
   - Click **cell C19**, click the **Sum arrow** in the Editing group, and then select **Average**.
   - Select the **range C6:C15** and click **Enter** (the checkmark between the Name Box and the Formula Bar).
h. Calculate the median number of passengers per day by doing the following:
   - Click **cell C20**.
   - Click **Insert Function**, type **median** in the **Search for a function box**, and then click **Go**.
   - Click **MEDIAN** in the **Select a function box** and click **OK**.
   - Select the **range C6:C15** to enter it in the **Number1 box** and click **OK**.
i. Calculate the least number of passengers on a daily flight by doing the following:
   - Click **cell C21**, click the **Sum arrow** in the Editing group, and then select **Min**.
   - Select the **range C6:C15** and press **Enter**.
j. Calculate the most passengers on a daily flight by doing the following:
   - Click **cell C22** if necessary, click the **Sum arrow** in the Editing group, and then select **Max**.
   - Select the **range C6:C15** and press **Enter**.
k. Calculate the number of flights for Sunday by doing the following:
   - Click **cell C23** if necessary, click the **Sum arrow** in the Editing group, and then select **Count Numbers**.
   - Select the **range C6:C15** and press **Enter**.
l. Calculate the average, median, least full, and most full percentages in **cells D19:D22**. Format the values with Percent Style with zero decimal places. Do not copy the formulas from column C to column D, as that will change the borders. Select **cells C18:D23**, copy the range, and then paste in these cells: **E18**, **G18**, **I18**, **K18**, **M18**, and **O18**. Press **Esc** after pasting.
m. Create a footer with your name on the left side, the sheet name code in the center, and the file name code on the right side.
n. Save and close the workbook, and submit based on your instructor's directions.

2 Steggel Consulting Firm Salaries

You work in the Human Resources Department at Steggell Consulting Firm. You are preparing a model to calculate bonuses based on performance ratings, where ratings between 1 and 1.9 do not receive bonuses, ratings between 2 and 2.9 earn $100 bonuses, ratings between 3 and 3.9 earn $250 bonuses, ratings between 4 and 4.9 earn $500 bonuses, and ratings of 5 or higher earn $1,000 bonuses. In addition, you need to calculate annual raises based on years employed. Employees who have worked five or more years earn a 3.25% raise; employees who have not worked at least five years earn a 2% raise. This exercise follows the same set of skills as used in Hands-On Exercises 1–4 in the chapter. Refer to Figure 2.41 as you complete this exercise.

a. Open *e02p2Salary* and save it as **e02p2Salary_LastFirst**.
b. Click **cell B4**, click the **FORMULAS tab**, click **Date & Time** in the Function Library group, select **TODAY**, and then click **OK** to enter today's date in the cell.
c. Enter a formula to calculate the number of years employed by doing the following:
   - Click **cell C11**, click **Date & Time** in the Function Library group, scroll through the list, and then select **YEARFRAC**.
   - Click **cell A11** to enter the cell reference in the **Start_date box**.
   - Press **Tab** and click **cell B4** to enter the cell reference in the **End_date box**.
   - Press **F4** to make **cell B4** absolute and click **OK**. (Although you could have used the formula =($B$4-A11)/365 to calculate the number of years, the YEARFRAC function provides better accuracy because it accounts for leap years and the divisor 365 does not. The completed function is =YEARFRAC(A11,$B$4).
   - Double-click the **cell C11 fill handle** to copy the YEARFRAC function down the Years Employed column. Your results will differ based on the date contained in cell B4.

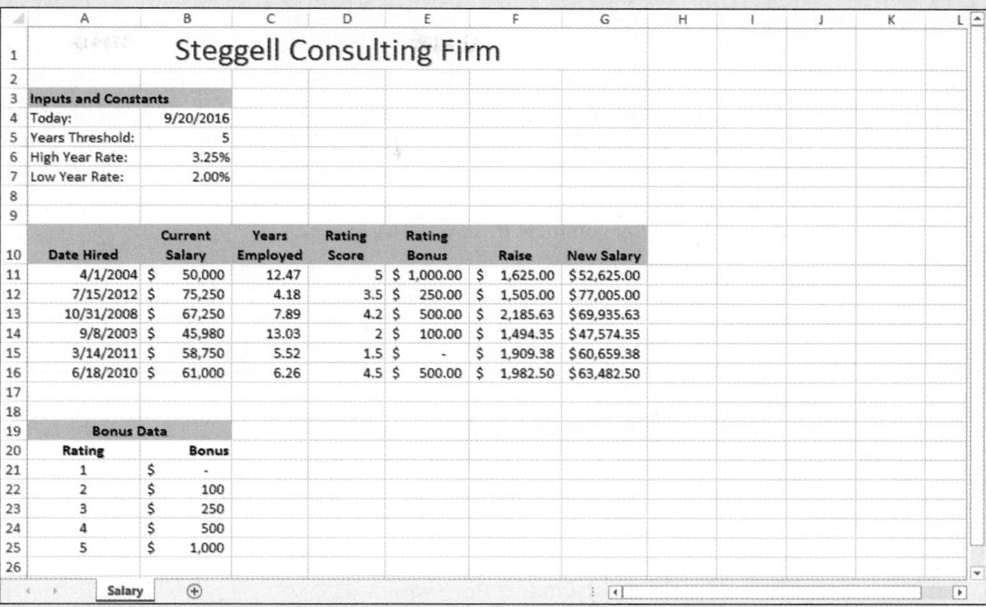

FIGURE 2.41 Steggell Consulting Firm

d. Enter the breakpoint and bonus data for the lookup table by doing the following:

- Click **cell A21**, type **1**, and then press **Ctrl+Enter**.
- Click the **HOME tab**, click **Fill** in the Editing group, and then select **Series**. Click **Columns** in the *Series in* section, leave the **Step value** at **1**, type **5** in the **Stop value box**, and then click **OK**.
- Click **cell B21**. Enter **0**, **100**, **250**, **500**, and **1000** down the column. The cells have been formatted with Accounting Number Format with zero decimal places.
- Select **range A21:B25**, click in the **Name Box**, type **Bonus**, and then press **Enter**.

e. Enter the bonus based on rating by doing the following:

- Click **cell E11** and click the **FORMULAS tab**.
- Click **Lookup & Reference** in the Function Library group and select **VLOOKUP**.
- Type **D11** in the **Lookup_value box**, type **Bonus** in the **Table_array box**, type **2**, and then click **OK**. The completed function is =VLOOKUP(D11,Bonus,2).
- Double-click the **cell E11 fill handle** to copy the formula down the Rating Bonus column.

f. Enter the raise based on years employed by doing the following:

- Click **cell F11**, click **Logical** in the Function Library group, and then select **IF**.
- Type **C11>=$B$5** to compare the years employed to the absolute reference of the five-year threshold in the **Logical_test box**.
- Press **Tab** and type **B11*$B$6** to calculate a 3.25% raise for employees who worked five years or more in the **Value_if_true box**.
- Press **Tab** and type **cell B11*$B$7** to calculate a 2% raise for employees who worked less than five years in the Value_if_false box. Click **OK**. The completed function is =IF(C11>=$B$5,B11*$B$6,B11*$B$7).
- Double-click the **cell F11 fill handle** to copy the formula down the Raise column.

g. Click **cell G11**. Type **=B11+E11+F11** to add the current salary, the bonus, and the raise to calculate the new salary. Double-click the **cell G11 fill handle** to copy the formula down the column.

h. Create a footer with your name on the left side, the sheet name code in the center, and the file name code on the right side.

i. Save and close the workbook, and submit based on your instructor's directions.

3 New Car Loan

After obtaining a promotion at work, you want to buy a luxury car, such as a Lexus or Infinity. Before purchasing a car, you want to create a worksheet to estimate the monthly payment based on the purchase price (including accessories, taxes, and license plate), APR, down payment, and years. You will assign range names and use range names in the formulas to make them easier to analyze. This exercise follows the same set of skills as used in Hands-On Exercises 1–4 in the chapter. Refer to Figure 2.42 as you complete this exercise.

	A	B	C
1	Car Loan		
2			
3	Inputs		
4	Cost of Car*	45000	
5	Down Payment	10000	
6	APR	0.0399	
7	Years	5	
8	Payments Per Year	12	
9	*Includes taxes, etc.		
10			
11	Outputs		
12	Loan	=Cost-Down	
13	Monthly Payment	=PMT(APR/Months,Years*Months,-Loan)	
14	Total to Repay Loan	=Years*Months*Payment	
15	Total Interest Paid	=Repaid-Loan	
16			

FIGURE 2.42 Car Loan

a. Open *e02p3CarLoan* and save it as **e02p3CarLoan_LastFirst**.

b. Name the input values by doing the following:

DISCOVER

- Select the **range A4:B8**.
- Click the **FORMULAS tab** and click **Create from Selection** in the Defined Names group.
- Make sure *Left column* is selected and click **OK**.
- Click each input value cell in the **range B4:B8** and look at the newly created names in the Name Box.

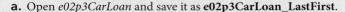

c. Edit the range names by doing the following:

- Click **Name Manager** in the Defined Names group.
- Click **Cost_of_Car**, click **Edit**, type **Cost**, and then click **OK**.
- Change *Down_Payment* to **Down**.
- Change *Payments_Per_Year* to **Months**.
- Click **Close** to close the Name Manager.

d. Name the output values in the **range A12:B15** using the *Create from Selection* method you used in step b to assign names to the empty cells in the range B12:B15. However, you will use the range names as you build formulas in the next few steps. Edit the range names using the same approach you used in step c.

- Change *Monthly_Payment* to **Payment.**
- Change *Total_Interest_Paid* to **Interest**.
- Change *Total_to_Repay_Loan* to **Repaid**.
- Click **Close** to close the Name Manager.

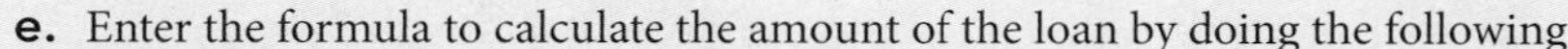

e. Enter the formula to calculate the amount of the loan by doing the following:
   - Click **cell B12**. Type **=Cos** and double-click **Cost** from the Function AutoComplete list. If the list does not appear, type the entire name **Cost**.
   - Press - and type **do**, and then double-click **Down** from the Function AutoComplete list.
   - Press **Enter** to enter the formula =Cost-Down.

f. Calculate the monthly payment of principal and interest by doing the following:
   - Click the **FORMULAS tab**. Click **cell B13**. Click **Financial** in the Function Library group, scroll down, and then select **PMT**.
   - Type **APR/Months** in the **Rate box**.
   - Press **Tab** and type **Years*Months** in the **Nper box**.
   - Press **Tab**, type **-Loan** in the **Pv box**, and then click **OK**. The completed function is =PMT(APR/Months,Years*Months,-Loan).

g. Enter the total amount to repay loan formula by doing the following:
   - Click **cell B14**. Type = to start the formula.
   - Click **Use in Formula** in the Defined Names group and select **Years**.
   - Type *, click **Use in Formula** in the Defined Names group, and then select **Months**.
   - Type *, click **Use in Formula** in the Defined Names group, and then select **Payment**.
   - Press **Enter**. The completed formula is =Years*Months*Payment.

h. Use the skills from step g to enter the formula **=Repaid-Loan** in **cell B15**.

i. Select the **range B12:B15**, click the **HOME tab**, and then click **Accounting Number Format** in the Number group.

j. Select the option to center the worksheet data between the left and right margins in the Page Setup dialog box.

k. Create a footer with your name on the left side, the sheet name code in the center, and the file name code on the right side.

l. Right-click the **Car sheet tab**, select **Move or Copy** from the menu, click **(move to end)** in the *Before sheet* section, click the **Create a copy check box**, and then click **OK**. Rename the Car (2) sheet **Formulas**.

m. Make sure the Formulas sheet is active. Click the **FORMULAS tab** and click **Show Formulas** in the Formula Auditing group. Widen column B to display entire formulas.

n. Click the **PAGE LAYOUT tab** and click the **Gridlines Print check box** and the **Headings Print check box** in the Sheet Options group to select these two options.

o. Insert a new sheet, name it **Names**, type **Range Name** in **cell A1**, and then type **Location** in **cell B1**. Apply bold to these column labels. Click **cell A2**, click the **FORMULAS tab**, click **Use in Formula**, select **Paste Names**, and then click **Paste List** to paste an alphabetical list of range names in the worksheet. Adjust the column widths. Apply the same Page Setup settings and footer to the Formulas and Cars worksheets.

p. Save and close the workbook, and submit based on your instructor's directions.

Mid-Level Exercises

1 Metropolitan Zoo Gift Shop Weekly Payroll

ANALYSIS CASE 

As manager of the gift shop at the Metropolitan Zoo, you are responsible for managing the weekly payroll. Your assistant developed a partial worksheet, but you need to enter the formulas to calculate the regular pay, overtime pay, gross pay, taxable pay, withholding tax, FICA, and net pay. In addition, you want to total pay columns and calculate some basic statistics. As you construct formulas, make sure you use absolute and relative cell references correctly in formulas and avoid circular references.

a. Open the *e02m1Payroll* workbook and save it as **e02m1Payroll_LastFirst**.

b. Study the worksheet structure and read the business rules in the Notes section.

c. Use IF functions to calculate the regular pay and overtime pay based on a regular 40-hour workweek in **cells E5** and **F5**. Pay overtime only for overtime hours. Calculate the gross pay based on the regular and overtime pay. Abram's regular pay is $398. With 8 overtime hours, Abram's overtime pay is $119.40.

d. Create a formula in **cell H5** to calculate the taxable pay. Multiply the number of dependents by the deduction per dependent and subtract that from the gross pay. With two dependents, Abram's taxable pay is $417.40.

e. Use a VLOOKUP function in **cell I5** to identify and calculate the federal withholding tax. With a taxable pay of $417.40, Abram's tax rate is 25% and the withholding tax is $104.35. The VLOOKUP function returns the applicable tax rate, which you must then multiply by the taxable pay.

f. Calculate FICA in **cell J5** based on gross pay and the FICA rate and calculate the net pay in **Cell K5**.

g. Calculate the total regular pay, overtime pay, gross pay, taxable pay, withholding tax, FICA, and net pay on row 17.

h. Copy all formulas down their respective columns.

i. Apply **Accounting Number Format** to the **range C5:C16**. Apply **Accounting Number Format** to the first row of monetary data and to the total row. Apply **Comma Style** to the monetary values for the other employees. Underline the last employee's monetary values and use the Format Cells dialog box to apply **Double Accounting Underline** for the totals.

j. Insert appropriate functions to calculate the average, highest, and lowest values in the Summary Statistics area (the **range I21:K23**) of the worksheet.

DISCOVER 

k. At your instructor's discretion, use Help to learn about the FREQUENCY function. The Help feature contains sample data for you to copy and practice in a new worksheet to learn about this function. You can close the practice worksheet containing the Help data without saving it. You want to determine the number (frequency) of employees who worked less than 20 hours, between 20 and 29 hours, between 30 and 40 hours, and over 40 hours. **Cells J28:J31** list the ranges. You need to translate this range into correct values for the Bin column in **cells I28:I31** and enter the FREQUENCY function in **cells K28:K31**. The function should identify one employee who worked between 0 and 19 hours and six employees who worked more than 40 hours.

l. Apply other page setup formats as needed.

m. Insert a new sheet named **Overtime**. List the number of overtime hours for the week. Calculate the yearly gross amount spent on overtime assuming the same number of overtime hours per week. Add another row with only half the overtime hours (using a formula). What is your conclusion and recommendation on overtime? Format this worksheet.

n. Insert a footer with your name on the left side, the sheet name code in the center, and the file name code on the right side of both worksheets.

o. Save and close the workbook, and submit based on your instructor's directions.

2 Mortgage Calculator

FROM SCRATCH

As a financial consultant, you work with people who are planning to buy a new house. You want to create a worksheet containing variable data (the price of the house, down payment, date of the first payment, and borrower's credit rating) and constants (property tax rate, years, and number of payments in one year). Borrowers pay 0.5% private mortgage insurance (PMI) on the loan amount if they do not make at least a 20% down payment. A borrower's credit rating determines the required down payment percentage and APR. For example, a person with an excellent credit rating may make only a 5% down payment with a 3.25% APR loan. A person with a fair credit rating will make a 15% down payment and have a higher APR at 5.25%. Your worksheet needs to perform various calculations. The filled cells in column F indicate cells containing formulas, not values. Refer to Figure 2.43 as you complete this exercise.

	A	B	C	D	E	F
1	Mortgage Calculator					
2						
3	Inputs				Intermediate Calculations	
4	Negotiated Cost of House		$ 375,000.00		APR Based on Credit Rating	3.25%
5	Additional Down Payment		$ 5,000.00		Min Down Payment Required	$ 18,750.00
6	Date of First Payment		5/1/2016		Annual Property Tax	$ 2,812.50
7	Credit Rating		Excellent		Annual PMI	$ 1,756.25
8						
9	Constants				Outputs	
10	Property Tax Rate		0.75%		Total Down Payment	$ 23,750.00
11	Down Payment to Avoid PMI		20.00%		Amount of the Loan	$351,250.00
12	PMI Rate		0.50%		Monthly Payment (P&I)	$1,528.66
13	Term of Loan in Years		30		Monthly Property Tax	234.38
14	# of Payments Per Year		12		Monthly PMI	146.35
15					Total Monthly Payment	$ 1,909.39
16	Credit	Down Payment	APR		Date of Last Payment	4/1/2046
17	Excellent	5%	3.25%			
18	Good	10%	3.50%			
19	Fair	15%	4.25%			
20	Poor	20%	5.25%			
21						

FIGURE 2.43 Mortgage Data

a. Start a new Excel workbook, save it as **e02m2Loan_LastFirst**, rename Sheet1 **Payment**, add a new sheet, and then rename it **Range Names**.

b. Select the **Payment sheet**, type **Mortgage Calculator** in **cell A1**, and then merge and center the title on the first row in the **range A1:F1**. Apply bold, **18 pt size**, and **Gold, Accent 4, Darker 25% font color**.

c. Create and format the Inputs and Constants areas by doing the following:
   - Type the labels in the **range A3:A20**. For each label, such as *Negotiated Cost of House*, merge the cells, such as the **range A4:B4**, and apply **Align Text Left**. You will have to merge cells for nine labels.
   - Enter and format the *Inputs* and *Constants* values in column C.

d. Create the lookup table in the **range A16:C20** to use the credit ratings to identify the appropriate required percentage down payment and the respective APR by doing the following:
   - Type **Credit**, **Down Payment**, and **APR** in the **range A16:C16**.
   - Type the four credit ratings in the first column, the required down payment percentages in the second column, and the respective APRs in the third column.
   - Format the percentages, apply **Align Text Right**, and then indent the percentages in the cells as needed.

e. Assign range names to cells containing individual values in the Inputs and Constants sections. Do *not* use the *Create from Selection* feature because the labels are stored in merged cells. Assign a range name to the lookup table.

f. Type labels in the *Intermediate Calculations* and *Outputs* sections in column E and assign a range name to each cell in the **ranges F4:F7** and **F10:F12**. Widen column E as needed.

g. Enter formulas in the *Intermediate Calculations* and *Outputs* sections using range names to calculate the following:

DISCOVER

- **APR** based on the borrower's credit rating by using a lookup function. Include the range_lookup argument to ensure an *exact match*. For example, a borrower who has an Excellent rating gets a 3.25% APR.
- **Minimum down payment required** amount by using a lookup function and calculation. Include the range_lookup argument to ensure an *exact match*. For example, a borrower who has an Excellent rating is required to pay a minimum of 5% down payment of the negotiated purchase price. Multiply the function results by the negotiated cost of the house. Hint: The calculation comes after the closing parenthesis.
- **Annual property tax** based on the negotiated cost of the house and the annual property tax rate.
- **Annual PMI**. If the borrower's total down payment (required and additional) is 20% or higher of the negotiated purchase price (multiply the cost by the PMI avoidance percentage), PMI is zero. If the total down payment is less than 20%, the borrower has to pay PMI based on multiplying the amount of the loan by the PMI rate.
- **Total down payment**, which is sum of the required minimum down payment (calculated previously) and any additional down payment entered in the Inputs section.
- **Amount of the loan**, which is the difference between the negotiated cost of the house and the total down payment.
- **Monthly payment** of principal and interest using the PMT function.
- **Monthly property tax**, the **monthly PMI**, and the **total monthly payment**.
- **Last payment date** using the EDATE function. The function's second argument must calculate the correct number of months based on the total length of the loan. For example, if the first payment date is 5/1/2016, the final payment date is 4/1/2046 for a 30-year loan. The last argument of the function must subtract 1 to ensure the last payment date is correct. If the last payment date calculated to 5/1/2046, you would be making an extra payment.

h. Format each section with fill color, bold, underline, number formats, borders, and column widths as shown in the figure.

i. Paste a list of range names in the Range Names worksheet. Insert a row above the list and type and format column labels above the two columns in the list of range names.

j. Center the worksheet data horizontally between the left and right margins.

k. Insert a footer with your name on the left side, the sheet name code in the center, and the file name code on the right side of both sheets.

l. Save and close the workbook, and submit based on your instructor's directions.

3 Professor's Grade Book

You are a teaching assistant for Dr. Denise Gerber, who teaches an introductory C# programming class at your college. One of your routine tasks is to enter assignment and test grades into the grade book. Now that the semester is almost over, you need to create formulas to calculate category averages, the overall weighted average, and the letter grade for each student. In addition, Dr. Gerber wants to see general statistics, such as average, median, low, and high for each graded assignment and test, as well as category averages and total averages. Furthermore, you need to create the grading scale on the documentation worksheet and use it to display the appropriate letter grade for each student.

a. Open *e02m3Grades* and save it as **e02m3Grades_LastFirst**.

b. Use breakpoints to enter the grading scale in the correct structure on the Documentation worksheet and name the grading scale range **Grades**. The grading scale is as follows:

95+	A
90–94.9	A–
87–89.9	B+
83–86.9	B
80–82.9	B–
77–79.9	C+
73–76.9	C
70–72.9	C–
67–69.9	D+
63–66.9	D
60–62.9	D–
0–59.9	F

c. Calculate the total lab points earned for the first student in **cell T8** in the Grades worksheet. The first student earned 93 lab points.

d. Calculate the average of the two midterm tests for the first student in **cell W8**. The student's midterm test average is 87.

e. Calculate the assignment average for the first student in **cell I8**. The formula should drop the lowest score before calculating the average. Hint: You need to use a combination of three functions: SUM, MIN, and COUNT. The argument for each function for the first student is B8:H8. Find the total points and subtract the lowest score. Then divide the remaining points by the number of assignments minus 1. The first student's assignment average is 94.2 after dropping the lowest assignment score.

f. Calculate the weighted total points based on the four category points (assignment average, lab points, midterm average, and final exam) and their respective weights (stored in the **range B40:B43**) in **cell Y8**. Use relative and absolute cell references as needed in the formula. The first student's total weighted score is 90.

g. Use a VLOOKUP function to calculate the letter grade equivalent in **cell Z8**. Use the range name in the function. The first student's letter grade is A–.

h. Copy the formulas down their respective columns for the other students.

i. Name the passing score threshold in **cell B5** with the range name **Passing**. Use an IF function to display a message in the last grade book column based on the student's semester performance. If a student earned a final score of 70 or higher, display *Enroll in CS 202*. Otherwise, display *RETAKE CS 101*. Remember to use quotation marks around the text arguments.

j. Calculate the average, median, low, and high scores for each assignment, lab, test, category average, and total score. Display individual averages with no decimal places; display category and final score averages with one decimal place. Display other statistics with no decimal places.

k. Insert a list of range names in the designated area in the Documentation worksheet. Complete the documentation by inserting your name, today's date, and a purpose statement in the designated areas.

DISCOVER 

l. At your instructor's discretion, add a column to display each student's rank in the class. Use Help to learn how to insert the RANK function.

m. Select page setup options as needed to print the Grades worksheet on one page.

n. Insert a footer with your name on the left side, the sheet name code in the center, and the file name code on the right side of each worksheet.

o. Save and close the workbook, and submit based on your instructor's directions.

4 Facebook and Blackboard

COLLABORATION CASE 

FROM SCRATCH

Social media extends past friendships to organizational and product "fan" pages. Organizations such as Lexus, Pepsi, and universities create pages to provide information about their organizations. Some organizations even provide product details, such as the Lexus ES350. Facebook includes a wealth of information about Microsoft Office products. People share information, pose questions, and reply with their experiences.

a. Log in to your Facebook account. If you do not have a Facebook account, sign up for one and add at least two classmates as friends. Search for Microsoft Excel and click **Like**.

b. Review postings on the Microsoft Excel wall. Notice that some people post what they like most about Excel or how much it has improved their productivity. Post a note about one of your favorite features about Excel that you have learned so far or how you have used Excel in other classes or on the job. Start Word and, using the Snipping Tool, insert a screenshot of your posting. Save the document as **e02t1_LastFirst**.

c. Click the **Discussions link** on the Microsoft Excel Facebook page and find topics that relate to IF or VLOOKUP functions. Post a response to one of the discussions. Take a screenshot of your posting and insert it into your Word document.

d. Create a team of three students. Create one discussion that asks people to describe their favorite use of any of the nested functions used in this chapter. Each team member should respond to the posting. Monitor the discussion and, when you have a few responses, capture a screenshot of the dialogue and insert it into your Word document.

e. Save and close the document. Submit it based on your instructor's directions.

f. Go to www.youtube.com and search for one of these Excel topics: absolute references, mixed references, semi-selection, IF function, VLOOKUP function, circular references, statistical functions shown in Table 2.2, date functions shown in Table 2.3, or range names.

g. Watch several video clips and find one of particular interest to you.

h. Post the URL on your Facebook wall. Specify the topic and describe why you like this particular video.

i. Watch videos from the links posted by other students on their Facebook walls. Comment on at least two submissions. Point out what you like about the video or any suggestions you have for improvement.

j. If required by your instructor, insert screenshots of your postings in a Word document. Save and submit based on your instructor's directions.

Beyond the Classroom

College Sports Scores

RESEARCH CASE

You want to create a spreadsheet to display data for your favorite college sports team. Conduct an Internet search to identify the game dates, your team's scores, the opponent, and the opponent's score for each game for the last complete season. Enter the data into a new workbook and save the workbook as **e02b2Sports_LastFirst**. Games are usually scheduled seven days apart. Enter this value on a second sheet, assign a range name, and then use the range name in a formula to calculate the game dates based on the original game date. In some instances, you may have to enter a date if more or fewer days exist between two game dates. In the fifth column, use an IF function to determine if your team won or lost each game; display either *Win* or *Lose*. In the sixth column, use an IF function to calculate by how many points your team won each game or display an empty string by entering "" in the value_if_false argument if your team lost.

Create a statistics area to calculate the average, median, low, and high scores for your team. Below the won-by points column, use two different count functions to count the number of games won and lost. Use Help to learn about the COUNTIF function and use this function to count the number of games won based on the number of *Win* entries. Use mixed references in the function's first argument, copy the function, and then edit the second argument of the copied COUNTIF function to calculate the number of games lost. The summary area should have four count functions. Add titles and column labels, format data within the columns, and then include the URL of where you got the data. Include a footer with your name on the left side, the date code in the center, and the file name code on the right side. Save and close the workbook, and submit based on your instructor's directions.

Park City Condo Rental

DISASTER RECOVERY

You and some friends are planning a Labor Day vacation to Park City, Utah. You have secured a four-day condominium that costs $1,200. Some people will stay all four days; others will stay part of the weekend. One of your friends constructed a worksheet to help calculate each person's cost of the rental. The people who stay Thursday night will split the nightly cost evenly. To keep the costs down, everyone agreed to pay $30 per night per person for Friday, Saturday, and/or Sunday nights. Depending on the number of people who stay each night, the group may owe more money. Kyle, Ian, Isaac, and Daryl agreed to split the difference in the total rental cost and the amount the group members paid. Open *e02b3ParkCity*, address the circular reference error message that displays, and save the workbook as **e02b3ParkCity_LastFirst**.

Review the worksheet structure, including the assumptions and calculation notes at the bottom of the worksheet. Check the formulas and functions, making necessary corrections. With the existing data, the number of people staying each night is 5, 7, 10, and 10, respectively. The total paid given the above assumptions is $1,110, giving a difference of $90 to be divided evenly among the first four people. Kyle's share should be $172.50. In the cells containing errors, insert comments to describe the error and fix the formulas. Verify the accuracy of formulas by entering an IF function in **cell I1** to ensure the totals match. Nick, James, and Body inform you they can't stay Sunday night, and Rob wants to stay Friday night. Change the input accordingly. The updated total paid is now $1,200, and the difference is $150. Include a footer with your name on the left side, the date code in the center, and the file name code on the right side. Save and close the workbook, and submit based on your instructor's directions.

Interview Walkthough

SOFT SKILLS CASE S

FROM SCRATCH 

After watching the video, create a workbook named **e02b4Interview_LastFirst** that lists five to seven common interview questions in the first column. In the second column, enter a percentage weight for each question. For example, the first question might count 5% of the total. The total weights should be 100%. Include columns to rate five interviewees on the questions using a scale of 1–5 where 1 is low and 5 is high. Incude a column label with a first name for each interviewee. At the bottom of the first interviewee's column, use the AVERAGE function with the argument to multiply that person's individual scores by their respective weights using relative and absolute references correctly. Copy the formula to the other candidates.

Add an input area for a minimum weighted score of 4.5. Assign a range name to the score. On the row below the weighted scores, add a row labeled *Second Interview?* Enter an IF function for the first candidate: If the weighted score is greater than or equal to 4.5, then display *Yes*; otherwise, display *No*. Copy the function for the other candidates. Include a footer with your name on the left side, the date code in the center, and the file name code on the right side. Save and close the workbook, and submit based on your instructor's directions.

Capstone Exercise

You are a sales representative at the local fitness center, Health & Fitness Gym. Your manager expects each representative to track weekly new membership data, so you created a spreadsheet to store data. Membership costs are based on membership type. Clients can rent a locker for an additional annual fee. You are required to collect a down payment based on membership type, determine the balance, and then calculate the monthly payment based on a standard interest rate. In addition, you need to calculate general statistics to summarize for your manager. Spot-check results to make sure you created formulas and functions correctly.

Perform Preliminary Work

You need to open the starting workbook you created, acknowledge the existing circular reference error, and assign a range name to the membership lookup table. You will correct the circular reference error later.

a. Open the *e02c1Gym* workbook, click **Help**, read about circular references, close the Help window that displays, and then save the workbook as **e02c1Gym_LastFirst**.

b. Assign the name **Membership** to the **range A18:C20**.

c. Insert a function to display the current date in **cell B2**.

Calculate Cost, Annual Total, and Total Due

You are ready to calculate the basic annual membership cost and the total annual cost. The basic annual membership is determined based on each client's membership type, using the lookup table.

a. Insert a lookup function in **cell C5** to display the basic annual membership cost for the first client.

b. Use an IF function in **cell E5** to calculate the annual total amount, which is the sum of the basic cost and locker fees for those who rent a locker. For people who do not rent a locker, the annual cost is only the cost shown in column C. The Locker column displays *Yes* for clients who rent a locker and *No* for those who don't.

c. Calculate the total amount due in **cell G5** for the first client based on the annual total and the number of years in the contract.

d. Copy the three formulas down their respective columns.

Determine the Down Payment and Balance

You need to collect a down payment based on the type of membership for each new client. Then you must determine how much each client owes.

a. Insert a lookup function in **cell H5** to display the amount of down payment for the first client based on the membership type.

b. Find and correct the circular reference for the balance. The balance is the difference between the total due and the down payment.

c. Copy the two formulas for the rest of the clients.

Calculate the Monthly Payment

Clients pay the remainder by making monthly payments. Monthly payments are based on the number of years specified in the client's contract and a standard interest rate.

a. Insert the function in **cell J5** to calculate the first client's monthly payment, using appropriate relative and absolute cell references.

b. Copy the formula down the column.

c. Edit the formula by changing the appropriate cell reference to a mixed cell reference. Copy the formula down.

Finalize the Workbook

You need to perform some basic statistical calculations and finalize the workbook with formatting and page setup options.

a. Calculate totals on row 14.

b. Insert the appropriate functions in the *Summary Statistics* section of the worksheet: **cells H18:H22**. Format the payments with **Accounting Number Format** and format the number of new members appropriately.

c. Format the other column headings on rows 4 and 17 to match the fill color in the **range E17:H17**. Wrap text for the column headings.

d. Format the monetary values for Andrews and the total row with **Accounting Number Format**. Use zero decimal places for whole amounts and display two decimal places for the monthly payment. Apply **Comma Style** to the internal monetary values. Underline the values before the totals and apply **Double Accounting Underline** (found in the Format Cells dialog box) for the totals.

e. Set **0.3"** left and right margins and ensure the page prints on only one page.

f. Insert a footer with your name on the left side, the date code in the center, and the file name code on the right side.

g. Save and close the workbook, and submit based on your instructor's directions.

Excel

Charts

CHAPTER 3

Depicting Data Visually

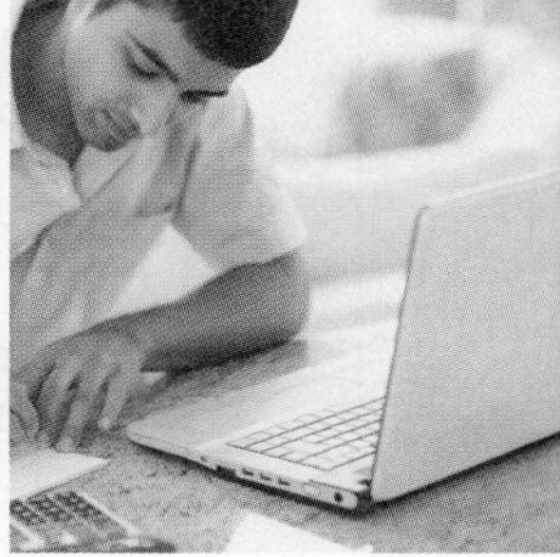

OBJECTIVES

AFTER YOU READ THIS CHAPTER, YOU WILL BE ABLE TO:

CASE STUDY | Computer Job Outlook

You are an academic advisor for the School of Computing at a private university in Seattle, Washington. You will be visiting high schools in the state over the next few weeks to discuss the computing programs at the university and to inform students about the job outlook in the computing industry.

Your assistant, Doug Demers, researched growing computer-related jobs in the *Occupational Outlook Handbook* published by the Bureau of Labor Statistics on the U.S. Department of Labor's Web site. In particular, Doug listed seven jobs, the number of those jobs in 2010, the projected number of jobs by 2020, the growth in percentage increase and number of jobs, and the 2010 median pay. This data set shows an 18%–31% increase in computer-related jobs in that 10-year time period.

To prepare for your presentation to encourage students to enroll in your School of Computing, you want to create several charts that depict the job growth in the computer industry. You know that different charts provide different perspectives on the data. After you complete the charts, you will be able to use them in a variety of formats, such as presentations, fliers, brochures, and press releases.

Chart Creation Basics

The expression "a picture is worth a thousand words" means that a visual can be a more effective way to communicate or interpret data than words or numbers. Storing, organizing, and performing calculations on quantitative data are important, but you must also be able to analyze the data. A ***chart*** is a visual representation of numerical data that compares data and helps reveal trends or patterns to help people make informed decisions. An effective chart depicts data in a clear, easy-to-interpret manner and contains enough data to be useful without overwhelming your audience.

A chart may include several chart elements. The ***chart area*** contains the entire chart and all of its elements, including the plot area, titles, legend, and labels. The ***plot area*** is the region containing the graphical representation of the values in the data series. Two axes form a border around the plot area.

The ***X-axis*** is a horizontal border that provides a frame of reference for measuring data horizontally. The ***Y-axis*** is a vertical border that provides a frame of reference for measuring data vertically. Excel refers to the axes as the category axis and value axis. The ***category axis*** displays descriptive group names or labels (such as college names, cities, or equal amounts of time) to identify data. Categories are usually defined by column or row labels (such as job titles or years) in the worksheet. The ***value axis*** displays incremental numbers to identify the worksheet values (such as number of jobs or revenue) used to create the chart. A ***legend*** is a key that identifies the color, gradient, picture, texture, or pattern assigned to each data series in a chart. For example, blue might represent values for 2010, and orange might represent values for 2020.

In this section, you will select the data source, choose the best chart type to represent numerical data, and designate the chart's location.

Selecting the Data Source

Before creating a chart, organize the worksheet data so that the values in columns and rows are on the same value system (such as dollars or units), make sure labels are descriptive, and delete any blank rows or columns that exist in the primary data set. Look at the structure of the worksheet—the column labels, the row labels, the quantitative data, and the calculated values. Decide what you want to convey to your audience by answering these questions:

- Does the worksheet hold a single set of data, such as average snowfall at one ski resort, or multiple sets of data, such as average snowfall at several ski resorts?
- Do you want to depict data for one specific time period or over several time periods, such as several years or decades?

Identify the data range by selecting values and labels that you want to include in the chart. If the values and labels are not stored in adjacent cells, hold Ctrl while selecting the nonadjacent ranges. Do not select worksheet titles or subtitles; doing so would add unnecessary data to the chart.

Figure 3.1 shows a worksheet containing computer-related job titles, the number of jobs in 2010, the projected number of jobs by 2020, and other details. Row 3 contains labels merged and centered over individual column labels in row 5. Row 4 is blank and hidden. It is a good practice to insert a blank row between merged labels and individual column labels. Without the blank row, you would not be able to correctly sort data; the column headings would be sorted with the data.

Each cell containing a value is a ***data point***. For example, the value 110,800 is a data point for the number of Database Administrators in 2010. A group of related data points that display in row(s) or column(s) in the worksheet create a ***data series***. For example, the values 110,800 and 144,800 comprise the Database Administrators data series. Row and column labels (such as job titles, years, growth, etc.) are used to create ***category labels*** in charts.

	A	B	C	D	E	F
1	**Computer-Related Jobs**					
2						
3		# of Jobs		Job Growth		Median Pay
5		2010	2020 Est.	% Growth	# of New Jobs	2010
6	Database Administrators	110,800	144,800	31%	34,000	$ 73,490
7	Info Security Analysts	302,300	367,900	22%	65,600	$ 75,600
8	CIS Managers	307,900	363,700	18%	55,800	$ 115,780
9	Network/System Admins	347,200	443,800	28%	96,600	$ 69,160
10	Programmers	363,100	406,800	12%	43,700	$ 71,380
11	Software App Developers	520,800	664,500	28%	143,700	$ 90,530
12	Systems Analysts	544,400	664,800	22%	120,400	$ 77,740
14	Source: Bureau of Labor Statistics, U.S. Department of Labor, *Occupational Outlook Handbook, 2012-13 Edition*, on the Internet at http://www.bls.gov/					

FIGURE 3.1 Sample Data Set

TIP Avoid Using Data Aggregates and Individual Values

Make sure that each data series uses the same scale. For example, do not include data aggregates (such as totals or averages) with individual values. The data source used to create the chart in Figure 3.2 mixes individual number of jobs by title with the total number of jobs, which distorts the scale from the comparison of the number of jobs for each job title.

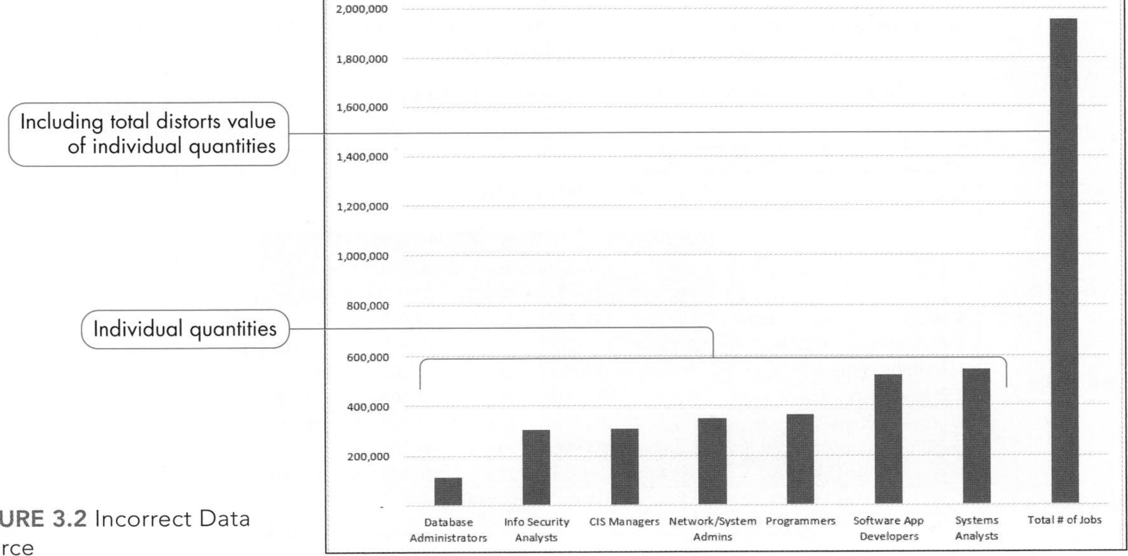

FIGURE 3.2 Incorrect Data Source

TIP Charts Update When Data Change

After you create a chart, you may need to change the worksheet data. When you change the worksheet data, Excel updates any charts that you created based on the data.

Choosing a Chart Type

When you select a range of cells and position the mouse pointer over that selected range, Excel displays the Quick Analysis button in the bottom-right corner of the selected area. The Excel 2013 Quick Analysis tool enables you to use analytical tools, such as charts, to quickly examine data. You should select a chart type that appropriately represents the data and tells a story. You can create different charts from the same data set, but each chart tells a different story. For example, one chart might compare the number of computer-related jobs between 2010 and 2020, and another chart might indicate the percentage of new jobs by job title. The most commonly used chart types are column, bar, line, and pie (see Table 3.1). Each chart type is designed to provide a unique perspective to the selected data.

TABLE 3.1 Common Chart Types

Chart	Chart Type	Description
	Column	Displays values in vertical columns where the height represents the value; the taller the column, the larger the value. Categories display along the horizontal (category) axis.
	Bar	Displays values in horizontal bars where the width represents the value; the wider the bar, the larger the value. Categories display along the vertical (category) axis.
	Line	Displays category data on the horizontal axis and value data on the vertical axis. Appropriate to show continuous data to depict trends over time, such as months, years, or decades.
	Pie	Shows proportion of individual data points to the sum of all those data points.

To create a chart, do the following:

1. Select the data and click the Quick Analysis button.
2. Click CHARTS in the Quick Analysis gallery (see Figure 3.3).
3. Position the mouse over each recommended chart thumbnail to see the type of chart that would be created from the selected data.
4. Click the thumbnail of the chart you want to create.

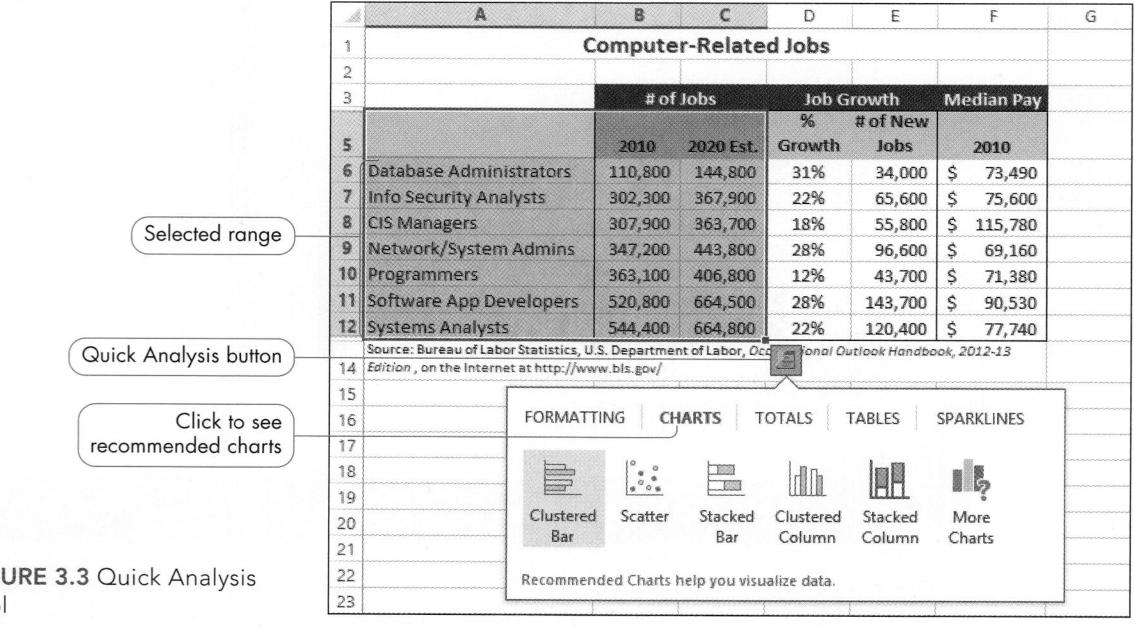

FIGURE 3.3 Quick Analysis Tool

Another way to create a chart is to click the Insert tab and do one of the following:

- Click the chart type (such as Column) in the Charts group and click a chart subtype (such as Clustered Column) from the chart gallery (see Figure 3.4).
- Click Recommended Charts in the Charts group to open the Insert Chart dialog box (see Figure 3.5), click a thumbnail of the chart you want, and then click OK.

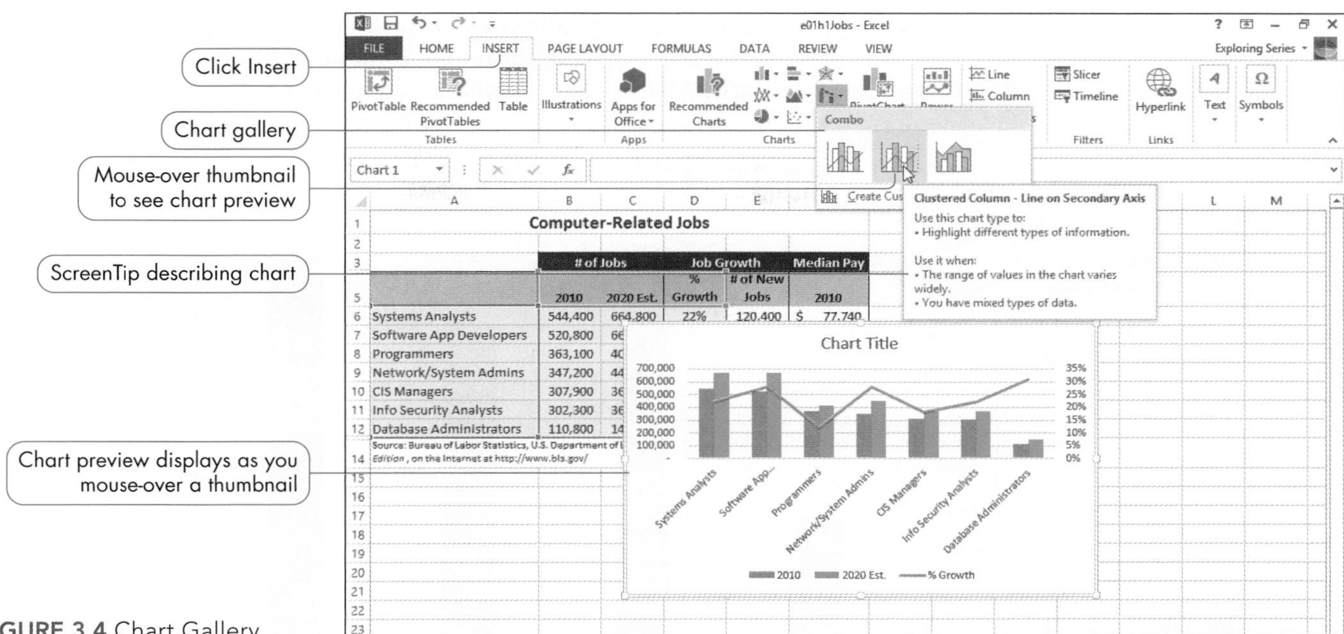

FIGURE 3.4 Chart Gallery

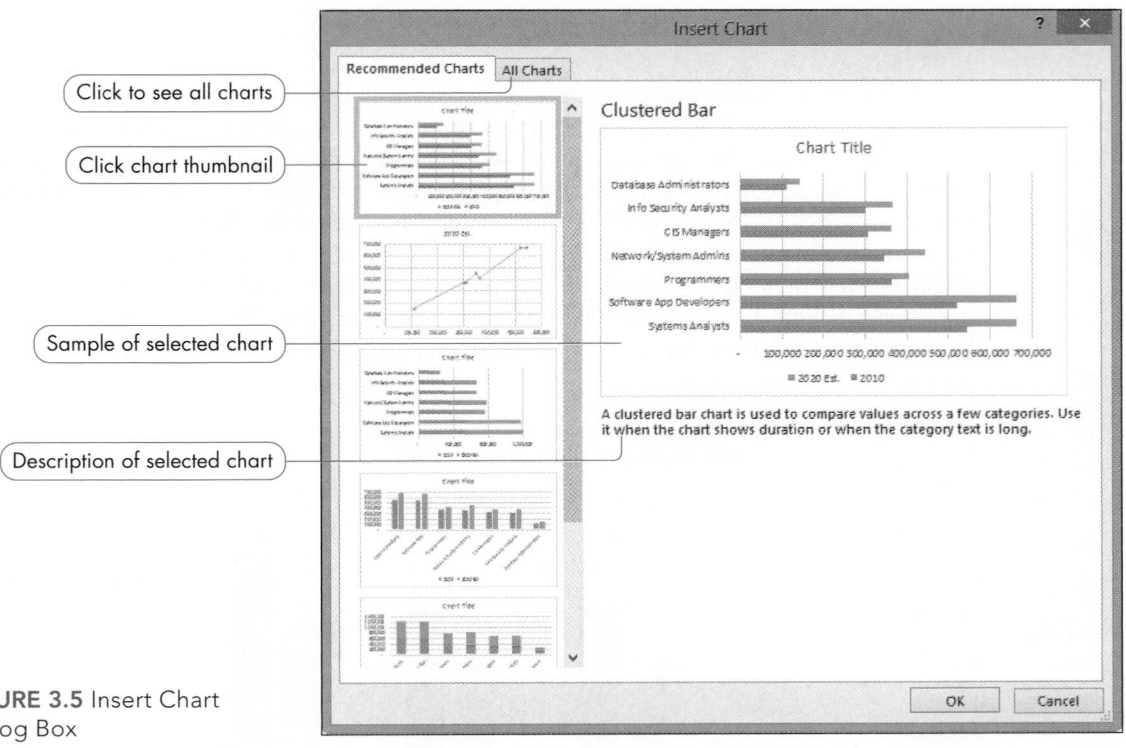

FIGURE 3.5 Insert Chart Dialog Box

Create a Column Chart

STEP 1

A ***column chart*** displays data vertically in columns. Create a column chart to compare values across different categories, such as population among cities in a state or number of computer-related jobs between two years. Column charts are most effective when they are limited to seven or fewer categories. If more categories exist, the columns appear too close together, making it difficult to read the labels.

The column chart in Figure 3.6 compares the number of projected jobs by job title for 2020 using the data in Figure 3.1. The first four job titles stored in the first column (range A6:A9) form the category axis, and the increments of the number of jobs in 2020 (range C6:C9) form the value axis. The height of each column represents the value of individual data points: The larger the value, the taller the column. For example, the Info Security Analysts column is taller than the Database Administrators column, indicating that more jobs are projected for Info Security Analysts than Database Administrators.

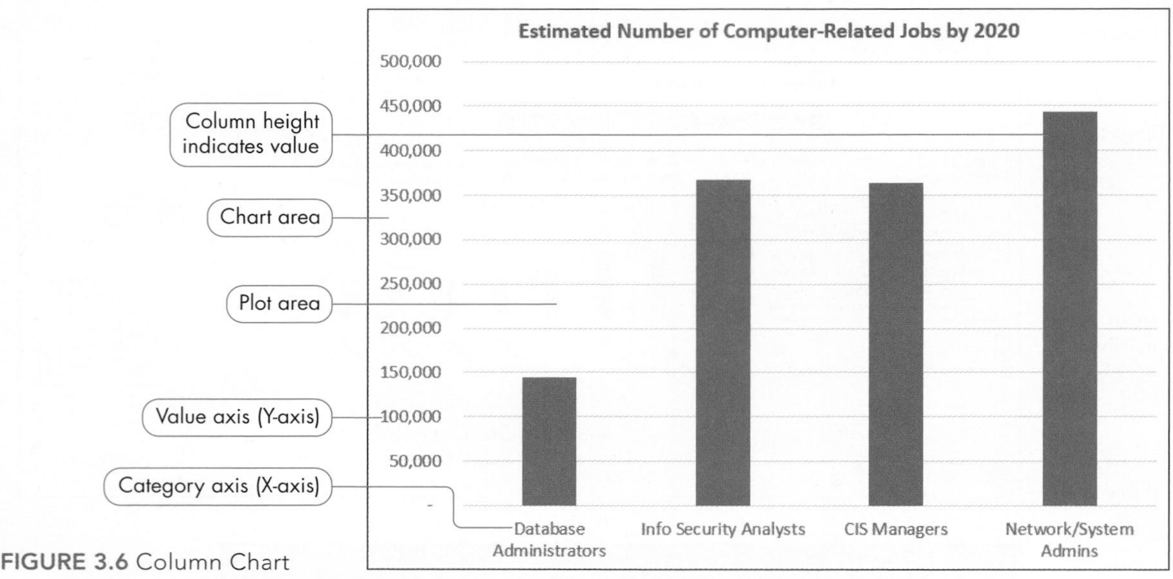

FIGURE 3.6 Column Chart

A ***clustered column chart*** compares groups—or clusters—of columns set side by side for easy comparison. The clustered column chart facilitates quick comparisons across data series, and it is effective for comparing several data points among categories. Figure 3.7 shows a clustered column chart created from the data in Figure 3.1. By default, the row labels appear on the category axis, and the yearly data series appear as columns with the value axis showing incremental numbers. Excel assigns a different color to each yearly data series and includes a legend so that you will know what color represents which data series. The 2010 data series is light blue, and the 2020 data series is dark blue. This chart makes it easy to compare the predicted job growth from 2010 to 2020 for each job title and then to compare the trends among job titles.

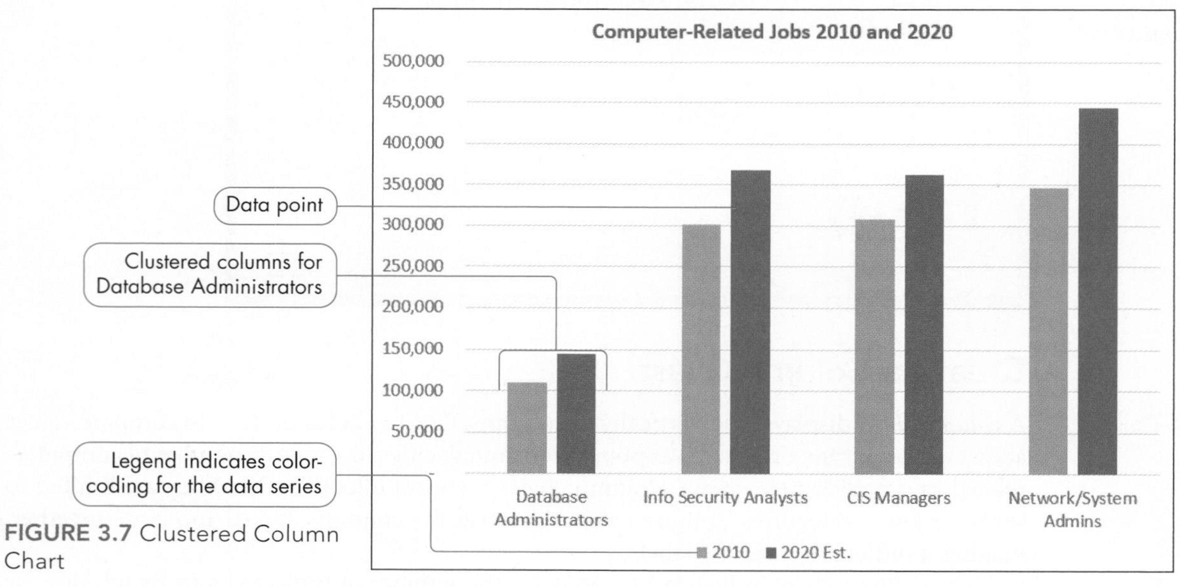

FIGURE 3.7 Clustered Column Chart

Figure 3.8 shows a clustered column chart in which the categories and data series are reversed. The years appear on the category axis, and the job titles appear as color-coded data series and in the legend. This chart gives a different perspective from that in Figure 3.7 in that it compares the number of jobs within a given year, such as 2010.

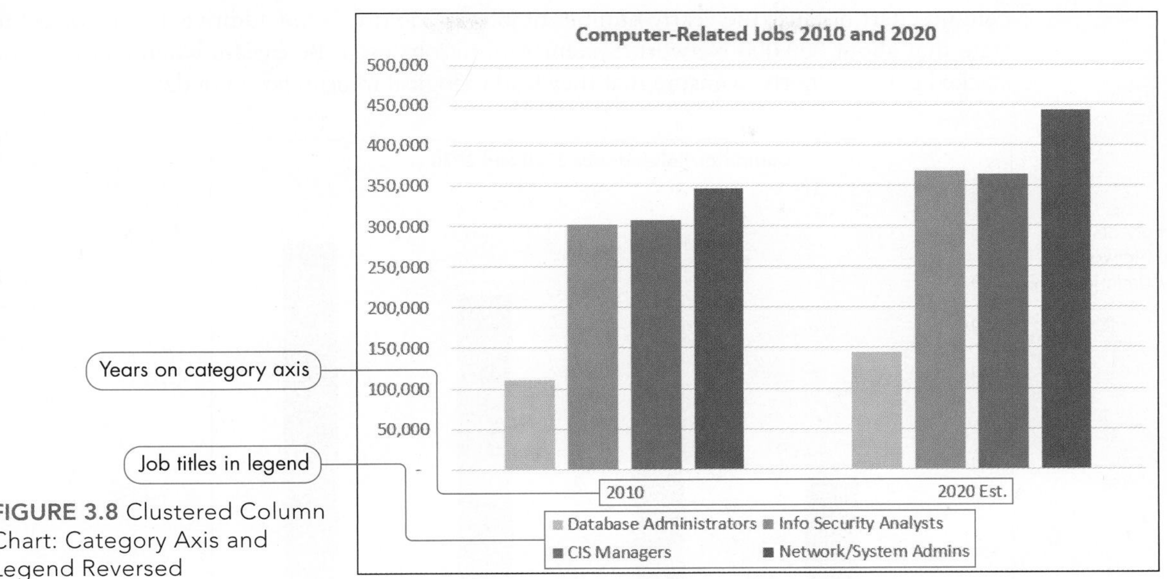

FIGURE 3.8 Clustered Column Chart: Category Axis and Legend Reversed

A ***stacked column chart*** shows the relationship of individual data points to the whole category. A stacked column chart displays only one column for each category. Each category within the stacked column is color-coded for one data series. Use the stacked column chart when you want to compare total values across categories, as well as to display the individual category values. Figure 3.9 shows a stacked column chart in which a single column represents each categorical year, and each column stacks color-coded data-point segments representing the different jobs. The stacked column chart enables you to compare the total number of computer-related jobs for each year. The height of each color-coded data point enables you to identify the relative contribution of each job to the total number of jobs for a particular year. A disadvantage of the stacked column chart is that the segments within each column do not start at the same point, making it more difficult to compare individual segment values across categories.

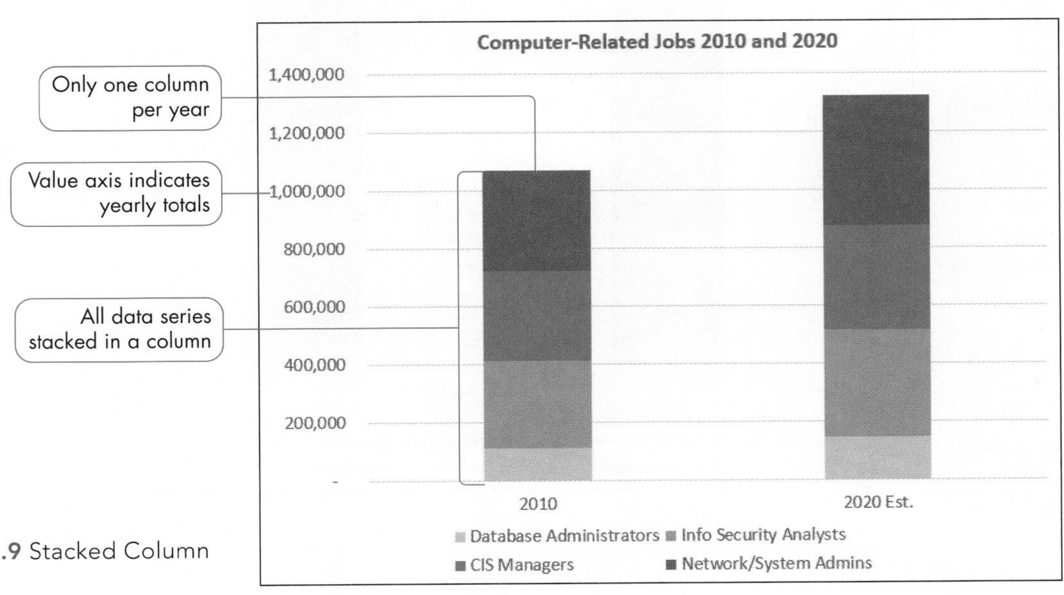

FIGURE 3.9 Stacked Column Chart

When you create a stacked column chart, make sure data are *additive*: each column represents a sum of the data for each segment. Figure 3.9 correctly uses years as the category axis and the jobs as data series. Within each year, Excel adds the number of jobs, and the columns display the total number of jobs. For example, the estimated total number of computer-related jobs in 2020 is about 1,300,000. Figure 3.10 shows an incorrectly constructed stacked column chart because the yearly number of jobs by job title is *not* additive. It is incorrect to state that about 800,000 Network/System Admin jobs exist. Be careful when constructing stacked column charts to ensure that they lead to logical interpretation of data.

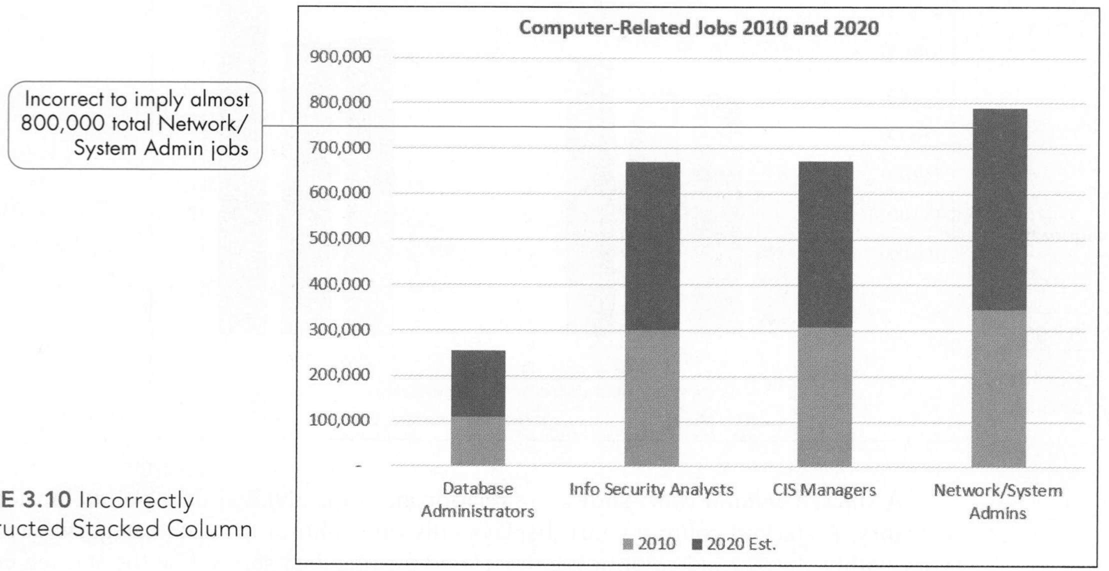

FIGURE 3.10 Incorrectly Constructed Stacked Column Chart

A ***100% stacked column chart*** converts individual data points into percentages of the total value. Each data series is a different color of the stack, representing a percentage. The total of each column is 100%. This type of chart depicts contributions to the whole. For example, the chart in Figure 3.11 illustrates that Network/System Admins account for over 30% of the computer-related jobs represented by the four job categories.

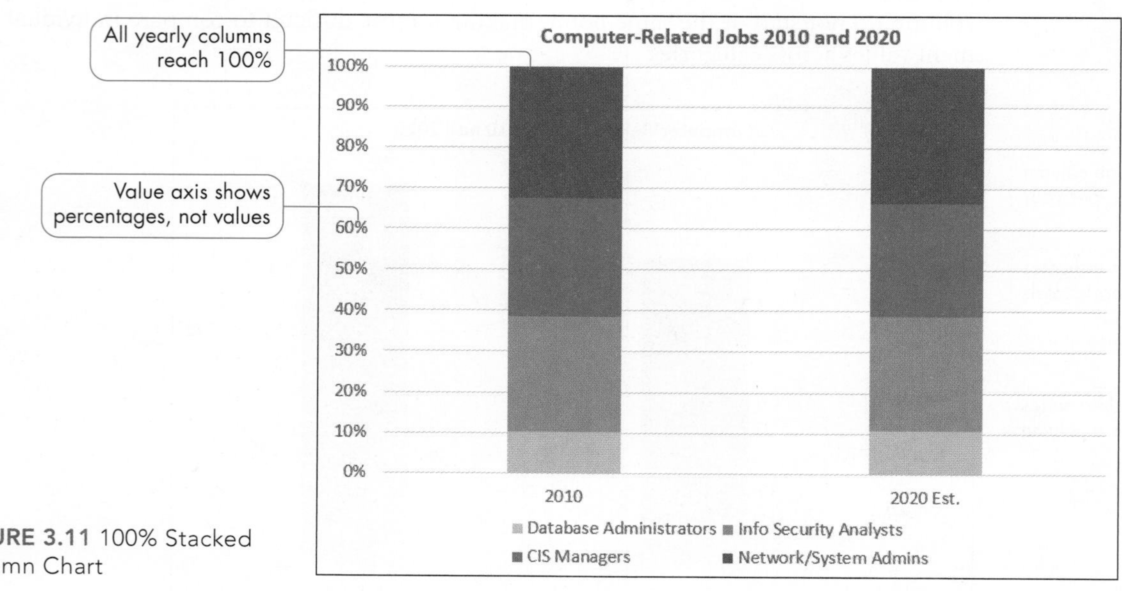

FIGURE 3.11 100% Stacked Column Chart

Avoid 3-D Charts

Avoid creating 3-D charts, because the third dimension is a superficial enhancement that usually distorts the charted data. For example, some columns appear taller or shorter than they actually are because of the angle of the 3-D effect, or some columns might be hidden by taller columns in front of them.

Create a Bar Chart

STEP 3»

A ***bar chart*** compares values across categories using horizontal bars. The horizontal axis displays values, and the vertical axis displays categories (see Figure 3.12). Bar charts and column charts tell a similar story: they both compare categories of data. A bar chart is preferable when category names are long, such as *Database Administrators*. A bar chart enables category names to appear in an easy-to-read format, whereas a column chart might display category names at an awkward angle or in a smaller font size. The overall decision between a column and a bar chart may come down to the fact that different data may look better with one chart type than the other.

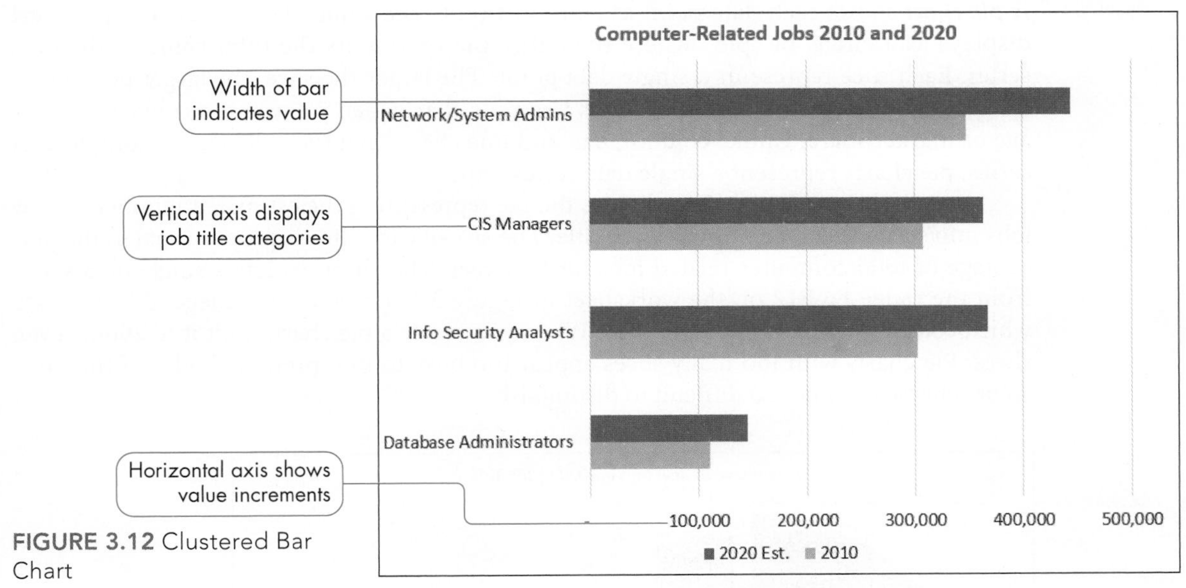

FIGURE 3.12 Clustered Bar Chart

Create a Line Chart

A ***line chart*** displays lines connecting data points to show trends over equal time periods. Excel displays each data series with a different line color. The category axis (X-axis) represents time, such as 10-year increments, whereas the value axis (Y-axis) represents the value, such as money or quantity. A line chart enables you to detect trends because the line continues to the next data point. To show each data point, choose the Line with Markers chart type. Figure 3.13 shows a line chart indicating the number of majors from 2005 to 2020 at five-year increments. The number of Arts majors remains relatively constant, but the number of Tech & Computing majors increases significantly over time, especially between the years 2010 and 2020.

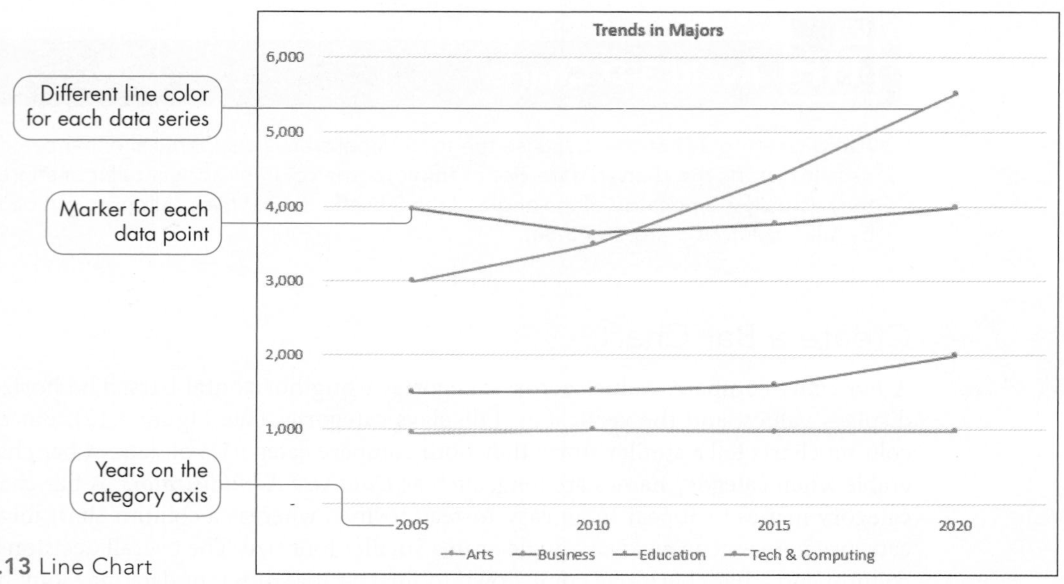

FIGURE 3.13 Line Chart

Create a Pie Chart

STEP 4

A ***pie chart*** shows each data point as a proportion to the whole data series. The pie chart displays as a circle, or "pie," where the entire pie represents the total value of the data series. Each slice represents a single data point. The larger the slice, the larger percentage that data point contributes to the whole. Use a pie chart when you want to convey percentage or market share. Unlike column, bar, and line charts that typically chart multiple data series, pie charts represent a single data series only.

The pie chart in Figure 3.14 divides the pie representing the estimated number of new jobs into seven slices, one for each job title. The size of each slice is proportional to the percentage of total computer-related jobs for that year. The chart depicts a single data series from the range E6:E12 on the worksheet in Figure 3.1. Excel creates a legend to indicate which color represents which pie slice. When you create a pie chart, limit it to about seven slices. Pie charts with too many slices appear too busy to interpret, or shades of the same color scheme become too difficult to distinguish.

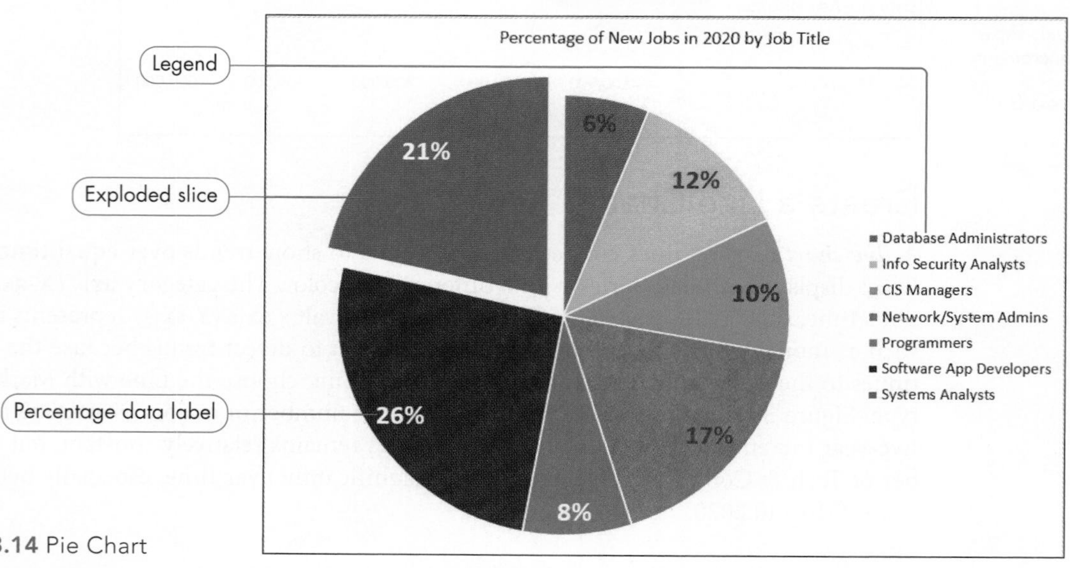

FIGURE 3.14 Pie Chart

The projected number of new Systems Analyst jobs is 33,900, which accounts for 21% of the new jobs. You can focus a person's attention on a particular slice by separating one or more slices from the rest of the chart in an ***exploded pie chart***, as shown in Figure 3.14.

Change the Chart Type

After you create a chart, you may decide that the data would be better represented by a different type of chart. For example, you might decide a bar chart would display the labels better than a column chart. When you select a chart, Chart Tools displays on the Ribbon with the Design and Format tabs. To change the type of an existing chart, do the following:

1. Select the chart and click the DESIGN tab.
2. Click Change Chart Type in the Type group to open the Change Chart Type dialog box, which is similar to the Insert Chart dialog box.
3. Click the ALL CHARTS tab within the dialog box.
4. Click a chart type on the left side of the dialog box.
5. Click a chart subtype on the right side of the dialog box and click OK.

Create Other Chart Types

Two other chart types that are used for specialized analysis are X Y (scatter) charts and stock charts.

An ***X Y (scatter) chart*** shows a relationship between two numerical variables using their X and Y coordinates. Excel plots one variable on the horizontal X-axis and the other variable on the vertical Y-axis. Scatter charts are often used to represent data in educational, scientific, and medical experiments. Figure 3.15 shows the relationship between the number of minutes students view a training video and their test scores.

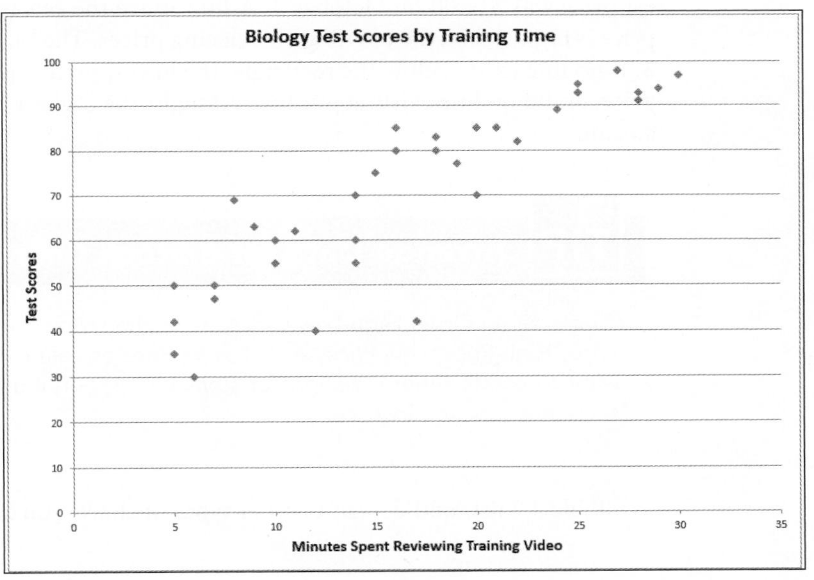

FIGURE 3.15 X Y (Scatter) Chart

A ***stock chart*** shows fluctuations in stock changes. You can select one of four stock subtypes: High-Low-Close, Open-High-Low-Close, Volume-High-Low-Close, and Volume-Open-High-Low-Close. The High-Low-Close stock chart marks a stock's trading range on a given day with a vertical line from the lowest to the highest stock prices. Rectangles mark the opening and closing prices. Figure 3.16 shows three days of stock prices for a particular company.

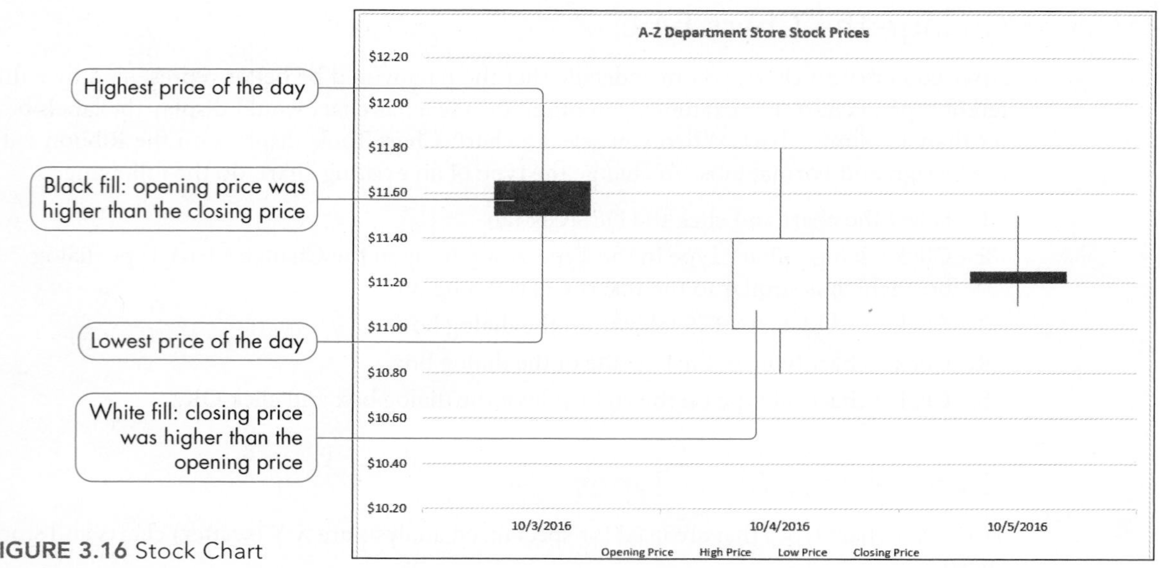

FIGURE 3.16 Stock Chart

The rectangle represents the difference in the opening and closing prices. If the rectangle has a white fill, the closing price is higher than the opening price. If the rectangle has a black fill, the opening price is higher than the closing price. In Figure 3.16, on October 3, the opening price was $11.65, and the closing price was $11.50. A line below the rectangle indicates that the lowest trading price is lower than the opening and closing prices. The lowest price was $11.00 on October 3. A line above the rectangle indicates the highest trading price is higher than the opening and closing prices. The highest price was $12.00 on October 3. If no line exists below the rectangle, the lowest price equals either the opening or closing price, and if no line exists above the rectangle, the highest price equals either the opening or closing price.

TIP Arrange Data for a Stock Chart

To create an Open-High-Low-Close stock chart, you must arrange data with Opening Price, High Price, Low Price, and Closing Price as column labels in that sequence. If you want to create other variations of stock charts, you must arrange data in a structured sequence required by Excel.

Table 3.2 lists and describes other types of charts you can create in Excel.

TABLE 3.2 Other Chart Types

Chart	Chart Type	Description
	Area	Similar to a line chart in that it shows trends over time; however, the area chart displays colors between the lines to help illustrate the magnitude of changes.
	Surface	Represents numeric data and numeric categories. Takes on some of the same characteristics as a topographic map of hills and valleys.
	Doughnut	A derivative of a pie chart showing relationship of parts to a whole, but the doughnut chart can display more than one data series.
	Bubble	A derivative of a scatter chart in which both the horizontal and vertical axes are value axes. The third value determines the size of the bubble, where the larger the value, the larger the bubble. Do not select the column labels, as they might distort the data.
	Radar	Uses each category as a spoke radiating from the center point to the outer edges of the chart. Each spoke represents each data series, and lines connect the data points between spokes, similar to a spider web. You can create a radar chart to compare aggregate values for several data series.
	Combo	Combines two chart types (such as column and line) to plot different data types (such as values and percentages).

Moving, Sizing, and Printing a Chart

Excel inserts the chart as an embedded object in the current worksheet, often to the right side of, but sometimes on top of and covering up, the data area. After you insert a chart, you usually need to move it to a different location, adjust its size, and prepare to print it.

Move a Chart

To move the chart on the active worksheet, position the mouse pointer over the chart area. When you see the Chart Area ScreenTip and the mouse pointer includes the white arrowhead and a four-headed arrow, drag the chart to the desired location.

You can place the chart in a separate worksheet, called a ***chart sheet***. A chart sheet contains a single chart only; you cannot enter data and formulas on a chart sheet. If you leave the chart in the same worksheet, you can print the data and chart on the same page. If you want to print or view a full-sized chart, move the chart to its own chart sheet. To move a chart to another sheet or a chart sheet, do the following:

1. Select the chart.
2. Click the DESIGN tab and click Move Chart in the Location group to open the Move Chart dialog box (see Figure 3.17).
3. Select one of these options to indicate where you want to move the chart:
    - Click *New sheet* to move the chart to its own sheet.
    - Click *Object in*, click the *Object in* arrow, and select the worksheet to which you want to move the chart. The default chart sheet is Chart1, but you can rename it in the Move Chart dialog box or similarly to the way you rename other sheet tabs. Click OK.

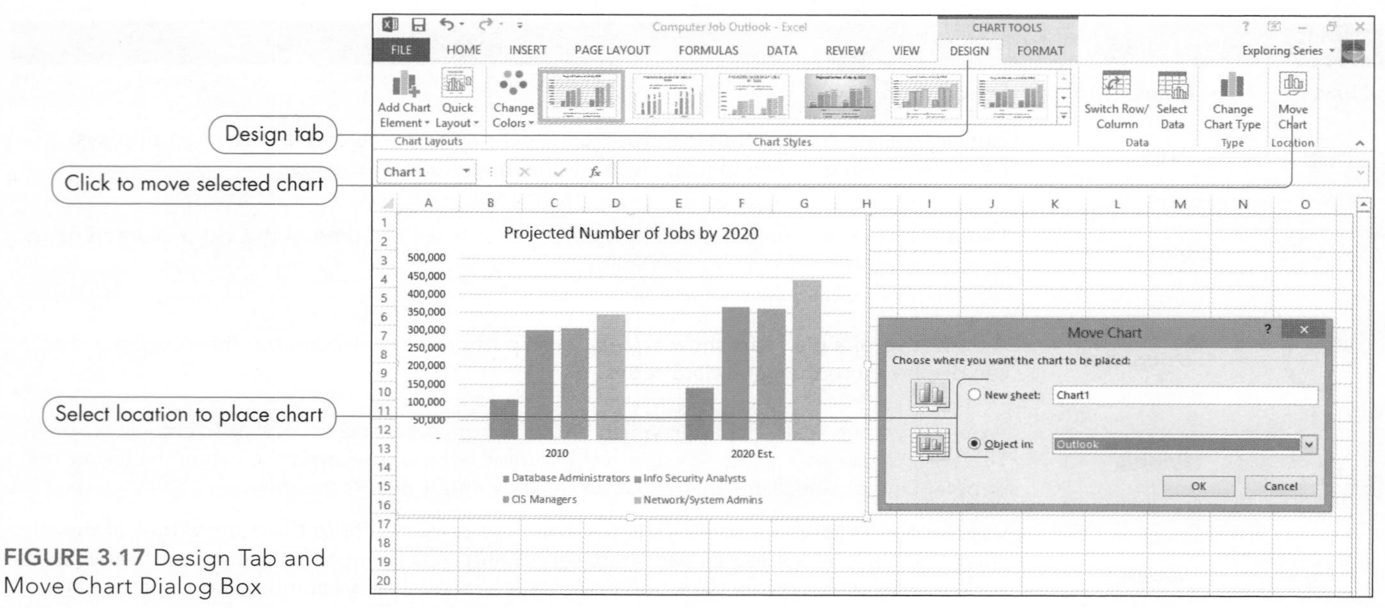

FIGURE 3.17 Design Tab and Move Chart Dialog Box

Size a Chart

If you keep a chart in a worksheet, you can size it to fit in a particular range or to ensure the chart elements are proportional. To change the chart size, do the following:

1. Select the chart.
2. Position the mouse pointer on the outer edge of the chart where you see eight small white-filled squares, called ***sizing handles***.
3. When the mouse pointer changes to a two-headed arrow, drag the border to adjust the chart's height or width. Drag a corner sizing handle to increase or decrease the height and width of the chart at the same time. Press and hold down Shift as you drag a corner sizing handle to change the height and width proportionately.

You can also change the chart size by clicking the Format tab and changing the height and width values in the Size group (see Figure 3.18).

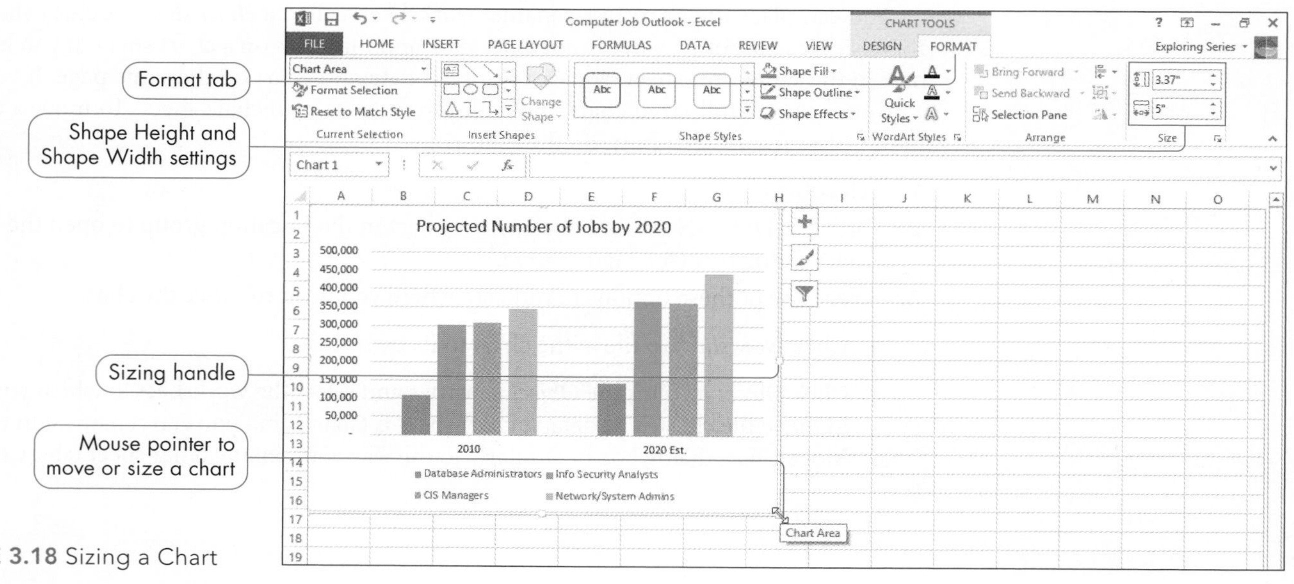

FIGURE 3.18 Sizing a Chart

Print a Chart

If you embedded a chart on the same sheet as the data source, you need to decide if you want to print the data only, the data *and* the chart, or the chart only. To print the data only, select the data, click the File tab, click Print, click the first arrow in the Settings section and select Print Selection, and then click Print. To print only the chart, select the chart, click the File tab, click Print, make sure the default setting is Print Selected Chart, and then click Print to print the chart as a full-page chart. If the data and chart are on the same worksheet, print the worksheet contents to print both, but do not select either the chart or the data before displaying the Print options. The preview shows you what will print. Make sure it displays what you want to print before clicking Print.

If you moved the chart to a chart sheet, the chart is the only item on that worksheet. When you display the print options, the default is Print Active Sheets, and the chart will print as a full-page chart.

1. Why should you not include aggregates, such as totals or averages, along with individual data series in a chart? ***p. 507***
2. What is the purpose of each of these chart types: (a) column, (b) bar, (c) line, and (d) pie? ***p. 508***
3. How can you use the Quick Analysis button to create a chart? ***p. 508***
4. After you create a chart, where is it located by default? What do you usually do to the chart immediately after creating it? ***p. 517***

Hands-On Exercises

MyITLab® HOE1 Training

1 Chart Creation Basics

Doug Demers, your assistant, gathered data about seven computer-related jobs from the *Occupational Outlook Handbook* online. He organized the data into a structured worksheet that contains the job titles, the number of jobs in 2010, the projected number of jobs by 2020, and other data. Now you are ready to transform the data into visually appealing charts.

Skills covered: Create a Clustered Column Chart • Create a Bar Chart • Change the Chart Position, Size, and Type • Create a Pie Chart

STEP 1 ›› CREATE A CLUSTERED COLUMN CHART

You want to compare the number of jobs in 2010 to the projected number of jobs in 2020 for all seven computer-related professions that Doug entered into the worksheet. You decide to create a clustered column chart to depict this data. After you create this chart, you will move it to its own chart sheet. Refer to Figure 3.19 as you complete Step 1.

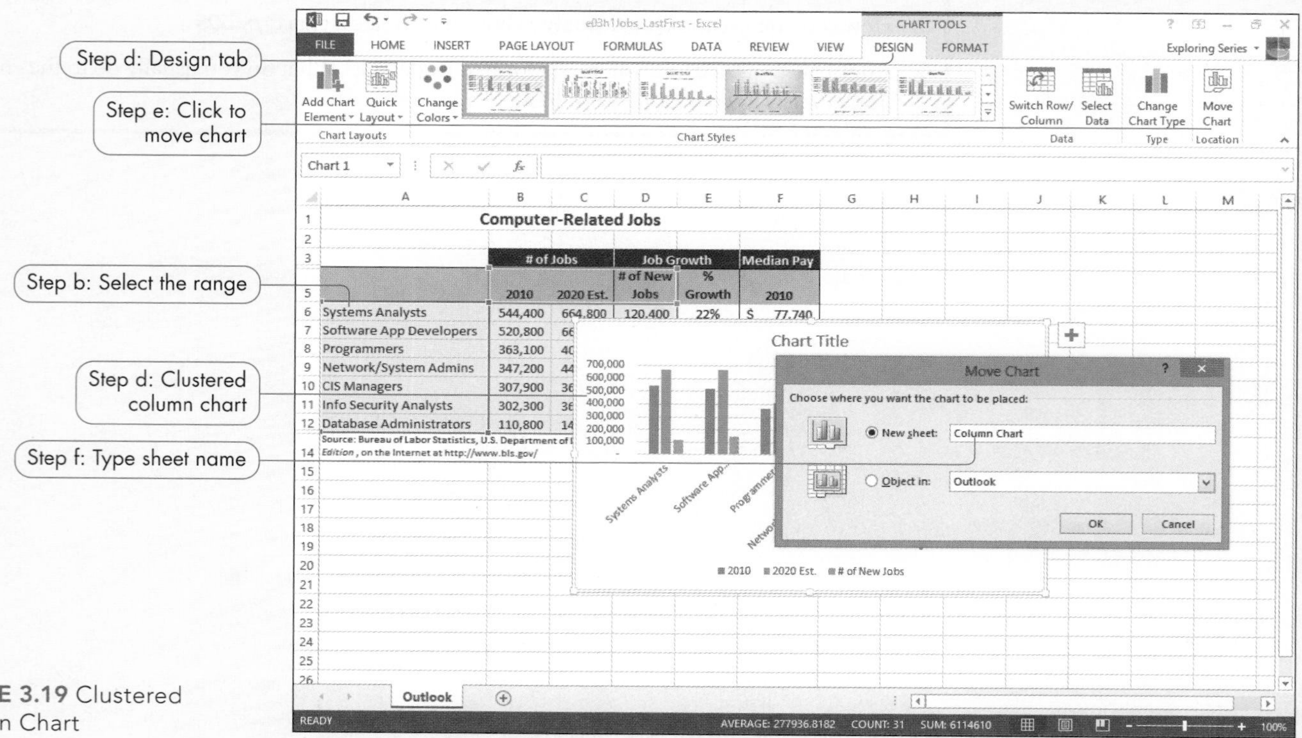

FIGURE 3.19 Clustered Column Chart

a. Open *e03h1Jobs* and save it as **e03h1Jobs_LastFirst**.

> **TROUBLESHOOTING:** If you make any major mistakes in this exercise, you can close the file, open *e03h1Jobs* again, and then start this exercise over.

b. Select the **range A5:D12**.

You selected the job titles, the number of jobs in 2010, the projected number of jobs in 2020, and the number of new jobs.

c. Click the **Quick Analysis button** at the bottom-right corner of the selected range and click **CHARTS**.

The Quick Analysis gallery displays recommended charts based on the selected range.

d. Position the mouse pointer over *Clustered Column* to see a live preview of what the chart would look like and click **Clustered Column**.

Excel inserts a clustered column chart based on the selected data.

The DESIGN tab displays on the Ribbon.

e. Click **Move Chart** in the Location group to open the Move Chart dialog box.

f. Click **New sheet**, type **Column Chart**, and click **OK**. Save the workbook.

Excel moves the clustered column chart to a new sheet called Column Chart. Later, you will modify the chart.

STEP 2 ›› CREATE A BAR CHART

You want to create a bar chart to depict the number of jobs in 2010 and the number of new jobs that will be created by 2020. Refer to Figure 3.20 as you complete Step 2.

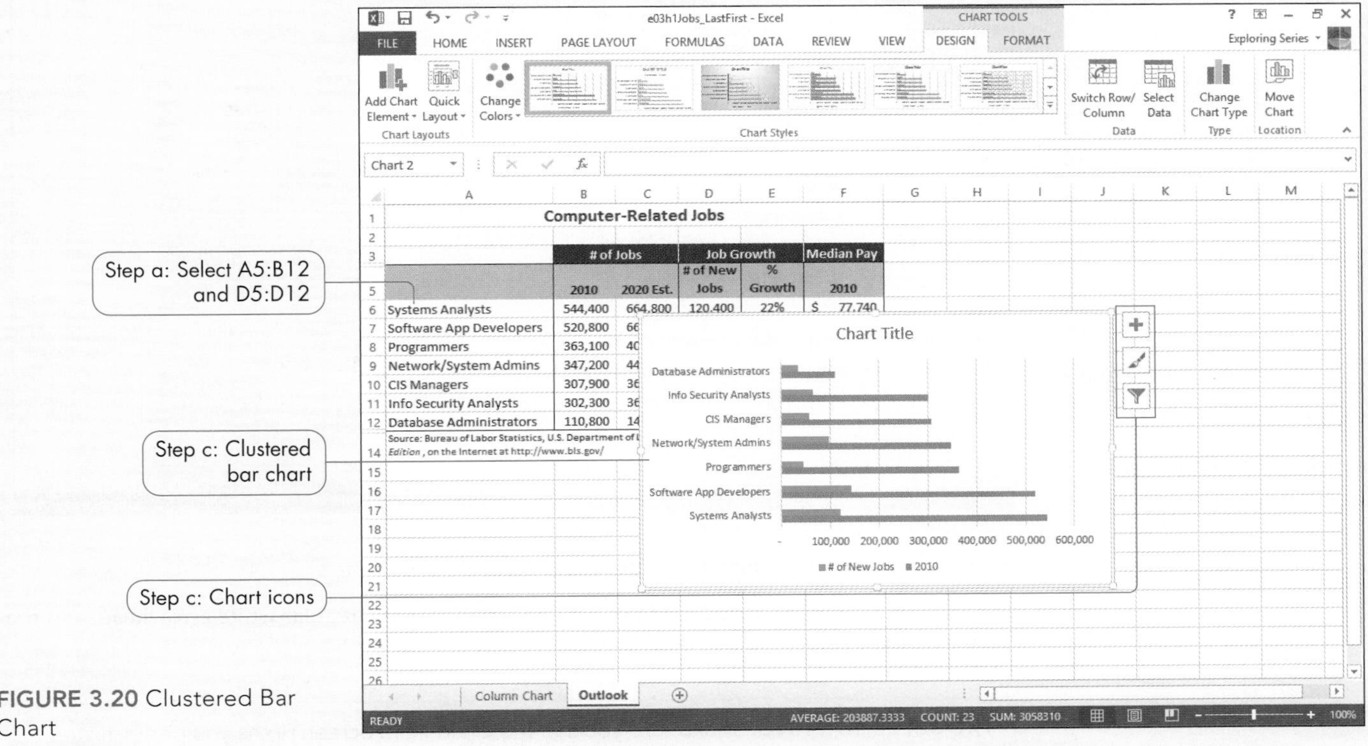

FIGURE 3.20 Clustered Bar Chart

a. Click the **Outlook sheet tab**, select the **range A5:B12**, press and hold **Ctrl**, and then select the range **D5:D12**.

You selected the job title labels, the number of jobs in 2010, and the number of new jobs.

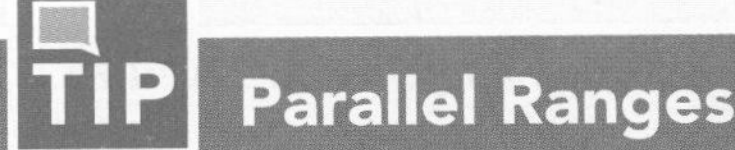

TIP Parallel Ranges

Nonadjacent ranges should be parallel so that the legend will correctly reflect the data series. This means that each range should contain the same number of related cells. For example, A5:A12, B5:B12, and D5:D12 are parallel ranges.

b. Click the **INSERT tab** and click **Insert Bar Chart** in the Charts group.

A gallery containing thumbnails of different bar charts displays.

c. Click **Clustered Bar** in the 2-D Bar group. Save the workbook.

Excel inserts the clustered bar chart in the worksheet. Three icons display to the right side of the selected chart: Chart Elements, Chart Styles, and Chart Filters.

STEP 3 » CHANGE THE CHART POSITION, SIZE, AND TYPE

Because the bar chart overlaps the data, you need to move it. You decide to position it below the job outlook data and adjust its size. Finally, you want to change the chart to a stacked bar chart to show the total jobs in 2020 based on the number of jobs in 2010 and the number of new jobs. Refer to Figure 3.21 as you complete Step 3.

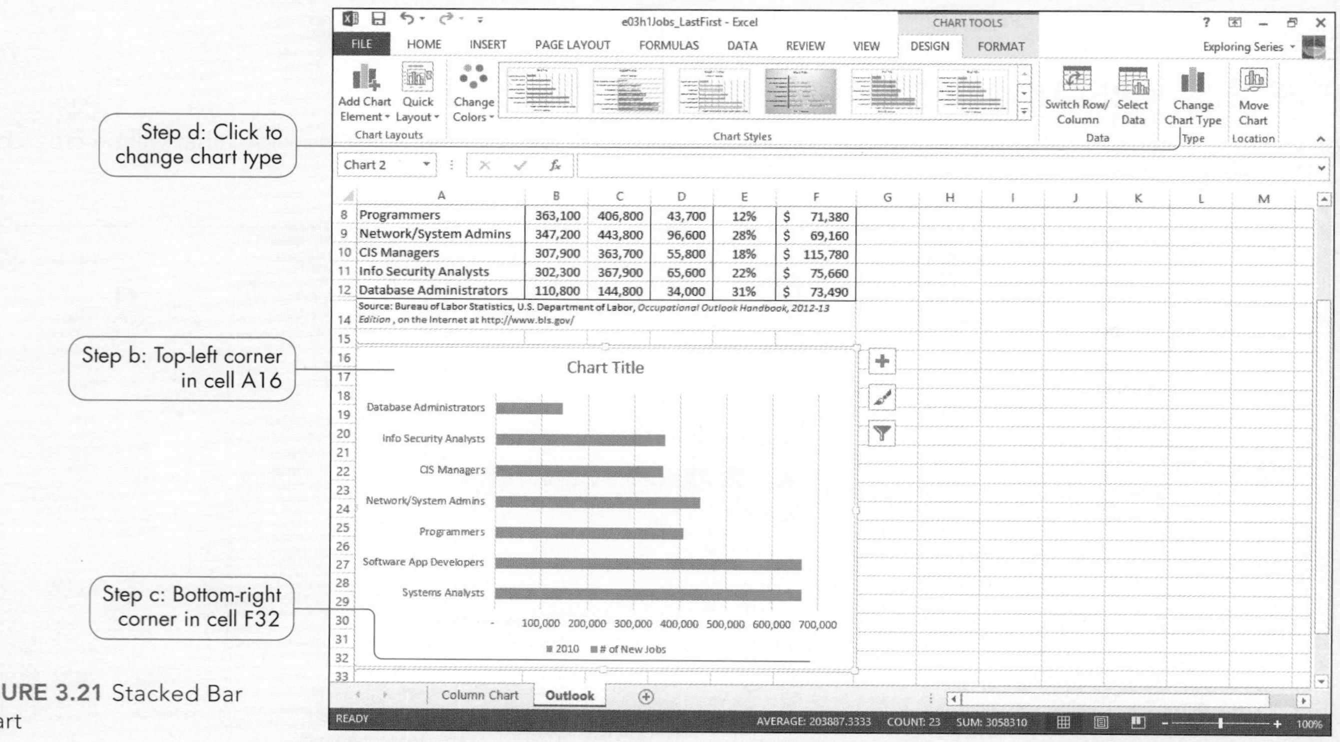

FIGURE 3.21 Stacked Bar Chart

a. Position the mouse pointer over the empty area of the chart area.

The mouse pointer includes a four-headed arrow with the regular white arrowhead, and the Chart Area ScreenTip displays.

TROUBLESHOOTING: Make sure you see the Chart Area ScreenTip as you perform step b. If you move the mouse pointer to another chart element—such as the legend—you will move or size that element instead of moving the entire chart.

b. Drag the chart so that the top-left corner of the chart appears in **cell A16**.

You positioned the chart below the worksheet data.

c. Drag the bottom-right sizing handle through **cell F32**.

You changed both the height and the width at the same time.

d. Click **Change Chart Type** in the Type group, click **Stacked Bar** in the top center of the dialog box, and then click **OK**. Save the workbook.

   Excel stacks the 2010 number of new jobs data series into one column per job title. This chart tells the story of where the projected number of jobs in 2020 come from: the number of existing jobs in 2010 (blue) and the number of new jobs (orange).

STEP 4 » CREATE A PIE CHART

You decide to create a pie chart that depicts the percentage of new jobs by job title created out of the total number of new jobs created, which is 559,800. After creating the pie chart, you will move it to its own sheet. Finally, you want to draw attention to the job that has the largest slice by exploding it. Refer to Figure 3.22 as you complete Step 4.

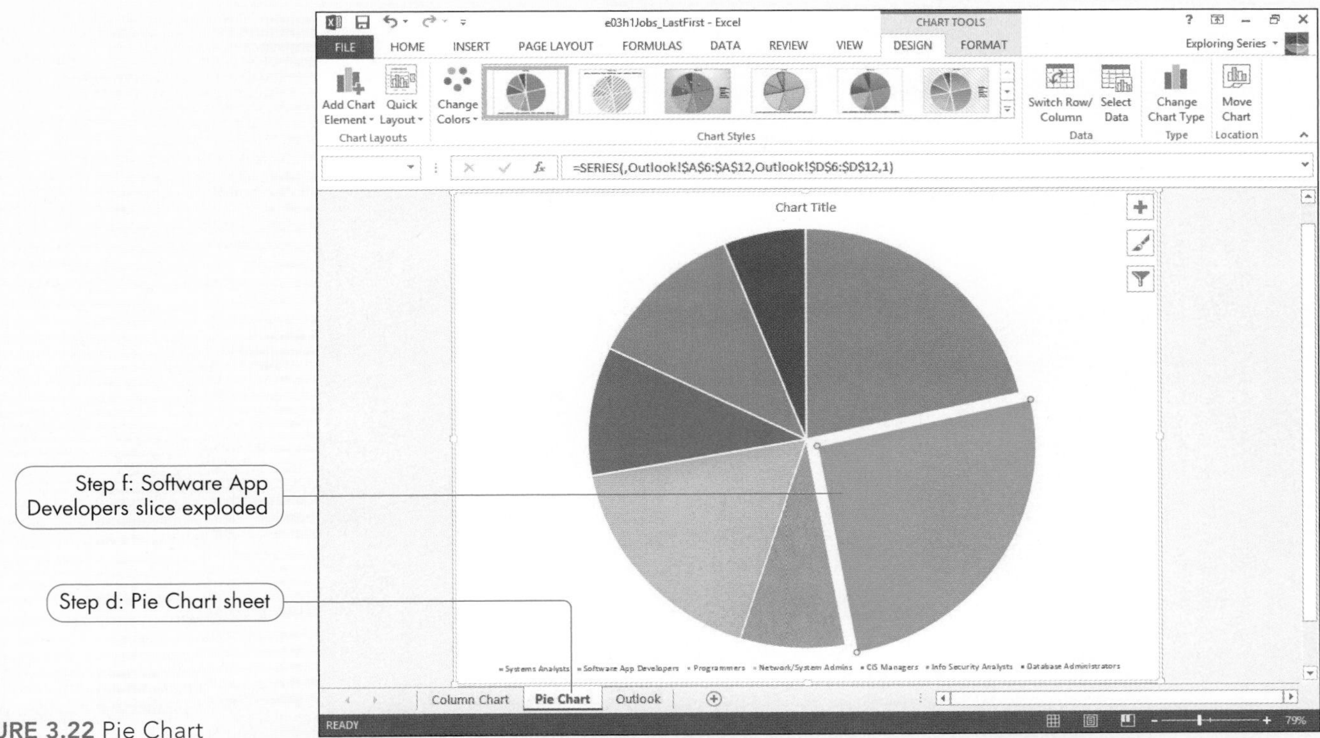

FIGURE 3.22 Pie Chart

a. Select the **range A6:A12** and press and hold **Ctrl** as you select the **range D6:D12**.

> **TROUBLESHOOTING:** Do not select cells A5 and D5 this time because you are creating a pie chart. Doing so would add unnecessary data to the chart.

b. Click the **INSERT tab**, click **Insert Pie or Doughnut** in the Charts group, and then select **Pie** in the 2-D Pie group on the gallery.

   The pie chart may overlap part of the worksheet data and the stacked bar chart.

c. Click **Move Chart** in the Location group on the DESIGN tab.

   The Move Chart dialog box opens.

d. Click **New sheet**, type **Pie Chart**, and then click **OK**.

   Excel creates a new sheet called Pie Chart. The pie chart is the only object on that sheet.

e. Click the **Software App Developers orange slice**, pause, and then click it again.

   The first click selects all slices of the pie. The second click selects only the Software App Developers slice.

TROUBLESHOOTING: If you double-click the pie chart, the Format Data Series task pane opens on the right side of the chart. Click its Close button and click the orange slice one time.

f. Drag the **Software App Developers orange slice** away from the pie a little bit.

g. Save the workbook. Keep the workbook open if you plan to continue with the next Hands-On Exercise. If not, close the workbook and exit Excel.

Chart Elements

After you create a chart, you usually need to add components to describe the chart. Adding descriptive text for labels provides information for the reader to comprehend the chart. When you create a chart, one or more components may display by default. For example, when you created the charts in Hands-On Exercise 1, Excel displayed a placeholder for the chart title and displayed a legend so that you know which color represents which data series.

When you select a chart, Excel displays three icons to the right side the chart, the first of which is Chart Elements. In addition, the Design tab contains the Chart Layouts group so that you can add and customize chart elements.

In this section, you will learn how to add and format chart elements.

Adding Chart Elements

A ***chart element*** is a component that completes or helps clarify the chart. Some chart elements, such as chart titles, should be included in every chart. Other elements are optional. Table 3.3 describes the chart elements, and Figure 3.23 illustrates several chart elements.

TABLE 3.3 Chart Elements

Element	Description
Axes	Category axis labels, such as job titles, and the value axis quantities in increments in column, bar, and line charts. Axes display by default.
Axis titles	Labels that describe the category and value axes. You can display axis titles, such as *In Millions of Dollars* or *Top 7 Computer Job Titles*, to clarify the axes. Axis titles are not displayed by default.
Chart title	Label that describes the entire chart. It should reflect the purpose of the chart. For example, *Houses Sold* is too generic, but *Houses Sold in Seattle in 2016* indicates the what (Houses), the where (Seattle), and the when (2016). The default is *Chart Title*.
Data labels	Descriptive labels that show exact value or name of a data point. Data labels are not displayed by default.
Data table	A grid that contains the data source values and labels. If you embed a chart on the same worksheet as the data source, you might not need to include a data table. Only add a data table with a chart that is on a chart sheet.
Error bars	Visuals that indicate the standard error amount, a percentage, or a standard deviation for a data point or marker. Error bars are not displayed by default.
Gridlines	Horizontal or vertical lines that span across the chart to help people identify the values plotted by the visual elements, such as a column. Excel displays horizontal gridlines for column, line, scatter, stock, surface, and bubble charts and vertical gridlines for bar charts. Gridlines may display by default, depending on the chart type.
Legend	A key that identifies the color, gradient, picture, texture, or pattern assigned to each data series. The legend is displayed by default for particular charts.
Trendline	A line that depicts trends or helps forecast future data, such as estimating future sales or number of births in a region.You can add a trendline to column, bar, line, stock, scatter, and bubble charts. Excel will analyze the current trends to display a line indicating future values based on the current trend.

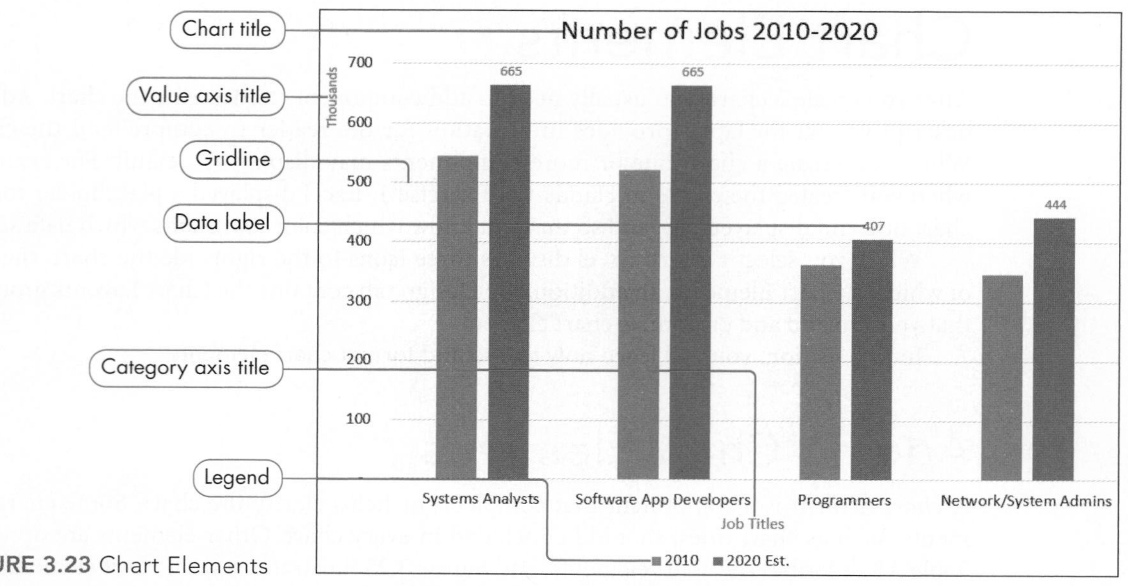

FIGURE 3.23 Chart Elements

To add a chart element, do the following:

1. Click the Chart Elements button to the right side of the chart (see Figure 3.24).
2. Click an empty check box to display an element, or position the mouse pointer on an element and click the triangle to select more specific chart elements. For example, if you click the triangle to the right of Axis Titles, you select on which axis to include a title.
3. If you selected a title, type the text for the title, and then press Enter.
4. Click the Chart Elements button again to close the menu.

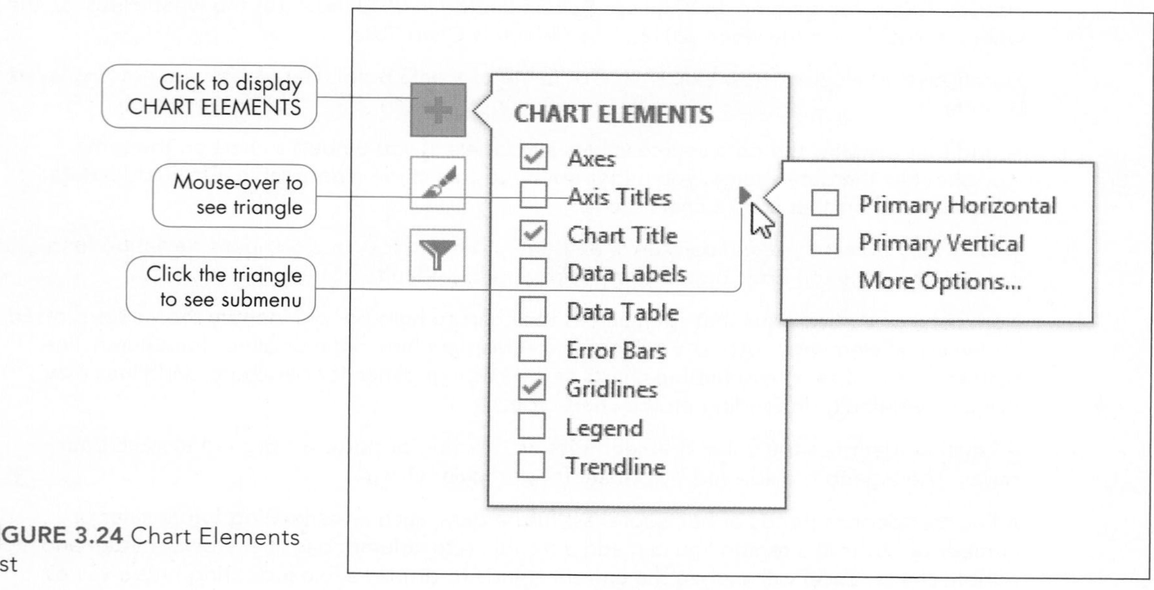

FIGURE 3.24 Chart Elements List

TIP Remove an Element

To remove an element, click Chart Elements and deselect a check box. Alternatively, click Add Chart Element in the Chart Layouts group on the Chart Tools Design tab, position the mouse pointer over the element name, and then select None.

To use the Design tab to add or remove a chart element, do the following:

1. Click the DESIGN tab.
2. Click Add Chart Element in the Chart Layouts group.
3. Point to an element and select from that element's submenu (see Figure 3.25).
4. If you selected a title, type the text for the title and press Enter.

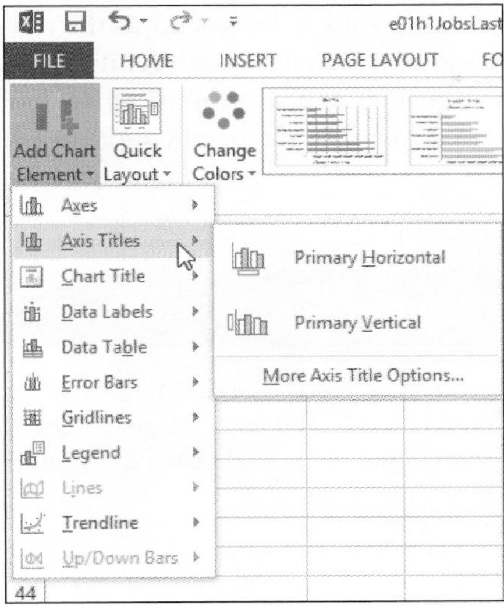

FIGURE 3.25 Chart Elements Menu and Submenu

Position the Chart Title

Excel includes the placeholder text *Chart Title* above the chart when you create a chart. You should replace that text with a descriptive title. To change the chart title text, click the Chart Title placeholder, type the text, and then press Enter. You can select the position of the title by doing the following:

1. Click the Chart Elements button to the right side of the chart.
2. Position the mouse pointer over Chart Title and click the triangle on the right side.
3. Select one of the options:
    - Above Chart: Centers the title above the plot area, decreasing the plot area size to make room for the chart title.
    - Centered Overlay: Centers the chart title horizontally without resizing the plot area; the title displays over the top of the plot area.
    - More Options: Opens the Format Chart Title task pane so that you can apply fill, border, and alignment settings.
4. Click the Chart Elements button to close the menu.

Include and Position Axis Titles

STEP 2» Excel does not include axis titles by default; however, you can display titles. When you click Chart Elements and click the triangle on the right side of Axis Titles, you can select Primary Horizontal and Primary Vertical. The horizontal axis title displays below the category labels, and the rotated vertical axis title displays on the left side of the value axis. After including these titles, you can click the respective title, type the text for the title, and then press Enter.

Include and Position Data Labels

STEP 3» Excel does not include data labels by default; however, you can display the exact values of the data points in the chart. When you click Chart Elements and click the triangle on the right side of Data Labels, you can select where the labels display.

By default, Excel adds data labels to all data series. If you want to display data labels for only one series, select the data labels for the other data series and press Delete. In Figure 3.23, data labels are included for the 2020 data series but not the 2010 data series.

Position the Legend

When you create a multiple series chart, the legend displays, providing a key to the color-coded data series. You can position the legend to the right, top, bottom, or left of the plot area. Choose the position based on how the legend's placement affects the chart. Make sure that the columns, bars, or lines appear proportionate and well balanced after you position the legend. You may need to adjust the height and/or width of the entire chart to achieve a balanced appearance.

TIP Quick Layout

Use Quick Layout to apply predefined layouts to a chart. Specifically, you can apply a layout to add several chart elements at one time. Click Quick Layout in the Chart Layouts group on the Design tab (see Figure 3.26) and select a layout. Each layout contains predefined chart elements and their positions.

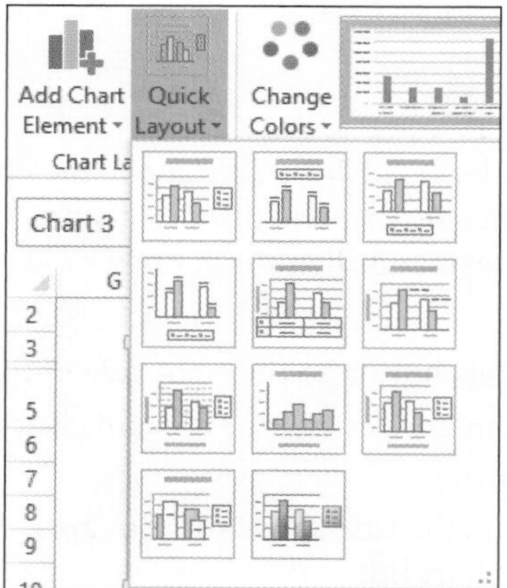

FIGURE 3.26 Quick Layout Gallery

Formatting Chart Elements

When you position the mouse pointer over the chart, Excel displays a ScreenTip with the name of that chart element. To select a chart element, click it when you see the ScreenTip, or click the Format tab, click the Chart Elements arrow in the Current Selection group, and then select the element from the list.

STEP 1»

After you select a chart element, you can format it. For example, you might want to apply 18-pt font size to the chart title. In addition, you might want to change the fill color of a data series to red. You can apply these formats from the Home tab:

- Font for titles, axes, and labels
- Font Size for titles, axes, and labels
- Font Color for titles, axes, and labels
- Fill Color for column, bar, and line data series or background fill color behind titles and labels

Format the Chart Area, Plot Area, and Data Series

STEP 4» You can apply multiple settings, such as fill colors and borders, at once using a Format task pane. To display a chart element's task pane, double-click the chart element. Figure 3.27 displays the Format Chart Area, Format Plot Area, and Format Data Series task panes. All three task panes include the same fill and border elements. After you select a fill option, such as *Gradient fill*, the remaining options change in the task pane.

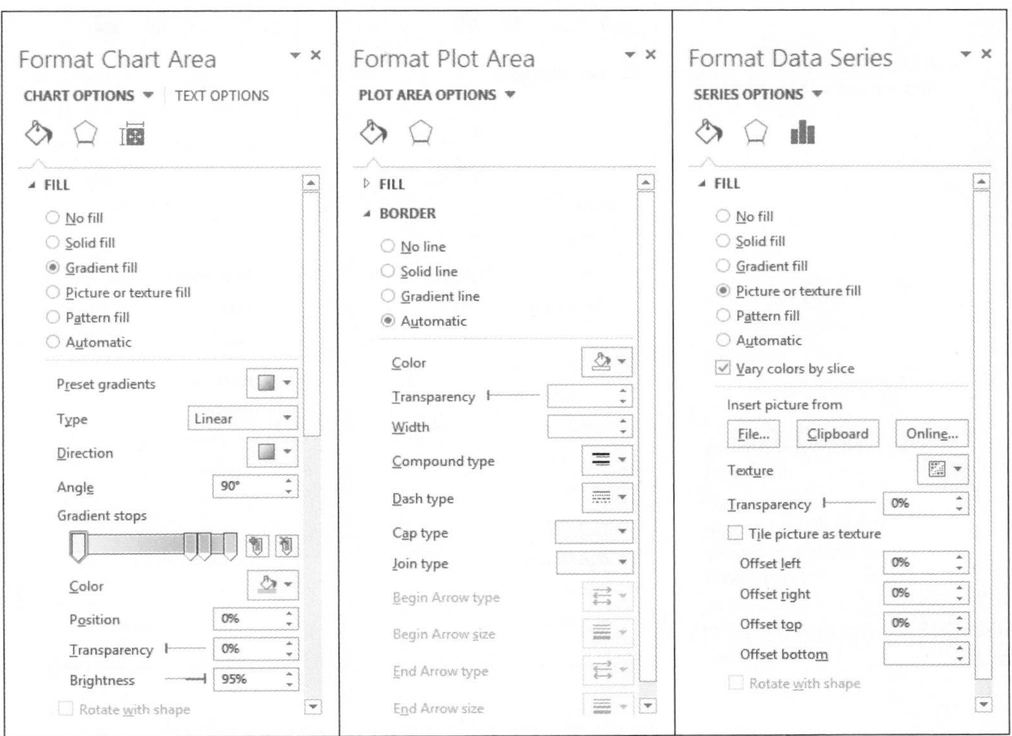

FIGURE 3.27 Format Task Panes

TIP Use Images or Textures

For less formal presentations, you might want to use images or a texture to fill the data series, chart area, or plot area instead of a solid fill color. To use an image or a texture, click the Fill & Line icon at the top of the task pane, click Fill, and then click *Picture or texture fill* in the Format Data Series task pane. Click File or Online in the *Insert picture from* section and insert an image file or search online to insert an image. The image is stretched by default, but you can select the Stack option to avoid distorting the image. To add a texture, click *Picture or texture fill*, click Texture, and then select a textured background from the gallery of textures. Generally, do not mix images and textures.

Format Axes

Based on the data source values and structure, Excel determines the starting, incremental, and stopping values that display on the value axis when you create the chart. You might want to adjust the value axis. For example, when working with large values such as 4,567,890, the value axis displays increments, such as 4,000,000 and 5,000,000. You can simplify the value axis by displaying values in millions, so that the values on the axis are 4 and 5 with the word *Millions* placed by the value axis to indicate the units. Figure 3.28 shows the Format Axis task pane. Diagonal black triangles, such as Axis Options, indicate all of a category's options are displayed (see the left task pane in Figure 3.28). Triangles with a white fill, such as Number, indicate the category options are not displayed (see the left task pane in Figure 3.28). You might need to scroll down and click a category name, such as Number, to see additional options. The task pane on the right side of Figure 3.28 shows the Number options after clicking the triangle.

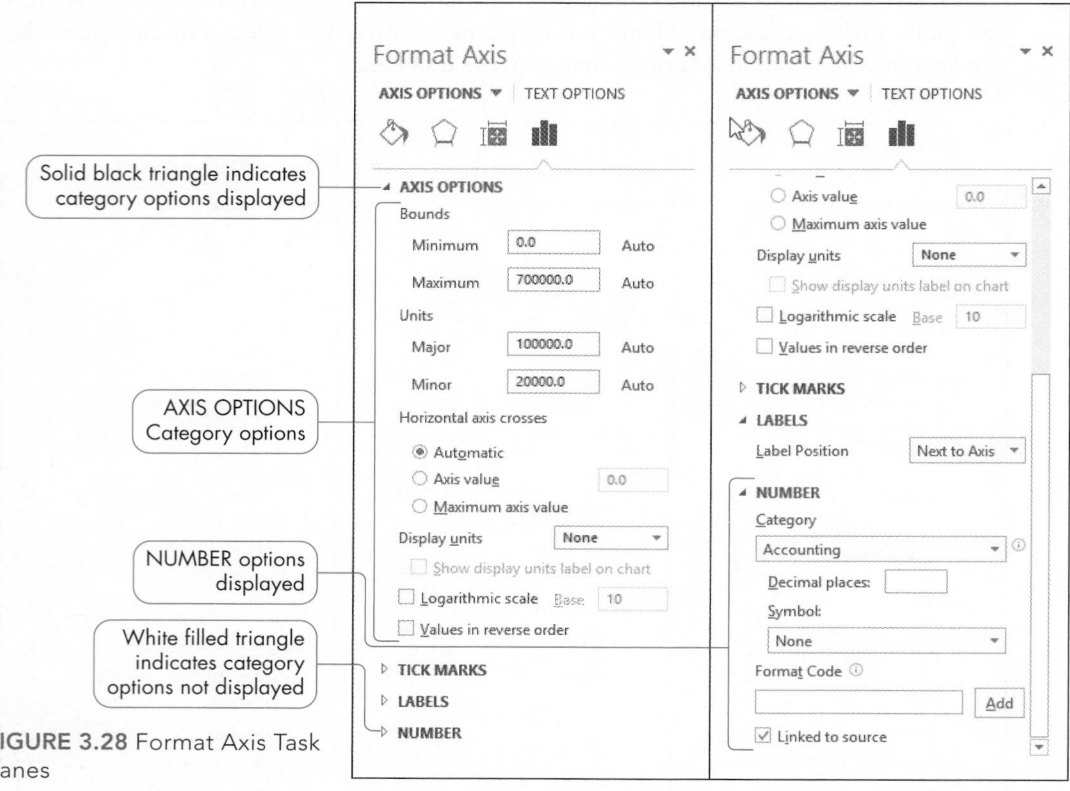

FIGURE 3.28 Format Axis Task Panes

Insert and Format Data Labels

When you select a data label, Excel selects all data labels in that data series. To format the labels, double-click a data label to open the Format Data Labels task pane (see Figure 3.29). The Format Data Labels task pane enables you to specify what to display as the label. The default setting for Label Contains options is Value, but you can display additional label contents, such as the Category Name. However, displaying too much label content can clutter the chart. You can also specify the Label Position, such as Center or Outside End. If the numeric data labels are not formatted, click Number and apply number formats.

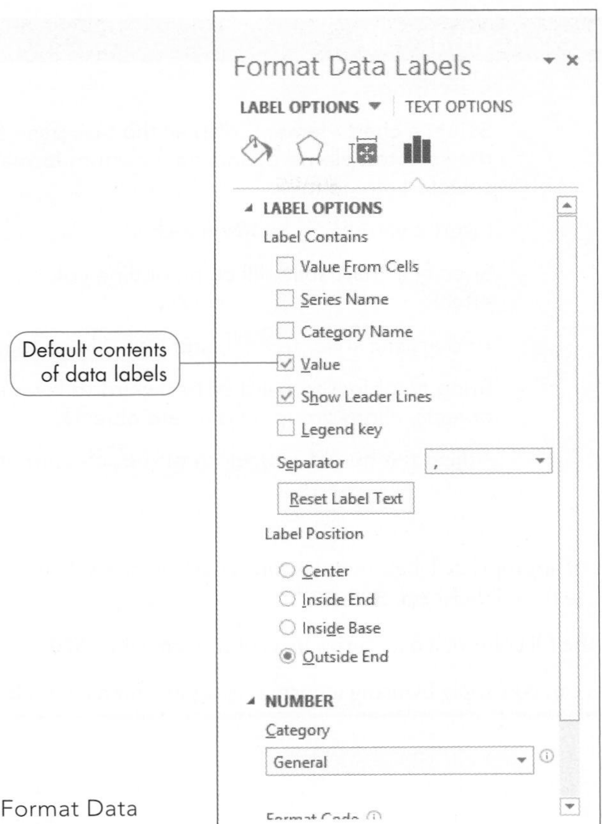

FIGURE 3.29 Format Data Labels Task Pane

TIP Pie Chart Data Labels

When you first create a pie chart, Excel generates a legend to identify the category labels for the different slice colors, but it does not display data labels. You can display Values, Percentages, and even Category Labels on or next to each slice. Pie charts often include percentage data labels. If you also include category labels, remove the legend to avoid duplicating elements.

Use the Chart Tools Format Tab

The Format tab contains options to select a chart element, insert shapes, apply shape styles, apply WordArt styles, arrange objects, and specify the size of an object. Table 3.4 lists and describes the groups on the Format tab.

TABLE 3.4 Chart Tools Format Tab

Group	Description
Current Selection	Select a chart element, display the task pane to format the selected element, and clear custom formatting of the selected element.
Insert Shapes	Insert a variety of shapes in a chart.
Shape Styles	Specify a chart style, fill color, outline color, and shape effect.
WordArt Styles	Add artistic style, text fill, and text effects to an object.
Arrange	Bring an object forward or backward to layer multiple objects; align, group, and rotate objects.
Size	Adjust the height and width of the selected object.

1. List at least four types of appropriate labels that describe chart elements. What types of things can you do to customize these labels? ***pp. 525–527***
2. How can you change the fill color of a data series in a column chart? ***p. 529***
3. What types of formats can you apply by using a Format task pane for a chart element? ***p. 529***

Hands-On Exercises

2 Chart Elements

You want to enhance the computer job column, bar, and pie charts by adding some chart elements. In particular, you need to enter a descriptive chart title for each chart, add and format axis titles for the bar chart, add and format data labels for the pie chart, and change fill colors in the pie chart.

Skills covered: Add and Format Chart Titles • Add and Format Axis Titles • Add and Format Data Labels • Apply Fill Colors

STEP 1 » ADD AND FORMAT CHART TITLES

When you created the column, bar, and pie charts in Hands-On Exercise 1, Excel displayed *Chart Title* at the top of each chart. You need to type chart titles that appropriately describe each chart. In addition, you want to format the chart titles by applying bold to them and enlarging their font sizes. Refer to Figure 3.30 as you complete Step 1.

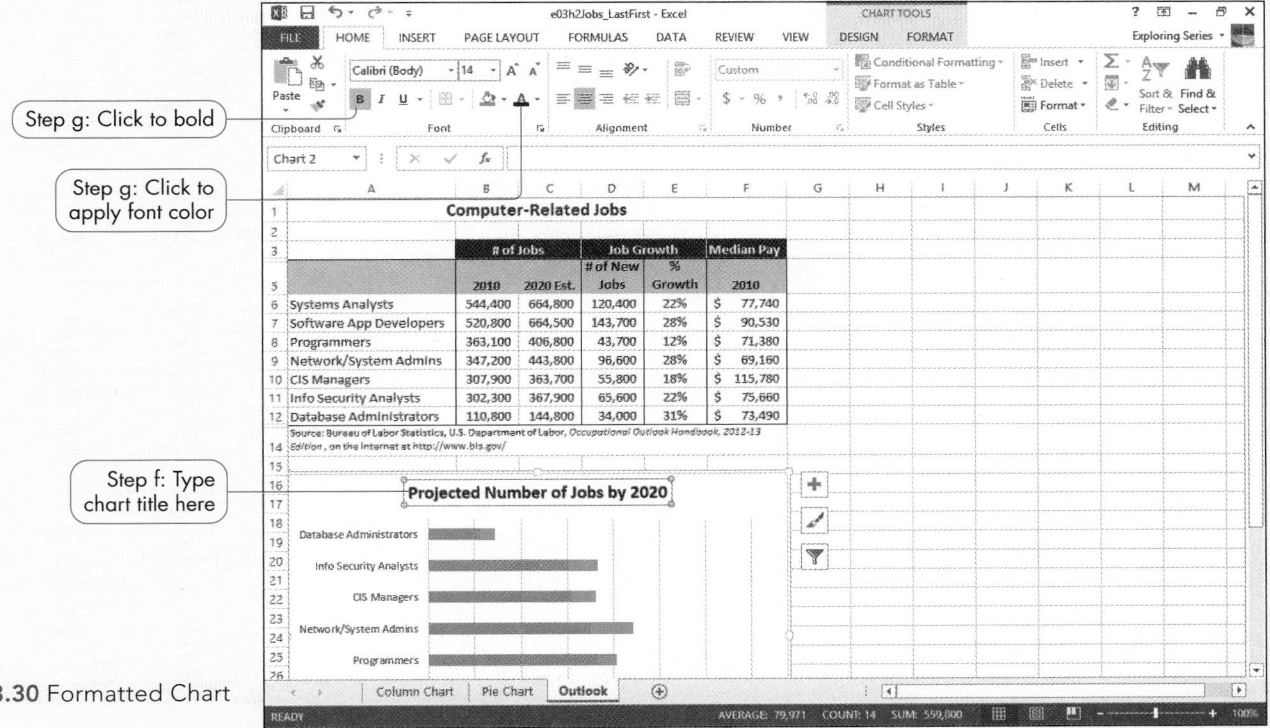

FIGURE 3.30 Formatted Chart Title

a. Open *e03h1Jobs_LastFirst* if you closed it at the end of Hands-On Exercise 1 and save it as **e03h2Jobs_LastFirst**, changing *h1* to *h2*.

b. Make sure the Pie Chart sheet is the active sheet, select the **Chart Title placeholder**, type **New Computer-Related Jobs by 2020** in the Formula Bar, and then press **Enter**.

Excel displays the text you typed in the chart title.

> **TROUBLESHOOTING:** If you double-click a title and type directly into the title placeholder, do *not* press Enter after typing the new title. Doing so will add a blank line. If you select the title placeholder only and type text, the text will appear in the Formula Bar.

c. Click the **HOME tab**, click **Bold**, click the **Font Size arrow**, and then select **18**.

You formatted the pie chart's title so that it stands out better.

d. Click the **Column Chart sheet tab**, select the **Chart Title placeholder**, type **Number of Computer-Related Jobs 2010 and 2020** in the Formula Bar, and then press **Enter**.

e. Click **Bold**, click the **Font Size arrow**, and then select **18**.

f. Click the **Outlook sheet tab**, select the **Chart Title placeholder**, type **Projected Number of Jobs by 2020**, and then press **Enter**.

g. Click **Bold**, click the **Font Size arrow**, and then select **14**. Click the **Font Color arrow** and click **Dark Blue** in the *Standard Colors* section. Save the workbook.

You formatted the bar chart title to be consistently formatted with the worksheet title.

STEP 2 » ADD AND FORMAT AXIS TITLES

For the bar chart, you want to add and format a title to describe the job titles on the vertical axis. In addition, you want to simplify the horizontal axis values to avoid *,000* for each increment and add the title *Thousands*. Refer to Figure 3.31 as you complete Step 2.

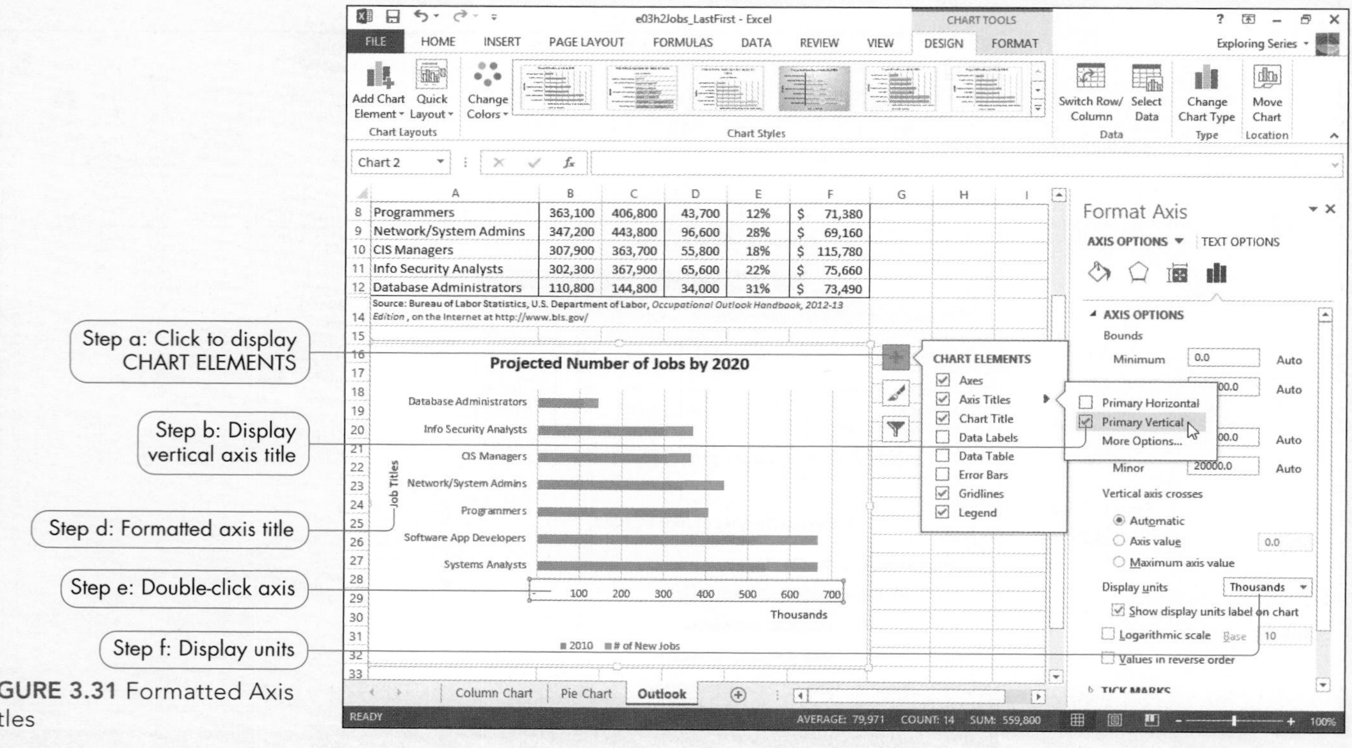

FIGURE 3.31 Formatted Axis Titles

a. Make sure the bar chart is selected in the Outlook worksheet and click the **Chart Elements button** to the right of the chart.

Excel displays the CHART ELEMENTS menu.

b. Position the mouse pointer over *Axis Titles*, click the **Axis Titles arrow**, and then click the **Primary Vertical check box**.

Excel displays *Axis Title* on the left side of the vertical axis.

c. Make sure the *Axis Title* placeholder is selected, type **Job Titles** in the Formula Bar, and then press **Enter**.

d. Click **Font Color** to apply the default Dark Blue font color to the selected axis title.

e. Double-click the values on the horizontal axis.

Excel displays the Format Axis task pane so that you can format the value axis.

f. Click **AXIS OPTIONS**, if necessary, click the **Display units arrow,** and then select **Thousands**.

The axis now displays values such as 700 instead of 700,000. The title *Thousands* displays in the bottom-right corner of the horizontal axis.

g. Click the **HOME tab**, make sure the title *Thousands* is selected, and then apply **Dark Blue font color** in the Font group. Close the task pane. Save the workbook.

STEP 3 » ADD AND FORMAT DATA LABELS

The pie chart includes a legend to identify which color represents which computer-related job; however, it does not include numerical labels to help you interpret what percentage of all computer-related jobs will be hired for each position. You want to insert and format percentage value labels. Refer to Figure 3.32 as you complete Step 3.

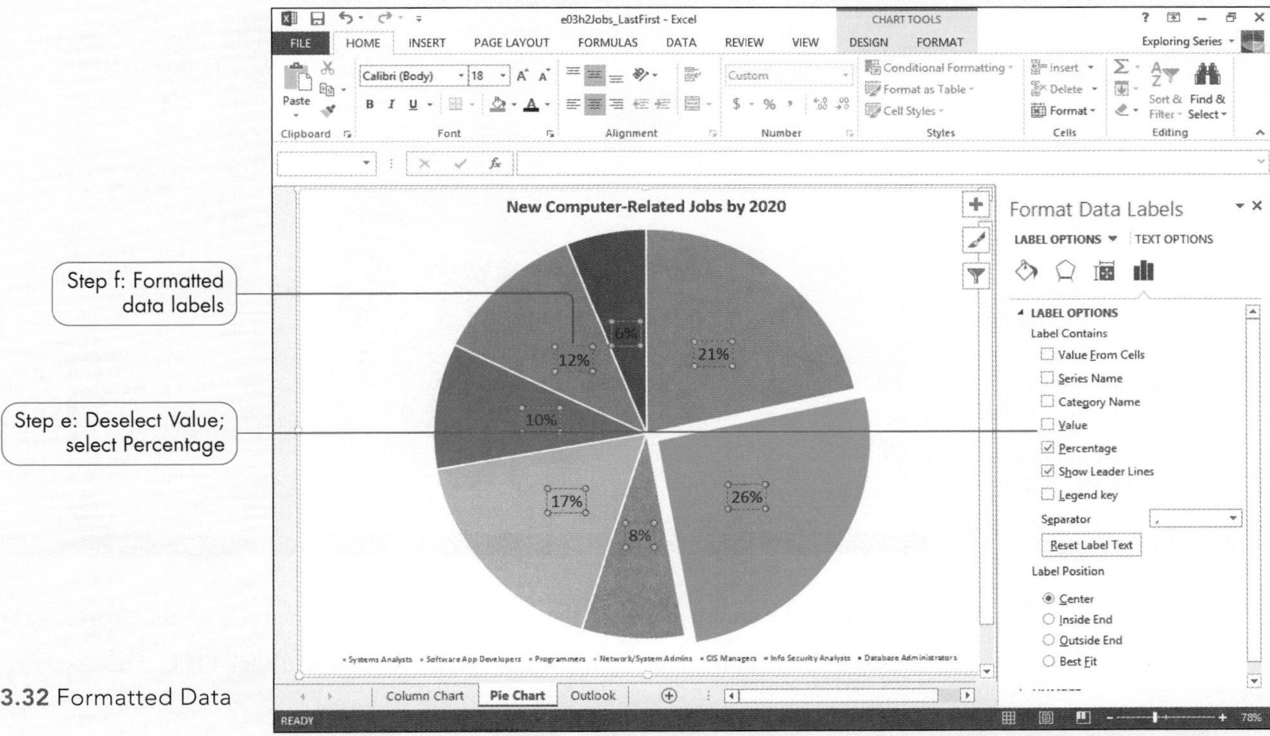

FIGURE 3.32 Formatted Data Labels

a. Click the **Pie Chart Sheet tab** and click the **Chart Elements button.**

b. Click the **Data Labels arrow** and select **Center.**

You added data labels to the pie slices.

TROUBLESHOOTING: If the Chart Elements menu remains open, click the Chart Elements button to close the menu.

c. Double-click one of the data labels to display the Format Data Labels task pane.

d. Click the **Label Options icon** in the Format Data Labels task pane, if necessary.

e. Click the **LABEL OPTIONS triangle**, if necessary, click the **Percentage check box** to select it, and then click the **Value check box** to deselect it.

   Typically, pie chart data labels show percentages instead of values.

f. Change the font size to **18** to make the data labels larger. Save the workbook.

STEP 4 ≫ APPLY FILL COLORS

You want to apply a texture fill to the chart area and change the fill colors for the Software Apps Developers' and the Database Administrators' slices. Refer to Figure 3.33 as you complete Step 4.

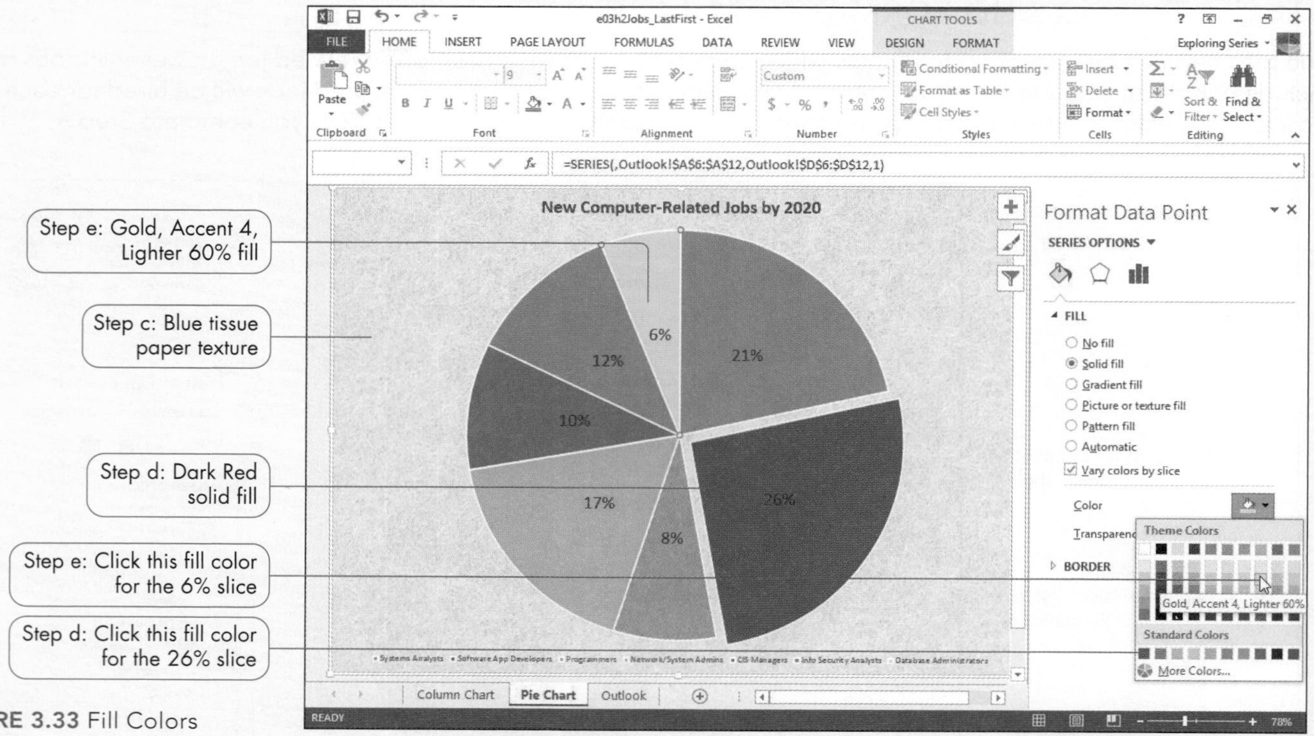

FIGURE 3.33 Fill Colors

a. Position the mouse pointer in the white space and click when you see the Chart Area ScreenTip.

b. Click **Fill & Line** in the Format Chart Area task pane and click **FILL**, if necessary.

   The task pane displays different fill options.

c. Click **Picture or texture fill**, click the **Texture arrow**, and then click **Blue tissue paper**.

   The chart area now has the blue tissue paper texture fill.

d. Click the pie chart, pause, and then click the **26% orange slice**. Click **Solid fill**, click the **Color arrow**, and then click **Dark Red** in the *Standard Colors* section.

   The Software Apps Developers slice is now dark red.

e. Click the **6% slice**, click **Solid fill**, click the **Color arrow**, and then click **Gold, Accent 4, Lighter 60%**.

   The new color for the Database Administrators slice makes it easier to read the percentage data label.

f. Save the workbook. Keep the workbook open if you plan to continue with the next Hands-On Exercise. If not, close the workbook and exit Excel.

Chart Design and Sparklines

After you add and format chart elements, you might want to experiment with other features to enhance a chart. The Chart Tools Design tab contains two other groups: Chart Styles and Data. These groups enable you to apply a different style or color scheme to a chart or manipulate the data that are used to build a chart. You can also click the Chart Styles and Chart Filters buttons to the right of a chart to change the design of a chart.

At times, you might want to insert small visual chart-like images within worksheet cells to illustrate smaller data series rather than a large chart to illustrate several data points. Excel enables you to create small chart-like images in close proximity to individual data points to help you visualize the data.

In this section, you will learn how to apply chart styles and colors, filter chart data, and insert and customize miniature charts (sparklines) within individual cells.

Applying a Chart Style and Colors

STEP 1» You can apply a different ***chart style***, a collection of formatting that controls the color of the chart area, plot area, and data series. Styles also affect the look of the data series, such as flat, 3-D, or beveled. Figure 3.34 shows the options when you click the Chart Styles button to the right side of the chart, and Figure 3.35 shows the Chart Styles gallery when you click Chart Styles on the Design tab.

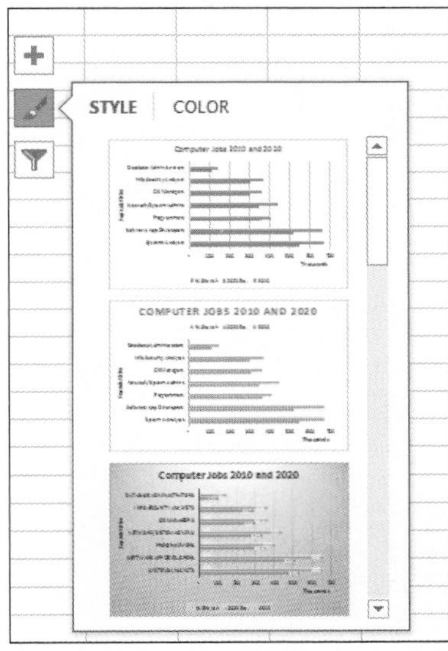

FIGURE 3.34 Chart Styles

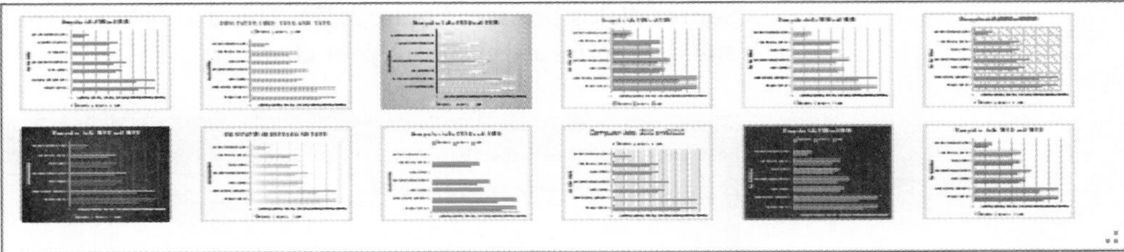

FIGURE 3.35 Chart Styles Gallery

TIP Choosing Appropriate Chart Styles

When choosing a chart style, make sure the style complements the chart data and is easy to read. Also, consider whether you will display the chart onscreen in a presentation or print the chart. If you will display the chart in a presentation, consider selecting a style with a black background.

You can change the color scheme by clicking the Chart Styles button on the right side of the chart and clicking Color or click Change Colors in the Chart Styles group on the Design tab. You can select from the Colorful and Monochromatic sections.

Modifying the Data Source

The data source is the range of worksheet cells that are used to construct a chart. Although you should select the data source carefully before creating a chart, you may decide to alter that data source after you create and format the chart. The Data group on the Design tab is useful for adjusting the data source.

Create Chart Filters

STEP 2»

A ***chart filter*** controls which data series and categories are visible in a chart. By default, all the data you selected to create the chart are used to construct the data series and categories. However, you can apply a chart filter to hide extraneous data. Click the Chart Filter button to the right side of the chart to display the options (see Figure 3.36). A check mark indicates the data series or category currently displayed in the chart. Click a check box to deselect or hide a data series or category.

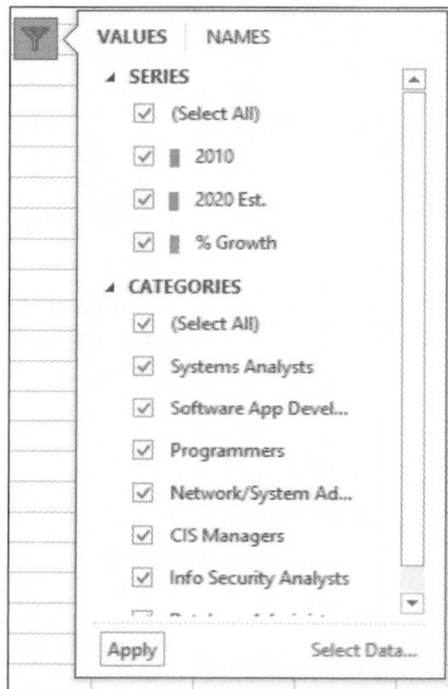

FIGURE 3.36 Chart Filter Options

You can click Select Data in the Data group on the Design tab to open the Select Data Source dialog box (see Figure 3.37). This dialog box is another way to filter which categories and data series are visible in your chart.

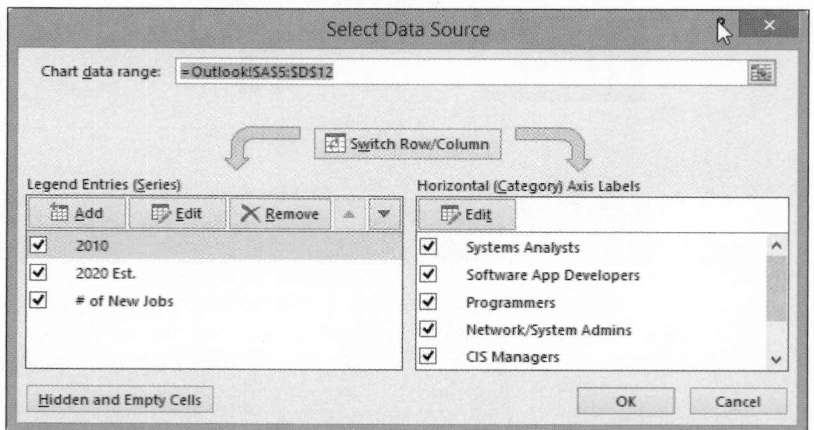

FIGURE 3.37 Select Data Source Dialog Box

Switch Row and Column Data

You can switch data used to create the horizontal axis and the legend. In Figure 3.38, the chart on the left uses the job titles to build the data series and legend, and the years display on the horizontal axis. The chart on the right shows the results after switching the data: the job titles build the horizontal axis, and the years build the data series and legend. To switch the data, click Switch Row/Column in the Data group on the Design tab.

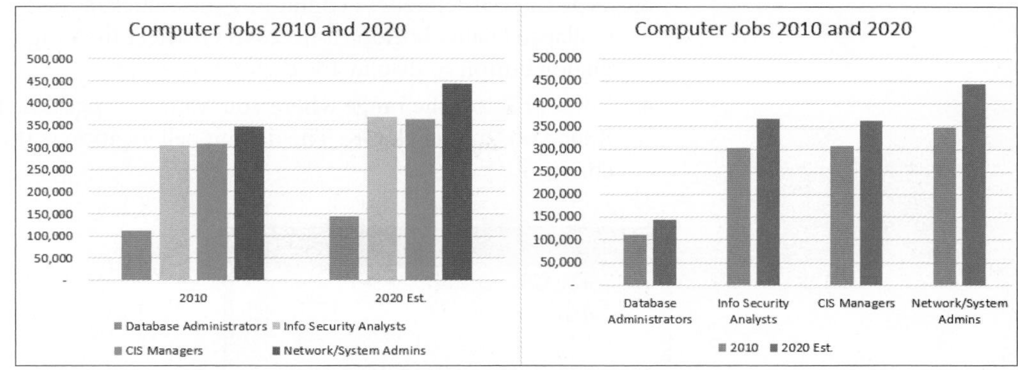

FIGURE 3.38 Original Chart and Chart with Reversed Rows/Columns

Creating and Customizing Sparklines

A ***sparkline*** is a small line, column, or win/loss chart contained in a single cell. The purpose of a sparkline is to present a condensed, simple, succinct visual illustration of data. Unlike a regular chart, a sparkline does not include a chart title or axis labels. Inserting sparklines next to data helps your audience understand data quickly without having to look at a full-scale chart.

Figure 3.39 shows three sample sparklines: line, column, and win/loss. The line sparkline shows trends over time, such as each student's trends in test scores. The column sparkline compares test averages. The win/loss sparkline depicts how many points a team won or lost each game.

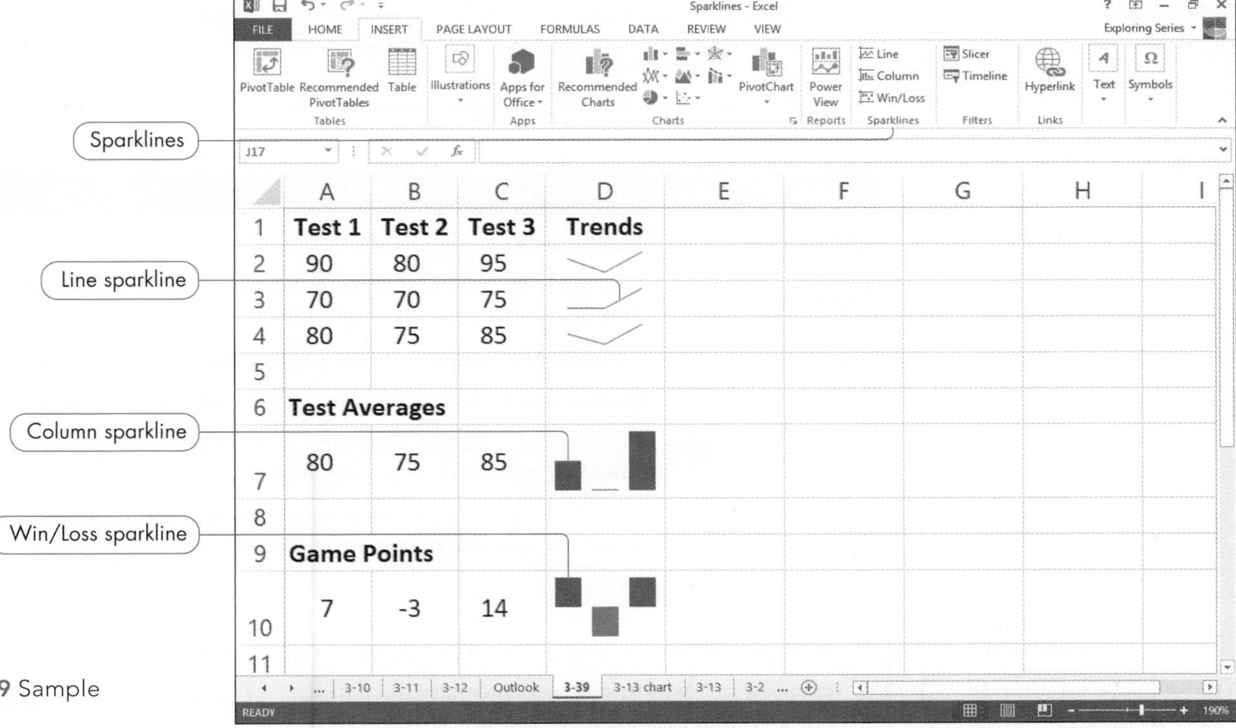

FIGURE 3.39 Sample Sparklines

Create a Sparkline

STEP 3» Before creating a sparkline, identify which data you want to depict and where you want to place them. To create a sparkline, do the following:

1. Click the INSERT tab.
2. Click Line, Column, or Win/Loss in the Sparklines group. The Create Sparklines dialog box opens (see Figure 3.40).
3. Type the cell references containing the values in the Data Range box, or click the Collapse Dialog button (if necessary), select the range, and then click the Collapse Dialog button to display the dialog box again.
4. Enter or select the range where you want the sparkline to display in the Location Range box and click OK. The default cell location is the active cell unless you change it.

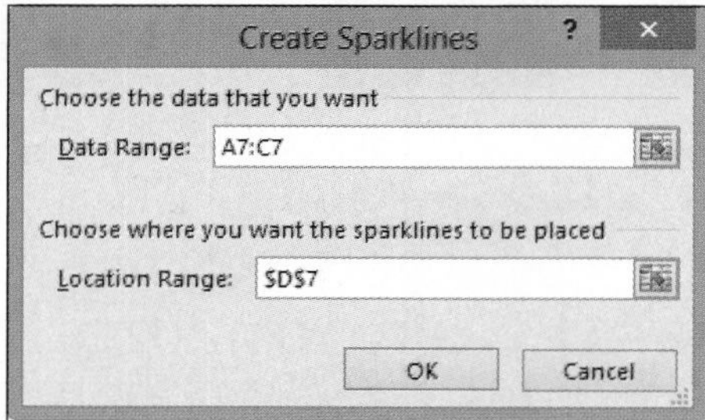

FIGURE 3.40 Create Sparklines Dialog Box

Customize a Sparkline

After you insert a sparkline, the Sparkline Tools Design tab displays (see Figure 3.41), with options to customize the sparkline.

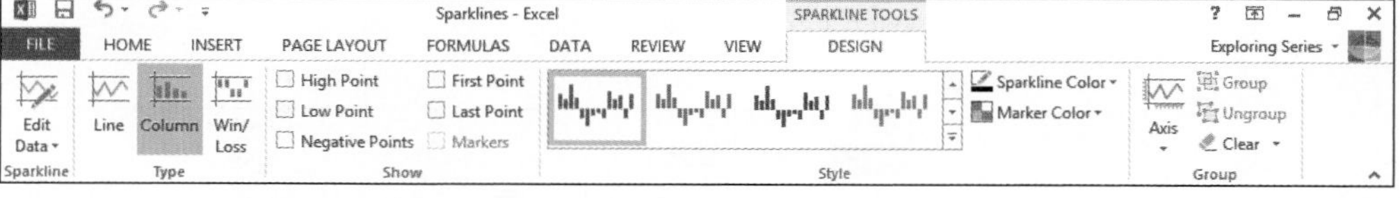

FIGURE 3.41 Sparkline Tools Design Tab

Table 3.5 lists and describes the groups on the Sparkline Tools Design tab.

TABLE 3.5 Sparkline Tools Design Tab

Group	Description
Sparkline	Edit the location and data source for a group or individual data point that generates a group of sparklines or an individual sparkline
Type	Change the selected sparkline type (line, column, win/loss)
Show	Display points, such as the high points, or markers within a sparkline
Style	Change the sparkline style, similar to a chart style, change the sparkline color, or change the marker color
Group	Specify the horizontal and vertical axis settings, group objects together, ungroup objects, and clear sparklines

Quick Concepts

1. What are two ways to change the color scheme of a chart? ***p. 537***
2. How can you change a chart so that the data in the legend are on the X-axis and the data on the X-axis are in the legend? ***p. 539***
3. What is a sparkline, and why would you insert one? ***pp. 539–540***

Hands-On Exercises

3 Chart Design and Sparklines

Now that you have completed the pie chart, you want to focus again on the bar chart. You are not satisfied with the overall design and want to try a different chart style. In addition, you would like to include sparklines to show trends for all jobs between 2010 and 2020.

Skills covered: Apply a Chart Style • Apply Chart Filters • Insert and Customize Sparklines

STEP 1 » APPLY A CHART STYLE

You want to give more contrast to the bar chart. Therefore, you will apply the Style 2 chart style. That style formats the chart area with a dark fill color and helps highlight the data series. Refer to Figure 3.42 as you complete Step 1.

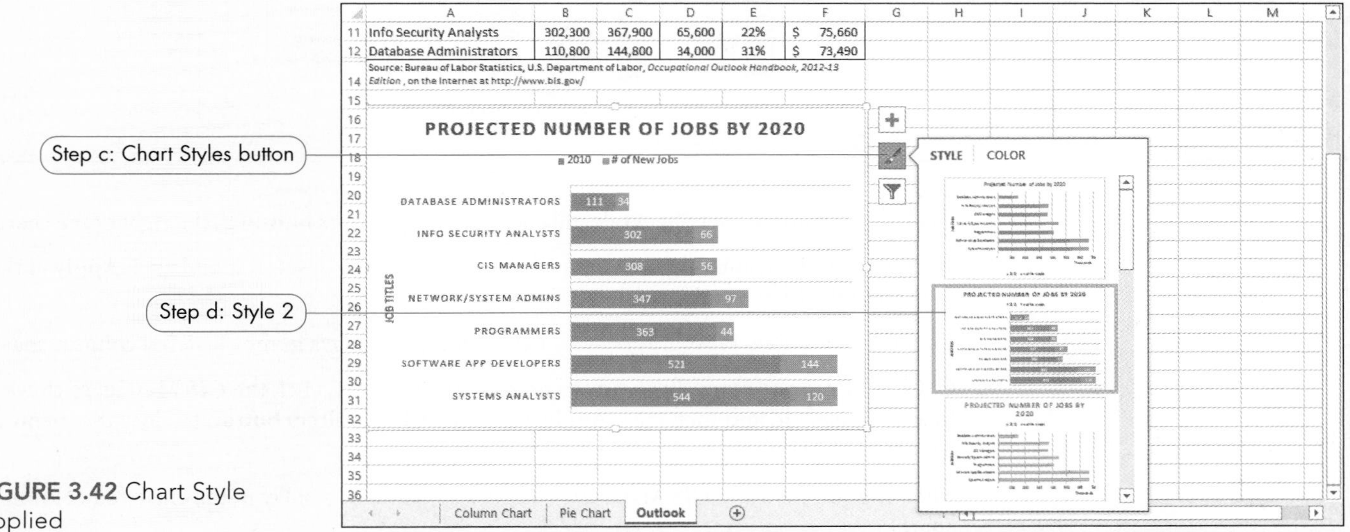

FIGURE 3.42 Chart Style Applied

a. Open *e03h2Jobs_LastFirst* if you closed it at the end of Hands-On Exercise 2 and save it as **e03h3Jobs_LastFirst**, changing *h2* to *h3*.

b. Click the **Outlook Sheet tab** and click the bar chart to select it.

c. Click the **Chart Styles button** to the right of the chart.

The gallery of chart styles opens.

d. Click **Style 2**. Click the **Chart Styles button** to close the gallery. Save the workbook.

Excel applies the Style 2 chart style to the chart, which displays value data labels in white font color within each stack of the bar chart. The chart title and the category labels display in all capital letters. The legend displays above the plot area.

STEP 2 » APPLY CHART FILTERS

When you first created the clustered column chart, you included the number of new jobs as well as the number of 2010 jobs and the projected number of 2020 jobs. However, you decide that the number of new jobs is implied by comparing the 2010 to the 2020 jobs. Therefore, you want to set a chart filter to exclude the number of new jobs. Refer to Figure 3.43 as you complete Step 2.

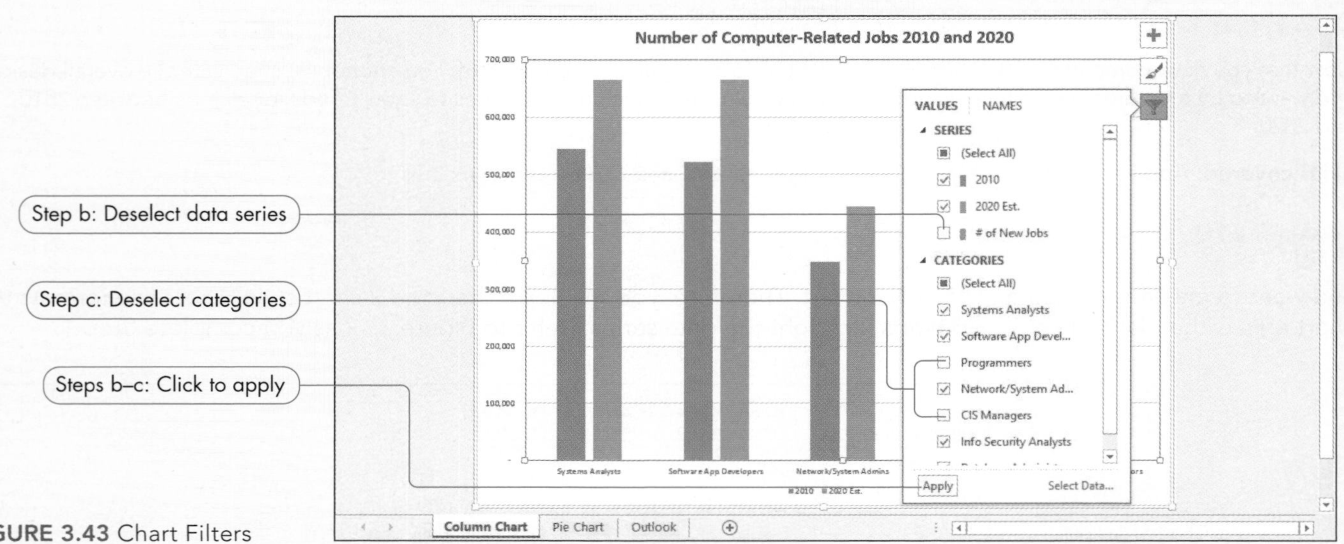

FIGURE 3.43 Chart Filters

a. Click the **Column Chart Sheet tab** and click the **Chart Filters button** to the right of the chart.

b. Click the **# of New Jobs check box** in the SERIES group to deselect it and click **Apply** at the bottom of the filter window.

The number of new jobs (gray) data series no longer displays in the clustered column chart.

c. Click the **Programmers check box** to deselect the category, click the **CIS Managers check box** to deselect it, and then click **Apply**. Click the **Chart Filters button** to close the menu. Save the workbook.

The Programmers and CIS Managers categories no longer display in the clustered column chart.

STEP 3 » INSERT AND CUSTOMIZE SPARKLINES

You want to insert sparklines to show the trends between 2010 and 2020. After inserting the sparklines, you want to display the high points to show that all jobs will have major increases by 2020. Refer to Figure 3.44 as you complete Step 3.

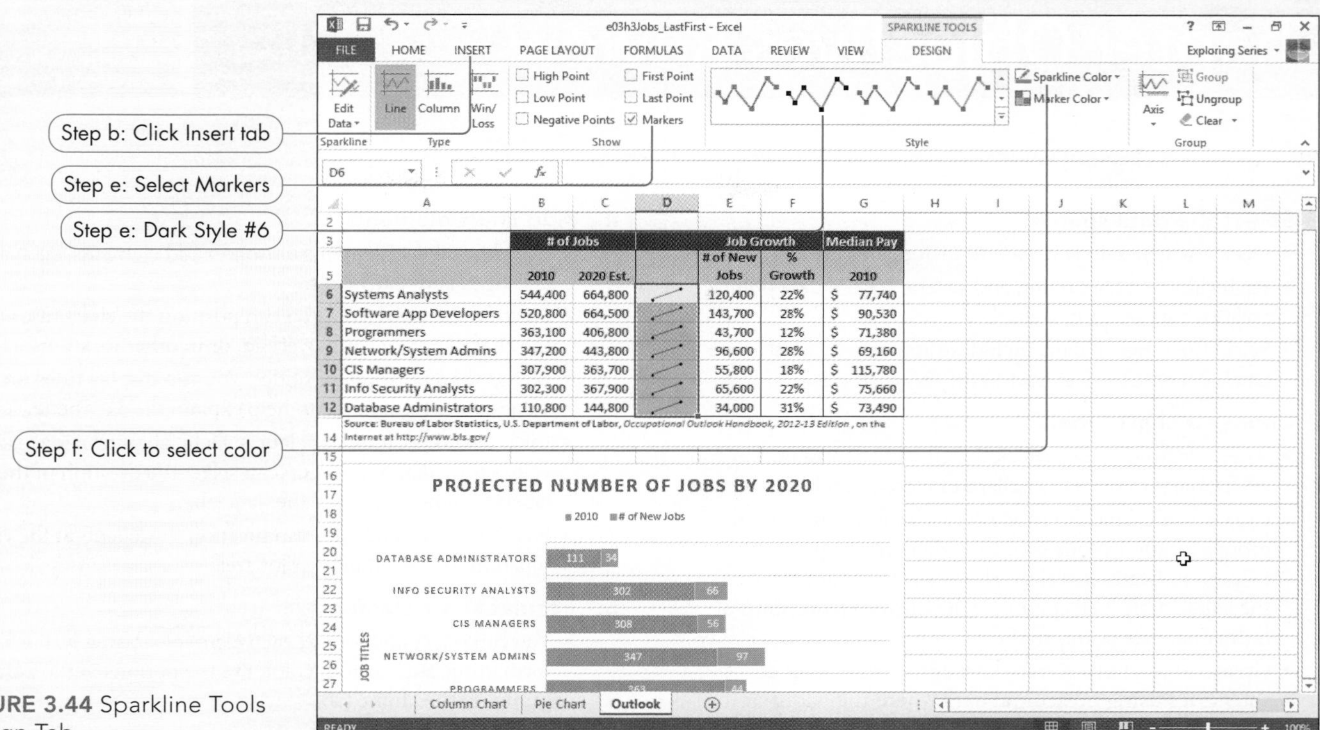

FIGURE 3.44 Sparkline Tools Design Tab

a. Click the **Outlook sheet tab**, select **cell D6**, click the **HOME tab**, click the **Insert arrow** in the Cells group, and then select **Insert Sheet Columns**.

   You inserted a new column to place the sparklines close to the data you want to visualize.

b. Click the **INSERT tab** and click **Line** in the Sparklines group.

c. Select the **range B6:C12** to enter that range in the Data Range box.

   You can select multiple rows at one time to create a group of sparklines.

d. Press **Tab** and select the **range D6:D12** to enter that range in the Location Range box. Click **OK**.

   Excel inserts sparklines in the range D6:D12 with each sparkline representing data on its respective row. The Sparkline Tools Design tab displays.

e. Click the **Markers check box** in the Show group to select it and click **Sparkline Style Dark #6** in the Style group.

f. Click **Sparkline Color** in the Style group and click **Red**.

g. Save and close the workbook, and submit based on your instructor's directions.

Chapter Objectives Review

After reading this chapter, you have accomplished the following objectives:

1. **Select the data source.**
   - Decide which data you want to include in a chart.
   - Each value is a data point, and several related data points create a data series in a chart.
   - Select the range of data, including appropriate labels. The labels become the legend and the category axis.
2. **Choose a chart type.**
   - After selecting a range, click the Quick Analysis button and click Charts to display a gallery of recommended chart types.
   - Create a column chart: A clustered column chart compares groups of side-by-side columns where the height of the column indicates its value. The taller the column, the larger the value. A stacked column chart shows relationships of individual data points to the whole.
   - Create a bar chart: A bar chart compares values across categories using horizontal bars where the width of the bar indicates its value. The wider the bar, the larger the value.
   - Create a line chart: A line chart compares trends over time. Values are displayed on the value axis, and time periods are displayed on the category axis.
   - Create a pie chart: A pie chart indicates proportions to the whole for one data series. The size of the slice indicates the size of the value. The larger the pie slice, the larger the value.
   - Select other chart types based on the intended purpose.
   - Change the chart type: After creating a chart, you can change it to a different type using the Change Chart Type command.
   - Create other chart types: An X Y (scatter) chart shows a relationship between two numerical variables. A stock chart shows fluctuations in prices of stock, such as between the opening and closing prices on a particular day.
3. **Move, size, and print a chart.**
   - Move a chart: The Move Chart dialog box enables you to select a new sheet and name the new chart sheet.
   - Size a chart: Adjust the chart size by dragging a sizing handle or specifying exact measurements in the Size group on the Format tab.
   - Print a chart: To print a chart with its data series, the chart needs to be on the same worksheet as the data source. To ensure both the data and the chart print, make sure the chart is not selected. If the chart is on its own sheet or if you select the chart on a worksheet containing other data, the chart will print as a full-sized chart.
4. **Add chart elements.**
   - Click the Chart Elements button to add elements, such as axis titles and data labels.
   - Position the chart title: You can position the chart title above the chart, centered and overlaid, or in other locations.
   - Include and position axis titles: You can display titles for the value and category axes to help explain the axes better.
   - Include and position data labels: Data labels provide exact values for a data series. You can select the position of the data labels and the content of the data labels.
   - Position the legend: You can position the legend to the right, top, bottom, or left of the plot area.
5. **Format chart elements.**
   - You can select and format each element separately. For basic formatting, such as font color, use the options in the Font group on the Home tab.
   - Format the chart area, plot area, and data series: The Format task panes enable you to apply fill colors, select border colors, and apply other settings.
   - Format axes: You can specify number formats for the value axis. You can specify measurement units, such as Millions, to simplify the value axis increments.
   - Insert and format data labels: You can specify what is displayed in data labels and how to format the labels.
   - Use the Chart Tools Format tab: This tab enables you to select a chart element and insert and format shapes.
6. **Apply a chart style and colors.**
   - You can apply a chart style, which determines formatting, such as the background color and the data series color.
7. **Modify the data source.**
   - You can add or remove data from the data source to change the data in the chart.
   - Create chart filters: The Select Data Source dialog box enables you to modify the ranges used for the data series.
   - Switch row and column data: Excel usually places the first column of data as the category axis and the first row of data as the legend, but you can switch these.
8. **Create and customize sparklines.**
   - Create a sparkline: A sparkline is a miniature chart in a cell representing a single data series.
   - Customize a sparkline: You can customize sparklines by changing the data source, location, and style. You can display markers and change line or marker colors.

Key Terms Matching

Match the key terms with their definitions. Write the key term letter by the appropriate numbered definition.

- **a.** Axis title
- **b.** Bar chart
- **c.** Category axis
- **d.** Chart area
- **e.** Chart title
- **f.** Clustered column chart
- **g.** Data label
- **h.** Data point
- **i.** Data series
- **j.** Gridline
- **k.** Legend
- **l.** Line chart
- **m.** Pie chart
- **n.** Plot area
- **o.** Sizing handle
- **p.** Sparkline
- **q.** Stock chart
- **r.** Task pane
- **s.** Value axis
- **t.** X Y (scatter) chart

1. ______ Chart type to compare multiple categories of data vertically. **p. 510**
2. ______ Miniature chart contained in a single cell. **p. 539**
3. ______ Chart type that shows trends over time in which the value axis indicates quantities and the horizontal axis indicates time. **p. 508**
4. ______ Label that describes the chart. **p. 525**
5. ______ Label that describes either the category axis or the value axis. **p. 525**
6. ______ Key that identifies the color, gradient, picture, texture, or pattern fill assigned to each data series in a chart. **p. 506**
7. ______ Chart type that compares categories of data horizontally. **p. 508**
8. ______ Chart that shows each data point in proportion to the whole data series. **p. 508**
9. ______ Numeric value that decribes a single value on a chart. **p. 506**
10. ______ Chart that shows the high, low, and close prices for individual stocks over time. **p. 515**
11. ______ Indicators that enable you to adjust the height and width of a selected chart. **p. 518**
12. ______ Horizontal or vertical line that extends from the horizontal or vertical axis through the plot area. **p. 525**
13. ______ Chart type that shows the relationship between two variables. **p. 515**
14. ______ Group of related data points that display in row(s) or column(s) in a worksheet. **p. 506**
15. ______ Window of options to format and customize chart elements. **p. 529**
16. ______ Provides descriptive group names for subdividing a data series. **p. 506**
17. ______ Section of a chart that contains graphical representation of the values in a data series. **p. 506**
18. ______ Boundary that contains the entire chart and all of its elements, including the plot area, titles, legends, and labels. **p. 506**
19. ______ Descriptive label that shows the exact value of the data points on the value axis. **p. 525**
20. ______ Displays incremental numbers to identify approximate values, such as dollars or units, of data points in a chart. **p. 506**

Multiple Choice

1. Which type of chart is the *least* appropriate for depicting yearly rainfall totals for five cities for four years?
   (a) Pie chart
   (b) Line chart
   (c) Column chart
   (d) Bar chart

2. What is the typical sequence for creating a chart?
   (a) Select the chart type, select the data source, and then size and position the chart.
   (b) Select the data source, size the chart, select the chart type, and then position the chart.
   (c) Select the data source, select the chart type, and then size and position the chart.
   (d) Click the cell to contain the chart, select the chart type, and then select the data source.

3. Which of the following applies to a sparkline?
   (a) Chart title
   (b) Single-cell chart
   (c) Legend
   (d) Multiple data series

4. If you want to show exact values for a data series in a bar chart, which chart element should you display?
   (a) Chart title
   (b) Legend
   (c) Value axis title
   (d) Data labels

5. The value axis currently shows increments such as 50,000 and 100,000. What do you select to display increments of 50 and 100?
   (a) More Primary Vertical Axis Title Options
   (b) Show Axis in Thousands
   (c) Show Axis in Millions
   (d) Show Right to Left Axis

6. You want to create a single chart that shows each of five divisions' proportion of yearly sales for each year for five years. Which type of chart can accommodate your needs?
   (a) Pie chart
   (b) Surface chart
   (c) Clustered bar chart
   (d) 100% stacked column chart

7. Currently, a column chart shows values on the value axis, years on the category axis, and state names in the legend. What should you do if you want to organize data with the states on the category axis and the years shown in the legend?
   (a) Change the chart type to a clustered column chart.
   (b) Click Switch Row/Column in the Data group on the Design tab.
   (c) Click Layout 2 in the Chart Layouts group on the Design tab and apply a different chart style.
   (d) Click Legend in the Labels group on the Layout tab and select Show Legend at Bottom.

8. Which tab contains commands to apply a predefined chart layout that controls which elements are included, where, and their color scheme?
   (a) Design
   (b) Layout
   (c) Format
   (d) Page Layout

9. Which icon does *not* display to the right of a selected chart?
   (a) Chart Elements
   (b) Chart Styles
   (c) Chart Filters
   (d) Chart Quick Analysis

10. What indicates that the closing price was higher than the opening price in a stock chart?
   (a) A double vertical line between the price markers
   (b) A positive data label above the data series for a particular day
   (c) A rectangle with a white fill color
   (d) A rectangle with a black fill color

Practice Exercises

1 Hulett Family Utility Expenses

Your cousin, Alex Hulett, wants to analyze his family's utility expenses for 2016. He gave you his files for the electric, gas, and water bills for the year. You created a worksheet that lists the individual expenses per month, along with yearly totals per utility type and monthly totals. You will create some charts to depict the data. This exercise follows the same set of skills as used in Hands-On Exercises 1–3 in the chapter. Refer to Figure 3.45 as you complete this exercise.

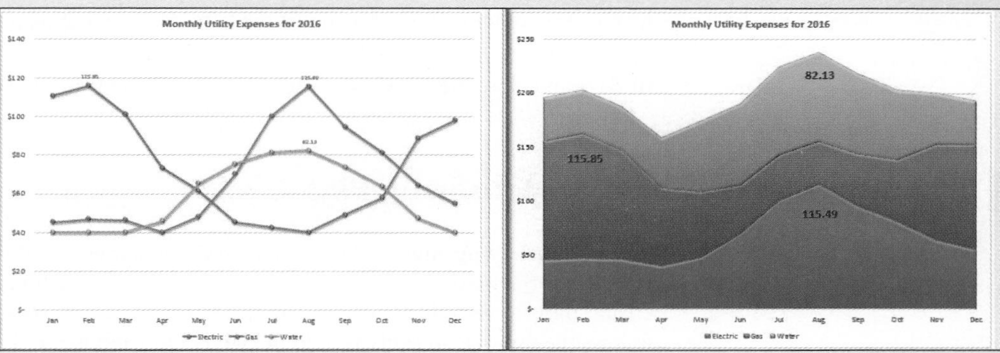

FIGURE 3.45 Hulett Family Utility Expenses

a. Open *e03p1Utilities* and save it as **e03p1Utilities_LastFirst**.

b. Select the **range A4:E17**, click the **Quick Analysis button**, and then click **CHARTS**.

c. Click **Clustered Column**, click the **Chart Filters button** to the right of the chart, and then do the following:
   - Deselect the **Monthly Totals check box** in the SERIES group.
   - Scroll through the CATEGORIES group and deselect the **Yearly Totals check box**.
   - Click **Apply** to remove totals from the chart. Click **Chart Filters** to close the menu.

d. Position the mouse pointer over the chart area. When you see the Chart Area ScreenTip, drag the chart so that the top-left edge of the chart is in **cell A19**.

e. Click the **FORMAT tab** and change the size by doing the following:
   - Click in the **Shape Width box** in the Size group, type **6"**, and then press **Enter**.
   - Click in the **Shape Height box** in the Size group, type **3.5"**, and then press **Enter**.

f. Click the **DESIGN tab**, click **Quick Layout** in the Chart Layouts group, and then click **Layout 3**.

g. Select the **Chart Title placeholder** and type **Monthly Utility Expenses for 2016**.

h. Click the **More button** in the Chart Styles group and click **Style 8**.

i. Select the chart, if necessary, click **Copy** on the HOME tab, click **cell A37**, and then click **Paste**. With the second chart selected, do the following:
   - Click the **DESIGN tab**, click **Change Chart Type** in the Type group, click **Line** on the left side of the dialog box, select **Line with Markers** in the top-center section, and then click **OK**.
   - Click the **Electric data series line** to select it and click the highest marker to select only that marker. Click the **Chart Elements button** and click **Data Labels**.
   - Repeat and adapt the previous bulleted step to add a data label to the highest Gas and Water markers. Click the **Chart Elements button** to close the menu.
   - Select the chart, copy it, and then paste it in **cell A55**.

j. Make sure the third chart is selected and do the following:
   - Click the **DESIGN tab**, click **Change Chart Type** in the Type group, select **Area** on the left side, click **Stacked Area**, and then click **OK**.
   - Click **Move Chart** in the Location group, click **New sheet**, type **Area Chart**, and then click **OK**.
   - Select each data label, click **Bold**, and select **18-pt font size**. Move the data label up closer to the top of the respective shaded area.
   - Select the value axis, select **12-pt font size**, and then select **Black, Text 1 font color**.

- Right-click the value axis and select **Format Axis**. Scroll down in the Format Axis task pane, click **NUMBER**, and then type **0** in the **Decimal places box**. Close the task pane.
- Apply **12-pt font size** and **Black, Text 1 font color** to the category axis and to the legend.

k. Click the **Expenses sheet tab**, select the line chart, and then do the following:

- Click the **DESIGN tab**, click **Move Chart** in the Location group, click **New sheet**, type **Line Chart**, and then click **OK**.
- Apply **12-pt font size** to the value axis, category axis, and legend.
- Format the vertical axis with zero decimal places.

l. Create a footer with your name on the left side, the sheet name code in the center, and the file name code on the right side of each sheet.

m. Save and close the workbook, and submit based on your instructor's directions.

2 Trends in Market Value of Houses on Pine Circle

You are considering buying a house on Pine Circle, a quiet cul-de-sac in a suburban area. Recently, you researched the market value and square footage of the five houses on Pine Circle. Now, you want to create charts to visually depict the data to determine which house you might want to buy. This exercise follows the same set of skills as used in Hands-On Exercises 1–3 in the chapter. Refer to Figure 3.46 as you complete this exercise.

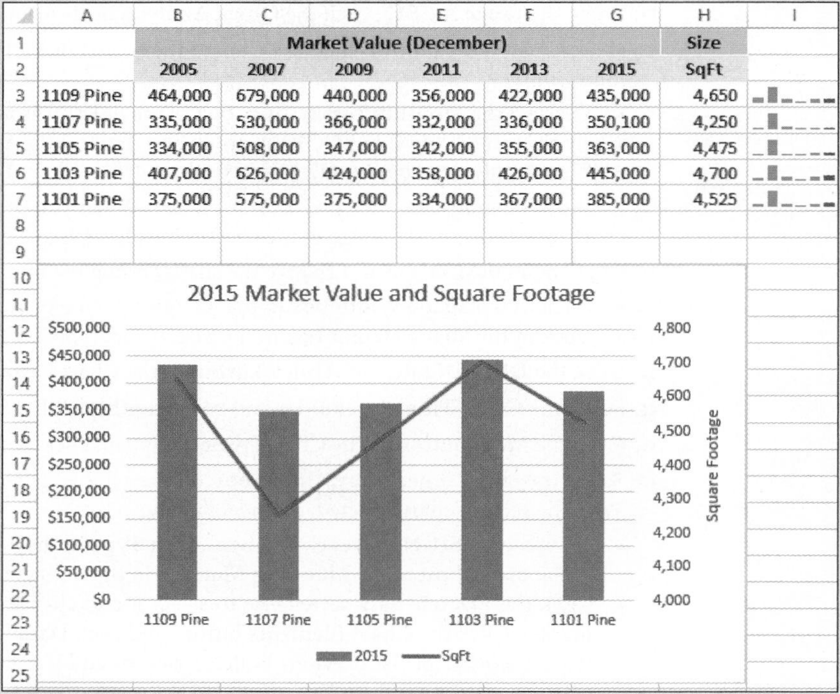

	A	B	C	D	E	F	G	H	I
1		Market Value (December)						Size	
2		2005	2007	2009	2011	2013	2015	SqFt	
3	1109 Pine	464,000	679,000	440,000	356,000	422,000	435,000	4,650	
4	1107 Pine	335,000	530,000	366,000	332,000	336,000	350,100	4,250	
5	1105 Pine	334,000	508,000	347,000	342,000	355,000	363,000	4,475	
6	1103 Pine	407,000	626,000	424,000	358,000	426,000	445,000	4,700	
7	1101 Pine	375,000	575,000	375,000	334,000	367,000	385,000	4,525	

FIGURE 3.46 Market Values

a. Open *e03p2Pine* and save it as **e03p2Pine_LastFirst**.

b. Select the **range A2:G7**, click the **Quick Analysis button**, click **CHARTS**, and then click **Line**.

c. Click **Move Chart** in the Location group, click **New sheet**, type **Line**, and then click **OK**.

d. Select the **Chart Title placeholder** and do the following:

- Type **Market Value of Pine Circle Houses** and press **Enter**.
- Bold the title, apply **20-pt size**, and select **Olive Green, Accent 3, Darker 50% font color**.

e. Click the value axis on the left side of the chart and do the following:
   - Apply **12-pt font size** and **Olive Green, Accent 3, Darker 50% font color**.
   - Double-click the value axis to display the Format Axis task pane. If necessary, click the **Axis Options icon** and click **AXIS OPTIONS** to display options.
   - Type **300000** in the **Minimum Bounds box** and press **Enter**. The Maximum Bounds box should change to 700000 automatically.
   - Scroll down in the Format Axis task pane and click **NUMBER** to display those options.
   - Click the **Category arrow** and select **Currency**.
   - Close the Format Axis task pane.

f. Click the **Chart Elements button**, click the **Axis Titles triangle**, and then click the **Primary Vertical check box**. Type **December Market Values** in the **Axis Title placeholder** and press **Enter**.

g. Make sure the Chart Elements menu is showing, click the **Gridlines triangle**, and then click the **Primary Minor Horizontal check box**. Click **Chart Elements** to close the menu.

h. Select the category axis, apply **12-pt font size**, and apply **Olive Green, Accent 3, Darker 50% font color**.

i. Right-click the legend and select **Format Legend**. Click **Top** in the *Legend Position* section of the Format Legend task pane and close the task pane.

j. Click the **Pine Circle Sheet tab** and select the **ranges A2:A7**, **G2:G7**, and **H2:H7**.

k. Click the **INSERT tab**, click **Insert Combo Chart** in the Charts group, and then click the **Clustered Column – Line on Secondary Axis thumbnail**.

l. Do the following to the chart:
   - Drag the chart to fill the **range A10:H25**.
   - Select the **Chart Title Placeholder** and type **2015 Market Value and Square Footage**.
   - Double-click the value axis on the left side, scroll down in the Format Axis task pane, click **NUMBER**, click the **Category arrow**, and then select **Currency**.
   - Click the **Chart Elements button**, click the **Axis Titles triangle**, click the **Secondary Vertical check box**, type **Square Footage**, and then press **Enter**. Close the Format Axis Title task pane.

m. Select the **range B3:G7**, click the **INSERT tab**, click **Column** in the Sparklines group, make sure B3:G7 displays in the Data Range box, type **I3:I7** in the **Location Range box**, and then click **OK**.

n. Customize the sparklines by doing the following:
   - Click **More** in the Style group and select **Sparkline Style Accent 6, Darker 25%**.
   - Click **Last Point** in the Show group.

o. Create a footer with your name on the left side, the sheet name code in the center, and the file name code on the right side of both sheets.

p. Save and close the workbook, and submit based on your instructor's directions.

Mid-Level Exercises

1 Airport Passenger Counts

ANALYSIS CASE 

As an analyst for the airline industry, you track the number of passengers at major U.S. airports. One worksheet you created lists the number of total yearly passengers at the top five airports for four years. To prepare for an upcoming meeting, you need to create a chart to compare the number of passengers for each airport. In addition, you want to insert sparklines to visually represent trends in passengers at each airport.

a. Open *e03m1Airports* and save it as **e03m1Airports_LastFirst**.

b. Create a clustered column chart for the **range A4:E9**. Position the chart to fit in the **range A15:F34**.

c. Customize the chart style by doing the following:
   - Apply **Style 8 chart style**.
   - Select **Color 6** in the *Monochromatic* section of the Change Colors gallery.
   - Change the fill color of the 2011 data series to **White, Background 1**.

d. Enter **Passengers by Top U.S. Airports** as the chart title.

e. Adjust the value axis by doing the following:
   - Change the display units to **Millions** for the value axis.
   - Edit the axis title to display **MILLIONS OF PASSENGERS**.

f. Display data labels above the columns for the 2011 data series only.

g. Insert Line sparklines in the **range F5:F9** to illustrate the data in the **range B5:E9**. This should insert a sparkline to represent yearly data for each airport.

h. Customize the sparklines by doing the following:
   - Show the high and low points in each sparkline.
   - Apply **Black, Text 1 color** to the high point marker in each sparkline.
   - Apply **Dark Red color** to the low point marker in each sparkline.

i. Merge cells in the **range A36:F41**, wrap text, and then apply **Top Align** and **Align Left** alignments.

j. Compose a paragraph that analyzes the trends depicted by the airport sparklines. Notice the overall trends in decreased and increased number of passengers and any unusal activity for an airport. Spell check the worksheet and correct any errors.

k. Insert a footer with your name on the left side, the sheet name code in the center, and the file name code on the right side on all worksheets.

l. Save and close the workbook, and submit based on your instructor's directions.

2 Grade Analysis

You are a teaching assistant for Dr. Monica Unice's introductory psychology class. You have maintained her grade book all semester, entering three test scores for each student and calculating the final average. Dr. Unice wants to see a chart that shows the percentage of students who earn each letter grade. You decide to create a pie chart. She wants to see if a correlation exists between attendance and students' final grades, so you will create a scatter chart.

a. Open *e03m2Psych* and save it as **e03m2Psych_LastFirst**.

b. Create a pie chart from the Final Grade Distribution data located below the student data and move the pie chart to its own sheet named **Grades Pie**.

c. Customize the pie chart with these specifications:
   - Style 7 chart style
   - Chart title: **PSY 2030 Final Grade Distribution - Fall 2016**
   - B grade slice exploded
   - Legend: none

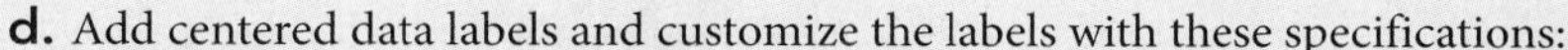

d. Add centered data labels and customize the labels with these specifications:
   - Label captions: **Percentage** and **Category Name**; no values
   - 28-pt size; Black, Text 1 font color, and bold

DISCOVER

e. Create a Scatter with only Markers chart using the attendance record and final averages from the Grades worksheet. Move the scatter chart to its own sheet named **Scatter Chart**.

f. Apply these label settings to the scatter chart:
   - Legend: none
   - Chart title: **Attendance-Final Average Relationship**
   - Primary horizontal axis title: **Percentage of Attendance**
   - Primary vertical axis title: **Student Final Averages**

g. Use Help to learn how to apply the following axis settings:
   - Vertical axis: 40 minimum bounds, 100 maximum bounds, 10 major units, and a number format with zero decimal places
   - Horizontal axis: 40 minimum bounds, automatic maximum bounds, automatic units

h. Apply **12 pt font size** to the vertical axis title, vertical axis, horizontal axis title, and horizontal axis.

i. Add the **Parchment texture fill** to the plot area and insert a linear trendline.

j. Insert a footer with your name on the left side, the sheet name code in the center, and the file name code on the right side for the two chart sheets.

k. Save and close the workbook, and submit based on your instructor's directions.

3 Box Office Movies

FROM SCRATCH

You and two of your friends like to follow the popularity of new movies at the theater. You will research current movies that have been showing for four weeks and decide which movies to report on. Work in teams of three for this activity. After obtaining the data, your team will create applicable charts to illustrate the revenue data. Team members will critique each other's charts.

a. Have all three team members log in to a chat client and engage in a dialogue about which movies are currently playing. Each member should research a different theater to see what is playing at that theater. Decide on six movies that have been in theaters for at least four weeks to research. Save a copy of your instant message dialogue and submit based on your instructor's directions.

b. Divide the six movies among the three team members. Each member should research the revenue reported for two movies for the past four weeks. Make sure your team members use the same source to find the data.

Student 1:

c. Create a new Excel workbook and enter appropriate column labels and the four-week data for all six movies. Name Sheet1 **Data**.

d. Format the data appropriately. Save the workbook as **e03t1CurrentMovies_GroupName**. Upload the workbook to a shared location, such as OneDrive, and contact the next student.

Student 2:

e. Create a line chart to show the trends in revenue for the movies for the four-week period.

f. Add a chart title, format the axes appropriately, select a chart style, and then apply other formatting.

g. Move the chart to its own sheet named **Trends**. Save the workbook, upload it to the shared location, and then contact the next student.

Student 3:

h. Add a column to the right of the four-week data and total each movie's four-week revenue.

i. Create a pie chart depicting each movie's percentage of the total revenue for your selected movies.

j. Add a chart title, explode one pie slice, add data labels showing percentages and movie names, and then apply other formatting.

k. Move the chart to its own sheet named **Revenue Chart**. Save the workbook, upload it to the shared location, and then contact the first student.

Student 1:

l. Critique the charts. Insert a new worksheet named **Chart Critique** that provides an organized critique of each chart. Type notes that list each team member's name and specify what each student's role was in completing this exercise.

m. Save the workbook, upload it to the shared location, and then contact the second student.

Student 2:

n. Read the critique of the line chart and make any appropriate changes for the line chart. On the critique worksheet, provide a response to each critique and why you made or did not make the suggested change.

o. Save the workbook, upload it to the shared location, and then contact the third student.

Student 3:

p. Read the critique of the pie chart and make any appropriate changes for the pie chart. On the critique worksheet, provide a response to each critique and why you made or did not make the suggested change.

q. Save and close the workbook. Submit based on your instructor's directions.

Beyond the Classroom

Historical Stock Prices

RESEARCH CASE 

FROM SCRATCH

You are interested in investing in the stock market. First, you need to research the historical prices for a particular stock. Launch a Web browser, go to money.msn.com/investing/, type a company name, such as Apple, and then select the company name from a list of suggested companies. Click the **Historical Prices link**. Copy the stock data (date, high, low, open, close, volume) for a six-month period and paste it in a new workbook, adjusting the column widths to fit the data. Save the workbook as **e03b2StockData_LastFirst**. Rename Sheet1 **Data**. Display data for only the first date listed for each month; delete rows containing data for other dates. Sort the list from the oldest date to the newest date. Use Help if needed to learn how to sort data and how to create a Volume-Open-High-Low-Close chart. Then rearrange the data columns in the correct sequence. Format the data and column labels. Insert a row to enter the company name and insert another row to list the company's stock symbol, such as AAPL. Copy the URL from the Web browser and paste it as a source below the list of data and the date you obtained the data. Merge the cells containing the company name and stock symbol through the last column of data and word-wrap the URL.

Create a Volume-Open-High-Low-Close chart on a new chart sheet named **Chart**. Type an appropriate chart title. Set the primary vertical axis (left side) unit measurement to millions and include an axis title **Volume in Millions**. Include a secondary vertical axis (right side) title **Stock Prices**. Apply **Currency number style** with 0 decimal places for the secondary axis values. Apply **11-pt size** to the vertical axes and category axis. Use Help to research how to insert text boxes. Insert a text box that describes the stock chart: white fill rectangles indicate the closing price was higher than the opening price; black fill rectangles indicate the closing price was lower than the opening price; etc. Create a footer with your name, the sheet name code, and the file name code on both worksheets. Save and close the workbook, and submit based on your instructor's directions.

Harper County Houses Sold

DISASTER RECOVERY 

You want to analyze the number of houses sold by type (e.g., rambler, two story, etc.) in each quarter during 2012. Your intern created an initial chart, but it contains a lot of problems. Open *e03b3Houses* and save it as **e03b3Houses_LastFirst**. Identify the errors and poor design for the chart. Below the chart, list the errors and your corrections in a two-column format. Then correct problems in the chart. Create a footer with your name, the sheet name code, and the file name code. Adjust the margins and scaling to print the worksheet data, including the error list, and the chart on one page. Save and close the workbook, and submit based on your instructor's directions.

Time Management

SOFT SKILLS 

FROM SCRATCH

After reviewing the video on time-management skills, start a new workbook and save it as **e03b4Time_LastFirst**. List the major activities you do each week (e.g., sleeping, attending classes, eating, etc.) in the first column. In the second column, enter the number of hours per week you spend on each task. For example, if you sleep 8 hours each night, enter 56 (8 hours × 7 nights). Insert the SUM function to total the hours. The total hours per week is 168, so the total time of all activities should be 168. Adjust any values until the total is correct.Create a pie chart based on this data, include and format percentage data labels, and include an appropriate chart title. Below the data and chart, type a recommendation for yourself to improve your time-management skills. Create a footer with your name, the sheet name code, and the file name code. Save and close the workbook, and submit based on your instructor's directions.

Capstone Exercise

You are an assistant manager at Premiere Movie Source, an online company that enables customers to download movies for a fee. You need to track movie download sales by genre. You gathered the data for November 2016 and organized it in an Excel workbook. You are ready to create charts to help represent the data so that you can make a presentation to your manager later this week.

Set Chart Filters, Position, and Size

You created a clustered column chart, but you selected too many cells for the data source. You need to open the workbook and set chart filters to exclude extraneous data sources. In addition, you want to position and size the chart below the data.

a. Open the *e03c1Movies* workbook and save it as **e03c1Movies_LastFirst**.

b. Set chart filters to remove the Category Totals and the Weekly Totals.

c. Position and size the chart to fill the **range A18:K37**.

d. Change the row and column orientation so that the weeks appear in the category axis and the genres appear in the legend.

Add Chart Labels

You need to enter text for the chart title and add a value axis title. In addition, you want to position the legend on the right side because it is easier to read a vertical, alphabetical list rather than a horizontal list of genres.

a. Enter the text **November 2016 Downloads by Genre** as the chart title, bold the title, and then apply **Black, Text 1 font color**.

b. Add a value axis title: **Number of Downloads**. Apply **Black, Text 1 font color**.

c. Move the legend to the right side of the chart.

Format Chart Elements

You are ready to apply the finishing touches to the clustered column chart. You will format the category axis by adjusting the font size and applying a darker font color. You will add and adjust data labels to the Drama data series to emphasize this series.

a. Format the category axis with **11-pt size** and **Black, Text 1 font color**.

b. Select the **Drama data series** and add data labels in the Outside End position.

c. Add a **Gradient fill** to the data labels.

Insert and Format Sparklines

You want to show weekly trends for each genre by inserting sparklines in the column to the right of Category Totals.

a. Click **cell G5** and insert Line Sparklines for the weekly data for each category and the weekly totals, but do not include the category totals for the data range. The location range should be **G5:G15**.

b. Apply the **Sparkline Style Accent 3 (no dark or light) sparkline style**.

c. Show the high point and markers.

d. Change the high point marker color to **Red**.

Create a Stacked Bar Chart

You want to create a bar chart to show how the weekly totals contribute to the month totals by genre.

a. Select the **range A4:E14**. Create a clustered bar chart.

b. Move the chart to its own sheet named **Bar Chart**.

c. Change the chart type to a stacked bar chart.

d. Add a chart title above the chart and enter **November 2016 Weekly Downloads**.

Format the Bar Chart

You want to enhance the appearance of the chart by applying a chart style and adjusting the axis values.

a. Apply bold and **Blue, Accent 5 font color** to the chart title.

b. Apply **11-pt font size** to the category axis, value axis, and the legend.

c. Use the AXIS OPTIONS to display the value axis in units of **Thousands**, set the Major Units to **500**, and apply the **Number format** with 1 decimal place.

d. Use the AXIS OPTIONS to format the category axis so that the category labels are in reverse order.

Finalizing the Charts

You want to prepare the workbook in case someone wants to print the data and charts. To ensure the worksheet data and chart print on the same page, you need to adjust the page setup options.

a. Create a footer on each worksheet with your name, the sheet name code, and the file name code.

b. Apply **landscape orientation** for the Data worksheet.

c. Set **0.2"** left, right, top, and bottom margins for the original worksheet.

d. Change the scaling so that the worksheet fits on only one page.

e. Save and close the workbook, and submit based on your instructor's directions.

Excel

Datasets and Tables

CHAPTER 4

Managing Large Volumes of Data

OBJECTIVES AFTER YOU READ THIS CHAPTER, YOU WILL BE ABLE TO:

CASE STUDY | Reid Furniture Store

Vicki Reid owns Reid Furniture Store in Portland, Oregon. She divided her store into four departments: Living Room, Bedroom, Dining Room, and Appliances. All merchandise is categorized into one of these four departments for inventory records and sales. Vicki has four sales representatives: Chantalle Desmarais, Jade Gallagher, Sebastian Gruenewald, and Ambrose Sardelis. The sales system tracks which sales representative processed each transaction.

The business has grown rapidly, and Vicki hired you to analyze the sales data in order to increase future profits. For example, which department generates the most sales? Who is the leading salesperson? Do most customers purchase or finance? Are sales promotions necessary to promote business, or will customers pay the full price?

You downloaded March 2016 data from the sales system into an Excel workbook. To avoid extraneous data that is not needed in the analysis, you did not include customer names, accounts, or specific product numbers. The downloaded file contains transaction numbers, dates, sales representative names, departments, general merchandise description, total price, payment type, transaction type, and the total price.

Large Datasets

So far you have worked with worksheets that contain small datasets, a collection of structured, related data in a limited number of columns and rows. In reality, you will probably work with large datasets consisting of hundreds or thousands of rows and columns of data. When you work with small datasets, you can usually view most or all of the data without scrolling. When you work with large datasets, you probably will not be able to see the entire dataset onscreen even on a large, widescreen monitor set at high resolution. You might want to keep the column and row labels always in view, even as you scroll throughout the dataset. Figure 4.1 shows the Reid Furniture Store's March 2016 sales transactions. Because it contains a lot of transactions, the entire dataset is not visible. You could decrease the zoom level to display more transactions; however, doing so decreases the text size onscreen, making it hard to read the data.

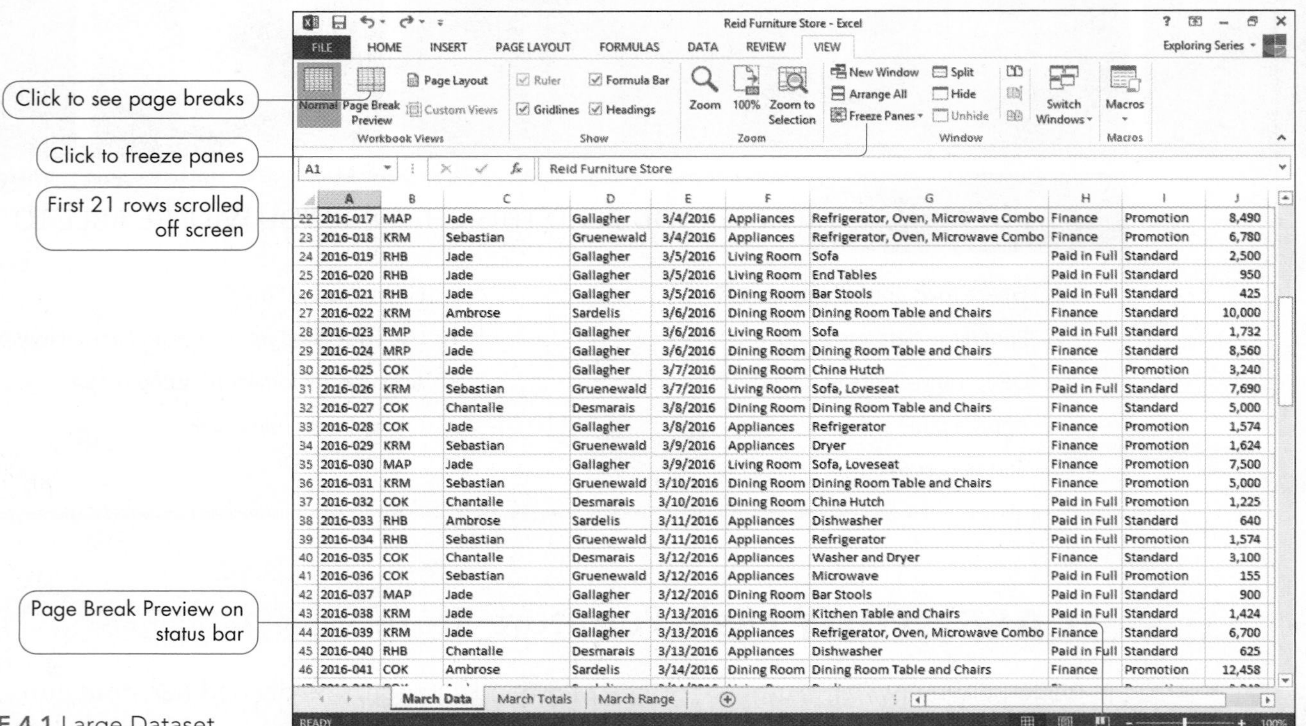

	A	B	C	D	E	F	G	H	I	J
22	2016-017	MAP	Jade	Gallagher	3/4/2016	Appliances	Refrigerator, Oven, Microwave Combo	Finance	Promotion	8,490
23	2016-018	KRM	Sebastian	Gruenewald	3/4/2016	Appliances	Refrigerator, Oven, Microwave Combo	Finance	Promotion	6,780
24	2016-019	RHB	Jade	Gallagher	3/5/2016	Living Room	Sofa	Paid in Full	Standard	2,500
25	2016-020	RHB	Jade	Gallagher	3/5/2016	Living Room	End Tables	Paid in Full	Standard	950
26	2016-021	RHB	Jade	Gallagher	3/5/2016	Dining Room	Bar Stools	Paid in Full	Standard	425
27	2016-022	KRM	Ambrose	Sardelis	3/6/2016	Dining Room	Dining Room Table and Chairs	Finance	Standard	10,000
28	2016-023	RMP	Jade	Gallagher	3/6/2016	Living Room	Sofa	Paid in Full	Standard	1,732
29	2016-024	MRP	Jade	Gallagher	3/6/2016	Dining Room	Dining Room Table and Chairs	Finance	Standard	8,560
30	2016-025	COK	Jade	Gallagher	3/7/2016	Dining Room	China Hutch	Finance	Promotion	3,240
31	2016-026	KRM	Sebastian	Gruenewald	3/7/2016	Living Room	Sofa, Loveseat	Paid in Full	Standard	7,690
32	2016-027	COK	Chantalle	Desmarais	3/8/2016	Dining Room	Dining Room Table and Chairs	Finance	Standard	5,000
33	2016-028	COK	Jade	Gallagher	3/8/2016	Appliances	Refrigerator	Finance	Promotion	1,574
34	2016-029	KRM	Sebastian	Gruenewald	3/9/2016	Appliances	Dryer	Finance	Promotion	1,624
35	2016-030	MAP	Jade	Gallagher	3/9/2016	Living Room	Sofa, Loveseat	Finance	Promotion	7,500
36	2016-031	KRM	Sebastian	Gruenewald	3/10/2016	Dining Room	Dining Room Table and Chairs	Finance	Promotion	5,000
37	2016-032	COK	Chantalle	Desmarais	3/10/2016	Dining Room	China Hutch	Paid in Full	Promotion	1,225
38	2016-033	RHB	Ambrose	Sardelis	3/11/2016	Appliances	Dishwasher	Paid in Full	Standard	640
39	2016-034	RHB	Sebastian	Gruenewald	3/11/2016	Appliances	Refrigerator	Paid in Full	Promotion	1,574
40	2016-035	COK	Chantalle	Desmarais	3/12/2016	Appliances	Washer and Dryer	Finance	Standard	3,100
41	2016-036	COK	Sebastian	Gruenewald	3/12/2016	Appliances	Microwave	Paid in Full	Promotion	155
42	2016-037	MAP	Jade	Gallagher	3/12/2016	Dining Room	Bar Stools	Paid in Full	Standard	900
43	2016-038	KRM	Jade	Gallagher	3/13/2016	Dining Room	Kitchen Table and Chairs	Paid in Full	Standard	1,424
44	2016-039	KRM	Jade	Gallagher	3/13/2016	Appliances	Refrigerator, Oven, Microwave Combo	Finance	Standard	6,700
45	2016-040	RHB	Chantalle	Desmarais	3/13/2016	Appliances	Dishwasher	Paid in Full	Standard	625
46	2016-041	COK	Ambrose	Sardelis	3/14/2016	Dining Room	Dining Room Table and Chairs	Finance	Promotion	12,458

FIGURE 4.1 Large Dataset

As you work with larger datasets, realize that the data will not always fit on one page. You will need to preview the automatic page breaks and probably insert some manual page breaks in more desirable locations, or you might want to print only a selected range within the large dataset to distribute to others.

In this section, you will learn how to keep labels onscreen as you scroll through a large dataset. In addition, you will learn how to manage page breaks, print only a range instead of an entire worksheet, and print column labels at the top of each page of a large dataset.

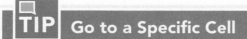

TIP Go to a Specific Cell

You can navigate through a large worksheet by using the Go To command. Click Find & Select in the Editing group on the Home tab and select Go To (or press F5 or Ctrl+G) to display the Go To dialog box, enter the cell address in the Reference box, and then press Enter to go to the cell.

You can also click in the Name Box, type the cell reference, and then press Enter to go to a specific cell.

Freezing Rows and Columns

When you scroll to parts of a dataset not initially visible, some rows and columns disappear from view. When the row and column labels scroll off the screen, you may not remember what each column represents. You can keep labels onscreen by freezing them. ***Freezing*** is the process of keeping rows and/or columns visible onscreen at all times even when you scroll through a large dataset. Table 4.1 describes the three freeze options.

TABLE 4.1 Freeze Options

Option	Description
Freeze Panes	Keeps both rows and columns above and to the left of the active cell visible as you scroll through a worksheet.
Freeze Top Row	Keeps only the top row visible as you scroll through a worksheet.
Freeze First Column	Keeps only the first column visible as you scroll through a worksheet.

STEP 1»

To freeze labels, click the View tab, click Freeze Panes in the Window group, and then select a freeze option. To freeze one or more rows and columns, use the Freeze Panes option. Before selecting this option, make the active cell one row below and one column to the right of the rows and columns you want to freeze. For example, to freeze the first five rows and the first column, make cell B6 the active cell before clicking the Freeze Panes option. As Figure 4.2 shows, Excel displays a horizontal line below the last frozen row (row 5) and a vertical line to the right of the last frozen column (column A). Unfrozen rows (such as rows 6–14) and unfrozen columns (such as columns B and C) are no longer visible as you scroll down and to the right, respectively.

Rows 1–5 and column A frozen

Vertical line to the right of last frozen column

Horizontal line below last frozen row

	A	D	E	F	G	H	I	J
1	Reid F							
2	Monthly T	March 2016						
3	Down Pay	25%						
4								
5	Trans_No	Sales_Last	Date	Department	Furniture	Pay_Type	Trans_Type	Amount
15	2016-010	Gallagher	3/2/2016	Dining Room	Dining Room Table and Chairs	Finance	Standard	6,780
16	2016-011	Desmarais	3/2/2016	Dining Room	Dining Room Table and Chairs	Finance	Standard	10,000
17	2016-012	Sardelis	3/2/2016	Appliances	Washer	Paid in Full	Promotion	1,100
18	2016-013	Desmarais	3/3/2016	Living Room	Recliners	Finance	Standard	2,430
19	2016-014	Gallagher	3/3/2016	Dining Room	Dining Room Table and Chairs	Paid in Full	Standard	4,550
20	2016-015	Desmarais	3/3/2016	Living Room	Sofa, Loveseat, Chair Package	Finance	Standard	6,784
21	2016-016	Gallagher	3/4/2016	Appliances	Dishwasher	Paid in Full	Standard	640
22	2016-017	Gallagher	3/4/2016	Appliances	Refrigerator, Oven, Microwave Combo	Finance	Promotion	8,490
23	2016-018	Gruenewald	3/4/2016	Appliances	Refrigerator, Oven, Microwave Combo	Finance	Promotion	6,780
24	2016-019	Gallagher	3/5/2016	Living Room	Sofa	Paid in Full	Standard	2,500
25	2016-020	Gallagher	3/5/2016	Living Room	End Tables	Paid in Full	Standard	950

FIGURE 4.2 Freeze Panes Set

To unlock the rows and columns from remaining onscreen as you scroll, click Freeze Panes in the Window group and select Unfreeze Panes, which only appears on the menu when you have frozen rows and/or columns. After you unfreeze the panes, the Freeze Panes option appears instead of Unfreeze Panes on the menu again.

When you freeze panes and press Ctrl+Home, the first unfrozen cell is the active cell instead of cell A1. For example, with column A and rows 1 through 5 frozen in Figure 4.2, pressing Ctrl+Home makes cell B6 the active cell. If you need to edit a cell in the frozen area, click the particular cell to make it active and edit the data.

Printing Large Datasets

For a large dataset, some columns and rows may print on several pages. Analyzing the data on individual printed pages is difficult when each page does not contain column and row labels. To prevent wasting paper, always use Print Preview. Doing so enables you to adjust page settings until you are satisfied with how the data will print.

The Page Layout tab (see Figure 4.3) contains options to help you prepare large datasets to print. Previously, you changed the page orientation, set different margins, and adjusted the scaling. In addition, you can manage page breaks, set the print area, and print titles.

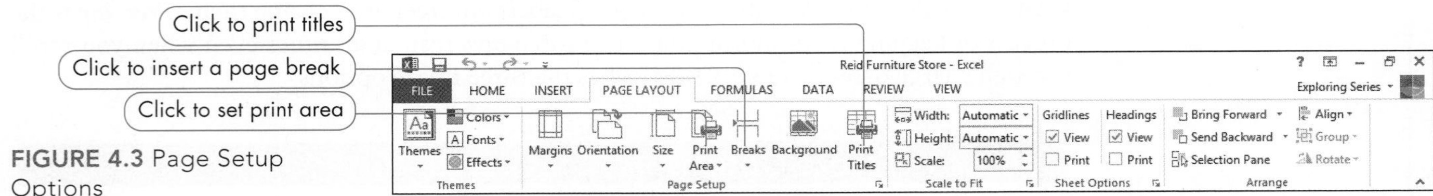

FIGURE 4.3 Page Setup Options

Display and Change Page Breaks

Based on the paper size, orientation, margins, and other settings, Excel identifies how much data can print on a page. Then it displays a ***page break***, indicating where data will start on another printed page. To identify where these automatic page breaks will occur, click Page Break Preview on the status bar or in the Workbook Views group on the View tab. In Page Break Preview, Excel displays watermarks, such as *Page 1*, indicating the area that will print on a specific page. Blue dashed lines indicate where the automatic page breaks occur, and solid blue lines indicate manual page breaks.

If the automatic page breaks occur in undesirable locations, you can adjust the page breaks. For example, if you have a worksheet listing sales data by date, the automatic page break might occur within a group of rows for one date, such as between two rows of data for 3/14/2016. To make all rows for that date appear together, you can either insert a page break above the first data row for that date or decrease the margins so that all 3/14/2015 transactions fit at the bottom of the page. To do this, drag a page break line to the desired location.

Manual Page Break: Do the following to set a manual break at a specific location:

STEP 2»

1. Click the cell that you want to be the first row and column on a new printed page. For example, click cell A50 if you want cell A50 to start a new page. If you click cell D50, you create a page for columns A through C, and then column D starts a new page.
2. Click the PAGE LAYOUT tab.
3. Click Breaks in the Page Setup group and select Insert Page Break. Excel displays a solid blue line in Page Break Preview or a dashed line in Normal view to indicate the manual page breaks you set. Figure 4.4 shows a worksheet with both automatic and manual page breaks.

Remove a Manual Page Break: To remove a manual page break, do the following:

1. Click a cell below a horizontal page break or a cell to the right of a vertical page break.
2. Click Breaks in the Page Setup group and select Remove Page Break.

Reset Page Breaks: To reset all page breaks back to the automatic page breaks, do the following:

1. Click Breaks in the Page Setup group.
2. Select Reset All Page Breaks.

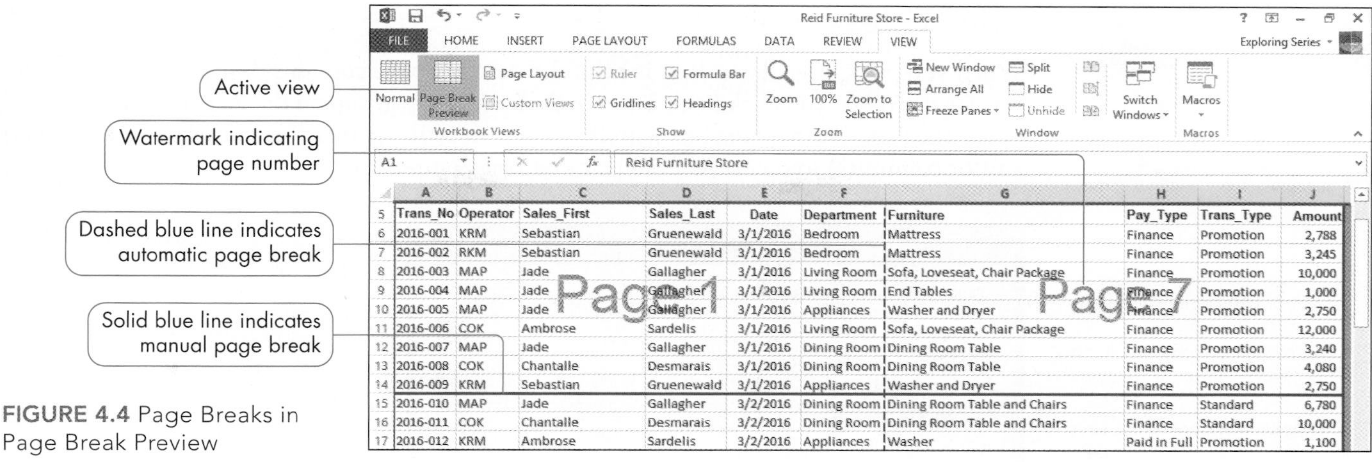

FIGURE 4.4 Page Breaks in Page Break Preview

Set and Clear a Print Area

The default Print settings send an entire dataset on the active worksheet to the printer. However, you might want to print only part of the worksheet data. If you display the worksheet in Page Break view, you can identify which page(s) you want to print. Then click the File tab and select Print. Type the number(s) of the page(s) you want to print. For example, to print page 2 only, type 2 in the Pages text box and in the *to* text box.

You can further restrict what is printed by setting the ***print area***, which is the range of cells that will print. For example, you might want to print only an input area or just the transactions that occurred on a particular date. To set a print area, do the following:

STEP 3

1. Select the range you want to print.
2. Click the PAGE LAYOUT tab and click Print Area in the Page Setup group.
3. Select Set Print Area.

In Page Break Preview, the print area has a white background and solid blue border; the rest of the worksheet has a gray background (see Figure 4.5). In Normal view or Page Layout view, the print area is surrounded by thin gray lines.

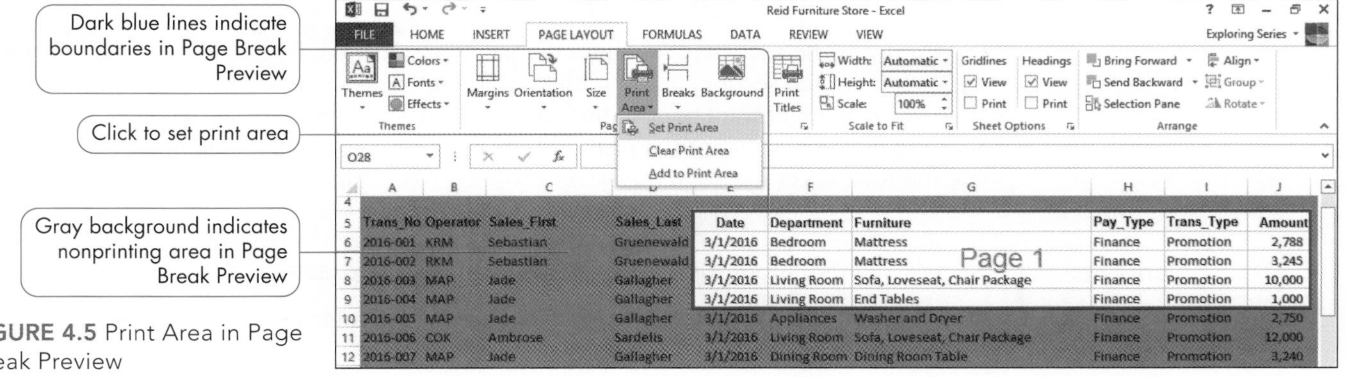

FIGURE 4.5 Print Area in Page Break Preview

To add print areas where each print area will print on a separate page, select the range you want to print, click Print Area, and then select *Add to Print Area*. To clear the print area, click Print Area in the Page Setup group and select Clear Print Area.

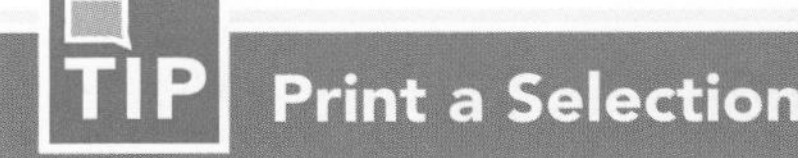

TIP Print a Selection

Another way to print part of a worksheet is to select the range you want to print. Click the File tab and click Print. Click the first arrow in the *Settings* section and select Print Selection.

Print Titles

STEP 4》 When you print large datasets, it is helpful that every page contains descriptive column and row labels. When you click Print Titles in the Page Setup group on the Page Layout tab, Excel opens the Page Setup dialog box with the Sheet tab active so that you can select which row(s) and/or column(s) to repeat on each printout (see Figure 4.6).

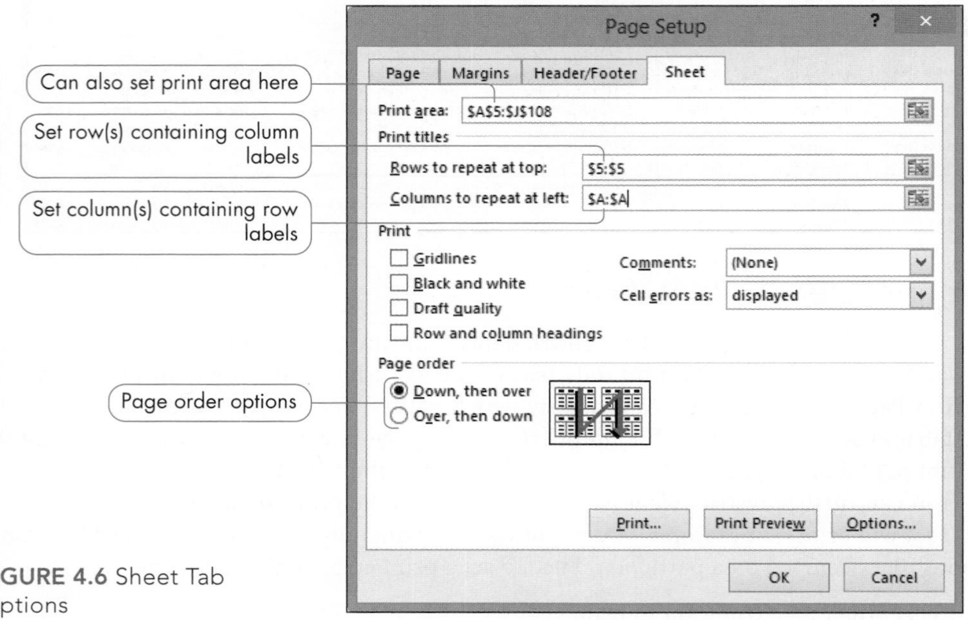

FIGURE 4.6 Sheet Tab Options

To print the column labels at the top of each page, select the row(s) that contain the labels or titles (such as row 5) in the *Rows to repeat at top* box to display $5:$5. To print the row labels at the left side of each page, select the column(s) that contain the labels or titles (such as column A) in the *Columns to repeat at left* box to display AA.

Control Print Page Order

Print order is the sequence in which the pages are printed. By default, the pages print in this order: top-left section, bottom-left section, top-right section, and bottom-right section. However, you might want to print the entire top portion of the worksheet before printing the bottom portion. To change the print order, open the Page Setup dialog box, click the Sheet tab, and then select the desired *Page order* option (see Figure 4.6).

Quick Concepts

1. What is the purpose of freezing panes in a worksheet? ***p. 557***
2. Why would you want to insert page breaks instead of using the automatic page breaks? ***p. 558***
3. What steps should you take to ensure that column labels display on each printed page of a large dataset? ***p. 560***

Hands-On Exercises

1 Large Datasets

You want to review the large dataset that shows the March 2016 transactions for Reid Furniture Store. You will need to view the data and adjust some page setup options so that you can print necessary labels on each page.

Skills covered: Freeze Rows and Columns • Manage Page Breaks • Set and Clear a Print Area • Print Titles

STEP 1 » FREEZE ROWS AND COLUMNS

Before printing the March 2016 transaction dataset, you want to view the data. The dataset contains more rows than will display onscreen at the same time. You decide to freeze the column and row labels to stay onscreen as you scroll through the transactions. Refer to Figure 4.7 as you complete Step 1.

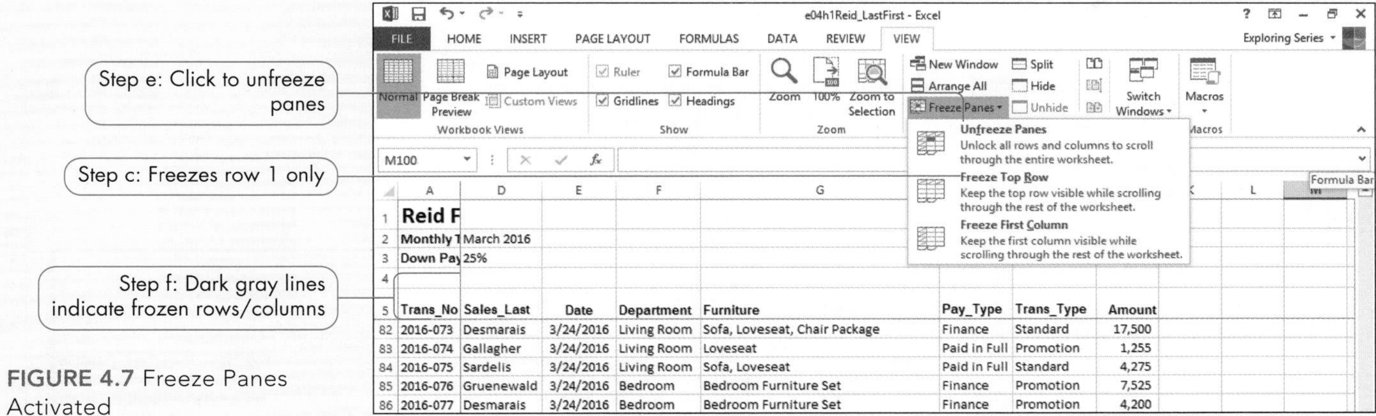

FIGURE 4.7 Freeze Panes Activated

a. Open *e04h1Reid* and save it as **e04h1Reid_LastFirst**.

> **TROUBLESHOOTING:** If you make any major mistakes in this exercise, you can close the file, open *e04h1Reid* again, and then start this exercise over.

The workbook contains three worksheets: March Data (for Hands-On Exercises 1–3), March Totals (for Hands-On Exercise 4), and March Range (for Hands-On Exercise 5).

b. Press **Page Down** four times to scroll through the dataset. Then press **Ctrl+Home** to go back to the top of the worksheet.

After you press Page Down, the column labels in row 5 scroll off the screen, making it challenging to remember what type of data are in some columns.

c. Click the **VIEW tab**, click **Freeze Panes** in the Window group, and then select **Freeze Top Row**.

A dark gray horizontal line displays between rows 1 and 2.

d. Press **Page Down** to scroll down through the worksheet.

As rows scroll off the top of the Excel window, the first row remains frozen onscreen. The title by itself is not helpful; you need to freeze the column labels as well.

e. Click **Freeze Panes** in the Window group and select **Unfreeze Panes**.

f. Click **cell B6**, the cell below the row and one column to the right of what you want to freeze. Click **Freeze Panes** in the Window group and select **Freeze Panes**.

Excel displays a vertical line between columns A and B, indicating that column A is frozen, and a horizontal line between rows 5 and 6, indicating the first five rows are frozen.

g. Press **Ctrl+G**, type **M100** in the **Reference box** of the Go To dialog box, and then click **OK** to make cell M100 the active cell. Save the workbook.

Rows 6 through 81 and columns B and C are not visible because they scrolled off the screen.

> **TROUBLESHOOTING:** Your screen may differ from Figure 4.7 due to different Windows resolution settings. If necessary, continue scrolling right and down until you see columns and rows scrolling offscreen.

STEP 2 » MANAGE PAGE BREAKS

You plan to print the dataset so that you and Vicki Reid can discuss the transactions in your weekly meeting. Because the large dataset will not fit on one page, you want to see where the automatic page breaks are and then insert a manual page break. Refer to Figure 4.8 as you complete Step 2.

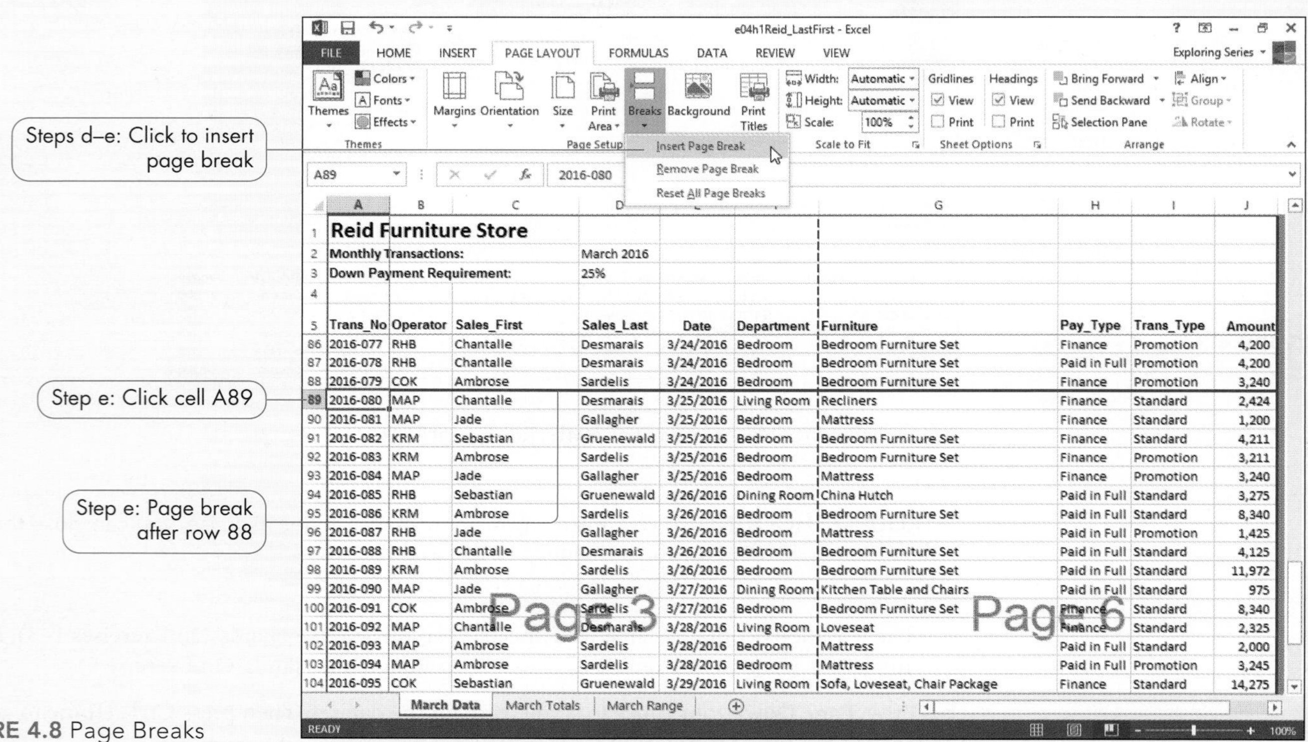

FIGURE 4.8 Page Breaks

a. Press **Ctrl+Home** to move to **cell B6**, the first cell in the unfrozen area. Click the **VIEW tab**, if necessary, and click **Page Break Preview** in the Workbook Views group or on the status bar.

Excel displays blue dashed lines to indicate the automatic page breaks.

b. Scroll down until you see row 44 below the frozen column labels.

The automatic horizontal page break is between rows 46 and 47 (or between rows 45 and 46). You do not want transactions for a particular day to span between printed pages, so you need to move the page break up to keep all 3/13/2016 transactions together.

c. Click **cell A45**, the first cell containing 3/13/2016 data and the cell to start the top of the second page.

d. Click the **PAGE LAYOUT tab**, click **Breaks** in the Page Setup group, and then select **Insert Page Break**.

You inserted a page break between rows 44 and 45 so that the 3/13/2016 transactions will be on one page.

e. Click **cell A89**, click **Breaks** in the Page Setup group, and then select **Insert Page Break**. Save the workbook.

You inserted a page break between rows 88 and 89 to keep the 3/25/2016 transactions on the same page.

TIP Using the Mouse Pointer to Move Page Breaks

To use the mouse pointer to adjust a page break, position the mouse pointer on the page break line to see the two-headed arrow and drag the line to where you want the page break to occur.

STEP 3 » SET AND CLEAR A PRINT AREA

You want to focus on the transactions for only March 1, 2016. To avoid printing more data than you need, you will set the print area to print transactions for only that day. Refer to Figure 4.9 as you complete Step 3.

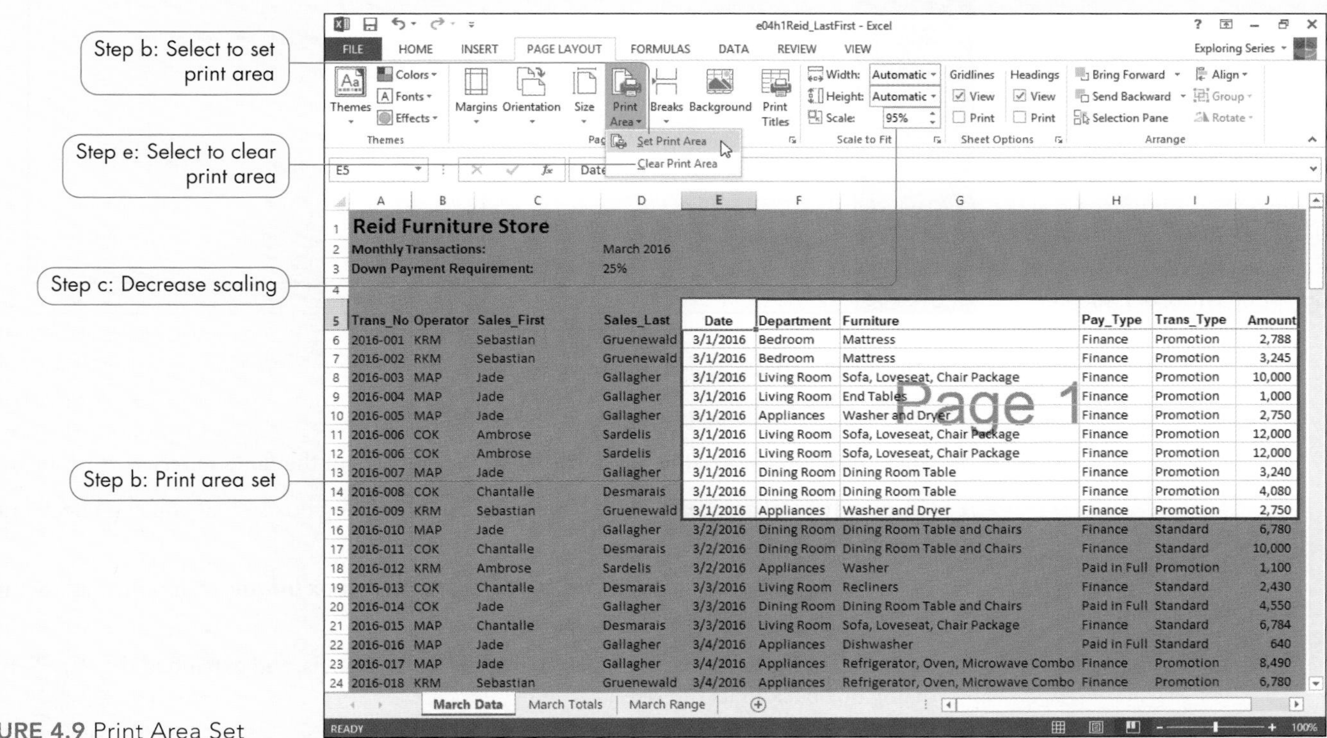

FIGURE 4.9 Print Area Set

a. Scroll up to see the first row of March data. Select the **range E5:J15**, the range of data for March 1, 2016.

b. Click the **PAGE LAYOUT tab**, if necessary, click **Print Area** in the Page Setup group, and then select **Set Print Area**.

Excel displays the print area with a solid blue border. A dotted blue line displays between columns I and J, indicating an automatic page break. The rest of the worksheet displays with a gray background.

c. Click **cell E5** and click the **Scale arrow** down one time in the *Scale to Fit* group.

The selected print area will print on one page.

d. Press **Ctrl+P** to see that only the print area will print. Press **Esc**.

e. Click **Print Area** in the Page Setup group and select **Clear Print Area**. Save the workbook.

STEP 4 » PRINT TITLES

Only the first page will print both row and column labels. Pages 2 and 3 will print the remaining row labels, Page 4 will print the remaining column labels, and Pages 5 and 6 will not print either label. You want to make sure the column and row labels print on all pages. To do this, you will print titles. Refer to Figure 4.10 as you complete Step 4.

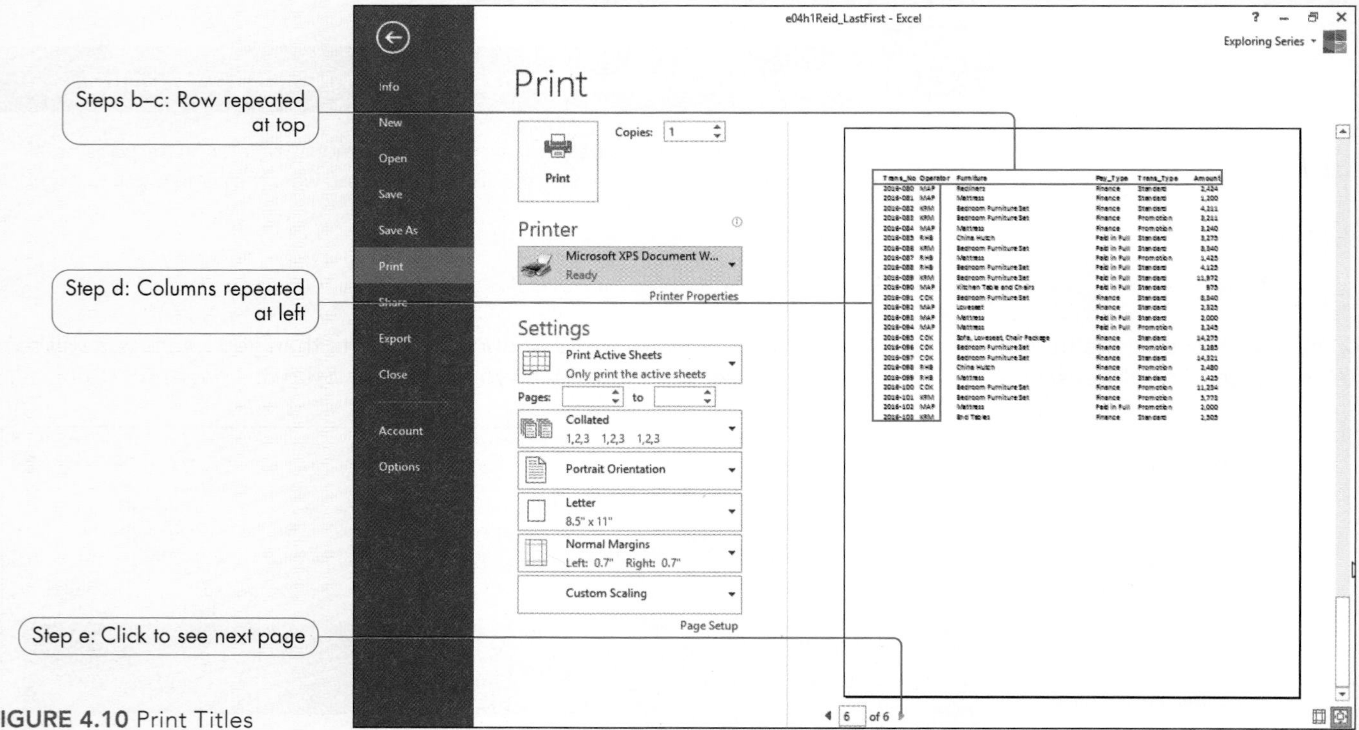

FIGURE 4.10 Print Titles

a. Click **Print Titles** in the Page Setup group.

   The Page Setup dialog box opens, displaying the Sheet tab.

b. Click the **Collapse Dialog box button** on the right side of the *Rows to repeat at top* box.

   Clicking the *Collapse Dialog box* button reduces the dialog box so that you can select a range in the worksheet easily.

c. Click the **row 5 heading** and click the **Collapse Dialog box button** within the Page Setup: Rows to repeat at top dialog box.

   You selected the fifth row, which contains the column labels, and expanded the Page Setup dialog box back to its full size.

d. Click in the **Columns to repeat at left box**, type **A:B**, and then click **Print Preview**.

e. Click **Next Page** at the bottom of the Microsoft Office Backstage view. Click **Next Page** until the sixth page displays.

   Figure 4.10 shows a preview of the sixth page. The column labels and the first two columns appear on all pages.

f. Click the **Back arrow** in the top-left corner of the Microsoft Office Backstage view.

g. Save the workbook. Keep the workbook onscreen if you plan to continue with the next Hands-On Exercise. If not, close the workbook and exit Excel.

Excel Tables

All organizations maintain lists of data. Businesses maintain inventory lists, educational institutions maintain lists of students and faculty, and governmental entities maintain lists of contracts. Although more complicated related data should be stored in a database-management program, such as Access, you can maintain structured lists in Excel tables. A ***table*** is a structured range that contains related data organized in such a way as to facilitate data management and analysis. Although you can manage and analyze a range of data, a table provides many advantages over a range of data:

- Column headings remain onscreen without having to use Freeze Panes.
- Filter arrows are available for efficient sorting and filtering.
- Table styles easily format table rows and columns with complementary fill colors.
- Calculated columns where the formulas copy down the columns automatically are available to create and edit.
- Calculated total row enables the user to implement a variety of summary functions.
- Structured references can be used instead of cell references in formulas.
- Table data can export to a SharePoint list.

In this section, you will learn table terminology and rules for structuring data. You will create a table from existing data, manage records and fields, and remove duplicates. Then you will apply a table style to format the table.

Designing and Creating Tables

A table is a group of related data organized in a series of rows and columns that is managed independently from any other data on the worksheet. Each column represents a ***field***, which is an individual piece of data, such as last names or quantities sold. Each field should represent the smallest possible unit of data. For example, instead of a Name field, separate name data into First Name and Last Name fields. Instead of one large address field, separate address data into Street Address, City, State, and ZIP Code fields. Separating data into the smallest units possible enables you to manipulate the data in a variety of ways for output. Each row in a table represents a ***record***, which is a collection of related data about one entity. For example, all data related to one particular transaction form a record in the Reid Department Store worksheet.

You should plan the structure before creating a table. The more thoroughly you plan, the fewer changes you will have to make to the table after you create it. To help plan your table, follow these guidelines:

- Enter field (column) names on the top row.
- Keep field names short, descriptive, and unique. No two field names should be identical.
- Format the field names so that they stand out from the data.
- Enter data for each record on a row below the field names.
- Do not leave blank rows between records or between the field names and the first record.
- Delete any blank columns between fields in the dataset.
- Make sure each record has something unique, such as a transaction number or ID.
- Insert at least one blank row and one blank column between the table and other data, such as the main titles. When you need multiple tables in one workbook, a best practice is to place each table on a separate worksheet.

Create a Table

STEP 1» When your worksheet data are structured correctly, you can easily create a table. To create a table from existing data, do the following:

1. Click within the existing range of data.
2. Click the INSERT tab and click Table in the Tables group. The Create Table dialog box opens (see Figure 4.11), prompting you to enter the range of data.
    - If Excel does not correctly predict the range, select the range for the *Where is the data for your table?* box.
    - If the existing range contains column labels, select the *My table has headers* check box.
3. Click OK to create the table.

FIGURE 4.11 Create Table Dialog Box

Quick Analysis Table Creation

You can also create a table by selecting a range, clicking the Quick Analysis button, clicking TABLES (see Figure 4.12) in the Quick Analysis gallery, and then clicking Table. While Quick Analysis is efficient for tasks such as creating a chart, it may take more time to create a table because you have to select the entire range first. Some people find that it is faster to create a table from the Insert tab.

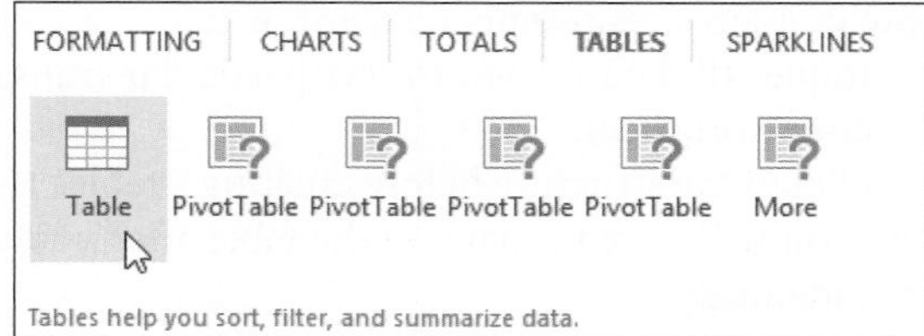

FIGURE 4.12 Quick Analysis Gallery

After you create a table, the Table Tools Design tab displays. Excel applies the default Table Style Medium 2 style to the table, and each cell in the header row has arrows, also called *filtering arrows* or *filtering buttons* in Excel Help (see Figure 4.13). This book uses the term *filter arrows* for consistency. Excel assigns a name to each table, such as Table 1. You can change the table name by clicking in the Table Name box in the Properties group, typing a new name using the same rules you applied when assigning range names, and then pressing Enter.

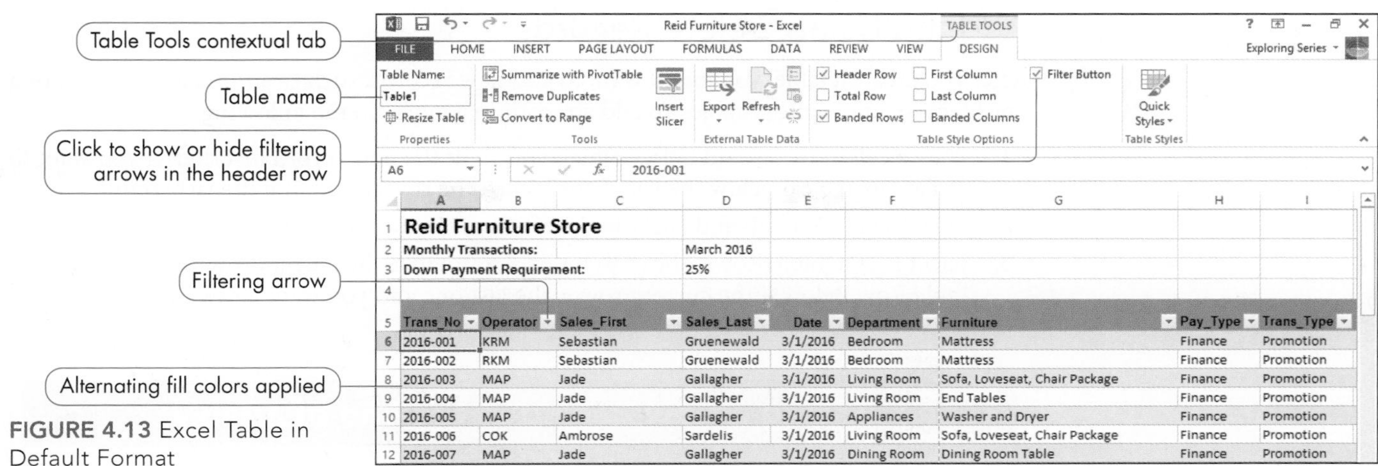

FIGURE 4.13 Excel Table in Default Format

Instead of converting a range to a table, you can create a table structure first and add data to it later. Select an empty range and follow the previously listed steps to create the range for the table. The default column headings are Column1, Column2, and so on. Click each default column heading and type a descriptive label. Then enter the data into each row of the newly created table.

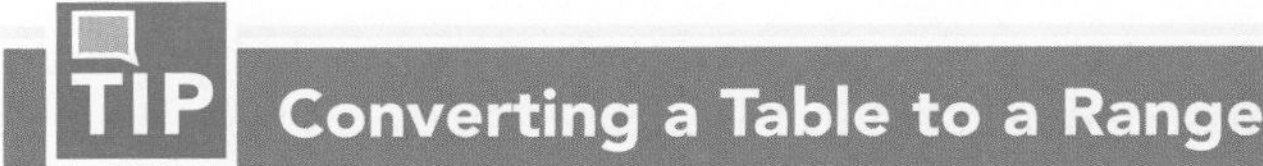

To convert a table back to a range, click within the table range, click the Table Tools Design tab, click *Convert to Range* in the Tools group, and then click Yes in the message box asking, *Do you want to convert the table to a normal range?*

Add and Delete Fields

STEP 2»

After creating a table, you might want to add a new field. For example, you might want to add a field for product numbers to the Reid Furniture Store transaction table. To insert a field:

1. Click in any data cell (but not the cell containing the field name) in a field that will be to the right of the new field. For example, to insert a new field between the fields in columns A and B, click any cell in column B.
2. Click the HOME tab and click the Insert arrow in the Cells group.
3. Select *Insert Table Columns to the Left*.

If you want to add a field at the end of the right side of a table, click in the cell to the right of the last field name and type a label. Excel will extend the table to include that field and will format the cell as a field name.

You can also delete a field if you no longer need any data for that particular field. Although deleting records and fields is easy, you must make sure not to delete data erroneously. If you accidentally delete data, click Undo immediately. To delete a field, do the following:

1. Click a cell in the field that you want to delete.
2. Click the Delete arrow in the Cells group on the HOME tab.
3. Select Delete Table Columns.

Add, Edit, and Delete Records

STEP 3» After you create a table, you might want to add new records, such as adding a new client or a new item to an inventory table. To add a record to a table, do the following:

1. Click a cell in the record below which you want the new record inserted. If you want to add a new record below the last record, click the row containing the last record.
2. Click the HOME tab and click the Insert arrow in the Cells group.
3. Select Insert Table Rows Above to insert a row above the current row, or select Insert Table Row Below if the current row is the last one and you want a row below it.

TIP Adding a New Record at the End of a Table

You can also add a record to the end of a table by clicking in the row immediately below the table and typing. Excel will extend the table to include that row as a record in the table and will apply consistent formatting.

You might need to change data for a record. For example, when a client moves, you need to change the client's address and phone number. You edit data in a table the same way you edit data in a regular worksheet cell.

Finally, you can delete records. For example, if you maintain an inventory of artwork in your house and sell a piece of art, delete that record from the table. To delete a record from the table:

1. Click a cell in the record that you want to delete.
2. Click the HOME tab and click the Delete arrow in the Cells group.
3. Select Delete Table Rows.

Remove Duplicate Rows

STEP 4» A table might contain duplicate records, which can give false results when totaling or performing other calculations on the dataset. For a small table, you might be able to detect duplicate records by scanning the data. For large tables, it is more difficult to identify duplicate records by simply scanning the table with the eye. To remove duplicate records, do the following:

1. Click within the table and click the DESIGN tab.
2. Click Remove Duplicates in the Tools group to display the Remove Duplicates dialog box (see Figure 4.14).
3. Click Select All to set the criteria to find a duplicate for every field in the record and click OK. If you select individual column(s), Excel looks for duplicates in the specific column(s) only and deletes all but one record of the duplicated data. Excel will display a message box informing you of how many duplicate rows it removed.

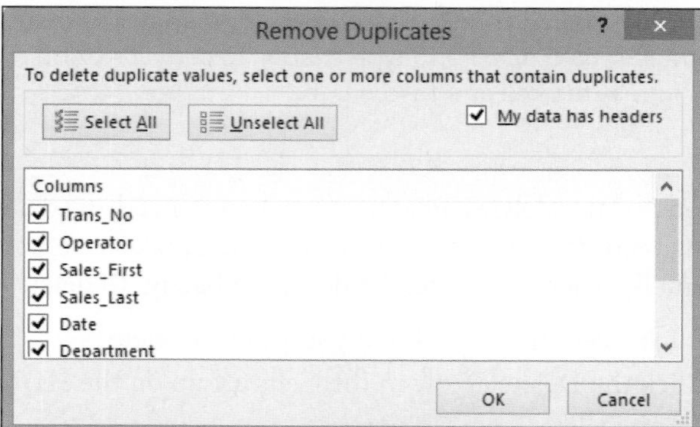

FIGURE 4.14 Remove Duplicates Dialog Box

TIP Data Tab to Delete Duplicates

You can also click the Data tab and click Remove Duplicates in the Data Tools group to open the Remove Duplicates dialog box.

Applying a Table Style

STEP 5»

Excel applies a table style when you create a table. ***Table styles*** control the fill color of the header row (the row containing field names) and rows of records. In addition, table styles specify bold and border lines. You can change the table style to a color scheme that complements your organization's color scheme or to emphasize data the header rows or columns. Click Quick Styles in the Table Styles group to display the Table Styles gallery (see Figure 4.15). To see how a table style will format your table using Live Preview, position the pointer over a style in the Table Styles gallery. After you identify a style you want, click it to apply it to the table.

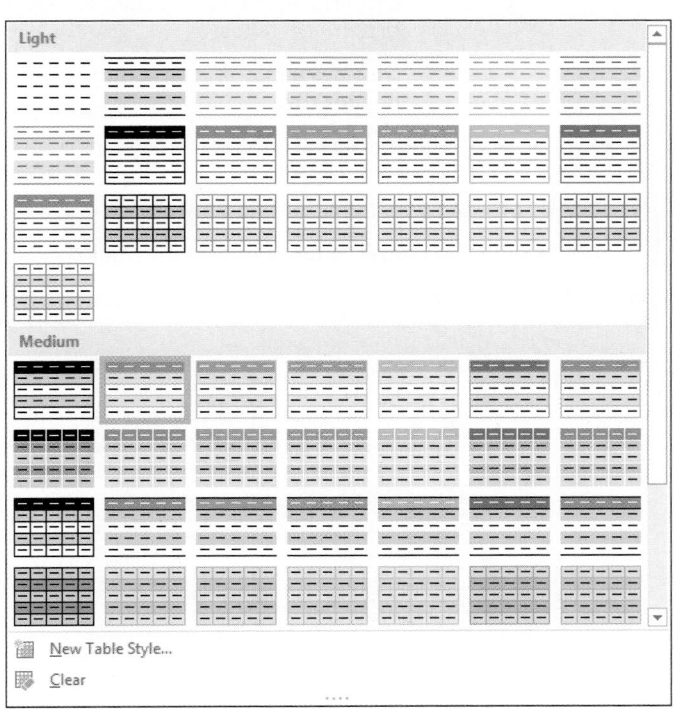

FIGURE 4.15 Table Styles Gallery

After you select a table style, you can control what the style formats. The Table Style Options group contains check boxes to select specific format actions in a table. Table 4.2 lists the options and the effect of each check box. Avoid overformatting the table. It is not good to apply so many formatting effects that the message you want to present with the data is obscured or lost.

TABLE 4.2 Table Style Options

Check Box	Action
Header Row	Displays the header row (field names) when checked; removes field names when not checked. Header Row formatting takes priority over column formats.
Total Row	Displays a total row when selected. Total Row formatting takes priority over column formats.
First Column	Applies a different format to the first column so that the row headings stand out. First Column formatting takes priority over Banded Rows formatting.
Last Column	Applies a different format to the last column so that the last column of data stands out; effective for aggregated data, such as grand totals per row. Last Column formatting takes priority over Banded Rows formatting.
Banded Rows	Displays alternate fill colors for even and odd rows to help distinguish records.
Banded Columns	Displays alternate fill colors for even and odd columns to help distinguish fields.
Filter Button	Displays a filter button on the right side of each heading in the header row.

1. List at least four guidelines for planning a table in Excel. ***p. 565***
2. Why would you convert a range of data into an Excel table? ***p. 565***
3. What are six options you can control after selecting a table style? ***p. 570***

Hands-On Exercises

2 Excel Tables

You want to convert the March data to a table. As you review the table, you will delete the unnecessary Operator field, add two new fields, insert a missing furniture sale transaction, and remove duplicate transactions. Finally, you will enhance the table appearance by applying a table style.

Skills covered: Create a Table • Add and Delete Fields • Add Records • Remove Duplicate Rows • Apply a Table Style

STEP 1 » CREATE A TABLE

Although the Reid Furniture Store's March transaction data are organized in an Excel worksheet, you know that you will have additional functionality if you convert the range to a table. Refer to Figure 4.16 as you complete Step 1.

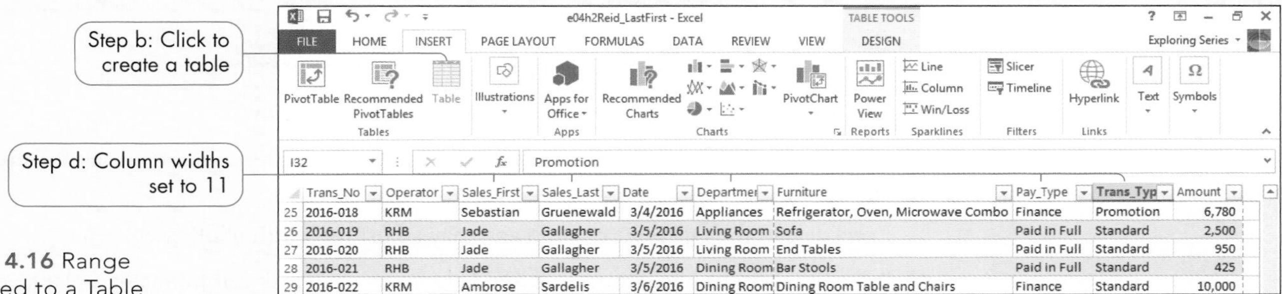

FIGURE 4.16 Range Converted to a Table

a. Open *e04h1Reid_LastFirst* if you closed it at the end of Hands-On Exercise 1 and save it as **e04h2Reid_LastFirst**, changing *h1* to *h2*. Click **Normal** on the status bar.

b. Click in any cell within the transactional data, click the **INSERT tab**, and then click **Table** in the Tables group.

The Create Table dialog box opens. The *Where is the data for your table?* box displays =$A$5:$I$112. Keep the *My table has headers* check box selected so that the headings on the fifth row become the field names for the table.

c. Click **OK** and click **cell A5**.

Excel creates a table from the data range and displays the DESIGN tab, filter arrows, and alternating fill colors for the records. The columns widen to fit the field names, although the wrap text option is still applied to those cells.

d. Set column width to **11** for the Sales_First, Sales_Last, Department, Pay_Type, and Trans_Type fields.

e. Unfreeze the panes and scroll through the table. Save the workbook.

With a regular range of data, column labels scroll off the top of the screen if you do not freeze panes. When you scroll within a table, the table's header row remains onscreen by moving up to where the Excel column (letter) headings usually display (see Figure 4.16).

STEP 2 ADD AND DELETE FIELDS

The original range included a column for the data entry operators' initials. You will delete this column because you do not need it for your analysis. In addition, you want to add a field to display down payment amounts in the future. Refer to Figure 4.17 as you complete Step 2.

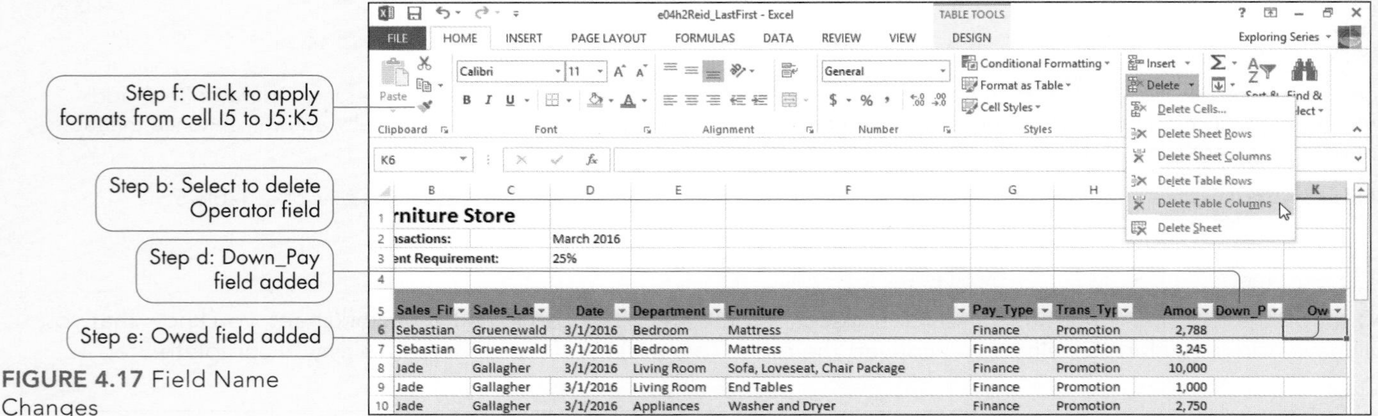

FIGURE 4.17 Field Name Changes

a. Click **cell B25** or any cell containing a value in the Operator column.

You need to make a cell active in the field you want to remove.

b. Click the **HOME tab**, click the **Delete arrow** in the Cells group, and then select **Delete Table Columns**.

Excel deletes the Operator column and may adjust the width of other columns.

c. Adjust the widths of columns E, F, and G as necessary. Click **cell J5**, the first blank cell on the right side of the field names.

d. Type **Down_Pay** and press **Ctrl+Enter**.

Excel extends the table formatting to column J automatically. A filter arrow appears for the newly created field name, and alternating fill colors appear in the rows below the field name. The fill color is the same as the fill color for other field names; however, the font color is White, Background 1, instead of Black Text 1.

e. Click **cell K5**, type **Owed**, and then press **Ctrl+Enter**.

f. Click **cell I5**, click **Format Painter** in the Clipboard group, and then select the **range J5:K5** to copy the format. Save the workbook.

STEP 3 » ADD RECORDS

As you review the March 2016 transaction table, you notice that two transactions are missing: 2016-68 and 2016-104. After finding the paper invoices, you are ready to add records with the missing transaction data. Refer to Figure 4.18 as you complete Step 3.

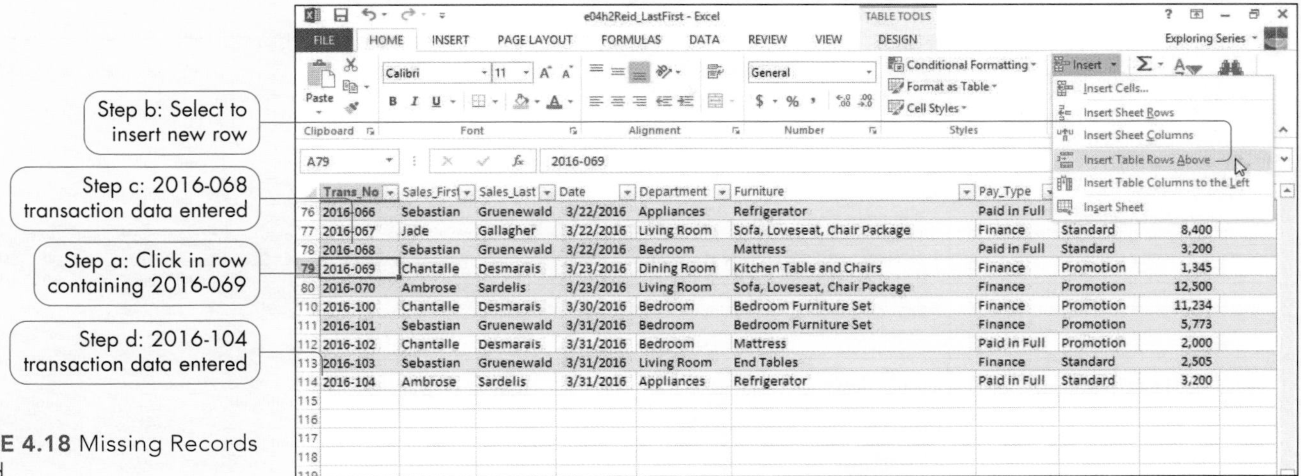

FIGURE 4.18 Missing Records Added

a. Click **cell A78** or any cell within the table range on row 78.

The missing record 2016-68 needs to be inserted between 2016-67 on row 77 and 2016-69 on row 78.

b. Click the **HOME tab**, click the **Insert arrow** in the Cells group, and then select **Insert Table Row Above**.

Excel inserts a new table row on row 78, between the 2016-67 and 2016-69 transactions.

c. Enter the following data in the respective fields on the newly created row.

2016-068, **Sebastian**, **Gruenewald**, **3/22/2016**, **Bedroom**, **Mattress**, **Paid in Full**, **Standard**, **3200**

d. Click **cell A114** and enter the following data in the respective fields. Save the workbook.

2016-104, **Ambrose**, **Sardelis**, **3/31/2016**, **Appliances**, **Refrigerator**, **Paid in Full**, **Standard**, **1500**

When you start typing 2016-104 in the row immediately below the last record, Excel immediately includes and formats row 114 as part of the table. Review Figure 4.18 to ensure you inserted the records in the correct locations. Rows 81–109 are hidden to display both new records in one screenshot.

STEP 4 » REMOVE DUPLICATE ROWS

You noticed that the 2016-006 transaction is duplicated on rows 11 and 12 and that the 2016-018 transaction is duplicated on rows 24 and 25. You think the table may contain other duplicate rows. To avoid having to look at the entire table row by row, you want to have Excel find and remove the duplicate rows for you. Refer to Figure 4.19 as you complete Step 4.

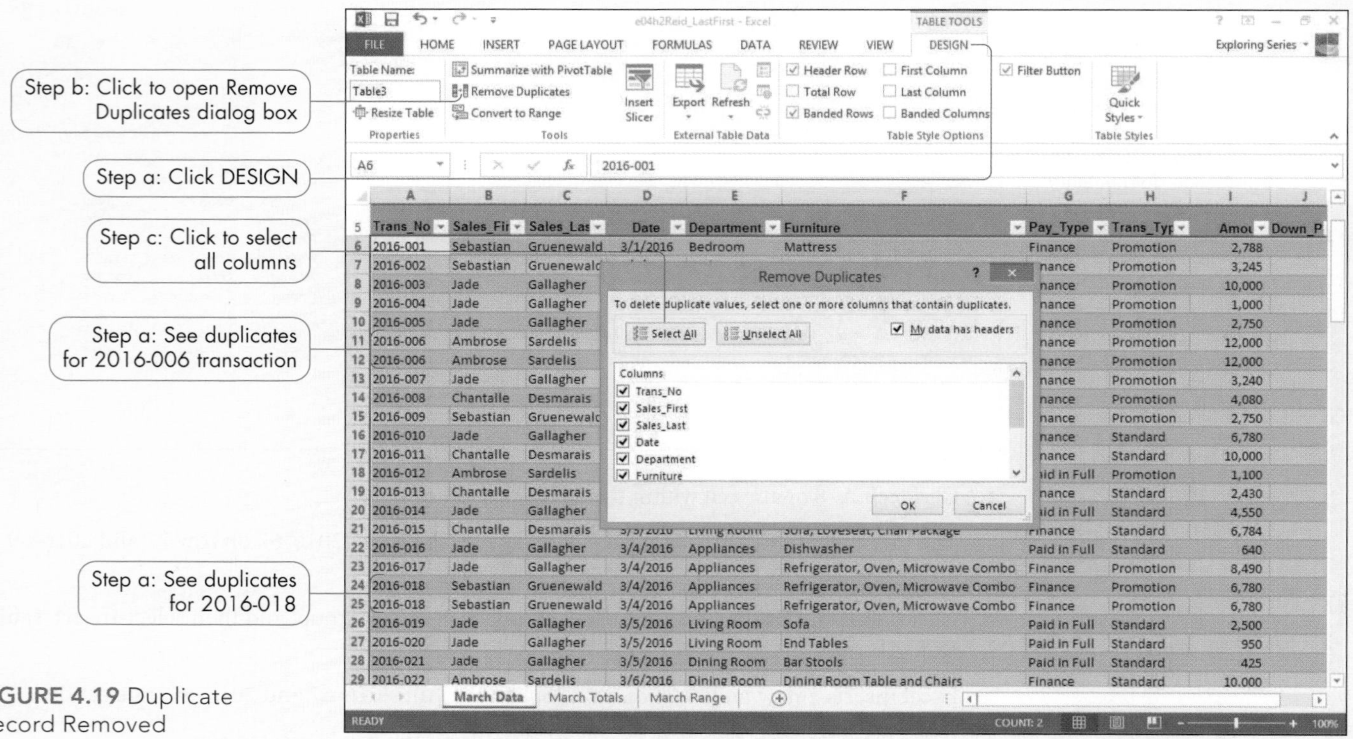

FIGURE 4.19 Duplicate Record Removed

a. Scroll to see rows 11 and 12. Click the **DESIGN tab**.

The records on rows 11 and 12 are identical. Rows 24 and 25 are also duplicates. You need to remove the extra rows.

b. Click **Remove Duplicates** in the Tools group.

The Remove Duplicates dialog box opens.

c. Click **Select All**, make sure the **My data has headers check box** is selected, and then click **OK**.

Excel displays a message box indicating *5 duplicate records found and removed; 104 unique values remain.*

d. Click **OK** in the message box. Press **Page Down** until you see the last record. Save the workbook.

Transaction 2016-104 is located on row 109 after the duplicate records are removed.

STEP 5 » APPLY A TABLE STYLE

Now that you have finalized the fields and added missing records to the March 2016 transaction table, you want to apply a table style to format the table. Refer to Figure 4.20 as you complete Step 5.

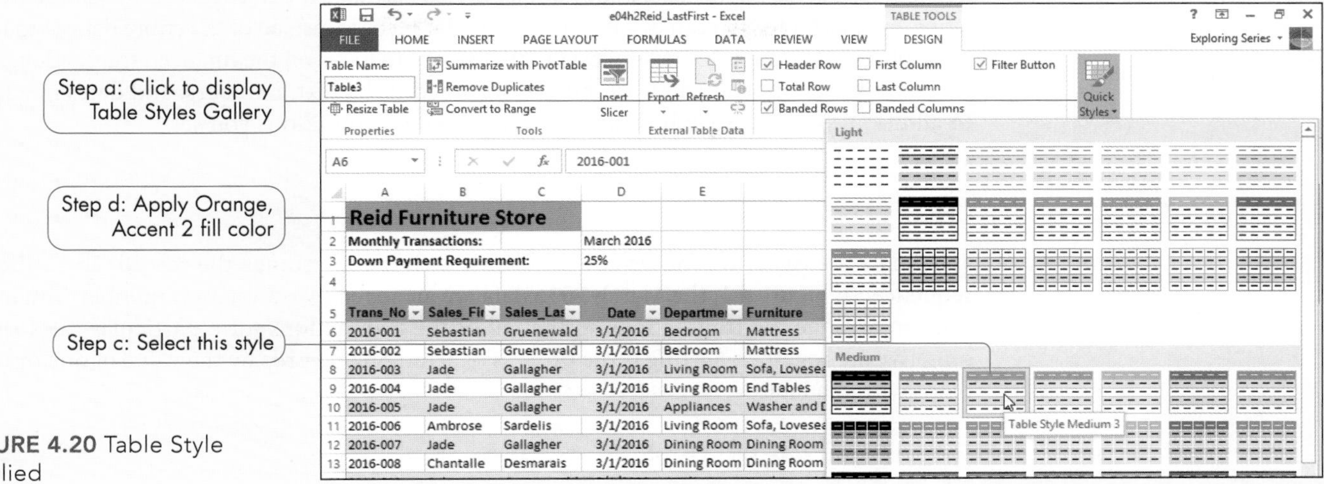

FIGURE 4.20 Table Style Applied

a. Click the **DESIGN tab** and click **Quick Styles** in the Table Styles group to open the Table Styles gallery.

b. Position the mouse pointer over the fourth style on the second row in the *Light* section.

Live Preview shows the table with the Table Style Light 10 style but does not apply it.

c. Click **Table Style Medium 3**, the third style on the first row in the *Medium* section.

Excel formats the table with the Table Style Medium 3, which applies Orange, Accent 2 fill color to the header row and Orange, Accent 2, Lighter 80% fill color to every other record.

d. Press **Ctrl_Home** to go to cell A1. Select the **range A1:C1**, click the **Fill Color arrow** in the Font group on the HOME tab, and then click **Orange, Accent 2**.

You applied a fill color for the title to match the fill color of the field names on the header row in the table.

e. Save the workbook. Keep the workbook onscreen if you plan to continue with the next Hands-On Exercise. If not, close the workbook and exit Excel.

Table Manipulation

You have a variety of options to manipulate table data, in addition to managing fields, adding records, and applying table styles. You can arrange the records in different sequences to get different perspectives on the data. For example, you can arrange the transactions by sales representative. Furthermore, you can display only particular records instead of the entire dataset to focus on a subset of the data. For example, you might want to focus on the financed transactions.

In this section, you will learn how to sort records by text, numbers, and dates in a table. In addition, you will learn how to filter data based on conditions you set.

Sorting Data

Table data are easier to understand and work with if you arrange the records in a different sequence. In Figure 4.1, the March 2016 data are arranged by transaction number. You might want to arrange the transactions so that all of the transactions for a particular sales representative are together. ***Sorting*** is the process of arranging records by the value of one or more fields within a table.

Sort One Field

STEP 1》 You can sort data in a table or a regular range in a worksheet. To sort by only one field, you can use any of the following methods for either a range of data or a table:

- Click in a cell within the field you want to sort and click Sort & Filter in the Editing group on the HOME tab.
- Click in a cell within the field you want to sort and click *Sort A to Z*, *Sort Z to A*, or Sort in the Sort & Filter group on the DATA tab.
- Right-click the field to sort, point to Sort on the shortcut menu, and then select the type of sort you want.
- Click the filter arrow in the header row and select the desired sort option.

Table 4.3 lists sort options by data type.

TABLE 4.3 Sort Options

Data Type	Options	Explanation
Text	Sort A to Z	Arranges data in alphabetical order.
	Sort Z to A	Arranges data in reverse alphabetical order.
Dates	Sort Oldest to Newest	Displays data in chronological order, from oldest to newest.
	Sort Newest to Oldest	Displays data in reverse chronological order, from newest to oldest.
Values	Sort Smallest to Largest	Arranges values from the smallest value to the largest.
	Sort Largest to Smallest	Arranges values from the largest value to the smallest.
Color	Sort by Cell Color	Arranges data together for cells containing a particular fill color.
	Sort by Font Color	Arranges data together for cells containing a particular font color.

Sort Multiple Fields

STEP 2》 At times, sorting by only one field yields several records that have the same information. For example, the same last name or the same department could display several times. In those instances, you may want to add a sort on a second field. A second sort will help to uniquely identify a record. You might need both last name and first name to identify an individual. Using multiple level sorts enables like records in the primary sort to be further organized by additional sort levels. For example, you might want to sort by department, then by sales representative, and finally by sales amount. Excel enables you to sort data on 64 different levels. To perform a multiple level sort:

1. Click in any cell in the table.
2. Click Sort in the Sort & Filter group on the Data tab to display the Sort dialog box.
3. Select the primary sort level by clicking the *Sort by* arrow, selecting the field to sort by, and then clicking the Order arrow and selecting the sort order from the list.
4. Click Add Level, select the second sort level by clicking the *Then by* arrow, select the column to sort by, click the Order arrow, and then select the sort order from the list.
5. Continue to click Add Level and add sort levels until you have entered all sort levels. See Figure 4.21. Click OK.

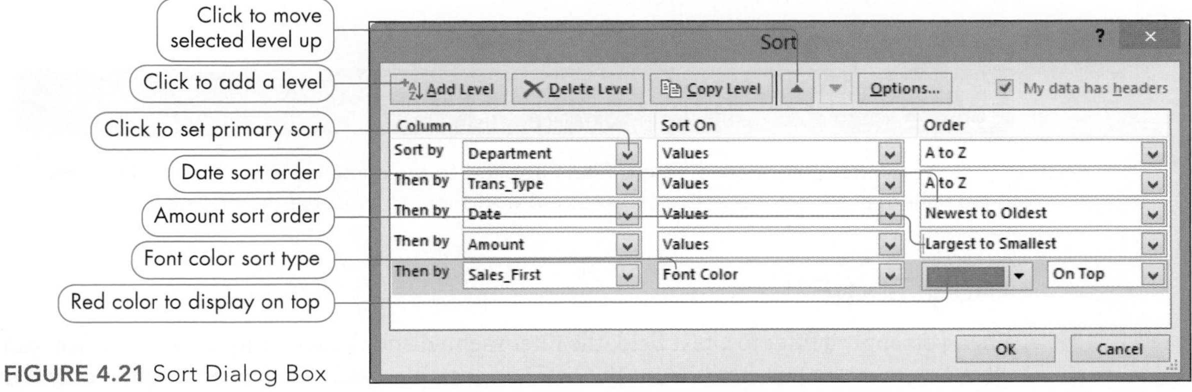

FIGURE 4.21 Sort Dialog Box

Create a Custom Sort

Excel arranges data in defined sequences, such as alphabetical order. For example, days of the week are sorted alphabetically: Friday, Monday, Saturday, Sunday, Thursday, Tuesday, and Wednesday. However, you might want to create a custom sort sequence. For example, you can create a custom sort to arrange days of the week in order from Sunday to Saturday.

To create a custom sort sequence:

1. Click Sort in the Sort & Filter group on the DATA tab.
2. Click the Order arrow and select Custom List to display the Custom Lists dialog box (see Figure 4.22).
3. Select an existing sort sequence in the *Custom lists* box, or select NEW LIST.
4. Click Add and type the entries in the desired sort sequence in the *List entries* box, pressing Enter between entries.
5. Click Add and click OK.

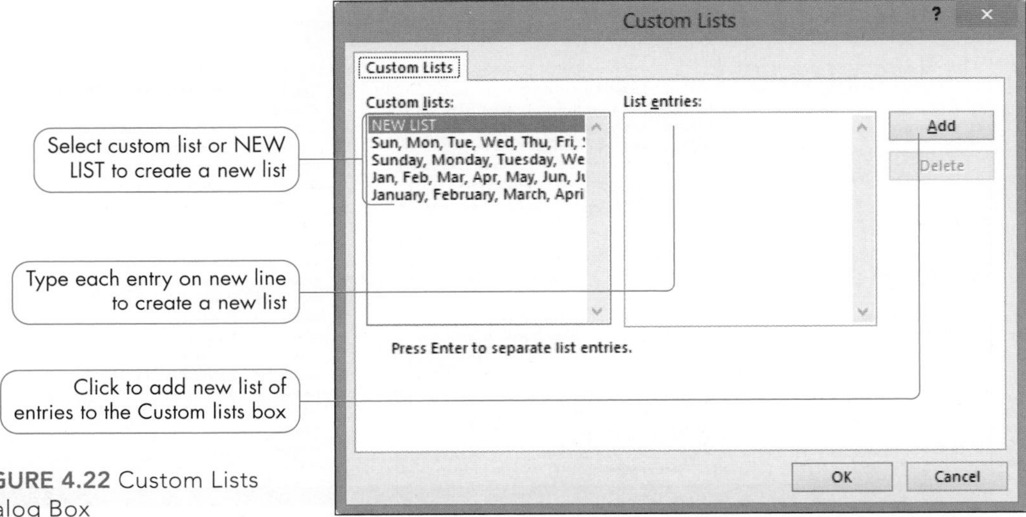

FIGURE 4.22 Custom Lists Dialog Box

Filtering Data

Filtering is the process of specifying conditions to display only those records that meet certain conditions. For example, you might want to filter the data to show transactions for only a particular sales representative. To filter records by a particular field, click the filter arrow for that field. The list displays each unique label, value, or date contained in the column. Deselect the (Select All) check box and click the check box for each value you want to include in the filtered results.

Often you will need to apply more than one filter to display the needed records. You can filter more than one field. Each additional filter is based on the current filtered data and further reduces a data subset. To apply multiple filters, click each field's filter arrow and select the values to include in the filtered data results.

Copying Before Filtering Data

Often, you need to show different filters applied to the same dataset. You can copy the worksheet and filter the data on the copied worksheet to preserve the original dataset.

Apply Text Filters

STEP 3»

When you apply a filter to a text field, the filter menu displays each unique text item. You can select one or more text items from the list. For example, select Gallagher to show only her records. To display records for both Gallagher and Sardelis, deselect the (Select All) check mark and click the Gallagher and Sardelis check boxes. You can also select Text Filters to see a submenu of additional options, such as *Begins With*, to select all records for which the name begins with the letter G, for example.

Figure 4.23 shows the Sales_Last filter menu with two names selected. Excel displays records for these two reps only. The records for the other sales reps are hidden but not deleted. The filter arrow displays a filter icon, indicating which field is filtered. Excel displays the row numbers in blue, indicating that you applied a filter. The missing row numbers indicate hidden rows of data. When you remove the filter, all the records display again.

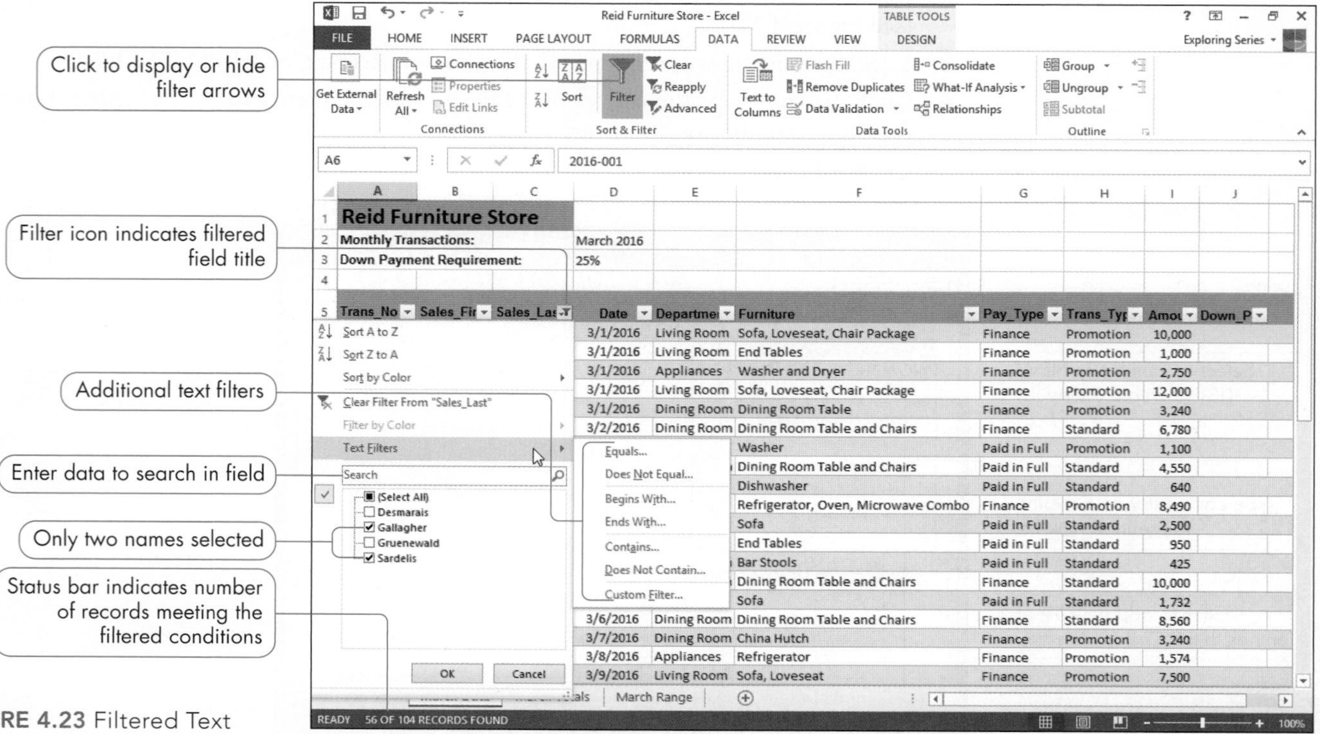

FIGURE 4.23 Filtered Text

TIP Filter Arrows

Click the Filter Button check box in the Table Style Options group on the Design tab to display or hide the filter arrows. For a range of data instead of a table, click Filter in the Sort & Filter group on the Data tab to display or hide the filter arrows.

Apply Number Filters

STEP 4

When you filter a field of numbers, you can select specific numbers. You might want to filter numbers by a range, such as numbers greater than $5,000 or numbers between $4,000 and $5,000. The submenu enables you to set a variety of number filters. In Figure 4.24, the amounts are filtered to show only those that are above the average amount. In this situation, Excel calculates the average amount as $4,512. Only records above that amount display.

If the field contains a large number of unique entries, you can click in the Search box and then type a value, text label, or date. Doing so narrows the visible list so that you do not have to scroll through the entire list. For example, if you enter $7, the list will display only values that start with $7.

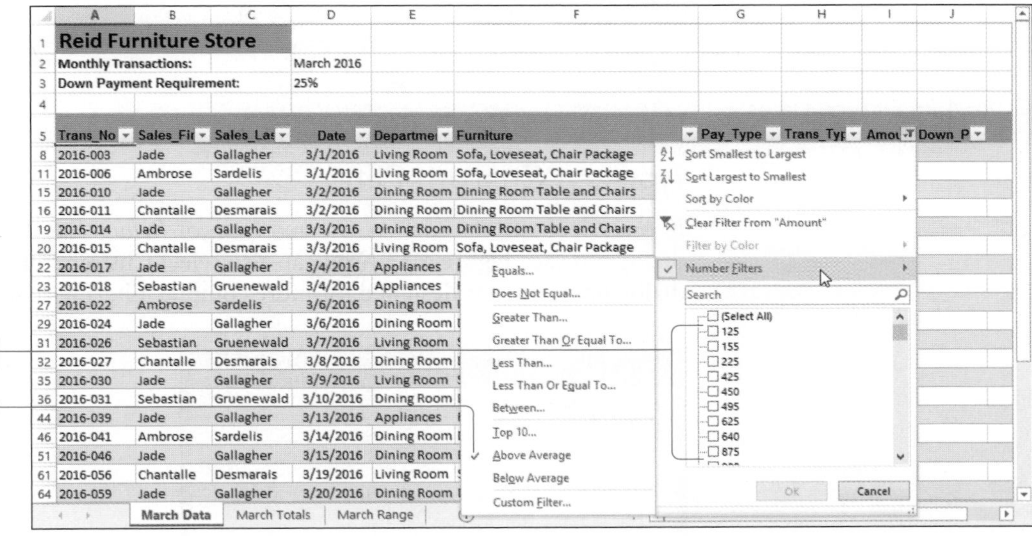

FIGURE 4.24 Filtered Numbers

The Top 10 option enables you to specify the top records. Although the option name is Top 10, you can specify the number or percentage of records to display. For example, you can filter the list to display only the top five or the bottom 7%. Figure 4.25 shows the Top 10 AutoFilter dialog box. Click the first arrow to select either Top or Bottom, click the spin arrows to indicate a value, and then click the last arrow to select either Items or Percent.

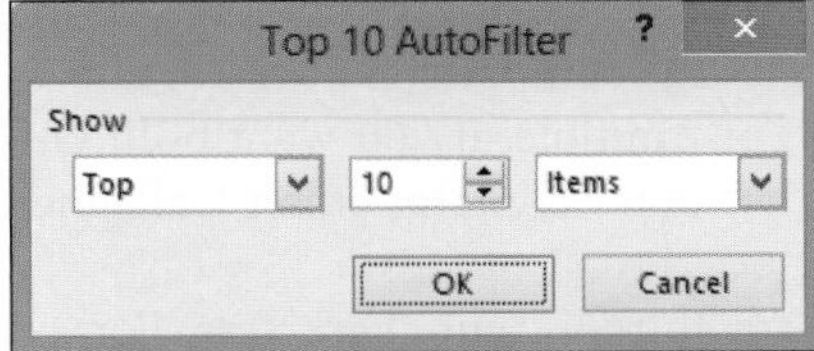

FIGURE 4.25 Top 10 AutoFilter Dialog Box

Apply Date Filters

STEP 5›› When you filter a field of dates, you can select specific dates or a date range, such as dates after 3/15/2016 or dates between 3/1/2016 and 3/7/2016. The submenu enables you to set a variety of date filters. For more specific date options, point to Date Filters, point to *All Dates in the Period*, and then select a period, such as Quarter 2 or October. Figure 4.26 shows the Date Filter menu.

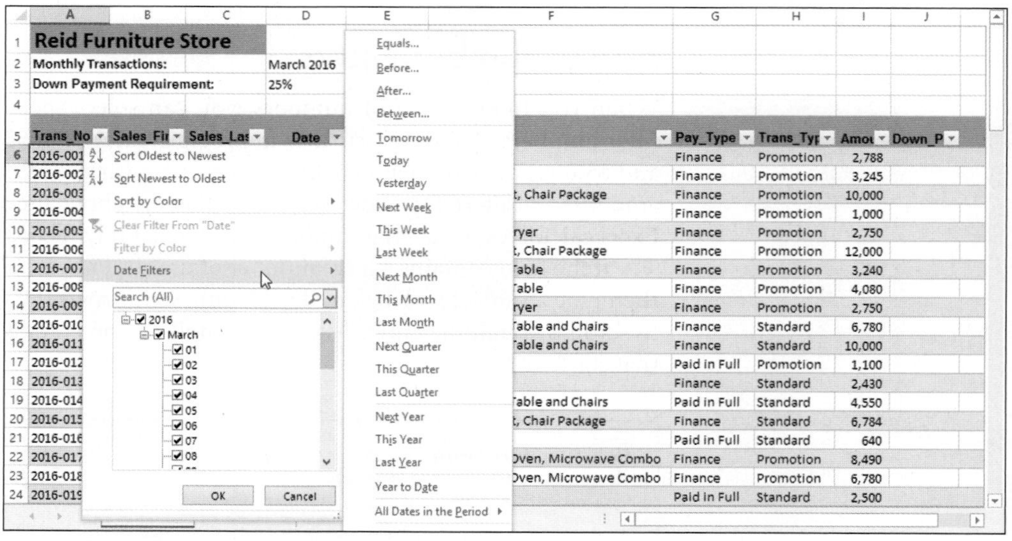

FIGURE 4.26 Filtered Dates

Apply a Custom Filter

If you select options such as *Greater Than* or *Before*, Excel displays the Custom AutoFilter dialog box (see Figure 4.27). You can also select Custom Filter from the menu to display this dialog box, which is designed for more complex filtering requirements.

Custom AutoFilter

Show rows where:

Amount

equals

And Or

Use ? to represent any single character

Use * to represent any series of characters

OK Cancel

FIGURE 4.27 Custom AutoFilter Dialog Box

The dialog box indicates the column being filtered. To set the filters, click the arrows to select the comparison type, such as equals or contains. Click the arrow on the right to select a specific text, value, or date entry, or type the data yourself. For ranges of dates or values, click And, and then specify the comparison operator and value or date for the next condition row. For text, click Or. For example, if you want both Gallagher and Desmarais, you must select Or because each data entry contains either Gallagher or Desmarais but not both at the same time.

You can use wildcards to represent characters. For example, to select all states starting with New, type *New* * in the second box to obtain results such as New York or New Mexico. The asterisk (*) represents any number of characters. If you want a wildcard for only a single character, type the question mark (?).

Clear Filters

You can remove the filters from one or more fields to expand the dataset again. To remove only one filter and keep the other filters, click the filter arrow for the field from which you wish to clear the filter and select Clear Filter From.

To remove all filters and display all records in a dataset, do one of the following:

- Click Filter in the Sort & Filter group on the DATA tab.
- Click Sort & Filter in the Editing group on the HOME tab and select Filter.

Quick Concepts

1. What is the purpose of sorting data in a table? ***p. 576***
2. What are two ways to arrange (sort) dates? ***p. 576***
3. List at least five ways you can filter numbers. ***p. 579***
4. Assume you are filtering a list and want to display records for people who live in Boston or New York. What settings do you enter in the Custom AutoFilter dialog box for that field? ***p. 580***

Hands-On Exercises

Watch the Video
for this Hands-
On Exercise!

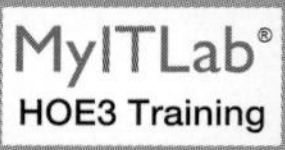
MyITLab®
HOE3 Training

3 Table Manipulation

You want to start analyzing the March 2016 transactions for Reid Furniture Store by sorting and filtering data in a variety of ways to help you understand the transactions better.

Skills covered: Sort One Field • Sort Multiple Fields • Apply Text Filters • Apply a Number Filter • Apply a Date Filter

STEP 1 ›› SORT ONE FIELD

First, you want to compare the number of transactions by sales rep, so you will sort the data by the Rep_Last field. After reviewing the transactions by sales reps, you want to arrange the transactions from the one with the largest purchase first to the smallest purchase last. Refer to Figure 4.28 as you complete Step 1.

Step b: Click to sort alphabetically by last name

Step c: Click to sort amount from largest to smallest

	A	B	C	D	E	F	G	H	I	J
5	Trans_No	Sales_Fir	Sales_Las	Date	Departme	Furniture	Pay_Type	Trans_Typ	Amou	Down_P
6	2016-073	Chantalle	Desmarais	3/24/2016	Living Room	Sofa, Loveseat, Chair Package	Finance	Standard	17,500	
7	2016-097	Sebastian	Gruenewald	3/29/2016	Bedroom	Bedroom Furniture Set	Finance	Standard	14,321	
8	2016-095	Sebastian	Gruenewald	3/29/2016	Living Room	Sofa, Loveseat, Chair Package	Finance	Standard	14,275	
9	2016-056	Chantalle	Desmarais	3/19/2016	Living Room	Sofa, Loveseat, Chair Package	Finance	Standard	12,500	
10	2016-070	Ambrose	Sardelis	3/23/2016	Living Room	Sofa, Loveseat, Chair Package	Finance	Promotion	12,500	
11	2016-041	Ambrose	Sardelis	3/14/2016	Dining Room	Dining Room Table and Chairs	Finance	Promotion	12,458	
12	2016-072	Ambrose	Sardelis	3/23/2016	Bedroom	Bedroom Furniture Set	Finance	Promotion	12,150	
13	2016-006	Ambrose	Sardelis	3/1/2016	Living Room	Sofa, Loveseat, Chair Package	Finance	Promotion	12,000	
14	2016-089	Ambrose	Sardelis	3/26/2016	Bedroom	Bedroom Furniture Set	Paid in Full	Standard	11,972	
15	2016-100	Chantalle	Desmarais	3/30/2016	Bedroom	Bedroom Furniture Set	Finance	Promotion	11,234	
16	2016-011	Chantalle	Desmarais	3/2/2016	Dining Room	Dining Room Table and Chairs	Finance	Standard	10,000	
17	2016-003	Jade	Gallagher	3/1/2016	Living Room	Sofa, Loveseat, Chair Package	Finance	Promotion	10,000	
18	2016-064	Sebastian	Gruenewald	3/21/2016	Appliances	Refrigerator, Oven, Microwave Combo	Finance	Promotion	10,000	
19	2016-022	Ambrose	Sardelis	3/6/2016	Dining Room	Dining Room Table and Chairs	Finance	Standard	10,000	
20	2016-060	Sebastian	Gruenewald	3/20/2016	Dining Room	Dining Room Table and Chairs	Finance	Standard	9,430	
21	2016-024	Jade	Gallagher	3/6/2016	Dining Room	Dining Room Table and Chairs	Finance	Standard	8,560	
22	2016-017	Jade	Gallagher	3/4/2016	Appliances	Refrigerator, Oven, Microwave Combo	Finance	Promotion	8,490	
23	2016-067	Jade	Gallagher	3/22/2016	Living Room	Sofa, Loveseat, Chair Package	Finance	Standard	8,400	
24	2016-086	Ambrose	Sardelis	3/26/2016	Bedroom	Bedroom Furniture Set	Paid in Full	Standard	8,340	
25	2016-091	Ambrose	Sardelis	3/27/2016	Bedroom	Bedroom Furniture Set	Finance	Standard	8,340	
26	2016-026	Sebastian	Gruenewald	3/7/2016	Living Room	Sofa, Loveseat	Paid in Full	Standard	7,690	
27	2016-059	Jade	Gallagher	3/20/2016	Dining Room	Dining Room Table and Chairs	Finance	Promotion	7,540	
28	2016-076	Sebastian	Gruenewald	3/24/2016	Bedroom	Bedroom Furniture Set	Finance	Promotion	7,525	
29	2016-061	Chantalle	Desmarais	3/21/2016	Appliances	Refrigerator, Oven, Microwave Combo	Finance	Promotion	7,500	

March Data | March Totals | March Range

FIGURE 4.28 Sorted Data

a. Open *e04h2Reid_LastFirst* if you closed it at the end of Hands-On Exercise 2. Save it as **e04h3Reid_LastFirst**, changing *h2* to *h3*.

b. Click the **Sales_Last filter arrow** and select **Sort A to Z**.

   Excel arranges the transactions in alphabetical order by last name, starting with Desmarais. Within each sales rep, records display in their original sequence by transaction number. If you scan the records, you can see that Gallagher completed the most sales transactions in March. The up arrow icon on the Sales_Last filter arrow indicates records are sorted in alphabetical order by that field.

TIP Name Sorts

Always check the data to determine how many levels of sorting you need to apply. If your table contains several people with the same last name but different first names, you would first sort by the Last Name field, then sort by First Name field. All the people with the last name Desmarais would be grouped together and further sorted by first name, such as Amanda and then Bradley.

c. Click the **Amount filter arrow** and select **Sort Largest to Smallest**. Save the workbook.

   The records are no longer sorted by Sales_Last. When you sort by another field, Excel arranges the data for that field. In this case, Excel arranges the transactions from the one with the largest amount to the smallest amount, indicated by the down arrow icon in the Amount filter arrow.

STEP 2 » SORT MULTIPLE FIELDS

You want to review the transactions by payment type (financed or paid in full). Within each payment type, you want to further compare the transaction type (promotion or standard). Finally, you want to compare costs within the sorted records by displaying the highest costs first. You will use the Sort dialog box to perform a three-level sort. Refer to Figure 4.29 as you complete Step 2.

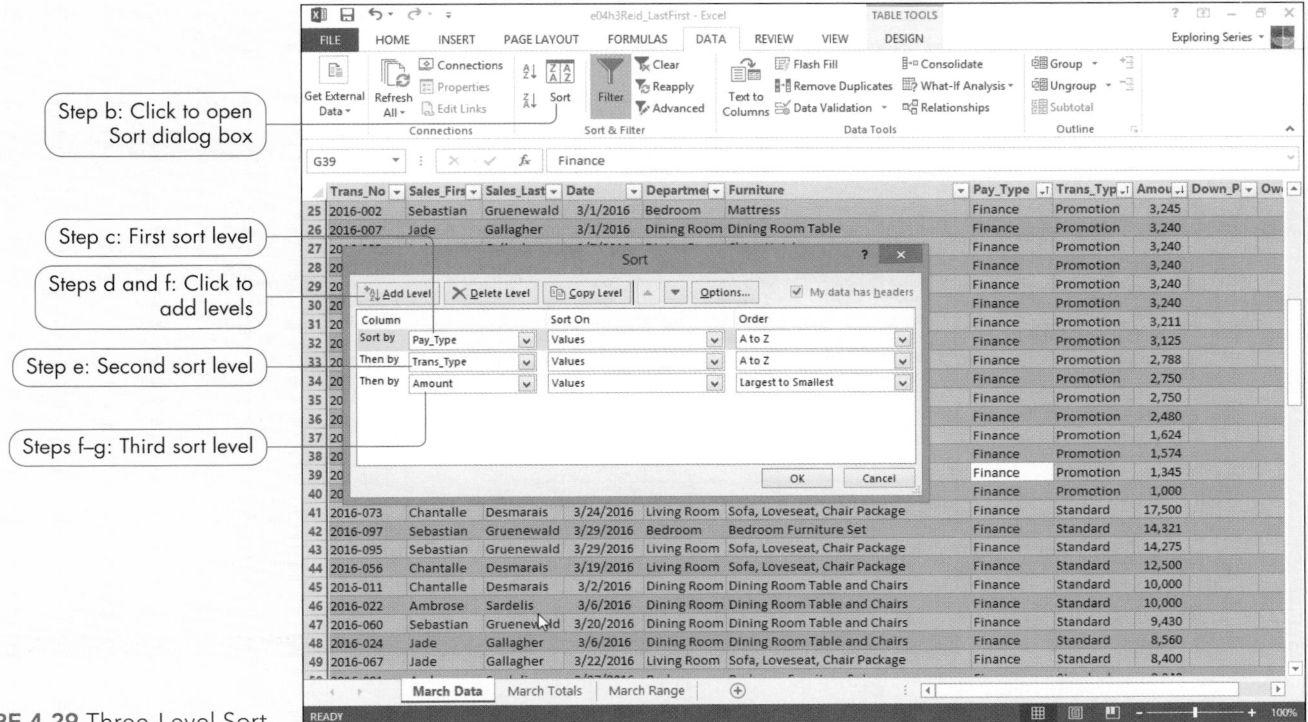

FIGURE 4.29 Three-Level Sort

a. Click inside the table and click the **DATA tab**.

   Both the DATA and HOME tabs contain commands to open the Sort dialog box.

b. Click **Sort** in the Sort & Filter group to open the Sort dialog box.

c. Click the **Sort by arrow** and select **Pay_Type**. Click the **Order arrow** and select **A to Z**.

   You start by specifying the column for the primary sort. In this case, you want to sort the records first by the Payment Type column.

d. Click **Add Level**.

   The Sort dialog box adds the *Then by* row, which adds a secondary sort.

e. Click the **Then by arrow** and select **Trans_Type**.

   The default order is A to Z, which will sort in alphabetical order by Trans_Type. Excel will first sort the records by the Pay_Type (Finance or Paid in Full). Within each Pay_Type, Excel will further sort records by Trans_Type (Promotion or Standard).

f. Click **Add Level** to add another *Then by* row. Click the second **Then by arrow** and select **Amount**.

g. Click the **Order arrow** for the Amount sort and select **Largest to Smallest**.

Within the Pay_Type and Trans_Type sorts, this will arrange the records with the largest amount first in descending order to the smallest amount.

h. Click **OK** and scroll through the records. Save the workbook.

Most customers finance their purchases instead of paying in full. For the financed transactions, more than half were promotional sales. For merchandise paid in full, a majority of the transactions were standard sales, indicating that people with money don't necessarily wait for a promotional sale to purchase merchandise.

STEP 3 » APPLY TEXT FILTERS

Now that you know Jade Gallagher had the most transactions for March, you will filter the table to focus on her sales. You notice that she sells more merchandise from the Dining Room department, so you will filter out the other departments. Refer to Figure 4.30 as you complete Step 3.

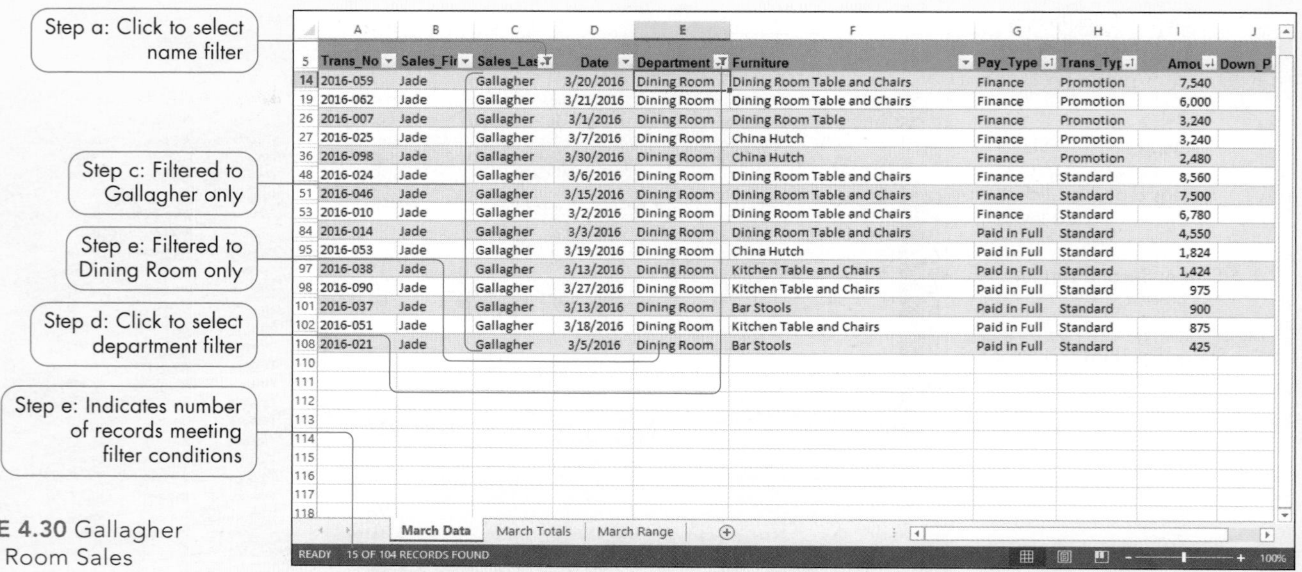

5	Trans_No	Sales_Fir	Sales_Las	Date	Department	Furniture	Pay_Type	Trans_Typ	Amou	Down_P
14	2016-059	Jade	Gallagher	3/20/2016	Dining Room	Dining Room Table and Chairs	Finance	Promotion	7,540	
19	2016-062	Jade	Gallagher	3/21/2016	Dining Room	Dining Room Table and Chairs	Finance	Promotion	6,000	
26	2016-007	Jade	Gallagher	3/1/2016	Dining Room	Dining Room Table	Finance	Promotion	3,240	
27	2016-025	Jade	Gallagher	3/7/2016	Dining Room	China Hutch	Finance	Promotion	3,240	
36	2016-098	Jade	Gallagher	3/30/2016	Dining Room	China Hutch	Finance	Promotion	2,480	
48	2016-024	Jade	Gallagher	3/6/2016	Dining Room	Dining Room Table and Chairs	Finance	Standard	8,560	
51	2016-046	Jade	Gallagher	3/15/2016	Dining Room	Dining Room Table and Chairs	Finance	Standard	7,500	
53	2016-010	Jade	Gallagher	3/2/2016	Dining Room	Dining Room Table and Chairs	Finance	Standard	6,780	
84	2016-014	Jade	Gallagher	3/3/2016	Dining Room	Dining Room Table and Chairs	Paid in Full	Standard	4,550	
95	2016-053	Jade	Gallagher	3/19/2016	Dining Room	China Hutch	Paid in Full	Standard	1,824	
97	2016-038	Jade	Gallagher	3/13/2016	Dining Room	Kitchen Table and Chairs	Paid in Full	Standard	1,424	
98	2016-090	Jade	Gallagher	3/27/2016	Dining Room	Kitchen Table and Chairs	Paid in Full	Standard	975	
101	2016-037	Jade	Gallagher	3/13/2016	Dining Room	Bar Stools	Paid in Full	Standard	900	
102	2016-051	Jade	Gallagher	3/18/2016	Dining Room	Kitchen Table and Chairs	Paid in Full	Standard	875	
108	2016-021	Jade	Gallagher	3/5/2016	Dining Room	Bar Stools	Paid in Full	Standard	425	

FIGURE 4.30 Gallagher Dining Room Sales

a. Click the **Sales_Last filter arrow**.

The (Select All) check box is selected.

b. Click the **(Select All) check box** to deselect all last names.

c. Click the **Gallagher check box** and click **OK**.

The status bar indicates that 33 out of 104 records meet the filtering condition. The Sales_Last filter arrow includes a funnel icon, indicating that this column is filtered.

d. Click the **Department filter arrow**.

e. Click the **(Select All) check box** to deselect all departments, click the **Dining Room check box** to focus on that department, and then click **OK**. Save the workbook.

The remaining 15 records show Gallagher's dining room sales for the month. The Department filter arrow includes a funnel icon, indicating that this column is also filtered.

STEP 4 » APPLY A NUMBER FILTER

Vicki is considering giving a bonus to employees who sold the high-end dining room furniture during a specific time period (3/16/2016 to 3/31/2016). You want to determine if Jade Gallagher qualifies for this bonus. In particular, you are interested in how much gross revenue she generated for dining room furniture that cost at least $5,000 or more. Refer to Figure 4.31 as you complete Step 4.

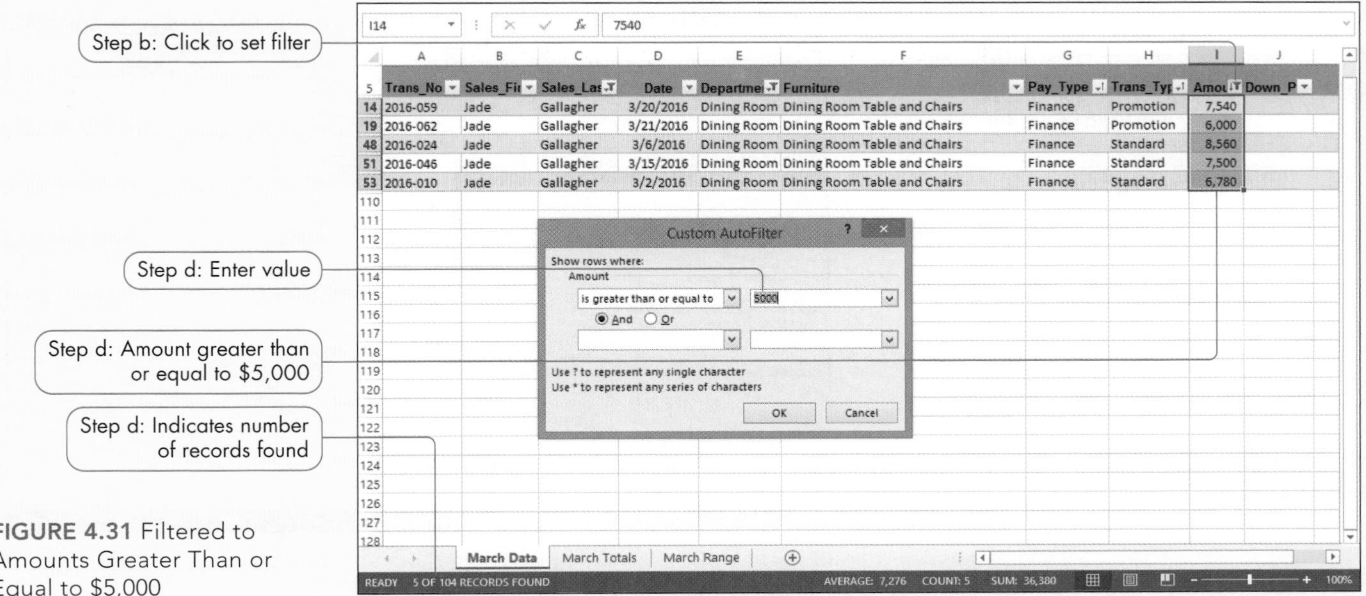

FIGURE 4.31 Filtered to Amounts Greater Than or Equal to $5,000

a. Select the **range I14:I108** of the filtered list and then view the status bar.

The average transaction amount is $3,754 with 15 transactions (i.e., 15 filtered records).

b. Click the **Amount filter arrow**.

c. Point to **Number Filters** and select **Greater Than Or Equal To**.

The Custom AutoFilter dialog box opens. The default comparison *is greater than or equal to* is displayed.

d. Type **5000** in the box to the right of *is greater than or equal to* and click **OK**. Save the workbook.

When typing numbers, you can type raw numbers such as 5000 or formatted numbers such as $5,000. Out of Gallagher's original 15 dining room transactions, only 5 transactions (one-third of her sales) were valued at $5,000 or more.

> **TROUBLESHOOTING:** If no records display or if too many records display, you might have entered 500000 or 500. Repeat steps b through d.

STEP 5 » APPLY A DATE FILTER

Finally, you want to study Jade Gallagher's sales records for the last half of the month. You will add a date filter to identify those sales records. Refer to Figure 4.32 as you complete Step 5.

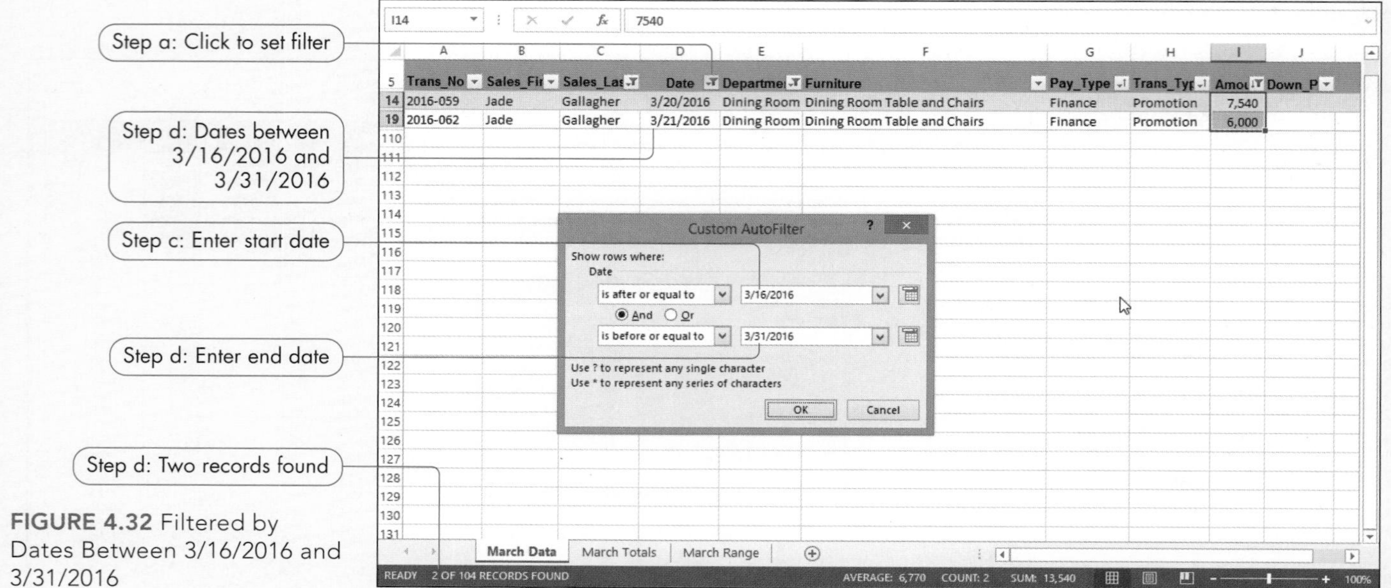

FIGURE 4.32 Filtered by Dates Between 3/16/2016 and 3/31/2016

a. Click the **Date filter arrow**.

b. Point to **Date Filters** and select **Between**.

The Custom AutoFilter dialog box opens. The default comparisons are *is after or equal to* and *is before or equal to*, ready for you to enter the date specifications.

c. Type **3/16/2016** in the box on the right side of *is after or equal to*.

You specified the starting date of the range of dates to include. You will keep the *And* option selected.

d. Type **3/31/2016** in the box on the right side of *is before or equal to*. Click **OK**.

Gallagher had only two dining room sales greater than $5,000 during the last half of March.

e. Save the workbook. Keep the workbook onscreen if you plan to continue with the next Hands-On Exercise. If not, close the workbook and exit Excel.

Table Aggregation

In addition to sorting and filtering tables to analyze the data, you might want to add fields that perform calculations using existing fields. For example, you might want to calculate a required down payment on the amount purchased. Furthermore, you might want to perform aggregate calculations, such as AVERAGE, for a field of numeric data.

In this section, you will learn how to insert structured references to build formulas within a table. In addition, you will learn how to add a row at the end of the table to display basic statistical calculations.

Using Structured References and a Total Row

Excel aids you in quantitative analysis. Your value to an organization increases with your ability to create sophisticated formulas, aggregate data in a meaningful way, and interpret those results. Although you can create complex formulas that you understand, you should strive to create formulas that other people can understand. Creating easy-to-read formulas helps you present self-documenting formulas that require less explanation on your part. When you create formulas for tables, you can use built-in functionality (such as structured references and a total row) that assists you in building understandable formulas.

Create Structured References in Formulas

Your experience in building formulas involves using cell references, such as =SUM(B1:B15) or =H6*$B$3, or range names, such as grades in =VLOOKUP(E5,grades,2). You can use cell references and range names in formulas to perform calculations in a table, as well as another type of reference for formulas in tables: structured references. A ***structured reference*** is a tag or use of a table element, such as a field heading, as a reference in a formula. Structured references in formulas clearly indicate which type of data is used in the calculations.

STEP 1

A structured reference requires brackets around column headings or field names, such as =[Amount]−[Down_Pay]. The use of field headings without row references in a structured formula is called an *unqualified reference*. Formula AutoComplete displays a list of field headings after you type the equal sign and the opening bracket (see Figure 4.33). Type or double-click the column name from the list and type the closing bracket. Excel displays a colored border around the referenced column. When you enter a formula using structured references, Excel copies the formula down the rest of the table column automatically, compared to typing references in formulas and manually copying the formula down a column.

Type =[to start structured reference

Formula AutoComplete displays field names

	Date	Departmen	Furniture	Pay_Type	Trans_Type	Amou	Down_P	Owed
98	3/28/2016	Bedroom	Mattress	Paid in Full	Standard	2,000	=[	
99	3/28/2016	Bedroom	Mattress	Paid in Full	Promotion	3,245	Trans_No	
100	3/29/2016	Living Room	Sofa, Loveseat, Chair Package	Finance	Standard	14,275	Sales_First	
101	3/29/2016	Bedroom	Bedroom Furniture Set	Finance	Promotion	3,285	Sales_Last	
102	3/29/2016	Bedroom	Bedroom Furniture Set	Finance	Standard	14,321	Date	
103	3/30/2016	Dining Room	China Hutch	Finance	Promotion	2,480	Department	
104	3/30/2016	Bedroom	Mattress	Finance	Standard	1,425	Furniture, Pay_Type	
105	3/30/2016	Bedroom	Bedroom Furniture Set	Finance	Promotion	11,234	Trans_Type	
106	3/31/2016	Bedroom	Bedroom Furniture Set	Finance	Promotion	5,773	Amount	
107	3/31/2016	Bedroom	Mattress	Paid in Full	Promotion	2,000	Down_Pay	
108	3/31/2016	Living Room	End Tables	Finance	Standard	2,505	Owed	
109	3/31/2016	Appliances	Refrigerator	Paid in Full	Standard	1,500		

FIGURE 4.33 Structured Reference Creation

You can also use the semiselection process to create a formula. As you point to cells to enter a formula in a table, Excel builds a formula like this: =[@Amount]−[@Down_Pay], where the @ indicates the current row. If you use the semiselection process to create a formula outside the table, the formula includes the table and field names, such as =Table1 [@Amount]−Table1[@Down_Pay]. Table1 is the name of the table; Amount and Down_Pay are field names. This structured formula that includes references, such as table numbers, is called a *fully qualified structured reference*. When you build formulas *within* a table, you can use either unqualified or fully qualified structured references. If you need to use table data in a formula *outside* the table boundaries, you must use fully qualified structured references.

Add a Total Row

At times, aggregating data provides more meaningful quantitative interpretation than individual values. For regular ranges of data, you use basic statistical functions, such as SUM, AVERAGE, MIN, and MAX, to provide meaning for a dataset. An Excel table provides the advantage of being able to display a total row automatically without creating the aggregate function yourself. A ***total row*** displays below the last row of records in an Excel table and enables you to display summary statistics, such as a sum of values displayed in a column.

To display and use the total row:

STEP 2

1. Click the DESIGN tab.
2. Click Total Row in the Table Style Options group. Excel displays the total row below the last record in the table. Excel displays *Total* in the first column of the total row. Excel either sums or counts data for the last field, depending on the type of data stored in that field. If the last field consists of values, Excel sums the values. If the last field is text, Excel counts the number of records.
3. Click a cell in the total row, click that cell's total row arrow, and then select the function results that you desire. To add a summary statistic to another column, click in the empty cell for that field in the total row and click the arrow to select the desired function. Select None to remove the function.

Figure 4.34 shows the active total row with totals applied to the Amount, Down_Pay, and Owed fields. A list of functions displays to change the function for the last field.

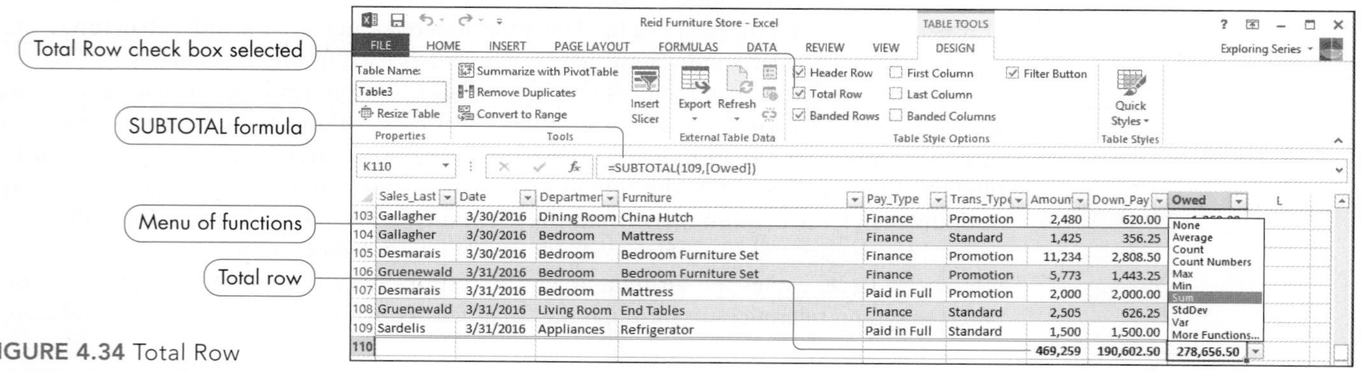

FIGURE 4.34 Total Row

TIP Filtering Data and Subtotals

If you filter the data and display the total row, the SUBTOTAL function's 109 argument ensures that only the displayed data are summed; data for hidden rows are not calculated in the aggregate function.

The calculations on the total row use the SUBTOTAL function. The ***SUBTOTAL function*** calculates an aggregate value, such as totals or averages, for values in a range or database. If you click in a calculated total row cell, the SUBTOTAL function displays in the Formula Bar. The function for the total row looks like this: =SUBTOTAL(function_num,ref1). The function_num argument is a number that represents a function (see Table 4.4). The ref1 argument indicates the range of values to calculate. The SUBTOTAL function to total the values in the Owed field would be =SUBTOTAL(109,[Owed]), where the number 109 represents the SUM function, and [Owed] represents the Owed field. A benefit of the SUBTOTAL function is that it subtotals data for filtered records, so you have an accurate total for the visible records.

```
=SUBTOTAL(function_num,ref1,...)
```

TABLE 4.4 SUBTOTAL Function Numbers

Function	Database Number	Table Number
AVERAGE	1	101
COUNT	2	102
COUNTA	3	103
MAX	4	104
MIN	5	105
PRODUCT	6	106
STDEV	7	107
STDEVP	8	108
SUM	9	109
VAR	10	110
VARP	11	111

1. What is a structured reference? What is the general format for including a field name in a formula? Give an example. ***p. 587***
2. What are the benefits of displaying a total row and selecting functions instead of adding functions yourself below a table? ***p. 588***

Hands-On Exercises

4 Table Aggregation

You further analyze the March 2016 transactions for Reid Furniture Store: You want to calculate the required down payment amount and how much customers owe for their purchases. Finally, you will convert the table back to a range.

Skills covered: Create Structured References in Formulas • Add a Total Row • Convert a Table to a Range

STEP 1 » CREATE STRUCTURED REFERENCES IN FORMULAS

To continue reviewing the March transactions, you need to calculate the required down payment for customers who financed their purchases. The required down payment is located above the table data so that you can change that value if needed. In addition, you want to calculate how much customers owe on their purchases if they did not pay in full. You will use structured formulas to perform these calculations. Refer to Figure 4.35 as you complete Step 1.

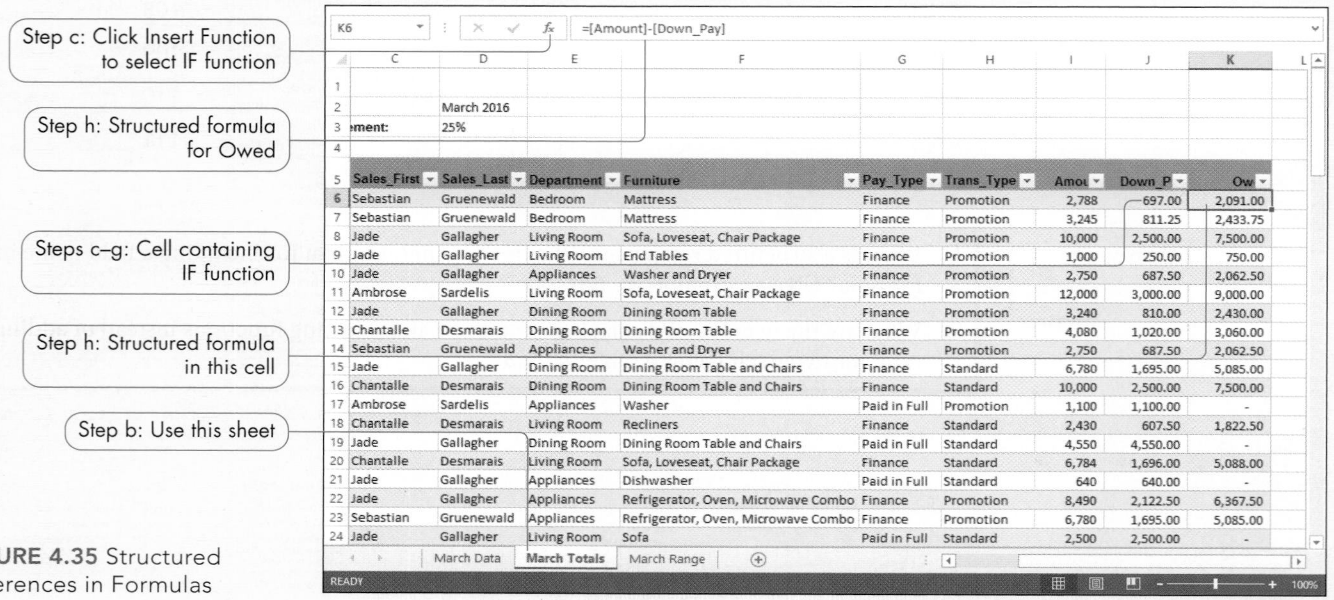

FIGURE 4.35 Structured References in Formulas

a. Open *e04h3Reid_LastFirst* if you closed it at the end of Hands-On Exercise 3. Save it as **e04h4Reid_LastFirst**, changing *h3* to *h4*.

b. Click the **March Totals worksheet tab** and make **cell J6** the active cell.

   To preserve the integrity of the sorting and filtering in case your instructor wants to verify your work, you will continue with an identical dataset on another worksheet.

c. Click **Insert Function** to open the Insert Function dialog box, select **IF** in the **Select a function list**, and then click **OK**.

d. Type **[Pay_Type]="Paid in Full"** in the **Logical_test box**.

   The logical test evaluates whether a customer paid in full, indicated in the Pay_Type field. Remember to type the brackets around the column label.

e. Type **[Amount]** in the **Value_if_true box**.

   If a customer pays in full, the down payment is the full amount.

f. Type **[Amount]*$D$3** in the **Value_if_false box.**

If a customer does not pay in full, he or she must pay a required down payment. You use [Amount] to refer to the Amount field in the table. Enclose the field labels in brackets. The amount is multiplied by the absolute reference to D3, the cell containing the required down payment percentage. Make this cell reference absolute so that it does not change when Excel copies the formula down the Down_Pay column.

g. Click **OK** to enter the formula.

The formula looks like this in the Formula Bar: =IF([Pay_Type]= "Paid in Full",[Amount],[Amount]*$D$3). Because you are entering formulas in a table, Excel copies the formula down the column automatically. The first customer must pay a $697 down payment (25% of $2,788). The columns in the current worksheet have been formatted as Comma Style for you.

> **TROUBLESHOOTING:** If the results seem incorrect, check your function. Errors will result if you do not enclose the field names in brackets, if you have misspelled a field name, if you omit the quotation marks around *Paid in Full*, and so on. Correct any errors.

h. Click **cell K6**. Type the formula =**[Amount]–[Down_Pay]** and press **Enter**. Save the workbook.

The formula calculates how much customers owe if they finance their purchases. Excel copies the formula down the column.

STEP 2 ADD A TOTAL ROW

You want to see the monthly totals for the Amount, Down_Pay, and Owed columns. Instead of entering SUM functions yourself, you will add a total row. Refer to Figure 4.36 as you complete Step 2.

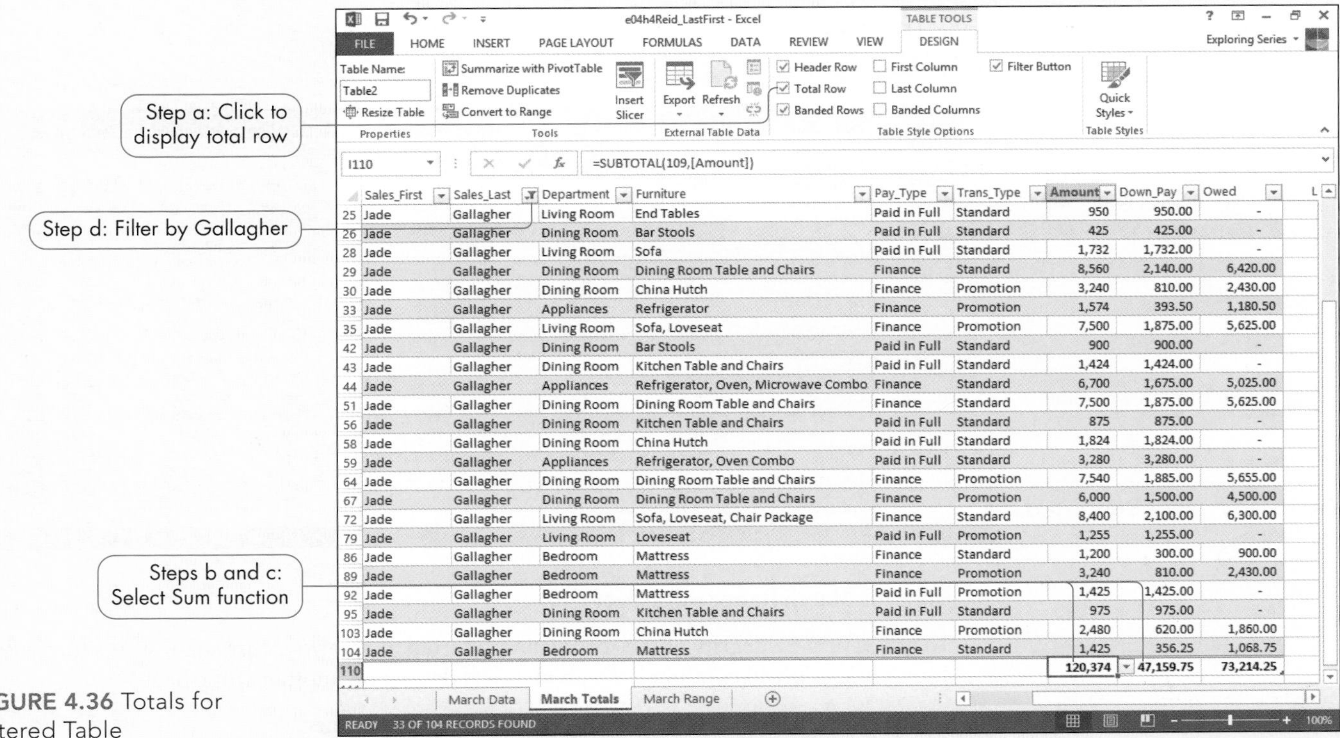

FIGURE 4.36 Totals for Filtered Table

a. Click the **DESIGN tab** and click **Total Row** in the Table Style Options group.

Excel displays the total row after the last record. It sums the last field of values automatically. The total amount customers owe is $278,656.50.

b. Click the **Down_Pay cell** in row 110, click the **total arrow**, and then select **Sum**.

You added a total to the Down_Pay field. The total amount of down payment collected is $190,602.50. The formula displays as =SUBTOTAL(109,[Down_Pay]) in the Formula Bar.

c. Click the **Amount cell** in row 110, click the **total arrow**, and then select **Sum**.

You added a total to the Amount column. The total amount of merchandise sales is $469,259. The formula displays as =SUBTOTAL(109,[Amount]) in the Formula Bar.

d. Filter by Gallagher again. Save the workbook.

The total row values change to display the totals for only Gallagher: $120,374 (Amount), 47,159.75 (Down_Pay), and 73,214.25 (Owed). This is an advantage of using the Total Row, which uses the SUBTOTAL function, as opposed to if you had inserted the SUM function manually. The SUM function would provide a total for all data in the column, not just the filtered data.

STEP 3 » CONVERT A TABLE TO A RANGE

Your last task for now is to convert a copy of the table to a range again so that you can apply other formats. Refer to Figure 4.37 as you complete Step 3.

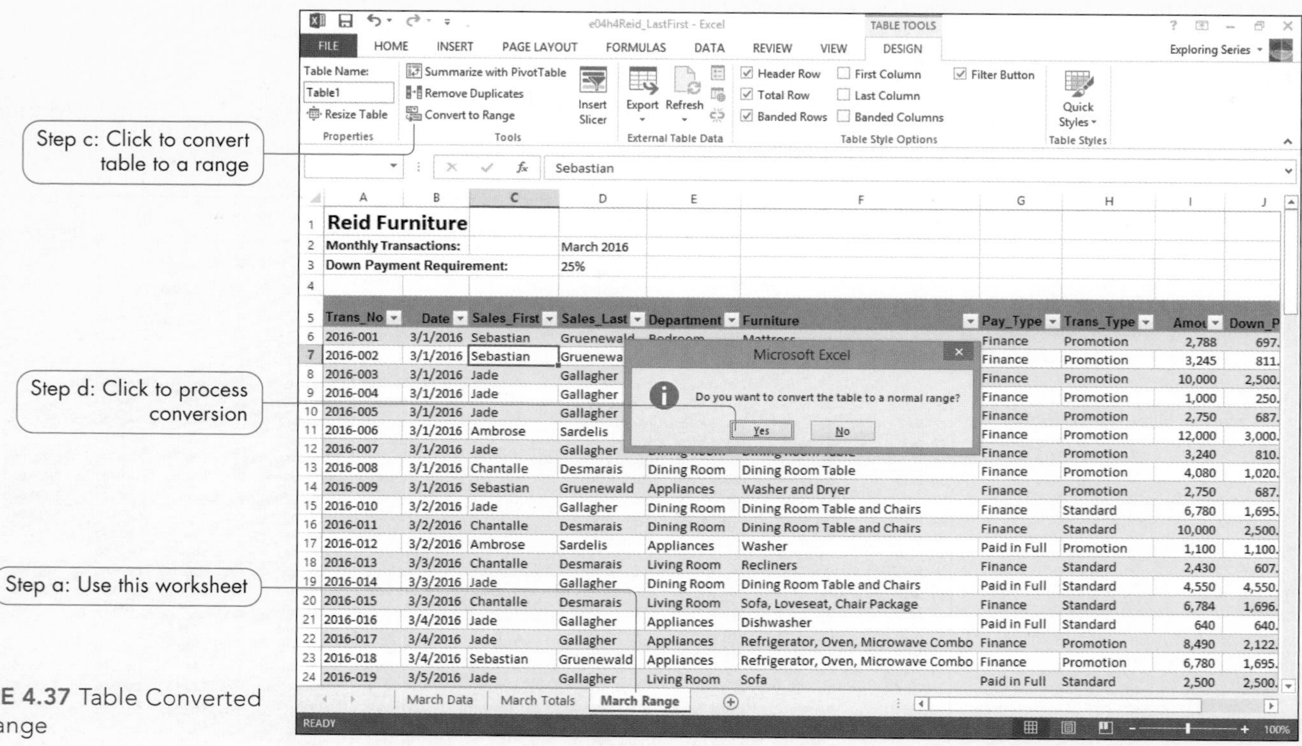

FIGURE 4.37 Table Converted to a Range

a. Click the **March Range worksheet tab**.

To preserve the integrity of the sorting and filtering in case your instructor wants to verify your work, you will continue with an identical dataset on another worksheet.

b. Click within the table and click the **DESIGN tab**, if necessary.

c. Click **Convert to Range** in the Tools group.

Excel displays a message box asking if you want to convert the table to a range.

d. Click **Yes**.

Excel converts the table to a range. The filter arrows disappear, and the Design tab no longer displays. The range is still formatted using a table style. The structured formula =[Amount]-[Down_Pay] in cell K6 changes to ='March Range'!$I$6:$I$109-'March Range'!$J$6:$J$109.

e. Save the workbook. Keep the workbook onscreen if you plan to continue with the next Hands-On Exercise. If not, close the workbook and exit Excel.

Conditional Formatting

You use table styles, or a variety of font, alignment, and number formats on the Home tab, to format a worksheet. You can also apply special formatting to cells that contain particular values or text using conditional formatting. ***Conditional formatting*** applies special formatting to highlight or emphasize cells that meet specific conditions. For example, a sales manager might want to highlight cells containing the top 10 sales amounts, or a professor might want to highlight test scores that fall below the average. You can also apply conditional formatting to point out data for a specific date or duplicate values in a range.

In this section, you will learn about the five conditional formatting categories and how to apply conditional formatting to a range of values based on a condition you set.

Applying Conditional Formatting

Conditional formatting helps you and your audience understand a dataset better because it adds a visual element to the cells. The term is called *conditional* because the formatting occurs when a condition is met. This is similar logic to the IF function you have used. Remember with an IF function, you create a logical test that is evaluated. If the logical or conditional test is true, the function produces one result. If the logical or conditional test is false, the function produces another result. With conditional formatting, if the condition is true, Excel formats the cell automatically based on that condition. If the condition is false, Excel does not format the cell. If you change a value in a conditionally formatted cell, Excel examines the new value to see if it should apply the conditional format.

Apply Conditional Formatting with the Quick Analysis Tool

When you select a range and click the Quick Analysis button, the FORMATTING options display in the Quick Analysis gallery. Position the mouse over a thumbnail to see how it will affect the selected range (see Figure 4.38). You can also apply conditional formatting by clicking Conditional Formatting in the Styles group on the Home tab.

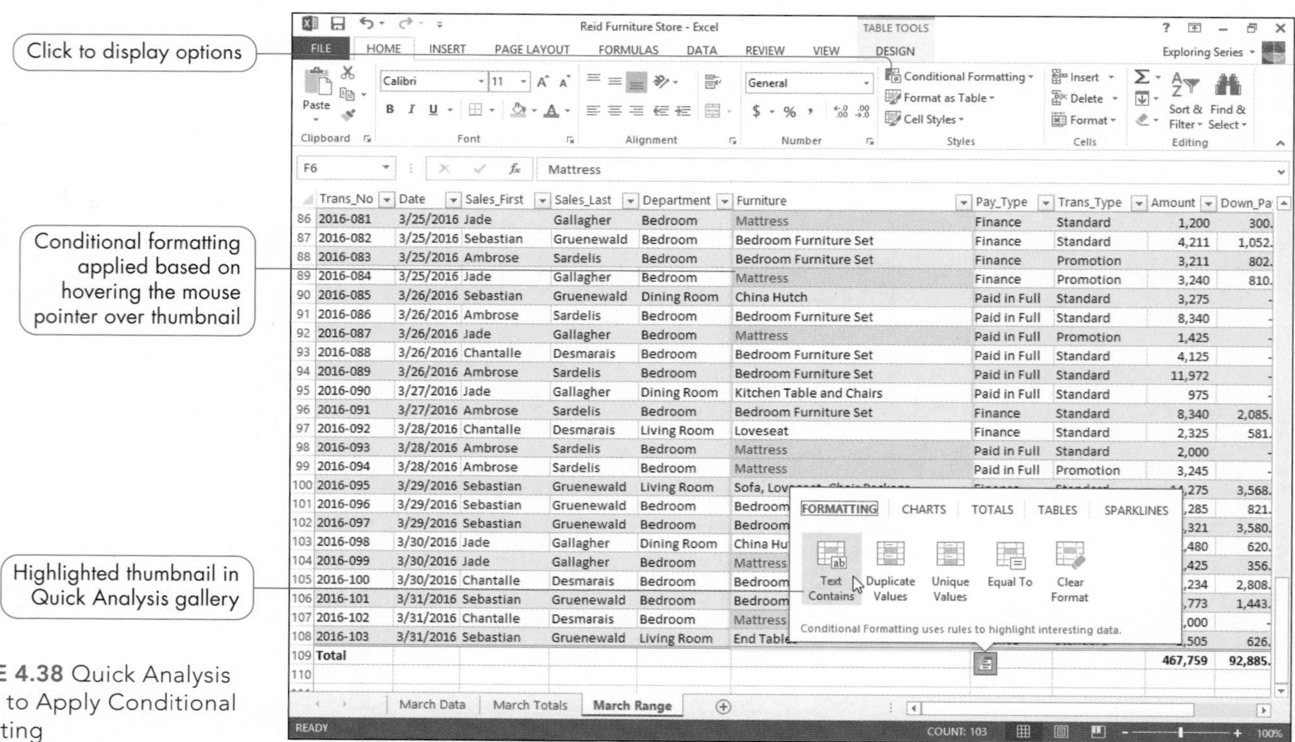

FIGURE 4.38 Quick Analysis Gallery to Apply Conditional Formatting

Table 4.5 describes the conditional formatting options in the Quick Analysis gallery.

TABLE 4.5 Conditional Formatting Options in Quick Analysis Gallery

Options	Description
Text Contains	Formats cells that contain the text in the first selected cell. In Figure 4.38, the first selected cell contains Mattress. If a cell contains Mattress and Springs, Excel would format that cell also because it *contains* Mattress.
Duplicate Values	Formats cells that are duplicated in the selected range.
Unique Values	Formats cells that are unique; that is, no other cell in the selected range contains the same data.
Equal To	Formats cells that are exactly like the data contained in the first selected cell.
Clear Format	Removes the conditional formatting from the selected range.

Table 4.6 lists and describes a number of different conditional formats that you can apply if you want more specific rules.

TABLE 4.6 Conditional Formatting Options

Options	Description
Highlight Cells Rules	Highlights cells with a fill color, font color, or border (such as Light Red Fill with Dark Red Text) if values are greater than, less than, between two values, equal to a value, or duplicate values; text that contains particular characters; or dates when a date meets a particular condition, such as *In the last 7 days*.
Top/Bottom Rules	Formats cells with values in the top 10 items, top 10%, bottom 10 items, bottom 10%, above average, or below average. You can change the exact values to format the top or bottom items or percentages, such as top 5 or bottom 15%.
Data Bars	Applies a gradient or solid fill bar in which the width of the bar represents the current cell's value compared to other cells' values.
Color Scales	Formats different cells with different colors, assigning one color to the lowest group of values and another color to the highest group of values, with gradient colors to other values.
Icon Sets	Inserts an icon from an icon palette in each cell to indicate values compared to each other.

To apply a conditional format, select the cells for which you want to apply a conditional format, click the Home tab, click Conditional Formatting in the Styles group, and then select the conditional formatting category you want to apply.

Apply the Highlight Cells Rules

STEP 1» The Highlight Cells Rules category enables you to apply a highlight to cells that meet a condition, such as a value greater than a particular value. This option contains predefined combinations of fill colors, font colors, and/or borders. This category is useful because it helps you identify and format automatically values of interest. For example, a weather tracker who developed a worksheet containing the temperatures for each day of a month might want to apply a conditional format to cells that contain temperatures between 70 and 75 degrees. To apply this conditional formatting, she would select Highlight Cells Rules and then select

Between. In the Between dialog box (see Figure 4.39), the weather tracker would type 70 in the *Format cells that are BETWEEN* box and 75 in the *and* box, select the type of conditional formatting, such as *Light Red Fill with Dark Red Text*, and then click OK to apply the formats.

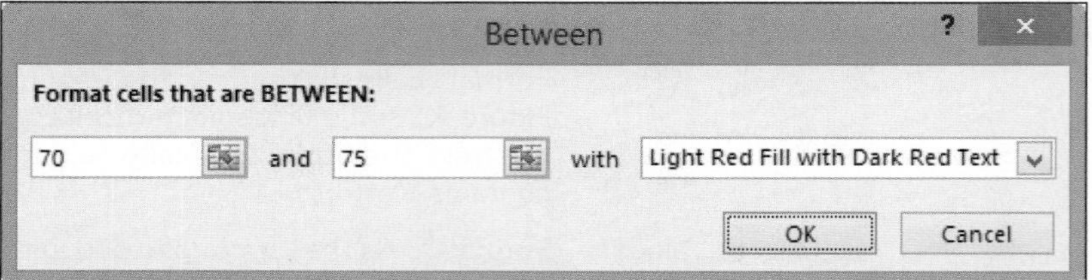

FIGURE 4.39 Between Dialog Box

Figure 4.40 shows two columns of data that contain conditional formats. The Department column is conditionally formatted to highlight text with a Light Red Fill with Dark Red Text for cells that contain *Living Room*, and the Amount column is conditionally formatted to highlight with Red Border values between $5,000 and $10,000.

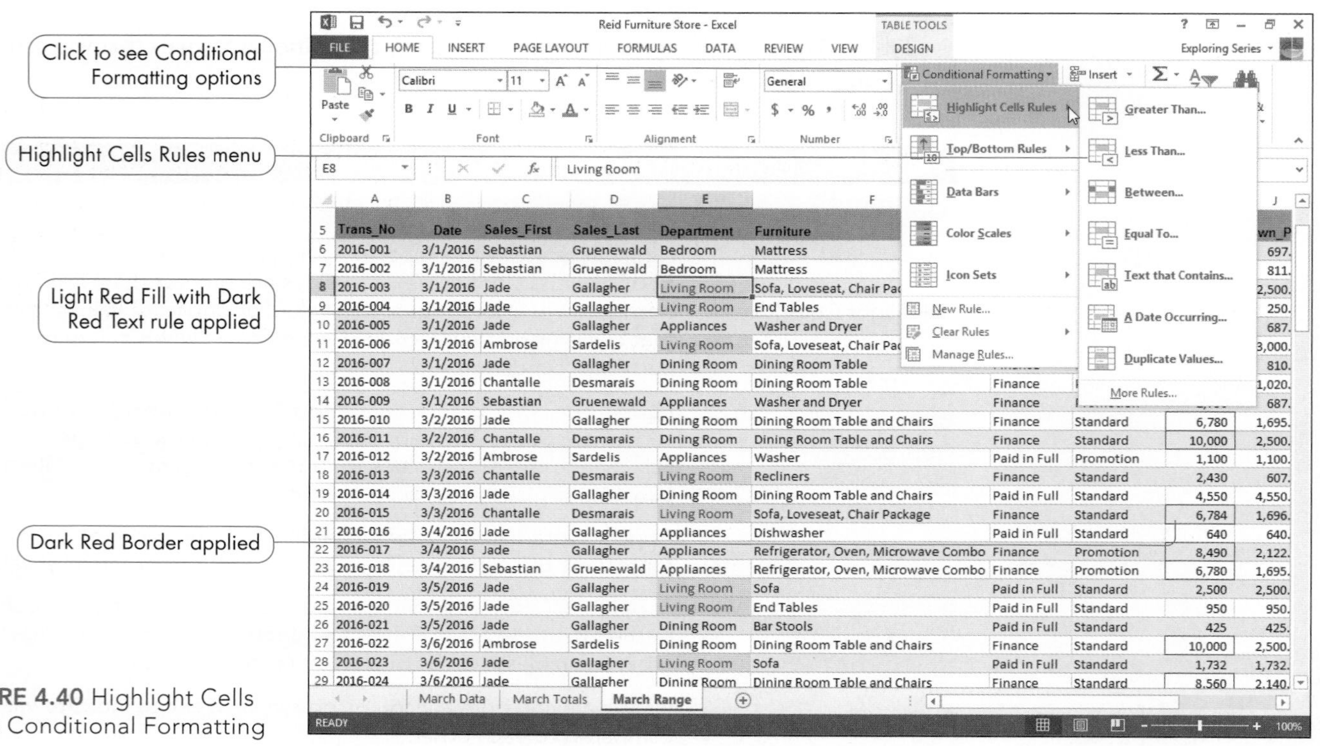

FIGURE 4.40 Highlight Cells Rules Conditional Formatting

Specify Top/Bottom Rules

STEP 2» You might be interested in identifying the top five sales to reward the sales associates, or want to identify the bottom 15% of automobile dealers so that you can close underperforming locations. The Top/Bottom Rules category enables you to specify the top or bottom number, top or bottom percentage, or values that are above or below the average value in that range. In Figure 4.41, the Amount column is conditionally formatted to highlight the top five amounts. (Some rows are hidden so that all top five values display in the figure.) Although the menu option is Top 10 Items, you can specify the exact number of items to format.

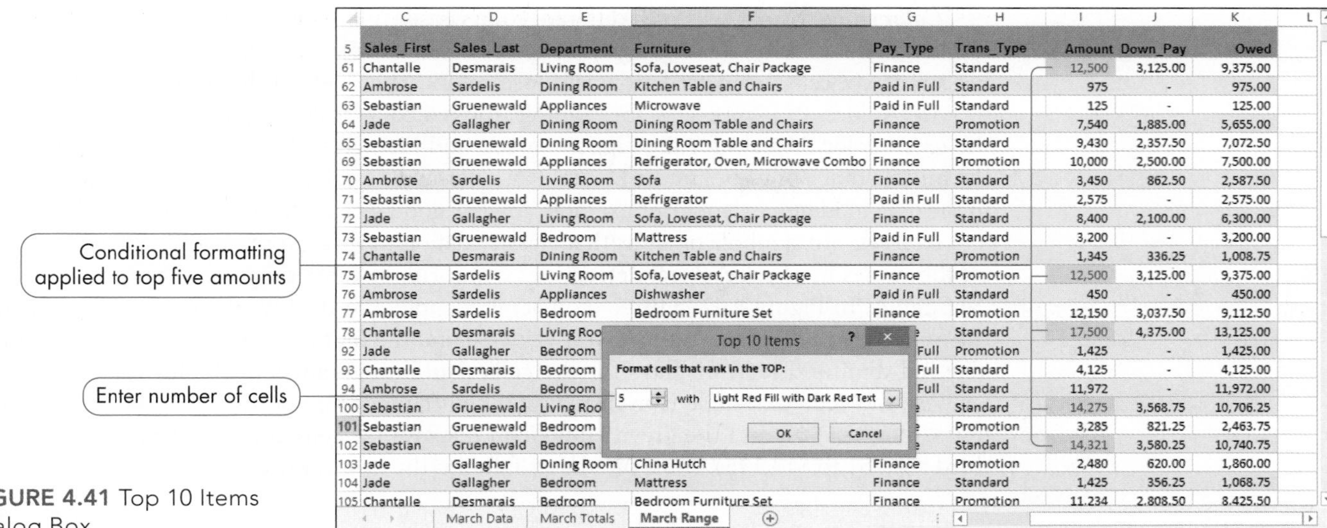

FIGURE 4.41 Top 10 Items Dialog Box

Display Data Bars, Color Scales, and Icon Sets

STEP 3»

Data bars indicate the value of a cell relative to other cells (see Figure 4.42). The width of the data bar represents the value in a cell, with a wider bar representing a higher value and a narrower bar a lower value. Use data bar conditional formatting to identify high and low values. Excel locates the largest value and displays the widest data bar in that cell. Excel then finds the smallest value and displays the smallest data bar in that cell. Excel sizes the data bars for the remaining cells based on their values relative to the high and low values in the column. If you change the values, Excel updates the data bar widths. Excel uses the same color for each data bar, but each bar differs in size based on the value in the respective cells.

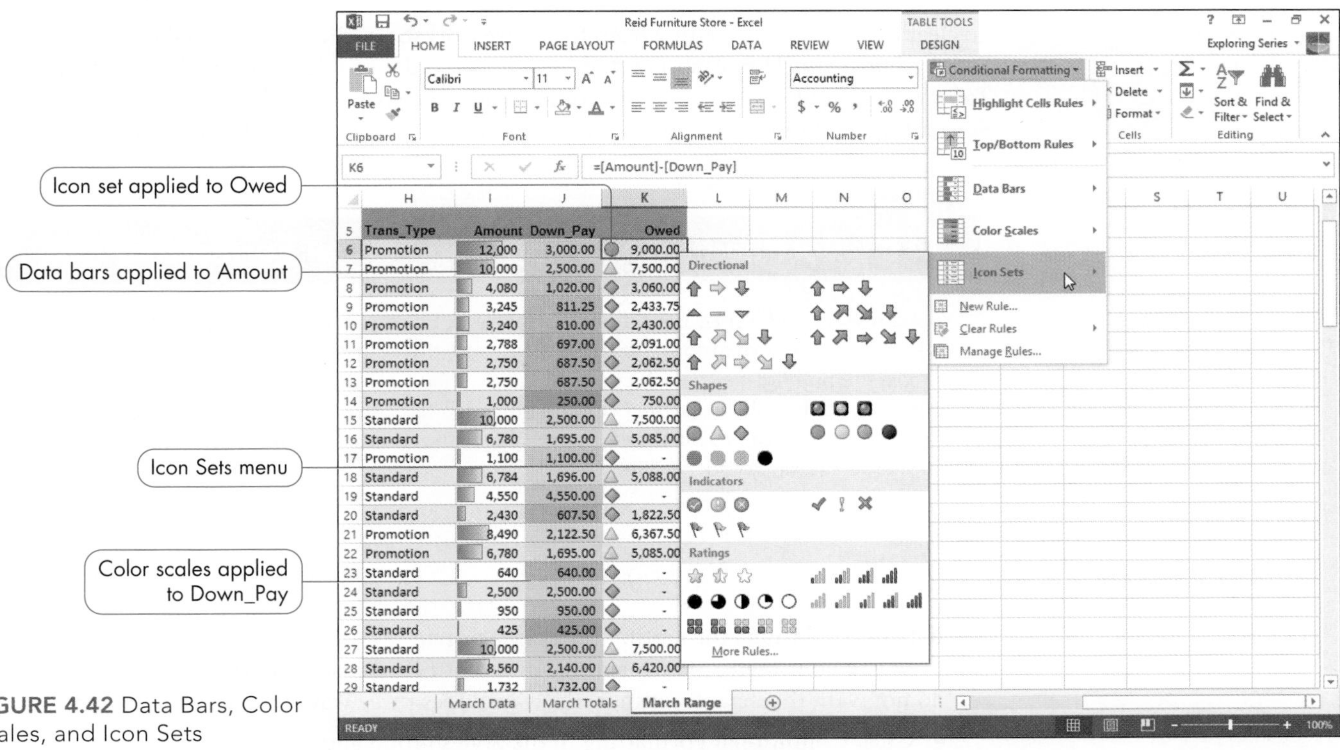

FIGURE 4.42 Data Bars, Color Scales, and Icon Sets

Color scales format cells with different colors based on the relative value of a cell compared to other selected cells. You can apply a two- or three-color scale. This scale assists in comparing a range of cells using gradations of those colors. The shade of the color represents higher or lower values. In Figure 4.42, for example, the red color scales display for the lowest values, the green color displays for the highest values, and gradients of yellow and orange represent the middle range of values in the Down_Pay column. Use color scales to understand variation in the data to identify trends, for example, to view good stock returns and weak stock returns.

Icon sets are symbols or signs that classify data into three, four, or five categories, based on the values in a range. Excel determines categories of value ranges and assigns an icon to each range. In Figure 4.42, a three-icon set was applied to the Owed column. Excel divided the range of values between the lowest value $0 and the highest value of $13,125 into thirds. The red diamond icon displays for the cells containing values in the lowest third ($0 to $4,375), the yellow triangle icon displays for cells containing the values in the middle third ($4,376 to $8,750), and the green circle icon displays for cells containing values in the top third ($8,751 to $13,125). Most purchases fall into the lowest third.

Don't Overdo It!

Although conditional formatting helps identify trends, you should use this feature wisely. Apply conditional formatting when you want to emphasize important data. When you decide to apply conditional formatting, think about which category is best to highlight the data. Sometimes simple highlighting will suffice when you want to point out data meeting a particular condition; other times, you might want to apply data bars to point out relative differences among values. Finally, do not apply conditional formatting to too many columns.

Clear Rules

To clear conditional formatting from the entire worksheet, click Conditional Formatting in the Styles group on the Home tab, point to Clear Rules, and then select *Clear Rules from Entire Sheet*. To remove conditional formatting from a range of cells, select cells. Then click Conditional Formatting, point to Clear Rules, and then select *Clear Rules from Selected Cells*.

Sort and Filter Using Conditional Formatting

You can sort and filter by conditional formatting. For example, if you applied the Highlight Cells Rules conditional formatting, you can sort the column by color so that all cells containing the highlight appear first or last. To do this, display the filter arrows, click the arrow for the conditionally formatted column you wish to sort, point to Sort by Color, and then click the fill color or No Fill in the *Sort by Cell Color* area. If you applied the Icon Sets conditional formatting, you can filter by icon.

Creating a New Rule

The default conditional formatting categories provide a variety of options. Excel also enables you to create your own rules to specify different fill colors, borders, or other formatting if you do not want the default settings. Excel provides three ways to create a new rule:

- Click Conditional Formatting in the Styles group and select New Rule.
- Click Conditional Formatting in the Styles group, select Manage Rules to open the Conditional Formatting Rules Manager dialog box, and then click New Rule.
- Click Conditional Formatting in the Styles group, select a rule category such as Highlight Cells Rules, and then select More Rules.

The New Formatting Rule dialog box opens (see Figure 4.43) so that you can define your new conditional formatting rule. First, select a rule type, such as *Format all cells based on their values*. The *Edit the Rule Description* section changes, based on the rule type you select. With the default rule type selected, you can specify the format style (2-Color Scale, 3-Color Scale, Data Bar, or Icon Sets). You can then specify the minimum and maximum values, the fill colors for color sets or data bars, or the icons for icon sets. After you edit the rule description, click OK to save your new conditional format.

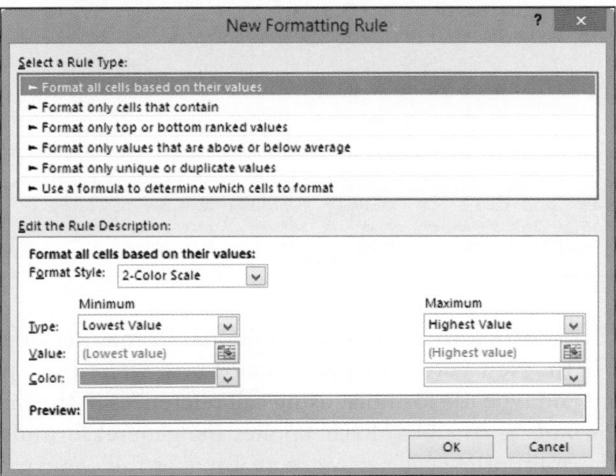

FIGURE 4.43 New Formatting Rule Dialog Box

If you select any rule type except the *Format all cells based on their values* rule, the dialog box contains a Format button. When you click Format, the Format Cells dialog box opens so that you can specify number, font, border, and fill formats to apply to your rule.

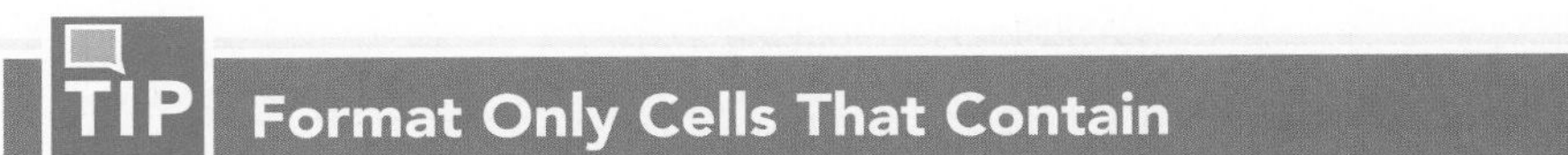

This option provides a wide array of things you can format: values, text, dates, blanks, no blanks, errors, or no errors. Formatting blanks is helpful to see where you are missing data, and formatting cells containing errors helps you find those errors quickly.

Use Formulas in Conditional Formatting

STEP 4

If you need to create a complex conditional formatting rule, you can select a rule that uses a formula to format cells. For example, you might want to format merchandise amounts of financed items *and* amounts that are $10,000 or more. Figure 4.44 shows the Edit Formatting Rule dialog box and the corresponding conditional formatting applied to cells.

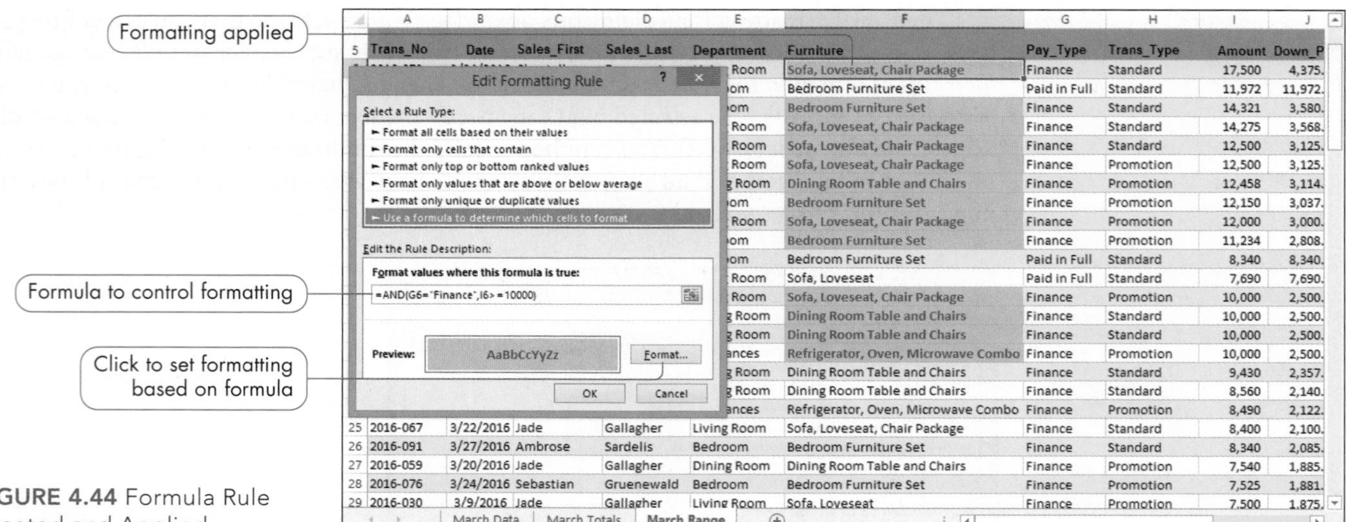

FIGURE 4.44 Formula Rule Created and Applied

To create a formula-based conditional formatting rule, select the data and create a new rule. In the New Formatting Rule dialog box, select *Use a formula to determine which cells to format* and type the formula, using cell references in the first row, in the *Format values where this formula is true* box. Excel applies the general formula to the selected range, substituting the appropriate cell reference as it makes the comparisons. In the Figure 4.44 example, =AND(G6="Finance",I6>=10000) requires that the text in the Pay_Type column (column F) contain *Finance* and the Amount column (column I) contain a value that is greater than or equal to $10,000. The AND function requires that both logical tests be met to apply the conditional formatting. Two logical tests are required; however, you can include additional logical tests. Note that *all* logical tests must be true to apply the conditional formatting.

= AND(logical1,logical2,...)

Manage Rules

To edit or delete conditional formatting rules you create, click Conditional Formatting in the Styles group and select Manage Rules. The Conditional Formatting Rules Manager dialog box opens (see Figure 4.45). Click the *Show formatting rules for* arrow and select from current selection, the entire worksheet, or a specific table. Select the rule and click Edit Rule or Delete Rule.

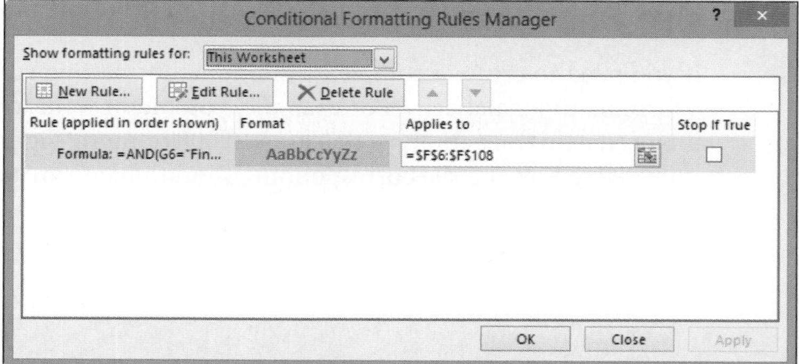

FIGURE 4.45 Conditional Formatting Rules Manager Dialog Box

1. How is conditional formatting similar to an IF function? ***p. 594***
2. What conditional formatting would be helpful to identify the three movies with the highest revenue playing at theaters? ***p. 596***
3. How is data bar conditional formatting helpful when reviewing a column of data? ***p. 597***

Hands-On Exercises

Watch the Video for this Hands-On Exercise!

MyITLab®
HOE5 Training

5 Conditional Formatting

Vicki Reid wants to review the transactions with you. She is interested in Sebastian Grunewald's sales record and the three highest transaction amounts. In addition, she wants to compare the down payment amounts visually. Finally, she wants you to analyze the amounts owed for sales completed by Sebastian.

Skills covered: Highlight Cells Rules • Specify Top/Bottom Rules • Display Data Bars • Use a Formula in Conditional Formatting

STEP 1 » HIGHLIGHT CELLS RULES

You want to identify Sebastian's sales for March 2016 without filtering the data. You will apply a conditional format to apply a fill and font color so that cells containing his first name stand out. Refer to Figure 4.46 as you complete Step 1.

Step c: Select Sales_First names

Step e: Type name here

Step e: Select this formatting

Step e: Conditional formatting applied

FIGURE 4.46 Text Formatted with Highlight Text Rules

a. Open *e04h4Reid_LastFirst* if you closed it at the end of Hands-On Exercise 4. Save the workbook as **e04h5Reid_LastFirst**, changing *h4* to *h5*.

b. Select **row headings 6 through 109** in the March Range worksheet. Click the **HOME tab**, if necessary, click the **Fill Color arrow**, and then select **No Fill**.

You removed the previous table style with banded rows. This will avoid having too many fill colors when you apply conditional formatting rules.

c. Select the **range C6:C109**, which is the column containing the sales representatives' first names.

d. Click **Conditional Formatting** in the Styles group, point to *Highlight Cells Rules*, and then select **Text that Contains**.

The Text That Contains dialog box opens.

e. Type **Sebastian** in the box, click the **with arrow**, and then select **Green Fill with Dark Green Text**. Click **OK**. Deselect the range and save the workbook.

Excel formats only cells that contain Sebastian with the fill and font color.

TIP Apply Multiple Formats to One Column

While the range is selected, you can apply another conditional format, such as Light Yellow with Dark Yellow text for another first name.

STEP 2 ›› SPECIFY TOP/BOTTOM RULES

Vicki is now interested in identifying the highest three sales transactions in March. Instead of sorting the records, you will use the Top/Bottom Rules conditional formatting. Refer to Figure 4.47 as you complete Step 2.

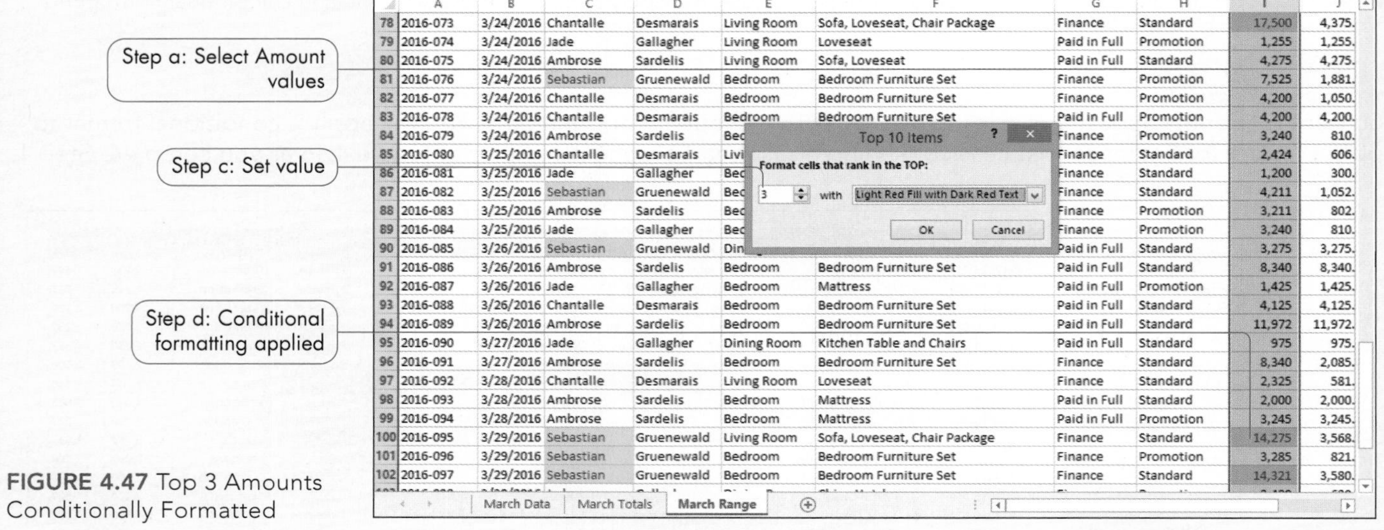

FIGURE 4.47 Top 3 Amounts Conditionally Formatted

a. Select the **range I6:I109**, the range containing the amounts.

b. Click **Conditional Formatting** in the Styles group, point to *Top/Bottom Rules*, and then select **Top 10 Items**.

The Top 10 Items dialog box opens.

c. Click the spin arrow to display *3* and click **OK**.

d. Scroll through the worksheet to see the top three amounts. Save the workbook.

STEP 3 ›› DISPLAY DATA BARS

Vicki wants to compare all of the down payments. Data bars would add a nice visual element as she compares down payment amounts. Refer to Figure 4.48 as you complete Step 3.

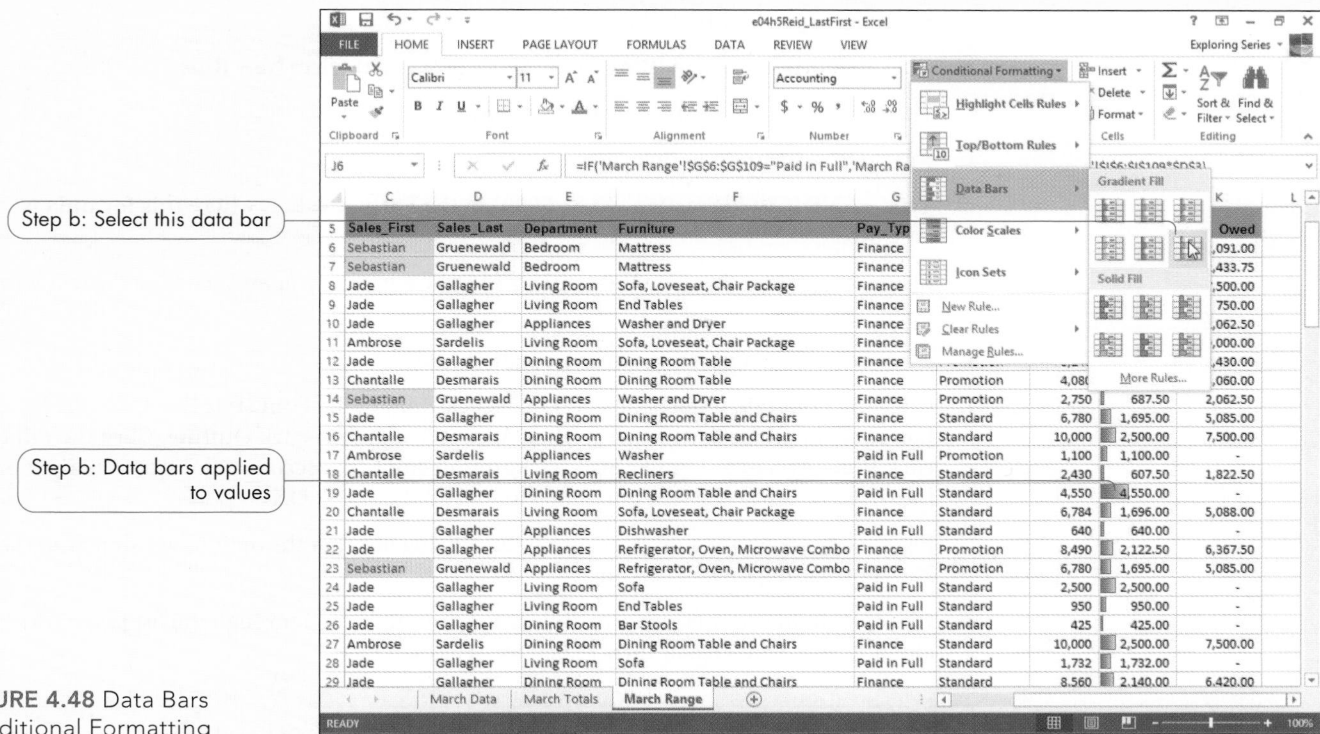

FIGURE 4.48 Data Bars Conditional Formatting

a. Select the **range J6:J109**, which contains the down payment amounts.

b. Click **Conditional Formatting** in the Styles group, point to *Data Bars*, and then select **Purple Data Bar** in the *Gradient Fill* section. Scroll through the list and save the workbook.

   Excel displays data bars in each cell. The larger bar widths help Vicki quickly identify the largest down payments. However, the largest down payments are identical to the original amounts when the customers pay in full. This result illustrates that you should not accept the results at face value. Doing so would provide you with an inaccurate analysis.

STEP 4 » USE A FORMULA IN CONDITIONAL FORMATTING

Vicki's next request is to analyze the amounts owed by Sebastian's customers. In particular, she wants to highlight the merchandise for which $5,000 or more is owed. To do this, you realize you need to create a custom rule that evaluates both the Sales_First column and the Owed column. Refer to Figure 4.49 as you complete Step 4.

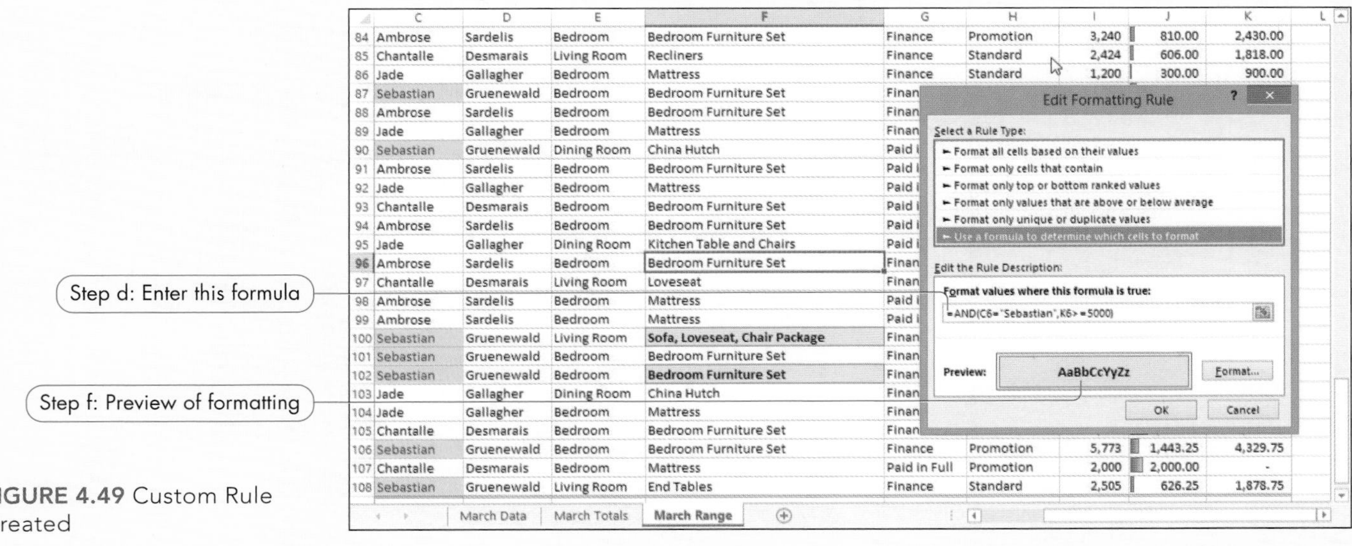

FIGURE 4.49 Custom Rule Created

a. Select the **range F6:F109**, which contains the merchandise.

b. Click **Conditional Formatting** in the Styles group and select **New Rule**.

The New Formatting Rule dialog box opens.

c. Select **Use a formula to determine which cells to format**.

d. Type **=AND(C6="Sebastian",K6>=5000)** in the **Format values where this formula is true box**.

Because you are comparing the contents of cell C6 to text, you must enclose the text within quotation marks.

e. Click **Format** to open the Format Cells dialog box.

f. Click the **Font tab**, if necessary, and then click **Bold** in the **Font style list**. Click the **Border tab**, click the **Color arrow**, select **Blue, Accent 5**, and then click **Outline**. Click the **Fill tab**, click **Blue, Accent 5, Lighter 80% background color** (the second color from the right on the first row below the first horizontal line), and then click **OK**.

Figure 4.49 shows the Edit Formatting Rule dialog box, but the options are similar to the New Formatting Rule dialog box.

g. Click **OK** in the New Formatting Rule dialog box and scroll through the list to see which amounts owed are greater than $5,000 for Sebastian only.

> **TROUBLESHOOTING:** If the results seem incorrect, click Conditional Formatting and select Manage Rules. Edit the rule you just created and make any corrections to the formula.

h. Save and close the workbook and submit based on your instructor's directions.

Chapter Objectives Review

After reading this chapter, you have accomplished the following objectives:

1. **Freeze rows and columns.**
   - The Freeze Panes setting freezes the row(s) above and the column(s) to the left of the active cell. When you scroll, those rows and columns remain onscreen.
   - Use Unfreeze Panes to clear the frozen rows and columns.
2. **Print large datasets.**
   - Display and change page breaks: Display the data in Page Break Preview to see the automatic page breaks. Dashed blue lines indicate automatic page breaks. You can insert manual page breaks, indicated by solid blue lines.
   - Set and clear a print area: If you do not want to print an entire worksheet, select a range and set a print area.
   - Print titles: Select rows to repeat at top and/or columns to repeat at left to print the column and row labels on every page of a printout of a large dataset.
   - Control print page order: You can control the sequence in which the pages will print.
3. **Design and create tables.**
   - A table is a structured range that contains related data. Tables have several benefits over regular ranges. The column labels, called *field names*, display on the first row of a table. Each row is a complete set of data for one record.
   - You should plan a table before you create it. Create unique field names on the first row of the table and enter data below the field names, avoiding blank rows.
   - Create a table: You can create a table from existing data. Excel applies the Table Style Medium 2 format and assigns a name, such as Table1, to the table. When the active cell is within a table, the Table Tools Design tab displays.
   - Add and delete fields: You can insert and delete table rows and columns to adjust the structure of a table.
   - Add, edit, and delete records: You can add table rows, edit records, and delete table rows.
   - Remove duplicate rows: Use the Remove Duplicates dialog box to remove duplicate records in a table. Excel will display a dialog box telling you how many records are deleted.
4. **Apply a table style.**
   - Table styles control the fill color of the header row and records within the table.
5. **Sort data.**
   - Sort one field: You can sort text in alphabetical or reverse alphabetical order, values from smallest to largest or largest to smallest, and dates from oldest to newest or newest to oldest. Click the filter arrow and select the sort method from the list.
   - Sort multiple fields: Open the Sort dialog box and add column levels and sort orders.
   - Create a custom sort: You can create a custom sort for unique data, such as ensuring the months sort in sequential order rather than alphabetical order.
6. **Filter data.**
   - Filtering is the process of specifying conditions for displaying records in a table. Only records that meet those conditions display; the other records are hidden.
   - Apply text filters: A text filter can find exact text, text that does not equal a condition, text that begins with a particular letter, and so forth.
   - Apply number filters: A number filter can find exact values, values that do not equal a particular value, values greater than or equal to a value, and so on.
   - Apply date filters: You can set filters to find dates before or after a certain date, between two dates, yesterday, next month, and so forth.
   - Clear filters: If you do not need filters, you can clear the filters.
7. **Use structured references and a total row.**
   - Create structured references in formulas: A structured reference uses field names instead of cell references, such as =[Amount]–[Down Payment]. Field names must display in brackets within the formula.
   - Add a total row: You can display a total row after the last record. You can add totals or select a different function, such as Average.
8. **Apply conditional formatting.**
   - Apply conditional formatting with the Quick Analysis Tool: After selecting text, click FORMATTING on the Quick Analysis gallery to apply a conditional format.
   - Apply the highlight cells rules: This rule highlights cell contents with a fill color, font color, and/or border color where the contents match a particular condition.
   - Specify top/bottom rules: This rule enables you to highlight the top *x* number of items or percentage of items.
   - Display data bars, color scales, and icon sets: Data bars compare values within the selected range. Color scales indicate values that occur within particular ranges. Icon sets display icons representing a number's relative value compared to other numbers in the range.
   - Clear rules: If you no longer want conditional formatting applied, you can clear a rule.
9. **Create a new rule.**
   - You can create conditional format rules. The New Formatting Rule dialog box enables you to select a rule type.
   - Use formulas in conditional formatting: You can create rules based on content in multiple columns.
   - Manage rules: Use the Conditional Formatting Rules Manager dialog box to edit and delete rules.

Key Terms Matching

Match the key terms with their definitions. Write the key term letter by the appropriate numbered definition.

- **a.** Color scale
- **b.** Conditional formatting
- **c.** Data bar
- **d.** Field
- **e.** Filtering
- **f.** Freezing
- **g.** Icon set
- **h.** Page break
- **i.** Print area
- **j.** Print order
- **k.** Record
- **l.** Sorting
- **m.** Structured reference
- **n.** SUBTOTAL function
- **o.** Table
- **p.** Table style
- **q.** Total row

1. ________ A conditional format that displays horizontal gradient or solid fill indicating the cell's relative value compared to other selected cells. **p. 597**

2. ________ The process of listing records or text in a specific sequence, such as alphabetically by last name. **p. 576**

3. ________ The process of specifying conditions to display only those records that meet those conditions. **p. 578**

4. ________ A set of rules that applies specific formatting to highlight or emphasize cells that meet specifications. **p. 594**

5. ________ A group of related fields representing one entity, such as data for one person, place, event, or concept. **p. 565**

6. ________ The rules that control the fill color of the header row, columns, and records in a table. **p. 569**

7. ________ An indication of where data will start on another printed page. **p. 558**

8. ________ A table row that appears below the last row of records in an Excel table and displays summary or aggregate statistics, such as a sum or an average. **p. 588**

9. ________ A conditional format that displays a particular color based on the relative value of the cell contents to the other selected cells. **p. 599**

10. ________ The sequence in which the pages are printed. **p. 560**

11. ________ A tag or use of a table element, such as a field label, as a reference in a formula. Field labels are enclosed in square brackets, such as [Amount] within the formula. **p. 587**

12. ________ A conditional format that displays an icon representing a value in the top third, quarter, or fifth based on values in the selected range. **p. 598**

13. ________ The range of cells within a worksheet that will print. **p. 559**

14. ________ A predefined formula that calculates an aggregate value, such as totals, for values in a range, a table, or a database. **p. 588**

15. ________ The smallest data element contained in a table, such as first name, last name, address, and phone number. **p. 565**

16. ________ A structure that organizes data in a series of records (rows), with each record made up of a number of fields (columns). **p. 565**

17. ________ The process of keeping rows and/or columns visible onscreen at all times even when you scroll through a large dataset. **p. 557**

Multiple Choice

1. You have a large dataset that will print on several pages. You want to ensure that related records print on the same page with column and row labels visible and that confidential information is not printed. You should apply all of the following page setup options *except* which one to accomplish this?
   (a) Set a print area.
   (b) Print titles.
   (c) Adjust page breaks.
   (d) Change the print page order.

2. You are working with a large worksheet. Your row headings are in column A. Which command(s) should be used to see the row headings and the distant information in columns X, Y, and Z?
   (a) Freeze Panes command
   (b) Hide Rows command
   (c) New Window command and cascade the windows
   (d) Split Rows command

3. Which statement is *not* a recommended guideline for designing and creating an Excel table?
   (a) Avoid naming two fields with the same name.
   (b) Ensure no blank columns separate data columns within the table.
   (c) Leave one blank row between records in the table.
   (d) Include field names on the first row of the table.

4. You have a list of all the employees in your organization. The list contains employee name, office, title, and salary. You want to list all employees in each office branch. The branches should be listed alphabetically, with the employee earning the highest salary listed first in each office. Which is true of your sort order?
   (a) Branch office is the primary sort and should be in A to Z order.
   (b) Salary is the primary sort and should be from highest to lowest.
   (c) Salary is the primary sort and should be from lowest to highest.
   (d) Branch office is the primary sort and should be in Z to A order.

5. You suspect a table has several identical records. What should you do?
   (a) Do nothing; a logical reason probably exists to keep identical records.
   (b) Use the Remove Duplicates command.
   (c) Look at each row yourself and manually delete duplicate records.
   (d) Find the duplicate records and change some of the data to be different.

6. Which check box in the Table Style Options group enables you to apply different formatting to the records in a table?
   (a) Header Row
   (b) Banded Rows
   (c) Banded Columns
   (d) Total Row

7. Which date filter option enables you to specify criteria for selecting a range of dates, such as between 3/15/2016 and 7/15/2016?
   (a) Equals
   (b) Before
   (c) All Dates in the Period
   (d) Between

8. You want to display a total row that identifies the oldest date in a field in your table. What function do you select from the list?
   (a) Max
   (b) Sum
   (c) Min
   (d) Count

9. What type of conditional formatting displays horizontal colors in which the width of the bar indicates relative size compared to other values in the selected range?
   (a) Color Scales
   (b) Icon Sets
   (c) Data Bars
   (d) Sparklines

10. When you select the _______ rule type, the New Formatting Rule dialog box does not show the Format button.
   (a) Format all cells based on their values
   (b) Format only cells that contain
   (c) Use a formula to determine which cells to format
   (d) Format only unique or duplicate values

Practice Exercises

1 Fiesta® Items and Replacement Values

FROM SCRATCH 

Marie Maier has collected Fiesta dinnerware, manufactured by the Homer Laughlin China Company, since 1986. Between 1986 and 2012, the company produced 30 colors, each with a unique name. Marie created a table in Word that lists the name, number, year introduced, and year retired (if applicable) for each color. She created another table in Word that lists the item number, item, replacement value, and source of information for each item in her collection. Her main sources for replacement values are Homer Laughlin (www.fiestafactorydirect.com), Replacements, Ltd. (www.replacements.com), eBay (www.ebay.com), and two local antique stores. She needs your help to convert the data to Excel tables, apply table formatting, delete duplicate records, insert functions, and sort and filter the data. This exercise follows the same set of skills as used in Hands-On Exercises 1–3 in the chapter. Refer to Figure 4.50 as you complete this exercise.

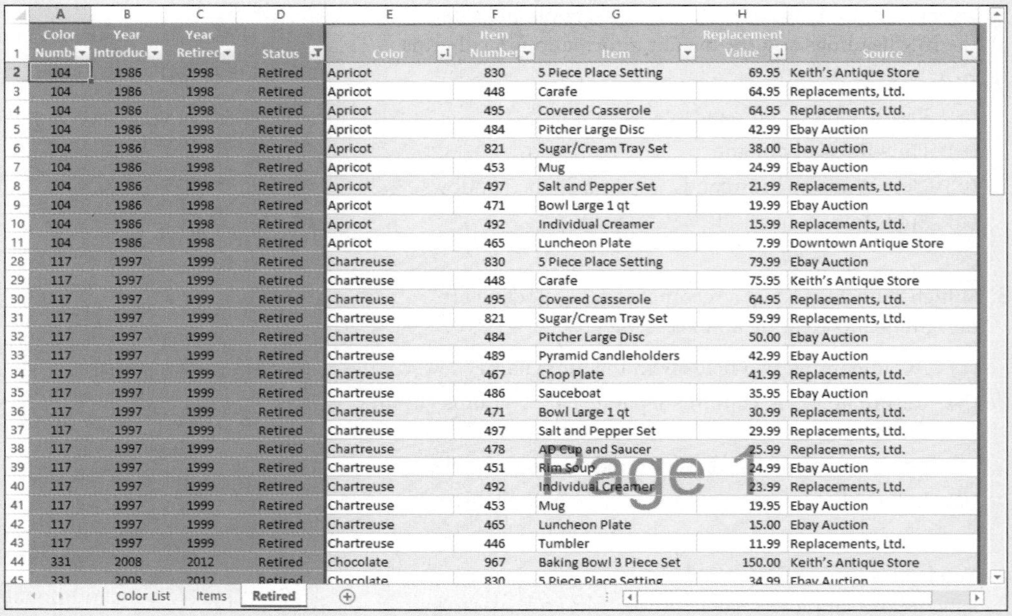

	A	B	C	D	E	F	G	H	I
1	Color Numb	Year Introduc	Year Retired	Status	Color	Item Number	Item	Replacement Value	Source
2	104	1986	1998	Retired	Apricot	830	5 Piece Place Setting	69.95	Keith's Antique Store
3	104	1986	1998	Retired	Apricot	448	Carafe	64.95	Replacements, Ltd.
4	104	1986	1998	Retired	Apricot	495	Covered Casserole	64.95	Replacements, Ltd.
5	104	1986	1998	Retired	Apricot	484	Pitcher Large Disc	42.99	Ebay Auction
6	104	1986	1998	Retired	Apricot	821	Sugar/Cream Tray Set	38.00	Ebay Auction
7	104	1986	1998	Retired	Apricot	453	Mug	24.99	Ebay Auction
8	104	1986	1998	Retired	Apricot	497	Salt and Pepper Set	21.99	Replacements, Ltd.
9	104	1986	1998	Retired	Apricot	471	Bowl Large 1 qt	19.99	Ebay Auction
10	104	1986	1998	Retired	Apricot	492	Individual Creamer	15.99	Replacements, Ltd.
11	104	1986	1998	Retired	Apricot	465	Luncheon Plate	7.99	Downtown Antique Store
28	117	1997	1999	Retired	Chartreuse	830	5 Piece Place Setting	79.99	Ebay Auction
29	117	1997	1999	Retired	Chartreuse	448	Carafe	75.95	Keith's Antique Store
30	117	1997	1999	Retired	Chartreuse	495	Covered Casserole	64.95	Replacements, Ltd.
31	117	1997	1999	Retired	Chartreuse	821	Sugar/Cream Tray Set	59.99	Replacements, Ltd.
32	117	1997	1999	Retired	Chartreuse	484	Pitcher Large Disc	50.00	Ebay Auction
33	117	1997	1999	Retired	Chartreuse	489	Pyramid Candleholders	42.99	Ebay Auction
34	117	1997	1999	Retired	Chartreuse	467	Chop Plate	41.99	Replacements, Ltd.
35	117	1997	1999	Retired	Chartreuse	486	Sauceboat	35.95	Ebay Auction
36	117	1997	1999	Retired	Chartreuse	471	Bowl Large 1 qt	30.99	Replacements, Ltd.
37	117	1997	1999	Retired	Chartreuse	497	Salt and Pepper Set	29.99	Replacements, Ltd.
38	117	1997	1999	Retired	Chartreuse	478	AD Cup and Saucer	25.99	Replacements, Ltd.
39	117	1997	1999	Retired	Chartreuse	451	Rim Soup	24.99	Ebay Auction
40	117	1997	1999	Retired	Chartreuse	492	Individual Creamer	23.99	Replacements, Ltd.
41	117	1997	1999	Retired	Chartreuse	453	Mug	19.95	Ebay Auction
42	117	1997	1999	Retired	Chartreuse	465	Luncheon Plate	15.00	Ebay Auction
43	117	1997	1999	Retired	Chartreuse	446	Tumbler	11.99	Replacements, Ltd.
44	331	2008	2012	Retired	Chocolate	967	Baking Bowl 3 Piece Set	150.00	Keith's Antique Store
45	331	2008	2012	Retired	Chocolate	830	5 Piece Place Setting	34.99	Ebay Auction

Color List | Items | Retired

Page 1

FIGURE 4.50 Fiesta® Collection

a. Open *e04p1Colors* in Word. Do the following to copy the Word table data into Excel and prepare the data to be used as a lookup table:

- Click the **table icon** in the top-left corner of the table and click **Copy** in the Clipboard group.
- Start a new Excel workbook, click the **Paste arrow** in the Clipboard group in Excel, and then select **Match Destination Formatting (M)**.
- Bold and horizontally center the labels on the first row. Center the data in the first, third, and fourth columns. Widen the second and third columns to fit the data.
- Select the **range A2:D31**, click in the **Name Box**, type **colors**, and then press **Enter** to assign a name to the selected range.
- Click **cell A2**, click **Sort & Filter** in the Editing group, and then select **Sort Smallest to Largest**. Remember that you must sort the first column in ascending order to use the table for an exact match for a VLOOKUP function.
- Save the Excel workbook as **e04p1Collection_LastFirst**. Close the Word document.

b. Open *e04p1Items* in Word. Select and copy the table, display the Excel workbook, add a new sheet, make sure **cell A1** is the active cell in the new sheet, and then paste the table in the same way you did in step a. Widen column E. Rename *Sheet2* **Items**. Close the Word document.

c. Click **cell A2** in the Items sheet, click the **VIEW tab**, click **Freeze Panes** in the Window group, and then select **Freeze Top Row**.

d. Press **Ctrl+End** to go to the last data cell. The first row is frozen so that the column labels remain onscreen. Press **Ctrl+Home** to go back to **cell A2**.

e. Click the **INSERT tab**, click **Table** in the Tables group, and then click **OK** in the Create Table dialog box.

f. Click **Quick Styles** in the Table Styles group and click **Table Style Medium 5**.

g. Click the **DATA tab**, click **Remove Duplicates** in the Data Tools group, and then click **OK** in the Remove Duplicates dialog box. Click **OK** in the message box that informs you that *12 duplicate values were found and removed; 356 unique values remain.*

h. Click **cell B2**, click the **HOME tab**, click the **Insert arrow** in the Cells group, and then select **Insert Table Columns to the Left**. Then insert two more columns to the left. Do the following to insert functions and customize the results in the three new table columns:

- Type **Year Introduced** in **cell B1**, **Year Retired** in **cell C1**, and **Color** in **cell D1**.
- Click **cell B2,** type **=VLOOKUP([Color Number],colors,3,False)**, and then press **Enter**. Excel copies the function down the Year Introduced column. This function looks up each item's color number using the structured reference [Color Number], looks up that value in the colors table, and then returns the year that color was introduced, which is in the third column of that table.
- Click **cell B2**, click **Copy**, click **cell C2**, and then click **Paste**. Change the *3* to **4** in the col_index_num argument of the pasted function. Excel copies the function down the Year Retired column. This function looks up each item's color number using the structured reference [Color Number], looks up that value in the colors table, and then returns the year that color was retired, if applicable, which is in the fourth column of that table. The function returns 0 if the retired cell in the lookup table is blank.

- Click the **FILE tab**, click **Options**, click **Advanced**, scroll down to the *Display options for this worksheet* section, click the **Show a zero in cells that have zero value check box** to deselect it, and then click **OK**. The zeros disappear. (This option hides zeros in the active worksheet. While this is not desirable if you need to show legitimate zeros, this worksheet is designed to avoid that issue.)
- Click **cell C2**, click **Copy**, click **cell D2**, and then click **Paste**. Change the *4* to **2** in the col_index_num argument of the pasted function. Excel copies the function down the Color column. This function looks up each item's color number using the structured reference [Color Number] to look up that value in the colors table and returns the color name, which is in the second column of that table.

i. Apply wrap text, horizontal centering, and **30.75 row height** to the column labels row. Adjust column widths. Center data horizontally in the Color Number, Year Introduced, Year Retired, and Item Number columns. Apply **Comma Style** to the Replacement Values. Deselect the data.

j. Click **Sort & Filter** in the Editing group and select **Custom Sort** to display the Sort dialog box. Do the following in the Sort dialog box:

- Click the **Sort by arrow** and select **Color**.
- Click **Add Level**, click the **Then by arrow**, and then select **Replacement Value**.
- Click the **Order arrow** and select **Largest to Smallest**. Click **OK**.

k. Right-click the **Items sheet tab**, select **Move or Copy**, click **(move to end)**, click the **Create a copy check box**, and then click **OK**. Rename the copied sheet **Retired**.

l. Make sure the active sheet is Retired. Insert a table column between the Year Retired and Color columns.

- Type **Status** in **cell D1** as the column label.
- Click **cell D2**, type **=IF([Year Retired]=0, "Current","Retired")**, and then press **Enter**. This function determines that if the cell contains a 0 (which is hidden), it will display the word *Current*. Otherwise, it will display *Retired*.

m. Click the **Status filter arrow**, deselect the **Current check box**, and then click **OK** to filter out the current colors and display only retired colors.

n. Click the **DESIGN tab** and click **Total Row** in the Table Style Options group. Press **Ctrl+End** to go to the total row, click the **Source total cell** (which contains a count of visible items), click the

Source total arrow, and then select **None**. Click **cell H358**, the *Replacement Value total* cell, click the **Replacement Value total arrow**, and then select **Sum**.

o. Prepare the Retired worksheet for printing by doing the following:
- Set **0.2**" left and right page margins.
- Select the **range E1:I358**, click the **PAGE LAYOUT tab**, click **Print Area** in the Page Setup group, and then select **Set Print Area**.
- Click **Print Titles** in the Page Setup group, click the **Rows to repeat at top Collapse Dialog box button**, click the **row 1 header**, and then click the **Collapse Dialog box button**. Click **OK**.
- Click the **VIEW tab** and click **Page Break Preview** in the Workbook Views group. Decrease the top margin to avoid having only one or two records print on the last page.

p. Create a footer with your name on the left side, the sheet name code in the center, and the file name code on the right side of each worksheet.

q. Save and close the workbook and submit based on your instructor's directions.

2 Dentist Association Donation List

The Midwest Regional Dentist Association is planning its annual meeting in Lincoln, Nebraska, this spring. Several members donated items for door prizes at the closing general session. You will organize the list of donations and format it to highlight particular data for your supervisor, who is on the conference board of directors. This exercise follows the same set of skills as used in Hands-On Exercises 2–5 in the chapter. Refer to Figure 4.51 as you complete this exercise.

	A	B	C	D	E	F	G	H	I	J	K
1	ID	First Name	Last Name	Address	City	State	Zip Code	Item Donated	Value	Category	
2	19	Tara	Huber	9507 Sandy Elms	Omaha	NE	68102	Laptop Computer	$1,000	Equipment	
3	20	Benjamin	Brown	143 Sunset Avenue	Tucson	AZ	85701	Digital Camera	$400	Equipment	
4	3	Kim	Jansen	6000 North Meridian	Oklahoma City	OK	73102	MP3 Player	$200	Equipment	
5	28	Vickie	Anderson	431 North Mulberry Lane	Greeley	CO	80634	MP3 Player	$145	Equipment	
6	31	Anita	Miller	832 East 3rd Street	Grand Junction	CO	81506	MP3 Player	$145	Equipment	
7	34	Brad	Foust	3434 Reno Street	Dodge City	KS	67801	Digital Camera	$125	Equipment	
8	15	Huong	Ngyun	P.O. Box DEF	Dallas	TX	75201	Gym Membership	$250	Other	
9	29	Ian	Parker	421 North 3rd Street	Lubbock	TX	79401	Gym Membership	$200	Gift Certificate	
10	4	Donna	Reed	P.O. Box ABC	Dumas	TX	79029	Hotel Accomodations	$100	Gift Certificate	
11	8	Catherine	McQuaide	31 Oakmont Circle	Dallas	TX	75201	10 pounds of Fresh Fish	$100	Product	
12	14	Dan	Reed	901 North Street	Austin	TX	78701	Yoga Class	$100	Service	
13	16	Robert	McMahon	912 South Front Street	Lincoln	NE	68504	Web Site Services	$100	Service	
14	23	Jennifer	Ward	377 Hillman Avenue	Houston	TX	77002	1-Year Free Coffee	$100	Product	
15	26	Bobby	Wilcox	3141 Lincoln Drive	Lincoln	NE	68504	Automotive Gift Certificate	$100	Gift Certificate	
16	2	Kelly	Kripton	444 East Walnut Grove	Dodge City	KS	67843	Football Tickets	$75	Product	
17	18	Emiko	Francani	800 North Street	Emporia	KS	66801	Floral Arrangement	$75	Gift Certificate	
18	24	Michael	Anderson	1 Clark Smith Drive	Topeka	KS	66603	Gift Basket	$75	Product	
19	27	Peggy	Jackson	140 Oak Circle	Grand Junction	CO	81503	Restaurant Gift Certificate	$75	Gift Certificate	
20	17	Dennis	Boothe	1100 Choctaw Lane	Alva	OK	73717	YMCA Swimming Lessons	$65	Service	
21	5	Huong	Pham	1401 Washington Circle	Colorado City	CO	81019	Restaurant Gift Certificate	$60	Gift Certificate	
22	1	Shelly	Martin	123 North Street	Amarillo	TX	79101	Massage	$50	Other	
23	6	George	Martin	555 Kaminini Street	Denver	CO	80022	Car Wash Card	$50	Other	
24	7	Marion	McMahon	2216 North Oklahoma Street	Tulsa	OK	74103	Automotive Gift Certificate	$50	Gift Certificate	

Donation List

FIGURE 4.51 Donation List

a. Open *e04p2Donate* and save it as **e04p2Donate_LastFirst**.

b. Click the **DESIGN tab**, click **Remove Duplicates** in the Tools group, and then click **OK**. Click **OK** in the message box that tells you that Excel removed three duplicate records.

c. Click **Convert to Range** in the Tools group and click **Yes** in the message box.

d. Select the **range A2:J35**, click the **HOME tab**, click the **Fill Color arrow** in the Font group, and then select **No Fill** to remove the table fill colors.

e. Select the **range I2:I35**. Click **Conditional Formatting** in the Styles group, point to *Highlight Cells Rules*, and then select **Greater Than**. Type **99** in the **Format cells that are GREATER THAN box** and click **OK**.

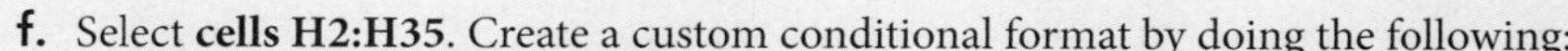

f. Select **cells H2:H35**. Create a custom conditional format by doing the following:
   - Click **Conditional Formatting** in the Styles group and select **New Rule**.
   - Click **Use a formula to determine which cells to format**.
   - Type =(J2="**Equipment**") in the **Format values where this formula is true box**. The basic condition is testing to see if the contents of cell J2 equal the word *Equipment*. You type *Equipment* in quotation marks because you are comparing text instead of a value.
   - Click **Format**, click the **Fill tab** if necessary, and then click **Red, Accent 2, Lighter 60%** (sixth background color on the second row below the first horizontal line).
   - Click the **Border tab**, click the **Color arrow**, click **Dark Red**, and then click **Outline**.
   - Click **OK** in each dialog box.

DISCOVER 

g. Click in the table to deselect the range. Click **Sort & Filter** in the Editing group and select **Custom Sort**. The dialog box may contain existing sort conditions for the State and City fields, which you will replace. Set the following sort conditions:
   - Click the **Sort by arrow** and select **Item Donated**. Click the **Sort On arrow** and select **Cell Color**. Click the **Order arrow** and select the **RGB(146, 205, 220) fill color**. The fill color displays for the Order.
   - Click the **Then by arrow** and select **Value**. Click the **Order arrow** and select **Largest to Smallest**.
   - Click **OK**.

h. Select **Landscape orientation**, set appropriate margins, and then adjust column widths so that all the data will print on one page. Do not decrease the scaling.

i. Create a footer with your name on the left side, the sheet name code in the center, and the file name code on the right side.

j. Save and close the workbook and submit based on your instructor's directions.

Mid-Level Exercises

1 Biology Department Teaching Schedule

As the department head of the biology department at a university, you prepare and finalize the faculty teaching schedule. Scheduling preparation takes time because you must ensure that you do not book faculty for different courses at the same time or double-book a classroom with two different classes. You downloaded the Spring 2015 schedule as a starting point and edited it to prepare the Spring 2016 schedule, and now you need to sort and filter the schedule to review it from several perspectives.

a. Open *e04m1Classes* and save it as **e04m1Classes_LastFirst**.
b. Freeze the panes so that the column labels do not scroll offscreen.
c. Convert the data to a table and name the table **Spring2016**.
d. Apply **Table Style Light 14** to the table.

DISCOVER

e. Sort the table by Instructor, then Days, and then Start Time. Create a custom sort order for Days so that it appears in this sequence: MTWR, MWF, MW, M, W, F, TR, T, R. (The day abbreviations are as follows: M = Monday, T = Tuesday, W = Wednesday, R = Thursday, F = Friday.)
f. Remove duplicate records from the table. Excel should find and remove three duplicate records.
g. Copy the Faculty sheet, place the copied worksheet to the right of the Faculty sheet, and then rename the duplicate worksheet **Rooms**. Sort the data in the Rooms sheet by Room in ascending order, then by Days using the custom sort order you created in step e, and finally by Start Time from earliest to latest time.
h. Copy the Rooms sheet, place the copied worksheet to the right of the Rooms sheet, and then rename the duplicate worksheet **Prime Time**.
i. Filter the table in the Prime Time sheet to show only classes scheduled on any combination of Monday, Wednesday, and Friday. Include classes that meet four days a week (MTWR). Do not include any other combination of Tuesday or Thursday classes, though. Also filter the table by classes that start between 9:00 AM and 12:00 PM. The status bar indicates 20 of 75 records found.
j. Insert a field on the right side of the Credits field in the Faculty sheet. Type the label **Capacity**. Insert a lookup function that looks up the room number, compares it to the lookup table in the Room Capacity worksheet, and returns the room capacity. Make sure the function copies down the entire column.
k. Select the first three sheet tabs and set **0.2**" left and right margins, **Landscape orientation**, and **95% scaling**. Repeat the column labels on all pages. On the Faculty sheet, decrease some column widths so that the Capacity column will print on the same page as the other columns.
l. Display the Faculty sheet in Page Break Preview. Adjust any page breaks so that classes for a particular instructor do not split between pages.
m. Display the Rooms sheet in Page Break Preview. Adjust any page breaks so that classes for a particular room do not split between pages, if necessary. Set the worksheet to print 1 page wide and 3 pages tall.
n. Insert a footer with your name on the left side, the sheet name code in the center, and the file name code on the right side of all four sheets.
o. Save and close the workbook and submit based on your instructor's directions.

2 Artwork

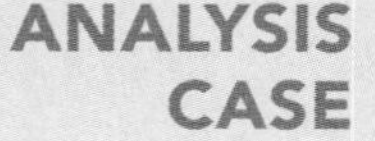

You work for a gallery that is an authorized Greenwich Workshop fine art dealer (www.greenwichworkshop.com). Customers in your area are especially fond of James C. Christensen's art. Although customers can visit the Web site to see images and details about his work, they have requested a list of all his artwork. Your assistant prepared a list of artwork: art, type, edition size, release date, and issue price. In addition, you included a column to identify which pieces are sold out at the publisher, indicating the rare, hard-to-obtain artwork that is available on the secondary market. You now want to convert the data to a table so that you can provide information to your customers.

a. Open *e04m2FineArt* and save it as **e04m2FineArt_LastFirst**.

b. Convert the data to a table and apply **Table Style Medium 5**.

c. Add a row (below the *The Yellow Rose* record) for this missing piece of art: **The Yellow Rose, Masterwork Canvas Edition**, **50** edition size, **May 2009** release date, **$895** issue price. Enter **Yes** to indicate the piece is sold out.

d. Sort the table by Type in alphabetical order and then by release date from newest to oldest.

e. Add a total row that shows the largest edition size and the most expensive issue price. Delete the Total label in **cell A205**. Add a descriptive label in **cell C205** to reflect the content on the total row.

DISCOVER

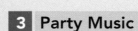

f. Create a custom conditional format for the Issue Price column with these specifications:

- 4 Traffic Lights icon set (Black, Red, Yellow, Green)
- Red icon when the number is greater than 1000
- Yellow icon when the number is less than or equal to 1000 and greater than 500
- Green icon when the number is less than or equal to 500 and greater than 250
- Black icon when the number is less than or equal to 250.

DISCOVER

g. Filter the table by the Red Traffic Light conditional formatting icon.

h. Answer the questions in the range D211:D215 based on the filtered data.

★ i. Set the print area to print the **range C1:H205**, select the **first row to repeat at the top of each printout**, set **1**" top and bottom margins, set **0.3**" left and right margins, and then select **Landscape orientation**. Set the option to fit the data to 1 page.

j. Wrap text and horizontally center column labels and adjust column widths and row heights as needed.

k. Create a footer with your name on the left side, the sheet name code in the center, and the file name code on the right side.

l. Save and close the workbook and submit based on your instructor's directions.

3 Party Music

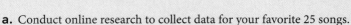

FROM SCRATCH

You are planning a weekend party and want to create a mix of music so that most people will appreciate some of the music you will play at the party. To help you decide what music to play, you have asked five classmates to help you create a song list. The entire class should decide on the general format, capitalization style, and sequence: song, musician, genre, year released, and approximate song length.

a. Conduct online research to collect data for your favorite 25 songs.

b. Enter the data into a new workbook in the format, capitalization style, and sequence that was decided by the class.

c. Save the workbook as **e04m3PlayList_LastFirst**.

d. Upload the file to a shared folder on OneDrive or Dropbox that everyone in the class can access.

e. Download four workbooks from friends and copy and paste data from their workbooks into yours.

f. Convert the data to a table and apply a table style of your choice.

g. Detect and delete duplicate records. Make a note of the number of duplicate records found and deleted.

h. Sort the data by genre in alphabetical order, then by artist in alphabetical order, and then by release date with the newest year first.

i. Set a filter to hide songs that were released before 2000.

j. Display the total row and select the function to count the number of songs displayed.

k. Insert comments in the workbook to indicate which student's workbooks you used, the number of duplicate records deleted, and number of filtered records.

l. Save and close the workbook. Submit the workbook based on your instructor's directions.

Beyond the Classroom

Flight Arrival Status

FROM SCRATCH

As an analyst for an airport, you want to study the flight arrivals for a particular day. Select an airport and find its list of flight arrival data. Some airport websites do not list complete details, so search for an airport that does, such as Will Rogers World Airport or San Diego International Airport. Copy the column labels and arrival data (airline, flight number, city, gate, scheduled time, status, etc.) for one day and paste them in a new workbook. The columns may be in a different sequence from what is listed here. However, you should format the data as needed. Leave two blank rows below the last row of data and enter the URL of the Web page from which you got the data, the date, and the time. Save the workbook as **e04b2Flights_LastFirst**. Convert the list to a table and apply a table style.

Sort the table by scheduled time and then by gate number. Apply conditional formatting to the Status column to highlight cells that contain the text *Delayed* (or similar text). Add a total row to calculate the MODE for the gate number and arrival time. You must select **More Functions** from the list of functions in the total row and search for and select **MODE**. Change the label in the first column from *Total* to **Most Frequent**. Use Help to refresh your memory on how to nest an IF function inside another IF function. Add a calculated column on the right side of the table using a nested IF function and structured references to display *Late* if the actual time was later than the scheduled time, *On Time or Early* if the actual time was earlier or equal to the scheduled time, or *Incomplete* if the flight has not landed yet.

Name the worksheet **Arrival Time**. Copy the worksheet and name the copied worksheet **Delayed**. Filter the list by delayed flights. Include a footer with your name on the left side, the sheet name code in the center, and the file name code on the right side of both worksheets. Adjust the margins on both worksheets as necessary. Save and close the workbook, and submit based on your instructor's directions.

U.S. Population

A colleague at an advertising firm downloaded U.S. population information from the government Web site. In the process of creating tables, he made some errors and needs your help. Open *e04b3Populate* and save it as **e04b3Populate_LastFirst**. As you find the errors, document them on the Errors worksheet and make the corrections. Your documentation should include these columns: Error Number, Location, Problem, and Solution. Both tables in the U.S. Population worksheet should show grand total populations per year. The state table should be sorted by region and then by state. Your colleague wants to emphasize the top 15% state populations for the most recent year in the state table. The last column should show percentage changes from year to year, such as 0.6%. Your colleague wants to print only the state data. Select the sorted data population for one region at a time to compare to the regional totals in the first table to crosscheck the totals. For example, when you select the July 1, 2008, Midwest values in the second table, the status bar should display the same value as shown for the Midwest July 1, 2008, values in the first table. Create a footer with your name, the sheet name code, and the file name code. Save and close the workbook, and submit based on your instructor's directions.

Performance Evaluation

SOFT SKILLS CASE

FROM SCRATCH

After watching the Performance Evaluation video, create a workbook that lists at least 10 performance traits mentioned in the video or other common performance traits, such as "arriving to work on time." Use the second column for a self-evaluation and the third column for manager evaluation. Below the list, create a description to describe ratings 1 through 5. For example, Exemplary—exceeds expectations is a 5, and Unacceptable—grounds for probation is a 1. Enter your own scores for each performance trait and enter scores based on your manager's review. Save the workbook as **e04b4Performance_LastFirst**.

Convert the list to a table and sort the table alphabetically by performance trait descriptions. Add a total row and select the AVERAGE function for the two ratings columns. Create a conditional formatting rule to highlight cells in the ratings columns for values less than 3. Insert three rows at the top for a title, your name, and the current date. Create a footer with your name on the left side, the date code in the center, and the filename code on the right side. Save and close the workbook, and submit based on your instructor's directions.

Capstone Exercise

You work at Mountain View Realty. A coworker developed a spreadsheet listing houses listed and sold during the past several months. She included addresses, location, list price, selling price, listing date, and date sold. You need to convert the data to a table. You will manage the large worksheet, prepare the worksheet for printing, sort and filter the table, include calculations, and then format the table.

Prepare the Large Worksheet as a Table

You will freeze the panes so that labels remain onscreen. You also want to convert the data to a table so that you can apply table options.

a. Open the *e04c1Houses* workbook and save it as **e04c1Houses_LastFirst**.

b. Freeze the first row on the Sales Data worksheet.

c. Convert the data to a table and apply the **Table Style Medium 17**.

d. Remove duplicate records.

Add Calculated Fields and a Total Row

The office manager asked you to insert a column to display the percentage of list price. The formula finds the sale price percentage of the list price. For example, if a house was listed at $100,000 and sells for $75,000, the percentage of list price is 75%. In some cases, the percentage is more than 100%. This happens when a bidding war occurs and buyers increase their offers, which results in the seller getting more than the list price.

a. Insert a new field to the right of the Selling Price field. Name the new field **Percent of List Price**.

b. Create a formula with structured references to calculate the percentage of the list price.

c. Format the field with **Percent Style** with one decimal place.

d. Insert a new field to the right of the Sale Date field. Name the new field **Days on Market**.

e. Create a formula with structured references to calculate the number of days on the market. Apply the **General number format** to the values.

f. Add a total row to display the average percentage of list price and average number of days on market. Format the average number of days on market as a whole number. Use an appropriate label for the total row.

Sort and Print the Table

To help the office manager compare house sales by city, you will sort the data. Then you will prepare the large table to print.

a. Sort the table by city in alphabetical order and add a second level to sort by days on market with the houses on the market the longest at the top within each city.

b. Adjust column widths so that the data are one page across (three pages total). Wrap the column labels.

c. Repeat the field names on all pages.

d. Change page breaks so that city data do not span between pages and change back to Normal view.

e. Add a footer with your name on the left side, the sheet name code in the center, and the file name code on the right side.

Copy and Filter the Data

The office manager needs to focus on houses that took longer than 30 days to sell within three cities. To keep the original data intact for the agents, you will copy the table data to a new sheet and use that sheet to display the filtered data.

a. Copy the Sales Data sheet and place the duplicate sheet to the right of the original sheet tab. Convert the table to a range of data and delete the average row.

b. Rename the duplicate worksheet **Filtered Data**.

c. Display the filter arrows for the data.

d. Filter the data to display the cities of Alpine, Cedar Hills, and Eagle Mountain.

e. Filter the data to display records for houses that were on the market 30 days or more.

Apply Conditional Formatting

To highlight housing sales to illustrate trends, you will apply conditional formatting. Because data are sorted by city, you will use an icon set to color-code the number of days on market. You will also apply data bar conditional formatting to the sale prices to help the office manager visualize the differences among the sales.

a. Apply the **3 Arrows (Colored) icon set** to the *Days on Market* values.

b. Apply the **Light Blue Data Bar conditional formatting** in the *Gradient Fill* section to the selling prices.

c. Create a new conditional format that applies yellow fill and bold font to values that contain 95% or higher for the *Percent of List Price* column.

d. Edit the conditional format you created so that it formats values 98% or higher.

Finalize the Workbook

You are ready to finalize the workbook by adding a footer to the new worksheet and saving the final workbook.

a. Add a footer with your name on the left side, the sheet name code in the center, and the file name code on the right side.

b. Remove all page breaks in the Filtered Data worksheet.

c. Select **Landscape orientation** and set appropriate margins so that the data will print on one page.

d. Save and close the workbook and submit based on your instructor's directions.

Access

Introduction to Access

CHAPTER 1

Finding Your Way Through an Access Database

OBJECTIVES

AFTER YOU READ THIS CHAPTER, YOU WILL BE ABLE TO:

1. Understand database fundamentals p. 618
2. Use an existing database p. 625
3. Sort table data on one or multiple fields p. 636
4. Create, modify, and remove filters p. 637
5. Know when to use Access or Excel to manage data p. 645
6. Understand relational power p. 646
7. Create a database p. 653

CASE STUDY | Managing a Business in the Global Economy

Northwind Traders* is an international gourmet food distributor that imports and exports specialty foods from around the world. Northwind's products include meats, seafood, dairy products, beverages, and produce. Keeping track of customers, vendors, orders, and inventory is a critical task. The owners of Northwind have just purchased an order-processing database created with Microsoft Office Access 2013 to help manage their customers, suppliers, products, and orders.

You have been hired to learn, use, and manage the database. Northwind's owners are willing to provide training about their business and Access. They expect the learning process to take about three months. After three months, your job will be to support the order-processing team as well as to provide detail and summary reports to the sales force as needed. Your new job at Northwind Traders will be a challenge, but it is also a good opportunity to make a great contribution to a global company. Are you up to the task?

*Northwind Traders was created by the Microsoft Access Team as a sample database for Access 2003. Access 2013 does not include a sample database, so you will use a modified version of Northwind Traders. The names of companies, products, people, characters, and/or data are fictitious.

Databases Are Everywhere!

A ***database*** is a collection of data organized as meaningful information that can be accessed, managed, stored, queried, sorted, and reported. You probably participate in data collection and are exposed to databases on a regular basis. For example, your community college or university uses a database to store registration data. When you enrolled at your institution, you created a profile that was saved in a database. When you registered for this course, your data was entered into a database. If you have a bank account, have a Social Security card, have a medical history, or have booked a flight with an airline, your information is stored in a record in a database.

If you use the Internet, you probably use databases often because the Internet can provide you with easy access to databases. For example, when you shop online or check your bank statement online, you connect to a database. Even when you type a search phrase into Google and click Search, you are using Google's massive database with all of its stored Web page references and keywords. Look for something on Amazon, and you are searching Amazon's database to find a product that you might want to buy. Need a new driver for golfing? Log on to Amazon, search for "golf clubs driver" (see Figure 1.1), and find the right driver with your preferred loft, hand orientation, flex, shaft material, and price range. All of this information is stored in Amazon's products database.

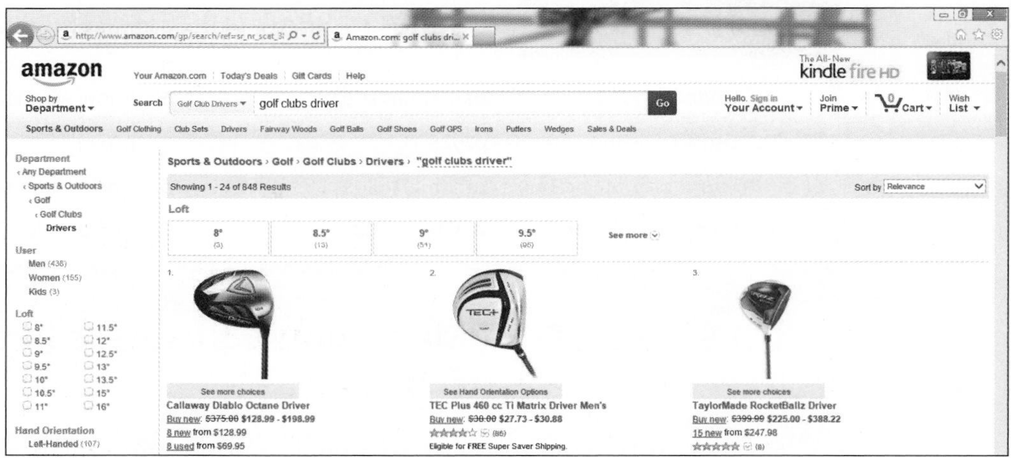

FIGURE 1.1 Amazon Web Site

Organizations rely on data to conduct daily operations, regardless of whether the organization exists as a profit or not-for-profit environment. Organizations maintain data about their customers, employees, orders, volunteers, activities, and facilities. Organizations maintain data about their customers, employees, orders, volunteers, activities, and facilities, and this data needs to be stored, organized, and made available for analysis. *Data* and *information* are two terms that are often used interchangeably. However, when it comes to databases, the two terms mean different things. *Data* is what is entered into a database. *Information* is the finished product that is produced by the database. Data is converted to information by selecting, calculating, sorting, or summarizing records. Decisions in an organization are usually based on information produced by a database, rather than raw data.

In this section, you will learn the fundamentals of organizing data in a database, explore what Access database objects are and what their purpose is, and examine the Access interface.

Understanding Database Fundamentals

People use databases to store collections of data. A ***database management system (DBMS)*** is a software system that provides the tools needed to create, maintain, and use a database. Database management systems make it possible to access and control data and display the information in a variety of formats such as lists, forms, and reports. ***Access*** is the database management system included in the Office 2013 Professional suite and the Office 2013 Professional Academic suite. Access is a valuable decision-making tool that many organizations are using. Advanced Access users and software developers can even use Microsoft Access to develop software applications for specific solutions to the needs of organizations. For example, a health organization uses Access to track and understand disease reports.

Organize Information in a Database and Recognize Access Objects

STEP 2»

An Access database is a structured collection of ***objects***, the main components that are created and used to make the database function. The main object types in an Access database are listed below and discussed in the following paragraphs.

- Tables
- Forms
- Queries
- Reports
- Macros
- Modules

The objects that make up an Access database are available from the ***Navigation Pane***. The Navigation Pane is an Access interface element that organizes and lists the database objects in an Access database. You will learn about the object types and their benefits in the remainder of this section. Later you will learn to create and use these objects.

The foundation of every database is a ***table***, the object in which data, such as a person's name or a product number, is stored. The other objects in a database are based on one or more underlying tables. To understand how an Access database works and how to use Access effectively, you should learn the structure of a table. Tables organize data into columns and rows. Columns display a ***field***, the smallest data element of a table. For example, in the Northwind database, a table containing information about customers would include a Customer ID field. Another field would contain the Company Name. Fields may be required or optional—a contact name may be required, for example, but a contact title may be optional.

Each row in a table contains a ***record***, a complete set of all the fields (data elements) about one person, place, event, or concept. A customer record, for example, would contain all of the fields about a single customer, including the Customer ID, the Company Name, Contact Name, Contact Title, Address, City, etc. Figure 1.2 shows the Northwind database with the Customers table selected in the Navigation Pane. The Customers table is open and shows the records of Northwind customers in the table rows. Each record contains multiple fields, with the field name displaying at the top of each column.

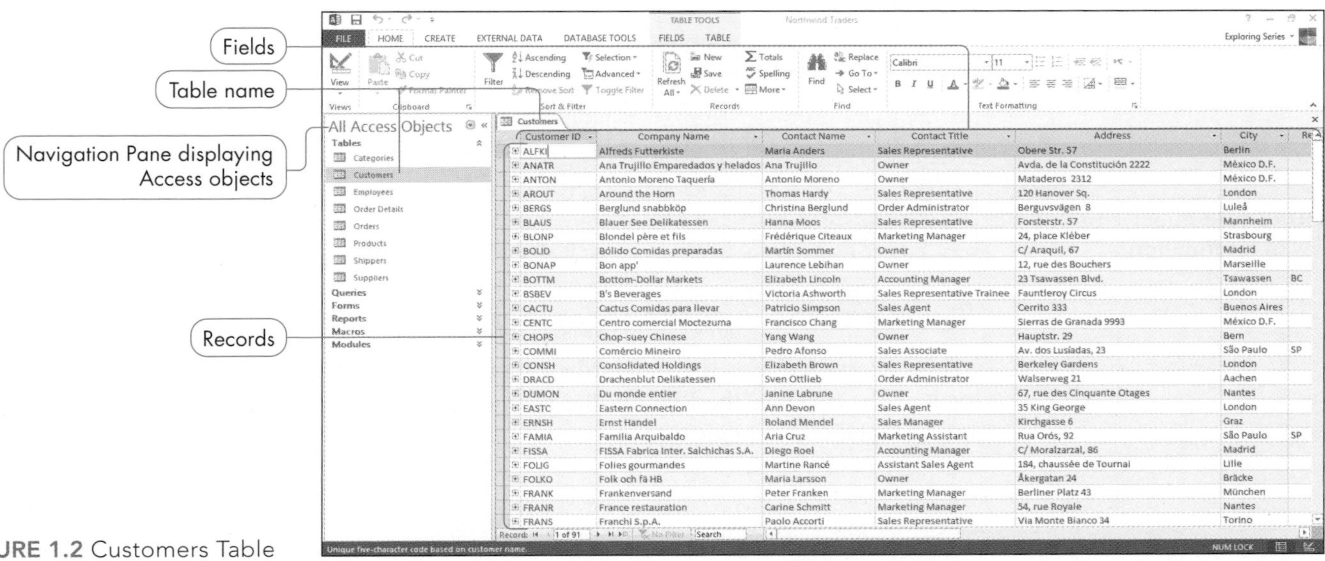

FIGURE 1.2 Customers Table

A ***form*** is an object that gives a user a way of entering and modifying data in databases. Forms enable you to enter, modify, or delete table data. They enable you to manipulate data in the same manner that you would in a table. The difference is that you can create a form that will limit the user to viewing only one record at a time. This helps the user to focus on the data being entered or modified and also provides for more reliable data entry. As an Access user, you will add, delete, and edit records in Form view. As the Access designer, you will create and edit the form structure.

A ***query*** is a question that you ask about the data in your database. For example, how many of our customers live in Boston? The answer is shown in the query results. A query can be used to display only records that meet certain conditions and only the fields that you require. In addition to helping you find and retrieve data that meets the conditions that you specify, you can use a query to update or delete records and to perform predefined or custom calculations with your data.

A ***report*** contains professional-looking formatted information from underlying tables or queries. Reports enable you to print the information in your database and are an effective way to present database information. You have control over the size and appearance of everything in a report. Access provides different views for designing, modifying, and running reports.

Two other object types, macros and modules, are used less frequently unless you are a power Access user. A ***macro*** object is a stored series of commands that carry out an action. You can create a macro to automate simple tasks by selecting an action from a list of macro actions. A ***module*** is similar to a macro, as it is an object that adds functionality to a database, but modules are written using the VBA (Visual Basic for Applications) programming language.

Figure 1.3 displays the different object types in Access with the foundation object—the table—in the center of the illustration. The purpose each object serves is explained underneath the object name. The flow of information between objects is indicated by single arrowhead arrows if the flow is one direction only. Two arrowhead arrows indicate that the flow goes both directions. For example, you can use forms to view, add, delete, or modify data from tables.

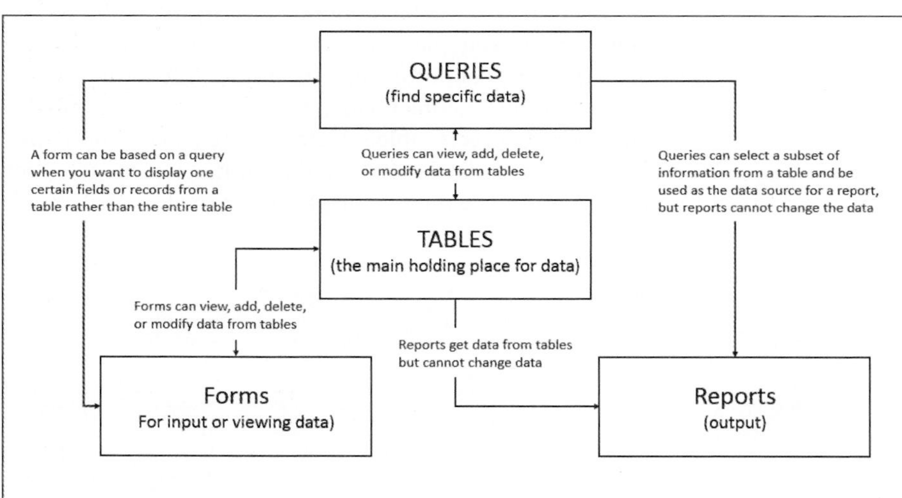

FIGURE 1.3 Object Types and Flow of Information

Examine the Access Interface

While Access includes the standard elements of the Microsoft Office applications interface such as the title bar, the Ribbon, the Home tab, the Backstage view, and scroll bars, it also includes elements unique to Access.

TIP Access Title Bar

By default, the Access 2013 title bar displays the full path name and file name for the Access database. Displaying just the file name can give the application a cleaner or simpler look. To customize the title bar, click the File tab, click Options, and then click Current Database. Type the file name or the name you wish to display in the Application Title box. The title bars of the Access databases in this book have been modified to display only the file names of the databases.

The Access Ribbon has five tabs that will always display, as well as contextual tabs that appear only when particular objects are open. The File tab leads to the Backstage view, which gives you access to a variety of database tools such as Save, Save As, Compact and Repair, Backup Database, and Print. The Home tab, the default Access tab, contains basic editing functions, such as cut and paste, filtering, find and replace, and most formatting actions. This tab also contains the features that enable you to work with record creation and deletion, totals, and spelling.

The Create tab contains all the tools used to create new objects in a database whereas the External Data tab contains all of the operations used to facilitate data import and export. Finally, the Database Tools tab contains the feature that enables users to create relationships between tables and enables use of the more advanced features of Access, such as setting relationships between tables, analyzing a table or query, and migrating data to SharePoint.

On the left side of the screen, you will see the Navigation Pane. The Navigation Pane organizes and lists all of the objects that are needed to make the current database function. You can open any object by double-clicking the object's name in the list. You can also open an object by right-clicking the object name and selecting Open from the shortcut menu. Right-clicking provides other options, such as renaming the object, cutting the object, and copying the object.

Most databases contain multiple tables, queries, forms, and reports. By default, the objects display in groups by object type in the Navigation Pane. If you wish, you can collapse the contents of an object group by clicking the group heading or the double arrows to the right of the group heading. To expand the contents of an object group that has been hidden, click the heading again or click the double arrows to the right of the group heading again. If you wish to change the way objects are grouped in the Navigation Pane, click the list arrow on the Navigation Pane title bar and select your preferred configuration of the available options.

TIP Navigation Pane Display

You may wish to expand the area available for an open object by changing the display of the Navigation Pane to a narrow vertical ribbon. You can toggle the display by clicking the Shutter Bar Open/Close button at the top-right corner of the Navigation Pane. The Shutter Bar Open/Close button looks like a double arrow. Click the button again to expand the Navigation Pane. F11 also toggles the display of the Navigation Pane.

By default, Access uses a Tabbed Documents interface. That means that each object that is open has its own tab beneath the Ribbon and to the right of the Navigation Pane. You can switch between open objects by clicking a tab to make that object active. Figure 1.4 shows the Access interface for the Northwind Traders database, which was introduced in the Case Study at the beginning of the chapter. The Navigation Pane is grouped by object type. The Tables and Reports groups in the Navigation Pane are expanded. The Table Tools contextual tab displays because the Employees table is open. The Employees table shows the records for nine employees. The employee records contain multiple fields about each employee, including the employee's Last Name, First Name, Hire Date, Region, and so on. Occasionally a field does not contain a value for a particular record. For example, one of the employees, Nancy Davolio, has not been assigned a title yet. The value of that field is missing. Access shows a blank cell when data is missing.

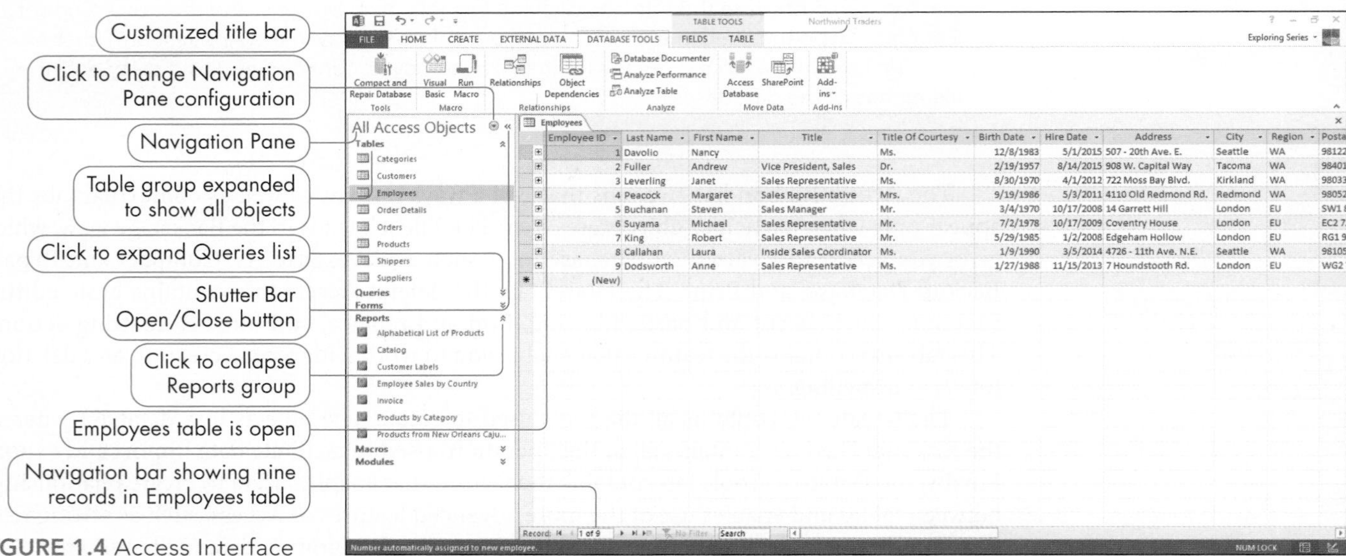

FIGURE 1.4 Access Interface

Explore Access Views

Access provides two different ways to view a table: the Datasheet view and the Design view. To switch between views:

- Click the HOME tab and click View in the Views group to toggle between the current view and the previous view.
- Click the HOME tab, click the View arrow in the Views group, and then select the view you want to use.
- Right-click the object tab and select the view you want to use.
- Right-click the object in the Navigation Pane and select the view you want to use.
- Click one of the view shortcuts in the lower-right corner of the Access window.

The ***Datasheet view*** is a grid containing fields (columns) and records (rows), similar to an Excel spreadsheet. You can view, add, edit, and delete records in the Datasheet view. Figure 1.5 shows the Datasheet view for the Northwind Customers table. Each row contains a record for a specific customer. Click the ***record selector*** at the beginning of a row to select the record. Each column represents a field or one attribute about a customer. Click the ***field selector***, or column heading, to select a column.

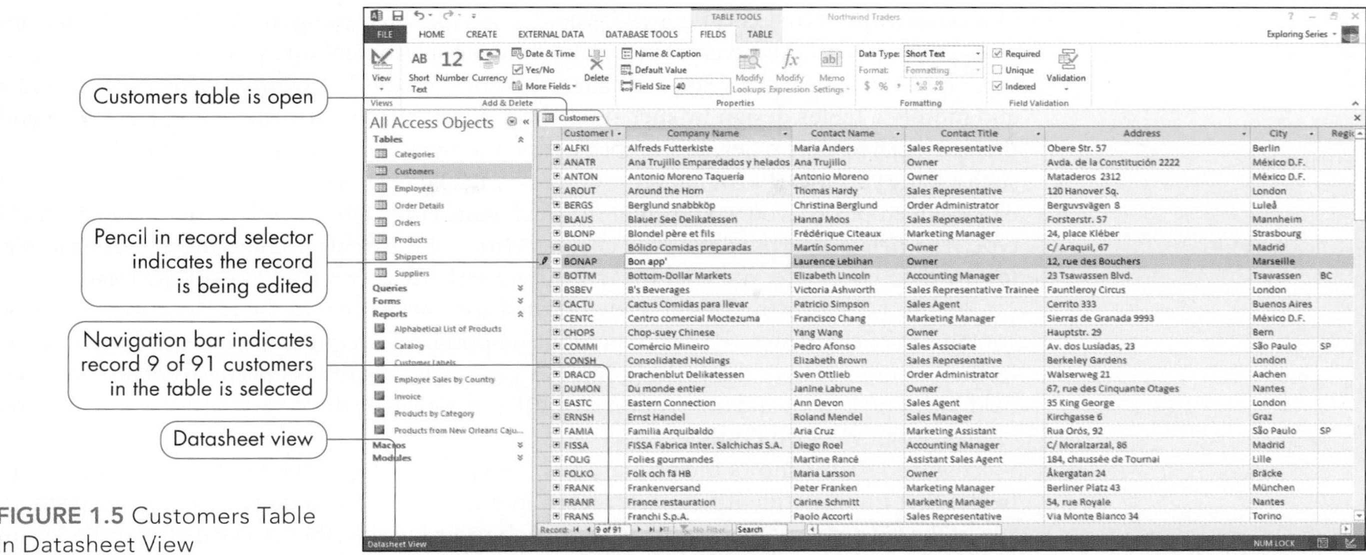

FIGURE 1.5 Customers Table in Datasheet View

The navigation bar at the bottom of Figure 1.5 shows that the Customers table has 91 records and that record number 9 is the current record. The vertical scroll bar on the right side of the window displays only when the table contains more records than can appear in the window at one time. Similarly, the horizontal scroll bar at the bottom of the window displays only when the table contains more fields than can appear in the window at one time.

The pencil symbol to the left of Record 9 indicates that the data in that record is being edited and that changes have not yet been saved. The pencil symbol disappears when you move to another record. It is important to understand that Access saves data automatically as soon as you move from one record to another. This may seem counterintuitive at first because other Office applications, such as Word and Excel, do not save changes and additions automatically.

Figure 1.6 shows the navigation buttons on the ***navigation bar*** that you use to move through the records in a table, query, or form. The buttons enable you to go to the first record, the previous record, the next record, or the last record. The button with the yellow asterisk is used to add a new (blank) record. You can also type a number directly into the current record field, and Access will take you to that record. Finally, the navigation bar enables you to find a record based on a single word. Type the word in the search box, and Access will locate the first record that contains the word.

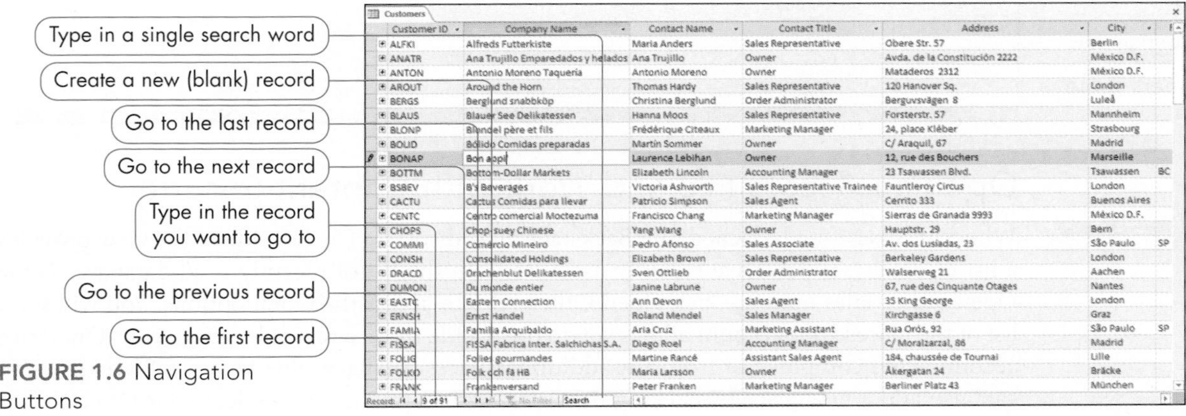

FIGURE 1.6 Navigation Buttons

You can also use the Find command in the Find group on the Home tab to locate specific records within a table, form, or query. You can search for a single field or the entire record, match all or part of the selected field(s), move forward or back in a table, or specify a case-sensitive search. The Replace command can be used to substitute one value for another. Select Replace All if you want Access to automatically search for and replace every instance of a value without first checking with you. Be careful when using the Replace All option for global replacement, however, because unintended replacements are possible.

The ***Design view*** gives you a detailed view of the table's structure and is used to create and modify a table's design by specifying the fields it will contain, the fields' data types, and their associated properties. Data types define the type of data that will be stored in a field, such as short text, long text, numeric, currency, etc. For example, if you need to store the hire date of an employee, you would enter the field name Hire Date and select the Date/Time data type. The ***field properties*** define the characteristics of the fields in more detail. For example, for the field Hire Date, you could set a field property that requires a Short Date format.

Figure 1.7 shows the Design view for the Customers table. In the top portion, each row contains the field names, the data type, and an optional description for each field in the table. In the bottom portion, the Field Properties pane contains the properties (details) for each field. Click on a field, and the properties for that field will be displayed in the bottom portion of the Design view window.

Figure 1.7 also shows the primary key. The ***primary key*** is the field (or combination of fields) that uniquely identifies each record in a table. The CustomerID field is the primary key in the Customers table; it ensures that each record in the table can be distinguished from every other record. It also helps prevent the occurrence of duplicate records. Primary key fields may be numbers, letters, or a combination of both. In Figure 1.7, the primary key has an ***AutoNumber*** data type (a number that is generated by Access and is automatically incremented each time a record is added). Another example of a primary key is an automatically generated Employee ID.

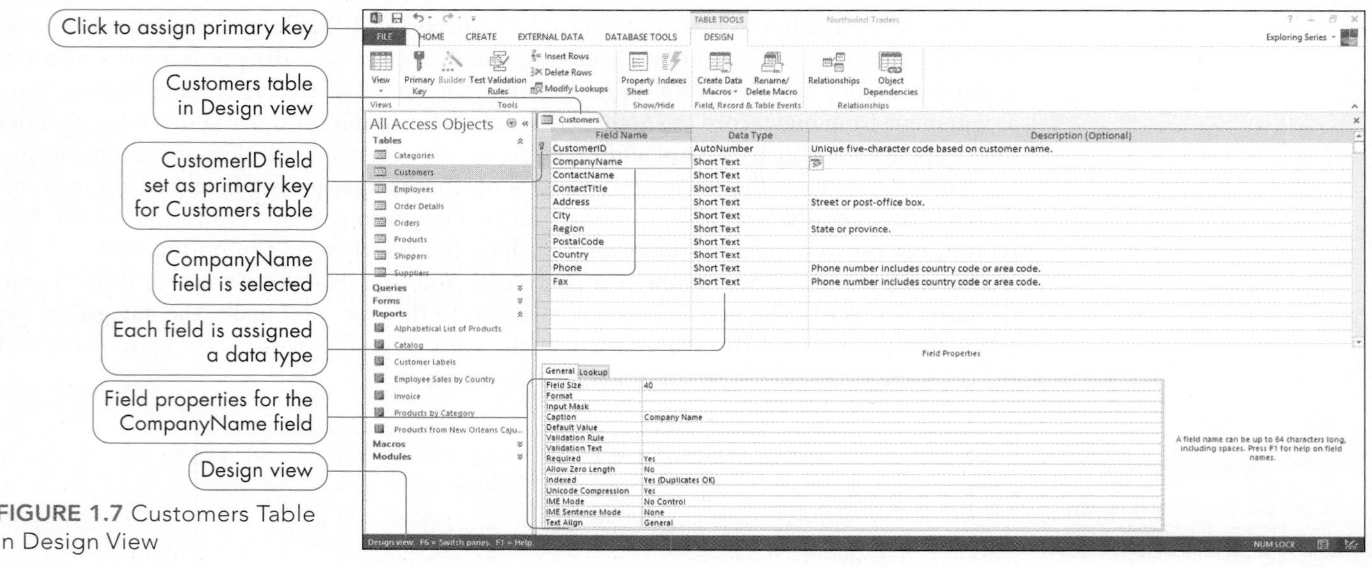

FIGURE 1.7 Customers Table in Design View

Open an Access File and Work with Content Security

STEP 1» When Access is first launched, the Backstage view displays. The left side of the view provides a list of databases you have recently used. Beneath the list of recently used databases is the Open Other Files option. Click Open Other Files to access the Open options. You will see a list of the places your account allows you to open a file from: a recent location, your OneDrive account, your computer, or from any additional places you have added to your Places list. You can also add a new place by clicking the *Add a Place* option. If you select your OneDrive or another place and the desired database is not in the recent list, you will need to click Browse to open the Open dialog box. Then you can locate and select the database and click Open.

If you are currently using Access and wish to open another database, do the following:

1. Click the FILE tab.
2. Click Open in Backstage view to access Open options.
3. Select the place where the database is stored.

4. Click Browse to open the Open dialog box.
5. Locate and select the database and click Open.

If you open a database from a location you have not designated as a trusted location or open a database that does not have a digital signature from a publisher you can trust, Access will display a message bar immediately below the Ribbon. The message bar displays a security warning designed to prevent you from opening a database that may contain harmful code that can be hidden in macros or VBA modules. Click the Enable Content button if you trust the database's source—it becomes a trusted location. After you click Enable Content, Access closes the database and reopens the file to enable the content. Access also adds the database to its list of trusted documents so you will not see the security message again. All content from this publisher and associated with this book can be trusted.

Using an Existing Database

Databases must be carefully managed to keep information accurate. Records need to be edited when changes occur and when new records are added, and records may need to be deleted on occasion. All of these processes are easily accomplished using Access. Managing a database also requires that you understand when data is saved and when you need to use the Save commands.

Understand the Difference Between Working in Storage and Memory

STEP 3»

The way Access performs its save function is different from the other Microsoft Office applications. Word, Excel, and PowerPoint all work primarily from memory. In those applications, your work is not automatically saved to your storage location. You must save your work. This could be catastrophic if you are working with a PowerPoint presentation and you forget to save it. If the power is lost, you may lose your presentation. Access, on the other hand, works primarily from storage. As you enter and update the data in an Access database, the changes are automatically saved to the storage location you specified when you saved the database. If a power failure occurs, you will lose only the changes to the record that you are currently editing.

When you make a change to a record's content in an Access table (for example, changing a customer's cell phone number), Access saves your changes as soon as you move the insertion point to a different record. However, you are required to save after you modify the design of a table, a query, a form, or a report. When you modify an object's design, such as widening a field display on the Customers form, and then close it, Access will prompt you with the message "Do you want to save changes to the design of form 'Customers'?" Click Yes to save your changes.

Also in Access, you can click Undo to reverse the most recent change (the phone number you just modified) to a single record immediately after making changes to that record. However, unlike other Office programs that enable multiple Undo steps, you cannot use Undo to reverse multiple edits in Access.

With an Access database file, several users can work in the same file at the same time. Databases are often located on company servers, making it easy to have multiple users working in the same database at the same time. As long as multiple users do not attempt to change the same record at the same time, Access will let these users access the database simultaneously. So one person can be adding records to the Customers table while another can be creating a query based on the Products table. Two users can even work on the same table as long as they are not working on the same record.

Add, Edit, and Delete Records

STEP 4» To add a new record, click New in the Records group on the Home tab or click *New (blank) record* on the navigation bar. In a table, you can also click the first column of the blank row beneath the last record. As soon as you begin typing, the asterisk record indicator changes to a pencil icon to show that you are in editing mode. Press Tab to move to the next column so that you can enter the data for the next field. Pressing Tab in the last column in the record saves the record and moves the insertion point to the next record. You can also press Shift+Enter at any time in the record to save the record. The easiest way to save the record is to press the up or down arrow on your keyboard, which moves you to another record. As soon as you move to another record Access automatically saves the changes to the record you created or changed.

To edit a record, tab to the field you want to modify and type the new data. When you start typing, you erase all existing data in the field because the entire field is selected. You can switch to Edit mode by pressing F2. In Edit mode, you will not automatically delete all the data in the field. Instead, you can position your insertion point and make the changes you want.

REFERENCE Keyboard Shortcuts for Entering Data

Keystroke	Result
Up arrow (↑)	Moves insertion point up one row.
Down arrow (↓)	Moves insertion point down one row.
Left arrow (←)	Moves insertion point left one field in the same row.
Right arrow (→)	Moves insertion point right one field in the same row.
Tab or Enter	Moves insertion point right one field in the same row.
Shift+Tab	Moves insertion point left one field in the same row.
Home	Moves insertion point to the first field in the current row.
End	Moves insertion point to the last field in the current row.
Page Up	Moves insertion point up one screen.
Page Down	Moves insertion point down one screen.
Ctrl+Home	Moves insertion point to the first field in the first row.
Ctrl+End	Moves insertion point to the last field in the last row.
Esc	Cancels any changes made in the current field while in Edit mode.
Ctrl+Z	Reverses the last edit.
Ctrl+semicolon (;)	Enters the current date.
Ctrl+Alt+Spacebar	Enters the default value of a field.
Ctrl+single quote	Enters the value from the same field in the previous record.
Ctrl+plus sign (+)	Moves to a new record row.
Ctrl+minus sign (–)	Deletes the current record.

STEP 5» To delete a record, click the row selector for the record you want to delete and click Delete in the Records group on the Home tab. You can also delete a selected record by pressing Delete on the keyboard, or by right-clicking the row selector and selecting Delete Record from the shortcut menu.

Deleting Records

Be careful about deleting records in a database. Deleting a record may result in the deletion of records in a related table. That information may be critical to the organization. For example, deleting an inactive customer may seem like a good idea, but if you delete the customer it could impact your order history.

Save As, Compact and Repair, and Back Up Access Files

STEP 6»

The Backstage view gives you access to the Save As command. When you click the Save As command, you can choose the file type you want to save: the database or the current object. Having the option of saving the entire database or just a component of it distinguishes Access from Word, Excel, and PowerPoint. Those applications have only one thing being saved—the primary document, workbook, or presentation. Save Database As enables you to select whether you want to save the database in the default database format (Access 2007–2013 file format), in one of the earlier Access formats, or as a template. Save Object As enables you to make a copy of the current Access object or publish a copy of the object as a PDF or XPS file. A PDF or XPS file looks the same on most computers because these file types preserve the object's formatting. PDF and XPS files also have a small file size. You can also click Save on the Quick Access Toolbar to save an active object—clicking Save on the Quick Access Toolbar does not save the database.

To help you manage your database so that it operates efficiently and securely, Access provides two utilities to help protect the data within a database: ***Compact and Repair***, which reduces the size of the database, and ***Back Up Database***, which creates a duplicate copy of the database.

Databases have a tendency to expand with everyday use and may become corrupt, so Access provides the *Compact and Repair Database* utility. Entering data, creating queries, running reports, and adding and deleting objects will all cause a database file to expand. This growth may increase storage requirements and may also impact database performance. When you run the Compact and Repair utility, it creates a new database file behind the scenes and copies all the objects from the original database into the new one. As it copies the objects into the new file, Access removes temporary objects and unclaimed space due to deleted objects, which results in a smaller database file. *Compact and Repair* will also defragment a fragmented database file if needed. When the utility is finished copying the data, it deletes the original file and renames the new one with the same name as the original. This utility can also be used to repair a corrupt database. In most cases, only a small amount of data—the last record modified—will be lost during the repair process. You should compact your database every day. To compact and repair an open database, do the following:

1. Close all open objects in the database.
2. Click the FILE tab.
3. Click *Compact and Repair Database* in the Info options.

As an alternative, you can click the Database Tools tab and click *Compact and Repair Database* in the Tools group.

Automatic Compact

You can have Access compact the open database each time you close it by using the *Compact and Close* option. To use this option, click File to open the Backstage view. Click Options and click Current Database. In the *Options for the current database* pane, click the *Compact on Close* check box under Application Options. Click OK.

The Back Up Database utility makes a copy of the entire database to protect your database from loss or damage. Imagine what would happen to a firm that loses the orders placed but not shipped, a charity that loses the list of donor contributions, or a hospital that loses the digital records of its patients. Making backups is especially important when you have multiple users working with the database. When you use the Back Up Database utility, Access provides a file name for the backup that uses the same file name as the database you are backing up, an underscore, and the current date. This makes it easy for you to keep track of databases by the date they were created. To back up a database, do the following:

1. Click the FILE tab and click Save As.
2. Click Save Database As under File Types, if necessary.
3. Click Back Up Database under the Advanced group.
4. Click Save As. Revise the location and file name if you want to change either and click Save.

In Hands-On Exercise 1, you will work with the Northwind Traders database discussed in the Case Study at the beginning of the chapter. You open the database and examine the interface and Access views, organize information, work with records, and save, compact, repair, and back up the database.

Quick Concepts

1. Name the six objects in an Access database and briefly describe the purpose of each. ***p. 619***
2. What is the difference between Datasheet view and Design view in a table? ***p. 622***
3. What is meant by the statement "Access works from storage"? ***p. 625***
4. What is the purpose of the *Compact and Repair* utility? ***p. 627***

Hands-On Exercises

1 Databases Are Everywhere!

Northwind purchases food items from suppliers around the world and sells them to restaurants and specialty food shops. Northwind depends on the data stored in its Access database to process orders and make daily decisions. In your new position with Northwind Traders, you need to spend time getting familiar with the Access database. You will open Northwind's database, examine the Access interface, review the existing objects in the database, and explore Access views. You will add, edit, and delete records using both tables and forms. Finally, you will compact and repair, and back up the database.

Skills covered: Open an Access File and Work with Content Security • Examine the Access Interface, Explore Access Views, Organize Information in a Database, and Recognize Access Objects and Edit a Record and Understand the Difference Between Working in Storage and Memory • Add a Record • Delete a Record • Save As, Compact and Repair, and Back Up the Database

STEP 1 » OPEN AN ACCESS FILE AND WORK WITH CONTENT SECURITY

This exercise introduces you to the Northwind Traders database. You will use this database to learn the fundamentals of working with database files. Refer to Figure 1.8 as you complete Step 1.

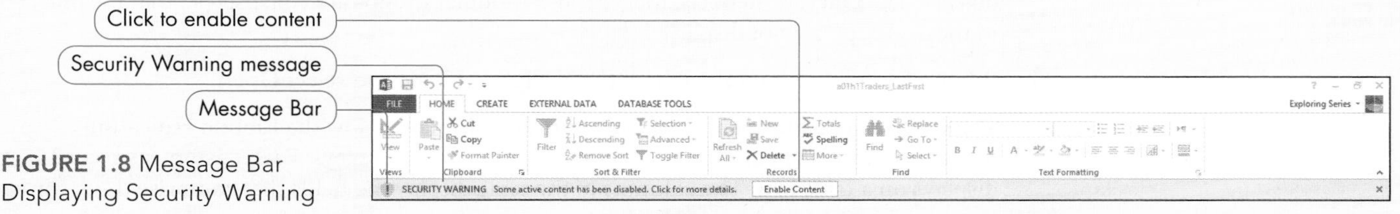

FIGURE 1.8 Message Bar Displaying Security Warning

a. Open Access, click **Open Other Files**, click **Computer**, and then click **Browse**. Navigate to the folder location designated by your instructor. Click *a01h1Traders* and click **Open**.

b. Click the **FILE tab**, click **Save As**, click **Save Database As**, and then verify *Access Database* is selected under *Database File Types*. Click **Save As** and save the file as **a01h1Traders_LastFirst**.

When you save files, use your last and first names. For example, as the Access author, I would save my database as *a01h1traders_KrebsCynthia*. The Security Warning message bar appears below the Ribbon, indicating that some database content is disabled.

c. Click **Enable Content** on the Security Warning message bar.

When you open an Access file from the student files associated with this book, you will need to enable the content. You may be confident of the trustworthiness of the files for this book. Keep the database open for the rest of the exercise.

STEP 2 » EXAMINE THE ACCESS INTERFACE, EXPLORE ACCESS VIEWS, ORGANIZE INFORMATION IN A DATABASE, AND RECOGNIZE ACCESS OBJECTS

Now that you have opened Northwind Traders, you examine the Navigation Pane, objects, and views to become familiar with these fundamental Access features. Refer to Figure 1.9 as you complete Step 2.

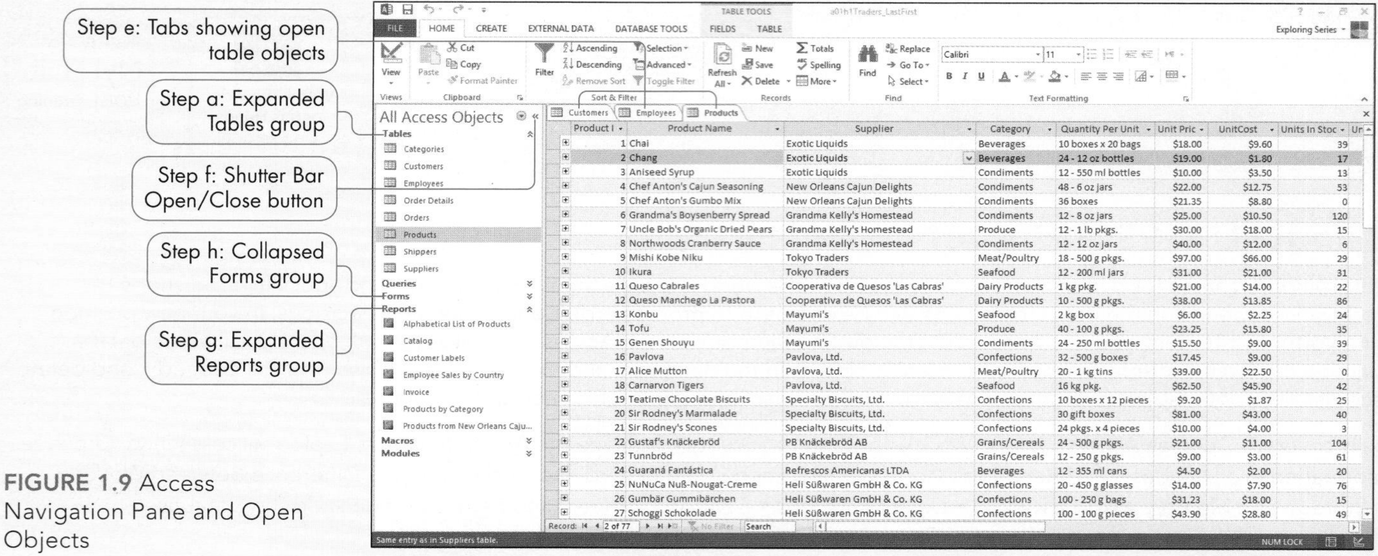

FIGURE 1.9 Access Navigation Pane and Open Objects

a. Scroll through the Navigation Pane and note the Access objects listed under each expanded group.

The Tables group and the Forms group are expanded, displaying all of the tables and forms objects. The Queries, Reports, Macros, and Modules groups are collapsed so that the objects in those groups are not displayed.

b. Right-click the **Customers table** in the Navigation Pane and select **Open**.

The Customers table opens. The Customers tab displays below the Ribbon indicating the table object is open. The data contained in the table displays. Each customer's record displays on a table row. The columns of the table display the fields that comprise the records. You are viewing the table in Datasheet view.

c. Click **View** in the Views group on the HOME tab.

The view of the Customers table switches to Design view. The top portion of the view displays each field that comprises a customer record, the field's data type, and an optional description of what the field should contain. The bottom portion of the view displays the field properties (attributes) for the selected field.

d. Click **View** in the Views group on the HOME tab again.

Because View is a toggle button, your view returns to the Datasheet view, which resembles an Excel worksheet.

e. Double-click **Employees** in the Navigation Pane Tables group and double-click **Products** in the same location.

The tabs for three table objects display below the Ribbon: Customers, Employees, and Products.

f. Click the **Shutter Bar Open/Close button** on the title bar of the Navigation Pane to contract the Navigation Pane. Click the button again to expand the Navigation Pane.

The Shutter Bar Open/Close button toggles to allow you to view more in the open object window, or to enable you to view your database objects.

g. Scroll down in the Navigation Pane and click **Reports**.

The Reports group expands, and all report objects display.

h. Click the arrows to the right of Forms in the Navigation Pane.

The Forms group collapses and individual form objects no longer display.

STEP 3 » EDIT A RECORD AND UNDERSTAND THE DIFFERENCE BETWEEN WORKING IN STORAGE AND MEMORY

You need to learn to edit the data in the Northwind database, because data can change. For example, employees will change their address and phone numbers when they move, and customers will change their order data from time to time. Refer to Figure 1.10 as you complete Step 3.

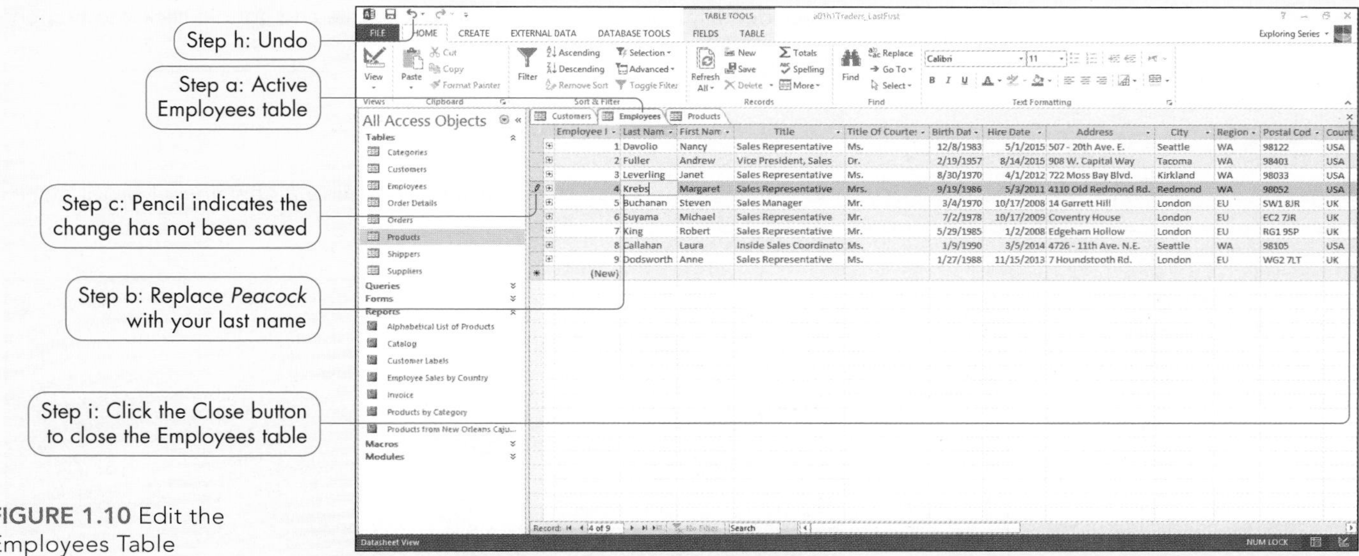

FIGURE 1.10 Edit the Employees Table

a. Click the **Employees tab** to activate the Employees table.

b. Click the **Last Name field** in the fourth row. Double-click **Peacock**; the entire name highlights. Type your last name to replace *Peacock*.

Your last name replaces Peacock. For example, as the Access author, my last name, Krebs, replaces Peacock.

c. Press **Tab** to move to the next field in the fourth row. Replace *Margaret* with your first name and press **Tab**.

Your first name replaces Margaret. For example, as the Access author, my first name, Cynthia, replaces Margaret. You have made changes to two fields in the same record. The pencil symbol in the row selector box indicates that the record has not yet been saved.

d. Click **Undo** on the Quick Access Toolbar.

Your first and last names revert back to *Margaret Peacock* because you have not yet left the record.

e. Type your first and last names again to replace *Margaret Peacock*. Press **Tab**.

You should now be in the title field and your title, *Sales Representative*, is selected. The record has not been saved, as indicated by the pencil symbol in the row selector box.

f. Click anywhere in the third row where Janet Leverling's data is stored.

The pencil symbol disappears, indicating your changes have been saved.

g. Click the **Address field** in the first record, Nancy Davolio's record. Select the entire address and then type **4004 East Morningside Dr**. Click anywhere on the second record, Andrew Fuller's record.

h. Click **Undo**.

Nancy Davolio's address reverts back to 507- 20th Ave. E. However, the Undo command is now faded. You can no longer undo the change that you made replacing Margaret Peacock's name with your own.

i. Click the **Close (X) button** at the top of the table to close the Employees table.

The Employees table closes. You are not prompted to save your changes; they have already been saved for you because Access works in storage, not memory. If you reopen the Employees table, you will see your name in place of Margaret Peacock's name.

> **TROUBLESHOOTING:** If you click the Close (X) button on the title bar at the top right of the window and accidentally close the database, locate the file and double-click it to reopen the file.

STEP 4 ›› ADD A RECORD

You need to add new products to the Northwind database because the company is adding a new line of products. Refer to Figure 1.11 as you complete Step 4.

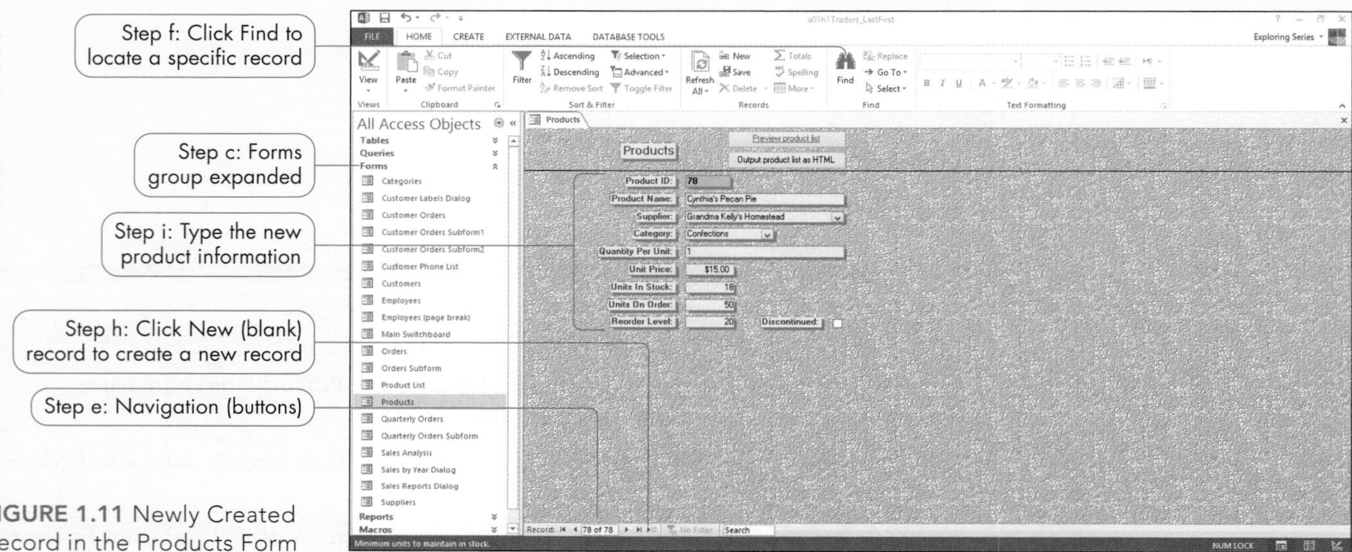

FIGURE 1.11 Newly Created Record in the Products Form

a. Right-click the **Customers tab** and click **Close All**.

b. Click the **Tables group** in the Navigation Pane to collapse it and collapse the **Reports group**.

c. Click the **Forms group** in the Navigation Pane to expand the list of available forms.

d. Double-click the **Products form** to open it.

e. Locate the navigation buttons at the bottom of the Access window. Practice moving from one record to the next. Click **Next record** and click **Last record**; click **Previous record** and click **First record**.

f. Click **Find** in the Find group on the HOME tab, type **Grandma** in the **Find What box**, click the **Match arrow**, and then select **Any Part of Field**. Click **Find Next**.

You should see the data for Grandma's Boysenberry Spread. Selecting the Any Part of the Field option will return a match even if it is contained in the middle of a word.

g. Close the Find dialog box.

h. Click **New (blank) record** on the navigation bar.

i. Enter the following information for a new product.

Field Name	Value to Type
Product Name	*Your name*'s Pecan Pie
Supplier	Grandma Kelly's Homestead (click the arrow to select from the list of Suppliers)
Category	Confections (click the arrow to select from the list of Categories)
Quantity Per Unit	1
Unit Price	15.00
Units in Stock	18
Units on Order	50
Reorder Level	20
Discontinued	No (leave the check box unchecked)

As soon as you begin typing in the product name box, Access assigns a Product ID, in this case 78, to the record. The Product ID is used as the primary key in the Products table.

j. Click anywhere on the Pecan Pie record you just entered. Click the **FILE tab**, click **Print**, and then click **Print Preview**.

The first four records display in the Print Preview.

k. Click **Last Page** in the navigation bar and click **Previous Page** to show the new record you entered.

The beginning of the Pecan Pie record is now visible. The record continues on the next page.

l. Click **Close Print Preview** in the Close Preview group.

m. Close the Products form.

STEP 5 » DELETE A RECORD

To help you understand how Access stores data, you verify that the new product is in the Products table. You also attempt to delete a record. Refer to Figure 1.12 as you complete Step 5.

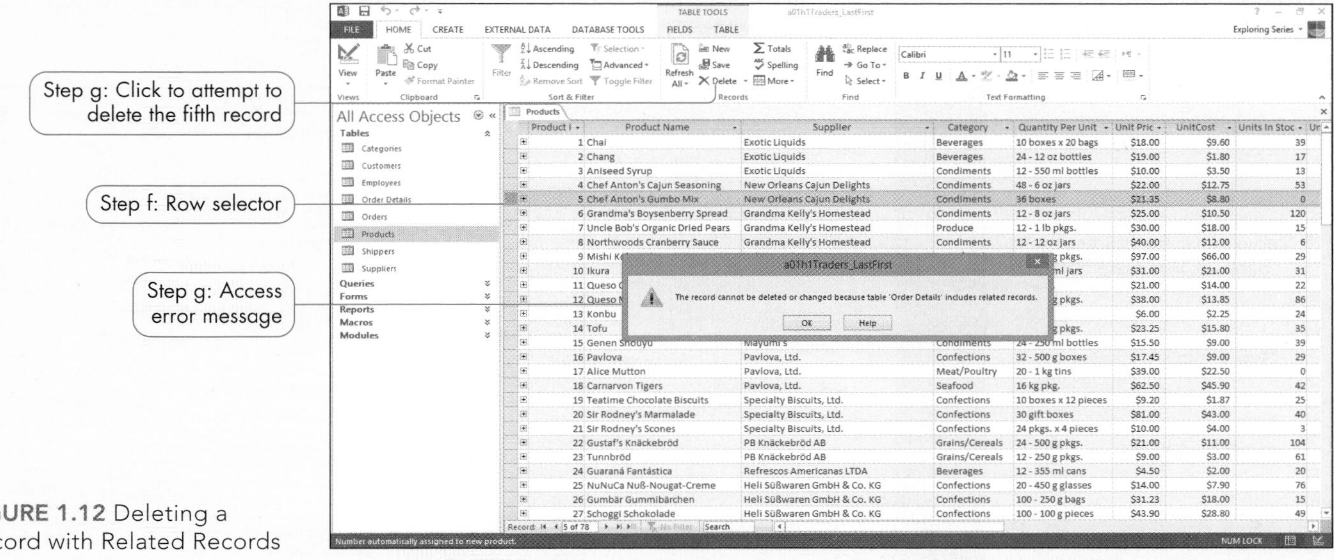

FIGURE 1.12 Deleting a Record with Related Records

a. Click the **Forms group** in the Navigation Pane to collapse it and expand the **Tables group**.

b. Double-click the **Products table** to open it.

c. Click **Last record** in the navigation bar.

The Pecan Pie record you entered in the Products form is listed as the last record in the Products table. The Products form was created from the Products table. Your newly created record, Pecan Pie, is stored in the Products table even though you added it using the form.

d. Navigate to the fifth record in the table, *Chef Anton's Gumbo Mix.*

e. Use the horizontal scroll bar to scroll right until you see the Discontinued field.

The check mark in the Discontinued check box tells you that this product has been discontinued.

f. Click the **row selector** to the left of the fifth record.

The row highlights with a red-colored border to show that it is selected.

g. Click **Delete** in the Records group and read the error message.

The error message that displays tells you that you cannot delete this record because the table 'Order Details' has related records. (Customers ordered this product in the past.) Even though the product is now discontinued and no stock remains, it cannot be deleted from the Products table because related records exist in the Order Detail table.

h. Click **OK**.

i. Navigate to the last record and click the **row selector** to highlight the entire row.

j. Click **Delete** in the Records group. Read the warning.

The warning box that appears tells you that this action cannot be undone. Although this product can be deleted because it was just entered and no orders were created for it, you do not want to delete the record.

k. Click **No**. You do not want to delete this record. Close the Products table.

> **TROUBLESHOOTING:** If you clicked Yes and deleted the record, return to Step i. Reenter the information for this record. You will need it later in the lesson.

STEP 6 ›› SAVE AS, COMPACT AND REPAIR, AND BACK UP THE DATABASE

You will protect the Northwind Traders database by using the two built-in Access utilities—Compact and Repair and Back Up Database. Refer to Figure 1.13 as you complete Step 6.

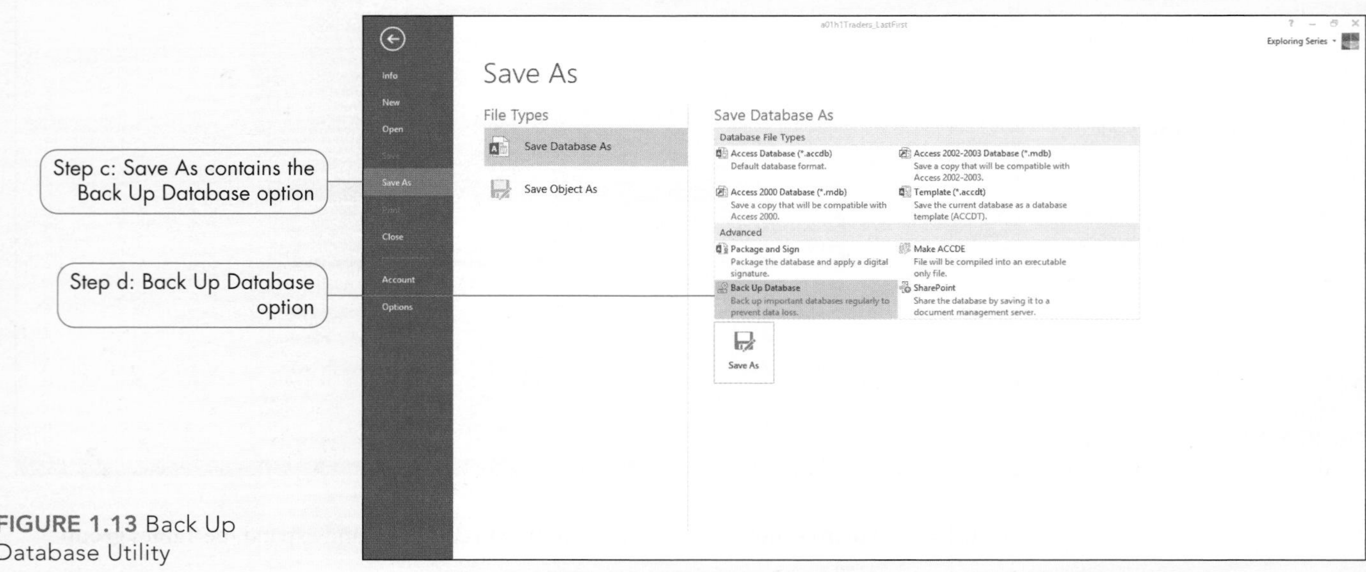

FIGURE 1.13 Back Up Database Utility

a. Click the **FILE tab** to open the Backstage view.

b. Click Compact & Repair Database.

Using the *Compact and Repair* utility helps improve the performance of your database.

c. Click the **FILE tab**, click **Save As**, and then click **Save Database As** under *File Types*, if necessary.

d. Double-click **Back Up Database** under the Advanced group to open the **Save As** dialog box.

   The backup utility assigns the default name by adding a date to your file name.

e. Verify the *Save in* folder displays the location where you want your file saved and click **Save**.

   You just created a backup of the database after completing Hands-On Exercise 1. The original database *a01h1traders_LastFirst* remains onscreen.

f. Keep the database open if you plan to continue with Hands-On Exercise 2. If not, close the database and exit Access.

Sorts and Filters

Access provides you with many tools that you can use to change the order of information and to identify and extract only the data needed at the moment. For example, you might need to display information by customer name in alphabetical order. Or you might need to know which suppliers are located in New Orleans or which customers have outstanding orders that were placed in the last seven days. You might use that information to identify possible disruptions to product deliveries or customers who may need a telephone call to let them know the status of their orders.

In this section, you will learn how to sort information and to isolate records in a table based on certain criteria.

Sorting Table Data on One or Multiple Fields

You can change the order of information by sorting one or more fields. A ***sort*** lists records in a specific sequence, such as alphabetically by last name or by ascending EmployeeID. To sort a table on one criteria, do the following:

STEP 4»

1. Click in the field that you want to use to sort the records.
2. Click Ascending or Descending in the Sort & Filter group on the HOME tab.

Ascending sorts a list of text data in alphabetical order or a numeric list in lowest to highest order. ***Descending*** sorts a list of text data in reverse alphabetical order or a numeric list in highest to lowest order. Figure 1.14 shows the Customers table for a bank sorted in ascending order by state.

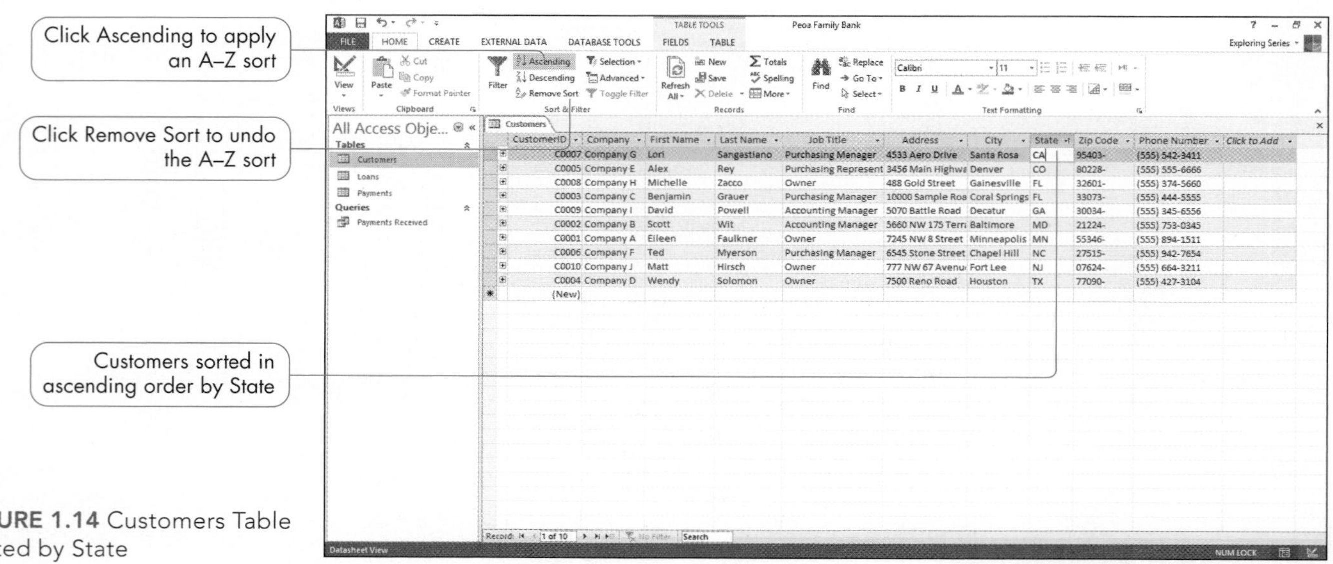
Click Ascending to apply an A–Z sort
Click Remove Sort to undo the A–Z sort
Customers sorted in ascending order by State

FIGURE 1.14 Customers Table Sorted by State

Access can sort records by more than one field. Access sorts multiple criteria by first sorting the column on the left. The column immediately to the right of that column is sorted next. Because of this, you must arrange your columns in this order. To move a column, select the column and hold down the left mouse button. A heavy black bar appears to the left of the column. Drag the column to the position where you want it for the multiple sort.

Creating, Modifying, and Removing Filters

In Hands-On Exercise 1, you added Pecan Pie to the Products table with a category of Confections, but you also saw many other products. Suppose you wanted to see a list of just the products in the Confections category. To obtain this list, you would open the Products table in Datasheet view and create a filter. A ***filter*** displays a subset of records based on specified criteria. A ***criterion*** (or criteria, plural) is a number, a text phrase, or an expression used to select records from a table. Therefore, to view a list of all Confections, you would need to filter the Category field of the Products table using Confections as the criterion.

You can use filters to analyze data quickly. Applying a filter does not delete any records; filters only *hide* records that do not match the criteria. Two types of filters are discussed in this section: *Filter by Selection* and *Filter by Form*.

Use, Modify, and Remove a Filter

Filter by Selection displays only the records that match a criterion you select. To use *Filter by Selection*, do the following:

STEP 1》

1. Click in any field that contains the criterion on which you want to filter.
2. Click Selection in the Sort & Filter group on the HOME tab.
3. Select *Equals "criterion"* from the list of options.

Figure 1.15 displays a Customers table with 10 records. The records in the table are displayed in sequence according to the CustomerID, which is also the primary key (the field or combination of fields that uniquely identifies a record). The navigation bar at the bottom indicates that the active record is the first row in the table. *Owner* in the Job Title field is selected.

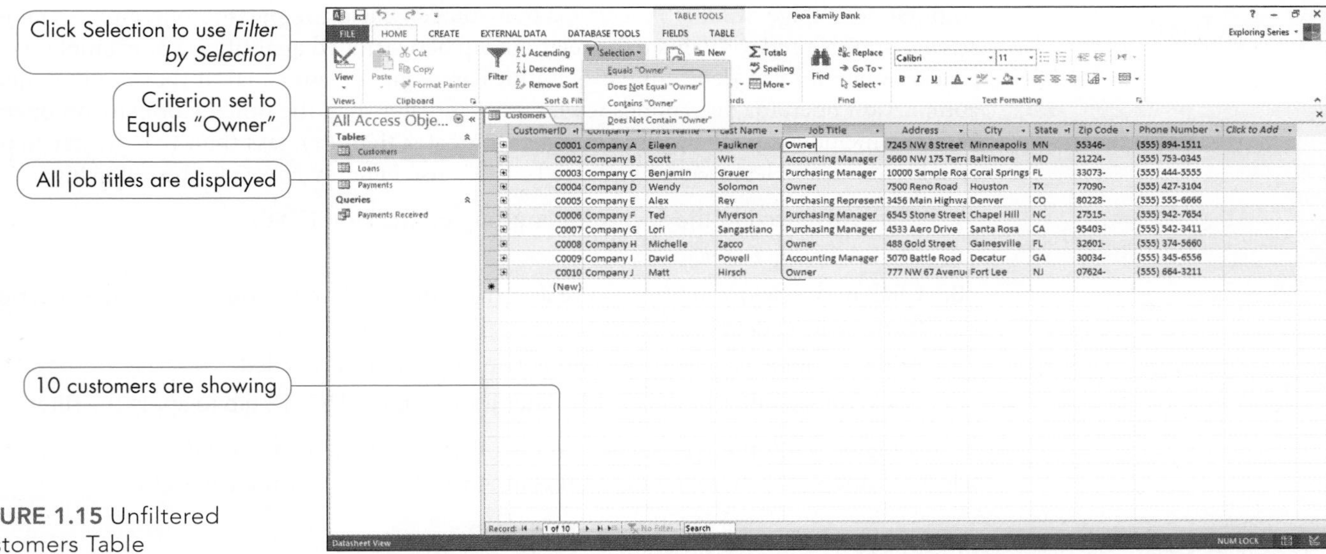

Click Selection to use Filter by Selection
Criterion set to Equals "Owner"
All job titles are displayed
10 customers are showing

FIGURE 1.15 Unfiltered Customers Table

Figure 1.16 displays a filtered view of the Customers table, showing records with the job title *Owner*. The navigation bar shows that this is a filtered list containing 4 records matching the criteria. (The Customers table still contains the original 10 records, but only 4 records are visible with the filter applied.)

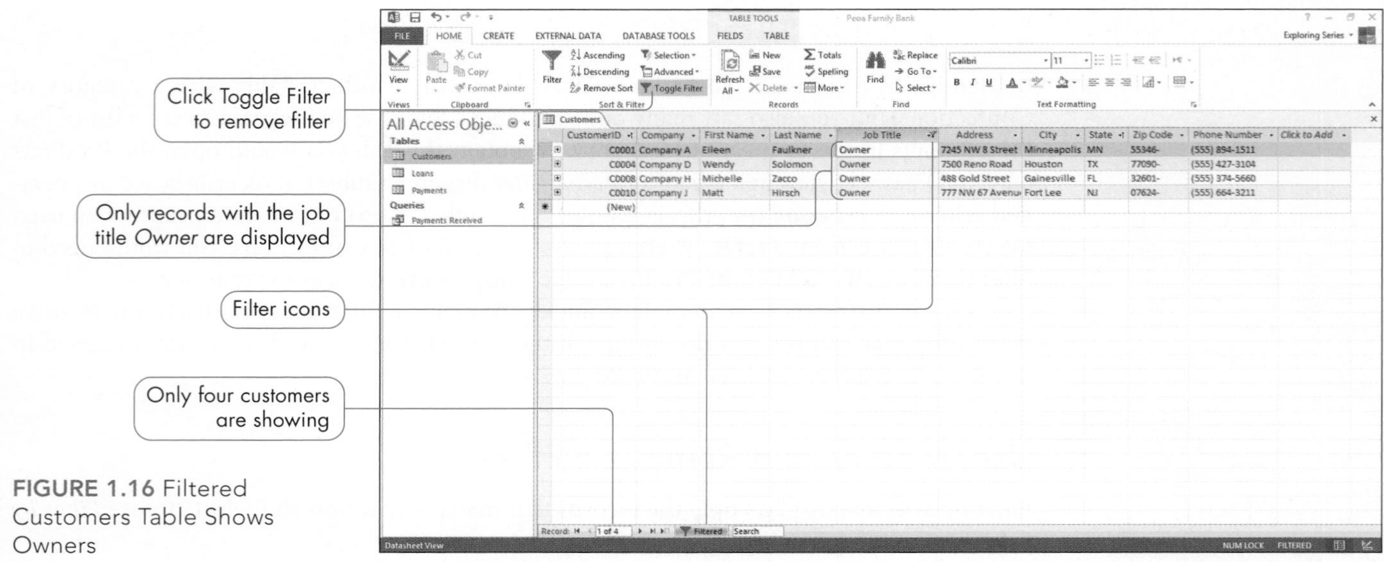
Click Toggle Filter to remove filter
Only records with the job title Owner are displayed
Filter icons
Only four customers are showing

FIGURE 1.16 Filtered Customers Table Shows Owners

Filter by Form is a more versatile method of selecting data because it enables you to display table records based on multiple criteria. When you use *Filter by Form*, all of the records are hidden and Access creates a blank form in a design grid. You see only field names with an arrow in the first field. Click on other fields and an arrow displays. Click an arrow and a list opens for you to use to specify your criterion. You can specify as many criteria as you need. When you apply the filter, Access displays the records that meet your criteria.

STEP 3» An advantage of using this filter method is that you can specify AND and OR logical operators. If you use the AND operator, a record is included in the results if all the criteria are true. If you use the OR operator, a record is included if at least one criterion is true. Another advantage of *Filter by Form* is that you can use a comparison operator. A ***comparison operator*** is used to evaluate the relationship between two quantities. For example, a comparison operator can determine if quantities are equal or not equal. If they are not equal, a comparison operator determines which one is greater than the other. Comparison operator symbols include: equal (=), not equal (<>), greater than (>), less than (<), greater than or equal to (>=), and less than or equal to (<=). To use *Filter by Form*, do the following:

1. Click Advanced in the Sort & Filter group on the HOME tab.
2. Click *Filter by Form*.
3. Click in the field you want to use as a criterion. Click the arrow to select the criterion from existing data.
4. Add additional criterion and comparison operators as needed.
5. Click Toggle Filter in the Sort & Filter group on the HOME tab to apply the filter.

In Figure 1.17, the Northwind Traders Products table is open. *Filter by Form* is set to select products with an inventory (Units in Stock) level greater than 30 (>30).

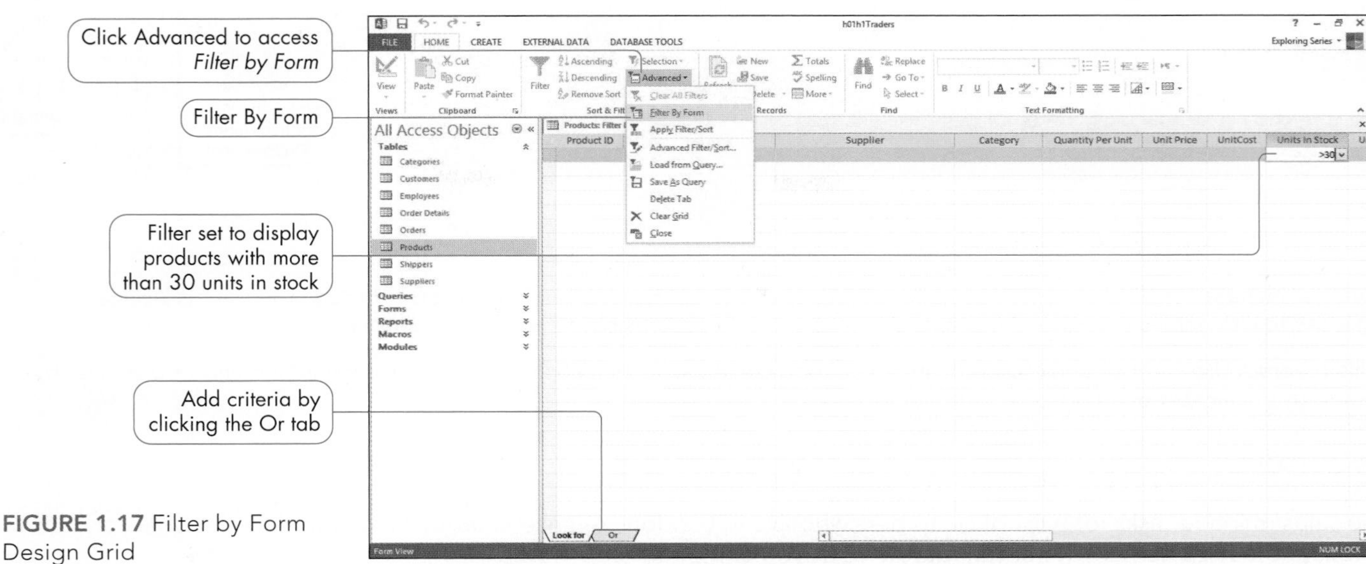
Click Advanced to access *Filter by Form*
Filter By Form
Filter set to display products with more than 30 units in stock
Add criteria by clicking the Or tab

FIGURE 1.17 Filter by Form Design Grid

The sort and filter operations can be done in any order; that is, you can sort a table first and apply a filter. Conversely, you can filter a table first to show only selected records and sort the filtered table to display the records in a certain order. It does not matter which operation is performed first.

STEP 2

You can also filter the table further by applying a second, third, or more criteria. For example, in the Products table shown in Figure 1.17, you can apply *Filter by Form* by clicking in the Supplier cell, selecting Exotic Liquids from the list, and then applying the filter. Then you could click Beverages and apply *Filter by Selection* to display all the beverages supplied by Exotic Liquids. You can also click Toggle Filter at any time to remove all filters and display all the records in the table. Filters are a temporary method for examining table data. If you close the filtered table and reopen it, the filter will be removed and all of the records will be restored.

TIP Use Undo After Applying a Filter by Selection

You can apply one *Filter by Selection* to a table, and then a second, and then a third to display certain records based on three criteria. If you click Toggle Filter, all three filters will be removed. What if you only want the last filter removed? Click Undo to remove only the last filter. Click Undo again and remove the second-to-last filter. This feature will help you apply and remove multiple filters, one at a time.

Quick Concepts

1. What are the benefits of sorting the records in a table? ***p. 636***
2. What is the purpose of creating a filter? ***p. 637***
3. What is the difference between *Filter by Selection* and *Filter by Form*? ***pp. 637–638***
4. What is a comparison operator and how is it used in a filter? ***p. 638***

Hands-On Exercises

MyITLab® HOE2 Training

2 Sorts and Filters

The sales manager at Northwind Traders needs quick answers to her questions about customer orders. You use the Access database to filter tables to answer these questions, then sort the records based on the manager's needs.

Skills covered: Use Filter by Selection with an Equal Condition • Use Filter by Selection with a Contains Condition • Use Filter by Form with a Comparison Operator • Sort a Table

STEP 1 ›› USE FILTER BY SELECTION WITH AN EQUAL CONDITION

The sales manager asks for a list of customers who live in London. You use *Filter by Selection* with an equal condition to locate these customers. Refer to Figure 1.18 as you complete Step 1.

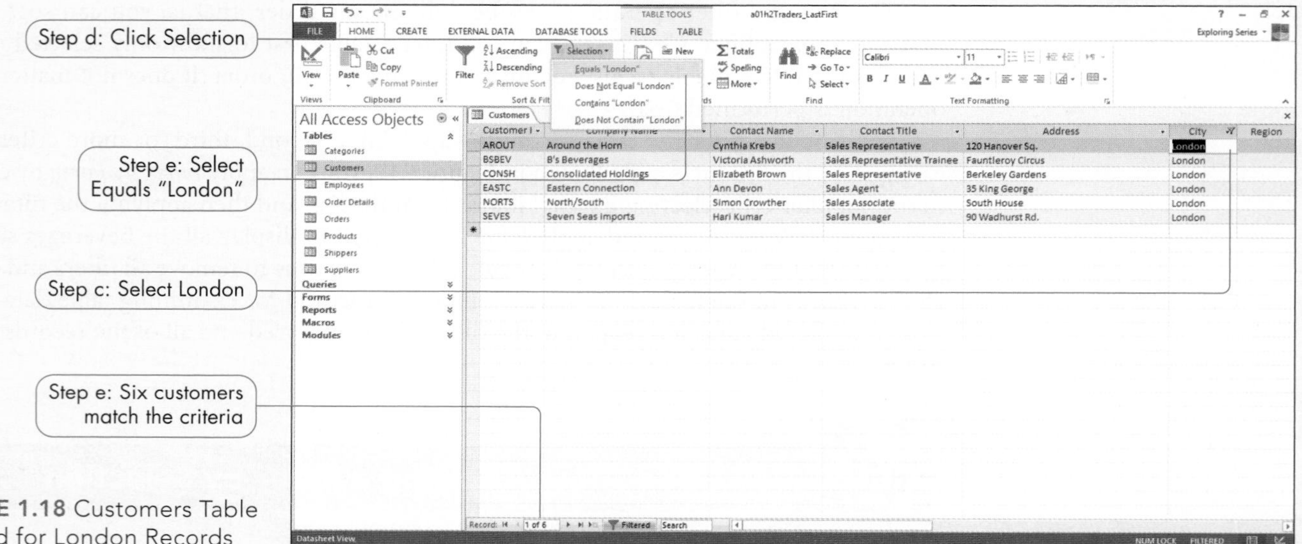

FIGURE 1.18 Customers Table Filtered for London Records

a. Open the *a01h1traders_LastFirst* database if you closed it after the last Hands-On Exercise and save it as **a01h2Traders_LastFirst**, changing *h1* to *h2*.

> **TROUBLESHOOTING:** If you make any major mistakes in this exercise, you can close the file, open *a01h1Traders_LastFirst* again, and then start this exercise over.

b. Double-click the **Customers table** in the Navigation Pane under *Tables*, navigate to record 4, and then replace *Thomas Hardy* with your name in the Contact Name field.

c. Scroll right until the City field is visible. The fourth record has a value of *London* in the City field. Click the field to select it.

d. Click **Selection** in the Sort & Filter group on the HOME tab.

e. Select **Equals "London"** from the menu. Note that six customers were located.

The navigation bar display shows that six records that meet the *London* criterion are available. The other records in the Customers table are hidden. The Filtered icon also displays on the navigation bar, indicating that the Customers table has been filtered.

f. Click **Toggle Filter** in the Sort & Filter group to remove the filter.

g. Click **Toggle Filter** again to reset the filter. Leave the Customers table open for the next step.

STEP 2 ≫ USE FILTER BY SELECTION WITH A CONTAINS CONDITION

The sales manager asks you to narrow the list of London customers so that it displays only Sales Representatives. To accomplish this task, you add a second layer of filtering using the *Filter by Selection* feature. Refer to Figure 1.19 as you complete Step 2.

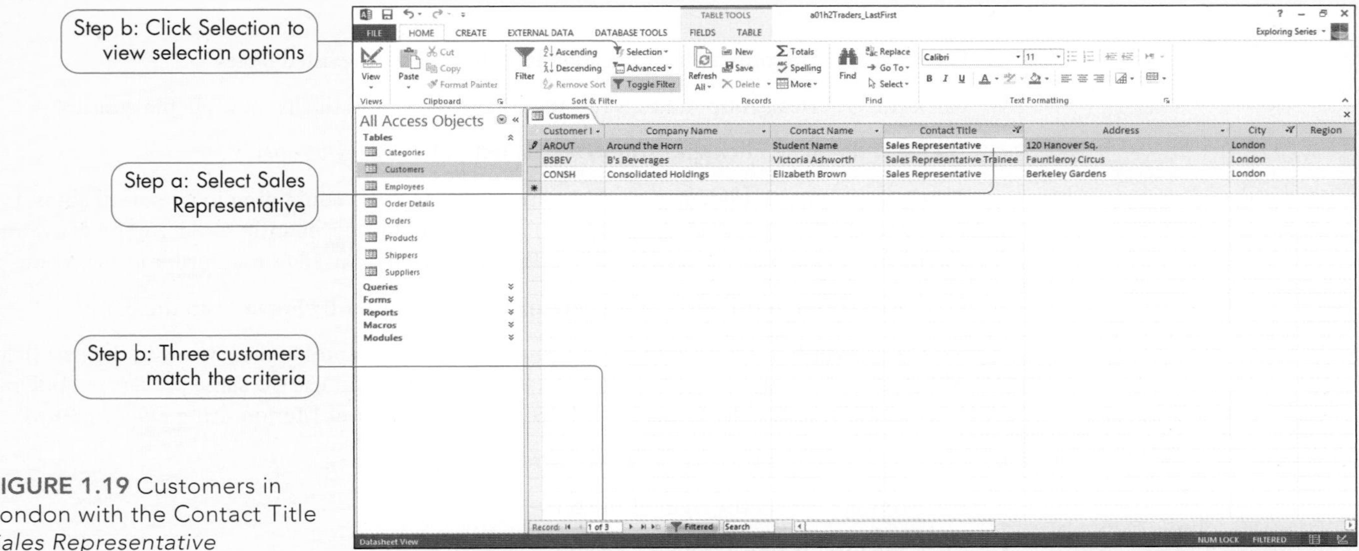
Step b: Click Selection to view selection options
Step a: Select Sales Representative
Step b: Three customers match the criteria

FIGURE 1.19 Customers in London with the Contact Title *Sales Representative*

a. Click in any field in the Contact Title column that contains the value *Sales Representative.*

b. Click **Selection** in the Sort & Filter group and click **Contains "Sales Representative"**. Locate your name in the filtered table. Compare your results to those shown in Figure 1.19.

Three records match the criteria you set. You have applied a second layer of filtering to the customers in London. The second layer further restricts the display to only those customers who have the words *Sales Representative* contained in their titles.

> **TROUBLESHOOTING:** If you do not see the record for Victoria Ashworth, you selected *Equals "Sales Representative"* instead of *Contains "Sales Representative"*. Repeat steps a and b, making sure you select *Contains "Sales Representative"*.

c. Close the Customers table. Click **Yes** if a dialog box asks if you want to save the design changes to the Customers table.

STEP 3 ≫ USE FILTER BY FORM WITH A COMPARISON OPERATOR

You are asked to provide a list of records that do not match just one set of criteria. You are asked to provide a list of all extended prices less than $50 for a specific sales representative. Use *Filter by Form* to provide the information when two or more criteria are needed. You also preview the results in Print Preview to see how the list would print. Refer to Figure 1.20 as you complete Step 3.

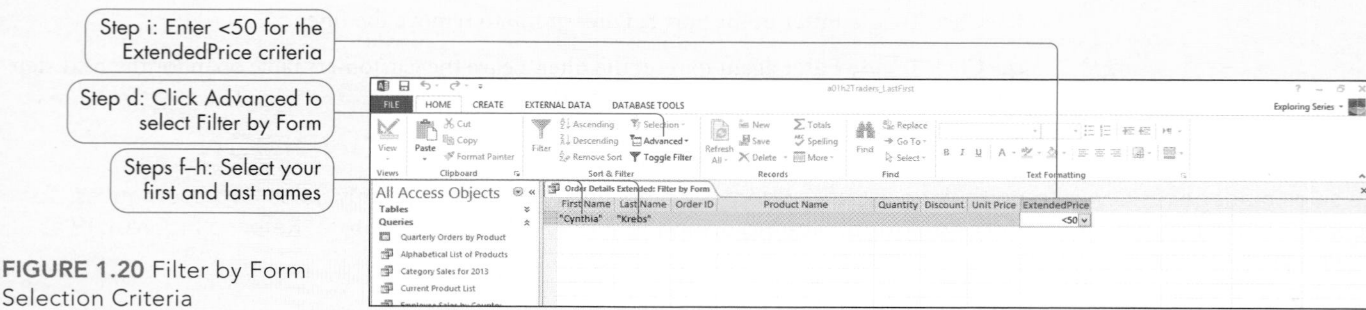
Step i: Enter <50 for the ExtendedPrice criteria
Step d: Click Advanced to select Filter by Form
Steps f–h: Select your first and last names

FIGURE 1.20 Filter by Form Selection Criteria

a. Click the **Tables group** in the Navigation Pane to collapse the listed tables.

b. Click the **Queries group** in the Navigation Pane to expand the list of available queries.

c. Locate and double-click the **Order Details Extended query** to open it.

   This query contains information about orders. It has fields containing information about the sales person, the Order ID, the product name, the unit price, quantity ordered, the discount given, and an extended price. The extended price is a field used to total order information.

d. Click **Advanced** in the Sort & Filter group and select **Filter by Form** from the list.

   All of the records are now hidden, and you see only field names and an arrow in the first field. Although you are applying *Filter by Form* to a query, you can use the same process as applying *Filter by Form* to a table. You are able to enter more than one criterion using *Filter by Form*.

e. Click in the first row under the First Name field, if necessary.

   An arrow appears at the right of the box.

f. Click the **First Name arrow**.

   A list of all available first names appears. Your name should be on the list. Figure 1.20 shows *Cynthia Krebs*, which replaced Margaret Peacock in Hands-On Exercise 1.

> **TROUBLESHOOTING:** If you do not see your name and you do see Margaret on the list, you probably skipped steps in Hands-On Exercise 1. Close the query without saving changes, return to the first Hands-On Exercise, and then rework it, making sure not to omit any steps. Then you can return to this location and work the remainder of this Hands-On Exercise.

g. Select your first name from the list.

h. Click in the first row under the Last Name field to reveal the arrow. Locate and select your last name by clicking it.

i. Scroll right until you see the Extended Price field. Click in the first row under the Extended Price field and type **<50**.

   This will select all of the items that you ordered where the total was under $50. You ignore the arrow and type the expression needed.

j. Click **Toggle Filter** in the Sort & Filter group.

   You have specified which records to include and have executed the filtering by clicking Toggle Filter. You should have 31 records that match the criteria you specified.

k. Click the **FILE tab**, click **Print**, and then click **Print Preview**.

   You instructed Access to preview the filtered query results. The preview displays the query title as a heading. The current filter is applied, as well as page numbers.

l. Click **Close Print Preview** in the Close Preview group.

m. Close the Order Details Extended query. Click **Yes** if a dialog box asks if you want to save your changes.

Deleting Filter by Form Criterion

While working with *Filter by Selection* or *Filter by Form*, you may inadvertently save a filter. To view a saved filter, open the table or query that you suspect may have a saved filter. Click Advanced in the Sort & Filter group and click *Filter by Form*. If criteria appear in the form, then a filter has been saved. To delete a saved filter, toggle the filter, click Advanced, and then click Close All Filters. Close and save the table or query.

STEP 4 » SORT A TABLE

The Sales Manager is pleased with your work; however, she would like some of the information to appear in a different order. You will now sort the records in the Customers table using the manager's new criteria. Refer to Figure 1.21 as you complete Step 4.

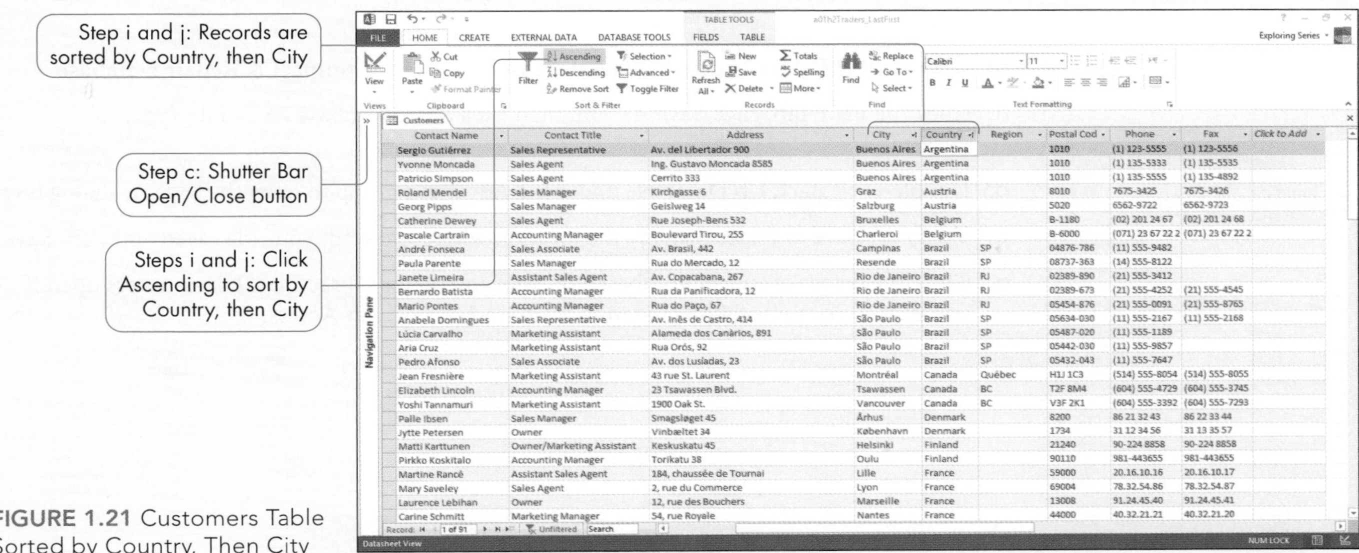

FIGURE 1.21 Customers Table Sorted by Country, Then City

a. Click the **Queries group** in the Navigation Pane to collapse the listed queries.

b. Click the **Tables group** in the Navigation Pane to expand the list of available tables and double-click the **Customers table** to open it.

This table contains information about customers. The table is sorted in alphabetical order by Company Name.

c. Click the **Shutter Bar Open/Close button** in the Navigation Pane to close the Navigation Pane.

It will be easier to locate fields in the Customer table if the Navigation Pane is closed.

d. Click any field in the Customer ID column, the first field in the table. Click **Descending** in the Sort & Filter group on the HOME tab.

Sorting in descending order on a character field produces a reverse alphabetical order.

e. Scroll right until you can see both the Country and City fields.

f. Click the **Country column heading**.

The entire column is selected.

g. Click the **Country column heading** again and hold down the **left mouse button**.

A thick dark blue line displays on the left edge of the Country field.

h. Check to make sure that you see the thick blue line. Drag the **Country field** to the left until the thick black line moves between the City and Region fields. Release the mouse and the Country field position moves to the right of the City field.

You moved the Country field next to the City field so that you can easily sort the table based on both fields. In order to sort by two or more fields, they need to be placed adjacent to each other.

i. Click any city name in the City field and click **Ascending** in the Sort & Filter group.

The City field displays the cities in alphabetical order.

j. Click any country name in the Country field and click **Ascending**.

The countries are sorted in alphabetical order. The cities within each country also are sorted alphabetically. For example, the customer in Graz, Austria, is listed before the customer in Salzburg, Austria.

k. Close the Customers table. Click **Yes** to save the changes to the design of the table.

l. Click the **Shutter Bar Open/Close button** in the Navigation Pane to open the Navigation Pane.

m. Click the **FILE tab** to open the Backstage view and click **Compact & Repair Database**.

n. Click the **FILE tab**, click **Save As**, and then click **Save Database As** in File Types, if necessary.

o. Double-click **Back Up Database** under the Advanced group to open the Save As dialog box.

p. Verify the *Save in* folder displays the location where you want your file saved and click **Save**.

q. Close the database and submit based on your instructor's directions. Leave Access open if you plan to continue with Hands-On Exercise 3. If not, exit Access.

Access Versus Excel, and Relational Databases

Both Access and Excel contain powerful tools that enable you to extract the information you need and arrange it in a way that makes it easy to analyze. An important part of becoming a proficient Office user is learning which of these applications to use to accomplish a task.

In this section, you will learn how to decide whether to use Access or Excel by examining the distinct advantages of each application. Ideally, the type of data and the type of functionality you require should determine which program will work best.

Knowing When to Use Access or Excel to Manage Data

You are probably familiar with working in an Excel spreadsheet. You type the column headings, enter the data, perhaps add a formula or two, and then add totals to the bottom. Once the data has been entered, you can apply a filter, sort the data, or start all over—similar to what you learned to do in Access with filters. It is true that you can accomplish many of the same tasks using either Excel or Access. Although the two programs have much in common, they each have distinct advantages. How do you choose whether to use Access or Excel? The choice you make may ultimately depend on how well you know Access. Users who know Excel only are more likely to use a spreadsheet even if a database would be better. When database features are used in Excel, they are generally used on data that is in one table. When the data is better suited to be on two or more tables, then using Access is preferable. Learning how to use Access will be beneficial to you because it will enable you to work more efficiently with large groups of data.

Select the Software to Use

A contact list (for example, name, address, phone number) created in Excel may serve your needs just fine in the beginning. Each time you enter a new contact, you can add another row to the bottom of your worksheet. You can sort the list by last name for easier look-up of names. In Excel, you can easily move an entire column, insert a new column, or copy and paste data from one cell to another. This is the "ease of use" characteristic of Excel.

If you need to expand the information in Excel to keep track of each time you contacted someone on your contact list, you may need an additional worksheet. This additional sheet would only list the contacts whom you have contacted and some information about the nature of the contact. Which contact was it? When was the contact made? Was it a phone contact or a face-to-face meeting? As you track these entries, your worksheet will contain a reference to the first worksheet using the contact name.

If a contact is deleted on the first worksheet, that contact's information will still remain on the second worksheet, unless someone remembers to remove it. Similarly, information could be added about a contact on the second worksheet without the contact being officially entered into the first worksheet. As the quantity and complexity of the data increase, the need to organize your data logically also increases.

Access provides built-in tools to help organize data better than Excel. One tool that helps Access organize data is the ability to create relationships between tables. A ***relationship*** is a connection between two tables using a field that is common to the two tables. The benefit of a relationship is the ability to efficiently combine data from related tables for the purpose of creating queries, forms, and reports. Relationships are the reason Access is referred to as a relational database.

Use Access

STEP 1 Use Access to manage data when you:

- Require multiple related tables to store your data.
- Have a large amount of data.
- Need to connect to and retrieve data from external databases, such as Microsoft SQL Server.
- Need to group, sort, and total data based on various parameters.
- Have an application that requires multiple users to connect to one data source at the same time.

Use Excel

Use Excel to manage data when you:

- Need only one worksheet to handle all of your data.
- Have mostly numeric data—for example, you need to maintain an expense statement.
- Require subtotals and totals in your worksheet.
- Want to primarily run a series of "what if" scenarios on your data.
- Need to create complex charts and/or graphs.

Understanding Relational Power

In the previous section, we compared Excel worksheets to Access relational databases. Access has the ability to create relationships between two tables, whereas Excel does not. Access is known as a ***relational database management system*** (RDBMS); using an RDBMS, you can manage groups of data (tables) and set rules (relationships) between tables. When relational databases are designed properly, users can easily combine data from multiple tables to create queries, forms, and reports.

Good database design begins with grouping data into the correct tables. This practice, known as ***normalization***, will take time to learn, but over time you will begin to understand the fundamentals. The design of a relational database management system is illustrated in Figure 1.22, which shows the table design of the Northwind Traders database. The tables have been created, the field names have been added, and the data types have been set. The diagram shows the relationships that were created between tables using ***join lines***. Join lines enable you to create a relationship between two tables using a common field. Figure 1.22 also shows the join lines between related tables as a series of lines connecting common fields. For example, the Suppliers table is joined to the Products table using the common field SupplierID. If you examine some of the connections, you will see that the EmployeeID is linked to the Orders table by a join line. This means that you can produce a report displaying all orders for a customer and the employee who entered the order. The Orders table is joined to the Order Details table where the OrderID is the common field. The Products table is joined to the Order Details table where the ProductID is the common field. These table connections enable you to query the database for information stored in multiple tables. This feature gives the manager the ability to ask questions like "How many different beverages were shipped last week?" or "What was the total revenue generated from seafood orders last year?"

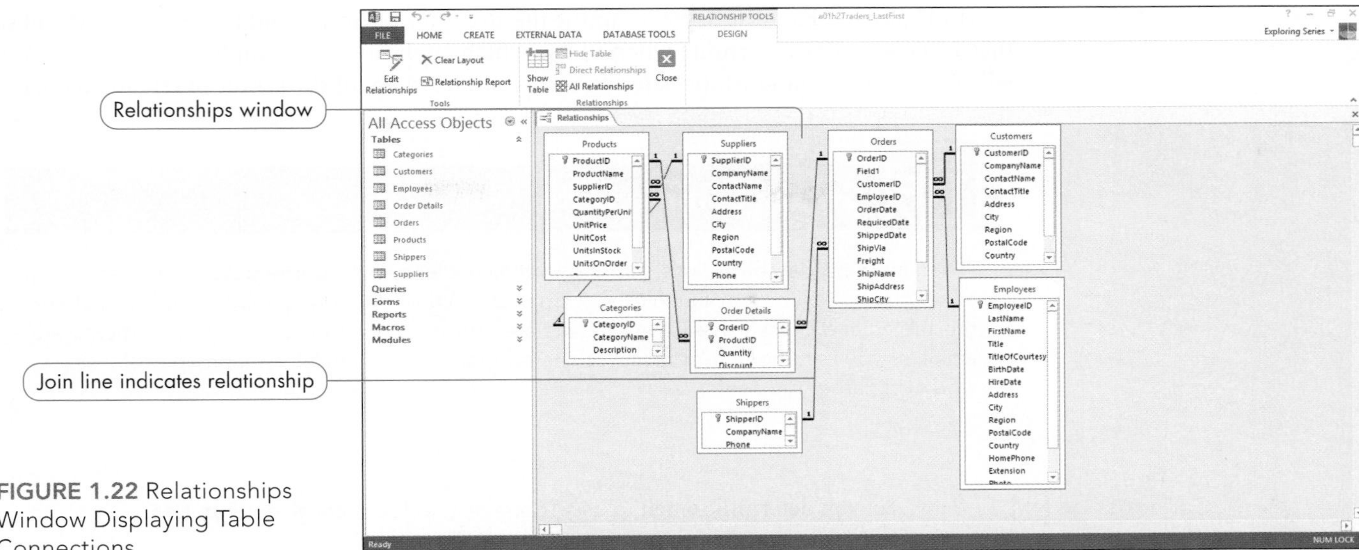

FIGURE 1.22 Relationships Window Displaying Table Connections

Use the Relationships Window

Relationships are set in the Relationships window by the database developer after the tables have been created but before any sample data is entered. The most common method of connecting two tables is to connect the primary key from one table to the foreign key of another. A ***foreign key*** is a field in one table that is also the primary key of another table. In the previous figure, Figure 1.22, the SupplierID (primary key) in the Suppliers table is joined to the SupplierID (foreign key) in the Products table. Remember, a primary key is a field that uniquely identifies each record in a table.

To create a relationship between two tables, follow these guidelines:

1. Click Relationships in the Relationships group on the DATABASE TOOLS tab.
2. Add the two tables that you want to join together to the Relationships window.
3. Drag the common field (e.g., SupplierID) from the primary table (e.g., Suppliers) onto the common field (e.g., SupplierID) of the related table (e.g., Products). The data types of the common fields must be the same.
4. Check the Enforce Referential Integrity check box.
5. Close the Relationships window.

STEP 2

TIP View Join Lines

Databases with many tables with relationships may make it difficult to see the join lines between tables. Tables may be repositioned to make it easier to see the join lines. To reposition a table, drag the table by its table name to the new position.

Enforce Referential Integrity

STEP 3

Enforce referential integrity is one of three options you can select when setting a table relationship. When ***enforce referential integrity*** is checked, Access ensures that data cannot be entered into a related table unless it first exists in the primary table. For example, in Figure 1.22 you cannot enter a product into the Products table using a SupplierID that does not exist in the Suppliers table. This rule ensures the integrity of the data in the database and improves overall data accuracy. Referential integrity also prohibits users from deleting a record in one table if it has records in related tables.

In Hands-on Exercise 3, you examine the strengths of Access and Excel in more detail so that you can better determine when to use which application to complete a given task. You will also explore relationships between tables and learn about the power of relational data.

TIP Create Sample Data

When learning database skills, starting with a smaller set of sample data prior to entering all company records can be helpful. A small amount of data gives you the ability to check the tables and quickly see if your results are correct. Even though the data amounts are small, as you test the database tables and relationships, the results will prove useful as you work with larger data sets.

Quick **Concepts**

1. How can you determine when to use Access or Excel to manage data? ***p. 645***
2. Explain the term RDBMS. ***p. 646***
3. What is the purpose of a join line? ***p. 646***

Hands-On Exercises

Watch the Video for this Hands-On Exercise!

MyITLab®
HOE3 Training

3 Access Versus Excel, and Relational Databases

In this exercise, you review the relationships set in the Northwind Traders database. This will help you learn more about the overall design of the database. Examining the relationships will also help you understand why Access rather than Excel is used by Northwind Traders for data management.

Skills covered: Know When to Use Access or Excel to Manage Data • Use the Relationships Window, Use Filter by Form with a Comparison Operator, and Reapply a Saved Filter • Enforce Referential Integrity

STEP 1 » KNOW WHEN TO USE ACCESS OR EXCEL TO MANAGE DATA

In this exercise, you examine the connections between the tables in the Northwind Traders database and review the reasons that Access was selected as the application for this data. Refer to Figure 1.23 as you complete Step 1.

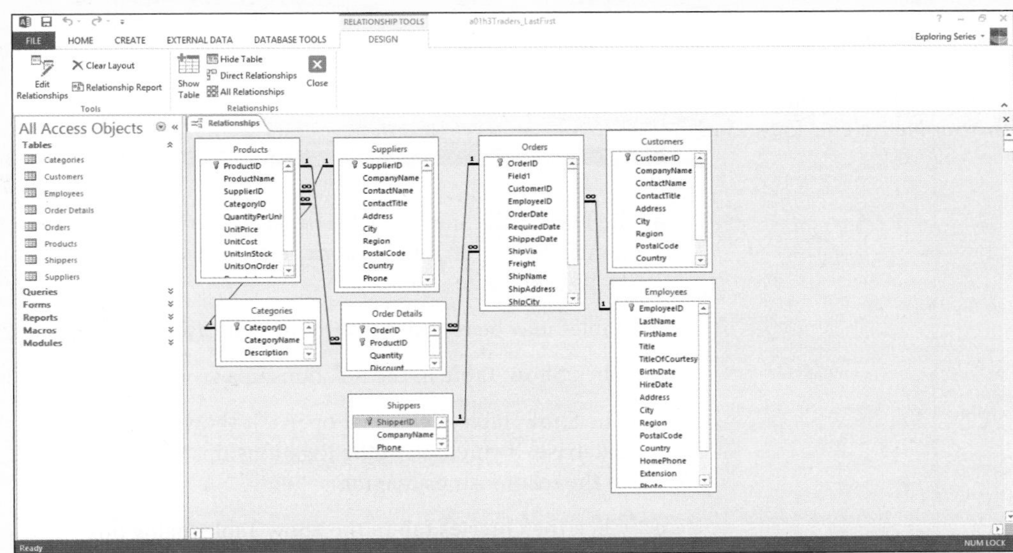

FIGURE 1.23 Relationships Window for the Northwind Database

a. Open the *a01h2Traders_LastFirst* database if you closed it after the last Hands-On Exercise and save it as **a01h3Traders_LastFirst**, changing *h2* to *h3*.

b. Click the **DATABASE TOOLS tab** and click **Relationships** in the Relationships group.

c. Examine the join lines showing the relationships that connect the various tables. For example, the Orders table is connected to the Order Details table.

   Examining the number of tables in a database and their relationships is a good way to determine whether you need to use Excel or Access for your data. Because this data needs more than one table, involves a large amount of connected data, needs to group, sort, and total data based on various parameters, and needs to allow multiple users to connect to one data source at the same time, it is better to manipulate this data using Access rather than using Excel.

STEP 2 » USE THE RELATIONSHIPS WINDOW, USE FILTER BY FORM WITH A COMPARISON OPERATOR, AND REAPPLY A SAVED FILTER

Use the Relationships window to move tables to make the join lines easier to view. To reinforce your filter skills, use *Filter by Form* to solve more complex questions about the Northwind data. After you retrieve the records, save the *Filter by Form* specifications so that you can reapply the filter later. Refer to Figure 1.24 as you complete Step 2.

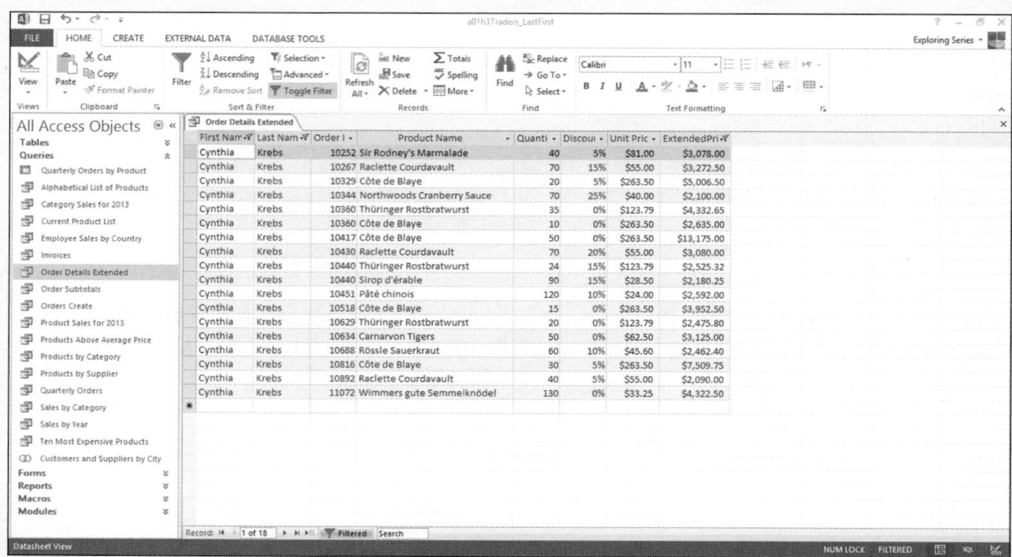

FIGURE 1.24 Query Results with Your Name and Extended Price >$2,000

a. Reposition the Shippers table beneath the Orders table by dragging it to the right by its table name. Reposition the Categories table beneath the Order Details table by dragging it to the right by its table name.

Tables may be repositioned to make it easier to see the join lines creating the relationships.

b. Click **Show Table** in the Relationships group on the RELATIONSHIPS TOOLS DESIGN tab.

The Show Table dialog box opens. It shows you the eight tables that are available in the database. If you look in the Relationships window, you will see that all eight tables are open in the relationships diagram.

c. Click the **Queries tab** in the Show Table dialog box.

All of the queries created from the tables in the database are listed in the Show Table dialog box. You could add all of the queries to the Relationships window. Things might become cluttered, but you could tell at a glance from where the queries get their information.

d. Close the Show Table dialog box.

e. Click the **Shutter Bar Open/Close button** in the Navigation Pane to open the Navigation Pane, if necessary.

f. Click **All Access Objects** on the Navigation Pane and click **Tables and Related Views.**

You now see each table and all the queries, forms, and reports that are based on each table. If a query is created using more than one table, it appears multiple times in the Navigation Pane.

g. Close the Relationships window. Save the changes to the design. Click **All Tables** on the Navigation Pane and click **Object Type**.

h. Collapse the Tables group in the Navigation Pane, expand the **Queries** group, and then double-click the **Order Details Extended query**.

i. Click **Advanced** in the Sort & Filter group, select **Filter by Form**, click in the first row under the Last Name field, and then select your last name.

j. Scroll right (or press **Tab**) until the Extended Price field is visible. Click in the first row in the Extended Price field and type **>2000**.

   The Extended Price field shows the purchased amount for each item ordered. If an item sold for $15 and a customer ordered 10, the Extended Price would display $150.

k. Click **Toggle Filter** in the Sort & Filter group. Examine the filtered results.

   Your comparison operator, >2000, identified 18 items ordered where the extended price exceeded $2,000.

l. Close the Order Details Extended query by clicking the **Close (X) button**. Click **Yes** to save changes.

m. Open the Order Details Extended query again.

   The filter disengages when you close and reopen the object. However, because you opted to save the changes before closing, the filter has been stored with the query. You may reapply the filter at any time by clicking the Toggle Filter command (until the next filter replaces the current one).

n. Click **Toggle Filter** in the Sort & Filter group. Compare your results to Figure 1.24.

o. Save and close the query.

STEP 3 ›› ENFORCE REFERENTIAL INTEGRITY

You need an additional relationship created between the Orders table and the Customers table. You create the relationship and enforce referential integrity. Refer to Figure 1.25 as you complete Step 3.

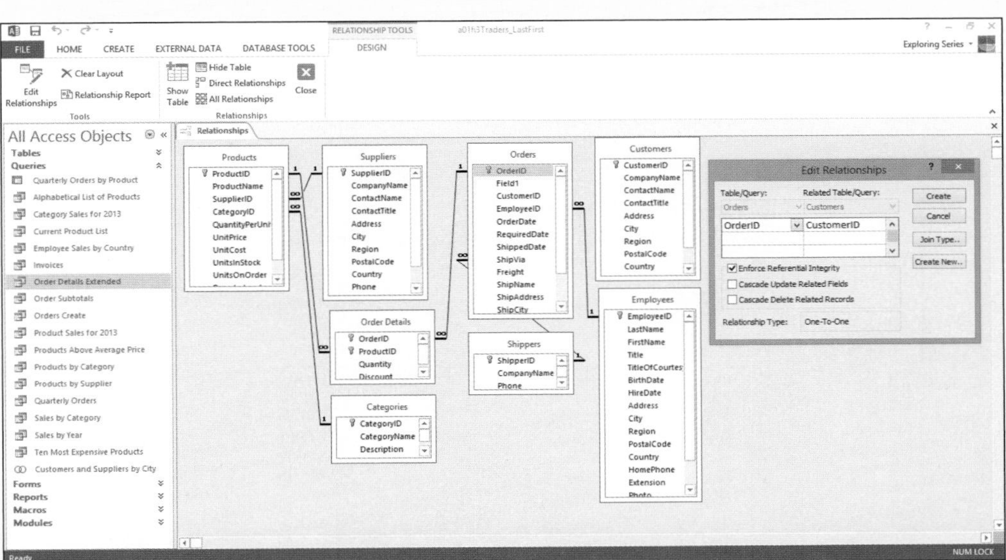

FIGURE 1.25 Relationship Created Between Orders Table and Customers Table

a. Click the **DATABASE TOOLS tab** and click **Relationships** in the Relationships group.

b. Locate the CustomerID field in the Orders table and drag it to the CustomerID field (primary key) in the Customers table.

   The Edit Relationships dialog box opens. It shows that the Table/Query is from the Customers table and the related Table/Query comes from the Orders table. The relationship type is displayed at the bottom of the dialog box and indicates that this will be a One-To-Many relationship.

c. Click **Enforce Referential Integrity**.

   Access will now ensure that data cannot be entered into the related table (Orders) unless it first exists in the primary table (Customers).

d. Click **Create**.

A join line displays between the Orders and Customers tables.

e. Click the **FILE tab** and click **Compact & Repair Database**. Click **Yes** if asked if you want to save changes to the layout of Relationships.

f. Click the **FILE tab**, click **Save As**, and then click **Save Database As** under *File Types* if necessary. Double-click **Back Up Database** in the Advanced group to open the Save As dialog box.

g. Verify the *Save in* folder displays the location where you want your backup file saved and click **Save**.

A duplicate copy of the database is saved with the default file name that is the original file name followed by the current date.

h. Exit Access.

Access Database Creation

Now that you have examined the fundamentals of an Access database and explored the power of relational databases, it is time to create one! In this section, you explore the benefits of creating a database using each of the methods discussed in the next section.

Creating a Database

When you first start Access, the Backstage view opens and provides you with three methods for creating a new database. These methods are:

- Creating a custom Web app
- Creating a blank desktop database
- Creating a database from a template

Creating a ***custom Web app*** enables you to create a database that you can build and then use and share with others through the Web. Creating a blank desktop database lets you create a database specific to your needs. Rather than starting from scratch by creating a blank desktop database, you may want to use a template to create a new database. An Access ***template*** is a predefined database that includes professionally designed tables, forms, reports, and other objects that you can use to jumpstart the creation of your database.

Figure 1.26 shows the options for creating a custom Web app, a blank desktop database, and multiple templates from which you can select the method for which you want to create a database.

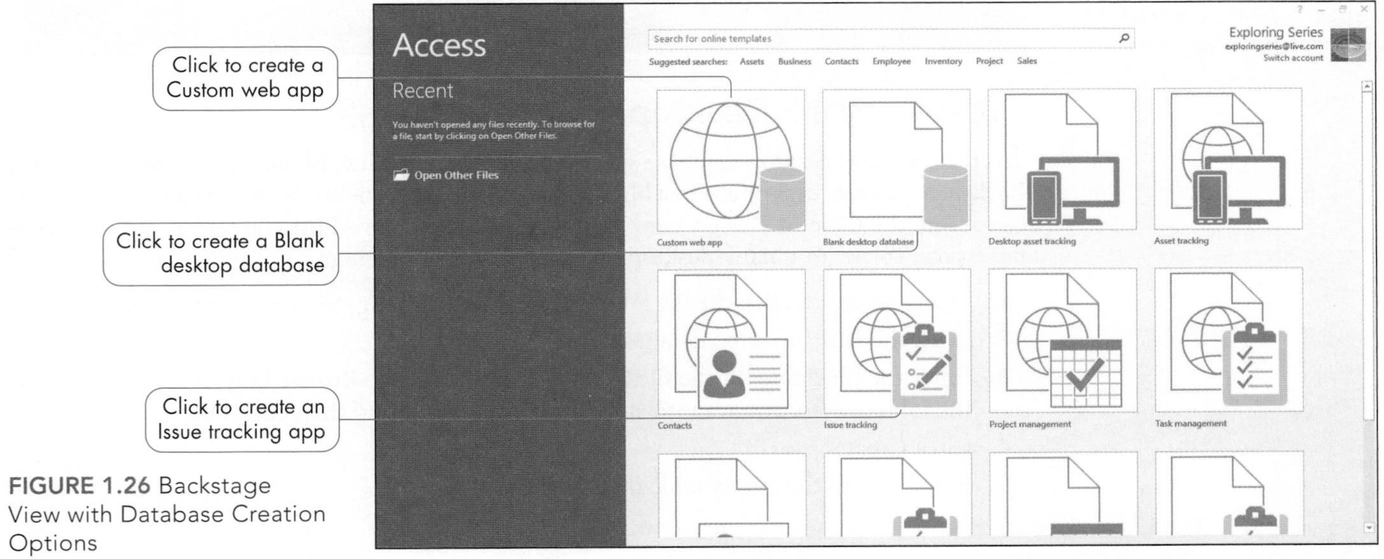

FIGURE 1.26 Backstage View with Database Creation Options

Create a Web Application Using a Template

Creating a Web app (application) is new in Access 2013. An Access Web app is a new type of database that lets you build a browser-based database application— you can create a database in the cloud that you and others can access and use simultaneously. This requires that you use a host server such as SharePoint (a Web application platform developed by Microsoft) or Office 365 (a cloud service edition of SharePoint).

To create a Web app, click *Custom web app* in the Backstage view, give your app a name, and then choose a location. Once you click Create, a blank database opens. You then create the tables that will serve as the foundation of your database. The easiest way to add a table is to use the Access library of Table Templates. Each of the templates in the library includes tables, fields, and views that you will need to create an app. Some templates also include related tables.

As an alternative to creating a Web app from scratch, you can select a Web app template from the Backstage view. These templates are fully functional Web databases. Click one of the Web app template tiles and an introduction screen appears that previews the datasheet, provides a description of the purpose of the datasheet, lets you know the download size of the database, and even displays how users like you have rated the database. You give the app a name and select the Web location where the app is to be saved. Finally, you create the app. When you have completed the database, click Launch App in the View group on the Home tab. You can then use it and share it on the Web. Figure 1.27 shows the introduction screen for the Asset tracking template. This template requires SharePoint so that you can share content with others.

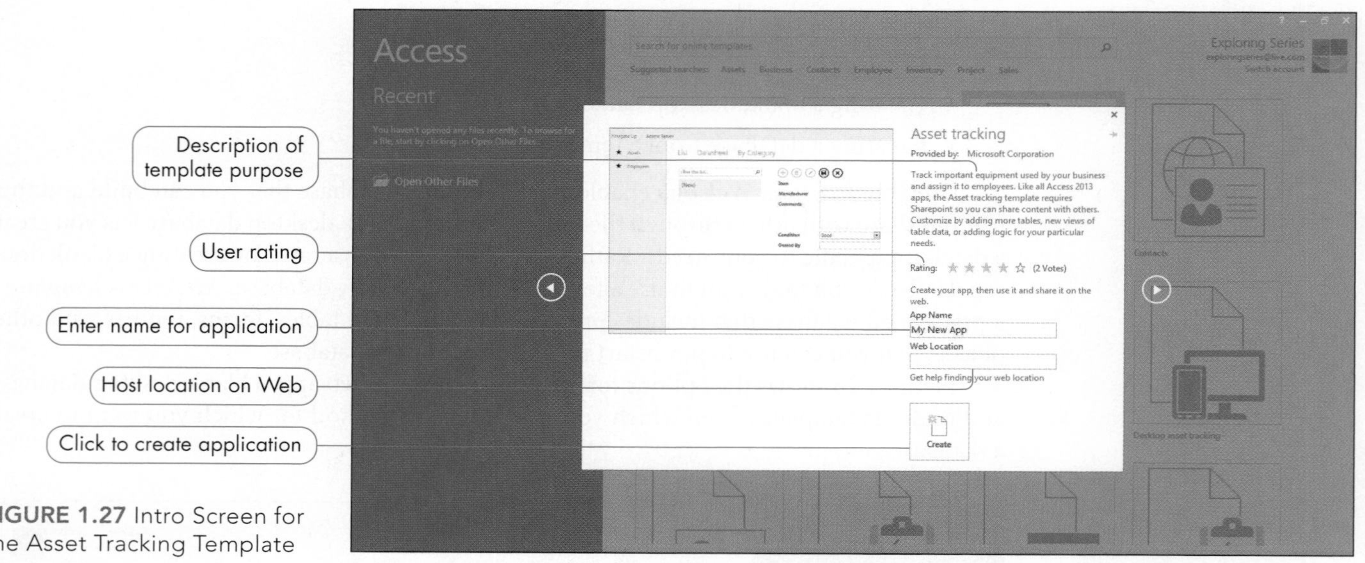

FIGURE 1.27 Intro Screen for the Asset Tracking Template

Create a Blank Desktop Database

To create a blank desktop database specific to your needs, click *Blank desktop database* in the Backstage view. Access opens to a blank table in Datasheet view where you can add data. You can refine the table in Design view. You would then create additional tables and objects as necessary. To create a blank desktop database, do the following:

1. Open Access or click the FILE tab to open the Backstage view and click New.
2. Click the *Blank desktop* database tile.
3. Enter the file name for the file in the text box, click the Browse button to navigate to the folder where you want to store the database file, and then click OK.
4. Click Create.
5. Enter data in the empty table that displays.

Create a Desktop Database Using a Template

Using a template to start a database saves you a great deal of creation time. Working with a template can also help a new Access user become familiar with database design. Templates are available from the Backstage view, where you can select from a variety of templates or search online for more templates.

Access also provides templates for desktop use. To create a desktop database from a template, do the following:

STEP 1

1. Open Access or click the FILE tab to open the Backstage view and click New.
2. Click the database template you want to use.
3. Enter the file name for the file in the text box, click the Browse button to navigate to the folder where you want to store the database file, and then click OK.

4. Click Create to download the template.
5. Open the database and click Enable Content in the Security Warning message bar if you trust the source of the database.

Once the database is open, you may see a Getting Started page that includes links you can use to learn more about the database. A new Access user can gain valuable information by watching any associated videos and clicking provided hyperlinks. When finished reviewing the learning materials, close the Getting Started page to view the database. Figure 1.28 displays the Getting Started page included with the *Desktop task management* template. Two videos are provided to aid you in using and modifying the database. Because this database contains a Contacts table, there is a hyperlink to a wizard that will import contacts from Microsoft Outlook (if you use Microsoft Outlook). Links are available that will connect you with experts, enable you to get free advice from a forum, and get more help from Microsoft .com. The Getting Started page also includes a button you can click to open a survey that provides feedback to Microsoft. Close the Getting Started page to return to the database.

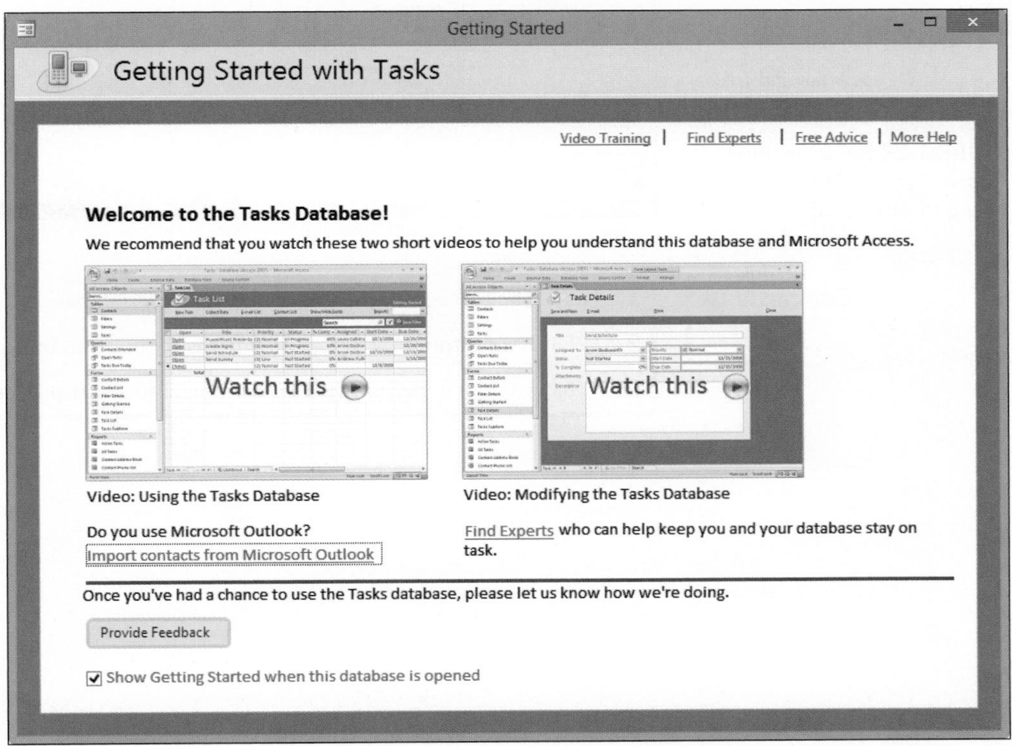

FIGURE 1.28 Getting Started Page for Desktop Task Management Template

STEP 2» Because you downloaded a template, some objects will have already been created. You can work with these objects just as you did in the first three sections of this chapter. For example, you can enter data directly into any existing table in the database by opening the table, clicking in the first empty field, typing the data, tabbing to the next empty field, and then typing the data for the next field. You can also open any form that is part of the downloaded template and enter the data directly in the forms. Some templates will include queries and reports. Edit any object to meet your requirements.

STEP 3» Once the database is opened, review the objects listed in the Navigation Pane. Change the Navigation Pane category from Object Type to *Tables and Related Views* to become familiar with the relationships between the tables and other database objects. Note the tables and the objects that are based on them.

After noting the objects in the database, open the Relationships window to see the connections between them. Once you are familiar with the database design, you can enter your data.

Figure 1.29 displays the open Task Management database with the Navigation Pane set to display *Tables and Related Views*. The Tasks table displays with its related queries, forms, and reports. The Relationships window shows the relationship between the Contacts table and the Tasks table.

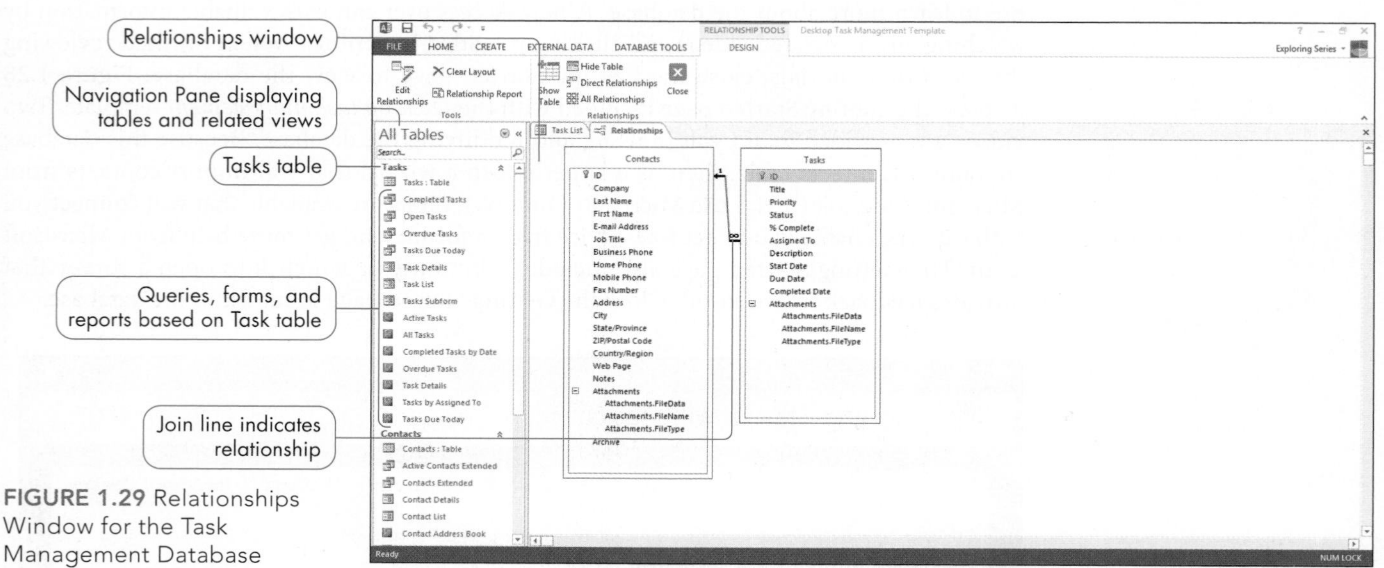

FIGURE 1.29 Relationships Window for the Task Management Database

1. Name the three methods for creating a new database. ***p. 653***
2. What is a custom Web app, and what is required to build a custom Web app? ***p. 653***
3. What are two benefits of using a template to create a database? ***p. 654***

Hands-On Exercises

4 Access Database Creation

After working with the Northwind Traders database on the job, you decide to use Access to create a personal contact database. Rather than start from scratch, you use an Access Contact Manager desktop template to jumpstart your database creation. A Web app is not necessary because you do not want to share your contacts with others.

Skills covered: Create a Desktop Database Using a Template • Add Records to a Downloaded Desktop Database Template • Explore the Database Objects in a Downloaded Desktop Database Template

STEP 1 » CREATE A DESKTOP DATABASE USING A TEMPLATE

You locate an Access desktop template that you can use to create your personal contact database. This template not only allows you to store names, addresses, telephone numbers, and other information, but also lets you categorize your contacts, send e-mail messages, and create maps of addresses. You download and save the template. Refer to Figure 1.30 as you complete Step 1.

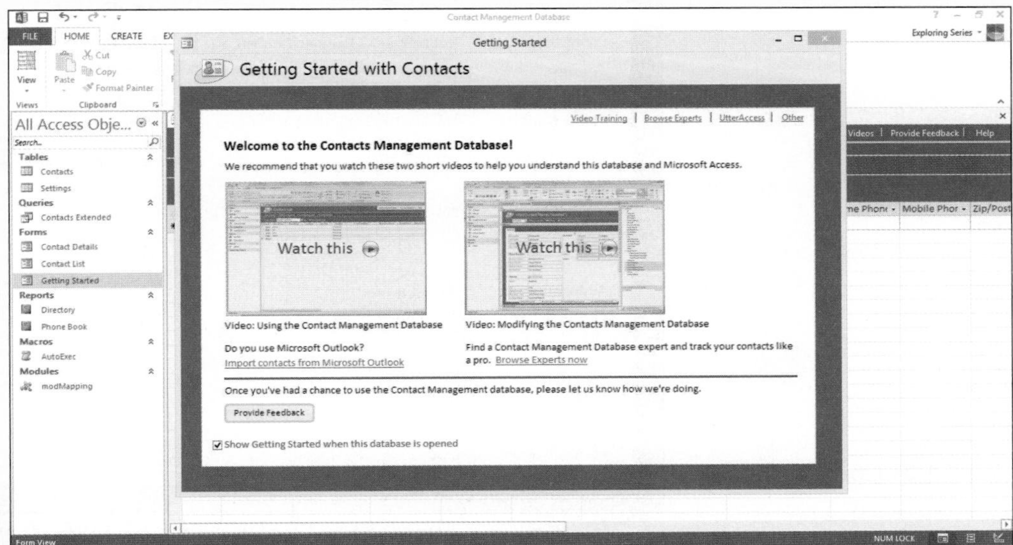

FIGURE 1.30 Desktop Contacts Intro Screen

a. Open Access. Click the Contacts link in the Suggested searches list. Click *Desktop contacts* from the available contacts.

The Create Intro Screen page for the Desktop contacts database opens.

b. Click the **Browse icon** to navigate to the folder where you are saving your files, enter **a01h4Contacts_LastFirst** as the file name, and then click **OK**.

c. Click **Create** to download the template.

d. Click **Enable Content** on the Security Warning message bar.

> **TROUBLESHOOTING:** If the Getting Started page does not display, click Getting Started in the Forms category on the Navigation Pane.

> **TROUBLESHOOTING:** The Getting Started page opens every time you open the Contacts Management database. To close this page until you want to view it again, clear the *Show Getting Started when this database is opened* check box at the bottom-left corner of the dialog box before closing the Getting Started page.

e. Close the Getting Started page.

The database displays with the Contact List table open.

STEP 2 ›› ADD RECORDS TO A DOWNLOADED DESKTOP DATABASE TEMPLATE

Because the database opens in the Contact List form, you decide to begin by entering a contact—your dentist—in the form. Refer to Figure 1.31 as you complete Step 2.

Step d: Open your dentist's record

FIGURE 1.31 Contact Details Form

a. Click in the empty first field of the first row. Enter the following information, pressing **Tab** between each entry. Do not press Tab after entering the ZIP/Postal Code.

Field Name	Value to Type
First Name	Tanya
Last Name	Machuca
Company	Hobblecreek Mountain Dentistry
Job Title	D.D.S.
Category	Business (select from list)
E-mail Address	HMDentistry@email.com
Business Phone	801-555-8102
Home Phone	(leave blank)
Mobile Phone	801-555-8921
ZIP/Postal Code	84664

b. Click **Save and Close**.

c. Double-click **Contact List** in the Forms group on the Navigation Pane.

d. Click **Open** in the first field of Dr. Machuca's record.

Open is a hyperlink to a different form in the database. The Contact Details form opens, displaying Dr. Machuca's information. More fields are available for you to use to store information.

e. Enter the following additional information to the record:

Field Name	Value to Type
Street	56 West 200 North
City	Mapleton
State/Province	UT
Country/Region	USA
Notes	Available Tuesday - Friday 7 a.m. to 4 p.m.

f. Click the **Click to Map hyperlink** to view a map to Dr. Machuca's office. Close the map.

Bing displays a map to the address in the record. You can get directions, locate nearby businesses, and use many other options.

g. Click **Save and Close** in the top center of the form to close the Contact Details form.

The record is saved.

h. Click **New Contact** beneath the Contact List title bar.

The Contact Details form opens to a blank record.

i. Enter the following information for a new record, pressing **Tab** to move between fields. Some fields will be blank.

Field Name	Value to Type
First Name	Rowan
Last Name	Westmoreland
Company	Phoenix Aesthetics
Job Title	Aesthetician
Mobile Phone	801-555-2221
Street	425 North Main Street
City	Springville
State/Province	UT
ZIP/Postal Code	84663
Category	Personal
E-mail Address	Rowan55W5@email.com
Notes	Recommended by Michelle

j. Click **Save and Close**.

STEP 3 » EXPLORE THE DATABASE OBJECTS IN A DOWNLOADED DESKTOP DATABASE TEMPLATE

You explore the objects created by the template so that you understand the organization of the database. Refer to Figure 1.32 as you complete Step 3.

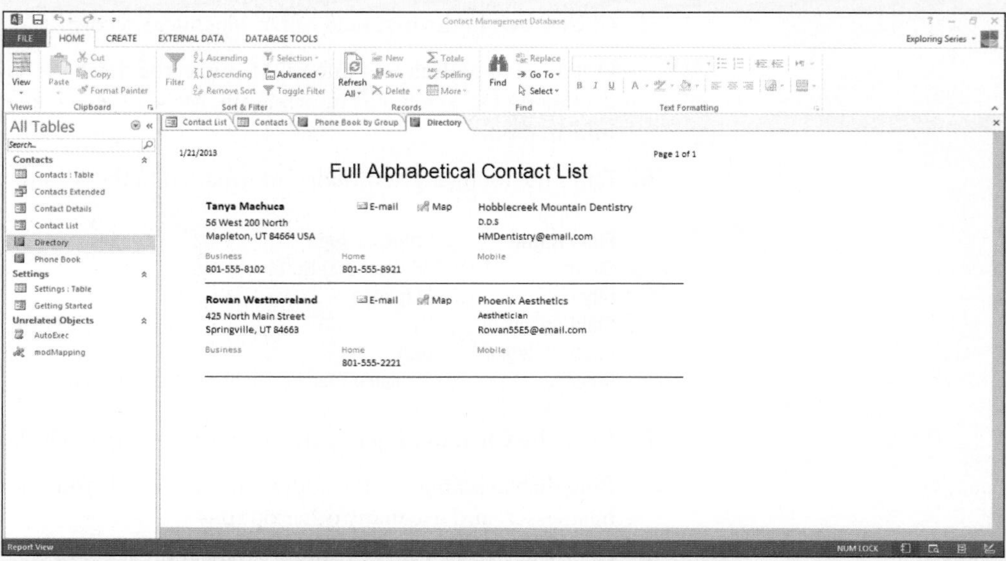

FIGURE 1.32 Directory Form

a. Double-click the **Contacts table** in the Navigation Pane to open it.

The information you entered using the Contact List form and the Contact Details form displays in the Contacts table.

b. Click the **Reports group** in the Navigation Pane to expand the list of reports, if necessary.

The list of reports contained in the database file opens.

c. Double-click **Phone Book** in the Navigation Pane to open it.

The Phone Book report opens displaying the contact name and phone information organized by category.

d. Double-click the **Directory report** in the Navigation Pane to open it.

The Directory report opens, displaying a full alphabetical contact list. The Directory report was designed to display more fields than the Phone Book, but it is not organized by category.

e. Click **All Access Objects** on the Navigation Pane and select **Tables and Related Views**.

You can now see the objects that are based on the Contacts table.

f. Right-click the **Directory report tab** and click **Close All**.

g. Exit Access and submit your work based on your instructor's directions.

Chapter Objectives Review

After reading this chapter, you have accomplished the following objectives:

1. **Understand database fundamentals.**
   - A database is a collection of data organized as meaningful information that can be accessed, managed, stored, queried, sorted, and reported.
   - Organize information in a database and recognize Access objects: An Access database is a structured collection of six types of objects—tables, forms, queries, reports, macros, and modules.
   - The foundation of a database is its tables, the objects in which data is stored. Each table in the database is composed of records, and each record is in turn comprised of fields.
   - The primary key in a table is the field (or combination of fields) that makes every record in a table unique.
   - Examine the Access interface: Objects are organized and listed in the Navigation Pane. Access also uses a Tabbed Documents interface in which each object that is open has its own tab.
   - Explore Access views: The Datasheet view enables the user to view, add, edit, and delete records, whereas the Design view is used to create and modify a table's design by specifying the fields it will contain, the fields' data types, and their associated properties.
   - Open an Access file and work with Content Security: When a database is opened from a location that has not been designated as a trusted location or that does not have a digital signature from a publisher you can trust, Access displays a message bar with a security warning. Click the Enable Content button if you trust the database's source.
2. **Use an existing database.**
   - Understand the difference between working in storage and memory: Access works primarily from storage. Records can be added, modified, or deleted in the database, and as the information is entered it is automatically saved.
   - Add, edit, and delete records: A pencil icon displays in the row selector box to indicate when you are in editing mode. Moving to another record or clicking Save on the Quick Access Toolbar saves the changes.
   - To add a new record, click *New (blank) record* on the navigation bar. To delete a record, click the row selector and click Delete in the Records group on the Home tab.
   - Save As, Compact and Repair, and Back Up Access files: *Compact and Repair* reduces the size of the database, and Back Up creates a duplicate copy of the database.
3. **Sort table data on one or multiple fields.**
   - Sorting changes the order of information, and information may be sorted by one or more fields.
4. **Create, modify, and remove filters.**
   - A filter is a set of criteria that is applied to a table to display a subset of records in that table.
   - *Filter by Selection* displays only the records that match the selected criteria.
   - *Filter by Form* displays records based on multiple criteria and enables the user to apply logical operators and use comparison operators.
5. **Know when to use Access or Excel to manage data.**
   - Use Access to manage data when you require multiple related tables to store your data; have a large amount of data; need to connect to and retrieve data from external databases; need to group, sort, and total data based on various parameters; and/or have an application that requires multiple users to connect to one data source.
   - Use Excel to manage data when you need one worksheet to handle all of your data; have mostly numeric data; require subtotals and totals in your worksheet; want to primarily run a series of "what if" scenarios on your data; and/or need to create complex charts and/or graphs.
6. **Understand relational power.**
   - Use the Relationships window: A relationship is a connection between two tables using a common field. The benefit of a relationship is to efficiently combine data from related tables for the purpose of creating queries, forms, and reports.
   - Enforce referential integrity: Enforcing referential integrity when setting a table relationship ensures that data cannot be entered into a related table unless it first exists in the primary table.
7. **Create a database.**
   - Create a Web application using a template: Creating a custom Web app enables you to create a database that you can build and use and share with others through the Web.
   - Creating a blank desktop database: Creating a blank desktop database lets you create a database specific to your needs.
   - Create a desktop database using a template: A template is a predefined database that includes professionally designed tables, forms, reports, and other objects that you can use to jumpstart the creation of your database.

Key Terms Matching

Match the key terms with their definitions. Write the key term letter by the appropriate numbered definition.

a. Back Up Database
b. Compact and Repair
c. Custom Web app
d. Datasheet view
e. Design view
f. Field
g. Filter by Form
h. Filter by Selection
i. Form
j. Navigation Pane
k. Object
l. Primary key
m. Query
n. Record
o. Relational database management system (RDBMS)
p. Relationship
q. Report
r. Sort
s. Table
t. Template

1. _______ View that enables you to add, edit, and delete the records of a table. **p. 622**

2. _______ An Access object that enables you to enter, modify, or delete table data. **p. 620**

3. _______ An Access utility that reduces the size of the database and can repair a corrupt database. **p. 627**

4. _______ A main component that is created and used to make a database function. **p. 619**

5. _______ A filtering method that displays records based on multiple criteria **p. 638**

6. _______ A system that uses the relational model to manage groups of data (tables) and rules (relationships) between tables. **p. 646**

7. _______ A database that can be built, used, and shared with others through the use of a host server. **p. 653**

8. _______ An object that contains professional-looking formatted information from underlying tables or queries. **p. 620**

9. _______ An object used to store data, and the foundation of every database. **p. 619**

10. _______ An Access utility that creates a duplicate copy of the database. **p. 627**

11. _______ A predefined database that includes professionally designed tables, forms, reports, and other objects. **p. 653**

12. _______ A filtering method that displays only records that match selected criteria. **p. 637**

13. _______ A connection between two tables using a common field. **p. 645**

14. _______ A method of listing records in a specific sequence. **p. 636**

15. _______ View that enables you to create tables, add and delete fields, and modify field properties. **p. 624**

16. _______ An Access interface element that organizes and lists the database objects in a database. **p. 619**

17. _______ A question you ask that can help you find and retrieve table data meeting conditions you specify. **p. 620**

18. _______ The smallest data element in a table, such as first name, last name, address, or phone number. **p. 619**

19. _______ Complete set of all the fields (data elements) about one person, place, event, or concept. **p. 619**

20. _______ The field (or combination of fields) that uniquely identifies each record in a table. **p. 624**

Multiple Choice

1. Which sequence represents the hierarchy of terms, from smallest to largest?
   (a) Database, table, record, field
   (b) Field, record, table, database
   (c) Record, field, table, database
   (d) Field, record, database, table

2. You edit several records in an Access table. When should you execute the Save command?
   (a) Immediately after you edit a record
   (b) When you close the table
   (c) Once at the end of the session
   (d) Records are saved automatically; the save command is not required.

3. Which of the following is *not* true of an Access database?
   (a) Short Text, Number, AutoNumber, and Currency are valid data types.
   (b) Every record in a table has the same fields as every other record.
   (c) Every table in a database contains the same number of records as every other table.
   (d) Each table should contain a primary key; however, a primary key is not required.

4. Which of the following is *true* regarding the record selector box?
   (a) An orange border surrounds the record selector box and the active record.
   (b) A pencil symbol indicates that the current record already has been saved.
   (c) An asterisk indicates the first record in the table.
   (d) An empty square indicates that the current record is selected.

5. Which of the following will be accepted as valid during data entry?
   (a) Adding a record with a duplicate primary key
   (b) Entering text into a numeric field
   (c) Entering numbers into a text field
   (d) Omitting an entry in a required field

6. You have finished an Access assignment and wish to turn it in to your instructor for evaluation. As you prepare to transfer the file, you discover that it has more than doubled in size. You should:
   (a) Delete extra tables or reports or fields to make the file smaller.
   (b) Zip the database file prior to sending it to your instructor.
   (c) Compact and repair the database before sending it to your instructor.
   (d) Turn it in; the size does not matter.

7. Which of the following conditions is available through *Filter by Selection*?
   (a) Equals condition
   (b) Delete condition
   (c) AND condition
   (d) OR condition

8. An Employees table is open in Datasheet view. You want to sort the names alphabetically by last name and then by first name (e.g., Smith, Andrew). To do this, you must:
   (a) First sort ascending on first name and then on last name.
   (b) First sort descending on first name and then on last name.
   (c) First sort ascending on last name and then on first name.
   (d) First sort descending on last name and then on first name.

9. Which of the following is *not* true when creating relationships between tables?
   (a) Join lines create a relationship between two tables.
   (b) The common fields used to create a relationship must both be primary keys.
   (c) The data types of common fields must be the same.
   (d) Enforcing referential integrity ensures that data cannot be entered into a related table unless it first exists in the primary table.

10. All of the following statements are *true* about creating a database *except*:
    (a) Creating a custom Web app requires that you use a host server.
    (b) When creating a blank desktop database, Access opens to a blank table in Datasheet view.
    (c) Using a template to create a database saves time because it includes predefined objects.
    (d) The objects provided in a template cannot be modified.

Practice Exercises

1 Hotel Rewards

FROM SCRATCH

The Lakes Hotel and Conference Center caters to upscale business travelers and provides stylish hotel suites, sophisticated meeting and reception facilities, and state-of-the-art media equipment. The hotel is launching a rewards club to help the marketing department track the purchasing patterns of its most loyal customers. All of the hotel transactions will be stored in an Access database. Your task is to create a member table and enter sample customers. You will practice filtering on the table data. This exercise follows the same set of skills as used in Hands-On Exercises 1 and 2 in the chapter. Refer to Figure 1.33 as you complete this exercise.

Members

ID	LastName	FirstName	Address	City	State	Zip	Phone	DateOfMembership
1	Guerassio	Janine	1012 TRADERS TRAIL	GRAHAM	NC	27253		1/26/2015
2	Gutierrez	Antonio	102 PENNYPACKER CT	ELIZABETH CITY	NC	27909	555-387-6394	1/29/2016
3	Sigman	Hanni	1922 WRIGHTSVILLE AVE	CARY	NC	27512	555-784-8851	7/30/2016
4	O'Brien	Lovie	3413 KISTLER COURT	WILMINGTON	NC	28409	555-227-8335	2/13/2015
5	Ratanaphruks	Kritika	4444 LLOYD CT	RALEIGH	NC	27609		3/18/2014
6	Koski	Janice	3904 HUNT CHASE CT	RALEIGH	NC	27612		7/3/2016
7	Tulowiecki	Jerry	775 BEAR RIDGE TRAIL	RALEIGH	NC	27607	555-762-9373	5/21/2016
8	Yingling	Bev	PO BOX 7045	SALISBURY	NC	28146		2/17/2014
9	Gray	Bob	100 BIRDIE COURT	RALEIGH	NC	27612	555-787-7688	9/1/2015
10	Hauser	Bob	10008 WHITESTONE RD	RALEIGH	NC	27612	555-783-8286	3/1/2015
(New)								

FIGURE 1.33 Enter Data into the Members Table

a. Open Access and click **Blank desktop database**.

b. Type **a01p1Rewards_LastFirst** in the **File Name box**. Click the **Browse icon**. Navigate to the location where you are saving your files in the File New Database dialog box, click **OK** to close the dialog box, and then click **Create** to create the new database.

c. Click **View** in the Views group on the TABLE TOOLS FIELDS tab to switch to Design view. Type **Members** in the **Save As dialog box** and click **OK**.

d. Type **LastName** under the ID field and press **Tab**. Accept **Short Text** as the Data Type. Type **FirstName** in the third row and press **Tab**. Accept **Short Text** as the Data Type.

e. Type the next five fields into the Field Name column: **Address**, **City**, **State**, **Zip**, and **Phone**. Accept **Short Text** as the Data Type for each of these fields.

f. Type **DateOfMembership** as the last Field Name and select **Date/Time** as the Data Type.

g. Click **View** in the Views group to switch to Datasheet view. Click **Yes** to save the table. Type the data as shown in Figure 1.33. Increase the column widths to fit the data as necessary. Press **Tab** to move to the next field.

h. Find a record that displays *Raleigh* as the value in the City field. Click **Raleigh** to select that data value.

i. Click **Selection** in the Sort & Filter group on the HOME tab. Select **Equals "Raleigh"**.

j. Find a record that displays *27612* as the value in the Zip field. Click **27612** to select that data value.

k. Click **Selection** in the Sort & Filter group on the HOME tab. Select **Equals "27612"**.

l. Click any value in the FirstName field. Click **Ascending** in the Sort & Filter group on the HOME tab. Click any value in the LastName field. Click **Ascending** in the Sort & Filter group on the HOME tab.

m. Click the **FILE tab**, click **Print**, and then click **Print Preview** to preview the sorted and filtered table.

n. Click **Close Print Preview** in the Close Preview group.

o. Close the table and save the changes.

p. Click the **FILE tab** and click **Compact and Repair Database** under *Advanced*.

q. Click the **FILE tab**, click **Save As**, and then double-click **Back Up Database**.

r. Click **Save** to accept the default backup file name with today's date.

s. Click the **FILE tab** and click **Exit** (to exit Access). Submit the database based on your instructor's directions.

2 Custom Coffee

The Custom Coffee Company provides coffee, tea, and snacks to offices in Miami. Custom Coffee also provides and maintains the equipment for brewing the beverages. The firm has a reputation for providing outstanding customer service. To improve customer service even further, the owner recently purchased an Access database to keep track of customers, orders, and products. This database will replace the Excel spreadsheets currently maintained by the office manager. The Excel spreadsheets are out of date, and they do not allow for data validation while data is being entered. The company hired you to verify and enter all the Excel data into the Access database. This exercise follows the same set of skills as used in Hands-On Exercises 1–3 in the chapter. Refer to Figure 1.34 as you complete this exercise.

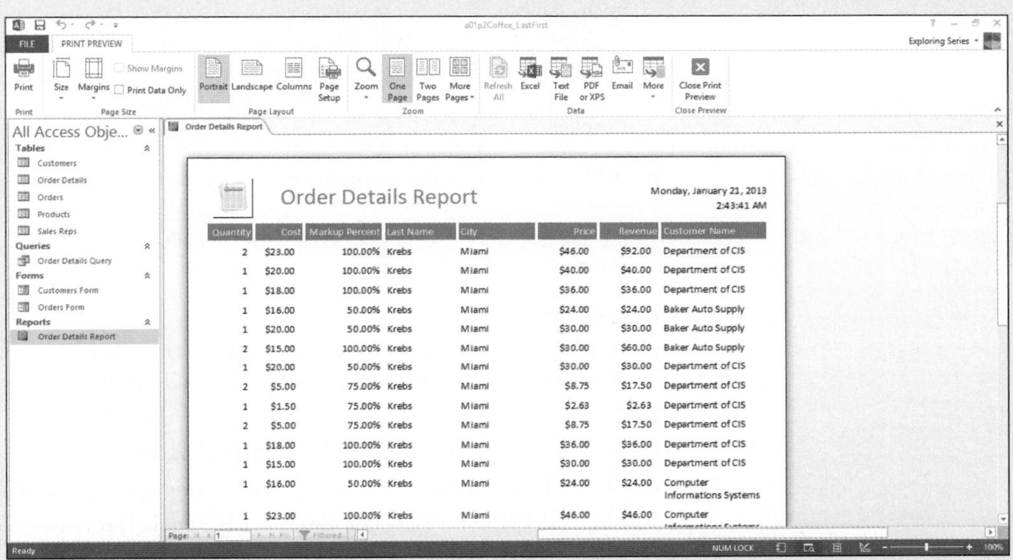

FIGURE 1.34 Order Details Report Filtered for *YourName* and *Miami*

a. Open the *a01p2Coffee* file and save the database as **a01p2Coffee_LastFirst**.

b. Click the **DATABASE TOOLS tab** and click **Relationships** in the Relationships group. Review the table relationships. Take note of the join line between the Customers and Orders tables.

c. Click **Close** in the Relationships group.

d. Double-click the **Sales Reps table** in the Navigation Pane to open it. Replace *YourName* with your name in both the LastName and FirstName fields. For example, as the Access author, I used the name Cynthia Krebs in place of FirstName LastName. Close the table by clicking the **Close (X) button** on the right side of the Sales Reps window.

e. Double-click the **Customers Form** to open it. Click **New (blank) record** in the navigation bar at the bottom of the window. Add a new record by typing the following information; press **Tab** after each field.

Customer Name:	*your name* Company
Contact:	*your name*
Email:	*yourname*@email.com
Address1:	123 Main St
Address2:	(leave blank)
City:	Miami
State:	FL
Zip Code:	33133
Phone:	(305) 555-1234

Fax: (leave blank)
Service Start Date: 01/17/2016
Credit Rating: A
Sales Rep ID: 2

Note the pencil in the top-left margin of the form window. This symbol indicates the new record has not been saved. Press **Tab**. The pencil symbol disappears, and the new customer is automatically saved to the table.

f. Close the Customers Form.

g. Double-click the **Orders Form** to open it. Click **New (blank) record** in the navigation bar at the bottom of the window. Add a new record by typing the following information:

Customer ID: 15 (Access will convert it to C0015)
Payment Type: Cash (select using the arrow)
Comments: Ship this order in 2 days
Product ID: 4 (Access will convert it to P0004)
Quantity: 2

h. Add a second product using the following information:

Product ID: 6 (Access will convert it to P0006)
Quantity: 1

i. Close the form.

j. Double-click the **Order Details Report** to open it in Report view. Click your name in the Last Name field, click **Selection** in the Sort & Filter group, and then click **Equals "Your Name"**.

k. Right-click **Miami** in the City field and select **Equals "Miami"** from the shortcut menu.

l. Click the **FILE tab**, click **Print**, and then click **Print Preview**.

m. Click **Close Print Preview** in the Close Preview group. Close the report.

n. Click the **FILE tab** and click **Compact & Repair Database**.

o. Click the **FILE tab**, click **Save As**, and then double-click **Back Up Database**. Use the default backup file name.

p. Close Access. Submit based on your instructor's directions.

3 Camping Trip

You and your friends have decided to spend your annual reunion camping at the Wawona Campground in Yosemite National Park. Wawona Campground is an extremely popular campground. Campground reservations are available in blocks of one month at a time, up to five months in advance, on the 15th of each month at 7 AM Pacific time. Nearly all reservations are filled the first day they become available, usually within seconds or minutes after 7 AM. Realizing that making reservations is a high-priority, critical task, and that there are many other tasks that must be completed before you can have a successful trip, your group decides to use the Access Task Management Database to begin getting organized for their trip on September 15, 2015. Other tasks can be entered at a later time. This exercise follows the same set of skills as used in Hands-On Exercises 3 and 4 in the chapter. Refer to Figures 1.35–1.38 as you complete this exercise.

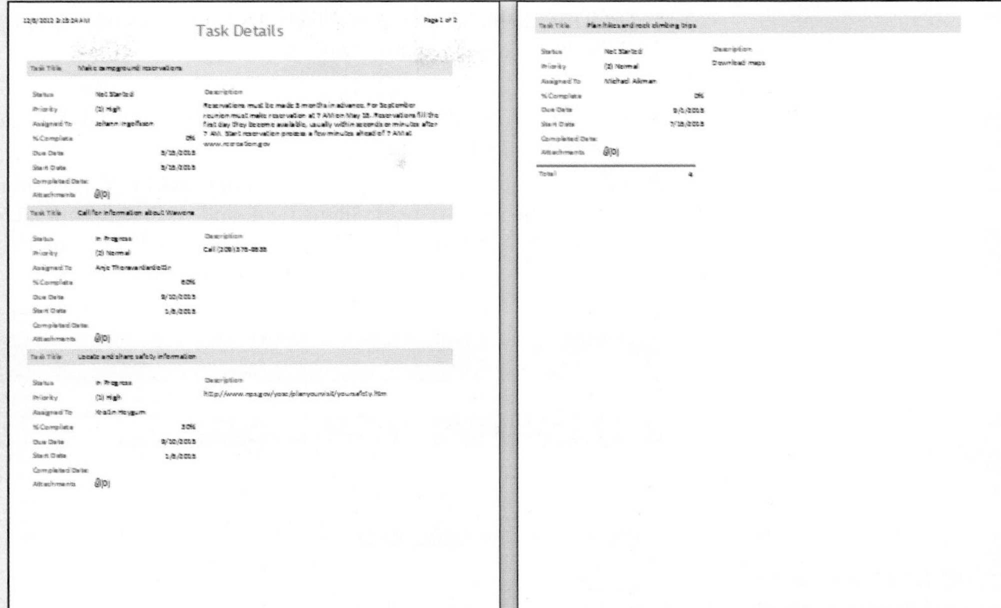

FIGURE 1.35 Task Details Report

a. Open Access and click the **Desktop task management template** in the Access Backstage view.

b. Type **a01p3Camping_LastFirst** in the **File name box**. Click the **Browse icon**. Navigate to the location where you are saving your files in the File New Database dialog box, click **OK** to close the dialog box, and then click **Create** to create the new database.

c. Click the **Watch this arrow** for the *Using the Tasks Database* template video on the left side of the Getting Started page. If the Getting Started page does not open, open the Getting Started form in the Forms group in the Navigation Pane. Click **Watch this>>** and watch the video. Close the video when you have finished watching it. Click **Close** again to return to the *Getting Started with Tasks* page.

d. Remove the check in the *Show Getting Started when this database is opened* check box so that the page does not automatically display in the future. If you want to view Getting Started again, you can click **Getting Started** in the Forms category on the Navigation Pane. Click the **Close (X) button**.

e. Click **Relationships** in the Relationships group on the DATABASE TOOLS tab and note the relationship between the Contacts table and the Tasks table. Close the Relationships window.

f. Double-click **Contact List** in the Forms category on the Navigation Pane. Type the information for each field in the Contact list form using the information displayed in Figure 1.36, pressing **Tab** between each field.

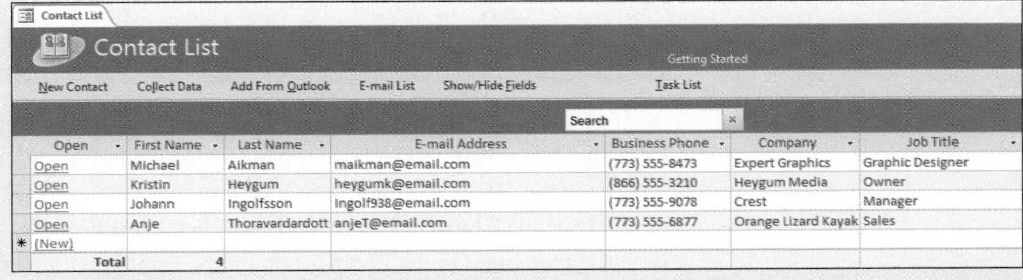

FIGURE 1.36 Contact List

g. Close the Contact List form. The Task List form displays because it was the form open when you downloaded the database.

> **TROUBLESHOOTING:** If the Task List form does not display, double-click the Task List form in the Navigation Pane to open it.

h. Click the **Shutter Bar Open/Close button** to close the Navigation Pane, which enables you to see more table fields.

i. Enter the information for each field in the Task List form using the information displayed in Figure 1.37. In the Priority field, Status field, and Assigned To field, click the arrow and select the list of options. When typing the Start Date and Due Date, type the date and add **7 AM** after the date. Although the date does not show in the table, it is required.

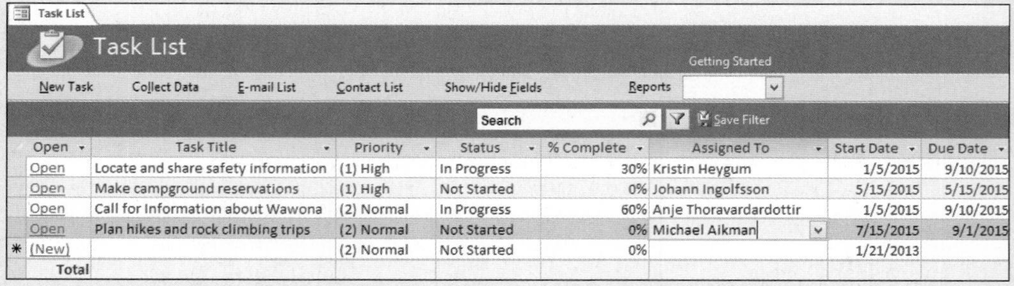

FIGURE 1.37 Task List Form

j. Close the Tasks table and click the **Shutter Bar Open/Close button** to open the Navigation Pane.

k. Double-click **Task Details** in the Forms category in the Navigation Pane.

l. Refer to Figure 1.38 to enter the information in the **Description box** and close the Task Details form.

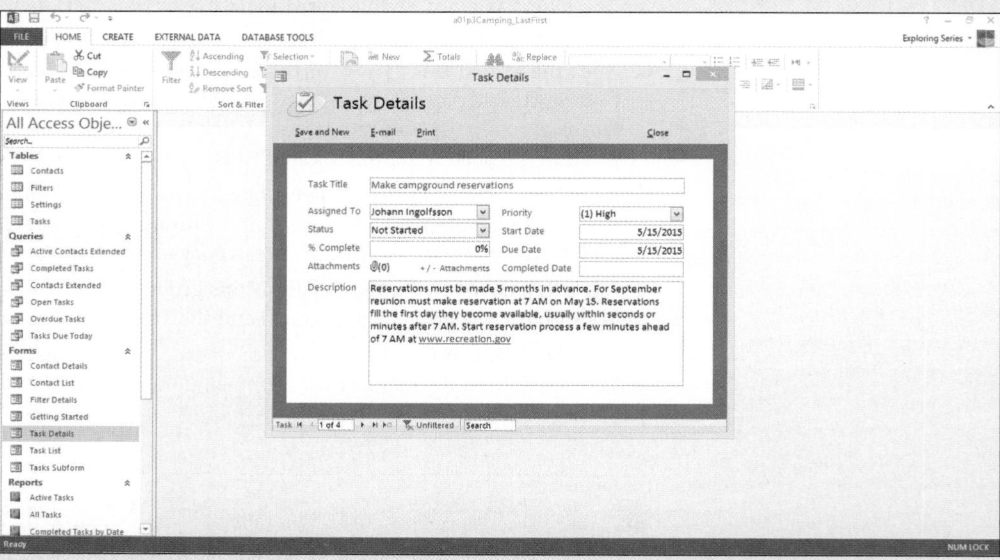

FIGURE 1.38 Description in Task Details Form

m. Refer to Figure 1.35 and continue entering the descriptions for each of the records.

n. Double-click **Task Details** in the Reports category in the Navigation Pane to view the report displaying the details about the tasks you have created. Scroll down to see all tasks.

o. Click the **FILE tab**, click **Print**, and then click **Print Preview**.

p. Click **Two Pages** in the Zoom group on the Print Preview tab. Note the report format groups the information by Task Title.

q. Click **Close Print Preview** in the Close Preview group. Close the report.

r. Click the **FILE tab** and click **Compact & Repair Database**.

s. Click the **FILE tab**, click **Save As**, and then double-click **Back Up Database**. Use the default backup file name.

t. Close Access. Submit based on your instructor's directions.

Mid-Level Exercises

1 Home Sales

FROM SCRATCH

You are the senior partner in a large, independent real estate firm that specializes in home sales. Most of your time is spent supervising the agents who work for your firm. The firm needs to create a database to hold all of the information on the properties it has listed. You will use the database to help find properties that match the goals of your customers. You will create the database, create two tables, add data to both tables, and create a relationship. Refer to Figure 1.39 as you complete this exercise.

Properties

ID	DateListed	DateSold	ListPrice	SalesPrice	SqFeet	Beds	Baths	Address	SubDivision	Agent	Style	Construction	Garage	YearBuilt
1	5/28/2015		$246,000.00		1928	2	2	1166 Avondale	3	1	Ranch	Brick	1 Car Attached	2010
2	7/22/2015		$263,600.00		1896	2	2	1684 Riverdale	3	2	2 Story	Frame	1 Car Attached	2009
3	6/7/2015		$270,000.00		2026	2	2	1166 So;verdate	3	4	Split Level	Stone	2 Car Attached	2007
4	6/7/2015		$298,000.00		1672	1	1	4520 Oakdale	3	3	Ranch	Brick	1 Car Attached	1997
5	6/22/2015		$312,000.00		2056	2	2	1838 Hillendale	3	4	Split Level	Frame	2 Car Attached	2003
6	7/24/2015		$339,600.00		2456	3	3	1255 Copperdale	3	5	Ranch	Brick	2 Car Attached	2008
7	6/22/2015		$339,600.00		2539	3	3	1842 Gardendale	3	3	2 Story	Stone	1 Car Detached	1983
8	8/12/2015		$239,600.00		2032	2	3	1605 Lakedale	3	2	Split Foyer	Frame	Carport	2002
9	6/22/2015		$379,000.00		2540	3	2	1775 Jerrydale	3	1	Ranch	Brick	3 Car Attached	2014
10	6/23/2015	9/14/2015	$172,500.00	$168,000.00	2030	3	2	213 Merrydale	3	3	Ranch	Stone	1 Car Attached	2010
* (New)			$0.00	$0.00	0	0	0		0	0				0

FIGURE 1.39 Properties Table

a. Open Access and click **Blank desktop database**. Type **a01m1Homes_LastFirst** in the **File Name box**. Click **Browse** and navigate to the location where you are saving your files. Click **OK** to close the dialog box and click **Create** to create the new database.

b. Switch to Design view. Type **Properties** in the **Save As dialog box** and click **OK**.

c. Type **DateListed** under the ID field and press **Tab**. Select **Date/Time** as the Data Type.

d. Type the remainder of the fields and Data Types as shown:

Field Name	Data Type
DateSold	Date/Time
ListPrice	Currency
SalesPrice	Currency
SqFeet	Number
Beds	Number
Baths	Number
Address	Short Text
SubDivision	Number
AgentID	Number
Style	Short Text
Construction	Short Text
Garage	Short Text
YearBuilt	Number

e. Switch to Datasheet view. Type the first 10 records as shown in Figure 1.39.

f. Open the *a01m1Properties.xlsx* workbook file in Excel. Click **row 2**, press and hold the **left mouse button**, and then drag through **row 70** so that all the data rows are selected. Click **Copy** in the Clipboard group on the HOME tab. Click **Yes** to save the data to the Clipboard when prompted. Close the Excel file.

g. Return to Access and click on the **asterisk (*)** on the first new row of the Properties table. Click **Paste** in the Clipboard group to paste all 69 rows into the Properties table. Save and close the table.

h. Click **Table** in the Tables group on the CREATE tab. Click **View** in the Views group on the TABLE TOOLS FIELDS tab to switch to Design view. Save the table as **Agents**. Change the primary key from ID to **AgentID**. Add the following fields and switch to Datasheet view. Save changes to the table design when prompted.

Field Name	Data Type
FirstName	Short Text
LastName	Short Text
Title	Short Text

i. Enter the following data in the Agents table and close the table.

AgentID	FirstName	LastName	Title
1	Kia	Hart	Broker
2	Keith	Martin	Agent
3	Kim	Yang	Agent
4	Steven	Dougherty	Agent in Training
5	Angela	Scott	Agent in Training
6	Juan	Resario	President

j. Click the **DATABASE TOOLS tab** and click **Relationships** in the Relationships group. Add both tables to the Relationships window and close the Show Table dialog box.

k. Drag the bottom border of the Properties table downward until all fields display. Drag the **AgentID field** from the Agents table and drop it onto the **AgentID field** in the Properties table. Click the **Enforce Referential Integrity check box** in the Edit Relationships dialog box to activate it. Click **Create** and close the Relationships window. Click **Yes** to save your changes.

l. Open the **Properties** table. Click **Advanced** in the Sort & Filter group and click **Filter By Form**. Set the criteria to identify properties with a list price less than $300,000 and with two bedrooms. (You will use the expression <300000 for the criteria of the list price.) Display the results and sort by ascending list price. Save and close the table.

m. Compact, repair, and back up the database.

n. Exit Access. Submit the database based on your instructor's directions.

2 National Conference

The Association of Higher Education will host its National Conference on your campus next year. To facilitate the conference, the information technology department has replaced last year's Excel spreadsheets with an Access database containing information on the rooms, speakers, and sessions. Your assignment is to create a room itinerary that will list all of the sessions, dates, and times for each room. The list will be posted on the door of each room for the duration of the conference. Refer to Figure 1.40 as you complete this exercise.

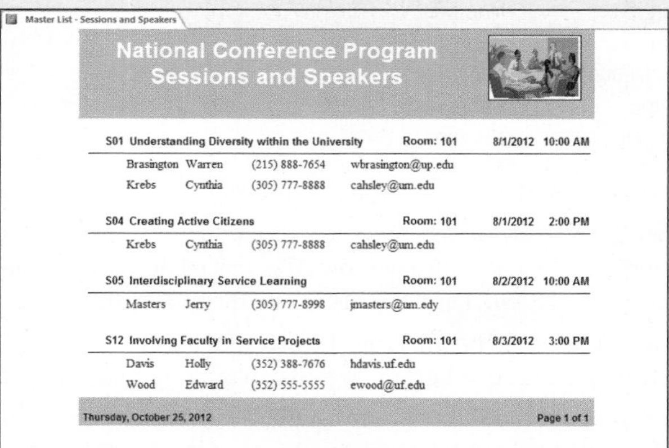

FIGURE 1.40 Sessions and Speakers Report—Room 101

a. Open the *a01m2NatConf* file and save the database as **a01m2NatConf_LastFirst**.

b. Open the Relationships window.

c. Review the objects in the database to see if any of the existing objects will provide the room itinerary information displayed in Figure 1.40.

DISCOVER 

d. Open the SessionSpeaker table. Scroll to the first blank record at the bottom of the table and enter a new record using SpeakerID **99** and SessionID **09**. (Note: Speaker 99 does not exist.) How does Access respond? Close the dialog box, recognizing that you are not saving this record. Close the SessionSpeaker table. In the Relationships window, right-click the join line between the Speakers table and SessionSpeaker table and click **Delete**. Click **Yes** to permanently delete the selected relationship from the database. Close the Relationships window. Open the SessionSpeaker table and enter the same record again. How does Access respond this time? Close the SessionSpeaker table.

e. Open the Speakers table. Find and replace *YourName* with your name. Close the Speakers table.

f. Open the Speaker–Session Query and apply a filter to identify the sessions where you or Holly Davis are the speakers. Use *Filter by Form* and the Or tab. (Nine records should display.)

g. Sort the filtered results in ascending order by the RoomID field and save and close the query.

h. Open the Master List–Sessions and Speakers report. Right-click the **Master List–Sessions and Speakers tab** and select **Report View**.

i. Apply a filter that limits the report to sessions in Room 101 only.

j. Click the **FILE tab**, click **Print**, and then click **Print Preview**. Compare the report to Figure 1.40 and make any corrections necessary. Close Print Preview and close the report.

k. Compact and repair the database.

l. Back up the database. Use the default backup file name.

m. Exit Access. Submit based on your instructor's directions.

3 Used Cell Phones for Sale

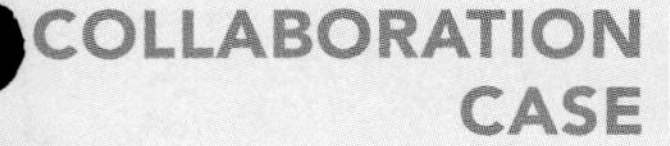
COLLABORATION CASE 

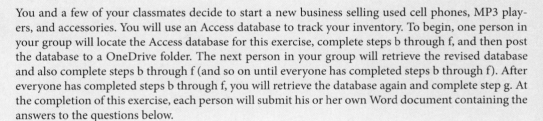

You and a few of your classmates decide to start a new business selling used cell phones, MP3 players, and accessories. You will use an Access database to track your inventory. To begin, one person in your group will locate the Access database for this exercise, complete steps b through f, and then post the database to a OneDrive folder. The next person in your group will retrieve the revised database and also complete steps b through f (and so on until everyone has completed steps b through f). After everyone has completed steps b through f, you will retrieve the database again and complete step g. At the completion of this exercise, each person will submit his or her own Word document containing the answers to the questions below.

a. Open the *a01m3Phones* database and save it as **a01m3PhonesGroupX_LastFirst**. (Replace *X* with the number assigned to your group by your instructor.)

b. Open the Inventory table and review the records in the table. Take note of the data in the TypeOfDevice column. Close the table and open the DeviceOptions table. Review the data and close the table.

c. Open the Relationships window. What is the benefit of the relationship between the Inventory table and the DeviceOptions table? Create a Word document with both the question and your answer. After you complete this exercise, you will submit this Word document to your instructor using the file name **a01m3PhonesAnswers_LastFirst**. Close the Relationships window.

d. Open the Inventory Form and add the information about your cell phone to the table (or search the Internet for any model if you do not have a cell phone) in the first new blank record. Enter your name in the SellerName field. With your information showing in the form, take a screenshot of the form using the Snipping Tool. Paste the image into the Word document you created in step c. Close the form.

e. Open the Inventory Report by Manufacturer in Report view. Filter the records for only items that have not been sold. Take a screenshot using the Snipping Tool and paste the image into the Word document. Close the report, close the database, and then exit Access.

f. Create a folder on your OneDrive account named **Exploring Access** and share the folder with other members in your group and the instructor. Upload the database to this new folder and notify another person in your group. The next person will complete steps b through f, and then the next person, until all group members have added their information.

g. After all the new phone records have been added, each person in the group should download the **a01m3PhonesGroupX** database again and use filters to answer the following questions. Add the questions and your answers to the Word document you created.

1. How many phones are still for sale? ___________
2. How many phones are made by Apple or Samsung? ___________
3. How many phones were sold in the first half of 2013? ___________ List the ID numbers ___________
4. Sort the phones from lowest to highest asking price. Which phone is the least expensive? ___________ Most expensive? ___________
5. How many items are not phones? ___________

h. Use e-mail or text messaging to communicate with the other members in your group if you have any questions.

i. Submit the Word document based on your instructor's directions.

Beyond the Classroom

Northwind Revenue Report

RESEARCH CASE

Open the *a01b2NWind* file and save the database as **a01b2NWind_LastFirst**. Open the Employees table and replace *YourName* with your first and last names. Before you can filter the Revenue report, you need to update the criterion in the underlying query to match the dates in the database. Right-click the **Revenue query** in the Navigation Pane and click **Design view** in the shortcut menu. Scroll to the right until you see *OrderDate*. Right-click in the **Criteria row** under *OrderDate* and click **Zoom**. Change the criterion to **Between#1/1/2015#And#3/31/2015#** and click **OK**. Click **Run** in the Results group on the Query Tools Design tab and save the query. Open the Revenue report. Use the tools that you have learned in this chapter to filter the report for only your sales of Confections. Close the report. Compact, repair, and back up your database and exit Access.

Lugo Computer Sales

DISASTER RECOVERY 

You are having trouble with an Access 2013 database. One of the employees accidentally changed the CustomerID of Lugo Computer Sales. This change caused a problem in one of the relationships. Open the *a01b3Recover* file and save the database as **a01b3Recover_LastFirst**. Open the Customers and Orders tables and examine the data. Change the Lugo Computer Sales CustomerID in the Customers table back to the original number of 6. Reset the relationship between the Customers table and the Orders table and enforce referential integrity. Compact, repair, and back up your database and exit Access. Submit the database based on your instructor's directions.

Financial Literacy

SOFT SKILLS CASE 

The Cambridge Resources Group stated that surveyed executives ranked the "toll on productivity caused by financial stress" as one of the "most critical unaddressed issues in the workplace today." Dr. E. Thomas Garman, the president of Personal Finance Employee Education Foundation, stated that "60% of employees live paycheck to paycheck" and that research shows that "those with more financial distress report poor health; financially distressed workers (40–50%) report that their financial problems cause their health woes; and that positive changes in financial behaviors are related to improved health."

Tracking your income and your expenses enables you to see where your money is going. With this information you can create a budget that will help you reach your goals. To aid you with this process, Microsoft created a downloadable Personal Account Ledger template. This database includes a form that enables you to record transactions; reports to display transactions, expenses by category, and income by category; and a tax report. Open *a01b4Ledger*, a database based on the Microsoft Personal Account Ledger, and save it as **a01b4Ledger_LastFirst**. Use the Account Transaction List to enter your income and expenses for the previous month. Then view the Income by Category report and the Expenses by Category report. Compact, repair, and back up your database and exit Access. Submit the database based on your instructor's directions.

Capstone Exercise

Your boss expressed concern about the accuracy of the inventory reports in the bookstore. He needs you to open the inventory database, make modifications to some records, and determine if the changes you make carry through to the other objects in the database. You will make changes to a form and verify those changes in a table, a query, and a report. When you have verified that the changes update automatically, you will compact and repair the database and make a backup of it.

Database File Setup

You will open an original database file and save the database with a new name, replace an existing author's name with your name, create a table, create table relationships, sort, and apply a filter by selection.

a. Open the *a01c1Books* file and save the database as **a01c1Books_LastFirst**.

b. Create a new table in Design view. Save the table as **Publishers**. Change the primary key from ID to **PubID** with a Data Type of **Short Text**. Add the following fields and switch to Datasheet view. Save changes to the table design when prompted.

Field Name	Data Type
PubName	Short Text
PubAddress	Short Text
PubCity	Short Text
PubState	Short Text
PubZIP	Short Text

c. Enter the following data in the Publishers table and close the table.

PubID	PubName	PubAddress	PubCity	PubState	PubZIP
BB	Bantam Books	1540 Broadway	New York	NY	10036
FS	Farrar, Straus and Giroux	12 Union Square West	New York	NY	10003
KN	Knopf	299 Park Avenue	New York	NY	10171
LB	Little, Brown and Company	1271 Avenue of the Americas	New York	NY	10020
PH	Pearson/ Prentice Hall	1 Lake Street	Upper Saddle	NJ	07458
SS	Simon & Schuster	100 Front Street	Riverside	NY	08075

d. Open the Maintain Authors form.

e. Navigate to Record 7 and replace *YourName* with your name.

f. Add a new Title: **Technology in Action**. The ISBN is **0-13-148905-4**, the PubID is **PH**, the PublDate is **2015**, the Price is $89.95 (just type **89.95**, no $), and StockAmt is **95** units. Move to any other record to save the new record. Close the form.

g. Open the Maintain Authors form again and navigate to Record 7. The changes are there because Access works from storage, not memory. Close the form again.

Sort a Query and Apply a Filter by Selection

You need to reorder a detail query so that the results are sorted alphabetically by the publisher name.

a. Open the Publishers, Books, and Authors Query.

b. Click in any record in the PubName column and sort the field in ascending order.

c. Check to make sure that four books list you as the author.

d. Click your name in the Author's Last Name field and filter the records to show only your books.

e. Close the query and save the changes.

View a Report

You need to examine the Publishers, Books, and Authors Report to determine if the changes you made in the Maintain Authors form appear in the report.

a. Open the Publishers, Books, and Authors Report.

b. Check to make sure that the report shows four books listing you as the author.

c. View the layout of the report in Print Preview.

d. Close the report.

Filter a Table

You need to examine the Books table to determine if the changes you made in the Maintain Authors form carried through to the related table. You also will filter the table to display books published after 2010 with fewer than 100 copies in inventory.

a. Open the Books table.

b. Use *Filter by Form* to create a filter that will identify all books published after 2010 with fewer than 100 items in stock.

c. Apply the filter and preview the filtered table.

d. Close the table and save the changes.

Compact and Repair a Database and Back Up a Database

Now that you are satisfied that any changes made to a form or query carry through to the table, you are ready to compact, repair, and back up your file.

a. Compact and repair your database.

b. Create a backup copy of your database, accept the default file name, and save it.

c. Exit Access. Submit based on your instructor's directions.

Tables and Queries in Relational Databases

Designing Databases and Extracting Data

OBJECTIVES AFTER YOU READ THIS CHAPTER, YOU WILL BE ABLE TO:

CASE STUDY | Bank Audit

During a year-end review, a bank auditor uncovers mishandled funds at Commonwealth Federal Bank in Wilmington, Delaware. In order to analyze the data in more detail, the auditor asks you to create an Access database so he can enter the compromised accounts, the associated customers, and the involved employees. Once the new database is created and all the data are entered, you will help the auditor answer questions by creating and running queries.

As you begin, you realize that some of the data are contained in Excel spreadsheets. After discussing this with the auditor, you decide importing these data directly into the new database would be best. Importing from Excel into Access is commonplace and should work well. Importing will also help avoid errors that are associated with data entry. Once the Excel data have been imported, you will use queries to determine which data do not belong in the database. Unaffected records will be deleted.

This chapter introduces the Bank database case study to present the basic principles of table and query design. You will use tables and forms to input data, and you will create queries and reports to extract information from the database in a useful and organized way. The value of that information depends entirely on the quality of the underlying data—the tables.

Table Design, Creation, and Modification

Good database design begins with the tables. Tables provide the framework for all of the activities you perform in a database. If the framework is poorly designed, the rest of the database will be poorly designed as well. Whether you are experienced in designing tables or just learning how, the process should not be done haphazardly. You should follow a systematic approach when creating tables for a database. This process will take practice; however, over time, you will begin to see the patterns and eventually see the similarities among all databases.

In this section, you will learn the principles of good table design. You will review essential guidelines used when creating tables. After developing and testing the table design on paper, you will implement that design in Access. The first step is to list all the tables you need for the database and list all the fields in each table. While you learned to create tables in the previous chapter, in this chapter you will learn to refine them by changing the properties of various fields. You will also be introduced to the concept of data validation. You want to make sure the data entered into the database are valid for the field and valid for the organization. Allowing invalid data into the tables will only cause problems later.

Designing a Table

Recall that a table is a collection of records, with each record made up of a number of fields. During the table design process, think of the specific fields you need in each table; list the fields under the correct table and assign each field a data type (such as short text, number, or date) as well as its size (length) or format. The order of the fields within the table and the specific field names are not significant because they can be changed later. What is important is that the tables contain all necessary fields so that the system can produce the required information.

For example, consider the design process necessary to create a database for a bank. Most likely you have a bank account and know that the bank maintains data about you. Your bank has your name, address, phone number, and Social Security number. It also knows what accounts you have (checking, savings, money market), if you have a credit card with that bank, and what its balance is. Additionally, your bank keeps information about its branches around the city or state. If you think about the data your bank maintains, you could make a list of the categories of data needed to store that information. These categories for the bank—customers, accounts, branches—become the tables in the bank's database. A bank's customer list is an example of a table: It contains a record for each bank customer.

After the tables have been identified, add the necessary fields using these six guidelines. (These guidelines are discussed in detail in the following paragraphs.)

- Include the necessary data.
- Design for now and for the future.
- Store data in their smallest parts.
- Add calculated fields to a table.
- Design to accommodate date arithmetic.
- Link tables using common fields.

Figure 2.1 shows a customer table and two other tables found in a sample bank database. It also lists fields that would be needed in each table record.

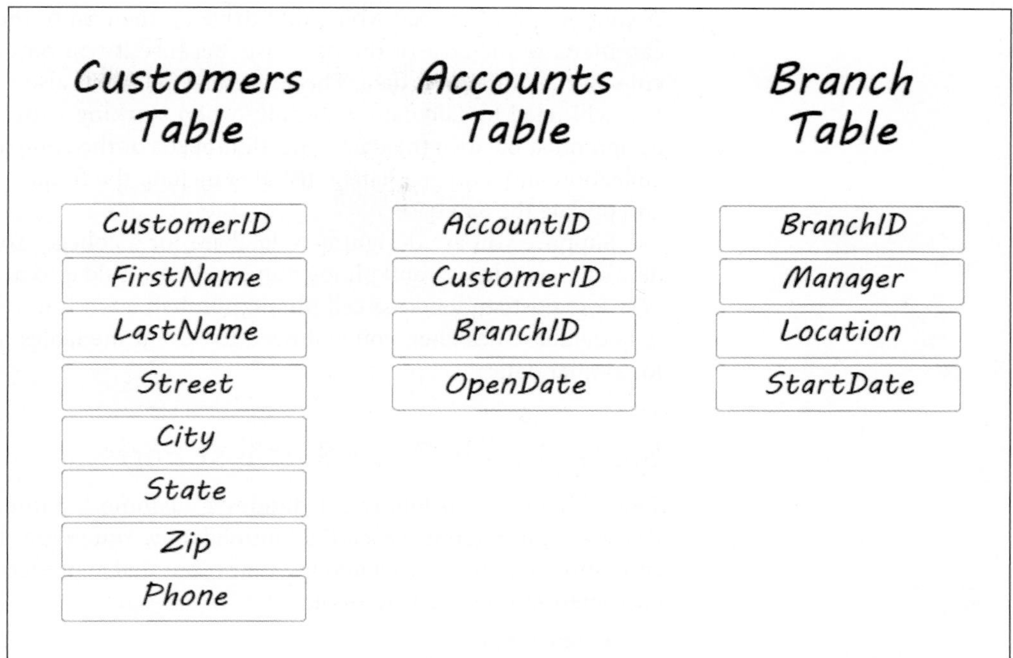

FIGURE 2.1 Rough Draft of Tables and Fields in a Sample Database

Include Necessary Data

A good way to determine what data are necessary in tables is to consider the output you need. It will probably be necessary for you to create professional-looking reports for others, so begin by creating a rough draft of the reports you will need. Then design tables that contain the fields necessary to create those reports. In other words, ask yourself what information will be expected from the system and determine the data required to produce that information. Consider, for example, the tables and fields in Figure 2.1. Is there required information that could not be generated from those tables?

- You can determine which branch a customer uses because the Accounts table includes the CustomerID and the BranchID.
- You can determine who manages a particular branch and which accounts are located there because the Branch table contains the Manager and Location fields.
- You can determine how long a customer has banked with the branch because the date he or she opened the account is stored in the Accounts table.
- You cannot generate the monthly bank statement. In order to generate a customer bank statement (showing all deposits and withdrawals for the month), you would need to add an additional table—an Account Activity table.
- You cannot e-mail a customer because the Customers table does not contain an E-mail field.

If you discover a missing field, such as the E-mail field, you can insert a row anywhere in the appropriate table and add the missing field. The databases found in a real bank are more complex, with more tables and more fields; however, the concepts illustrated here apply both to our sample bank database and to real bank databases.

Design for Now and for the Future

As the data requirements of an organization evolve over time, the information systems that hold the data must change as well. When designing a database, try to anticipate the future needs of the system and build in the flexibility to satisfy those demands. For example, when you add a text field, make sure that the number of characters allocated is sufficient to accommodate future expansion. On the other hand, if you include all the possible fields that anyone might ever need, you could drive up the cost of the database. Each additional field can increase the cost of the database, because it will require additional employee time to enter and maintain the data. The additional fields will also require more storage space, which you will need to calculate, especially when working with larger databases. Good database design must balance the data collection needs of the company with the cost associated with collection and storage. Plans must also include the frequency and cost necessary to modify and update the database.

Suppose you are designing a database for a college. You would need to store each student's name, address, and phone number. You would also need to store multiple phone numbers for most students—a cell phone number, a work number, and an emergency number. As a database designer, you will need to design the tables to accommodate multiple entries for similar data.

Store Data in Their Smallest Parts

The table design in Figure 2.1 divides a customer's name into two fields (FirstName and LastName) to reference each field individually. You might think it easier to use a single field consisting of both the first and last name, but that approach is too limiting. Consider a list of customers stored as a single field:

- Sue Grater
- Rick Grater
- Nancy Gallagher
- Harry Weigner
- Barb Shank
- Pete Shank

The first problem in this approach is the lack of flexibility: You could not easily create a salutation for a letter of the form *Dear Sue* or *Dear Ms. Gallagher* because the first and last names are not accessible individually.

A second difficulty is that the list of customers cannot be easily displayed in alphabetical order by last name because the last name begins in the middle of the field. The names could easily be alphabetized by first name because the first name is at the beginning of the field. However, the most common way to sort names is by the last name, which can be done more efficiently if the last name is stored as a separate field.

Think of how an address might be used. The city, state, and postal code should always be stored as separate fields. Any type of mass mailing requires you to sort on ZIP codes to take advantage of bulk mail. Other applications may require you to select records from a particular state or postal code, which can be done more efficiently if you store the data as separate fields. Often database users enter the postal code, and the database automatically retrieves the city and state information. You may need to direct a mailing only to a neighborhood or to a single street. The guideline is simple: Store data in their smallest parts.

Add Calculated Fields to a Table

A ***calculated field*** produces a value from an expression or function that references one or more existing fields. Access enables you to store calculated fields in a table using the calculated data type. An example of a calculated field can be found in the bank database. Suppose the bank pays its customers 1.0% interest on the principal each month. A calculated field, such as Monthly Interest, could store the expression Principal × 0.01. The interest amount would then appear on the customer's monthly bank statement.

Storing calculated data in a table enables you to add the data easily to queries, forms, and reports without the trouble of an additional calculation. Storing calculated data in a table may increase the size of the database slightly, but the benefits may outweigh this drawback. In the chapters ahead, you will examine calculations and calculated fields in greater detail. You will learn when to add calculated fields to a table and when to avoid them.

Design to Accommodate Date Arithmetic

Calculated fields are frequently created with numeric data, as the preceding Monthly Interest field example illustrates. You can also create calculated fields using date/time data. If you want to store the length of time a customer has been a customer, you would first create a field to hold the start date for each customer. Next, you would create a calculated field that contains an expression that subtracts the start date from today's date. The resulting calculation would store the number of days each customer has been a customer. Divide the results by 365 to convert days to years. If you want to calculate days to years and account for leap year, you could divide the results by 365.25.

This same concept applies to bank accounts; a bank is likely to store the OpenDate for each account in the Accounts table, as shown in Figure 2.1. Using this date, you can subtract the open date from today's date and calculate the number of days the account has been open. (Again, divide the results by 365 to convert to years.) If you open the Accounts table at least one day later, the results of the calculated field will be different.

A person's age is another example of a calculated field using date arithmetic—the date of birth is subtracted from today's date and the result is divided by 365. It might seem easier to store a person's age rather than the birth date to avoid the calculation. But that would be a mistake because age changes over time and would need to be updated each time age changes. Storing the date of birth is much better because the data remains ***constant***. You can use ***date arithmetic*** to subtract one date from another to find out the number of days, months, or years that have lapsed between them. You can also add or subtract a constant from a date.

Plan for Common Fields Between Tables

As you create the tables and fields for the database, keep in mind that the tables will be joined in relationships using common fields. Draw a line between common fields to indicate the joins, as shown in Figure 2.2. These join lines will be created in Access when you learn to create table relationships later in the chapter. For now, you should name the common fields the same and make sure they have the same data type. For example, CustomerID in the Customers table will join to the CustomerID field in the Accounts table. CustomerID must have the same data type (in this case number/long integer) in both tables; otherwise, the join line will not be allowed.

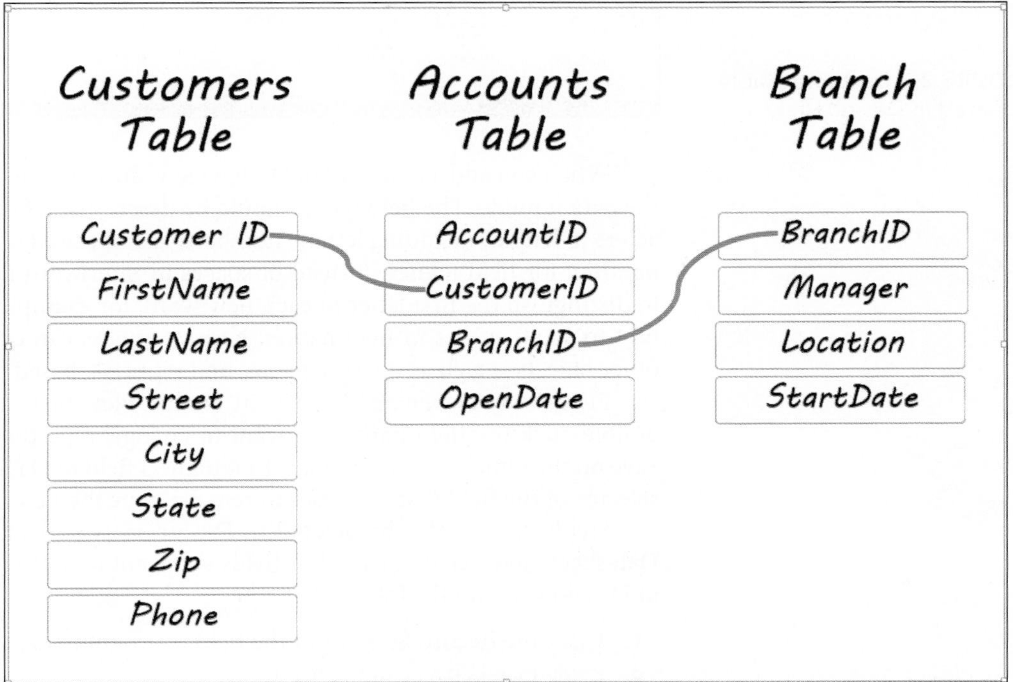

FIGURE 2.2 Create Relationships Using Common Fields

Avoid ***data redundancy***, which is the unnecessary storing of duplicate data in two or more tables. You should avoid duplicate information in multiple tables in a database, because errors may result. Suppose the customer address data were stored in both the Customers and Accounts tables. If a customer moved to a new address, it is possible that the address would be updated in only one of the two tables. The result would be inconsistent and unreliable data. Depending on which table served as the source for the output, either the new or the old address might be given to someone requesting the information. Storing the address in only one table is more reliable.

Creating and Modifying Tables

Tables can be created in a new blank database or in an existing database. You can create a table by:

STEP 1»

- Typing a field name in a row in Design view.
- Entering table data into a new row in Datasheet view.
- Importing data from another database or application such as Excel.

Regardless of how a table is first created, you can always modify it later to include a new field or change an existing field. Figure 2.3 shows a table created by entering fields in Design view.

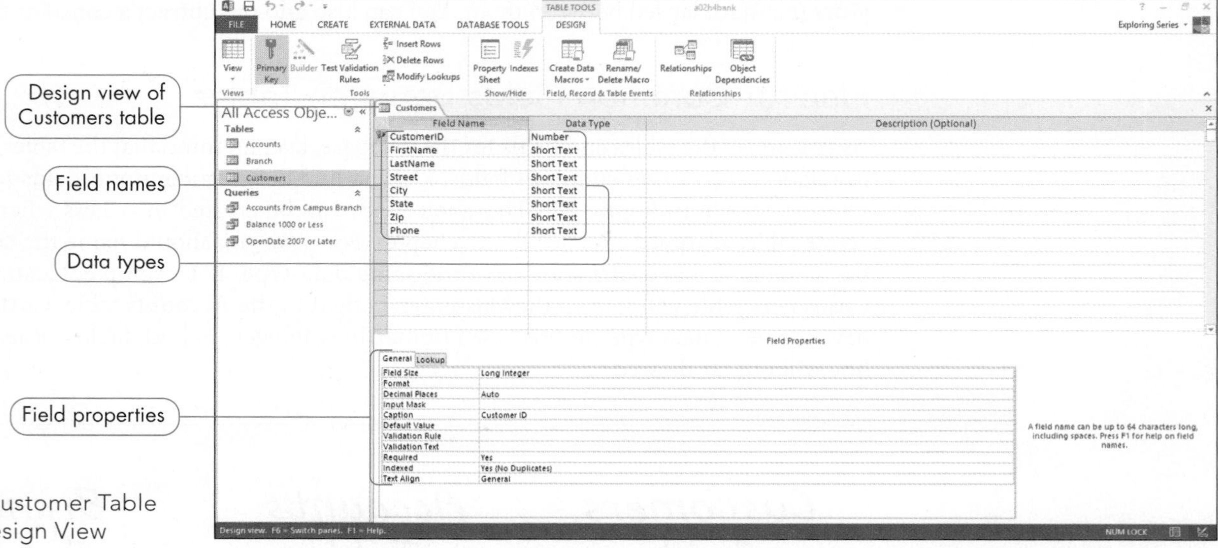

FIGURE 2.3 Customer Table Created in Design View

STEP 4»

When you add a new field in Design view, the field must be given a field name to identify the data it holds. The field name should be descriptive of the data and can be up to 64 characters in length, including letters, numbers, and spaces. Database developers use ***CamelCase notation*** for field names. Instead of spaces in multiword field names, use uppercase letters to distinguish the first letter of each new word, for example, ProductCost or LastName. It is best to avoid spaces in field names, because spaces can cause problems when creating the other objects—such as queries, forms, and reports—based on tables.

Fields may be renamed either in Design view or in Datasheet view. In Design view, double-click the field name you want to change, type the new field name, and then click Save on the Quick Access Toolbar. To rename a field in Datasheet view, double-click the field selector of the field that you want to rename, type the new field name, and then press Enter.

Fields can be also be deleted in Design view or Datasheet view. To delete a field in Datasheet view, select the field or fields you want to delete and press Delete. To delete fields in Design view, do the following:

1. Click the Record Selector of the field you want to delete to select it.
2. Click Delete Rows in the Tools group.

3. Click Yes in the message box that appears if you want to permanently delete the field(s). Click No if you do not want to delete the field(s).
4. Click Yes in the second message box that will appear if the selected field you are deleting is a primary key. Click No if you do not want to delete the primary key.

TIP Freeze Fields in an Access Database

To keep a field viewable while you are scrolling through a table, select the field or fields you want to freeze, right-click, and then click Freeze Fields. If you want the field(s) to remain frozen when you are finished working, save the changes when you close the table. To unfreeze all fields, right-click the field(s) and select Unfreeze All Fields.

Determine Data Type

Every field also has a ***data type*** property that determines the type of data that can be entered and the operations that can be performed on that data. Access recognizes 12 data types. Table 2.1 lists these data types, their uses, and examples of the data type.

TABLE 2.1 Data Types and Uses

Data Type	Description	Example
Short Text	Stores alphanumeric data, such as a customer's name or address. It can contain alphabetic characters, numbers, and/or special characters (e.g., an apostrophe in O'Malley). Social Security numbers, telephone numbers, and postal codes should be designated as text fields since they are not used in calculations and often contain special characters such as hyphens and parentheses. A short text field can hold up to 255 characters. Formerly Text data type.	2184 Walnut Street
Long Text	Lengthy text or combinations of text and numbers, such as several sentences or paragraphs; used to hold descriptive data. Formerly Memo data type.	A description of product packaging
Number	Contains a value that can be used in a calculation, such as the number of credits a course is worth. The contents are restricted to numbers, a decimal point, and a plus or minus sign.	12
Date/Time	Holds dates or times and enables the values to be used in date or time arithmetic.	10/31/2016 1:30:00 AM
Currency	Used for fields that contain monetary values.	$1,200
AutoNumber	A special data type used to assign the next consecutive number each time you add a record. The value of an AutoNumber field is unique for each record in the file.	1, 2, 3
Yes/No	Assumes one of two values, such as Yes or No, True or False, or On or Off (also known as a Boolean). For example, is a student on the Dean's list: Yes or No.	Yes
OLE Object	Contains an object created by another application. OLE objects include spreadsheets, pictures, sounds, and graphics.	JPG image
Hyperlink	Stores a Web address (URL) or the path to a folder or file. Hyperlink fields can be clicked to retrieve a Web page or to launch a file stored locally.	http://www .keithmast.com
Attachment	Used to store multiple images, spreadsheet files, Word documents, and other types of supported files.	An Excel workbook
Calculated	The results of an expression that references one or more existing fields.	[IntRate] + 0.25
Lookup Wizard	Creates a field that enables you to choose a value from another table or from a list of values by using a list box or a combo box.	Customers table with an AccountID field that looks up the Account ID from an Accounts table

Establish a Primary Key

STEP 2» As you learned earlier, the primary key is the field (or combination of fields) that uniquely identifies each record in a table. Access does not require that each table have a primary key. However, good database design usually includes a primary key in each table. You should select unique and infrequently changing data for the primary key. For example, a complete address (street, city, state, and postal code) may be unique but would not make a good primary key because it is subject to change when someone moves.

You probably would not use a person's name as the primary key, because several people could have the same name. A customer's account number, on the other hand, is unique and is a frequent choice for the primary key, as in the Customers table in this chapter. The primary key can be easily identified in many tables—for example, a PartNumber in a parts table, the ISBN in the book database of a bookstore, or a StudentID that uniquely identifies a student. When no primary key occurs naturally, you can create a primary key field with the AutoNumber data type. The ***AutoNumber*** data type is a number that automatically increments each time a record is added.

In Figure 2.4, the book's ISBN is the natural primary key for the book table because no two book titles can have the same ISBN. This field uniquely identifies the records in the table. Figure 2.5 depicts the Speakers table, where no unique field can be identified from the data. Because of this, you can add the SpeakerID field with an AutoNumber data type. Access automatically numbers each speaker record sequentially with a unique ID as each record is added.

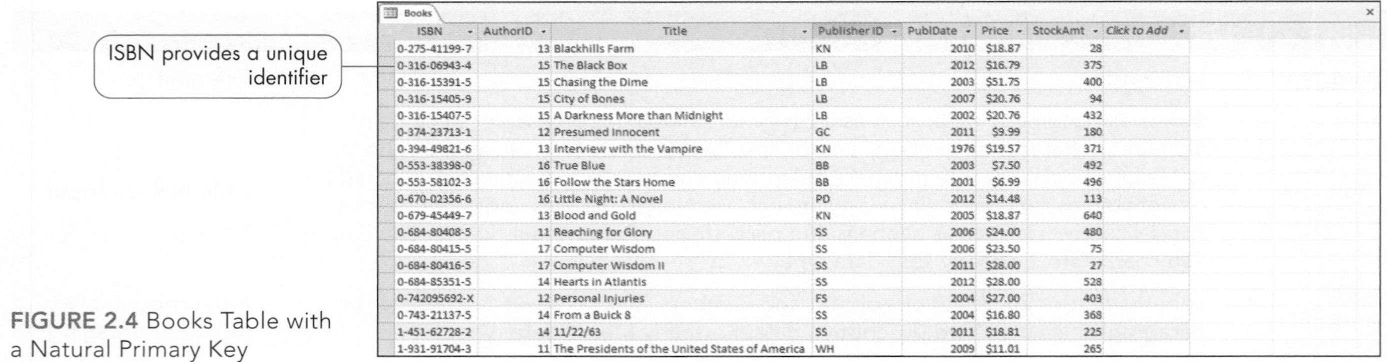
ISBN provides a unique identifier
Books

ISBN	AuthorID	Title	Publisher ID	PublDate	Price	StockAmt	Click to Add
0-275-41199-7	13	Blackhills Farm	KN	2010	$18.87	28	
0-316-06943-4	15	The Black Box	LB	2012	$16.79	375	
0-316-15391-5	15	Chasing the Dime	LB	2003	$51.75	400	
0-316-15405-9	15	City of Bones	LB	2007	$20.76	94	
0-316-15407-5	15	A Darkness More than Midnight	LB	2002	$20.76	432	
0-374-23713-1	12	Presumed Innocent	GC	2011	$9.99	180	
0-394-49821-6	13	Interview with the Vampire	KN	1976	$19.57	371	
0-553-38398-0	16	True Blue	BB	2003	$7.50	492	
0-553-58102-3	16	Follow the Stars Home	BB	2001	$6.99	496	
0-670-02356-6	16	Little Night: A Novel	PD	2012	$14.48	113	
0-679-45449-7	13	Blood and Gold	KN	2005	$18.87	640	
0-684-80408-5	11	Reaching for Glory	SS	2006	$24.00	480	
0-684-80415-5	17	Computer Wisdom	SS	2006	$23.50	75	
0-684-80416-5	17	Computer Wisdom II	SS	2011	$28.00	27	
0-684-85351-5	14	Hearts in Atlantis	SS	2012	$28.00	528	
0-742095692-X	12	Personal Injuries	FS	2004	$27.00	403	
0-743-21137-5	14	From a Buick 8	SS	2004	$16.80	368	
1-451-62728-2	14	11/22/63	SS	2011	$18.81	225	
1-931-91704-3	11	The Presidents of the United States of America	WH	2009	$11.01	265	

FIGURE 2.4 Books Table with a Natural Primary Key

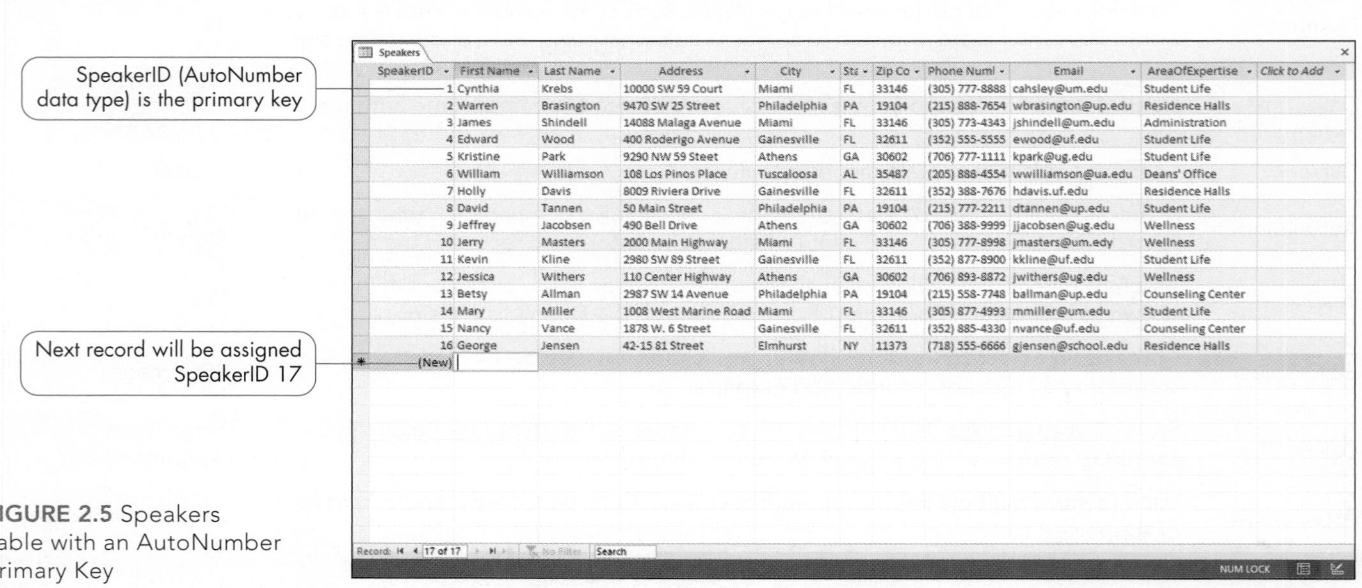
SpeakerID (AutoNumber data type) is the primary key
Next record will be assigned SpeakerID 17
Speakers
Record: 17 of 17
No Filter
Search
NUM LOCK

SpeakerID	First Name	Last Name	Address	City	State	Zip Co	Phone Numl	Email	AreaOfExpertise	Click to Add
1	Cynthia	Krebs	10000 SW 59 Court	Miami	FL	33146	(305) 777-8888	cahsley@um.edu	Student Life	
2	Warren	Brasington	9470 SW 25 Street	Philadelphia	PA	19104	(215) 888-7654	wbrasington@up.edu	Residence Halls	
3	James	Shindell	14088 Malaga Avenue	Miami	FL	33146	(305) 773-4343	jshindell@um.edu	Administration	
4	Edward	Wood	400 Roderigo Avenue	Gainesville	FL	32611	(352) 555-5555	ewood@uf.edu	Student Life	
5	Kristine	Park	9290 NW 59 Steet	Athens	GA	30602	(706) 777-1111	kpark@ug.edu	Student Life	
6	William	Williamson	108 Los Pinos Place	Tuscaloosa	AL	35487	(205) 888-4554	wwilliamson@ua.edu	Deans' Office	
7	Holly	Davis	8009 Riviera Drive	Gainesville	FL	32611	(352) 388-7676	hdavis.uf.edu	Residence Halls	
8	David	Tannen	50 Main Street	Philadelphia	PA	19104	(215) 777-2211	dtannen@up.edu	Student Life	
9	Jeffrey	Jacobsen	490 Bell Drive	Athens	GA	30602	(706) 388-9999	jjacobsen@ug.edu	Wellness	
10	Jerry	Masters	2000 Main Highway	Miami	FL	33146	(305) 777-8998	jmasters@um.edy	Wellness	
11	Kevin	Kline	2980 SW 89 Street	Gainesville	FL	32611	(352) 877-8900	kkline@uf.edu	Student Life	
12	Jessica	Withers	110 Center Highway	Athens	GA	30602	(706) 893-8872	jwithers@ug.edu	Wellness	
13	Betsy	Allman	2987 SW 14 Avenue	Philadelphia	PA	19104	(215) 558-7748	ballman@up.edu	Counseling Center	
14	Mary	Miller	1008 West Marine Road	Miami	FL	33146	(305) 877-4993	mmiller@um.edu	Student Life	
15	Nancy	Vance	1878 W. 6 Street	Gainesville	FL	32611	(352) 885-4330	nvance@uf.edu	Counseling Center	
16	George	Jensen	42-15 81 Street	Elmhurst	NY	11373	(718) 555-6666	gjensen@school.edu	Residence Halls	
(New)										

FIGURE 2.5 Speakers Table with an AutoNumber Primary Key

Explore a Foreign Key

A ***foreign key*** is a field in one table that is also the primary key of another table. The CustomerID is the primary key in the Customers table. It serves to uniquely identify each customer. It also appears as a foreign key in a related table. For example, the Accounts table contains the CustomerID field to establish which customer owns the account. A CustomerID can appear only once in the Customers table, but it may appear multiple times in the Accounts table (when viewed in Datasheet view) because one customer may own multiple accounts (checking, money market, home equity). Therefore, the CustomerID is the primary key in the Customers table and a foreign key in the Accounts table.

If you were asked to create an Access database for the speakers at a national conference, you would create a database with the tables Speakers and SessionSpeaker. You would add a primary key field to the Speakers table (SpeakerID) along with a speaker's FirstName and LastName fields; you would also add two fields to the SessionSpeaker table (SpeakerID and SessionID). The SpeakerID field in the Speakers table is a primary key and would not allow duplicates; the SpeakerID field in the SessionSpeaker table is a foreign key and would allow duplicates so that a speaker may speak more than once at the conference. The SpeakerID in the SessionSpeaker table enables you to join the two tables in a relationship. Figure 2.6 shows portions of the Speakers and SessionSpeaker tables.

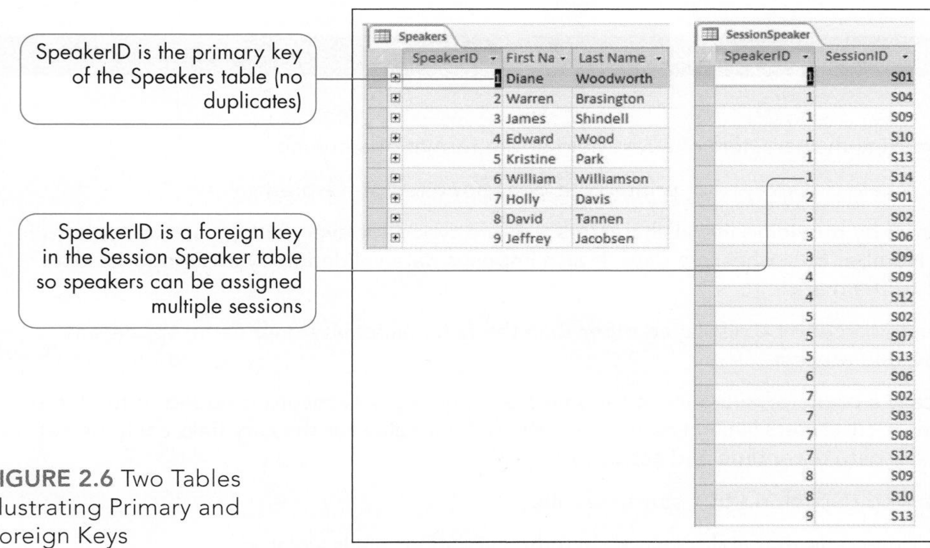
SpeakerID is the primary key of the Speakers table (no duplicates)
SpeakerID is a foreign key in the Session Speaker table so speakers can be assigned multiple sessions

Speakers

SpeakerID	First Na	Last Name
1	Diane	Woodworth
2	Warren	Brasington
3	James	Shindell
4	Edward	Wood
5	Kristine	Park
6	William	Williamson
7	Holly	Davis
8	David	Tannen
9	Jeffrey	Jacobsen

SessionSpeaker

SpeakerID	SessionID
1	S01
1	S04
1	S09
1	S10
1	S13
1	S14
2	S01
3	S02
3	S06
3	S09
4	S09
4	S12
5	S02
5	S07
5	S13
6	S06
7	S02
7	S03
7	S08
7	S12
8	S09
8	S10
9	S13

FIGURE 2.6 Two Tables Illustrating Primary and Foreign Keys

Work with Field Properties

STEP 3

While a field's data type determines the type of data that can be entered and the operations that can be performed on that data, it is its ***field properties*** that determine how the field looks and behaves.

Field Size is a commonly changed field property. A field with a ***short text data type*** can hold up to 255 characters; however, you can limit the characters by reducing the field size property. For example, you would limit the State field to only two characters because all state abbreviations are two letters. A field with a ***number data type*** can be set to Integer to display the field contents as integers from –32,768 to 32,768 or to Long Integer for larger values.

You can set a ***caption property*** to create a label more readable than a field. The caption displays at the top of a table or query column in Datasheet view and when the field is used in a report or form. For example, a field named ProductCostPerUnit could have the caption *Per Unit Product Cost*. Even if a caption is used, however, you must use the actual field name, ProductCostPerUnit, in any calculation.

Best Fit Columns

If a field name is cut off in Datasheet view, you can adjust the column width by positioning the pointer on the vertical border on the right side of the column. When the pointer displays as a two-headed arrow, double-click the border. You can also click More in the Records group on the Home tab. Select Field Width and click Best Fit in the Column Width dialog box.

Set the validation rule property to restrict data entry in a field to ensure the correct type of data are entered or that the data do not violate other enforced properties. The ***validation rule*** checks the data entered when the user exits the field. If the data entered violate the validation rule, an error message displays and prevents the invalid data from being entered into the field. For example, if you have set the data type for a field as Number and then try to enter text in the field, you will receive an error message telling you that the value you entered does not match the Number data type in the column.

The field properties are set to default values according to the data type, but you can modify them if necessary. Common property types are defined in Table 2.2.

TABLE 2.2 Common Access Table Property Types and Descriptions

Property Type	Description
Field Size	Determines the maximum characters of a text field or the format of a number field.
Format	Changes the way a field is displayed or printed but does not affect the stored value.
Input Mask	Simplifies data entry by providing literal characters that are typed for every entry, such as hyphens in a Social Security Number or slashes in a date. It also imposes data validation by ensuring that data entered conform to the mask.
Caption	Enables an alternate name to be displayed other than the field name; alternate name appears in datasheets, forms, and reports.
Default Value	Enters automatically a predetermined value for a field each time a new record is added to the table. For example, if most customers live in Los Angeles, the default value for the City field could be set to Los Angeles to save data entry time and accuracy.
Validation Rule	Requires data entered to conform to a specified rule.
Validation Text	Specifies the error message that is displayed when the validation rule is violated.
Required	Indicates that a value for this field must be entered.
Allow Zero Length	Allows entry of zero length text strings ("") in a Hyperlink, or Short or Long Text fields.
Indexed	Increases the efficiency of a search on the designated field.
Expression	Used for calculated fields only. Enters the expression you want Access to evaluate and store.
Result Type	Used for calculated fields only. Enters the format for the calculated field results.

Enter Table Records in Datasheet View

STEP 5»

While Design view is used to create and modify the table structure by enabling you to add and edit fields and set field properties, Datasheet view is used to add, edit, and delete records. As you have learned, the Datasheet view of an Access table resembles an Excel spreadsheet and displays data in a grid format—rows represent records and columns represent fields. Datasheet view indicates the current record using a gold border; you can select a record by clicking the record selector on the left side of each record. Use the new blank record (marked with an asterisk) at the end of the table to add a new record.

In Hands-On Exercise 1, you will create a new database and enter fields into a table. Then you will switch to the table's Design view to add additional fields and modify selected field properties of various fields within the table. Finally, you will enter data in the table in Datasheet view.

Quick Concepts

1. What is meant by "Design for now and the future" when designing database fields? ***p. 677***
2. What is the difference between a primary key and a foreign key? ***p. 683***
3. What is a field property? Which field property creates a more readable label that displays in the top row in Datasheet view and in forms and reports? ***p. 683***

Hands-On Exercises

MyITLab® HOE1 Training

1 Table Design, Creation, and Modification

Assisting the bank auditor at Commonwealth Federal Bank as he investigates the mishandled funds will be a great opportunity for you to showcase your Access skills. Be sure to check your work each step of the way, because your work will come under substantial scrutiny. Do a good job with this Access project and more opportunities might come your way.

Skills covered: Create a Table in Datasheet View • Delete a Field and Set a Table's Primary Key • Work with Field Properties • Create a New Field in Design View • Modify the Table in Datasheet View

STEP 1 » CREATE A TABLE IN DATASHEET VIEW

You create a new desktop database to store information about the mishandled funds database. You enter the data for the first record (BranchID, Manager, and Location). Refer to Figure 2.7 as you complete Step 1.

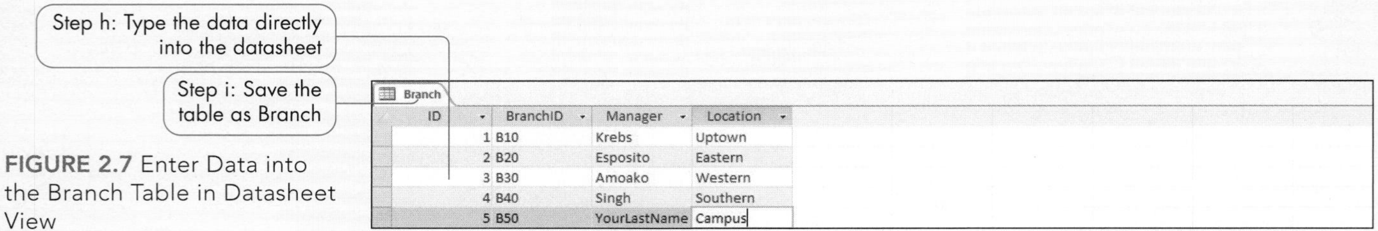

FIGURE 2.7 Enter Data into the Branch Table in Datasheet View

a. Start Microsoft Office Access 2013 and click **Blank desktop database**.

b. Type **a02h1Bank_LastFirst** into the **File Name box**.

c. Click **Browse** to find the folder location designated by your instructor and click **OK**. Click **Create** to create the new database.

Access will create the new database named *a02h1Bank_LastFirst* and a new table will automatically open in Datasheet view.

d. Click **Click to Add** and select **Short Text** as the Data type.

Click to Add changes to *Field1*. *Field1* is selected to make it easier to change the field name.

e. Type **BranchID** and press **Tab**.

A list of Data types for the third column opens so that you can select the data type for the third column.

f. Select **Short Text**, type **Manager**, and then press **Tab**.

g. Select **Short Text**, type **Location**, and then click in the first column next to the New Record asterisk.

h. Enter the data for the new table as shown in Figure 2.7, letting Access assign the ID field for each new record. Replace *YourLastName* with your own last name.

Entering data in Datasheet view provides an easy way to create the table initially. You can now modify the table in Design view as described in the next several steps.

i. Click **Save** on the Quick Access Toolbar. Type **Branch** in the **Save As dialog box** and click **OK**.

STEP 2 ≫ DELETE A FIELD AND SET A TABLE'S PRIMARY KEY

It is possible to modify tables even after data have been entered; however, pay attention to the messages from Access after you make a design change. In this step, you will be modifying the Branch table. You examine the design of the table and realize that the BranchID field is a unique identifier, making the ID field redundant. You delete the ID field and make the BranchID field the primary key field. Refer to Figure 2.8 as you complete Step 2.

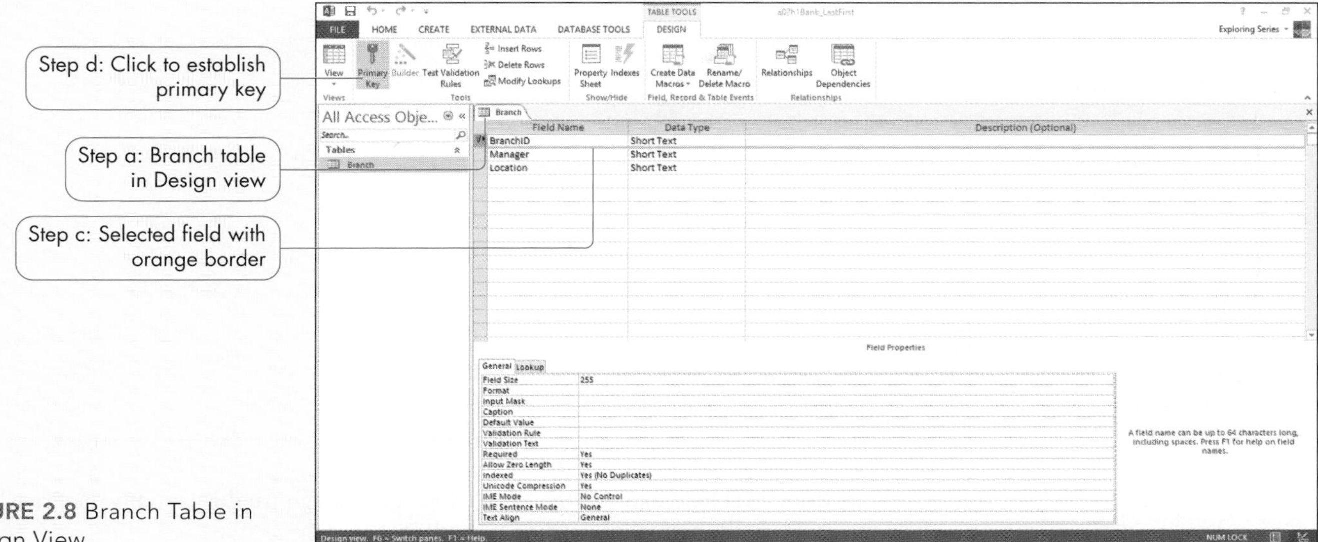

FIGURE 2.8 Branch Table in Design View

a. Click **View** in the Views group to switch to the Design view of the Branch table.

The Field Name for each of the four fields displays along with the Data Type.

b. Click the **ID field** to select it, if necessary. Click **Delete Rows** in the Tools group. Click **Yes** to both warning messages.

Access responds with a warning that you are about to permanently delete a field and a second warning that the field is the primary key. You delete the field because you will set the BranchID field as the primary key.

c. Click the **BranchID field,** if necessary.

The cell field name now has a orange border, as shown in Figure 2.8.

d. Click **Primary Key** in the Tools group on the DESIGN tab.

You set the BranchID as the primary key. The Indexed property in the *Field Properties* section at the bottom of the design window displays *Yes (No Duplicates)*.

e. Click **Save** on the Quick Access Toolbar to save the table.

TIP Shortcut Menu

You can right-click a row selector to display a shortcut menu to copy a field, set the primary key, insert or delete rows, or to access field properties. Use the shortcut menu to make these specific changes to the design of a table.

STEP 3 ≫ WORK WITH FIELD PROPERTIES

You need to modify the table design further to comply with the bank auditor's specifications. Be aware of messages from Access that indicate you may lose data. Refer to Figure 2.9 as you complete Step 3.

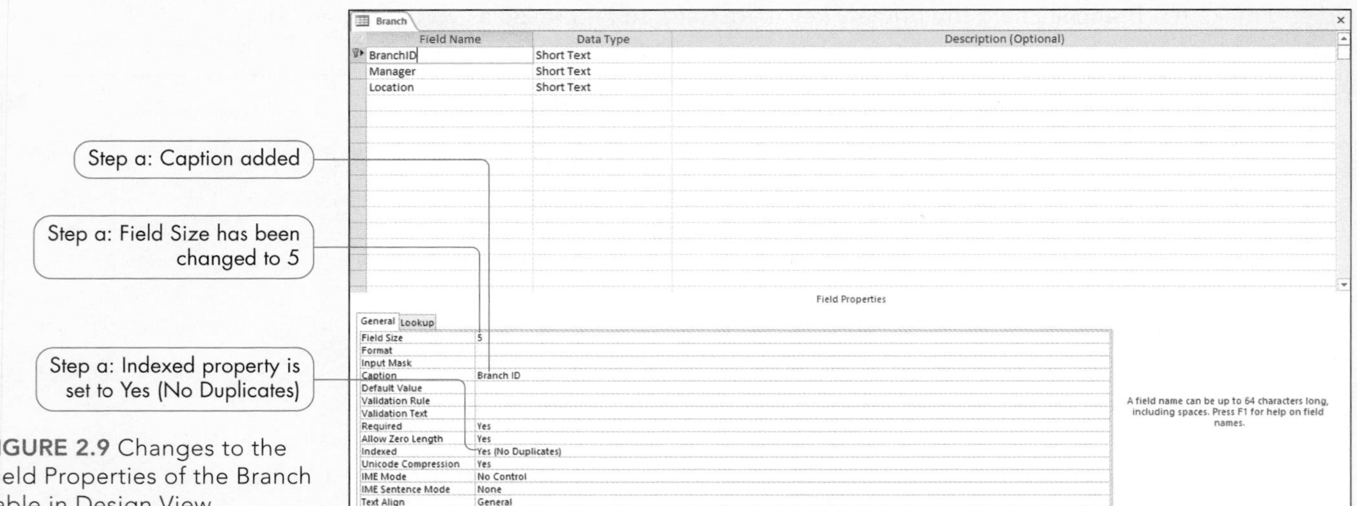

FIGURE 2.9 Changes to the Field Properties of the Branch Table in Design View

a. Click the **BranchID field name** in the top section of the design window; modify the BranchID field properties in the bottom of the design window.

- Click in the **Field Size property** and change *255* to **5**.
- Click in the **Caption property** and type **Branch ID**. Make sure *Branch* and *ID* have a space between them.
  A caption provides a more descriptive field name. It will appear as the column heading in Datasheet view.
- Check the Indexed property; confirm it is *Yes (No Duplicates)*.

b. Click the **Manager field name** at the top of the window; modify the following field properties:

- Click in the **Field Size property** and change *255* to **30**.
- Click in the **Caption property** and type **Manager's Name**.

c. Click the **Location field name** and modify the following field properties:

- Click in the **Field Size property** and change *255* to **30**.
- Click in the **Caption property** and type **Branch Location**.

STEP 4 ≫ CREATE A NEW FIELD IN DESIGN VIEW

You notify the auditor that a date field is missing in your new table. Modify the table to add the new field. The data can be entered at a later time. Refer to Figure 2.10 as you complete Step 4.

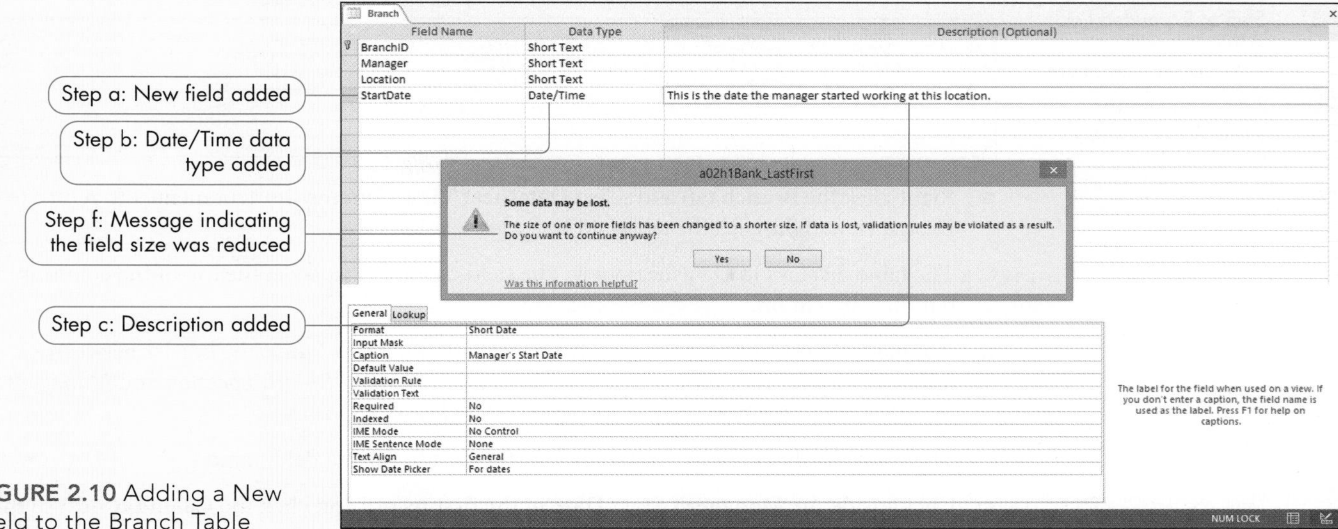

FIGURE 2.10 Adding a New Field to the Branch Table

a. Click in the first blank row below the Location field name and type **StartDate**.

   You added a new field to the table.

b. Press **Tab** to move to the Data Type column. Click the **Data Type arrow** and select **Date/Time**.

> **TIP Keyboard Shortcut for Data Types**
>
> You also can type the first letter of the data type, such as d for Date/Time, s for Short Text, or n for Number. To use the keyboard shortcut, click on the field name and press Tab to advance to the Data Type column. Next, type the first letter of the data type.

c. Press **Tab** to move to the Description column and type **This is the date the manager started working at this location.**

d. Click the **Format property**, click the arrow, and then select **Short Date** from the list of date formats.

e. Click in the **Caption property** and type **Manager's Start Date**.

f. Click **Save** on the Quick Access Toolbar.

   A warning dialog box opens to indicate that "Some data may be lost" because the size of the BranchID, Manager, and Location field properties were shortened. It asks if you want to continue anyway. Always read the Access warning! In this case, you can click Yes to continue because you know that the existing data are no longer than the new field sizes.

g. Click **Yes** in the warning box.

STEP 5 》 MODIFY THE TABLE IN DATASHEET VIEW

As you work with the auditor, you will modify tables in the bank database from time to time. To modify the table, you will need to switch between Design view and Datasheet view. Refer to Figure 2.11 as you complete Step 5.

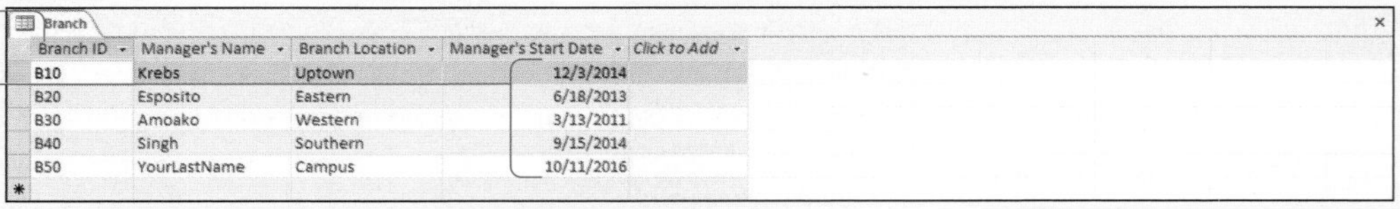

Step b: Expanded fields

Step d: Start dates

Branch ID	Manager's Name	Branch Location	Manager's Start Date	Click to Add
B10	Krebs	Uptown	12/3/2014	
B20	Esposito	Eastern	6/18/2013	
B30	Amoako	Western	3/13/2011	
B40	Singh	Southern	9/15/2014	
B50	YourLastName	Campus	10/11/2016	
*				

FIGURE 2.11 Start Dates Added to the Branch Table

a. Right-click the **Branch tab** and select **Datasheet View** from the shortcut menu. (To return to Design view, right-click the tab again and select Design view.)

The table displays in Datasheet view. The field captions display at the top of the columns, but they are cut off.

b. Double-click the border between *Branch ID* and *Manager's Name*, the border between *Manager's Name* and *Branch Location*, the border between *Branch Location* and *Manager's Start Date*, and the border after *Manager's Start Date.*

The columns shrink or expand to display the best fit for the field name.

c. Click inside the **Manager's Start Date** in the first record and click the **Calendar** next to the date field. Use the navigation arrows to find and select **December 3, 2014** from the calendar.

You can also enter the dates by typing them directly into the StartDate field.

d. Type the start date directly in each field for the rest of the managers, as shown in Figure 2.11.

e. Click the **Close (X) button** at the top-right corner of the datasheet, below the Ribbon.

> **TROUBLESHOOTING:** If you accidentally click the Close (X) button on top of the Ribbon, you will exit Access completely. To start again, launch Access and click the first file in the Recent list.

f. Double-click the **Branch table** in the Navigation Pane to open the table. Check the start dates.

The start dates are still there even though you did not save your work in the previous step. Access saves the data to your storage location as soon as you move off the current record or close an object.

g. Click the **FILE tab**, click **Print**, and then click **Print Preview**.

Occasionally, users will print an Access table. However, database developers usually create reports to print table data.

h. Click **Close Print Preview** and close the Branch table.

i. Keep the database open if you plan to continue with Hands-On Exercise 2. If not, close the database and exit Access.

Multiple-Table Databases

In Figure 2.1, the sample bank database contains three tables—Customers, Accounts, and Branch. You created one table, the Branch table, in the previous section using the Datasheet view and modified the table fields in Design view. You will create the two remaining tables using a different method—importing data from Excel. In this section, you will learn how to import data from Excel, modify tables, create indexes, create relationships between tables, and enforce referential integrity.

Sharing Data

Most companies store some type of data in Excel spreadsheets. Often, the data stored in those spreadsheets can be more efficiently managed in an Access database. Fortunately, Access provides you with a wizard that guides you through the process of importing data from Excel. The wizard can also guide you as you import data from other Access databases. You can import tables, queries, forms, reports, pages, macros, and modules from another database.

Import an Excel Spreadsheet

STEP 1»

STEP 2»

Figures 2.12 through 2.17 show the steps of the Get External Data – Excel Spreadsheet feature. Launch the feature by clicking the External Data tab and clicking Excel in the Import & Link group. Figure 2.12 shows the first screen of the Get External Data – Excel Spreadsheet feature. In this step, you specify the source of the data. Locate the Excel file you want to import by clicking Browse. Then choose between three options for the incoming data: *Import the source data into a new table in the current database*; *Append a copy of the records to the table*, which adds the data to an existing table; or *Link to the data source by creating a linked table*, which creates a link to the Excel source. Importing or appending data stores a copy of the data in Access, whereas linking the data keeps the data in the original file and Access retrieves the data each time the database is opened.

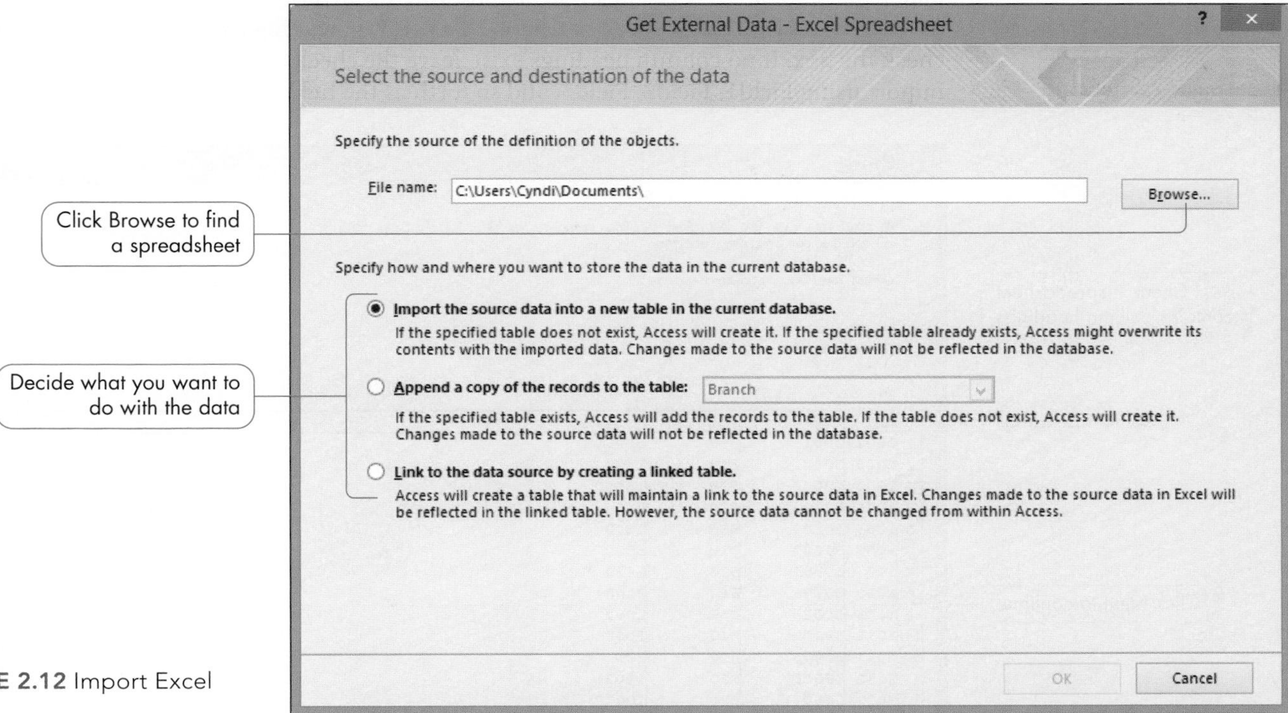

FIGURE 2.12 Import Excel Data

After you locate and select an Excel workbook, accept the default option (*Import the source data into a new table in the current database*) and click OK. The Import Spreadsheet Wizard dialog box launches and displays a list of the worksheets in the specified workbook.

Select the worksheet you want to import and click Next. Figure 2.13 shows the Accounts worksheet selected. The bottom of the Import Spreadsheet Wizard dialog box displays a preview of the data stored in the specified worksheet.

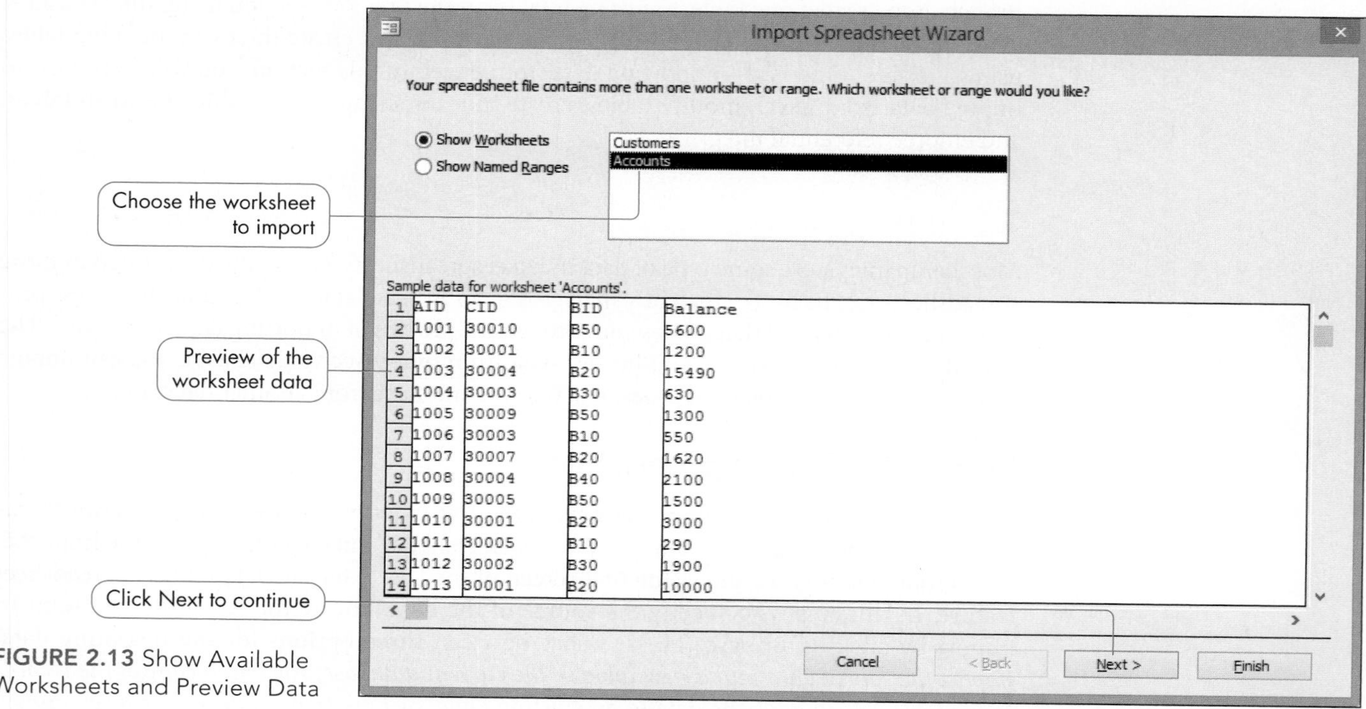

FIGURE 2.13 Show Available Worksheets and Preview Data

Although a well-designed spreadsheet may include descriptive column headings that can be used as field names, not all spreadsheets are ready to import. You may have to revise the spreadsheet before importing it. The second window of the Import Spreadsheet Wizard dialog box contains a check box that enables you to convert the first row of column headings to field names in Access (see Figure 2.14). If a column heading row exists in the spreadsheet, check the box. If no column headings exist, leave the check box unchecked, and the data will import using Field1, Field2, Field3, and so forth as the field names.

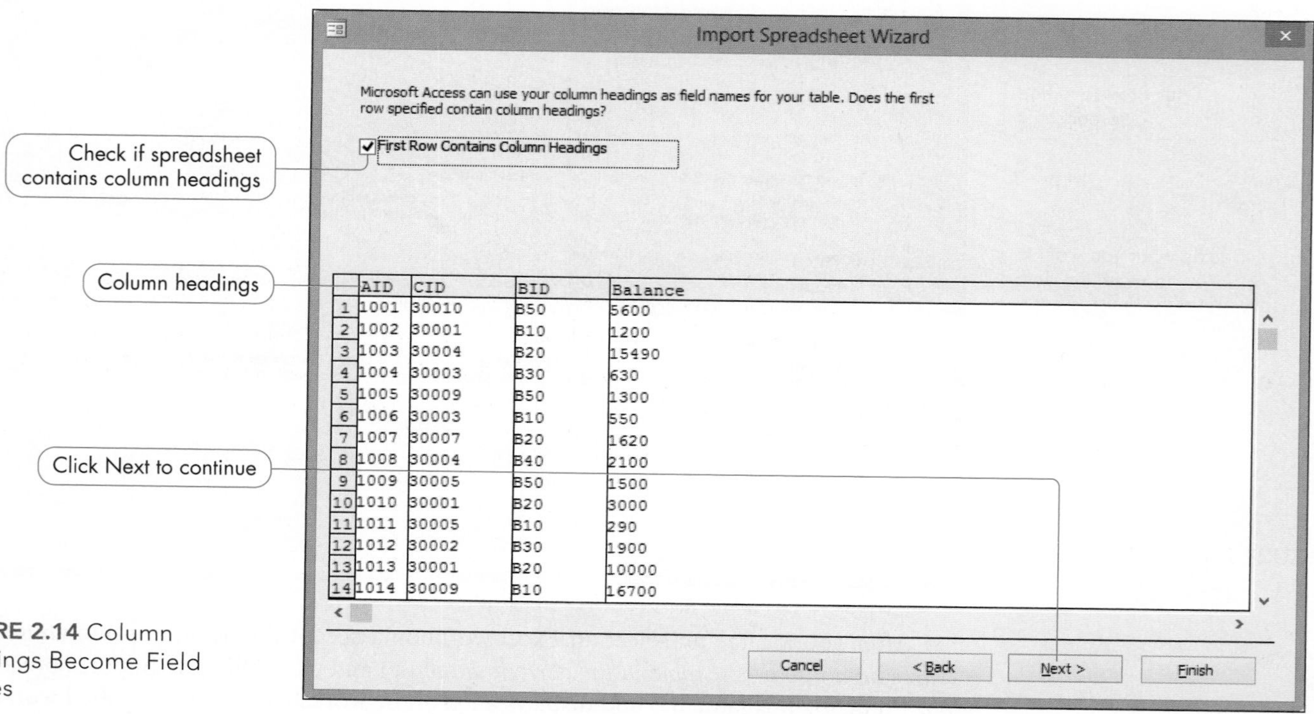

FIGURE 2.14 Column Headings Become Field Names

The third window of the Import Spreadsheet Wizard dialog box enables you to specify field options (see Figure 2.15). The AID field is highlighted in this figure. Because it will become this table's primary key, you need to set the Indexed Property to *Yes (No Duplicates)*. To modify the field options of the other fields, click the Field Name column heading and make the changes. Not all Access table properties are supported by the wizard. You may need to open the table in Design view after importing it to make any additional field property changes.

TIP Retrieve Data Quickly with Indexing

When you set the primary key in Access, the ***indexed property*** is automatically set to *Yes (No Duplicates)*. The indexed property setting enables quick sorting in primary key order and quick retrieval based on the primary key. For non–primary key fields, it may be beneficial to set the Indexed property to *Yes (Duplicates OK)*. Again, Access uses indexing to sort and retrieve data quickly based on the indexed field. As a general rule, indexed fields are usually foreign keys and are numeric.

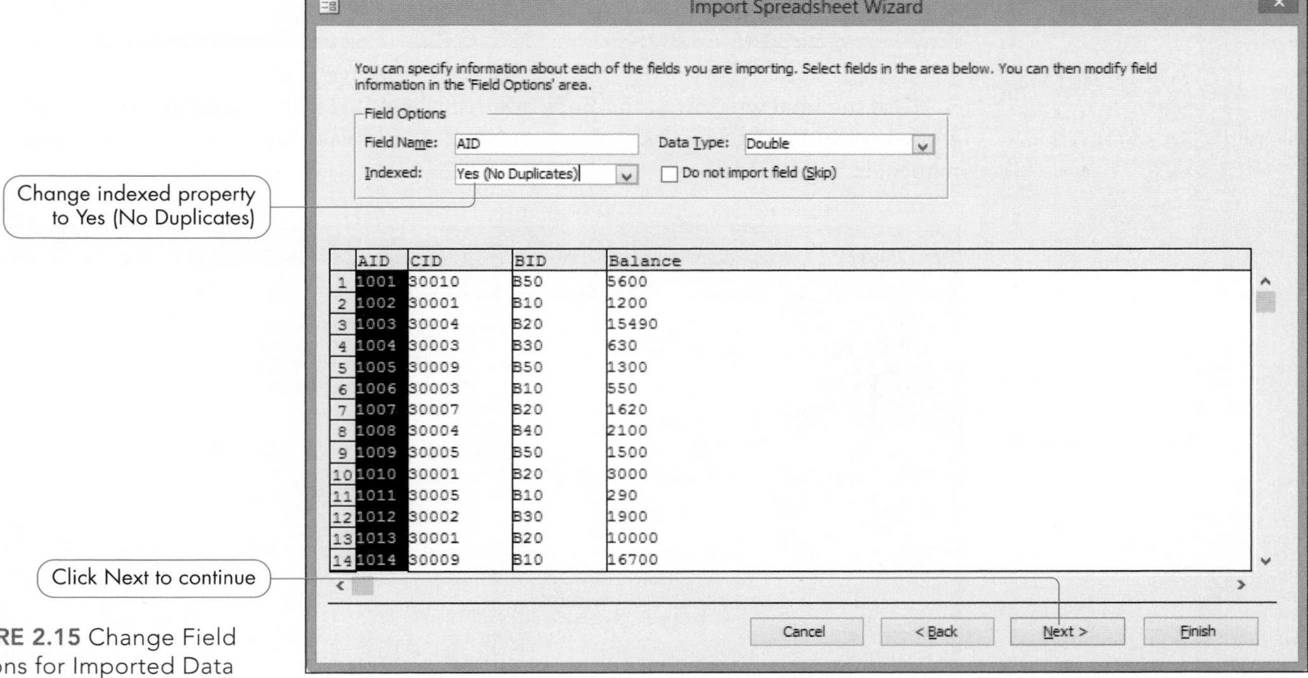

	AID	CID	BID	Balance
1	1001	30010	B50	5600
2	1002	30001	B10	1200
3	1003	30004	B20	15490
4	1004	30003	B30	630
5	1005	30009	B50	1300
6	1006	30003	B10	550
7	1007	30007	B20	1620
8	1008	30004	B40	2100
9	1009	30005	B50	1500
10	1010	30001	B20	3000
11	1011	30005	B10	290
12	1012	30002	B30	1900
13	1013	30001	B20	10000
14	1014	30009	B10	16700

FIGURE 2.15 Change Field Options for Imported Data

The fourth window of the Import Spreadsheet Wizard dialog box enables you to choose a primary key before the import takes place (see Figure 2.16). If the option *Let Access add primary key* is selected, Access will generate an AutoNumber field and designate it as the primary key. Otherwise, you can designate a field to be the primary key or choose to have no primary key. In the import depicted in the Figure 2.16, the Excel data have a unique identifier (AID) that will become the table's primary key.

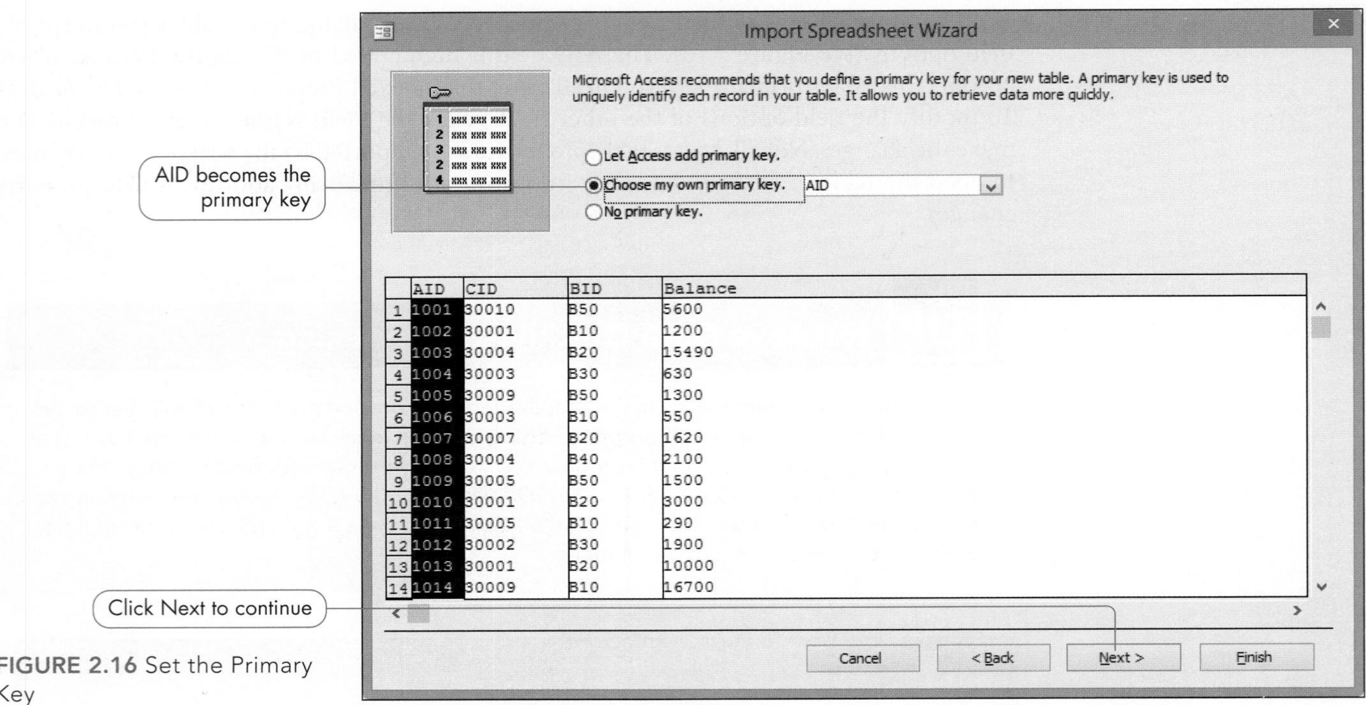

FIGURE 2.16 Set the Primary Key

Use the final window of the Import Spreadsheet Wizard to name the Access table. If the worksheet in the Excel workbook was named, Access uses the worksheet name as the table name (see Figure 2.17).

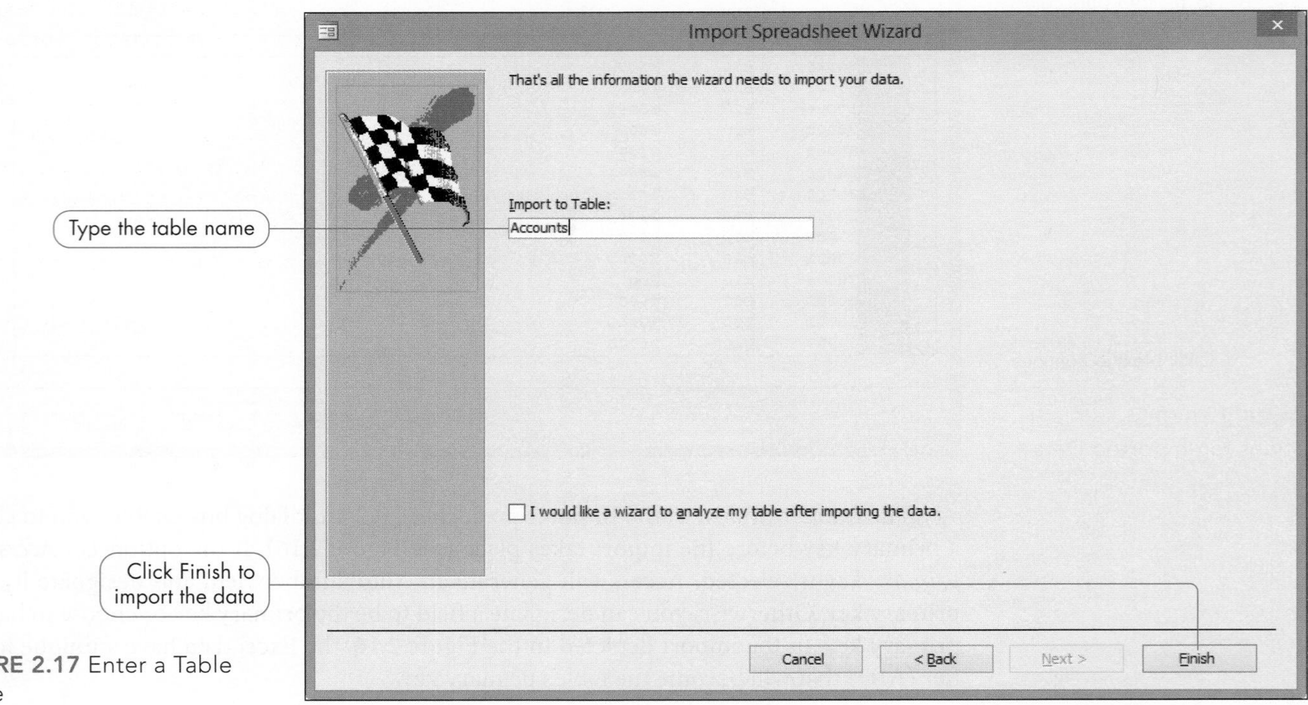

FIGURE 2.17 Enter a Table Name

Finally, the Wizard will ask if you wish to save the import steps. If the same worksheet is imported from Excel to Access on a recurring basis, you could save the parameters and use them again. To save the import steps, such as the indexing option and any new field names, click Save Import Steps in the Save Import Steps group. Saving the import steps will help you import the data the next time it is needed.

Modify an Imported Table's Design and Add Data

STEP 3 Importing data saves typing and prevents errors that may occur while entering data, but modifications will usually be required. After you have imported a table, open the table and examine the design to see if changes need to be made. You may need to modify the table by renaming fields so that they are more meaningful. To rename a field in Datasheet view, right-click the arrow next to the field name and click Rename Field. Type the new field name. To rename a field in Design view, select the field name and type the new name. In the bank example, you would change the name of the AID field to AccountID. Switch to Design view to modify the data type and field size.

STEP 4 You may need to add new fields or delete unnecessary fields. To add a new field in Datasheet view, right-click the field name to the right of where you want the new field to be added. Click Insert Field. To delete a field in Datasheet view, right-click the name of the field you want to delete and click Delete Field. To create a new field in Design view, click in the row below where you want the new field to be added and click Insert Rows in the Tools group on the Design tab. To delete a row in Design view, click in the row you want to delete and click Delete Rows in the Tools group on the Design tab. After making the modifications, you can add any data needed to the table.

Establishing Table Relationships

As previously discussed, the benefit of a relationship is to efficiently combine data from related tables for the purpose of creating queries, forms, and reports. Because this is such an important concept in designing and creating relational databases, this chapter reviews creating relationships and enforcing referential integrity. To ensure you are creating redundancy, you should store like data items together in the same table. In the example we are using, the customer data are stored in the Customers table. The Branch table stores data about the bank's branches, management, and locations. The Accounts table stores data about account ownership and balances.

STEP 5 Once you have created the tables by storing like data items together, you will be able to recognize that some tables have common fields with others. Our Accounts table shares a common field with the Customers table—the CustomerID. It also shares a common field with the Branch table—BranchID. These common fields can be used to establish relationships between two tables.

Once you determine the common fields, you drag the field name from one table to the field name on the table you want to be joined.

Figure 2.18 shows the Bank database with relationships created by joining common fields.

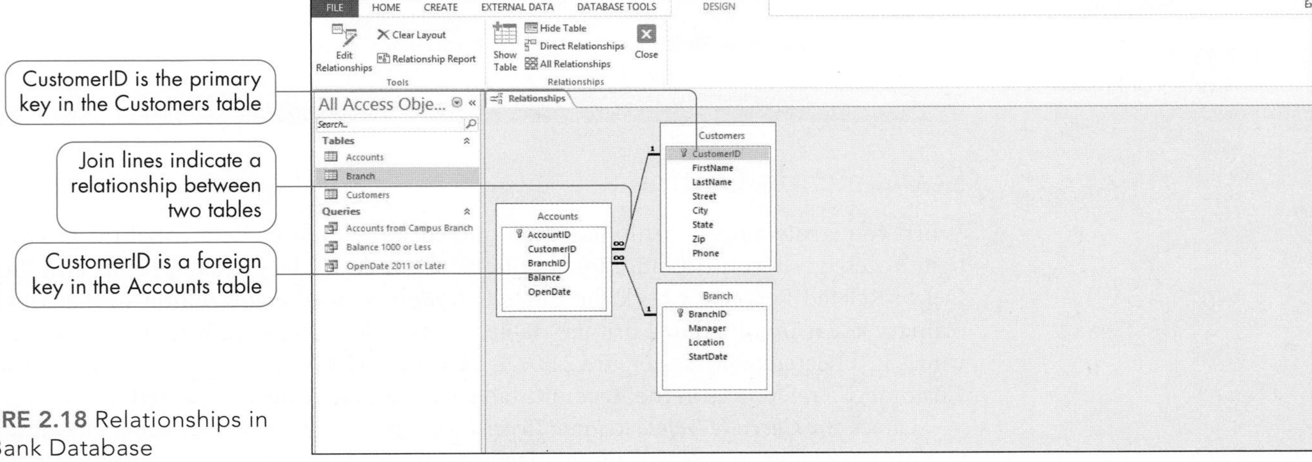

FIGURE 2.18 Relationships in the Bank Database

The primary key of a table plays a significant role when setting relationships. You cannot join two tables unless a primary key has been set in the primary table. In our Bank database, the CustomerID has been set as the primary key in the Customers table. Therefore, a relationship can be set between the Customers table and the Accounts table. Similarly, the Branch table can be joined to the Accounts table because BranchID has been set as the primary key in the Branch table.

The other side of the relationship join line is most often a foreign key of the related table. A foreign key is a field in one table that is also the primary key of another table. In the previous example, CustomerID in the Accounts table is a foreign key; BranchID in the Accounts table is a foreign key. Relationships between tables will almost always be set using primary and foreign keys.

Establish Referential Integrity

When you create a relationship in Access, the Edit Relationships dialog box displays. The first check box, Enforce Referential Integrity, should be checked in most cases. Remember, referential integrity enforces rules in a database that are used to preserve relationships between tables when records are changed.

STEP 6» When referential integrity is enforced, you cannot enter a foreign key value in a related table unless the primary key value exists in the primary table. In the case of the Bank database, a customer's account information (which includes CustomerID) cannot be entered into the Accounts table unless the customer information is first entered into the Customers table. If you attempt to enter an account prior to entering the customer information, an error will appear, as shown in Figure 2.19. When referential integrity is enforced, you cannot delete a record in one table if it has related records.

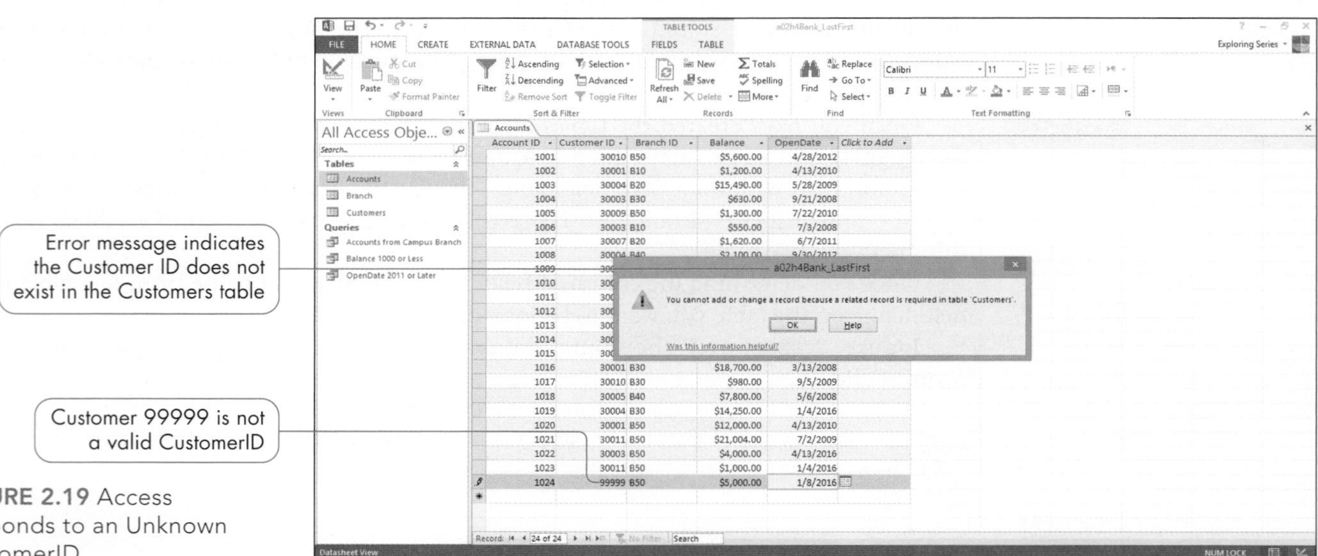

FIGURE 2.19 Access Responds to an Unknown CustomerID

Set Cascade Options

When you create a relationship in Access and click the Enforce Referential Integrity checkbox, Access gives you two additional options: Cascade Update Related Fields and Cascade Delete Related Records. Check the ***Cascade Update Related Fields*** option so that when the primary key is modified in a primary table, Access will automatically update all foreign key values in a related table (see Figure 2.20). If a CustomerID is updated for some reason, all the CustomerID references in the Accounts table will automatically be updated.

Check the ***Cascade Delete Related Records*** option so that when the primary key is deleted in a primary table, Access will automatically delete all records in related tables that reference the primary key (see Figure 2.20). If one branch of a bank closes and its record is deleted from the Branch table, any account that still remains with this branch would be deleted. Access will give a warning first and enable you to avoid the action. This may be a desired business rule, but it should be set with caution.

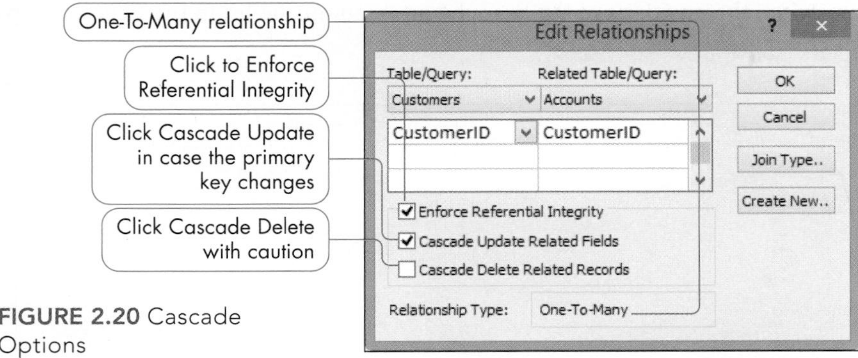

FIGURE 2.20 Cascade Options

Establish a One-to-Many Relationship

Figure 2.20 also shows that the relationship that will be created will be a one-to-many relationship. Access provides three different relationships for joining your data: one-to-one, one-to-many, and many-to-many. The most common type by far is the one-to-many relationship. A ***one-to-many relationship*** is established when the primary key value in the primary table can match many of the foreign key values in the related table.

For example, a bank customer will be entered into the Customers table once and only once. The primary key value, which is also the customer's CustomerID number, might be 1585. That same customer could set up a checking, savings, and money market account. With each account, the CustomerID (1585) is required and therefore will occur three times in the Accounts table. The value appears once in the Customers table and three times in the Accounts table. Therefore, the relationship between Customers and Accounts would be described as one to many.

Table 2.3 lists and describes all three types of relationships you can create between Access tables.

TABLE 2.3 Relationship Types

Relationship Type	Description
One-to-Many	The primary key table must have only one occurrence of each value. For example, each customer must have a unique identification number in the Customers table, or each employee must have a unique EmployeeID in the Employee table. The foreign key field in the second table may have repeating values. For example, one customer may have many different account numbers, or one employee can perform many services.
One-to-One	Two different tables use the same primary key. Exactly one record exists in the second table for each record in the first table. Sometimes security reasons require a table be split into two related tables. For example, anyone in the company can look in the Employee table and find the employee's office number, department assignment, or telephone extension. However, only a few people need to have access to the employee's network login password, salary, Social Security number, performance review, or marital status. Tables containing this information would use the same unique identifier to identify each employee.
Many-to-Many	This is an artificially constructed relationship giving many matching records in each direction between tables. It requires construction of a third table called a junction table. For example, a database might have a table for employees and one for projects. Several employees might be assigned to one project, but one employee might also be assigned to many different projects. When Access connects to databases using Oracle or other software, you find this relationship type.

Figure 2.21 shows the Relationships window for the Bank database and all the relationships created using referential integrity. The join line between the CustomerID field in the Customers table and the CustomerID field in the Accounts table indicates that a one-to-many relationship has been set. You can rearrange the tables by dragging the tables by the title bar. You can switch the positions of the Branch and Accounts tables in the Relationships window without changing the relationship itself.

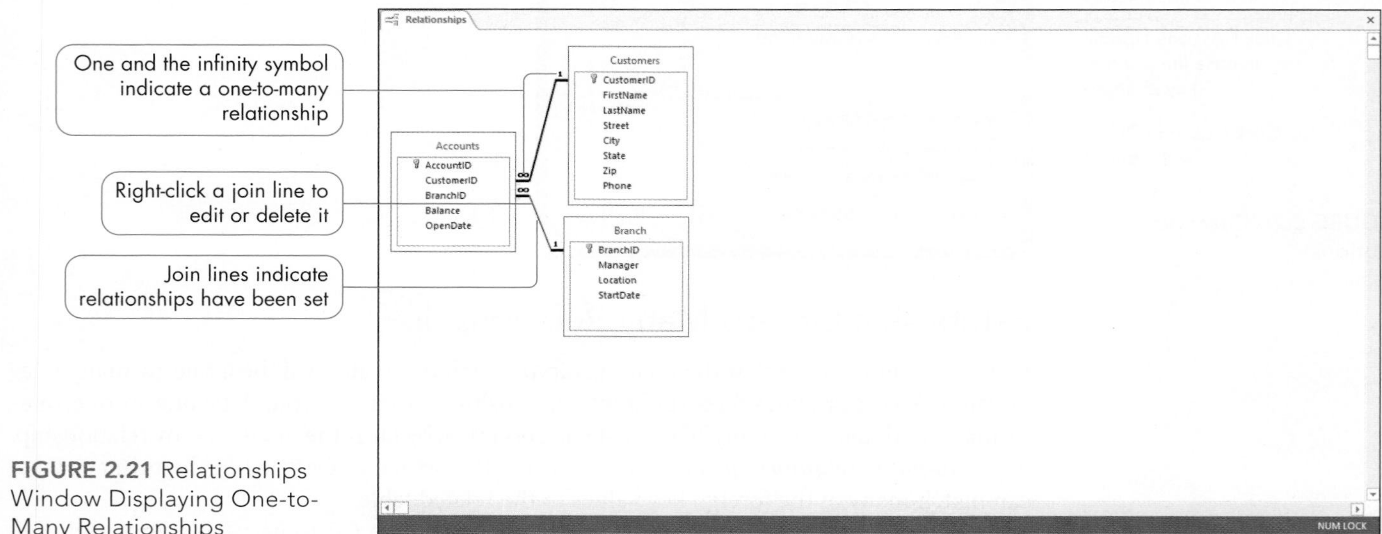

FIGURE 2.21 Relationships Window Displaying One-to-Many Relationships

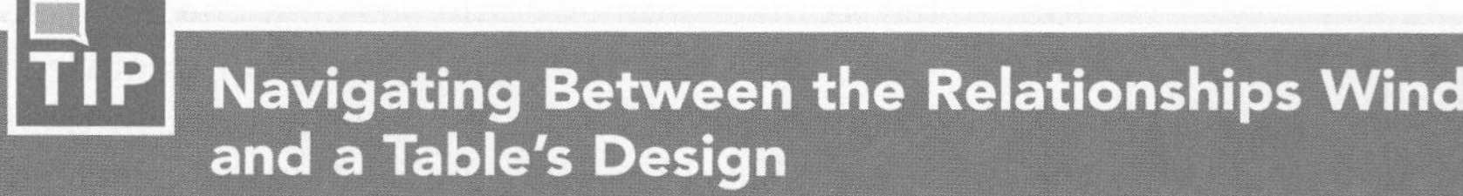

TIP Navigating Between the Relationships Window and a Table's Design

When you right-click on a table's title bar in the Relationships window, the shortcut menu offers you a chance to open the table in Design view. This is a convenient feature because if you want to link one table to another table, the joined fields must have the same data type. This shortcut enables you to check the fields and revise them if necessary if a table contains a field with the wrong data type.

In the following Hands-On Exercise, you will create two additional tables in the Bank database by importing data from an Excel spreadsheet and from an Access database. You will establish and modify field properties. Then you will connect the newly imported data to the Branch table by establishing relationships between the tables.

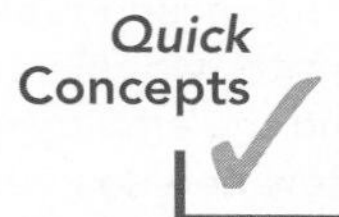

Quick Concepts

1. Describe a scenario that may require you to import Excel data into Access. ***p. 691***
2. What is the purpose of setting a relationship between two tables? ***p. 695***
3. Why would you enforce referential integrity when setting a relationship? ***p. 696***
4. Give an example of two database tables that would contain a one-to-many relationship. Describe the relationship. ***p. 697***

Hands-On Exercises

Watch the Video
for this Hands-
On Exercise!

MyITLab®
HOE2 Training

2 Multiple-Table Databases

You created a new Bank database, and you created a new Branch table. Now you are ready to import additional tables—one from an Excel spreadsheet and one from an Access database. Assume that the data are formatted correctly and are structured properly so that you can begin the import process.

Skills covered: Import Excel Data • Import Data from an Access Database • Modify an Imported Table's Design and Add Data • Add Data to an Imported Table • Establish Table Relationships • Test Referential Integrity

STEP 1 » IMPORT EXCEL DATA

You and the auditor have discovered several of Commonwealth's files that contain customer data. These files need to be analyzed, so you decide to import the data into Access. In this exercise, you import an Excel spreadsheet into the Bank database. Refer to Figure 2.22 as you complete Step 1.

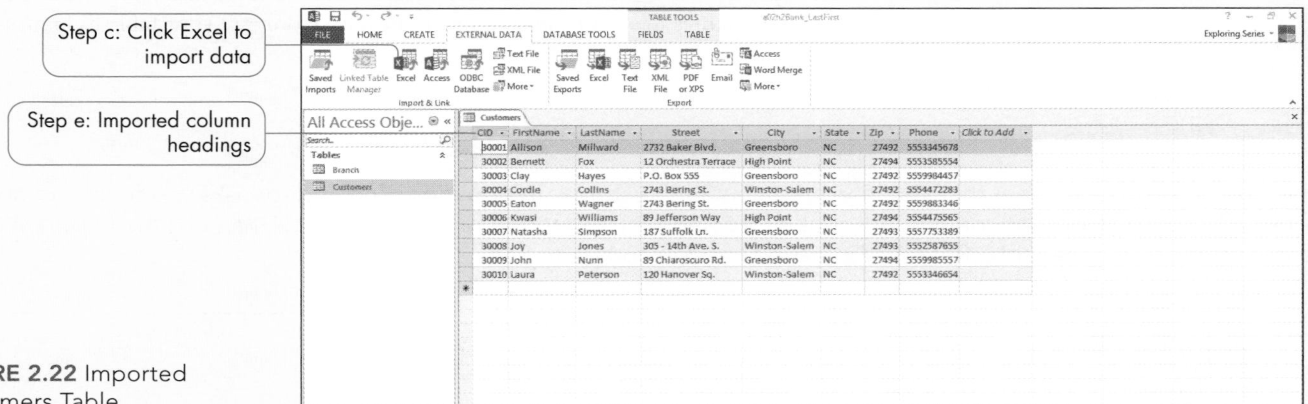
Step c: Click Excel to import data
Step e: Imported column headings

FIGURE 2.22 Imported Customers Table

a. Open *a02h1Bank_LastFirst* if you closed it at the end of Hands-On Exercise 1. Click the **FILE tab**, click **Save As**, and then click **Save As** in the *Save Database As* section. Type **a02h2Bank_LastFirst**, changing *h1 to h2*. Click **Save**.

b. If necessary, click **Enable Content** below the Ribbon to indicate you trust the contents of the database

TROUBLESHOOTING: If you make any major mistakes in this exercise, you can close the file, open *a02h1Bank_LastFirst* again, and then start this exercise over.

c. Click the **EXTERNAL DATA tab** and click **Excel** in the Import & Link group to launch the Get External Data – Excel Spreadsheet feature. Select the **Import the source data into a new table in the current database option**, if necessary.

d. Click **Browse** and go to the student data folder. Select the *a02h2Customers* workbook. Click **Open** and click **OK** to open the Import Spreadsheet Wizard.

e. Ensure that the *First Row Contains Column Headings* check box is checked to tell Access that column headings exist in the Excel file.

The field names CID, FirstName, LastName, Street, City, State, ZIP, and Phone will import from Excel along with the data stored in the rows in the worksheet. The field names will be modified later in Access.

f. Click **Next**.

g. Ensure that *CID* is displayed in the Field Name box in Field Options. Click the **Indexed arrow** and select **Yes (No Duplicates)**. Click **Next**.

The CID (CustomerID) will become the primary key in this table. It needs to be a unique identifier, so we must change the properties to no duplicates.

h. Click the **Choose my own primary key option**. Make sure that the CID field is selected. Click **Next**.

The final screen of the Import Spreadsheet Wizard asks you to name your table. The name of the Excel worksheet was Customers, and Access defaults to the worksheet name. It is an acceptable name.

i. Click **Finish** to accept the Customers table name.

A dialog box opens asking if you wish to save the steps of this import to use again. If this were sales data that was collected in Excel and updated to the database on a weekly basis, saving the import steps would save time. You do not need to save this example.

j. Click the **Close (X) button**.

The new table displays in the Navigation Pane and resides in the Bank database.

k. Open the imported Customers table in Datasheet view and double-click the border between each of the field names to adjust the columns to Best fit. Compare your table to Figure 2.22.

l. Close the table.

STEP 2 ›› IMPORT DATA FROM AN ACCESS DATABASE

The Customers spreadsheet that you imported contains customer information. The auditor asks you to import an Access database table that contains account information related to the mishandled funds. You use the Import Wizard to import the database table. Refer to Figure 2.23 as you complete Step 2.

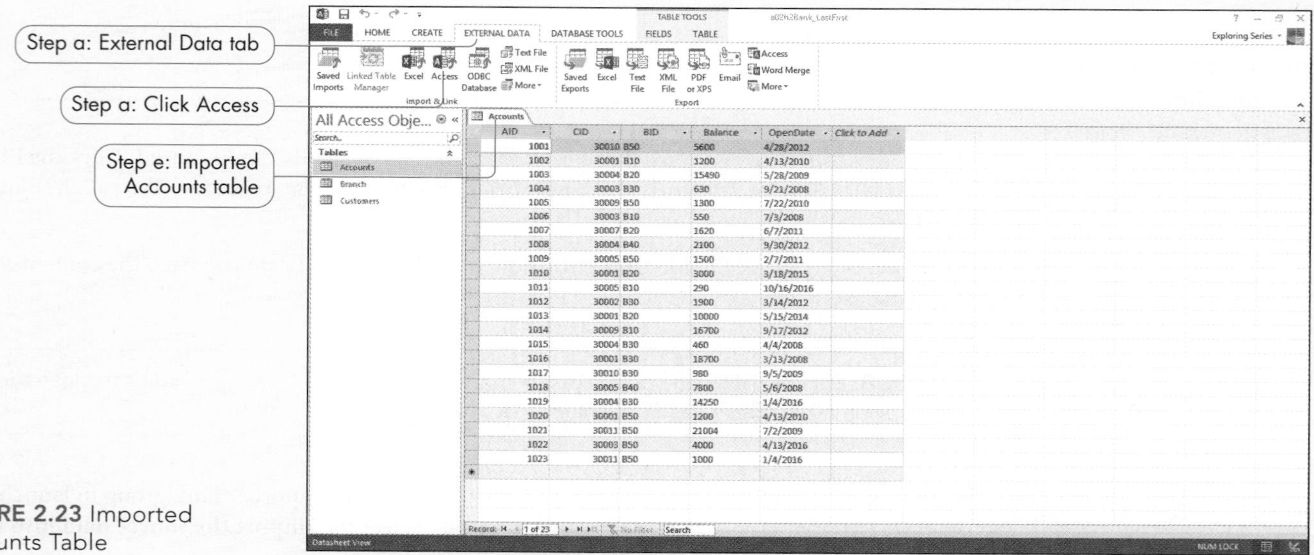

FIGURE 2.23 Imported Accounts Table

a. Click the **EXTERNAL DATA tab** and click **Access** in the Import & Link group to launch the Get External Data – Access Database feature. Select the **Import tables, queries, forms, reports, macros, and modules into the current database option**, if necessary.

b. Click **Browse** and go to the student data folder. Select the *a02h2Accounts* database. Click **Open** and click **OK** to open the Import Objects dialog box.

The Accounts table is active; you will import this table.

c. Ensure that the Accounts table is selected and click **OK**.

d. Click **Close** on the Save Import Steps dialog box.

The Navigation Pane contains three tables: Accounts, Branch, and Customers.

e. Open the imported Accounts table in Datasheet view and compare it to Figure 2.23.

STEP 3 » MODIFY AN IMPORTED TABLE'S DESIGN AND ADD DATA

When importing tables from either Excel or Access, the fields may have different data types and property settings than required to create table relationships. You need to modify the tables so that each field has the correct data type and field size. Refer to Figure 2.24 as you complete Step 3.

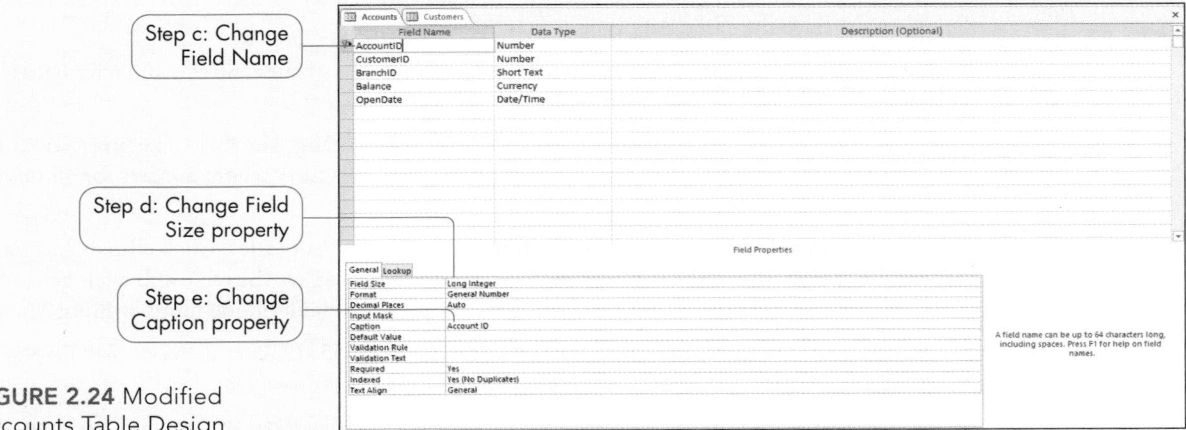

FIGURE 2.24 Modified Accounts Table Design

a. Right-click the **Accounts table** in the Navigation Pane.

b. Click **Design View** to open the table in Design view.

The Accounts table displays with the primary key AID selected.

c. Change the AID field name to **AccountID**.

d. Change the Field Size property to **Long Integer** in the Field Properties at the bottom of the Design window.

Long Integer ensures that there will be enough numbers as the number of customers grows over time and may exceed 32,768 (the upper limit for Integer values).

e. Type **Account ID** in the **Caption property box** for the AccountID field. The caption contains a space between *Account* and *ID*.

f. Change the CID field name to **CustomerID**.

g. Change the Field Size property to **Long Integer** in the Field Properties at the bottom of the Design window.

You can select the Field Size option using the arrow, or you can type the first letter of the option you want. For example, type l for Long Integer or s for Single. Make sure the current option is completely selected before you type the letter.

h. Type **Customer ID** in the **Caption property box** for the CustomerID field. The caption contains a space between *Customer* and *ID*.

i. Click the **BID field**. Change the BID field name to **BranchID**.

j. Type **5** in the **Field Size property box** in the Field Properties.

k. Type **Branch ID** in the **Caption property box** for the Branch ID field.

l. Change the Data Type of the Balance field to **Currency**.

The Currency data type is used for fields that contain monetary values.

m. Change the Data Type of the OpenDate field to **Date/Time** and add **Short Date** in the Format field property. Type **Open Date** in the **Caption property box**.

The OpenDate field stores the date that each account was opened.

n. Click **View** in the Views group to switch to Datasheet view. Read the messages and click **Yes** twice.

   In this case, it is OK to click Yes because the shortened fields will not cut off any data. Leave the table open.

o. Right-click the **Customers table** in the Navigation Pane and select **Design View** from the shortcut menu.

p. Change the CID field name to **CustomerID**. Change the Field Size property of the CustomerID field to **Long Integer** and add a caption, **Customer ID**. Take note of the intentional space between *Customer* and *ID*.

   The Accounts table and the Customers table will be joined using the CustomerID field. Both fields must have the same data type.

q. Change the Field Size property to **20** for the FirstName, LastName, Street, and City fields. Change the Field Size for State to **2**.

r. Change the data type for ZIP and Phone to **Short Text**. Change the Field size property to **15** for both fields. Remove the @ symbol from the Format property where it exists for all fields in the Customers table.

s. Click the **Phone field name** and click **Input Mask** in Field Properties. Click **ellipsis (...)** on the right side to launch the Input Mask Wizard. Click **Yes** to save the table and click **Yes** to the *Some data may be lost* warning. Click **Finish** to apply the default phone number Input Mask.

   The phone number input mask enables users to enter 6105551212, and Access will display it as (610)555-1212.

t. Click **Save** to save the design changes to the Customers table. Read the warning box and click **Yes**.

STEP 4 » ADD DATA TO AN IMPORTED TABLE

Now that you have created the Access tables, you add records. You may also need to update and delete records if you and the auditor decide the information is no longer needed. Refer to Figure 2.25 as you complete Step 4.

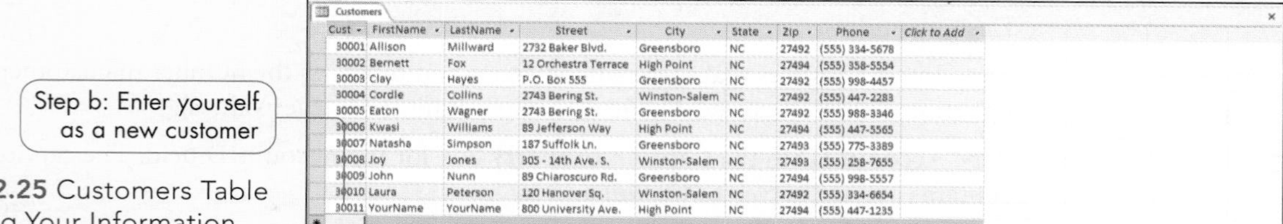

Customers

Cust	FirstName	LastName	Street	City	State	Zip	Phone	Click to Add
30001	Allison	Millward	2732 Baker Blvd.	Greensboro	NC	27492	(555) 334-5678	
30002	Bernett	Fox	12 Orchestra Terrace	High Point	NC	27494	(555) 358-5554	
30003	Clay	Hayes	P.O. Box 555	Greensboro	NC	27492	(555) 998-4457	
30004	Cordle	Collins	2743 Bering St.	Winston-Salem	NC	27492	(555) 447-2283	
30005	Eaton	Wagner	2743 Bering St.	Greensboro	NC	27492	(555) 988-3346	
30006	Kwasi	Williams	89 Jefferson Way	High Point	NC	27494	(555) 447-5565	
30007	Natasha	Simpson	187 Suffolk Ln.	Greensboro	NC	27493	(555) 775-3389	
30008	Joy	Jones	305 - 14th Ave. S.	Winston-Salem	NC	27493	(555) 258-7655	
30009	John	Nunn	89 Chiaroscuro Rd.	Greensboro	NC	27494	(555) 998-5557	
30010	Laura	Peterson	120 Hanover Sq.	Winston-Salem	NC	27492	(555) 334-6654	
30011	YourName	YourName	800 University Ave.	High Point	NC	27494	(555) 447-1235	

Step b: Enter yourself as a new customer

FIGURE 2.25 Customers Table Displaying Your Information

a. Click **View** in the Views group to display the Customers table in Datasheet view.

   The asterisk at the bottom of the table data in the row selector area is the indicator of a place to enter a new record.

b. Click the **Customer ID field** in the record after *30010*. Type **30011**. Fill in the rest of the data using your information as the customer. You may use a fictitious address and phone number.

   Note the phone number format. The input mask you set formats the phone number.

c. Close the Customers table. The Accounts table tab is open.

> **TROUBLESHOOTING:** If the Accounts table is not open, double-click Accounts in the Navigation Pane.

d. Locate the new record indicator—the * in the row selector—and click in the **Account ID column**. Type **1024**. Type **30011** as the Customer ID and **B50** as the Branch ID. Type **14005** for the Balance field value. Type **8/7/2015** for the OpenDate.

e. Add the following records to the Accounts table:

Account ID	Customer ID	Branch ID	Balance	Open Date
1025	30006	B40	$11,010	3/13/2013
1026	30007	B20	$7,400	5/1/2014

f. Close the Accounts table; keep the database open.

STEP 5 » ESTABLISH TABLE RELATIONSHIPS

The tables for the bank investigation have been designed. Now you will need to establish connections between the tables. Look at the primary and foreign keys as a guide. Refer to Figure 2.26 as you complete Step 5.

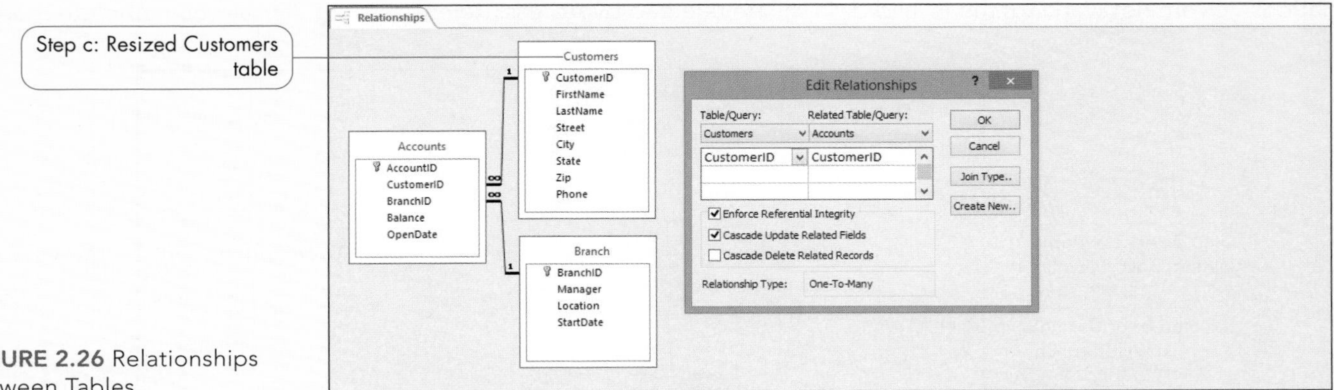

FIGURE 2.26 Relationships Between Tables

a. Click the **DATABASE TOOLS tab** and click **Relationships** in the Relationships group.

The Relationships window opens and the Show Table dialog box appears.

> **TROUBLESHOOTING:** If the Show Table dialog box does not open, click Show Table in the Relationships group on the Relationships Tools Design tab.

b. Double-click each of the three tables displayed in the Show Table dialog box to add them to the Relationships window. (Alternatively, click a table and click **Add**.) Click **Close** in the Show Table dialog box.

> **TROUBLESHOOTING:** If you have a duplicate table, click the title bar of the duplicated table and press Delete.

c. Resize the Customers table box so all of the fields are visible. Arrange the tables as shown in Figure 2.26.

d. Drag the **BranchID field** in the Branch table onto the BranchID field in the Accounts table. The Edit Relationships dialog box opens. Click the **Enforce Referential Integrity** and **Cascade Update Related Fields check boxes**. Click **Create**.

A black line displays, joining the two tables. It has a 1 at the end near the Branch table and an infinity symbol on the end next to the Accounts table. You have established a one-to-many relationship between the Branch and Accounts tables.

e. Drag the **CustomerID field** in the Customers table onto the CustomerID field in the Accounts table. The Edit Relationships dialog box opens. Click the **Enforce Referential Integrity** and **Cascade Update Related Fields check boxes**. Click **Create**.

You have established a one-to-many relationship between the Customers and Accounts tables. A customer will have only a single CustomerID number. The same customer may have many different accounts: Savings, Checking, CDs, and so forth.

TROUBLESHOOTING: If you get an error message when you click Create, verify that the data types of the joined fields are the same. To check the data types from the Relationships window, right-click the title bar of a table and select Table Design from the shortcut menu. Modify the data type and field size of the join fields if necessary.

f. Click **Save** on the Quick Access Toolbar to save the changes to the relationships. Close the Relationships window.

STEP 6 ›› TEST REFERENTIAL INTEGRITY

The design of the Bank database must be 100% correct; otherwise, data entry may be compromised. Even though you are confident that the table relationships are correct, you decide to test them by entering some invalid data. If the relationships are not working, the invalid data will be rejected by Access. Refer to Figure 2.27 as you complete Step 6.

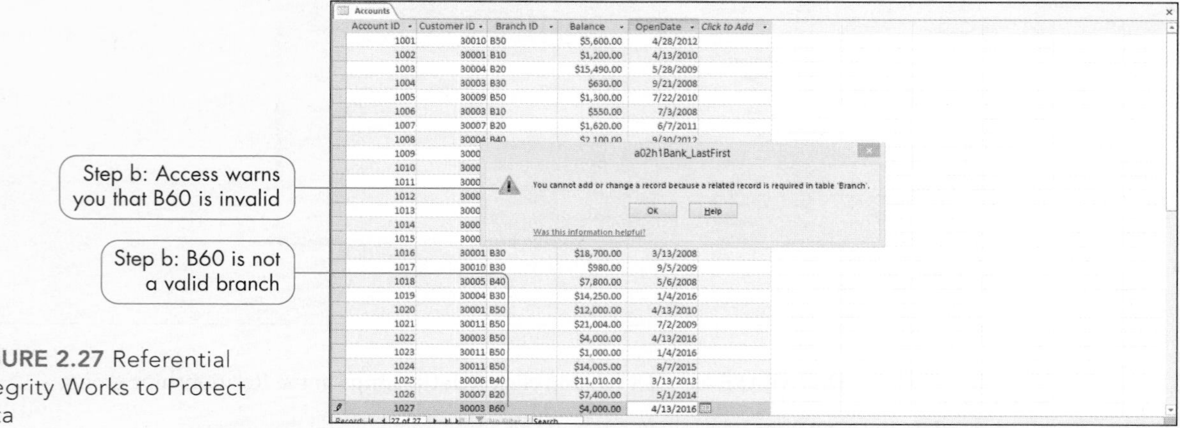

FIGURE 2.27 Referential Integrity Works to Protect Data

a. Double-click the **Accounts table** to open it in Datasheet view.

b. Add a new record, pressing **Tab** after each field: Account ID: **1027**, Customer ID: **30003**, Branch: **B60**, Balance: **4000**, OpenDate: **4/13/2016**.

   You attempted to enter a nonexistent BranchID and were not allowed to make that error. A warning message is telling you that a related record in the Branch table is required because the Accounts table and the Branch table are connected by a relationship with Enforce Referential Integrity checked.

c. Click **OK**. Double-click the **Branch table** in the Navigation Pane and examine the data in the BranchID field. Notice the Branch table has no B60 record. Close the Branch table.

d. Replace *B60* with **B50** in the new Accounts record and press **Tab** three times. As soon as the focus moves to the next record, the pencil symbol disappears and your data are saved.

   You successfully identified a BranchID that Access recognizes. Because referential integrity between the Accounts and Branch tables has been enforced, Access looks at each data entry item in a foreign key and matches it to a corresponding value in the table where it is the primary key. In step b, you attempted to enter a nonexistent BranchID and were not allowed to make that error. In step d, you entered a valid BranchID. Access examined the index for the BranchID in the Branch table and found a corresponding value for B50.

e. Close the Accounts table. Reopen the Accounts table; you will find that the record you just entered for 1027 has been saved. Close the table.

   You have established a one-to-many relationship between the Customers and Accounts tables. A customer will have only a single CustomerID number. The same customer may have many different accounts: Savings, Checking, CDs, and so forth.

f. Close all open tables, if necessary.

g. Keep the database open if you plan to continue with Hands-On Exercise 3. If not, close the database and exit Access.

Single-Table Queries

If you wanted to see which customers currently have an account with a balance over $5,000, you could find the answer by creating an Access query. A ***query*** enables you to ask questions about the data stored in a database and then provides the answers to the questions by providing subsets or summaries of data. Because data are stored in tables in a database, you always begin a query by asking, "Which table holds the data I want?" For the question about account balances over $5,000, you would reference the Accounts table. If you want to invite customers in a certain ZIP code to the Grand Opening of a new branch, you could create a query based on the Customers table.

You use the ***Query Design view*** to create queries. The Query Design view is divided into two parts: The top portion displays the tables, and the bottom portion (known as the query design grid) displays the fields and the criteria. You select only the fields you want arranged in the order that you want the resulting data displayed. The design grid also enables you to sort the records based on one or more fields. You can also create calculated fields to display data based on expressions that use the fields in the underlying table. For example, you could calculate the monthly interest earned on each bank account.

In this section, you will use the Query Design view and the Query Wizard to create queries that display only data that you select. Multitable queries will be covered in the next section.

Creating a Single-Table Query

You can create a single-table query in two ways—by using the Simple Query Wizard or the Query Design tool in the Queries group on the Create tab. The Query Design tool is the most flexible way to create a query. You can add criteria to a query while in the Query Design view. After you design a query, you can display the results of the query by switching to Datasheet view. A query's datasheet looks and acts like a table's datasheet, except that it is usually a subset of the records found in the entire table. The subset shows only the records that match the criteria that were added in the query design. The subset may contain different sorting of the records than the sorting in the underlying table. Datasheet view allows you to enter a new record, modify an existing record, or delete a record. Any changes made in Datasheet view are reflected in the underlying table that the query is based upon.

STEP 3»

Be aware that query results display the actual records that are stored in the underlying table(s). Being able to correct an error immediately while it is displayed in query results is an advantage. You save time by not having to close the query, open the table, find the error, fix it, and then run the query again. However, you should use caution when editing records in query results since you will be changing the table data.

Create a Single-Table Select Query

The Query Design tool is used to create ***select queries***, a type of query that displays only the records that match criteria entered in Query Design view. To create a select query using the Query Design tool, do the following:

STEP 2»

1. Click the CREATE tab.
2. Click Query Design in the Queries group.
3. Select the table you need in your query from the Show Table dialog box.
4. Click Add to add the table to the top section of the query design and close the Show Table dialog box.
5. Drag the fields needed from the table to the query design grid (or alternatively, double-click the field names); then add criteria and sorting options.
6. Click Run in the Results group to show the results in Datasheet view.

Use Query Design View

The Query Design view consists of two parts. The top portion contains tables with their respective field names. If a query contains more than one table, the join lines between tables will be displayed as they were created in the Relationships window.

The bottom portion (known as the query design grid) contains columns and rows. Each field in the query has its own column and contains multiple rows. The rows permit you to control the query results.

- The ***Field row*** displays the field name.
- The ***Table row*** displays the data source.
- The ***Sort row*** enables you to sort in ascending or descending order.
- The ***Show row*** controls whether the field will be displayed in the query results.
- The ***Criteria row*** is used to set the rules that determine which records will be selected, such as customers with account balances greater than $5,000.

Figure 2.28 displays the query design grid with the Show Table dialog box open. The Accounts table has been added from the Show Table dialog box. Figure 2.29 shows the Design view of a sample query with four fields, with a criterion set for one field and sorting set on another. The results of the query are shown in Datasheet view, as shown in Figure 2.30.

TIP Examine the Records

An experienced Access user always examines the records returned in the query results. Verify that the records in the query results match the criteria that you specified in Design view. As you add additional criteria, the number of records returned will usually decrease.

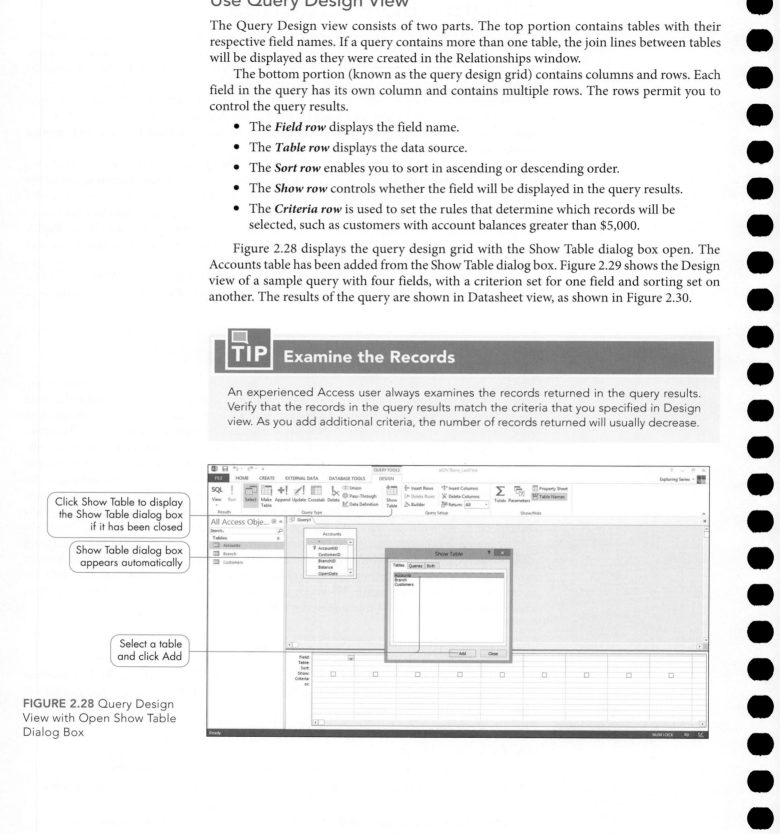

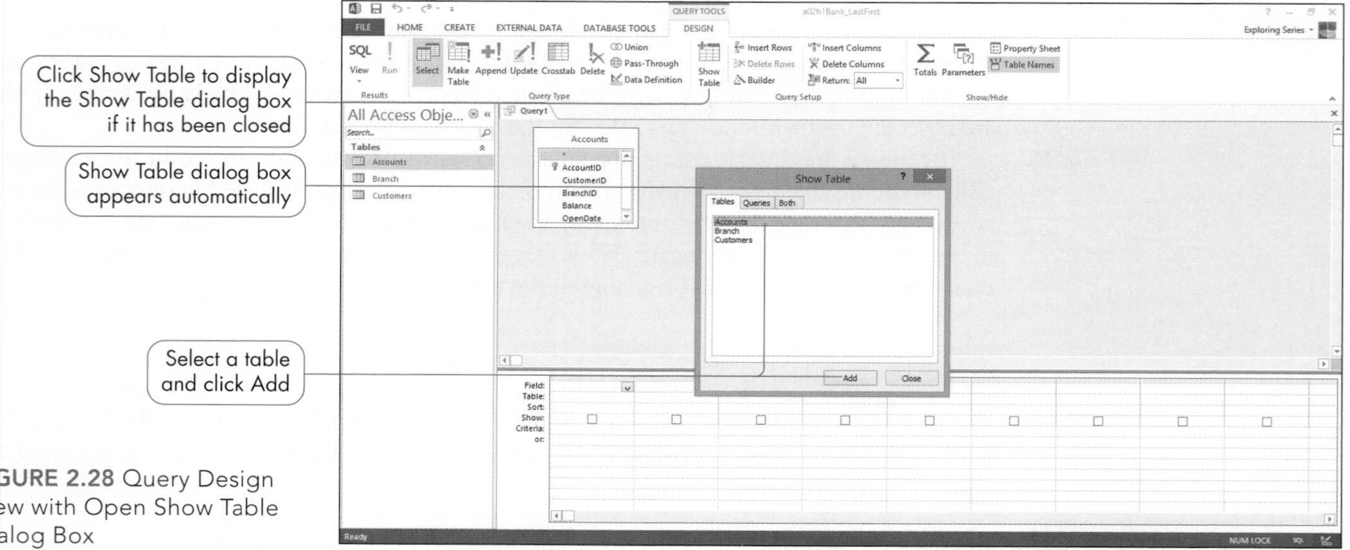

Click Show Table to display the Show Table dialog box if it has been closed
Show Table dialog box appears automatically
Select a table and click Add

FIGURE 2.28 Query Design View with Open Show Table Dialog Box

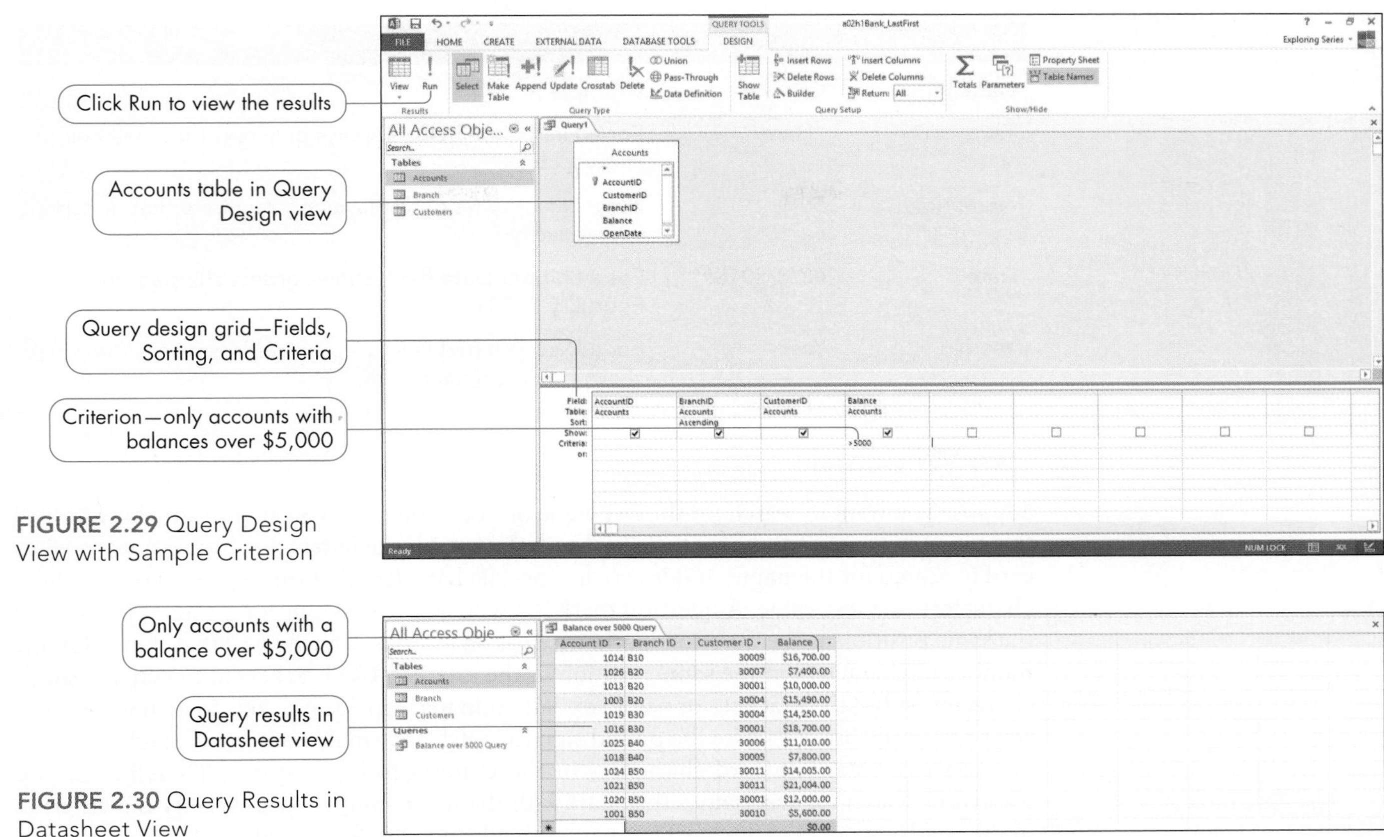

FIGURE 2.29 Query Design View with Sample Criterion

FIGURE 2.30 Query Results in Datasheet View

When you developed the tables, you toggled between the Design view and Datasheet view. Similarly, you will toggle between Design view and Datasheet view when you create queries. Use Design view to specify the criteria; you can use the results that display in Datasheet view to answer a question or to make a decision about the organization. Use Datasheet view to see the results of your query. Each time you need to fine-tune the query, switch back to Design view, make a change, and then test the results in Datasheet view. After you are satisfied with the query results, you may want to save the query so it can become a permanent part of the database and can be used later.

Specifying Query Criteria for Different Data Types

When specifying the criteria for a query, you may need to include a ***delimiter***—a special character that surrounds a criterion's value. The delimiter needed is determined by the field data type, and Access will automatically enter the delimiter for you for some data types. Text fields require quotation marks before and after the text. Access automatically adds the quotation marks around text, but to ensure that the correct delimiter is used, you may want to include the delimiters yourself.

Use plain digits (no delimiter) for the criteria of a numeric field, currency, or AutoNumber. You can enter numeric criteria with or without a decimal point and with or without a minus sign. Commas and dollar signs are not allowed.

When the criterion is in a date field, you enclose the criterion in pound signs, such as #10/14/2016#. Access accepts a date with or without the pound signs, but if you enter 1/1/2016 without the pound signs, Access will automatically add the pound signs when you move to another column in the design grid. The date value can be entered using any allowed format, such as February 2, 2016, 2/2/2016, or 2-Feb-16. You enter criteria for a Yes/No field as Yes or No. See Table 2.4 for query criteria and examples.

TABLE 2.4 Query Criteria		
Data Type	**Criteria**	**Example**
Text	"Harry"	For a FirstName field, displays only text that matches Harry exactly.
Numeric	5000	For a Quantity field, displays only numbers that match 5000 exactly.
Date	#2/2/2015#	For a ShippedDate field, shows orders shipped on February 2, 2015.
Yes/No	Yes	For a Discontinued field, returns records where the check box is selected.

Use Wildcards

Suppose you want to search for the last name of a customer, but you are not sure how to spell the name; however, you know that the name starts with the letters Sm. You can use a wildcard to search for the name. ***Wildcards*** are special characters that can represent one or more characters in a text value. A question mark is a wildcard that stands for a single character in the same position as the question mark, whereas an asterisk is a wildcard that stands for any number of characters in the same position as the asterisk. Use brackets to match any single character within the brackets, or use an exclamation mark inside brackets to match any character not in the brackets. Use the pound sign to match any single numeric character.

You can enter wildcard characters in the Criteria row of a query. Therefore, if you wanted to search for just names that start with the letters Sm, you can specify the criterion in the LastName field as Sm*. All last names that begin with Sm would display. For example, H?ll will return Hall, Hill, and Hull, whereas S*nd will return Sand, Stand, and StoryLand. Table 2.5 shows more query examples that use wildcards.

TABLE 2.5 Query Criteria Using Wildcards			
Character	**Description**	**Example**	**Result**
*	Matches for any number of characters in the same position as the asterisk	Sm*	Small, Smiley, Smith, Smithson
?	Matches for a single character in the same position as the question mark	H?ll	Hall, Hill, Hull
[ ]	Matches any single character within the brackets	F[ae]ll	Fall and Fell, but not Fill or Full
[!]	Matches any character not in the brackets	F[!ae]ll	Fill and Full, but not Fall or Fell

Use Comparison Operators in Queries

A comparison operator, such as equal (=), not equal (<>), greater than (>), less than (<), greater than or equal to (>=), and less than or equal to (<=), can be used in the criteria of a query. Comparison operators enable you to limit the query results to only those records that meet the criteria. For example, if you only want to see accounts that have a balance greater than $5,000, you would type >5000 in the Criteria row. Table 2.6 shows more comparison operator examples as well as other sample expressions.

TABLE 2.6 Comparison Operators in Queries

Expression	Example
=10	Equals 10
<>10	Not equal to 10
>10	Greater than 10
>=10	Greater than or equal to 10
<10	Less than 10
<=10	Less than or equal to 10

Work with Null

Sometimes finding what is missing is an important part of making a decision. For example, if you need to know which orders have been completed but not shipped, you would create a query to find the orders with a missing ShipDate. Are there missing phone numbers or addresses for some of your customers? Create a query to find customers with a missing PhoneNumber. The term that Access uses for a blank field is ***null***. Table 2.7 gives two illustrations of when to use the null criterion in a query.

TABLE 2.7 Establishing Null Criteria Expressions

Expression	Description	Example
Is Null	Use to find blank fields	For an Employee field in the Customers table when the customer has not been assigned a sales representative.
Is Not Null	Used to find fields with data	For a ShipDate field; a value inserted indicated the order was shipped to the customer.

Establish AND, OR, and NOT Criteria

Remember the earlier question, "Which customers currently have an account with a balance over $5,000?" This question was answered by creating a query with a single criterion, as shown in Figure 2.29. At times, questions are more specific and require queries with multiple criteria. For example, you may need to know "Which customers from the Eastern branch currently have an account with a balance over $5,000?" To answer this question, you need to specify criteria in multiple fields using the ***AND logical operator***. When the criteria are in the same row of the query design grid, Access interprets the instructions using the AND operator. This means that the query results will display only records that match *all* criteria.

When you have multiple sets of criteria and you need to satisfy one set only, use the ***OR logical operator***. The query results will display records that match any of the specified criteria. To use the OR operator, type your expression into the Criteria row, separating the criteria with the OR operator. Table 2.8 shows an example of an OR operator created using this method. You can also type the first expression into the Criteria row and then type the subsequent expression by using the Or row in the design grid. Figure 2.31b displays an example of an OR operator using this method.

The ***NOT logical operator*** returns all records except the specified criteria. For example, "Not Eastern" would return all accounts except those opened at the Eastern branch.

TABLE 2.8 AND, OR, and NOT Queries

Logical Operator	Example	Result
AND	"Eastern" AND "Campus"	For a Branch field, returns all records for the Eastern and Campus branches.
AND	>5000 AND <10000	For a Balance field, returns all accounts with a balance greater than $5,000 and less than $10,000.
OR	5000 OR 10000	For a Balance field, returns all accounts with a balance of exactly $5,000 or $10,000.
NOT	Not "Campus"	For a Branch field, returns all records except those in the Campus branch.

The first example in Figure 2.31 shows a query with an AND logical operator (criteria on the same row are implicitly joined by AND). It will return all of the B20 branch accounts with balances over $5,000. (Both conditions must be met for the record to be included.) The second example in Figure 2.31 shows a query with an OR logical operator. It will return all of the B20 branch accounts regardless of balance plus all accounts at any branch with a balance over $5,000. (One condition must be met for a record to be included.) The third example in Figure 2.31 shows a query that uses the NOT logical operator. It will return all of the accounts—excluding the B20 branch—with a balance over $5,000. The last example in Figure 2.31 shows a query that combines AND and OR logical operators. The top row will return B20 branch accounts with a balance over $5,000, and the second row will return B30 branch accounts with a balance over $15,000.

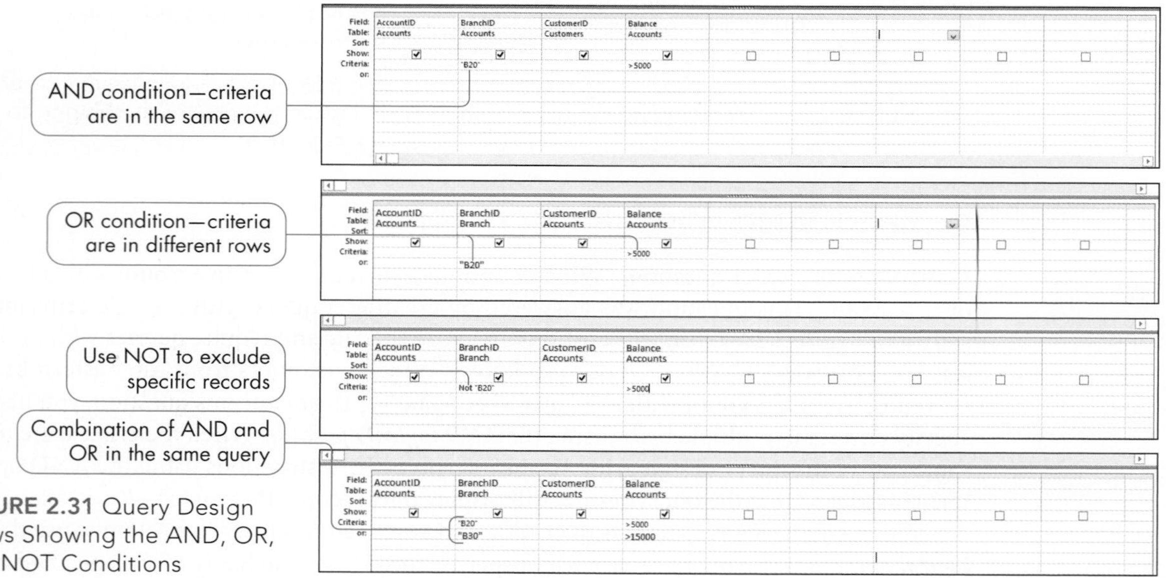

FIGURE 2.31 Query Design Views Showing the AND, OR, and NOT Conditions

TIP Finding Values in a Date Range

To find the values contained within a data range, use the > (greater than) and < (less than) operators. For example, to find the values of a date after January 1, 2015, and before December 31, 2015, use the criterion >1/1/2015 and <12/31/2015. You can also use the BETWEEN operator. For example BETWEEN 1/1/2015 and 12/31/2015.

Understanding Query Sort Order

The ***query sort order*** determines the order of records in a query's Datasheet view. You can change the order of records by specifying the sort order in the Design view. When you want to sort using more than one field, the sort order is determined from left to right. The order of columns should be considered when first creating the query. For example, a query sorted by LastName and then by FirstName must have those two fields in the correct order in the design grid. You can change the order of the query fields in the design grid to change the sort order of the query results.

STEP 2》 To change the order of fields, select the column you want to move by clicking the column selector. Release the mouse, then click again and drag the selected field to its new location. To insert additional columns in the design grid, select a column and click Insert Columns in the Query Setup group. The inserted column will insert to the left of the selected column. To delete a column, click the column selector to select the column and click the Delete Columns button on the Design tab or press Delete on the keyboard.

Running, Copying, and Modifying a Query

Several ways exist to run a query. One method is to click Run in the Results group when you are in Design view. Another method is to locate the query in the Navigation Pane and double-click it. A similar method is to select the query and press Enter.

After you create a query, you may want to create a duplicate copy to use as the basis for creating a similar query. Duplicating a query saves time when you need the same tables and fields but with slightly different criteria.

Run a Query

After you create a query and save it, you can run it directly from the Design view. You run a query by clicking the Run command (the red exclamation point) in the Results group on the Query Tools Design tab. You can also run a query from the Navigation Pane. Locate the query you want to run and double-click the query. The results will display as a tab in the main window.

Copy a Query

Sometimes you have a one-of-a-kind question about your data. You would create a query to answer this question and then delete the query. However, sometimes you need a series of queries in which each query is similar to the first. For example, you need a list of accounts in each branch. In a case like this, you create a query for one branch and then save a copy of the query and give it a new name. Finally, you would change the criteria to match the second branch. To accomplish this, do the following:

1. Open the query you want to copy.
2. Click the FILE tab and click Save As.
3. Click Save Object As in the *File Types* section.
4. Ensure Save Object As is selected in the *Database File Types* section and click Save As.
5. Type the name you want to use for the new query in the Save As dialog box and click OK (see Figure 2.32).
6. Switch to Design view and modify the query criteria.

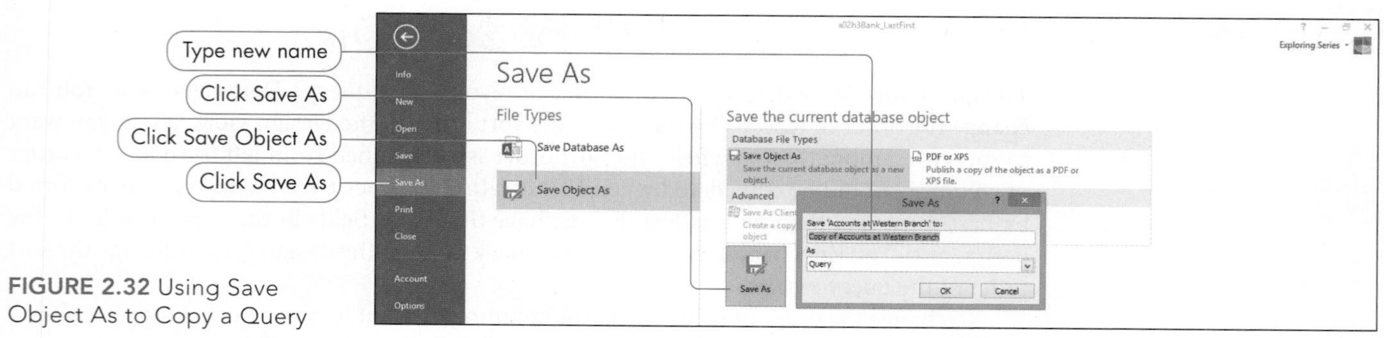

FIGURE 2.32 Using Save Object As to Copy a Query

You can also right-click the original query in the Navigation Pane and click Copy. Click in the Navigation Pane again and click Paste. Type a name for the new query in the Paste As dialog box.

Using the Query Wizard

STEP 1》 You may also create a query using the Query Wizard. Like all of the Microsoft wizards, the ***Simple Query Wizard*** guides you through the query design process. The wizard is helpful for creating basic queries that do not require criteria. After the query is created using the Wizard, you can switch to Design view and add criteria manually. Even if you initiate the query with a wizard, you will need to learn how to modify it in Design view. Often, copying an existing query and making slight modifications to its design is much faster than starting at the beginning with the wizard. You also will need to know how to add additional tables and fields to an existing query when conditions change. To launch the Query Wizard, click the Create tab and click Query Wizard in the Queries group (see Figure 2.33).

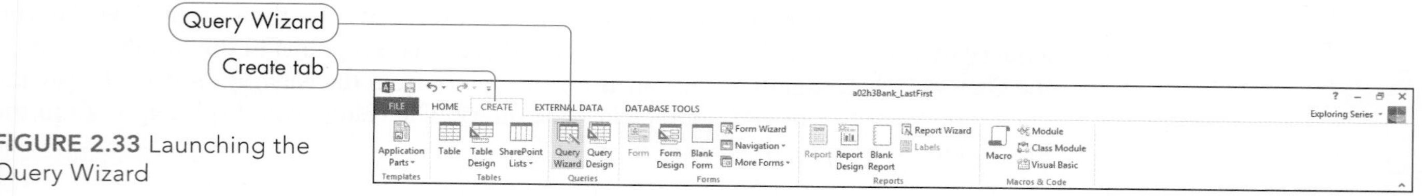

FIGURE 2.33 Launching the Query Wizard

Select the Simple Query Wizard in the Query Wizard dialog box, as shown in Figure 2.34.

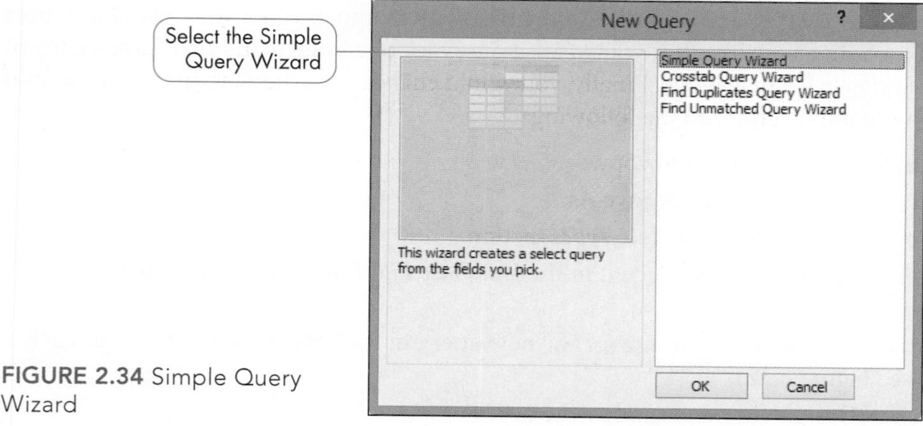

FIGURE 2.34 Simple Query Wizard

In the first step of the Simple Query Wizard dialog box, you specify the tables or queries and fields needed in your query. When you select a table from the Tables/Queries arrow (queries can also be based on other queries), a list of the table's fields displays in the Available Fields list box. See Figures 2.35 and 2.36.

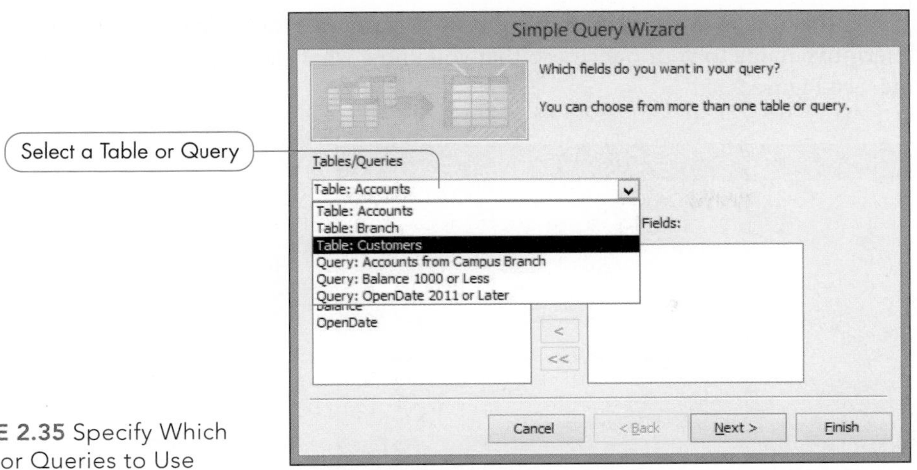

FIGURE 2.35 Specify Which Tables or Queries to Use

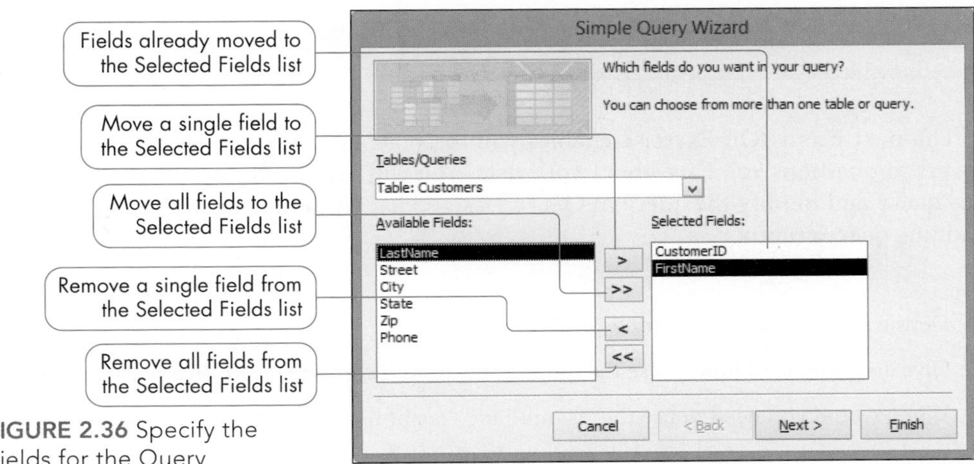

FIGURE 2.36 Specify the Fields for the Query

Select the necessary fields and add them to the Selected Fields list box using the directional arrows shown in Figure 2.36.

In the next screen (shown in Figure 2.37), you choose between a detail and a summary query. The detail query shows every field of every record in the result. The summary query enables you to group data and view only summary records. For example, if you were interested in the total funds deposited at each of the bank branches, you would set the query to Summary, click Summary Options, and then click Sum on the Balance field. Access would then sum the balances of all accounts for each branch.

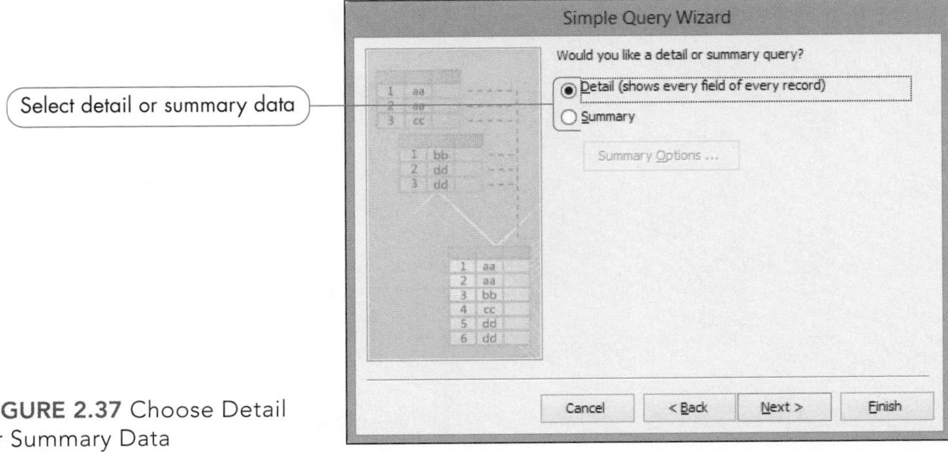

FIGURE 2.37 Choose Detail or Summary Data

The final dialog box of the Simple Query Wizard asks for the name of the query. Assign a descriptive name to your queries so that you know what each does by looking at the query name. See Figure 2.38.

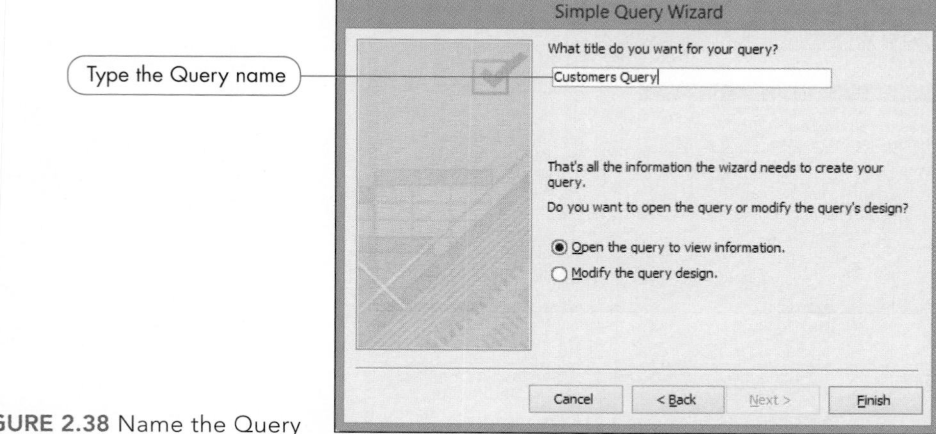

FIGURE 2.38 Name the Query

The next Hands-On Exercise enables you to create and run queries in order to find answers to questions you have about your data. You will use the Query Wizard to create a basic query and modify the query in Query Design view by adding an additional field and by adding query criteria.

1. Define a query. Give an example. ***p. 704***
2. Give an example of how to use the criteria row to find certain records in a table. ***p. 706***
3. When would you need to use the "is null" and "is not null" criteria? ***p. 709***
4. When would you want to copy a query? ***p. 711***

Hands-On Exercises

3 Single-Table Queries

The tables and table relationships have been created, and some data have been entered. Now, you need to begin the process of analyzing the bank data for the auditor. You will do so using queries. You decide to begin with the Accounts table.

Skills covered: Create a Query Using a Wizard • Specify Query Criteria and Query Sort Order • Change Query Data

STEP 1 ≫ CREATE A QUERY USING A WIZARD

You decide to start with the Query Wizard, knowing you can always alter the design of the query later in Query Design view. You will show the results to the auditor using Datasheet view. Refer to Figure 2.39 as you complete Step 1.

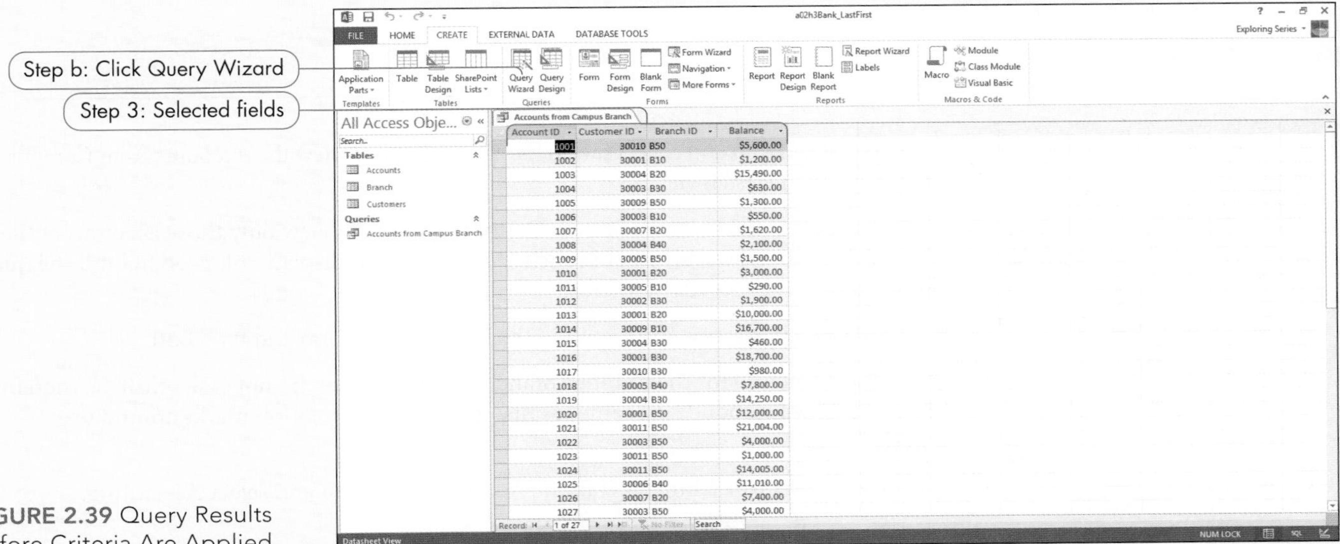

FIGURE 2.39 Query Results Before Criteria Are Applied

a. Open *a02h2Bank_LastFirst* if you closed it at the end of Hands-On Exercise 2. Save the database as **a02h3Bank_LastFirst**, changing *h2* to *h3*.

b. Click the **CREATE tab** and click **Query Wizard** in the Queries group to launch the New Query wizard.

The New Query Wizard dialog box opens. Simple Query Wizard is selected by default.

c. Click **OK.**

d. Verify that *Table: Accounts* is selected in the Tables/Query box.

e. Select **AccountID** from the **Available Fields list** and click >. Repeat the process with CustomerID, BranchID, and Balance.

The four fields should now display in the Selected Fields list box.

f. Click **Next**.

g. Confirm *Detail* is selected and click **Next**.

h. Name the query **Accounts from Campus Branch**. Click **Finish**.

This query name describes the data in the query results. Your query should have four fields: AccountID, CustomerID, BranchID, and Balance. The Navigation bar indicates 27 records meet the query criteria.

STEP 2 ≫ SPECIFY QUERY CRITERIA AND QUERY SORT ORDER

The auditor indicated that the problem seems to be confined to the Campus branch. You use this knowledge to revise the query to display only Campus accounts. Refer to Figure 2.40 as you complete Step 2.

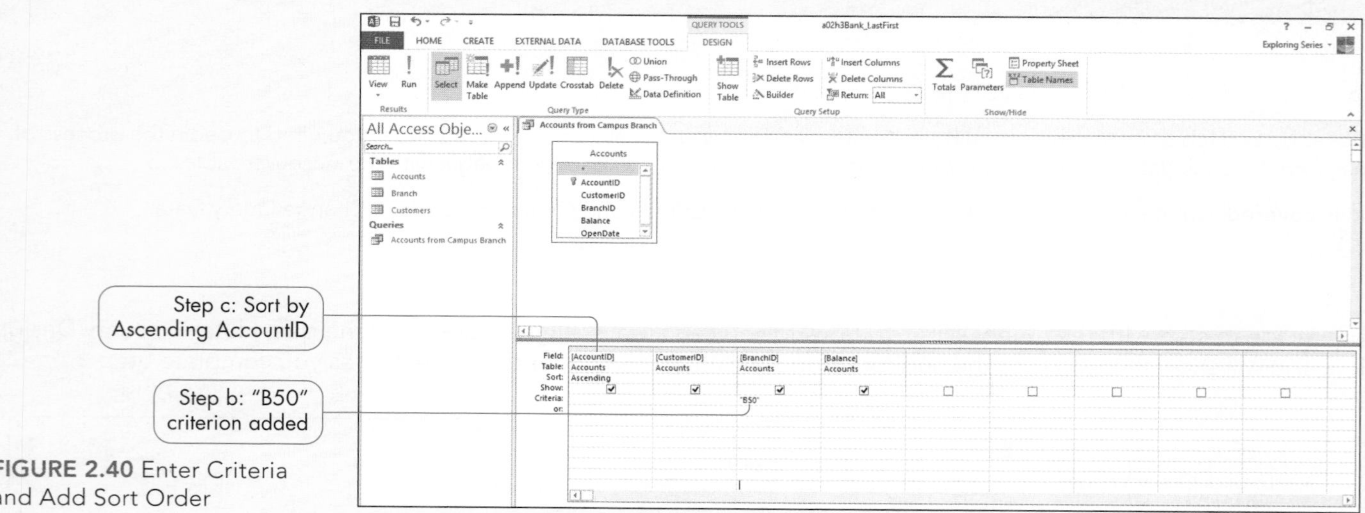

FIGURE 2.40 Enter Criteria and Add Sort Order

a. Click the **HOME tab** and click **View** in the Views group to view the Accounts from Campus Branch query in Design view.

   You have created the Campus Branch Customers query to view only those accounts at the Campus branch. However, other branches' accounts also display. You need to limit the query results to only the records of interest.

b. Click in the **Criteria row** (fifth row) in the BranchID column and type **B50**.

   B50 is the BranchID for the Campus branch. Access queries are not case sensitive; therefore, b50 and B50 will produce the same results. Access adds quotation marks around text criteria.

c. Click in the **Sort row** (third row) in the AccountID column and select **Ascending**.

d. Click **Run** in the Results group.

   You should see nine records, all from Branch B50, in the query results.

STEP 3 ≫ CHANGE QUERY DATA

When the query results are on the screen, the auditor notices that some of the data are incorrect, and one of the accounts is missing. From your experience with Access, you explain to the auditor that the data can be changed directly in a query rather than switching back to the table. Refer to Figure 2.41 as you complete Step 3.

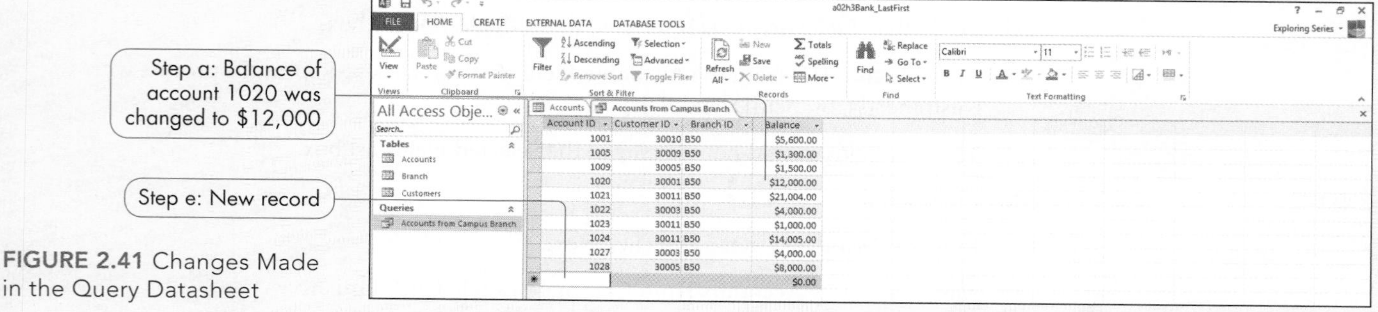

FIGURE 2.41 Changes Made in the Query Datasheet

a. Click on the **Balance field** in the record for account 1020. Change *$1,200* to **$12,000**. Press **Enter**. Save and close the query.

   You are modifying the record directly in the query results.

b. Double-click the **Accounts table** in the Navigation Pane to open it.

   Only one account shows a $12,000 balance. The Account ID is 1020 and the Customer ID is 30001. The change you made in the Accounts table from the Campus Branch query datasheet automatically changed the data stored in the underlying table.

c. Open the Customers table. Find the name of the customer whose CustomerID is 30001. Note that the account belongs to Allison Millward. Close the Customers table.

d. Add a new record to the Accounts table with the following data: **1028** (Account ID), **30005** (Customer ID), **B50** (Branch ID) **8/4/2016** (Open Date) , and $8,000 (Balance). Press **Tab**.

> **TROUBLESHOOTING:** If the Accounts table is not open, double-click Accounts in the Navigation Pane.

   The new record is added to the Accounts table.

e. Double-click the **Accounts from Campus Branch query** in the Navigation Pane.

   Customer 30005 now shows two accounts: one with a balance of $1,500 and one with a balance of $8,000.

f. Close the Accounts from Campus Branch query and close the Accounts table.

g. Keep the database open if you plan to continue with Hands-On Exercise 4. If not, close the database and exit Access.

Multitable Queries

Multitable queries contain two or more tables. They enable you to take advantage of the relationships that have been set in your database. When you need to extract information from a database with a query, most times you will need to pull the data from multiple tables to provide the answers you need. One table may contain the core information that you need, while another table may contain the related data that makes the query relevant to the users.

For example, the sample bank database contains three tables: Customers, Accounts, and Branch. You connected the tables through relationships in order to store data efficiently and enforce consistent data entry. The Accounts table lists the balances of each account at the bank—the key financial information. However, the Accounts table does not list the contact information of the owner of the account. Therefore, the Customers table is needed to provide the additional information.

Creating a Multitable Query

STEP 2»

Creating a multitable query is similar to creating a single-table query; however, choosing the right tables and managing the table relationships will require some additional skills. First, you should only include related tables in a multitable query. ***Related tables*** are tables that are joined in a relationship using a common field. As a rule, related tables should already be established when you create a multitable query. Using Figure 2.42 as a guide, creating a query with the Accounts and Branch tables would be acceptable, as would using Accounts and Customers tables, or Accounts, Branch, and Customers tables. All three scenarios include related tables. Creating a query with the Branch and Customers tables would not be acceptable because these tables are *not* directly related. To create a multitable query, do the following:

1. Click the CREATE tab.
2. Click Query Design in the Queries group.
3. Select the table you need in your query from the Show Table dialog box.
4. Click Add to add the table to the top section of the query design.
5. Select the next table you want to add to the query and click Add. Continue selecting and adding tables to the top section of the query design until all the tables you need display.
6. Drag the fields needed from the tables to the query design grid (or alternatively, double-click the field names); then add criteria and sorting options.
7. Click Run in the Results group to show the results in Datasheet view.

When creating a multitable query, you should only include related tables. As a guide, you can print the Relationship Report in the Tools group on the Relationship Tools Design tab when the Relationships window is open. This report will help you determine which tables are related in your database.

Refer to Figure 2.31 (the top image) showing the results of the query "Which customers from the Campus branch have an account with a balance over $5,000?" To make this report more understandable to others, we can modify the query by adding the Branch Location (in place of the BranchID) and the Customer LastName (in place of the CustomerID). To make these changes, we would need to add the Branch table (which contains the Location field) and the Customers table (which contains the LastName field) to the query design.

Add Additional Tables to a Query

STEP 1

To modify a saved query, open the query in Design view. If you wanted to change the Balance Over $5000 query as discussed earlier, first open the query in Design view. To add additional tables to a query, open the Navigation Pane (if necessary) and drag tables directly into the top portion of the query design grid. For example, the Branch and Customers tables were added to the query, as shown in Figure 2.42. The join lines between tables indicate that relationships were previously set in the Relationships window.

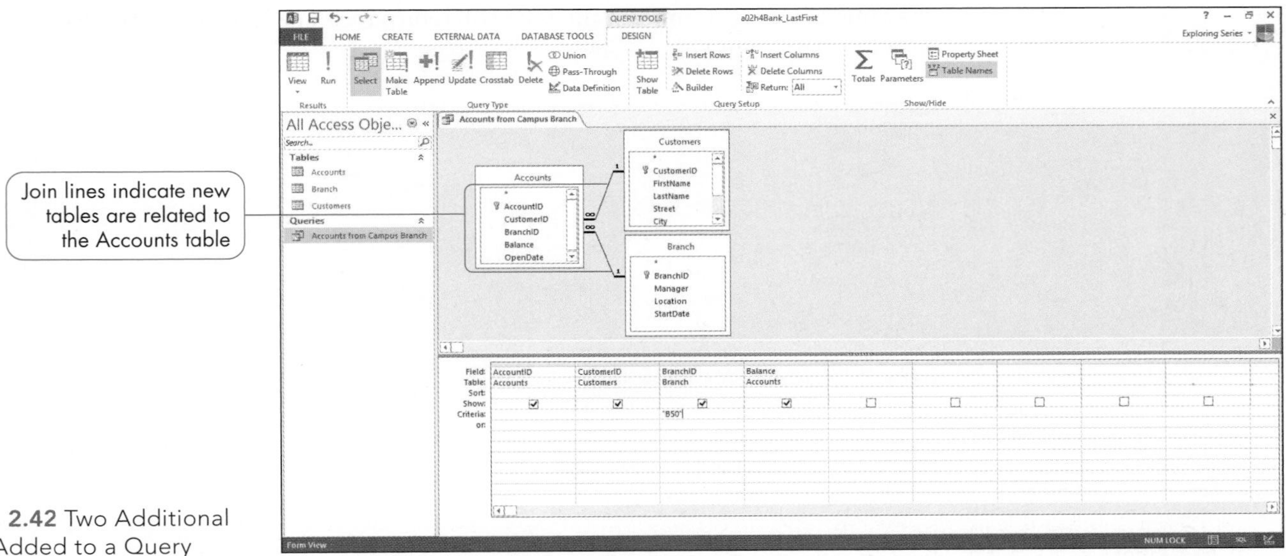

FIGURE 2.42 Two Additional Tables Added to a Query

Modifying a Multitable Query

STEP 3

After creating a multitable query, you may find that you did not include all of the fields you needed, or you may find that you included fields that are unnecessary and complicate the results. You may find that other fields could be included that would make the results more understandable to others. To modify multitable queries, you use the same techniques you learned for single-table queries. Add tables using the Show Table dialog box; remove tables by clicking the unwanted table and pressing Delete. Add fields by double-clicking the field you want; remove fields by clicking the column selector and pressing Delete. Join lines between related tables should display automatically in a query if the relationships were previously established, as shown in Figure 2.42.

TIP Changes in Multitable Queries Do Not Affect Relationships

When you add two or more tables to a query, join lines appear automatically. You can delete the join lines in a query with no impact on the relationships themselves. Deleting a join line only affects the relationships in the individual query. The next time you create a query with the same tables, the join lines will be restored. And, if you open the Relationships window, you will find the join lines intact.

Add and Delete Fields in a Multitable Query

In Figure 2.43, three tables, as well as the join lines between the tables, display in the top pane of the Query Design view. All the fields from each of the tables are now available to be used in the query design grid. Figure 2.43 shows that Location (from the Branch table) replaced BranchID and LastName (from the Customers table) replaced CustomerID to make the results more useful. The BranchID was deleted from the query; therefore, the "B50" criterion was removed as well. "Campus" was added to the Location field's criteria row in order to extract the same results. Because criteria values are not case sensitive, typing "campus" is the same as typing "Campus," and both will return the same results. The results of the revised query are shown in Figure 2.44.

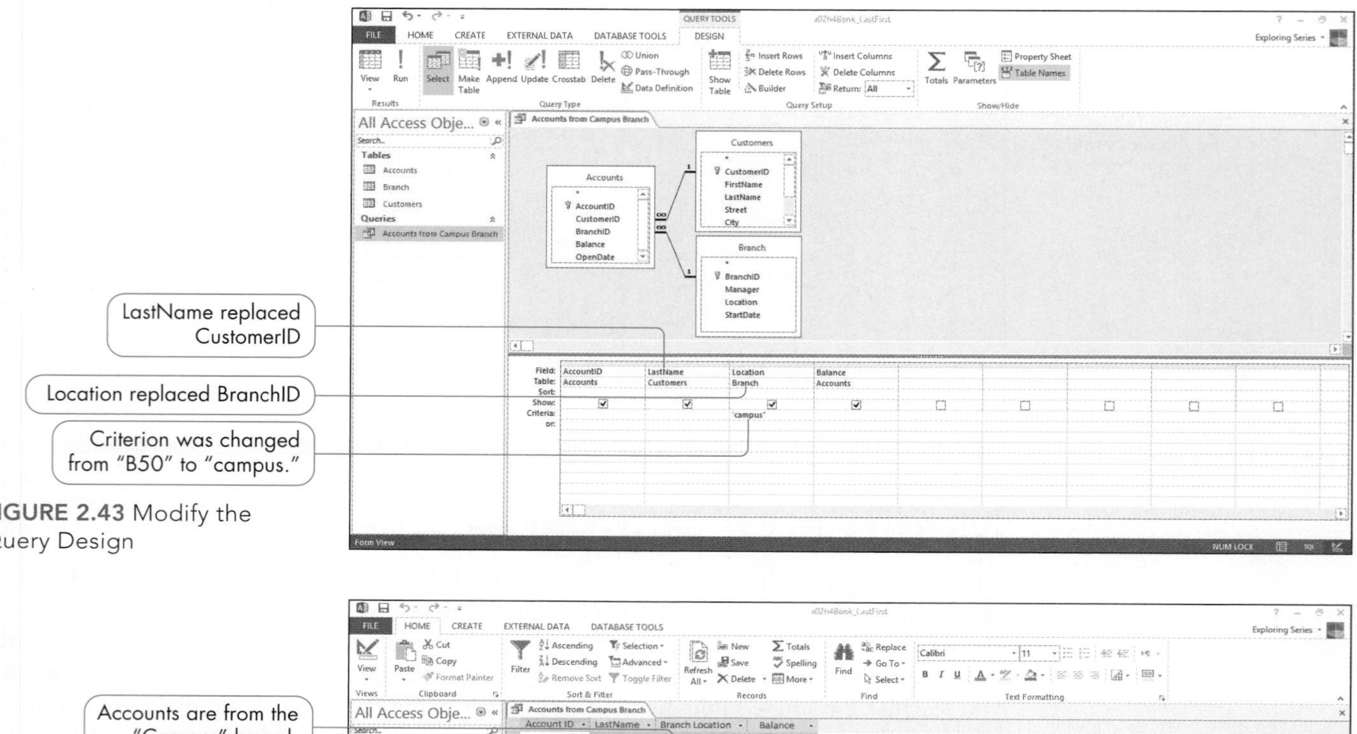

FIGURE 2.43 Modify the Query Design

Accounts are from the "Campus" branch

Account ID	LastName	Branch Location	Balance
1001	Peterson	Campus	$5,600.00
1005	Nunn	Campus	$1,300.00
1009	Wagner	Campus	$1,500.00
1020	Millward	Campus	$12,000.00
1021	YourName	Campus	$21,004.00
1022	Hayes	Campus	$4,000.00
1023	YourName	Campus	$1,000.00
1024	YourName	Campus	$14,005.00
1027	Hayes	Campus	$4,000.00
1028	Wagner	Campus	$8,000.00

FIGURE 2.44 Datasheet View of a Multitable Query

Add Join Lines in a Multitable Query

In Figure 2.45, two tables are added to the query design, but no join line connects them. The results of the query will be unpredictable and will display more records than expected. The Customers table contains 11 records, and the Branch table contains 5 records. Because Access does not know how to interpret the unrelated tables, the results will show 55 records—every possible combination of customer and branch (11 × 5). See Figure 2.46.

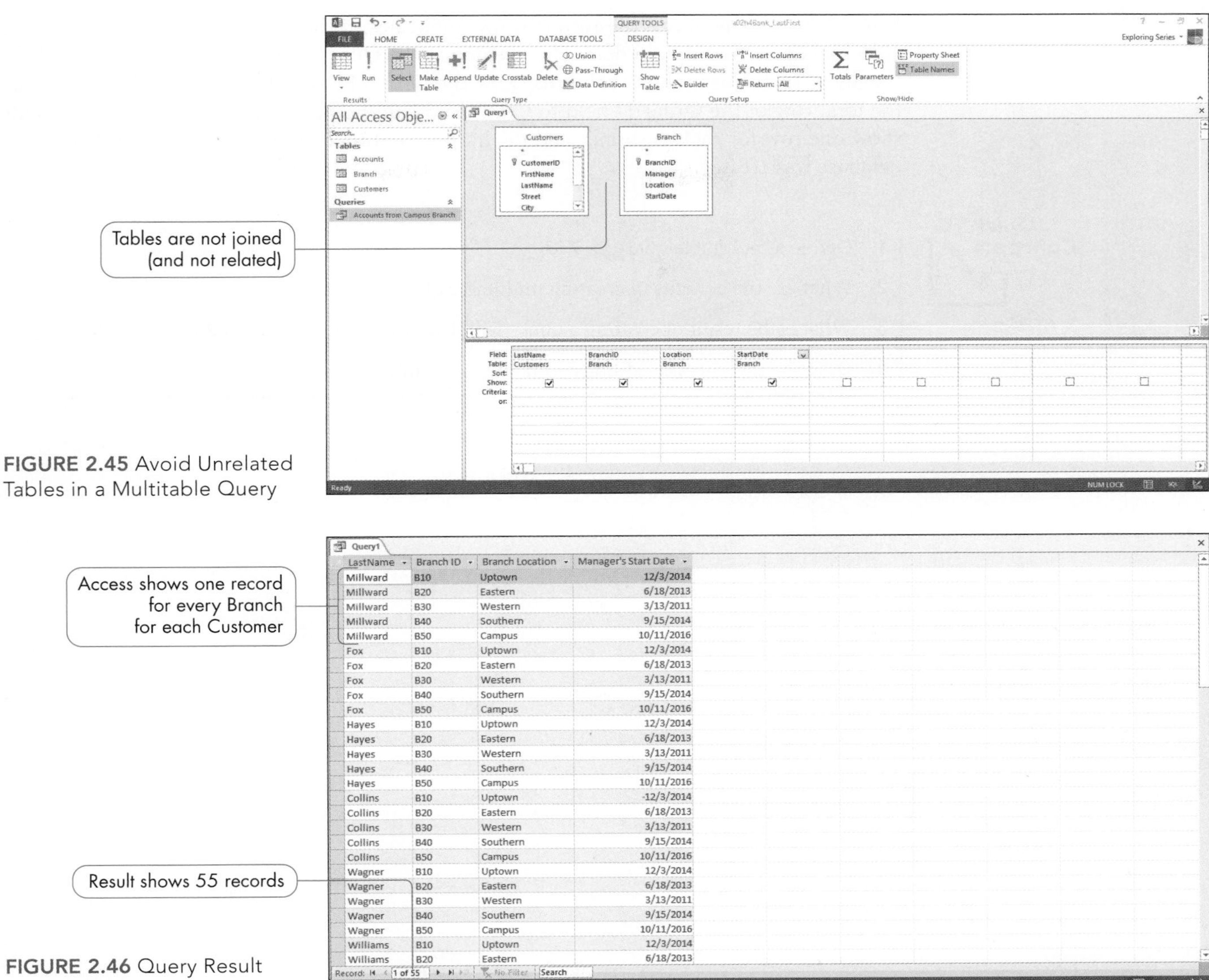

FIGURE 2.45 Avoid Unrelated Tables in a Multitable Query

FIGURE 2.46 Query Result with Unrelated Tables

To fix this problem, you can create join lines using the existing tables if the tables facilitate this by having common fields. In a situation like this, in which there are no common fields, you must add an additional table that will provide a join between all three tables. In the Branch query, you can add the Accounts table, which will facilitate a join between the two existing tables, Customers and Branch. As soon as the third table is added to the query design, the join lines appear automatically, as shown in Figure 2.43.

Over time, your database will grow, and additional tables will be added. Occasionally, new tables are added to the database but not added to the Relationships window. When queries are created with the new tables, join lines will not be established. When this happens, add join lines to the new tables. Or you can create temporary join lines in the query design. These join lines will provide a temporary relationship between two tables and enable Access to interpret the query properly.

Get Answers Using a Multitable Query

STEP 4»

You can get key information from your database using a multitable query. For example, if you want to know how many orders each customer placed since the database was created, you would create a new query and add the Customers and Orders tables to the Query Design view. After you verify that the join lines are correct, you add the CustomerID field from the Customers table and the OrderID field from the Order table to the query design grid.

When you run the query, the results show duplicates in the CustomerID column because customers place multiple orders. Then return to the Query Design view and click Totals in the Show/Hide group. Both columns show the Group By option in the Total row. Change the total row of the OrderID field to Count and run the query again. This time the results show one row for each customer and the number of orders each customer placed since the database was created.

1. Define a multitable query. ***p. 718***
2. What are the benefits of creating multitable queries? ***p. 718***
3. What is the result of creating a query with two unrelated tables? ***p. 720***
4. Describe the purpose adding a join line in a multitable query. ***p. 721***

Hands-On Exercises

4 Multitable Queries

Based on the auditor's request, you will need to evaluate the data further. This requires creating queries that are based on multiple tables rather than on a single table. You decide to open an existing query, add additional tables, and then save the query with a new name.

Skills covered: Add Additional Tables to a Query • Create a Multitable Query • Modify a Multitable Query • Get Answers Using a Multitable Query

STEP 1 » ADD ADDITIONAL TABLES TO A QUERY

The previous query was based on the Accounts table, but now you need to add information to the query that is in the Branch and Customers tables. You will need to add the Branch and Customers tables to the query. Refer to Figure 2.47 as you complete Step 1.

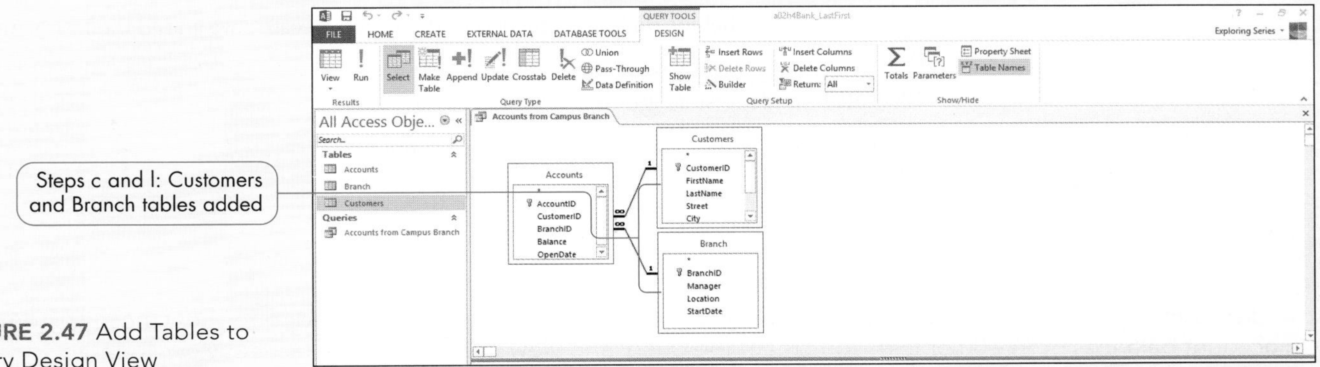

FIGURE 2.47 Add Tables to Query Design View

a. Open *a02h3Bank_LastFirst* if you closed it at the end of Hands-On Exercise 3. Save the database as **a02h4Bank_LastFirst**, changing *h3* to *h4*.

b. Right-click the **Accounts from Campus Branch query** in the Navigation Pane and select **Design View** from the shortcut menu.

c. Drag the **Branch table** from the Navigation Pane to the top pane of the query design grid next to the Accounts table.

   A join line connects the Branch table to the Accounts table. The query inherits the join lines from the relationships created in the Relationships window.

d. Drag the **Location field** from the Branch table to the first empty column in the design grid.

   The Location field should be positioned to the right of the Balance column.

e. Click the **Show check box** under the BranchID field to clear the check box and hide this field in the results.

   The BranchID field is no longer needed because the Location field provides the same information. Because you unchecked the BranchID show check box, the BranchID field will not display the next time the query is opened.

f. Delete the B50 criterion in the BranchID field.

g. Type **Campus** as a criterion in the Location field and press **Enter**.

   Access adds quotation marks around *Campus* for you; quotes are required for text criteria. You are substituting the Location criterion *(Campus)* in place of the BranchID criterion (B50).

h. Remove Ascending from the AccountID sort row. Click in the **Sort row** of the Balance field. Click the arrow and select **Descending**.

i. Click **Run** in the Results group.

   The BranchID field does not display in the Datasheet view because you hid the field in step e. Only Campus accounts should display in the datasheet (10 records). Next, you will add the Customer LastName and delete the CustomerID from the query.

j. Save the changes to the query design.

k. Click **View** in the Views group to return to the Design view.

   The BranchID field no longer displays on the field as it has been hidden.

l. Drag the **Customers table** from the Navigation Pane to the top section of the query design grid and reposition the tables so that the join lines are not blocked (see Figure 2.47).

   The one-to-many relationship lines automatically connect the Customers table to the Accounts table (similar to step c above)

m. Drag the **LastName field** in the Customers table to the second column in the design grid.

   The LastName field should be positioned to the right of the AccountID field.

n. Click the column selector in the CustomerID field to select it. Press **Delete**.

   The CustomerID field is no longer needed in the results because we added the LastName field.

o. Click **Run** in the Results group.

   The last names of the customers now display in the results.

p. Save and close the query.

STEP 2 » CREATE A MULTITABLE QUERY

After discussing the query results with the auditor, you realize that another query is needed to show those customers with account balances of $1,000 or less. You create the query and view the results in Datasheet view. Refer to Figure 2.48 as you complete Step 2.

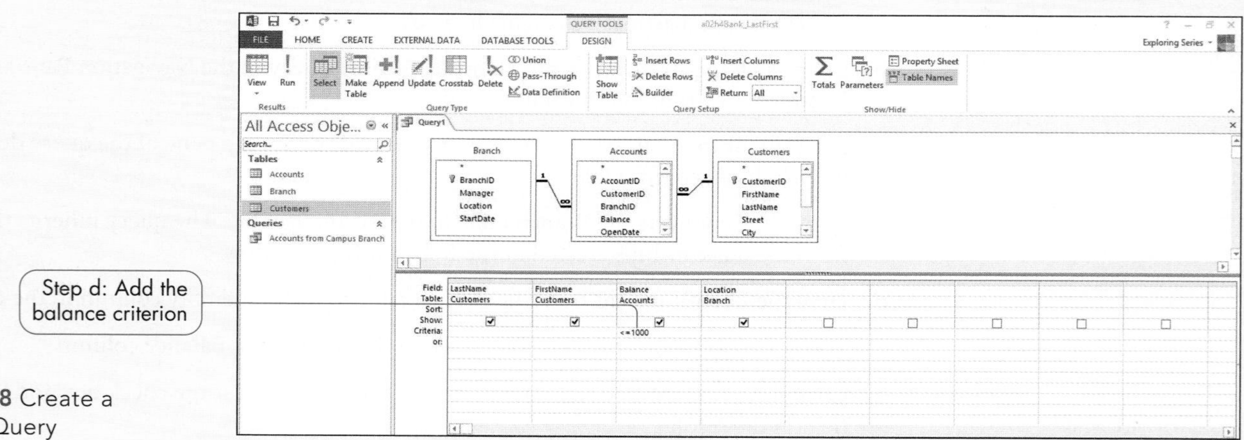

FIGURE 2.48 Create a Multitable Query

a. Click the **CREATE tab** and click **Query Design** in the Queries group.

b. Double-click the **Branch table name** in the Show Table dialog box and double-click **Accounts** and **Customers** to add all three to the Query Design view. Click **Close** in the Show Table dialog box.

   Three tables were added to the query.

c. Double-click the following fields to add them to the design grid: **LastName**, **FirstName**, **Balance**, and **Location**.

d. Type **<=1000** in the **Criteria row** of the Balance column.

e. Click **Run** in the Results group to see the query results.

Six records that have a balance of $1,000 or less display.

f. Click **Save** on the Quick Access Toolbar and type **Balance 1000 or Less** as the Query Name in the **Save As dialog box**. Click **OK**.

STEP 3 ›› MODIFY A MULTITABLE QUERY

The auditor requests additional changes to the Balance 1000 or Less query you just created. You will modify the criteria to display the accounts that were opened after January 1, 2011, with balances of $2,000 or less. Refer to Figure 2.49 as you complete Step 3.

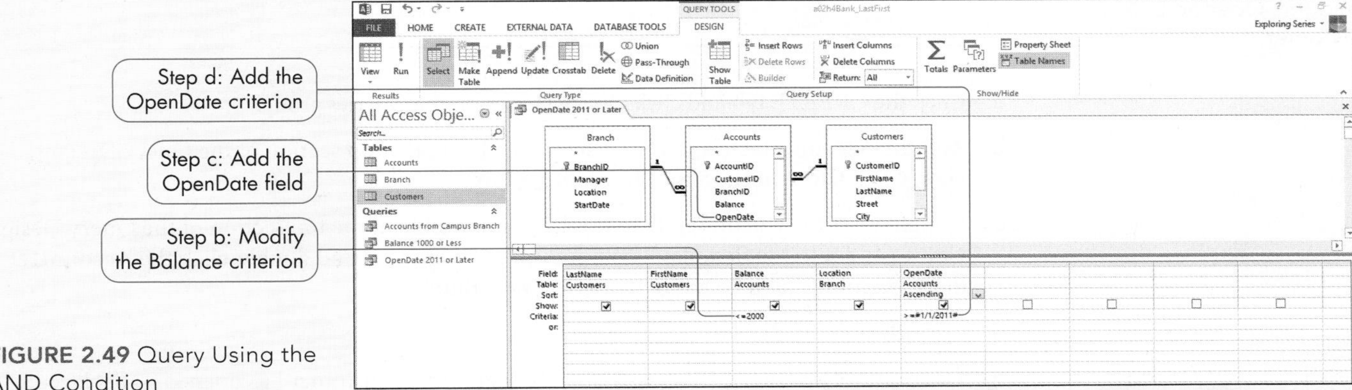

FIGURE 2.49 Query Using the AND Condition

a. Click **View** in the Views group to switch the *Balance 1000 or Less* query to Design view.

b. Type **<=2000** in place of *<=1000* in the **Criteria row** of the Balance field.

c. Double-click the **OpenDate field** in the Accounts table in the top section of the Query Design view to add it to the first blank column in the design grid.

d. Type **>=1/1/2011** in the **Criteria row** of the OpenDate field to extract only accounts that have been opened since January 2011.

After you type the expression and then move to a different column, Access will add the # symbols around the date automatically.

e. Click **Run** in the Results group to display the results of the query.

Five records display in the query results.

f. Click the **FILE tab**, click **Save As**, click **Save Object As**, and then click **Save As**. Type **OpenDate 2011 or Later** as the query name. Click **OK**.

g. Click **View** in the Views group to return to the Design view of the query.

h. Click in the **Sort row** of the OpenDate field and select **Ascending**.

i. Click **Run** in the Results group.

The records are sorted from the earliest open date after January 1, 2011, to the most recent open date.

j. Save and close the query.

STEP 4 » GET ANSWERS USING A MULTITABLE QUERY

The auditor wants to know the number of accounts each customer has opened. You create a query using a Totals row to obtain these data. Refer to Figure 2.50 as you complete Step 4.

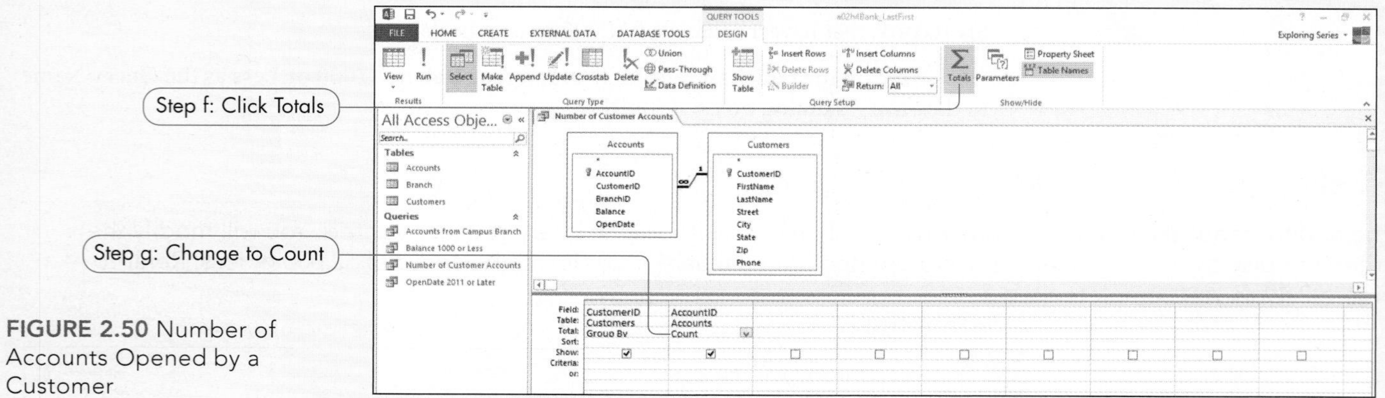

FIGURE 2.50 Number of Accounts Opened by a Customer

a. Click the **CREATE tab** and click **Query Design** in the Queries group.

b. Add the Accounts table and the Customers table to the top section of the Query Design view. Click **Close** in the Show Table dialog box.

c. Double-click the **CustomerID** in the Customers table in the top section of the Query Design view to add it to the first blank column in the design grid and double-click the **AccountID** in the Accounts table to add it to the second column.

d. Click **Run** in the Results group.

   The results show there are 28 records. Every account a customer has opened is displayed. The auditor only wants the total number of accounts a customer has, so you need to modify the query.

e. Click **View** in the Views group to return to the Design view of the query.

f. Click **Totals** in the Show/Hide group.

   Both columns show the Group By option in the Total row.

g. Click **Group By** in the Total row of the AccountID field and select **Count**.

h. Click **Run** in the Results group.

   The results show one row for each customer and the number of accounts each customer has opened since the database was created.

i. Click **Save** on the Quick Access Toolbar and type **Number of Customer Accounts** as the query name. Close the query.

j. Submit based on your instructor's directions and close Access.

Chapter Objectives Review

After reading this chapter, you have accomplished the following objectives:

1. **Design a table.**
   - Include necessary data: Consider the output requirements when creating table structure. Determine the data required to produce the expected information.
   - Design for now and for the future: When designing a database, try to anticipate the future needs of the system and build in the flexibility to satisfy those demands.
   - Store data in its smallest parts: Store data in its smallest parts to make it more flexible. Storing a full name in a Name field is more limiting than storing a first name in a separate FirstName field and a last name in a separate LastName field.
   - Add calculated fields to a table: A calculated field produces a value from an expression or function that references one or more existing fields. Storing calculated data in a table enables you to add the data easily to queries, forms, and reports without the trouble of an additional calculation.
   - Design to accommodate date arithmetic: Calculated fields are frequently created with numeric data. You can use date arithmetic to subtract one date from another to find out the number of days, months, or years that have lapsed between them. You can also add or subtract a constant from a date.
   - Plan for common fields between tables: Tables are joined in relationships using common fields. Name the common fields with the same name and make sure they have the same data type.

2. **Create and modify tables.**
   - Create tables: Create tables in Datasheet view or Design view. You can also import data from another database or an application such as Excel.
   - Determine data type: Data type properties determine the type of data that can be entered and the operations that can be performed on that data. Access recognizes 12 data types.
   - Establish a primary key: The primary key is the field that uniquely identifies each record in a table.
   - Explore a foreign key: A foreign key is a field in one table that is also the primary key of another table.
   - Work with field properties: Field properties determine how the field looks and behaves. Examples of field properties are the field size property and the caption property.
   - Enter table records in Datasheet view: Datasheet view is used to add, edit, and delete records. Design view is used to create and modify the table structure by enabling you to add and edit fields and set field properties.

3. **Share data.**
   - Import data: You can import data from other applications such as an Excel spreadsheet or import data from another database by using the Import Wizard.
   - Modify an imported table's design and add data: After importing a table, examine the design and make necessary modifications. Modifications may include changing a field name, adding new fields, or deleting unnecessary fields.

4. **Establish table relationships.**
   - Set relationships in the Relationships window: Use Show Table to add tables to the Relationships window. Drag a field name from one table to the corresponding field name in another table to join the tables.
   - Establish referential integrity: Referential integrity enforces rules in a database that are used to preserve relationships between tables when records are changed.
   - Set cascade options: The Cascade Update Related Fields option ensures that when the primary key is modified in a primary table, Access will automatically update all foreign key values in a related table. The Cascade Delete Related Records option ensures that when the primary key is deleted in a primary table, Access will automatically delete all records in related tables that reference the primary key.
   - Establish a one-to-many relationship: A one-to-many relationship is established when the primary key value in the primary table can match many of the foreign key values in the related table. One-to-one and many-to-many are also relationship possibilities, but one-to-many relationships are the most common.

5. **Create a single-table query.**
   - Create a single-table select query: A single-table select query uses fields from one table to display only those records that match certain criteria.
   - Use Query Design view: Use Query Design view to create and modify a query. The top portion of the view contains tables with their respective field names and displays the join lines between tables. The bottom portion, known as the query design grid, contains columns and rows that you use to control the query results.

6. **Specify query criteria for different data types.**
   - Different data types require different syntax: Date fields are enclosed in pound signs (#) and text fields in quotations (""). Numeric and currency fields require no delimiters.
   - Use wildcards: Wildcards are special characters that can represent one or more characters in a text value. A question mark is a wildcard that stands for a single character in the same position as the question mark, while an asterisk is a wildcard that stands for any number of characters in the same position as the asterisk.
   - Use comparison operators in queries: Comparison operators such as equal (=), not equal (<>), greater than (>), less than (<), greater than or equal to (>=), and less than or equal to (<=) signs can be used in the criteria of a query to limit the query results to only those records that meet the criteria.

- Work with null: Access uses the term *null* for a blank field. Null criteria can be used to find missing information.
- Establish AND, OR, and NOT criteria: The AND, OR, and NOT logical operators are used when queries require multiple criteria. The AND logical operator returns only records that meet all criteria. The OR logical operator returns records meeting any of the specified criteria. The NOT logical operator returns all records except the specified criteria.

7. Understand query sort order.

- Query sort order: The query sort order determines the order of records in a query's Datasheet view. You can change the order of records by specifying the sort order in Design view.
- Determining sort order: The sort order is determined from the order of the fields from left to right. Move the field columns to position them in left to right sort order.

8. Run, copy, and modify a Query.

- Run a query: To obtain the results for a query, you must run the query. To run the query, click Run in the Results group when you are in Design view. Another method is to locate the query in the Navigation Pane and double-click it. A similar method is to select the query and press Enter.
- Copy a query: To save time, after specifying tables, fields, and conditions for one query, copy the query, rename it, and then modify the fields and criteria in the second query.

9. Use the Query Wizard.

- Create a query using the Query Wizard: The Query Wizard is an alternative method for creating queries. It enables you to select tables and fields from lists. The last step of the wizard prompts you to save the query.

10. Create a multitable query.

- Creating a multitable query: Multitable queries contain two or more tables enabling you to take advantage of the relationships that have been set in your database.
- Add additional tables to a query: Open the Navigation Pane and drag the tables from the Navigation Pane directly into the top section of the Query Design view.

11. Modify a multitable query.

- Add and delete fields in a multitable query: Multitable queries may need to be modified. Add fields by double-clicking the field name in the table you want; remove fields by clicking the column selector and pressing Delete.
- Add join lines in a multitable query: If the tables have a common field, create join lines by dragging the field name of one common field onto the field name of the other table. Or you can add an additional table that will provide a join between all three tables.
- Get answers using a multitable query: Use the total row options of a field such as Count to get answers.

Key Terms Matching

Match the key terms with their definitions. Write the key term letter by the appropriate numbered definition.

- **a.** AND logical operator
- **b.** AutoNumber
- **c.** CamelCase notation
- **d.** Caption property
- **e.** Cascade Update Related Fields
- **f.** Criteria row
- **g.** Data redundancy
- **h.** Data type
- **i.** Field property
- **j.** Foreign key
- **k.** Multitable query
- **l.** Number data type
- **m.** Null
- **n.** One-to-many relationship
- **o.** OR logical operator
- **p.** Query
- **q.** Referential Integrity
- **r.** Simple Query Wizard
- **s.** Sort row
- **t.** Wildcard

1. _____ A special character that can represent one or more characters in the criterion of a query. **p. 708**
2. _____ A characteristic of a field that determines how a field looks and behaves. **p. 683**
3. _____ Returns only records that meet all criteria. **p. 709**
4. _____ A row in the Query Design view that determines which records will be selected. **p. 706**
5. _____ Determines the type of data that can be entered and the operations that can be performed on that data. **p. 681**
6. _____ Used to create a more readable label that displays in the top row in Datasheet view and in forms and reports. **p. 683**
7. _____ Enables you to ask questions about the data stored in a database. **p. 705**
8. _____ The term *Access* uses to describe a blank field. **p. 709**
9. _____ A data type that is a number that automatically increments each time a record is added. **p. 682**
10. _____ The unnecessary storing of duplicate data in two or more tables. **p. 680**
11. _____ A data type that can store only numerical data. **p. 683**
12. _____ A relationship established when the primary key value in the primary table can match many of the foreign key values in the related table. **p. 697**
13. _____ A field in one table that is also the primary key of another table. **p. 683**
14. _____ An option that directs Access to automatically update all foreign key values in a related table when the primary key value is modified in a primary table. **p. 696**
15. _____ Rules in a database that are used to preserve relationships between tables when records are changed. **p. 696**
16. _____ Uses no spaces in multiword field names, but uses uppercase letters to distinguish the first letter of each new word. **p. 680**
17. _____ A row in the Query Design view that enables you to reorder data in ascending or descending order. **p. 706**
18. _____ Contains two or more tables, enabling you to take advantage of the relationships that have been set in your database. **p. 718**
19. _____ Returns records meeting any of the specified criteria. **p. 709**
20. _____ Provides dialog boxes to guide you through the query design process. **p. 712**

Multiple Choice

1. All of the following are suggested guidelines for table design *except*:
   (a) Include all necessary data.
   (b) Store data in its smallest parts.
   (c) Avoid date arithmetic.
   (d) Link tables using common fields.

2. Which of the following determines the type of data that can be entered and the operations that can be performed on that data?
   (a) Field properties
   (b) Data type
   (c) Caption property
   (d) Normalization

3. When entering, deleting, or editing table data:
   (a) The table must be in Design view.
   (b) The table must be in Datasheet view.
   (c) The table may be in either Datasheet or Design view.
   (d) Data may only be entered in a form.

4. When importing data into Access, which of the following statements is *true*?
   (a) The Import Wizard only works for Excel files.
   (b) The Import Wizard is found on the Create tab.
   (c) You can assign a primary key while you are importing Excel data.
   (d) The wizard will import the data in one step after you select the file.

5. The main reason to enforce referential integrity in Access is to:
   (a) Limit the number of records in a table.
   (b) Make it possible to delete records.
   (c) Keep your database safe from unauthorized users.
   (d) Keep invalid data from being entered into a table.

6. An illustration of a one-to-many relationship would be a:
   (a) Person changes his/her primary address.
   (b) Customer may have multiple orders.
   (c) Bank branch location has an internal BranchID code.
   (d) Balance field is totaled for all accounts for each person.

7. A query's specifications providing instructions about which records to include must be entered on the:
   (a) Table row of the query design grid.
   (b) Show row of the query design grid.
   (c) Sort row of the query design grid.
   (d) Criteria row of the query design grid.

8. When adding Value criteria to the Query Design view, the value you enter must be delimited by:
   (a) Nothing ().
   (b) Pound signs (#).
   (c) Quotes (" ").
   (d) At signs (@).

9. It is more efficient to make a copy of an existing query rather than create a new query when which of the following is *true*?
   (a) The existing query contains only one table.
   (b) The existing query and the new query use the same tables and fields.
   (c) The existing query and the new query have the exact same criteria.
   (d) The original query is no longer being used.

10. Which of the following is *true* for the Query Wizard?
    (a) You can only select tables as a source.
    (b) No criteria can be added.
    (c) Fields from multiple tables are not allowed.
    (d) You do not need a summary.

Practice Exercises

1 Our Corner Bookstore

FROM SCRATCH

Tom and Erin Mullaney own and operate a bookstore in Philadelphia, Pennsylvania. Erin asked you to help her create an Access database because of your experience in this class. You believe that you can help her by creating a database and importing the Excel spreadsheets they use to store the publishers and the books that they sell. You determine that a third table—for authors—is also required. Your task is to design and populate the three tables, set the table relationships, and enforce referential integrity. If you have problems, reread the detailed directions presented in the chapter. This exercise follows the same set of skills as used in Hands-On Exercises 1 and 2 in the chapter. Refer to Figure 2.51 as you complete this exercise.

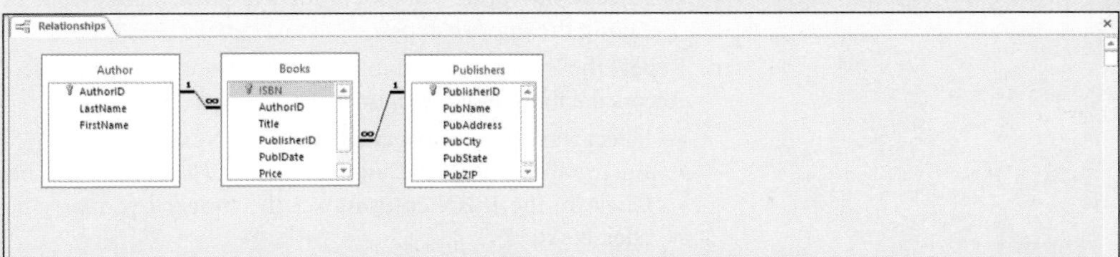

FIGURE 2.51 Books Relationships Window

a. Open Access and click **Blank desktop database**. Type **a02p1Books_LastFirst** in the **File Name box**. Click **Browse** to locate your student data files folder in the File New Database dialog box, click **OK** to close the dialog box, and then click **Create** to create the new database.

b. Type **11** in the **Click to Add column** and click **Click to Add**. The field name becomes *Field1*, and *Click to Add* now appears as the third column. Click in the third column, type **Benchloss**, and then press **Tab**. The process repeats for the fourth column; type **Michael R.** and press **Tab** twice.

c. The cursor returns to the first column where *(New)* is selected. Press **Tab**. Type the rest of the data using the following table. These data will become the records of the Author table.

ID	Field1	Field2	Field3
1	11	Brenchloss	Michael R.
(New)	12	Turow	Scott
	13	Rice	Anne
	14	King	Stephen
	15	Connelly	Michael
	16	Rice	Luanne
	17	*your last name*	*your first name*

d. Click **Save** on the Quick Access Toolbar. Type **Author** in the **Save As dialog box** and click **OK**.

e. Click **View** in the Views group to switch to the Design view of the Author table.

f. Select **Field1**—in the second row—in the top portion of the table design and type **AuthorID** to rename the field. In the *Field Properties* section in the lower portion of the table design, type **Author ID** in the **Caption property box** and verify that *Long Integer* displays for the Field Size property.

g. Select **Field2** and type **LastName** to rename the field. In the *Field Properties* section in the bottom portion of the Design view, type **Author's Last Name** in the **Caption property box** and type **20** as the field size.

h. Select **Field3** and type **FirstName** to rename the field. In the *Field Properties* section in the bottom portion of the table design, type **Author's First Name** as the caption and type **15** as the field size.

i. Click the **ID field row selector** (which shows the primary key) to select the row and click **Delete Rows** in the Tools group. Click **Yes** twice to confirm both messages.

j. Click the **AuthorID row selector** and click **Primary Key** in the Tools group to reset the primary key.

k. Click **Save** on the Quick Access Toolbar to save the design changes. Click **Yes** to the *Some data may be lost* message. Close the table.

l. Click the **EXTERNAL DATA tab** and click **Excel** in the Import & Link group to launch the Get External Data – Excel Spreadsheet feature. Verify the *Import the source data into a new table in the current database* option is selected, click **Browse**, and then go to the student data folder. Select the *a02p1Books* workbook, click **Open**, and then click **OK**. This workbook contains two worksheets. Follow these steps:

- Select the **Publishers worksheet** and click **Next**.
- Click the **First Row Contains Column Headings check box** and click **Next**.
- Select the **PubID field**, click the **Indexed arrow**, select **Yes (No Duplicates)**, and then click **Next**.
- Click the **Choose my own primary key arrow**, select **PubID**, if necessary, and then click **Next**.
- Accept the name *Publishers* for the table name, click **Finish**, and then click **Close** without saving the import steps.

m. Repeat the Import Wizard to import the Books worksheet from the *a02p1Books* workbook into the Access database. Follow these steps:

- Select the **Books worksheet** and click **Next**.
- Ensure the *First Row Contains Column Headings* check box is checked and click **Next**.
- Click on the **ISBN column**, set the Indexed property box to **Yes (No Duplicates)**, and then click **Next**.
- Click the **Choose my own primary key arrow**, select **ISBN** as the primary key field, and then click **Next**.
- Accept the name *Books* as the table name. Click **Finish** and click **Close** without saving the import steps.

n. Right-click the **Books table** in the Navigation Pane and select **Design View**. Make the following changes:

- Change the PubID field name to **PublisherID**.
- Change the Caption property to **Publisher ID.**
- Change the PublisherID Field Size property to **2**.
- Click the **ISBN field** and change the Field Size property to **13**.
- Change the AuthorCode field name to **AuthorID**.
- Change the AuthorID Field Size property to **Long Integer**.
- Click the **ISBN field row selector** (which shows the primary key) to select the row. Drag the row up to the first position.
- Click **Save** on the Quick Access Toolbar to save the design changes to the Books table. Click **Yes** to the *Some data may be lost* warning.
- Close the table.

o. Right-click the **Publishers table** in the Navigation Pane and select **Design View**. Make the following changes:

- Change the PubID field name to **PublisherID**.
- Change the PublisherID Field Size property to **2**.
- Change the Caption property to **Publisher's ID**.
- Change the Field Size property to **50** for the PubName and PubAddress fields.
- Change the Pub Address field name to **PubAddress** (remove the space).
- Change the PubCity Field Size property to **30**.
- Change the PubState Field Size property to **2**.
- Change the Pub ZIP field name to **PubZIP** (remove the space).
- Click **Save** on the Quick Access Toolbar to save the design changes to the Publishers table. Click **Yes** to the *Some data may be lost* warning. Close all open tables.

p. Click the **DATABASE TOOLS tab** and click **Relationships** in the Relationships group. Click **Show Table** if necessary. Follow these steps:

- Double-click each table name in the Show Table dialog box to add it to the Relationships window and close the Show Table dialog box.
- Drag the **AuthorID field** from the Author table onto the AuthorID field in the Books table.

- Click the **Enforce Referential Integrity** and **Cascade Update Related Fields check boxes** in the Edit Relationships dialog box. Click **Create** to create a one-to-many relationship between the Author and Books tables.
- Drag the **PublisherID field** from the Publishers table onto the PublisherID field in the Books table.
- Click the **Enforce Referential Integrity** and **Cascade Update Related Fields check boxes** in the Edit Relationships dialog box. Click **Create** to create a one-to-many relationship between the Publishers and Books tables.
- Click **Save** on the Quick Access Toolbar to save the changes to the Relationships window and click **Close**.

q. Click the **FILE tab** and click **Close** to exit Access.
r. Submit based on your instructor's directions.

2 Morgan Insurance Company

The Morgan Insurance Company offers a full range of insurance services in four locations: Miami, Boston, Chicago, and Philadelphia. They store all of the firm's employee data in an Excel spreadsheet. This file contains employee name and address, job performance, salary, and title. The firm is converting from Excel to Access. A database file containing two of the tables already exists; your job is to import the employee data from Excel for the third table. Once imported, you need to modify field properties and set new relationships. The owner of the company, Victor Reed, is concerned that some of the Atlanta and Boston salaries may be below the guidelines published by the national office. He asks that you investigate the salaries of the two offices and create a separate query for each city. If you have problems, reread the detailed directions presented in the chapter. This exercise follows the same set of skills as used in Hands-On Exercises 2–4 in the chapter. Refer to Figure 2.52 as you complete this exercise.

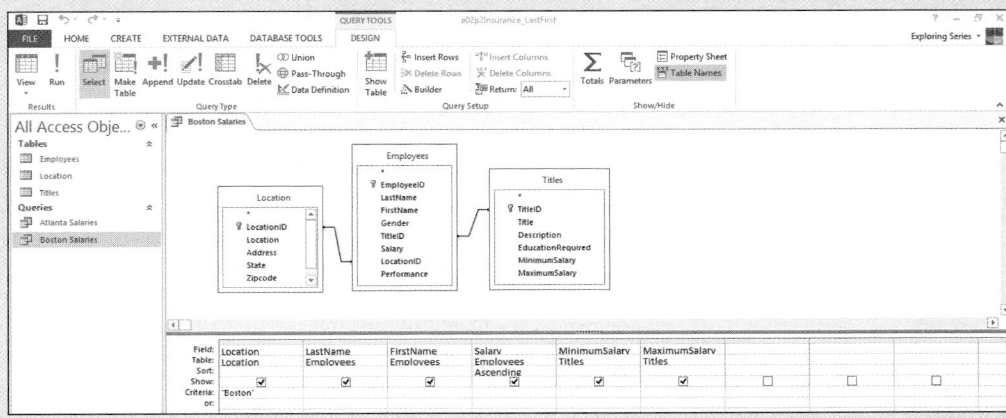

FIGURE 2.52 Boston Salaries Query Design

a. Open *a02p2Insurance*. Click the **FILE tab**, click **Save As**, and then click **Save As** again to save the database as **a02p2Insurance_LastFirst**. Double-click the **Location table** and look at the contents to become familiar with the field names and the type of information stored in the table. Repeat with the Titles table.

b. Click the **EXTERNAL DATA tab**, click **Excel** in the Import & Link group, and then do the following:
- Click **Browse** and locate the *a02p2Employees* workbook in your student data files location. Select the file, click **Open**, and then click **OK**.
- Select the **Employees worksheet**, if necessary, and click **Next**.
- Click the **First Row Contains Column Headings check box** and click **Next**.
- Click the **Indexed arrow** for the EmployeeID field, select **Yes (No Duplicates)**, and then click **Next**.

- Click **Choose my own primary key arrow**, select the **EmployeeID** as the primary key, and then click **Next**.
- Accept the name *Employees* for the table name, click **Finish**, and then click **Close** without saving the import steps.

c. Double-click the **Employees table** in the Navigation Pane, click the **HOME tab**, and then click **View** in the Views group to switch to the Design view of the Employees table. Make the following changes:

- Click the **LastName field** and change the Field Size property to **20**.
- Change the Caption property to **Last Name**.
- Click the **FirstName field** and change the Field Size property to **20**.
- Change the Caption property to **First Name**.
- Click the **LocationID field** and change the Field Size property to **3**.
- Change the Caption property to **Location ID**.
- Click the **TitleID field** and change the Field Size property to **3**.
- Change the Caption property to **Title ID**.
- Change the Salary field data type to **Currency** and change *General Number* in the Format property in field properties to **Currency**.
- Save the design changes. Click **Yes** to the *Some data may be lost* warning.

d. Click **View** in the Views group to view the Employees table in Datasheet view and examine the data. Click any record in the Title ID and click **Ascending** in the Sort & Filter group on the HOME tab. Multiple employees are associated with the T01, T02, T03, and T04 titles.

e. Double-click the **Titles table** in the Navigation Pane to open it in Datasheet view. Notice the T04 title is not in the list.

f. Add a new record in the first blank record at the bottom of the Titles table. Use the following data:

- Type **T04** in the **TitleID field**.
- Type **Senior Account Rep** in the **Title field**.
- Type **A marketing position requiring a technical background and at least three years of experience** in the **Description field**.
- Type **Four-year degree** in the **Education Requirements field**.
- Type **45000** in the **Minimum Salary field**.
- Type **75000** in the **Maximum Salary field**.

g. Close all tables. Click **Yes** if you are asked to save changes to the Employees table.

h. Click the **DATABASE TOOLS tab** and click **Relationships** in the Relationships group. Click **Show Table** if necessary. Follow these steps:

- Double-click each table name in the Show Table dialog box to add them to the Relationships window and close the Show Table dialog box.
- Adjust the height of the tables so that all fields display.
- Drag the **LocationID field** in the Location table onto the LocationID field in the Employees table.
- Click the **Enforce Referential Integrity** and **Cascade Update Related Fields check boxes** in the Edit Relationships dialog box. Click **Create** to create a one-to-many relationship between the Location and Employees tables.
- Drag the **TitleID field** in the Titles table onto the TitleID field in the Employees table.
- Click the **Enforce Referential Integrity** and **Cascade Update Related Fields check boxes** in the Edit Relationships dialog box. Click **Create** to create a one-to-many relationship between the Titles and Employees tables.
- Click **Save** on the Quick Access Toolbar to save the changes to the Relationships window and close the Relationships window.

i. Click the **CREATE tab** and click the **Query Wizard** in the Queries group. Follow these steps:

- Select **Simple Query Wizard** and click **OK**.
- Select **Table: Employees** in the Tables/Queries box, if necessary.
- Double-click **LastName** in the **Available Fields list** to move it to the Selected Fields list.
- Double-click **FirstName** in the **Available Fields list** to move it to the Selected Fields list.

- Double-click **LocationID** in the **Available Fields list** to move it to the Selected Fields list.
- Click **Next**.
- Select the **Detail (shows every field of every record) option**, if necessary, and click **Next**.
- Type **Employees Location** as the query title and click **Finish**.

j. Click the **CREATE tab** and click the **Query Wizard** in the Queries group. Follow these steps:

- Select **Simple Query Wizard** and click **OK**.
- Select **Table: Location** in the Tables/Queries box.
- Double-click **Location** in the **Available Fields list** to move it to the Selected Fields list.
- Select **Table: Employees** in the Tables/Queries box.
- Double-click **LastName**, **FirstName**, and **Salary**.
- Select **Table: Titles** in the Tables/Queries box.
- Double-click **MinimumSalary** and **MaximumSalary**. Click **Next**.
- Select the **Detail (shows every field of every record) option**, if necessary, and click **Next**.
- Type **Atlanta Salaries** as the query title and click **Finish**.

k. Click the **HOME tab** and click **View** to switch to the Design view of the Atlanta Salaries Query. In the Criteria row of the Location field, type **Atlanta**. Click in the **Sort row** in the Salary field and select **Ascending**. Click **Run** in the Results group on the DESIGN tab. Visually inspect the data to see if any of the Atlanta employees have a salary less than the minimum or greater than the maximum when compared to the published salary range. These salaries will need to be updated later. Save and close the query.

l. Right-click on the **Atlanta Salaries query** in the Navigation Pane and select **Copy**. Right-click a blank area in the Navigation Pane and select **Paste**. In the Paste As dialog box, type **Boston Salaries** for the query name. Click **OK**.

m. Right-click on the **Boston Salaries query** in the Navigation Pane and select **Design View**. In the Criteria row of the Location field, replace *Atlanta* with **Boston**. Click **Run** in the Results group on the DESIGN tab. Visually inspect the data to see if any of the Boston employees have a salary less than the minimum or greater than the maximum when compared to the published salary range. Save and close the query.

n. Click the **FILE tab** and click **Close** to exit Access.

o. Submit based on your instructor's directions.

Mid-Level Exercises

1 My Game Collection

ANALYSIS CASE 

Over the years, you have collected quite a few video games, so you cataloged them in an Access database. After opening the database, you create two tables—one to identify the game system that plays your game and the other to identify the category or genre of the game. Then, you will join each table in a relationship so that you can query the database. Refer to Figure 2.53 as you complete this exercise.

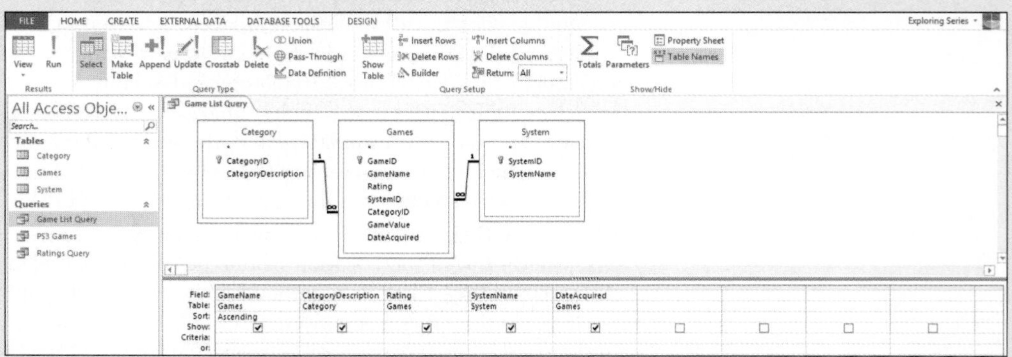

FIGURE 2.53 Game List Query

a. Open *a02m1Games* and save the database as **a02m1Games_LastFirst**. Open the *Games* table and review the fields containing the game information.

b. Click the **CREATE tab** and click **Table Design** in the Tables group. To save time, you opened Table Design to create the fields for a new table rather than creating a table and switching to Design View.

c. Type **SystemID** for the first Field Name and select **Number** as the Data Type.

d. Type **SystemName** for the second Field Name and accept **Short Text** as the Data Type.

e. Change to Design view. Delete the ID row. Make **SystemID** the primary key and change the Data Type to **AutoNumber**. Add the caption **System ID**.

f. Change the SystemName Field Size property to **15**. Add the caption **System Name**, making sure there is a space between System and Name. Save the table as **System**, saving the changes to the table design. Switch to Datasheet view.

g. Add the system names to the System table as shown below, letting Access use AutoNumber to create the SystemID field. Close the table.

System ID	System Name
1	XBOX 360
2	PS3
3	Wii
4	NES
5	PC Game
6	Nintendo 3DS

h. Click the **CREATE tab** and click **Table Design** in the Tables group. Delete the existing ID row. Type **CategoryID** for the first Field Name and select **AutoNumber** as the Data Type. Set the CategoryID as the **Primary Key**.

i. Type **CategoryDescription** for the second Field Name and accept **Short Text** as the Data Type. Change the Field Size property to **25**. Add the caption **Category Description**, making sure there

j. Add the category descriptions to the Category table as shown below, letting Access use AutoNumber to create the CategoryID field. Close the table.

CategoryID	Category Description
1	Action
2	Adventure
3	Arcade
4	Racing
5	Rhythm
6	Role-playing
7	Simulation
8	Sports

k. Click the **DATABASE TOOLS tab** and click **Relationships** in the Relationships group. Add all three tables to the Relationships window and close the Show Table dialog box. Create a one-to-many relationship between CategoryID in the Category table and CategoryID in the Games table. Enforce referential integrity and cascade update related fields.

l. Create a one-to-many relationship between SystemID in the System table and SystemID in the Games table. Enforce referential integrity and cascade update related fields. Close the Relationships window, saving changes.

m. Use the Query Wizard to create a simple query using the Games table. Use the following fields in the query: GameName, Rating. Save the query using the title **Ratings Query**.

n. Switch to Query Design view. Sort the rating field in ascending order and run the query. Close the query, saving the changes to the design of the Ratings Query.

o. Create a multitable query in Design view using all three tables. Use the following fields: GameName, CategoryDescription, Rating, SystemName, and DateAcquired.

p. Sort the query in Ascending order by GameName and run the query. Save the query as **Game List Query** and close the query.

q. Copy the **Game List Query** and paste it in the Navigation Pane using the name **PS3 Games**. Modify the query in Design view by using **PS3** as the criteria for SystemName. Remove the sort by GameName and sort in ascending order by CategoryDescription. The query results should include 7 records.

r. Close the PS3 Games query, saving the changes to the design.

s. Assume you are going home for Thanksgiving and you want to take your Wii gaming system and games home with you—but you only want to take home games with a rating of Everyone. Create a query named **Thanksgiving Games** that shows the name of the game, its rating, the category description of the games, and the system name. The results of the query will tell you which games to pack.

t. Submit based on your instructor's directions.

2 The Prestige Hotel

The Prestige Hotel chain caters to upscale business travelers and provides state-of-the-art conference, meeting, and reception facilities. It prides itself on its international, four-star cuisine. Last year, it began a member reward club to help the marketing department track the purchasing patterns of its most loyal customers. All of the hotel transactions are stored in the database. Your task is to help the managers of the Prestige Hotel in Denver and Chicago identify their customers who stayed in a room last year and who had three persons in their party. Refer to Figure 2.54 as you complete this exercise.

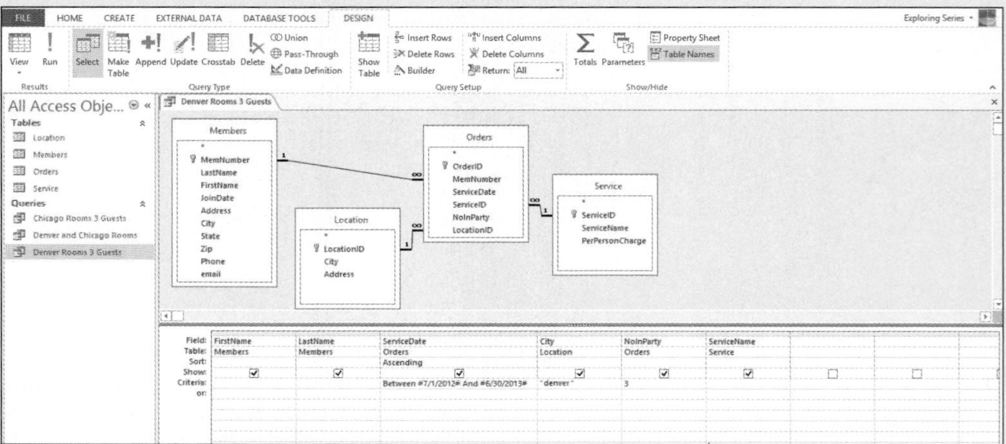

FIGURE 2.54 Denver Rooms 3 Guests Query

a. Open *a02m2Hotel* and save the file as **a02m2Hotel_LastFirst**. Review the data contained in the three tables. Specifically, look for the tables and fields containing the information you need: dates of stays in Denver suites, the members' names, and the numbers in the parties.

b. Import the location data from the Excel file *a02m2Location* into your database as a new table. The first row does contain column headings. Set the LocationID Indexed property to **Yes (No Duplicates)** and set the Data Type to **Long Integer**. Select the **LocationID field** as the primary key. Name the table **Location**. Do not save the import steps.

c. Open the Relationships window and create a relationship between the Location table and the Orders table using the LocationID field. Enforce referential integrity and select **Cascade Update Related Fields**. Create a relationship between the Orders and Members tables using the MemNumber field, ensuring that you enforce referential integrity and cascade update related fields. Create a relationship between the Orders and Service tables using the ServiceID field, ensuring that you enforce referential integrity and cascade update related fields. Save and close the Relationships window.

d. Open the Members table and find Bryan Gray's name. Replace his name with your own first and last names. Use Find to locate Nicole Lee's name and replace it with your name. Close the table.

DISCOVER

e. Create a query using the following fields: ServiceDate (Orders table), City (Location table), NoInParty (Orders table), ServiceName (Service table), FirstName (Members table), and LastName (Members table). Set the criteria to limit the output to **Denver**. Use the Between command to only show services from **7/1/2012** to **6/30/2013**. Set the Number in Party criterion to **3**. Sort the results in ascending order by the Service Date. Compare your query to Figure 2.54.

f. Run the query and examine the number of records in the status bar at the bottom of the query. It should display *154*. If your number of records is different, examine the criteria.

g. Change the order of the query fields so that they display as FirstName, LastName, ServiceDate, City, NoInParty, and ServiceName.

h. Save the query as **Denver Rooms 3 Guests**. Close the query and copy and paste it, renaming the new query **Chicago Rooms 3 Guests**; one of your colleagues in Chicago asked for your help in analyzing the guest data.

i. Open the Chicago Rooms 3 Guests query in Design view and change the criterion for Denver to **Chicago**. Run and save the changes. You should have 179 results.

DISCOVER

j. Combine the two previous queries into a third query named **Denver and Chicago Rooms 3 Guests**. Use the criteria from the two individual queries to create a combination AND–OR condition. The records in the combined query should equal the sum of the records in the two individual queries (333 records).

k. Submit based on your instructor's directions.

3 Used Cell Phones for Sale

COLLABORATION CASE 

ANALYSIS CASE 

You and a few of your classmates started a new business selling used cell phones, MP3 players, and accessories. You have been using an Access database to track your inventory. You decide to improve the data entry process by adding three additional tables. After the new tables are added and the relationships set, you will create several queries to analyze the data. In order to collaborate with the other members of your group, you will post an Access database and two Excel files to a OneDrive folder. At the completion of this exercise, each person will submit his or her own Word document containing the answers to the questions below.

a. Open the *a02m3Phones* database and save the file as **a02m3Phones_GroupX**. Close the database. (This step will be completed by only one person in your group. Replace *X* with the number assigned to your group by your instructor.) Create a folder on your OneDrive account named **Exploring Access** and share the folder with the other members in your group and the instructor. Upload the database to this new folder and notify the other members in your group.

★ b. Download the database from the Exploring Access OneDrive folder created in step a and save it locally as **a02m3Phones_GroupX_LastFirst**. (Everyone in the group will complete this step.) Open the database, open the Inventory table, and than review the records in the table. Take note of the data in the TypeOfDevice column; this field is joined to the DeviceOptions table, and the *enforce referential integrity* option has been set. Only the options in the DeviceOptions table are allowed to be entered. What other fields in this table could be joined to a table in the same way? Type your answer into a Word document named **a02m3Phones_Answers_LastFirst**.

c. Import the data in the *a02m3Carriers* Excel spreadsheet into a new table named **Carriers**. Let Access add a primary key field (ID). Open the table and verify that the data imported correctly. Change the ID field to **CarrierID**. Save and close the Carriers table.

d. Open the Inventory table in Design view and add a new field under the Carrier field named **CarrierID**. Set the Data Type to **Number**. Save and close the table. Open the Relationships window and the Carriers table. Create a relationship between the Carriers table and the Inventory table using the CarrierID field. Enforce referential integrity. Take a screen shot of the Relationships window using the Snipping Tool and paste the image into the Word document you created in step b. Close the Relationships window.

e. Open the Inventory table and the Carriers table. Using the CarrierID field in the Carriers table, enter the correct CarrierID into each record in the Inventory table.

f. Repeat steps c, d, and e for the fields Manufacturer and Color. To do this, one member of the group must create an Excel spreadsheet named **a02m3Manufacturers**, which contains all the manufacturers found in the Inventory table. Another member of the group must create an Excel spreadsheet named **a02m3Colors**, which contains all the colors found in the Inventory table. Both of these Excel spreadsheets must be saved to the Exploring Access folder created in step a so all members can access the data.

g. Create relationships between the tables based on common fields. Take a screen shot of the Relationships window using the Snipping Tool and paste the image into the Word document. Close the Relationships window.

h. After all the new tables have been added, each person in the group should create all of the following queries. Make sure the text fields from the supporting tables appear in the queries (not the ID fields). Save each query as noted below. Take a screen shot of the datasheet of each query using the Snipping Tool and paste the image into the Word document.
   1. Display all the phones that are still for sale (SellDate is Null). Save as **qry1 Phones For Sale**.
   2. Display all the phones that are not made by Apple. Save as **qry2 Not Apple Phones**.
   3. List the Manufacturer and Model and asking price of sold phones; also include phones that are less than $50. Sort by asking price; only include tables that are required. Save as **qry3 Phones Sold or less than $50**.
   4. Display the phones that were purchased before 4/1/2012. Exclude the sold phones. Sort by purchase date. Save as **qry4 Obsolete Phones**.

i. Use e-mail or text messaging to communicate with other members in your group if you have any questions.

j. Exit all applications. Submit both the Word document and the database based on your instructor's directions.

Beyond the Classroom

Database Administrator Position

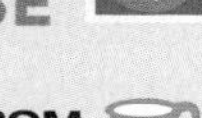

You arrive at Secure Systems, Inc., for a database administrator position interview. After meeting the human resources coordinator, you are given a test to demonstrate your skills in Access. You are asked to create a database from scratch to keep track of all the candidates for the positions currently open at Secure Systems. Use the Internet to search for information about database management. One useful site is published by the federal government's Bureau of Labor Statistics. It compiles an Occupational Outlook Handbook describing various positions, the type of working environment, the education necessary, salary information, and the projected growth. The Web site is http://www.bls.gov/ooh. After researching the database administrator position requirement, create a database using these requirements:

a. Name the database **a02b2Admin_LastFirst**.

b. Create three tables including these fields: Candidates (CandidateID, FirstName, LastName, Phone, Email), JobOpenings (Job OpeningID, JobName, Required Skill, HourlyPayRate, DataPosted, Supervisor), and Interviews (InterviewSequenceID, CandidateID, JobOpeningID, InterviewedBy, DateOfInterview, Rank).

c. Set the table relationships.

d. Add 10 candidates—yourself and 9 other students in your class.

e. Add the Database Administrator job and four other sample jobs.

f. Add eight sample interviews—four for the Database Administrator position and four others. Rank each candidate on a scale of 1 to 5 (5 is highest).

g. Create a query that lists the LastName, FirstName, JobOpeningID, InterviewedBy, DateofInterview, and Rank fields. Display only Database Administrator interviews with a ranking of 4 or 5. Sort by last name and first name. Run the query.

h. Compact and repair the database. Close Access. Submit based on your instructor's directions.

May Beverage Sales

A coworker called you into his office, explained that he was having difficulty with Microsoft Access 2013, and asked you to look at his work. Open *a02b3Traders* and save it as **a02b3Traders_LastFirst**. It contains two queries, *May 2015 Orders of Beverages and Confections* and *2015 Beverage Sales by Ship Country*. The May 2015 Orders of Beverages and Confections query is supposed to have only information from May 2015. You find other dates included in the results. Change the criteria to exclude the other dates. The 2015 Beverage Sales by Ship Country query returns no results. Check the criteria in all fields and modify so that the correct results are returned. After you find and correct the error(s), compact and repair the database. Close Access. Submit based on your instructor's directions.

Conflict Database

SOFT SKILLS S

After watching the Conflict: Sexual Harassment video, search the Web for the Equal Employment Opportunities Commission (EEOC) government site. Open the EEOC site and read the *About EEOC: Overview* information. Open a Word document and save it as **a02b4Harrassment_Answers_LastFirst**. Type a paragraph about the responsibilities of the EEOC.

Locate the *EEOC Laws, Regulations, Guidance & MOUs* page. The *Discrimination by Type* section includes a list of hyperlinks to discrimination type pages—pages that include laws, regulations and policy guidance, and also fact sheets, Q&As, best practices, and other information organized by basis of discrimination. Select a discrimination link and review the material on the page. Type two to three additional paragraphs in the Word document to summarize what you have read. Be sure to use good grammar, punctuation, and spelling in your document. Save the Word document and submit based on your instructor's directions.

Capstone Exercise

The Morris Arboretum in Chestnut Hill, Pennsylvania, tracks donors in Excel. They also use Excel to store a list of plants in stock. As donors contribute funds to the Arboretum, they can elect to receive a plant gift from the Arboretum. These plants are both rare plants and hard-to-find old favorites, and they are part of the annual appeal and membership drive to benefit the Arboretum's programs. The organization has grown, and the files are too large and inefficient to handle in Excel. Your task will be to begin the conversion of the files from Excel to Access.

Create a New Database

You need to examine the data in the Excel worksheets to determine which fields will become the primary keys in each table and which fields will become the foreign keys. Primary and foreign keys are used to form the relationships between tables.

a. Open the *a02c1Donors* Excel workbook.

b. Open the *a02c1Plants* Excel workbook.

c. Examine the data in each worksheet and identify the column that will become the primary key in an Access table. Identify the foreign keys in each table.

d. Create a new, blank database named **a02c1Arbor_LastFirst**.

Create a New Table

Use the new blank table created automatically by Access to hold the donations as they are received from the donors.

a. Switch to Design view and save the table as **Donations**.

b. Add the remaining field names in Design view. Note: The data for this table will be added later in this exercise.

- Change *ID* to **DonationID** with the **AutoNumber Data Type**.
- Add **DonorID** (a foreign key) with the **Number Data Type** and a field size of **Long Integer**.
- Add **PlantID** (a foreign key) as **Number Data** and a field size of **Long Integer**.
- Enter two additional fields with an appropriate data type and field properties. Hint: You need the date of donation and the amount of donation.

c. Verify the primary key is *DonationID*.

d. Save the table. Close the table.

Import Data from Excel

You need to use the Import Spreadsheet Data Wizard twice to import a worksheet from each Excel workbook into Access. You need to select the worksheets, specify the primary keys, set the indexing option, and name the newly imported tables (see Figures 2.12 through 2.17).

a. Click the **EXTERNAL DATA tab a**nd click **Excel** in the Import & Link group.

b. Locate and select the *a02c1Donors* workbook.

c. Set the DonorID field Indexed option to **Yes (No Duplicates)**.

d. Select **DonorID** as the primary key when prompted.

e. Accept the table name *Donors*.

f. Import the *a02c1Plants* file, set the **ID field** as the primary key, and then change the indexing option to **Yes (No Duplicates)**.

g. Accept the table name *Plants*.

h. Open each table in Datasheet view to examine the data.

i. Change the ID field name in the Plants table to **PlantID**.

Create Relationships

You need to create the relationships between the tables using the Relationships window. Identify the primary key fields in each table and connect them with their foreign key counterparts in related tables. Enforce referential integrity and cascade and update related fields.

a. Open the Donors table in Design view and change the Field Size property for DonorID to **Long Integer** so it matches the Field Size property of DonorID in the Donations table.

b. Open the Plants table in Design view and change the Field Size property for PlantID to **Long Integer** so it matches the Field Size property for PlantID in the Donations table.

c. Close the open tables and open the Relationships window.

d. Add the three tables to the Relationships window using the Show Table dialog box. Close the Show Tables dialog box.

e. Drag the **DonorID field** in the Donors table onto the DonorID field in the Donations table. Enforce referential integrity and cascade and update related fields. Drag the **PlantID field** from the Plants table onto the PlantID field of the Donations table. Enforce referential integrity and check the **Cascade Update Related Fields option**.

f. Close the Relationships window and save your changes.

Add Sample Data to the Donations Table

Add 10 records to the Donations table.

a. Add the following records to the Donations table.

Donation ID	Donor ID	Plant ID	Date Of Donation	Amount Of Donation
10	8228	611	3/1/2015	$150
18	5448	190	3/1/2015	$15
6	4091	457	3/12/2015	$125
7	11976	205	3/14/2015	$100
1	1000	25	3/17/2015	$120
12	1444	38	3/19/2015	$50
2	1444	38	4/3/2015	$50
4	10520	49	4/12/2015	$460
5	3072	102	4/19/2015	$450
21	1204	25	4/22/2015	$120

b. Sort the Donations table by the AmountOfDonation field in descending order.

Use the Query Wizard

Use the Query Wizard to create a query of all donations greater than $100 in the Donations table. Use the following guidelines:

a. Include the DonorID and AmountOfDonation fields.

b. Name the query **Donations Over 100**.

c. Add criteria to include only donations of more than $100.

d. Sort by ascending AmountOfDonation.

e. Save and close the query.

Create a Query in Design View

You need to create a query that identifies the people who made a donation after April 1, 2015. The query should list the date of the donation, donor's full name (LastName, FirstName), phone number, the amount of the donation, and name of the plant they want. Sort the query by date of donation, then by donor last name. This list will be given to the Arboretum staff so they can notify the donors that a plant is ready for pickup.

a. Click the **CREATE tab** and click **Query Design** in the Queries group.

b. Add the tables and fields necessary to produce the query as stated previously. Name the query **Plant Pickup List**.

c. Run and print the query from Datasheet view.

Modify a Query in Design View

a. Copy the Plant Pickup List query on the Navigation Pane and paste it using **ENewsletter** as the query name.

b. Open the ENewsletter query in Design view and delete the DateofDonation column.

c. Add the ENewsletter field to the design and set it to sort in Ascending order. Position the ENewsletter field on the grid so that the query sorts first by ENewsletter and then by LastName.

d. Compact and repair the database. Close Access.

e. Submit based on your instructor's directions.

Customize, Analyze, and Summarize Query Data

Creating and Using Queries to Make Decisions

OBJECTIVES

AFTER YOU READ THIS CHAPTER, YOU WILL BE ABLE TO:

1. Create a calculated field in a query p. 746
2. Format and save calculated results p. 749
3. Create expressions with the Expression Builder p. 757
4. Use built-in functions in Access p. 759
5. Add aggregate functions to datasheets p. 767
6. Create queries with aggregate functions p. 768

CASE STUDY | Housing Slump Means Opportunity for College Students

Two students from Passaic County Community College (PCCC) decided they would take advantage of the declining housing market. After taking several business courses at PCCC and a weekend seminar in real estate investing, Donald Carter and Matthew Nevoso were ready to test their skills in the marketplace. Don and Matt had a simple strategy—buy distressed properties at a significant discount, then resell the properties for a profit one year later when the market rebounds.

As they drove through the surrounding neighborhoods, if they noticed a For Sale sign in a yard, they would call the listing agent and ask for the key information such as the asking price, the number of bedrooms, square feet, and days on the market. Because they were just starting out, they decided to target houses that were priced at $150,000 or below and only houses that had been on the market at least six months.

For the first two months, they gathered lots of information and began to get a feel for the houses and prices in the area. Some neighborhoods were definitely more distressed than others! But they still had not made any offers. The two PCCC investors realized they needed a more scientific approach to finding an investment property. Based on a tip from the real estate seminar, they decide to create a database using Access 2013, using data from free lists of homes for sale. They would then like to use Access to help them find houses that meet their criteria. Once the data is in Access, you can help Don and Matt easily identify the qualifying properties. This new database approach should help them become more successful and hopefully help them acquire their first investment property.

Calculations and Expressions

One reason you might choose Excel over a program like Word is for the ability to perform calculations. At first glance, you may not see an obvious location for you to enter a calculation in Access. However, Access includes many of the same built-in calculations and functions that Excel does.

So, why do you need to create calculated fields? Similar to Excel, there are going to be times when you have to process data into information. For example, it could be as simple as needing to calculate a paycheck amount. If you have one field storing the number of hours worked and another field storing the hourly pay rate, you would be able to multiply them together to get the total amount the person is owed. Basic calculations such as these can be done using a query, so you do not have to rely on doing calculations by hand, which can lead to mistakes.

Unfortunately, calculations may not always be that easy. We did not consider some of the common deductions, such as Social Security, Medicare/FICA, federal and state income taxes, unemployment insurance, and possibly union dues. Some of these may be a flat rate, and others may be calculated based on your paycheck amount.

Expressions go beyond simple mathematical functions. Access includes extremely powerful logical functions as well. For example, your employees will claim a certain number of allowances. Based on the number of allowances an employee claims, the amount deducted from the paycheck will be different. This advanced topic will not be covered in this chapter.

When working with Access, there will be times when you need to create arithmetic calculations—using expressions and functions—in your database. In Access 2013, you can add calculations to tables, queries, forms, and reports. Often, rather than storing a calculated value, you would instead store the components of it and calculate the field when necessary. For example, if you have a list price and amount ordered, you would not need to also store the total amount due, because this is the list price multiplied by the amount ordered. Calculating fields rather than storing them will reduce the likelihood of errors and inconsistencies and also save space, as you are storing less information.

In this section, you will learn about the order of operations and how to create a calculated field in a query.

Creating a Calculated Field in a Query

When creating a query, in addition to using fields from tables, you may also need to create a calculation based on the fields from one or more tables. For example, a table might contain the times when employees clock in and out of work. You could create a calculated field (as defined in an earlier chapter) to determine, or calculate, how many hours each employee worked by subtracting the ClockIn field from the ClockOut field. You create calculated fields in the Design view of a query. A formula used to calculate new fields from the values in existing fields is known as an ***expression***. An expression can consist of a number of different elements to produce the desired output. The elements used in an expression may include the following:

- Identifiers (the names of fields, controls, or properties)
- Arithmetic operators (for example, *, /, +, or –)
- Functions (built-in functions like Date or Pmt)
- Values that do not change, known as ***constants*** (numbers such as 30 or 0.5)

You can use calculations to create a new value based on an existing field, verify data entered, set grouping levels in reports, or help set query criteria.

Understand the Order of Operations

The ***order of operations*** determines the sequence by which operations are calculated in an expression. You may remember PEMDAS from a math class, or the mnemonic device "Please Excuse My Dear Aunt Sally." Evaluate expressions in parentheses first, then exponents, then multiplication and division, and, finally, addition and subtraction. Table 3.1 shows some examples of the order of operations. You must have a solid understanding of these rules in order to create calculated fields in Access. Access, like Excel, uses the following symbols:

- Parentheses ( )
- Exponentiation ^
- Multiplication *
- Division /
- Addition +
- Subtraction –

TABLE 3.1 Examples of Order of Operations

Expression	Order to Perform Calculations	Output
=2+3*3	Multiply first and then add.	11
=(2+3)*3	Add the values inside the parentheses first and then multiply.	15
=2+2^3	Evaluate the exponent first, 2^3=2*2*2 (or 8). Then add.	10
=10/2+3	Divide first and then add.	8
=10/(2+3)	Add first to simplify the parenthetical expression and then divide.	2
=10*2–3*2	Multiply first and then subtract.	14

Build Expressions with Correct Syntax

Expressions are entered in the first row of the query design grid. You must follow the correct ***syntax***, which dictates the structure and components required to perform the necessary calculations in an equation or evaluate expressions. You can create expressions to perform calculations using field names, constants, and functions. If you use a field name, such as Balance, in an expression, you must spell the field name correctly; otherwise, Access displays an error. Access ignores spaces in calculations.

For example, if you worked at a company that was planning on allowing customers to pay off their balance in 12 monthly payments, you would divide the balance by 12. However, let's say you wanted to add a 3.5% surcharge. In this case, you would multiply the balance by 0.035 (3.5%) and then divide that total by 12. An example of an expression with correct syntax is:

STEP 1

```
Balance*0.035/12
```

If you type the preceding function into a line in a query and save the query, you may be surprised to see Access add a few things to the line (see Figure 3.1):

```
Expr1: [Balance]*0.035/12
```

Access made a few changes to your entry. First, it removed extra spaces. Secondly, Access added brackets *[ ]* around the Balance field, which Access uses to indicate a field name. In addition, you see that Access added *Expr1:* to the start of the line. This is how Access assigns a column heading to this field. If you were to run the query, the column heading would be *Expr1*. As this is not a descriptive name, it would probably be better to include your own title. If you wanted to name this column MonthlySurcharge, you would start the expression with the name, followed by a colon, followed by the expression:

```
MonthlySurcharge: Balance*0.035/12
```

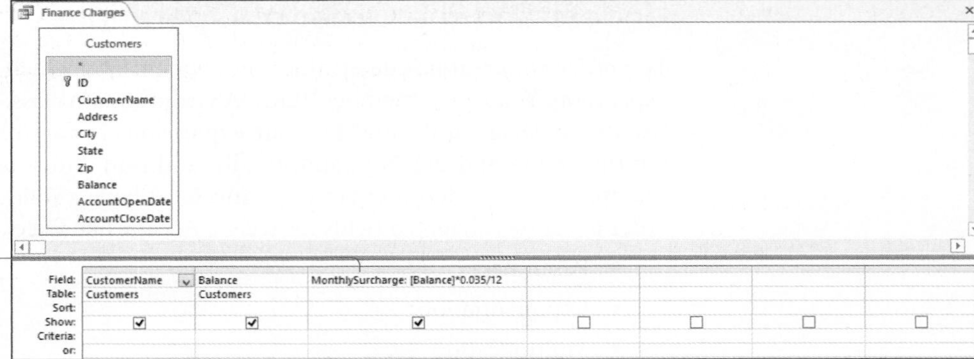

FIGURE 3.1 Calculated Field in a Query Design

TIP Avoid Spaces in Calculated Field Names

Although you can use spaces in calculated field names, it is a good habit not to use spaces. For example, use NewPrice: [Price]*1.1 rather than New Price: [Price]*1.1. If you avoid spaces in calculated field names, it will be easier to reference these fields in other queries, related forms, and related reports. If you want a column heading to have spaces in it, you should set the Caption property, which will be discussed later in this section.

Again, if you saved the query, Access would add brackets around the Balance field.

In calculated fields, the parts of the formula are usually a constant (for example, 0.035 and 12 in the preceding example), a field name (for example, Balance), or another calculated field. Figure 3.1 shows the MonthlySurcharge field, calculated by multiplying the Balance field by 0.035 (or 3.5%) and dividing by 12. This calculation shows what a customer would pay as a monthly surcharge if you offered him or her the monthly payments and added a 3.5% fee.

The arithmetic operators, the * symbol (multiply) and the / symbol (divide), first multiply [Balance] by 0.035 and then divide the result by 12. There is no real issue in this example with order of operations because the order of operations states that multiplication and division are at the same level of precedence. In other words, if you state 12*3/3, whether you do the multiplication or division first, the result will be exactly the same (12).

The query results, as shown in Figure 3.2, display a decimal number in the MonthlySurcharge column. Notice the results are not formatted well. This will be addressed later in this section.

Finance Charges

CustomerName	Balance	MonthlySurcharge
Terri Mccoy	$24,286.00	70.8341666666667
Willie Mann	$47,041.00	137.202916666667
Michael Warren	$26,888.00	78.4233333333333
Tammy Mason	$28,255.00	82.4104166666667
Ashley Smith	$38,108.00	111.148333333333
Paul Johnson	$38,664.00	112.77
Leroy Morrison	$8,070.00	23.5375
Phyllis Daniel	$19,166.00	55.9008333333333
Ryan Weaver	$34,000.00	99.1666666666667
Aaron Jordan	$39,889.00	116.342916666667
Howard Hernandez	$2,296.00	6.69666666666667
Francisco Byrd	$17,146.00	50.0091666666667
Jacob Santos	$49,218.00	143.5525
Willie Anderson	$40,940.00	119.408333333333
Oscar Porter	$12,064.00	35.1866666666667
Evelyn Moore	$42,199.00	123.080416666667
Cheryl Carr	$40,620.00	118.475
Ana Keller	$49,509.00	144.40125
Glenn Brewer	$24,820.00	72.3916666666667
Peter Dean	$48,987.00	142.87875
Sheila Turner	$32,572.00	95.0016666666667
Jason Rodgers	$28,864.00	84.1866666666667
Joel Gonzales	$31,350.00	91.4375
Dolores Hayes	$13,745.00	40.0895833333333
Nancy Daniels	$4,639.00	13.5304166666667
Vivian Cannon	$24,358.00	71.0441666666667

MonthlySurcharge shows many digits

FIGURE 3.2 Results of a Calculated Field in a Query

Another example of when to use a calculated field is calculating a price increase for a product or service. Suppose you need to calculate a 10% price increase on certain products you sell. You could name the calculated field NewPrice and use the expression (CurrentPrice) + (CurrentPrice × 0.10). The first segment represents the current price, and the second segment adds an additional 10%. (Recall that to get 10% of a number, you would multiply by 0.10.) The expression would be entered into the query design grid as follows:

```
NewPrice: [CurrentPrice] + [CurrentPrice]*0.10
```

Note that if you are adept at math, you may find other ways to calculate this increase.

TIP Use Zoom (Shift+F2) to View Long Expressions

To see the entire calculated field expression, click the field in Query Design view and press Shift+F2. A new window will appear to enable you to easily see and edit the entire contents of the cell. Access refers to this window as the Zoom dialog box, as shown in Figure 3.3.

Zoom can also be used in a number of other contexts. If you are ever having trouble viewing the entirety of a text box, try using Shift+F2 to expand it. Once you are done modifying a field, click the X in the top-right corner of the Zoom dialog box.

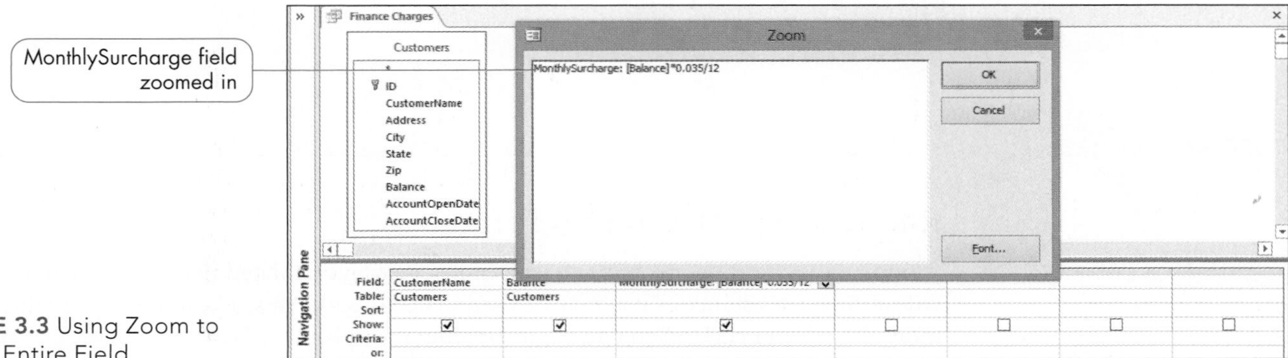

FIGURE 3.3 Using Zoom to See an Entire Field

Formatting and Saving Calculated Results

In the previous example, we saw inconsistent results in the formatting, with some results showing only two decimal places and others showing many decimal places. In Figure 3.2, the MonthlySurcharge field was extremely difficult to read. Part of the purpose of queries is to perform calculations, but an overlooked portion of that is the formatting. You can create a clever calculation, but if it is not labeled and formatted correctly, it may leave your users confused. Spending a few moments formatting your output will make your query more usable.

There is a way to give Access instructions as to how to format the field. You can use the ***Property Sheet*** to do so. The Property Sheet enables you to change settings such as number format, number of decimal places, and caption, among many others. You can select a predefined format (for example, currency), change the number of decimal places, and also change the caption, as you did in the earlier chapter on tables. To format the calculated results:

STEP 2»

1. Open the query in Design view.
2. Click in the calculated field cell (the cell you just created).
3. On the QUERY TOOLS DESIGN tab, click Property Sheet in the Show/Hide group.
4. To change the format, click the *Format property* arrow and select your desired format. For numeric fields, the Decimal Places property will allow you to choose exactly how many decimal places display.

5. To change the caption, click in the text box next to the caption and type your desired column heading. This will override the column name, much like the caption property does for a field name in a table, as shown in a previous chapter.

Formats vary based on the data type. A currency field will have options related to number format, whereas a date/time field will have options related to changing the display of the date and/or time. Figure 3.4 shows the Property Sheet options related to a numeric field.

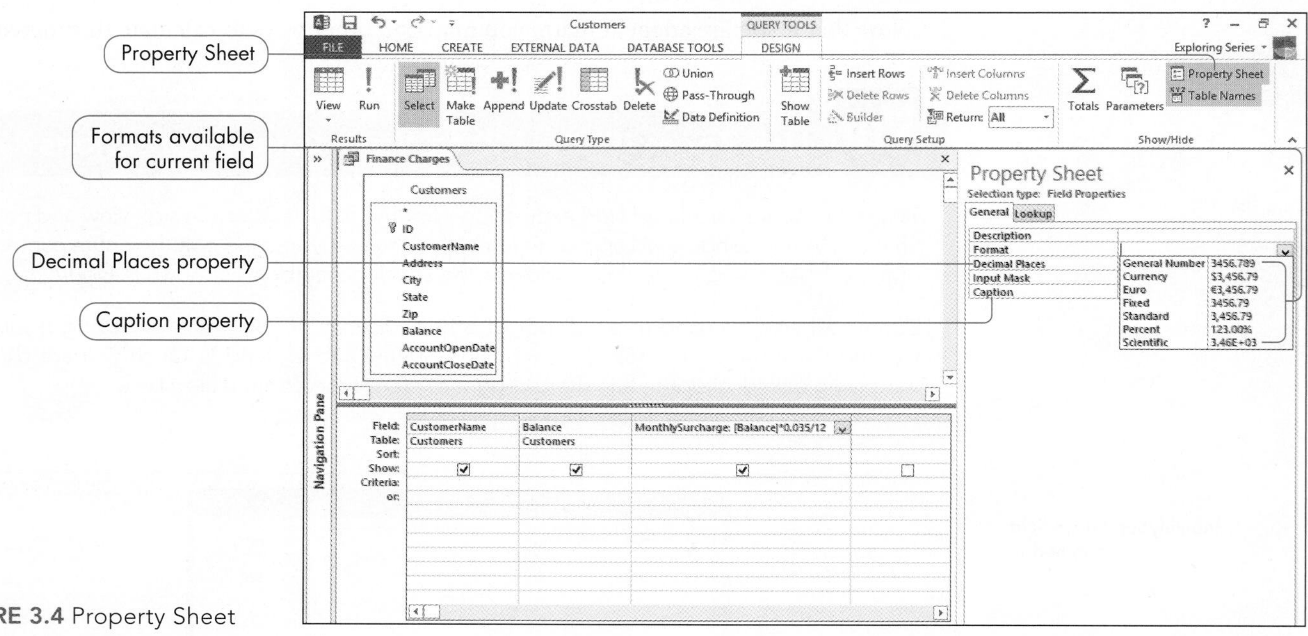

FIGURE 3.4 Property Sheet

Recover from Common Errors

A number of common errors can occur while creating calculated fields. Access may not provide as much assistance as you may be used to in cases like this. The following are three common errors that occur when you begin creating formulas.

STEP 3

- Forgetting the colon between the column title and the formula
  - A correct formula would look like this:

    Expr1: [Balance]*0.035/12

    If you forget the colon, the formula looks like this instead:

    Expr1 [Balance]*0.035/12

    and you will get an error about invalid syntax.
- Typing a field name incorrectly
  - If your field name is Balance and you mistype it, you will not get an error until you attempt to run the query. You may end up with a formula that looks like this:

    Expr1: [Baalnce]*0.035/12
  - When you run the query, you will be prompted by Access to give a value for Baalnce.
- Forgetting the order of operations
  - If you do not check your formulas, you may get bad values. For example, the following would not produce the expected output:

    Expr2: [NumberOfDays] + 7/365
  - If you need addition to be done before division, you must remember the parentheses:

    Expr2: ([NumberOfDays] + 7)/365

d. Select the **Agents table** and click **Add**. Select the **Properties table** and click **Add**. Close the Show Table dialog box.

e. Double-click the **FirstName** and **LastName fields** in the Agents table to add them to the design grid.

f. Double-click the **ListPrice**, **SqFeet**, and **Sold fields** in the Properties table to add them to the query design grid.

g. Click **Run** in the Results group to display the results in Datasheet view.

   You should see 303 properties in the results.

h. Switch to Design view. Type **No** in the Criteria row of the Sold field.

i. Select **Ascending** from the Sort row of the ListPrice field.

j. Click **Run** to see the results.

   You only want to see properties that were not sold. There should now be 213 properties in the datasheet.

k. Click **Save** on the Quick Access Toolbar and type **Price Per Sq Ft** as the Query Name in the Save As dialog box. Click **OK.**

l. Switch to Design view. Click in the top row of the first blank column of the query design grid and use **Shift+F2** to show the Zoom dialog box. Type **PricePerSqFt: ListPrice/SqFeet** and click **OK**.

   Access inserts square brackets around the fields for you. The new field divides the values in the ListPrice field by the values in the SqFeet field. The *:* after *PricePerSqFt* is required.

m. Click **Run** in the Results group to view the results.

   The new calculated field, PricePerSqFt, is displayed. Compare your results to those shown in Figure 3.5.

TROUBLESHOOTING: If you see pound signs (#####) in an Access column, use the vertical lines between column indicators to increase the width.

TROUBLESHOOTING: If, when you run the query, you are prompted for PricePerSqFt, cancel and return to Design view. Ensure you have entered the formula from step l to the field line of the query, not the criteria line.

n. Save the changes to the query and close the query.

STEP 2 » FORMAT AND SAVE CALCULATED RESULTS

Don and Matt would like the field formatted differently. You will change the format to Currency and add a caption to the calculated field. Refer to Figure 3.6 as you complete Step 2.

Steps d–e: PricePerSqFt field formatted as Currency with added caption

Price Per Sq Ft Formatted

First Name	Last Name	List Price	Square Feet	Sold	Price Per Sq Ft
StudentFirst	StudentLast	$109,140.00	1133	No	$96.33
Bill	Sabey	$119,990.00	1202	No	$99.83
Anny	Almonte	$122,220.00	1235	No	$98.96
Robert Allen	Dickey	$129,780.00	1132	No	$114.65
Bill	Sabey	$136,680.00	1375	No	$99.40
Karean	Eissler	$138,990.00	1276	No	$108.93
Anny	Almonte	$140,693.00	1490	No	$94.42
Karean	Eissler	$140,904.00	1301	No	$108.30
Anny	Almonte	$150,200.00	1652	No	$90.92
StudentFirst	StudentLast	$163,737.00	1476	No	$110.93
StudentFirst	StudentLast	$164,436.00	1850	No	$88.88
Pradeep	Rana	$166,530.00	1676	No	$99.36
StudentFirst	StudentLast	$166,552.00	1623	No	$102.62
Anny	Almonte	$166,800.00	1598	No	$104.38
Anny	Almonte	$168,354.00	1651	No	$101.97
StudentFirst	StudentLast	$168,504.00	1625	No	$103.69
Anny	Almonte	$172,458.00	1798	No	$95.92
Bill	Sabey	$174,230.00	1771	No	$98.38
StudentFirst	StudentLast	$174,720.00	1694	No	$103.14
Robert Allen	Dickey	$174,720.00	1610	No	$108.52
Anny	Almonte	$174,720.00	1667	No	$104.81
Robert Allen	Dickey	$175,560.00	1562	No	$112.39
StudentFirst	StudentLast	$177,984.00	1707	No	$104.27
Bill	Sabey	$179,712.00	1854	No	$96.93
Bill	Sabey	$182,385.00	2014	No	$90.56
Anny	Almonte	$183,312.00	1721	No	$106.51
Anny	Almonte	$184,473.00	1791	No	$103.00

FIGURE 3.6 Results of Calculated Field Creation

a. Make a copy of the Price Per Sq Ft query. Name the copy **Price Per Sq Ft Formatted.**

b. Open the Price Per Sq Ft Formatted query in Design view.

c. Click in the **PricePerSqFt calculated field cell**. Click **Property Sheet** in the Show/Hide group on the DESIGN tab.

The Property Sheet displays on the right side of your screen.

d. Click the **Format box**. Click the **Format property arrow** and select **Currency**.

e. Click in the **Caption box** and type **Price Per Sq Ft**. Press **Enter**. Close the Property Sheet.

f. Click **Run** to view your changes.

The calculated field values are formatted as Currency, and the column heading displays *Price Per Sq Ft* instead of *PricePerSqFt*.

g. Save the changes to the query.

STEP 3 » RECOVER FROM COMMON ERRORS

A few errors arise as you test the new calculated fields. You check the spelling of the field names in the calculated fields because that is a common mistake. Refer to Figure 3.7 as you complete Step 3.

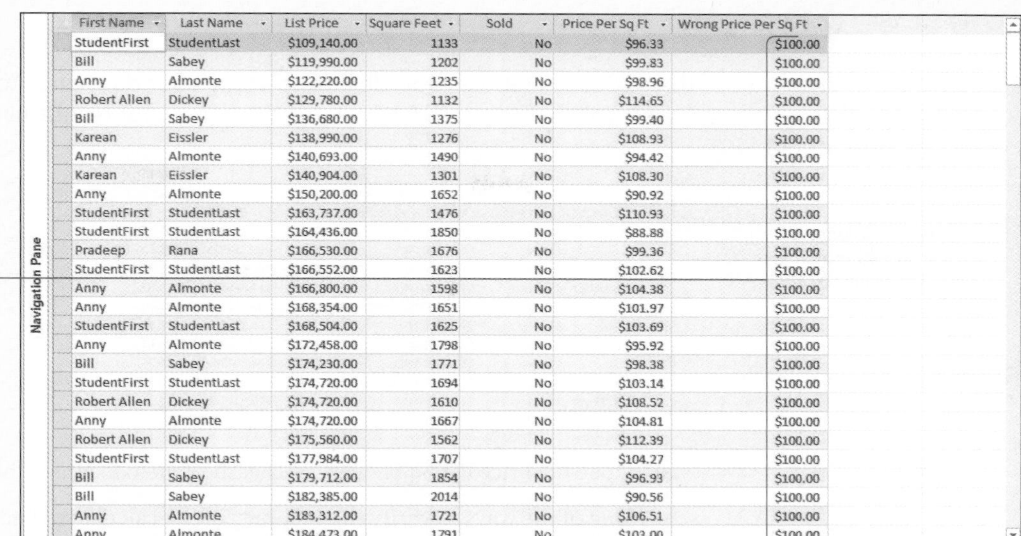

First Name	Last Name	List Price	Square Feet	Sold	Price Per Sq Ft	Wrong Price Per Sq Ft
StudentFirst	StudentLast	$109,140.00	1133	No	$96.33	$100.00
Bill	Sabey	$119,990.00	1202	No	$99.83	$100.00
Anny	Almonte	$122,220.00	1235	No	$98.96	$100.00
Robert Allen	Dickey	$129,780.00	1132	No	$114.65	$100.00
Bill	Sabey	$136,680.00	1375	No	$99.40	$100.00
Karean	Eissler	$138,990.00	1276	No	$108.93	$100.00
Anny	Almonte	$140,693.00	1490	No	$94.42	$100.00
Karean	Eissler	$140,904.00	1301	No	$108.30	$100.00
Anny	Almonte	$150,200.00	1652	No	$90.92	$100.00
StudentFirst	StudentLast	$163,737.00	1476	No	$110.93	$100.00
StudentFirst	StudentLast	$164,436.00	1850	No	$88.88	$100.00
Pradeep	Rana	$166,530.00	1676	No	$99.36	$100.00
StudentFirst	StudentLast	$166,552.00	1623	No	$102.62	$100.00
Anny	Almonte	$166,800.00	1598	No	$104.38	$100.00
Anny	Almonte	$168,354.00	1651	No	$101.97	$100.00
StudentFirst	StudentLast	$168,504.00	1625	No	$103.69	$100.00
Anny	Almonte	$172,458.00	1798	No	$95.92	$100.00
Bill	Sabey	$174,230.00	1771	No	$98.38	$100.00
StudentFirst	StudentLast	$174,720.00	1694	No	$103.14	$100.00
Robert Allen	Dickey	$174,720.00	1610	No	$108.52	$100.00
Anny	Almonte	$174,720.00	1667	No	$104.81	$100.00
Robert Allen	Dickey	$175,560.00	1562	No	$112.39	$100.00
StudentFirst	StudentLast	$177,984.00	1707	No	$104.27	$100.00
Bill	Sabey	$179,712.00	1854	No	$96.93	$100.00
Bill	Sabey	$182,385.00	2014	No	$90.56	$100.00
Anny	Almonte	$183,312.00	1721	No	$106.51	$100.00
Anny	Almonte	$184,473.00	1791	No	$103.00	$100.00

FIGURE 3.7 Results of a Misspelled Field Name

a. Switch to Design view of the Price Per Sq Ft Formatted query. Scroll to the first blank column of the query design grid and click in the top row.

b. Use **Shift+F2** to display the Zoom dialog box. Type **WrongPricePerSqFt: xListPrice/ xSqFeet**. Click the **OK button** in the Zoom dialog box.

Be sure that you added the extra *x*'s to the field names. You are intentionally misspelling the field names to see how Access will respond. Access inserts square brackets around the field names for you.

c. Click **Property Sheet** in the Show/Hide group of the DESIGN tab. Click the **Format box**. From the menu, select **Currency**. Click in the **Caption box** and type **Wrong Price Per Sq Ft**. Close the Property Sheet.

d. Click **Run** in the Results group.

You should see the Enter Parameter Value dialog box. The dialog box indicates that Access does not recognize xListPrice in the tables defined for this query in the first record. When Access does not recognize a field name, it will ask you to supply a value.

e. Type **100000** in the first parameter box. Press **Enter** or click **OK**.

Another Enter Parameter Value dialog box displays, asking that you supply a value for xSqFeet. Again, this error occurs because the tables defined for this query do not contain an xSqFeet field.

f. Type **1000** in the second parameter box and press **Enter**.

The query has the necessary information to run and returns the results in Datasheet view.

g. Examine the results of the calculation for *Wrong Price Per Sq Ft*. You may have to scroll right to see the results.

All of the records show 100 because you entered the values 100000 and 1000, respectively, into the parameter boxes. The two values are treated as constants and give the same results for all the records.

h. Return to Design view. Press **Shift+F2** to zoom. Correct the errors in the WrongPricePerSqFt field by changing the formula to **WrongPricePerSqFt: [ListPrice]/ [SqFeet]**. Click the **Close (X) button** in the top-right corner of the Zoom dialog box to close it.

i. Run and save the query. Close the query.

The calculated values in the last two columns should be the same.

STEP 4 » VERIFY THE CALCULATED RESULTS

Because you are in charge of the Access database, you decide to verify your data prior to showing it to the investors. You use two methods to check your calculations: estimation and checking your results using Excel. Refer to Figure 3.8 as you complete Step 4.

Step e: Column G results should match first 10 results in column F

1	First Name	Last Name	List Price	Square Feet	Sold	PricePerSqFt	
2	StudentFirst	StudentLast	$109,140.00	1133	FALSE	96.32833186	$96.33
3	Bill	Sabey	$119,990.00	1202	FALSE	99.82529118	$99.83
4	Anny	Almonte	$122,220.00	1235	FALSE	98.96356275	$98.96
5	Robert Allen	Dickey	$129,780.00	1132	FALSE	114.6466431	$114.65
6	Bill	Sabey	$136,680.00	1375	FALSE	99.40363636	$99.40
7	Karean	Eissler	$138,990.00	1276	FALSE	108.9263323	$108.93
8	Anny	Almonte	$140,693.00	1490	FALSE	94.42483221	$94.42
9	Karean	Eissler	$140,904.00	1301	FALSE	108.3043812	$108.30
10	Anny	Almonte	$150,200.00	1652	FALSE	90.92009685	$90.92
11	StudentFirst	StudentLast	$163,737.00	1476	FALSE	110.9329268	$110.93

FIGURE 3.8 Results Validated in Excel

a. Open the Price Per Sq Ft query in Datasheet view. Examine the PricePerSqFt field.

One of the ways to verify the accuracy of the calculated data is to ask yourself if the numbers make sense.

b. Locate the second record with *Bill Sabey* as the listing agent, an asking price of *$119,990*, and square footage of *1202*. Ask yourself if the calculated value of *$99.83* makes sense.

The sale price is $119,990, and the square footage is 1202. You can verify the calculated field easily by rounding the two numbers (to 120,000 and 1,200) and dividing the values in your head (120,000 divided by 1,200 = 100) to verify that the calculated value, $99.83 per square foot, makes sense.

> **TROUBLESHOOTING:** If the second record is not the one listed above, ensure you have sorted the query by the List Price in ascending order, as specified in Step 1i.

c. Open a new, blank workbook in Excel and switch to Access. Drag over the record selector for the first 10 records (the tenth record has a list price of $163,737). Click **Copy** in the Clipboard group on the HOME tab.

You will verify the calculation in the first 10 records by pasting the results in Excel.

d. Switch to Excel and, click **Paste** in the Clipboard group on the HOME tab.

The field names display in the first row, and the 10 records display in the next 10 rows. The fields are located in columns A–F. The calculated field results are pasted in column F as values rather than as a formula.

> **TROUBLESHOOTING:** If you see pound signs (#####) in an Excel column, use the vertical lines between column indicators to increase the width.

e. Type **=C2/D2** in **cell G2** and press **Enter**. Copy the formula from **cell G2** and paste it into **cells G3 to G11**.

The formula divides the list price by the square feet. Compare the results in columns F and G. The numbers should be the same, except for a slight difference due to rounding.

> **TROUBLESHOOTING:** If the values differ, look at both the Excel and Access formulas. Determine which is correct, and then find and fix the error in the incorrect formula.

f. Save the Excel workbook as **a03Property_LastFirst**. Exit Excel.

g. Keep the database open if you plan to continue with the next Hands-On Exercise. If not, close the database and exit Access.

The Expression Builder and Functions

In the last Hands-On Exercise, you calculated the price per square foot for real estate properties. That simple calculation helped you to evaluate all the properties on the investment list. You were able to type the expression manually.

When you encounter more complex expressions, you can use the ***Expression Builder*** tool to help you create more complicated expressions. When you create an expression in the field cell, you must increase the column width to see the entire expression. The Expression Builder's size enables you to easily see complex formulas and functions in their entirety. In addition, it provides easy access to objects, operators, functions, and explanations for functions.

In this section, you will learn how to create expressions using the Expression Builder. You also will learn how to use built-in functions.

Creating Expressions with the Expression Builder

Launch the Expression Builder while in the query design grid to assist with creating a calculated field (or other expression). (See "Launch the Expression Builder" later in this section for directions.) The Expression Builder helps you create expressions by supplying you with the fields, operators, and functions you need to create them. When you use the Expression Builder to help you create expressions, you can eliminate spelling errors in field names. Another advantage is when you are inserting functions; functions require specific arguments in a specific order. When you insert a function using the Expression Builder, the builder gives you placeholders that tell you which values belong where.

You may not always need the Expression Builder. As you become familiar with programs like Access, some of the more common tasks may become second nature to you. Rather than clicking to find what you need, you may be able to do your day-to-day work without the aid of the Expression Builder. However, when working with a less familiar calculation, having this tool gives you extra support.

Though you will learn about the Expression Builder in queries in this chapter, this tool can be used in many other areas. You can also use the Expression Builder when working with forms and reports. For example, if you need to perform a calculation in a form or report, you can launch the Expression Builder to assist you with this task. The same skills you learn here can be applied there as well.

Missing Field Names

If you have not yet saved your query, you may not see the names of the fields you are working with. This is especially true of any calculated fields you want to use as part of another expression. If you cannot see a field you need to use, exit the Expression Builder, save the query, and close and reopen the query. Once you reenter the Expression Builder, you should see the missing fields.

Create an Expression

The left column of the Expression Builder dialog box contains Expression Elements (see Figure 3.9), which include the built-in functions, the tables and other objects from the current database, and common expressions. Select an item in this column.

The middle column displays the Expression Categories based on the item selected in the Expression Elements box (see Figure 3.9). For example, when the Built-In Functions item is selected in the Expression Elements box, the available built-in function categories, such as the Math category, are displayed in the Expression Categories box.

The right column displays the Expression Values, if any, for the categories that you selected in the Expression Categories box (see Figure 3.9). For example, if you click Built-In Functions in the Expression Elements box and click Date/Time in the Expression Categories box, the Expression Values box lists all of the built-in functions in the Date/Time category.

You can create an expression by manually typing text in the expression box or by double-clicking the elements from the bottom section in the Expression Builder dialog box. For example, to create a calculated field using the fields in the tables, type the calculated field name and type a colon. Next, click the desired table listed in the Expression Elements section and double-click the field you want. Click the Operators item in the Expression Elements section and choose an operator (such as + or *) from the Expression Categories section (or just type the operator). The Expression Builder is flexible and will enable you to find what you need while still enabling you to modify the expression manually.

Calculated fields are relatively simple to create, and most Access developers can create them without the Expression Builder. The main reason to use the builder for a calculated field is to eliminate spelling errors in field names. Using functions in Access almost always requires the Expression Builder because the syntax of functions can be difficult to remember. When you double-click the Functions command in the Expression Elements box and click Built-In Functions, the Expression Categories box lists all the available functions in Access. The Expression Values box lists the functions in each of the categories. When you find the function you need, double-click it and the function displays in the expression box. You can see the «placeholder text» where the arguments belong; replace each placeholder text with the argument values, either numbers or fields from a table.

Launch the Expression Builder

STEP 1» To launch the Expression Builder:

1. Open a query in Design view (or create a new query).
2. Verify the QUERY TOOLS DESIGN tab is selected on the Ribbon.
3. Click the top cell of a blank column (also known as the Field cell, because it appears in the row labeled Field) where you would like your expression to appear.
4. Click Builder in the Query Setup group, and the Expression Builder launches (see Figure 3.9). (You can also launch the Expression Builder by right-clicking the cell where you want the expression and selecting Build from the shortcut menu.)

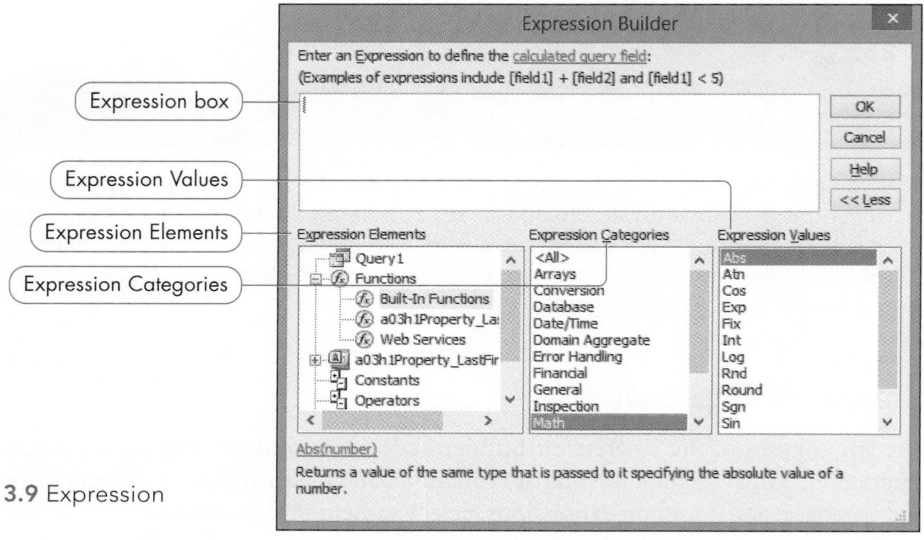

FIGURE 3.9 Expression Builder

5. The top section of the Expression Builder dialog box contains a rectangular area (known as the *expression box*) where you create an expression. You can type your expression in the expression box manually, or you can use the Expression Elements, Expression Categories, and Expression Values in the bottom portion of the Expression Builder. The bottom area allows you to browse for functions, tables, queries, and more. Refer to Figure 3.9.
6. Double-click an item in the *Expression Categories* or *Expression Values* section to add it automatically to the expression box, thus allowing you to use this interface to avoid typographical errors.
7. After you create the expression, click OK to close the Expression Builder window. The expression is then entered into the current cell in the query design grid. From the query design, click Run in the Results group to view the results (in Datasheet view). If the results are incorrect, you can return to Design view and use the Expression Builder again to correct the expression.

Using Built-In Functions in Access

STEP 2»

Similar to Excel, a number of functions are built into Access. A ***function*** is a predefined computation that performs a complex calculation. It produces a result based on inputs known as arguments. An ***argument*** is any data that is needed to produce the output for a function. The term *argument*, outside of computers, can mean a fact. For example, in court, you may have a judge ask a lawyer to present his argument. Similarly, Access will need arguments, or facts, to execute a function. Arguments can be a variable (such as a field name) or a constant (such as a number). Some functions require no arguments, but many require at least one. Some functions have optional arguments, which are not required but may be necessary for your task.

Many of the tasks that are built in are tasks that would otherwise be difficult to perform. If you had to figure out the payment of a loan or determine the year portion of a date without functions, it would not be an easy task.

Once you identify what you need a function to do, you can check the Built-In Functions in the Expression Builder to see if the function exists. If it does, add the function to the expression box and replace the «placeholder text» with the argument values. Functions work the same in Access and Excel and other programming languages (such as Visual Basic). There are nearly 150 built-in functions in Access, and many of them will not apply to the task you are performing. Be aware that if you want to perform complex operations, there may be a function that can do it for you. In cases like this, search engines or Microsoft Help are extremely useful. This chapter will demonstrate one function.

Calculate Payments with the Pmt Function

Figure 3.10 shows the ***Pmt function***, which calculates the periodic loan payment given the interest rate per period (for example, monthly), term of the loan (in months), and the original value of the loan (the principal). To use this function, you will need to supply at least three arguments as field names from underlying tables or as constants:

- The first argument is the interest rate per period. Interest rates are usually stated as annual rates, so you will need to convert the annual interest rate to the rate per period. For example, if a loan is paid monthly, you can calculate the rate by dividing the yearly rate by 12.
- The second argument is the number of periods. Because loan terms are usually stated in years, you will need to multiply the number of years by the number of payments per year. For example, a monthly payment would be calculated as the number of years multiplied by 12.
- The third argument is the present value—or principal—of the loan. It is the amount a customer is borrowing.

- The last two arguments—future value and type—are both optional, so they are usually 0 or blank. The future value shows the amount the borrower will owe after the final payment has been made. The type tells Access whether the payment is made at the beginning or the end of the period.

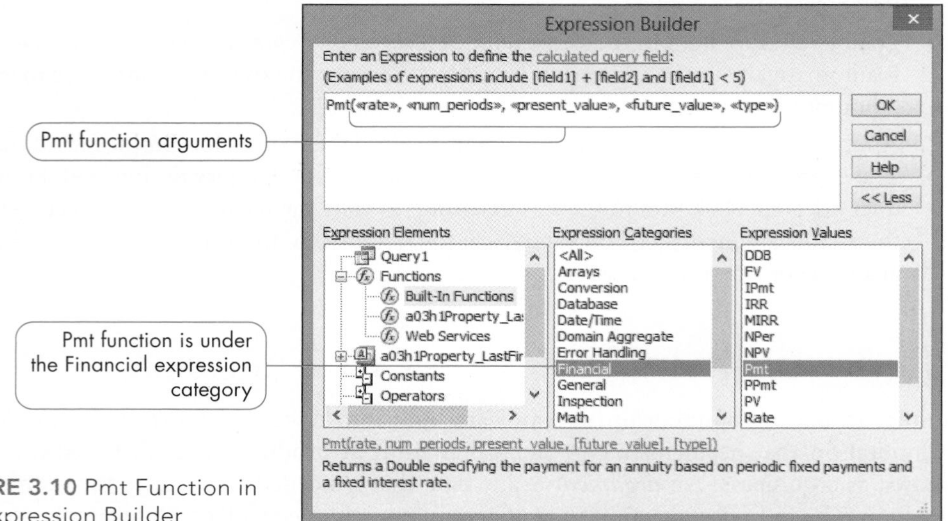

FIGURE 3.10 Pmt Function in the Expression Builder

The following example shows how to use the Pmt function to calculate the monthly payment on a $12,500 loan, at a 5.0% interest rate, with a four-year loan term.

Function: Pmt(*rate, num_periods, present_value, future_value, type*)

Example: Pmt(0.06/12, 5*12, 12500)

The Pmt function will return a negative value (as a loan payment is considered a debit). If you would like to display this as a positive number, you will need to negate it.

Table 3.2 describes the arguments for the Pmt function in more detail.

TABLE 3.2 Arguments of the Pmt Function

Part	Description
( )	Items inside the parentheses are arguments for the function. The arguments are separated by commas. Some arguments are optional; some arguments have a default value. In the Pmt function, the first three arguments are required and the last two are optional.
rate	Required. Expression or value specifying interest rate per period, usually monthly. A mortgage with an annual percentage rate of **6.0%** with monthly payments would have a rate entered as **0.06/12**, since the rate of 6% would be entered as .06, and because there are 12 months in a year. A loan with a 4% interest rate paid quarterly would be expressed as .04/4 for the same reason. A common cause of issues with this function is that people forget to divide the annual percentage rate by the number of periods in a year.
num_periods	Required. Expression or integer value specifying total number of payment periods in the loan. For example, monthly payments on a five-year car loan give a total of 5 * 12 (or 60) payment periods. Quarterly payments on a six-year loan would give a total of 6 * 4 (or 24) payment periods.
present_value	Required. Expression or value specifying the present value of the money you borrow. If you borrow $12,500 for a car, the value would be 12500.
future_value	*Optional* (can be left blank). Expression or value specifying the future value after you've made the final payment. Most consumer loans have a future value of $0 after the final payment. However, if you want to save $50,000 over 18 years for your child's education, then 50000 is the future value. Zero is assumed if left blank.
type	*Optional* (can be left blank). Value (0 or 1) identifying when payments are due. Use 0 if payments are due at the end of the payment period (the default), or 1 if payments are due at the beginning of the period. Zero is assumed if left blank.

In the second Hands-On Exercise, you will practice using the Expression Builder to add and modify a field, and use a built-in function.

Quick Concepts

1. List two benefits of creating expressions with the Expression Builder. ***p. 757***
2. Give an example of a built-in function. ***p. 759***
3. What is an argument in a function? Give an example. ***p. 759***
4. Describe a scenario where you might use the Pmt function. ***p. 759***

Hands-On Exercises

MyITLab®
HOE2 Training

2 The Expression Builder and Functions

When Don and Matt ask you to calculate the price per bedroom and the price per room for each property, you use the Expression Builder to make the task easier. You also add two additional fields that calculate the days on market and the estimated commission for each property.

Skills covered: Use the Expression Builder to Add and Modify a Field • Use Built-In Functions

STEP 1 » USE THE EXPRESSION BUILDER TO ADD AND MODIFY A FIELD

You create a copy of the Price Per Sq Ft Formatted query from the previous Hands-On Exercise and paste it using a new name. You will add a few more calculated fields to the new query. You will create one calculation to determine the price per bedroom for each house. You will create a second field to calculate the price per room. For this calculation, you will assume that each property has a kitchen, a living room, a dining room, and the listed bedrooms and bathrooms. The calculations you will create are shown in Figure 3.11. Your expected output is shown in Figure 3.12.

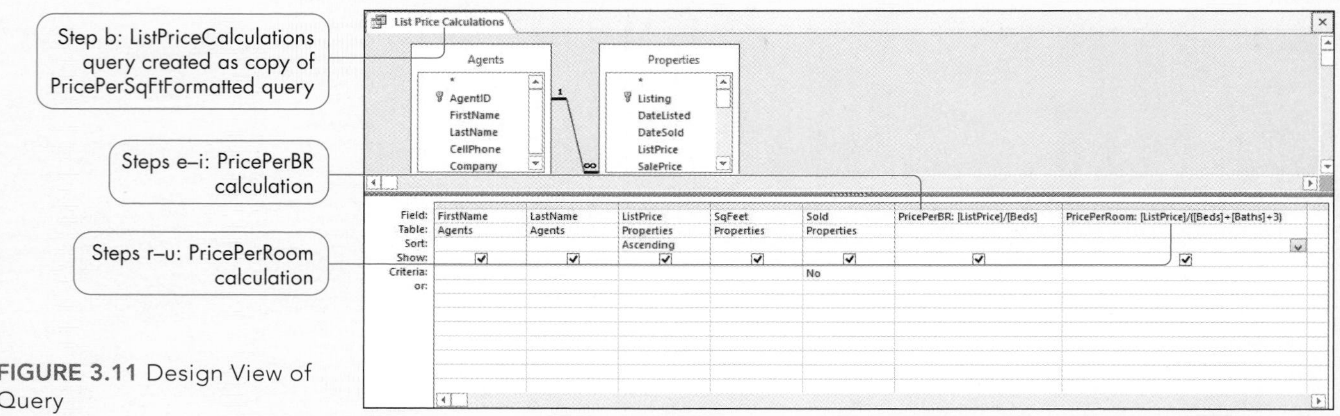

FIGURE 3.11 Design View of Query

a. Open *a03h1Property_LastFirst* if you closed it at the end of Hands-On Exercise 1 and save it as **a03h2Property_LastFirst**, changing *h1* to *h2*.

b. Create a copy of the Price Per Sq Ft Formatted query with the name **List Price Calculations**.

The new query is displayed in the Navigation Pane. The name of the query suggests it should contain calculations based on each property's list price.

c. Open the List Price Calculations query in Design view. Click the **WrongPricePerSqFt field**. Click **Delete Columns** in the Query Setup group on the QUERY TOOLS DESIGN tab.

> **TROUBLESHOOTING:** If instead of the column being deleted, a new row named *Delete* appears on the bottom half of the screen, close the query without saving, open in Design view once more, and ensure you are clicking Delete Columns in the Query Setup group. If you click Delete under Query Type, you will get very different results.

d. Click in the top cell in the PricePerSqFt column and click **Builder** in the Query Setup group.

The Expression Builder dialog box opens, displaying the current formula.

TROUBLESHOOTING: If the Builder is gray and cannot be clicked, ensure you have clicked in the top cell of the column.

e. Change the PricePerSqFt field name to **PricePerBR**.

f. Double-click the **[SqFeet] field** in the expression and press **Delete**.

g. Click the **plus sign** (+) under Expression Elements, next to the *a03h2Property_LastFirst* database in the Expression Elements box, to expand the list. Click + next to *Tables* and click the table named **Properties**.

   The fields from the Properties table are now listed in the middle column (Expression Categories).

h. Double-click the **Beds field** to add it to the expression box.

   The expression now reads *PricePerBR: [ListPrice]/[Properties]![Beds].*

i. Highlight the **[Properties]! prefix** in front of *Beds* and press **Delete**.

   The expression now reads *PricePerBR: [ListPrice]/[Beds].* As the Beds field name is unique within our query, the table name is not necessary. Removing this makes the query easier to read. If a field named Beds appeared in more than one table in our query, removing the table name would cause problems.

j. Click **OK** and click **Run** to view the query results.

   Notice the column heading still reads Price Per Sq Ft. Also notice the column's contents are formatted as Currency. These settings were copied when we copied the query.

k. Switch to Design view and ensure the **PricePerBR field** is selected. Click **Property Sheet** in the Show/Hide group and change the **Caption** to **Price Per Bedroom**. Close the Property Sheet. Run the query and examine the changes.

   The PricePerBR column now has an appropriate caption.

l. Switch to Design view. Select the entire **PricePerBR expression**, right-click the selected expression, and then select **Copy**. Right-click in the top cell of the next blank column and select **Paste**.

   You will edit the copy so that it reflects the price per room. As stated already, you assume the kitchen, living room, dining room, and the bedrooms and bathrooms will make up the number of rooms. Your final formula would be the list price divided by the total number of rooms, which is the number of bedrooms (in the Beds field), plus the number of bathrooms (found in the Baths field), plus 3 (a constant representing the kitchen, living room, and dining room).

m. Click **Builder** in the Query Setup group.

n. Change the PricePerBR field name to **PricePerRoom**.

o. Add **parentheses** before the [Beds] portion of the formula. Type a **plus sign** (+) after *[Beds].*

   As you want the addition to be done first, the order of operations states we must enclose the addition in parentheses. The expression box should read *PricePerRoom: [ListPrice]/([Beds]+*

p. Click the **plus sign** (+) next to the *a03h2Property_LastFirst* database in the Expression Elements box to expand the list. Click the **plus sign** (+) next to *Tables* and click the **Properties table**.

   The fields from the Properties table are now listed in the Expression Categories box.

q. Double-click the **Baths field** to add it to the expression box.

   The expression now reads *PricePerRoom: [ListPrice]/([Beds]+[Properties]![Baths].*

r. Type another plus sign after *[Baths]* and type **3)**.

The expression now reads *PricePerRoom: [ListPrice]/([Beds]+[Properties]![Baths]+3)*.

s. Delete the [Properties]! portion of the expression and click **OK** to close the Expression Builder.

The expression now reads *PricePerRoom: [ListPrice]/([Beds]+[Baths]+3)*.

t. Click **Property Sheet**. Type **Price Per Room** in the **Caption box**. Close the Property Sheet.

u. Run the query. Widen the PricePerRoom column if necessary in order to see all the values.

Step i: Price Per Bedroom results

Step u: Price Per Room results

List Price Calculations

First Name	Last Name	List Price	Square Feet	Sold	Price Per Bedroom	Price Per Room
StudentFirst	StudentLast	$109,140.00	1133	No	$54,570.00	$18,190.00
Bill	Sabey	$119,990.00	1202	No	$59,995.00	$17,141.43
Anny	Almonte	$122,220.00	1235	No	$61,110.00	$17,460.00
Robert Allen	Dickey	$129,780.00	1132	No	$64,890.00	$18,540.00
Bill	Sabey	$136,680.00	1375	No	$68,340.00	$22,780.00
Karean	Eissler	$138,990.00	1276	No	$69,495.00	$19,855.71
Anny	Almonte	$140,693.00	1490	No	$70,346.50	$20,099.00
Karean	Eissler	$140,904.00	1301	No	$70,452.00	$23,484.00
Anny	Almonte	$150,200.00	1652	No	$75,100.00	$21,457.14
StudentFirst	StudentLast	$163,737.00	1476	No	$81,868.50	$27,289.50
StudentFirst	StudentLast	$164,436.00	1850	No	$82,218.00	$27,406.00
Pradeep	Rana	$166,530.00	1676	No	$83,265.00	$27,755.00
StudentFirst	StudentLast	$166,552.00	1623	No	$83,276.00	$27,758.67
Anny	Almonte	$166,800.00	1598	No	$83,400.00	$27,800.00
Anny	Almonte	$168,354.00	1651	No	$84,177.00	$24,050.57
StudentFirst	StudentLast	$168,504.00	1625	No	$84,252.00	$28,084.00
Anny	Almonte	$172,458.00	1798	No	$86,229.00	$24,636.86
Bill	Sabey	$174,230.00	1771	No	$87,115.00	$29,038.33
StudentFirst	StudentLast	$174,720.00	1694	No	$87,360.00	$29,120.00
Robert Allen	Dickey	$174,720.00	1610	No	$87,360.00	$29,120.00
Anny	Almonte	$174,720.00	1667	No	$87,360.00	$29,120.00
Robert Allen	Dickey	$175,560.00	1562	No	$87,780.00	$25,080.00
StudentFirst	StudentLast	$177,984.00	1707	No	$88,992.00	$29,664.00
Bill	Sabey	$179,712.00	1854	No	$89,856.00	$25,673.14
Bill	Sabey	$182,385.00	2014	No	$45,596.25	$22,798.13
Anny	Almonte	$183,312.00	1721	No	$91,656.00	$30,552.00
Anny	Almonte	$184,473.00	1791	No	$92,236.50	$26,353.29

Record: 1 of 213 No Filter Search

FIGURE 3.12 Final Results of Query

v. Save and close the query.

TIP Switching Between Object Views

You can switch between object views quickly by clicking View, or you can click the View arrow and select the desired view from the list. Another way to switch between views is to right-click the object tab and select the view from the shortcut menu.

TIP Expression Builder and Property Sheet

You can launch the Expression Builder by either clicking Builder in the Query Setup group on the Design tab or by right-clicking in the top row of the query design grid and selecting Build. Similarly, you can display the Property Sheet by clicking Property Sheet in the Show/Hide group on the Design tab or by right-clicking the top row of the query design grid and selecting Properties from the shortcut menu.

STEP 2 » USE BUILT-IN FUNCTIONS

Don and Matt feel like they are close to making an offer on a house. They would like to restrict the query to houses that cost $150,000 or less. They would also like to calculate the estimated mortgage payment for each house. You create this calculation using the Pmt function. You will use the Pmt function to calculate an estimated house payment for each of the sold properties. You make the following assumptions: 80% of the sale price will be financed, a 30-year term, monthly payments, and a fixed 6.0% annual interest rate. Refer to Figures 3.13 and 3.14 as you complete Step 2.

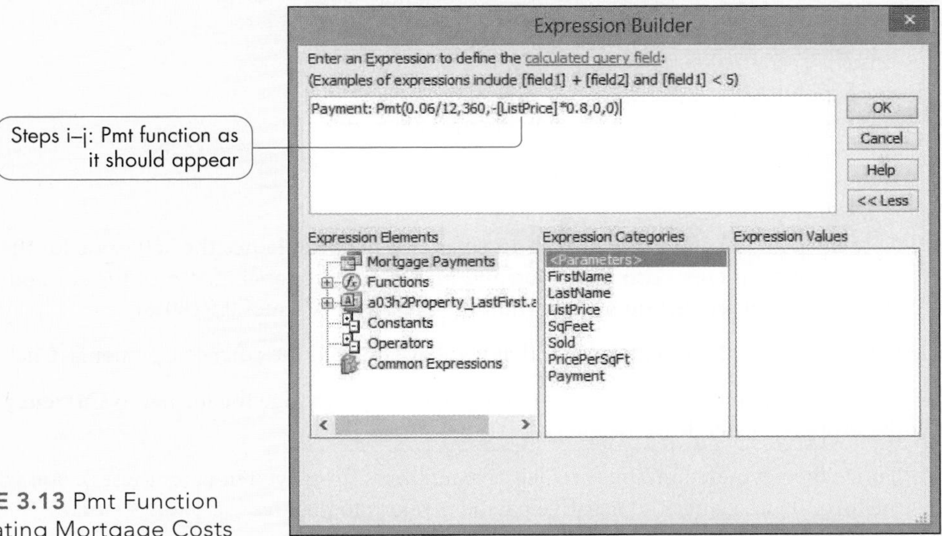

FIGURE 3.13 Pmt Function Calculating Mortgage Costs

a. Create a copy of the Price Per Sq Ft Formatted query named **Mortgage Payments**.

The new query is displayed in the Navigation Pane.

b. Right-click **Mortgage Payments** and select **Design View**.

c. Delete the WrongPricePerSqFt field.

The WrongPricePerSqFt field is not needed for this query.

> **TROUBLESHOOTING:** If you do not see the WrongPricePerSqFt field, ensure you copied the correct query.

d. Type **<=150000** in the Criteria row of the ListPrice column. Press **Enter**.

The query, when it is run, will show only the houses that cost $150,000 or less.

e. Click in the top cell of the first blank column. Click **Builder** in the Query Setup group to open the Expression Builder dialog box.

f. Double-click **Functions** in the Expression Elements box and click **Built-In Functions**.

g. Click **Financial** in the Expression Categories box.

h. Double-click **Pmt** in the Expression Values box.

The expression box displays:

Pmt(«rate», «num_periods», «present_value», «future_value», «type»)

i. Position the insertion point before the Pmt function. Type **Payment:** to the left of the Pmt function.

The expression box now displays:

Payment:Pmt(«rate», «num_periods», «present_value», «future_value», «type»)

TROUBLESHOOTING: If you forget to add the calculated field name to the left of the expression, Access will add *Expr1* to the front of your expression for you. You can edit the Expr1 name later, after the Expression Builder is closed.

j. Click each argument to select it and substitute the appropriate information. Make sure there is a comma between each argument.

Argument	Replacement Value
«rate»	0.06/12
«num_periods»	360
«present_value»	[ListPrice]*0.8
«future_value»	0
«type»	0

Note the loan is a 30-year loan with 12 payments per year, hence the 360 value for the number of payments. Also note, Don and Matt plan on financing 80% of the cost, putting 20% down. Therefore, you need to multiply the list price times 0.8 (80%).

k. Examine Figure 3.13 to make sure that you have entered the correct arguments. Click **OK**.

l. Click **OK**. Open the **Property Sheet** for *Payment* and change the format to **Currency**. Close the Property Sheet. **Run** the query.

Notice the payment amounts are negative numbers (displayed in parentheses). You will edit the formula to change the negative payment values to positive.

m. Right-click the **Mortgage Payments tab** and select **Design View**. Click **Builder**. Add a **minus sign** (–) to the left of *[ListPrice]* and click **OK**.

By adding the negative sign in front of the ListPrice field, you ensure the value is displayed as a positive number. The expression now reads *Payment: Pmt(0.06/12,360, –[ListPrice]*0.8,0,0)*.

The calculated field values should now appear as positive values formatted as currency, as shown in Figure 3.14.

Mortgage Payments

First Name	Last Name	List Price	Square Feet	Sold	Price Per Sq Ft	Payment
StudentFirst	StudentLast	$109,140.00	1133	No	$96.33	$523.48
Bill	Sabey	$119,990.00	1202	No	$99.83	$575.52
Anny	Almonte	$122,220.00	1235	No	$98.96	$586.22
Robert Allen	Dickey	$129,780.00	1132	No	$114.65	$622.48
Bill	Sabey	$136,680.00	1375	No	$99.40	$655.57
Karean	Eissler	$138,990.00	1276	No	$108.93	$666.65
Anny	Almonte	$140,693.00	1490	No	$94.42	$674.82
Karean	Eissler	$140,904.00	1301	No	$108.30	$675.83

Steps l–n: Payment field displayed as a positive number, formatted as Currency

FIGURE 3.14 Results of Mortgage Payments Query

n. Click **OK**. Run the query and examine the results.

The query displays a column containing the calculated monthly mortgage payment, formatted as currency.

o. Save and close the query. Keep the database open if you plan to continue with the next Hands-On Exercise. If not, close the database and exit Access.

Aggregate Functions

Aggregate functions perform calculations on an entire column of data and return a single value. Aggregate functions—such as Sum, Avg, and Count—are used when you need to evaluate a group of record values rather than the individual records in a table or query.

Access refers to aggregate functions as Totals. Totals can be added to the Datasheet view of a query, or they can be added to a query's Design view. Based on the data type, different aggregate functions will be available. Numeric fields are eligible for all of the functions, whereas Short Text fields are not. A list of common aggregate functions is shown in Table 3.4.

A car dealer's monthly inventory report is a good example of a report that might contain aggregate information. The cars would be grouped by model, then by options package and color. At the end of the report, a summary page would list the count of cars in each model for quick reference by the sales reps. In the property database, aggregate information could be grouped by county or by subdivision. For example, the average home price per county could be presented in a query or a report. This would give prospective buyers a good idea of home prices in their target counties. Almost every company or organization that uses a database will require some type of aggregate data.

TABLE 3.4 Common Aggregate Functions

Function	Description	Use with Data Type(s)
AVG	Calculates the average value for a column. The function ignores null values.	Number, Currency, Date/Time
COUNT	Counts the number of items in a column. The function ignores null values.	All data types except a column of multivalued lists.
MAXIMUM	Returns the item with the highest value. For text data, the highest value is "Z." The function ignores null values.	Number, Currency, Date/Time, Short Text
MINIMUM	Returns the item with the lowest value. For text data, the lowest value is "a." The function ignores null values.	Number, Currency, Date/Time, Short Text
SUM	Adds the items in a column. Works only on numeric and currency data.	Number, Currency

In this section, you will learn how to create and work with aggregate functions. Specifically, you will learn how to use the Total row and create a totals query.

Adding Aggregate Functions to Datasheets

Aggregate functions are most commonly used in tables, queries, and reports. Occasionally, aggregate functions are also added to the *form footer* section of forms. Aggregate data helps users evaluate the values in a single record as compared to the aggregate of all the records. If you are considering buying a property in Bergen County, New Jersey, for $150,000, and the average price of a property in that county is $450,000, you know you are getting a good deal (or buying a bad property).

Access provides two methods of adding aggregate functions to a query—a ***Total row***, which displays the results of the aggregate function as the last row in the Datasheet view of a table or query, and a totals query created in Query Design view.

The first method enables you to add a Total row to the Datasheet view. This method is quick and easy and has the advantage of showing the total information while still showing the individual records. Adding a Total row to a query or table can be accomplished by most users, even those who are not familiar with designing a query. Note the Total row values cannot be modified; you can change the aggregate function displayed there, but you cannot overwrite the numbers.

Add a Total Row in a Query or Table

STEP 1

Figure 3.15 shows the Total row added to the Datasheet view of a query. You can choose any of the aggregate functions that apply to numeric fields. Follow these steps to add a Total row to a query or table:

1. Ensure you are viewing the query in Datasheet view.
2. Click Totals in the Records group on the HOME tab. The Total row is added at the bottom of the datasheet, below the new record row of the query or table.
3. In the new Total row, you can select one of the aggregate functions by clicking in the cell and clicking the arrow. The list of aggregate functions includes Sum, Avg, Count, and others.

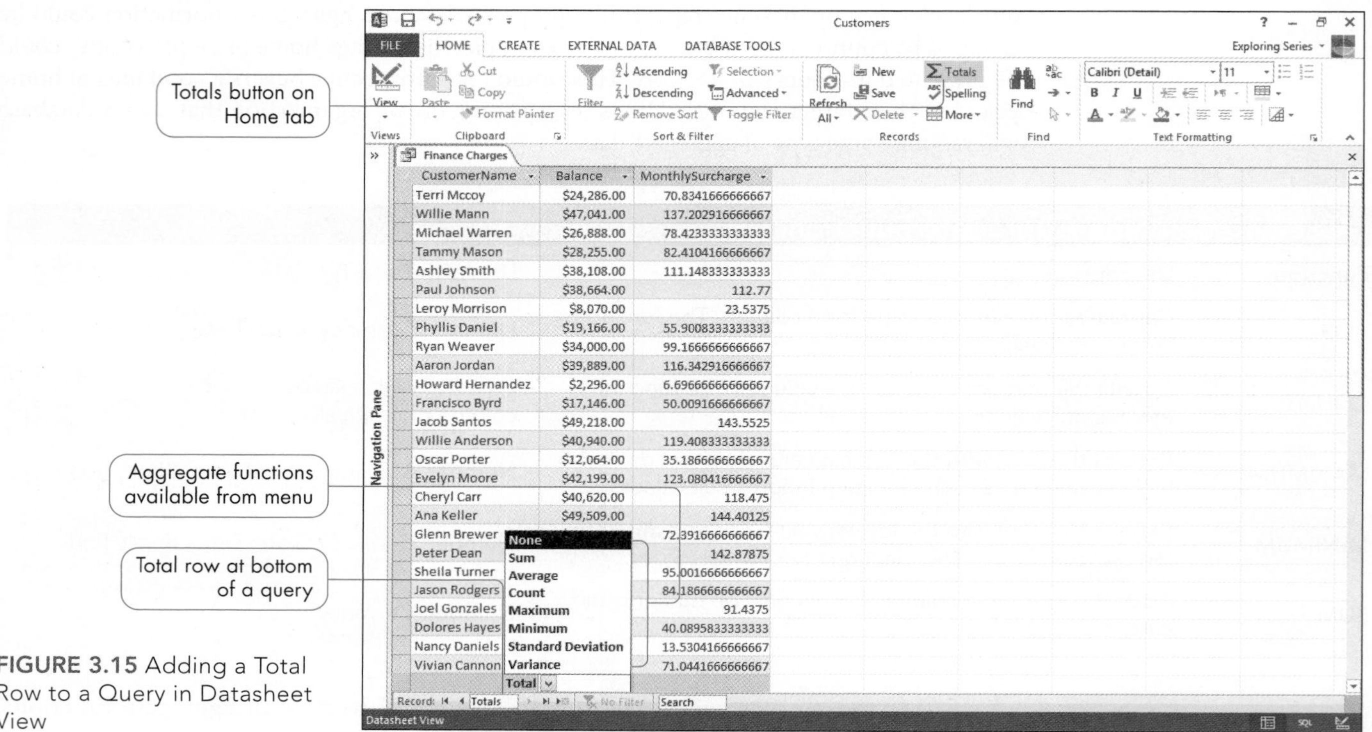

FIGURE 3.15 Adding a Total Row to a Query in Datasheet View

Creating Queries with Aggregate Functions

The second method to display aggregate functions requires you to alter the design of a query and add a Total row in the Query Design view. Once the totals data is assembled, you can use it to make decisions. For example, you can use the Count function to show the number of houses sold. You could also use the Avg function to show the average sale price for houses. This method has the advantage of enabling you to group your data by categories.

Many times, you will need to find some sort of averages for fields, and you may need to do more in-depth statistics than just an overall set as we did in the previous few pages. Instead of wanting to see the average sale price for houses, you may want to see the average sale price by city. Using the total row in the previous example, this is not feasible. Another limitation of the previous example is that I might want to see the average sale price, minimum sale price, and maximum sale price. Using the previous method, we would have to put the sale price field into our query three times, leading to repeated columns.

Instead of showing detail, we can quickly see the overall statistics for the entire table or query. For example, if you want to see the number of listings, average value, and the average size in square feet for all properties in your table, you can run a totals query to get that data and not see details. Instead of doing that, we can create a different type of query to summarize our data.

Create a Basic Totals Query

A ***totals query*** contains an additional row in the query design grid and is used to display aggregate data when the query is run. Figure 3.16 shows a totals query in Design view, and Figure 3.17 shows the results.

To create a Totals query:

1. Create a query in Design view and add the fields for which you want to get statistics. For example, in the preceding example, we would add the Listing, List Price, and Square Feet fields.
2. Click Totals in the Show/Hide group on the QUERY TOOLS DESIGN tab to display the total row. A new row should display in your query between the Table and Sort options. You will notice it defaults to Group By.
3. For each field, select the menu next to Group By and select the aggregate function you want applied to that field. For example, we want to count the number of listings and average both the list price and square feet values.
4. If you would like to apply specific formats, display the Property Sheet (as we did earlier in this chapter) and adjust the settings for each field.
5. Run the query to see your results.

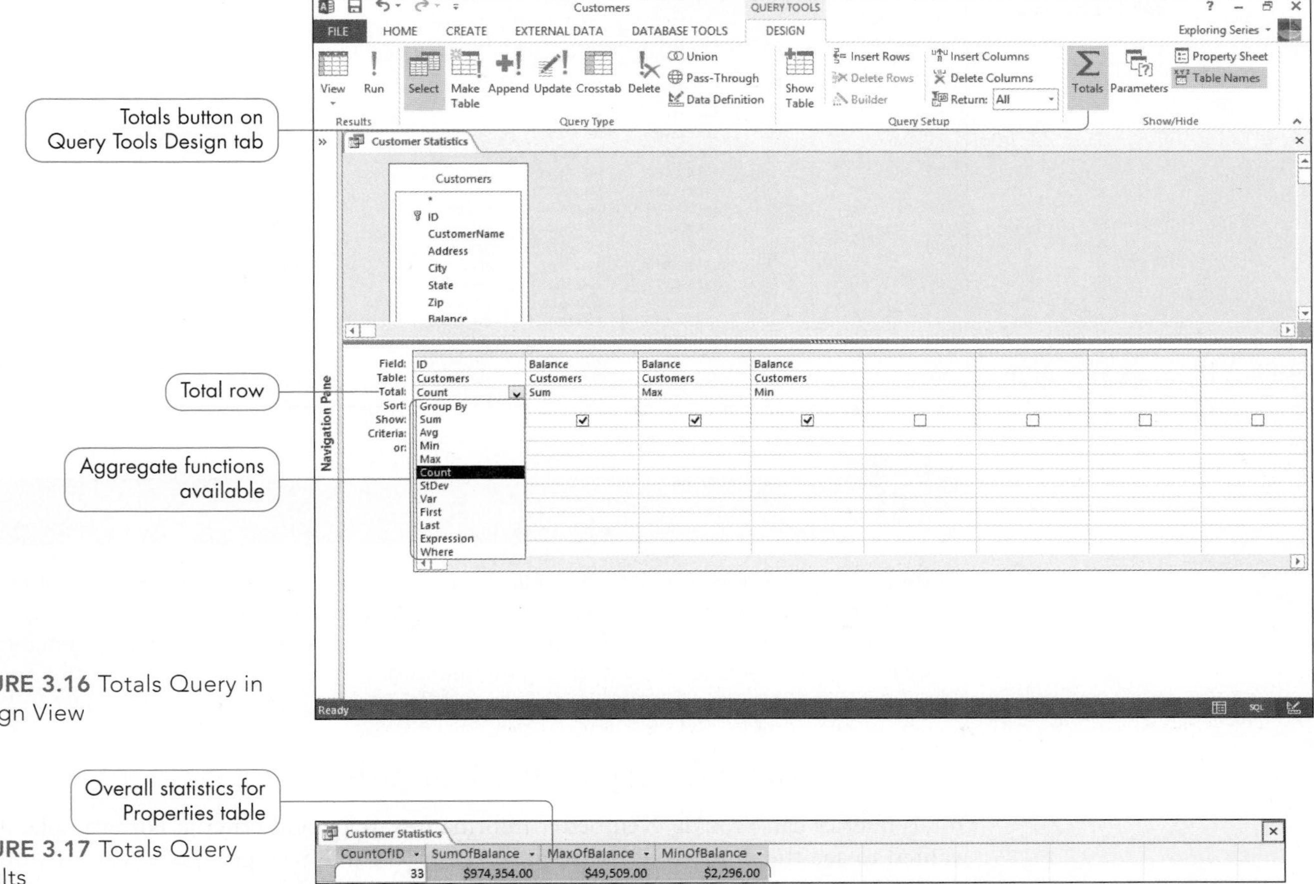

FIGURE 3.16 Totals Query in Design View

FIGURE 3.17 Totals Query Results

Create a Totals Query with Grouping

Grouping a query allows you to summarize your data by the values of a field. For example, you want to see the results not for the entire table, but instead by state. You can add the State field as a grouping level, and Access will show you the statistics you request for each state.

To group an existing query, add the field you wish to group by to the query in Design view. You would then verify the Total row displays Group By (see Figure 3.18). So if you want to see the results by state, add the State field to the query and leave the Total with the default of Group By. You may want to move this column to the beginning, as it will make your query easier to read.

Figure 3.18 shows the Design view of a totals query with five columns, one of which is the grouping field. Figure 3.19 shows the results of this query.

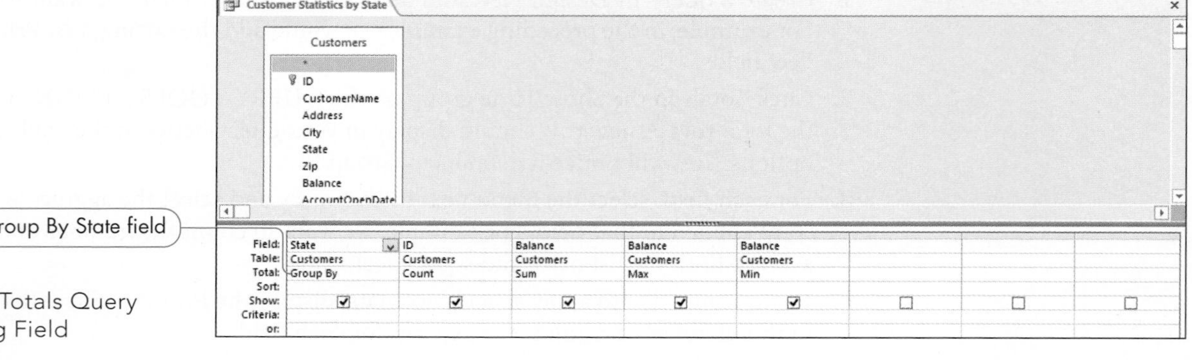

FIGURE 3.18 Totals Query with Grouping Field

Statistics by state

Customer Statistics by State

State	CountOfID	SumOfBalance	MaxOfBalance	MinOfBalance
AK	3	$105,936.00	$40,940.00	$26,888.00
AL	1	$8,070.00	$8,070.00	$8,070.00
CA	2	$45,095.00	$31,350.00	$13,745.00
GA	2	$14,360.00	$12,064.00	$2,296.00
IA	2	$50,982.00	$35,609.00	$15,373.00
IL	2	$57,830.00	$38,664.00	$19,166.00
MA	1	$48,987.00	$48,987.00	$48,987.00
MN	1	$32,572.00	$32,572.00	$32,572.00
MO	1	$28,255.00	$28,255.00	$28,255.00
MS	1	$30,631.00	$30,631.00	$30,631.00
NC	1	$28,864.00	$28,864.00	$28,864.00
NM	1	$39,889.00	$39,889.00	$39,889.00
NY	1	$24,358.00	$24,358.00	$24,358.00
OH	2	$65,440.00	$40,620.00	$24,820.00
OK	4	$127,393.00	$49,218.00	$17,146.00
OR	1	$4,639.00	$4,639.00	$4,639.00
PA	1	$49,509.00	$49,509.00	$49,509.00
SC	1	$34,000.00	$34,000.00	$34,000.00
TN	1	$47,041.00	$47,041.00	$47,041.00
WA	2	$69,498.00	$45,212.00	$24,286.00
WI	1	$29,730.00	$29,730.00	$29,730.00
WV	1	$31,275.00	$31,275.00	$31,275.00

FIGURE 3.19 Query Grouped by State Field

TIP Too Much Grouping

Beware that the more grouping levels you add, the less valuable the data is probably going to be; a typical totals query will group by only a few columns. As the purpose of grouping is to get some sort of aggregate data (such as a sum) for related data, grouping by more fields leads to less data being summarized.

Create a Totals Query with a Condition

Totals queries can provide even better information if you add criteria. For example, if you wanted to see the number of houses, average price, and average square feet for only the unsold properties, grouped by state, you can add the Sold field to the query. You would set the criteria to No to indicate that the Sold field is no. You should select Where from the menu in the Total row for any field you add to which you wish to apply criteria. Figure 3.20 shows a query with a condition added, and Figure 3.21 shows the results. You can compare this to Figure 3.19 to see the change in results.

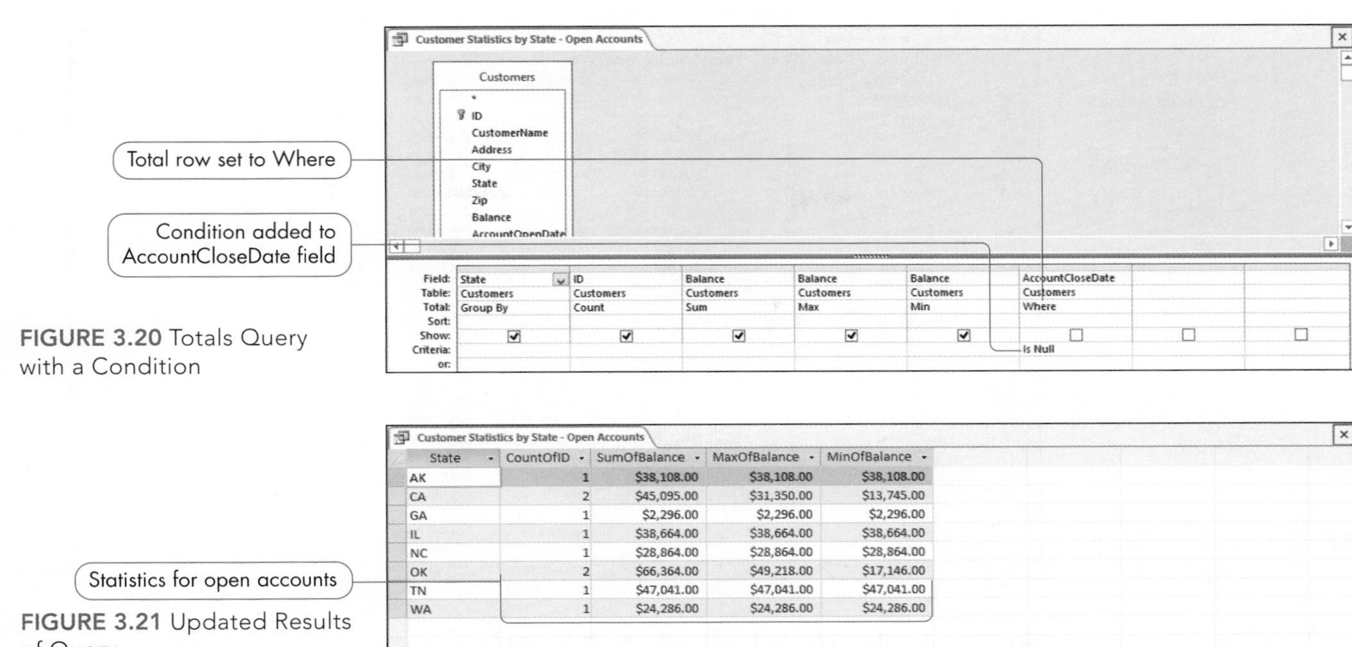

Field:	State	ID	Balance	Balance	Balance	AccountCloseDate
Table:	Customers	Customers	Customers	Customers	Customers	Customers
Total:	Group By	Count	Sum	Max	Min	Where
Criteria:						Is Null

FIGURE 3.20 Totals Query with a Condition

State	CountOfID	SumOfBalance	MaxOfBalance	MinOfBalance
AK	1	$38,108.00	$38,108.00	$38,108.00
CA	2	$45,095.00	$31,350.00	$13,745.00
GA	1	$2,296.00	$2,296.00	$2,296.00
IL	1	$38,664.00	$38,664.00	$38,664.00
NC	1	$28,864.00	$28,864.00	$28,864.00
OK	2	$66,364.00	$49,218.00	$17,146.00
TN	1	$47,041.00	$47,041.00	$47,041.00
WA	1	$24,286.00	$24,286.00	$24,286.00

FIGURE 3.21 Updated Results of Query

Create a Totals Query with Multiple Grouping Levels

At times, you may want to add multiple grouping fields. For example, instead of grouping by State, you might want to group by City. However, if you group by city, customers with the same city name in different states would be grouped together. For example, all 50 states have a location named Greenville. If you grouped by city, all customers with a city of Greenville, regardless of state, would appear as a group. This is probably not your intention. Instead, you probably would want to see results by City and State, and thus would want to add multiple grouping levels. Figure 3.22 shows a second grouping level, and Figure 3.23 shows the results of the query if we group by State and then by City. Notice the multiple Greenville results.

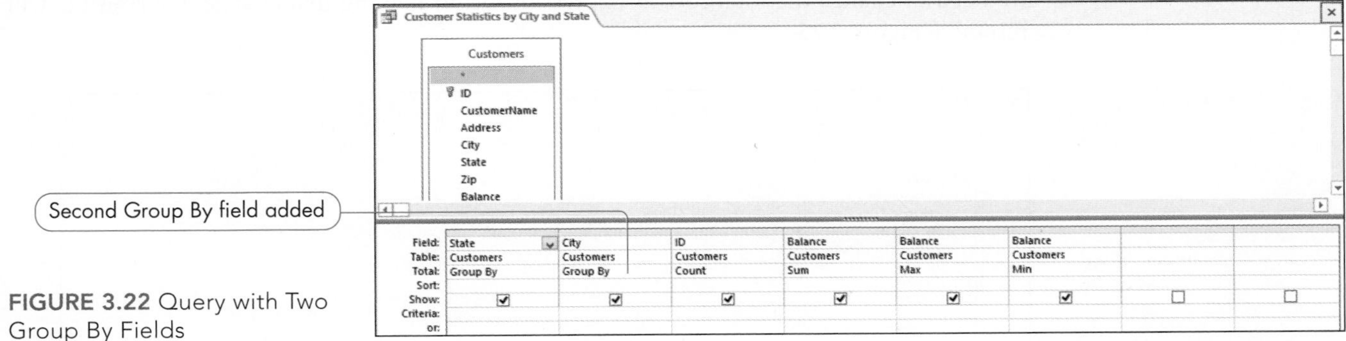

Field:	State	City	ID	Balance	Balance	Balance
Table:	Customers	Customers	Customers	Customers	Customers	Customers
Total:	Group By	Group By	Count	Sum	Max	Min

FIGURE 3.22 Query with Two Group By Fields

Each state may have multiple entries

City field added to query

State	City	CountOfID	SumOfBalance	MaxOfBalance	MinOfBalance
AK	Greenville	2	$67,828.00	$40,940.00	$26,888.00
AK	Kaktovik	1	$38,108.00	$38,108.00	$38,108.00
AL	Greenville	1	$8,070.00	$8,070.00	$8,070.00
CA	Los Angeles	1	$13,745.00	$13,745.00	$13,745.00
CA	San Diego	1	$31,350.00	$31,350.00	$31,350.00
GA	Austell	1	$2,296.00	$2,296.00	$2,296.00
GA	Leary	1	$12,064.00	$12,064.00	$12,064.00
IA	Albert City	1	$15,373.00	$15,373.00	$15,373.00
IA	Iowa City	1	$35,609.00	$35,609.00	$35,609.00
IL	Champaign	2	$57,830.00	$38,664.00	$19,166.00
MA	Southampton	1	$48,987.00	$48,987.00	$48,987.00
MN	Beltrami	1	$32,572.00	$32,572.00	$32,572.00
MO	De Kalb	1	$28,255.00	$28,255.00	$28,255.00
MS	Meridian	1	$30,631.00	$30,631.00	$30,631.00
NC	Raleigh	1	$28,864.00	$28,864.00	$28,864.00
NM	Bard	1	$39,889.00	$39,889.00	$39,889.00
NY	Saint Bonavent	1	$24,358.00	$24,358.00	$24,358.00
OH	Canton	1	$40,620.00	$40,620.00	$40,620.00
OH	Cincinnati	1	$24,820.00	$24,820.00	$24,820.00
OK	Albany	1	$17,146.00	$17,146.00	$17,146.00
OK	Canadian	1	$42,199.00	$42,199.00	$42,199.00
OK	Lahoma	1	$18,830.00	$18,830.00	$18,830.00
OK	Rufe	1	$49,218.00	$49,218.00	$49,218.00
OR	Fall Creek	1	$4,639.00	$4,639.00	$4,639.00
PA	Pine Bank	1	$49,509.00	$49,509.00	$49,509.00
SC	Clemson	1	$34,000.00	$34,000.00	$34,000.00
TN	Auburntown	1	$47,041.00	$47,041.00	$47,041.00

FIGURE 3.23 Results of Query with Two Group By Fields

Add a Calculated Field to a Totals Query

STEP 3» Once you have created a totals query, you can create calculated fields as you did earlier in the chapter. Often, you will want to apply an aggregate function to an existing field, such as summing up the values in a field. However, there may be times when you would prefer to apply an aggregate function to a calculation rather than a field.

We will use a customer purchases database to demonstrate this. When working with a customer order database, you may have a field for each order containing the total order cost and another field for each order containing the shipping cost. If you use the Sum aggregate function and group by the customer ID, you would have the total amount of their orders, and then as a separate column the total cost of the shipping they have paid. Instead of doing that, you may prefer to first create a calculated field that adds the total order cost and shipping cost for each order, and then group by a CustomerName. You will notice in Figure 3.24 we need to change the total row to Expression. After making that change, your results will resemble Figure 3.25.

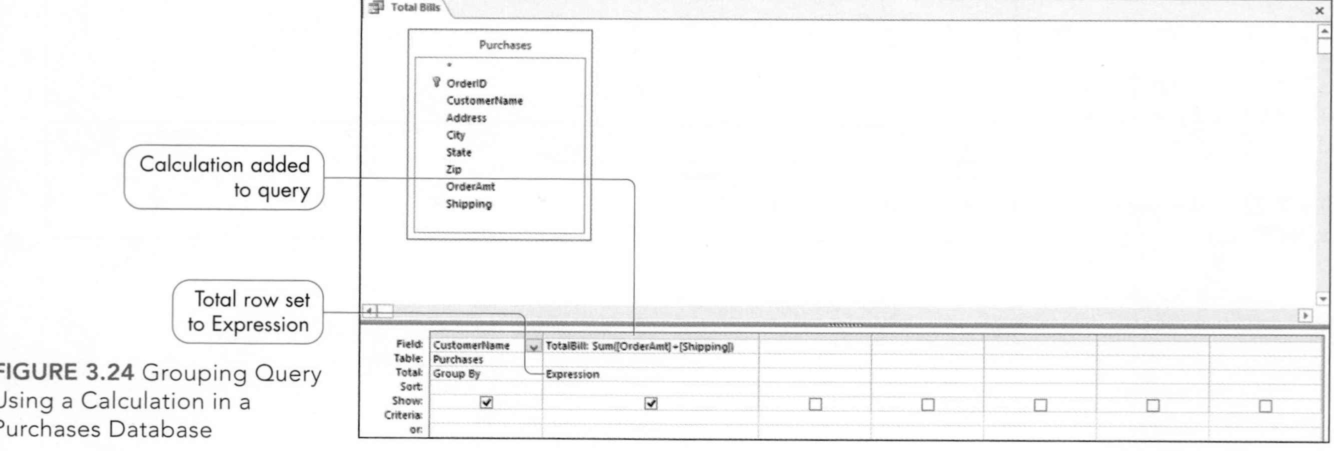

FIGURE 3.24 Grouping Query Using a Calculation in a Purchases Database

Results are each customer's total bill

Total Bills

CustomerName	TotalBill
Alice Ray	$688.99
Alicia Byrd	$810.50
Amber Ingram	$506.50
Annette Gibson	$720.99
Arthur Powell	$477.99
Beth Vaughn	$203.99
Carla Black	$478.50
Crystal Delgado	$166.99
Esther Bennett	$198.50
Eva Turner	$673.99
Florence Douglas	$633.99
Frances Foster	$317.50
Gina West	$629.99
Gloria Medina	$615.99
Harold Wolfe	$432.50
Heather Davidson	$343.50
Jamie Wheeler	$243.99
Jeanette Griffin	$436.50
Keith Strickland	$349.50
Lawrence Payne	$390.50
Leonard Delgado	$161.50
Lynn Brooks	$363.50
Marvin Santiago	$757.98
Megan Wheeler	$720.99
Phillip Medina	$676.50
Steve Mills	$674.50
Thelma Burgess	$529.99

FIGURE 3.25 Results of Grouping Query with a Calculation in a Purchases Database

In the third Hands-On Exercise, you will add aggregate functions to datasheets, create a totals query, and add grouping, conditions, and calculated fields to totals queries.

Quick Concepts

1. What are the benefits of aggregate functions? Give an example. ***p. 767***
2. How do you add a Total row to a datasheet? ***p. 768***
3. What is a totals query? ***p. 769***
4. What is the difference between a query with a Total row and a totals query? ***p. 769***

Hands-On Exercises

Watch the Video for this Hands-On Exercise!

MyITLab® HOE3 Training

3 Aggregate Functions

The investors decide it would be helpful to analyze the property lists they purchased. Some of the lists do not have homes that match their target criteria. The investors will either need to purchase new lists or alter their criteria. You create several totals queries to evaluate the property lists.

Skills covered: Add Aggregate Functions to Datasheets • Create a Totals Query with Grouping and Conditions • Add a Calculated Field to a Totals Query

STEP 1 » ADD AGGREGATE FUNCTIONS TO DATASHEETS

You begin your property list analysis by creating a total row in the Datasheet view of the Mortgage Payments query. This will give you a variety of aggregate information for each column. Refer to Figure 3.26 as you complete Step 1.

Step g: Average of PricePerSqFt

Step f: Count of Listing

Step e: Average of ListPrice

Step c: Total row

Mortgage Payments

First Name	Last Name	List Price	Square Feet	Listing	Sold	Price Per Sq Ft	Payment
StudentFirst	StudentLast	$109,140.00	1133	10004	No	$96.33	$523.48
Bill	Sabey	$119,990.00	1202	10091	No	$99.83	$575.52
Anny	Almonte	$122,220.00	1235	10036	No	$98.96	$586.22
Robert Allen	Dickey	$129,780.00	1132	10028	No	$114.65	$622.48
Bill	Sabey	$136,680.00	1375	10008	No	$99.40	$655.57
Karean	Eissler	$138,990.00	1276	10016	No	$108.93	$666.65
Anny	Almonte	$140,693.00	1490	10069	No	$94.42	$674.82
Karean	Eissler	$140,904.00	1301	10061	No	$108.30	$675.83
*							
Total		$129,799.63		8		$102.60	

FIGURE 3.26 Total Row Added to Query Datasheet

a. Open *a03h2Property_LastFirst* if you closed it at the end of Hands-On Exercise 2 and save it as **a03h3Property_LastFirst**, changing *h2* to *h3*.

b. Right-click the **Mortgage Payments query** in the Navigation Pane and select **Design View**. Drag the **Listing field** from the Properties table to the fifth column.

   The Listing field is now in the fifth column, between the SqFeet and Sold fields. The other columns shift to the right.

> **TROUBLESHOOTING:** If you drag the Listing field to the wrong position, you can drag it again to the correct location.

c. Switch to Datasheet view. Click **Totals**, in the Records group on the HOME tab to display the Total row.

   The Total row displays as the last row of the query results.

d. Click in the cell that intersects the Total row and the List Price column.

e. Click the arrow and select **Average** to display the average value of all the properties that have not sold. Widen the List Price column if you can't see the entire total value.

   The average list price of all properties is $129,799.63.

f. Click the arrow in the Total row in the Listing column and select **Count** from the list.

   The count of properties in this datasheet is 8.

g. Click in the **Total row** in the Price Per Sq Ft column. Click the arrow and select **Average** to display the average price per square foot.

   The average price per square foot is $102.60.

h. Save and close the query.

STEP 2 » CREATE A TOTALS QUERY WITH GROUPING AND CONDITIONS

You create a totals query to help Don and Matt evaluate the properties in groups. Refer to Figure 3.27 and Figure 3.28 as you complete Step 2.

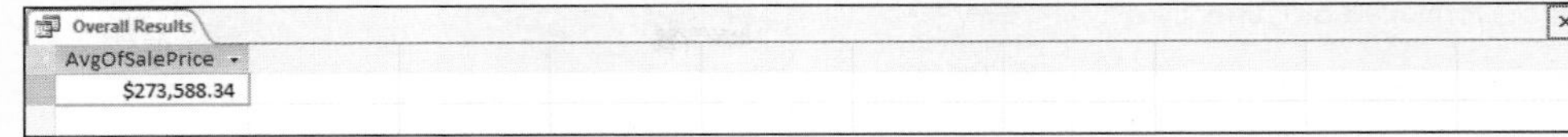

FIGURE 3.27 Overall Results Query

a. Click **Query Design** in the Queries group of the CREATE tab.

You create a new query in Query Design; the Show Table dialog box opens.

b. Add the Properties table from the Show Table dialog box. Close the Show Table dialog box.

c. Add the SalePrice and Sold fields from the Properties table to the query design grid.

d. Click **Totals** in the Show/Hide group of the QUERY TOOLS DESIGN tab to show the Total row.

A new row labeled Totals displays at the bottom of the screen in the design grid, between the Table and Sort rows. Each field will have Group By listed in the new row by default.

e. Click the **Group By arrow** in the SalePrice column Total row and select **Avg.**

f. Click the **Group By arrow** in the Sold column Total row and select **Where**. Type **Yes** in the Criteria row.

This criterion will limit the results to sold houses only.

g. Click in the **SalePrice field** and click **Property Sheet** in the Show/Hide group. Change the SalePrice format to **Currency**. Close the Property Sheet. Run the query and compare your results to Figure 3.27.

The results show an overall average of $273,588.34 for the sold properties in the database.

h. Click **Save** on the Quick Access Toolbar and type **Overall Results** as the Query Name in the Save As dialog box. Click **OK**. Close the query.

i. Click **Query Design** in the Query group of the HOME tab to create a new query.

j. Add the Properties table and the Lists table from the Show Table dialog box. Close the Show Table dialog box.

k. Add the NameOfList field from the Lists table and the SalePrice, Listing, and Sold fields from the Properties table to the query design grid.

l. Click **Totals** on the QUERY TOOLS DESIGN tab in the Show/Hide group to show the Total row.

A new row labeled Total appears at the bottom of the screen in the design grid between the Table and Sort rows.

m. Change the Total row for *SalePrice* to **Avg.**

n. Change the Total row for *Listing* to **Count**.

o. Change the Total row for *Sold* to **Where**. Type **Yes** in the Criteria row.

This criterion will limit the results to sold houses only.

p. Click in the **SalePrice field** and click **Property Sheet** in the Show/Hide group. Change the SalePrice format to **Currency**.

q. Change the caption of the Listing column to **Number Sold**. Run the query and widen the columns as shown in Figure 3.28.

Notice Major Houses has the only average sale price under $200,000. As Don and Matt are hoping to focus on inexpensive properties, they will focus on properties offered by this source. Notice the query results show the number of properties sold in each source, in addition to the average sale price. This will help determine which sources have been more effective.

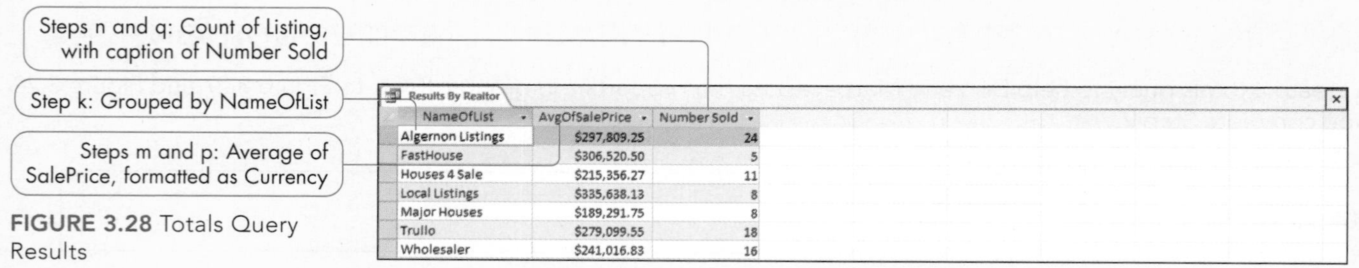

NameOfList	AvgOfSalePrice	Number Sold
Algernon Listings	$297,809.25	24
FastHouse	$306,520.50	5
Houses 4 Sale	$215,356.27	11
Local Listings	$335,638.13	8
Major Houses	$189,291.75	8
Trullo	$279,099.55	18
Wholesaler	$241,016.83	16

FIGURE 3.28 Totals Query Results

r. Click **Save** on the Quick Access Toolbar and type **Results By Realtor** as the Query Name in the Save As dialog box. Click **OK**. Keep the query open for the next step.

STEP 3 » ADD A CALCULATED FIELD TO A TOTALS QUERY

The previous query shows the average value of the properties by realtor. However, Don and Matt learned at the seminar they attended that the longer a property has been on the market, the better your chances of negotiating a better price. You will revise the query to include the average number of days on the market for each realtor. Refer to Figure 3.29 as you complete Step 3.

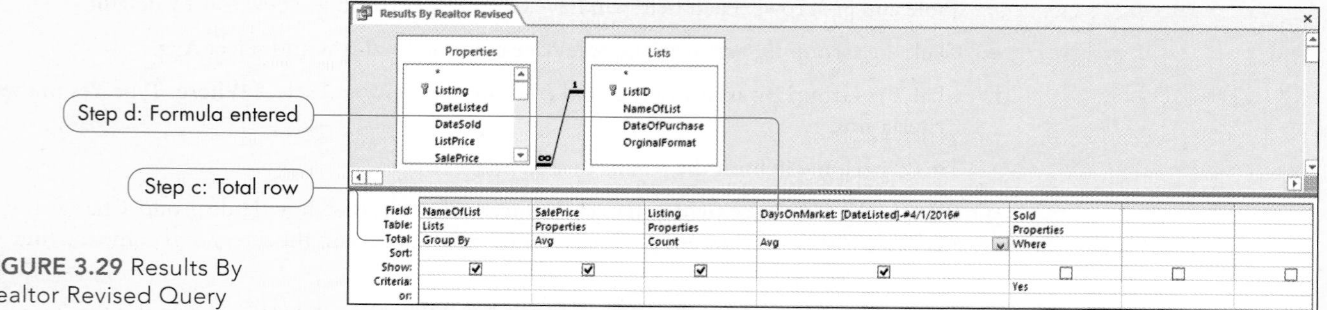

FIGURE 3.29 Results By Realtor Revised Query

a. Click the **FILE tab**, click **Save As**, and then click **Save Object As**. Click **Save As**, and in the *Save 'Results By Realtor' to:* box, type **Results By Realtor Revised.**

b. Switch to the Datasheet view for the new Results By Realtor Revised query, if necessary.

c. Click **Totals** in the Records group of the HOME tab. Change the Total to **Sum** in the Number Sold column.

The total number of houses sold (90) now displays at the bottom of the Number Sold column.

d. Switch to Design view. In the first blank column, type **DaysOnMarket: [DateListed] – #4/1/2016#** to create a new calculated field. Change the Total row to **Avg.**

The DaysOnMarket field will show the average number of days on the market for each realtor's listings.

e. Display the Property Sheet for the DaysOnMarket field and change the Format property to **Fixed**. Change the Decimal Places property to **0**. Close the Property Sheet.

> **TROUBLESHOOTING:** If you do not see a Decimal Places property immediately beneath the Format property, change the format to Fixed, save and close the query, and then reopen the query. Refer to Figure 3.4 for the location of Decimal Places.

f. Run the query and examine the DaysOnMarket field.

Major Houses listings have an average of 117 days on the market. The combination of inexpensive prices and properties that do not sell quickly may help Don and Matt negotiate with the realtor.

g. Save and close the query.

h. Exit Access. Submit based on your instructor's directions.

Chapter Objectives Review

After reading this chapter, you have accomplished the following objectives:

1. **Create a calculated field in a query.**
    - Calculations can be based on fields, constants, and/or functions.
    - Understand the order of operations: Calculated fields follow the same order of operations as mathematical equations—parentheses, then exponentiation, then multiplication and division, and finally addition and subtraction.
    - Build expressions with correct syntax: Expressions must be written using proper syntax—the rules governing the way you give instructions to Access.
2. **Format and save calculated results.**
    - Calculated results may not have the format you want; change the properties of a calculated field using the Property Sheet.
    - Recover from common errors: Common errors include forgetting the colon in the appropriate location, spelling errors, and misuse of the order of operations.
    - Verify calculated results: Always check the results of your equation; Access will check for syntax errors, but not logic errors.
3. **Create expressions with the Expression Builder.**
    - Expression Builder helps create complex expressions.
    - Create an expression: Expression Builder allows you to choose fields and built-in functions easily, and gives you a larger screen to view your expression.
    - Launch the Expression Builder: Clicking the Builder button will open the tool.
4. **Use built-in functions in Access.**
    - Access includes functions, or predefined computations that perform complex calculations.
    - There are almost 150 built-in functions in Access.
    - Some require arguments: inputs (often fields or constants) given to a function.
    - Calculate payments with the Pmt Function: The Pmt function accepts the rate per term, number of payments, and loan amount and calculates a loan payment.
5. **Add aggregate functions to datasheets.**
    - Aggregate functions perform calculations on an entire column of data and return a single value.
    - Include functions such as Sum, Avg, and Count.
    - Add a total row in a query or table: The total row displays at the bottom of a query or table; it can perform any aggregate function on each column.
6. **Create queries with aggregate functions.**
    - This gives you more control over application of your aggregate functions.
    - Create a basic totals query: Create a query as usual and click the Totals button in Design view.
    - Create a totals query with grouping: Grouping allows you to summarize your data by the values of a field; instead of showing overall averages, add state as a grouping field and see averages for each state.
    - Create a totals query with a condition: Conditions can be added to totals queries, such as only showing listings with the Sold field equal to No.
    - Create a totals query with multiple grouping levels: You can add multiple grouping levels; for example, you could group by State and then by City to get more detailed results.
    - Add a calculated field to a totals query: You can apply an aggregate function to the results of a calculation; for example, subtract a date from today's date to get the number of days a listing is active and calculate the overall average of days listings are active.

Key Terms Matching

Match the key terms with their definitions. Write the key term letter by the appropriate numbered definition.

- **a.** Aggregate Function
- **b.** Argument
- **c.** Constant
- **d.** Expression
- **e.** Expression Builder
- **f.** Function
- **g.** Grouping
- **h.** Order of Operations
- **i.** Pmt Function
- **j.** Property Sheet
- **k.** Syntax
- **l.** Total Row
- **m.** Totals Query

1. ______ A value that does not change. **p. 746**
2. ______ A formula used to calculate new fields from the values in existing fields. **p. 746**
3. ______ Determines the sequence by which operations are calculated in an expression. **p. 747**
4. ______ Dictates the structure and components required to perform the necessary calculations in an equation or evaluate expressions. **p. 747**
5. ______ Enables you to change settings such as number format, number of decimal places, and caption. **p. 749**
6. ______ An Access tool that helps you create more complicated expressions. **p. 757**
7. ______ A predefined computation that performs a complex calculation. Almost 150 are built into Access. **p. 759**
8. ______ Any data needed to produce output for a function. **p. 759**
9. ______ Calculates the periodic loan payment given the interest rate per period, term of the loan in months, and the original value of the loan. **p. 759**
10. ______ Performs calculations on an entire column of data and returns a single value. Includes functions such as Sum, Avg, and Count. **p. 767**
11. ______ Displays aggregate function results as the last row in the Datasheet view of a table or query. **p. 767**
12. ______ Makes an additional row available in the query design grid. Used to display aggregate data when the query is run. **p. 769**
13. ______ Allows you to summarize your data by the values of a field. **p. 769**

Multiple Choice

1. Which of the following correctly identifies the rules for the order of operations?
   (a) Parentheses, exponentiation, addition, subtraction, multiplication, division
   (b) Exponentiation, parentheses, addition, subtraction, multiplication, division
   (c) Addition, subtraction, multiplication, division, exponentiation, parentheses
   (d) Parentheses, exponentiation, multiplication, division, addition, subtraction

2. What is the result of the following expression?
   (3 * 5) + 7 – 2 – 6 / 2
   (a) 17
   (b) 7
   (c) 14.5
   (d) 13

3. Which of the following *cannot* be adjusted in the Property Sheet?
   (a) Number of decimal places
   (b) Mathematical expression
   (c) Caption
   (d) Number format (for example, Currency)

4. Which of the following is *not* an aggregate function?
   (a) Pmt
   (b) Avg
   (c) Count
   (d) Min

5. Which of the following can be added to a totals query?
   (a) Conditions
   (b) Grouping fields
   (c) Aggregate functions
   (d) All of the above can be added to a totals query

6. Which statement about a totals query is *true*?
   (a) A totals query is created in Datasheet view.
   (b) A totals query may contain several grouping fields but only one aggregate field.
   (c) A totals query is limited to only two fields, one grouping field and one aggregate field.
   (d) A totals query may contain several grouping fields and several aggregate fields.

7. Which of the following statements is *true*?
   (a) A total order cost would be a common field to group by.
   (b) A last name would be a common field to group by.
   (c) For best results, add as many group by fields as possible.
   (d) None of the above statements is true.

8. After creating a calculated field, you run the query and a Parameter dialog box appears on your screen. How do you respond to the Parameter dialog box?
   (a) Click OK to make the parameter box go away.
   (b) Look for a possible typing error in the calculated expression.
   (c) Type numbers in the Parameter box and click OK.
   (d) Close the query without saving changes. Reopen it and try running the query again.

9. A query contains student names. You run the query and while in Datasheet view, you notice a spelling error on one of the student's names. You correct the error in Datasheet view. Which statement is *true*?
   (a) The name is correctly spelled in this query but will be misspelled in the table and all other queries based on the table.
   (b) The name is correctly spelled in this query and any other queries, but will remain misspelled in the table.
   (c) You cannot edit data in a query.
   (d) The name is correctly spelled in the table and in all queries based on the table.

10. Which of the following about the Total row in the query design grid is *false*?
    (a) The Total row enables you to apply aggregate functions to the fields.
    (b) The Total row does not display by default in all new queries.
    (c) The Total row is located between the Table and Sort rows.
    (d) The Total row cannot be applied to numeric fields.

Practice Exercises

1 Comfort Insurance

The Comfort Insurance Agency is a mid-sized company with offices located across the country. Each employee receives a performance review annually. The review determines employee eligibility for salary increases and the annual performance bonus. The employee data is stored in an Access database, which is used by the human resources department to monitor and maintain employee records. Your task is to calculate the salary increase for each employee; you will also calculate the average salary for each position. This exercise follows the same set of skills as used in Hands-On Exercises 1 and 2 in the chapter. Refer to Figure 3.30 as you complete this exercise.

Raises and Bonuses

Last Name	First Name	Performance	Salary	2016 Increase	New Salary
Lacher	Tom	Good	$31,200.00	3.00%	$32,136.00
Fantis	Laurie	Good	$28,000.00	3.00%	$28,840.00
Fleming	Karen	Average	$41,100.00	3.00%	$42,333.00
Mc Key	Boo	Good	$39,600.00	3.00%	$40,788.00
Daniels	Phil	Good	$42,600.00	3.00%	$43,878.00
Park	Johnny	Excellent	$48,400.00	3.00%	$49,852.00
Johnson	Debbie	Excellent	$39,700.00	3.00%	$40,891.00
Drubin	Lolly	Good	$37,000.00	3.00%	$38,110.00
Titley	David	Good	$40,200.00	3.00%	$41,406.00
Grippando	Joan	Average	$26,100.00	3.00%	$26,883.00
Block	Leonard	Excellent	$26,200.00	3.00%	$26,986.00
Mills	Jack	Average	$44,600.00	3.00%	$45,938.00
Nagel	Mimi	Average	$46,200.00	3.00%	$47,586.00
Rammos	Mitzi	Excellent	$32,500.00	3.00%	$33,475.00
Vieth	Paula	Good	$40,400.00	3.00%	$41,612.00
Novicheck	Deborah	Good	$46,800.00	3.00%	$48,204.00
Brumbaugh	Paige	Average	$49,300.00	3.00%	$50,779.00
Abrams	Wendy	Good	$47,500.00	3.00%	$48,925.00
Harrison	Jenifer	Excellent	$44,800.00	3.00%	$46,144.00
Gander	John	Average	$38,400.00	3.00%	$39,552.00
Sell	Mike	Excellent	$43,500.00	3.00%	$44,805.00
Smith	Denise	Average	$45,200.00	3.00%	$46,556.00
Pawley	Eleanor	Excellent	$42,700.00	3.00%	$43,981.00
Harris	Jennifer	Average	$34,900.00	3.00%	$35,947.00
North	Randy	Excellent	$31,700.00	3.00%	$32,651.00
Shuffield	Jan	Good	$33,700.00	3.00%	$34,711.00
Barnes	Jeb	Excellent	$46,900.00	3.00%	$48,307.00

Record: 1 of 311 No Filter Search

FIGURE 3.30 Raises and Bonuses Query

a. Open *a03p1Insurance*. Save the database as **a03p1Insurance_LastFirst**.

b. Examine the Relationships for the database. Notice the table structure, relationships, and fields. Once you are familiar with the database, close the Relationships window.

c. Create a new query in Design view. Add the Employees and Titles tables.

d. Add the LastName, FirstName, Performance, and Salary fields from the Employees table to the query. Add the 2016Increase field from the Titles table to the query.

e. Click the top row of the first blank column in the query design grid and type **NewSalary:[Salary]+[Salary]*[2016Increase]** to create a calculated field that adds the existing salary to the increase. You may opt to use the Expression Builder if you prefer.

f. Click **Run** in the Results group to run the query. Look at the output in the Datasheet view. Verify that your answers are correct. Notice that the fourth column heading displays *2016 Increase*.

   This is the caption for the 2016Increase field in the Titles table that was carried over to the query. When a caption exists for a field in the table Design view, the caption also displays in the Query Datasheet view instead of the field name in the query.

g. Switch back to Design view. Click in the **NewSalary calculated field**, display the Property Sheet, and then change the format to **Currency**. Type **New Salary** in the **Caption box**. Close the Property Sheet.

h. Save the query as **Raises and Bonuses**. Close the query.

i. Create a new query in Design view. Add the Employees and Titles tables.

   You will create a query to show the average salary by position.

j. Add the TitleName field from the Titles table. From the Employees table, add the Salary field.

k. Display the Total row. Change the Total row for Salary to **Avg**. Leave the TitleName field set to **Group By**.

l. Click the **Salary field** and display the Property Sheet. Change the format for the field to **Currency**.

m. Run the query. Save the query as **Average Salary By Position** and close the query.

n. Exit Access and submit based on your instructor's directions.

2 Analyze Orders

FROM SCRATCH

You are the marketing manager of your company, and you must use the order information from an Access database to analyze sales trends. You need to determine the order revenue for all orders, grouped by Ship Country. The company would also like to check to see if there are order delays related to a specific employee. You must analyze shipping performance based on the number of days it takes to ship each order. This exercise follows the same set of skills as used in Hands-On Exercises 2 and 3 in the chapter. Refer to Figure 3.31 as you complete this exercise.

Shipping Issues

EmployeeID	TimeToShip
1	26
2	47
3	44
4	50
4	29
5	50
6	29
9	80

FIGURE 3.31 Shipping Issues Query

a. Create a new blank desktop database named **a03p2Orders_LastFirst**.
You will be shown a blank table in Datasheet view.

b. Click **View** in the Views group to switch to Design view. Save the table as **Orders**.

c. Change the first Field Name to **OrderID** and change the Data Type to **Number**. Type **CustomerID** in the second row and press **Tab**. Accept **Short Text** as the Data Type. Type **EmployeeID** in the third row and press **Tab**. Select **Number** for the Data Type.

d. Type and format the remainder of the fields as follows:

OrderDate	Date/Time
ShippedDate	Date/Time
ShipVia	Number
Revenue	Currency
ShipCountry	Short Text

e. Click **View** in the Views group to switch to Datasheet view. Click **Yes** to save the table. Add the three records as shown in the following table. Press **Tab** to move to the next field.

Order ID	Customer ID	Employee ID	Order Date	Shipped Date	Ship Via	Revenue	Ship Country
10248	WILMK	5	1/6/2017	1/19/2017	1	$142.86	Belgium
10249	TRADH	6	1/7/2017	1/10/2017	2	$205.38	Germany
10250	HANAR	4	1/10/2017	1/30/2017	2	$58.60	Venezuela

f. Open the *a03p2Orders* Excel file and click **Enable Editing**, if necessary. Click and hold **row 2** and drag through **row 828** so that all of the data rows are selected. Click **Copy** in the Clipboard group.

g. Return to Access and click on the **asterisk** (*) on the fourth row of the Orders table. Click **Paste** in the Clipboard group and click **Yes** to confirm that you want to paste all 827 rows into the Orders table. Save and close the table, and then close the spreadsheet and Excel. If prompted to save the data in the clipboard, click **No**.

h. Click the **CREATE tab** and click **Query Design** in the Queries group to start a new query. The Show Table dialog box opens. Add the Orders table and close the Show Table dialog box.

i. Add EmployeeID to the query and sort the table by EmployeeID in ascending order.

j. Use the Expression Builder to create a new calculated field. Type the following: **TimeToShip: [ShippedDate]-[OrderDate]**

   Run the query and verify that TimeToShip is displaying valid values.

k. Switch back to Design view. Add the criteria **>21** to the TimeToShip field. Run the query and compare your results with Figure 3.31.

   The results do not show a pattern of one employee's orders being delayed.

l. Save the query as **Shipping Issues**. Close the query.

m. Click the **CREATE tab** and click **Query Design** in the Queries group to start a new query. The Show Table dialog box opens. Add the Orders table and close the Show Table dialog box. Click **Totals** in the Show/Hide group.

n. Insert the ShipCountry and Revenue fields from the Orders table.

o. Verify the value for ShipCountry is set to **Group By** in the Totals row in Design view and verify that the value for the Revenue field is set to **Sum**.

p. Click in the **Revenue field**. Display the Property Sheet and change the caption to **Total Revenue**.

q. Click **Run** to see the results and save the query as **Revenue by Ship Country**. Close the query.

r. Exit Access and submit based on your instructor's directions.

Mid-Level Exercises

1 Small Business Loans

You are the manager of the small business loan department for the U.S. government. You need to calculate the payments for the loans that are currently on the books. To do this, you will need to create a query and add the Pmt function to calculate the loan payments for each loan. You will also summarize each loan by loan type (M=Mortgage, C=Car, and O=Other). Refer to Figure 3.32 as you complete this exercise.

Loan Payments

Company	LoanID	Amount	InterestRate	Term	LoanClass	Payment
Jones and Co	1	29,000.00	5.90%	15	M	$243.15
Elements, Inc.	2	23,000.00	5.25%	5	C	$436.68
Godshall Meats, LLC	3	24,000.00	4.50%	3	C	$713.93
Godshall Meats, LLC	4	12,000.00	3.99%	10	O	$121.44
Godshall Meats, LLC	5	60,000.00	5.50%	30	M	$340.67
Elements, Inc.	6	4,000.00	6.50%	5	O	$78.26
Jones and Co	7	43,000.00	5.50%	5	O	$821.35
Jones and Co	8	37,000.00	5.80%	30	M	$217.10
Jones and Co	9	15,000.00	4.75%	3	O	$447.88
Jones and Co	10	8,000.00	5.50%	15	M	$65.37
Godshall Meats, LLC	11	34,000.00	5.00%	3	C	$1,019.01
Godshall Meats, LLC	12	13,000.00	7.99%	5	O	$263.53
Jones and Co	13	46,000.00	6.50%	5	C	$900.04
Godshall Meats, LLC	14	56,000.00	5.99%	15	M	$472.26
Godshall Meats, LLC	15	54,000.00	6.25%	15	M	$463.01
Jones and Co	16	39,000.00	6.50%	15	M	$339.73
Jones and Co	17	21,000.00	6.00%	30	M	$125.91
Godshall Meats, LLC	18	27,000.00	5.50%	3	O	$815.29
Elements, Inc.	19	44,000.00	5.50%	5	C	$840.45
Godshall Meats, LLC	20	22,000.00	6.25%	4	C	$519.20
Godshall Meats, LLC	21	6,000.00	6.75%	4	C	$142.98
Godshall Meats, LLC	22	46,000.00	6.50%	15	M	$400.71
Jones and Co	23	25,000.00	5.00%	15	M	$197.70
Jones and Co	24	11,000.00	5.55%	30	M	$62.80
Jones and Co	25	52,000.00	4.99%	15	M	$410.94
*						
Total		751,000.00	5.74%	12		

FIGURE 3.32 Loan Payments Query Results

a. Open Access and create a new blank desktop database named **a03m1Loans_LastFirst**. Access will display a table named Table1 with one field, ID.

b. Switch to Design view. Type **Customers** in the **Save As dialog box** and click **OK**.

c. Change the first Field Name to **CustomerID** and accept **AutoNumber** as the Data Type. Type **Company** in the second row and press **Tab**. Accept **Short Text** as the Data Type. Type **FirstName** in the third row and press **Tab**. Accept **Short Text** as the Data Type.

d. Type the remainder of the fields:

LastName	Short Text
City	Short Text
State	Short Text
Zip	Short Text

e. Verify the first field is set as the primary key.

f. Switch to Datasheet view. Click **Yes** to save the table. Add the records as shown in the following table. Note you will allow Access to assign an ID. Once you have entered the records, close the Customers table.

Company	FirstName	LastName	City	State	Zip
Jones and Co	Robert	Paterson	Greensboro	NC	27401
Elements, Inc.	Merve	Kana	Paterson	NJ	07505
Godshall Meats, LLC	Francisco	De La Cruz	Beverly Hills	CA	90210

g. Click the **External Data tab** and click **Excel** in the Import & Link group. Click **Browse** to locate the *a03m1Loans* spreadsheet. Select the database and click **Open** at the bottom of the dialog box.

h. Ensure the *Import the source data into a new table in the current database option* is selected and click **OK**. Click **Next** three times, until you are asked to add a primary key. From the *Choose my own Primary Key* menu, select **LoanID** (this should be the default option). Click **Next** once more and click **Finish**. Click **Close** in the Save Import Steps dialog box.

i. Open the Loans table in Design view. Select the **InterestRate field** and change the format to **Percent**. Change the field size for the CustomerID field to **Long Integer**. Click **Yes** when prompted that some data may be lost. Save and close the table.

j. Click the **Database Tools tab** and click **Relationships** in the Relationships group. Add both tables to the Relationships window and close the Show Table dialog box.

k. Drag the **CustomerID field** from the Customers table and drop it onto the CustomerID field in the Loans table. Check the **Enforce Referential Integrity check box** in the Edit Relationships dialog box and click **Create**. Save and close the Relationships window.

l. Create a query using the two tables that will calculate the payment amount for each loan. Add the following fields: **Company**, **LoanID**, **Amount**, **InterestRate**, **Term**, and **LoanClass**. Sort the query by LoanID in ascending order. Save the query as **Loan Payments**.

★ m. Add a calculated field named **Payment** in the first blank column to calculate the loan payment for each loan, using the Expression Builder. Use the Pmt function. Insert the appropriate field names in place of the placeholder arguments. Assume the loans have monthly payments (12 payments per year). Ensure the payment displays as a positive number. Run the query.

The first loan should have a value of approximately $243.15 (the extra decimal places will be removed shortly). Refer to Figure 3.32. If your number does not match up, reexamine your formula.

TROUBLESHOOTING: If you cannot see the fields from your current query, ensure you have saved the query. Try closing and reopening the query.

n. Switch to Design view and change the display to **Currency format**. Run the query again to verify your changes. Compare your results to Figure 3.32.

o. Switch to Datasheet view and add a **Totals row**. Use it to calculate the sum of the amount column, the average interest rate, and the average term. Save and close the query.

p. Create a copy of Loan Payments. Save the new query as **Loan Payments Summary**.

q. Open the Loan Payments Summary query in Design view and rearrange the columns as follows: LoanClass, LoanID, Amount, and InterestRate. Delete columns CompanyName, Term, and Payment. Click **Totals** in the Show/Hide group. Change the Total row from left to right as follows: Group By, Count, Sum, and Avg. Run the query.

As we sorted the previous query by LoanID in Ascending order, this query will have the same sort by default.

r. Switch to Design view and display the Property Sheet. For the LoanID field, change the caption to **Loans**. For the Amount field, change the caption to **Total Amount** and change the format to **Currency**. For the InterestRate field, change the caption to **Avg Interest Rate** and change the format to **Percent**. Run the query. Save and close the query.

s. Exit Access, and submit based on your instructor's directions.

2 Investment Properties

You are in charge of LGS Investment's database, which contains all of the information on the properties your firm has listed and sold. Your task is to determine the length of time each property was on the market before it sold. You also need to calculate the sales commission from each property sold. Two agents will receive commission on each transaction: the listing agent and the selling agent. You also need to summarize the sales data by employee and calculate the average number of days each employee's sales were on the market prior to selling and the total commission earned by the employees. Refer to Figure 3.33 as you complete this exercise.

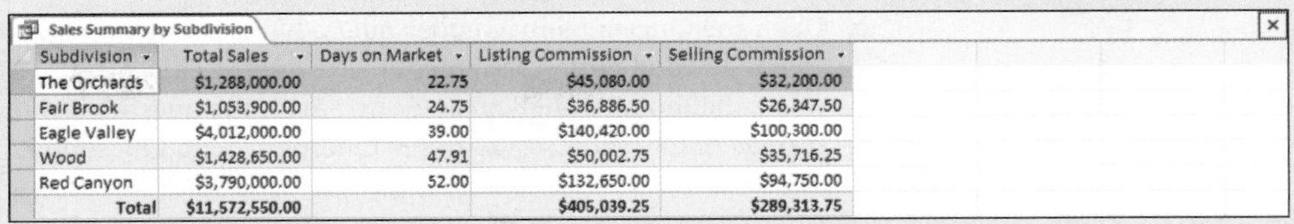

Sales Summary by Subdivision

Subdivision	Total Sales	Days on Market	Listing Commission	Selling Commission
The Orchards	$1,288,000.00	22.75	$45,080.00	$32,200.00
Fair Brook	$1,053,900.00	24.75	$36,886.50	$26,347.50
Eagle Valley	$4,012,000.00	39.00	$140,420.00	$100,300.00
Wood	$1,428,650.00	47.91	$50,002.75	$35,716.25
Red Canyon	$3,790,000.00	52.00	$132,650.00	$94,750.00
Total	$11,572,550.00		$405,039.25	$289,313.75

FIGURE 3.33 Sales Summary Query

a. Open *a03m2Homes*. Save the database as **a03m2Homes_LastFirst**.

b. Create a new query, add the necessary tables, and then add the following fields: from the Agents table, add the LastName field; from the Properties table, the DateListed, DateSold, SalePrice, SellingAgent, and ListingAgent fields; and from the SubDivision table, the Subdivision field.

c. Add criteria to the table to ensure the DateSold field is not empty (in other words, properties that have not been sold). Format the SalePrice field as **Currency**. Save the query as **Sales Report**.

d. Create a calculated field using the Expression Builder named **DaysOnMarket** by subtracting DateListed from DateSold. This will calculate the number of days each sold property was on the market when it sold. Add a caption of **Days on Market**.

e. Calculate the commissions for the selling and listing agents using two calculated fields. The listing commission rate is **3.5%** of the sale price, and the selling commission rate is **2.5%** of the sale price. You can type these in directly or use the Expression Builder. Name the newly created fields **ListComm** and **SellComm**. These fields contain similar expressions. They need to be named differently so that the proper agent—the listing agent or the selling agent—gets paid. Add captions and format the fields as **Currency**.

f. Save the query after you verify that your calculations are correct. In Datasheet view, add the Total row. Calculate the average number of days on the market and the sum for the SalePrice and the two commission fields. Save and close the query.

g. Create a copy of the Sales Report query named **Sales Summary by Last Name**. Remove the DateListed, SellingAgent, ListingAgent, and Subdivision fields.

h. Display the Total row. Group by LastName and change the DateSold field Total row to **Where**, so the condition carries over. Show the sum of SalePrice, the average of DaysOnMarket, and the sum for both ListComm and SellComm. Change the caption for the SalePrice field to **Total Sales** and format the DaysOnMarket field as **Fixed**. Run the query. Adjust column widths as necessary.

i. Adjust the Total row in the Datasheet view so it shows the sum of TotalSales. Save the query.

DISCOVER

j. Create a copy of the Sales Summary by Last Name query named **Sales Summary by Subdivision**. Modify the query so the grouping is based on the Subdivision field, not LastName. Sort the query results so the fewest Days on Market is first and the most Days on Market is last. Limit the results to the top five rows.

k. Exit Access and submit based on your instructor's directions.

3 Political Pollsters

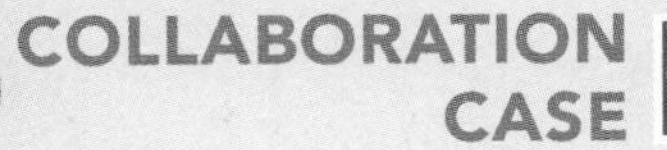

You are working with a group that would like to analyze survey results. You are specifically looking for trends in the data based on gender, political affiliation, and income level. To demonstrate the power of Access, you and your group will perform a small survey, add the results to a database, and create some queries to demonstrate how grouping can help get results.

a. Individually, open the *a03t1Survey.docx* file. Collect 10 responses each (unless directed to do otherwise by your instructor). You should try to survey a diverse group of people. You can do this survey via e-mail, Facebook, or another appropriate method. Bring the collected data to your group.

b. Open the *a03t1Survey* database and save the database as **a03t1Survey_GroupName**. Use the Enter New Survey Result form to enter all of your information into the existing database. There are four records to start your database.

c. Open the Questions By Gender query. Notice your average for question 1 is a number between 1 and 3. As your survey document listed Agree as a 3, Neutral as 2, and Disagree as 1, the higher the value, the more strongly people agree with the question. Modify the query so that you display the average of Question2, Question3, Question4, and Question5. Change the format for the new fields to **Fixed**.

d. Create a query named **Questions By Party**, using the Questions By Gender query as a guide, grouping by the PoliticalAffiliation field rather than the Gender field.

e. Create a query named **Questions By Income Level**, using the Questions By Gender query as a guide, grouping by the IncomeLevel field rather than the Gender field.

f. Examine your results. Discuss the results with your group and type up your conclusions in a new Word document named **a03t1SurveyResults_GroupName**. You should be able to make around five conclusions. An example of a conclusion might be that people of lower income levels are less interested in being taxed to support free Internet than people of higher income.

g. Exit Access and Word and submit based on your instructor's directions.

Beyond the Classroom

Too Many Digits

RESEARCH CASE

This chapter introduced you to calculated fields. Open the database *a03b2Interest* and save the database as **a03b2Interest_LastFirst**. Open the Monthly Interest query in Datasheet view. Notice the multiple digits to the right of the decimal in the Monthly Interest column; there should only be two digits. Search the Internet to find a function that will resolve this rounding problem. You only want to display two digits to the right of the decimal (even when you click on a Monthly Interest value). Apply your changes to the Monthly Interest field, change the format to **Currency**, and then run the query to test your changes. Save the query as **Monthly Interest Revised**. If you manage to find a solution, add a second column named **MonthlyInterestRounded** that rounds to the nearest dollar. Close the query, close the database, and then exit Access. Submit your work based on your instructor's directions.

Payroll Summary Needed

DISASTER RECOVERY 

You were given an Excel spreadsheet that contains paycheck information for your company. Your task is to summarize this data by employee Social Security Number (SSN) and report your results to your supervisor. Open the spreadsheet *a03b3Paychecks* and examine the data. Select all the data and copy the data. You will use Access to summarize the data in this spreadsheet. Open the Access database named *a03b3Payroll* and save it as **a03b3Payroll_LastFirst**. Open the Payroll table, select the first row, and then paste the records. Create a new totals query that summarizes the data by SSN; include the count of pay periods (using the ID field) and the sum of each currency field. Do not include the PayDate field in this query. Create a calculated field named **Total Compensation**, which totals all assets the employees have, including pay, 401(k) retirement, and health benefits. Add appropriate captions to shorten the default captions. Run the query and save it as **Payroll Summary**. Close the query, close the database, and then exit Access. Submit the database based on your instructor's directions.

Customer Service Dialog

SOFT SKILLS CASE

Passaic County Technology Services (PCTS) provides technical support for a number of local companies. Part of their customer service evaluation involves logging how calls are closed and a quick, one-question survey given to customers at the end of a call, asking them to rate their experience from 1 (poor) to 5 (excellent). To evaluate the effectiveness of their operation, they have asked you to create some queries to help evaluate the performance of the company. Open the database *a03b4PCTS* and save the database as **a03b4PCTS_LastFirst**.

1. Create a query to show each technician and his or her effectiveness.
   - List each technician's first and last names, the number of calls, and the average of the customer's satisfaction for all calls assigned to the rep.
   - Format the average in Standard format and sort by the average so the highest average customer satisfaction appears first.
   - Save the query as **Tech Effectiveness**.
2. Create a query to show how effective the company is by call type.
   - List the call type's description (for example, Hardware Support) and the number of calls and average customer satisfaction for all calls of that type.
   - Format the average in Standard format and sort by the average so the highest average customer satisfaction appears first.
   - Save the query as **Call Type Effectiveness**.

3. Create a query to show how satisfied each customer is.
   - List the company name and the number of calls and average customer satisfaction for all calls.
   - Format the average in Standard format and sort by the average so the highest average customer satisfaction appears first.
   - Save the query as **Customer Happiness**.

Now that you have created these queries, your supervisor should be able to quickly determine which technicians have the happiest customers, which call types the company is most effective on, and which customers are less happy than others. Close the queries, close the database, and then exit Access. Submit the database based on your instructor's directions.

Capstone Exercise

Northwind Traders, an international gourmet food distributor, is concerned about shipping delays over the past six months. Review the orders over the past six months and identify any order that was not shipped within 30 days. Each customer that falls within that time frame will be called to inquire about any problems the delay may have caused. In addition, you will create an order summary and an order summary by country.

Database File Setup

Open the food database, use Save As to make a copy of the database, and then use the new database to complete this capstone exercise. You will add yourself to the employee database.

a. Locate and open *a03c1Food* and save the database as **a03c1Food_LastFirst**.

b. Open the Employees table. Add yourself as an employee. Fill in all information, with the hire date as today. Set your *Title* to **Technical Aide**, extension to **1144**, and the Reports To field to **Buchanan, Steven**. Leave the EmployeePicture field blank.

c. Close the Employees table.

Shipping Efficiency Query

You need to create a query to calculate the number of days between the date an order was placed and the date the order was shipped for each order. As you create the query, run the query at several intervals so you can verify that the data look correct. The result of your work will be a list of orders that took more than three weeks to ship. The salespeople will be calling each customer to see if there was any problem with their order.

a. Create a query using Query Design. From the Customers table, include the fields CompanyName, ContactName, ContactTitle, and Phone. From the Orders table, include the fields OrderID, OrderDate, and ShippedDate.

b. Run the query and examine the records. Save the query as **Shipping Efficiency**.

c. Add a calculated field named **DaysToShip** to calculate the number of days taken to fill each order. (*Hint*: The expression will include the OrderDate and the ShippedDate; the results will not contain negative numbers.)

d. Run the query and examine the results. Does the data in the DaysToShip field look accurate? Save the query.

e. Add criteria to limit the query results to include any order that took more than 30 days to ship.

f. Add the Quantity field from the Order Details table and the ProductName field from the Products table to the query. Sort the query by ascending OrderID. When the sales reps contact these customers, these two fields will provide useful information about the orders.

g. Switch to Datasheet view to view the final results. This list will be distributed to the sales reps so they can contact the customers. In Design view, add the caption **Days to Ship** to the DaysToShip field.

h. Save and close the query.

Order Summary Query

You need to create an Order Summary that will show the total amount of each order in one column and the total discount amount in another column. This query will require four tables: Orders, Order Details, Products, and Customers. Query to determine if employees are following the employee discount policy. You will group the data by employee name, count the orders, show the total dollars, and show the total discount amount. You will then determine which employees are following the company guidelines.

a. Create a query using Query Design and add the four tables above. Add the fields OrderID and OrderDate. Set both fields' Total row to **Group By**.

b. Add a calculated field in the third column. Name the field **ExtendedAmount**. This field should multiply the number of items ordered by the price per item. This will calculate the total amount for each order. Format the calculated field as **Currency** and change the caption to **Total Dollars**. Change the Total row to **Sum**.

c. Add a calculated field in the fourth column. Name the field **DiscountAmount**. The field should multiply the number of items ordered, the price per item, and the discount field. This will calculate the total discount for each order. Format the calculated field as **Currency** and add a caption of **Discount Amt**. Change the Total row to **Sum**.

d. Run the query. Save the query as **Order Summary**. Return to Design view.

e. Add criteria to the OrderDate field so only orders made between 1/1/2016 and 12/31/2016 are displayed. Change the Total row to **Where**. This expression will display only orders that were created in 2016.

f. Run the query and view the results. Save and close the query.

Order Financing Query

Northwind is considering offering financing options to their customers with 5% interest, to be paid over 12 months.

a. Create a copy of the Order Summary query named **Order Financing**.

b. Switch to Design view of the new query and remove the DiscountAmount field.

c. Add a new field using the Expression Builder named **SamplePayment**. Insert the Pmt function with the following parameters:

- Use **.05/12** for the rate argument (5% interest, paid monthly)
- Use the number **12** for the num_periods argument (12 months)
- Use the calculated field **ExtendedAmount** for the present_value

d. Change the Total row to **Expression** for the SamplePayment field.

e. Change the Format for the SamplePayment field to **Currency**.

f. Save and close the query.

Order Summary by Country Query

You need to create one additional query based on the Order Summary query you created in a previous step. This new query will enable you to analyze the orders by country.

a. Create a copy of the Order Summary query named **Order Summary by Country**.

b. Replace the OrderID field with the Country field in Design view of the new query.

c. Run the query and examine the summary records; there should be 21 countries listed.

d. Switch to Design view and change the sort order so that the country with the highest ExtendedAmount is first and the country with the lowest ExtendedAmount is last.

e. Run the query and verify the results.

f. Save and close the query.

g. Exit Access and submit based on your instructor's directions.

Creating and Using Professional Forms and Reports

Moving Beyond Tables and Queries

OBJECTIVES AFTER YOU READ THIS CHAPTER, YOU WILL BE ABLE TO:

1. Create forms using form tools p. 792
2. Use form views p. 799
3. Work with a form layout control p. 802
4. Sort records in a form p. 804
5. Create reports using report tools p. 812
6. Use report views p. 819
7. Modify a report p. 821
8. Sort records in a report p. 824

CASE STUDY | Coffee Shop Starts New Business

The La Vida Mocha coffee shop in Paterson, New Jersey, once was an ordinary coffee shop selling retail coffee, tea, and pastries to its loyal customers in northern New Jersey. Then, in 2012, owner Ryung Park decided to use her knowledge of the coffee industry to sell coffee products to businesses in her area. This new venture grew quickly and soon became 25% of her annual revenue. Realizing that this new business would need more of her time each day, she decided to create an Access database to help track her customer, product, and order information.

With the help of a student from Passaic County Community College, she created a database with tables to hold data for customers, products, sales reps, and orders. She is currently using these tables to enter and retrieve information.

Ryung wants to have one of her employees, Nabil, manage the database. However, she does not want him to work in the tables; she wants him to work with forms. Ryung heard that forms have an advantage over tables because they can be designed to show one record at a time—this will reduce data-entry errors. Ryung would also like to create several reports for her own benefit so she can stay on top of the business by reviewing the reports each week.

You have been hired to help Ryung create the new forms and reports that she needs for the business. She will describe the forms and reports to you in detail and also provide written instructions. You will be expected to work independently to create the forms and reports.

Form Basics

A *form* is a database object that is used to add data into or edit data in a table. Most Access database applications use forms rather than tables for data entry and for looking up information. Three main reasons exist for using forms rather than tables for adding, updating, and deleting data. They are:

- You are less likely to edit the wrong record by mistake.
- You can create a form that shows data from more than one table simultaneously.
- You can create Access forms to match paper forms.

If you are adding data using a table with many columns, you could jump to the wrong record in the middle of a column accidentally. For example, you could enter the data for one record correctly for the first 10 fields but then jump to the row above and overwrite existing data for the remaining field values unintentionally. In this case, two records would have incorrect or incomplete data. A form will not allow this type of error because most forms restrict entry to one record at a time.

Many forms require two tables as their record source. For example, you may want to view a customer's details (name, address, e-mail, phone, etc.) as well as all of the orders he or she has placed. This would require using data from both the Customers and the Orders tables in one form. Similarly, you may want to view the header information for an order while also viewing the detail line items for the order. This would require data from both the Orders and Order Details tables. Both of these examples enable a user to view two record sources at the same time and make changes—additions, edits, or deletions—to one or both sources of data.

Finally, when paper forms are used to collect information, it is a good idea to design the electronic forms to match the paper forms. This will make data entry more efficient and reliable and ease the transition from paper form to computer form. Access forms can be designed to emulate the paper documents already in use in an organization. This facilitates the simultaneous use of both paper forms and electronic data. Databases do not necessarily eliminate paper forms; they supplement and coexist with them.

In this section, you will learn the basics of form design. You will discover multiple methods to create and modify Access forms.

Creating Forms Using Form Tools

Access provides a variety of options for creating forms. There are a number of built-in layouts that you can choose from. Database designers may eventually develop a preference for one or two types of form layouts, but keep in mind you have a lot of options if needed. You will want to find a balance between creating a form that is simple while still powerful enough to be of use.

Access provides 14 different tools for creating forms. You can find these options in the Forms group on the Create tab. The Forms group contains four of the most common form tools (Form, Form Design, Blank Form, and Form Wizard), a list of Navigation forms, and More Forms, as shown in Figure 4.1. Navigation forms provides a list of six templates to create a user interface for a database; the More Forms command lists four additional form tools (Multiple Items, Datasheet, Split Form, and Modal Dialog). Select a table or query, click one of the tools, and Access will create a form using the selected table or query. The most common of these tools, the *Form tool*, is used to create data-entry forms for customers, employees, products, and other primary tables.

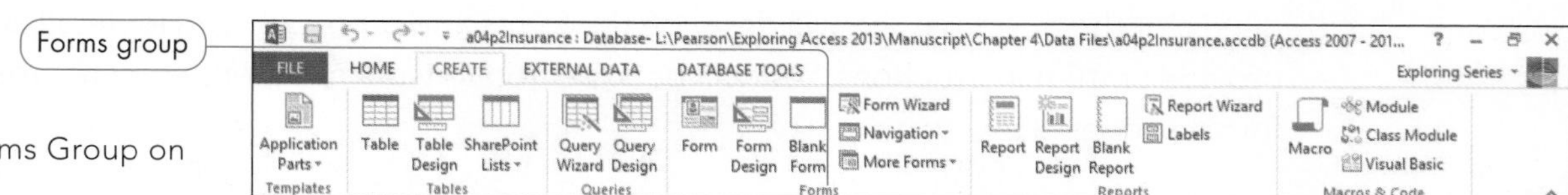

FIGURE 4.1 Forms Group on Create Tab

A complete list of all the Form tools available in Access is found in the Form Tools Reference at the end of this section. Many of the tools will be covered in this chapter. Some tools will not be covered, however, because they are not commonly used or because they are beyond the scope of this chapter (e.g., Form Design, Blank Form, Navigation forms, and Modal Dialog form). Use Microsoft Access Help to find more information about Form tools not covered in this chapter.

TIP Usability Testing

After a database object (such as a form) is finalized, it should be tested by both the database designer and the end users. The designer should be certain the report meets any criteria the users have given him or her. The designer should also browse through the records to make sure the values in all records (and not just the first record) display correctly. Likewise, the end users should have the opportunity to test the form and provide feedback. After all, they will be the ones using it, so the database designer has a responsibility to ensure the end users are comfortable with the object.

Ideally, a form should simplify data entry. Creating a form is a collaborative process between the form designer and the form users. This process continues throughout the life of the form, because the data needs of an organization may change. Forms designed long ago to collect information for a new customer account may not have an e-mail field; the form would have to be modified to include an e-mail field. The form designer needs to strike a balance between collecting the information users need to do their jobs and cluttering the form with extraneous fields. The users of the data know what they need and usually offer good feedback about which fields should be on a form. If you listen to their suggestions, your forms will function more effectively, the users' work will be easier, and your data will contain fewer data-entry errors.

After discussing the form with the users, it will help you to create the form in Access if you sketch the form first. After sketching the form, you will have a better idea of which form tool to use to create the form. After the form is created, use the sketch to determine which fields are required and in what the order of fields should be.

Identify a Record Source

Before you create a form, you must identify the record source. A ***record source*** is the table or query that supplies the records for a form or report. You may also see the record source referred to as a data source in certain help files and instructions. Use a table if you want to include all the records from a single table. Use a query if you need to filter the records in a table, if you need to combine records from two or more related tables, or if you do not want to display all fields.

For example, if a sales rep wants to create a form that displays customers from a single state only—where his customers reside—he should base the form on a query. Or, if a parts manager needs to review only parts with a zero on-hand quantity, he could create a form based on a query that includes only records with on-hand equal to zero.

Use the Form Tool

STEP 1» As noted earlier, the Form tool is the most common tool for creating forms. To use the Form tool:

1. Select a table or query from the Navigation Pane
2. On the CREATE tab, in the Forms group, click Form.

Based on that table or query, Access automatically creates a new form. You may need to modify the form slightly, but you can create a stacked layout form in a just one click. A ***stacked layout*** displays fields in a vertical column. Because this is a form, it will display one record at a time, as shown in Figure 4.2. The other type of layout you may use is a ***tabular layout***, which displays data horizontally across the page.

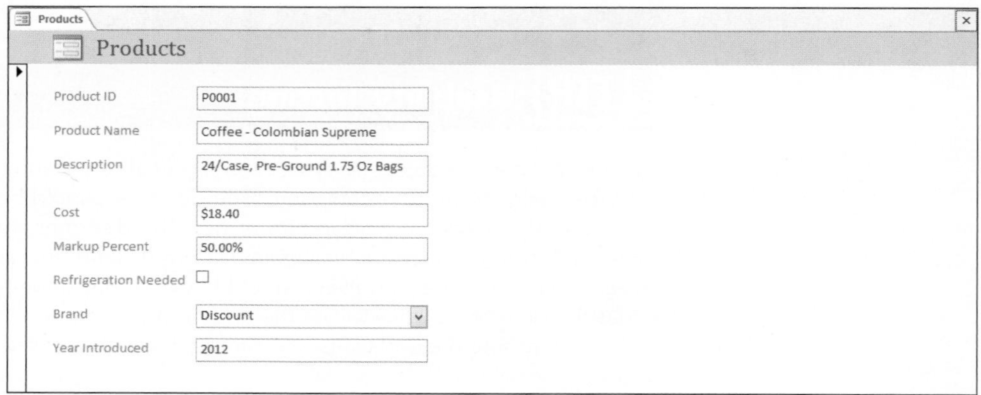

FIGURE 4.2 Form with a Stacked Layout

Understand Controls

Notice in Figure 4.3 that each field has a label on the left and a text box on the right. These are referred to as controls. ***Controls*** are the text boxes, buttons, boxes, and other tools you use to add, edit, and display the data in a form or report. In Figure 4.3, Product ID, Product Name, Description, and the rest of the field labels are controls. In addition, the boxes containing the values for each field (P0001, Coffee–Colombian Supreme, etc.) are all controls. More specifically, the form locations that hold data are generally text box controls, and the text in front of those, marking what the field means, are label controls.

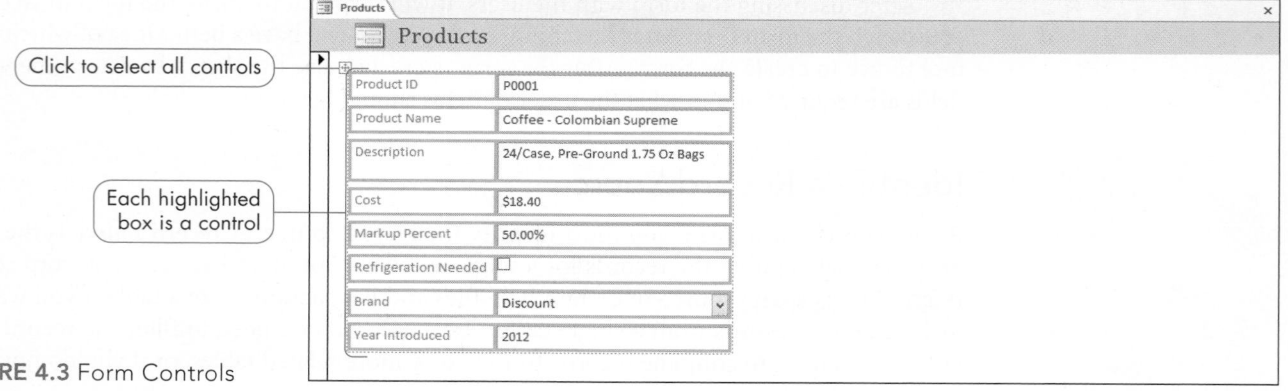

FIGURE 4.3 Form Controls

A ***layout control*** provides guides to help keep controls aligned horizontally and vertically and give your form a uniform appearance. The fields are all aligned in Figure 4.3 because a layout control keeps them that way. Picture the layout control as a bookcase, with each field being a shelf on the bookcase.

Work with Form Views

There are three different views of a form available. The first, ***Form view***, is a simplified interface primarily used for data entry. This view does not enable you to make changes to the layout. As such, the Form view is an excellent way for users to interact with the form. This ensures they do not accidentally change the form layout. Figure 4.4 shows a form in Form view. Notice forms can include features such as drop-down lists.

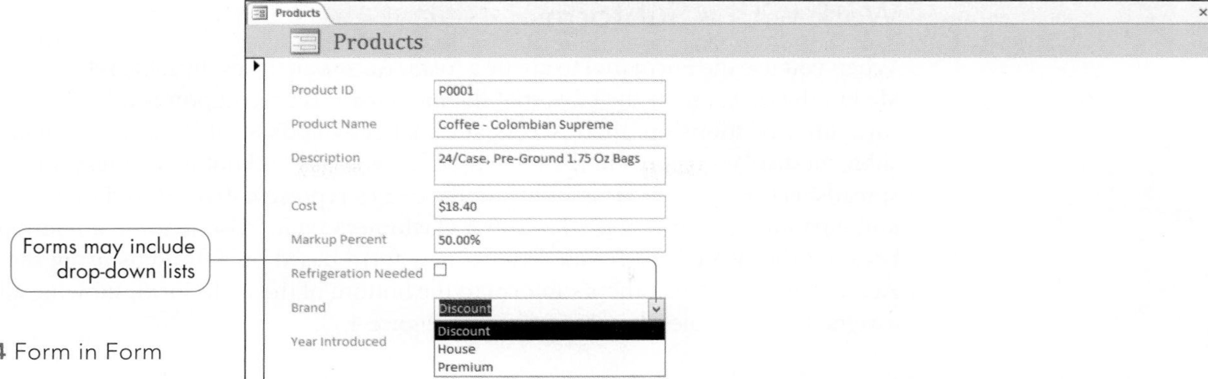

FIGURE 4.4 Form in Form View

The second view, ***Layout view***, enables users to make changes to the layout while viewing the data on the form. Reports have a similar view with the same name. This will be discussed later in the chapter. Layout view is useful for testing the functionality of the form and adjusting sizes of fields as needed. In the previous section, you were shown how to create a form using the Form Tool. When you do this, Access opens the form in Layout view ready for customizing. Figure 4.5 shows a form in Layout view.

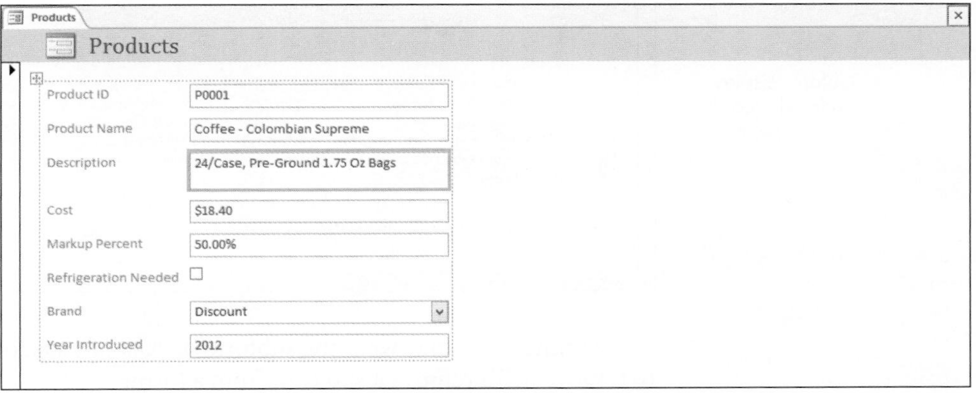

FIGURE 4.5 Form in Layout View

The third view, ***Design view***, allows you to change advanced design settings you cannot see in the Layout view, such as a background image. Reports also have a Design view, which will also be discussed later in this chapter. Design view is a much more powerful way of changing the form layout. It is more complex than Layout view, so you would likely use Design view only when you need to perform advanced form layout adjustments. Figure 4.6 shows a form in Design view.

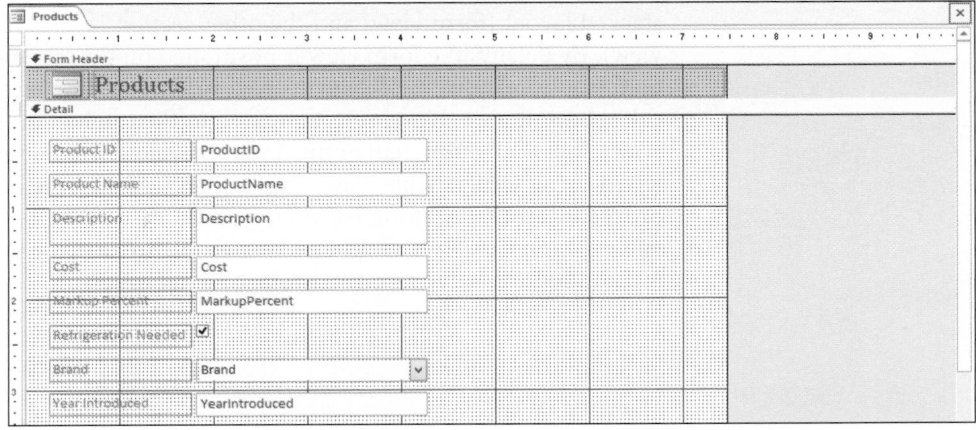

FIGURE 4.6 Form in Design View

These three views will be described in more detail later in this chapter.

Work with a Subform

When you use the Form tool to create a form, Access analyzes the table relationships you created in the database. If the table that the main form is based upon is related to another table through a relationship, then Access automatically adds a subform to the main form. The subform displays records in the related table, generally laid out in a table, similar to an Excel spreadsheet. For example, assume you have sales representatives stored in a SalesReps table and customer information stored in a Customers table. Also assume a relationship exists between the two tables. If you create a new form based on SalesReps using the Form tool, Access will add a Customers subform to the bottom of the main form, showing all customers assigned to each sales representative (see Figure 4.7).

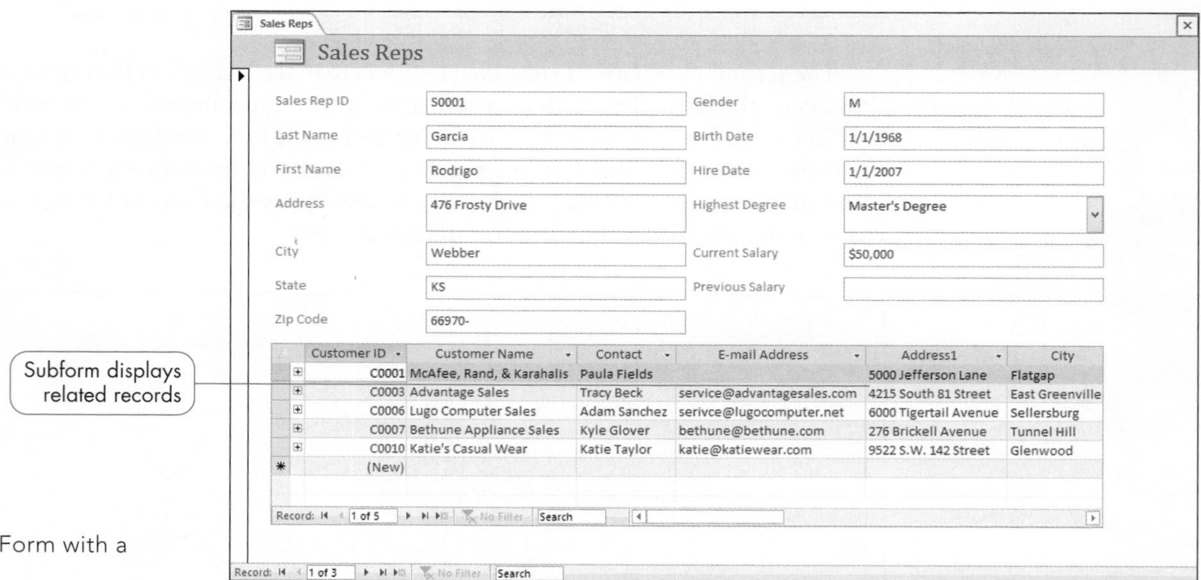

FIGURE 4.7 Form with a Subform

At times, you may want the subform as part of your form; at other times, you may want to remove it. To remove a subform from a form:

1. Switch to Design view.
2. Click anywhere inside the subform.
3. Press Delete.

Create a Split Form

A ***split form*** combines two views of the same record source—one section is displayed in a stacked layout (form view) and the other section is displayed in a tabular layout (datasheet view). By default, the form view is positioned on the top and the datasheet view is displayed on the bottom; however, the form's page orientation can be changed from horizontal to vertical in Layout view. If you select a record in the top half of the form, the same record will be selected in the bottom half of the form and vice versa. For example, if you create a split form based on an Orders table, you can select an Order in the datasheet section and then see the order's information in the *Form view* section (see Figure 4.8). This gives you the option to enter data in the Form view while being able to navigate between orders more quickly. The top and bottom halves are synchronized at all times.

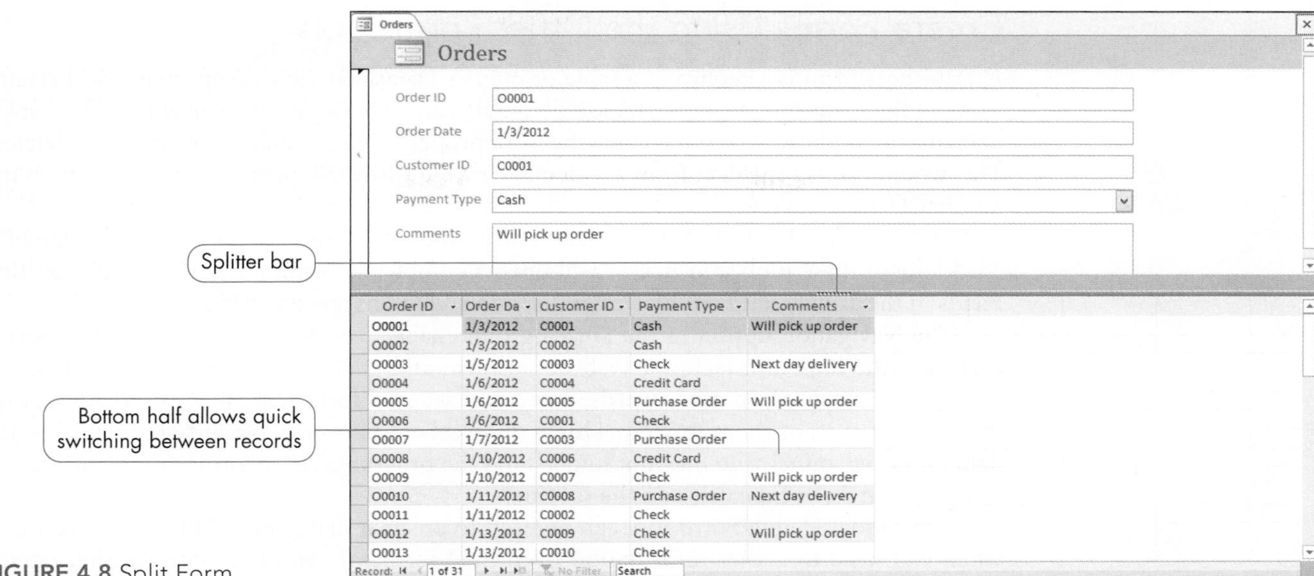

Order ID	Order Da	Customer ID	Payment Type	Comments
O0001	1/3/2012	C0001	Cash	Will pick up order
O0002	1/3/2012	C0002	Cash	
O0003	1/5/2012	C0003	Check	Next day delivery
O0004	1/6/2012	C0004	Credit Card	
O0005	1/6/2012	C0005	Purchase Order	Will pick up order
O0006	1/6/2012	C0001	Check	
O0007	1/7/2012	C0003	Purchase Order	
O0008	1/10/2012	C0006	Credit Card	
O0009	1/10/2012	C0007	Check	Will pick up order
O0010	1/11/2012	C0008	Purchase Order	Next day delivery
O0011	1/11/2012	C0002	Check	
O0012	1/13/2012	C0009	Check	Will pick up order
O0013	1/13/2012	C0010	Check	

FIGURE 4.8 Split Form

To create a split form, do the following:

1. Select a table or query in the Navigation Pane.
2. Click the CREATE tab.
3. Click More Forms in the Forms group.
4. Select Split Form.

Once you have completed those steps, a new split form displays. You can add, edit, or delete records in either section. The ***splitter bar*** divides the form into two halves. Users can adjust the splitter bar up or down unless the form designer disables this option.

Create a Multiple Items Form

A ***Multiple Items form*** displays multiple records in a tabular layout similar to a table's Datasheet view. However, a Multiple Items form gives you more customization options than a datasheet, such as the ability to add graphical elements, buttons, and other controls. Figure 4.9 shows a Multiple Items form created from the Employees table.

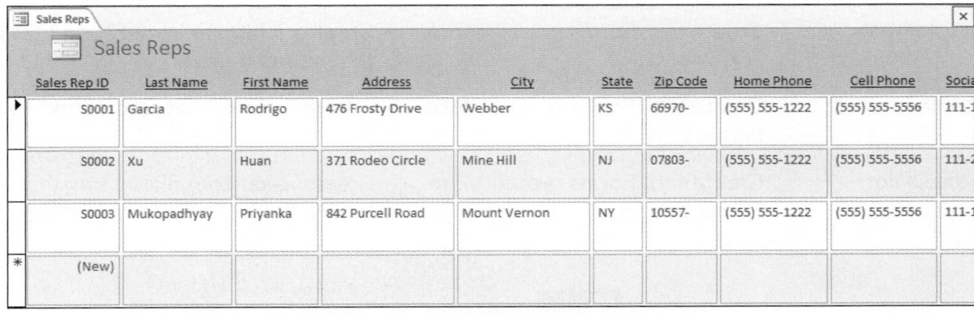

Sales Rep ID	Last Name	First Name	Address	City	State	Zip Code	Home Phone	Cell Phone	Socia
S0001	Garcia	Rodrigo	476 Frosty Drive	Webber	KS	66970-	(555) 555-1222	(555) 555-5556	111-1
S0002	Xu	Huan	371 Rodeo Circle	Mine Hill	NJ	07803-	(555) 555-1222	(555) 555-5556	111-2
S0003	Mukopadhyay	Priyanka	842 Purcell Road	Mount Vernon	NY	10557-	(555) 555-1222	(555) 555-5556	111-1
(New)									

FIGURE 4.9 Multiple Items Form

To create a Multiple Items form, do the following:

1. Select a table or query from the Navigation Pane.
2. Click the CREATE tab.
3. Click More Forms in the Forms group.
4. Select Multiple Items from the list of options.

Create Forms Using the Other Form Tools

A Datasheet form is a replica of a table or query's Datasheet view except that it still retains some of the form properties. Database designers can also use the Datasheet form to display data in a table-like format but change the form properties to not allow a record to be deleted. This would protect the data from accidental damage while still providing the users with the familiar Datasheet view.

The Form Design tool and the Blank Form tools can be used to create a form manually. Click one of these tools and Access will open a completely blank form. Click Add Existing Fields in the Tools group on the Design tab and add the necessary fields.

The Navigation option in the Forms group enables you to create user interface forms that have the look and feel of a Web-based form and enable users to open and close the objects of a database. In other words, you could set up a form that allows users to click on the forms you want them to view. This is an excellent option to simplify the database for data-entry personnel who may not understand the program. These forms are also useful for setting up an Access database on the Internet.

The Modal Dialog Form tool can be used to create a dialog box. This feature is useful when you need to gather information from the user before working with another object. Dialog boxes are common in all Microsoft Office applications.

REFERENCE Form Tools

Form Tool	Location	Use
Form	Create tab, Forms group	Creates a form with a stacked layout displaying all of the fields in the record source.
Form Design	Create tab, Forms group	Create a new blank form in Design view.
Blank Form	Create tab, Forms group	Create a new blank form in Layout view.
Form Wizard	Create tab, Forms group	Answer a series of questions and Access will create a custom form for you.
Navigation	Create tab, Forms group, Navigation button	Create user-interface forms that can also be used on the Internet. Six different Navigation form layouts are available from the drop-down list.
Split Form	Create tab, Forms group, More Forms button	Creates a two-part form with a stacked layout in one section and a tabular layout in the other.
Multiple Items	Create tab, Forms group, More Forms button	Creates a tabular layout form that includes all of the fields from the record source.
Datasheet	Create tab, Forms group, More Forms button	Creates a form that resembles the datasheet of a table or query.
Modal Dialog	Create tab, Forms group, More Forms button	Creates a custom dialog box that forces the user to respond before working with another object.

TIP Print with Caution!

Users can print a form by clicking the File tab and selecting the Print option. However, printing from a form should be done with caution. Forms are not generally designed for printing, so you may end up with hundreds of pages of printouts. A form with a stacked layout of 1,000 records could print thousands of pages unless you choose the Selected Record(s) option in the Print dialog box. The Selected Record(s) option, as shown in Figure 4.10, will only print the current record (or selected records).

FIGURE 4.10 Printing Selected Records

Using Form Views

Access provides different views for a form, similar to the different views in tables and queries. Tables and queries have Design view and Datasheet view. Most forms have Layout view, Form view, and Design view.

As you work with the form tools to create and modify forms, you will often need to switch between the three form views in Access: Layout view, Form view, and Design view. Most of your design work will be done in Layout view; occasionally, you will switch to Design view to add a more advanced feature, such as a background, or to use a layout option that is otherwise unavailable. Users of the form will only work in Form view. There should be no reason for a user to switch to Layout or Design view. Modifications to the form should be done by the designated form designer.

After a form is generated by a Form tool, you may need to modify it. Commonly, you may add a field, remove a field, change the order of fields, change the width of a field, modify the theme, or modify label text. These changes can be made in a form's Layout view. Advanced changes, such as changing headers or footers or adding a background image, can be made in a form's Design view.

Edit Data in Form View

STEP 2»

Use Form view to add, edit, and delete data in a form; the layout and design of the form cannot be changed in this view. Recall from a previous chapter that you can move from one field to another field by pressing Tab on your keyboard or clicking the desired field with your mouse.

Alter a Form in Layout View

Use Layout view to alter the form design while still viewing the data. You use Layout view to add or delete fields in a form, modify field properties, change the column widths, and enhance a form by adding a color scheme or styling. While you are working in Layout view, you can see the data as it would appear in Form view, but you cannot edit the data in Layout view. Seeing the data in Layout view makes it easier to size controls, for example, to ensure the data is visible. It is good practice to test a form in Form view after making changes in Layout view.

Use the Form Layout Tools Tabs

Forms have a number of options you can use to format. Once you are in Layout or Design view, you will have access to the report layout tools. You have three tabs available:

- Design: Use this tab to make changes to the design of the form, such as adding sorting, changing themes, and inserting additional controls.
- Arrange: Use this tab to change the layout of a form, to move fields, or to insert space.
- Format: Use this tab to change the font; add or remove bolding, italics, or underlining; change font size; change font color or background; adjust text alignment; or add a background image.

Add a Field to a Form

STEP 3» To add a field to a form, do the following:

1. Open the form in Layout view.
2. Click Add Existing Fields in the Tools group on the DESIGN tab to reveal the available fields from the form's record source. A Field List pane appears at the right of your screen.
3. For a single-table form, you will be presented with a list of fields. For a multiple-table form, you will first need to click the + (plus) next to the appropriate table to locate the desired field.
4. Drag the new field to the precise location on the form, using the shaded line (the color may vary, based on your Office configuration) as a guide for the position of the new field. The other fields will automatically adjust to make room for the new field.

Depending on the layout of the form, the shaded line will appear vertically (tabular layouts) or horizontally (stacked).

Delete a Field from a Form

To delete a field, do the following:

1. Switch to Layout view.
2. Click the text box control of the field to be deleted (note the shaded border around the control).
3. Click the Select Row option on the Layout tab in the Rows & Columns group.
4. Press Delete. The other fields will automatically adjust to close the gap around the deleted field.

Adjust Column Widths in a Form

When column widths are adjusted in a form with a stacked layout, all columns will increase and decrease together. Therefore, it is best to make sure that field columns are wide enough to accommodate the widest value in the table. For example, if a form contains information such as a customer's first name, last name, address, city, state, ZIP, phone, and e-mail address, you will need to make sure the longest address and the longest e-mail address are completely visible (because those fields are likely to contain the longest data values).

To decrease column widths in a form with a stacked layout, do the following:

1. Open the form in Layout view.
2. Click the text box control of the first field to select it.
3. Move the mouse over the right border of the field until the mouse pointer turns into a double arrow.
4. Drag the right edge to the left or right until you arrive at the desired width.

You will notice that all the fields change as you change the width of the first field. All fields that are part of the layout will have a standard width. If you wanted to resize one specific field, you would need to remove that field from the layout control. Note that "removing a field from the layout control" does not mean "removing a field from the form." Recall that the layout control keeps each field in place. If you remove a field from the layout control, it stays on the form but can be moved more freely.

Modify Form Controls using the Format Tab

When you view a form in Layout view, the Form Layout Tools tab displays the Design tab, Arrange tab, and Format tab. The Format tab, shown in Figure 4.11, contains a series of commands that enable you change the font, display, and alignment of the controls on a form. This is useful if you need to quickly change the look of one cell. For example, if you have a form that shows the information about the sale of a vehicle, you might want to emphasize the net profit of each transaction.

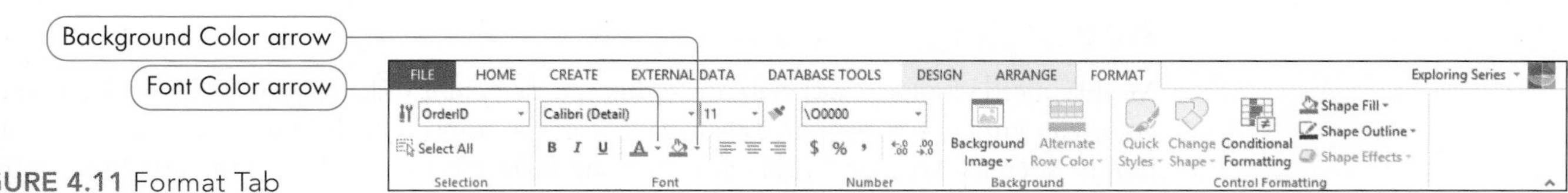

FIGURE 4.11 Format Tab

From this tab, you can change a number of properties. For example, you can perform these tasks, and more:

- Change the font size: Click the Font Size arrow in the Font group.
- Change emphasis: In the Font group, add bold, italics, or underlining.
- Change alignment: In the Font group, choose left, center, or right align.
- Change a control's background color: Click the Background Color arrow (refer to Figure 4.11) and select a color for the background.
- Change a control's font color: Click the Font Color arrow (refer to Figure 4.11) and select a color for the cell's font.
- Change number format: In the Number group, change to currency, percentage, or add commas; increase or decrease decimal places.

Selecting Controls

Controls, as mentioned, include both the labels identifying a field and the text box displaying field values. There may be times you want to select multiple controls. You will notice when you click on one control and click on another that the original control is deselected. If you need to select multiple controls, click on the first control you wish to select, hold down CTRL on your keyboard, and then click on the other controls you wish to select. Once they are selected, you can perform many tasks, such as formatting or deletion.

Add a Theme to a Form

You can apply a theme to a form in order to give the form a more professional finish. A ***theme*** is a defined set of colors, fonts, and graphics that can be applied to a form (or report). Click Themes in the Themes group on the Design tab, select a theme from the Themes Gallery, and Access will apply the theme to the form. Each theme has a name; you can determine the name of a theme by pointing the mouse to a theme and waiting for the tip to pop up, showing the name.

You can apply a theme to a single form or to all the forms in your database that share a common theme. Applying the same theme to all forms will provide a consistent look to your database; most users prefer a consistent theme when using Access forms. The same themes found in Access are also available in Excel, Word, and PowerPoint. Therefore, you can achieve a uniform look across all Office applications. Themes can be customized and saved so that the theme you create can be used again. Click the Save Current Theme command as shown in Figure 4.12 to do so.

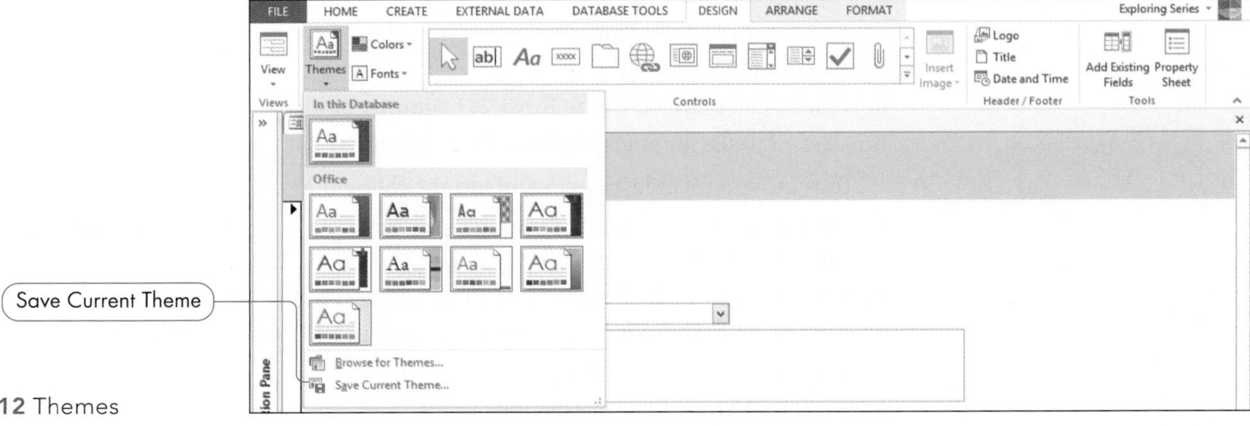

FIGURE 4.12 Themes

Add Styling to a Form

Modifying the font size of labels, changing the font color of labels, and adding a background color can enhance a form and also make it more usable. It is best to choose a familiar font family, such as Arial or Calibri, for both the form label controls and the text box controls. Apply bold to the labels in order to help the user distinguish labels from the text boxes. You should also consider right-aligning the labels and left-aligning the text box controls to reduce distance between the label and field, as illustrated in Figure 4.13. You may also want to separate the primary key field from the rest of the form by providing a sufficient visual boundary.

One note of caution: Try to avoid what graphic artists refer to as the "ransom note effect." Using too many font families, font sizes, colors, and other effects can take away from your design.

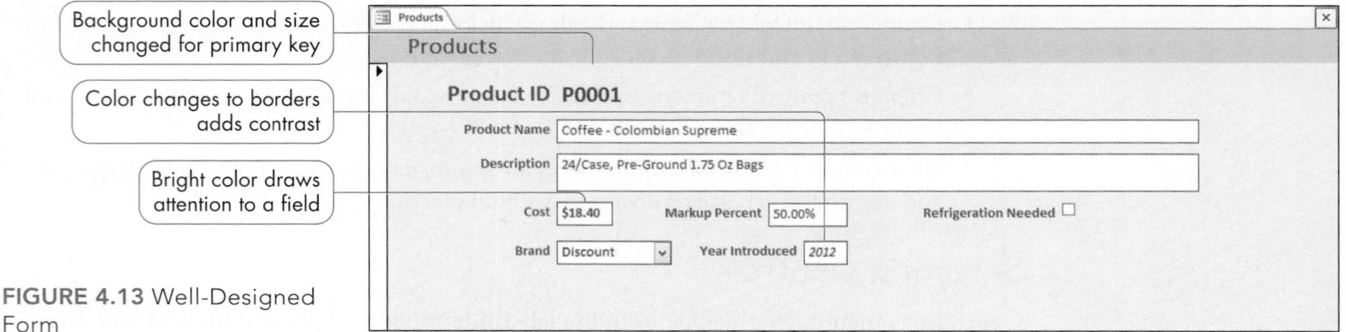

FIGURE 4.13 Well-Designed Form

Working with a Form Layout Control

Whenever you use one of the form tools to create a new form, Access will add a layout control to help align the fields. Recall that the layout control helps keep controls aligned in order to give your form a uniform appearance. The layout control provides structure for the fields but is restrictive. If you wish to have more control over the location of your fields, you can remove the layout control and position the controls manually on the grid.

Modify a Form Using the Arrange Tab

The Arrange tab appears in both Layout view and Design view. Use this tab to change the layout of a form, to move fields up and down, to insert a space above or below your current position, or to insert a space to the left or the right of the current field. To use these commands, first open a form in Layout view or Design view and click the Arrange tab. Next, select a field or fields and click the appropriate command.

The Table group contains commands that enable you to add gridlines to a form's layout, to change a form's layout from stacked to tabular (and vice versa), or to remove a form's layout. The Remove Layout command is only available in Design view.

STEP 4

To change the arrangement of a form, do the following:

1. Open the form in Layout view.
2. Click any of the field text boxes.
3. Click the ARRANGE tab.
4. Click Select Layout in the Rows & Columns group.
5. Click Tabular or Stacked in the Table group.

To remove a form layout control, do the following:

1. Switch to Design view (if you are not in Design view, you will not see the Remove Layout option).
2. Click on one of the fields that is currently part of the layout.
3. On the ARRANGE tab, click Select Layout in the Rows & Columns group.
4. Click Remove Layout in the Table group.
5. Switch to Layout view to arrange fields.

If you have removed the layout control or have a form that never had one, you can add one if you do the following:

1. Switch to Layout view or Design view (you can switch in either view).
2. Select all the controls you would like added back to the layout control, such as the field labels and text boxes. Hold down CTRL on your keyboard and click on each control, or click the FORMAT tab and in the Selection group, click Select All if you want to add everything to a layout.
3. On the ARRANGE tab, in the Table group, click Tabular or Stacked

The Rows & Columns group contains commands that enable you to insert rows and columns inside a form's layout. For example, in a form with a stacked layout, you may want to separate some fields from the rest of the fields. To do this, you could select a text box and click Insert Below. This will create a space after the selected field. This group also contains the Select Layout, Select Column, and Select Row commands. In Figure 4.14, three rows have been inserted above the Cost field.

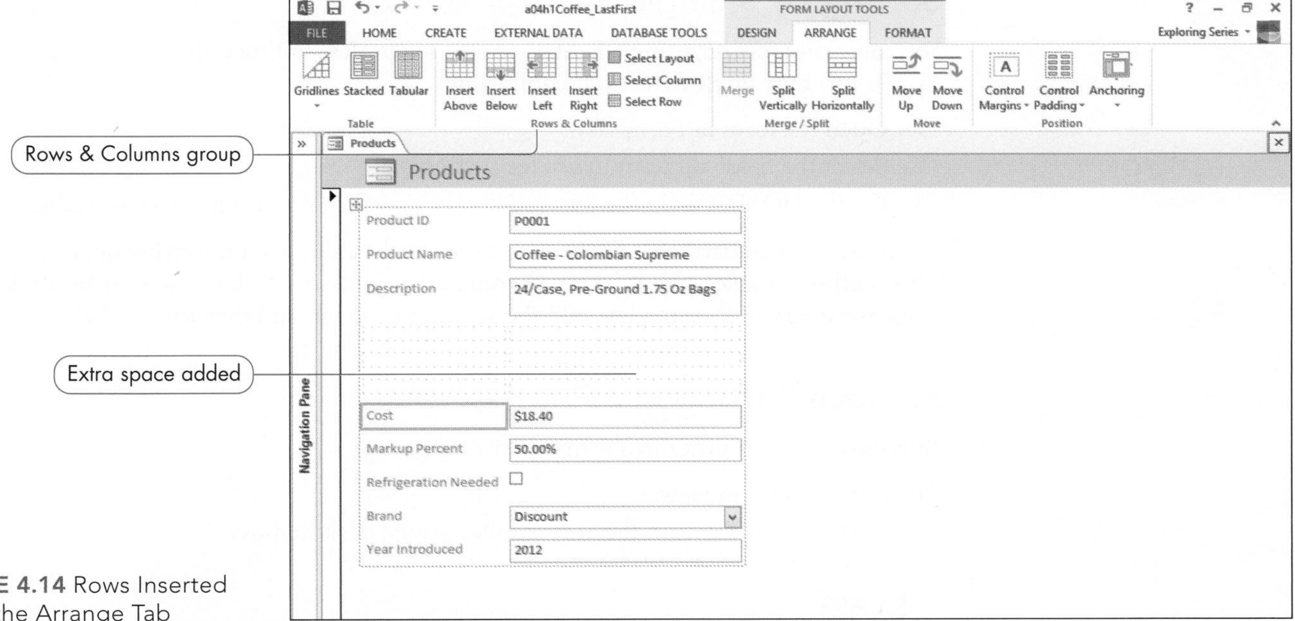

FIGURE 4.14 Rows Inserted Using the Arrange Tab

The Move group contains two commands that enable you to move a field up or down in a stacked layout. For example, if you want to move the second field in a stacked layout to the first position, select the second field's text box and label and click Move Up in the Move group. Moving fields up or down in a form may cause unexpected results; you can always use the Undo command if you need to revert back to a previous layout.

The Position group contains commands that enable you to modify the margins and the padding of controls in a form. This group also contains the Anchoring command, which enables you to change where the form's controls appear on the screen. By default, forms are anchored at the top left; however, you can change this to any of the nine options using the anchoring command.

TIP Apply a Background Image to a Form

To apply a Background Image to a form, open the form in Design view, click the Format tab, and then click Background Image in the Background group. Next, click Browse to locate the image you want to apply to the form. Once the image has been applied to the form, you can change the properties of the image so that the image is anchored and sized correctly.

Sorting Records in a Form

When a form is created using a Form tool, the sort order of the records in the form is dependent on the sort order of the record source—a table or a query. Tables are usually sorted by the primary key, whereas queries can be sorted in a variety of ways. Adding and removing sorts are shown in Figure 4.15.

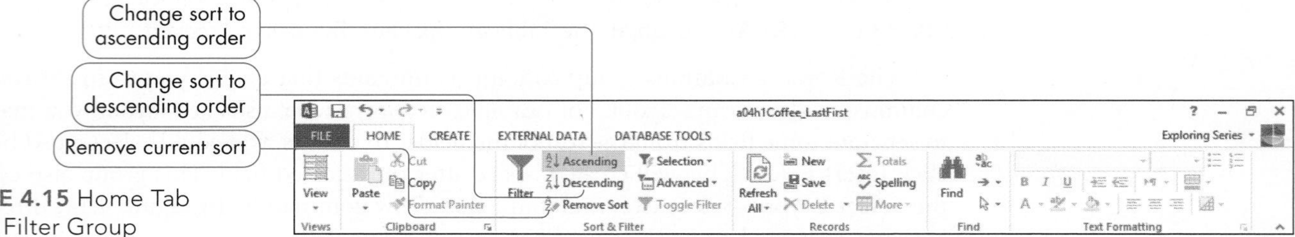

FIGURE 4.15 Home Tab Sort & Filter Group

Sorting by a Single Field

You can easily sort on a single field, in ascending or descending order.

To sort by a single field, do the following:

1. Open the form in Form view.
2. Select the field you want to use for sorting.
3. On the HOME tab, in the Sort & Filter group, click Ascending or Descending.

If the form is based on a query, you can instead modify the underlying query's sort order. This method enables you to create a more advanced sort order based on multiple fields. Open the query in Design view, add the sorting you want, and then save and close the query.

Remove Sorting in a Form

To remove the sort order in a form, do the following:

1. Switch to Form view.
2. On the HOME tab, in the Sort & Filter group, click Remove Sort.

TIP Inconsistent Sorting Due to Spaces

Including extra spaces when you enter values into fields can cause issues with sorting. To Access, the following values are not the same:

Little Falls, NJ 07424

Little Falls, NJ 07424

Notice the extra space after the word *Little*. If you attempt to sort, these cities will end up in different places in the sort. The first Little Falls (without the extra space) would appear between Little Egg Harbor Township and Little Ferry. However, the second version would end up above Little Egg Harbor Township, because Access treats the space as a different character.

Inconsistent spacing can cause inconsistent sorting. Try to remember that when performing data entry. If you inherit a database with this issue, you might consider performing a Replace, replacing two spaces with one.

1. How does a form simplify data entry (when compared to entering data into a table)? ***p. 792***
2. What is the record source of a form? ***p. 793***
3. What is the difference between Layout view and Design view? ***pp. 794–795***
4. What is the difference between a form with a subform and a split form? ***p. 796***
5. What is a layout control? What are the pros and cons of a layout control? ***p. 802***

Hands-On Exercises

1 Create and Modify Forms

It is your first day on the job at La Vida Mocha. After talking with Ryung about her data-entry needs, you decide to create several sample forms with different formats. You will show each form to Ryung and Nabil to get feedback and see if they have a preference.

Skills covered: Create Forms Using Form Tools • Use Form Views • Work with a Form Layout Control • Sort Records in a Form

STEP 1 » CREATE FORMS USING FORM TOOLS

You will create some forms to help Ryung and Nabil with their data entry process. After discussing their needs, you created some sketches that you will implement. Refer to Figure 4.16 as you complete Step 1.

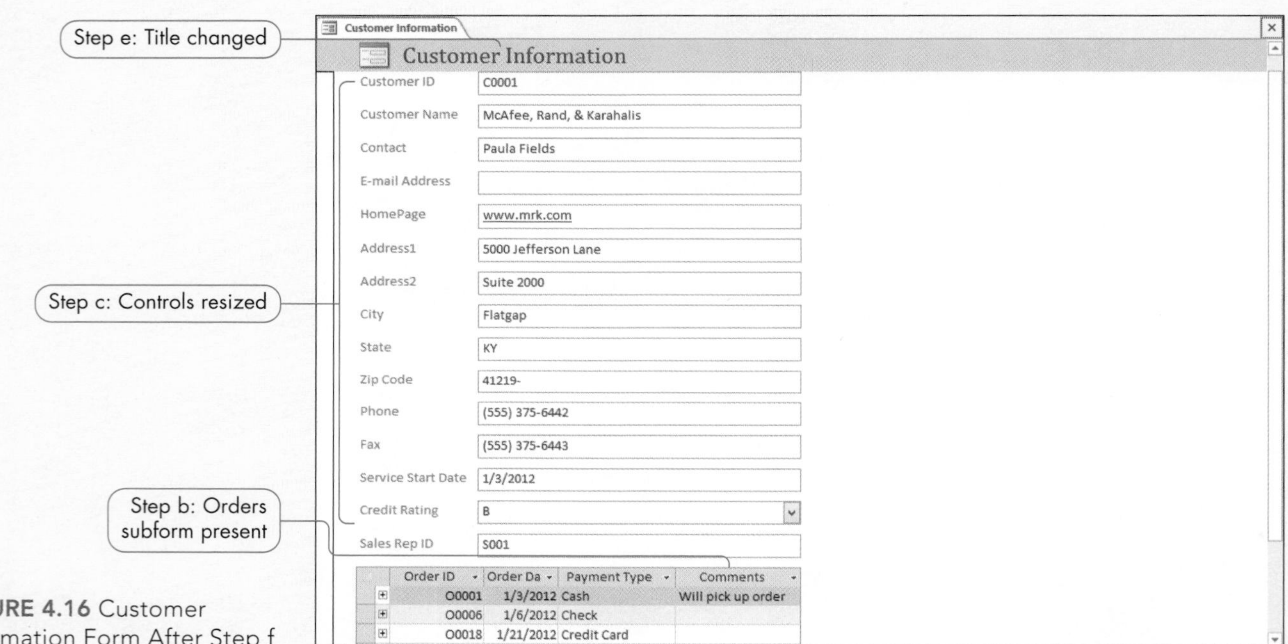

FIGURE 4.16 Customer Information Form After Step f

a. Open *a04h1Coffee*. Click the **FILE tab**, select **Save As**, and click **Save As**. Type **a04h1Coffee_LastFirst** as the file name. Click **Save**.

> **TROUBLESHOOTING:** Throughout the remainder of this chapter and textbook, click Enable Content whenever you are working with student files.

> **TROUBLESHOOTING:** If you make any major mistakes in this exercise, you can close the file, repeat step a above, and then start over.

b. Click the **Customers table** in the Navigation Pane. Click the **CREATE tab** and click **Form** in the Forms group.

   Access creates a new form with two record sources—Customers (with stacked layout, on top) and Orders (with datasheet layout, below). Access found a one-to-many relationship between the Customers and Orders tables. The form opens in Layout view.

c. Click the top text box containing *C0001* if it is not already selected. The text box is outlined with a shaded border. Move the mouse to the right edge of the shaded border until the mouse pointer changes to a double-headed arrow. Drag the right edge to the left until the text box is approximately half of its original size.

   All the text boxes and the subform at the bottom adjust in size when you adjust the top text box. This is a characteristic of Layout view—enabling you to easily modify all controls at once.

> **TROUBLESHOOTING:** You may need to maximize the Access window or close the Navigation Pane if the right edge of the text box is not visible.

d. Ensure the labels at the left all appear without being cut off. If they are cut off, adjust the size of the labels like you did in step c.

e. Click **Save** in the Quick Access Toolbar, and then type **Customer Information** as the form name in the **Save As dialog box**. Click **OK**.

f. Click the **Customers title** at the top of the form to select it, click again, and then change the title to **Customer Information**. Press **Enter** to accept the change. Your form should now look like Figure 4.16. Close the form.

> **TROUBLESHOOTING:** If you make a mistake that you cannot easily recover from, consider deleting the form and starting over. The Form tool makes it easy to start over again.

g. Verify the Customers table is selected in the Navigation Pane. Click the **CREATE tab** and click **More Forms** in the Forms group. Select **Split Form**.

   Access creates a new form with a split view, one view in stacked layout and one view laid out like a datasheet.

h. Click anywhere on the Coulter Office Supplies customer record in the bottom portion of the form (record 14). Note: You may need to scroll down to see this record.

   The top portion shows all the information for this customer.

i. Click the **Customers title** at the top of the form to select it, click **Customers** again, and then change the title to **Customers - Split View**. Press **Enter** to accept the change.

j. Click **Save** on the Quick Access Toolbar and type **Customers - Split View** in the **Form Name box**. Click **OK**. Close the form.

k. Click the **Products table** in the Navigation Pane. Click the **CREATE tab**, click **More Forms** in the Forms group, and then select **Multiple Items**.

   Access creates a new multiple-item form based on the Products table. The form resembles a table's Datasheet view.

l. Click the **Products title** at the top of the form to select it, click again on **Products**, and then change the title to **Products - Multiple Items**. Press **Enter** to save the title.

m. Save the form as **Products - Multiple Items** and close the form.

n. Click the **Orders table** in the Navigation Pane. Click **Form** in the Forms group on the CREATE tab.

   A form with a subform showing each line of the order is created.

o. Switch to Design view. Click anywhere inside the subform and press **Delete** on your keyboard.

   The subform is removed.

p. Save the form as **Order Information**. Close all open objects.

STEP 2 » USE FORM VIEW TO CHANGE DATA

Now that you have created three forms, you will show Nabil how to use the forms to perform data entry.

a. Right-click the **Customer Information** form in the Navigation Pane and click **Open**. Advance to the sixth customer, *Lugo Computer Sales*, using the **Next Record button** on the Navigation Bar at the bottom of the form.

> **TROUBLESHOOTING:** Two Navigation bars exist, one for the main form and one for the subform. Make sure you use the bottom-most one that shows 14 records.

b. Double-click the **Customers table** in the Navigation Pane.

   Two tabs now display in the main window. You will compare the table data and the form data while you make changes to both.

c. Verify the sixth record of the Customers table is *Lugo Computer Sales*, which corresponds to the sixth record in the Customer Information form. Click the tabs to switch between the table and the form.

d. Click the **Customer Information tab** and replace *Adam Sanchez*, the contact for Lugo Computer Sales, with your name. Advance to the next record to save the changes. Click the **Customers tab** to see that the contact name changed in the table as well.

   The contact field and the other fields on the Customer Information form automatically change the data in the underlying table.

> **TROUBLESHOOTING:** If the change to Adam Sanchez does not display in the Customers table, check the Customer Information form to see if the pencil displays in the left margin. If it does, save the record by advancing to the next customer and recheck to see if the name has changed.

e. Close the Customer Information form and the Customers table.

f. Open the Customers – Split View form. In the bottom portion of the split form, click **Lugo Computer Sales**, the sixth record. Notice the top portion now displays the information for Lugo Computer Sales. Notice there is an error in the e-mail address—*service* is misspelled. In the top portion of the form, change the e-mail address to **service@lugocomputer.net**.

g. Click another record in the bottom pane and click back on **Lugo Computer Sales**.

   The pencil disappears from the record selector box and the changes are saved to the table.

STEP 3 » USE LAYOUT VIEW TO MODIFY A FORM LAYOUT

You will make some changes to the layouts based on recommendations Nabil gave you after seeing the forms in action. You will also add a missing field to the main table and add it to the form. Refer to Figure 4.17 as you complete Step 3.

Step d: Refrig? column resized

Products - Multiple Items

Product ID	Product Name	Description	Refrig?	Brand	Year Introduced
P0001	Coffee - Colombian Supreme	24/Case, Pre-Ground 1.75 Oz Bags	☐	Discount	2012
P0002	Coffee - Hazelnut	24/Case, Pre-Ground 1.75 Oz Bags	☐	Premium	2012
P0003	Coffee - Mild Blend	24/Case, Pre-Ground 1.75 Oz Bags	☐	House	2012
P0004	Coffee - Assorted Flavors	18/Case. Pre-Ground 1.75 Oz Bags	☐	House	2012
P0005	Coffee - Decaf	24/Case, Pre-Ground 1.75 Oz Bags	☐	Discount	2012
P0006	Tea Bags - Regular	75/Box, Individual Tea Bags	☐	House	2012
P0007	Tea Bags - Decaf	75/Box, Individual Tea Bags	☐	House	2012
P0008	Creamers - Assorted Flavors	400/Case, 8 50-count Boxes	☐	Discount	2012
P0009	Creamers - Liquid	200/Case, Individual Creamers	☑	Premium	2012
P0010	Sugar Packets	2000/Case	☐	House	2012
P0011	Ceramic Mug	SD Company Logo	☐	House	2012
P0012	Sugar Substitute	500/Case, 1-Serving Bags	☐	Discount	2012
P0013	Coffee Filters	500/Case, Fits 10-12 Cup Coffee Mal	☐	House	2012
P0014	Napkins	3000/Case, White	☐	House	2012
P0015	Stirrers - Plastic	1000/Box	☐	Discount	2012
P0016	Stirrers - Wood	1000/Box	☐	Discount	2012
P0017	Spoons	500/Box, White Plastic	☐	House	2012
P0018	Popcorn - Plain	36/Case, 3.75 Oz Microwave Bags	☐	House	2012
P0019	Popcorn - Buttered	36/Case, 3.75 Oz Microwave Bags	☐	House	2012
P0020	Soup - Chicken	50 Envelopes	☐	Premium	2012
P0021	Soup - Variety Pak	50 Envelopes	☐	Premium	2012
P0022	Styrofoam Cups - 10 ounce	1000/Case	☐	House	2012

Record: 1 of 25 | No Filter | Search

FIGURE 4.17 Final Version of Products—Multiple Items Report

a. Switch the Customers – Split View form to Layout view. Move your mouse over the splitter bar, the border between the top and bottom portions of the window. When the pointer shape changes to a double-headed arrow, drag the **splitter bar** up until it almost touches the Sales Rep ID field. Save and close the form.

b. Open the Products – Multiple Items form in Layout view. Move the mouse over the bottom edge of cell P0001 until the pointer shape changes to a two-headed arrow. Drag the bottom edge up to reduce the height of the rows so they are as tall as they need to be to accommodate the information.

Changing the height of one row affects the height of all the rows.

c. Click anywhere on the Cost column and click **Select Column** in the Rows & Columns group on the ARRANGE tab. Press **Delete** to remove the column. Repeat the process to delete *MarkupPercent*.

d. Click the **Refrigeration Needed label** to select it. Change the label to the abbreviation **Refrig?**. Shrink the field so it is as wide as necessary. Save and close the form.

You removed fields from the Products – Multiple Items form and the other fields adjust to maintain an even distribution (after you remove the blank space).

e. Open the Customer Information form in Layout view.

f. Click **Themes** in the Themes group on the DESIGN tab. Right-click the **Slice theme** and click **Apply Theme to This Object Only**.

The font and color scheme adjust to match this theme.

TROUBLESHOOTING: Recall that you can determine which theme is named Slice by pointing the mouse to a theme and waiting for a tip to display. Themes are displayed in alphabetical order.

g. Click **Shape Fill** in the Control Formatting group on the FORMAT tab. Click **Light Turquoise, Background 2.**

The background color of the CustomerID field changes to light turquoise.

TROUBLESHOOTING: If you do not see a Light Turquoise, Background 2 in the first row, ensure you have selected the Slice theme.

TROUBLESHOOTING: If the entire background changes to blue, undo and ensure you have selected the control containing *C0001*.

h. Select the **Customer Name field** (which should be *McAfee, Rand, & Karahalis*). Change the font size to **16**.

   The customer name appears in a larger font, setting it apart from the other fields.

i. Save and close the form.

j. Right-click the **Customers table** in the Navigation Pane and click **Design View**.

   You will add the HomePage field to the Customers table.

k. Click the **Address1 field** and click **Insert Rows** in the Tools group.

   A new row is inserted above the Address1 field.

l. Type **HomePage** in the blank **Field Name box** and choose **Hyperlink** as the Data Type.

m. Save and close the Customers table.

n. Right-click the **Customer Information form** in the Navigation Pane and click **Layout View**.

   You will add the HomePage field to the Customer Information form.

o. Click **Add Existing Fields** in the Tools group on the DESIGN tab to display the Field List pane (if necessary).

p. Click the **HomePage field**. Drag the field from the Field List pane to the form, below the E-mail Address field, until a shaded line displays between *E-mail Address* and *Address1*, and release the mouse. Close the Field List pane.

   Access shows a shaded line to help you place the field in the correct location.

TROUBLESHOOTING: If the placement of this field does not look correct, you can use the Undo button and try again.

q. Switch to Form view. Press **Tab** until you reach the HomePage field and type www.mrk.com into the field. Save and close the form.

r. Click the **Revenue query** in the Navigation Pane. Click **Form** in the Forms group on the CREATE tab to create a new form based on this query.

s. Display the form in Design view. Select all text box field controls (from *Last Name* down to *Revenue*) by clicking on the first field (Last Name), holding down **CTRL** on your keyboard, and clicking on each of the other controls. Click **Remove Layout** in the Table group on the ARRANGE tab. Switch to Layout view.

TROUBLESHOOTING: Recall the Remove Layout option only appears in Design view, so if you do not see the option, ensure you are in Design view.

t. Resize the controls individually so they are approximately the same size as shown in Figure 4.18.

u. Click the **Price control**. Hold down **CTRL** and click the **Revenue control**, the **Price label**, and the **Revenue label**. Drag the fields to the locations shown in Figure 4.18. Switch to Form view.

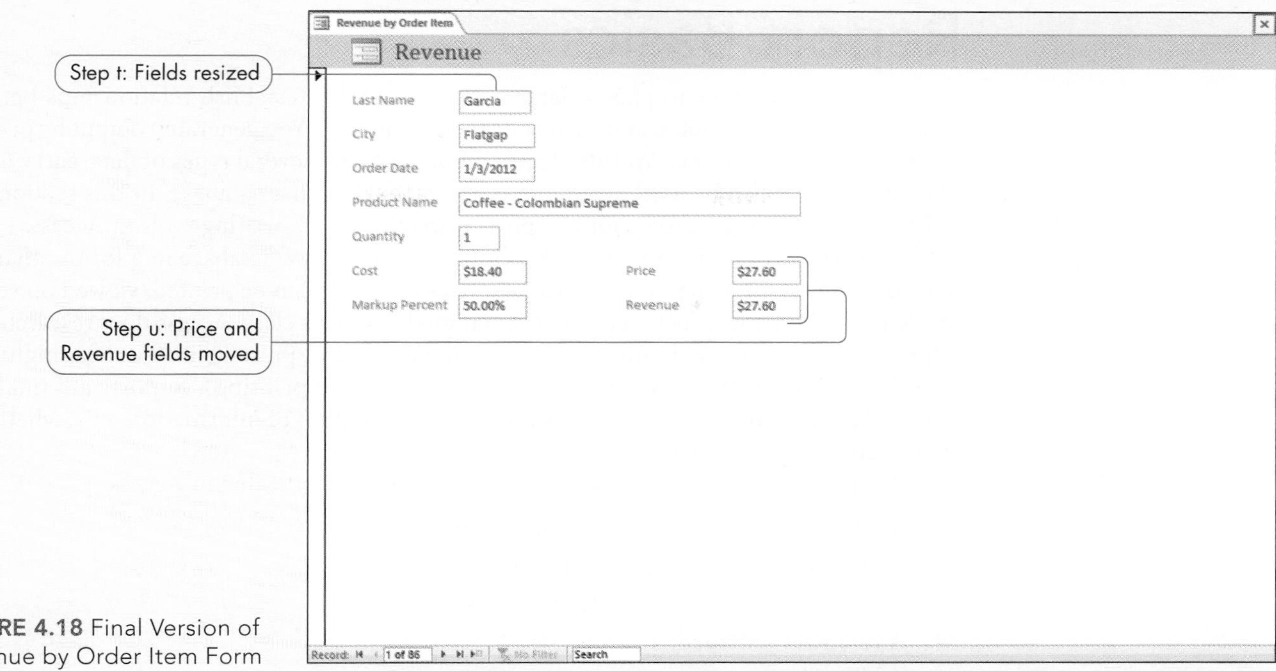

FIGURE 4.18 Final Version of Revenue by Order Item Form

v. Save the form as **Revenue by Order Item**. Close the form.

STEP 4 » USE A CONTROL LAYOUT AND SORT RECORDS IN A FORM

Ryung tested the Customer Information form and likes the way it is working. She asks you to change the sorting to make it easier to find customers with a similar customer name. She also has an old form that she hopes you can make easier to read but keep in the vertical format.

a. Open the Sales Reps form in Layout view. Notice the form is not laid out well.

b. Click **Select All** in the Selection group on the FORMAT tab.

   All 14 controls are outlined.

c. Click **Tabular** in the Table group on the ARRANGE tab.

   The controls are lined up horizontally.

d. Click **Stacked** in the Table group on the ARRANGE tab. Switch to Form view.

   Ryung wanted the form laid out vertically. The controls are lined up vertically and are much easier to read.

e. Save and close the form.

f. Open the Customer Information form in Form view. Click **Next record** in the Navigation bar at the bottom several times to advance through the records.

   Take note that the customers are in Customer ID order.

g. Click **First record** in the Navigation bar to return to customer *McAfee, Rand, & Karahalis.*

h. Click the **Customer Name field** and click **Ascending** in the Sort & Filter group on the HOME tab.

   Advantage Sales displays, as they are the first customer name in alphabetical order.

i. Click **Next record** in the Navigation bar at the bottom to advance through the records.

   The records are in Customer Name order.

j. Save and close the Customer Information form.

k. Keep the database open if you plan to continue with the next Hands-On Exercise. If not, close the database and exit Access.

Report Basics

By now, you know how to plan a database, create a table, establish relationships between tables, enter data into tables, and extract data using queries. You generated output by printing table and query datasheets. You also learned how to create several types of data-entry forms. These forms can also be used for inquiries about the data in a database. In this section, you will learn how to create professional reports using the report-writing tools in Access.

A ***report*** is a document that displays information from a database in a format that outputs meaningful information to its readers. Access reports can be printed, viewed on screen, or even saved as a file. Much like a report you might do for a class, Access does research (gets information from the tables or queries) and organizes and presents it in a meaningful way (the final report, formatted for on-screen viewing or for printing). Reports are unable to change data in your database; a report is designed for output of information only, whether to the screen, to the printer, or to a file.

The following are all examples of reports that might be created in Access:

1. A telephone directory sorted by last name
2. A customer list grouped by sales rep
3. An employee list sorted by most years of service
4. A financial statement
5. A bill or invoice
6. A bar chart showing sales over the past 12 months
7. A shipping label
8. A letter to customers reminding them about a past due payment

Although you can print information from forms, information printed may not be easily understood or economical in terms of paper use. Most of the printed documents generated by Access will come from reports. Reports can be enhanced to help the reader understand and analyze the data. For example, if you print the Datasheet view from the Customers table, you will be able to locate the key information about each customer. However, using report tools, you can group the customers by sales rep and highlight the customers who have not placed an order in six months. This is an example of converting a list of customers into an effective business tool. To increase business, the sales reps could contact their customers who have not ordered in six months and review the findings with the sales manager. A sales report could be run each month to see if the strategy has helped produce any new business.

In this section, you will create reports in Access by first identifying a record source, then sketching the report, and finally choosing a Report tool. You will learn how to modify a report by adding and deleting fields, resizing columns, and adding a color scheme. You will also learn about the report sections, the report views, and controls on reports. After having worked through forms in the earlier section on forms, you will discover that there are many similarities between forms and reports.

Creating Reports Using Report Tools

Access provides five different report tools for creating reports. The report tools are found on the Create tab, in the Reports group, as shown in Figure 4.19. Click one of these tools and Access will base the report using the table or query that is currently selected. The most common of the tools, the ***Report tool***, is used to instantly create a tabular report based on the table or query currently selected. The Report Design tool is used to create a new blank report in Design view. This tool is used by advanced users who want to create a blank report with no help from Access. The Blank Report tool is used to create a new blank report so that you can insert fields and controls manually and design the report. The Report Wizard tool will ask a series of questions and help you create a report based on your answers. The Labels tool is used to create a page of labels using one of the preformatted templates provided by Access. Table 4.1 provides a summary of the five report tools and their usage.

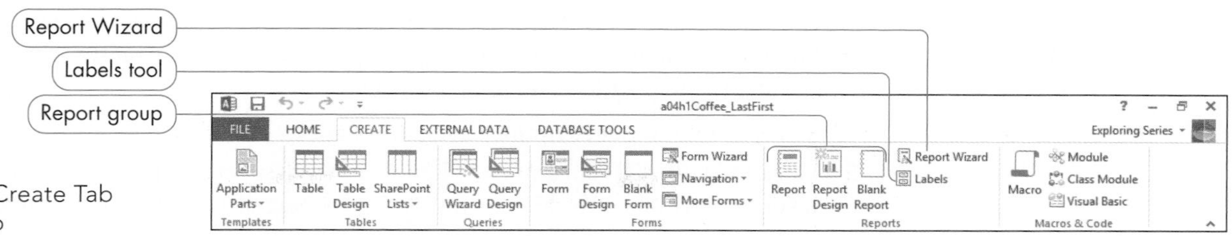

FIGURE 4.19 Create Tab Reports Group

After you create a report using one of the report tools, you can perform modifications in Layout view or Design view.

TABLE 4.1 Report Tools and Their Usage

Report Tool	Usage
Report	Create a tabular report showing all of the fields in the record source.
Report Design	Create a new blank report in Design view. Add fields and controls manually.
Blank Report	Create a new blank report in Layout view. Add fields and controls manually.
Report Wizard	Answer a series of questions and Access will design a custom report for you.
Labels	Choose a preformatted label template and create a sheet of labels.

Before you create a report in Access, you should ask these questions:

- What is the purpose of the report?
- Who will use the report?
- Which tables are needed for the report?
- What information needs to be included?
- How will the report be distributed? Will users pull the information directly from Access, or will they receive it through e-mail, fax, or the Internet?
- Will the results be converted to Word, Excel, HTML, or another format?

In the *Forms* section of this chapter, you learned that it is helpful to talk to users and sketch an Access form before you launch Access. The same holds true for creating an Access report. Users can give you solid feedback, and creating a sketch will help you determine which report tool to use to create the report.

The first step in planning your report is to identify the record source. You may use one or more tables, queries, or a combination of tables and queries as the report's record source. Sometimes, a single table contains all of the records you need for the report. Other times, you will need to incorporate several tables. When multiple tables are needed to create a report, you can add all the necessary tables into a single query and then base the report on that query. (As stated earlier, multiple tables in a query must be related, as indicated with join lines. Tables with no join lines usually indicate an incorrect record source.)

Reports can also contain graphics as well as text and numeric data. For example, you can add a company logo. After you identify the record source, you also need to specify which graphic images are needed (and the location of the images).

Use the Report Tool

STEP 1»

After you sketch the report, you can decide which report tool is appropriate to produce the desired report. Access provides several tools that you can use to create a report (refer to Figure 4.20). Which one you select depends on the layout of the report, the record source, and the complexity of the report design.

The easiest way to create a report is with the Report tool. The ***Report tool*** is used to instantly create a tabular report based on the table or query currently selected. To create a report using the Report tool, do the following:

1. Select a table or query in the Navigation Pane.
2. Click the CREATE tab and click Report in the Reports group. Access creates a tabular layout report instantly. Notice, this type of report displays data horizontally across the page in a landscape view, as shown in Figure 4.20.

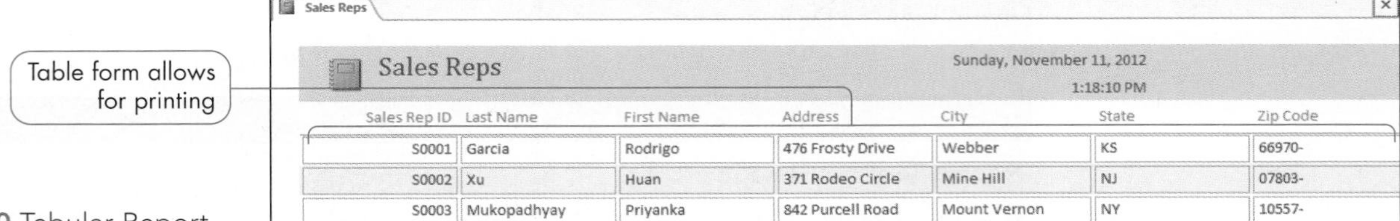

FIGURE 4.20 Tabular Report

If you prefer, you can display a report using a stacked layout, which displays fields in a vertical column. This type of report is less common, as it would result in longer printouts. The number of records on one page depends on the number of records in the record source. You can also force a new page at the start of each record.

Use the Report Wizard to Create a Basic Report

You can also create a professional report with the Report Wizard. The ***Report Wizard*** asks you questions and then uses your answers to generate a customized report. The wizard uses six dialog boxes to collect information about your report. After thinking through the structure, the layout, and the record source, you are ready to launch the Report Wizard.

1. Select the report's record source in the Navigation Pane and click Report Wizard in the Reports group on the CREATE tab.
   The wizard opens with the table or query (the record source) displayed in the first dialog box. Although you chose the record source before you started, the first dialog box enables you to select fields from additional tables or queries.
2. Choose the fields you want to include in the report. Click the Tables/Queries drop-down list to display a list of available tables or queries. As with the query wizard you used in a previous chapter, you can click > to choose a single field, >> to choose all fields, < to remove a field, and << to remove all fields from the report. See Figure 4.21. Set the desired fields and click Next.

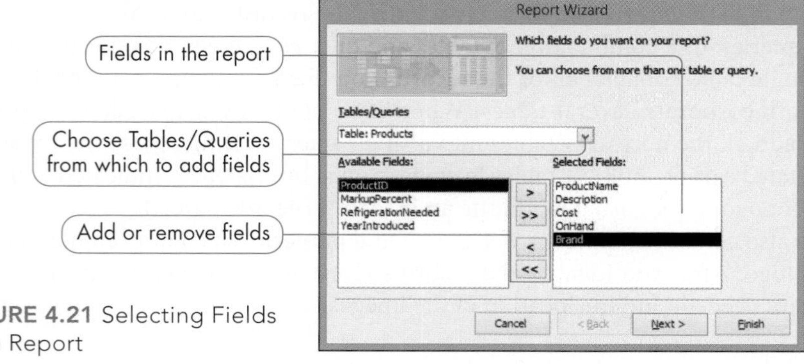

FIGURE 4.21 Selecting Fields for a Report

3. The next dialog box, shown in Figure 4.22, asks, "Do you want to add any grouping levels?" As you learned in a previous chapter, grouping lets you organize and summarize your data, based on values in a field. For a basic report, you will not select any grouping fields and instead just click Next.

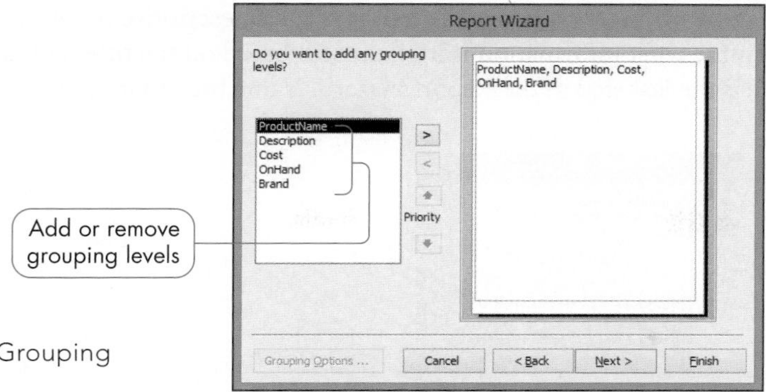

FIGURE 4.22 Grouping Options

4. The next dialog box, shown in Figure 4.23, asks "What sort order do you want for your records?" For the sort options, specify which field you want to sort by first and optionally add a second, third, and fourth sort. For each field, choose ascending order and/or descending order. Click on the word Ascending and it will toggle to Descending; clicking again will switch back to Ascending. Set the desired sort options and click Next.

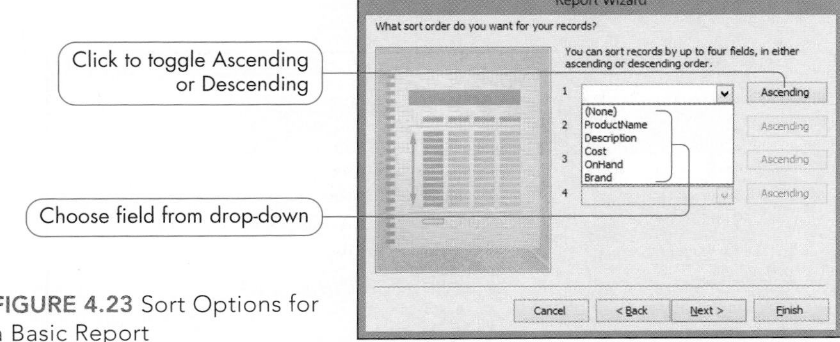

FIGURE 4.23 Sort Options for a Basic Report

5. The next dialog box will determine the report's appearance. You will be given the option to select Columnar, Tabular, or Justified as the layout.

   - Columnar will display the information in a column. This leads to reports that are easier to read, but long printouts.
   - Tabular will display the data in a table format. This is good for saving space, but it may be difficult to fit all fields on one printed page.
   - Justified will display the information in a column as well. If you have Long Text fields, this is a good option to ensure all your data fits.

   Tabular is the option you choose to fit the report on as few pages as possible. Clicking an option will give you a general preview in the preview area. You can also select the orientation for the report, either Portrait or Landscape (see Figure 4.24). Select an appropriate format for the report. Set the desired options and click Next.

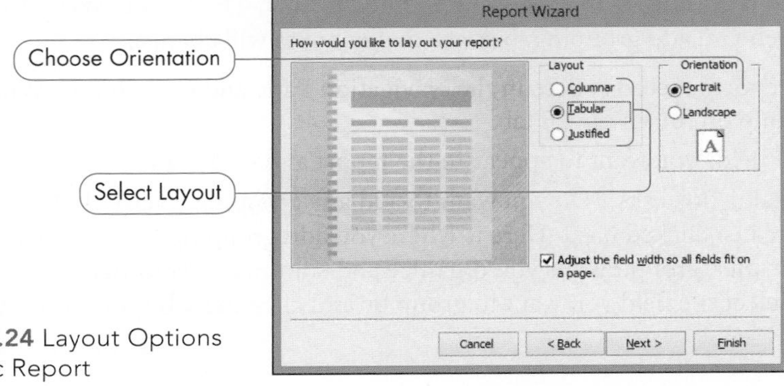

FIGURE 4.24 Layout Options for a Basic Report

6. Decide on an appropriate name for the report. Type a descriptive report name so you can easily determine what information is in the report based on the title. This step, shown in Figure 4.25, is the last step in the Report Wizard. Name the report and click Finish.

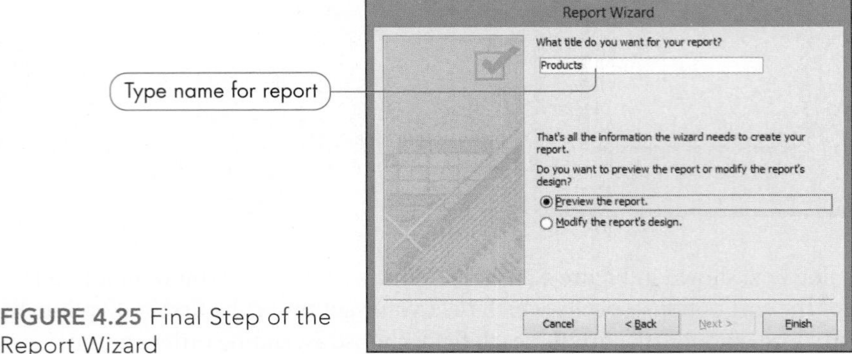

FIGURE 4.25 Final Step of the Report Wizard

Now that you have stepped through the wizard, you will get a report incorporating all the options you chose, as shown in Figure 4.26. You may need to adjust the size of fields, as some may not be fully displayed.

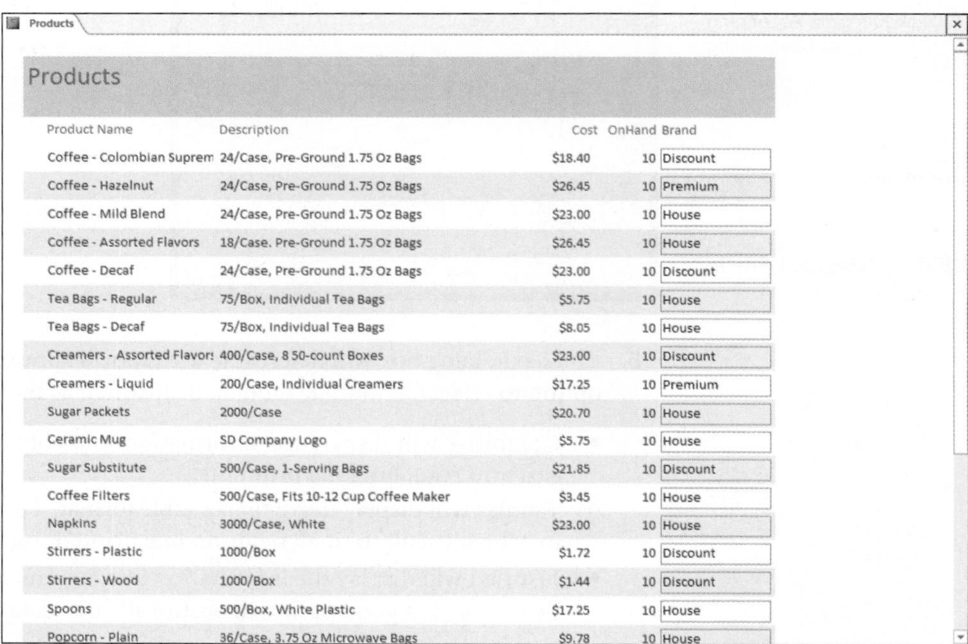

Products

Product Name	Description	Cost	OnHand	Brand
Coffee - Colombian Suprem	24/Case, Pre-Ground 1.75 Oz Bags	$18.40	10	Discount
Coffee - Hazelnut	24/Case, Pre-Ground 1.75 Oz Bags	$26.45	10	Premium
Coffee - Mild Blend	24/Case, Pre-Ground 1.75 Oz Bags	$23.00	10	House
Coffee - Assorted Flavors	18/Case. Pre-Ground 1.75 Oz Bags	$26.45	10	House
Coffee - Decaf	24/Case, Pre-Ground 1.75 Oz Bags	$23.00	10	Discount
Tea Bags - Regular	75/Box, Individual Tea Bags	$5.75	10	House
Tea Bags - Decaf	75/Box, Individual Tea Bags	$8.05	10	House
Creamers - Assorted Flavor:	400/Case, 8 50-count Boxes	$23.00	10	Discount
Creamers - Liquid	200/Case, Individual Creamers	$17.25	10	Premium
Sugar Packets	2000/Case	$20.70	10	House
Ceramic Mug	SD Company Logo	$5.75	10	House
Sugar Substitute	500/Case, 1-Serving Bags	$21.85	10	Discount
Coffee Filters	500/Case, Fits 10-12 Cup Coffee Maker	$3.45	10	House
Napkins	3000/Case, White	$23.00	10	House
Stirrers - Plastic	1000/Box	$1.72	10	Discount
Stirrers - Wood	1000/Box	$1.44	10	Discount
Spoons	500/Box, White Plastic	$17.25	10	House
Popcorn - Plain	36/Case, 3.75 Oz Microwave Bags	$9.78	10	House

FIGURE 4.26 Results of Report Wizard

Use the Report Wizard with Grouping

In the previous example, we created a basic report using the Report Wizard. However, we can use grouping if we want to summarize our report by a certain field. We can also display overall totals and percentages based on a predefined format. The Report Wizard still has six dialog boxes when you add grouping, but two dialog boxes will change.

1. Select the report's record source in the Navigation Pane and click Report Wizard in the Reports group on the CREATE tab.
2. Choose the fields you want to appear in the report and click Next.
3. The next dialog box asks, "Do you want to add any grouping levels?" In the previous example, we just clicked Next. Here is where you add grouping. As we learned in a previous chapter, grouping lets you organize and summarize your data based on values in a field. Select the field you want to group by and click the > button to add the new

group. If you need a second or third grouping level, add those field names in order. The order in which you select the groups dictates the order of display in the report. Figure 4.27 shows the sort options for a grouped report. In this specific example, records are being grouped by the Brand. Once you have selected the appropriate options, click Next.

4. Because we have specified grouping, the next dialog box asks, "What sort order and summary information do you want for detail records?" Here, you can click Summary Options if you want to add aggregate functions (e.g., sum, average, minimum, and maximum) and to specify whether you want to see detail records on the report or only the aggregate results (see Figure 4.28). You can also choose to calculate percentages, so if you had one group that made up half your sales, you would see 50%. Click OK to return to the Report Wizard. The sort options are the same as before. Set the appropriate options and click Next.

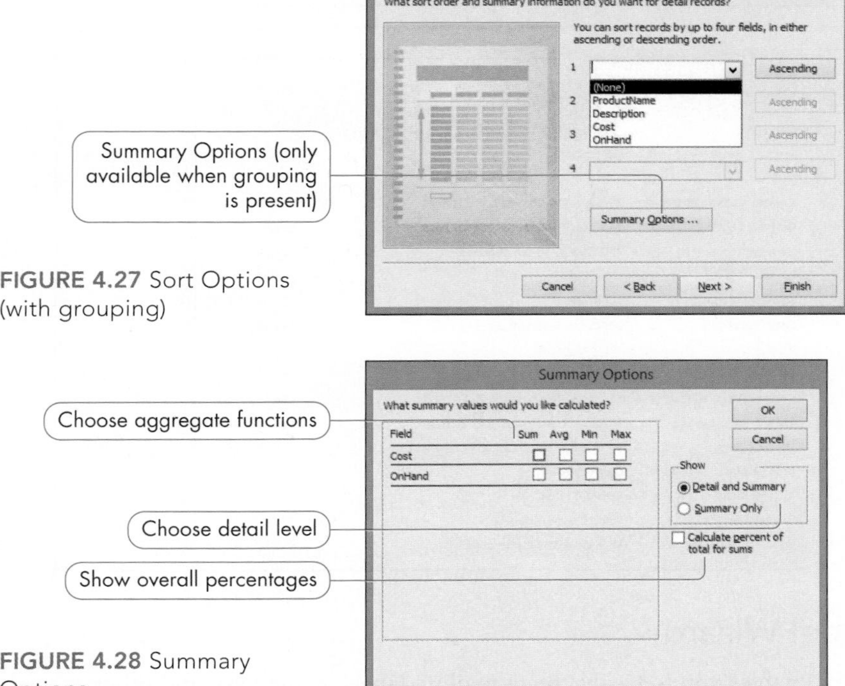

FIGURE 4.27 Sort Options (with grouping)

FIGURE 4.28 Summary Options

5. The next dialog box, shown in Figure 4.29, will determine the report's appearance. If you have selected grouping, you will be prompted to select the layout from three options:

   - Stepped Layout will display column headings at the top of the page and keep the grouping field(s) in their own row.
   - Block Layout will include the grouping field(s) inline with the data, saving some space when printing. It has one set of column headings at the top of each page.
   - Outline Layout will display the grouping field(s) on their own separate rows and has column headings inside each group. This leads to a longer report when printing but may help make the report easier to read.

   Clicking any of these layouts will give you a general preview in the preview area. The option to choose Portrait or Landscape is still available. Click Next.

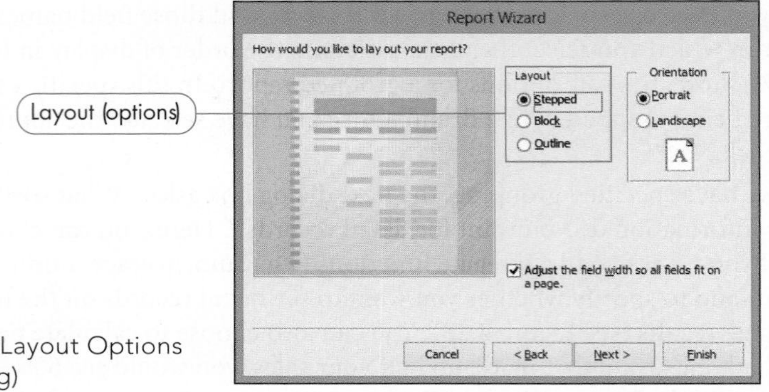

FIGURE 4.29 Layout Options (with grouping)

6. Decide on an appropriate name for the report. Type a descriptive report name. Click Finish. Your grouped report will resemble Figure 4.30.

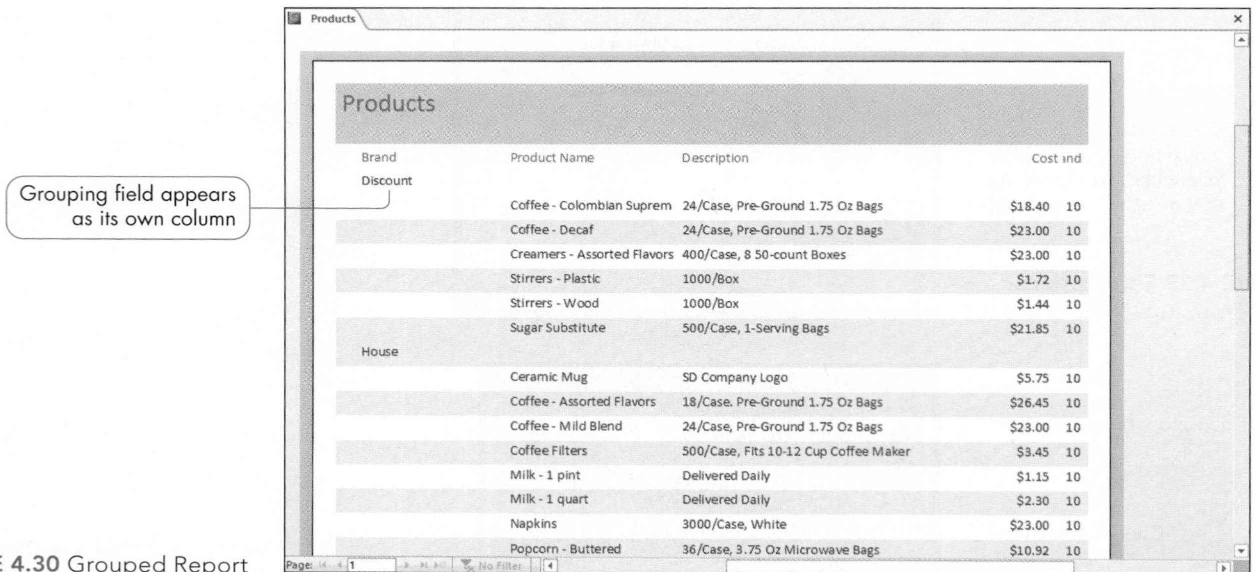

FIGURE 4.30 Grouped Report

Use the Label Wizard

The ***Label Wizard*** enables you to easily create mailing labels, name tags, and other specialized tags. A ***mailing label report*** is a specialized report that comes preformatted to coordinate with name-brand labels, such as Avery. Access includes most common labels built into the program. Even if you purchase a store brand from an office supply store, they will generally state the comparable Avery label number.

To use the Label Wizard, do the following:

1. Select the table or query that will serve as the record source for the report.
2. Click Labels in the Reports group on the CREATE tab.
3. Select the manufacturer, the product number, and the label type and click Next.
4. Choose the font type and size and click Next.
5. Add the fields to the label template, as shown in Figure 4.31. You will need to place the fields exactly as you wish them to appear, including adding a comma between City and State and pressing Enter after the CustomerName.
6. Add any sort fields and click Next.
7. Name the report and click Finish to generate your labels. The results are shown in Figure 4.32.

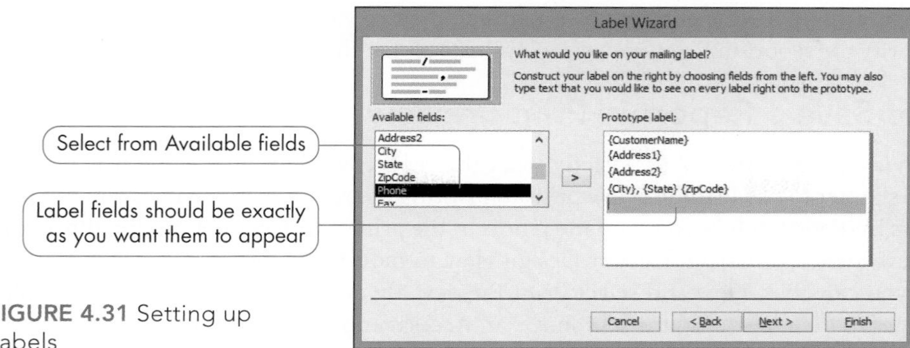

FIGURE 4.31 Setting up Labels

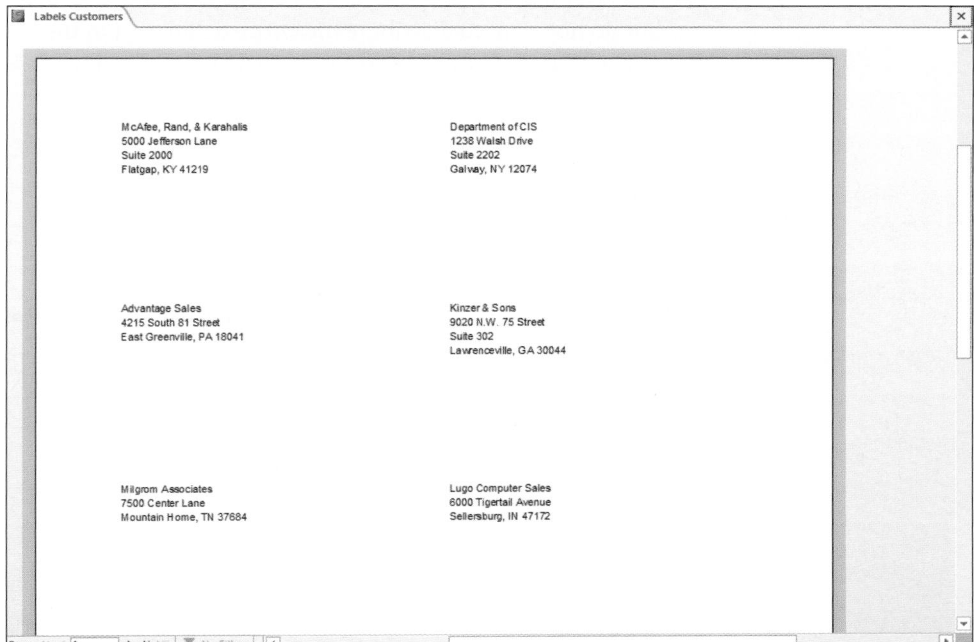

FIGURE 4.32 Output of Label Wizard

Using Report Views

As you work with the report tools to create and modify reports, you will find the need to frequently switch between the four report views in Access—Layout view, Print Preview, Design view, and Report view. Most of your design work will be done in Layout view, but occasionally, you will need to switch to Design view to apply a more advanced feature, such as a calculated field. Users of the report will use Print Preview or Report view. There should be no reason for a user to switch to Layout view or Design view. Modifications to the report should be done by the designated report designer. To switch between the four views, click the View arrow in the Views group and select the desired view.

View a Report in Report View

Report view enables you to view a report onscreen in a continuous page layout. Report view is similar to Form view for forms. However, because the data shown in a report cannot be changed, it is simply a way of viewing the information without having to worry about accidentally moving a control. In addition, using report view allows quick access to filtering options.

Alter a Report in Layout View

Use Layout view to alter the report design while still viewing the data. You should use Layout view to add or delete fields in the report, modify field properties, change the column widths, sort, and filter data by excluding certain records. Although Layout view appears similar to Print

Preview, you will find sufficient variations between the two views, so that you will still always need to verify the report in Print Preview to evaluate all the changes made in Layout view.

Print or Save a Report in Print Preview

STEP 2》 ***Print Preview*** enables you to see exactly what the report will look like when it is printed. Most users prefer to use Print Preview prior to printing the report. This enables you to intercept errors in reports before you send the report to the printer. You cannot modify the design in this view; switch to Layout view or Design view to modify the design. To switch to Print Preview, you can click View and select Print Preview. By default, Print Preview will display all the pages in the report. Figure 4.33 shows an Access report in Print Preview.

Once you are in Print Preview, you have the option to save the report to a file as well. This is a useful option if you plan on distributing some of your information electronically but do not want to distribute the entire database. On the Print Preview tab in the Data group, you will find a number of different data types. See Figure 4.33. Simply choose the type of file you wish to create, and choose the directory and file name.

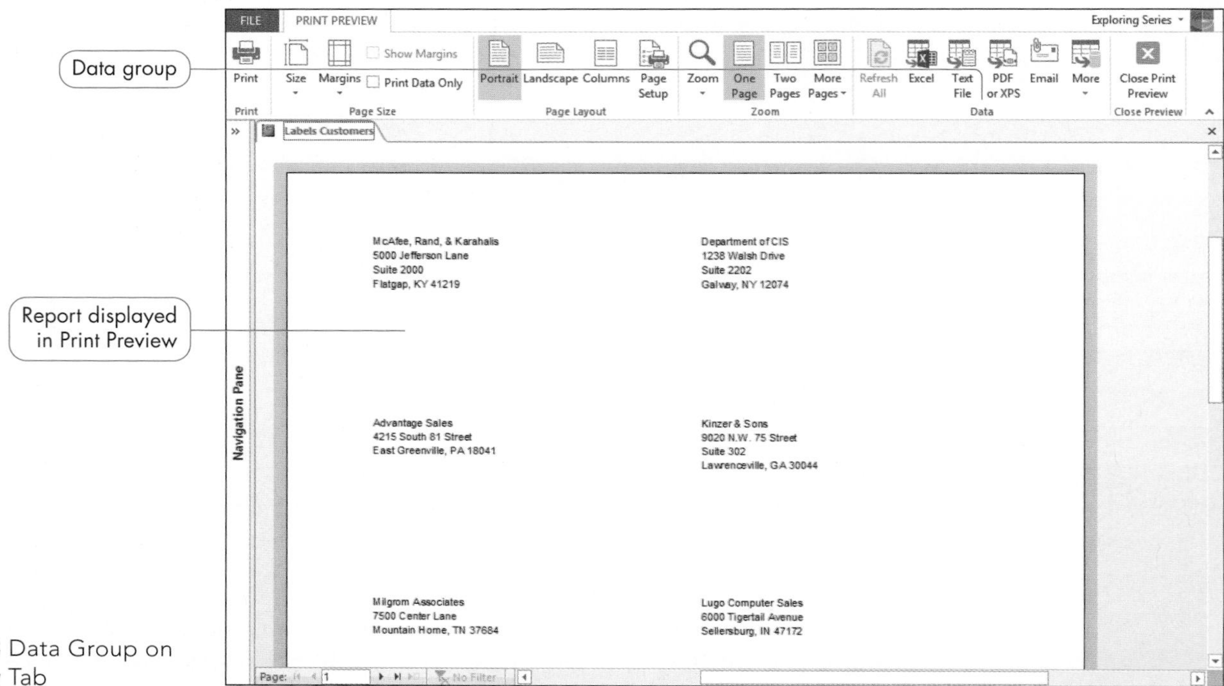

FIGURE 4.33 Data Group on Print Preview Tab

Commonly used formats include Excel, Word, or Portable Document Format (PDF). ***Portable Document Format (PDF)*** is a file type that was created for exchanging documents independent of software applications and operating system environment. In other words, you can e-mail files in this format to users running Mac operating system or a Linux operating system, and they can open it, even if they do not have Microsoft Office. Acrobat files often open in a program called Adobe Reader, a free tool that displays PDF files.

Because databases contain a great deal of information, Access reports may become very long, requiring many pages to print. Experienced Access users always use Print Preview prior to printing their reports. Some reports may require hundreds of pages to print. Other reports may be formatted incorrectly, and a blank page may print after each page of information. It would be better to correct this problem prior to sending it to the printer.

Modifying a Report

After a report is generated by one of the report tools, you may need to modify it. Similar to forms, the common changes to a report are add a field, remove a field, change the order of fields, change the width of a field, and modify the title. Much like a form, the Report has many options you can use to format a report. Once you are in Layout or Design view, you will have access to the report layout tools. You have four tabs available:

- Design: Use this tab to make changes to the design of the report, such as adding sorting, changing themes, and inserting additional controls.
- Arrange: Use this tab to change the layout of a report, to move fields up and down, to insert a space above or below your current position, or to insert a space to the left or the right of the current field.
- Format: Use this tab to change the font; add or remove bolding, italics, or underlining; change font size; change font color or background; adjust text alignment; or add a background image.
- Page Setup: Use this tab to change paper size, margins, page orientation, or to add columns.

Modify a Report Using the Arrange Tab

The Arrange tab displays in both Layout view and Design view. To use these commands, first open a report in Layout view or Design view and click the Format tab. Next, select a field or fields and click the appropriate command. Some key commands are highlighted in Figure 4.34.

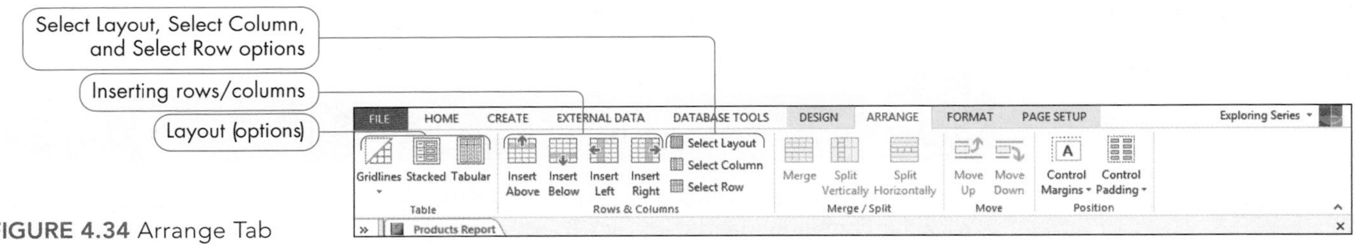

FIGURE 4.34 Arrange Tab

The Table group contains commands that enable you to add gridlines to a report's layout, to change a report's layout from stacked to tabular (and vice versa), or to remove a report's layout. The Remove Layout command is available in Design view only. For example, if a report was created with a tabular layout, you could change it to a stacked layout by doing the following:

STEP 3»

1. Open the report in Layout view.
2. Click the ARRANGE tab.
3. Click on any text box in the *Detail* section.
4. Click Select Layout in the Rows & Columns group.
5. Click Stacked in the Table group.

The Rows & Columns group contains commands that enable you to insert rows and columns inside a report's layout. For example, in a report with a stacked layout, you may want to separate the first three fields from the rest of the fields. To do this, you could select the third text box and click Insert Below. This will create a space after the third field. This group also contains the Select Layout, Select Column, and Select Row commands.

The Merge/Split group contains commands that enable you to merge and split the cells on a report. There are times when you may want to deviate from the basic row and column formats that the Access Report Wizards create. In this case, you can change the layout of the report using the merge cells and split cell commands. These commands do not change the actual controls, only the layout of the controls.

The Move group contains two commands that enable you to move a field up or down in a stacked layout. For example, if you want to move the second field in a stacked layout to the first position, select the second field's text box and label, and then click Move Up in the Move group. Moving fields up or down in a report may cause unexpected results; you can always use the undo command if you need to revert back to the beginning.

The Position group contains commands that enable you to modify the margins and the padding of controls in a report. This group also contains the Anchoring command, which enables you to change where the report's controls appear on the screen. By default, reports are anchored at the top left; however, you can change this to any of the nine options using the anchoring command.

Modify Report Controls using the Format Tab

The Format tab contains a series of commands that enable you change the font, display, and alignment of the controls on a report, as shown in Figure 4.35. This is useful if you need to quickly change the look of one cell. For example, you may have an important field you want to emphasize. To do so, do the following:

1. Switch to Layout view (or Design view).
2. Select the field you wish to format.
3. Click the FORMAT tab.
4. Change the format as desired. You can format the text as you would in Microsoft Word.

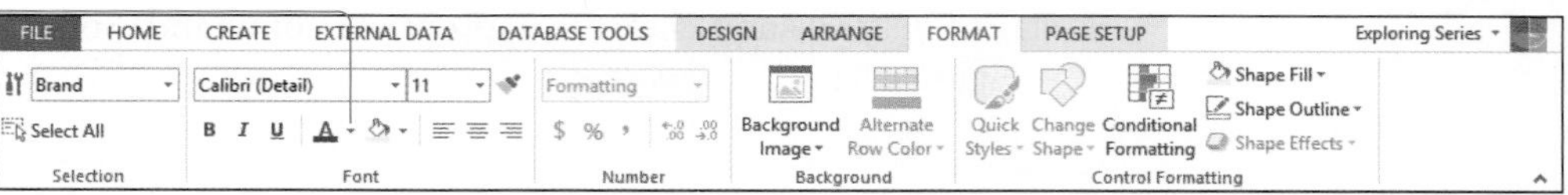

FIGURE 4.35 Format Tab

TIP Apply a Background Image to a Report

To apply a Background Image to a report, open the report in Layout view (or Design view), click the Format tab, and then click Background Image in the Background group. Next, click Browse to locate the image you want to apply to the report. Once the image has been applied to the report, you can change the properties of the image so that the image is anchored and sized correctly.

Add a Field to a Report

Adding a field to a report with a tabular layout is similar to adding a field to a form with a tabular layout. To add a field to a report, do the following:

1. Switch to Layout view.
2. On the DESIGN tab, in the Tools group, click Add Existing Fields to reveal the available fields in the report's record source. The Field List pane will display on the right-hand side of your screen.
3. For a single-table report, you will be presented with a list of fields. For a multiple-table report, you will first need to click the + (plus) next to the appropriate table to locate the desired field.
4. Drag the new field to a precise location on the report, using the vertical shaded line as a guide for the position of the new field, and release the mouse. The other fields will automatically adjust to make room for the new field.

The process of adding a field to a report with a stacked layout is the same as a tabular layout. The only difference is the shaded line will appear horizontally.

Delete a Field from a Report

To delete a field from the *Detail* section of a tabular report, do the following:

1. Switch to the Layout view (or Design view) of the report.
2. Click the text box of the field to be deleted. Click Select Column in the Rows & Columns group on the ARRANGE tab. Note the shaded border appears around the field and the label for the field.
3. With the shaded border visible, press Delete on your keyboard. The field disappears and the other fields fill in the gap.

Adjust Column Widths in a Report

You can adjust the width of each column in a tabular report individually so that each column is wide enough to accommodate the widest value. For example, if a report contains first name, last name, address and city, and email address, you will need to make sure the longest value in each field is completely visible. Scroll through the records to make sure this is the case.

To modify column widths in a tabular report, do the following:

1. Switch to the Layout view (or Design view) of the report.
2. Click the text box of the field you want to adjust. The field will have a shaded border around it, indicating it is selected.
3. Move the mouse to the right border of the selected field; when the mouse pointer turns to a double arrow, drag the edge to the right (to increase) or the left (to decrease) until you arrive at the desired width.

Changing Margins and Orientation

Sometimes, you may wish to print a page in Landscape or adjust the margins rather than adjusting widths. You will notice the Page Setup tab has these options. In the Page Size group, you can change the margins, and in the Page Layout group, you can choose Portrait or Landscape. See Figure 4.36 for locations of commonly used tools on this tab.

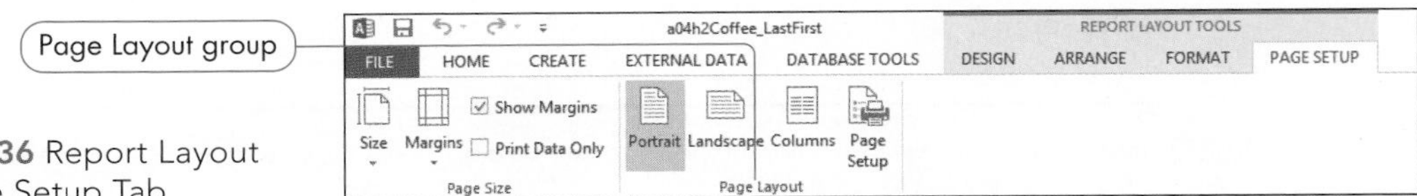

FIGURE 4.36 Report Layout Tools Page Setup Tab

Add a Theme to the Report

You can enhance the report's appearance by applying one of the themes provided by Access. To apply a theme, do the following:

1. Switch to Layout view (or Design view).
2. Click Themes in the Themes group on the DESIGN tab. Scroll through the themes until you find a theme you like; hover over one of the options to see a quick preview of the current report using the current theme. (This is easier to preview in Layout view.)
3. Right-click a theme and select *Apply Theme to This Object Only*. You can also apply the theme to all objects.

Work with a Report Layout Control

Whenever you use one of the report tools to create a new report, Access will add a layout control to help align the fields. Layout controls in reports work the same as layout controls in forms. As discussed earlier in this chapter, the layout control provides guides to help keep controls aligned horizontally and vertically and give your report a uniform appearance.

There are times when you may want to remove the layout control from a report in order to position the fields without aligning them to each other. If you want to remove the layout control from a report, do the following:

1. Switch to Design view (this is not available in Layout view).
2. Click anywhere inside the layout control you want to remove.
3. Click Select Layout in the Rows & Columns group on the ARRANGE tab.
4. In the Table group, click Remove Layout and the layout control is gone. All of the controls are still on the report, but the rectangle binding them together is gone.

You can add a layout control to a report by first selecting all the controls you want to keep together. Then, click Stacked or Tabular in the Table group and the layout control appears.

Sorting Records in a Report

When a report is created using the Report tool, the sort order of the records in the report is initially dependent on the sort order of the record source—similar to the way records are sorted in a form. The primary key of the record source usually dictates the sort order. However, a report has an additional feature for sorting. While in Layout view or Design view, click Group & Sort in the Grouping & Totals group on the Design tab. The Group, Sort, and Total pane displays at the bottom of the report. This section enables you to set the sort order for the report and override the sorting in the report's record source. Note that if you did not use the Report Wizard, this is how you would add grouping and totals to a report.

Sorting is important because sorting by a primary key may not be intuitive. For example, sorting by a field like LastName might be a better choice than a primary key so users see the records are in alphabetical order by LastName.

Change the Sorting in a Report

STEP 4»

If you want to change the sorting in the report, do the following:

1. Switch to Layout view.
2. On the DESIGN tab, in the Grouping & Totals group, click Group & Sort to display the *Group, Sort, and Total* section, as shown in Figure 4.37. This will appear at the bottom of the report.

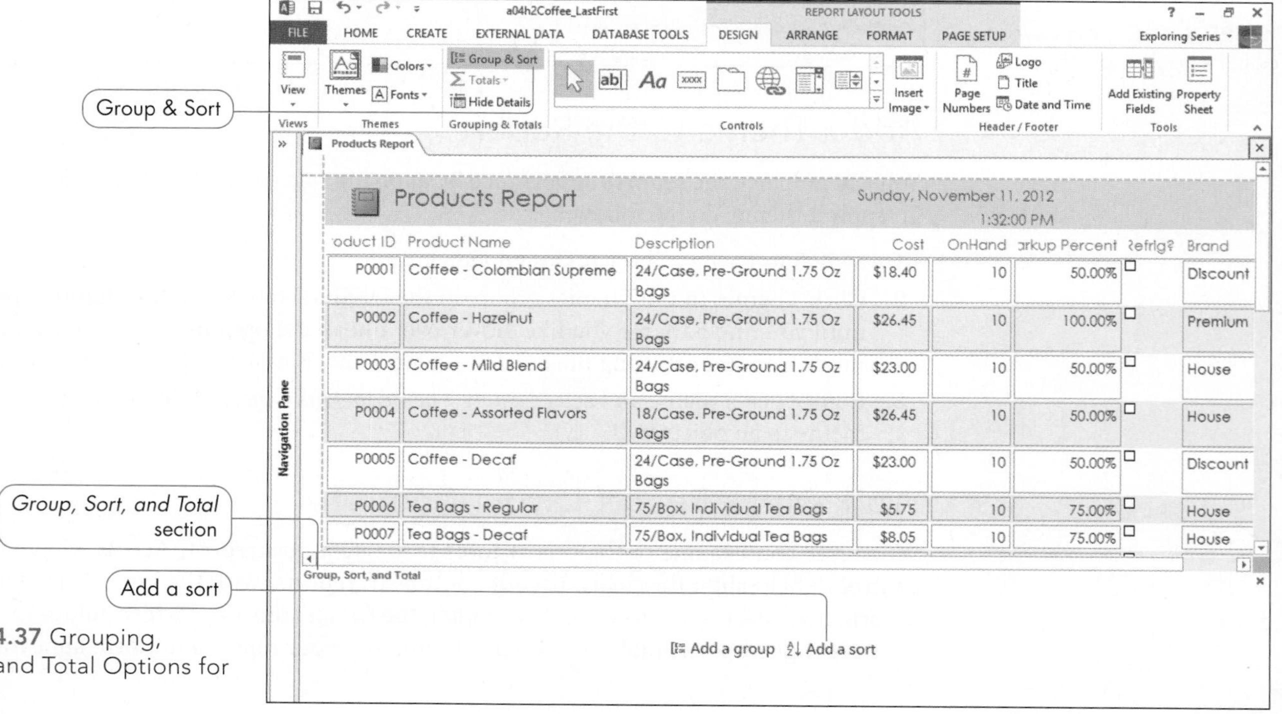

FIGURE 4.37 Grouping, Sorting, and Total Options for Reports

3. Click *Add a sort* and select the field you wish to sort by, which you can change as shown in Figure 4.38. The default sort order is ascending.

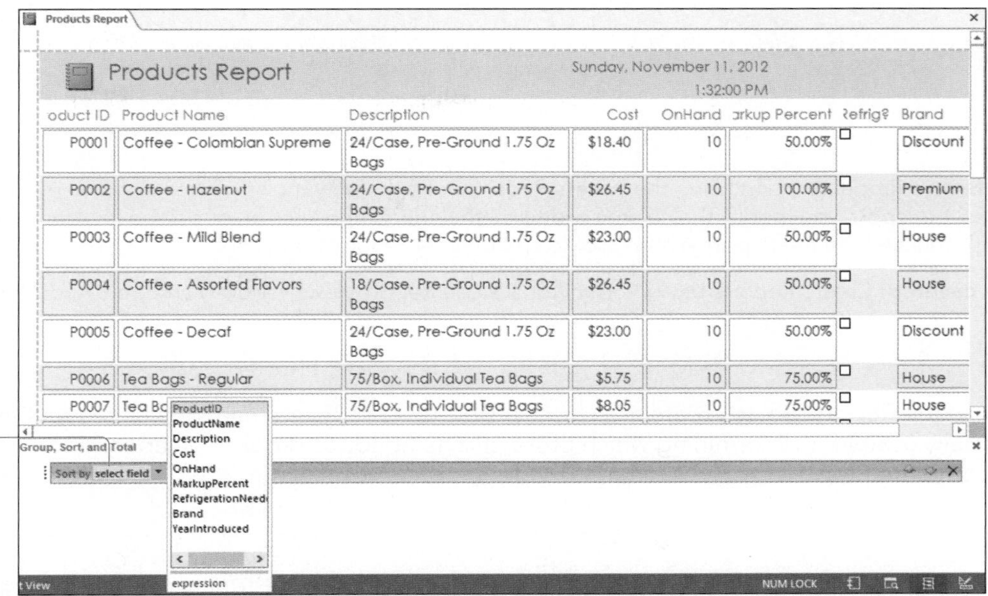

Select sort field

FIGURE 4.38 Adding a Sort to a Report

4. If you wish to add a second sort, click *Add a Sort* again. For example, you could sort first by Brand and then by ProductName, as shown in Figure 4.39.

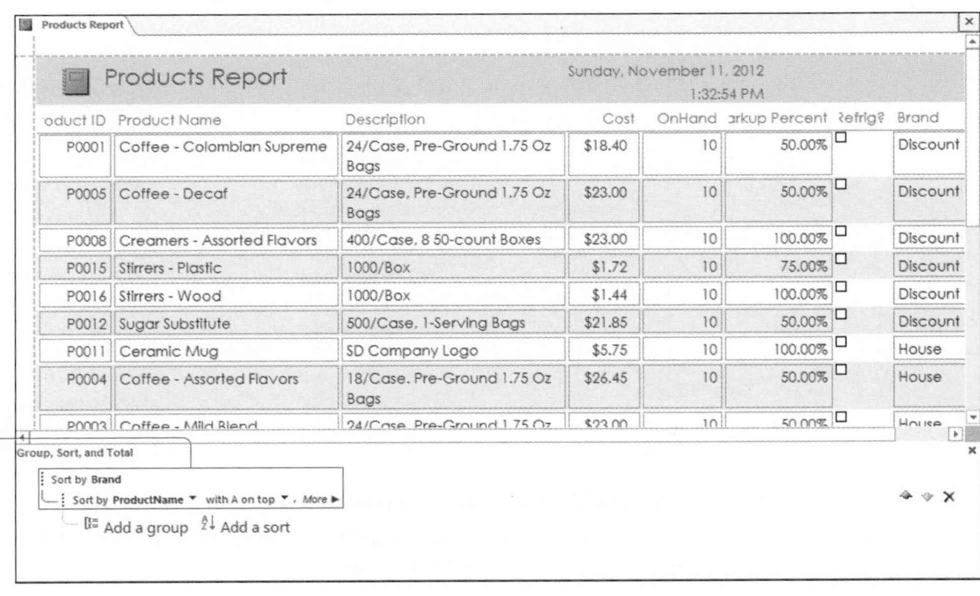

Multiple sort fields

FIGURE 4.39 Report with Multiple Sort Fields

Quick Concepts

1. Compare controls in forms and controls in reports. ***pp. 794, 812***
2. What are the benefits of using the report wizard? ***p. 814***
3. What is the difference between Print Preview and Report view? ***pp. 819–820***
4. What are the benefits of a report layout control when modifying a report? ***pp. 823–824***
5. Why is sorting the records in a report important? ***p. 824***

Hands-On Exercises

MyITLab® HOE2 Training

2 Report Basics

You create a Products report using the Access Report tool to help Ryung stay on top of the key data for her business. After Access creates the report, you modify the column widths so the entire report fits on one page (portrait or landscape, depending on the report). You also use the Report Wizard tool to create other reports for Ryung.

Skills covered: Create Reports Using Report Tools • Use Report Views • Modify a Report • Sort Records in a Report

STEP 1 ≫ CREATING REPORTS USING REPORT TOOLS

You use the Report tool to create an Access report to help Ryung manage her product information. This report is especially useful for determining which products she needs to order to fill upcoming orders. Refer to Figure 4.40 as you complete Step 1.

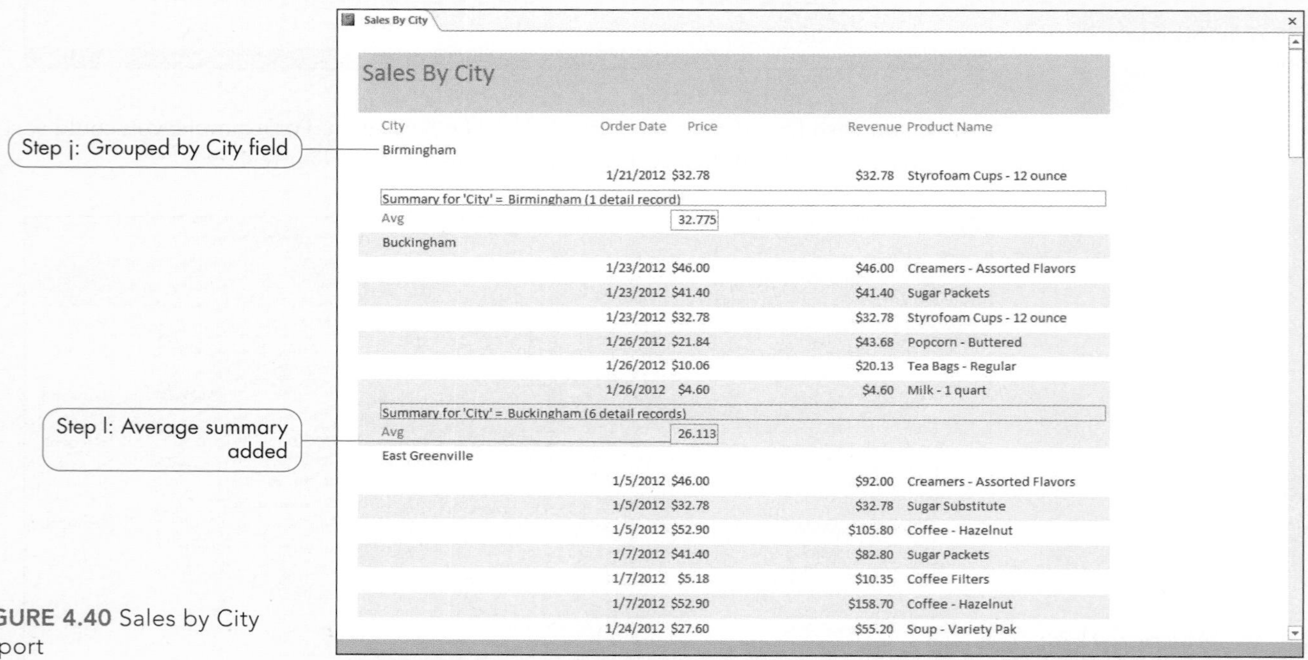

FIGURE 4.40 Sales by City Report

a. Open *a04h1Coffee_LastFirst* if you closed it at the end of Hands-On Exercise 1. Click the **FILE tab**, select **Save As**, and then click **Save As**. Type **a04h2Coffee_LastFirst** as the file name, changing *h1* to *h2*. Click **Save**.

b. Select the **Products table** in the Navigation Pane. Click the **CREATE tab** and click **Report** in the Reports group.

   Access creates a new tabular layout report based on the Products table. The report opens in Layout view ready to edit.

c. Click the **Products title** at the top of the report to select it, click again on **Products**, and then change the title to **Products Report**. Press **Enter** to accept the change.

d. Right-click the **Products report tab** and select **Print Preview**.

   The report is too wide for the page; you will exit Print Preview and change the orientation to Landscape.

e. Click **Close Print Preview**.

f. Click the **PAGE SETUP tab** and click **Landscape** in the Page Layout group.

   The report changes to Landscape orientation. Most of the columns now fit onto one page. You will make further revisions to the report later on so that it fits on one page.

g. Save the report as **Products Report**. Close the report.

h. Select the **Revenue query** in the Navigation Pane. Click the **CREATE tab** and click **Report Wizard** in the Reports group.

   The Report Wizard launches.

i. Click the **City field** and click the > **button** to add the City field to the report. Repeat the same process for the **OrderDate**, **Price**, **Revenue**, and **ProductName fields**. Click **Next**.

j. Select **City** and click the > **button** to add grouping by city. Click **Next**.

k. Select **OrderDate** for the sort order and leave the order as **Ascending**. Click **Summary Options**.

l. Click the **Avg check box** on the Price row to summarize the Price field. Click **OK**.

m. Click **Next**. Click **Next** again to accept the default layout.

n. Type **Sales by City** for the title of the report. Click **Finish**.

   The report is displayed in Print Preview mode. Some of the data values and labels cannot be seen. Next, you will adjust the controls.

o. Click **Close Print Preview**.

p. Switch to Layout view if necessary and adjust the controls so all the field values are visible as shown in Figure 4.40.

q. Display the report in Print Preview to verify your changes.

r. Save and close the report.

STEP 2 » USING REPORT VIEWS

The Products report you created for La Vida Mocha looks very good, according to Ryung. However, she does not have Access at home and would like to have a copy of the report saved so she can bring it home. You will save a copy of the report for her.

a. Open the **Products Report** and switch to **Print Preview**. Click **PDF or XPS** in the Data group on the PRINT PREVIEW tab. Enter the file name **a04h2Products_LastFirst** and click **Publish**.

   Windows will open the report in your system's default PDF viewer, which may be Adobe Reader or the Windows 8.1.1 Reader app.

b. Switch back to Access, if necessary. Click **Close** when asked if you want to save the export steps.

c. Click **Close Print Preview** and close the report.

STEP 3 » MODIFYING A REPORT

Ryung realized the Products table is missing a field. She would like you to add this to the table and update the report to reflect the new field. She would also like to make sure the report fits nicely onto one landscape page. She has also asked you to show her some sample color schemes.

a. Right-click the **Products table** and select **Design view**.

   You need to add the OnHand field to the Products table.

b. Click the **MarkupPercent field** and click **Insert Rows** in the Tools group on the DESIGN tab.

   A new blank row displays above the MarkupPercent field.

c. Type **OnHand** in the **Field Name box** and select **Number** as the Data Type.

d. Save the table. Click **View** to change to Datasheet view.

The new OnHand column appears empty in each row. Next, you will add sample data to the new field.

e. Fill in the number **10** for each item's OnHand field.

f. Close the Products table.

g. Right-click the **Products Report** and select **Layout view**.

h. Click **Add Existing Fields** in the Tools group on the DESIGN tab unless the Field List already appears on the right of your screen.

i. Drag the **OnHand field** from the Field List pane between the Cost and MarkupPercent fields. Close the Field List pane.

Because of the tabular layout control, Access adjusts all the columns to make room for the new OnHand field.

j. Display the report in Print Preview.

The report is still too wide for a single page.

k. Click **Close Print Preview**. Switch to Layout view if necessary.

l. Click anywhere on the **Year Introduced column**. Click the **ARRANGE tab** and click **Select Column** in the Rows & Columns group. Press **Delete** to remove the column.

The Year Introduced column is removed from the report and the other fields fill the empty space.

> **TROUBLESHOOTING:** If you cannot see the Year Introduced column, try scrolling to the right.

m. Click the **ProductID column heading** and drag the right border to the left until the Product ID heading still fits, but any extra white space is removed.

n. Click the **Refrigeration Needed column heading** and rename the column **Refrig?**. Adjust the column width of the Refrig? column so any extra white space is removed.

o. Click **Themes** in the Themes group on the DESIGN tab.

The available predefined themes display.

p. Right-click the **Organic theme** and choose **Apply Theme to This Object Only**. Display the report in Print Preview.

Access reformats the report using the Organic theme.

> **TROUBLESHOOTING:** If you cannot figure out which theme is which, you can hover the mouse over each theme and a ScreenTip will display the theme name.

q. Click **Close Print Preview**. Click the **FILE tab**, select **Save As**, select **Save Object As**, and then click **Save As**. Type **Products Organic** as the report name and click **OK**.

You saved the report with one theme. Now, you will apply a second theme to the report and save it with a different name.

r. Switch to Layout view and click **Themes** in the Themes group to apply a different theme.

s. Right-click the **Retrospect theme** and choose **Apply Theme to This Object Only**. Display the report in Print Preview.

If we do not tell Access to apply the theme to this object only, all objects will change.

t. Click **Close Print Preview**. Click the **FILE tab**, select **Save As**, select **Save Object As**, and then click **Save As**. Type **Products Retrospect** as the report name and click **OK**. Close the report.

You will be able to show Ryung two different themes.

STEP 4 » SORTING RECORDS IN A REPORT

Ryung would like the Products Report report to be sorted by Product Name order (rather than ProductID order). You change the sort order and preview again to see the results.

a. Open **Products Report** in Layout view.

> **TROUBLESHOOTING:** If you cannot see the Products Report, click the Shutter Bar to maximize the Navigation Pane.

b. Click **Group & Sort** in the Grouping & Totals group on the DESIGN tab.

The *Add a group* and *Add a sort* options appear at the bottom of the report.

> **TROUBLESHOOTING:** If the options do not appear, they may have been showing. Try clicking Group & Sort again.

c. Click **Add a sort**.

A new Sort bar displays at the bottom of the report.

d. Select **Brand** from the list.

The report is now sorted by Brand in Ascending order (with Discount on top).

e. Click **Add a group**.

f. Select **Brand** from the list.

The report is now grouped by Brand.

g. Display the report in Print Preview.

h. Close Print Preview and save and close the report.

i. Close the database. Submit the database and the PDF file *a04h2Products_LastFirst* based on your instructor's directions.

Chapter Objectives Review

After reading this chapter, you have accomplished the following objectives:

1. **Create forms using form tools.**
   - A form is used to add data to or edit data in a table.
   - Access provides 14 different tools for creating forms.
   - If you use a form, you are less likely to edit the wrong record.
   - Forms can show data from multiple tables at once.
   - Forms can be customized to match a paper form.
   - Identify a record source: A record source is the table or query that supplies the records.
   - Use the Form tool: The Form tool creates a basic form.
   - Understand controls: Controls are the text boxes, buttons, boxes, and other tools you use to add, edit, and display data in a form or report.
   - Work with form views: Form view is a simplified interface used for data entry, but it allows no changes. Layout view allows users to make changes to the layout while viewing the data on the form. Design view allows you to change advanced design settings you cannot see in the Layout view.
   - Work with a subform: A subform displays data from a related table for each record in the main table.
2. **Create a split form: A split form combines two views of the same record source—one section is displayed in a stacked layout and the other section is displayed in a tabular layout.**
   - Create a multiple-item form: This form displays multiple records in a tabular layout similar to a table's Datasheet view, with more customization options.
   - Create forms using the other form tools: A Datasheet form is a replica of a table or query's Datasheet view except that it still retains some of the form properties. The Form Design tool and the Blank Form tools can be used to create a form manually. The Navigation option in the Forms group enables you to create user interface forms that have the look and feel of a Web-based form and enable users to open and close the objects of a database. The Modal Dialog Form tool can be used to create a dialog box.
3. **Use form views.**
   - Edit data in Form view: Most users will work in Form view. This allows changes to data but not to design elements.
   - Alter a form in Layout view: Layout view allows you to change the design of a form while viewing data.
   - Add a field to a form: Fields can be added to an existing form using the Field List.
   - Delete a field from a form: Fields can be removed, but you may need to select the entire control to avoid leaving empty space in the form.
   - Adjust column widths in a form: Column widths often need to be adjusted. Numeric fields may show up as #### if the value cannot be displayed in the box.
   - Use the Form Layout tools tabs: There are three Form Layout tabs that allow you to manipulate the design of a form.
   - Modify form controls using the Format tab: The Format tab allows changes to the font, including bold, italic, underlining, font size, font color, font background, and alignment.
   - Select controls: Controls can be selected manually or by using the Arrange tab.
   - Add a theme to a form: Themes can be applied to a single form or to all objects in the database.
   - Add styling to a form: Forms can have many types of styles applied. Take care to avoid too many styles on a single form, as it can distract from the form.
4. **Work with a form layout control.**
   - Modify a form using the Arrange tab: The Arrange tab appears in both Layout view and Design view and allows you to change form layout, field order, and spacing options.
   - The Table group lets you add gridlines, change from stacked to tabular layout (and vice versa), or remove a form's layout.
   - The Move group contains lets you move fields.
   - The Position group lets you modify the margins and the padding of controls in a form.
5. **Sort records in form.**
   - Default sort order is the sort order of the data source (table, query, etc.).
   - Sort by a single field: Forms can be sorted by a single field in either ascending or descending order.
   - Remove sorting in a form: Sorts can be removed from a form at any point.
6. **Create reports using report tools.**
   - A report is a document that displays information from a database in a format that outputs meaningful information to its readers.
   - Access reports can be printed, viewed on screen, or saved as files.
   - Reports cannot change data in your database.
   - Use the Report tool: Access has five report tools: The Report tool instantly creates a tabular report based on the table or query currently selected. The Report Design tool creates a new blank report in Design view. The Blank Report tool creates a new blank report so that you can insert fields and controls manually and design the report. The Report Wizard tool helps you create a report. The Labels tool creates a page of mailing labels using a template.
   - Use the Report Wizard to create a report: The Report Wizard will guide you step by step through creating a report, asking questions and generating output.
   - Use the Report Wizard with grouping: The Report Wizard options will change when you add grouping. It will also allow summary options such as creating a sum of a field for each grouping level.
   - Use the Label Wizard: The Label Wizard can produce printable labels. Access includes predefined standard formats for common labels.

7. **Use report views.**
   - View a report in Report view: Report view is ideal for viewing data onscreen. Neither data nor design can be changed.
   - Alter a report in Layout view: Layout view allows you to change the design of a report while viewing data.
   - Print or save a report in Print Preview: Print Preview shows the way the report will display when printed. It also allows you to save the report as a file in a number of formats.

8. **Modify a report.**
   - Modify a report using the Design tab: The Design tab allows you to add or change sorting, change report theme, and insert additional controls.
   - Modify a report using the Arrange tab: The Arrange tab allows you to change the report layout, move fields, and insert spaces.
   - Modify report controls using the Format tab: The Format tab allows changes to the font, including bold, italic, underlining, font size, font color, font background, and alignment.
   - Add a field to a report: Fields can be added to an existing report using the Field List.
   - Delete a field from a report: Fields can be removed, but you may need to select the entire control to avoid leaving empty space in the report.
   - Adjust column widths in a report: Column widths often need to be adjusted. Numeric fields may show up as #### if the value cannot be displayed in the box.
   - Change margins and orientation: You can display the report in portrait or landscape format and increase or decrease margin size.
   - Add a theme to the report: Themes can be applied to a single report or to all objects in the database.
   - Work with a Report Layout control: The Layout control keeps the fields neatly spaced, making it harder to place fields in an exact location but keeping a standard format.

9. **Sort records in a report.**
   - Default sort order for reports is the sort order of the record source.
   - Change the sorting in a report: Sorting can be done by a single or by multiple fields.

Key Terms Matching

Match the key terms with their definitions. Write the key term letter by the appropriate numbered definition.

- **a.** Controls
- **b.** Design view
- **c.** Form
- **d.** Form tool
- **e.** Form view
- **f.** Label Wizard
- **g.** Layout control
- **h.** Layout view
- **i.** Multiple Items form
- **j.** Portable Document Format (PDF)
- **k.** Print Preview
- **l.** Record source
- **m.** Report
- **n.** Report tool
- **o.** Report view
- **p.** Report Wizard
- **q.** Split form
- **r.** Stacked layout
- **s.** Tabular layout
- **t.** Theme

1. ______ A database object that is used to add data into or edit data in a table. **p. 792**

2. ______ Used to create data entry forms for customers, employees, products, and other primary tables. **p. 792**

3. ______ The table or query that supplies the records for a form or report. **p. 793**

4. ______ Displays fields in a vertical column. **p. 794**

5. ______ Displays data horizontally. **p. 794**

6. ______ The text boxes, buttons, boxes, and other tools you use to add, edit, and display the data in a form or report. **p. 794**

7. ______ Provides guides to help keep controls aligned horizontally and vertically and give your form a uniform appearance. **p. 794**

8. ______ A simplified interface primarily used for data entry; does not allow you to make changes to the layout. **p. 794**

9. ______ Enables users to make changes to a layout while viewing the data on the form or report. **p. 795**

10. ______ Enables you to change advanced design settings you cannot see in the Layout view, such as a background image. **p. 795**

11. ______ Combines two views of the same record source—one section is displayed in a stacked layout and the other section is displayed in a tabular layout. **p. 796**

12. ______ Displays multiple records in a tabular layout similar to a table's Datasheet view, with more customization options. **p. 797**

13. ______ A defined set of colors, fonts, and graphics that can be applied to a form or report. **p. 801**

14. ______ A document that displays information from a database in a format that outputs meaningful information to its readers. **p. 812**

15. ______ Used to instantly create a tabular report based on the table or query currently selected. **p. 814**

16. ______ Asks you questions and then uses your answers to generate a customized report. **p. 814**

17. ______ Enables you to easily create mailing labels, name tags, and other specialized tags. **p. 818**

18. ______ Enables you to see what a printed report will look like in a continuous page layout. **p. 819**

19. ______ Enables you to see exactly what the report will look like when it is printed. **p. 820**

20. ______ A file type that was created for exchanging documents independent of software applications and operating system environment. **p. 820**

Multiple Choice

1. The table or query that supplies the records for a form or report is also known as the:
   (a) Control.
   (b) Record Source.
   (c) Theme.
   (d) Tabular Layout.

2. Which of the following statements is *false*?
   (a) Both forms and reports can use tabular and stacked layouts.
   (b) A stacked layout displays data in a vertical column.
   (c) A tabular layout displays data horizontally.
   (d) Stacked layouts are more common for reports because they will use less paper when printed.

3. Which of the following is *not* an example of a control?
   (a) A text box on a form
   (b) Buttons on a report
   (c) A report
   (d) A box on a report

4. The simplest interface you can use to modify control widths in a form is in:
   (a) Layout view.
   (b) Form view.
   (c) Design view.
   (d) Report view.

5. Which of the following views is the most powerful, but also the most complicated?
   (a) Design view.
   (b) Layout view.
   (c) Form view/Report view.
   (d) Print Preview.

6. Which of the following statements about reports are *false*?
   (a) Reports can be saved to a file on your computer.
   (b) Reports are primarily used to modify data.
   (c) Reports can produce output in a number of ways, including mailing labels.
   (d) Reports can be created simply using the Report tool.

7. Use the ____________ to see exactly what the printed report will look like before printing.
   (a) Report tool
   (b) Report Wizard
   (c) Report view
   (d) Print Preview

8. If you have a client working on a Mac system, which of the following file formats would be the best choice to use to ensure the client can open it?
   (a) Microsoft Word
   (b) Microsoft Excel
   (c) Microsoft Access
   (d) Portable Document Format (PDF)

9. Which of the following statements is *false*?
   (a) Reports are generally used for printing, emailing, or viewing data on the screen.
   (b) Layout controls for forms and reports are the defined sets of colors, fonts, and graphics.
   (c) Forms are often used for inputting data.
   (d) Forms and reports both include controls, such as text boxes, that can be resized.

10. Which of the following statements is *false*?
    (a) You can use grouping to show a list of properties by state.
    (b) Sorting can be done on both forms and reports.
    (c) Sorting can be done in ascending or descending order.
    (d) You can either group or sort (but not both).

Practice Exercises

1 Financial Management

You are working as a customer service representative for a financial management firm. Your task is to contact a list of prospective customers and introduce yourself and the services of your company. You will create a form to help you view one customer at a time while also helping add and update the data. After creating the form, you will customize it and add sorting. You will also create a report to show you all the data on one screen, for viewing purposes. This exercise follows the same set of skills as used in Hands-On Exercises 1 and 2 in the chapter. Refer to Figure 4.41 as you complete this exercise.

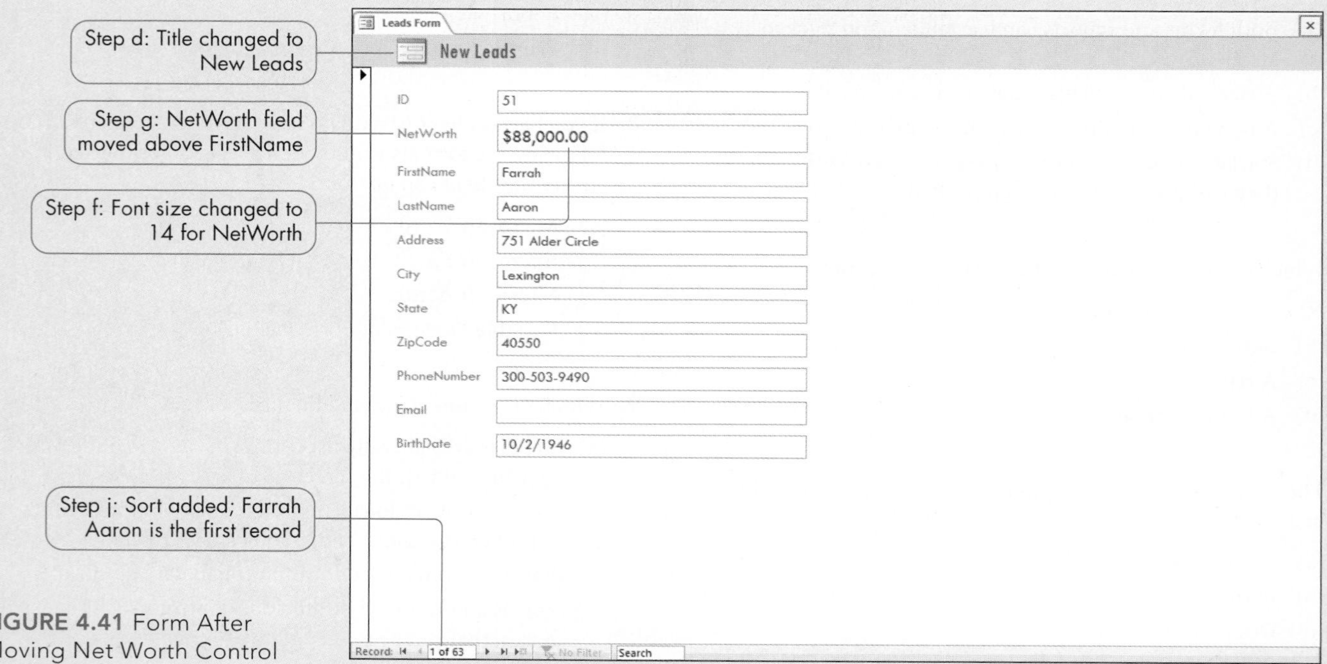

FIGURE 4.41 Form After Moving Net Worth Control

a. Start Access and open **a04p1Prospects**. Save the database as **a04p1Prospects_LastFirst**.

b. Click the **Leads table**. Click the **CREATE tab** and click **Form** in the Forms group.

   A new form based on the Leads table displays in Layout view.

c. Click the **ID text box** and drag the right border of the first field to the left to shrink the column by approximately half of its original size.

   The other columns will shrink as well.

d. Change the title of the form to **New Leads**.

e. Click **Themes** in the Themes group of the DESIGN tab. Select the **Integral theme** (first row, third column).

f. Change the font size to **14** for the NetWorth text box control.

g. Click **Select Row** in the Rows & Columns group on the ARRANGE tab. Click **Move Up** in the Move group on the ARRANGE tab until *NetWorth* appears above *First*.

> **TROUBLESHOOTING:** If both items do not move together, undo, ensure both are selected, and then follow the instructions in step g.

   NetWorth should now appear above the FirstName. See Figure 4.41.

h. Save the form as **Leads Form**. Switch to Form view.

i. Navigate to record 63. Enter your first and last names in the appropriate fields. Leave the e-mail address blank.

j. Click in the **Last field** (if necessary) and click **Ascending** in the Sort & Filter group of the HOME tab

   Farrah Aaron should be the first record displayed unless your last name appears before hers alphabetically.

k. Save and close the form.

l. Click the **Leads table**. Click **Report** in the Reports group on the CREATE tab.

   A new report is created based on the Leads table.

m. Make fields as small as possible to remove extra white space. Do not try to fit the entire report all on one page, as you will be using this for on-screen viewing only.

n. Save the report as **Leads Report**. Close the report.

o. Exit Access. Submit the database based on your instructor's directions.

2 Comfort Insurance

The Human Resources department of the Comfort Insurance Agency has initiated its annual employee performance reviews. You will create a form for them to help organize input and a report showing employee salary increases and bonuses. The employee data, along with forms and reports, are stored in an Access database. You need to prepare a report showing employee raises and bonuses by city. This exercise follows the same set of skills as used in Hands-On Exercises 1 and 2 in this chapter. Refer to Figure 4.42 as you complete this exercise.

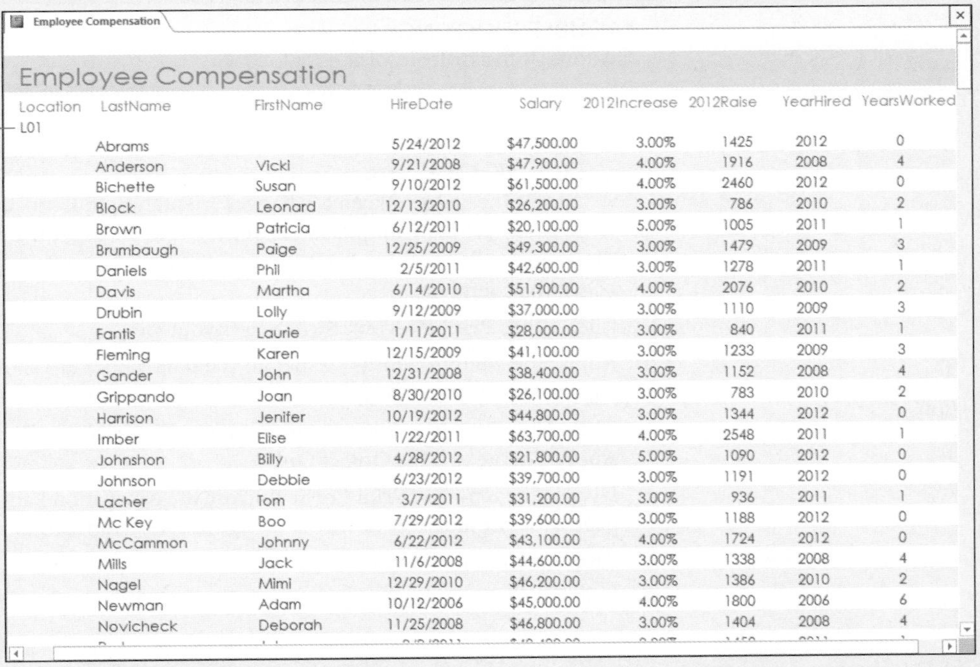

Step k: Location is a grouping level

Employee Compensation

Employee Compensation

Location	LastName	FirstName	HireDate	Salary	2012Increase	2012Raise	YearHired	YearsWorked
L01								
	Abrams		5/24/2012	$47,500.00	3.00%	1425	2012	0
	Anderson	Vicki	9/21/2008	$47,900.00	4.00%	1916	2008	4
	Bichette	Susan	9/10/2012	$61,500.00	4.00%	2460	2012	0
	Block	Leonard	12/13/2010	$26,200.00	3.00%	786	2010	2
	Brown	Patricia	6/12/2011	$20,100.00	5.00%	1005	2011	1
	Brumbaugh	Paige	12/25/2009	$49,300.00	3.00%	1479	2009	3
	Daniels	Phil	2/5/2011	$42,600.00	3.00%	1278	2011	1
	Davis	Martha	6/14/2010	$51,900.00	4.00%	2076	2010	2
	Drubin	Lolly	9/12/2009	$37,000.00	3.00%	1110	2009	3
	Fantis	Laurie	1/11/2011	$28,000.00	3.00%	840	2011	1
	Fleming	Karen	12/15/2009	$41,100.00	3.00%	1233	2009	3
	Gander	John	12/31/2008	$38,400.00	3.00%	1152	2008	4
	Grippando	Joan	8/30/2010	$26,100.00	3.00%	783	2010	2
	Harrison	Jenifer	10/19/2012	$44,800.00	3.00%	1344	2012	0
	Imber	Elise	1/22/2011	$63,700.00	4.00%	2548	2011	1
	Johnshon	Billy	4/28/2012	$21,800.00	5.00%	1090	2012	0
	Johnson	Debbie	6/23/2012	$39,700.00	3.00%	1191	2012	0
	Lacher	Tom	3/7/2011	$31,200.00	3.00%	936	2011	1
	Mc Key	Boo	7/29/2012	$39,600.00	3.00%	1188	2012	0
	McCammon	Johnny	6/22/2012	$43,100.00	4.00%	1724	2012	0
	Mills	Jack	11/6/2008	$44,600.00	3.00%	1338	2008	4
	Nagel	Mimi	12/29/2010	$46,200.00	3.00%	1386	2010	2
	Newman	Adam	10/12/2006	$45,000.00	4.00%	1800	2006	6
	Novicheck	Deborah	11/25/2008	$46,800.00	3.00%	1404	2008	4

FIGURE 4.42 Final Employee Compensation Report

a. Open *a04p2Insurance*. Save the database as **a04p2Insurance_LastFirst**.

b. Select the **Locations table**. Click the **CREATE tab** and click **Form** in the Forms group.

   A new form based on the Locations table opens in Layout view.

c. Click the **LocationID text box** containing *L01*. Move the mouse to the right edge of the shaded border until the mouse pointer changes to a double-headed arrow. Drag the right edge to the left to reduce the size of the text box to approximately half of its original size.

   The LocationID field and all the other fields should become smaller.

d. Click the subform at the bottom of the form. Press **Delete** to delete the subform.

e. Click **Themes** in the Themes group on the DESIGN tab. Right-click the **Wisp theme** (third row, first column) and select **Apply Theme to This Object Only**.

f. Save the form as **Locations**. Close the form.

g. Select the **Locations table**. Click the **CREATE tab** and click **Report** in the Reports group.

   A new tabular layout report based on the Locations table opens in Layout view.

h. Click the **LocationID label** and drag the right border of the label to the left to reduce the size of the control to approximately half of its original size.

i. Repeat the sizing process with the **Zipcode label** and the **OfficePhone label**. Adjust the other columns if necessary until there are no controls on the right side of the vertical dashed line.

j. Display the report in Print Preview. Verify that the report is only one page wide. Save the report as **Locations** and close the report.

k. Select the **Employees Query**. Click the **CREATE tab** and click **Report Wizard** in the Reports group to launch the Report Wizard. Respond to the questions as follows:

   - Click (>>) to add all the fields to the Selected Fields box. Click **Next**.
   - Accept grouping by Location. Click **Next**.
   - Select **LastName** for the first sort order and **FirstName** for the second. Click **Summary Options**.

> **TROUBLESHOOTING:** If you do not see summary options, click Back and click Summary Options at the bottom of the dialog box.

   - Click **Sum** for Salary, **Avg** for 2012Increase, and **Avg** for YearsWorked. Accept all other defaults. Click **OK**. Click **Next**.
   - Accept the Stepped layout. Change Orientation to **Landscape**. Click **Next**.
   - Type **Employee Compensation** for the title of the report. Click **Finish**.

   The report is displayed in Print Preview mode. Some of the columns are too narrow. Next, you will adjust the columns.

l. Click **Close Print Preview**. Switch to Layout view.

m. Adjust the column widths so that all the data values are showing and the report appears on one page. Some of the columns will need to be reduced, and some will need to be widened.

n. Click **Themes** in the Themes group on the DESIGN tab. Right-click the **Slice theme** and choose **Apply Theme to This Object Only**.

o. Display the report in Print Preview. Close the Navigation Pane and verify that the report is still one page wide. Compare your report to Figure 4.42. Adjust column widths to display all values.

p. Save and close the Employee Compensation report. Close the database.

q. Exit Access. Submit based on your instructor's directions.

Mid-Level Exercises

1 Hotel Chain

ANALYSIS CASE

You are the general manager of a large hotel chain. You track revenue by categories, such as conference room rentals and weddings. You need to create a report that shows which locations are earning the most revenue in each category. You will also create a report to show you details of your three newest areas: St. Paul, St. Louis, and Seattle.

a. Open *a04m1Rewards*. Save the database as **a04m1Rewards_LastFirst**.

b. Select the **Members table** and create a Multiple Items form. Save the form as **Maintain Members**.

c. Modify the form in Layout view as follows:
   - Change the MemNumber label to **MemID** and reduce the MemNumber column width.
   - Adjust the column widths to eliminate extra white space.
   - Delete the form icon (the picture next to the title of the form) in the Form Header.

d. Change the sorting on the MemberSince control so that the members who joined most recently are displayed first.

DISCOVER

e. Click on the **LastName field**. Change the Control Padding to **Wide**. Hint: Search **Control Padding Wide** in Access Help.

   The controls have some extra space between them.

f. Save and close the form.

g. Select the **Revenue query** and create a report using the Report Wizard. Answer the wizard prompts as follows:
   - Include all fields.
   - Add grouping by City and by ServiceName.
   - Add a Sum to the Revenue field and check the **Summary Only option**.
   - Choose **Outline Layout**.
   - Name the report **Revenue by City and Service**.

h. Scroll through all the pages to check the layout of the report while in Print Preview mode.

i. Exit Print Preview. Switch to Layout view and delete the NumInParty and PerPersonCharge controls.

j. Change the font size, font color, and/or background color of the Sum control (not the Revenue control) so the control stands out from the other controls.

k. Change the font size, font color, and/or background color of the Grand Total control (found at the end of the report) so the control stands out as well.

l. Change the sort on the report, so that it sorts by city in descending order—that is, so that the last city alphabetically (St. Paul) is displayed first.

★ m. Examine the data in the report to determine which city of St. Paul, St. Louis, and Seattle has the highest Sum of event revenue. You will use this information to modify a query.

★ n. Modify the Totals by Service query so the criteria for the City field is the city you determined had the highest sum from St. Paul, St. Louis, or Seattle. Save and close the query.

o. Create a report using the Report tool based on the Totals by Service query. Name the report **Targeted City**.

p. Close the report. Close the database.

q. Exit Access. Submit based on your instructor's directions.

2 Benefit Auction

You are helping to organize a benefit auction to raise money for families who lost their homes in a natural disaster. The information for the auction is currently stored in an Excel spreadsheet, but you have volunteered to migrate this to Access. You will create a database that will store the data from Excel in an Access database. You will create a form to manage the data-entry process. You also need to create two reports: one that lists the items collected in each category and one for labels so you can send the donors a thank-you letter after the auction.

a. Open Access and create a new database named **a04m2Auction_LastFirst**.
   A new table appears with an ID column.
b. Switch to Design view. Type **Items** in the **Save As dialog box** and click **OK**.
c. Change the ID Field Name to **ItemID**. Type **Description** in the second row and press **Tab**. Accept **Short Text** as the Data Type. Type **50** in the **Field Size property** in Field Properties.
d. Type the remainder of the fields and adjust the data types as shown:

Field Name	Data Type
DateOfDonation	Date/Time
Category	Short Text
Price	Currency
DonorName	Short Text
DonorAddress1	Short Text
DonorAddress2	Short Text

e. Open Excel. Open the **a04m2_Items** file. Examine the length of the Category, DonorName, DonorAddress1, and DonorAddress2 columns. Determine how many characters are needed for each field, and round to the nearest 5. For example, if a field needs 23 characters, you would round up to 25. You will use this to change field sizes in the table.
f. Change the field size for the Category, DonorName, DonorAddress1, and DonorAddress2 to the sizes you chose in step e. Save the table.
g. Copy and paste the rows from the Excel file into the table. Resize the columns so all data is visible. Close the table.

TROUBLESHOOTING: Recall that you must click the Record Selector (pencil icon, to the left of a blank row) to paste data.

TROUBLESHOOTING: Once you have pasted the data, ensure your chosen field sizes did not cause you to lose data. If so, update the field size, delete the records you pasted in, and then repeat step g.

h. Verify that the Items table is selected. Create a new form using the Form tool.
i. Change the layout of the form to a **Tabular Layout**. Resize field widths to reduce extra space. It is acceptable for field values to appear on two lines.
j. Change the title of the form to **Items for Auction**.

DISCOVER

k. Add conditional formatting so that each Price that is greater than 90 has a text color of **Green**. Use the Green color in the first row of the options.
l. Save the form as **Auction Items Form**.
m. Switch to Form view. Create a new record with the following information. Note it will automatically assign an ItemID of 27 for you.

Description	DateOfDonation	Category	Price	DonorName	DonorAddress1	DonorAddress2
iPad	12/31/2016	House	$400	Staples	500 Market St	Brick, NJ 08723

n. Add a sort to the form, so the lowest priced items appear first. Close the form.
o. Select the **Items table** in the Navigation Pane and create a report using the Report Wizard. Include all fields except the donor address fields, group by Category, include the Sum of Price as a Summary Option, accept the default layout, and then save the report **Auction Items by Category**.

p. Switch to Layout view and adjust the controls so all data is visible. Preview the report to verify the column widths are correct.

q. Sort the report so the least expensive items are shown first. Save and close the report.

r. Create mailing labels based on the Avery 5660 template. Place the donor name on the first line, address on the second, and city, state, and ZIP on the third line. Sort the labels by DonorName. Name the report **Donor Labels**. After you create the labels, display them in Print Preview mode verify everything will fit onto the label template. Close the label report.

s. Exit Access. Submit the database based on your instructor's directions.

3 Used Cell Phones for Sale

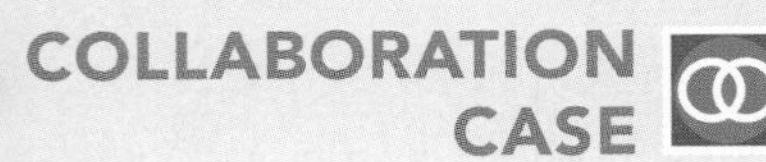

You and a few of your classmates started a new business selling used cell phones, MP3 players, and accessories. You have been using an Access database to track your inventory. You need to create several forms and reports to increase database efficiency and analysis. You have used Access forms and reports as part of your classwork, but you would like to experiment with them as they apply to you in a real-world scenario.

a. Choose one unique type of form and one unique type of report each. Based on your experience in class, you saw there were a number of different types of forms and reports that can be created. Choose one each from the following:

   Forms: Form tool, Form Wizard, Multiple Items Form, Split Form

   Reports: Report Tool, Report Wizard, Label Wizard

b. Open Access and open the *a04t1Phones* database individually. Save the file as **a04t1Phones_LastFirst**. Each of you will create your forms and reports in an individual database.

c. Create a form and a report based on the Inventory table, using the type of form and report you chose in step a, unless you chose Label Wizard. If you chose Label Wizard, you should create a report based on the Mailing List table, using Avery 8660 as your destination label.

d. Save the form and report as **LastFirst**, replacing Last and First with your last and first names.

e. Make the report as attractive and useful as possible. You may want to change sorting, add grouping (to reports), remove or add a layout control, change formatting options, and/or change the background color. Modify the form and report, save the changes, and exit Access.

f. Meet as a group. Open the *a04t1Phones* database and save the file as **a04t1Phones_GroupName**.

g. Import the form and report from each of your databases.

   Your *a04t1Phones_GroupName* file will now have one form and one report for each student.

h. Examine the forms and reports each of you created.

i. Examine your results. Determine which forms and reports you would keep, if this were the real world. Rename the forms and reports you would keep as **Keep_LastFirst** and rename the ones you would discard as **Discard_LastFirst**. Do not delete the forms and reports you will not use.

j. Modify the forms and reports you plan to keep as a group, if necessary. Save the changes and close all forms and reports. Ensure each student has a copy of the final *a04t1Phones_GroupName* database.

k. Exit Access and submit both the *a04t1Phones_GroupName* and *a04t1Phones_LastFirst* databases based on your instructor's directions.

Beyond the Classroom

Create a Split Form

FROM SCRATCH

This chapter introduced you to Access forms, including the split form. It is possible to turn an existing form into a split form if you modify a few form properties. Perform an Internet search to find the steps to convert a form to a split form. First, create a new database and name the file **a04b2Split_LastFirst**. Next, import *only* the Books table and Books form from the *a04b2BooksImport* database. To import the objects, click the **External Data tab** and click **Access** in the Import & Link group. After the new objects have been imported, use the information from the Internet to convert the Books form into a split form. Make sure the datasheet is on the bottom half. Change the form so it sorts by Title in ascending order. Save the form as **Split Form Books**. Close Access. Submit the database based on your instructor's directions.

Properties by City

Munesh, a co-worker, is having difficulty with an Access report and asked you for your assistance. He was trying to fix the report and seems to have made things worse. Open the *a04b3Sales* database and save the file as **a04b3Sales_LastFirst**. In the new database, open Properties Report in Report View. Notice Munesh moved fields around and the report does not fit on one page. In addition, there is a big gap between two fields and he moved the Bed and Bath fields so they are basically on top of one another. Add all of the fields to a Tabular Layout. Add grouping by City. Sort the report by Year Built in descending order. Change the report to Landscape orientation and adjust the column widths so they all fit onto one page. Save the new report as **Properties by City**. Close Access. Submit the database based on your instructor's directions.

Performance Reviews

SOFT SKILLS CASE

Passaic County Medical Monitoring provides visiting nurse care for patients in and around Passaic County, New Jersey. They have recently moved their records into an Access database. The director of Human Resources, Farrah Hassan, brings the nurses in yearly for a performance review. Employees are rated by a survey given to patients, asking them to rate the nurses on a scale of 1 (poor) to 5 (superb). You have been asked to create a one-page summary report to show the average of each employee's ratings. You will open her *a04b4Perform* database and save it as **a04b4Perform_LastFirst**. Use the Report Wizard to create a report based on the Performance and Nurses tables, group by the nurse, and add summary options to average the results for Promptness, Attitude, Knowledge, and Gentleness. The final report should display the NurseID, NurseFirst, and NurseLast fields and the averages for each of the four columns. You will also want to format each of the columns in the final report so they show two decimal places. You calculated the results by hand for nurse 1, Lan Wang, and her averages were 3.00 for Promptness, 3.11 for Attitude, 3.67 for Knowledge, and 3.67 for Gentleness, so when you create your report, you can check that it shows the correct data. Save the report as **Overall Ratings**, close Access, and submit the database based on your instructor's directions.

Capstone Exercise

Your boss asked you to prepare a schedule for each speaker for the national conference being hosted next year on your campus. She wants to mail the schedules to the speakers so that they can provide feedback on the schedule prior to its publication. You assure her that you can accomplish this task with Access.

Database File Setup

You need to copy an original database file, rename the copied file, and then open the copied database to complete this capstone exercise. After you open the copied database, you replace an existing employee's name with your name.

a. Open *a04c1_NatConf*.

b. Save the database as **a04c1NatConf_LastFirst**.

c. Open the Speakers table.

d. Find and replace *YourName* with your name. Close the table.

Create and Customize a Form

You need to create a form to add and update Speakers. Use the Form tool to create the form and modify the form as explained. You will also add a layout to an existing form.

a. Select the **Speakers table** as the record source for the form.

b. Use the Form tool to create a new stacked form.

c. Change the title to **Enter/Edit Speakers**.

d. Reduce the width of the text box controls to approximately half of their original size.

e. Delete the Sessions subform.

f. View the form and data in Form view. Sort the records by LastName in ascending order.

g. Save the form as **Edit Speakers**. Close the form.

h. Open the Room Information form in Layout view. The form does not have a Form Layout. Select all controls and apply the **Stacked Layout**.

i. Save and close the form.

Create a Report

You need to create a report based on the Speaker and Room Schedule query. You decide to use the Report Wizard to accomplish this task. You will also need to email the schedule to the presenters, so you will save the report as a PDF.

a. Select the **Speaker and Room Schedule query** as the record source for the report.

b. Activate the **Report Wizard** and use the following options as you go through the Wizard:

- Select all of the available fields for the report.
- View the data by Speakers.
- Accept LastName and FirstName as grouping levels.
- Use **Date** as the primary sort field in ascending order.
- Accept the Stepped and Portrait options.
- Save the report as **Speaker Schedule**.
- Switch to Layout view and apply the **Organic theme** to only this report.

c. Preview the report. Switch to Layout view. Adjust the column widths if necessary.

d. Switch to Print Preview and save the report as a PDF named **a04c1Speaker_LastFirst**.

e. When the PDF displays, close the program that displays it and return to Access. Exit Print Preview. Close the report.

Add an Additional Field

You realize the session times were not included in the query. You add the field to the query and then start over with the Report Wizard.

a. Open the Speaker and Room Schedule query in Design view.

b. Add the **StartingTime field** in the Sessions table to the design grid, after the Date field. Run the query.

c. Save and close the query.

d. Click the **Speaker and Room Schedule query**. Start the Report Wizard again and use the following options:

- Select all of the available fields for the report.
- View the data by Speakers.
- Use the LastName, FirstName fields as the primary grouping level.
- Use Date as the primary sort field in ascending order.
- Use StartingTime as the secondary sort field in Ascending order.
- Select the **Stepped** and **Portrait options**.
- Name the report **Speaker Schedule Revised**.
- Switch to Layout view and apply the **Facet theme** (first row, second column) to only this report.

e. Adjust the column widths in Layout view so that all the data is visible.

f. Add a space to the column heading labels as needed. For example, the column LastName should read Last Name.

g. Save and close the report. Close the database.

h. Exit Access. Submit the database and PDF based on your instructor's directions.

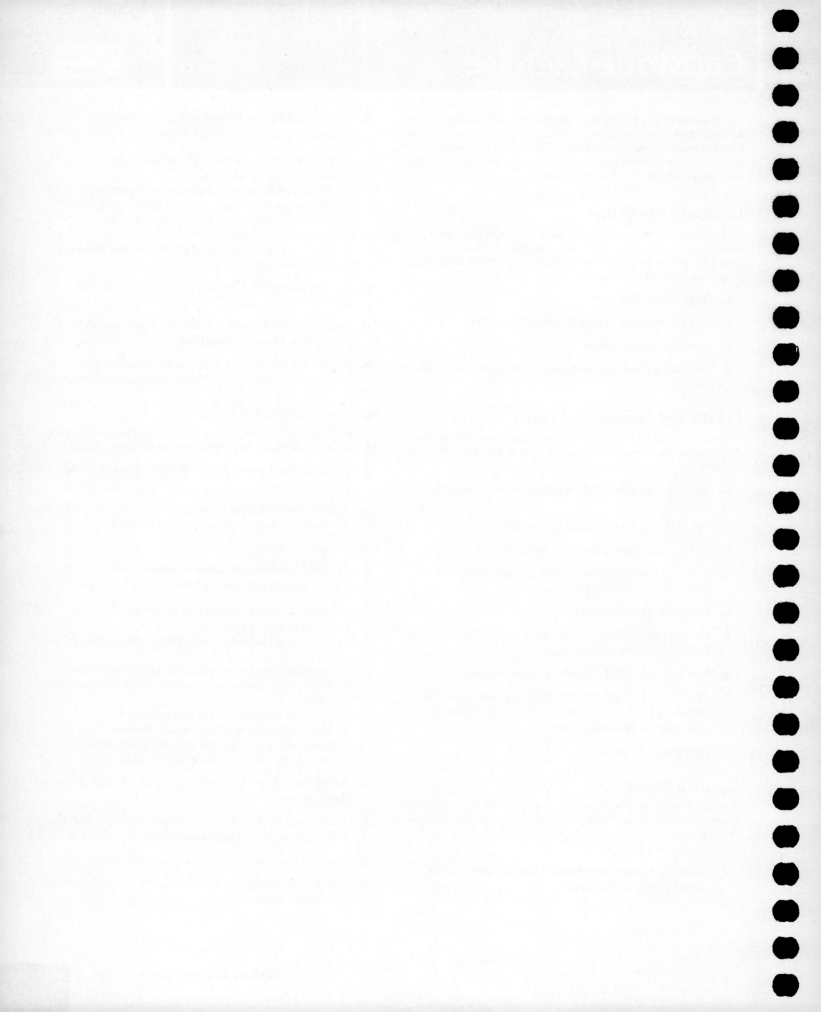

PowerPoint

Introduction to PowerPoint

CHAPTER 1

Creating a Basic Presentation

OBJECTIVES AFTER YOU READ THIS CHAPTER, YOU WILL BE ABLE TO:

CASE STUDY | Be a Trainer

You teach employee training courses for the Training and Development department of your State Department of Human Resources. You begin each course by delivering an electronic presentation. The slide show presents your objectives for the course, organizes your content, and aids your audience's retention. You prepare the presentation using Microsoft Office PowerPoint 2013.

Because of the exceptional quality of your presentations, the director of the State Department of Human Resources has asked you to prepare a new course on presentation skills. In the Hands-On Exercises for this chapter, you will work with two presentations for this course. One presentation will focus on the benefits of using PowerPoint, and the other will focus on the preparation for a slide show, including planning, organizing, and delivering.

Introduction to PowerPoint

You can use Microsoft PowerPoint 2013 to create an electronic slide show or other materials for use in a professional presentation. A ***slide*** is the most basic element of PowerPoint (similar to a page being the most basic element of Microsoft Word). Multiple slides may be arranged to create a presentation, called a ***slide show***, that can be used to deliver your message in a variety of ways: you can project the slide show on a screen as part of a presentation, run it automatically at a kiosk or from a DVD, display it on the World Wide Web, or create printed handouts. A ***PowerPoint presentation*** is an electronic slide show saved with a .pptx extension after the file name.

Figure 1.1 shows a PowerPoint presentation with slides containing content, such as text, online pictures, and images. The presentation has a consistent design and color scheme. It is easy to create presentations with consistent and attractive designs using PowerPoint.

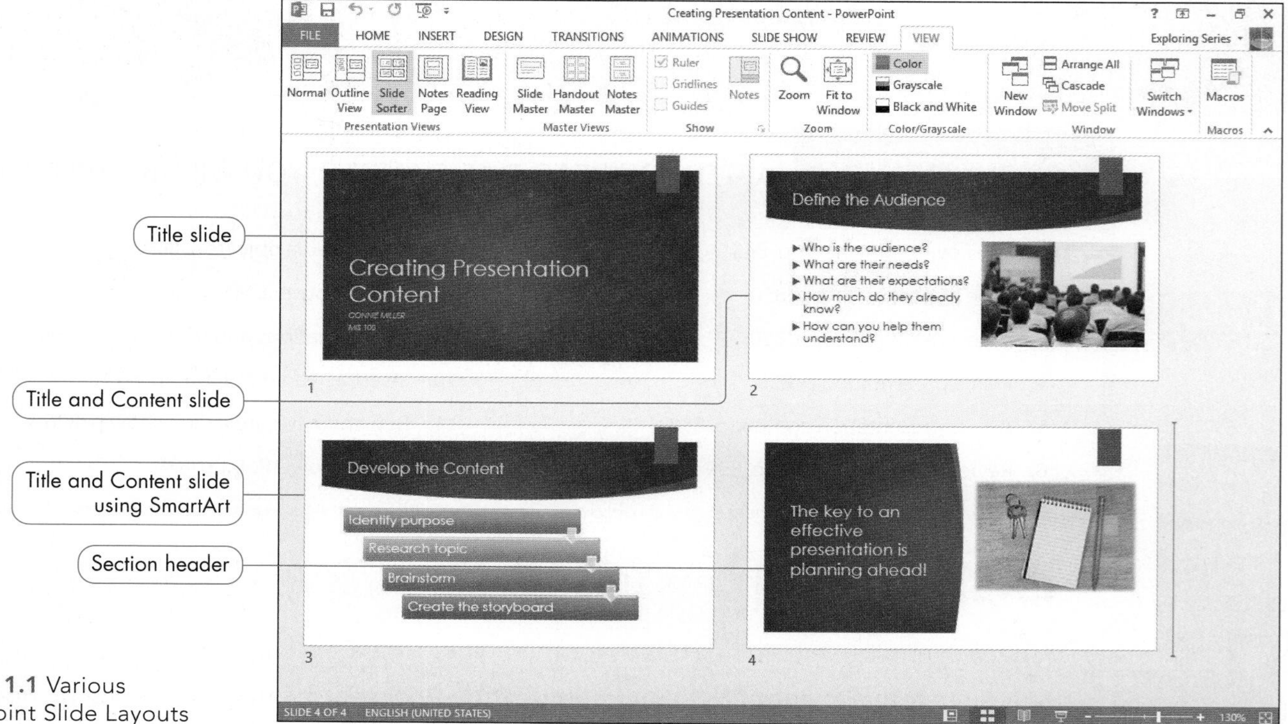

FIGURE 1.1 Various PowerPoint Slide Layouts

In this section, you will start your exploration of PowerPoint by viewing a previously completed presentation so that you can appreciate the benefits of using PowerPoint. You will modify the presentation and add identifying information, examine PowerPoint views to discover the advantages of each view, and save the presentation.

The speaker is the most important part of any presentation. Poor delivery will ruin even the best presentation. Speak slowly and clearly, maintain eye contact with your audience, and use the information on the slides to guide you. Do not just read the information on the screen, but expand on each sentence or image to give your audience the intended message.

Using PowerPoint Views

STEP 1» Figure 1.2 shows the default PowerPoint view, ***Normal view***, with two panes that provide maximum flexibility in working with the presentation. The pane on the left side of the screen shows ***thumbnails*** (slide miniatures), and the Slide pane on the right displays the current slide. This is where you make edits to slide content.

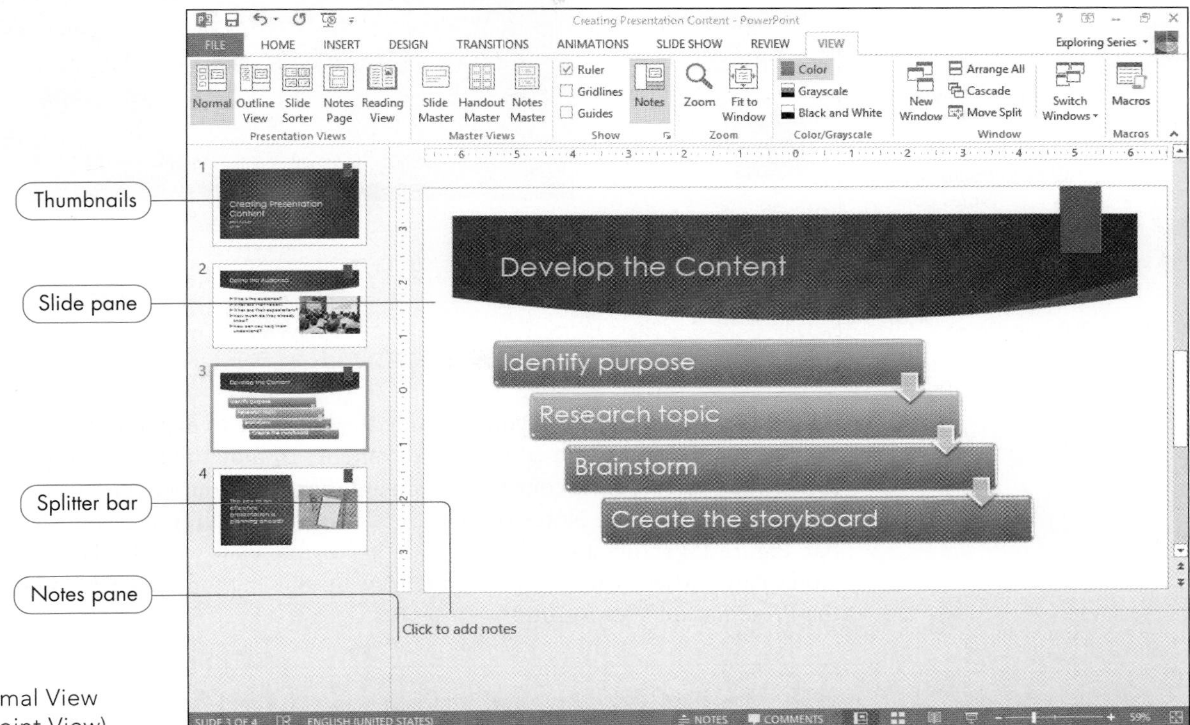

FIGURE 1.2 Normal View (Default PowerPoint View)

TIP Showing the Notes Pane

When you open PowerPoint, the Notes pane may be hidden from view. The Notes pane is where you enter notes pertaining to the slide or the presentation. You can change the size of these panes by dragging the splitter bar that separates one pane from another. To show the pane, click the View tab, and then click Normal in the Presentation Views group. Alternatively, you can click Notes on the status bar.

Figure 1.3 shows PowerPoint's ***status bar***, which contains the slide number and options that control the view of your presentation: Notes button, Comments button, View buttons, a Zoom slider, the Zoom level button, and the *Fit slide to current window* button. The status bar is located at the bottom of your screen and can be customized. To customize the status bar, right-click it, and then click the options you want displayed from the Customize Status Bar list.

FIGURE 1.3 PowerPoint Status Bar

While in Normal view, you can hide the left pane to expand the Slide pane so that you can see more detail while editing slide content. To hide the left Thumbnails pane, drag the splitter bar that separates one pane from another until you see the word *Thumbnails* appear. You can also hide the Notes pane at the bottom by clicking the Notes button in the Status bar. Figure 1.4 shows an individual slide in Normal view with the Thumbnails pane and the Notes pane closed. You can restore the view by clicking the View tab and clicking Normal in the Presentation Views group.

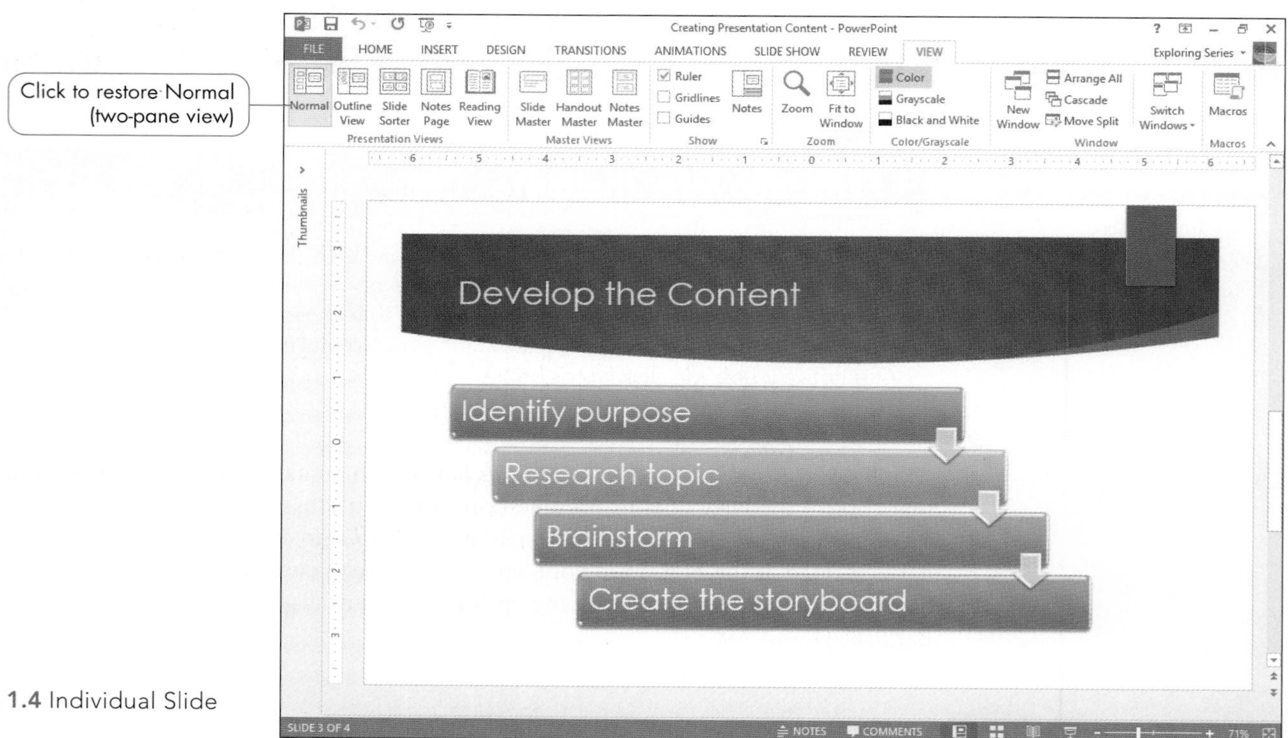

FIGURE 1.4 Individual Slide View

PowerPoint offers views in addition to Normal view, including Outline View, Slide Sorter view, Notes Page view, Reading View, and Slide Show view. Access Outline View, Slide Sorter, Notes Page, and Reading View from the Presentation Views group on the View tab. Access options for the Slide Show view from the Start Slide Show group on the Slide Show tab. For quick access, many of these views are available on the status bar.

Add-Ins Tab

You may see an Add-Ins tab on the Ribbon. This tab indicates that additional functionality, such as an updated Office feature or an Office-compatible program, has been added to your system. Add-Ins are designed to increase your productivity.

Outline View is used when you would like to enter text into your presentation using an outline. In other words, rather than having to enter the text into each placeholder on each slide separately, you can type the text directly into an outline. Figure 1.5 shows an example of the Outline View.

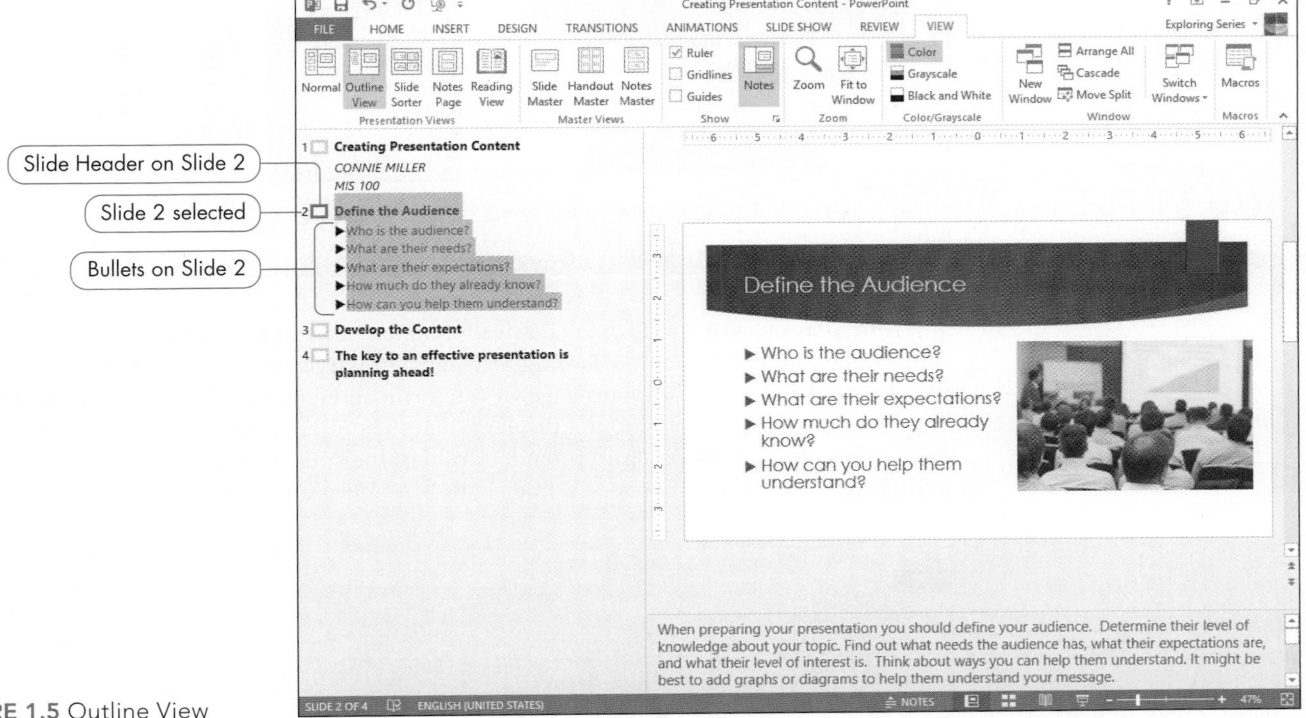

FIGURE 1.5 Outline View

Slide Sorter view displays thumbnails of your presentation slides, which enables you to view multiple slides simultaneously (see Figure 1.6). This view is helpful when you wish to change the order of the slides or to delete one or more slides. You can set transition effects (the way the slides transition from one to another) for multiple slides in Slide Sorter view. If you are in Slide Sorter view and double-click a slide thumbnail, PowerPoint returns the selected slide to Normal view. To rearrange slides in Slide Sorter view:

1. Move the mouse pointer over the slide thumbnail of the slide you wish to move.
2. Drag the slide to the new location.

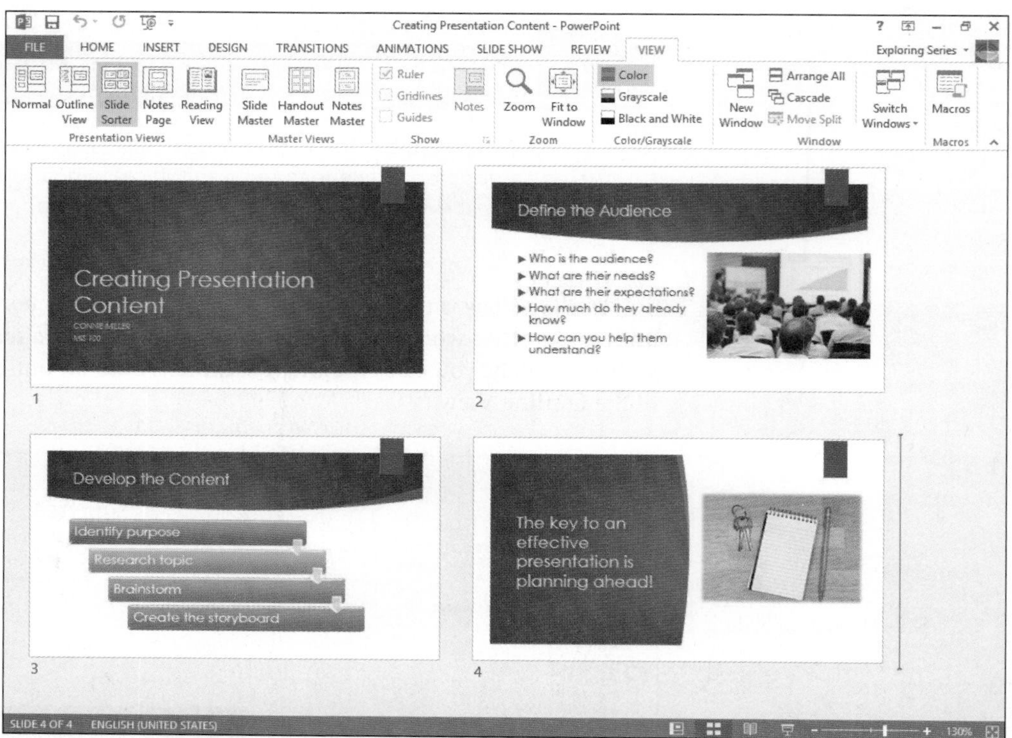

FIGURE 1.6 Slide Sorter View

Notes Page view is used when you need to enter and edit large amounts of text to which the speaker can refer when presenting. If you have a large amount of technical detail in the speaker notes, you can use Notes Page view to print audience handouts that include the slide and associated notes. Notes do not display when the presentation is shown (except when the Presenter view is used), but are intended to help the speaker remember the key points or additional information about each slide. Figure 1.7 shows an example of the Notes Page view.

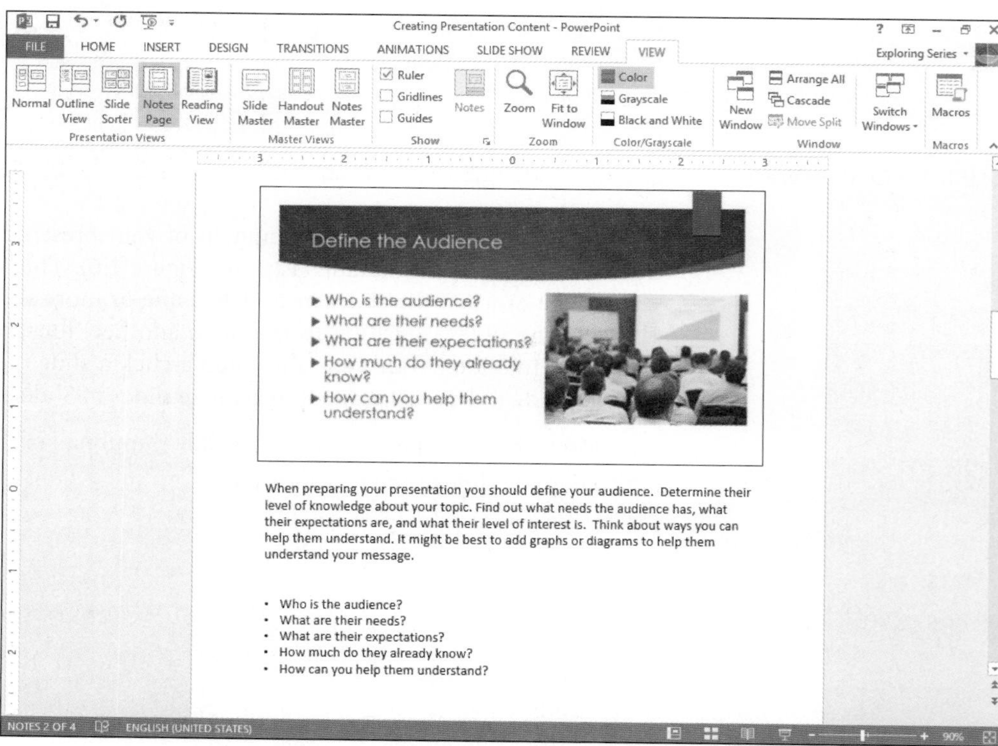

FIGURE 1.7 Notes Page View

Reading View is used to view the slide show full screen, one slide at a time. Animations and transitions are active in the Reading View. A title bar including the Minimize, Maximize/Restore (which changes its name and appearance depending on whether the window is maximized or at a smaller size), and Close buttons is visible, as well as a modified status bar (see Figure 1.8). In addition to View buttons, the status bar includes navigation buttons for moving to the next or previous slide, as well as a menu for accomplishing common tasks such as printing. Press Esc to quickly return to the previous view.

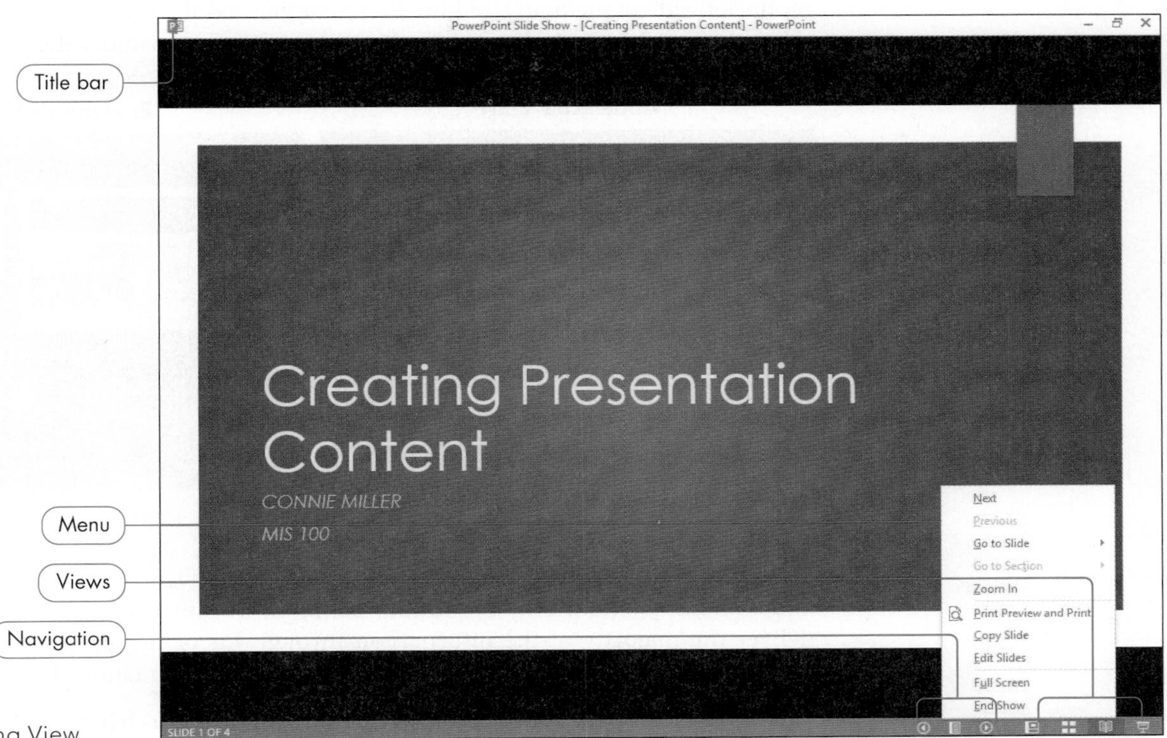

FIGURE 1.8 Reading View

Slide Show view is used to deliver the completed presentation full screen to an audience, one slide at a time, as an electronic presentation (see Figure 1.9). The slide show can be presented manually, where the speaker clicks the mouse to move from one slide to the next, or automatically, where each slide stays on the screen for a predetermined amount of time, after which the next slide appears. A slide show can contain a combination of both methods for advancing to the next slide. You can insert transition effects to impact the look of how one slide moves to the next. To end the slide show, press Esc.

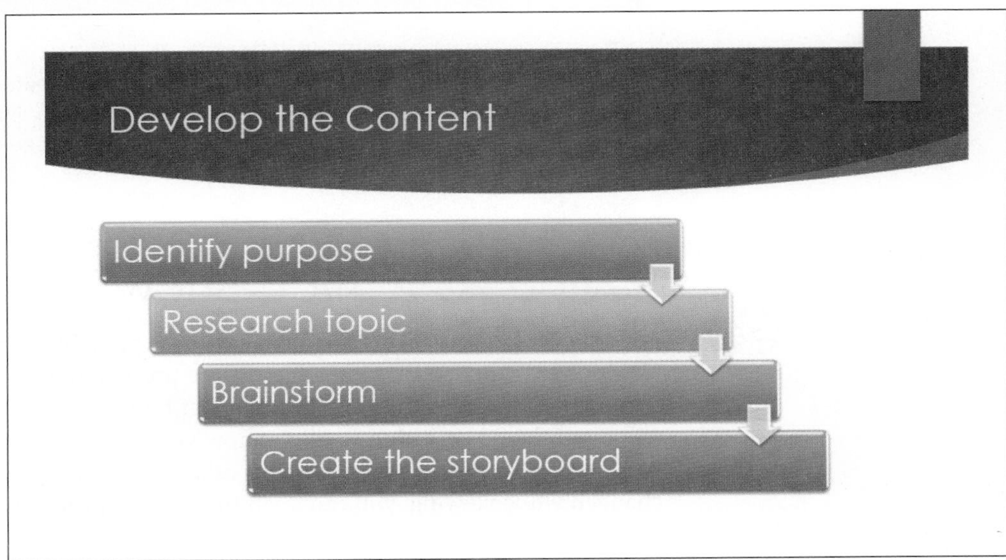

FIGURE 1.9 Slide Show View

Presenter view is a specialty view that delivers a presentation on two monitors simultaneously. Typically, one monitor is a projector that delivers the full-screen presentation to the audience; the other monitor is a laptop or computer so that the presenter can see the slide, speaker notes, and a thumbnail image of the next slide. This enables the presenter to move between slides as needed, navigate to the previous or next slide using arrows, or write on the slide with a marker. A timer displays the time elapsed since the presentation began so that the presenter can keep track of the presentation length. Figure 1.10 shows the audience view on the left side of the figure and the Presenter view on the right side. To use Presenter view, select the Use Presenter View option in the Monitors group under the Slide Show tab.

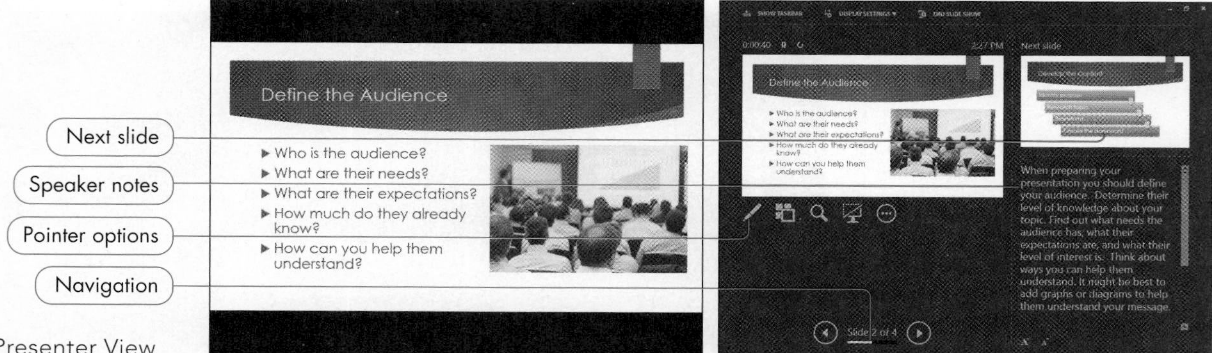

FIGURE 1.10 Presenter View

Typing a Speaker Note

Slides should contain only a minimum amount of information, and the speaker should deliver the majority of the information through his or her presentation. Consequently, speaker notes can be a most useful tool when giving a presentation. To create a speaker note:

STEP 2》

1. If the Notes pane is not visible, click Notes on the status bar.
2. Drag the splitter bar between the Slide pane and the Notes pane up to expand the Notes pane.
3. Click in the Notes pane to begin typing. To modify the text, click the HOME tab and apply formatting using the tools in the Font and Paragraph groups.

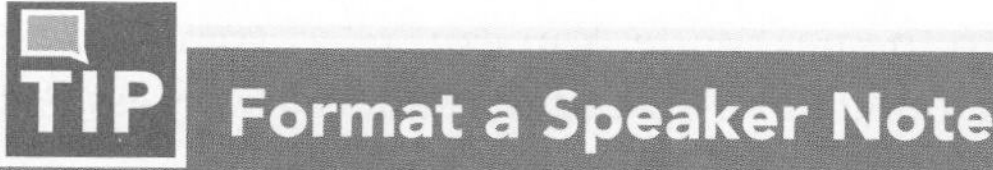

TIP Format a Speaker Note

The speaker's notes can be formatted much like a Word document. You can create bulleted lists and italicize or bold key words you want to feature, among other things to help you stay organized and on track with your presentation. Not all text modifications will be visible in the Normal view or in the Presenter view. To see modifications such as font and font size, switch to the Notes Page view.

Saving As a Slide Show

STEP 3》

PowerPoint presentations are saved with a .pptx file extension and opened in Normal view so that you can make changes to the presentation. You can save your presentation as a ***PowerPoint show*** with a .ppsx extension by using the Save As command. This file type will open the presentation in Slide Show view and is best for distributing an unchangeable version of a completed slide show to others for viewing. Whereas the .ppsx file cannot be changed while viewing, you can open the file in PowerPoint and edit it.

1. Describe the main advantage for using each of the following views: Normal view, Notes Page view, Slide Sorter view, and Slide Show view. ***pp. 845–849***
2. Explain the difference between a PowerPoint presentation (.pptx) and a PowerPoint show (.ppsx). ***pp. 844–850***
3. Discuss the purpose of a speaker note. ***p. 850***

Hands-On Exercises

Watch the Video
for this Hands-
On Exercise!

MyITLab®
HOE1 Training

1 Introduction to PowerPoint

You have been asked to create a presentation on the benefits of PowerPoint for the Training and Development department. You decide to view an existing presentation to determine if it contains material you can adapt for your presentation. You view the presentation, add a speaker note, and then save the presentation as a PowerPoint show.

Skills covered: Open, View, and Save a Presentation • Type a Speaker Note • Save as a PowerPoint Show

STEP 1 » OPEN, VIEW, AND SAVE THE PRESENTATION

In this step, you open and save the slide show created by your colleague. You will also review your presentation. You experiment with various methods of advancing to the next slide and then return to Normal view. As you use the various methods of advancing to the next slide, you find the one that is most comfortable to you and then use that method as you view slide shows in the future. An audio clip of audience applause will play when you view Slide 4: The Essence of PowerPoint. You will want to wear a headset if you are in a classroom lab so that you do not disturb classmates.

a. Start PowerPoint and open the *p01h1Intro* file.

b. Save the file as **p01h1Intro_LastFirst**.

> **TROUBLESHOOTING:** If you make any major mistakes in this exercise, close the file, open *p01h1Intro* again, and then start this exercise over. When you save files, use your last and first names. For example, as the PowerPoint author, I would name my presentation *p01h1Intro_RutledgeAmy.*

c. Click **Slide Show** on the status bar.

The presentation begins with the title slide, the first slide in all slide shows. The title has an animation assigned, so it comes in automatically.

d. Press **Spacebar** to advance to the second slide and read the slide.

The title on the second slide automatically wipes down, and the arrow wipes to the right.

e. Position the pointer in the bottom-left corner side of the slide, and click the **right arrow** in the Navigation bar to advance to the next slide. Read the slide content.

The text on the third slide, and all following slides, has the same animation applied to create consistency in the presentation.

f. Click the **left mouse button** to advance to the fourth slide, which has a sound icon displayed on the slide.

The sound icon on the slide indicates sound has been added. The sound has been set to come in automatically so you do not need to click anything for the sound to play.

> **TROUBLESHOOTING:** If you do not hear the sound, your computer may not have a sound card or your sound may be muted.

g. Continue to navigate through the slides until you come to the end of the presentation (a black screen).

h. Press **Esc** to return to Normal view.

STEP 2 » TYPE A SPEAKER NOTE

In this step, you add a speaker note to a slide to help you remember to mention some of the many objects that can be added to a slide. You also view the note in Notes view to see how it will print. Refer to Figure 1.11 as you complete Step 2.

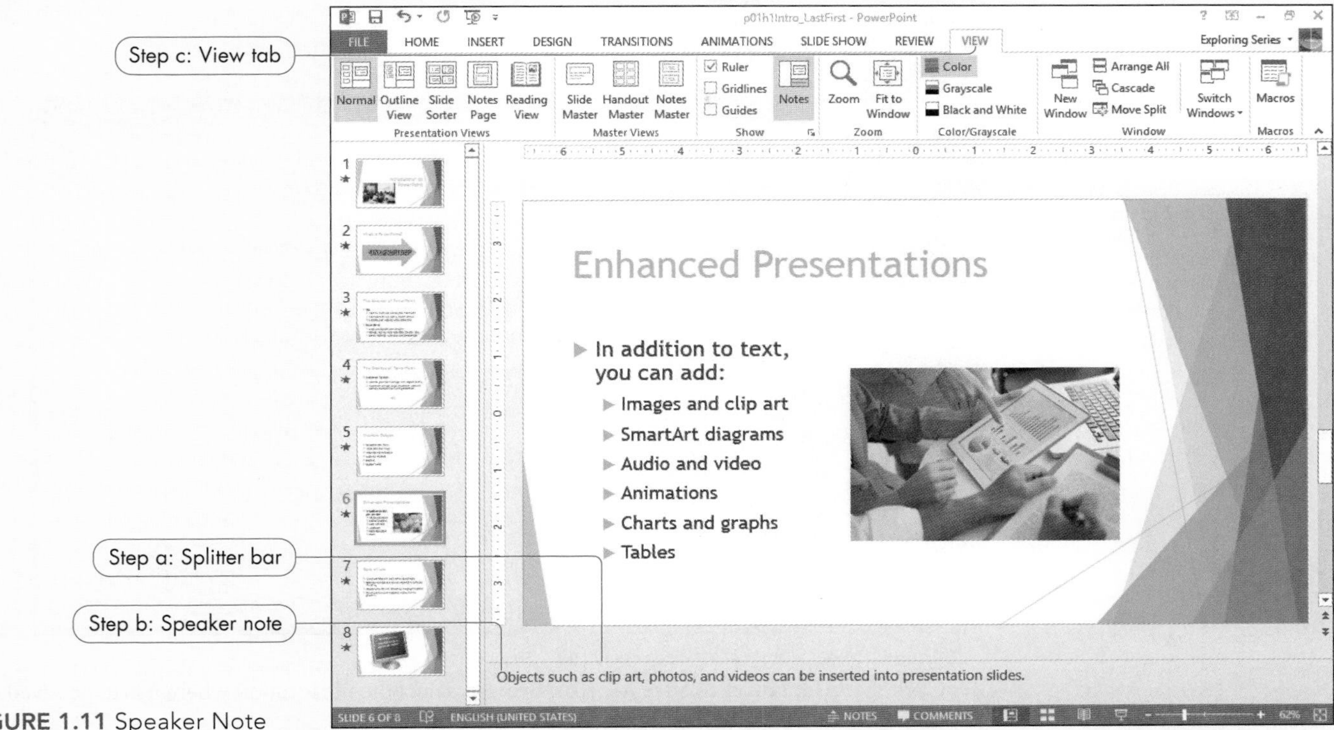

FIGURE 1.11 Speaker Note

a. Click the **Slide 6 thumbnail** and drag the splitter bar between the Slide pane and the Notes pane up to expand the Notes pane, if necessary.

Slide 6 is selected, and the slide displays in the Slide pane.

TROUBLESHOOTING: If the Notes pane is not visible, click Notes on the Status bar.

b. Type **Objects such as clip art, photos, and videos can be inserted into presentation slides.** in the **Notes pane**.

c. Click the **VIEW tab** and click **Notes Page** view in the Presentation Views group.

The slide is shown at a reduced size and the speaker note is shown below the slide.

d. Click **Normal** in the Presentation Views group.

This returns the presentation to the Normal view.

e. Save the presentation.

STEP 3 » SAVE AS A POWERPOINT SHOW

You want to save the slide show as a PowerPoint show so that it opens automatically in Slide Show view rather than Normal view. Refer to Figure 1.12 as you complete Step 3.

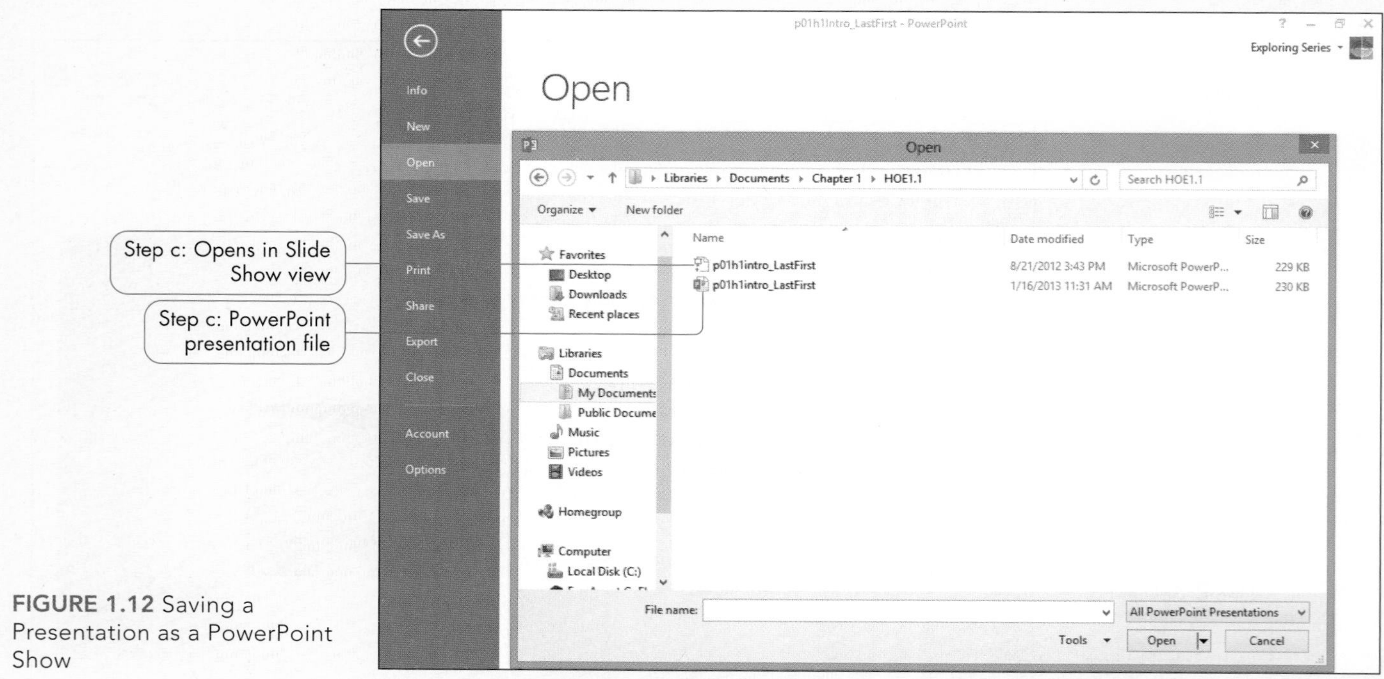

FIGURE 1.12 Saving a Presentation as a PowerPoint Show

a. Click the **FILE tab**, click **Save As**, click **Browse**, select the file location where it is to be saved, click **Save as type**, and then select **PowerPoint Show**.

b. Leave the file name *p01h1Intro_LastFirst* for the PowerPoint show.

   Although you are saving this file with the same file name as the presentation, it will not overwrite the file, as it is a different file type.

c. Click **Save**.

   You have created a new file, a PowerPoint Show, in your folder. A gray icon is used to indicate the PowerPoint Show file that opens in Slide Show view. The orange icon listed is used to indicate the PowerPoint Presentation file. See Figure 1.12 to view these icons.

d. Close the *p01h1Intro_LastFirst* presentation and submit based on your instructor's directions. Exit PowerPoint.

Presentation Creation

You are ready to create your own presentation by choosing a theme, adding content, and applying formatting. You should create the presentation by adding the content first and then applying formatting so that you can concentrate on your message and its structure without getting distracted by the formatting of the presentation.

Planning a Presentation

Creating an effective presentation requires advance planning. First, determine the goal of your presentation. An informative presentation could notify the audience about a change in policy or procedure. An educational presentation could teach an audience about a subject or a skill. Sales presentations are often persuasive calls to action to encourage the purchase of a product, but they can also be used to sell an idea or process. A goodwill presentation could be used to recognize an employee or acknowledge an organization. You could even create a certificate of appreciation using PowerPoint.

Next, research your audience—determine their level of knowledge about your topic. Find out what needs the audience has, what their expectations are, and what their level of interest is.

After determining your purpose and researching your audience, brainstorm how to deliver your message. Before using your computer, you may wish to sketch out your thoughts on paper to help you organize them. After organizing your thoughts, add them as content to the slide show, and then format the presentation.

In this section, you will create a visual plan called a *storyboard*. You will also learn to polish your presentation by using layouts, applying design themes, and reviewing your presentation for errors.

Prepare a Storyboard

A ***storyboard*** is a visual plan for your presentation that helps you plan the direction of your presentation. It can be a very rough draft that you sketch out while brainstorming, or it can be an elaborate plan that includes the text and objects drawn as they would appear on a slide.

A simple PowerPoint storyboard is divided into sections representing individual slides. The first block in the storyboard is used for the title slide. Subsequent blocks are used to introduce the topics, develop the topics, and then summarize the information. Figure 1.13 shows a working copy of a storyboard for planning presentation content. The storyboard is in rough-draft form and shows changes made during the review process. A blank copy of the document in Figure 1.13 has been placed on the student CD should you wish to use this for presentation planning. The PowerPoint presentation shown in Figure 1.14 incorporates the changes.

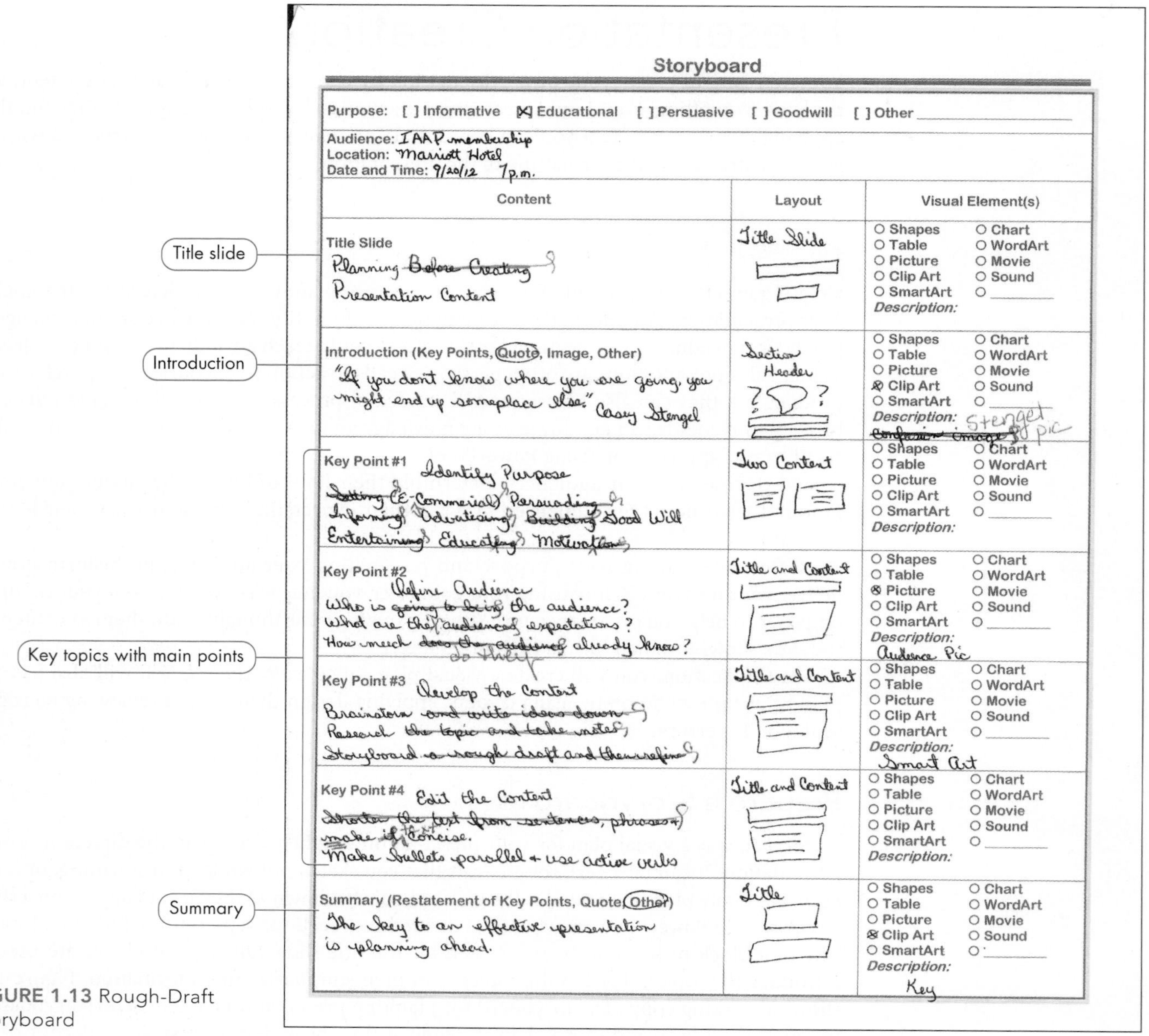

Title slide

Introduction

Key topics with main points

Summary

Storyboard

Purpose: [ ] Informative [X] Educational [ ] Persuasive [ ] Goodwill [ ] Other ____________

Audience: IAAP membership
Location: Marriott Hotel
Date and Time: 9/20/12 7p.m.

Content	Layout	Visual Element(s)
Title Slide Planning ~~Before Creating~~, Presentation Content	Title Slide	O Shapes O Chart O Table O WordArt O Picture O Movie O Clip Art O Sound O SmartArt O ______ *Description:*
Introduction (Key Points, Quote, Image, Other) "If you don't know where you are going, you might end up someplace else." Casey Stengel	Section Header	O Shapes O Chart O Table O WordArt O Picture O Movie ☒ Clip Art O Sound O SmartArt O ______ *Description:* ~~Confusion image~~ Stengel pic
Key Point #1 Identify Purpose ~~Setting~~ (E-Commercial) Persuading, Informing, Advertising, ~~Building~~ Good Will Entertaining, Educating, Motivating	Two Content	O Shapes O Chart O Table O WordArt O Picture O Movie O Clip Art O Sound O SmartArt O ______ *Description:*
Key Point #2 Define Audience Who is ~~going to be~~ the audience? What are ~~the~~ their ~~audience's~~ expectations? How much ~~does the audience~~ do they already know?	Title and Content	O Shapes O Chart O Table O WordArt ☒ Picture O Movie O Clip Art O Sound O SmartArt O ______ *Description:* Audience Pic
Key Point #3 Develop the Content Brainstorm ~~and write ideas down~~, Research ~~the topic and take notes~~, Storyboard ~~a rough draft and then refine~~,	Title and Content	O Shapes O Chart O Table O WordArt O Picture O Movie O Clip Art O Sound O SmartArt O ______ *Description:* Smart Art
Key Point #4 Edit the Content ~~Shorten the text from sentences, phrases,~~ ~~make it~~ text concise. Make bullets parallel + use active verbs	Title and Content	O Shapes O Chart O Table O WordArt O Picture O Movie O Clip Art O Sound O SmartArt O ______ *Description:*
Summary (Restatement of Key Points, Quote, Other) The key to an effective presentation is planning ahead.	Title	O Shapes O Chart O Table O WordArt O Picture O Movie ☒ Clip Art O Sound O SmartArt O ______ *Description:* Key

FIGURE 1.13 Rough-Draft Storyboard

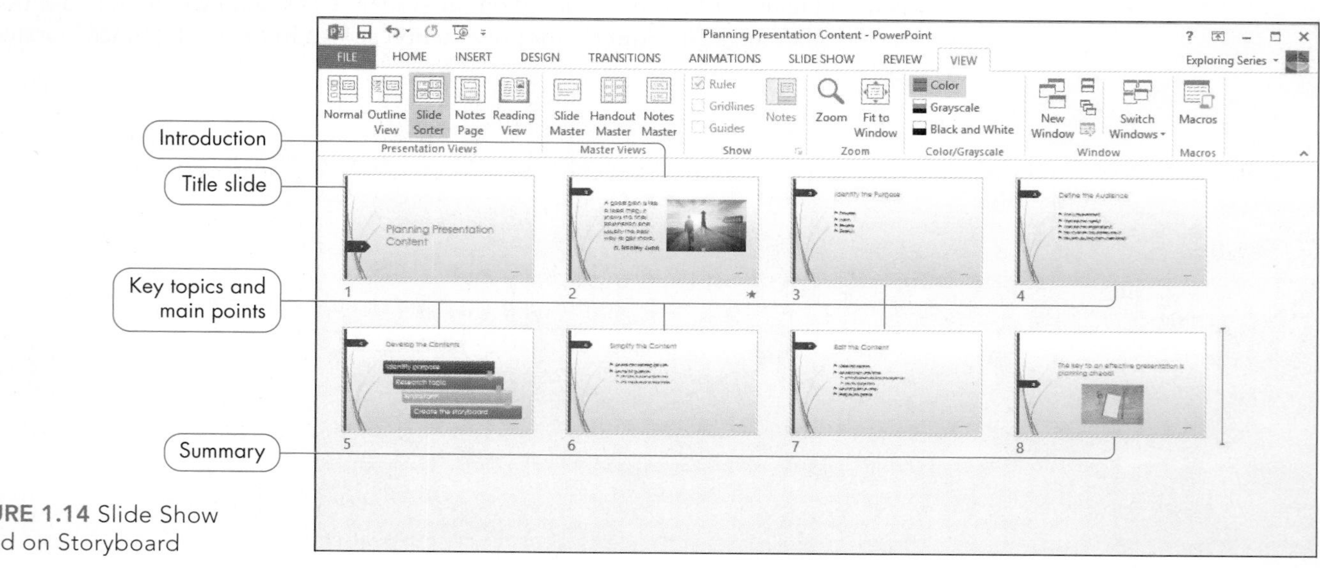

FIGURE 1.14 Slide Show Based on Storyboard

STEP 1» Begin with a Theme or Template

When you first open PowerPoint 2013, you are presented with the opportunity to choose from several themes. A ***theme*** is a file that includes the formatting elements like a background, a color scheme, and slide layouts that position content placeholders. Some presentations, or ***templates***, include suggestions for how to modify the slide show, whereas others include ideas about what you could say to inform your audience about your topic. PowerPoint 2013 has added widescreen themes in addition to the standard sizes to accommodate widescreen monitors and wide-format projectors. If you don't want to use one of the pre-created, widescreen themes, you can choose to open a different presentation.

Once you have chosen a theme, you will see the variants for the theme. A ***variant*** is a variation of the theme design you have chosen. Each variant uses different color palettes and font families. Figure 1.15 shows the Ion theme with four variant options for this theme. Click Create to choose your theme and begin your presentation. Even though you choose your theme first, your decision is not final as you can always change a theme later. (To change a theme or variant, click the Design tab. Additional themes and variants will display.)

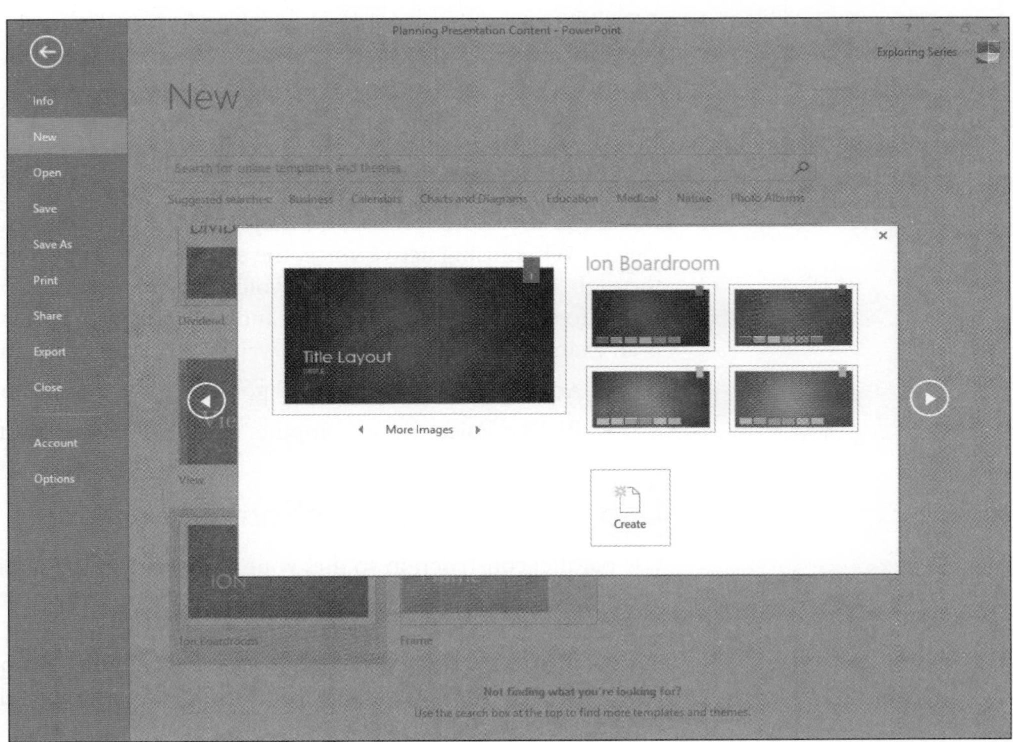

FIGURE 1.15 Ion Theme with Variant Options

Create a Title Slide and Introduction

The title slide should have a short title that indicates the purpose of the presentation. Try to capture the title in two to five words. The title slide should also contain information such as the speaker's name and title, the speaker's organization, the organization's logo, and the date of the presentation. This information is typically included in the subtitle placeholder.

After the title slide, you may want to include an introduction slide that will get the audience's attention. The introduction could be a list of topics covered in the presentation, a thought-provoking quotation or question, or an image that relates to the topic. Introduction slides can also be used to distinguish between topics or sections of the presentation.

Create the Main Body of Slides

The content of your presentation follows the title slide and the introduction. Each key thought should be a separate slide with the details needed to support that thought. Present the details as bullets or a short paragraph that relates to the content. When determining the content, ask yourself what you want your audience to learn and remember. Support the content with facts, examples, charts or graphs, illustrations, images, or video clips.

Create the Conclusion

End your presentation with a summary or conclusion that reviews the main points, restates the purpose of the presentation, or invokes a call to action. You may also want to repeat your contact information at the end of the presentation so the audience knows how to follow up with any questions or needs.

Assessing Presentation Content

After you create the storyboard, review what you wrote. Edit your text to shorten complete sentences to phrases that you can use as bulleted points by eliminating excess adverbs and adjectives and using only a few prepositions.

Use Active Voice

Review and edit the phrases so they begin with active voice when possible to involve the viewer. When using active voice, the subject of the phrase performs the action expressed in the verb. In phrases using passive voice, the subject is acted upon. Passive voice needs more words to communicate your ideas and can make your presentation seem flat. The following is an example of the same thought written in active voice and passive voice:

- Active Voice: Students need good computer skills for problem solving.
- Passive Voice: Good computer skills are needed by students for problem solving.

Use Parallel Construction

Use parallel construction so that your bullets are in the same grammatical form to help your audience see the connection between your phrases. If you start your first bullet with a noun, start each successive bullet with a noun; if you start your first bullet with a verb, continue with verbs. Parallel construction also gives each bullet an equal level of importance and promotes balance in your message. In the following example, the fourth bullet is not parallel to the first three bullets because it does not begin with a verb. The fifth bullet shows the bullet in parallel construction.

- Find a good place to study.
- Organize your study time.
- Study for tests with a partner.
- Terminology is important so learn how to use it properly. (Incorrect)
- Learn and use terminology properly. (Correct)

Follow the 7 × 7 Guideline

Remember, the slides will be read by your audience, not you. Therefore, you should not put entire paragraphs on your slides. Keep the information on your slides concise. You will expand on the slide content when delivering your presentation with the use of notes. Follow the 7 × 7 guideline, which suggests that you use no more than seven words per line and seven lines per slide. Although you may be forced to exceed this guideline on occasion, follow it as often as possible.

After you complete the planning and review process, you are ready to prepare the PowerPoint slide show to use with your presentation.

Use Slide Layouts

STEP 2 » PowerPoint provides a set of predefined slide ***layouts*** that determine the position of the objects or content on a slide. Slide layouts contain several combinations of placeholders. When you click the New Slide arrow on the Home tab, a gallery from which you can choose a layout displays. All of the layouts except the Blank layout include placeholders. ***Placeholders*** are objects that hold specific content, such as titles, subtitles, or images. Placeholders determine the position of the objects on the slide.

After you select a layout, click a placeholder to add your content. When you click a placeholder you can edit it. The border of the placeholder becomes a dashed line and you are able to enter content. If you click the dashed line placeholder border, the placeholder and its content are selected. The border changes to a solid line. Once selected, you can drag the placeholder to a new position or delete the placeholder. Any change you make impacts all content in the placeholder. Unused placeholders in a layout do not show when you display a slide show.

A new, blank presentation includes a title slide layout with a placeholder for the presentation title and subtitle. Add new slides using the layout from the layout gallery. By default, text on slides following the title slide appears as bullets.

Using Bullets

To increase or decrease indents for bulleted items, use Tab. To increase an indent, press Tab. To decrease an indent, hold down Shift+Tab.

You can change the layout of an existing slide by dragging placeholders to a new location or by adding new placeholders and objects. To format the text in the slide, use the controls in the Paragraph group found on the Home tab. You can make basic edits such as changing font, color, and size by using these controls.

New Slide Button

The New Slide button has two parts, the New Slide button and the New Slide arrow. Click the New Slide arrow when you want to choose a layout from the gallery. Click New Slide, which appears above the New Slide arrow, to quickly insert a new slide. If you click New Slide when the Title slide is selected, the new slide uses the Title and Content layout. If the current slide uses any layout other than Title slide, the new slide uses the same layout.

Reviewing the Presentation

After you create the presentation, check for spelling errors and incorrect word usage. Nothing is more embarrassing or can make you appear more unprofessional than a misspelled word enlarged on a big screen.

STEP 3 » Use a four-step method for checking spelling in PowerPoint. First, read the slide content after you enter it. Second, use the Spelling feature located in the Review tab to check the entire presentation. Third, ask a friend or colleague to review the presentation. Finally, display the presentation in Slide Show view or Reading View and read each word on each slide out loud. Although proofreading four times may seem excessive, it will help ensure your presentation is professional.

Proofing Options

The Spelling feature, by default, does not catch contextual errors like *to*, *too*, and *two*, but you can set the Proofing options to help you find and fix this type of error. To modify the proofing options, click File and click Options. Click Proofing in the PowerPoint Options window and click Check Grammar and Spelling. With this option selected, the spelling checker will flag contextual mistakes with a red wavy underline. To correct the error, right-click the flagged word and select the proper word choice.

Use the Thesaurus

As you create and edit your presentation, you may notice that you are using one word too often, especially at the beginning of bullets. Use the Thesaurus so your bulleted lists do not constantly begin with the same word and so you make varied word choices.

Reorder Slides

As you develop your presentation, you may realize that your need to reorder your slides. This can easily be done using the Slide Sorter view. To reorder slides:

STEP 5»

1. Click the VIEW tab.
2. Click Slide Sorter in the Presentation Views group.
3. Select the slide you wish to move and drag the slide to the new location.
4. Double-click any slide to return to the Normal view.

Quick Concepts

1. Identify the three advanced planning steps you should follow before adding content to a slide show. ***p. 855***
2. Define "storyboard" and describe how a storyboard aids you in creating a slide show. ***p. 855***
3. Describe two guidelines you should follow when assessing your slide content. ***p. 858***
4. Explain the difference between a slide layout and a presentation theme. ***pp. 857 and 859***

Hands-On Exercises

2 Presentation Creation

To help state employees learn the process for presentation creation, you decide to give them guidelines for determining content, structuring a slide show, and assessing content. You create a slide show to deliver these guidelines.

Skills covered: Create a New Presentation and Edit the Title Slide • Add New Slides • Use Spell Check and the Thesaurus • Modify Text and Layout • Reorder Slides

STEP 1 » CREATE A NEW PRESENTATION AND EDIT THE TITLE SLIDE

You are creating a Training and Development presentation for your employees. As you progress through the steps, you will add and edit several slides. You begin by choosing the Ion theme with a specific variation color.

a. Start PowerPoint.

b. Choose the **Retrospect theme** with the **orange variant**. Click **Create**.

c. Save the presentation as **p01h2Content_LastFirst**.

d. On the title slide, click in the **title placeholder** and type **Creating Presentation Content**.

e. Type your name in the **subtitle placeholder**.

f. Click **Notes** on the status bar. Add the text **Training and Development** to the **Notes pane**.

g. Save the presentation.

STEP 2 » ADD NEW SLIDES

You continue creating your presentation by adding a second slide with the Title and Content layout. After adding a title to the slide, you create a bulleted list to develop your topic. After adding the presentation content, you proofread the presentation to ensure no errors exist. Refer to Figure 1.16 as you complete Step 2.

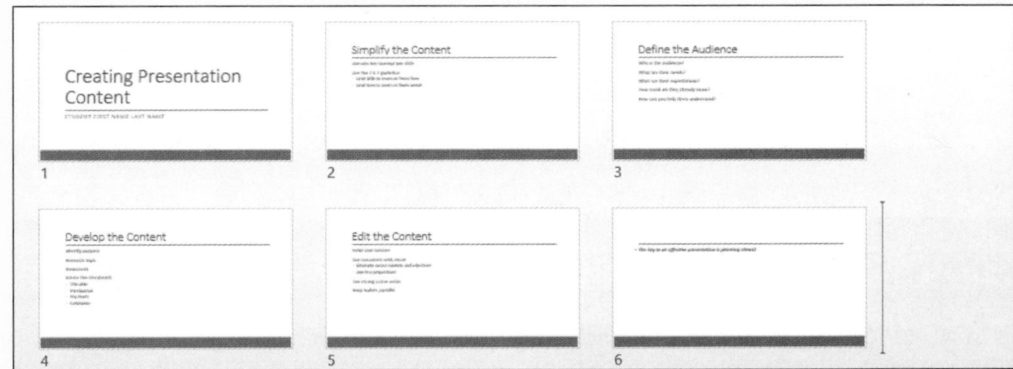

FIGURE 1.16 New Slides with Text Content

a. Click **New Slide** in the Slides group on the HOME tab.

The new Slide 2 contains two placeholders: one for the title and one for body content. You can insert an object, such as a table or image, by clicking a button in the center of the content placeholder. To enter text in a list, type the text in the content placeholder.

b. Type **Simplify the Content** in the **title placeholder**.

c. Click in the **content placeholder** below the title placeholder, type **Use one main concept per slide**, and then press **Enter**.

   By default, the list level is the same as the previous level. Notice that the Retrospect theme does not automatically place bullets into the body of the presentation.

d. Type **Use the 7 × 7 guideline** and press **Enter**.

e. Click **Increase List Level** in the Paragraph group.

   The list level indents, the font size is reduced, and a bullet appears indicating this is a subset of the main level.

f. Type **Limit slide to seven or fewer lines** and press **Enter**.

g. Type **Limit lines to seven or fewer words**. (Do not include the period.)

   By default, the list level is the same as the previous level.

h. Click **New Slide** in the Slides group four times to create four more slides with the Title and Content layout.

i. Type the following text in the appropriate slide. Use **Increase List Level** and **Decrease List Level** in the Paragraph group to change levels.

Slide	**Slide Title**	**Content Data**
3	Define the Audience	Who is the audience?
		What are their needs?
		What are their expectations?
		How much do they already know?
		How can you help them understand?
4	Develop the Content	Identify purpose
		Research topic
		Brainstorm
		Create the storyboard
		Title slide
		Introduction
		Key points
		Conclusion
5	Edit the Content	Make text concise
		Use consistent verb tense
		Eliminate excess adverbs and adjectives
		Use few prepositions
		Use strong active verbs
		Keep bullets parallel
6		The key to an effective presentation is planning ahead!

j. Save the presentation.

STEP 3 » USE SPELL CHECK AND THE THESAURUS

It is important to proofread your presentation, making sure that you did not make any errors in spelling or grammar. Additionally, it is important not to use the same words too frequently. In this step, you check for spelling errors and substitute the word *key* for the word *main*.

a. Click **Spelling** in the Proofing group on the REVIEW tab and correct any errors. Carefully proofread each slide.

   The result of the spelling check depends on how accurately you entered the text of the presentation.

b. On Slide 2, use the Thesaurus to change *main* in the first bulleted point to **key** and click the **Close (X) button** on the Thesaurus.

c. Save the presentation.

STEP 4 » MODIFY TEXT AND LAYOUT

You want to end the slide show with a statement emphasizing the importance of planning and decide to modify the text and layout of the slide to give it more emphasis. You also leave space on the slide so that later you can add clip art. Refer to Figure 1.17 as you complete Step 4.

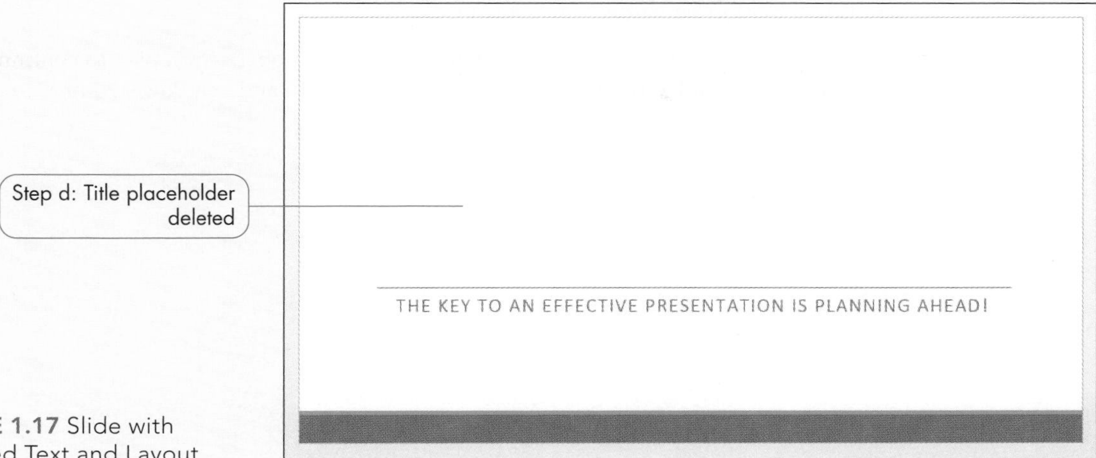

FIGURE 1.17 Slide with Modified Text and Layout

a. Click the **Slide 6 thumbnail** in the Slides pane.

b. Click the **HOME tab** and click **Layout** in the Slides group.

c. Click **Section Header** from the Layout gallery.

   The layout for Slide 6 changes to the Section Header layout. The Section Header layout can be used on any slide in a slide show if its format meets your needs.

d. Click the border of the title placeholder and press **Delete**.

   The dotted line border becomes a solid line, which indicates the placeholder is selected. Pressing Delete removes the placeholder and the content of that placeholder.

e. Click the **subtitle placeholder** and click **Center** in the Paragraph group on the HOME tab.

   The layout of Slide 6 has now been modified.

f. Save the presentation.

STEP 5 » REORDER SLIDES

You notice that the slides do not follow a logical order. You change the slide positions in Slide Sorter view. Refer to Figure 1.18 as you complete Step 5.

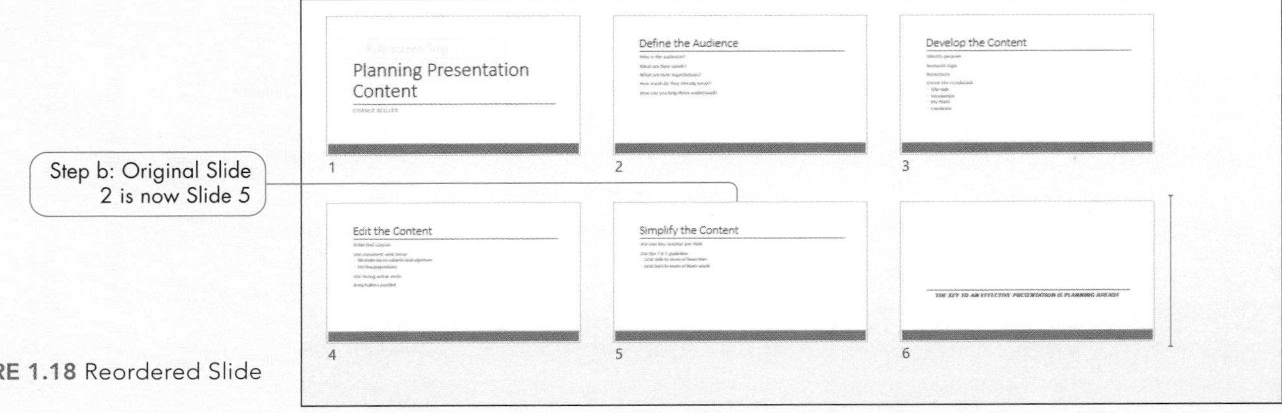

FIGURE 1.18 Reordered Slide Show

a. Click the **VIEW tab** and click **Slide Sorter** in the Presentation Views group.

b. Select **Slide 2** and drag it before the summary (last) slide so that it becomes Slide 5.

   After you drop the slide, all slides renumber.

c. Double-click **Slide 6**.

   Your presentation returns to Normal view.

d. Save the *p01h2Content_LastFirst* presentation and keep it open if you plan to continue with the next Hands-On Exercise. If not, close the presentation and exit PowerPoint.

Presentation Enhancement

You can strengthen your slide show by adding graphics and media objects that relate to the message and support the text. PowerPoint enables you to include a variety of visual objects to add impact to your presentation. You can add online pictures, WordArt (stylized letters), sound, animated clips, and video clips to increase your presentation's impact. You can add tables, charts and graphs, and SmartArt diagrams created in PowerPoint, or you can insert objects that were created in other applications, such as a chart from Microsoft Excel or a table from Microsoft Word. You can add animations and transitions to catch the audience's attention. You can also add identifying information on slides or audience handouts by adding headers and footers.

In this section, you will add a table to organize data in columns and rows. You will insert clip art objects that relate to your topics and will move and resize the clip art. You will apply transitions to control how one slide changes to another and add animations to text and clip art to add visual interest. You will finish by adding identifying information in a header and footer.

Inserting Media Objects

Adding media objects such as pictures, clip art, audio, and/or video is especially important in PowerPoint, as PowerPoint is a visual medium. In addition to using the Insert tab to insert media objects in any layout, the following layouts include specific buttons to quickly insert objects:

- Title and Content
- Two Content
- Comparison
- Content with Caption
- Picture with Caption

STEP 2» Clicking the Pictures icon in the content placeholder (or the Pictures button on the Insert tab) opens a dialog box you can use to browse for picture files on your hard drive or a removable storage device. Clicking Online Pictures opens the Insert Pictures dialog box that allows you to search Office.com Clip Art or elsewhere on the World Wide Web. Figure 1.19 displays the layout buttons.

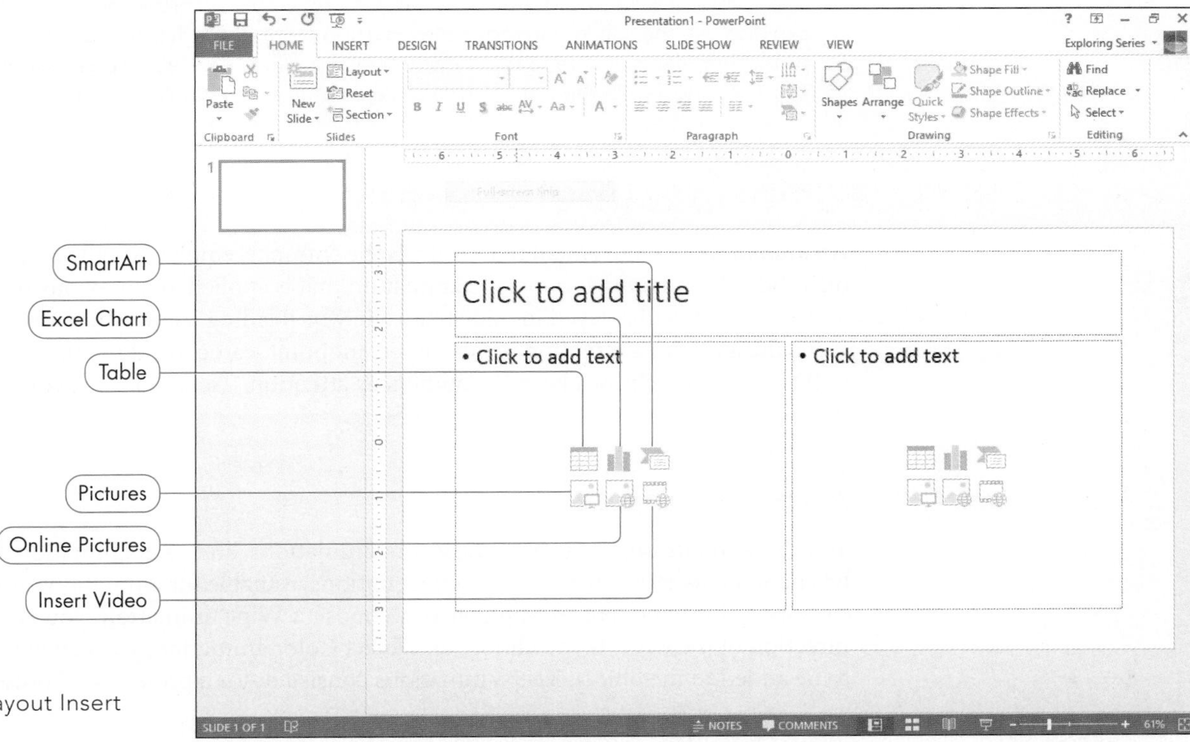

FIGURE 1.19 Layout Insert Buttons

Adding a Table

A ***table*** organizes information in columns and rows. Tables can be simple and include just a few words or images, or they can be more complex and include structured numerical data.

STEP 1»

To create a table on a new slide, you can select any layout, click the Insert tab, click Table in the Tables group, and then specify the number of rows and columns you would like to have. You can also click the Insert Table icon on any slide layout that includes it. Figure 1.20 shows a table added to a slide. Once a table is created, you can resize a column or a row by positioning the pointer over the border you wish to resize and then dragging the border to the desired position.

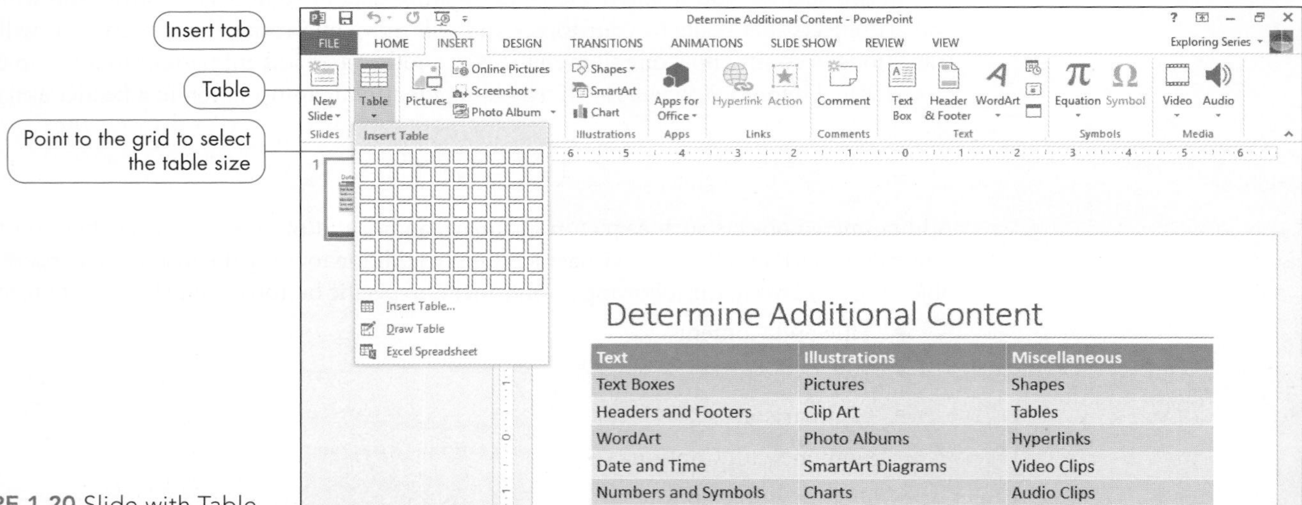

FIGURE 1.20 Slide with Table

TIP Movement within a Table

The insertion point will show you where the text you type will appear in the table. Use the arrow keys or click anywhere in the table to move the insertion point to a new cell. You can also use the Tab key to move the insertion point. Press Tab to move to the next cell or press Shift+Tab to move to the previous cell. Pressing Ctrl+Tab inserts an indent within the cell. Pressing Tab in the last cell of a table creates a new blank row at the end of the table.

Using Animations and Transitions

An ***animation*** is a movement that controls the entrance, emphasis, exit, and/or path of objects on a slide. A ***transition*** is a specific animation that is applied as a previous slide is replaced by a new slide while displayed in Slide Show view or Reading View. Animating objects can help focus the audience's attention on an important point, can control the flow of information on a slide, and can help you keep the audience's attention. Transitions provide visual interest as the slides change.

Animate Objects

You can animate objects using a variety of animations, and each animation can be modified by changing its effect options. The effect options available for animations are determined by the animation type. For example, if you choose a Wipe animation, you can determine the direction of the wipe. If you choose an Object Color animation, you can determine the color to be added to the object. Keep animations consistent for a professional presentation.

STEP 4» To apply an animation to text or other objects, do the following:

1. Select the object you want to animate.
2. Click the ANIMATIONS tab.
3. Click More in the Animation group to display the Animation gallery.
4. Click an animation type to apply.
5. Click Effect Options to display any available options related to the selected animation type.

The slide in Figure 1.21 shows an animation effect added to the picture. A tag with the number 1 is attached to the picture to show that it will run first. A quote on the slide (not pictured) has a number 2 to show that it will play after the first animation.

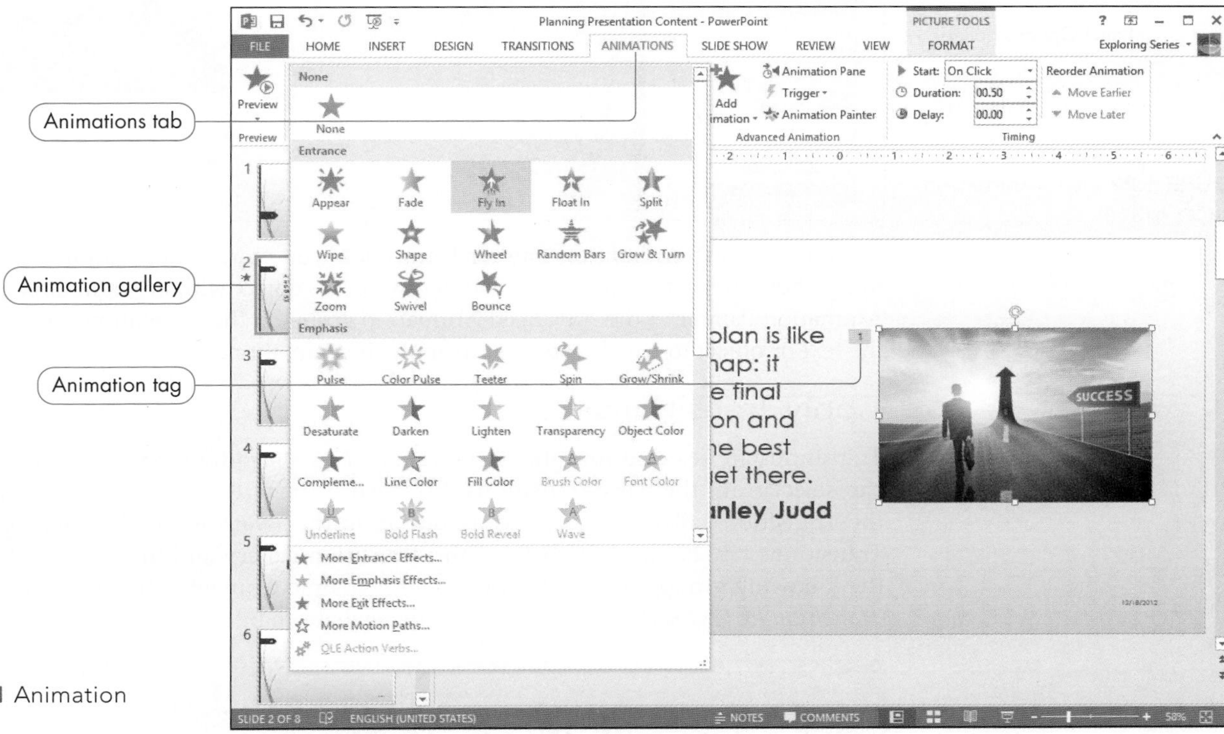

FIGURE 1.21 Animation Gallery

The slide in Figure 1.22 shows Fly In animation effects added to the quotation and name line. Tags with the numbers 2 and 3 are attached and are shaded pink to show that they are selected. The Effect Options gallery for the Fly In Effect is open so that a direction for the image to fly in from can be selected. Click Preview in the Preview group to see all animations on the slide play. You can also see the animations in Reading View and in Slide Show view. Slides that include an animation display a star icon beneath the slide when viewing the slides in Slide Sorter view.

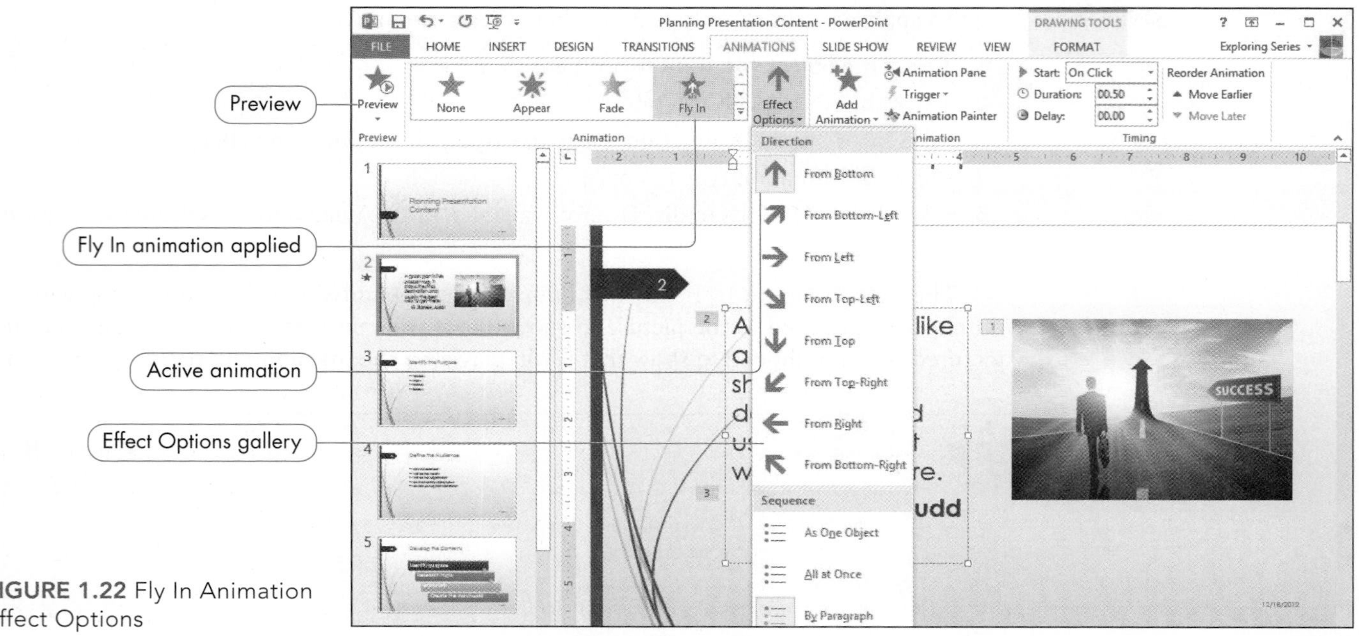

FIGURE 1.22 Fly In Animation Effect Options

PowerPoint's Animation Painter feature lets you copy an animation from one object to another. To use the Animation Painter, select an object with an animation applied, click Animation Painter in the Advanced Animation group on the Animations tab, and then click the text or object to which you want to apply the animation.

Apply Transitions

STEP 3

Transitions are selected from the *Transition to This Slide* group on the Transitions tab. You can select from the basic transitions displayed or from the Transition gallery. To display the Transition gallery, click the More button in the *Transition to This Slide* group on the Transitions tab. Figure 1.23 displays the Transition gallery and the available transitions in the following groups: Subtle, Exciting, and Dynamic Content. Click Effect Options in the *Transition to This Slide* group to see any effects that can be applied to the transition.

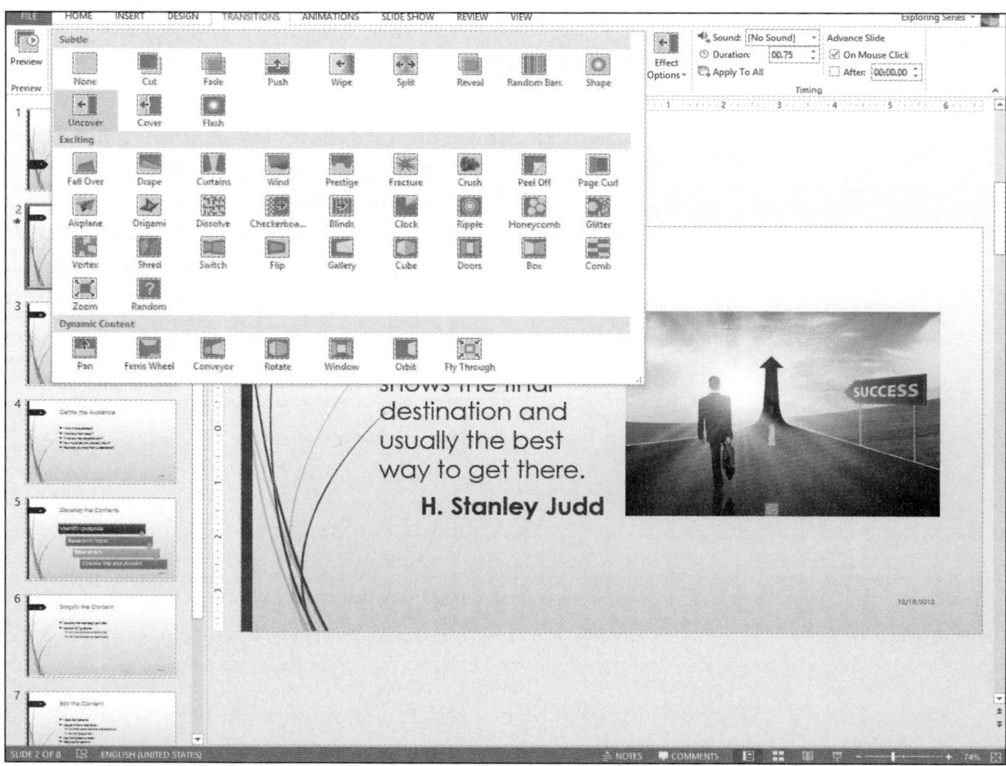

FIGURE 1.23 Transition Gallery

Slide Sorter View and Transitions

Transition effects and transition effect options also can be applied from the Slide Sorter view. Applying transitions in Slide Sorter view is helpful when you want to apply the same transition to multiple slides. Do so by selecting the slides prior to applying the effect.

After you choose a transition effect, you can select a sound to play when the transition takes effect. You can choose the duration of the transition in seconds, which controls how quickly the transition takes place. You can also control whether the transition applies to all the slides or just the current slide. The sound can be added by choosing an option in the Sound menu found in the Timing group on the Transitions tab.

Another determination you must make is how you want to start the transition process. Use the Advance Slide options in the Timing group to determine whether you want to manually click or press a key to advance to the next slide or if you want the slide to automatically advance after a specified number of seconds. You can set the number of seconds for the slide to display in the same area.

To delete a transition, click the Transitions tab and click None in the *Transition to This Slide* group. If you wish to remove all transitions, click the Transitions tab, click None in the *Transition to This Slide* group, and then click *Apply to All* in the Timing group.

Effectively Adding Transitions, Animations, and Sound

When you select your transitions, sounds, and animations, remember that too many transition and animation styles can be distracting. The audience will be wondering what is coming next rather than paying attention to your message. The speed of the transition is important, too—very slow transitions will lose the interest of your audience. Too many sound clips can be annoying. Consider whether you need to have the sound of applause with the transition of every slide. Is a typewriter sound necessary to keep your audience's attention, or will it grate on their nerves if it is used on every word? Ask someone to review your presentation and let you know of any annoying or jarring elements.

Inserting a Header or Footer

The date of the presentation, the presentation audience, a logo, a company name, and other identifying information are very valuable, and you may want such information to appear on every slide, handout, or notes page. Use the *Header and Footer* feature to do this. A ***header*** contains information that generally appears at the top of pages in a handout or on a notes page. A ***footer*** contains information that generally appears at the bottom of slides in a presentation or at the bottom of pages in a handout or on a notes page. Because the slide master (Slide Master View) of the theme controls the placement of the header/footer elements, you may find headers and footers in various locations on the slide.

STEP 5 To insert text in a header or footer, do the following:

1. Click the INSERT tab.
2. Click Header & Footer in the Text group.
3. Click the Slide tab or the *Notes and Handouts* tab.
4. Click desired options and enter desired text, if necessary.
5. Click *Apply to All* to add the information to all slides or pages, or if you are adding the header or footer to a single slide, click Apply.

Figure 1.24 shows the Slide tab of the *Header and Footer* dialog box.

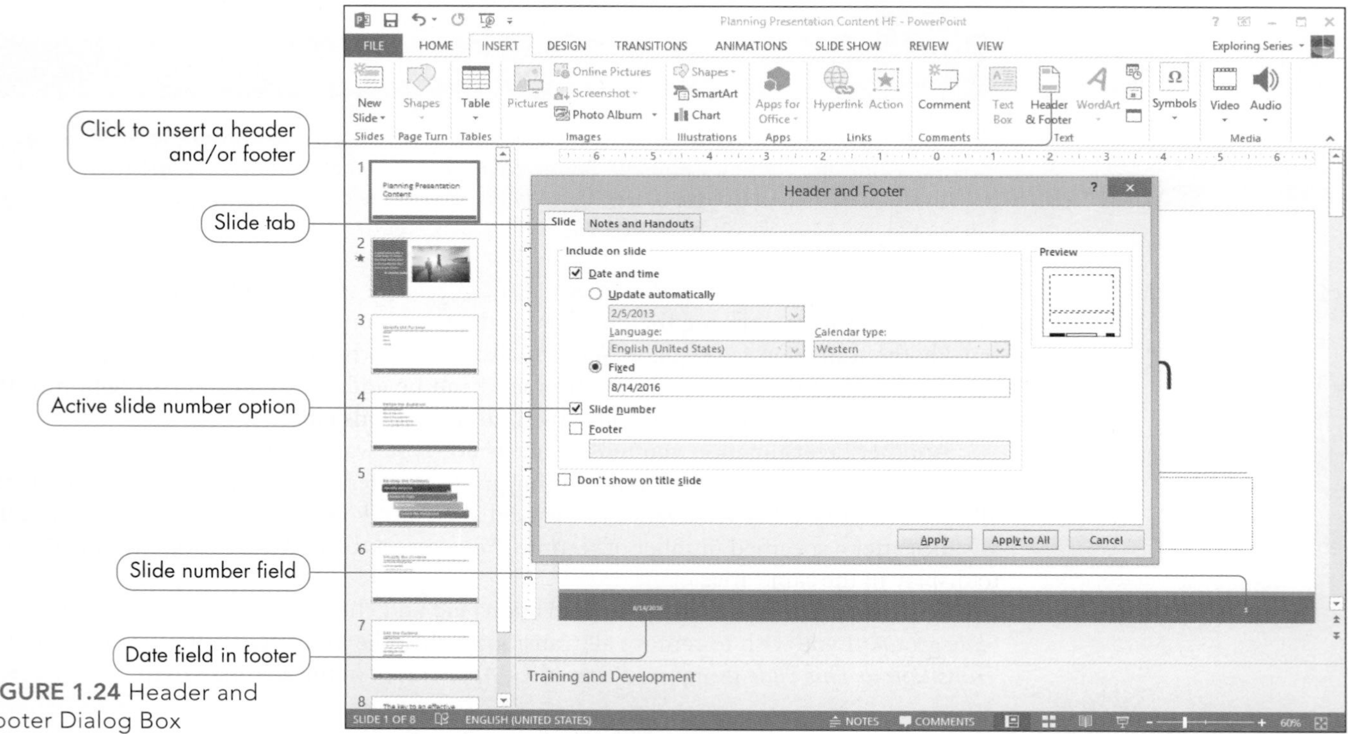

FIGURE 1.24 Header and Footer Dialog Box

With the *Header and Footer* dialog box open, click the *Date and time* check box to insert the current date and time signature. Click *Update automatically* if you wish the date to always be current. Once you select *Update automatically*, you can select the date format you prefer. Alternatively, you can choose the option to enter a fixed date to preserve the original date, which can help you keep track of versions. Click the Slide Number check box to show the slide number on the slide. Click in the Footer box to enter information. The Preview window allows you to see the position of these fields. Always note the position of the fields, as PowerPoint layouts vary considerably in *Header and Footer* field positions. If you do not want the header or footer to appear on the title slide, select *Don't show on title slide.*

The *Notes and Handouts* tab gives you an extra field box for the Header field. Because this feature is used for printouts, the slides are not numbered, but the pages in the handout are. As you activate the fields, the Preview window shows the location of the fields. The date and time are located on the top right of the printout. The Header field is located on the top left. The page number is located on the bottom right, and the Footer field is on the bottom left.

Quick Concepts

1. Explain why adding media objects to a PowerPoint slide show is important. ***p. 865***
2. How does a table organize information? ***p. 866***
3. Describe three benefits that can occur when objects are animated in a slide show. ***p. 866***
4. Give an example of when you would use the *Update automatically* option in the *Header and Footer* feature. When would you use the *Fixed date* option? ***p. 870***

Hands-On Exercises

3 Presentation Enhancement

You decide to strengthen the slide show by adding objects. You know that adding clip art and additional information in a table will help state employees stay interested and retain information. You insert a table, add clip art, apply a transition, and animate the objects you have included. Finally, you enter a slide footer and a *Notes and Handouts* header and footer.

Skills covered: Add a Table • Insert Online Pictures • Apply a Transition • Animate Objects • Create a Handout Header and Footer

STEP 1 » ADD A TABLE

To organize the list of objects that can be added to a PowerPoint slide, you create a table on a new slide. Listing these objects as bullets would take far more space than a table takes. Refer to Figure 1.25 as you complete Step 1.

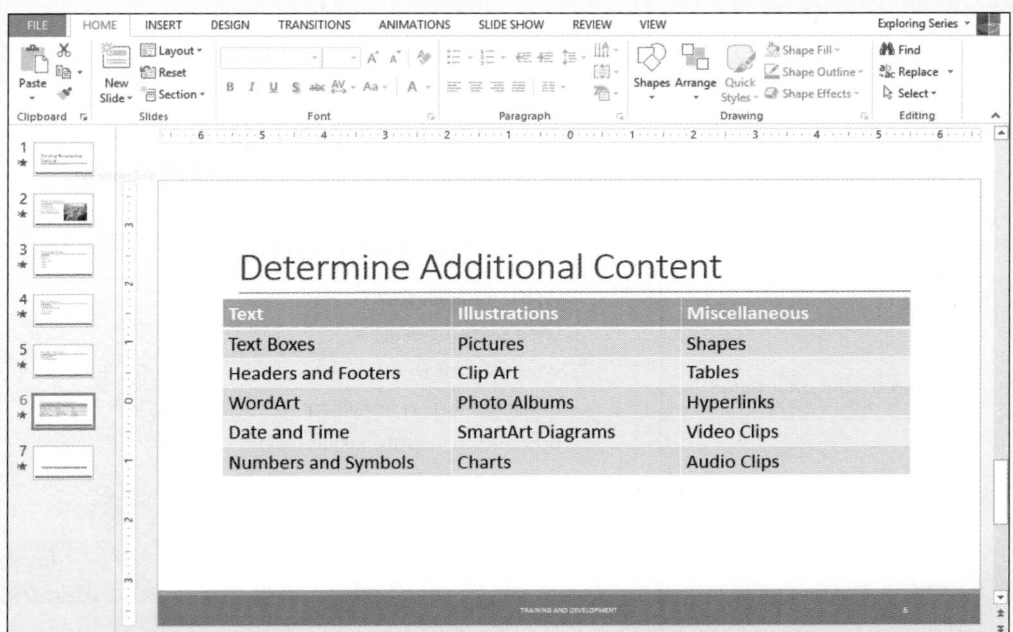

FIGURE 1.25 PowerPoint Table

a. Open *p01h2Content_LastFirst* if you closed it after the last Hands-On Exercise and save it as **p01h3Content_LastFirst**, changing *h2* to *h3*.

> TROUBLESHOOTING: If you make any major mistakes in this exercise, you can close the file, open *p01h2Content_LastFirst* again, and then start this exercise over.

b. Click **Slide 5** and click **New Slide** in the Slides group.

A new slide with the *Title and Content* layout is inserted after Slide 5.

c. Click the **title placeholder** and type **Determine Additional Content**.

d. Click **Insert Table** in the content placeholder in the center of the slide.

The Insert Table dialog box opens.

e. Set the number of columns to **3** and the number of rows to **6** and click **OK**.

   PowerPoint creates the table and positions it on the slide. The first row is formatted differently from the other rows so that it can be used for column headings.

f. Click the top-left cell in the table and type **Text**. Press **Tab** to move to the next cell and type **Illustrations**. Press **Tab**, type **Miscellaneous**, and then press **Tab** to move to the next row.

g. Type the following text in the remaining table cells, pressing **Tab** after each entry.

Text Boxes	Pictures	Shapes
Headers and Footers	Clip Art	Tables
WordArt	Photo Albums	Hyperlinks
Date and Time	SmartArt Diagrams	Video Clips
Numbers and Symbols	Charts	Audio Clips

h. Save the presentation.

STEP 2 ›› INSERT ONLINE PICTURES

In this step, you insert clip art from Office.com and then resize it to better fit the slide. The clip art you insert relates to the topic and adds visual interest. Refer to Figure 1.26 as you complete Step 2.

FIGURE 1.26 Inserted and Resized Clip Art

a. Display **Slide 2**, click **Layout** on the HOME tab, and then click the **Two Content layout**.

   Changing the layout for this slide will better accommodate the photo you will add in the next step.

b. Click the **Online Pictures icon** in the right content placeholder, click the **Office.com Clip Art search box**, and then type the keyword **audience**. Press **Enter**. Select the image shown in Figure 1.26. Click **Insert**.

> **TROUBLESHOOTING:** If you cannot locate the picture shown in Figure 1.26, choose another photo showing an audience.

c. Save the presentation.

STEP 3 » APPLY A TRANSITION

To add motion when one slide changes into another, you apply a transition to all slides in the presentation. You select a transition that is not distracting but that adds emphasis to the title slide. You will also include a sound as the transition occurs. Refer to Figure 1.27 as you complete Step 3.

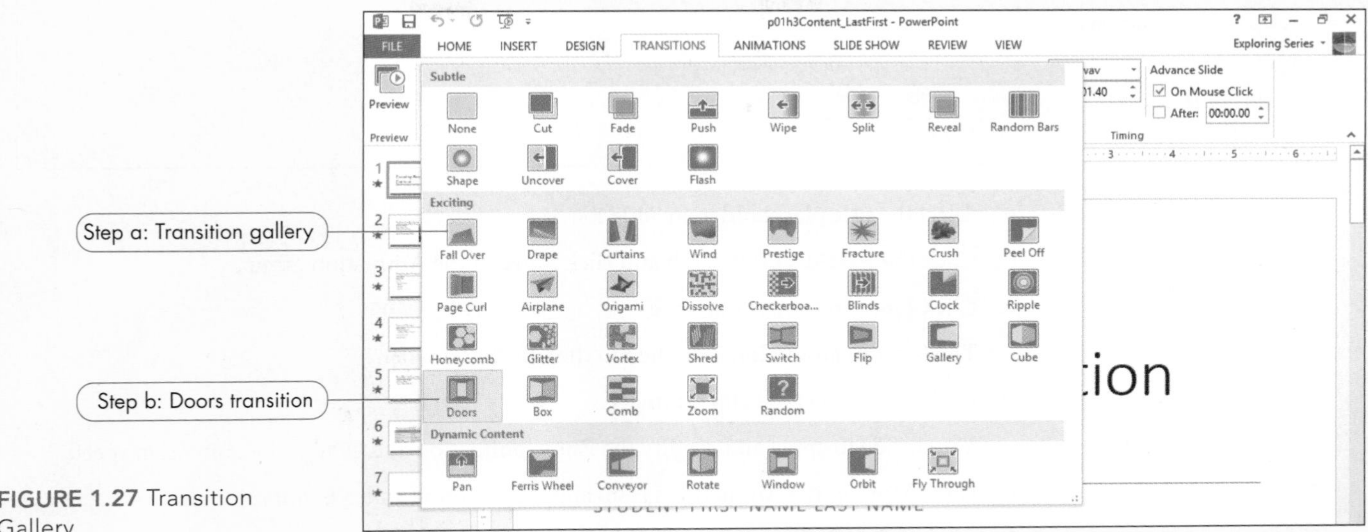

FIGURE 1.27 Transition Gallery

a. Click the **TRANSITIONS tab** and click **More** in the *Transition to This Slide* group.

The Transition gallery displays.

b. Click **Doors** under *Exciting*.

The transition effect will apply to all of the slides in the presentation. Notice that a star has been added next to the thumbnail of any slide where a transition has been applied.

c. Click **Apply to All** in the Timing group.

d. Select the **Slide 1 thumbnail**, click the **Sound arrow** in the Timing group, and then select **Push**.

The Push sound will play as Slide 1 enters when in Slide Show view.

e. Click **Preview**.

The Transition effect will play along with the sound for the first slide.

> **TROUBLESHOOTING:** If you are completing this activity in a classroom lab, you may need to plug in headphones or turn on speakers to hear the sound.

f. Save the presentation.

STEP 4 » ANIMATE OBJECTS

You add animation to your slide show by controlling how individual objects such as lines of text or images enter or exit the slides. Refer to Figure 1.28 as you complete Step 4.

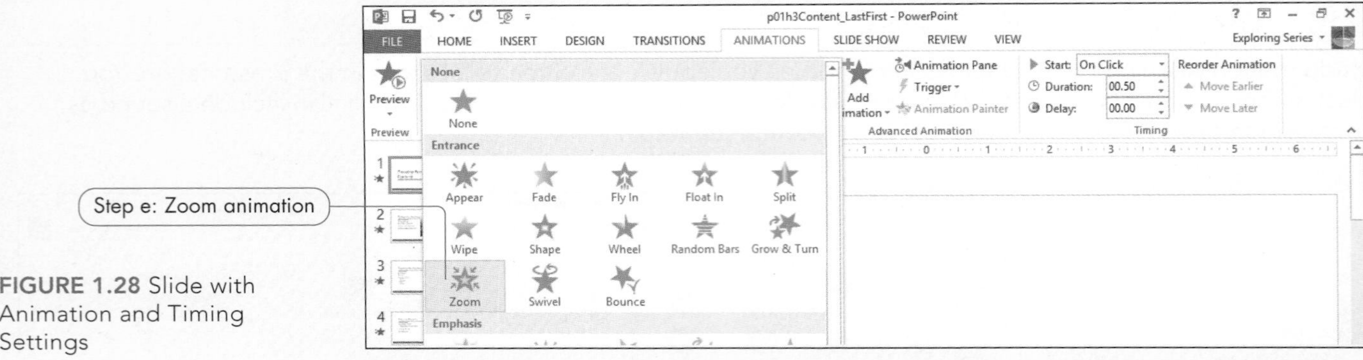

FIGURE 1.28 Slide with Animation and Timing Settings

a. Select the **title placeholder** on Slide 1.

b. Click the **ANIMATIONS tab** and click **More** in the Animation group.

c. Click **Float In** (under *Entrance*).

   The Float In animation is applied to the title placeholder.

d. On Slide 2, select the clip art image.

   You decide to apply and modify the Zoom animation and change the animation speed.

e. Click **More** in the Animation group and click **Zoom** (under *Entrance*).

f. Click **Effect Options** in the Animation group and select **Slide Center**.

   The clip art now grows and zooms from the center of the slide.

g. Save the presentation.

STEP 5 ›› CREATE A HANDOUT HEADER AND FOOTER

Because you are creating this presentation for the Training and Development department, you include this identifying information in a slide footer. You also decide to include your personal information in a Notes and Handouts header and footer. Refer to Figure 1.29 as you complete Step 5.

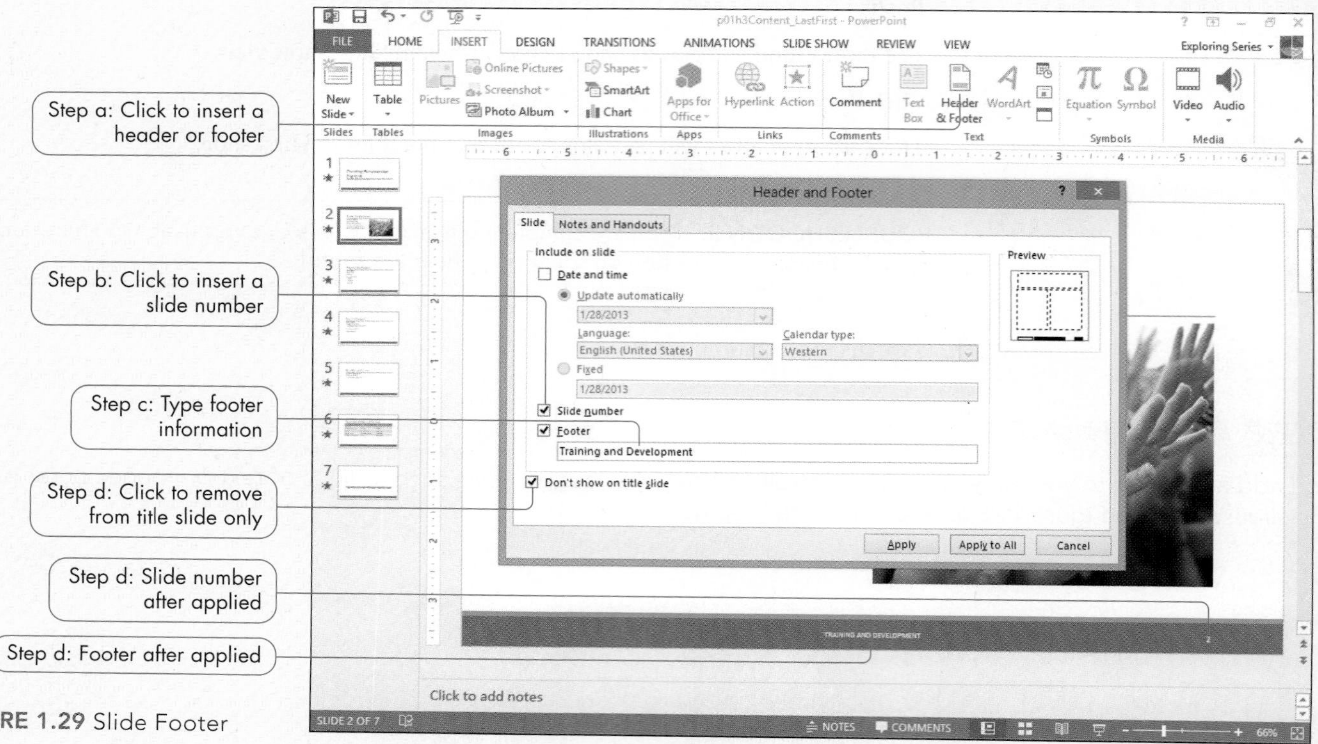

FIGURE 1.29 Slide Footer

a. Click the **INSERT tab** and click **Header & Footer** in the Text group.

The Header and Footer dialog box opens, with the Slide tab active.

b. Click **Slide number**.

The slide number will now appear on each slide. Note the position of the slide number in the Preview window: top right of the slide. The template determined the position of the slide number.

c. Click the **Footer check box** and type **Training and Development**.

Training and Development will appear on each slide. Note the position of the footer in the Preview window: bottom right of the slide.

d. Click **Don't show on title slide** and click **Apply to All**.

The slide footer displays at the bottom right on all slides except the title slide.

e. Save the **p01h3Content_LastFirst** presentation and keep it open if you plan to continue to the next Hands-On Exercise. Close the file and exit PowerPoint if you will not continue with the next exercise at this time.

Navigation and Printing

STEP 1》 In the beginning of this chapter, you opened a slide show and advanced one by one through the slides by clicking the mouse button. Audiences may ask questions that can be answered by going to another slide in the presentation. As you respond to the questions, you may find yourself needing to jump back to a previous slide or needing to move to a future slide. You may even find that during your presentation you wish to direct your audience's attention to a single area of a slide (a new feature of PowerPoint 2013). PowerPoint's navigation options enable you to maneuver through a presentation easily.

To help your audience follow your presentation, you can choose to provide them with a handout. Various options are available for audience handouts. Be aware of the options, and choose the one that best suits your audience's needs. You may distribute handouts at the beginning of your presentation for note taking or provide your audience with the notes afterward.

In this section, you will run a slide show and navigate within the show. You will practice a variety of methods for advancing to new slides or returning to previously viewed slides. You will annotate slides during a presentation and will change from screen view to black-screen view. Finally, you will print handouts of the slide show.

Running and Navigating a Slide Show

PowerPoint provides multiple methods to advance through the slide show. You can also go backward to a previous slide, if desired. Use Table 1.1 to identify the navigation options, and then experiment with each method for advancing and going backward. Find the method that you are most comfortable using and stay with that method.

TABLE 1.1 Navigation Options

Navigation Option	Navigation Method
Advance Through the Slide Show	Press the Spacebar. Press Page Down. Press N for next. Press → or ↓. Press Enter.
Return to a Previous Slide or Animation	Right-click and choose Previous from the shortcut menu. Press Page Up. Press P for previous. Press ← or ↑. Press Backspace.
End the Slide Show	Press Esc.
Go to a Specific Slide	Type the slide number and press Enter. Right-click, point to See All Slides, and then click the slide desired.
Zoom into a Specific Area of a Slide	Right-click, point to Zoom In, and then choose the desired area of the slide. To zoom out, press Esc.

TIP Slide Show Controls

In addition to the slide controls at the bottom left of your slide, you can also press F1 at any time during your presentation to see a list of slide show controls. Familiarize yourself with these controls before you present to a group.

After the last slide in your slide show displays, the audience sees a black slide. This slide has two purposes: It enables you to end your show without having your audience see the PowerPoint design screen, and it cues the audience to expect the room lights to brighten. If you need to blacken the screen at any time during your presentation, you can type B. (If you blacken the screen in a darkened room, you must be prepared to quickly brighten some lights.) When you are ready to start your slide show again, simply type B again.

If you prefer bringing up a white screen, type W. White is much harsher on your audience's eyes, however. Only use white if you are in an extremely bright room. Whether using black or white, you are enabling the audience to concentrate on you, the speaker, without the slide show interfering.

If an audience member asks a question that is answered in another slide on your slide show, you can go to that specific slide by using the See All Slides command. The See All Slides command is found on the shortcut menu, which displays when you right-click anywhere on the active slide during your presentation. The See All Slides command displays all of your slides so you can easily identify and select the slide to which you want to go. This shortcut menu also lets you end the slide show as well as access other features.

If an audience member asks you a question that is best explained by a graph or diagram you have on a slide in your presentation, you can zoom in on a single section of the slide to answer the question. To enlarge a section of a slide on the screen, do the following:

1. Navigate to the slide.
2. Click the magnifying glass icon. This will bring up a highlighted rectangular area on your slide.
3. Move the rectangular box over the area of the slide you want to emphasize. (Figure 1.30 shows the rectangular box.)
4. Click Esc to return to Normal view.

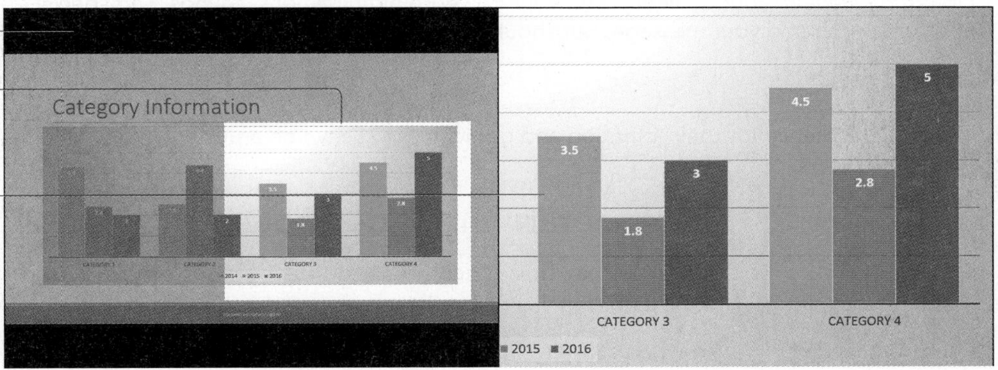

FIGURE 1.30 Zoom to Emphasize Part of a Slide

REFERENCE Delivery Tips

Practice the following delivery tips to gain confidence and polish your delivery.

Before the presentation:

- Practice or rehearse your PowerPoint presentation at home until you are comfortable with the material and its corresponding slides.
- Do not read from a prepared script or your PowerPoint Notes. Presenting is not karaoke. Know your material thoroughly. Glance at your notes infrequently. Never post a screen full of small text and then torture your audience by saying, "I know you can't read this, so I will …"
- Arrive early to set up so you do not keep the audience waiting while you manage equipment.
- Have a backup in case the equipment does not work: Overhead transparencies or handouts work well.
- If appropriate, prepare handouts for your audience so they can relax and participate in your presentation rather than scramble taking notes.
- Make sure your handouts acknowledge and document quotes, data, and sources.

During the presentation:

- Speak to the person farthest away from you to be sure the people in the last row can hear you. Speak slowly and clearly.
- Vary your delivery. Show emotion or enthusiasm for your topic. If you do not care about your topic, why should the audience?
- Pause to emphasize key points when speaking.
- Look at the audience, not at the screen, as you speak to open communication and gain credibility.
- Use the three-second guide: Look into the eyes of a member of the audience for three seconds and then scan the entire audience. Continue doing this throughout your presentation. Use your eye contact to keep members of the audience involved.
- Blank the screen by typing B or W at any time during your presentation when you want to solicit questions, comments, or discussion.
- Do not overwhelm your audience with your PowerPoint animations, sounds, and special effects. These features should not overpower you and your message, but should enhance your message.

After the presentation:

- Thank the audience for their attention and participation. Leave on a positive note.

Annotate the Slide Show

STEP 2» You may find it helpful to add ***annotations*** (notes or drawings) to your slides during a presentation. To add written notes or drawings, do the following:

1. Right-click a slide in Slide Show view.
2. Point to Pointer Options.
3. Click Pen or Highlighter.
4. Hold down the left mouse button and write or draw on the screen.

If you want to change the ink color for the Pen or Highlighter, right-click to bring up the shortcut menu, point to Pointer Options, and then click your pen type and ink color. To erase what you have drawn, press E. Your drawings or added text will be clumsy efforts at best, unless you use a tablet computer that includes a stylus and drawing screen. With each slide, you must again activate the drawing pointer, in order to avoid accidentally drawing on your slides. The annotations you create are not permanent unless you save the annotations when exiting the slide show and then save the changes upon exiting the file. You may want to save the annotated file with a different file name from the original presentation.

Rather than annotate a slide, you may simply want to point to a specific section of the screen. The laser pointer feature will allow you to do this. To use the laser pointer, do the following:

1. Right-click a slide in Slide Show view.
2. Point to Pointer Options.
3. Click Laser Pointer.
4. Move the mouse to the desired position.
5. Press Esc to end the laser pointer.

Annotating Shortcuts

Press Ctrl+P to change the pointer to a drawing pointer while presenting, and click and draw on the slide, much the same way your favorite football announcer diagrams a play. Use Page Down and Page Up to move forward and backward in the presentation while the annotation is in effect. Press Ctrl+A to return the mouse pointer to an arrow.

Printing in PowerPoint

A printed copy of a PowerPoint slide show can be used to display speaker notes for reference during the presentation, for audience handouts or a study guide, or as a means to deliver the presentation if there were an equipment failure. A printout of a single slide with text on it can be used as a poster or banner. Figure 1.31 shows the print options. Depending on your printer and printer settings, your button names may vary. To print a copy of the slide show using the default PowerPoint settings, do the following:

1. Click the FILE tab.
2. Click Print.
3. Click Printer to choose the print device you want to use.
4. Click Print All Slides to select the print area and range.
5. Click Full Page Slides to select the layout of the printout.
6. Click to select Collated or Uncollated.
7. Click Color to select color, grayscale, or pure black and white.
8. Click Print.

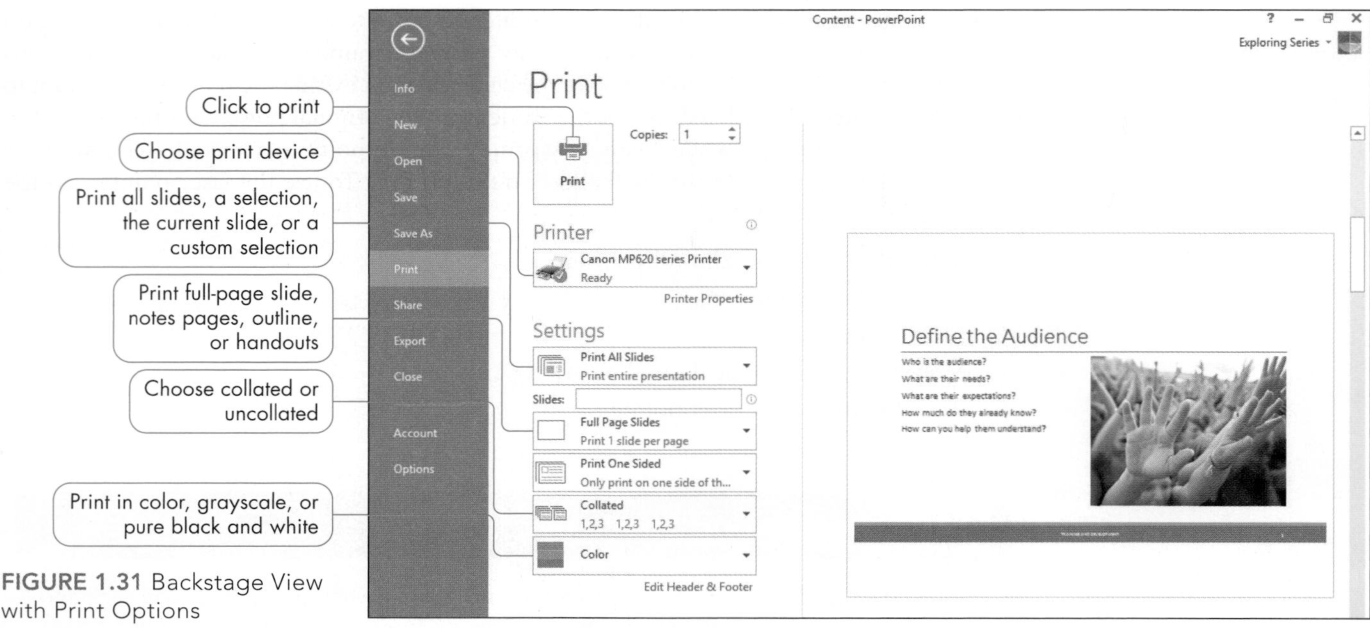

FIGURE 1.31 Backstage View with Print Options

Print Full Page Slides

Use the Print Full Page Slides option to print the slides for use as a backup or when the slides contain a great deal of detail the audience needs to examine. You will be grateful for the backup if your projector bulb blows out or if your computer quits working during a presentation.

If you are printing the slides on paper smaller than the standard size, be sure to change the slide size and orientation before you print. By default, PowerPoint sets the slides for landscape orientation for printing so that the width is greater than the height (11" × 8 1/2"). If you are going to print a flyer or overhead transparency, however, you need to set PowerPoint to portrait orientation, to print so that the height is greater than the width (8 1/2" × 11").

To change your slide orientation:

1. Click the DESIGN tab.
2. Click Slide Size in the Customize group.
3. Click Customize Slide Size.
4. Click Portrait or Landscape in the *Slides* section. Here, you can also change the size of the slide as well as the orientation. If you want to create a custom size of paper to print, enter the height and width.

After you click the File tab and click Print, you can determine the color option with which to print.

- Color: prints your presentation in color if you have a color printer or grayscale if you are printing on a black-and-white printer.
- Grayscale: prints in shades of gray, but be aware that backgrounds do not print when using the Grayscale option. By not printing the background, you make the text in the printout easier to read and you save a lot of ink or toner.
- Pure Black and White: prints in black and white only, with no gray color.

When you click Full Page Slides, several print options become available:

- Frame Slides: puts a black border around the slides in the printout, giving the printout a more polished appearance.
- Scale to Fit Paper: ensures that each slide prints on one page even if you have selected a custom size for your slide show, or if you have set up the slide show so that it is larger than the paper on which you are printing. If you have applied shadows to text or objects, click High Quality so that the shadows print.
- Print Comments and Ink Markup: prints any comments or annotations. This option is active only if you have used this feature.

Print Handouts

STEP 3»

The principal purpose for printing handouts is to give your audience something they can use to follow and take notes on during the presentation. With your handout and their notes, the audience has an excellent resource for the future. Handouts can be printed with one, two, three, four, six, or nine slides per page. Printing three handouts per page is a popular option because it places thumbnails of the slides on the left side of the printout and lines on which the audience can write on the right side of the printout. Figure 1.32 shows the option set to Handouts and the *Slides per page* option set to 6.

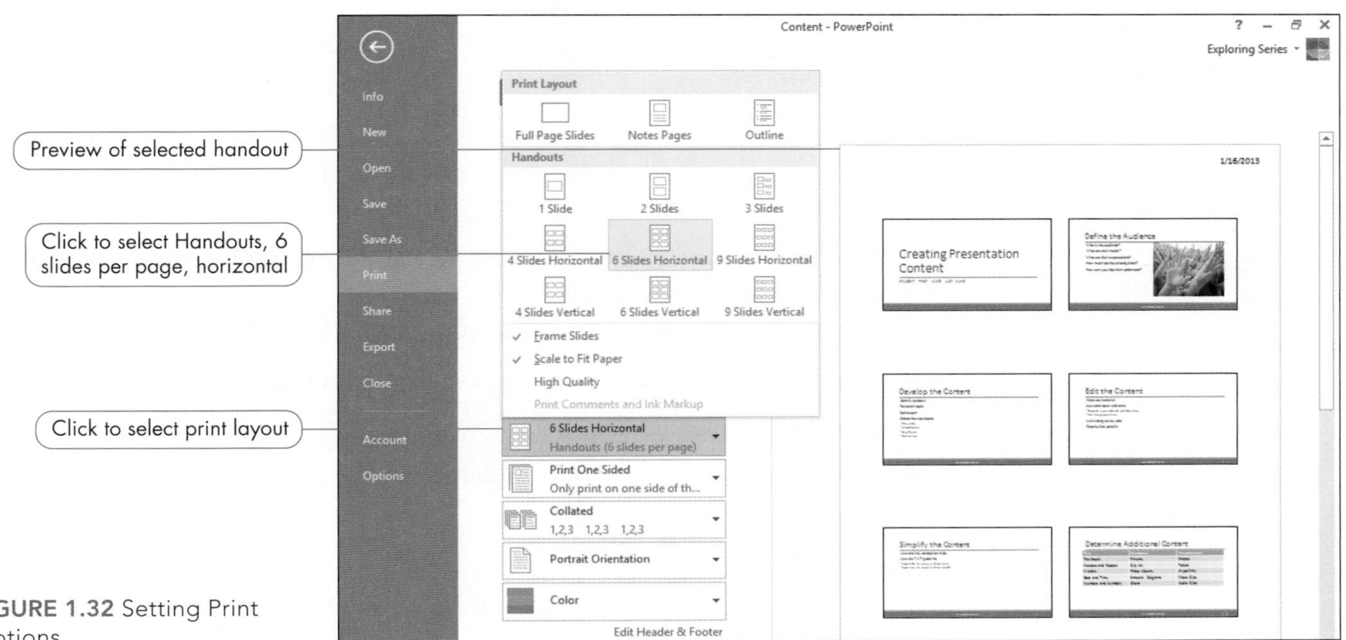

FIGURE 1.32 Setting Print Options

Print Notes Pages

If you include charts, technical information, or references in a speaker note, you will want to print a Notes Page if you want the audience to have a copy. To print a specific Notes Page, change the print layout to Notes Pages and click the Print All Slides arrow. Click Custom Range and enter the specific slides to print.

Print Outlines

You may print your presentation as an outline made up of the slide titles and main text from each of your slides if you only want to deal with a few pages. The outline generally gives you enough detail to keep you on track with your presentation, but does not display speaker notes.

Quick Concepts

1. How do you access the *Go to Slide* command when displaying a slide show, and what does it do? ***p. 876***
2. Discuss three presentation delivery do's and three presentation don'ts. ***p. 878***
3. Describe at least three uses for a printed copy of a PowerPoint slide show. ***p. 879***

Hands-On Exercises

Watch the Video
for this Hands-
On Exercise!

MyITLab®
HOE4 Training

4 Navigation and Printing

To prepare for your presentation to Training and Development department employees, you practice displaying the slide show and navigating to specific slides. You also annotate a slide and print audience handouts.

Skills covered: Start a Slide Show • Annotate a Slide • Print Audience Handouts

STEP 1 » START A SLIDE SHOW

In this step, you practice various slide navigation techniques to become comfortable with their use. You also review the Slide Show Help feature to become familiar with navigation shortcuts.

a. Open *p01h3Content_LastFirst* if you closed it at the end of Hands-On Exercise 3 and save it as **p01h4Content_LastFirst**, changing *h3* to *h4*.

b. Click the **SLIDE SHOW tab** and click **From Beginning** in the Start Slide Show group.

   Note the transition effect and sound you applied in Hands-On Exercise 3.

c. Press **Spacebar** to display the animation.

d. Click the **left mouse button** to advance to Slide 2.

e. Press **Page Down** to advance to Slide 3.

f. Press **Spacebar** to play the animation.

   Note that the clip art animation plays on click.

g. Press **Page Up** to return to Slide 2.

h. Click the **Magnifying glass icon** and zoom in only on the text for Slide 2.

i. Press **Enter** to advance to Slide 3.

j. Press **N** to advance to Slide 4.

k. Press **Backspace** to return to Slide 3.

l. Press the number **5** and press **Enter**.

   Slide 5 displays.

m. Press **F1** and read the Slide Show Help window showing the shortcut tips that are available during the display of a slide show. Practice moving between slides using the shortcuts shown in Help.

n. Close the Help window.

STEP 2 » ANNOTATE A SLIDE

You practice annotating a slide using a pen, and then you remove the annotations. You practice darkening the screen and returning to the presentation from the dark screen.

a. On Slide 3, press **Ctrl+P**.

   The mouse pointer becomes a pen.

b. Circle and underline the words *Research topic* on the slide.

c. Press **E**.

   The annotations erase.

d. Press **B**.

   The screen blackens.

e. Press **B** again.

   The slide show displays again.

f. Press **Esc** to end annotations.

g. Press **Esc** to end the slide show.

STEP 3 » PRINT AUDIENCE HANDOUTS

To enable your audience to follow along during your presentation, you print handouts of your presentation. You know that many of the audience members will also keep your handouts for future reference.

a. Click the **FILE tab** to display the Backstage view and click **Print**.

b. Click **Full Page Slides** and select **4 Slides Horizontal** in the *Handouts* section.

> **TROUBLESHOOTING:** If you have previously selected a different print layout, Full Page Slides will be changed to that layout. Click the arrow next to the displayed layout option.

c. Click **Print** to print the presentation if requested by your instructor.

d. Save and close the file, and submit based on your instructor's directions.

Chapter Objectives Review

After reading this chapter, you have accomplished the following objectives:

1. **Use PowerPoint views.**
   - Slide shows are electronic presentations that enable you to advance through slides containing content that will help your audience understand your message.
   - Normal view displays either thumbnail images or an outline in one pane, the slide in one pane, and a Notes pane.
   - Slide Sorter view displays thumbnails of slides to enable you to organize your presentation.
   - Outline View enables you to easily create a presentation from an outline.
   - Notes Page view displays a thumbnail of the slide and speaker notes.
   - Slide Show view displays the slide show in full-screen view for an audience.
   - Presenter view gives the presenter options such as a timer and notes, whereas the audience views the full-screen presentation.
2. **Type a speaker note.**
   - Slides should contain only a minimum amount of information, and the speaker should deliver the majority of the information throughout the presentation.
   - Speaker notes can be added to the PowerPoint presentation to provide the speaker with additional notes, data, or other comments that will be useful during the presentation.
3. **Save as a slide show.**
   - You can save a presentation as a slide show, so that when the file opens it is in Slide Show mode. Slide shows cannot be edited and are saved with the file extension .ppsx.
4. **Plan a presentation.**
   - Prepare a storyboard: Organize your ideas on a storyboard, and then create your presentation in PowerPoint.
   - Create a title slide and introduction: The title slide should have a short title that indicates the purpose. An introduction slide will get the audience's attention.
   - Create the main body of slides: The content of your presentation follows the title slide and the introduction.
   - Create the conclusion: End your presentation with a summary or conclusion that reviews the main points, restates the purpose, or invokes a call to action.
5. **Assess presentation content.**
   - Use active voice: Review and edit the phrases so they begin with active voice when possible.
   - Use parallel construction: Use parallel construction so that your bullets are in the same grammatical form.
   - Follow the 7 × 7 guideline: Use no more than seven words per line and seven lines per slide.
   - When you add a slide, you can choose from a set of predefined slide layouts that determine the position of the objects or content on a slide.
   - Placeholders hold content and determine the position of the objects on the slide.
   - Reorder slides: You can easily reorder your slides using the Slide Sorter view.
6. **Review the presentation.**
   - Use the Spelling and Thesaurus features, and review the presentation in Normal and Slide Show views to ensure no errors exist.
7. **Insert media objects.**
   - Media objects such as clip art, images, movies, and sound can be added to enhance the message of your slides and to add visual interest.
8. **Add a table.**
   - Tables organize information in rows and columns.
9. **Use animations and transitions.**
   - Animate objects: Animations control the movement of an object on the slide.
   - Apply transitions: Transitions control the movement of slides as one slide changes to another.
10. **Insert a header or footer.**
    - Headers and footers are used for identifying information on the slide or on handouts and note pages. Header and footer locations vary depending on the theme applied.
11. **Run and navigate a slide show.**
    - Various navigation methods advance the slide show, return to previously viewed slides, or go to specific slides.
    - Slides can be annotated during a presentation to add emphasis or comments to slides.
12. **Print in PowerPoint.**
    - Print handouts: Handouts print miniatures of the slides using 1, 2, 3, 4, 6, or 9 slide thumbnails per page.
    - Print notes pages: Notes Page method prints a single thumbnail of a slide with its associated notes per page.
    - Print outlines: Outline View prints the titles and main points of the presentation in outline format.

Key Terms Matching

Match the key terms with their definitions. Write the key term letter by the appropriate numbered definition.

- **a.** Animation
- **b.** Annotation
- **c.** Layout
- **d.** Normal view
- **e.** Notes Page view
- **f.** Placeholder
- **g.** PowerPoint presentation
- **h.** PowerPoint show
- **i.** Presenter view
- **j.** Reading View
- **k.** Slide
- **l.** Slide show
- **m.** Slide Show view
- **n.** Slide Sorter view
- **o.** Status bar
- **p.** Storyboard
- **q.** Theme
- **r.** Thumbnail
- **s.** Transition
- **t.** Variant

1. _______ Defines containers, positioning, and formatting for all of the content that appears on a slide. **p. 859**
2. _______ The default PowerPoint view, containing two panes that provide maximum flexibility in working with the presentation. **p. 845**
3. _______ A container that holds content. **p. 859**
4. _______ The movement applied to an object or objects on a slide. **p. 866**
5. _______ The most basic element of PowerPoint, analogous to a page in a Word document. **p. 844**
6. _______ A note or drawing added to a slide during a presentation. **p. 878**
7. _______ Located at the bottom of the screen, this contains the slide number, a spell check button, and options that control the view of your presentation. **p. 845**
8. _______ Used to view a slide show full screen, one slide at a time. **p. 849**
9. _______ A presentation saved with a .pptx extension. **p. 844**
10. _______ A method to deliver your message in a variety of ways using multiple slides. **p. 844**
11. _______ Used if the speaker needs to enter and edit large amounts of text for reference in the presentation. **p. 848**
12. _______ Uses a .ppsx extension. **p. 850**
13. _______ A specialty view that delivers a presentation on two monitors simultaneously. **p. 850**
14. _______ A variation of the theme you have chosen, using different color palettes and font families. **p. 857**
15. _______ Used to deliver a completed presentation full screen to an audience, one slide at a time. **p. 849**
16. _______ A slide miniature. **p. 845**
17. _______ A specific animation that is applied when a previous slide is replaced by a new slide. **p. 866**
18. _______ Displays thumbnails of your presentation slides, allowing you to view multiple slides simultaneously. **p. 847**
19. _______ A visual design that helps you plan the direction of your presentation slides. **p. 855**
20. _______ A collection of formatting choices that includes colors, fonts, and special effects. **p. 857**

Multiple Choice

1. Which of the following will display a list of shortcuts for navigating when presenting a slide show?
   (a) F1
   (b) F11
   (c) Ctrl+Enter
   (d) Esc

2. What is the name for PowerPoint's predefined slide arrangements?
   (a) Placeholder views
   (b) Slide layouts
   (c) Slide guides
   (d) Slide displays

3. What is the term for a variation of the theme using different color palettes and font families?
   (a) Palette
   (b) Design
   (c) Variant
   (d) Layout

4. When making a presentation that includes a large detailed table, which print method should you use?
   (a) Handout, 6 Slides Horizontal
   (b) Outline
   (c) Notes Pages
   (d) Full Page Slide

5. Which of the following components are contained in Normal view?
   (a) Slide Sorter pane, Thumbnails pane, and Reading pane
   (b) Thumbnails pane, Slide pane, and Reading pane
   (c) Thumbnails pane and Slide pane
   (d) Slide pane, Notes pane, and Slide Sorter pane

6. What view is the best choice if you want to reorder the slides in a presentation?
   (a) Presenter view
   (b) Reading View
   (c) Slide Sorter view
   (d) Slide Show view

7. Regarding themes, which of the following is a *true* statement?
   (a) A theme must be applied before slides are created.
   (b) The theme can be changed after all of the slides have been created.
   (c) Themes control placeholder location but not fonts and backgrounds.
   (d) Placeholders positioned by a theme cannot be moved.

8. In reference to content development, which of the following points is *not* in active voice and is not parallel to the others?
   (a) Identify the purpose of the presentation.
   (b) Storyboards are used to sketch out thoughts.
   (c) Brainstorm your thoughts.
   (d) Research your topic.

9. The animation effect that controls how one slide changes to another slide is called:
   (a) Transition.
   (b) Timing.
   (c) Animation.
   (d) Advance.

10. During a slide show, which of the following would best be used to focus audience attention on a specific object?
    (a) Put nothing on the slide but the object.
    (b) Apply an animation to the object.
    (c) Use the Pen tool to circle the object.
    (d) Apply a transition to the object.

Practice Exercises

1 Student Success

FROM SCRATCH

The slide show you create in this practice exercise covers concepts and skills that will help you be successful in college. You create a title slide, an introduction, four slides containing main points of the presentation, and a conclusion slide. Then, you review the presentation and edit a slide so that the text of the bulleted items is parallel. Finally, you print a title page to use as a cover and notes pages to staple together as a reference. This exercise follows the same set of skills as used in Hands-On Exercises 1–4 in the chapter. Refer to Figure 1.33 as you complete the exercise.

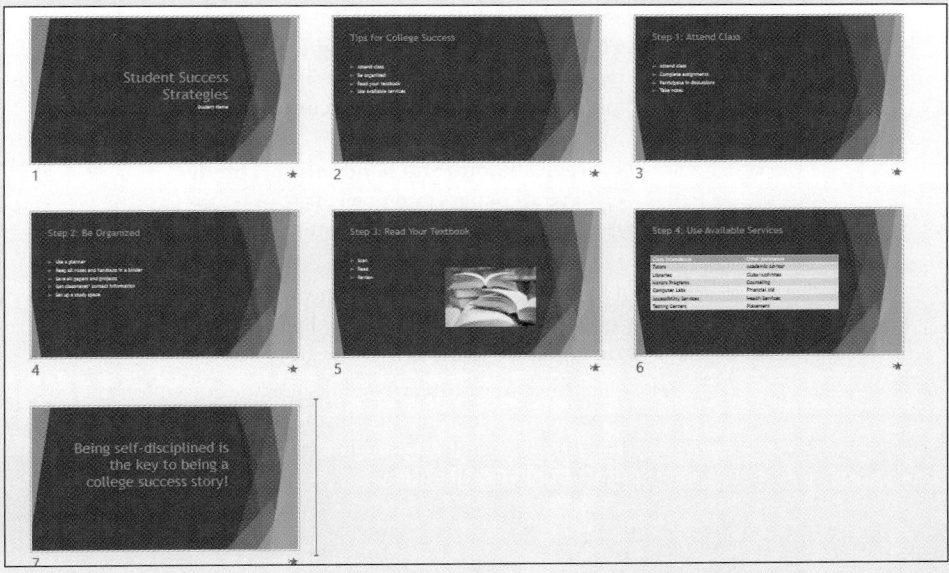

FIGURE 1.33 Student Success Strategies

a. Open PowerPoint.
b. Click the **Facet theme**. Click the variant with the dark blue background (bottom-right corner) and click **Create**.
c. Save the presentation as **p01p1Success_LastFirst**.
d. Click the **Slide 1 thumbnail**. Click the **INSERT tab**, click **Header & Footer** in the Text group, and then click the **Notes and Handouts tab** in the *Header and Footer* dialog box. Make the following changes:
   - Select the **Date and time check box** and click **Update automatically** (if necessary).
   - Click to select the **Header check box** and type your name in the **Header box**.
   - Click the **Footer check box** and type your instructor's name and your class name in the **Footer box**. Click **Apply to All**.
e. On Slide 1, click in the **title placeholder** and type **Student Success Strategies**. Click in the **subtitle placeholder** and type your name.
f. Click **New Slide** in the Slides group on the HOME tab to create a new slide (Slide 2) for the introduction of the slide show. Type **Tips for College Success** in the **title placeholder** and type the following bulleted text in the **content placeholder**:
   - **Class attendance**
   - **Be organized**
   - **Read your textbook**
   - **Use available services**

g. Click **New Slide** in the Slides group on the HOME tab to create a new slide (Slide 3) for the first main point of the slide show. Type **Step 1: Attend Class** in the **title placeholder** and type the following bulleted text in the **content placeholder**:

- **Attend class**
- **Complete assignments**
- **Participate in discussions**
- **Take notes**

h. Click **Notes** on the status bar. Type the following in the **Notes pane**: **When you miss class, you lose the opportunity to listen to the lecture, take notes, participate in discussions, and you also miss assignments, quizzes, and tests.**

i. Click **New Slide** in the Slides group on the HOME tab to create a new slide (Slide 4) for the second main point of the slide show. Type **Step 2: Be Organized** in the **title placeholder** and enter the following bulleted text in the **content placeholder**:

- **Use a planner**
- **Keep all notes and handouts in a binder**
- **Save all papers and projects**
- **Get classmates' contact information**
- **Set up a study space**

j. Type the following in the **Notes pane** for Slide 4: **Record every assignment, quiz, and exam date in a planner. Keep all returned papers, quizzes, to use as a resource for studying for a final exam and as a record of your grades for the course.**

k. Click the **New Slide arrow** in the Slides group on the HOME tab. Click **Two Content** to create a new slide (Slide 5) for the third main point of the slide show. Type **Step 3: Read Your Textbook** in the **title placeholder** and enter the following text in the **content placeholder** on the left side of the slide following the title:

- **Scan**
- **Read**
- **Review**

l. Click the **Online Pictures icon** in the content placeholder on the right side of the slide. Type **textbook** in the **Office.com Clip Art box**. Press **Enter.** Click an image of stacked textbooks on the slide, as shown in Figure 1.34, and click **Insert** to insert the image.

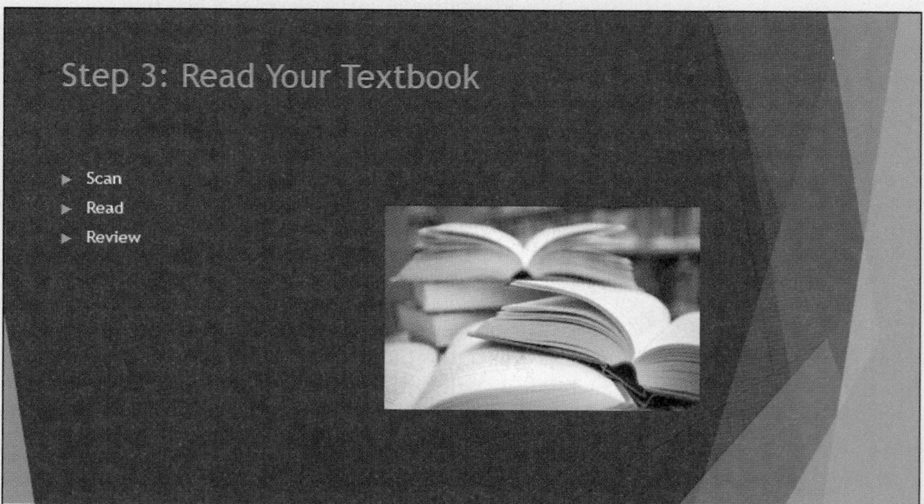

FIGURE 1.34 Inserted Image

> **TROUBLESHOOTING:** If you cannot locate the image in Figure 1.34, select another clip art image of a textbook or textbooks. Expand your search terms to include other result types if necessary.

m. Type the following in the **Notes pane**: **Read the chapter summary and review questions. Next, read the entire chapter for detail and to increase your comprehension.**

n. Click the **New Slide arrow** in the Slides group on the HOME tab. Click **Title and Content** to create a new slide (Slide 6) for the last main point of the slide show. Type **Step 4: Use Available Services** in the **title placeholder**.

o. Click the **Insert Table icon** in the content placeholder. Set *Number of columns* to **2** and *Number of rows* to **7**. Click **OK**. Type the following text in the columns, pressing **Tab** after each entry except the last:

Class Assistance	**Other Assistance**
Tutors	Academic Advisor
Libraries	Clubs/Activities
Honors Programs	Counseling
Computer Labs	Financial Aid
Accessibility Services	Health Services
Testing Centers	Placement

p. Type the following in the **Notes pane** for Slide 6: **You can use campus facilities like computer labs without charge because typically the cost is covered through fees you pay. You can also get questions answered and problems resolved by talking to personnel in campus offices.**

q. Click the **New Slide arrow** in the Slides group on the HOME tab. Click **Title Slide** to create a new slide (Slide 7) for the conclusion slide of the slide show. Type **Being self-disciplined is the key to being a college success story!** in the **title placeholder**. Select the border of the subtitle placeholder and press **Delete**.

r. Review Slide 2 and note that the slide bullets are not in parallel construction. The first bulleted point needs to be changed to active voice. Select **Class attendance** and type **Attend class**.

s. Click the **TRANSITIONS tab** and click **More** in the *Transition to This Slide* group. Click **Push** in the Transition gallery.

t. Click **Apply to All** in the Timing Group.

u. Click the **FILE tab**, click **Print**, and then click in the box marked *Slides*. Type **2-7** as the slide range. Click **Full Page Slides** and select **Notes Pages**. Click **Frame Slides** and click **Print**, if your instructor asks you to submit printed slides.

v. Staple the title page you printed to the front of the Notes Pages to use as a cover page, if your instructor asked you to print this exercise.

w. Click the **REVIEW tab** and click **Spelling**. Click **Save** to save the presentation. Click the **FILE tab**, click **Save As**, and then choose the location where you will save the file. In the Save As dialog box, change the *Save as type* to **PowerPoint Show** and click **Save**. Close the presentation. Submit files based on your instructor's directions.

2 Tips for a Successful Presentation

FROM SCRATCH

Your employer is a successful author who has been asked by the local International Association of Administrative Professionals (IAAP) to give tips for presenting successfully using PowerPoint. He created a storyboard of his presentation and has asked you to create the presentation from the storyboard. This exercise follows the same set of skills as used in Hands-On Exercises 2 and 3 in the chapter. Refer to Figure 1.35 as you complete this exercise.

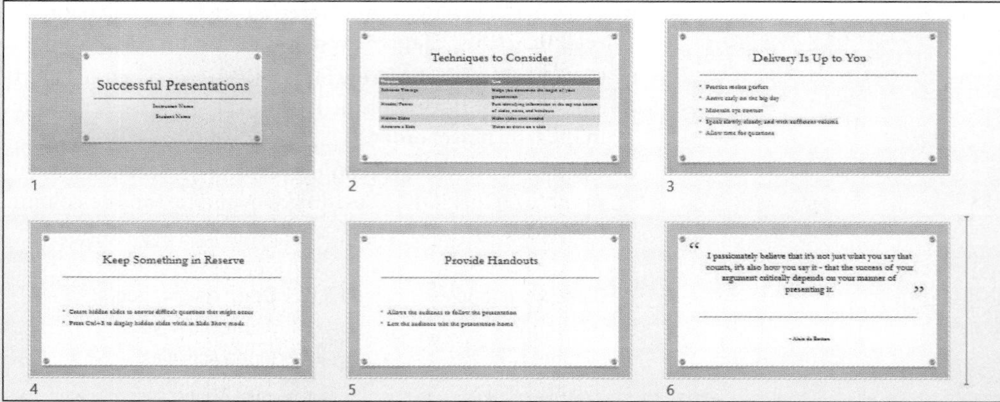

FIGURE 1.35 Successful Presentations

a. Open PowerPoint.

b. Select the **Organic** theme, select the variant in the bottom-right corner, and then click **Create**.

c. Save the presentation as **p01p2Presenting_LastFirst**.

d. Click the **INSERT tab**, click **Header & Footer**, and then click the **Notes and Handouts tab** in the *Header and Footer* dialog box.

- Click to select the **Date and time check box** and click **Update automatically**, if necessary.
- Click to select the **Header check box** and type your name in the **Header box**.
- Click to select the **Footer check box** and type your instructor's name and your class name. Click **Apply to All**.

e. On Slide 1, click in the **title placeholder** and type **Successful Presentations**. Click in the **subtitle placeholder** and type your instructor's name. Press **Enter**. On the new line, type your name.

f. Click the **HOME tab** and click **New Slide** in the Slides group.

g. Click in the **title placeholder** and type **Techniques to Consider**.

h. Click the **Insert Table icon** in the content placeholder and enter **2** columns and **5** rows.

i. Type the following information in the table cells, pressing **Tab** after each item except the last.

Feature	**Use**
Rehearse Timings	Helps you determine the length of your presentation
Header/Footer	Puts identifying information on the top and bottom of slides, notes, and handouts
Hidden Slides	Hides slides until needed
Annotate a Slide	Writes or draws on a slide

j. Click the **HOME tab** and click **New Slide** in the Slides group. Type **Delivery Is Up to You** in the **title placeholder**.

k. Click in the **content placeholder** and type the following bulleted text:

- **Practice makes perfect**
- **Arrive early on the big day**
- **Maintain eye contact**
- **Speak slowly, clearly, and with sufficient volume**
- **Allow time for questions**

l. Click **New Slide** and type **Keep Something in Reserve** in the **title placeholder**.

m. Click in the **content placeholder** and type the following bulleted text:

- **Create hidden slides to answer difficult questions that might occur**
- **Press Ctrl+S while in Slide Show view to display hidden slides**

n. Click **New Slide** and type **Provide Handouts** in the **title placeholder**.

o. Click in the **content placeholder** and type the following bulleted text:
   - **Allows the audience to follow the presentation**
   - **Lets the audience take the presentation home**

p. Click the **New Slide arrow** and click **Quote with Caption**.

q. Type **I passionately believe that it's not just what you say that counts, it's also how you say it - that the success of your argument critically depends on your manner of presenting it.** in the **title placeholder**.

r. Click the **center placeholder** and press **Delete**.

s. Type - **Alain de Botton** in the **bottom placeholder**.

t. Click the **REVIEW tab** and click **Spelling** in the Proofing group. Accept *Lets* in Slide 5, if necessary. Review the presentation in Slide Show view to fix any spelling errors.

u. Click the **SLIDE SHOW tab** and click **From Beginning** in the Start Slide Show group. Press **Page Down** to advance through the slides. When you reach the last slide of the slide show, press the number **3** and press **Enter** to return to Slide 3.

v. Right-click, point to *Pointer Options*, and then click **Highlighter**. Highlight **Speak slowly, clearly, and with sufficient volume**.

w. Press **Page Down** to advance through the remainder of the presentation. Press **Esc** when you reach the black slide at the end of the slide show and click **Keep** to keep your slide annotations.

x. **Save** the presentation. Close the file and submit based on your instructor's directions.

Mid-Level Exercises

1 Planning Presentation Content

Brainstorming a topic and creating a storyboard with ideas is the first step in slide show development. After creating the slide show from a storyboard, however, the information should be accessed and edited so that the final slide show is polished and professional. In this exercise, you create a slide show from a storyboard and then edit the slide show following the tips contained in the content.

a. Open PowerPoint. Create a new presentation, applying the design theme of your choice to the presentation. Save the presentation as **p01m1Refine_LastFirst**.

b. Create the following slides with the content contained in the following table:

Slide Number	Slide Layout	Slide Title	Slide Content
1	Title	Refining Presentation Content	(type your name) (type your class)
2	Title and Content	Principles for Refining Content	• Simplify content • Reduce text • Edit text • Make text readable • Emphasize main points • Create consistency • Create a mood with color

3	Title and Content	Simplify Content	• Plan 3 to 5 text slides per major concept
			• Use one main concept per slide
			• Use 7 × 7 guideline
			  • Limit slide to 7 or fewer lines
			  • Limit words in lines to 7 or fewer

4	Title and Content	Reduce Text	• First Edit
			  • Reduce paragraph text to sentences
			• Second Edit
			  • Reduce sentences to phrases
			• Third Edit
			  • Edit phrase text

5	Title and Content	Edit Text	• Make text concise • Use consistent verb tense • Use strong, action verbs • Use few adverbs and adjectives • Use few prepositions

6	Title and Content	Make Text Readable	• Consider font attributes
			  • Font style
			  • Font size
			• Choose a typeface that depicts the content
			• Limit the number of fonts on slide

7	Title and Content	Emphasize Main Points	• Use images and objects that relate to topic • Animate text and charts • Use bullets for items of equal importance • Use numbers for ranking or sequencing

Slide Number	Slide Layout	Slide Title	Slide Content
8	Title and Content	Create Consistency	• Use same fonts, sizes, and attributes • Apply consistent alignment • Use same paragraph spacing • Utilize color scheme
9	Two Content	Create a Mood with Color	*(In the left placeholder)* • Yellow—Optimism, Warmth • White—Peace, Quiet • Green—Growth • Red—Action, Enthusiasm • Blue—Calm, Traditional • Black—Power, Strength • Grey—Neutral
10	Title Slide	The key to success is to make certain your slide show is a visual aid and not a visual distraction.	Dr. Joseph Sommerville Peak Communication Performance

c. Show the slide number on the slides. Apply to all slides except on the title slide. (Note: the slide number will appear at the top of the slides for this theme.)

d. On Slide 9, insert a clip art image in the empty placeholder that illustrates the concept of color. Add other visual objects if you choose, but make sure the objects enhance the message.

e. Review the slide show and adjust font size, image size, and placeholder location until all elements fit attractively and professionally on the slides.

f. Assign the transition of your choice to all slides in the slide show, and then animate at least one individual object of your choice.

g. Save the presentation. Close the file and submit based on your instructor's directions.

2 Wireless Network Safety

You volunteer at the local community center. You have been asked to present to a group of young teens about staying safe when using wireless computer networks. You have researched the topic and using your notes you are ready to prepare your presentation.

a. Open PowerPoint and start a new presentation. Apply the design theme of your choice. Save the presentation as **p01m2Wifi_LastFirst**.

b. Add **WiFi Safety** as a footer on all slides except the title slide. Also include an automatically updated date and time and a slide number. (Note: The placement of Wifi Safety footer text, dates, and slide numbers will vary based on the theme chosen.)

c. Create a *Notes and Handouts* header with your name and a footer with your instructor's name and your class name. Include the current date. Apply to all.

d. On the title slide, add the title **WiFi Safety** in the **title placeholder**. Type **Keeping Your Personal Information Safe** in the **subtitle placeholder**.

e. Insert a new slide using the **Two Content layout**. Type **Wireless Fidelity (WiFi)** as the title.

f. Type the following into the **left content placeholder**:
- **Uses radio waves to exchange data wirelessly via a computer network**
- **Commonly found at coffee shops and other public places**
- **Also called hotspots**

g. Add a clip art photograph to the right content placeholder: Search for **WiFi** in the Office.com clip art box. Insert the photo of your choosing. Move the photo so it is positioned attractively.

h. Insert a new slide using the **Title and Content layout** as the third slide in the presentation. Type **WiFi Hotspot Security** as the title.

i. Type the following into the **content placeholder**:
   - **Avoid unsecured networks if possible**
   - **Don't access confidential information**
   - **Set network locations to "Public"**
   - **Keep firewall and antivirus software up-to-date**

j. Click **Notes** on the status bar. Add the following text to the **Notes pane**:

   Although a number of threats exist when using public WiFi hotspots, there are several ways you can protect yourself and your computer.

k. Insert a new slide using the **Blank layout** as the fourth slide in the presentation.

l. Click the **INSERT tab**, click **Table**, and then draw a table with four rows and four columns. Type the following text in the table.

Threat	Explanation
Identity Theft	Criminal act involving the use of your personal information for financial gain.
Hacking	Unauthorized access to a computer or network.
Malware	Software programs that are designed to be harmful. A virus is a type of malware.

m. Position the table attractively on the page.

n. Apply the **Fade transition** from the Subtle category to all slides in the slide show.

o. Add the **Bounce animation** from the Entrance category to the content placeholder and the image on Slide 2. Set the animations so they bounce at the same time.

p. Move Slide 4 so that it becomes Slide 3.

q. Review the presentation and correct any errors you find.

r. Print the handouts, three per page, framed.

s. Save the presentation. Close the file and submit based on your instructor's directions.

3 Creating a Free Web Site and Blog for Your Powerpoint Experiences

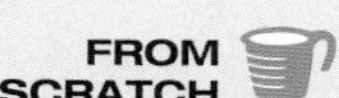

Web 2.0 technologies make it easy for people to interact using the Internet. Web applications often combine functions to help us create our online identity, share information, collaborate on projects, and socialize. In this exercise, you will create an online identity for your use in your PowerPoint class, share information about your PowerPoint experience with others, and get to know a few of your classmates. You will create a Web site for use during your PowerPoint class, add information to the pages in your Web site, and then share the address of your site with others. You will also visit the Web sites of others in your class.

a. Open a Web browser and go to **www.weebly.com**.

b. Enter your full name as the Username in the Sign Up box, enter your e-mail address, and then enter a password.

c. Select the text in the Welcome to Weebly box and enter a title for your Web site as follows: use your first name followed by PPT to indicate this is your PowerPoint site, select the Education category, and then Class Project for your site type.

d. Select **Use a Subdomain of Weebly.com** in the Choose Your Website Domain box to set up the address where people will find your Web site online. Using a subdomain of Weebly.com is free. Click **Continue**. You have created your Web site and you should note your Web site address as you will be sharing this address with your instructor and/or selected classmates.

e. Select the **Elements tab**, if necessary, and drag elements from the top bar to the page to create your site. Add an element that can be used to introduce yourself to others (such as Paragraph with Title or Paragraph with Picture). Also, add a contact form so other students can get in touch with you if they have a comment or question.

f. Click the **Design tab** and select the Design theme of your choice for your site.

g. Click the **Pages tab** and click **Add Blog**. Click in the **Page Name box**, select **Blog Remove!**, type the name you want to use for your blog, and then click **Save Settings**. The left panel of the screen now shows that your Web site has two pages: your home page and your blog site.

h. Edit your blog by adding text that explains your previous experience with PowerPoint and why you have registered for this class. Search YouTube for a video about PowerPoint or presentation skills. Create a second blog entry about what you learned and include the link for others to view if interested.

i. Publish your Web site. Type the security words in the verification box as requested. Click the **X** in the Website Published box to finish.

j. Exchange Web site addresses with at least three other students in your class. Visit your classmates' Web sites and use the contact form on their Home pages to leave your information and a comment. Then, revisit your Web site to see what comments your classmates entered.

k. E-mail your instructor the Web site address you created in step e so your instructor can visit your site.

Beyond the Classroom

Taking Online Courses

RESEARCH CASE

Many colleges and universities are offering online courses as an alternative to face-to-face classroom instruction. Use the Internet to research the pros and cons of taking a class online, explain why some courses may be better suited to this format, and discuss some strategies to succeed in an online course. Create a storyboard on paper or using Microsoft Word. Include a title slide and at least four slides related to this topic. Include a summary reviewing the success strategies. Choose a theme, transitions, and animations. Insert at least one appropriate clip art image. Include slide notes as necessary. Create a handout header with your name, page numbers, and the current date. Include a handout footer with your instructor's name and your class name. Review the presentation to ensure there are no errors by viewing each slide in Slide Show view. Print as directed by your instructor. Save the presentation as **p01b2OnlineSuccess_LastFirst**. Close the file and submit based on your instructor's directions.

Polishing a Business Presentation

DISASTER RECOVERY

A neighbor has created a slide show to present to a local business explaining his company's services. He has asked you to refine the slide show so it has a more professional appearance. Open *p01b3Green* and save the file as **p01b3Green_LastFirst**. View the slide show. Note that the text is difficult to read because of a lack of contrast with the background, there are capitalization errors and spelling errors, the bulleted points are not parallel, and images are positioned and sized poorly. Select and apply a design theme and a colors scheme. Modify text following the guidelines presented throughout this chapter. Reposition placeholders as needed. Size and position the images in the presentation or replace them with your choice of images. Text may be included in speaker notes to emphasize visuals, if desired. Apply a transition to all slides. Add a minimum of two animations. Make other changes you choose. Create a handout header with your name and the current date. Include a handout footer with your instructor's name and your class name. Review the presentation to ensure there are no errors by viewing each slide in Slide Show view. Save your file and then save it again as a PowerPoint show. Close the file and submit based on your instructor's directions.

Preparing for an Interview

SOFT SKILLS

FROM SCRATCH

Research the profession you are most interested in pursuing upon graduation. Create a storyboard on paper or using Microsoft Word outlining job search strategies for the profession. Then, create a PowerPoint presentation based on this outline. Include a title slide and at least four slides related to this topic. Choose a theme, transitions, and animations. Insert at least one appropriate clip art image. Include slide notes on most slides as necessary. Create a handout header with your name and the current date. Include a handout footer with your instructor's name and your class name. Review the presentation to ensure there are no errors by viewing each slide in Slide Show view. Print as directed by your instructor. Save the presentation as **p01b3Search_LastFirst**. Close the file and submit based on your instructor's directions.

Capstone Exercise

Gamerz is a successful retail store. The company sells video games as well as traditional games such as puzzles and board games, and is renowned for hosting game nights and competitions. Gamerz is a place where customers can find gaming resources, supplies, gaming news, and a good challenge. The store has been in operation for six years and has increased its revenue and profit each year. The partners are looking to expand their operation and need to prepare a presentation for an important meeting with financiers.

Create a Title Slide

You add your name to the title slide, apply a theme, and create a slide for the Gamerz mission statement.

a. Open *p01c1Capital* and save it as **p01c1Capital_LastFirst**.

b. Create a *Notes and Handouts* header with your name and a footer with your instructor's name and your class name. Include the current date. Apply to all.

c. On Slide 1, replace *Your name* in the **subtitle placeholder** with your name.

d. Apply the **Retrospect design theme** with the gray background variant.

e. Insert a new slide using the **Title Only layout** after Slide 1. Type the following in the **title placeholder**: **Gamerz provides a friendly setting in which customers can purchase game equipment and resources as well as participate in a variety of challenging gaming activities.**

f. Change the font size to **30 pt** and apply **Italic**.

Create Tables to Display Sales Data

You create tables to show the increase in sales from last year to this year, the sales increase by category, and the sales increase by quarters.

a. On Slide 5, create a table of six columns and three rows. Type the data from Table 1 below in your table.

b. Format the table text font to **20 pt**. Center align the column headings and right align all numbers. Position the table on the slide so it is approximately centered.

c. On Slide 6, create a table of five columns and three rows. Type the data from Table 2 below in your table and apply the same formatting to this table that you applied in step b.

d. Check the spelling in the presentation, and review the presentation for any other errors. Fix anything you think is necessary.

e. View the presentation, and as you navigate through the slides, note that the presentation plan included the mission statement as the introduction slide, included supporting data in the body of the presentation, and included a plan for the future as the conclusion (summary) slide.

Add Clip Art and Animation

Gamerz uses a video game controller in its logo. You use a video game controller on the title slide to continue this identifying image.

a. On Slide 1, open Online Pictures. Use **video game controller** as your search keyword in the Office.com Clip Art search box and locate the image of a video game controller. Size and position the image appropriately.

b. Use the same clip art of a video game controller on the last slide of your slide show. Position the clip in the bottom-right portion of your slide, and increase its size.

c. On Slide 4, select the **Our first year was profitable box** and apply the **Fly In entrance animation**.

d. Select the **Our second year was significantly better box** and apply the **Fly In entrance animation**. Change the Start option to **After Previous**.

TABLE 1

Year	New Video Games	Used Video Games	Board Games	Puzzles	Events
Last Year	$120,200	$90,200	$75,915	$31,590	$25,755
This Year	$128,200	$110,700	$115,856	$38,540	$46,065

TABLE 2

Year	Qtr 1	Qtr 2	Qtr 3	Qtr 4
Last Year	$64,761	$55,710	$34,292	$72,101
This Year	$75,594	$68,497	$69,057	$119,551

Use Presentation View

You proofread the presentation in Slide Show view and check the animations. You print a handout with four slides per page.

a. Start the slide show and navigate through the presentation.

b. Annotate the conclusion slide, *The Next Steps*, by underlining *detailed financial proposal* and circling *two* and *ten* with a red pen.

c. Exit the presentation and keep the annotations.

d. Save and close the file, and submit based on your instructor's directions.

Presentation Development

Planning and Preparing a Presentation

OBJECTIVES AFTER YOU READ THIS CHAPTER, YOU WILL BE ABLE TO:

1. Create a presentation using a template p. 900
2. Modify a presentation based on a template p. 902
3. Create a presentation in Outline view p. 908
4. Modify an outline structure p. 909
5. Print an outline p. 911
6. Import an outline p. 916
7. Reuse slides from an existing presentation p. 916
8. Use sections p. 920
9. Examine slide show design principles p. 921
10. Modify a theme p. 923
11. Modify the slide master p. 924

CASE STUDY | The Wellness Education Center

The Wellness Education Center at your school promotes overall good health to students and employees. The director of the Center has asked you to create two slide shows that she can use to deliver presentations to the campus community.

You create a presentation to inform campus groups about the Center by downloading a template with a wellness theme from Microsoft Office Online. You modify several of the layouts the template provides to customize the template to your needs. To concentrate on the content of the slides, you use the Outline view to enter slide text and edit the presentation outline.

You create a second presentation for the Center using an outline the director created in Microsoft Word. You import the outline, supplement it with slides you reuse from another presentation, and divide the presentation into sections. Using standard slide show design guidelines, polish the presentation by editing the content and the theme.

Templates

One of the hardest things about creating a presentation is getting started. You may have a general idea of what you want to say but not how to organize your thoughts. Or you may know what you want to say but need help designing the look for the slides. PowerPoint's templates enable you to create professional-looking presentations and may even include content to help you decide what to say. In this section, you will learn how to create a presentation using a template that you modify to fit your needs.

Creating a Presentation Using a Template

A ***template*** is a file that includes the formatting elements like a background, a theme with a color scheme and font selections for titles and text boxes, and slide layouts that position content placeholders. Some templates include suggestions for how to modify the template, whereas others include ideas about what you could say to inform your audience about your topic. These suggestions can help you learn to use many of the features in PowerPoint.

PowerPoint offers templates for you to use. You can quickly and easily download additional professional templates in a variety of categories. These templates were created by Microsoft, a Microsoft partner, or a member of the Microsoft community. For example, you can select a suggested search term or type your own search term in the Search box. Then you can filter by category to narrow your search further. For example, you can download a template for a renewable energy presentation created by a Microsoft partner, an active listening presentation created by a Microsoft community member, or a business financial report created by Microsoft. Figure 2.1 shows four PowerPoint templates.

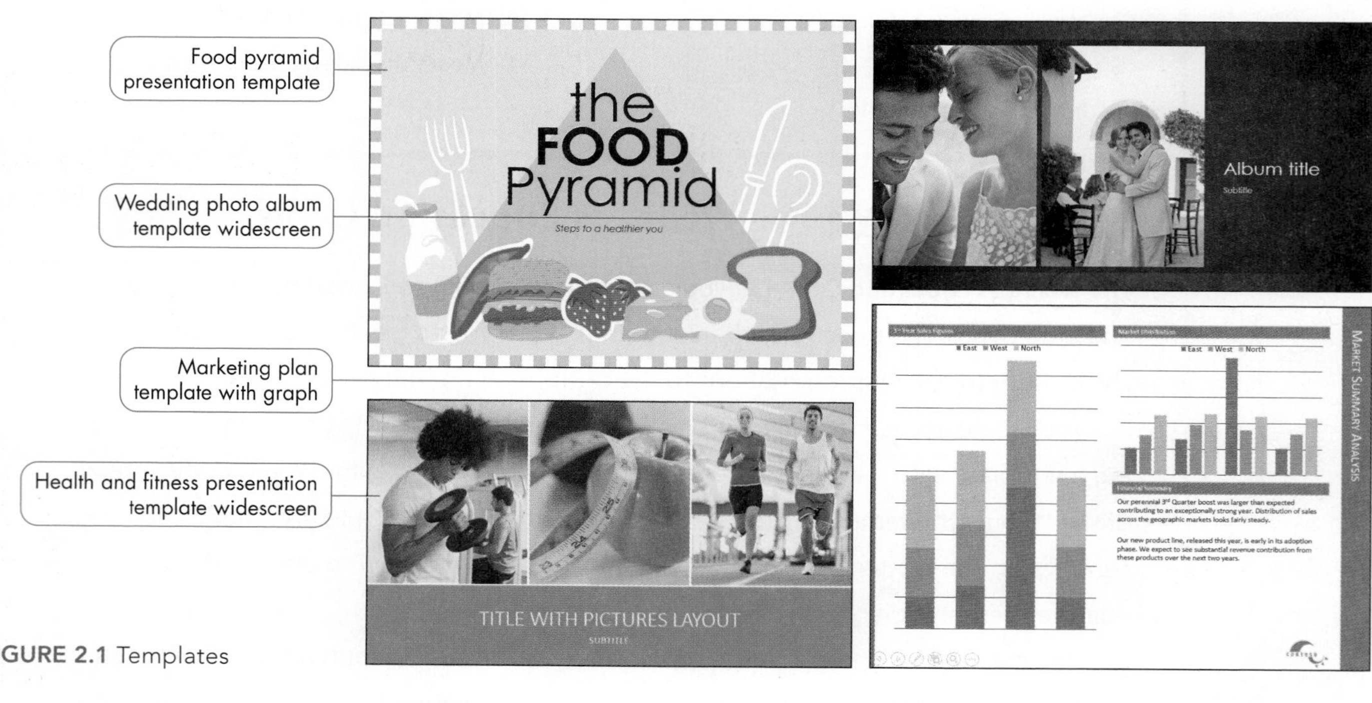

FIGURE 2.1 Templates

TIP Searching for a Template

When you search for a template, you are searching those located on your computer as well as online from Microsoft.com. With Office 2013, templates are no longer installed on your computer with the program but rather are located online. Consequently, your computer must be connected to the Internet to search for Office 2013 templates.

STEP 1

When you create a new presentation, you typically choose a template with a theme and variant that suits your project. To begin a presentation using a template, do the following:

1. Start PowerPoint.
2. Click one of the suggested search terms or click in the search box and type the text for which you would like to search. Press Enter.

   For example, you may wish to search for Marketing templates, and thus you would type *Marketing* as your search term.
3. Click a template or theme to preview it in a new window.
4. Click Create to open the template.

Figure 2.2 displays the Backstage view of *Templates and Themes*. Your view may show different template options, as Microsoft frequently updates the available templates.

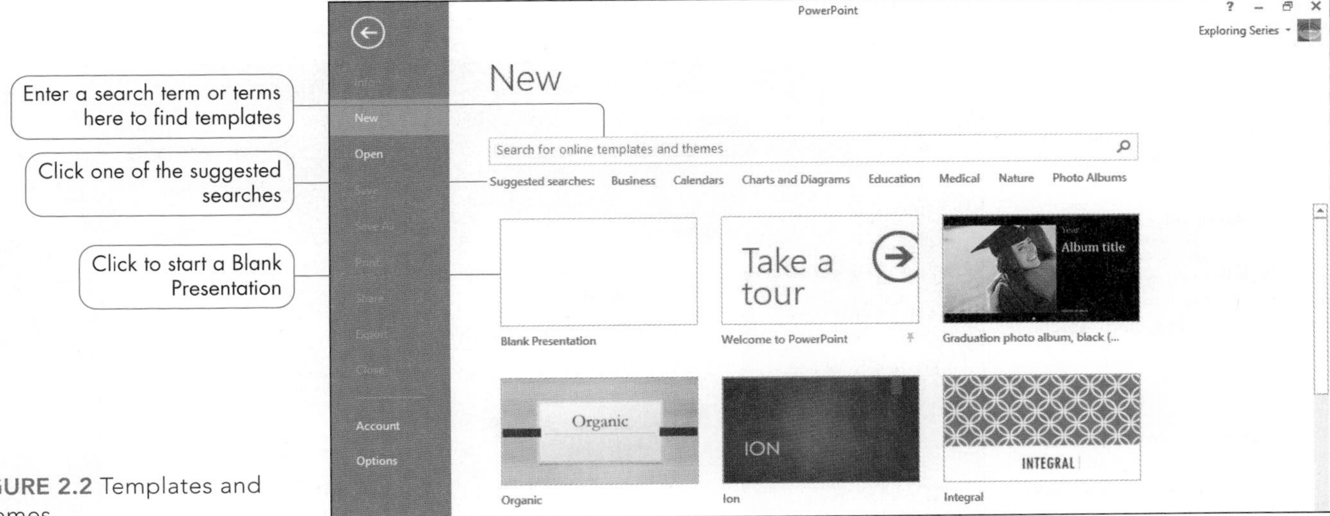

FIGURE 2.2 Templates and Themes

You can filter your results further by using one of the filter categories on the right side of the screen. For example, Figure 2.3 shows a Photo Albums template search further narrowed to presentations with the criteria of Family. Depending on your search criteria, you may also see non–PowerPoint templates in your search results.

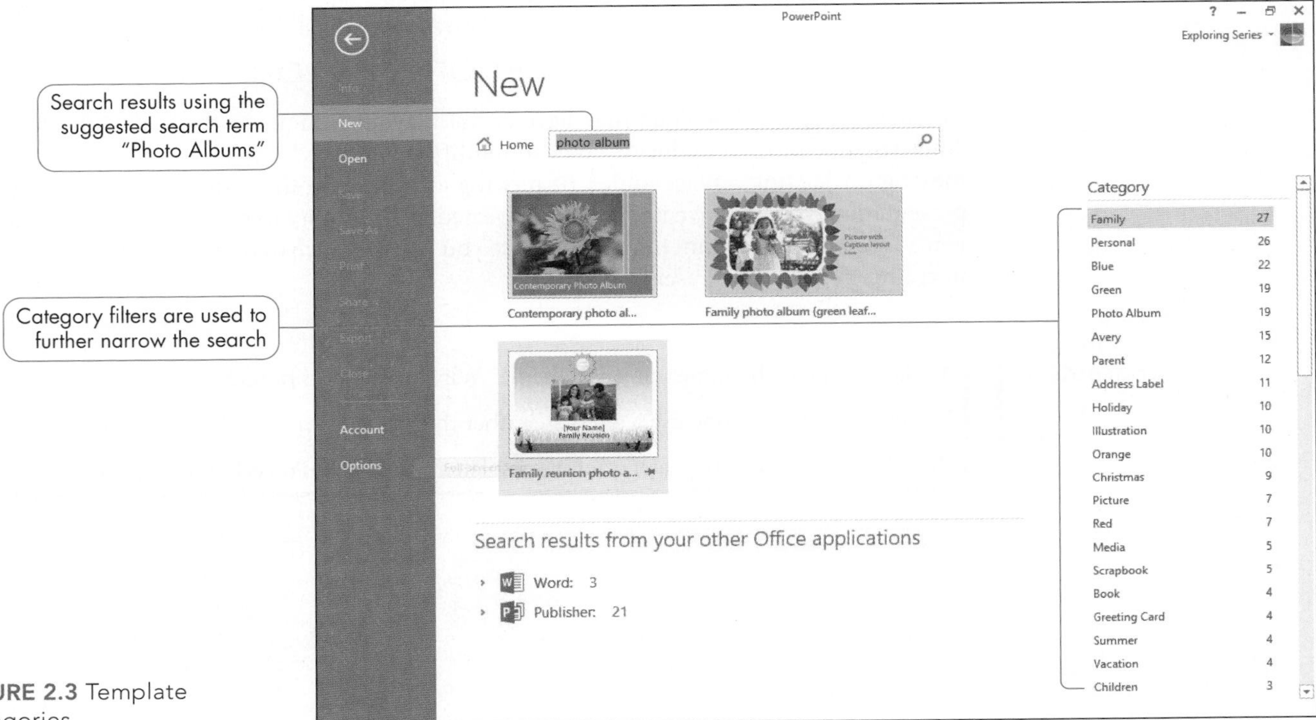

FIGURE 2.3 Template Categories

Searching by Template Dimensions

In the category list, you can search by 4:3 for templates with the typical screen dimensions or 16:9 for widescreen templates. Since most screens and televisions have moved to the widescreen format, you may wish to choose the 16:9 dimension size.

Click once on the template to preview the template. Double-click the template to open the presentation. In Figure 2.4, the Family Photo Album template is selected. The title slide for the template displays in the new screen. You can view the other slides in the template by clicking the More Images arrows. Click Create to select the template or click the left or right red arrows to preview other templates.

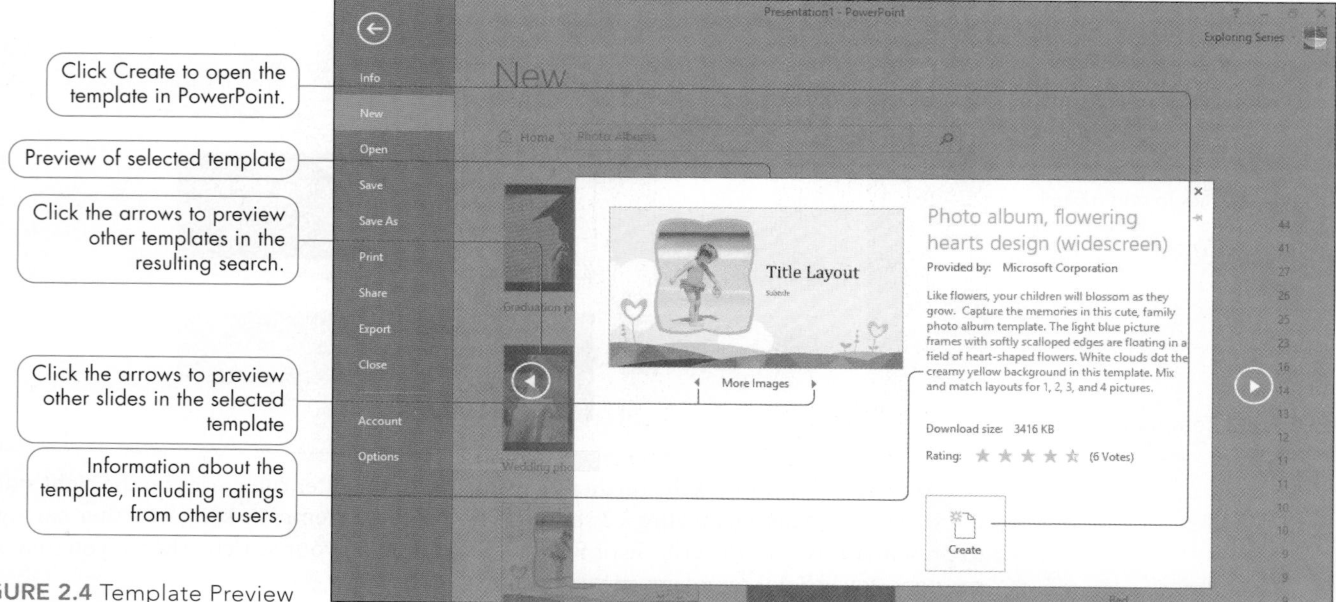

FIGURE 2.4 Template Preview

Modifying a Presentation Based on a Template

STEP 2

The templates you download may have custom layouts unique to that particular template. After you download a template, you can modify it, perhaps by changing a font style or size, moving or deleting a placeholder, or moving an object on the slide. After you modify the presentation, you can save it and use it repeatedly. The ability to save these changes can save you a tremendous amount of time, because you will not have to redo your modifications the next time you use the presentation.

***Quick* Concepts**

1. Is a template the same thing as a theme? Why or why not? ***p. 900***
2. Why might someone use a template rather than start from a blank presentation? ***p. 900***
3. What are some of the categories of templates available in PowerPoint 2013? ***p. 901***

Hands-On Exercises

1 Templates

To promote the Wellness Education Center at your school, you decide to create a presentation that can be shown to campus groups and other organizations to inform them about the Center and its mission.

Skills covered: Create a New Presentation Based on a Template • Modify a Placeholder • Modify a Layout • Add Pictures and Modify a Caption

STEP 1 » CREATE A NEW PRESENTATION BASED ON A TEMPLATE

You begin the Wellness Education Center presentation by looking for a template that is upbeat and that will represent the idea that being healthy makes you feel good. You locate the perfect template (a photo album with warm sunflowers on the cover) from the Photo Albums category. You open a new presentation based on the template and save the presentation. Refer to Figure 2.5 as you complete Step 1.

Step c: Contemporary photo album. Click to open

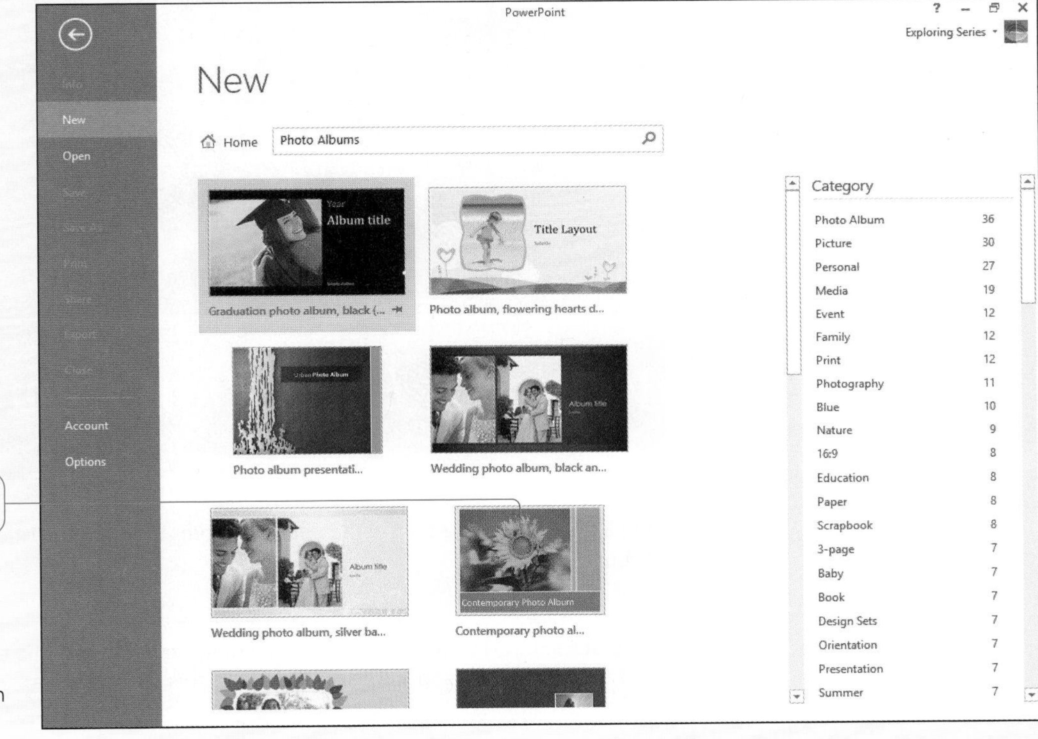

FIGURE 2.5 New Presentation Dialog Box

a. Start PowerPoint.

b. Click the **Photo Albums** category in Suggested searches.

Thumbnails of sample Photo Album templates will display.

c. Click **Contemporary photo album** and click **Create** in the Preview window.

d. View the slide show and read each of the instructions included in the template.

Templates may include instructions for their use or tips on the content that may be added to create a specific presentation. For example, Slide 2 includes instructions to follow for adding your own pages to the album.

e. Click the **INSERT tab** and click **Header & Footer** in the Text group. Click the **Notes and Handouts tab** in the Header and Footer dialog box. Create a handout header with your name and the current date and a handout footer with your instructor's name and your class. Include the current date. The page number feature can remain active. Click **Apply to All**.

f. Save the presentation as **p02h1Center_LastFirst**.

STEP 2 » MODIFY A PLACEHOLDER

The template you selected and downloaded consists of a Title Slide layout you like, but the text in the placeholders needs to be changed to the Wellness Center information. You edit the title slide to include the Center's name and slogan. You also modify the title placeholder to make the Center's name stand out. Refer to Figure 2.6 as you complete Step 2.

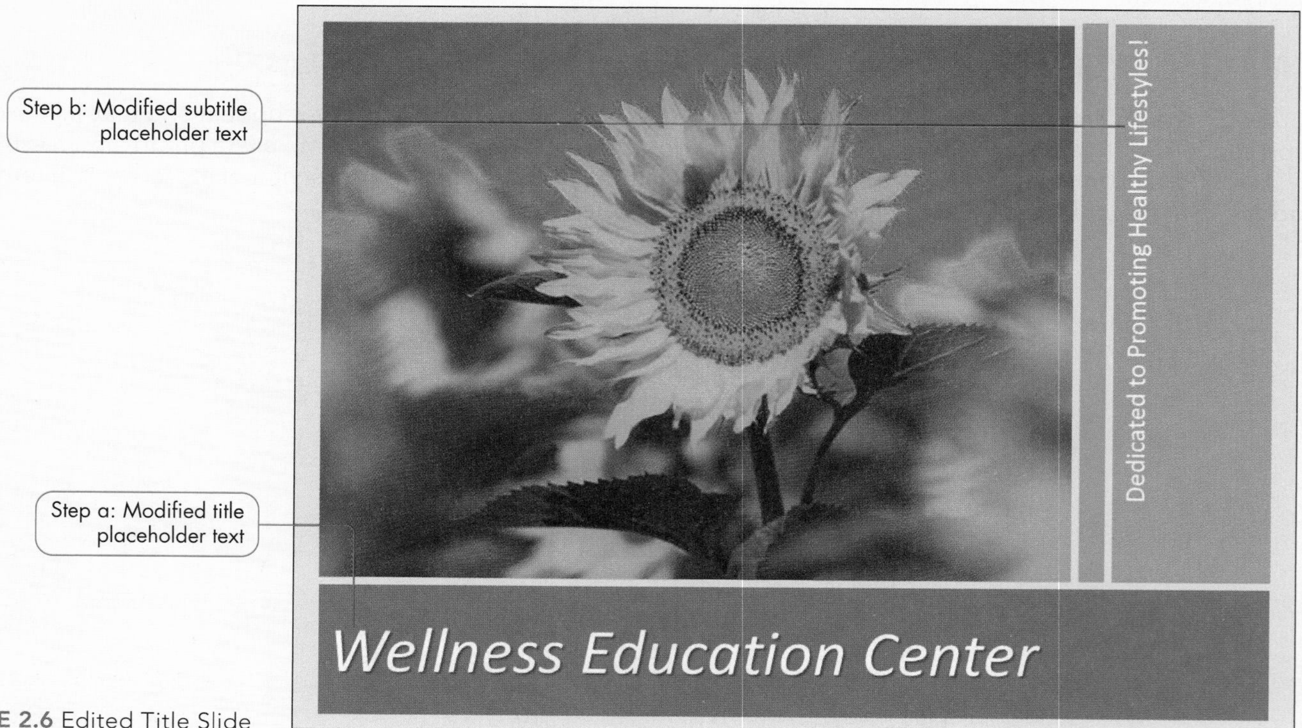

FIGURE 2.6 Edited Title Slide

a. On Slide 1, select the text *Contemporary Photo Album* in the title placeholder and type **Wellness Education Center**.

> **TROUBLESHOOTING:** If you make any major mistakes in this exercise, close the file, open *p02h1Center_LastFirst* again, and then start this exercise over.

b. Click the subtitle text *Click to add date or details* and type **Dedicated to Promoting Healthy Lifestyles!**.

c. Select the title text and click **Italic** and **Text Shadow** in the Font group on the HOME tab.

The template's title placeholder is modified to make the title text stand out.

d. Save the presentation.

STEP 3 » MODIFY A LAYOUT

The Contemporary Photo Album template includes many layouts designed to create an interesting photo album. Although the layout you selected conveys the warm feeling you desire, the layouts need to be modified to fit your needs. You modify a section layout and add a new slide with the layout of your choice. You also delete unnecessary slides. Refer to Figure 2.7 as you complete Step 3.

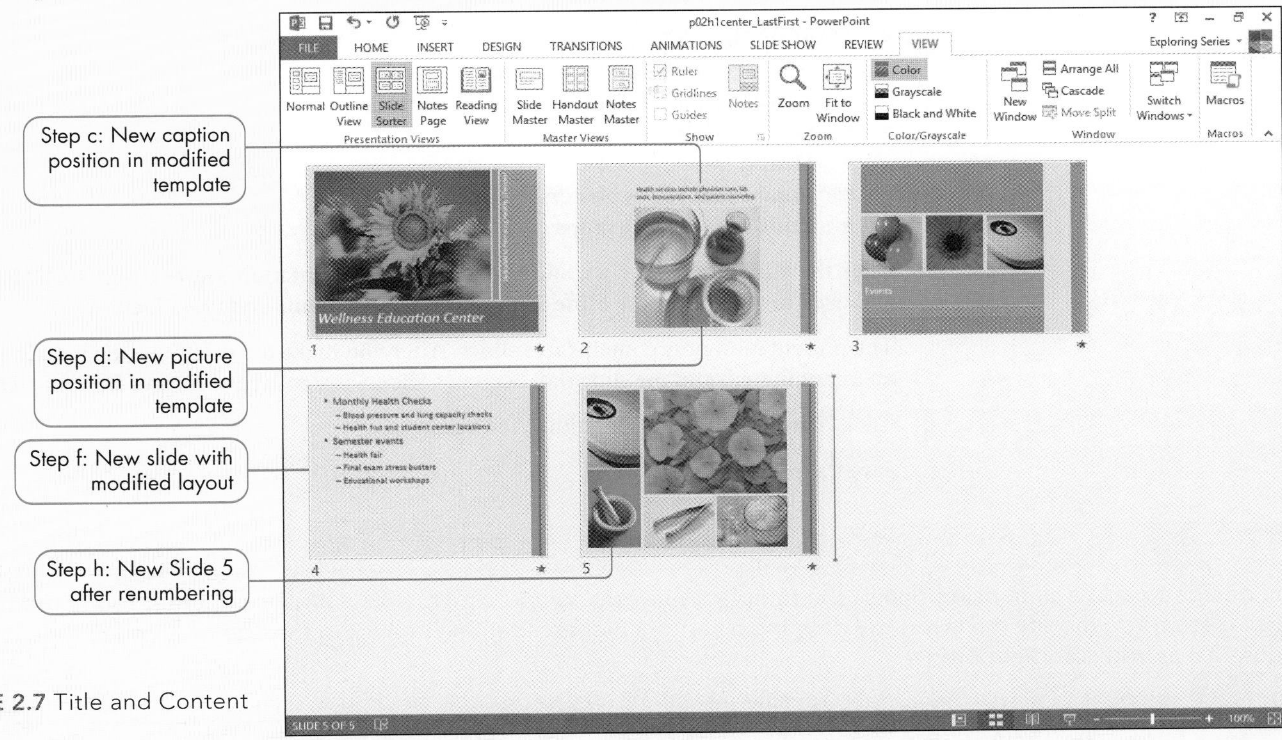

FIGURE 2.7 Title and Content Layout

a. On Slide 2, replace the sample text with **Health services include physician care, lab tests, immunizations, and patient counseling.**

b. Click the **Layout arrow** in the Slides group and click the **Square with Caption layout**.

Note that the Contemporary Photo Album template has many more layouts than the default Office Theme template. The number of layouts provided with a template varies, so always check to see your options.

c. Click the caption and drag the caption to the top of the picture (not above it). As you drag, you will notice red line guides appear to help you as you move the object.

Shift constrains the movement of the caption as you drag so that the new position of the caption is aligned left with its original position.

d. Select the picture and drag the picture below the caption.

The template layout is modified to show the caption above the picture.

e. On Slide 3, select the placeholder text that reads *Choose a layout…*, and then type **Events**. Delete the subtitle text.

When you delete existing text in a new template placeholder, it is replaced with instructional text such as *Click to add subtitle*. It is not necessary to delete this text, as it will not display when the slide show is viewed.

f. Click the **New Slide arrow** and click the **Title and Content layout**.

TROUBLESHOOTING: Clicking the New Slide arrow opens the Layout gallery for you to select a layout. Clicking New Slide directly above the New Slide arrow creates a new slide using the layout of the current slide.

g. Delete the title placeholder in the new slide and drag the content placeholder to the top of the slide. Enter the following information:

- **Monthly Health Checks**
  - **Blood pressure and lung capacity checks**
  - **Health Hut and Student Center locations**
- **Semester Events**
  - **Health fair**
  - **Final exam stress busters**
  - **Educational workshops**

h. Click the **VIEW tab** and click **Slide Sorter** in the Presentation Views group. Hold down **Ctrl** and click to dual select the **Slide 5** and **Slide 6 thumbnails** and press **Delete.**

The presentation now contains five slides. After you make the deletions, the remaining slides are renumbered, and the slide that becomes Slide 5 is a collage of images from the template.

i. Click **Normal** in the Presentation Views group.

j. Save the presentation.

STEP 4 » ADD PICTURES AND MODIFY A CAPTION

You decide to add a slide using one of the template's layouts to add a picture of a Wellness Center room and the nursing staff. You modify the layout by deleting a caption placeholder and changing the size of another. Refer to Figure 2.8 as you complete Step 4.

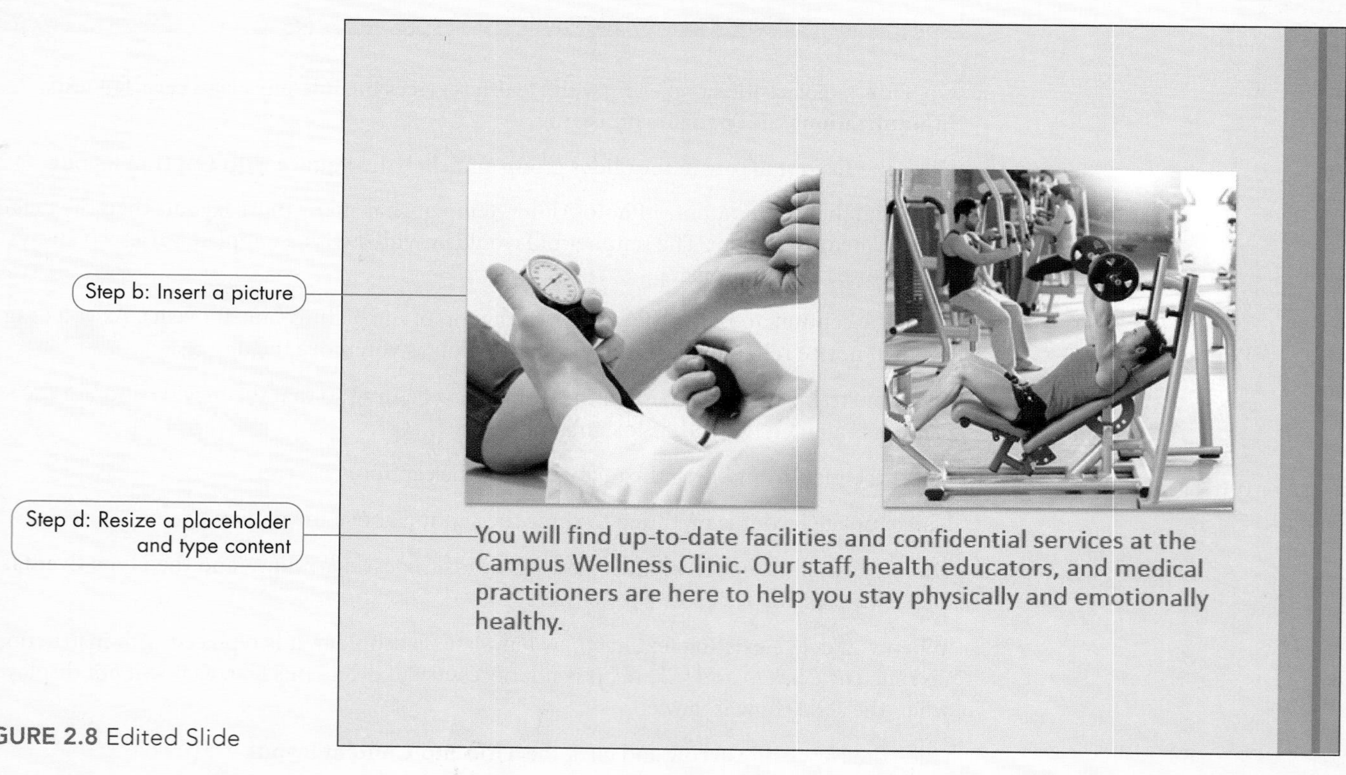

FIGURE 2.8 Edited Slide

a. On Slide 4, click the **New Slide arrow** on the HOME tab and click **2-Up Square with Caption**.

   A new slide is created. The layout includes two picture placeholders and two caption placeholders.

b. Select the **left picture placeholder** and click **Online Pictures** on the INSERT tab. In the **Office.com Clip Art search box**, type **Blood Pressure Check**, press **Enter**, and then insert a picture of your choice.

   The image is added to the placeholder.

c. Select the **right picture placeholder** and click **Online Pictures** on the INSERT tab. In the **Office.com Clip Art search box**, type **Gym**, press **Enter**, and then insert a picture of your choice.

TROUBLESHOOTING: Clicking the icon in the center of the picture placeholder will open the Insert Picture dialog box. If this happens, press Cancel. Select somewhere in the white space around the icon to select the placeholder. Once the placeholder is selected, you will be able to continue with the instructions for adding an Online Picture.

d. Delete the right caption placeholder and select the remaining caption placeholder. Click the **FORMAT tab** located under *DRAWING TOOLS*. In the size group, change the width to 7.7". The caption placeholder will now be the length of both pictures.

e. Type the following in the **caption placeholder**: **You will find up-to-date facilities and confidential services at the Campus Wellness Clinic. Our staff, health educators, and medical practitioners are here to help you stay physically and emotionally healthy.**

f. Spell check and save the presentation. Keep the presentation open if you plan to continue with Hands-On Exercise 2. If not, save and close the presentation and exit PowerPoint.

Outlines

An ***outline*** organizes text using a ***hierarchy*** with main points and subpoints to indicate the levels of importance of the text. When you use a storyboard to determine your content, you create a basic outline. An outline is the fastest way to enter or edit text for a presentation. Think of an outline as the road map you use to create your presentation. Rather than having to enter the text in each placeholder on each slide separately, you can type the text directly into an outline, and it will populate into the slides automatically.

In this section, you will add content to a presentation in Outline view. After creating the presentation, you will modify the outline structure. Finally, you will print the outline.

Creating a Presentation in Outline View

STEP 1» To create an outline for your presentation you must be in ***Outline view***. To change to Outline view:

1. Click the VIEW tab.
2. Click Outline View in the Presentations Views group.

In Outline view, the presentation is displayed as a list of all slides that illustrates the hierarchy of the titles and text in each individual slide. Beside each slide is a slide number, next to which is a slide icon, followed by the slide title if the slide contains a title placeholder. The slide title is bolded. Slide text is indented under the slide title. A slide with only an image (no text) will not have a title in the outline and will display only the slide number and icon.

One benefit of working in Outline view is that you get a good overview of your presentation without the distraction of design elements, and you can move easily from one slide to the next. You can copy text or bullets from one slide to another and rearrange the order of the slides or bullets. Outline view makes it easy to see relationships between points and to determine where information belongs. Figure 2.9 shows a portion of a presentation in Outline view.

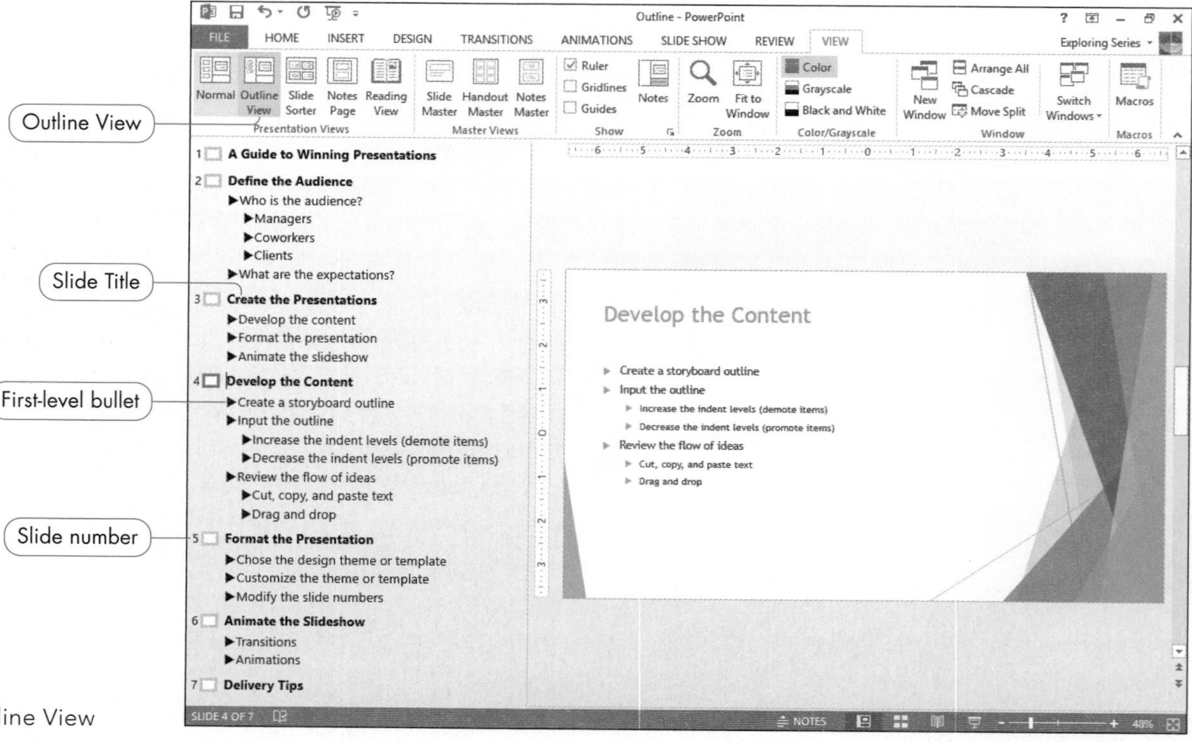

FIGURE 2.9 Outline View

PowerPoint accommodates nine levels of indentation, although you will likely only use two or three per slide. Levels make it possible to show hierarchy or relationships between the information on your slides. The main points appear on Level 1; subsidiary items are indented below the main point to which they apply, and their font size is decreased.

You can promote any item to a higher level or demote it to a lower level, either before or after the text is entered, by clicking Increase List Level or Decrease List Level in the Paragraph group on the Home tab. When designing your slides, consider the number of subsidiary or lower-level items you add to a main point; too many levels within a single slide make the slide difficult to read or understand because the text size becomes smaller with each additional level.

TIP Changing List Levels in an Outline

As a quick alternative to using Increase and Decrease List Level commands on the Home tab, press Tab to demote an item or press Shift+Tab to promote an item.

On Slide 4 in Figure 2.9, the title of the slide, *Develop the Content*, appears immediately after the slide number and icon. The first-level bullet, *Create a storyboard outline*, is indented under the title. The next first-level bullet, *Input the outline*, has two subsidiary, or second-level, bullets. The following bullet, *Review the flow of ideas*, is moved back to Level 1, and it also has two subsidiary bullets.

STEP 2»

Outline view can be an efficient way to create and edit a presentation. To use the Outline view to create a presentation, use the Outline pane located on the left:

1. Press Enter to create a new slide or bullet at the same level.
2. Press Tab to demote or Shift+Tab to promote items as you type to create a hierarchy of information on each slide.
3. Use the Cut, Copy, and Paste commands in the Clipboard group on the HOME tab to move and copy selected text.

Modifying an Outline Structure

Because Outline view shows the overall structure of your presentation, you can use it to move bullets or slides until your outline's organization is refined. You can collapse or expand your view of the outline contents to see slide contents or just slide titles. A ***collapsed outline*** view displays only slide icons and the titles of the slides, whereas the ***expanded outline*** view displays the slide icon, the title, and the content of the slides. You can collapse or expand the content in individual slides or in all slides.

Figure 2.10 displays a collapsed view of the outline displaying only the icon and title of each slide. When a slide is collapsed, a wavy line appears below the slide title, letting you know additional levels exist but are not displayed. The collapsed view makes it easy to move slides. To move a slide, position the pointer over a slide icon until the pointer changes to a four-headed arrow, and then drag the icon to the desired position.

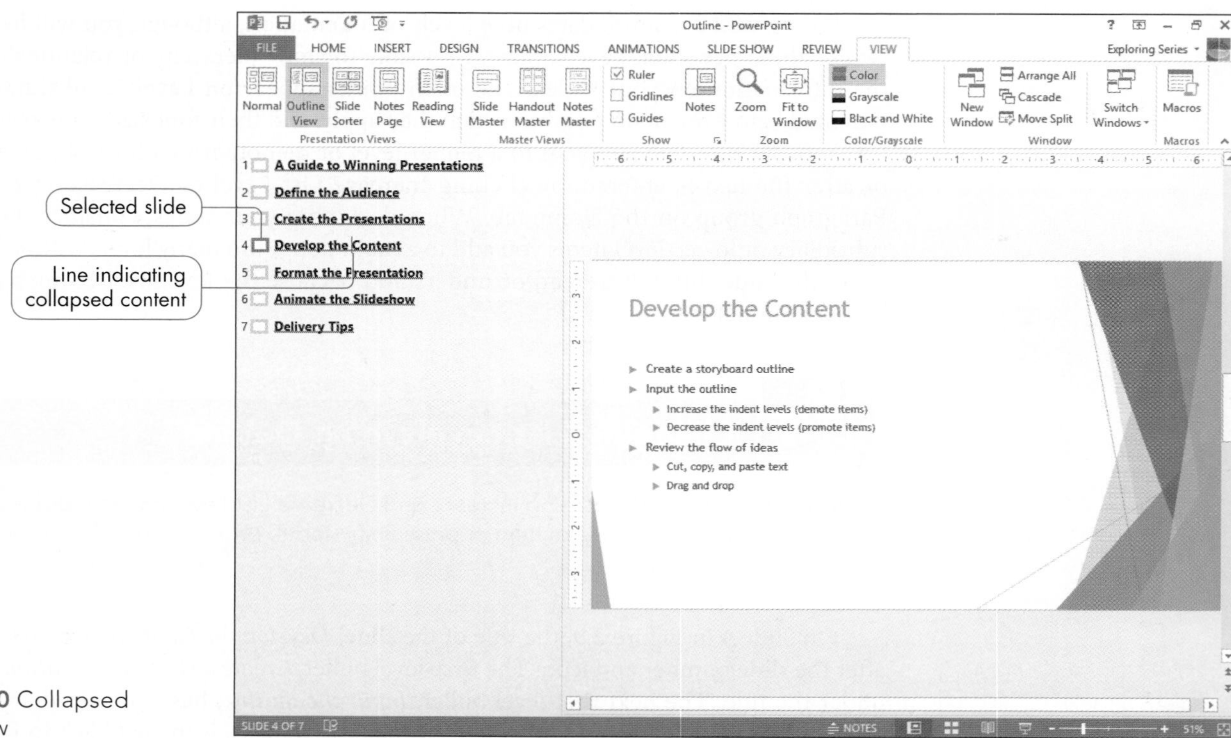

FIGURE 2.10 Collapsed Outline View

STEP 3

To collapse or expand a slide:

1. In the Outline pane, double-click the slide icon. Doing this action expands the slide contents in the pane.
2. Right-click the text following an icon to display a shortcut menu with options for collapsing or expanding the selected slides or all slides.

Figure 2.11 shows the shortcut menu options.

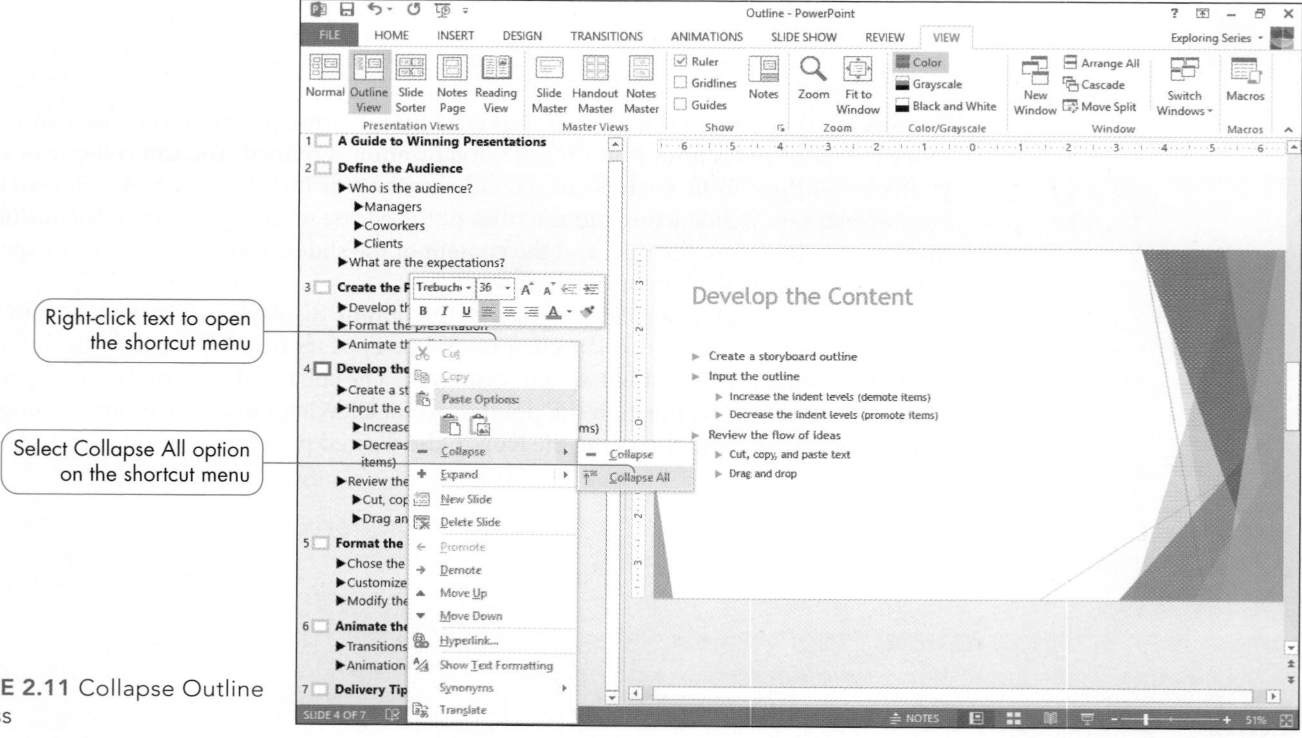

FIGURE 2.11 Collapse Outline Process

Printing an Outline

You can print an outline in either expanded or collapsed view. Figure 2.12 displays a preview of an expanded view of the outline ready to print. The slide icon and slide number will print with the outline. To print the outline, do the following:

1. Click the FILE tab.
2. Click Print.
3. Click Full Page Slides, Notes Pages, or Outline (whichever displays) to open a gallery of printing choices.
4. Click Outline.
5. Click Print.

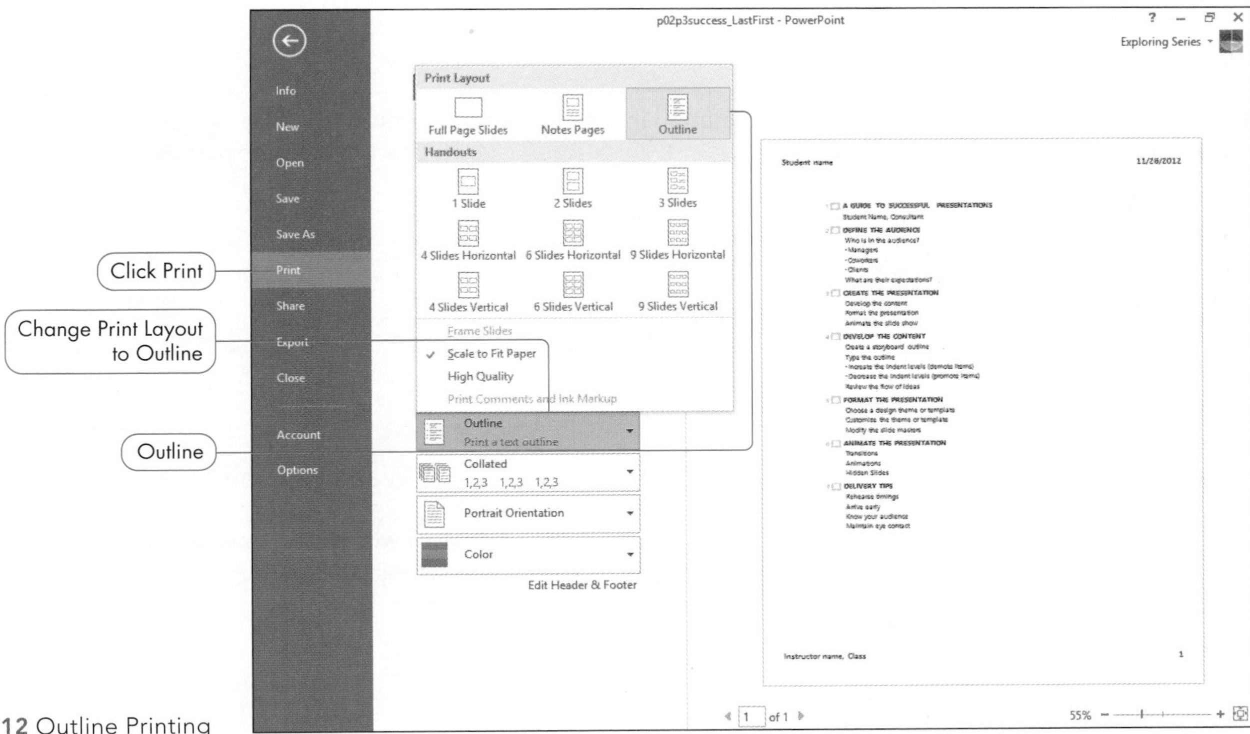

FIGURE 2.12 Outline Printing

Quick Concepts

1. What is a hierarchy? ***p. 908***
2. What are two benefits of creating a presentation in Outline view? ***p. 908***
3. Why would you collapse the view of an outline while in Outline view? ***p. 909***

Hands-On Exercises

2 Outlines

The Wellness Center sponsors a Walking Wellness group to help campus members increase their physical activity and cardiovascular fitness. The director of the Wellness Center believes that joining a group increases a member's level of commitment and provides an incentive for the member to stay active. She asks you to edit the slide show you created in Hands-On Exercise 1 to include information about the walking group.

Skills covered: Use Outline View • Edit the Outline • Modify the Outline Structure and Print

STEP 1 » USE OUTLINE VIEW

Because you want to concentrate on the information in the presentation rather than the design elements, you use Outline view. You add the information about the walking group as requested by the director. Refer to Figure 2.13 as you complete Step 1.

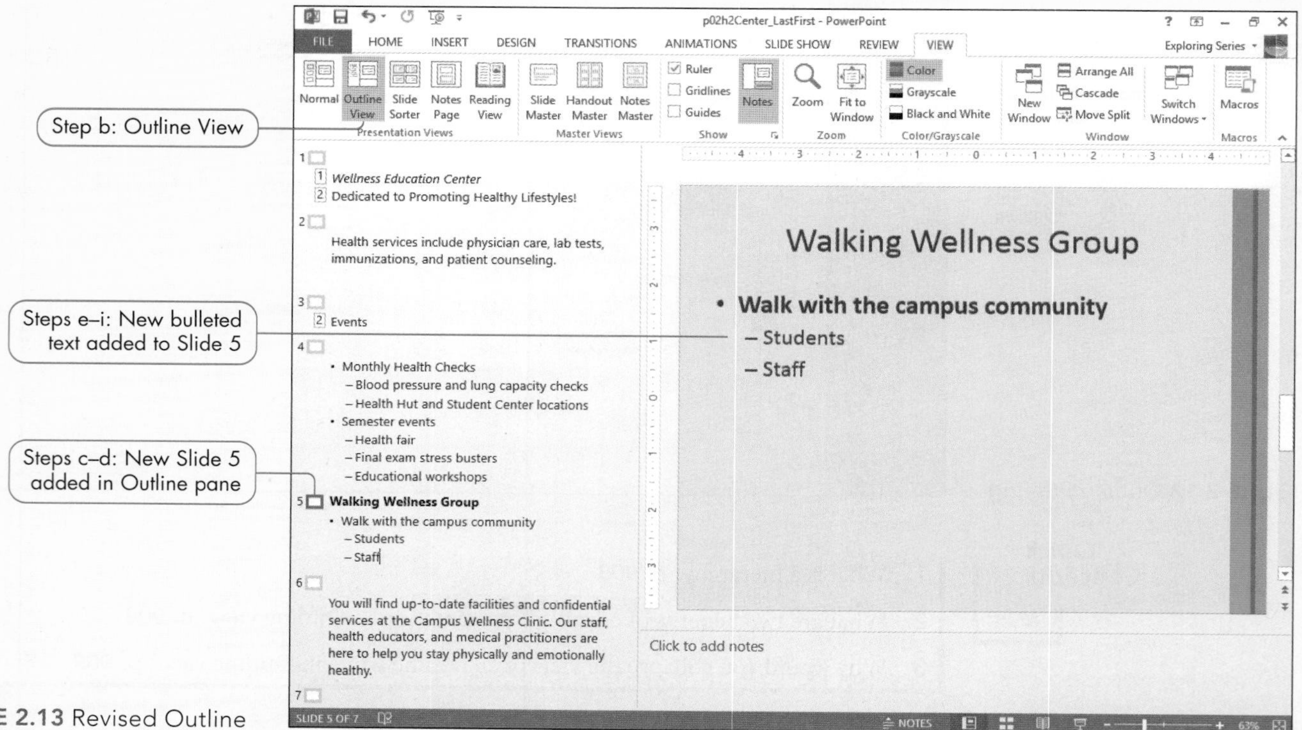

FIGURE 2.13 Revised Outline

a. Open *p02h1Center_LastFirst*, if necessary, and save the presentation as **p02h2Ccenter_LastFirst**, changing *h1* to *h2*.

b. Click the **VIEW tab** and click **Outline View** in the Presentation Views group.

   Note that each slide in the presentation is numbered and has a slide icon. Slides 1 through 5 include text on the slides. Slide 6 contains images only, so no text is displayed in the outline.

c. Click at the end of the last bullet on Slide 4 and press **Enter**.

   The text in the outline is also displayed on the slide in the Slide pane. The insertion point is now positioned to enter text at the same level as the previous bullet point. To create a new slide at a higher level, you must decrease the indent level.

d. Click **Decrease List Level** in the Paragraph group on the HOME tab twice.

   A new Slide 5 is created, the previous Slide 5 is renumbered as Slide 6, Slide 6 is renumbered as Slide 7, etc.

e. Type **Walking Wellness Group** and press **Enter**.

   Pressing Enter moves the insertion point to the next line and creates a new slide, Slide 6.

f. Press **Tab** to demote the text in the outline.

   The insertion point is now positioned to enter bulleted text.

g. Type **Walk with the campus community** and press **Enter**.

h. Press **Tab** to demote the bullet and type **Students**.

   Students becomes Level 3 text.

i. Press **Enter** and type **Staff**.

j. Save the presentation.

STEP 2 » EDIT THE OUTLINE

While proofreading your outline, you discover that you did not identify one of the campus community groups. Finally, you notice that you left out one of the most important slides in your presentation: why someone should walk. You edit the outline and make these changes. Refer to Figure 2.14 as you complete Step 2.

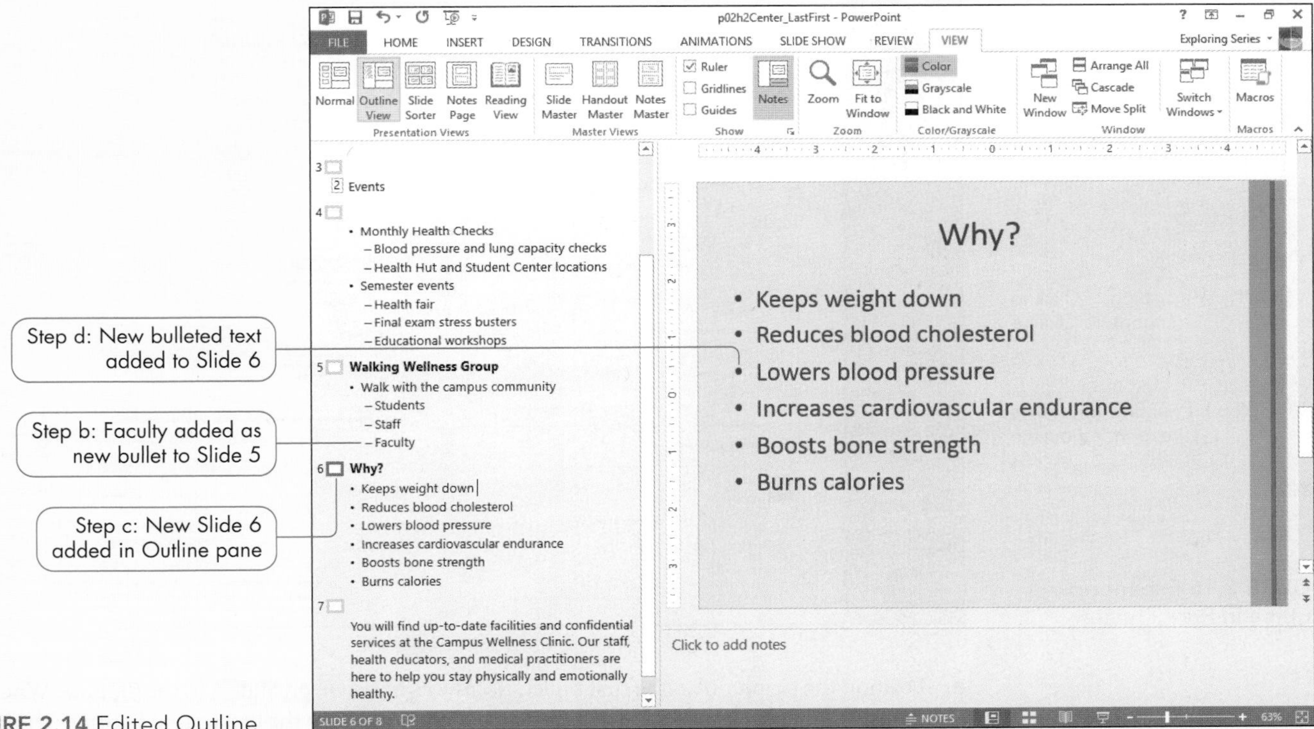

FIGURE 2.14 Edited Outline

a. Click at the end of the word *Staff* on Slide 5 of the outline.

b. Press **Enter** and type **Faculty**.

> **TROUBLESHOOTING:** If your text does not appear in the correct position, check to see if the insertion point was in the wrong location. To enter a blank line for a new bullet, the insertion point must be at the end of an existing bullet point, not at the beginning.

c. Press **Enter** and press **Shift+Tab** twice.

Pressing Shift+Tab promotes the text to create a new Slide 6.

d. Using the Outline pane, type the information for Slide 6 as shown below:

Why?

- **Keeps weight down**
- **Reduces blood cholesterol**
- **Lowers blood pressure**
- **Increases cardiovascular endurance**
- **Boosts bone strength**
- **Burns calories**

e. Save the presentation.

STEP 3 » MODIFY THE OUTLINE STRUCTURE AND PRINT

The director of the Wellness Clinic has reviewed the slide show and made several suggestions about its structure. She feels that keeping weight down belongs at the bottom of the list of reasons for walking and asks you to reposition it. Refer to Figure 2.15 as you complete Step 3.

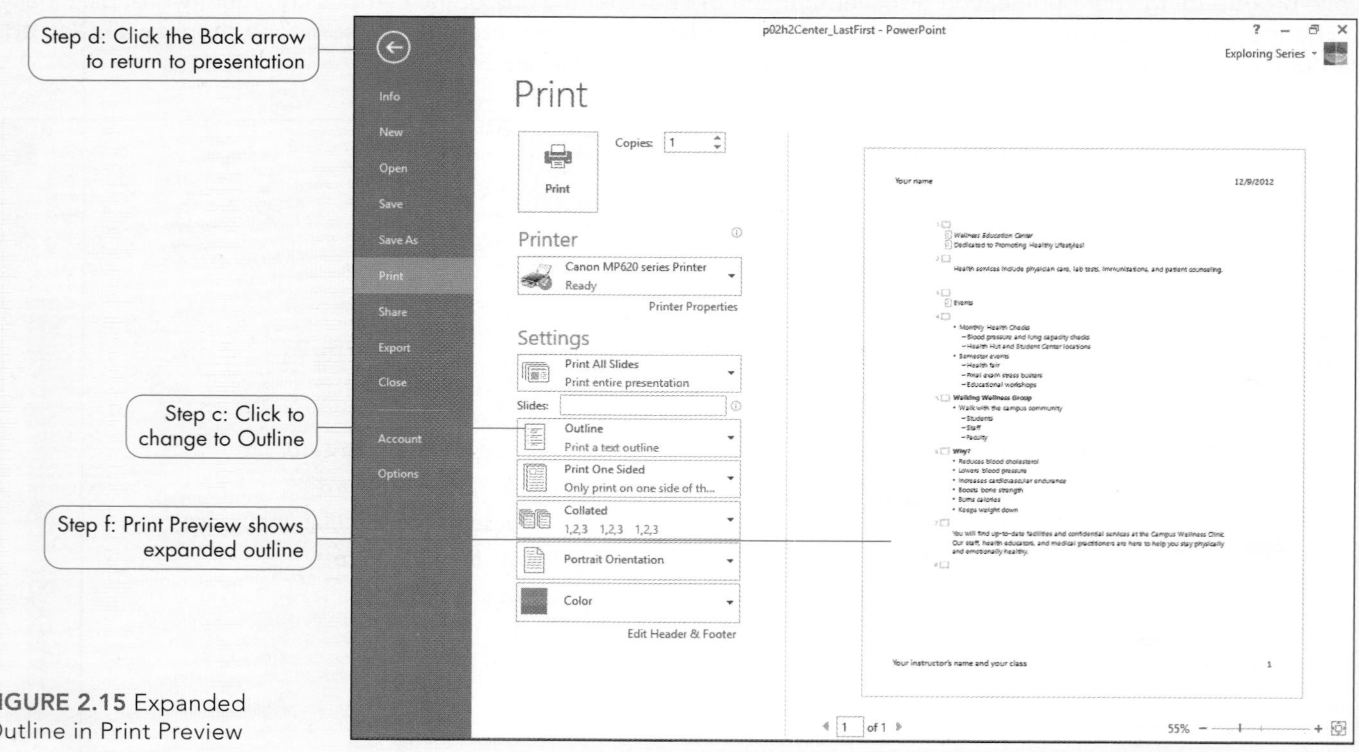

FIGURE 2.15 Expanded Outline in Print Preview

a. Position the pointer over the first bullet, *Keeps weight down*, on Slide 6 in the Outline. When the mouse pointer looks like a four-headed arrow, click and drag the text until it becomes the last bullet on the slide.

b. Right-click the Slide 6 text, point to *Collapse*, and then click **Collapse All**.

Only the slide titles will be shown in the Outline.

c. Click the **FILE tab**, click **Print**, and then click the **Full Page Slides arrow**, if necessary. Click **Outline**.

A preview of the collapsed outline shows in the Preview pane. Because so few slides contain titles, the collapsed outline is not helpful.

d. Click the **back arrow** to return to the presentation.

The Outline pane is once again visible.

e. Right-click any text visible in the Outline pane, point to *Expand*, and then select **Expand All**.

f. Click the **FILE tab** and click **Print**.

The Outline Print Layout is retained from step d and the expanded outline shows in the Preview pane.

g. Click the **back arrow** to return to the presentation.

h. Spell check the presentation. Save and close the presentation and submit based on your instructor's directions.

Data Imports

You can add slides to a presentation in several ways if the content exists in other formats, such as an outline in Word or slides from other presentations. PowerPoint can create slides based on Microsoft Word outlines (.docx or .doc formats) or outlines saved in another word-processing format that PowerPoint recognizes. You can import data into a slide show to add existing slides from a previously created presentation. This is a very efficient way to add content to a slide show.

In this section, you will learn how to import an outline into a PowerPoint presentation and how to add slides from another presentation into the current presentation.

Importing an Outline

Outlines created in Microsoft Word created specifically in an outline format can be imported to quickly create a PowerPoint presentation. To create an outline in Word, you must click the View tab, click Outline, and then enter your text. A list in Word that was not created in the Outline view will not import easily to PowerPoint.

PowerPoint recognizes outlines created and saved in ***rich text format (.rtf)***, a file format you can use to transfer formatted text documents between applications such as word-processing programs and PowerPoint. You can even transfer documents between different platforms such as Macintosh and Windows. The structure and most of the text formatting are retained when you import the outline into PowerPoint.

PowerPoint also recognizes outlines created and saved in a ***plain text format*** (which uses the file extension ***.txt***), a file format that retains text without any formatting. Because .txt outlines have no saved hierarchical structure, each line of the outline becomes a slide. Another alternative is to import a Web document (.htm), but in this case all the text from the file appears in one placeholder on one slide. Avoid saving outlines you create in these formats, but if you receive an outline in a .txt or .htm format, you can create a hierarchy in PowerPoint without having to retype the text.

STEP 1>> To create a new presentation from an outline, do the following:

1. Click the New Slide arrow on the HOME tab.
2. Click *Slides from Outline.*
3. Locate and select your file and click Insert.

TIP Problems Importing a Word Outline

If you import a Word document that appears to be an outline and after importing, each line of the Word document becomes a title for a new slide, the Word document is actually a bulleted list rather than an outline. These two features are separate and distinct in Word and do not import into PowerPoint in the same manner. Open the bulleted list in Word in the Outline View, apply outline formatting, save the file in the RTF format, and then re-import it to PowerPoint.

Reusing Slides from an Existing Presentation

STEP 2>> You can reuse slides from an existing PowerPoint presentation when creating a new presentation. To import existing slides without having to open the other file, do the following:

1. Click the New Slide arrow in the Slides group on the HOME tab.
2. Click Reuse Slides.

3. Click Browse, click Browse File, and then navigate to the folder containing the presentation that has the slides you want to use.
4. Click Open.
5. Click a slide to add it to the presentation or right-click any slide and select Insert All Slides to add all of the slides to the presentation.

By default, when you insert a slide into the presentation, it takes on the formatting of the open presentation. If the new slides do not take on the formatting of the open presentation, select the imported text in Outline view and click Clear all Formatting in the Font group of the Home tab. It will format the slides using the active theme. If you wish to retain the formatting of the original presentation, click the *Keep source formatting* check box at the bottom of the Reuse Slides pane, shown in Figure 2.16.

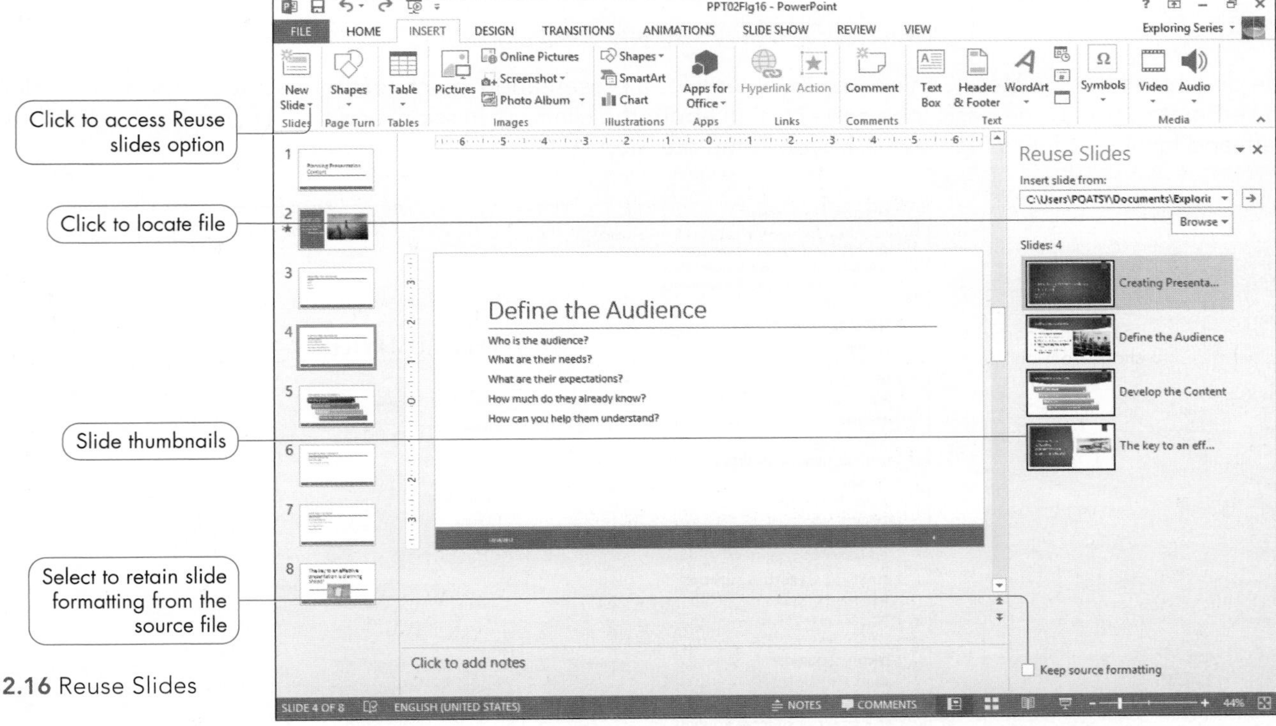

FIGURE 2.16 Reuse Slides Pane

Quick Concepts

1. What are the two types of text formats for outlines that PowerPoint recognizes? ***p. 916***
2. Do you need to have another presentation open to reuse its content in your current presentation? ***p. 916***
3. When you insert a slide into a presentation, what formatting does it use—the formatting from the open presentation or its original formatting? ***p. 917***

Hands-On Exercises

MyITLab®
HOE3 Training

3 Data Imports

The director of the Wellness Clinic is impressed with the clinic overview presentation you created. She gives you an electronic copy of an outline she created in a word-processing software package and asks if you can convert it into a slide show. You create a slide show from the outline and then supplement it with content from another slide show.

Skills covered: Import a Rich Text Format Outline • Reuse Slides from Another Presentation

STEP 1 »» IMPORT A RICH TEXT FORMAT OUTLINE

The director of the Wellness Clinic saves an outline for a presentation in rich text format. You import the outline into PowerPoint to use as the basis for a presentation about the clinic, its mission, and the services it provides to students, staff, and faculty. Refer to Figure 2.17 as you complete Step 1.

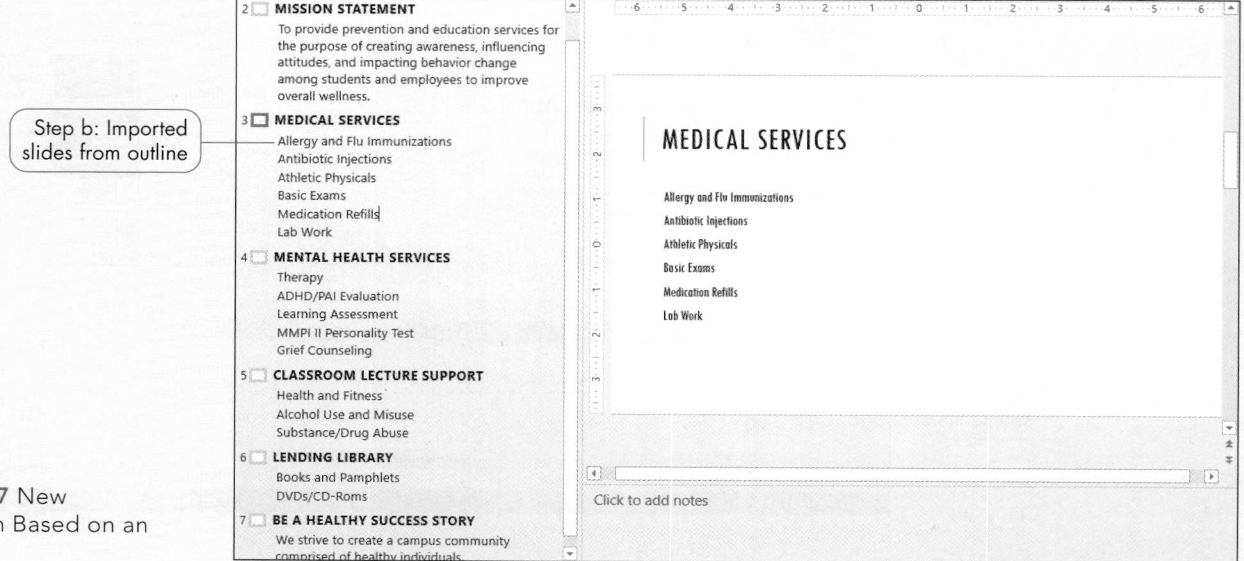

FIGURE 2.17 New Presentation Based on an Outline

a. Click the **FILE tab**, click **New**, and then double-click **Blank Presentation**.

A new blank presentation opens.

b. Click the **New Slide arrow**, click **Slides from Outline**, and then navigate to the location of your Chapter 2 student data files.

c. Browse and open file *p02h3MedOutline.*

The outline is opened and new slides are added to the presentation.

d. Click the **VIEW tab** and click **Outline View** in the Presentation Views group.

The outline retains its hierarchy. Each slide has a title and bulleted text.

e. Create a handout header with your name and a handout footer with your instructor's name and your class. Include the current date.

f. Apply the **Integral theme** to all slides.

The Integral theme adds a subtle blue line next to the title.

g. Save the presentation as **p02h3Mission_LastFirst**.

STEP 2 ⟫ REUSE SLIDES FROM ANOTHER PRESENTATION

While reviewing the Wellness Center presentation, you realize you do not have a title slide or a final slide inviting students to contact the Center. You reuse slides from another presentation created for the Center containing slides that would fit well in this presentation. Refer to Figure 2.18 as you complete Step 2.

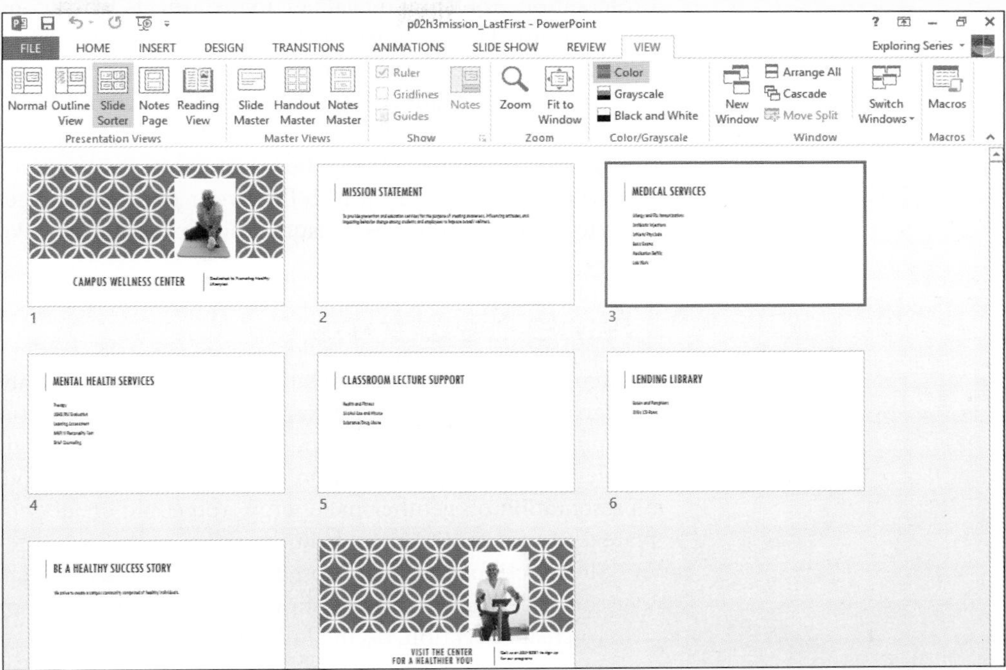

FIGURE 2.18 Reused Slides Added to Presentation

a. On Slide 1, click the **New Slide arrow** in the Slides group on the HOME tab. Click **Reuse Slides** at the bottom of the New Slides gallery.

b. Click **Browse**, click **Browse File**, and then locate your student data files. Select *p02h3Wellness.pptx*, and then click **Open**.

> **TROUBLESHOOTING:** If you do not see the *p02h3Wellness* file, click *Files of type* and select All PowerPoint Presentations.

c. Click the **Keep source formatting check box** at the bottom of the Reuse Slides pane.

   With Keep source formatting selected, the images and design of the slides you reuse will transfer with the slide.

d. Click the first slide (*Campus Wellness…*) in the Reuse Slides pane.

   The slide is added to your presentation after the current slide, Slide 1.

e. Delete the blank title slide that is currently Slide 1.

   The newly reused slide needs to be in the Slide 1 position to serve as the title slide of your presentation.

f. Click the **Slide 7 icon** (*BE A HEALTHY SUCCESS STORY*) in the original presentation.

g. Click **Slide 7** in the Reuse Slides pane and close the Reuse Slides pane.

h. Keep the presentation open if you plan to continue with the next Hands-On Exercise. If not, save and close the presentation and exit PowerPoint.

Design

When working with the content of a presentation, it can be helpful to work with the blank Office Theme. Working in the blank template lets you concentrate on what you want to say. After you are satisfied with the content, then you can consider the visual aspects of the presentation. You should evaluate many aspects when considering the visual design of your presentation. Those aspects include layout, background, typography, color, and animation, as well as dividing the content into sections.

Because the majority of people using PowerPoint are not graphic artists and do not have a strong design background, Microsoft designers created a variety of methods to help users deal with design issues. Using these features, you can create a slide show using a professional design and then modify it to reflect your own preferences. Before doing so, however, you need to consider some basic visual design principles for PowerPoint.

Using Sections

Content organization is an effective design element. Content divided into ***sections*** can help you group slides meaningfully. When you create a section, it is given the name *Untitled Section*. You will want to change the section name to give it a meaningful name, which enables you to jump to a section quickly. For example, you may be creating a slide show for a presentation on geothermal energy. You could create sections for Earth, plate boundaries, plate tectonics, and thermal features.

Slide sections can be collapsed or expanded. Use either Normal view or Slide Sorter view to create sections. Figure 2.19 shows a section added to a presentation in Normal view.

STEP 1» To create a section, do the following:

1. Select the first slide of the new section.
2. Click Section in the Slides group on the HOME tab.
3. Click Add Section.
4. Right-click Untitled Section and select Rename Section.
5. Type a new name for the section.

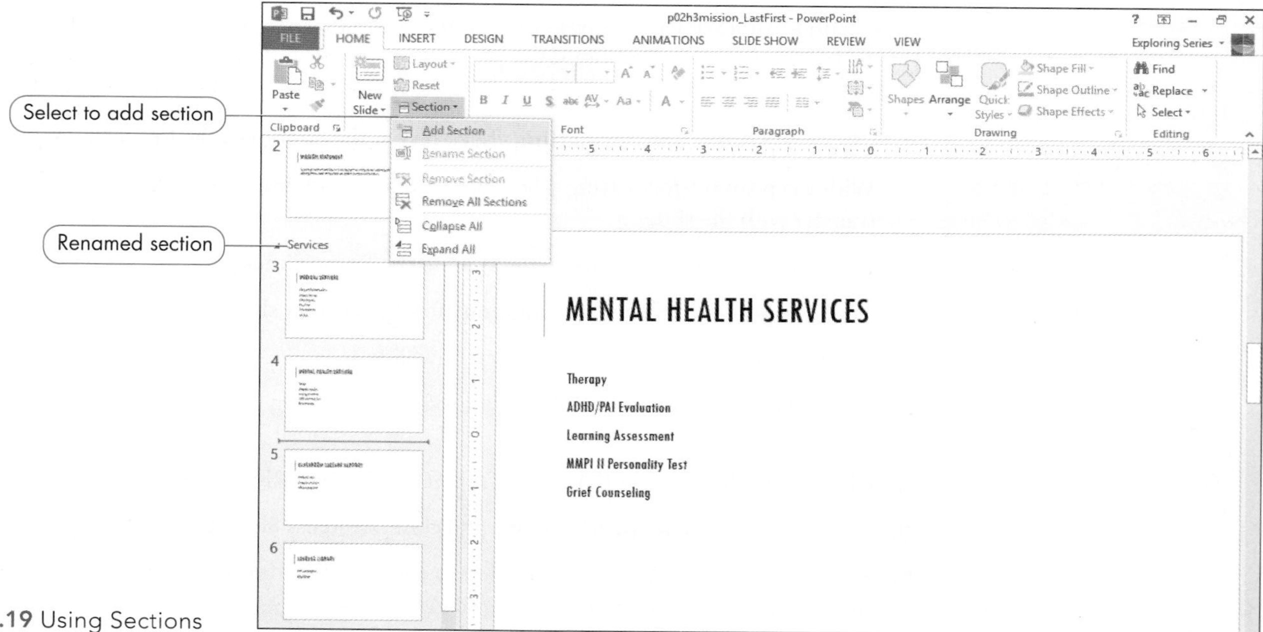

FIGURE 2.19 Using Sections

Examining Slide Show Design Principles

STEP 2» When applied to a project, universally accepted design principles can increase its appeal and professionalism. Some design aspects may be applied in specific ways to the various types of modern communications: communicating through print media such as flyers or brochures, through audio media such as narrations or music, or through a visual medium such as a slide show. The following reference table focuses on principles that apply to slide shows and examines examples of slides that illustrate these principles.

REFERENCE Slide Show Design Principles

Example	Design Tip
 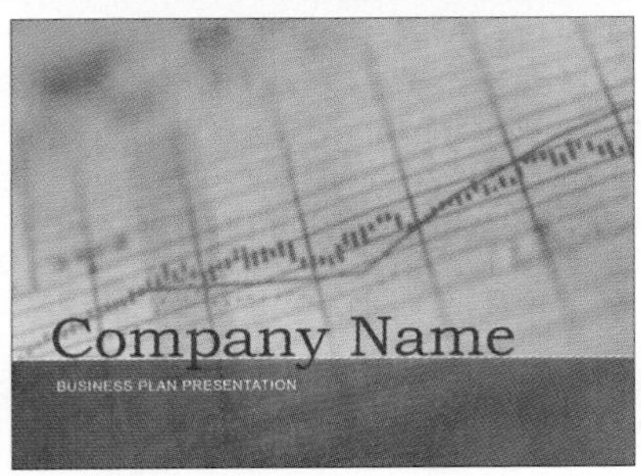 **FIGURE 2.20** Examples of Templates Appropriate for Different Audiences	• **Choose design elements appropriate for the audience.** Consider the audience's background. A presentation to elementary students might use bright, primary colors and cartoon-like clip art. Fonts should be large and easy to read. For an adult audience, choose muted earth tones and use photographs rather than cartoon-like clip art to give the slide show a more professional appearance. Figure 2.20 shows design examples suitable for grade school and business audiences, respectively.
  **FIGURE 2.21** Examples of a Cluttered Design (top) and a Clean Design (bottom)	• **Keep the design neat and clean.** This principle is often referred to as KISS: Keep it sweet and simple! Figure 2.21 shows an example of a cluttered and a clean design. Avoid using multiple fonts and font colors on a slide. Do not use more than three fonts on a slide. Avoid using multiple clip art images. Use white space (empty space) to open up your design.

Example	Design Tip
Delivery Tips • Rehearse timings • Arrive early • Maintain eye contact • Know your audience  **FIGURE 2.22** Examples of an Effective Focal Point (top) and an Ineffective Focal Point (bottom)	• **Create a focal point that leads the viewer's eyes to the critical information on the slide.** The focal point should be the main area of interest. Pictures should always lead the viewer's eyes to the focal point, not away from it. Images should not be so large that they detract from the focal point, unless your goal is to make the image the focal point. Figure 2.22 illustrates examples of ineffective and effective focal points.
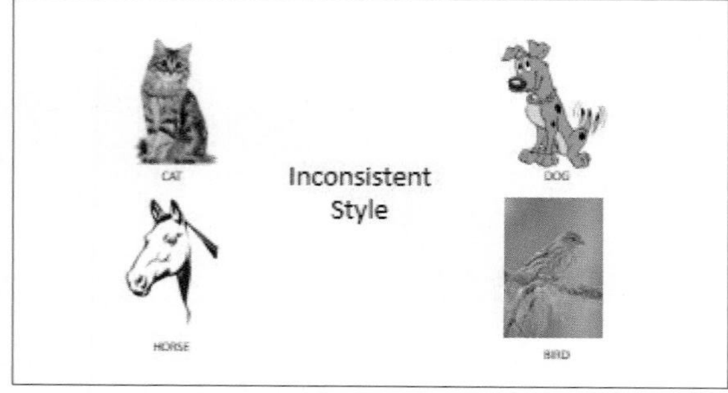 Consistent Style **FIGURE 2.23** Examples of Disjointed (top) and Unified (bottom) Design Elements	• **Use unified design elements for a professional look.** Visual unity creates a harmony between the elements of the slide and between the slides in the slide show. Unity gives the viewer a sense of order and peace. Create unity by repeating colors and shapes. Use clip art in only one style. Figure 2.23 shows a disjointed and a unified design.
 **FIGURE 2.24** Sans Serif (left) and Serif (right) Fonts	• **Choose fonts appropriate for the output of your presentation.** If a presentation is to be delivered through a projection device, consider using sans serif fonts with short text blocks. If your presentation will be delivered as a printout, consider using serif fonts. Serif fonts help guide the reader's eyes across the page. You may use longer text blocks in printed presentations. Figure 2.24 displays an example of a sans serif font—a font that does not have serifs, or small lines, at the ends of letters. It also shows an example of a serif font with the serifs on the letter *S* circled. Decorative fonts are also available but should be used sparingly. When choosing a font, remember that readability is critical in a presentation.

REFERENCE Continued

Example	Design Tip
Text Guidelines • Do not underline text. • DO NOT USE ALL CAPS. • Use **bold** and *italics* sparingly. • Avoid text that leaves one word on a line on its own. • Avoid using multiple spaces after punctuation. Space once after punctuation in a text block. Spacing more can create rivers of white. The white "river" can be very distracting. The white space draws the eye from the message. It can throb when projected. **FIGURE 2.25** Appropriate and Inappropriate Text Examples	• **Do not underline text.** Underlined text is harder to read, and it is generally assumed that underlined text is a hyperlink. • **Avoid using all capital letters.** In addition to being difficult to read, words or phrases in all caps are considered to be "yelling" at the audience. • **Use italics and bold sparingly.** Too much emphasis through the use of italics and bold is confusing and makes it difficult to determine what is important. • **Avoid creating lines of text that leave a single word hanging on a line of its own.** Modify the placeholder size so that more than one word is on a subsequent line. • **Use just one space after punctuation in text blocks.** Using more than one space can create distracting white space in the text block. Figure 2.25 illustrates these principles.
Title Text ▸ Title text should be in title case and 36pt or more ▸ Bulleted text should be in sentence case and 28pt or more **FIGURE 2.26** Readable Text Guidelines	• **Make text readable.** Title text should use title case and be 36 pt or higher. Bulleted text should be in sentence case and be 28 pt or higher. Figure 2.26 illustrates readable text.

Remember that these design principles are guidelines. You may choose to avoid applying one or more of the principles, but you should be aware of the principles and carefully consider why you are not following them. If you are in doubt about your design, ask a classmate or colleague to review the design and make suggestions. Fresh eyes can see things you might miss.

Modifying a Theme

STEP 3» Themes can be modified once they have been applied. You can change the variants, colors, fonts, and effects used in the theme. You can even change the background styles. Each of these options is on the Design tab, and each has its own gallery. Figure 2.27 shows the locations for accessing the galleries.

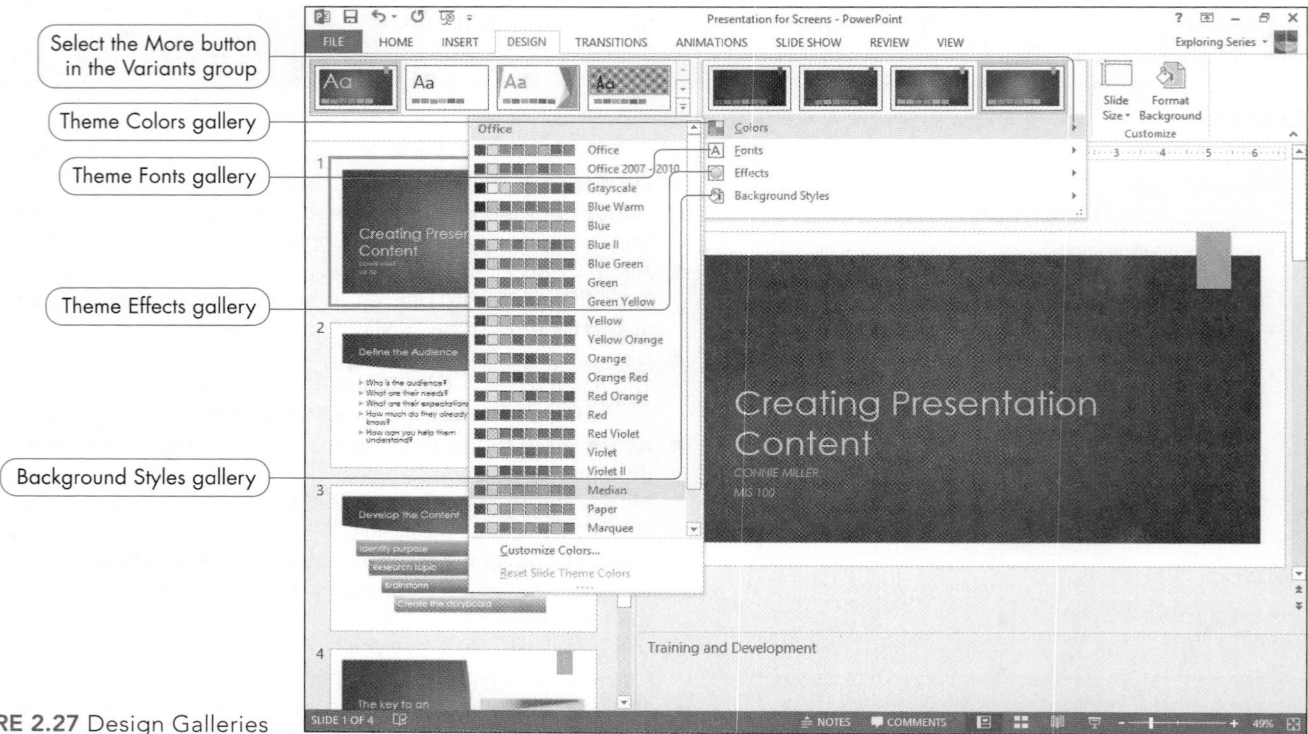

FIGURE 2.27 Design Galleries

Each PowerPoint theme includes a ***Colors gallery***, a gallery that provides a set of colors with each color assigned to a different element in the theme design. Once the theme is selected, you can click Colors to display the built-in gallery. Click one of the Theme Colors to apply it. You can even create your own color theme set by clicking Customize Colors at the bottom of the gallery.

Selecting a font for the title and another for the bullets or body text of your presentation can be difficult. Without a background in typography, determining which fonts go together well is difficult. The ***Fonts gallery*** is a gallery that pairs a title font and a body font. Click any of the samples in the Fonts gallery, and the font pair is applied to your theme.

The ***Effects gallery*** displays a full range of special effects that can be applied to all shapes in the presentation. Using effects aids you in maintaining a consistency to the appearance of your presentation. The gallery includes effects such as a soft glow, soft edges, shadows, or three-dimensional (3-D) look.

You can change the background style of the theme by accessing the ***Background Styles gallery***, a gallery containing backgrounds consistent with the selected Theme Colors. Simply changing your background style can liven up a presentation and give it your individual style.

Some of the themes include background shapes to create the design. If the background designs interfere with other objects on the slide, such as tables, images, or charts, you can select Hide Background Graphics by clicking Format Background, and the background shapes will not display for that slide.

To access these galleries, do the following:

1. Click the DESIGN tab.
2. In the Variants group, click More and choose the gallery you wish to change (Colors, Fonts, Effects, or Background Styles).

Modifying the Slide Master

STEP 4» You can further modify and customize your presentation through the slide master. ***Masters*** control the layouts, background designs, and color combinations for handouts, notes pages, and slides, giving the presentation a consistent appearance. By changing the masters, you make selections that affect the entire slide show and the supporting materials. This is more efficient than changing each slide in the presentation. The design elements you already know about, such as themes and layouts, can be applied to each type of master. Masters control the consistency of your presentations, notes, and handouts. Slide masters can be reused in other presentations. In this section, you learn how to modify the slide masters. Specifically, you will learn how to customize the slide master and slide layouts controlled by the slide master.

Each of the layouts available to you when you choose a design theme has consistent elements that are set by a ***slide master*** containing design information. The slide master is the top slide in a hierarchy of slides based on the master. As you modify the slide master, elements in the slide layouts related to it are also modified to maintain consistency. A slide master includes associated slide layouts such as a title slide layout, various content slide layouts, and a blank slide layout. The associated slide layouts designate the location of placeholders and other objects on slides as well as formatting information.

To modify a slide master or slide layout based on a slide master, do the following:

1. Click the VIEW tab.
2. Click Slide Master in the Master Views group.
3. Click the slide master at the top of the list or click one of the associated layouts.
4. Make modifications.
5. Click Close Master View in the Close group on the SLIDE MASTER tab.

In Slide Master view, the slide master is the larger, top slide thumbnail shown in the left pane. The Title Slide Layout is the second slide in the pane. The number of slides following it varies depending upon the template. Figure 2.28 shows the Organic Theme Slide Master and its related slide layouts. The ScreenTip for the slide master indicates it is used by one slide because the slide show is a new slide show composed of a single title slide.

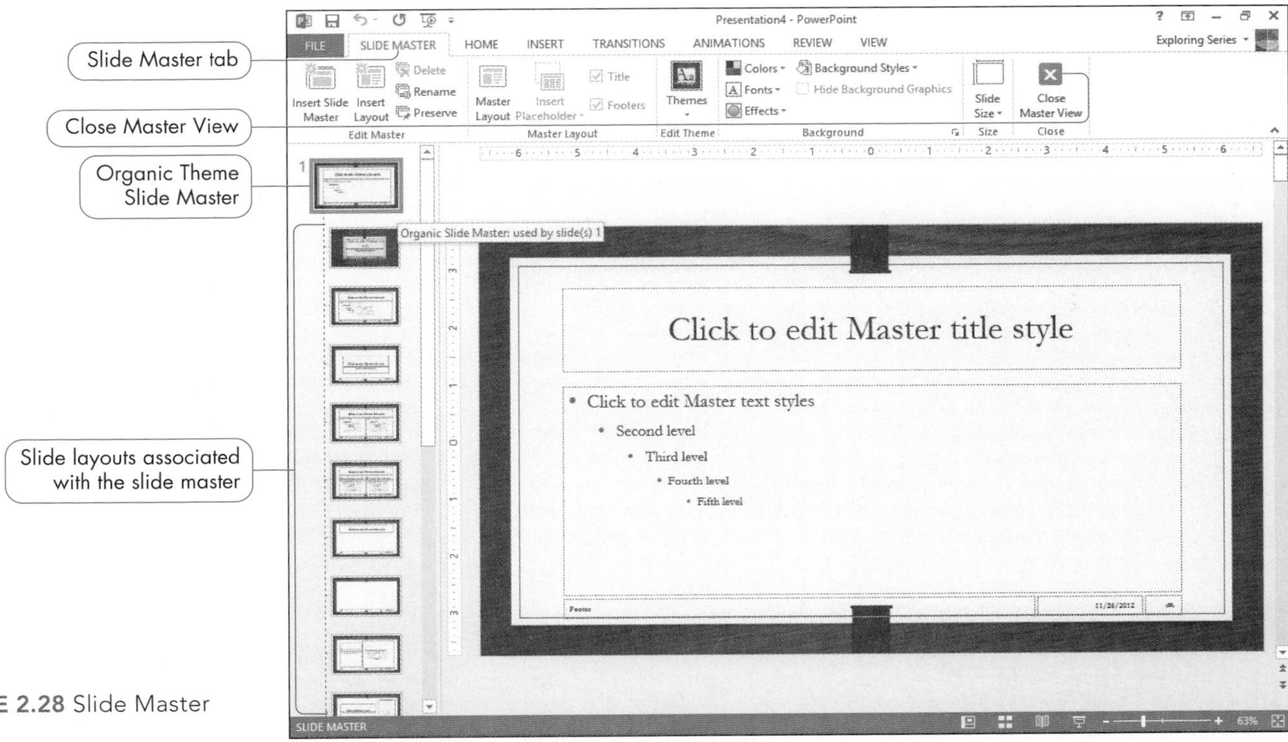

FIGURE 2.28 Slide Master View

The slide master is the most efficient way of setting the fonts, color scheme, and effects for the entire slide show. For example, you may wish to add a small company logo to the right corner of all slides. To set these choices, click the slide master thumbnail in the slide pane to display the slide master. The main pane shows the placeholders for title style, text styles, a date field, a footer field, and a page number field. Double-click the text in the Master title style or any level of text in the Master text styles placeholder and modify the font appearance. You can also make adjustments to the footer, date, and page number fields.

You can move and size the placeholders on the slide master. The modifications in position and size will be reflected on the associated slide layouts. This may conflict with some of the slide layout placeholders, however. The placeholders can be moved on the individual slide layouts as needed.

1. How are sections in a presentation similar to tabs in a binder? *p. 920*
2. Locate a PowerPoint presentation online and then use the Slide Show Design Principles described in this chapter to identify principles the creator used or failed to use. *p. 921*
3. Which elements of a theme can be modified? Why would you modify a theme? *p. 923*

Hands-On Exercises

4 Design

The director of the Wellness Center plans to add more content to the Campus Wellness Center mission presentation. To help her organize the content, you create sections in the slide show. You apply your knowledge of design principles to make the text more professional and readable. Finally, you change the theme and make modifications to the presentation through the slide master.

Skills covered: Create Sections • Apply Design Principles • Modify a Theme • Modify the Slide Master

STEP 1 » CREATE SECTIONS

After reviewing the Campus Wellness Center mission slide show, you decide to create four sections organizing the content. Refer to Figure 2.29 as you complete Step 1.

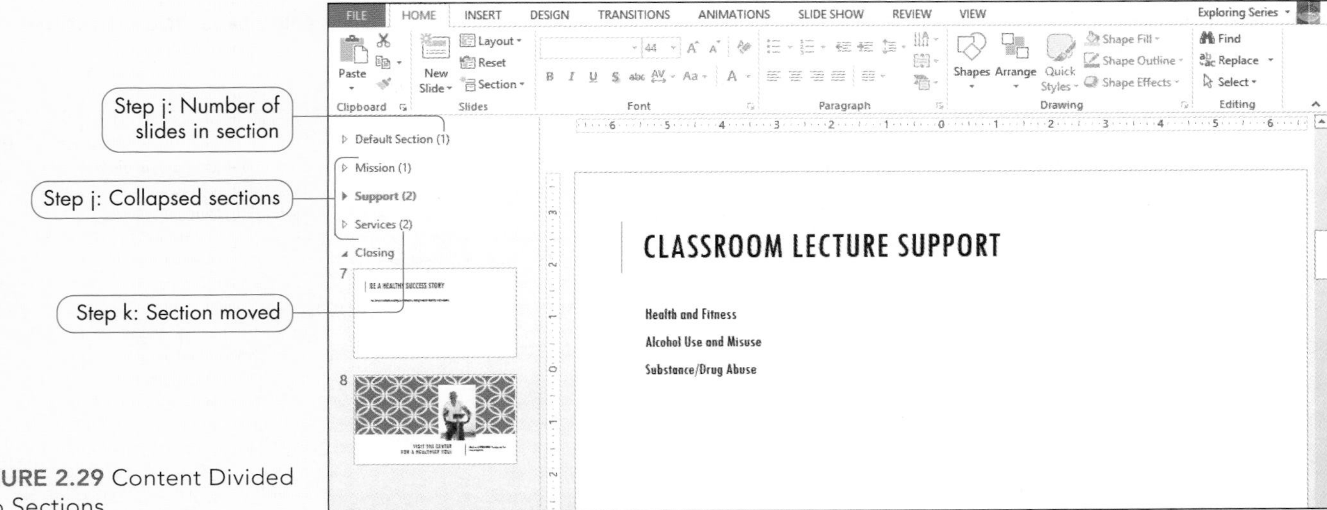

FIGURE 2.29 Content Divided into Sections

a. Open *p02h3Mission_LastFirst*, if necessary, and save the presentation as **p02h4Mission_LastFirst**, changing *h3* to *h4*.

b. Click the **VIEW tab**, click **Normal**, and then click the **Slide 2 icon**.

c. Click **Section** in the **Slides group** on the HOME tab and select **Add Section**.

A section divider is positioned between Slide 1 and Slide 2 in the Slides tab. It is labeled *Untitled Section*.

d. Right-click the **Untitled Section divider** and select **Rename Section**.

The Rename Section dialog box opens.

e. Type **Mission** in the **Section name box** and click **Rename**.

The section divider name changes and displays in the Slides tab.

f. Create a new section between Slides 2 and 3.

g. Right-click **Untitled Section**, click **Rename**, and then name the section **Services**.

h. Right-click between Slide 4 and Slide 5, click **Add Section**, and then rename the section **Support**.

i. Right-click between **Slide 6** and **Slide 7** and create a section named **Closing**.

The slide show content is divided into logical sections.

j. Right-click any section divider and select **Collapse All**.

The Slides tab shows the four sections you created: *Mission*, *Services*, *Support*, and *Closing*, as well as the *Default* section. Each section divider displays the section name and the number of slides in the section.

k. Right-click the **Support section** and click **Move Section Up**.

The *Support* section and all its associated slides are moved above the *Services* section.

l. Right-click any section divider and click **Expand All**.

m. Click the **VIEW tab** and click **Slide Sorter** in the Presentation Views group.

Slide Sorter view displays the slides in each section.

n. Click **Normal** in the Presentation Views group. Save the presentation.

STEP 2 » APPLY DESIGN PRINCIPLES

You note that several of the slides in the presentation do not use slide show text design principles. You edit these slides so they are more readable. Refer to Figure 2.30 as you complete Step 2.

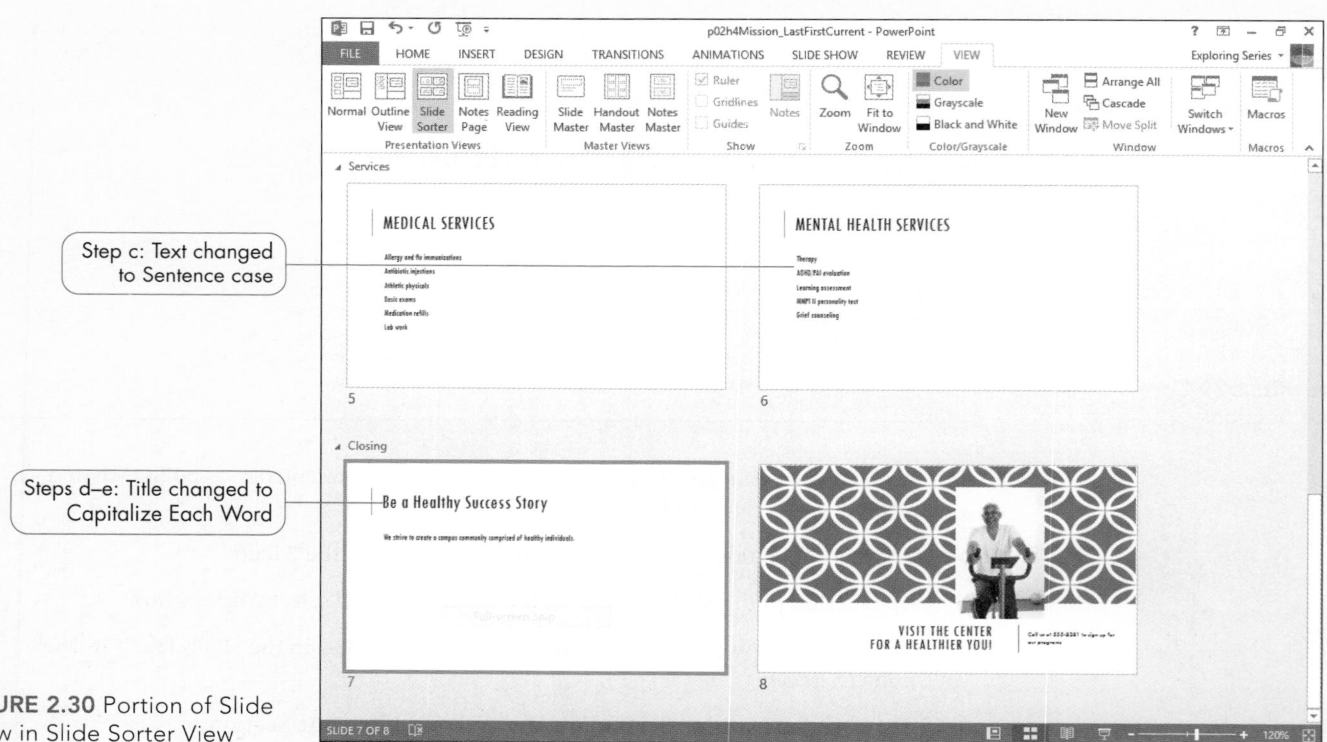

FIGURE 2.30 Portion of Slide Show in Slide Sorter View

a. On Slide 3, select the text below the title placeholder, click the **Change Case arrow** in the **Font group** of the HOME tab, and then select **Sentence case**.

The text now meets the guideline and is more readable.

b. Change the text below the titles in Slides 4, 5, and 6 to **Sentence case**.

c. On Slide 4, change the second line to **DVDs/CDs**.

Always proofread to ensure that the case feature accurately reflects proper capitalization.

d. On Slide 7, select the **title text**, click **Change Case** in the Font group, and then click **Capitalize Each Word**.

   Each word in the title begins with a capital letter.

e. Change the uppercase *A* in the title to a lowercase *a*.

   Title case capitalization guidelines state that only significant parts of speech of four or more letters should be capitalized. Minor parts of speech including articles and words shorter than four letters should not be capitalized.

f. Click the **VIEW tab** and click **Slide Sorter** in the Presentation Views group.

   Note the sentence case in the *Services* section.

g. Save the presentation.

STEP 3 » MODIFY A THEME

Although you are satisfied with the opening and closing slides, you think the main body of slides should be enhanced. You decide to change the theme and then modify the new theme to customize it. Refer to Figure 2.31 as you complete Step 3.

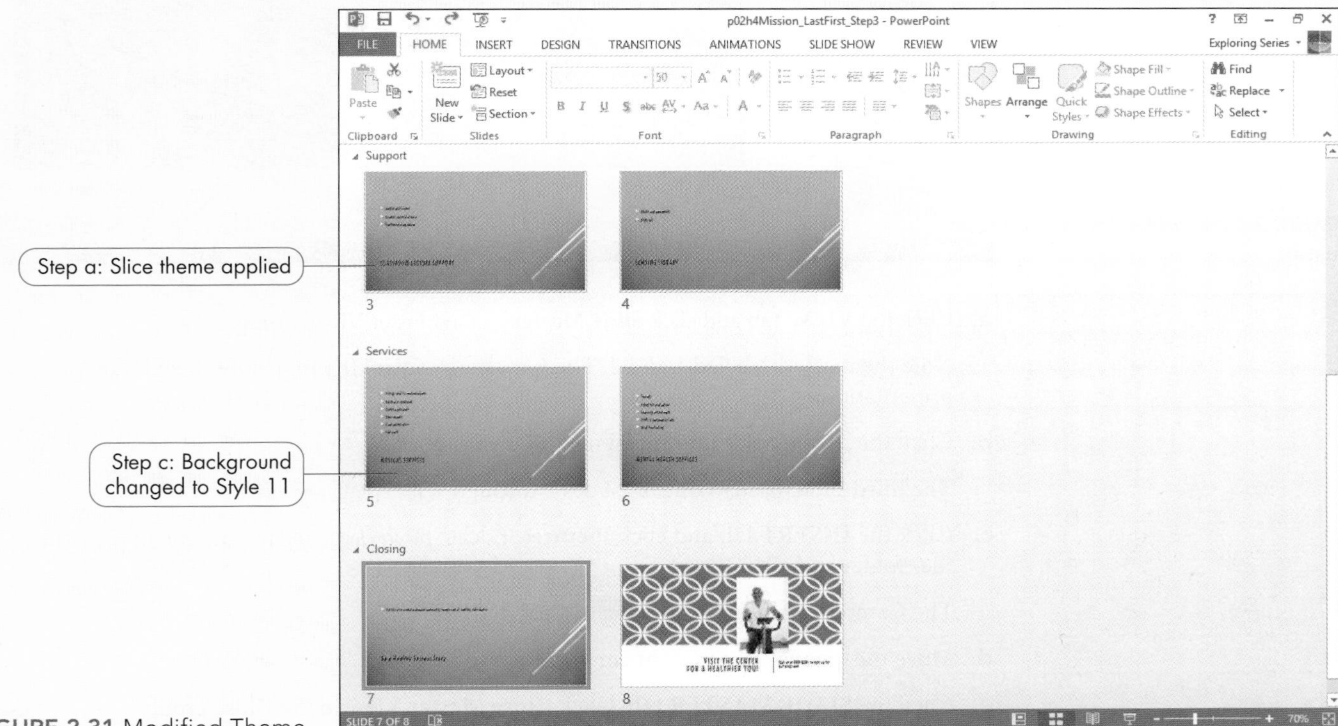

FIGURE 2.31 Modified Theme

a. Click the **DESIGN tab** and click **Slice** in the Themes gallery.

   The Slice theme, which provides a new background, is applied to the slide show except for the title and conclusion slides.

b. Click the **DESIGN tab** and click **More** in the Variants group.

   The Variants Gallery opens.

c. Select **Background Styles** and click **Style 11**.

d. Save the presentation.

STEP 4 ›› MODIFY THE SLIDE MASTER

You want to add the Campus Wellness Center logo to slides 2 through 7 using the slide master. Refer to Figure 2.32 as you complete Step 4.

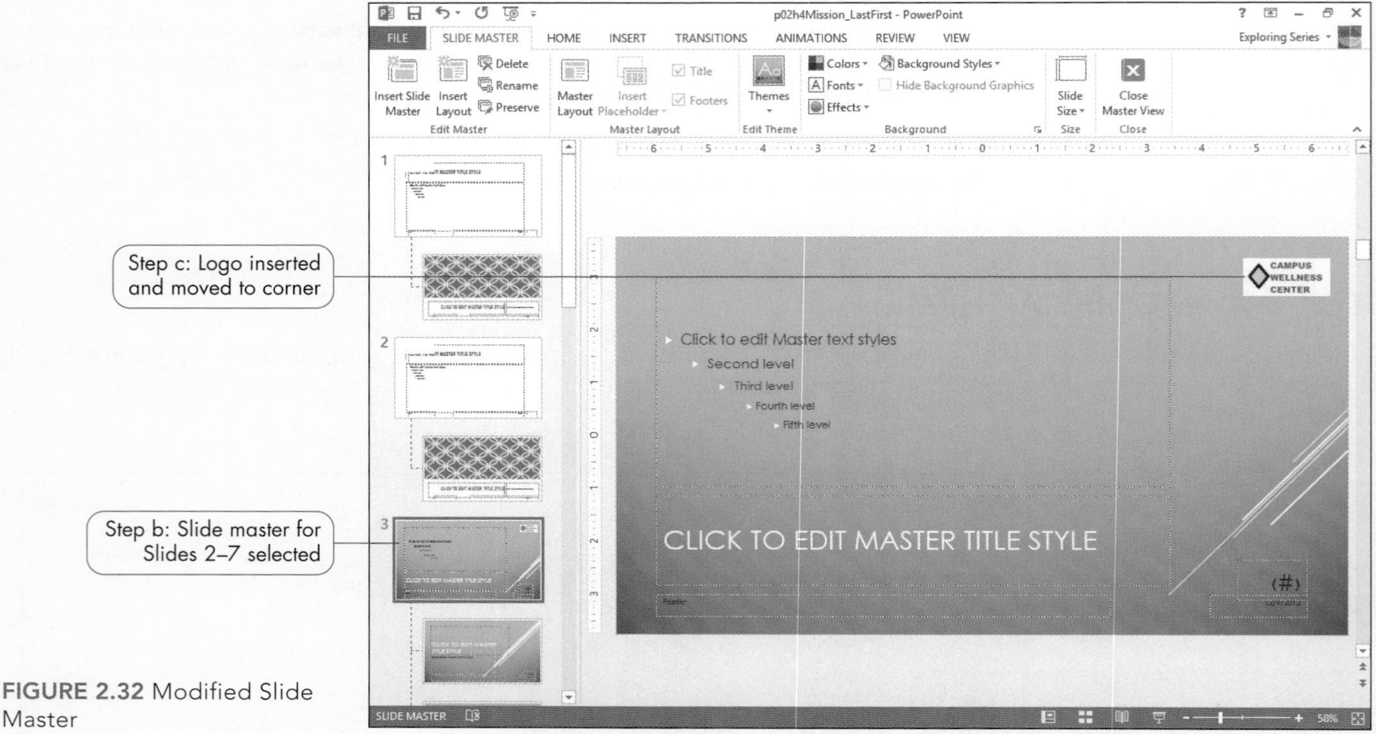

FIGURE 2.32 Modified Slide Master

a. Click the **VIEW tab** and click **Slide Master** in the Master Views group.

   Note the masters labeled 1 and 2. These masters control the first and last slides of the presentation.

b. Click the slide master thumbnail next to the number 3.

   The third slide master controls slides 2 through 7.

c. Click the **INSERT tab** and click **Pictures**. Locate *p02h4Logo.jpg* picture file in the student files folder and click **Insert**.

   The Campus Wellness Center logo is inserted.

d. Move the logo to the top right corner of the slide master.

e. Click the **SLIDE MASTER tab**. Click **Close Master View** in the Close group.

   Observe that the logo has been inserted on Slides 2 through 7 in the presentation.

f. Spell check the presentation. Save and close the file and submit based on your instructor's directions.

Chapter Objectives Review

After reading this chapter, you have accomplished the following objectives:

1. **Create a presentation using a template.**
   - Using a template saves time and enables you to create a more professional presentation.
   - Templates incorporate a theme, a layout, and content that you can modify.
   - You can download templates from Office.com or elsewhere on the Web.
2. **Modify a presentation based on a template.**
   - You can modify the structure of a template. The structure is modified by changing the layout of a slide.
   - To change the layout, drag placeholders to new locations or resize placeholders.
3. **Create a presentation in Outline view.**
   - When you use a storyboard to determine your content, you create a basic outline.
   - Entering your presentation in Outline view enables you to concentrate on the content of the presentation and saves time because you can enter information efficiently without moving from placeholder to placeholder.
4. **Modify an outline structure.**
   - Because Outline view helps you see the structure of the presentation, you are able to see where content needs to be strengthened or where the flow of information needs to be revised.
   - If you decide a slide contains content that would be presented better in another location in the slide show, use the Collapse and Expand features to easily move it.
   - By collapsing the slide content, you can drag the slide to a new location and then expand it.
   - To move individual bullet points, cut and paste the bullet points, or drag and drop them.
5. **Print an outline.**
   - An outline can be printed in either collapsed or expanded form to be used during a presentation.
6. **Import an outline.**
   - You can import any outline that has been saved in a format PowerPoint can read.
   - In addition to a Word outline, you can use the common generic formats rich text format and plain text format.
7. **Reuse slides from an existing presentation.**
   - Slides that have been previously created can be reused in new slide shows for efficiency and continuity.
8. **Use sections.**
   - Sections help organize slides.
   - Each section can be named to help identify the contents of the sections.
   - Sections can be collapsed or expanded.
9. **Examine slide show design principles.**
   - Using basic slide show principles and applying the guidelines make presentations more polished and professional.
10. **Modify a theme.**
    - In addition to layouts, a template includes themes that define its font attributes, colors, and backgrounds.
    - Themes can be changed to customize a slide show.
11. **Modify the slide master.**
    - A slide master controls the design elements and slide layouts associated with the slides in a presentation.

Key Terms Matching

Match the key terms with their definitions. Write the key term letter by the appropriate numbered definition.

- **a.** Background styles gallery
- **b.** Collapsed outline
- **c.** Colors gallery
- **d.** Effects gallery
- **e.** Expanded outline
- **f.** Fonts gallery
- **g.** Hierarchy
- **h.** Master
- **i.** Outline
- **j.** Outline view
- **k.** Plain text format (.txt)
- **l.** Slide Master
- **m.** Rich text format (.rtf)
- **n.** Template

1. ________ A file that incorporates a theme, a layout, and content that can be modified. **p. 900**
2. ________ A method of organizing text in a hierarchy to depict relationships. **p. 908**
3. ________ Indicates levels of importance in a structure. **p. 908**
4. ________ Shows the presentation in an outline format displayed in levels according to the points and any subpoints on each slide. **p. 908**
5. ________ Displays only the slide number, icon, and title of each slide in Outline view. **p. 909**
6. ________ Displays the slide number, icon, title, and content of each slide in Outline view. **p. 909**
7. ________ A file format that retains structure and most text formatting when transferring documents between applications or platforms. **p. 916**
8. ________ A file format that retains only text but no formatting when transferring documents between applications or platforms. **p. 916**
9. ________ Provides a set of colors for every available theme. **p. 924**
10. ________ Contains font sets for the content. **p. 924**
11. ________ Includes a range of effects for shapes used in the presentation. **p. 924**
12. ________ Provides both solid color and background styles for application to a theme. **p. 924**
13. ________ The top slide in a hierarchy of slides based on the master. **p. 925**
14. ________ Controls the layouts, background designs, and color combinations for handouts, notes pages, and slides, giving the presentation a consistent appearance. **p. 924**

Multiple Choice

1. A template is a format that can be modified and incorporates all of the following *except*:
   (a) Theme.
   (b) Layout.
   (c) Margins.
   (d) Content.

2. To create a presentation based on a template, click the:
   (a) FILE tab and search for a template.
   (b) FILE tab, click New, and then search for a template.
   (c) INSERT tab and select Add Template.
   (d) DESIGN tab and select New.

3. What is the advantage to collapsing the outline so only the slide titles are visible?
   (a) Transitions and animations can be added.
   (b) Graphical objects become visible.
   (c) More slide titles are displayed at one time, making it easier to rearrange the slides in the presentation.
   (d) All of the above.

4. Which of the following is *true*?
   (a) The slide layout can be changed after the template has been chosen.
   (b) Themes applied to a template will not be saved with the slide show.
   (c) Placeholders downloaded with a template cannot be modified.
   (d) Slides cannot be added to a presentation after a template has been chosen.

5. Which of the following is the fastest and most efficient method for reusing a slide you have customized in another presentation?
   (a) Open the slide, delete the content, and then enter the new information.
   (b) Save the custom slide and reuse it in the new presentation.
   (c) Open the slide and cut and paste the placeholders to a new slide.
   (d) Drag the placeholders from one slide to the next.

6. Which of the following is not an efficient method for adding existing content to a presentation?
   (a) Retype the content from an existing slide show into a new slide show.
   (b) Insert content by adding slides from an outline.
   (c) Copy and paste slides from an existing slide show into a new slide show.
   (d) Insert content by reusing slides.

7. All of the following are true *except*:
   (a) Pressing TAB demotes a bullet point from the first level to the second level.
   (b) Pressing SHIFT+TAB promotes a bullet point from the second level to the first level.
   (c) Pressing SHIFT+TAB demotes a bullet point from the first level to the second level.
   (d) Pressing Increase List Level demotes a bullet point from the first level to the second level.

8. Which of the following is *not* true of sections?
   (a) Sections can be renamed.
   (b) Sections can be created in Normal view or Slide Sorter view.
   (c) Sections can be collapsed.
   (d) A slide show can be divided into only six logical sections.

9. Which of the following formats cannot be imported to use as an outline for a presentation?
   (a) .jpg
   (b) .docx
   (c) .txt
   (d) .rtf

10. You own a small business and decide to institute an Employee of the Month award program. Which of the following would be the fastest way to create the award certificate with a professional look?
    (a) Enter the text in the title placeholder of a slide, change the font for each line, and then drag several clip art images of awards onto the slide.
    (b) Select a Theme, modify the placeholders, and then enter the award text information.
    (c) Create a table, enter the award text in the table, and then add clip art.
    (d) Access Microsoft Office Online and download an Award certificate template.

Practice Exercises

1 Certificate of Excellence

Figure 2.33 displays a Certificate of Excellence, created from a template downloaded from Microsoft Office Online for K&H Design, a small concrete design shop. You are the owner of K&H Design, and you want to present your employee, Juan Carlos Sanchez, with the Certificate of Excellence. This exercise follows the same set of skills as used in Hands-On Exercises 1 and 4 in the chapter. Refer to Figure 2.33 as you complete this exercise.

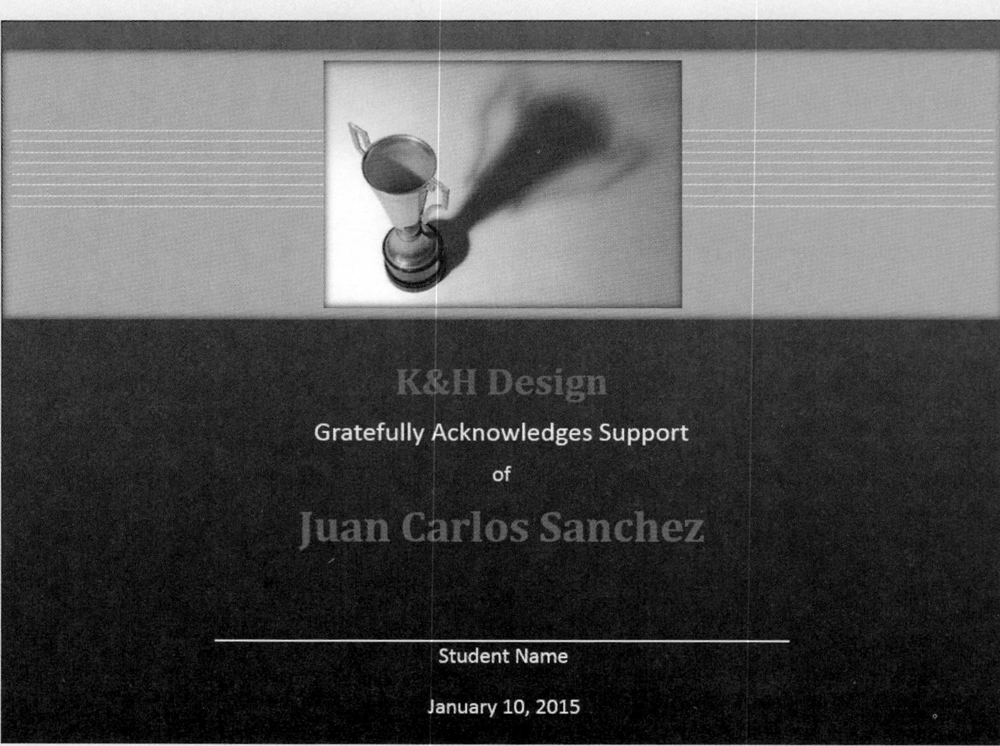

FIGURE 2.33 Downloaded and Modified Template

- **a.** Start PowerPoint. Click in the **Search online templates and themes search box**. Search for **Certificate of appreciation**.

  Thumbnails of sample templates will display.
- **b.** Click **Certificate of appreciation to donor** and click **Create** in the Preview pane.
- **c.** Save the file as **p02p1Donor_LastFirst**.
- **d.** Create a *Notes and Handouts* header with your name and a footer with your instructor's name and your class. Include the current date set to update automatically. The page number feature can remain active. Click **Apply to All**.
- **e.** Select the text *Organization Name* and type **K&H Design**.
- **f.** Select the text *Name* and type **Juan Carlos Sanchez**.
- **g.** Select the box containing the words *Presenter Name and Title* and replace the text with your first and last names.
- **h.** Select the text *Date* and type today's date.
- **i.** Click the **DESIGN tab** and click **More** in the Variants group. Select **Background Styles** and click **Style 12** (third row, fourth column).
- **j.** Save and close the file and submit based on your instructor's directions.

2 Classic Photo Album

You enjoy using your digital camera to record nature shots during trips you take on weekends. You decide to store these pictures in an electronic slide show that you can display for your family. You use the Classic Photo Album template. This exercise follows the same set of skills as used in Hands-On Exercises 1 and 4 in the chapter. Refer to Figure 2.34 as you complete this exercise.

FIGURE 2.34 Classic Photo Album in Slide Sorter View

a. Start PowerPoint.

b. Click **Photo Albums** at the end of the row of Suggested searches.
Thumbnails of sample templates will display.

c. Click **Classic photo album** and click **Create**.

d. Save the presentation file as **p02p2Album_LastFirst**.

e. Create a *Notes and Handouts* header with your name and a footer with your instructor's name and your class. Include the current date set to update automatically. The page number feature can remain active. Click **Apply to All**.

f. Select the word *CLASSIC* in the **title placeholder** of the first slide and type **Nature**.

g. Change the case of the title to **Capitalize Each Word**.

h. Replace the text in the **subtitle placeholder**, *Click to add date and other details*, with **Favorite Pictures in 2016**.

i. Click the **New Slide arrow** to display the Layout gallery.

j. Click the **Portrait with Caption layout** to add a new Slide 2.

k. Click the **picture icon**, locate the image *p02p2Nature* from your student data files, and then click **Insert**.

l. Click in the **caption placeholder** and type **Our way is not soft grass, it's a mountain path with lots of rocks. But it goes upwards, forward, toward the sun.** Press **Enter** twice and type **Ruth Westheimer**.

m. On Slide 3, read the text in the placeholder and click anywhere in the text.

n. Click the border of the caption placeholder and press **Delete** to remove the content. Select the placeholder again and press **Delete** to remove the placeholder. Modify the layout of the slide by dragging the picture placeholder to the right side of the slide.

o. Select the **Slide 4 thumbnail**, click **Layout** in the Slides group, and then click the **2-Up Landscape with Captions layout** to apply it to the slide.

p. Select the extra photograph (the smaller one) and press **Delete**. Select a border surrounding one of the caption placeholders and press **Delete**. Repeat selecting and deleting until all caption placeholders have been deleted. Delete the CHOOSE A LAYOUT placeholder.

q. Select the **Slide 5 thumbnail**, hold down **Ctrl**, and select the **Slide 7 thumbnail** in the Slides tab, and then press **Delete** to delete Slides 5 and 7 entirely.

r. Click the **SLIDE SHOW tab** and click **From Beginning** in the Start Slide Show group to view your presentation. Note the variety of layouts. Press **Esc** when you are done viewing the presentation.

s. Save and close the file and submit based on your instructor's directions.

3 A Guide to Successful Presentations

Your community's Small Business Development Center (SBDC) asks you to provide training to local small business owners on preparing and delivering presentations. You create an outline and then supplement it by reusing slides from another presentation and by adding slides from an outline. Because the slides come from different sources, they have different fonts, and you change the fonts to match, one of the design principles discussed in the chapter. You create sections to organize the presentation and then polish the presentation by adding and modifying a theme. This exercise follows the same set of skills as used in Hands-On Exercises 2–4 in the chapter.

a. Create a new, blank presentation. Click the **VIEW tab** and click **Outline View**. Click next to the Slide 1 icon and type **A Guide to Winning Presentations**. Press **Enter** and press **Tab**. Type your name and add the title **Consultant**.

b. Save the new presentation as **p02p3Success_LastFirst**.

c. Create a *Notes and Handouts* header with your name and a footer with your instructor's name and your class. Include the current date set to update automatically. The page number feature can remain active.

d. Click the **New Slide arrow** in the Slides group, click **Slides from Outline**, locate *p02p3TipsOutline* in your student data files, and then click **Insert**.

e. Switch to Outline view, select the word *Winning* on Slide 1, and type **Successful**.

f. Click at the end of the last bulleted text on Slide 3, press **Enter**, and then press **Shift+Tab** to create a new Slide 4. Type **Develop the Content** and press **Enter**.

g. Press Tab, type **Create a storyboard outline**, and then press **Enter**.

h. Type **Type the outline** and press **Enter**.

i. Press **Tab** to create a subpoint and type **Increase the indent levels (demote items)**. Press **Enter**.

j. Type **Decrease the indent levels (promote items)** and press **Enter**.

k. Press **Shift+Tab** to return to the previous level and type **Review the flow of ideas**.

l. Click at the end of the last bulleted text on Slide 4 and click the **New Slide arrow** in the Slides group.

m. Click **Reuse Slides** at the bottom of the gallery to open the Reuse Slides pane. Click **Browse**, click **Browse File**, select *p02p3Reuse*, and then click **Open**.

> **TROUBLESHOOTING:** If you do not see the *p02p3Reuse* file, change the *Files of type* option to All PowerPoint Presentations.

n. Double-click each of the slides in the Reuse Slides pane to insert the slides into the slide show. Close the Reuse Slides pane.

o. Press **Ctrl+A** to select all text in the outline, change the font to **Calibri (Body)**, and then deselect the text.

p. Right-click any bullet point to collapse, point to *Collapse*, and then select **Collapse All**.

- **q.** Drag the Slide 5 icon below the Slide 7 icon.
- **r.** Right-click one of the slide titles, point to *Expand*, and then select **Expand All**.
- **s.** Click the **VIEW tab**, click **Normal**, and then click the **DESIGN tab**. Click **More** in the Themes group and click **Integral**. Choose the green variant (the second variant from the left).
- **t.** On Slide 2, click the **HOME tab**, click **Section**, and then select **Add Section**.
- **u.** Right-click **Untitled Section**, select **Rename Section**, select **Untitled Section** (if necessary), and then type **Create**. Click **Rename**.
- **v.** Repeat steps t and u to create a section named **Refine** before Slide 5 and a section named **Deliver** before Slide 7.
- **w.** Click **VIEW tab** and click **Slide Master**. Click the top slide (numbered Slide 1) in the slide pane.
- **x.** Click the **INSERT tab** and click **Pictures**. Locate *p02p3PresenterLogo* and click **Insert**. Move the image to the bottom-right corner of the slide. Click the **SLIDE MASTER tab** and click **Close Master View**.
- **y.** Click the **FILE tab**, click **Print**, click **Full Page Slides**, and select **Outline**. View the outline in the Preview pane and press **Cancel** to close the Print dialog box.
- **z.** Save and close the file and submit based on your instructor's directions.

Mid-Level Exercises

1 Nutrition Guide

You have been asked to help create a presentation for a local Girl Scout troop that is featuring good nutrition as its theme for the month. You locate a Microsoft Office Online template for nutrition that has some fun animations that you think the young girls will enjoy. Since you've given similar presentations, you decide to reuse basic slide content you've previously created on standard nutritional guidelines supported by the U.S. Department of Agriculture. Lastly, you modify the presentation using the Slide Master so all the changes are easily implemented to all slides.

a. Start PowerPoint, and in **Search online templates and themes box**, type **Nutrition**.

b. Select **Health nutrition presentation** and click **Create**.

c. Save the presentation as **p02m1Food_LastFirst**.

d. Create a *Notes and Handouts* header with your name and a footer with your instructor's name and your class. Include the current date.

e. View the slides in Slide Show view.

f. You notice that there are cute animations on the first and last slides, but some modifications need to be made.

g. On Slide 1, replace the word *Fruit* in the triangle with **Food**.

h. Click Slide 6 and make a similar change, replacing *Fruit* with **Food**.

i. Make the following changes to Slide 1:
   - Replace *Feb – 2010* with the current month and year.
   - Replace *Title of the Presentation* with **Nutritional Guide**.
   - Delete the subtitle of the presentation.

j. Delete Slides 2 through 5.

k. Click the **New Slide arrow** in the Slides group of the HOME tab and select **Reuse Slides**.

l. Browse to locate and select the *p02m1Diet* presentation from the student data files in the Reuse Slides pane.

m. Select all seven slides in the Reuse Slides pane. Close the Reuse Slides pane.

n. Move Slide 2 so it becomes the last slide of the presentation.

o. Click the **VIEW tab** and click **Slide Master** from the Master Views group.

p. Click the top slide in the left pane and make the following changes to the Title and Content Layout slide master:
   - Select the five levels of text in the content placeholder, click the **Font Color arrow** in the Mini Toolbar, select the **Eyedropper**, and then click the grapes image in the bottom-right corner to select the color of the grapes.
   - Select the text in the title (*Click to edit Master title style*), click the **Font Color arrow** in the Mini Toolbar, select **Lime, Text 1, Darker 25%** (fifth row, second column).
   - Increase the font size of the slide title to **36**.
   - Change *www.funFruit.com* to **www.funFood.com** in the bottom-right corner of the slide.
   - Click the center text box at the bottom of the slide, delete *Coming to Fruition*, and then type **for Everyone**.
   - Close the Slide Master and close the Reuse Slides pane.

q. View Slides 2 through 8 to ensure the changes in the slide master are reflected in the slides.

r. Select Slide 9 and make the following changes
   - Replace *Pears, not for squares* with **Food is fun for everyone!**
   - Delete the text box content.

s. Save and close the file and submit based on your instructor's directions.

2 Go Digital

The local senior citizens' center has asked you to speak on photography. The center has many residents interested in learning about digital photography. You decide to create a presentation with sections on learning the advantages of a digital camera, choosing a camera, taking pictures with a digital camera, and printing and sharing photos. In this exercise, you begin the presentation by creating the sections and completing the content for the first section.

a. Create a new blank PowerPoint presentation and create slides from the *p02m2Outline.docx* outline. Save the slide show as **p02m2Digital_LastFirst**.

b. Apply the **Wisp theme** to the slides.

c. Delete the blank Slide 1 and change the layout of the new Slide 1 to **Title Slide**.

d. Review the presentation in PowerPoint's Outline view and add the following information as the last bullets on Slide 2:
   - **Instant feedback**
   - **Sharing**

e. Promote the text *Free Experimentation* on Slide 4 so that it creates a new slide.

> **TROUBLESHOOTING:** If you cannot select a bullet, place your insertion point at the end of the bullet and click to select the bulleted line.

f. Select all text in Outline view and click **Clear All Formatting** in the Font group on the HOME tab.

g. Open the Reuse Slides pane and browse to locate and open the *p02m2Slides* presentation. Click the last slide in the original presentation. Right-click any slide and click **Insert All Slides**. The new slides should be inserted as Slides 6 and 7. Close the Reuse Slides pane.

h. Select **More in the Variants Gallery** on the DESIGN tab and change the presentation font to **Corbel**. Using the Colors gallery, change the presentation colors to **Red**.

i. Return to Normal view.

j. Create a section between Slides 1 and 2 named **Advantages**.

k. Create a section after Slide 7 named **Choosing a Digital Camera**.

DISCOVER

l. Use the Web to research things to consider when purchasing a digital camera. Be sure to include the major types of cameras available.

m. Insert a new Slide 8 in the **Choosing a Digital Camera** section to explain your findings.

n. Create a *Notes and Handouts* header with your name and a footer with your instructor's name and your class. Include the current date.

o. Save and close the file and submit based on your instructor's directions.

3 Using Social Technologies for Ideas and Resources

COLLABORATION
CASE

FROM
SCRATCH

Social networking enables us to connect with others who share common interests via the Internet. Social networking also helps businesses connect with their customers. Give an overview of some of the popular social media technologies such as Facebook, Twitter, LinkedIn, etc. and discuss how businesses can utilize them to engage their customers. Choose a business that interests you and discuss which social media technologies it uses and how they are used to connect with its customers. In this exercise, you will visit Microsoft's Office.com website, download a template from the Design Gallery, modify the template with your information, and then post the PowerPoint presentation you create to a Web site for others to view.

a. Access the Internet and go to http://office.microsoft.com/en-us/templates. Click **PowerPoint**. Click to see all available PowerPoint 2013 templates.

b. The page you view displays a series of slides created by Microsoft and some of its partners. Microsoft provides these slides as an exclusive benefit for its users. Click the thumbnail to see further details about the presentation.

c. Select one of the presentations and download the slides to the location you use to store your files for this class. Save the file as **p02m3Resources_GroupName**. Open the saved slide show and modify the slides so they reflect your information and ideas. Be sure to follow the design principles discussed in the chapter. Your presentation should be approximately 6–9 slides in length, including the title and credit slides. Delete any unnecessary slides found in the template. Make sure you create a final slide that credits the source for the slide design. Provide the URL for the location from where you downloaded the presentation.

d. Load your edited presentation to an online location for others to review. Upload your presentation to your Microsoft OneDrive account or use another method for sharing your presentation with your instructor and classmates. (If you do not already have a OneDrive account, you can create a free account at https://onedrive.live.com.)

e. Invite three classmates to go to the site, view the presentation you saved, and then add a comment about your presentation. If using OneDrive, to add comments, click the **Comment button** in PowerPoint Online. If you saved to another online storage location, share the location with three classmates and ask them to download the presentation. After viewing the presentation, ask them to e-mail you with their comments.

f. Visit three of your classmates' presentations from their storage locations. Leave a comment about their presentations or e-mail your classmates, sharing a comment about their presentations.

g. Review the comments of your classmates.

h. Submit based on your instructor's directions.

Beyond the Classroom

Social Media Marketing

RESEARCH CASE

You have a bright, creative, and energetic personality, and you are using these talents in college as a senior majoring in marketing. You hope to work in social media marketing. The Marketing 405 course you are taking this semester requires every student to create a social media marketing plan for a fictional company and to present an overview of the company to the class. This presentation should include the company purpose, the company's history, and past and present projects—all of which you are to "creatively invent." Include a final slide giving the resources you used to create your presentation.

Search Office.com for an appropriate template to use in creating your presentation. Research what a social media marketing campaign entails, and use what you learn to add your own content to comply with the case requirements. Add clip art, transitions, and animations as desired. Organize using sections. Create a handout header with your name and a handout footer with your instructor's name and your class. Include the current date. Save the presentation as **p02b2Marketing_LastFirst** and submit as directed by your instructor.

Michigan, My State

DISASTER RECOVERY

Your sister spent a lot of time researching and creating a presentation on the state of Michigan for a youth organization leader and team members. She does not like the presentation's design and has asked for your help. You show her how to download the state history report presentation template from Office.com, Presentations category, Academic subcategory. Save the new presentation as **p02b3State_LastFirst**. Reuse her slides, which are saved as *p02b3Michigan*. Cut and paste the images she gathered into the correct placeholders and move bulleted text to the correct slide. Resize placeholders as needed. You tell your sister that mixing clip art with pictures is contributing to the cluttered look. Choose one format based on your preference. Create new slides with appropriate layouts as needed. You remind her that although federal government organizations allow use of their images in an educational setting, your sister should give proper credit if she is going to use their data. Give credit to the State of Michigan's Web site for the information obtained from Michigan.gov (http://michigan.gov/kids). Give credit to the U.S. Census Bureau (www.census.gov) for the Quick Facts. Finalize the presentation by deleting unneeded slides, adding appropriate sections, modifying themes, proofreading, and applying transitions. Create a handout header with your name and a handout footer with your instructor's name and your class. Include the current date. Print the outline as directed by your instructor. Save the presentation and submit as directed by your instructor.

Time Management Skills

SOFT SKILLS CASE

Time management is an important skill for both students and professionals. Review the time management lesson found at the following Web site: http://www.gcflearnfree.org/jobsuccess/2. Using Word in Outline View, create an outline discussing the major points of the lesson. Your outline should have four headings with supporting bullets for each. Create a PowerPoint presentation based on your outline and add design elements to enhance your presentation. Be sure to follow the design rules discussed in this chapter. Add a small clock or hourglass to one corner of your slides using the slide master. Create a handout header with your name and a handout footer with your instructor's name and your class. Include the current date. Save the presentation as **p02b4TimeManagement_LastFirst** and submit as directed by your instructor.

Capstone Exercise

Your neighbors in your small southwestern subdivision are concerned about drought, fire danger, and water conservation. You volunteer to gather information about possible solutions and share the information with them in a PowerPoint presentation at the next neighborhood association meeting. In this capstone project, you concentrate on developing the content of the presentation.

Design Template

You download an Office.com template to create the basic design and structure for your presentation, save the presentation, and create the title slide.

a. Create a new presentation using one of the available templates. Search for the template using the search term **Ecology** and locate and download the **Ecology photo panels template**.

b. Save the presentation as **p02c1Wise_LastFirst**.

c. Type **Conserve** as the title on the title slide.

d. Type the subtitle **Waterwise Landscaping**.

e. Delete the blank Slides 7 through 11.

f. Create a handout header with your name and a handout footer with your instructor's name and your class. Include the current date. Apply to all slides.

Outline and Modifications

Based on the storyboard you created after researching water conservation on the Internet, you type the outline of your presentation. As you create the outline, you also modify the outline structure.

a. Open the Outline View.

b. Type **Waterwise Options** as the title for Slide 2.

c. Enter each of the following as Level 1 bullets for Slide 2: **Zeroscaping**, **Xeriscaping**. Remove the third bullet, which is blank.

d. Delete Slides 3, 4, and 5.

e. Change the layout of the new Slide 3 to **Title and Content**.

f. Type **Purpose of Landscaping** as the title for Slide 3.

g. Type each of the following as Level 1 bullets for Slide 3: **Beauty**, **Utility**, **Conservation**.

h. Add this speaker note to Slide 3: **With water becoming a limited resource, conservation has become an additional purpose of landscaping.**

i. Modify the outline structure by reversing Slides 2 and 3.

Imported Outline

You have an outline on zeroscaping that was created in Microsoft Word and a slide show on xeriscaping. You reuse this content to build your slide show.

a. Position the insertion point at the end of the outline.

b. Use the **Slides from Outline option** to insert the *p02c1Zero* outline.

c. Delete any blank slides.

d. Change the layout of Slide 4 to **Picture with Caption**.

e. Insert *p02c1Zeropic* in the **picture placeholder**.

f. Position the point of insertion at the end of the outline.

g. Reuse all of the slides, using the same order, from *p02c1Xeri* to add four slides to the end of the presentation.

h. Insert *p02c1Xeripic* in the **picture placeholder** on Slide 8.

Design

The outline slides do not match the design of the other slides. You want to remove the formatting from those slides to create a uniform look. Additionally, the room in which you will be displaying the slide show is very light. You decide to darken the slides, which will increase the slide visibility. You also adjust the font size of two captions to increase their readability.

a. Select **Slides 4 through 7** in the outline and clear all formatting from the slides.

b. Change the background style for all four slides to **Style 4** (first row, fourth column).

c. Increase the font size of the title and caption text two levels on Slides 4 and 8.

d. Use the spelling checker and proofread the presentation.

Sections

To facilitate moving between the slides concerning zeroscaping and the slides concerning xeriscaping, you create sections.

a. Add a section before Slide 4 and rename it **Zeroscaping**.

b. Add a section before Slide 8 and rename it **Xeriscaping**.

c. Print the outline as directed by your instructor.

d. Save and close the file and submit based on your instructor's directions.

Presentation Design

Illustrations and Infographics

OBJECTIVES AFTER YOU READ THIS CHAPTER, YOU WILL BE ABLE TO:

CASE STUDY | Illustrations and Infographics Mini-Camp

As an information technology (IT) project manager, you must often create presentations for senior management. Your presentations detail current team projects, which often require flow charts and diagrams.

This summer, you are working with several IT interns. You have been requested to introduce the interns to drawing using computer-based drawing tools, creating infographics, and working with online pictures. You decide to teach a PowerPoint mini-camp because you want to introduce the participants to PowerPoint's many tools for creating and modifying illustrations.

You begin the camp by teaching the participants how to create and modify lines and shapes, how to use shapes to create flow charts, how to use SmartArt diagrams, and how to modify online pictures to meet their needs. You also teach participants WordArt manipulation as a creative way to enhance text used in illustrations and infographics.

Shapes

Text can be very effective when giving a presentation, but sometimes it is simply not enough. Illustrations and diagrams can and usually do add additional clarity to the idea that is being presented. One type of visual element is a ***shape***, a geometric or non-geometric object used to create an illustration or to highlight information. For example, on a slide containing a list of items, you could include a quote related to the items and create the quote inside a shape to call attention to it. You can combine shapes to create complex images. Figure 3.1 shows three PowerPoint themes using shapes in each of these ways. The Striped Black Border theme uses a rectangular shape to draw attention to the information in the title placeholder. The Currency design theme uses curved lines to create an interesting design. The ListDiagram theme uses rounded rectangles to emphasize each concept.

FIGURE 3.1 Using Shapes in Themes

Infographics, a shortened term for information graphics, are visual representations of data or knowledge. Infographics typically use shapes to present complex data or knowledge in an easily understood visual representation. PowerPoint includes powerful drawing tools you can use to create lines and shapes, which are the basis for infographics. Because drawn images are created with shapes, you should learn to modify the shapes used for drawn images to meet your needs. In addition to using the drawing tools, you can enhance shapes by adding effects such as 3-D, shadow, glow, warp, bevel, and others. These effects are accessible through style galleries. Using these visual effects makes it easy for you to create professional-looking infographics to enhance your presentation.

In this section, you will create and modify various shapes and lines. You will also customize shapes and apply special effects to objects. Finally, you will learn how to apply and change outline effects.

Creating Shapes

STEP 1» PowerPoint provides tools for creating shapes. You can insert a multitude of standard geometric shapes such as circles, squares, hearts, or stars. You can insert equation shapes, such as + and ÷, and a variety of banners. After you create a shape, you can modify it and apply fills and special effects.

To create a shape, do the following:

1. Click the INSERT tab.
2. Click Shapes in the Illustrations group.
3. Click the shape you desire from the Shapes gallery.
4. Click the desired position in which to place the shape, or drag the cross-hair pointer to control the approximate size of the shape as desired.
5. Release the mouse button.

To resize the shape, drag any of the sizing handles that surround the shape after it is created. Figure 3.2 shows the Shapes gallery and the many shapes from which you can choose. Notice that the most recently used shapes are at the top of the list so you can conveniently reuse them.

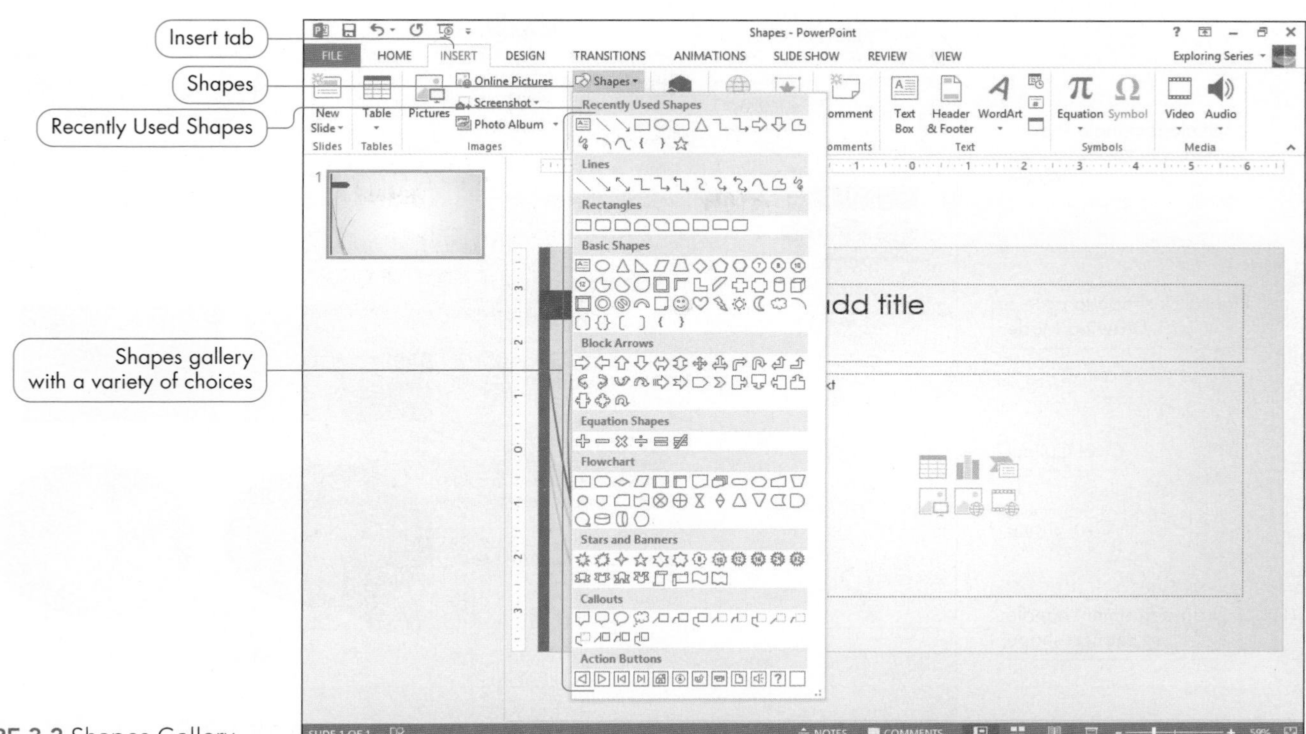

FIGURE 3.2 Shapes Gallery

TIP Using the Drawing Group

You can also access the Shapes gallery from the Drawing group on the Home tab. This group allows you to choose a shape, arrange its order and position, apply a Quick Style, and then change properties of the shape. If you have a widescreen monitor or if your monitor is set for a higher resolution, the Drawing group displays individual shapes instead of one Shapes command. If this is the case, click the More button to open the Shapes gallery.

The Shapes command deactivates the selected shape after you draw it once, forcing you to reselect the shape each time you want to use it. By activating the ***Lock Drawing Mode*** feature, you can add several shapes of the same type on your slide without selecting the shape each time.

To activate Lock Drawing Mode:

1. Right-click the shape you want to use in the Shapes gallery and select Lock Drawing Mode.
2. Click anywhere on the slide or drag to create the first shape.
3. Click or drag repeatedly to create additional shapes of the same type.
4. To release the Lock Drawing Mode, press Esc.

Figure 3.3 shows a series of squares created with the Lock Drawing Mode activated. Additionally the figure shows a basic oval and Smiley Face both located in the Basic Shapes category, and a ***callout*** created using the Oval Callout located in the Callouts category. A callout is a shape that includes a line with a text box that can be used to add notes, often used in cartooning. Notice that the Smiley Face shape is selected on the slide. The sizing handles display around the shape. This yellow square is an ***adjustment handle*** that you can drag to change the shape. If you drag the adjustment handle upward, the smile becomes a frown. Some shapes have an adjustment handle, and some do not.

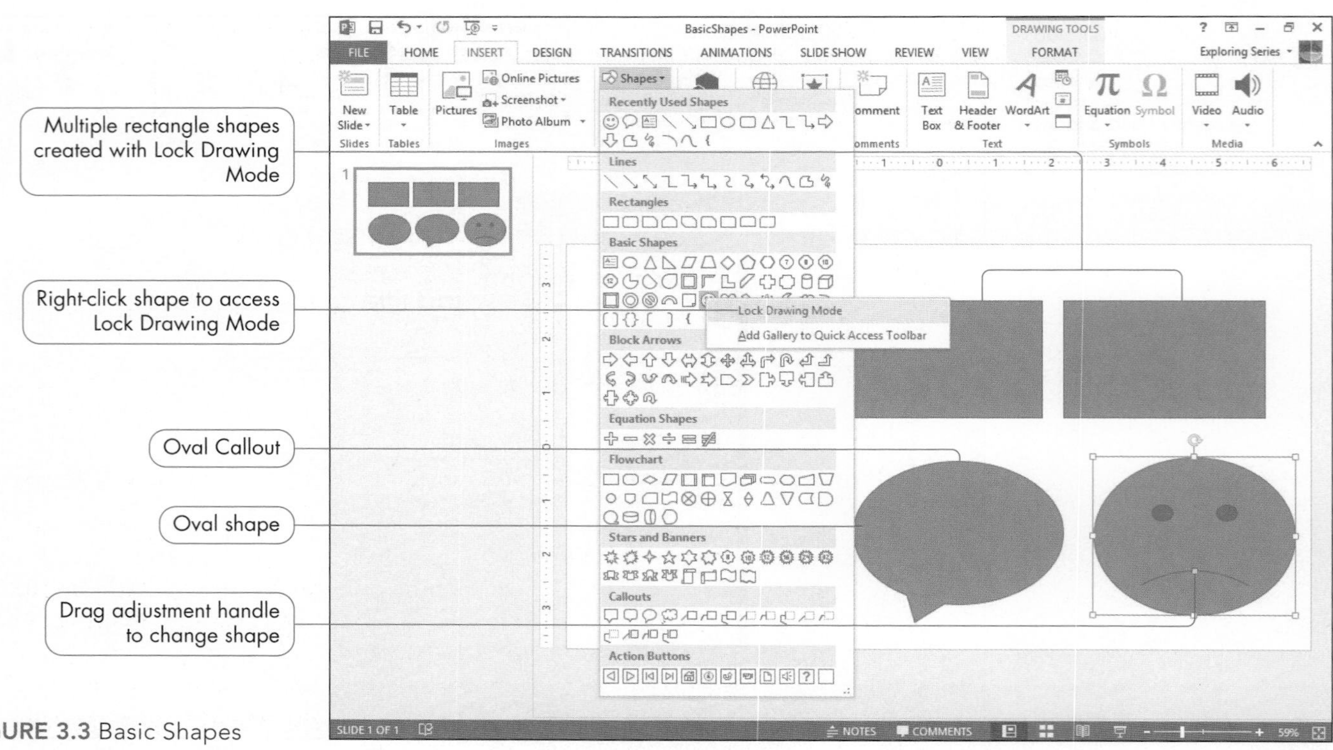

FIGURE 3.3 Basic Shapes

TIP Constrain a Shape

A rectangle can be constrained or forced to form a perfect square, and an oval or ellipse can be constrained to form a perfect circle. To constrain a shape, press and hold Shift as you drag to create the shape.

Draw Lines and Connectors

STEP 2» Lines are shapes that can be used to point to information, to connect shapes on a slide, or to divide a slide into sections. Lines also are often used in slide design. To draw a straight line:

1. Select the line in the Lines category of the Shapes gallery.
2. Position the pointer on the slide where you want the line to begin.
3. Drag to create the line. Hold Shift as you drag to constrain to a perfectly horizontal, vertical, or any multiple of a 45-degree angle line.

You can also create curved lines. These may take a little practice to get the curve you want. To create a curved line:

1. Click the curve shape in the Lines category of the Shapes gallery.
2. Click the slide at the location where you want to start the curve.
3. Click again where the peaks or valleys of the curve occur and continue to click and move the mouse to shape the curve in the desired pattern.
4. Double-click to end the curve.

As you click while creating the curve, you set a point for the curve to bend around. To draw a shape that looks like it was drawn with a pen, select the Scribble shape.

In addition to drawing simple lines to create dividing lines and waves, you may need ***connectors***, or lines that attach to the shapes you create. Connector lines move with shapes when the shapes are moved. The three types of connectors are straight, elbow (to create angled lines), and curved. To determine which line shapes are connectors, point to the line in the gallery and a ScreenTip will appear with the shape name, such as Curved Arrow Connector.

The first step in working with connectors is to create the shapes you want to connect with lines.

To connect shapes:

1. Create the shapes you wish to connect.
2. Select a connector line from the Lines category of the Shape gallery.
3. After you select the connector, squares appear around the previously created shapes when you move your pointer over them. These are the locations where you can attach the connector.
4. Click one of the squares to connect with the circle of the connector line that will appear on the next shape. You can also drag to control the direction and size of the connector line.
5. The two shapes are now connected. You can also connect placeholders with a connector line.

If you move a shape that is joined to another shape using a connector line, the connecting line moves with it, extending or shortening as necessary to maintain the connection. Sometimes when you rearrange the shapes, the connectors may no longer extend to the shape that was not moved, or the connectors may cross shapes and be confusing. If that happens, you can use the yellow adjustment handle located on the connector line to reshape the connectors. Select the connector lines and drag the handles to obtain a clearer path.

A ***flow chart*** is an illustration that shows a sequence to be followed or a plan containing steps (see Figure 3.4). For example, you could use a flow chart to illustrate the sequence to follow when implementing a new product. Connector lines join the shapes in a flow chart.

The typical flow chart sequence includes start and end points shown in oval shapes, steps shown in rectangular shapes, and decisions to be made shown in diamond shapes. Connectors with arrows demonstrate the order in which the sequence should be followed to accomplish the goal. Each shape has a label to which you can add text, indicating what the shape represents. When you select a shape and type or paste text into it, the text becomes part of the shape.

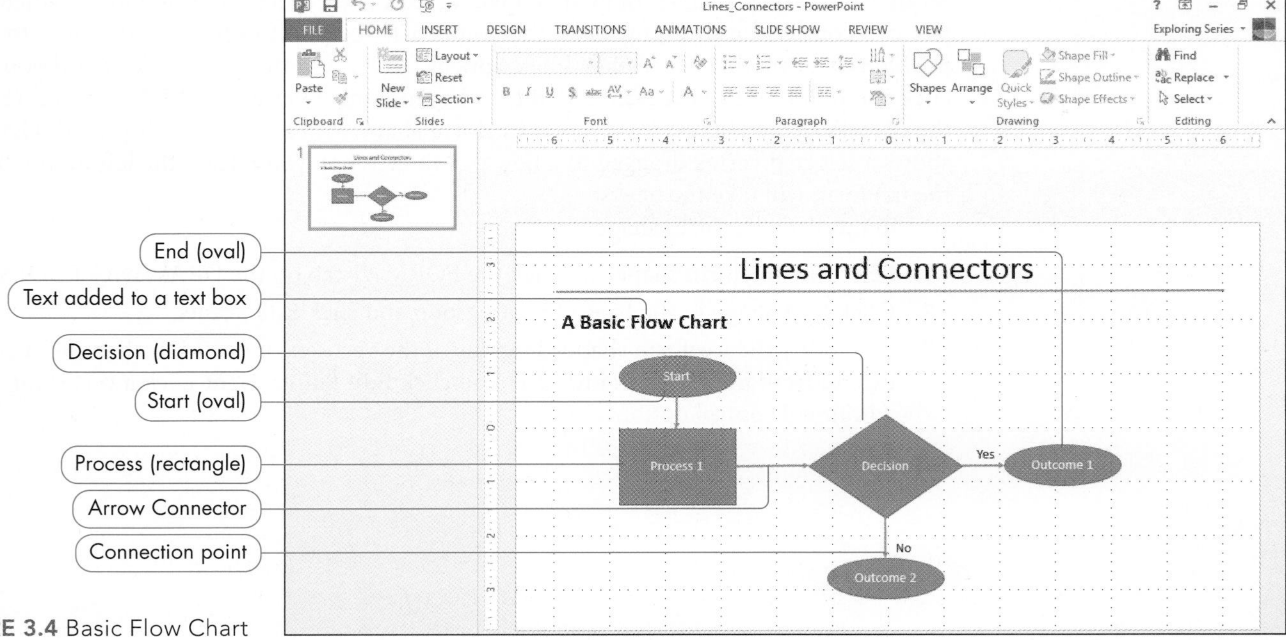

FIGURE 3.4 Basic Flow Chart

Sometimes it is necessary to add a text box to a slide. ***Text boxes*** can be more flexible than content placeholders or can be added to slides in which the chosen layout doesn't include a content placeholder, but text is still necessary. For example, use a text box to add a quote to a slide that is separate from the slide content placeholder. Text inside a text box can be formatted just as text in placeholders is formatted. You can even add a border, fill, shadow, or 3-D effect to the text in a text box. Figure 3.4 shows a basic flow chart created with shapes, connectors, and text boxes.

Create and Modify Freeform Shapes

A ***freeform shape*** is a shape that can be used to create customized shapes using both curved and straight-line segments.

To create a freeform shape:

1. Select the Freeform shape in the Lines category of the Shapes gallery and click the slide.
2. Click to draw straight lines and drag to create curves.
3. Double-click to end the freeform shape. If you end by clicking the starting point of the shape, you create a closed shape.

Create a Closed Shape

If you use the Curve, Freeform, or Scribble line tool to create a shape and end the shape at its starting point, the starting point and ending points join to create a closed shape. The advantage of joining the ends of the line and creating a closed shape is that you can include a fill, or interior content.

Sometimes, the freeform shape you have drawn is not exactly as you desired. You can modify the freeform shape to achieve the desired shape. This can be achieved through the help of a vertex. ***Vertexes***, also known *as anchor points*, which are the black squares that control the curve line segments, indicate where two line segments meet or end. If you will recall, from early principles of math, it takes at least two points to define a line segment; thus you can control the shape by using the points. Click a point to move and drag it to a new position or to modify the shape's line segment curve. A vertex can be deleted if you right-click the point and select Delete Point. Either moving a vertex or deleting it will redefine the object's shape. Figure 3.5 shows a freeform shape with its vertexes displayed. Figure 3.6 shows a selected vertex dragged to a new position. When you release the left mouse button, the freeform will take the new shape.

To modify a freeform shape:

1. Select the freeform shape and click the FORMAT tab on the DRAWING TOOLS tab.
2. Click Edit Shape in the Insert Shapes group and click Edit Points.
3. To modify the freeform shape, drag one of the vertexes or one of the handles that extend from the vertex point. After you click Edit Points, right-click a vertex for additional control options.

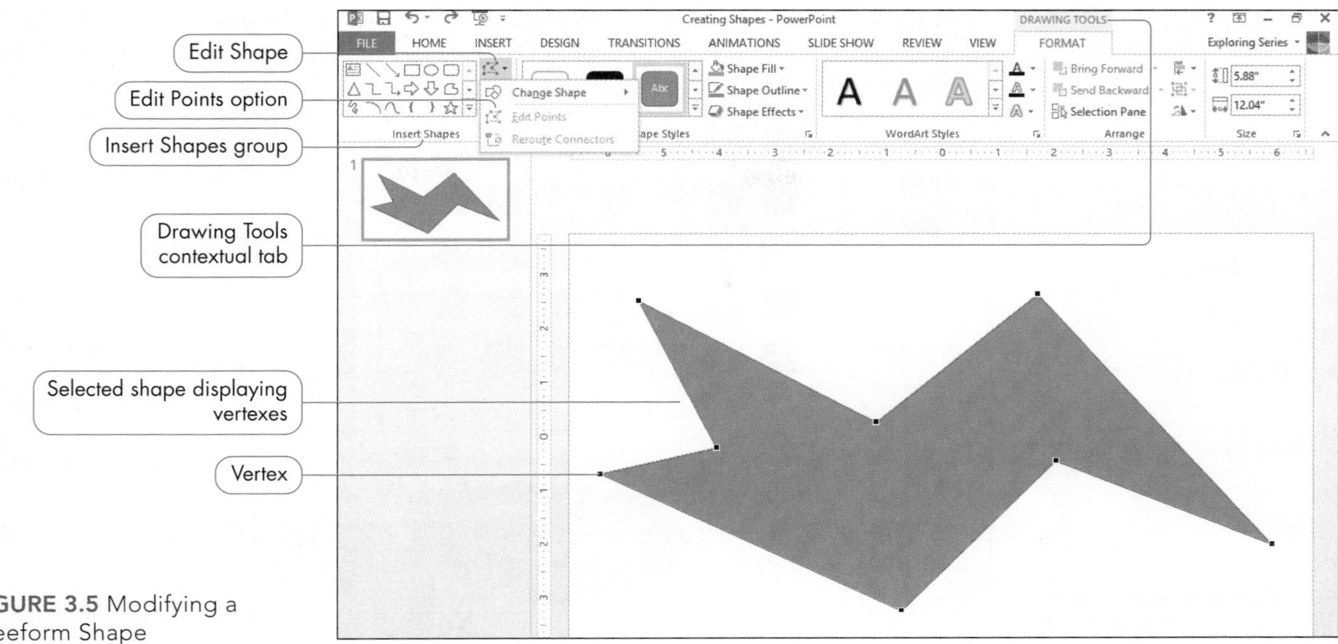

FIGURE 3.5 Modifying a Freeform Shape

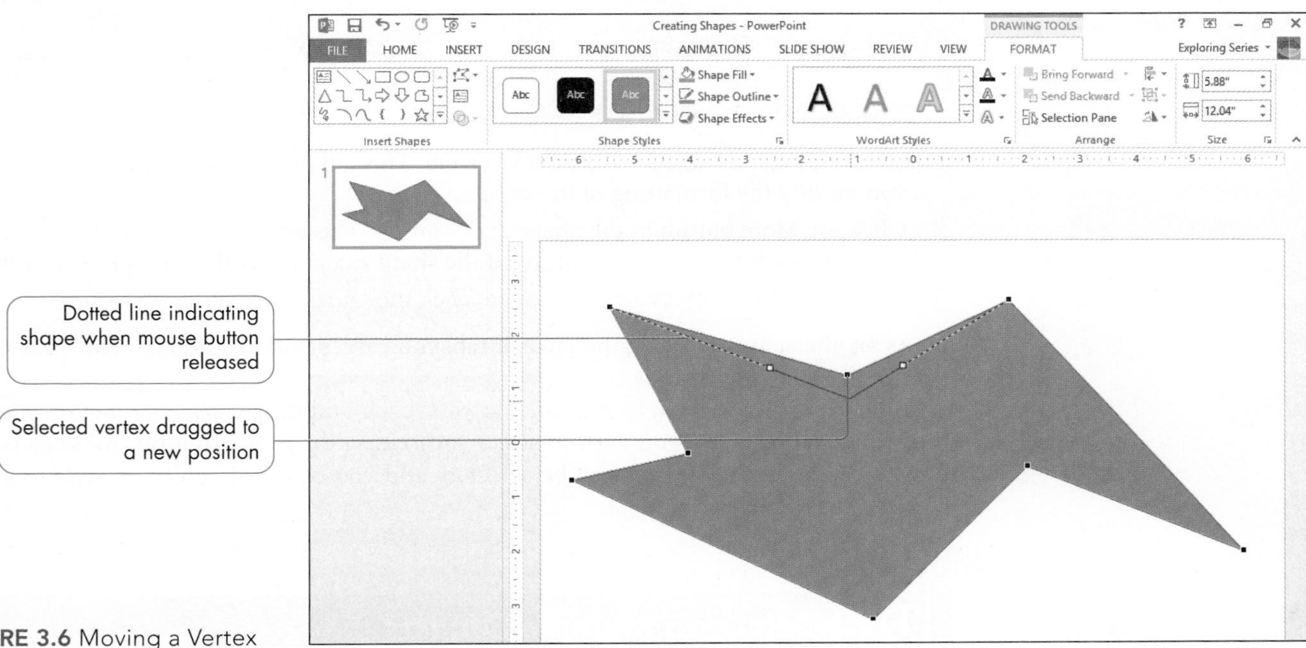

FIGURE 3.6 Moving a Vertex

Applying Quick Styles and Customizing Shapes

STEP 3

A ***Quick Style*** is a combination of different formats that can be selected from the Quick Style gallery and applied to a shape or other objects. To see how a Quick Style would look when applied, position your pointer over the Quick Style thumbnail. When you identify the style you want, click to apply the style to a selected object. Options in the gallery include edges, shadows, line styles, gradients, and 3-D effects. Figure 3.7 shows the Quick Style gallery and several shapes with a variety of Quick Styles applied to them.

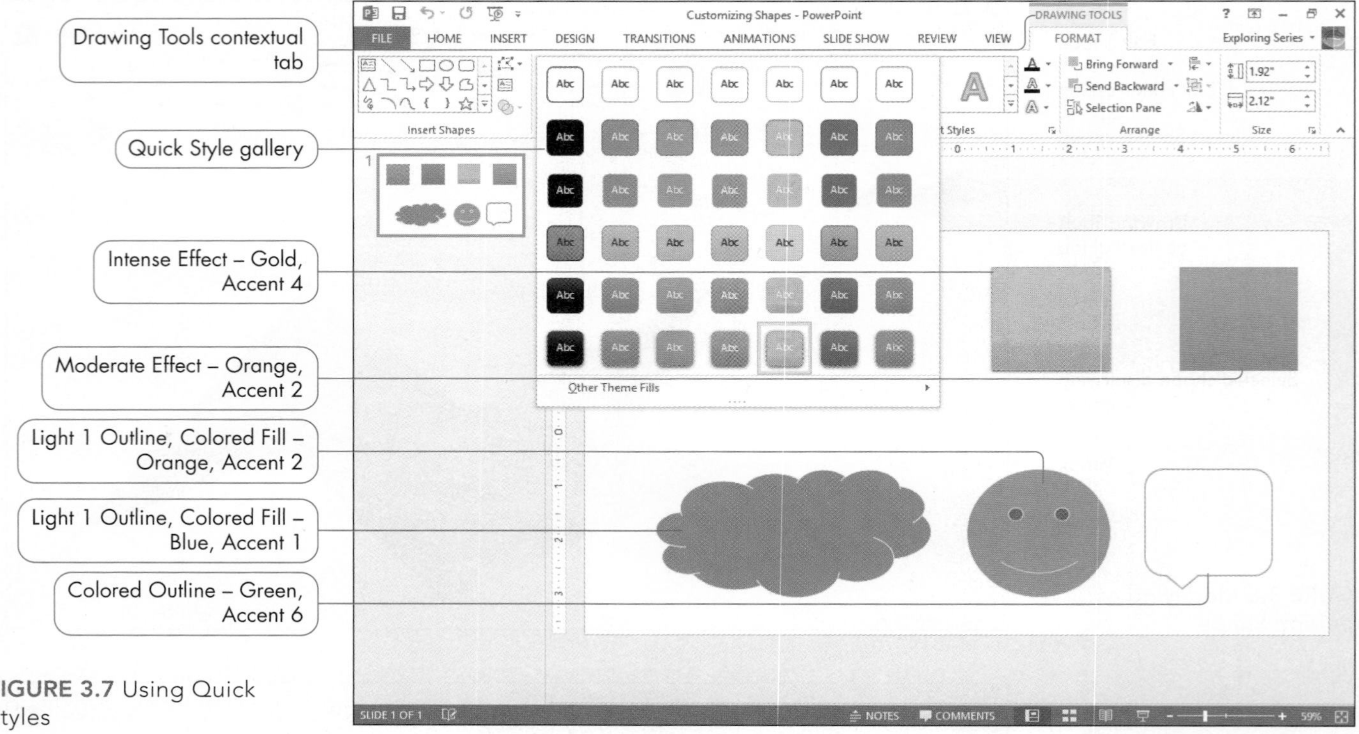

FIGURE 3.7 Using Quick Styles

To apply a Quick Style to a shape:

1. Select the shape and click the FORMAT tab. This tab provides the tools to work with as you modify the formatting of the selected shape.
2. Click the More button in the Shape Styles group. This enables you to apply a Quick Style or to select the fill and outline of the shape manually and apply special effects.
3. When the Quick Styles gallery is open, click the Quick Style you wish to apply.

As an alternative to using the Format tab, you can click the Home tab and click Quick Styles in the Drawing group.

To apply a Quick Style to multiple objects, click and drag a ***selection net*** or ***marquee*** around all of the objects you wish to select and release the mouse button. All objects contained entirely within the net will be selected, and you can apply a Quick Style to all the objects at the same time.

TIP Selecting Multiple Objects

If objects are difficult to select with a selection net because of their placement or because they are nonadjacent, press and hold Ctrl or Shift as you click each object. While the Ctrl or Shift keys are pressed, each mouse click adds an object to the selection. When you have selected all objects, choose the style or effect you want, and it will apply only to the selected objects.

Change Shape Fills

One way to customize a shape is by changing the shape ***fill***, or the interior of the shape. You can choose a solid color fill, no fill, a picture fill, a ***gradient fill*** (a blend of one color to another color or one shade to another shade), or a texture fill. To change the fill of a selected object, click Shape Fill in the Shape Styles group on the Format tab. The Shape Fill gallery provides color choices that match the theme colors or color choices based on Standard Colors. Figure 3.8 shows the Shape Fill options and a shape filled with the Yellow Standard Color.

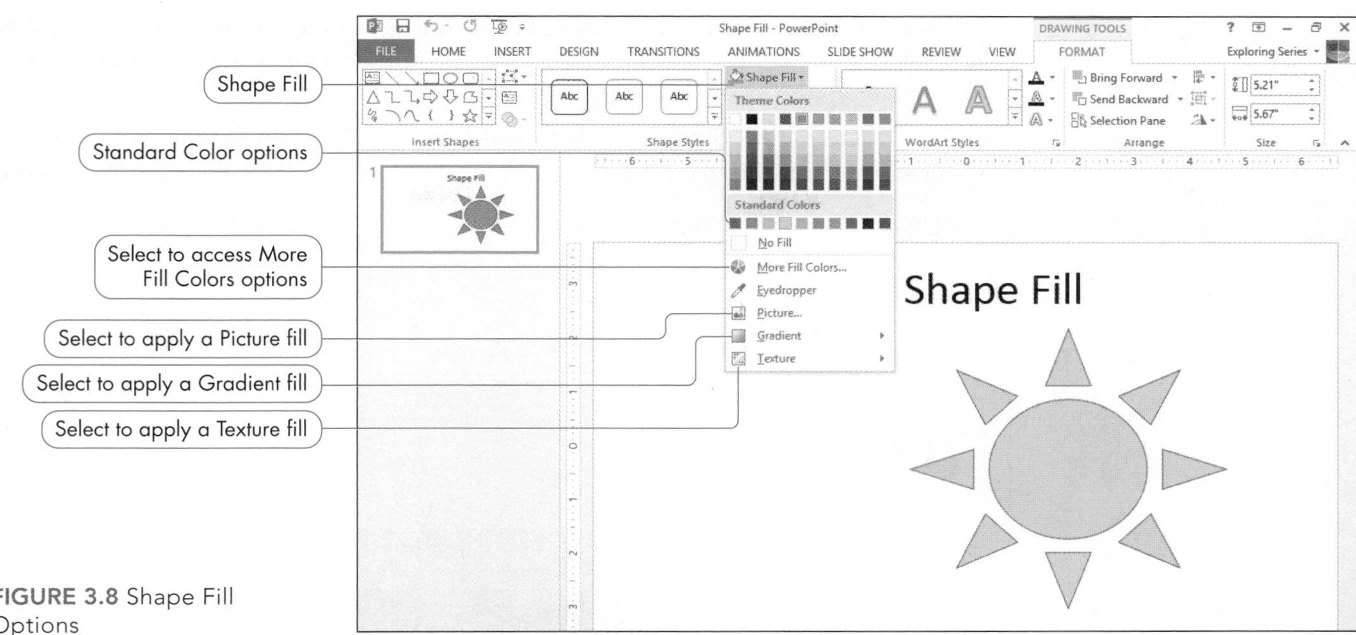

FIGURE 3.8 Shape Fill Options

If the color choices do not meet your needs, you can recreate an exact color in another part of your presentation by using the Eyedropper tool. Perhaps you want to recreate the red in the picture of a sunset you have in your presentation. To use the Eyedropper:

1. Click the shape you want to fill, click the Shape Fill arrow, and then select Eyedropper.
2. Hover over the color you want to recreate and press Enter.
3. The shape will now be filled with that color.

Alternatively, you may also select More Fill Colors to open the Colors dialog box where you can mix colors based on an RGB color model (Red Green Blue) or an HSL color model (Hue Saturation Luminosity). The default RGB color model gives each of the colors red, green, and blue a numeric value that ranges from 0 to 255. The combination of these values creates the fill color assigned to your shape. When all three RGB values are 0, you get black. When all three RGB values are 255, you get white. By using different combinations of numbers between 0 and 255, you can create more than 16 million shades of color.

The Colors dialog box also enables you to determine the amount of ***transparency***, or visibility of the fill. At 0% transparency, the fill is ***opaque*** (or solid), while at 100% transparency, the fill is clear. The Colors dialog box enables you to drag a slider to specify the percentage of transparency. Figure 3.9 shows the Colors dialog box with the RGB color model selected, Red assigned a value of 236, Green assigned a value of 32, Blue assigned a value of 148, and a transparency set at 0%.

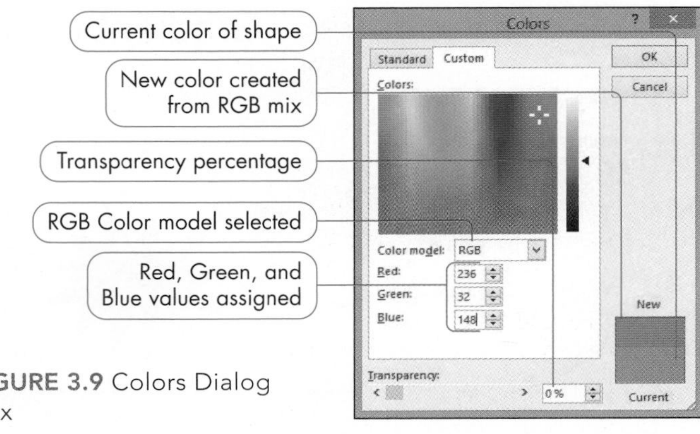

FIGURE 3.9 Colors Dialog Box

You can fill shapes with images using the ***picture fill*** option. This option enables you to create unusual frames for your pictures and can be a fun way to vary the images in your presentation. To insert a picture as a fill:

1. Select Picture in the Shape Fill gallery, which is accessible from the FORMAT tab.
2. Browse to locate the picture that you want to add and double-click the picture to insert it.

Figure 3.10 shows the Plaque shape filled with a casual snapshot taken with a digital camera.

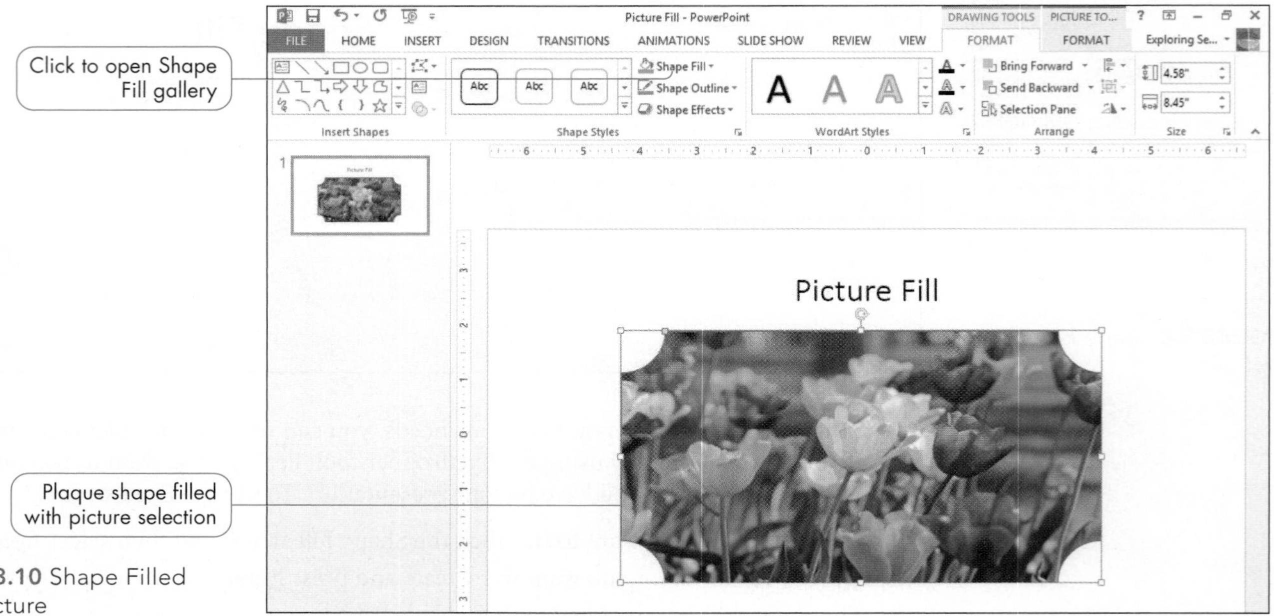

FIGURE 3.10 Shape Filled with a Picture

As discussed earlier in the chapter, you can fill shapes with gradient fills, a blend of two or more colors. When you select Gradient from the Shape Fill gallery, another gallery of options opens, enabling you to select Light and Dark Variations that blend the current color with white or black in linear or radial gradients. Figure 3.11 shows the gradient options for a selected object.

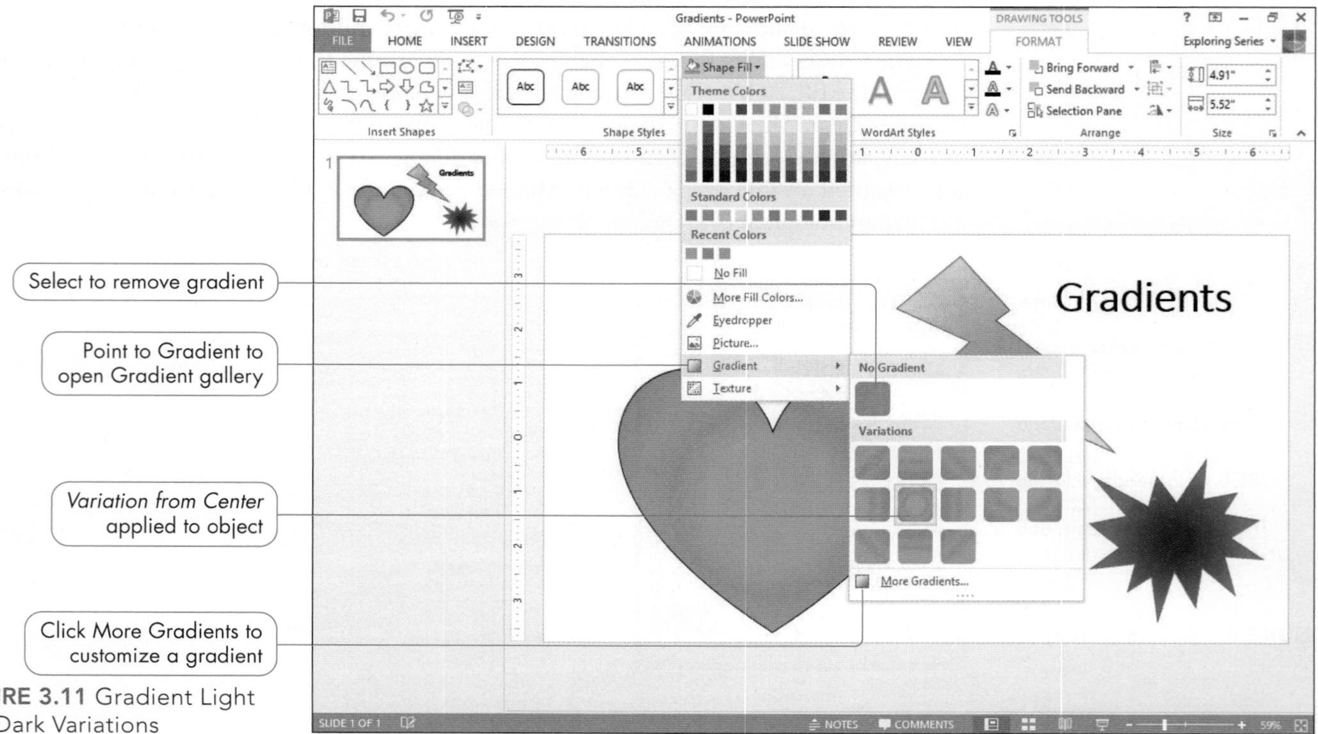

FIGURE 3.11 Gradient Light and Dark Variations

When you select More Gradients at the bottom of the Gradients gallery, the Format Shape pane displays. The Gradient fill option in the *Fill* section provides access to the Preset gradients gallery. This gallery gives you a variety of gradients using a multitude of colors to create truly beautiful impressions. Figure 3.12 shows the Preset gradients gallery.

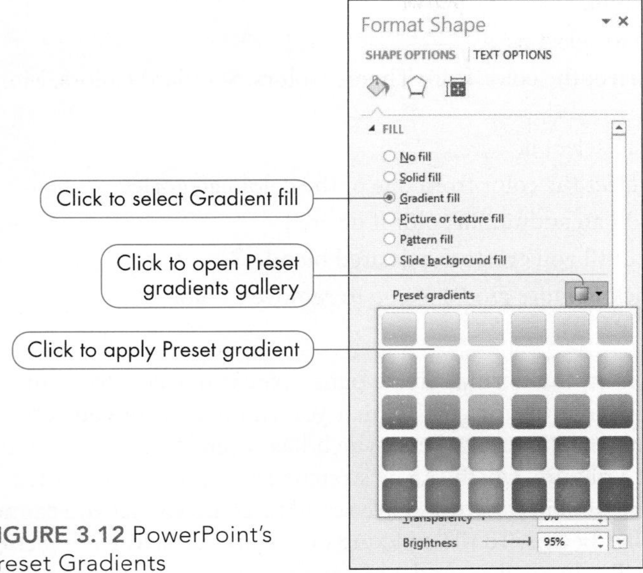

FIGURE 3.12 PowerPoint's Preset Gradients

You can create a custom gradient in the Format Shape pane. You can select the colors to blend for the gradient, the direction and angle of the gradient, the brightness of the colors, and the amount of transparency to apply. Figure 3.13 shows a custom gradient created for a heart image.

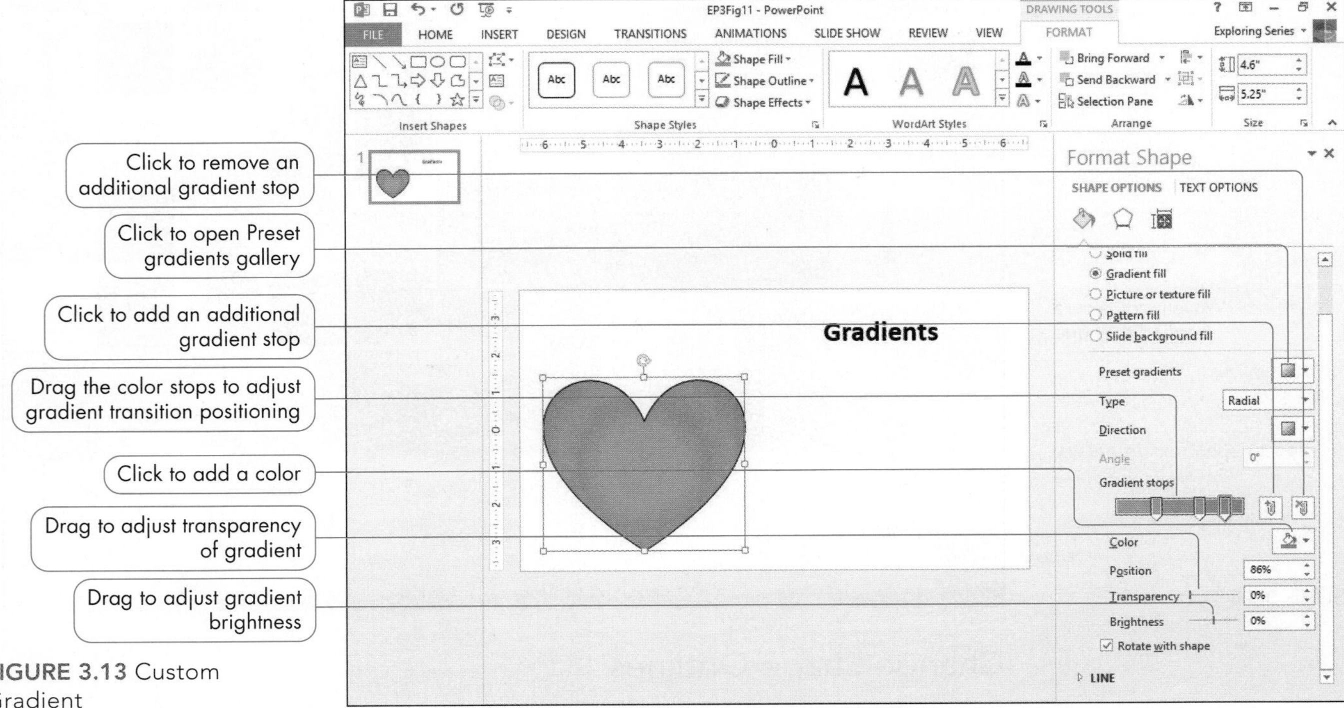

FIGURE 3.13 Custom Gradient

To create a custom gradient:

1. Select the shape you want to contain the gradient.
2. Click the FORMAT tab.
3. Click the Format Shape dialog box launcher in the Shape Styles group.
4. Click Fill and click Gradient Fill.
5. Click the first Gradient stop to select it.
6. Click the Color arrow and select the color from Theme Colors, Standard Colors, More Colors, or the Eyedropper.
7. Click the last Gradient stop to select it.
8. Click the Color arrow and select the color from one of the color categories.
9. Click *Add gradient stop* to add an additional color if desired.
10. Drag the new gradient stop until you create the desired blend.
11. Click a gradient stop and click *Remove gradient stop* to remove a color.
12. Click Close.

Selecting *Picture or texture fill* in the Format Shape pane gives you access to common ***texture fills***, such as canvas, denim, marble, or cork, which you can use to fill your object. Selecting the Texture button opens the Texture gallery, which has several options. Click the File button to navigate and insert a picture, which can be stretched to fit the shape or tiled so the picture is repeated to fill the shape. Tiled textures have seamless edges so that you cannot tell where one tile ends and another begins. To tile a picture or texture fill, select *Tile picture as texture*. Figure 3.14 shows the Texture gallery and a rectangle used as a background that contains the woven mat fill.

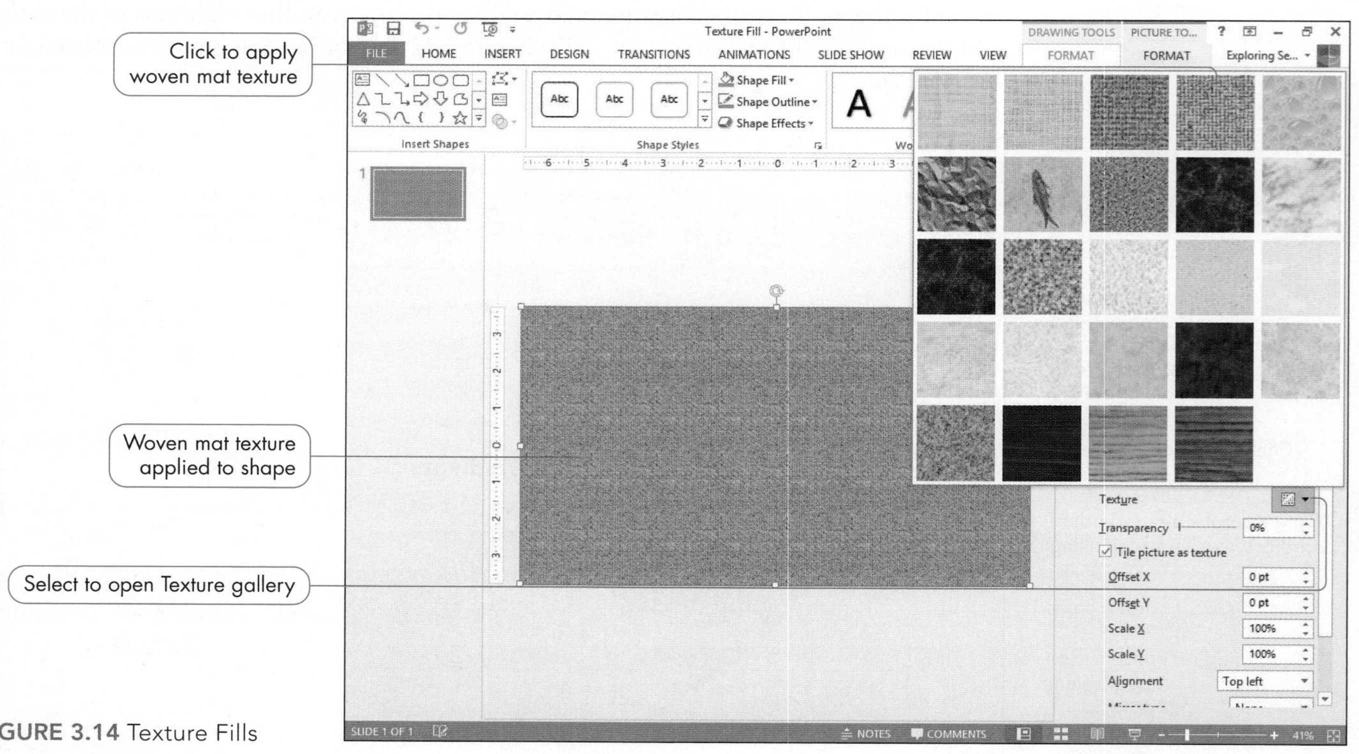

FIGURE 3.14 Texture Fills

Change Shape Outlines

By default, outlines form a border around the shape. You can modify a shape's outline by changing its color, style, or ***line weight*** (thickness). You can modify outlines using the Shape Styles feature accessible in the Shape Styles group or by clicking the Shape Styles dialog box launcher to open the Format Shape pane. You can customize outlines using the Shape Outline gallery options available in the Shape Styles group or the Line options in the Format Shape pane. First, select the line or object and open the Shape Outline gallery by clicking Shape Outline. The same color options used to change the color of fills are available to change the color of outlines. If you wish to remove an outline, select the No Outline option. In Figure 3.15, the outline surrounding the shape with the picture fill has been removed so that it does not detract from the image.

The width or thickness of a line is measured in ***points*** (pt), the smallest unit of measurement in typography. One vertical inch contains 72 pt.

To set the line width:

1. Click Shape Outline in the Shape Styles group on the DRAWING TOOLS FORMAT tab.
2. Point to Weight to display line weight choices from 1/4 pt to 6 pt.

To access additional line weight options, select More Lines to open the Format Shape pane with the Line options displayed. The Format Shape pane enables you to change the line weight using the spin arrows in the Width box or by typing the weight directly into the Width box. You can also use the Format Shape pane to create Compound type outlines, which combine thick and thin lines. Figure 3.15 displays lines and an outline for a shape in various weights.

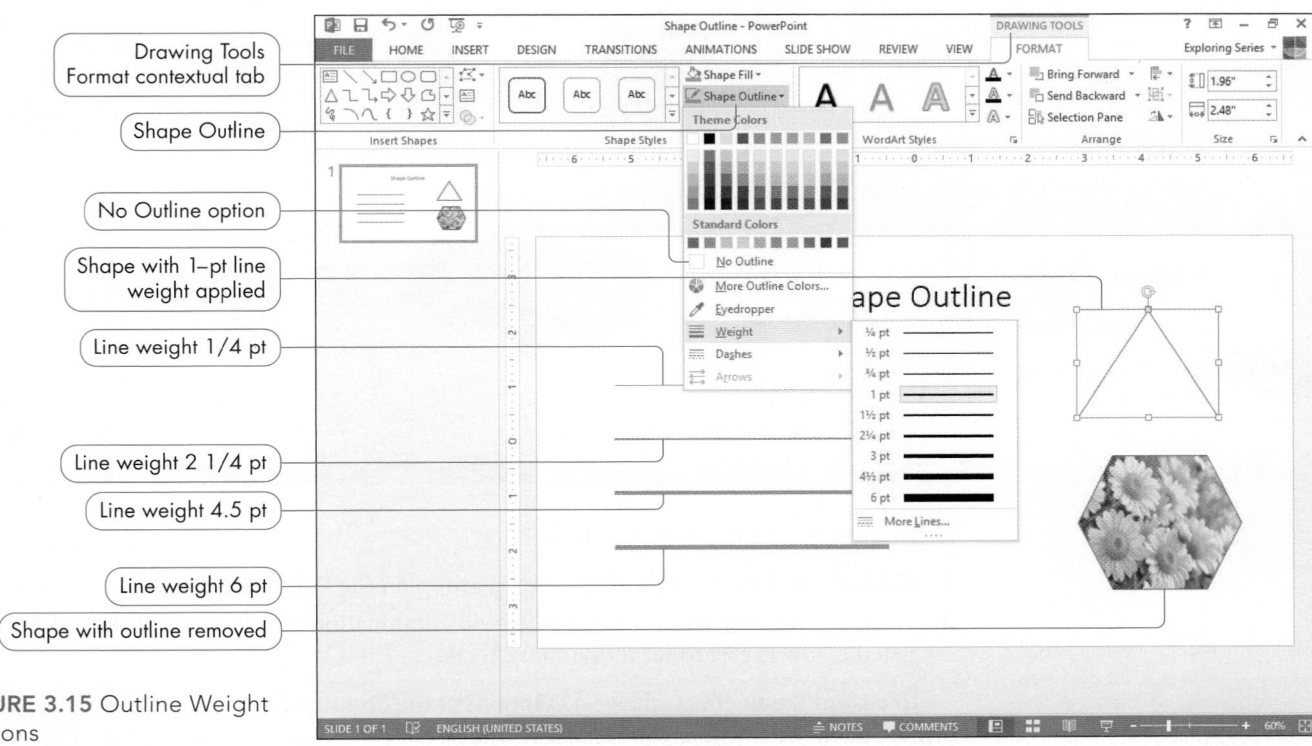

FIGURE 3.15 Outline Weight Options

For variety, you can change a solid line to a dashed line. Dashed lines make interesting boxes or borders for shapes and placeholders by using round dots, square dots, and combinations of short dashes, long dashes, and dots. To make a line or object outline dashed:

1. Select the object.
2. Click Shape Outline on the FORMAT tab.
3. Point to the Dashes option and click the desired line style.

You can add an arrowhead to the beginning or end of a line to create an arrow that points to critical information on the slide. The Shape Outline feature enables you to create many different styles of arrows using points, circles, and diamonds. To add an arrowhead:

1. Select a line.
2. Click Shape Outline on the FORMAT tab.

3. Point to the Arrows option.
4. Click the desired style.

Change Shape Effects

STEP 4 You do not need an expensive, high-powered graphics editor for special effects because PowerPoint enables you to apply many stunning effects to shapes: preset three-dimensional effects, shadow effects, reflections, glows, soft edge effects, bevels, and 3-D rotations. One of the greatest strengths of PowerPoint is its ability to immediately update any shape effects if you choose a new theme. Figure 3.16 shows an example of some of the shape effects available.

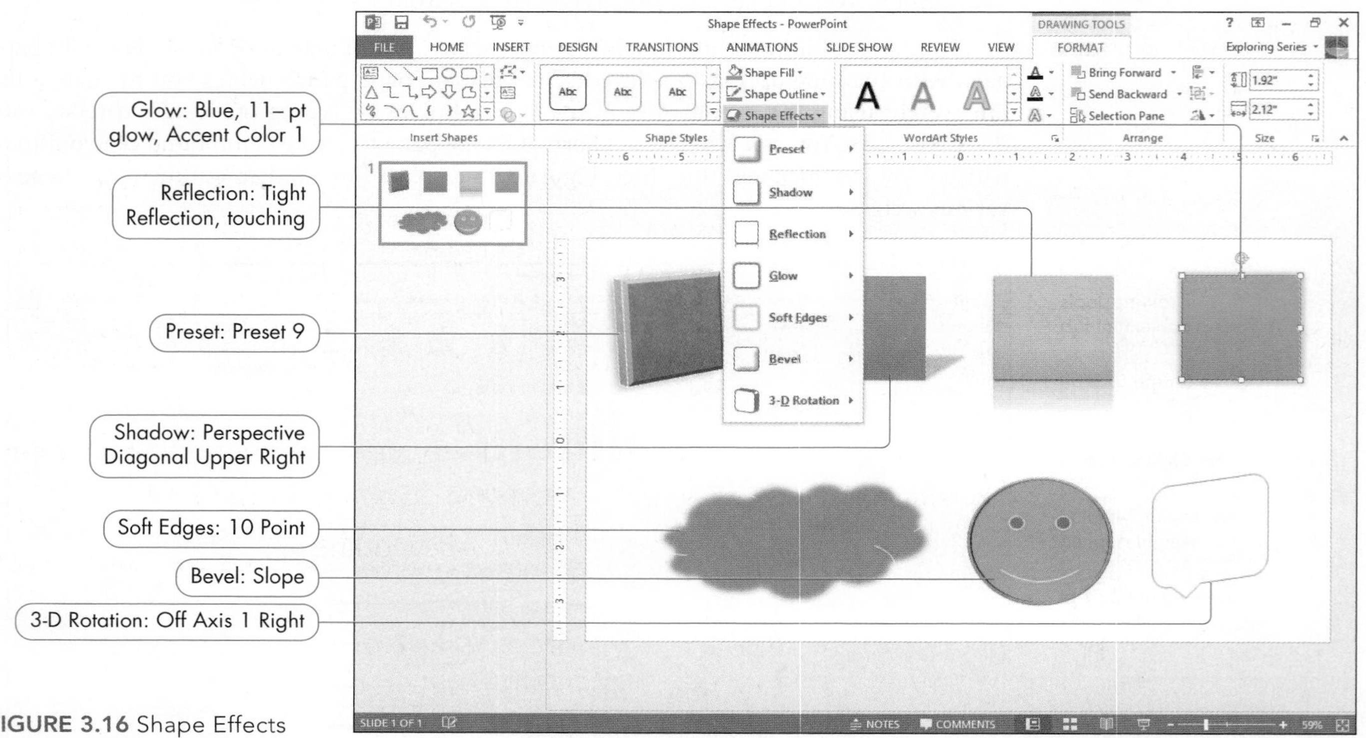

FIGURE 3.16 Shape Effects

To apply effects to a selected shape:

1. Click Shape Effects in the Shape Styles group on the FORMAT tab.
2. Point to *Preset effects* and select a built-in combination or select one of the options listed below Preset to set individual effects.

To customize an effect, click 3-D Options at the bottom of the Preset gallery to open the Format Shape pane, where you can define the bevel, depth, contour, and surface of the effect. Figure 3.17 displays the Format Shape options and the Material options for the surface of a shape.

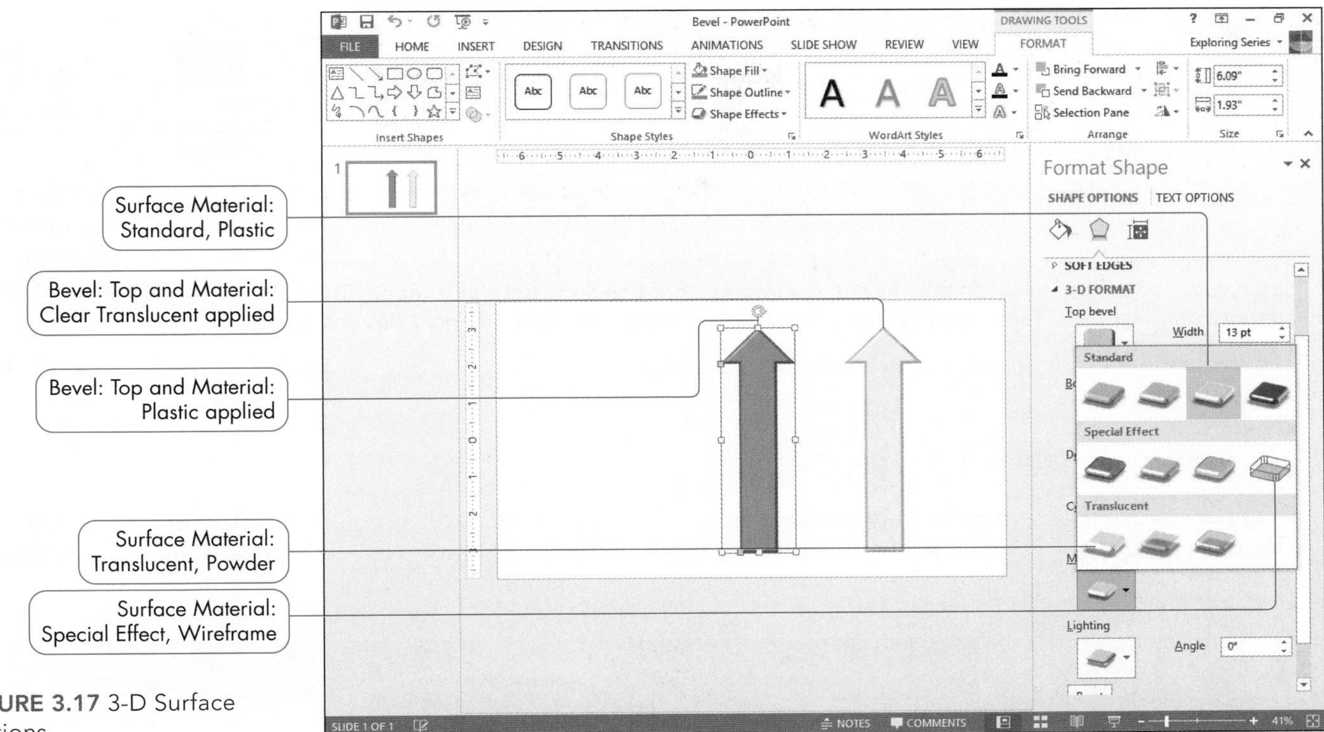

FIGURE 3.17 3-D Surface Options

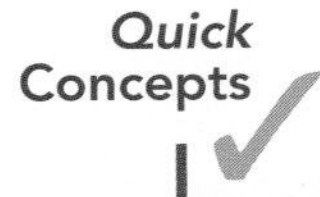

1. Describe the purpose and effectiveness of incorporating shapes into a presentation. ***p. 944***
2. What is the value of using connector lines when creating a flow chart? ***p. 946***
3. List three types of fills that can be applied to a shape. ***p. 952***

Hands-On Exercises

1 Shapes

You begin your PowerPoint mini-camp by having the interns work with a project status report. They will create basic shapes using PowerPoint's drawing tools. You also ask the group to customize the shapes by adding styles and effects.

Skills covered: Create Basic Shapes • Draw and Format Connector Lines • Apply a Quick Style and Customize Shapes • Use Shape Effects

STEP 1 » CREATE BASIC SHAPES

Knowing how to use a flow chart to diagram the processes or steps needed to complete a project or task is a valuable skill. To teach participants how to create multiple shapes using the Lock Drawing Mode, you have them create several ovals as part of a project flow chart. Refer to Figure 3.18 as you complete Step 1.

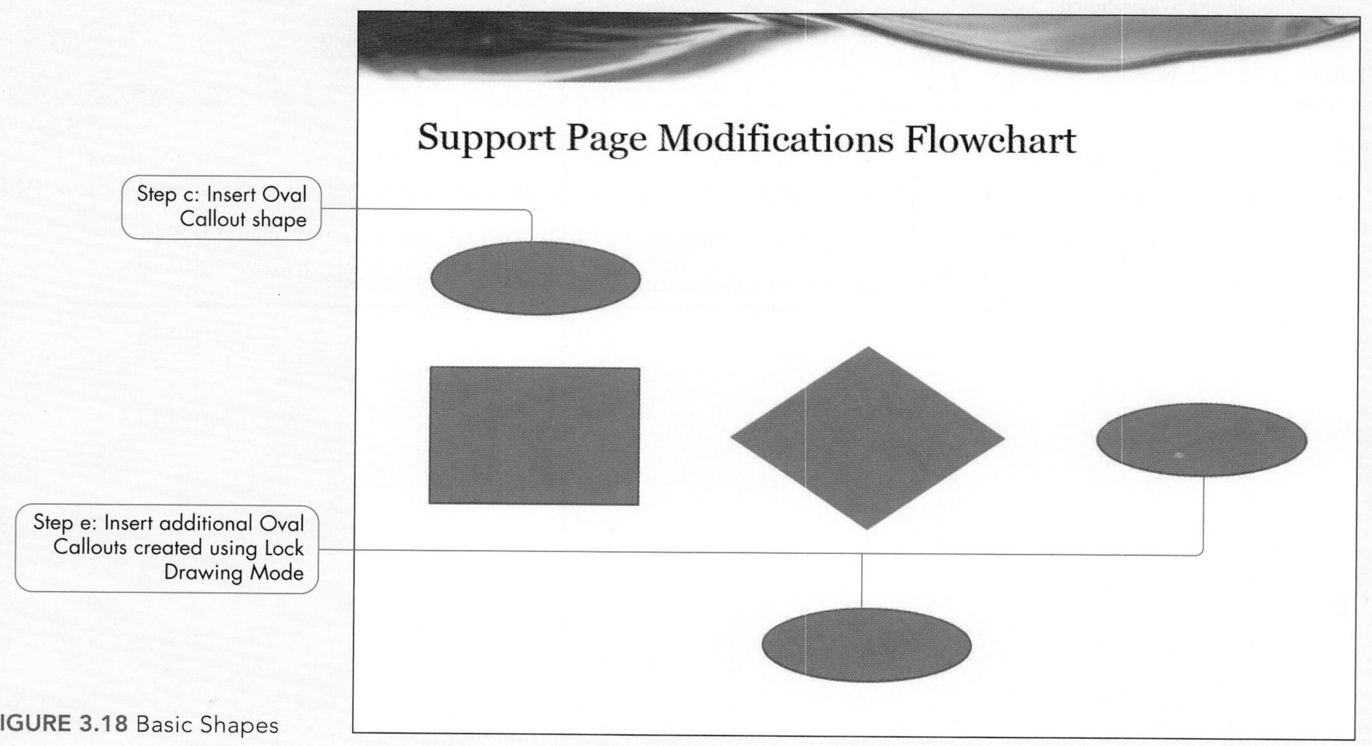

FIGURE 3.18 Basic Shapes

a. Start PowerPoint, open *p03h1Project*, and then save it as **p03h1Project_LastFirst**.

> **TROUBLESHOOTING:** If you make any major mistakes in this exercise, you can press Ctrl+Z to undo as many steps as needed, or close the file, open *p03h1Project*, and then start this exercise over.

b. On Slide 1, replace *First Name Last Name* with your name. Create a handout header with your name and a handout footer with your instructor's name and your class. Include the current date. Apply to all.

c. On Slide 6, click **Oval** in the Basic Shapes in the Drawing group on the HOME tab. Position your pointer on the top-left side of the slide above the square shape and below the title and drag to create the shape.

> **TROUBLESHOOTING:** If you do not see the Oval shape, click the More button for the Basic Shapes or click the Insert tab and click Shapes in the Illustrations group.

Do not worry about the exact placement or size of the shapes you create at this time. You will learn how to precisely place and size shapes in the steps to follow.

d. Click the **INSERT tab** and click **Shapes** in the Illustrations group. Right-click **Oval** in the Basic Shapes category and select **Lock Drawing Mode**.

You activate Lock Drawing Mode so that you can create multiple shapes of the same kind.

e. Position the pointer to the right of the diamond and drag to create the oval. Repeat this process below the diamond to mimic Figure 3.18. Press **Esc** to turn off Lock Drawing Mode.

You create two additional Oval callouts.

f. Save the presentation.

STEP 2 » DRAW AND FORMAT CONNECTOR LINES

To continue building the flow chart, the mini-camp interns need to practice creating connecting lines between shapes. You also teach the group how to add a text box to a slide so they can add text, because the title only template is being used. Refer to Figure 3.19 as you complete Step 2.

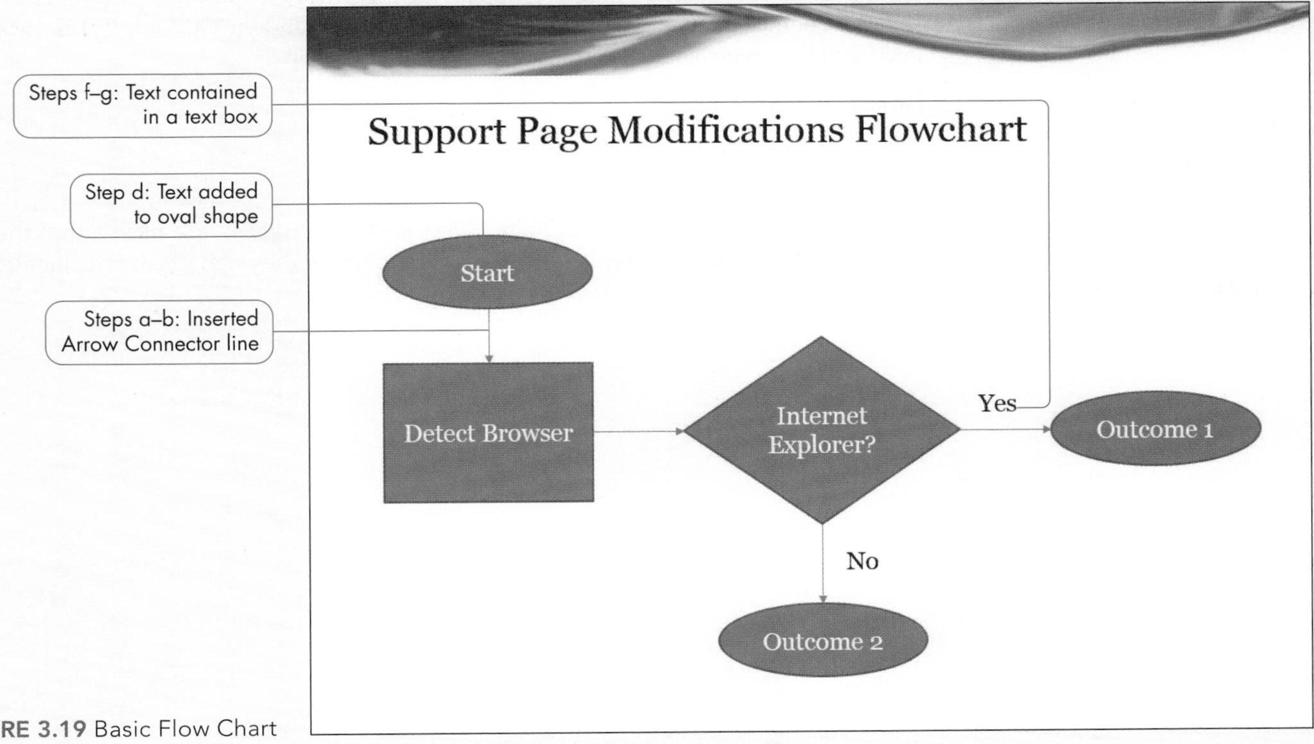

FIGURE 3.19 Basic Flow Chart

a. Click **Shapes** in the Illustrations group, click **Arrow** in the Lines category, move the cross-hair pointer over the oval on the left side of the slide, and then position the pointer on the bottom-center handle.

The shape's connector handles appear when a connector line is selected and the cross-hair pointer is moved onto the shape.

b. Drag a connecting line that attaches the bottom-center connecting handle of the oval to the top center connecting handle of the rectangle below it.

A connector arrow is placed between the oval and the rectangle. The default line weight is very thin at 1/2 pt.

c. Click **Shapes** in the Illustrations group on the FORMAT tab, right-click the **Arrow**, and then select **Lock Drawing Mode**. Create connecting arrows using the technique just practiced that will attach the rectangle to the diamond and the diamond to the two remaining ovals, as shown in Figure 3.19. Press **Esc**.

d. Right-click the oval on the top-left of the slide, select **Edit Text**, and then type **Start**.

The text you typed becomes part of the oval shape.

e. Select the square shape and type **Detect Browser**. Use either of the practiced methods to select each of the remaining shapes and type the text shown in Figure 3.19.

f. Click the **INSERT tab** and click **Text Box** in the Text group.

Clicking Text Box enables you to create text that is not contained in a shape or in a placeholder on the slide.

g. Position the pointer above the connector between the *Decision* diamond and the *Outcome 1* oval, click once, and then type **Yes**.

> **TROUBLESHOOTING:** If the text box is not positioned above the connector line between the *Decision* diamond and the *Outcome 1* oval, click the border (not the sizing handle) of the text box and drag it into position.

h. Click **Text Box** in the Insert Shapes group on the FORMAT tab, position the pointer to the right side of the connector between the *Decision* diamond and the *Outcome 2* oval, click once, and then type **No**. Reposition the text box if necessary.

i. Save the presentation.

STEP 3 ›› APPLY A QUICK STYLE AND CUSTOMIZE SHAPES

You encourage participants of the mini-camp to experiment with Quick Styles and to modify shape fills so that they are able to customize shapes. Then they set the shapes to styles of your choice to show they can meet specifications when asked. Refer to Figure 3.20 as you complete Step 3.

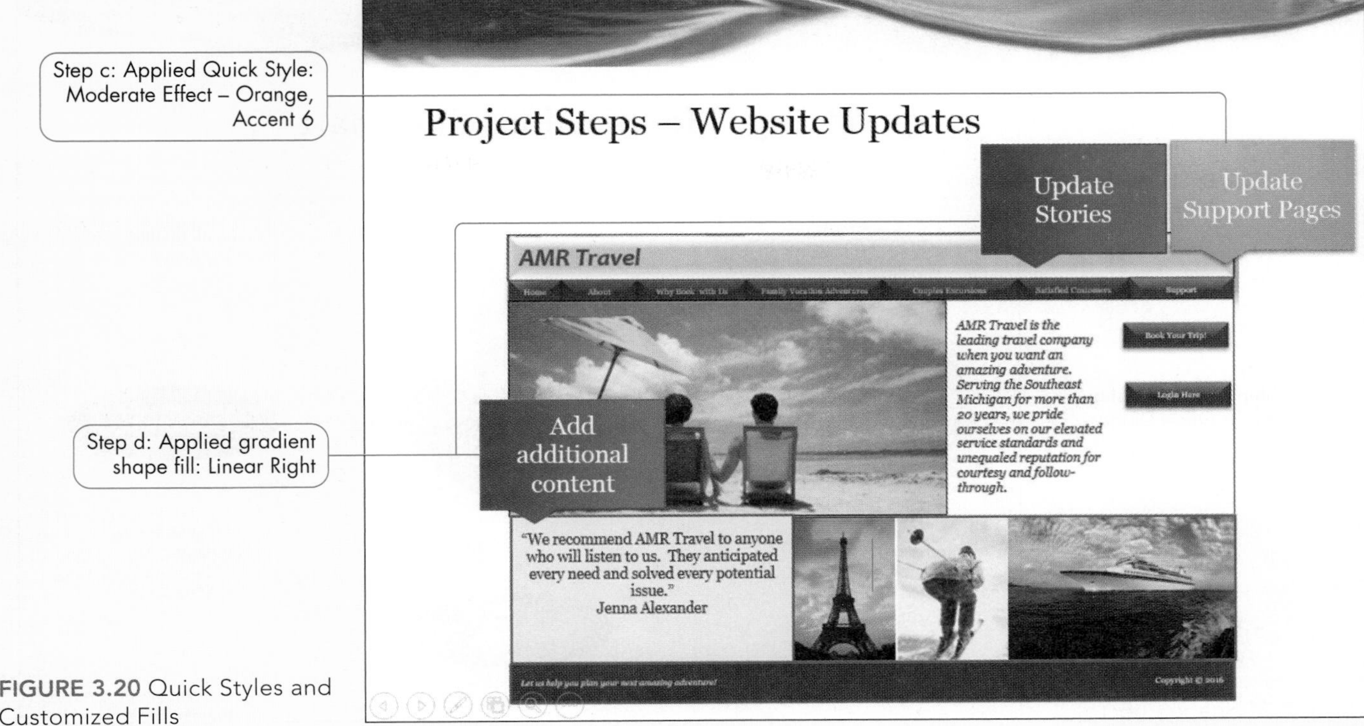

FIGURE 3.20 Quick Styles and Customized Fills

a. On Slide 5, select the far-right callout shape.

b. Click the **FORMAT tab** and click **More** in the Shape Styles group.

The Quick Style gallery opens.

c. Move your pointer over the Quick Styles and note the changes in fill, outline, and effects to the shape as you do so. After you are through experimenting, click **Moderate Effect - Orange, Accent 6** (fifth row, seventh column). Click in an empty area to deselect the callout.

Live Preview shows the effects on your object as you move the pointer over the Quick Style options.

d. Press and hold **Ctrl** and click the remaining two callout shapes to select them. Click the **FORMAT tab**, click **Shape Fill** in the Shape Styles group, and then click **Blue, Accent 1** (first row, fifth column). Click **Shape Fill** again, point to *Gradient*, and then click **Linear Right** under *Dark Variations*. Click **Text Fill** in the WordArt Styles group and click **White, Background 1** to change the text to a white color.

You apply a gradient fill to more than one shape at a time.

e. Save the presentation.

STEP 4 » USE SHAPE EFFECTS

PowerPoint provides many shape effects that you can use for emphasis. You ask the participants to apply effects to the flow chart shapes so they become familiar with the options available. Refer to Figure 3.21 as you complete Step 4.

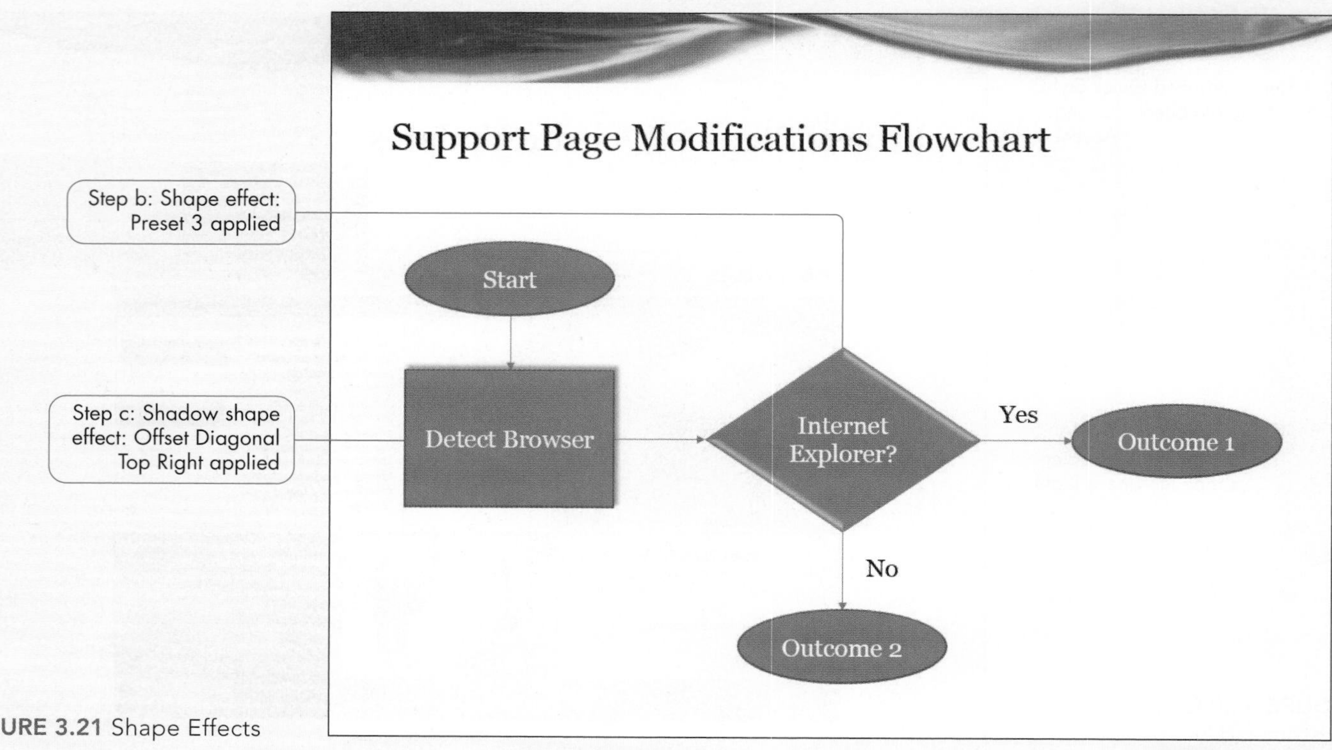

FIGURE 3.21 Shape Effects

a. Click **Slide 6** and click the diamond shape.

b. Click the **FORMAT tab**, click **Shape Effects** in the Shape Styles group, point to *Preset*, and then click **Preset 3**.

   Preset 3 combines a bevel type, a depth, contours, and a surface effect.

c. Select the rectangle shape, click **Shape Effects** in the Shape Styles group, point to *Shadow*, and then click **Offset Diagonal Top Right** (Outer category).

   The Offset Diagonal option applies a 4-pt soft shadow to the top right of the rectangle.

d. Spell check the presentation. Save the presentation and submit the file based on your instructor's directions. Close the file and exit PowerPoint.

SmartArt and WordArt

Diagrams are infographics used to illustrate concepts and processes. PowerPoint includes a feature to create eye-catching diagrams: SmartArt. Attention is drawn to an infographic using text created by another eye-catching PowerPoint feature: WordArt. In this section, you will create and modify SmartArt diagrams and WordArt text.

Creating SmartArt

STEP 1 The ***SmartArt*** feature enables you to create a diagram and to enter the text of your message in one of many existing layouts. SmartArt helps to create a visual representation of your information. The resulting illustration is professional looking and complements the theme you selected. You can also convert existing text to SmartArt. Figure 3.22 compares a text-based slide in the common bullet format to a second slide showing the same information converted to a SmartArt diagram. The arrows and colors in the SmartArt diagram make it easy for the viewer to understand the message and remember the concept of a cycle. It is especially effective when you add animation to each step.

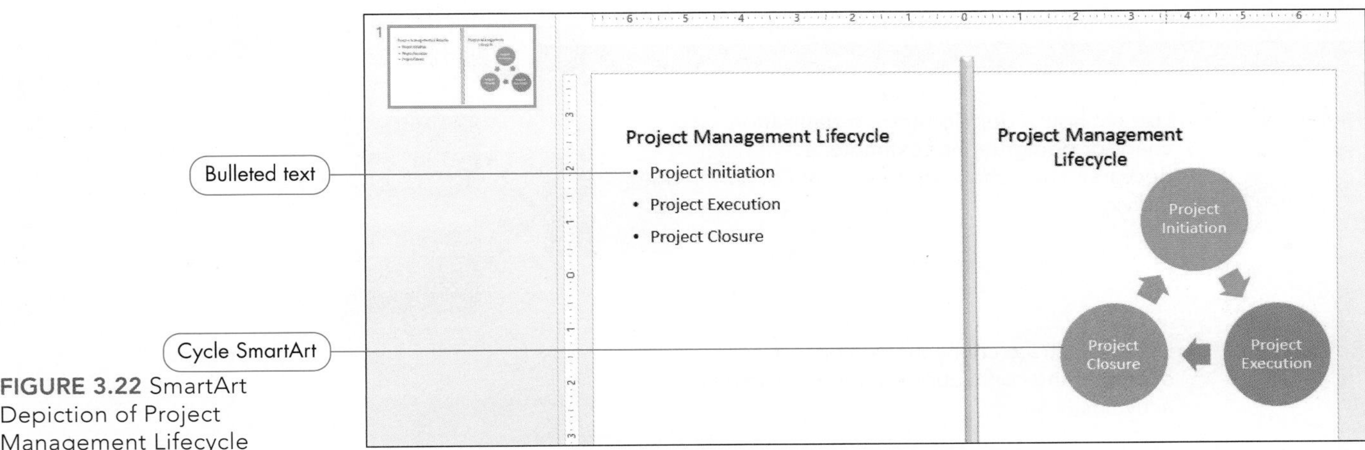

FIGURE 3.22 SmartArt Depiction of Project Management Lifecycle

A SmartArt diagram creates a layout for your information, provides a pane for quickly entering information, automatically sizes shapes and text, and gives you the ability to switch between layouts, making it easy to choose the most effective layout. Some layouts can be used for any type of information and are designed to be visually attractive, while other layouts are created specifically for a certain type of information, such as a process or hierarchy. SmartArt types include options for presenting lists of information in ordered (steps to complete a task) or unordered (features of a product) formats.

To create a SmartArt diagram, choose a diagram type that fits your message. The SmartArt gallery has nine different categories of diagrams: List, Process, Cycle, Hierarchy, Relationship, Matrix, Pyramid, Picture, and Office.com. At the top of the list of categories is All, which you can click to display the choices from all categories. Each category includes a description of the type of information appropriate for the layouts in that category. The following reference table shows the SmartArt categories and their purposes.

REFERENCE SmartArt Diagram

Type	Purpose	Sample SmartArt
List	Use to show nonsequential information. For example: a list of items to be checked on a roof each year.	Flashing Shingles Soffits
Process	Use to show steps in a process or a timeline. For example: the steps involved in washing a car.	Hose → Sponge → Rinse
Cycle	Use to show a continual process. For example: the recurring business cycle.	Expansion Downturn Recession Recovery
Hierarchy	Use to show a decision tree, organization chart, or pedigree. For example: a pedigree chart showing the parents of an individual.	Reed J. Olsen Ivan Olsen Gladys Jones
Relationship	Use to illustrate connections. For example: the connections among outdoor activities.	Camping Hiking Fishing
Matrix	Use to show how parts relate to a whole. For example: the Keirsey Temperament Theory of four groups describing human behavior.	Rationals Idealists Keirsey Temperaments Artisans Guardians
Pyramid	Use to show proportional relationships with the largest component on the top or bottom. For example: an ecology chart.	Indirect Consumers Direct Consumers Producers

REFERENCE Continued

Type	Purpose	Sample SmartArt
Picture	Use to show nonsequential or grouped blocks of information. Maximizes both horizontal and vertical display space for shapes.	Xeriscaping Zeroscaping
Office.com	Miscellaneous shapes for showing blocks of information.	Images Audio Video

Figure 3.23 shows the Choose a SmartArt Graphic dialog box. The pane on the left side shows the types of SmartArt diagrams available. Each type of diagram includes subtypes that are displayed in the center pane. Clicking one of the subtypes enlarges the selected graphic and displays it in the preview pane on the right side. The preview pane describes purposes for which the SmartArt subtype can be used effectively. Some of the descriptions include tips for the type of text to enter.

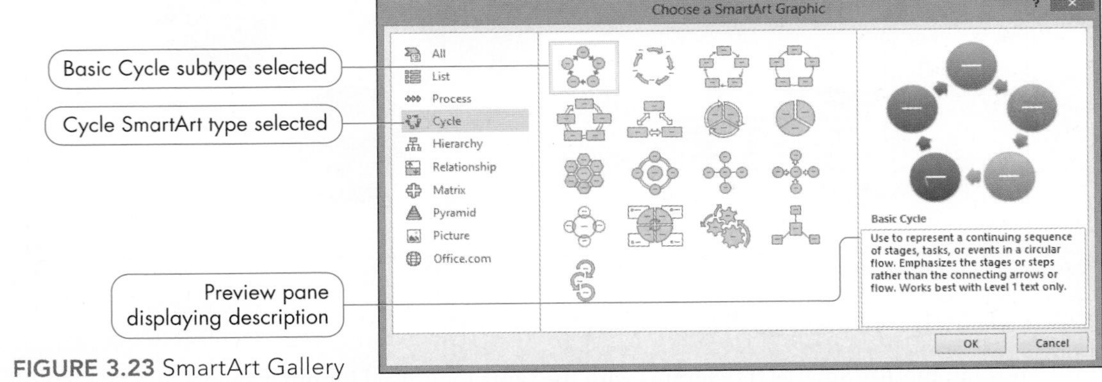

FIGURE 3.23 SmartArt Gallery

To create a SmartArt diagram:

1. Click the INSERT tab.
2. Click SmartArt in the Illustrations group.
3. Click the type of SmartArt diagram you want in the left pane.
4. Click the SmartArt subtype you want in the center pane.
5. Preview the selected SmartArt and subtype in the right pane.
6. Click OK.

Text in SmartArt

Some SmartArt layouts allow only one level of text, while others are set up for one or two levels of text. So, if there are main and subpoints that need to be displayed, a SmartArt graphic that allows two levels of text is necessary. Also, be sure to keep the text short and limit it to key points to create a visually appealing diagram.

Once you select the SmartArt diagram type and the subtype, a ***Text pane*** opens in which you can enter text. If the Text pane does not open, click Text Pane in the Create Graphic group on the SmartArt Tools Design tab. The Text pane works like an outline—enter a line of text, press Enter, and then press Tab or Shift+Tab to increase or decrease the indent level. The font size will decrease to fit text inside the shape, or the shape may grow to fit the text, depending on the size and number of shapes in your SmartArt diagram. The layout accommodates additional shapes as you enter text unless the type of shape is designed for a specific number of shapes, such as the Relationship Counterbalance Arrows layout, which is designed to show two opposing ideas. If you choose a diagram with more shapes than you need, you may need to delete the extra shapes; then PowerPoint will automatically rearrange the shapes to eliminate any blank space. Figure 3.24 shows text entered into the Text pane for a Basic Cycle SmartArt diagram. Because four lines of text were entered, four shapes were created.

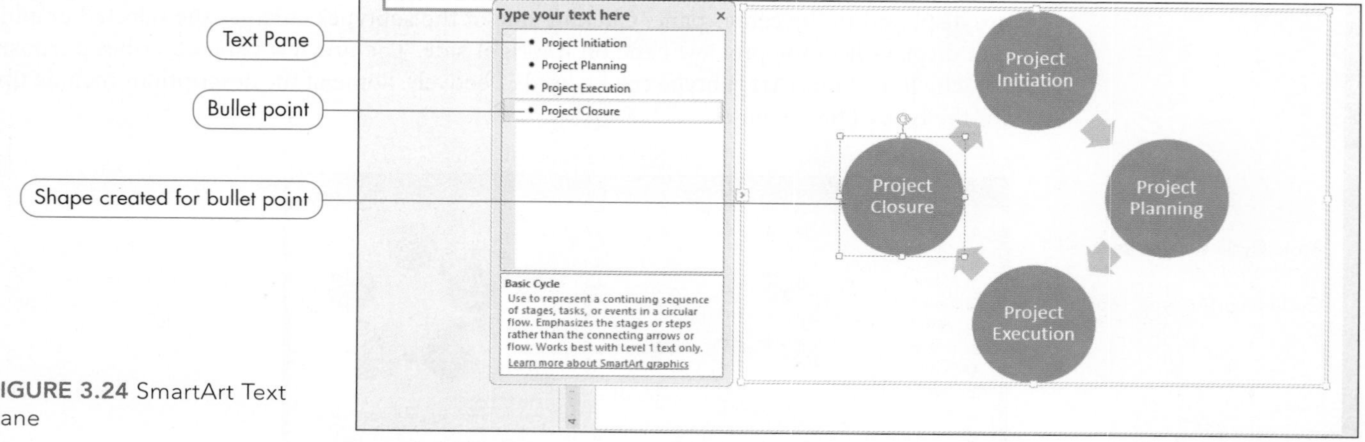

FIGURE 3.24 SmartArt Text Pane

Modifying SmartArt

You can modify SmartArt diagrams with the same tools used for other shapes and text boxes. You can reposition or resize a SmartArt diagram by dragging its borders. You also can modify SmartArt text in the Text pane just as if it is in a placeholder, or you can modify the text in the shape itself. If you need an additional shape, click to position your insertion point in the Text pane at the beginning or end of the text where you want to add a shape, press Enter, and then type the text.

An alternative method for adding shapes is to use the Add Shape command. To use the Add Shape command, do the following:

1. Click an existing shape in the SmartArt diagram.
2. Click the SMARTART TOOLS DESIGN tab.
3. Click the Add Shape arrow in the Create Graphic group.
4. Select Add Shape After, Add Shape Before, Add Shape Above, Add Shape Below, or Add Assistant when available.

SmartArt diagrams have two galleries used to enhance the appearance of the diagram, both of which are located under the SmartArt Tools Design tab in the SmartArt Styles group. One gallery changes colors, and the other gallery applies a combination of special effects.

Change SmartArt Theme Colors

STEP 2» To change the color scheme of your SmartArt diagram, click Change Colors to display the Colors gallery (see Figure 3.25). The gallery contains Primary Theme Colors, Colorful, and Accent color schemes. Click a color variation to apply it to the SmartArt diagram.

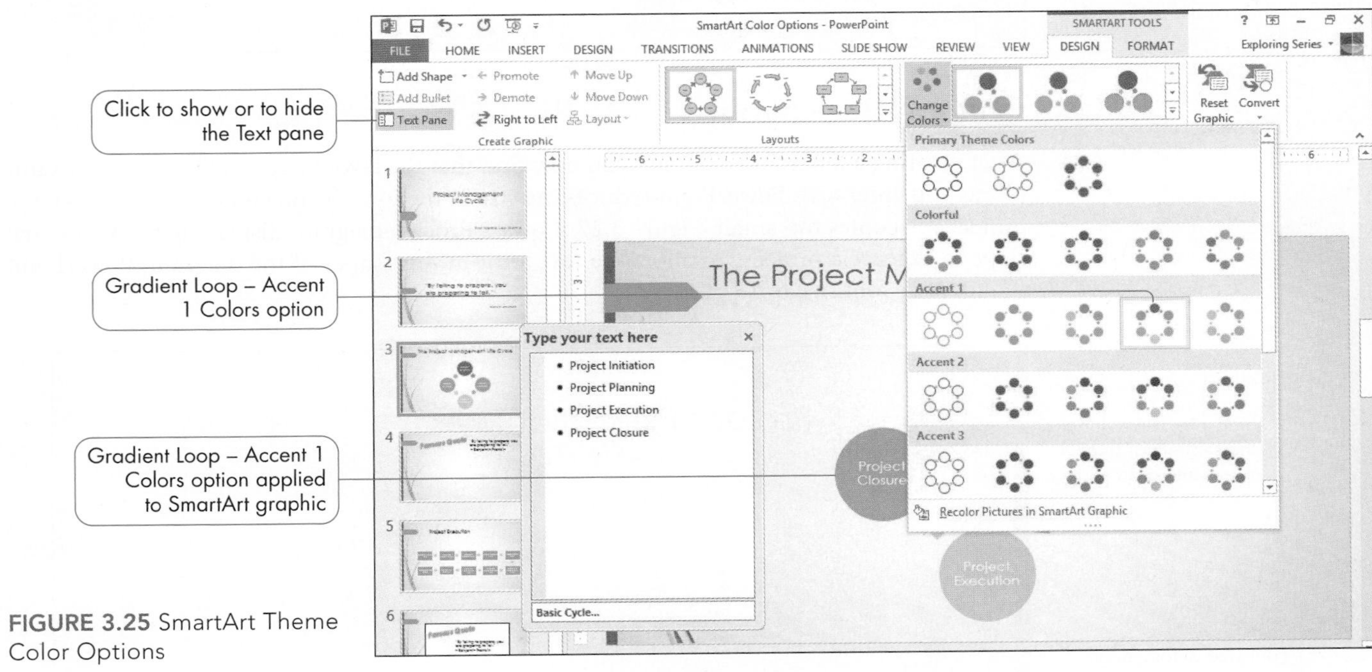

FIGURE 3.25 SmartArt Theme Color Options

Use Quick Styles with SmartArt

After creating the diagram, you can use Quick Styles to adjust the style to match other styles you have used in your presentation or to make the diagram easier to understand. To apply a Quick Style to a SmartArt diagram, click the diagram and click the Quick Style from the SmartArt Styles gallery. To see the complete gallery, click the More button in the SmartArt Styles group on the SmartArt Tools Design tab. The gallery opens and displays simple combinations of special effects, such as shadows, gradients, and 3-D effects, that combine perspectives and surface styles. Figure 3.26 displays the SmartArt Quick Styles gallery.

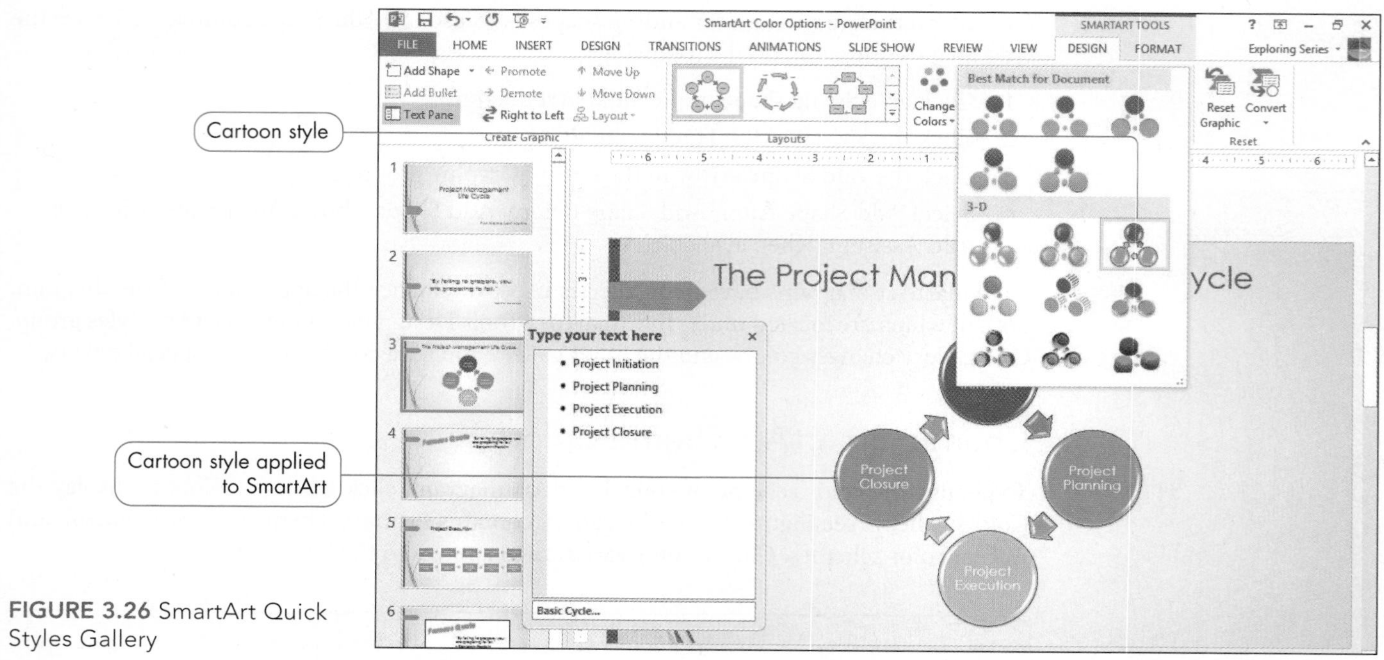

FIGURE 3.26 SmartArt Quick Styles Gallery

Change the Layout

STEP 3

After creating a SmartArt diagram, you may find that the layout needs adjusting. For example, as you enter text, PowerPoint reduces the size of the font. If you enter too much text, the font size becomes too small. Figure 3.27 shows a Process diagram displaying the sequential steps to execute a project. To allow the text to fit in the shapes of the diagram, PowerPoint reduced the font size to 13 pt.

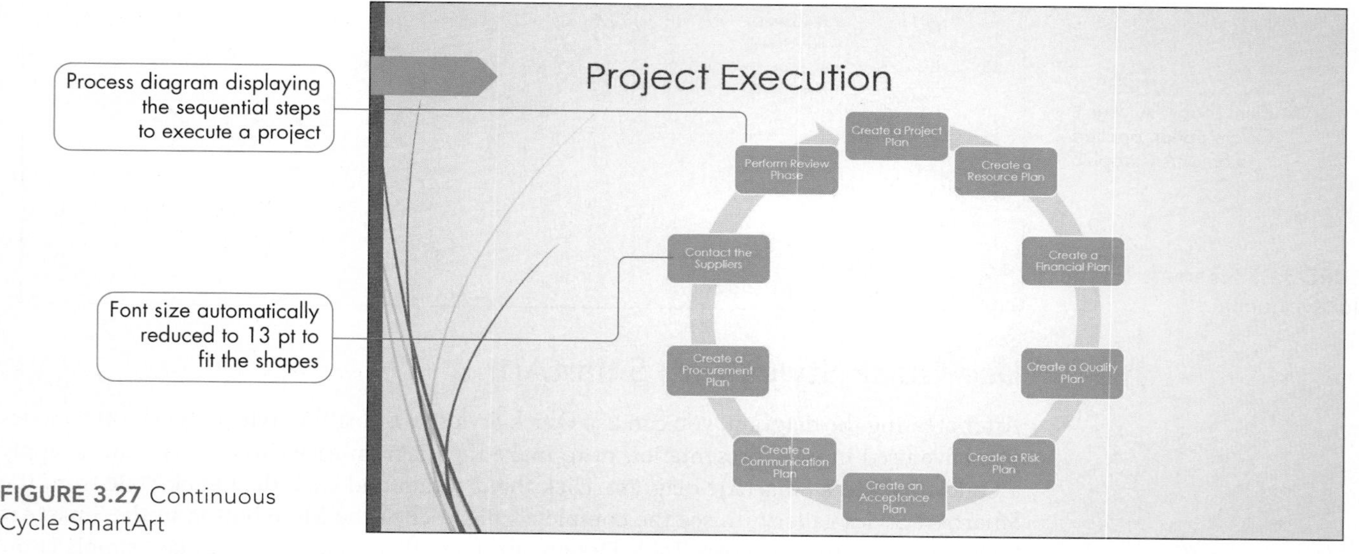

FIGURE 3.27 Continuous Cycle SmartArt

By adjusting the layout, you can make the Project Execution diagram easier to read. First, select the SmartArt diagram and the SmartArt Tools Design tab. Click the More button in the Layouts group to display the Layouts gallery. Layouts display the various subtypes for the SmartArt layout type currently applied. In addition, Live Preview will reflect the current color and styles applied for any layout subtype changes. Figure 3.28 shows the same process from Figure 2.27 only modified to utilize the Basic Bending Process layout.

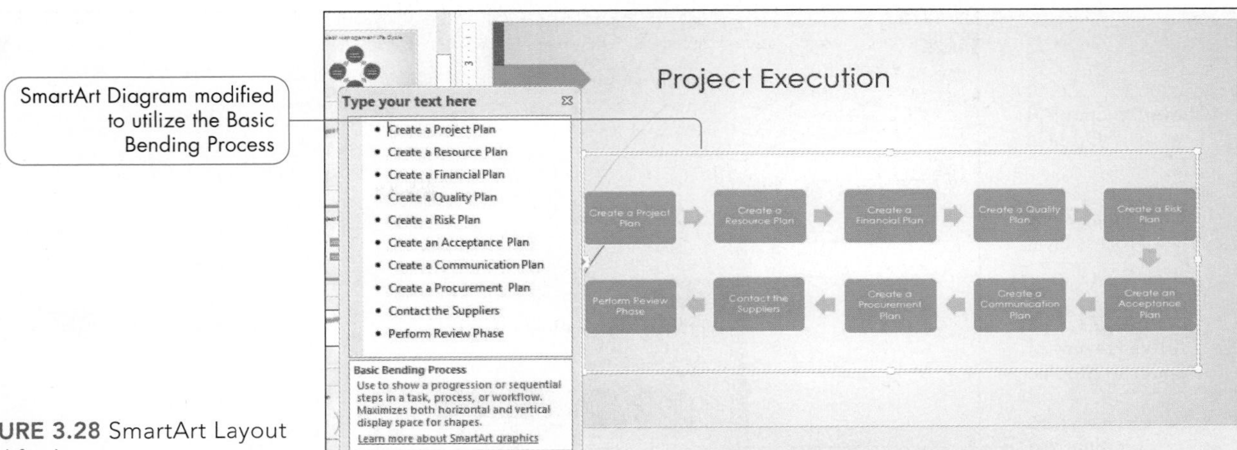

FIGURE 3.28 SmartArt Layout Modified

Change SmartArt Type

You can change the SmartArt diagram type if you decide a different diagram would be better. The process is similar to changing the SmartArt layout subtypes. Changing the diagram type may affect the audience's perception of your diagram. For example, if you have created a list of unordered items, switching to a cycle diagram implies that a specific order to the items exists. Also, if you have customized the shapes, keep in mind that changes to colors, line styles, and fills will transfer from the old diagram to a new one. However, some effects, such as rotation, do not transfer.

To change the SmartArt diagram type:

1. Click to select the SmartArt diagram.
2. Click the More button in the Layouts group on the DESIGN tab and click More Layouts.
3. The *Choose a SmartArt Graphic* gallery opens, displaying all the layouts grouped by category. Click the type and layout you desire.

Convert Text to a SmartArt Diagram

You can also convert existing text to a SmartArt diagram by selecting the placeholder containing the text and clicking *Convert to SmartArt Graphic* in the Paragraph group on the Home tab. When the gallery opens, click the desired layout for the SmartArt diagram (see Figure 3.29).

To quickly convert text to a SmartArt graphic, select the text, right-click, and then select *Convert to SmartArt*. The *Convert to SmartArt* gallery opens so you can select a SmartArt style.

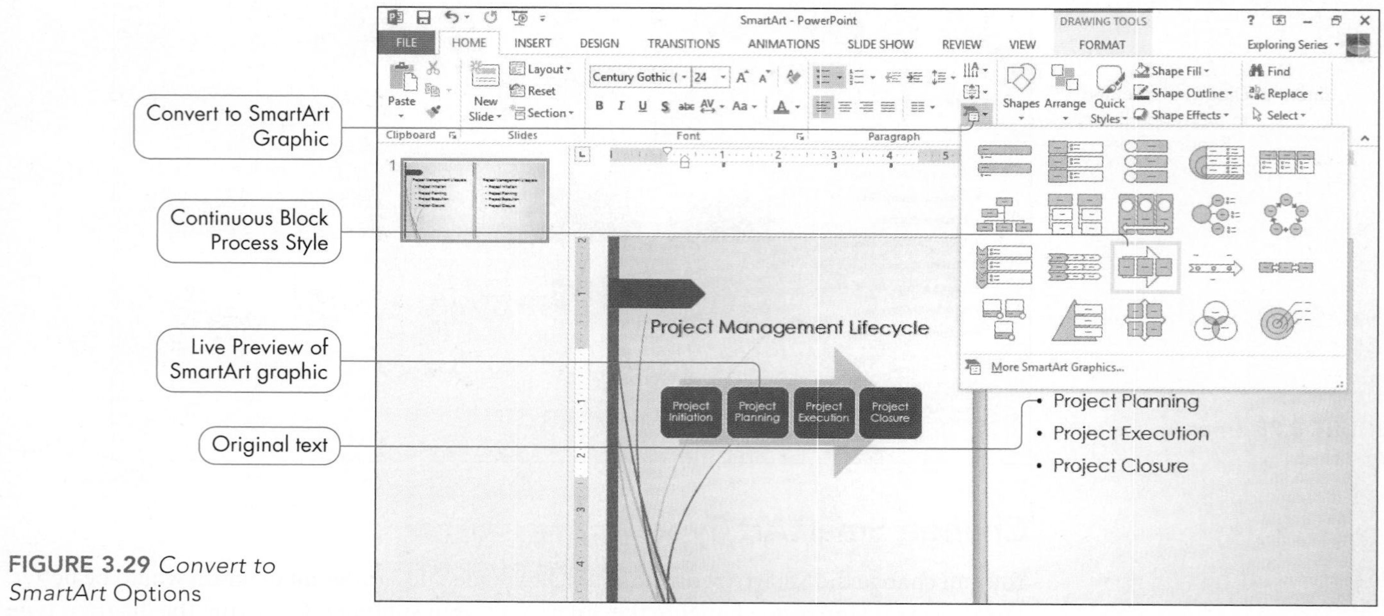

FIGURE 3.29 *Convert to SmartArt Options*

Creating WordArt

STEP 4

WordArt is text that uses special effects based on styles in the WordArt gallery to call attention to the text. In WordArt, special effects apply to the text itself, not to the shape surrounding the text. For example, in a WordArt graphic the text would have a 3-D reflection rather than the box surrounding the text. By applying special effects, such as curves or waves, directly to the text, you can create text that emphasizes the information for your audience.

The WordArt gallery has a variety of text styles to choose from, as well as the option to change individual settings or elements to modify the style. You can convert existing text to WordArt text, or you can create a WordArt object and then enter text.

To create WordArt:

1. Click the INSERT tab.
2. Click WordArt in the Text group.
3. Click the WordArt style of your choice.
4. Enter your text in the WordArt placeholder.

To convert existing text to a WordArt graphic:

1. Select the text to convert to WordArt text.
2. Click the More button in the WordArt Styles group on the FORMAT tab.
3. Click the WordArt style of your choice.

Modifying WordArt

You can change the style of a WordArt object by clicking a Quick Style located in the WordArt Styles group on the Format tab. Alternatively, you can modify the individual elements of the WordArt by clicking Text Fill, Text Outline, or Text Effects in the WordArt Styles group. WordArt Text Effects includes a unique Transform option. Transform can rotate the WordArt text around a path or add a warp to stretch, angle, or bloat letters. Figure 3.30 shows the WordArt gallery options, and Figure 3.31 shows the warp options available in the WordArt Transform category.

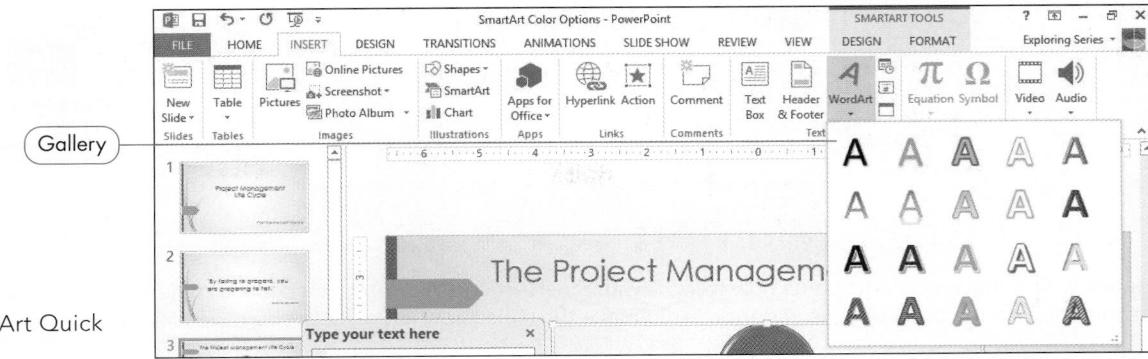

FIGURE 3.30 WordArt Quick Styles Gallery

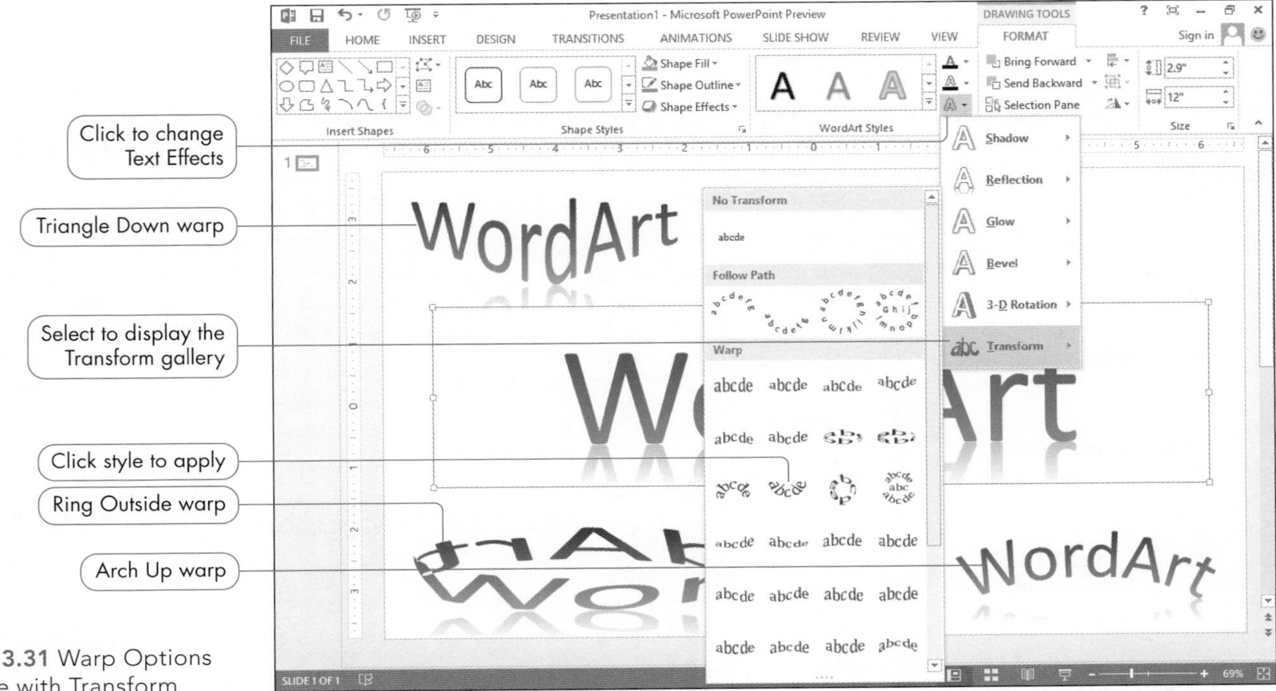

FIGURE 3.31 Warp Options Available with Transform

Quick Concepts

1. Which SmartArt diagram type would be most effective to show a timeline? ***p. 964***
2. How does entering text in a SmartArt Text Pane work like an outline? ***p. 966***
3. How would you convert existing text to a SmartArt diagram? ***p. 969***
4. List three text effects that can be modified when using WordArt. ***p. 970***

Hands-On Exercises

2 SmartArt and WordArt

To teach your mini-camp participants how to work with SmartArt and WordArt, you choose to have the group work with a presentation about a process—the water cycle. To make the slide show interesting, you have included fun, interesting water facts.

Skills covered: Create SmartArt • Modify a SmartArt Diagram • Change SmartArt Type and Modify the SmartArt Layout • Create and Modify WordArt

STEP 1 ≫ CREATE SMARTART

A SmartArt diagram is perfect for introducing the concept of the project management life cycle and is an example of a simple infographic explaining a complex concept. You teach your students to diagram using PowerPoint's SmartArt feature. Refer to Figure 3.32 as you complete Step 1.

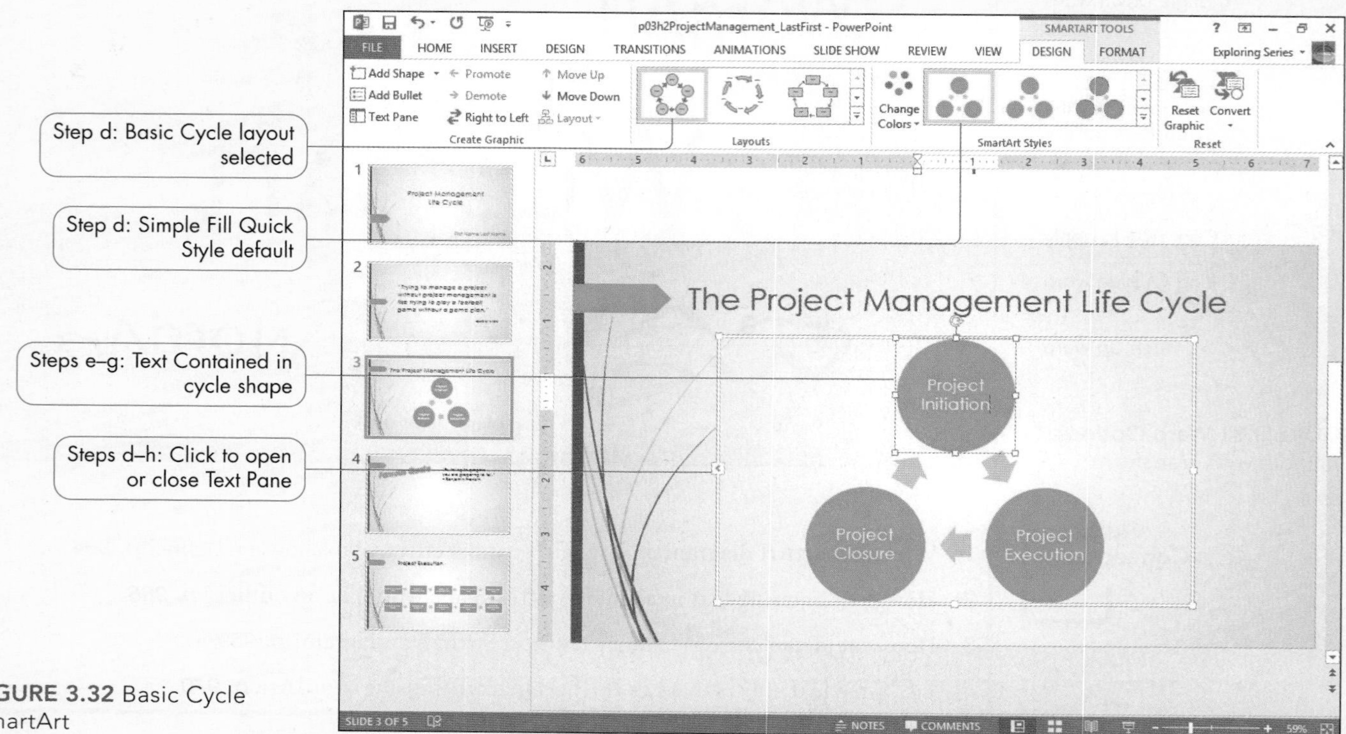

FIGURE 3.32 Basic Cycle SmartArt

a. Open the *p03h2ProjectManagement* presentation and save it as **p03h2ProjectManagement_LastFirst**.

b. On Slide 1, replace *First Name Last Name* with your name. Create a handout header with your name and a handout footer with your instructor's name and your class. Include the current date.

c. Click **Slide 3**. Click the **INSERT tab** and click **SmartArt** in the Illustrations group.

   The *Choose a SmartArt Graphic* dialog box opens.

d. Click **Cycle**, click the subtype **Basic Cycle**, and then click **OK**.

   The Text pane opens with the insertion point in the first bullet location so that you can enter the text for the first cycle shape.

TROUBLESHOOTING: If the Text pane is not displayed, click Text Pane in the Create Graphic group or click the arrow on the center-left side of the SmartArt boundary.

e. Type **Project Initiation.**

As you type, the font size for the text gets smaller so the text fits in the shape.

f. Press ↓ to move to the second bullet and type **Project Execution**. Repeat this technique to add a third bullet and type **Project Closure.**

g. Press ↓ to move to the blank bullet point and press **Backspace**. Repeat to remove the second blank bullet point.

The extra shapes in the Basic Cycle SmartArt are removed.

h. Click the **Close (X) button** on the top right of the Text pane to close it.

i. Drag the SmartArt object down so that it does not overlap with the title.

j. Resize the SmartArt object by selecting the outside object border, dragging the corners of the object, and then respositioning it until the object fits comfortably under the title. See Figure 3.32.

k. Save the presentation.

STEP 2 » MODIFY A SMARTART DIAGRAM

You need to modify the structure of the SmartArt diagram because a step in the cycle was omitted. The diagram could be enhanced with a color style change. You teach your participants these skills. Refer to Figure 3.33 as you complete Step 2.

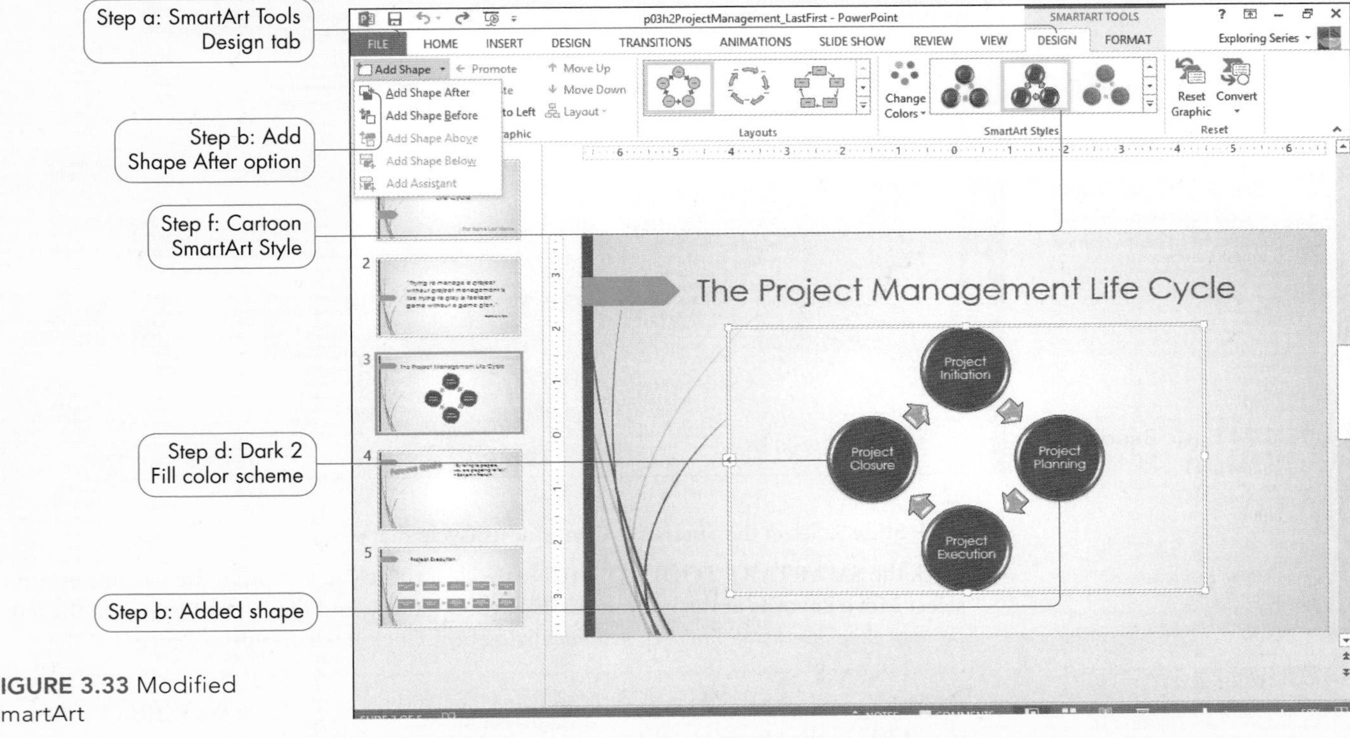

FIGURE 3.33 Modified SmartArt

a. Click the **Project Initiation shape** and click the **SMARTART TOOLS DESIGN tab**, if necessary.

b. Click the **Add Shape arrow** in the Create Graphic group and select **Add Shape After.**

You have added a new shape after *Project Initiation* and before *Project Execution.*

> **TROUBLESHOOTING:** If you had clicked Add Shape, you would have automatically added a shape after the selected shape. Using the Add Shape arrow gives you a choice of adding before or after.

c. Type **Project Planning** in the new shape.

d. Click the SmartArt border to select all the shapes in the SmartArt diagram, click **Change Colors** in the SmartArt Styles group, and then click **Dark 2 Fill** in the Primary Theme Colors category.

e. Click the **More button** in the SmartArt Styles group and move the pointer over the styles.

   Live Preview shows the impact each style has on the shapes and text in the SmartArt diagram.

f. Click **Cartoon** in the 3-D category (first row, third column).

   This choice makes the text readable and enhances the appearance of the SmartArt diagram.

g. Save the presentation.

STEP 3 » CHANGE SMARTART TYPE AND MODIFY THE SMARTART LAYOUT

Many different layouts are available for SmartArt diagrams, and you teach the mini-camp group that for an infographic to be effective, it must be understood quickly. You ask the group to note the reduced font size on the process SmartArt showing the Project Execution. You teach them to change the layout of the SmartArt to make it more effective. Refer to Figure 3.34 as you complete Step 3.

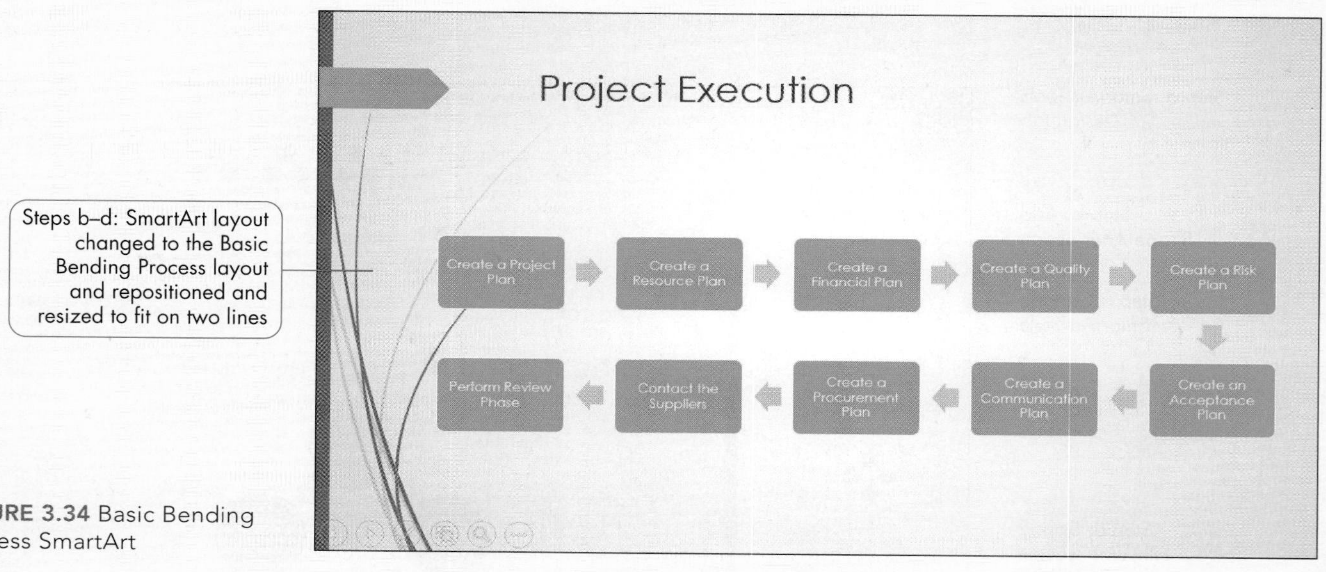

FIGURE 3.34 Basic Bending Process SmartArt

a. Click **Slide 5**. Select the **SmartArt Continuous Cycle shape** by clicking any shape.

b. Click the **SMARTART TOOLS DESIGN tab**, click the **More button** in the Layouts group, select **More Layouts** at the bottom of the Layouts gallery, and then click **Process** in the left pane of the *Choose a SmartArt Graphic* dialog box. Click **Basic Bending Process** in the center pane and click **OK**.

c. Click the **SmartArt border** to select all the shapes, if necessary. Click the **FORMAT tab**, type **4.03"** in the **Shape Height box** in the Size group, and then press **Enter**.

d. Open the Size Dialog Box Launcher. Click **POSITION** and **type 1.6"** in the **Horizontal Position box** and **2.44"** in the **Vertical Position box**.

   Deselect the SmartArt diagram by clicking outside of the SmartArt.

e. Save the presentation.

STEP 4 » CREATE AND MODIFY WORDART

You teach the participants how to use WordArt to call attention to text and how to modify the Text effects applied to the WordArt. You also have them insert text in a text box so they can compare the options available with each method for adding text to a slide. Refer to Figure 3.35 as you complete Step 4.

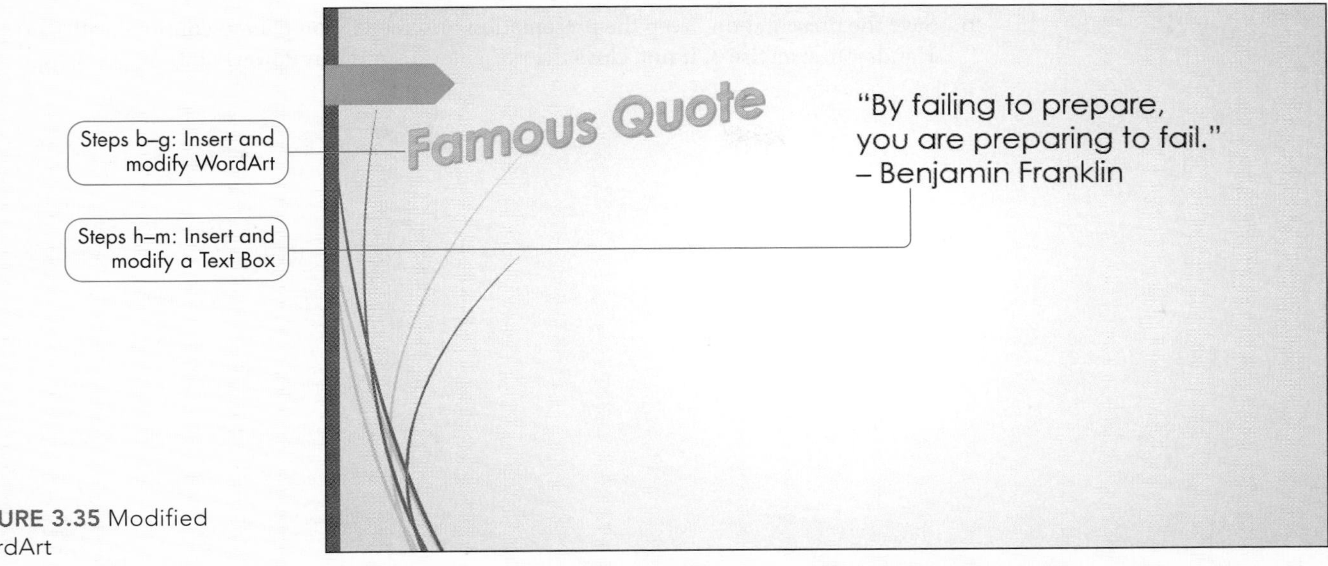

FIGURE 3.35 Modified WordArt

a. Click **Slide 4**. Click the **INSERT tab** and click **WordArt** in the Text group.

b. Click **Pattern Fill - Orange, Accent 1, 50%, Hard Shadow - Accent 1** (fourth row, third column).

   A WordArt placeholder is centered on the slide.

c. Type **Famous Quote** in the **WordArt placeholder**.

d. Click the **FORMAT tab**, if necessary, click **Text Effects** in the WordArt Styles group, and then point to *3-D Rotation*.

   The 3-D Rotation gallery opens, showing No Rotation, Parallel, Perspective, and Oblique categories.

e. Click **Off Axis 1 Right** (under Parallel category, second row, second column).

f. Type **1.5"** in the **Shape Height box** in the Size group and press **Enter**.

   The height of the WordArt shape adjusts to 1.5".

g. Open the Size Dialog Box Launcher and click **POSITION** to expand. Type **0.69"** in the **Horizontal Position box** and **1.08"** in the **Vertical Position box**. Drag the WordArt shape to the top-left corner of the slide as shown in Figure 3.35. Close the Size Dialog Box Launcher and deselect the shape.

h. Click the **INSERT tab** and click **Text Box** in the Text group.

i. Click to the bottom right of the WordArt shape and type **"By failing to prepare, you are preparing to fail." – Benjamin Franklin**.

   The text box expands to fit the text, with the result that the text is contained in one long line that flows off the slide.

j. Click the **FORMAT tab**, type **5.1"** in the **Shape Width box** in the Size group, and then press **Enter**.

k. Click the **Size Dialog Box Launcher**, click to expand the TEXT BOX options, and then click the **Wrap text in shape check box**.

l. Click the border of the text box to select all the text. Click the **HOME tab** and change the font size of the text to **28 pt**.

m. Click the **Size Dialog Box Launcher**. Click **POSITION**. Type **6.98"** in the **Horizonal Position box** and type **1.08"** in the **Vertical Position box**.

The top of the text box is now aligned with the top of the WordArt, as shown in Figure 3.35.

n. Save the presentation. Keep the presentation onscreen if you plan to continue with Hands-On Exercise 3. If not, close the presentation and exit PowerPoint.

Object Manipulation

As you add objects to your slides, you may need to manipulate them by arranging them differently on the slide or recoloring them. Perhaps you have several shapes created, and you want them to align at their left edges, or you want to arrange them by their center points and then determine the order of the shapes. You may have inserted a drawn image, and the colors used in the image do not match the color of the SmartArt on a slide. You may have added a drawn image that includes something you do not want.

In this section, you will learn to modify objects. You will isolate objects, flip and rotate objects, group and ungroup objects, and recolor the image. You will also learn to determine the order of objects and align objects to one another and to the slide.

Modifying Objects

Many clip art images are made from a series of combined shapes. You can modify existing drawings by breaking them into individual shapes and removing pieces you do not need, changing or recoloring shapes, rotating shapes, and combining shapes from several objects to create a new object. Figure 3.36 shows a picnic illustration available from Microsoft Office Online. The illustration was broken apart; the fireworks, flag, fries, and tablecloth removed; the hamburger, hotdogs, and milkshake flipped and resized; and the hamburger and chocolate milkshake recolored.

FIGURE 3.36 Modified Drawn Images

STEP 1» Resizing objects is the most common modification procedure. You have learned to resize an object by dragging a sizing handle; however, you may need a more precise resizing method. For example, you use PowerPoint to create an advertisement for an automobile trader magazine, and the magazine specifies that the ad must fit in a 2" by 2" space. You can specify the exact height and width measurement of an object or adjust to a specific proportion of its original size.

The controls to resize an object to an exact measurement are found in the Size group on the Format tab or the Format pane. The Size group contains controls to change the height and width of an object quickly. The Format pane also contains boxes for entering exact measurements for shape height and width, but additionally allows you to use a precise rotation angle and to scale an object based on its original size (note that not all Online Pictures entered are added at full size).

To keep the original height and width proportions of an image, make sure the *Lock aspect ratio* check box is selected. ***Aspect ratio*** is the ratio of an object's width to its height. The image in Figure 3.37 was proportionally sized to more than twice its original size.

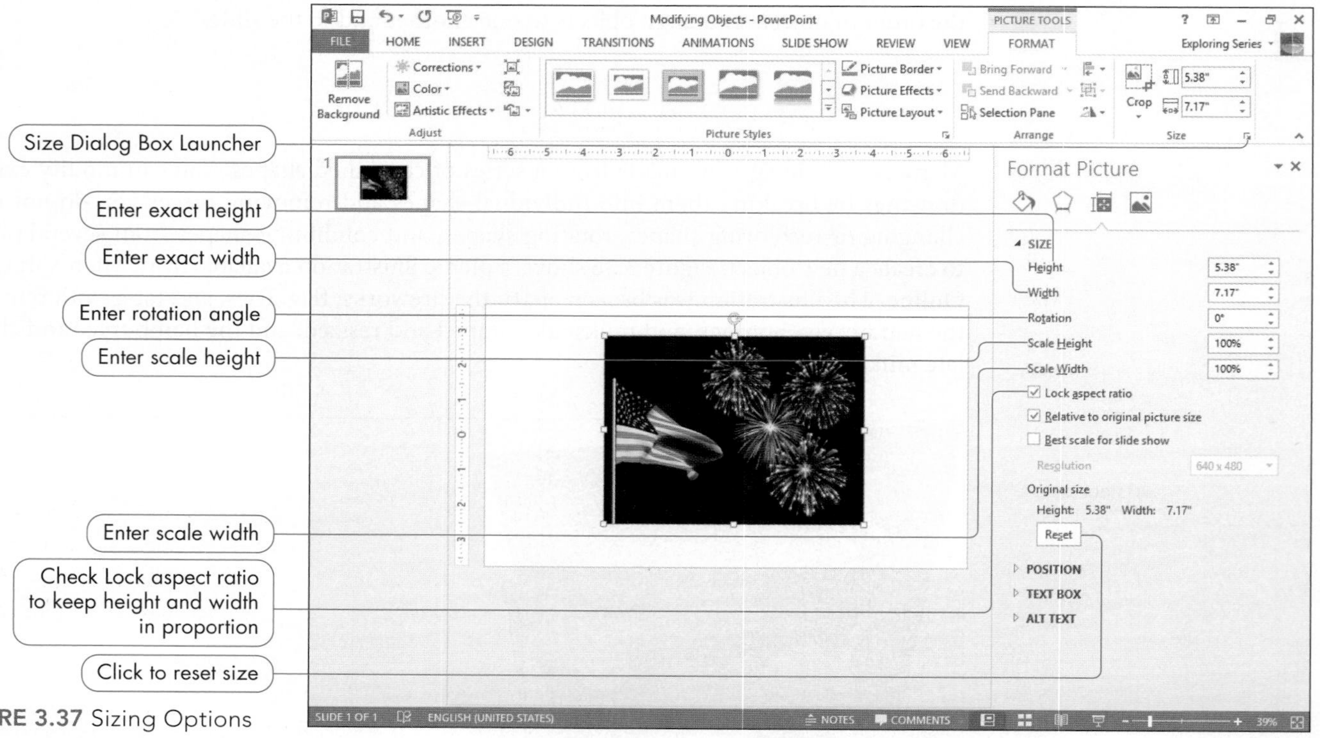

FIGURE 3.37 Sizing Options

Flip and Rotate

STEP 2»

Sometimes you will find that an object is facing the wrong way and you need to reverse the direction it faces, or ***flip*** it. You can flip an object vertically or horizontally to get a mirror image of the object. You may find that you need to ***rotate*** an object, or move the object around its axis. Perhaps you took a photograph with your digital camera sideways to get a full-length view, but when you download the image, it displays sideways. You can quickly rotate an object left or right 90°, flip it horizontally or vertically, or freely rotate it any number of degrees.

You rotate a selected object by dragging the rotation handle located at the top of the object in the direction you want it to rotate. To constrain the rotation to 15° angles, press and hold Shift while dragging. To rotate exactly 90° to the left or the right, click Rotate in the Arrange group on the Format tab. If you need a mirror image, click Rotate and select Flip Vertical or Flip Horizontal. You can also drag one of the side sizing handles over the opposite side and flip it. However, this method will cause distortion if you do not drag far enough to keep the height and width measurements proportional. Figure 3.38 shows rotate options and an image that has been flipped.

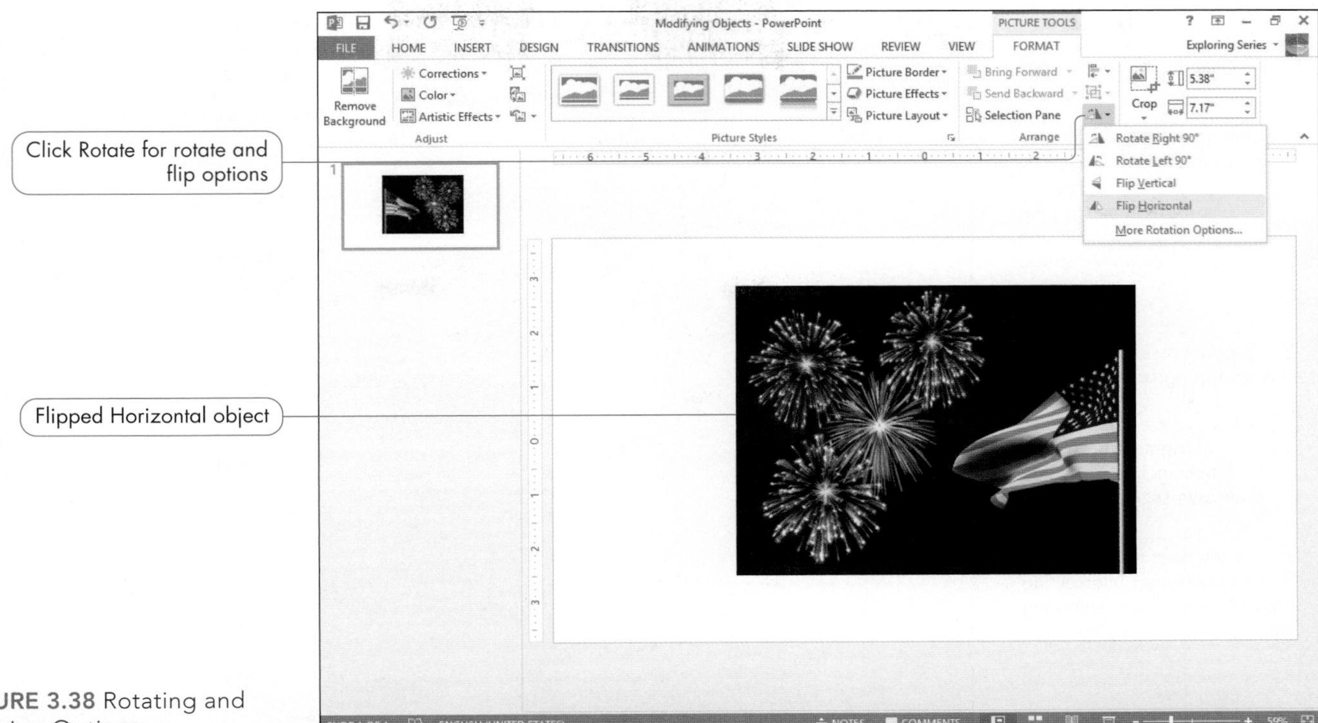

FIGURE 3.38 Rotating and Flipping Options

Merge Shapes

The Merge Shapes feature allows you to take shapes that you have inserted and merge them together. There are five different merging options: Union, Combine, Fragment, Intersect, and Subtract. Figure 3.39 shows the five different merging option results of a heart and a lightning bolt created using Shapes in the Insert Shapes group on the Format tab. To merge shapes:

1. Arrange the shapes so they are overlapping as desired.
2. Select the overlapping shapes by dragging a selection net around all of the shapes.
3. Click the FORMAT tab.
4. Click Merge Shapes in the Insert Shapes group.
5. Click the merge option of your choice.

TIP Using Subtract Shapes

When applying the Subtract Shapes merging option, you will have a different result depending on the shape you select first. In Figure 3.39, the heart was selected first, and the lightning bolt second.

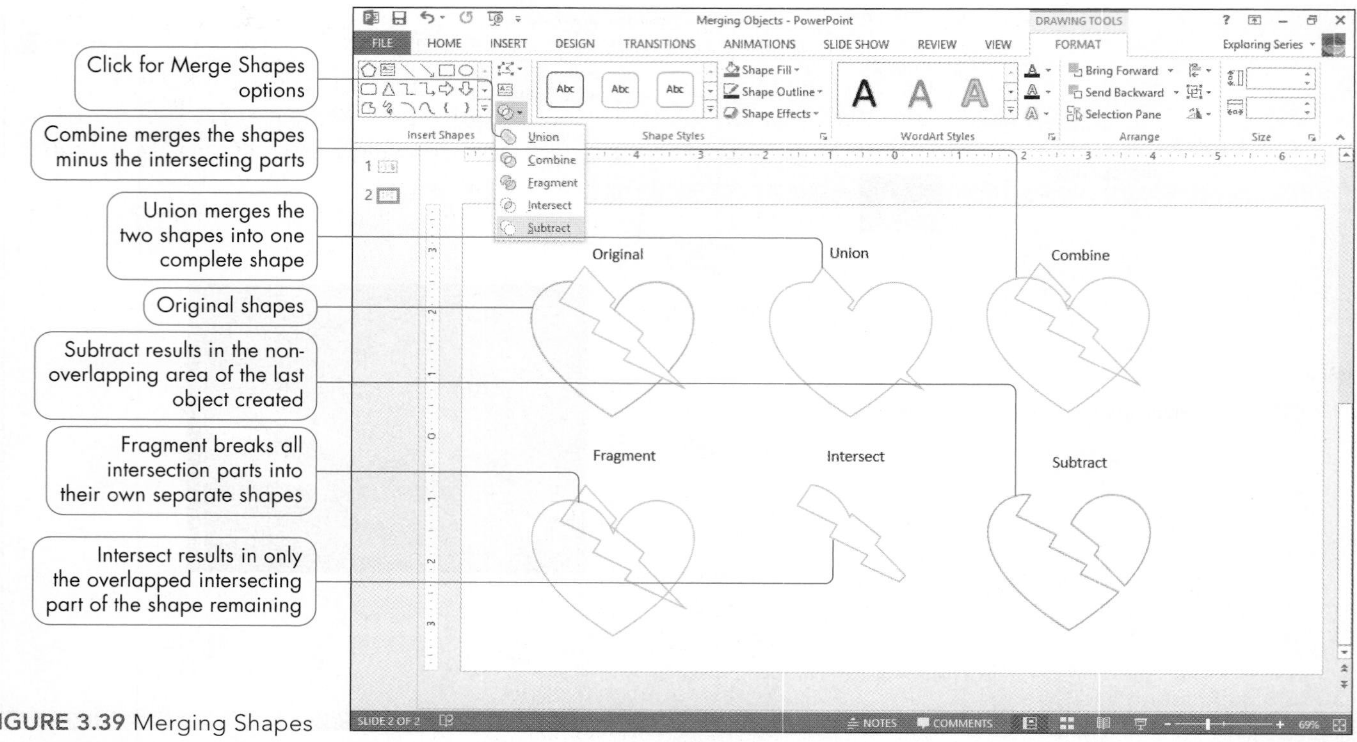

FIGURE 3.39 Merging Shapes

Group and Ungroup Objects

STEP 3

A drawn object is usually created in pieces, layered, and then grouped to create the final image. These images can be ***ungrouped***, or broken apart, so you can modify or delete the individual pieces. ***Grouping*** enables multiple objects to act or move as though they were a single object, whereas ungrouping separates an object into individual shapes. Grouping is different from merging a shape. Grouping simply makes it easier to move the newly grouped object or apply formatting, whereas merging may create a new object altogether.

Clip art images are typically created and saved as ***vector graphics***, which are math-based. Drawing programs such as Adobe Illustrator and CorelDRAW are used to create vector graphic images. The advantage of vector files is that they retain perfect clarity when edited or resized due to the fact that the computer simply recalculates the math. Vector files also use a smaller amount of storage space compared to their pixel-based counterparts such as photographs. Many company logos or the drawn clip art images available from the Online Pictures on Microsoft.com are vector graphics, which leads to another advantage of vector images: If a vector clip art image is inserted, it is automatically a grouped image, and thus, the option to ungroup is available. This ability to ungroup (or group) the image enables you to separate the parts of the image and edit or adjust the image to tailor it to your needs.

TIP An Image That Will Not Ungroup

If your selected imported image will not ungroup for editing, it is not in a vector format. Online Pictures from Microsoft.com also contains clip art in bitmap, .jpg, .gif, and .png formats, which are not vector-based images and cannot be ungrouped.

Some non-vector graphics can be converted into drawing objects. Right-click the image on the slide and select Edit Picture if the option is available. If the option is not available, the graphic cannot be converted into a drawing object. After you select Edit Picture, a message opens asking if you want to convert the picture into a drawing object. Click Yes. This action converts the object into a vector graphic.

Once converted into a drawing object, right-click the image again, point to Group, and then select Ungroup. The object ungroups and the individual pieces are selected. Some images may have more than one grouping. The artist may create an image from individual shapes, group it, layer it on other images, and then group it again. If this occurs, the ungroup option will be available to repeat again. Figure 3.40 is an example of a complex file that has been ungrouped with some of the pieces selected.

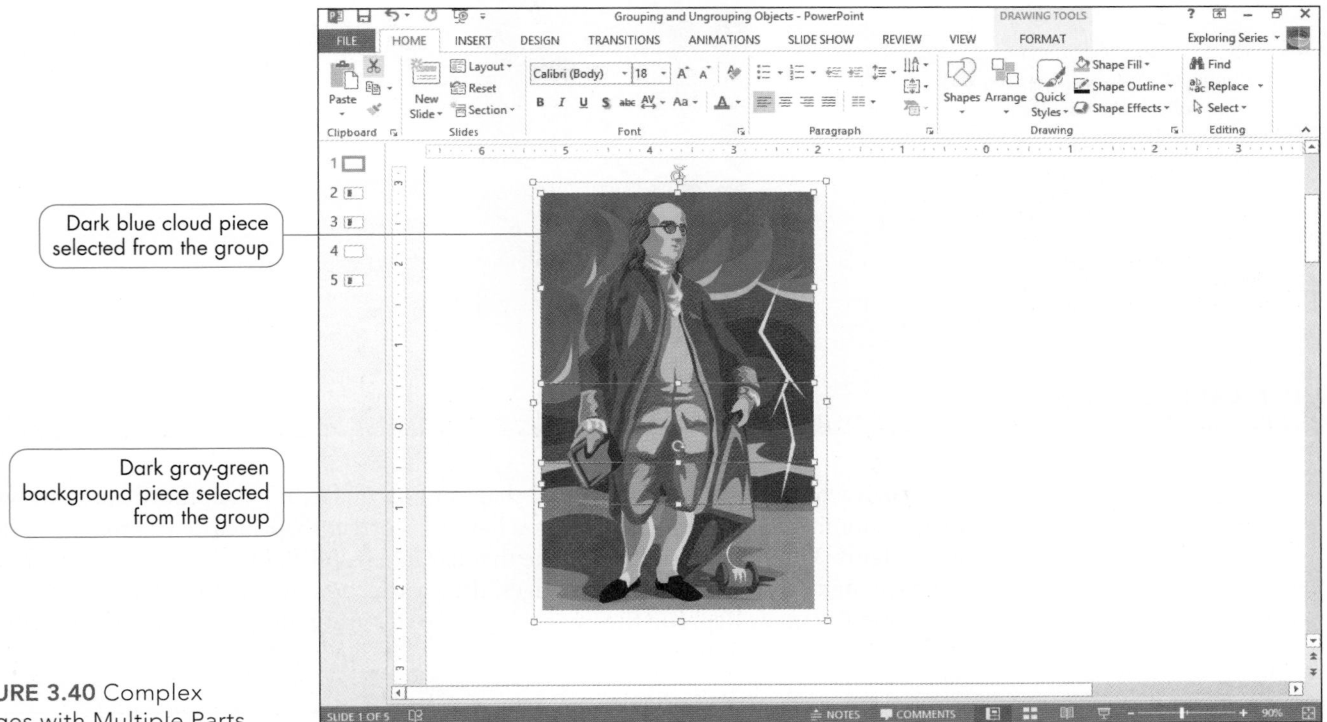

FIGURE 3.40 Complex Images with Multiple Parts

If necessary, to continue ungrouping, select the image, right-click, click Group, and then click Ungroup as many times as necessary to break the image down to all shapes. You can also select the image and click the Format tab. Click Group in the Arrange group, and if the image can be broken down further, the Ungroup option will be active with Group and Regroup grayed out. Select Ungroup, and each individual shape is surrounded by adjustment handles. Click outside of the image borders to deselect the shapes and click the individual shape you wish to change. Figure 3.41 shows a graphic that has been ungrouped. All of the individual parts are selected.

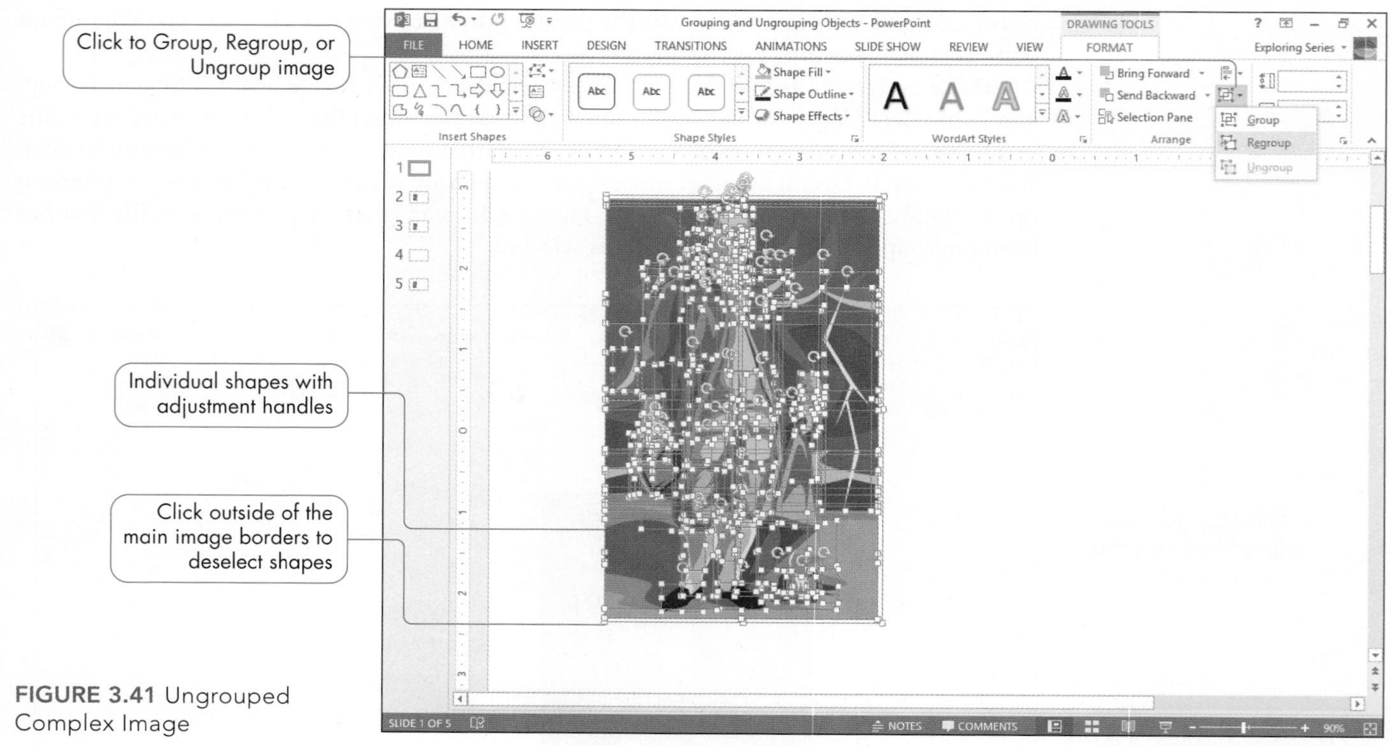

FIGURE 3.41 Ungrouped Complex Image

When working with the individual shapes of an image, it is helpful to zoom in on the image. Zooming helps you make sure you have the correct shape before you make modifications. Figure 3.42 shows a selected shape that has had its fill changed to a theme color. Once you have made all of your needed changes, drag a selection net around all the shapes of the image and Group or Regroup the image. If you do not group the image, you risk moving the individual pieces inadvertently.

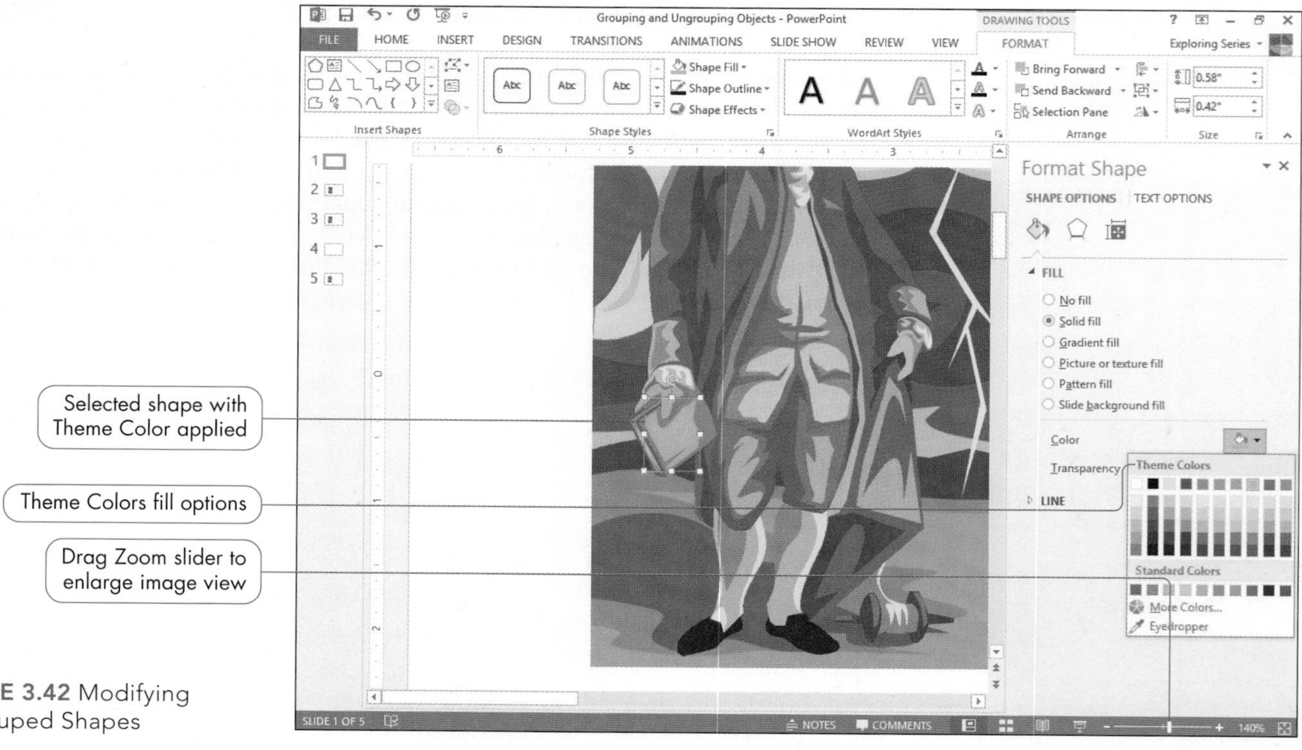

FIGURE 3.42 Modifying Ungrouped Shapes

Recolor Objects

STEP 4» You can quickly change the colors in an image using the Recolor Picture option regardless of image file type, which enables you to match your image to the color scheme of your presentation without the ability or need for ungrouping the image and changing the color of each shape. You can select either a dark or a light variation of your color scheme.

You also can change the color mode of your picture to Grayscale, Sepia, Washout, or Black and White. Grayscale changes your picture up to 256 shades of gray. Sepia gives you that popular golden tone often used for an old-fashioned photo look. Washout is used to create watermarks, whereas *Black and White* is a way to reduce image color to black and white. Figure 3.43 shows an image and three variations of color.

FIGURE 3.43 Recoloring Objects

To change the colors of your image:

1. Select the image you want to change.
2. Click the FORMAT tab.
3. Click Color in the Adjust group.
4. Click the color variation of your choice, or select More Variations to open the Theme Colors options and select a theme color.

The Recolor gallery includes a Set Transparent Color option that is extremely valuable for creating a transparent area in many pictures. When you click Set Transparent Color, the pointer changes shape and includes an arrowhead for pointing. Move the pointer until the arrowhead is pointing directly at the color you wish to make transparent and click. The color becomes transparent so that anything underneath shows through. In Figure 3.44, the sky is set to transparent so the white background shows.

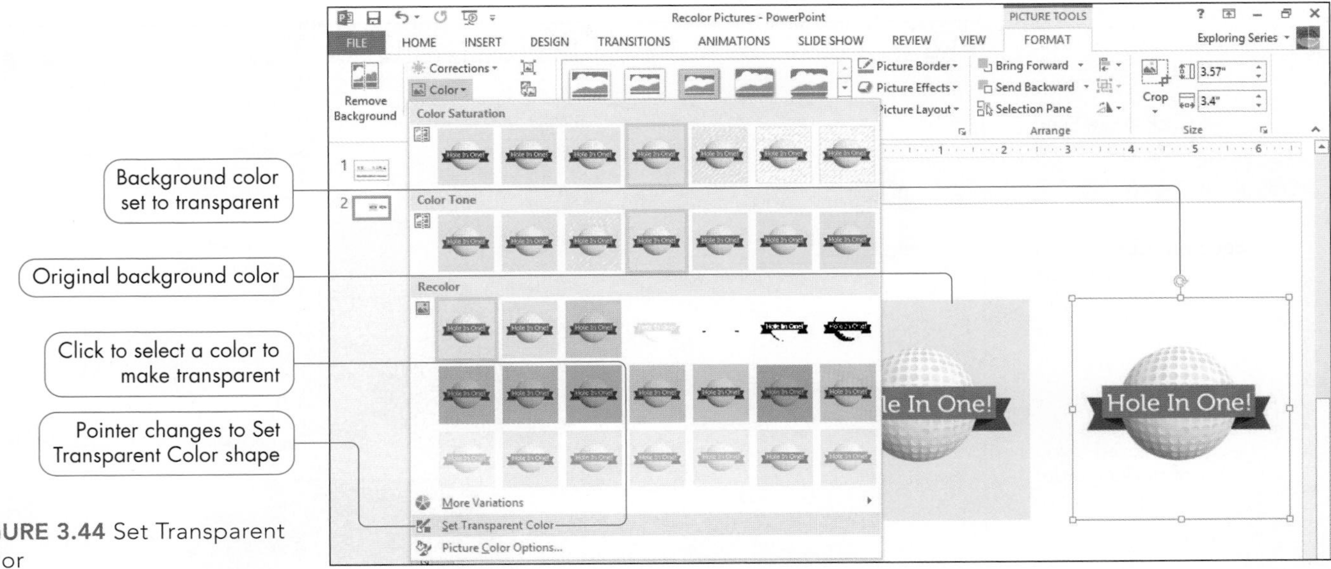

FIGURE 3.44 Set Transparent Color

Arranging Objects

When you have multiple objects such as shapes, Online Pictures, SmartArt, and WordArt on the page, it can become challenging and time consuming to arrange them. Smart Guides (discussed in Chapter 2) are good for simple alignment; however, this does not work for all situations. For more complex siutations, PowerPoint has several features to control the order and position of the objects, how the objects align to one another, and how they align to the slide. Before using any of these features, you must select the object(s). You can select the object(s) by using the ***Selection Pane***. The Selection Pane, found in the Arrange group on the Format tab, contains a list of all objects on the slide. Click Selection Pane to open the Selection Pane if an object is selected. Click any object on the list to select it and make changes to it. The object you selected is highlighted in the Selection Pane. If an object is not selected, click the Home tab, click Select in the Editing group, and then select Selection Pane.

Order Objects

STEP 5»

You can layer shapes by placing them under or on top of one another. The order of the layers is called the ***stacking order***. PowerPoint adds shapes or other objects in a stacking order as you add them to the slide. The last shape you place on the slide is on top and is the highest in the stacking order. Drawn images are comprised of shapes that have been stacked. Once you ungroup an image and modify it, you may need to change the stacking order. You can open the Selection Pane to see the order in which objects are placed. The topmost object on the list is at the top of the stacking order.

To change the order of a stack of shapes:

1. Select a shape.
2. Click the FORMAT tab.
3. The Arrange group on the FORMAT tab includes the Bring Forward and Send Backward arrows to open a submenu for each that includes the following options:

Bring to Front	Moves the shape to the top of the stacking order
Send to Back	Moves the shape to the bottom of the stacking order
Bring Forward	Moves the shape up one layer
Send Backward	Moves the shape down one layer

Figure 3.45 shows the results of changing a square in the middle of a stacking order to the top of a stacking order.

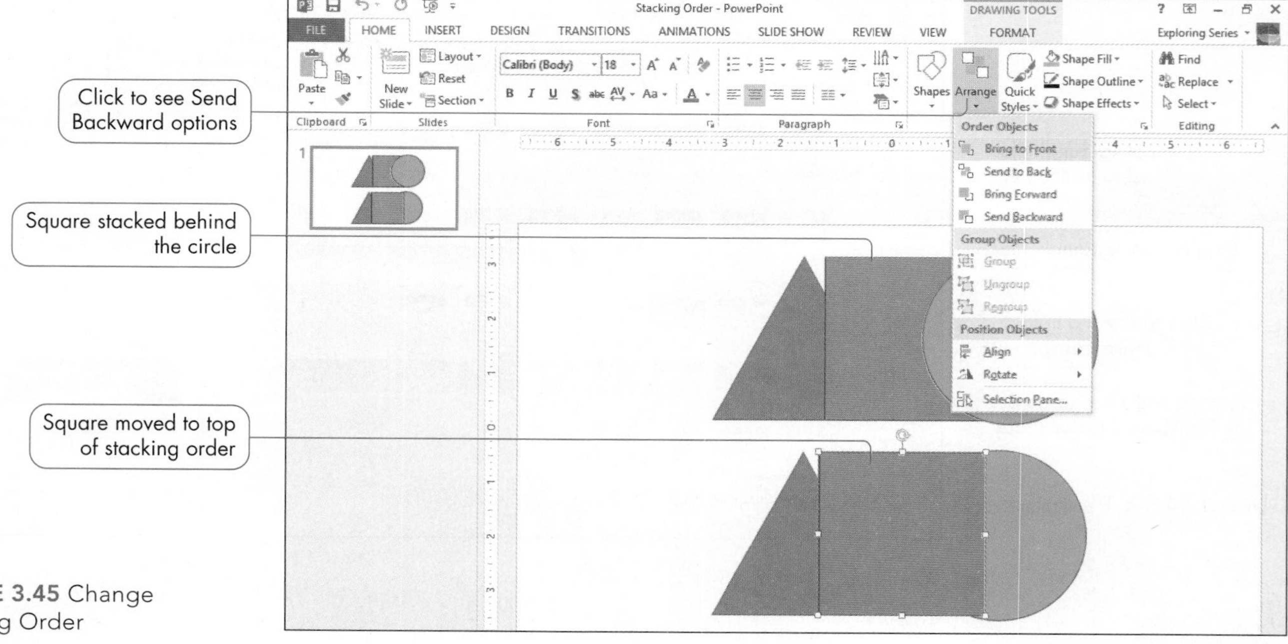

FIGURE 3.45 Change Stacking Order

TIP Ordering Shortcuts

You can right-click a shape and select *Bring to Front* or *Send to Back*. Using this method, you can still choose whether to move one layer or all layers. You also can open the Selection Pane, select the object, and then click the Re-order Bring Forward arrow or the Send Backward arrow to move the object up the list or down the list.

Align Objects

You can position objects precisely on the slide. For example, you can align a series of boxes at their tops or adjust the amount of space between the boxes so that they are evenly spaced. PowerPoint has rulers, a grid, and drawing guides that enable you to complete the aligning process quickly.

Each slide can display a ***grid*** containing intersecting lines, similar to traditional graph paper. Grids are hidden and are nonprinting, but you can display the grid to align your objects and to keep them evenly spaced. When you activate the grid, you will not see it in Slide Show view, and it will not print. Rulers can also help keep your objects aligned by enabling you to see the exact size of an object or the distance between shapes.

To view the grid and the ruler, click the View tab and click the check boxes for *Gridlines and Ruler*. To change the grid settings:

1. Click the VIEW tab.
2. Click the Show Dialog Box Launcher in the Show group.
3. Adjust the settings and click *Display grid on screen.*
4. Click OK.

By default, objects snap to the gridlines and measurement lines on the rulers. The *Snap to* feature forces an object to align with the grid by either the center point or the edge of the object, whichever is closer to the gridline. You can turn off the *Snap to* feature or change the setting so that objects snap to other objects. To change the grid settings, select an object and click the Show Dialog Box Launcher on the View tab.

Figure 3.46 displays the *Grid and Guides* dialog box options.

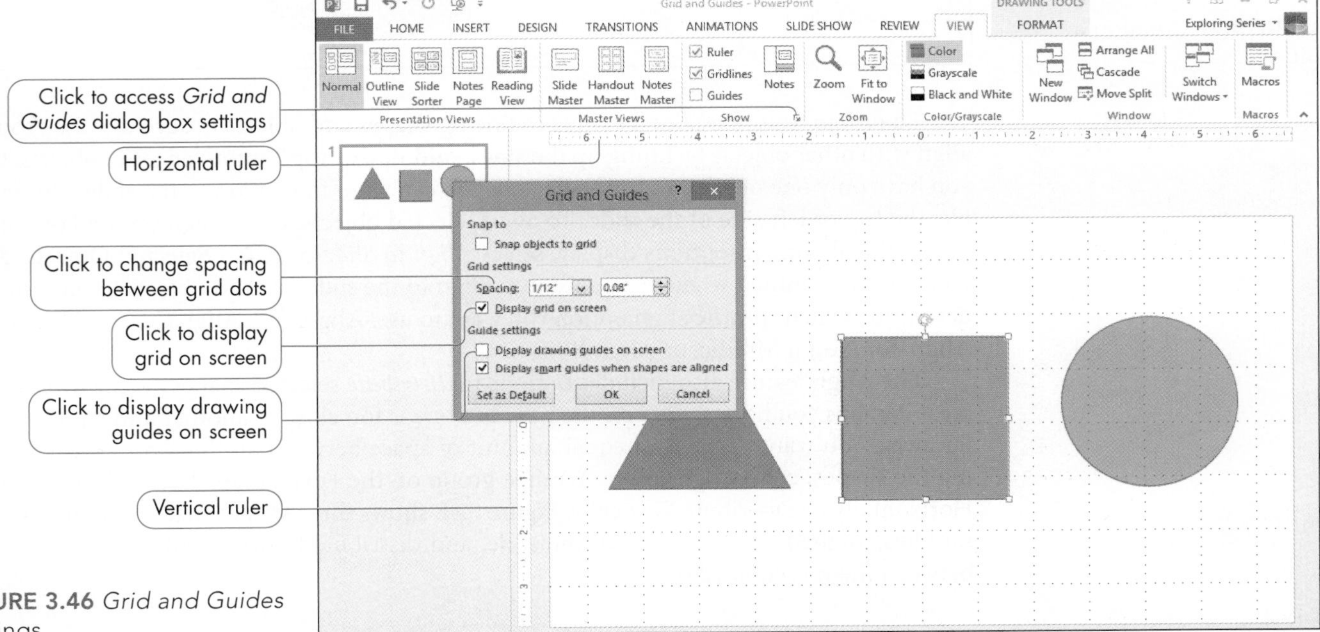

FIGURE 3.46 *Grid and Guides* Settings

Guides are nonprinting, temporary vertical or horizontal lines that you can place on a page to help you align objects or determine regions of the slide. New to PowerPoint 2013 are ***SmartGuides***. You will notice the red-line SmartGuides display when you move objects on your slide. These simple guides help you quickly align objects in relation to other objects. For more precise positioning of objects, you can use guides to mark margins on a slide.

To activate guides:

1. Click the VIEW tab.
2. Click the check box next to Guides.
3. Click the Show Dialog Box Launcher.
4. Click *Display drawing guides on screen.*
5. Click OK.

When you first display the guides, you see two guides that intersect at the center of the slide (the zero setting on both the horizontal and vertical rulers). To move a guide, position your cursor over it and drag. A directional arrow will appear as well as a measurement telling you how far from the center point you are moving the guide. To create additional guides, press Ctrl+Shift while dragging. To remove guides, drag them off the slide. Figure 3.47 displays the default horizontal and vertical guides.

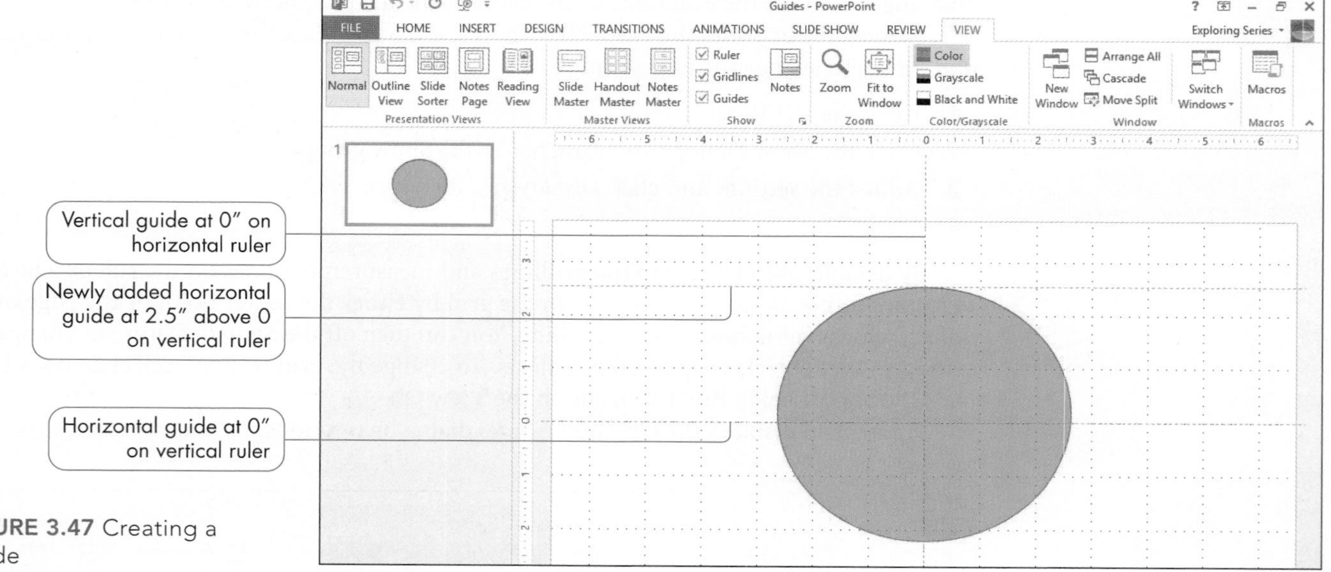

FIGURE 3.47 Creating a Guide

The ***Align*** feature makes it simple to line up shapes and objects in several ways. You can align with other objects by lining up the sides, middles, or top/bottom edges of objects. Or, if you have only one object or group selected, you can align in relation to the slide—for example, the top or left side of the slide. To align selected objects, click Align on the Format tab. When the alignment options display, select *Align to Slide* or Align Selected Objects. After you have determined whether you want to align to the slide or align objects to one another, determine which specific align option you want to use: Align Left, Align Center, Align Right, Align Top, Align Middle, or Align Bottom.

The Align feature also includes options to ***distribute*** selected shapes evenly over a given area. Perhaps you have shapes on the page but one is too close to another and another is too far away. You want to have an equal amount of space between all the shapes. After selecting the shapes, click Align in the Arrange group on the Format tab. Then select Distribute Horizontally or Distribute Vertically. Figure 3.48 shows three shapes that are aligned at their middles, aligned to the middle of the slide, and distributed horizontally so that the space between them is equidistant.

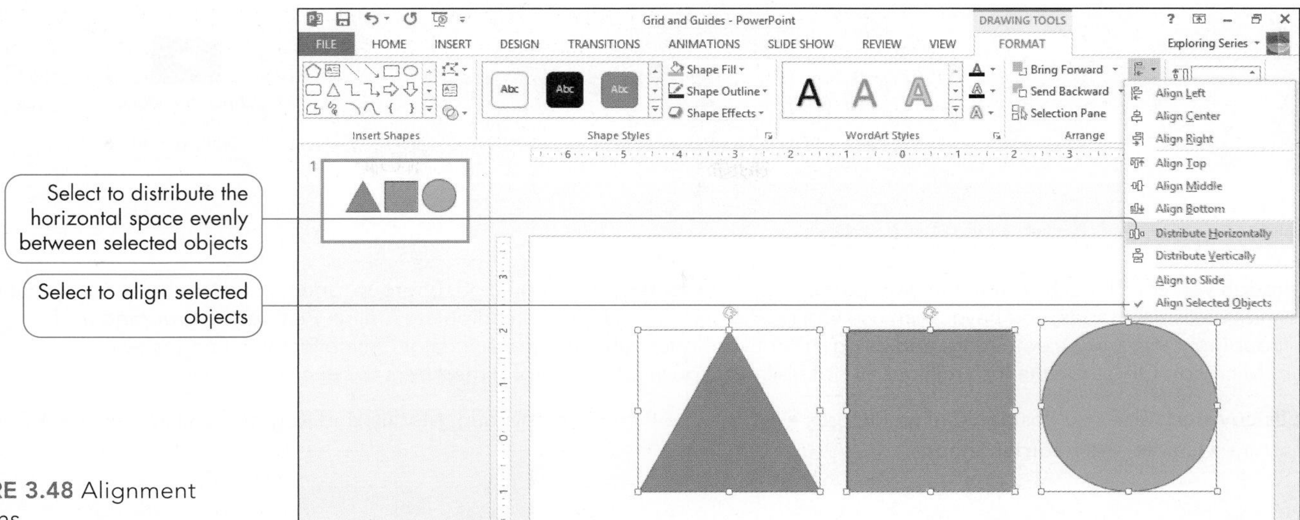

FIGURE 3.48 Alignment Options

Quick Concepts

1. What is the name for the process of breaking apart an image so that individual shapes can be modified? ***p. 980***
2. What PowerPoint feature allows you to quickly change the colors in an image? Why would you do this? ***p. 983***
3. How are rulers, a grid, and drawing guides used when aligning objects? ***p. 985***

Hands-On Exercises

3 Object Manipulation

Although you could teach your mini-camp participants how to size, position, align, ungroup, and use other object manipulation techniques using shapes, you have them use Online Pictures. The ability to manipulate Online Pictures by grouping and ungrouping, recoloring, combining, and using other techniques turns the thousands of Online Pictures images available from Microsoft Office Online into millions of possibilities. You want your group members to have these skills.

Skills covered: Size and Position Online Pictures • Flip Online Pictures • Ungroup, Modify, and Regroup Online Pictures • Recolor a Picture • Create and Reorder Shapes

STEP 1 ›› SIZE AND POSITION ONLINE PICTURES

You teach your mini-camp participants to use the Size Dialog Box Launcher. You want them to be able to precisely size and position objects on the slide. Refer to Figure 3.49 as you complete Step 1.

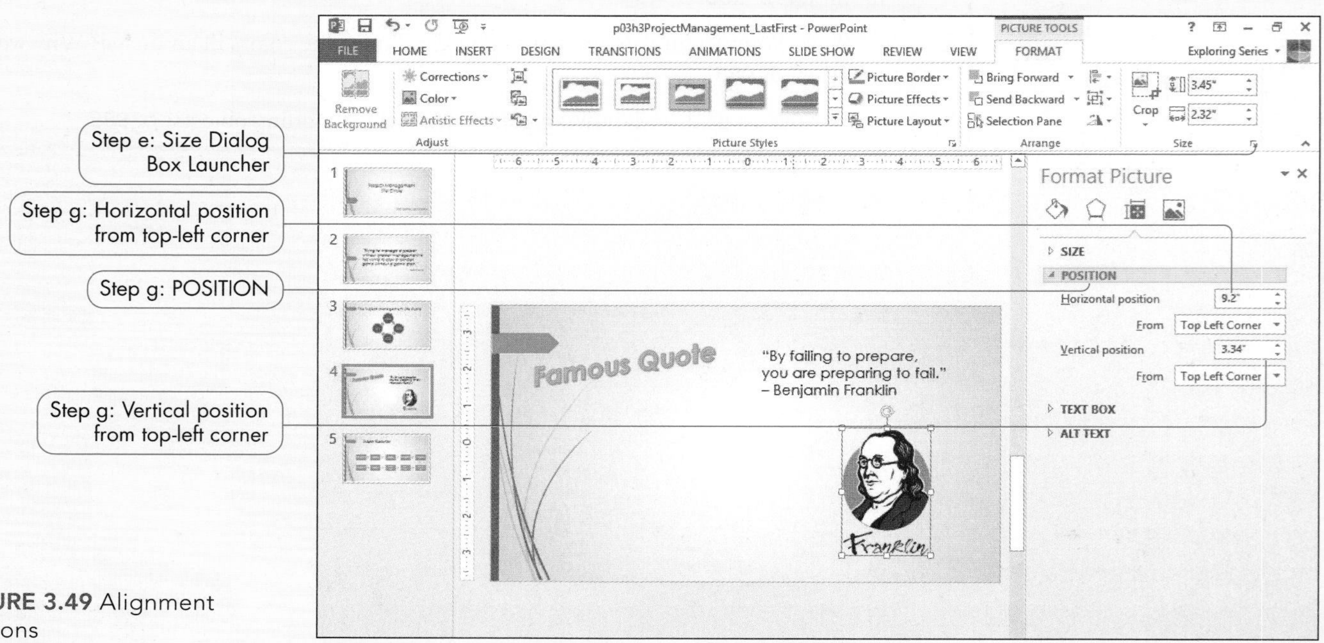

FIGURE 3.49 Alignment Options

a. Open the *p03h2ProjectManagement_LastFirst* presentation if you closed it after the previous exercise. Save the presentation as **p03h3ProjectManagement_LastFirst**, changing *h2* to *h3*.

b. Click **Slide 4**. Click the **INSERT tab** and click **Online Pictures** in the Images group.

The Insert Pictures pane opens.

c. Type **Benjamin Franklin** in the **Office.com Clip Art search box** and press **Enter**.

A few images of Benjamin Franklin display. Entering the keywords *Benjamin Franklin* narrowed your search more than if you had entered the generic keyword *Franklin*.

d. Insert the Online Pictures image of Benjamin Franklin as shown in Figure 3.49.

You have inserted the Online Pictures image in the center of Slide 4.

TROUBLESHOOTING: If you cannot locate the image in Figure 3.49, select another Online Pictures image of Benjamin Franklin. Expand your search terms to include other result types if necessary.

e. Click the **Size Dialog Box Launcher** in the Size group on the FORMAT tab.

The Format Picture pane opens with the SIZE option expanded.

f. Type **3.45"** in the **Height box** and click in the **Width box**.

Because *Lock aspect ratio* is selected, the width of the image changes to 2.32", keeping the image in proportion.

g. Click the **POSITION arrow** in the Format Picture pane to expand the options. Type **9.2"** in the **Horizontal position box**, type **3.34"** in the **Vertical position box**, press **Enter**, and then close the Format Picture pane.

The picture is moved to a new position.

h. Save the presentation.

STEP 2 》 FLIP ONLINE PICTURES

Rotating and flipping are both ways to angle an object on the slide. You can rotate using precise measurements or, for an imprecise method of rotation, you can rotate the object using the Rotation handle. You ask your participants to use these methods so that they are familiar with the benefits of each. Refer to Figure 3.50 as you complete Step 2.

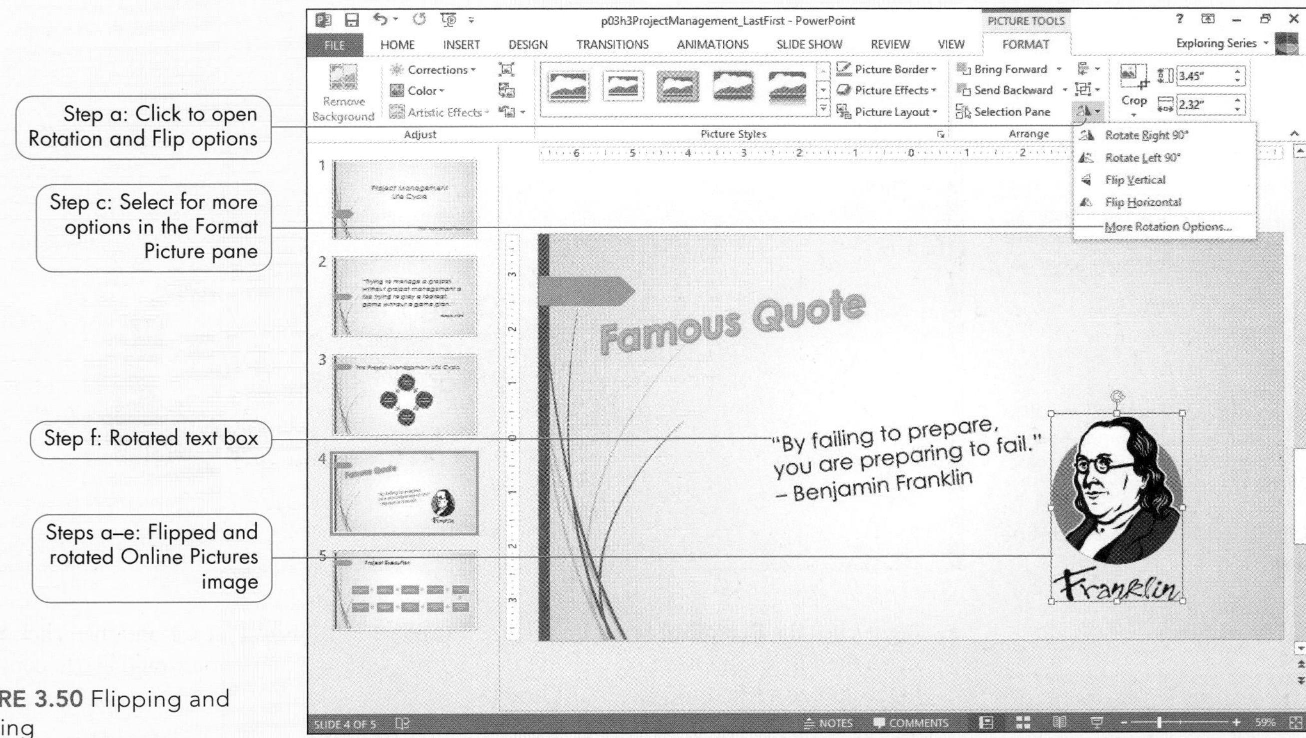

FIGURE 3.50 Flipping and Rotating

a. Click the **Benjamin Franklin image** and click **Rotate** in the Arrange group on the FORMAT tab.

The rotate and flip options appear.

b. Click **Flip Horizontal**.

c. Click **Rotate** in the Arrange group and select **More Rotation Options**.

d. Type **180** in the **Rotation box** and press **Enter**.

The picture is rotated upside down.

e. Click **Rotate** and select **Flip Vertical**. Close the Format Shape pane.

The Online Pictures picture appears to be in its original position, but the rotation angle is still set at 180°.

f. Select the text box in the top right of the slide and drag it down and to the left to the approximate center of the slide. Position the insertion point over the rotation handle and drag the rotation handle to the left until the text box is rotated to approximately match the slant in the *Famous Quote* WordArt.

> **TROUBLESHOOTING:** As you change the angle of rotation for the text box, you will need to reposition it on the slide. An easy way to make small position adjustments is to press the arrow keys on the keyboard.

g. Save the presentation.

STEP 3 » UNGROUP, MODIFY, AND REGROUP ONLINE PICTURES

Being able to change colors, remove shapes, add shapes, and group and regroup Online Pictures images are important skills you want your participants to master. You ask the participants to change the color of the letters in Franklin, move grouped items, and regroup the Ben Franklin Online Pictures image. Refer to Figure 3.51 as you complete Step 3.

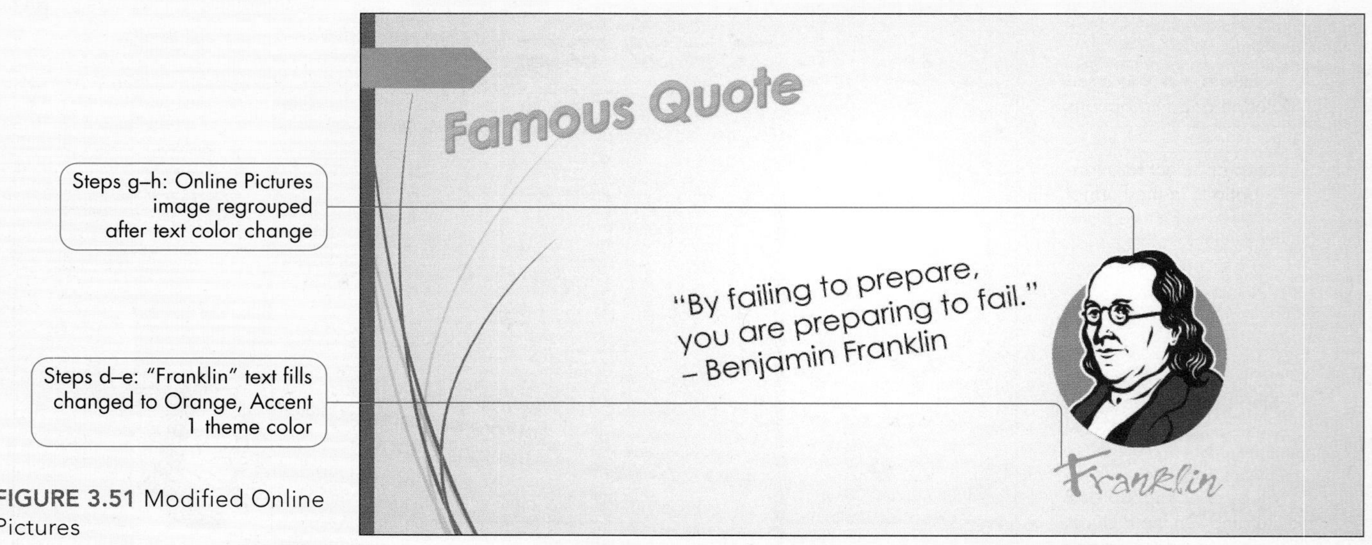

FIGURE 3.51 Modified Online Pictures

a. Right-click the **Benjamin Franklin picture** on Slide 4, select **Edit Picture**, and then click **Yes** when the Microsoft Office PowerPoint message box opens asking if you would like to convert the picture to a Microsoft Drawing Object.

The image has been converted to a drawing object and flips back to its original rotation angle.

b. Click the **FORMAT tab**, click **Group** in the Arrange group, select **Ungroup**, and then click outside the Online Pictures border.

When you ungroup the Online Pictures image, each shape comprising the image is selected and surrounded with adjustment handles. Clicking outside the border deselects the shapes so that you can select just the one you wish to modify.

c. Drag the **Zoom slider** until the image is at a level with which you are comfortable and drag the scroll bars to locate the name *Franklin* at the bottom of the Online Pictures image.

   Zooming in makes selecting the individual shape you wish to modify easier.

d. Select the **F** in *Franklin*, click the **FORMAT tab** if necessary, click **Shape Fill** in the Shape Styles group, and then click **Orange, Accent 1** (first row, fifth column).

   You change the black *F* in the original Online Pictures image to a color that matches your theme color.

e. Drag a selection around all the remaining letters in *Franklin* and click the **Shape Fill button** (not the arrow) to change the fill color of the other letters to **Orange, Accent 1**.

   The Shape Fill button will default to the last color selected.

f. Click the **VIEW tab** and click **Fit to Window** in the Zoom group.

g. Drag a selection net around all the shapes used to make the Benjamin Franklin Online Pictures image. It may be easier to start at the outside top-right area and drag down to the bottom-left corner area to avoid including the text box.

   All the shapes are selected. Pressing Ctrl and clicking the shapes individually would be time consuming because of the many shapes involved.

h. Click the **FORMAT tab**, click **Group** in the Arrange group, and then select **Regroup**.

   Because the WordArt and the text box were not part of the original group, they do not become part of the group.

i. Save the presentation.

STEP 4 » RECOLOR A PICTURE

You teach your mini-camp participants to recolor an Online Pictures image so that it matches the color scheme of the presentation. Refer to Figure 3.52 as you complete Step 4.

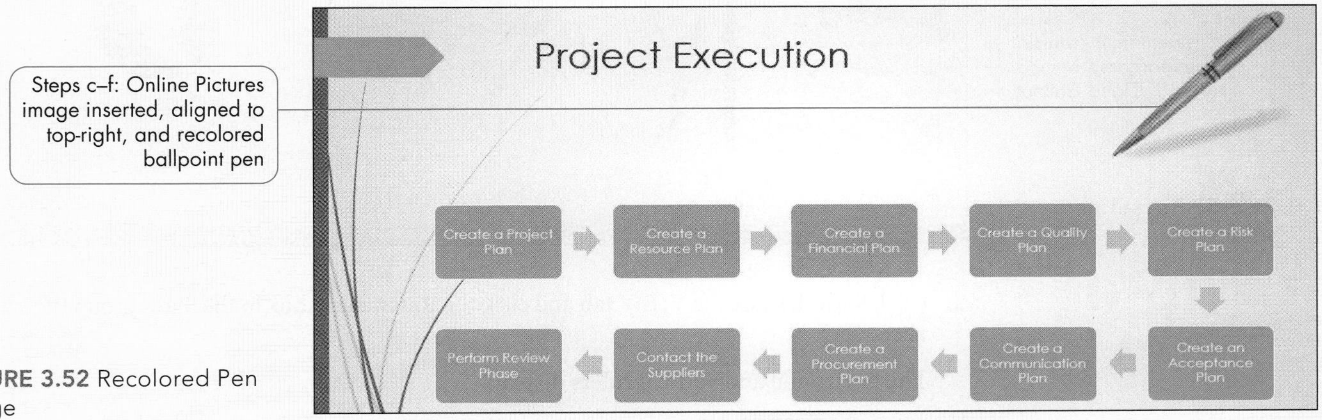

FIGURE 3.52 Recolored Pen Image

a. Click **Slide 5**. Click the **INSERT tab** and click **Online Pictures** in the Images group.

b. Type **Pen** in the **Office.com Clip Art search box** and press Enter.

c. Choose the gray ballpoint pen. Refer to Figure 3.52 to determine which pen to insert.

d. While the Online Picture image is selected, click the **FORMAT tab** under *PICTURE TOOLS*. In the Size group, change the height to **3"**.

   The width will change to 3" automatically.

e. Click the **FORMAT tab** under *PICTURE TOOLS* again, if not already selected. Click **Align** in the Arrange group and select **Align Top** to move the object to the top of the slide. Once the Online Picture image is aligned to the top, click **Align** again and select **Align Right**.

   The Online Picture image is now aligned to the top right of the slide.

f. Click **Color** in the Adjust group located under the FORMAT tab and click **Green, Accent color 6 Dark** under the Recolor category (second row, seventh column).

Online Pictures images do not need to be converted to a drawing object; you can use the picture tools to modify them. Recoloring an image can be applied to any image, and therefore it does not require Online Pictures images to be ungrouped or to be vectors.

The color of the Online Pictures image now matches the colors in the theme.

g. Save the presentation.

STEP 5 ›› CREATE AND REORDER SHAPES

Being able to create and reorder shapes allows you to be creative, enabling you to create backgrounds, borders, and corners. You ask your group to create a background for three Online Pictures images, which unifies the images. Refer to Figure 3.53 as you complete Step 5.

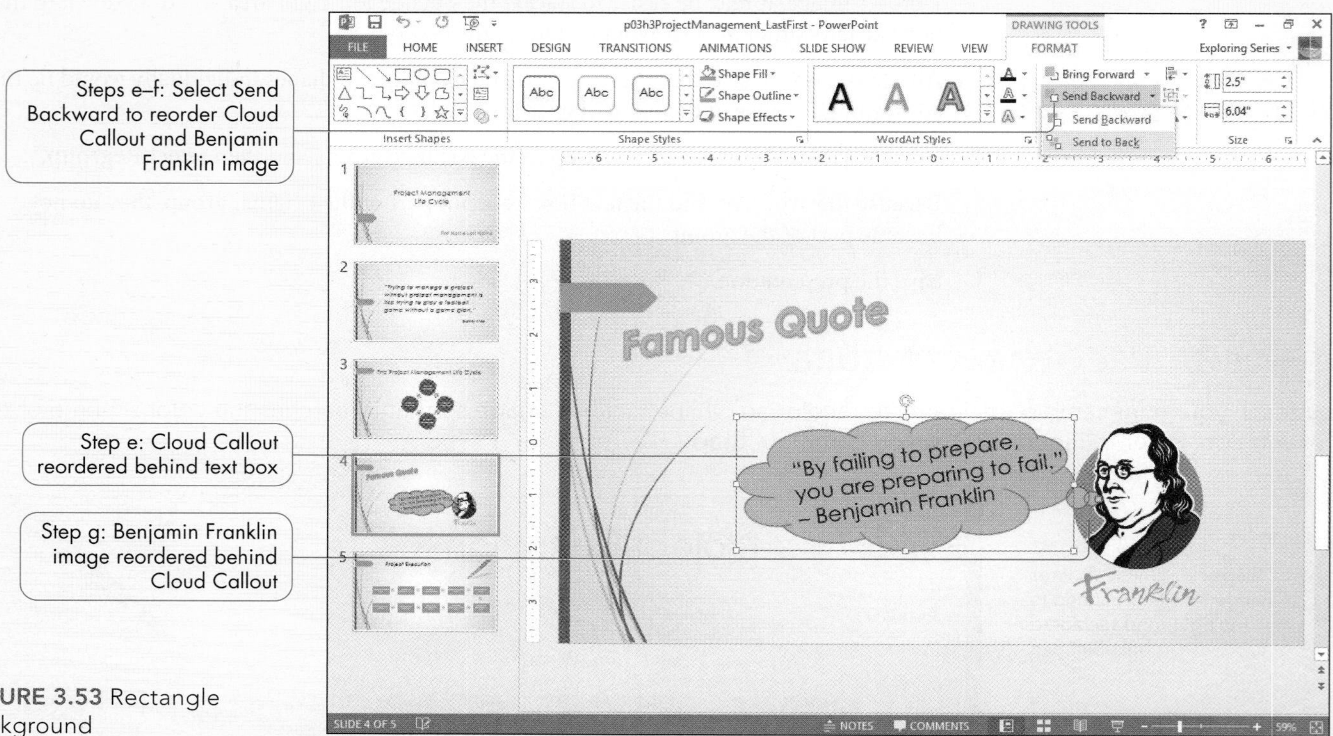

FIGURE 3.53 Rectangle Background

a. Click **Slide 4**. Click the **VIEW tab** and click the **Ruler check box** in the Show group (if necessary).

The horizontal and vertical rulers display.

b. Click the **INSERT tab**, click **Shapes** in the Illustrations group, and then click the **Cloud Callout** in the Callouts category.

c. Position the cross-hair pointer on the slide so that the indicator on the ruler is at the 3.5" mark to the left of the zero point on the horizontal ruler and the 0.5" mark above the zero point on the vertical ruler.

This is the beginning point for the cloud callout.

d. Drag to the 2.5" mark to the right of the zero point on the horizontal ruler and the 2" mark below the zero point on the vertical ruler and release.

A large cloud callout shape in the theme color is created on top of the text box on the slide. You will use the cloud callout as a background for the Online Pictures image. Currently, it is hiding the quote and must be reordered.

e. Drag the yellow square at the bottom of the callout shape to the 3" mark to the right of the zero point on the horizontal ruler and the 1" mark below 0 on the vertical ruler until it looks similar to the position shown in Figure 3.53.

f. Click the **FORMAT tab**, click **Shape Fill arrow** in the Shape Styles group, and then click **Orange, Accent 1, Lighter 40%** (fourth row, fifth column). Click **Send Backward** in the Arrange group of the FORMAT tab and select **Send to Back**.

g. Select the **Benjamin Franklin Online Pictures image**. Click **Send Backward** in the Arrange group and select **Send to Back**. If necessary, nudge the Franklin image and text box into position as seen in Figure 3.53.

h. Save and submit the file based on your instructor's directions. Close the file and exit PowerPoint.

Chapter Objectives Review

After reading this chapter, you have accomplished the following objectives:

1. **Create shapes.**
   - You can use shapes to highlight information, as a design element, as the basis for creating illustrations, or to contain information in infographics.
   - Draw lines and connectors: Lines are shapes that can be used to point to information, or to divide a slide into sections. Connectors are lines that attach to the shapes you create and move with shapes when the shapes are moved.
   - Create and modify freeform shapes: PowerPoint provides tools for creating, sizing, and positioning shapes. A freeform shape is a shape that can be used to create customized shapes using both curved and straight-line segments. Sometimes, the freeform shape you have drawn is not exactly as you desired. You can modify the freeform shape to achieve the desired shape through the help of a vertex. Vertexes are the black squares that control the curve line segments, indicating where two line segments meet or end.
2. **Apply Quick Styles and customize shapes.**
   - Change shape fills: A shape can be customized by changing its default fill to another color, to a picture, to a gradient, to a texture, or to no fill.
   - Change shape outlines: The shape outline color, weight, or dash style can be modified.
   - Change shape effects: Special effects such as shadows, reflections, and glows may be added.
   - Applying a Quick Style enables you to apply preset options.
3. **Create SmartArt.**
   - SmartArt graphics are diagrams that present information visually to effectively communicate your message.
   - SmartArt can be used to create effective infographics.
   - You can convert text to a SmartArt diagram.
4. **Modify SmartArt.**
   - Change SmartArt theme colors: SmartArt diagrams can be modified to fit nearly any color scheme.
   - Use Quick Styles with SmartArt: After creating the diagram, you can use Quick Styles to adjust the style to match other styles you have used in your presentation or to make the diagram easier to understand.
   - Change the layout: Once a SmartArt diagram type has been chosen, it can easily be converted to another type.
   - Change SmartArt type: You can change the SmartArt diagram type if you decide a different type would be better.
   - Convert text to a SmartArt diagram: Bullets and other text can be converted directly to a SmartArt diagram.
   - SmartArt can be modified to include additional shapes, to delete shapes, to apply a SmartArt style, to revise the color scheme, or to add special effects.
   - The direction of the SmartArt can be changed.
   - SmartArt can be resized and repositioned.
5. **Create WordArt.**
   - WordArt is text with decorative effects applied to draw attention to the text.
   - Select a WordArt style and type the text you desire.
6. **Modify WordArt.**
   - WordArt can be modified by transforming the shape of the text and by applying special effects and colors.
   - Text created as WordArt can be edited.
   - Among the many special effects available are 3-D presets and rotations.
7. **Modify objects.**
   - Flip and rotate: An object may be flipped horizontally or vertically, or rotated by dragging its green rotation handle.
   - Merge shapes: The Merge Shapes feature allows you to take shapes that you have inserted and merge them together. There are five different merging options: Union, Combine, Fragment, Intersect, and Subtract.
   - Group and ungroup objects: Vector images can be ungrouped so basic shapes can be customized, and objects can be regrouped so they can be moved as one object.
   - Recolor objects: Pictures can be recolored by changing their color mode or by applying dark or light variations of a theme color or custom color.
8. **Arrange objects.**
   - Objects are stacked in layers.
   - The object at the top of the layer is the one that fully displays, while other objects in the stack may have some portions blocked.
   - Order objects: The stacking order of shapes can be reordered so that objects can be seen as desired.
   - Align objects: Features such as rulers, grids, guides, align, and distribute can be used to arrange objects on a slide and arrange objects in relation to one another.

Key Terms Matching

Match the key terms with their definitions. Write the key term letter by the appropriate numbered definition.

- a. Adjustment handle
- b. Aspect ratio
- c. Callout
- d. Connector
- e. Distribute
- f. Flow chart
- g. Freeform shape
- h. Gradient fill
- i. Group
- j. Guide
- k. Infographic
- l. Line weight
- m. Lock Drawing Mode
- n. Picture fill
- o. Selection net
- p. SmartArt
- q. Stacking order
- r. Texture fill
- s. Vector graphic
- t. Vertex

1. ______ Inserts an image from a file into a shape. **p. 952**
2. ______ A blend of two or more colors or shades. **p. 950**
3. ______ A marquee that selects all objects in an area you define by dragging the mouse. **p. 950**
4. ______ A yellow square that enables you to modify a shape. **p. 945**
5. ______ Enables the creation of multiple shapes of the same type. **p. 945**
6. ______ An illustration showing the sequence of a project or plan. **p. 947**
7. ______ A visual representation of data or knowledge. **p. 944**
8. ______ A line shape that is attached to and moves with other shapes. **p. 946**
9. ______ Diagram that presents information visually to effectively communicate a message. **p. 963**
10. ______ Refers to keeping an object's proportion the same with respect to width and height. **p. 978**
11. ______ Combines two or more objects. **p. 980**
12. ______ Point where a curve ends or the point where two line segments meet in a freeform shape. **p. 948**
13. ______ To divide or evenly spread shapes over a given area. **p. 986**
14. ______ Inserts a texture such as marble into a shape. **p. 954**
15. ______ A shape that combines both curved and straight lines. **p. 948**
16. ______ A shape that includes a text box you can use to add notes. **p. 945**
17. ______ The order of objects placed on top of one another. **p. 984**
18. ______ An object-oriented graphic based on geometric formulas. **p. 980**
19. ______ A straight horizontal or vertical line used to align objects. **p. 986**
20. ______ The width or thickness of a line. **p. 954**

Multiple Choice

1. Which of the following is text that has a decorative effect applied?
   (a) Text box
   (b) WordArt
   (c) Text pane
   (d) SmartArt

2. To rotate a shape on your slide:
   (a) Do nothing, because shapes cannot be rotated.
   (b) Drag one of the corner adjustment handles.
   (c) Double-click the lightning bolt and enter the number of degrees to rotate.
   (d) Drag the handle at the top of the image.

3. Which of the following is a reason for ungrouping a drawn object?
   (a) To resize the group as one piece
   (b) To move the objects as one
   (c) To add text on top of the group
   (d) To be able to individually change shapes used to create the composite image

4. Which of the following is a reason for grouping shapes?
   (a) To be able to change each shape individually
   (b) To create a relationship diagram
   (c) To move or modify the objects as one
   (d) To connect the shapes with connectors

5. You have inserted an Online Pictures image of the ocean with a sailboat on the right side. If you flip the image vertically, what would the resulting image look like?
   (a) The image would show right side up, but the sailboat would be on the left side.
   (b) The image would be upside down with the sailboat pointing down.
   (c) The image would be rotated 270°, and the sailboat would be at the top.
   (d) The image would be rotated 90°, and the sailboat would be on the bottom.

6. You have items needed for a camping trip in a bullet placeholder. Which of the following SmartArt diagrams would you use to display the data as an infographic?
   (a) Hierarchy
   (b) Cycle
   (c) List
   (d) Relationship

7. Which of the following is *not* available from the SmartArt gallery?
   (a) Data table
   (b) Horizontal bullet list
   (c) Process graphic
   (d) Cycle matrix

8. Which of the following might be a reason for changing the stacking order of shapes?
   (a) To show a relationship by placing shapes in front of or behind each other
   (b) To hide something on a shape
   (c) To uncover something hidden by another shape
   (d) All of the above

9. Which of the following is used to show a continual process?
   (a) Hierarchy
   (b) Matrix
   (c) Cycle
   (d) Relationship

10. Which of the following may be used to add emphasis to text on a slide?
    (a) Apply a WordArt Quick Style to the selected text.
    (b) Create the text using the WordArt feature.
    (c) Apply a Text Effect to the selected text.
    (d) All of the above

Practice Exercises

1 Cloud Computing Infographic

FROM SCRATCH

To help explain cloud computing to employees, you decide to create an infographic using a SmartArt Hierarchy diagram. You want the infographic to show the three categories of cloud computing: IaaS (Infrastructure-as-a-Service), PaaS (Platform-as-a-Service), and SaaS (Software-as-a-Service). You also want to show common providers in each category to help employees recognize the differences in the categories. This exercise follows the same set of skills as used in Hands-On Exercise 2 in the chapter. Refer to Figure 3.54 as you complete this exercise.

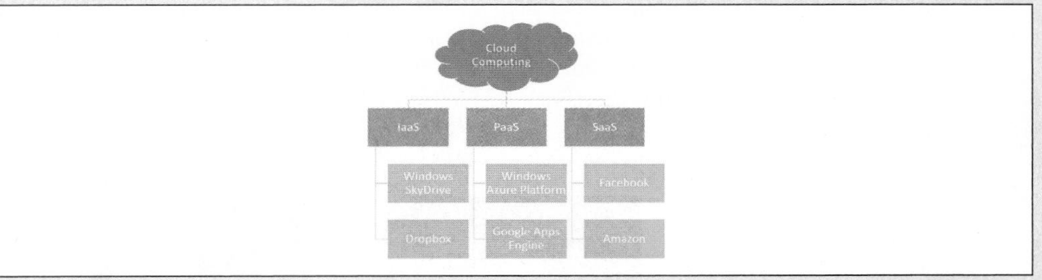

FIGURE 3.54 Cloud Computing Infographic

a. Open a blank presentation file and save it as **p03p1Cloud_LastFirst**. Create a *Notes and Handouts* header with your name and a footer with your instructor's name and your class. Include the current date.

b. Click the **HOME tab** and click **Layout** in the Slides group. Select the **Blank layout**.

c. Click the **INSERT tab** and click **SmartArt** in the Illustrations group. Click **Hierarchy** in the left pane of the *Choose a SmartArt Graphic* dialog box. Click **Lined List** (fourth row, third column) and click **OK**.

d. Change the size of the shape by doing the following:
   - Click the **FORMAT tab**, click **Size**, and then click the **Size Dialog Box Launcher** to open the Format Shape pane.
   - Click the SmartArt shape.
   - Click in the **Height box** and type **6.5"**.
   - Click in the **Width box** and type **8"**.
   - Click the **POSITION arrow**, if necessary, and type **2.8"** in the **Horizontal position box** and **0.5"** in the **Vertical position box**.
   - Close the Format Shape pane.

e. Click the **DESIGN tab** and click **Text Pane** in the Create Graphic group to open the text pane (if necessary).

f. Type **Cloud Computing** in the first bulleted level in the Text pane.

g. Select the second bullet point and type **IaaS**. Press **Enter**, press **Tab**, and then type **Windows OneDrive**. Press **Enter** and type **Dropbox**. Press **Enter**.

h. Press **Shift+Tab** and type **PaaS**. Press **Enter**, press **Tab**, and then type **Windows Azure Platform**. Press **Enter** and type **Google Apps Engine**.

i. Select the first [Text] bullet point and type **SaaS**. Select the remaining [Text] bullet point, press **Tab**, and then type **Facebook**. Press **Enter** and type **Amazon**.

j. Close the Text pane.

k. Click the **More button** in the Layouts group on the DESIGN tab and click **Organization Chart** (first row, first column).

l. Click **Change Colors** in the SmartArt Styles group and click **Colorful Range - Accent Colors 2 to 3**.

m. Click the **More button** in the SmartArt Styles group and click **White Outline** in the *Best Match for Document* section.

n. Select the **Cloud Computing shape** and click the **FORMAT tab**. Click **Change Shape** in the Shapes group and click **Cloud** in the *Basic Shapes* section. Click **Larger** in the Shapes group six times.

o. Apply the **Fill - White, Outline - Accent 1, Shadow WordArt style** to the Cloud Computing text box. Then, apply the **Tight Reflection, touching Reflection Text Effect** to the WordArt.

p. Save and close the file. Submit based on your instructor's directions.

2 Principles of Pilates

You have created a slide show about Pilates for your Pilates instructor to show prospective students. You use infographics, shapes, and Online Pictures to share his message. This exercise follows the same set of skills as used in Hands-On Exercises 1–3 in the chapter. Refer to Figure 3.55 as you complete this exercise.

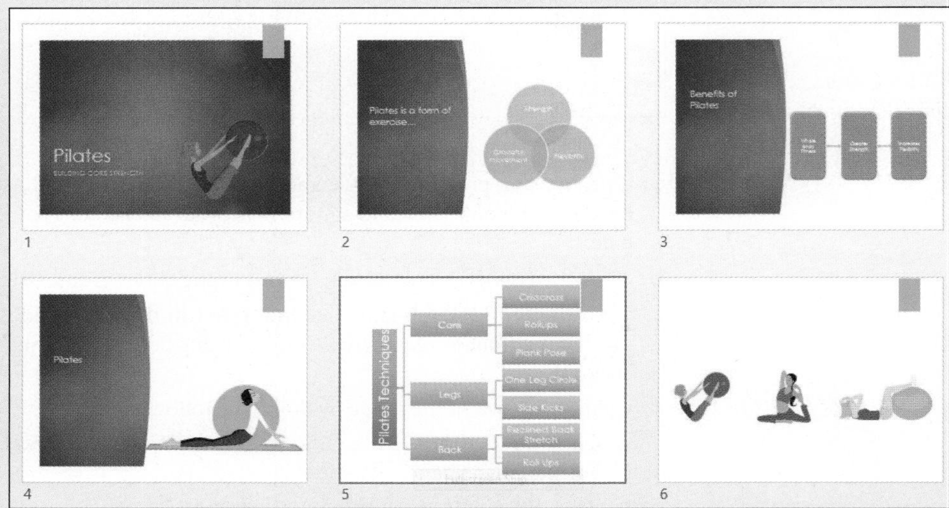

FIGURE 3.55 Pilates, Strengthening the Core

a. Open *p03p2Pilates* and save it as **p03p2Pilates_LastFirst**.

b. Create a handout header with your name and a handout footer with your instructor's name and your class. Include the current date.

c. Click **Slide 2**. Click the placeholder containing the bullet points and click the **HOME tab**.

d. Click **Convert to SmartArt** in the Paragraph group and click **Basic Venn**.

e. Click **Change Colors** in the SmartArt Styles group. Click **Transparent Gradient Range - Accent 1** in the *Accent 1* section.

f. Click **Slide 3**. Click the **INSERT tab**, click **Shapes** in the Illustrations group, and then select **Double Arrow** in the *Lines* section. Drag an arrow from the right-center connecting point on the *Whole Body Fitness* shape to the left-center connecting point on the *Creates Strength* shape. Repeat this step to create a connector between the *Creates Strength* shape and the *Increases Flexibility* shape.

g. Click **Slide 5**. Select the **Hierarchy SmartArt** and click the **SMARTART TOOLS DESIGN tab**.

h. Select the **Core shape** and click the **Add Shape arrow** in the Create Graphic group. Select **Add Shape Below** and type **Plank Pose**.

i. Click the **More button** in the Layouts group on the DESIGN tab and select **More Layouts**. Click **Horizontal Multi-Level Hierarchy** in the Hierarchy category.

j. Click **Intense Effect** in the SmartArt Styles group.

k. Click **Slide 1**. Select the image, click the **FORMAT tab**, and then click **Color** in the Adjust group. Click **Sepia** in the Recolor variations category (first row, third column).

l. Click **Slide 4**. Right-click the image and select **Edit Picture**. Click **Yes** to convert the picture into a drawing object. Select the image again.

m. Click the **FORMAT tab** and click **Group** in the Arrange group. Select **Ungroup**.

n. Click the **VIEW tab** and click **Zoom** in the Zoom group. Select **200%** and click **OK**. Deselect the shapes and select the circle.

o. Click the **FORMAT tab** and click **Shape Fill**. Select **Lime, Accent** 1 (top row, fifth column).

p. Click **Fit to Window** in the Zoom group.

q. Drag a selection net around all the shapes comprising the clip art image, click the **FORMAT tab**, click **Group** in the Arrange group, and then select **Regroup**.

r. Click the **INSERT tab** and click **Shapes** in the Illustrations group. Click **Freeform** in the *Line* section.

s. Click approximately 0.5" from the foot of the woman to create the first point of a freeform shape you create to resemble a mat (see Figure 3.55).

t. Click approximately 0.5" from the right hand of the woman to create the second point of the freeform shape.

u. Click approximately 1/4" vertically and horizontally from the bottom right of the slide.

v. Click approximately 1/4" vertically and horizontally from the bottom left of the slide.

w. Click the starting point of the freeform shape to complete the shape.

x. Click the **FORMAT tab**, click the **Send Backward arrow**, and then select **Send to Back**.

y. Click **Slide 6**. Line up the three figures in a horizontal line beginning with the woman with the red ball and ending with the woman with the purple ball. Drag a selection net around all the images and click the **FORMAT tab**. Click **Align,** click **Align Middle**. Click **Align,** click **Distribute Horizontally** to evenly distribute the images.

z. View the slide show. Save and close the file and submit based on your instructor's directions.

Mid-Level Exercises

1 SmartArt and Online Pictures Ideas

To help you become familiar with the SmartArt Graphic gallery and the types of information appropriate for each type of diagram, you create a slide show of "SmartArt ideas." You also manipulate clip art. In this activity, you work extensively with sizing, placement, and fills.

a. Open *p03m1Ideas* and save it as **p03m1Ideas_LastFirst**. On Slide 1, replace *First Name Last Name* with your name.

b. Create a handout header with your name and a handout footer with your instructor's name and your class. Include the current date.

c. View the gridlines.

d. Click **Slide 2**. Insert a **Vertical Box List SmartArt diagram** (second row, second column in the List category) and make the following modifications:
   - Apply the **Subtle Effect** from SmartArt Styles.
   - Type the following list items into the **Text Pane**:
     - **List**
     - **Process**
     - **Cycle**
     - **Hierarchy**
     - **Relationship**
     - **Matrix**
     - **Pyramid**
     - **Picture**
   - Change the text font size to **24 pt**.
   - Size the SmartArt diagram to **7"** wide and drag it so that it is at the horizontal center of the slide using the grid to help you determine placement.
   - Align the bottom border of the SmartArt diagram with the last line of the gridline.

e. Click **Slide 3**. Convert the text to an **Upward Arrow SmartArt diagram** and make the following modifications:
   - Apply the **Simple Fill SmartArt Style**.
   - Change the height of the SmartArt diagram to **6.17"** and the width to **10"**.
   - **Align Center** the diagram. Then **Align Middle** the diagram.

f. Click **Slide 4**. Insert a **Diverging Radial SmartArt diagram** and make the following modifications:
   - Apply the **3-D Polished SmartArt Style**.
   - Change the SmartArt colors to **Colorful - Accent Colors** (first row, first column in the *Color* section).
   - Type **Residential College** as the center hub and type **Build Community**, **Promote Personal Growth**, and **Support Academic Success** as the spokes around the hub. Remove the extra shape.
   - Set the height of the SmartArt to **5.5"** and the width to **6.67"**.

g. Click **Slide 5**. Insert a **Horizontal Hierarchy SmartArt diagram** (third row, fourth column in the Hierarchy category) and make the following modifications:
   - Apply the **Flat Scene SmartArt Style**.
   - Type **School of Business** as the first-level bullet in the **Text Pane**. Enter **M&M** and **DIS** as the second-level bullets and type the following in the third-level bullets: **Marketing**, **Management**, **MIS**, and **POM**.
   - Click **Right to Left** in the Create Graphic group to change the orientation of the diagram.
   - Drag the borders of the SmartArt graphic until it fits the page and the text is large enough to read.

h. Click **Slide 6**. Insert a **Basic Venn SmartArt diagram** (tenth row, fourth column in the Relationship category) and make the following modifications:

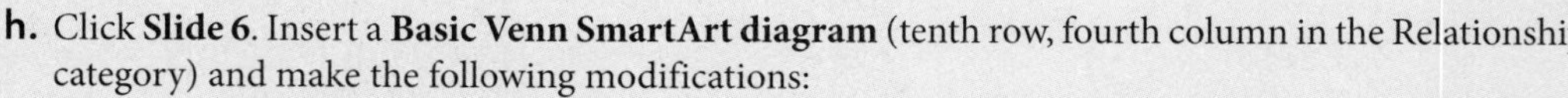

   - Type the following as three bullets in the **Text Pane**: **Anesthesiology**, **Nurses**, and **Surgeon**.
     - Insert a picture fill in the *Anesthesiology* shape using an Online Picture with *Doctor* as the key term.

    - Insert a picture fill in the *Nurses* shape using an Online Picture with *Nurse* as the key term.
    - Insert a picture fill in the *Surgeon* shape using an Online Picture with *Surgeon* as the key term.
  - Recolor all images using the **Grayscale variation**.
  - Format the SmartArt text with the **Fill - White, Outline - Accent 2, Hard Shadow - Accent 2 Style**.
  - Set the height of the SmartArt to **4.5"** and the width to **5.5"**.
  - Use the grid to center the Venn diagram in the available space.

i. Click **Slide 7**. Insert a **Basic Matrix SmartArt diagram** (first row, first column in the Matrix category) and make the following modifications:
  - Apply the **Subtle Effect SmartArt Style**.
  - Change the colors to **Colorful - Accent Colors**.
  - Type the following text in the **Text Pane**:
    - **Urgent & Important**
    - **Not Urgent & Important**
    - **Urgent & Not Important**
    - **Not Urgent & Not Important**

j. Click **Slide 8**. Insert a **Basic Pyramid SmartArt diagram** (first row, first column in the Pyramid category) and make the following modifications:
  - Apply the **Subtle Effect SmartArt Style**.
  - Enter a blank space at the top pyramid level and add the following text to the remaining levels. You will add the text for the top pyramid level in a text box in a later step so that the font in the SmartArt is not reduced to a difficult-to-read font size.
    - **Esteem**
    - **Belonging and Love**
    - **Safety**
    - **Biological Needs**
  - Drag the border of the SmartArt diagram until it fills the available white space on the slide. Deselect the pyramid.
  - Create a text box on the top left of the slide and type **Self-Actualization** in the **text box**. Change the font size to **39 pt**. Drag the text box so it is centered over the top of the empty pyramid.
  - Apply the **Fill - Brown, Text 1, Shadow WordArt Style** to the text box *Maslow's Hierarchy of Needs*.
  - Apply the **Deflate Transform Text Effect** to the WordArt text.

k. Click **Slide 9**. Ungroup the complex clip art image until all grouping is undone. Make the following changes:
  - Change the color of the bird so it is red.
  - Regroup the pieces of the clip art image.

l. View the slide show. Save and close the file and submit based on your instructor's directions.

2 The Arts

A presentation created by a local arts volunteer can be improved using shapes and SmartArt. You will update the presentation using the Organic design theme, Inset SmartArt style.

a. Open *p03m2Perform* and save it as **p03m2Perform_LastFirst**. Create a *Notes and Handouts* header with your name and a footer with your instructor's name and your class. Include the current date.

b. Click **Slide 4**. Select the bulleted text and convert it to a **Process Arrows SmartArt diagram** available in the Process SmartArt category. Apply the **Polished SmartArt Style** available in the 3-D category.

c. Click **Slide 5**. Select the existing SmartArt diagram and change the layout to a **Segmented Pyramid** in the Pyramid SmartArt category. Apply the **Inset SmartArt Style** available in the 3-D category. Resize the SmartArt to fit the available area and horizontally center the SmartArt.

d. Click **Slide 6**. Create an **Organization Chart SmartArt diagram** available in the Hierarchy category. The top level of management is the *Executive Committee*. The Executive Committee has the following subcommittees: **Finance Committee**, **Program Committee**, and **Marketing Committee**.

e. Add two shapes beneath each. Add the following committees to the Finance Committee: **Investments** and **Financial Oversight**. Add the following committees to the Program Committee: **Grants** and **Distribution**. Add the following committees to the Marketing Committee: **Public Relations** and **Fundraising**.

f. Apply the **Inset SmartArt Style** available in the 3-D category.

g. Click **Slide 7**. Insert your choice of music clip art. Ungroup the clip art image and change the fill color of several shapes to theme colors. Resize and position the image as appropriate. Regroup the clip art.

> **TROUBLESHOOTING:** If you choose an image that you cannot ungroup and modify, choose another image.

h. Use the Freeform tool or Curve tool to create a shape that covers the title, subtitle, and the clip art image. Move the shape you created to the back so all other objects on the slide are visible. Edit the shape fill and outline, and move the objects on the slide until you are satisfied with your slide.

i. Save and close the presentation and submit based on your instructor's directions.

3 Learning from an Expert

Video-sharing sites such as YouTube.com make it possible to learn from PowerPoint industry experts as well as everyday PowerPoint users. You can learn through step-by-step instructions or by inspiration after seeing others use PowerPoint. The video source may also refer you to a professional Web site that will provide you with a wealth of tips and ideas for creating slide shows that move your work from ordinary to extraordinary. In this exercise, you will view a YouTube video featuring the work of Nancy Duarte, a well-known PowerPoint industry expert. After viewing the video and related Web site, you will use shapes and animation to recreate one of the effects in Duarte's presentation. Finally, you will post the slide you created to your Web site and blog about your experience. Note: This exercise assumes you have done the collaboration exercise for Chapter 1. If you have not completed that exercise, use OneDrive.com or another method for sharing your presentation with your instructor and classmates.

a. Access the Internet and go to www.youtube.com. Search for the video *Duarte Design's Five Rules for Presentations by Nancy Duarte*. View the video, click the supporting link beneath the video (http://blog.duarte.com/), and note the additional resources available to viewers of the video. Close the Web site.

b. Advance to 2:29 in the video clip on YouTube and rewatch Duarte's Rule 4—Practice Design Not Decoration.

c. Open *p03m3Duarte.pptx*, which contains the slide *Duarte's Rule 4*. Apply animations to the shapes and text contained in the file to reproduce the effect of Duarte's slide. If you prefer, create your own slide reproducing any of Duarte's rules for effective presentations and animate it as desired. Save the file as **p03m3Duarte_LastFirst**.

d. Load your animated slide to your Weebly Web site if you completed Collaboration Exercise 1. Open the site and click the Multimedia link on the Elements tab. Drag the File element to your home page and upload the *p03m3Duarte_LastFirst* file. If you are not using the Weebly.com site created during Collaborative Exercise 1, upload your animated slide to OneDrive.com or another online storage site.

e. Create a blog entry about this experience if you are using the Weebly.com site created in Collaborative Exercise 1. Discuss Duarte's rules and whether you have seen good examples and/or bad examples of these rules used in presentations. Ask three classmates to go to your Weebly Web site, view the presentation you saved, and then add a comment about your presentation or blog entry. If you saved to OneDrive.com or another online storage location, share the location with three classmates and ask them to download the presentation. Ask your classmates to view the presentation and ask them to e-mail you with their comments.

f. Visit three of your classmates' Web sites after the due date for this exercise and use the contact form on their home pages to leave your information and a comment about their presentations or blogs. Revisit your Web site to see what comments your classmates entered. Or, download and view three of your classmates' animated slides from the storage location they used.

g. E-mail your instructor your Web site address or storage location so your instructor can review your presentation.

Beyond the Classroom

Predators

Create a presentation about a predator of your choice, such as a shark or lion. After an appropriate title slide, include an introduction slide using a Pyramid SmartArt that shows the levels in a food chain. Use the following levels from top level to bottom level to create the pyramid: **Predators**, **Secondary Consumers**, **Primary Consumers**, and **Primary Producers**. The food chain is shown as a pyramid to show that meat-eating predators at the top of the food chain are more rare than plant-eating primary consumers, which are more rare than primary producers such as plants. Type a speaker note for the introduction slide that summarizes how the levels of the food chain work. After the introductory slide, research the predator of your choice and include a minimum of four slides sharing information about the predator. For example, create a presentation about sharks that could include where sharks are located, their classification, their prey, their hunting methods and tools, and their conservation status. Add at least one additional slide that includes shapes and add shape effects to the shapes. Include speaker notes to clarify information. On the title slide, add a title using WordArt of your choice. Apply a design theme and modify it as desired. In addition to the Food Chain Pyramid, include several Online Pictures images or pictures in appropriate locations. Add a transition and animations to enhance the show. Include a *Notes and Handouts* header with your name and a handout footer with your instructor's name and your class. Save your presentation as **p03b2Predator_LastFirst**. Submit based on your instructor's directions.

My Nation

Your student teaching supervisor has asked you to change the presentation she created about America's symbols to make it more visually and emotionally interesting for her students. If you desire, you may select another country, but be sure to include the inspirational symbols of the country you choose. Open *p03b3Symbols* or create your own presentation and save the new presentation as **p03b3Symbols_ LastFirst**. Apply the design theme of your choice and change other themes as desired. Add shapes, SmartArt, pictures, and clip art to add visual interest. Text can be moved to speaker notes, if desired, so that you can showcase symbols. Align and order objects attractively. Finalize the presentation by proofreading and applying transitions and animations. Create a *Notes and Handouts* header with your name and a footer with your instructor's name and your class. Include the current date. Save the presentation and submit based on your instructor's directions.

Personal Financial Management

SOFT SKILLS CASE

FROM SCRATCH

Research personal financial management practices. You may wish to use one of the lessons found on CNN Money: http://money.cnn.com/magazines/moneymag/money101/. Then, create a PowerPoint presentation based on your research. Include a title slide and at least five slides related to the topic you have chosen. Choose a theme, transitions, and animations. Insert at least one appropriate clip art image and incorporate a SmartArt diagram into your presentation to better demonstrate your point. Also incorporate WordArt into your presentation. Include slide notes on most slides as necessary and add your sources to the notes. Create a handout header with your name and the current date. Include a handout footer with your instructor's name and your class name. Review the presentation to ensure there are no errors. Save the presentation as **p03b4Money_LastFirst** and submit based on your instructor's directions.

Capstone Exercise

You began a presentation on waterwise landscaping and concentrated on the content of the presentation. You decide to use the SmartArt feature to create infographics to demonstrate a process and to incorporate shapes to demonstrate concepts.

Create a "Fire Aware" Landscape

You decide to create shapes to explain the concept of creating zones to protect a home from fire and indicate the depth of the zones on the landscape. You stack three oval shapes to create the zones, and you use a combination of text boxes and online pictures to create the landscape. Refer to Figure 3.57 as you complete this exercise.

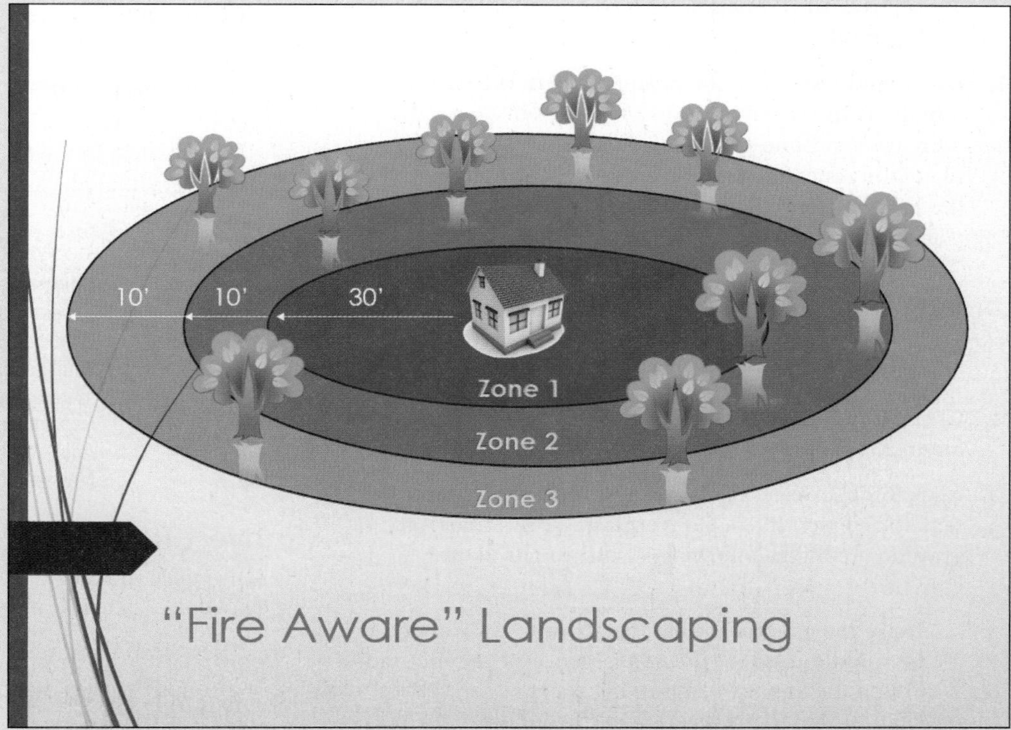

FIGURE 3.57 Fire Aware Landscaping

a. Open *p03c1Xeri* and save it as **p03c1Xeri_LastFirst**. Create a handout footer with your name and your class.

b. Click **Slide 12**. Insert an oval shape in the approximate center of the blank area of the slide. This will be the center oval in a stack of ovals used to define the zones. Apply the following modifications to the shape:
   - Change the Shape Fill, under more colors, to a custom RGB color: **Red:51, Green:102, and Blue:0**, and a **Transparency** of **50%**.
   - Change the oval size to a height of **1.67"** and width of **5"**.

c. Make a copy of the oval you created in step b. Change the second oval size to a height of **2.92"** and width of **7.08"**.

d. Make a third copy of the oval. Change the third oval size to a height of **4"** and width of **9"**.

e. Select the largest oval and send to back. Select the middle-sized oval and send backward so that the smallest oval is the top layer, followed by the middle and largest ovals.

f. Select all three ovals and **Align Center** and **Align Middle**. Using the *POSITION* section in the Format Shapes Pane, group the three ovals so they will move as one. Position the group at horizontal position **0.58"** from the top-left corner and vertical position **1.33"** from the top-left corner.

g. Insert a text box, type **Zone 1**, and then drag it to the bottom center of the small oval. Apply the **Fill - Sky Blue, Background 2, Inner Shadow WordArt Style** to the text. Make two copies of the text box and edit them to read *Zone 2* and *Zone 3*. Drag **Zone 2** to the bottom center of the medium-sized oval and drag **Zone 3** to the bottom center of the large oval.

h. **Align Center** the text boxes.

i. Locate and insert an online picture of a house, and position it in the center of Zone 1. Size it appropriately.

j. Create an arrow that begins near the left edge of the house image and points left to the edge of the Zone 1 oval (see Figure 3.57). Create another arrow that begins near the end of the first arrow and ends at the edge of the Zone 2 oval, and a similar arrow for Zone 3. Set the weight for the arrows at **1 pt**. Set the arrow color to **White, Background 1**.

k. Create three text boxes and center one above each arrow. Label the Zone 1 text box **30'** and label the Zone 2 and 3 text boxes **10'**. Format the text color to **White, Background 1**.

l. Locate and insert an online picture of a tree. Duplicate it multiple times and position a few trees in Zone 2 and more trees in Zone 3. Position smaller trees toward the top of the zones and larger trees nearer the bottom of the zones. Refer to Figure 3.57, but your tree and tree placement can vary.

Convert Text to SmartArt

To add visual interest to slides, you go through the slide show and convert some of the bulleted lists to SmartArt graphics.

a. Click **Slide 2**. Convert the bulleted text to a **Basic Venn SmartArt graphic**.

b. Click **Slide 3**. Select the **Waterwise Options bulleted text** and convert it to a **Converging Arrow SmartArt graphic**. Apply the following modifications to the graphic:

- Resize the graphic so that the arrows almost touch in the middle to show the convergence of the methods around the theme of conserving water.
- Align the SmartArt diagram in the middle of the horizontal space for *Waterwise Options*.
- Apply the **Polished SmartArt Style** to arrows.

c. Select the **Wildfire Aware Options bulleted text** and convert it to a **Continuous Arrow Process SmartArt graphic** to indicate that the creation of defensible landscaping leads to zones. Apply the **Polished SmartArt Style** and change the text color for each text block in the arrow to **White, Background 1**.

Create SmartArt

You have a list of waterwise landscaping principles that you decide would present well as a SmartArt list.

a. Add a new slide after Slide 12 using a **Title Only layout**.

b. Type **Principles for Waterwise Landscaping** in the **title placeholder**. Change the title font size to **29 pt** and resize the placeholder so the title displays on one line.

c. Insert a text box and type **Tips from the Office of Community Services, Fort Lewis College** inside. Center the text under the title.

d. Insert a **Vertical Bracket List SmartArt** to show the steps, or work flow, in the waterwise landscaping process. Type the text in the following table in the **Text Pane**. The number should be at Level 1, and the process text should be at Level 2.

Number	Process Text
1	Develop Landscape Plan
2	Condition Your Soil
3	Limit Lawn Size
4	Irrigate Efficiently
5	Use Appropriate Plants
6	Apply Mulches
7	Maintain

Convert Text to WordArt

The last graphic you want to insert is a WordArt object. After inserting the WordArt, you will apply an animation scheme.

a. Click **Slide 1** and select the title.

b. Apply the **Pattern Fill - Dark Blue, Accent 3, Narrow Horizontal, Inner Shadow WordArt Style** to the title.

c. Apply the **Fill - Dark Blue, Accent 3, Angle Bevel Style** to the subtitle.

d. Apply the **Fly In animation** to the title and apply the **Fade animation** to the subtitle.

e. Check the spelling in the slide show and accept or correct all spellings on the slide.

f. View the slide show. Save and close the file and submit based on your instructor's directions.

PowerPoint

PowerPoint Rich Media Tools

CHAPTER 4

Enhancing with Multimedia

OBJECTIVES AFTER YOU READ THIS CHAPTER, YOU WILL BE ABLE TO:

CASE STUDY | Engagement Album

Your sister was recently married. As a gift to the couple, you decide to create two memory slide shows to celebrate. The first slide show will feature images of the couple in a few engagement photos and on their honeymoon in Europe. The second slide show will display photos taken during a family vacation.

As you prepare the first slide show, you edit the images using PowerPoint's Picture Tools. Each slide in the first slide show is created individually, and each image is manipulated individually. You download an image from the Internet representing the couple's honeymoon and insert a video of fireworks recorded by the groom during the honeymoon. You insert a fireworks sound clip and music file to complement the fireworks display. Finally, you create the second slide show, a family vacation, using PowerPoint's Photo Album feature. You utilize the Photo Album options for image manipulation.

Pictures

Multimedia refers to multiple forms of media, such as text, graphics, sound, animation, and video, that are used to entertain or inform an audience. You can use any of these types of media in PowerPoint by placing the multimedia object on a slide. You already have placed text and graphics in presentations, and you have applied animations to objects and transitions to slides. In this chapter, you will expand your experience with multimedia by inserting pictures, sound, and video in slides.

Multimedia graphics include clip art, objects created using drawing programs, diagrams and illustrations, pictures or photographs, scanned images, and more. You have worked extensively with clip art, diagrams, and illustrations. In this section, you will concentrate on pictures.

Pictures are bitmap images that computers can read and interpret to create a photorealistic image. Unlike clip art ***vector images***, which are created by mathematical statements, ***bitmap images*** are created by bits or pixels placed on a grid or map. In a bitmap image, each pixel contains information about the color to be displayed. A bitmap image is required to have the realism necessary for a photograph. Think of vector images as connect-the-dots and bitmap images as paint-by-number, and you begin to see the difference in the methods of representation.

Each type of image has its own advantages and disadvantages. Vector graphics can be sized easily and still retain their clarity but are not photorealistic. Bitmap images represent a much more complex range of colors and shades but can become pixelated (individual pixels are visible and display square edges for a "jaggies" effect) when they are enlarged. A bitmap image can also be a large file, so ***compression***, a method applied to data to reduce the amount of space required for file storage, may be applied. The compression may be lossy (some data may be lost when decompressed) or lossless (no data is lost when decompressed).

TIP Compression: Lossy Versus Lossless

Depending on the image's use, you may want to choose a specific image format so that images don't appear pixelated when enlarged. Certain formats can be either lossy or lossless. Lossy compression reduces a file by permanently eliminating certain data, especially redundant data. This makes the file size smaller. However, when the file is uncompressed, only a part of the original data is still there. Pixelation may not even be noticeable for certain image uses, so it might not be an issue. The JPEG image file, a common format, is an image that has lossy compression.

Alternatively, with lossless compression, data that was originally in the file remains after the file is uncompressed. All of the information is completely restored. The Graphics Interchange File (GIF) is an image format that provides lossless compression.

Figure 4.1 displays a pumpkin created as a vector image and one created as a bitmap image. Note the differences in realism. The boxes show a portion of the images enlarged. Note the pixilation, or jaggedness, in the enlarged portion of the bitmap image.

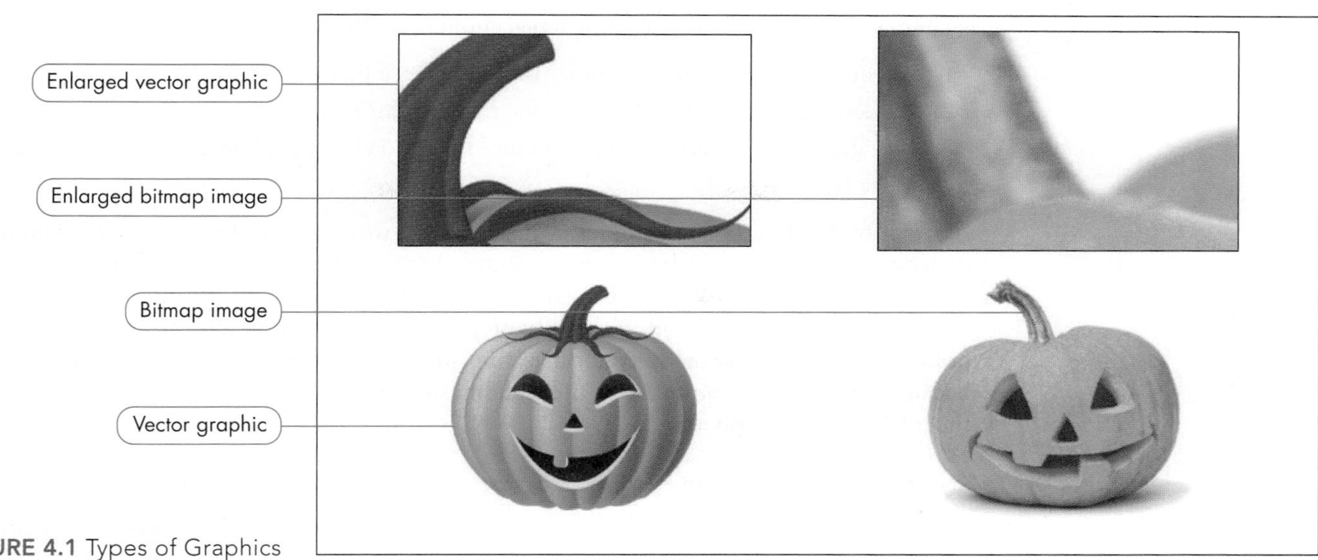

FIGURE 4.1 Types of Graphics

Inserting a Picture

PowerPoint does not have to be all bullets; a good image can be more memorable than a simple list of words. You can accomplish this task by scanning and saving a photograph or piece of artwork, by downloading images from a digital camera, by downloading a previously created bitmap image from Office.com Clip Art or the Internet, or by creating an image in a graphics-editing software package like Adobe Photoshop. Table 4.1 displays the types of graphic file formats that you can add to a PowerPoint slide in alphabetical order by file extension.

TABLE 4.1 Types of Graphic File Formats Supported by PowerPoint

File Format	Extension	Description
Windows Bitmap (Device Independent Bitmap)	.bmp, .dib	A representation consisting of rows and columns of dots. The value of each dot is stored in one or more bits of data. Uncompressed and creates large file size.
Windows Enhanced Metafile	.emf, .wmf	A Windows 32-bit file format.
Graphics Interchange Format	.gif	Limited to 256 colors. Effective for scanned images such as illustrations rather than for color photographs. Good for line drawings and black-and-white images. Supports transparent backgrounds.
Joint Photographic Experts Group	.jpg, .jpeg	Supports 16 million colors and is optimized for photographs and complex graphics. Format of choice for most photographs on the Web. Uses lossy compression.
Macintosh PICT	.pict, .pic, .pct	Holds both vector and bitmap images. PICT supports 8 colors; PICT2 supports 16 million colors.
Portable Network Graphics	.png	Supports 16 million colors. Approved as a standard by the World Wide Web Consortium (W3C). Intended to replace .gif format. Uses lossy compression.
Tagged Image File Format	.tif, .tiff	Best file format for storing bitmapped images on personal computers. Can be any resolution. Lossless image storage creates large file sizes. Not widely supported by browsers.
Microsoft Windows Metafile	.wmf	A Windows 16-bit file format.

STEP 1 To add a picture to a slide using a placeholder, do the following:

1. Select a layout with a placeholder that includes a Pictures button.
2. Click the Pictures button to open the Insert Picture dialog box.
3. Navigate to the location of your picture files and click the picture you want to use.
4. Click Insert.

Figure 4.2 shows two examples of placeholders with Pictures buttons. When you insert a picture in this manner, the picture is centered within the placeholder frame and is sometimes cropped to fit within the placeholder. This effect can cause unwanted results, such as the tops of heads cropped off. If this situation occurs, undo the insertion, enlarge the placeholder, and then repeat the steps for inserting an image. Use this method sparingly, however, because any changes you make to the slide master or theme may not appear correctly once those changes are applied.

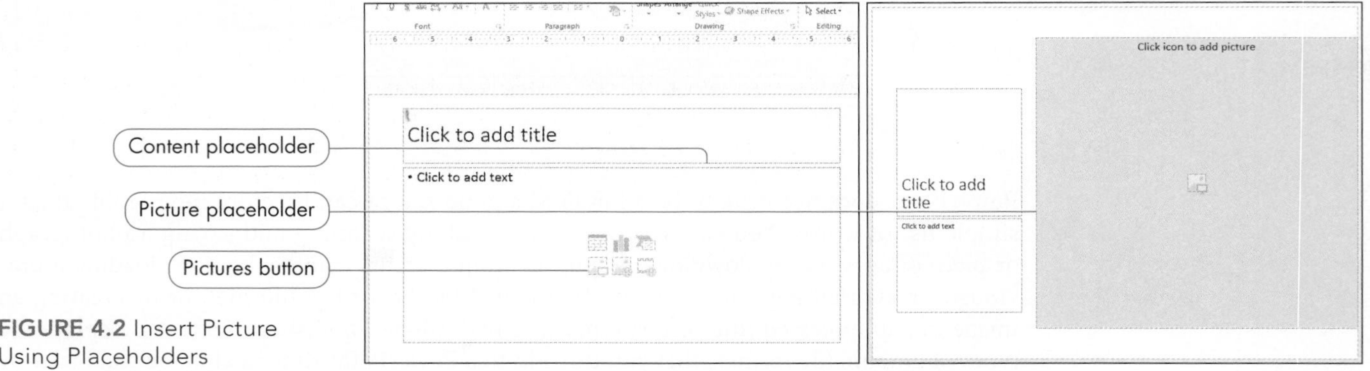

FIGURE 4.2 Insert Picture Using Placeholders

Another way to insert an image is to click Pictures on the Insert tab. The advantage of this method is that your image comes in at full size rather than centered and cropped in a placeholder, and you do not need a picture placeholder. You can then resize the image to fit the desired area. The disadvantage is the time you spend resizing and positioning the image.

To add a picture using the Insert tab, do the following:

1. Click the INSERT tab.
2. Click Pictures in the Images group.
3. Navigate to the location of your picture files and click the picture you want to use.
4. Click Insert.
5. Adjust the size and position of the picture as necessary.

If you are adding multiple images to a slide show, you can speed up the process by inserting images directly from File Explorer. Open File Explorer and navigate to the folder where the images are located. Position the File Explorer window next to the PowerPoint window and drag the images from the Explorer window onto the slides of your choice.

Transforming a Picture

Once you insert a picture onto a slide, PowerPoint provides powerful tools that you can use to adjust the image. Found on the Picture Tools Format tab (see Figure 4.3), Picture Tools are designed to adjust an image background, correct image problems, manipulate image color, or add artistic or stylized effects. You can also arrange, crop, or resize an image using Picture

Tools. Additionally, when you right-click on the picture and select Format Picture, you will open the Format Picture task pane, where you can also access these same tools.

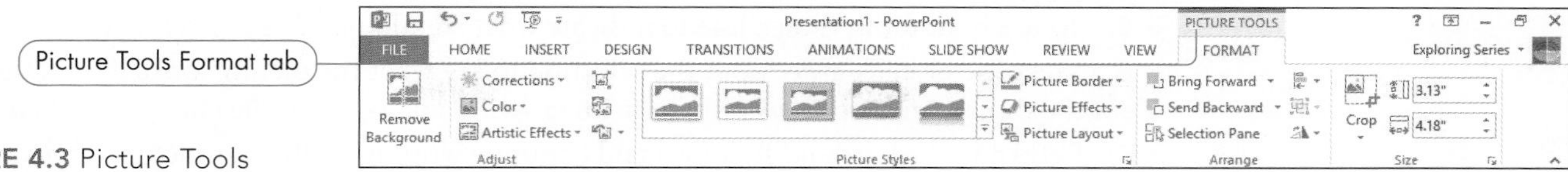

FIGURE 4.3 Picture Tools

Remove a Picture Background

The Remove Background tool in the Adjust group on the Format tab enables you to remove portions of a picture you do not want to keep. Rather than have a rectangle-shaped picture on your slide, you can have an image that flows into the slide. When you select a picture and click the Remove Background tool, PowerPoint creates an automatic marquee selection area in the picture that determines the ***background***, or area to be removed, and the ***foreground***, or area to be kept. PowerPoint identifies the background selection with magenta coloring. You can then adjust PowerPoint's automatic selection by marking areas you want to keep, marking areas you want to remove, and deleting any markings you do not want. You can discard any changes you have made or keep your changes. Figure 4.4 shows a picture in which the Remove Background tool has created a marquee identifying the foreground and background.

FIGURE 4.4 Remove Background Marquee, Foreground, and Background

Once the background has been identified by the marquee, you can refine the marquee size and shape so that it contains everything you want to keep without extra areas. To resize the marquee:

1. Drag a marquee handle (the same process you use to resize clip art).
2. Refine the picture further by using the tools available on the Background Removal tab (see Figure 4.5).

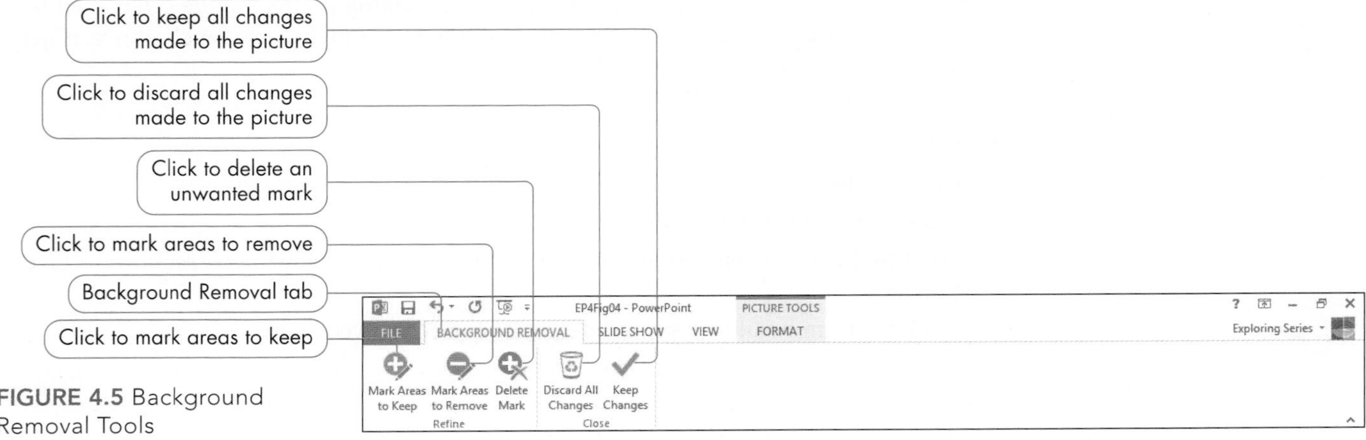

FIGURE 4.5 Background Removal Tools

3. Use the *Mark Areas to Keep* tool to add to the foreground, which keeps the area.
4. Use the *Mark Areas to Remove* tool to add to the background, which eliminates the area.
5. To use both tools, drag a line to indicate what should be added or removed.
6. Press Esc or click away from the selection to see what the picture looks like. Note that the thumbnail also shows what the image will look like with the changes applied.
7. Return to Background Removal and continue working with your picture. Figure 4.6 shows a resized marquee with enlarged areas marked to show areas to keep and to remove. Figure 4.7 shows the flower picture with the background removed.

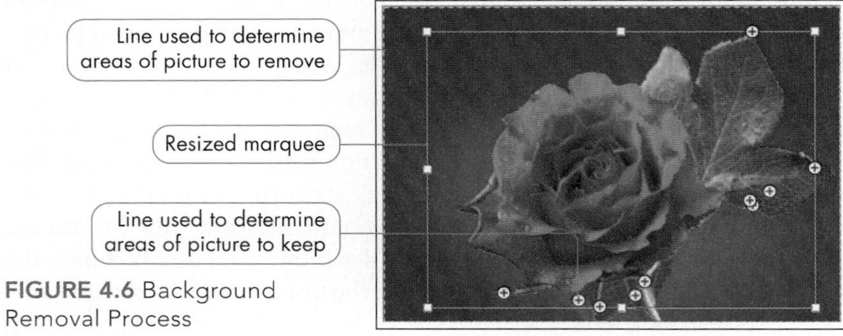

FIGURE 4.6 Background Removal Process

FIGURE 4.7 Background Removed from Flower

Correct a Picture

PowerPoint 2013 includes Corrections, a set of tools in the Adjust group. As well as being able to adjust brightness and contrast as in previous versions, you can now soften or sharpen a picture. You can see what a correction will look like by previewing it in Live Preview.

You can enhance a picture by ***sharpening*** it—bringing out the detail by making the boundaries of the content more prominent. Or you may want to ***soften*** the content—blur the edges so the boundaries are less prominent. Sharpening a picture can make it clearer, but oversharpening can make the picture look grainy. Softening is a technique often used for a more romantic image or to make skin appear softer, but applying too much blur can make the picture difficult to see.

STEP 2»

To sharpen or soften a picture, do the following:

1. Select the picture.
2. Click the FORMAT tab.
3. Click Corrections in the Adjust group.
4. Point to the thumbnails in the *Sharpen/Soften* section to view the corrections in Live Preview.
5. Click the thumbnail to apply the degree of correction you want.

You can make fine adjustments to the amount of sharpness and softness you apply to a picture. To make adjustments, follow Steps 1–3 above and click Picture Corrections Options at the bottom of the gallery. The Format Picture pane opens. Drag the *Sharpness* slider or enter a percentage in the box next to the slider. Figure 4.8 shows the Corrections gallery, a picture that has been softened, and a picture that has been sharpened.

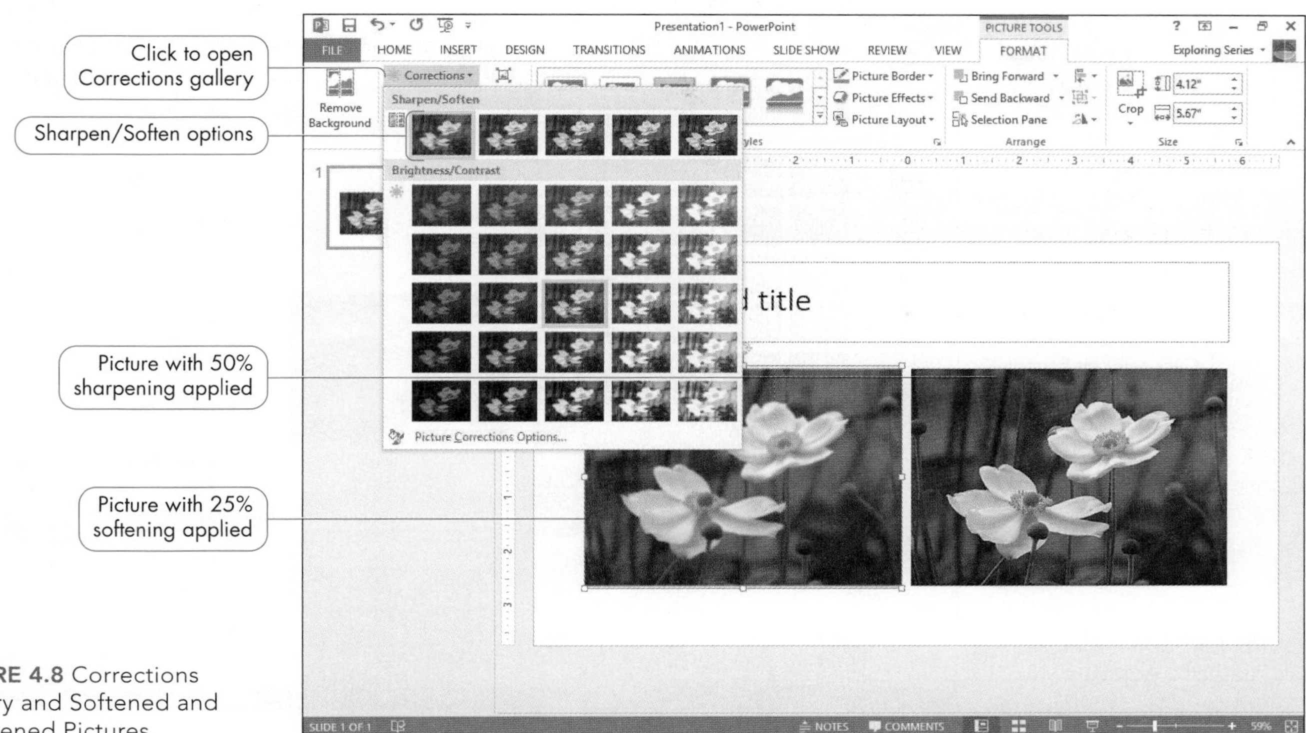

FIGURE 4.8 Corrections Gallery and Softened and Sharpened Pictures

The ***brightness*** (lightness or darkness) of a picture is often a matter of individual preference. You might need to change the brightness of your picture for reasons other than preference, however. For example, sometimes printing a picture requires a different brightness than is needed when projecting an image. This situation occurs because during printing, the ink may spread when placed on the page, making the picture darker. Or, you might want a picture as a background and need to reduce the brightness so that text will show on the background.

Contrast refers to the difference between the darkest area (black level) and lightest area (white level). If the contrast is not set correctly, your picture can look washed out or muddy; too much contrast, and the light portion of your image will appear to explode off the screen or page. Your setting may vary depending on whether you are going to project the image or print it. Projecting impacts an image because of the light in the room. In a very light room, the image may seem to need a greater contrast than in a darker room, and you may need to adjust the contrast accordingly. Try to set your control for the lighting that will appear when you display the presentation.

To adjust the brightness and contrast of a picture, do the following:

1. Select the picture.
2. Click the FORMAT tab.
3. Click Corrections in the Adjust group.
4. Point to the thumbnails in the *Brightness/Contrast* section to view the corrections in Live Preview.
5. Click the thumbnail to apply the degree of correction you want.

You can make fine adjustments to the amount of brightness or contrast you apply. To make adjustments, follow Steps 1–3 above and click Picture Corrections Options at the bottom of the gallery. The Format Picture task pane opens. Drag the Brightness and Contrast sliders until you get the result you want or enter percentages in the boxes next to the sliders. Figure 4.9 shows the Corrections gallery displaying the original picture as well as the same picture that has been adjusted for brightness.

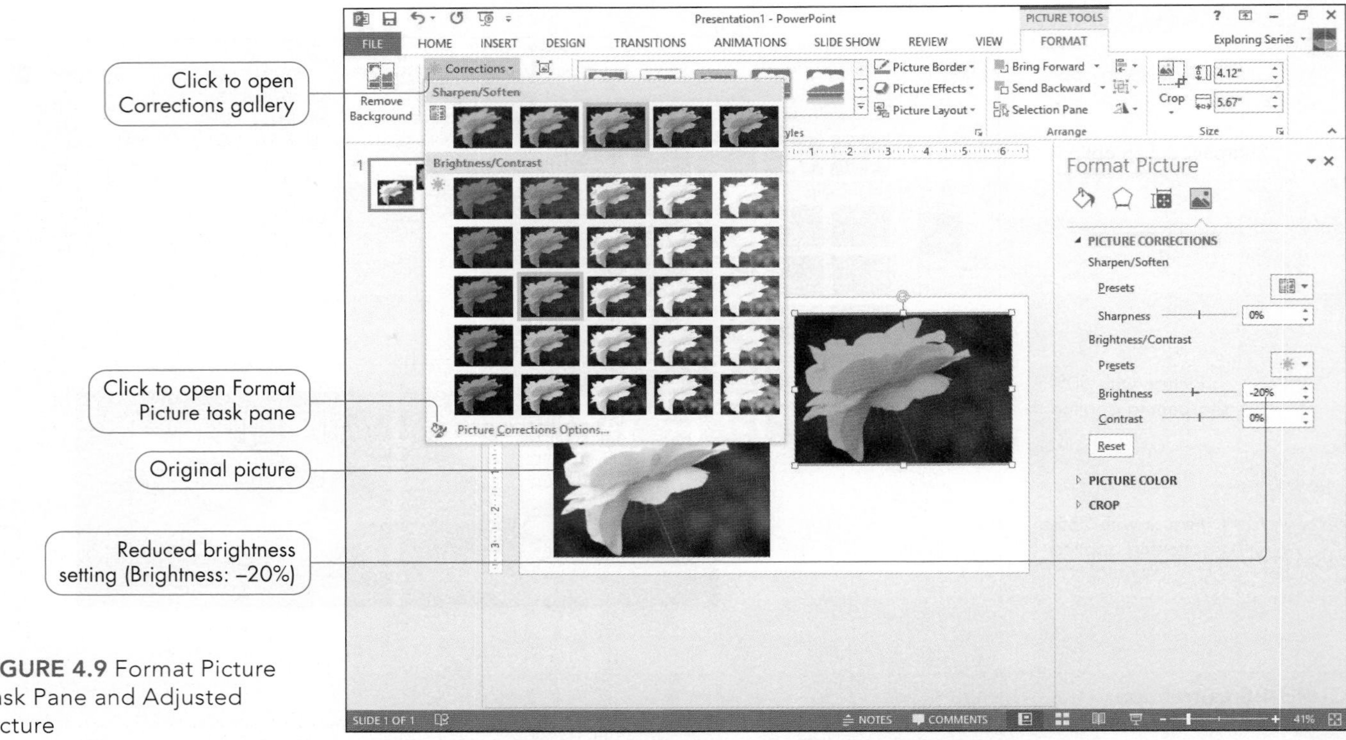

FIGURE 4.9 Format Picture Task Pane and Adjusted Picture

Change Picture Color

You can change the colors in your picture by using PowerPoint's color tools. To access the color tools, do the following:

1. Select the picture.
2. Click the FORMAT tab.
3. Click Color in the Adjust group.
4. Point to the thumbnails in the gallery to view the corrections in Live Preview.
5. Click the thumbnail to apply the color effect you want.

You can change a picture's ***saturation*** or the intensity of the colors in an image. A high saturation level makes the colors more vivid, whereas 0% saturation converts the picture to grayscale. Figure 4.10 shows a picture at its original (100%) intensity and with various levels of intensity.

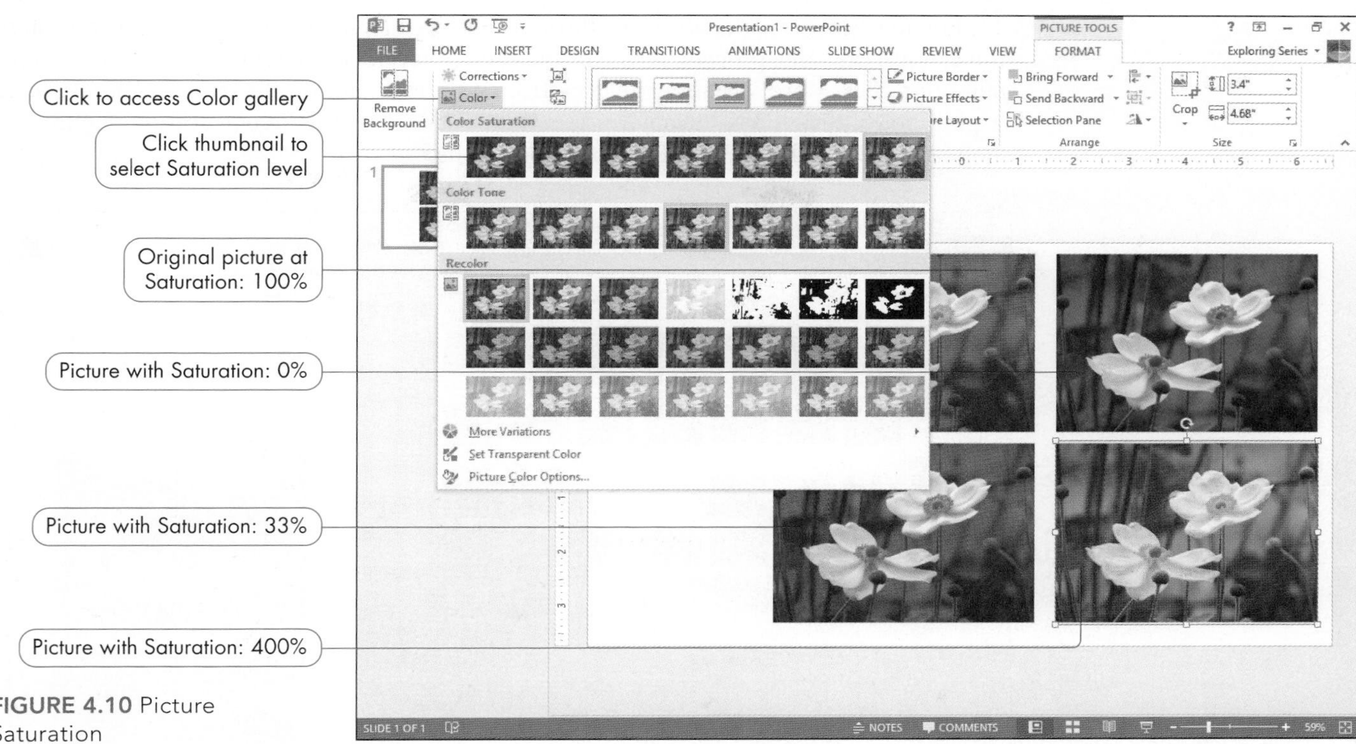

FIGURE 4.10 Picture Saturation

The ***tone***, or temperature, of a color is a characteristic of lighting in pictures. It is measured in ***kelvin*** (K) units of absolute temperature. Lower color temperatures are cool colors and appear blueish white, whereas higher color temperatures are warm colors and appear yellowish to red. PowerPoint enables you to increase or decrease a picture's temperature to enhance its details. Point to a thumbnail to see the amount of temperature in Kelvin units that would be applied. Figure 4.11 shows a picture with its original cooler tone and a copy of the picture at a higher temperature with a warmer tone.

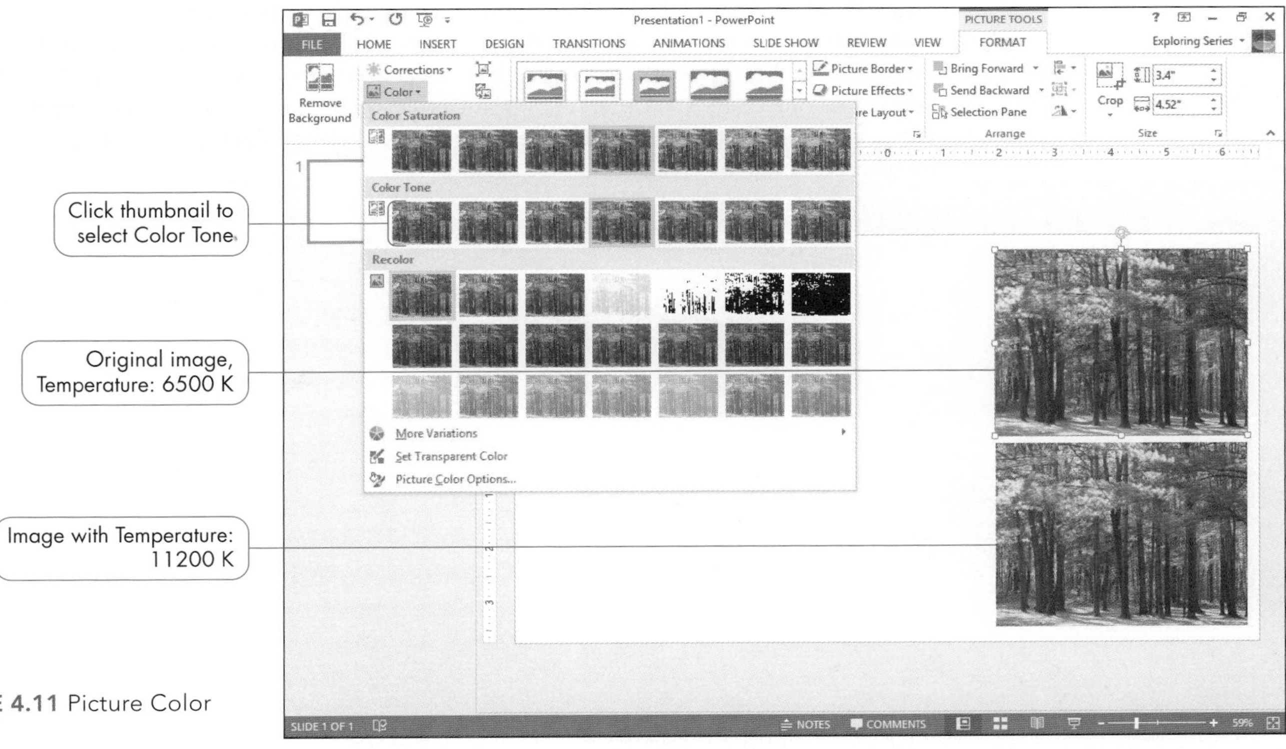

FIGURE 4.11 Picture Color Tone

Previously, you ***recolored*** clip art illustrations by changing multiple colors to two colors. You can use the same process to recolor pictures. You can click a preset thumbnail from the gallery or click More Variations to pick from additional colors. To return a picture to its original color, click the No Recolor preset thumbnail under the *Recolor* section. Figure 4.12 shows a picture with the Sepia Recolor preset applied.

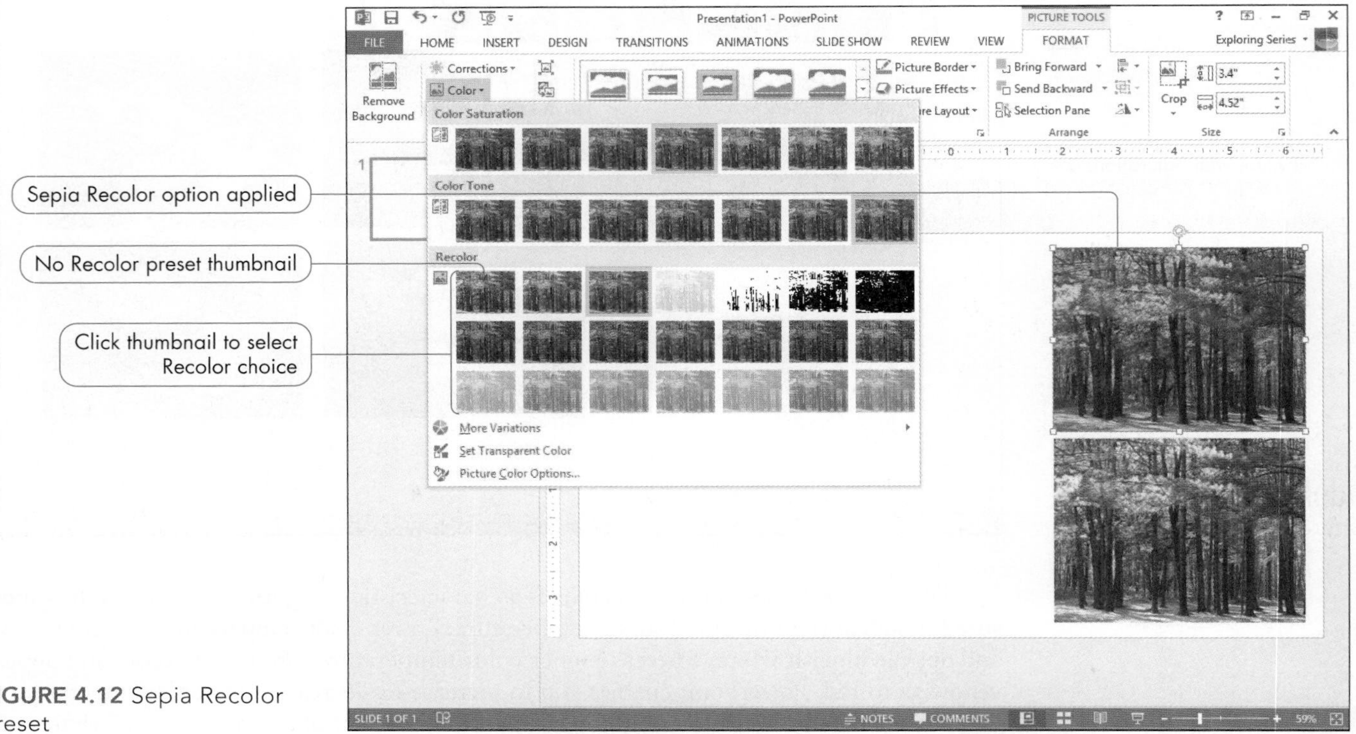

FIGURE 4.12 Sepia Recolor Preset

Use Artistic Effects

PowerPoint's artistic effects enable you to change the appearance of a picture so that it looks like it was created with a marker, as a pencil sketch or watercolor painting, or using other effects. Use Live Preview to see how an artistic effect changes your picture. You can apply only one effect at a time. Any artistic effects that you have previously applied are lost when you apply a new effect. Figure 4.13 shows a Glow Edges artistic effect applied to a picture.

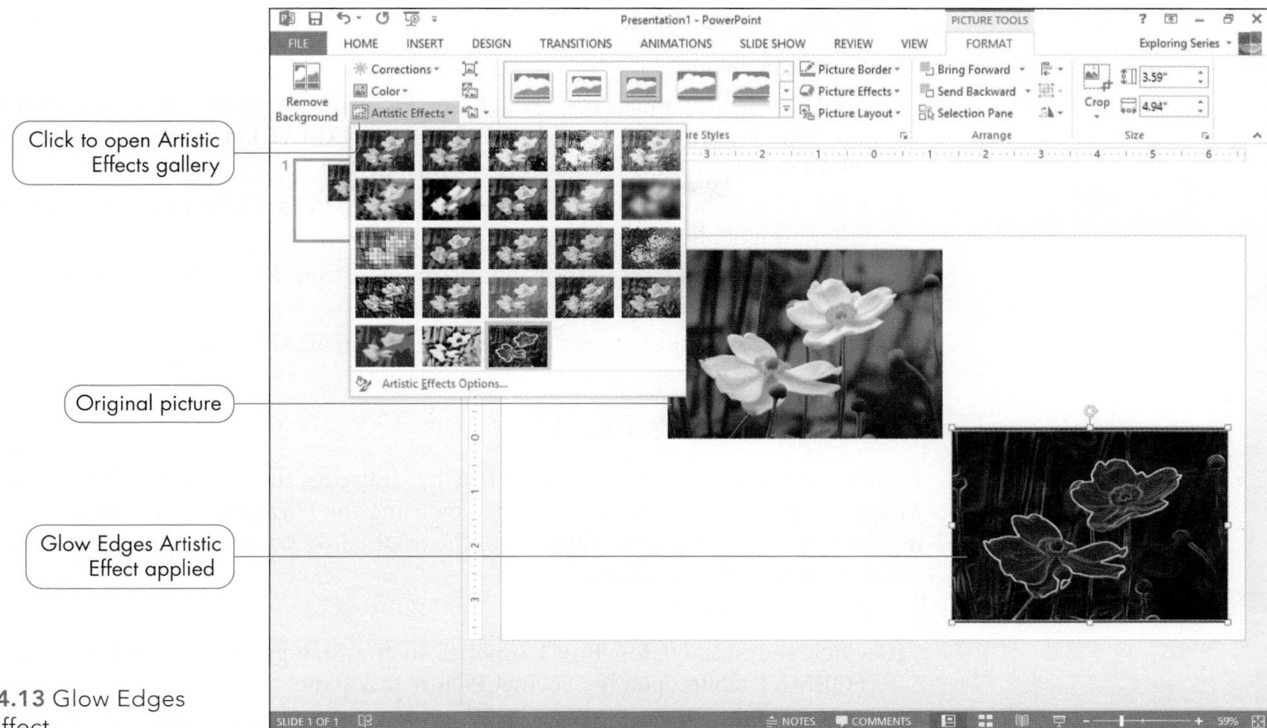

FIGURE 4.13 Glow Edges Artistic Effect

STEP 3» To use an artistic effect, do the following:

1. Select the picture.
2. Click the FORMAT tab.
3. Click Artistic Effects in the Adjust group.
4. Point to the thumbnails in the gallery to view the artistic effects in Live Preview.
5. Click the thumbnail of the artistic effect you want to use.

Apply Picture Styles

With Picture Styles, you can surround your picture with attractive frames, soften the edges of pictures, add shadows to the edges of pictures, apply 3-D effects to pictures, and add glossy reflections below your pictures. Many other effects are possible with Picture Styles, and when you consider that each of these effects can be modified, your creative opportunities are endless! Figure 4.14 shows a few of the possibilities.

FIGURE 4.14 Picture Style Applications

To apply a picture style:

1. Select the picture.
2. Point to a gallery image displayed in the Picture Styles group (to see more styles, click the More button) on the PICTURE TOOLS FORMAT tab to see a Live Preview and click the gallery image to select the picture style.
3. Click Picture Border in the Picture Styles group to enable you to select your border color, weight, or dash style.
4. You can use the Picture Effects option to select from Preset, Shadow, Reflection, Glow, Soft Edges, Bevel, and 3-D Rotation effects.
5. Use Picture Layout to apply your picture to a SmartArt diagram.

Resize or Crop a Picture

Resizing a picture can be accomplished by dragging the sizing handles for the image. Moreover, this can also be accomplished by using the Format Picture task pane and changing the size of the picture to a percent of the original. When *Lock aspect ratio* is checked, the image is resized proportionally.

To resize a picture:

1. Click the Size Dialog Box Launcher in the Size group on the PICTURE TOOLS FORMAT tab to open the Format Picture task pane.
2. Click in the Scale Height or Scale Width box, select 100, and then type the new size.

Cropping a picture using the Crop tool lets you eliminate unwanted portions of an image, focusing the viewer's attention on what you want him or her to see. Remember that if you crop an image and try to enlarge the resulting picture, pixelation may occur that reduces the quality of the image. Figure 4.15 shows a picture with the areas to be cropped from view displayed in gray.

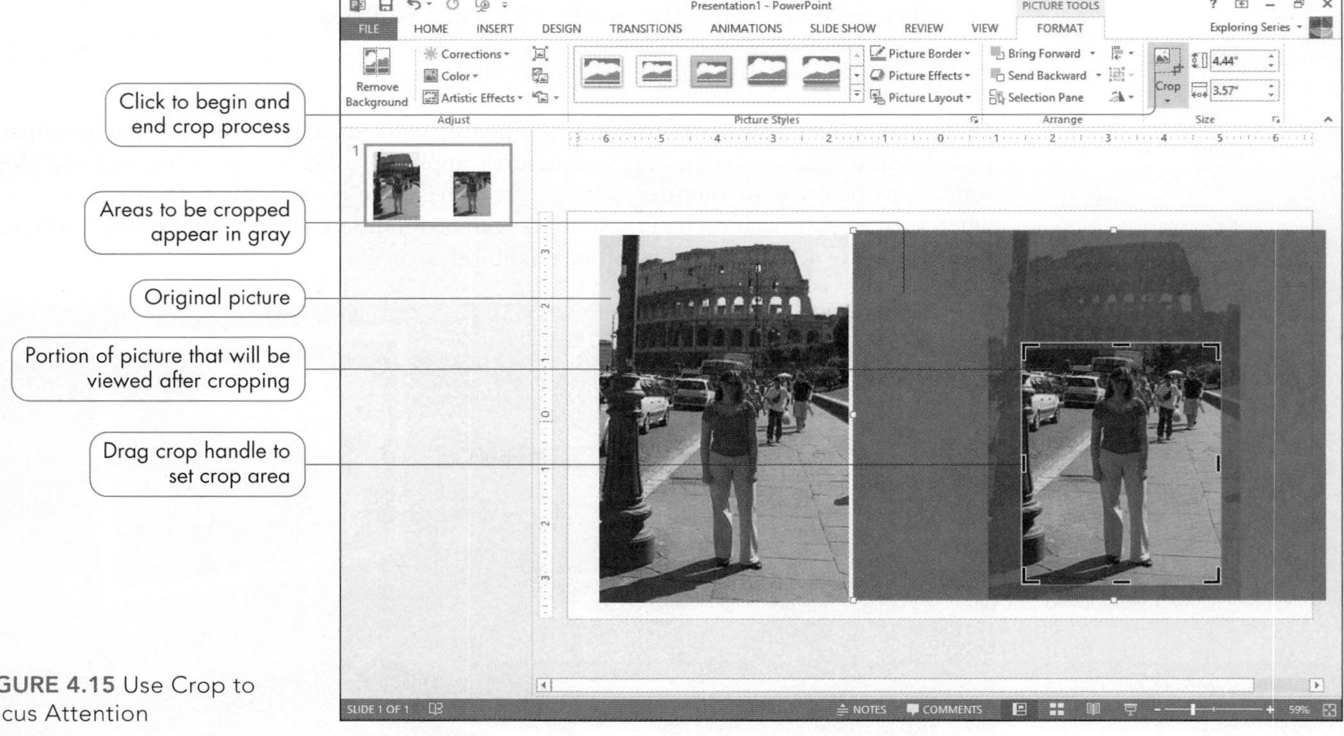

FIGURE 4.15 Use Crop to Focus Attention

To crop a picture, do the following:

1. Select the picture.
2. Click the FORMAT tab.
3. Click Crop in the Size group.
4. Position the mouse pointer over a cropping handle and drag inward to eliminate the portion of the image you do not want to view. Use a corner handle to crop in two directions at once.
5. Repeat Step 4 for the remaining sides of the picture.
6. Click Crop again to toggle it off.

When you crop a picture, the cropped portion does not display on the slide, but it is not removed from the presentation file. This is helpful in case you decide later to reset the picture to its original state. When you crop an image, because the unwanted portions of the image are not deleted, the file size is not reduced. Use the Compress Pictures feature to reduce the file size of the image, or all images at once, to reduce the file size of the presentation.

Compress Pictures

When you add pictures to your PowerPoint presentation, especially high-resolution pictures downloaded from a digital camera, the presentation file size dramatically increases. It may increase to the point that the presentation becomes slow to load and sluggish to play. The increase in the file size depends on the resolution of the pictures you add. Use the Compress Pictures feature to eliminate a large part of this problem. The Compress Pictures feature is in the Adjust group on the Picture Tools Format tab.

The Compress Pictures feature can help you manage large image files by changing the resolution of pictures and by permanently deleting any cropped areas of a selected picture. By default, you apply compression to only the selected image. If you remove the check, all pictures in the presentation are compressed. You select the amount of compression applied by determining your output. Select 220 pixels per inch (ppi) to ensure you will obtain a good quality printout. Select 150 ppi, however, if you will be displaying the slide show only onscreen or using it for a Web page. Select 96 ppi if you plan to e-mail the slide show. Figure 4.16 shows the Compress Pictures dialog box.

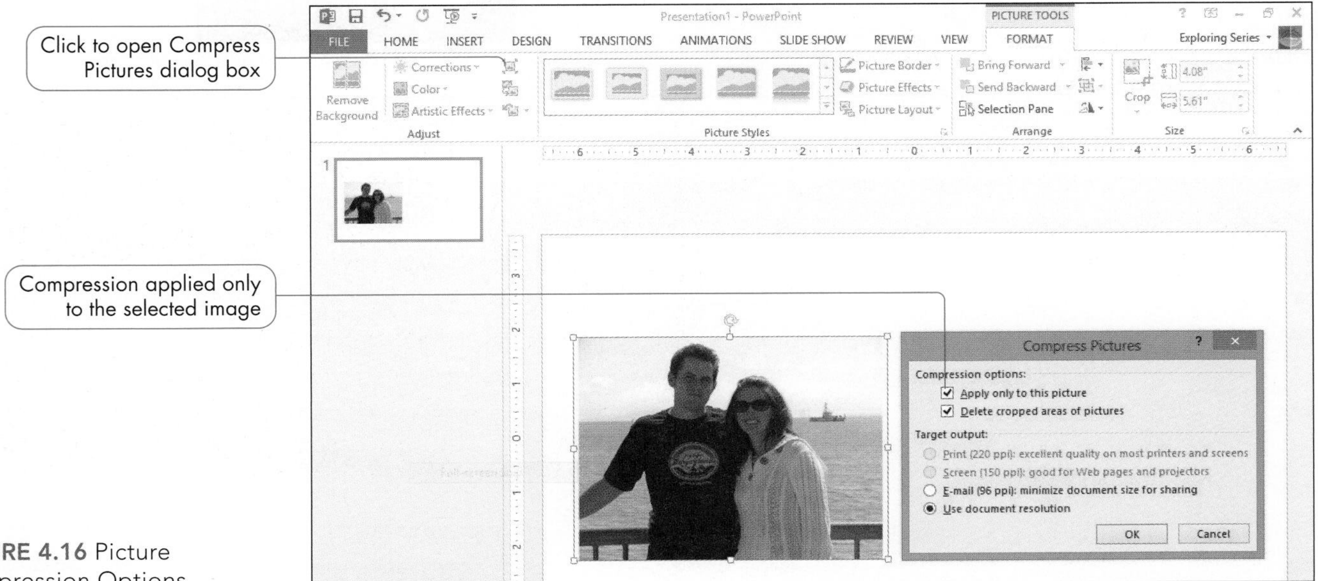

FIGURE 4.16 Picture Compression Options

Create a Background from a Picture

Pictures can make appealing backgrounds if they are transparent enough that text on top of them can be easily read. Picture backgrounds personalize your presentation. To use a photograph as a background, use the Format Background command rather than the Insert Picture feature. Using Insert Picture involves more time because when the picture is inserted it must be resized and the order of the objects on the screen has to be changed to prevent the photograph from hiding placeholders. Figure 4.17 shows an image inserted using Insert Picture that must be resized if it is to be used as a background. It hides the placeholders, so it needs to be positioned at the back and its transparency must be adjusted. Figure 4.18 shows the same picture as Figure 4.17, but in this figure, it was inserted as a background. It is automatically placed behind placeholders and resized to fit the slide, and the transparency is adjusted.

If the background image is too busy or not transparent enough, it can make the presentation difficult to read or distract the audience. You may need to test several images and settings if its color does not contrast enough with the text.

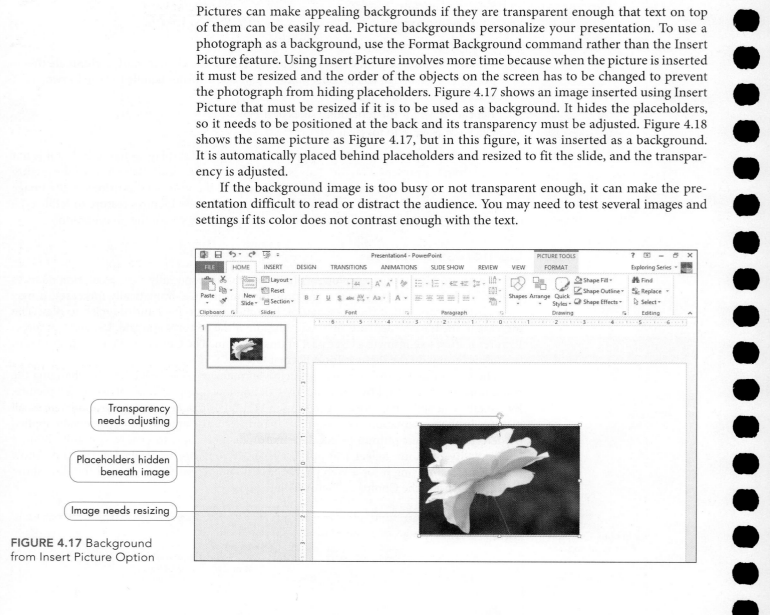

FIGURE 4.17 Background from Insert Picture Option

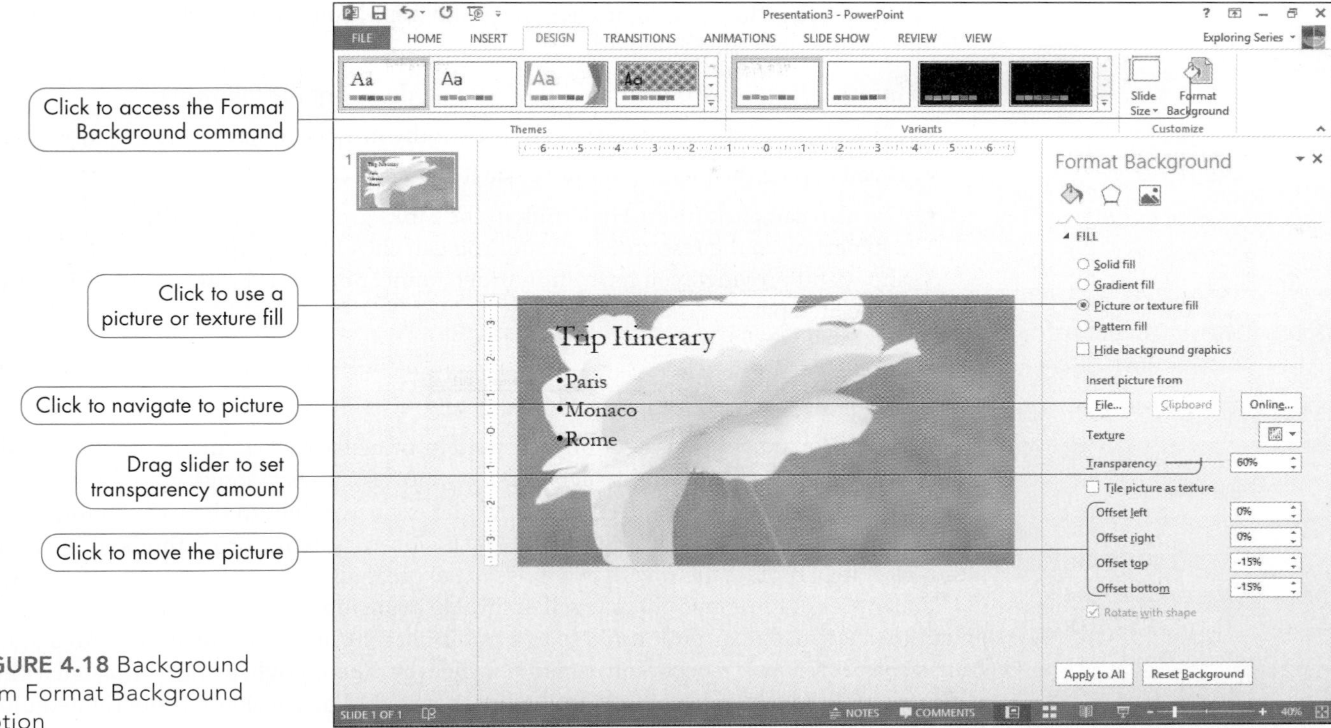

FIGURE 4.18 Background from Format Background Option

To create a background from a picture using the Background command, do the following:

1. Click the DESIGN tab.
2. Click Format Background in the Customize group. The Format Background task pane displays.
3. Click *Picture or texture fill.*
4. Click File and navigate to the location where your picture is stored.
5. Click the picture file and click Insert.
6. Adjust the transparency for the picture.
7. Click Close to apply the picture background to the current slide or click *Apply to All* to apply it to all slides in the presentation.

The task pane also includes options for moving the picture by offsetting it to the left or right or the top or bottom, and for adjusting the transparency amount.

Using the Internet as a Resource

In this chapter, you will use the Internet as a resource for pictures, video, and audio. PowerPoint interacts with the Internet in three important ways:

1. You can download resources from any Web page for inclusion in a PowerPoint presentation. Note, however, that some images may not be used without permission or license from the creator.
2. You can insert hyperlinks into a PowerPoint presentation and click those links to display the associated Web page in your browser.
3. You can convert any PowerPoint presentation into a Web page.

STEP 5» Regardless of how you choose to use a photograph, your first task is to locate the required image. To download an image:

1. Right-click the image to display a shortcut menu and select Save Picture As to save the file. (This command may vary among Web broswers.)

2. Alternatively, when you right-click the photograph, you can also select Copy to copy the picture onto the Clipboard.

To insert a downloaded picture in PowerPoint, do any of the following:

- Click the INSERT tab and click Pictures in the Images group.
- If you copied the picture, simply paste it onto the slide.
- You also can click Insert Hyperlink in the Links group on the INSERT tab to insert a hyperlink to the resource Web site. You can click the hyperlink during the slide show, and provided you have an Internet connection, your browser will display the associated page.

Understand Copyright Protection

A ***copyright*** provides legal protection to a written or artistic work, including literary, dramatic, musical, and artistic works such as poetry, novels, movies, songs, computer software, and architecture. It gives the author of a work the exclusive right to the use and duplication of that work. A copyright does not protect facts, ideas, systems, or methods of operation, although it may protect the way these things are expressed.

The owner of the copyright may sell or give up a portion of his or her rights; for example, an author may give distribution rights to a publisher and/or grant movie rights to a studio. ***Infringement of copyright*** occurs anytime a right held by the copyright owner is violated without permission of the owner. Anything on the Internet should be considered copyrighted unless the site specifically says it is in the ***public domain***, in which case the author is giving everyone the right to freely reproduce and distribute the material, thereby making the work owned by the public at large. A work also may enter the public domain when the copyright has expired. Facts themselves are not covered by copyright, so you can use statistical data without fear of infringement. Images are protected unless the owner gives his or her permission for downloading.

TIP Using Media Elements

Photos, clip art, fonts, sounds, and videos available from Microsoft and its partners through Office.com are part of Microsoft's Media Elements and are copyright protected by Microsoft. To see what uses of Media Elements are prohibited, go to http://www.office.com and search for *What Uses of Photos, Clip Art, and Font Images are Prohibited?*

The answer to what you can use from the Web depends on many things, including the amount of the information you reference, as well as the intended use of that information. It is considered fair use, and thus not an infringement of copyright, to use a portion of a work for educational or nonprofit purposes, or for critical review or commentary. In other words, you can use quotes, facts, or other information from the Web in an educational setting, but you should cite the original work in your footnotes, or list the resource on a bibliography page or slide. The following reference table presents guidelines for students and teachers to help determine what multimedia can be used in an educational project based on the Proposal for Fair Use Guidelines for Educational Multimedia created in 1996. These guidelines were created by a group of publishers, authors, and educators who gathered to interpret the Copyright Act of 1976 as it applies to educational and scholarly uses of multimedia. You should note that although these guidelines are part of the Congressional Record, they are not law. They can, however, help you determine when you can use multimedia materials under Fair Use principles in a noncommercial, educational use.

REFERENCE Multimedia Copyright Guidelines for Students and Teachers

The following guidelines are based on Section 107 of the U.S. Copyright Act of 1976 and the Proposal for Fair Use Guidelines for Educational Multimedia (1996), which sets forth fair use factors for multimedia projects. These guidelines cover the use of multimedia based on Time, Portion, and Copying and Distribution Limitations. For the complete text of the guidelines, see www.uspto.gov/web/offices/dcom/olia/confu/confurep.pdf.

General Guidelines

- Student projects for specific courses may be displayed and kept in personal portfolios as examples of their academic work.
- Students in specific courses may use multimedia in projects with proper credit and citations. Full bibliographic information must be used when available.
- Students and teachers must display copyright notice if copyright ownership information is shown on the original source. Copyright may be shown in a sources or bibliographic section unless the presentation is being used for distance learning. In distance learning situations, copyright must appear on the screen when the image is viewed.
- Teachers may use media for face-to-face curriculum-based instruction, for directed self-study, in demonstrations on how to create multimedia productions, for presentations at conferences, and for distance learning. Teachers may also retain projects in their personal portfolios for personal use such as job interviews or tenure review.
- Teachers may use multimedia projects for educational purposes for up to two years, after which permission of the copyright holder is required.
- Students and teachers do not need to write for permission to use media if it falls under multimedia guidelines unless there is a possibility that the project could be broadly distributed at a later date.

Text Guidelines

- Up to 10 percent of a copyrighted work, or up to 1,000 words, may be used, whichever is less.
- Up to 250 words of a poem, but no more than five poems (or excerpts) from different poets or an anthology. No more than three poems (or excerpts) from a single poet.

Illustrations

- A photograph or illustration may be used in its entirety.
- Up to 15 images, but no more than 15 images from a collection.
- No more than 5 images of an artist's or photographer's work.

Motion Media

- Up to 10 percent of a copyrighted work or 3 minutes, whichever is less.
- Clip cannot be altered in any way.

Music and Sound

- Up to 10 percent of a copyrighted musical composition, not to exceed 30 seconds.
- Up to 10 percent of a sound recording, not to exceed 30 seconds.
- Alterations cannot change the basic melody or fundamental character of the work.

Distribution Limitations

- Multimedia projects should not be posted to unsecured Web sites.
- No more than two copies of the original may be made, only one of which may be placed on reserve for instructional purposes.
- A copy of a project may be made for backup purposes, but may be used only when the original has been lost, damaged, or stolen.
- If more than one person created a project, each person may keep only one copy.

In the following Hands-On Exercise, you will insert pictures (bitmap images) into slides, both with and the use of content placeholders. You will use Picture Tools to remove a background from an image, to soften and sharpen an image, and to adjust the brightness, contrast, saturation, and tone of a picture. You will apply a picture style and modify its effects. You will crop a picture and compress all the images in the slide show. You will also create a background for a slide from a picture. Finally, you will learn about using the Internet as a resource for images and review the Fair Use guidelines relating to student use of media downloaded from the Internet. You will download a picture from the Internet and insert the picture into a slide show.

1. What is the difference between bitmap images and vector graphics? Name one advantage and disadvantage of each type of graphic. ***p. 1008***
2. Why would you compress an image? ***p. 1019***
3. List five ways to transform an image by using PowerPoint's Picture Tools. ***p. 1010***
4. What is infringement of copyright? What is "fair use?" ***p. 1022***

Hands-On Exercises

MyITLab® HOE1 Training

1 Pictures

You decide to create a memories slide show for your sister and her husband, who were recently married. You include their engagement and honeymoon pictures.

Skills covered: Insert Pictures and Remove a Background • Correct a Picture and Change Picture Color • Apply an Artistic Effect and a Picture Style • Create a Background from a Picture, Crop and Compress • Insert a Picture from the Internet

STEP 1 » INSERT PICTURES AND REMOVE A BACKGROUND

You start the memory album with a picture from the couple's engagement. Because the Title Slide layout does not include a placeholder for content, you add a picture using the *Insert Picture from File* feature. You then insert images into content placeholders provided in the album layout. Refer to Figure 4.19 as you complete Step 1.

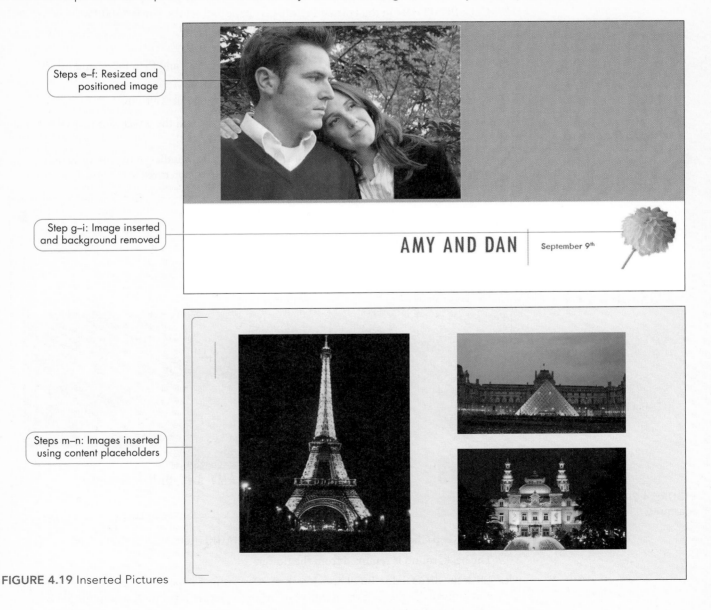

Steps e–f: Resized and positioned image

Step g–i: Image inserted and background removed

AMY AND DAN

September 9th

Steps m–n: Images inserted using content placeholders

FIGURE 4.19 Inserted Pictures

a. Open *p04h1Memory* and save it as **p04h1Memory_LastFirst.**

> **TROUBLESHOOTING:** If you make any major mistakes in this exercise, you can close the file, open *p04h1Memory* again, and then start this exercise over.

b. Create a handout header with your name and a handout footer with your instructor's name and your class. Apply to all slides. Include the current date.

c. On Slide 1, click the **INSERT tab** and click **Pictures** in the Images group.

   You add a picture using the Insert Picture command because the Title Slide layout does not include a placeholder for content. The Insert Picture dialog box opens.

d. Locate the *p04h1Mem1.jpg* picture in the *p04h1Memory_Media* folder and click **Insert**.

   The picture is inserted and centered on the slide.

e. Click the **Size Dialog Box Launcher** in the Size group on the FORMAT tab to open the Format Picture task pane. Click in the **Scale Height box**, select **100**, and then type **96**. Press **Enter**.

   Typing 96 in the Scale Height box automatically sets the Scale Width to 96% because the *Lock aspect ratio* check box is selected.

f. Click **POSITION** in the Format Picture task pane and set the **Horizontal Position** to **1.00"** from the Top Left Corner. Set the **Vertical Position** to **0.11"** from the Top Left Corner. Click the **Close (X) button**.

g. Click the **INSERT tab**, click **Pictures** in the Images group, and then locate and insert *p04h1Mem2.jpg*.

h. Click **Remove Background** in the Adjust group on the FORMAT tab.

   A marquee that includes most of the flower appears around the image. Some petals are cut off and need to be added back in.

i. Drag the left-center, left-bottom, and right-center sizing handles of the marquee as necessary until all petals and the stem are included in the picture (see Figure 4.20).

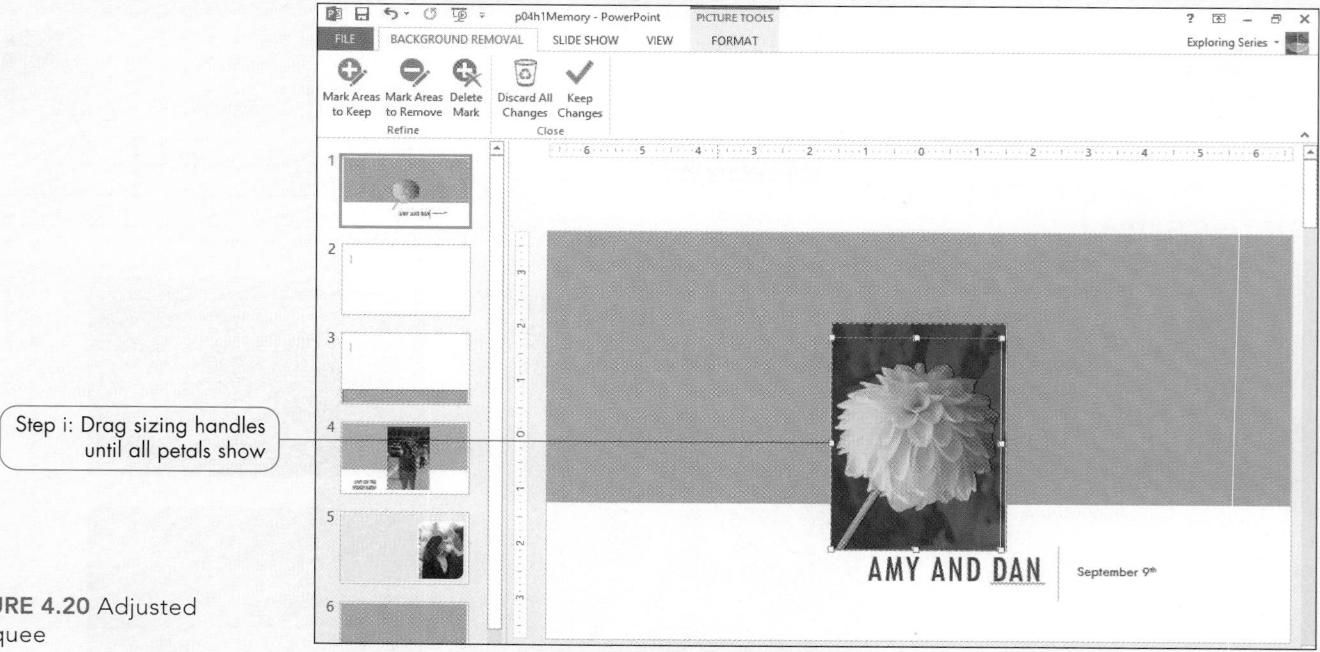

Step i: Drag sizing handles until all petals show

FIGURE 4.20 Adjusted Marquee

j. Click **Keep Changes** in the Close group on the BACKGROUND REMOVAL tab.

   The background is removed from the flower.

k. Click the **Size Dialog Box Launcher** in the Size group to open the Format Picture task pane and remove the check in the **Relative to original picture size check box** in the *SIZE* section. Click in the **Scale Height box** and type **50**. Press **Enter**.

l. Click **POSITION** in the Format Picture task pane, if necessary, and set the **Horizontal Position** to **11.59"** from the Top Left Corner. Set the **Vertical Position** to **4.79"** from the Top Left Corner. Click the **Close (X) button** to close the Format Picture task pane.

   The flower is now positioned in the right lower section of the slide. Refer to Figure 4.19.

m. Click **Slide 2**. Click **Pictures** in the large content placeholder on the left side of the slide. Click the *p04h1Mem3.jpg* file to select it and click **Insert**.

n. Use the Pictures buttons in the two small content placeholders on the right side of the screen to insert *p04h1Mem4.jpg* and *p04h1Mem5.jpg* into your presentation.

   Note that the images were centered inside the placeholders.

o. Save the presentation.

STEP 2 » CORRECT A PICTURE AND CHANGE PICTURE COLOR

You want to include two pictures of the couple in the memory album, but the pictures were taken in different lighting conditions. You decide to use PowerPoint's correction tools to enhance the pictures. You also change the color tone of a picture to warm it up to match the warm color of the background graphic color on the slide where it appears. Refer to Figure 4.21 as you complete Step 2.

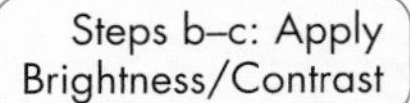

FIGURE 4.21 Picture Correction and Color Tone Adjustment

a. Click **Slide 3**. Click the **Pictures button** in the content placeholders to insert *p04h1Mem6.jpg* into the left placeholder and *p04h1Mem7.jpg* into the right placeholder.

b. Select the image on the left and click **Corrections** in the Adjust group on the FORMAT tab. Click **Brightness: –20% Contrast: +20%** (fourth row, second column of the *Brightness/Contrast* section).

   The image becomes slightly darker, and the increased contrast brings out the picture detail.

c. Select the image on the right and click **Corrections** in the Adjust group on the FORMAT tab. Click **Brightness: –20% Contrast: 0% (Normal)** (third row, second column of the *Brightness/Contrast* section).

   The image becomes more contrasted, and the brightness is reduced.

d. Click **Slide 4** and select the picture of the woman.

e. Click **Color** in the Adjust group and click **Temperature: 11200 K** in the Color Tone gallery. Next, click **Corrections** in the Adjust group and click **Brightness: +40% Contrast: 0%** (third row, fifth column).

   The cooler tones in the image are converted to warmer tones, which casts a gold hue over the picture. The picture is also brighter, emphasizing the colosseum in the background.

f. Click the **More button** in the Picture Styles group and click **Rotated, White**.

g. Save the presentation.

STEP 3 » APPLY AN ARTISTIC EFFECT AND A PICTURE STYLE

The title slide includes a picture of the couple that you want to stand out. The Artistic Effects gallery includes many picture effects, and the Picture Styles gallery includes a variety of Picture Border effects. You decide to experiment with the options available in the galleries to see the impact they have on the title slide picture. You also apply an artistic effect. Refer to Figure 4.22 as you complete Step 3.

Steps c–e: Artistic effects and picture styles applied to image

Steps f–i: Artistic effects and picture styles applied to image

FIGURE 4.22 Applied Artistic Effect and Picture Styles

a. Click **Slide 1**, select the picture of the couple, and then click the **FORMAT tab**, if necessary.

b. Click **Artistic Effects** in the Adjust group.

The Artistic Effects gallery opens. Point to the effects and watch how each effect impacts the image.

TROUBLESHOOTING: Some of the artistic effects involve extensive changes, so expect a slowdown as the preview is created.

c. Click **Texturizer** (fourth row, second column).

A light texture is applied to the picture.

d. Click the **More button** in the Picture Styles group.

The Picture Styles gallery opens. Point to the styles and watch how each style impacts the image.

e. Click **Center Shadow Rectangle**.

A gray shadow displays evenly around the picture.

f. Click the **HOME tab**, click **Format Painter** in the Clipboard group, and then click the **flower picture**.

You copied the artistic effect and picture style and applied them to the flower.

g. Select the picture of the couple again and click the **FORMAT tab**.

h. Click **Picture Border** in the Picture Styles group and click **Brown, Text 2** (first row, fourth column) in the *Theme Colors* section.

i. Click **Picture Effects** in the Picture Styles group, point to *Bevel*, and then click **Cool Slant** (first row, fourth column of the *Bevel* section).

The Bevel effect is applied to the outer edges of the picture.

j. Save the presentation.

STEP 4 ›› CREATE A BACKGROUND FROM A PICTURE, CROP, AND COMPRESS

The honeymooners stayed in a suite with a gorgeous view of a garden, and you want to include a picture of one of the flowers as the background setting of a picture of the honeymooners. Refer to Figure 4.23 as you complete Step 4.

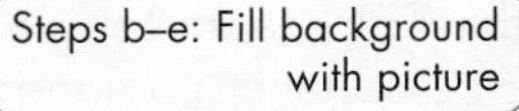

FIGURE 4.23 Background from a Picture

a. Click the **DESIGN tab**.

b. Click **Slide 5** and click **Format Background** in the Customize group.

   The Format Background task pane displays.

c. Click the **Hide background graphics check box** in the Format Background task pane.

d. Click **Picture or texture fill** and click **File** to open the Insert Picture dialog box.

e. Select *p04h1Mem8.jpg*, click **Insert**, and then close the Format Background task pane.

f. Examine the picture on the far right of the slide.

g. Click the **VIEW tab** and click **Ruler** in the Show group, if necessary.

   Activating the ruler will make it easier for you to determine the area to crop.

h. Select the picture, click the **FORMAT tab**, and then click **Crop** in the Size group.

i. Drag the top-left corner down and to the right until the vertical ruler reaches approximately the +2 1/2" mark and the horizontal ruler reaches approximately the +2" mark.

   The resulting size of the image is 5.81" high and 4.25" wide—yours may differ.

j. Click **Crop** in the Size group again to crop the area from view and to turn off the Crop feature.

k. Select the cropped picture and click the **FORMAT tab**, if necessary.

l. Click **Compress Pictures** in the Adjust group.

   The Compress Pictures dialog box opens.

m. Click **Use document resolution** in the *Target output* section.

n. Click the **Apply only to this picture check box** to deselect it.

   You need to compress all the pictures you have used in the presentation to reduce the presentation file size, not just the selected picture.

o. Click **OK**.

The portions of the image that were cropped from view are deleted, and all pictures in the slide show are compressed.

p. Save the presentation.

STEP 5 » INSERT A PICTURE FROM THE INTERNET

The couple visited Rome, Italy, during their honeymoon, so you want to insert a picture of the Colosseum to end the slide show. You insert an image from Image*After, a Web site that provides pictures free for personal or commercial use. Refer to Figure 4.24 as you complete Step 5.

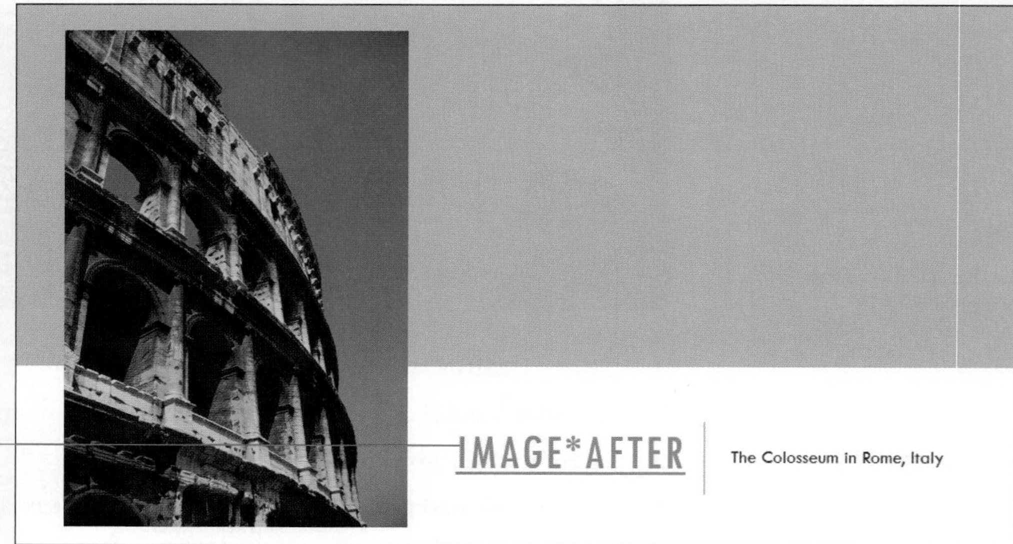

FIGURE 4.24 Hyperlink to ImageAfter.com

a. Click **Slide 6**. Note the text *Image*After* (imageafter.com) is a hyperlink.

The hyperlink will display if you view the presentation in Slide Show view.

b. Right-click the link and select **Open Hyperlink** to launch the Web site in your default browser.

> **TROUBLESHOOTING:** If you are not connected to the Internet, the hyperlink will not work. Connect to the Internet and repeat step b.

The Image*After Web site displays thumbnails of images pertaining to the Colosseum in Rome.

c. Click the thumbnail of your choice to display a larger image. Right-click the image, select **Copy**, and then close the browser.

The Copy command may be named something else depending on the Web browser you are using.

d. Right-click anywhere on Slide 6 and paste the image using the Picture paste option in the submenu.

e. Depending on the size of the image you insert, you may need to adjust the image size to appropriately fit in the presentation.

f. Drag the picture to position it on the left side of the slide, leaving the Image*After text box visible.

The Image*After text box should be visible to give credit to the image source.

g. Save the presentation. Keep the presentation open if you plan to continue with the next Hands-On Exercise. If not, close the presentation and exit PowerPoint.

Video

With video added to your project, you can greatly enhance and reinforce your story, and your audience can retain more of what they see. For example, a video of water tumbling over a waterfall would stir the emotions of a viewer far more than a table listing the number of gallons of water falling within a designated period of time. Anytime you can engage a viewer's emotions, he or she will better remember your message.

In this section, you will learn the types of video file formats that PowerPoint supports, examine the options available when using video, and insert a video clip into the memories presentation.

Adding Video

Table 4.2 displays the common types of video file formats you can add to a presentation, listed in alphabetical order by file extension. Different file formats use different types of ***codec*** (coder/decoder) software, which use algorithms to compress or code videos, and then decompress or decode the videos for playback. Video playback places tremendous demand on your computer system in terms of processing speed and memory. Using a codec reduces that demand. In order for your video file to be viewed correctly, the video player must have the appropriate software installed and the correct version of the software. Even though your video file extension is the same as the one listed in Table 4.2 or in Help, the video may not play correctly if the correct version of the codec software is not installed.

TABLE 4.2 Types of Video File Formats Supported by PowerPoint

File Format	Extension	Description
Windows Media File	.asf	**Advanced Streaming Format** Stores synchronized multimedia data. Used to stream audio and video content, images, and script commands over a network.
Windows Video File	.avi	**Audio Video Interleave** Stores sound and moving pictures in Microsoft Resource Interchange File Format (RIFF).
Movie File	.mpg or .mpeg	**Moving Picture Experts Group** Evolving set of standards for video and audio compression developed by the Moving Picture Experts Group. Designed specifically for use with Video-CD and CD-i media.
Adobe Flash Media	.swf	**Flash Video** File format generally used to deliver video over the Internet. Uses Adobe Flash Player.
Windows Media Video File	.wmv	**Windows Media Video** Compresses audio and video by using Windows Media Video compressed format. Requires minimal amount of storage space on your computer's hard drive.

When you add video to your presentation, you can ***embed*** the video and store the video within the presentation, or you can ***link*** to the video, which creates a connection from the presentation to another location such as a storage device or Web site. The advantage of embedding video is that a copy of the video file is placed in the slide, so moving or deleting the original video will not impact your presentation. The advantage of linking a video file is that your presentation file size is smaller. A linked video is stored in its own file. Another advantage of linking over embedding is that the presentation video is updated automatically if the original video object is changed. One caution for using a linked video from a file—the video is not part of the presentation, and if you save the presentation file to a different location, such as a flash drive, you must make sure you save the video to the new location, too. If you change the location of the video, you must make sure to change the link to the video file in the presentation.

STEP 1》 To insert a video in a presentation, do the following:

1. Click the INSERT tab.
2. Click Video in the Media group.
3. Click *Video on My PC*.
4. Browse, locate, and select the video you want to use in the presentation.
5. Click Insert to insert the video in your presentation or click the Insert arrow and select *Link to File* to link the video to your presentation.

PowerPoint 2013 has made it even easier to add online video, such as a video from YouTube, to a presentation. You can search for an online video from within PowerPoint, and the video will be inserted directly into your slide. You can then move the video to the location on the slide or resize the video just as you would a photograph. Figure 4.25 shows the search box options for Online Video. Video can be inserted from anywhere on the Web, your OneDrive account (if you have video saved there), YouTube, or from a Web site where you have been given the embed code for the video.

Figure 4.26 shows the results of the TED video search. The search term *TED Talks* in the YouTube Search box was used for the search. (TED.com is a popular Web site for videos relating to technology, entertainment, and design.) These videos can also be viewed from TED.com.

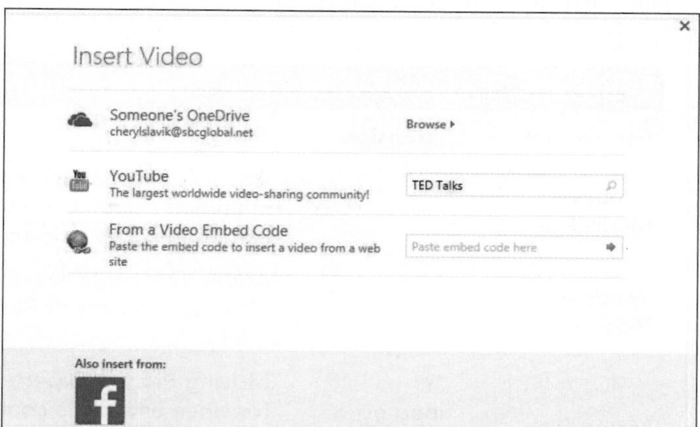

FIGURE 4.25 Online Video Search Options

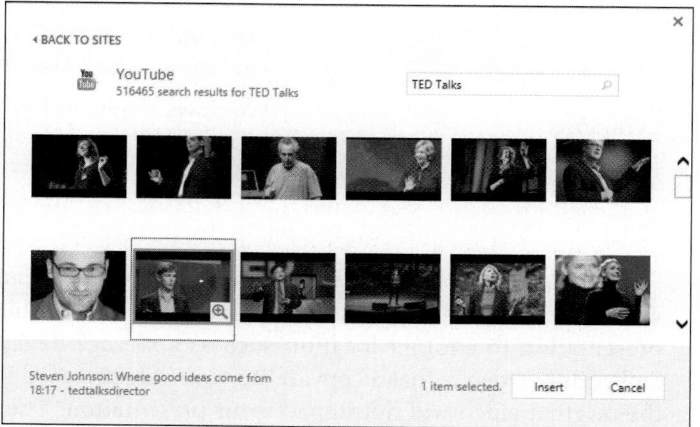

FIGURE 4.26 Search Results for YouTube Search

To search for and insert an online video in a presentation, do the following:

1. Click the INSERT tab.
2. Click Video in the Media group.
3. Click Online Video.

4. Browse, locate, and select the video you want to use in the presentation.
5. Click Insert to insert the video in your presentation.

You can also embed video from an online Web site. When you embed video from the online site, you have to copy and paste the embed code from the online site into the *From a Video Embed Code* box. Figure 4.27 shows embed code inserted into PowerPoint's *From a Video Embed Code* box. If you have embedded video from an online site, you must be connected to the Internet when you display the presentation.

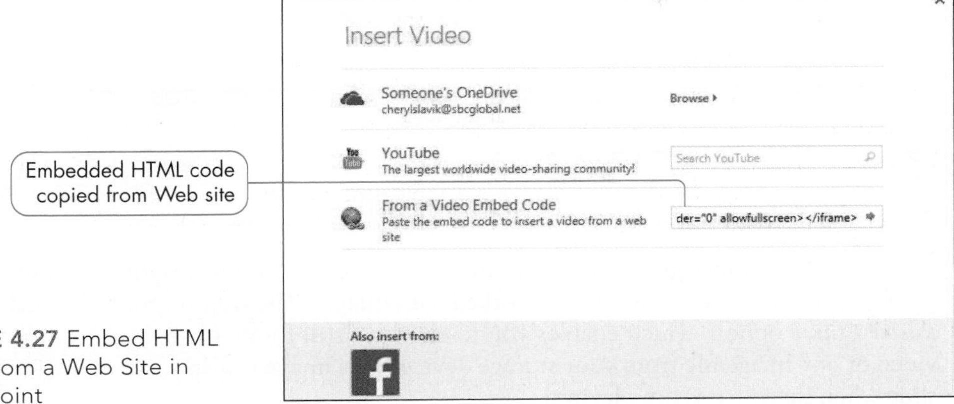

FIGURE 4.27 Embed HTML Code from a Web Site in PowerPoint

To insert embed code from an online video site, do the following:

1. Locate video on an online video site.
2. Copy the embed code.
3. Click the INSERT tab in PowerPoint.
4. Click Video in the Media group.
5. Click Online Video.
6. Paste the embed HTML code into the *From a Video Embed Code* box.
7. Click Insert.

Whether you have inserted your own video or video from a Web site, the video will include a Media Controls bar with a Play/Pause button, a Move Back button, a Move Forward button, a time notation, and a Mute/Unmute control slider. The Move Back and Move Forward buttons aid you when editing your own video. The Media Controls bar is shown in Figure 4.28.

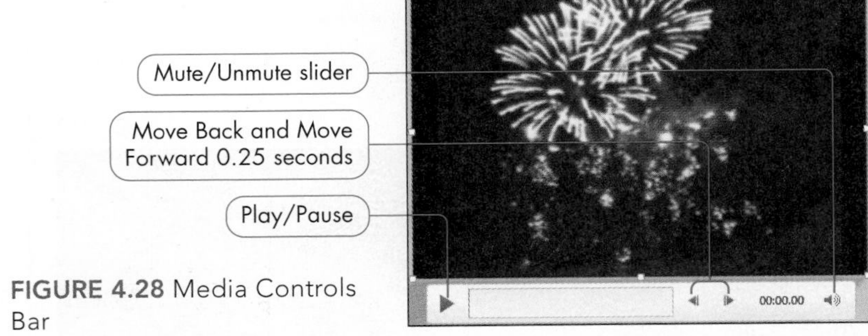

FIGURE 4.28 Media Controls Bar

Using Video Tools

PowerPoint includes wonderful tools for working with video. You can format the video's brightness and contrast, color, and style. You can apply most artistic image effects, add or remove bookmarks, trim the video, and set fade in or fade out effects. When you select an inserted video, the Video Tools tab displays with two tabs: the Format tab and the Playback tab.

Format a Video

The Format tab includes options for playing the video for preview purposes, adjusting the video, applying a style to the video, arranging a video on the slide, and cropping and sizing the video. Figure 4.29 displays the Video Tools Format tab. Some of these tools will not work with embedded Web site videos.

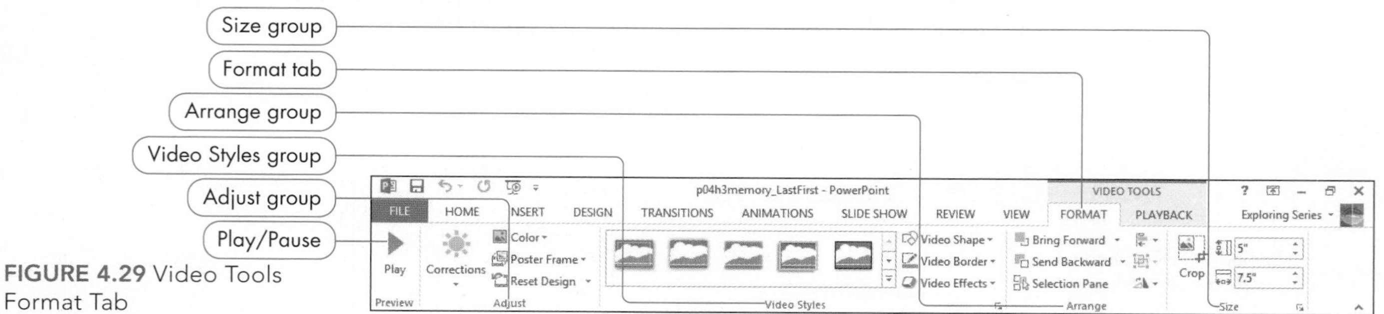

FIGURE 4.29 Video Tools Format Tab

Using the Adjust group, you can adjust video contrast and brightness, and you can recolor a video as you did when you worked with images. The Adjust group also includes the ***Poster Frame*** option, which enables you to choose a still frame (or image) from within the video or any image file from your storage device. This image is displayed on the PowerPoint slide when the video is not playing.

STEP 2

To create a poster frame from a video, do the following:

1. Click Play in the Preview group to display the video.
2. Pause the video when the frame you want to use as the poster frame appears.
3. Click Poster Frame in the Adjust group.
4. Click Current Frame.

To create a poster frame from an image stored in your storage device, do the following:

1. Click Poster Frame in the Adjust group.
2. Click *Image from File*.
3. Locate and select desired image.
4. Click Insert.

Figure 4.30 shows a video using with a Poster Frame option set to the current frame.

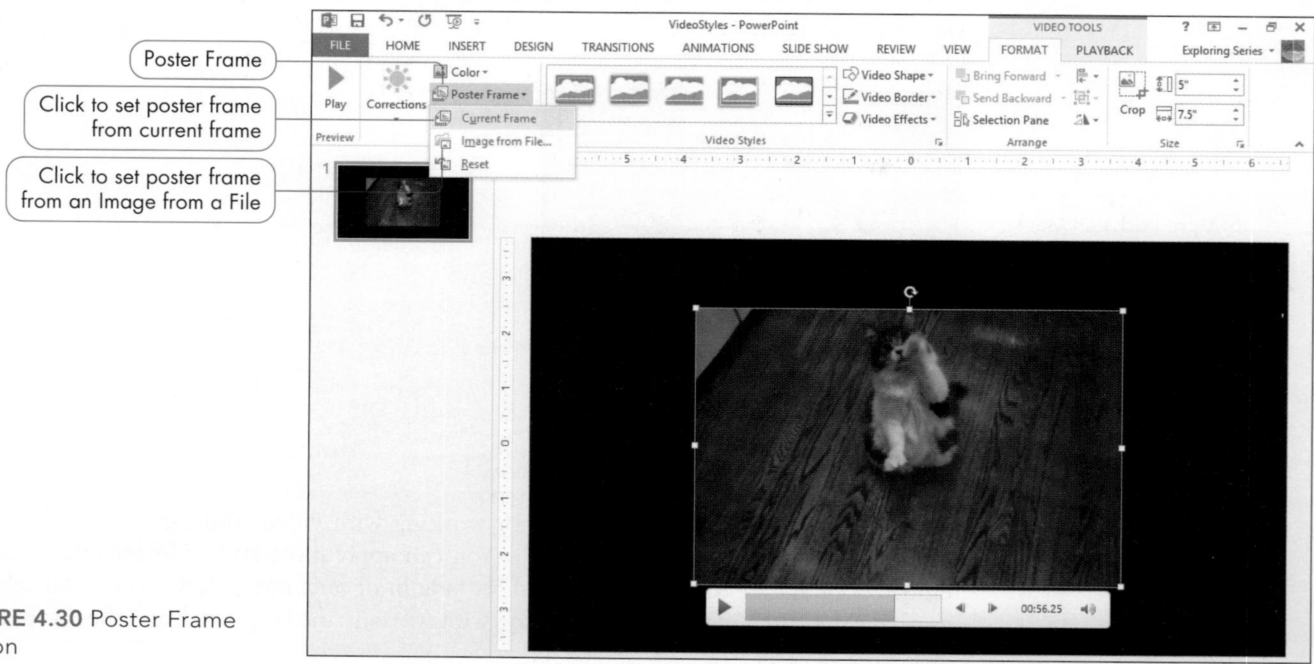

FIGURE 4.30 Poster Frame Option

The Style effects available for images are also available for videos. In addition to the styles in the Video Styles gallery, you can edit the shape of a video, change the border of the video, and add video effects such as Shadow, Reflection, Glow, Soft Edges, Bevel, and 3-D Rotation. Figure 4.31 shows a video formatted to fit a PowerPoint shape, with a gray border and reflection added.

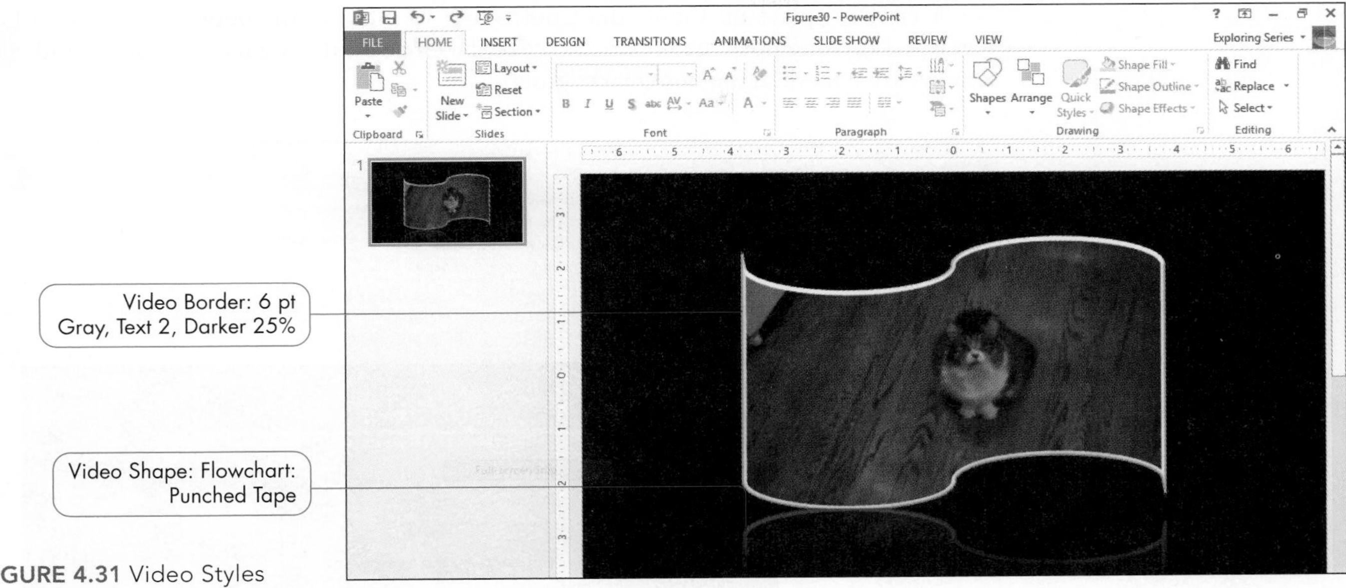

FIGURE 4.31 Video Styles

TIP Resetting a Video

To discard all formatting changes from a selected video, click the Reset Design arrow in the Adjust group on the Format tab and select Reset Design or Reset Design & Size.

Set Video Playback Options

The Playback tab includes options used when viewing a video. These tools can be used to bookmark, edit, and control the video, and can eliminate the need to use any outside video-editing software for basic video-editing functions. Figure 4.32 displays the Video Tools Playback tab.

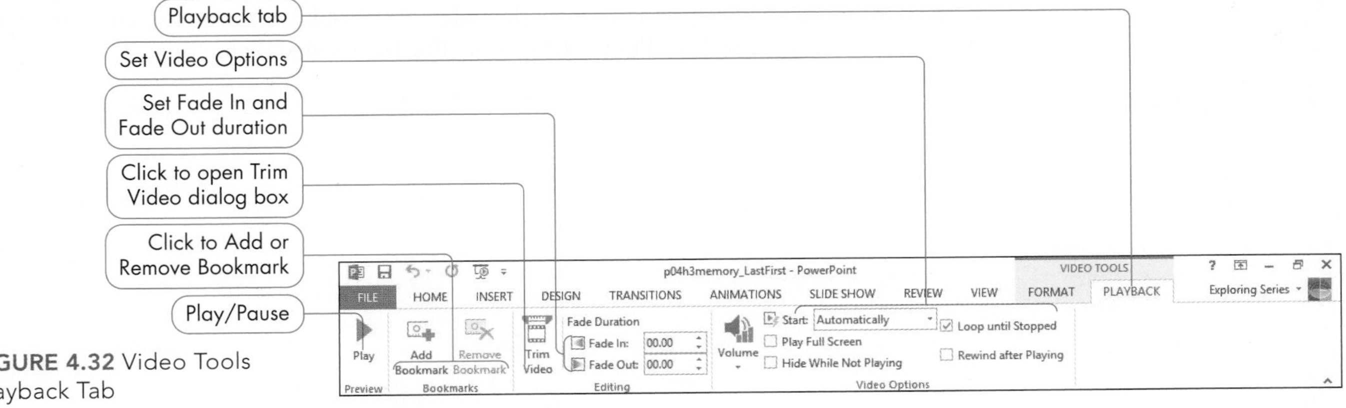

FIGURE 4.32 Video Tools Playback Tab

You can use ***bookmarks*** to mark specific locations in a video, making it possible to quickly advance to the part of the video you want to display or to trigger an event in an animation.

STEP 3

To bookmark a video, do the following:

1. Select the video and click the PLAYBACK tab.
2. Click Play on the Media Control bar. Pause the video at the desired frame.
3. Click Add Bookmark in the Bookmarks group when the video reaches the location you want to quickly move to during your presentation.

A circle displays on the Media Control bar to indicate the bookmark location (see Figure 4.33). To remove the bookmark, click the circle on the Media Control bar and click Remove Bookmark in the Bookmarks group.

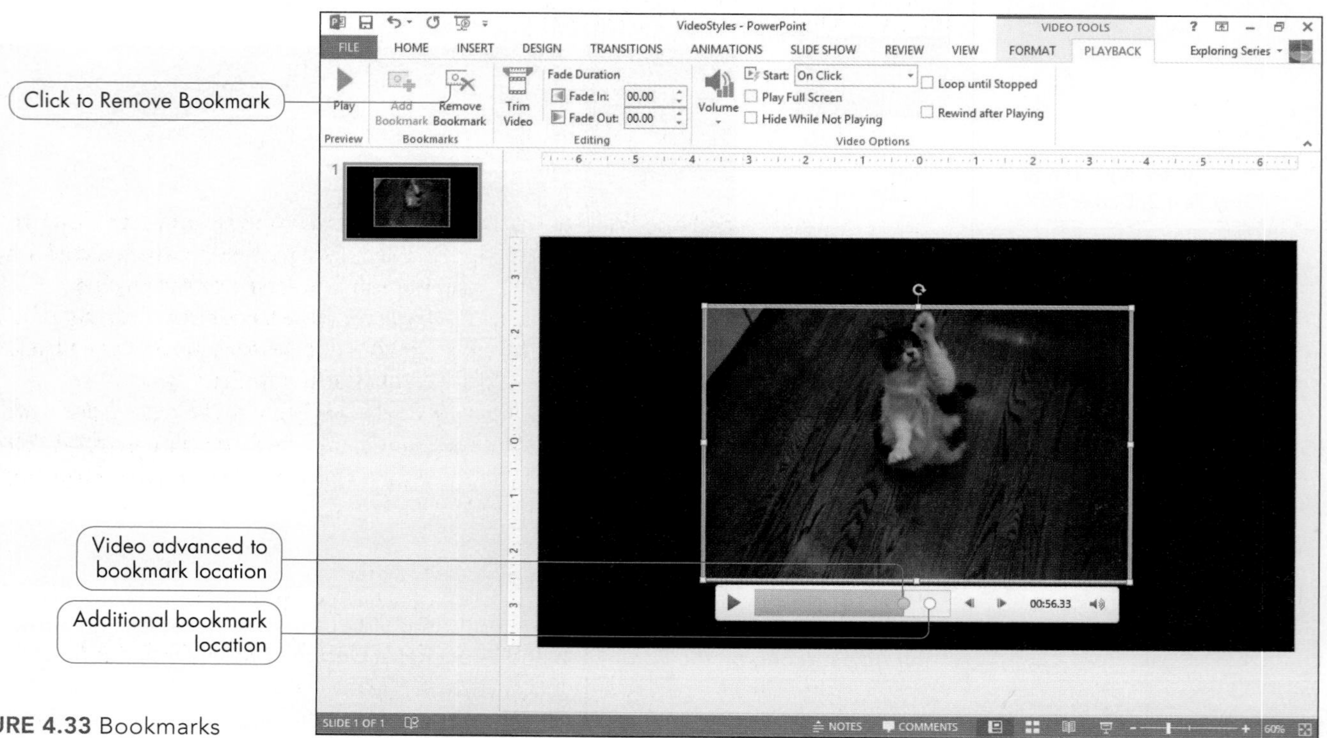

FIGURE 4.33 Bookmarks

PowerPoint enables you to perform basic video editing by enabling you to determine the starting and ending of a video and set a Fade In and Fade Out duration. In the Trim Video dialog box, which you access in the Editing group on the Playback tab, you can use the Trim option to specify the Start Time and End Time for a video, or you can drag the Start marker and the End marker on the Timing slide bar to select the time. The advantage to dragging the markers is that as you drag, you can view the video. Any bookmarks you set will also display in the Trim Video dialog box. Figure 4.34 shows the Trim Video dialog box.

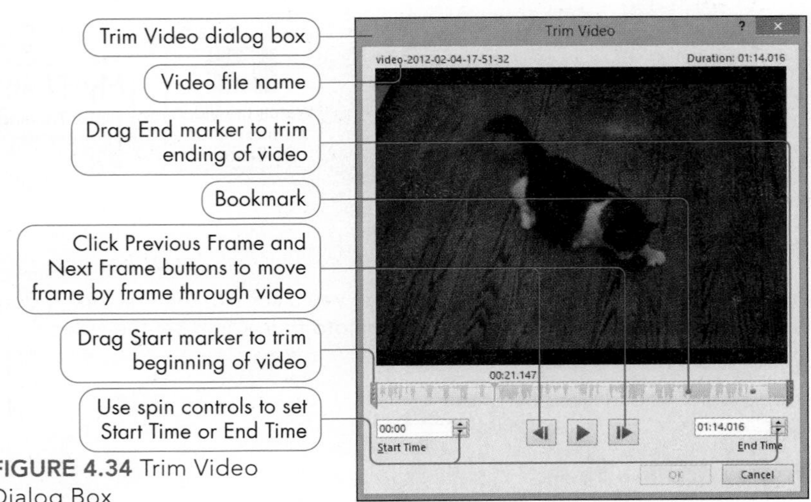

FIGURE 4.34 Trim Video Dialog Box

To set a Fade In or Fade Out duration, click the spin arrows or enter an exact time in the appropriate boxes in the Editing group on the Playback tab. If you have selected a poster frame for your video, the poster frame will fade into the first frame of your video.

The Video Options group of the Playback tab enables you to control a variety of display options. You can control the volume of the video by clicking the Volume arrow and selecting Low, Medium, or High. You can also mute any sound attached to the video.

The Video Options group also enables you to determine whether the video starts on the click of the mouse (the default setting) or automatically when the slide displays. You can choose to play the video at full screen, hide the video when it is not playing, loop continuously until you stop the playback, and rewind after playing.

1. What is a video codec, and why is it usually necessary? ***p. 1031***
2. Explain the difference between embedding a video and linking a video. ***p. 1031***
3. Why would you add a bookmark to a video? ***p. 1035***

Hands-On Exercises

Watch the Video for this Hands-On Exercise!

MyITLab®
HOE2 Training

2 Video

In Europe, the couple recorded some fireworks displayed during a sports event. The groom gave you a copy of the fireworks video because you think it would be an excellent finale to the slide show. You insert the video, add a photo frame, and set the video playback options.

Skills covered: Insert a Video from a File • Format a Video • Set Video Playback Options

STEP 1 ›› INSERT A VIDEO FROM A FILE

You create a copy of the previous presentation and insert the fireworks video. Refer to Figure 4.35 as you complete Step 1.

FIGURE 4.35 Inserted Windows Media Video File

a. Open the *p04h1Memory_LastFirst* presentation and save it as **p04h2Memory_LastFirst**, changing *h1* to *h2*.

b. Click **Slide 7**. Click the **INSERT tab** and click Video in the Media group.

c. Select **Video on My PC**, open the *p04h1Memory_Media* folder, select *p04h2Fireworks.wmv*, and then click **Insert**.

d. Save the presentation.

STEP 2 ›› FORMAT A VIDEO

The first image of the video shows the fireworks in the beginning stages. You decide to use a poster frame of the fireworks while they are fully bursting so the slide has an attractive image on display before the video begins. You also decide that a shape removing the edges of the video would be an improvement. Finally, you add a shadow video effect. Refer to Figure 4.36 as you complete Step 2.

FIGURE 4.36 Formatted Video File

a. Click **Move Forward 0.25 Seconds** on the Media Controls bar located beneath the video to advance the video to the frame at 2.00 seconds.

b. Click the **FORMAT tab**, if necessary, click **Poster Frame** in the Adjust group, and then click **Current Frame**.

   The frame you selected becomes the poster frame and displays on the slide.

c. Click **Video Shape** in the Video Styles group and click **Hexagon** in the Basic Shapes category.

   The video shape changes to a hexagon.

d. Click **Video Effects**, point to *Shadow*, and then click **Perspective Diagonal Lower Left** in the Perspective category.

   The shadow displays in a hexagon shape with a perspective view.

e. Click the **SLIDE SHOW tab** and click **From Current Slide** in the Start Slide Show group.

   Slide 7 opens with the video displayed on the slide. The poster frame shows the fireworks at full cascade with the video shadow.

f. Move the pointer to the bottom of the video to display the Media Controls bar and click **Play**. Press **Esc** when you are finished.

g. Save the presentation.

STEP 3 ›› SET VIDEO PLAYBACK OPTIONS

The last burst of fireworks does not finish its crescendo, so you decide to trim away this last portion of the video. Because you do not want the viewers of the presentation to have to click to begin the video, you change the start setting to start automatically. You decide to loop the video to play continuously until stopped because it is so short. Refer to Figure 4.37 as you complete Step 3.

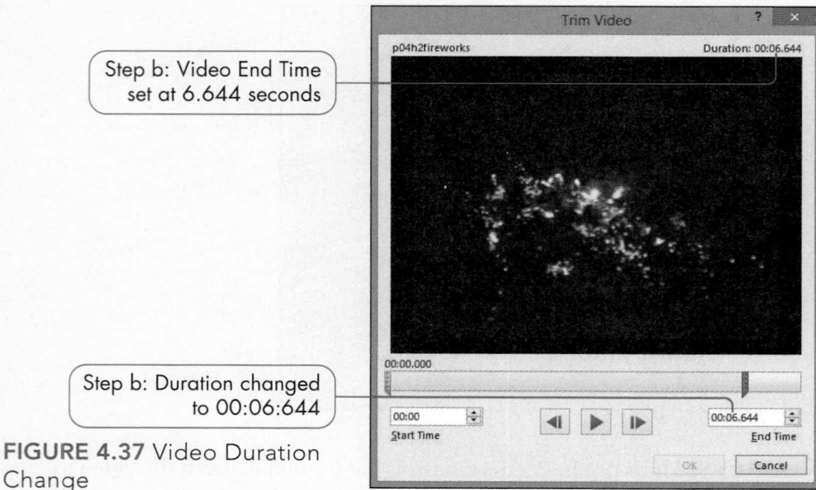

FIGURE 4.37 Video Duration Change

a. Select the video object, if necessary, click the **PLAYBACK tab**, and then click **Trim Video** in the Editing group.

The Trim Video dialog box opens.

b. Drag the red **End Time marker** on the slider until *00:06.644* appears in the End Time box, or type **00:06.644** in the **End Time box**, and click **OK**.

The duration of the video changes from 7.755 seconds to 6.644 seconds.

c. Click the **Start arrow** in the Video Options group and select **Automatically**.

d. Select the **Loop until Stopped check box** in the Video Options group.

The fireworks video will continue to play until you advance to end the slide show.

e. Click the **SLIDE SHOW tab** and click **From Beginning** in the Start Slide Show group.

Advance through the slide show. Note the video plays in the hexagon shape.

f. Save the presentation. Keep the presentation open if you plan to continue with the next Hands-On Exercise. If not, close the presentation and exit PowerPoint.

Audio

Audio can draw on common elements of any language or culture—screams, laughs, sobs—to add excitement, provide a pleasurable background, set the mood, or serve as a wake-up call for the audience. Harnessing the emotional impact of sound in your presentation can transform your presentation from good to extraordinary. On the other hand, use sound incorrectly, and you can destroy your presentation, leaving your audience confused or distracted. Keep in mind the guideline emphasized throughout this book—any object you add to the presentation should enhance, not detract from, your message.

In this section, you will review the methods for inserting sound and tips for each method. You insert sound from the Insert Audio dialog box or saved audio file and learn how to determine the number of times a sound clip plays, the number of slides through which the sound plays, and the method for launching the sound.

Adding Audio

Your computer needs a sound card and speakers to play audio. In a classroom or computer laboratory, you will need a headset or headphones/earbuds for playback so that you do not disturb other students. You can locate and play sounds and music from the Insert Audio dialog box, or from a hard drive, flash drive, or any other storage device. You can also record your own sounds, music, or narration to play from PowerPoint.

Insert Audio from a File

Table 4.3 lists the commonly used types of audio file formats supported by PowerPoint, listed in alphabetical order by extension.

TABLE 4.3 Commonly Used Audio File Formats Supported by PowerPoint

File Format	Extension	Description
MIDI File	.mid or .midi	**Musical Instrument Digital Interface** Standard format for interchange of musical information between musical instruments, synthesizers, and computers.
MP3 Audio File	.mp3	**MPEG Audio Layer 3** Sound file that has been compressed by using the MPEG Audio Layer 3 codec (developed by the Fraunhofer Institute).
Windows Audio File	.wav	**Wave Form** Stores sounds as waveforms. Depending on various factors, one minute of sound can occupy as little as 644 kilobytes or as much as 27 megabytes of storage.
Windows Media Audio File	.wma	**Windows Media Audio** Sound format used to distribute recorded music, usually over the Internet. Compressed using the Microsoft Windows Media Audio codec.

STEP 1» To insert audio from a file, do the following:

1. Click the INSERT tab.
2. Click Audio in the Media group.
3. Click *Audio on My PC.*
4. Browse, locate, and select the desired file.
5. Click Insert.

A gray speaker icon representing the file displays in the center of the slide with a Media Controls bar beneath it. The same controls are available when you select audio as when you select video.

Add Audio from Office.com Clip Art

You can search for and insert Office.com Clip Art files, which include a number of royalty-free sounds. These audio files are typically short in duration.

STEP 3»

To insert sound from an Online Site:

1. Click the INSERT tab, click Audio in the Media Group, and then click Online Audio.
2. When the search box opens, enter a term in the Office.com Clip Art box and press Enter.
3. Point to a sound clip in the results pane to display a tip showing the length of the sound track.
4. Hover over the clip to hear a preview.
5. Select the desired clip and click Insert.

TIP Hiding the Sound Icon During a Presentation

When audio is added to a presentation, the sound icon shows on the slide. You may not want the icon to display during the presentation, however. To hide the icon during a presentation, click the icon, click the Audio Tools Playback tab, and select Hide During Show in the Audio Options group.

Record and Insert Audio

Sometimes you may find it helpful to add recorded audio to a slide show. Although you could record music, ***narration*** (spoken commentary) is more common. One example of a need for recorded narration is when you want to create a self-running presentation, such as a presentation displaying in a kiosk at the mall or online. Other examples include creating an association between words and an image on the screen for a presentation to a group learning a new language and vocabulary building for young children. Rather than adding a narration prior to a presentation, you could create the narration during the presentation. For example, recording the discussion and decisions made during a meeting would create an archive of the meeting.

Before creating the narration, keep in mind the following:

- Your computer will need a sound card, speakers, and a microphone.
- Comments on selected slides may be recorded rather than narrating the entire presentation.
- Voice narration takes precedence over any other sounds during playback, making it possible for a voice to play over inserted audio files.
- PowerPoint records the amount of time it takes you to narrate each slide, and if you save the slide timings, you can use them to create an automatic slide show.
- You can pause and resume recording during the process.

To record audio, do the following:

1. Click the INSERT tab.
2. Click Audio in the Media group.
3. Click Record Audio.
4. Click Record (see Figure 4.38).
5. Record your message.
6. Click Stop.
7. Click Play to check the recording.
8. Type a name for the recording and click OK.

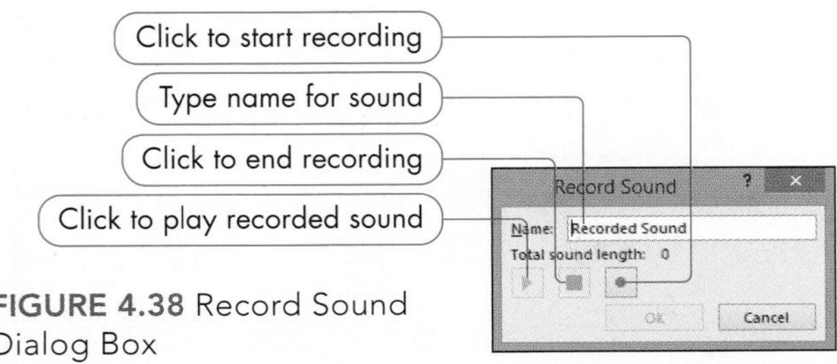

FIGURE 4.38 Record Sound Dialog Box

TIP Create Notes of Your Narration

A transcript of your narration should be available for those in your audience who are hearing impaired. Providing the transcript lets this audience gain from your presentation, too. Put the transcript in the Notes pane and print the notes to provide a transcript.

Changing Audio Settings

When the icon for an inserted audio clip is selected, the Audio Tools tab appears with two tabs: Format and Playback. The Format tab is not relevant, as it provides options relating to images. The Playback tab provides options for playing and pausing the audio clip, adding a bookmark, trimming, fading in and out, adjusting volume, determining starting method, hiding the audio icon while playing, looping, and rewinding after playing. All of these features work similarly to the video features, except that the *Trim audio* feature provides an audio time line rather than a video preview window.

Animate an Audio Sequence

Although the Playback tab gives you only two options for starting—On Click or Automatically—you have other options available through the Timing group on the Animations tab. You can choose whether the audio plays with a previous event or after a previous event; for example, you can have the audio play as a picture appears or after.

STEP 2» To set the audio to play with or after a previous event:

1. Select the sound icon.
2. Click the ANIMATIONS tab.
3. Click the Start arrow in the Timing group.
4. Click With Previous or After Previous.

The Timing group on the Animations tab also includes a Delay spin box that you can use to delay the play of an audio clip (see Figure 4.39).

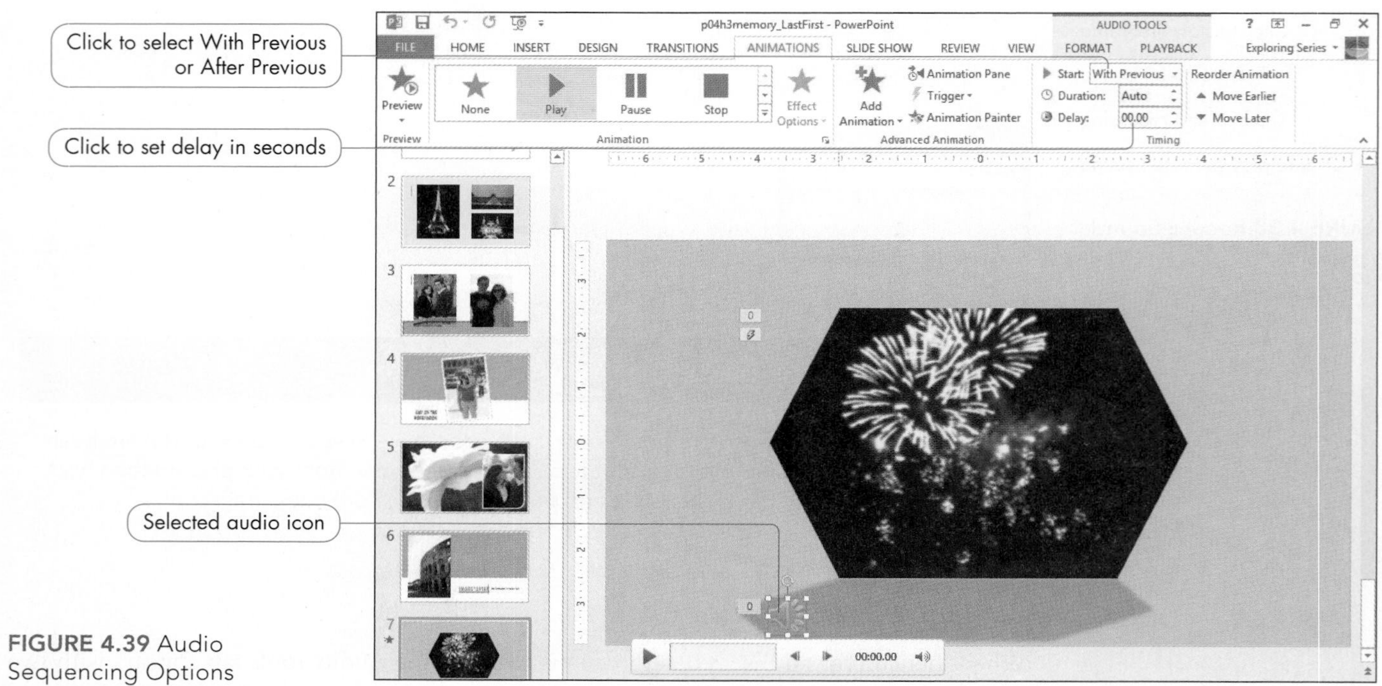

FIGURE 4.39 Audio Sequencing Options

Play a Sound over Multiple Slides

By default, audio plays until it ends or until the next mouse click. If you are playing background music, this means the music ends when you click to advance to the next slide.

To continue audio over multiple slides, do the following:

1. Select the sound icon and click the ANIMATIONS tab.
2. Click Animation Pane in the Advanced Animation group.
3. Select the sound you want to continue over multiple slides.
4. Click the arrow to the right of the sound.
5. Click Effect Options.
6. Click the After option in the *Stop playing* section of the Effect tab.
7. Enter the number of slides during which you want the sound to play (see Figure 4.40).

If the background music stops before you get to the last slide, use the Loop Until Stopped feature to keep the sound repeating. Click the Playback tab and click the Loop Until Stopped check box in the Audio Options group.

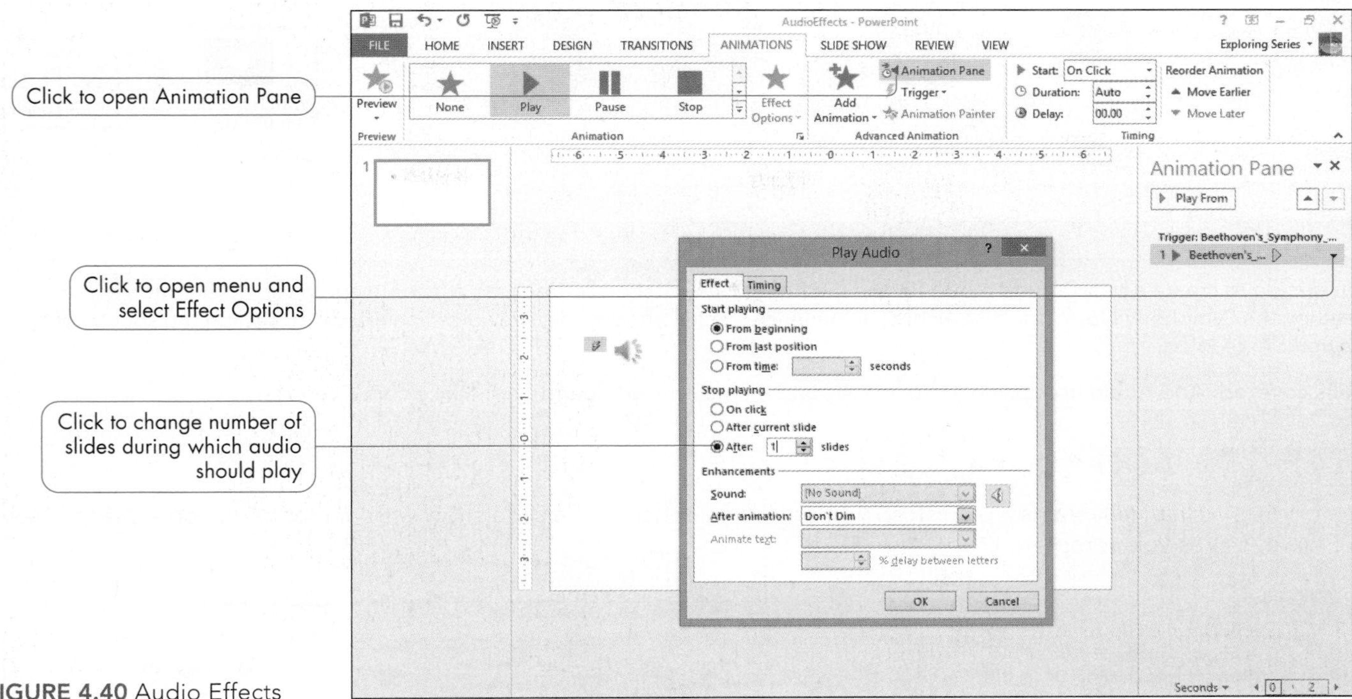

FIGURE 4.40 Audio Effects

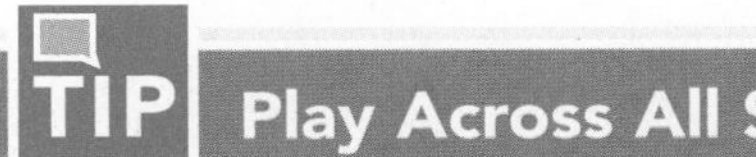

TIP Play Across All Slides

You can set an audio clip to play across slides easily by clicking the Playback tab and selecting the Play Across Slides check box. This option does not let you set the number of slides over which you want the audio to play, however.

***Quick* Concepts**

1. What are the three methods for inserting audio into a presentation? ***p. 1041***
2. Describe a situation where a narrated PowerPoint presentation would be advisable. ***p. 1042***
3. What audio options are available from the Audio Tools Playback tab? ***p. 1043***

Hands-On Exercises

MyITLab®
HOE3 Training

3 Audio

You decide to create a background mood for the memories presentation by inserting a favorite audio clip of the bride—Beethoven's Symphony No. 9. You also want to experience the full effect of the fireworks finale slide by adding the sounds of fireworks exploding.

Skills covered: Add Audio from a File • Change Audio Settings • Insert Sound from Office.com Clip Art

STEP 1 » ADD AUDIO FROM A FILE

The bride is a classically trained pianist, so you decide to enhance the slide show with one of her favorite pieces. Refer to Figure 4.41 as you complete Step 1.

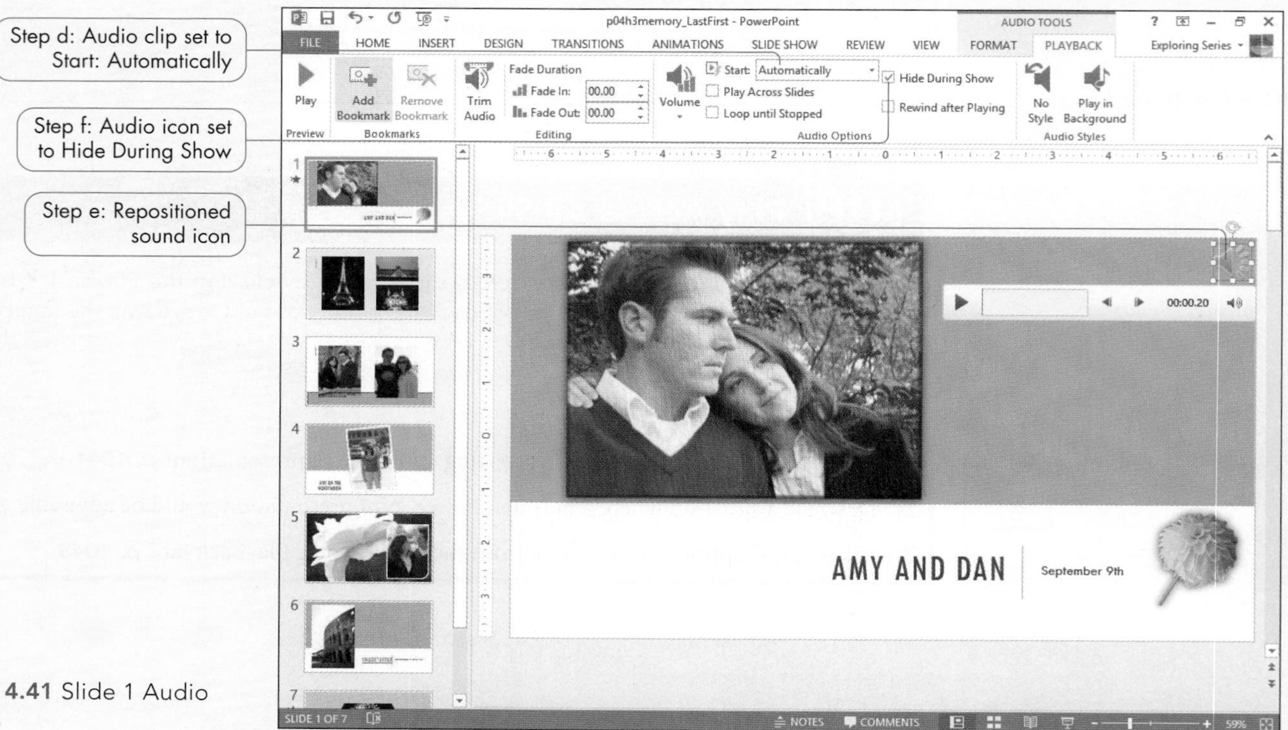

FIGURE 4.41 Slide 1 Audio Settings

a. Open the *p04h2Memory_LastFirst* presentation if you closed it after the last exercise and save it as **p04h3Memory_LastFirst**, changing *h2* to *h3*.

> **TROUBLESHOOTING:** To complete this exercise, it is best that you have a sound card and speakers. Even if this equipment is not available, however, you can still perform these steps to gain the knowledge.

b. Click **Slide 1**. Click the **INSERT tab**, click **Audio** in the Media group, and then select **Audio on My PC**.

The Insert Audio dialog box opens.

c. Locate the *p04h1Memory_Media* folder, select **Beethoven's_Symphony_No_9**, and then click **Insert**.

   The sound icon and Media Controls bar are displayed in the center of the slide.

d. Click the **PLAYBACK tab**, click the **Start arrow** in the Audio Options group, and then select **Automatically**.

e. Drag the **sound icon** to the top-right corner of the slide.

f. Click the **Hide During Show check box** in the Audio Options group.

g. Click **Play** in the Preview group.

h. Save the presentation.

STEP 2 ›› CHANGE AUDIO SETTINGS

Because PowerPoint's default setting ends a sound file when a slide advances, the Beethoven file is abruptly cut off when you advance to the next slide. You adjust the sound settings so the file plays continuously through all slides in the slide show. Refer to Figure 4.42 as you complete Step 2.

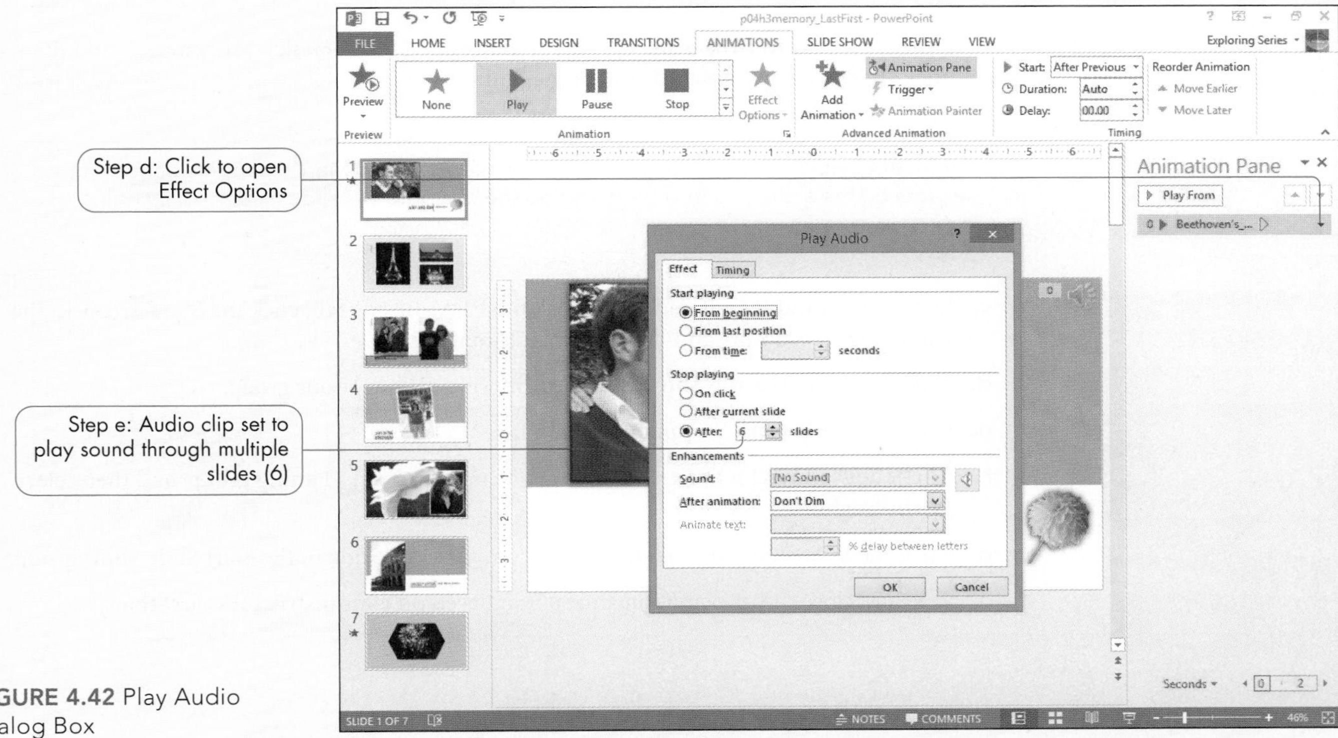

FIGURE 4.42 Play Audio Dialog Box

a. Click the **SLIDE SHOW tab** and click **From Beginning** in the Start Slide Show group. Advance through the slides and end the slide show.

   Note that the sound clip on Slide 1 discontinues playing as soon as you click to advance to the next slide.

b. Select the **sound icon** on the top-right of Slide 1.

c. Click the **ANIMATIONS tab** and click **Animation Pane** in the Advanced Animation group.

d. Click the **Beethoven's Symphony sound arrow** in the animation list and select **Effect Options**.

e. Click **After** in the *Stop playing* section, type **6** in the box, and then click **OK**. Close the Animation Pane.

f. Save the presentation.

g. Play the slide show and note the music plays through the sixth slide.

STEP 3 ≫ INSERT SOUND FROM OFFICE.COM CLIP ART

The sound of fireworks exploding would make the finale slide more effective. You locate a fireworks audio clip, add it to the fireworks slide, set it to start automatically, and set it to loop until the presentation ends. After adding the audio clip, you modify its setting so it plays concurrently with the video. You move the audio icon so that it does not block the view of the fireworks. You also hide the audio icon during the presentation. Refer to Figure 4.43 as you complete Step 3.

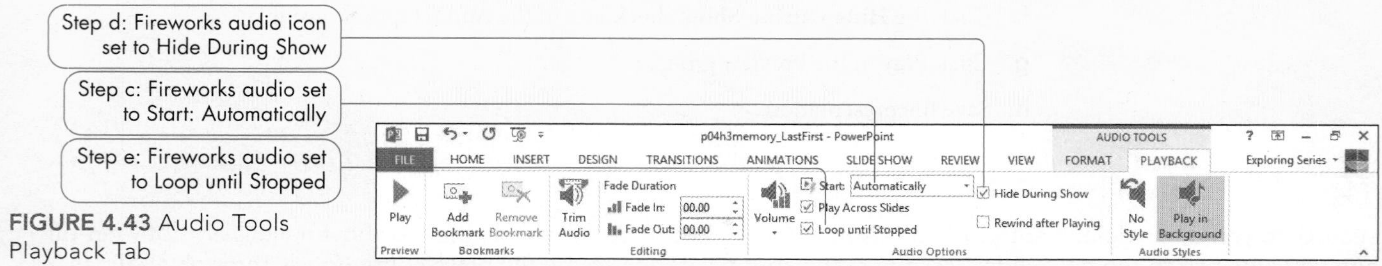

FIGURE 4.43 Audio Tools Playback Tab

a. Click **Slide 7**. Click the **INSERT tab**, click **Audio** in the Media group, and then select **Online Audio**.

b. Type the keyword **fireworks** in the **Search box**, press **Enter**, click **Fireworks 2**, and then click **Insert**. Drag the sound icon to the bottom-left corner.

> **TROUBLESHOOTING:** If the sound clip speaker icon and Media Controls bar do not appear on the slide, you may be dragging the clip onto the slide instead of inserting the clip.

c. Select the **sound icon** if necessary, click the **PLAYBACK tab**, click the **Start arrow** in the Audio Options group, and then select **Automatically**.

d. Click the **Hide During Show check box** in the Audio Options group.

e. Click the **Loop until Stopped check box**.

f. Click the **ANIMATIONS tab**, click the **Start arrow** in the Timing group, and then select **With Previous.**

g. Click the **SLIDE SHOW tab** and click **From Current Slide** in the Start Slide Show group.

h. Save and close the presentation and submit based on your instructor's directions.

Photo Albums

PowerPoint has a Photo Album feature designed to speed up the album creation process. This feature takes the images you select and arranges them on album pages based on selections you make.

In this section, you will use the Photo Album feature to create an album and use the feature settings to customize your album.

Creating a Photo Album

A PowerPoint ***Photo Album*** is a presentation that contains multiple pictures that are imported and formatted through the Photo Album feature. Because each picture does not have to be formatted individually, you save a considerable amount of time. The photo album in Figure 4.44 took less than two minutes to create and assign a theme. Because a four-per-page layout was selected, images were reduced to fit the size of the placeholder. This setting drastically reduced the size of some images.

FIGURE 4.44 PowerPoint Photo Album

STEP 1

To create a photo album, do the following:

1. Click the INSERT tab.
2. Click Photo Album in the Images group.
3. Click File/Disk.
4. Navigate to your pictures and select the pictures to include in the album.
5. Click Insert.
6. Select the Photo Album options you want.
7. Click Create.

If you click the Photo Album arrow, you may choose between creating a new album and editing a previously created album. When you select the pictures you want to include in the album, do not worry about the order of the pictures. You can change the order later. Once an album has been created, you can edit the album settings by clicking the Photo Album arrow in the Images group on the Insert tab and selecting Edit Photo Album.

TIP Creating Family Albums

After creating an album, add transitions and you have a beautiful presentation for a family gathering or special event. Loop the presentation and let it run so people can watch as they desire. Burn the presentation to a CD and send it as a holiday greeting.

Setting Photo Album Options

Using the photo album features can save you some time formatting and setting various design options. Several tools allow you to do things such as selecting picture order, rotating images, changing contrast and brightness, inserting captions for your photos, and finally selecting an album layout. Figure 4.45 shows the location of these tools. Each is discussed in detail in the following sections.

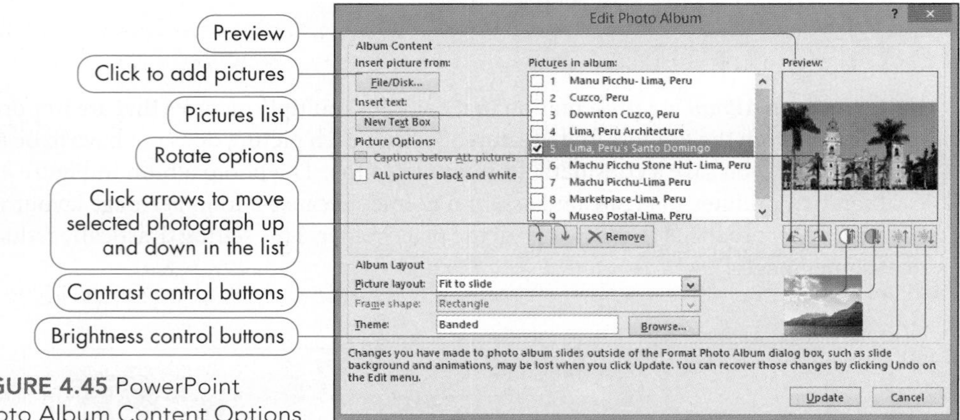

FIGURE 4.45 PowerPoint Photo Album Content Options

Selecting Pictures and Setting the Picture Order

After pictures are selected, they will display in a list in the *Album Content* section of the Photo Album dialog box. Click the name of a picture to display a preview to help you determine the order of pictures in the album.

To set the picture order:

1. Use the *Move up* arrow and the *Move down* arrow to reposition a selected photograph.
2. Use Ctrl or Shift to select more than one image.
3. Delete any unwanted photographs by selecting them and clicking Remove.

If you have downloaded photographs from a digital camera, you may need to rotate some images. Click the check box of the photo you want to rotate and click the rotate left or rotate right button. Rotate buttons are included in the *Album Content* section under the image preview.

Changing Picture Contrast and Brightness

STEP 2»

Contrast and brightness controls enable you to fine-tune your pictures. To set the contrast or brightness:

1. Click the check box next to the photo you want to modify.
2. Click the contrast or brightness controls until the photo is modified as desired.

Inserting Captions

The New Text Box button allows you to insert a text box with the photo caption in the album. The text placeholder is the same size as the placeholders for pictures. The *Captions below ALL pictures* option will not become available until you choose an album layout, which is discussed next. When this option is active, the file name of the picture displays as a caption below the picture in the album. You can modify the caption text once the album is created.

Setting an Album Layout

STEP 3 The *Album Layout* section of the Photo Album dialog box gives many options for personalizing the album. First, you can select a Picture layout: a single picture fitted to a full slide; one, two, or four pictures on a slide; or one, two, or four pictures and a title placeholder per slide. When you fit a single picture per slide, the image is maximized on the slide.

STEP 4 You can select from a variety of frame shapes in the *Album Layout* section. Options include rectangles, rounded rectangles, simple black or white frames, a compound black frame, a center shadow rectangle, or a soft edge rectangle.

STEP 5 You can apply a theme for the background of your album while in the Photo Album dialog box. This helps to personalize the album. If you are in a networked lab situation, it may be difficult to navigate to the location where themes are stored. If this is the case, create the album and in the main PowerPoint window, click the Design tab, click the More button in the Themes group, and then select your theme from the gallery.

1. What advantages does the Photo Album feature offer? ***p. 1050***
2. List two image transformation tools available in the *Album Content* section of the Photo Album dialog box. ***p. 1050***
3. Describe one way to personalize an album. ***p. 1051***

Hands-On Exercises

MyITLab®
HOE4 Training

4 Photo Albums

The bride and groom also took a trip to Peru, capturing photos of the gorgeous scenery. You prepare a photo album to help them preserve their memories. You take the time to improve the picture quality by adjusting the brightness and contrast. You also apply an album layout, apply frame shapes, and apply a theme to further personalize the album.

Skills covered: Create an Album, Select and Order Pictures • Adjust Contrast and Brightness • Set Picture Layout • Select Frame Shape • Edit Album Settings and Apply a Theme

STEP 1 » CREATE AN ALBUM, SELECT AND ORDER PICTURES

You have a folder in which you have saved the images you want to use for the vacation album. In this step, you add the images to the album and order the images by the date during which the trip was taken. Refer to Figure 4.46 as you complete Step 1.

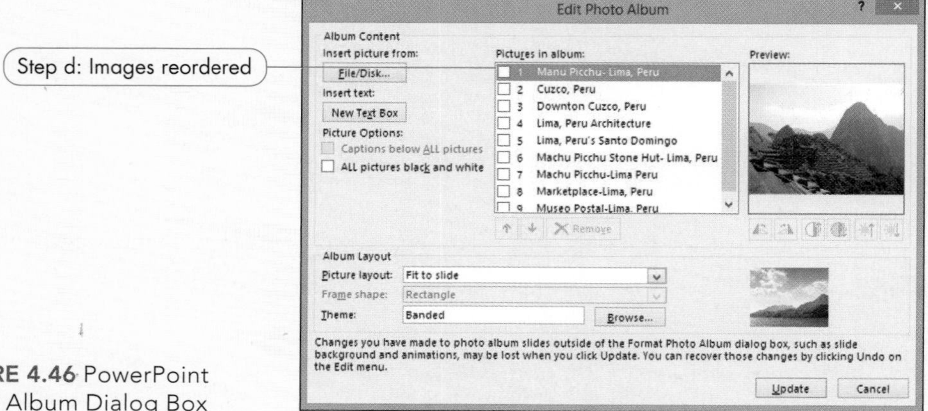

FIGURE 4.46 PowerPoint Photo Album Dialog Box

a. Open a new blank presentation. Click the **INSERT tab** and click **Photo Album** in the Images group.

The Photo Album dialog box opens.

b. Click **File/Disk**. Open the *p04h4Album_Media* folder.

c. Click one of the files in the list, press **Ctrl+A** to select all pictures in the folder, and then click **Insert**.

The list of pictures displays in the *Pictures in album* box.

d. Click to select the *Manu Picchu- Lima, Peru* picture and click the **Move up arrow** to reposition the picture so that it is the first picture in the list. Refer to Figure 4.46 to ensure your images are in the correct order and click **Create**.

STEP 2 » ADJUST CONTRAST AND BRIGHTNESS

The Photo Album feature includes buttons that enable you to adjust the contrast and brightness of images without having to access PowerPoint's Picture Tools. You use the Photo Album buttons to adjust the contrast in one of the Isle of Skye pictures. Refer to Figure 4.47 as you complete Step 2.

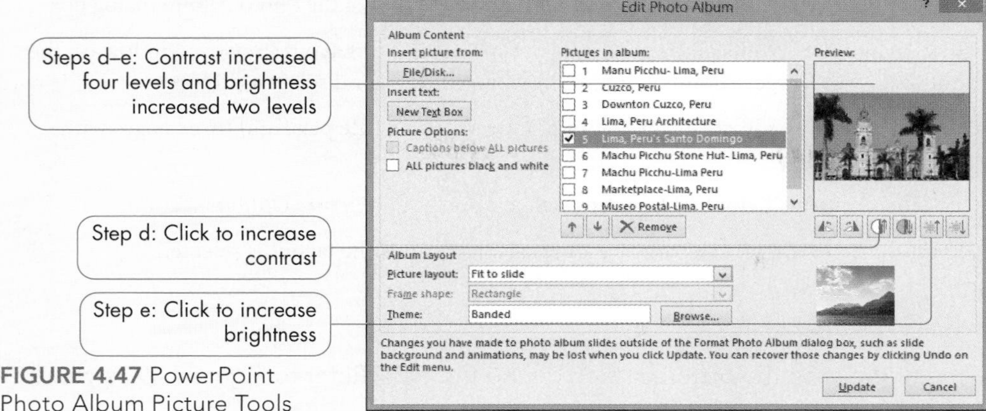

FIGURE 4.47 PowerPoint Photo Album Picture Tools

a. Click the **Photo Album arrow** located in the Images group under the INSERT tab.

b. Select Edit Photo Album.

> **TROUBLESHOOTING:** If the list of photos does not display, you have selected the Photo Album button and not the Photo Album arrow.

c. Select **Lima, Peru's Santo Domingo** by placing a check mark in its check box in the **Pictures in album list**.

d. Click **Increase Contrast** (third button from the left) four times.

e. Click **Increase Brightness** (fifth button from the left) twice.

The adjusted image can be viewed in the Preview window. If you had changed brightness only, the image would be washed out.

STEP 3 ›› SET PICTURE LAYOUT

You change the layout of the album pages to four pictures per page. Then, to help identify the location the image was taken from during the trip, you include captions. Refer to Figure 4.48 as you complete Step 3.

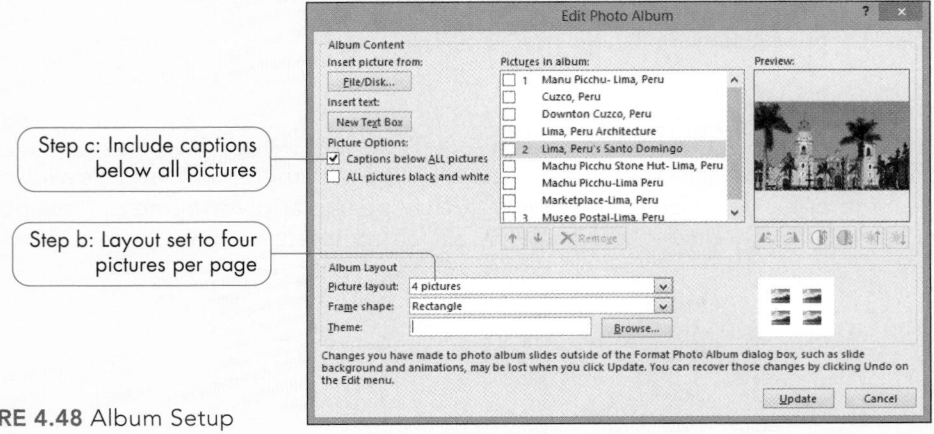

FIGURE 4.48 Album Setup

a. Click the **Picture layout arrow** in the *Album Layout* section of the Photo Album dialog box.

b. Click each of the layouts and view the layout in the Album Layout Preview window on the right (below the larger Album Content Preview window) and select **4 pictures**.

   Clicking *4 pictures* will create an album of four pages—a title page and three pages with pictures.

c. Click the **Captions below ALL pictures check box** in the *Picture Options* section.

   Captions below ALL pictures only becomes available after the layout is selected.

STEP 4 ›› SELECT FRAME SHAPE

You decide to use a simple white frame to enhance the pictures taken during the trips. Refer to Figure 4.49 as you complete Step 4.

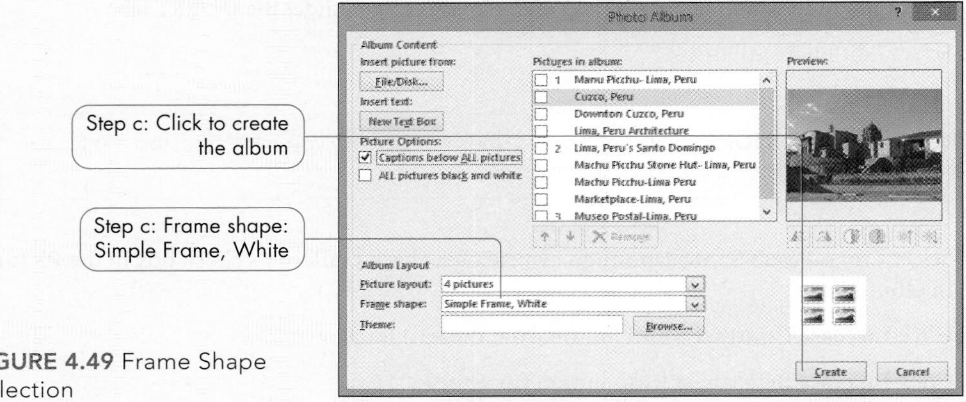

FIGURE 4.49 Frame Shape Selection

a. Click the **Frame shape arrow** in the *Album Layout* section.

b. Select each of the frames and view the layout in the Preview window on the right.

c. Select **Simple Frame, White** and click **Update**.

d. Create a handout header with your name and a handout footer with your instructor's name and your class. Include the current date.

e. On Slide 1, enter your name in the **subtitle placeholder**, if necessary.

f. Save the presentation as **p04h4Album_LastFirst**.

STEP 5 ›› EDIT ALBUM SETTINGS AND APPLY A THEME

You decide to edit your album settings so that you include only one picture per page rather than four. This allows more space for the pictures to show more detail. You also change the frame shape and apply a theme to the album. Finally, you correct one of the captions for an image. Refer to Figure 4.50 as you complete Step 5.

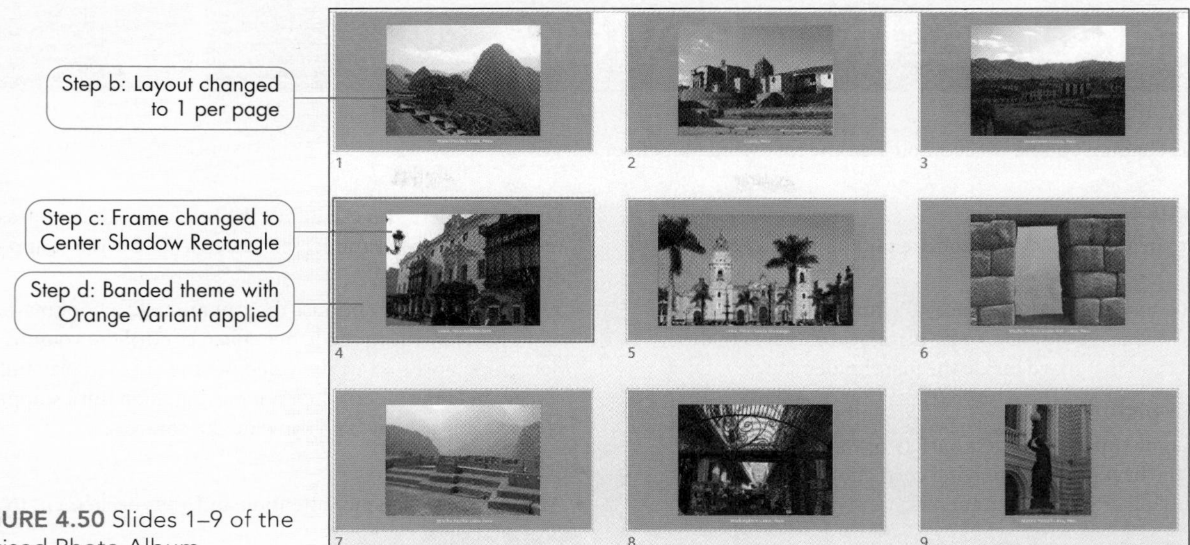

FIGURE 4.50 Slides 1–9 of the Revised Photo Album

a. Click the **INSERT tab**, click the **Photo Album arrow** in the Images group, and then select **Edit Photo Album**.

The Edit Photo Album dialog box opens displaying the current settings, which you may now change.

b. Click the **Picture layout arrow** and select **1 picture**. If necessary, delete any blank slides.

c. Click the **Frame shape arrow** and select **Center Shadow Rectangle**. Click **Update**.

The pictures now display one per page.

d. Click the **DESIGN tab**, apply **Banded theme** in the Themes group, and then click the **Orange Variant** in the Variants group.

e. Click **Slide 4**. Edit the text box to correct the spelling of *Downtown*.

The text box caption below the image has been corrected, since the picture file name was misspelled.

f. Save and close the file and submit based on your instructor's directions.

Chapter Objectives Review

After reading this chapter, you have accomplished the following objectives:

1. **Insert a picture.**
   - Pictures are in a bitmap format and are photorealistic portrayals.
   - They can be inserted using the Insert Picture option, which centers the image on the slide, or by using placeholders that center and crop the image inside the placeholder.
2. **Transform a picture.**
   - Pictures can be transformed in a variety of ways, including removing the background, applying corrections, changing colors, applying artistic effects and picture styles, and cropping.
   - Remove a background: The Remove Background tool enables you to remove portions of a picture you do not want to keep.
   - Correct a picture: You can enhance a picture by sharpening or softening it, or you can increase or decrease a picture's brightness and contrast.
   - Change picture color: Use the color tools to adjust the saturation and tone of your pictures.
   - Use artistic effects: With artistic effects you can change the appearance of a picture so that it looks like it was created with a marker, as a pencil sketch, and more.
   - Apply picture styles: You can surround your picture with attractive frames, soften the edges of pictures, add shadows to the edges of pictures, apply 3-D effects to pictures, add glossy reflections, and more.
   - Resize or crop a picture: You can resize pictures or crop them to remove unwanted portions of the image.
   - Compress pictures: Pictures can be compressed to save file storage space.
   - Create a background from a picture: Pictures can make appealing backgrounds when you adjust the transparency.
3. **Use the Internet as a resource.**
   - The Internet can be extremely valuable when searching for information for a presentation.
   - Understand copyright protection: Although students and teachers have rights under the Fair Use Act, care should be taken to honor all copyrights.
   - Before inserting any information or clips into your slide show, research the copyright ownership.
   - To be safe, contact the Web site owner and request permission to use the material.
   - Any information used should be credited and include hyperlinks when possible, although attribution does not relieve you of the requirement to honor copyrights.
4. **Add video.**
   - You can insert video located on your hard drive or storage device or YouTube, or embed HTML coding from an online site.
5. **Use Video Tools.**
   - PowerPoint includes video editing tools.
   - Format a video: You can adjust the brightness and contrast, recolor, set a poster frame, select a style, and arrange and size a video.
   - Set video playback options: You can also add a bookmark, trim, set a fade in and fade out effect, control the volume, determine how to start the video, set the video to play full screen, hide the video when not playing, loop until stopped, rewind after playing, and show media controls.
6. **Add audio.**
   - Audio catches audience attention and adds excitement to a presentation.
   - Take care when adding sound that it enhances your message rather than detracts from it.
   - Insert audio from a file: PowerPoint supports many different audio file formats that enable you to include sounds with your presentation.
   - Add audio from Office.com clip art: Office.com provides a number of short, royalty-free sounds.
   - Record and insert audio: You may find it helpful to add recorded audio to a slide show by using narration (spoken commentary).
7. **Change audio settings.**
   - Animate an audio sequence: You can also add a bookmark, trim, set a fade in and fade out effect, control the volume, and determine how to start audio.
   - You can hide the speaker icon when not playing, loop until stopped, rewind after playing, and show media controls.
   - Play a sound over multiple slides: By default, audio plays during one slide and stops when you advance to a new slide, but it can be set to play over multiple slides.
8. **Create a Photo Album.**
   - When you have multiple images to be inserted, using the Photo Album feature enables you to quickly insert the images into a slide show.
   - After identifying the images you want to use, you can rearrange the order of the pictures in the album.
   - You also can choose among layouts for the best appearance.
9. **Set Photo Album options.**
   - Select pictures and set the picture order: PowerPoint enables you to determine the order of pictures in the album.
   - Album options for contrast and brightness enable you to make image changes without having to leave the Photo Album dialog box.
   - In addition to adjusting contrast and brightness, you can change the pictures to black and white.
   - Insert captions: File names can be turned into captions for the pictures.
   - Set an album layout: A frame shape can be selected and a theme applied to complete the album appearance.

Key Terms Matching

Match the key terms with their definitions. Write the key term letter by the appropriate numbered definition.

a. Background
b. Bitmap image
c. Brightness
d. Compression
e. Contrast
f. Copyright
g. Cropping
h. Embed
i. Foreground
j. Link
k. Multimedia
l. Narration
m. Photo Album
n. Poster frame
o. Public domain
p. Recolor
q. Saturation
r. Sharpening
s. Softening
t. Tone

1. ______ An image created by bits or pixels placed on a grid to form a picture. **p. 1008**
2. ______ Spoken commentary that is added to a presentation. **p. 1042**
3. ______ Process of changing picture colors to a new temperature. **p. 1016**
4. ______ Temperature of a color. **p. 1015**
5. ______ The intensity of a color. **p. 1014**
6. ______ Enhances the edges of the content in a picture to make the boundaries more prominent. **p. 1012**
7. ______ Legal protection afforded to a written or artistic work. **p. 1022**
8. ______ To store an object from an external source within a presentation. **p. 1031**
9. ______ The difference between the darkest and lightest areas of a picture. **p. 1013**
10. ______ The process of eliminating any unwanted portions of an image. **p. 1018**
11. ______ The rights to a literary work or property owned by the public at large. **p. 1022**
12. ______ Method applied to data to reduce the amount of space required for file storage. **p. 1008**
13. ______ The portion of the picture that is kept, which is also the main subject of the picture. **p. 1011**
14. ______ Multiple forms of media used to entertain or inform an audience. **p. 1008**
15. ______ Presentation containing multiple pictures organized into album pages. **p. 1049**
16. ______ The portion of a picture that is removed because it is not desired in the picture. **p. 1011**
17. ______ A connection from the presentation to another location such as a storage device or Web site. **p. 1031**
18. ______ The frame that displays on a slide when a video is not playing. **p. 1034**
19. ______ Blurs the edges of the content in a picture to make the boundaries less prominent. **p. 1012**
20. ______ The lightness or darkness of a picture. **p. 1013**

Multiple Choice

1. Which of the following file formats supports transparent backgrounds, is limited to 256 colors, and is effective for scanned images such as illustrations rather than color photographs?
   (a) .bmp
   (b) .jpg
   (c) .gif
   (d) .tiff

2. Which of the following is *not* permitted for a student project containing copyrighted material?
   (a) The student markets the project on a personal Web site.
   (b) Only a portion of copyrighted material is used, and the portion was determined by the type of media used.
   (c) The student receives permission to use copyrighted material to be distributed to classmates in the project.
   (d) The educational project is produced for a specific class and then retained in a personal portfolio for display in a job interview.

3. Which of the following Picture Tools would help you manage large image files by permanently deleting any cropped areas of a selected picture and by changing the resolution of the pictures?
   (a) Brightness
   (b) Contrast
   (c) Recolor
   (d) Compress Pictures

4. Which of the following picture adjustments is *not* found in the corrections tools?
   (a) Sharpness
   (b) Contrast
   (c) Tone
   (d) Soften

5. Which of the following stores sound and moving pictures in Microsoft Resource Interchange File Format (RIFF)?
   (a) .gif
   (b) .wmv
   (c) .avi
   (d) .bmp

6. All of the following can be used to play a selected sound clip for preview *except*:
   (a) Click Play/Pause on the Media Controls bar.
   (b) Click Play in the Preview group on the Audio Tools Playback tab.
   (c) Click the blue bar on the right side of the clip in the Insert Audio dialog box and select Preview/Properties.
   (d) Click Play in the Preview group on the Audio Tools Playback tab.

7. Which of the following is a *false* statement regarding recording a narration?
   (a) Narrations cannot be paused during recording.
   (b) You can pause and resume recording during the process.
   (c) PowerPoint records the amount of time it takes you to narrate each slide.
   (d) Voice narration takes precedence over any other sounds during playback.

8. The Photo Album dialog box enables you to make all of the following edits to pictures *except*:
   (a) Rotate.
   (b) Contrast.
   (c) Crop.
   (d) Brightness.

9. Which of the following formatting options is *not* available for video?
   (a) Brightness
   (b) Cropping
   (c) Background Removal
   (d) Soft Edges

10. Audio Playback tools enable you to do all of the following *except*:
    (a) Add a bookmark.
    (b) Fade the audio in.
    (c) Rewind after playing.
    (d) Apply an artistic effect.

Practice Exercises

1 Geocaching Slide Show

The slide show in Figure 4.51 is designed to be used with a presentation introducing a group to the sport of geocaching. Geocaching became a new sport on May 2, 2000, when 24 satellites around the globe stopped the intentional degradation of GPS signals. On May 3, Dave Ulmer hid a bucket of trinkets in the woods outside Portland, Oregon, and the sport was born! It continues to grow at remarkable speed. Your geocaching presentation is designed to teach the basics of taking something, leaving something, and signing the logbook. This exercise follows the same set of skills as used in Hands-On Exercises 1 and 3 in the chapter. Refer to Figure 4.51 as you complete this exercise.

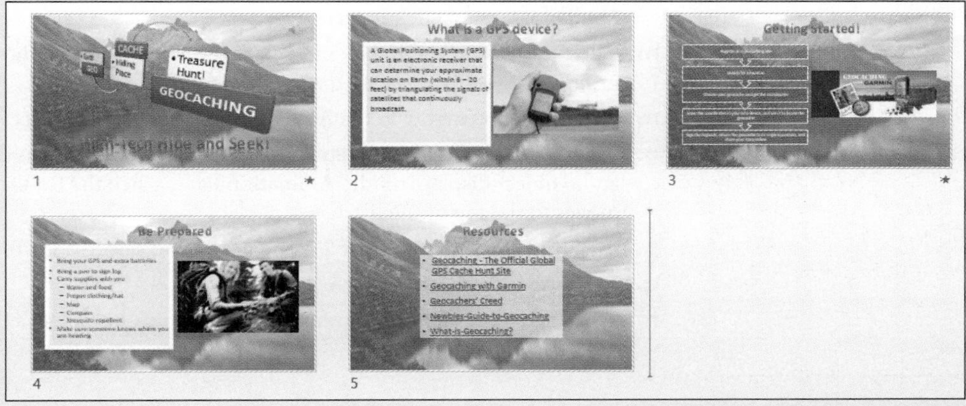

FIGURE 4.51 Geocaching Slide Show

a. Open the *p04p1Cache* slide show and save it as **p04p1Cache_LastFirst**.

b. Create a handout header with your name and a handout footer with your instructor's name and your class. Include the current date.

c. Click the **DESIGN tab** in any slide and click **Format Background** in the Customize group to open the Format Background task pane.

d. Click **Picture or texture fill**, click **Online...**, type **mountain lake** in the **Office.com Clip Art search box**, and press **Enter**. Select the photo shown in the background of Figure 4.51 (or a similar photo) and click **Insert**. Drag the **Transparency slider** to 30% or type **30** in the **Transparency box**. Click **Apply to All** and click **Close** to close the Format Background task pane.

e. Click **Slide 2**. Click the **Pictures button** in the right placeholder. In the *p04p1Cache_Media* folder, click and examine the **p04p1gps picture**. Click **Insert** and examine the image on Slide 2 and note the resizing of the placeholder to keep the image in proportion.

f. Click **Color** in the Adjust group and change the **Color Saturation** to **0%**.

g. Click the border of the text box on the left side of the slide, click the **HOME tab**, click **Format Painter** in the Clipboard group, and then click the **gps picture**.

h. Open your browser and type **garminuk.geocaching.com** in the address bar to open the *Geocaching with Garmin* Web site. Right-click **Geocaching with Garmin** and select **Save background as**. Save the image as **p04p1garminlogo** (used with permission) to your student data folder for this chapter. Close your browser.

> **TROUBLESHOOTING:** The Save Background As option is available in Internet Explorer. If you are using Firefox, click View Background Image and right-click and save the image. If you are using another browser, right-click the image and select the appropriate option from the menu.

i. Click **Slide 3**. Click the **Pictures button** in the placeholder on the right. Locate the *p04p1garmin-logo* image and click **Insert**.
j. Click **Slide 4**. Click the picture of the geocachers and click the **FORMAT tab**. Click **Artistic Effects** in the Adjust group and select **Paint Strokes**.
k. Click **Slide 1**. If you are able to record narration in your computer lab, click the **INSERT tab**, click the **Audio arrow** in the Media group, and then select **Record Audio**. Click the red **Record Sound button** and read the Speaker Note at the bottom of Slide 1. When finished reading, click the blue **Stop button** and click **OK**. If you are not able to record narration, proceed to step l.
l. If you are not able to record narration in your computer lab, click **Insert**, click the **Audio arrow** in the Media group, and then select **Audio on My PC**. Locate *p04p1Narration* in the p04p1Cache_Media folder and click **Insert**.
m. Click the **PLAYBACK tab** and select the **Hide During Show check box** in the Audio Options group. Drag the audio icon to the top right of the slide.
n. Click the **Start arrow** in the Audio Options group and select **Automatically**.
o. Click the **ANIMATIONS tab** and click **Animation Pane** in the Advanced Animation group. The audio object displays on the Animation Pane. Click the **Re-Order up arrow** until the sound object moves to the top of the list.
p. Click the **Start arrow** in the Timing group and select **With Previous**. Close the Animation Pane.
q. View the slide show.
r. Save and close the file and submit based on your instructor's directions.

2 Geocaching Album

FROM SCRATCH

Geocachers are asked to share their geocaching experience in the geocache logbook. The *Geocaching—The Official Global GPS Cache Hunt Site* includes some easy steps for logging a geocache find and even enables you to upload a photo with your log entry. Often, geocachers also put their geocaching stories, photos, and videos online in the form of slide shows using a variety of software packages. In this exercise, you create a geocache slide show quickly and easily using the PowerPoint Photo Album feature and add video and text to the slide show. This exercise follows the same set of skills as used in Hands-On Exercises 2 and 4 in the chapter. Refer to Figure 4.52 as you complete this exercise.

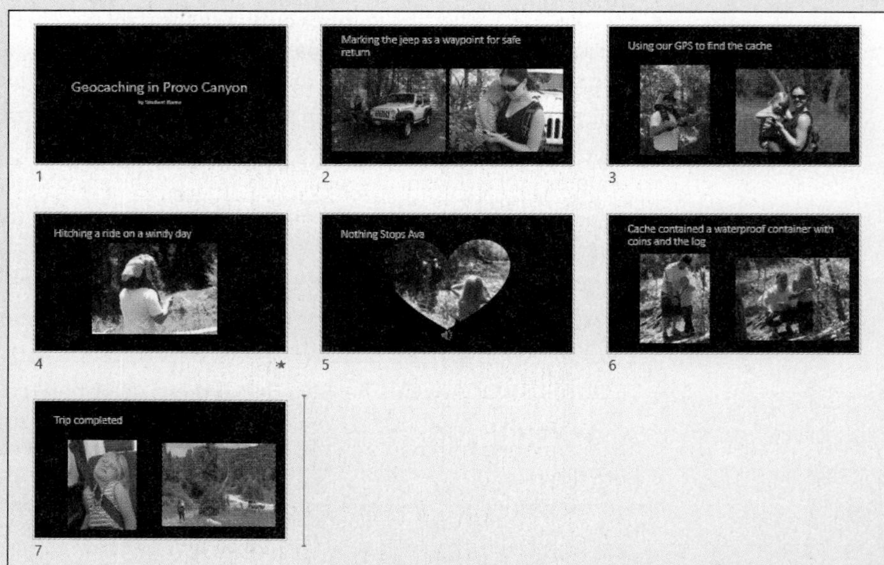

FIGURE 4.52 Geocaching Album

a. Open a new blank presentation. Click the **INSERT tab** and click **Photo Album** in the Images group.

b. Click **File/Disk** in the *Insert picture from* section, open the p04p2Geo_Media folder, click one of the files, and then press **Ctrl+A** to select all pictures in the folder. Click **Insert**.

c. Select *p04p2Img3* in the *Pictures in album* section and click **Rotate Right** (second option from the left). Repeat to rotate *p04p2Img5* and *p04p2Img8* to the right.

d. Click the **Picture layout arrow** in the *Album Layout* section and select **2 pictures with title**.

e. Click the **Frame shape arrow** in the *Album Layout* section and select **Center Shadow Rectangle**.

f. Click **Create** and save the album as **p04p2Geo_LastFirst**.

g. Create a handout header with your name and a handout footer with your instructor's name and your class. Include the current date.

h. Click **Slide 1**, if necessary. Change the title to **Geocaching in Provo Canyon**. Change the subtitle to include your name, if necessary.

i. Click the **DESIGN tab**, click the **More button** in the Themes group, and then click the **Office Theme Dark theme**.

j. Enter the following slide titles:

Slide 2	Marking the jeep as a waypoint for safe return
Slide 3	Using our GPS to find the cache
Slide 4	Cache contained a waterproof container with coins and the log
Slide 5	Trip completed

k. Click **Slide 3**. Click the **HOME tab**, click the **New Slide arrow**, and then select **Title Only**. Change the title of the slide to **Hitching a ride on a windy day**.

l. Click the **Insert tab**, click the **Video arrow** in the Media group, and then select **Video on My PC**. Click *p04p2Vid1* from the p04p2Geo_Media folder and click **Insert**.

m. Click the **PLAYBACK tab** and click **Trim Video** in the Editing group. Type **00:17.491** in the **Start Time box** and click **Play**. Type **00:22.337** in the **End Time box** and click **OK**.

n. Type **00.01** in the **Fade Out box** in the Editing group.

o. Click the **Start arrow** in the Video Options group and select **Automatically**.

p. Click the **FORMAT tab** and move to the video frame at 4.75 seconds. Click **Poster Frame** in the Adjust group and select **Current Frame**.

q. Insert a new Title Only slide, change the title to **Nothing Stops Ava**, and then insert *p04p2Vid2* from the p04p2Geo_Media folder.

r. Click the **PLAYBACK tab** and click **Move Forward 0.25 Seconds** on the Media Controls bar to advance the video to the frame at 14 seconds. Click **Add Bookmark** in the Bookmarks group.

s. Click the **FORMAT tab**, click **Video Shape** in the Video Styles group, and then click **Heart** in the Basic Shapes gallery.

t. Click **Slide 7**, click the **INSERT tab**, click **Audio** in the Media group, and then click **Online Audio**. Type the keyword **lullaby**, and press **Enter**. Click the **Music Box Melody**. Click **Insert**.

u. Drag the audio icon to the bottom of the screen.

v. Select one of the images in your album, click the **FORMAT tab**, click **Compress Pictures** in the Adjust group, and then click the **Apply only to this picture check box** to deselect it. Click **OK**.

w. View the slide show. On Slide 5, point to the Media Controls bar, click the bookmark, and then click **Play** to begin the video at the bookmark site.

x. Save and close the file and submit based on your instructor's directions.

3 Accident Record

You are involved in an accident on your bullet bike on the way to school one morning. You take pictures with your cell phone to keep a record of the damage to send to your insurance agent. You decide the quickest way to assemble the photographs is to create a Photo Album that is suitable for sending by e-mail. You then edit the Photo Album to include a text box so that you have a location in which to enter the accident details. This exercise follows the same set of skills as used in Hands-On Exercises 1 and 4 in the chapter. Refer to Figure 4.53 as you complete this exercise.

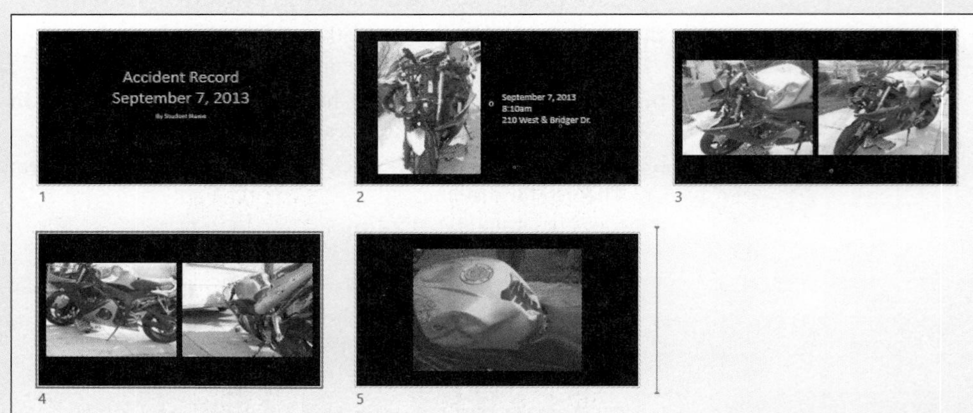

FIGURE 4.53 Accident Record Compressed for E-Mail

a. Open a blank presentation document, click the **INSERT tab**, and then click **Photo Album** in the Images group.

b. Click **File/Disk**, navigate to the p04p3Accident_Media folder, press **Ctrl+A**, and then click **Insert**.

c. Click **Create** to create the album and save the album as **p04p3Accident_LastFirst**.

d. Review the slides and note that each picture is placed on its own slide, that the photograph is dark in Slide 6, and that the photograph of the bullet bike is sideways in Slide 7.

e. Click the **INSERT tab**, click the **Photo Album arrow**, and then select **Edit Photo Album**.

f. Select the **p04p3Accident6 picture** and click the **Move up arrow** to reposition it so that it is the first picture in the *Pictures in album* list.

g. Click the **Rotate left button** once to rotate the picture so that the bullet bike is upright.

h. With *p04p3Accident6* still selected, click **New Text Box**.

i. Select **p04p3Accident5**, click the **Increase Contrast button** five times, and then click the **Increase Brightness button** seven times.

j. Click the **Picture layout arrow** in the *Album Layout* section and click **2 pictures**.

k. Click the **Frame shape arrow** in the *Album Layout* section and select **Center Shadow Rectangle**.

l. Click **Update**.

m. Create a handout header with your name and a handout footer with your instructor's name and your class. Include the current date.

n. Move to Slide 1 and change the Photo Album title to **Accident Record** on one line and **September 7, 2016** on the following line. Change the subtitle to include your name, if necessary.

o. Move to Slide 2, select the words *Text Box*, and then type the following information:
   - **September 7, 2016**
   - **8:10 a.m.**
   - **210 West & Bridger Dr.**

p. Select the image on Slide 5 and click the **FORMAT tab**. Change the height to **6"** in the Size group. The width automatically adjusts to 8".

q. Click **Align** in the Arrange group and click **Align Center**. Click **Align** in the Arrange group again and click **Align Middle**.

r. With the image still selected, click **Compress Pictures** in the Adjust group and deselect the **Apply only to this picture check box** so all pictures in the album will be compressed.

s. Click **E-mail** in the *Target output* section and click **OK**.

t. Spell check the presentation. Save and close the file and submit based on your instructor's directions.

Mid-Level Exercises

1 ATV for Sale

FROM SCRATCH

You have enjoyed riding your four wheeler ATV but now decide that you want to sell it to purchase a snowmobile. Using PowerPoint, you create a flyer advertising the four wheeler that you can reproduce to hang on bulletin boards at the college. Refer to Figure 4.54 as you complete this exercise.

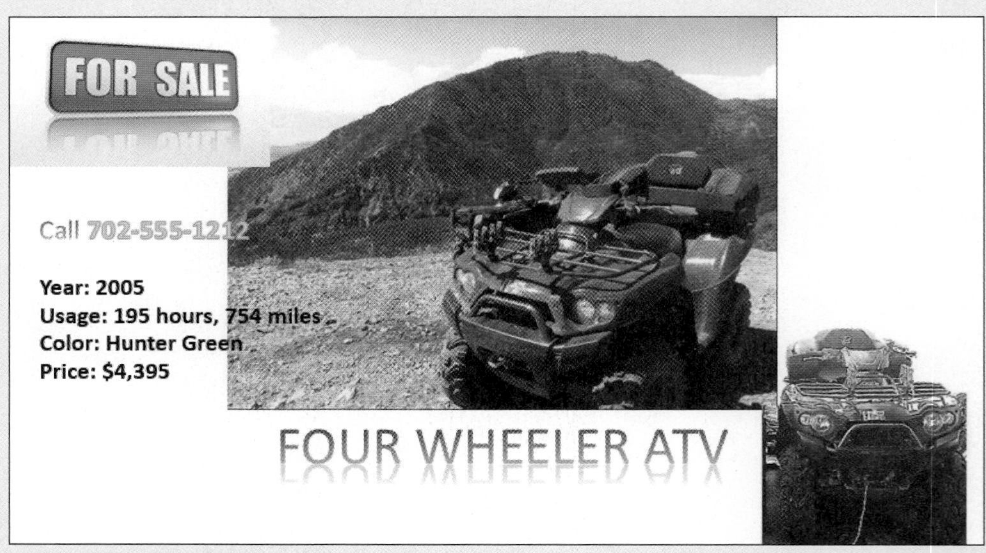

FIGURE 4.54 ATV Sales Flyer

a. Open a blank presentation and save it as **p04m1Flyer_LastFirst**.
b. Create a handout header with your name and a handout footer with your instructor's name and your class. Include the current date.
c. Change the layout to **Blank layout**.
d. Insert the *p04m1Atv1* image located in your student files in the p04m1Flyer_Media folder. Drag the image so that it aligns with the top edge of the page.
e. Insert a WordArt object in the Text group by clicking the **INSERT tab**, clicking **WordArt, Gradient Fill - Gray** (second row, first column), and then typing **FOUR WHEELER ATV**. Apply the Text Effect **Tight Reflection, touching** (first row, first column under *Reflection Variations*).
f. Center the text below the picture.
g. Click the **INSERT tab**, click **Online Pictures** to locate the *For Sale* sign shown in Figure 4.54, and then insert the image.
h. Change the scale of the *For Sale* image to 75% of its original size. Position the *For Sale* sign in the top-left corner.
i. Create a text box and type **Call 702-555-1212**. Apply a WordArt Style to the text using the FORMAT tab: **WordArt Fill - Orange, Accent 2, Outline - Accent 2** (first row, third column). Change the font size to **28 pt**.
j. Insert the *p04m1Atv2* image located in your student files in the p04m1Flyer_Media folder. Drag the image so that the image borders align with the bottom-right corner of the flyer.
k. Adjust the sharpness of the image to +**50%**. Adjust the brightness and contrast to **Brightness: +40% Contrast: +40%**.
l. Create a text box and type the following information inside it:

   Year: 2005

   Usage: 195 hours, 754 miles

   Color: Hunter Green

   Price: $4,395

m. Change the font size of the text box to **24 pt**. Position the text box below the *Call 702-555-1212* text.

n. Compress all the photographs on the flyer.

o. Spell check the presentation. Save and close the file and submit based on your instructor's directions.

2 Impressionist Paintings

CREATIVE CASE 

In this exercise, you will use the Internet to obtain images of paintings by some of the masters of the Impressionist style. The paintings may be viewed at the Web Museum (www.ibiblio.org/wm/paint) that is maintained by Nicolas Pioch for academic and educational use. On the Famous Artworks exhibition page, click the Impressionism Theme (or search for Impressionist paintings or painters).

a. Open the *p04m2Painting* presentation and save it as **p04m2Painting _LastFirst**.

b. Create a handout header with your name and a handout footer with your instructor's name and your class. Include the current date. On Slide 1, change the subtitle *First Name Last Name* to your name.

c. View the slide show and click the hyperlink to *The Web Museum* on Slide 1 to open the Famous Artworks exhibition. Locate the images you will copy and paste into the slide show.

d. When you locate a painting, click the thumbnail image to enlarge it, then right-click it and save the image to a new folder on your storage device named **Impressionist Paintings**. If necessary, change the name of the file to include the artist and the name of the painting. Repeat this process until you have saved each of the images of the paintings shown in the table below and close the browser.

Slide #	Artist	Title
Slide 1	Alfred Sisley	*Autumn: Banks of the Seine near Bougival*
Slide 2	Claude Monet	*Impression: soleil levant*
Slide 4	Edgar Degas	*Ballet Rehearsal*
Slide 5	Claude Monet	*Waterlilies, Green Reflection, Left Part*
Slide 6	Berthe Morisot	*The Artist's Sister at a Window*
Slide 7	Pierre-Auguste Renoir	*On the Terrace*

e. Return to your slide show. Insert the picture for Slide 1 as a background and insert each of the remaining pictures on the appropriate artist's slide. Resize and position the images as needed. Use picture styles. You do not need to compress the images, as they are already low resolution.

f. Change the font on the Slide 1 Subtitle Placeholder to **White Bold**.

g. Insert an audio clip of your choice in Slide 1. As an alternative to providing your own audio clip, search for the keyword **classical** in the Insert Audio dialog box. Find *Nocturne in Es-Dur* in the search results and insert it in Slide 1.

h. Position the audio icon on the slide and hide it during show. Loop the audio clip and set the song so it plays continuously across slides and does not stop with the next mouse click.

i. Insert a blank slide after Slide 7. Search the Web for a video clip on Impressionist art, copy the embed code for the video, and then insert the embed code in PowerPoint. Apply a **Video Style** and choose other video settings as desired.

j. Spell check the presentation. Save and close the file and submit based on your instructor's directions.

3 Red Butte Garden

You visited Red Butte Garden, a part of the University of Utah, and enjoyed the natural gardens and the botanical garden. You want to create a Photo Album of the pictures you took that day.

a. Create a new Photo Album and insert all of the pictures in the p04m3Garden_Media folder.
b. Remove the *p04m3Img1* (Red Butte Garden & Arboretum) picture.
c. Locate *p04m3Img2*, increase the brightness six times, and then increase the contrast twice.
d. Locate *p04m3Img14*, increase the brightness twice, and then increase the contrast six times.
e. Apply a **2 pictures layout** and the **Simple Frame, White frame** shape style.
f. Create the album and save it as **p04m3Garden_LastFirst**.
g. Create a handout header with your name and a handout footer with your instructor's name and your class. Include the current date.
h. Edit the album so only one picture per page displays and click **Update**.
i. Insert *p04m3Img1* as the background for Slide 1 and remove the title and subtitle placeholders.
j. Move Slide 2 to the end of the slide show and apply the **Paint Brush Artistic Effect**.
k. Click **Slide 14**. Apply a **Sharpen: 50% correction**.
l. Apply the **Reveal transition** on any slide and set the advance to automatically advance after **00:02:00**. Apply to all slides.
m. Save and close the file and submit based on your instructor's directions.

4 Collaborating on a Group Project

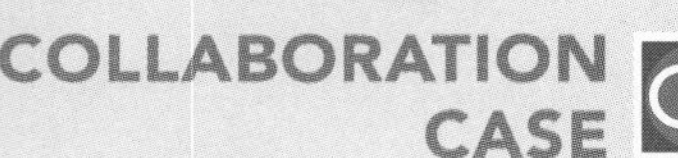

In this exercise, you will collaborate with two to three students from your class to create a PowerPoint presentation advertising a product. Your group will determine the product you want to sell. Be inventive! Find an existing product that you can use as a prop to represent your new product (see example in second paragraph). Create a storyboard for that product and use a digital camera or cell phone to capture images for the product. You will upload your version of the pictures to a location all team members can access, such as a OneDrive account. You will then view your team's pictures, download the ones you want to use, and create a presentation based on the storyboard—each group member prepares his or her own storyboard and presentation. Only the images are shared. You will insert the images you want to use in the slides. You will edit the images as needed. You will create a final slide that lists all of the team members in your group. Finally, you will upload your version of the presentation to your Web site and blog about your experience.

For example, after talking using chat technology, a group decides to use green mouthwash as their product. But rather than have it represent mouthwash, they are going to use it as a "brain enhancer." They create a storyboard that lists Slide 1 as a Title and Content slide using the image of the mouthwash and the name of the product—Brain ++. For the second slide, they decide to illustrate the problem by having a picture of a person holding a test paper with the grade F plainly visible. For the third slide, they decide to illustrate the solution by having the same person pretending to drink the Brain ++. The fourth slide demonstrates the result by showing the same person holding a test paper with the grade A plainly visible. The last slide lists all members of the group. Note: This exercise assumes you have done the Collaboration exercise for Chapter 1. If you have not completed that exercise, use OneDrive.com or another method for sharing your presentation with your instructor and classmates.

a. Create a group with two to three class members and exchange contact information so you will be able to message each other. For example, have each member create a Microsoft account, a Yahoo! account, a Facebook account, or use Oovoo or some other text or video chat technology.
b. Determine, as a group, the product you will be advertising and its use. Discuss the story line for your product with the group, then each member should create a storyboard.

c. Each member should use a digital camera or cell phone to take pictures of the product.
d. Upload your images to OneDrive, which will allow all group members to access the pictures.
e. View all of the images your group uploaded, determine which ones you want to use in your presentation, and then download those images.
f. Create a PowerPoint presentation and insert the product images into slides following the storyboard you created. Edit the slides and images as needed. Enhance slides as desired.
g. Save the completed presentation as **p04m4Product_GroupName** to OneDrive.
h. Create a blog posting about this experience, or write an essay using Microsoft Word. Was collaborating with others through a chat tool a good experience or was it difficult? What did you like about the experience? How could it have been improved? How easily did your group reach agreement on your product?
i. If you stored your presentation on OneDrive, share the folder with your instructor so he or she can download and view the presentation.

Beyond the Classroom

Zeroscaping Versus Xeriscaping

RESEARCH CASE

While on a trip through the Southwest, you took pictures of zeroscaping examples. You plan to use them in an existing slide show on waterwise landscaping. You want to know more about xeriscaping, however, so you research xeriscaping online. One site, XericUtah (xericutah.com), has beautiful images of xeriscaping, so you contact them and receive permission to use images from their Web site.

Open *p04b2Landscape* and save it as **p04b2Landscape_LastFirst**. Add a handout header with your name and a handout footer with your instructor's name and your class. Include the current date. Research zeroscaping and xeriscaping online and include the Web sites on a Resources slide at the end of the slide show. Please remember that giving credit to your source does not mean you are released from copyright requirements. Create several speaker notes with information you find during your research. Use the zeroscaping images located in the p04b2Landscape_Media folder where appropriate, but visit xericutah.com to obtain images for the xeriscaping portion of the slide show. Use a xeriscaping picture for the background of the Title slide. You may change the template and add animations as desired. Add an audio clip and set it to play across all slides. Insert a related video on its own slide. Save and close the file and submit based on your instructor's directions.

Cascade Springs Ecosystem

DISASTER RECOVERY

You and another fifth-grade teacher are working together to create slide shows for your science students. The other teacher visited Cascade Springs, took pictures, and created a PowerPoint Photo Album of the pictures. Open *p04b3Springs* and save the new presentation as **p04b3Springs_LastFirst**. Review the album and read the speaker notes created from National Forest Service signs available to hikers to help them understand the fragile ecosystem. Your role is to review the presentation created by the album and determine which slides and speaker notes to keep. When necessary, rotate images. You may also change the template or slides as desired. If it is possible to record narration in your classroom lab, read and record shortened versions of at least three speaker notes and add the audio files to the slides. If you are unable to record the narration, insert the audio files in the p04b3Springs_Media folder in appropriate locations. Set the audio files to play when the sound icon is clicked. This allows a teacher to determine if he or she wants to use recordings during the presentation or lecture himself or herself. Finalize the presentation by proofreading, applying transitions and animations, and testing sound icons to ensure they work properly. Compress all images to Screen Target Output. Finally, create a handout header with your name and a handout footer with your instructor's name and your class. Include the current date. Save the album and submit as directed by your instructor.

Dress for Success

SOFT SKILLS CASE S

FROM SCRATCH

First impressions are important when job hunting, so it is essential to dress professionally. Professions and companies vary, but following a basic set of rules will ensure that you make a good impression. Watch the Soft Skills Dress for Success Video on myITlab or as provided by your instructor. Create a PowerPoint presentation with photos to demonstrate the dos and don'ts. You may choose to create your presentation for either men, women, or both combined. Apply several of the photo-editing techniques discussed in the chapter to the photos. Indicate your modifications in the speaker notes on each slide. Locate a video to coincide with this topic and insert the video on its own slide. Add a handout header with your name and a handout footer with your instructor's name and your class. Include the current date. Be sure to include the Web sites on a Resources slide at the end of the slide show. Please remember that giving credit to your source does not mean you are released from copyright requirements. Finalize the presentation by proofreading, applying transitions and animations, and testing sound icons to ensure they work properly. Compress all images to Screen Target Output. Save the presentation as **p04b4Dress_LastFirst** and submit as directed by your instructor.

Capstone Exercise

Your parents recently visited Washington, DC. You volunteer to create a slide show that they can e-mail to family and friends. You use a modified version of Microsoft's Contemporary Photo Album template. The album has been modified to use a Green theme. In this activity, you will create the content, insert the photos, modify the photos, add sound, and insert a video clip of the soldier in Arlington. All media for this activity are located in the p04c1DC_Media folder.

Insert Pictures

Using template layouts and picture placeholders, you insert photos of the city. You modify template placeholders for better fit.

a. Open the file named *p04c1DC* and save it as **p04c1DC_LastFirst**.

b. Create a handout header with your name and a handout footer with your instructor's name and your class. Include the current date.

c. Click **Slide 1**, if necessary. Locate the p04c1DC_Media folder and insert *p04c1DC1* into the picture placeholder.

d. Change the subtitle to your first and last name.

e. Click **Slide 2** and insert *p04c1DC2*. Replace the caption *Click to add title* with **World War II Memorial**.

f. Click **Slide 3**. Insert *p04c1DC3* in the picture placeholder and replace the caption Click to add text with **The Capitol Building**.

g. Crop out the vehicles in the bottom of the photo of the Capitol building. Reposition the photo as needed.

h. Click **Slide 4**. Change the layout to **Left Two Pictures with Caption**.

i. Replace the text in the title placeholder with **Washington Monument and Lincoln Memorial** and delete the subtitle placeholder. Insert *p04c1DC4* in the left picture placeholder and insert *p04c1DC5* in the right placeholder.

j. Click **Slide 5**. Replace the text in the caption placeholder with **Arlington National Cemetery**. Insert *p04c1DC6* in the top-left picture placeholder, insert *p04c1DC7* in the top-right placeholder, insert *p04c1DC8* in the bottom-left placeholder, and then insert *p04c1DC9* in the bottom-right placeholder.

k. View and save the presentation.

Apply and Modify a Picture Style, Change Images

The pictures on Slides 1 and 4 would stand out better if they had a frame. You apply and modify a Picture Style.

a. Click **Slide 4**. Select the left picture and apply the **Metal Oval picture style**.

b. Apply the **Preset 5 Picture Effect** to the left picture (second row, first column).

c. Use the Format Painter to copy the effects applied to the left photo and apply them to the photo on the right.

d. Click **Slide 1** and select the picture. Apply the **Rotated, White picture style** and apply the **Watercolor Sponge artistic effect**.

e. Save the presentation.

Adjust and Compress Images

Some pictures on Slide 5 need the brightness, contrast, and color tones adjusted. You use Picture Tools to adjust the pictures, and you apply an e-mail compression to all photographs.

a. Click **Slide 5**, select the bottom-left picture, and then increase the image brightness **+20%**.

b. Select the top-left picture, set the saturation to **200%**, and then set the color tone to **7200 K**.

c. Compress all images for e-mail output.

d. Save the presentation.

Insert a Video and Add Sound

You insert a video clip of the changing of the guard for the Tomb of the Unknown Soldier and modify the settings. Finally, you add a soft music clip that plays continuously through all slides.

a. Click **Slide 6**. Add the title text **Changing of the Guard**. Center the text.

b. Search for and insert a YouTube video showing the changing of the guard at Arlington National Cemetery. Resize the video to a height of **5"**.

c. Set the video to play automatically.

d. Change the Video Options to **Hide While Not Playing** and to **Rewind after Playing**.

e. Click **Slide 1**. Search for an audio clip using **yankee doodle** as the keyword for your search.

f. Insert *Yankee Doodle 2* on Slide 1 and have it **Play across Slides** and start **Automatically**.

g. Hide the audio icon during the show.

h. Spell check the presentation. Save and close the file and submit based on your instructor's directions.

Create a Photo Album

Your friend asks you for a printed copy of all of the images. You prepare a photo album and print it.

a. Create a New Photo Album using the images in the p04c1DC_Media folder.

- **b.** Rearrange the pictures so they appear in the following order: DC1, DC3, DC2, and then the remaining pictures in numerical order.
- **c.** Create the album using two pictures per slide and a **Simple Frame, White frame shape**.
- **d.** Save the album as **p04c1Washington_LastFirst**.
- **e.** Delete the last slide.
- **f.** Create a handout header with your name and a handout footer with your instructor's name and your class. Include the current date.
- **g.** Apply *DC1* at 50% transparency as the background image for the title slide.
- **h.** Modify the title on the Title Slide to **Washington Sights** and type your name in the subtitle. Change the text color to **Black**. Bold the text.
- **i.** Spell check the presentation. Save and close the file and submit based on your instructor's directions.

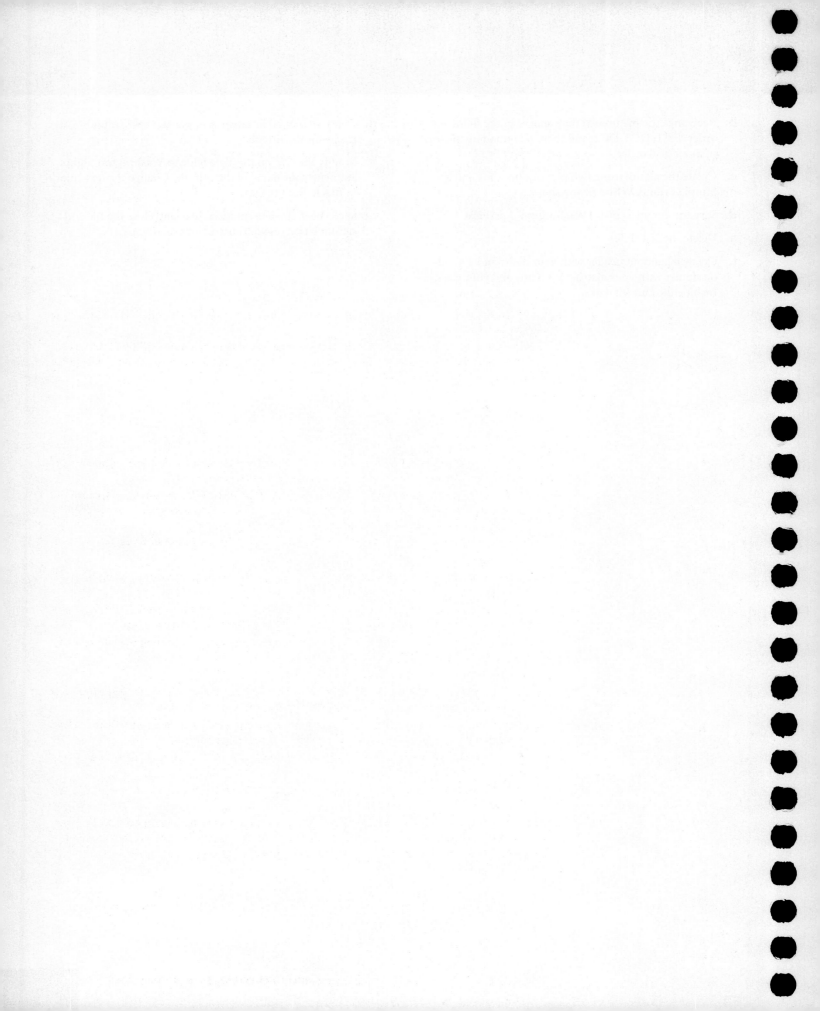

Word Application Capstone Exercise

You are an employee of Calypso Travel Club, which is a timesharing resort management company. Your position requires that you encourage owner participation and promote travel programs. You are also involved with providing new owners with all the information they need to begin planning vacations and taking advantage of club ownership. One of the first things you send each new owner is a Quick Start Guide. You typically create a mailing once each month, with a welcome letter and the Quick Start Guide. You have prepared that material and are ready to merge the document with a database table of new owners. You will format the letter and the Quick Start Guide to produce a mailing that is both attractive and informative.

Review Comments

You will review and respond to comments left by your supervisor.

a. Start Word. Open *w00ac1Travel*. Note: You may notice some spelling errors; you will fix these later in this exercise.

b. Ensure that all of the markup is shown. Track Changes should not be on. You will find three comments on page 2 of the document. Read and act on each comment. There is no need to reply to the comments; just take the action required.

c. Delete all comments in the document.

Format Characters and Paragraphs

You will improve the appearance of the document by adjusting line and paragraph spacing and modifying the font. In addition, bullets will draw attention to selected paragraphs.

a. Select all text from *Welcome to the Club!* on page 2 to the end of the document. (Because the WordArt object is anchored to the first paragraph, it will be selected as well.) Change the line spacing to **1.5** and ensure that paragraph spacing before and after is **0**.

b. With all document text selected, change the font to **Georgia** with a font size of **12 pt**.

c. Add solid round bullets to the following paragraphs:
   - The three paragraphs under the *Flexibility* heading near the end of page 2, beginning with *Experience exotic destinations* and ending with *Bonus Time*.
   - The three paragraphs under the *Convenience* heading at the bottom of page 2 and the top of page 3, beginning with *Automatically receive* and ending with *vacation planning*.
   - The three paragraphs under the *Affordability* heading on page 3, beginning with *Enjoy vacations* and ending with *from your taxes*.

d. Add checkmark bullets to the following paragraphs:
   - The three paragraphs in the *Purchase Points* section on page 3, beginning with *Determine your family's vacation needs* and ending with *A Calypso resort is never far away*.
   - The two paragraphs in the *Plan Your Vacation* section on page 3, beginning with *Choose when, where, and for how long* and ending with *make and cancel reservations*.
   - The two paragraphs near the top of page 4, beginning with *With each reservation* and ending with *as your vacation needs change*.
   - The two paragraphs in the *Take Off!* section on page 4, beginning with *Not only are you entitled* and ending with *Take your pick!*.

e. Apply a hollow round bullet to the first five paragraphs on page 4, beginning with *Make points reservations* and ending with *Access frequently questions*. Indent the five paragraphs with hollow round bullets so they appear as a sublevel of the checkmarked bullets on the previous page.

Review Word Usage

You will check for spelling and grammatical errors, correcting any that are identified. You will also use the thesaurus to identify an alternate word.

a. Use Word's Spelling & Grammar feature to check for spelling and grammatical errors, making any necessary corrections. The word *Your* is used correctly in the document, as is the word *later*.

b. Use Word's Thesaurus to identify an alternate word for *globally* in the fourth paragraph on page 2. Replace *globally* with *worldwide*.

Apply and Modify Styles

Headings are used in the document but are not clearly delineated. You will apply heading styles to the headings and modify a heading style.

a. Apply **Heading 1** style to the following headings, beginning on page 2:

Explore the World with the Leader in Vacation Club Ownership

Vacation Club Points

The Points System

Ready to Begin Your Experience?

b. Apply **Heading 2** style to the following headings, beginning on page 2:

Flexibility

Convenience

Affordability

Purchase Points

Plan Your Vacation

Take Off!

c. Modify the Heading 1 style to include an underline and a font color of **Orange, Accent 2, Darker 25%**. Modify the Heading 2 style to include a font color of **Orange, Accent 2, Darker 25%**.

Insert Features that Improve Readability

You will insert symbols to improve readability. You will also include a page number, adjust margins, and insert a page break.

a. Place the insertion point to the left of the heading *Purchase Points* on page 3. Insert a number 1 symbol from the (normal text) font, character code **2776**. Similarly, insert a number 2 symbol (character code **2777**) at the left of the heading *Plan Your Vacation* heading, and a number 3 symbol (character code **2778**) at the left of the heading *Take Off!*.

b. Replace the hyphen between the words *program* and *Calypso* in the third multiline paragraph on page 2 with an **em dash symbol**.

c. Insert a page number footer, using a center-aligned **Plain Number 2 selection**.

d. Change the margins on all sides to **1"**. Insert a page break before the *The Points System* heading on page 4.

Work with Columns and Section Breaks

You will format sections of the document differently, including a two-column format for some areas and a one-column format for others. In addition, you will add a page border to one section of the document. You will insert section breaks appropriately so that formatting can differ.

a. Place the insertion point after the word *Team* (before the Page Break) at the end of the text on page 1. Add a **Continuous section break** at the location of the insertion point.

b. Click anywhere on page 2 and add a page border. Select a **Box border** with a color of **Orange, Accent 2, Darker 25%**. Apply the border to **This section**. Accept all other default border settings.

c. Select text on pages 5 and 6, beginning with *Destinations Plus* and ending with *Calypso Vacation Services* (before the final line in the document). Format the selection in two columns.

d. Center the final paragraph in the document, beginning with *For more information*.

Insert and Format Graphics

You will modify the WordArt object at the beginning of page 2 so that it coordinates with other elements of the document. You will also insert a graphic in the two-columned section near the end of the document.

a. Select the WordArt object at the top of page 2. Change the font size of the second line in the WordArt object, *Relax with Us*, to **24 pt**. Change the WordArt style to **Fill – Orange, Accent 2, Outline – Accent 2**. Change the WordArt Shape Style to **Colored Fill – Orange, Accent 2**. Apply a Shape Effect of **Bevel, Riblet**. Visually center the WordArt object horizontally, using the green alignment guides to assist.

b. Click to the left of the *Explorer* heading on page 5. Insert an online picture, using **Airplane** as a search term and selecting the picture of a jet in flight titled *Airplane in sunny sky* (also included in your data files). Change the height to **0.8"** and wrap text as **Tight**. Remove the background from the picture, keeping the suggested changes. Drag to position the graphic at the top right corner of the left column, using the green alignment guides to position it in the top-right corner of the column.

Insert Tables

You will create two tables to describe the vacation club points system.

a. Insert a blank paragraph after the *The Points System* section (not the heading, but the paragraph following, ending in *Calypso Points ownership levels*). Insert a 4 × 6 table and populate it as follows:

Calypso Club Points	Purchase Price (one-time)	Maintenance Fees	Annual Club Dues
1,500 points	$11,700	$325	$175
2,500 points	$19,250	$575	$175
3,500 points	$25,300	$785	$175
5,000 points	$30,250	$1,015	$175
6,500 points	$34,890	$1,500	$215

b. Select a table style of **Grid Table 4 – Accent 2**. AutoFit the contents of the table. Center align all dollar amounts in the last three columns.

c. Select the second, third, and fourth columns. Change the properties of the selected columns to include a width of **1.3"**. Insert a column at the right of the Annual Club Dues column and add the column heading **Total Fees and Dues**. Include a formula in the new column for each points level, adding Maintenance Fees and Annual Club Dues. Delete the extra paragraph mark below the table.

d. Click before the last line in the document, beginning with *For More Information*, and press **Enter**. Click before the new blank paragraph, clear all formatting, and then insert a 3 × 4 table. Create the following table, merging all cells in the first row. Bold entries in rows 1 and 2 and center items in columns 2 and 3 (and row 1).

Bonus Time Reservation Window		
	La Sonora and Wailaki	All Other Resorts
Book Online	83 days	36 days
Call Vacation Services	80 days	32 days

e. Shade row 1 with **Orange, Accent 2, Darker 25%**. Shade remaining rows with **Orange, Accent 2, Lighter 40%**. Select the entire table. Select a Pen Color of **Orange, Accent 2, Darker 50%** and apply the color to **Outside Borders**. Select a **double-underline Line Style** and apply it to the border dividing row 1 and row 2. Press **Esc**.

Insert Captions and a Footnote

You will add captions to the two tables and provide additional information in a footnote.

a. Click anywhere in the first table and insert a caption below the table: **Table 1: Calypso Points System**. Insert a caption below the second table: **Table 2: Bonus Time Reservations**.

b. Modify the Caption style to include a font color of **Orange, Accent 2, Darker 25%**.

c. Click after the words *Calypso Club Points* in the top-left cell of Table 1. Insert a footnote: **The examples in this table are for illustrative purposes only. The number of points required for club rentals may change from time to time**. Save as **w00ac1Travel_LastFirst**.

Complete a Mail Merge

You will prepare a mailing to new owners, merging the document you have prepared with a data source.

a. Move to the beginning of the document. Begin a new mail merge, creating letters using the current document. The data source is the *NewOwners* workbook, using the Sheet1 worksheet.

b. Insert an Address Block, using default settings, in the identified area on page 1. Include the number of points (Points Purchased) in place of the bracketed area on page 2. Insert or type the current date at the top of the letter on page 1.

c. Merge all records, resulting in an 18-page document, with letters and a Quick Start Guide going to each of the three new owners. Save the new document as **w00ac1MergedTravel_LastFirst**.

d. Submit *w00ac1MergedTravel_LastFirst* according to your instructor's directions. Close *w00ac1Travel_LastFirst* without saving it.

Excel Application Capstone Exercise

You work for a travel company that specializes in arranging travel accommodations for student tours and vacations in exciting destinations such as Canada, Rome, and the Czech Republic. You created a workbook to store agent names, student IDs, and tour codes. The workbook also contains a worksheet to store lookup tables. You will complete the workbook for your manager's approval. You will insert formulas and a variety of functions, convert data to a table, sort and filter the table, and prepare a chart.

Name the Lookup Tables

The Lookup Tables worksheet contains two lookup tables: one to look up the base price to find the commission rate and the other table to look up the tour package code to find the tour description, departure date, and base cost. You need to assign a range name to each lookup table.

a. Start Excel. Open *e00a1Trips* and save the workbook as **e00a1Trips_LastFirst**. Make sure the Lookup Tables sheet is active.

b. Assign the range name **rates** to the base price and commission range.

c. Assign the range name **tours** to the data for the package, tour description, departure, and base cost.

Insert Functions and Formulas

You need to insert lookup functions that look up the tour code, compare it to the lookup table, and then return the tour description, departure date, and base cost of the trip. Then you need to insert a formula to calculate the cost with taxes and fees, the monthly payment, and the agents' commissions.

a. Click **cell D13** on the Data sheet and insert a VLOOKUP function that looks up the tour code, compares it to the tours table, and returns the description.

b. Click **cell E13** and insert a lookup function that looks up the tour code, compares it to the tours table, and returns the departure date.

c. Click **cell F13** and insert a lookup function that looks up the tour code, compares it to the tours table, and returns the base cost of the trip.

d. Click **cell G13** and insert a formula that adds taxes and fees to the base cost of the trip (in cell F13) by using the percentage value in the input area. Use a mixed reference to the cell containing 20% in the input area above the data.

e. Click **cell H13** and insert the PMT function to calculate the payments for students who want to pay for their trips in three installments. Use the interest rate and months in the input area above the data. Use appropriate relative, mixed, and/or absolute cell references in the formula. Make sure the result is a positive value.

f. Click **cell I13** and calculate the agent commission using the base cost of the trip and a VLOOKUP function that returns the commission rate based on the base cost of the trip using the rates lookup table. The function should then calculate the monetary value of the commission.

g. Copy the formulas and functions down their respective columns.

Format Data

You need to format the titles and numeric data in the Data sheet. In addition, you want to freeze the column labels so that they do not scroll offscreen. You also want to apply conditional formatting to emphasize values above the average value.

a. Merge and center the main title on the first row over all data columns on the Data sheet. Apply bold and **18 pt font size**.

b. Merge and center the subtitle on the second row over the data columns.

c. Apply **Currency number format** to the monetary values in columns F, G, H, and I.

d. Hide the Tour Code column.

e. Wrap text in the **range F4:I4**. Set the column widths for these columns to **11**, if necessary. Adjust the row height, if necessary.

f. Freeze the panes so that the row of column labels does not scroll offscreen.
g. Apply the **Light Red Fill with Dark Red Text conditional formatting** to values in the *Total Cost with Taxes* column when the values are above average.

Add Summary Statistics

The Data worksheet contains a section for Summary Statistics. You insert functions to perform these calculations. Use the total cost, including taxes and fees, for the range in the functions.

a. Insert a function to calculate the total for all trips in **cell G5**, the average trip cost in **cell G6**, and the median trip cost in **cell G7**.
b. Insert a function to calculate the lowest trip cost in **cell G8** and the highest trip cost in **cell G9**.
c. Click **cell G10** and enter a function to display today's date.

Sort and Filter the Data

To preserve the integrity of the original data, you copy the worksheet. You will then convert the data in the copied worksheet to a table, apply a table style, sort and filter the data, and then display totals.

a. Copy the Data sheet and place the copied sheet before the Summary sheet. Remove the conditional formatting rule on the Data (2) sheet.
b. Convert the data range in the Data (2) sheet to a table.
c. Apply the **Table Style Medium 21 style** to the table.
d. Sort the table by departure date from oldest to newest and then alphabetically by trip description.
e. Apply a filter to display trips arranged by agents Avery and Ross only.
f. Display a total row. Add totals for all monetary columns.

Create Sparklines and Insert a Chart

The Summary sheet provides a six-month summary of sales. You want to insert sparklines to display trends for each agent and provide a $500 bonus if the sales were greater than the average combined sales. Finally, you want to create a chart.

a. Create Line sparklines in column H in the Summary sheet to display six-month trends for each agent. Show the high point in each sparkline. Apply the **SparkLine Style Accent 1, Darker 50% style**. If needed, apply the **Blue, Accent 1 high point marker color**.
b. Insert an IF function in column I that displays a $500 bonus if an agent's average sales are greater than the average of all sales for the six months. Use two nested AVERAGE functions in the logical_test argument of the IF function to make the comparison.
c. Create a clustered column chart of the agents and their six-month sales, using the chart type that displays the months on the category axis.
d. Move the chart to a chart sheet named **Sales Chart**.
e. Apply the **Layout 1 chart layout**.
f. Type **January–June 2016 Sales by Agent** for the chart title.
g. Apply the **Style 14 chart style**.
h. Create a footer with your name on the left side, the sheet tab code in the center, and the file name code on the right side of each sheet.
i. Apply **0.2**" left and right margins and scale to one page for the Data and Data (2) sheets. Select **Landscape orientation** for the Data (2) sheet.
j. Save the workbook. Close the workbook and exit Excel. Submit the workbook as directed by your instructor.

Access Application Capstone Exercise

You were recently hired by your local college to help with registering all transfer students. The college's Transfer Counseling Department is a one-stop location for transfer students to come with questions. They have been working with Excel spreadsheets generated by the Information Technology department, but they are hoping to do more with an Access database. They have had a number of problems, including employees putting information in the wrong fields, putting information in the wrong format, and creating incorrect formulas. They are also hoping for more consistent ways of finding information, as well as being able to generate reports. Your tasks include importing an existing Excel worksheet as a table into your Access database; modifying the table; creating a relationship between two tables; creating queries with calculated fields, functions, and totals; creating a form for input; and creating a report.

Set Up the Database File and Import an Excel Worksheet

To start, you have been provided with a database the Information Technology department created. The database has one table and one form. You will be importing an Excel spreadsheet into a table and creating a primary key.

a. Start Access. Open *a00c1College* and save the database as **a00c1College_LastFirst**.

b. Import the *a00c1Transfer* Excel workbook into a table named **Transfer Schools**. While importing the data, choose **StudentID** as the primary key field. Ensure *StudentID* has a data type of Short Text.

Modify a Table

Now that you have imported the data from the spreadsheet, you will modify the field properties in the Transfer Schools table and demonstrate sorting.

a. Set the StudentID field size to **10**.

b. Remove the @ symbol from the StudentID format property.

c. Change the AdmittingSchool field size to **75**.

d. Change the RegistrationFee and TuitionDue fields to have **0** decimal places.

e. Switch to Datasheet View. Resize all columns so all data are displayed.

f. Sort the Transfer Schools table on the CreditsTransferred field in ascending order.

g. Save and close the table.

Create Relationships

Now that the table is imported and modified, you will create a relationship between the two tables.

a. Add the Transfer Schools and Transfer Students tables to the Relationships window.

b. Create a one-to-one relationship between the StudentID field in the Transfer Students (primary) table and the StudentID field in the Transfer Schools (related) table. Enforce referential integrity between the two tables.

c. Save the changes and close the Relationships window.

Modify Data in a Form

You will demonstrate changing information in a form.

a. Open the Transfer Students Data Entry form.

b. Change the major for *Cornelius Kavanaugh* to **Elementary Education**. Close the form.

Create a Query

Rey Rivera, a counselor in the center, would like your assistance in helping him find certain information. You will create a query for him and demonstrate how he can change information.

a. Create a new query using Design view. This query will access fields from both the Transfer Schools and Transfer Students tables. From the Transfer Students table, add the FirstName, LastName, Major, Class, and GPA fields. From the Transfer Schools table, add the AdmissionDate, TuitionDue, CreditsEarned, and CreditsTransferred fields.
b. Save the query as **Transfer Credits**.
c. Set the criteria in the AdmissionDate field to **8/1/2015**. Run the query (144 records will display).
d. Enter the TuitionDue for Diana Sullivan as **$1500** and the GPA for Audrey Owen as **3.51**.
e. Save the query.

Create Calculated Fields

Now that you have created the query, you will create a second query for Rey that will calculate the number of credits students lost upon transfer, the tuition payments for which they will be responsible (assuming three payments per semester), and the payment due date.

a. Switch to Design view of the Transfer Credits query. Save the query as **Transfer Credit Calculations**.
b. Remove the criteria from the AdmissionDate field.
c. Create a calculated field in the first empty field cell of the query named **LostCredits** that subtracts CreditsTransferred from CreditsEarned.
d. Create another calculated field named **TuitionPayments** that determines tuition paid in three installments. Using the Pmt function, replace the rate argument with **0.025/3**, the num_periods argument with **3**, and the present_value argument with the student's tuition payment. Use **0** for the future_value and type arguments. Ensure the payment appears as a positive number.
e. Format the TuitionPayments calculated field as **Currency**.
f. Create another calculated field named **DueDate** after the TuitionPayments field. To calculate the due date, add **30** to their AdmissionDate. Run the query and verify that the three calculated fields have valid data.
g. Add a total row to the query. Average the GPA column and sum the LostCredits column. Save and close the query.

Create a Totals Query

Cala Hajjar, the director of the center, needs to summarize information about the transfer students for the 2015–2016 academic year to present to the College's Board of Trustees. You will create a totals query for her to summarize the number of transfer students, average number of credits earned and transferred, and total tuition earned by transfer institution.

a. Create a new query in Design view. Add the Transfer Schools table.
b. Add the AdmittingSchool, StudentID, CreditsEarned, CreditsTransferred, and TuitionDue fields.
c. Sort the query by AdmittingSchool in ascending order.
d. Show the Total row. Group by AdmittingSchool and show the count of StudentID, the average CreditsEarned, the average of CreditsTransferred, and the sum of TuitionDue.
e. Format both average fields as **Standard**.
f. Change the caption for the StudentID field to **NumStudents**, the caption for the CreditsEarned average to **AvgCreditsEarned**, the caption for the CreditsTransferred average to **AvgCredits Transferred**, and the caption for SumOfTuitionDue to **TotalTuition**.
g. Run the query. Resize columns so all data are shown.
h. Save the query as **Transfer Summary**.
i. Close the query.

Create a Form

Hideo Sasaki, the department's administrative assistant, will handle data entry. He has asked you to simplify the way he inputs information into the new table. You will create a form based on the new Transfer Schools table.

a. Create a Split Form using the Transfer Schools table as the source.
b. Change the height of the AdmittingSchool field to reduce extra space.
c. Remove the layout. Shrink each field so it is only as large as it needs to be.
d. Click on record 123455 in the bottom half of the split form. Make sure all fields are still visible. If not, adjust the controls so all values are visible.
e. Move the CreditsTransferred field so it is to the right of the CreditsEarned field on the same row.
f. Change the format of the TuitionDue field so the font size is **18** and the font color is **Red** (last row, second column in the *Standard Colors* section).
g. Change the fill color of the StudentID field to be **Yellow** (last row, fourth column in the *Standard Colors* section).
h. Save the form as **Transfer Schools Form**. Save and close the form.

Create a Report

Cala Hajjar, the director of the center, saw the query you created for Rey. She is hoping you can create a more print-friendly version for her to distribute to the Board of Trustees. You will create a report based on the Transfer Credits Calculations query.

a. Create a report using the Report Wizard. Add the Class, FirstName, LastName, Major, GPA, and LostCredits fields from the Transfer Credit Calculations query. Do not add any grouping or sorting. Ensure the report is in Landscape orientation.
b. Save the report as **Transfer Students Report** and view the report in Layout view.

Format a Report

Now that you have included the fields Cala has asked for, you will work to format the report to make the information more obvious.

a. Apply the **Wisp theme** (third row, first column) to this object only.
b. Group the report by the Class field. Sort the records within each group by LastName then by FirstName, both in ascending order.
c. Change the font size of the Class field to **16.**
d. Adjust the text boxes so the values are completely visible.
e. Switch to Print Preview mode and verify the report is only one page wide (note: it may be a number of pages long).
f. Export the results as a PDF document using the file name **a00c1Transfer_LastFirst**.
g. Save and close the report.

Close and Submit Database

a. Compact and repair the database.
b. Create a backup of the database. Accept the default name for the backup.
c. Close all database objects and exit Access.
d. Submit the database, backup, and PDF based on your instructor's directions.

PowerPoint Application Capstone Exercise

You are a student employee of your college's Student Success department. A previous employee created a presentation for students to view while they are waiting for their advisor. The goal of the presentation is to raise student awareness about available savings and discounts. You decide to modify the original slide show to add additional information and visual impact. You will insert and modify an image, a SmartArt graphic, and a reused slide containing a table.

Presentation Setup and Slide Creation

You need to open the original slide show, rename the file, and save it. You insert a new slide for additional information.

a. Start PowerPoint. Open *p00ac1Discounts* and save the file as **p00ac1Discounts_LastFirst**.

b. Create a *Notes and Handouts* header and footer with the date, your name in the header, and your instructor's name and your class in the footer.

c. Insert a new slide after Slide 4 with the *Title and Content* layout.

d. Move to the new Slide 5 if necessary and type **Travel Savings** in the **title placeholder**.

e. Type the following as Level 1 bullets for Slide 5: **Airfare discounts**, **Rail passes**, **Global phones**.

f. Apply the **Quotable Theme** and select the **lime green variant**. Change the color theme to **Green Yellow**.

Insert and Modify a Picture

You need to insert, resize, and position a picture. You also add a picture frame to the image.

a. On Slide 5, insert the picture file **p00ac1Rooftops.jpg**.

b. Change the width of the picture to **3"** and the height to **2"**. Deselect the **Lock aspect ratio option**, if necessary.

c. Move the picture to the bottom-right corner of the slide so that it aligns with the bottom and right edges of the slide.

d. Apply the Picture Style **Simple Frame, Black**.

Add a Shape

To draw attention to an instruction, you decide to add a shape to a slide and insert text. After adding the shape, you group it with another shape to form an attention-grabbing graphic.

a. Click **Slide 2** and insert the **Horizontal Scroll shape** (second row, sixth column in the *Stars and Banners* category).

b. Change the width of the shape to **2.5"** and the height to **1.75"**.

c. Position the shape horizontally at **4.5"** to the right of 0 and vertically at **1.5"** below 0.

d. Type **Use a search engine to find "Software Discounts"** in the shape.

e. Select both the **Explosion1 shape** and the **Horizontal Scroll shape** and align them by their middles. Group the shapes.

f. Make sure the shapes are still selected and apply the shape style **Light 1 Outline – Colored Fill – Blue Accent 6**.

Use WordArt, Format a Background, and Insert Audio

You decide to enhance the Title slide by changing text to WordArt, formatting the background to add an image, and then adding an audio clip.

a. Click **Slide 1**. Select the text in the title placeholder and apply the WordArt style **Fill - White, Text 1, Outline – Background 1, Hard Shadow – Background 1**.

b. Switch to the VIEW tab, select the **Outline View**, select the **subtitle placeholder** on Slide 1, and then delete it. Switch to Normal view.

c. Click the **DESIGN tab** and access the Format Background options so that you can select a picture fill.
d. Insert a picture from online by searching the term *Dollars* and inserting a picture of your choosing. Change the transparency to **20%**.
e. Insert online audio by searching for the term *Techno* and looking for Techno pop music. Apply a **02.00 Fade Out duration**.
f. Change the audio clip playback from *On Click* to **Play Across Slides** and to start automatically. Check the **Loop until Stopped audio option**.
g. Align the sound icon to the bottom left corner of the slide.

Add Content and Animation

You reuse a previously created slide to add content, and then you format the table on the reused slide. Next, you create a SmartArt graphic to include information about "free stuff" for students and animate the graphic.

a. Switch to the HOME tab and use the Reuse Slides feature to add the slide in *p00ac1Tips.pptx* to the end of the presentation.
b. Select the table on the new Slide 6 and set the height of all the rows to **1"**.
c. Center align the text in the table. Apply the **Medium Style 1 table style** to the table.
d. Move the table so that its top-left corner is at the 1" mark above the 0 on the vertical ruler. Center align the table on the slide.
e. Insert a new slide after Slide 6 using the *Title and Content* layout. Type **Free Stuff** in the **title placeholder**.
f. On the new Slide 7, insert a Vertical Box List SmartArt graphic. Type **Ringtones** in the top shape, **Online video games** in the middle shape, and **Magazines and samples** in the bottom shape.
g. Change the SmartArt layout to a **Horizontal Bullet List** and change the SmartArt style to **Inset** (3-D category).
h. Align the SmartArt graphic to the bottom of the slide and resize as necessary so that it fits on the slide.
i. Apply the **Fly In animation** (Entrance category) to the SmartArt. Change the sequence of the animation to the **One by One effect**.

Finalize the Presentation

To ensure the professionalism of the presentation, you review the presentation and make changes.

a. Spell-check the presentation and correct any misspelled words. Ignore the message that appears for *PacSun*.
b. Click **Slide 2**. Use the Thesaurus to replace the word generally with an appropriate synonym.
c. Apply the **Cube transition** to all slides.
d. Change the transition timing so that all slides advance automatically after 8 seconds.
e. View the presentation.
f. Save the presentation. Close the presentation and exit PowerPoint. Submit the presentation as directed by your instructor.

Glossary

100% stacked column chart A chart type that places (stacks) data in one column per category, with each column the same height of 100%.

Absolute cell reference A designation that provides a permanent reference to a specific cell. When you copy a formula containing an absolute reference, the cell reference in the copied formula does not change, regardless of where you copy the formula. An absolute cell reference appears with a dollar sign before both the column letter and the row number, such as $B$4.

Access (Office Fundamentals) Relational database management software that enables you to record and link data, query databases, and create forms and reports. (Access) A database management system included in the Microsoft Office 2013 Professional suite.

Accounting Number Format A number format that displays $ on the left side of a cell and formats values with commas for the thousands separator and two decimal places.

Action Center A feature in Windows 8.1.1 that monitors your system for various maintenance and security settings.

Active cell The current cell in a worksheet. It is indicated by a dark green border onscreen.

Adjustment handle A yellow diamond that enables you to modify a shape.

Aero Peek A sneak preview of any open window, even if it is obscured by another, by placing the mouse pointer over the program's icon on the taskbar.

Aggregate function Performs calculations on an entire column of data and returns a single value. Includes functions such as Sum, Avg, and Count.

Align To arrange in a line to be parallel with other objects or in relation to the slide.

Alignment Placement of data within cell boundaries.

Alignment guide A horizontal or vertical green bar that appears as you move an object, assisting with aligning the object with text or with another object.

AND logical operator Returns only records that meet all criteria.

Animation A movement that controls the entrance, emphasis, exit, and/or path of objects in a slide show.

Annotation A written note or drawing on a slide for additional commentary or explanation.

APA (American Psychological Association) Writing style established by the American Psychological Association with rules and conventions for documenting sources and organizing a research paper (used primarily in business and the social sciences).

App bars Bars, such as the Tabs bar and Address bar, that float on the screen above the application when summoned.

Area chart A chart type that emphasizes magnitude of changes over time by filling in the space between lines with a color.

Argument (Word) A positional reference, contained in parentheses within a function. (Access) Any data needed to produce output for a function.

Ascending A sort that lists text data in alphabetical order or a numeric list in lowest to highest order.

Aspect ratio The ratio of an object's width to its height.

Auto Fill A feature that enables you to copy the contents of a cell or a range of cells or to continue a sequence by dragging the fill handle over an adjacent cell or range of cells.

AutoComplete A feature that searches for and automatically displays any other label in that column that matches the letters you typed.

AutoNumber A number data type that is generated by Access and is incremented each time a record is added.

AutoRecover A feature that enables Word to recover a previous version of a document.

AVERAGE function A predefined formula that calculates the arithmetic mean, or average, of values in a range.

Axis Category or incremental value labels to identify the measurements along the horizontal and vertical axes of a chart.

Axis title A label that describes either the category axis or the value axis. Provides clarity, particularly in describing the value axis.

Back Up Database An Access utility that creates a duplicate copy of the database.

Background The portion of a picture that is deleted when removing the background of a picture.

Background Styles gallery Provides both solid color and background styles for application to a theme.

Backstage view A component of Office 2013 that provides a concise collection of commands related to common file activities and provides information on an open file.

Backup A copy of a file or folder on another drive.

Bar chart A chart type that compares values across categories using horizontal bars. In a bar chart, the horizontal axis displays values and the vertical axis displays categories.

Bibliography A list of works cited or consulted by an author in his or her work.

Bitmap image An image created by bits or pixels placed on a grid to form a picture.

Border (Word) A line that surrounds a paragraph, page, or a table or table element. (Excel) A line that surrounds a cell or a range of cells to offset particular data from the rest of the data in a worksheet.

Border Painter A feature that enables you to choose border formatting and click on any table border to apply the formatting.

Breakpoint The lowest value for a specific category or series in a lookup table.

Brightness The lightness or darkness of a picture.

Bubble chart A chart type that shows relationships among three values by using bubbles to show a third dimension. The third dimension is indicated by the size of the bubble; the larger the bubble, the larger the value.

Bullet A graphic element that itemizes and separates paragraph text to increase readability; often used to identify lists.

Calculated field Produces a value from an expression or function that references one or more existing fields.

Calculator A tool that lets you perform simple addition, subtraction, multiplication, and division to advanced scientific, programming, and statistical functions.

Callout A shape that includes a text box you can use to add notes.

CamelCase notation Uses no spaces in multiword field names but uses uppercase letters to distinguish the first letter of each new word.

CAPTCHA A scrambled code used with online forms to prevent mass sign-ups. It helps to ensure that an actual person is requesting the account.

Caption A descriptive title for a table.

Caption property Used to create a more readable label that appears in the top row in Datasheet view and in forms and reports.

Cascade Delete Related Records An option that directs Access to automatically delete all records in related tables that match the primary key that is deleted from a primary table.

Cascade Update Related Fields An option that directs Access to automatically update all foreign key values in a related table when the primary key value table is modified in a primary table.

Category axis The chart element that displays descriptive group names or labels, such as city names or departments, to identify data.

Category label Text that describes a collection of data points in a chart.

Cell The intersection of a column and row in a table.

Cell address The unique identifier of a cell, starting with the column letter and then the row number, such as A9.

Center alignment Positions text horizontally in the center of a line, an equal distance from both the left and right margins.

Charms A toolbar for Windows 8.1.1 made up of five icons (Search, Share, Start, Devices, and Settings) that enables you to search for files and applications, share information with others within an application that is running, return to the Start screen, control devices that are connected to your computer, or modify various settings depending on which application is running when accessing the Setting icon.

Charms bar Provides quick access to actions that most users perform frequently in Windows 8.1.1.

Chart A visual representation of numerical data.

Chart area A boundary that contains the entire chart and all of its elements, including the plot area, titles, legends, and labels.

Chart element A component of a chart that helps complete or clarify the chart.

Chart filter A setting that controls what data series are displayed or hidden in a chart.

Chart sheet A sheet within a workbook that contains a single chart and no spreadsheet data.

Chart style A collection of formatting that controls the color of the chart area, plot area, and data series.

Chart title The label that describes the entire chart. The title is usually placed at the top of the chart area.

Chicago Writing style established by the University of Chicago with rules and conventions for preparing an academic paper for publication.

Circular reference A situation that occurs when a formula contains a direct or an indirect reference to the cell containing the formula.

Citation A note recognizing a source of information or a quoted passage.

Clip art An electronic illustration that can be inserted into an Office project.

Clipboard An Office feature that temporarily holds selections that have been cut or copied and allows you to paste the selections.

Cloud storage A technology used to store files and to work with programs that are stored in a central location on the Internet.

Clustered column chart A type of chart that groups, or clusters, similar data into columns to compare values across columns.

Codec (coder/decoder) A digital video compression scheme used to compress a video and decompress for playback.

Collapsed outline Displays only the slide number, icon, and title of each slide in Outline view.

Color scale A conditional format that displays a particular color based on the relative value of the cell contents to the other selected cells.

Colors gallery Provides a set of colors for every available theme.

Column A format that separates document text into side-by-side vertical blocks, often used in newsletters.

Column chart A type of chart that displays data vertically in columns to compare values across different categories.

Column heading The alphabetical letters above the columns in a worksheet.

Column index number The number of the column in the lookup table that contains the return values.

Column width The horizontal measurement of a column in a table or a worksheet. In Excel, it is measured by the number of characters or pixels.

Combo chart A chart that combines two chart types, such as column and line, to plot different types of data, such as quantities and percentages.

Comma Style A number format that formats values with commas for the thousands separator and two decimal places.

Command A button or area within a group that you click to perform tasks.

Comment A note, annotation, or additional information to the author or another reader about the content of a document.

Compact and Repair An Access utility that reduces the size of the database and can repair a corrupt database.

Comparison operator An operator used to evaluate the relationship between two quantities.

Compression A method applied to data to reduce the amount of space required for file storage.

Conditional formatting A set of rules that applies specific formatting to highlight or emphasize cells that meet specifications.

Connector A Lines shape that is attached to and moves with other shapes.

Constant A value that does not change.

Contextual tab A Ribbon tab that displays when an object, such as a picture or table, is selected. A contextual tab contains groups and commands specific to the selected object.

Contrast The difference between the darkest and lightest areas of a picture.

Controls The text boxes, buttons, boxes, and other tools you use to add, edit, and display the data in a form or report.

Copy To duplicate an item from the original location and place the copy in the Office Clipboard.

Copyright The legal protection afforded to a written or artistic work.

COUNT function A predefined formula that tallies the number of cells in a range that contain values you can use in calculations, such as the numerical and date data, but excludes blank cells or text entries from the tally.

COUNTA function A predefined formula that tallies the number of cells in a range that are not blank; that is, cells that contain data, whether a value, text, or a formula.

COUNTBLANK function A predefined formula that tallies the number of cells in a range that are blank.

Cover page The first page of a report, including the report title, author or student, and other identifying information.

Criteria row A row in the Query Design view that determines which records will be selected.

Criterion A number, text phrase, or an expression used to select records.

Crop The process of reducing an image size by eliminating unwanted portions of an image or other graphical object.

CSE (Council of Science Editors) Writing style providing rules and conventions for preparing reports in the sciences.

Current List Includes all citation sources you use in the current document.

Custom Web app A database that can be built, used, and shared with others through the use of a host server (e.g., SharePoint or Office 365).

Cut To remove an item from the original location and place it in the Office Clipboard.

Data bar A conditional format that displays horizontal gradient or solid fill indicating the cell's relative value compared to other selected cells.

Data label An identifier that shows the exact value of a data point on the value axis in a chart. Appears above or on a data point in a chart. May indicate percentage of a value to the whole on a pie chart.

Data point A numeric value that describes a single value in a chart or worksheet.

Data redundancy The unnecessary storing of duplicate data in two or more tables.

Data series A group of related data points that display in row(s) or column(s) in a worksheet.

Data source A list of information that is merged with a main document during a mail merge procedure.

Data table A grid that contains the data source values and labels to plot data in a chart. A data table may be placed below a chart or hidden from view.

Data type Determines the type of data that can be entered and the operations that can be performed on that data.

Database A collection of data organized as meaningful information that can be accessed, managed, stored, queried, sorted, and reported.

Database management system (DBMS) A software system that provides the tools needed to create, maintain, and use a database.

Datasheet view A view that enables you to add, edit, and delete the records of a table.

Date arithmetic The process of adding or subtracting one date from another, or adding or subtracting a constant from a date.

Default Office settings that remain in effect unless you specify otherwise.

Delimiter A special character that surrounds the criterion's value.

Descending A sort that lists text data in reverse alphabetical order or a numeric list in highest to lowest order.

Design view A view that enables you to create tables, add and delete fields, and modify field properties; or to change advanced design settings not seen in Layout view, such as a background image.

Desktop A modified version of the desktop in previous editions of Windows. Serves the purpose of a desk, on which multiple tasks can be completed.

Dialog box A window that displays when a program requires interaction with you, such as inputting information, before completing a procedure. This window typically provides access to more precise, but less frequently used, commands.

Dialog Box Launcher An icon in a Ribbon group that you can click to open a related dialog box. It is not found in all groups.

Distribute To divide or evenly spread selected shapes over a given area.

Document Inspector Checks for and removes certain hidden and personal information from a document.

Document Panel Provides descriptive information about a document, such as a title, subject, author, keywords, and comments.

Document theme A unified set of design elements, including font style, color, and special effects, that is applied to an entire document.

Doughnut chart A chart type that displays values as percentages of the whole but may contain more than one data series.

Draft view View that shows a great deal of document space, but no margins, headers, footers, or other special features.

Effects gallery Includes a range of effects for shapes used in the presentation.

Embed To store an object from an external source within a presentation.

Endnote A citation that appears at the end of a document.

Enforce referential integrity A relationship option that ensures that data cannot be entered into a related table unless it first exists in a primary table.

Enhanced ScreenTip A feature that provides a brief summary of a command when you point to the command button.

Error bar Visual that indicates the standard error amount, a percentage, or a standard deviation for a data point or marker.

Excel A software application used to organize records, financial transactions, and business information in the form of worksheets.

Expanded outline Displays the slide number, icon, title, and content of each slide in Outline view.

Exploded pie chart A chart type in which one or more pie slices are separated from the rest of the pie chart for emphasis.

Expression A formula used to calculate new fields from the values in existing fields.

Expression Builder An Access tool that helps you create more complicated expressions.

Field The smallest data element in a table, such as first name, last name, address, or phone number.

Field property A characteristic of a field that determines how a field looks and behaves.

Field row A row in the Query Design view that displays the field name.

Field selector The column heading of a datasheet used to select a column.

File Electronic data such as documents, databases, slide shows, worksheets, digital photographs, music, videos, and Web pages.

File Explorer A component of the Windows operating system that can be used to create and manage folders.

Fill The interior contents of a shape.

Fill color The background color that displays behind the data in a cell.

Fill handle A small square at the bottom-right corner of a cell used to copy cell contents or text or number patterns to adjacent cells.

Filter Displays a subset of records based on a specified criterion.

Filtering The process of specifying conditions to display only those records that meet those conditions.

Filter by Form A filtering method that displays records based on multiple criteria.

Filter by Selection A filtering method that displays only records that match selected criteria.

Find An Office feature that locates a word or phrase that you indicate in a document.

Firewall A software program that helps to protect against unauthorized access (hacking) to your computer.

First line indent Marks the location to indent only the first line in a paragraph.

Flip To reverse the direction an object faces.

Flow chart An illustration showing the sequence of a project or plan containing steps.

Folder A directory into which you place data files in order to organize them for easier retrieval.

Font A combination of typeface and type style.

Fonts gallery Contains font sets for title text and bulleted text.

Footer Information that generally displays at the bottom of a document page, worksheet, slide or database report.

Footnote A citation that appears at the bottom of a page.

Foreground The portion of the picture that is kept when removing the background of a picture.

Foreign key A field in one table that is also a primary key of another table.

Form A database object that is used to add, edit, or delete table data.

Form letter A letter with standard information that you personalize with recipient information, which you might print or e-mail to many people.

Form tool Used to create data entry forms for customers, employees, products, and other primary tables.

Form view A simplified interface primarily used for data entry. Does not allow you to make changes to the layout.

Format Painter A command that copies the formatting of text from one location to another.

Formatting The process of modifying text by changing font and paragraph characteristics.

Formula A combination of cell references, operators, values, and/or functions used to perform a calculation.

Formula AutoComplete A feature that displays a list of functions and defined names that match letters as you type a formula.

Formula Bar An element in Excel that appears below the Ribbon and to the right of the Insert Function command. It shows the contents of the active cell.

Freeform shape A shape that combines both curved and straight-line segments.

Freezing The process of keeping rows and/or columns visible onscreen at all times even when you scroll through a large dataset.

Full Screen Mode Provides a completely clear document space in which to edit a document.

Function A predefined computation that simplifies creating a complex calculation and produces a result based on inputs known as arguments.

Function ScreenTip A small pop-up description that displays the arguments for a function as you enter it directly in a cell.

Gallery A set of selections that displays when you click a More button, or in some cases when you click a command, in a Ribbon group.

Gradient fill A fill that contains a blend of two or more colors or shades.

Grid A set of intersecting lines used to align objects.

Gridline A horizontal or vertical line that extends from the horizontal or vertical axis through the plot area to guide the reader's eyes across the chart to identify values.

Group A subset of a tab that organizes similar tasks together; to combine two or more objects.

Grouping Allows you to summarize your data by the values of a field.

Guide A straight nonprinting horizontal or vertical line used to align objects.

Hanging indent Aligns the first line of a paragraph at the left margin, indenting remaining lines in the paragraph.

Header Information that generally displays at the top of a document page, worksheet, slide or database report.

Header row The first row in a data source, which contains labels describing the data in rows beneath.

Help and Support A feature that provides answers to questions about a process or tool on almost any Windows topic.

Hierarchy Indicates levels of importance in a structure.

HLOOKUP function A predefined formula that looks up a value in a horizontal lookup table where the first row contains the values to compare with the lookup value.

Homegroup A Windows 8.1.1 feature that enables you to share resources on a home network.

Horizontal alignment The placement of cell data between the left and right cell margins in a worksheet.

Icon A picture or image on the desktop that represent programs, files, folders, or other items related to your computer.

Icon set A conditional format that displays an icon representing a value in the top third, quarter, or fifth based on values in the selected range.

IF function A predefined logical formula that evaluates a condition and returns one value if the condition is true and a different condition if the value is false.

Indent (Word) A setting associated with the way a paragraph is distanced from one or more margins. (Excel) A format that positions cell contents to the right of the left cell margin to offset the data.

Index An alphabetical listing of topics covered in a document, along with the page numbers on which the topic is discussed.

Indexed property Setting that enables quick sorting in primary key order and quick retrieval based on the primary key.

Infographic Information graphic that is a visual representation of data or knowledge.

Infringement of copyright Occurs when a right of the copyright owner is violated.

Input area A range of cells in a worksheet used to store and change the variables used in calculations.

Insert control An indicator that displays between rows or columns in a table; click the indicator to insert one or more rows or columns.

Insertion point Blinking bar that indicates where text that you next type will appear.

Join line A line used to create a relationship between two tables using a common field.

Jump List A list of program shortcuts, which shows recently opened files, the program name, an option to pin or unpin an item, and a close option.

Justified alignment Spreads text evenly between the left and right margins, so that text begins at the left margin and ends uniformly at the right margin.

Kelvin The unit of measurement for absolute temperature.

Key Tip The letter or number for the associated keyboard shortcut that displays over features on the Ribbon or Quick Access Toolbar.

Label Wizard Enables you to easily create mailing labels, name tags, and other specialized tags.

Landscape An orientation for a displayed page or worksheet that is wider than it is tall.

Layout Determines the position of the objects or content on a slide.

Layout control Provides guides to help keep controls aligned horizontally and vertically and give your form a uniform appearance.

Layout view Enables users to make changes to a layout while viewing the data on the form or report.

Left alignment Begins text evenly at the left margin, with a ragged right edge.

Left indent A setting that positions all text in a paragraph an equal distance from the left margin.

Legend A key that identifies the color, gradient, picture, texture, or pattern assigned to each data series in a chart.

Library A collection of files from different locations that is displayed as a single unit.

Line chart A chart type that displays lines connecting data points to show trends over equal time periods, such as months, quarters, years, or decades.

Line spacing The vertical spacing between lines in a paragraph.

Line weight The width or thickness of a shape's outline.

Link A connection from the presentation to another location such as a storage device or Web site.

Live Layout The feature that enables you to watch text flow around an object as you move the object.

Live Preview An Office feature that provides a preview of the results of a selection when you point to an option in a list or gallery. Using Live Preview, you can experiment with settings before making a final choice.

Lock Drawing Mode Enables the creation of multiple shapes of the same type.

Logical test An expression that evaluates to true or false; the first argument in an IF function.

Lookup table A range that contains data for the basis of the lookup and data to be retrieved. In a vertical lookup table, the first column contains a list of values to compare to the lookup value. In a horizontal lookup table, the first row contains a list of values to compare to the lookup value.

Lookup value The cell reference of the cell that contains the value to look up within a lookup table.

Macro A stored series of commands that carry out an action.

Mail Merge A process that combines content from a main document and a data source.

Mailing label report A specialized report that comes preformatted to coordinate with name-brand labels.

Main document Contains the information that stays the same for all recipients in a mail merge.

Margin The area of blank space that displays to the left, right, top, and bottom of a document or worksheet.

Markup balloon A bordered area in the margin of a report that contains a comment and any replies to the comment.

Marquee A pane designed to help select objects from a listing of all objects on a slide.

Masters Controls the layouts, background designs, and color combinations for handouts, notes pages, and slides, giving the presentation a consistent appearance.

Master List A database of all citation sources created in Word on a particular computer.

MAX function A predefined formula that finds the highest value in a range.

MEDIAN function A predefined formula that finds the midpoint value, which is the value that one half of the values in a list are above or below.

Merge field Serves as a placeholder for the variable data that will be inserted into the main document during a mail merge procedure.

Microsoft Office A productivity software suite including four primary software components, each one specializing in a particular type of output.

MIN function A predefined formula that finds the lowest value in a range.

Mini toolbar The feature that provides access to common formatting commands, displayed when text is selected.

Mixed cell reference A designation that combines an absolute cell reference with a relative cell reference.

MLA (Modern Language Association) Writing style established by the Modern Language Association, with rules and conventions for preparing research papers (used primarily in the area of humanities).

Module An object that is written using Visual Basic for Applications (VBA) and adds functionality to a database.

Multimedia Multiple forms of media used to entertain or inform an audience.

Multiple Items form Displays multiple records in a tabular layout similar to a table's Datasheet view, with more customization options such as the ability to add graphical elements, buttons, and other controls.

Multitable query Contains two or more tables. It enables you to take advantage of the relationships that have been set in your database.

Name Box An identifier that displays the address of the current cell in an Excel worksheet.

Narration Spoken commentary that is added to a presentation.

Navigation bar Bar located at the bottom of a table, query, or form that is used to move through records.

Navigation Pane (Office Fundamentals) A section of the File Explorer interface that provides ready access to computer resources, folders, files, and networked peripherals. (Access) An interface element that organizes and lists database objects.

Nested function A function that contains another function embedded inside one or more of its arguments.

Nonadjacent range A collection of multiple ranges that are not positioned in a contiguous cluster in an Excel worksheet.

Normal view The default view of a document, worksheet or presentation.

Normalization The practice of good database design involving grouping data into the correct tables.

NOT logical operator Returns all records except the specified criteria.

Notepad A program that enables you to create documents.

Notes Page view A view used for entering and editing large amounts of text to which the speaker can refer when presenting.

Notification area An area of the taskbar where icons are displayed that indicate tasks that need the user's attention.

NOW function A predefined formula that uses the computer's clock to display the current date and time in a cell.

Nper The number of payment periods over the life of a loan or investment; the second argument in the PMT function.

Null The term Access uses to describe a blank field.

Number data type A data type that can store only numerical data.

Number formats Predefined settings that control how values appear in cells.

Numbering Sequences items in a list by displaying a successive number beside each item.

Object (Word) An item, such as a picture or text box, that can be individually selected and manipulated in a document. (Access) A main component that is created and used to make a database function.

One-to-many relationship A relationship established when the primary key value in the primary table can match many of the foreign key values in the related table.

OneDrive An application used to store, access, and share files and folders.

OneDrive for Windows app A downloadable app that synchronizes documents between a computer and OneDrive storage so that documents in both locations remain up to date.

Opaque A solid fill, one with no transparency.

Operating system Software that directs computer activities such as checking all components, managing system resources, and communicating with application software.

OR logical operator Returns records meeting any of the specified criteria.

Order of operations (order of precedence) Determines the sequence by which operations are calculated in an expression.

Outline A method of organizing text in a hierarchy to depict relationships.

Outline View (Word) A structural view of a document that can be collapsed or expanded as necessary. (PowerPoint) Shows the presentation in an outline format displayed in levels according to the points and any subpoints on each slide.

Output area The range of cells in an Excel worksheet that contain formulas dependent on the values in the input area.

Page break An indication where data will start on another printed page. The software inserts automatic page breaks based on data, margins, and paper size. Users can insert additional page breaks.

Page Break Preview The display that shows the worksheet data and page breaks within the worksheet.

Page Layout view The display that shows the worksheet data, margins, headers, and footers.

Paint A Windows 8 program that enables you to create drawings and to open digital pictures.

Paragraph spacing The amount of space before or after a paragraph.

Paste To place a cut or copied item in another location.

Paste Options button An icon that displays in the bottom-right corner immediately after using the Paste command. It enables the user to apply different paste options.

PDF Reflow Word feature that converts a PDF document into an editable Word document.

Percent Style A number format that displays values as if they were multiplied by 100 and with the % symbol.

Photo Album A presentation containing multiple pictures organized into album pages.

Picture A graphic file that is retrieved from storage media or the Internet and placed in an Office project.

Picture fill Inserts an image from a file into a shape.

Pie chart A chart type that shows each data point in proportion to the whole data series as a slice in a circle. A pie chart depicts only one data series.

Pinning Adding a tile to the Start screen.

Placeholder A container that holds text, images, graphs, videos, or other objects to be used in the presentation.

Plagiarism The act of using and documenting the works of another as one's own.

Plain Text Format (.txt) A file format that retains only text but no formatting when you transfer documents between applications or platforms.

Plot area The region of a chart containing the graphical representation of the values in the data series.

PMT function A predefined formula in Excel that calculates the periodic loan payment.

Pmt function A predefined formula in Access that calculates the periodic loan payment.

Point The smallest unit of measurement in typography.

Pointing The process of using the mouse pointer to select cells while building a formula. Also known as *semi-selection*.

Portable Document Format (PDF) A file type that was created for exchanging documents independent of software applications and operating system environment.

Portrait An orientation for a displayed page or worksheet that is taller than it is wide.

Poster frame The frame that displays on a slide when a video is not playing.

PowerPoint A software application used to create dynamic presentations to inform groups and persuade audiences.

PowerPoint presentation A presentation that can be edited or displayed on a computer.

PowerPoint show An unchangeable electronic slide show format used for distribution.

Presenter view A specialty view that delivers a presentation on two monitors simultaneously.

Primary key The field (or combination of fields) that uniquely identifies each record in a table.

Print area The range of cells within a worksheet that will print.

Print Layout view View that closely resembles the way a document will look when printed.

Print order The sequence in which the pages are printed.

Print Preview Enables you to see exactly what the report will look like when it is printed.

Property sheet Enables you to change settings such as number format, number of decimal places, and caption, among many others.

Public domain The rights to a literary work or property owned by the public at large.

Pv The present value of a loan or an annuity; the third argument in the PMT function and refers to the original amount of the loan.

Query Enables you to ask questions about the data stored in a database and then provides the answers to the questions by providing subsets or summaries of data.

Query Design view Enables you to create queries; the Design view is divided into two parts—the top portion displays the tables and the bottom portion (known as the *query design grid*) displays the fields and the criteria.

Query sort order Determines the order of records in the query's Datasheet view.

Quick Access Toolbar A component of Office 2013, located at the top-left corner of the Office window, that provides handy access to commonly executed tasks such as saving a file and undoing recent actions.

Quick Analysis A tool that provides a fast way to analyze a selected range of data by inserting basic calculations, charts, convert the data to a table, or apply conditional formatting or other analytical features.

Quick Style A combination of formatting options that can be applied to a shape or graphic.

Radar chart A chart type that compares aggregate values of three or more variables represented on axes starting from the same point.

Range A group of adjacent or contiguous cells in an Excel worksheet.

Range name A word or string of characters assigned to one or more cells. It can be up to 255 letters, characters, or numbers but must start with a letter or underscore and have no spaces or special symbols.

Rate The periodic interest rate; the percentage of interest paid for each payment period; the first argument in the PMT function.

Read Mode View in which text reflows automatically between columns to make it easier to read.

Reading View A view that displays the slide show full screen, one slide at a time, complete with animations and transitions.

Recolor The process of changing picture colors to a duotone style.

Record A group of related fields representing one entity, such as data for one person, place, event, or concept.

Record selector A small box at the beginning of a row used to select a record.

Record source The table or query that supplies the records for a form or report.

References A list of works cited or consulted by an author in his or her work; the list is titled *References*.

Referential integrity Rules in a database that are used to preserve relationships between tables when records are changed.

Related tables Tables that are joined in a relationship using a common field.

Relational database management system (RDBMS) A database management system that uses the relational model to manage groups of data (tables) and rules (relationships) between tables.

Relationship A connection between two tables using a common field.

Relative cell reference A designation that indicates a cell's relative location within the worksheet using the column letter and row number, such as B5. When a formula containing a relative cell reference is copied, the cell references in the copied formula change relative to the position of the copied formula.

Replace An Office feature that finds text and replaces it with a word or phrase that you indicate.

Report An object that contains professional-looking formatted information from underlying tables or queries.

Report tool Used to instantly create a tabular report based on the table or query currently selected.

Report view Enables you to see what a printed report will look like in a continuous page layout.

Report Wizard Asks you questions and uses your answers to generate a customized report.

Revision mark Indicates where text is added, deleted, or formatted while the Track Changes feature is active.

Ribbon The long bar of tabs, groups, and commands located just beneath the Title bar.

Rich Text Format (.rtf) A file format that retains structure and most text formatting when transferring documents between applications or platforms.

Right alignment Begins text evenly at the right margin, with a ragged left edge.

Right indent A setting that positions all text in a paragraph an equal distance from the right margin.

Rotate To move an object around its axis.

Row heading The numbers to the left side of rows in a worksheet.

Row height The vertical measurement of the row in a worksheet.

Run command Used to produce query results (the red exclamation point).

Sans serif font A font that does not contain a thin line or extension at the top and bottom of the primary strokes on characters.

Saturation The intensity of a color.

Screen saver A moving series of pictures or images that displays when your computer has been idle for a specified period of time.

Section A division to presentation content that groups slides meaningfully.

Section break An indicator that divides a document into parts, enabling different formatting for each section.

Select query A type of query that displays only the records that match criteria entered in Query Design view.

Selection net A pane designed to help select objects from a listing of all objects on a slide.

Selection Pane A pane designed to help select objects.

Semi-selection The process of using the mouse pointer to select cells while building a formula. Also known as *pointing*.

Serif font A font that contains a thin line or extension at the top and bottom of the primary strokes on characters.

Shading A background color that appears behind text in a paragraph, page, or table element.

Shape A geometric or non-geometric object, such as a rectangle or an arrow, used to create an illustration or highlight information.

Sharpening Enhances the edges of the content in a picture to make the boundaries more prominent.

Sheet tab A visual element that shows the name of a worksheet contained in the workbook.

Sheet tab navigation Visual elements that help you navigate to the first, previous, next, or last sheet within a workbook.

Shortcut An icon, identified by a small arrow in the bottom left-hand corner, that provides quick access to programs or features just like the tiles on the Start screen.

Short text data type A text field that can store up to 255 characters but has a default field size of 50 characters.

Shortcut menu Provides choices related to the selection or area at which you right-click.

Show row A row in the Query Design view that controls whether the field will be displayed in the query results.

Simple Markup Word feature that simplifies the display of comments and revision marks, resulting in a clean, uncluttered look.

Simply Query Wizard Provides dialog boxes to guide you through the query design process.

Sizing handles A series of faint dots on the outside border of a selected chart or object; enables the user to adjust the height and width of the chart or object.

Slide The most basic element of PowerPoint.

Slide master The top slide in a hierarchy of slides based on the master.

Slide show A series of slides displayed onscreen for an audience.

Slide Show view A view used to deliver the completed presentation full screen to an audience, one slide at a time, as an electronic presentation.

Slide Sorter view A view that displays thumbnails of presentation slides, which allows you to view multiple slides simultaneously.

SmartArt A diagram that presents information visually to effectively communicate a message.

SmartGuide A dotted line that appears automatically to assist with lining up images or text.

Snap A process with Windows 8 in which two apps can be displayed on the screen at once.

Snip The output of using the Snipping Tool.

Snipping Tool A Windows 8 accessory program that provides users the ability to capture an image of all (or part of) their computer's screen.

Softening Blurs the edges of the content in a picture to make the boundaries less prominent.

Sort The process of listing records or text in a specific sequence, such as alphabetically by last name.

Sort row A row in the Query Design view that enables you to sort in ascending or descending order.

Source A publication, person, or media item that is consulted in the preparation of a paper and given credit.

Sparkline A small line, column, or win/loss chart contained in a single cell to provide a simple visual illustrating one data series.

Split form Combines two views of the same record source—one section is displayed in a stacked layout, and the other section is displayed in a tabular layout.

Splitter bar Divides a form into two halves.

Spreadsheet An electronic file that contains a grid of columns and rows used to organize related data and to display results of calculations, enabling interpretation of quantitative data for decision making.

Spyware Software that is usually downloaded without your awareness and collects personal information from your computer.

Stacked column chart A chart type that places stacks of data in segments on top of each other in one column, with each category in the data series represented by a different color.

Stacked layout Displays fields in a vertical column.

Stacking order The order of objects placed on top of one another.

Start screen The display that you see after you turn on your computer and respond to any username and password prompts.

Status bar A horizontal bar found at the bottom of the program window that contains information relative to the open file.

Stock chart A chart type that shows fluctuations in stock changes.

Storyboard A visual plan of a presentation that displays the content of each slide in the slide show.

Structured reference A tag or use of a table element, such as a column label, as a reference in a formula. Column labels are enclosed in square brackets, such as [Amount], within the formula.

Style A named collection of formatting characteristics that can be applied to text or paragraphs.

Style manual A guide to a particular writing style outlining required rules and conventions related to the preparation of papers.

Style set A combination of title, heading, and paragraph styles that can be used to format all of those elements in a document at one time.

Subfolder A folder that is housed within another folder.

SUBTOTAL function A predefined formula that calculates an aggregate value, such as totals, for values in a range, a table, or a database.

SUM function A predefined formula that calculates the total of values contained in two or more cells.

Surface chart A chart type that displays trends using two dimensions on a continuous curve.

Switch list A list of thumbnails of previous programs.

Symbol A character or graphic not normally included on a keyboard.

Syntax The rules that dictate the structure and components required to perform the necessary calculations in an equation or to evaluate expressions.

Tab (Office Fundamentals) A component of the Ribbon that is designed to appear much like a tab on a file folder, with the active tab highlighted, that is used to organize groups by function. (Word) A marker that specifies the position for aligning text in a column arrangement, often including a dot leader.

Table (Word) A grid of columns and rows that organizes data. (Access) An object used to store and organize data in a series of records (rows) with each record made up of a number of fields (columns) and is the foundation of every database.

Table alignment The position of a table between the left and right document margins.

Table array The range that contains the body of the lookup table, excluding column labels. The first column must be in ascending order to find a value in a range, or it can be in any order to look up an exact value. It is the second argument within a VLOOKUP or HLOOKUP function.

Table of Contents Page that lists headings in the order in which they appear in a document and the page numbers on which the entries begin.

Table row A row in Query Design view that displays the data source.

Table style A named collection of color, font, and border design that can be applied to a table.

Tabular layout Displays data horizontally.

Taskbar A tool for keeping track of open computer programs or files.

Template A predesigned file that incorporates formatting elements, such as theme and layouts, and may include content that can be modified.

Text Any combination of letters, numbers, symbols, and spaces not used in Excel calculations.

Text box An object that provides space for text and graphics; it can be formatted with a border, shading, and other characteristics.

Text pane A pane for text entry used for a SmartArt diagram.

Texture fill Inserts a texture such as canvas, denim, marble, or cork into a shape.

Theme A collection of design choices that includes colors, fonts, and special effects used to give a consistent look to a document, workbook, database form or report, or presentation.

Thesaurus A tool used to quickly find a synonym (a word with the same meaning as another).

Thumbnail A miniature view of a slide that appears in the Slides tab and Slide Sort view.

Tile A colorful block on the Start screen that when clicked will launch a program, file, folder, or other Windows 8 app.

Title bar A component of Microsoft Office that identifies the current file name and the application in which you are working and includes control buttons that enable you to minimize, maximize, restore down, or close the application window.

TODAY function A predefined formula that displays the current date in a cell.

Toggle The action of switching from one setting to another. Several Home tab tasks, such as Bold and Italic, are actually toggle commands.

Tone The temperature of a color.

Toolbar Provides shortcuts to Web resources.

Total row A table row that displays below the last row of records in an Excel table, or in Datasheet view of a table or query, and displays summary or aggregate statistics, such as a sum or an average.

Totals query Makes an additional row available in the query design grid. Used to display aggregate data when the query is run.

Track Changes Word feature that monitors all additions, deletions, and formatting changes you make in a document.

Transition A specific animation that is applied as a previous slide is replaced by a new slide while displayed in Slide Show view or Reading view.

Transparency The visibility of fill.

Trendline A line that depicts trends or helps forecast future data in a chart. For example, if the plotted data includes 2005, 2010, and 2015, a trendline can help forecast values for 2020 and beyond.

Turabian Writing style that originated with the Chicago style but omits much of the information that is relevant for publishing.

Ungroup To break a combined grouped object into individual objects.

User interface The screen display through which you communicate with the software.

Validation rule Prevents invalid data from being entered into a field.

Value A number that represents a quantity or a measurable amount.

Value axis The chart element that displays incremental numbers to identify approximate values, such as dollars or units, of data points in a chart.

Variant A variation on a chosen design theme.

Vector graphic An object-oriented graphic that is math-based.

Vector image An image created by a mathematical statement; a form of clip art.

Vertex The point where a curve ends or the point where two line segments meet in a shape.

Vertical alignment The position of data between the top and bottom cell margins.

View The way a file appears onscreen.

View controls Icons on the right side of the status bar that enable you to change to Normal, Page Layout, or Page Break view to display the worksheet.

Virus A computer program that attaches itself to another computer program (known as the *host program*) and attempts to spread to other computers when files are exchanged.

VLOOKUP function A predefined formula that looks up a value and returns a related result from the lookup table.

Watermark Text or graphic that displays behind text.

Web Layout view View that displays how a document will look when posted on the Internet.

Wildcard A special character that can represent one or more characters in the criterion of a query.

Window An area of space on the desktop.

Windows 8.1.1 A Microsoft operating system released in 2012 that can operate on touch-screen devices as well as laptops and desktops because it has been designed to accept multiple methods of input.

Windows 8.1.1 app An application specifically designed to run in the Start screen interface of Windows 8 that is either already installed and ready to use or can be downloaded from the Windows Store.

Windows 8.1.1 interface The name given to the Start screen that features large type with clean, readable block images inspired by metropolitan service signs such as those found on bus stations and subways.

Windows Defender Antispyware and antivirus software included with Windows 8.1.1.

Windows Updates Automatically downloaded updates provided by Microsoft to enhance Windows security or fix problems.

Wizard A tool that makes a process easier by asking a series of questions, then creating a structure based on your answers.

Word A word processing software application used to produce all sorts of documents, including memos, newsletters, forms, tables, and brochures.

Word processing software A computer application, such as Microsoft Word, used primarily with text to create, edit, and format documents.

Word Online An online component of Office Online presenting a free, although limited, version of Word 2013.

Word wrap The feature that automatically moves words to the next line if they do not fit on the current line.

WordArt A feature that modifies text to include special effects, such as color, shadow, gradient, and 3-D appearance.

WordPad A program that enables you to create documents.

Workbook A collection of one or more related worksheets contained within a single file.

Works Cited A list of works cited or consulted by an author in his or her work; the list is titled *Works Cited*.

Worksheet A single spreadsheet that typically contains descriptive labels, numeric values, formulas, functions, and graphical representations of data.

Wrap text An Excel feature that makes data appear on multiple lines by adjusting the row height to fit the cell contents within the column width.

Writing style Writing a paper as directed by a style manual such as MLA or APA.

X Y (scatter) chart A chart type that shows a relationship between two variables using their X and Y coordinates. Excel plots one coordinate on the horizontal X-axis and the other variable on the vertical Y-axis. Scatter charts are often used to represent data in educational, scientific, and medical experiments.

X-axis A horizontal border that provides a frame of reference for measuring data horizontally on a chart.

Y-axis A vertical border that provides a frame of reference for measuring data vertically on a chart.

Zoom control A control that enables you to increase or decrease the size of the worksheet data onscreen.

Zoom slider A horizontal bar on the far right side of the status bar that enables you to increase or decrease the size of file contents onscreen.

Index

E

F

G

H

I

P

Q

R

S

T

U

V

W

X

Y

Z

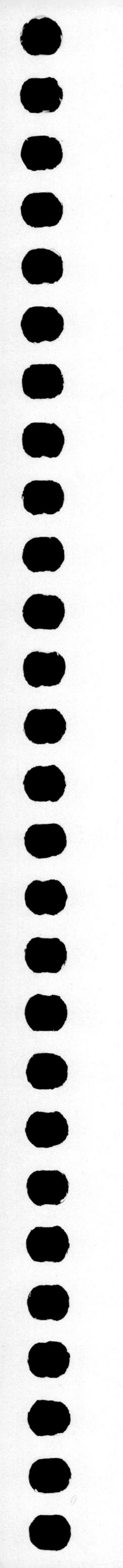